The Vocabulary of the Greek Testament

Illustrated from the papyri and other non-literary sources

James Hope Moulton, George Milligan

Alpha Editions

This edition published in 2020

ISBN : 9789354037511

Design and Setting By
Alpha Editions
www.alphaedis.com
email - alphaedis@gmail.com

THE VOCABULARY
OF THE
GREEK TESTAMENT

*ILLUSTRATED FROM THE PAPYRI AND OTHER
NON-LITERARY SOURCES*

BY

JAMES HOPE MOULTON, D.D., D.THEOL.

Late Fellow of King's College, Cambridge ; Greenwood Professor of Hellenistic
Greek and Indo-European Philology, Manchester University

AND

GEORGE MILLIGAN, D.D.

Regius Professor of Divinity and Biblical Criticism,
Glasgow University

HODDER AND STOUGHTON
LIMITED   LONDON
1914–1929

PREFATORY NOTE

Upwards of twenty years ago Professor J. H. Moulton asked me to join with him in an effort to illustrate the *Vocabulary of the Greek Testament* from recently discovered non-literary texts. First came a series of joint articles in the *Expositor* during 1908 to 1911 dealing with certain representative words. In 1914 we found it possible to publish the First Part of the *Vocabulary*: Part II followed in the next year. Our collaboration was then cut short by Dr. Moulton's tragic death, though I have done my utmost to utilize any notes or references that he left behind him. The grasp and range of Dr. Moulton's Greek scholarship are too well known to require acknowledgment here, but I may be allowed to record my own deep sense of personal loss in the removal at the height of his powers of one who was always the truest of friends and the most loyal of colleagues.

It may be well, perhaps, to emphasize that it was in no way our aim to provide a complete *Lexicon* to the Greek New Testament, but rather to show the nature of the new light cast upon its language by the rich stores of contemporary papyri discovered in recent years. (See further the General Introduction to the present volume.) Apart from the papyri, considerable use has been made of the Greek inscriptions, and evidence from other non-literary sources has been freely cited, wherever it seemed likely to be useful. Very often words have been included for which our non-literary sources provide no illustration, in order to show from literary evidence, if forthcoming, or from its very absence, the relation of such words to the popular Greek.

The use of Professor J. H. Thayer's monumental edition of Grimm's *Lexicon* (Edinburgh, 1886), has been assumed throughout. Professor Souter's *Pocket Lexicon to the Greek New Testament* (Oxford, 1916), a marvellous *multum in parvo*, and the excellent *Manual Greek Lexicon of the New Testament* by Professor G. Abbott-Smith (Edinburgh, 1922) have been of the utmost value. In the later Parts of the *Vocabulary* frequent reference has also been made to W. Bauer's revised and enlarged edition of E. Preuschen's *Griechisch-Deutsches Wörterbuch zu den Schriften des Neuen Testaments* (Giessen, 1928), and to F. Preisigke's comprehensive *Wörterbuch der griechischen Papyrusurkunden*, I.–III. i. (Berlin, 1925–1929). Other books of reference will be found detailed in Abbreviations I. General.

For the ready assistance of many friends, too numerous to mention, in the carrying through of this book, I am deeply grateful; but a special word of thanks is due to Professor W. G. Waddell, now of the Egyptian University, Cairo, who has read all the proofs with the most meticulous care, and has in addition furnished important suggestions.

It remains only to acknowledge the generosity and enterprise of Messrs. Hodder & Stoughton in undertaking the publication of the work, and to express my sense of the singular skill and accuracy with which the compositors and readers of the firm of Messrs. R. Clay & Sons, Bungay, have carried through an extremely intricate piece of printing.

G. Milligan.

The University, Glasgow.
July, 1929.

GENERAL INTRODUCTION

FEW archæological discoveries in recent years have awakened more widespread interest than the countless papyrus documents recovered from the sands of Egypt, and as it is from them that our principal non-literary illustrations of the *Vocabulary of the Greek Testament* have been drawn, it may be well to describe briefly by way of Introduction what these papyri are, and what is the nature of their value for the New Testament student.

Papyrus as Writing Material.—In itself, the word papyrus is the name of a reed-plant (*Cyperus papyrus*, L.) which at one time grew in great profusion in the river Nile, and gave its name to the writing material or "paper" of antiquity formed from it. The pith (βύβλος) of the stem of the papyrus plant was cut into long thin strips, which were laid down on a flat table and soaked with Nile water. A second layer was then placed crosswise on the top of the first, and the two layers were pressed together to form a single web or sheet. After being dried in the sun, and scraped with a shell or bone to remove any roughness, a material not unlike our own brown paper was produced.[1]

The size of the papyrus sheets varied considerably, but for non-literary documents a common size was from nine to eleven inches in height, and from five to five and a half inches in breadth. When more space than that afforded by a single sheet was required, a number of sheets were joined together to form a roll, which could easily be extended or shortened as desired. Thus, to take the case of the New Testament autographs, which were almost certainly written on separate papyrus rolls, a short Epistle, like the Second Epistle to the Thessalonians, would be a roll of about fifteen inches in length with the contents arranged in some five columns, while St. Paul's longest Epistle, the Epistle to the Romans, would run to about eleven feet and a half. The shortest of the Gospels, St. Mark's, would occupy about nineteen feet; the longest, St. Luke's, about thirty-one or thirty-two feet. And the Apocalypse of St. John has been estimated at fifteen feet. Taking the other books on the same scale, Sir F. G. Kenyon, to whom the foregoing figures are also due, has calculated that if the whole New Testament was written out in order on a single roll, the roll would extend to more than two hundred feet in length, obviously an utterly unworkable size.[2] This alone makes it clear that not until the papyrus stage in their history was past, and use was made of both sides of parchment or vellum leaves, was it possible to include all the books of the New Testament in a single volume.

The side of the papyrus on which the fibres ran horizontally, or the *recto*, as it came to be technically known, was from its greater smoothness, generally preferred for writing, while the back, or the *verso*, was reserved for the address, at any rate in the case of letters. But when space failed, the *verso* could also be utilized, as shown in a long

---

[1] See further Pliny, *N.H.* xiii. 11–13, and cf. F. G. Kenyon, *The Palaeography of Greek Papyri* (Oxford, 1899), p. 14 ff.

[2] *Handbook to the Textual Criticism of the New Testament*, 2nd edit. (London, 1912), p. 35 ff.

magical papyrus in the British Museum, in which nineteen columns are written on the *recto*, and the remaining thirteen on the *verso*.[1]

In any case we have abundant evidence of the use of the *verso*, when fresh papyrus was not available, as when a man writes a letter on the back of a business document, explaining that he had been unable at the moment to find a "clean sheet" ($\chi\alpha\rho\tau\iota\sigma\nu$ $\kappa\alpha\theta\alpha\rho\sigma\nu$),[2] or as when the back of the official notification of the death of a certain Panechotes is used for a school-exercise or composition, embodying such maxims as "do nothing mean or ignoble or inglorious or cowardly," written in a beginner's hand and much corrected.[3]

In other cases, before the *verso* has been so used, the original contents of the *recto* have been effaced or washed out, a practice which adds point to a familiar verse. In Col 2[11], we read that our Lord "blotted out the bond written in ordinances that was against us, which was contrary to us," and the verb used for "blotted out" ($\dot{\epsilon}\xi\alpha\lambda\epsilon\dot{\iota}\psi\alpha\varsigma$) is the technical term for "washing out" the writing from a papyrus sheet. So complete was the forgiveness which Christ by His work secured, that it completely cancelled the old bond, that had hitherto been valid against us, for it bore our signature ($\chi\epsilon\iota\rho\sigma\gamma\rho\alpha\phi\sigma\nu$). He made the bond as though it had never been (cf. Exod 32[32f.], Rev 3[5]).

As regards other writing materials, a reed pen ($\gamma\rho\alpha\phi\iota\kappa\dot{\sigma}\varsigma$ $\kappa\dot{\alpha}\lambda\alpha\mu\sigma\varsigma$; cf. 3 Macc 4[20]) was prepared, much as we now prepare a quill, while the ink ($\tau\dot{\sigma}$ $\mu\dot{\epsilon}\lambda\alpha\nu$: cf. 2 John [12]) was made from a mixture of charcoal, gum and water. The marvellous way in which the ink has preserved its colour invariably attracts attention, and shows that anything in the nature of adulteration must have been unknown. A first-century letter, chiefly about writing materials, refers to "the ink pot" ($\tau\dot{\sigma}$ $\beta\rho\dot{\sigma}\chi\iota\sigma\nu$ $\tau\sigma\hat{\upsilon}$ $\mu\dot{\epsilon}\lambda\alpha\nu\sigma\varsigma$).[4]

The character of the handwriting naturally varies with the nature of the document and the education of the scribe. But the task of decipherment can rarely be said to be easy, partly owing to the frequent use of contractions and partly to the numerous *lacunae* or gaps caused by the brittle nature of the material. The restoration of the letters or words which have thus dropped out demands the exercise of the utmost patience and skill. And those who have had an opportunity of inspecting some of the originals can only marvel that intelligible transcriptions have been made from them at all.

When, then, we speak of papyri, we are to think simply of rolls or sheets of paper of this character, which had been put to all the many and various purposes to which paper as a writing material is put amongst ourselves, while the addition of "Greek" distinguishes the papyri written in that language from the Aramaic or Latin or Coptic papyri which have been similarly recovered. We need only add that the earliest dated Greek papyrus we possess belongs to the year B.C. 311-310,[5] and that from that time an almost continuous chain of documents carries us far down into Byzantine times.

Papyrus Discoveries.—With the exception of some calcined rolls from Herculaneum, which were brought to light as far back as 1752 and the following years, papyri have been found only in Egypt, the marvellously dry climate of that country being especially favourable to their preservation. A certain number, more particularly those of a literary character, have been recovered from their original owners' tombs. The *Persae* of Timotheos, for example, the oldest Greek literary manuscript in existence, dating, as it does, from the fourth century B.C., was found near Memphis in the coffin of a Greek soldier, by whose side it had been deposited in a leathern bag. And an Homeric roll,

---

[1] P Lond 121 (iii/A.D.) (= I. p. 83 ff.). For the abbreviations used in the citation of papyrus passages, see Abbreviations II. Papyri.

[2] P Gen I. 52[3] (iv/A.D.): cf. *Archiv* iii. p. 399.   [3] P Oxy I. 79 (A.D. 181-192).

[4] P Oxy II. 326 (c. A.D. 45).   [5] P Eleph 1 (= *Selections*, No. 1).

now in the Bodleian Library, Oxford, used to be exhibited along with a lock of the hair of the lady with whom it had been buried. Other rolls have been found in earthen jars in the ruins of temples or houses, thus strangely recalling the prophecy of Jeremiah: "Thus saith the Lord of hosts, the God of Israel: Take these deeds, this deed of the purchase, both that which is sealed, and this deed which is open, and put them in an earthen vessel; that they may continue many days" (chap. 32¹¹ RV).

But the great mass of papyri come from the rubbish heaps, rising sometimes to a height of twenty to thirty feet, on the outskirts of old Egyptian towns and villages. Possibly out of a feeling of reverence for the written word, the inhabitants did not as a rule burn their old papers, but threw them out on these heaps. There they were quickly covered over with the fine desert sand, and, so long as they were above the damp level of the Nile, have remained practically uninjured down to the present day. For the most part they consist of single sheets, or fragments of sheets, sometimes no larger than a postage stamp, but occasionally whole baskets of official documents are found, which had been cleared out *en masse* from public archives or record offices. And everyone will recognize the absorbing interest attaching to these scraps of paper, discarded as useless by their first writers and owners, on which no eye has looked for many hundreds of years, but which now, as original documents, recreate and revivify the past for us in a way which nothing else could do.

The earliest finds in Egypt of which we have knowledge took place in 1778, when some Arabs, digging for their own purposes in the Fayûm district, accidentally came upon some fifty rolls in an earthen pot; but, unable to find purchasers, they destroyed them on account, it is said, of the aromatic smell they gave forth in burning. Only one roll was saved which, passing into the hands of Cardinal Stefano Borgia, came to be known as the *Charta Borgiana*. The contents are of little general interest, being merely an account of the forced labours of the peasants on the Nile embankment at Arsinoë in the year A.D. 191–2, but the papyrus will always have the significance of being the first Greek papyrus to be published in Europe.[1]

In the year 1820 further finds, dating from the second century B.C., were made in the neighbourhood of Memphis and Thebes, but it was not until 1889–90 that a beginning was made in systematic exploration, when at Gurob Professor Flinders Petrie extracted a large number of papyri from Ptolemaic mummy-cases, and brought them home to England.

To the same period of exploration belong such important literary finds as the lost work of Aristotle on *The Constitution of Athens*, copied on the back of a farm-bailiff's accounts, which are dated in the eleventh year of Vespasian, that is A.D. 78–9; the *Mimiambi* or *Mimes* of Herodas, which reproduce with photographic exactness the ordinary, and often sordid, details of the everyday life of the third century B.C.; and about thirteen hundred lines of the *Odes* of Bacchylides, a contemporary of Pindar, and a nephew of the Simonides for the recovery of whose works Wordsworth longed in a well-known poem:

> O ye, who patiently explore
> The wreck of Herculanean lore,
> What rapture! could ye seize
> Some Theban fragment, or unroll
> One precious, tender-hearted, scroll
> Of pure Simonides.

[1] It was published under the title *Charta Papyracea Graece scripta Musei Borgiani Velitris*, ed. N. Schow, Romae, 1778

But significant though these discoveries were, their interest was largely eclipsed by the results of the digging carried on by Dr. Grenfell and Dr. Hunt at Oxyrhynchus, the ancient Behneseh, in the winter of 1896-97 and the following years. The two English explorers had been attracted to the spot by the expectation that early fragments of Christian literature might be found there, in view of the important place which Oxyrhynchus occupied in Egyptian Christianity in the fourth and fifth centuries. And their prescience was rewarded, for, amongst the papyri recovered on the second day, was a crumpled leaf written on both sides in uncial characters, amongst which Dr. Hunt detected the somewhat rare Greek word for "mote" (κάρφος). This suggested to him the "mote" of our Lord's Sayings in the Sermon on the Mount (Matt 7³⁻⁵); and, on further examination, he found that he had in his hand a leaf out of a very early collection of Sayings attributed to Jesus, some of which corresponded closely with the canonical Sayings of the Gospels, while others were new.[1] We are not at present concerned with the many questions which were thus raised,[2] but the importance of the discovery was undeniable, especially when it was followed next day by the finding of another uncial fragment containing the greater part of the first chapter of St. Matthew's Gospel, written not later than the third century, and therefore a century older than the oldest manuscript of the New Testament previously known.[3] Both leaves, Dr. Grenfell suggests, may not improbably have formed "the remains of a library belonging to some Christian who perished in the persecution during Diocletian's reign, and whose books were then thrown away."[1]

Along with these, and other almost equally sensational finds, Oxyrhynchus yielded an enormous mass of documents of the most miscellaneous character dating from the Roman Conquest of Egypt to the tenth century after Christ, when papyrus was superseded by paper as a writing material.

Other noteworthy collections come to us from the British Museum, Berlin, Florence, and various other sources, and the general result is that there are now available about ten thousand published documents, and that these are being constantly added to.[5] Whether the still unedited papyri have any great surprises in store for us it is vain even to conjecture. But even if they have not, they will serve a useful purpose in illustrating and confirming the lexical and other results that have already been reached, and in increasing still further our stock of first-hand documentary evidence regarding the most important period in the world's history.

Classification of Papyri.—The papyri are generally classified under the two main heads, literary and non-literary, with the biblical and theological texts occupying a position about mid-way between the two. It is with the non-literary texts that we are concerned just now, and a glance at the citations on one or two pages of the following *Vocabulary* is sufficient to show the miscellaneous character of these texts, comprising as they do all manner of official documents, such as Imperial rescripts, accounts of judicial proceedings, tax and census papers, contracts of marriage and divorce, notices of birth and death,

---

[1] P Oxy I. 1.

[2] Reference may be made to *The Sayings of Jesus from Oxyrhynchus*, edited with Introduction, Critical Apparatus, and Commentary by Hugh G. Evelyn White (Cambr. Univ. Press, 1920).

[3] P Oxy I. 2.

[4] Egypt Exploration Fund: *Archaeological Report*, 1896-97, p. 6. See further an article by the present writer on "The Greek Papyri and the New Testament" in *The History of Christianity in the Light of Modern Knowledge* (Blackie and Son, 1929), p. 300 ff.

[5] A list of the principal papyrus collections will be found under Abbreviations II.

and so forth, along with a number of private letters touching upon all sides of family and everyday life.

And as the contents of these *documents humains* are wide as life itself, so they supply materials for the most varied fields of human learning. Their value to the historian and the jurist is apparent on the surface, while with their aid the geographer can reconstruct the map of ancient Egypt with a precision previously impossible. To the palaeographer again, who has hitherto been sadly hampered by *lacunae* in the development of ordinary script, they offer an uninterrupted series of examples, many of them exactly dated by year and month and day, from the third century before Christ to the eighth century after Christ. And to the philologist they show the true place of the Κοινή, the Common Greek of the period, as distinguished from the dialects of the classical period, in the development of the Greek language. Examples of the Κοινή on its literary side had not, indeed, been previously wanting, but now, for the first time, it was possible to see it in undress, as it was spoken and written by the ordinary men and women of the day.

"**New Testament Greek**."—It is with this aspect of the papyri that we are primarily concerned. Alike in Vocabulary and Grammar the language of the New Testament exhibits striking dissimilarities from Classical Greek; and in consequence it has been regarded as standing by itself as "New Testament Greek." In general it had been hastily classed as "Judaic" or "Hebraic" Greek; its writers being Jews (with the probable exception of St. Luke), and therefore using a language other than their own, a language filled with reminiscences of the translation-Greek of the Septuagint on which they had been nurtured.[1] But true as this may be, it does not go far to explain the real character of the Greek which meets us in the New Testament writings. For a convincing explanation we have in the first instance to thank the German scholar, Adolf Deissmann, now Professor of New Testament Exegesis in the University of Berlin. While still a pastor at Marburg, Dr. (then Mr.) Deissmann happened one day to be turning over in the University Library at Heidelberg a new section of a volume containing transcripts from the collection of Greek Papyri at Berlin. And, as he read, he was suddenly struck by the likeness of the language of these papyri to the language of the Greek New Testament. Further study deepened in his mind the extent of this likeness, and he realized that he held in his hand the real key to the old problem.

So far from the Greek of the New Testament being a language by itself, or even, as one German scholar called it, "a language of the Holy Ghost,"[2] its main feature was that it was the ordinary vernacular Greek of the period, not the language of contemporary literature, which was often influenced by an attempt to imitate the great authors of classical times, but the language of everyday life, as it was spoken and written by the ordinary men and women of the day, or, as it is often described, the Κοινή or Common Greek, of the great Graeco-Roman world.

That, then, is Deissmann's general conclusion, which quickly found an enthusiastic

---

[1] Cf. W. F. Howard's Appendix "Semitisms in the New Testament" in *Grammar of New Testament Greek* by J. H. Moulton and W. F. Howard (Edinburgh, 1929), Vol. II. p. 411 ff.

[2] R. Rothe, *Zur Dogmatik* (Gotha, 1863), p. 238: "We can indeed with good right speak of a language of the Holy Ghost. For in the Bible it is manifest to our eyes how the Divine Spirit at work in revelation always takes the language of the particular people chosen to be the recipient, and makes of it a characteristic religious variety by transforming existing linguistic elements and existing conceptions into a shape peculiarly appropriate to that Spirit. This process is shown most clearly by the Greek of the New Testament" (quoted by Deissmann, *The Philology of the Greek Bible* (London, 1908), p. 42 f.).

and brilliant advocate in this country in the person of Dr. J. H. Moulton. And though the zeal of the first discoverers of the new light may have sometimes led them to go rather far in ignoring the Semitisms, on the one hand, and the literary culture of the New Testament writers, on the other, their main conclusion has found general acceptance, and we have come to realize with a definiteness unknown before that the book intended for the people was written in the people's own tongue. Themselves sprung from the common people, the disciples of One Whom the common people heard gladly, its writers, in their turn, wrote in the common tongue to be "understanded of the people."

Anticipations of this View.—It is somewhat strange that this discovery was so long deferred. Publications of papyri go back as far as 1826, but there is nothing to show that this particular way of utilizing their documents ever occurred to the first editors. At the same time it is interesting to notice certain anticipations from other sources of what such discoveries might mean, or, as it has been called, of Deissmannism before Deissmann.

In the *Prolegomena* to his translation of Winer's well-known *Grammar of New Testament Greek*, published in 1859, Professor Masson, at one time Professor in the University of Athens, writes : "The diction of the New Testament is the plain and unaffected Hellenic of the Apostolic Age, as employed by Greek-speaking Christians when discoursing on religious subjects. . . . Perfectly natural and unaffected, it is free from all tinge of vulgarity on the one hand, and from every trace of studied finery on the other. Apart from the Hebraisms—the number of which have, for the most part, been grossly exaggerated—the New Testament may be considered as exhibiting the only genuine *facsimile* of the colloquial diction employed by *unsophisticated* Grecian gentlemen of the first century, who spoke without pedantry—as ἰδιῶται (' private persons '), and not as σοφισταί (' adepts ')" (p. vii. f.).[1]

A second statement to much the same effect will be found in the article "Greek Language (Biblical)," contributed by Mr. (afterwards Principal Sir James) Donaldson to the third edition of Kitto's *Cyclopaedia of Biblical Literature*, edited by Dr. W. Lindsay Alexander (Edinburgh, 1876). In Vol. ii. p. 170, the writer states : "Now it seems to us that the language used by the Septuagint and N(ew) T(estament) writers was the language used in common conversation, learned by them, not through books, but most likely in childhood from household talk, or, if not, through subsequent oral instruction. If this be the case, then the Septuagint is the first translation which was made for the great masses of the people in their own language, and the N(ew) T(estament) writers are the first to appeal to men through the common vulgar language intelligible to all who spoke Greek. The common Greek thus used is indeed considerably modified by the circumstances of the writers, but these modifications no more turn the Greek into a peculiar dialect than do Americanisms or Scotticisms turn the English of Americans and Scotsmen into peculiar dialects of English."[2]

---

[1] Cf. J. Rendel Harris, *Exp T*, xxv. p. 54 f., and notes by the present writer in *ib.* xxxi. p. 421, and xxxii. p. 231 f.

Of a much more general character, but interesting from its early date, is Dr. John Lightfoot's comment on the Preface to the Lord's Prayer in Mt 6⁹, in his *Horae Hebraicae et Talmudicae*, first published as far back as 1658: "In interpreting very many phrases and histories of the New Testament, it is not so much worth, what we think of them from notions of our own, feigned upon I know not what grounds, as in what sense these things were understood by the hearers and lookers on, according to the usual custom and vulgar dialect of the nation."

[2] I owe the reference to a note by W. L. Lorimer in *Exp T*, xxxii. p. 330, where attention is also drawn to the position taken up by Salmasius in his *Funus linguae Hellenisticae* and his *De Hellenistica Commentarius*, both published in 1643.

Still more interesting is the prophecy ascribed to Professor (afterwards Bishop) J. B. Lightfoot in the year 1863. Lecturing to his class at Cambridge, Dr. Lightfoot is reported to have said: "You are not to suppose that the word [some New Testament word which had its only classical authority in Herodotus] had fallen out of use in the interval, only that it had not been used in the books which remain to us : probably it had been part of the common speech all along. I will go further, and say that if we could only recover letters that ordinary people wrote to each other without any thought of being literary, we should have the greatest possible help for the understanding of the language of the N(ew) T(estament) generally."[1]

The significance of this quotation is unmistakable, and it is followed, twenty-one years later, by what is, so far as I know, the first definite mention in this country of the papyri in connexion with New Testament study. It occurs in Dean Farrar's well-known volume, *The Messages of the Books* (London, Macmillan, 1884), where, in a footnote to his chapter on the "Form of the New Testament Epistles," the writer remarks: "It is an interesting subject of inquiry to what extent there was at this period an ordinary form of correspondence which (as among ourselves) was to some extent fixed. In the papyrus rolls of the British Museum (edited for the trustees by J. Forshall [in 1839]) there are forms and phrases which constantly remind us of St. Paul" (p. 151).

The hint, thus thrown out, was unfortunately not followed up at the time, but if the full significance of the papyri for the study of the New Testament was long in being recognized, no one can complain of lack of attention to the subject at the present day. It is leading to the re-writing of our Lexicons and Grammars of the New Testament, and no modern Commentary on any of its books fails to avail itself of the help afforded by these new treasures from Egypt.

Gains from the Study of the Papyri.—Abundant proof of this will be forthcoming in the pages which follow. Meanwhile, it may be helpful to those who have made no special study of the subject if I attempt to indicate some of the ways in which the new evidence can be applied to the elucidation of the words of the New Testament.

Orthography and Accidence.—We may begin with Orthography and Accidence. In these particulars the New Testament writings have not yet been subjected to the same searching comparison with the new evidence which Helbing and Thackeray have applied to the Old Testament ; but enough has already been done by Blass, Schmiedel, Moulton, and Deissmann, following on the notable work of Westcott and Hort, to show that we are in a better position to-day for recovering the *ipsissima verba* of the New Testament autographs than many modern textual critics are ready to admit. There was a constant tendency on the part of the later copyists to improve on the "vulgarisms" or "colloquialisms" of the original, and it cannot but help us to determine what is due to this refining process when we have such abundant evidence in our hands as to how the common people of the time actually wrote and spelt.

The form $\gamma\acute{\epsilon}\nu\eta\mu\alpha$, for example, which Westcott and Hort prefer for the five occurrences of this word in the New Testament (Mt 26[29], Mk 14[25], Lk 12[18] (marg.), 22[18], 2 Cor 9[10]), as against the $\gamma\acute{\epsilon}\nu\nu\eta\mu\alpha$ of the Textus Receptus (except in Lk 12[18]), is now fully established on the evidence both of the Ptolemaic papyri, and of those belonging to the first four centuries after Christ. The aspirated $\sigma\phi\upsilon\rho\acute{\iota}\varsigma$, again, for $\sigma\pi\upsilon\rho\acute{\iota}\varsigma$ (Mt 15[37], 16[10], Mk 8[8, 20], Ac 9[25]) is amply, though not universally, attested in the vernacular documents ; while the syncopated form $\tau\alpha\mu\epsilon\hat{\iota}o\nu$ (for $\tau\alpha\mu\iota\epsilon\hat{\iota}o\nu$) as in Mt 6[6], 24[26], Lk 12[3, 24], is the prevailing form in the papyri from i/A.D. onwards, though the fuller form occurs in various passages from

[1] Quoted by Moulton *Prolegomena*[3], p. 242

Ptolemaic times. The very indifference, indeed, of the writers of our documents to symmetrical forms or to unified spelling may in itself be taken as a warning against the almost feverish haste with which a "redactor," or later author, is sometimes brought in to explain similar phenomena in the different parts of a New Testament book.

Morphology.—In the same way, when we pass to Morphology, it is again to discover that many verbal forms, with which our best New Testament texts have made us familiar, can here be amply attested. One of the commonest of these is the attaching of 1st aorist forms to the 2nd aorist, as when in Mt 10²³ we read ἐλθάτω for ἐλθέτω, and in Mk 3⁸ ἦλθαν for ἦλθον. The practice, already present in the Attic εἶπον, meets us repeatedly in the papyri, as well as in late Hellenistic writers generally. Similarly, γέγοναν for γεγόνασι, which Westcott and Hort read in Rom 16⁷, in accordance with ℵ A, receives frequent corroboration, as in an almost contemporary papyrus letter from the Fayûm.[1] An interesting form, which may cause trouble, if it is not watched, is the substitution of ἐάν for ἄν after ὅς, ὅπου, etc., which the same editors have faithfully reproduced from the leading manuscripts in such passages as Mt 12³² ὃς ἐὰν εἴπῃ and Mk 14⁹ ὅπου ἐὰν κηρυχθῇ. Professor J. H. Moulton has carefully examined the evidence of the papyri on this point, and has found that in the first and second centuries of the Christian era ἐάν greatly predominated, but that, as a form of ἄν, it had almost died out in ordinary usage before the great uncials were written. The fact, therefore, that their scribes preserved ἐάν may be taken as showing that they "faithfully reproduce originals written under conditions long since obsolete."[2]

Syntax.—This last example may fittingly introduce us to the field of Syntax, and to Moulton and Howard's invaluable *Grammar*, where at every turn the evidence of the newly-discovered vernacular documents is called in to decide corresponding usages in the New Testament writings. One or two examples will show how rich and suggestive that evidence is.

Take, for instance, the prepositions, and an impartial survey can hardly fail to lead us to the conclusion that the laxer usage which is everywhere observable in later Greek hardly justifies many of the over-niceties of interpretation in which New Testament expositors have been apt to indulge. The free interchange of εἰς and ἐν is a case in point. This may be carried back to the fact that both words are originally forms of the same root; but what we are especially concerned with is that they are largely interchanged in ordinary usage, as when in a letter of A.D. 22 the writer tells us that when he came to Alexandria (ἐπὶ τῷ γεγονέναι ἐν Ἀλεξανδρίᾳ), he learnt so and so from certain fishermen at Alexandria (εἰς Ἀλεξάνδρι[αν]).[3] When, then, in commenting on Jn 1¹⁸ ὁ ὢν εἰς τὸν κόλπον τοῦ πατρός, Bishop Westcott speaks of the phrase as implying "the combination (as it were) of rest and motion, of a continuous relation, with a realisation of it," is he not pressing the phraseology farther than contemporary evidence warrants, however doctrinally true the deduction may be? Nor can those who advocate the rendering "immersing them into the name of the Father and of the Son and of the Holy Spirit" for the baptismal formula in Mt 28¹⁹ do so on the ground that the more familiar rendering is philologically inaccurate. Without entering on the question as to the exact shade of meaning underlying βαπτίζοντες, it is clear that εἰς τὸ ὄνομα may be understood as practically equivalent to ἐν τῷ ὀνόματι, the new light thus joining

---

[1] BGU II. 597¹⁹ (A.D. 75).   [2] *Prolegomena*, p. 421.
[3] P Oxy II. 294⁵·⁶ (A.D. 22) (= *Selections*, p. 34).

hands with, and lending support to, the almost unanimous tradition of the Western Church.[1]

A corresponding caution must be observed in connexion with the construction of ἵνα. Classical Greek has taught us to expect that ἵνα construed with the subjunctive denotes purpose, but in Hellenistic Greek this has been extended to include a consecutive usage, and sometimes, as in modern Greek, a simple statement of fact. When, therefore, in Jn 17³ the Fourth Evangelist writes—αὕτη δέ ἐστιν ἡ αἰώνιος ζωὴ ἵνα γινώσκωσι σὲ τὸν μόνον ἀληθινὸν θεὸν καὶ ὃν ἀπέστειλας Ἰησοῦν Χριστόν it is of course possible that by the latter clause he means us to understand our Lord as pointing to the knowledge of God as the aim and end of eternal life. But it is equally permissible, and more in accord with contemporary usage, to interpret the words as defining the contents of the life eternal : this life is a life consisting in, and maintained by, the knowledge of God, and of Him whom God had sent.

It would be easy to go on multiplying examples in this direction, but enough has been said to show that the syntax of the New Testament is not modelled on strictly classical lines, and that this must be kept steadily in view in the work of interpretation.

Vocabulary.—It is, however, in the matter of Vocabulary that the new gains make themselves most fully felt, and prove most clearly that we are dealing with a book written in the common speech of its day.

This is seen, for example, in the large reduction in the number of so-called " Biblical " words, that is, words which have hitherto been regarded as the special property of the Biblical writers, no evidence of their use having hitherto been procurable from profane sources.

Thayer, at the end of his edition of Grimm's Lexicon, gives a long list of these " Biblical " words, the very length of which tends to confirm that feeling of the isolated or peculiar character of the New Testament writings, to which reference has already been made. The list is unnecessarily long even from Thayer's point of view, as it includes not a few words for which he himself supplies references from non-Christian sources, which, though sometimes later in point of time than the New Testament itself, nevertheless show unmistakably that the words belong to the ordinary stock then in use. And now the new evidence comes in to extend these references in so many directions that Deissmann is able to reduce the number of words peculiar to the New Testament to something like fifty, or about one per cent. of the whole vocabulary.[2]

Our new sources do not merely reduce the number of words hitherto regarded as peculiar to the New Testament writings ; they also confirm the meanings traditionally assigned to others, sometimes on somewhat slender grounds.

A familiar instance is the Pauline word λογεία. According to Grimm-Thayer, the word is " not found in profane authors," but for its meaning in 1 Cor 16¹⁻², the only places where it occurs in the New Testament, the translation " a collection " is suggested. Such a translation is in harmony with the context, and is now conclusively established by the fact that from the second century B.C. the word is found in the papyri in this sense. It is sufficient to refer to a curious letter from Tebtunis, in which a tax-gatherer, after naively describing his unprincipled efforts to defeat a rival in the collection of a certain tax, adds, " I bid you urge on Nicon regarding the collection (περὶ τῆς λογε‹ί›ας). " [3]

---

[1] See the discussion between Bishop Chase and Dean Armitage Robinson in *J T S* vi. p. 481 ff., vii. p. 186 ff., and viii. p. 161 ff., and on the phrase generally, cf. Heitmüller, *Im Namen Jesu*, Göttingen, 1903.

[2] See *Light from the Ancient East*,² p. 78.   [3] P Tebt I. 58⁵⁵ (B.C. 111).

c

Or, to take a wholly different example, when in a letter of A.D. 41,[1] a man counsels a friend in money-difficulties to plead with one of his creditors μὴ ἵνα ἀναστατώσῃς ἡμᾶς, "do not unsettle us," that is "do not drive us out from hearth and home," he little thought that he would supply future students of the New Testament with an apt parallel for the metaphorical use of the same verb in Gal 5¹², where St. Paul expresses the hope that οἱ ἀναστατοῦντες, "those who are unsettling" his Galatian converts, "would even mutilate themselves." So too the naughty boy's admission from Oxyrhynchus that his mother complains "that he is upsetting me" (ὅτι ἀναστατοῖ με)[2] throws light upon the description of the brethren at Thessalonica by their Jewish opponents, "These that have turned the world upside down (οἱ τὴν οἰκουμένην ἀναστατώσαντες) have come hither also" (Ac 17⁶).[3]

Similar aid is given in the choice of meaning where more than one rendering is possible. In Mt 6²⁷, for example, both the Authorized and Revised Versions agree in rendering ἡλικία by "stature," "And which of you by being anxious can add one cubit unto his stature?" but the margin of the Revised Version has "age"; and if we are to follow the almost unanimous testimony of the papyri, this latter sense should be adopted throughout the New Testament occurrences of the word, except in Lk 19³, where the context makes it impossible. Thus in the important verse, Lk 2⁵² καὶ Ἰησοῦς προέκοπτεν τῇ σοφίᾳ καὶ ἡλικίᾳ, the meaning is not that Jesus "advanced in wisdom and stature," that is "in height and comeliness" (as Grimm-Thayer), but "in wisdom and age," a description to which an excellent parallel is now afforded by an inscription of ii/B.C., in which a certain Aristagoras is praised as—ἡλικίᾳ προκόπτων καὶ προαγόμενος εἰς τὸ θεοσεβεῖν.[4]

Again, in not a few instances, our new documents supply us with the true meaning of words only imperfectly understood before.

In commenting on 1 Pet 1⁷ ἵνα τὸ δοκίμιον ὑμῶν τῆς πίστεως πολυτιμότερον χρυσίου τοῦ ἀπολλυμένου διὰ πυρὸς δὲ δοκιμαζομένου εὑρεθῇ εἰς ἔπαινον καὶ δόξαν καὶ τιμὴν ἐν ἀποκαλύψει Ἰησοῦ Χριστοῦ Dr. Hort (Comm. ad l.) saw that the meaning required was "the approved part or element of the faith," that is, the pure faith that remained when the dross had been purged away by fiery trial; but unable to find any warrant for this sense of δοκίμιον, he was driven to suspect that the true reading was δόκιμον, for which he had the support of a few cursives. There was no need, however, for any such conjecture. Ever since Deissmann[5] first drew attention to the importance of the evidence of the papyri in this connexion, examples have been rapidly accumulating to show that δοκίμιος, as well as δόκιμος, means "proved," "genuine," in such a phrase as χρυσὸς δοκίμιος, "tested gold," and we need no longer have any hesitation in so translating the word both in the Petrine passage and in Jas 1³.

Or, to take another example, where the appearance of a hitherto unestablished usage has again done away with the need of textual emendation. In Ac 16¹² ἥτις ἐστὶν πρώτη τῆς μερίδος Μακεδονίας πόλις, the reading μερίδος was objected to by Dr. Hort, on the ground that μερίς never denotes simply a region or province, and he proposed accordingly to read Πιερίδος in its stead, "a chief city of Pierian Macedonia."[6] But while it is true that μερίς in the sense of a geographical division does not occur in classical writers, it is regularly so used in documents of the Apostolic age, so that the rendering "district" in the Revised Version, however arrived at, need no longer raise any qualms.

[1] BGU IV. 1079 (= Selections, No. 15).   [2] P Oxy I. 119 (= Selections, No. 42).

[3] It may be noted that the phrase ἆρον αὐτόν, "Away with him," applied to the boy in the above document, supplies a striking linguistic parallel to Jn 19¹⁵ ἆρον, ἆρον, σταύρωσον αὐτόν.

[4] Syll 325 (= ³ 708)¹⁸.   [5] See BS p. 259 ff.   [6] Notes on Select Readings,² p. 96 f.

It is, however, by imparting a fresh life and reality to many of our most ordinary New Testament terms that the new authorities render their most signal service. We know how our very familiarity with Scriptural language is apt to blind us to its full significance. But when we find words and phrases, which we have hitherto associated only with a religious meaning, in common, everyday use, and employed in circumstances where their meaning can raise no question, we make a fresh start with them, and get a clearer insight into their deeper application.

Take, for instance, the common designation of Christians as "brethren" or "brothers" (ἀδελφοί). The practice no doubt was taken over from Judaism (Ac 2²⁹, ⁷, al.) and from the example of our Lord Himself (cf. Mt 12¹⁸, 23⁸); but we can at least see how the adoption of such a term was rendered easier by its application to the members of a funeral society, whose duty it was to take part in the embalming of dead bodies, or again to the "fellows" of a religious corporation in the Serapeum of Memphis.[1]

So with the title "presbyter" (πρεσβύτερος). Without entering on the question of the presbyter's place and authority in the early Christian Church, it is obvious that the use of the word in civil life to denote a local or village officer must have prepared the way in Gentile circles for its acceptance in its new connotation. Thus in the year B.C. 117 a tax-farmer petitions the village-scribe and "the elders of the cultivators," that he may be assured of official "protection."[2] Or, again, in A.D. 114 a woman lodges a complaint of assault and robbery against another woman whose husband as "elder" was responsible for the peace and order of the village.[3] Or once more, in a document of A.D. 159–60, mention is made of the priests of the Soenopaeus temple as being divided into five tribes under the rule of five "elder-priests"—clearly a title not of age but of dignity.[4] It is in this same document, we may note in passing, that the charge is laid against a fellow-priest "of letting his hair grow too long and of wearing woollen garments"—the former item recalling the fact that in the Early Church short hair was considered the mark of a Christian teacher, as compared with the unshorn locks of the heathen philosopher.

Keeping still to words with an ecclesiastical ring about them, the term "liturgy" has an interesting history. In classical times it was used of public services rendered gratuitously to the State, but later it came to be applied to all kinds of work or service, including those of a religious character, such as the "liturgy" of the Twin Sisters Thaues and Thaus, who held some position as attendants in the temple of Serapis at Memphis, with a corresponding right to certain allowances of oil and bread, which were apparently frequently in arrears.[5] Similarly the corresponding verb is used in a contract of the year A.D. 8–9 with an *artiste* who undertakes to give her "services" (λειτουργεῖν) on certain specified occasions, including the festivals of Isis and Hera, at a salary of forty drachmae a year, along with a further wage or present (ὀψώνιον) of thirteen drachmae two obols.[6]

Other more general uses of the word occur in connexion with the maintenance of the banks of the Nile, or with the release of persons from some public service "because it is not at present their turn to serve (διὰ τὸ μὴ ἐκπεσ[τ]εῖ]ν αὐτοῖς τὸ νῦν λειτουργῆσαι)."[7] Very interesting too is a doctor's claim for exemption, on the ground that he was a doctor by profession, and had "treated medically" (ἐθεράπευσα: cf. Ac 28⁹ and Ramsay, *Luke*,

---

[1] P Tor I. 1⁵·²⁹ (B.C. 116); P Par 42¹ (B.C. 156) (but see *UPZ* i. p. 319).

[2] P Tebt I. 40 (= *Selections*, No. 10).

[3] BGU I. 22 (= *Selections*, No. 29).   [4] BGU I. 16 (= *Selections*, No. 33).

[5] The story of the Twins has been graphically reconstructed by Sir F. G. Kenyon in P Lond I. p. 2 ff.

[6] P Oxy IV. No. 731.   [7] P Hib I. 78¹¹ (B.C. 244–3).

p. 16 f.) the very persons who were now attempting to lay this new "liturgy" upon him (οἵτινές με εἰς λειτο[υ]ρ[γ]ίαν δεδώκασι).[1]

I admit, of course, that none of these instances adds materially to our knowledge of the word's connotation, but they give it fresh point, and enable us to understand how well-adapted it was to describe the "liturgy" or "ministry" of Christian fellowship (cf. 2 Cor 9¹², Phil 2¹⁷·³⁰), and all the more so, because the word has now come to be almost wholly limited to a particular form of public worship.

Its occurrence in the current phraseology of the time adds again a fresh reality to the Greek word (ἀρραβών), which is usually translated "earnest" in our English Versions. We have all been taught that by the "earnest" of the Spirit in such passages as 2 Cor 1²², 5⁵, Eph 1¹⁴, we are to understand a part given in advance of what will be bestowed fully afterwards. But how increasingly clear this becomes when a woman who is selling a cow receives a thousand drachmae as an "earnest" (ἀρραβῶνα) on the total purchase-money,[2] or when certain dancing girls at a village entertainment receive so many drachmae "by way of earnest" (ὑπὲρ ἀραβῶνος) on their promised salary![3]

Much help can also be derived from the legal documents, which are so common amongst the papyri. Thus in his pioneer *Bible Studies* (p. 104 ff.), Deissmann has shown that the Greek adjective (βέβαιος) usually translated "sure" or "steadfast" in our English Versions, along with its cognate verb (βεβαιόω) and substantive (βεβαίωσις), is the regular technical term in the papyri to denote legally guaranteed security. This sense occurs, of course, in classical Greek, but its constant reappearance in the papyri gives fresh point to the New Testament usage. Two examples will make this clear. In an application for a lease belonging to the year A.D. 78, and therefore practically contemporary with the New Testament writings, provision is made for the publication of the lease for the legal period of ten days "in order that if no one makes a higher bid (ἐπίθεμα), the lease may remain guaranteed (βεβαία) to us for the period of five years without change,"[4] and, similarly, in a somewhat later document (A.D. 266), connected with the registration of a deed, it is laid down, "I will further guarantee the property always against all claims with every guarantee" (ἔτι τε καὶ παρέξομαί σοι βέβαια διὰ παντὸς ἀπὸ πάντων πάσῃ βεβαιώσει).[5] Read, then, the verb with this technical sense in view, and what added assurance it gives to the promise of 1 Cor 1⁷ : "Thus you lack no spiritual endowment during these days of waiting till our Lord Jesus Christ is revealed ; and to the very end he will guarantee (βεβαιώσει) that you are vindicated on the day of our Lord Jesus Christ" (Moffatt), just as another legal term (ὑπόστασις), which was used to denote the collection of papers bearing upon the possession of a piece of property, or as we would now say, the title-deeds, imparts a new certainty to the familiar definition—"Faith is the title-deed (ὑπόστασις) of things hoped for" (Heb 11¹).

In what are probably the earliest of his letters that have come down to us, the two Epistles to the Thessalonians, St. Paul finds it necessary to rebuke his converts for walking "in a disorderly manner" (2 Thess 3¹¹). The word (ἀτάκτως), with its cognates, is confined to these Epistles in the New Testament, and what exactly is meant by it is by no means clear at first sight. Is St. Paul referring to actual sin or moral disorder, or to something less heinous? The papyri have supplied the answer in a striking manner. Among them is a contract of A.D. 66 in which a father arranges to apprentice his son with a weaver for one year. All the conditions of the contract as regards food and clothing

[1] P Oxy I. 40⁶ (ii/iii A.D.).　　　　[2] P Par 58¹⁴ (B.C. 153) (= *UPZ* i. p. 325).
[3] P Grenf II. 67¹⁷ (A.D. 237) (= *Selections*, No. 45).
[4] P Amh II. 85²⁰⁶.　　　　[5] P Oxy IX. 1200²⁴.

are carefully laid down. Then follows the passage which specially interests us. If there are any days during this period on which the boy "fails to attend" or "plays truant" (ὅσας δ' ἐὰν ἐν τούτῳ ἀτακτήσῃ ἡμέρας), the father has to produce him for an equivalent number of days after the period is over. And the verb which is used to denote playing truant is the same verb which St. Paul uses in connexion with the Thessalonians.[1] This then was their fault. They were idling, playing truant. The *Parousia* of the Lord seemed to them to be so close at hand that it was unnecessary for them to interest themselves in anything else. Why go to their daily work in the morning, when before night Christ might have come, they thought, forgetting that the best way to prepare for that coming was to show themselves active and diligent in the discharge of their daily work and duty.

The reference to the *Parousia* may suggest a last example. *Parousia*, as applied to the Return of the Lord, is simply the anglicizing of a Greek word (παρουσία) which literally means "presence." But in late Greek the word had come to be applied in a quasi-technical sense to the "visit" of a king or great man. Thus in a papyrus of iii/B.C. we read of a district that was mulcted to provide a "crown" for one of the Ptolemaic kings on the occasion of his "visit"; and in a letter of about the same date a certain Apenneus writes that he has made preparations for the "visit" of a magistrate Chrysippus (ἐπὶ τὴν παρουσίαν τοῦ Χρυσίππου) by laying in a number of birds for his consumption, including geese and young pigeons.[2]

It would seem, therefore, that as distinguished from other words associated with Christ's Coming, such as His "manifestation" (ἐπιφάνεια) of the Divine power and His "revelation" (ἀποκάλυψις) of the Divine plan, the "parousia" leads us rather to think of His "royal visit" to His people, whether we think of the First Coming at the Incarnation, or of the Final Coming as Judge.

The Literary Character of the New Testament.—These examples are sufficient to show that it is often from the most unlikely quarters that light is shed upon our New Testament vocabulary, and that a scrap of papyrus may be the means of settling some long-standing *crux interpretum*. I would not, however, be understood to say that the later Greek which we associate with the papyri has no rules of its own, or that, in the hands of the New Testament writers, it is not often employed with marked literary grace and power. The writers, of course, differ largely in this connexion, in keeping with their individual education and culture. At one end of the scale, we have the rude Greek of St. Mark's Gospel, or of the Apocalypse: at the other, the polished periods of the author of the Epistle to the Hebrews. But even in the case of the least literary writings of the New Testament we must beware of so emphasizing their popular character as to lose sight of the dignity and beauty imparted to them in virtue of the subject-matter with which they deal and the spiritual genius of their authors. "In the Gospels," as Professor Wellhausen has pointed out, "spoken Greek, and even Greek as spoken amongst the lower classes, has made its entry into literature."[3] And Professor Jülicher has borne similar testimony with reference to the Pauline Epistles. "These Epistles," he writes, "in spite of the fact that they are always intended as writings of the moment addressed to a narrow circle of readers, yet approach much more nearly to the position of independent literary works than the average letters of great men in modern times. . . . Without knowing or intending it, Paul became by his letters the creator of a Christian literature." And more than that, Paul, as

[1] P Oxy II. No. 275 (= *Selections*, No. 20).
[2] P Petr II. 39 (e)[18] (as read by Wilcken *Ostr.* i. p. 275); P Grenf II. 14 (h)[2].
[3] *Einleitung in die drei ersten Evangelien* (Berlin, 1905), p. 9.

the same authority admits, "must be ranked as a great master of language, . . . and it is because his innermost self breathes through every word that most of his Epistles bear so unique a charm."[1] It is utterly unnecessary to labour the point. Such passages as the triumphant Hymn of Hope in Rom 8 and the glorious Hymn of Love in 1 Cor 13 are moved by a heart-felt eloquence which makes them, regarded as literature, as notable as anything ever penned. And if we are told that the Pauline letters "differ from the messages of the homely Papyrus leaves from Egypt not as letters, but only as the letters of *Paul*,"[2] we can accept the statement (though hardly in the sense the writer intended it), because it is just " Paul," and what Paul stands for, that does make all the difference.

G. MILLIGAN.

[1] *An Introduction to the New Testament*, translated by Janet Penrose Ward (London, 1904), pp. 48 f., 51.

[2] Deissmann, *BS*, p. 44.

ABBREVIATIONS

I. GENERAL

Abbott *Fourfold Gospel* .... = *The Fourfold Gospel*, Section II. *The Beginning*, by E. A. Abbott. Cambridge, 1914.

„ *Joh. Gr.*...... = *Johannine Grammar*, by the same. London, 1906.

„ *Joh. Voc.*.... = *Johannine Vocabulary*, by the same. London, 1905.

Abbott *Songs* .... = *Songs of Modern Greece*, by G. F. Abbott. Cambridge, 1900.

Aegyptus .... = *Aegyptus. Rivista Italiana di Egittologia e di Papirologia.* Ed. A. Calderini. Milan, 1920- .

AJP .... = *The American Journal of Philology.* Baltimore, 1880- .

AJT .... = *The American Journal of Theology.* Chicago, 1897- .

Anz *Subsidia* .... = *Subsidia ad cognoscendum Graecorum sermonem vulgarem e Pentateuchi versione Alexandrina repetita* (being *Diss. philolog. Halenses*, xii. 2), by H. Anz. Halle, 1894.

Archiv. .... = *Archiv für Papyrusforschung.* Ed. U. Wilcken. Leipzig, 1901- .

Aristeas .... = *Aristeae ad Philocratem Epistula.* Ed. P. Wendland. Leipzig, 1900.

Artemidorus or Artem. = *Artemidori Daldiani Onirocriticon Libri V.* Ed. R. Hercher. Leipzig, 1864.

BCH .... = *Bulletin de Correspondance Hellénique.* Paris and Athens. 1877- .

Berger *Strafklauseln* = *Die Strafklauseln in den Papyrusurkunden*, von A. Berger. Leipzig, 1911.

Berichtigungen .... = *Berichtigungsliste der Griechischen Papyrusurkunden aus Ägypten*, herausgegeben von F. Preisigke. Berlin und Leipzig, 1922.

Birt *Buchrolle*......... = *Die Buchrolle in der Kunst*, von Theodor Birt. Leipzig, 1907.

Blass *Gr.* .... = *Grammar of New Testament Greek*, by F. Blass. Eng. tr. by H. St. John Thackeray. Second edit. London, 1905.

Blass *Philology* ...... = *Philology of the Gospels*, by Friedrich Blass. London, 1898.

Blass-Debrunner...... = *Friedrich Blass' Grammatik des neutestamentlichen Griechisch.* Fünfte Aufl. von A. Debrunner. Göttingen, 1921.

Boisacq *Dict. Etym.*.. = *Dictionnaire Étymologique de la Langue Grecque*, par Émile Boisacq. Heidelberg and Paris, 1916.

Boll *Offenbarung* .... = *Aus der Offenbarung Johannis: Hellenistische Studien zum Weltbild der Apokalypse*, von Franz Boll. Leipzig, 1914.

Bonhöffer *Epiktet.* = *Epiktet und das Neue Testament* (being *Religionsgeschichtliche Versuche und Vorarbeiten*, herausgegeben von R. Wünsch und L. Deubner, X), von Adolf Bonhöffer. Giessen, 1911.

Brugmann *Grundriss*² = *Grundriss der vergleichenden Grammatik der indogermanischen Sprachen*, von Karl Brugmann. Zweite Bearbeitung. Strassburg, 1897.

Brugmann-Thumb.... = *Griechische Grammatik*, von Karl Brugmann. Vierte vermehrte Aufl., von Albert Thumb. Munich, 1913.

BS. .... See under Deissmann.

Burkitt *Syriac Forms* = *The Syriac Forms of New Testament Proper Names*, by F. C. Burkitt. London, [1912].

BZ. .... = *Byzantinische Zeitschrift.* Ed. K. Krumbacher. Leipzig, 1892- .

Cadbury *Diction* ...... = *The Style and Literary Method of Luke.* I. *The Diction of Luke and Acts.* II. *The Treatment of Sources in the Gospel* (being *Harvard Theological Studies*, VI.), by Henry J. Cadbury. Harvard University Press, 1919, 1920.

Conybeare and Stock *LXX Selections*.... = *Selections from the Septuagint*, by F. C. Conybeare and St. George Stock. Boston, [1905].

CQ .... = *The Classical Quarterly.* London, 1907- .

CR............ = *The Classical Review.* London, 1887- .

CRE............ See under Ramsay.

Cronert or Cronert
Lex............ = *Passow's Worterbuch der griechischen Sprache,* völlig neu bearbeitet von W. Crönert. 3 parts. Göttingen, 1912-14.

Cronert *Mem. Herc.* = *Memoria Graeca Herculanensis,* by W. Cronert. Leipzig, 1903.

Deissmann *BS*......... = *Bible Studies,* by G. Adolf Deissmann. Engl. ed. by A. Grieve. Edinburgh, 1901.

,, *Festgabe...* = *Festgabe für Adolf Deissmann zum 60. Geburtstag 7. November 1926.* Tübingen, 1927.

,, *in Christo* = *Die neutestamentliche Formel " in Christo Jesu,"* von G. Adolf Deissmann. Marburg, 1892.

,, *LAE* and *LAE²*...... = *Light from the Ancient East,* by Adolf Deissmann. English translation by Lionel R. M. Strachan. London, 1910 and 1927.

,, *Philology* ... = *The Philology of the Greek Bible: its Present and Future,* by Adolf Deissmann. English translation by Lionel R. M. Strachan. London, 1908.

,, *Sprachliche Erforschung..* = *Die sprachliche Erforschung der griechischen Bibel* (being *Vorträge der theologischen Konferenz zu Giessen. XII. Folge*), von G. Adolf Deissmann. Giessen, 1898.

,, *Urgeschichte* = *Die Urgeschichte des Christentums im Lichte der Sprachforschung,* von Adolf Deissmann. Tübingen, 1910.

Dieterich *Abraxas* ... = *Abraxas: Studien zur Religionsgeschichte des Spätern Altertums,* von Albrecht Dieterich. Leipzig, 1891.

,, *Mithrasliturgie* = *Eine Mithrasliturgie* erläutert von Albrecht Dieterich. 2te Aufl. Leipzig and Berlin, 1910.

Dieterich *Untersuch* = *Untersuchungen zur Geschichte der Griechischen Sprache, von der Hellenistischen Zeit bis zum 10. Jahrh. n. Chr.,* von Karl Dieterich. Leipzig, 1898.

Diog. Oenoand...... = *Diogenis Oenoandensis fragmenta* Ed. I. William. Leipzig, 1907.

Documents .... See under Milligan.

Durham, D. B.
Menander .... = *The Vocabulary of Menander, considered in its relation to the Koine.* Princetown, 1913.

EB .... = *Encyclopedia Biblica.* London, 1899-1903.

EEF .... = Egypt Exploration Fund.

EGT .... = *The Expositor's Greek Testament,* edited by W. Robertson Nicoll. 5 vols. London, 1897-1910.

Epicurea ...... See under Usener.

Erman und Krebs ... = *Aus den Papyrus der Königlichen Museen [zu Berlin],* von A. Erman und F. Krebs. Berlin, 1899.

Exler *Epistolography* = *The Form of the Ancient Greek Letter. A Study in Greek Epistolography.* By Francis Xavier J. Exler. Catholic University of America, Washington D.C. 1923.

Exp. .... = *The Expositor.* London, 1875- . Cited by series, volume, and page.

ExpT .... = *The Expository Times.* Edinburgh, 1889- .

Ferguson, W. D.
Legal Terms...... = *The Legal Terms Common to the Macedonian Inscriptions and the New Testament* (being *Historical and Linguistic Studies in Literature related to the New Testament.* 2nd Series, Vol. II., Part 3), by W. D. Ferguson. Chicago, 1913.

Field *Notes..........* = *Notes on the Translation of the New Testament* (being *Otium Norvicense* iii.), by F. Field. Cambridge, 1899.

Foucart *Associations Religieuses* .... = *Des Associations Religieuses chez les Grecs.* Par P. Foucart. Paris, 1873.

Gerhard *Erbstreit* .... = *Ein grako-ägyptischer Erbstreit aus dem zweiten Jahrhundert vor Chr.* (being *Sitzungsberichte der Heidelberger Akademie der Wissenschaften,* 8. Abhandlung), von G. A. Gerhard. Heidelberg, 1911.

GH............ = Grenfell and Hunt. See further under Abbreviations II. Papyri.

Ghedini *Lettere*........ = *Lettere Christiane dai Papiri Greci del III e IV Secolo.* Ed. G. Ghedini. Milan, 1923.

Giles *Manual..........* = *A Short Manual of Comparative Philology for Classical Students,* by P. Giles, M.A. Second edit. London, 1901.

Glaser *De ratione....* = *De ratione, quae intercedit inter sermonem Polybii et eum, qui in titulis saeculi III, II, I apparet,* by Otto Glaser. Giessen, 1894.

Gradenwitz *Einführung* .... = *Einführung in die Papyruskunde,* von O. Gradenwitz. Heft i. Leipzig, 1900.

Grimm or Grimm-
Thayer............... = *A Greek-English Lexicon of the
New Testament*, being Grimm's
Wilke's *Clavis Novi Testamenti*,
tr. and enlarged by J. H. Thayer.
Second edit. Edinburgh, 1890.
[Thayer's additions are usually
cited under his name.]

Hatch *Essays*.......... = *Essays in Biblical Greek*, by E.
Hatch. Oxford, 1889.

Hatzidakis *Einl.* ... = *Einleitung in die Neugriechische
Grammatik*, von G. N. Hatzi-
dakis. Leipzig, 1892.

Heinrici *Litt. Char.* = *Der litterarische Charakter der
neutestamentlichen Schriften*,
von C. F. Georg Heinrici.
Leipzig, 1908.

Helbing *Gr.*........... = *Grammatik der Septuaginta: Laut-
und Wortlehre*, von R. Hel-
bing. Göttingen, 1907.

Herwerden or Her-
werden *Lex.*.......... = *Lexicon Graecum Suppletorium et
Dialecticum²*, by H. van Her-
werden. 2 vols. Leiden, 1910.

Hesychius.............. = *Hesychii Alexandrini Lexicon*,
ed. M. Schmidt. Jena, 1867.

Hobart................. = *The Medical Language of St. Luke*,
by W. K. Hobart. Dublin and
London, 1882.

Hohlwein *L'Égypte
Romaine*............... = *L'Égypte Romaine. Recueil des
Termes Techniques relatifs aux
Institutions Politiques et Admin-
istratives de l'Égypte Romaine,
suivi d'un choix de Textes
Papyrologiques*, par N. Hohl-
wein. Brussels, 1912.

HR.................... = *A Concordance to the Septuagint*,
by E. Hatch and H. A. Redpath.
Oxford, 1897.

HZNT................. = *Handbuch zum Neuen Testament*,
ed. H. Lietzmann. Tübingen,
1906- .

ICC.................. = *International Critical Commentary*.
Edinburgh. Various dates.

Jannaris *Gr.*........... = *An Historical Greek Grammar*, by
A. N. Jannaris. London, 1897.

JBL.................. = *The Journal of Biblical Literature*.
Middletown, 1881- .

J.Eg.Arch. .... = *The Journal of Egyptian Archæ-
ology*. London, 1914- .

JHS .... = *The Journal of Hellenic Studies*.
London, 1880- .

Jouguet *Vie municipale* = *La Vie Municipale dans l'Égypte
Romaine* (being *Bibliothèque des
Écoles Françaises d'Athènes et
de Rome*, 104), par P. Jouguet.
Paris, 1911.

JTS.................. = *The Journal of Theological Studies*,
London, 1900- .

Kaelker *Quaest* ...... = *Quaestiones de Elocutione Polybiana*
(being *Leipziger Studien* III.

ii.). by F. Kaelker. Leipzig,
1880.

Kennedy *Sources*... = *Sources of New Testament Greek*,
by H. A. A. Kennedy. Edin-
burgh, 1895.

Krebs *Präp.*.......... = *Die Präpositionen bei Polybius*
(being *Beiträge zur Historischen
Syntax der Griechischen Sprache*,
ii. von F. Krebs. Würzburg,
1882.

Kühner³. or Kühner-
Blass, Kühner-Gerth = *Ausführliche Grammatik der
Griechischen Sprache*, von R.
Kühner, besorgt von F. Blass
(Formenlehre) und B. Gerth
(Satzlehre). Hanover and Leip-
zig, 1890-1904.

Kuhring.............. = *De Praepositionum Graecarum in
Chartis Aegyptiis Usu Quaes-
tiones Selectae*, by G. Kuhring.
Bonn, 1906.

LAE. .... See under Deissmann.

Lafoscade *De epi-
tulis* .... = *De epistulis (aliisque titulis) im-
peratorum magistratuumque Ro-
manorum quas ab aetate Augusti
usque ad Constantinum Graece
scriptas lapides papyrive rexa-
verunt*, par Léon Lafoscade.
Paris, 1902.

Laqueur *Quaestiones* = *Quaestiones Epigraphicae et Papyro-
logicae Selectae*, by R. Laqueur.
Strassburg, 1904.

Lewy *Fremdwörter*.. = *Die Semitischen Fremdwörter im
Griechischen*, von H. Lewy.
Berlin, 1895.

Lietzmann *Gr. Pap.* = *Griechische Papyri* (in *Kleine Texte
für theologische Vorlesungen und
Übungen*, 14). Ed. H. Lietzmann. Bonn, 1905. English
edition, Cambridge, 1905.

Linde *Epic* .... = *De Epicuri Vocabulis ab optima
Atthide alienis* (being *Breslauer
Philologische Abhandlungen*, ix.
3), by P. Linde. Breslau,
1906.

Lob. *Par.*........... = *Paralipomena Grammaticae Graecae*,
by C. A. Lobeck. Leipzig,
1837.

,, *Phryn.*........... = *Phrynichi Ecloga*. Ed. C. A. Lobeck. Leipzig, 1820.

LS⁸ and LS⁹ .... = *A Greek-English Lexicon*, com-
piled by H. G. Liddell and
R. Scott. Eighth edition. Oxford, 1901. Ninth edition.
Oxford, 1925- .

Luckhard *Privathaus* = *Das Privathaus im ptolemäischen
und römischen Ägypten*, by F.
Luckhard. Giessen, 1914.

Lumbroso *Raccolta*... = Raccolta di scritti in onore di
Giacomo Lumbroso (1844-1925).
Milan, 1925.

Magie .... = *De Romanorum iuris publici sacrique vocabulis sollemnibus in Graecum sermonem conversis,* by D. Magie. Leipzig, 1905.

Maidhof *Begriffsbestimmung* .... = *Zur Begriffsbestimmung der Koine, besonders auf Grund des Attizisten Moiris* (being *Beiträge zur Historischen Syntax der Griechischen Sprache,* 20), von A. Maidhof. Würzburg, 1912.

Martin *Épistratèges* = *Les Épistratèges, Contribution à l'Étude des Institutions de l'Égypte Gréco-Romaine,* par Victor Martin. Geneva, 1911.

Mayser *Gr.* .... = *Grammatik der Griechischen Papyri aus der Ptolemäerzeit. Laut- und Wortlehre,* von E. Mayser. Leipzig, 1906.

,, *Gr.* II. i. ... = *Ib.* II. *Satzlehre, Analytischer Teil* i., von E. Mayser. Berlin u. Leipzig, 1926.

Meecham *Letters* ...... = *Light from Ancient Letters.* By Henry G. Meecham. London, [1923].

Meisterhans *Gr.* ...... = *Grammatik der attischen Inschriften,* von K. Meisterhans. Dritte Auflage von E. Schwyzer. Berlin, 1900.

Mél. Chatelain .... = *Mélanges offerts à M. Émile Chatelain.* Paris, 1910.

Mél. Nicole .... = *Mélanges . . . offerts à Jules Nicole.* Geneva, 1905.

Menander *Fragm.* ... = *Comicorum Atticorum Fragmenta,* III. Ed. Th. Kock. Leipzig, 1888.

,, *Selections* = *Selections from Menander,* edited by W. G. Waddell, M.A. Oxford, 1927.

Menandrea .... = *Menandrea ex papyris et membranis vetustissimis.* Ed. A. Körte. Leipzig, 1912.

Meyer *Gr.* .... = *Griechische Grammatik*[3], von Gustav Meyer. Leipzig, 1896.

Meyer *Heerwesen* .... = *Das Heerwesen der Ptolemäer und Römer in Ägypten,* von Paul M. Meyer. Leipzig, 1900.

,, *Jur. Pap.* ...... = *Juristische Papyri. Erklärung von Urkunden zur Einführung in die Juristische Papyruskunde,* von Paul M. Meyer. Berlin, 1920.

MGr .... = Modern Greek.

Milligan *Documents* = *The New Testament Documents: Their Origin and Early History,* by George Milligan. London, 1913. [Out of print.]

,, *Here and There* ... = *Here and There among the Papyri,* by the same. London, 1923. [Out of print.]

,, *Selections* ... = *Selections from the Greek Papyri,*

by the same. New edit. Cambridge, 1927.

,, *Thess.* .... = *St. Paul's Epistles to the Thessalonians,* by the same. London, 1908.

Mitteis or Wilcken *Papyruskunde* ...... = *Grundzüge und Chrestomathie der Papyruskunde* I. i. ed. U. Wilcken, and II. i. ed. L. Mitteis. Leipzig and Berlin, 1912. See also Abbreviations II. *Papyri* s.v. *Chrest.*

Modica *Introduzione* = *Introduzione allo Studio della Papirologia Giuridica,* by M. Modica. Milan, [1913].

Moeris .... = *Moeridis Atticistae Lexicon Atticum.* Ed. J. Pierson. Leiden, 1759.

Moulton *Proleg.* ...... = *A Grammar of New Testament Greek.* Vol. I. Prolegomena[3], by James Hope Moulton. Edinburgh, 1908.

,, *Gr.* ii. = *A Grammar of New Testament Greek.* Vol. II. *Accidence and Word-Formation with an Appendix on Semitisms in the New Testament,* by James Hope Moulton and Wilbert Francis Howard. Edinburgh, 1929.

,, *Egyptian Rubbish-heaps* = *From Egyptian Rubbish-heaps,* by James Hope Moulton. London, 1916.

,, *Einleitung..* = *Einleitung in die Sprache des Neuen Testaments.* (Translated with additions from the third edition of *Prolegomena.*) Heidelberg, 1911.

Musonius .... = *C. Musonii Rufi Reliquiae.* Ed. O. Hense. Leipzig, 1905.

Nachmanson .... = *Laute und Formen der Magnetischen Inschriften,* von E. Nachmanson. Uppsala, 1903.

Nägeli .... = *Der Wortschatz des Apostels Paulus,* von Th. Nägeli. Göttingen, 1905.

Norden *Agnostos Theos* .... = *Agnostos Theos,* von Eduard Norden. Leipzig und Berlin, 1913.

Oertel *Liturgie* ...... = *Die Liturgie. Studien zur Ptolemäischen und Kaiserlichen Verwaltung Ägyptens,* von F. Oertel. Leipzig, 1917.

Otto *Priester* .... = *Priester und Tempel im Hellenistischen Ägypten,* von Walter Otto, 2 vols. Leipzig and Berlin, 1905, 1908.

Pelagia-Legenden .... = *Legenden der heiligen Pelagia.* Ed. H. Usener. Bonn, 1879.

Plaumann *Ptolemais.* = *Ptolemais in Oberägypten. Ein Beitrag zur Geschichte des Hellenismus in Ägypten,* von Gerhard Plaumann. Leipzig, 1910.

Poland *Vereinswesen* = *Geschichte des Griechischen Vereinswesens*, von Franz Poland. Leipzig, 1909.

Preisigke *Fachwörter* = *Fachwörter des öffentlichen Verwaltungsdienstes Ägyptens in den griechischen Papyrusurkunden der ptolemäisch-römischen Zeit*, von Friedrich Preisigke. Göttingen, 1915.

„ *Namenbuch* = *Namenbuch enthaltend alle griechischen, lateinischen, ägyptischen, hebräischen, arabischen und sonstigen semitischen und nichtsemitischen Menschennamen, soweit sie in griechischen Urkunden (Papyri, Ostraka, Inschriften, Mumienschildern usw.) Ägyptens sich vorfinden*, von Friedrich Preisigke. Heidelberg, 1922.

„ *Wörterbuch* = *Wörterbuch der griechischen Papyrusurkunden*, von Friedrich Preisigke (und E. Kiessling). Vols. I. II. III. i. Berlin, 1925-29.

Preuschen-Bauer *Wörterbuch* = *Griechisch-Deutsches Wörterbuch zu den Schriften des Neuen Testaments* (being an entirely new edition of E. Preuschen's *Handwörterbuch zu den Schriften des Neuen Testaments*), von W. Bauer. Giessen, 1928.

Proleg .... See under Moulton.

Psaltes *Gr.* .... = *Grammatik der Byzantinischen Chroniken* (being *Forschungen zur griechischen und lateinischen Grammatik*, 2), von Stamatios B. Psaltes. Göttingen, 1913.

Radermacher *Gr.* and
Gr.² .... = *Neutestamentliche Grammatik* (being *Handbuch zum Neuen Testament* I. i.), von L. Radermacher. Tübingen, 1911 and 1925.

Ramsay *Cities* .... = *The Cities of St. Paul*, by W. M. Ramsay. London, 1907.

„ *CRE* .... = *The Church in the Roman Empire before A.D. 170*, by the same. Fifth edition. London, 1897.

„ *Letters* .... = *The Letters to the Seven Churches of Asia*, by the same. London, 1904.

„ *Luke* .... = *Luke the Physician*, by the same. London, 1908.

„ *Paul* .... = *S. Paul the Traveller and the Roman Citizen*, by the same. Third edition. London, 1897.

„ *Recent Discovery* .... = *The Bearing of Recent Discovery on the Trustworthiness of the New Testament*, by the same. London, 1915.

„ *Stud. in the E. Rom. Prov.* = *Studies in the History and Art of*

the Eastern Provinces of the Roman Empire (being *Aberdeen University Studies*, 20), edited by the same. Aberdeen, 1906.

„ *Teaching* .... = *The Teaching of Paul in Terms of the Present Day*, by the same. London, [1913].

Regard *Prépositions* = *Contribution à l'Étude des Prépositions dans la Langue du Nouveau Testament*, par Paul F. Regard. Paris, 1919.

REGr .... = *Revue des Études Grecques*. Paris, 1888- .

Reinhold .... = *De Graecitate Patrum Apostolicorum Librorumque Apocryphorum Novi Testamenti Quaestiones Grammaticae* (being *Diss. Phil. Hal.* xiv. 1.), by H. Reinhold. Halle, 1898.

Reitzenstein *Poimandres* .... = *Poimandres: Studien zur Griechisch-Ägyptischen und Frühchristlichen Literatur*, von R. Reitzenstein. Leipzig, 1904.

„ *Hellen. Mysterienrelig.* = *Die Hellenistischen Mysterienreligionen, ihre Grundgedanken und Wirkungen*, by the same. Leipzig, 1910.

Revillout *Mélanges* .... = *Mélanges sur la métrologie, l'économie politique, et l'histoire de l'ancienne Égypte*, by Eugène Revillout. Paris, 1895.

Robertson *Gr.³* .... = *A Grammar of the Greek New Testament in the Light of Historical Research*, by A. T. Robertson. New York, [1914].

Rossberg .... = *De Praepositionum Graecarum in Chartis Aegyptiis Ptolemaeorum Aetatis Usu*, by C. Rossberg. Jena, 1909.

Rostovtzeff *A Large Estate* .... = *A Large Estate in Egypt in the Third Century B.C. A Study in Economic History* (being *University of Wisconsin Studies in the Social Sciences and History*, 6), by Michael Rostovtzeff. Madison, 1922.

Rouffiac *Recherches* = *Recherches sur les caractères du grec dans le Nouveau Testament d'après les inscriptions de Priène*, par J. Rouffiac. Paris, 1911.

Rutherford *NP* .... = *The New Phrynichus*, by W. G. Rutherford. London, 1881.

SAM .... = *Studi della Scuola Papirologica, R. Accademia Scientifico-Letteraria in Milano*. Milano, 1915- .

Schlageter .... = *Der Wortschatz der ausserhalb Attikas gefundenen attischen Inschriften*, von J. Schlageter. Strassburg, 1912.

Schmid *Atticismus...* = *Der Atticismus in seinen Haupt-vertretern von Dionysius von Halikarnass bis auf den Zweiten Philostratus*, by W. Schmid. 4 vols. and Register. Stuttgart, 1887-97.

Schmidt *Jos.* = *De Flavii Josephi Elocutione Observationes Criticae*, by W. Schmidt. Leipzig, 1893.

Schubart *Buch* = *Das Buch bei den Griechen und Römern*, von W. Schubart. Berlin, 1907.

„ *Einführung* = *Einführung in die Papyruskunde*, von W. Schubart. Berlin, 1918.

Schulze *Gr. Lat.* = *Graeca Latina*, scripsit Gulielmus Schulze. Göttingen.

Schürer *Geschichte* = *Geschichte des Jüdischen Volkes im Zeitalter Iesu Christi*, von E. Schürer. 3te u. 4te Aufl. Leipzig, 1901.

„ *HJP* = The above *History of the Jewish People in the Time of Jesus Christ*, translated from the second German edition. Edinburgh, 1890-1.

Schweizer *Perg.* = *Grammatik der Pergamenischen Inschriften*, von E. Schweizer. Berlin, 1898.

Searles *Lexicographical Study* = *A Lexicographical Study of the Greek Inscriptions* (being *Chicago Studies in Classical Philology*. II.). By Helen M. Searles. Chicago, 1898.

SH = *The Epistle to the Romans*, by W. Sanday and A. C. Headlam. Fifth Edition. Edinburgh, 1902.

Sharp *Epict.* = *Epictetus and the New Testament*, by Douglas S. Sharp. London, 1914.

Slaten *Qualitative Nouns* = *Qualitative Nouns in the Pauline Epistles and Their Translation in the Revised Version* (being *Historical and Linguistic Studies in Literature related to the New Testament*. Second Series, Vol. IV., Part 1), by Arthur Wakefield Slaten. Chicago, 1918.

Sophocles *Lex.* = *Greek Lexicon of the Roman and Byzantine Periods*, by E. A. Sophocles. New York, 1887.

Souter *Lex.* = *A Pocket Lexicon to the Greek New Testament*, by A. Souter. Oxford, 1916.

Studi della Scuola Pap. ... See s.v. *SAM*.

Sudhoff *Ärztliches* = *Ärztliches aus griechischen Papyrus-Urkunden* (being *Studien zur Geschichte der Medizin*, 5/6), von Karl Sudhoff. Leipzig, 1909.

Suidas *Lex.* = *Suidae Lexicon*. Ed. I. Bekker. Berlin, 1854.

Teles ed. Hense = *Teletis Reliquiae* ed. O. Hense. Editio secunda. Tübingen, 1909.

Thackeray *Arist.* = *The Letter of Aristeas translated into English*, by H. St. J. Thackeray. London, 1917.

„ *Gr.* = *A Grammar of the Old Testament in Greek* i., by H. St. John Thackeray. Cambridge, 1909.

Thayer = See under Grimm.

Thieme = *Die Inschriften von Magnesia am Maander und das Neue Testament*, von G. Thieme. Göttingen, 1906.

Thumb *Dial.* = *Handbuch der Griechischen Dialekte*, von Albert Thumb. Heidelberg, 1909.

„ *Handbook* = *Handbook of the Modern Greek Vernacular*, by Albert Thumb. Translated from the second German edition by S. Angus. Edinburgh, 1912.

„ *Hellen.* = *Die Griechische Sprache im Zeitalter des Hellenismus*, von A. Thumb. Strassburg, 1901.

„ *Spiritus asper* = *Untersuchungen uber den Spiritus asper im Griechischen*, von A. Thumb. Strassburg, 1889.

Trench *Syn.* = *Synonyms of the New Testament*, by Richard Chenevix Trench. New edit. London, 1901.

Usener *Epic.* = *Epicurea*, ed. H. Usener. Leipzig, 1887.

Vettius Valens = *Vettii Valentis Anthologiarum Libri*. Ed. W. Kroll. Berlin, 1908.

Viereck *SG* = *Sermo Graecus quo S.P.Q.R. magistratusque populi Romani usque ad Tib. Caesaris aetatem in scriptis publicis usi sunt*, by Paul Viereck. Göttingen, 1888.

Völker *Art.* = *Syntax der griechischen Papyri*. I. *Der Artikel*, von F. Völker. Münster, 1903.

Wackernagel *Anredeformen* = *Über einige antike Anredeformen* (Einladung zur akadem. Preisverkündigung), von J. Wackernagel. Göttingen, 1912.

„ *Hellenistica* = *Hellenistica* (Einladung zur akadem. Preisverkündigung), von J. Wackernagel. Göttingen, 1907.

Wendland *Literaturformen* = *Die Urchristlichen Literaturformen* (being *Handbuch zum Neuen Testament*, I. 3), von Paul Wendland. Tübingen, 1912.

Wenger *Stellvertretung* = *Die Stellvertretung im Rechte der Papyri*, von L. Wenger. Leipzig, 1906.

WH .... = *The New Testament in the Original Greek*, by B. F. Westcott and F. J. A. Hort. Vol. i. *Text*. Vol. ii. *Introduction*. Revised editions. London, 1898 and 1896.

White *Sayings*........ = *The Sayings of Jesus from Oxyrhynchus*. Ed. Hugh G. Evelyn White. Cambridge, 1920.

Winer-Moulton *Gr*... = *A Treatise on the Grammar of New Testament Greek*. Translated from G. B. Winer's 7th edition, with large additions, by W. F. Moulton. 3rd edition. Edinburgh, 1882.

Winer-Schmiedel *Gr*. = *Grammatik des neutestamentlichen Sprachidioms*, von G. B. Winer. 8te Aufl. von P. W. Schmiedel. Göttingen, 1894- .

Zahn *Introd*.......... = *Introduction to the New Testament*, by Theodore Zahn. English tr. Edinburgh, 1909.

Ziemann *Epist*...... = *De epistularum Graecarum formulis sollemnibus quaestiones selectae* (being *Diss. philolog. Halenses* xviii. 4), by F. Ziemann. Halle, 1911.

ZNTW .. .. = *Zeitschrift für die Neutestamentliche Wissenschaft*. Giessen, 1900- .

Zorell .... = *Novi Testamenti Lexicon Graecum* (being *Cursus Scripturae Sacrae* I. vii.), auctore Francisco Zorell, S.J. Paris, 1911.

II. PAPYRI

BGU................ = *Aegyptische Urkunden aus den königlichen Museen zu Berlin: Griechische Urkunden* I.—VII. Berlin, 1895-1926.

Chrest. I. and II...... = *Grundzüge und Chrestomathie der Papyruskunde*. I. ii. ed. U. Wilcken, and II. ii. ed. L. Mitteis. Leipzig and Berlin, 1912.

Ghedini *Lettere* ...... = *Lettere Christiane dai Papiri Greci del III. e IV. Secolo*. Ed. G. Ghedini. Milan, 1923.

Gnomon or *Gnomon* = BGU V. 1.

Olsson *Papyrusbriefe* = *Papyrusbriefe aus der frühesten Römerzeit*. Ed. Bror Olsson. Uppsala, 1925.

P Alex................ = *Papyrus ptolémaïques du Musée d'Alexandrie*, ed. G. Botti in *Bulletin de la Société Archéol. d'Alexandrie*, p. 65 ff. Alexandria, 1899.

P Amh................ = *The Amherst Papyri* I. II. Edd. B. P. Grenfell and A. S. Hunt. London, 1900-1.

P Bad................ = *Griechische Papyri* (= *Veröffentlichungen aus den badischen Papyrus-Sammlungen* ii. and iv.). Ed. Friedrich Bilabel. Heidelberg, 1923 and 1924.

P Bouriant .... = *Les Papyrus Bouriant*, par Paul Collart. Paris, 1926.

P Cairo Preis......... = *Griechische Urkunden des Ägyptischen Museums zu Kairo*. Ed. F. Preisigke. Strassburg, 1911.

P Cairo Zen........... = *Catalogue Général des Antiquités Égyptiennes du Musée du Caire*. Nos. 59001-59531. *Zenon Papyri*, I. II. III. Ed. C. C. Edgar. Cairo, 1925-28.

P Catt .... = P Cattaoui, ed. G. Botti in *Rivista Egiziana* vi. p. 529 ff.

P Cornell .... = *Greek Papyri in the Library of Cornell University*. Edd. William Linn Westermann and Casper J. Kraemer, Jr. New York, 1926.

P Eleph.............. = *Elephantine-Papyri*. Ed. O. Rubensohn. Berlin, 1907.

P Eud................ = *Eudoxi ars astronomica, qualis in Charta Aegyptiaca superest*, ed. F. Blass. Kiliae, 1887.

P Fay .... = *Fayûm Towns and their Papyri*. Edd. B. P. Grenfell, A. S. Hunt, and D. G. Hogarth. London, 1900.

P Flor .... = *Papiri Fiorentini* I.-III. Edd. G. Vitelli and D. Comparetti. Milan, 1906-15.

P Frankf.............. = *Griechische Papyri aus dem Besitz des Rechtswissenschaftlichen Seminars der Universität Frankfurt* (being *Sitzungsberichte der Heidelberger Akademie der Wissenschaften, Philosophisch-historische Klasse*, 14 *Abhandlung*), von H. Ewald. Heidelberg, 1920.

P Gen .... = *Les Papyrus de Genève* I. Ed. J. Nicole. Geneva, 1896-1900.

P Giss................ = *Griechische Papyri zu Giessen* I. Edd. O. Eger, E. Kornemann, and P. M. Meyer. Leipzig, 1910-12.

P Goodsp .... = *A Group of Greek Papyrus Texts*. Ed. Edgar J. Goodspeed (being *Classical Philology*, I. 2.) Chicago, 1906.

P Goodsp Cairo ...... = *Greek Papyri from the Cairo Museum*. Ed. E. J. Goodspeed. Chicago, 1902.

P Goodsp Chicago ... = *Chicago Literary Papyri*. Ed. E. J. Goodspeed. Chicago, 1908.

P Grad................ = *Griechische Papyri der Sammlung Gradenwitz*. Ed. G. Plaumann. Heidelberg, 1914.

P Grenf I. .... = *An Alexandrian Erotic Fragment, and other Greek Papyri, chiefly Ptolemaic*. Ed. B. P. Grenfell. Oxford, 1896.

P Grenf II. .... = *New Classical Fragments, and other Greek and Latin Papyri.* Edd. B. P. Grenfell and A. S. Hunt. Oxford, 1897.

P Hal I. .... = *Dikaiomata,* herausgegeben von der *Graeca Halensis.* Berlin, 1913.

P Hamb. .... = *Griechische Papyrusurkunden der Hamburger Staats- und Universitätbibliothek* I. Ed. P. M. Meyer. Leipzig u. Berlin, 1911–1924.

P Hawara. .... = Flinders Petrie, *Hawara, Biahmu, and Arsinoe.* London, 1889.

P Heid .... = *Veröffentlichungen aus der Heidelberger Papyrus-Sammlung* I. Ed. A. Deissmann. Heidelberg, 1905.

CP Herm .... = *Corpus Papyrorum Hermopolitanorum* I. Ed. C. Wessely. Leipzig, 1905.

P Hib. .... = *The Hibeh Papyri,* I. Edd. B. P. Grenfell and A. S. Hunt. London, 1906.

P Iand .... = *Papyri Iandanae* Parts i.–iv. Edd. E. Schäfer, L. Eisner, L. Spohr, and G. Spiess. Leipzig, 1912–14.

P Karanis .... = *Papyri from Karanis.* Ed. E. J. Goodspeed. Chicago, 1900.

P Leid .... = *Papyri Graeci Musei antiquarii publii Lugduni-Batavi,* 2 vols. Ed. C. Leemans. 1843, 1885.

P Lille .... = *Papyrus Grecs de Lille* I. Parts i. ii. iii. Ed. P. Jouguet. Paris, 1907–23.

P Lips .... = *Griechische Urkunden der Papyrussammlung zu Leipzig* I. Ed. L. Mitteis. Leipzig, 1906.

P Lond .... = *Greek Papyri in the British Museum.* Vols. I. and II. ed. F. G. Kenyon; Vol. III. edd. F. G. Kenyon and H. I. Bell; Vols. IV., V., ed. H. I. Bell. London, 1893–1917.

P Lond 1912–1929 ...... being *Greek Papyri in the British Museum,* ed. by H. I. Bell in *Jews and Greeks in Egypt.* London, 1924.

P Magd. .... = *Papyrus de Magdola* being *Papyrus Grecs de Lille* II. Ed. J. Lesquier. Paris, 1912.

P Masp. .... = *Papyrus Grecs d'Époque Byzantine* (being *Catalogue Général des Antiquités Égyptiennes du Musée du Caire,* Nos. 67001—67359), par Jean Maspero, I.–III. Cairo, 1911–16.

P Meyer .... = *Griechische Texte aus Ägypten,* ed. P. M. Meyer. Berlin, 1916.

P Michigan .... = *Classical Philology,* xxii. 3 (July, 1927), pp. 237 ff.

P Mon .... = *Veröffentlichungen aus der Papyrus-Sammlung der K. Hof- und Staatsbibliothek zu München.* I. *Byzantinische Papyri.* Leipzig, 1914.

P Osl I. .... = *Papyri Osloenses.* I. *Magical Papyri.* Ed. S. Eitrem. Oslo, 1925.

P Oxy .... = *The Oxyrhynchus Papyri.* Vols. I.–VI. edd. B. P. Grenfell and A. S. Hunt; Vols. VII.–IX. ed. A. S. Hunt; Vols. X.–XV., edd. B. P. Grenfell and A. S. Hunt; Vol. XVI., edd. B. P. Grenfell, A. S. Hunt, and H. I. Bell; Vol. XVII., ed. A. S. Hunt. London, 1898–1927.

P Par .... = Paris Papyri in *Notices et Extraits* XVIII. ii. Ed. Brunet de Presle. Paris, 1865.

P Par 574 .... = The Paris Magical papyrus edited by C. Wessely in *Denkschriften der philosophisch-historischen Classe der Kaiserlichen Akademie der Wissenschaften zu Wien* XXXVI (1888), p. 75 ff.

P Petr .... = *The Flinders Petrie Papyri* in the Proceedings of the Royal Irish Academy—"Cunningham Memoirs," Nos. viii., ix., and xi. Parts I. II. ed. J. P. Mahaffy; Part III. edd. J. P. Mahaffy and J. G. Smyly. Dublin, 1891–4.

CPR. .... = *Corpus Papyrorum Raineri. Griechische Texte* I. Ed. C. Wessely. Vienna, 1895.

P Rein .... = *Papyrus Grecs et Démotiques.* Ed. Th. Reinach. Paris, 1905.

P Rev L .... = *Revenue Laws of Ptolemy Philadelphus.* Ed. B. P. Grenfell with an Introduction by J. P. Mahaffy. Oxford, 1896.

P Ryl .... = *Catalogue of the Greek Papyri in the John Rylands Library.* Manchester I., ed. A. S. Hunt; II. edd. J. de M. Johnson, V. Martin, and A. S. Hunt. Manchester, 1911–15.

P Sa'íd Khan .... = Greek Parchments from Avroman in Media, discovered by Dr. Sa'íd Khan, published in *JHS* xxxv. pp. 22–65, by E. H. Minns. London, 1915.

PSI .... = *Pubblicazioni della Società Italiana per la ricerca dei Papiri greci e latini in Egitto: Papiri Greci e Latini* I.–IX. i. Florence, 1912–28.

P Strass .... = *Griechische Papyrus zu Strassburg* I, II. Ed. F. Preisigke. Leipzig, 1912–1920.

P Tebt .... = *The Tebtunis Papyri.* Vol. I. edd.
B. P. Grenfell, A. S. Hunt,
and J. G. Smyly: Vol. II.
edd. B. P. Grenfell, A. S. Hunt,
and E. J. Goodspeed. London,
1902-7.

P Thead.................. = *Papyrus de Théadelphie.* Ed. P.
Jonguet. Paris, 1911.

P Tor .... = *Papyri Graeci Regii Taurinensis
Musei Aegyptii.* 2 vols. Ed. A.
Peyron. Turin, 1826-7.

P Vat .... = A. Mai, *Classicorum auctorum e
Vaticanis codicibus editorum
Tomi IV. et V.* Rome, 1831-33.

Preisigke .... = Papyri in *Sammelbuch:* see under
Abbreviations III.

Selections... ... . = *Selections from the Greek Papyri,*
by George Milligan. Cambridge,
1927.

UPZ .... = *Urkunden der Ptolemäerzeit.* (*Äl-
tere Funde*). I. *Papyri aus
Unterägypten.* Ed. U. Wilcken.
Berlin u. Leipzig, 1927.

Witkowski² or Wit-
kowski *Epp²*....... = *Epistulae Privatae Graecae²*. Ed.
S. Witkowski. Leipzig, 1911.

III. INSCRIPTIONS AND OSTRACA

Audollent .... = *Defixionum Tabellae.* Ed. A.
Audollent. Paris, 1904.

Brit. Mus. Inscrr.... = *The Collection of Ancient Greek
Inscriptions in the British
Museum.* Oxford, 1874- .

Cagnat.................. = *Inscriptiones Graecae ad Res
Romanas pertinentes,* ed. R.
Cagnat. I. III. IV. 1-5. Paris,
1911-14.

C. and B. .... = *Cities and Bishoprics of Phrygia,*
by W. M. Ramsay. Vol. I.
Parts i. ii. Oxford, 1895, 1897.

CIA..................... = *Corpus Inscriptionum Atticarum.*
Berlin, 1873-97.

CIG................... = *Corpus Inscriptionum Graecarum.*
Berlin, 1828-77.

CIL................... = *Corpus Inscriptionum Latinarum.*
Berlin, 1862-1909.

Calder................. = (unpublished) Greek Inscriptions
from Phrygia, ed. W. M. Calder.

Cauer................... = *Delectus Inscriptionum Graecarum²*.
Ed. P. Cauer. Leipzig, 1883.

Cos..................... = *The Inscriptions of Cos,* edd. W. R.
Paton and E. L. Hicks. Oxford,
1891.

Duchesne et Bayet.... = *Mémoire sur une Mission au Mont
Athos,* par L'Abbé Duchesne et
M. Bayet. Paris, 1876.

Fay Ostr .... = *Fayûm Towns and their Papyri,*
pp. 317-332.

GDI .... = *Sammlung der griechischen Dialekt-*

Inschriften. Ed. H. Collitz.
Göttingen, 1884- .

IG..................... = *Inscriptiones Graecae,* ed. cons. et
auct. Acad. Regiae Borussicae.
Berlin, 1873- .

IG Sept............... = *Corpus Inscriptionum Graecae
Septentrionalis.* Ed. W. Ditten-
berger. Berlin, 1892.

IGSI.................. = *Inscriptiones Graecae Siciliae et
Italiae.* Ed. G. Kaibel. Berlin,
1890.

IMAe.................. = *Inscriptiones Graecae Insularum
Maris Aegaei.* Edd. H. von
Gaertringen and W. R. Paton.
Berlin, 1895- .

IosPE .... = *Inscriptiones Oris Septentrionalis
Ponti Euxini,* being Inscriptions
from Olbia on the Euxine in the
Appendix to *Scythians and
Greeks,* by E. H. Minns. Cam-
bridge, 1913.

Kaibel .... = *Epigrammata Graeca ex lapidibus
collecta.* Ed. G. Kaibel. Berlin,
1878.

Latyschev.............. = *Inscriptiones Antiquae Orae Septentrionalis Ponti Euxini Graecae
et Latinae,* ed. B. Latyschev.
I, II. Petropolis, 1885, 1890.

Letronne............... = *Recueil des inscriptions grecques
et latines de l'Égypte,* by M.
Letronne. 2 vols. Paris, 1842-8.

Magn .... = *Die Inschriften von Magnesia am
Maander.* Ed. O. Kern. Berlin,
1900.

Meyer Ostr............. = *Ostraka der Sammlung Deissmann,*
ed. Paul M. Meyer in *Griechische
Texte aus Ägypten,* p. 107 ff.
Berlin, 1916.

Michel................. = *Recueil d'Inscriptions Grecques.*
Ed. Ch. Michel. Paris, 1900.
Supplément i. Paris, 1912.

Milne *Theb. Ostr*........ See under *Theb. Ostr.*

OGIS.................. = *Orientis Graeci Inscriptiones Selectae.* 2 vols. Ed. W. Ditten-
berger. Leipzig, 1903-5.

Ostr or Wilcken Ostr = *Griechische Ostraka aus Aegypten
und Nubien.* 2 vols. Ed. U.
Wilcken. Leipzig, 1899.

PAS .... = *Papers of the American School of
Classical Studies at Athens.*
Boston.

Perg.................. = *Die Inschriften von Pergamon* I.
II. (in *Altertümer von Pergamon
viii.*). Ed. M. Fränkel. Berlin,
1900-05.

Preisigke.............. = *Sammelbuch Griechischer Urkunden aus Ägypten.* I. II. III.
Ed. F. Preisigke. Strassburg
and Berlin, 1915-27. [Includes
many papyri: when these are
cited the abbreviation is "Preisigke" in Roman type.]

Preisigke Ostr......... = Die Prinz-Joachim-Ostraka, edd. F. Preisigke and W. Spiegelberg. Strassburg, 1914.

Priene................. = Die Inschriften von Priene. Ed. H. von Gaertringen. Berlin, 1906.

Roberts-Gardner...... = Introduction to Greek Epigraphy, Part ii. The Inscriptions of Attica. Edd. E. S. Roberts and E. A. Gardner. Cambridge, 1905.

Syll. and Syll.³ .... = Sylloge Inscriptionum Graecarum². 2 vols. and index. Ed. W. Dittenberger. Second edition. Leipzig, 1888-1901. References are also given to the third edition, 3 vols. and index. Leipzig, 1915-24.

Theb. Ostr............. = Theban Ostraca, pp. 68-161. Greek Texts, ed. J. G. Milne. Oxford, 1913.

Waddington Inscriptions .... = Inscriptions grecques et latines recueillies en Grèce et en Asie Mineure. Edd. Ph. Le Bas et W. H. Waddington. Paris, 1870.

Wilcken Ostr ....See under Ostr.

Wünsch AF............ = Antike Fluchtafeln (in Kleine Texte für theologische Vorlesungen und Ubungen, 20). Ed. R. Wünsch. Bonn, 1907.

NOTE ON METHOD OF PUBLICATION.

Quotations from Papyri and Inscriptions are printed as in the editions from which they come, except for the notation used to show that the modern editor wishes to insert or delete. Here the text is given as found in the original document, with a note in brackets if necessary. Square brackets [ ] denote a gap in the original; round brackets ( ) the resolution of an abbreviation (as (ἔτους) for ∠), except in some inscriptions where the editor uses them to denote faint or missing letters; angular brackets < > a mistaken omission in the original; braces { } a superfluous letter or letters; and double square brackets [[ ]] a deletion. Letters which are not read with certainty are indicated by dots underneath. Interlineations and erasures in the original are generally pointed out in a note. The line given for a cited word is that which contains the beginning of the word.

A

ἀβαρής—ἀγαπάω

ἀβαρής.

For ἀβαρής in a metaphorical sense, as in 2 Cor 11⁹, Nägeli (p. 38) cites *CIG* 5361⁵ (Berenice, i/B.C.) ἀ. ἑαυτὸν παρέσχηται, and BGU I. 248²⁶ (ii/A.D.) ἐὰν δέ σοι ἀβα[ρὲ]ς ᾖ, χρῆσόν μοι ὀνάριον. Add P Oxy VI. 935²⁹ (late ii/A.D.) and BGU IV. 1080¹⁷ᶠ (iii/A.D. ?) εἴ σοι ἀβ[α]ρές ἐστιν καὶ δυνα[τόν, σ]υναπόστιλόν μοι κτλ. The physical sense is cited from Aristotle ; the metaphysical appears in Plutarch (59C).

Ἀβραάμ.

For a Græcised form Ἄβραμος, cf. BGU II. 585ⁱⁱ·³ (after A.D. 212) Πααβῶς Ἀβράμου. The non-Græcised form is common in Fayûm documents of the Christian period, e.g. BGU I. 103¹¹ (vi/vii A.D.) Ἀβραάμ ; see further Deissmann *BS*, p. 187. A Jew Ἀβράμ[ιος ? is named in BGU II. 715ⁱⁱ·² (Fayûm A.D. 101-2).

ἄβυσσος.

As a substantive (Rom 10⁷, Rev 9¹ etc.) ἀ. is common in the magic papyri, e.g. P Lond 121²⁵ (iii/A.D.) (= I. p. 93) ἐπὶ τῆς ἀβύσσου, *ib.*⁵¹⁷ (= I. p. 100) τῇ καλουμένῃ ἀβύσσῳ. See also Nägeli, p. 46.

ἀγαθοποιός.

This rare adjective, which in the NT is confined to 1 Pet 2¹⁴, is found as an astrological term in a magical papyrus of iv/A.D., P Lond 122¹⁶ (= I. p. 116) ἀγαθοποιὲ τῆς οἰκουμένης : cf. *ib.* 46⁴⁸ (iv/A.D.) (= I. p. 66) μετὰ ἀγαθοποιῶν, with reference to stars of benign influence. The verb is found in Aristeas (ed. Wendland) 242, ἀλλὰ δέον (*l.* δέον θεὸν) ἱκετεύειν, πάντα ἀγαθοποιεῖν.

ἀγαθός.

The comparative βελτίων (in the LXX about 20 times for the commoner κρείσσων) occurs in the fragmentary P Petr III. 42 H (8) 1¹⁵ (middle of iii/B.C.) (= Witkowski *Epp.*², p. 16). In a votive inscription discovered at Cos (Paton and Hicks, 92), Nero is described as ἀγαθὸς θεός (cf. Deissmann *LAE*, p. 349). For ἀγαθὸς δαίμων, see 57 in the same collection (= *CIG* 2510)—Τύχᾳ Ἀγαθᾷ καὶ Ἀγαθῷ Δαίμονι καὶ τῶ(ι) δάμω(ι), etc., etc. One other phrase is worth quoting : P Oxy II. 298¹⁴ (i/A.D.) ἐὰν ἐπ' ἀγαθῷ παραγένῃ, "if you arrive happily," *ib.* III. 531⁶ (ii/A.D.) ἕως ἐπ' ἀγαθῷ πρὸς σὲ παραγένομαι, BGU III. 835¹⁹ᶠ (beginning of iii/A.D.) εἰς τὴν ἐπ' [ἀ]γαθοῖς γεναμένης κατασποράν, P Flor I. 21¹⁰ (A.D. 239) *al.* The neuter pl., as in Lk 12¹⁹, may be illustrated by P Ryl I. 28¹⁸² (iv/A.D.) ποὺς δεξιὸς ἐὰν ἅλληται, δεσπότης ἔσται πολλῶν ἀγαθῶν καὶ κτημάτων, "if the right foot quiver, the man will be master of many blessings and possessions" (Ed.).

PART I.

ἀγαθωσύνη.

The word is "found only in Bibl. and eccl. writers" (Grimm-Thayer). But the abstract suffix -σύνη (on which cf. Brugmann-Thumb *Griech. Gramm.*⁴, p. 224) was productive in the Hellenistic period. About a dozen noun occur in NT, and ἁγιωσύνη and μεγαλωσύνη come under the same condemnation in Grimm-Thayer : so would ταπεινοφροσύνη, but Thayer quotes Josephus and Epictetus against Grimm. Nägeli (p. 43) has "profane" warrant for ἁγιωσύνη, which is none the worse for being later than NT times. Any writer was free to coin an abstract of this sort, just as we can attach the suffix -ness to any adjective we please ; and the absence of attestation signifies nothing that could carry any weight.

ἄγαμος.

BGU I. 86¹⁵ (ii/A.D.) ἐφ' ὃν χρόνον ἄγαμός ἐσ[τιν, *ib.* 113⁴ (ii/A.D.) εἴ τινες ἄγαμοι εἶεν, P Ryl I. 28⁻⁹ (iv/A.D.) ἀγάμῳ δὲ γάμον δηλοῖ. *Preisigke* 374 (i/B.C.–i/A.D.) has ἄγαμε on a gravestone.

ἀγανακτέω.

P Lond 44²⁰ (B.C. 161) (= I. p. 34) ἀγανακτοῦντα ἐφ' οἷς διετελοῦντο ἐν τοιούτωι ἱερῶι. P Oxy VIII. 1119⁸ (A.D. 254) ἥτις ἀγανακτήσασα ἐπέστειλεν κτλ. *Syll* 803⁹ᶠ iii/B.C. πρᾶτον ἀγανακτῶν τ[ᾶι πρά[ξει . . . In *ib.* 356³⁵ B.C. ὁ τὴν κοινὴν ἁπάντων ὑμῶν ἀσφάλειαν ἀναιροῦντων ἀγανακτοῦντες, it takes a gen., which might however be a gen. abs. : the inscription, a rescript of Augustus, is in the high style. P Magd 24⁵ (iii/B.C.) ἀγανακτήσαντος δέ μου καὶ ἐπιτιμῶντος αὐτ[ῆι. P Thead 15¹⁰ (iii/A.D., in an advocate's pleading. A curious use of the passive occurs in the late P Lond IV. 1397³ (A.D. 710) μέλλεις ἀγανακτηθῆναι, "you will incur our anger." The word is also found in the apocryphal Gospel of Peter 4 (ed. Swete), where on one of the malefactors upbraiding the Jews for their treatment of Jesus on the Cross, we read ἀγανακτήσαντες ἐπ' αὐτῷ ἐκέλευσαν ἵνα μὴ σκελοκοπηθῇ, ὅπως βασανιζόμενος ἀποθάνοι.

ἀγανάκτησις.

This NT ἅπ. εἰρ. (2 Cor 7¹¹) may be illustrated by P Grenf II. 82¹⁷ᶠ (*c.* A.D. 400) μεταγνῶναι ἔχετε ὥστε καὶ ἀγανακτήσεως δικαστικῆς πειραθῆναι, where certain offenders are threatened with legal proceedings and penalties, if they disregard the writer's demand.

ἀγαπάω.

The Pauline phrase in 1 Th 1⁴ ἀδελφοὶ ἠγαπημένοι ὑπὸ [τοῦ] θεοῦ, which in this exact form is not found elsewhere in the NT (cf. in the LXX Sir 45¹ ἠγαπημένον ὑπὸ (ἀπὸ ℵ) θεοῦ καὶ ἀνθρώπων), is well illustrated by a similar

i

use in connexion with Ptolemy on the Rosetta stone, *OGIS* 90⁴ (B.C. 196) ἠγαπημένου ὑπὸ τοῦ Φθᾶ. Cf. a Munich papyrus in *Chrest.* I. 109¹² (end of iii/B.C.), where Wilcken restores [Πτολεμαῖ]ος αἰωνόβιος ἠγα[πημένος ὑπὸ τῆς Ἰσιδος]. It may be noted that in Mk 10²¹ Field (*Notes*, p. 34) suggests the translation "caressed" for ἠγάπησεν, comparing Plut. *Pericl.* 1 : ξένους τινὰς ἐν Ῥώμῃ πλουσίους, κυνῶν τέκνα καὶ πιθήκων ἐν τοῖς κόλποις περιφέροντας καὶ ἀγαπῶντας (*fondling*) ἰδὼν ὁ Καῖσαρ . . . ἠρώτησεν εἰ παιδία παρ᾽ αὐτοῖς οὐ τίκτουσιν αἱ γυναῖκες. B. L. Gildersleeve (*Justin Martyr*, p. 135) suggests that "the larger use of [ἀγαπᾶν] in Christian writers is perhaps due to an avoidance of φιλεῖν in the sense of 'kissing.'" He says Xenophon made the two words absolute synonyms, comparing *Memorabilia* ii. 7. 9 with 12 ; while he deprecates refinements in Jn 21¹⁵⁻¹⁷, since "the Evangelist himself did not see the point, as Augustin notes (*Civ. Dei* vii. 11)." This seems undeniable in Xenophon *l.c.*, though in so severely simple a writer as Jn it is extremely hard to reconcile ourselves to a meaningless use of synonyms, where the point would seem to lie in the identity of the word employed. Gildersleeve's remark that "ἀγαπᾶν is a colder word than φιλεῖν and less intimate" will hold for "profane" Greek ; but this is emphatically a case where the needs of a new subject take up a rather colourless word and indefinitely enrich it. In NT ἀγαπᾶν is purged of all coldness, and is deeper than φιλεῖν, though the latter remains more human. See R. H. Strachan's references and discussion in *Expos.* VIII. vii. 203-7 (March 1914). A Christian metrical epitaph (*Cagnat* 600 after midd. iv/A.D.) has ἀ. with infin. as in Class. Grk : νῦν ἀγαπᾷς σὺ μαθεῖν τίς ἐγὼ ξένος ἢ πόθεν ἤλθα.

ἀγάπη.

Though it would be going too far to say that this important Biblical word was "born within the bosom of revealed religion," it is remarkable that there have been only three supposed instances of its use in "profane" Greek, two of which are now read otherwise and the third is doubtful. Deissmann originally cited P Par 49³ (B.C. 164–58) in this connexion (*Bibelstudien*, p. 80 f.) ; but in the English edition (*BS*, p. 198 f.) he admitted that the restoration ταραχήν must be substituted. Next Hatch in *JBL* xxvii. 2, p. 134 ff. cited an inscription of the Imperial period, from Tefeny in Pisidia, giving the mantic significance of various throws of the dice : πέμψει δ᾽ εἰς ἀγά[πη]ν σε φιλομμειδὴς Ἀφροδείτη. But Prof. Deissmann now calls our attention to a Breslau dissertation by F. Heinevetter *Würfel-und Buchstabenorakel in Griechenland und Kleinasien* (1912), where it seems to be proved (p. 10) that εἰς ἀγαθόν must be read in the line we have quoted. There remains only the citation (Crönert, *Lex. s.v.*) of δι᾽ ἀ[γ]άπης ἐ[ναρ]γοῦς from the Herculaneum papyri of Philodemus the Epicurean (i/B.C.), with the note "(sicher?)."

The history of this word is so crucial for the orientation of the Biblical Greek vocabulary that we must pursue it in some detail. Deissmann's argument from Thayer's Philonic citation of ἀγάπη is repeated in the English *BS* (p. 199) without regard to Ramsay's criticism (*ExpT* ix. p. 568). And Deissmann certainly seems justified in asserting that in the *Quod Deus immut.* (p. 283 M = Cohn-Wendland, ed.

min., p. 69) Philo is not taking the word from the LXX, unless Wisd 3⁹ (love towards God) 6¹⁸ (love of Wisdom) may be taken as the models for his ennobled use of the word. For in LXX it is used 14 times of sexual love (Jer 2² figuratively), and twice in antithesis to μῖσος : Sir 48¹¹ ℵ is the only other occurrence besides those from *Wisdom*. Aristeas (ii/i B.C.) has the word (§ 229) in the higher sense, and may stand with the author of *Wisdom* as the earliest to adapt it to this purpose. In its redemption from use as a mere successor to the archaic ἔρως, Alexandrian Jews of i/B.C. seem to have led the way. The fact that its use was very restricted made it easier to annex for a special purpose. Since the *Song of Songs* (where it occurs 11 times) could hardly be proved to have existed for the NT writers, there were virtually no other associations before their minds ; and the appropriation of ἀγαπᾶν and ἀγάπη proceeded side by side. As the record of its use in Aquila, Symmachus and Theodotion shows (see HR), the word retained in independent circles the connotations we find in Cant and Eccl, and grew slightly more common. In late Christian papyri we find it narrowed like our "charity" : Crönert cites P Gen I. 14⁷ (iv/v A.D.) and P Lond 77⁵⁸ (viii/A.D.) (= I. p. 234). On the Christian use of Ἀγάπη as a proper name see W. M. Ramsay *C. and B.*, ii. p. 492 f.

It should finally be remarked that there is no reason for postulating ἀγάπη as the origin of a denominative ἀγαπάω, as τιμή produces τιμάω, etc. Ἀγάπη is in any case a backformation from the verb, replacing the older ἀγάπησις, and originating doubtless in a restricted dialectic area. Cf. the case of οἰκοδομή, *q.v.*

ἀγαπητός.

For the use of this characteristic NT designation in the Christian papyri, see for example the address of the muchdiscussed letter of Psenosiris P Grenf II. 73 (late iii/A.D.) (= *Selections*, p. 117), Ἀπόλλωνι πρεσβυτέρῳ ἀγαπητῷ ἀδελφῷ ἐν Κ(υρί)ῳ χαίρειν. So P Lond 417¹ (c. A.D. 346) (= II. p. 299, *Selections*, p. 123), P Heid 6⁷ (iv/A.D.) (= *Selections*, p. 125) al. The word is also found in a horoscope of A.D. 20–50 addressed to a certain Tryphon—P Oxy II. 235². Τρύφων ἀγαπέτε : he may of course have been a Jew— see on the fem. Τρύφαινα below.

ἀγγαρεύω.

Ptolemaic examples of this interesting old Persian word are P Petr II. 20ⁱᵛ·⁵ (B.C. 252) τοῦ . . . λέμβου . . . ἀγγαρευθέντος ὑπὸ σοῦ with reference to a "post boat," and P Tebt I 5¹⁸², ²⁵² (B.C. 118) where for the editors' ἐπαρετεῖν Wilcken (*Archiv* iii. p. 325) reads ἐγγαρεύειν. From A.D. 42 add P Lond 1171 (t)² (= III. p. 107) μηδενὶ ἐξέστω ἐνγαρεύειν τοὺς ἐπὶ τῆς χώρας—a prefect's rescript. Cf BGU I. 21ⁱⁱⁱ·¹⁶ (A.D. 340) οἴνου ἐνγαρίας, and from the inscriptions *Syll* 932⁴ (beginning of iii/A.D.) ἀγγαρειῶν ἄνεσιν with Dittenberger's note, "vehicula cursus publici ponderosissima et lentissima, quae bubus vehebantur (*cursus clabularis* Cod Theod. VI. 29, 5, 1, VIII. 5, 11), *angariarum* nomine utebantur." Herwerden *Lex.* cites a form ἀνενγάρευτος = ἀναγγάρευτος, from an inscr. which Mayser (p. 56) refers to *Arch. Zeit.* 1890, p. 59. See further Zahn *Intr.* i. p. 66, Deissmann *BS* p. 86 f., and Rostowzew "Angariae" in *Klio* vi. (1906) p. 249 ff. For the spelling with ἰ. in Mk 15²¹ ℵ* B* Deissmann (*BS* p. 182) compares BGU I. 21ⁱⁱⁱ·¹⁶ (A.D. 340—coeval with the MSS.) ἐνγαρίας. The noun ἄγγαρος appears in Greek as early as Æschylus *Agam.* 294 ἀγγάρου πυρός, "the *courier* flame": it is probably the Iranian cognate of ἄγγελος. It survives in vernacular MGr ἀγγαρεμένος, "put to compulsory labour" (Thumb *Handbook*, p. 315). In his note on P Lond IV. 1376¹ (A.D. 711) the editor suggests that in the late Aphrodito papyri ἀγγαρευτής is used in the general sense of "foreman," "superintendent."

ἀγγεῖον.

is found in P Tor I. 1ⁱⁱ·⁸ (ii/B.C.) for the "casket" or "chest" in which plaintiffs in the court of the Chrematistae, or Greek judges of Egypt, were in the habit of placing their petitions (*Archiv* iii. p. 26 ff). See also P Gen I. 74⁸ ff (probably iii/A.D.) διὸ ἐρωτηθεὶς ἐκλαβὼν ἀντίγραφον καὶ βαλὼν εἰς ἀγγῖον σφράγι[σ]ον: similarly in *Syll* 790⁴¹ (i/B.C.) of oracular πινάκια, which are put εἰς ἀγγεῖον and sealed (κατασφραγισάσθωσαν) with various officers' seals. In BGU I. 248 (ii/A.D.) a note is added on the margin— χρῆσον Σαβείνῳ ἀγγείῳ, εἰς ὃ κόμιζέ μοι ἔλαιον, where ἀ. is a jar for oil, as in Mt 25⁴: cf. P Oxy VII. 1070⁸⁰ (iii/A.D.) ἀγγείῳ ἡμιχόῳ, P Hamb I. 23³⁴ (A.D. 569) μεστὰ ἀγγῖα τριάκοντα, P Lond 1036⁹ (vi/A.D.) (= III. p. 269) οἴνο(υ) ἀγγῖον μέγα ἕν, P Leid Wⁱⁱⁱ·⁵ ἀ. μέλιτος μεστόν.

The form ἄγγος, which is found in the true text of Mt 13⁴⁸, may be illustrated from *Michel* 1361ᵈ (Thasos, iv/B.C.) ἢν δέ τις ἐγβάλλη[ι τῶν δούλων κόπρον, ὥστε] τὸ χωρίον εἶναι τὸ ἄγγος τοῦ ἀναιρερημένου τὸν κῆπο[ν] κτλ. The word is used of a cinerary urn (as in Herod. i. 113) in CIG 3573.

ἀγγελία.

In the curious pamphlet on omens drawn from involuntary twitchings, P Ryl I. 28¹⁶¹ (iv/A.D.), we find σφυρ[ὸ]ν δεξιὸν ἐὰν ἄλληται, ἀγγελίαν αὐτῷ σημαίνι ἀπροσδόκητον, "if the right ankle quiver, it signifies that the person will have unexpected news." The word is common in literature.

ἄγγελος.

In *Syll* 512⁷¹, a dialect inscr. of ii/B.C. from Calymna, ἄγγελοι are envoys whose names are given. The word is used in the sense of "intermediary" (cf. Gal 3¹⁹) in *Syll* 122²⁵ (iv/B.C.) ὀμόσαι δ]ὲ ἀγγέλλων. For the presumably Christian "angel" inscriptions from Thera see Deissmann *LAE*, p. 279 with accompanying facsimile, and the paper "It is his Angel" (J. H. M.) in *JTS* 1902, p. 519 f. Add (from Crönert) *IG* XII. iii. 933. In *Archiv* iii. p. 445. No. 67, is published a Greek inscription from Assouan of the time of M. Aurelius, which begins—Μεγάλη τύχη τοῦ [θε]ο[ῦ . . . τ]ῶν ἀνγέλων τῆς [ἱ]ερεί[ας]: cf. also p. 451 No. 94 (time of Diocletian), Ὑπὲρ εὐχῆς τῶν ἀνγέλων Ἐμεσηνοὶ ἀνέθηκαν κτλ. Οἱ ἄγγελοι θεοῦ, as in 1 Tim 5²¹, occurs in the extremely interesting Jewish inscription *Syll* 816¹⁰ κύριε ὁ πάντα ἐ[φ]ορῶν καὶ οἱ ἄγγελοι θεοῦ. Dittenberger assigns it to i/A.D. and yet apparently prefers to regard it as Christian: there does not, however, seem to be anything distinctive of Christianity—it is a Jewish prayer for vengeance upon unknown murderers: see Deissmann *LAE*, p. 423 ff. It is interesting to observe that the special meaning "angel" is

apparently a reversion to the oldest signification, for in Homer the ἄγγελος is often a messenger of the gods. The two branches of the Aryan language-group diverge here. In Vedic Indian the *Aṅgirasaḥ* are "higher beings intermediate between gods and men," as Macdonell rather tentatively concludes (*Vedic Mythology*, 143). In Persian *angara* (?—see on ἀγγαρεύω) is a human messenger. Perhaps both meanings coexisted in the corner of the Indo-Germanic area to which the word is restricted. See also Hatzidakis on ἄγγελος in *Sitz. Ber. d. Wien. Akad.* 1913, 2.

ἀγγέλλω.

For ἀγγέλλω = "proclaim," "summon to an office," see the summons to celebrate the accession of Hadrian, P Giss I. 3²ᶠᶠ (A.D. 117) ἥκω (*sc.* Φοῖβος θεός) . . . ἄνακτα καινὸν Ἀδριανὸν ἀγγέλλω[ν]: cf. P Flor I. 2⁴·⁸ᶠᶠ· (A.D. 265) ὁ ἀγγελεὶς ἀντι[λά]βηται τῆς ἐνχειρισθείσης αὐτῷ χρείας [ὑ]γι[ῶς] καὶ πιστῶς. It is hardly accidental that the words quoted from the Giessen papyrus form an iambic line: the document has a strong literary flavour. Ἀγγέλλω is one of those verbs which became practically obsolete in the vernacular except in their compounds. Nine of these are found in NT, while the simplex only occurs in Jn 4⁵¹ ℵD, 20¹⁸ ℵ*ABIX. Jn is a writer who likes uncompounded verbs; see *Camb. Bibl. Essays.* p. 492.

ἄγγος.

See *s.v.* ἀγγεῖον.

ἀγέλη.

The noun occurs twice in a farm account, P Lond 1171 (B.C. 8) (= III. p. 177). For the adjective ἀγελαῖος, see *Syll* 587²⁰⁹ (iv/B.C.) κεραμίδες ἀγελαῖαι, with Dittenberger's note.

ἀγενεαλόγητος.

"Nowhere found in prof. auth.," says Grimm, nor are we able to supply the gap—which is not surprising! It is a good sample of a class of words which any author might coin for a special purpose.

ἀγενής.

Ἀγενής, as opposed to εὐγενής, is well illustrated by P Oxy I. 33ᵛ·⁵ (late ii/A.D.) where, in a dramatic interview with the Emperor, in all probability M Aurelius—though Wilcken (*Chrest.* I. p. 34 f.) decides for Commodus—a certain Appianus, who had been condemned to death, appeals to his nobility (εὐγένεια) in such a way as to lead the Emperor to retort—Φῇς οὖν ὅτι ἡμεῖς ἀγενεῖς ἐσμεν; For the more general sense of "mean," "base," see the *verso* of the illiterate P Oxy I. 79³ (not earlier than ii/A.D.), perhaps a school composition (Edd.), μηδὲν ταπινὸν μηδὲ ἀγενὲς . . . πρᾶξις. In *Syll* 855¹¹ (a dialect inscr. from Delphi, recording the "sale" of a slave to the god for freedom—ii/B.C.) εἰ δέ τι Μνασὼ (the slave) πάθοι ἀγενὴς ὑπάρχουσα, τὰ καταλειφθέντα ὑπὸ Μνασῶς Ἀγησαβούλας (the mistress) ἔστω: here ἀγενής must mean "childless," as in the similar phrase in *Syll* 862²², an inscr. of the same period, place and subject. The word was used in this sense by Isaeus, according to Harpocration.

ἁγιάζω.

Clear evidence for the verb and noun outside bibl. and eccl. writings appears to be wanting : cf. Anz *Subsidia*, p. 374 f. The suffix -άζειν was as active as our *-fy* in producing new words, and the abstract -ασμός accompanied it, as *-fication* accompanies our verb. When therefore ἅγιος was appropriated in Jewish circles to represent their special idea of "holiness," it was natural that the factitive derivative should be coined from it, as a technical term which would be immediately understood by any Greek, even if he had never met with the actual form. The series was the more needed, as Greek religion had already the forms ἁγίζω, ἁγισμός, ἁγιστεύω, ἁγιστήριον, etc., with their technical meanings : the variant words with the added -α- answered to them in function, but were free from pagan association.

ἅγιος.

The adjective is common as a title of the gods in the inscriptions, e. g. *OGIS* 378[1] (A.D. 18 9) θεῷ ἁγίῳ ὑψίστῳ : cf. *ib.* 721[1] ὁ δᾳδοῦχος τῶν ἁγιωτάτων Ἐλευσῖνι μυστηρίων. The superlative may be further illustrated (cf. Jude[20]) from the oldest recovered Christian letter P Amh I. 3[1] iii 22f. (between A.D. 264 (265) and 282 (281)) τοῖς κατ᾽ αὐτὸν ἁγιω[τ]άτοις προ[ε]στῶσι : cf. Deissmann *LAE* p. 102 ff. For τὸ ἅγιον as "temple" cf. *OGIS* 56[2] (the Canopus inscr. of Ptolemy III. B.C. 239) καθιδρῖσαι [. . ἄγαλμα χρυσοῖς διάλιθον] ἐν τῶι ἁγίωι.

ἁγιότης, ἁγιωσύνη.

Ἁγιότης, as a title, is found in the late P Giss I. 55[5] (vi/A.D.) addressed by one "papa" or "bishop" to another —ἠξιώθην . . . γράψαι πρ[ὸ]ς τὴν σὴν ἁγιότητ[α]. For a similar use of ἡ ἁγιωσύνη with reference to an ἐπίσκοπος, see the *Pelagia-Legenden* (ed. Usener) p. 16[2], cf. p. 8[11]. On the "profane" warrant for ἁγιωσύνη, and the naturalness of coining (with ἱερ(ε)ωσύνη for model), see the remarks on ἀγαθωσύνη above.

ἀγκάλη.

With the use of ἀγκάλη in Lk 2[28] cf. *OGIS* 56[60] (Canopus decree, B.C. 239) (τις) τῶν . . . ἱερέων πρὸς τὸν στολισμὸν τῶν θεῶν οἴσει ἐν ταῖς ἀγκαλαῖς. For the derived sense of "bundle" (*i. e.* "armful") see P Lond 131 *recto* 47 (A.D. 78–9) (=I. p. 183) δεσμεύων ἀγκάλας. P Oxy VI. 935[18] ff (iii/A.D.) ἡ μεταφ[ορ]ὰ τῶν ἀνκαλῶν ἔστε εἰθ[έ]ως ὑπὸ τοῦ πατρός, "the transport of the bundles will be performed immediately by my father" (Edd.).

ἄγκυρα.

P Lond 1164 (*h*)[9] (A.D. 212) (=III. p. 164) ἀνκύραις σιδηραῖς δυσὶ σὺν σπάθαις σιδηραῖς (the two teeth of the anchor). *Syll* 588[108, 171] (ii/B.C.) ἄγκυρα σιδηρᾶ. For the figurative sense, as Heb 6[19], cf. ἁ. γῆρως. *IG* XII. vii. 123[b].

ἄγναφος.

In P Lond 193 *verso* 22 (ii/A.D.) (=II. p. 246) a borrower pledges her κιτῶν(α) ἄγναφο[ν] λευκό[ν], "new white shirt," for an advance of 11 drachmas. P Hamb I. 10[24] (ii/A.D.) has it in a list of garments that had been stolen, including

an *abolla* ἄγναφος : P. M. Meyer renders "ungewalkt, frisch vom Webstuhl, rudis," and gives some other references. Plutarch 169C, 691D, has ἄγναπτος, "undressed, uncarded."

ἁγνεία.

OGIS 56[32] (decree of Canopus, B.C. 239) μετέχειν δὲ καὶ τοὺς ἐκ τῆς πέμπτης φυλῆς τῶν Εὐεργετῶν θεῶν τῶν ἁγνειῶν καὶ τῶν ἄλλων ἁπάντων τῶν ἐν τοῖς ἱεροῖς, *ib.* 573[6] (i/A.D.) τῶι δὲ ποιήσαντι ἔσται ἁγνεία, an inscription cut in the rock near a temple in Cilicia. Cf. *Syll* 655[6] (A.D. 83), μετὰ πολλῆς ἁγνείας καὶ νομίμων ἐθῶν, and the celebrated Epidaurian inscription quoted under ἁγνός. P Par 5[xiv. 10] (B.C. 114) couples ἁγνει[ῶν] and λειτουργιῶν following [τ]άφων. BGU IV. 1198[12] (i/B.C.) ποιούμενοι ἁγνήας καὶ θυσίας. The verb is found BGU I. 149 (ii/iii A.D.), temple accounts, including καὶ ταῖς κωμασίαις τῶν θεῶν (processions of images of the gods) τοῖς ἁγνεύουσι ἐκ περιτροπῆς (according to rota) ἱερεῦσι· Θωθ ᾱ ὑπὲρ ἁγνείας ἡμερῶν ζ ἑξ ἡμερησιῶν [so much]. A very similar entry appears in BGU I. 1[17] (ii/A.D.).

In P Oxy V. 840[8], the fragment of an uncanonical gospel composed before A.D. 200, we read that the Saviour brought His disciples εἰς αὐτὸ τὸ ἁγνευτήριον καὶ περιεπάτει ἐν τῷ ἱερῷ, "into the very place of purification, and was walking in the temple." For the verb ἁγνεύω see BGU IV. 1201[6] (A.D. 2) τῶν ἁγνευόν[τ]ων ἱερέων διαπεραιωμένων πρὸς τὰς λιτουργείας καὶ θυσείας τῶν θεῶν, P Tebt II. 298[63] (A.D. 107–8) ἱερεῦσι[ ] ἴσαις ἁγνεύου[σ]ι καθ᾽ ἡμέραν (πυροῦ) δ, "to officiating priests ¼ art. of wheat daily" (Edd.).

ἁγνίζω, ἁγνισμός.

The verb occurs in the Leyden *Papyrus magica* (ed. Dieterich) VI. 36 ποιήσας βόθρον ἐπὶ ἡγνισμένῳ τόπῳ. For the subst. see *Syll* 879[18] f. (end of iii/B.C.) τὸν δὲ γυναικονόμον τὸν ὑπὸ τοῦ δήμου αἱρούμενον τοῖς ἁγνισμοῖς κτλ. Cf. Anz *Subsidia*, p. 283.

ἀγνοέω.

A good parallel to the Pauline phrase 1 Th 4[13] οὐ θέλομεν δὲ ὑμᾶς ἀγνοεῖν occurs in P Tebt II. 314[3] (ii/A.D.) πιστεύω σε μὴ ἀγνοεῖν, which also illustrates the use with the negative in 2 Cor 2[11]. The construction in P Tebt I. 43[25] (B.C. 118) ὑφ᾽ ἡμῶν ἐν τισιν ἠγνοηκότων may help the difficult 2 Pet 2[12] ἐν οἷς ἀγνοοῦσιν βλασφημοῦντες. The suggestion of wilful ignorance (see ἄγνοια) appears in P Oxy IX. 1188[5] (A.D. 13) στοχα(σάμενος) τοῦ μηδ(ὲν) ἀγνοη(θῆναι) μηδὲ πρὸς χά(ριν) οἰκονομηθ(ῆναι), "making it your aim that nothing be concealed or done by favour" (Edd.). For ἀγνοεῖν of a person, cf. P Giss I. 69[4] (A.D. 118–9) Χαιρήμονα τὸν ἀναδιδόντα τὸ ἐπιστό[λι]ον τοῦτο οὐκ ἀγνοεῖς, ἄδελφε.

ἀγνόημα.

The royal decree of Euergetes II. and the two Cleopatras, P Tebt I. 5[3] (B.C. 118), proclaims an amnesty for all their subjects for ἀγνοημάτων ἁμαρτημ[άτ]ων [ἐ]γκλημάτων καταγνωσμάτων (see note), where the difference between the first two words is brought out by the editors' rendering, "errors," "crimes" : cf. *Archiv* ii. p. 483 ff. An inscription from Egypt, *OGIS* 116[2] (ii/B.C.), has συγγνώ[μην . . .] αν γεγονόσιν ἀγνοήμα[σιν . . .] in a broken context, but the meaning seems clear. The combination quoted above from P Tebt I. 5 apparently recurs in BGU IV. 1185[7] (i/B.C.) ἀγνοημ[ά]των ἁμαρτημάτων καταγνωσμάτω[ν . . .]ν σκεπεστικῶν αἰτιῶν πασῶν κτλ. Similarly in P Par 63[xiii.2] one of the Ptolemies writes ἀπολελυκότες πάντας τοὺς ἐνεσχημένους ἔν τισιν ἀγνοήμασιν ἢ ἁμαρτήμασιν ἕως τῆς ιθ τοῦ ἐπείφ. (On ἐνέχεσθαι ἐν see *Proleg.* p 61 f.). The Seleucid Demetrius uses a like combination in 1 Macc 13[39], and it is further found in Tob 3[3], and Sir 23[2] (cited by Thayer). Ἀγνόημα is accordingly marked by this association as meaning an offence of some kind, and "error" is its natural equivalent : so in Heb 9[7].

ἄγνοια.

The connotation of wilful blindness, as in Eph 4[18], is found in P Tebt I. 24[33] (B.C. 117), where an official reports the misconduct of certain persons whose plans he had frustrated, so that λήγοντες τῆς ἀγνοίας they left the district. The writer had ἀνοίας first, and then added γ above the line. In the ordinary sense of inadvertence it is common : e.g BGU IV. 1114[9] (B.C. 8-7) γέγονεν δὲ κατ' ἄγνοιαν εἰς τὸ αὐτοῦ Κοΐντου Καικιλίου Κάστορος ὄνομα. [ὁ κατεχλους] With a gen. the same phrase occurs in P Oxy VI. 925[5] (ii/iii A.D.) ἐπεὶ κατ' ἄγνοιαν τῶν φροντίδων αὐτῶν ἠργάσατο, *ib.* I. 78[23 ff.] (iii/A.D.) ἵν' οὖν μὴ δόξω συνθέσθαι τῇ τοῦ πραγματικοῦ ἀγνοίᾳ ἐπιδίδωμι τὰ βιβλίδια κτλ. The simple dat. appears with same sense in P Flor II. 132[8] (iii/A.D.) ἐλε[ξ]αν πεποιηκέναι ταῦτα ἀγνοίᾳ. For κατὰ ἄγνοιαν, as in Ac 3[17], see P Oxy II. 237[viii. 36] (A.D. 186) ἵνα οἱ συναλλάσσοντες μὴ κατ' ἄγνοιαν ἐνεδρεύωνται, "in order that persons entering into agreements may not be defrauded through ignorance" (Edd.).

ἁγνός.

In its narrower sense we may compare a psephism from Assos, dated A.D. 37, *Syll* 364[2] τὴν πάτριον ἁγνὴν Παρθένον (cf. 2 Cor 11[2]), *i.e.* Athena Polias, as Dittenberger notes— the "Blessed Virgin" of Greek religion : cf. *Preisigke* 2481 (i/A.D.) Ἰουλία ἁγνή, ἐτῶν κγ, εὐψύχι. It is applied to holy places in P Tebt II. 616 (ii/A.D.), a letter from a προφήτης.—[ὅ]τι ἔξεσ[τι] πᾶσι ἐν ἁγνοῖς τόπο.ς γενέσθαι. For the ceremonial use of ἁ. see *Priene* 205, εἰσίναι εἰς τ[ὸ] ἱερὸν ἁγνὸν ἐ[ν] ἐσθῆτι λευκ[ῆ], an inscription at the entrance to a ἱερὸς οἶκος. Routiac (*Recherches*, p. 62), who cites the passage, aptly recalls the inscription of the temple of Epidaurus mentioned by Clement Alex. (*Strom.* V. 1. 13, 3) to illustrate the transition from the ritual to the moral sense—

> ἁγνὸν χρὴ νηοῖο θυώδεος ἐντὸς ἰόντα
> ἔμμεναι· ἁγνείη δ' ἐστὶ φρονεῖν ὅσια.

(Also in Porphyry *de abst.* ii. 19, *ap. Syll* ii. p. 267.) There is also a noteworthy usage in the Chian dialectic inser., *Syll* 570[9] (iv/B.C.) [ὁ ἰ]δὼν κατειπάτω πρ[ὸς] τὸς βασιλέας ἁγ[νῶς] πρὸς τὸ θεό, "give information . . . if he would be blameless before the God." An interesting example of the adj. occurs in P Oxy I. 41[29 f.] (the report of a public meeting, iii/iv A.D.), where at a popular demonstration in honour of the prytanis the people are described as shouting—ἁγνοὶ

πιστοὶ σύνδικοι, ἁγνοὶ πιστοὶ συ[ν]ή̣ γορο]ι, ἰς ὥρας πᾶσι τοῖς τὴν πόλιν φιλοῦσιν, "True and upright advocates, true and upright assessors ! Hurrah for all who love the city !" (Edd.). Ἀγνῶς in the sense of Phil 1[17], "honestly," is common in honorific inscriptions, as OGIS 485[13] (Magnesia, Roman age) τὰς λοιπὰς δὲ φιλοτειμίας τελιάσαντα ἁγνῶς καὶ ἀμέμπτως, *ib.* 524[5] (Thyatira, do.) ἀγορανομήσαντα τετράμηνον ἁγνῶς : so as early as Pindar (*O.* iii. 37).

The adjective and its derivatives may accordingly take a wide meaning, as wide as our *pure* in the ethical sense. But a starting-point must not be overlooked : cf. the Avestan *yasna* "ritual," Sanskrit *yaj*, Av. *yas* "to worship," showing that it originally denoted "in a condition prepared for worship." The uses noted under ἁγνεία and in this article show that this meaning persisted ; and it is not out of sight in NT times. In pagan technical language it definitely connoted twofold abstinence, as a necessary condition of entrance into a temple. The definition of Hesychius gives us the condition in its oldest form : "ἁγνεύειν· καθαρεύειν ἀπό τε ἀφροδισίων καὶ ἀπὸ νεκροῦ."

ἁγνότης.

IG IV. 588[15] (Argos, ii/A.D.) δικαιοσύνης ἔνεκεν καὶ ἁγνότητος (cited by Grimm).

ἀγνωσία.

BGU II. 614[22] (A.D. 217), ἵν' οὖν μὴ ἀγνωσία ᾖ. P Hawara (*Archiv* v. p. 383) 69[11] (i/ii A.D.) ἴτε ἀνισθησίαν ἴτε ἀγνωσίαν αἰτιᾶσθαι. The latter instance has the suggestion of disgraceful ignorance which attaches to both the NT occurrences.

ἄγνωστος.

Deissmann (*St Paul*, p. 251 ff.) supplies an interesting parallel to the Greek inscription which St Paul read on an altar at Athens, Ac 17[23] ἀγνώστῳ θεῷ, from a votive inscription, probably of ii/A.D., on an altar discovered at Pergamon in 1909. The inscription is mutilated, but may probably be restored as follows—

> θεοῖς ἀγν[ώστοις]
> Καπίτω[ν]
> δᾳδοῦχο[ς].

"To unknown gods Capito torchbearer." See also P Giss I. 3[21] (A.D. 117) ἥκω σοι, ὦ δῆμ[ε], οὐκ ἄγνωστος Φοῖβος θεός, where the description of Φοῖβος as οὐκ ἄγνωστος may be due, as the editor suggests, to the fact that he was the god of the special district in question. Cf. also BGU II. 590[6] (A.D. 177-8), where γε[ν]ομένων ἀγνώστων ἡμεῖν refers to two (divine ?) Caesars, Commodus and his great father. "Agnostos Theos" is the title of an elaborate monograph by E. Norden (Leipzig, 1913), in which he makes the Areopagus speech in Ac 17 the starting-point for a series of discussions on the history of the forms of religious speech.

ἀγορά.

The ordinary meaning "market" does not need illustrating. That bankers were to be found there may be seen in BGU III. 986[5] (Hadrian's reign) διὰ τῆς Ἀ . . . τοῦ

Θεογείτονο[ς τρ]απέ(ζης) ἀγορᾶς. It denotes "provisions," "supplies," in P Petr II. 13 (17)⁶ (B.C. 258–3), and *ib.* 15 (2)⁶ (B.C. 241–39) [τ]ὴν γινομένην ἀγορὰν εἰς . . . "provisions up to a certain amount." Cf. P Amh II. 29¹¹ (*c.* B.C. 250) ἢ εἴ τιν]ες ἄλλαι ἀγοραὶ συντάσ[σονται, as restored by Wilcken, *Archiv* ii. p. 119. In an important article on the system of the *conventus*, or official circuit of the Prefect in Roman Egypt (*Archiv* iv. p. 366 ff.), Wilcken states that ἀγορά is often used = *forum* in its more pregnant sense of a judicial assembly (cf. *OGIS* 517 note 7). So in BGU III. 888¹ (A.D. 109) we find a man described as νομογράφος ἀγορᾶς.

ἀγοράζω.

The verb (MGr = "buy") is common in deeds of sale, e.g. P Lond 882²⁴ (B.C. 101) (= III. p. 14) ἣν ἠγόρασεν παρὰ Θ., *ib.* 1208¹⁰ (B.C. 97) (= III. p. 19). It is used of the purchase of slaves in *OGIS* 338²³ (the will of Attalus III.—B.C. 133): cf. 1 Cor 6²⁰, 7²³ τιμῆς ἠγοράσθητε (Deissmann *LAE*, p. 328). So P Oxy VIII. 1149⁵ ff. (ii/A.D.) ἀ[γο]ράσαι παρὰ Τασαρ[α]πίωνος ὃν ἔχει δοῦλον Σαραπίωνα, "to buy from Tasarapion her slave Sarapion," *al.* Both the verb and the corresponding substantive are found in P Oxy II. 298¹¹, ⁴⁸, a long letter by a tax-collector of i/A.D., στατῆρας πορφύ[ρ]ας ἀγόρασον . . . ἐὰν εὕρης ἀγ[ο]ραστὴν τοῦ μέρ[ους] τῆς οἰκίας. For ἀγοραστός, see also P Petr II. 20ⁱⁱ ⁵,⁸ (B.C. 252) τοῦ ἀγοραστοῦ = "(wheat) for sale," and P Tebt I. 30¹¹ (A.D. 123) (= *Selections*, p. 78) ἀγοραστὴν παρὰ Θενπετεσούχου . . . οἰκίαν, "the house as purchased from Thenpetesuchus," *al.* Ἀγοράζειν παρά is illustrated above (P Lond 1208¹⁰, P Oxy 1149⁵, etc.): for ἀ. ἀπό cf. P Flor II. 175¹¹ (A.D. 255) δήλοι (for δήλου) ἀπὸ τίνος τέκτονος ἠγοράσθη. For the gen. of price cf. P Par 59⁵ (= Witkowski *Epp.²*, p. 75—B.C. 60) τούτων (*sc.* 1 talent 140 drachmae) ἠγώρακα σίτου ἀρ ταβας) β (δραχμῶν) χλ κτλ.

ἀγοραῖος.

Prof. Lake (*Earlier Epistles of St. Paul*, p. 69 n³) regards ἀγοραίων in Ac 17⁵ as "agitators," in view of Plutarch *Aemil. Paul.* 38, ἀνθρώπους ἀγενεῖς καὶ δεδουλευκότας, ἀγοραίους δὲ καὶ δυναμένους ὄχλον συναγαγεῖν, a neat double parallel. In *Syll* 553²³ (ii/B.C.) it is used of "merchants," "dealers." The grammarian Ammonius (iv/A.D.) would distinguish ἀγοραῖος = ἐν ἀγορᾷ τιμώμενος from ἀγόραιος = ἐν ἀγορᾷ τεθραμμένος: Crönert remarks that the MSS. vary. For the special use seen in Ac 19³⁸, ἀγοραῖοι ἄγονται καὶ ἀνθύπατοί εἰσιν, Wilcken (*Archiv* iv. *l.c.* under ἀγορά can only cite from the papyri P Oxy III. 471¹²⁶ (an advocate's speech, ii/A.D.) [τὰ] τοῦ . [. . . . .] ἀγοραίον κριτήρ[ια, where it is derived from ἀγορά = *forum*. (He quotes a striking parallel to the whole phrase of Ac *l.c.* from P Flor I. 61⁴⁶ (A.D. 86–8) ὅπου διαλογισμοὶ καὶ ἡγέμονες παραγενόμενοι.) In *OGIS* 484⁶⁹ (ii/A.D.), however, an imperial rescript addressed to the Pergamenes, we find ταῖς ἀγοραίοις πιπρασκομένων: unfortunately there are gaps on each side, but the gender shows that ἡμέραι is understood, denoting in this connexion "market days." See also Ramsay's notes on the ἀγοραία (σύνοδος), *conventus iuridicus*, at Apamea, *C. and B.* nos. 294, 295 (ii. p. 461, also p. 428): also *Cagnat* IV. 790 and note.

ἀγράμματος.

Ἀ. is of constant occurrence in the formula used by one person signing a deed or letter on behalf of another who cannot write—ἔγραψα ὑπέρ τινος ἀγραμμάτου, e.g. BGU I. 118 ff. 17, *ib.* 152⁶ (both ii/A.D.): cf. P Oxy II. 275⁴³ (A.D. 66) (= *Selections* p. 58) Ζωίλος . . . ἔγραψα ὑπὲρ αὐτοῦ μὴ ἰδότος γράμματα. The great frequency of ἀγράμματος, invariably in this sense, suggests that the sneer in Ac 4¹³ is intended to picture the Apostles as "illiterate," and not merely "unversed in the learning of the Jewish schools" (Grimm). For the place which dictation had in the composition of the NT writings, see Milligan *NT Documents*, pp. 21 ff., 241 ff.

ἀγρεύω.

In the literal sense this verb occurs in P Louvre 10632 (= *Chrest.* I. 107¹³, B.C. 131) ἐὰν τῆς ταραχῆ[ς . . . . o]ἱ ἁλιεῖς δυνηθῶσι ἀγρεύειν τὸν [αὐτὸν τρόπον, ὃν καὶ] πρότερον εἰθ[ι]σμένοι ἐ[ν] τόποις [ἦ]σαν, and P Oxy I. 122⁹ (iii/iv A.D.) ἡμεῖ[ς] δὲ ἀγρεύειν τῶν θηρίων δυνά[με]θα οὐδὲ ἕν, "and we cannot catch a single animal" (Edd.).

ἀγριέλαιος.

In view of Sir W. M. Ramsay's recent discussion of the meaning of ἀ. in Rom 11¹⁷ (see *Pauline Studies*, p. 219 ff.), the occurrence of the adjective in *Syll* 540¹⁸⁹ (ii/B.C.) may be noted – κύβους κατασκευ[ασάμε]νος ξύλων ξηρῶν ἀγριελαίνων.

ἄγριος.

P Tebt II. 612 (i/ii A.D.) θήρας ἀγρίων: cf. BGU IV. 1123⁹ (time of Augustus) ἢ ἰχθύας ἢ ἀγρίας ἢ ξυλείας. The adjective is used of a "malignant" sore or wound in *Syll* 802¹¹¹ (iii/B.C.) ὑπὸ τοῦ ἀγρίου ἕλκεος δεινῶς διακείμ[εν]ος: *ib.* 806⁶ (Roman age).

ἀγρός.

This old and once common word is unexpectedly rare in papyri. P Strass I. 52⁵, ¹⁴ (A.D. 151) concerns 2½ arourae of "catoecic land," ἃς καὶ παρα[δώσει ἡ δεδανισμ]ένη κατ' ἀγρὸν σπ[ορί]μας, "will transfer these as they lie in good condition for sowing," as the edd. render the same formula in P Ryl II. 164⁵ (A.D. 171): Preisigke, "in einem landwirtschaftlich brauchbaren Zustande, saatfähig." The same connotation of "agricultural land" appear in a few instances we can quote. P Amh II. 68⁶⁷ (i/A.D.) τῆς νυνεὶ κατ' ἀγρὸν θεωρίας. *Ib.* 134⁵ (ii/A.D.) ὄντα ἐν ἀγρῷ μετὰ τῶν θρεμμάτων, "in the fields with the cattle"; and as late as iv/A.D., *ib.* 143⁴ ὁ γὰρ ἀγρὸς Ἀβίου ἐξῆλθεν εἰς σπ[ο]ράν. In P Oxy III. 506⁴² (A.D. 143) ἀπογράφεσθαί τινα ἐπὶ τῶν ἀγρῶν, "register any one as owning those lands": ἐπὶ τοῦ ἀγροῦ has apparently been erased. *Ib.* VI. 967 (ii/A.D.) καλῶς δὲ ποιήσεις ἐπιστείλασα εἰς ἀγρὸν ἄρξασθαι τῶν εἰς τοὺς ἀμπελῶνας ποτισμῶν. P Eleph 13⁶ (B.C. 223–2), περὶ δὲ τοῦ οἰναρίου Πραξιάδης οὔπω εἰσελήλυθεν ἐξ ἀγροῦ: this resembles the ἀπ' ἀγροῦ ("from field labour" probably) in Mk 15²¹. Apart from one Byzantine document, the two instances quoted are the only occurrences of ἀγρός in P Oxy I.–X., and in the indices to P Fay, P Hib, P Tebt, P Grenf and the Revenue Law it never appears at all, nor in vols. III. and IV. of BGU. It is not worth while to present the scattered instances that are found in some other collections. Crönert's remark that **ἀγρός** is obsolete in MGr, except in Cyprian, having been progressively supplanted by χώρα and χωρίον, falls in o line with its relative infrequency in the papyri. It is, however, very common throughout the LXX, and in the Synoptic Gospels (Mt 16, Mk 8, Lk 9). In Acts it only comes once, and it may be significant that Luke has χώρα (Lk 12[16], 21[21]) or χωρίον (Ac 1[18 f.], 4[34], 5[3, 8], 28[7]) where **ἀγρός** might have been expected. So also Jn 4[35], 4[5], Jas 5[4]. It is difficult to draw a clear inference, but it looks as if for some reason **ἀγρός** was a favourite word with translators from Hebrew or Aramaic. We shall meet with other words, rare or comparatively rare in vernacular documents, which have secured a good deal of space in bibl. concordances in this way.

ἀγρυπνέω.

P Giss I. 19[7] (early ii/A.D.) συν]εχῶς ἀγρυπνοῦσα νυκτὸς ἡ[μέρας]. P Ryl II. 62[9] (iii/A.D.) ἀγρυπνεῖται καὶ κολάζεται. For the construction with ἐπί (as in Prov 8[34], Job 21[32]), see the Septuagint Memorial from Adrumetum of iii/A.D., cited by Deissmann *BS.* p. 275, l. 6 f., ἀγρυπνο[ῦν]τα ἐπὶ τῇ φιλίᾳ αὐτῆς κτλ. Cf. P Giss I. 67[6] (ii/A.D.) οἷς ὀφείλω ἐπιτεταγμέ[νως (*l.* -ταμ-) ἐπ]αγρυπνεῖν.

ἀγρυπνία.

This word, in NT only 2 Cor 6[5], 11[27], is found in *Syll* 803[50] (iii/B.C.) οὗτος ἀγρυπνίαις συνεχόμενος διὰ τὸμ πόνον τᾶς κεφαλᾶ[ς]—a passage which also throws light on the NT usage of συνέχομαι, e.g. Mt 4[24] νόσοις καὶ βασάνοις συνεχομένους. For the adverb of the primary ἄγρυπνος, see *OGIS* 194[21] (i/B.C.) ἄ[γρ]ύπνως . . . [ἐφ]ρόντισεν.

ἀγυιά.

This word, very common in papyri, is claimed for NT vocabulary by an acute conjecture of Mr A. Pallis (*A few Notes on St Mark and St Matthew, based chiefly on Modern Greek*, Liverpool, 1903, p. 12). In Mk 6[56] ἐν ἀγοραῖς appears as ἐν πλατείαις in D 565 700; and the Old Syriac, Latin and Gothic versions have "streets," which is preferable in sense. Pallis suggests that ἐν ἀγυιαῖς was the original, from which by a very slight corruption came ἀγοραῖς in the Greek MSS, and by paraphrase πλατείαις in D and its fellows. In Oxyrhynchus papyri ἐν ἀγυιᾷ is a recurrent legal formula, describing documents drawn up "in the street": see Grenfell and Hunt, P Oxy IV. p. 202, and Mitteis in Mitteis-Wilcken *Papyruskunde*, II. i. p. 61 n[4]

ἄγω.

The spread (mostly in the compounds) of the late and vulgar sigmatic aor. act. is well seen in uneducated writers of papyri. Thus P Grenf II. 44[11] (A.D. 101) and BGU II. 607[16] (A.D. 163) κατῆξαν, BGU I. 81[20] (A.D. 189) κατήξαμεν, P Ryl I. 27[35] (iii/A.D.) συνάξας. P Hawara 312[4] (ii/A.D.) (in *Archiv* v. p. 393) ἄξαι, P Giss I. 27[9] (ii/A.D.) ἄξω: cf. P Tebt I. 22[16] διάξησθε (B.C. 112). Thackeray *Gr.* p. 233 gives LXX evidence; Crönert *Mem. Herc.*, p. 232 n[2] has passages from late papyri, together with ἄξωσιν from Herculaneum (i/A.D.). Cf. also 2 Pet 2[5], Ac 14[27] D, and below.

W. G. Rutherford *New Phrynichus*, p. 217 f., shows that ἠξάμην is Homeric, and survives in Herodotus and early Attic. Whether its appearance in (mostly illiterate) papyri is due to survival in dialects, especially Ionic, or to independent recoinage of a very obvious type, need not be discussed here. The importance of the form for the NT was emphasized by Moulton in *Camb. Bibl. Essays*, p. 485 (1909), (cf. *Einleitung*, p. 84). In Lk 3[17] ℵ* reads συνάξαι, as do all authorities in 13[34] ἐπισυνάξαι). We may be quite sure that Luke never emended the normal strong aorist into this colloquial, if not uneducated form. It was therefore in Q, and Mt 3[12], 23[37] represent emendations—one to the future, which appeared in the last clause of the verse (κατακαύσει), the other to the "correct" infinitive ἐπισυναγαγεῖν: the latter emendation figures in all MSS. except ℵ* in Lk 3[17]. The point has important results, when set among others of like nature, in the discussion of the synoptic problem: see *Expos.* VII. vii. p. 413. The active perfect of ἄγω does not appear in NT; but we may note that ἀγήγοχα (Tobit 12[9]) can be quoted from *OGIS* 219[35] (iii/B.C.), 267[12] (ii/B.C.). There are many varieties here: -αγέοχα P Tebt I. 5[94] (B.C. 118) and *Letronne* 84 (i/B.C.); ἀγείοχα (or cpd.) P Tebt I. 10[6] (B.C. 114), P Par 15[67] (B.C. 120), P Ryl II. 67[5] (ii/B.C.), P Oxy II. 283[14] (A.D. 45), P Leid B[4] (ii/B.C.); -ἀγόοχα P Tebt I. 124 (c. B.C. 118). We have not attempted to make this list exhaustive.

For ἄγω in the sense of "fetch," "carry away," see P Oxy IV. 742[7] (B.C. 2), where instructions are given to deposit certain bundles of reeds in a safe place ἵνα τῇ ἀναβάσει αὐτὰς ἄξωμεν. Wilcken's proposal (*ap.* Witkowski *Epp.*[2], p. 128) that ἄξωμεν should be assigned to ἄγνυμι seems to us improbable. For the construction with μετά (2 Tim 4[11]) cf. P Petr II. 32 (2a)[13] ἄγων μεθ' αὐτοῦ. For " bring before " a court of justice, as Mt 10[18], Ac 18[12], cf. BGU I. 22[31 f.] (A.D. 114) (= *Selections*, p. 76) διὸ ἀξιῶ ἀκθῆναι τοὺς ἐνκαλουμένους ἐπὶ σὲ πρὸς δέουσ(αν) ἐπέξοδον.—a petition to the Strategus. So also P. Tebt II. 331[16 f.] (c. A.D. 131) ἀξιῶ ἀχθῆναι αὐτοὺς ἐπὶ σέ: the constr. with ἐπί is regular, as in NT. Note P Oxy X. 1279[25] (A.D. 139) μετὰ δὲ τὴν πενταετίαν οὐκ ἀχθήσομαι εἰς τὴν μίσθωσιν " I shall not be forced to take the lease " (Edd.). Ἄγειν for "keeping," "holding" a special day or festival (as Tob 11[19]: cf. Ac 19[38] ἀγοραῖοι ἄγονται—see *s.v.* ἀγοραῖος) appears in *OGIS* 456[10] καταγγελεῖς τῶν πρώτων ἀ(χ)θησο[μένων ἀγώνων], "heralds of the first games that shall be held." So with ἐ[νιαυσίας ἑ]ο[ρ]τάς in *OGIS* 111[26]; P Oxy VII. 1025[17] (iii/A.D.) pass. with θεωρίαι; P Giss I. 27[9] (ii/A.D.) στεφανηφορίαν ἄξω. More generally we have σχολὴν ἄγειν in P Tebt II. 315[17] (ii/A.D.), and ἄγοντος τὰ κατ' ἔ[το]ς γεωργικὰ ἔργα in P Ryl II. 154[20] (A.D. 66). Somewhere under this heading will come Lk 24[21] τρίτην ταύτην ἡμέραν ἄγει, where if the verb is not impersonal, ὁ Ἰησοῦς might be supplied as subject. The intransitive ἄγειν may be seen in the meaning " lead," of a road or canal, as P Petr I. 22 (2); and a rather similar intransitive use occurs in an Egyptian inscr. of Augustus (*Preisigke* 401, A.D. 10-1) who records that he ποταμ[ὸν] . . . ἤγαγεν . . . ῥέοντα δι' ὅλης τῆς πόλεως: in the Latin equivalent *flumen . . . induxit*. Ἄγωμεν (as in Jn 14[3]) survives in MGr ἄμε, "go " (Thumb).

ἀγωγή.

The figurative sense of ἀγωγή, as in 2 Tim. 3[10], may be paralleled from P Par 61[11 f.] (B.C. 156) πάντα ἐστὶν ἀλλότρια τῆς τε ἡμῶν ἀγωγῆς, P Tebt I. 24[57] (B.C. 117) μ[ο]χθηρὰν ἀγωγήν. Cf. OGIS 223[15] (iii/B.C.) φαίνεσθε γὰρ καθόλου ἀγωγῆι ταύτῃ χρῆσθαι, and ib. 474[9] (i/A.D.) διὰ [τὴν κο σμιωτάτην αὐτῆς] ἀγωγήν with Dittenberger's note. A good example is also afforded by Magn 164[2] (i/ii A.D.) ἤθει καὶ ἀγωγῇ κόσμιον. As action-noun to ἄγειν, it means "freightage" in Syll 587[17] (B.C. 329-8, Attic) τῆς τομῆς τῶν λίθων καὶ τῆς ἀγωγῆς καὶ τῆς θέσεως. Hence "load," "freight," cf. Wilcken Ostr. ii. 797 (Ptol.) ἀχύρου ἀγω(γὴν) ἕνα (sic), ib. 1168 εἰς τὰς καμείνους ἀγω(γαί) (sc. ἀχύρου): so P Oxy IX. 1167[10] (A.D. 211), P Lond 1164(h)[7 and 24] (A.D. 212) (= III. p. 164 f.). Ἀγωγὴν ποιεῖσθαι "carry off," "arrest," is found in P Tebt I. 39[22 f.] (B.C. 114) and ib. 48[22 f.] (c. B.C. 113), and in P Fay 12[31] (c. B.C. 103) the substantive occurs in the sense of "abduction." For ἀ. as a legal term see P Lond 951[4] (A.D. 249) (= III. p. 221) ὁμολογῶ μηδεμίαν ἀγωγὴν ἔχειν κατὰ μηδένα τρ[όπ]ον πρός σε, and cf. Archiv iv. p. 400.

ἀγών.

The ethical meaning of ἀγών is frequent in late Greek, e.g. P Flor I. 36[26] (iv/A.D.) τ ὸ ν περὶ ψυχῆς ἀγῶ[ν]α. In Col 2[1], however, Field (Notes, p. 195) prefers to think of outward, rather than of inward, conflict, and compares Plut. Vit. Flam. XVI. πλεῖστον δ' ἀγῶνα καὶ πόνον αὐτῷ παρεῖχον αἱ περὶ Χαλκιδέων δεήσεις πρὸς τὸν Μάνιον, where Langhorne translates, "but he had much greater difficulties to combat, when he applied to Manius in behalf of the Chalcidians." In a petition of B.C. 5, BGU IV. 1139[17], we find διὸ ἀξιοῦμέν [σε] τὸν πάντων σωτῆρα καὶ ἀντιλήμπτορα ὑπὲρ σπλάγχνου τὸν ἀγῶνα ποιούμενοι to compel restitution of a stolen daughter. For the literal meaning, see Syll 524 where various τῶν τε παίδων καὶ τῶν ἐφήβω[ν] . . . ἀγῶνες in reading, music, etc., are enumerated: BGU IV. 1074[15] (iii/A.D.) of great games at Oxyrhynchus, etc., etc.

ἀγωνία.

P Tebt II. 423[13 f.] (early iii/A.D.) ὡς εἰς ἀγωνίαν με γενέσθαι ἐν τῷ παρόντι, "so I am at present very anxious" (Edd.). The corresponding verb is common with the meaning "to be distressed," "to fear." Thus P Petr II. 11 (1) ἵνα εἰδῶμεν ἐν οἷς εἶ καὶ μὴ ἀγωνιῶμεν, "that we may know what you are about, and we may not be anxious" (Ed.): ib. III. 53 (?)[15 f.] οὐ γὰρ ὡς ἔτυχεν ἀγωνιῶμεν, "for we are in a state of no ordinary anxiety" (Edd.); P Oxy IV. 744[4] (B.C. 1) (= Selections, p. 32), μὴ ἀγωνιᾷς, "do not worry"; ib.[14] ἐρωτῶ σε οὖν ἵνα μὴ ἀγωνιάσῃς, "I urge you therefore not to worry." An almost contemporary instance is afforded by BGU IV. 1078[5] (A.D. 39) ὅτι ἀγωνιῶ περὶ ὑμῶν : of a later date are P Giss I. 17[6,12] (time of Hadrian), ib. 19[3] μεγάλως ἀγωνῶσα περί σου, PSI 94[16] (ii/A.D.) μὴ ἀγωνία δὲ περὶ τῶν ἱματίων. The verb is found twice in the apocryphal Gospel of Peter 5, ἠγωνίων μή ποτε ὁ ἥλιος ἔδυ, and 10 ἀγωνιῶντες μεγάλως καὶ λέγοντες Ἀληθῶς υἱὸς ἦν θεοῦ. On the translation of ἀγωνία in Lk 22[44] see a note by Moffatt in Exp. VIII. vii. p. 91 ff.

ἀγωνίζομαι

is very common in the inscriptions, e.g. Syll 213[33] (iii/B.C.) ἀγωνιζόμενος ὑπὲρ τῆς κοινῆς σωτηρίας, where the reference is to warfare. So ib. 163[18] (B.C. 318-7) προείλετο τελευτῆσαι ὑπὸ τῶν ἐναντίων ἀγ[ωνιζόμεν]ος ὑπὲρ τῆς δημοκρατίας : ib. 199[7] (iii/B.C.) and 108[17] (B.C. 281) ἀγωνιζόμενος ὑπ[ὲρ αὐτοῦ], etc. Cf. an Athenian inscription of B.C. 268-6, Syll 214[10], ἐπειδὴ πρότερομ μὲν Ἀθηναῖοι καὶ Λακεδαιμόνιοι καὶ οἱ σύμμαχοι οἱ ἑκατέρων φιλίαν καὶ συμμαχίαν κοινὴν ποιησάμενοι πρὸς ἑαυτοὺς πολλοὺς καὶ καλοὺς ἀγῶνας ἠγωνίσαντο μετ' ἀλλήλων πρὸς τοὺς καταδουλοῦσθαι τὰς πόλεις ἐπιχειροῦντας. The phrase here hardly differs from 2 Tim 4[7], and when taken along with the preceding inscription makes it decidedly less clear that the figure there is drawn from the games, as Deissmann thinks (LAE, p. 312), illustrating the passage from a ii/A.D. inscription from the theatre at Ephesus—ἠγωνίσατο ἀγῶνας τρεῖς, ἐστέφθη δύο (Greek Inscriptions in the British Museum III. 604). For the rare use of ἀ. with an inf as in Lk 13[24] ἀγωνίζεσθε εἰσελθεῖν, Field (Notes, p. 66) compares Diod. Sic. X., p. 25, ed. Bip. : ὥστε ὁ μὲν πατὴρ ἐξίστασθαι τῆς ὅλης ἀρχῆς ἠγωνίζετο τῷ παιδί. The verb is MGr.

ἀδάπανος.

This NT ἅπ. εἰρ. (1 Cor 9[18]) is found in Michel 1006[3] (Teos, ii/B.C.) ἀδάπανον τὴν συμμορίαν καθιστάνειν : cf. Priene 111[145] (end of i/B.C.).

ἀδελφή.

P Oxy IV. 744[1] (B.C. 1) (= Selections, p. 32). Ἱλαρίων (λ. -ων) Ἄλιτι τῆι ἀδελφῆι πλεῖστα χαίρειν, "Hilarion to Alis, his sister, heartiest greetings," Alis being doubtless wife as well as sister, by a not uncommon Egyptian practice. It figured in Egyptian religion : cf. P Oxy VI. 886[7] (iii/A.D.) ἡ Ἶσις ζητοῦσα ἑαυτῆς τὸν ἀδελφὸν κὲ ἄνδρα Ὄσιρειν. Cf. for this an Egyptian inscr. of the reign of Augustus, Archiv v. p. 164 Ἀ[ρ]τεμίδωρος Ἀνουβᾶτος καὶ ἡ γυνὴ ἀδελφὴ Ἡρακλία . . . καὶ ὁ υἱὸς Ἑρμανοῦβ(ι)ς, and still more clearly P Tebt II 320[3] (A.D. 181) τῆ[ς] . . . γυναικὸς . . [οὔσης μο]υ ὁμοπ[ατρίου) καὶ ὁμ[ομ(ητρίου] ἀδ]ελ(φῆς). But there seem to be places where the word means simply "wife"; see under ἀδελφός, and cf. P Oxy VII. 1070 (iii/A.D.), where a man addresses his wife as ἀδελφή and speaks of "our child and your brother and your father and your mother and all our (relations)"—clearly she was not "sister" literally. Dittenberger on OGIS 60[6] (B.C. 247-21) Βερενίκη, ἡ ἀδελφὴ καὶ γυνὴ αὐτοῦ (Ptolemy Euergetes), shows that ἀδελφή was an honorary title : Berenice was her husband's cousin. For the later metaphorical use of the word (1 Cor 7[15], etc.), cf. the Paris magical papyrus l. 1135 ff. χαίρετε οἷς τὸ χαίρειν ἐν εὐλογίᾳ δίδοται ἀδελφοῖς καὶ ἀδελφαῖς ὁσίοις καὶ ὁσίαις.

ἀδελφός.

For the literal and the more general derived sense we may quote Syll 474[10] ἀδελφοὶ οἷς κοινὰ τὰ πατρῷα, and 276[26] διὰ τὸ Μεσσαλιήτας εἶναι ἡμῖν ἀδελ[φούς]. In P Lond 42[1] (B.C. 168) (= I. p. 30, Selections p. 9) Ἰσίας Ἡφαιστίωνι τῶι ἀδελφῶ[ι χαί(ρειν)], it seems probable that Isias is

addressing her *husband*, not *brother* : see Kenyon's note *ad l.*
where Letronne's statement that the Ptolemies called their
wives ἀδελφαί even where they were not actually so is
quoted. Witkowski *Epp.*[2] p. 61 maintains this against
Wilcken, quoting Wilamowitz (*Gr. Lesebuch* I. p. 397), and
noting that Isias says ἡ μήτηρ σου, showing that Isias and
Hephaestion were not children of the same mother. Cf.
also P Par 45 and 48 (ii/B.C.) where men address with τῷ
ἀδελφῷ χαίρειν men who are no relation to them. For the
use of ἀδελφοί to denote members of the same religious community cf. P Tor I. 1ᵇ ²⁰ (ii/B.C.) where the members of a
society which had to perform a part of the ceremony of
embalming bodies are described as ἀδελφῶν τῶν τὰς
λειτουργίας ἐν ταῖς νεκρίαις παρεχομένων, and in P Par
42¹ ᵉᵗᶜ. (ii/B.C.) the same designation is applied to the
"fellows" of a religious corporation established in the
Serapeum of Memphis. In P Tebt I. 12 (B.C. 118) Crönert
assumes that one town clerk addresses another as ἀδελφός :
Grenfell and Hunt take it literally—see their introduction.
Crönert quotes also *Syll* 607 (iii/iv A.D.), where it is used
between two δεκάπρωτοι, and *OGIS* 257² (B.C. 109), where
one king so addresses another. In this last case the kings
were the sons of sisters, but Dittenberger warns us against
taking ἀδελφός as used loosely for ἀνεψιός. He refers to
OGIS 138¹ (ii/B.C.), where Ptolemy Euergetes II. addresses
as "brother" one Lochus, who in other inscriptions is
συγγενής—"our trusty and well-beloved cousin," as an
English king would have put it. Ἀδελφέ as a term of
address may be illustrated by P Flor II. 228 (iii/A.D.), where
Palas thrice calls Heroninus ἀδελφέ : in four other letters to
him, from about the same time, he only calls him φίλτατος.
So P Tebt II. 314¹² (ii/A.D.) ἔρρωσό μοι ἀδελφε, in a letter
addressed at the beginning τῷ] τιμιωτάτῳ. (The voc. survives
in Pontic MGr ἄδελφε—elsewhere ἀδερφέ—says Thumb.)
A clear case is BGU IV. 1209² (B.C. 23), where Tryphon
addresses τῶι ἀδελφῶι, and goes on to write of his correspondent's late brother as his own former friend : τοῦ εὐκλήρου
ἀδελφοῦ σου ἡμῶν δὲ φίλου γενομένου Πετεχῶντος. Ἀδελφός
as a title of address is discussed in *Rhein. Mus.* N.F. lv.
p. 170. From the Christian papyri we may note P Grenf
II. 73² (late iii/A.D.) (= *Selections* p. 117) Ἀπόλλωνι
πρεσβυτέρῳ ἀγαπητῷ ἀδελφῷ ἐν Κ(υρί)ῳ χαίρειν, P. Lond
417¹ ᶠ. (c. A.D. 346) (= II. p. 299, *Selections* p. 123) τῷ
δεσπότῃ μου καὶ ἀγαπητῷ ἀδελφῷ Ἀβιννέῳ πραι ποσίτῳ),
and P Iand 11⁹ (iii/iv A.D.) τῷ κυρίῳ μου ἀδελφῷ Πέτρῳ (cf.
Wilcken, *Archiv* vi. p. 295). For the Christian use of the
word see Harnack *Mission and Expansion of Christianity*[2] I.
p. 405 ff. On ἀδελφός "improperly" used in the LXX, see
a note by Hort *The Epistle of St. James*, p. 102 f.

ἀδελφότης.

This word, which is confined to 1 Pet 2¹⁷, 5⁹ in the NT.
occurs in the late P Giss I. 57² (vi/vii A.D.), P Oxy I. 158²
(same date) παρακαλῶ τὴν ὑμετέραν λαμπρὰν γνησίαν ἀδελφότητα, "I urge you, my true and illustrious brother." From
an earlier date may be quoted Ramsay *C. and B.*, ii. p. 720,
no. 655 (prob. iii/A.D.) εἰρήν[η] πάσῃ τῇ ἀδελ[φότητ]ι :
the inscription is the dedication of a κοιμητήριον, which
Ramsay notes as a Christian term appearing as early as A.D.
251. Ramsay's remark, "It is noteworthy that the collective ἀδελφότης had already been formed," betrays forgetfulness

of 1 Pet *ll.cc.*, as well as of occurrences in Dion Chrysostom
and 1 and 4 Maccabees : see Grimm. Crönert adds Vettius
Valens, whom Kroll dates under the Antonines—see his
index *s.v.*

ἄδηλος.

P Lond 946²³ (A.D. 226) (=III. p. 118) ἀδήλου ὄντος εἰ
ὑμεῖν διαφέρει ἡ κληρονομία, P Oxy I. 118⁵ ᶠ (late iii/A.D.)
διὰ τὸ ἄδηλον τῆς ὁδοιπορίας.

ἀδημονέω.

Lightfoot's translation of ἀδημονῶν, "distressed," in Phil
2²⁶, is borne out by P Oxy II. 298⁴⁵ ᶠ. (i/A.D.) λίαν ἀδημονοῦμεν
χάρ[ι]ν τῆς θρεπτῆς Σαραποῦτος, where the editors render,
"I am excessively concerned on account of the foster-child
Sarapous." Towards the etymology of this word, T. W. Allen
(*CR* xx. p. 5) traces an adj. δήμων in the *Iliad* (Μ 211),
with the meaning "knowing" "prudent," so that ἀδημονεῖν
would suggest originally bewilderment. The adj. must be
independent of δαήμων, though ultimately from the same
root (*dens*, as in δέδαε, Skt *dasmáḥ* : cf. Boisacq *Dict.
Etym.*, p. 168).

ᾅδης.

Without suggesting that there is anything to be called a
real parallel with Rev 21⁸, it may be worth while to quote P
Oxy I. 33ⁱᵛ ³ ᶠᶠ. (late ii/A.D.), an interesting papyrus describing
an interview between M. Aurelius or Commodus and a rebel,
τίς ἤδη τὸν δεύτερόν μου ᾅδην προσκυνοῦντα καὶ τοὺς πρὸ
ἐμοῦ τελευτήσαντας . . . μετεκαλέσατο, *i.e.* "facing death
for the second time." The word does not appear in the
indices of any papyrus collection, so far as non-literary
documents go : the magic papyrus, P Leid Vᵛⁱⁱ ²⁰ (οὗ ἡ
γῆ ἀκούσασα ἐλεύσεται, ὁ ᾅδης ἀκούων ταράσσεται) will
serve as exception to prove the rule. Except for its appropriation from the literary language to represent *Sheol* in the
LXX, we should probably not find it in NT. It is significant that Paul substitutes θάνατε for ᾅδη when quoting Hos
13¹⁴ in 1 Cor 15⁵⁵. Prof. W. M. Calder tells us the word is
common on tombstones in Asia Minor—doubtless a survival
of its use in the old Greek religion.

ἀδιάκριτος.

OGIS 509⁸ (ii/A.D.) οὐδὲ τοῦτο τὸ μέρος κατέλιπον
ἀδιάκριτον. For the adv. see P Oxy IV. 715³⁶ (A.D. 131)
where a registration of property is certified with the words
κ[α]τακεχώ(ρικα) ἀδιακ(ρίτως ?). The editors translate ἀ.
"jointly," as = κοινῶς ἐξ ἴσου in l. 7, but Wilcken (*Archiv*
iv. p. 254) prefers "ohne Untersuchung"—a rendering
which may help us in Jas 3¹⁷.

ἀδιάλειπτος.

Syll 732³⁶ (c. B.C. 34) ἐφ' ᾗ ἔσχηκεν πρὸς τὴν σύνοδον
ἀδιαλίπτωι φιλοτιμία. In the adverb we have an early
example of this Hellenistic compound in P Tebt I. 27⁴⁵
(B.C. 113), τ]ὴν ἀδιαλίπτως προσφερομέ[ένη]ν σ]π[ο υδὴν : cf.
BGU I. 180¹⁰ (ii/iii A.D.) ἐν λειτουργίᾳ εἰμ[ὶ] ἀδιαλεί-
[ππ]ως, *Syll* 732¹⁵ (i/B.C.) ἀδιαλίπτως δὲ ἐπαγωνιζόμενος,
ib. 805⁴ (Roman period) of a cough. Other citations are
needless.

2

ἀδιάφθορος.

In *Syll* 168²⁵ (iv/B.C.) the Athenian statesman Lycurgus is praised as ἀδιάφθορον κ[αὶ] ἀνεξέλεγκτον αὐτὸν ὑπὲρ] τῆς πατρίδος . . . παρ[έχων]. Some late MSS. give the derived noun (-ία) in Tit 2⁷, and Grimm ingeniously traces our adjective to the verb ἀδιαφθείρω!

ἀδικέω.

The verb is common in petitions, as P Tebt I. 42⁶ (c. B.C. 114) ἠ̓δικημένος καθ' ὑπερβολὴν ὑπ[ὸ] Ἁρμιύσιος, P Eleph 27(1)⁵ (iii/B.C.) τούτου δὲ γενομένου ἐσόμεθα οὐκ ἠδικημένοι; so P Passal⁸ (Ptol.) (Witkowski *Epp.*² p. 53) φρόντισον οὖν, ὅπως μὴ ἀδικηθῆι ὁ ἄνθρωπος. With cognate acc., as in Col 3²⁵, BGU IV. 1138¹³ (i/B.C.) ὃ ἠδίκησεν ἐμαρτυρήσατ.ενή. In the sense of *harming* something inanimate (Rev 6⁶ 7²·³—the latter paralleled in Thucydides) see *Syll* 557⁸ τὴν δὲ λοιπὴν χώραν τὴν ἱερὰν τοῦ Ἀπόλλωνος τοῦ Πτωΐου μὴ ἀδικεῖν μηδένα, and cf. *BCH* 1902. p. 217: ἐάν τις τὴν στήλην ἀδικήσει, κεχολωμένον ἔχοιτο Μῆνα καταχθόνιον. The wider sense of ἀδικεῖν "injure" is well illustrated by Swete on Rev 2¹¹.

ἀδίκημα.

The concrete noun from ἀδικεῖν, defined in Aristotle (ap. Thayer) as τὸ ἄδικον ὅταν πραχθῇ, occurs frequently. So BGU IV. 1008²² (i/B.C.), a marriage contract, of a "wrong" done to the wife (εἰς αὐτὴν ἀδίκημα). P Lille I. 29¹ (iii/B.C.) ἐὰν δέ τις περὶ ἀδικήματος ἑτέ[ρο]υ οἰκέτηι ὄντι δίκην γραψάμενος ὡς ἐλευθέρωι καταδικάσηται, P Amh II. 33¹³ (c. B.C. 157) ἐνφανισμὸν περί τινων ἀδικημάτω[ν] καὶ παραλογιῶν σίτου τε καὶ χαλκοῦ "misdeeds and peculations," *Archiv* 472¹⁹ ᶠ·, 884⁸ ᶠ·, 1009⁸⁷, etc.

ἀδικία.

P Oxy IX. 1203²¹ (i/A.D.) τὰ ὑπὸ τοῦ πατρὸς Λεωνίδου ἐπὶ τῇ ἡμῶν ἀδικίᾳ πραχθέντα "done by his father L. to our hurt." BGU IV. 1123¹¹ (i/B.C.) μηδ' ἄλλο μηδὲν ἐπιτελεῖν ἐπὶ τῇ τοῦ ἑτέρου ἀδικίᾳ. P Tebt I. 104²¹ (B.C. 92) the husband may not alienate the property, ἐπ' ἀδικίαι τῆι Ἀπολλωνίαι. P Magd 14¹¹ (iii/B.C.) συγγρα[φὴ] ἐπ' ἀδικίαι γεγρ.μμένη. It is curious that this recurrent combination should not appear in NT (except in 1 Cor 13⁶, which is quite different), among two dozen instances of the noun. For the concrete sense we find in papyri the neuter ἀδίκιον, which is also Attic, and quotable from Ionic inscriptions: see instances in Mayser *Gr.* p. 432.

ἄδικος.

P Tebt II. 286⁷ (A.D. 121–38) νομὴ ἄδικος [οὐ]δὲν ἰσχύει, "unjust possession is invalid"; *ib.* 302¹³ (A.D. 71–2) ἄδικον [ἐστιν ἡμᾶς ἀπαιτεῖσθαι]. Of a person, BGU IV. 531²⁰ ᶦᶦ (ii/A.D.) πέπεισαι [γὰρ] μού τῇ γνώμῃ ὡς οὔτε εἰμὶ ἄδικος οὔτε ἀ[λ]λοτρίων ἐπιθυμητής. Instances need not be multiplied.

ἄδολος.

The sense of this adjective in 1 Pet 2² is now set at rest by its constant occurrence in the papyri in the sense of "pure," "unadulterated." Thus P Hib I. 85¹⁴ (B.C.

261–0) σῖτον καθαρὸν ἄδολον ἀπὸ πάντων μετρήσει, *ib.* 98¹⁹ (B.C. 251–0) σῖτον κα[θαρὸν ἄ]δ[ο]λον κεκοσκιν[ευμένον] ("sifted"). Six examples come from this volume of iii/B.C. all referring to "unadulterated" corn. From i/A.D. we may cite P Oxy VIII. 1124¹¹ (A.D. 26) πυρὸν νέο[ν] καθαρὸν ἄδολον ἄκρειθον, "wheat that is new, pure, unadulterated, and unmixed with barley." PSI 31²¹ (A.D. 104) τὰ ἐκφόρια παραδώσω ἐν τῇ κώμῃ καθαρὰ καὶ ἄδωλα gives the adj. a general application to all farm produce. P Oxy IV. 729¹⁹ (A.D. 137) ἀπ[οδότωσαν τῷ μεμισθ[ω]κότι τὸν μὲν οἶνον παρὰ ληνὸν νέον ἄδολον gives the rare application to liquids: cf. P Ryl II. 97 (A.D. 139), of oil. The word is used of λαχανοσπέρμον, "vegetable seed," in P Fay 89¹¹ (A.D. 0), and of λάχανον in BGU IV. 1015¹² (A.D. 222–3). Cf. *Syll* 653¹⁰⁰ (i/B.C.) οἱ πωλοῦντες ἄδολα καὶ καθαρά. So of χρῖμα in Aeschylus *Agam.* 95 (but cf. Verrall), and in MGr of wine (Abbott, *Songs of Modern Greece*, p. 68). The figurative use appears in the late P Par 21¹⁵ (a deed of sale, A.D. 616), ὁμολο γοῦμεν . . . ἀδόλῳ συνειδήσει.

ἁδρότης.

In Wilcken *Ostr.* ii. 1600 (ii/A.D.) ἁδρο⁸ appears twice, representing presumably something from ἁδρός The adjective occurs in BGU III. 781ᵛⁱ·² (i/A.D.) πατέλλον ἁδρόν.

ἀδυνατέω.

Applied to persons this verb retains its classic sense, "to be incapable," in late Greek: cf. P Par 35¹⁶ (B.C. 163), διὰ τὸ ἐμὲ ἐν κατοχεῖ εἶτα ἀδυνατεῖν, *ib.* 63¹·⁴ (B.C. 165) ὅπως μήτεν τῶν ἀδυνατούντων γεωργεῖν περισπᾶται μηθείς, and ⁹·¹ τοὺς ἀδυνατοῦντας ἀναγκάζειν ἐπιδέχεσθαι τὰ τῆς γεωργίας. The neuter sense, "to be impossible," when applied to things, appears in the LXX, which seems to tell in favour of the AV rendering in Lk 1³⁷, as against the RV: see Hatch *Essays* p. 4, Field *Notes* p. 46 f., where the true reading παρὰ τοῦ θεοῦ (RV) is rendered "for from God no word (or, nothing) shall be impossible."

ἀδύνατος.

In P Par 66²⁰ (late Ptol.) πρεσβύτεροι καὶ ἀδύνατοι are men "not strong enough" to work: cf. also P Lond 971⁴ (iii/iv A.D.) (III. p. 128) ἀδύνατος γάρ ἐστιν ἡ γυνὴ διὰ ἀσθένειαν τῆς φύσε[ως] and *ib.* 678⁸ (B.C. 99–8) (= III. p. 18) ἀ]δύνατ[ος ὄμμ]ασι. In *Syll* 802⁵ (iii/B.C.) ἀδύνατος is associated with ἀπίθανος, applied to ἰάματα, *ib.* 512²⁴ (ii/B.C.) of witnesses unable to appear.

ᾄδω.

For the dative construction as in Eph 5¹⁹, Col 3¹⁶, cf. from the LXX Judith 16 ¹³ ᾄσατε τῷ κυρίῳ, and such passages as Philostr. *Imag.* i. xi. 780 Καΰστρῳ ταῦτα καὶ Ἴστρῳ ᾄσονται, Heliod. *Aethiop.* v. 15 ἐμβατήρια ᾄδ. Διονύσῳ (Nageli, p. 42). For the passive see P Giss I. 97⁸ (ii/iii A.D.) ὕμνοι μὲν ᾄ[δονται] γλώττῃ ξενική.

ἀεί.

It may be well to note that ἀεί, whose oldest form is αἰϜεί, is the locative of a neuter noun identical with Lat. *aevom*: αἰών is the same word in a different declension. The papyrus form is ἀεί, as Mayser shows, p. 103 f. : αἰεί, which Brugmann *Griech. Gram.*[4] p. 57 thinks to be re-formed under the influence of αἰών, crept in after the Ptolemaic period. It occurs however as early as B.C. 22 in the new parchment from Avroman in Western Media (P Saïd Khan 2 ᵃ⁹), described by E. H. Minns at the Hellenic Society (Nov. 11, 1913 : τελέσουσι δ' αἰεὶ κατ' ἐνιαυτ[ὸ]ν κτλ. It figures in the standing formula of the Decian libelli (A.D. 250) : as P Ryl II. 112 aⁱ, ᵇⁱ, cⁱ. The word comes most frequently in similar formal phrases, like ἐπὶ or εἰς τὸν ἀεὶ χρόνον (e.g. P Oxy III. 503⁹—A.D. 118, or P Lips I. 3ⁱ⁻⁸—A.D. 256), or in the stiff language of legal documents, as BGU IV. 1108²⁵ (B.C. 5) etc. It only occurs in this one place in BGU I.-IV. : in P Oxy I.-X. its total is 7, for the non-literary texts, and of these only two (iii/ or ii/iii A.D.) are dissociated from formulae. It may be seen also eight times in CPR in a standing formula. It is significant in this connexion that it is greatly outnumbered in NT by πάντοτε, which replaces it in MGr. Note the petition P Ryl II. 114²³ (c. A.D. 280) οἰκίωται . . τῷ Σ. [ἐμὲ τὴν χηρὰ]ν . . ἀεὶ ἀποστερεῖν, "it has become a habit with S. on all occasions to rob me" (Edd.).

ἀετός.

Michel 833¹² (Delos, inventory of temple treasures, B.C. 279), ἀετὸς ἀργυροῦς τῶν ἀρχαίων διαπεπτωκώς. As a constellation name it appears twice in a calendar, P Hib I. 27¹⁰⁵⁻¹⁸ (c. B.C. 300), and rather later in the Eudoxus papyrus. Mayser (p. 104) cites instances of its appearance as a proper name, by way of showing that the old Attic spelling αἰετός did not survive : it may be seen in *Syll* 537⁹ (second half of iv/B.C.), where the word is an architectural term (= gable). In *Syll* 583¹⁷ (i/A.D.) we have a marble altar of Zeus at Smyrna, ἔχων ἀετὸν ἐν ἑαυτῷ : so *ib.* 588¹⁹¹ (Delos, c. B.C. 180) ἀετοῦ κεφαλὴ ἀργυρᾶ ἐπίχρυσος.

ἄζυμος.

To the instances of this word from profane authors in Grimm-Thayer, add Hippocrates Περὶ Διαίτης III. 79, where it is used along with ἄρτος.

ἀηδία.

This vernacular word (Lk 23¹² D) is supported by P Par 11²⁴ (B.C. 157) καταπεφευγότας διὰ τὴν ἀηδίαν. *ib.* 48ⁱⁱ (B.C. 153) τοῦ πρός σε τὴν ἀηδείαν ποήσαντος, "who had that disagreement with you," P Lond 342⁹ f. (A.D. 185) (= II. p. 174) ἄλογον ἀηδίαν συνεστήσαντο, and almost identically BGU I. 22¹⁴ f. (A.D. 114) (= *Selections*, p. 75) ; cf. P Tebt II. 304⁹ (A.D. 167-8) ἀητίαν [*i.e.* -δίαν] συνῆψαν (*l.* συν-), "they picked a quarrel." The verb ἀηδίζομαι occurs in P Lond 42ⁱ·²⁷ (B.C. 172) (= I. p. 30, *Selections*, p. 10 f.) in the sense "I am troubled, distressed." For the adverb see BGU II.665ⁱⁱⁱ·¹⁰ f. (i/A.D.) ἀηδῶς δὲ ἔσχον περὶ τοῦ ἵππου, *ib.* III. 801³ f. (ii/A.D.) λείαν ἀ[η]δῶς ἥ[κο]υσα παρὰ κτλ. Instances of these words are frequent : we need not cite more.

ἀήρ.

A very late (vi/A.D.) citation may be made from an illiterate document which fairly proves the word in continued vernacular use : P Lond 991¹⁰ (= III. p. 258) ἀπὸ θημελίου ἕως ἀέρως. Vettius Valens p. 330¹⁹ has ὅ τε περικεχυμένος

ἀὴρ ἄφθαρτος ὑπάρχων καὶ διήκων εἰς ἡμᾶς ἀπόρροιαν καιρικὴν ἀθανασίας ἀπονέμει κτλ. In Wünsch *AF* 4³⁷ (iii/A.D.) we have ἀέρος τὴν ἐξουσίαν ἔχοντα Ωη Ἰάω εεαφ—but in syncretic documents of this kind a reminiscence of Eph 2² is not excluded. Add P Leid Wˣᵛⁱⁱⁱ·³⁸ ὁ ἀέρα βλέπων. In BGU IV. 1207⁶ (B.C. 28) we find some gauzy fabrics described as ἀερο[ι]δῆ. The noun survives in MGr.

ἀθανασία.

This word, which in the NT is confined to 1 Cor 15⁵⁴ f., 1 Tim 6¹⁶, occurs several times in Wisdom, but not elsewhere in the Greek OT : cf. however, Sirach 51⁹ Α καὶ ἀπὸ ἀθανάτου ῥύσεως ἐδεήθην, "and to the Immortal One did I pray for deliverance," and see also Didache 4⁸. As showing the wider connotation of the word in early times, cf. the description of Caligula in *Syll* 395¹ (i/A.D.) τὸ μεγαλεῖον τῆς ἀθανασίας, and the use of the formula οὐδεὶς ἀθάνατος in sepulchral epitaphs, where, as Ramsay (*Luke the Physician*, p. 273) has shown, the meaning is "no one is free from death" rather than "no one is immortal." Pagan examples of this usage can be cited (Ramsay, *ut supra*), but it is generally Christian. One interesting instance may be cited where the formula has been expanded into two lines : οὐδὶς [ἀθά]νατος, εἰ μὴ μόνον ἶς θεὸς αὐτός, ὁ πάντων γεν[ετὴ]ς κὲ πᾶσι τὰ πάντα μερίζων, "no one is immortal except only the one God Himself, who is father of all and gives all things to all" (*Studies in the Eastern Roman Provinces*, p. 120). Wünsch *AF* 5²⁴ (Deissmann's "LXX Memorial"—iii/A.D.) has τοῦ Κυρίου α[ὐ]ω[νίου] ἀθανάτου παντεφόπτου. *Preisigke* 304ᵇ (iii/iv A.D.), where a tomb is forbidden to be used for any παρὲξ τῶν γαμβρῶν ἀθανάτων, shows a strange sense as well as irregular grammar. As illustrating the vernacular usage, reference may be made to P Strass I. 30⁶ (A.D. 276), where the epithet is applied to she-goats—αἶγας θηλείας τε[λ]είας ἀθανάτους, obviously in the sense of "very strong, hardy": see the editor's introduction, where he translates ἀ. "von eiserner Bestand," and cites Herod. vii. 31, μελεδωνῷ ἀθανάτῳ ἀνδρὶ κτλ.: cf. also P Cairo Preis 41³ (iv/A.D.)]. γείου ἀθανά[του . . .]. ἀρούρας. Crönert, however (*Lex. s.v.*), takes it in the sense to be mentioned next. In BGU IV. 1058²⁵ (B.C. 13) μηθὲ[ν τ]ὸ καθόλου λαβοῦσα διὰ τὸ ἀθάνατον αὐτὴν ἐπιδεδέχθαι τροφεύειν (*l.* -ειν) the word appears to imply that the person providing a slave as wet-nurse undertook to carry out the contract for the two stipulated years "apart from the death of" the infant, whose place could be filled by another : cf. the Persian Guard, the "Immortals," so called because their numbers were kept up to the same figure. Antiochus of Commagene uses the adjective as an epithet of κρίσις in his famous inscription, *OGIS* 383²⁰⁷ (i/B.C.), meaning presumably "unalterable": cf. *Syll* 365⁷ (i/A.D.) τῆς ἀθανάτου χάριτος of Caligula. From the sixth century we may quote P Oxy I. 130²¹, where a petitioner says that he will send up ὕμνους ἀθανάτους "unceasing hymns" to the Lord Christ for the life of the man with whom he is pleading. See also Vettius above *s.v.* ἀήρ).

ἀθέμιτος.

This late form is found in P Tor I. 1ⁱ·²² (B.C. 120) αἷς [*sc.* θεαῖς] ἀθέμιτά ἐστιν νεκρὰ σώματα, a passage which seems to support the rendering "abominable" in 1 Pet 4³, and in consequence perhaps the Gentile destination of the Epistle: see Bigg's note *ad l.* Vettius Valens the astrologer (ii/A.D.) tells us that under the influence of Saturn, Mars and Venus some people **ἀθεμίτοις μίξεσι καὶ ἀδιαφόροις** ("reckless") **ἀνεπιστρεπτοῦσι** (p. 43⁵⁷): the same writer (p. 184⁷) speaks of men who **ἀρνοῦνται τὰ θεῖα καὶ ἑτεροσεβοῦσι ἢ ἀθεμιτοφαγοῦσιν** The word is thus equivalent to *nefastus.*

ἄθεος.

OGIS 569²² (iv/A.D.) **τῆς τῶν ἀθέων ἀπεχθοῦς ἐπιτηδεύσεως.** For the popular cry **αἶρε τοὺς ἀθέους.** "Away with the atheists," directed against the early Christians, see the account of the martyrdom of Polycarp in Eus. *H.E.* iv. 15, 19: cf. *ib.* ix. 10, 12, **παρ' ᾧ γε** (Maximinus) **μικρῷ πρόσθεν δυσσεβεῖς ἐδοκοῦμεν καὶ ἄθεοι καὶ παντὸς ὄλεθροι τοῦ βίου.** See also the Logion P Oxy I. 1 *recto*³ **ἐὰν ὦσιν [β' οὐκ] εἰσὶ]ν ἄθεοι.**

ἄθεσμος.

An instance of this word, which in the NT is confined to 2 Peter (2⁷, 3¹⁷), may be quoted from the late P Oxy I. 129⁷ (vi/A.D.) where a man breaks off the engagement of his daughter to a certain Phoebammon, because it had come to his ears that the latter was giving himself over to "lawless" deeds—**ἀκηκόεναι σε παρεμβάλλοντα ἑαυτὸν ἐν τοῖς αὐτοῖς ἀθέσμοις πράγμασιν.**

ἀθετέω.

This verb, which is not approved by the Atticists (frequent in Polybius), occurs five times in the Pauline writings, always with reference to things, except 1 Th 4⁸ **ὁ ἀθετῶν οὐκ ἄνθρωπον ἀθετεῖ ἀλλὰ τὸν θεόν.** In the LXX it represents no fewer than seventeen Hebrew originals. It appears in the new Median parchment of B.C. 22, P Saïd Khan 2 ᴬ ¹¹. For its use in the papyri, cf. P Tebt I. 74⁵⁹ (B.C. 114–3) **ἐν τῆι ἠθετημένηι ἱερᾷ,** BGU IV. 1123¹¹ (time of Augustus) **ἀθετεῖν τῶν ὡμολογημένων,** P Oxy IV. 808 (i/A.D.), **ἠθέ[τισται** of loans repaid and cancelled, *ib.* VIII. 1120⁸ (ii/A.D.) **ἐξεῖσχυσεν τὰ βιβλείδια ἀθετηθῆναι,** "procured the failure of the petition"; and in the inscriptions, *OGIS* 444¹⁸ **ἐὰν δέ τινες τῶν πόλεων ἀθετ[ῶσι]** τὸ **σύμφωνον.** This is fairly near the meaning suggested from the LXX in Mk 6²⁶, "break faith with her," by Abbott *Joh. Voc.* p. 322: see also Field *Notes,* p. 30. The adjective is found in P Amh II. 64¹²⁴ (A.D. 107) where certain officials are described as **ἀ]θέτους . . . κ[αὶ] μὴ ἀναλογοῦντας τὴν ἐ[π]ιμέλειαν,** "inefficient and incapable of doing their duties" (Edd.): cf. P Lond 237²³ (c. A.D. 346) (= II. p. 291) **τὸν ἐν ἀθέτῳ σιτόκριθον,** with reference to corn (wheat and barley) rejected by the inspector as unfit for food.

ἀθέτησις.

The force of **ἀθέτησις** in Heb 7¹⁸, 9²⁶ is well brought out by Deissmann's reference (*BS* p. 228 f.) to the technical legal formula in the papyri **εἰς ἀθέτησιν καὶ ἀκύρωσιν,** as in BGU I. 44¹⁶ (A.D. 102) **τὴν δ[ια]γραφὴν εἰς ἀθέτησιν καὶ ἀκύρωσιν,** "the decree to be annulled and cancelled." So

P Amh II. 111¹⁹·¹ (A.D. 132), P. Tebt II. 307¹³ (A.D. 198), P Saïd Khan 2ᵇ ¹⁴ (B.C. 22), etc.

ἄθλησις.

IG XIV. 1102 (Rome, ii/A.D.). CP Herm 119 *verso* iii 13 (a rescript of Gallienus), **εὐδοκίμων κατὰ τὴν ἄθλησ[ιν] γενομένων.** *Syll* 686²⁴ (ii/A.D.) **ἀξίως καὶ τοῦ Διὸς τοῦ Ὀλυμπίου καὶ τῆς ἀθλήσεως.** Other words of this family are well evidenced. Thus *OGIS* 339⁷⁹ (Sestos, ii/B.C.) **τιθεὶς ἆθλα πάντων τῶν ἀθλημάτων,** with **ἀθλητής, ἀθλόφορος,** etc.

ἀθροίζω.

OGIS 764⁹ (c. B.C. 127) **τὸ . . . ἀθρο[ισθὲν πλῆθος].** P Par 40⁴² (B.C. 156) **χρή[ματα ἠ]θροικότες.** For the adjective see P Petr II. xi(1)⁷ (iii/B.C.) (= *Selections,* p. 8) **ἀθροῦν,** "in a lump sum." Cf. P Amh II. 79⁶⁴ (ii/A.D.) **ἀθρόον ἀργύριον.** On its form see Crönert *Mem. Herc.,* p. 166.

ἀθυμέω.

P Amh II. 37⁷·ᶜᶠ·¹⁰ (B.C. 196 or 172) **μὴ ἀθύμει.** P Giss I. 79ⁱⁱⁱ ¹¹ (ii/A.D.) **οὐ χ[άρι]ν οὐδ[εὶ]ς ἀθυμεῖ πωλεῖν κτῆμα.** The substantive is found P Par 22¹¹⁴ (ii/B.C.) **τῷ δὲ μὴ ἡμᾶς εἶναι σὺν αὐτῷ ὑπὸ τῆς ἀθυμίας μετήλλαχεν τὸν βίον.** The adverb **ἀθύμως** occurs in *Syll* 220¹⁰⁹ (iii/B.C.) **πολλῶν ἐχόντων ἀ. καὶ παρεσκευασμένων ἐγλείπειν τὴν πόλιν.**

ἀθῷος.

P Oxy II. 237ᵛⁱⁱⁱ·¹⁷ (ii/A.D.) **ο[ὐ]δ[ὲ] τότε ἀθῷος ἐσόμενος, ἀλλὰ τοῖς τεταγμένοις ἐπιτίμοις ἐνεχόμενος,** "and even so he shall not escape his liabilities, but shall be subject to the legal penalties"—a legal opinion quoted in the lengthy Petition of Dionysia. An earlier example is afforded by P Tebt I. 44²¹ (ii/B.C.) where certain precautions are taken lest an assailant **ἀθῷος διαφύγῃ,** "should escape unpunished." Cf. *Syll* 790⁵⁹ (i/B.C.) **ἃ ἐὰν ὁμό[σω]σιν, ἔστωσαν ἀθῷοι.**

αἴγειος.

P Fay 107²·ᶠ· (A.D. 133) **ὑφείλαντο δέρματα αἴγειαν** (*i.e.* -α) **τέσσαρα,** "carried off four goat skins" P Oxy II. 234¹⁶ (ii/iii A.D.) **χολὴ ταυρεία [ἢ κ]αὶ αἰγεία ἢ προβατεία.** P Leid Xˣᵛ·¹⁹ (iii/iv A.D.) **μιγνυμένη αἵματι αἰγείῳ** For a form **αἰγικός,** see P Grenf II. 51¹⁵ (A.D. 143) **ἀ[πέ]χειν αὐτοὺς τιμὴν δερμάτων αἰγικῶν τεσσάρων.** Also **δέρματα αἴγινα** P Lond 236⁸ (A.D. 346) (= II. p. 291).

αἰγιαλός.

The word is common (MGr = "seashore") ; but it may be noted that in P Tebt I. 79 (c. B.C. 148) it refers to the shore of Lake Moeris; in *ib.* 82 (B.C. 115) and 83 (late ii/B.C.) to the shore of a marshy lake then covering the neighbourhood of Medinet Nehâs (see the editors' note on p. 346). So P Fay 82¹ (A.D. 145), P Tebt II. 308⁵ (A.D. 174). On the use of the term in Ac 27³⁹, see W. M. Ramsay *St Paul,* p. 341, and *Expositor* V. vi. p. 154 ff. P Fay 222 (iii/A.D.) is the beginning of a document addressed **Φιλίππῳ αἰγιαλοφύλακι Ἀρσινοί[του].** We find **γῆ αἰγιαλῖτις** mentioned in P Oxy VI. 918ᵛⁱⁱⁱ·¹⁰ (ii/A.D.), P Lond 924⁷ (A.D. 187–8) (= III. p. 134): Sir F. G. Kenyon renders "land on the border of the lake."

Αἰγύπτιος.

In P Lond 43² ᶠ (ii/B.C.) (= I. p. 48) a mother congratulates her son because he had been learning Αἰγύπτια γράμματα, or the demotic speech: cf. P Tebt II. 291⁴² (A.D. 162) where a priest gives practical proof of his qualifications by his knowledge of ἱερατικὰ [καὶ] Αἰγύπτ.α γρόμμ[ματ]α.

ἀΐδιος.

Syll 306¹⁵ (ii/B.C.—Delphi) ὅπως ὑπάρχῃ ἁ δωρεὰ εἰς πάντα τὸν χρόνον ἀίδιος. In OGIS 56³⁴ (iii/B.C., the Canopus inscription of Ptolemy III.) it is ordained to pay τιμὰς ἀιδίους in all the temples to Queen Berenice, who εἰς θεοὺς μετῆλθεν shortly before. So ib. 248²⁶ (ii/B.C., Antiochus Epiphanes) τὰ καλὰ τῶ[ν] ἔργων εἰς ἀίδιομ μνήμην ἀνάγων. In ib. 383⁷⁶ Antiochus I. of Commagene (i/B.C.) claims περὶ δὲ ἱερουργιῶν ἀιδίων διάταξιν πρέπουσαν ἐποιησάμην. The phrase τ. ἀίδιον χρόνον is common in the inscriptions, e.g. Syll 96⁸ (iv/B.C.). The adjective has been restored in the late P Lond 113⁶³ (vi/A.D.) (= I. p. 202) τὴν ἀϊδί[α]ν ἰσχύν: otherwise we cannot quote papyri—possibly the word was only appropriate to the stiffer language of inscriptions.

αἰδώς.

We can supply no papyrus references for this expressive word (1 Tim 2⁹, Heb 12²⁸ MPω), but it is found in 3 Maccabees and in Epictetus: also OGIS 507⁸ (ii/A.D.) (with ἐπιείκεια). The verb occurs P Fay 12³ (c. B.C. 103) οὐκ αἰδεσθεὶς δὲ το[ῦτο], "so far from being abashed" (Edd.), and often elsewhere: it is curious that Nägeli (p. 57) should make it absent from the papyri as from NT—a glance at the indices would suffice. The adj. αἰδέσιμος and its abstract -ότης came into common use in late times.

αἷμα.

An interesting parallel to the common Biblical phrase αἷμα ἐκχέω, especially as it appears in Deut 19¹⁰ καὶ οὐκ ἐκχυθήσεται αἷμα ἀναίτιον, is afforded by an inscription found on a tombstone at Rheneia, containing a Jewish "prayer for vengeance," Syll 816² ᶠ (i/A.D.) ἐγχέαντας αὐτῆς τὸ ἀναίτιον αἷμα ἀδίκως: see the full discussion in Deissmann LAE p. 423ᶠᶠ. For the use of αἷμα, as in Jn 1¹³, cf. P Lips I. 28¹⁶ (A.D. 381) πρ[ὸ]ς τὸ εἶναί σου υἱ[ὸ]ν γνήσιον καὶ πρωτότοκον ὡς ἐξ ἰδίου αἵματος γεννηθέντα σοι. In P Leid C (verso) ⁱⁱ·⁹ (p. 118—B.C. 161) two men appear in a dream saying Πτολεμαῖος, λαβὲ το[ὺς] χαλκοὺς τοῦ αἵματος: they count out a purseful and say to one of the Twins εἰδοὺ τοὺς χαλκοὺς τοῦ αἵματος. Leemans quotes an opinion that this meant the price of a victim, and compares Mt 27⁶. In the sense of murder or blood-guiltiness it finds modern support in the Pontic dialect (Thumb BZ xxii. p. 489), which is evidence for its place in the Eastern Κοινή, apart from any Semitic influence.

αἱμορροέω.

The noun occurs in BGU IV. 1026¹⁵ (magical text, iv/v A.D.) αἱμάροιαν ἰᾶται—following a spell from Homer, described as αἱμαροικόν (Il. 1⁷⁵). Thumb (BZ xxii.

p. 489) compares αἱματορροῦσα "hemorrhage" in MGr (Rhodes).

αἶνος.

Syll 452⁴ (c. B.C. 240, Epidaurus, in dialect) κατὰ τὸν αἶνον τὸν τῶν Ἀ[χαι]ῶν is explained by Dittenberger as a "decree" of the Achaean Council. He compares ib. 306²⁹ (ii/B.C.) μήτε κατὰ ψάφισμα μήτε κατ' αἶνον, the former being a decree of the people, the latter of the Senate (Delphi): and he cites Hesychius αἶνος· γνώμη, παροιμία, παράδειγμα, ἔπαινος· καὶ ἡ χειροτονία καὶ ψήφισμα.

αἰνέω.

Dittenberger, in his note on Syll 835⁸ (iv/B.C., Elatea) [ὁ δᾶμ]ος αἰνεῖ, observes that the use of the verb belongs to the older language. But Plutarch has it occasionally: and in the LXX it is four times as frequent as ἐπαινέω, especially in the sense of praising God.

αἵρεσις.

In Michel 1001ᵛⁱⁱ·³³ (Thera, c. B.C. 200) αἱρείσθω τὸ κοινὸν . . . ἄνδρας κτλ· καὶ ἐγγραφέτω καὶ τὰν τούτων αἵρεσιν ὁ ἐπίσσοφος, the noun is the nomen actionis of αἱρεῖσθαι, "choose." The two meanings (1) animus, sententia, and (2) secta, factio, are both illustrated by Dittenberger in OGIS: for (1) he gives fourteen examples from i/B.C. or earlier, for (2) only three of equal antiquity, viz. 176 τῆς Ἀμμωνίου αἱρέσεως, 178 similar (both from reign of Ptolemy XI. ii/B.C), and 442 (a senatus consultum of i/B.C. apparently) Σύλλ]ας αὐτοκράτωρ συνεχώρησεν [π]ό̣λ[εις ὅπως ἰδί]οις τοῖς νόμοις α̣ἱρέσιν τε ὦσιν. (Note the effect of slavish translation from Latin ablative.) 2 Pet 2¹ is the only NT passage assigned by Grimm to the first head, and there the RV has a margin assigning it to (2). Herwerden cites an inscription from Delphi of iii/B.C. (BCH xx. p. 478) where the word equals εὔνοια: ἐνεφάνισε τὰν αἵρεσιν, ἃν ἔχει ποτί τε τὸ ἱερὸν καὶ τὰν πόλιν. Cf. Roberts-Gardner 55¹⁹ (a decree of the Senate and people) καὶ αὐτὸς δὲ Φαῖδρος τὴν αὐτὴν αἵρεσιν ἔχων τοῖς προγόνοις (l. προγόνοις) διατετέλεκεν ἑαυτὸν ἄξιον παρασκευάζων τῆς πρὸς τὸν δῆμον εὐνοίας. The editors note that this sense of αἵρεσις = "propensus animus," "kindly feeling towards a person," is very common in later inscriptions.

In the papyri the meaning seems generally "choice": in wills it is used = "voluntas," or "disposition," e.g. P Oxy VI. 907¹ (A.D. 276) αἱρέσει τῇ ὑποτεταγμένῃ, "according to the disposition below written." P Tebt I. 27⁶⁸ (B.C. 113) ἐπὶ τὴν αἵρεσιν τῶν ἐπιγενη[μ]άτων shows the pure verbal noun "receiving," and in P Oxy IV. 716²² (A.D. 186) τὴν ἀμείνονα αἵρεσιν διδόντι it is a "bid" (at an auction); so also BGU II. 656⁵ (ii/A.D.) προσερχέσθωσαν (i.e. -θωσαν) τοῖς πρὸς τούτοις ἔρεσιν (i.e. αἵρεσιν) διδόντες. Other examples of the word are P Petr II. 1⁶ τὴν τῶν ἀνθρώπων αἵρεσιν, P Par 63ᵛⁱⁱⁱ·⁵ᶠ (c. B.C. 164) προαιρούμενος ἵνα μετακληθῇς ἔτι πρὸς τὴν ἐμὴν αἵρεσιν, and BGU IV. 1070⁸ (A.D. 218) εὐδοκοῦντα τῇ αἱρέσει τῆς ἐπιτροπῆς. P Tebt I. 28⁹ᶠ (B.C. 114) comes nearest to the meaning (1)—καὶ κατὰ τὸ παρὸν δ[ι]ὰ τῶν ἀναφ[ορῶν] τῆι αὐτῆι αἱρέσει κεχρημένων, which the editors render "since they show the same behaviour in their reports." This use gives us a foretaste of the development in malam partem, producing "factiousness" and then "heresy": cf. *Syll* 308²³ (ii/B.C.) γίνωνται δὲ καὶ ἄλλοι ζ[ηλ]ωταὶ τῆς αὐτῆς αἱρέσεως. In *Syll* 367¹¹ (i/A.D) αἱρεσιάρχης means the chief of the profession (medical).

αἱρετίζω.

Syll 633² (ii/A.D.) αἱρετίσαντος (το)ῦ (θ)εοῦ.

αἱρέω.

The middle usage of this word, which alone occurs in the NT, may be illustrated from P Par 26⁴ (B.C. 163-2) (= *Selections*, p. 18) ὑμῖν δὲ γίνοιτο κρατεῖν πάσης ἧς ἂν αἱρῆσθε χώρας, P Lips I. 104¹¹ (c. B.C. 96-5) περὶ ὧν ἂν αἱρῆσθε γράφετέ μοι, P Oxy III. 489⁴ (a will, A.D. 117) καθ' ὃν ἐὰν αἱρῶμαι [τρόπον], P Ryl II. 153¹³ (A.D. 138-61) κ]ύριος γὰρ ὢν τῶν ἰδίων οὕτως ᾕρημαι διατέσθαι, P Tebt II. 319²⁰ (A.D. 248) ὃ ἐὰν αἱρῆται, and so frequently. It is a sign of the gradual disappearance of the subtler meanings of the middle, that so early as B.C. 95 we find ἐὰν αἱρῆτε and ἐὰν αἱρεῖσθε used side by side for "if you like," P Grenf II. 36¹⁴,¹⁸; see further *Prolegomena*, p. 159. For other uses of the active cf. P Fay 34¹⁴ (A.D. 161) τὸ αἱροῦν ἐξ ἴσου, "equal instalments," the same in *ib.* 93¹⁷ (A.D. 161), P Oxy III. 502²⁸ (A.D. 164) τὰς αἱρούσας τῶν ἐνοικίων δραχμὰς ἑκατόν, "the proportionate amount of the rent, 100 drachmae" (Edd.), BGU II. 405¹⁰ (A.D. 348) πέπρακα εἰς τὸ ἑροῦν (*i.e.* αἱροῦν) μοι μέρος.

αἴρω.

For αἴρω, "raise," "lift up," as in Rev 10⁵, cf. *Syll* 807³ (ii/A.D.) ἄραι τὴν χεῖρα, and so *ib.* 807²⁰,²⁷. One passage for αἴρειν χεῖρας may be specially noted, the Alexandrian inscr. in *Preisigke* 1323 (ii/A.D.): θεῷ ὑψίστῳ καὶ πάντων ἐπόπτῃ καὶ Ἡλίῳ καὶ Νεμέσεσι αἴρει Ἀρσινόη ἄωρος τὰς χεῖρας. The inscr. is heathen, but has striking similarity to the Jewish prayer for vengeance on which Deissmann comments in *LAE* p. 423 ff.: is its thought partly due to Jewish suggestion? In P Fay 103³ (iii/A.D.) payment is allotted to the bearers of a corpse—τοῖς ἠρκάσι (*l.* -όσι) αὐτόν: cf. P Grenf II. 77⁹ (iii/iv A.D.) (= *Selections*, p. 120). In a magical formula of iii/A.D. instructions are given to take twenty-nine palm leaves, on which the names of the gods have been inscribed, and then —ἆρε (= αἶρε) κατὰ δύο δύο, "lift them up two by two," P Oxy VI. 886¹⁹ (= *Selections*, p. 111). A good parallel to Col 2¹⁴ is afforded by BGU II. 388ⁱⁱ·²³ (ii/iii A.D.) ἆρον ταῦτα ἐκ τοῦ μ[έ]σ[ου]. In 19¹⁵ ἆρον, ἆρον, σταύρωσον αὐτόν may be illustrated from a strangely incongruous source, the well-known school-boy's letter, where the boy's mother is represented as saying—ἀναστατοῖ με· ἀρρον αὐτόν, "he upsets me: away with him!" P Oxy I. 119¹⁰ (ii/iii A.D.) (= *Selections*, p. 103): cf. *Syll* 737¹⁴² (ii/A.D.) ἐὰν δὲ ἀπειθῇ, αἱρέτωσαν αὐτὸν ἔξω τοῦ πυλῶνος. A parallel of a different kind is found in the *defixio* from Cnidus, *Audollent* no. 1¹⁸ (p. 6—ii/i B.C.) ἵναι αὐτὸν ἐκ τῶν ζώντων ἄρῃ —which the editor should not (p. 550) assign to αἴρειν! In the curious nursery alphabet, P Tebt II. 278 (early i/A.D.) αἴρειν is used six times for stealing (a garment). So in the passive BGU IV. 1201¹⁸ (A.D. 2) εὕροσαν τὸν στροφέα τοῦ ἑνὸς μέρους [τ]ῆς θύρας ἠρμένον χ[ε]ρσεῖν. The use is common. With εἰς it can express "removing to" a place, as P Tebt II. 308⁹ (A.D. 174)—a man has paid for 20,000

papyrus stalks "which he has had transported to Tebtunis by Heracleides" (εἰς T. ἄρας διὰ Ἡ.). The classical use of the middle may be seen in P Lond 854⁶ (i/ii A.D.) (= III. p. 206, *Selections*, p. 70) ἀράμενος ἀνάπλο[υν], of a tourist going up the Nile. To Wetstein's parallels for Lk 16²¹ αἴρεις ὃ οὐκ ἔθηκας C. Taylor (*JTS* ii. p. 432) adds the Jewish precepts quoted by Philo (Mangey II. 620) ἅ τις παθεῖν ἐχθαίρει μὴ ποιεῖν αὐτόν, ἃ μὴ κατέθηκεν μηδ' ἀναιρεῖσθαι, and Plato *Leg.* xi. (913 C) κάλλιστον νόμων διαφθείρων καὶ ἀπλούστατον καὶ οὐδαμῇ ἀγεννοῦς ἀνδρὸς νομοθέτημα, ὃς εἶπεν· Ἃ μὴ κατέθου μὴ ἀνέλῃ. In MGr only as compounded, παίρνω = ἀπαίρω.

αἰσθάνομαι.

This verb, in NT only Lk 9⁴⁵, is asserted by Nägeli (p. 57) to be absent from the papyri. This is a still more remarkable oversight than that noted under αἰδώς. A few examples will suffice. P Eleph 13³ (B.C. 223-2) ἐχάρην ἐπὶ τῶι με αἰσθέσθαι τὰ κατά σε, P Oxy III. 472³ (c. A.D. 130) οὔτ' ἔφη πρός τινα αἰσθέσθαι οὐδενός ("noticed anything"), BGU II. 372¹·¹⁶ (A.D. 154) ἵστωσαν [μ]ὲν τ[ὸ]ν . . . ἐκ ταύ[της] τῆς αἰτ[ίας ἔ]τι κατεχόμενον α[ἰσ]θήσεσθαι τῆς τοῦ μεγίστου Αὐτοκράτορος εὐ[μ]εν[εί]ας (see *Chrest.* I. p. 33), *ib.* 417¹ (ii/iii A.D.) αἰσθόμε(νον) τὴν τοῦ καιροῦ πικρίαν (note the accus. in a vernacular document), *ib.* 531ⁱⁱ·¹⁹ (ii/A.D) α[ἰ]σθόμενος πῶς με φιλεῖς, and an ostrakon in *Archiv* vi. p. 220 (iii/B.C.) ἀπόστειλον τοῖς ὑπογεγραμμένοις τὰς πεταλίας κρυφῇ καὶ μηθεὶς αἰσθανέσθω. But it is hardly necessary to go on to the other five or six volumes in which the index contains this verb. It survives in MGr.

αἴσθησις.

P Leid Wxiv·⁴⁴ πάσαις ταῖς αἰθήσεσι, Wunsch *AF* 18ⁱⁱ (iⁱ/ii A.D.) τούτους ἀναθεμα[τί]ζομεν· σῶμα, πνεῦμα ψ[υ]χήν, [δι]άνοιαν, φρόνησιν, αἴσθησιν, ζωήν, καρδίαν, and *ib.* 4²⁵ (iii/A.D.) βασάνισον αὐτῶν τὴν διάνοιαν, τὰς φρένας, τὴν αἴσθησιν. Prof. H. A. A. Kennedy, following Klöpper, quotes a good passage from Hippocrates to illustrate Phil 1⁹: *de Off. Med.* 3 ᾧ καὶ τῇ ὄψι καὶ τῇ ἁφῇ καὶ τῇ ἀκοῇ καὶ τῇ ῥινὶ καὶ τῇ γλώσσῃ καὶ τῇ γνώμῃ ἔστιν αἰσθέσθαι.

αἰσθητήριον.

For this word (Heb 5¹⁴) see Linde, *Epic.* p. 32, who cited Epicurus, Aristotle, etc., but shows that it came into the vernacular.

αἰσχρολογία.

BGU III. 909¹² (A.D. 359) πολλὰς ἔ[σ]χρολογίας εἰς πρόσωπόν μου ἐξειπών. A literary citation is P Oxy III. 410⁷⁶ (Doric, iv/B.C.) τὸ δὲ φεύγεν τὰς αἰσχρολογίας με-γ[αλ]οπρεπὲς καὶ κόσμος λόγω, 'the avoidance of abuse is a mark of high-mindedness and an ornament of speech" (Edd). The adj. is generally associated with foul or filthy rather than abusive speaking in Col 3⁸: cf. Didache 3³, where after a warning against ἐπιθυμία the Christian is counselled to be μηδὲ αἰσχρολόγος μηδὲ ὑψηλόφθαλμος (" one who casts lewd eyes"): cf. 2 Pet 2¹⁴) ἐκ γὰρ τούτων ἁπάντων μοιχεῖαι γεννῶνται.

αἰσχρός.

BGU IV. 1024ⱽⁱⁱ·²⁰ (ii/iii A.D.), where a judge says to a scoundrel ἀπέσφα[ξ]ας γυναῖκα, Διόδιμε, αἰσχρῶς, P Tebt

I. 24⁹⁹ (B.C. 117) αἰ]σχρά without context, *ib.* II. 276⁴ (ii/iii A.D.—an astrological work) ἀπὸ αἰσχρᾶς περιστά-[σεως?] "an unfavourable position." The word is not common, and is peculiar to Paul in NT.

αἰσχύνη.

In P Eleph 1⁶ (a marriage contract, B.C. 311–10) (= *Selections*, p. 2) provision is made that if the bride κακοτεχνοῦσα ἁλίσκηται ἐπὶ αἰσχύνηι τοῦ ἀνδρός, "shall be detected doing anything wrong to the shame of her husband," he shall be entitled to take certain steps against her: cf. P Gen 21¹¹ (ii/B.C.) (as completed, *Archiv* iii. p. 388) μηδ' αἰ[σ]χύνειν Μενεκράτην ὅσα φέρει ἀνδρὶ αἰσχύνην—the same formula in P Tebt I. 104²⁰ (B.C. 92). So P Par 47²⁵ (c. B.C. 153) (= *Selections*, p. 23) ὑπὸ τῆς αἰσχύνης, "for very shame," P Oxy III. 471⁷⁸ (ii/A.D.) ἅπαξ γὰρ ἐν ἔθει τῆς ο[ἰσ]χύνης γενόμενον, "for when once accustomed to his shame."

αἰσχύνομαι.

P Par 49²⁵ (B.C. 164–58) ὁ δέ, φαίνεται, τὴν ἡμέραν ἐκείνην ἀσχοληθείς, ἤσχυνται συμμεῖξαί μοι: we may either suppose φαίνεται parenthetical or emend ἠσχύνθαι. *ib.* ²⁸ οὐκέτι ἥκει πρὸς ἐμὲ αἰσχυνθείς, *Syll* 802¹²² (iii/B.C., Epidaurus) αἰσχυνόμενος δ[ὲ ἅτε] καταγελάμενος ὑπ[ὸ] τῶν ἄλλων. For the active (not in NT) see P Oxy III. 407⁴ (early ii/A.D.) αἰσχύνειν Θέωνα, P Gen 21¹¹, as quoted under αἰσχύνη.

αἰτέω.

The ordinary meaning of this word "to make a request," "to ask for something" is borne out by the papyri, e.g. P Fay 109¹² (early i/A.D.) αἴτησον Σάραν τὰς τοῦ (δραχμὰς) ιβ̅, "ask Saras for the twelve (silver) drachmae." In *ib.* 121¹²ff. (c. A.D. 100) it is construed with the accusative of the thing and παρά, τὸ δ[έρ]μα τοῦ μόσχου οὗ ἐθύ[σ]αμεν αἴτησον πα[ρὰ τοῦ] κύρτου βυρσέως, "ask the hunch-backed tanner for the hide of the calf that we sacrificed" (Edd.): cf. Ac 3². See further *s.v.* ἐρωτάω, and for the distinction between active and middle *Proleg.* p. 160 f. If the middle connotes a greater degree of earnestness, it is natural that it should be more frequent than the active, as for example in the phrases αἰτούμενος λόγον δηλῶ . . . (P Hamb I. 6⁸ (A.D. 129), αἰτούμενος . . . ὀνόματα . . . δίδομει (BGU I. 91⁵ff. A.D. 170–1), and see the list of passages in the index to *Syll* (iii. p. 245). The verbal occurs negatived in P Ryl II. 163⁴ (A.D. 130) γῆς κατοικικοῦ ἀναιτήτου, "not subject to demand" (Edd.—see the note on 164⁴).

αἴτημα.

Syll 418⁶² (iii/A.D.) οὐδεὶς ἡμεῖν ἐνόχλησεν οὔτε ξενίας (αἰτή)ματι οὔτε παροχῆς ἐπιτηδείων. For αἴτησις see P Oxy I. 56²¹⁶ (A.D. 211) διέγραψα δὲ τὸ ὡρισμένον τῆς αἰτήσ[εω]ς τέλος: "I have paid the appointed tax for making such a request" (Edd.): the word is fairly common.

αἰτία.

P Petr III. 53 (n) (iii/B.C.) ἀπέσταλται εἰς Ἀλεξανδρείαν πρὸς αἰτίαν ὑπὲρ ἧς [ἀπ]ολογίζεται ἀ[λ]λ' οὐ τυχὼν ἐπι-δείξειν (? 1st -δεῖξαι) [π]ρὸς βίαν ἔχεται, "he was sent to Alexandria to meet a charge against him and make his

defence; but since he did not succeed in clearing himself he is forcibly detained" (Edd.). So BGU I. 207³ (A.D. 199) τοῖς δικαία[ν] αἰτ[ί]αν ἐσχηκόσι, and so identically P Strass I. 22³ᶠ (iii/A.D.)—it was a legal formula. Note P Ryl II. 144²² (A.D. 38) ἐτόλμησεν φθόνους (= φθόνου) μοι ἐπαγαγεῖν αἰτίας τοῦ μὴ ὄντος, "to bring baseless accusations of malice" (Edd.). In *ib.* 63³ (iii/A.D.—an astronomical dialogue) τίς δὲ ἡ αἰτία τούτων [τ]ῶ̣ν [εἰ]δώλων ("What is the cause of these images?"—Edd.) we might possibly render "case": Prof. Hunt paraphrases "What is the meaning?" If so, it comes fairly near Mt 19¹⁰ εἰ οὕτως ἐστὶν ἡ αἰτία τοῦ ἀνθρώπου μετὰ τῆς γυναικός. Cf. P Par 49²⁷ (B.C. 164–58) εἴπερ οὖν ἐστιν αὕτη ἡ αἰτία. A more general use in P Tbi I. 43⁷ (B.C. 201 (200)) ἵνα μὴ αἰτίας ἔχῃς, "lest you be blamed." P Giss I. 40¹ ² (A.D. 212) joined with λ[ιβ]έλλου[s] in the sense of *querelae* (Ed.). The more ordinary meaning "reason," "excuse," like Mt 19³, etc., hardly needs illustration, but cf. BGU I. 136²⁵ᶠ (A.D. 135) κατὰ ταύτην [τὴν αἰ]τίαν, P Oxy III. 472² (c. A.D. 130) εἴχεν μὲν οὖν αἰτίας, and frequently in the inscriptions, e.g. *Michel* 456¹¹ (ii/B.C.) διὰ ταύτας τὰς αἰτίας. BGU IV. 1205⁷ (B.C. 28) τὴν αἰτίαν τοῦ φακοῦ has an insufficiently clear context. Ἄνευ αἰτίας, *sine causa*, appears in PSI 41¹⁶ (iv/A.D.).

αἰτιάομαι.

In Rom 3⁹ D*G ᾐτιασάμεθα is read for προῃτιασάμεθα of the printed texts: cf. P Tebt I. 35¹⁹ (B.C. 111) παρὰ ταῦτα ποιῶν ἑαυτὸν αἰτιάσεται, "any one disobeying these orders will render himself liable to accusation," and OGIS 484⁹ (ii/A.D.) ᾐτιάθησαν. In P Oxy VII. 1032⁵¹ (A.D. 162) τὸν ὑπηρέτην αἰτιᾶς, we have an abnormal active. The verb is not uncommon.

αἴτιος.

For the absolute use = "guilty," cf. BGU II. 651¹⁰ (A.D. 192) and P Flor I. 6¹⁶f. (A.D. 255) πρὸς τοὺς φανησομένους αἰτίους: so P Tebt II. 330⁴ᶠ (ii/A.D.) πρὸς τὸ φανέντος τινὸς αἰτ[ίο]υ μένιν μοι τὸν λόγο[ν, "if any one is proved to be the culprit, he may be held accountable to me" (Edd.), *ib.* 333¹⁵ (A.D. 216), etc. A more neutral sense, "responsible," occurs three times in the Revenue Papyrus (B.C. 259–8), where sundry officials "shall, each of them who is responsible (ἕκαστος τῶν αἰτίων), pay a fine to the Treasury," if on inspection it appears that the proper acreage has not been sown. It is used wholly *in bonam partem* in Heb 5⁹, with which cf. Diodorus Siculus iv. 82 αἴτιος ἐγένετο τῆς σωτηρίας. For the dependent genitive cf. also *Syll* 737⁸⁰ (ii/A.D.) ὁ αἴτιος γενόμενος τῆς μάχης. The Lukan use of the neuter = "cause," shading into "crime," may be illustrated from P Hib I. 73¹⁵ (B.C. 243–2) ὅπως εἰδῇς εἶναι αἴτιον τοῦ μὴ γενέσθαι τῶι Δω[ρ]ίωνι ἀπόδοσιν τὴν] Πάτρωνος βίαν, "the reason . . . is the violence of P." (Edd.).

αἰτίωμα.

So in Ac 25⁷ (all uncials), hitherto without external parallel: the confusion between -αω and -οω forms recalls ἠσσᾶσθαι and (Ion.) ἐσσοῦσθαι. It is now supported by P Fay 111⁸ (A.D. 95–6) (= *Selections*, p. 66) ὁ [ὀν]ηλάτης τὼ αἰτίωμα περιέπυησε, "the donkey-driver shifted the blame from himself." The generally illiterate character of the document somewhat discounts the value of its evidence.

αἰφνίδιος.

The adverb occurs in P Fav 123²¹ ff. (c. A.D. 100), an uneducated letter—αἰφνιδί[.]ως (with a letter erased) εἴρηχεν ἡμῖν σήμερον : cf. Syll 324²⁰ (i/B.C.) αἰφνίδιον σ(υ)μφορὰν θεασάμενος, also ib. 326⁷ αἰφνιδίως ἐπιβαλόντος and OGIS 339¹⁵ (ii/B.C.) ἐκ τῆς αἰφνιδίου περιστάσεως.

αἰχμαλωτίζω.

Syll 348⁷˙¹⁰ (Cyzicus, i/B.C.) ὃν αἰχμα]λωτισθέντα ἐκ Λιβύης . . . [ὅ]τι ἠχμαλώτισται Μάρκος. Phrynichus (ed. Lobeck, p. 442) characterizes the verb as ἀδόκιμον (i. e. good vernacular !).

αἰχμάλωτος.

The word is found in P Lille I. 3⁶⁶ (after B.C. 241–0) αἰχμαλώτοις εἰς τὴν γινομένην σύ[νταξιν ?] In their note the editors think that the reference is to certain prisoners brought from Asia by Philadelphus (cf. P Petr II. 29(6)) to some of whom a regular "allowance" or "grant" (σύνταξις) may have been made. Dittenberger's indices show seven inscriptions in Syll and one in OGIS containing the word, all in the Hellenistic period. For the subst. see Michel 965⁶ (beginning ii/B.C.) ἔ]σωισεν ἐκ τῆς αἰχμαλωσίας.

αἰών.

Magn 180³ ff. (ii/A.D.) μόνος τῶν ἀπ᾽ αἰῶνος νεικήσας Ὀλύμπια, etc.—the athlete is claiming to have made a record : cf. the description of a certain ἀρχιερεὺς τῶν θεῶν in Syll 365⁶ (i/A.D.), as διὰ βίου πρῶτον τῶν ἀπ᾽ αἰῶνος, and ib. 680⁴⁸ (ii/A.D.) ἣν μόνος ἀπ᾽ αἰῶνος ἀνδρῶν ἐποίησεν. P Oxy I. 33³ⁱⁱⁱ·⁶ (ii/A.D.) θεωρήσατε ἕνα ἀπ᾽ αἰῶνος ἀπαγόμ[ενο]ν, "behold one led off to death," literally "from life." Minns IosPE i. 22³⁵ τῶν ἀπ᾽ αἰῶνος. Preisigke 1105 (i/A.D.) ἐπ᾽ ἀγαθῷ εἰς τὸν (l. τὸν) αἰῶνα. P Giss I. 13¹⁹ (ii/A.D.) ὅπω[s] πλουτή[σ]ῃς εἰς αἰῶ[να] "for the rest of your life." P Oxy I. 41 (iii/iv A.D.) is a curious report of a public meeting at Oxyrhynchus, punctuated with cries of Ἄγουστοι κύριοι εἰς τὸν αἰῶνα, "the Emperors for ever !": cf. OGIS 515⁵⁵ (iii/A.D.) Succlam(atum) est : is αἰῶ[να] with Dittenberger's note. So Syll 376⁵⁰ (i/A.D.) Διὶ Ἐλευθερίῳ [Νέρων]ι εἰς αἰῶνα : also Magn 130⁷ ff (i/B.C.) εὐεργέτην δὲ [γ]εγονότα τοῦ δήμου κατὰ πολλοὺς [τ]ρόπους πρὸς τὸν αἰῶνα, OGIS 383⁴⁴ (i/B.C.) εἰς τὸν ἄπειρον αἰῶνα—passages which are sufficient to show how thoroughly "Greek" the prepositional combinations with αἰών are. Reference should be made to Syll 757 (i/A.D.), an interesting inscription dedicated to Αἰών as a deity. For αἰών = period of life, cf. Syll 364⁹ (A.D. 37) ὡς ἂν τοῦ ἡδίστου ἀνθρώποις αἰῶνο(s) νῦν ἐνεστῶτος. On the Rosetta stone, OGIS 90 (B.C. 196), Ptolemy V is described as αἰωνόβιος : cf. P Lond 3¹⁹ (B.C. 146 or 135) (= I. p. 46) ἐπὶ βασιλέως αἰωνοβίου. So P Giss I. 36²⁰ (B.C. 161) βασιλεύ(οντος) αἰωνοβίο(υ) of Ptolemy Philometor. See below on αἰώνιος, where also there are remarks on etymology.

αἰώνιος.

Without pronouncing any opinion on the special meaning which theologians have found for this word, we must note that outside the NT, in the vernacular as in the classical

Greek (see Grimm-Thayer), it never loses the sense of perpetuus (cf. Deissmann BS p. 363, LAE p. 368). It is a standing epithet of the Emperor's power : thus Cagnat IV. 144³ τ αἰ οἶκον of Tiberius, BGU I. 176 τοῦ αἰωνίου κόσμου of Hadrian. From the beginning of iii/A.D. we have BGU II. 362ⁱᵛˑ¹¹ ff. ὑπὲρ σωτηρίων καὶ αἰω[νίου] διαμο[νῆ]s τοῦ κυρίου ἡμῶν Αὐτοκρά[τορος] Σεουή[ρου Ἀ]ντωνίνου. Two examples from iv/A.D. may be quoted addressed to the Emperor Galerius and his colleagues : ὑμετέρῳ θείῳ καὶ αἰωνίῳ [νεύματι], and [ὑπὲρ] τῆς αἰωνίου καὶ ἀφθάρτου βασιλείας ὑμῶν, OGIS 569²⁰˙²⁴. Ultimately it becomes a direct epithet of the Emperor himself, taking up the succession of the Ptolemaic αἰωνόβιος (see above under αἰών sub fin.). The earliest example of this use we have noted is BGU IV. 1062²⁷ (A.D. 236), where it is applied to Maximus : so in P Grenf II. 67²⁷, a year later. (In both the word is said to be very faint.) P Lond 233⁸ (= II. p. 273) παρὰ τῆς θιότητος τῶν δεσποτῶν ἡμῶν αἰωνίων Αὐγούστων, referring to Constantius and Constans, is the precursor of a multitude of examples of the epithet as applied to the Christian Emperors. The first volume of the Leipzig Papyri alone has twenty-seven instances of the imperial epithet, all late in iv/A.D. Even in BGU I. 303² (A.D. 586) and ib. 309⁴ (A.D. 602) we have still τοῦ αἰωνίου Αὐγούστου (Maurice). In Syll 757¹² (i/A.D.—see under αἰών) note θείας φύσεως ἐργάτης αἰωνίου (of Time). Syll 740¹⁸ (iii/A.D.) joins it with ἀναφαίρετον. P Grenf II. 71¹¹ (ii/A.D.) ὁμολογῶ χαρίζεσθαι ὑμῖν χάριτι αἰωνίᾳ καὶ ἀναφαιρέτῳ is a good example of the meaning perpetuus ; and from a much earlier date (i/B C.) we may select OGIS 383⁸˙⁶ (a passage in the spirit of Job 19²¹) : Ἀντίοχος . . . ἐπὶ καθωσιωμένων βάσεων ἀσύλοις γράμμασιν ἔργα χάριτος ἰδίας εἰς χρόνον ἀνέγραψεν αἰώνιον. Add BGU II. 531ⁱⁱˑ²⁰ (ii/A.D.) ἐὰν δὲ ἀστοχήσῃς [αἰω]γίαν μοι λοίπην (i. e. λύπην) [π]αρέχιν μέλλις. In his Index to OGIS Dittenberger gives fourteen instances of the word.

The etymological note on αἰών in Grimm-Thayer, though less antiquated than usual, suggests the addition of a statement on that side. Αἰέν is the old locative of αἰών as αἰές is of αἰώς (acc. αἰῶ in Aeschylus), and αἰεί, ἀεί of *αἰϜόν (Lat. aevum), three collateral declensions from the same root. In the Sanskrit āyu and its Zend equivalent the idea of life, and especially long life, predominates. So with the Germanic cognates (Gothic aiws). The word, whose root it is of course futile to dig for, is a primitive inheritance from Indo-Germanic days, when it may have meant " long life " or "old age"—perhaps the least abstract idea we can find for it in the prehistoric period, so as to account for its derivatives.

In general, the word depicts that of which the horizon is not in view, whether the horizon be at an infinite distance, as in Catullus' poignant lines—

> Nobis cum semel occidit brevis lux,
> Nox est perpetua una dormienda,

or whether it lies no farther than the span of a Caesar's life.

ἀκαθαρσία.

In a literal sense the noun occurs in a formula used in agreements for renting houses, which the tenant undertakes to leave in good condition. Thus P Oxy VIII. 1128⁵ (A.D. 173) παραδότω τοὺς τόπους καθαροὺς ἀπὸ κοπρίων καὶ πάσης ἀκαθαρσίας : ib. VI. 912²⁶ (A.D. 235). BGU II. 393¹⁶ (A.D. 168) ἄν[ευ] ἀκαθαρσία[s], P Lond 216²⁸ ᶠ (A.D. 94)

(= II. p. 187). P Lips I. 16¹⁰ (A.D. 158) where ἀπό stands without καθαρούς (see under ἀπό). Vettius Valens, p. 2¹⁹, has it in conjunction with κιναιδία : Kroll takes it as "*oris impudicitia* (?)."

ἀκάθαρτος.

The adjective is found in a moral sense of an unclean demon in the long magical papyrus P Par 574¹²⁹⁸ (= *Selections*. p. 113). It occurs in the correspondence of the architect Cleon (B.C. 255-4), P Petr II. 4. (3)⁵ (p. 8), εἰλήφαμεν δὲ τοῦ ἀκαθάρτου καὶ τὸ [. . ., where the ganger Apollonius seems to be writing about a supply of iron for quarrymen, but the mutilation prevents our determining the reference. Vettius Valens, p. 70¹, has πάθεσιν ἀκαθάρτοις καὶ παρὰ φύσιν ἡδοναῖς, where the ethical sense is completely developed : half way comes *Syll* 633³ (ii/A.D. according to Michel), where a Lycian named Xanthus dedicates a shrine to Mên Tyrannus and says καὶ [μηθένα] ἀκάθαρτον προσάγειν · καθαριζέστω δὲ ἀπὸ σ(κ)όρδων κα[ὶ] χοιρέων] κα[ὶ] γ[υ]ναικός—the impurity is ritual.

ἀκαιρος.

The well-known letter of a prodigal son, BGU III. 846¹¹ᶠ (ii/A.D.) (= *Selections*, p. 94) has the adverb ἀκαιρίως πάντα σοι διήγηται, "unseasonably related all to you." For the adjective cf. *Syll* 730¹² (ii/B.C.) αἱ λίαν ἄκαιροι δαπάναι. The derived noun appears in P Par 63ˣˡ· ⁹⁴ᶠ (B.C. 165) διά τε τὴν περιέχουσάν μει (*l.* με) κατὰ πολλοὺς τρόπους ἀκ[αι]ρίαν.

ἄκακος.

BGU IV. 1015¹¹ᶠ (A.D. 222-3) λ[άχαν]ον νέον νέον καθαρὸν ἄδολ(ον) . [. . ἄ]κακ[ον] must have a passive sense "undamaged." So P Oxy I. 142⁵ (A.D. 534), a similar formula. For ἄ. = "simple" rather than "innocent" in Rom 16¹⁸, see the quotations from Wetstein recalled by Field *Notes*, p. 166.

ἄκανθα.

In P Oxy III. 646 (time of Hadrian) a legacy includes κλείνη ἀκανθίνη, *i.e.* a couch made of acantha-wood (Herod. ii. 96, Strabo 175). Sir F. G. Kenyon (P Lond I. p. 140), calls it "the Egyptian acacia from which gum arabic is obtained, and whose branches were in early times used for boat-building." Its pods are mentioned in P Leid X (iii/iv A.D.), a long list of chemical prescriptions : ˣⁱⁱ· ³⁵ (p. 237) ἀκάνθης κεράτια. The name, or derivatives of it, may be seen in P Lond 214¹³ ᶠᶠ· (A.D. 270-5) (= II. p. 162), *ib.* 1177¹⁷⁷ (A.D. 113) (= III. p. 186), P Oxy I. 121⁴ (iii/A.D.), *ib.* VI. 909¹⁷ (A.D. 225), *ib.* VIII. 1112⁵ (A.D. 188), P Flor I. 50⁷² (A.D. 268), etc. This evidence isolates further the word as used in Mark and John (Isa 34¹³) ; but the meaning there is not shaken. We need not discuss the identification of ἄκανθα, ἄκανθος (so MGr ἀγκάθι, Pontic ἀχάντι, "thorn"), and the derived adjective, as occurring in Egypt : in the NT the exact nature of the thorny plant indicated is indeterminate : see *Enc. Bibl.* 5059 f.

ἄκαρπος.

The adj. may be cited from P Oxy I. 53⁹ (A.D. 316) ὅθ[εν] ἐφῖδον τὴν περσέαν ἄκαρπον οὖσαν πολλ[ῶ]ν ἐτῶν

διόλου ξηραντῖσαν. For the subst. see *Syll* 42·³⁰ (ii/A.D.) διὰ τὰς γενομένας ἐφ᾽ ἐξ᾽ ῆς ἀκαρπίας τῶν ἐλαιων.

ἀκατάγνωστος.

To illustrate this NT ἄπ. εἰρ. (Tit 2⁸) Deissmann (*BS* p. 200 f.) cites from the inscriptions a sepulchral epitaph *CIG* 1971 *b⁵* (Thessalonica, A.D. 165), where the word is applied to the deceased, and a similar usage in an inscription at Rome *IGSI* 2139³ (date ?) (ἄμεμπτος, ἀκατάγνωστος), also a deed of tenure from the Fayum, BGU I. 308⁵ (Byz.) (= *Chrest.* II. 278) ἐπάναγκες ἐπιτελέσωμεν τὰ πρὸς τὴν καλλιεργίαν τῶν ἀρουρῶν ἔργα πάντα ἀκαταγνώστ[ως]. Add P Oxy I. 140¹⁵, P Lond 113¹⁵ (= I. p. 209), P Grenf I. 57¹⁶ and *ib.* 58¹¹ (all vi/A.D.) : also P Giss I. 56⁵ (vi/A.D.) where the editor cites similar expressions, such as ἀκαταφρονήτως, ἀναμφιβόλως. Nageli (p. 47) compares εὐκατάγνωστος in P Tor I. 1ᵛⁱⁱⁱ· ¹¹ (ii/B.C.).

ἀκατάκριτος.

This word has hitherto been found only in Ac 16⁷, 22²⁵, and though "uncondemned" (AV, RV) is its natural meaning, this does not suit the context. Accordingly Blass thinks that it may there = Attic ἄκριτος, which can be used of a cause *not yet tried*. See also Ramsay *St Paul*, p. 225, where it is pointed out that Paul in claiming his rights would probably use the Roman phrase *re incognita*, "without investigating our case," and that this was inadequately rendered by the Lucan ἀκατάκριτος.

ἀκατάπαστος.

For the genitive construction after this neuter adjective in 2 Pet 2¹⁴ ἀκαταπάστους ἁμαρτίας, cf. such examples from the papyri as P Tebt I. 124²⁶ (*c.* B.C. 118) ἀσυκοφαντή(τους) καὶ ἀδιστάστους ὄντος πάσης αἰ[τ]ίας, BGU III. 970⁷ᶠ (A.D. 177) τῆς εἰς ἄπαντας εὐεργεσίας . . . ἀβοήθητος : see *Proleg.* p. 235. In view of the common vulgar change of αυ to ᾰ (as in Ἄγουστος, ᾰτός, etc.—see *Proleg.* p. 47) it is not improbable that ἀκατάπαυστος may be the word intended, so that the mass of the MSS. have glossed correctly. Prof. Thumb suggests that the influence of ἐπάην may have affected the form. For this word cf. PSI 28⁵² (iii/iv A.D.—magic) ἔρωτι ἀκαταπαύστῳ.

ἀκαταστασία.

A literary citation for this Stoic word may be made from P Grenf I. 1⁴ (ii/B.C.), the Erotic fragment, where the faithless lover is called ἀκαταστασίης εὑρέτης. See also the astrological papyrus published in *Archiv* i. p. 493 f. τῆς συ[μβ]ίου σῆς ἀκαταστασί(αν) (l. 25 f.). It occurs nearly a dozen times in Vettius Valens, coupled with πλάνη καὶ ἀλητεία (p. 4¹⁸), ἀνωμαλία (p. 44¹⁸—one MS.), στάσις, ἔχθρα, συνοχή, κρίσις, ταραχή, etc. : it several times has οἰκείων dependent on it. The verb ἀκαταστατέω also occurs three times. That the astrologers had so thoroughly domesticated it does not prove that Paul, James and Luke were using a word of the higher culture.

ἀκατάστατος.

Audollent no. 4 (*b*)¹² (a curse on a leaden tablet from Cnidus) ἀνατίθημι Δάματρι καὶ Κόραι τὸν τὴν οἰκίαν) μου ἀκατά[σ]τατον ποιοῦ(ν)τα. The date (*op. cit.* p. 5) is given as B.C. 300-100, though the series may be later (Newton).

ἀκέραιος.

Syll 210[13] (ii/B.C.) τὴν χώραν ἀκέραιον. P Par 60[iii 28] (A.D. 232) (= *Chrest.* I. p. 64) . . .] αὐτῷ τὸ πρᾶγμα ἀκέραιον ὡς ἦλθεν . . . In PSI 86[6] (A.D. 367 75) a man named Aurelius Sneus is bailed out of prison on certain conditions, ἀκέραιον καὶ ἐκτὸ[ς] φυ[λακῆς ἀ]ναδοθέντα. Much earlier comes an instance of the adverb, in BGU IV. 1208[47] (B.C. 27–6) ἐξηγή[σατό μ]οι ἀκεραίως an outrage (ὕβρις) set forth in the petition which these words close. It is associated with ἀσινής in *IG* III. 1418 (ii/A.D.), and in a Delphian inscr. of ii/B.C. (*BCH* xxvii. p. 109[23]) πρᾶγμα ἀ. — οὐ κεκριμένον. Cronert, to whom these two passages are due, cites also *IG* XIV. 951[21] (Rome, B.C. 78) εἰς ἀκέραιον ἀποκαθιστάναι — *in integrum restituere.* In P Lips I. 13[11] (A.D. 366) ἀ]κεραίων ὄντων καὶ ἀκινδύνων is applied to a loan, in the promise to pay interest. (MGr ἀκέριος.)

ἀκλινής.

This NT ἅπ. εἰρ. (Heb 10[23]) occurs in a petition (v/A.D.) of stilted style but far from accurate : P Oxy VI. 904[9] ταῖς ἀκλεινεῖς (*l.* -έσιν) ἀκοαῖς τῆς ὑμετέρας ἐξουσίας, "the impartial ears of your highness."

ἀκμάζω.

In his famous speech at Corinth, announcing freedom to the Greeks, Nero expresses regret that it had not been in his power to offer it ἀκμαζούσης τῆς Ἑλλάδος, so that more might have shared in his bounty (*Syll* 376[17]). The more literal sense appears in P Lond 46[220] (a magical papyrus, iv/A.D.) (= I. p. 72) ὅσα ἀκμάζει τῶν ὀπωρῶν. According to Moeris ("ἥβαν Ἀττ., ἀκμάζειν Ἑλλ."). Nero's composition-master must have allowed a vernacular word to sully the purity of the oration.

ἀκμήν.

In *OGIS* 201[13] (vi/A.D.) οὐκ ἀπῆλθον ὅλως ὀπίσω τῶν ἄλλων βασιλέων, ἀλλὰ ἀκμὴν ἔμπροσθεν αὐτῶν, the adverb seems to have the meaning "valde, magnopere, longe," in accordance with the original meaning of ἀκμή (see Dittenberger's note). Cf. *Syll* 326[12] (i/A.D.) παραλαβὼν τοὺς ἐν ἀκμαι τῶν πολιτᾶν : similarly P Oxy III. 473[8] (A.D. 138 (6)) παρὰ τὴν πρώτην ἀκμήν. A compound adjective ἴσακμον, "with an even edge," is applied to a weaver's instrument in P Oxy VII. 1035[14] (A.D. 143) See on the later history of this word (MGr ἄκμα = ἔτι) K. Krumbacher's important article in Kuhn's *Zeitschrift* xxvii. pp. 498–521. The noun was in Hellenistic use, according to Moeris : "ὡραία γάμων Ἀττ., ἐν ἀκμῇ γάμου Ἑλλ." The adverbial accus. was banned by the same grammarian in favour of ἔτι : so also Phrynichus (Rutherford *NP*, p. 203). In the NT, however, except for Mt 15[16], all writers conspired to Atticize here : ἔτι was clearly quite good "bad Greek," as well as ἀκμήν !

ἀκοή.

The word is sometimes concrete, denoting "the ear": so in the late document cited above under ἀκλινής, and in P Oxy I. 129[4] (vi/A.D.) εἰς ἀκοὰς ἐμὰς ἦλθεν. Much earlier is Wunsch *AF* 1[7] (i/ii A.D.) where ἀκοάς stands between ἐνκέφαλον [πρόσω]πον and ὀφρ[ῦς] μυκτῆρας. Its more normal sense of "hearing" appears in a would-be cultured letter, BGU IV. 1080[6] (iii/A.D.) (= *Chrest.* I. p. 564) καὶ ἡμεῖς δὲ ἀκοῇ ἀπόντες ὡς παρόντες διαθέσει ηὐφράνθημεν :

the writer is able to quote Homer. It is joined with ὄσφρησις (as in 1 Cor 12[17]) in the quasi-literary P Ryl II. 63[5] (ii/A.D.—an astrological dialogue).

ἀκολουθέω

is still the word for "following," in MGr (ἀκλουθῶ) : it is noteworthy that in a large batch of petitions in P Ryl II. 124–152, from Euhemeria (A.D. 28–42) we find the MGr form anticipated four times (ἐπηκλούθησε or -ηκότος). In the papyri the verb takes the place of ἔπομαι, which is also wanting in the NT, and in the LXX is confined to 3 Maccabees. In the most literal sense we have such passages as P Lond 131 *recto*[59] (A.D. 78–9) (= I. p. 171) παιδ(ῶν) β ἀκολουθούντων τοῖς ὄνοις. P Lille I. 1 *verso*[18] (B.C. 259) has an inanimate object : ἀκολουθήσουσι δὲ τοῖς προυπάρχουσι χώμασι, "they will follow up, continue, the existing banks." For the thought of "following" to get a favour see BGU IV. 1079[10] (A.D. 41) (= *Selections*, p. 39), ἀκολούθει δὲ Πτολλαρίωνι πᾶσαν ὥραν, "stick to Pollarion constantly": cf. l. 26 μᾶλλον ἀκολουθῶ· αὐτῷ δύνῃ φιλιάσαι αὐτῷ, "rather stick to him, and so you may become his friend." In P Petr III. 128[10] the verb is used of journey-money assigned to an official, ἐφόδοις τοῖς ἀκολουθοῦσι τῶ [ἐπιστά]τηι. A striking parallel to the language of Mt 19[27], and parallels, is to be found in an early papyrus Latin letter of recommendation discovered at Oxyrhynchus, P Oxy I. 32[10 ff.] (ii/A.D.), "reliquit enim su[o]s [e]t rem suam et actum et me secutus est." If the letter can be regarded as a Christian letter, its value, in view of its age, would be unique : see Deissmann *LAE*, p. 182. For the adjective, see P Tebt II. 290[14] (A.D. 123) ἀκόλουθ ὄν) ἐστι, "it is consequently right" (Edd.), and for the adverb, see P Tebt I. 33[2] (B.C. 112) (= *Selections*, p. 39) φρόν]τισον οὖν ἵνα γένη ται) ἀκολούθως, "take care therefore that action is taken in accordance with it," P Oxy I. 38[13] (A.D. 49–50) ἀκολούθως τοῖς ὑπὸ σοῦ, "in accordance with what had been enacted by you":—the word is very common. The verb normally takes the dative. P Amh II. 62[2] (ii/B.C.) shows it absolute : εἰσὶν οἱ ἀκολουθοῦντες μαχαιρο φόροι) Δίδυμος Λυσίμαχος κτλ. In P Lille I. 26[4] (iii/B.C.) we have an adverbial accus., εἰ μὴ ἀκολουθεῖς ἅπαντα. Note P Par p. 411 (Ptol.) Ἀμ]μώνιον ἀκολουθοῦντά σοι ὀφθαλ[μοῖς. For ἀκ. μετά cf. Rutherford *NP*, p. 458 f., where the construction is shown to be Attic.

ἀκούω.

The verb is of course common enough, and needs little or no illustration, having few peculiarities. Its use for a judicial hearing (as Ac 25[22]) may be paralleled with P Iand 9[10] (ii/A.D.) καὶ [μέ]χ[ρι] τούτου οὔπω ἠκούσθ ημ]εν, and P Oxy VII. 1032[59] (A.D. 162), where the epistrategus endorses a petition with ἀκουσθήσεται. So in BGU II. 511[ii. 2] (= *Chrest.* I. p. 26), an account written about A.D. 200 of a trial before Claudius, we have ἀκούει Κλαύδιος Καῖσα[ρ Σέβαστος Ἰσιδώρου] γυμνασιάρχου πόλεως Ἀ[λεξανδρέων] κατὰ Ἀγρίππου βασιλέω[ς. The last example will illustrate ἀκούειν with normal gen. of person : P Par 48[4] (B.C. 153) (= Witkowski[2] p. 91) ἀκούσαντες . . τὰ περὶ σοῦ συνβεβηκότα will serve for *accus. rei*, and will also illustrate the common use with περί, since the phrase is a mixture of ἀκ. περὶ σοῦ and ἀκ. τὰ σοι συνβεβηκότα (Witk.). The

same papyrus shows us the participial object clause, l. ¹²
ἀκούσαντες δὲ ἐν τῷ μεγάλῳ Σαραπιείου ὄντα σε. In
P Amh II. 37⁸ (ii/B.C.) ἐκούομεν δὲ μὴ παραγεγονέ[ναι . . .
we have apparently the infin. construction, and so in
P Grenf II. 36¹⁵ (B.C. 95), ἠκούσαμεν τὸν μὲν καταβεβρωκέναι τὸν σπόρον—Witkowski (² p. 120, cf. p. xiv.)
allows the writer to be "modice eruditus." For ἀκούειν
ὡς cf. CPHerm 22⁵: for the commoner ὅτι, P Tebt II.
416⁸ (iii/A.D.) μὴ οὖν ἀκούσῃς ἀνθρώπων ὅτι μέλλω μένιν
ἐνθάδε. With the introductory imper., as in Mk 4³, cf. the
dialogue in P Ryl II. 63³ iii/A.D.) where ἄκουε precedes an
exposition.

ἀκρατής

in the sense of "impotent" is found in Syll 802, 803
(iii/B.C.), inscriptions from Asclepios' temple, e.g. 802²²
ἀνὴρ τοὺς τᾶς χηρὸς δακτύλους ἀκρατεῖς ἔχων. Vettius
Valens (p. 30³³) associates ἀστάτους ταῖς γνώμαις καὶ
ἀκρατεῖς.

ἄκρατος

P Oxy II. 237ⁱⁱ⁴⁰ (A.D. 186) παρ' οἷς ἄκρατός ἐστιν ἡ
τῶν νόμων ἀποτομ[ί]α, "amongst whom the severity of
the law is untempered" Edd.). It is said to mean "un-
diluted" in MGr: cf. Od. ix. 297 ἄκρητον γάλα.

ἀκρίβεια

P Par 63ⁱⁱ⁴⁵ (ii/B.C.) μετὰ πάσης ἀκριβείας, τὴν ἐκτ[ε]νε-
[σ]τάτην [ποι]ήσασθαι πρόνοιαν combines some characteristic Lucan and Pauline words. P Lond 121⁸⁴¹ (iii/A.D.)
(= I. p. 111), has ἐπ' ἀκριβίας, an adverbial phrase like ἐπ'
ἀληθείας. A rather literary document, an advocate's speech
for prosecution—suspected by the editors of being a rhetorical
exercise—contains the sentence ἄμεινον δ' αὗται καὶ σαφέστερον τὴν περὶ τοῦτο ἀκρείβειαν καὶ τὴν ἐπιμέλειαν Μαξίμ[ο]υ
δηλώσουσιν (P Oxy III. 471³³ ᶠᶠ., ii/A.D.), which the editors
translate, "These letters will still better and more clearly
exhibit Maximus' exactness and care in this matter." Near
the end of the petition of Dionysia (P Oxy II. 237ᵛⁱⁱⁱ²⁹,
A.D. 186) we have μετὰ πάσης ἀκρειβείας φυλασσέσθωσαν
(sc. αἱ ἀπογραφαί) : and in P Petr III. 3) (a) recto²⁶ ᶠ. a
prisoner complains to the Epimeletes that it was on account
of the "punctiliousness" of his predecessor in office that he
had been confined—[ἀ]κριβείας ἕνεκεν ἀπήχθην. The verb
ἀκριβεύειν, "to get exact instructions," appears in P Amh
II. 154⁷ (vi/vii A.D.) ἐὰν μὴ ἀκριβεύσωμαι ἀφ' ὑμῶν περὶ
ἑκάστου πράγματος: Cronert's earliest citation for this verb
is "Barnabas" 2¹⁰. It may be formed by association with
ἀκρίβεια, by the influence of the close relation of -εια and
-εύω.

ἀκριβής

In P Oxy VI. p. 226 part of a document is given which
forms the first column of no. 899 (A.D. 200): ὅπως ἐξετά-
σαντ(ες) κατὰ τὸ ἀκρειβέστερον τῷ (a gap follows) This
is a good example of an elative comparative (Proleg. pp. 78
and 236), for the meaning is clearly "having most carefully
examined": cf. also P Petr II. 16¹³. A late iv/A.D. inscription, Syll 423¹⁵, has βρέβιον (= breve, a précis) τῶν
εἰρημένων ἀπάντων ἀκριβῆ διδασκαλίαν ἐπέχον. The
neuter as a noun occurs in the Magnesian inscr. Syll 929³²

(ii/B.C.) τῶι μὲν ἀκριβεῖ τῆς ψήφου βραβευθῆναι τὴν κρίσιν
οὐκ ἠβουλόμεθα, of counting a vote exactly: and P Tebt II.
287¹⁹ (A.D. 161-9) τὸ ἀκρειβὲς μάθῃς. The adverb is treated
separately below.

ἀκριβόω

This fairly common classical and Hellenistic verb does not
happen to occur in the papyri, so far as we have noticed.
We might add to the literary record Vettius Valens p. 295²
τούτων οὕτως κατ' ἐξέτασιν ἠκριβωμένων, which has exactly
the same sense as in Mt 2¹⁶.

ἀκριβῶς

For ἀ. with οἶδα, as 1 Th 5², cf. P Goodsp Cairo 5¹¹
(iii B.C.) ὅπως ἀκριβῶς εἰδῇς, P Petr II. 15 (1)¹¹ (iii/B.C.)
εἰδῆσαι ἀκριβῶς: cf. P Hib I. 40⁶ᶠ (iii/B.C.) ἐπίστασο μέντοι
ἀκριβῶς. P Par 44⁷ (B.C. 153) (= Witkowski EPP.² p. 83)
διασάφη[σ]όν μοι . . . τὰ περὶ σαυτὸν ἀκριβῶς. P Lond
354²³ (c. B.C. 10) (= II. p. 165) ἐπιγνόντα ἀκριβῶς ἕκαστα.
The comparative is used very much as in Ac 23¹⁵, ²⁰ in
P Oxy VIII. 1102¹² (c. A.D. 146), the strategus ἀκρειβέστερον
ἐξετάσει ἢ κατοικ[, and again BGU II. 388ⁱⁱⁱ⁴¹ (ii/iii A.D.).
ἥξει Ἅρπαλος καὶ ἐξετασθήσεται περὶ τούτου ἀκριβέσ τε-
ρον: the combination was evidently a formula. With
πυνθάνεσθαι (as in Ac 23²⁰) cf. P Petr II. 16⁵⁴ (iii B.C.)
πευσόμεθα ἀκριβέστερον. The superlative occurs in P Hib
I. 27ⁱⁱ ³⁴ (early iii/B.C.) ὡς οὖν ἠδυνάμην ἀκριβέστατα.

ἀκροατής

The verb occurs in the magic papyrus P Lond I. 46¹⁷⁷
(iv/A.D.) (= I. p. 70) φρικτὸς μὲν ἰδεῖν, φρικτὸς δὲ
ἀκροᾶσθαι.

ἀκροβυστία

We have (naturally enough) no citations to illustrate this
technical word of Jewish ritual, but a note on its formation
might be given (from J. H. Moulton's forthcoming Grammar
of NT Greek, vol. II.): "Ἀκροποσθία, a normal descriptive
cpd. from ἄκρος and πόσθη with a fresh suffix, is found in
Hippocrates, and is obviously the original of the LXX word.
When a word containing a vox obscena was taken from
medical vocabulary into popular religious speech, it was
natural to disguise it: a rare word βύστρα βύσμα may
supply the model."

ἀκρογωνιαῖος

may very well have been coined by the LXX (Isa 28¹⁶).
The Attic word was γωνιαῖος: see inscriptional citations in
J. A. Robinson Ephesians, p. 164. Cronert (p. 253) has
several other compounds of ἄκρος, some of which may be in
the same category. W. W. Lloyd in CR iii. p. 419a (1889)
among some architectural notes on Eph 2²⁰ ²², says: "The
acrogoniaios here is the primary foundation-stone at the angle
of the structure by which the architect fixes a standard for
the bearings of the walls and cross-walls throughout."

ἀκροθίνιον

The word is doubtfully restored in Syll 633⁴ (ii/A.D.)
where it is prescribed that the worshippers shall bring
among other offerings κολλύβων χοίνικες δύο καὶ ἀκρο-
[θίνιον?]. Cf. GDI 2501ᵈ⁴⁷ (Delphi, c. B.C. 305) τὠπόλλωνι
τὰ ἀκρόθινα (pointed out by Prof. Thumb).

ἄκρος.

P Tebt II. 380[17] (i/A.D.) οὐλὴ ὀφρύει δεξιᾳ ἄκρᾳ, "a scar at the tip of the right eyebrow," P Oxy I. 43 (*verso*) i[17] (iii/A.D.) ἐπʼ ἄκρῳ ῥύμης Σεύθον. In P Oxy I. 108[i. 3] (A.D. 183 or 215), the meat bill of a cook, ἄκρα β are translated by the editors "two trotters." Cf. *Preisigke* 358[4] (iii/B.C.) τὸ ἄκρον τῆς σκιᾶς, of the shadows on a sundial, and *Syll* 804[9] (? ii/A.D.) κιτρίου προλαμβάνειν (= "eat," see *s.v.*) τὰ ἄκρα : *ib.* 425[7. 9] (iii/B.C.) κατὰ τῶν ἄκρων, "down the heights" (as often).

Ἀκύλας.

Thayer's doubts regarding the existence of the genitive of this proper name may be set at rest by its occurrence in the papyri, where it is found in two forms—Ἀκύλου (BGU II. 484[6], A.D. 201–2) and Ἀκύλα (*ib.* I. 71[21], A.D. 189, P Strass 22[10], iii/A.D., Σουβατιανοῦ Ἀ.). Much earlier is Γαίου Ἰουλίου Ἀκύλα, on the inser. of Augustus in *Preisigke* 401, A.D. 10–1. See Deissmann *BS*, p. 187, where the doubling of the λ in certain manuscripts of Ac 18[2] and Rom 16[3] is further illustrated by the occurrence of both Ἀκύλας and Ἀκύλλας in duplicate documents of the end of ii/A.D. with reference to the veteran C. Longinus Aquila (BGU I. 326). An Aquila of Pontus occurs on an inscription of Sinope, Φλ]αμιν[ίʼ]ον Ἀκύλα, as noted by D. M. Robinson in the *Prosopographia* to his monograph on Sinope, *Am. Journ. of Philology* xxvii. p. 269 (1906).

ἀκυρόω.

The adjective ἄκυρος is common in legal phraseology (e.g. it comes *quater* in the Ptolemaic Hibeh papyri). It occurs in the new Median parchment, P Saʻid Khan 1[a. 23] (B.C. 88) ὃς ἂν δὲ ἐγβάλῃ κτλ. [ἔ]στω ἄκυρος applied to a *person*, whose action is voided by illegality, a classical use. In the second parchment (B.C. 22) τὴν τε ἀθέτησιν εἶναι αὐτὴν ἄκυρον, it has its normal Hellenistic force. Ἀκύρωσις goes with ἀθέτησις (see *s.v.*), or is used by itself, especially in the phrase εἰς ἀκύρωσιν of a will or an I.O.U. received back to be *cancelled* : so P Oxy I. 107[4. 6] (A.D. 123) ἀνέλαβον παρὰ σοῦ εἰς ἀκύρωσιν, *ib.* III. 490[3. 6] (A.D. 124) πρὸς ἀκύρωσιν ἄγειν τήνδε τὴν διαθήκην, "to revoke this will." The verb occurs in the same sense P Oxy III. 491[3] (A.D. 126), 494[4] (A.D. 156), 495[3] (A.D. 181–9), etc.: cf. *Syll* 329[9] (i/B.C.) ἠκυρῶσθαι τὰς κ[α]τ' αὐτῶν ἐκγραφὰς καὶ ὀφειλήμ[ατα].

ἀκωλύτως.

The adjective occurs rarely B.C., and one citation from Plato stands in Crönert as warrant for classical antiquity. The adverb becomes very common from ii/A.D. It is of constant occurrence in legal documents, e.g. P Oxy III. 502[31] (A.D. 164) ὡς πρόκειται ἐπὶ τὸν χρόνον ἀκωλύτως, "as aforesaid for the appointed time without hindrance" of the lease of a house, *ib.* VI. 912[19] (A.D. 235), *ib.* VIII. 1127[16] (A.D. 183) and VII. 1036[27] (A.D. 273) : see exx. of this combination in the note to P Giss I. 49[27] (p. 74). So P Lips I. 26[11] (beginning iv/A.D.) P Gen 11[16] (A.D. 350), and the Edmonstone papyrus, P Oxy IV. p. 203 (A.D. 354), νέμεσθε εἰς οὓς ἐὰν βούλητε τόπους ἀκωλύτως καὶ ἀνεπιλήμπτως. Add the sixth century P Lond 991[15] (= III. p. 258) ἀκολύτως καὶ

ἄκων.

This common Greek word, which in the NT is found only 1 Cor 9[17], occurs several times in the long petition of Dionysia, P Oxy II. 237[vi. 18, vii. 5, 12, 22] (A.D. 186), : cf. the fourth century Christian letter P Oxy VI. 939[12] (= *Selections*, p. 129) ἐς τηλικαύτην σε [ἀγωνία]ν ἄκων ἐνέβαλον, "unwillingly I cast you into such grief." Add from the inscriptions, *Syll* 350[5] (time of Augustus) εἴτε ἑκόντα εἴτε ἄκοντα, *ib.* 415[8] (iii/A.D.), etc.

ἀλάβαστρον.

The word is found with μύρου, as in Mk 14[3], in *OGIS* 629[35] (A.D. 137) μύρου [ἐν ἀλαβάσ]τροις, according to the editor's restoration. In P Petr II. 47[8] the words ἐν Ἀλαβάστρων πόλει, "in Alabastropolis," occur in the subscription to a contract for a loan. From v/B.C. may be quoted *Syll* 44[8], ἀλά[βαστ[οι], according to the Attic form : cf. *Michel* 823[11] (B.C. 220), *ib.* 833[9] (B.C. 279), σὺν τοῖς ἀλαβάστροις, in an inventory of temple treasures. From a much later period we have mention of a quarry near Alexandria, or at any rate belonging to Alexandria—P Théad 36[3] (A.D. 327) ἐπιμελητὴς τεχνιτῶν ἀποστελλομένων ἐν ἀλαβαστρίῳ Ἀλεξανδρίας, *ib.* 35[3] (A.D. 325) ἐπιμελητὴς ἐργατῶν τῶν [κατ]ὰ τὴν ἀλαβαστρίνην μεγάλ(ην), *ib.* 34[2] and editor's note (p. 182). Earlier than this is P Ryl II. 92 (ii/iii A.D.) a list of persons designated for employment εἰς ἀλαβάστρινα, and other works. The alabaster quarry may also be recognized in P Petr II. 9 (2)[5] (B.C. 241–39) μετα[πορεύ]εσθαι εἰς ἀλαβα[στί]θιδα : see the editor's note, p. [23], as to the locality. Finally, there is an inventory in P Lond 402 *verso* (ii/B.C.) (= II. p. 12) which includes among a good many utensils and articles known and unknown ἀλαβαστρο(υ)θῆκαι : we may infer that the writer first meant to coin a compound, and then changed his mind and wrote the genitive. (See also under ἀσκός.)

ἀλαζονεία.

To its later literary record may be added *Test. xii. patr., Jos.* 17 οὐχ ὕψωσα ἐμαυτὸν ἐν ἀλαζονείᾳ διὰ τὴν κοσμικὴν δόξαν μου, ἀλλʼ ἤμην ἐν αὐτοῖς ὡς εἷς τῶν ἐλαχίστων (cited by Mayor on Jas 4[16]).

ἅλας.

As early as iii/B.C. the neuter form is proved to have been in existence, e.g. P Petr III. 140 (*x*)[2] ἔλαιον ῡ ἅλας ῡ ξύλα, and may therefore be acknowledged in P Hib I. 152 (B.C. 250) ἐμβαλοῦ εἰς τὸ πλοῖον ἅλας καὶ λωτόν, though there the editors treat the word as accusative plural. A clear example seems to be quotable from P Par 55 *bis* i. 29 (ii/B.C.) καὶ ἄρτοι καὶ ἅλας. From later times we can quote P Leid X i. 8 (iii/iv A.D.) ἅλας Καππαδοκικόν, P Oxy IX. 1222[2] (iv/A.D.) τὸ ἅλας. The ambiguity of earlier exx. attaches itself even to P Leid C *verso* iv. 5 (p. 93 of part i.), where ἅλας may as well be acc. pl., since the items are acc. as well as nom. in this λόγος of provisions supplied to the Twins of the Serapeum (ii/B.C.). Mayser (*Gr.* p. 286)

ἄκων.

βεβη[ίως] : the word is legal to the last. For the triumphant note on which it brings the Acts of the Apostles to a close, see Harnack *Lukas der Arzt* p. 116, Eng. Tr. p. 163 f., and cf. Milligan *Documents*, p. 168.

quotes a conjectural reading ἅλατος for ἅμτος in the same document; but the Petrie and the Paris papyri cited give us our only certain exx. from Ptolemaic times, to set beside 2 Esd 7[22], Sir 39[26]. Cf. MGr ἁλάτι. Mr Thackeray (in a letter) would now regard ἅλας in LXX as probably neuter : "the only indubitable cases of the plural are in the local plural phrases ἡ θάλασσα (etc.) τῶν ἁλῶν. This looks as if the plural was the regular form for salt-*areas*." In the fourteen LXX instances of ἅλα and ἅλας the article is absent, and we are free to assume that a new neuter noun was already developing, perhaps under analogy of other food names like γάλα and κρέας. Ἁλός lived on in the papyri as late as A.D. 258-9, P Lond 1170 *verso*[124] (= III. p. 196). By σταθμίον ἁλις in P Tebt II. 331[11] (*c.* A.D. 131) we are apparently to understand ἁλός, "a quantity of salt." BGU III. 731[ii. 9] (A.D. 180) ἁλὸς πλεῖστον will serve as a further instance. Note ἁλική, "salt tax," common in early papyri : see ἁλυκός below.

ἀλείφω.

Passim in papyri, e.g. P Fay 121[6] (*c.* A.D. 100) ὃ καὶ ἀλείψεις ἐπιμελῶς, "which you will carefully grease," of a yoke-band. We find statues (ἀνδριάντες) the objects in BGU II. 362[vii. 16, x. 17] (A.D. 215). In P Oxy III. 528[10 f.] (ii/A.D.) a man, whose wife had gone away, writes to her that since they had bathed together a month before, he had never bathed nor anointed himself—οὐκ ἐλουσάμην οὐκ ἥλιμε (*l.* ἥλειμμαι). A curiously spelt perfect ἐνήλεπα from ἐναλείφω is found in a somewhat similar connexion in P Oxy II. 294[15] (A.D. 22). Cf. also a third-century inscription in honour of a gymnasiarch, φιλοτίμως ἀλείφοντι (Milne *JHS* 1901. p. 284), noted by the editors on P Oxy III. 473[3] (A.D. 138-60), where we find the substantive ἄλειμμα. Cf. also *OGIS* 59[18] (iii/B.C.) ὅπως ἔχωσιν εἴς τε τὰς θυσίας καὶ τὸ ἄλειμμα δαπανᾶν. For the phrase "free from erasure" cf. BGU II. 666[31] (A.D. 177) ἐστὶν δὲ καθαρὸν ἀπὸ ἀλείφατος καὶ ἐπιγραφῆς : cf. P Ryl II. 165[17] (A.D. 136). As against the contention that ἀλείφω is the "mundane and profane" and χρίω the "sacred and religious" word (Trench), see P Petr II. 25 (*a*)[13], where χρίσιν is used of the lotion for a sick horse.

ἀλέκτωρ.

See Rutherford *NP* p. 307 for the history of this word (MGr ἀλόχτερας) in classical Greek. It is found in P Tebt I. 140 (B.C. 72) τι[μὴ]ν ἀλέκτορος καὶ ἀρτοπίνακος. Add P Ryl II. 166[18] (A.D. 26) ἀ. ἕνα (which, as in 167[18], is promised as a yearly offering, in the proposal to take up a lease), P Fay 119[29] (*c.* A.D. 100) ἀλέκτορας δέκα, BGU I. 269[1] (ii/iii A.D.) and IV. 1067[11 f.] (A.D. 101-2) ἀλεκτόρων. From a later time (iii/iv A.D., according to Leemans) comes P Leid V[ix. 31, 32, x. 1], where we have (τὸν) ἀλέκτορα *bis*, and then ἀλεκτόρου : so Wünsch *AF* 3[16] (imperial) ὁ ἀλέκτωρ. It was clearly the normal Κοινή form ; but ἀλεκτρυόνων may still be seen in P Oxy IX. 1207[8] (A.D. 175-6?) ἀ. τελείων τεσσάρων, in the same phrase as BGU IV. 1067 *l.c.* It is noteworthy that ἀλεκτρύων occurs in the well-known Gospel fragment (*Mitteilungen* of the Rainer Papyri I. i. 54) ὁ ἀλεκτρύων δὶς κοκ[κύξει]. Cf. *Michel* 692[5] (i/A.D.) ἀλεκτρύονα, but in l. 27 of the same inscription ἀλέκτορας.

ἄλευρον.

The word (MGr ἀλεύρι) is found in the long magical papyrus P Lond 121[5. 9] (iii/A.D.) (= I. p. 101) : cf. *ib.* 1170 *verso* [490] (A.D. 258-9) (= III. p. 204) σάκκον ἀλεύρ[ο]υ, and *ib.* 988[13] (= III. p. 244) (iv/A.D.) αὐτὸς γὰρ τὰ ἑαυτοῦ ἔχι ἄλευρα.

ἀλήθεια.

The noun occurs frequently in prepositional phrases, μετὰ πάσης ἀληθείας, etc. Ἐπ' ἀληθείας is found in P Amh II. 68[33] (late i/A.D.) ὀμνύομεν . . . εἰ μὴν ἐξ ὑγειοῦς καὶ ἐπ' ἀληθείας ἐπιδεδωκ[έ]ναι : so P Oxy III. 480[9] (A.D. 132), and *Syll* 226[174] (iii/B.C.) οὐ γεγενημένον τούτου ἐπ' ἀληθείας, etc. This NT phrase is thoroughly idiomatic, we see, and not "translation Greek" in Mark. Other combinations are ἐξ ἀ., P Oxy VII. 1032[33] (A.D. 162) ἐ[κ] τῆς ἀ., P Flor I. 32[11] (A.D. 298) ἐξόμνυμι . . . ἐξ ἀ. καὶ πίστεως. (For this collocation of nouns, cf. P Oxy I. 70[5] (iii/A.D.) πίστιν καὶ ἀλήθ[ειαν ἔχει, "is credited and accepted," of a contract Edd.) With 2 Jn[1], 3 Jn[1] ὃν ἐγὼ ἀγαπῶ ἐν ἀληθείᾳ, cf. the Gemellus letters, P Fay 118[26] (A.D. 110) ἀσπάζου τοὺς φιλοῦντές σε πάντες πρὸς ἀλήθιαν, and *ib.* 119[26] (*c.* A.D. 100) τοὺς φιλοῦντες ἡμᾶς πρὸς ἀλήθιαν. In much the same sense we find ταῖς ἀληθεί(αις), P Ryl II. 105[26] (A.D. 136). For the noun without prepositions we may quote P Oxy II. 283[13 f.] (A.D. 45) ἐξ οὗ δεήσει γνωσθῆναι πᾶσαν τὴν περὶ τῶν προγεγραμμένων ἀλήθειαν, P Giss I. 84[11] (ii/A.D.) φι]λοῦσι νῦν οὗτοι τὴν ἀλήθ[ε]ιαν εἰπεῖν, P Lond 412[5] (A.D 351) = (II. p. 280) εἰ μὴ ὑπῆρχεν ἡμεῖν ἡ τῶν νόμων ἀλήθει[α], *ib.* 807[3] (A.D. 84) (= III. p. 206) νυνεὶ δὲ ὑμεῖς τὴν ἀλήθειαν γράψαται, etc. From v/vi A.D. comes an interesting Christian prayer in P Oxy VI. 925[5] φανέρωσόν μοι τὴν παρὰ σοὶ ἀλήθιαν εἰ βούλη με ἀπελθεῖν εἰς Χιούτ. The form of the petition closely follows those of paganism.

ἀληθεύω.

We have noticed no early occurrence, but cf. P Amh II. 142[1] (iv/A.D.) ἀληθευοντ . . ., before a gap.

ἀληθής.

The adjective is common in formulæ : thus in the 42 documents (Ptolemaic) of the P Magd there are 17 instances, all like 1[16] καὶ ἐὰν ἦι ἃ γράφω ἀληθῆ, or to the same purport. So P Strass I. 41[18] (*c.* A.D. 250) δεῖ γὰρ τὰ ἀληθῆ λέγειν. etc. It seems always to bear the normal meaning of "true in fact" ; so ὅρκος, Wilcken *Ostr* 1150 (Ptol.). In P Tebt II. 285[3] (A.D. 239) it is applied to "legitimate" children : cf. *ib.* 293[17] (*c.* A.D. 187), where, with reference to an application to circumcise a boy, it is declared ἀληθῆ εἶναι αὐτὸν ἱερατικοῦ [γέ]νους, "that he is in truth of priestly family." In BGU IV. 1024[vi. 17] (iv/v A.D.) οὐκ ἀληθής is applied to a person. For the adverb we need cite only P Gen I. 55[6] (iii/A.D.) καλοκαγαθίαν ὡς ἀληθῶς ἀσύνκριτον ἐπίπαν.

ἀληθινός

is less common still than ἀληθής, but is found in MGr. In P Petr II. 19 (*1a*)[6] (iii/B.C.) it is used in a petition by a prisoner who affirms that he has said nothing μηδέποτε ἄτοπον, ὅπερ καὶ ἀληθινόν ἐστι, and again (*si vera lectio*) *ib.* 2 (3) (B.C. 260), where the writer assures his father εἰ ἐν ἄ]λλοις ἀλύπως ἀπαλλάσσεις εἴη ἂν ὡς ἐγὼ τοῖς θεοῖς ἔσχομεν [χάριν ἀληθ]ινόν, "if in other matters you are getting on without annoyances, there will be, as we have given, true gratitude to the gods": cf. *Syll* 316¹⁷ (ii/B.C.) πα]ρασχομένων τῶν κατηγόρων ἀληθινὰς ἀποδείξεις, and the same phrase in BGU IV. 1141¹² (time of Augustus). Caracalla's edict, P Giss I. 40 ⁱⁱ·²⁷, speaks of οἱ ἀληθινοὶ Αἰγύπτιοι as "easily distinguished by their speech." The word is also found in the fragmentary BGU III. 742ⁱⁱ·¹¹ (A.D. 122) ἐν ταῖς ἀληθ[ι]ναῖς ἀντὶ φερνῆς ἡ παραχώρησις ἐγένετο. In an obscure letter concerning redemption of garments etc. in pawn, P Oxy I. 114⁷ (ii/iii A.D.), we have ἀληθινοπόρφυρον translated by the editors "with a real purple (border?)." In *OGIS* 223¹⁷ (iii/B.C.) the Seleucid Antiochus Soter writes ἀπλάστως καὶ ἀληθινῶς ἐμ πᾶσι προσφερομένους. In Wünsch *AF* 4⁴⁴ (iii/A.D.) we find εἴπω σοι καὶ τὸ ἀληθινὸν ὄνομα ὃ τρέμει Τάρταρα κτλ. For Christian examples of ἀληθινός from the papyri, see P Oxy VI. 925² (v/vi A.D.) (=*Selections*, p. 131) Ὁ θ(εὸ)s ... ὁ ἀληθινός, and the Christian amulet of vi/A.D. edited by Wilcken in *Archiv* i. p. 431 ff. (= BGU III. 954, *Selections*, p. 132), where at l. 28 ff. we find—ὁ φῶς ἐκ φωτός, θ(εὸ)s ἀληθινὸς χάρισον ἐμὲ κτλ.

ἁλιεύς.

The word is too common in itself to need illustrating, unless we recorded the appearance of the epithet ποτάμιος to indicate a fisherman who exercised his calling on the Nile. It is, however, a good example of the rule by which in Hellenistic of the second period (*i.e.* A.D.) two *i*-sounds are not allowed to come together: see *Proleg.*³ p. 44 f. In this one case, in the nom. and accus. pl. of ἁλιεύς, dissimilation instead of contraction has taken place: ἁλεεῖς occurs in NT and in P Flor I. 127¹⁵ (A.D. 256), but note 119² ἁλι(εῖs and 275⁸, from the same correspondence, and BGU IV. 1035⁶ (v/A.D.). Of course P Petr III. 59ⁱⁱ·⁸ belongs to a period when the phonetic difficulty was not felt. Another expedient was ἁλιέας, P Flor II. 201⁸ (iii/A.D.). Hellenistic does not follow the Attic contractions (Δωριᾶς, -ῶν): cf. ἁλιέων BGU III. 756⁸ (A.D. 199), Ἐριέως P Petr III. 59 (*d*)¹⁴. We find ἁλιείων in P Amh II. 30²⁹ (ii/B.C.).

ἁλιεύω.

The verb occurs in P Flor II. 275²¹, from the Heroninus correspondence (middle iii/A.D.).

ἀλλά.

The closeness of ἀλλά to πλήν appears in more uses than one. Armitage Robinson, *Ephesians*, p. 205, has a note on a quasi-resumptive use of ἀλλά in Eph 5²⁴ which is closely paralleled by that of πλήν in ver. 33. Then there are instances of ἀλλά = "except." This is clear where we have ἀλλ' ἤ (as in 2 Cor 1¹³): thus P Petr II. 9 (3 ᵇ (B.C. 241–39) ὥστε μηθένα εἶναι ἐνταῦθα ἀλλ' ἢ ἡμᾶς, "There is no one left here except ourselves" (Ed.), *ib.* 46 (*a*)⁵ (B.C. 200) καὶ μὴ ὑποκεῖσθαι πρὸς ἄλλο μηδὲν ἀλλ' ἢ τὴν προγεγραμ-[μέν]ην ἐγγύην, "has not been pledged for any other purpose than the aforesaid security" (*id.*), P Lond 897¹³ (A.D. 84) (=III. p. 207) ὁ μέντοιγε οὐ θέλωι ἀλλὰ ἢ ἀνάγκηι. In P Tebt I. 104¹⁹ (B.C. 92) μὴ ἐξέστω Φιλίσκωι γυναῖκα ἄλλην

ἐπ[α]γ[α]γέσθαι ἀλλὰ Ἀπολλωνίαν, "any other wife but A." (Edd.), shows the same use for ἀλά alone. See *Proleg.*³ p. 241 (with some additional remarks in the German ed., p. 269). G. C. Richards (*JTS* x. p. 288) observes on the note in *Proleg.*, "In Mk 4²² ἐὰν μή and ἀλλά are parallel, a usage which Aramaic explains but Greek does not." (Cf. the variants in Mk 9⁸.) Without doubting that an Aramaic background makes the usage all the easier, we can assert that Hellenistic Greek does admit this use of ἀλλά. For ἀλλὰ μήν (not in NT) cf. P Oxy III. 472³⁷ (*c.* A.D. 130) ἀ. μὴν . υτων πίστεως περὶ τούτων οὔσης, P Flor I. 89¹² (iii/A.D.) ἀ. μ. καὶ πρὸς τὴν παρακομι-[δὴν τ]ούτων [π]λοῖον παρασχεῖν σπούδασον. It is hardly necessary to illustrate the conjunction further.

ἀλλάσσω.

As so often happens, the simple verb (MGr ἀλλάζω) is outnumbered greatly by its compounds. We may cite *Syll* 178¹⁴·²² (iv/B.C.) κεκτῆσθαι καὶ ἀλλάσσεσθαι καὶ ἀποδόσθαι, P Oxy IV. 729⁴³ (A.D. 137) ἐὰν δὲ αἱρώμεθα ἀλλάσσειν κτήνη ἢ πωλεῖν ἐξέσται ἡμεῖν, P Lips I. 107³ (middle iii/A.D.) ἀλλάξας τὸν λόγον, BGU IV. 1141⁴¹·⁴⁴ (Augustus), where a πορφύρα has been "bartered," P Oxy IV. 729⁴¹ (A.D. 137) in association with πωλεῖν. In P Tebt I. 124³¹ (*c.* B.C. 118) "ἡλλαγμένοι seems to be equivalent to ἀπηλλαγμένοι rather than to have the meaning 'exchange'" (Edd.). An illiterate papyrus of A.D. 75 may be cited for the construction: BGU II. 597¹⁰ ἀλλαξέτω σε αὐτὸν (*sc.* a sack of wheat) Πασίων καλοῖς σπέρμασει. Σέ here is we suppose for σοί: the dative σπέρμασι reminds us of the NT ἐν ὁμοιώματι (Rom 1²³, from LXX), since the addition of ἐν to a dative is nothing out of the way. (Of course we are not questioning the influence of literal translation here.) The verb is also found in the fragment of the uncanonical Gospel, P Oxy V. 840¹⁷ ff. τοῦτο τὸ ἱερὸν τ[όπον ὄν]τα καθαρόν, ὃν οὐδεὶς ἄ[λλος εἰ μὴ] λουσάμενος καὶ ἀλλά[ξας τὰ ἐνδύ]ματα πατεῖ. For the substantive, see P Eleph 14⁹ (late iii/B.C.) τὴν εἰθισμένην ἀλλαγήν: it is fairly common.

ἀλλαχόθεν.

P Oxy II. 237ᵛ·¹⁵ (A.D. 186) οὐκ ἀλλαχόθεν ἡγήσατο τὴν ἐξέτασιν ἔσεσθαι serves to support Jn 10¹. The word is classical, though assailed by Atticists (Thayer).

ἀλλαχοῦ.

For this form (= ἄλλοσε or ἀλλαχόσε), which is found in the NT only in Mk 1³⁸, cf. *Syll* 418⁸⁸ (iii/A.D.) ἀλλαχοῦ πεμπόμενοι. In P Lips I. 104²⁹ (i/ii A.D.) Wilcken *Archiv* iv p. 484 proposes now to read εἰ καὶ ἐφ' ἀλλαχῇ βαδίζετε, where ἀλλαχῇ is treated like an adjective (= ἄλλῃ) with ὁδῷ supplied. If the reading is accepted, we should place it with ἐκ τότε, ἀπὸ πέρυσι, etc.

ἀλληλούϊα.

For this word which is generally used as a title in the Psalms, but occurs at the end of Ps 150, cf. the closing words of a strophe in a liturgical fragment of v/vi A.D., P Ryl I. 9¹¹ εὐλογήσ[ω t[ὸν] λαόν μου εἰς τὸν ἀῶνα ἀλ(ληλούϊα?) with the editor's note. It is also found at the end of an amulet (P Berol 6096): τὸ σῶμα καὶ τὸ δέμα (? αἷμα) τοῦ Χ(ριστο)ῦ, φεῖσαι τοῦ δούλου σου τὸν φοροῦντα τὸ φυλακτήριον τοῦτο. ἀμήν, ἀλληλούϊα ‡α ‡ω‡ (Schaefer in P Iand I. p. 29).

ἀλλογενής.

This word, frequent in the LXX and once in the NT (Lk 17[18]), is, according to Grimm, found "nowhere in profane writers." But note should be taken of the famous inscription on the Temple barrier, OGIS 598 (i/A.D.), beginning μηθένα ἀλλογενῆ εἰσπορεύεσθαι ἐντὸς τοῦ περὶ τὸ ἱερὸν τρυφάκτου καὶ περιβόλου, "let no foreigner enter within the screen and enclosure surrounding the sanctuary." Josephus, in his description of the tablet (Bell. Jud. v. 193) substitutes μηδένα ἀλλόφυλον παριέναι, a good example of his methods of mending the vernacular Greek he heard and read. Mommsen argued that the inscription was cut by the Romans. We might readily allow the word to be a Jewish coinage, without compromising the principle that Jewish Greek was essentially one with vernacular Greek elsewhere. The word is correctly formed, and local coined words must be expected in every language that is spoken over a wide area.

ἅλλομαι.

The verb is used in P Ryl II. 138[15] (A.D. 34) of a thief's incursion, just as εἰσπηδάω: κατέλαβα τοῦτον διὰ νυκτὸς ἡλμένον εἰς κτλ. "I detected him when under cover of night he had sprung into the farmstead" (Edd.). It is recurrent in the curious document P Ryl I. 28 (iv/A.D.), on divination by "quivering" of various parts of the body.

ἄλλος.

The differentia of ἄλλος as distinguished from ἕτερος may be left to the latter article. With ἡ ἄλλη Μαρία in Mt 27[61] cf. P Petr III. 59 (c) (Ptol.), where a great many names appear as Θάησις ἄλλη, Κόνρης ἄλλος, even where no duplicate appears in the document itself—its fragmentary character presumably accounts for this. (Grimm's article on Μαρία (3) suggests the remark that the repetition of the same name within a family is paralleled in papyri: thus P Petr III. 117 (g) [ii 17 f.] [Μ]άνρης μικρὸς Τεῶτος καὶ Μάνρης ἀδελφὸς ὡσαύτως—we quote without prejudicing the discussion as to the Maries!) The form τἄλλα with crasis is frequent: see Witkowski[2] (Index) p. 162 for several instances. For ἄλλος used = alter, see Proleg. p. 80 n.[1], where an ex. is quoted from a Doric inscr. as early as B.C. 91. An idiomatic use of ἄλλος may be quoted from P Oxy VII. 1070[52] μὴ . . . , ὃ μὴ εἴη, ἀλ' ἐξ ἄλλων γένηται, "lest . . . , what heaven forbid, we find ourselves at sixes and sevens" (Edd.): the note is, "ἀλλ' ἐξ ἄλλων, if the letters are rightly so interpreted, seems to be a phrase meaning out of harmony, one person doing one thing and another another."

ἀλλοτριοεπίσκοπος.

For the formation of this rare word (in NT only 1 Pet 4[15]) cf. μελλοέφηβος P Oxy IX. 1202[7] (A.D. 217), δειγματοάρτ(ην) and χωματοεπιμ(ελητής) P Lond 1150[37 and 39] (A.D. 145-7) (=III. p. 113), the former also P Oxy I. 63[3] (ii/iii A.D.) τοὺς δειγματοάρτας καθ' αὑτὸν ἀναπέμψαι πρὸς ζυγοστα[σ]ίαν, "send up the inspectors yourself to the examination" (Edd.). For the meaning of ἀ. Deissmann (BS p. 224) cites a synonymous phrase from BGU II.

531[ii. 22] (ii/A.D.) οὔτε εἰμὶ ἄδικος οὔτε ἀ[λ]λοτρίων ἐπιθυμητής, and see further Zeller Sitzungsberichte der Berliner Akademie, 1893, p. 129 ff., where the word is explained from parallels out of the popular philosophy of the day, e.g. Epict. iii. 22, 97 οὐ γὰρ τὰ ἀλλότρια πολυπραγμονεῖ, ὅταν τὰ ἀνθρώπινα ἐπισκοπῇ, ἀλλὰ τὰ ἴδια. See also ZNTW vii. p. 271 ff. On the possible bearing of the word on the date of 1 Pet, see Jülicher Introduction to the NT, p. 213.

ἀλλότριος.

P Oxy VII. 1067[8 ff.] (a very ungrammatical letter of iii/A.D.), μάθε οὖν ὅτι ἀλλοτρίαν γυναῖκαν (l. ἀλλοτρία γυνή) ἐκληρονόμησεν αὐτόν, "know then that a strange woman is made his heir" (Ed.). The adjective is common in the sense of alienus, "belonging to others": one or two special applications may be cited. A rescript of Gordian (P Tebt II. 285[6]), which Wilcken marks as suffering from translation out of Latin, uses τοὺς ἀλλοτρίους for "outsiders," as against legitimate children. P Giss I. 67[19] (ii/A.D.) τὸ γὰρ ἀλλ[ότ]ριον ἐποίησα ξυ [. . . seems to imply "I did what was foreign to me," but the lost context may change this entirely. Ib. 99[6] (ii/iii A.D.) κατὰ τὸ τῶν αὐτο[χθόνω]ν Αἰγυπτίων ἀλλότρια ταῦ[τα ἦν], ἑδρᾶτο δὲ ὅμως. P Tor I. 1[viii. 3] (Ptol. Euergetes) προέφερετο ἀλλότριον εἶναι τὸ παρεισαγόμενον ὑπ' αὐτοῦ. P Oxy II. 282[9] (A.D. 30-5) ἡ δὲ ἀλλοτρία φρονήσασα τῆς κοινῆς συμβ.ώ.σεως, "became dissatisfied with our union" (Edd.): so P Ryl II. 125[10] (c. A.D. 30) ἀλλότρια φρονήσασα, "changed her mind," of a mill-hand leaving her work. BGU II. 405[11] (A.D. 348), ξένον με εἶναι καὶ ἀλλότριον αὐτῆς, gives the genitive dependent on it, and ib. IV. 1121[22] (B.C. 5) μήτε ἴδια μήτ' ἀλλότρια has the antithesis which characterizes best its meaning.

ἀλλοτριόω.

P Tebt I. 105[38] (B.C. 103) καὶ μὴ ἐξέστω αὐτ[ῶι] ἀλλοτρ[ιοῦν . . .] τὴν μίσθωσιν. BGU IV. 1024[iv. 10] (iv/v A.D.) σὺ δὲ ἐπεβούλευσας σῶμα (l. σώματι) ἀλλοτρ[ι]ωθέντι ὑπὸ τοῦ [γ]ένους τῶν ἀνθρώπων. This last has the sense which in NT is expressed more strongly by the perfective compound ἀπαλλοτριοῦν.

ἀλλόφυλος.

For this classical word (Ac 10[28]) cf. BGU I. 31[ii 8. 11], ib. II. 411[2] (A.D. 314) Αὐρηλίῳ Ἀτρῇ ἀλλοφύλου γεωργῷ χαίρε[ιν], ib. III. 270-7) Α[ὐρ.]ήλιος . . . ἀλλόφυλος ἀπὸ κώμης Φ[ι]λαδελφίας, and ib. III. 858[2. 5] (A.D. 294). Preisigke 3441 (from Elephantine) τὸ προσκύνημα τ[ῶ]ν ἀλλοφύλ[ω]ν. See also the citation from Josephus (s.v. ἀλλογενής).

ἄλλως

was common, though it curiously occurs only once in NT. Thus P Tebt II. 450[2] (B.C. 5) καὶ μὴ ἀλ[λ]ως ποήσῃς—a frequent phrase in letters conveying an urgent request. P Flor II. 151[10] (A.D. 267) μὴ ἐπ' αὐτοὺς στρατιώτης ἀποσταλῇ καὶ ἄλλως ἐφόδιον βλαβῶσιν, etc.

ἀλοάω.

With the substantive ἀλοητός, which is found as a variant in LXX Lev 26[5], Amos 9[13], may be compared P Tebt I.

48¹⁶ᶠ· (c. B.C. 113) ὄντων πρὸς τῆι παραδόσει τῶν ἐκφορίων
καὶ τοῦ ἀλοητοῦ, where however from its dependence on
παραδόσει, the editors understand ἀ. to refer to a payment
of some kind, probably to various minor taxes at the ἅλως.
See also BGU IV. 1031¹¹ (ii/A.D.) ὅρα μὴ ἀμελήσῃς τὸν
ἀλοητὸν τῆς νησοῦ. (It is better with Crönert s.v. to write
the word with smooth breathing, instead of following the
abnormal ἀ. of the Attic cognate ἅλως.)

ἄλογος.

The adverb occurs in the curious acrostic papyrus of early
i/A.D., P Tebt. II. 278³⁰ᶠ·, where the story of the loss of a
garment is told in short lines, beginning with the successive
letters of the alphabet—

> ζητῶι καὶ οὐχ εὑρίσκωι.
> ἦρτε ἀλόγως.

"I seek, but do not find it. It was taken without cause."
In P Fay 19²ᶠᶠ· (Hadrian's letter) the writer asserts that his
death took place ο]ὔτε ἀω[ρεὶ οὔτ]ε ἀλόγως οὔτε οἰκτρῶς
οὔτε ἀπ[ροσ]δοκήτω[ς οὔτε ἀνοή]τως, the sense of "unreasonably" seems clear, ἀλόγως being emphasized by
ἀνοήτως, as ἀωρεί is by ἀπροσδοκήτως. So BGU I. 74⁸
(A.D. 167) καὶ γὰρ ἂν ἄλογον εἴη κτλ., P Lond 973 ⁴¹ᶠ·
(iii/A.D.) (= III. p. 213) μὴ δόξῃς με ἀλόγως [. . . ., P Tebt
II. 420⁵ (iii/A.D.) ἄλογος (l. -ως) ἐξήλθατε ἀπ' ἐμοῦ. Later
examples are P Lips I. 111²⁹ (iv/A.D.) and P Amh II.
145¹⁶ (iv/v A.D.) ἐλυπήθην διότι ἀπεδήμησας ἀλόγως, "I
am grieved because you went away without cause." There
is a curious use of a derived verb in P Tebt I. 138 (late
ii/B.C.), where an assailant σπασάμενος ταύτην (sc. μάχαιραν)
βουλόμενός με ἀλογῆσαι κατήνεγκε [πλ]ηγαῖς τρισὶ κτλ.—
a rather aggressive "neglect" or "contempt"! Cf. BGU
I. 22¹⁴ᶠ· (A.D. 114) (= Selections, p. 75) ἄλογόν μοι ἀηδίαν
συνεστήσατο, "picked a senseless quarrel against me," and
similarly P Ryl II. 144¹⁶ (A.D. 38), P Lond 342⁶ (A.D. 185)
(= II. p. 174), ib. 214⁸ (A.D. 270-5) (= II. p. 161), χθὲς
ἀλόγως γενόμενος εἰς ἀμπελικὸν χωρίον, "entered violently" or "without authorisation." Similarly P Flor I.
58⁷ (iii/A.D.) ἀλόγως ἐπελθ[ό]ντες δίχα παντὸς νόμου, a
"brutal" assault. We shall see a similar activity developed
in καταφρονεῖν. On the other hand BGU IV. 1024ᵛⁱⁱ· ¹⁵
(iv/v A.D.) ἔδοξεν τῷ Ζ. ἄλογον εἶναι τὴν ἀξίωσιν shows the
sense "unreasonable." P Grenf II. 77⁹ (iii/iv A.D.) ἀλόγως
ἀπέστητε μὴ ἄραντες [τὸ σ]ῶμα τοῦ ἀδελφοῦ ἡμῶν is not
far from "unfeelingly." P Oxy III. 526⁴ (ii/A.D.) οὐκ
ἤμην ἀπαθὴς ἀλόγως σε καταλείπιν, "so unfeeling as to
leave you without reason" (Edd.). And so on, always with
a sense going decidedly beyond "unreasonably" and
shading into "brutally." Hence the noun use of the
modern Greek ἄλογο, "horse": it is nearly approached in
P Oxy I. 138²⁹ (early vii/A.D.), χορηγῆσαι ἄλογα εἰς τὰς
γεουχικὰς χρείας, where animals in harness are meant, if
not horses exclusively. Prof. Thumb remarks that as early
as Dion Cassius the word = "animal": cf. Hatzidakis Einl.,
p. 34 f. Ps 32⁹ supplies the line of development.

ἁλυκός.

BGU I. 14ⁱᵛ ²² (iii/A.D.) τυρῶν ἁλυκῶν, ib. IV. 1060
verso⁹ τιμὴ ζύτου εὐπρατικ[οῦ] καὶ ἁλυκῆς: the last
two words are interlinear, and their relation is not clear—

the writer is illiterate enough to mean "cheap and salted
beer," no doubt a popular beverage then as now. But
query? Mayser Gr. p. 102 shows that ἁλικός, really a
distinct word, supplants the earlier ἁλυκός in Hellenistic.

ἄλυπος.

For this common Greek word, which in the NT is confined to Phil 2²⁸, cf. P Petr II. 13¹³ (B.C. 258-3) πᾶν ἐ[μοὶ
ἔστ]αι πεφροντισμένον τοῦ σε γενέσθαι ἄλυπον [πάντως?],
"I have used every forethought to keep you free from
trouble" (Ed.): so BGU I. 246¹⁷ (ii/iii A.D.) πῶς ἄλυπος
ἦν. For this adverb see P Petr II 2 (3)¹ᶠ· (iii/B.C.) (= Witkowski, Epp² p. 22) εἰ ἔρρωσαι καὶ ἐν τοῖς ἄ]λλοις ἀλύπως
ἀπαλλάσσεις, εἴη ἄν, ὡς ἐγὼ τοῖς θεοῖς εὐχόμεν[ος διατελῶ].

ἅλυσις.

Syll 586⁵⁶ (iv/B C.), 588³² (ii/B.C.) al. P Leid Wⁱⁱ· ³² πᾶσα
ἅλυσις ἀνυχθήτω. Two diminutives may be quoted Ἀλυσί-
διον (MGr ἁλυσίδα) occurs in P Oxy III. 406³ (A.D. 127)
and 528²⁰ (ii/A.D.). A simpler form appears in P Hib I.
121³ (B.C. 250) ἁλύσιον.

ἁλυσιτελής.

P Tebt I. 68³¹ (B.C. 117-6) τῶ[ν] ἀλυσιτελῶν γενῶν of
inferior crops, "unprofitable" by comparison with wheat.

ἅλων.

The old form ἅλως, in the "Attic" declension, is still
very much more common in papyri, e.g. P Fay 112¹⁸ ᶠ· (A.D.
99) μὴ σπουδασέτωσαν ἅλω, "do not let them be in a hurry
with the threshing-floor," P Lond 314¹⁷ (A.D. 149) (= II.
p. 109) ἐφ' ἅλω τῶν ἐδαφῶν, i.e. as soon as the corn is
threshed: but the NT third declension form is found in
P Tebt I. 84⁸ (B.C. 118) ἁλώνωι (= ων, see Proleg. p. 49),
PSI 37¹ (A.D. 82) ἐφ' ἁλώνων, BGU II. 651⁵ (ii/A.D.). ib.
III. 759¹¹ (ii/A.D.), P Strass I. 10²⁰ (iii/A.D.) P Lond 1239¹³
(A.D. 278-81) (= II. p. 52), and ib. 976⁷ (A.D. 315)
(= III. p. 231). See further Crönert Mem. Herc., p. ix.
The derivative ἡ ἁλωνία, the space reserved for a threshing-
floor, occurs P Tebt II. 346⁶ (early i/A.D.), BGU I. 146⁸
(ii/iii A.D.), P Lond 1170 verso³⁹¹ (A.D. 258-9) (= III. p.
202), and P Oxy X. 1255⁸ (A.D. 292).

ἅμα.

The adverbial use seen in Mt 20¹ may be illustrated by
P Flor I. 36⁵ (c. iv/A.D., init.) μνηστευσαμένου μου . . . τὴν
. . . [θ]υγατέρα . . . [ἅ]μα ἐκ νηπίας ἡλικίας, P Oxy VII.
1025¹⁶ (late iii/A.D.) τῶν θεωριῶν ἅμ' αὔ[ρ]ιον ἥτις ἐστὶν ι
ἀγομ[έν]ων. For ἅμα = "at the same time," see P Giss I.
13⁸ (ii/A.D.) πέμψεις ἅμα τὰς γ̄ ἐπιστολάς, P Oxy IV. 798
(probably B.C. 183) ὡς δ' ἂν παραγένωνται οἱ σιτολόγοι ἐπὶ
τὴν παράληψιν τῶν σιτικῶν ἀπομετρήσομεν ἅμα καὶ ταῦτα,
al. With ἅμα c. dat. "together with," cf. P Oxy IV. 658¹³
(A.D. 250) τῶν ἱερῶν ἐγευσάμην ἅμα τῷ υἱῷ μου, so with a
dat. P Rein 26¹⁴ (B.C. 104) ἅμα τῆι συγγραφῆι ταύτηι
ἀναφερομένηι, P Oxy VI. 975 (i/A.D.) a loan to be repaid
ἅμα τῇ μῇ τρύ[γ]η, P Petr I. 24 (3) (c. B.C. 249) ἅμα
τῆι λοιπῆι ἀγορᾶι ἧι εἰλήφασι ἐγ βασιλικοῦ, P Flor I. 6¹⁵
(A.D. 210) ἐχειροτονήθην ἅμ' ἄλλοις, ib. 21¹⁵ (A.D. 239) ἅμα
τοῖς τῆς κώμης δημοσίοις (neuter) πᾶσι. The use of ἅμα
therefore as an "improper" preposition was not unusual.

Paul however prefers to keep it as an adverb, adding
σύν (1 Th 4[17], 5[10]) : for the preposition only Mt 13[29] is
quotable from NT, and even there D adds σύν. We may
compare ὁμόσε c. dat. in P Lips Inv 266 (ii/A.D.—*Archiv* v.
245) ὁμόσε ταῖς ἄλλαις εὐεργεσίαις. Thayer's note that "ἅμα
is temporal and ὁμοῦ local, in the main" (from Ammonius),
has support from most of our examples. Both usages are
illustrated in the Ptolemaic Pathyris papyrus (*Archiv* ii.
p. 515 f.) ἐπεὶ γέγραφεν ὁ πατὴρ συνμίσγειν ἄγων τοὺς
Κροκοδιλοπολίτας καὶ ὑμᾶς ἅμα, ὀρθῶς ποιήσετε καὶ κε-
χαρισμένως ἑτοίμους γενέσθαι ὡς ἅμα ἡμῖν συνεξορμήσητε.

ἀμαθής.

From the Hellenistic period, but in the local dialect, is the
well-known Epidaurus inscription, *Syll* 802 (iii/B.C.) : here
in l.[39] we have ὑπόμναμα τᾶς ἀμαθίας, of a votive silver pig
offered in the shrine. The adj. (2 Pet 3[16]) might from its
NT record be literary. J. B. Mayor (*in loc.*) remarks.
"It is strange that so common a word as ἀμαθής should not
be found elsewhere in the NT or LXX, its place being
taken by such words as ἰδιώτης (Ac 4[13], 1 Cor 14[16, 23]), or
ἀγράμματος (Ac 4[13]), or ὁ ἀγνοῶν (Heb 5[2])." But our failure
to find exx. from Hellenistic sources agrees with this absence.

ἀμάραντος.

With the use of this adjective in 1 Pet 1[4] κληρονομίαν . . .
ἀμάραντον may be compared a passage in the Apocalypse of
Peter 5. καὶ ὁ κύριος ἔδειξέ μοι . . . τὴν γῆν αὐτὴν ἀνθοῦσαν
ἀμαράντοις ἄνθεσι. See also a poem engraved on a sepulchral monument erected by Euergetes II. (B.C. 145–16), in
honour of his wife Aphrodisia, where the following words
occur, μένοιτ' ἐπὶ γῆς ἀμάραντοι, ὅσσον ἐγὼ ναίω δώματα
Φερσεφόνης (*Archiv* i. 220). Wisd 6[12] reinforces this rare
Petrine word (cf. ἀμαράντινος 5[4]) : for its outside record see
Thayer, who quotes *CIG* II. 2942 (?)[3], a iii/iv A.D. inscription
on a gladiator's tomb, ending ἔσχ[α] τέ[λος] βιότου χερσὶν
φονίαις ἀμάραντο[ν]. It is a proper name in P Ryl II. 166[30]
(A.D. 26) Γάιος Ἰούλιος Ἀμάρ[α]ντου.

ἀμαρτάνω.

It will be convenient to give (non-Christian) citations for
this important word fully. In a private letter of the time of
Augustus the writer complains—ἐγὼ μὲν οὐ δοκῶι ἄξιος εἶναι
ἱβρίζεσθαι . . . οὐδὲ γὰρ ἡμάρτηκά τι εἰς σέ (cf. Ac 25[8], etc.),
BGU IV. 1141[14 ff.] : cf. l. 8 ἐν τῇ πρώτῃ μου ἐπιστολῇ οὐθὲν
ἁμάρτημα ἔνει (*l.* ἔνι = ἔνεστι). BGU III. 846 (ii/A.D.)
(= *Selections*, p. 93, *Documents*, p. 259) is an illiterate
appeal from Antonius Longus to his mother entreating her to
be reconciled to him. He makes his daily prayer to Serapis
for her, etc.—λοιπὸν οἶδα τί αἱμαυτῷ παρέσχημαι, παιπαίδδευμαι καθ' ὃν δὴ (corrected from δι) τρόπον, οἶδα, ὅτι
ἡμάρτηκα (l. 10 ff.), "But I know I have been punished with
what I have brought upon myself, in a way that I know, for
I have sinned": cf. Lk 15[18, 21] In the interesting rescript
of an Emperor to the Jews, P Par 68[60 ff.], we read, καὶ γὰρ
τ[οὺς εἰς ἡμᾶς] ἁμαρτάνοντας δε[όντως κολάζεσθαι] εἰκές.
In P Oxy I. 34[iii. 4] (A.D. 127) a Roman prefect uses some
strong language about infringement of his instructions regarding certain archives : ἄδειαν ἑαυτοῖς ὧν ἁμαρτάνουσι ἔσεσθ[α]ι
νομίζοντες, "imagining that they will not be punished for
their illegal acts" (Edd.).

ἀμάρτημα.

In P Oxy I. 34[iii. 13] (cf. under ἁμαρτάνω) we read τοὺς
παραβάντας καὶ τοὺ[ς] διὰ ἀπείθιαν κ[αὶ] ὡς ἀφορμὴν ζητοῦντας ἁμαρτημάτω[ν] τειμωρήσομαι, "any persons who violate
it, whether from mere disobedience or to serve their own
nefarious purposes, will receive condign punishment." The
substantive is also found in conjunction with ἀγνόημα (see *s.v.*)
in P Tebt I. 5[3] (B.C. 118) and BGU IV. 1185[7] late i/B.C.) :
cf. P Par 63[xii. 2 ff.], a letter of Ptolemy Euergetes II. (B.C.
165), ἀπολελυκότες πάντας τοὺς ἐνεσχημένους ἔν τισιν
ἀγνοήμασιν ἢ ἁμαρτήμασιν κτλ. See also BGU IV. 1141[8],
quoted under ἁμαρτάνω, and P Flor II. 162[10] (midd. iii/A.D.)
τὰ παλαιά σου ἁμαρ[τ]ήματα ἐπεξελεύσε[ω]ς τείξεται.

ἁμαρτία.

In an inscription of Cyzicus territory (*JHS* xxvii. (1907)
p. 63), which F. W. Hasluck supposes to belong to iii/B.C.,
we find ἁμαρτίαν μετανόει, and the word is also found in
the interesting *Syll* 633[14 ff.] (ii/A.D.) which illustrates so
many NT words, ὃς ἂν [*εἰ leg.*] δὲ πολυπραγμονήσῃ τὰ
τοῦ θεοῦ ἢ περιεργάσηται, ἁμαρτίαν ὀφιλέτω Μηνὶ
Τυράννωι, ἣν οὐ μὴ δύνηται ἐξειλάσασθαι. See also P
Lips I. 119 *recto*[3] (A.D. 274) . . . τ]ῶν ἁμαρτιῶ[ν] τὰς
πονηρίας συνεχῶ[ς ἀ]νορθουμένων. P Oxy VIII. 1119[11] (A.D.
254) αὐτὸς ὑπέσχετο ἀντὶ τῆς ἁμαρ[τ]ίας, ἀγνοίας πρ[ό]φασιν
ὑποτειμησάμενος, ὑποστήσεσθαι τὸ [με]τὰ τοῦτο τὰς
λειτουργίας. On the Greek conception of ἁμαρτία see *CR*
xxv. pp. 105–7, and xxiv. pp. 88, 234.

ἁμάρτυρος.

P Flor I. 59[13] (A.D. 225 or 241) ἵνα μὴ ἁμάρτυρον ᾖ. To
its literary record may be added Callimachus *Frag.* 442
ἁμάρτυρον οὐδὲν ἀείδω.

ἁμαρτωλός

appears in *OGIS* 55[50] (B.C. 240) ἐὰν [δὲ] μὴ συντελῇ ὁ
ἄρχων καὶ οἱ πολῖται τὴν [θυσί]αν κατ' ἐνιαυτόν, ἁμαρτωλοὶ
ἔστωσαν [θεῶ]ν πάντων, "sinners *against* all the gods." Cf.
also the common phrase in sepulchral epitaphs in the south-
west of Asia Minor containing a threat against any one
who shall desecrate the tomb, ἁμαρτωλὸς ἔστω θεοῖς (κατα)-
χθονίοις, "let him be as a sinner before the (sub)terranean
gods": see Deissmann *LAE* p. 115, who regards the
genitive after ἁμαρτωλός as a possible "provincialism of
S.W. Asia Minor." (See under ἔνοχος.) He cites another
occurrence, from the same locality, with the formula as in
OGIS 55 (p. 116 n.). Schlageter p. 24 adds *IG* III. 461 a.
These instances are sufficient to prove the "profane" use of
the word, as Cremer (*ap.* Deissmann *ut s.*) admitted in his
Appendix.

ἄμαχος.

Cos 325[9] ἄμαχος ἄζηλος χρόνος πᾶς ἦν ἐν εἶπον, οὐδ'
ἐχω[ρ]ίσθημέν ποτε—a sepulchral inscription by a husband
in memory of his wife—illustrates the non-military use of the
word found twice in the Pastorals (1 Tim 3[3], Tit 3[2]). So
also an epitaph from Apameia (c. iii/A.D.) in *Kaibel* 387,
ἄμαχος ἐβίωσα με[τὰ φί]λων κὲ συνγενῶν.

ἀμάω.

The word is almost entirely poetical in earlier Greek,
though found in Herodotus. Plutarch has it, and P Hib I.

47¹² (an uneducated letter of B.C. 256), θερίζειν δὲ καὶ ἀμᾶν, "to mow and to reap," which indicates its place in the vernacular

ἀμελέω.

This common vernacular word is used absolutely in P Tebt I. 37²³ ᶠᶠ (B.C. 73) ἐὰν δὲ ἀμελήσῃς ἀναγκασθήσομαι ἐγὼ ἐ[λθεῖ]ν αὔριο[ν, P Oxy IV. 742¹¹ (B.C. 2) μὴ ἀμελήσῃς, P Giss I. 13²² ᶠ ἐὰν ἐξετάσῃς περὶ τῶν ἔργω[ν], οὐκ ἀμελῶ, al. For the construction with the genitive, see P Fay 112⁹ (A.D. 99) ἠμέληκας αὐτοῦ, ib. 125³ (ii/A.D.) μὴ ἀμελήσας το[ῦ] κλήρου τοῦ στρατηγικοῦ. "do not neglect the ballot for the strategus," P Oxy I. 113¹⁶ (ii/A.D.) μὴ δόξῃς με ἠμεληκότα τῆς κλειδός, "do not think that I took no trouble about the key" (Edd.), P Tebt II. 289⁸ (A.D. 23) ὡς ἀ[με]-λοῦντα τῆς εἰσπρά[ξεως, ib. 421¹⁰ (iii/A.D.), etc., and even with the dative in the illiterate P Par 18⁴ μὴ ἀμελήσις (l. ἀμελήσῃς) τῷ υἱῷ μου. For the passive may be quoted P Giss I. 41 ii. ²⁴ (time of Hadrian) ὑπὸ τῆς μακρᾶς ἀποδη-μίας τὰ ἡμέτε[ρα] πα[ντ]άπασιν ἀμεληθέντα τυγχ[άνει, and P Lond Inv. Nr. 1885 v. ¹² (in Archiv vi. p. 102) (A.D. 103) ἵν' οὖν τὰ βιβλία ἀνανκεῶτατα ὄντα μὴ ἀμεληθῇ. Ἀμελέω is followed by the infinitive in P Grenf II. 38⁴ (B.C. 81) μὴ ἀμελήσ[α]ς α[. . ἀγο]ράσαι. For the sub-stantive, see P Oxy I. 62⁹ (iii/A.D.) ἐκ τῆς σῆς ἀμελείας, "through any neglect of yours"; and for the adj. a letter from Hermopolis Inv. Nr. 74 (quoted P Giss I. 13²³ note) Ἐπαφρόδειτος ἕως τούτου οὐδὲν ἀμελέστερον ποιεῖ, ἀλλὰ προσκαρτερεῖ ἡμῖν καὶ πᾶσι τοῖς πράγμασί σου.

ἄμεμπτος.

In a private letter of the time of Augustus the writer remarks κἀγὼ τὴ[ς] φιλίαν σου [θέλωι] ἄμεμπτ[ον] ἐματὸν ἐτήρησα (BGU IV. 1141²⁵). For the adjective in a marri-age contract see CPR I. 27¹³ (A.D. 190) αὐτῆς δὲ τῆς Θ. ἄμεμπτον καὶ ἀκατηγόρη[τον ἑαυτὴν παρ]εχομένην (sic) It is common in sepulchral epitaphs in conjunction with χρηστός. OGIS 443⁹ (i/B.C.) has τήν τε τῶν . . . νεανίσκων ἐνδημίαν εὔτ[ακτ]ον π[αρέχεται καὶ ἄμεμπ]τον—Ditten-berger's supplement is at least plausible. For the adverb see P Giss I 98⁵ (ii/A.D.) τὰ τέσσερα οὖν κολοφώνια τὰ ἐπιβάλ-λοντά μοι δότε αὐτῇ ἀμέμπτως, ἀλλ' ἐν τάχει, P Lond 924⁶ (A.D. 187-8) (= III. p. 134) ἀ. πληρουμένων—little more than "duly paid," P Oxy III. 473⁴ (A.D. 138-60). ib. 496⁸ (A.D. 127) συμβιούτωσαν οὖν ἀλλή'λο]ις ἀμέμπτω[ς οἱ γ]α-μοῦντες, and V. 724¹⁰ (A.D. 155), a contract of apprenticeship to a shorthand writer, where provision is made that the pupil shall be taught not only to write fluently, but to read what he has written ἀμέμπτως. From the inscriptions cf. OGIS 485¹² ᶜ τὰς λοιπὰς δὲ φιλοτειμίας τελιάσαντα ἁγνῶς καὶ ἀμέμπτως.

ἀμέριμνος.

BGU II. 372 ii. ²⁶ (A.D. 154), "let them come down ἀμ[έ]ριμνοι." The same papyrus l. 7 shows the subst. ἀμεριμνία united with ἀσφάλεια as frequently in the papyri. For the adjective see also P Fay 117²² (A.D. 108) ἐκτίναξον τὸ διειρον (?) ἵνα ἀμέριμνος ᾖς, P Oxy VI. 933¹⁹ ᶜ (late ii/A.D.) καὶ περὶ τοῦ οἴκου ἀμέριμνος γείνου ὡς σοῦ παρόντος, "have no more anxiety about your household than you would if you were present" (Edd.), and P Flor II. 157

(iii/A.D.), where instructions are given to supply certain workmen with provisions, in order that they may be able to work heartily—ἔχοντες τὸ ἀμέριμνον τῶν τρόφων. For the adverb cf. P Iand 8¹³ (ii/A.D.) διαπέμψ[ομαι διὰ το]ῦ ὀνολάτου ἀμερίμνω[ς, "mittam secure" (Ed.). P Lips I. 105²⁰ (i/ii A.D.) has ἵνα μέντοι ἀμεριμνότερον ἔχῃς, γράφω σοι. Cf. ib. 110¹⁴ (iii/iv A.D.) ἵνα ἀμέριμνος ὦμε (= ὦμαι, a middle form), BGU II. 417⁷ (ii/iii A.D.), etc.: the formula, with slight variations, is common. An adjective ἀμεριμνικός is found P Fay 130¹⁰ (iii/A.D.). P Amh II. 136 (iii/A.D.) has both [ἀμ]ε[ρί]μνως and the derived verb ἀμεριμνῶ in the sense "free from anxiety": cf. P Oxy VI. 930⁸ ᶠᶠ (ii/iii A.D.) ἠμερίμνουν γὰρ περὶ αὐτοῦ εἰδυῖα ὅτι κατὰ δύν[α]μιν μέλλει σοι προσέχειν, "for I had no anxiety about him, knowing that he intended to look after you to the best of his ability." Ἀμεριμνία also occurs in an almost unintelligible sentence at the beginning of P Oxy I. 34 i. ³ (A.D. 127): cf. BGU IV. 1082⁷ (iv/A.D.) ὑπὲρ ἀμερ(ιμνίας). It will be seen that the NT meaning alone is attested from the vernacular docu-ments. Its tone in them suggests that "anxiety" rather exaggerates the word. So in Mt 28¹⁴ we might paraphrase "we will put it right with the Procurator, so that you need not trouble"; and in 1 Cor 7³² the verb that follows clearly does not suggest anxious care.

ἀμετάθετος.

In OGIS 331⁵⁴ (ii/B.C.) King Attalus II of Pergamon, writing to the Pergamenes, orders his rescript to be placed in the temples, ὅπως ἂν εἰς τὸν ἅπαντα χρόνον ἀκίνητα καὶ ἀμετάθετα μένῃ: cf. ib. 335⁷³ (an Aeolic inscription, ii/i B.C.) [τὰ δὲ κρίθεντα ὑ]π[ά]ρξοισι κύρια καὶ ἀμετάθετα. A letter from Sutenas Verus in Laforcade, no. 105¹¹ (A.D. 131) has βεβαιῶ ἐπί τε τῷ ἀσαλεύτον [. . τὴν δωρεὰν] καὶ ἀμετάθετον εἰς τὸν ἀεὶ χρόνον εἶναι καὶ κτλ. P Oxy I. 75¹³ (A.D. 129) ἐφ' ᾗ [. . διαθήκη] ἀμεταθήκῳ ἀμφότεροι ἐτελεύτησαν, and ib. III. 482⁵ ᶜ (A.D. 109) διαθήκῃ, ἐφ' ᾗ καὶ ἀμεταθέτῳ ἐτελεύτα ("which will was unchanged at his death"), show that the word was used as a technical term in connexion with wills. The connotation adds considerably to the force of Heb 6¹⁷ ᶠ.

ἀμετακίνητος.

The adjective ἀκίνητος occurs P Gen I. 11⁸ (A.D. 350) ἐκ δικαίου καὶ ἀκινήτου κλήρου, and in OGIS 331⁵³, cited under ἀμετάθετος.

ἀμετανόητος.

P Lips I. 206 ᶠ is late (beginning of iv/A.D.), but ὁμολο-γοῦμεν [ἐκο]υσία καὶ α[ὐ]θαιρέτῳ καὶ ἀμε[τα]νοήτῳ γνώμῃ seems to be a legal formula, such as would presumably suffer little change with time: it occurs a little earlier (A.D. 289) in P Strass I. 29³¹, the same three words (adverb form) in the same order. Its active force agrees with that in Rom 2⁵. (Norden Agnostos Theos p. 135 translates the word here "unbussfertig," and refers to Bonhöffer Ep ktet u. das NT p. 106 f., who claims that in this word (as in μετάνοια, -νοεῖν) "gewissermassen der Gegensatz des antiken und des christ-lichen Denkens spiegle.") But in CPR I. 216⁵ (i/ii A.D.) κυρίαν καὶ βεβαίαν καὶ ἀμετανόητον, P Grenf II. 68, 70 (iii/A.D.) duplicate deeds of gift—ὁμολογῶ χαρίζεσθαί σοι χάριτι ἀναφαιρέτῳ καὶ ἀμετανοήτῳ . . . μέρος τέταρτον κτλ. there is a passive sense "not affected by change of mind," like ἀμεταμέλητος in Rom 11²⁹. So P Lond 1164 (ⅇ)⁵ (A.D. 212) (=III. p. 166) κυρίως καὶ ἀναφαιρέτως καὶ [ἀ]μετανοήτως.

ἄμετρος.

The form ἀμέτρητος occurs in a touching sepulchral inscription regarding a husband and wife from Rhodes *IMAe* 149 (ii/B.C.) : ταὐτὰ λέγοντες ταὐτὰ φρονοῦντες ἤλθομεν τὰν ἀμέτρητον ὁδὸν εἰς ᾿Αΐδαν.

ἀμήν.

ϙθ is a common symbol in the Christian papyri for ἀμήν, 99 being the sum of the numerical equivalents of the letters (1 + 40 + 8 + 50) : see e.g. P Oxy VI. 925⁷ (v/vi A.D.), where a prayer for guidance regarding a certain journey concludes—γένοιτο, ϙθ, "so be it ; Amen," and P Iand I. 6¹⁶ (a Christian amulet—v/vi A.D.) with the editor's note. In P Oxy VII. 1058 (iv/v A.D.) the word is written out in full, ὁ θ(εὸ)ς τῶν παρακειμένων σταυρῶν, βοήθησον τὸν δοῦλόν σου ᾿Απφουᾶν. ἀμήν, "O God of the crosses that are laid upon us, help thy servant Apphouas. Amen." (Ed.)

ἀμήτωρ

does not happen to occur in our documents. For its connotation in Heb 7³ see ἀπάτωρ, and note Grimm's citations from Philo : the evidence is quite sufficient to dispose of Grimm's own note that the signification is "unused by the Greeks." For the word cf. also the line from Euripides (drama unknown) cited by Wilamowitz *Sitz. d. Berl. Ak.*, 1907, p. 7—῎Αφιδνε, γαίας υἱὲ τῆς ἀμήτορος.

ἀμίαντος.

The use of the word in the NT is probably to be traced to the LXX, rather than to the influence of the mystery religions as Perdelwitz (*Die Mysterienreligion und das Problem des I. Petrusbriefes*, Giessen, 1911, pp. 45-50) ingeniously suggests, contrasting the ἀμίαντος inheritance of the Christian with the blood-stained *Himmelskleid*, with which the initiate is robed as he ascends from the grave in the Taurobolium.

A new literary citation for this word may be given from the Bacchylides papyrus, iii. 86, βαθὺς μὲν αἰθὴρ ἀμίαντος, where Jebb translates "the depths of air receive no taint."

ἄμμος.

P Petr II. 4 (9)⁵ (iii/B.C.) ὥστε ἀνακαθᾶραι τὴν ἄμμον, *ib.* III. 43 (2) *recto* ii. ¹² (2nd year of Euergetes I.) ἐργάσασθαι τὴν ἄμμον τοῦ ὑδραγωγοῦ ἐπὶ τῆς κατὰ ῾Ηφαιστιάδα διώρυγος, " to clear out the sand from the water-course of the canal near Hephaistias," BGU II. 530¹⁹ ᶠᶠ. (i/A.D.) (= *Selections*, p. 61) ὁ ὑδραγωγὸς συνεχώσθη ὑπὸ τῆς ἄμμου, "the water-course was choked with sand," P Tebt II. 342²⁷ (late ii/A.D.) εἰς ἐκσκαφὴν χοὸς . . . καὶ ἄμμου, P Flor II. 157⁵ (iii/A.D.) εἰς τ[ὸ] ἔργον ἐκεῖνο τὸ τῆς Θεω[ξ]ενίδος, τούτεστιν τὸ τῆς ἄμμου. From the inscriptions it is sufficient to cite *Syll* 587¹⁹⁷ (iv/B.C.) ἄμμου ἀγωγαὶ πέντε. In BGU I. 108¹ (A.D. 203-4) (= *Chrest.* I. 227) Wilcken reads ἀμμόχοστος (*l.* ἀμμόχωστος), "covered with sand," with reference to a plot of land, and compares the similar use of ὕφαμμος in P Amh II. 85¹⁶ (A.D. 78).

ἀμνός.

Syll 615⁹ (iii/A.D.) ἀμνὸς λευκὸς ἐνόρχης. Herwerden (*s.v.* ἀρήν) quotes an inscription from *Cey* 40⁸. ἀμνὰν καὶ ἀμνόν. The noun (etymologically identical with Lat. *agnus*, our *yean*) is only four times found in NT, always with the sacrificial connotation which is abundant in LXX. See under ἀρήν.

ἀμοιβή.

The phrase in 1 Tim 5⁴ ἀμοιβὰς ἀποδιδόναι τοῖς προγόνοις, "to make a fitting requital to one's parents," is well illustrated by *Priene* 112¹⁷, where a certain Zosimus having received the title of citizen "has made no fruitless return for the honour"—[οὐκ ἄκαρπον τὴν τῆς τιμῆς] δέδειχεν ἀμοιβήν : cf. *Cagnat* IV. 293 ⁱⁱ ³⁹ (ii/B.C.) κομιζόμενος τῶν εὐεργεσιῶν ἀξίας τὰς ἀμοιβάς, *Syll* 305⁵ (i/A D.) βασιλέων κἂν πάνυ ἐπινοῶσιν εἰς εὐχαριστίαν τηλικούτου θεοῦ εὑρεῖν ἴσας ἀμοιβὰς οἷς εὐηργέτηνται μὴ δυναμένων. In P Oxy IV. 705⁶¹ (A.D. 200-2) the Emperors Septimius Severus and Caracalla reply to a certain Aurelius Horion who desired to confer benefactions on Oxyrhynchus—ἀποδεχόμεθά σε καὶ ταύτης τῆς ἐπιδόσεως ἣν ἀξιοῖς ἐπιδοῦναι ταῖς κώμαις τῶν ᾿Οξυρυγχειτῶν ἀποδιδοὺς ἀμοιβὴν ἐνκτήσεως, "we approve of this benefaction also which you request leave to confer upon the villages of the Oxyrhynchite nome, giving (to different persons) a succession in the enjoyment of it (?) " (Edd.). P Giss I. 22⁶ (ii/A.D.) νῦν ὄντως ἀμοιβ[ὴ]ν [. . .] τῆς εὐσεβείας μου ἀ[ναλ]αμβανούσης σε ἀπρόσ[κοπ]ον καὶ ἱλαρώτατον.

ἄμπελος

is amply vouched for in the papyri, as in BGU IV. 1119¹⁰, 1123² (both time of Augustus), and P Lond 921³ (late ii/iii A.D.) (= III. p. 134) ἦσαν ἐν ἀμπέλῳ, "planted with vines." In P Petr I. 29⁴ (iii/B.C.) πεφύτευται δὲ καὶ ἡ ἄμπελος πᾶσα, ἅ. is used in a collective sense : cf. P Flor I. 50² (A.D. 268) ἐξ ἴσου τῆ[ς ἀμπέ]λου μεριζομένης. This use of ἄμπελος (so MGr ἀμπέλι) which makes it equivalent to ἀμπελών, occurs also in the Median parchments, P Said Khan (B.C. 88 and 22), deeds concerning the transfer of a "vineyard," which is never called ἀμπελών in the documents. We may probably apply this use in Rev 14¹⁸·¹⁹, and perhaps in Didache 9².

ἀμπελουργός.

Syll 535¹⁷ (B.C. 46-5) ἀμπελουργὸν δ᾿ ἐπάγειν Αἰξωνέας τοῖς ἔτεσι τοῖς τελευταίοις πέντε may serve to illustrate this NT ἅπ. εἰρ. (Lk 13⁷).

ἀμπελών.

Nothing earlier than Diodorus (i/B.C.) in "profane" Greek is cited for this word by Grimm. It occurs in five documents of P Tebt I., three of them ii/B.C., and two a little later : cf. also the Ptolemaic P Eleph 14² τῶν μὲν ἀμπελώνων τοὺς καθήκοντας ἀργυρικοὺς φόρους. Its appearance in P Hib I. 151 (*c.* B.C. 250) is presumably coeval with the LXX ; nor does the language (. . . μὴ παραγίνεσθαι . . . τρυγήσοντα τὸν ἀμπελῶνα, from a fragment of a letter) suggest that the word was new. It occurs indeed frequently in Rev L, a few years older still. For an instance contemporary with its NT appearances, see PSI 82³ (A.D. 65) τῶι ὑπάρχοντι ἡμῖν . . . ἀμπελῶνι : cf. P Tebt II. 357[15] (A.D. 107) τέλ(η) . . . ἀμπελῶνο(ς) κατοικ(ικοῦ) (ἀρούρας) ᾱ, "taxes upon 1 aroura of catoecic vine-land." The suffix -ών (like -etum in Latin) denoting plantations of trees was productive in Hellenistic : see under ἐλαιών.

Ἀμπλίας.

As showing the widespread occurrence of this name in its longer form Ἀμπλιᾶτος, and the impossibility therefore of connecting it specially with the Imperial household at Rome (cf. Lightfoot, *Philippians*, p. 172), Rouffiac *Recherches sur les caractères du Grec dans le NT* p. 90 gives the following instances of its use—at Rome, *CIL* VI. 14918, 15509, but also at Pompeii *CIL* IV. 1182, 1183, and *ib.* Suppl. I. Index, p. 747 ; in Spain *CIL* II. 3771 ; at Athens *IG* III. 1161[8], 1802 ; and at Ephesus *CIL* III. 436. See further Milligan *Documents*, p. 183.

ἀμύνομαι.

Syll 356[15] (rescript of Augustus) καὶ [ὅτε ἡ]μύνοντο. The word may have almost fallen out of the colloquial language, to judge from its rarity in LXX and NT, and the absence of occurrences in papyri.

ἀμφιάζω.

See under ἀμφιέννυμι.

ἀμφιβάλλω.

This word, which is used absolutely in Mk 1[16], is construed with an accusative in the Bacchylides papyrus xvii. 5 ff. ἢ τις ἀμετέρας χθονὸς δυσμενὴς ὅρι᾿ ἀμφιβάλλει στραταγέτας ἀνήρ ; "Is the leader of a hostile army besetting the borders of our land?" (Jebb). From non-literary papyri we have a citation two centuries after Mark— P Flor II. 119[3] (A.D. 254) ἐπέδωκάν μοι οἱ ἁλι[εῖς οἳ περὶ διατα?]γὴν ἀμφιβάλλουσι. The supplement is wholly conjectural, but the verb must mean "to fish" as in Mark, and may be used absolutely.

ἀμφιέννυμι.

The full form in Mt 6[30] is a survival of the literary language, and must have been nearly obsolete even in cultivated colloquial. It is clear therefore that Luke (12[28]) represents Q, whether we read ἀμφιάζει with B or -έζει with the rest : as elsewhere (cf. *Cambridge Biblical Essays*, p. 485 f.). Luke faithfully preserves a vernacular form which he would not have used in his own writing. For the form with α cf. Vettius Valens p. 64[9] (ἀμφιάσαι), and *OGIS* 200[24] (Aethiopia, iv/A.D.) ἀμφιάσαντες : Blass (Kühner *Gramm.*[3] ii. p. 366) quotes several instances from post-classical literature, including Plutarch (ἀπημφίαζε) and even Lucian (μεταμφιάσομαι). So ἠμφιασμένον Mt 11[8] D. The classical aorist appears in *Syll* 197[24] (iii/B.C.) ἀμφιέσας. The back-formation ἀμφιέζω is an obvious first step towards ἀμφιάζω, which shows the influence of the large class of -άζω verbs (so W. Schmid *ap.* Schweizer *Perg.*, p. 37). But though ε forms are predominantly attested in NT (with significant revolts on the part of B and D—see above), it seems doubtful whether ἀμφιέζω can be confidently claimed for the Κοινή, unless as a local survival. A grammarian in Cramer *Anecd. Ox.* II. 338 says τὸ μὲν ἀμφιέζω ἐστὶ κοινῶς, τὸ δὲ ἀμφιάζω δωρικόν, ὥσπερ τὸ ὑποπιέζω καὶ ὑποπιάζω.

This may be true for πιάζω (*q. v.*), but the other record is too scanty for much assurance. See Radermacher *Gramm.*, p. 35, and references in Brugmann-Thumb[4], p. 78.

ἄμφοδον.

This word is quoted by LS from Aristophanes and Hyperides, in both cases only as cited by later writers. Its appearance in Mark (11[4]) and the δ-text of Acts (19[28] D etc.) is in accord with its frequency in the papyri of the Roman age, e. g. PSI 38[2] (A.D. 101) ἀ]ναγ[ραφό(μενος) ἐ]π᾿ ἀμφόδ(ου) Φρο[υρίου), P Fay 28[4] (A.D. 150-1) (= *Selections*, p. 81) Τασουχαρίου τῆς Διδᾶ ἀπ[ὸ ἀ]μφόδου Ἑρμουθιακῆς. Grenfell and Hunt translate the word "quarter," *vicus*. A large number of these are named, and residents are registered in the ἀπογραφαί as ἀπ᾿ ἀμφόδου Ἀπολλωνίου Ἱερακίου and the like, or ἀπὸ Μακεδόνων with ἀμφόδου omitted. Cf. *Syll* 528, τοὺς ἐν τῶι ἀνφόδωι τετάχ(θ)αι ἀπὸ τοῦ πύργου τοῦ τῆς Ἀγαθῆς Τύχης ἕως τοῦ τῆς Εὐετηρίας, where Dittenberger defines ἄ. as "pars oppidi domibus inter se contingentibus exaedificata, quae undique viis circumdatur." On its gender cf. Mayser *Gr.* p. 261 n.

ἀμφότεροι.

On P Lond 336[13] (A.D. 167) (= II. p. 221) Kenyon observes, "ἀμφότεροι = πάντες in late Byzantine Greek . . . and it is possible that colloquially the use existed earlier." The text here has the names of five men—ἀμφότεροι ἱερεῖς θεοῦ κώμης Σοκνοπαίου Νήσου. In P Théad 26[4] (A.D. 296) Αὐρήλιοι [Ἡ]ρωνῖνος καὶ Ἀθανάσιος κ[αὶ Φιλάδελφος καὶ Σερηνίων ἀμφότεροι ἐξηγ(ητεύσαντες) makes ἀμφ. apply to three persons, if with the Ed. (and no. 27[7]) we read ὁ καὶ Ἀθανάσιος : in no. 27 we find the first two characterized as having been exegetae, while Serenion is κοσμ(ητεύσας), two years later. Prof. Thumb refers to *BZ* xi. p. 111 for ἀμφ. = "alle zusammen." In the London papyrus, despite Bury's paper on this late usage (*CR* xi. p. 393), it is hard to disagree with Kenyon's suspicion that it was not only the last two of these five who were priests : cf. P Lond 353[7] (A.D. 221) (= II. p. 112) where again we find five representatives of the πενταφυλία of Socnopaei Nesus.

This usage is further strengthened by P Gen I. 67[5] (A.D. 382), and *ib.* 69[4] (A.D. 386) where ἀμφότεροι is used of four men. A similar extension of the word to the seven sons of Sceva in Ac 19[16] undoubtedly simplifies the narrative. See further Moulton *CR* xv. p. 440, and *Proleg.* p. 80, where other exx. are noted. Radermacher (*Gramm.* p. 64) is in favour of making ἀμφ. mean "all" in Acts.

ἀμώμητος,

only found in 2 Pet 3[14] and in literary Hellenistic (Anthology), may be quoted from an Alexandrian epitaph in Preisigke 332, Π[. . . .]αικ[. . ἀμ]ώμητε, εὐψύχι, (ἐτῶν) γ̄ : so the word is used here of a little child. In *ib.* 367, Κλέοβι ἀμώμητε, εὐψύχι, (ἐτῶν) κ̄ε̄, it belongs to a young man, dying prematurely. Add the "Apocrypha Moisis," P Leid W[iii.] [4] ἧκε κύριε ἀμώμητος καὶ ἀπήμαντος.

ἄμωμος.

The word is found in a sepulchral epitaph from Thessalonica *CIG* 1974, also in the sepulchral poem referred to under ἀμάραντος—δικνὺς σέλας αἰὲν ἄμωμον. Nägeli (p. 25) further cites the Paris magical papyrus, l. 1311. For the use of Ἄμωμος as a proper name, see Fick-Bechtel *Die griechischen Personennamen*, p. 213.

Hort (on 1 Pet. 1¹⁹) points out that the Biblical use of ἄμωμος, properly "without blame," was affected by the Hebrew מוּם "blemish," for rendering which the LXX translators caught at the curiously similar μῶμος.

ἄν.

For the rapid decay of this particle in Hellenistic vernacular, reference may be made to *Proleg.* pp. 165-9, 197-201 : a few additional points may be brought in. First comes the use with relatives and conjunctions, normally but by no means universally taking the subjunctive. Here in i/ and ii/A.D. ἐάν greatly predominated over ἄν, except with ὅπως, ὡς and ἕως. Thackeray (*Gr.* p. 68), collecting statistics from more extensive material than had been available in *Proleg.* p. 43, sums up the results to the same purpose : about B.C. 133 "ὅς [etc.] ἐάν begins to come to the front, and from i/B.C. onwards the latter is always the predominant form : the figures in both columns decrease in iii/–iv/A.D., when the use of the indefinite relative in any form was going out of use." The ultimate result of this process is seen in MGr, where the only traces left of ἄν are in the compounds σάν "as," "as soon as," and ἄν "if," with κάν (= κἄν) "even." Σάν is from ὡς ἄν, which in papyri is used in the same senses : thus BGU IV. 1098⁴⁴ (end of i/B.C.) ὡς ἂν ἐπὶ το[ῦ κα]ιροῦ κοινῶς κρίνωσι (according as), *ib.* 1209¹³ (B.C. 23) ὡς ἂν λάβῃς τὸ γράμμα (as soon as), P Hib I. 66⁴ (B.C. 228-7), ὡ[ς δ'] ἂν παραγένωμαι (do.). Several instances are collected by Witkowski (² p. 87), and Phil 2²³, 1 Cor 11³⁴, Rom 15²⁴ noted as parallel, as in *Proleg.* p. 167. The MGr ἄν inherits the uses of ἐάν. The latter in vernacular Hellenistic is stable, or even reverts to εἰάν by re-composition ; but the form ἄν is found in many illiterate documents of the Κοινή (as for instance in the boy's letter, P Oxy I. 119 (ii/iii A.D.)), and may be the direct ancestor of the MGr. See *Proleg.* p. 43 n.². On ἄν with opt., or *ind. in realis*, see *Proleg.* pp. 197-201. A reference should be added to Goodspeed's convincing suggestion (*ExpT* xx. 471 f.) that in Mk 7¹¹ we should read ὃ ἂν (so D) ἐξ ἐμοῦ ὠφεληθῇς, indic., "what you would have gained from me." Two or three additional instances of ἄν in "unreal" clauses may be given from the papyri :— P Tor I. 1ᵛⁱⁱⁱ·³⁵ᶠᶠ· (B.C. 116) (= *Chrest.* II. p. 39), καὶ εἴπερ γε δὴ ἐνόμιζεν ἔχειν τι δίκαιον κτλ., οὐκ ἄν ποτε προαχθῆναι (depending on ὥστ' εὔβηλον εἶναι l. 31), P. Giss I. 47¹⁷ (early ii/A.D.) τὸ ὀνάριον τὸ χαλκοῦν εἰ ἐπωλεῖτο δραχμῶν κδ, ἔκτοτε ἂν ἔπεμψά σοι, *ib.* 79ⁱⁱ·⁶ (same period) εἰ δυνατόν μ[ο]ι ἦν κτλ., οὐκ ἄν ὠ[κ]νήκειν, BGU IV. 1141²⁷ᶠ· (end of i/B.C.) ἣ (*l.* εἰ) ἦν δάκρυά σοι γράφειν, γεγραφήκειν ἂν ἀπὸ τῶν δακρύων, CPHerm I. 7⁷ᶠ· εἰ μὲν δὴ χορηγία τις [ἦ]ν κτλ. (a gap of 21 letters included), οὐδὲν ἄν ἡμᾶ[ς ἔδει πε]ρὶ τού-[τ]ων δεῖσθαι. To the papyrus exx. of ἄν dropped (*Proleg.*³ p. 200 n.¹), add PSI 71⁹ᶠ· (vi/A.D.) εἰ μὴ ἡ θεία πρόνοια ἐβοήθησεν κτλ., εἶχαν ἀλλήλ[ους] ἀναιλῖν (*l.* ἀνελεῖν). The fewness of our exx. shows that the NT omissions of ἄν, practically confined to Jn, are not normal Κοινή grammar, except in clauses where omission was classical : the construction itself was dying out, but the ἄν was preserved while the locution lasted. MGr uses a periphrastic conditional mood (Thumb *Handbook*, p. 195).

ἀνά

survives almost exclusively in the limited uses seen in NT. The new "improper preposition" ἀνὰ μέσον is common : cf. MGr ἀνάμεσα. Thus P Magd 2³ (B.C. 221) ἀνὰ μέσον τοῦ τε Πωώριος [*l.* τοίχου] καὶ τοῦ τοῦ ἀνδρός μου. *Syll* 929⁴⁶ (ii/B.C.) τῆς κειμένης ἀνὰ μέσον Ἰτανίων τε καὶ Ἱεραπυτνίων, P Petr I. 11¹⁹ (iii/B.C.) οὐλὴ ἀνὰ μέσον ὀφρύων, *ib.* III. 37(a)ⁱⁱ·¹⁸ (B.C. 257) χώματος τοῦ ἀνὰ μέσον τοῦ κλήρου, *OGIS* 50⁶² (iii/B.C.) ὧν ἀνὰ μέσον ἔσται ἡ ἀσπιδοειδὴς βασιλεία (a crown adorned with serpents), P Oxy I. 99⁹ (A.D. 55) ἀνὰ μέσον οὔσης τυφλῆς ῥύμης, etc. In *Syll* 334⁴ (B.C. 73) περὶ ἀντιλογιῶν τῶν ἀνάμ[εσον] θεῶι Ἀμφιαράωι καὶ τῶν δημοσιωνῶν γεγονότων Dittenberger (who here prints as one word) comments on the barbarous grammar, the preposition taking dative and genitive together. Ἀνὰ λόγον "in proportion" is not rare : e.g. P Ryl II. 96¹⁴ (A.D. 117-8) (ἀρούρας) δή (= ⅔) ἀνὰ λόγον τῆς ἀρούρας "at a rate per aroura." Note *ib.* 88²¹ (A.D. 156) οὐδὲν δέ μοι ὀ[φείλεται ὑπὲρ τ]ῶν ἀνὰ χεῖρα χρόνων, "the current period" (Edd., who cite *ib.* 99⁷, BGU I. 155¹³ and IV. 1049²³). The distributive use of ἀνά is often found in papyri : thus P Oxy IV. 819 (c. A.D. 1) τὰ δὲ προκείμενα χ(όας) δ πεπρᾶσθαι δι' ἐμοῦ ἀνὰ δραχ(μὰς) πέντε. Radermacher (*Gr.* p. 16) remarks on its appearance in doctors' prescriptions to mark the dose, and gives some other vernacular instances, noting that it began to figure in colloquial Attic in the classical age. It serves to express multiplication, as in P Petr II. 30(b)²⁰ (iii/B.C.) β(ασιλικοῦ) ι̅ ἀφόρου κ̅/λ ἀνὰ γ̅ ζ̅ ρ̅ε̅ "10 of Crown land + 20 of unproductive = 30 × 3½ = 105." Cf. a papyrus cited by Wilcken in *Archiv* v. p. 245. Note P Ryl II. 168⁷ (A.D. 120) ἀνὰ λαχάνου μέτρωι ἐλαιουργικῶι ἀρτάβας τρεῖς. Ἀνὰ πλέο[ν occurs in P Tebt II. 344¹⁰ (ii/A.D.). On the possibly corrupt solecism in 1 Cor 6⁵ see *Proleg.* p. 90. Nachmanson *Beiträge*, p. 97 cites an inscription in which distrib. ἀνά c. acc. has the same sense as a simple acc. with κατ' ἄνδρα δόντα ἐπὶ δὶς τοῖς μὲν πολείταις κατ' ἄνδρα δην(άρια) δ̅, τοῖς δὲ λοιποῖς ἐλευθέροις ἀν[ὰ] δην(άρια) β̅ (*IG* iv. 597⁹ ff.—Argos, "spät").

ἀναβαθμός.

Syll 587³⁰⁸ (iv/B.C.) ἀναβαχμ[ο]ύς (*l.* -σμούς, apparently parts of a τροχιλεία, on which see Dittenberger's note. For examples of ἀ. in late Greek, cf. Aelian vi. 61, xi. 31 ; Dion Cass. lxv. 21, lxviii. 5 (Lobeck *Phryn.*, p. 324). Rutherford (*NP*, p. 372) adds the note of Moeris, βαθμὸς Ἀττικῶς, βαθμὸς Ἑλληνικῶς, in confirmation of Phrynichus, who tells us that the θ is Ionic : for the relation of the -σμός and -θμός suffixes see Brugmann-Thumb⁴ p. 2184.

ἀναβαίνω.

Wilcken (*Archiv* v. p. 268), commenting on POxy VI. 898⁹·¹⁵ (A.D. 123) εἰς Ὄασιν καταβῆναι—ἀναβάντα εἰς τὸν Ὀξυρυγχείτην, notes that this may either be literal or refer to Oxyrhynchus as the county town : ἀναβαίνειν εἰς πόλιν, καταβαίνειν εἰς κώμην. P Par 49 (B.C. 164-58) gives us instances of the verb as used in NT for "going up" to the Temple : l. 32 οὐκ ἔχω σχολὴν ἀναβῆναι πρὸς ὑμᾶς (*sc.* the recluses in the Serapeum), *ib.* 34 ἐὰν ἀναβῶ κἀγὼ προσκυνῆσαι. So P Par 47¹⁹ᶠ· (c. B.C. 153) ὁ στρατηγὸς ἀναβαίνει αὔριον εἰς τὸ Σαραπιῆν. Witkowski (² p. 72) remarks that the Serapeum was situated above the town, so that the verb was appropriate, as in Lk 18[10]. The common phrase ἀ. εἰς Ἱεροσόλυμα, etc., may be illustrated from P Lond 1170 *verso*[48] (A.D. 258–9), (= III. p. 194), where an account of labourers "off work" (ἀργησάντων) describes one as ἀναβὰς εἰς τὴν πόλιν and another ἀναβὰς ἐπὶ τῆς πόλ. The same meaning, or something near it, may be seen recurring in P Oxy VIII. 1157 (late iii/A.D.), as [25]ἀντίγραψον κἀγὼ ἀναβαίνω καὶ ἀπογράφομαι, *ib.* [7] ἐπιδὴ οὖν οὐ δύναμαι ἀναβῆναι ἴδε ἡ (*l.* εἰ) δύνῃ ἡμᾶς ἀπογράψε: we should use "come up" in the same connotation. So *ib.* VI. 935[13] (iii/A.D.) ἔμελλον δ[ὲ] καὶ α[ὐτὸ]ς ἀναβῆναι, BGU IV. 1007[3] (i/A.D.) ἐὰν δὲ ὁ ἀντίδικος ἀναβῇ, περίβλεπε αὐτόν. In *ib.* 1141[35] (late i/B.C.) ἡμέρας δὲ ἐν αἷς ἀναβαίνωσι, εὑρίσκωσι αὐτὸν καθήμενο(ν) it perhaps means "go upstairs." In P Petr II. 9 (3)[8] (iii/B.C.) πλήρωμα ἀναβέβηκεν is "the gang has gone away." Cf. MGr ἀνεβαίνω.

For the substantive cf. P Grenf II. 67[15 f.] (A.D. 237) (= *Selections*, p. 109) where three asses are provided ὑπὲρ καταβάσεως καὶ ἀναβάσεως, "for the conveyance down and up again" of dancing girls for a village festival. Ἀνάβασις is common in the papyri and the inscriptions of the "rising" of the Nile, e.g. BGU I. 12[4] (A.D. 181–2) [τῆς τοῦ] ἱερωτάτου Νείλου ἐπ' ἀγαθῷ ἀναβάσεως, OGIS 666 (*c.* A.D. 55) ἡ Αἴγυπτος, τὰς τοῦ Νείλου δωρεὰς ἐπαυξομένας κατ' ἔτος θεωροῦσα, νῦν μᾶλλον ἀπέλαυσε τῆς δικαίας ἀναβάσεως τοῦ θεοῦ, where Dittenberger draws attention to the fact that δικαία ἀνάβασις is a "solenne vocabulum" in this connexion. So in the papyri, BGU IV. 1208[17] (B.C. 27) τ]ὴν ἀποτομίαν (see *s.v.*) τῆς ἀναβάσεως. There are some other instances in Meyer's note on P Giss I. 37, intro. n[3]. In *Cagnat* III. 975 (? i/A.D.) ἀ. is part of a house: τὴν ἀ. ταύτην σὺν τῇ ἀψεῖδι.

ἀναβάλλω,

in something like the forensic sense "defer" a case, occurs in P Tebt I. 22[9] (B.C. 112) ἀναβαλλόμενος εἰς τὸν φυλακίτην, "referring the matter to the inspector": cf. P Par 66[21] (i/B.C.) ὧν τὰ ἔργα ἀναβάλουσιν (*l.* -λλ-), "whose work is postponed." Elsewhere it is generally = "cast up" or "send back": in Ostr 1154 (Rom.) ἀναβαλεῖν τὰ ἱμάτιά σου appears to be used of the "setting up" of a weaver's warp. Cf. P Giss I. 20[15 ff.] (ii/A.D.) εἰ θέλεις ἀναβληθῆναί σ[ου τ]ὴν ἰσχνὴν [λε]υκὴν στολὴν, φρόντισον τῆς πορφύρας. In Ostr 1399 (A.D. 67–8) ἀνεβ(άλετε) εἰς τὸ κενὸν (*l.* καινὸν χῶ(μα) ναύβ(ια) δέκα πέντε, 1567 (A.D. 105) ἀναβ(εβλήκατε) εἰς χῶ(μα) Ἀθην(αίων) ν αύβιον) (ἥμισυ). it may mean "throw up," of a measure of earth excavated (cf. Mahaffy *Petrie Papyri*, III. p. 344): this is a return to its most primitive sense—cf. *Syll* 587[165] (B.C. 329–8) τέκτοσιν τοῖς ἀναβάλουσιν τὰς πλίνθους. Another physical sense appears in P Flor II. 233[8] (A.D. 263), where Comparetti renders ἵνα ... [ἀ]ναβληθῶσι "'vi si adattino' (le spalliere)." The verb is MGr. The expressive compd. διαναβάλλομαι "procrastinate" occurs P Tebt I. 50[27] (B.C. 112–1).

ἀναβιβάζω.

P Oxy III. 513[27] (A.D. 184) ἀναβεβίσθαι (*l.* -βιβάσθαι) εἰς δραχμὰς χειλίας [ὀκ]τακοσίας, "raised the price to eighteen hundred drachmas." (MGr ἀνεβάζω.)

ἀναβλέπω.

Syll 807[17] (ii/A.D.) καὶ ἀνέβλεψεν καὶ ἐλήλυθεν καὶ ηὐχαρίστησεν δημοσίᾳ τῷ θεῷ, of a blind man "recovering sight" in the temple of Asclepios, as in Jn 9[11, 15] (cf. *Documents*, p. 154). So at the beginning of the same inscr., καὶ ὀρθὸν ἀνέβλεψε.

ἀναβοάω.

In the interview between Marcus Aurelius (?) and a condemned criminal, P Oxy I. 33[iii 7] (= *Chrest.* I. p. 35), we read of the latter that ἀνεβόησεν [μ]έσης Ῥώμης, summoning the Romans to see him led off to death. Beyond this rather *outré* document, we have no other evidence of the Κοινή use of the word, an interesting confirmation of WH's rejection of it in Mt 27[46]—unless indeed the more literary Matthew was emending Mark (15[34])!

ἀναβολή.

The word is used with a large variety of meanings. Thus P Amh II. 34 (*d*)[5] (*c.* B.C. 157) ἐκθεῖναι τὴν κατάστασιν εἰς μηδεμίαν ἀναβολὴν ("without delay") ποιησαμένους: cf. *Syll* 425[22] (iii/B.C.) ἀναβολὰν λαβόντες ἔτη τρία. In P Oxy IV. 729[7] (A.D. 137) τὴν δὲ ἀν[α]βολὴν ποιήσονται ἀπὸ τῶν ἐθίμων ἀναβολῶν, and P Goodsp Cairo 15[9] (A.D. 362) τὴν ἀναβολὴν πεποίημαι, we have the same phrase as in Ac 25[17] (*plus* the article), but in a wholly different sense, "to make an embankment." In P Tebt II. 378[20] (A.D. 265) τοὺς [δι]ωρύγων τε κ[αὶ ὑδ]ραγωγῶν [ἀ]ναβολὰς is rendered by the editors "banking up of canals and conduits," and probably a similar rendering, rather than "dredging," should be given to P Amh II. 91[11] (A.D. 159) ἀναβολὰς διωρύγω(ν): cf. CP Herm 41 χώμασι καὶ ἀναβολαῖς, and P Lond 1171[60] (B.C. 8) (= III. p. 179) ἀναβολῆς ναυβίων (see on ἀναβάλλω, and Kenyon's note here). In P Oxy VI. 909[25] (A.D. 225) τὴν προκειμένων ἀκανθῶν ἀναβολήν, the word is used in the unusual sense of digging up or uprooting (see the editors' note). In P Tebt II. 413[10] (ii/iii A.D.) the editors translate τέρα ἀνβολὰ (*l.* τέσσαρας ἀναβολάς), "4 bags," and compare P Oxy IV. 741[14] (ii/A.D.) where ἀναβολή, in the sense of ἀναβολίδιον, occurs next before προχείρια in a list of articles. Further in a legal document P Petr III. 21 (*g*)[21] (iii/B.C.) we have τῆς ἀναβολῆς τοῦ ἱματίου with hiatus before and after, so that we cannot certainly join the words. In P Théad Inv. 15, a receipt of Constantine's time, those who grant the receipt name themselves ἀποδέκται λίνου τοῦ ἱεροῦ ἀναβολικοῦ, where Jouguet finds a reference to the linen for a military mantle ("ἀναβολικοῦ *de* ἀναβολή = ἀμβολή = *abolla*, etc."): but see Wilcken *Archiv*, iv. p. 185.

ἀνάγαιον.

This form of the word is supported by κατάγ(ε)ιον, P Oxy I. 75[19] (A.D. 129), and VI. 911[15] (iii/A.D.), 912[12] (*ib.*); καταγαίῳ, P Lond 1164 (*c*[8] A.D. 212) (= III. p. 160), καταγαία, P Oxy VI. 903[1] (iv/A.D.), κατάκεον, P Rein 43[9] (A.D. 102, illiterate). Τῶν ἀνωγαίων occurs at the end of vi/A.D., P Par 21[3], and ἀνώγιον in CPR 28[16] (A.D. 110), after a lacuna: cf. MGr ἀνώγι "upper storey."

ἀναγγέλλω,

which in Hellenistic Greek is found much in the sense of the Attic ἀπαγγέλλω, is illustrated by P Petr III. 42 H (8f)[7]

(iii/B.C.) τὰ γεγενημέ̓να σοι ἐμοὶ ἀνήγγελλον, *ib.* 56 (*h*)[12]
(Ptol.) ἀναγγέλειν σοι αὐθήμερον : cf. *Syll* 263[7] (*c.* B.C.
200) ἐντέταλμαι αὐτῶι ἀναγγεῖλαι ὑμῖν ἃ ἠβουλόμην ὑμᾶς
εἰδῆσαι. Further instances in P Eleph 13[6] (B.C. 223-2, —
Witkowski[2] p. 43), P Petr II. 11, 2[5] (iii/B.C.—*ib.* p. 7) ; see
also *Syll* index (III. p. 249). For the use of the word in the
LXX, see Anz *Subsidia*, p. 283.

ἀναγεννάω.

The word, as well as the thought, is found in the Hermetic
writings, e.g. Reitzenstein *Poimandres* p. 339[11] ἀγνοῶ, ὦ
τρισμέγιστε, ἐξ οἴας μήτρας ἀνεγεννήθης, σποράς δὲ ποίας :
cf. Bauer on Jn 3[3] (in *HZNT*) and Reitzenstein *Die hell.
Mysterienreligionen* pp. 26, 31.

ἀναγινώσκω.

For this word — "read aloud," as generally in classical
Greek, cf. P Grenf I. 37[15] (late ii/B.C.) ἐπιλέγματος ἀναγνωσθέντος, of the reading aloud of a petition, and P Goodsp Cairo
29 [iii. 1] (*c.* A.D. 150) ἧς ἀναγνωσθείσης, of a will. So P Oxy
I. 59[8] (A.D. 292) ἐπίσταλμα ἐν ἡμῖν ἀνεγνώσ[θη], "at a
meeting of our body a despatch was read," and *Michel* 699[5]
(end of iii/B.C.) τό τε ψήφισμα ἀνέγνωσαν. The word is
used absolutely in P Amh II. 94[2] (A.D. 107) ἀναγνωσθέντος,
"a report was read." On the other hand it must mean
simply "read" in P Eleph 9[3] (B.C. 222) ὡς ἂν οὖν ἀναγνῶις
[τὴ]ν ἐπιστολήν, and similarly *ib.* 13[3], also BGU IV. 1079[6 ff.]
(a private letter — i/A.D.) λοιπὸν οὖν ἔλαβον παρὰ το[ῦ]
Ἀραβος τὴν ἐπιστολὴν καὶ ἀνέγνων καὶ ἐλυπήθην, and
P Fay 20[23] (iii/iv A.D.) where it refers to copies of an edict
set up in public places σύνοπτα τοῖς ἀναγινώσκουσιν, "in
full view of those who wish to read." Ἀνέγνων is a common
formula for an authenticating signature, like the *Legimus*
of the Roman Emperors : see e.g. P Par 69[8, 10, 14] (B.C. 233).
The play on two compounds of γινώσκω in 2 Cor 1[13] may be
paralleled by P Oxy VII. 1062[13] (ii/A.D.) αὖ[τ]ὴν δέ σοι τὴν
ἐπιστολὴν πέμψω διὰ Σύρου ἵνα αὐτὴν ἀναγνοῖς νήφων καὶ
σαυτοῦ καταγνοῖς. It is interesting to note from the literary
record of the verb that the meaning "read" is essentially
Attic, Ionic (Herod.) using ἐπιλέγεσθαι : see LS and
Schlageter p. 24. In *Preisigke* 1019, 1020, 1022, 1023,
all προσκυνήματα from the same Egyptian temple (Kalab-
schah), also 1065 (Abydos)—we find the record of the
adoration of a number of persons from one family, to which
is appended καὶ τοῦ ἀναγινώσκοντος, in one case following
καὶ τοῦ γράψαντος. This inclusion of the reader, whoever
he may be, distantly reminds us of Rev 1[3].

ἀναγκάζω.

P Oxy IV. 717[14] (late i/B.C.) ἠν]άγκασμαι βοᾶν αὐτῶι.
A somewhat weakened sense is seen in P Fay 110[4] (A.D. 94)
εὖ ποιήσεις . . ἀναγκάσας ἐκχωσθῆναι τὸ ἐν αὐτῶι κόπριον,
"please have the manure there banked up" (Edd.) : cf. the
use in Lk 14[23], where ἀνάγκασον describes the "constraint"
of hospitality which will not be denied. Other occurrences
are BGU IV. 1042[5, 6] (iii/A.D.) ἐ[ν]έτυχ[ε τ]ῷ δικαιοδότη
καὶ ἀ[ν]ή[γκ]αξέ με προσκαρτερεῖν τῷ βήμ[ατ]ι αὐτοῦ·
so we venture to restore the text, in accordance with the
meaning clearly needed—the augment will be a blunder like
that which secured permanent footing in διηκόνουν, etc. A
similar aor. is apparently intended in P Amh II. 133[12] (early

ii/A.D.) καὶ μετὰ πολλῶν κόπων ἀνηκάσαμεν (*l.* ἀνηγκ-)
αὐτῶν (for αὐτούς) ἀντασχέσθαι κτλ. "and with great
difficulty I made them set to work" (Edd.). The contracted future occurs in an edict of Germanicus on a Berlin
papyrus (*Archiv* vi. p. 280) ἐάμ μοι μὴ πεισθῆτε, ἀναγκάτέ
με κτλ. BGU IV. 1141[7] (end of i/B.C.) ἀναγκάζομαι μηκέτι
σοι μηδὲν γράψαι, [ἵνα] νοήσης. P Lond 951 *verso* [3] (late
iii/A.D) (= III. p. 213) ἤκουσ[α] ὅ[τ]ι θηλάζειν αὐτὴν
ἀναγκάζεις. The verb is MGr.

ἀναγκαῖος.

P Fay 10 [,1] (early i/A.D.) πρὸς ἀναγκαῖν (= -αῖον).
Ordinary uses may be seen in P Tor I. 1[vii. 6] (B.C. 110) κατὰ
τὸ ἀναγκαῖον "necessitate coactus," P Leid B[iii. 3] (ii/B.C.)
εἰς τὸ μηθὲν τῶν ἀναγκαίων ἡμᾶς ὑστερεῖν, P Flor II. 132[11]
(A.D. 257) ὅπερ ἀναγκαῖόν σε ἦν γνῶναι (as Ac 13[46]), *ib.* 170[8]
(A.D. 255) εἰ περὶ τῶν οὐδαμινῶν ἀμελεῖτε, πόσῳ μᾶλλον
τῶν ἀναγκαιοτέρων. In combination with φίλος, meaning
"intimate," as in Ac 10[24], we have P Flor II. 142[2] (A.D.
264) ἐπειδήπερ ἐντολικὸν ἔχω ἀναγκαίου φίλου : cf. *Syll*
737[51] (ii/A.D.) (εἰ) σφόδρα ἀναγκαῖός τις ἦν. For the Pauline
phrase ἀναγκαῖον ἡγεῖσθαι, as 2 Cor 9[5], Phil 2[25], cf. P Fay
111[19] (A.D. 95-6) (= *Selections*, p. 67) [ἀ]νανκαῖν ἡγησα[ς],
"considering that it is essential," *Syll* 656[8] (ii/A.D.) ὅθεν
ἀναγκαῖον ἡγησάμην (c. inf.) : cf. ὑπολαμβάνομεν ἀ. εἶναι,
ib. 700[74]. The RV margin at Tit 3[14] εἰς τὰς ἀναγκαίας
χρείας, "for necessary wants," that is "for the necessities
of life," is supported by P Oxy VII. 1068[16] (iii/A.D.) χάριν
ἀναγκέας χρίας, and by *Priene* 108[80] (*c.* B.C. 120), where
Moschion is thanked for having given a certain sum εἰς
χρείας ἀναγκαίας. Cf. P Grenf II. 14 (*c*)[1 f.] (iii/B.C.)
χρείαν ἔχομεν ἀναγκαίαν Τιμοξένου ὥστε ἀποστεῖλαι αὐτὸν
εἰς τὴν πόλιν. The superlative is found P Par 46[7] (B.C 153)
ἐν τοῖς ἀναγκαιοτάτοις καιροῖς, and P Giss I. 25[3] (ii/A.D.)
πάντων τῶν εὐχῶν μου ἀναγκαιοτάτην ἔχω τὴν τῆς ὑγείας
σου, *al.* Cf. the elative in P Lond 42[31] (B.C. 168) (= I. p. 30)
εἴπερ μὴ ἀναγκαιότερόν σ[ε] περισπᾶι, "unless urgent business detains you," P Flor I. 61[15] (A.D. 86-8) ἐντυγχάνει σοι
τὸ πρῶτον κ[ὰ]ι ἀναγκαιότατον. For the adverb, cf. P Flor
II. 138[5] (A.D. 264) ἐπεὶ ἀναγκαίως σου χρήζω, *OGIS* 669[8]
(i/A.D.) προέγραψα ἀναγκαίως περὶ ἐκάστου τῶν ἐπιζητουμένων, P Giss I. 68[8] (early ii/A.D.) ἀναγκαίως γράφω σοι·
οὐδένα ᾿χω (*l.* ἔχω) [μ]ετὰ τὸν θεὸν εἰ μή σε, etc.

ἀναγκαστός.

The derived adj. ἀναγκαστικός occurs eight times in Vettius
Valens, with the meaning "*potens*," "*efficax*" (Ed.).

ἀνάγκη.

For ἔχειν ἀνάγκην followed by the infinitive, as Lk 14[18],
cf. P Oxy VII. 1061[4] (B.C. 22) ἀνάγκην ἔσχον παρακαλέσαι,
"I have been obliged to urge," P Flor II. 278[v. 23] (iii/A.D.)
ἀνάγκην ἔσχον ἐ[ντ]υχεῖν. The converse appears in BGU
IV. 1141[47] (B.C. 14) διὸ ἀνάγκη με ἔσχηκε ἐνφανίσαι. The
word = "calamity" occurs in *Syll* 255[27] (iii B.C.) ἐν
ἀνάγκαις καὶ κακοπαθίαις γένηται—cf. 2 Cor 6[4], etc. In
a leaden tablet found at Carthage, Wünsch *AF* 4[4] (iii/A.D.)
ἐξορκίζω σε] τὸν θεὸν τῆς ἀνάγκης τὸν μέγαν Ἀρουρο-
βααρζαγραν, we have, as Wünsch thinks, the Orphic conception surviving : he compares P Lond 121[648] (iii/A.D.)
(= I. p. 105) θεὸς ὁ ἐπὶ τῆς ἀνάγκης τεταγμένος Ἰακούβ
Ἰαιβω (? = יהוה) Σαβαώθ Ἀδωναϊ—in neither of these

however can we speak exactly of "the great goddess of Necessity." She figures in Vettius Valens, p. 173 (top), αὐτήν τε τὴν πρόνοιαν καὶ τὴν ἱερὰν Ἀνάγκην. For the ordinary use of the word we may quote *Ostr* 1153 (Rom.) μὴ ἄλλως ποιήσητ(ε) εἰδότ(ες) τὴν ἀνάγκην, P Flor II. 177[10] (A.D. 257) ἐπεὶ δὲ οἶδα ὅτι καὶ ἀνάγκης καὶ ὑπομνήσεως χρῄζεται, "you need compulsion and reminder," *ib.* 186[9] (A.D. 259), διὰ τὴν ἀνάνκην τῶν ἀναιλωμάτων, "the pressure of expenses," *ib.* 222[9] (A.D. 256) εἰς τὰ ἀναλώματά μου τῆς φροντίδος ἐν ἀνάγκῃ, etc. The word is MGr.

ἀνάγνωσις.

Syll 552[81] (Magnesia, late ii/B.C.) ἐὰν δὲ μὴ ποιήσωνται τὴν ἀνάγνωσιν [αὐ]τοῦ καθότι προστέτακται: several instances might be quoted from iii/A.D. in the normal sense of "reading." In P Tebt I. 61 (*b*)[3] (B.C. 118–7) we have the survival of an earlier meaning: ἐπὶ τῆς ἀναγνώ[σ]ε[ως] τῆς κα[τ]ὰ [φύ]λλ[ον γε]ωμετρίας, "at the revision of the survey of the crops" (Edd.).

ἀνάγω.

The use of ἀ. in Ac 12[4] finds a ready parallel in *Syll* 366[24] (i/A.D.) ἀναχθέντα εἰς τὸν δῆμον ἐὰν μὲν πολείτης ᾖ, ἀποξενοῦσθαι. For the meaning "restore," "bring back," cf. P Par 10[12] τοῦτον ὃς ἂν ἀναγάγῃ, with reference to a runaway slave, and Wilcken's restoration (*Archiv* iv. p. 548) of P Lond 021[5] (ii/iii A.D.) (= III. p. 134) ἀναγαγεῖν ε[ἰς ἄμπελον] of bringing back certain arourai to use as a vineyard. See the editor's note on P Oxy VII. 1032[8] (A.D. 162) ἀνήξαμεν κτλ. "we converted out of our own ancient plots . . . τ̄ο̄ of an aroura of vine-land," and *ib.* IV. 707[23] (*c.* A.D. 136) γῆν ἀνάξαι ἀμπέλω. (On the vulgar 1st aor. see above under ἄγω.) P Flor II. 134[6] (A.D. 260) ἵν[α] τὸ ἀναγόμενον ἐν Βουβάστω κτημάτιων ὑποσχισθῇ, is rendered by Comparetti "perchè la terra *annessa* in Bubasto venga dissodata." *Syll* 936[6] καὶ καταβαλέτω τὰμ πεντηκοστὰν π[ρὶ]ν ἀνάγειν τι ἢ πωλεῖν seems to mean "before he brings (the merchandise) into the town or sells it," *i. e.* "bring up" from the landing stage. The familiar use of ἀνάγειν for "putting out to sea" is found in BGU IV. 1200[14] (B.C. 1) τοῦ τὴν πρόσοδον ἀνηγμένου εἰς Ἰταλίαν, modified in a transitive direction. For its sacrificial use (as in Ac 7[41]) cf. *OGIS* 764[47] (*c.* B.C. 127) ἀναγαγὼν ἐκ τοῦ ἰδίου ταύρους δύο καὶ καλλιερή[σας κτλ: so elsewhere in this inscr. (= *Cagnat* IV. 294).

ἀναδείκνυμι.

Frequent in inscr., in a sacrificial sense, e. g. *Syll* 553[14] (iii/ii B.C.) ἀναδεικνύωσι τῷ Διὶ ταῦρον. Nearer to the sense of Ac 1[24] is the astrological phrase in Vettius Valens, p. 119[25] ἐὰν δὲ Ζεὺς μαρτυρήσῃ Κρόνῳ, νόμιμος γάμος ἀναδειχθήσεται ἢ καί τινας ἐξευγενίσουσιν. Note *Syll* 329[12] (B.C. 86) κέκρικεν ἀναδείξαι τὸν πρὸς Μιθραδάτην πόλεμον, which comes near our "*declare* war": so in *OGIS* 441[49] *ex suppl.*).

ἀναδέχομαι.

There is a legal sense of this word which is not uncommon —P Oxy III. 513[57 ff.] (A.D. 184) ἐάν τις ζήτη[σις] περὶ τούτου γένηται πρὸς αὐτὸν . . . [ἐγὼ] αὐτὸς τοῦτο ἀναδέξομαι, "if any action is brought against him in connexion with this, I will take the responsibility upon myself" (Edd.).

So P Tebt I. 98[27] (*c.* B.C. 112) ὧν ἀδεδί̈γμεθα (*l.* ἀναδ-), "for whom we are security," and the late P Grenf II 99 (*a*)[1 ff.] (vi/vii A.D.) Δανεὶτ ἀνεδέξατο Θαησίαν ὥστε αὐτὴν ἀπελθῖν εἰς διαίτην καὶ τὰ ἀπὸ διαίτης ποιήσῃ, "David has become surety for Thaesia on condition that she return to her home and busy herself with its duties." The verb is followed by the infinitive, P Tebt I. 75[6] (B.C. 112) ἀναδέχομαι πόρον δώσιν τῆς (ἀρτάβης), "I undertake to provide for the artaba tax": P Hib I. 58[9 ff.] (B.C. 245-4) ἀναδίδεκται γὰρ ἡμῖν ἀπομετρήσειν σῖτον: cf. *OGIS* 339[30] (ii/B.C.) τάς τε πρεσβείας ἀνεδέχετο προθύμως, *ib.* 441[9] (i/B.C.) καὶ διὰ ταῦτα κινδύνους πολλοὺς [. . .] ὑπὲρ τῶν ἡμετέρων δημοσίων [. . . προθυμό]τατα ἀ[ν]αδεδειγμένους. *Syll* 929[30] (ii/B.C.) πᾶσαν ἀναδεχόμενοι κακοπαθίαν χάριν τοῦ μηθενὸς ὑστερῆσαι δικαίου μηθένα τῶν κρινομένων, of judges who say they have given not only the day but τὸ πλεῖον τῆς νυκτός to their work. Add *Syll* 530[63] (late iv/B.C.) = "undertake"; so P Eleph 29[12] (iii/B.C.), P Tebt II. 329[19] (A.D. 139), and BGU I. 194[11] (A.D. 177), and P Ryl II. 77[38] (A.D. 192) ἀναδεξάμενος τὴν μείζονα ἀρχὴν οὐκ ὀφείλει τὴν ἐλάττον' ἀποφεύγειν. The predominance of this meaning suggests its application in Heb 11[17]. The statement that Abraham had "undertaken," "assumed the responsibility of" the promises, would not perhaps be alien to the thought. In Ac 28[7] it is "hospitio excepit" (Blass), Attic ὑποδέχεσθαι.

ἀναδίδωμι.

On P Fay 26[13 ff.] (A.D. 150) ἵν' οὖν τοὺς συνοψιοῦντας . . . ἀναδῶτε, the editors remark that "ἀναδιδόναι (or εἰσδιδόναι) is the regular word for presenting a list of well-to-do persons (εὔποροι) from whom a certain number were to be selected for a λειτουργία," and compare P Oxy I. 82[2] (middle iii/A.D.) τὰς ἀναδόσεις τῶν λειτουργῶν, and BGU I. 194[2] (A.D. 177). See the note on P Ryl II. 91[3]. See also P Flor I. 2[2·37] (A.D. 265) οἱ ἀναδοθέντες, men whose names had been "sent up"; *ib.* 25[30] (ii/A.D.) ἣν καὶ ἀναδέδωκε εἰς ἀκύρωσιν, of a document; and so P Tebt II. 397[13] (A.D. 198). In *Syll* 279[7] (ii/B.C.) we find τό τε ψήφισμα ἀνέδωκεν according to the best reading. P Tebt II. 448 (ii/iii A.D.) τῷ ἀναδιδόντι σοι τὸ ἐπιστόλιον "the bearer": cf. *IGSI* 830[22] ἀνεγνώσθη ἐπιστολὴ Τυρίων στατιωναρίων ἀναδοθεῖσα ὑπὸ Λάχητος, ἑνὸς αὐτῶν. In P Oxy VII. 1063[14] (ii/iii A.D.) τὸ πιττά[κ]ιον ἀναγνοὺς μὴ ἀναδῷς τῷ Ἡρώ[δ]ῃ we may render "pass on." Note in *ib.* 1033[5] (A.D. 392) the strange form ἀναδεδοιημένοι. In Vettius Valens p. 21[1] τὰς ἀναδοθείσας ὥρας = "the given hours," in a mathematical sense.

ἀναζάω.

For ἀ., as in Rom 7[9], Nägeli p. 47 cites *CIG* 2566 (Crete, date?) Ἀρχονίκα Ζαύλω . . . ἀναζῶσα Ἀρτέμιδι εὐακ[ό]ῳ, where Archonica fulfils a vow to Artemis, "being alive once more." Other instances of the verb from profane sources will be found in Deissmann *LAE* p. 94 ff.

ἀναζητέω.

The verb is capable of general use, as in P Oxy VII. 1066[18] (iii/A.D.) ἀναζήτησον [ῥίνην] "look for a file." But it is specially used of searching for human beings, with an implication of difficulty, as in the NT passages. So P Hib I. 71[b] (B.C. 245-4) τὴν πᾶσαν σπουδὴν ποιήσαι ὅπ[ως ἀνα|ζητηθέντες ἀποσταλῶσι, "make every effort to search for them" etc. with reference to certain slaves who had deserted. P Rein 17¹³ (B.C. 109) has nearly the same phrase: cf. *Syll* 220¹⁸ (iii/B.C.) *ex suppl.*, P Flor I. 83¹² (iii/iv A.D.) ἀναζητηθέντα ἀναπεμφθήσεσθαι πρὸς τὸν κράτιστον ἐπίτροπον. P Tebt I. 138 (late ii/B.C.) ἀναζητούμενος Ὀννῶφρις οὐχ εὑρίσκεται, *ib.* 53²² (B.C. 110) οἱ εὐθυνόμενοι ἀναζητηθ[έ]ντες, "the culprits having been searched for." For the noun ἀναζήτησις, cf. P Fay 107³ (A.D. 133) ποήσασθαι τὴν καθήκουσαν ἀναζήτησιν, "to hold the due inquiry." P Tebt II. 423¹² (early iii/A.D.) πρ[ὸς] ἀναζήτην (*l.* -ησιν) χόρτου, "to look for hay," and P Ryl II. 78³² (A.D. 157) περὶ ἀναζητήσεως Πάνθηρος.

ἀναζωπυρέω.

A characteristic compound of the Pastorals (2 Tim 1⁶), but vouched for in the common speech of the day: P Leid Wˣᵛⁱ·⁴⁰ (ii/iii A.D.)—an occult pamphlet—αὐτὸ γάρ ἐστιν τὸ ἀναζωπυροῦν τὰς πάσας βίβλους, cf. *ib.* Vˣ·⁷ (iii/iv A.D.) δι' οὗ ζωπυρεῖται πάντα πλάσματα. See further Anz *Subsidia*, p. 284 f., and cf. F. C. Conybeare in *Exp* VII. iv. p. 40.

ἀναθάλλω

is one of the words that Nägeli cites (p. 81) to prove that in Phil 4¹⁰ ἀνεθάλετε τὸ ὑπὲρ ἐμοῦ φρονεῖν, Paul has taken vocabulary from the more cultured Κοινή, through his later intercourse with Greeks. It should be noted, however, that the word is not rare in the LXX (especially in Sirach), five times in this rare tense and four times transitively. It is a curious problem whence the LXX derived it. The simplex occurs in BGU IV. 1112¹⁸ (B.C. 4) παρείληφεν δὲ καὶ ἡ Εὐγένεια τὸ παιδίον θάλλουσαν.

ἀνάθεμα.

Deissmann's discovery of ἀνάθεμα in the "Biblical Greek" sense, in a source entirely independent of Jewish influence, is a remarkable confirmation of his general thesis. At the end of a heathen curse from Megara, belonging to i/ii A.D., there is a separate line of large letters ΑΝΕΘΕΜΑ which he (*LAE* p. 92 f.) interprets as = ἀνάθεμα—"curse!" The weakening of the accented α to ε is explained as a vulgar Greek extension of the augment to a derivative (cf. Nägeli p. 49, following Wackernagel). See on this the plentiful material in Hatzidakis *Einleitung*, p. 64 f. The verb occurs three times in the same curse, l. 5 ἀναθεματί-ζ[ομ]εν αὐτούς, l. 8 ἀναθεμα[τί]ζομεν, and on the back l. 8 f. ἀναθεματ[ί]ζομεν τούτο[υς]. For the complete text, as originally edited by Wünsch, see *IG* III. 2. and also his *Antike Fluchtafeln*, p. 4 ff. Newton (*Essays in Archaeology*, p. 193 f.) describes a number of leaden tablets of about B.C. 150 discovered at Knidos, in a sacred precinct dedicated to Persephone and other deities, which were graven with similar *anathemata*. The person on whom the curse was to fall was always devoted to the vengeance of the two Infernal Goddesses, Demeter and her daughter, "May he or she never find Persephone propitious!" With 1 Cor 16²¹ may be compared the ending of a sepulchral inscription (iv/v A.D.) from Attica, where on any one's interfering with the remains the curse is called down—ἀνάθεμα ἤτω μαρὰν ἀθάν (see *Roberts-Gardner* 387): the meaning

of the Aramaic σύμβολον being wholly unknown, it could be used as a curse—like unknown words in later days? It should be noted that the new meaning "curse" naturally attached itself to the late form ἀνάθεμα rather than to the older ἀνάθημα. Nouns in -μα tended to develop weak root-form by association with those in -σις, which always had it. The noun is MGr: thus ἀνάθεμα ἐσένα, "a curse on you" (Thumb, *Handbook* p. 38).

ἀναθεματίζω.

For the meaning see under ἀνάθεμα. The form may be illustrated by ἐκθεματίζω in P Tebt I. 27⁴⁷ (B.C. 113) ἐκθεματισθῆι, "be proclaimed a defaulter." There is also a simplex in BGU IV. 1127³⁰ (B.C. 18) ἐξῖναι τῶι Εὐαγγέλωι θεματίσαντι ἐπὶ τραπέζαν ἔνθεσμον . . . παραχώρησιν ποιεῖσθαι, *Syll* 329³⁶ (i/B.C.), meaning "to deposit."

ἀνάθημα.

See Index to *Syll* III. p. 206, which shows how the old form and the later ἀνάθεμα (like ἀνάδημα and ἀνάδεμα, etc.) lived on side by side. In his index to *OGIS* Dittenberger is content with "ἀνάθημα, ἀναθήματα *passim*." That the alternative lived on in Semitic districts as well as in Greece itself, in the same sense, is well shown in a trilingual inscr. —Latin, Greek and Punic—in G. A. Cooke's *North Semitic Inscriptions*, p. 109 (ii/B.C.), Ἀσκληπιῶι Μηρρή ἀνάθεμα βωμὸν ἔστησε Κλέων. This answers to *donum dedit* in the Latin, נדר in the Punic.

ἀναίδεια.

OGIS 665¹⁶ (A.D. 48–9) ὑπὸ τῶν πλεονεκτικῶς καὶ ἀναιδῶς ταῖς ἐξουσίαις ἀποχρωμένων associates the original adj. from which ἀναίδεια comes with another which well illustrates its connotation—audacious "desire to get": cf. Lk 11⁸ and for a slightly different connotation Sir 25²². In P Lond 342¹⁴ (A.D. 185) (= II. p. 174) the adj. is used of a man who proves himself ἀναιδὴς ἐν τῇ κώμῃ by levying contributions on the inhabitants etc.; and for the verb see P Ryl II. 141¹⁷ (A.D. 37) ἀναιδενόμενοι μὴ ἀποδῦναι, "shamelessly refusing to pay" (Edd.).

ἀναίρεσις.

Field (*Notes*, p. 116) remarks that "killing" or "slaying" would be more adequate than "death" (AV, RV) as a rendering. Since even the AV of 2 Macc 5¹³, which he notes, does not make "unto the killing of him" English, we must either keep "death" or substitute "murder," which the tone of ἀναιρῶ would fairly justify: see *sub voce*.

ἀναιρέω.

The commercial sense of ἀναιρέω seems the commonest. P Lond 1168⁶ᶠ· (A.D. 18) (= III. p. 136) ἀντὶ τοῦ τόκου [ὧ]ν ἀνείρηται, "the interest on what she has borrowed," *ib.* 1164¹⁷ (A.D. 212) (= III. p. 158) ἀνηρῆσθαι τὸν πωλοῦντα π[αρ]ὰ τοῦ ὠνουμένου τὴν συνπεφωνημένην πρὸς ἀλλ[ή]λους τιμήν, BGU IV. 1130² (= B.C. 11): cf *ib.* 1135⁶ (*do.*) ἀνείλαν[το. P Fay 100¹⁹· ²⁶ (A.D. 99) ἀνίρημαι, of "receiving" money: so P Flor I. 1⁶·¹² (A.D. 153), *ib.* 81⁵ (A.D. 103). In the more general sense of "take up," P Tebt I. 138 (late ii/B.C.) ἀνελόμενος τὴν ἑαυτοῦ μάχαιραν, and the interesting imperial letter, now dated in the time of

Hadrian (*Hermes* xxxvii. p. 84 ff.), BGU I. 140¹⁰ ᶠᶠ· with reference to τ[ο]ύτους, ε[ὖ]s οἱ γονεῖς αὐτῶν τῷ τῆς στρατείας ἀνείλα[ν]το χρόνῳ. For the active cf. P Oxy I. 37⁶ (A.D. 49) (= *Selections*, p. 49), ἀνείλεν ἀπὸ κοπρίας ἀρρενικὸν σωμάτιον, "picked up from the dung-heap a male foundling"; the corresponding passive is used of the same transaction in *ib.* 38³ (A.D. 49-50) (= *Selections*, p. 52), ὃ ἀνείρηται ἀπὸ κοπρίας. The recurrent formula δουλικὸν παιδίον ἀναίρετον ὑποτίτθιον (as BGU IV. 1107⁸—B.C. 13) shows how technical the term had become: cf. Ac 7²¹. For the meaning "kill," cf. P Amh II. 142³ (iv/A.D.) βουλόμενοι ἀναιρῆσαί με : in *Syll* 929⁴⁶ of a city "destroyed." So also, seemingly, in P Par 68ᵇ ⁵ (Rom.) ἀναιρεθῆναι μέλλω[ν]: the context is fragmentary, but the general subject—an apology for the Jews—makes it probable. The compound ἀναταναιρεῖν (cf. ἀντανπληροῦν) occurs frequently in P Tebt I., as 61(b)²¹⁴ (B.C. 118-7) [ἀν]ταναιρεθείσης, "subtracted." So P Petr III. 76ⁱⁱⁱ ¹ (ii/B.C.), *ib.* 104³ τοῦ ἀνειλημμένου, of a farm-holding "confiscated" to the state, BGU III. 776ⁱ· ⁷ (i/A.D.).

ἀναίτιος.

Syll 816⁷ ἐγχέαντας αὐτῆς τὸ ἀναίτιον αἷμα ἀδίκως, *ib.*¹² ἵνα ἐγδικήσῃς τὸ αἷμα τὸ ἀναίτιον. This interesting inscription, containing phrases from the LXX, is given by Dittenberger as of Jewish or Christian origin. The latter alternative has been rightly excluded, since there is no sign of the NT visible. The prayer is a Jewish prayer for vengeance belonging to the end of the second, or the beginning of the first century B.C. See the full discussion in Deissmann *LAE*, p. 423 ff., and note the remarkably similar but pagan prayer from Alexandria in *Preisigke* 1323 (ii/A.D.).

ἀνακαθίζω.

This term, common in medical writings (Lk 7¹⁵, Ac 9⁴⁰), is found in a Christian letter of iv/A.D., which is full of NT echoes—P Oxy VI. 939²⁵ (= *Selections*, p. 130) ἔδοξεν . . . ἀνεκτότερον ἐσχηκέναι ἀνακαθεσθεῖσα, νοσηλότερον δὲ ὅμως τὸ σωμάτιον ἔχει, "she seems . . . to be in a more tolerable state in that she has sat up, but nevertheless she is still in a somewhat sickly state of body." See Hobart, p. 11 f.

ἀνακαινίζω.

See s.v. ἀνακαινόω.

ἀνακαινόω

and its noun ἀνακαίνωσις have not been traced in any source earlier than Paul, who might very well coin a word of this sort—there is however no proof that he really did so. Nägeli, p. 53, remarks on these and other "new words" of Paul that they answer in formation to that of other Κοινή words, going back to old Greek stems and only combining them afresh. Here the similar ἀνακαινίζειν (Heb 6⁶) exists in literature, as does ἀνακαίνισις. Did Paul not know them, so that he had to form words for his purpose, on such an analogy as ἀνανεόω? Or were his words current in a limited district only? Thayer notes that Hermas used ἀνακαίνωσις (*Vis.* iii. 8⁹): ἡ ἀ. τῶν πνευμάτων ὑμῶν looks like a reminiscence of Rom 12², and is no warrant for independent use.

ἀνακαλέπτω.

Syll 803¹² (iii/B.C.) ἐδόκει αὐτοῦ [τὸ ἔσθος ὁ θε]ὸς (Asclepios) ἀγκαλύψαι. P Oxy X. 1297⁹ (iv/A.D.) of a vessel of oil.

ἀνακάμπτω.

In connexion with the metaphorical use in Lk 10⁶, we may quote BGU III. 896⁶ (ii/A.D.) πάντα τὰ ἐμὰ ἀνακάμψει εἰς τὴν προγεγραμμ[ένην θυγατέρα]. For the ordinary sense "return," cf. P Magd 8¹⁰ (iii/B.C.), μετὰ δὲ ταῦτ' ἀνακάμ[ψαντός μου]. See also Anz *Subsidia*, p. 314 f.

ἀνάκειμαι.

For the sense *accumbere* (Jn 6¹¹, etc.), which does not seem to be older than the Macedonian period, may be cited BGU I. 344 (ii/iii A.D.), a list of names of οἱ ἀνακίμενοι, and ending γίνονδαι ἄνδρες ἀναγείμενον (!) μ̄χ̄. The verb occurs in the more ordinary sense, as passive to ἀνατίθημι, in the great Ephesian inser., *Syll* 656⁴⁶ (ii/A.D.) ἀνακεῖσθαι τῇ θεῷ (" be dedicated "), of the month Artemision (so also I. ⁵²). The same meaning appears in *ib* 827⁴ καθιερωμένων καὶ ἀνακειμένων τῆι Οὐρανίαι ᾿Αφροδίτει (i/B.C.).

ἀνακεφαλαιόω

naturally does not figure in our non-literary sources: it belongs to a more cultivated stratum of thought—see its record in Grimm. But the commonness of κεφάλαιον, "sum," total," would make the meaning obvious even to ordinary readers.

ἀνακλίνω.

The NT writers use ἀνακλίνεσθαι, "to recline at a table," instead of the classical παρα- and κατα-κλίνεσθαι, in a way which suggests that this usage was characteristic of the common speech, though we are unable to illustrate it. Sir W. M. Ramsay has drawn our attention to the fact that in the anti-Christian Society of Tekmoreioi at Pisidian Antioch the President was πρωτανακλίτης, who sits in the chief place at table, and he takes this as an indication that the ritual feast was moulded on the Eucharist. For such imitations as marking the pagan reaction about A.D. 304-13, see his *Pauline and other Studies*, p. 103 ff.

ἀνακόπτω.

P Flor I. 36³ (early iv/A.D.) crimes ὑφ' οὐδενὸς ἄλλου ἀνακόπτεται, but by the punishment of the criminal; a similar connotation probably may be recognised in the fragmentary P Giss I. 87¹⁰ (ii/A.D.) . .] παραγγέλλειν ἀνακοπῆναι [. ., from what the scanty context suggests. So also in P Thead 19¹⁵ (iv/A.D.) δέομαι τῆς σῆς ἀρε[τῆ]s κελεύσαι . . . τὴν παιδιὰν τῆς γυναικὸς ἀνακοπῆναι δι' οὐ εὐδοκιμάσῃς. The word obviously does not encourage us to approve the few cursives that show it in Gal 5⁷.

ἀνακράζω.

The vernacular character of this compound is sufficiently established by our one citation, BGU IV. 1201¹¹ (ii/A.D.) καὶ ἡμῶν ἀνακράξαντες (for -ων !) εἰς τὴν κώμην πρὸς βοήθιαν κατεπήδησεν ὁ γυμνασίαρχος κτλ.: the temple of Serapis was on fire, so that the word on this occasion no doubt implies considerable vigour, as we should expect from its record elsewhere.

ἀνακρίνω.

For the judicial sense "examine," as in 1 Cor 9³, cf. *Michel* 409⁹ (beginning of iii/B.C.) τοὺς μὲν πλεί[στους τῶν διαφερομένων ἀνα[κρινάμ]ενοι πολλάκις ἐφ᾽ αὑτοὺς διέλυον συμφ[ερόντως], *Syll* 512⁴⁸ (ii/B.C.) ἀνακρινάντω δὲ καὶ το[ὺ]ς μάρτυρας. The substantive (*q.v.*) is found in the previous line of the latter inscription.

ἀνάκρισις.

See on ἀνακρίνω. In *OGIS* 374 (i/B.C.), which commemorates a certain Papias, a privy councillor and chief physician of Mithradates Eupator, King of Pontus, we find him described as τεταγμένον δὲ καὶ ἐπὶ τῶν ἀνακρίσεων. Dittenberger gives reasons for thinking that "non tam iudicem quam inquisitorem hoc significat," one who presided over the examination of men suspected of conspiracy: cf. *Syll* 356⁵⁸ (B.C. 6), a rescript of Augustus, who says πέπονφα δὲ ὑμεῖν καὶ α[ὐτ]ὰς τὰς ἀνακρίσεις, the *précis* of a preliminary inquiry, cf. also *Preisigke* 1568 ᾽Α. τὸν συγγενῆ καὶ κτλ. καὶ ἐπιστράτηγον καὶ πρὸς ταῖς ἀνακρίσεσι (reign of Euergetes II.). The noun occurs again in P Tebt I. 86¹ ᶠᶠ (late ii/B.C.), where a man is described as ὁ πρὸς τα[ῖ]ς ἀ]νακρίσεσι. In P Lips I. 4¹⁵ (A.D. 293) the word follows ἀπογραφή, and Mitteis notes that it occurs in P Lond 251 (A.D. 337–50) (= II. p. 317) likewise in connexion with the purchase of a slave: "since ἀνάκρισις means a preliminary examination (*Voruntersuchung*), one thinks of a trial made before the purchase of the slave." Cf. the use of the word in Ac 25²⁶.

ἀνακύπτω.

P Par 47²³ ᶠᶠ. (*c.* B.C. 153) (= *Selections*, p. 23), a very grandiloquent but ill-spelt letter, will illustrate Lk 21²⁸: οὐκ ἔστι ἀνακύψα (*l.* -κύψαι) πόποτε ἐν τῇ Τρικομίαι ὑπὸ τῆς αἰσχύνης, "it is not possible ever to look up again in Triconia for very shame." It appears also in P Ryl I. 28²³ (iv/A.D.), on omens drawn from twitching—one sort portends that the man "will suffer loss for a time and will emerge again from his troubles" (Ed.—ἐκ τῶν κακῶν ἀνακύψει).

ἀναλαμβάνω.

Syll 329⁴⁹ (i/B.C.) ἀναλαβόντας τὰ ὅπλα, "taking up," literally. P Tebt II. 296⁴ ¹⁵ (A.D. 123) has the verb twice = "receive." *OGIS* 383¹³⁵ (see under ἀνάλημψις) κόσμον Περσικῆς ἐσθῆτος ἀ[ν]αλαμβάνων, uses it for the first investiture (with the sacred thread of Parsism, presumably: cf. on this inscr. the Hibbert Lectures, 1912, pp. 106–8). PSI 74⁵ ᶠᶠ (iii/A.D.) ἀξιῶ ἀναλαβόντας παρ᾽ ἐμοῦ τὴν ὁμολογίαν ὑπογεγραμμένην. In P Lille 1. 14⁵ (B.C. 243–2) ἀνάλαβε δ᾽ [οὖν α]ὐτοῦ τὸν κλῆρον εἰς τὸ βασιλικόν. and P Oxy III. 471⁹⁹ (ii/A.D.) τὴν οὐσίαν αὐτοῦ . . . ἀναλημφθῆναι (μ erased) κελεύεις, the verb has the meaning "confiscate": so *Perg* I. 249²⁴ (*ap.* Schweizer *Perg* p. 203). In P Oxy VI. 899³⁷ (A.D. 200) ᾧ ἀνείλημπται ἐπιστολὴ τοῦ κρα[τίστου] δι[ο]ικητοῦ, the editors translate "to which is joined a letter of his highness the dioecetes," and quote *ib.* 985 and BGU I. 168²⁴ τοῖς ὑπομνήμασι ἀνελήμφθη. The participle τὰ ἀνειλημμένα = "obligations" is found P Oxy IV. 707²⁵, ³⁵ (*c.* A.D. 136). Cf. the phrase ἔρανον ἀ., in BGU IV. 1165¹⁵ (B.C. 19), ᾧ ἀγίληφαν [κατὰ συν]γραφὴν

ἐράνῳ. P Lond 905 (ii/A.D.) (= III. p. 219) has ἀναλημπ-θῆναι and the noun ἀνάλημπτες in a very illiterate document. "Repeat," of an advocate setting forth his case, is the meaning in P Tor I. 1ˣⁱ ²⁰ (B.C. 116) (= *Corpⁱ.* II. p. 36) ἀναλαβὼν ἐξ ὧν παρέκειτο ὁ Ἑρμίας "repetens quae Hermias protulit" (Peyron). The Biblical use of "take up" for an ascension into heaven is naturally not paralleled in our sources: for exx. in Jewish writings see Charles's note on *Apoc. of Baruch*, p. 73.

ἀνάλημψις.

P Tebt II. 296¹³ (A.D. 123) is the receipt for money paid for a priestly office, ἐξ ἀναλή[ψεως] ἐν αὐτῷ "as payable by himself" (Edd.): cf. reference to this document under the verb. It means "entertainment" (*s.* one form of "reception") in *Syll* 418³⁶ (iii/A.D.), ἀναγκάζουσιν ἡμᾶς ξενίας αὐτοῖς παρέχειν καὶ ἕτερα πλεῖστα εἰς ἀνάλημψιν αὐτῶν ἄνευ ἀργυρίου χορηγεῖν. P Oxy VI. 086ⁱⁱⁱ. (early ii/A.D.) αὐλὴ δηλ(ωθεῖσα) ἐπικεκρατῆσθαι πρὸ τῆς ἀναλήμψεως ὑπὸ Πετεσούχου. *OGIS* 383¹⁰² —the inscription of Antiochus I. of Commagene (i/B.C.) —ὑπὲρ ἀναλήψεως διαδήματος, his coronation: see also the verb above. The substantive follows the verb's wide range of meaning, which we have only partially illustrated, as needless for the NT. Dr Charles (*l. c.* above) quotes Ryle and James as claiming *Ps. Sol.* 4²⁰ to be the earliest instance of its use (as in Lk 9⁵¹) for "ascension" into heaven.

ἀναλίσκω.

P Flor II. 212⁴ (A.D. 254) εἰς τοσαύτην ἀτυχίαν ἦλθες τοσαῦτα λήμματα ἀναλίσκων ὡς μὴ ἔχειν σε ἀρτά[β]ην μίαν λωτίνου. P Eleph 5²² οἴνου ἀνηλώθησαν κ(εραμία) μγ, P Par 49¹⁹ (B.C. 164–58) μηδὲ ἀναλίσκειν χαλκοῦς, etc. Notice ἀναλουμένων in the same sense, P Lond 1177¹¹ (B.C. 113) (= III. p. 181). P Grenf II. 77¹⁵ (iii/iv A.D.) (= *Selections*, p. 121) φροντίσατε οὖν τὰ ἀναλωθέντα ἑτοιμάσαι, "see to it therefore that you furnish the sums expended." P Oxy I. 58²⁰ (A.D. 288) τὰ μάταια ἀναλώματα π[α]ύσεται, "useless expense will be stopped," with reference to a proposed reduction in the number of treasury officials. The noun ἀνάλωμα (often ἀνήλωμα), which does not happen to occur in NT, is exceedingly common. The verb is an early compound of Ϝαλίσκω, whose simplex survives in the passive ἁλίσκομαι: the ᾱ is due to contraction of -αϜα- after loss of digamma. The meaning *destroy* is therefore parallel with ἀναιρέω. Note aor. ἀνάλωσα P Oxy X. 1295⁸ (ii/iii A.D.).

ἀναλογία.

A iii/A.D. citation may be made from P Flor I. 50⁹¹ κατ[ὰ τὸ] ἥμισυ κατ᾽ ἀναλογίαν τῶν φοινίκων (once πρὸς ἀ.). "proportionately." The verb is found in P Amh II. 64¹³ (A.D. 107) μὴ ἀναλογοῦντας τὴν ἐ[π]ιμέλειαν, which the editors translate "incapable of doing their duties." For adjective see P Amh II. 85¹⁷ ᶠ. (A.D. 78) παραδεχθήσεται ἡμῖν—ἀπὸ τοῦ προκειμένου φόρου κατὰ τὸ ἀνάλογον, "a proportionate allowance shall be made to us from the aforesaid rent" (Edd.): so in *Syll* 329⁶¹ (B.C. 86), and (without τὸ) P Ryl II. 99⁷ (iii/A.D.). Cf. *Syll* 371¹² (i/A.D.) ἀνάλογον πεποίηται τὴν ἐπιδημίαν τῇ . . σεμνότητι. It is open to us to write τὸ ἀνὰ λόγον (Aristotle, etc.), as the editors do in P Ryl II. 154³² (A.D. 66) κατὰ τὸ ἀ. λ. τ[ῶν μ]ηνῶν.

The adjective is only in the first stages of evolution : see LS. The adverb is found in the modern sense "analogously" in Wisd 15[5].

ἀναλογίζομαι.

P Tor I. 1 [v. 30] (B.C. 116) (= *Chrest.* II. p. 35) καὶ ἔφη, ἀναλογιζομένων τῶν χρόνων, ἀπὸ μὲν τοῦ Ἐπιφάνους ἐτῶν κδ κτλ., "told off," "reckoned up." This arithmetical sense —cf. λόγος— "a/e"—is the oldest for the whole group and it would seem that the metaphor was conscious even when the use was widened. So in Heb 12[3] ἀναλογίσασθε immediately follows the reference to the "balancing," as it were, of the προκειμένη χαρά against the tremendous cost. Cf. the simplex in Phil 4[8], where we are bidden to "count over" our spiritual treasure.

ἀναλύω.

For the intransitive meaning "depart" (Polybius and later), cf. P Tor I. 1 [ii. 16] (B.C. 116) (= *Chrest.* II. p. 32) ἐγὼ δὲ ἐφ' ἱκανὰς ἡμέρας καταφθαρεὶς ἠναγκάσθην, τῶν ἀνθρώπων μὴ ἐρχομένων εἰς τὰς χεῖρας, ἀναλῦσαι εἰς τὸ τεταγμένον, "demandatam mihi stationem repetere" (Peyron, and so Mitteis). Closely parallel is the contemporary P Par 15[29] (B.C. 120) οἰομένων ἐφ' ἱκανὸν χρόνον καταφθαρέντα με ἐντεῦθεν ἀναλύσειν. So *ib.* 22[29] (ii/B.C.) ἀποσυλήσας ἡμᾶς ἀνέλυσε, P Lond 44[17] (B.C. 161) (= I. p. 34) μετὰ κραυγῆς τε διαστελλομένου μεθ' ἡσυχίας ἀναλύειν. In a Ptolemaic papyrus published by Grenfell-Hunt in *Archiv* i. p. 59 ff. we find λύσαντες ἐκχρήματα θ ἀνέλυσαν, where the editors note that ἀνέλυσαν may = "they returned" (cf. Lk 12[36]) or may refer to the preceding βασιλικὸν χῶμα, "they destroyed it." For the meaning "die" Nageli, p. 34, cites the memorial inscription *IGSI* 1794[2] (Rom.) καὶ πῶς μοι βεβίωται καὶ πῶς ἀνέλυσα μαθήσ(η), cf. *ib.* 159 ἀναλύειν τὸν βίον.

ἀναμάρτητος.

For ἀ. "sinless," as in Jn 8[7], cf. Musonius, p. 6[16], where it is laid down— μηδένα ἀπαιτεῖσθαι εἶναι ἀναμάρτητον, ὅστις ἀρετὴν μὴ ἐξέμαθεν, ἐπείπερ ἀρετὴ μόνη ποιεῖ μὴ ἁμαρτάνειν ἐν βίῳ. See also Aristeas 252 (*bis*).

ἀναμένω

occurs several times in the Alexandrian papyri of the reign of Augustus, collected in BGU IV. Thus 1151[35] (B.C. 13) μὴ ἀναμείναντας τὸν μεμερισμ(ένον) αὐτοῖς χρό(νον) μέχρι τοῦ ἐκτῖσαι τὸ ὅλον κεφάλ(αιον), and in almost the same terms 1053[i. 33] (*id.*), 1055[29] (*id.*), 1150[18] (B.C. 15), 1167[54] (B.C. 12), of debtors who are to pay up without "waiting for" the time allowed them. The word is MGr.

ἀναμιμνήσκω.

Syll 256[26] (ii/B.C.) ἀναμιμ]νησκόμενοι πατρίων. P Grenf I. 1[ii. 2] (ii/B.C.—literary) ὀδύνη με ἔχει ὅταν ἀναμνησθῶ ὡς κτλ.: so also in [i. 22] μαίνομ' ὅταν ἀναμ[νη]σθῶμ' εἰ μονοκοιτήσω—for the form see Mayser *Gr.* p. 383.

ἀνάμνησις.

In the Magnesian inscr. *Syll* 920[106] (ii/B.C.), unfortunately in this part exceedingly imperfect, we have . . .](σ)ίας καὶ μέχρι τοῦ συστάντος ἐν Κρήτῃ πολέμου, ὧν ἀνά(μνησ)ιν . . . .] (ἐπ)οι(οῦν)το [. . .

ἀνανεόω

occurs very frequently in *Syll* and *OGIS* : its record as an Attic word is noted by Schlageter, p. 25. Nearest to Eph 4[23] is *Syll* 722[13] (later than B.C. 167—from Cnosus, in dialect) ὁμοίως δὲ καὶ τὰν εὔνοιαν ἂν ἔχει ποτὶ (*i. e.* πρὸς) τὰν πόλιν ἀνανεώμενος αὐτῶς (*l.* αὐτός Edd.) τὰν προγονικὰν ἀρετὰν δι' ἐγγράφω ἐπ[έδειξ]ε. So *ib.* 481[30] (iii/ii B.C.) τά τε ἐξ ἀρχῆ[ς] οἰκεῖα ὑπάρ[χοντα Σελευκεῦσι]ν ἐκ προγόνων ἀνε[νε]ώσατο, *ib.* 654[b. 1] (? ii/B.C.) διότι ἁ πόλις τῶν Ἑρμιονέων ἀνανεοῦταί τε τὰν συγγένειαν καὶ φιλίαν κτλ., *OGIS* 90[35] (Rosetta stone, B.C. 196) προσπυνθανόμενός τε τὰ τῶν ἱ[ερῶν τιμιώτατα ἀνανεοῦτο ἐπὶ τῆς ἑαυτοῦ βασιλείας ὡς καθήκει. The substantive may be quoted from papyri. Thus P Oxy II. 274[20] (A.D. 89-97) Σαραπίων τέτακται τε[λος] ἀνανεώ[σ]εως τῆς προκειμένης ὑποθήκης, the charge for a renewal of a mortgage, P Strass I. 52[7] (A.D. 151) μὴ προσδεομένοις ἀνανε[ώ]σεως, and similarly P Flor I. 1[b] (A.D. 153), and *ib.* 81[11] (A.D. 103) : cf. also P Magd 31[7, 12] (B.C. 217). The word seems to be confined to legal phraseology.

ἀναντίρρητος.

So spelt in *OGIS* 335[138] (Pergamon, ii/i B.C.), with the meaning "beyond possibility of dispute," as in Ac 19[36]. Grimm notes that the word begins in Polybius, where the active sense of Ac 10[29] is also paralleled : so in xxiii. 8[11], where Schweighauser renders "summo cunctorum consensu."

ἀνάξιος.

P Strass I. 5[8] (A.D. 262), ἀνάξια [τ]ῆς ὑπὸ σοῦ πᾶσιν ἡμῖν πρυτανευομένης εἰρή[ν]ης ὁ πρεσβύτης παθών. Cf. also Aristeas 217 ἠρώτα δέ, πῶς ἂν μηδὲν ἀνάξιον ἑαυτῶν πράσσοιμεν. The word survives in MGr = "incapable."

ἀνάπαυσις.

In P Flor I. 57[56] (A.D. 223-5) a septuagenarian pleads for "relief" (ἀναπαύσεως) from public duties (λειτουργίαι) ; and in BGU I. 180[6] (ii/iii A.D.) we read of the πεντ[α]ετῆ χρό[ν]ον ἀνα[παύσε]ως accorded to veterans μετὰ τ[ὴν ἀπό]λυσιν from military service. As will be seen from the record of the verb below, the essential idea is that of a respite, or *temporary* rest as a preparation for future toil, which Lightfoot (on Philem[7]) finds in ἀναπαύω. This brings out all the better the differentia of κατάπαυσις in Heb 4, the Sabbath followed by no weekday.

ἀναπαύω.

The verb is a technical term of agriculture in P Tebt I. 105[23] (B.C. 103), to rest land by sowing light crops upon it. Cf P Lond 314[15. 1] (A.D. 149) (= II. p. 189 f.), σπείρων . . . ἀρ]ούρας δύο ἀπὸ νότου ἀναπαύμεσι γέ[νε]σι, P Amh II. 91[16] (A.D. 159) γένεσι ἀναπαύματος, "with light crops" (Edd.), and the full discussion by Wilcken *Archiv* i. p. 157 f. Land thus rested was ἐν ἀναπαύματι, P Tebt I. 72[389] (B.C. 114-3), P Lond 1223[8] (A.D. 121) (= III. p. 139), or could be called ἀνάπαυμα itself, as P Fay 112[4] (A.D. 99) [τὰ] ἀναπαύματα ὑπόσχεισον, "hoe the fallows" (Edd.). A wider use may be seen in P Oxy VIII. 1121[12] (A.D. 295), with the "temporary" connotation gone : ταύτης πρὸ ὀλίγων τούτων ἡμερῶν τὸν βίον ἀναπαυσαμένης ἀδιαθέτου, "a few days ago she died intestate" (Edd.) So in

Preisigke 1205, upon a mummy, ἐν Ἀλεξανδρείᾳ ἀναπαυσά-μενος, and *ib.* 609, 611, two "R.I.P." Christian gravestones — κ(ύρι)ε, ἀνάπα[υ]σον [? τὴν ψυχὴν τοῦ δούλου σου, or the like], followed by date of death, and Ἀθ(α)νασία, ἀναπα[ύ]ου. The date of these instances saves us from the necessity of reconsidering Lightfoot's definition for NT times.

ἀναπείθω.

This verb = "persuadendo excitare, sollicitare," which in the NT is found only in Ac 18[13], is well illustrated by P Magd 14[3 f.] (B.C. 221) where a father lodges a complaint against a courtesan who had induced his son to sign a bill in her favour for 1000 drachmas—παραστησαμένη γάρ τινας [τῶν παρ'] αὐτῆς, ἀνέπεισεν τὸν υἱόν μου . . . συγγράψασθαι αὐτῆι κτλ. So P Oxy X. 1205[10] (ii/iii A.D.). The sense of evil persuasion equally underlies the use in LXX Jer 36 (29)[8], 1 Macc 1[11]. In P Ryl II. 114[8] (c. A.D. 280) the *nuance* is weaker, but survives in the complaining tone of the aggrieved widow who writes Συρίων . . . ἀναπίσας τὸν ἄν[δ]ρα Γανίδα ὀνό[μ]ατι ποιμένιν αὐτοῦ τὰ πρόβατα, "persuaded my husband G. to pasture his flock" (Edd.).

ἀναπέμπω.

To Deissmann's examples of this word (*BS* p. 229) = "remittere," "to send up to a higher authority," as in Lk 23[7], Ac 25[21], add P Hib I. 57[1] (B.C. 247), *Syll* 177[51,107] (end of iii/B.C.), *OGIS* 194[-3] (i/B.C.), *ib.* 329[51] (ii/B.C.). *Priene* 111[147] (i/B.C.) περὶ ὧν ὁ στρατηγὸς Λεύκιος Λε[υ]κίλιος ἔγραψεν] καὶ ἀνέπεμψεν [πρὸς τὴν σ]ύγκλητον, P Tebt I. 7[7] (B.C. 114), *ib.* II. 287[6] (A.D. 161-9) ἐνέτυχον τῷ ἡγεμόνι καὶ ἀνέπεμψεν αὐτοὺς ἐπὶ Κρασσὸν τὸν κράτιστον [ἐπιστράτη-γ]ον, "they appealed to the prefect, who referred them to his highness the epistrategus Crassus" (Edd.), *ib.* 504 (iii/A.D.) a warrant for arrest, *al.* Similarly the phrase ἐξ ἀναπομπῆς is used of the "delegation" of a case from one authority to another, e.g. BGU I. 19[2] (A.D. 135), CPR 18[2] (A.D. 124): see further *Archiv* iii. p. 74. For the alternative meaning "to send back" (Lk 23[15], Philem[12]). Cf. P Par 13[24] (B.C. 157) οὐκ ἀναπέμψαντες τὴν φερνήν. P Oxy VII. 1032[50] (A.D. 162) ἀνέπεμψεν καὶ τοῦτο ἐπί σε.

ἀναπίπτω.

For the later meaning "lie down," "recline," of which there is no instance in Attic Greek (Rutherford *NP* p. 294), see P Par 51[4 ff.] (B.C. 160) (= *Selections* p. 19), ἀναπίπτο-μαι ἐπ' ἄχυρον . . . ἀναπίπτει καὶ αὐτός. (On the irregular voice, see *Proleg.* p. 159.) Cf. LXX Gen 49[9] ἀναπεσὼν ἐκοιμήθης ὡς λέων : see Anz *Subsidia*, p. 301 f.

ἀναπληρόω.

OGIS 56[18] (B.C. 238) ὅπως ἅπαντες εἰδῶσιν διότι τὸ ἐνλεῖπον πρότερον (as to the calendar) διωρθῶσθαι καὶ ἀναπεπληρῶσθαι συμβέβηκεν διὰ τῶν Εὐεργετῶν θεῶν : the first word describes *correction*, the second *intercalation*. On P Par 62[v.3] (ii/B.C.) τοῖς δ' ἀναπληρώσουσιν τὰς ὠνὰς δο-θήσεται ὀψώνια, ἐάνπερ ἐκπληρώσουσιν κτλ, "those who complete the contracts," see Wilcken *Ostr.* i. p. 532 f., who explains the ὀψώνια (against Grenfell) as a commission of 10%. The noun occurs in P Lond 890[4] (B.C. 6) (= III. p. 168) εἰς ἀναπλήρωσιν τιμῆς, and the verb in *Syll* 510[62] (ii/B.C.) τὸ γενόμενον διάπτωμα ἀναπληρούτωσαν : cf. P Petr III.

54 (a) (3)[4] (Philadelphus) ἀναπληρούτωσα[ν], but with a hiatus both before and after. In P Lille I. 8[14] (iii/B.C.) a petitioner demands the restoration of certain cattle that had been taken from him, that he may "make up" his rent— ὅ[π]ως δύνωμαι ἀναπληροῦν τὰ ἐ[κ]φόρια τῆς γῆς. P Giss I. 48[39] (A.D. 203) ἵν' εἰδῆτε καὶ ἕκαστος τὰ ἴδια μέρη ἀνα-πληρώσει seems from the context to have the same meaning ("pay"), though a more general sense is also possible. The same formula is found in *Chrest.* I. 52[8] (A.D. 194). The meaning "fulfil" may be seen in P Oxy VIII. 1121[11] (A.D. 295) οὐκ ἐπαυσάμην τὰ πρέποντα γείνεσθαι ὑπὸ τέκνων γονεῦσι ἀναπληροῦσα.

ἀνάπτω.

P Giss I. 3[8] (meant to be literary—A.D. 117) τοιγαροῦν θύοντες τὰς ἑστίας ἀνάπτωμεν. P Leid W[xx.35] (occult) ἀνάψας τῷ βωμῷ (*l.* τὸν βωμόν. (MGr ἀνάφτω.)

ἀνασείω.

P Tebt I. 28[20] (c. B.C. 114) ὑπ' αὐτ[ῶν] τούτων ἀνασιόμενοι εὐμαρεστέρα[ν] ἀσχολί[αν], "may be thereby incited to make easier for us the performance of our duty" (Edd.), *i.e.* to the Government—a curious contrast to the normal connotation of the verb, as in Mk 15[11], Lk 23[5]. For the literal meaning see *Syll* 789[36] (iv/B.C.) ὁ δ' ἐπ[ι]σ[τ]ά[τη]ς [ἀνασ]είσας τ[ὴ]ν ὑδρίαν τὴν χαλκὴν ἑλκέτω τὸν καττ[ό]-τ[ε]ρον ἑκάτερον ἐμ μέρει.

ἀνασκευάζω.

P Oxy IV. 745[5] (c. A.D. 1) μ[ὴ] . . . πάλιν ἑατοὺς ἀνα-σκευάζωμε[ν] μὴ οὔσης χρής, "and we go bankrupt again without any necessity" (Edd.). This really involves the meaning "subvert" found in Ac 15[24], drawn from the military sense, "to plunder," "dismantle" a town. Vettius Valens has the word twice : p. 212[20], ἐὰν δόξῃ τις ἐν αὐταῖς ταῖς ἡμέραις ἐκπλοκήν τινα πεποιηκέναι πράγματός τινος, ἀνασκευασθήσεται καὶ ἐπιτάραχον γενήσεται καὶ ἐπιζήμιον ἢ εὐκαθαίρετον καὶ προσκοπτικόν, and 283[23] τῷ δὲ λθ ἔτει τοῦ πράγματος ἀνασκευασθέντος διὰ τὴν προϋπάρχουσαν ἔχθραν εἰς νῆσον κατεδικάσθη. Kroll (Index *s.v.*) makes it here "t. t. iudiciorum," the "reversal" of a judgement presumably. The noun (p. 228[27]) ἀνασκευασμοὺς τηκτῶν πραγμάτων does not look technical—"upset" would seem to represent it, as in the phrase ἀνασκευαὶ πραγμάτων (four times).

ἀνασπάω.

In P Tebt II. 420[25] (iii/A.D.) ἀνασπασθῇ is used with regard to the "pulling up" (?) of barley, with which the editors compare BGU III. 1041[8] (ii/A.D.) ἔτι δὲ καὶ ἀνεσπά-σθη σου ἡ κριθὴ ἀρτ[ά]β[αι] ιε̄ : we may add P Flor II. 235[5] (A.D. 266) ἀνασπῶντι πυρόν.

ἀνάστασις.

The verb is frequent in inscriptions with the sense "erec-tion" of a monument, see *Syll* 324[8], 342[48] (both i/B.C.), *C. and B.* ii. p. 637 (A.D. 70-80), *IMAe* iii. 478, 479, 481 (all ii/A.D.), *Magn* 179[24 f.], 193[25], and for the verb *Syll* 656[71], 686[4] (both ii/A.D.), *al.* So still in A.D. 215, BGU I. 362[vii.3] (= *Chrest.* I. p. 128) ὑπὲρ ἀνα[στάσεω]ς the "setting up" of a statue of Severus, and probably *ib.* IV. 1028[6] (ii/A.D.) ὁλκῆς μν[ῶ]ν δ πρὸς ἀ[νά]στασιν [. . ., but the context is not clear. The narrative of Ac 17 (see v. ³²) prepares us for the total novelty of the meaning "resurrection": it was a perfectly natural use of the word, but the idea itself was new. We find this meaning in *C. and B.* no. 232 (= *Cagnat* IV. 743, Alexander Severus), where an Epicurean Jew of Eumeneia in Phrygia begins to tell us what he thought of ο]ἵ δὴ δ[είλ]αιοι πάντ[ες] εἰς ἀ[νά]στασιν . . . (βλέποντες or the like): see Ramsay's interesting notes.

ἀναστατόω.

"Nowhere in profane authors," says Grimm. Its place in the vernacular is proved, however, with singular decisiveness by a private letter almost contemporary with the Biblical citations. BGU IV. 1079²⁰ (A.D. 41) (= *Selections,* p. 40), μὴ ἵνα ἀναστατώσῃς ἡμᾶς, "do not drive us out," and later by the boy's letter, P Oxy I. 119¹⁹ (ii/iii A.D.) (= *Selections,* p. 103) ἀναστατοῖ με · ἄρρον (*l.* ἆρον) αὐτόν, "he quite upsets me—off with him": cf. also P Strass I. 5¹⁶ (A.D. 262) ἀν[άσ]τατον τὸν πρ[ε]σβύτην π[ε]ποίηντα[ι]—a reversion to the classical locution.

ἀναστρέφομαι.

The old meaning "reverti" may be seen in P Tebt I. 25¹³ (B.C. 117) ἀνεστραμμένως δαινεκθέντες (*l.* διενεχ·), "perversely." Deissmann (*BS* pp. 88, 194) has shown that for the meaning "behave," which Grimm compared with the moral signification of הָלַךְ "walk," it is unnecessary to postulate Semitic influence. As his examples are all from Pergamon, we may add others to show that it was no local peculiarity. OGIS 48⁸ (iii/B.C.) ὁρῶντές τινας τῶν πολιτῶν [μ]ὴ ὀρθῶς ἀνα[στρ]ε[φ]ομένους καὶ θόρυβον οὐ τὸν τυχόντα παρ[έχ]οντας is from Egypt, and *Syll* 521⁹⁵ (B.C. 100) τοῖς καλῶς καὶ εὐσεβῶς ἀναστραφεῖσιν is from Athens. In *JBL* xxvii. ii. p. 136 Hatch cites the following instances from the *Proceedings of the American School of Classical Studies at Athens,* iii. 73 (Dulgerler, ancient Artanada, in Cilicia, Imperial period) ἀγνῶς ἀναστραφέντα, iii. 423 (Kara Baulo in Pisidia, probably Imperial) ἀναστραφέντας . . . μεγαλοπρεπῶς καὶ εὐσχημόνως. Cf. also *Priene* 108²²⁴ (after B.C. 129) τῆι πόλε(ι) συμφερόντως ἀνεστράφη, *ib.* 115⁵ (i/B.C.) ἀναστρεφόμενος ἐν πᾶσιν φιλ[ανθρώπως]. P Amh II. 131¹¹ (early ii/A.D.) has ἀ. περί in the sense "attend to": cf. P Gen I. 6⁸ (A.D. 146), ἀναστρ[α]φέντος μου πε[ρὶ] τὴν τούτων ἀπαίτησιν, P Fay 12⁷ (*c.* B.C. 103) τῶν . . . οὐ ἀπὸ τοῦ βελτ[ί]στου ἀναστρεφομένων, "being of the less reputable class" (Edd.). In P Oxy II. 237 ⁷¹ ²¹ (A.D. 186) μεταπαθῶς ἀναστραφ[έν]τα is translated "being sympathetically disposed," *ib.* VI. 907¹⁷ (A.D. 276) πρεπόντως περὶ τὴν συμβίωσιν ἀναστραφείσῃ is "who has conducted herself becomingly in our married life" (Edd.), and *ib.* I.71 ii. 12 (A.D. 303) μὴ ὀρθῶς ἀναστραφέντες is "behaved dishonestly," P Lond 358¹² (*c.* A.D. 150) (= II. p. 172) αὐθάδως ἀναστραφέντων. Instances can be multiplied. Vettius Valens (see Kroll's Index) has the verb in this sense in the active, as well as in the middle.

ἀναστροφή.

The somewhat formal use of ἀ., with the meaning "behaviour, conduct," is not balanced by occurrences in colloquial papyri: an edict of Caracalla (A.D. 215) has the word—ἔτι τε

καὶ ζω[ὴ] δεικνύει ἐναντία ἔθη ἀπὸ ἀναστροφῆς [πο]λειτικῆς εἶναι ἀγροίκους Α[ἰ]γυπτίους (P Giss I. 40ii. ²⁸). Bp E. L. Hicks's pioneer paper in *CR* i. (1887), p. 6. drew attention to the inscriptional use of the term: he noted the frequency of its association with words like πάροικοι and παρεπίδημοι, a curious parallel to 1 Pet 2¹¹ ʳ. Kälker *Quaest.,* p. 301 says "apud Polybium primum accipit notionem *se gerendi,*" quoting iv. 82¹ κατὰ τ. λοιπὴν ἀ. τεθαυμασμένος, and referring to three inscrr. with ἀ. ποιεῖσθαι. This last phrase however occurs in five Doric inscrr. of ii/B.C., to look no further than *Syll* (314²¹, 654¹⁹, 663⁹, 718⁴, 927²¹), as well as in the Attic inscr. cited by Kälker (*l.c.*) (*CIA* 477ᵇ ¹²); so that we may safely assume that the locution had become widely current in the Κοινή before Polybius used it. Apart from ἀ. ποιεῖσθαι as a periphrasis for ἀναστρέφεσθαι, we can quote *Syll* 491⁵ κατά τε τὰν ἐμπειρίαν καὶ τὰν ἄλλαν ἀνα[σ]τροφάν, and 663¹⁴ ἀ. ἔχειν (as in 1 Pet 1¹²)—both ii/B.C. The Index to OGIS has "ἀναστροφή—*passim.*" In view of this frequency, and the plentiful record of ἀναστρέφεσθαι, the absence of the noun from papyri is rather marked. It may only mean that it was not current in Egypt.

ἀνατάσσομαι.

The only passage from profane literature which has as yet been cited for this verb, Plut. *Moral.* 968 CD, where an elephant is described as "rehearsing" by moonlight certain tricks it had been taught (πρὸς τὴν σελήνην ἀνατατττόμενος τὰ μαθήματα καὶ μελετῶν), makes it probable that it is to be understood = "bring together," "repeat from memory" in Lk 1¹: see Blass *Philology of the Gospels,* p. 14 ff., and cf. *ExpT* xviii. p. 396. In OGIS 213²⁴ (iv/iii. B.C.) the hitherto unknown substantive ἀνατάκται is found as the designation of certain magistrates at Miletus, whom Dittenberger gathers to have been charged with disbursements to the authorities for their several public works.

ἀνατέλλω.

Michel 466¹⁰ (iii/B.C.) ἄμα τῶι ἡλίωι [ἀν]ατέλλοντι. "at daybreak." It is curious that the astrologer Vettius Valens has no instance of the verb, though he uses its derivatives freely. It survives in MGr. The cpd ἐπανατέλλω occurs in some would-be verse on the wall of a sepulchral vault at Ramleh, age of the Antonines: *Preisigke* 2134—

Ἀστὴρ οὐράνιος ὁ ἐπὶ ἀστέρι ἐπανατέλλων
ἐσπάσθη.

ἀνατίθημι.

Note the perfect active ἀνατέθηκα in *Syll* 604¹⁰ (Pergamon, end of iii/B.C.). This is a later example of what is now known to be the classical form of the perfect of τίθημι, which only in the Hellenistic age was replaced by τέθεικα. The late sense "impart," "communicate," with a view to consultation, found in the two NT occurrences of the word (Ac 25¹⁴, Gal 2² ; cf. 2 Macc 3⁹) seems to appear in P Par 60ii ²³ (A.D. 233) ἀναθέμενοι τὸ πρᾶγμα ἀκ[έραιον]. In P Strass I. 41⁷ (A.D. 250) ὥστε οὐκ ἂν ἔχοι ἀναθέσθαι τὴν δίκη[ν εἰς ἑτέραν ἡμέραν] the verb = "postpone." The active = "dedicate" occurs everywhere.

ἀνατολή.

For the use of the plural to denote "the east," found unambiguously in Mt 2¹ (cf. 8¹¹, 24²⁷, Lk 13²⁹), we can quote the new parchment from Media, presumably the home of these Magi, P Saïd Khan 2[a].8 (B.C. 22), where we read ὅρια καὶ γειτνίαι ἀπὸ τῶν ἀνατολῶν. Cf. also the Alexandrian sundial inscription in *Preisigke* 358[2] (iii/B.C.) περιφερειῶν τῶν ἐφεξῆς τῶν διατεινουσῶν ἀπ' ἀνατολῶν ἐπὶ δύσεις. For the same phrase without the ellipsis, as in Rev 7[2] Α ἀπὸ ἀνατολῶν ἡλίου, cf. *OGIS* 225[41] (iii/B.C.) ἀπὸ ἡλίου ἀνατολῶν. For the singular in the same sense see *OGIS* 199[2] (i/A.D.), where ἀπὸ ἀνατολῆς is opposed to ἀπὸ δύσεως, and *Syll* 740[25] (A.D. 212) ᾧ γείτον[ε]ς [ἀπ]ὸ μὲν ἀνατολῆς [οἱ]'Επαφρᾶ κληρ[όνομοι]. The more literal sense—which seems probable in Mt 2[2, 9], from the otherwise motiveless substitution of sing. for plural—appears in the calendar of P Hib I. 27[45] (B.C. 301–240) πρὸς τὰς δόσεις (*l.* δύσεις) καὶ ᾇ[να]τολὰς τῶν ἄστρω[ν], and in P Tebt II. 276[38] (ii/iii A.D.) [ἐν τῇ ἑ]ῴα ἀνατολῇ, the heliacal rising of Venus. Time, instead of point of compass, is indicated in P Oxy IV. 725[12] (A.D. 183) ἀπὸ ἀν[ατολῆς] ἡ[λίου] μέχρι δύσεως, P Ryl I. 27[63] (astronomical—iii/A.D.) μετὰ ᾱ ὥραν ἔγγιστα τῆς τοῦ (ἡλίου) ἀνα[το]λῆς, "1 hr. approximately after sunrise" (Ed.). Similarly in BGU IV. 1021[13] (iii/A.D.) where, in apprenticing a slave to a hairdresser for instructions, his master undertakes to produce him daily ἀπὸ ἀνατολῆς ἡλίου μέχρι δύσεως τρεφόμενον καὶ ἱμ[α]τιζόμενον. A nearly identical phrase in the "shorter conclusion" of Mark presumably has the other meaning—αὐτὸς ὁ Ἰησοῦς ἀπὸ ἀνατολῆς καὶ ἄχρι δύσεως ἐξαπέστειλεν δι' αὐτῶν τὸ ἱερὸν καὶ ἄφθαρτον κήρυγμα τῆς αἰωνίου σωτηρίας. In MGr it means either "east" or "Asia Minor."

ἀνατρέπω.

With Tit 1[11] οἵτινες ὅλους οἴκους ἀνατρέπουσιν διδάσκοντες ἃ μὴ δεῖ αἰσχροῦ κέρδους χάριν, we may compare P Par 63[ix. 35] (ii/B.C.) τῆς πατρικῆς οἰκίας . . . ἔτι ἔνπροσθεν ἄρδην [ἀ]νατετραμμένης δι' ἀσ[ω]τίας. The literal meaning is found in P Oxy I. 69[2] (A.D. 190) φέρουσαν εἰς δημοσίαν ῥύμην ἀνατρέψαντας, "they broke down (a door) leading into the public street," and *Syll* 801[9] (ii/A.D.) εἰς γῆν ἀνατρέψαι: the inscription quotes the LXX. but is pagan. For the subst. see P Oxy VI. 902[11] (*c.* A.D. 465) εἰς τελείαν γὰρ ἀνατροπὴν . . . περιέστην, "I have been reduced to complete ruin" (Edd.).

ἀναφαίνω.

The verb occurs in the interesting Christian letter, P Oxy VI. 939[1] (iv/A.D.) θεοῦ γνῶσις ἀνεφάνη ἅπασιν ἡμῖν: cf. Lk 19[11] παραχρῆμα μέλλει ἡ βασιλεία τοῦ θεοῦ ἀναφαίνεσθαι. From iii/A.D. comes the *defixio* in Wünsch *AF*, no. 4[37], τὸν μονογενῆ, τὸν ἐξ αὐτοῦ ἀναφανέντα, of a god who receives the names Ωη Ἰάω εεηαφ.

ἀναφάλαντος.

This LXX word (Lev 13[41]) in the sense of "bald on the forehead" frequently recurs in personal descriptions in Ptolemaic wills, e. g. P Petr I. 20(1)[10] (B.C. 225) θ]ρὶξ ἀναφάλανθος.

ἀναφέρω.

With reference to the use of this verb in 1 Pet 2[24], Deissmann has argued (*BS* p. 88 ff.) that the writer may have had in view the forensic usage to denote the imposing

of the debts of another upon a third, in order to free the former from payment: he compares P Petr I. 16(2)[10] (B.C. 237) περὶ δὲ ὧν ἀντιλέγω ἀναφερομέν[ων εἰς ἐμὲ] ὀφειλημάτων κριθήσομαι ἐπ' Ἀσκληπιάδου, "as to the debts laid upon (or against) one, against which I protest, I shall let myself be judged by Asclepiades." Any direct suggestion of substitution or expiation would thus be foreign to the Petrine passage, the writer's thought being simply that the sins of men were removed from them, and *laid upon* the cross. On *Syll* 813[11] ἀνένεγκα[ι] αὐτὸς παρὰ Δ[άμ]ατρα (*sc.* garments deposited with some one who refused to return them), Dittenberger suggests somewhat doubtfully that the objects are, as it were, brought to the goddess as evidence of the wrong done. The meaning would then be closely akin to that in P Petr II 38 (*b*)[5] ὅπως ἀνενέγκωμεν ἐπὶ Θεογένην, "that we may report it to Theogenes," *ib.* III. 46 (1)[5] ἕως ἂν ἐπὶ τὸν διοικητὴν ἀνενέγκωμεν, 104[5] ἀνενήνοχεν ἐφ' ἡμᾶς . . . συγγραφήν, "has submitted to us a contract" (Edd.), *et alibi*. Here we have the verb followed by ἐπί c. accusative, but the accusative is of a *person*, a difference which also seriously weakens the applicability of the parallel drawn by Deissmann for 1 Pet 2[24]. We must not further discuss this difficult passage here.

One or two miscellaneous examples of the verb may be added. It is used of "transference" from a village prison to the prison of the metropolis in P Lille I. 7[15] (iii/B.C.) νυνὶ δὲ ἀνενήνοχέν με εἰς τὸ ἐν Κροκοδίλων πό[λει] δεσμωτήριον, and of the "registration" of the death of a priest in the official list in P Lond 281[15] (A.D. 66) = (II. p. 66) ὅπως ἀνενεχθῇ ἐν [τοῖς] τετελευτη᾽κό᾽σι. In P Ryl II. 163[13] (A.D. 139) ὁπηνίκα ἐὰν αἱρῇ ἀνοίσω δημοσίῳ [χρηματισμῷ] is rendered "whenever you choose, I will make the notification by an official deed": see parallels in the note, showing ἀναφέρω and ἀναφορά to be "vague terms" covering a variety of forms of documentation where an official reference is implied. The verb is common in connexion with the payment of monies, e. g. P Lille I. 11[6] (iii/B.C.) of grain; P Gen I. 22[4] (A.D. 37–8), P Flor I. 1[.3 30] (A.D. 153), P Tebt II. 399[13] (both ii/A.D.). Other occurrences are *Syll* 588[115] (ii/B.C.), *Michel* 1007[10] (ii/B.C.) οὐδεμίαν ἀνενέγκαντες τῶι κοινῶι δαπάνην, P Rein 26[15] (B.C. 104) ἅμα τῇ συγγραφῇ ταύτῃ ἀναφερομένῃ, BGU IV. 1124[5] (B.C. 18) ἣν ἀνενηόχασιν αὐτῶι . . . συνχώρησιν (cf. 1157[8]), P Lond 1170 *verso* [81] (A.D. 258–9) (= III. p. 195).

The subst. **ἀναφορά** (which is MGr) is common in the sense of "instalment," e. g. P Hib I. 114[4] (B.C. 244) [ἔσ]τιν δὲ ἡ ἀναφορὰ ἀπὸ Μεχεὶρ [ἕω]ς Φαῶφι μηνῶν θ κτλ., "the instalment for the nine months from Mecheir to Phaophi is . . ." P Eleph 17[19 ff.] (B.C. 223–2) ἧς τὴν πρώτην ἀναφορὰν καταβεβλήκασιν . . . διὰ τὸ μὴ ἰσχύειν αὐτοὺς καταβαλεῖν τὰς λοιπὰς ἀναφοράς, P Lond 286[18] (A.D. 88) (= II. p. 184) ἃς κ(αὶ) διαγράψωμεν ἐν ἀναφοραῖς δέκα κατὰ μ[ῆνα], P Iand 26[18] (A.D. 98) τὸν [δὲ] φόρον ἀποδόσω ἐ[ν ἀν]αφοραῖς τέσσαρσι. In P Oxy I. 67[4] (A.D. 338) it means "petition"—ἐνέτυχον διὰ ἀναφορᾶς τῷ κυρίῳ μου κτλ.

ἀναφωνέω.

A weakened meaning occurs in P Fay 14[2] (B.C. 124) τοῦ ἀναπεφωνημένου Νουμηνίῳ στεφάνου, "the crown tax decreed for Numenius."

ἀναχρονίζω

in the sense of χρονίζω occurs in the illiterate P Tebt II. 413[11] (ii/iii A.D.) ἀναχρονίζομεν [σ]οι πέμποντες ἐπιστόλια, "we are late in sending you letters" (Edd.). The papyrus has other examples of the tendency of uneducated persons to use compounds: NT critics may remember this when they assume the *littérateur's* hand in some of Luke's "emendations" (?) of Q.

ἀνάχυσις

For the metaphorical use of this word in 1 Pet 4[4] εἰς τὴν αὐτὴν τῆς ἀσωτίας ἀνάχυσιν we may cite Philo *Somn.* II. 42 ἀ. τοῦ ἀλόγου πάθους. We have no vernacular parallels.

ἀναχωρέω

is applied to the "falling" of the Nile in P Magd 11[15] (B.C. 221) τοῦ ὕδατος ἀναχωροῦντος, as is the substantive in P Petr II. 13 (19)[9] (c. B.C. 252) (= Witkowski[2], p. 10) τὴ]ν ἀνα[χώ]ρησιν τοῦ ποταμοῦ. In the census return BGU II. 447[6] (A.D. 173–4) the name of a man is included who was at the time ἐν ἀναχωρήσει, "away from home" ("bleibende Entfernung," Wessely *Karanis*, p. 34). See Wilcken *Ostr.* i. p. 448, and for the same meaning of "absence" cf. P Tebt II. 353[6] (A.D. 192) ἀπ' ἀναχωρήσεως κατισεληλυθώς. In P Tebt I. 41[14] (c. B.C. 119) certain βασιλικοὶ γεωργοί petition against one Marres, stating that on account of his extortion they had gone on strike and taken refuge in the neighbouring villages—ἀνακεχωρήκαμεν εἰς τὰς περιοίκας κώμας: cf. P Oxy II. 252[9] (A.D. 19–20) ἀνεχώρησεν [εἰς τὴν] ξένην, *Syll* 802[117] (iii/B.C.) τοῦτο ποιήσας εἰς τὸ ἄβατον ἀνεχώρησε, and the late Sileo rescript *OGIS* 201[9] (vi/A.D.) ἀναχωρήθην εἰς τὰ ἄνω μέρη μου. P Lille I. 3[26] (B.C. 241) ἀνακεχώρηκε[ν . . .] ἔτη is rendered by Wilcken "er is geflohen" (*Archiv* v. p. 222): he remarks that the Christian ἀναχωρηταί were those who "fled" from the world— "retire" is too weak for ἀναχωρέω. The connotation of "taking refuge" from some peril will suit most of the NT passages remarkably well.

ἀναψύχω

In P Lond 42[18] (B.C. 168) (= I. p. 30, *Selections* p. 10) we have an urgent appeal to a man who has become a recluse in the Serapeum: his wife writes to him, δο[κο]ύσα ν[ῦ]γ [γ]ὲ σοῦ παραγενομένου τεύξεσθαί τινος ἀναψυχῆς, "thinking that now at last on your return I should obtain some relief." The noun, which is classical and occurs several times in the LXX along with the corresponding verb (cf. 2 Tim 1[16]), is found also in P Vat A[15] (B.C. 168) (= Witkowski[2], p. 65)—a letter to the same recluse by his brother, obviously in collusion with the wife. For the verb see P Oxy X. 1296[7] (iii/A.D.) φιλοπονοῦμεν καὶ ἀναψύχομεν "I am industrious and take relaxation" (Edd.). See Anz *Subsidia*, p. 303.

ἀνδραποδιστής

For the original noun cf. BGU IV. 1059[9] (Aug.) ταξαμένη τὸ τέλος εἰς τὰ ἀ., "having paid the slave-duty," and *Syll* 825[2] (iv/B.C.) ὅρος ἐργαστηρίου καὶ ἀνδραπόδων πεπραμένων ἐπὶ λύσει: workshop and slaves attached to it, sold "à réméré" (Michel). *OGIS* 218[62], [110] (iii/B.C.) has ἀνδράποδα in a catalogue of property, *ib.* 773[1] (iv/iii B.C.) τῶν ἀ. [τ]ῶν ἀποδράντων, also *ib.* 629[22] (A.D. 137) *ex suppl.* It also

occurs in a psephism of Apamea (or a neighbouring town) of the reign of Augustus: ἀνδράποδα δὲ καὶ τετράποδα καὶ λοιπὰ ζῷα ὁμοίως πωλείσθω. This last combination reminds us of the etymology of the word, which is merely an analogy-formation from τετράποδα, with which it is so often associated—just as *electrocute* is made out of *execute*, to take a modern instance of a common resource of language. The word, which was normally plural (sing. in P Cattaoui [5.16] = *Chrest.* II. p. 423, ii/A.D.), was never an ordinary word for *slave*: it was too brutally obvious a reminder of the principle which made quadruped and human chattels differ only in the number of their legs. The derivative ἀνδραποδίζω, "kidnap" supplied an agent noun with the like odious meaning, which alone appears in NT (1 Tim 1[10]). See also Philo *de Spec. Leg.* IV. 13 (p. 338 M.) κλέπτης δέ τίς ἐστι καὶ ὁ ἀνδραποδιστής, ἀλλὰ τοῦ πάντων ἀρίστου, ὅσα ἐπὶ γῆς εἶναι συμβέβηκεν.

Ἀνδρέας

To the occurrences of this Greek name we may add *Syll* 391[1], a memorial inscription of ii/B.C. —Ἀνδρέας καὶ Ἀριστό-μαχος Ἀργεῖοι ἐποίησαν. The form Ἀνδρήας is found in *Priene* 313[50] (i/B.C.).

ἀνδρίζομαι

P Petr II. 40 (a)[12] (c. B.C. 233) (= Witkowski[2], p. 41) μὴ οὖν ὀλιγοψυχήσητε, ἀλλ' ἀνδρ.ζεσθε—a good parallel to 1 Cor 16[13]. Cf. also BGU IV. 1205[13] (B.C. 28) μόνον ἀνδρα-γάθι ἐν τῆι ἀριθμήσε[ι, "work hard" or the like (διανδρ. in *ib.* 1205[13], etc., P Oxy II. 291[8] (A.D. 25–6) καὶ προέγραψ[ά σοι] ἀνδραγαθί[ν], "I have already written to you to be firm" (Edd.). The adj. ἀνδρεῖος is found in a eulogy on the good deeds of the Emperor Aurelian, P Lips I. 119[ii. 3] (A.D. 274) τηλικαῦτα ἀθρόως ἔχοντας ἀγαθὰ παρὰ τῆς ἀκηράτου μεγαλοδωρίας τοῦ ἀνδριστάτου τῶν πώποτε Αὐτο-κρατόρων Αὐρηλιανοῦ. The subst. is defined in Aristeas 199 (ed. Wendland) τί πέρας ἀνδρείας ἐστίν; ὁ δὲ εἶπεν· εἰ τὸ βουλευθὲν ὀρθῶς ἐν ταῖς τῶν κινδύνων πράξεσιν ἐπιτελοῖτο κατὰ πρόθεσιν, "'What is the the true aim of courage?' And he said, 'To execute in the hour of danger, in accord-ance with one's plan, resolutions that have been rightly formed'" (Thackeray). Cf. *OGIS* 339[71] (c. B.C. 120) προ-τρεπόμενος δὲ διὰ τῆς τοιαύτης φιλοδοξίας πρὸς ἄσκησιν καὶ φιλοπονίαν τοὺς νέους, ἐξ ὧν αἱ τῶν νεωτέρων ψυχαὶ πρὸς ἀνδρείαν ἁμιλλώμεναι καλῶς ἄγονται τοῖς ἤθεσιν πρὸς ἀρετήν.

Ἀνδρόνικος

A proper name widely used throughout the Empire: cf. *Syll* III. Index p. 11, and *Priene* 313 (i/B.C.).

ἀνδροφόνος

For this NT ἄπ. εἰρ. (1 Tim 1[9]) cf. *OGIS* 218[99] (iii/B.C.) τοὺς τὴμ ψῆφ[ον προσθεμ]ένους ἀνδροφόνους εἶναι. It appears in a metrical epitaph from Corcyra (before B.C. 227), *Kaibel* 184[4] λῃστὰς ἀνδροφόνους.

ἀνέγκλητος

In P Oxy II. 281[12] (A.D. 20–50), a petition to the ἀρχι-δικαστής, a woman who had been deserted by her husband claims—παντελῶς ὄντα ἀνέγκλητον ἐματὴν ἐν ἅπασει παρει-χόμην, "I for my part conducted myself blamelessly in all respects" (Edd.): cf. *Syll* 429[14] (iii/B.C.) ἀνένκλητον ἑαυτὸν παρεσχηκὼς πρὸς πάντας τοὺς φυλέτας. For the adverb see P Magd 15³ (B.C. 221), where a barber states that he has been wronged by one of his clients, notwithstanding that he has treated him in an irreproachable manner – τεθεραπευκὼς ἀνεγκλή[τως]. A wider sense is found *Syll* 925¹⁶ (B.C. 207 (?)) τοὺς στρατιώτας εὐτάκτους παρεσκεύαξαν καὶ ἀνενκλήτους, and *ib.* 540¹⁶³ B.C. 175-1), where the epithet is applied to stones. Bp E. L. Hicks in *CR* i. (1887) p. 65, citing a Prienean inscr. to illustrate another word, observed that ἀ. was a common word in Greek decrees: the phrase in this one was ἐπῄνεσεν ἐπί τε τῷ σωφρόνως καὶ ἀνεγκλήτως παρεπιδημῆσαι. Prof. Calder has an inscr. (no. 8) in which a son commemorates his mother in the forms of public honorific monuments—with ἐπειδή, ἔδοξε, etc.: he says τήν τε [οἰκί]αν κυβερνήσασα ἀνενκλήτως καὶ τὸ παιδίον ἐκθρέψασα. It is from the southern cemetery at Karabunar (Hyde). Other instances are needless.

ἀνεκδιήγητος

is a word which Paul might have coined (2 Cor 9¹⁵). But it is found as a variant in Aristeas 99 θαυμασμὸν ἀδιήγητον (ἀνεκδιήγητον BL), "wonder beyond description."

ἀνέκλειπτος

In *OGIS* 383⁷⁰ (i/B.C.) Antiochus of Commagene declares θεραπείαν τε ἀνέγλειπτον καὶ ἱερεῖς ἐπιλέξας σὺν πρεπούσαις ἐσθῆσι Περσικῶι γένει κατέστησα. (The spelling γλ, where ἐκ is concerned, is usual in Hellenistic: see Brugmann-Thumb, *Gr.* p. 148.) In P Lond 1166⁷ (A.D. 42) (= III. p. 105) contractors undertake to provide τὰ καύματα ἀνέγλειπτα for a bath during the current year. The adverb is found *IGSI* 2498⁷. For a form ἀνεκλιπής, see Wisd 7¹⁴, 8¹⁸.

ἀνεκτός

Cagnat IV. 293ⁱⁱ ⁴ (Pergamon, ii/B.C.) πάντα δὲ κίνδυν]ο[ν κ]αὶ κακοπαθίαν ἀνεκτὴν ἡγούμενος. If the reading can be accepted, the word occurs in the dialect inscription *Syll* 793 αἰ ἀ(ν)εκτό]ν ἐστι τᾶ Θεμί[σ]τι καὶ βέλτιον ἐ(σ)κιχρέμεν. Its appearance in the Christian letter P Oxy VI. 939²⁵ (iv/A.D.) (= *Selections*, p. 130) ἀνεκτότερον ἐσχηκέναι, "to be in a more tolerable state," counts naturally for little, as NT echoes abound.

ἀνέλεος

This remade form in Jas 2¹³ may be illustrated from P Lips I. 39²² (A.D. 390) τύψας με [ἀν]ελεῶς—though, of course, thus accented, it comes from ἀνελεής. Whether this last is any better Attic than ἀνέλεος may, however, be questioned, unless we postulate it as the alternative to νηλεής, from which the Attic ἀνηλεής came by mixture. But the solitary grammarian whom Lobeck (*Phryn.*, p. 710 f.) quotes for it is not very solid ground

ἀνεμίζω

Mayor on Jas 1⁶ suggests that the ἅπ. εἰρ. may have been coined by the writer, who is fond of -ίζω verbs. The suffix was at least as available for making a new verb in Hellenistic as its derivative -ize is in English. Of course the parallels in Grimm-Thayer are far later.

PART I.

ἄνεμος.

To Deissmann's example (*BS.* p. 248) CPR 115⁶ (ii/A.D.) γείτο]νες ἐκ τεσσάρων ἀνέμων, where the phrase clearly refers to the four cardinal points as in Zech 11⁶, Mt 24³¹, Mk 13²⁷, we may add P Flor I. 50¹⁰⁴ (A.D. 268) ἐκ τῶν τεσσάρων ἀνέμων. The same use of ἄνεμος is implied in P Flor I. 20⁹ (A.D. 127) ἐξ οὗ ἐὰν ὁ Ὧρος αἱρῆται ἀνέμου: Vitelli compares Catullus xxvi, where the poet says his bungalow is " exposed " (*opposita*) not to S. or W. wind, N. or E., but to a mortgage of £63. In P Oxy I. 100⁹ (A.D. 133) a declaration regarding the sale of land, we find ὧν ἡ τοποθεσία καὶ τὸ κατ' ἄνεμον διὰ τῆς καταγραφῆς δεδήλωται, where the editors understand by τὸ κατ' ἄνεμον the boundaries on the four sides. For the ordinary sense we need quote nothing, unless we may note the combination in Wünsch *AF* 4⁶ (p. 15—iii/A.D.) τὸν θεὸν τῶν ἀνέμων καὶ πνευμάτων Λαιλαμ. (It is MGr.)

ἀνεξεραύνητος.

For this NT ἅπ. εἰρ. (Rom 11³³), Nägeli (p. 23) cites, in addition to the references in Grimm-Thayer, a fragment of Heraclitus in Clem. Alex. *Strom.* II. 17, p. 437 P (fr. 18 Diels). On the spelling see *Proleg.* p. 46.

ἀνεξίκακος.

P Tebt II. 272¹⁹ (a medical fragment, late ii/A.D.), gives a literary citation for the word, εἰ γὰρ ἀνεξί[κ]ακος ἐν τοῖς [λ]οιποῖς ὢν μὴ ἑπόμενοι τὸ δίψ[ος], "for if he has general endurance but is nevertheless unable to bear the thirst " (Edd.). Vettius Valens has it, p. 38²¹, οὐκ ἄποροι καθίστανται, ἐπιτάραχοι δὲ καὶ ἀνεξίκακοι, ἐγκρατεῖς περὶ τὰς τῶν αἰτίων ἐπιφοράς. Though Lucian (*iud. voc.* 9) is posterior in date to Paul and to Wisd 2¹⁹ (ἀνεξικακία), he is adequate evidence for the earlier use of the word in " profane " Greek!

ἀνεξιχνίαστος.

This word seems to have been borrowed by Paul (Rom 11³³, Eph 3⁹) from Job (5⁹, 9¹⁰, 34²⁴), and is re-echoed in early Fathers.

ἀνεπαίσχυντος.

Josephus (*Ant.* xviii. 243 μηδὲ δευτερεύειν ἀνεπαίσχυντον ἡγοῦ, cited by Thayer) did not borrow this from his earlier contemporary, the writer of 2 Tim 2¹⁵; but a word can hardly be called a coinage which only involves putting *un-* before an existing word (cf. αἰσχυντικός).

ἀνεπίλημπτος.

For this word, which is found *ter* in 1 Tim (3², 5⁷, 6¹⁴), cf. P Tor I. 1ᵛⁱⁱⁱ ¹⁵ (ii/B.C.), where one of the conditions of a decree of amnesty for offences is stated to be τὰς παρακειμένας ὑπ' αὐτοῦ συγγραφὰς ἀνεπιλήπτους εἶναι. See also P Tebt I. 5⁴⁸ (B.C. 118) ἀκατηγο[ρήτου]ς καὶ ἀνεπιλήπτους, *ib.* 61(*b*)²⁰⁷⁴ (B.C. 118-7) κλήρους ἀ.σ.υκοφαντή[τους] καὶ ἀκατηγορήτους καὶ ἀνεπιλήπτου]ς πάσαις αἰτίαις ὄντ]ας; and so *ib.* 72¹⁷⁵ (B.C. 114-3). Dibelius (on 1 Tim 6¹⁴) quotes a Jewish deed of manumission, Latyschev *IosPE.* II. 52⁸ᶠᶠ κατὰ εὐχή[ν] μου ἀνεπίληπτον καὶ ἀπα[ρ]ενόχλητον ἀπὸ παντὸς κληρονόμου.

6

ἀνέρχομαι

of "going up" to the capital is illustrated by the illiterate P Tebt II. 412³ (late ii/A.D.), ἀνελθε εἰς τὴν μητρόπολιν τοῦ νέου ἔτους ἐπὶ καίγὼ ἀνέρχομε εἰς τὴν πόλιν : cf. *ib.* 411⁵ (ii/A D.) αὐτῇ ὥρᾳ ἄνελθε, ὁ γὰρ κράτιστος ἐπιστράτηγος ἱκανῶς σε ἐπεζήτησε, "come up instantly, for his highness the epistrategus has made several inquiries for you" (Edd.), and P Lond 948 *verso* ³ (A.D. 257) (= III p. 210) ἀνερχέστω. Other citations are hardly required, but we may add the almost contemporary BGU II. 595¹⁵ (*c.* A.D. 70-80) ὅτι ὁ υἱός μου ἀσθενεῖ δινῶς, τούτου ἕνεκα ἀνηρχόμην.

ἄνεσις.

This word, which with the exception of Ac 24²³ is used in the NT only by Paul, and always with the contrast to θλίψις either stated or implied (see Milligan on 2 Thess 1⁷), is found in a more general sense in P Tebt I. 24³³ (B.C. 117) ἀν[έ]σει γεγονότας, "becoming remiss," as in the paradoxical phrase ἐμπειρίᾳ ἀνέσεως, Wisd 13¹³ : cf. also *Syll* 533¹⁶ (iii/A.D. *init.*), 932⁵³ (*ib.*), where it is used of "relief" from taxation. P Ryl II. 84⁶ (A.D. 146) ὅπως φροντίσῃς . . . τὴν ἄνεσιν τὴν διὰ τοῦτο γενομένην τῶν ὑπαρχόντων γενέσθαι, "in order that . . . the ensuing remission of the lands be effected" (Edd., comparing *Chrest.* I. 363 introd.). For the phrase in Ac 24²³ ἔχειν τε ἄνεσιν, where the RV renders "should have indulgence," cf. P Giss I. 59 (A.D. 119-20), where a number of persons are enrolled as having *vacatio munerum* (λειτουργιῶν), as ἄνεσιν ἐσχηκότες ἑπταετίας τῆς ἀπὸ ι̅ς̅ (ἔτους) [16th year of Trajan] ἕως νῦν, and others, one of a τριετία. Can the ἄνεσις in Ac *l.c.* be a kind of *libera custodia*? Moffatt renders the clause, "allow him some freedom."

ἀνετάζω.

In P Oxy I. 34ⁱ. ¹³ (A.D. 127) a prefect uses this word in directing Government clerks whose business it was to "examine" documents and glue them into τόμοι. This is one of the words which Grimm characterizes as "not found in prof. auth.," occurring first in LXX. The compound (Ac 22²⁴·²⁹), now vindicated as sufficiently "profane," was as rare as its simplex (cf. Wisd 2¹⁹) : it may be suspected that the common ἐξετάζω "to get out the truth," (ἐτεός – see Boisacq *Dict. Etym.*, p. 291) was the original from which both ἐτάζω and ἀνετάζω (and παρετάζω in Arcadian) were devised.

ἄνευ.

P Par 45⁴ (B.C. 153) ἄνευ τῶν θεῶν οὐθὲν γίνεται, BGU I. 267⁶ (A.D. 199) ἄνευ τινὸς ἀμφισβητήσεως. Quotations are hardly needed, but see Wilcken *Ostr.* i. p. 559 f., where it is shown that in certain connexions ἄνευ must have the meaning of "without the knowledge of" rather than "in the absence of," e.g. P Petr II. Appendix. p. 3, ὅτι ἄνευ ἡμῶν καὶ τῶν μετ' Ἀριστοκρίτους λογευτῶν [προ]ξενεῖ τοὺς ὑποτελεῖς τοῦ φυλακ[τι]κοῦ εἰς τὸ ἴδιον, where Wilcken translates "ohne unser Wissen und ohne Wissen jener Logeuten lädt er die Steuerzahler zu sich in's Haus." In sepulchral inscriptions the preposition is often used in the sense "apart from," "except," as in the formula ἐάν τις τολμήσῃ ἀνύξε (*l.* ἀνοῖξαι) τὸν σορὸν τοῦτον ἄνευ τῶν ἰδίων αὐτοῦ, see *IGSI* 3225, 2327, *al.* cited by Herwerden. See further Kuhring, p. 46 f.

ἀνεύθετος.

ἅπ. εἰρ. in Ac 27¹², is another new word made with *un-* which may or may not have been first used by Luke. The simplex is found in Lk 9⁶², 14³⁵, and in Heb 6⁷.

ἀνευρίσκω.

Syll 154 *bis* (late iv/B.C.), 803²⁶ (iii/B.C.). The adjective ἀνεύρετος is found on the *recto* of P Amh II. 125 (late i/A.D.), where a petition concludes, οἱ δὲ λοιποὶ αὐτῶ[ν ἐν] συνώδῳ ἄνδ(ρες) κ̅ε̅ ἀνεύρητοι ἐγένοιτο (*l.* ἀνεύρετοι ἐγένοντο), καὶ ἀφήλπακαν (*l.* ἀφήρπακαν) ἡμῶν ἱμάτια κτλ.

ἀνέχω.

The verb is not common in early papyri, but cf. P Strass I. 22²² (iii/A.D.) σιωπήσαντος τοῦ νομίζοντος αὐτῷ διαφέρειν καὶ ἀνασχομένου ὑπὲρ δεκαετίαν (a statute of limitations comes in), P Gen I. 76¹⁴ (iii/iv A.D.), P Lips I. 5 ⁱⁱ·⁸ (iii/A.D.), 55¹¹ (iv/A.D.), and P Oxy VI. 903³⁶ (iv/A.D.) κἀγὼ οὐκ ἠνεσχόμην ἐκβαλεῖν αὐτήν, "but I refused to send her away" (Edd.). Later examples are P Oxy I. 130¹⁵ (vi/A.D.) οἱ διαφέροντες τοῦ ἐμοῦ δεσπότου οὐκ ἠνέσχετο (*l.* ἠνέσχοντο) ποιῆσαι κατὰ τὴν κέλευσιν τοῦ ἐμοῦ ἀγαθοῦ δεσπότου, "the servants of my lord refused to do my kind lord's bidding" (Edd.), and P Grenf I. 64² (vi/vii A.D.) οὐκ ἠνέσχετο τοῦτο ποιῆσαι. There is a note on the syntax of the verb in W. Schmidt *Jos.*, p. 424 f., and one on the complexities of its augment in Crönert *Mem. Herc.*, p. 207.

It may be noted that Nestle (*ExpT* xix. p. 284) has drawn attention to the interesting reading ἀνέξεται (for ἀνθέξεται) in Mt 6²⁴ = Lk 16¹³, as supported by the OLat (*sustinebit* or *patietur*) and OSyr ("endure," Burkitt) : it was familiar from the common Stoic formula ἀνέχου καὶ ἀπέχου, "Put up with the one, and take advantage of the other" (see *s.v.* καταφρονέω) will be the meaning.

ἀνεψιός.

This word, which in Greek writers is regularly applied to cousins german whether on the father's or on the mother's side (see Lightfoot on Col 4¹⁰, may be illustrated from P Lond 1164 (*k*)²⁰ (A.D. 212) (= III. p. 167) τὸ καταλειφθὲν ὑπὸ [το]ῦ κατὰ πατέρα μου ἀνεψιοῦ Ἰσιδώρου and P Tebt II. 323¹³ (A.D. 127) μετὰ κυρίου τοῦ ἑαυτῆς κ[α]τὰ μητέρα ἀνεψιοῦ Ὀρσέως. *Preisigke* 176 (reign of M. Aurelius) has ἀνεψιὸς πρὸς πατρός and πρὸς μητρός. See also P Oxy I. 99³·¹⁵ (A.D. 55), P Fay 99⁵ (A.D. 159), BGU II. 648⁹ (A.D. 164 or 196), and from the inscriptions *OGIS* 544⁷ (ii/A.D.), where, however, the editor notes, "Graecos non distinguere fratres patrueles et consobrinos, sed utrosque aeque ἀνεψιούς appellare." Phrynichus (ed. Lobeck) p. 306 praises ἀνεψιός as against the form ἐξάδελφος, which is found in the LXX (Tob 1², 11¹⁸) and in Christian writers. Both occur in MGr, ἀνιψιός for "nephew," and ἐξάδερφος for "cousin (male)." The fem. ἀνεψιά may be cited from PSI 53¹⁴⁵ (A.D. 132-3) ἐπιγέγραμμαι [τῆς ἀν]εψιᾶς μου κύριος. Ἀνεψιάδης, "cousin's son," occurs in *Preisigke* 176 (see above).

ἄνηθον.

Syll 804²⁶ (perhaps ii/A.D.) ἅ. μετ' ἐλαίου, for headache. P Oxy VIII. 1088⁶⁷ (early i/A.D.), a collection of prescriptions, commends for a ὑπνωτικὸν πότημα · ιοσκ[νάμου . .,] ἀννήσου (δρ.) ᾱ, ὀπίου (τριωβολον) · μείξ[ας δός, "soporific:

henbane . . ., anise 1 dr. etc." (Ed.) This spelling is also found in P Ryl II. 148[19] (A.D. 40).

ἀνήκω.

The ethical meaning of this word "to be due" is by no means confined to the Biblical literature, as the following citations will show. OGIS 532[17] (B.C. 3), the Paphlagonians' oath of allegiance to Augustus, has the undertaking **παν]τὶ τρόπωι ὑπὲρ τῶ[ν] ἐκείνοις ἀνηκό[ντων]** (for the rights of Augustus and his heirs) **πάντα κίνδυνον ὑπομενεῖν.** Other examples of this use, which is found in 1 and 2 Maccabees, are given in the index. From the Magnesian inscriptions we may quote 53[63] (end of iii/B.C.) **οὐθενὸς ἀποστήσεται** (sc. ὁ δῆμος **τῶν ἀνηκόντων τῇ πόλει τῶν Μαγνήτων πρὸς τιμὴν ἢ χάριτος ἀπόδοσιν,** where Thieme (p. 15) renders, "was man der Stadt der Magneten zu erweisen schuldig ist." Similarly from the papyri: P Fay 94 (iii/A.D.) has twice **περὶ τῶν [τῇ ἐπιτροπείᾳ] ἀνηκόντων,** as the editors restore it, "his duties in the period of guardianship, functions pertaining to it." In P Tebt I. 6[41] (ii/B.C.) **τῶν ἀνηκόντων τοῖς ἱερο[ῖς κομίζεσθαι,** "the dues which belong to the temples," it is unfortunately not clear whether the infinitive depends on ἀνηκόντων or on the main verb **προστετάχαμεν:** cf. P Tebt I. 43[25] (B.C. 118) **ἐν τοῖς ὑμῖν ἀνήκουσι,** "in your interests". In P Flor I. 1[4 al.] (A.D. 153) **ἀνηκόντων πάντων** is simply "all that belongs." A technical use based on this appears in a Rainer papyrus in Chrest. I. 72, p. 101, (A.D. 234) **δηλοῦμεν μηδὲν δεῖν ἀνῆ[κον σ]ημάναί ποτε τῇ τοῦ ἰδιολόγου κ[αὶ ἀρχ]ιερέως ἐπιτροπ ῇ,** where Wilcken explains it as the "Kompetenzkreis" of these two officials.

ἀνήμερος.

A good example of this NT ἅπ. εἰρ. (2 Tim 3[3]) is afforded by Epictetus' description (I. iii. 7) of those who forget their divine origin as like to lions—**ἄγριοι καὶ θηριώδεις καὶ ἀνήμεροι**

ἀνήρ.

The special differentia of **ἀνήρ : ἄνθρωπος** survives in MGr (**ἄντρας, ἄθρωπος**), where even the old gen. sing. (**ἀντρός**) may still be found beside the "regular" **τοῦ ἄντρα** (Thumb Handbook, p. 48). Naturally there is nothing particular to record in the uses of this everyday word, which has in NT and Hellenistic generally much the same range as in class. Gk. Thus, taking the index to BGU IV., we can illustrate many of the uses noted for the NT in Grimm from documents of the Augustan period. So (1) husband by the perpetual phrase **μετὰ κυρίου τοῦ ἀνδρός** after the name of a woman, as 1126[4] (where **ἀνδρός** is written over an erased **ὁμομητρίου ἀδελφοῦ**), or in a marriage contract as 1098[33] **τηρεῖν τὰ πρὸς τὸν ἄνδρα καὶ τὸν κοινὸν βίον δίκαια,** while the document will also use **ἀνήρ** for irregular relations in the pledge **μηδ' ἄλλωι ἀνδρὶ συνεῖναι.** Then under Grimm's (3) we have 1189[11] **οἱ σημαινόμενοι ἄνδρες** "the persons named," 1061[7] where Patellis and **ἄλλοι ἄνδρες ιε̄** committed a burglary: the common phrase (**τὸ**) **κατ' ἄνδρα,** "viritim," in 1047[iii. 11] (A.D. 131); and (from A.D. 196) 1022[7] **ἄνδρες κράτιστοι** in address (cf. II. 646[20]— A.D. 193—**ὦ ἄνδρ]ες 'Αλεξανδρεῖς**) accounts for another use. 'Ανήρ in distinction from **νήπιος** or **παιδίον** alone remains: of this less common use we do not happen to notice an

example, but literature supplies them in plenty. We might add as an instance of technical use **ἀνδρῶν καὶ ἱππέω[ν],** P Flor II. 278[18. 29] (iii/A.D.).

ἀνθίστημι.

P Petr II. 37 2 (a) verso[14] **οὐ γὰρ δύναμαι ἀνθ[Οστάνειν,** BGU III. 747[ii. 10] **ἐνιαχοῦ δὲ καὶ τολμῶσιν ἀντίστασθαι** (l. ἀνθ-), P Hawara 69[4] (ii/A.D.) (= Archiv v. p. 383) . .]οὐκ **ἀντέστην π[. .,** P Leid W[xii 40] **ἰσχυρότερον ἀντέστη αὐτῷ.**

ἀνθομολογέομαι.

P Oxy IV. 743[34 and 40] (B.C. 2) (= Witkowski[2]. p. 130) **ὡς ἀνθομολογη[σομένω] ὑπέρ σου ὡς ὑπ(έρ) μου,** where the Edd. render "as he will agree in everything for you just as for me": cf. P Giss I. 71[7] (ii/A.D.) **ὥσ τε . . α]ὐτὸν παραγενόμενον ἀν[θομο]λογήσασθαί σου τῇ εἰς [με σπου]δῇ** "may answer to, come up to," and P Tebt I. 21[6] (B.C. 115) **καὶ 'Αρίστιππον αὐτῶι ἀνθομολογήσεσθαι** "and that A. will come to an understanding with him " (Edd.), P Par 42[7] (B.C. 156) **καὶ ὁ ἀδελφός σου ἀνθωμολογεῖτο μὴ ἠδικεῖσθαι ὑπ' αὐτοῦ.** Add P Tebt II. 410[14] (A.D. 16) **ἀνθο]μολογήσηται περὶ τῆς σπ[ο]υδῆς,** "he may answer for your activity." In P Grenf II. 71[ii. 14] (A.D. 244-8) **καὶ ἐπερωτηθέντες ἀνθωμολογήσαμεν περὶ τ[ο]ῦ ταῦθ' οὕτως ὀρθῶς καὶ καλῶς γεγηνῆσθαι,** the active appears with the meaning "acknowledge," "formally admit," the correctness of a legal form.

ἄνθος.

Syll 930[11] **μηδὲ ἄνθεα παρφέρην (ἐν τὸ ἱερόν).** OGIS 365[7] (ii/B.C.) has **ἀνθεών,** "viridarium," and Vettius Valens, p. 15[4]. speaks of **ἀνθηραὶ (μοῖραι).** The noun in its two NT occurrences only repeats Isai 40[6 f.], but it is fairly common in LXX, and survives in MGr. It recurs in P Leid W.

ἄνθραξ.

P Petr III. 107(d)[29], P Lond 1159[59] (A.D. 145-7) (= III. p. 113) **ἐπὶ ξυλ καὶ ἀνθράκων καὶ φαν∞ καὶ λαμπά[δ],** P Fay 348 (ii/iii A.D.) **ἀνθρακο(ς).** The word also occurs ter in Michel 594 (B.C. 270), a long inscription from Delos containing the receipts and expenses of the ἱεροποιοί. It is MGr **ἄνθρακας.**

ἀνθρωπάρεσκος.

which starts in LXX and Pss. Sol., was presumably as much a coinage as our own "men-pleasers," but made in a language where compounds are more at home than in ours. If this is a "Bibl." word, it is only an instance of the fact that every Greek writer made a new compound when his meaning required one. Lobeck on Phryn., p. 621, cites **αὐτάρεσκος** from Apoll. de Conjunct., p. 504.

ἀνθρώπινος.

This significant adj. is found in Wilcken Ostr. ii. no. 1218 (Rom.) **μέλη ἰαϊκά** (l. ἰατρ.) **ἀνθρώπι(να),** with reference apparently to certain healing charms. In wills of the Ptolemaic period **ἀνθρώπινόν τι πάσχειν** is the stereotyped form for "to die," e.g. P Petr I. 11[9 ff.] (the will of a cavalry officer) **ἐὰν δέ τι ἀνθρώπινον πάθω καταλείπω τ[ὰ μοι ὑπάρχοντα ἐγ] τοῦ βασιλικοῦ καὶ τὸν ἵππον καὶ τὰ ὅπλα κτλ.:** cf. also the important marriage contract P Gen I. 21[15] (ii/B.C.) ἐὰν δέ τις αὐτῶν ἀνθρώπινόν τι πάθῃ καὶ τελευτήσῃ κτλ., and BGU IV. 1149³⁴ (a loan—B.C. 13) ἐὰν δὲ συνβῇ τὸν δοῦλον διαδρᾶναι ἢ καὶ παθεῖν τι ἀνθρώπινον, καὶ οὕτως εἶναι τὰ ὀφιλόμενα ἀκίνδυνα κτλ. So P Tebt II. 333¹¹ (A.D. 216), Syll 635¹³ (Rom.—note the unusual present πάσχῃ), etc. Various uses of the adj. are illustrated in Syll: thus 347⁸ (B.C. 48), an Asian decree in honour of Julius Caesar, τὸν ἀπὸ Ἄρεως καὶ Ἀφροδε[ί]της θεὸν ἐπιφανῆ καὶ κοινὸν τοῦ ἀνθρωπίνου βίου σωτῆρα, 305¹⁰ (c. A.D. 37)—a grandiloquent adulatory oration from Cyzicus—θεῶν δὲ χάριτες τούτῳ διαφέρουσιν ἀνθρωπίνων διαδοχῶν, ᾧ ἡ νυκτὸς ἥλιος κτλ., 462³⁰ (iii/B.C., Crete) καὶ θ.[νων ("divine") κ]αὶ ἀνθρωπίνων πάντων (cf. 722³³). 463¹³² (late iii/B.C.) οἱ ἐ[ρ]ευταὶ οἱ τῶν ἀνθρωπίνων, "the comptrollers of secular revenues". The strong pervading antithesis with "divine" in the uses of this word lends emphasis to such a phrase as ἀ. κτίσις in 1 Pet 2¹³ (where see Hort). It is MGr.

ἀνθρωποκτόνος,

for which only Euripides is cited, will be one of the words Hellenistic prose has taken over from poetical vocabulary. Murray gives the lines thus (*Iph. Taur.* 389)—

This land of murderers to its god hath given
Its own lust ; evil dwelleth not in heaven.

ἄνθρωπος.

like ἀνήρ, has kept its differentia practically unchanged from Homer to MGr. It is interesting to notice its philosophical abstract ἀνθρωπότης vouched for as fairly popular Greek by Vettius Valens (p. 346⁵⁹, in antith. to ἀθανασία), passing into Christian theology (see LS and Sophocles *Lex.*), and current in MGr. The NT has no trace of the curious misuse by which the principal difference between ἀ and ἀνήρ is ignored : Tob 6⁸ ἀνθρώπου ἢ γυναικός. P Flor I. 61⁶⁰ (A.D. 86-8) ἄξιος μ[ὲ]ν ἧς μαστιγωθῆναι, διὰ σεαυτοῦ [κ]ατασχὼν ἄνθρωπον εἰσχήμονα καὶ γυν[αῖ]κας is not parallel, as ἀ. only means "person": as little is Jn 7²² f. (Grimm). Another case of ἄνθρωπος invading the sphere of ἀνήρ is the Matthaean locution ἄ. οἰκοδεσπότης, βασιλεύς, φαγός etc. As Grimm's passages show, this is Greek, though not Attic : Mt may have got it from LXX (so Lev 21⁹ ἀνθρώπου ἱερέως). Some papyrus passages may be cited, though little is needed. The antithesis with θεός has figured under ἀνθρώπινος : the complementary one comes out well in BGU IV. 1024ⁱᵛ⁶ (iv/v A.D.), where a judge pronounces sentence of death with the words σύ μοι δοκεῖς [ψυχὴ]ν ἐ]χειν θηρίου καὶ [ο]ὐκ ἀνθρώπου, [μᾶλλον δ]ὲ οὐδὲ θηρίου— he proceeds to give reasons. *Ib.* 1030⁷ (iii/A.D.) ἐπίγοντες τοὺς ἀνθρώπους καὶ τοὺς τέκτονας—ἀ. is general and τ. special. *ib.* 1031¹³ (ii/A.D.) ἔκδος ἀνθρώποις ἀσφα[λέσ]ι. Its anaphoric use with the article (as Mt 12¹³ etc.) may be seen in *ib.* 1208ⁱ·²⁵ (B.C. 27-6)ἵνα δὲ εἰδῆς τὸ ὄρθριον ("scin Morgengruss," "seine erste Tat" says Schubart) τοῦ ἀνθρώ(που), πέπομφά σοι ἣν τίθεται μίσθωσιν. This particular instance may perhaps serve as an illustration of "the adjunct notion of contempt (Jn 5¹²)," on which Grimm remarks (*l.d.*). Under the same heading, with commiseration instead of contempt, will come πρεσβύτης ἄνθρωπός εἰμι in P Strass I. 41⁴⁰ (A.D. 250). In the edict of Caracalla, P Giss I. 40ⁱ·⁶ (A.D. 212-5) ὀσ]άκις ἐὰν ὑ[π]εισέλθ[ωσ]ιν εἰς τοὺς ἐμοὺς ἀν[θρ]ώπους the

---

editor notes the tone as characteristic of his dynasty. The general sense in the plural may be illustrated by Syll 424¹ (A.D. 361-3) τὸν γῆς καὶ θαλάσσης καὶ παντὸς ἀνθρώπων ἔθνους δεσπότην of the brief Emperor Julianus, *ib.* 806²² (ii/A.D.) of a series of diseases κ]α[ὶ] ὅσα κακὰ κ[αὶ πά]θη ἀνθρώποι[ς γί]γνεται.

ἀνθύπατος.

Syll 656² (ii/A.D.) presents Gaius Papillius Carus Pedo ἀνθύπατος replying to a resolution of the Ephesian Βουλή, who had referred him to his predecessors' practice (τοὺς πρὸ ἐμ[οῦ] κρατίστους ἀνθυπάτους). *Ib.* 316³ (ii/B.C.) has Q. Fabius Q. f. Maximus, ἀνθύπατος Ῥωμαίων, addressing the authorities of a town in Achaia. So *passim*, except in Egypt : since this country was governed by a prefect, we do not hear of proconsuls in the papyri.

ἀνίημι.

P Petr III. 53 (*b*)⁴ (iii/B.C.) ἀνεῖεται λοιπογραφεῖσθαι, "he is permitted to remain in arrears" (Edd.). Syll 552²⁹·⁵⁹ (late i/B.C.) of school-boys "let off" ἐκ τῶν μαθημάτων. P Amh II. 90 (*b*)⁹ (A.D. 179) βορρᾶ ἀνιμένη λιβὸς ἰδιωτικά, "on the north dedicated land, on the west private properties" (Edd.) So *Cagnat* IV. 292³⁹ (Pergamon, c. B.C. 130) ἀνεῖναι δ[ὲ] αὐτοῦ κ[αὶ τ]έμενος, *consecrare* Ed. P Oxy III. 471⁸⁶ (ii/A.D.) γέλωτα πολὺν καὶ ἀνειμένον . . . γελᾶν, "laughed long and freely" (Edd.), *ib.* 505¹⁸ (A.D. 118) ἀνεῖναι "admit," *ib.* 533³⁰ (ii/iii A.D.) ἐὰν ἀνεθῶσι, "if they are neglected." P Ryl II. 77³⁰ (A.D. 192) κελεύσατε ὃ ἔδωκα ἱκανὸν ἀνεθῆναι. P Grenf II. 78²¹ (A.D. 307) ἀξιῶ . . . ἀνεθῆνα[ι] "released." P Cattaoui ⁶·¹⁸ (ii/A.D.) (= *Chrest.* II. p. 423) τὰ ἄλλα σοι ἀνίημι, "concede." A literary effort celebrating the accession of Hadrian, P Giss I. 3⁸ff shows us loyal subjects γέλωσι καὶ μέθαις ταῖς ἀπὸ κρήνης τὰς ψυχὰς ἀνέντες γυμνασίων τε ἀλείμμασι (see Wilcken on the document, *Archiv* v. p. 249).

ἀνίστημι.

P Amh II. 68⁴³ (late i/A.D.) has ἀρούρας . . . ὑπὸ ἀμφοτέρων τῶν πρὸς χρείαις διὰ τῶν λόγων ἀνασταθείσας = "reported" or the like. The transitive tenses are common in the sense of "setting up" a statue : cf. P Oxy IV. 707²⁵ (c. A.D. 136) ἀνασ[τῆ]σαί τε τὰς τοῦ κτήματος καὶ πωμαρίου πλάτας ἐπὶ μέτροις, "that he should restore on a certain scale the walls (?) of the vineyard and orchard" (Edd.), BGU II. 362ⁱⁱ·⁴ (A.D. 215) (= *Chrest.* I. p. 127) εἰς ὑπηρεσίαν τοῦ ἀναστ[αθ]έντος θείου κ[ολοσ]σιαίου ἀνδριάντος. The formula became so common for setting up a gravestone that ἀνέστησα alone, with accus. of person buried, became current in E. Phrygia and Lycaonia (Ramsay *C. and B.*, ii. p. 732). P Oxy VIII. 1161⁹ (Christian letter, iv/A.D.) μὴ δυναμένη ἀναστῆναι ἐκ τῆς κοίτης μου, will serve as an instance of the intransitive use. One very interesting passage is added by a restoration of Wilcken's in P Tebt II. 285¹⁵ (A.D. 121-38)—see *Archiv* v. p. 232: ἀνασ[τὰ]ς εἰς [σ]υμ[βούλιον κ]αὶ σκεψάμ[ενος με]τ[ὰ τ]ῶν [. . . With this reference to assessors Wilcken compares Ac 26³⁰.

ἀνόητος.

The adv. is supplied by the editors in the Hadrian letter, P Fay 19⁴ (ii/A.D.), οὔτε ἀνοή]τως ἀπαλλάσσομαι τοῦ βίο[υ]. It is current in MGr, meaning "unreasonable" (Thumb).

ἀνοίγω.

That ancient scribes were almost capable of sympathy with modern school-boys in writing the augmented forms of this intractable verb is shown by frequent misspellings in late papyri: thus PSI II. 132[9] (iii/A.D.) ἀνῴχθαι. From Ptolemaic papyri we have the regular forms ἠνώξαμεν P Petr II. 37 1[a. 12], and ἀνεῳγμένον ib. 2[a 5], also ἀνοῖξαι ib. III. p. 133. The phrase of Mt 2[11] is nearly paralleled in Syll 601[32] (iii/B.C.) ἀνοιγόντων δὲ οἱ ἐξετασταὶ κατ' ἐνιαυτὴν (l. -τὸν) τὸν θησαυρόν: so ib. 653[93] (the Andania "Mysteries" inscr., in dialect—B.C. 91), 587[302] B.C. 320–8) τῶι τοὺς θησαυροὺς ἀνοίξαντι. That of Rev 5[9] etc. occurs in Syll 790[47] (i/A.D.) τὰς σφραγῖδας ἀνοιξάτω. Close to this is its use for the "opening" of a will, as P Ryl II. 109[9] (A.D. 235—a stilted document with δυεῖν and υίέας!) ἐκ διαθήκης τῆς καὶ ἀνοιχθε[ίσ]ης κατὰ τὸ ἔθος. We may quote OGIS 222[26] (B.C. 266–1) ἀνοῖξαι δ'ε] τοὺς ἱερεῖς καὶ τὰς ἱερείας τὰ ἱερά, cf. 332[28] (B.C. 138–2) ἀ. τοὺς ναούς, and Dittenberger's note, with parallels showing that the solemn "opening" of shrines was a conspicuous feature in ritual—cf. 1 Regn 3[15] καὶ ὤρθρισεν τὸ πρωῒ καὶ ἤνοιξεν τὰς θύρας οἴκου Κυρίου, and Rev 11[19]. 15[5]. Something akin to our "opening" a building may be seen in OGIS 529[11] (A.D. 117–38) πρῶτον μὲν ἀνοίξαντα τὸ γυμνάσιον—he had evidently been prime mover in its establishment. The Neoplatonists appropriated the NT phrase "heavens opened": cf. Kaibel 882 (Athens—c. iii/A.D.) Θειολόγου Λαίτοιο μετάρσιον ὕμνον ἀκούσας οὐρανὸν ἀνθρώποις εἶδον ἀνοιγόμενον. Laetus, a contemporary of Plotinus (Ed.), is acclaimed as a reincarnation of Plato. The word is common on later tombstones for violating a grave. The frequency of the spelling ἀνύγω has been thought to go rather beyond the mere blundering substitution of an identically pronounced symbol: Radermacher (Gr. p 35 n.[2]) would attribute it to the influence of ἀνύω, which is however a decidedly rarer word (not in NT). But Prof. Thumb regards it as purely graphic. We may quote two illiterate papyri of ii/B.C., written by the same hand, P Par 51[7] (= Selections p. 19) and 50[7]: see Mayser Gr., p. 110. So also P Tebt II. 383[29] (A.D. 46) (the entrance and the exit) εἰς ἣν καὶ ἀνίξι ἑαυτῇ . . . . θύραν. The late 2 aor. pass. ἠνοίγη (as Mk 7[35], Ac 12[10] etc.) is illustrated by BGU I. 32[ii. 10] (as amended p. 359) (A.D. 194) ἠνύγη [κ]αὶ ἀνεγνώσθη—of a will: cf. also the amended reading in l. 21 ἠνύγησαν. The verb is MGr.

ἀνοικοδομέω.

In P Lond 887[2] (iii/B.C.) (= III. p. 1) a complaint is lodged against a neighbour who has "built" (ἀνοικοδόμηκεν) a staircase in a mutual courtyard, and thereby caused some injury to the petitioner: cf. P Magd 2[2] (ii/B.C.) ἀνοικοδομήσαντος ἐν τῶι αὐτοῦ τόπωι ἱερόν κτλ., and P Oxy IV. 707[27] (c. A.D. 136) ἀνοικοδομῆσαι τρόχον ἐκ καινῆς ἐξ ὀ[πτῆς] πλίνθου ἐπὶ μέτροις ὡρισμένοις, "should build on a fixed scale a new wheel of baked brick" (Edd.). In P Petr II. 12 (1)[15] (B.C. 241) καὶ ἀνοικοδομῆσαι βελτίους τῶν προϋπαρχόντων βωμῶν the meaning is "rebuild": cf. Syll 220[12] (iii/B.C.) καὶ τῶν τειχῶν τῶν ἐν τῆι νήσωι πεπτωκότων συνεπεμελήθη ὅπως ἀνοικοδομηθεῖ, and Chrest. I. 96[viii. 4]

(A.D. 215) οἰκοδόμ οις ἵ κατασπῶσι καὶ ἀνοικοδομ οῦσι . ib. II. 68[11] (A.D. 14) οὓς καὶ ἀνοικοδόμησα ἐπὶ τῶι [ἀρχ[α[ί ωι θεμελίωι. Omission of augment is frequent in these ol- words. For a Christian use of ἀ. see the interesting epitaph of the fourth-century bishop of Laodicea, M. Julius Eugenios, who describes himself as during his episcopate πᾶσαν τὴν ἐκλησίαν ἀνοικοδο[μ ἤσας ἀπὸ θεμελίων, W. M. Calder in Exp VII. vi. p. 387.

ἄνοιξις

occurs in the magical papyrus P Lond 46[274] (iv/A.D.) (= I. p. 73). In MGr it means "springtime."

ἀνομία.

P Par 14[27] (ii/B.C.) they assaulted me ἀφορήτῳ ἀνομ[ᾳ ἐξενεχθέντες. P Oxy VIII. 1121[20] (A.D. 295) ἅπαντα ὡς ἐν ἀνομία[ι]ς ἀπεσύλησαν, "lawlessly carried them all off" (Ed.).

ἄνομος.

P Oxy II. 237[vii. 11] (A.D. 186), the Dionysia petition, has ἀνόμου κατοχῆς, "an illegal claim." The closeness of ἀνομία and ἀδικία may be seen in the associated adjectives of P Lond 358[13] (c. A.D. 150) (= II. p. 172), where ἄνομα καὶ ἄδικα are complained of. Cf. IGSI 1047[3] τοῦ ἀνόμου Τυφῶνος. For the adverb see P Magd 6[11] (B.C. 221) μὴ περιδεῖμ με ἀνόμως ὑβριζόμενον ὑπὸ τῶν ποιμένων, and BGU IV. 1200[20] (B.C. 2–1) ἐξουσίαν ἔχοντες τῶι Ἀσκληπιάδου ἀ. ἀποδέδωκαν κτλ. The construction in 1 Cor 9[21] μὴ ὢν ἄνομος θεοῦ is illustrated in Proleg. p. 235 f. The verb ἀνομέω as a transitive appears in P Par 37[18] (ii/B.C.) ἀξιῶ . . . μὴ ὑπεριδεῖν με ἠνομημένον καὶ ἐγκεκλειμένον: cf. ib. 35[21] (by the same writer), with the same combination in the present (passive).

ἀνορθόω

occurs in the fragmentary P Lips I. 119 recto[3] (A.D. 274) τ]ῶν ἁμαρτιῶ[ν] τὰς πονηρίας συνεχῶ]ς ἀ νορθουμένων. For the sense of "rear again," as Ac 15[16], cf. OGIS 710[4] (ii/A.D.) τὸ π[ρ]οπύλα[ιον χρόνῳ [διαφθαρὲ]ν [ἀ]νώρθωσεν ἐκ τοῦ ἰδίου Ἀπολλώνιος ἐπ' ἀγαθῶι. The noun occurs in P Ryl II. 157[13] (A.D. 135) ἔσται δὲ ἡ ἀνόρθωσις τῶν [νῦν ἀποκαθι]στανομένων κοινῶν (τ)ει[χ]ῶ[ν] ἀ[πὸ κ]οινῶν λ[η]μμάτων "the restoration of the common walls" (Edd.).

ἀνόσιος.

This adjective, which in the NT is confined to 1 Tim 1[9], 2 Tim 3[2], is frequently applied to the Jews in connexion with the great Jewish war in Egypt A.D. 115–7. See e.g. P Giss I. 41[ii. 4] παρὰ τὴν τῶν ἀνοσίων ['Ιου]δαίω[ν ἔ]φοδον, with the editor's introduction. So P Brem 40[4] (Trajan) (= Chrest. I. 16) μία ἦν ἐλπὶς καὶ λοιπὴ προσδοκία ἡ τῶν ἀπὸ τοῦ νομοῦ ἡμῶν ἀθρόων κωμ[η]τῶν [πρὸ]ς τοὺς ἀνοσίους 'Ιο[υδα]ίους, who had just won a victory. From a later time comes the fragment of a letter in the correspondence of Heroninus (mid. iii/A.D.), P Flor II. 268[6], . . .]ενοις ἀνοσείους [. . ., with θεῶν ἐπιτρε[πόντων] in the next line, but no other context to help.

ἀνοχή.

P Oxy VII. 1068[15] (iii/A.D.) ἀλλὰ ἡμερῶν ἀνοχὴν ἔχω, "and I have a delay of some days" (Ed.).

ἀνταγωνίζομαι.

For the derived noun cf. P Oxy III. 519²¹ (ii/A.D.) . . .]ανωνι ἀνταγ(ωνιστῇ) (δραχμαὶ) [. ., in a list of payments to gymnastic performers. The verb construed with πρός, as in Heb 12⁴, occurs in *Priene* 17¹⁵ (soon after B.C. 278) πρὸς τοὺς βαρβάρους ἀνταγωνίζεσθαι.

ἀναναπληρόω.

With this expressive compound (Col 1²⁴) cf. the similarly formed ἀναναγινώσκω in the fragmentary P Petr II. 17 (1)¹⁶, where with reference apparently to certain ἐγκλήματα we read, ἀναναγνώσθη μοι καθότι ἀξιῶ. Its opposite ἀναναιρέω is common in Ptolemaic land-surveys = "subtract". In P Tebt I. alone there are over twenty instances of this use (see Index: cf. also P Eleph 28⁶ (iii/B.C.), and from i/A.D BGU III. 770ⁱⁱ ¹⁸ αἱ εἰς ἀτέλ(ειαν) ἀναναιρ[ού]μεναι . . . . Grimm's citations sufficiently warrant ἀναναπληρόω itself. Linde (p. 49) cites the noun (-ωσις) from Epicurus 11⁵.

ἀνταποδίδωμι.

P Par 34²² (ii/B.C.) χαλκίαν τηροῦντες ἀν[τ]απ[ο]δώσωσι αὐτοῖς. *Chrest.* II. 372ⁱⁱ. ¹¹ (ii/A.D.) δεῖσθαι οὐ[ν] ἃ ὑφείλατο ἐπαναγκασθῆναι ἀ[ν]τα[π]οδοῦναι. P Leid W ˣˣⁱ. ³⁴.

ἀνταπόδομα.

figures in LXX and in Didache 5² μάταια ἀγαπῶντες, διώκοντες ἀνταπόδομα: we have no citations to make.

ἀνταπόδοσις.

Dr Nägeli (cf. p. 36) kindly supplies us with the following instances of the use of this word in the inscrr. and papyri: *Michel* 913 (ii/B.C.) (= CIG 3088) . . . ὑποβολῆς ἀνταποδόσεως, Ζωΐλος Ζωΐλου ἀναγνώσεως, Ζωΐλος Ζωΐλου κτλ. (according to the commentary in CIG ὑποβολῆς, in sense of ῥαψῳδίας, is dependent on ἀνταποδόσεως): CPR I., p. 59 (a loan on a house—beginning of iv/A.D.) ἐπὰν μὴ ἀποδῶ τοκΐν (fut. of τοκίζω, with -ΐν for -ιεῖν, and act. for mid.) σοι ἐπιγνώσωμαι (l. -ομαι) τοῦ ὑπερπίπτοντος χρόνου ἄχρις ἀνταποδώσεως, where the editor translates, "wenn nicht, so verstehe ich mich für die Überzeit bis zur Rückerstattung dazu, sie Dir zu verzinsen." Its literary record is unexceptionable.

ἀντέχομαι.

For ἀ. in its more primary NT sense "hold firmly to" Mt 6²⁴, Lk 16¹³ (but see *s.v.* ἀνέχω), 1 Th 5¹⁴, Tit 1⁹, cf. such passages from the Κοινή as P Par 14²² (ii/B.C.) οὐθενὸς δικαίου ἀντεχόμενοι (so BGU IV. 1187²⁰, in Augustus' reign, and P Tor 3²⁴ (ii/B.C.), and 1ⁱⁱ. ¹⁴ (B.C. 116)), P Tebt I. 49⁹ (B.C. 117 (= *Selections*, p. 28) τοὺς ἐκ τῆς κώμης ὁμοθυμαδὸν ἀντέχεσθαι τῆς σῆς σκέπης, "that the inhabitants of the village are with one accord holding fast to your protection," and P Amh II. 133¹¹ ff. (early ii/A.D.) καὶ μετὰ πολλῶν κόπων ἀνηκάσαμεν (= ἠναγκ-—see under ἀναγκάζω) αὐτῶν ἀντασχέσθαι (l. ἀντισχ-) τῆς τούτων ἐνεργίας ἐπὶ τῷ προτέρῳ ἐκφορίου, "and with great difficulty I made them set to work at the former rent" (Edd.). The verb is very common in petitions, as implying that, notwithstanding the course taken, other claims are not lost sight of: e.g. P Oxy II. 281³⁰ (A.D. 20–50), *ib.* 282²⁰ (A.D. 30–5) τῶν μὲν γὰρ ἄλλων τῶν ὄντων μο[ι] πρ[ὸς] αὐτὴν ἀνθέξομα[ι] (l. ἀντέχ-) κα[ὶ ἀ]νθέξομαι, "this petition is without prejudice to the other

claims which I have or may have against her" (Edd.), and *ib.* IX. 1203⁵⁰ (late i/A.D.) τῶν γὰρ ὑπόντων ἡμεῖν δικαίων πάντων ἀντεχόμεθα καὶ ἀνθεξόμεθα, "for we maintain and shall maintain all our subsisting rights" (Ed.). The same combination of tenses is found in P Strass I. 74¹⁸ (A.D. 126) τῶν μὲν πρὸ ἄλλων τῶν κατ' ἐμαυτὸν δικα[ί]ων ἀντέχωμαι καὶ ἀνθέξ[ο]μαι ἐν οὐδενεὶ ἐλλατού[μενος], and in P Flor I. 86²⁸ (i/A.D.): see also *ib* 51²² (A.D. 138–61). In P Tebt I. 41²¹ ff. (c. B.C. 119) αὐτ[οὶ] τε ἀπαρενόχλητοι ὄντες δυν[ώ]μεθα ἀντέχεσθαι τῆς εἰσαγωγῆς καὶ οὐθὲν τῶι βασιλεῖ διαπέσῃ, the editors render "that we being undisturbed may be enabled to attend to the collection of the revenues and the interests of the king may suffer no harm." Similarly BGU IV. 1116¹⁶ (B.C. 13) ἀ. τῆς μισθώ(σεως). P Tebt II. 309² (A.D. 116–7) ἀντεχό[μενοι καὶ ἑτέροι]ς μεταμισθοῦντες is rendered "resuming the land and leasing it to others." It will be noticed that the instances (which might be added to) are all *c. gen. rei: gen. pers.*, as in the Gospels, does not occur among them.

ἀντί.

The primitive local force, surviving in ἔναντι and the Latin cognate *ante*, and conspicuous in the old Cretan dialect, leaves traces in the Κοινή: there is an interesting discussion of its *provenance* in Wackernagel's pamphlet, *Hellenistica* (Göttingen, 1907), p. 5 f. Its solitary appearance in an Attic inscr., and in one passage of the "Halbattiker" Xenophon, make quite natural such an abnormality in the Κοινή as P Par 1⁴⁰⁶ (the astronomical treatise of Eudoxus) ὅταν ἡ σελήνη τῷ ἡλίῳ ἐπισκοτήσ[η] ἀντὶ τῆς ὄψεως ἡμῶν. Closely akin is the temporal use in *Syll* 616⁴³ (dialect of Cos, iii/B.C.) ἁγνεύεσθαι . . ἀντὶ νυκτός, "ea ipsa nocte": so Dittenberger, who compares 438⁴⁵ (Delphi, before B.C. 400) ἀντὶ Ϝέτεος, and Hesychius "ἀντέτους· τοῦ αὐτοῦ ἔτους." This may be seen still in P Lond 1171⁹ (B.C. 8) (= III. p. 177) τιμ(ῆς) οἴνου ἀντὶ τῆς ε̄ τῶν ἐπαγομένων "to cost of wine *for* the 5th of the intercalary days." By far the commonest meaning of ἀντί is the simple "instead of." P Tebt II. 343²¹ (ii/A.D.) ὥστε ἀντὶ ἐλαιῶνο[ς] φ[ο(ρίμου)] ἄρουραι κτλ. "making 2½ arourae converted from productive oliveyard" (Edd.). P Giss I. 47¹⁰ (ii/A.D.) a corslet bought for 300 dr. ἀντὶ πλείονος, "under its value." P Rein 7⁴ (B.C. 141?) ἀντ' ἐλευθέρου δούλο[ς] γενέσθαι. P Oxy VIII. 1119²⁰ (A.D. 254) ἑτέρους ἀντ' αὐτῶν. P Hib I. 170 (B.C. 247) ἵνα μὴ ἀντὶ φιλίας ἔχθραν [ποιώ]μεθα. P Tebt II. 302⁵ (A.D. 71–2) τυγχάνομεν μερισθ[έντες ἐκ τοῦ δημοσί[ο]υ ἀντὶ συντάξεως κτλ. "instead of a subvention" (Edd.). This shades into "in exchange for" or "in return for": *Calder* 455 (c. mid. iii/A.D.) τόνδε σε Μυγδονίη Διονύσιον ἀντὶ β[ίου πολλῶν καὶ τῆς εἰρήνης στέμμα, "thy statue here, a Dionysius (in marble), M. (erected, thus honouring thee with) a crown in return for guarding the life of many and for preserving the peace" (Ed.). Preisigke 628 (A.D. 216)—the writer begs to have the stipulated 7 artabae of wheat ἀντὶ πλειόνων τῶν κλεπέντων. BGU III. 822¹² (iii/A.D.) ὀφείλ[ι] γάρ μοι
ἀντὶ
χαλκὸν τῶν ἐνοικίων. Kuhring p. 20 remarks that ὑπέρ has mostly superseded ἀντί. The formula ἀνθ' οὗ with names, as Ἑρμίας ἀνθ' οὗ Ἑρμῆς [ὁ καὶ Εὐδαίμων, BGU IV. 1062¹ (A.D. 236–7), has raised some discussion: see note and reff. there—Cronert took it as "adoptive son of," Viereck (fol.

lowing Wilcken) makes it = ὁ καί. In that case what are we to make of P Lond 1170⁷²⁷ (iii/A.D.) (= III. p. 102) Ἐκύσεως ἀνθ' οὗ Ἐκύσεως, "Smith *alias* Smith"? For ἀνθ' ὧν "wherefore" or "because" we may quote *OGIS* 90³⁵ (the Rosetta stone—B.C. 196) ἀνθ' ὧν δεδώκασιν αὐτῶι οἱ θεοὶ ὑγίειαν κτλ., similarly 56¹⁹ (the Canopus inscr. of Ptolemy III. B.C. 247–21), P Leid D²¹ (mid. ii/B.C.) σοὶ δὲ γίνοιτο, ἀνθ' ὧν (= because) πρὸς τὸ θεῖον ὁσίως διάκ[ει]σαι καὶ τῶν ἱεροδούλων . . . ἀντιλαμβάνῃ, ἐπαφροδίσια χάρις μορφῇ κτλ. In P Tebt I. 120⁴³ (i/B.C.) Πακύσι ἀνθ' ὧ(ν) κέχρη(κε) τιμῇ[ς] κτλ., ἀντί has the ordinary commercial sense. P Ryl II. 159¹⁸ (A.D. 31-2) . . . ἀνθ'] ὧν ἔλαβε παρὰ τῆς Τα[χ]οῖτος . . . . τοῖς δέο]υσι καιροῖς "in return for the . . . which he received from T. at the proper times." The supplement depends on the parallel document P Oxy III. 504¹⁷ (early ii/A.D.), and is seen to be no instance of the conjunctional phrase ἀνθ' ὧν.

ἀντιβάλλω.

The subst. ἀντιβλήματα is found in P Oxy III. 498¹⁶ (ii/A.D.), a contract with stone-cutters, where the editors understand it of small stones used to insert in vacant places between larger ones. Vettius Valens p. 351²⁰ ἐπειράθημεν καὶ τὰς ἀντιβαλλούσας μοίρας τῇ εὑρεθείσῃ ἐπισυντιθέναι, ὅπως ἡ ἑτέρα χρηματίσει μοῖρα, "the corresponding parts" presumably.

ἀντιδιατίθημι.

A literary citation may be given for this NT ἅπ. εἰρ. (2 Tim 2²⁵): Longinus *de Sublim.* 17 has πρὸς τὴν πειθὼ τῶν λόγων πάντως ἀντιδιατίθεται, "steels himself utterly against persuasive words" (Roberts).

ἀντίδικος.

For this common legal word we may refer to the interesting lawsuit regarding the identity of a child, which recalls so vividly 1 Kings 3¹⁶ff.: the prosecuting advocate states that his client had put the foundling in the defendant's charge— τοῦτο ἐνεχείρισεν τῆι ἀντιδίκωι (P Oxy I. 37¹·⁵ (A.D. 49) (= *Selections*, p. 49). Cf. P Ryl II. 65¹⁵ (B.C. 67?), P Oxy II. 237ᵛⁱⁱ·²⁴,²²·ᵛⁱⁱⁱ·¹² (A.D. 186), BGU II. 592⁷ (ii/A.D.), P Strass I. 41⁷·²⁶ᶠ· (c. A.D. 250). Ἀντίδικος may be used of public opponents, as when the citizens of Abdera appealing to Rome against annexation by Cotys the Thracian speak of τ[οὺς προ]νοουμένους τοῦ ἀντιδίκου ἡμῶν (*Syll* 303²⁴, before B.C. 146), and also in the plural, of a body of opponents, as several times in *Syll* 512 (ii/B.C.), the case of the children of Diagoras of Cos *versus* the town of Calymnus; also of the two parties, as in P Lille I. 20²⁴ (iii/B.C.), παρόντων τῶν ἀ. Silco, king of Nubia (vi/A.D.), concludes his ambitious effort at Greek with a terrible threat against οἱ ἀντίδικοί μου: this is the wider use found in 1 Pet 5⁸ and the LXX, with classical warrant. The verb appears in *Preisigke* 2055² (iv/v A.D.) . . .]Ἄρεως ἀντιδικησαντ[. . ., and the abstract in P Tor I. 1ᵛⁱ·⁸ᶠ· (B.C. 117) αὐτοὶ καὶ τὴν πρὸς τὸν Ἑρμίαν κρίσιν]γδικάσαντες ἐκστήσωσιν αὐτὸν τῆς πρὸς αὐτοὺς ἀντιδικίας.

ἀντίθεσις.

The verbal adj. is used in a report of ii/B.C. regarding the peculations of certain officials, P Tebt I. 24⁶³, one of the

charges against them being that they had "wormed themselves" (αὐτοὺς ἐνειληκότων) into certain positions ἀντιθέταις τῆς καθ' ἑαυτοὺς ἀσχολία (*l.*– as, "inconsistent with their own work" (Edd.).

ἀντικαθίστημι.

P Oxy I. 97⁹ (A.D. 115-6) περὶ ἧς ἀντ[ε]κατέστη αὐτοῖς ἐπὶ τοῦ τοῦ νομοῦ [σ]τρ(ατηγοῦ) Ἀπολλωνίο[υ], BGU I. 168¹¹ (probably A.D. 169) πρ[ὸ]ς ἥ[ν] καὶ ἀν[τ]ικατές[την] ἐπὶ Αἰλίου, and l.²¹ ἐφ' οὗ καὶ ἀντικατέ[σ]την . . . πρὸς τὸν Οὐαλέριον. For the subst. see P Oxy II. 260⁸ᶠᶠ (A.D. 59) ἐξ ἧς ἐποιησάμε[θα] πρὸ[ς] ἑαυτοῦ (*l.* -οὺς) ἐπὶ τοῦ στρατηγοῦ . . . ἀντικαταστάσεως, "in consequence of our confronting each other before the strategus" (Edd.); BGU III. 808⁷ (ii/A.D.) ἐν] δ[ὲ] τῇ γενομένῃ ἐπὶ σοῦ, κύριε, ἀ[ν]τικατα-[στάσει, and *Syll* 355⁷ (Chios, c. A.D. 3) ὕστερον δὲ ἑκατέρου μέρους ἐξ ἀντικα[τα]στάσεως περὶ τῶν κατὰ μέρος ζητημάτων ἐν[τ]υχόντος διή[κου]σα.

ἀντίκειμαι.

P Par 45⁶ (c. B.C. 153) (= Witkowski², p. 85) Μενέδημον ἀντικείμενον ἡμῖν.

ἄντικρυς.

Thackeray, *Gr.* p. 136, notes its use for "opposite" (3 Macc 5¹⁶, Ac 20¹⁵) as "late": see his note on these words with movable s. Cf. P Oxy I. 43 *verso* ¹¹·²⁰ (A.D. 295) καταμένων ἄντικρυς οἰκίας Ἐπιμάχου, P Tebt II. 395⁴ (A.D. 150) ἄντικρυς Τυχαίου, "opposite the temple of Fortune," P Oxy III. 471⁸¹ (ii/A.D.) ἄντικρυς ἁπάντων, "in the presence of all." P Lond 978⁵ (A.D. 331) (= III. p. 233) καὶ κατ' ἄντικρυ[. . . is before a hiatus. The (Attic) compound καταντικρύ(ς) occurs in Apoc Petr 6, εἶδον δὲ καὶ ἕτερον τόπον καταντικρὺς ἐκείνου αὐχμηρὸν πάνυ, καὶ ἦν τόπος κολάσεως, "over against that other." In P Hawara 116 *verso* ²¹¹ (= *Archiv* v. p. 385 f.) (Antoninus Pius) we read ἀντικ[ρὺ Τυχαίου]: clearly this may as well have been ἄντικρυς.

ἀντιλαμβάνομαι.

This common verb is found in the general sense of "lay hold of," "undertake," in P Lond 301⁶ᶠᶠ (A.D. 138-61) (= II. p. 256) ὀμνύω . . . ἀντιλήμψασθαι τῆς χρείας πιστῶς καὶ ἐπιμελῶς: so P Iand 33¹² (Commodus), rendered "se officio suo bene functuros esse." P Oxy IX. 1190¹² ᶠᶠ (A.D. 211-2) ὀμνύω . . . ἀντιλήμψασθαι (*l.* -ε- ἔσθαι τῷ προσήκοντι χρόνῳ τῆς δηλουμένης χρείας, καὶ ταύτην ἐκτελέσειν, "I do swear that I will take up at the proper time the said office and will discharge it" (Ed.): in the first two -ασθαι has intruded into the weakened future inf., now getting rare. P Flor I. 47a¹² (A.D. 213-7) ἐντεῦθεν δὲ ἑκάτερο]ν ἀντιλαμβάνε-σθαι καὶ χρᾶσθαι καὶ οἰκονομεῖν καὶ διοικ[εῖν. Cf. P Rein 47⁴ (ii/A.D.) τῆς] γ[εωρ]γίας ἀ. P Oxy VIII. 1123⁵ (A.D. 158-9) ὁμολογῶ ἀπὸ τοῦ νῦν ἀντιλήμψεσθαι τῆς . . .]της ἀναγρα-φομένης εἰς τὸν μετηλ[λαχότα σου] πατέρα, "I agree that I will henceforward undertake all the public land registered in the name of your departed father" (Ed). So BGU II. 531ⁱⁱ·²² (ii/A.D.) παρακαλῶ δέ σε, ἄδελφε, ἀντιλα[β]έσθαι τῆ[ς τ]ρυγί[ας] to "set to" the vintage, and P Tebt II. 303¹² (A.D.150) ἐπ[ὶ] τῷ Ἅρπα[λον ἀ]ντιλαβέσθαι ταύτης ποιοῦντα πᾶσαν τὴν ὑπηρε[σία]ν, "on condition that H. shall occupy this post performing all the duties." From this come two derived senses, of which only the first is represented in the NT, (1) "aid," "succour" of a friend, (2) "seize" of an opponent. Good examples of (1) are P Petr II. 3 (*b*)[7] (iii/B.C.) σὺ δὲ ἀφιλοτίμως μου ἀντιλαμβάνηι, P Par 27[22] καθότι οὐ διαλείπεις ἡμῶν ἀντιλαμβανόμενος, P Grenf I. 30[6] (B.C. 103) ἐ[φ]' οἷς ἂν οὖν ὑμῶν προσδέωνται ἀντιλαμβανόμενοι, BGU IV. 1138[24] (Aug.) ἵν' ὧι ἀντιλημμέ(νος), and the expressive double compound in P Hib I 82[17] (B.C. 239-8) καλῶς οὖν π]οιήσεις συναν[τι]λ[α]μβανόμενος προθύμως περὶ τῶν εἰς ταῦτα συγκυρόντων, "please therefore to give your zealous co-operation in all that concerns this" (Edd.). Cf. *OGIS* 697[1] (a Roman inscription from Egypt, on the graves of murdered men) ἀντιλα(β)οῦ, κύριε Σάραπι. Dittenberger quotes P Fay 12[14] (B.C. 103) τούτων δὲ γενομένων ἔσομαι ἀντειλημμένος, the passive. In *OGIS* 51[b] (iii/B.C.) καὶ κατ' ἰδίαν ἑκάστου καὶ κατὰ κοινὸν πάντων ἀντιλαμβάνεται, the verb must have the same sense. *Ib.* 339[2] (ii/B.C.) shows gen. of thing, τῆς τε ἄλλης εὐσχημοσύνης τῆς κατὰ τὸ γυμνάσιον ἀντελάβετο. For (2), where the meaning is *in malam partem*, see such passages as BGU II. 648[10] (ii/A.D.) βιαίως ἀντι[λ]αμβάνονται τ[ο]ῦ πατρικοῦ μου μέρους, P Lond 924[12] (A.D. 187-8) (= II. p. 135) βιαίως ἀντέλαβον τὸ τῆς γῆς : other examples in Gradenwitz, *Einführung* i. p. 18. For the subst. ἀντιλήμπτωρ, formerly regarded as "peculiar to the LXX" (Cremer[7]) Deissmann (*BS* p. 91) cites P Lond 23 (B.C. 158-7) (= I. p. 38), in which a petitioner claims the King and Queen as his ἀντιλήμπτορες, and says he finds his καταφυγή in them : cf. for the same conjunction of words LXX 2 Regn 22[3]. Add BGU IV. 1138[8] (cited above), where a Roman official is invoked as τὸν πάντ(ων) σωτῆ(ρα) καὶ ἀντιλ(ήμπτορα)—the same phrase without abbreviations occurs in a papyrus of the same collection cited in *Archiv* v. p. 81 n[2].

ἀντιλέγω.

The strong sense of ἀ. in Rom 10[21], "contradict," "oppose" may be illustrated by P Oxy VIII. 1148[6] (i/A.D.) where an oracle is consulted as to whether it is better for a certain man and his wife μὴ συμφωνῆσαι νῦν τῷ πατρὶ α(ὐτοῦ) ἀλλὰ ἀντιλέγειν καὶ μὴ διδόναι γράμματα, "not to agree now with his father, but to oppose him and make no contract" (Ed.). A somewhat weaker usage appears in *Syll* 523[31] (iii/B.C.) ἐὰν δὲ οἱ γραμματοδιδάσκαλοι ἀντιλέγωσιν πρὸς αὐτοὺς περὶ τοῦ πλήθους τῶν παίδων, *ib.* 540[43] (ii/B.C.), ἐὰν δὲ πρὸς αὐτοὺς ἀντιλέγωσιν οἱ ἐργῶναι περὶ τινος τῶν γεγραμμένων. Cf. also P Oxy I. 67[19] (a dispute regarding property, A.D. 338) εἰ πρὸς τὴν τῶν . . . οἰκοπ[έ]δ[ων] ἀποκατάστασιν . . . οἱ ἐ[— αἰ]τιαθ[έν]τες ἀντιλέγοιεν, "if the accused persons protest against the restoration of the estates" (Edd.), *ib.* X. 1252 *verso*[37] (A.D. 288-95) ἀντιλέγοντες ἔρρωνται, "persist in their refusal" (Edd.), and *ib.* II. 237[viii. 15] (petition of Dionysia, A.D. 186) ὁ δὲ παρὼν ἀναγνωσθέντος τοῦ βιβλειδίου πρὸ βήματος ἐσιώπησεν, οὐδὲν ἀντειπεῖν δυνά[με]νο[ς]: so CP Herm 7[ii. 15] (? ii/A.D.) εἰ δὲ θέλετε ἑτέραν γενέσθαι οὐκ ἀντιλέγω, οὐ γὰρ δύναμαι.

ἀντίλη(μ)ψις.

Like the verb, the subst. frequently has the meaning "help" in petitions, e.g. P Par 26[9] (B.C. 163-2) (= *Selections*, p. 17) δεόμεθα οὖν ὑμῶν, μίαν ἔχουσαι ἐλπίδα τὴν

ὑφ' ὑμῶν ἐσομένην ἀντίληψιν, ἀποστείλαι ἡμῶν τὴν ἔντευξιν ἐπὶ Διονύσιον, "we beg you, therefore, having as our one hope the assistance that lies in your power, to send away our petition to Dionysius," P Amh II. 35[57] (B.C. 132) τυχόντες τῆς παρὰ σ[ο]ῦ ἀντιλήψεως, P Grenf I. 15[1] (not later than B.C. 146 or 135) σῆς δικαίας ἀντιλήψεως, BGU IV. 1187[27] (i/B.C.). For the extension of this meaning to religious matters in the LXX and in 1 Cor 12[28], see *BS* p. 92. It should be noted that the μ which WH insert in the noun in this last passage begins to invade it even in the earlier documents: cf. *Proleg.* p. 56. Thus P Lond 23[20] (B.C. 158) (= I. p. 38) ἧς ἔχετε πρὸς πάντας . . . ἀντιλήμψεως, and the same phrase in P Tebt I. 43[29] (B.C. 118) : cf. P Tebt II. 283[30 ff.] (B.C. 93 or 60) τούτου δὲ γενομ[έ]νου ἔσομαι τετευχὼς [τῆ]ς παρὰ σοῦ ἀντιλήμψεως, "for if this is done I shall have gained succour from you" (Edd.). Later examples of the word are P Fay 206 (A.D. 113) διὸ ἐπὶ σὲ τὴν καταφ[υ]γὴν ποιησάμενος ἀξιῶ ἐάν σοι φαίνηται ἀντιλήμψεως τυχεῖν πρὸς τὸ δύνασθαί με ἐπιμένιν ἐν τῇ ἰδίᾳ διευθύνων τὰ δημοσία, and BGU II. 613[12] (time of Antoninus Pius) δεόμενος τῆς ἀπὸ σοῦ ἀντιλήμψεως τ[υχεῖ]ν.

ἀντιλογία.

The disputed meaning "opposition" in *act* (see Thayer) finds fresh confirmation in P Petr II. 17 (3)[7] (iii/B.C.) where ἀντιλογίαν γενομένην Ἀττάλωι refers to an "assault." The word is fairly common, meaning "quarrel," as P Grenf I. 38[3] (ii/i B.C.) ἀντιλογίαν πρός με συνστησάμενος, P Ryl II. 68[10] (B.C. 89) ἐμπεσοῦσα] ἐξ ἀντιλο[γ]ίας ἐ[πληξέν] με, "attacking me in consequence of a dispute" (Edd.), and P Tebt I. 138 (late ii/B.C.). So in the formula ἄνευ (χωρὶς) πάσης ἀντιλογίας, "without dispute," in formal promises to pay money, etc. : BGU IV. 1133[15] (Aug.), P Strass I. 75[10] (A.D. 118), P Lond 310[16] (A.D. 146) (= II. p. 208) (ἀντιλογίας γεινομένης), Wilcken *Ostr* 1151 (iii/A.D.), P Flor I. 43[14] (A.D. 370) and *ib.* 94[13] (A.D. 491). Cf. *Syll* 929[115] (ii/B.C.) ὑπ' οὐδενὸς ἀντιλογίας, *ib.* 334[b. 32] (i/B.C.).

ἀντιλοιδορέω.

P Petr III. 21 (*g*)[20] (late iii/B.C.) ἐμοῦ δέ σε ἀντιλοιδοροῦντος follows ἐλοιδόρησας φαμένη κτλ. : cf. 1 Pet 2[23].

ἀντιμετρέω.

For this rare NT word (Lk 6[38]) Herwerden refers to the Byzantine Theophyl. Sim. p. 48, 25 (1 5, 5) ἀ. ἀμοιβὴν ἀξίαν τοῖς βεβιωμένοις. Grimm cites Lucian, *Amor.* 19, which is stronger evidence for its "profaneness."

ἀντιμισθία.

No instance of this Pauline word (Rom 1[27], 2 Cor 6[13]) seems as yet to have been found outside Christian literature. This, however, may be wholly accidental ; and there is certainly nothing in the word itself to exclude it from the ordinary terminology of the day : see for further examples of the same kind Nägeli p. 50 ff.

ἀντιπαρέρχομαι.

Lk 10[31] can hardly have acquired this word from Wisd 16[10], where the sense is markedly different. It is quoted from Straton (ii/A.D. ?), who writes (*Anth. Pal.* 12[8]) ἀντιπαρερχόμενος τὰ στεφανηπλόκια : Meineke took the rather needless trouble to emend ἄρτι παρ.—did he know that the word occurred in Biblical literature? If the compound is rightly read there, it might be a new coinage, as it may well be in Wisdom and in Luke. Any writer was free to make a fresh compound like this for a special purpose. Straton was morally the most tainted writer in the Anthology, and we may be quite sure he owed as little to Holy Writ as it owed to him!

'Αντίπας.

Deissmann (*BS* p. 187) calls attention to the appearance of ['Α]ντιπάτρου in *Perg* II. 524² (" not older than Caracalla?"): that the full form of the name is used may be evidence that this later Pergamene was not called after the martyr.

ἀντιπέρα.

This NT ἅπ. εἰρ., warranted from Polybius, is perhaps to be supplied in P Oxy I. 141⁵ (A.D. 303) τοῖς ἀγροφύλαξ(ι) . . . φυλάττουσ(ι) τὸ ἀντιπελ ( ), with reference to guards who protected estates on the further bank (probably of the Baḥr Yusuf).

ἀντιπίπτω.

P Leid D²¹ (ii/B.C.), one of the letters of Ptolemaeus in the cause of the Serapeum Twins, has μηδὲν ἀντιπεσόν[τ]α, "not opposing me."

ἀντιτάσσω.

The verb occurs twice in P Oxy IV. 707ⁱⁱ. ¹⁷, ²⁸ (*c.* A.D. 136), a report of legal proceedings, with reference to the opposing party. P Cattaoui *verso* ⁱ. ⁷ (mid. ii/A.D.) (= *Chrest.* II. p. 98) τῆς ἀντιτεταγμένης ἀρτίως Δρουσίλλας. There are several instances in *OGIS* in a military sense, which was of course the earliest.

ἀντίτυπον.

The meaning "impress" is rightly given by LS for τύπος as the first that arises from the etymology, and it is well supported in classical and post-classical writers. Hence, though "profane" examples for ἀντίτυπος(-ον) = "corresponding" (adj.) or "image" (noun) are rare, we can take the use in Heb 9²⁴ and 1 Pet 3²¹ (" answering to ") as the survival of a primitive meaning. Note also Polyb. vi. 31⁸ τοῖς δ' ἱππεῦσι τούτοις ἀντίτυποι τίθενται, of auxiliary infantry posted "opposite" the cavalry, in a corresponding position. In MGr written language ά. means "copy" of a book.

ἀντίχριστος.

Grimm suggests that John (1 Jn 2¹⁸ etc.) coined the word : Bousset (*Antichrist Legend* p. 136) says it "is not older than the NT." It seems obvious, from the manner of its first introduction, that it was at any rate quite familiar to the readers of 1 Jn and 2 Jn; but it might easily have been introduced by the author in his earlier teaching. The most probable model would be ἀντίθεος (" aemulus Dei " in Lactantius), for which Cumont (*Les Religions Orientales*² p. 387) cites a magical papyrus, πέμψον μοι τὸν ἀληθινὸν Ἀσκληπιὸν δίχα τινὸς ἀντιθέου πλανοδαίμονος. It was a term applied to the *daēva* of Magian religion, on whom see

Early Zoroastrianism (Hibbert Lectures 1912), ch. iv.: they were "counter-gods." Whether John means primarily "a rival Christ" or "an opponent of Christ" or "a substitute for Christ" may be left to the commentators. The first and third may be paralleled by the two senses of ἀντιστράτηγος, "the enemy's general" and "pro-praetor": cf. ἀντισύγκλητος, the name Marius gave to his bodyguard, as an "opposition Senate," ἀντιχόρηγος "rival choregus," and ἀντιταμίας "pro-quaestor" etc. The second is less easily paralleled: Caesar's 'Αντικάτων, a counterblast to Cicero's *Cato*, may serve. Generally speaking, ἀντι-.x suggested (1) the claim to be x, (2) opposition to, equivalence to (cf. Homeric ἀντίθεος, and the name 'Αντίπατρος), substitution for an existing x.

ἀντλέω.

P Oxy VI. 985 (i/A.D., second half) ἀνηλώμα(τος) Φαύστῳ ἀντλοῦντι μηχα(νήν), P Lond 1177⁶⁹ (A.D. 113) (= III. p. 183) ἀντλούντων ἀπὸ πρωίας ἕως ὀψέ. In the late P Oxy I. 147 (A.D. 556) we have a receipt for a "rope" or "coil" provided by the monks for the machine in the garden of the Holy Mary ἐπὶ τῷ ἀντλῆσαι ὕδωρ εἰς τὴν ἁγί(αν) κολυμβήθραν, "for raising water to fill the holy font." The subst. ἀντλητής occurs in P Lond 1177 (cited above), P Tebt I. 241 (B.C. 74) and P Strass I. 52¹⁴ (A.D. 151); and ἀντλία in BGU IV. 1120⁴⁷ᶠ (B.C. 5). For the compound ἀναντλέω used metaphorically, see P Vat A¹³ (B.C. 108) (= Witkowski², p. 65) τοιούτους καιροὺς ἀνηντληκυῖα: similarly P Hawara 56²⁰ (? late i/A.D.) (*Archiv* v. p. 382) ἀρρωστίαν ἰσοθάνατο(ν) [ἐξ]ήντλησα—presumably [ἀν]ήντλησα as is likely, in view of the parallel just cited.

ἀντοφθαλμέω.

"Verbum elegantius = resistere," so Blass on Ac 6¹¹, where the word is found in his "β-text," μὴ δυνάμενοι οὖν ἀντοφθαλμεῖν (ἀντιλέγειν) τῇ ἀληθείᾳ: cf. the Polybian passage cited by Schweighauser (with a wrong reference in *Lex Polyb. s.v.*, μὴ δύνασθαι τοῖς χρήμασιν ἀντοφθαλμεῖν. In the ordinary text of the NT ά. occurs only in Ac 27¹⁵ of a vessel's not being able to "face" the wind: cf. Wisd 12¹⁴, of a king or prince who cannot "look God in the face" (ἀντοφθαλμῆσαί σοι), and *Apoc. Baruch* 7 (p. 80, ed. James) οὖ τὴν θέαν οὐκ ἠδυνήθημεν ἀντοφθαλμῆσαι καὶ ἰδεῖν. For a similar usage see Barnab. 5¹⁰, and cf. Clem. Rom. 34 of an idle workman—ὁ νωθρὸς καὶ παρειμένος οὐκ ἀντοφθαλμεῖ τῷ ἐργοπαρέκτῃ αὐτοῦ, "does not look his employer in the face."

The word was read in the printed text of P Par 63⁴³, but is removed by Mahaffy (P Petr III. p. 23), who reads ἀντ' ὀφθαλμ[ῶ]ν (θεμένου)ς, "keeping it before your eyes." The parallel compound ἐ[π]οφθαλμήσασα occurs in P Théad 19⁹ (iv/A.D.) "ayant jeté un œil d'envie sur le troupeau" (Ed.).

ἄνυδρος.

OGIS 199²¹ (i/A.D.) οἰκοῦντα ἐντὸς πεδίων μεγάλων ἀνύδρων—the "waterless" deserts stretching to the south and west of Abyssinia. P Oxy VI. 918ⁱⁱ ¹⁰ (a land-survey, ii/A.D.) μεθ' (ἣν) γύη[ς ἄ]νυδρ(ος). P Lips Inv 348⁶ (A.D. 376-8) (= Chrest. II. p. 86) ἀνέδραμον . . . δι' ἀνύδρων ὁρῶν. The subst. is found in the petition of certain quarrymen to be transferred to the alabaster quarries on account of the want of water in the place where they were working—διὰ τὴν ἀνυδρίαν τῶν τόπων [τῶνδ]ε (P Petr II. 9(2)⁶ (iii/B.C.)).

ἀνυπόκριτος.

To the literary citations for this word given by Nägeli, p. 43, we may add Demetrius *de Eloc.* 194.

ἀνυπότακτος.

In the great Paris magic papyrus (edited by Wessely, *Wien. Denkschr.* XXXVI. ii. pp. 44 ff.) 1367 we find ἀνυποτάκτους following σιδηροψύχους ἀγριοθύμους. Moeris (ed. Pierson), p. 34, defines ἀφηνιαστής by ἀνυπότακτος, ὑπερήφανος. See further Nägeli, p. 45.

ἄνω.

Tob Sᵃ ℵ ἀπέδραμεν τὸ δαιμόνιον ἄνω εἰς τὰ μέρη Αἰγύπτου—other authorities for this recension have εἰς τὰ ἄνω μέρη —raises some problems, on which reference may be made to *Early Zoroastrianism*, p. 338, and D. C. Simpson *in loc.* (Oxford Apocrypha). For the text as it stands good illustration may be found in the Egyptian documents, P Leid Dᵃ¹⁶ εἰς τοὺς ἄνω τόπους, "ad loca superiora," and the contemporary *OGIS* 111¹⁷ (after B.C. 163) ἐπὶ τῶν ἄνω τόπων [ταχθείς]. Cf. P Petr II. 33 (a) ᴬ·¹·¹⁰ (a steward's account) ἄρτων τῶν ἀποσταλέντων σοι ἄνω, P Oxy IV. 744⁸ (B.C. 1) (= *Selections*, p. 33) ἀποστελῶ σε ἄνω, "I will send them up to you" (from Alexandria): on σέ = σοί, cf. *Proleg.* p. 64. For ἡ ἄνω κλῆσις in Phil 3¹⁴ the RV *mg* (= "the call, Come up!") is apparently presumed in *Apoc. Baruch* 4 (p. 87³³, ed. James) ἐν αὐτῷ μέλλουσιν τὴν ἄνω κλῆσιν προσλαβεῖν, καὶ τὴν εἰς παράδεισον εἴσοδον. A curious metrical epitaph (no. 69) in Prof. Calder's Phrygian collection, dated by him after the middle of iv/A.D., begins

νῦν ἀγαπᾷς σὺ μαθεῖν τίς ἐγὼ ξένος, ἢ πόθεν ἦλθα ;
ἐγ λεγεῶνος ἄνω θεμέν[ων] βασιλέα μέγιστον,

which he renders "from the legion of those that have set the mighty king on high." In P Fay 101 *verso* ᴵ·¹⁵ (an account, about B.C. 18) we find ἄνω· Παῦνι δ ἕως Ἐπεὶφ ῑε, where the editors explain ἄνω as indicating that the following dates "Pauni 4 to Epeiph 15" should have headed the account, instead of coming at the end. The superlative ἀνωτάτω occurs in P Lond 1170 *verso* (c)¹¹ (A.D. 42) (= III. p. 107) τῇ ἀνωτάτω χρήσομαι τειμωρίᾳ, "the highest penalty"— an unusual application : cf. Epict. iii. 24⁸¹ ἡ ἀνωτάτω καὶ κυριωτάτη (*sc.* ἄσκησις). The compound ἐπάνω (*q.v.*) is represented in MGr.

ἄνωθεν.

In P Petr III. 43(2)ⁱᵛ·¹⁷ (B.C. 246) ἄνωθεν is found in opposition to κάτω : *hiat contextus.* P Hib I. 110⁶⁵ (records of postal service, *c.* B.C. 255) ὥρας πρώτης παρέδωκεν Θεύχρ[η]στος ἄνωθεν Δινίαι κυ[λιστο]ὺς γ̄, "1st hour, Theochrestus delivered to Dinias 3 rolls from the upper country" (Edd.). "Ανωθεν appears again twice in this document, and κάτωθεν "from the lower country." (This is a very early example of the approximation of ο and ω, on which see *Proleg.*³ pp. 244 and 35 f.). BGU IV. 1208² (Aug.) καταντή[σα]ς ἐκ τῶν ἄνωθεν [τόπων] . . . ἐκομισά[μη]ν διὰ Σωτηρίχου κτλ. In P Tebt I. 59⁶ ᶠᶠ·¹⁰ (B.C. 99) ἣν ἔχετε πρὸς ἡμᾶς ἄνωθεν πατρικὴν φιλίαν, and διὰ τὸ ἄνωθεν

φοβεῖσθαι καὶ σέβεσθαι τὸ ἱερόν, the editors translate "of old." P Oxy II. 237ᵛⁱⁱⁱ·³¹ (A.D. 186) ὅπερ οὐ καλῶς ἐνδέχεται, εἰ μὴ ἄνωθεν γένοιτο ἀντίγραφα, "this cannot be done adequately unless copies are made from the beginning" (Edd.). In P Oxy IV. 718²¹ (A.D. 180-92) ἔτι δὲ ἄνωθ[ε]ν τῶν δημοσίων ἀποδιδομένων, the editors translate "although the imposts have for years been paid." But "completely," "from the beginning" may equally be the sense of ἄνωθεν : cf. *ib.* 745ᵗ·ᶠᶠ (*c.* A.D. 1) μ[ὴ . . .]νε[.] . η[. .]να ἄνωθεν γείνηται πάντα καὶ πάλιν ἑατοὺς ἀνασκευάζωμε[ν] μὴ οὔσης χρήας, "in order that everything may not be completely . . . and we go bankrupt again without any necessity" (Edd.). In BGU II. 595⁵ ᶠᶠ (A.D. 70-80) the meaning "again," "a second time," seems best to suit the context. A certain Sochotes, wishing to repay a loan, did not find his creditor— τοῦ δὲ σὲ μὴ εὑρεθῆναι ἀποδέδωκε αὐτὰς ἄνωθον (for ἄνωθεν) ἵνα φιλάνθρωπον εἰς δύο τόπους μὴι χορηγῆι, where Lietzmann (*Gr. Pap.* p. 14) understands by φιλάνθρωπον a gratuity : "S. has once paid it and would have to pay it again, if he went back home with the borrowed money ; therefore he returns it immediately." Other examples of the word are CPR 1¹⁹ (i/A.D.) καθὼς ἄνωθεν εἴθιστο, P Tebt II. 298⁶¹ (A.D. 107) ἀκολούθως τῇ ἄν[ωθ]εν συνηθείᾳ, BGU IV. 1074² (iii/A.D.) τοῖς ἄνωθεν προγόνοις, and P Oxy IX. 1204¹⁴ (A.D. 299) δεδέηται τῆς θείας τύχης ἔτι ἄνωθεν τῶν δεσποτῶν ἡμῶν. The usage of the inscriptions follows on similar lines. Dittenberger (*Syll* III. p. 256) enumerates three meanings—(1) *de supero* 537⁶³ ἐπεργάσεται ὀρθὸν καὶ ὁμαλὲς ἄνωθεν, (2) *antiquitus* 929³¹ νόμοις γὰρ ἱεροῖς . . . ἄνωθεν διεκεκώλυτο ἵνα μηθεὶς κτλ., (3) *denuo* 732¹¹ γενηθεὶς δ[ὲ] καὶ παραίτιος τῆς ἄνωθεν συλλογῆς, a decree of i/B.C. referring to the revival of certain sacred practices which had ceased for some time.

ἀνώτερος.

For this comparative with reference to time, cf. *Syll* 307⁵⁵ (ii/B.C.) ἔτει ἀνώτερον τρί[τῳ], *ib.* 318⁶ (B.C. 118) τὸν ἀνώτερον μὲν χρόνον πάντα διατετέλεκεν. In P Giss I. 48²⁴ (A.D. 202-3) we find the -ω form, τοῖς ἀνωτέρω ἔτεσι.

ἀνωφελής.

P Lond 908³¹ (A.D. 139) (= III. p. 133) ὅπως εἰδῇ ἄκυρον καὶ ἀνωφελὲς κριθησόμενον ὃ μετέδωκεν ὑπόμνημα. The same document has κενῶς καὶ [ἀ]νωφελῶς (l. 28). In P Hawara 56²⁹ (?late i/A.D.) (= *Archiv* v. p. 382) we find a derived subst., ὅτι ἀρρωστίαν ἰσοθάνατο(ν) [ἐξ]ήντλησα καὶ ἄλλας πολλὰς ἀνωφελίας.

ἀξίνη.

P Magd 8⁶ (B.C. 218) δρέπανον θεριστικὸν οὗ τιμὴ (δραχμὰς) β, ἀξίνη (δραχμὰς) β. Herwerden *s.v.* κλής recalls the proverbial saying—τῇ κλειδὶ τὰ ξύλα σχίζειν, τῇ δ' ἀξίνη τὴν θύραν ἀνοίγειν (Plut. *Mor.* 43 C). Cf. MGr ἀξινάρι.

ἄξιος

appears with infin. in BGU IV. 1141¹³ (B.C. 14) ἐγὼ μὲν οὐ δοκῶι ἄξιος εἶναι ὑβρίζεσθαι. For the absolute use (as Mt 10¹¹·¹³) see P Petr II. 15 (3)⁷ (B.C. 241-39) τοῦτο δὲ ποιήσας εὐχαριστήσεις ἡμῖν κ[αὶ?] ἄξιος γάρ ἐστιν ὁ ἄνθρωπος ἐν χρείαι[. . . where the editor translates, "By doing this you will oblige us, [. .] for the man is worthy of it, [but] in need—." The sense of "worth," "value," is illustrated by P Lille I. 6[8] (iii/B.C.), where a certain Petesuchos complains that robbers ἐξέδυσαν χιτῶνα ἄξιον (δραχμὰς) ϛ "a tunic worth six drachmas." So the fem. became a noun = "value": BGU IV. 1118[30] (B.C. 22) πείθεσθαι περὶ τῆς τούτων ἀξίας, ib. 1126[14] (B.C. 8) ἐκτίνιν τὴν ἑκάστου ἀξίαν πλὴν συμφανοῦς ἀπ[ωλείας]. For ἀξίως τοῦ θεοῦ (as in 1 Th 2[12], 3 Jn[6] etc.) see Deissmann BS p. 248 f., who shows that "the formula was a very popular one in Pergamus (and doubtless also in other localities)." He cites five inscrr., as Perg I. 248[7] ff. (ii/B.C.), where Athenaios, a priest of Dionysios and Sabazios, is extolled as συ[ν]τετελεκότος τὰ ἱερά . . . εὐσεβῶς [μ]ὲγ καὶ ἀξίως τοῦ θεοῦ. We may add Magn 33[20] (Gounos in Thessaly, iii/B.C.) ἀξίως [τ]ῆ[ς] θε[ε]ᾶς, ib. 85[10 f.] (Tralles) ἀξίως τῆς τε Ἀρτέμιδος . . . καὶ [τοῦ] . . δήμου, and Priene 110[15] (end of i/B.C.) πομπεύσας τῆ προστάτιδι τῆς] πόλεως Ἀθηνᾶι τῆς θεᾶς ἀξί[ως]. So P Petr II. 13 (19)[4] (c. B.C. 252) (= Witkowski,[2] p. 18) οὐ] μὴν οὐδὲν ἐμοὶ [ἔσται με]ῖζον ἢ σοῦ προστατῆσα[ι τὸν] ἐ[π]ίλοιπον βίον, ἀξίως [μὲ]ν σοῦ, ἀξίως δ' ἐμοῦ, where the dependent gen. is neither divine nor a community, but has the dignity characteristic of the *pietas* of this charming letter. A combination may be seen in the letter of Aline to her husband, P Giss I. 20[24] (ii/A.D.), following the citation under ἀξιόω below, ἵνα ἀξίως σοῦ καὶ τῶν θεῶν ἀόκνως προσέλθη. The word survives in MGr.

ἀξιόω

is very common in legal documents = "claim," e.g. P Oxy I. 37[i. 21] (A.D. 49) (= Selections, p. 50) ἀξιῶι ταῦ[τα] φυλαχθῆ[ν]αι, "I demand that these (documents) be preserved (in the record)," ib. II. 237[vi. 14] (A.D. 186) ἀξιῶν τότε ἃ προσήνεγκα αὐτῆ ἀνακομίσασθαι, "claiming to recover what I had made over to her." It also frequently occurs in the weakened sense "request," "ask," as P Eleph 19[18] (iii/B.C.) ἀξιῶ σε ἀνακαλέσασθαι Μίλωνα, P Par 49[10 ff.] (B.C. 164–58) (= Witkowski[2], p. 70) τοῦ δὲ ἀδελφοῦ σου συμπεσόντος μοι . . . καὶ ἀξιώσαντός με, P. Oxy IV. 805 (B.C. 25) ἀξιῶ δὲ ἀντιφωνεῖν [μ]οι πυκνότερον, P Giss I. 20[22] (ii/A.D.) ἀξιώσεις οὖν δίστιχον αὐτῶι γραφῆναι (can this mean "you will arrange that . . ."?). For ἀξιόω of prayer (as LXX Jer 7[16], 11[14]) cf. P Par 51[22] (a dream from the Serapeum, B.C. 160) (= Selections, p. 20) ἡξίωκα τὸν Σάραπιν καὶ τὴν Ἶσιν λέγων· Ἐλθέ μοι, θεὰ θεῶν κτλ., and Syll 816[1] (ii/i B.C.) ἐπικαλοῦμαι καὶ ἀξιῶ τὸν θεὸν τὸν ὕψιστον . . . ἐπὶ τοὺς δόλωι φονεύσαντας κτλ. (See Deissmann LAE p. 423 ff.) The verb occurs in OGIS 201[7] (the Silco inscription, vi/A.D.) αὐτοὶ ἡξίωσάν με, where Dittenberger renders, "dignitatem meam regian agnoverunt." For a similar use of the noun ἀξίωμα, see P Tebt I. 33[4] (B.C. 112) (= Selections, p. 30) ἐν μίζονι ἀξιώματι κα[ὶ] τιμῆι. For the LXX usage of ἀξίωμα = "request, petition" (Esther 5[3·8], 7[2 f.] etc.), Deissmann (BS p. 92 f.) refers to the confirmation afforded by the inscriptions, e.g. Syll 303[6] (before B.C. 146) περὶ ἧς (χώρας) ἐπιδοὺς ἀξίωμα βασιλεὺς Θρακῶν Κότ[υς] . . . ἤτει τ[ὴν π]άτριον ἡμῶν χώραν. Fränkel on Perg I. 13[1] (iii/B.C.) describes it as very rare: see his exx.

ἀόρατος.

P Leid W[ii. 27] (occult) has ἀ. among divine epithets, also vii. 41 of fire (!). From Hellenistic times comes the Milesian epitaph Kaibel 223 ἀνύσαντά σε τὰν ἀόρατον . . ἀτρατατου (ἀτραπιτὸν Ed.) βιότου: "videtur via dici quam qui sequitur nescit quo ducit." The subst. occurs in Magn 114[1] διὰ τὴν . . . ἀορασίαν τῶν ἀρτοκόπων.

ἀπαγγέλλω.

The verb = "report," "announce" (as Mk 6[30]) is found in P Lond 42[25 ff.] (B.C. 168) (= I. p. 30, Selections, p. 11) ἔτι δὲ καὶ Ὥρου τοῦ τὴν ἐπιστολὴν παρακεκομικό[το]ς ἀπηγγελκότος ὑπὲρ τοῦ ἀπολελύσθαι σε ἐκ τῆς κατοχῆς παντελῶς ἀηδί-ζομαι, "and now that Horus who brought the letter has reported about your having been released from your retreat, I am utterly distressed." So P Tebt II. 297[7] (c. A.D. 123) ἀπήνγ[ει]λεν τὴν τάξιν ὡς ὀφείλουσαν πραθῆναι, "reported that the office ought to be sold." Abbott, Joh. Voc. p. 164, has a good note on the force of ἀπ. = "report, bring word" in Jn 16[25]: he illustrates it from Epictetus. In the interesting proceedings before a Roman Emperor, P Oxy I. 33 (late ii/A.D.), the word seems almost to have the legal sense of "appeal," as when the accused man exclaims, v. 6 ff.: ὑπὲρ τῆς ἐμαυτοῦ εὐγενείας . . . ἀπαγγέλλ[ω], "I appeal on behalf of my nobility" (Edd.).

ἀπάγω.

The verb is found four times in P Oxy I. 33 (late ii/A.D.), of one being "led off" to death, which may perhaps determine the meaning in Ac 12[19]: the guards were not merely "imprisoned," but "led away to death" (RV mg). Lk 23[26], with the Vulgate duci and the gloss ἀποκτανθῆναι in D*, are probably decisive for this (the Attic) meaning. On the other hand, it should be noted that ἀ. is the ordinary word for "arresting" (cf. Gen 39[22] τοὺς ἀπηγμένους = "the prisoners") as P Petr III. 36 (a) verso[8] ἀδίκως ἀπηγμένον and ib.[27] ἀ]κριβείας ἕνεκεν ἀπήχθην: so P Lille 7[13] (iii/B.C.) οὗτος δὲ ἀπήγαγέν με εἰς τὸ αὐθι δεσμωτήριον, P Petr II. 10 (2)[12] συνέταξεν ὁ ὑπηρέτης ἀπαγαγεῖν με, "the apparitor gave directions to arrest me" (Ed.), and OGIS 90[14] (the Rosetta stone, B.C. 196) τοὺς ἐν ταῖς φυλακαῖς ἀπηγμένους . . . ἀπέλυσε τῶν ἐνκεκλ(η)μένων. Cf. also P Oxy II. 237[vi. 18] (A.D. 186), where Chaeremon claims the right of taking away his daughter even against her will from her husband's house—ἀπάγοντι αὐτὴν ἄκουσαν ἐκ τῆς τοῦ ἀνδρὸς οἰκίας, BGU IV. 1139[15] (B.C. 5) ἐτόλμησε . . . ἀποστερεῖν ἀπαγαγεῖν τὴν θυγατέρα ἡμῶν . . . καὶ ἔχειν παρ' ἑαυτῶι ἐν εἱρκτ[ῆ ἐπὶ] μῆνας ἕ. In the dialect inscription Syll 271[6, 23] (ii/B.C.) it denotes apparently the "capture" of youths in a raid.

ἀπαίδευτος.

In P Oxy I. 33[ii. 13] (late ii/A.D.) Appianus does not hesitate to charge the Emperor (? Marcus Aurelius) with τυραννία ἀφιλοκαγαθία ἀπαιδία as contrasted with the virtues of his deified father Antoninus who was φιλόσοφος . . . ἀφιλάργυρος . . . φιλάγαθος. See Archiv i. p. 37.

ἀπαίρω.

For the intransitive sense of ἀ. = "depart," as in Gen 37[17], cf. P Petr II. 13 (5)[5] (B.C. 258–3) ἀπ[ηρμ]ένον "on your departure." In the Paris magical papyrus 3082 Deissmann (LAE p. 254) ingeniously proposes to substitute for the meaningless ἀφαιρων of the MS. ἀπαίρων in the sense of "make to go forth" (as LXX Ps 77²⁶,⁵²)—ὁρκίζων δὲ φύσα ἀπὸ τῶν ἄκρων καὶ τῶν ποδῶν ἀπαίρων τὸ φύσημα ἕως τοῦ προσώπου καὶ εἰσκριθήσεται. MGr παίρνω (also παίρω) is given as "take," "fetch" in Thumb's Glossary: it might equally well come from ἐπαίρω, but the meaning suits ἀπαίρω better.

ἀπαιτέω.

BGU II. 530³⁶ (i/A.D.) (= *Selections*, p. 62) ἄλλως τε καὶ ἀπαιτεῖται ὑπὸ τῶν πρακτόρων ἱκανόν, "especially security is demanded by the taxgatherers": cf. P Fay 39¹⁴ᶠᶠ (A.D. 183) ἐκ τίνος ἀπαιτεῖται τὸ προκείμενον ἀπότακτον, where the editors state that ἀ. "may imply that the payment was in arrear or have a quite general meaning." The former alternative is clearly implied in P Fay 11²⁰ (c. B.C. 115) ὁ ἐνκαλούμενος πλεονάκις ἀπῃτημένος [ο]ὐχ ὑπομένει ἑκουσίως ἀποδιδόναι, "the accused, though frequent demands have been made, persistently refuses to pay voluntarily" (Edd.). Other examples of the verb, which is common, are P Flor I. 61⁴² (A.D. 86–8) διὰ τί ἕως σήμερον οὐκ ἀπῄτησας, and again ⁶¹ ἐπεὶ σιτόλογοι ἦσαν καὶ ἀπητ[οῦ]ντο εἰς τὸν Κ[α]ίσαρος λόγον, P Lond 856¹⁹ (late i/A.D.) (= III. p. 92) ὁ δὲ λήμπτωρ ἀπαιτεῖ certain taxes, P Tebt II. 327¹⁹ᶠᶠ (late ii/A.D.) οὐ δεόντως ἀπαιτοῦμα[ι] τὰ ὑπὲρ τῶν ὑπαρχόν[τω]ν τελούμενα δημόσια, "demands have wrongfully been made upon me for the government dues payable on behalf of the property" (Edd.): a very similar phrase occurs in CPHerm 52ⁱ,¹⁶. In P Oxy VIII. 1157¹⁵ (late iii/A.D.) καὶ μάθε ὅτι τὸ ἐπεικεφάλαιον ἀπαιτοῦσιν "find out also about the collection of the poll-tax" (Ed.): the idiomatic impersonal plural curiously contrasts with the translation Greek, showing the same word, in Lk 12²⁰. In the Christian letter P Oxy VI. 939¹⁶ (iv/A.D.) (= *Selections*, p. 129) we have the phrase τοῦτο τοῦ καθήκοντος ἀπ[α]ι-[τοῦντ]ος, "this being what duty demanded." For the subst. see BGU IV. 1103¹⁸ (B.C. 14) περὶ ἀπαιτήσεως τοῦ φερναρίου, P Oxy I. 104²⁸ (a will, A.D. 96) ἀπαίτη[σι]ν ποιήσεσθαι, etc., and for the adj. ἀπαιτήσιμος various land-surveys of ii/B.C.—P Tebt I. 61, 64, 72. The noun ἀπαιτητής occurs in Wilcken *Ostr* 1460 (A.D. 185–6) δι' ἐμοῦ Μάρκου . . . ἀπαιτ(ητοῦ).

ἀπαλγέω.

To Grimm-Thayer's reff. for this NT ἅπ. εἰρ. (Eph 4¹⁹ ἀπηλγηκότες, but ἀπηλπικότες DG etc.) in its Hellenistic sense of "to despair" or "become callous," add Dion Cass. xlviii. 37 ἀ. πρὸς τὴν ἐλπίδα.

ἀπαλλάσσω.

In one of the oldest marriage-contracts hitherto discovered among the Greek papyri, P Gen I. 21¹² (ii/B.C.), provision is made for what will take place if the wife of her own accord βούληται ἀπαλλάσσεσθαι, "desires to be released": so P Tebt I. 104³¹ (B.C. 92), P Oxy I. 104²⁶ (a will, A.D. 96) ἡνίκα ἐὰν ἀπαλλαγῇ τοῦ ἀνδρός, ib. II. 265¹⁷ (A.D. 81–95), ib. II. 207¹⁷,²⁰ (A.D. 36), al, and for the subst. in a similar sense P Oxy VI. 905¹¹ (A.D. 170) ἐ]ὰν δ[ὲ ἀ]παλλαγὴ γένη[τα]ι. The correlative is well seen in P Ryl II. 154²⁶ (A.D. 66) ἐὰν δὲ διαφορᾶς αὐτοῖς γεναμένης [χ]ωρίζονται ἀπ' ἀλλήλων, ἤτοι τοῦ Χ. ἀποπέμποντος τ[ὴ]ν Θ. ἢ καὶ αὐτῆς ἑκουσίω[ς ἀ]παλλασσομέν[η]ς [ἀ]π' αὐτοῦ: the correspond-

ing nouns ἀποπομπή and ἑκούσιος ἀπαλλαγή appear in l. ²⁹. A more general use of the verb is afforded by P Petr II. 2 (3)¹ᶠ (B.C. 260) (= Witkowski², p. 22) εἰ ἔρρωσαι καὶ ἐν τοῖς [ἄ]λλοις ἀλύπως ἀπαλλάσσεις, "if you are well and in other respects are getting on without annoyance." P Petr II. 20ⁱᵛ·⁸ (as amended P Petr III.) (B.C. 252) λυσιτε-λέστερον ἀπαλλάξει, "it will be more profitable for you to release (the boat from ἀγγαρία)." P Ryl II. 77³⁵ (A.D. 192) καὶ ἀπαλλαγῆναι ἐπιτηρήσεως "released from the super-intendence of land under lease" (Edd.). The perf. partic. mid. means "dead" in P Lond 015¹³ (A.D. 160 or 161) (= III. p. 27): cf. μετηλλαχώς. P Tebt II. 315 (ii/A.D.) twice shows the word, as ¹⁵ [μη]δὲν ταραχ[θ]ῇς, ἐγὼ γάρ [σ]ε [ἀ]παλλάξω (and so²⁹) "I will get you off" (Edd.). Ib. 385²⁴ (A.D. 117) ᾧ καὶ δώσι ἀπαλλασσομένῳ . . . "on his release (from apprenticeship)": cf. the subst. in P Oxy IX. 1204¹³ (A.D. 299) ἀπαλλαγὴν εὕρασθαι πειρώμενος . . . τῶν πολει-τικῶν λειτουργιῶν, "endeavouring to find a release from municipal offices." The τοῦ βίου, which produces the use noted above, is expressed in Hadrian's dying letter (or what purports to be such), P Fay 19¹⁹ [οὔτε ἀ]νοήτως ἀπαλλάσσομε τοῦ βίου. From inscriptions may be cited *Syll* 510⁸⁹ (ii/B.C.) ὅσοι δὲ ἐγκαταλιπόντες τὰ κτήματα ἀπηλλαγμένοι εἰσίν, οἱ δὲ τοκισταὶ γεγεωργήκασιν, εἶναι τὰ κτήματα τῶν τοκιστῶν, apparently "have absconded." So P Fay 12¹⁹ (c. B.C. 103) ἀπηλλάγησαν. There is a curious use in P Flor II. 262¹⁴ (iii/A.D.) ἀπήλαξεν γὰρ τότε τὸν πῆχιν δραχμῶν δέκα, which Comparetti renders "poichè allora valutò il cubito a dieci dramm:"—so we say "he let it go for a shilling."

ἀπαλλοτριόω.

Syll 226¹⁸⁴ (Olbia on Euxine, iii/B.C.) οὐδενὸς δ' ἀπηλλοτρί-ωσε οὐδὲν τῶν ὑπαρχόντων. Ib. 860¹²,¹³ (in dialect, Delphi, ii/B.C.) ὡσα[ύτω]ς δὲ μηδὲ ἀπαλλοτριωσάτω 'Ασία . . . , εἰ δὲ ἀπαλλοτριωοίη καθ' ὁποίον τρόπον κτλ. *OGIS* 383¹⁸³ (i/B.C.) μήτε αὐτὼι καταδουλώσασθαι, μήτε εἰς ἕτερον ἀπαλ-λοτριῶσαι. Dittenberger (*Syll* II. p. 10, n⁹) cites another Delphian inscr. with ἀπαλλοτριώουσα. Cf. also *Syll* 226¹² (iii/B.C., Orchomenus in Arcadia—in dialect) μὴ ἐξέστω μηθενὶ ἀπαλλοτριῶ[σαι ἐντὸς ἐτ]έων εἴ[κ]οσι (sc. γᾶν κλᾶρον ἢ οἰκίαν), P Lond 1157 *verso*(b)³ (illiterate, A.D. 246) (= III. p. 111) ἀπολοτριοῦσται, apparently for ἀπαλλοτριοῦσθαι (Edd.). The compound ἐξαλλ. is more common: thus P Giss I. 2ⁱ·²⁴ (B.C. 173), BGU IV. 1167⁶² (B.C. 12), ib. 1187¹³ (i/B.C.), P Oxy VIII. 1118²⁰ (i/ii A.D.), of the "alienation" of property. Note also the verbal ἀνεξαλλοτρίωτον in P Ryl II. 177¹¹ (A.D. 246), "unalienated": we might say of this what we said of ἀνεπαίσχυντος and other like words. The noun occurs in Vettius Valens p. 2³⁷, where Mars is said to produce a host of evils, including γονέων ἀπαλ-λοτριώσεις, "estrangements of parents."

ἀπαντάω.

The verb is very common of "attendance" before a magistrate. It is sufficient to cite P Petr III. 30⁵ καὶ φαμένη καταστήσεσθαι πρὸς [με] τ[ὴ]... οὐκ ἀπήντη[σέ] σε, "though she said that she would appear against me on the . . . she did not present herself" (Edd.), P Tor II. 13¹⁵ (B.C. 147) ἀ. ἐπὶ τὸ κριτήριον, P Grenf I. 13⁵ (B.C. 152 or 141) ἀπαντᾶν ἐπὶ σέ, P Oxy I. 59⁸ᶠᶠ (A.D. 292) αἱρεθέντος Θεοδώρου ἀντὶ 'Αρείονος σκρείβα ἀπαντῆσαι ἐπὶ τὴν ἡγεμονίαν καὶ προσεδρεῦσαι τῷ ἀχράντῳ αὐτοῦ δικαστηρί[ῳ], "Theodorus, who was recently chosen in place of Arion the scribe to proceed to his highness the prefect and attend his immaculate court" (Edd.), P Cairo Preis 4²⁰ (A.D. 320) ἀπαντησάτωσαν [ἐπ]ὶ τὸ ἡγ[ε]μονικὸν δικαστήριον, and from the inscriptions, *Syll* 737⁹⁴ (ii/iii A.D.) εἰ δέ τις τῶν ἰοβάκχων, εἰδὼς ἐπὶ τοῦτο ἀγορὰν ὀφείλουσαν ἀχθῆναι, μὴ ἀπαντήσῃ, ἀποτεισάτω τῷ κοινῷ λεπτοῦ δρ[α]χμὰς ν̄. P Lond 42²ᶠ· B.C. 168) (= I. p. 30, *Selections* p. 9) εἰ ἐρρωμένοι τἆλλα κατὰ λόγον ἀπαντᾷ, "if you are well, and things in general are going right," shows a common epistolary formula: cf. P Vat A² (B.C. 168) (= Witkowski², p. 64), P Par 45²ᶠ· (B.C. 153) *al.* In MGr the verb means "answer."

ἀπάντησις.

The word is used absolutely (as Mt 25⁶ and LXX 1 Regn 13¹⁵) in P Tebt I. 43⁶· ⁷ (B.C. 118) παρεγενήθημεν εἰς ἀπάντησιν (a newly arriving magistrate)—a passage which may demolish the Semitism sometimes found lurking in the word. For εἰς ἀ. construed with the gen. (as Mt 27³² δ-text and 1 Th 4¹⁷) cf. BGU II. 362ˣⁱⁱ ¹⁷ (A.D. 215) πρὸς [ἀ]πάντη[σιν τοῦ] ἡγεμόνος, and the *Pelagia-Legenden* (ed. Usener) p. 19 εἰς ἀπάντησιν τοῦ ὁσίου ἀνδρός. A Ptolemaic inscription edited by Strack (*Archiv* iii. p. 129) has ἵν' εἰδῇ[ἣν ἔσχηκεν πρὸς αὐτὸν ἡ πόλις εὐχάριστον ἀπάντησιν. The word seems to have been a kind of *t.t.* for the official welcome of a newly arrived dignitary—a usage which accords excellently with its NT usage. See *Proleg.*³ pp. 14, 242.

For a subst. ἀπαντητήριον, *deversorium*, see P Iand 17³ (vi/vii. A.D.).

ἅπαξ.

P Oxy III. 471⁷⁷ (ii/A.D.) ἅπαξ γὰρ ἐν ἔθει τῆς α[ἰσ]χύνης γενόμενον, "for when once accustomed to his shame" (Edd.). In P Lond 417⁸ (c. A.D. 346) (= III. p. 299, *Selections*, p. 124), we find συνχωρῆσε αὐτοῦ τούτω τὸ ἄβαξ (= συνχωρῆσαι αὐτῷ τοῦτο τὸ ἅπαξ) "pardon him this once"—a substantival use of ἅπαξ, which has been traced perhaps to Coptic influence (Deissmann *LAE*, pp. 206, 209): cf. below. Note also P Giss I. 48¹⁰ (A.D. 202–3) οὐχ ἅπαξ παρεγράφη, "not once alone," ἀλλ' ὁποσάκις ἕκαστα προσηνέχθη, and P Oxy VIII. 1102⁸ (c. A.D. 146) ἐπεὶ ἅπαξ προσῆ[λθε] τῇ κληρονομίᾳ, "having once entered on the inheritance" (Ed.). Vettius Valens, p. 285³⁰ has ἅπαξ τε καὶ ἀπαραιτήτως δαμάζουσιν (Ed.). *OGIS* 201 (vi/A.D.), an inscr. of King Silco of Nubia, which is very instructive for the study of foreigners' Greek, has ἅπαξ in a curious idiom: thus ἐν ἅπαξ is *semel*, τὸ πρῶτον ἅπαξ = *primum*, ἅπαξ δύο = *bis*. Dittenberger quotes Lepsius to show that it is an effort to render a Coptic word answering to Ger. *Mal*, Fr. *fois*. In P Oxy VIII. 1138¹³ (v/vi A.D.) the words πρὸς ἅπαξ occurring at the end of a receipt are translated "once for all" by the editor, who compares BGU IV. 1020¹⁵ (vi/A.D.): so εἰς ἅπαξ P Oxy X. 1294¹⁴ (ii/iii A.D.).

ἀπαράβατος.

In P Ryl II. 65¹⁸ (B.C. 67?—in any case Ptol.) a judgement ends with καὶ τἆλλα τὰ δι' αὐτῆ[ς δι]ωρισμένα μένειν κύρια καὶ ἀπαράβατα, "valid and inviolate" (Edd.). The legal formula, thus established for an early period, survives six centuries later in P Grenf I. 60⁷ (A.D. 581) ἀπαραβάτῳ

πράσει: "inviolable" must be the sense, though the words follow a hiatus. Another example, also vi A.D., is in P Lond 1015¹² (= III. p. 257) ἄτρωτα καὶ ἀσάλευτα καὶ ἀπαράβατα. . . , a contract for the surrender of property. See also P Catt recto⁸· ¹³ (ii/A.D.) (= *Chrest.* II. p. 422) ἔνια ἀπαράβατά ἐστιν, "es gibt Dinge, an denen sich nichts andern lasst" (Ed.). It is clear that the technical use, compared with the late literary (ap. Lobeck *Phryn.* p. 313), constitutes a very strong case against the rendering "not transferable". Phrynichus himself prescribed ἀπαραίτητος: what sense that would have made in Heb 7⁴ passes comprehension. Vettius Valens has the adverb five times (see index), always as "validly" or "inevitably." It occurs in P Strass I. 45²⁰ (A.D. 569), rendered "unverbrüchlich" (Ed.).

ἀπαρνέομαι.

A literary citation for this word may be given from the recently recovered *Mimes* of Herodas, IV. 74 οὐδ' ἐρεῖς "κεῖνος ὤνθρωπος ἐν μὲν εἶδεν, ἐν δ' ἀπηρνήθη," where Nairn prefers to render ἀ. "failed to see" rather than "was denied": cf. Mk 8³⁴ εἴ τις θέλει ὀπίσω μου ἐλθεῖν, ἀπαρνησάσθω ἑαυτόν, "let him lose sight of himself and his own interests," as Grimm renders. But this involves a needless distinction from Mk 14⁷², where the verb means "disown."

ἀπαρτί

is to be written as two words, the combination matching such familiar Hellenistic locutions as ἕως ἄρτι, ἐκ πότε, ἀπὸ πέρυσι, etc. The two Attic quotations which Thayer takes over from LS are denied by Lobeck *Phryn.* p. 21, who takes ἀπαρτί by preference in the extant passage: Rutherford *NP* p. 71 agrees with him. Ἀπαρτί = "exactly" in Ionic, and (by irony) "quite the contrary" in Attic (Rutherford): it has a totally different history from ἀπ' ἄρτι. On the practice of the critical editors, see Nestle *Einf. in das Gr. NT³*, p. 27

ἀπαρτισμός.

We can only cite two instances of this rare noun, one from P Catt verso⁹· ²⁵ (ii/A.D.) (= *Chrest.* II. p. 90) μέχρι τοῦ τῆς λογοθεσίας ἀπαρτισμοῦ "till the completion of the audit," and the other from P Giss I. 67⁷ ᶠᶠ· (time of Trajan or Hadrian) ἤδη κα[τ]ὰ τὰς ἐντολάς σου Ἡράκλειος ὁ ἐπίτρ[ο]πος χωρὶς τῶν ξενικῶν ξύλων τὸν ἀπαρτισ[μ]ὸ[ν] τῶν ἐπὶ [τό]πων [ἔργων πρ]ὸ ὀφθαλμῶν ἔχει. But the verbal phrase εἰς τὸ ἀπαρτίζειν is so completely equivalent to εἰς ἀπαρτισμόν (Lk 14²⁸) that the verb may be illustrated. P Oxy I. 117⁴ ⁷ (ii/iii A.D.) has the aor. pass. twice, the "completing" of a horoscope (?) and of a sale of slaves: cf. *ib.* VI. 908²³ (A.D. 199) ὥστε ὑφ' ἑκάστου ὑμῶν ἀρτοκοπεῖον ἓν ἀπαρτισθῆναι, "that one bakery be fitted out by each of you" (Edd.), *ib.* 936²² (iii/A.D.) οὐκ ἔχω ἄρτι σεῖτον οὐδὲ τὰ βιβλίδια ἀπήρ[τ]ισται ἕως ἄρτι, "I have no food now, and the petitions have not yet been got ready" (Edd.). P Oxy IV. 724¹¹ (A.D. 155) ἐὰν δὲ ἐντὸς τοῦ χ[ρ]όνου αὐτὸν ἀπαρτίσῃς οὐκ ἐκδέξομαι τὴν προκειμένην προθεσμ[ί]αν "if you make him perfect [in shorthand] within the period, I will not wait for the aforesaid limit" (Edd.) is a close parallel to the NT use of καταρτίζω (Gal 6¹, 1 Th 3¹⁰ *al.*).

P Lips I. 105¹¹ (i/ii A.D.) μόγις τὸν τῆς βεβρεγμένης ἀπήρτισα, "I have with difficulty completed the account of the irrigated land." BGU II. 448²³ ᶠᶠ. (ii/A.D.) πρὸς τὸ τὴν π[ρ]οα[ί]ρεσ[ι]ν τῶν [διαθεμέ]νων φανερὰν [κ]ατα- στῆ[ναι καὶ ἕκασ]τα ἀπαρτισθῆναι τοῖς ἐν[γ]εγρα[μμ]έν[ο]ις ἀκολούθως. In P Catt *verso*ᶦᶦᶦ·¹³ (as cited above) we find the expression μετὰ τὴν χειροτονίαν ἐντὸς ἓ ἡμερῶν ἀπαρτι- οῦσιν τὰς δίκας. P Ryl II. 74⁴ (A.D. 133–5) shows the verb in a proclamation of M. Petronius Mamertinus, prefect of Egypt, where [τὸν διαλο]γισμὸν ἀπαρτίσαι is rendered by the editors "to complete the *conventus*." We could cite many more exx.: the relative frequency of the ἀπό and the κατά compounds of this verb in NT and papyri is quite reversed.

ἀπαρχή.

In P Tor I. 1ᵛᶦᶦ·¹⁰ (B.C. 117) the word is used for "legacy-duty": see Wilcken *Ostr.* i. p. 345 f., *Archiv* iii. p. 7 f. and Mitteis in *Chrest.* II. p. 421. In P Tebt II. 316¹⁰ (A.D. 99) καὶ μὴ ἀλλοτρίᾳ ἀπαρχῇ μηδὲ ὁμωνυμίᾳ κεχρῆ- σται, the editors understand it of the "entrance-fee" paid by ephebi on enrolment in the Alexandrian demes, and suggest the same meaning for P Flor I. 57⁸¹ (A.D. 100) τοῦ παιδὸς ἀπαρχή, where, however, Vitelli refers it to "la tassa di successione," and Wilcken (*Chrest.* I. p. 168) regards the sense as still obscure. See also BGU I. 30 ἡ ἀπαρχὴ Μάρκου Ἀντωνίου Διοσκύρου, and *ib.* IV. 1150¹¹ (B.C. 11) ἀνακεκόμισται δὲ ἡ Ὀπώρα παρὰ τῇ(ς) Ἀρτέμιδ[ο]ς ἃς ἔδωκεν αὐτῇ ἐν ὑπ(αλλάγματι) ἀπαρχὰς δύο κατὰ δου- λικ[ῶν] σωμάτων Δ. καὶ Ἐ. οἴας καὶ ἔλαβεν. The editor (Schubart) compares P Tebt II. 316 and the note there (see above), but observes that the meaning will not suit the present passage: neither "legacy-duty" nor "entrance-fee" will serve, nor "an impost upon Jews." Schubart suggests it was some pecuniary rights in these slaves which Artemis had "deposited in pledge" with Opora. In the Magnesian inscriptions the word is very common in the sense of a personal "gift" to the goddess: thus in 83, ἀ. τῇ θεᾷ Ἀρ[τέμιδι. It is a very old use of the word, as may be seen from the lines inscribed by an Athenian potter of vi/B.C. on a base intended for a vase (*Syll* 772)—Νέαρχος ἀν[έ]θη- κε[ν ὁ κεραμε]ὺς ἔργον ἀπαρχὲ[ν τ]ἀθεναίαι. Thieme (p. 26) throws out the suggestion that this sense might possibly be recognized in Rom 8²³. From *Syll* we may also cite 526²¹ (i/B.C.—"i. e. sacrificium," notes Dittenberger); 587²⁶³·ᵃˡ (B.C. 329—ἀπαρχῆς, as throughout this long inscription, except in ²⁹⁷: it is ἀ. τοῦ σίτου, first-fruits given to Demeter and Kore at Eleusis); 588¹¹⁴ (ii/B.C.); 611²¹ (i B.C.—see note). So OGIS 179¹² (B.C. 95) δίδοσθαι . . κατ' ἐνιαυτὸν ἀπαρχὴν εἰς τὸ ἱερὸν . . πυροῦ ἀρτά βας ρπβ∠ (182½), *i. e.* ½ art. of wheat for each day of the year. It is clear that the connotation "*first*-fruits" could not be pressed in our exegesis of the term when it appears in NT, apart from associations wholly outside the field surveyed in this article; and we are perhaps at liberty to render "sacrifice" or "gift" where it improves the sense. The uses of this liberty must not be discussed here. For a discussion of the word, see Gradenwitz in *Berl. Philol. Woch.* 1914, p. 135 ff.

ἅπας.

The use of ἅπας for πᾶς appears to be largely determined by considerations of euphony, and is confined principally to literary documents: see Mayser *Gr.* p. 161 f., where it is shown that in seventeen out of twenty-one occurrences in Ptolemaic papyri ἅπας follows a consonant, and only in four cases a vowel. As examples of ἅπας from Roman times we may cite P Oxy III. 471⁸² (official—ii/A.D.) ὥστε ἄντικρυς ἁπάντων συνπαίζειν, and *ib.* 642 (official—ii/A.D.) πρὸ παντὸς γὰρ πεφροντίκαμεν τῆς πρὸς ὑμᾶς . . . εὐνοίας καὶ ἀρετῆς ἢ τῶν ἄλλων ἁπάντων. P Ryl II. 68¹² (B.C. 89) [πλη]ξέν] με . . . [πλη]γαῖς πλεί[στα]ις εἰς ἅπαν [μέρος] τοῦ σώμα[τό]ς μου answers to Mayser's rule, but has no suspicion of literariness. So such a phrase as εἰς τὸν ἅπαντα χρόν[ον], P Tebt I. 567 (late ii/B.C.).

ἀπατάω.

PSI II. 152²¹ (ii/A.D.) may show ἠπάτ[ων in a frag- mentary line at the end, with practically no context: ψεῦδος occurs a line higher up. It is surprising that this is the only citation we can make. The verb is absent from Polybius and only occurs twice in Plutarch, but is fairly fre- quent in LXX, and found in early Christian writers. It was evidently falling into disuse in most quarters.

ἀπάτη.

For ἀ. = "deceit" (as 4 Macc 18⁸, 2 Th 2¹⁰, Heb 3¹³) cf. P Oxy VII. 1020⁷ ᶠ· (A.D. 198–201) εἰ τὴν ἐκ τῆς ἡ[λικίας] ἔχεις βοήθιαν, τὸν ἀγῶνα τῆς ἀπάτης ὁ ἡγούμε[ε]νος τοῦ ἔθνους ἐκδι[κ]ήσει, "if you can claim the assistance due to immature age, the prefect of the province shall decide the suit for fraud" (Ed.). So CPHerm 6⁹ νῦν δὲ οἱ μὲν [μετ' ἀπά]της εἰσποιοῦ[ντ]αι, if the supplement is right. Atten- tion may be called to Deissmann's note in his *Hellenisierung des semitischen Monotheismus* (*Neue Jahrb. f. d. klass. Altertum,* 1903), p. 165 n.: he recalls the fact that ἀπάτη in popular Hellenistic had the meaning "pleasure," and finds this in Mt 13²² = Mk 4¹⁹ (cf. Lk 8¹⁴) and 2 Pet 2¹³: cf. Polyb. ii. 56¹² and Moeris' definition (p. 65)—Ἀπάτη ἡ πλάνη παρ' Ἀττικοῖς . . . ἡ τέρψις παρ' Ἕλλησιν. Of this rare sense Rouffiac (p. 38 f.) cites a probable instance from *Priene* 113⁶⁴ (B.C. 84) κα[τατιθ]εὶς δὲ μὴ μόνον τὰ πρὸς ἡδον[ήν, ἀλλὰ καὶ βουλόμενος ἐκ[τ]ὸς ἀπάτην χορη- γῆσαι [τοῖς θεαταῖς, αὐλητήν?], where he renders, "il ne fit pas seulement ce qui était agréable, mais voulant en outre offrir une réjouissance aux spectateurs (il fit venir [un joueur de flûte?])." It may be added that in P Petr III 11²¹ Ἀπάτη appears as a proper name, where (as in other cases) we may safely assume the "Hellenistic" meaning. But the word must have really covered both, like our verb "be- guile"; and ἀπατάω would tend to keep the older sense to the front. If it is derived from a root akin to our *find* (see Boisacq *s. v.*), it meant "invention, discovery" at the start, and was then turned *in malam partem,* to be partially reformed in later vernacular.

ἀπάτωρ.

The word is common in papyri in such a formula as BGU I. 88⁴ (ii/A.D.) Χαιρῆ μων' ἀπάτωρ μητ ρὸς Θασῆτος, *ib.* III. 971¹⁰ (ii/A.D.) Θερμουθάριον ἀπάτορα μ(ητρὸς) [Θερμουθαρίου]. Krebs (*Aus den Papyrus d. Königlichen Museen,* p. 160) renders BGU II. 410¹³ (A.D. 159–60) Ἰσάρι[ο]ν ἀπάτορα μητρὸς Τανεφ[ρ]έμμεως, as "the ille- gitimate daughter of Tanephremmis," and *ib.* 392¹⁰ (A.D. 208) Πᾶις ἀ(πάτωρ) μητ ρὸς Τελβάβεως, as "Pais, father unknown" (p. 175). The editors translate similarly in P Fay 39⁵ (A.D. 183) and in P Tebt II 397¹¹ (A.D. 198). Without the mother's name we have P Ryl I. 12² (A.D. 250) Δημῶτος ἀπάτορος, and P Lond 1170⁵⁶² (iii/A.D.) (= III. p. 98) Πολυδεύκους ἀπάτορος, also ⁴⁹⁶ Σωτήριδος [ἀπ]άτορος—in a long list of names in which the rest have the father's name given: we must assume the same sense. It does not seem to be used for "fatherless." See *Archiv* ii. p. 97. Deissmann (*LAE* p. 39 f.) has drawn attention to the fact that so far back as 1808 W. Sturz (in his *De Dialecto Macedonica et Alexandrina Liber*, Lipsiae, p. 146 f.) made use of the Charta Borgiana (the first papyrus ever brought to Europe, in 1778) to explain the use of ἀ. in Heb 7³. That a word meaning "father unknown" should be available for use in a passage where the thought is so far from the beaten track, is quite natural: the ἀμήτωρ following, which by association shares its special sense, protected ἀπάτωρ from its common implication.

ἀπείθεια.

That this noun, with ἀπειθέω and ἀπειθής, connotes invariably "disobedience, rebellion, contumacy," is made abundantly clear from papyri and inscriptions: Grimm's assumption that ἀπειθέω (instead of ἀπιστέω) is the antithesis to πιστεύω, though supported by the RV mg (= AV) in Jn 3³⁶, has no warrant whatever. For the noun see P Oxy I. 34³ⁱⁱⁱ·⁹ᶠᶠ· (A.D. 127) τούτους τε οὖν κελεύω καὶ τοὺς πολειτικοὺς πάντας τὰ ἀκόλουθα τοῖ[ς] προστεταγμένοις ποιεῖν, εἰδότας ὅ[τι] τοὺς παραβάντας καὶ τοὺ[ς] διὰ ἀπείθιαν κ[αὶ] ὡς ἀφορμὴν ζητοῦντας ἁμαρτημάτω[ν] τειμωρήσομαι, "These therefore I command, and all the civil servants, to do what is in accord with the instructions given, knowing that those who have transgressed, and those who (have done wrong) deliberately (*lit.* by way of disobedience), and as seeking an occasion for wrong-doing, I shall punish." (In the very elliptical phrase τοὺς διὰ ἀπείθειαν it is possible that the Eparch accidentally omitted ἁμαρτάνοντας, though it can be translated without: we can hardly get help from Rom 3²⁶ τὸν ἐκ πίστεως—cf. 4¹⁴ c.—as the preposition is much easier). Add P Fay 21⁷ (A.D. 134) [ὅπ]ως τῆς ἀποθίας ἐκῖνοι τὴν προσήκουσαν δίκην ὑ]πόσχωσι, where the Edd. conjecture ἀπειθίας or ἀπαθείας, BGU III. 747ⁱⁱ·¹⁴ (A.D. 139) ὑπόδιγμα τῆς ἀπειθίας, and P Rein 51²¹ (iii/A.D.), where τῆς τούτων ἀπιθείας follows μὴ πιθόμενοι νόμοι[ς]

ἀπειθέω.

For ἀ. = "disobey" in its later as in its earlier history see *s.v.* ἀπείθεια and cf. P Hib I. 73¹⁹ (B.C. 243–2) τὴν Πάτρωνος βίαν, ὃς ἀπειθῶν διατετέλεκε τοῖς πα]ρὰ σοῦ προστάγμασιν, "the violence of Patron, who has continued to disobey your orders" (Edd.), P Tebt I. 6⁴⁶ (B.C. 139—decree of Euergetes II) τοὺς δὲ ἀπειθοῦντας ἐπαναγκάζετε εὐτάκτω[ς] ἕκαστ' ἀποδιδόναι, "compel those who disobey to pay all the sums regularly" (Edd.), *ib.* 49¹⁷ (B.C. 113) ἐὰν δὲ ἀπειθῆι, "if he refuses" (Edd.). So Rev L 43¹⁰ (ii/B.C.) [τ]ῶν γεωργῶν τῶν ἠπειθηκότων, P Tebt I. 183 (late ii/B.C.) ἐ[ὰ]ν δὲ ἀπειθ[ῶσι κ]αταστῆσαι ἐπ[ὶ] τὸν στρατη[γό]ν, and from Roman times P Tebt II. 315³⁹ (ii/A.D.) ἔχι γὰρ συστατικὰς [ὅ]πως τὸν ἀπιθοῦντα μετὰ φρουρᾶς τῷ ἀρχιερῖ πέμπιν, "he has instructions to send recalcitrants under

guard to the high-priest" (Edd.), P Oxy IX. 1185³¹ (c. A.D. 200) εἰ δὲ μή γε, ὃς ἂν ἀπειθήσει τούτῳ μου τῷ διατά[γματι], "otherwise, if any one disobeys this my order," P Ryl II. 153³⁷ (A.D. 138–61) ἐὰν δ[ὲ] ἀπιθῇ ὁ [Μύρων καὶ μὴ ἀπ]οδοῖ ταύτας, of disobedience to the terms of a will. Add from the inscriptions *Syll* 614¹¹⁰ (Cos, dialect. iii/B.C.) αἰ δέ κά τις . . . ἀπειθῇ, let him be fined, *ib.* 510³² (Ephesus. ii/B.C.) ὡς ἀπειθοῦντα καὶ ἐπιβουλεύοντα τοῖς συ(μ)φέρουσι τῆς πόλεως, *ib.* 737⁹⁹ (ii/A.D., Athens) ἐὰν δὲ ἀπειθῇ πρασσόμενος, he is to be denied entrance to the Bacchium, and similarly ¹⁴², *ib.* 653⁴⁰ (Andania. B.C. 91) τὸν δὲ ἀπειθοῦντα ἢ ἀπρεπῶς ἀναστρεφόμενον εἰς τὸ θεῖον μαστιγούντω οἱ ἱεροί, and so ⁴³. We have not sought for more instances, but it has seemed desirable to give rather plentiful illustration to prove a case which is very important for doctrine.

ἀπειθής

occurs in *Syll* 810⁸ (Phlius) δίκη δὲ ἐπικρέματα[ι] τιμωρὸς ἀπελθόν[τι] ἀπειθὴς Νεμέσε[ως], where Dittenberger renders "implacabilis Nemeseos deae vindicta tibi imminet."

ἀπειλέω.

P Oxy II. 237ᵛⁱ·⁴ (A.D. 186) μήτε ἐμοὶ ἔτι ἀπει[λεῖν]. P Grenf I. 53⁹ (iv/A.D.) (= *Chrest.* I. 131) ἀσπάζεται τὰ παιδία σου καὶ Ἀλλοῦς πολλά σοι ἀπειλ(εῖ). Vettius Valens. p. 5³¹, has ἀπειλητικοί "men given to using threats," which comes from a verbal ἀπειλητός. Since this verb, with its rather commoner noun, might have had a large use in the innumerable papyrus petitions, we seem bound to infer that it was going out of popular speech. It occurs nine times in LXX and twice in NT. Its use in Ac 4¹⁷, where one is strongly tempted to accept from E and P the characteristic ἀπειλῇ ἀπειλησώμεθα, clearly reflects the literal rendering of a Semitic original reported to Luke from an eye-witness—was it Paul? Homoeoteleuton and unfamiliarity to Greek ears would account for the loss of the noun in אABD Pesh., etc. (so Blass).

ἀπειλή.

P Ryl II. 114¹² (c. A.D. 280) μετ'] ἀπιλῆς με ἀπέπεμψεν "drove me away with a threat." BGU IV. 1060⁵ (B.C. 23–2) ὅθεν καταπεπονημένοι προήγμεθα πρὸς ἀπειλαῖς. CP Herm 25ⁱⁱ·², a law report, makes an advocate say οὔτε συσκευα[ὶ οὔτε] ἀπειλαὶ κατεσίγησαν μ[. . . . . . .]. P Ryl I. 28¹¹⁷ (iv/A.D.) the "quivering" (see under ἅλλομαι) of the left shin means for a slave ἀπειλαὶ καὶ μόχθοι. In the vi/A.D. inscr. *OGIS* 521¹⁴ (Abydos) we have ἀεὶ τὴν ἀπιλὴν ἐν τοῖς πράγμασιν ὁρῶντα: Dittenberger accepts the emendation γράμμασιν.

ἄπειμι.

P Par 45² (B.C. 153) ἀπόντος μου πεφρόντικα ὑπέρ σου. P Tebt II. 317¹² (A.D. 174–5) ἕκαστα ἐπιτελοῦντι ἐκ τοῦ ἐμοῦ ἀπούσης ὀνόματος καθὰ καὶ ἐμοὶ παρούσηι ἐξῆν, "while carrying out everything in my name during my absence, just as I should have the right to do if I were present" (Edd.). BGU IV. 1080⁶ ᶠᶠ· (iii/A.D. ?) καὶ ἡμεῖς δὲ ἀκοῇ ἀπόντες ὡς παρόντες διαθέσι ηὐφράνθημεν. CP Herm 26⁷⁶ εἰ βούλει καὶ ἀπόντων αὐτ[ῶν . . . . (a fragmentary law report). P Oxy IX. 1204²³ (A.D. 299) Παῦνι ‾κ‾ ἀπήμην ἐν Ὀάσει ὅτε ἔγνων ἀπήντησα.

ἀπεῖπον.

The middle (as in 2 Cor 4²) appears in *Ostr* 1156 ἀπειπόμεθα παρ᾽ ἡμῶν χρήσασθαι ᾧ βούλει γερδ(ιείῳ). The perfect may be cited from BGU IV. 1113ʳ (B.C. 14) τοῦ Κανοληίο[υ ἀπε]ειρημένου τὴν ἐπιτροπείαν, and pres. with aor. in P Giss I. 82²¹ (A.D. 117) . . ἀπο]λ[ε]γομένων καὶ ἀπειπομένων πάσας τὰς μέχρι νῦν δαπά[νας . . . In the new uncanonical Gospel fragment, P Oxy X. 1224 ⁱⁱ·ᵛᵉʳˢᵒ (p. 7) (iv/A.D.) we find τί οὖν ἀ]πεῖπας : "What then hast thou forbidden ?" (Edd.).

ἀπείραστος.

For the gen. constr. after this negative adj. in Jas 1¹³ ὁ γὰρ θεὸς ἀπείραστός ἐστιν κακῶν, cf. P Tebt I. 124²⁶ (c. B.C. 118), where certain allotments are described as ἀσυκοφαντή(τους) καὶ ἀδιστάστους ὄντας πάσης αἰ[τ]ίας, "subject to no dispute or question on any ground" (Edd.). The citation may also help to support the neuter sense which Hort assigns to ἀπείραστος in the NT passage. For similar gen. construction with negative adjectives numerous passages may be quoted : cf. *Proleg.* p. 235 f.

ἄπειρος.

According to Meisterhans *Gr.* p. 150 the Attic inscriptions use ἀπείρων, not ἄπειρος, in the sense of "endless." It might be read, if worth while, in *OGIS* 383₅¹³ (Commagene–i/B.C.) εἰς τὸν ἄπειρον (or ἀπείρον ?) αἰῶνα κοιμήσεται, but χρόνος ἄπειρος in l. ¹¹³ (= Avestan *zervan akarana*—see J. H. Moulton, *Hibbert Lectures*, p. 107) is decisive. For ἀ. construed with the gen., as Heb 5¹³, cf. P Giss I. 68¹⁷ (ii/A.D.) ἐπὶ Φιβᾶς ὁ αὐτοῦ ἄπειρός ἐστιν τῶν τόπων καὶ οὐ δύναται μόνος προσε[λθε]ῖν, "since Phibas, his slave, is unacquainted with the places, and cannot come alone." Ἄπειρος in this sense is the opposite of ἔμπειρος (cf. πεῖρα) : meaning "endless," as a substitute for the Epic ἀπείρων, it is connected with πέρας.

ἀπεκδέχομαι.

This rare word is used in the apocryphal *Acta Pauli* iii. of Onesiphorus on the outskirts of Lystra "waiting for" Paul's arrival from Iconium—εἰστήκει ἀπεκδεχόμενος αὐτόν. Nageli (p. 43) and LS *s.v.* give late "profane" citations which make it perhaps possible that Paul was not the first to use a regularly formed perfective of ἐκδέχομαι, which becomes a favourite word with him : it also figures in 1 Pet and Heb, where of course borrowing from Paul is possible. But if late writers who never could have read him use the word, it is obviously conceivable that they coined it independently, as we may very probably suppose him to have done. See the next article.

ἀπέκδυσις

is admittedly a word first used by Paul, so far as our present knowledge goes : only one MS of Josephus (*Antt.* vi. 14²) saves its verb from the same category. There can be little doubt that Lightfoot (on Col 2¹⁵) rightly treats them both as minted by the Apostle. It was evidently for the special purpose in his mind when writing this letter ; and if Nageli (p. 50) asks why he should have coined a word not needed to express some specially Christian conception, the answer is surely that a new compound, formed by prefixing a per-

fectivizing preposition in an entirely normal way, was a resource available for and generally used by any real thinker writing Greek. What else are we to infer from the list of ἅπαξ εἰρημένα which any writer's *inter verborum* will afford, even if the majority were really only ἅπαξ εὑρημένα? The case of ἀπεκδέχομαι (*q.v.*) may be taken with this : but there, if Paul coined the word, he used it again, which he did not with these. On the problem of Col 2¹⁵ we have nothing to contribute that would be relevant in this work.

ἀπελαύνω.

P Giss I. 70⁷ (Hadrian) ἀπελα[σ]α τὸ πλοῖον περὶ ὥραν ἐνάτην, "I caused the boat to sail about the ninth hour." P Tor I. 1 ⁱⁱⁱ ³² (B.C. 116) (= *Chrest.* II. p. 33) καὶ κατὰ μὲν τὸν τρόπον τοῦτον φήσας ἀπελαύνεσθαι αὐτοὺς τῆς κρατήσεως τῆς οἰκίας. P Par 37¹⁷ ἀπελάσαντό με, with mid. for act. : note the dropped augment in the two aorist forms cited here. BGU III. 759¹⁸ (A.D. 125) ἀπήλασαν αἶγας τρεῖς (of robbers), P Lips I. 37²⁸ (A.D. 389) ζῷα ἀπελακότας (sc. ἀπεληλ.) πολλάκις.

ἀπελεγμός

is a ἅπ. εἰρ. of Luke (Ac 19²⁷), being an easy derivative from ἀπελέγχω "repudiate," on the model of ἐλεγμός (LXX) from ἐλέγχω.

ἀπελεύθερος.

For the Pauline phrase ἀπελεύθερος Κυρίου in 1 Cor 7²², Deissmann (*LAE* p. 332 f.) compares the common title "freedman of the Emperor," Σεβαστοῦ ἀπελεύθερος or ἀπελεύθερος Καίσαρος : see e. g. *Syll* 371⁷ (time of Nero), and the numerous examples in Magie *De vocabulis solemnibus* p. 70. The adjective is very common in the papyri, e. g. P Oxy I. 98³ (A.D. 141–2) Ἀρχίᾳ ἀπελευθέρῳ Ἀμοιτᾶτος, *ib.* 104⁴ (A.D. 96) Σο(ή)ρις Ἁρποχρᾶτος ἀπελευθέρου *al.* For the light thrown by the ancient rites of manumission on the Pauline teaching regarding spiritual freedom see Deissmann's valuable discussion referred to above, and *Archiv* v. p. 117 f.

Ἀπελλῆς.

Priene 248 (c. B.C. 1) has the acc. Ἀπελλῆν, as in Rom 16¹⁰ : a similar name Ἀπελλᾶς, gen. -ᾶ, is cited by Hatch in *JBL* xxvii., part ii., p. 145, from a Carian inscr. concerning a *tribunus militum* who served under Vespasian against the Jews. The name Ἀπελλῆς is widely spread : on some confusions with Ἀπολλῶς cf. Zahn *Intr.* i. p. 270, and Blass-Debrunner § 29. 4.

ἀπελπίζω.

This late compound generally takes the acc. instead of the natural gen., as in Lk 6³⁵ if we read μηδένα with ℵ W etc., and the Lewis Syriac : see *Proleg.* p. 65. The passive is found *Syll* 807¹⁰ (ii/A.D.) αἷμα ἀναφέροντι . . . ἀφηλπισμένῳ ὑπὸ παντὸς ἀνθρώπου, the "faith-cure" of a man who had been "given up." (For the φ, which occurs in Lk *l c.* DP, and twice in this inscription, see *Proleg.* p. 44.) The editor restores the verb in *OGIS* 194²⁰ (i/B.C.) ὥσπερ λαμπρὸς ἀστὴρ καὶ δαίμων ἀγαθ[ὸς τοῖς ἀπελπίζουσι]ν ἐπέλαμψε. There is a good collection of instances from literature in Linde *Epicurus* p. 31 f., beginning with Hyperides. His passage from Epicurus himself is worth quoting : 62⁶ τὸ μέλλον . . . μήτε . . προσμένωμεν ὡς ἐσόμενον μήτε ἀπελπίζωμεν ὡς πάντως οὐκ ἐσόμενον. It survives in MGr.

ἀπέναντι.

'A., construed with the gen. in the sense of "over against," "opposite," as in Mt 27³¹, is well illustrated by P Grenf. I. 21⁴ (B.C. 120) ἀπέναντι τῆς θύ(ρας) αὐ(τοῦ) and *Syll* 558¹⁷ (i/A.D.) τὸν ναὸν τὸν ἀπέναντι τῆ[s] ἐσόδου. See also P Petr II. 17 (3)³ (iii/B.C.), and from the inscriptions *Priene* 37¹⁶⁵ (beginning of ii/B.C.) ἀπὸ δὲ τῶν ἐγκολαπτῶν ὅρων εἰς τὸν ἀπέναντι βουνὸν τὸν λεπρὸν ἐθήκαμεν ὅρον, *ib.* 42⁵⁹ ἐπὶ τὴν ἀ. ὀφρύν and *Preisigke* 3556 (on a mummy). On P Ryl I. 30¹² (i/B.C.), a few lines from a historical work, Prof. Hunt observes that "the use of the preposition ἀπένα[ν]τι, of which Stephanus quotes no example earlier than Polybius," may perhaps give "some indication of the date of the work." Wackernagel, *Hellenistica*, p. 3 ff., quotes ἵναντι c. gen. from a very old Cretan inscr., and ἔναντι from Delphi (B.C. 198) : in both dialects ἀντί was still used in the old local sense. From this Doric Greek it passed into the Κοινή about B.C. 300. He goes on to discuss its relations with ἐναντίον, etc.

ἀπερισπάστος.

The adj. is common. Thus P Grenf. I. 11ⁱⁱ·³ (B.C. 157) τούτου δὲ γενομένου καὶ ἀπερίσπαστος ὢν δυνήσομαι ἀπροφασίστως εἰς τὸ βασιλικὸν τὰ ἐκφόρια ἀπομετρῆσαι. P Oxy II. 286¹⁷ (A.D. 82) ὅπως παρέχωνται ἡμᾶς ἀπερισπάστους [καὶ] ἀπαρενοχλήτους ὑπὲρ τῆς προκειμένης ὀφειλῆς καὶ ἀποδώσειν ταῦτα, "in order that they may secure us against any liability or trouble in connexion with the aforesaid debt, and may repay it" (Edd.). In P Oxy VI. 898⁵ (A.D. 123) ὑποθέσθαι ὅσα ἔχω ἐν τῇ Ὀάσε[ι] κτήματα [λα]βόντα τοῦ Διοσκόρο[υ] γράμματα ἀπερι σπ]άστου, the editors translate "to mortgage all my property in the Oasis in return for a deed of release received from Dioscorus," and explain γράμματα ἀπερισπάστου as a deed of indemnification, distinguished by the formula ἀπερίσπαστον παρέξεσθαι or some equivalent phrase. In l. 18 of this same papyrus the deed is called ἡ ἀπερίσπαστος simply. The development of meaning is exactly like that of our "security," in the commercial sense. Other examples of the word are P Rein 18⁴⁰ (B.C. 108), BGU IV. 1057²² (Aug.), P Lond 932² (A.D. 211) (=III. p. 149), and P Amh II. 101¹⁰ (early iii/A.D.), etc.

ἀπερίτμητος.

On the possibility that this harsh word may have been coined by the Greek Jews of Alexandria to express the contempt with which they regarded the uncircumcised, see Deissmann *BS*, p. 153. Of course it must be remembered that περιτέμνω itself is familiar in papyri, in connexion with the circumcision of priests in Egyptian temples : see Otto *Priester* i. p. 214.

ἀπέρχομαι

occurs in a special sense in the affectionate letter of Philonides to his father the "architect" Cleon, P Petr II. 13 (19)⁷ (middle of iii/B.C.) (= Witkowski², p. 19), ζῶντός σου καὶ εἰς θεοὺς ἀπελθόντος. So, much later, in the beautiful simplicity of a Christian epitaph, *Preisigke* 1190 : Τἄησαι ἐβίωσεν

εἴκουσι ὀκτώ, γ(ίνονται) (ἔτη) κη' Εἰς λαμπρὰν (sc. γῆν) ἀπῆλθεν—a striking contrast to the monotonous ὥρε χαῖρε on the pagan tombs of the young. For the ordinary use of the word, it is sufficient to cite P Par 32⁵·⁶ (B.C. 162) γινώσκετε, ἀφ᾽ οὗ ἀφ᾽ ὑμῶν ἀπελήλυθα, μὴ ἐσχολα[κέν]αι με . . . [ποιεῖν ὅσα] ἐνέτειλας, BGU III. 884³·¹⁹⁶ (ii/iii A.D.) πρὶν οὖν ἀπέλθης πρὸς Χαιρήμονα, ἀνάβαινε πρός με, ἵνα σοι ἀποτάξωμαι. It may be noted that "in later times the idea of the word goes forward to the goal" (Usener, *Pelagia-Legenden*, p. 49). So in *Pelagia*, p. 7³ ἀπήλθαμεν ἐν τῇ μεγάλῃ ἐκκλησίᾳ, "we arrived at the great church"; and much earlier in BGU III. 814³⁰ (iii/A.D.) γείνωσκε ὅτι λοιποῦμαι ὅτι οὐκ ἀπῆλθα ἐγγὺς τοῦ ἀδελφοῦ, "have never come near my brother," *ib.*²² ἔλεγε ὅτι ἐὰν ἀπέλθω εἰς οἶκον, πέμπω σ[οι] πάντα· οὐδέν μ[ο]ι ἐπέμψατε — τε). διὰ τεί : The ἀπό has thus done for this word what it did in early times for ἀφικνέομαι, *perfectivizing* the action : see *Proleg.* p. 111 ff. So also with ἀποβαίνω.

ἀπέχω.

Deissmann (*BS* p. 229 and *LAE* p. 110 ff.) has already shown how much light is thrown on the NT use of this word (Mt 6²·⁵·¹⁶, Phil 4¹⁸) by the papyri and ostraca. There it is constantly found in the sense of "I have received," as a technical expression in drawing up a receipt. Consequently in the Sermon on the Mount we are led to understand ἀπέχουσιν τὸν μισθὸν αὐτῶν, *they can sign the receipt of their reward*: their right to receive the reward is realised, precisely as if they had already given a receipt for it" (*BS* p. 229). To the almost contemporary instances of this usage which Deissmann gives, BGU II. 584⁵ᶠ· (A.D. 44) καὶ ἀπέχω τὴν συγκεχωρημένην τιμὴν πᾶσαν ἐκ πλήρους, and *ib.* 612²ᶠ (A.D. 57) ἀπέχω παρ᾽ ὑμῶν τὸν φόρον τοῦ ἐλα[ι]ουργίου, ὧν ἔχετέ [μο]υ ἐν μισθώσει, we may add a few exx. which might be multiplied almost indefinitely : P Par 52³ (B.C. 163-2) ἀπέχι παρ᾽ ἐμοῦ τιμῆς ὀθόνια, P Tebt I. 109¹⁷ (B.C. 93) τάλαντον ἕν, ὃ ἀπέχουσιν οἱ προγεγραμμένοι π[α]ρὰ Πετεσούχου, BGU III 075²⁰ᶠᶠ· (A.D. 45) (= *Selections*, p. 43) ἀ]πέχι ἡ Τεσεν[ο]ῦφις τὴν ὀφίλη[μένην] ὁ Πα[οῦς] φερνὴ[ν] ἀργυρίου : we might suggest τὴν ὀφίλη (*i. e.* ει) [αὐτῇ] as a rather simpler emendation than the editor's ὑπὸ τοῦ Παοῦτος—the substitution of η for (ε)ι has a parallel in l. ⁵ of this illiterate deed of divorce. Also PSI 39⁸ (A.D. 148) ἀπέχειν τὴν συμπεφωνημένην τιμὴν ἀργυρίου δραχμὰς ἑκατὸν ὀγδοηκονταοκτώ, etc. For the subst. ἀποχή, which is used exactly in the sense of our "receipt," cf. P Oxy I. 91²⁵ (A.D. 187) κυρία ἡ ἀποχή, "the receipt is valid," *ib.* II. 269ⁱⁱ·⁸ (A.D. 57) ἐάν σοι δῦ τὸ ἀργύριον δὺς αὐτῷ ἀποχήν, "if he gives you the money, give him the receipt," *Ostr* 50 (i/A.D.) τὴν προτ(έραν) ἀποχ(ήν). and often. An important note by Albert Thumb (in *Neue Jahrbücher f. d. kl. Altertum*, 1906, p. 255) shows that the function of the *perfectivizing* preposition is to supply a present answering to the past ἔσχον. In receipts we find regularly ἀπέχω and ἔσχον, hardly ever (as *Ostr* 1417, 1430) ἀπέσχον, still less ἀπέσχηκεν, as in BGU IV. 1058¹⁸ (Augustus). See further Wilcken *Ostr.* i. p. 85 f. and H. Erman in *Archiv* i. p. 77 ff.

For the intransitive sense of the verb "to be away, distant," cf. P Strass I. 57⁶ (ii/A.D.) μηδὲ μεῖλιον ἀπεχουσῶν ἀλλήλ[ων], and *Michel* 466⁹ (iii/B.C.) ἀπέχον ἀπὸ τῆς γῆς [ἐ]φ' [ὅ]σον ποδῶν ἐπ[τ]ά, a vessel "distant from the shore as much as seven feet," P Lille I. 1⁵ (B.C. 259-8) χώματα ῇ ᵀᵃ ἀπέχον ἀπ' ἀλλήλων σχοινία κε̄, ib. 2² (iii/B.C.) ἀπέχει δὲ ἡ γῆ αὐτή [why not αὕτη?] ἀπὸ τῆς κώμης στάδια ιε, etc. It may be added that the impersonal sense of "it is enough," "it is sufficient," often given to ἀπέχει in the difficult passage Mk 14⁴¹ is rejected by de Zwaan (Exp. VI. xii. p. 452 ff.), who understands the word in the usual commercial sense referred to above—"He (Judas) did receive (the promised money)"—and refers to P Leid I. p. 97, for similar instances of ἀπέχει with this meaning standing by itself. For the middle, as in 1 Th 4³, etc., cf. Syll 356²⁶, a rescript of Augustus (B.C. 31) τῆς τῶν πολεμίων ὠμότητος οὐδὲ τῶν ναῶν οὐδὲ τῶν ἱερῶν τῶν ἁγιωτάτων ἀποσχομένης.

ἀπιστέω.

P Oxy III. 471⁴ (ii/A.D.) π]ροσθήσω τι κύριε περ[ὶ οὗ] θαυμάσεις οἶμαι καὶ ἀπι[στήσ]εις ἕως ἂν τὰ γράμμ[ατα ἀνα]γνῶμεν (with 2nd ν deleted and μεν written above), "I will add a fact, my lord, which will, I expect excite your wonder and disbelief until we read the documents" (Edd.). P Oxy II. 237ᵛ·⁵ (A.D. 186) has τάχα ἀπιστεύσας εἰ κτλ. : here we must assume a momentary slip of spelling with πιστεύω in mind—of course ἀπιστεύω is an impossible word even in papyri. Syll 802²¹ (dialect, iii/B.C.) ἀπίστει τοῖς ἰάμασιν καὶ ὑποδιέσυρε τὰ ἐπιγράμμα[τ]α, said of a sceptic at the Asclepios temple in Epidaurus. So lines 30. 1. The appearance of the word for "incredulity" helps the case for ἀπειθέω as retaining its proper force.

ἀπιστία

appears in the quasi-Ionic of the illiterate P Par 25 (B.C. 165) κατ' ἀπιστήην : ἀπιστίη was the real Ionic, and we have to take this as a mere blunder—see Mayser Gr. pp. 11 f., 130.

ἄπιστος

may be cited from Syll 802³² (iii/B.C.) meaning first "incredible" and then "incredulous" : ὅτι τοίνυν ἔμπροσθεν ἀπιστεῖς αὐτο[ῖς] (the inscriptions recording cures), οὐκ ἐοῦσιν ἀπίστοις, τὸ λοιπὸν ἔστω τοι, φάμεν, "Ἄπιστος ὄν[ομα]. It is MGr.

ἁπλότης.

Kaibel 716⁵ (Rome) ἤσκι τὴν ἁπλότητα, φίλους ὑπὲρ ἁτὸν ἐτίμα. The word is found OGIS 764⁷ (ii/A.D.) unfortunately with a hiatus both before and after. On its biblical use see Charles's note on Test. xii. patr. Iss. iii. 1.

ἁπλοῦς.

The papyri have sundry uses of this word which effectively dispose of the contention that "the moral sense is the only one lexically warranted" (see Grimm-Thayer). Thus P Gen I. 21¹¹ (ii/B.C.), the marriage-contract already referred to (under ἀπαλλάσσω), where it is enacted that in the event of the wife's being set free, the husband shall repay τὴν φερνὴν ἁπλῆν, "the marriage-dowry pure and simple," but that in the event of his not doing so at the proper time he shall repay it with interest. In this sense we often find ἁπλοῦς contrasted with σὺν ἡμιολίᾳ, as in BGU IV. 1059⁸ (Augustus) ἐκτεῖσαι τὸ μὲν δάνηον σὺν ἡμιολίᾳ, τοὺς δὲ

τόκους ἁπλοῦς, ib. 1147¹⁷ (B.C. 13). P Cairo Preis 1¹⁸ (ii/A.D.) πρᾶσις ἦν ἁπλῆ ἀνεύθυνος, P Tebt II. 340¹⁴ (A.D. 206) τὸ δὲ συναίρεμα τοῦτο δισσὸ[ν] γρα φὲν ἐπὶ τῷ ἁπλοῦν συνηγηθῆναι "to be considered as one," P Oxy VI. 921 recto (iii/A.D.) where mention is made of different kinds of πήχεις- ἁπλοῖ, καμαρωτικοί (or -ωτοί) and ἐμβαδοί (see the editors' introduction), with the reference to a ἁπλοῦν οἴκημα in OGIS 483¹¹¹ (ii/B.C.), will serve to illustrate the variety of "non-moral" senses left to the word in the vernacular. In P Petr I. 12²⁰ (iii/B.C.) ἁπλοίδιον (for the Homeric ἁπλοΐς) is used to denote a single garment. The moral sense is well illustrated by Syll 633¹² (ii/A.D.) καὶ εὐείλατος γένοι[τ]ο ὁ θεὸς τοῖς θεραπεύουσιν ἁπλῆ τῇ ψυχῇ. For the adverb see the separate article. In MGr ἁπλός means "simple, naive, natural."

ἁπλῶς.

The adverb is frequent in legal documents to lend emphasis to a statement : P Oxy II. 237ᵛⁱ·²¹ (A.D. 186) ἄλλο ἀδίκημα εἰς αὐτὸν ἁπλῶς, "any other single act of injustice against himself," cf. P Flor I. 28¹⁵ (ii/A.D.) παντὸς ἁπλῶς εἴδους, and similarly P Amh II. 96³ (A.D. 213). So with the negative P Lond 1218¹⁰ (A.D. 39) (= III. p. 130) οὐκ εἶχον ἁπλῶς πρᾶγμα, P Oxy II. 268¹⁶ (A.D. 58) περὶ ἄλλου μηδενὸς ἁπλῶς ἐγγράπτου ἢ ἀγράφου πράγματος, "concerning any other matter whatever written or unwritten," ib. VI. 900⁵ (iii/iii A.D.) μηδὲ περὶ ἄλλου μηδενὸς ἁπλῶς μέχρι τῆς ἐνεστώσης ἡμέρας, "or on any other subject whatever up to the present day"; and the short P Tebt II. 400 (B.C. 92 or 50) μὴ κατεγγύα μηδὲν τὸν Κόμωνος τοῦ Κόμωνος πρὸς μηδὲν ἁπλῶς. In a philosophic letter of iv/A.D., P Oxy I. 120⁵ ᵗ., the editors translate χρὴ γάρ τινα ὁρῶντα αἰαυτὸν ἐν δυστυχίᾳ κἂν ἀναχωρεῖν καὶ μὴ ἁπλῶς μάχαισθαι τῷ δεδογμένῳ, "when a man finds himself in adversity he ought to give way and not fight stubbornly against fate." Reference should be made to Hort's abundant illustrations in his note upon Jas 1⁵.

ἀπό.

In this and the other prepositions of very wide and general use we have not pretended to any fullness : they would afford abundant material for a fair-sized treatise. We only notice such special uses as we have remarked in our reading, and have therefore passed over most of the common and obvious uses. On ἀπό there are some illustrations in Proleg. which may be recalled with some additions. There is the partitive use (pp. 102, 245), still current in MGr : so P Petr III. 11²⁹ (B.C. 234) ἀφεῖσθ[ω] ἀπὸ τῶν ὑπαρχόντων μοι [σ]ωμάτων [ἐ]ὶ εὐθερα Δ. καὶ Ἀ., ib. II. 11 (1)⁵ (= Selections p. 7) (iii/B.C.) ἀπὸ τούτου τὸ μὲν ἥμισυ . . . τὸ δὲ λοιπόν κτλ. P Tebt II. 299¹³ (c. A.D. 50) ἀπολυσίμ[ο]υ ἀπὸ ἀνδ[ρῶν πεντή]κοντα "one of the 50 exempted persons" (Edd.), P Iand 8⁶ (ii/A.D.) διεπεμψάμην σοι . . ἀ[πὸ τοῦ ο]ἴνου Κνίδια τρία, etc. To Kuhring's scanty exx. (p. 37) for ἀπό of agent (cf. Proleg. pp. 102, 246) add Syll 655³ A.D. 83) συντετηρημένα ἀπὸ βασιλέων καὶ Σεβαστῶν, P Lond 1173¹² (A.D. 125) (= III. p. 208) ἕως πεισθῆς ἀπ' αὐτοῦ, P Flor II. 150⁵ (A.D. 267) ἀ. τῶν μυῶν κατεσθιόμενα, BGU IV. 1185²⁶ (Augustus or earlier) μηδὲ κατακαλεῖσθαι ἀπὸ μηδεν ός. It is universal in MGr, but its very limited use in papyri and NT suggests that in the Hellenistic period it had only local currency. Various uses under the general heading of *source* are collected in Kuhring p. 35 f. : add the remarkable BGU IV. 1079[25] (A.D. 41) (= *Selections* p. 40) ὡς ἂν πάντες καὶ σὺ βλέπε σατὸν ἀπὸ τῶν Ἰουδαίων "like everybody else, you too must beware of the Jews." The familiar NT idiom (Mk 8[15] *al*) may be translation Greek still, but it is evidently possible enough in vernacular untouched by Semitic influence. Kuhring's instances cover the categories of *cause, authorship, receipt, inheritance*, but not *instrument* : there are numerous exx. of καθαρὸς ἀπό and the like (once regarded as Semitism !). Sometimes the καθαρός is dropped, and ἀπό is practically = ἄνευ : see Kuhring p. 53 f., and add P Lips I. 16[19] (A.D. 138) πα[ρ]αδώσω σο]ι σὺν ταῖς ἐφαιστώσαις θ[ύραις] κ[αὶ] κλεισὶ καὶ ἀπὸ πάσης ἀκαθαρσίας : on P Fay 345 the edd. note " cf. CPR 38[21], BGU I. 30[21], etc., where these phrases occur without καθαρός." Not that καθαρός is really to be supplied : the *privative* ἀπό, as Kuhring calls it, is quite naturally developed. Cf. P Tebt II. 420[4] (iii/A.D.) ἀπὸ ζημίας "blameless." In P Oxy VIII. 1103[3] (A.D. 360 a certain Eutrygius is called ἀπὸ λογιστῶν "ex-logistes": Prof. Hunt notes "On the titular use of *ex* and ἀπό see Mommsen *Ephem. Epigr.* v. p. 128-9, and cf. e.g. 133[4] ἀπὸ ὑπάτων [A.D. 550], 895[2] ἀπὸ μειζόνων [vi/vii A.D.], P [Lond] 233[5] [= II. p. 273—A.D. 345] ἀπὸ ἐπάρχων, P Flor I. 71 *passim* [iv/A.D.]." On its relations with ἐκ, παρά and ὑπό see *Proleg.* p. 237 : add *Preisigke* 997 and 998, two προσκυνήματα from the same place, dated respectively A.D. 4 and A.D. 16-7, with ὑπὸ χειμῶνος ἐλασθείς in the first and ἀπὸ χιμῶνος ἐλασθείς in the other. We may further note the idiomatic use of ἀπό in Mk 7[4] ἀπ' ἀγορᾶς, 15[21] ἀπ' ἀγροῦ, "fresh from market," "from field-work," which is well illustrated by such phraseology as that in *Syll* 567 (ii/A.D.), a tariff prescribing the number of days of ceremonial impurity following certain acts, described as τὰ ἐκτός : thus ἀπὸ τυροῦ ἡμέ(ρας) α, ἀπὸ φθορείων ἡμε ρῶν μ, ἀπὸ κήδους [οἰκ]είου ἡμε ρῶν μ, ἀπὸ συνουσίας νομίμου they may enter the shrine the same day after washing and anointing. Cf. Deissmann *BS* p. 227. Among phrases with ἀπό we may note one in P Ryl II. 157[21] (A.D. 135) εἰ χρεία γείνοιτο [ποτίσαι ἐ]ν ἀναβάσει [y.z.] ἀπὸ ποδὸς τὴν αὐτὴν νοτίνην μερίδα, "if need arises at the inundation to water the same southern portion by foot." It seems clear that this refers to the same method of irrigation which appears in Deut 11[10] LXX ὅταν σπείρωσιν τὸν σπόρον καὶ ποτίζωσιν τοῖς ποσὶν αὐτῶν ὡσεὶ κῆπον λαχανίας : see Driver *in loc.* The editors in their note cite a papyrus with ἀπὸ ποδὸς ποτισ[μ]οῦ. In ἁλιεῖς ἀπὸ ποδός (BGU I. 220, 221, III. 756) the sense is different, perhaps "from the bank" (lit. "on foot"). In P Rein 18[11] (B.C. 108) we note μέχρι [ἂν ἀπὸ] τοῦ σπόρου γένηται until he has finished his sowing." For ἀπό denoting *matter* or *material*, as Mt 3[4], cf. *Priene* 117[23] (i/B.C.) στεφανῶσα[ι . . . στεφ]άνῳ χρυσέωι ἀπὸ χρυσοῦ. The phrase ἀπὸ μέρους may be provisionally illustrated by P Ryl II. 133[17] (A.D. 33) αὐθάδως κατέσπασεν ἀπὸ μέρους "ventured to pull it partly down" : see further under μέρος. On ἀπ' αἰῶνος we gave some parallels under αἰών : add *Preisigke* 176[4] A.D. 161-80, πρώτου τῶν ἀπ' αἰῶνος. Ἀπὸ τοῦ νῦν is illustrated by Deissmann *BS* p. 253, and ἀπὸ τοῦ βελτίστου *ib.* 93 : add P Tebt I. 5[59] (B.C. 118, II. 282[3] (late ii/B.C.), P Fay 12[5] (B.C. 103). See further *Proleg.* p. 9 for Rev 1[4], on which

more may be said under εἰμί. Rossberg's dissertation systematically illustrates papyrus usages of ἀπό, as far as its date (1908) allows : it ought perhaps to be observed that the extracts are not always correctly transcribed. There is an elaborate dissertation on later uses of ἀπό in composition by K. Dieterich in *Int. Forsch.* xxiv. pp. 87-158, on which cf. Fränkel, *Wochenschr. f. klass. Philol.*, 1909 p. 399 ff.

ἀποβαίνω.

For the metaphorical sense (as in Lk 21[13], Phil 1[19]) cf. P Petr III. 42 H (8) f[5] (iii/B.C.) (= Witkowski[2], p. 15) νυνὶ [δὲ ἐν φόβωι ε]ἰμὶ οὐ μετρίωι, πῶ[ς] τε σοὶ ἀποβήσεται καὶ ἡμῖν. *Syll* 406[19] (A.D. 147—a reply of M. Aurelius to an address of congratulation on the birth of a son who had died after it was sent) εὔνοια ὑμῶν, ἣν ἐνεδείξασθε συνησθέντες μοι γεννηθέντος υἱοῦ, εἰ καὶ ἑτέρως τοῦτο ἀπέβη, οὐδὲν ἧττον φανερὰ ἐγένετο. The literal sense may be illustrated by the use of the verb, with its nouns ἀπόβασις and ἀποβατικόν, to denote a kind of chariot race in which one of two men in a car had to jump off : see *Syll* 670 i/ii A.D. and notes. Schlageter p. 50 quotes ἀπόβασις from a Delos inscr. in *BCH* xiv. p. 399[115] B.C. 270?, where it means "place of exit," the classical meaning having been "landing."

ἀποβάλλω.

Syll 324[20] (i/B.C.) τῆς πόλεως ἀποβεβλημένη[ς] ἀγαθὸν [πολείτην. The words τὰ ἀποβάλλοντα are used as a designation for certain δημόσια ἐδάφη in P Flor I. 20[18] (A.D. 127) (= *Chrest.* I. p. 422), but the reason for the designation is by no means clear : see the note by Vitelli, who favours a sense = "fruitful," and compares the somewhat similar usage in P Gen I. 6[10] (ii/A.D.) μήτε ἐκ τ[οῦ] κεφαλαίου τι αὐτοὺς [ἀ]ποβεβληκέναι. P Ryl I. 28[12] (iv/ A.D.) tells us that one kind of "quivering" means that pollà ἀποβάλλει ὁ τοιοῦτος, and in [190] one whose left shin quivers ἀποβαλεῖν πρόσωπον ὑποτακτικόν, "will lose a subordinate person." PSI 32[17] (A.D. 208) μὴ ἐξεῖναι δὲ ἡμεῖν ἀποβαλέσθαι σε τῆ[ς μι]σθώσεως.

ἀποβλέπω.

For this NT ἅπ. εἰρ. (Heb 11[26] cf. *Syll* 656[19] Ephesus, ii/A.D.) ἀποβλέπων εἴς τε τὴν εὐσέβειαν τῆς θεοῦ καὶ εἰς τὴν τῆς λαμπροτάτης Ἐφεσίων πόλεως τειμήν.

ἀπογίνομαι.

P Ryl II. 65[9] (B.C. 67?) has ἀπογεγονότα πλείονα σώματα, "several corpses." P Grenf II. 69[19] (A.D. 265) τῷ ἀπογεγονότι πατρὶ αὐτοῦ, "his departed father." P Lips I. 29 (A.D. 295) has aor. partic. *ter* in the same sense— so *Syll* 727[15] (ii/B.C.) and 850[22] (ii/B.C.) : but three or four iv/A.D. documents in the same collection show the general meaning "depart" c. gen.

ἀπογραφή.

It is hardly necessary to observe that a very large number of the papyri are census papers, and that by their aid a fourteen years' period has been established during the Imperial age : the discovery was first made by Wilcken, *Hermes* xxviii. p. 230 ff. (1893). The oldest certainly dated census paper is one of A.D. 34, published in *Philologus* lxxi. p. 24 ff. : ἀπογράφομαι εἰς τὸ ἐν[εσ]τὸς κ ἔτος Τιβερίου Καίσαρος

Σεβαστοῦ. The editor, S. Eitrem, remarks that P Oxy II. 254 probably belongs to A.D. 20. See Grenfell and Hunt's long introduction to that document, discussing the argument of Sir W. M. Ramsay in his *Was Christ Born at Bethlehem?* (1898); and note that they think P Oxy II. 256 might even go back to A.D. 6. For the κατ᾽ οἰκίαν ἀπογραφή of the Ptolemaic period, see P Petr III. 59 (*d*), a very early example. They were made every year, and included the name of the owner and other occupants of each house, then the total number of inhabitants, and the number of males. In later times we find in the ἀπογραφή a return of property, as in P Oxy I. 72 (A.D. 90),—of a slave, as *ib.* 73 (A.D. 94), and of sheep and goats, etc., as 74 (A.D. 116)—the two latter are examples of the annual registration. See Wilcken, *Grundzüge* I. p. 175 f., and for the Imperial census pp. 192 f. and 202 f. He accepts P Oxy II. 254 and 255 as belonging to the census of A.D. 19-20 and 47-8 respectively; and agrees with Grenfell and Hunt that "this census was established in B.C. 10-9 or A.D. 5-6." In favour of this is the fact that the new λαογραφία, poll-tax, which was closely connected with the census, was in operation in B.C. 10-8. Wilcken's points must not be repeated here, for we cannot spare room for the *Realien*. He shows that the purpose of the census was to determine the total population of Egypt, and each person according to his residence, ἴδια : this is specially brought out by the edict of Vibius Maximus (P Lond 904 = *Selections* no. 28), in which the Prefect orders all to return to their homes for the census of A.D. 104. (See further on this Wilcken's introduction to the document in *Chrest.* I. 202, p. 235 f., and Deissmann *LAE* p. 268 f. There seems to be an unnoticed reference to this requirement in the late iii/A.D. document, P Oxy VIII. 1157 : the writer asks his sister to register him in his absence if possible, and if not to let him know, that he may come and do it.) Wilcken shows that personal attendance to the duty of εἰκονισμός (cf. P Oxy VII. 1022) was necessary, and brings into connexion the story of Lk 2. The only thing he does not explain is his own use of the term "legend" (*l.c.* p. 194). The deduction so long made from Luke's shocking blunders about the census apparently survives the demonstration that the blunder lay only in our lack of information : the microbe is not yet completely expelled. Possibly the salutary process may be completed by our latest inscriptional evidence that Quirinius was a legate in Syria for census purposes in B.C. 8-6 (see *Expositor* VIII. iv. pp. 385, 481 ff.).

ἀπογράφομαι.

On the general subject we have included everything under the noun above. The verb is used as a "vox sollennis" in P Petrie II. 11 (2 ³ (mid. iii/B.C.) (= Witkowski², p. 6) ἀπογέγραμμαι δὲ ἐπὶ τελώνιον τὸ οἰκόπεδον κτλ, "I have registered as subject to tax the site bringing 17½ dr. rent." So P Oxy I. 36ⁱⁱ ¹¹ (ii/iii A.D.), where, in connexion with the payment of customs, it is laid down that ἐὰν μὲν εὑρεθῇ τ[ι] ἕτερον ἢ ὁ ἀπεγράψατο, στερήσιμον ἔστω, "if anything be discovered other than what was declared, it shall be liable to confiscation." If not, the τελώνης had to repay to the merchant the cost of unloading his ship for examination. It is usually the middle voice that is employed—a fact not unconnected with the personal responsibility already noticed. But in P Ryl II. 103¹⁷·²⁰ (A.D. 134) we have ἀπεγρά φη),

[ἀπεγ]ρά[φ]ησαν, as against ἀπεγράψατο (-αντο) in other places in the document : the former simply gives the fact of the registration, which indeed in one case, that of a slave's child, was effected by the head of the family.

With the use of the verb in Heb 12²³ may be compared *Apoc. Pauli* (ed. Tischendorf), p. 39 f. : γνῶτε, υἱοὶ τῶν ἀνθρώπων, ὅτι πάντα τὰ πραττόμενα παρ᾽ ὑμῶν καθ᾽ ἡμέραν ἄγγελοι ἀπογράφονται ἐν οὐρανοῖς.

ἀποδείκνυμι.

P Alex 4⁶ (iii/B.C.) (= Witkowski², p. 51) ἀποδείξομέν σε, "we shall report you." For the middle cf. *Syll* 521¹⁹ (B.C. 100) the newly admitted *ephebi* ποιησάμενοι . . . μελέτην ἐν τοῖς ὅπλοις ἀπεδείξαντο τοῖς . . . Θησείοις. The verb is very common in the sense of "appoint" or "nominate": in P Ryl II. 153¹⁷ (A.D. 138-61) ἀποδίγνυμι τὸν υἱόν as heir to my estate. Generally it is used of "proclaiming" an appointment to public office. Thus in the rough draft of a public proclamation of the accession of Nero we are told ὁ δὲ τῆς οἰκουμένης καὶ προσδοκηθεὶς καὶ ἐλπισθεὶς Αὐτοκράτωρ ἀποδέδεικται, "the expectation and hope of the world has been declared Emperor" (P Oxy VII. 1021⁵ᶠᶠ·, A.D. 54), and in the same Emperor's speech to the Greeks he describes himself as δ[η]μαρχικῆς ἐξουσίας τὸ τρισκαιδέκατον ἀποδεδειγμένος = *designatus* (*Syll* 376³³, A.D. 67, with Dittenberger's note). Other examples are P Petr III. 36 (*a*) *verso* ¹⁷ ἐπ[ὶ] τῶν ἀποδεδειγμένων ἐπισκόπων "in the presence of the appointed supervisors," P Gen I. 36² (ii/A.D.) Ἀνουβίωνι ἀποδ[εδε]ιγμένῳ γυμνασιάρχῳ, and from the inscriptions *OGIS* 437⁹² (i/B.C.) οἱ ὑφ᾽ ἑκατέρων τῶν δήμων ἀποδειχθέντες ἄνδρες ἐπὶ τῶν συλλύσεων Σαρδιανῶν, *Syll* 409¹¹ (ii/A.D.) ἀποδειχ[θέν]τος ὑπὸ θεοῦ Ἀδριανοῦ, etc.

This use of the verb adds point to 2 Thess 2⁴, where the man of lawlessness is described as ἀποδεικνύντα ἑαυτὸν ὅτι ἔστιν θεός—he actually "proclaims" himself as God (see further Milligan *ad l.*). For the other meaning, "demonstrate," as in Ac 25⁷, cf. P Par 15³¹⁴ (B.C. 120) ἠρώτησεν τὸν Ἑρμίαν εἴ τινα ἀπόδειξιν παράκειται (so Radermacher *Gr.* p. 152 f.) ὡς ἔστιν αὐτοῦ προγονική, P Lond. 904³⁴ (A.D. 104—see above, under ἀπογραφή) (= III. p. 126) οἱ ἀποδ[εί]ξαντες ἀναγκ[αίαν α]ὑτῶν τὴν παρου[σίαν, who have "proved" their inability to return home for the census, P Fay 32¹⁵ (A.D. 131) πρότερον ἀποδίξω ὑπάρχειν "I will first establish my title to the ownership" (Edd.), and BGU II. 388ⁱⁱ ¹⁹ (ii/iii A.D.) ἐκ τῆς κατ᾽ οἰκίαν ἀπογραφῆς ἀποδείκνυται, τίνος ἐστιν δοῦλος. The verb in MGr (ἀποδείχνω) means "prove."

ἀπόδειξις.

P Lond 921¹⁰ (ii/iii A.D.) (= III. p. 134) καὶ εἰς ἀπόδιξιν [ὑπε]θέμην σοι τὰ ὑπογεγρ αμμένα) "in proof thereof." P Oxy II. 257¹⁹ (A.D. 94-5) καθ᾽ [ἃς] ἐπήνεγκεν ἀποδείξεις, "in accordance with the proofs he produced." P Amh II. 77³² (A.D. 139) ἵνα δυνηθῶ τὴν ἀπόδιξιν ἐπ᾽ αὐτοὺς π[ο]ιησ[ά]. μενο[ς τυχεῖν καὶ τῆς ἀπὸ σοῦ εὐεργεσίας, "in order that I may produce the proofs against them and obtain your beneficence" (Edd.). P Tebt II. 291⁴¹ (A.D. 162) (= *Chrest.* I. p 163) [ἀπ]όδειξιν δοὺς τοῦ ἐπίστασθαι [ἱε]ρατικὰ [καὶ] Αἰγύπτια γράμ[ματ]α, a priest gives proof of his qualifications by his knowledge of hieratic and Egyptian writing. *Syll* 521⁴² (see above under ἀποδείκνυμι ἐπο[ι]ή-σαντο . . . ἐπ' ἐξόδωι τῆς ἐφηβείας τὴν ἀπόδει[ξιν τ]ηι βουλῆι. In P Tor I. 1ᵛⁱⁱ ⁸ (B.C. 116) (= *Chrest.* II. p. 37) it is closely connected with another compound: καὶ μετὰ τὰς ἐπιδείξεις ταύτας αἰτεῖσθαι αὐτὸν τὰς περὶ τῆς οἰκίας ἀποδείξεις. "tandem, hisce demonstratis, iam ipsi licuisset a nobis documenta petere, quae ad domum attinent" (Peyron). BGU IV. 1141¹² (c. B.C. 14) καὶ δέδωκα ἀποδείξεις ἀληθινάς "genuine proofs." P Catt iii. 9 (ii/A.D.) (= *Chrest.* II. p. 421) ἐὰν τ[ι]να[ς] ἐναργεῖς ἀποδ[εί]ξεις ἔχῃς, ἐὰν ἐπενέ[γ]κῃς. ἀκούσομαί σου (οσον was first written). Cf. *Syll* 726²⁰ (ii/B.C.) ἀ. σαφεῖς. For the sense "election" (the *nomen actionis* to ἀποδείκνυμι), cf. *Syll* 206²⁹ (B.C. 274) γίνεσ[θαι δὲ εἰς τὸ λοιπὸν] τὴν ἀπόδειξιν τῶν θεωρῶν καθ' ἑκάστην πενταετηρίδα. For a "display," cf. *Syll* 923⁹³ (ii/B.C.) . . . ποιη[τ]ῶν καὶ ἱστοριαγράφων ἀποδείξεις.

ἀπόδεκτος.

OGIS 441¹⁰⁰ (i/B.C.) ἀπόδεκ[τα ὑπάρχει]ν δεῖν. (Ἀπρόσ-δεκτος is found in the contrary sense P Oxy II. 268¹⁸ (A.D. 58) τὴν ἐσομένην ἔφ[ο]δον ἄκυρον καὶ πρόσδεκτον (*l.* ἀπρ.) ὑπάρχειν, "any claim that is made shall be void and inadmissible" (Edd.): cf. the Xanthos inscription *Syll* 633⁹ (ii/A.D.) ἐὰν δέ τις βιάσηται, ἀπρόσδεκτος ἡ θυσία παρὰ τοῦ θεοῦ.) Ἀποδεκτέος "laudandus" occurs in Vettius Valens: see under ἀποδέχομαι. The noun ἀποδέκτης, following σίτ[ου], occurs in *Ostr* 1217 (iii/A.D.), *a.*

ἀποδέχομαι.

P Oxy VI. 939¹⁰ ᶠᶠ. (iv/A.D.), a letter from a Christian dependent to his master regarding the illness of his mistress, has the following: συνγνώμην δέ, κύριέ μου, σχοίης μοι [καὶ εὔνους] ἀποδέξει με εἰ καὶ ἐς τηλικαύτην σε [ἀγωνία]ν ἄκων ἐνέβαλον γράψας περὶ αὐτῆς ὅσα [ἐκομίσω], "please pardon me, my lord, and receive me kindly, though I unwillingly caused you so much anxiety by writing to you the messages which you received" (Edd.). *Syll* 603⁶¹ (ii/B.C.) ἐμφανίζειν δὲ αὐτοῖς ὅτι καὶ νῦν πρῶτοι τὸν ἀγῶνα ταῖς Μούσαις στεφα[ν]ίτην ἀποδέχοντ[αι . . ., *ib.* 790⁴¹ (i/B.C.) ἁγνεύοντες καὶ νήφοντες καὶ ἀποδεχόμενοι τὰ πινάκια παρὰ τῶν μαντευομένων. *OGIS* 602¹ Egypt οὐκ ἀπεδεξάμην σε τ(ῆς) ἐ[ν λόγοις] τριβῆς [ἕνεκεν]. Vettius Valens p. 250²² τινὲς μὲν εὐχερεῖς καὶ ἐπακτικοὶ τῆς ἀληθείας ἀποδέχονται, which Kroll renders "laudantur," comparing p. 329¹⁶ ὅθεν ἀποδεκτέος ὁ τοιοῦτος. Gildersleeve (*Just. M.* p. 230) remarks on the "respectful" tone of the verb in Ac 24³ πάντη τε καὶ πανταχοῦ ἀποδεχόμεθα. It survives in MGr.

ἀποδημέω.

Early examples of this verb are afforded by P Petr III. 42¹⁵ (iii/B.C.) εἰμὶ γὰρ πρὸς τῶι ἀποδημεῖν, "for I am on the point of departure" (Edd.), and P Par 46⁸ (B.C. 153) ἐνκατελέλοιπε με ἀποδημήσας. An antithesis which verbally resembles 2 Cor 5⁹ may be seen in P Tebt I. 104¹⁷ (B.C. 92) ἐνδημῶν καὶ ἀποδημῶν, in a marriage contract: similarly BGU I. 183⁷ (A.D. 85), P. Giss I. 2ⁱ ¹⁹ (B.C. 173), and cf. P Par 69 (iii/A.D.) where the arrivals and departures of a strategus are recorded in his day-book by ἐπι- and ἀποδημέω respectively (cf. *Archiv* iv. p. 374). On P Catt⁰ 20 (ii/A.D.) (= *Chrest.* II. p. 422) ἐὰν γένηταί με ἀποδημεῖν, P. M. Meyer observes (*Archiv* iii. p. 84) that the verb is the antithesis

of ἐνδημεῖν, as especially in marriage contracts. Add P Oxy I. 41⁴⁸ (late i/A.D.) ἀποδημοῦντός σου, "in your absence," *ib.* II. 326⁷ (c. A.D. 45) οὐκ ἔλαβον ἀργύριον παρὰ [τῶν πρ]οπόλων ἀφ' οὗ ἀπεδήμη[σα]. *ib.* III. 471⁸ (ii/A.D.) ἀποδη[μοῦντ]ες ἠγνοήσατε τὰς [π]ερὶ τούτων γεγραμ-μένας ὑμ[εῖ]ν ἐπιστολάς, P Tebt II. 333⁷ (A.D. 216) τοῦ πατρός μου . . . ἀποδημήσαντος . . . πρὸς κυνηγίαν λα-γοῶν, "my father set off to hunt hares," and P Amh II. 145¹⁶ (iv/v A.D.) ἐλυπήθην διότι ἀπεδήμησας ἀλόγως, "I am grieved because you went away without cause" (Edd.). In *Syll* 633¹³ (Rom.) ἐὰν δέ τινα ἀνθρώπινα πάσχῃ ἢ ἀσθενήσῃ ἢ ἀποδημήσῃ που gives us a good combination. For the subst. cf. P Oxy III. 471¹³¹ (ii/A.D.) τάς τε ἀποδημίας, P Tebt II. 336³ (ii/A.D.) ἐμοῦ ἐν ἀποδημίᾳ ὄντος, and P Giss I. 41ⁱⁱ· ³ (Hadrian) ὑπὸ τῆς μακρᾶς ἀποδημίας τὰ ἡμέτε[ρα] πα[ντ]άπασιν ἀμεληθέντα τυγχ[άνει].

ἀπόδημος.

Syll 154²⁴ (age of Alexander) τοὺς δὲ ἀποδήμους, ἐπειδὰν ἔλθωσι ἐς τὴμ πόλιν, ἀποδοῦναι τὴν τιμὴν διὰ μηνός. *ib.* 427³⁰ (iv/iii B.C.) (Crete, in dialect) καὶ τ[ο]ὺς ἄλλο[υ]ς πολίτας ἐξορκιῶ, τοὺ[ς] μὲν ἐνδάμους αὐτίκα μάλα, τοὺς δ' ἀποδάμους αἴ κα ἔλθωντι, [ὡ]ς ἄ[ν] δύνωμαι τάχιστα].

ἀποδίδωμι.

It is unnecessary to illustrate at length this very common verb, the uses of which are on familiar lines. Thus ἀπόδος τῷ δεῖνι is the direction on the back of a letter, e.g. P Oxy II. 293²⁰ (A.D. 27) ἀπόδο[ς] παρὰ Διον[υσίου] Διδύμῃ τῆι ἀδε[λφῆ]: see also Wilcken *Archiv* v. p. 238 for the use of ἀπόδος to denote the transmission of an official document. Similarly the verb is the appropriate one everywhere for the "paying" of a debt, or "restoring" of a due of any kind—P Eleph 1¹¹ (B.C. 311-0) (= *Selections*, p. 3) of a dowry, Ἡρακλείδης Δημητρίαι τὴμ φερνὴν ἣν προσηνέγκατο [δραχμὰς Ᾱ], an observance due to the gods P Giss I. 27¹⁰ (ii/A.D.) ἵνα . . . τοῖς θεοῖς τὰς ὀφειλομένα[ς] σπονδὰς ἀποδῶ, rent *ib.* 46⁴ (Hadrian) τὰ [ἐ]κφόρια οὐκ ἀπέδοσαν, P Oxy I. 37ⁱⁱ· ⁸ (A.D. 49) (= *Selections*, p. 51) of wages for services that have not been fully rendered, ἀποδοῦσαν αὐτὴν ὃ εἴληφεν ἀργύριον, and *ib.* II. 269⁶ (A.D. 57) of a loan of money, ἃς ἀποδώσω σοι τῇ τριακάδι τοῦ Κα[ισαρε]ίου μηνός. In P Grenf I. 43⁵ ᶠᶠ· (ii/B.C.) [α]ὐτοῦ δὲ μηδ' ἀπο-δεδωκότος ἡμῖν μ[ηδ]ὲ ἵππον μηδὲ τὴν πορείαν αὐτῆς ἐπ[ιδε]-δωκότος, we have two compounds well distinguished. For some notes on its flexion see under δίδωμι. The middle ἀποδόσθαι "sell" (Ac 5⁸ etc.) may be illustrated from P Tor I. 1ⁱᵛ ²² B.C. 116) (= *Chrest.* II. p. 34, ᵛⁱ ²⁴ (p. 36) etc. Cf. MGr ἀποδίδω.

ἀποδιορίζω.

The simplex (if we may so call what is already a compound) may be seen in Wünsch *AF* 3²⁵ (p. 12) (Carthage, leaden tablet) ἐξορκίζω ὑμᾶς κατὰ τοῦ ἐπάν[ω] τοῦ οὐρανοῦ θεοῦ, τοῦ καθημένου ἐπὶ τῶν Χερουβί, ὁ διορίσας τὴν γῆν καὶ χωρίσας τὴν θάλασσαν: the writer has got enough Judaism to curse with. For his grammar cf. *Proleg.* p. 60 n.¹.

ἀποδοκιμάζω.

P. Giss I. 47¹⁴ ᶠᶠ· (Hadrian) παραζώ[ν]ιον γὰρ πρὸς τὸ παρὸν γνήσιον οὐχ εὑρέθη, ἀλλ' οὐδὲ ἐδικαίωσα ἀγοράσαι ἀποδοκιμασθῆναι δυνάμενον, "a girdle-dagger suitable for the present purpose has not been found, and I have not thought it right to buy one that might be rejected." On the use in 1 Pet 2⁷ of the LXX ἀποδοκιμάζω instead of ἐξουθενέω as in Ac 4¹¹ for the Heb סאמ in Ps 118²², as indicating a progress on Peter's part in Greek ways and speech, see Ramsay *Pauline Studies*, p. 254 f. Vettius Valens uses it twice: p. 278¹⁸ ἐὰν δὲ τοὺς κακοποιούς (= εὔρωμεν χρηματίζοντας καὶ τὸν Ἥλιον ἢ τὴν Σελήνην ἐπιθεωροῦντας [καὶ] τὸν ὡροσκόπον, ἀποδοκιμάζομεν τὴν γένεσιν, p. 313²⁶ πρὸς τὸ μὴ πλέκεσθαί τινας ἢ ἀποδοκιμάζειν τὴν αἵρεσιν.

ἀποδοχή.

Syll 371²¹ (Magnesia, i/A.D.) δεδόχθαι . . τετιμῆσθαι . . Τύραννον καὶ εἶναι ἐν ἀποδοχῇ τῷ δήμῳ. In *ib.* 656²⁰¹ (Ephesus, c. A.D. 148) an ἀγωνοθέτης named Priscus is styled ἀνδρὸς δοκιμωτάτου καὶ πάσης τειμῆς καὶ ἀποδοχῆς ἀξίου. Field's examples (*Notes*, p. 203) show how much of a formula this ἀποδοχῆς ἄξιος (as 1 Tim 1¹⁵) had become. The inscription is quoted, with other epigraphic examples, by Bishop Hicks in *CR* i. p. 4, from which may be selected *OGIS* 339¹¹ (c. B.C. 120) τῆς καλλίστης ἀποδοχῆς ἀξιούμενος παρ' αὐτῶι. *Priene* 108³¹² (after B.C. 120), 109²³¹ (c. B.C. 120) ἐν ἀποδοχῆι τῆι μεγίστηι εἶναι, "to enjoy the highest esteem" (see Fouillac, p. 39).

The derivative ἀποδοχεῖον, which is found in the LXX, occurs in Rev L 31¹⁹, 32², 54¹⁸ (B.C. 258), and is apparently to be restored in the much mutilated P Petr III 36 (*b*) ii ¹² (B.C. 252) βουκόλων κ(ώμης) ἀποδοχίω[ι], "in the granary of the herdsmen's village." So P Hib I 85²¹ (B.C. 261).

The phrase μετὰ πάσης ἀποδοχῆς (cf. 1 Tim 1¹⁵) occurs in *Cagnat* IV. 144⁸ (Cyzicus, ii/A.D.), of the "general appreciation" of an act of the Princess Antonia Tryphaena.

ἀπόθεσις.

BGU II. 606⁵ (A.D. 306) πρὸς ἀ]πόθεσιν ἀχύρου. *Syll* 420¹⁶ (iv/A.D. init.) τῇ ἀποθέσει τῶν στεφάνων, the ceremony of resigning a priesthood, the inauguration to which was παράληψις τοῦ στεφάνου (so Ed.). Ἀπόθετος occurs in a petition P Oxy I. 71ⁱⁱ ¹⁹ (A.D. 303), but unfortunately the passage is much mutilated. With the idea of 2 Pet 1¹⁴ we might compare σῶ]μ' ἀποδυσάμενος in *Kaibel* 403⁵ (iv/v A.D., but not Christian).

ἀποθήκη.

The word is by no means so common as might have been expected. In the Indexes to *Oxyrhynchus Papyri* I.-X. it is only noted once, namely P Oxy I. 43 *verso* iii ³⁴ (A.D. 295). See also BGU I. 32³, *ib.* III. 816⁵ (iii/A.D.), and *ib.* 931² (iii/iv A.D.) ἐμετρήθη ἀπὸ ἀποθήκης τῆς μέσης ἐλαίου μετρητὰς γ̄—these are the only occurrences in BGU I.-IV. In P Tebt II. 347 (a banking account, ii/A.D.) the word is repeatedly prefixed to different items, "the sums so indicated being apparently 'deposited' (in a bank?)" (Edd.). Add *Syll* 734⁵¹ (Cos) μηδ' ἀποθήκηι χρᾶσθαι τ[ῆι αὐλ]ῆι τῆι ἐν τῶι ἱερῶι, and *Chrest.* II. 96⁶ (after A.D. 350), where counsel pleads that the defendant should give up ¼ of δωρεᾶς καὶ ἀποθήκης, ἢ τὴν ἀποκατάστασιν ἡμῖν ποιήσασθαι τούτων: Mitteis (p. 116) explains these as "donatio propter nuptias?" and "ein Geschäftsladen." Prof. Thumb notes that the

noun survived in Romance (Span. *bodega*, Fr. *boutique*): this reinforces its ancient Hellenistic record.

ἀποθησαυρίζω

appears twice in Vettius Valens: p. 162²¹ ἀνεύφραντοι ἀποθησαυριζομένων, 181² ἡδέως ἀποθησαυριζόντων πρὸς τὰ μέτρα τῶν γενέσεων.

ἀποθλίβω.

P Tor I. 1ⁱⁱ ¹⁴ (B.C. 116) (= *Chrest.* II. p. 32) οἱ ἐγκαλούμενοι ἀποθλιβέντες τῶι μηθενὸς δικαίου ἀντέχεσθαι.

ἀποθνήσκω.

On the reason why the perfect of this verb was τέθνηκα, not ἀποτέθνηκα, see *Proleg.* p. 114. Marcus Aurelius, it is true, uses ἀποτέθνηκα, a natural result of levelling when the simplex had become obsolete; but the editor of P Iand 9⁵ (ii/A.D.) is not thereby justified in restoring ἀπο]τεθνῶτ[ος. No other part of the simplex survives, and no other compound. An interesting instance of the word occurs in P Par 47⁷ᶠᶠ (c. B.C. 153) (= *Selections*, p. 22) οἱ παρὰ σὲ θεοὶ . . . ὅτι ἐνβέβληκαν ὑμᾶς εἰς ὕλην μεγάλην καὶ οὐ δυνάμεθα ἀποθανεῖν, "your gods (are false) because they have cast us into a great forest, where we may possibly die." As a parallel to the Pauline usage in 1 Cor 15³¹ may be noted the touching letter P Giss I 17⁹ (time of Hadrian), where a slave writes to her absent master, ἀποθνήσκομεν ὅτι οὐ βλέπομέν σε καθ' ἡμέραν. The use of the present tense justifies one more citation, BGU IV. 1024ⁱᵛ ⁹ (iv/v A.D.), where a ἡγεμών, passing sentence of death on a man who had disinterred a corpse, says he is less than a beast, καὶ γὰρ τὰ θηρία [τ]οῖς μὲν ἀνθρώποις πρόσισιν, τῶν δὲ [ἀ]ποθνησκόντων φίδοντα[ι. Here the meaning is "spare them when they die": the pres. is frequentative, as in Heb 7³ or Rev 14¹³. The MGr is ἀποθαίνω (or πεθαίνω etc.).

ἀποκαθίστημι.

For the meaning "restore," "give back," see P Petr III. 53 (*p.* ¹²), where in connexion with certain arrears into which a priest had fallen provision is made πρᾶξαι τοὺς ἐγγύους αὐτοῦ καὶ ἡμῖν ἀποκαταστῆσ[α]ι, "that payment be exacted from his sureties and restitution made to us" (Edd.). P Rein 17¹⁵ (B.C. 109) may be cited for its grammar, noteworthy at this early date: ὅπως οἱ αἴτιοι ἀναζητηθέντες ἐξαποσταλῶ[σ]ι ἐπὶ τὸν στρατηγόν, [καὶ] ἐμοὶ μὲν διαπεφωνημένα ἀποκατασ[τα]θείη, οἱ δὲ αἴτιοι τύχωσι τῶν ἐξακολουθούντων. The passive ἀποκατασταθήσεται occurs in BGU IV. 1060²⁸ (B.C. 23-2). *OGIS* 90¹³ (Rosetta stone—B.C. 196) ἀποκατέστησεν εἰς τὴν καθήκουσαν τάξιν. *Syll* 540³⁴ (B.C. 175-1) if a workman breaks a stone, ἕτερον ἀποκαταστήσει δόκιμον. P Revill Mél p. 295⁵ (B.C. 131-0) = Witkowski², p. 96) μέχρι τοῦ τὰ πράγματ' ἀποκαταστῆναι, P Amh II. 48¹⁰ (B.C. 106) καὶ ἀποκαταστησάτω εἰς οἶκο[ν] [π]ρὸς αὐτὴν τοῖς ἰδίοις, "shall deliver it to her at her house at his own expense" (Edd.). P Oxy I. 38¹² (A.D. 49-50) (= *Selections*, p. 53) ὑφ' οὗ καὶ ἀποκατεστάθη μοι ὁ υἱός, *ib.* II. 278¹⁷ (hire of a mill—A.D. 17) καὶ μετὰ τὸν χρόνον ἀπ[οκα]ταστησάτω ὁ μάνης (the servant) τὸν μύλον ὑγιῆι καὶ ἀσινῆι, οἷον καὶ παρείληφεν, *ib.* VI. 929¹⁷ (ii/iii A.D.) ἀποκαταστῆσαί μοι εἰς Ὀξυρυγχείτην ἐξ ὧν ἔσχον τὰ προκείμενα πάντα, etc. In the long land survey

P Tebt I. 61 *b*²²¹ (B.C. 118-7) the question is asked with regard to certain land, εἰ [α]ὐτὴ [ἀνταναι]ρετέα [ἄλλη δὲ] ἀπὸ ὑπολόγου ἀνταναιρεθεῖσα ἀποκαταστατέα, "whether it should be deducted (from the cleruchic land) and other land subtracted from that in the unprofitable list should be substituted" (Edd.: cf. a land survey of the second century, where a holding that had become καθ' ὕδατος ἀποκατεστάθ(η) τῷ ἐνεστ(ῶτι) (ἔτει), was "reclaimed" in the year in which the survey was written (P Oxy VI. 918 intr.). Note the passive in Vettius Valens, p. 68²⁴ = *ex captivitate redire* (Ed.).

For the double augment, which is found in the NT (Mt 12¹³, Mk 8²⁵, Lk 6¹⁰, cf. such an occasional occurrence in the inscriptions as *Calder* 8⁸ ἀπεκατέστησεν, *Letronne* 525⁸ (ii/A.D.) ἀπεκατεστάθη, and similarly *Archiv* ii. p. 436. no. 31 (i/A.D.); also P Tebt II. 413⁴ (ii/iii A.D.) ἀπεκατέστησα. By the Byzantine period it had become very common. See further Winer-Schmiedel *Gr.* p. 103, and Brugmann-Thumb *Gr.* p. 311. Note the perf. ἀποκαθέστακεν, *Syll* 365⁷ (i/A.D.).

ἀποκαλύπτω.

For the literal sense of this significant word cf. P Gen I. 16¹³ (A.D. 207), as amended *Add.* p. 37, ὁ[πό]ταν ἡ τοια[ύ]τη γῆ ἀποκαλυ[φθ]ῇ, μισθοῦται καὶ σπείρεται: cf. BGU II. 640⁷ (i/A.D.) βουλόμεθα μισθώσασθαι ἀποκαλυφῆς (*l.* -εῖσης) αἰγιαλοῦ, and CPR I. 239⁵ (A.D. 212) βούλομαι μισθώσασθαι ἀποκαλυφείσης χέρσου αἰγειαλοῦ, both as amended by Spohr in his note on P Iand 27⁶ (A.D. 100-1). He remarks that the phrase denotes "agri litorales," which could only be cultivated when the water had receded. Since two of Spohr's passages have ἀποκαλυφῆς (BGU II. 640 and CPR 32⁷) αἰγιαλοῦ, one is tempted to postulate rather an adjective ἀποκάλυφος, which would be quite regular in formation. A further instance might be sought in CPHerm 45⁶, where we would read ὀψ[ὶ] μως ἀποκάλυφο[ι] (ἄρουραι) ε̄. We may add for the other form P Iand 30¹⁵ (A.D. 105-6) ἐκ τῶν ἀποκαλυ[φέντω]ν ἀπ' αἰγ[ια]λοῦ ἐδα[φ]ῶν. To the classical and late Greek instances of the verb given by the dictionaries may now be added the new literary fragment in P Oxy III. 413¹⁶⁶ ἀ[ποκ]άλυψον ἵνα ἴδω αὐτήν.

ἀποκάλυψις.

The Biblical history of ἀποκάλυψις along with the foregoing verb is discussed by Milligan *Thess.* p. 149 ff. Jerome's assertion (*Comm. in Gal.* 1¹²) that the word "proprie Scripturarum est: a nullo sapientum saeculi apud Graecos usurpatum" cannot, however, be substantiated, if only because of its occurrences in Plutarch, who, like the NT writers, drew from the common vocabulary of the time. see e.g. *Mor.* 70 F.

ἀποκαραδοκία.

For the verb see Polyb. xviii. 31 ἀποκαραδοκεῖν τὴν Ἀντιόχου παρουσίαν, al. Cf. the interesting sixth-century papyrus from Aphrodite in Egypt (cited by Deissmann *LAE* p. 377 f.; cf. *Archiv* v. p. 284) in which certain oppressed peasants petition a high official whose παρουσία they have been expecting: assuring him that they await (ἐκδέχομεν) him—οἶον οἱ ἐξ Ἅδου καραδοκοῦντες τὴν τότε τοῦ Χριστοῦ ἀενάου θ(εο)ῦ παρουσίαν, "as those in Hades watch eagerly for the parousia of Christ the everlasting God." While the perfectivized verb is well supported in literary Κοινή, the noun is so far peculiar to Paul, and may quite possibly have been his own formation: cf. what we have said above under ἀπεκδέχομαι and ἀπέκδυσις.

ἀποκατάστασις.

This subst., which in the NT is found only in Ac 3²¹, occurs in the sense of "restitution" in P Par 63¹¹¹·⁴⁰ ᵈ· (B.C. 164) παντάπασιν δὲ μετὰ τὴν ἀπὸ τῶν πραγμάτων νυνεὶ ἀποκατάστασειν ἑρμῶμεν ἀπὸ βραχέων μόλις εὐσχημονεῖν, P Leid Bⁱⁱⁱ ¹⁵ καὶ τούτων τὴν ἀποκατάστασιν ἡμῖν γενηθῆναι. So in *Syll* 552 (late ii/B.C.) twice with reference to the "renewal" of the temple cell of the goddess Artemis at Magnesia—¹³ εἰς τὴν ἀποκατάστασιν τοῦ ναοῦ συντέλειαν εἴληφεν, and ²³ συντελέσαι τὴν ἀποκατάστασιν τῆς θεοῦ, and in OGIS 483⁵ (ii/B.C.) of the "repair" of a public way—ἔκδοσιν ποιησάμενοι τῆς ἀποκαταστάσεως τοῦ τόπου. In P Oxy I. 67⁹ a dispute concerning property—A.D. 338) it is laid down, εἰ πρὸς τὴν τῶν ὑπὸ τῶν αἰτιαθέντων διακατέχεσθαι λ[εγο]μένων οἰκοπ[έ]δ[ω]ν ἀποκατάστασιν κτλ., "if the accused persons protest against the restoration of the estates of which they are said to be in occupation," etc. In the third century petition, P Oxy I. 70, the editors render ¹⁶ ff· συνέβη δὲ ἀποκατάστασιν με ποιήσασθαι πρὸς αὐτὸν τῷ διελθόντι κ̄ ἔτει, by "it happened that a balancing of accounts took place between us in the past 20th year." Add P J Jor I. 43¹³ (A.D. 370) χειρο-γ[ρα]φείαν ἤτοι ἀσφάλειαν τῆς ἀποκαταστάσεως τούτων, P Strass I. 29⁷ (iv/A.D.) μετὰ τὴν ἀποκατάστασιν τούτων παρὰ Φοιβάμμωνος Παπνουθίου λάμβανε τὴν πρᾶσιν, and *Chrest.* II. p. 117, printed above under ἀποθήκη. Another noun-formation occurs in P Tebt II. 424⁸ (late iii/A.D.) ὡς ἐὰ (*l.* ἐὰν) μὴ ἀποκαταστασίας [δ]ὴ πέμψῃς [ο]ἶδάς σου τὸ[ν] κίνδυνον, "so unless you now send discharges (of debts) you know your danger" (Edd.). To the literary record may be added Epicurus 8⁹ (Linde *Epic.* p. 32). On the astrological use of ἀποκατάστασις (= the final point of agreement of the world's cyclical periods) as underlying the NT idea, see J. Lepsius in *Exp.* VIII. iii. p. 158 ff., where reference is also made to Brandes *Abhandl. z. Gesch. des Orients*, p. 123, "The Egyptian Apokatastasis-years."

ἀπόκειμαι.

P Par 63¹⁸·⁴⁷ (ii/B.C.) ἀπόκειται γὰρ παρὰ θ[εοῦ] μῆνις τοῖς μὴ κατὰ τὸ βέλτιστον [προαι]ρουμένοις ζῆν: there is a suggestion of Rom 2⁵. Closely parallel with the NT use of the verb is OGIS 383¹⁸⁹ (the important inscription of Antiochus I., the quasi-Zoroastrian king of Commagene in i/B.C.) οἷς ἀποκείσεται παρὰ θεῶν καὶ ἡρώων χάρις εὐσεβείας (see Dittenberger's note). For a similar use of the simplex cf. *Magn* 115¹⁵ (ii/A.D.) διὰ ταῦτά σοι κείσεται μεγάλη χάρις ἐμ βασιλέως οἴκωι, and see *XVII* xv. p. 94 ff. With Heb 9²⁷ cf. *Kaibel* 416⁶ (late, Alexandria) ὡς εἰδὼς ὅτι πᾶσι βροτοῖς τὸ θανεῖν ἀπόκειται: there are no signs of Christianity in the epitaph. A more literal use, serving as transition to the next, is in BGU IV. 1023⁷ (A.D. 185-6) γραφὴ θεακῶν (*l.* -γῶν): see reff. in *Tebt. Pap.* I. p. 610) καὶ τῶν ἐν τῷ ἱερῷ ἀποκειμένων. The word is common in the sense "to be stored," e.g. P Oxy I. 69⁵ (A.D. 190) ἀπὸ τῶν ἐν τῇ οἰκίᾳ ἀποκειμένων, BGU I. 275²

(A.D. 215) ἐν ᾗ αὐλῇ ἐστὶν ἀποκειμένη μηχανή, P Tebt II.
340¹³ (A.D. 200) αἱ καὶ ἀποκείμεναι ἐν θησ αυρῷ ἐπὶ σφραγίδι
Ἀμμωνίου, "which are stored at the granary under the
seal of A." (Edd.), and P Lond Inv. no. 1885⁷ (A.D.
114-5—published by Bell in *Archiv* vi. p. 102) τὰ ἐν αὐτῇ
βιβλία ἀποκείμενα, documents "housed" in the βιβλιοθήκη
ἐγκτήσεων.

In Deut 32³⁴ οὐκ ἰδοὺ ταῦτα συνῆκται παρ' ἐμοί, καὶ
ἐσφράγισται ἐν τοῖς θησαυροῖς μου, Symmachus substitutes ἀπόκειται for συνῆκται.

ἀποκλείω.

P Oxy II. 265¹⁴ (a marriage contract, A.D. 81-95) μηδ'
ἀποκλεῖν (= ἀποκλείειν) μηδενὸς τῶν ὑπαρχόντω[ν. (For
the Hellenistic contraction of two *i*-sounds, see *Proleg*³
p. 45.) *ib.* X. 1272⁵ (A.D. 144) ἀπέκλε[ισα τὴν θύ]ρ[αν
τῆς . . .] οἰκίας μου καὶ τὴν τοῦ πεσσοῦ (terrace) ·θύ[ραν.

ἀποκόπτομαι.

On this word, taken in the sense of Deut 23¹ (supported
by several instances in literary Κοινή—see Grimm-Thayer)
Nageli has some good remarks (p. 78 f.): he brings together
several phrases which show Paul using a more vernacular
style in Gal than anywhere else, the startling passage 5¹²
being the climax—"Der zürnende Apostel lasst auch seiner
Wortwahl freien Lauf; die starksten Ausdrücke der
Umgangsprache sind 'etzt die geeignetsten." Cf. *Proleg.*
pp. 163, 201.

ἀπόκριμα.

OGIS 335⁹⁵ (ii/B.C.) τὰ ἀ]ποσταλέντα ὑπ [αὐ]τῶν
ἀποκρίματα and ¹¹⁹ καθό[τ]ι καὶ αὐτοὶ διὰ τῶν ἀποκριμά-
τω[ν] ἐνεφάνισαν. Still nearer in point of time to the sole
NT occurrence of the word (2 Cor 1⁹) is *IMAe* 2⁴ (Rhodes,
A.D. 51) in which τὰ εὐκταιότατα ἀποκρίματα refer to
favourable *decisions* of the Emperor Claudius (Deissmann,
BS p. 257): cf. *IG* VII. 2711⁶¹ᶠᶠ (A.D. 37) προσενδεξάμενος
κατὰ δωρεὰν [πρεσ]βεύσιν πρὸς τὸν Σεβαστὸν . . .
ἤνενκεν ἀπόκριμα πρὸς τὸ ἔθνος πάσης [φιλαν]θρωπίας καὶ
ἐλπίδων ἀγαθῶν πλήρες. *OGIS* 494¹³ (? i/iiA.D.) joins
ἐπιστολαί, ἀποκρίματα, διατάγματα: Dittenberger defines
these successively in the context as dispatches addressed by
the proconsul to the Emperor, the Senate, etc., replies
given to deputations of provincials to him, and *edicta*, or
documents addressed to the people at large, and not to
individuals. See also his note on *Syll* 368⁵ (i/A.D.), where
C. Stertinius, chief physician to the Imperial family, is also
ἐπὶ τῶν Ἑλληνικῶν ἀποκριμάτων. In P Tebt II. 286¹
(A.D. 121-38) ἀ. is a "rescript" of Hadrian. Paul (*l.c.*) may
be taken as meaning that he made his distressed appeal to
God, and kept in his own heart's archives the answer—
"ἀποθάνῃ· τὸ δὲ ἀποθανεῖν κέρδος," as we might reconstruct it.

ἀποκρίνομαι.

Syll 928¹² (Magnesia, early ii/B.C.) περὶ ταύ[της τῆς] χώρας
τῆς παρὰ Πριηνέων ἀποκεκριμένης οὔσης shows the old
ἀποκρίνω in passive. For the combination of pf. partic. and
ὤν, cf. Col 1²¹. In P Ryl II. 122¹¹ (A.D. 127) εἰς τὸ κἀμὲ
δύνασθαι ἀποκριθῆναι τῶι δημοσίωι, "enabling me thus to
fulfil my duties towards the Treasury" (Edd.), we have an

isolated ex. of the passive aor. not meaning "answer." This
latter, so overwhelmingly predominant in NT, is rather
surprisingly uncommon in the non-literary Κοινή. Early
inscriptional instances are *Syll* 328¹¹ (B.C. 84) ἀπεκρίθ[ην
κα]λῶς [αὐτ ὁν [τε δεδω]κέναι καὶ κτλ., *ib.* 307⁶¹ (B.C. 150-47)
ἔδοξεν . . . τούτοις φιλανθρώπως ἀποκριθῆναι, *ib.* 930⁵⁴ (B.C.
112), same phrase: the last two are *senatus consulta*, starting
in Latin. Similarly the dialectic *Syll* 654⁵ (? ii/B.C.) ἀποκρι-
θῆμεν τοῖς πρεσβευταῖς διότι κτλ. Mayser, p. 379, pronounces it "die eigentliche κοινή-form," but he only has
five instances, P Par 34¹⁰ (B.C. 157), 35³⁰ (B.C. 163), 15³⁵
(B.C. 120), P Leid U⁶⁸ ¹¹ (ii/B.C.), and P Grenf I. 37¹⁴ (B.C.
108—ἐκρίθη for ἀπεκρ.): he cannot, however, quote any
cases of ἀπεκρινάμην. On the other hand we cannot find
any more instances of ἀπεκρίθην from later papyri, except
P Lond 121³⁵⁰ (iii/A.D.) (= I. p. 95), and two Christian
documents, P Grenf II. 112²⁰ (a Festal Epistle, A.D. 577?)
and PSI 26¹ (see Addenda) (v/A.D.—acts of a martyrdom). Since MGr ἀποκρίθηκα shows that it lived on, its
disappearance in the post-Ptolemaic period outside NT is
hard to explain. It is not, however, replaced by ἀπεκρινάμην, as to which subsequent information has antiquated
the statement in *Proleg.* p. 161 f. (corrected in *Einleitung*
p. 254 n.¹). For the middle aorist occurs very often in
papyri, but they are without exception legal reports, in which
ἀπεκρείνατο (so usually—also ptc. or inf.) means "replied,"
of an advocate or a party in a suit. The references had
better be appended: P Hib I. 31²¹ (c. B.C. 270) . . . ἀ]πεκρίνα-
[το . . . , no context, but the whole document proves its
connotation), P Amh II. 66³⁷ (A.D. 124), P Catt¹ ²² (= *Chrest.*
II. p. 419) (ii/A.D.), P Oxy II. 237ᵛⁱⁱ ²⁵ ³³ (A.D. 186),
ib. III. 653 (A.D. 162-3), BGU I. 114ⁱ ²² (ii/A.D.), 136¹⁵
(A.D. 135), and 361ⁱⁱ ⁶,¹² (ii/A.D.), *ib.* II. 388ⁱⁱ ¹⁷,³⁰
(ii/iii A.D.), *ib.* III. 660ⁱ ¹⁵ (A.D. 142?), P Lips I. 32¹,⁵,⁶
(iii/A.D.), *ib.* 33ⁱⁱ ¹⁶ and 36⁵ (iv/A.D.), *Chrest.* II. 78⁹ (p. 86,
A.D. 376-8), P Théad 14²¹ (iv/A.D.) δι' ἑρμηνέ[ως] ἀπεκρεί-
ναν[το (in a *procès verbal*), PGU III. 936¹³ (A.D. 426),
PSI 52³³ (vi/A.D.) and 61³³, 62²⁴ (early vii/A.D.)—all three
πᾶσιν τοῖς πρὸς αὐτὸν (or -ἦν) ἐπιζητουμένοις ἀποκρίνασθαι.
The only one that need be noted specially is P Giss I. 40ⁱⁱ ⁸
(A.D. 212), where Caracalla says ἵνα μή τις στενότερον
παρερμηνεύσῃ τὴν χάριτά μου ἐκ τῶν ῥη[μά]των το[ῦ]
προτέρου διατάγματος, ἐν ᾧ οὕτως ἀπεκριν[ά]μην κτλ.
This may represent *rescripsi*, but in any case we cannot miss
the formal and weighty tone of the verb.

We proceed to compare these facts with those of Biblical
Greek. Thackeray tells us (*Gr.* p. 239) that ἀπεκρίθην "is
employed throughout the LXX: the classical ἀπεκρινάμην
in the few passages where it occurs seems to be chosen as
suitable for solemn or poetical language." Such a passage as
3 Regn 2¹, the last charge of King David to his heir,
might be compared with Caracalla's use of the form. The
fairly clear use in the fragment of a law report from P Hib
above tells us that the legal use was already possible at the
time when the LXX was growing. So we may take its
meaning throughout as being (1) "uttered solemnly," (2)
"replied in a court of law." These two meanings cover all
the NT passages: (1) accounts for Lk 3¹⁶, Jn 5¹⁷·¹⁹, Ac 3¹²,
(2) for Mt 27¹², Mk 14⁶¹, Lk 23⁹, with Jn 5¹¹ (אᵃ) not far
away. With the absence of ἀπεκρίθην from the Pauline and
other Epistles, and the Apocalypse except for one passage,

we may compare the silence of the papyri after ii/B.C. We are inclined to suggest that the word belongs only to early Hellenistic, whence it was taken by the LXX translators to render a common Hebrew phrase, passing thence into the narrative parts of NT as a definite "Septuagintalism." From the Gospels and Acts it passed into ecclesiastical diction (cf. Reinhold, p. 77), and so ultimately into MGr. The contrast between the two halves of the NT will thus be parallel with that noted above under **ᾅδης**.

ἀπόκρισις.

Syll 276²⁸ (Lampsacus, c. B.C. 195) . . . ὅταν παρ' αὐτοῦ λ]άβωσιν ἀποκρίσεις τὰς ἁρμοζούσας τ[. . ., *ib.* 177⁶² (Teos, B.C. 303) οἰόμεθα δὲ [δεῖν ἀποδειχθῆ]ναι τρεῖς ἄνδρας εὐθὺς ὅταν [ἡ] ἀπόκ[ρι]σις ἀναγνωσθῆι, *ib.* 314¹⁵ (ii/B.C., Messenian dialect) ἔδοξε τοῖς συνέδροις ἀπόκρισιν δόμεν διότι κτλ., *ib.* 928²¹ (Magnesia, ii/B C. *init.*) τὴν Μυλασέων ἀπόκρισιν to the praetor M. Aemilius. From the papyri we can only cite P Oxy VI. 941⁹ (vi/A.D.), and other late exx.; like the verb, this word for "answer" clearly suffered eclipse, and returned into the language at a late period.

ἀποκρύπτω.

P Strass I. 42¹⁷ (census return—A.D. 310) ὄμνυμει θεοὺς ἅπαντας . . . μηδένα ἀποκεκρυφέναι. *Syll* 801 (Ephesus, vi/B.C.) has the verb thrice, of a bird flying out of sight: this early Ionic lies far behind the Hellenistic period, but may be added to the literary record of the verb, which we have not noticed in our sources. Vettius Valens has it p. 15²⁶ (not in index) ζητητικαὶ τῶν ἀποκεκρυμμένων — cf. Paul's use of the participle.

ἀπόκρυφος

is a favourite word with Vettius Valens. It denotes p. 2¹⁶ the "hidden" organs of the body (τῶν ἐντὸς ἀ.). The influence of Gemini (p. 7³⁴) produces κριτικοὶ κακῶν καὶ ἀγαθῶν, φρόνιμοι, περίεργοι, ἀποκρύφων μύσται, etc. In p. 108³ περὶ δεσμῶν καὶ συνοχῶν καὶ ἀποκρύφων πραγμάτων καὶ κατακρίσεως καὶ ἀτιμίας it suggests unknown disasters of the future. P. 170⁶ περὶ θεμελίων ἢ κτημάτων (? κτισμάτων ed.) ἢ ἀποκρύφων ἢ περὶ νεκρικῶν, subjects on which signs are sought ἀπὸ τοῦ ὑπογείου. In p 170²¹ (so 301²¹, 335⁴) μυστικῶν ἢ ἀποκρύφων πραγμάτων suggests "mysteries" again. The adverb is joined with ἐφθονημένως p. 301⁵, of "mystifying and grudging" expositions. See also *Kaibel* 1028¹⁰ (Andros, iv/A.D., a hymn to Isis) ἀπόκρυφα σύνβολα δέλτων εὑρομένα. P Leid W is Μουσέως ἱερὰ βίβλος ἀπόκριφος (ᵛⁱⁱⁱ·³⁹) : cf. i. 18.

ἀποκτείνω.

P Magd 4⁵ (iii/B.C.) ἀπέκτειναν, P Par 23⁶ (B.C. 165) ἀποκτῖναι, *ib.* 11 *verso* ² (B.C. 157) ἀποκτέναι (see Mayser, p. 70). The verb only occurs eleven times in *Syll* index. In later papyri we can quote P Oxy VI. 903⁶ (iv/A.D.) ἀποκτίνας αὐτοὺς τῶν π[λ]ηγῶν "half killed them with blows" (Edd.), PSI 27²¹ (v/A.D., Acts of a martyr), P Lips I. 40ⁱⁱⁱ ² (law report, iv/v A.D.) ἠθέλησεν αὐτὸν ἀποκρῖναι (*sic*), P Gen I. 49²⁰ (iv/A.D.) [π]ληγὲς ἀπέ[κτ]εινάν με —as in P Oxy VI. 903, the complainant was obviously not "kilt ent...ely"! P Lond 240¹⁰ (A.D. 346) (= II. p. 278)

ἀπέκτινέν μέ τε εἰ μὴ γ´ ἐς φυγὴν ἐχρησάμην, BGU IV. 1024ⁱⁱⁱ ³⁹ (iv/v A.D.) ξίφι ἀπέκ[τεινε. For five centuries then we have no trace of this supposed common verb from popular sources : yet in the middle of this period it abounds in the NT texts, developing a whole series of curious forms in the present stem. Meanwhile it was flourishing in literature, to which perhaps it owes its return to the popular speech in the Byzantine age. A more extensive search in the older inscriptions outside Egypt is desirable, as it might prove that the word was in popular use in other countries. Indeed the NT is evidence of this by itself.

ἀποκυέω.

BGU II. 665ⁱⁱ ¹⁹ (i/A.D.) ἡτοιμάσθη αὐτῇ πάντα [π]ρὸς [τ]ὴν λοχ[ε]ίαν αὐτάρκως, ἐρωτῶσι δ' ε̣ καί, κύριε (*sc.* πάτερ), [ἡ] μήτηρ [α]ὐτοῦ, ὅπως ἀποκυή[σ]ῃ ω[. . . The word, accordingly, notwithstanding Hort's attempt (on Jas 1¹⁵) to apply it specially to cases of abnormal birth, would seem to have been an ordinary synonym of τίκτω, but definitely "perfectivized" by the ἀπό, and so implying delivery. For the simplex cf. *Syll* 797 (ii/B.C.) τὸ παιδάριον ὃ Ἀννύλα κύει, 802³, 803²⁷.

ἀπολαμβάνω.

The use of ἀπολαβέσθαι in Mk 7³³ = "draw aside," "separate," is well illustrated by P Lond 42¹² ᶠᶠ (B.C. 168) (= I. p. 30, *Selections*, p. 10) ἐπὶ δὲ τῶι μὴ παραγίνεσθαί σε [πάντω]ν τῶν ἐκεῖ ἀπειλημμένων παραγεγο[νό]των ἀηδίζομαι, " but that you did not return when all those who were shut up with you arrived distresses me "—with reference to the "recluses" of the Serapeum. So P Vat A¹⁰ (B.C. 168) (= Witkowski², p. 65) ἠβουλόμην δὲ καὶ σὲ παραγεγονέναι εἰς τὴν πόλ[ι]ν, καθάπερ . . . οἱ ἄλλοι οἱ ἀπειλη[μμένοι] π[ά]ντες. The word is of course very common. It is found in the sense of "receive," "welcome" (as in the TR of 3 Jn⁸) in P Lips I. 110⁶ (iii/iv A.D.) εὐχόμενος ὅπως ὁλοκληροῦσάν σε καὶ ὑγιαίνουσαν ἀπολάβω (cf. Lk 15²⁷, and P Iand 13¹⁷ ἵνα μετὰ χαρᾶς σε ἀπολάβωμεν. The full force of the ἀπό — as pointing to a "promise made centuries before "—is probably to be retained in Gal 4⁵ (see F. B. Westcott, *St Paul and Justification*, p. 75). It is the ordinary correlative of ἀποδίδωμι. For the simple sense of "receiving " what is due, cf. P Tor I. 1ᵛⁱⁱⁱ ²⁹ (B.C. 116) (= *Chrest.* II. p. 38) τὴν τιμὴν ἀπολαβεῖν.

ἀπόλαυσις.

OGIS 383¹¹ ᶠᶠ (Commagene inscription, i/B.C.) οὐ μόνον κτῆσιν βεβαιοτάτην, ἀλλὰ καὶ ἀπόλαυσιν ἡδίστην ἀνθρώποις ἐνόμισα τὴν εὐσέβειαν, *ib.*¹⁵⁰ κοινὴν ἀπόλαυσιν ἑορτῆς παρεχέτω, *ib.* 669⁵ (i/A.D.) τά τε πρὸς σωτηρίαν καὶ τὰ πρὸς ἀπόλαυσιν, IG XII. iii. 326¹² (Thera, time of Antonines) πρὸς [ἀπ]όλαυσιν. Cf. εἰς ἀπόλαυσιν in Didache 10⁶. A derived adjective occurs in Vettius Valens p. 15⁴ αἱ δὲ ἑξῆς ε̄ (*sc.* μοῖραι) Ἀφροδίτης εὐκρατότεραι ἀνειμέναι πολύσοφοι ἀπολαυστικαί, "given to enjoyment."

For the verb cf. OGIS 669³ (i/A.D.) τὴν πόλιν ἀπολαύουσαν τῶν εὐεργεσιῶν ἃς ἔχει κτλ, P Fay 125⁹ ᶠᶠ (ii/A.D.) εὔχομαι [γὰρ] μείζονος ἀξίας γενέσθαι [ἀφ' ο]ὖ ἀπολαύομεν τῶν δώ[ρων], "for I hope to be better off now that we are enjoying presents (?)" (Edd.), BGU I 248¹³ (ii/A.D.) τῶν ἠθῶν σου ἀπολαῦσαι, P Oxy I 41⁸ (iii/iv A.D.) πολλῶν ἀγαθῶν ἀπολαύομεν. The sepulchral inscr., *Preisigke* 2004, Ἀντωνεῖνε, πάντων ἀπέλουσας, must presumably mean ἀπέλαυσας. *Syll* 891[19]—a curious funeral inscription composed by a heathen by a proselyte, who quotes the LXX— μηδὲ καρπῶν ἀπολαύοι. Cf Herm 119 *verso* [iii.16] (iii/A.D.), where Aelius Asclepiades receives ἄφεσις from public services from Gallienus ἵν]α διὰ τὴν [τῶν προγόνων] ἀρετὴν ἀπολαύσῃ τῆς ἐμῆς φιλανθρωπίας.

ἀπολείπω.

P Par 22[6] (ii/B.C.) ἡ γὰρ δηλουμένη Νέφορις ἀπολιποῦσα τὸν πατέρα ἡμῶν συνῴκησε Φιλίππῳ τινί. The word is apparently a *term. techn.* in wills, etc., e.g. P Oxy I. 105[3,4] (A.D. 117–37) κληρόνομον ἀπολείπω τὴν θυγατέρα[ν] μου . . . τὰ δὲ ὑπ᾽ ἐμοῦ ἀπολειφθησόμενα σκεύη κτλ., P Catt[iv.9] (ii/A.D.) (= *Chrest.* II. p.421), BGU IV. 1098[49] (c. B.C. 18). *ib* 1148[22] (B.C. 13), *ib.* 1164[18] (B.C. 15–1), and *Michel* 1001[ii. 4] (c. B.C. 200 —the Will of Epicteta). In BGU IV. 1158[17] (B.C. 19–18) (= *Chrest.* II. p. 123) ἀπόλειπέ μοι τὸν Παπία (*i. e.* -αν) ἐκ τῆ(ς) φυλακῆ(ς), a jailor reports what the offending party said to him, asking him to "leave" the imprisoned debtor to him. The verb occurs in a Phrygian tombstone of A.D. 114, *C. and B.* 599 (ii. p. 656) υἱοὺς ὑπὲρ γῆς ἀπολιποῦσ[α] τέσσαρας καὶ θυγατέρα. It is MGr.

ἀπόλλυμι.

One or two instances of the literal use of this common verb will suffice—P Petr III. 51[5] τὸ ἀργύριον ὃ ᾤοντο ἀπολωλέναι, "the money which they thought had been lost," P Oxy IV. 743[23] (B.C. 2) ἐγὼ ὅλος διαπονο[ῦ]μαι εἰ Ἕλενος χαλκοῦς ἀπόλε[σ]εν, "I am quite upset at Helenos' loss of the money" (Edd.). In P Fay 111[3 d] (A.D. 95–6) we have it of destroying life : μέμφομαί σαι μεγάλως ἀπολέσας χ[υ]ρίδια δύο ἀπὸ τοῦ σκυλμοῦ τῆς ὁδοῦ, "I blame you greatly for the loss of two pigs owing to the fatigue of the journey" (Edd.). (Probably the writer meant ἀπολέσαντα, but the nom. will construe.) So in the dreams of Ptolemy, son of Glaucias, the helper of the Temple twins, P Par 50[9] (B.C. 160) Λέγω· Μηθαμῶς ἐργῇς (?) ἡ ἀπολέσῃ σον τὸν παῖδα· κύριος οὐκ ἀπολύει (= ἀπολλύει, presumably) τὸν αὐτοῦ παῖδα. Cf. P Petr III. 36 (*a*) *verso* [28] δεόμενος μή με ἀπολέσηι τῶι λιμῶι ἐν τῆι φυλακῆι : so Lk 15[17]. In the curious nursery acrostic, P Tebt II. 278[5 f.] belonging to early i/A.D. in which the story of the loss of a garment is told in lines beginning with the letters of the alphabet in order, we find :

λέων ὁ ἄρας

μωρὸς ἀπολέσας

"a lion he was who took it, a fool who lost it " (Edd., who would read ὁ ἀ., as in the other lines). In P Ryl II. 141[21] (A.D. 37) καὶ ἀπώλεσα ἃς εἶχον ἀπὸ τιμ(ῆς) ὀπίου "I lost 40 silver drachmae which I had with me from the sale of opium" (Edd.), it connotes robbery ; and so in *Syll* 237[7] (iii/B.C.) χρήματα τῶι θεῶι ἐμάννυσαν ἃ ἦσαν ἐκ τοῦ ἱεροῦ ἀπολωτα (*l.* ἀπολωλότα) ἀπὸ τοῦ ἀναθέματος τῶν Φωκέων, καὶ ἐξήλεγξαν τοὺς ἱεροσυληκότας. The -μι forms of the mid. are unchanged : thus P Petr II. 4 (1)[4] (B.C. 255–4) νυνὶ δὲ ἀπολλύμεθα (quarrymen "worked to death" over exceedingly hard stone), P Tebt II. 278[26] (see above) ἀπόλλυται, etc.

Ἀπολλῶς

has gen. Ἀπολλῶτος in an inscr. from the Serapeum at Memphis. See *Preisigke* 1917, who accents the nom. Ἀπολλῶς : since it is probably short for Ἀπολλώνιος (which occurs in Codex Bezae), this accords with analogy. The name can be quoted from *Ostr* 1319 (B.C. 7), 1577 (A.D. 132), *Preisigke* 1113 (A.D. 147–8), P Lond 929[44,66] (ii/iii A.D.) (= III. p. 42 f.), *ib.* 1233[6] (A.D. 211) (= III. p. 58), where the editors would like to make Ἀπολλῶς gen., and P Goodsp 37[7,11,20] (A.D. 143) Ἀπολλῶτι. Without seeking for more exx., we may observe that Ἀπολλώνιος was an extraordinarily common name, no fewer than 39 persons bearing it in the inscrr. of *Syll.* (Naturally the abbreviated name does not figure in the more formal inscriptional style.) Ἀπολλόδωρος has over 50, and Ἀπολλωνίδης (-δας) half as many : Ἀπολλῶς might be a short form of these also. So apart from the very precise identification available we might not be sure that there was only one Apollos in NT.

ἀπολογέομαι.

A good example of this judicial verb is afforded by P Par 35[1 ff.] (a petition to King Ptolemy Philometor, B.C. 163) ἐάν σοι φαίνηται, συντάξαι καταστῆσαι ἐπί σε ὑπὲρ μὲν [ἐμο]ῦ ἀπολογιούμενον Δημήτριον "to make my defence" : cf. P Strass I. 5[15] (A.D. 262) ἀπολο]γησομένους πρὸς τὰ [ἀ]εὶ αἱ]ρόμενα αὐτοῖς and *OGIS* 609[39] (A.D. 231) μή τις ὡς ἀγνοήσας ἀπολογήσηται. Vettius Valens p. 209[13] βασιλεῖ ἀπολογήσεται, καὶ ἐὰν μὴ ὑπὲρ ἑαυτοῦ, ὑπὲρ ἑτέρου δέ (cf. p. 269[29]). Cf. for a cognate verb P Petr III. 53 (*n*)[8] (iii/B.C.) (= Witkowski[2], p. 45) πρὸς αἰτίαν, ὑπὲρ ἧς ἀπ᾽ολογίζεται, "to meet a charge against him, and make his defence" (Edd.), *OGIS* 315[33] (B.C. 164–3) καὶ αὐτὸς ὑπὲρ ὧν ἔφησεν ἔχειν τὰς ἐντολὰς διὰ πλειόνων ἀπελογίσατο. P Leid A[31] (Ptol) ἀπολογίσωμαι (needlessly corrected to -ήσωμαι by Leemans), *al.* See Hatzidakis *Einl.* p. 395, "sagte man auch im Alterthum sowohl ἀπολογέομαι als ἀπολογίζομαι," and Mayser *Gr.* p. 83 f. The verb is found in MGr.

ἀπολογία.

P Tor I. 1[vii. 1] (B.C. 116) (= *Chrest.* II. p. 36) τὴν δ᾽αὐτὴν ἀπολογίαν ἔχειν, BGU II. 531[ii. 21] (ii/A.D.) ἀπέχεις οὖν τὴν ἀπολογίαν, P Lips I. 58[18] (A.D. 371) αὐτὰ τὰ ἐν[τ]άγια πρὸς ἀπολογίαν ἐπὶ τοῦ δικαστηρίω (= ίου), and for ἀπολογισμός in a weakened sense, P Oxy II. 297[3 ff.] (A.D. 54) καλῶς ποιήσεις γράψεις διὰ πιττακίων τὸν ἀπολογισμὸν τῶν [π᾽ρ]ο[β]άτων, "kindly write me in a note the record of the sheep" (Edd.). Ἀπολογία occurs several times in Vettius Valens.

ἀπολύω.

This common verb, in the sense "dismiss," "send away on a mission" (as Ac 13[3], and probably Heb 13[23]) may be illustrated by P Par 49[19] (B.C. 164–58) (= Witkowski[2] p. 70) ἀπέλυσα εἴπας αὐτῶι ὀρθρίτερον ἐλθεῖν. In P Lond 42[26] (see above under ἀπολαμβάνω) it is used of departure from seclusion in the Serapeum—ὑπὲρ τοῦ ἀπολελύσθαι σε ἐκ τῆς κατοχῆς: cf. P Petr II. 11(i)[3] (iii/B.C.) (= *Selections*, p. 7) ὅπως τῆς ἐπὶ τοῦ παρόντος σχολῆς ἀπολυθῶ, "in order that I may be relieved from my present occupation," BGU I. 27[14] (ii/A.D.) (= *Selections*, p. 101) ὥστε ἕως σήμερον μηδέν᾽ ἀπολελύσθαι τῶν μετὰ σίτου, "so that up till to-day no one of us in the corn service has been let go." Release from prison is implied in P Giss I. 65a[1]. 66[11] (ii/A.D.): see Kornemann's note. P Oxy X. 1271[5] (A.D. 246) is in a request to the Prefect for a permit to leave the country by ship from Pharos: ἀξιῶ γράψαι σε τῷ ἐπιτρόπῳ τῆς Φάρου ἀπολῦσαί με κατὰ τὸ ἔθος. The sense of "grant an amnesty to" underlies P Par 63[xiii 2ff.] (B.C. 165) ἀπολελυκότες πάντας τοὺς ἐνεσχημένους ἔν τισιν ἀγνοήμασιν ἢ ἁμαρτήμασιν, and P Tor I. 1[vii.13] (B.C. 116) (= Chrest. II. p. 37): see Mitteis in loc. Akin to this is the use in BGU IV. 1106[31] (B.C. 13) πλὴν συνφανοῦς ἀπωλήας, ἧς καὶ φανερᾶς γενηθείσ[ης ἀ]πολελύσθω. In P Tebt II. 490[3] (B.C. 92 or 59) ἀπολύσομαι τὸν χαλκόν the verb is used in the sense of "pay." cf. P Rein 54[7] (iii/iv A.D.) διεπεμψάμην σοι (κτήνη) . . . ὅπως γεμίσῃς αὐτὰ οἴνου ἐκ τῶν ἀπολυθέντων μοι ὑπὸ Ἰσχυρίωνος, "afin que tu les charges de vin, acheté sur la somme que m'a remboursée Ischyrion" (Ed.): so elsewhere of delivering goods. The index to OGIS gives a long list of citations in various senses, which need not be further illustrated. But the idea of a veteran "released" from long service, suggestive for Lk 2[29], may be noted in the t.t. ἀπολύσιμος ἀπὸ στ[ρ]ατείας, CPR 1[3] (A.D. 83-4): cf P Tebt II. 292[6] (A.D. 189-90) ἱερέως ἀπολυσίμου, P Lond 345[1] (A.D. 193) (= II. p. 114) ἀπολυσί(μων) τῆς λαογρ(αφίας). We may also compare Wünsch AF 4[30] (iii/A.D.) ὁρκίζω σε τὸν θεὸν τὸν τὴν κοίμησίν σοι δεδωρημένον καὶ ἀπολύσαντά σε ἀπὸ δ[εσμῶ]ν τοῦ βίου Νεθμομαω, and a tombstone of ii/A.D. (Al-xandria). Preisigke 2477 Ἡλιόδωρε οὐετρανὲ ἐντίμως ἀπολελυμένε, εὐψύχει: the perfect here might perhaps encourage us to take the phrase metaphorically—or literally, with a secondary application. It occurs with the aorist in Preisigke 423[3], seemingly a ii/A.D. papyrus: οὐετρα[νῷ] τῶν ἐντείμως ἀπολυθέντων. Whether or no we may recognize the figurative sense in the veteran's epitaph above, we may certainly illustrate the *Nunc dimittis* by this familiar term of military life.

ἀπομνημόνευμα.

though not a NT word, claims attention because of Justin's calling Gospel records ἀπομνημονεύματα τῶν ἀποστόλων (*Apol.* i. 67[3]). It may be cited from PSI 85 (a fragment on rhetoric, ii/A.D.), where ἡ χρεία—later described as so called because it is χρειώδης—is defined as ἀπομνήμευμα σύντομον ἐπὶ προσώπου τινὸς ἐπενετόν. The fragment proceeds διὰ τί ἀπομνημόνευμα ἡ χρία: ὅτι ἀπομνημονεύεται ἵνα λεχθῇ. If ἐκταθέν it may become διήγησις (cf. Lk 1[1]), and if not ἐπὶ προσώπου τινός it may become γνώμη ἢ ἄλλο τι. The note of the "memoir" accordingly is that it is *practical* (χρεία), *concise* (σύντομον), intended for *oral delivery* (ἵνα λεχθῇ), and relating to some *person* (ἐπὶ προσώπου τινός). All this suits excellently Justin's description of the Gospels as read in the Church meeting on Sunday morning. The epithet ἐπαινετόν may possibly be taken actively, so that it excludes criticism or invective. See also P Leid W[xxii 16]; and for the verb a very fragmentary Ptolemaic inscr. in *Archiv* v. p. 416 (Wilcken), where line [10] has]παρὰ τῶν σεμνοτάτων βασιλίων ἀπομνημονεύ[— apparently "that [somebody or something] may be had in remembrance."

ἀπονέμω.

In P Oxy I. 71[ii. 3] (A.D. 303) a Prefect is praised as rendering to all their due—πᾶσι τὰ ἴ[δ]ια ἀπονέμις: cf. ib.

IX. 1185[6] (c. A.D. 200) τὰς περὶ τῶν γυμνασιαρχιῶν καὶ ἀγορανομιῶν ἐφέσις τοῖς κρατίστοις ἐπιστρατίγοις ἀπένειμα, the "assigning" of appeals to the strategi. See also OGIS 90[19] (Rosetta stone, B.C. 196) τὸ δίκαιον πᾶσιν ἀπένειμεν, ib. 110[19] (ii/B.C.) ἐπ᾽[αὐταῖς τὰς ἀξίας] χάριτας ἀπονέμοντες [ἀεὶ τοῖς εὐεργετήσασιν], and Syll 325[33] (i/B.C.) βουλόμενος τὰς τῆς εὐσεβε[ί]ας χάριτας τοῖς θεοῖς ἀπονέμειν, which come near the use in 1 Pet 3[7].

ἀπονίπτω.

Syll 802[3] (iii/B.C.): a fraudulent patient at the Asclepieum is told to take off the bandage and ἀπονίψασθαι τὸ πρόσωπον ἀπὸ τᾶς κράνας, in which he sees the penalty of his deceit branded on his face.

ἀποπίπτω.

This word, which in the NT is found only once (Ac 9[18]) in its literal meaning of "fall off," occurs in a derived sense in P Par 47[27] (c. B.C. 153) (= Witkowski[2] p. 90, *Selections* p. 23) ὶ καὶ αὐτοὺς δεδώκαμεν καὶ ἀποπεπτώκαμεν "(one can never again hold up one's head in Triconia for very shame), if we have both given ourselves up and collapsed." Witkowski compares Polyb. i. 87[1] πίπτω ταῖς ἐλπίσιν. The verb also occurs in the philosophical fragment P Flor II. 113[iii 19] (ii/A.D.) ἀποπείπτειν τὰ ὦ[τα καὶ αὐ]τὰς ἀχρείους γενέσθαι: cf. *Archiv* vi. p. 230.

ἀποπνίγω.

Herwerden cites from BCH xvi. p. 384, no. 81, a deed of manumission from Delphi in which the inhuman clause is inserted—εἰ δέ τι γένοιτο ἐγ Διοκλέας τέκνον ἐν τῶι τᾶς παραμονᾶς χρόνωι, εἴ κα μὲν θέληι ἀποπνεῖξαι, ἐξουσίαν ἔχειν. A literary citation may be added from the new fragments of Callimachus, P Oxy VII. 1011[294] (late iv/A.D.),

ὡς δὴ μί᾽ ἡμέων σὺ μή με ποιῆσαι
εὔστεκτον, ἡ γὰρ γειτονεῦσ᾽ ἀποπνίγεις

which Prof. Hunt renders, "Don't you prescribe patience to me, as if you were one of us; your very presence chokes me."

ἀπορέω.

P Oxy III. 472[8] (c. A.D. 130) ὑπὸ δανειστῶν ὤλλυτο καὶ ἠπόρει, "he was ruined by creditors and at his wit's end" (Edd.): cf. the Christian letter of a servant to his master regarding the illness of his mistress, P Oxy VI. 939[31] (iv/A.D.). (= *Selections*, p. 130) νῦν δὲ πῶς πλίονα γράψω περὶ αὐτῆς ἀπορῶ, ἔδοξεν μὲν γὰρ ὡς προεῖπον ἀνεκτότερον ἐσχηκέναι, "but now I am at a loss how to write more regarding her, for she seems, as I said before, to be in a more tolerable state." Syll 303[18] (Abdera, i. B.C. 166) ἀρατὴν ἅμα καὶ σωτήριον [περὶ τῶν ἀπορουμένων ἀεὶ π[ρο]τιθέντες γνώμην "perplexed matters" (passive). The adj. ἄπορος, from which the verb is a denominative, occurs in the sense "without resources," which may be absolute or relative. Thus P Ryl II. 75[2] (late ii/A.D.) Ἀρχ[έλ]αος ῥήτωρ εἶπεν· "Ἄπορός ἐστιν ὁ Γλύκων καὶ ἐξίσταται" "G. has no revenue and resigns his property": so the editors render, explaining in the introduction the legal conditions of what answers roughly to a bankruptcy certificate. In P Lond 911[1] (A.D.

149) (= III. p 127. *Selections*, p. 80) the editors, following Wilcken's original suggestion, incline to make γραφῆς ἀπόρων "a certificate of poverty," qualifying for ἐπιμερισμὸς ἀπόρων, "poor relief." Now Wilcken makes it rather a list of men who have insufficient πόρος, "income," for the performance of public "liturgies," entailing an additional levy, ἐπιμερισμὸς ἀπόρων, upon the εὔποροι: see *Archiv* iv. p. 545, also p. 548, where Wilcken points out (on P Lond 846⁹ᶠᶠ⋅ = III. p. 131) that the ἄπορος is no pauper, but a weaver depending on his craft for livelihood, which he claims to be insufficient to qualify him for the presbyterate of a village. If this interpretation be adopted, it can readily be applied to three passages in P Fay where the same tax is mentioned—viz , 53⁶ (A.D. 110–1), 54¹³ (A.D. 117–8), and 256 (ii/A.D.)—and also to BGU III. 881⁷ (ii/A.D.) as amended in *Berichtigungen*, p. 7, ἐπι[μερισμοῦ] ἀπόρω[ν]. See also under ἀπορία.

ἀπορία.

Syll 529⁶ (i/B.C.) τῶν μὲν διὰ τὴν ἀπ[ο]ρίαν ἐκλελοιπότων τὴν πόλιν, τῶν δὲ διὰ τὴν γενομένη[ν λοι]μικὴν περίστασιν καὶ τὰς ἀρρωστίας μὴ δυναμένων [φυ]λάσσειν τὴν πατρίδα, where we naturally think of ἀ. as = "poverty," but the interpretation given in the last article is applicable. In P Fay 20⁵ (an imperial edict, iii/iv A.D.), which is restored εἴ γε μὴ τὸ τῆς π[α]ρὰ τοῖς καὶ τοῖς δημοσίας ἀπορίας ἐμποδὼν ἦν, πολὺ ἂν φανερωτέραν τὴν ἐμαυτοῦ μεγαλοψυχίαν ἐπιδεικ[ν]ύμενος, the editors translate "if the fact of the public embarrassment existing in various parts had not stood in my way, I should have made a much more conspicuous display of my magnanimity:" but they remark that the δημοσίους of the ill-spelt text should perhaps be emended δημοσίοις, with a lost word after the first τοῖς. Cf. also P Lips I. 36⁷ (A.D. 376 or 378). In CPHerm 6¹⁰ we have ἀπορίᾳ δὲ πλοίων "from shortage of ships."

ἀπορρίπτω.

In a petition regarding the division of a piece of land, P Magd 29¹⁰ (B.C. 218), the appellant asks that the defendant should be forced to give him a proper entrance and exit (εἴσοδον καὶ ἔξοδον) instead of throwing him into a hidden corner— εἰς ἐσώτερόν με ἀπερρίφθαι. Another petition, P Lond 106¹³ and ²⁹ (B.C. 261 or 223) (= I. p. 61), gives us both ἐκρίπτω and ἀπορρίπτω—τά τε σκεύη μου ἐξέρριψεν εἰς τὴν ὁδὸν . . . ., ἐγὼ δὲ τὰ σκεύη τὰ ἀποριφέντα μου εἰς τὴν ὁδὸν εἰσήνεγκα. See also Moulton in *C R* xx. p. 216, where the fairly accessible variant of Ac 27⁴³ is produced against two classical scholars who strained at ἀπορρίπτειν intrans. in Charito iii. 5⁶.

ἀποσκευάζω.

For the subst. see the important P Par 63¹¹ ³⁰ (B.C. 165) καὶ τὰς ἀποσκευὰς τῶν ἐν τῆι πόλει περισπᾶν, where Mahaffy (P Petr III. p. 27) renders, "and that you should distrain the furniture of those in the city"; cf. *ib.* ᵛⁱⁱ ⁷ ταῖς ἀποσκευαῖς αὐτῶν ἐπιγεγράφθαι γῆν. The verb is not a NT word (Ac 21¹⁵ in 33 and a few cursives).

ἀποσκίασμα.

With this compound we may compare ἀποσκότωσις in Vettius Valens, p. 279²¹, of the waning moon. Mayor (on

Jas 1¹⁷) quotes ἀποσκιασμός from Plut. *Pericl.* 7, γνωμόνων ἀποσκιασμούς of shadows thrown on the dial, and ἀποσκιάζω from Plato *Rep.* vii. 532c: the -μα form is ἅπ. εἰρ.

ἀποσπάω.

For the use of this verb in Ac 20³⁰ ἀποσπᾶν τοὺς μαθητὰς ὀπίσω ἑαυτῶν, cf. P Petr III. 43(3)¹² (iii/B.C.), ἔγραψάς μοι μὴ ἀποσπάσαι τὸ π[λή]ρωμα ἐκ Φιλωτερίδος ἕως οὗ τὰ ἔργα συντελέσαι, "you wrote me not to withdraw the gang (of workmen engaged in the copper mines) from Philoteris before they had finished the work" (Edd.). "Withdraw," with no suggestion of violence, though with breach of contract, is the sense in numerous formal documents. Thus P Oxy IX. 1206¹³ (A.D. 335) in a case of adoption. BGU IV. 1125⁹ (B.C. 13), in the indenture of a slave : οὐκ ἀποσπάσω αὐτὸν ἀπὸ σοῦ [ἐντὸ]ς τοῦ χρόνου. P Oxy II. 275²² (A.D. 66), where in a contract of apprenticeship a father is not to have the power of removing his son from his master until the completion of the period— οὐκ ἐξόντος τῷ Τρύφωνι ἀποσπᾶν τὸν παῖδα ἀπὸ τοῦ Πτολεμαίου μέχρι τοῦ τὸν χρόνον πληρωθῆναι, so ²⁸ and *ib.* IV. 724¹³ (A.D. 155), also X. 1295⁴⋅⁶ (ii/iii A.D.), where a widow threatens to take away her son from a man in whose charge he had been left. Add the illiterate P Gen I. 54²¹, [ο]ὐκ αἰδυνήθημεν ἕνα ἄνθροπον ἀποσπάσαι ἐκεῖθεν, and BGU I. 176⁹ (Hadrian). In the marriage contract, P Oxy III. 496⁹ (A.D. 127), provision is made that in the event of a separation taking place, the bride shall have the power to "withdraw" a certain female slave, who forms part of her dowry—ἐπει[δὰν] ἡ ἀπαλλαγὴ [γ]ένηται γαμου[μέ]νη (*sc.* ἡ γ. μὲν ἀποσπάτω τὴν δ[ο]ύλην, and so ¹⁵. Perhaps the verb itself must not be credited with the stronger sense imparted by the context in P Oxy I. 37¹ ¹⁴ (A.D. 49) λειμανχουμέν[ο]υ τοῦ σωματ[ίο]υ ἀπέσπασεν ὁ Πεσοῦρις, "as the foundling was being starved Pesouris carried it off," so ᵢⁱ⋅¹ and still more in *ib.* 38⁹ (A.D. 49–50), ἐπικεχειρηκότος ἀποσπάσαι εἰς δουλαγωγία[ν] τὸν ἀφήλικά μου υἱόν. The passive, as in Lk 22⁴¹, Ac 21¹, appears in an inscr. from the Fayûm (B.C. 57–6) in *Chrest.* I. 70²⁴ (p. 99), οὐ δυνάμενοι δὲ τοῦ ἱεροῦ ἀποσπᾶσθαι, which in Wilcken's opinion means no more than the detention of these priests in the temple by ritual duties, preventing them from appearing in person. It would seem that the ordinary use of this verb does not encourage the stronger meaning Grimm finds in the Lucan passages, where the RV is adequate. For ἀποσπᾶν *c. acc. rei*, see Gosp. Petr. 6¹ (ed. Swete), ἀπέσπασαν τοὺς ἥλους.

ἀποστασία.

The noun ἀποστάτης (cf. LXX Dan 3³²) occurs in P Revill Mél (B.C. 130) (= Witkowski,² p. 96) χρήσασθαι δ'αὐτοῖς ὡς ἀποστάταις (*sc.* τοῖς ἐν Ἑρμώνθει ὄχλοις), whom a certain Paon μετὰ δυνατῶν ἱκανῶν is sailing up the Nile to reduce (καταστῆσαι). So in *Syll* 930³⁹ (B.C. 112) τινες τῶν ἐγ Βοιωτίας ἀποστά[ται] γεγενημένοι. In P Amh II. 30²³ᶠᶠ (ii/B.C.) we read of the burning of title-deeds by Egyptian "rebels," ἠναγκάσθην ὑπὸ τῶν Αἰγυπτίων ἀποστατῶν ἐνέγκαι τὰς συνγραφὰς καὶ ταύτας κατακαῦσαι. The old word ἀπόστασις, equivalent to -σία (cf. 1 Macc 2¹⁵, Ac 21²¹, and see Nägeli, p 31), occurs in P Par 36¹³ (ii/B.C.), where a temple recluse petitions the strategus against the conduct of certain persons who had forced their way into the temple. βουλόμενοι ἐξσπάσαι με καὶ ἀγαγῆσαι, καθάπερ καὶ ἐν τοῖς πρότερον χρόνοις ἐπεχείρησαν, οὔσης ἀποστάσεως. For the adj. ἀποστατικός, see P Tor 8^68 (B.C. 110) ἀποστατικῶι τρόπωι. In the same line αὐτοκρασίαι occurs. an illustration of the Hellenistic tendency to form new nouns in -σία: see Lobeck, *Parerga*. p. 528 f.

ἀποστάσιον.

BGU IV. 1002^16 (B.C. 55, a copy of a demotic bill of sale "μεθηρμηνευμένης κατὰ τὸ δυνατόν") has ἀποστασίου συνγραφή, "bond of relinquishing" (the sold property). The phrase is found as early as B.C. 258 in P Hib I. 96^3, "a contract of renunciation" between two military settlers, one of whom at least was a Jew. The editors remark, "This expression has hitherto always been found in connexion with the translations of demotic deeds concerning the renunciation of rights of ownership, the συγγραφὴ ἀποστασίου being contrasted with the πρᾶσις, the contract concerning the receipt of the purchase-price: cf. Wilcken, *Archiv* ii. p. 143 and pp. 388-9 [and now iv. p. 183]. This note does not seem to cover the passage in P Grenf I. 11^ii. 19 (B.C. 157) καὶ ἀποστασίου ἐγράψατο τῶι Παναῖ μὴ ἐπελεύσεσθαι, μήθ᾽ ἄλλον μηθένα τῶν παρ᾽ αὐτοῦ, "he had a bill of ejectment drawn against Panas, that neither he nor any person connected with him should trespass on the property." We may add P Ryl II. 160^9 (A.D. 28-9) πρᾶ[σ]ις καὶ ἀποστα[σίου] μέρη (*l.* μερῶν) κτλ. "sale and cession of two parts out of five" (Edd.).— so other documents in this set: also P Tebt II. 561 (early i/A.D.) πρᾶσις καὶ ἀποστασίου δούλου . ., and Preisigke 995 (B.C. 245-4) συνγραφή, ἣν ἐποιήσατο Κᾶπις Ταστῖτι ἀποστασίου περὶ ὧν ἐν[εκά]λει αὐτῆι. In P Giss I. 36^21 (ii/B.C.) we have καὶ ἀνενη[γ]νόχατε συγγρα φὰς ὠνῆς καὶ ἀποστασίου κατ᾽ αὐτῶν, and in BGU III. 910^23 (ii/A.D.) we have ἀκολο[ύ]θως ᾧ π[α]ρεθ[έ]μ(ην) ὑμῖν ἀ[ν]τιγράφω ἀποστασίου τ[οῦ πα]τρός μου Ὀνησικράτους κληρον[όμου τ]ῶν προγεγρα μμένων μου ἀδελφῶν τετ[ελ] ευτηκότων. In this last instance ἀποστασίου may be short for συγγραφῆς ἀποστασίου, or it may be the gen. of ἀποστάσιον used as in Mt 5^31, an abbreviation of the fuller phrase. (It might even be conjectured that in Mt *l. c.* the original reading was ἀποστασίου and not -ον: in its presumed original. Deut 24^, βιβλίον was expressed.) A good parallel for this kind of abbreviation is ἡ ἀπερίσπαστος in P Oxy VI. 898^18 (A.D. 123), for what is called in ^15 γράμματα ἀπερ[ισπ]άστου: it is "a deed of indemnification. distinguished by the formula ἀπερίσπαστον παρέξεσθαι or an equivalent phrase" (Edd.)—just as we talk of *nisi prius* actions. The specializing of this term for divorce is not paralleled in our documents, but it was clearly the nearest word to use to represent the Hebrew phrase. See also Wilcken *Archiv* iv. p. 456.

It may be added that in *Coptic Ostraca* 72 (ed. Crum), as translated on p. 13, we find an abbreviation of ἀποστάσιον used with reference to "a deed of divorce" in an episcopal circular.

ἀποστέλλω.

The verb is common in the sense of *mitto*. Thus P Par 32^0 (B.C. 162) (= Witkowski^2, p. 68) Καβάτοκον δ᾽ ἐπιτηρῶ, ἂν κατα[π]λῇ, ἀποστεῖλαί σοι, P Oxy IV. 744^8 (B.C. 1) (= *Selections*, p. 33) ἐὰν εὐθὺς ὀψώνιον λάβωμεν ἀποστελῶ σε ἄνω, "as soon as we receive wages I will send them up to you," and P Oxy I. 87^15 (A.D. 342) ἀπαντῆσαι ἅμα τοῖς εἰς τοῦτον ἀποσταλ[εῖσ]ι [ὀ]φ[ικιαλίοις, "to proceed with the officers sent for this purpose." which may illustrate the frequent NT sense of "commissioning." e. g. Mt 11^10, 13^41, Jn 20^21, Rev 1^1. So BGU IV. 1141^12 (c. B.C. 13) ἐρώτα οὓς ἀπέσταλκας καθ᾽ ἕκαστον εἶδος, and in passive CPHerm 101^5 (ii/A.D. or later, apparently) ἐνγράφω[ς ἀ]πεσταλμένος ὑφ᾽ ὑμῶν. "To send for" something is ἀ. ἐπί c. acc. in P Flor II. 120^8 (A.D. 254) ἐπεὶ αὔριον αὐτοὺς βούλομαι ἀποστεῖλαι εἰς Βερνεικίδα ἐπὶ τὸν σῖτον. Cf. *Preisigke* 174 (iii/B.C.) ἀποσταλεὶς ἐπὶ τὴν θήραν τῶν ἐλεφάντων τόδε δεύτερον.

For ἀποστέλλω = *rescribo*, see P Par 60^4 ff. (B.C. 154) = Witkowski^2, p. 78 ἀπόστιλόν μοι, πόσον ἔχει Πετευσοράπιος καὶ ἀπὸ ποίου χρόνου, P Oxy IV. 742^31 (B.C. 2) ἀπόστειλόν μ[ο]ι πόσας δέσμας παρείληφας. "send me word how many bundles you have received" (Edd.).

For the possibility in Ac 7^34 ἀποστείλω NABCDE is not a hortatory conjunctive (cf. Kühner-Gerth p. 219), but a present indicative, see Thumb *Hellen.* p. 18, where reference is made to a present form στείλω in the Pontic dialect. The form ἀφέσταλκα (*et sim.*) may be seen in the Κοινή: Meyer *Gr.* 320 gives five inscriptions containing it— add OGIS 5^6 (B.C. 311 – letter of Antigonus to Scepsians), *ib.* 6^4 (their reply), and *Magn* 45^, 87^6 (after B.C. 159). It does not seem impossible. despite the late date of its appearance. that this form should be the survival of the original ἔστ. (for σεστ.).

ἀποστερέω.

In the Cnidian *defixio*, Syll 814^5, we find τοὺς λαβόντας παρὰ Δ. παραθή[καν] καὶ μὴ ἀποδιδόντας ἀλλ᾽ ἀποστεροῦντας: this brings together correlate verbs. Παραθήκην ἀ. will answer to the phrase in Pliny's letter to Trajan 106^7 on the Christians' oath "ne depositum appellati abnegarent." C. H. Turner (*JTS* xi. p. 10 n.^ notes that in Mk 10^19 ℵ reads "ne abnegaveris." and *ac* "non abnegatus." which he regards as the key to the formula in Pliny. For ἀ. absolute, as in Mk *l. c.* and 1 Cor 7^5, cf. the petition of the Serapeum Twins P Par 26^33 ff. (B.C. 163-2) = *Sanction.* p. 17 ἕτεροι τῶν ἐκ τοῦ Ἀσκληπιείου ὄντες πρὸς χειρισμοῖς, παρ᾽ ὧν ἔθος ἐστὶν ἡμᾶς τὰ δέοντα κομίζεσθαι, ἀποστεροῦσιν, "others connected with the Asclepieum in the administration. from whom it is usual for us to receive what we need. are demanding." It is construed with an acc. as 1 Cor 6^8, in P Par 31^5 (ii/B.C.) ἀποστεροῦντες [ἡμ]ᾶς: cf. P Oxy II. 237^viii. 22 (A.D. 186) τῆς ὑπολειπομένης ἐμοὶ κατοχῆς τῆς οὐσίας ἵνα μ᾽ αὐτὴν ἀποστῆται (*l.* στερῇ) "a desire to deprive me of the right which I retain over the property" (Edd.). For the more normal constr. c. acc. pers. and gen. rei, see BGU IV. 1024^iv. 14 (iv/v A.D.) ποίας δὲ ἔσχεν ἐνθυμήσεις τὸν ἤδη κληθέντα (*for* κλιθέντα "lying dead" καὶ τῆς ἐσχάτης ἐλπίδας (*l.* -ος. of sepulture) ἀποστερ[ῆ]σαι; P Ryl II. 114^26 (c. A.D. 280) οἰκίωται δὲ τῷ προκειμένῳ Σ. [ἐμὲ τὴν χήρα]ν μετὰ νηπίων τέκνων ἀεὶ ἀποστερεῖν, *ib.* 110^16 (A.D. 194) βουλόμενοι ἀποστερέσαι τῶν ἐμῶν. The simplex occurs in the earliest dated papyrus, P Eleph 1^7 (B.C. 311-0) (= *Selections*, p. 3) στερέσθω ὧμ προσηνέγκατο πάντων. For the subst. see P Oxy I. 71^ii.10 (A.D. 303) ἐπὶ ἀποστερέσει τῇ ἡμετέρᾳ, "to my detriment" (Edd.).

ἀποστολή.

P Tebt I. 112⁶ (an account—B.C. 112) ὄψου εἰς ἀποστολὴν Μουσαίωι ρξ, P Oxy IV. 736¹² (c. A.D. 1) μύρου εἰς ἀποστολὴν ταφῆς θυγατρὸς Φνᾶς, "perfume for the despatch of the mummy of the daughter of Phna;" and from the inscriptions *Syll* 924²⁹ (end of iii/B.C.) ἐπὶ τᾶι ἀποστολᾶι τοῦ ἀνδρός, *ib.* 929.⁹⁹ (? B.C. 139), *ib.* 210¹¹ iii/B.C.) τῶν χρη]μάτων συναγωγῆς τε καὶ ἀποστ[ολῆς. It is thus the *nomen actionis* of ἀποστέλλω.

ἀπόστολος.

It is not easy to point to an adequate parallel for the NT usage of this important word, but it may be noted that in Herod. i. 21 (cf. v. 38) it is found = "messenger," "envoy," and with the same meaning in LXX 3 Regn 14⁶ A ἐγώ εἰμι ἀπόστολος πρὸς σὲ σκληρός, cf. Symm. Isai 18.². Reference may also be made to the interesting fragment in P Par p. 411 f. (B.C. 191), where, if we can accept the editor's restoration of the missing letters, we read of a public official who had sent to a delinquent a messenger bearing the orders he had disregarded—ἐπεσ]ταλκότων ἡμῶν πρός σε τὸν ἀπ[όστολον]. Cf. also a lexical extract cited by Nageli. p. 23, ὁ ἐκπεμπόμενος μετὰ στρατιᾶς καὶ παρασκευῆς ἀπόστολος καλεῖται: this is interesting as being coloured with the association found in Attic, though applied to a person.

Apart from its use in Attic inscriptions, as *Syll* 153 (B.C. 325) = "fleet," "naval expedition," ἀπόστολος is used for a "ship" in P Oxy III. 522 (ii/A.D.). In this document (cf. also P Tebt II. 486, ii/iii A.D.), which is an account of the expenses of corn-transport, it is of interest to notice that each ἀπόστολος is known by the name of its owner, e.g. λόγος ἀποστόλου Τριαδέλφου, "account—for the ship of Triadelphus." In P Oxy IX. 1107¹ (A.D. 211) a different sense is required—ὁπόταν τὰ ἐξ ἀποστόλων πλοῖα παραγέη̣ται, where Hunt renders, "whenever the boats collected in accordance with the orders of lading arrive," and cites P Amh II. 138¹⁰ (A.D. 326) (as amended by Mitteis, *Chrest.* II., p. 391) ἐξ ἀποστόλου τῆς τάξεως, where a ship-master embarks certain loads "in accordance with the bill of lading of the Officium," also P Lond 256 a.¹⁰ (A.D. 15) (= II., p. 99) ἀκολούθως τῷ [18 letters]ου ἀποστόλῳ, and CPHerm 6¹¹ cf. Wilcken *Chrest.* I., p. 522) ἐπ[εὶ οἱ σοὶ ἐπίτροπο[ι τοὺς καλο]υμένους ἀποστόλους [. . . . . . δι᾽] ὧν κελεύειν α[ὐτο]ῖς ἔθος [τὴν] τοῦ σείτου ἐμ[β]ο[λὴν ποιεῖσ]ται (l. -θαι). In P Oxy X. 1259¹⁰ (A.D. 211-2) ἐξ ἀποστόλου τοῦ κρατίστου ἐπιτρόπου τῆς Νέας πόλεως "in accordance with the message of his excellency" (Edd.), the noun seems to be more general; but the papyrus concerns the shipment of corn to Alexandria. See further *Archiv* iii. p. 221 f. Since in early times the non-specialized and etymological meaning is found in Herodotus, and the other only in Attic writers, we see in the NT use the influence of Ionic on the **Κοινή**: cf. *Proleg.* pp. 37, 81.

ἀποστοματίζω.

We have no citations for this word, which is literary in classical and post-classical times. The difficulty in Lk 11⁵³ is the factitive sense, *qs.* "to *make* repeat answers," for which the only adequate parallel in Wetstein's long list is a use of the passive assigned by Pollux (i. 102) to Plato, — ὑπὸ τῶν διδασκάλων ἐρωτᾶσθαι τὰ μαθήματα, ὡς ἀπὸ στόματος

λέγειν τὸ αὐτό. It may be added that Grimm's reference to "στοματίζω—not extant" is misleading: the verb was formed directly from ἀπὸ στόματος, just as ἐνωτίζομαι from ἐν ὠτί, etc.

ἀποστρέφω.

P Leid Wˣˣ.²³ has the prayer Σάραπι . . μὴ ἀποστραφῇς με. An amulet, the opening lines of which were published by Wilcken in *Archiv* i. 427, and tentatively dated iii/v A.D., is given in BGU III. 955. Κύριε Σαβαὼθ ἀπόστρεψον ἀπ᾽ ἐμοῦ ͗οτον (?) νόσον τῆς κεφαλ[ῆς. That these should be the only occurrences of so common a word we can cite from papyri is not a little perplexing. It occurs once in *Syll* 380¹¹ (A.D. 129), where Ephesus offers thanks to Hadrian as ἀποστρέψαντά τε καὶ τὸν βλά[πτοντα τοὺς] λιμένας ποταμὸν Καΰστρον. Its literary record is plentiful, and it requires nine columns in HR, with nine occurrences in NT, and a good number in the early patristic writers included in Goodspeed's indices. It is also found in Apoc. Peter 8 of men who "pervert" righteousness—ἀποστρέφοντες τὴν δικαιοσύνην.

ἀποσυνάγωγος

is "not found in prof. auth." (Grimm): it is as naturally not quotable from our sources. This is of course just the sort of word that would have to be coined for use in the Jewish community.

ἀποτάσσομαι.

For the NT meaning "take leave of," "bid farewell to," as 2 Cor 2¹³, cf. BGU III. 884¹² (ii/iii A.D. πρὶν οὖν ἀπέλθης πρὸς Χαιρήμονα, ἀνάβαινε) πρός με, ἵνα σοι ἀποτάξομαι, "may say goodbye to you," P Oxy VII. 1070⁵⁵ (iii/A.D.). Εὐδ[αίμων αὐτῷ ἀπετάξατο [λ]έγων ὅτι ἐν τῷ παρόντι οὐ σχολάζομεν ἑτέροις ἐξερχόμενοι, "Eudaemon parted with him, saying, 'At present we are not at leisure and are visiting others'" (Ed.). The meaning is stronger in P Oxy II. 298³¹ (i/A.D.) ἐπεὶ ἀποτάξασθαι αὐτῷ θέλω, where the context shows that the idea is "get rid of."

The active ἀποτάσσω, which is not found in the NT, is "to appoint," as in P Oxy III. 475²⁷ (A.D. 182) ἀποτάξαι ἕνα τῶν περὶ σὲ ὑπηρετῶν εἰς τὴν Σενέπτα, and in passive P Fay 12²⁷ (c. B.C. 103) τοὺς ἀποτεταγμένους τῆι κατοικίᾳ χρηματιστάς, "the assize-judges appointed for the settlement," or "command." BGU IV. 1061⁹ (B.C. 14) τὴν ἀποτεταγμένην πρὸς τῆι τηρήσει θυρωρόν, P Fay 20²⁰ iii/iv A.D.) εἰ ἀποτέτακται τὸν Αὐτοκράτορα ὁρᾶν πᾶσιν αὐτοῖς . . τὰ τῆς βασιλείας διοικοῦντα, "if they have all been commanded to watch the Emperor administering the affairs of his kingdom."

ἀποτελέω.

The verb occurs P Tebt II. 276 ii/iii A.D.), an astrological document, describing the effects (ἀποτελέσματα) due to the positions of the planets. Thus ¹⁴ Jupiter in conjunction with Mars (etc.) μεγάλας [βασιλεία]ς καὶ ἡγεμονίας ἀποτελεῖ, "makes." This is in accord with the use in Lk 13³² ἰάσεις ἀποτελῶ, and also in Jas 1¹⁵ ἡ δὲ ἁμαρτία ἀποτελεσθεῖσα ἀποκυεῖ θάνατον, where Hort (*ad l.*) has shown that ἀ. is "fully formed" rather than "full-grown." In PSI 101¹¹ (ii/A.D.) ἀποτελεσθῆναι (l. -ναι) γὰρ τὴν κώμην πάλαι ἀπὸ ἀνδρῶν κ̄ζ̄, νυνεὶ δὲ εἰς μόνους κατηντηκέναι ἄνδρας γ̄ (who had emigrated from inability to meet the heavier taxation) it seems to mean "the village once had a full strength of 27 contributors." (It should be noted that Prof. Hunt, in *The Year's Work* for 1912, p. 135, included this document among transcriptions which "show signs of inexperience.")

ἀποτίθημι.

The phrase of Mt 14[3] (LXX *al.*) is found nearly in P Eleph 12 (B.C. 223–2) γεγράφαμεν . . . τῶι φυλακίτηι . . . ἀποθέσθαι αὐτοὺς εἰς τὴν φυλακήν. The label on a mummy, *Preisigke* 3553, has ἀποτεθ(ειμένη) following ἔνδον ἐστίν, "is enclosed within." In P Flor II. 125[2] (A.D. 254) τὰ ἀποτεθέντα γένη ἐν Φιλαγρίδι is "the goods that were stored at P." So P Ryl II. 125[14] (A.D. 28–9) τὰ ὑπὸ τῆς μητρός μου ἀποτεθειμένα ἐν πυξιδίῳ ἔτι ἀπὸ τοῦ ιϛ [ἔτους Καίσαρος, "certain articles deposited in a little box by my mother as far back as in the 16th year of Augustus" (Edd.). A weakening of the sense of the verb is seen in the fourth century P Oxy I. 120[13] παραμένοντά μοι ἄχρις ἂν γνῶ πῶς τὰ κατ' αἱμαὶ ἀποτίθαιται, "to stay with me until I know the position of my affairs" (Edd.).

ἀποτίνω.

The verb is very common—P Petr I. 16 (2[13] iii/B.C.) ἐὰν δὲ μὴ διαγράψω [καὶ] μὴ παράσχωμαι τὸ λοιπὸν ἐμφανὲς ἀποτείσω ἡμιόλιον, P Par 13[14] (B.C. 157) ἀποτίνειν αὐτὸν τὴν φερνὴν παραχρῆμα σὺν τῇ ἡμιολίᾳ, P Oxy I. 101[43] (lease of land, A.D. 142) ὃ δ'ἂν προσοφειλέσῃ ὁ μεμισθωμένος ἀποτεισάτω μεθ' ἡμιολίας, *ib.* IV. 730[26] (A.D. 130) *al.* In an interesting contract of apprenticeship, P Oxy II. 275[27] (A.D. 66) (= *Selections.* p. 57) the father comes under a "forfeit" for each day of his son's absence from work— ἀ[πο]τεισάτω ἑκάσ[τ]ης ἡμέρας ἀργυρίου [δρ]αχμὴν μίαν. The verb is thus stronger than ἀποδίδωμι, and carries with it the idea of repayment by way of punishment or fine (cf. Gradenwitz *Eint.* i. p. 85 n[4]), a fact which lends emphasis to its use in Philem[19]. For the contrast between the two verbs, see P Gen I. 21[14] (ii/B.C.), as restored by Wilcken *Archiv* iii. p. 388, ἐὰν δὲ μὴ ἀποδῶι καθὰ γέγραπται, ἀποτε[ι]σάτω [παραχ]ρῆμα ἡμι[ό]λιον, cf. BGU I. 190[3] ff. 2nd fragment (Domitian), ἐὰν δὲ μὴ ἰσαποδῶι, ἀποτισάτωι παραχρῆμα μεθ' ἡμιολία[ς], and a similar use of προσαποτίσω in P Leid C[11].

From the inscriptions cf. *Kaibel* 509[2] where a certain physician of Nicaea records—πολ[λ]ὴν θάλασσα[ν] καὶ γαῖαν [π]ερ[ι]νοστήσας τὸ π[επρω]μένον ὧδ' [ἀπέ]τεισα, *i. e.* "I died here," *Syll* 737[97] (ii/A.D.) of an ἰόβακχος "fined," etc. The word occurs in P Said Khan I[b] 26 (B.C. 88) ἐὰν [δὲ κ]αὶ ὁ Γαθάκης ὀλιγωρήσῃ τὴν [ἄμπε]λον καὶ μὴ ποιήσῃ αὐτὴ[ν] ξπαφον ?, ἀποτειννύετω τὸ α[ὐτὸ ἐπί]τειμον : Radermacher *Gr.* p. 81 n[2] mentions ζέννυμι for ζέω, and ἀποτίννυμι in *Passio Scillitanorum* 6.

ἀποτολμάω.

Dittenberger prints the verb in *Syll* 805[94], but the context is so mutilated that the citation is at best only probable. The word has warrant from classical and Hellenistic literature.

ἀποτομία.

A rather curious use of the noun occurs in BGU IV. 1208[i] 17 (B.C. 27) τ]ὴν ἀποτομίαν τῆς ἀναβάσεως (the inundation of the Nile). P Oxy II. 237[viii] 40 (A.D. 186) παρ' οἷς ἄκρατός ἐστιν ἡ τῶν ν[ό'μων ἀποτομ[ί]α, "amongst whom the severity of the law is untempered" (Edd.). Counsel is pleading a native statute, admittedly harsh, which he claims was enforced rigidly ; the word does not suggest straining a statute, but simply exacting its provisions to the full. Wilcken (*Archiv* iii. p. 303) compares with this passage BGU IV. 1024[13] (iv/v A.D.)—a collection of judgements in capital cases, where he reads ἐνόμισας λανθάνειν τ[ὴ]ν νόμων (he would emend τῶν ν.) ἀπο[τ]ομίαν καὶ τὴν τοῦ δικάζοντος ἐξουσίαν. Cf. Plutarch *De liberis educ.* 18 (p. 13D) δεῖ τοὺς πατέρας τὴν τῶν ἐπιτιμημάτων ἀποτομίαν τῇ πρᾳότητι μιγνύναι. A further literary citation may illustrate the harsher side of the word—Demetrius *De Eloc.* 292 (ed. Roberts) κατὰ Φαλάριδος τοῦ τυράννου ἐροῦμεν καὶ τῆς Φαλάριδος ἀποτομίας, "we shall inveigh against the tyrant Phalaris and his cruelty."

ἀπότομος.

For the adj. in its literal sense "cut off," cf. an inscription from Delos *BCH* xxvii. p. 102[149] B.C. 250 τῶν στροφέων ἀπότομον μῆκος πήχεων πέντε. In *Cagnat* III. 366[9] Pamphylia, Imperial ὀξέσι σιδηροῖς καὶ ἀποτόμοις is believed to describe regular sharp weapons dealt out to gladiators for combat, in place of the blunt ones which the base populace found insufficiently exciting. In Wisd 11[10] it denotes God's retributive purposes towards Egypt, in contrast with His fatherly attitude to Israel at the Exodus.

ἀποτρέπω.

P Giss I. 20[6] (ii/A.D.) ἡ ἐπιστολή σου τὴν [μέριμναν ? . . .] που ἀπέτρεψεν [. . . It is unfortunate that this solitary citation for a verb common in literature should have no reliable context ; but it is something that the word itself seems clear, and occurs in a woman's private letter, which proves it vernacular.

ἀπουσία.

For ἀ. in the NT sense of "absence" (Phil 2[12]), see P Amh II. 135[5] (early ii/A.D.) μὴ ἀμελεῖν μου ἐν ἀπουσίᾳ τοιαύτῃ, "not to forget me in my long absence," BGU I. 195[38] (A.D. 161) κατα[φ]ρονηθεὶς ἐκ τῆς περὶ [τὴ]ν στρατίαν ἀπου[σί]α[ς] μου, *ib.* 242[5] (Commodus) κατὰ τὴν ἐμὴ[ν] ἀπουσίαν, P Gen I. 3[11] (A.D. 175–80) κατὰ ἀπουσίαν. Elsewhere it is used in the sense of "waste," "deficiency," e.g. BGU IV. 1065[15] (A.D. 97) δώσει ἑκάστου μναιαίου [ὑπ]ὲρ ἀπουσίας τετάρτην μίαν, P Oxy X. 1273[32] (A.D. 260—a marriage contract) τ]ὴν τούτων πάντων τρίψιν καὶ ἀπουσίαν εἶναι πρὸς τὸν γαμοῦντα "the responsibility for the wear and loss of all these" (Edd.). Cf. the use of the corresponding verb in Artem. I. 78, ὁ δὲ εἰς τὴν ἑαυτοῦ θυγατέρα ἀπουσιάσει, cited by Suidas *Lex.*, where ἀπρεπές is given as a meaning of ἀποῦν. Ἀπουσία was borrowed in Syriac to express a similar sense, as in the Acts of Thomas (iii/A.D.), according to Prof. R. H. Kennett (in a letter). The corresponding Greek (*Acta Thomae*, ed. Tischendorf, p. 196) has βρῶσιν μηδεμίαν ὅλως ἀπουσίαν ἔχουσαν. But as late as P Oxy IX. 1223[20] (late iv A.D.) διὰ τὴν ἀπουσίαν τοῦ γεούχου is still "owing to the absence of the landlord" (Ed.).

ἀποφέρω.

P Par 49[23f.] (B.C. 164–58) (= Witkowski[2], p. 71) διὰ τὸ εἰς τὴν πόλιν με θέλειν δοῦναι ἀπενεγκεῖν. The verb occurs *ter* in the boy's letter P Oxy I. 119 (ii/iii A.D.) (= *Selections*, p. 102 f.), e.g. καλῶς ἐποίησες οὐκ ἀπένηχές (*l.* ἀπήνεγκες) με μετʼ ἐσοῦ εἰς πόλιν, "*So* kind of you not to have taken me off with you to town !" For the verb with the added idea of violence, as Mk 15[1], see P Oxy I. 37[i.18] (A.D. 49) (= *Selections*, p. 50) βούλεται ὀν[ό]ματι ἐλευθέρου τὸ σωμάτιον ἀπενέγκασθαι, "she wishes to (defend herself on the ground) that the foundling was carried off in virtue of its being freeborn," BGU I. 22[29ff.] (A.D. 114) (= *Selections*, p. 76) ἀνέβη εἰς τὴν οἰκίαν μου, ἀπενέγκατο οἰχό(μενος) κίμενον ζεῦγος ψελλίω(ν) ἀργυρῶν, "he went up into my house, and carried off with him a pair of silver bracelets that were lying there" : cf. also P Magd 1[9] (B.C. 221) κατέσπειραν (τὸν κλῆρον) σησάμωι καὶ σίτωι καὶ ἀπενηνεγμένοι εἰσὶν παρὰ πάντα δίκαια. (The editor would read τὰ δίκαια.) Similarly P Ryl II. 153[21] (A.D. 66) κατασπείροντας καὶ ἀποφέροντας τὰ περιεσ[ύμεν]α ἐκ τ[ούτω]ν, and P Leid B[ii. 17] (ii/B.C.), where two persons are reported to have carried some oil off for their own use (ἀπενηνεγμένοι εἰσίν), BGU IV. 1006[21] (B.C. 14), al. The active seems to be used in the same sense in CPHerm 6[10], but the context is fragmentary. For the subst. see P Tebt II. 424[6] (late iii/A.D.) ἴσθι δὲ ὅτι ὀφίλις φόρους καὶ ἀποφορὰς ἑπτὰ ἐτῶν, "let me tell you that you owe seven years' rents and dues." (Edd.)

ἀποφεύγω.

P Ryl II. 77[39] (A.D. 192) ἀναδεξάμενος τὴν μείζονα ἀρχὴν οὐκ ἐφείλει τὴν ἐλάττον᾽ ἀποφεύγειν.

ἀποφθέγγομαι

occurs thrice in Vettius Valens, where the editor renders *vaticinari* : p. 75[21] ἐν ἱεροῖς κάτοχοι γίνονται ἀποφθεγγόμενοι ἢ καὶ τῇ διανοίᾳ παραπίπτοντες, 112[15] ἀποφθεγγομένους ἢ μανιώδεις ἢ προγνωστικοὺς ἀποτελοῦσιν, and 113[5] μανιώδεις ἐκστατικοὺς πτωματικοὺς ἀποφθεγγομένους ἀπεργάζονται—he refers to Manetho i. 237. This is an extension *in malam partem* of the mantic note which Winer (*ap.* Grimm-Thayer) finds in the verb.

ἀπόχρησις.

One or two instances of the verb ἀποχράομαι may be cited to illustrate the expressive ἀπόχρησις, which is found in the Greek Bible only in Col 2[22]. OGIS 665[16] (A.D. 49) ὑπὸ τῶν πλεονεκτικῶς καὶ ἀναιδῶς ταῖς ἐξουσίαις ἀποχρωμένων = *abutentibus* : the Prefect Cn. Vergilius Capito issues an edict against the abuse of the *libera vectio*. P Hib I. 52[7] (c. B.C. 245) κ[αὶ ὠ]ρυτίνων κλήρων ἀποκέχρηνται ταῖς νομαῖς, "the holdings in which they have used up the pastures" (Edd.).

ἀποχωρέω.

In the interesting census return P Lond 260[120] (A.D. 72–3) (= II. p. 51) reference is made to the son of a man who had acquired the Alexandrian citizenship and ἀποκεχ[ώ]ρηκε εἰς τὴ[ν] ἰδίαν, "had returned to his own country," who consequently was to be reckoned as Alexandrian. Cf. P Lond 44[18] (B.C. 161) (= I. p. 34 ἀπεχώρουν, and the illiterate P Fay 110[20]

A.D. 194 αἰὰν [ἀπο]χωρῶι πέμσωι πρὸς [σὲ εἴ]να σε ἀσπάσωμαι, "if I leave I will send to you to greet you."

ἀπρόσκοπος.

In the letter of a slave to her master, P Giss I. 17[5ff.] (Hadrian) ἠγωνίασα, κύριε, οὐ μετρίως, ἵνα ἀκούσω ὅτι ἐνώθρευσας, ἀλλὰ χάρις τοῖς θεοῖς πᾶσι ὅτι σε διαφυλάσσουσι ἀπρόσκοπον, the context implies that ἀ. must be understood in the sense of "free from hurt or harm." So in the same family correspondence, *ib.* 22[9] ἀ[να]λαμβανούσης σε ἀπρόσ[κοπ]ον καὶ ἱλαρώτατον. In the same again, *ib.* 79[iv. 8] ἵνα μετὰ φιλίας καὶ ἀπροσκόπως ἐξέλθωμεν ἀπʼ αὐτῶν ἐπʼ ἀγαθῶι "in Freundschaft und ohne Ärger und Anstoss" (Ed.). Under the form ἀπρόσκοπτος, it is found in the late (apparently heathen) inscription from Messana, IGSI 404 Ἀνδρόβιος Λύκιος ναύκληρος ἔζησε ἀπρόσκοπτος ἔτη λε̄ (see Nageli, p. 43) in the metaphorical sense of Phil 1[10] "blameless." It is clear that we need not be longer concerned with Grimm's note, already discounted by Thayer, that the adj. is "not found in profane authors."

ἀπροσωπολήμπτως

naturally does not appear. It is witness only to the firm hold of πρόσωπον λαμβάνειν as a *term. techn.* in the vocabulary of Jews, derived from a literal translation.

ἄπταιστος.

In the lack of other citations this NT ἅπ. εἰρ. (Jude[24]) may be illustrated from M. Aur. v. 9 τὸ ἄπταιστον καὶ εὔρουν ἐν πᾶσι, "the security and happy course of all things," which depend on the faculty of understanding and knowledge. See also 3 Macc 6[39] ὁ τῶν πάντων δυνάστης ἀπταίστους αὐτοὺς ἐρρύσατο ὁμοθυμαδόν.

ἅπτομαι.

The sense of eagerness comes out well in the royal letter to Attis, priest of Pessinus, OGIS 315[56] (B.C. 164–3) μετὰ δὲ ταῦτα ἐν ἄλλαις καὶ ἄλλαις ἡμέραις ἀεὶ διασκοποῦσιν (for -οὔντων) ἥπτετο μᾶλλον ἡμῶν, "urged his view upon us." In *Syll* 840[8] (Delphi, B.C. 177–6, in dialect) εἰ δέ τίς κα ἅπτηται Σωσίχας ἐπὶ καταδουλισμῶι, it means "lay hold of, appropriate." The active sense of "kindle," "set fire to," is illustrated by the magical papyrus P Lond 121[543] (iii/A.D.) (= I. p. 101) ἅπτε δὲ λιβάνῳ, and appears thrice in a very illiterate iv/A.D. letter, P Oxy X. 1297[12] ἀπέστιλά σοι . . . διὰ Ἴλιτος σφυρίδιον ἕν, ἅψαι αὐτὸν κεῖται (so *l.* 4,7) "I sent you . . by His one basket for you to burn" (Edd.). The middle occurs in the recently recovered Greek Acts of the martyr Christina—PSI 27[15 ff.] (v/A.D.) εὐχαριστῶ σο[ι ὁ] πατὴρ τοῦ κ̄ῡ Ῑῡ Χ̄ῡ, μὴ ἐνκατα[λίπῃς με εἰ]ς] τὸν αἰῶν[α᾽, ἀλλὰ ἐκ]τεινον] τὴν χεῖράν σου καὶ ἅψαι τοῦ πυρὸ[ς τούτου καὶ σ]βέσον τὸ ἐπ[αναστὰν] ἐπάνω μου, [μ]ήποτε ἐπιχαρῇ Οὐρβανὸς ὁ τύρα[ννος ἐπ᾽ ἐμέ]. The familiar ἅπτεσθαι of healing wrought by touch may be illustrated by *Syll* 803[62] (iii/B.C.—the Asclepieum at Epidaurus) ἐδόκει αὐτᾶι . . . τὸν θεὸν ἅψασ[θ]αί οὐ τᾶ[ς κοιλίας ᾽ ἐκ τού]του τᾶι Ἀνδρομάχαι (the suppliant) υἱ[ὸς ἐξ ᾽Αρύββα ἐγίνε[τ]ο. The opposite sense comes in *ib.* 804[21] (*ibidem*, perh. ii/A.D.) ἥψατο δέ μου (*sc.* ἡ νόσος) καὶ τῆς δεξιᾶς χιρὸς καὶ τοῦ μαστοῦ. MGr has ἀνάφτω "kindle," and the simplex in a special phrase, ἄψε σβύσε.

Ἀπφία.

To the examples from the inscriptions of this Phrygian proper name given by Lightfoot *Colossians*[6] p. 306 f. add *Perg* II. 513 Ἰουλίαν Ἀπφίαν Λικιαννήν, and *C. and B.* no. 309 (ii. p. 470—Apamea, pagan) Ἀπφία Παπίου μήτηρ. In *JBL* xxvii. pt. ii. p. 145 Hatch cites three instances of the form Ἀφία from *PAS* iii. 482, 508, 504 (Pisidia and Phrygia) In noting that the name is not to be found in the Magnesian inscriptions Thieme (p. 39) quotes K. Buresch *Aus Lydien*, Leipzig, 1898, p. 44, to the effect: "Der Name (Ἀφίας) gehört einer grossen in W(est)-Kleinasien und besonders N(ord) Lydien sehr verbreiteten Namenfamilie an, deren Mitglieder mit ππ, πφ, φφ, φ geschrieben erscheinen." See also Radermacher *Gr.* p. 40 n[1]. who supports from an early Lycian inscr. the spelling Ἀφφία (found in D).

ἀποθέω

occurs in P Fay 124[19] (ii/A.D.) ἄνευ νομίμων ἡμᾶς ἀποθεῖσθαι: the editors render "illegally ousted." The compound προσαποθέω is found in a papyrus of Magdola (B.C. 221—published in *Mélanges Nicole*, p. 285) προσαπώσατό με εἰς τὴν φυλακήν.

ἀπώλεια.

The weaker sense of ἀ. is illustrated by P Tebt II. 276[24] (an astrological fragment—ii/iii A.D.), where one who has acquired certain possessions ἐξωδιασμὸν αὐτῶν [ποιήσ]εται καὶ ἀπώλειαν, "will spend and lose them" (Edd.). Similarly in a series of nursing-contracts of the time of Augustus in BGU IV. we find the phrase ἐκτίνειν τὴν ἑκάστου ἀξίαν πλὴν συμφανοῦς ἀπωλείας, e.g. 1058[31] (= *Chrest.* II. 170), 1106[33], *al.* For the stronger meaning which we associate with NT usage, cf. the close of an ancient Coptic spell from the iii/A.D. Paris magical papyrus 1245 ff. (= *Selections*, p. 114) ἔξελθε δαῖμον, ἐπεί σε δεσμεύω δεσμοῖς ἀδαμαντίνοις ἀλύτοις, καὶ παραδίδωμί σε εἰς τὸ μέλαν χάος ἐν ταῖς ἀπωλίαις, "give you over to black chaos in utter destruction."

ἆρα.

For εἰ ἄρα, *si forte*, as in Mk 11[13], Ac 8[22], cf. P Petr II. 13 (19)[9] (middle of iii/B.C.) (= Witkowski,[2] p. 19) εἰ δ ἄρα μὴ ὁρᾶις ὃν δυνατόν, P Hal I[viii. 172] (middle of iii/B.C.) εἰ δὲ ἄρα δεῖ αὐτοῖς σταθμοὺς δίδο[σθ]αι π[α]ρὰ τῶν οἰκονόμων, διδότωσαν α[ὐ]τοῖς τοῖς ἀναγκαίοις. See also P Oxy VII. 1070[50] (iii/A.D.) μὴ ἀμελήσῃς μὴ ἄρα ποτὲ θέλῃς μ[ε]τὰ σ[ο]ῦ [Ἡρ]αε[ίδι τὴν τήρησιν τῆς ὅλης οἰκίας παραδιδόναι, "do not neglect this, lest indeed you choose to hand over the keeping of the whole house to Herais" (Ed.): cf. P Amh II. 84[20] (ii/iii A.D.) . . .]μενος μὴ ἄρα τι πάθω.

ἆρα.

The interrogative ἆρα occurs in a curious interview with a Roman emperor, P Oxy I. 33[iii. 7] (late ii/A.D.), where a condemned man asks who had recalled him, ἆρα ἡ σύνκλητος ἢ σὺ ὁ λήσταρχος; "Was it the senate, or you, the arch-pirate?" (Edd.). For the MGr use of ἀρά (ἄραγε[ς]) in questions implying doubt (or refusal), see Thumb's *Handbook*, p. 180 f.

ἀρά.

A sepulchral inscr. from S.W. Phrygia, *C. and B.* no. 466 (ii. p. 565), which Ramsay thinks Christian, mainly because of the name Ammerimnos, has ἐὰν δέ τις αὐτῶν μὴ φοβηθῇ τούτων τῶν καταρῶν, τὸ ἀρᾶς δρέπανον εἰσέλθοιτο εἰς τὰς οἰκήσις αὐτῶν καὶ μηδίναν ἐνκαταλείψετο. Here ἀρά might represent κατάρα, by the principle illustrated for verbs in *Proleg.* p. 115: but this does not apply in the closely similar no. 563 (Akmonia), where Jewish origin is argued. The noun may be quoted from a source where no suspicion of Jewish or Christian influence can come in—the end of the great inscr. of Antiochus I. of Commagene, *OGIS* 383[236] (i/B.C.), παρανόμωι δὲ γνώμηι κατὰ δαιμόνων τιμῆς καὶ χωρὶς ἡμετέρας ἀρᾶς παρὰ θεῶν ἐχθρὰ πάντα: cf. *Magn* 105[93] (ii/B.C.) νό[μοις γ]ὰρ ἱεροῖς καὶ ἀραῖς καὶ ἐπιτίμοις ἄνωθεν διεκεκώλ[υ]το ἵνα μηθεὶς ἐν τῷ ἱερῷ τοῦ [Διὸς] . . . [μ]ήτε ἐννέμῃ κτλ. For ἀρατός see *Syll* 303[17] (ii/B.C.), ἀρατὴν ἅμα καὶ σωτήριον [περὶ τῶ]ν ἀπορουμένων ἀεὶ π[ρο]τιθέντες γνώμην.

Ἀραβία.

For Ἀ. as the name of an Egyptian nome situated on the east side of the Nile, see P Lond 401[19] (B.C. 116-11) (= II. p. 14), P Oxy IV. 709[5] (c. A.D. 50). There would seem to be a reference to an Ἀραβία ἄνω in PSI 50[11] (A.D. 107), where see the editor's note.

ἀργέω.

In P Petr II. 4 (9)[4] (B.C. 255-4) certain quarrymen complain νυνὶ δὲ ἀργοῦμεν διὰ τὸ μὴ ἔχαν σώμ[α]τα ὥστε ἀνακαθᾶραι τὴν ἄμμον, "but now we are idle ('playing') for want of slaves to clear away the sand": cf. *ib.* 9 (3)[7] (B.C. 241-39), ἐὰν ἀργῶσιν, and 14 (1a[8]). Later instances of the verb are afforded by P Lond 131[*] (farm-accounts, A.D. 78) (= I. p. 190 f.), P Oxy IV. 725[35] (A.D. 183), a contract of apprenticeship where provision is made that the apprentice shall have twenty days' holiday in the year, ἀργήσει δὲ ὁ παῖς εἰς λόγον ἑορτῶν κατ᾽ ἔτος ἡμέρας εἴκοσι: cf. [40] ἐὰν δὲ πλείονας τούτων ἀργήσῃ, if he exceeds this number from idleness he is to make it good afterwards, *ib.* I. 121[18 f.] (iii A.D.) μὴ ἀφῇς αὐτοὺς ἀργῆσε ὅλους, "do not let them be wholly idle," and P Fay 131[25] (iii/iv A.D.) τὰ ταυρκὰ (*l.* -ικὰ) μὴ ἀργείτω. Add P Flor I. 101[9] (late i/A.D.) ἐπεὶ ἀργήσῃ[ται?] εἰς ἐξ ἡμῶν, P Lond 1170 *verso*[45] (A.D. 258-9) (= III. p. 194) λόγος ἐργατῶν ἀργησάντων, *ib.* 1173[10] (A.D. 125) (= III. p. 208) *al.* For ἀργ in P Lond 131 *recto*[49] (A.D. 78-9) (= I. p. 171) the editor conjectures ἀργίζει, or some other variant of ἀργεῖ, in the sense of "taking holiday": cf. Mayser, *Gr.* p. 84. The absence of the suggestion implied in our "idle" is well seen in P Oxy VIII. 1160[14] (iii/iv A.D.) διμήνου δὲ ἤργηκα ὧδη, εἰ μή, ἤμελλα ὑμῖν πάει (*i.e.* πᾶσι) ἄλλα πέμπιν, where there is no thought of apology for the two months. The word may be used of inanimate things, as of ships in P Petr II. 20[ii. 11] (B.C. 252) ὅπως . . . μὴ ἀργῇ τὰ πλοῖα, and of a garden in P Flor II. 262[9] (iii/A.D.) ἐπὶ ὁ κῆπος ἀργεῖ: this is correlate with the use of the causative καταργεῖ in Lk 13[7]. In MGr the verb means "delay, come too late," an easy development from the idea of "idling, dawdling": this might indeed be taken as corroborative evidence for the connotation of blameworthy "idling" which appears in NT, but not in our vernacular sources, as noted above.

ἀργός.

The various connotations of the verb appear in its source, the adj. ἀργός (ἀϝεργός), the opposite of ἐνεργός, "at work"). Thus in P Lond 015[5] (a census-return of A.D. 160–1) (= III. p. 27) a certain Apollonius is described as belonging to the "leisured" class of Memphis (τῶν ἀπὸ Μέμφεως ἀργῶν, a "practically certain" reading): cf. for the same description BGU III. 833[5] (A.D. 173–4). In BGU IV. 1078[6 ff.] (A.D. 39) a man writes to his sister, ἐὰν λάβω τὰ κερμάμια (?κεράμια), ὄψομαι τί με δεῖ ποιεῖν· οὐ γὰρ ἀργὸν δεῖ με καθῆσθαι. P Lond 1170 verso[174, 183] (see below) has ὄνος a ἀργός, "travelling light," as against others with loads. In P Flor I. 1[4nd] and P Amh II. 97[2] (both ii/A.D.) ἐλαιουργίου ἀργοῦ = "an oil-press which is out of working order": similarly P Oxy X. 1200[22] (early ii/A.D.) ἑτέρα (sc. κιβωτός) ἀργή "another out of use" (Edd.). In Syll 533[21] (iii/A.D.), τὸ ἀργόν is opposed to τὸ πεφυτευμένον: so ib. 233[8] (soon after B.C. 220) τῆς χώρας διὰ] τοὺς πολέμους ἀργοῦ καὶ ἀσπόρου οὔ[σης. In MGr ἀργά = "too late": cf. the note on the development of MGr ἀργῶ above.

The derived noun ἀργία "holiday" may be seen in P Petr III. 40 (a)[v 12], and in a diary of Heroninus, steward of property at Theadelphia (A.D. 258–9), P Lond 1170 verso[84 etc.] (= III. p. 202): against each day of the month is entered the work done thereon, but we have the 10th, 21st, and 24th marked ἀργία. It is open to question whether this neutral meaning should not be applied in Wisd 13[13], where ἀργίας and ἀνέσεως seem to stand by parallelism alike for "leisure": cf. RV mg. and our note on ἄνεσις. In that case the workman spends his working hours and the best parts of the wood in making something useful: the leavings of the wood are carved into an idol by his "holiday diligence" and the "skill of his spare time." Notice might be taken of the neat word-play on ἀργά . . . ἔργα in the context (14[5]): it recalls Henry Bradshaw's brilliant and convincing emendation in 2 Pet 3[10], τὰ ἐν αὐτῇ ἔργα < ἀργὰ > εὑρεθήσεται.

ἀργύρεος.

The adj. in its contracted form (as in 2 Tim 2[20], Rev 9[20]) is found in P Lond 101[11] (an inventory of household furniture, A.D. 103–17) (= II. p. 265) φύλλια ἀργυρᾶ ὀκτώ: cf. P. Lond 124[26] (iv/v A.D.) (= I. p. 122). Constant association with χρυσοῦς produced a mixture of flexion in the fem.: thus ἀργυρῆ BGU II. 388[ii. 22] (ii/iii A.D.), -ῆν P Leid W xxiii.[22] (ii/iii A.D.), but χρυσᾶν Rev 1[13], P Lond 124[26] (iv/v A.D.) = I. p. 122). For the uncontracted forms, which do not seem to occur in the Ptolemaic papyri (Mayser Gr. p. 293), see 1 Esr 6[17] Α τὰ χρυσᾶ καὶ τὰ ἀργύρεα (ἀργυρᾶ B), and cf. the long British Museum magic papyrus P Lond 121[581] (iii/A.D.) (= I. p. 102) ἐπιγραφόμενον ἐπὶ χρυσέου πετάλου ἢ ἀργυρέου, and OGIS 480[6] (Ephesus, ii/B.C.) Ἄρτεμιν ἀργυρέαν καὶ εἰκόνας ἀργυρέας δύο. See further Helbing Gr., p. 34 f.

The form ἀργυρικός = "of money" generally is common both in the papyri and the inscriptions, e.g. P Amh II. 31[6] (B.C. 112) τὴν σιτικὴν μίσθωσιν καὶ τὴν ἀργυρικὴν πρόσοδον

"rents in corn and taxes in money" (Edd.), P Grenf I. 21[16] (B.C. 126) ὑ]πάρχοντά μοι πάντα σύμβο[λά) τε σιτικὰ [κα]ὶ ἀργυ ρικὰ) "all contracts belonging to me of corn and of money," OGIS 90[21] (the Rosetta stone, B.C. 196) δαπάνας ἀργυρικάς τε καὶ σιτικὰς μεγάλας: cf. BGU I. 14[iii. 2] (A.D. 255) λόγος ἀργυρικὸς λημμάτων καὶ ἀναλωμάτων, ib. 15[i. 13] (A.D. 194) πράκτορα ἀργυρικῶν.

ἀργύριον.

In the marriage contract P Eleph 1[11] (B.C. 311–10) (= Selections, p. 3) provision is made that in certain circumstances the bridegroom shall repay the bride ἀργυρίου Ἀλεξανδρείου (δραχμὰς) Α, "1000 drachmas of Alexander's coinage." According to the editor, this is "perhaps the earliest documentary mention of Alexander's coinage," unless Syll 176 is about two years older. In P Amh II. 46[21] (ii/B.C.) mention is made of a bribe consisting of ἀργυρίου στα(τῆρας) ῃ, "eight staters of silver," by means of which a certain Epiodorus secured a fresh division of land in the interests of the temple of Soenopaeus. For a similar use of ἀργυρισμός and ἀργυρίζομαι see Wilcken Archiv iv. p. 174.

ἀργυροκόπος.

For this designation in Ac 19[24] (cf. LXX Jud 17[4], Jer 6[29]) of Demetrius, who was probably master of the guild for the year, see Ramsay CRE[5], p. 128, and cf. an order of payment of early ii/A.D. published by Milne amongst the Hawara Papyri, Archiv v. p. 382, no. 68, χρημάτισο ν) Ἀ [. .] Ἀπολλωνίου ἀργυροκ[όπῳ], and BGU III. 781[iv. 5] (i/A.D.) ἄλλα (sc. πινάκια) ὠτία μὴ ἔχοντα, κατασκευασθέντα ἐν Ἀρσινοΐτηι διὰ Ἀπολλωνίου ἀργ[υρο]κόπου, P Giss I. 47[22] (Hadrian) Διονυσ[ί]ου τοῦ ἀργυροκόπου. P Flor I. 71[659], P Oxy VIII. 1146[12], P Lond 083[1] (= III. p. 229) (all iv/A.D.), and Syll 873[1] (ἡ συνεργασία τῶν ἀργυροκόπων καὶ χρυσοχόων) also show it. For ἀργυροκοπεῖον see CIA II. 476[30] (c. B.C. 100).

ἄργυρος.

The distinction between ἄργυρος "s ver" and ἀργύριον "silver used as money," which in classical Greek has exceptions on both sides, is generally observed in NT: ἀργύριον in 1 Cor 3[12] and ἄργυρος in Mt 10[9] are the only clear exceptions. In the papyri ἄργυρος is as rare as ἀργύριον is ubiquitous. It figures frequently in P Leid X, a very long document dealing with metallurgical subjects (iii/iv A.D.). P Par 60 bis[32] (c. B.C. 200) has ἀργύρου στατήρων, and BGU III. 992[i. 5, 10] (B.C. 100) χαλκοῦ πρὸς ἄργυρον, but in P Lips I. 64[27] (iv/A.D.) ἄ[ργ]υρον (curiously abbreviated) is "Geld". Silver as a metal is thus the prevailing sense in the few occurrences we can report from papyri, while ἀργύριον for money appears many hundred times. The differentiation affects a well-known compound in C. and B. no. 300[14] (ii. p. 466—Apamea) ἀργυροταμιεύσαντα for ἀργυροτ. There are sundry derivatives of ἄργυρος, of which we might mention ἀργυρώνητος, occurring in P Saïd Khan 1[a 16] (B.C. 88) τὴν ἀ. ἄμπελον, P Lond 198[11] (A.D. 169–77) (= II. p. 173), BGU IV. 1105[21] (B.C. 11) καθυβρίζει καὶ τὰς χεῖρας ἐπιφέρων χρῆται ὡς οὐδὲ ἀργυρωνήτωι "treats me as he would not treat a thing he had bought"—the reading is not certain.

In the LXX the disparity between the frequency of ἄργυρος and ἀργύριον is just what it is in papyri. In MGr ἄργυρος is the metal.

Ἀρεοπαγίτης.

The form Ἀρευπαγίτης is found *Michel* 687[52] (end of iii/B.C.), *ib.* 823[7] (B.C. 220).

ἀρέσκεια.

For the bad sense which prevails in classical writers (see Lightfoot on Col 1[10]) a new literary citation may be made from Philodemus (i/B.C.) Περὶ κολακείας (in *Rhein. Mus.* lvi. 623) ἄνευ τῆς τοιαύτης ἀρεσκείας. But P Oxy IV. 729[21] (A.D. 137) is a close parallel for Paul's use: ποιῆσονται τοὺς ποτισμοὺς τοῦ [κτή]ματος καὶ τῆς καλαμ[είας] πεμπταίους πρὸς ἀρεσκί[αν] τοῦ Σαραπίωνος, "they shall irrigate the vine-land and the reed-land every fifth day to the satisfaction of Sarapion" (Edd.). We spell -εια on historical grounds, regarding the MSS. as inadequate witnesses for ει and ι: see *Proleg.* p. 47). Deissmann *BS* p. 224 cites an additional witness from an inscription, testifying with many passages in Philo to a use of ἀρέσκεια in a good sense—including even a relation towards God—wholly independent of NT. We may compare his inscription with a nearly identical phrase in *Priene* 113[73] (i/B.C.) τελειῶν δ' ὁ μετὰ ταῦτα χρόνος ἐθεωρεῖτο πρὸς τὴν εἰς τὸ πλῆ[θος] ἀρέσκειαν.

ἀρέσκω.

For the idea of *service* in the interests of others which underlies several of the NT occurrences of this verb (1 Th 2[5], Rom 15[1, 3], 1 Cor 10[33]), we may compare its use in monumental inscriptions to describe those who have proved themselves of use to the commonwealth, as *OGIS* 641 (A.D. 246-7) Ἰούλιον Αὐρήλιον . . . οἱ σὺν αὐτῷ κατελθόντες . . . ἀνέστησαν ἀρέσαντα αὐτοῖς, τειμῆς χάριν, *ib.* 646[12] (iii/A.D.) Σεπτίμ[ιον Οὐορώδην] . . . ἀναλώσαντα καὶ ἀρέσαντα τῇ τε αὐτῇ βουλῇ καὶ τῷ δήμῳ. For a wider sense see the interesting petition of a Jew of Alexandria in the 26th year of Augustus, who, after describing himself as μεταλαβὼν καθ' ὃ δυνατὸν καὶ τῷ πατρὶ [τῆ]ς ἀρεσκούσης παιδείας, goes on to state that he runs the risk τῆς ἰδίας πατρίδος στερηθῆναι (BGU IV. 1140[5 ff.]). In PSI 94[ff.] (ii/A.D.) a woman writes gratefully ὅτι ἤρεσε καὶ τῷ παιδὶ ἡ ποδίς, καὶ προσεδρεύει ἰς τὰ μαθήματα: cf. BGU IV. 1141[24] (Aug.) ὡς δοῦλος ἐπ' ἐλευθερίᾳ θέλει ἀρέσαι οὕτω κἀγὼ τὴν φιλίαν σου θέλων ἄμεμπτ[ον] ἐμᾶτον ἐτήρησα. In P Oxy VIII. 1153[25] (i/A.D.) a man sends his son a piece of fabric, telling him to show it to a third man and write as to the colour, ἐὰν αὐτῷ ἀρέσκῃ. Similarly in P Giss I. 20[15] (ii/A.D.) ὁποῖον δέ σοι χρῶ[μ]ᾳ ἀρέσκει, [δήλω]σον δι' ἐπι[σ]τολῆς ἢ μεικρὸν ἔρ[γο]ν αὐτοῦ π[έμψο]ν—a woman is writing to her husband about some wool she is working for him. (Ought we perhaps to supplement ἔρ[ιο]ν from the previous line, instead of ἔρ[γο]ν, "a little wool of that (colour)"?) The same lady's mother writes to the husband in 22[12] ταῦτα καὶ θεοῖς [ἀρέ]σκε[ι], but then unfortunately becomes illegible, though a small space suggests to the editor that the sentence ends there: in that case ταῦτα is her earnest wish to see her son-in-law safe home. The verb remains in the

vernacular to-day with meaning unchanged, but (normally) a less irregular present ἀρέζω.

ἀρεστός.

The adj. is very common. P Hib I. 51[1] (B.C. 245) πρι[ά]μενος λάμβανε ἀρεστὰς τ[ῶ]ν ὑπογεγραμμένων, "accept, if satisfactory, and buy at the prices below written" (Edd.). P Grenf II. 24[11] (B.C. 105) παρεχέσθω (*sc.* τὸν οἶνον) μόνιμον καὶ ἀρεστὸν ἕως Ἀθὺρ ᾱ, "wine that will keep and be satisfactory till Athyr 1st." P Amh II. 48[8] (B.C. 106) χορηγοῦντες κενώματα ἀρεστά, "providing acceptable vessels" (Edd.). In P Tebt II. 342[17] (late ii/A.D.) a pottery is described as λίθοις ἀρεστοῖς ἐξηρτισμένον), "newly fitted with stones in good order": so [22, 25]. Cf. *Syll* 522[17] (iii/B.C.) οἶνο[υ] παρέχειν ἀρεστόν, and for the adverb *Michel* 450[13 ff.] (ii/B.C.) ἀποδεδείχασιν οἱ ἐπιμεληταὶ τῆι βουλ[ῆι] συντετελεσμένα πάντα τὰ ἔργα ἀρεστῶς, BGU IV. 1119[21] (B.C. 5) τὰ προσήκοντα ἔργα πάντα καθ' ὥρα[ν] καὶ κατὰ καιρὸν ἀρεστῶς. The collocation of εὐάρεστος and δόκιμος in Rom 14[18] is closely paralleled in P Amh II. 89[8] (A.D. 121) τὸ (*l.* τὸν δὲ ἀργυρικὸν φόρον δόκιμον ἄριστον (*l.* ἀρεστόν), if the editors' certain emendation be accepted. So P Flor I. 1[6] (A.D. 153) ἀργύριον δόκιμον νομειτευόμενον ἀρεστόν: P Lond 938[5] (A.D. 225) (= III. p. 150), *al.*

Ἀρέτας.

The form Ἀρέτας (for rough breathing see WH *Intr.*[2] p. 313) instead of Ἀρέθας may, as Deissmann (*BS* p. 183 f.), following Schürer *Geschichte* i. p. 738, has suggested, be due to a desire to Hellenize the barbaric name by assimilation to ἀρετή.

ἀρετή.

The limitation of this word to four occurrences in NT—and two of them in 2 Pet—may possibly be connected with the very width of its significance in non-Christian ethics: it had not precision enough for large use in Christian language. If Brugmann is right in connecting it with ἀρέσκω *Kurzgef. vergl. Gr.* p. 519, this vagueness was there from the first. Our "virtue" is too narrow for a word which had nearly all the forces of our adj. "good": cf. Prof. G. Murray, *Greek Epic*, p. 57. Some Κοινή instances may be quoted. P Hib I. 15[55 ff.] (a rhetorical exercise, about B.C. 280-40): the younger men are exhorted to employ their bodies εὐκαίρως τὴν ἀπόδειξιν ποιησαμένους τῆς αὐτῶν ἀρετῆς, "in a timely display of their prowess" (Edd.). In the ordinance of Ptolemy Euergetes II., P Tebt I. 5[165 ff.] (B.C. 118) certain officials are warned not τὴν ἐν ἀρετῆι κειμένην βασιλικὴν) γῆν παραιρεῖσθαι τῶν γεωργῶν μηδὲ ἐπὶ ἐγλογῆι γεωργεῖν, "to take the richest Crown land from the cultivators by fraud or cultivate it at choice." The editors quote Hesychius ἀρετῶσιν· ἀρεταίνωσιν, εὐδαιμονῶσιν, ἐν ἀρετῆ ὦσιν. It is thus possible that we have here earlier evidence for ἀρεταί = *laudes* in the LXX (see Deissmann *BS* p. 95 f., Hort *1 Pet* p. 128 f.) as if "land in esteem." The other new meaning brought out by Deissmann (*ut supra*) "manifestation of power" (as 2 Pet 1[3]) may also be further illustrated. Thus in *Syll* 782[4] (iv/B.C.) Ἀθηναίαι Μένεια ἀνέθηκεν ὄψιν ἰδοῦσα ἀρετὴν τῆς θεοῦ. Dittenberger quotes with approval Foucart's definition of ἀρετή as signifying "vim divinam quae mirabilem in modum hominibus laborantibus salutem afferret." Cf. ib. 800^10 (Crete, early Empire) πλείονας ἀρετὰ[ς] τοῦ θεοῦ] and ib. 807^5 (c. ii/A.D.) where after a miraculous restoration of a blind man the people rejoice ὅτι ζῶσαι ἀρεταὶ ἐγένοντο ἐπὶ τοῦ Σεβαστοῦ ἡμῶν Ἀντωνείνου. There is suggestive force in this rejoicing of the pagan crowd to find that "powers" of Asclepios were still "alive" in those dark days.

A few miscellaneous references may be added. With the list of virtues in 2 Pet 1^5f., cf. OGIS 438^6ff. (i/B.C.) ἄνδρα ἀγαθὸν γενόμενον καὶ διενένκαντα πίστει καὶ ἀρετῇ καὶ δ[ικ]αιοσύνῃ καὶ εὐσεβείᾳ καὶ περὶ το[ῦ κ]ο[ι]ν[οῦ] συμφέροντος τὴν πλείστ[η]ν εἰσενηνεγμένον σπουδήν (see BS p. 360ff., LAE p. 322). In the invitation to celebrate Hadrian's accession to the Imperial throne, the new Emperor is described as one ᾧ πάντα δοῦλα [δι'] ἀρετὴν κ[αὶ] πατρὸς τύχην θεοῦ (P Giss I. 3^5f.). A sepulchral epigram from Hermupolis (PSI 17^vi.2, iii/A.D.) begins —[Ο]ὐ γὰρ ἐν ἀνθρώποισιν ἐὼν ἐβάδιζεν ἐκείνην τὴν ὁδὸν ἣν ἀρετῆς οὐκ ἐκάθηρε θέμις. And in the later papyri the word is frequent as a title of courtesy, e.g. P Oxy I. 60^4ff. (A.D. 323) ἀκολούθως τοῖς κελευσθεῖσι ὑπὸ τῆς ἀρετῆς τοῦ κυρίου μου διασημοτάτου ἡγεμόνος Σαβινιανοῦ, ib. 71^ii.18 (A.D. 303) εἴ σου δόξειεν τῇ ἀρετῇ : cf. P Lips I. 40^ii.20,iii.9,18 (iv/v A.D.), P Grenf II. 90^11 (vi/A.D.) al. The same usage is found in Jos. Antt. xii. 53 : cf. our "Excellency."

ἀρήν.

Of the nominative of this word (Ϝαρήν, declined according to the primitive model still normal in Sanskrit, and traced in κύων κυνός, caro carnis, etc.), we have no occurrences except in early times (Attic, Coan and Cretan inscriptions) : see Searles, Lexicographical Study (Chicago, 1898), p. 21. The oblique cases, although there is only one occurrence in the NT (Lk 10^3 ἄρνας), are by no means obsolete in the Κοινή : thus ἀρνός P Tebt I. 117^35 (B.C. 99), and even P Lond 125 verso^2 (magical, v/A.D.) (= I. p. 123) αἵματι ἀ[ρ]νὸς μέλανος ; ἄρνες P Hib I. 32^11 (B.C. 246) ; ἄρν(ασι) P Amh II. 73^5 (A.D. 129-30) ; ἄρνας BGU I. 133^8 (ii/A.D.), PSI 40^3 (A.D. 129), P Oxy I. 74^2 etc. (A.D. 116) ; PSI 56^8 (A.D. 107) ἄρνες, and so P Hawara 322^6 (Antoninus) (in Archiv v. p. 304). Mayser's instance from P Magd 21^4 must be dropped : see the new edition. Kaibel 1038^3a (Attalia, an oracle of Cybele) ὡ]ς ἄρνα[ς] κα[τ]έχουσι λύκοι : cf. Lk 10^3. The replacing of this irregular noun by the only formally diminutive ἀρνίον is normal. The distinction in use between this word and ἀμνός seems beyond our power to trace : van Herwerden (s.v. ἀρήν) cites a grammarian who makes this a lamb less than a year old, ἀμνός one over a year.

ἀριθμέω.

The ordinary use of the verb is for "payment" ; cf. P Giss I. 8^2 (A.D. 119) τὴ[ν συμ]φωνηθεῖαν (l. -σαν) τιμὴν τῷ Ἀπολλωνίῳ ἀρ[ιθ]μήσας, P Oxy III. 486^23 (A.D. 131) ἀριθμήσασα τιμὴν αὐτῆς, P Lille I. 3^40 (after B.C. 240) καλῶς ποι ήσεις] [συ]ντάξας ἀρ[ι]θμῆσαι ἡμῖν τὸ γινόμενον ὀψώ[νιον] τοῦ Λωΐο[υ μ]ηνός, al. In P Leid C^ii.19 (p. 118) (the dream of Ptolemaeus, ii/B.C.) οἴομαι ἀρεθμεῖν με seems to refer to "counting" days : ten lines higher the verb means "pay." BGU II. 620^6 (ii/A.D.) ἠριθμήθημε[ν has a lacuna following, but has reference apparently to numeration. The subst. ἀρίθμησις occurs in P Ryl II. 99^12 (iii/A.D.) διαγράψω . . ταῖς εἰθισμέναις ἀριθμήσεσιν "in the customary instalments" (Edd.). It is common in the phrase εἰς ἀρίθμησιν μηνός, as BGU I. 25^6, 41^6 (both i/iii A.D.), Preisigke 1090^2 (ostracon, A.D. 161). There is a further derivative ἀριθμητικός : Wilcken (Ostr. i. p. 351, cf. Archiv iv. p. 174) makes τὸ ἀ. an impost for the maintenance of the ἀριθμηταί, but GH (P Tebt II. p. 197) regard it rather as a tax on land : cf. BGU I. 236^9, 330^7 (both ii/A.D.). It is MGr, as is ἀριθμός. We may take the opportunity of noting the remarkable parallel to Mt 10^30, Lk 12^7 in the new fragment of Alcaeus (vii/vi B.C.), P Oxy X. 1233. fr. 8^10 . .]s παρὰ μοῖραν Διὸς οὐδὲ τρίχ[. . (see the note).

ἀριθμός.

P Petr II. 16^13 (middle iii/B.C.) (= Witkowski^2, p. 12) ἠκούσ]αμεν ἀριθμὸν ἔσεσθαι ἐκ τῶν Ἀρσινοε[ίω]ν, P Gen I. 16^22 (A.D. 207) τοῦ τούτου ἀδελφοὶ ὄντες τὸν ἀριθμὸν πέντε. For the LXX ἀριθμῷ = "few" in Num 9^20, Ezek 12^16 (Thackeray, O.T. Gram. p. 39), cf. P Oxy IV. 742^7f. (B.C. 2) (= Witkowski^2, p. 128) παράδος δέ τινι τῶν φίλων ἀριθμῷ αὐτάς (sc. δεσμάς), "deliver a few of them," rather than "deliver them accurately counted" (as Wilcken ap. Witkowski). But note the combination in P Oxy X. 1276^36 (A.D. 159) ἀριθμῷ πλήρεις : so ib. 1273^21 (A.D. 260) with ἀριθμοῦ, and 1291^10 (A.D. 325). Another use appears in BGU IV. 1085^25 (A.D. 171) where P. M. Meyer restores περὶ τῶν . . . ἀρι]θμῷ τριά[κο]ντα ἔντυχε τῷ στρατηγῷ : ἀριθμῷ is "a kind of rubric"—"heading no. 30," or the like. OGIS 266^6 (iii/B.C.) ὑπὲρ τῶν τὸν ἀριθμὸν ἀποδόντων τὸν κύριον, "as regards those who had completed the fixed number of years." It may be worth while to call attention to Wessely's paper on Gnostic numbers in the Mittheilungen of the Rainer Collection I. i. p. 113 ff. : thus 99 is the ἀριθμός of ἀμήν (α + μ + η + ν = 99) and the mystic Ἀβρασάξ is the number of the year, since its letters numerically total 365 (see P Leid W^iv.30). For the application of this principle to the "number" of the Beast (Rev 13^18), with illustrations from Greek graffiti from Pompeii (so before A.D. 79), see Deissmann LAE p. 276 f. : one of them is φιλῶ ἧς ἀριθμὸς φμε, "I love her whose number is 545." The case for a Greek rather than a Hebrew gematria in a Greek book is undeniably strong. Deissmann, l.c. refers to the dictionaries under ἰσόψηφος. We may cite from Cagnat IV. 743^7f. (= C. and B. no. 232—a metrical epitaph by a Jew of the time of Alexander Severus) a good instance of the gematria in Greek—ἰσόψηφος δυσὶ τούτοις Γάϊος ὡς ἅγιος ὡς ἀγαθὸς προλέγω : both adjectives total 284, agreeing with the number of his own name.

ἀριστερός.

For the phrase ἐξ ἀριστερῶν (as Lk 23^33) cf. P Ryl II. 153^47 (A.D. 138-61). BGU I. 86^7 (ii/A.D.), P Gen I. 43^4 (A.D. 226). The adj., it need hardly be said, is very common in the personal descriptions of appellants, witnesses, etc., in legal documents. Cf. also for the sake of the curious sidelight which it throws upon the daily life of Arsinoe the complaint which a woman lodges against Petechon, the male attendant in the women's baths, that he threw hot water over her and κατέκαυσεν τήν τε κοιλίαν καὶ τὸν ἀριστερὸν μηρὸν ἕως τοῦ γόνατος (P Magd 33 recto[4], B.C. 221). The adj. is still in use.

Ἀριστόβουλος.

A widely spread name : cf. Michel 372[6] (Leros, ii/B.C.), ib. 504[19] (Delos, B.C. 279), Magn 304[4], Priene 313[140].

ἄριστον.

P Oxy III. 519[17] (ii/A.D.) παιδίοις ἀρίστου ὀβ(ολοὶ) ϛ is presumably the account of a meal, which from the price was probably a light one ! So ib. IV. 736[8] (c. A.D. 1) πράσων ἀρίστῳ γερδί(ου) (ὀβολός) "leeks for the weaver's breakfast" (Edd.). P Tebt I. 112 introd. [17] (B.C. 112) ἀρίστου σὺν Ἡλιοδώ(ρωι) Ἀθη( ) κ̄, ib. 116[36] (late ii/B.C.) σῦκα ἐπὶ ἀρίστου ι. A more considerable meal seems intended in P Tebt I. 120[62] (i/B.C.) εἰς τὸ Ἰσιῆν τοῦ ἀρίστ[ο]υ ῑϛ̄ —it was a repast in the temple of Isis. Ib. 121[93] (i/B.C.) ὄψου ἐπ᾽ ἀρίστῳ ξ. We have not noticed the verb ἀριστάω.

ἀρκετός.

To the occurrences of this rare word we can now add BGU I. 33[5] (ii/iii A.D.) περὶ τῶν λοιπῶ[ν] ἔργων σου ἀρκετός γ[ε]νοῦ. We seem to have the adverb in the mutilated conclusion of BGU II. 531[ii.24] (ii/A.D.) ἐὰν δ[ὲ . . .] ἀρκετὸς [ἔ]χηι [. . . Vettius Valens, p. 304[25], has καὶ ἦν ἀρκετὸν κατὰ τοὺς λοιποὺς ἐᾶσαι. Kaibel Praef. 288c[10] shows ἀ[ρ]κετὰ τρι[—these three deaths suffice : the god is entreated to be satisfied. (The word is MGr.)

ἀρκέω.

For an impersonal use of ἀρκέω, as in Jn 14[8], see P Lond 964[13] (ii/iii A.D.) (= III. p. 212: λαβὼν κοτύλας τ[ό]σας φακῶν ἵνα ἀρκέσ[η] ἡ[μ]ῖν, and cf. the late P Oxy I. 131[11] (vi/vii A.D.) where, with reference to a disputed inheritance, it is stated that a father bequeathed half an acre of his land to a son, saying that it "is enough" for him— ὅτι ἀρκεῖ αὐτῷ τὸ ἡμιαρούριον. For the middle and passive. cf. P Giss I. 68[12 ff.] (ii/A.D.) ἠγόρασα γὰρ ἐνθάδε τριακοσίων δραχμῶν κ[α]ὶ οὐκ ἀρκεῖται, and P Goodsp 5[9] (ii/A.D.) ἀρκουμένων ἡμῶν τῆδε τῇ διαστολῇ) with the simple dative, as Lk 3[14]: so P Lips I. 33[ii.11] A.D. 308) Νεμεσίλλᾳ καὶ Διονυ[σίαν] ἀρκεσθῆναι προ[ι]ξεὶ β[ο]υλόμενος, CP Herm 9[11] οὐδὲ τούτοις ἀρκεσθέντες, cf. It has ἐπί as 3 Jn[10] in P Lond 45[13] (B.C. 160–59) (= I. p. 36) οὐκ ἀρκεσθέντες ἐφ᾽ οἷς ἦσαν διαπεπραγμένοι, and P Tor I. 1[ii.18] (B.C. 116) (= Chrest II. p. 32) οὐκ ἀρκεσθέντες δὲ ἐπὶ τῶι ἐνοικεῖν ἐν τῇ ἐμῇ οἰκίᾳ, ἀλλὰ καὶ κτλ. (indic.). Add P Amh II. 77[19] (A.D. 139) πλείσ[τ]α[ι]ς πληγαῖς με ᾐκίσατο, καὶ μὴ ἀρκεσθε[ὶ]ς ἐπή[ν]εγκέ μοι κτλ., P Ryl II. 145[19] (A.D. 38) ἔτι καὶ μὴ ἀρκ[εσ]θεὶς κτλ., "not content with heaping insults on my dependants," etc. (Edd.) (following a present ptc.). P Oxy I. 114[14] (ii/iii A.D.) ἐὰν οὖν μὴ ἀρκεσθῇ τὸ κέρμα, "if the cash is not sufficient." With the last citation under ἀρκετός cf. Kaibel 413[7] ἄρκεο μοῖρα θανόντι νέω[ι].

ἄρκτος.

Ἄρκος for ἄρκτος, as in Rev 13[2] (cf. 1 Regn 17[34]) is found in the later inscriptions, as in a Praenestine mosaic, IGSI 1302 (= CIG III. 6131b) (time of Hadrian ?) : cf. ib. 2325, 2328, 2334. The still more contracted ἄρξ occurs in the

---

Silko inscription OGIS 201[17] (vi/A.D.), ἐγὼ γὰρ εἰς κάτω μέρη λέων εἰμί, καὶ εἰς ἄνω μέρη ἄρξ εἰμι : where see Dittenberger's note. MGr ἀρκούδα "she-bear," as Thumb remarks, owes its origin to this bv-form : he also (Handb. p. 320) gives ἄρκος as current in Pontus.

ἅρμα.

P Petr. II. 25(a)[6] εἰς ἄρματα τὰ ἀκολουθοῦντα αὐτῶι. OGIS 533[18] (i/B.C.) ἁρμάτων καὶ κελ[ή]των. Magn 127[4] (i/B.C.) ἅρματι τελείωι. A half-literary citation from P Giss I. 3 may be permitted in view of the interest of the document, which is a call to celebrate the accession of Hadrian. The sun-god Phoebus Apollo is the speaker, and announces himself as having just come from accompanying Trajan on high in his white-horsed chariot—

Ἅρματι λευκοπώλωι ἄρτι Τραιαν[ῶι]
συνανατείλας ἥκω σοι, ὦ δῆμ[ε],
οὐκ ἄγνωστος Φοῖβος θεὸς ἄνακτα καινὸν Ἀδριανὸν ἀγγελῶ[ν].

ἁρμόζω.

We have found no direct parallel in the Κοινή to the use of ἡρμοσάμην in 2 Cor 11[2], where the middle is probably used purposely to bring out the Apostle's deep personal interest in this spiritual προμνηστική (see Proleg. p. 160) : but the use of μνηστεύεσθαι in P Flor I. 36[4] (iv/A.D. init.) of a mother making a match (μνηστευσαμένου μου) for her son with a cousin, is essentially on the same lines. In P Oxy VI. 906[7] (a deed of divorce, ii/iii A.D.) it is provided that the separating parties shall be free to marry as they choose without incurring any penalty—ἀπὸ δὲ τοῦ νῦν ἐξεῖναι τῷ Διογένει καὶ τῇ Πλουτάρχῃ ἑκάτερος αὐτῶν ἁρμόζεσ[θαι] ὡς ἐὰν αἱρῆται γάμῳ ἀνευθύνῳ ὄντι. In MGr ἁρμοστός-ή is the name of a betrothed pair. Cf. also Aristeas 250 πῶς ἁρμόσαι γυναικί (where the fact that the archaic optative is "incorrect" does not justify the editors in inserting ἄν).

In the active the verb is common = "to be suitable, fitting." P Fay 12[33] (c. B.C. 103) περὶ αὐτῶ[ν γ]ενομένης [ἀ]νάγκης ἁρμοζούσης διὰ δημοσίων, "suitable pressure being applied on this account by public officials" (Edd.). OGIS 335[159] (ii i B.C.) τοὺς ἁρ]μόζοντας λό[γ]ους, ib. 383[98] (i/B.C.) ὡς ἥρμοζεν ἕκαστος. BGU IV. 1120[32] (B.C. 5) τὴν ἁρμόζουσαν ἐπιμέλ[ειαν]. P Lond 256 recto[5] (A.D. 11–5) (= II. p. 97) τοῖς ἁρμόζουσι [κατὰ καιρὸν σπέρ]μασι. P Giss I 67[5] (ii/A.D.) δι᾽ ἧς (sc. ἐπιστολῆς) τὰ πρέποντά σου τῇ ἀξίᾳ καὶ [τῷ] ἤθει ἁρμόζοντά δηλοῖς. P Lips I. 38[i] (A.D. 390) αἱ ἐκ νόμων ἁρμό[ζ]ουσαι δικαιο[λ]ογίαι, etc. The prominence of the participle reminds us of our own fitting : it has its adverb ἁρμοζόντως, as in P Par 63[iii.77] (ii/B.C.), τοῖς καιροῖς πρεπόντως καὶ τοῖς ἀν[θρ]ώποις ἁρμο-ζόντως, Syll 258[5] (c. B.C. 200) ἁρμοζόντος (l. -ως) ἐν τοῖς (l. τοῖ) ψαφίσματι γεγραμμένοις. On the forms ἁρμόζειν and -ττειν, see Cronert Mem. Herc. pp. 135, 245 : the former is the true Hellenistic.

ἁρμός.

Syll 538[9] (? B.C. 353) συντιθέντα τοὺς ἁρμοὺς στερίφους, ἁρμόττοντας πανταχῆι, of the walls of a temple. Ib. 540[106] (B.C. 175–1) ἐκ τοῦ προσιόντος ἁρμοῦ : see Dittenberger's note. The word occurs in connexion with wrenching limbs out of their sockets (ἐξ ἁρμῶν ἀναμοχλεύοντες) in 4 Macc 10[5].

ἀρνέομαι.

Syll 356[25] (B.C. 6—a letter of Augustus) αὐτὸς μὲν γὰρ ἐνέμεινεν ἀρνούμενο[ς] "persisted in his denial." *OGIS* 484[31] (ii/A.D.) ἅπερ ἀρνουμένων αὐτῶν ἡδέως ἐπίστενον. For the aor. midd. (rare in Attic: cf. Veitch *Grk Verbs s.v.*) cf. BGU I. 195[22] (ii/A.D. ὑπὲρ δὲ τοῦ μὴ ἀρνήσασθαι ἐφ᾽ ἑκάστῳ τοῦτον . . . . P Flor I. 61[ii] [49] A.D. 86–8) ἠρνήσατο οὗτος [τὴ]ν κλη[ρ]ονομίαν τοῦ πατρὸς καὶ ἐγὼ τὴν (these three words interlineated) τοῦ ἰδίου πατρός. See also Helbing *Gr.* p. 90, and Mayor *Ep. of Jude*, p. 72, where it is stated that ἀρνέομαι (*denego*) with acc. of a person ("to disown") is unclassical, and seems to be confined to Christian literature. The verb is MGr.

ἀρνίον.

P Théad 8[14] (A.D. 306) ἀρνία ἐνιαύσια,[19] ἀρνία καὶ ἐρύφια. BGU II. 377[2,7] (early vii/A.D.), with other animal names, many in the -ιον form—καμήλι α), ὀρνίθ ια), perh. χοίρ(ια), etc. P Strass I. 24[7f] (A.D. 118) ἀρνίων ἐπιγονή ς) . . . ἀριθμῶι ἀρνίω ν). P Gen I. 68[7] (A.D. 382) ἀρνία ἔνδεκα. Its choice by the author of the Apocalypse as an exclusive term, for very frequent use, is part of a general tendency of the vernacular, in which nouns in -ιον multiplied fast: it is interesting to note that he has followed that tendency much earlier than our papyrus writers did in the case of this word. The complete absence of diminutive force in ἀρνίον as against ἀρήν may be noted. (MGr ἀρνί.)

ἀροτριάω

is found P Petr III. 31[7] τοῦ ζεύγους τῶν βοῶν μου πορευομένου ἐπὶ τῆς βασιλικῆς ὁδοῦ ὥστε ἀροτριᾶν. It is sometimes replaced by ὑποσχίζω, see the editors' note on P Lond 1170 *verso*[303] (A.D. 258–9) (=III. p. 200). The verb is found in the derived sense of "devise," like Heb. שֶּׂהָ, in Sir 7[12].

ἄροτρον

occurs in P Rein 17[20] (B.C. 109) ἄροτρον ᾱ ζυγὸν ᾱ (or ἄροτρον ἄζυγον α), P Flor II. 134[1] (A.D. 260) τὸ ταυρικὸν ἅμα τῷ ἀρότρῳ, P Strass I. 32[2] (a business letter, A.D. 261) Μάξιμον . . . ἀπέστειλα πρὸς σέ, ἵνα αὐτῷ ἄροτρον γένηται. Ἀροτήρ (contracted ἀρ᾽) is found in P Lond 257[200] (A.D. 94) (= II. p. 26): cf. *OGIS* 519[21] (iii/A.D.) τοὺς ἀροτῆρας βόας, where Dittenberger refers to Hesiod *Op.* 405 βοῦν ἀροτῆρα. MGr ἀλέτρι starts from ἀρέτριον, as Prof. Thumb notes.

ἁρπαγή.

Syll 928[85] (Magnesia, ii/B.C. *init.*) ἡ τῶν κτηνῶν ἁρπαγὴ γεγενημένη. BGU III. 871[5] (ii/A.D.) β[ί]ας καὶ ἁρπαγ[ῆς]. P Lips I. 64[55] (c. A.D. 368) δι᾽ ἁρπαγῆς.

ἁρπαγμός

occurs in the MS. of Vettius Valens, p. 122[1], ἐὰν Ἄρης κληρώσηται τὸν δαίμονα, Σελήνη δὲ τὸν γαμοστόλον, ἁρπαγμὸς ὁ γάμος ἔσται. Kroll says "nempe ἁρπάγιμος," but why not render "the marriage will be one of force," or perhaps "will be a great catch"? The closely parallel ἅρπαγμα, which modern commentators generally regard as a practical synonym of the rare ἁρπαγμός in Phil 2[6], may be cited from a magical text. The leaden tablet from Adru-

metum, printed with a commentary by Deissmann, *BS* pp. 274–300, and with slightly amended text by Wünsch *AF* no. 5, has in l. [31] δι᾽ ὃν ὁ λέων ἀφείησιν τὸ ἅρπασμα, the noun denoting the lion's "prey" as in LXX of Ezek 22[25]. One apt though not exact literary parallel seems to have escaped Lightfoot's net: Pindar *Pyth* 8[65] ἁρπαλέαν δόσιν "a gift to be eagerly seized" (Gildersleeve, who compares Phil *l. c.*), "the keen-sought prize" (Myers). This comes very near to the meaning *res rapienda* (rather than *res rapta*) by which ἁρπαγμόν seems best explained if really equivalent to ἅρπαγμα "spoil, prize." Against the solitary profane instance of ἁρπαγμός, in Plutarch 2. 12 A τὸν ἐκ Κρήτης καλούμενον ἁ., "*seizure*, rape," may be set a very close parallel also quoted by Lightfoot, οὐκ ἔστιν ἁρπαγμὸς ἡ τιμή (from a *catena* on Mk 10[41ff.]). Without discussing the *crux interpretum*, we might supply a list of the -μός nouns parallel to ἁρπαγμός in formation, as found in NT, such as may be cited to support the practical identity of ἁ. with ἅρπαγμα, and its distinctness from it, respectively. (1) Nouns which are or may be passive, like ἅρπαγμα = τὸ ἁρπακτόν or τὸ ἁρπακτέον: ὑπογραμμός, ψαλμός, θερισμός, ἱματισμός, ἐπισιτισμός, χρηματισμός. In these the abstract has become concrete, as our *writing, clothing, warning* have done, so that they are what the noun in -μα would have been. (Brugmann Thumb pp. 218, 222, defines the -μός and -μή nouns and the -μα as "verbal abstracts" and "nomina actionis" respectively; but both "partially pass into names of things.") (2) By far the larger number, some forty or more, denote the action of the verb—βρυγμός "gnashing," σεισμός "shaking," which in concrete development produces ἀσπασμός "a greeting," δεσμός "chain," etc. The statement that Plut. *Mor.* p. 12 is "the only instance of its use noted in prof. auth." as a matter of fact overlooks an instance of the identical ἁρπασμός given in Wyttenbach's *index verborum*—viz. p. 644 A (*Symposiaca* II. 10), where ὑφαίρεσις καὶ ἁρπασμὸς καὶ χειρῶν ἅμιλλα καὶ διαγκωνισμός are mentioned as conduct not tending to friendliness or convivial enjoyment; we may render "snatching and grabbing, fisticuffs and elbowing." Here again, therefore, the word is a *nomen actionis*, as in the other Plutarch passage.

ἁρπάζω.

P Lond 357[8] (A.D. 14–5) (= II. p. 166) ἁ]ρπάσαι τὰ ἐπιβάλλοντα. *OGIS* 665[18] (A.D. 49) ὅτι ἀναλίσκεταί τινα ἁρπαζόντων ἀδεῶς τῶν ἐπὶ ταῖς χρείαις. In P Par 68[8f.] (a document relating to the Jewish war of Trajan, ii/A.D.) we have τινὰς ἐπὶ κωστωδίαν ἥρπασαν καὶ [τοὺς ἁρπασθέν-τ]ας ἐτραυμάτισαν: cf. BGU I. 341[3], which deals with the same events, ἐκ κωστω]δίας ἥρπασαν. In l. [12] of the last papyrus ἡρπάγησαν is the true reading: see *Berichtigungen* p. 359. A common use may be illustrated by the petition BGU III. 759[23] (A.D. 125) ὅπως παραστήσω[σ]ι τοὺς αἰτ[ίους καὶ] ἀποτείσωσι τὰ ἡρπασμένα. According to Wilcken (*Archiv* i. p. 164) the verb is to be understood causatively in P Lond 408[11] (c. A.D. 346) (= II. p. 284) ἥρπαξας αὐτοὺς ὡς ἐν ἀνομίᾳ, "du hast sie plündern lassen." On this general tendency, cf. Hatzidakis *Einl.* p. 200 f. For ἁρπάζω, used of death, see the epitaph in *BCH* xxvii. p. 370, no. 101, ὑπὸ σκορπίου ἡρπά[σθ]η. The compound ἀφαρπάζω is found P Oxy I. 37[i.17] (A.D. 49) τὸ σωμάτιον ἀφήρπασεν, "carried the foundling off," P Strass I. 5[15] (A.D. 202) τὰ τετράποδα τὰ ἡμέτερα ἀφήρπασ[α]ν, and often in petitions complaining of robbery. For the double conjugation of this and similar verbs—due to the fact that both dental and guttural before -γω will make -ζω—see *Proleg.* p. 56. The verb survives in MGr.

ἅρπαξ.

Deissmann (*LAE* p. 321 n [1]) notes that ἅ. was current as a loan-word in Latin comedy: in Paul "it should probably not be translated 'robber' but rendered by some other word like 'swindler' ('extortioner,' AV, RV)."

ἀρραβών.

A word of undoubted Semitic origin (Heb. עֵרָבוֹן, cf. Lagarde *Mittail.* I. p. 212, Lewy *Fremdworter* p. 120), spelt ἀρραβών and ἀραβών: see *Proleg.* p. 45 and Thackeray *Gr.* I. p. 110, and cf. P Lond 334[14, 31] (A.D. 166) (= II. p. 211 f.), where both forms occur. The meaning of "earnest-money" (Scottice "arles") is well illustrated by P Par 58[14] (ii/B.C.) (= Witkowski[2], p. 81), where a woman who was selling a cow received 1000 drachmas as ἀραβῶνα. Similarly P Lond 143[13] (A.D. 97) (= II. p. 204), a receipt for 160 drachmas, being the residue of the earnest-money (200 drachmas) for 2 9/16 arourae of land, ἀπὸ λόγου ἀρρα βῶνος κλήρου κτλ., P Fay 91[14] (A.D. 99) ἀργυρίου δραχ[μὰς] δέκα ἐξ ἀρραβῶνα ἀναπόριφον, "16 drachmae of silver as unexceptionable earnest-money" (Edd.). P Oxy II. 299[2] (late i/A.D.) Λάμπωνι μυοθηρευτῇ ἔδωκα αὐτῷ διὰ σοῦ ἀραβῶνα (δραχμὰς) η ἵνα μυοθηρεύσει ἔντοκα, "regarding Lampon the mouse-catcher I paid him for you as earnest money 8 drachmae in order that he may catch the mice while they are with young" (Edd.), *ib.* VI. 920[12] (ii/iii A.D.) ἰς λόγ[ον] ἀραβῶ[νος] (δραχμαὶ) ιβ, Syll 226[131] (Olbia, iii/B.C.) ἐνέγκας εἰς τὴν ἐκλησίαν χρυσοῦς πεντακοσίους εἰς τοὺς ἀρραβῶνας. Additional examples are *Ostr* 1168, P Magd 20[5] (B.C. 217), P Lond 1229[16] (A.D. 145) (= III. p. 143), *ib.* 1170 *verso* [123] (A.D. 258-9) (= III. p. 106), BGU I. 240[6] (ii/A.D.), *ib.* II. 601[11] (ii/A.D.), and P Grenf II. 67[17 ff.] (A.D. 237) (= *Selections*, p. 109) where in the engagement of certain dancing girls for a village festival provision is made that they are to receive so many drachmas ὑπὲρ ἀραβῶνος [τῇ τ]ιμῇ ἐλλογουμέν[ο]υ, "by way of earnest-money to be reckoned in the price." The above vernacular usage amply confirms the NT sense of an "earnest," or a part given in advance of what will be bestowed fully afterwards, in 2 Cor 1[22], 5[5], Eph 1[14].

It may be added that in MGr ἡ ἀρραβωνι(α)σμένη = "the betrothed bride," "an interesting reminiscence," as Abbott (*Songs*, p. 258) remarks, "of the ancient custom of *purchasing* a wife." In the same way ἡ ἀρραβῶνα is used for "the engagement-ring." In the island of Cyprus we find the form ἀραῶνα (Thumb *Hellen.*, p. 23).

ἄρρητος

is common in sacred inscriptions, e.g. *Michel* 992[21] (Mantinea, B.C. 61) ἐσκέπασεν καὶ εὐσχημόνισεν τὰ περὶ τὰν θεὸν ἄρρητα μυστήρια. The word is thus associated with the Mysteries, and in 2 Cor 12[4] (ἄρρητα ῥήματα) suggests words too sacred to be uttered. Vettius Valens p. 19[1] has περὶ τὰ ἄρρητα ποιητικαί. P Leid W[xviii. 16], with κρυπτόν.

ἄρρωστος.

Syll 858[17] (Delphi, in dialect, ii/B.C.) ἀτελὴς ἁ ὠνὰ ἔστω, εἰ μὴ ἄρρωστος γένοιτο Σῶσος. We do not happen to have noticed any instance of the adj. in the papyri, but both verb and subst. are common. For the verb cf. P Petr I. 30[14] (middle of iii B.C.) (= Witkowski[2], p. 5) τὸν ὄν[τ]α ἐν Μέμφει ἀρρωστοῦντα, P Hib I. 73[15] (B.C. 243-2) εἰ οὖν μὴ ἠρρωστήσαμεν, P Par 49[31] (B.C. 164-58) (= Witkowski[2], p. 71) ἀγωνιῶ, μή ποτε ἀρ ρ ωστεῖ τὸ παιδάριον, P Ryl II. 68[15] (B.C. 89) ὥ[στε] διὰ τὰς πληγὰς ἀρρωστήσασα κατα κεῖσαι (*i.e.* -σθαι) κινδυνεύουσα τῶι βίωι (which shows that ἁ. may represent something very serious), BGU IV. 1125[7] (time of Augustus) ἅς (*sc.* ἡμέρας) δὲ ἐὰν ἀρτακτήσηι (*l.* ἀτακτήσηι) ἢι ἀρρωστήσηι. For the subst. see the very interesting petition which the priests of the temple at Soenopaei Nesus present to the Strategus, asking for certain favours at his hands, seeing that "in his sickness" he was healed by their god—ἐπεὶ οὖν σέσωσαι ἐν τῆι ἀρρωστίαι ὑπὸ τοῦ Σοκνοπαίτος θεοῦ μεγάλου (P Amh II. 35[32], B.C. 132), also P Tebt I. 44[5 f.] (B.C. 114) χάριν τῆς περιεχούσης με ἀρρωστίας, "on account of the sickness from which I am suffering," *ib.* 52[10 ff.] (*c.* B.C. 114) δι με (*l.* διὰ τό με) ἐν βαρυ[τε ρ]α (see *Proleg.* p. 78) ἀρρωστίᾳ κῖσ[θαι] ἐνδεὴς ουσα τῶν ἀναγ[καίων, "since I am seriously ill, being in want of the necessaries of life" (Edd.), and P Hawara 56[18 ff.] (probably late i/A.D.) (= *Archiv* v. p. 382) μαρτυρήσει δέ σ(οι) [Ἰ]σίδωρος, ὅτι ἀρρωστίαν ἰσοθάνατο(ν) [ἐξ]ήν τλησα. See also *Syll* 400[6] (iii/B.C.) ἐν[π]ετό[ν]των πολλῶν ἄγαν ὀλεθρί[ων ἀρρω στη]ημάτων καὶ τῶν ἰατρῶν τῶν [δαμ]οσ[ιευόν]των ἐν τᾶι πόλει ἀρρωστησάντων. The adj. is MGr, as are the derived verb and noun.

ἀρσενοκοίτης.

According to Nägeli (p. 46) this word is first found among the poets of the Imperial period, e.g. Epigr. adesp. *Anthol. Pal.* IX. 686[5]. Cf. for the verb *Or. Sib.* ii. 73 μὴ ἀρσενοκοιτεῖν, μὴ συκοφαντεῖν, μήτε φονεύειν.

ἄρσην.

The form ἄρσην, which WH read throughout, is illustrated by P Oxy IV. 744[9] (B.C. 1) (= *Selections*, p. 33) where with reference to the birth of a child it is directed ἐὰν ἦν (*l.* ᾖ) ἄρσενον ἄφες (or ἐὰν ἦν (*l.* ᾖ) θήλεα ἔκβαλε: cf. also P Gen I. 35[6] (A.D. 161) κ[αμήλους] [τε]λείους ἄρσενας δύο λευκούς. In P Oxy I. 37[17] (A.D. 49) (= *Selections*, p. 49) we have ἀρρενικὸν σωμάτιον, but in *ib.* 38[5] (a document dealing with the same incident, A.D. 49-50) (= *Selections*, p. 53) it is ἀρσενικὸν σωμάτιον. For ἄρρην see further CPR 28[12] (A.D. 110) τῶν δὲ ἀρρένων υἱῶν, BGU I. 88[6] (A.D. 147) κάμηλ(ον) ἄρρενον [λ]ευκόν, P Strass I. 30[16] (A.D. 276) ἀρρενικὰ ἑπτά, P Lond 46[105] (magic, iv/A.D.) (= I. p. 68) θῆλυ καὶ ἄρρεν. *Ostr* 1601 has παιδίον ἀρσενικοῦ: cf. P Oxy IX. 1216[14] (ii/iii A.D.) ἡ καὶ ἀρσε νεικὸν ἡμῖν ἀφίκατα[ι:]. "Have you produced us a male child?" (Ed.), and the MGr ἀρσενικός. There is an important investigation into the rationale of the variation between ρσ and ρρ in the Κοινή in Wackernagel *Hellenistica*, p. 12 ff.; also see Thumb *Hellen.*, p. 77 f. A further orthographic difference appears in P Petr III. 59 *b* (iii/ii B.C.) σώματα ἐρσενικά: see other instances, and a discussion on dialect points involved, in Mayser *Gr.* p. 5 ; and cf. Thumb's *Gr. Dial.* (index *s.v.* ἔρσην).

ἀρτέμων.

What particular sail is to be understood by ἀ. in Ac 27⁴⁰ is uncertain.   Sir W. M. Ramsay (Hastings' *DB* V. p. 399) refers to the case mentioned by Juvenal (*Sat* 12⁶⁹) where a disabled ship made its way into harbour *velo prora suo*, which the scholiast explains *artemone solo.* According to this, the ἀρτέμων would be a sail set on the bow.   See also Breusing *Die Nautik der Alten,* p. 79 f. (cited by Preuschen, *ad* Ac 27⁴⁰ in *HZNT*).

ἄρτι.

For ἄρτι of strictly *present* time (as Gal 1⁹⁶, 1 Th 3⁶, etc.) cf. BGU II. 594⁵ (*c.* A.D. 70-80) λέγων ὅτι μετὰ τὸν θερισμὸ[ν ἐργολ]αβήσομα[ι], ἄρτι γὰρ ἀσθενῶι, P Lond 937 *b*⁶ff (iii/A.D.) (= III. p. 213) δικάζομαι χάριν τῶν τοῦ ἀδελφοῦ μου καὶ οὐ δύναμαι ἄρτι ἐλθεῖν πρὸς σ[έ], *Syll* 387⁸ A.D. 127—a rescript of Hadrian) δίκαια ἀξιοῦν μοι δοκεῖτε καὶ ἀναγκαῖα ἄ[ρ]τι γενομένῃ πόλει : Stratonicea (in Lydia) was just "incorporated."   The word is very common in magical formulas, e.g. P Lond 121³⁷³ (iii/A.D.) (= I. p. 96) ἐν [τ]ῇ ἄρτι ὥρᾳ ἤδη ἤδη ταχὺ ταχύ, *ib.*⁶¹⁶ ἐν τῇ σήμερον ἡμέρᾳ ἐν τῇ ἄρτι ὥρα, and the incantation in the long Paris papyrus 574¹²⁴⁵ (iii/A.D.) (= *Selections*, p. 114) ἔξελθε, δαῖμον, . . . καὶ ἀπόστηθι ἀπὸ τοῦ δῖ(να) ἄρτι ἄρτι ἤδη, "depart from so and so at once, at once, now." For the combination of Mt 11¹², etc., cf. P Oxy VI. 936²³ (iii/A.D.) οὐκ ἔχω ἄρτι σεῖτον οὐδὲ τὰ βιβλίδια ἀπήρ[τ].σται ἕως ἄρτι, "the petitions have not yet been got ready" (Edd.).   According to Moeris p. 68 : "Ἄρτι, οἱ μὲν Ἀττικοὶ τὸ πρὸ ὀλίγου, οἱ δὲ Ἕλληνες καὶ ἐπὶ τοῦ νῦν λέγουσι. See also Lobeck *Phryn.* p. 18 ff , Rutherford *NP,* p. 70 ff., and Nägeli, p. 78, where the word is cited as a mark of the non-literary Κοινή.

ἀρτιγέννητος.

Cf. the late imperial inscr. in *Archiv* v. p. 166 (no. 17²—a metrical epitaph) Σαραπίωνα νέον τε καὶ ἀρτιγένειον ἔοντα. Lucian is sufficient warrant for Peter's adj. (1 Pet 2²).   See also Herwerden *Lex. s.v.*

ἄρτιος.

For ἄ. = τέλειος, see *Kaibel Praef 222 b*⁴ ἐτῶν ἀριθμὸν ὀγδοήκοντ' ἀρτίων.   In the difficult passage Herodas iv. 95, Nairn renders ἀρτίης μοίρης, "adequate" share.   The companion adjectives help to define the word in Vettius Valens, p. 14¹⁵, αἱ δὲ ϛ̄ Ἀφροδίτης (*sc.* μοῖραι) ἱλαραί, εὔτεχνοι, διαυγεῖς, ἄρτιοι, καθαροί, εὔχροοι   The adverb is found in P Lips I. 40 iii. 16 (iv/v A.D.) where a scribe is directed ἀκολουθεῖν τῷ νυκτοστρατήγῳ ἀρτίως κατὰ πρόσταγμα τῆς σῆς [λα[μ]π[ρότητος], and BGU III. 749⁹ (Byz.) ἀπὸ νεομηνίας τοῦ ἀρτίως [? ἀρχομένου] μηνός.

ἄρτος

is frequently found with καθαρός = "pure or "white bread," e.g. P Tebt II. 468 οἴνου κε(ράμιον) ᾱ, ἄρτων κα(θαρῶν) χ̄ (= 10 Choenices? Edd.).   P Oxy IV. 736³⁶ (a lengthy private account, *c.* A.D. 1) ἄρτου καθαροῦ παιδ(ῶν) ἡμιωβέλιον) "pure bread for the children ½ obol," P Giss

I. 14⁵ (ii. A.D.) ἔγραψάς μοι περὶ ἄρτων καθαρῶν πεγμφθῆναί σοι διὰ Διοσκύρου.   Other instances of the word are P Leid B i. 12 (ii/B.C.) ἄρτων πεπτῶν (in provision claimed for the Serapeum Twins), P Oxy VI. 936¹⁵ f. (iii/A.D.) σφυρίδιον Κανωπικὸν ὅπου ζεύγη ἄρτων δ̄, "a Canopic basket with four pairs of loaves," P Gen I. 74²⁵ f. (probably iii/A.D.) λήκυθον ἐλαίου καὶ ἄρτους μεγάλο[υ]ς τέσσαρας   In P Oxy VI. 908²²f (A.D. 199) ἀρτοκοπεῖον = "bakery"—ὥστε ὑφ' ἑκάστου ὑμῶν ἀρτοκοπεῖον ἐν ἀπαρτισθῆναι.   Ἄρτος is the common and only word for "bread" during the period we are concerned with : towards the end of it ψωμίον (*q. v.*) begins to acquire this meaning and takes its place.

ἀρτύω.

For ἀρτύω = "season," and not "restore" in Mk 9⁵⁰, Lk 14³², as in Col 4⁶, Wackernagel (*ThLZ* 1908, col 36 n¹) cites Athen. III. 113. 13 ἄρτος ἁπαλός, ἀρτυόμενος γάλακτι ὀλίγῳ καὶ ἐλαίῳ καὶ ἁλσὶν ἀρκετοῖς. Dioscor. II. 76 ἀρτυτοῖς (ἀρτυτικοῖς?) ἁλσί, *salibus condimento inservientibus.* P Tebt II. 375²⁷ (A.D. 140) ζύμης ἡρτυμένης. Ἀρτύματα "spices" are mentioned in an account P Amh II 126⁴⁰ (early ii/A.D.): cf. P Giss I 47¹⁴ (ii/A.D.) τὰ δύο μάτια (= ½ ataba) τῶν ἀρτυμάτων (δραχμῶν) π̄. A subst. ἀρτυματατᾶς occurs BGU IV. 1087 ii. 9 (iii/A.D.): cf. *ib.* I. 9 iv. 5 : cf. also ἀρτυματοπώλης on a tombstone, *Preisigke* 699 (ii/A.D.), and ἀρτυτήρ in *Michel* 1001 iv. 37, v. 4 (Epicteta's Will, Thera, *c.* B.C. 200).   In a lexicon to *Iliad* xviii., P Ryl I. 25¹⁰ (ii/A.D.) ἤρτυε is glossed [κατεσκεύα]ζε : for supplement see Hunt's note.

ἀρχάγγελος.

This title, which is found in the Greek Bible only in 1 Th 4¹⁶, Jude ⁹, passed into the magical papyri, e.g. P Lond I. 121²⁵⁷ (iii/A.D.) (= I. p. 92) τῷ κυρίῳ μου τῷ ἀρχαγγέλῳ Μιχαήλ, and the Paris papyrus 574¹²⁰⁰ (iii/A.D.) ὁ κτίσας θεοὺς καὶ ἀρχαγγέλους.   In addition to other references to the syncretic literature of the Imperial period Nägeli (p. 48 n¹) cites a gnostic inscription from Miletus *CIG* 2895 ἀρχάγγελον φυλάσσεται ἡ πόλις Μιλησίων.   That the word was coined in Judaism to express a Jewish idea is of course obvious : it need only be mentioned that the prefix ἀρχ(ι-) (*q. v.*) could be attached to any word at will.   On Grimm's note upon the archangelic Heptad reference might be made to the Hibbert Lectures (1912) on *Early Zoroastrianism,* p. 241.

ἀρχαῖος.

That this word retains in general the sense of *original,* as distinguished from παλαιός = *old,* is seen commonly in vernacular sources as in the NT.   Thus Ac 21¹⁶, where Mnason is described as an ἀρχαῖος μαθητής, "an *original* disciple," one who belongs to the "beginning of the Gospel" (Phil 4¹⁵), is illustrated by *Magn* 215*b*, a contemporary inscription, where an ἀρχαῖος μύστης inscribes an ἀρχαῖος χρησμός : the "ancient initiate" is opposed to the neophyte, the "ancient oracle" to one just uttered—the citation is made by Thieme, p. 26.   So BGU III. 992 ii. 6 (B.C. 160) καθὰ καὶ οἱ ἀρχαῖοι κύριοι ἐκ[έκ]τηντο, "the original owners."   It is from the meaning "original" that τὸ ἀρχαῖον becomes a term for "capital," as in Epicteta, *Michel* 1001 viii. 8 (Thera, *c.* B.C. 200), or "principal," as *Syll* 517¹⁶ f.

(ii/B.C., Amorgos), opposed to τόκος. For the more general sense of "ancient," recurrent in Mt 5²¹, etc., we may compare the horoscope P Oxy II. 235⁶ (A.D. 20–50) where a date is given κατ᾽ ἃ δὲ τοὺς] ἀρχαίους χρόνους, i.e. "old style": see also P Fay 139⁶ (late ii/A.D.), *Preisigke* 1011 (ii/A.D.), 3462 (A.D. 154–5), and P Grenf II. 67¹⁰ (A.D. 237) (= *Selections*, p. 108). The reference is to the old Egyptian system of reckoning 365 days to the year without a leap-year, which continued to be used in many non-official documents even after the introduction of the Augustan calendar. The neuter = "original condition" may be seen in *OGIS* 672⁶ ᶠᶠ (A.D. 80) where a river is dredged, etc., καὶ ἐπὶ τὸ ἀρχαῖον ἀπεκατεστάθη : similarly in 2 Cor 5¹⁷, the "original conditions" pass away before the fiat that καινὰ ποιεῖ πάντα (Rev 21⁵). The standard of "antiquity" may be illustrated by *Syll* 355¹¹ (c. A.D. 3), where ἀρχαιοτάτου δόγμα[τος refers to a *senatus consultum* of B.C. 80. We find towns partial to the adj.: cf. P Lond 1157 *verso* ² (A.D. 246) (= III. p. 110) Ἑρμουπόλεως τῆς μεγά ἀρχαίας καὶ λαμπρᾶς καὶ σεμνοτάτης. The standing title of Heracleopolis (as BGU III. 924¹—iii/A.D.), ἀ. καὶ θεόφιλος, reminds us of "ancient and religious foundations" at Oxford or Cambridge to-day. Reference may also be made to a payment for ἀρχαίων ἱππέων, *Ostr* 323 (c. i/B.C.), evidently a cavalry regiment (the "Old Guard"), see *ib.* i. p. 101 f., *Archiv* ii. p. 155 : and to a land survey, P Tebt II. 610 (ii/A.D.) [ἄλ]λης ποταμοφο[ρήτου) ἀρχαίας. In P Par 60 *bis* ² (c. B.C. 200) we find τὸ ἀνήλωμα εἰς Ἀλεξάνδρειαν ἀπὸ τῶν πληρωμάτων [ἀρ]χαίων : on the grammar cf. *Proleg.* p. 84 n¹. The distinction between ἀ. and παλαιός is naturally worn thin on occasion, as in BGU III. 781 (i/A.D.), an inventory including sundry "old" crockery, as πινάκια βωλητάρια ἀρχαῖα ¹ ¹, ἄλλα ἀρχαῖα ὠτάρια ἔχοντα ¹¹·⁴. Ἀ. of *relative* antiquity is well illustrated by *Kaibel* 241a⁸ (p. 521) ἀρχαίων κηδομένη λεχέων. Note further the comparative in a British Museum papyrus, cited in *Archiv* vi. p. 103 (A.D. 103), ἀπὸ τῶν ἀρχεωτέρων χρόνων. The adj. survives in MGr.

ἀρχή.

The double meaning, answering to ἄρχειν and ἄρχεσθαι severally, can be freely paralleled. The great difficulty of Jn 8²⁵ τὴν ἀρχὴν ὅτι καὶ λαλῶ ὑμῖν ; makes it desirable to quote P Oxy III. 472¹⁶ ᶠ (c. A.D. 130) οὐ δύναται γὰρ κεκλέφθαι τὸ μηδ᾽ ἀρχὴν γενόμενον μὴ δυνατὸν δ᾽ εἶναι, "for it is impossible for that to have been stolen which neither ever existed at all nor could exist" (Edd.); but the absence of the article, and the fact that we cannot quote other examples of this once familiar usage, makes the quotation of little weight for confirming the RV mg. here ("How is it that I even speak to you at all?"), though it is probably right. For τὴν ἀ. = "originally" (without negative) we may quote *Syll* 256²³ (c. B.C. 200, Magnesia) τῶν ἄλλων ἀ[γ]ώνων τ.ὴ]ν ἀρχὴ(ν) μὲν ἐπ᾽ ἀργ[ύρωι τε]θέντων—later they had wreaths for prizes. So without article *ib.* 921² (Thera, iii/B.C.) *ex suppl.* For ἀρχή, as in Jn 1¹, we may quote the remarkable inscr. of Q. Pompeius A.f. from Eleusis, dated by Dittenberger not later than Augustus, dedicated to Αἰών, ἀρχὴν μεσότητα τέλος τε οὐκ ἔχων, μεταβολῆς ἀμέτοχος (*Syll* 757). Some prepositional phrases may be illustrated. Ἀπὸ τῆς ἀρχῆς P Tor I. 1ˣ·⁴ (B.C. 116) (= *Chrest.* II., p. 39),

Syll 929²³ (?B.C. 139) τῶν διὰ προγόνων ἀπὸ τ. ἀ. γεγενημένων, *ib.*⁵⁷ οὖσαν δὲ καὶ ἀπὸ τ. ἀ. Ἰτανίων : usually anarthrous, as BGU IV. 1141⁴⁴ (c. B.C. 14) διὰ τί ἀπ᾽ ἀρχῆς ἐτυι (?) οὐκ ἐνεφάνισας ταῦτα :—so P Tor II. 2¹⁵ (B.C. 131) τ[ὴ]ν κατοικίαν [ἔ]χοντες ἐν τ[οῖς Μεμνο[ν]είοις ἔτι [ἀ]π᾽ ἀρ[χ]ῆς, and *Syll* 328²⁰ (B.C. 84) ἀπ᾽ ἀρχῆς τε τ[οῖς ἐκχθίστοις πολεμίοις [ἐβοήθ]ει. Ἐξ ἀρχῆς is more frequent : thus P Gen I. 7⁸ (ii/A.D.) κατὰ τὸ ἐξ ἀρχῆς ἔθος, BGU IV. 1118¹ (B.C. 22) τοὺς ἐξ ἀ. ἐθ[ισμούς, P Thead 1⁸ (A.D. 306) κατὰ τὴν ἐξ ἀ. καὶ μέχρι νῦν συνήθειαν, *Syll* 246⁹ (B.C. 220–16) ὅπως ἂν . . . ἡ πόλις [ἀ]ποκατασταθεῖ εἰς τὴν ἐξ ἀρχῆς εὐδαιμονίαν, *ib.* 292¹ (B.C. 179, Olympia, in dialect) εἰς τὰν ἐξ ἀρχᾶς ἐ[οῦσαν] φιλίαν ἀποκ[αταστάσαντα, *ib.* 540¹⁷⁴ (B.C. 175–1) πάλιν τε ἐξ ἀρχῆς ἄρας ποιήσει "do it over again," P Oxy VII. 1032⁴⁹ (A.D. 162) τὰ ἐξ ἀ. ἐπιζητηθέντα, "the statement originally required." Ed.V. Ἐν ἀρχῇ occurs P Petr II. 37 2b *verso*¹ (p. [120]) ἐπισκεψάμενος ἐν ἀρχῆι ἃ δεῖ γενέσθαι (Ed. p. 245). For ἀρχὴν λαβεῖν (Heb 2³) add to Wetstein's exx. Diog. Laert. *Proem.* iii. 4.

Ἀρχή, "beginning, foundation," may be illustrated by Wünsch *AF* 4³⁵ ὁρκίζω σε τὸν θεὸν . . . τῶν πελάγων τὴν ἀρχὴν συνβεβλημένον. P Oxy VII. 1021¹⁰, a document notifying the accession of Nero, calls the new Emperor "good genius of the world," and [ἀρ]χὴ πάντων ἀγαθῶν, "source of all good things" (Ed.); but unfortunately the reading (which is followed by an erasure) is noted as extremely doubtful. For the meaning "office, authority," cf. *Preisigke* 176¹⁵ (A.D. 101 80) ἄρξαντος τὰς αὐτὰς ἀρχάς, etc., etc. Deissmann *BS*, p. 267 n³, notes a use of τόπος (vid. s.v.) parallel with ἀρχή in this sense, and compares Jude⁶. P Hal 1²²⁶ (iii/B.C.) μαρτυρείτω ἐ[π]ὶ [τῆ]ι ἀρχῆι καὶ ἐπὶ τ[ῶι] δικαστηρίωι shows us ἀρχή in a concrete sense = "magistrate," as in Tit 3¹. In MGr it means "beginning."

ἀρχηγός.

To determine between "founder" and "leader" in Heb 2¹⁰, 12², Ac 3¹⁵, 5³¹, is a complex question which would carry us beyond the limits of a lexical note. But our few citations go to emphasize the closeness of correspondence with *auctor*, which it evidently translates in a Proconsul's edict, *Syll* 316³ (ii/B.C.) ἐγεγόνει ἀρχηγὸς τῆς ὅλης συγχύσεως,¹⁷ τὸν γεγονότα ἀρχηγὸν [τ]ῶν πραχθέντων. So P Oxy I. 41⁵·⁶ (iii/iv A.D.), where a crowd shouts repeatedly in honour of the prytanis, ἀρχηγὲ τῶν ἀγαθῶν, "source of our blessings," *auctor bonorum*. The phrase is found five centuries earlier in the Rosetta stone, *OGIS* 90⁴⁷ . . . anniversaries which are πολλῶν ἀγαθῶν ἀρχηγοὶ (π)ᾶσι. In *OGIS* 212¹³ Apollo is ἀ. τοῦ [γένους] of Seleucus Nicator (B.C. 306–280) whose mother was said to have dreamed that she conceived by Apollo : so in 219²⁶ of his son Antiochus I. (Soter). P Oxy X. 1241ⁱⁱⁱ·³⁵ (ii/A.D., lit.) ἀ. φόνου "the first shedder." The other meaning "leader" is seen in *Kaibel* 585 (Gaul) ἱερέων ἀρχηγοῦ, of a high priest of Mithras. So still in MGr.

ἀρχι-.

A specimen list of new words formed with this prefix will illustrate what was said above (s.v. ἀρχάγγελος) of the readiness with which any writer might coin a compound of this class. Ἀρχικυνηγός *Ostr* 1530, 1545, ἀρχυπηρέτης *Ostr* 1538, *Preisigke* 599⁶¹, ἀρχιδικαστής P Tebt II. 286¹⁴

(Hadrian), etc., ἀρχιπροφήτης P Gen I. 7⁵ (i/A.D.), P Tebt II. 313¹ (A.D. 216-1 , *Preisigke* 326 (Alexandria, ii/B.C. or Roman), P Ryl II. 110¹ (A.D. 259), etc (ἀρχιπροστάτης whence) ἀ[ρ]χιπρ[ο]στατοῦντος *Preisigke* 626 (Ptol.) : cf. *ib.* 639 (B.C. 25) συ[να]γογοῦ προστατήσας (pagan), ἀρχιθυρωρός *ib.* 327, ἀρχιβουλευτής *ib.* 1106 (Ptol.), ἀρχιμηχανικός *ib.* 1113 (A.D. 147-8), ἀρχισωματοφύλαξ *ib.* 1164 (ii/B.C.), ἀρχίατρος *Cahier* 129, ἀρχιγέρων *Preisigke* 2100 (i/B.C.), ἀρχιπρύτανις *ib.* 226; (i/B.C.). We have made no effort to enlarge the list, or to find additional instances of those quoted, which are enough to prove our case. Five of the twelve are not in L.S.

ἀρχιερατικός.

OGIS 470²¹ (time of Augustus) ὡς καὶ συνγε[νι]κοῖς ἀρχιερατικοῖς στεφάνοις κεκοσμῆσθαι. For the LXX verb ἀρχιερατεύω (1 Macc 14⁴⁷) see BGU II. 362ⁱⁱⁱ·²⁰ *al.* (A.D. 215), P Amh II. 82² (iii/iv A.D.) Διδαροῦ ἀρχιερατεύσαντος τῆς Ἀρσινοιτῶν πόλεως, *OGIS* 485⁴ (Roman—Magnesia) ἀρχιερατεύσαντα καὶ γραμματεύσαντα τῆς πόλεως, *etc.*

ἀρχιερεύς.

P Leid G⁴ (end of ii/B.C.) τοῖς ἐπιστάταις τῶν ἱερ[ῶ]ν καὶ ἀρχιερεῦσι seems to define the term in Egypt, but it had also more special use. P Tebt II. 315³¹ (ii/A.D.) τὸν ἀπιθοῦντα μετὰ φρουρᾶς τῷ ἀρχιερῖ πέμπιν is indeterminate. But in *ib.* 294², according to Wilcken and the editors, the same official, known as ἀρχιερεὺς Ἀλεξανδρείας καὶ Αἰγύπτου πάσης, is addressed as idiologus, "administrator of the Private accounts" (Edd.). *Preisigke* 305⁹ has υἱοῦ Τρήσεως ἀρχιερέως (A.D. 210), in a dedication. *Mi h. I* 1231 (early i/B.C.) Ἀρχιερεὺς μέγ̣ας rededicates to Ζεὺς Ὄλβιος (of Olba in Cilicia) buildings once constructed by Seleucus Nicator : we are reminded of the phrase in Heb 4¹⁴.

Ἀρχιερεύς and ἀρχιερεὺς μέγιστος were the regular terms in the East for translating the title *pontifex maximus*, borne by the Emperors : see *LAE*, p. 369 f., where Deissmann refers to the evidence from the inscriptions collected by Magie, p. 64. A word common in classical and later literature, though only once in the Gk OT, apart from Apocr. (esp. Macc), needs no further illustration. But we may note the form with γ in P Hib I. 62⁸ (B.C. 245) τῷ ἀρχιγερεῖ ἐν Θώλτει (see the editors' note), and the unelided ἀρχιερεύς in P Petr III. 53 (*p.²* (iii/B.C.)

ἀρχιποίμην.

Deissmann (*LAE*, p. 97 ff.) has shown that this NT ἅπ. εἰρ. (1 Pet 5⁴) can no longer be regarded as a Christian invention : it is found on the mummy label of an Egyptian peasant (*Preisigke* 3507), of the Roman period, which runs : Πλῆνις νεώτερος ἀρχιποίμενος (*l.* -μην) ἐβίωσεν ἐτῶν . . . "Plenis, the younger, chief shepherd. Lived . . . years." Cf. P Lips I. 97ˣⁱ·⁴ (A.D. 338) where a list of ποιμένες is headed by Κάμητι ἀρχιποιμένι.

ἀρχισυνάγωγος.

Preisigke 623 (B.C. 80-69) ὧν ἀρχισυνα]γωγὸς καὶ ἀρχιερεὺς [name presumably followed] : the previous mention of θε]ῶν Φιλοπατόρων suffices to show that a "profane" writer uses the term. Thayer's inscriptional and literary quotations had already corrected the implication of Grimm's note.

Cagnat I. 782 (Thrace) τὸν βω[μ]ὸν τῇ συναγω[γ]ῇ τῶν κουρέω[ν] ("collegio tonsorum," Ed.) [π]ερὶ ἀρχισυνά- γ[ωγ]ον Γ. Ἰούλιον [Ο]ὐάλεντα δῶ[ρ]ον ἀποκατέστη[σα]ν : C. Julius Valens is the Master of the Barbers' Company. See further Ziebarth *Vereinswesen*, p. 55 ff. For Jewish exx. see the Alexandrian inscr. of the time of Augustus in *Archiv* ii. p. 430, no. 5* and *C. and B.*, no. 559 (ii. p. 649), ὁ διὰ βίου ἀρχι[συν]άγωγος, with Ramsay's remarks, showing that one Julia Severa (A.D. 60-80), who figures in this Akmonian inscr., was a Jewess with the honorary title of "ruler of the synagogue" : cf. also Ramsay *CRE*, p. 68, and Lake, *Earlier Epistles of S. Paul*, p. 104 n¹.

ἀρχιτέκτων.

The word occurs several times in the correspondence (middle iii/B.C.) of Cleon the architect in P Petr II. (Wit- kowski,² nos. 1-10), *e. g.* 4 (1)¹, 15 (2)². In 42 (*a*)⁶ we read that one Theodorus, who had previously worked under Cleon (Θεόδωρον τὸν ὑπαρχιτέκτονα), was appointed Cleon's successor. For the use of the corresponding verb in the inscriptions, cf. *OGIS* 39² (iii/B.C.) ἀρχιτεκτονήσ[αντα] τὴν τριακοντήρη καὶ εἰκ[οσήρη], *al.* This example shows that the word is wider than our "architect." In P Tebt II. 286¹⁹ (A.D. 121-38) the editors translate ἐ[κ] τῆς τῶν ἀρτεκτόνων (*l.* ἀρχιτ.) πρ[ο]σφωνήσεως, "as the result of the declaration of the chief engineers" with reference to a dispute regarding a house. The RV is of course shown to be right by the context in 1 Cor 3¹⁰. It is worth while to remember that τέκτων in its turn is wider than "carpenter."

Other occurrences of ἀρχιτέκτων will be found in *Syll* 540¹⁶⁰ (ii/B.C.), a long inscription about the building of a temple, where the ἀ. has a ὑπαρχιτέκτων under him ; 545⁶·²⁶, 552²², 588²·⁷, etc. (all ii/B.C.) ; 653⁹⁰ (the Mysteries inscrip- tion from Andania, dated B.C. 91—in dialect) ; 248³ (Delphi, iii/B.C.—dialect) ὁ ἀρχιτέκτων τοῦ ναοῦ, *Cagnat* I. 925 (iii/A.D.) of the designer of a tower, 926 of a well, etc.

ἄρχομαι.

For the participle in a quasi-adverbial position (see *Proleg.*³ p. 240) cf. P Ryl II. 150¹³ (i/A.D.) λιβὸς [δὲ] ὧν κεκλήρων[ται λιβὸς ἐπ᾿ ἀπηλιώ]την ἀρξάμενοι ἀπὸ τῆς λιβικῆς γωνίας τοῦ πύργο[υ, *ib.* 157⁷ (A.D. 135) ἧς ἐστιν σχοινισμὸς [. . . . . . . ἀ]ρχομένου νότου ε[ἰ]ς β[ο]ρρᾶ, "its measurements are . . . beginning from south to north " etc. *Syll* 537⁵ (iv B.C.) σκευοθήκην οἰκοδομῆσαι . . ἀρξάμενον ἀπὸ τοῦ προπυλαίου. P Tebt II. 526 (ii/A.D.) ἀπηλ(ιώτου) ἐχόμ(εναι) ἀρχόμ(εναι) ἀπὸ βορρᾶ Πανκράτης (ἄρουραι) [.] Πρῖσκος (ἄρουραι) β (cited in Moulton, *Einleitung* p. 287). In reply to a suggestion from one of us that the frequent abbreviation of this participle might have occasioned some of the grammatical confusion found in NT passages (*Proleg.* 182, 240), Dr A. S. Hunt wrote (Sept. 1909) that ἀρχόμενος was "commonly abbreviated αρχ in land-survey lists, from Ptolemaic times downwards . . . So it was a stereotyped phrase which might have influenced Lk 24⁴⁷ : at any rate it is an ingenious suggestion."

The ordinary use of ἄρχομαι "begin" hardly needs illustrating. In P Giss I. 15⁵ (ii/A.D.) τῆς ἄλλης ἀρχόμεθα we see it c. gen. : so P Tebt II. 417⁸ (iii/A.D.) πλὴν ἀρξό- μεθ[α] τοῦ ἔργου. The familiar NT use in a quasi-auxiliary sense, by its significant absence from Paul and presence in such abundance in those books where OT language is imitated or Aramaic originals translated, seems to belong to the alien elements in NT Greek: see *Proleg.* p. 14 f. It does not however follow that Luke used it, as Mark seems to do, with no more force than the Middle English *gan*: we may refer to a note by Archdeacon Allen in a forthcoming work on the Gospel of Mark.

The act. ἄρχω "rule" only occurs twice in NT, and is too common in Greek to need quotations. It takes dat. in *Syll* 319[7] (ii/B.C.) οἶς [ἂν ὁ δῆμος ὁ Μηθυμναίων] ἄρχῃ, perhaps under Latin influence (cf. *impero* c. dat.): the recurrent δόλωι πονηρῶι "dolo malo" is suggestive in this regard. For the very common use = "hold office" may be cited P Oxy III. 471[145] (ii/A.D.) ἄρξας δὲ καὶ τὴν τ[ῶν ἐκεῖ] ἀρχιδικαστῶν ἀρ[χ]ὴν ἔτη δέ]κα.

ἄρχων.

The official uses of ἄ. are fully classified by Dittenberger in the index to his *OGIS*, where he cites instances of its application to (1) *summus magistratus*, (2) *praefectus in urbem aut regionem subditam missus*, (3) *magistratus provincialis Romanorum*, and (4) *magistratus quilibet*. To these for the NT we have to add "ruler of a synagogue," which is illustrated, according to de Rossi, in an Italian inscr. of the reign of Claudius, *Cagnat* I. 588 (= *IGSI* 949) Κλαύδιος Ἰωσῆς ἄρχων ἔζησεν ἔτη λε. *Ib.* 1024[21] (i/B.C.?) —the inscr. from Berenice in Cyrenaica cited above under ἀβαρής—ἔδοξε τοῖς ἄρχουσι καὶ τῷ πολιτεύματι τῶν ἐν Βερενίκῃ Ἰουδαίων: a list of these Jewish ἄρχοντες is given at the beginning of the inscr., which is dated at the σκηνο-πηγία. (See Schürer as cited below.) So in P Lond 1177[57] (A.D. 113) (= III. p. 183), in accounts for the water-works of the μητρόπολις (? Hermopolis)—Ἀρχόντων Ἰου]δαίων προσευχῆς Θηβαίων μηνιαίω < ρκη "The rulers of the *proseucha* of Theban Jews 128 drachmae a month" (see further s.v. προσευχή). For Jewish ἄρχοντες generally see Schürer's inscriptional evidence and discussion in *Geschichte* iii. p. 38 ff. (= *HJP* II. ii. p. 243 ff.). In P Lond 1178[60] (A.D. 194) (= III. p. 217) the designation is applied to the "presidents" of an athletic club known as "The Worshipful Gymnastic Society of Nomads" (ἡ ἱερὰ ξυστικὴ περιπολιστικὴ . . . σύνοδος). Miscellaneous references are P Oxy III. 473[2] (A.D. 138–60) of the magistrates of Oxyrhynchus, *ib.* 592 (A.D. 122–3) of Sarapion γενομένῳ πρυτανικῷ ἄρχοντ(ι) ἱερεῖ καὶ ἀρχιδικασῇ, BGU II. 362[v.2] (A.D. 214–5), *ib.* 388[ii.26] (ii/iii A.D.), P Fay 20[22] (iii/iv A.D.) τοῖς καθ' ἑκάστην πόλιν ἄρχουσιν, *Cagnat* I. 118[30] (B.C. 78) ἐάν τε ἐν ταῖς πατρίσιν κατὰ τοὺς ἰδίους νόμους βούλωνται κρίνεσθαι ἢ ἐπὶ τῶν ἡμετέρων ἀρχόντων ἐπὶ Ἰταλικῶν κριτῶν. In P Oxy III. 592 we have a πρυτανικὸς ἄρχων, which Wilcken (*Archiv* iv. p. 118 f.) regards as equivalent to πρύτανις. Note also P Giss I. 19[17] (ii/A.D.), where Aline commends to her husband, a στρατηγός, the example of ὁ ἐ]νθάδε στρατηγός, who τοῖς ἄρχου[σι ἐπιτί]θησι τὸ βάρος: these ἄρχοντες were accordingly subordinates. MGr οἱ ἄρχοντες or ἡ ἀρχοντιά = the local aristocracy.

ἄρωμα.

In *Syll* 939[17] (an undated decree from Arcadia, containing regulations about the mysteries, in strongly dialectic form, and therefore presumably not late) we find μάκων[σ]ι λευκαῖς,

λυχνίοις, θυμιάμασιν, [ζ]μύρναι, ἀρώμασιν all governed by χρέεσθαι (= χρῆσθαι). So *OGIS* 383[141] (i. B.C.) ἐπιθύσεις . . . ἀρωμάτων ἐν βωμοῖς τούτοις ποιείσθω. P Oxy IX. 1211[10] (ii/A.D.) πᾶν ἄρωμα χωρὶς λιβάνου, "every spice except frankincense," in a list of articles for a sacrifice, BGU I. 149[1] (ii/iii A.D.) (= *Chrest.* I. 93) ἰς τιμὴν [τῶν ἀρ]ωμάτων, in temple-accounts, and P Leid W[vi. 16].

For the adj. see P Fay 93[5 al.] (a lease of a perfumery business, A.D. 161) (= *Chrest.* I. 317) βούλομαι μισθώσασθαι παρά σου τὴν μυροπωλαικὴν (*l.* μυροπωλικὴν) καὶ ἀρωματικὴν (*l.* ἀρωματικὴν) ἐργασίαν κτλ. Add the inscription on a seal of the time of the Antonines ἀρωματικῆς τῶν κυρίων Καισάρων, where Rostowzew supplies ὠνῆς after ἀ.: see *Archiv* ii. p. 443, and for the ἀρωματική tax, *ib.* iii. p. 192, iv. p. 313 ff. The verb occurs *Priene* 112[62] (after B.C. 84) ἠρωματισμένον . . . ἔλαιον.

ἀσάλευτος.

For the metaph. use of ἀ. (as Heb 12[28]) cf. *Magn* 116[28 f.] (ii/A.D.) ἀ](σ)άλευτο[ν] καὶ ἀμετάθετον τὴν περὶ τούτων διάταξιν. *Kaibel* 1028[1] (Andros, hymn to Isis, iv/A.D.) στάλαν ἀσάλευτον, *ib.* 855[1] (Locris, Macedonian age) τὰν ἀσάλευτον νίκαν ἀρνύμενος. P Lips I. 34[13] (c. A.D. 375) διὰ τοῦτο δέομαι τῆς οὐρανίου ὑμῶν τύχης ἐπινεῦσαι [β]έβαια καὶ ἀσάλευτα [μέ]νειν τὰ περὶ ταύτης τῆς ὑποθέσεως πεπραγμένα ἐξ ἀντικαθεστώτων [ὑ]πομνη[μά]τω[ν], and similarly *ib.* 35[20]. Add the late Byzantine papyrus P Lond 483[81 f.] (A.D. 616) (= II. p. 328) ἄτρωτα καὶ ἀσάλευτα καὶ ἀπαράβατα, and the eighth century P Lond 77[61] (= I. p. 235) and P Par 21 *bis*[29] where ἀ. is coupled with ἀρραγής. It survives in MGr.

ἀσέβεια.

In P Eleph 23[1 ff.] (B.C. 223–2) we find the characteristic phrase ἔνοχον εἶναι τῆι ἀσεβείαι τοῦ ὅρκου: cf. *Syll* 566[20] (Rhodian dialect, iii/B.C.) ἢ ἔνοχος ἔστω τᾶι ἀσεβείαι (of violating certain taboos concerning a temple—the last of them μηδὲ ὑποδήματα ἐσφερέτω μηδὲ ὕειον μηθέν), and of a much later date *OGIS* 262[15] (iii/A.D.) ἔνοχον εἶναι ἀσεβείᾳ. In *Syll* 100[10] we have ἀ. with a genitive, εἰσ]πηδήσαντας νύκτωρ ἐπ' ἀδικίαι [καὶ] ἀσεβείαι τοῦ ἱεροῦ: King Lysimachus (B.C. 306–281) is decreeing penalties against men who tried to burn a temple. In the "*Apologia pro vita sua*" of Antiochus I, *OGIS* 383[115] (middle of i/B.C.) it is stated that χαλεπὴ νέμεσις βασιλικῶν δαιμόνων τιμωρὸς ὁμοίως ἀμελίας τε καὶ ὕβρεως ἀσέβειαν διώκει, and almost immediately afterwards there is a reference to the toilsome burdens of impiety—τῆς δὲ ἀσεβείας ὀπισθοβαρεῖς ἀνάγκαι.

ἀσεβέω.

OGIS 765[10] (iii/B.C.) τὸ θεῖον ἠσέβουν, with external accus., as in Aeschylus *Eum.* 270: the more regular construction occurs a few lines further down—εἰς τὸ θεῖον ἀσ[ε]-βοῦντα[ς]. So *Syll* 199[4] (see above) τ]οὺς ἀσεβήσαντας εἰς τὸ ἱερόγ, al. A iv/B.C. inscription in Boeotian dialect, *Syll* 120[7] π]οττὰς ἀσεβίοντας τὸ ἱαρό[ν] may be added for the accus. construction, also a late inscription from Lyttus, *Syll* 889[2] τῷ ἀσεβήσαντι τοὺς δαίμονας. The internal accus. appears in *Syll* 887 ἀσεβήσ(ει) τὰ περὶ τοὺς θεούς, as in Jude [15], the only NT occurrence of the verb (according to WH).

ἀσεβής

is found in P Tor 1. 1[iii 8] (B.C. 116) (= *Chrest* II. p. 33) τὴν γεγενημένην μοι καταφθορὰν ὑπὸ ἀσεβῶν ἀνθρώπων, and in the magical P Lond 121[604] (iii/A.D.) (= I. p. 103). It occurs also in *Syll* 789[52] (iv/B.C.) ὅπ]ως ἄ[ν] . . . μ[ηδ]ὲν ἀσεβὲς γένηται, and twice in *OGIS* 90[23, 26] (Rosetta stone, B.C. 196) τοῖς ἐπισυναχθεῖσιν εἰς αὐτὴν ἀσεβέσιν . . . τοὺς ἐν αὐτῆι ἀσεβεῖς πάντας διέφθειρεν of those who had created sedition, involving the majesty of the θεός on the throne, as Dittenberger explains. Several exx. of the adjective in Josephus are put together by Schmidt *Jos.* p. 357. For the adverb, see P Oxy II. 237[vi. 13] (A.D. 186) ἀσεβῶς καὶ παρανόμως.

ἀσέλγεια

appeared in P Magd 24[5] according to the original reading, but has been corrected in the new edition. The adj. appears among a number of technical epithets of ζῴδια in Vettius Valens p. 335[31]—ἢ χερσαία ἢ ἀσελγῆ ἢ λατρευτικὰ καὶ τὰ λοιπά. An obscure and badly-spelt document of iv/v A.D., BGU IV. 1024[v. 17], seems to contain this noun in the form ἀθελγία–ἀλλὰ ˊναντία καὶ ταύτης ὑπὸ σοῦ γενόμενον ἀθελγία ἐλενλέχ[ο]υσα τὰ πεπραγμένα, which the editor understands as = ἀλλ' ἐναντία ταύτῃ ἡ ὑπὸ σοῦ γενομένη ἀθελγία ἐλέγχουσα κτλ. But we mention this passage only to note how early the popular etymology was current connecting it with θέλγω. It is dubious at best, and the history of the word is really unknown; but cf. Havers in *Indogerm. Forschungen* xxviii (1911) p. 194 ff., who, adopting the foregoing etymology, understands ἀσελγής as = "geschlagen," then "wahnsinnig," and then "liebestoll, wollustig." He has not convinced Prof. Thumb. For the idea of sensuality associated with the word in late Greek, see Lightfoot on Gal 5[19].

A cognate noun appears in P Oxy VI. 903[1] (iv/A.D.) πολλὰ ἀσελγήματα λέγων εἰς πρόσωπόν μου καὶ διὰ τῆς ῥινὸς αὐτο[ῦ], "using many terms of abuse to my face, and through his nose" (Edd.). The complainant is a Christian.

ἄσημος

This word occurs perpetually in the papyri to denote a man who is "not distinguished" from his neighbours by the convenient scars on eyebrow or arm or right shin which identify so many individuals in formal documents. Thus in P Oxy I. 73[28 f.] (A.D. 94) a slave is described as μελίχρωτ[α μακρ]οπ[ρ]όσωπον ἄσημον, and similarly in P Fay 28[13 f] (A.D. 150–1) (= *Selections*, p. 82) the parents in giving notice of the birth of a son sign themselves—

Ἰσχυρ]ᾶς (ἐτῶν) μδ ἄσημος
Θαισάριον (ἐτῶν) κδ ἄσημος.

From the fact that in BGU I. 347 (ii/A.D.), an as yet uncircumcised boy is twice described as ἄσημος, Deissmann (*BS* p. 153) conjectures that ἄ. may have been the technical term for "uncircumcised" among the Greek Egyptians, but cites Krebs (*Philologus* liii. p. 586), who interprets it rather as = "free from bodily marks owing to the presence of which circumcision was forborne": cf. Preisigke 16[15] (A.D. 155–6), where formal enquiry is made as to a priest's sons, εἴ τινα σημεῖ[α ἔχουσιν, and leave for circumcision is

apparently given if these signs are not conspicuous (Wilcken *Archiv* v. p. 435 f.).

In BGU I. 22[32] (A.D. 114) (= *Selections*, p. 76) a pair of silver bracelets are described as of ἀσήμου "unstamped" silver, and the same epithet is applied to a δακτυριτριω, apparently some kind of a ring, in P Lond 193 *verso*[4] (ii/A.D.) (= II. p. 245). So *Syll* 586[72] (early iv/B.C., Athens) ἀργύριον σύμμεικτον ἄσημον, weighing so much, followed by χρυσίον ἄσημον, so much. The word became technical in commerce, so that Middle Persian borrowed it as *asīm* "silver" (P. Horn, in *Grundriss d. iran. Philol.* I. ii. p. 20). So MGr ἀσήμι, with the same meaning.

The only NT instance of ἄσημος is in Ac 21[39] (cf. 3 Macc 1[3]), where it = "undistinguished, obscure," as sometimes in classical writers, as Euripides *Ion* 8, οὐκ ἄσημος Ἑλλήνων πόλις (i. e. Athens). Cf. *Chrest* I. 14[iii 10] (p. 27—c. A.D. 200) ἐγὼ μὲν οὐκ εἰμι δοῦλος οὐδὲ μουσικῆς [υἱ]ός, ἀλλὰ διασήμου πόλεως [Ἀ]λεξαν[δρ]εί[ας] γυμνασίαρχος. For the evidence that Tarsus was "no mean city" see Ramsay, *Cities*, p. 85 ff., and more recently Böhlig, *Die Geisteskultur von Tarsos im augusteischen Zeitalter* (Göttingen, 1913). The adj. is applied to a ship in P Lond 948[2] (A.D. 236) (= III. p. 220), "without a figurehead" (παράσημος—*q.v.*).

ἀσθένεια

P Ryl II. 153[45] (A.D. 138–61) I have directed Eudaemon γράψαι ὑπὲρ ἐμο[ῦ] τῆς ὑπογραφῆς τὸ σῶμα διὰ τὴν περὶ ἐμὲ ἀσθένιαν. BGU I. 220[3] (ii/iii A.D.) illustrates the practice of consulting the local oracle in times of difficulty or sickness —ἢ μὲν σοθήσωμαι (= εἰ μὲν σωθήσομαι) ταύτης, ἧς (? for τῆς, or an extreme case of attraction) ἐν ἐμοὶ ἀσθενίας, τοῦτόν μοι ἐξένικον (= τοῦτό μοι ἐξένεγκον). P Lond 971[4] (iii/iv A.D.) (= III. p. 128) ἀδύνατος γάρ ἐστιν ἡ γυνὴ διὰ ἀσθένιαν τῆς φύσε[ω]ς. P Flor I. 51[5] (A.D. 138–61) σ]ωματικῆς ἀσθ ενεί]ας, in an incomplete context. The prepositional phrase of Gal 4[13] may be further illustrated by P Oxy IV. 726[10] (A.D. 135) οὐ δυνάμενος δι' ἀ[σ]θένειαν πλεῦσαι. Add BGU IV. 1109[11] (B.C. 5) τῆς Καλλιτύχης ἐν ἀσθενείᾳ διατεθείσης, and *OGIS* 244[10] (iii/B.C.) τὴν περὶ τὸ σῶμα [γε]γενημένην ἀσθένειαν διὰ τὰς συνεχεῖς κακο[π]αθίας, where the editor notes that there is no tautology, as κακοπαθία is to be understood in its later sense of laborious and troublesome work.

ἀσθενέω

is too common to need many citations. There is a pathetically laconic Ἀσθενῶ between some household details and concluding salutations in an undated letter, BGU III. 827[24]. P Oxy IV. 725[40] (A.D. 183) is typical: a boy apprenticed to a weaver is to have 20 holidays a year for festivals, without loss of wages, ἐὰν δὲ πλείονας τούτων ἀργήσῃ [ἢ ἀσ]θενήσῃ ἢ ἀτακτήσῃ κτλ, "from idleness or ill-health or disobedience" (Edd.), they must be made up. With the use of the verb in Mt 10[8] may be compared *Syll* 503[16] where a certain man is extolled because, in addition to other benefactions, παρέσχεν ἰατ]ρὸν τὸν θεραπεύσοντ[α τοὺς ἀσθε]νοῦντας ἐν τῇ[ι] παν[ηγύρει. See also P Par 5[3. 5] (B.C. 114) ἀσθενῶν τοῖς ὄμμασι (so also P Leid M[b. 6]), *ib.* 63[iv. 122] (B.C. 165) κατὰ τῶν ἀσθενούντων καὶ μὴ δυναμένων ὑπουργεῖν, BGU III. 844[12] (A.D. 83) κόπους γάρ μο[ι] παρέχει ἀσθενοῦντει. In

P Lond 144 (? i/A.D.) (=II. p. 253) a servant complains that he had been without food (**ἀσειτήσαντος** for two days, as the boy who brought his provisions "was sick," **ἀσθενήσαντος**: cf. P Lond 22⁹ (B.C. 164-3) (=I. p. 7) where **ἀσθενῶς διακειμένας** is used to describe the "sorry plight" of the twins in the Serapeum owing to the withholding of their allowances of oil and bread. In *Proleg.* p. 11 the very vernacular letter BGU III. 948⁷ (Christian, iv/v A.D.) is quoted for its closeness to Lk 13¹⁶: **ἡ μήτηρ σου Κ. ἀσθενῖ, εἰδοῦ, δέκα τρῖς μῆνες.** (See under **ἰδού.**) **Ἠσθένηκα** is answered by **ἐὰν κομψῶς σχῶ** in P Tebt II. 414¹⁰ (ii/A.D.). The compound **ἐξασθενέω** is found in BGU III. 903¹⁵ (ii/A.D.) as now amended, **τοὺς πλείστους ἐξασθενήσαντας ἀνακεχωρηκέναι κτλ.**: cf. also P Tebt I. 50⁶³ (B.C. 112-1), where for **ἐξησθενηκώς** the editors hesitate between the meanings "was impoverished" or "fell ill." Add PSI 101¹¹ (ii/A.D.) **οὕσπερ ἐξασθενήσαντας ἀνακεχωρηκέναι**: the last three substantial men of the village had emigrated because they could not stand the taxation.

ἀσθένημα.

BGU III. 903¹⁵ (ii/A.D.) was formerly read **ἐξ ἀσθενήματος**, but see the last article. The noun is warranted by Aristotle: Paul has developed the sense in his own way.

ἀσθενής.

P Amh II. 78¹¹ (A.D. 184) **μ[ου] πλεονεκτῖ ἄνθρωπος ἀ[σ]θενής** (for -ου -ούς!), *ib.* 141¹⁵ (A.D. 350) **οὐ δυναμένη ἀφησυχάσαι γυνὴ [ἀσθε]νὴς καὶ χήρα κτλ.** P Flor I. 58¹⁴ (iii/A.D.) **καταφρονο῀υντές μου ὡς γυναικὸς ἀσ[θ]ε[νο]ῦς.** P Thead 20¹·¹⁵ (iv/A.D.) **τὰς ἀσθενεστέρας κώμα[ς]**, "weaker" financially. For the adv. see OGIS 751⁸ (ii/B.C.) **ἐπεὶ θλιβέντες ἐμ πλείοσιν ἀσθενῶς [σχή]σετε.** The definitely moral character of the adj. in Rom and 1 Cor may be illustrated by Epict. *Diss.* i. 8. 8, where the **ἀσθενεῖς** are coupled with the **ἀπαίδευτοι.** The adj. is curiously rare by comparison with its derivative verb and noun.

Ἀσιάρχης.

For inscriptional light on the meaning of this term it will be enough to refer to the archaeologists: see esp. Ramsay's bibliography in his art. *sub voce* in Hastings *DB.*

ἀσιτία.

We can only add to the literary record the late P Ryl I. 16⁶ (cf. ¹²), a hagiographical fragment of vi/A.D., containing a discourse by a saint condemned to death by starvation—**δι' ὃν τὴν ἀσιτίαν κατεκρίθην.** See next article.

ἄσιτος.

We can illustrate the derived verb from the curious letter quoted under **ἀσθενέω**, where the context points clearly to absence of food, and not abstinence therefrom—P Lond 144³·⁷· (i/A.D.?) (=II. p. 253) **νωθρευσαμένου μου καὶ ἀσειτήσαντος ἡμέρας δύο ὥστε με μετὰ τῶν νομάρχων μηδὲ συνδιπνῆσαι.** The editor conjectures that the writer may have been in the desert, and that the nomarchs with whom he "did not even dine" were the officials who superintended the transport of goods from one village to another. The vernacular evidence therefore does not go far to decide the much discussed significance of the subst. in Ac 27²¹. And,

on the whole, in view of the undoubted use of **ἀσιτία** in medical phraseology to denote "loss of appetite" from illness (as Hipp. *Morb.* 454 **τήκεται ὁ ἀσθενῶν ὑπὸ ὀδυνέων ἰσχυρῶν καὶ ἀσιτίης καὶ βηχός**: other exx. in Hobart, *Medical Language of St. Luke*, p. 276, it seems best to understand it so here, and to think of Paul's companions as abstaining from food owing to their physical and mental state, and not because no food was forthcoming. See further Knowling in *EGT ad l.*, and the note by J. R. Madan in *JTS* vi. p. 116 ff.

ἀσκέω.

P Par 63⁸·²⁴ (ii/B.C.) **ε[ὐ]σέβειαν ἀσκήσαντα.** Lewy (*Fremdwörter*, p. 131) notes the use in the Hebrew Mishna and Aramaic Targum of עסק 'āsaq = "sich mit etwas beschäftigen, Mühe geben, sich befleissigen."

ἀσκός.

P Lond 402 *verso*¹⁰ (B.C. 152 or 141) (=II. p. 11) **ἀσκός** = "leathern bag or bottle." The word is used in the general sense "hide" or "skin" in P Fay 121⁹ (c. A.D. 100) where a new and strong yoke-band is to be selected **ἐκ τῶν ἐν τῆι κειβωτῶι τῶν ἀσκῶν**, "from those in the box of skins." Add OGIS 629⁴⁵ (ii/A.D.) **ἐν ἀσκοῖς] αἰγείοις.** Cagnat III. 1056ⁱⁱⁱ·⁴⁶ (Palmyra, Trajan's reign) **τοῦ ἐν] ἀ[σ]κοῖς δυσὶ αἰγείοις ἐπὶ κ[αμήλου εἰσ]κομισθέντος**: cf. above, ²⁶·³⁰, where the tax is defined on a load of **μύρον, ἐ[ν ἀλαβασ]τροῖς** and one **ἐν ἀσκοῖς] αἰγείοις** respectively— the supplements come from the Latin. Cf. MGr **ἀσκί** (Zaconian *aská*).

ἀσμένος.

P Grenf II. 14 (a)¹²ᵗ (iii/B.C.) **ἀξμένως [ἂν συ]νέταξεν τὸ παρ' αὐτῶι ἀποδοῦναι**, Syll 329⁵² (i B.C.) **ἀσμένως καὶ ἑκουσίως**, Magn 17⁴¹ **ἄσμενος ὑπήκουσεν Λ εὔκιππος.**

ἄσοφος.

occurs in P Ryl II. 62¹² (iii/A.D.), a translation of an unknown Latin literary work: **δύναμαι χαρίσασθαι καὶ πένητι [πλοῦ]τον καὶ ἄσοφον ἀρετῆς στεφανῶσαι**—"unskilled in wisdom," unless we should drop one s and read **ἀρετῃ** "crown with virtue."

ἀσπάζομαι.

The papyri have shown conclusively that this common NT word was the regular *term. tech.* for conveying the greetings at the end of a letter. Examples are BGU IV. 1079⁸ᶠᶠ (A.D. 41) (=*Selections*, p. 40) **ἀσπάζου Διόδωρον μ[ετ'] ἄλων** (*l.* ἄλλων) ... **ἀσπάζου Ἁρποχράτη[ν]**, *ib.* II. 423¹⁸ᶠᶠ (ii/A.D.) (=*Selections*, p. 91) **ἄσπασαι Καπίτων[α πο]λλὰ καὶ το[ὺ]ς ἀδελφούς [μ]ου καὶ Σε[ρῆνι]λλαν καὶ το[ὺ]ς φίλους [μ]ου**, etc. As showing how much the absence of these greetings was felt, we may quote P Giss I. 78⁷ (ii/A.D.) **ἡ μικρά μου Ἡραιδ[ο]ῦς γράφουσα τῶι πατρὶ ἐμὲ οὐκ ἀσπάζεται κ[α]ὶ διὰ τί οὐκ οἶδα**, and P Grenf I. 53⁸ᶠᶠ (iv A.D.) **Ἀλλοῖς πολλά σοι ἀπειλ(εῖ), ἐπὶ γὰρ πολλάκις γράψας καὶ πάντας ἀσπασάμενος αὐτὴν μόνον οὐκ ἠσπάσου.** The use of the 1st pers. **ἀσπάζομαι** by Tertius in Rom 16²¹, the only ex. of this exact formula in the NT, may be paralleled from P Oxy VII. 1067²⁵ (iii/A.D.) where to a letter from a certain Helene to her brother, their father Alexander adds the post-script—**κἀγὼ Ἀλέξανδρος ὁ π[α]τὴρ ὑμῶν ἀσπάζομαι ὑμᾶς** πολλά. (As there is no change of hand, both Helene and her father would seem to have employed an amanuensis: see the editor's note). When several persons are included in a greeting, the phrase κατ' ὄνομα often occurs (as in 3 Jn¹⁵) e. g. BGU I. 276²⁵ᶠ· (ii/iii A.D.) ἀσπάζομαι ὑμᾶς πάντες κατ' ὄνομ α, καὶ Ὡριγ[έ]νης ὑμᾶς ἀσπάζεται πάντες, P Oxy III. 533²⁷ᶠ· (ii/iii A.D.) ἀσπάσασθε τὸν μεικρὸν Σερῆνον καὶ Κοπρέα καὶ το[ὺ]ς ἡμῶν πάντας κατ' ὄνομα. Add P Fay 118²³ (A.D. 110) ἀσπάζου τοὺς φιλοῦντές σε πάντες πρὸς ἀλήθιαν (cf. 2 Jn¹, 3 Jn¹) and the Christian Psenosiris letter P Grenf II. 73⁴ᶠᶠ· (late iii/A.D.) (= Selections, p. 117) where immediately after the address we find πρὸ τῶν ὅλων πολλά σε ἀσπάζομαι καὶ τοὺς παρὰ σοὶ πάντας ἀδελφοὺς ἐν Θ(ε)ῷ.

For ἀ. = "pay one's respects to," as in Ac 25¹³, see BGU I. 376ⁱ·³ (A.D. 171) ἠσπάσατο τὸν λαμπρότατον ἡγ[εμό]να, and ib. 248¹² (ii/A.D.) θεῶν δὲ βουλομένων πάν[τ]ως μετὰ τὰ Σουχεῖα σὲ ἀσπάσομαι (cited by Deissmann, BS p. 257), and from the inscriptions OGIS 219⁴³ (iii/B.C.) ἀσπασάμενοι αὐτὸν παρὰ τ[οῦ δήμου]. Syll 318⁴¹ (B.C. 118) a deputation is sent οἵτινες πορευθέντες πρὸς αὐτὸν καὶ ἀσπασάμενοι παρὰ τῆς πόλεως καὶ συνχαρέντες ἐπὶ τῶι ὑγιαίνειν αὐτόν τε καὶ τὸ στρατόπεδον κτλ.

ἀσπασμός.

P Oxy III. 471⁶⁷ (ii/A.D.) μαρτύρονται κύριε τὴν σὴν τύχην [εἰ] μὴν ἀναμενόντων αὐτῶν (corr. from ἡμῶν) τὸν ἀσπασμόν[. . . The noun is curiously rare: the above is apparently its only occurrence in P Oxy I.–X., nor have we noticed any other instance of it in the ordinary papyrus collections.

ἄσπιλος.

Hort's remark on Jas 1²⁷ that "this is quite a late word, apparently not extant before NT" must be corrected in view of the fact that it is found already in IG II. v. 1054 c.⁴ (Eleusis, c. B.C. 300), where it is applied to stones—ὑγιεῖς λευκοὺς ἀσπίλους: cf. also Symm. Job 15¹⁵. For its use in the magic papyri see P Leid V viii. 11 ff. (as amended by Dieterich) ἐπίδος φοροῦντί μοι τήνδε τὴν δύναμιν ἐν παντὶ τόπῳ ἐν παντὶ χρόνῳ ἄπληκτον, ἀκαταπόνητον, ἄσπιλον ἀπὸ παντὸς κινδύνου τηρηθῆναι, ib. W ix ²⁶ᶠ· θῦε δὲ λυκὸν (l. λευκὸν) ἀλέκτορα, ἄσπελλον (l. ἄσπιλον). A deacon's litany of viii/ix A.D., P Grenf II. 113, commemorating the Virgin, is headed—[Περὶ τῆ]ς πρεσβείας καὶ ἱκετείας τῆς ἀσπίλου [δεσποίντ]ς τῶν ἀπάντων.

ἀσπίς.

In OGIS 90⁴³ (Rosetta stone—B.C. 196) ἀσπίς is used of the "asp" or "serpent" with which the golden βασιλεῖαι of the King were adorned—αἷς προσκείσεται ἀσπίς. see Dittenberger's note, and cf. τῶν ἀσπιδοειδῶν βασιλειῶν in the following line.

The etymology of the word is very obscure, but Lewy (Fremdwörter, p. 13) thinks that it may have been formed from the Heb פֶתֶן under the influence of ἀσπίς, "shield." Boisacq records this guess with a query, which Thumb endorses.

ἄσπονδος.

Priene has the combination ἀσυλεὶ καὶ ἀσπονδεὶ seven times, in the common sense "without formal treaty"—the

reverse of the meaning applied metaphorically in 2 Tim 3³: friends need no treaty, and implacable foes will not make one. Literary parallels suffice for the Pauline use.

ἀσσάριον.

The ordinary value of the ἀσσάριον was ¹⁄₁₆ of the δηνάριον, but Dittenberger OGIS ii. p. 108 n. ¹⁴ shows that the imperial silver denarius might be exchanged for 17 or even 22 provincial copper asses. The word can be quoted from Syll 869⁵ (Calymna, Rom.) ἐὰν δὲ μὴ [παραμείνῃ] (sc. the slave whose manumission is in question), ἀποδώσει ἑκάστης ἡμέρας ἀσσάρι(α) δ, ib. 871⁶ (Smyrna)—a decree regarding a Trust which had reduced a ferry fare from two obols to two ἀσσάρια, or ¼ denarius to ⅕ den. so as to undercut competitors (Dittenberger). Other instances are needless.

ἀστατέω.

In Isai 58⁷ Aquila substitutes ἀστατοῦντας for LXX ἀστέγους, while in Gen 4¹² Symmachus translates נָע וָנָד "a fugitive and a vagabond" by ἀνάστατος καὶ ἀκατάστατος. There would seem therefore to be a certain degree of "unsettlement" associated with the word; and accordingly Field (Notes, p. 170) proposes to render 1 Cor 4¹¹ καὶ ἀστατοῦμεν by "and are vagabonds," or "and lead a vagabond life." Grimm gives no profane warrant but a passage in the Anthology. We can add Vettius Valens, p. 116³⁹: the entrance of Mercury into a certain horoscope will produce πρακτικοὶ . . . καὶ εὐεπίβολοι καὶ φρόνιμοι καὶ ἐπαφρόδιτοι, πολύκοιτοι δὲ καὶ ἐπὶ πολὺ ἀστατοῦντες περὶ τοὺς γάμους, "very inconstant." He has the adj. p. 57⁶ ἄστατος καὶ ἐπίφοβος διάξει "he will live an unsettled life and liable to panic." It occurs also in Epicurus 65¹⁰ τὴν δὲ τύχην ἄστατον ὁρᾶν (Linde Epic. p. 36, where literary parallels are given).

ἀστεῖος.

As early as P Hib I. 54¹⁵ᶠᶠ· (c. B.C. 245) we find this word developed: ἐχέτω δὲ καὶ ἱματισμὸν ὡς ἀστειότατον, "let him wear as fine clothes as possible" (Edd.): cf. LXX Exod 2², Judith 11²³, and differently Judg 3¹⁷. Its connexion with the "city" was forgotten, and indeed ἄστυ itself had fallen out of common use (still in P Hal 1 ter (iii/B.C.)). By the Stoics it seems to have been used in a sense almost = σπουδαῖος. The noun ἀστειότης occurs in Vettius Valens, p. 101¹⁷, among τὰ σωματικὰ εὐημερήματα, the others being εὐμορφία, ἐπαφροδισία, μέγεθος, εὐρυθμία. The adj. means "witty" in MGr.

ἀστήρ.

Syll 140¹¹¹ (late iv/B.C.), a list of payments on account of the temple at Delphi, has το[ῦ ξ]υλ[ί]νου ἀστέρος τοῦ παρδείγματος "the pattern of the wooden star": see note. In OGIS 194¹⁹ (i/B.C.) it is said of the Egyptian Amon Ra that ὥσπερ λαμπρὸς ἀστὴρ καὶ δαίμων ἀγαθ[ὸς τοῖς ἀπελπί]ζουσι]ν ἐπέλαμψε. The use made of the same figure in the Apocalypse undoubtedly suggested the fourth century epitaph which Ramsay (Luke, p. 366) discovered on a stone now built into the wall of an early Turkish Khan in Lycaonia—

Νεστόριος πρεσβύτερος ἐνθάδε κῖτε
ἀστὴρ ὃς ἐνέλαμπεν ἐν ἐκλησίεσιν θεοῦ.

"Nestorius, presbyter, lies here, who shone a star among the Churches of God." One might suspect the ultimate origin of the phrase in Plato's exquisite epitaph on his friend Aster—

> Ἀστὴρ πρὶν μὲν ἔλαμπες ἐνὶ ζωοῖσιν ἑῷος,
> νῦν δὲ θανὼν λάμπεις ἕσπερος ἐν φθιμένοις.

Other instances of ἀστήρ are P Petr III. 134² (an astronomical fragment relating to the 36 decans presiding over the ten days' periods), P Par 1 (Eudoxus treatise, ii/B.C.) in the opening acrostic ¹⁰ χρόνος διοικῶν ἀστέρων γνωρίσματα, P Leid Wxiii.¹¹ τῶν ζ ἀστέρων (magic), ib. Vxiii.²⁹ ἀστὴρ ἀπὸ κεφαλῆς, etc. But we cannot quote it from papyri outside those on astrological or astronomical subjects and magic. It survives, however, in MGr ἀστέρας.

ἀστήρικτος.

Mayor (on 2 Pet 2¹⁴) cites Longinus ii. 2, ἀστήρικτα καὶ ἀνερμάτιστα "unstable and unballasted (Roberts): this should be added to Grimm's Anthology citation. We do not trouble much about vernacular warrant for words in 2 Pet. It occurs six times in Vettius Valens, in the phrase ἀ. λογισμοῦ "unstable in judgement."

ἄστοργος.

Kaibel 146⁶ (iii/iv A.D.) ἀστόργου μοῖρα κίχεν θανάτου: the epitaph is among the Elgin marbles. In ib. 1028¹⁴ (Andros, hymn to Isis, iv/A.D.), it means "amorem non expertus." Στοργή is found in Chrest. II. 361⁹ (A.D. 360) εὐνοίας καὶ στοργῆς ἔτι τε καὶ ὑπηρεσίας.

ἀστοχέω.

In the NT confined to the Pastorals, but quotable from iii/B.C. Thus Syll 239³ (B.C. 214) εἴπερ οὖν ἐγεγόνει τοῦτο, ἠστοχήκεισαν οἱ συνβουλεύσαντες ὑμῖν καὶ τοῦ συμφέροντος τῆι πατρίδι καὶ τῆς ἐμῆς κρίσεως, and P Par 35²⁶ (B.C. 163) ἀστοχήσαντες τοῦ καλῶς ἔχοντος—a close parallel to 1 Tim 1⁶. (For the gen. constr. cf. also Sir 7¹⁹.) From a later date we may quote the ill-spelt BGU II. 531ii.¹⁹ (ii/A.D.) ἐὰν δὲ ἀστοχήσῃς [αἰω]νίαν μοι λοίπην (l. λύπην [π]αρέχειν μέλλις, where the meaning seems to be "fail" or "forget." This the verb retains in MGr: so the Klepht ballad in Abbott's Songs, p. 34.

> Μὴν ἀστοχῇς τὴν ὁρμηνεία, τῆς γυναικὸς τὰ λόγια.
> Forget not thy wife's advice, forget not her words.

From the literary side we may quote P Oxy II. 219 (a)²¹ (i/A.D.), where in extravagant terms a man bewails the loss of a pet fighting-cock, ψυχομαχῶν, ὁ γὰρ ἀ[λ]έκτωρ ἠστόχηκε, "I am distraught, for my cock has failed me" (Edd.), and the adverb in the philosophical P Fay 337 (ii/A.D.) δεῖ τῶν [ἀν]θρώπων ἄρχειν [τῶν] πράξεων ἐκεί[νου]ς δὲ εὐθὺς ἐφέπεσθαι, οὐκ ἀτάκτως μέντοι ἀλλ᾽ εἱμα[ρ]μέ[νως]. τοῦ γὰρ ἀστόχως[. . .

ἀστραπή.

We can only cite the magical P Lond 121⁷⁸⁵ (iii/A.D.) (= I. p. 109). It is MGr.

ἀστράπτω.

The MGr ἀστράφτει, "it lightens," reinforces the literary record. The word was vernacular, though, as in the case of the noun, we know of no exx. except in the magic papyri,

P Lond 46¹⁵⁰ (iv/A.D.) (= I. p. 70) ἐγώ εἰμι ὁ ἀστράπτων: so ib. 121²³¹ (iii A.D.) and 122⁹² (iv/A.D.) (= I. pp. 92, 119).

ἄστρον.

In P Hib I. 27⁴¹ ff. (a calendar, B.C. 301-240) χρῶντ[αι] ταῖς κατὰ σελήνη[ν] ἡμέραις οἱ ἀστρολό[γοι] καὶ οἱ ἱερογραμματε[ῖς] πρὸς τὰς δόσεις καὶ ἀ[να]τολὰς τῶν ἄστρω[ν], "the astronomers and sacred scribes use the lunar days for the settings and risings of the stars" (Edd.): cf. ⁵⁰ f. οὐθὲν πα[ραλ]λάσσοντες ἐπ᾽ ἄστρω[ι] ἢ δύνοντι ἢ ἀνατ[ελ]λοντι, "without alterations owing to the setting or rising of a star" ib.). From the Adrumetum tablet (Wünsch AF, no. 5²³), on which Deissmann has written in BS, pp. 271 ff., we may quote ὁρκίζω σε τὸν φωστῆρα καὶ ἄστρα ἐν οὐρανῷ ποιήσαντα διὰ φωνῆς προστάγματος. Deissmann compared Gen 1¹⁶ f.; since there we have ἀστέρας, the substitution of ἄστρα suggests the suspicion that the simpler 2nd decl. noun was beginning to be preferred in the vernacular. (Both, however, figure in MGr, and ἀστήρ is more often found in NT.) Add P Grenf. I. 1⁶ (literary - ii/B.C.). ἄστρα φίλα καὶ συνερῶσα πότνια νύξ μοι, P Oxy IV. 731⁶ (A.D. 8-9) καὶ τοῖς ἄστροις Ἥρας τρίς, "three days at the time of the stars of Hera" (Edd., who note that the "star of Hera" was Venus, but the plural is unexplained), Syll 686²⁵ (early ii/A.D.) μέχρι νυκτός, ὡς ἄστρα καταλαβεῖν, διεκαρτέρησε, of a competitor in the pancration, OGIS 56³⁶ (B.C. 239-8), τὸ ἄστρον τὸ τῆς Ἴσιος, i.e. Sirius, the date of whose heliacal rising is defined in the succeeding lines. This last passage agrees with the NT in making ἄστρον a complete equivalent of ἀστήρ. It is MGr ἄστρο.

Ἀσύγκριτος.

This proper name is by no means peculiar to Rome (Rom 16¹⁴), though as yet it has not been very widely attested: see, however CIL VI. 12505 (Rome), IX. 114 (Brundisium), IX. 224 (Uria). and perhaps IG III. 1093 b⁵ (Attica) Ἀ]σύγκρ[ιτος]: cf. Rouffiac, p. 90 f., following Lietzmann (HZNT ad l.). For the adj. from which it is derived cf. BGU II. 613²⁰ (ii/A.D.) ἐκ τῆς ἀσυνκρίτ(ου) ἐπιστροφῆς, and one of the letters in the Abinnaeus correspondence, P Gen I. 55⁴ ff. (iv/A.D.) ἔσπευσα προσαγορεῦσέ σου τὴν ἀμίμητον καλοκαγαθίαν ὡς ἀληθὼς ἀσύνκριτον ἐπίπαν, P Oxy X. 1298² (iv/A.D.. Christian) τῷ δεσπότῃ καὶ ἀσυνκρίτῳ καὶ παραμυθίᾳ τῶν φίλων, "to my incomparable master, the consolation of his friends" (Edd.).

ἀσύμφωνος.

Vettius Valens has it often as a term. tech., e. g. p. 38¹⁵ Κρόνος μὲν οὖν καὶ Ἥλιος ἀσύμφωνοι.

ἀσύνετος.

P Oxy III. 471⁶⁹ (ii/A.D.), ἣν δὲ οὐκ ἀσύνετον, "and he was not stupid." Kaibel 225³ (near Ephesus) ἀξυνέτων δὲ βουλαῖς ἀνθρώπων τοῦδε ἔτυχον θανάτου; it seems clear that "foolish" here does not primarily denote lack of brains but moral obliquity.

ἀσύνθετος.

To other citations for the meaning "faithless" appearing in the derivative verb may be added three from Ptolemaic papyri for εὐσυνθετέω, "to keep faith"—P Petr II. 9 (2)[2] (B.C. 241-39), εὐσυνθετῆσαι αὐτοῖς, P Tebt I. 61 (a)[32] (B.C. 118-7), διὰ τὸ μὴ εὐσυνθετηκέναι ἐν τῆι διορθώσ[ε]ι τοῦ ἐπιβληθέντ[ος α]ὐτῶι στεφάνου, and similarly ib. 64 (a)[113] (B.C. 116-5). Add a British Museum papyrus quoted in *Archiv* vi. p. 101 (A.D. 114-5) τῶν β[ι]βλίων . . . ἐπαλλήλ[ων] κα[ὶ] ἀσυνθέτων διὰ τὸ πλῆθος κειμένων, which can only mean that these records were "closely packed together and not in order"—a meaning which follows well from that of συντίθημι, but does not seem to occur elsewhere.

ἀσφάλεια.

P Amh II. 78[16] (A.D. 184) ἀσφάλιαν γ[ρ]απτήν, "written security," P Tebt II. 293[19] (c. A.D. 187) τὰς παρατεθείσας ὑπὸ αὐτο ῦ [ἀσ]φα[λ]είας, "the proofs submitted by him" (Edd.), P Flor I. 25[28] (ii/A.D.), κατ' ἐ]νγράπτους ἀσφαλίας. In the inscriptions the word is very common united with ἀσυλία, ἀτέλεια, etc., e.g. OGIS 81[16] (iii/B.C.) ἀσφάλε[ιαν καὶ ἀ]συλίαν: cf. 270[11] (iii/B.C.), 352[60] (ii/B.C.). In ib. 669[10] (i/A.D.) we find τῶν θεῶν ταμιευσαμένων εἰς τοῦτον τὸν ἱερώτατον καιρὸν τὴν τῆς οἰκουμένης ἀσφάλειαν. As this illustrates the use of ἀ. found in 1 Th 5[3], so is that of Lk 1[4] paralleled by the papyrus instances cited above. The noun occurs innumerable times in the commercial sense, "a security." In P Tebt II. 407[10] (A.D. 199?) αἱ ὠναὶ καὶ ἀσφάλειαι is rendered "the contracts and title-deeds." For the phrase of Ac 5[23] cf. *Syll* 246[30], ὅπως μετὰ πάσης ἀσφαλε[ίας] συντελεσθεῖ (sc. ἡ τῶν μυστηρίων τελετή). For the idea of "security" against attack from outside cf. C. and B. 559[9] (ii. p. 650) ἐποίησαν τὴν τῶν θυρίδων ἀσφάλειαν καὶ τὸν λυπὸν πάντα κόσμον: the date is A.D. 60-80. Cf. P Fay 107[11] (A.D. 133) τοὺς φανέντας αἰτίους ἔχιν ἐν ἀσφαλείᾳ, "to keep the persons found guilty in a safe place" (Edd.). Personal "safety" comes in *Syll* 192[56] (B.C. 290-87) τὴν τοῦ ἑαυτοῦ σώματος ἀσφάλειαν. The word is MGr.

ἀσφαλής.

BGU III. 909[24] (A.D. 359) ἐν ἀσφαλεῖ παρὰ σε[αυ]τ[ῷ] αὐτοὺς τούτους ἔχιν. P Oxy III. 530[21] (ii/A.D.) ἀποδοῦσα οὖν αὐτῶι ἀπολήμψῃ τὰ ἱμάτια ὑγῆ καὶ ἐν ἀσφαλεῖ ποιήσῃς. "get my clothes back safe, and put them in a secure place" (Edd.), ib. 433[9] (ii/iii A.D.) ἐν ἀσφαλεῖ [ἥ]τω. *Priene* 114[10] (i/B.C.) τὴν] δὲ πίστιν καὶ φυλ[ακὴν] τῶν παραδοθέντων αὐτῶι γραμμάτων ἐποι[ήσ]ατο ἀσφαλῆ. Ib. 118[8] (i/B.C.) ἀσφαλέστατα πρὸς πάντα τὸν χρόνον γενηθῆναι τὰ βραβεῖα. For the adverb, cf. P Giss I. 19[14] (ii/A.D.) παρα]καλῶ σε οὖν ἀσφαλῶς σεαυτὸν [τηρεῖν *vel sim.*). P Hib I. 53[3] (B.C. 246) ἀσφαλῶς διεγγυᾶν, "to get good security," P Oxy IV. 742[5 f] (B.C. 2) θ[ὲ]ς αὐτὰς εἰς τόπον ἀσφαλῶς, "set them (sc. bundles of reeds) in a safe place." The word was common.

ἀσφαλίζομαι.

For the physical meaning of this very common verb, the only meaning which occurs in NT, may be quoted P Ryl II. 68[19] (B.C. 89) ὅπως ἀναχθεῖσα ἡ Τ. ἀσφαλισθῆι μέχρι τοῦ κτλ, "be brought up and secured until . . ." (Ed.), P Tebt II. 283[19] (i/B.C.) τὸν προγεγραμμένον Π. ἀσφαλίσασθαι, "to secure (arrest) the aforesaid P.," ib. I. 53[29] (B.C. 110)

ἀσφαλίσασθαι τὰ γενή[ματα), "seize the produce" (Edd.). Ib. II. 407[1] (A.D. 199?) ἀσφαλιζόμενος τὰ μέλλ[ο]ντα πρὸς ἐμ[ὲ ἐλθεῖν ὑπάρχο]ντα, "securing the property coming to me" (Edd.) has the commoner applied sense: cf. also P Oxy VII. 1033[19] (A.D. 392) διὰ τοῦτο ἑαυτοὺς ἀσφαλιζόμενοι τούσδε τοὺς λιβέλλους ἐπιδίδομεν, "therefore to safeguard ourselves we present this petition" (Ed.), P Lips I. 106[10 ff.] (A.D. 98) ἐὰν οὖν ὅ γε γνώστης σὺν τῷ μετόχῳ ἀσφαλίζηταί σε διὰ τοῦ γράμματος (l. -τος) τῶν γεωργῶ(ν). Add P Ryl II. 77[40] (A.D. 192) αὐτὰ ταῦτα ἀσφαλίσομαι κτλ., "I will certify these very facts by means of your minutes (Ed.), BGU III. 829[9] (A.D. 100) ἀσφ[άλισο]ν δὲ τ[ὴ]ν ἐ[μὴ]ν ὑπογραφήν, P Hamb I. 29[12] (A.D. 29), where the editors take it as "enter a protest." Demetrius *de Eloc.* 193 says the best "literary" style is συνηρτημένη καὶ οἷον ἠσφαλισμένη τοῖς συνδεσμοῖς, "compacted and (as it were) consolidated by the conjunctions" (Roberts). Ἀσφάλισμα "pledge" occurs BGU I. 248[8], II. 601[7] (?) (both ii/A.D.): cf. also ib. I. 246[14] (ii/iii A.D.) [π]αρασφαλίσματα. Cf. MGr (ἀ)σφαλίζω "shut."

ἀσχημονέω.

In P Tebt I. 44[17] (B.C. 114). a petition concerning a violent assault, the complaint is made that the aggressor ἕως [μέν τ]ινος ἐλοιδ[όρησέν με] καὶ ἀσχημο[νεῖ] ὕστερον δὲ ἐπιπηδήσας ἔδωκεν πληγὰς πλείους ἣι [ε]ἶχεν ῥάβδωι, where foul language at least is suggested. (Is ἀσχημόνει an unaugmented imperfect? The present is rather oddly sandwiched between two aorists, unless we are to call in the help of parallels noted *Proleg.* p. 121.) In the great Mysteries inscription from Andania, *Syll* 653[4] (B.C. 91), the candidate has to swear μήτε αὐ[τ]ὸς μηθὲν ἄσχημον μηδὲ ἄδικον ποιήσειν ἐπὶ καταλύσει τῶν μυστηρίων μήτε ἄλλωι ἐπιτρέψειν: in this case anything irreverent or improper would be included. Perhaps "behave dishonourably" is the meaning in 1 Cor 7[36], but the word seems to take the colour of its context. We find it in antithesis with εὐσχημονεῖν in the pompous but ungrammatical letter (a begging letter?), P Par 63[ix 78 f] (B.C. 165) παρὰ τὴν περιοῦσαν ἀγωγὴν ἀσχημονοῦντα προσδεῖσθαι τῆς παρ' ἑτέρων ἐπικουρείας, "since I cannot meet the conditions of life creditably I need external assistance": in the next sentence, after a fresh start, ὁρμώμεν ἀπὸ βραχείων μόλεις εὐσχημονεῖν.

ἀσχημοσύνη.

For ἀ. in Rom 1[27]=*opus obscaenum*, Lietzmann (*HZNT* III. i. *ad l.*) refers to Philo *Legg. Alleg.* II. 66, p. 78 τῆς . . ἀναισχυντίας παραδείγματα αἱ ἀσχημοσύναι πᾶσαι: cf. III. 158, p. 118. Vettius Valens p. 61[31] ἐν ἀσχημοσύναις καὶ κατακρίσεσι, apparently "scandals and condemnations."

ἀσχήμων.

Syll 653[4] (B.C. 91) μηθὲν ἄσχημον μηδὲ ἄδικον ποιήσειν. A "late form" of the adj. (LS, who quote Polemo, a writer of ii/A.D.) is found in P Ryl II. 144[18] (A.D. 38) παρεχρήσατό μοι πολλὰ καὶ ἄσχημα, "subjected me to much shameful mishandling" (Edd.). The ordinary form occurs in another petition of the same group, ib. 150[11] (A.D. 40-1) ἐκακολόγησεν πολλὰ καὶ ἀ[σ]χήμονα. So Vettius Valens p. 62[16] ἀτυχεῖς καὶ ἀσχήμονας.

ἀσωτία.

A good instance of this expressive word occurs in P Par 63[ix. 35] (B.C. 165) in the clause preceding that quoted above under ἀσχημονέω:—ἄλλως τε δὴ τῆς πατρικῆς οἰκίας, ὥσπερ καὶ σὺ γινώσκεις, ἔτι ἔνπροσθεν ἄρδην [ἀ]νατετραμμένης δι᾽ ἀσ[ω]τίας. It occurs after a hiatus in P Petr III. 21 (b)[11] (B.C. 225). A somewhat weaker sense is found in P Fay 12[24] (c. B.C. 103), where it is used of men who had pawned a stolen garment πρὸς ἀσωτείαν "incontinently." For the corresponding verb see P Flor I. 99[7] (i/ii A.D.) (=Selections, p. 71), a public notice which his parents set up regarding a prodigal son who ἀσωτευόμενος ἐσπάνισε τὰ αὐτοῦ πάντα, "by riotous living [cf. ἀσώτως, Lk 15[13]] had squandered all his own property," and PSI 41[12] (iv/A.D.), where a wife lays a complaint against her husband for misuse of her property καὶ ἀσωδ[εύ]ων καὶ πράττων [ἃ μὴ τοῖς ε]ὐγενέσι πρέπι. The word survives in the written MGr.

ἄσωτος.

Vettius Valens p. 18 joins ἀσώτων λάγνων καὶ κατωφερῶν ἀκρίτων ἐπιψόγων, εὐμεταβόλων περὶ τὰ τέλη, οὐκ εὐθανατούντων οὐδὲ περὶ τοὺς γάμους εὐσταθῶν. The use of the maxim noscitur a sociis here, as so often, makes the astrologer valuable for the delineation of a word's meaning. It is MGr.

ἀτακτέω.

For its original connotation of riot or rebellion cf. OGIS 200[6] (iv/A.D.) ἀτακτησάντων κατὰ καιρὸν τοῦ ἔθνους τῶν Βουγαειτῶν. So Syll 153[81] (B.C. 325-4) τοὺς ἀτακτοῦντας τῶν τριηράρχων, al. Like its parent adjective ἄτακτος, and the adverb, this verb is found in the NT only in the Thessalonian Epp., where their context clearly demands that the words should be understood metaphorically. Some doubt has, however, existed as to whether they are to be taken as referring to actual moral wrong-doing, or to a certain remissness in daily work and conduct. Chrysostom seems to incline to the former view, Theodoret to the latter : see the passages quoted in full with other illustrative material in Milligan Thess. p. 152 ff. The latter view is now supported by almost contemporary evidence from the Κοινή. In P Oxy II. 275[24f.] (A.D. 66), a contract of apprenticeship, a father enters into an undertaking that if there are any days when his son "plays truant" or "fails to attend"—ὅσας δ᾽ ἐὰν ἐν τούτῳ ἀτακτήσῃ ἡμέρας—he is afterwards to make them good ; and similarly in P Oxy IV. 725[39 ff.] (A.D. 183) a weaver's apprentice is bound down to appear for an equivalent number of days, if from idleness or ill-health or any other reason he exceeds the twenty days' holiday he is allowed in the year—ἐὰν δὲ πλείονας τούτων ἀργήσῃ [ἢ ἀσ]θενήσῃ ἢ ἀτακτήσῃ ἢ δι᾽ ἄλλην τιν[ὰ αἰ]τ[ίαν ἡμέρας κτλ. From an earlier date we may cite BGU IV. 1125[8] (B.C. 13), another contract, where the words occur ἅς δὲ ἐὰν ἀρτακτήσῃ ἢι ἀρρωστήσῃι : the strange word is what Lewis Carroll would call a "portmanteau," compounded of ἀργήσηι and ἀτακτήσηι. On the other hand in P Eleph 2[13] (a will, B.C. 285-4) καὶ ἡ πρᾶξις ἔστω ἐκ τοῦ ἀτακτοῦντος καὶ μὴ ποιοῦντος κατὰ τὰ γεγραμμένα the verb has the stronger sense, "to be contumacious." Its opposite εὐτακτέω is not uncommon. Thus Syll 519[27] (Athens, B.C. 334-3), where the ἔφηβοι of the year are formally praised for having been good

boys—ἐπειδὴ . . εὐτακτοῦσιν and obey the laws and the master appointed for them. In BGU IV. 1106[6] (B.C. 13) a wet-nurse is bound εὐτακτουμένην αὐτὴν τοῖς λο[ιποῖς κατ]ὰ μῆνα τροφήοις ποιεῖσθαι τήν τε ἑατῆς [καὶ τοῦ] παιδίου προσήκουσαν ἐπιμέλειαν : note the middle.

ἄτακτος.

See the discussion of ἀτακτέω. For the adj. (and adv.) we may quote P Fay 337[16 f.] (ii/A.D.) δεῖ τῶν [ἀν]θρώπων ἄρχειν [τῶν] πράξεων ἐκεί[νου]ς δὲ εὐθὺς ἐφέπεσθαι, οὐκ ἀτάκτως μέντοι ἀλλ᾽ εἱμα[ρ]μέ[ν]ως : the document is a fragment of " a philosophical work concerning the gods " (Edd.). In Vettius Valens p. 336[21] ἄτακτον φάσιν ἢ βελτίονα, the antithesis suggests a markedly bad meaning for ἄ. The same implication underlies the subst. in p. 116[13] πολλὰ καὶ τῶν ἀτακτημάτων κρυβήσεται καὶ οὐκ ἔσται αἰσχρά -which they would have been but for the kindly influence of Jupiter. The next sentence identifies the ἀτακτήματα as secret intrigues which will not be found out. In Syll 510 (see under ἀτακτέω), where four sets of ἔφηβοι and their σωφρονισταί get their meed of praise and garlands, εὐτ]άκτους αὐτοὺς παρέχουσιν replaces the verb in one place out of three. BGU IV. 1056[13] (B.C. 13) διδόντες τὸν μὲν τόκον κατὰ μῆνα εὐτάκτως, "regularly" : so 1156[14] (B.C. 15).

ἄτεκνος.

P Lond 23[13] (B.C. 158-7) (= I. p. 38) διὰ τὸ ἄτεκνόν με εἶναι. The word is common in connexion with dispositions of property, etc., e. g. P Oxy II. 249[10 ff.] (A.D. 80) τοῦ ὁμογνησίου μου ἀδελφοῦ Ποπλίου . . . μ[ε]τηλλαχότος ἀτέκνου, P Amh II. 72[5] (A.D. 246) ἄτεκνον καὶ ἀδιαθέτου "childless and intestate." P Strass I. 29[33] (A.D. 284), al. Cf. also BGU II. 648[15] (A.D. 164 or 196) ἐπεὶ καὶ ἄτεκν[ός] εἰμι καὶ οὐδὲ ἐμαυτῆι ἀπαρκεῖν δύναμαι.

ἀτενίζω.

For this characteristically Lukan word cf. the Leiden occult papyrus W[xvi. 8 f.] εἰσελθόντος δὲ τοῦ θεοῦ μὴ ἐνατένιζε τῇ ὄψει, ἀλλὰ τῆς (l. τοῖς) ποσί. The intensive meaning, which underlies the NT usage, comes out in the description of Thecla's rapt attention to Paul's teaching—ἀτενίζουσα ὡς πρὸς εὐφρασίαν (Acta Pauli viii.).

ἄτερ.

For this (originally) poetic word which is found in the Grk Bible only 2 Macc 12[15], Lk 22[6 and 35], cf. Priene 109[106] (c. B.C. 120) ἄτερ ὀψωνίου, "without salary." It occurs in P Oxy VI. 936[18] (iii/A.D., a rather uneducated letter) ὁ ἠπητὴς λέγει ὅτι οὐ δίδω οὔτε τὸν χαλκὸν οὔτε τὸ φαινόλιν ἄτερ Ἰούστου, "the cobbler says that he will not give up either the money or the cloak without Justus " (Edd.). Cf. also P Leid W[iii. 12] (Apocrypha Moisis) ἄτερ γὰρ τούτων (the ω corrected from ο) ὁ ἐὸς (l. θεὸς) οὐκ ἐπακούσεται. To the references in the Lexicons may be added Vettius Valens pp. 136[9], 271[9], 341[3], and Cleanthes hymn. Orph. 68, 8.

ἀτιμάζω.

P Petr II. 4 (6)[15f.] (B.C. 255-4) διϊον (l. δεινὸν) γάρ ἐστιν ἐν ὄχλωι ἀτιμάζεσθαι, "for it is a dreadful thing to be insulted before a crowd" (Ed.). Cf. OGIS 383[119] (i/B.C.)

12

καθωσιωμένων τε ἡρώων ἀτιμασθεὶς νόμος ἀνειλάτους ἔχει ποινάς, *Syll* 891²ᶠᶠ (ii/A.D.—pagan, but with phrases from LXX) ἐπικατάρατος ὅστις μὴ φείδοιτο . . . τοῦδε τοῦ ἔργου (a tomb and statue) . ., ἀλλὰ ἀτειμάσει ἢ μεταθήσει ὅρους ἐξ ὅρων (Dittenberger emends ἐξορύσσων) κτλ., BGU IV. 1024ᵛⁱⁱ·²⁸ (iv/v A.D.) πωλοῦσ[α αὐτὴν πρὸς] ἀτιμάζουσαν τιμήν (of a girl sold to shame). The connotation of the last ex. survives in MGr, to "seduce" a girl.

ἀτιμία.

P Giss I. 40ⁱⁱ ⁵, an edict announcing an amnesty of Caracalla A.D. 212, μετὰ τ[ὸ] π[λ]ηρωθῆναι τὸ τοῦ χρ[ό]νου διάστημα οὐκ ὀνειδισθήσεται ἡ τῆς ἀτιμ[ί]ας παρασημεί[ω]σις. The word is found in a hitherto unknown fragment, perhaps of Euripides, published in P Par p. 86—

> οὐκ ἦν ἄρ᾽ οὐθὲν πῆμ᾽ ἐλευθέραν δάκνον
> ψυχὴν ὁμοίως ἀνδρός, ὡς ἀτιμία.

(But Euripides did not write οὐθέν!)

ἄτιμος.

Its old technical meaning, familiar in Attic law—cf., for example, *Roberts-Gardner* no. 32ᴬ ³⁵, dated B.C. 377, ὑπαρχέτω μ[ὲν] αὐτῷ ἀτίμῳ εἶναι καὶ [τὰ χρ]ήμα[τα αὐτ]οῦ δημόσια ἔστω—is seen in *OGIS* 338²⁹ (ii/B.C.) εἶναι αὐτοὺς κα[ὶ] αὐτὰς ἀτίμους τε καὶ τὰ ἑκατέρων ὑπάρχοντα τῆς πόλεως: in 527⁸ ἄτι[μον] δὲ εἶναι the context seems to require the meaning of "contrary to law," though the editor admits that this cannot be found in the word itself. In the Acts of the martyrdom of Christina, PSI 27⁷ (v/A.D.) the Saint is described as addressing Urbanus as βάρος πάσ[ης ἀνομίας ἔχων καὶ] ἀτίμ[ο]υ σπέρματος. It is MGr.

ἀτιμόω.

In a fragmentary Decree of the Senate and People, *Roberts-Gardner* p. 69 ff., prescribing the conditions upon which Selymbria, after its capture in B.C. 409-8 by Alcibiades, was restored to the Athenian alliance, provision is made that disfranchised persons should be restored to their privileges—¹⁰ εἴ τις ἠτίμωτ[ο, ἔντιμον εἶναι].

ἀτμίς.

The long British Museum magical papyrus, P Lond 121⁶³⁹ and ⁷⁴⁸ (iii/A.D.) (= I. pp. 104, 108), shows this word twice—περιένεγκον τὸ δακ[τ]ύλιον ἐπὶ τῆς ἀτμίτος τοῦ λιβάνου) and περὶ τὴν ἀτμίδα. Cf. *Syll* 804¹⁹ (ii/A.D.?—Epidaurus) θυμιατήριον ἀτμίζο[ν.

ἄτοπος.

With ἐν ἀτόμῳ (1 Cor 15⁵²) cf. Symm. Isai 54⁸ ἐν ἀτόμῳ ὀργῆς, where the LXX has ἐν μικρῷ θυμῷ. This will suffice to make Paul's dependence for the word on Plato and Aristotle less assured than it might have been.

ἄτοπος.

From its original meaning "out of place," "unbecoming," ἄτοπος came to be used especially in Plato of what was "marvellous," "odd" (e. g. *Legg.* i. 646 B τοῦ θαυμαστοῦ τε καὶ ἀτόπου), and from this the transition was easy in later Grk to the ethical meaning of "improper," "unrighteous," e. g. Philo *Legg. Alleg.* iii. 17 παρ᾽ ὃ καὶ ἄτοπος λέγεται εἶναι ὁ φαῦλος ἄτοπον δέ ἐστι κακὸν δύσθετον. It

is in this sense that the word is always used in the LXX and in the NT (except Ac 28⁶—and even there it = κακόν), and the usage can be freely illustrated from the Κοινή. Thus in the early P Petr II. 19 (1 a) ⁵ᶠ· (iii/B.C.) a prisoner asserts "in the name of God and of fair play" (οὕνεκα τοῦ θεοῦ καὶ τοῦ καλῶς ἔχοντος) that he has said nothing ἄτοπον, ὅπερ καὶ ἀληθινόν ἐστι, and in *ib.* III. 43 (3) ¹⁷ᶠ· (iii/B.C.) precautions are taken against certain discontented labourers ἵνα μὴ ἄτοπ[ό]ν τι πράξωσιν. Similarly *Chrest.* I. 238¹² (c. A.D. 117) παραφυλάξε τε εἰς τὸ μηδὲν ἄτοπον ὑπ᾽ αὐτῶν πραχθῆναι. In BGU III. 757²¹ (A.D. 12) ἕτερα ἄτοπα are attributed to some marauders who had pulled to pieces a farmer's sheaves of wheat, and thrown them to the pigs; and the parents of the prodigal (P Flor I. 99¹⁰—see *s. v.* ἀσωτία) announce that they are giving publicity to his misdeeds μήποτε ἐ[π]ηρεάσῃ ἡμεῖν ἢ ἕτερο[ν] ἢ (? omit) ἄτοπόν τι πράξῃ[ι, "lest he should insult us, or do anything else amiss." P Flor II. 177¹⁶ (A.D. 257) ἄτοπον γάρ ἐστιν αὐτοὺς ὠνεῖσθαι is less clear. The subst. ἀτόπημα is found P Tebt II. 303¹¹ (A.D. 176-80) περὶ ὧν εἰς ἡμᾶς διεπράξατο ἀτοπημάτων, "concerning the outrages which he committed against us" (Edd.): cf. P Lips I. 39⁷ (A.D. 390) καὶ μ[η]κέτι κατὰ μηδενὸς ἀτόπημα διαπράξασθαι. A curious use of the adverb (if the restoration is correct) occurs in the Acts of Christina, where the saint is represented as addressing Urbanus, after having looked up into heaven καὶ [ἀτ]όπως γελάσασα (PSI 27⁷, v/A.D.); perhaps "with a strange" or "forced laugh." It may be added that in *CR* xvii. p. 265 οὐκ ἀτόπως is cited from Thucydides (vii. 30²) with the meaning "not badly"—"an uncommon use," the writer adds.

αὐγάζω.

Nageli (p. 25) translates this verb by "see, see clearly" in the Pauline passage 2 Cor 4⁴ εἰς τὸ μὴ αὐγάσαι τὸν φωτισμὸν τοῦ εὐαγγελίου τῆς δόξης τοῦ Χριστοῦ, holding that there is no reason why this old poetic sense (Soph. *Ph.* 217) should not have passed into the Κοινή. It should be noticed that in the LXX (Lev 13²⁵ *al*) the word has the wholly different meaning of "appear white or bright." For the compd. διαυγάζω see the horoscope P Lond 130⁷⁰ (i/ii A.D.) (= I. p. 135) διηύγαζεν.

αὐγή.

The choice of this word as a proper name in Egypt is witnessed by *Preisigke* 1995, 1999, 2003, 2006, 2008, from a set of sepulchral inscrr. of Alexandria. This is a better warrant of vernacular use than the fulsome laudation with which the Cyzicenes greeted the first acts of Gaius (A.D. 37), *Syll* 365³, ἐπεὶ ὁ νέος Ἥλιος Γάιος (κτλ.) συναναλάμψαι ταῖς ἰδίαις αὐγαῖς καὶ τὰς δορυφόρους τῆς ἡγεμονίας ἠθέλησεν βασιλήας, *i. e.* surrounded himself with satellites in the shape of vassal kings restored to thrones from which Tiberius expelled them (Dittenberger). Αὐγή is the MGr for "dawn," and probably superseded the irregular noun ἕως very early in the Κοινή history: Ac 20¹¹ ἄχρι αὐγῆς is thus good vernacular. So P Leid Wˣⁱ· ³⁵ ἐφάνη φῶς, αὐγή (cf. ⁱᵛ· ³⁹). Cf. also the dimin. αὐγούλα in MGr, as in the Klepht ballad (Abbott, *Songs* p. 26)—

> Κ᾽ ἐκεῖ πρὸς τὰ χαράγματα, κ᾽ ἐκεῖ πρὸς τὴν αὐγούλα,
> And there, towards daybreak, towards early morn.

Αὔγουστος

is usually replaced by the translation Σεβαστός: it is well to remember that the title meant a great deal more than "august," being connected essentially with the apotheosis of the Emperor. Since Σεβαστός enters into the style of every Emperor till Constantine (when in the papyri Αὔγουστος significantly replaces it), the original Latin word could be retained in an early writer (see *per contra* exx. from iv/A.D. below) as the personal name of Octavian: so Lk 2¹ against Ac 25²¹·²⁵. The spelling Ἀγούστου in אC*Δ represents a genuine Hellenistic pronunciation (see *Proleg.* p. 47): but in the case of this Latin word it is probably (so Prof. Thumb) conditioned by the influence of vulgar Latin: cf. Ital. *agosto.* Ἀ[γ]ούστων occurs in P Lond 407²¹ (A.D. 346) (= II. p. 274), which is roughly coeval with א: the Edd. note it is thus spelt in many of the papyri of the period. So P Oxy I. 41² (iii/iv A.D.) Ἄγουστοι κύριοι, BGU IV. 1049¹ (A.D. 342), P Goodsp Cairo 12ⁱ ¹¹ (A.D. 340) τῶν τὰ πάντα νικόντων Σεβαστῶν ἡμῶν Ἀγούστων, *ib.* 15² (A.D. 362) Ἀ[γο]ύστου. The tendency arose in Greek centuries earlier—Mayser *Gr.* p. 114 cites Γλακίου from P Par 41⁶ (B.C. 158), and σατοῦ and the like appear in Ptolemaic times.

αὐθάδης.

In P Amh II. 78¹³ᶠ. (A.D. 184) it seems certain that we should read μ[ου] πλεονεκτεῖ ἄνθρωπος α[ὐ]θάδης (not ἀσθενής). A few lines lower we find τοιαύτης ο[ὔ]ν αὐθαδίας ἐν αὐτῷ οὔσης οὐ δυνάμενος [ἐν]καρτερεῖν, "his audacity having reached this pitch I can endure no longer" (Edd.). According to Crönert *Mem. Herc.,* p. 32, the form αὐθαδία, which in Attic is confined to the poets, "linguae pedestris auctoribus sine dubio reddenda est." Its vernacular character may be further established by P Tebt I. 16¹⁰ (B.C. 114) αὐθαδίᾳ χρώμενοι "persisting in their violent behaviour" (Edd.). *Syll* 803²⁷ (ii/A.D.) καὶ τοὺς ὑβρίσαντας τοὺς ἥρωας (the *Di Manes*) τῶν τέκνων ἡμῶν καὶ ἐμὲ καὶ τὸν ἄνδρα μου Π. καὶ ἐπιμένοντας τῇ αὐθαδίᾳ, CP Herm 1³ (no context), BGU III. 747ⁱⁱ· ¹¹ (A.D. 139) μέχρι αὐθαδίας ἐπ[ι]χειροῦσιν φθάνειν, *ib.* IV. 1187²¹ (i/B.C.) τῆι δὲ περὶ ἑαυτὰς βίαι καὶ αὐθαδίᾳ [συ]νχρησάμενοι, P Gen I. 31⁹ (A.D. 145-6) τῇ αὐτῇ αὐθαδίᾳ χρώμενος. The subst. is not found in the NT, but see LXX Isai 24⁸, Didache 5¹. The adverb is quotable from P Tebt II. 331⁷ (c. A.D. 131) ἐπῆλθο[ν α]ὐθάδως εἰς ἣν ἔχω ἐν τῇ κώμῃ οἰκίαν, P Grenf I. 47¹⁰ (A.D. 148) ἐπιγνοὺς αὐθάδως τεθε[ρ]ῶσθαι ὑπ[ὸ] Ὧρους κτλ., P Ryl II. 133¹⁶ (A.D. 33) αὐθάδως κατέσπασεν ἀπὸ μέρους "ventured to pull it partly down" (Ed.), P Lond 358¹² (c. A.D. 150) (= II. p. 172) αὐθάδως ἀναστραφέντων, and P Oxy X. 1242ⁱⁱⁱ· ⁴⁴ (iii/A.D.—a semi-literary piece), where Trajan says to an anti-Semite advocate, Ἴδε, δεύτερόν σοι λέγω, Ἑρμαῖσκε, αὐθάδως ἀποκρείνῃ πεποιθὼς τῷ σεαυτοῦ γένει.

αὐθαίρετος.

In *OGIS* 583⁸ (i/A.D.) a certain Adrastus is praised as δωρεὰν καὶ αὐθαίρετος γυμνασίαρχος, *i.e.* he had provided oil at his own expense for the combatants, and exercised the office voluntarily (see the editor's note): cf. also the late P Par 21¹⁵ (A.D. 616) αὐθαιρέτῳ βουλήσει καὶ ἀδόλῳ συνειδήσει. For the adverb see *Magn* 163¹⁵ ᶠ. πᾶσάν τε λειτουργίαν . . . τελέσαντος τῇ πατρίδι αὐθαιρέτως, and the common technical phrase ἑκουσίως καὶ αὐθαιρέτως, *as* P Lond 280⁷ (A.D. 55) (= II. p. 193), BGU II. 581⁹ (A.D. 133), P Lips I. 17⁹ (A.D. 377), P Giss I. 56² (vi/A.D.), *al.*: the phrase may also be expressed adjectivally, as with γνώμῃ in P Oxy X. 1280⁹ (iv/A.D.).

αὐθεντέω.

The history of this word has been satisfactorily cleared up by P. Kretschmer, in *Glotta* iii. (1912), p. 289 ff. He shows that αὐθέντης "murderer" is by haplology for αὐτοθέντης from θείνω, while αὐθέντης "master" (as in literary MGr) is from αὐτ-έντης (cf. συνέντης· συνεργός in Hesychius, root *sen* "accomplish," ἁνύω). The astonishing sense-development described in Grimm may accordingly disappear. So likewise may his description of the verb as a "bibl. and eccl. word," after the evidence (given below) that the adj. αὐθεντικός is very well established in the vernacular. "Biblical"—which in this case means that the word occurs *once* in the NT (1 Tim 2¹²)—seems intended to hint what ἅπαξ εἰρημένον in a "profane" writer would not convey. We may refer to Nägeli, p. 49, for evidence which encourages us to find the verb's *provenance* in the popular vocabulary. The Atticist Thomas Magister, p. 18, 8, warns his pupil to use αὐτοδικεῖν because αὐθεντεῖν was vulgar (κοινότερον): so Moeris, p. 58—αὐτοδίκην (*l.* -εῖν) Ἀττικοι, αὐθέντην (*l.* -εῖν) Ἕλληνες. The use in 1 Tim 2¹² comes quite naturally out of the word "master, autocrat." Cf. P Leid W⁹¹ ⁴⁶ ὁ ἀρχάγγελος τῶν ὑπὸ τὸν κόσμον, αὐθέντα ἥλιε. For the adj. cf. *ib.* ᵛⁱ· ⁴⁶, P Oxy II. 260²⁰ (A.D. 59), a document signed by the assistant of the strategus to give it legal sanction — Θε[ω]ν Ὀννώφριος ὑπηρέτης ἐπηκολ[ού]θ[η]κα τῇ[αὐ]θεντι[κ]ῆι χιρ[ογρ]α(φίᾳ), "I, Theon, son of O., assistant, have checked this authentic bond" (Edd.): so *ib.* IV. 719²⁰· ³³ (A.D. 193). In BGU I. 326ⁱⁱ ²³ (ii/A.D.) a scribe declares the ἀντίγραφον before him to be σύμφωνον τῇ αὐθεντικῇ διαθήκῃ: cf. Wilcken *Ostr* 1010 (Roman) ὁμολ[ογοῦμεν] ἔχιν τὴν αὐθεντικὴν ἀποχὴν ἀχύρ[ου], P Hamb I. 18ⁱⁱ ⁶ (A.D. 222) αὐθ(εντικῶν) ἐπιστολ(ῶν) καὶ βιβλ(ιδίων) ὑποκεκολ(λημένων), P Giss I. 34⁴ (A.D. 205-6) τὰ αὐθεντικ[ά], and P Lond 985¹⁸ (iv/A.D.) (= III. p. 229) ἔδωκα τὸ ἴσον κ[αὶ] ἔχω τὴν αὐθε[ν]τικὴν ἀποχὴν παρ' ἐμαυτῷ. The subst. is found P Lips I. 33ⁱⁱ ⁶· ⁷· ²⁸ (A.D. 368), BGU II. 669¹⁸ (Byz.) ἰδίᾳ αὐθεντίᾳ ὄργανον ἔστησεν εἰ[ς] τὸν αὐτὸν λάκκον. For αὐθεντίζω, "take in hand," see *Chrest.* I. ii. p. 160. The noun produces ultimately the common MGr ἀφέντης (*Effendi*) "Mr."

αὐλή.

A Cairo papyrus (iii/B.C.), *Chrest.* I. 224⁷· ¹¹, has ἀπογεγράμμεθα τὴν [ὑ]πάρχουσα (*l.* -αν) ἡμῖν οἰκίαν [κ]αὶ αὐλὴν καὶ ἄλλο [ο]ἴκημα. P Lond 45¹⁵ (B.C. 160-59) (= I. p. 36) has a complaint against marauders who had not only sacked a house, but had appropriated to their own uses τὴν προσοῦσαν αὐλὴν καὶ τὸν τῆς οἰκίας τόπον ψιλόν. These will serve as good specimens of the normal use in the papyri, where the word is extremely common, denoting the "court" attached to a house: cf. BGU I. 275⁶ⁱ (A.D. 215) αὐλὴ προσκυρούσῃ οἰκίᾳ μου. It could be used for "lumber": see the ostracon from Syene, *Archiv* v. p. 179, no. 34⁵ τὸ ξύλον τὸ [μυρί]κινον τὸ ἐν τῇ αὐλῇ. Note that οἶκος could include both : P Fay 31[16] (c. A.D. 129) πέμπτον μέρος ὅλης τῆς οἰκίας καὶ αὐλῆς καὶ τοῦ ὅλου οἴκου "the fifth part of the whole house and court and of the whole tenement." So far as we have observed, there is nothing in the Κοινή to support the contention that in the NT αὐλή ever means the house itself : see Meyer on Mt 26[3]. The plural is used of "guest-chambers," as in the interesting P Tebt I. 33[9] (B.C. 112) (= Selections, p. 28) where, amongst the preparations for a Roman visitor, we read—φρόντισον ὡς ἐπὶ τῶν καθηκόντων τόπων αἵ τε αὐλαὶ κατασκευασ[θ]ήσο[ν]ται.

Like the Latin aula and our own court, the word readily comes to denote a Royal entourage, e.g. P Par 49[17] (B.C. 164-58) (= Witkowski[2], p. 70) δόξαντα ἀδελφὸν αὐτοῦ ἐν τῇ αὐλῇ εἶναι, "since he has a brother at Court"; OGIS 735[4] (ii/B.C.) τῶν περὶ αὐλὴν διαδόχων, referring to certain officials attached to the court of Ptolemy Philometor ; Vettius, p. 89[15], ἐν βασιλικαῖς αὐλαῖς : so also Preisigke 1568 (B.C. 146-17) πρῶτοι φίλοι καὶ χιλίαρχοι καὶ ἄλλοι οἱ περὶ αὐλήν. When, therefore, Suidas defined αὐλή as ἡ τοῦ βασιλέως οἰκία, he was not far out, though αὐλή seemingly cannot mean an ordinary house. BGU IV. 1008[1] (c. B.C. 17) τῷ δεῖν]ι τῶι ἐπὶ τοῦ ἐν τῆι αὐλῆι κριτηρίου presents a court sitting in the αὐλή, as against Mk 14[66], where the αὐλή is clearly outside the room where the Sanhedrists were in session. Syll 102[28] (B.C. 290-87) ἐν τῆι αὐλεῖ τοῦ ἱεροῦ (al.) illustrates Ps 84[2. 10] (LXX 83[3. 11]) : cf. also ib. 734[8 4] (Cos), where it is forbidden ἀποθήκηι χρᾶσθαι τ[ῆι αὐλ]ῆι τῆι ἐν τῶι ἱερῶι μηδ᾽ ἐν τῶι περιπάτω[ι, ἂ]μ μὴ πόλεμος ἦι. In MGr = "court."

αὐλητής

is found in P Hib I. 54[6] (c. B.C. 245) where the writer gives instructions regarding a forthcoming festival—ἀπό[σ]τειλον . . . τὸν αὐλητὴν Πετῶιν ἔχοντ[α] τούς τε Φρυγίους αὐλ[ο]ὺς καὶ τοὺς λοιπούς. So in P Oxy X. 1275[9] (iii/A.D.), where ὁ προεστὼς συμφωνίας αὐλητῶν καὶ μουσικῶν is engaged with his "company" (συμφωνία) for a five days' village festival. The festival for which the flute-player is wanted is more unmistakably secular in the fragmentary menu, P Giss I. 93[14]. Generally he belongs to the apparatus of religion. So apparently in Cagnat IV. 135[4] (B.C. 46—a revision of Syll 348), recording the prayer of Σωτηρίδης Γάλλος—a priest of the Magna Mater at Cyzicus —on behalf of his "partner" (σύμβιος) M. Stlaccius, an αὐλητής, who had been taken captive in a military expedition and sold. Syll 612[18] (B.C. 24) gives us an αὐλητής in a list of functionaries connected with the temple of Zeus at Olympia ; Dittenberger tells us this was the vernacular for σπονδαύλης, a title found always in ii/A.D. An αὐλητὴς τραγικός is mentioned in OGIS 51 (iii/B.C.) amongst the ἀδελφοί who formed the "synod" of the priest Zopyrus for ceremonial purposes. In Magn 98[45] the στεφανηφόρος has to provide αὐλητὴν συριστὴν κιθαριστήν for a festival of Zeus Sosipolis ; while ib. 237 is illustrated by an interesting sketch showing the triclinium ἱερῶν αὐλητρίδων καὶ ἀκροβατῶν attached to the temple of Archegetis of Chalchis. In the fragment of an uncanonical Gospel, composed before A.D. 200, reference is made to the washing of the outside skin ὑπερ [κα]ὶ αἱ πόρναι καὶ α[ἱ] αὐλητρίδες μυρί[ζ]ου[σιν κ]αὶ λούουσιν κτλ. (P Oxy V. 840[35 ff.]).

αὐλίζομαι.

OGIS 730[7] (iii/B.C.) ὥστε αὐλίσ[ασθα]ι [αὐτόθι ἐν ἡ]μ[έ]ραις δυσί(ν). We may note Didache 11[6], where it is laid down that a wayfaring apostle, on leaving any house where he has been entertained, is to take nothing with him except bread ἕως οὗ αὐλισθῇ, "until he reach his (next night's) lodging" : cf. the expressive use in LXX Ps 29[6] τὸ ἑσπέρας αὐλισθήσεται κλαυθμός, "weeping may come in to lodge (like a passing stranger) at even." In Preisigke 1579, a bracelet of Byzantine date, we find LXX Ps 90[1] as an amulet, with αὐλισθίσεται : there are no variants except of spelling.

αὐλός.

See the first citation s.v. αὐλητής. In BGU IV. 1125 ὑπαυλισμός is a flute accompaniment.

On a possible connexion of αὐλός with Heb לֹל "bore," "pierce," and then "pipe," see Lewy Fremdworte, p. 165 f. But Lithuanian and Slavonic words given in Boisacq s.v. are much closer ; and there is ἔναυλος, "ravine," to be reckoned with.

αὐξάνω.

According to Mayser, Gr. p. 465, the form αὐξάνω, which is found in the LXX (Gen 35[11], Sir 43[8]) and NT, occurs in the Ptolemaic papyri only in P Leid B[i. 8] (ii/B.C.) μᾶλλον αὐξάνεσθαι ἀκολούθως τῇ τῶν προγόνων [προαιρέσει] : elsewhere, as in the Attic inscriptions up to Imperial times (Meisterhans Gr. p. 176), we find only αὔξω. The latter, contrary to general NT usage (as Eph 2[21], Col 2[19]) is transitive in such passages as Michel 551[7] (the Canopus decree, B.C. 238) τὰς τι[μὰς τῶν θεῶν] ἐπὶ πλεῖον αὔξοντες, Cagnat IV. 247[35] (Stratonicea, c. B.C. 150) ἐπὶ πλεῖον αὔξειν τ[ὴν] φιλίαν, and Magn 33[7] αὔξοντες τὴν πρὸς τοὺς θεοὺς εὐσέβειαν, ib. 50[24] ἐπὶ πλεῖον αὔξων, after a hiatus. So, at a later time, the fuller form : P Ryl II. 77[36] (A.D. 192) τῆς πόλ(εως) αὐξάνε[ι] τὰ πράγματα. The same is implied in the use of the mid. in Syll 891[18] μηδὲ οἶκος αὔξοιτο—a pagan curse which quotes the LXX. For the intrans. usage cf. Aristeas 208 θεωρῶν, ὡς ἐν πολλῷ χρόνῳ καὶ κακοπαθείαις μεγίσταις αὔξει τε καὶ γεννᾶται τὸ τῶν ἀνθρώπων γένος. Of the moon, P Leid W[ii 21]. In MGr αὐξαίνω.

αὔξησις.

Cirest. I. 70[12] (an inser. of B.C. 57-c) τούτου πρὸς αὔξησιν ἀγομένου, of a temple for which the priests ask the privilege of ἀσυλία.

αὔριον.

P Par 47[19 f.] (c. B.C. 153) (= Selections, p. 23) ὁ στρατηγὸς ἀναβαίν᾽ αὔριον εἰς τὸ Σαραπιῆν, P Tebt I. 37[23 ff.] (B.C. 73) ἐὰν δὲ ἀμελήσῃς ἀναγκασθήσομαι ἐγὼ ἐ[λθεῖ]ν αὔριο[ν], and BGU I. 38[21] (i/A.D.) where a boy writes to his father that he goes daily to a certain seller of barley-beer (ζυθόπωλις) who daily says σήμερον αὔρ[ε]ιν (-(ε)ιν for -ιον, as often), "to-day, to-morrow (you shall get it)," but never gives it. The full phrase, which is contracted in Mt 6[31], Ac 4[3], is seen in BGU I. 286[10] (A.D. 306) ἀπὸ τῆς αὔριον ἡμέρας, and Wünsch AF 3[19] (Imperial) ἐν τῇ αὔριν ἡμέρᾳ. It appears without ἡμέρα in P Flor II. 118[5] (A.D. 254) μετὰ τὴν α., P Tebt II. 417[7] and 419[2] (iii/A.D.) ἐν τῇ α., BGU II. 511[i 19]

(c. A.D. 200) εἰς αὔ]ριον (or εἰς τὴν α.), etc. Mayser *Gr.* p. 200, quotes P Tebt I. 110¹⁷ (B.C. 105–4) τὸ ἐφαύρι[ο]ν for ἐφ' αὔριον as proof of the living character of the strong aspirate : here the analogy of ἐφ' ἡμέραν is an obvious influence. Note also the formula of invitation to dinner, as P Oxy III. 524³ α[ὔριον], ἥτις ἐστὶν λ, *ib.* I. 110³ (also ii/A.D.) αὔριον ἥτις ἐστὶν ιε̄, *ib.* 111³ (iii A.D.) αὔριον, ἥτις ἐστὶν πέμπτη : so *ib.* VII. 1025¹⁶ (late iii/A.D.), where an actor and a Homeric reciter are engaged to come for a festival "on the birthday of Cronus the most great god," τῶν θεωριῶν ἅμ' αὔ[ρ]ιον ἥτις ἐστὶν ι ἀγομ.έν]ων. It is MGr.

αὐστηρός.

The epithet of Lk 19²¹ is poorly rendered by the word we have borrowed. It obviously means "strict, exacting," a man who expects to get blood out of a stone. This sense is well seen in P Tebt II. 315¹⁹ (ii/A.D.), in which the writer warns his friend, who was evidently connected with the temple finance, to see that his books were in good order, in view of the visit of a government inspector, ὁ γὰρ ἄνθρωπος λείαν ἐστὶ[ν] αὐστηρός, "a regular martinet." Cf. BGU I. 140¹⁷ ff., the copy of a military letter or diploma of the time of Hadrian, in which, with reference to certain regulations affecting his soldiers, the Emperor rejoices that he is able to interpret in a milder manner (φιλανθρωπότερ[ον]) τὸ αὐστηρότερον ὑπὸ τῶν πρὸ ἐμοῦ αὐτοκρατόρων σταθέν. In the curious rhetorical exercise (?) P Oxy III. 471⁹² ff. (ii/A.D.) we find τί οὖν ὁ κατηφὴς σὺ καὶ ὑπεραύ[σ]τηρος οὐκ ἐκώλυες ; "why then did not you with your modesty and extreme austerity stop him ?" (Edd.). Here (as the context shows) a rigorous Puritanism is sarcastically attributed to a high Roman official, whose scandalous relations with a favourite ill became a *vir gravis* : this is nearer to the English *austere*. Four centuries earlier, it describes "rough" country, OGIS 168⁵⁷ αὐστηροῖς τόποις παρορίοις τῆι Αἰθιοπίαι. So in a metrical epitaph from Cos (i/B.C.), *Kaibel* 201⁵ γυμνάδος αὐστηρὸν διετῆ πόνον ἐκτελέσαντα, of "exacting" physical work. We may add that the connotation of the adj. in its later sense is very well given by the combination in Vettius Valens, p. 75¹¹, where a particular conjunction of Venus and Saturn produces αὐστηροὺς ἀγελάστους ἐπισκύνιον ἔχοντας, πρὸς δὲ τὰ ἀφροδίσια σκληροτέρους : the sequel however admits vice, but of a gloomy and bizarre type.

αὐτάρκεια

occurs in P Oxy IV. 729³⁰ (A.D. 137) τὴν δὲ αὐτάρκιαν κόπρον περιστερῶν, "guano, the necessary amount," P Flor II. 122¹¹ (A.D. 253–4) πάρεχε τὸ[ὀψώνιον ?] κατ' αὐτά[ρ-κειαν ?, *ib.* 242⁸ (same date) ἵνα δυνηθῇς ἔχειν τὴν αὐτάρ-κιαν ἔστ' ἂν τὰ σὰ ἐν ἑτοίμῳ γένηται. It is thus only concrete, "a sufficiency" : see next article. Vettius Valens (p. 289⁵²) has the noun, apparently with the meaning "a competence."

αὐτάρκης.

We have several quotations, but only in the simple sense of "enough." Thus P Oxy IV. 729¹³ (A.D. 137) τὸν αὐτάρκη κέραμον, "a sufficient number of jars," P Lond 1166⁶ (A.D. 42) (= III., p. 104) τὰ αὐτάρκη καύματα for a bath house, P Flor I. 25¹² (ii/A.D.) χ[ο]ρηγοῦντος τὰ αὐτάρκη σπέρματα,

P Strass I. 22²⁴ (iii/A.D.) ἡ [δ]ι' ἐνιαυτοῦ νομὴ αὐτάρκης ἐστίν, "the tenure of one year is sufficient," P Lond 948¹¹ (A.D. 236) παρεχόμενος ὁ κυβερνήτης τοὺς αὐτάρκεις ναύτας, "the full number of men," *ib.* 1171 *verso* ⁵ (A.D. 42) τὰ αὐταάρκει ἐπιδήτια (so Wilcken for αὐτάρκη ἐπιτήδεια) (severally = III., p. 220, 107), P Lips I. 26¹² (A.D. 205) α]ὐτάρκης γὰρ καὶ ὑπ' αὐ[τ]ῆς ἔπαθον : this is for αὐταρκες (or αὐτάρκη)—"I have suffered enough from her," etc. So in the adverb BGU II. 665¹¹⁻¹⁸ (i/A.D.) ἠτοιμάσθη αὐτῇ πάντα [π]ρὸς [τ]ὴν λοχ[ε]ίαν αὐταρκῶς, P Flor II. 247¹¹ (A.D. 256) αὐταρκῶς δὲ ἔχεις ἅπαξ ἐπιστέλλων κτλ., "it will be sufficient if you . . ." The participle of the derived verb is given in BGU IV. 1122¹⁸ (Aug.) τὰ αὐταρκ[οῦντα).

The record lends some emphasis to the Pauline use of the word in the philosophic sense of "self-sufficient, contented." For all his essentially popular vocabulary, on which Nägeli rightly lays stress, Paul could use the technical words of thinkers in their own way (cf. Nägeli's summing up, p. 44 f., and Milligan, *Documents*, p. 56 f.). We have to go to literary sources for parallels to Phil 4¹¹ and Sir 40¹⁸ : Kennedy *EGT* on Phil 4¹¹ well quotes Plato *Rep* 369 B οὐκ αὐτάρκης ἀλλὰ πολλῶν ἐνδεής, "we are not individually independent', but have many wants" (Davies and Vaughan). In Marcus Aurelius (i⁶) τὸ αὐταρκες ἐν παντί is mentioned as a characteristic of Antoninus Pius.

αὐτοκατάκριτος

is, for all we know to the contrary, a genuine new coinage in Tit 3¹¹. It is built on a model which any writer or speaker was free to use at will.

αὐτόματος.

CPHerm 119 *verso* i.¹⁶ (Gallienus) . .]αὐτόματο. καὶ [. . ., unfortunately in hiatus. Vettius Valens twice uses the adverb with προβιβάζων (or its passive), "advancing of its own accord." With the use of this word in Mk 4²⁸, Abbott (*Joh. Voc.* p. 54) compares Philo's description of Isaac the self-taught (αὐτομαθής) i. 571–2 ἔστι δὲ καὶ τρίτος ὅρος τοῦ αὐτομαθοῦς τὸ ἀναβαῖνον αὐτόματον (that which cometh up of itself). Cf. also Wisd 17⁵, where with reference to the plague of darkness it is said that no power of the fire or the stars could give the Egyptians light, διεφαίνετο δ' αὐτοῖς μόνον αὐτομάτη πυρὰ φόβου πλήρης, "but there appeared to them the glimmering of a fire self-kindled, full of fear." On Jn 16²⁷ αὐτὸς γὰρ ὁ πατὴρ φιλεῖ ὑμᾶς Field remarks (*Notes*, p. 104) that αὐτός is here = αὐτόματος *ultro, me non commendante*, and cites Callim. *H. Apoll.* ὁ αὐτοὶ νῦν κατοχῆες ἀνακλίνεσθε, where the Scholiast has αὐτόματοι.

αὐτόπτης.

In P Oxy VIII. 1154³ (late i/A.D.) a man, who was perhaps absent on military service, writes to his sister not to be anxious, αὐτόπτης γάρ εἰμι τῶν τόπων καὶ οὐκ εἰμὶ ξέν[ο]ς τῶν ἐνθάδε, "for I am personally acquainted with these places and am not a stranger here" (Edd.). Note Vettius Valens, p. 260²⁰, ἐγὼ δὲ οὐ λόγῳ καλῷ χρησάμενος, πολλὰ δὲ καμὼν καὶ παθὼν αὐτόπτης γενόμενος τῶν πραγμάτων δοκιμάσας συνέγραψα. The spell for procuring the visible appearance of the god invoked is introduced in the magical P Lond 122⁸ (iv/A.D.) (= I. p. 119) by the words ἐὰν θέλῃς καὶ αὐτοψαν αὐτὸν ἐκάλεσε, the evident intention being to correct **αυτοψαν** into the passive verbal **αυτοπτον**. Cf. also ib. 121⁷˙⁹ (ii/A.D.) (= I. p. 94), and the derived adj. **αὐτοπτικός** in the same papyrus in a spell for raising one's own "double," ³³⁵ **αὐτοπτικὴ ἐὰν βούλῃς σεαυτὸν [ἰ]δεῖν.** For the subst. cf. P Tebt II. 286²⁰ (A.D. 121–38) **ἐ[κ] τῆς α[ὐ]τοψ[ί]ας ἣν ἐγὼ ἐπεῖδον** "my own personal observation" (Edd.), P Amh II. 142¹² (iv/A.D.) **γενάμενοι ἐπὶ τὴν αὐτοψίαν καὶ ἀναμετρήσαντες τὸν κλῆρον,** P Oxy X. 1272¹⁹ (A.D. 144) **ἀξιῶ ἐὰν δόξῃ σοι παραγενέσθαι ἐπὶ τὴν αὐτοψίαν,** "come for a personal inspection" (Edd.), and P Leid W^xvi. 38.

αὐτός.

The weakening of the old distinction between **αὐτὸς ὁ** and **ὁ αὐτός,** especially in Luke, is noted in *Proleg.* p. 91, and paralleled from Hellenistic. We may add (cf. *Einleitung* p. 145 f.) *Syll* 807¹ (ii/A.D.) **αὐταῖς ταῖς ἡμέραις,** where Dittenberger remarks "expectaveris **ταῖς αὐταῖς,**" *OGIS* 383¹¹ (Antiochus of Commagene, i/B.C.) **τὴν αὐτήν τε κρίσιν,** for which Ditt. desiderates **ταύτην τὴν κρίσιν,** P Hib I. 30⁶ (B.C. 265) **αὐτὸς Ὧρος** "the said H.," P Lille I. 25⁷ (B.C. 221) **οὖ μ[ισ]θωτὴς Ἡρώδ[ης]** = **αὐτός** "ce même H.," P Oxy VI. 892³ (A.D. 338) **τῆς αὐτῆς πόλεως,** ib. VIII. 1119⁸ (A.D. 254) **τοῦ αὐτοῦ ἀμφοδογραμματέως** "the said a.": all these seem to be practically identical, with **αὐτός** differing little from **ἐκεῖνος.** The combination **αὐτὸ τοῦτο** may be illustrated by P Grenf I. 1¹⁴ (literary, ii/B.C.) "for this reason" (Ed.) as in 2 Pet 1⁵, P Ryl II. 77⁴⁹ (A.D. 192) **καὶ αὐτὰ ταῦτα ἀσφαλίσομαι** "I will certify these very facts" (Edd.), P Oxy VIII. 1119¹¹ (see above) **ὑπὲρ τοῦ μὴ καὶ τὸν νυνεὶ φύλαρχον δοκεῖν ἀγνοεῖν αὐτὰ ταῦτα** [. . .

For the phrase **ἐπὶ τὸ αὐτό** = "together," as apparently in Lk 17³⁵, see P Tebt I. 14²⁰ (B.C. 114), where the "total" value of certain property is one talent of copper—**ἀξίας ἐπὶ τὸ αὐτὸ χα(λκοῦ) (ταλάντου) ᾱ**: cf. II. 319⁸ (A.D. 248) **ἐπὶ τὸ αὐτὸ (ἄρουραι) ιε̅,** "a total of 15 arourae." 336¹⁰ (c. A.D. 190), al. This arithmetical use may be applied in Ac 2⁴⁷, if we may render "was daily heaping up the total of . . ." **Κατὰ τὸ αὐτό** with the same meaning, as in Ac 14¹, may be illustrated from the early marriage contract P Eleph 1⁵ (B.C. 311–10) (= *Selections* p. 2) **εἶναι δὲ ἡμᾶς κατὰ ταὐτό,** "and that we should live together." In P Eleph 2⁶ (B.C. 285–4) **κατὰ ταὐτά** = "in the same way." Vettius Valens, p. 57²⁸, uses **τὸ δ' αὐτό** to express the same meaning (**ὡσαύτως**).

On the redundant use of unemphatic **αὐτός** (in oblique cases) see *Proleg.* p. 84 f. We might add that possessive **αὐτοῦ** (like **ἐμοῦ,** etc.) becomes emphatic when placed between art. and noun: e.g. BGU IV. 1098³⁶ (c. B.C. 17) **ἄνευ τῆς αὐτο[ῦ] γν[ώ]μης,** and so ib. 1120¹² (B.C. 8). On the extent to which **αὐτός** (in oblique cases again) may have enlarged its functions at the expense of **ἑαυτοῦ** see next article. In MGr it is the personal pronoun "he" etc., or means "this."

αὐτοῦ.

How far this form is to be recognized in the sense of **ἑαυτοῦ** has been much debated: see the older literature in Grimm-Thayer. It is not *a priori* likely to be common. Meisterhans, *Gr.* p. 154, estimates that between B.C. 300 and 30 **ἑαυτοῦ** outnumbers **αὐτοῦ** in Attica by 100 : 7. But

Mayser, *Gr.* p. 305, makes **αὐτοῦ** three times as common as **ἑαυτοῦ** in iii/B.C. papyri (that is, those published before 1906, therefore excluding P Hib and many other Ptolemaic documents): in ii/B.C. the proportion is reversed, and in i/B.C. **ἑαυτοῦ** stands alone. Mayser's analysis of the documents—official, private letters, inscriptions, etc.—may also be noted. The fact emerges very clearly that both **σαυτοῦ** and **αὐτοῦ** have a certain place during the earlier Ptolemaic period, **αὐτοῦ** being certified by syntactical necessity or by **ἀφ΄, μεθ΄** etc., preceding. That in Egypt **αὐτοῦ** passed out of use is seen from later papyri: Moulton *Einleitung,* p. 139, mentions P Tebt II. 303⁷ (A.D. 176–80) **τῶν ϛ δι' αὐτῶν ἱερέων** ("independent"—Edd.) as the only quotable instance up to date (1910). "Outside Egypt, however, instances are not altogether wanting. Thus *Syll* 371¹⁵ (Magnesia, i/A.D.) **ὑφ' αὐτοῦ** (see however Nachmanson, p. 84), 507⁸ (Lindos, ii/A.D.) **μηδὲν αὐτοῖς δεινὸν συνειδότας.** Dieterich, *Untersuch.* p. 46, gives some inscriptional exx. of the vulgar **ἀτοῦ** (see *op. cit.* p. 78, and above p. 69 [= *Proleg.* p. 47], which show the occasional survival of forms without **ε.**" It may be added that some nine exx. of **αὐτοῦ** appear in the index of *Priene,* against about three times as many of **ἑαυτοῦ.** A good instance may be cited from *Kaibel* 716, the epitaph of a young man (Rome), **φίλους ὑπὲρ ἀτὸν ἐτίμα.** The progressive weakening of *h* would make the clearer form preferable. It is further suggested that the existence of **αὐτοῦ** in LXX (Thackeray *Gr.* p. 190), though far less common than **ἑαυτοῦ,** might help to produce occasional revivals of the obsolete form. We certainly cannot do violence to the sense by forcing **αὐτοῦ** into places where a reflexive is needed: it would be less objectionable to read **ἑαυτοῦ,** assuming **αὐτοῦ** due to some would-be Atticist scribe. See further Kennedy's note, *EGT* III. p. 404, which sums up in favour of a minimum admittance of **αὐτοῦ.**

αὐτόφωρος.

BGU II. 372²˙¹¹ (A.D. 154) (= *Chrest.* I. 19) **το[ὺς] λημφθέντας ἐπ' αὐτ[ο]φ[ώρ]ῳ κακούργους.**

αὐτόχειρ

is warranted in literature: we have not noticed it in our sources, except Vettius Valens. He uses it absolutely, p. 126²¹, = "suicides," and so 127¹⁹: it may have the same sense p. 39³³.

αὐχέω.

For **αὐχέω** construed with an acc. in Jas 3⁵ Hort *in l.* compares Aristid. i. 103 **μόνοις δ' ὑμῖν ὑπάρχει καθαρὰν εὐγένειάν τε καὶ πολιτείαν αὐχῆσαι,** and translates "hath great things whereof to boast," or shortly "great are its boasts" (*i.e.* the concrete subjects for boasting, **αὐχήματα,** not the boastings, **αὐχήσεις.**) Vettius has the verb with **ἐπί τινι,** p. 241⁹ **ὅτε οἱ πρὸ ἡμῶν ἐπὶ τούτῳ ηὔχουν καὶ ἐμακαρίζοντο.** It has a personal accus. in *Kaibel* 507³ (ii/A.D.) **αὐχῶ σώφρονα . . . Σεβῆραν** and similarly ib. 822⁶ (ii/iii A.D.) **Κεκροπίην αὐχεῖ πόλιν** (cf. 932⁷—iii/A.D.): in the passive, ib. 192¹ (Rom. age, Thera) **οὐ μόνον [ἡ] ὑχούμην Λακεδαίμονος ἐκ βασιλήων.** A Theban epitaph (iv/A.D.), ib. 489¹, has the very phrase of Jas 3⁵, **ὃν μεγάλ' αὐ]χήσασα πατρὶς Θή[β]η ποτ' ἔτω[. . :** Kaibel reads **ἐφώλπει,** remarking that digamma survived long in Boeotia (but surely not into iv/A.D., even in poetry). It is unfortunate that the opening words are lost. The record shows that the verb lived on mostly in the language of poetry.

αὐχμηρός.

We can quote only verse parallels for this word of 2 Peter (cf. Apoc Petr 6). *Kaibel* 548, a pretty epitaph on a boy of 16 (Nemausus in Gaul—Nismes) begins after Latin dedication—

> Ἄνθεα πολλὰ γένοιτο νεοδμήτῳ ἐπὶ τύμβῳ,
> μὴ βάτος αὐχμηρή, μὴ κακὸν αἰγίπυρον.

The epithet will imply "dark," "funereal" colour.

The combination quoted by Grimm from Aristotle recurs in *Kaibel* 431³ (Antioch, not before ii/A.D.)—

> κεῖμαι ἐς [αὐ]χμηροὺς καὶ ἀλαμπέας Ἀΐδος εὐνάς.

ἀφαιρέω.

This very common verb is found with the simple gen. in P Hib I. 63¹⁶ (c. B.C. 265) τούτων ἄφελε, "deduct from this"; cf. Rev 22¹⁹ with ἀπό added. *Passim* in the same sense in P Lond 265 (= II. p. 257), a mathematical papyrus of i/A.D. For the more general sense of "carry off," "take away." cf. P Petr III. 53 (j)¹⁵ ὥστε ἀφελέσθαι ἡμῶν βία[ι τὸ κτῆμα], P Magd 6⁶ (B.C. 221) ἀφείλοντο (a garment), *ib.* 42⁵ (B.C. 221) τό τε περιτραχηλίδιον ἐκ καθορμίων λιθίνων ἀφείλετό μ[οι], and so in P Lond 41²³ and 15 (B.C. 161) (= I. p. 28), one of the papyri dealing with the grievances of the Serapeum Twins—ἀφελεῖν α[ὐ]τῶν τοὺς ἄρτους and ἀφίλεσαν τοὺς αὐτῶν διδύμων ἄρτους. It has an extreme meaning in *IosPE* i. 22³¹, ὑπὸ τοῦ βασκάνου δαίμονος ἀφῃρέθη, by death. In BGU I. 74⁸ (ii/A.D.) καὶ γὰρ ἂν ἄλογον εἴη ὁπόσων μὲν υ̅] ἀφερετείητε, we are apparently to understand ἀφαιρεθείητε "you might be robbed." It may be noted that the middle could be used for the meaning "rob," as BGU III. 750¹⁵ (A.D. 125) ἀφελ[ό]μενοί μοι χιτῶνα, etc. We need only add the occurrence of the word in the vi/A.D. Christian amulet edited by Wilcken in *Archiv* i. p. 431 ff. (cf. *Selections*. p. 132 ff.) where the prayer occurs,¹² πᾶσαν δὲ νόσον καὶ πᾶσαν μαλακίαν ἄφελε ἀπ᾽ ἐμοῦ, ὅπως ὑγιανῶ, "take away from me all manner of disease and all manner of sickness that I may be in health."

ἀφανής.

P Gen I. 28¹⁶ (A.D. 136) ἀ]φανὴς ἐγένετο: similarly P Grenf II. 61¹⁶, P Lond 342⁹ (= II. p. 174), BGU I. 165⁶, *ib.* II. 467¹⁵ (all ii/A.D.), *Syll* 923¹⁶ (late iii/B.C.) τὰ μὲν ἐμφανέα . . τῶν δὲ ἀφανέων κτλ. (Aetolia—in dialect). *Ib.* 544² (Aug.) ἀφανοὺς γεγενημένου τοῦ πα[ρατειχίσ]ματος, 891¹⁸ καὶ εἴη ἀφανῆ τὰ κτήματα αὐτοῦ, 809¹¹ (iv/iii B.C.) ἀνόνητα αὐτῷ γένοιτο καὶ ἄχωρα καὶ ἄμοιρα καὶ ἀφανῆ αὐτῷ [ἅ]παντα γένοιτο.

ἀφανίζω.

For the ordinary sense cf. (e. g.) BGU I. 38¹² πάντα ἠφάνισται. For the later meaning "disfigure." "destroy," cf. P Oxy IX. 1220²⁰ iii/A.D.) οὐδὲν ἠφάνισεν ὁ ἱπποπόταμις, "the hippopotamus has destroyed nothing," P Ryl II. 152¹⁴ (A.D. 42) κατενέμησαν καὶ κατέφαγαν καὶ τοῖς ὅλοις ἠφάνισαν "overran, cropped, and utterly destroyed [my pasturage]" (Edd.), and P Lond 413¹⁴ f (c. A.D. 346)

(= II. p. 302) a request for nets since the gazelles were "spoiling" the writer's crops—ἐπιδὴ τὰ δορκάδι[α] ἀφανίζουσειν τὸ ἰ. τὰ] σπόριμα. A near parallel to Mt 6¹⁶ is afforded by the Christian hymn P Amh I. 2³ (iv/A.D.) Γάμον ἤλυθες βασιλῆος, Γάμον . . . ἵνα μή σ᾽ ἀφανίσῃς "Thou hast come to the marriage of the King, the marriage . . . that thou mayst not disfigure thy face." In a fragment of a Gnostic Gospel of early iv/A.D., P Oxy VIII. 1081²⁵ ᵃ, the Saviour in answer to the disciples' question, "How then can we find faith?" is represented as replying διελθο[ῦσιν ἐκ τῶν] ἀφανῶν κα]ὶ εἰ]ς τὸ [φῶ]ς τῶν φαινο[μέ]νων, "if ye pass from the things that are hidden," etc. (Ed.)

In *Kaibel* 376⁸ (Aezani, ii/A.D.) the verb is used of the "defacing" of a relief, ὅστις νεκρὰν πρόσοψιν ἀφανίσει τέκνου: cf. *ib.* 531² (Thrace) μου τὸ κάλλος ἠφάνισ[ε]ν (presumably Death is the subject). In 492³ (Thebes, i/B.C. or A.D.) Fortune ἠφάνισε a young athlete. A British Museum papyrus printed in *Archiv* vi, p. 102 (A.D. 114–5) has (l. 7) μετέδωκέν μοι . . . τὰ ἐν αὐτῇ (sc. the record office) βιβλία ἀφανί[σ]εσθαι, τὰ δὲ πλεῖστα καὶ ἀνεύρετα εἶναι: the present tense suits best the meaning "are being ruined."

ἀφανισμός.

Vettius Valens p. 55⁷ ὅπως τε οἱ ἀφανισμοὶ (sc. fetus) καὶ τὰ ἐκτρώματα γίνονται.

ἄφαντος.

This poetic word, which reappears in the later prose writers (e. g. Diod. Sic. iv. 65. 9). is found in the NT only in Lk 24³¹ ἄφαντος ἐγένετο ἀπ᾽ αὐτῶν. The addition of a complement such as ἀπ᾽ αὐτῶν is not in accordance with the usual Greek usage of the word, and is explained by Psichari (*Essai sur le Grec de la LXX*, p. 204 ff.) as a Hebraism. This would presumably mean that Luke imitated the occasional LXX ἀφανίζειν or -εσθαι ἀπό, but used the Hellenistic ἄφαντος γενέσθαι instead of the verb: clearly this combination was thoroughly vernacular prose by this time—it survives in MGr.

ἄφεδρων.

This rare word is found in *OGIS* 483²²⁰ ᵇ (ii/B.C.) in the same sense as in Mt 15¹⁷, Mk 7¹⁸, the only two occurrences of the word in Biblical Greek—Cod.D substitutes ὀχετόν in Mk. In LXX Lev 12² ἡ ἄφεδρος is used in another connexion.

ἀφειδία.

For the adj. see *OGIS* 383¹⁴² (i/B.C.) ἐπιθύσεις ἀφειδεῖς λιβανωτοῦ καὶ ἀρωμάτων, and the fine epitaph of a Sergius, martyred under Galerius, *Kaibel* 1064 (Justinian), referring to the ἀφειδέες ἀγῶνες of the Empress. The adv. is found P Tebt I. 24⁷⁶ (B.C. 117) ἀφει[δ]ῶς, *Syll* 342²⁹ (c. B.C. 48) ἀφειδῶς ἑαυτὸ[ν ἐπιδ]ιδούς. For the verb see *OGIS* 640¹² (iii/A.D.) οὐκ ὀλίγων ἀφειδήσαντα χρημάτων.

ἀφελότης.

Vettius Valens dispels Grimm-Thayer's aspersions once more: see p. 240¹⁵, the cultured man ῥᾳδίως ἁλίσκεται ὡς ἄπειρος τῶν παθῶν ὑπ᾽ ἀφελότητος καὶ ἀδιοικησίας προδεδομένος, "betrayed by simplicity and lack of practical capacity." So p. 153³⁹, if Kroll's conjecture is sound, οὐ φθόνῳ φερόμενοι οὐδὲ ἀφελότητι. So here is one writer neither "biblical" nor "ecclesiastical" who agrees with Luke in preferring this abstract to ἀφέλεια, which however he uses once, p. 42³⁴ εἰς ἀ. τὸν τρόπον ἐμφαίνοντες. The astrologer may further be quoted for the adverb ἀφελῶς. p. 168²³ πολλὰ δὲ ἀ. πιστεύσας ἀπώλεσεν, again confirming the colour of unworldly simplicity which appears in Ac 2⁴⁶. The same adverb may be quoted from an inser., IosPE i. 22²¹, ἑαυτὸν ἀ. τῇ πατρίδι ἐς ἅπαντα ἐπεδ.δον, as well as in Hellenistic literature. Thus Preuschen (HZNT ad Ac 2⁴⁶) cites Athenaeus, Deipnos. X. 419² (II. 412¹⁶ Kaibel) ἐστιαθεὶς ἀφελῶς καὶ μουσικῶς, where "simple" meals are contrasted with τὰ πολυτελῆ δεῖπνα. Add Kaibel 727¹⁴ (Christian?) εἰκοστὸν δὲ βιώσασαν ἀφελῶς ἐνιαυτόν : the same epitaph speaks of a ψυχὴν ἀφελῆ.

ἄφεσις.

In Egypt ἄφεσις τοῦ ὕδατος was apparently a technical expression for the "release" of the water from the sluices or canals for the purpose of irrigation, e.g. P Petr II. 13(2)¹² ff. (B.C. 258-3) ἵνα ἐπισκευασθῶσι πρὸ τῆς τοῦ ὕδατος ἀφέσεως, "in order that they (sc. bridges) may be finished before the letting down of the water" (Ed.), ib. III. 39¹², and 44 verso ¹¹ ¹⁹ f. τ[ῶν κατ]ὰ Πτολεμαίδα ἀ φ.έσεων ἠνοίξαμεν β θύ[ρας]. In this sense the noun may be concrete, meaning apparently a "channel" or "sluice" : P Oxy VI. 918ᵛ ²⁰(ii/A.D.) ἀπηλ(ιώτου) ὁδὸ(ς) δημοσί(α) ἐν ᾗ ἄφεσις λιθίνη. Hence, as Deissmann has shown (BS p. 98 ff.), the increased vividness for the Egyptians of the pictures in Joel 1²⁰, Lam 3⁴⁷ through the use of ἀφέσεις by the LXX translators. The word is similarly employed to denote the official "release" of the harvest after the taxes had been paid, in order that the cultivators might then use it for their own purposes, as P Petr II. 2(1)⁹ f. (B.C. 260-59) τῆς μ̣.ισθώσεως διαγορενούσης κομίσασθαι [αὐτὸ]ν τ[ὰ] ἐκφόρια ὅταν ἡ ἄφεσις δοθῇ, P Amh II. 43⁵ (B.C. 173) ὅταν ἡ ἄφεσις τῶν πυρίνων καρπῶν γένηται, "whenever the release of the wheat crops takes place" (Edd. : see their note ad l. and cf. Archiv iv. p. 65). The editors regard it as very doubtful whether the difficult phrase γῆ ἐν ἀφέσει, P Tebt I. 5³⁷ ff. (B.C. 118), is to be explained in the same way, and in their note on P Tebt II. 325⁵ they suggest "in reduction," or "on reduced terms" as a possible rendering. Mahaffy (P Petr III. p. 35) translates the same phrase in P Par 63¹⁷⁷ (B.C. 165) by "privileged land." A nearer approach to the Pauline use for "forgiveness" is afforded by the occurrence of the word in inscriptions for remission from debt or punishment, e.g. Michel 1340ᵇ ⁷ (Cnidus, ii/B.C.) τὰς τε ἀφέσιος τοῦ ταλάντου ὃ φαν[τι] ἀφεῖσθαι Καλύμνιοι ὑπὸ Παυσιμάχου, Syll 226¹⁶⁶ (Olbia on the Euxine, iii/B.C.) τοῖς μὲν ἀφέσεις ἐποιήσατο τῶν χρημάτων (and exacted no interest from other debtors), Magn 93(c)¹⁴ ff. τὰ γὰρ ὀφειλόμενα κατὰ τ]ὴν καταδίκην τῆς καθηκούσης τετευχέναι ἐξαγωγῆς ἤτοι εἰσ[πραχθείσης τ]ῆς καταδίκης ἢ ἀφέσεως γενομένης : see also CIG 2058ᵇ ⁷⁹ (Olbia, ii/i B.C.), 2335⁶ (Delos, time of Pompey) (Nageli, p. 56). With a gen. pers. it denotes the "release" of prisoners or captives, as Lk 4¹⁸, Syll 197²¹ (B.C. 284-3) ὅσοι δὲ αἰχμάλωτοι ἐγένοντο, ἐμφανίσας τῷ βα[σιλεῖ καὶ] λαβὼν αὐτοῖς ἄφε[σ]ιν κτλ., or "release" from some public duty, as P Oxy VII. 1020⁶ (A.D. 198-201) ὁ ἡγούμ[ενος] τοῦ ἔθνους τὸν ἀγῶνα τῆς ἀφέσεως ἐκδικ[ήσει.

In P Tebt II. 404¹ (late iii/A.D.) what seems to be the heading of a set of accounts runs Λόγο[ς] ἀφέσεως στατήρων ρλ : the editors render "expenditure (?)." It should also be noted that the word was a term. techn. in astrology : see index to Vettius, p. 377. Thus p. 225¹⁶ χρὴ ταῖς λοιπαῖς τῶν ἀστέρων ἀφέσεσι καὶ μαρτυρίαις καὶ ἀκτινοβολίαις προσέχειν. See also Abbott Joh. Voc. p. 178 f., with a correction in Fourfold Gospel, p. 59.

ἀφή.

For the special sense of "kindling" see P Tebt I. 88¹² f. (B.C. 115-4) εἴς τε τὰς θυσίας καὶ λύχνων ἀφῶν, "for sacrifices and for the kindling of lamps" (cf. λυχναψία, BGU II. 362ⁱ·¹·¹²·ᵉᵗᶜ·); and for the meaning "sand" or "dust" as a technical term of the arena see Syll 804¹¹ (? ii/A.D.) ἀφῇ πηλώσασθαι (with the editor's note). It is, however, a wholly different connexion with wrestling that is associated with the NT meaning of the word. Dean Robinson (on Eph 4¹⁶) has shown how from the ἀφὴ ἄφυκτος with which the wrestler fastened on his opponent ἀφή came to be used of the union of the Democritean atoms, and further of a band or ligament in ancient physiology. Hence in the Pauline usage, the thought is not so much of "touch" as of "fastening,"—the whole body is compacted διὰ πάσης ἀφῆς τῆς ἐπιχορηγίας "by every ligament of the whole apparatus" (Eph 4¹⁶), which in Col 2¹⁹ is expanded into διὰ τῶν ἀφῶν καὶ συνδέσμων "by the ligaments and sinews." A mysterious ἔπαφος occurs in the new Median parchment, P Saïd Khan 1ᵃ ²⁶ (B.C. 88) : the assignee of a vineyard is to be fined ἐὰν . . ὀλιγωρήσῃ τὴν ἄμπελον καὶ μὴ ποιήσῃ αὐτὴν ἔπαφον. Can this mean "properly tied up"—the branches being tied to the poles or trees on which they are trained ? The adj. will thus be formed from ἐπὶ ἀφαῖς "depending on fastenings"—a formation well paralleled in Hellenistic.

ἀφθαρσία.

An interesting example of this word occurs in the fragment of the Gnostic Gospel from the beginning of iv/A.D., P Oxy VIII. 1081¹⁴ ff., where in contrast to the perishing of everything born of corruption (ἀπὸ φθορᾶς) we find τὸ] δὲ γε[ι]νόμεν[ον ἀπὸ ἀφ θ]αρσίας [οὐκ ἀπο γείν[εται] ἀλλ[ὰ μ]έν[ει] ἀφ[θαρ]τον ὡς ἀπὸ ἀ[φ θ]αρσία]ς γεγονός. It is also quoted from Epicurus (60³) τὴν μετὰ ἀφθαρσίας μακαριότητα : see Linde, p. 43, where other literary parallels are noted.

ἄφθαρτος.

As an antithesis to "mortal," the term is well seen in Syll 365¹⁰ (c. A.D. 37) θεῶν δὲ χάριτες τούτῳ διαφέρουσιν ἀνθρωπίνων διαδοχῶν, ᾧ ἡ νυκτὸς ἥλιος καὶ (for ἢ) τὸ ἄφθαρτον θνητῆς φύσεως, OGIS 569²⁴ (A.D. 312) ὑπὲρ] τῆς αἰωνίου καὶ ἀφθάρτου βασιλε.ας ὑμῶν, with reference to the Imperial rule. The adj. occurs ter in the magic papyrus P Lond 121 (iii/A.D.) (= I. p. 83 ff.) : see also P Leid Wxx.³⁷ οὐρανὸν μέγαν ἀένναον ἄφθαρτον. Cf. s.v. ἀφθαρσία. The record hardly proves a vernacular currency.

ἀφθορία.

The adj. from which this abstract is formed occurs in the formula of contract with a wet-nurse, who is to feed the child τῶι ἰδίωι] αὐτῆς γάλακτι καθαρῶι καὶ ἀφθόρωι, BGU IV. 1107[7] (B.C. 13): so 1106[11] (suppl.), 1108[7], 1109[7] (all Aug., from Alexandria). For ἄφθορος = "chaste" see the magic papyri P Lond 46[376] (iv/A.D.) (= I. p. 77) ὑπὸ παιδὸς ἀφθόρου, and ib. 121[644] (iii/A.D.) (= I. p. 101) where similarly the vision is granted to a boy who is ἄφθορος καθαρός: cf. for the same meaning Justin *Apol.* i. 15[6], and *Dialog.* 100 (p. 327 c.) παρθένος γὰρ οὖσα Εὔα καὶ ἄφθορος (cited by Dibelius on Tit 2[7] in *HZNT*). Between 1 Pet 2[2] and our papyri, we should think of freedom from "taint"—the spiritual milk has gathered no microbes!

ἀφίημι.

Some abnormal NT forms of this very "irregular" verb may be illustrated: cf. Moulton, *Einleitung*, p. 82 f. The unaugmented aor. pass. ἀφέθησαν in Rom 4[7] (from Ps 31[1]) where ℵ has ἀφείθησαν) is matched by OGIS 435[9] (ii/B.C.) ἀφέθη; but BGU IV. 1022[8] (A.D. 196) ἀφθείθημεν (i.e. ἀφείθ.). Ἀφέωνται is to be compared with the imper. ἀφεώσθω in *Michel* 585[14] (Arcadian ? iii/B.C.), as well as with the Herodotean ἀνέωται: see *Proleg.* p. 38 n. Against this note imper. ἀφείσθω in CPHerm 119 *verso* iii. 14 (Gallienus). The pres. ἀφείς in Rev 2[20] and Ex 32[32] is best taken as a regular contraction of ἀφίεις, from ἀφίω (not a contract verb), which is the normal conjugation into which the -μι verb tends here to merge itself: evidence for ἀφιέω seems to be wanting. The assumption of an ἀφέω, formed by proportion from ἀφήσω, is insufficiently supported by the barbarous Silco inscr., OGIS 201[13] (vi/A.D.). The MGr is ἀφήνω, with aor. ἄφησα and ἀφῆκα.

Proleg. p. 175, may be referred to for the quasi-auxiliary use of ἄφες, MGr ἄς. We may quote P Amh II. 37[10] (B.C. 172) ἄφες αὐτὸν χαίρειν, P Hib I. 41[8] (c. B.C. 261) ἀφ[ε]ς αὐτὸν εἰσαγαγεῖν "allow him to collect" (Edd.); but P Oxy III. 413[184] (literary, i/A.D.) ἄφες ἐγὼ αὐτὴν θρηνήσω (literary, i/A.D.). The Latin *sine, sinite videamus* in Mt 27[49] and Mk 15[36] severally, may well mean "Let us see," as Pallis renders it (ἂς δοῦμε) in both cases, only differing in the speakers. The verb has not yet become a mere auxiliary: it may still be rendered "allow me to," etc. For the same use in another part of the verb cf. P Oxy VII. 1067[6] (iii/A.D.) ἀφῆκες αὐτὸν μὴ κηδεῦσαι αὐτόν, "you have allowed his burial to be neglected" (Ed.). So, with infin. again, in P Par 47[14] (c. B.C. 153) (= Witkowski[2], p. 89) ὅτι περάσεται ὁ δραπέ[τη]s μὴ ἀφῖναι ἡμᾶς ἐ[πὶ τ]ῶν τόπων ἶναι.

The uses of ἀφίημι start from the etymological sense "throw" seen in the cognate *abicio*. Thus in *Syll* 356[26] (B.C. 6) ἀφεῖναι τὴν γάστραν = "let the pot drop." From this primitive physical meaning may be derived the common meaning "leave, let go." So with dat. (as in Mt 5[40]) P Tebt II. 421[9] (iii/A.D.) θέλις αὐτὸν ἀφεῖναι τῆι θυγατρί σ[ον] ἄφες "if you wish to let your daughter have it, do so" (Edd.). P Grenf I. 26[9] (B.C. 113) τὴν δὲ ἡμιολίαν ἀφῆκε, "waived the extra 50%," will serve as an ex. of the use seen in Mt 18[27], which leads to the general idea of "forgiveness." Similarly in OGIS 90[12] (Rosetta stone—B.C. 196) εἰς τέλος ἀφῆκεν, of the "total remission" of certain taxes. (See for the NT usage of the word in this sense Brooke *Joh. Epp.* p. 20 f.) Not far from this is the use seen in P Oxy IV. 744[10] (B.C. 1) (= *Selections*, p. 33) ἐὰν . . τέκῃς

ἐὰν ἦν ἄρσενον ἄφες, ἐὰν ἦν θήλεα ἔκβαλε, "if it is a boy, let it be; if a girl, expose it." "To let alone" may mean "neglect" or "leave undone," as BGU III. 775[18] (ii/A.D.) τὰ ἤδη πρόλημα ἄφες ἄχρης ἂν γένομε ἐκῖ καὶ συνάρωμεν λόγον "leave the preparations (?) till I get there and we can confer together," or again as in P Lond 144[14] (? i/A.D.) (= II. p. 253) μὴ ἀφεῖναί με ἐπὶ ξένης ἀδιαφορηθῆναι, "not to leave me to be neglected in a strange land." It has an explanatory clause in a letter of Hadrian's age, P Oxy X. 1293[18] μὴ θελήσῃ τις ἀφεῖναι μέρος μὴ ἐνένκας, "lest one of them should want to leave part behind and not bring it" (Edd.). BGU III. 814 (iii/A.D.), a very ungrammatical complaint from a son to his mother, three times shows the verb meaning "abandon, desert," with an irregular dative object: [16] ἀφ[ῆ]κ[έ]ς μοι οὕ]τως μηδὲν ἔχων (for ἔχοντι), [18] ἀφῆκές [μοι οὔ]τ[ως] ὡς κύων (for κυνί), [27] μὴ ἀφήσις μοι οὗτος. So in the "Erotic Fragment," P Grenf I. 1[18] (literary, ii/B.C.) κύριε, μή μ᾽ ἀφῇς—an appeal from a forsaken girl to her lover. P Lille 29[ii. 32] (iii/B.C.) ἀφεῖσθα[ι τῆς κατα]δίκης will illustrate its use with a gen. of "releasing from": so P Oxy VIII. 1119[17] (A.D. 254) ὑμεῖς οἱ κράτιστοι οὐ μόνον ἀφίεται [ἡμᾶς πασῶν παρ᾽ ἄλλοις ἀρχῶν]—the suppl. seems sure. P Petr II. 13 (19)[7 f.] (middle of iii/B.C.) (= Witkowski *Epp.*[2], p. 19) μάλιστα μὲν οὖν τὴν πᾶσαν σπονδὴν πόησαι [το]ῦ ἀφεθῆναι σε διὰ τέλους, "above all things, then, make every effort to be finally relieved of your duties" (Ed.). Witkowski (*in loc.*) says ἀφιέναι is "vox sollemnis de missione militum." It may be that a similar "formal" dismissal or sending away of the multitudes is to be found in Mt 13[36] Mk 4[36]; but it may just as well mean simply "let go," as in ordinary colloquial speech. The equivalence of the Latin *mittere* is seen in the compound, P Ryl II. 126[14] (A.D. 28-9) ἐπαφεὶς τὰ ἑατοῦ πρόβατα καὶ βοικὰ κτήνη εἰς ἃ γεωργῶ . . ἐδάφ(η) "let his sheep and cattle into . . fields which I cultivate" (Ed.): cf. "liquidis immisi fontibus apros" in Vergil (*Ecl.* 2[59]). Finally, for the use of ἀφιέναι with a predicative adj. placed with the object, cf. P Fay 112[12] (A.D. 99) ἄθέρις (*sc.* -στον) αὐτὸν ἕως σήμερον ἀφίκας, "up to to-day you have left it unharvested" (Edd.), P Oxy III. 494[6] (A.D. 156) ἐλεύθερα ἀφίημι . . δοῦλά μου σώματα, of manumission under a will.

ἀφικνέομαι.

BGU II. 614[20] (A.D. 217) εἰς τοὺς τόπο[υς ἀφι[κέσθαι . ., and l. [27]; P Giss I. 34[7] (A.D. 265-6) εἴστω μέντοι, ὅτι ἐὰν μὴ ἀφίκηται σὺν τῇ [. . . A προσκύνημα from El-Kab in Egypt, *Preisigke* 158, has Ἀνδρόμαχος Μακεδὼν ἀφίκετο πρὸς Ἀμενώθην χρηστὸν θεόν—he records his immediate cure: so ib. 1049 (Abydos) Πειθαγόρας Πειθαγόρου ὅτ᾽ ἀφίκετο ἐπὶ σωτηρίαι, ib. 1052, *al*. It is almost a technical word in describing these "pilgrimages" to sacred places. So in verse, *Kaibel* 981[9], from the island of Philae (i/A.D.):—

Νῆσον ἔ[π]᾽ Αἰγύπτ[ο]ιο πέρας, περικαλλέα, σεμνήν
Ἴσιδος, Αἰθιόπων πρόσθεν, ἀφιξάμενοι
εἴδομεν ἐν Νείλωι ποταμῶι νέας ὠκυπορούσας.

In ordinary use it is hardly known, and in NT it only appears metaphorically, in Rom 16[19]. In *Preisigke* 1052 (Abydos) Κλεαίνετος ἐπὶ σωτηρίαι Ῥόδων ἀφίκετο, it seems as if the meaning is "arrived from Rhodes," involving a reanimation of the ἀπό in a new sense (instead of the perfectivizing force): cf. the problem of ἄφιξις below.

ἀφιλάγαθος.

In P Oxy I. 33[ii. 13] (ii/A.D.) (= Chrest I. 20) a certain Ap, ianus charges the Emperor Marcus Aurelius (?) with τυραννία ἀφιλοκαγαθία ἀπαιδία (presumably ἀπαιδευσία), after extolling his deified father as φιλόσοφος, ἀφιλάργυρος, and φιλάγαθος. Vettius Valens has the negative of a similar compound ἀφιλόκαλος, also found in Plutarch. Nägeli (p. 52) cites from an inscr. of ii/iii A.D. (Tanais) the strengthened compound παραφιλάγαθος.

ἀφιλάργυρος.

For this word, which according to Grimm-Thayer is found "only in the NT" (?), see (in addition to Didache 15[1]) the quotation from P Oxy I. 33 s.v. ἀφιλάγαθος. Add Priene 137[5] (probably ii/B.C.) : also Syll 732[25] (Athens, B.C. 36-5), 325[17] (Istropolis. i/B.C.), both of which have the adverb ἀφιλαργύρως. Cf. Nägeli, p. 31, Deissmann LAE, p. 81 f.

ἄφιξις.

One early citation may be made from P Petr II. 13 (18 a)[6] (B.C. 258-3) ἵνα ἀναχωσθῆι καὶ ὁμαλισθῆ πρὸς [τὴ]ν τοῦ βασιλέως ἄφιξιν, where the word certainly means arrival (the reference is to the filling up and levelling of some excavated place in view of a visit from King Ptolemy II.): so also in Aristeas (ed. Wendland) 173 ὡς δὲ παρεγενήθημεν εἰς Ἀλεξάνδρειαν. προσηγγέλη τῷ βασιλεῖ περὶ τῆς ἀφίξεως ἡμῶν, and Magn 17[11] ὡς δὲ περὶ ὀγδοήκονθ' ἔτη μετὰ τὴν ἄφιξιν ἐφά[νησαν οἱ λευκοὶ] κόρακες, and as late as iv/A.D. in P Lips I. 64[35] πρὸς (l. πρὸ) τῆς ἀφίξεως τοῦ δικαστηρίου and [47], and in the Christian letter P Oxy VI. 939[26ff.] (= Selections, p. 130) παραμυθούμ[ε]θα δὲ αὐτὴν ἑκάστης ὥρας ἐκδεχόμενοι τὴν [σ]ὴν ἄφιξιν, "we comfort her by hourly expecting your arrival" (Edd.). But Josephus Antt. ii. 18 fin., μὴ προδηλώσαντες τῷ πατρὶ τὴν ἐκεῖσε ἄφιξιν — not included among Grimm's citations—can hardly mean anything but "departure," or at least "journey": Whiston renders "removal." It must be admitted that Jos. uses the word also for "arrival," as Apion i. 18 (127), 25 (223) and 27 (275). See Proleg. p. 26 n[1] on the question of Ac 20[29].

ἀφίστημι.

The transitive tenses recur in formulæ upon contracts of sale, etc.: the vendor is to "repel" any claimant or trespasser. Thus BGU IV. 1127[19] (B.C. 18) καὶ πάντα τὸν ἐπελευσόμενον ἢ ἐμποιησόμενον αὐτὸν Ἀ. ἀφιστάσιν παραχρῆ[μα τοῖς ἰδίοις δαπανή]μασιν. Generally it is ἀποστήσειν, as P. M. Meyer notes on P Giss I. 51[20], where is a list of instances. Cf. P Lond 3[27] (B.C. 146 or 135) (= I., p. 46) ἐὰν δὲ μὴ ἀποστήσωσι, ἀποστήσω ἐπάναγκον, "if I do not repel him, I will go under compulsion" (Ed.). In P Par 59[2] (B.C. 160) (= Witkowski[2], p. 75) τὸν λόγον τῶν χαλκῶν (sc. λαβέ)· ἀπέστηκα (δραχμὰς) ἢ ἀργυρίου (δραχμὰς) Δσ̅ξ̅, Grenfell-Hunt-Smyly and Wilcken suspect a mistake for ἀπέσχηκα: Witkowski objects that ἀπέχω would have been enough, and would render "solutum accepi." But ἀπέσχηκα is quite common. Witkowski shows that even in Homer ἀφίσταμαι could mean "solvo pecuniam debitam." It also means "renounce a claim to" or "give up occupation" etc., c. gen. rei, with or without ἀπό: thus in P Grenf II. 28[3 ff] (B.C. 103) ἀφίσταται Σεννῆσις . . . ἀπὸ τῆς ἐωνημένης ὑπ' αὐτῆς παρὰ Πετεαρσεμθέως . . .

(τετάρτην) μερίδα ἀμπελῶ(νος) συνφύτου, the meaning seems to be that Sennesis "renounces" all claim to a piece of land she had sold to Petearsemtheus (but see the introduction to P Lips I. 1, and Wilcken in Archiv iv. p. 456). For a similar use of the middle cf. OGIS 763[46] (ii/B.C.) πειράσομαι καὶ νῦν τῆς τοιαύτης προθέσεως μὴ ἀφίστασθαι, and Magn 53[6] οὐθενὸς ἀποστήσεται τῶν ἀνηκόντων τῆι πόλει, al. For various uses of the intrans. active, cf. P Grenf II. 77[9] (iii/iv A.D.) ἀλόγως ἀπέστητε μὴ ἄραντες [τὸ σ]ῶμα τοῦ ἀδελφοῦ ὑμῶν, "you unfeelingly went off without taking your brother's body," but only (as appears later) his effects, P Lond 1209[2] (B.C. 89) (= III. p. 20) ὦτα ἀφεστηκότα, "ears standing out (from the head)," P Giss I. 9[3] τοῦ ἀνδρός μου . . . ἀποστάντ[ο]ς εἰς Ὄασιν ἐνπορίας χάριν. BGU I. 159[4] (A.D. 216) ἀπέστ[η]ν τῆς κώμης, OGIS 654[2] (i/B.C.) τὴν Θηβαίδα [ἀ]ποστᾶσαν . . . νικήσας, BGU III. 920[31] (A.D. 180) οὐκ ἐξόντος μοι ἀποστῆναι τῆς μισ[θ]ώσεως (cf. 1 Tim 4[1]), P Rein 7[18] (B.C. 141?) ἐμπλεκεὶς τέ μοι οὐκ [ἀ]πέστη καὶ μὴ ἠνάγκασε κτλ., "only left me after he had forced me to sign," etc. This last use, with which may be compared Lk 13[27], etc., is seen in an incantation of the great Paris magical papyrus, 574[1241] (iii/A.D.) (= Selections, p. 114) ἔξελθε δαῖμον, . . καὶ ἀπόστηθι ἀπὸ τοῦ δῖ(να), ἄρτι ἄρτι ἤδη.

ἄφοβος.

P Tebt I. 24[74] (B.C. 117). P Ryl II. 62[17] (iii/A.D.) (a literary effort) ἀ. καὶ πεπαρησιασμένως (i. e. πεπαρρ.)

ἀφοράω.

With ἀφορᾶν εἰς = "look away from [other things] to" in Heb 12[2], Abbott (Joh. Voc. p. 28) aptly compares Epict. ii. 19, 29 εἰς τὸν θεὸν ἀφορῶντας ἐν παντὶ καὶ μικρῷ καὶ μεγάλῳ, and iii. 24, 16 where Epictetus says of Herakles' attitude to Zeus—πρὸς ἐκεῖνον ἀφορῶν ἔπραττεν ἃ ἔπραττεν. On the form ἀφίδω (Phil 2[23] ℵ AB* D* FG 33) see Proleg. p. 44: in spite of Thackeray's note (Gr. p. 124 f.—which see for further exx.) we cannot allow the long-lost digamma any influence in determining this Hellenistic type—see Brugmann-Thumb p. 143, and further under ἔτος. In this word at any rate the levelling of ἀπιδεῖν to ἀφορᾶν is a certain explanation.

ἀφορίζω.

BGU III. 915[15, 21] (A.D. 49-50) τὰς ἀφωρισθείσας ὑπ' Ἑρμαίου (sc. ἀρούρας), ib. IV. 1060[33] (B.C. 14) τὸν ἀφωρικό(τα) τὸ ἔδαφος, in a technical sense: cf. much earlier OGIS 6[20] (iv/B.C.) ἀφορίσαι αὐτῶι τέμενος. Similarly in Rev L ἡ ἀφωρισμένη was the part of the Libyan nome, the produce of which was reserved for Alexandria: see the editor's note, p. 169. For the word, as in Mt 13[49], we may add a citation from the Pelagia-Legenden, p. 6[5], μή με ἀφορίσῃς ἀπὸ τοῦ οὐρανίου σου θυσιαστηρίου. In Kaibel 244[3], an epitaph from near Cyzicus, written in a conventional Doric, τᾷ κάλλος ἀφώρισε Κύπρις ἐν ἀστοῖς means "set apart" as incomparable.

ἀφορμή.

This Pauline word is well established in the vernacular with meanings varying from "incitement" or "prompting" (P Oxy II. 237[vii. 21], A.D. 186, ἐκ μη[τ]ρὸς ἀφορμῆς) to the more ordinary "occasion" or "opportunity." Thus the edict of an Eparch of Egypt, P Oxy I. 34[iii.12 ff] (A.D. 127) runs τοὺ[ς] διὰ ἀπείθίαν κ[αὶ] ὡς ἀφορμὴν ζητοῦντας ἁμαρτημάτω[ν] τειμωρήσομαι (see under ἀπείθεια). So in Caracalla's edict (A.D. 215), P Giss I. 40[ii. 11] ἵνα μ[ὴ] π[αρ'] α ὑτοῖς ἡ δειλίας αἰτία ἢ παρὰ το[ῖ]ς κακοήθεσιν ἐπηρ[ε]ίας ἀφορμὴ ὑπολειφθῇ. The last clause recalls Rom 7[8], and other passages where ἀφορμή and ἁμαρτία are brought together. (Ζητεῖν ἀφορμήν is a Western reading in Lk 11[54]). See also BGU II. 615[8] (ii/A.D.) ἀφορμὴν εὑρών (l. εὑροῦσα) —a daughter "finds an opportunity" to write to her father, ib. 632[11] (ii/A.D.) καὶ 'γὼ διὰ πᾶσαν ἀφορμὴν ο[ὐ]χ ὀκνῶ σοι γράψαι περὶ τῆ[ς] σωτηρίας μου καὶ τῶν ἐμῶν, "and on every opportunity I do not delay to write you regarding the health of myself and of mine," ib. III. 923[22] (iii/A.D.) καλῶς οὖν ποιήσεις, ἐὰν εὕρῃς ἀφορμή[ν] διαγραψάμενος κτλ., P Strass I. 22[20 f] (iii/A.D.) ἔχοντός τινος ἀφορμὴν κἂν βραχεῖαν δικαίαν κατοχῆς. "if any one has a just occasion of possession for however brief a period," and from the inscriptions Priene 105[12] (c. B.C. 9) ὄ[φ]ελος εὐτυχεστέρα[ς] λάβοι ἀφορμάς, and [16] ἵνα ἀφορμὴ γένοιτο τῆς εἰς τὸν Σεβαστὸν τειμῆς. The more literal sense of the word is seen in the iv/A.D. letter P Amh II. 143[14 ff] μὴ θελήσῃς οὖν, κύριε, μίνε (= μεῖναι) ἐκτὸς ἡμῶν αὔριον διὰ τὴν ἀφορμὴν τοῦ ὕδατος εἶνα δυνηθῶμεν ποτίσαι τ[ὸ]ν μέγαν κλῆρον, "so please, sir, do not stay away from us to-morrow, because of the flow of water, so that we may be able to irrigate the large holding" (Edd.). It is common in Vettius, esp. with πράξεως or πραγμάτων: thus p. 238[2] περὶ τὰς πράξεις καὶ βιωτικὰς ἀφορμάς. An apparently new verb ἀφορμάζεται is found in the late P Lond IV. 1360[7] (A.D. 710), in the sense of "make excuses" (Ed.). In MGr the noun means "occasion, cause."

ἀφρός.

The adj. ἀφριόεντι, as an epithet of the sea, occurs in a late hymn to Isis, Kaibel 1028[74]. For the medical writers' use of ἀφρός (Lk 9[39]) see Hobart's plentiful evidence, Med. Language of St Luke, p. 171. The word is MGr.

ἄφρων.

P Fay 124[13] (ii/A.D.) πάνυ γάρ μοι δοκεῖς ἄφρων τις εἶ[ν]αι, "indeed you appear to me to be quite mad" (Edd.) —a remonstrance addressed to a man who was defrauding his mother of some allowance. The adj. occurs in the literary P Grenf I. 1[19] (ii/B.C.) ἐὰν δ' ἐνὶ προσκαθεῖ μόνον, ἄφρων ἔσει: see note.

ἀφυπνόω.

Plummer on Lk 8[23] says the use = "fall asleep" is "medical and late": unfortunately he gives no evidence of the former (nor does Hobart mention it), but the citation from Heliodorus is to be noted. Lobeck Phryn. p. 224 gives others. The transference of an ἀπό compound from the end of an action to the beginning of it is seen also in ἄφιξις (q.v.): in neither case is Luke likely to have started the change of meaning, but our evidence is still scantier here than there.

ἀφυστερέω.

P Flor I. 3[17] (A.D. 301) ἐὰν δὲ ἀφυστερή[σ]ωσι καὶ μὴ παραστήσωμε[ν] ἡμεῖς αὐτ[ο]ὶ τὸν [ὑπὲρ] αὐτῶν λόγον ὑπο-

μ[εν]οῦμεν, "but if they fail, or if we do not make the arrangement, we hold ourselves responsible." A similar phrase is found ib. 34[11] (A.D. 342), P Lips I. 54[11] (A.D. 376), ib. 50[12] (A.D. 398), and PSI 86[4] (A.D. 367-75). P Lond 1166[13] (A.D. 42) (= III. p. 105) ἐὰν δὲ ἀφυστερῇ τὸ βαλανεῖον καὶ ὕ]μασι, of a bath insufficiently warmed, gives us the word from the NT epoch itself.

ἄφωνος.

In Syll 802[41] (iii/B.C., from the Asclepieum of Epidauros) one of the cures effected is that of a παῖς ἄφωνος. For its application to a dumb idol in 1 Cor 12[2], cf. Kaibel 402[4], from Sebastopolis in Galatia, where the marble pillar is made to say Γαῖά με τίκεν (l. τίκτεν) ἄφωνο[ν]: now through the inscription it speaks. The word is MGr.

ἀχάριστος.

In Syll 226[139] (Olbia, on Euxine—iii/B.C.) the verb ἀχαριστεῖν occurs in the normal sense: see also BGU IV. 1026[xvii. 16] (iv/v A.D. magical) τοὺς δὲ ἀπαλλαγέντος (l. ας) καὶ ἀχαριστήσαντα[ς]. In P Grenf I. 52[12] (iii A.D.) ἀχάριστον = "antidote" "id est sine gratia," as a Latin writer in Grenfell's note explains it, assigning a reason. A poem dated A.D. 94 (Kaibel 618, Rome) is inscribed on the tomb of its precocious author, a boy of eleven: it has the line σπείρων εἰς ἀχάριστα μάτην θ' ὑπὸ κυφὸν ἄροτρον ταῦρον ὑποζεύξας. Vettius also may be cited for adj. and verb, and the abstract ἀχαριστία.

ἀχειροποίητος.

This negative of a well-warranted word is said by Grimm to exist neither in profane authors nor in LXX. Its appearance, therefore, at once in Mark and in Paul is—cateat quantum—support for the inference that a genuine Logion about a "house not made with hands" underlies the perversion of Mk 14[58], and is quoted by Paul (and Heb 9[11. 24]): it would be probably a coinage for the occasion in the earliest source.

ἀχρεῖος.

With Lk 17[10] may be compared the fragmentary P Par 68[51] ἀχρείους δούλους: see also P Magd 29[6] (B.C. 217) τόπ[ον] ὄντα καί μοι ἀχρεῖον καὶ στενὸν ἐπὶ μῆκος δέδωκεν. The one occurrence of the adj. in NT may quite possibly be a mistaken gloss: the Lewis Syriac presumes simply δοῦλοί ἐσμεν, a very plausible reading.

Herwerden cites the abnormal feminine ἀχρεία from IG Sept 303[10] (iii/B.C.) φιάλην . . . ἀχρείαν.

ἀχρειόω.

In OGIS 573[18], a Cilician inscr of i/A.D., it is forbidden μήτε ἀπαλείψαι μήτε ἀχρεῶσαι μήτε μετᾶραι the inscription and votive offerings of an adjoining temple. The verb occurs in a quotation of Vettius, p. 200[1], where a king says ὁ τοιοῦτος . . . ἄτεκνος τῶν ἀναγκαίων στερηθήσεται καὶ πάντα ἀχρειώσας τρόπον ἐπαίτου ζήσεται.

ἄχρηστος.

P Tebt I. 74[30. 70], 75[56. 86] (both ii/B.C.) of "unproductive" land. So in CP Herm 7[ii. 9] (ii/A.D.), but hiat contextus.

15*

It describes a pig in P Flor II. 127[14] (A.D. 256) ἀλλὰ καλὸν πάλιν ἔστω, μὴ ὡς πρώην καὶ λεπτὸν καὶ ἄχρηστον. *Ib.* 185[7] (A.D. 254) κατεαγμένα καὶ ἄχρηστα, of panniers, and P Oxy X. 1346 (ii/A.D. ?) ἄχρηστος [γ]έγωναι (*l.* γέγονε), of a garment. *Cagnat* IV. 293[14] (Pergamon, B.C. 127–6) κατεφθαρμέ[νον . . . καὶ] . . . γεγονὸς ἄχρησ[τον, of a gymnasium. The moral sense of the word comes out in P Oxy VII. 1070[50 ff.] (iii/A.D.) μὴ ἀμελήσῃς μὴ ἄρα ποτὲ θέλῃς μ[ε]τὰ σ[ο]ῦ ['Ηρ]αεΐδι τὴν τήρησιν τῆς ὅλης οἰκίας παραδιδόναι ἀχρήστου οὔσης αὐτῆς. "do not neglect this, lest indeed you choose to hand over the keeping of the whole house to Herais, who is unworthy" (Ed.). The resemblance to Philem [11] is obvious. Vettius (p. 62[7]) speaks of ἄχρηστα βρέφη.

ἄχρι, ἄχρις.

No example of ἄχρις has yet been produced from the Ptolemaic papyri. In the Roman period both forms are found, their usage being apparently determined as a rule by the same considerations of euphony as in the NT. For ἄχρι οὗ cf. P Oxy I. 104[18] (a will, A.D. 96) ἄχρι οὗ ἐκπληρώσωσι ἀργυρίου δραχμαὶ τριακόσιαι, BGU I. 19[i. 5] (A.D. 135) ἄχρι οὗ γράψω τῷ κρατίστῳ ἡγεμόνι and P Oxy III. 507[30] (A.D. 169) ἄχρι οὗ ἀποδῶ σοι τὸ κεφάλαιον, etc. Without οὗ, cf. P Oxy III. 491[8] (A.D. 126) οὐ]δ' ἄλλως καταχρηματίζειν ἄχρι ἑκάτερος αὐτῶν πληρώσῃ ἔτη εἴκ[οσι πέντε, *ib.* IX. 1215 (ii/iii A.D.) (please come to me) ἄχρι τὰ πράγματα κατασταλῇ (illit. letter). For ἄχρις ἄν cf. BGU III. 830[13] (i/A.D.) ἄχρις ἄν σοι ἔλθω, *al.* Ἄχρι of manner is illustrated by *Ostr* 1129[5] (A.D. 207) ἄχρι τοῦ ὀψωνίου, P Tebt II. 301[21] (A.D. 190) ἔσχον τούτου [τὸ ἴ]σον ἄχρι ἐξετάσεως, "I have received a copy of this for investigation" (Edd.). With the phrase ἄχρι τοῦ νῦν in Rom 8[22], Phil 1[5], cf. BGU I. 256[9] (time of Antoninus Pius) μέχρ[ι] τ[οῦ] νῦν:

ἄχρι is only an *ablaut* variant of μέχρι—see Brugmann-Thumb, p. 631.

ἄχυρον.

A few citations suffice for this very common word, which survives in MGr. One shows that "bricks without straw" were as abnormal in the Ptolemaic period as in the days of the Exodus: P Petr II. 14 (2)[12] (as amended III. p. 139) shows directions ἐς τὰ ἄχυρα πρὸς τὴν πλινθολκίαν. So in *Syll* 587[73] (B.C. 329–8, Attica) ἀχύρων σάκοι εἰς τὴν οἰκοδομίαν τοῦ τείχους: Ditt. cites another Attic inscr. which mentions πηλὸς ἠχυρωμένος. This use of chaff was accordingly not limited to Egypt. The practice exemplified typically in the Ptolemaic ostracon, *Ostr* 1168—λό(γος) ἀχύρου, an account for fuel εἰς τὰς καμείνους, and in BGU III. 760[8] (ii/A.D.) ἄ. τὰ καὶ χωροῦντα ἰς ὑπόκαυσιν τοῦ με[γά]λου γυμ(νασίου), P Fay *Ostr* 21 (A.D. 306) ἀχύρου καυσίμου σάκ(κον) a- reminds us that (brickmaking apart) feeding the fire was the *normal use* of the "chaff." The stern theology of earlier days may have glossed the Baptist's words with Prov 16[4]!

ἀψευδής.

P Lond 121[570 f.] (magic, iii/A.D.) (= I. p. 102) ἐπὶ τῷ ἀχράντῳ φωτὶ ὀχούμενος ἀψευδής. The adverb is restored in BGU II. 432[ii. 1] (A.D. 190) λεγομενο[ἀψ]ευδῶς πρὸς κτλ : cf. also the late P Lond IV. 1343[8] (A.D. 709) ἀψευδῶς καὶ ἀσυμπαθῶς. The passive adj. occurs in *Preisigke* 1070 (a προσκύνημα from Abydos) . . . καὶ ἄψευστον καὶ δι' ὅλης οἰκουμέν(ης) μαρτυρούμενον οὐράνιον θεὸν [Βησᾶν ἐ]δείσα-[μεν, and P Leid W[xvii. 42] ὁ ἔχον τὴν ἄψευστον ἀλήθειαν.

ἄψυχος.

P Lond 121[441] (magic, iii/A.D.) (= I. p. 98) ἡσύχαζον ἀψύχοις τροφαῖς χρώμενος. It is MGr, = "lifeless."

B

Βάαλ—βαίνω

Βάαλ.

Τῇ Βάαλ in Rom 11[4] is paralleled in LXX four times outside Prophets and Apocrypha, where it is feminine without variant: correct thus the note in *Proleg.*[3], p. 59, where see also a reference to the usual explanation (Dillmann's).

Βαβυλών.

P Iand 15[iii. 5] (iv/A.D.) has Βαβ[υ]λ[ῶν]α in a fragmentary context. See also P Flor II. 278[ii. 8] (ii/A.D.), a letter addressed στρατ]ηγῶι 'Αραβία ς), where he is instructed καμήλους οὓς προσέ]ταξεν ἄρρενας καὶ ῥωμαλέους, δυναμένους ταῖς πορείαις ὑπηρετεῖν, ἢ αὐτὸς ἄγαγε ἢ διά τινος τῶν σῶν πέμψον εἰς Βαβυλῶνα.

βαδίζω.

For this common LXX verb reference may be made to P Par 51[3] (B.C. 160) (= *Selections*, p. 19) ᾦμ[ην] βατ(-δίζειν με [ἀπ᾽ὸ λειβὸς ἕως ἀ[πηλι᾽ώτου, "I dreamt that I was going from West to East," P Lips I. 104[28] (c. B.C. 96–5) (= Witkowski[2], p. 118) εἰκῆ ἐφ᾽ ἀλλαχῆ βαδίζετε, P Oxy IV. 743[29] (B.C. 2) τὸ βαδίσαι εἰς Τακόνα, and PSI I. 95[9] (iii/A.D.) κἂν σε δῆ (l. δέη) βαδίσαι εἰς . . . The subst. is found P Grenf II. 14 (b)[5] (B.C. 264 or 227) ὄνους βαδιστὰς πέντε. In P Flor III. 376[23] (iii/A.D.) ὑπὸ τοὺς βαδιστὰς [. . . has the note "sc. ὄνους": that the noun is really understood, and not latent in the hiatus, is shown by the word βαδιστηλάτας above (l. [13])—cf. P Tebt I. 262 (late ii/B.C.), PSI II. 205[7] (A.D. 295). A donkey was apparently regarded as "what will go," which is not a unanimously accorded estimate: does βαδιστής as epithet of ὄνος suggest that the verb connoted a kind of gait seen typically in a donkey? See also the editor's note on P Ryl II. 236[8] (A.D. 256).

βαθμός.

The thought of a "vantage ground, a 'standing' (RV) a little, as it were, above the common level," which Hort (*Christian Ecclesia*, p. 202) suggests for this word in 1 Tim 3[13], may be illustrated from the Mytilene inscription *IG* II. 243[16] τοῖς τὰς ἀξίας βασμοῖς ἀνελόγησε, "er wurde durch sein Verhalten dem Ehrenamte gerecht" (Nägeli, p. 20). See also R. M. Pope *Exp T* xxi. p. 112 ff. The word is found in the mystery religions, e.g. Reitzenstein *Poimandres* 13[9], p. 343, ὁ βαθμὸς οὗτος, ὦ τέκνον, δικαιοσύνης ἐστὶν ἕδρασμα. Immisch in *Philologus* xvii. (N.F.) p. 33 n.[1] cites βαθμός as a technical expression in philosophy, denoting a step towards the goal, and compares Olympiodorus *Proleg.* (*Comm. in Aristotelem Graeca* XII. 1), ed. Busse, p. 9[31], and *ib. Scholia in Platonis Phaedonem*, ed Finckh, p. 5[16].

The rule which the grammarians lay down that βαθμός is the Ionic form of the Attic βασμός (so Lob. *Phryn.* p. 324)

is not borne out by the evidence of the inscriptions: see Thumb *Hellen.* p. 73.

βάθος.

The literal meaning is illustrated by P Fay 110[5] (A.D. 94) σκάψον ἐπὶ βάθος, "dig a deep trench": cf. BGU II. 647[13, 25] (A.D. 130) ἐπὶ βάθους, *ib.* IV. 1122[16] (B.C. 14) . . .] ἔχον τὸ καθῆκον βάθος, of the setting of plants in trenches in a garden—cf. Mk 4[5]. The ordinary use in connexion with πλάτος is seen, e.g., in measurements for excavations in the construction of a canal, P Giss I. 42 (A.D. 117) *passim*, as [5] βο ρρᾶ, ἐχόμ(ενα) σχοι(νία) δ ξύλ(α) ρκ[η], πλ άτος ε. ν(αύβια) ξδ. Herwerden *Lex. s.v.* cites *Papiers du Louvre* ed. Letronne 64 (ii/B.C.) μὴ σ᾽ ἐπὶ βάθος ᾱ παντελῶς?) τοῦτο πεποηκέναι. The astrological use of β. to denote the space below the horizon out of which the stars rise e.g. Dieterich *Mithrasliturgie*, p. 8[5], ἐγώ εἰμι σύμπλανος ὑμῖν ἀστὴρ καὶ ἐκ τοῦ βάθους ἀναλάμπων) may throw some light on Rom 8[39] see Lietzmann in *HZNT ad loc.* For the true "Greek" character of the Pauline phraseology in Rom 11[33] ὦ βάθος πλούτου κτλ., see Norden *Agnostos Theos*, p. 243 f.

βαθύνω.

For this verb = "go deep," as in Lk 6[48], we can only point to Philo I. 248, 15 (cited in Sophocles *Lex. s.v.*): see Radermacher *Gr.* p. 19, for other solitary instances of transitive verbs used intransitively.

βαθύς.

For β. associated with time (class.), as in Lk 24[1], cf. P Lips I. 40[iii. 19] (iv/v A.D.) ὀψὲ πάνυ βαθ[εί]ας ἑσπέρ[ας. So in the fragment of an epithalamium (iv/A.D.) P Ryl I. 17[b]—

ὁμοφροσύνην δ᾽ ὀπάσ[ει]ε
ἤδη που θεὸς ἄμμι καὶ αὐτίκα τέκνα γενέ[σ]θαι
καὶ πα[ί]δων παῖδας καὶ ἐς βαθὺ γῆρας ἱκέσθ[αι.

It is applied to colour in P Lond 890[4] (ii/A.D.) (= III. p. 208) τὸ οὖν βαθύτερον (sc. πορφύριον) πεποίηται εἰς τὸ σπανοῦ (?) καὶ τὸ ὀξύτερον εἰς τ[ὸ] ἄλλ[ο]. The comparative βαθύτερον is also found P Petr III. 43 (2) *recto* [ii. 13] (B.C. 245) p. 121). Note a new compound, recalling the combination in Lk 6[48], P Hal I. 1[ii. 83] (iii B.C.), where a πολιτικὸς νόμος is headed φυτ[εύσ]εως καὶ οἰκοδομ[ίας] καὶ β[αθ]ορυ[γῆς.

βαίνω.

The simplex of this old verb, whose compounds are ubiquitous, has perhaps not quite disappeared from use, though not to be found in NT. Its present appears in Dt 28[56], its perfect in Wisd (*bis*) and 3 Macc: cf. BGU IV.

1192¹⁰ (i/B.C.), where τῶν [μ]ὲν β[αι]νόν[των] τὴν ἀπα[ίτησιν is read by Schubart, who regards the supplement as "unvermeidlich." Less noteworthy is its appearance in a long builder's specification for a temple at Lebadea, *Syll* 540¹⁶³ (B.C. 175-1) βεβηκότας (sc. τοὺς λίθους) ὅλους ἀσχάστους, ἀνε[γκλή]τους κτλ.

βαΐον.

This word, apparently of Egyptian origin, which is found in Bibl. Grk only in 1 Macc 13⁵¹, Jn 12¹³, occurs in the late P Flor I. 37³ (v/vi A.D.) δικαίῳ βαΐῳ, of a palm branch used as a measuring rod. **βαΐα** is quoted in P Tebt II. p. 69 from a text edited by Wessely; and **βαΐων** occurs in P Leid Vᵛⁱⁱ·²⁷, but with **βαΐς** as nom. in preceding line. The form **βαΐον** is presumed in the compounds **βαιοφορεῖν** and **βαιοφορία**: see P Tebt II. 294¹⁰ (application for the purchase of a priestly office—A.D. 146), where the writer promises "to carry the β." and perform all the other needful offices, also 295¹¹ (A.D. 126-38) and 599 (ii/A.D.). For the form **βαΐς** see P Lond 131 *recto*³⁸⁴ (A.D. 78-9) (= I. p. 181) βαεῖς, P Oxy IX.1211⁸ (ii/A.D.) **βαΐς χλωρᾶς ιϛ** (cf. P Leid Wᵛⁱ·⁵⁰—ii/iii A.D. λαβὼν βαῖν χλωράν), and BGU II. 362 (A.D. 215) *ter* in the phrase ὑπὸ δένδρα καὶ βαῖς: Wilcken *Chrest.* I. p. 128 prints β[αῖς]—ought it to be acc. pl. βαεῖς? In view of the above evidence the word makes yet another deduction from the fast vanishing list of "bibl. and eccles." words in Grimm.

βάλλω.

That the verb does not necessarily imply *casting* or *thrusting* with some degree of violence is clear already from the NT itself; and there are vernacular parallels to negative the assumption of "Jewish Greek." Thus in BGU II. 597⁴ (A.D. 75) ἵνα βάληι τὸν μόσχον πρὸ τῶν προβάτων the verb does not suggest a violent "flinging" of the helpless calf before the ferocious beasts afterwards named. Cf. P Oxy VII. 1069²⁶ (iii/A.D.) κ[α]λὰ μέτρα αὐτῷ βαλέτωσαν, "let them put good measure into it" with reference to the making of a tunic, and *ib.* VI. 934⁹ (iii/A.D.) μὴ οὖν ἀμελήσῃς τοῦ βαλεῖν τὴν κόπρον, "do not fail therefore to throw the manure on the land" (Edd.): cf. P Fay 118²¹ (A.D. 110) βάλλωι ἐξ ἀρούρας εἰς τὴν Ψεννῶφριν, "I am manuring six arourae at Psennophris" (Edd.). For a similar absolute usage see *Syll* 522⁷ (iii/B.C.) θύειν δὲ τὸμ μὲν βοῦν βεβληκότα, τὴν δὲ οἶν βεβληκ[υ]ῖαν, of animals that have "cast" their first teeth. A very curious absolute use occurs in *Syll* 380¹¹ (A.D. 129), where the Ephesians honour Hadrian as διδόντα τῇ θεῷ τῶν κληρονομιῶν καὶ βεβληκότων τὰ δίκαια: Dittenberger tentatively suggests that it may be a rendering of *bona caduca*, property without an heir. P Lond 1177¹⁵ (A.D. 113) (= III. p. 182) αἱ πλείω βληθεῖσαι [? sc. ὕδατος χορηγίαι] βαλανείου Σευηριανοῦ will illustrate Mt 9¹⁷ and other places where β. is used of liquids. With the phrase of Mt 5²⁵ etc. cf. P Tebt II. 567 (A.D. 53-4) εἰς δεσμευτήριον βληθήσεται. P Flor II. 148¹¹ (A.D. 266-7) τὰ δὲ τεμνόμενα φυτὰ εὐθέως εἰς ὕδωρ βαλλέσθω ἵνα μὴ ξηρανθῇ, "be put in water that they may not wither," is a further instance of the unemphatic use. The intransitive βάλλειν, in NT found only in Ac 27¹⁴, occurs in a much milder sense in Epict. ii. 20. 10 βαλὼν κάθευδε καὶ τὰ τοῦ σκώληκος ποίει, "lie down and sleep and play the part of the worm," *ib.* iv. 10. 29 τί οὖν οὐ

ῥέγκω βαλών: and Enoch 18⁶ ὄρη εἰς νότον βάλλοντα, (mis)quoted by Radermacher *Gr.* p. 18. For the aor. indic. ἐβλήθη used of present time in Jn 15⁶ cf. *Proleg.* pp. 134, 247, and Abbott *Joh. Gr.* p. 327. On βεβλῆσθαι, used of sick persons, as Mt 8¹⁴, Lk 16²⁰, see Field *Notes.* pp. 7, 70.

βάλλω is the only verb to form a gerundive in NT, and that only once (Lk 5³⁸ βλητέον): the gerundive in -τέος is rare, though not unknown, in papyri, and is generally found in formulae, so that we should hardly credit it to popular speech.

βαπτίζω.

As late as iv/A.D. the word is used in a magic papyrus, P Lond 46⁶⁹ (= I. p. 67) of a "submerged" boat—ἀπὸ νεναυαγηκ ὅτος) πλοίου ἀπὸ πάκτωνος βεβαπτισμ(ένου). Lucian *Timon* 44 makes the Misanthrope threaten ὠθεῖν καὶ ἐπὶ κεφαλὴν βαπτίζοντα. So in a fragment of Epictetus (Stobaeus no. 47—Schenkl p. 474), quoted by D. S. Sharp, *Epictetus and the NT*, p. 66, ὥσπερ οὐκ ἂν ἐβούλου ἐν νηὶ μεγάλῃ καὶ γλαφυρᾷ καὶ πολυχρύσῳ πλέων βαπτίζεσθαι. With its use to express ceremonial ablution—as Lk 11³⁸ and the new Gospel-fragment P Oxy V. 840¹⁵ μ[ή]τε μὴν τῶν μαθητῶν σου τοὺς π[όδας βα]πτισθέντων—we may compare another magic papyrus P Lond 121⁴¹¹ (iii/A.D.) (= I. p. 98) λουσάμενος καὶ βαπτισάμενος. Our earliest quotation is from P Par 47¹³ (c. B.C. 153) (= *Selections*, p. 22) κἂν ἴδῃς ὅτι μέλλομεν σωθῆναι, τότε βαπτιζώμεθα. The translation of the letter, which is very illiterate, is by no means clear, but βαπτιζόμεθα must mean "flooded," or overwhelmed with calamities. That the word was already in use in this metaphorical sense (cf. Diod. i. 73. 6), even among uneducated people, strikingly illustrates our Lord's speaking of His Passion as a "baptism" (Mk 10³⁸).

βάπτισμα.

The word is restored by the editor in the new fragment of an uncanonical Gospel, P Oxy X.1224, Fr. 2 *verso* ⁱ·⁴ (iv/A.D.) τί β]ά[πτισμ]α καινὸν [κηρύσσειν (sc. φασὶν) "what is the new baptism that they say thou dost preach?" —where for β. κηρύσσειν he compares Mk 1⁴, and for the likelihood of questions concerning a "new baptism," Jn 4¹¹. That the noun is "peculiar to NT and eccl. writ." (Grimm) is of course natural: the new use to which the verb was put as a *term. techn.* demanded a corresponding noun. The same may be said of βαπτισμός and βαπτιστής, which only occur certainly in Josephus's account of John the Baptist: see further *s.v.* βαπτισμός.

βαπτισμός.

Grimm's statement that "among prof. writ. Josephus alone (*Antt.* xviii. 5. 2) uses the word, and of John's baptism" is traversed by the ordinary text of Plutarch's *Moralia*: see the *De Superstitione* 3, p. 166 A, where he names among superstitions πηλώσεις καταβορβορώσεις βαπτισμούς, ῥίψεις ἐπὶ πρόσωπον, αἰσχρὰς προκαθίσεις, ἀλλοκότους προσκυνήσεις. But, unfortunately, the word is only Bentley's emendation for σαββατισμούς, according to Bernadakis' apparatus —was the change necessary?

As distinguished from βάπτισμα in which the result is included, βαπτισμός is the act of immersion (Blass *Gr.* p. 62):

and hence in Heb 6² Chase (*Confirmation in the Apost. Age*, p. 44 f.) understands διδαχὴ βαπτισμῶν as = "'the teaching about acts of washing,' the exposition of the truths and spiritual principles embodied and expressed in the baptism of this disciple and of that."

βάπτω.

In P Tebt II. 287³ (A.D. 161-9) the fullers and dyers of the Arsinoite nome appeal against a tax that had been imposed upon their trades—οἱ μέ]ν εἰ[σι] γναφεῖς ο[ἱ δὲ] βαφεῖς τὴν ἐργασίαν, δίδονται δὲ ὑπὲρ τέλους κτλ. For the τέλος βαφέων see also *Ostr* 700, 1068 (both ii/A.D.), and 1516 (ii/B.C.). In P Par 52¹⁰, 53⁵ (B.C. 163-2) βαπτά = "coloured garments": cf. P Oxy X. 1293²⁴ (A.D. 117-38) εἰς βαφὴν ἐρ[ί]δια, "wool to be dyed." A late instance of the verb in this sense may be cited from P Iand 17⁷ (vi/vii A.D.).

The verb is restored by the editors in the uncanonical Gospel fragment, P Oxy V. 840⁴³ ἐγὼ δὲ καὶ οἱ [μαθηταί μου] οὓς λέγεις μὴ βε[βα πτίσθαι βεβά]μμεθα ἐν ὕδασι ζω[ῆς αἰωνίου : cf. Epict. ii. 9. 20 ὅταν δ' ἀναλάβῃ τὸ πάθος τὸ τοῦ βεβαμμένου καὶ ᾑρημένου, τότε καὶ ἔστι τῷ ὄντι καὶ καλεῖται Ἰουδαῖος, where βεβαμμένου seems to refer to baptism and ᾑρημένου to circumcision (see Sharp *Epictetus and the NT*, p. 134 f.).

βάρβαρος.

For the contrast with Ἕλλην see *OGIS* 765¹⁶ (iii/B.C.) αὐτὸς δὲ ἀντετά[ξ]ατο πρὸς τοὺς βαρβάρους ἀ[τ]ιμ]άζοντάς τε ἡμᾶς] . . . καὶ εἰς τοὺς Ἕλληνας [παρανομοῦντας], cf. 15, 19, 21, 32; *ib*. 763¹⁰ (letter of Eumenes II. ii/B.C.) ἀναδείξας ἐμαυτὸν εὐεργέτην τῶν Ἑλλήνων πολλοὺς μὲν καὶ μεγάλους ἀγῶνας ὑπέστην πρὸς τοὺ[ς] βαρβάρους—apparently the Galatae, see Dittenberger's note, and for a similar reference *Magn* 46¹⁰. *Berber* is used in the same way by Egyptians to denote non-Egyptian peoples. In P Lond 410⁶ (c. A.D. 346) (= II. p. 298) a mother beseeches Abinnaeus to release from service her son—ἀπῆλθεν οὖν μετὰ τὸν βάρβαρον. P Par 10⁹ (B.C. 145) tells of a Syrian slave ἐστιγμένος τὸν δεξιὸν καρπὸν γράμμασι βαρβαρικοῖς, presumably Syrian. The more ethical sense of the word (as Ezra 21³¹⁽³⁸⁾) may be illustrated from Aristeas 122 τὸ τραχὺ καὶ βάρβαρον τῆς διανοίας.

βαρέω.

The verb is only found in perf. pass. in LXX, and only twice (Exod 7¹⁴, 2 Macc 13⁹ : see Thackeray *Gr.* i. p. 261. Similarly in NT we have only the passive, but the present and aorist are used. The record fits its early history, for βεβαρημένος is the oldest form after the Homeric βεβαρηώς; and Hippocrates is the first to use βαρέεται. See Anz *Subsidia*, p. 266 ff. Instances of the active are late in appearing. Anz quotes Lucian's censure on βαρεῖν for βαρύνειν, and mentions *CIG* 5853¹⁵ (A.D. 174) ἵνα μὴ τὴν πόλιν βαρῶμεν. MGr has βαρῶ, "strike," as well as βαρειοῦμαι. "be weary of" (Thumb *Handbook*, p. 321).

The use of the verb in the papyri tallies with this record. Thus P Tebt II. 327²⁵ (late ii/A.D.) γ]υνὴ οὖσα ἀβοήθητος πο[λλο]ῖς ἔτεσι βεβαρημένη, "a defenceless woman weighted with many years" (Edd.), P Oxy VI. 939²³ iv/A.D.) ἡνίκα ἐβαρεῖτο τῇ νόσῳ. It becomes a formula in

---

a group of documents relating to taxation. P Giss I.4¹¹ (A.D. 118) αὐτοί τε βεβαρημένοι πολλῶι χρόνωι δημοσίοις [. . .]. *ib*. 6⁵ (A.D. 117) αὐτὸς δὲ βαροῦμαι τῷ ἐκφορίῳ : so *ib*. 6⁹·¹⁰, two documents in *Archiv* v. p. 245 f., and another in P Ryl II. 96⁸, all with the same phraseology, and dated about the same time. Similarly P Brem 73⁵ (in *Chrest*. I. p. 277) (c. A.D. 117) ὅπως μὴ βαρηθῶσιν ἢ παραπραχθῶσιν οἱ ἐγχώριοι ἢ συκοφαντηθῶσιν, *Syll* 418⁸) (A.D. 238) ἐὰν βαρούμεθα (needlessly emended ὤμεθα , φευξόμεθα ἀπὸ τῶν οἰκείων (query οἰκ[ειῶν ?) καὶ μεγίστην ζημίαν τὸ ταμεῖον περιβληθήσεται. *ib*. 422³ (iv/A.D.) ὁ νομίζων βαρῖσθαι δέει τοῦ δικαστοῦ. These illustrate the use in 1 Tim 5¹⁶ : cf. also *CIG* 5853¹⁵ (= *OGIS* 595⁵⁵) as above. Other examples of the verb from the inscriptions are *Kaibel* 335⁴ θνήσκω δ' οὐχὶ ν[όσ]ῳ βεβαρημένος, 608⁶ (ii/iii A.D.) κεῖτε δ[ὴ] γήρᾳ βεβαρη[μέ]νος. In *Anth. Pal.* vii. 290 we have πυμάτῳ βεβαρημένον ὕπνῳ : cf. Mt 26⁴³, Lk 9³². The curious list of prognostications to be drawn from involuntary twitchings, P Ryl I. 28¹⁶⁴ᶠᶠ (iv/A.D.), has σφυρὸν εὐώνυμον ἐὰν ἅληται ἐν κρίσει βαρη[θ]εὶς ἔσται καὶ ἐκφεύξεται, "if the left ankle quiver he will be burdened with a trial, and will be acquitted" (Ed.). This metaphorical usage, as in 2 Cor 1⁸, 5⁴, may be further illustrated from P Oxy III. 525³ (early ii/A.D.) where, with reference to a voyage he was undertaking, the writer complains καθ' ἑκάστην ἡμέραν βαροῦμαι δι' αὐτὸν καὶ λείαν τῷ πράγματι καταξύομαι, "every day I am burdened on account of it and I am extremely worn out with the matter" (Edd.). Further instances of the active are P Oxy VIII. 1159² (late iii/A.D.) ἵνα μὴ βαρήσω αὐτῷ ὀψωνίου, "that I may not trouble him about provisions" (Ed.), and the late *ib*. 1. 126⁶ (A.D. 572), where one Stephanous undertakes βαρέσαι τὸ ἐμὸν ὄνομα, "to burden herself," with certain imposts hitherto paid by her father. See also *ib*. X. 1224 Fr. 2 *recto*ⁱⁱ ² (uncanonical Gospel—iv/A.D.) με ἐβάρησεν, "overcame me," where the editor suggests φόβος or λύπη as a possible subject, as well as ὕπνος (cf. the citation from the *Anth. Pal.* above).

Βαραββᾶς.

As against the popular etymology given in Ac 4³⁶. Deissmann has shown on the evidence of certain inscriptions that this proper name is Graecized from the Semitic ‏בר נבו‏ = "Son of Nebo": see *BS* pp. 187 ff., 307 ff., *ZNTW* vii. 1906) p. 91 f. This derivation has been accepted by Dalman *Words*, p. 40 f., and G. B. Gray *ExpT* x. p. 233 f.

βάρος.

BGU I. 159³ᶠᶠ (A.D. 216) (= *Chrest*. I. p. 486) μετὰ δὲ ταῦτα ἀναδο[θέντο]ς μου εἰς δη[μοσ]ί[α]ν λειτουργίαν βαρυτάτην οὖσαν ἀπέστ[η]ν τῆς κώμης οὐ δυνάμενος ὑποστῆναι τὸ βάρος τῆς λειτουργίας is a good example of the ordinary use of this noun with the corresponding adjective : cf. P Oxy VII. 1062¹⁴ (ii/A.D.) εἰ δὲ τοῦτό σοι βάρος φέρει, "if it is troublesome" (Ed.). A "burden" of oppression is referred to in *Syll* 418⁶⁷ (A.D. 238) ἐπεὶ οὖν οὐκέτι δυνάμεθα φέρειν τὰ βάρη, and one of taxation in P Giss I. 7¹³ (A.D. 117) ἐπεὶ οὖν ὁ κύριος ἡμῶν Ἁδριανὸς . . . ἐκούφισεν τῶν ἐγχωρίων τὰ βάρη καθολικῶς διὰ προγράμματος, ἀξιῶ τοιούτου ὄντος τοῦ βάρους κτλ. It denotes responsibility in *ib*. 19¹⁸ (ii/A.D.) ἀλλὰ ὡς [καὶ ὁ ἐ]νθάδε στρατηγὸς τοῖς ἄρχου[σι ἐπιτ]θησι τὸ βάρος, καὶ σὺ τὸ αὐ[τὸ ποίει. In reference to moral faults (cf. Gal 6[2]), see the Acts of the martyrdom of Christina, PSI 27[7] (v/A.D.) (as amended p. xi) βάρος πάσης ὀργῆς καὶ ἀτίμ[ο]υ σπέρματος. The word is found in the astrologer Vettius Valens, p. 292[6] ἐν συνοχαῖς καὶ βάρεσι γίνονται ἢ τραυμάτων περιπλοκαῖς : in the Index βάρος is rendered *molestia*.

βαρύνω.

The replacement of this classical verb by βαρέω was progressive, as is seen in the fact that βαρύνω is common in LXX, but never occurs in the NT according to WH, except in its compound καταβαρύνω: the vernacular record of βαρέω (*q.v.*) makes this very clear. For the older word cf. P Tebt I. 23[6] (*c.* B.C. 119 or 114) καθ' ὑπερβολὴν (cf. 2 Cor 1[8]) βεβαρυμμένοι, "excessively vexed" (Edd.), P Oxy II. 298[26] (i/A.D.) περὶ Ἑρμοδώρου γράφε[ι]s μοι λίαν αὐτὸν βαρύνομαι, "you write to me about Hermodorus that I am too severe with him" (Edd.), and OGIS 669[5] (i/A.D.) μὴ βαρυνομένην καιναῖς καὶ ἀδίκοις εἰσπράξεσι, *ib.*[18] ἵνα δὲ μηδαμόθεν βαρύνηι τὰς πρὸς ἀλλήλους συναλλαγάς.

βαρύς.

See the first reference *s.v.* βάρος and cf. P Tebt I. 52[11] (*c.* B.C. 114) δι (*l.* διὰ τό) με ἐν βαρυ[τέ]ρᾳ ἀρρωστίᾳ κῖσ[θαι, "since I am seriously ill" (Edd.). In P Goodsp Cairo 15[15] (A.D. 362) β. = "pregnant"—τὴν μὲν Τάησιν βαρέαν οὖσαν ἐκ τῶν πληγῶν αὐτῶν ἐξέτρωσεν (= -αν) τὸ βρέφος, "to Taesis who was pregnant they occasioned by their violence the miscarriage of her child" (Ed.) : see *Archiv* iii. p. 116 on the passage. For the adverb see P Lond 42[29] (B.C. 168) (= I. p. 31) ἡ μήτηρ σου τυγχάνει βαρέως ἔχουσα.

βασανίζω.

P Oxy VI. 903[10] (iv/A.D.) βασανιζόμενοι οὖν εἶπαν, "they under torture said "—of slaves. Cf. *Audollent* I.[27] (Cnidus tablet) μεγάλας βασάνους βασανιζόμενα, and the imprecatory tablet 35[6] μετὰ κυνῶν βασανίσαι in Bliss and Macalister, *Excavations in Palestine* (1902), p. 176. The verb also occurs *ter* in PSI I. 28, a magic tablet of iii/iv A.D. : another late instance is P Lips Inv 244[6] (in *Chrest.* II. p. 81) (A.D. 462) καὶ παρε[κ]λήθην καὶ ἐκλείσθην εἰς [τ]ὴν δη[μο]σ[ίαν] ε[ἱ]ρκτ[ὴ]ν τῶν χρεῶν ἕνεκα καὶ πολλα[. .]ον, ὅπερ ἀπηγορ[ε]υμένον τοῖς νόμοις, ἐβασανίσθην. A compound may be quoted from BGU IV. 1141[47] (B.C. 14), where ἐγὼι οὖν ἠρώτασα οὖν τὸν γέροντα is corrected above to ἐγβασανίσας οὖν ἠρώτων κατ' ἰδίαν. The curious imprecation in Wünsch *AF* no. 4 (iii/A.D.), where various infernal powers are invoked to prevent a rival's winning a horserace, has (v.[55]) βασάνισον αὐτῶν τὴν διάνοιαν τὰς φρένας τὴν αἴσθησιν ἵνα μὴ νοῶσιν τί π[ο]ιῶσιν.

βάσανος.

The original sense of "touchstone," "test," appears in P Oxy I. 58[25] (A.D. 288), where provision is made that only such persons are appointed to certain offices as are in a position to stand the test—οἳ καὶ βασάνοις ὑποκείσονται. In P Leid W[vii. 26 ff.] (ii/iii A.D.) λέγε· Κλῦτί μοι, ὁ χρηστὸς ἐν βαζάνοις, βοήθησον ἐν ἀνάγκαις, ἐλέημον ἐν ὥραις βιαίος (*i.e.* -αις), πολοὶ (*i.e.* -ὺ) δυνάμενος ἐν κόσμῳ, ὁ κτίσας τὴν ἀνάγκη (καὶ) τιμωρίαν, καὶ τὴν βάσανον, Leemans renders *exploratio*. For the derived sense, reference may be made

to the fragment of a legal code of iii/B.C., P Lille I. 29[i. 22], where the judges are empowered to employ "torture" in the case of slaves giving evidence, should it be found necessary— τῶν δὲ δούλων τῶν μαρτυρησάντων, οἱ δικασταὶ τὴν βάσανον ἐκ τῶν σωμάτων ποεί<σθωσαν, παρόντων τῶν ἀντιδίκων, ἐὰμ μὴ ἐκ τῶν τιθέντων δικαιωμάτων δύνωνται κρίνειν. So in a rescript of Augustus, *Syll* 356[12] (B.C. 6) ἐξετάσαι προστάξας . . . διὰ βασάνων = *quaerere tormentis*, of slaves after the murder of their master. See also the new uncanonical Gospel, P Oxy V. 840[6] κόλασιν ὑπομένουσιν καὶ πολ[λ]ὴν βάσανον, where the editors strangely remark that this use of β., as relating to punishment in the next world, is not found in NT ; but cf. Lk 16[23, 28]. Vettius Valens, p. 182[19], has the phrase ψυχικὰς βασάνους : cf. p. 201[32] ἐπὶ βασάνῳ καὶ ζημίᾳ καὶ κινδύνῳ, and p. 211[28] ὀδυνηρὰν ἐπάγρυπνον βάσανον.

βασιλεία.

As *kingship* or *sovranty* in the abstract is necessarily the root meaning of this word, it is easy to see how the passage into the concrete could either be on the lines of our *dominion* (cf. "our Sovereign and his dominions"), or follow the outward and visible *sign of royalty*. All these three meanings are fully illustrated from the inscriptions by Dittenberger in the Index to OGIS, e.g. (1) 331[4] (ii/B.C.) ὑῆ ἔτει τῆς ἐκείνου βασιλείας, (2) 248[15] (ii/B.C.) μέχρι τῶν ὁρίων τῆς ἰδίας βασιλείας, and (3) 90[4] (Rosetta Stone, B.C. 196) τὰς τοῦ βασιλέως χρυσᾶς βασιλείας δέκα. It is possible that some passages in the NT might gain in force if this last meaning "a sign of royalty" were substituted for "royalty" in the abstract—one might compare the line taken by the Revisers with ἐξουσία in 1 Cor 11[10]. But it may be doubted whether the change can be made very plausible in any case.

For β. in its original sense we may cite from the papyri P Par 61[6] (B.C. 156) πάντας τοὺς ὑπὸ τὴν βασιλείαν δικαιοδοτεῖσθαι, P Tor I. 1[vii. 14] (B.C. 114) τῶν μεγίστων βασιλέων ἀπολελυκότων τοὺς ὑπὸ τὴν βασιλείαν πάντας αἰτιῶν πασῶν. For the sense "reign" see P Oxy X. 1257[7] (iii/A.D.) ἐπὶ τοῦ (ἔτους) ᾱ ἔτους τῆς εὐτυχαιστάτης ταύτης βασιλείας. Deissmann *BS*, p. 361 f., compares with τὴν αἰώνιον βασιλείαν τοῦ κυρίου ἡμῶν καὶ σωτῆρος (2 Pet 1[11]) the phrase ἐπὶ τῆς τῶν κυρίων Ῥωμαίων αἰωνίου ἀρχῆς in the decree of Stratonicea (CIG II. no. 2715a, b).

βασίλειος.

Syll 220[45] (iii/B.C.) πραθέντος τε τοῦ στόλου εἰς βασίλεια, the palace of the satrap Saitaphernes. Dittenberger quotes Boeckh as arguing from the absence of the article that β. was here almost a proper name, as in Herod. iv. 20 : D. however is not convinced that the reference is to the same place. P Petr II. 23 (2)[1] shows βασίλειος qualifying γραμματεύς, instead of the regular βασιλικός. In the magic papyrus P Lond 46[48] (iv/A.D.) (= I. p. 79) βασίλιον is used with a symbol which the editor understands as = "sceptre": cf. Wisd 5[16] τὸ βασίλειον τῆς εὐπρεπείας, "the crown of royal dignity."

βασιλεύς.

In a letter written not later than B.C. 334 the title of βασιλεύς is adopted by Alexander the Great (*Priene* 1), and it was a favourite designation of his successors in the Syrian and Egyptian monarchies. In this way it became familiar to the Jews of the Dispersion; and when found in the Septuagint as the translation of their vernacular title would be "instinct with present meaning and full of absorbing associations," as Hicks (*CR* i. p. 7) has pointed out. In the NT it was transferred to the Roman Emperor (1 Tim 2², 1 Pet 2¹³·¹⁷) in accordance with common usage, as borne out by the inscriptions, e.g. *IG* III. 12¹⁵·¹⁷ (time of Hadrian), *CIG* II. 2721¹¹ (time of the Antonines), and the other examples cited by Magie, p. 62. Similarly Deissmann (*LAE*. p. 367 f.) brings forward evidence to show that the full title βασιλεὺς βασιλέων (as Rev 17¹⁴, 19¹⁶) was again "in very early Eastern history a decoration of actual great monarchs and also a divine title." The former has of course as its most obvious example the title of the Persian Kings, as at Behistan—χšāyaθiya χšāyaθiyānām : cf. the verbal phrase in the next article. For the latter, cf. the occult document P Leid Wˣˡᵛ·⁸ (ii iii A.D.) ἐπικαλοῦμαί σε, βασιλεῦ βασιλέων, τύραννε τυράννων, ἔνδοξε ἐνδοξοτάτων, δαίμων δαιμώνων, ἄλκιμε ἀλκιμωτάτων, ἅγιε ἁγίων. The similarity and at the same time contrast in the Christian usage would thus be full of significance to the Early Church, as in the case of the title κύριος (*q.v.*). On *OGIS* 35¹ (iii/B.C.) βασίλισσαν Φιλωτέραν βασιλέως Πτολεμαίου *sc.* II, Philadelphus, Dittenberger (p. 648) contests Strack's attempt to claim βασιλεύς as well as βασίλισσα as a term applicable to non-regnant members of a royal family: he notes that there is all the difference between βασιλεύς and its feminine. Wilcken *Archiv* iii. p. 319 supports him, and notes inscriptions where βασιλεύς is promptly dropped when a mere H.R.H. is named after the king and his consort. He also commends Dittenberger's remark that Augustus and Augusta had the same difference after Domitian's time.

βασιλεύω.

A good example of the ingressive aorist is afforded by the new Agraphon as restored by the editors—P Oxy IV. 654⁹ θαμ[βηθεὶς βασιλεύσει κα]ὶ βασιλεύσας ἀναπα]ήσεται, "astonished he shall reach the Kingdom, and having reached the Kingdom he shall rest": see *Proleg.* p. 130. The verb is used to render the Persian title (see under βασιλεύς) in P Saʿid Khan 1 (*a*)¹ (B.C. 88) βασιλεύοντος βασιλέων Ἀρσάκου : 1 (*b*)¹ and 2¹ (B.C. 22-1) have the same formula. CP Herm 125ⁱⁱ·³ (A.D. 260-8) διατρίβοντός σο[υ] ἐπὶ τῆς βασιλευούση[ς Ῥώμης supplies an illustration for Rev 18⁷. For the relation of the Pauline conception of "the saint as king" (Rom 5¹⁷, 2 Tim 2¹²) to the Greek philosophic ideal, see Ramsay *Teaching*, p. 157 ff.

βασιλικός.

is exceedingly common, but we may note P Petr III. 31⁵ (B.C. 240) πορευομένου ἐπὶ τῆς βασιλικῆς ὁδοῦ as coeval with the almost identical phrase of the LXX in Num 20¹⁷. This phrase at a later time was used to render *via regalis*, a Roman road built by the Emperor: see Ramsay *CRE*. p. 32 f., where a Latin inscr. from Pisidia brings the original back to the time of Augustus. The adj. is applied to the revenue in P Petr III. 26¹⁵ ὁ πράκτωρ ὁ ἐπὶ τῶν βασιλικ[ῶ]ν προσόδων τεταγμένος, "the officer appointed to collect the royal revenues": *Chrest.* I. 198¹⁹ (B.C. 240) τῶι ἐμ Βουβάστωι βασιλικῶι θησαυρῶι. In a papyrus of

the latter half of ii/A.D., edited by Comparetti in *Mél. Nicole*, p. 57 ff., we find ⁱᵛ·¹⁹ βασιλικῷ Ὀξυρυγχείτου. The editor remarks (p. 67) that in the absence of the Strategus his functions were fulfilled by his deputy, the βασιλικὸς γραμματεύς. So P Oxy IX. 1219¹⁵ (iii/A.D.) Ἀπ[ί]ωνα τὸν τοῦ Προσωπείτου βασιλικόν, "A. the basilicogrammateus of the Prosopite nome" (Ed.) ; the addressee, another Apion, held the same office in the Letopolite nome—cf. l.²⁰ βασιλικ(ῷ) γρ[αμματεῖ). If we might apply the Egyptian analogy, we might assume that γραμματεύς should similarly be supplied in Jn 4⁴⁶ : but the τις raises a difficulty. For the full title cf. *Chrest.* I. 224 (iii/B.C.), where a man registers his house πρὸς Καλλικράτην τὸν οἰκονόμον καὶ Ἰμούθην τὸν βασιλικὸν γραμματέα, etc. In *Chrest.* I. 308, an ostracon of ii/B.C., a certain Psenchousis, apparently a clerk in the office of the royal οἰκονόμος, pays 2000 dr. into the bank ἀπὸ τιμῆς ὀθονίων βασιλικῶν τοῦ λᾱ (ἔτους) : linen was a royal monopoly. There was in the imperial period a β. τραπεζίτης, as at Heptacomia in P Giss I. 59ⁱⁱⁱ·¹⁸ (A.D. 118-9). We need not illustrate such a word more fully, but we might quote *Syll* 846³¹ (B.C. 197-6) ἐπὶ τοῖσδε ἀπέδοτο Δαμέας ὁ παρὰ τοῦ βασιλέως Ἀττάλου ὁ ἐπὶ τῶν ἔργων τῶν βασιλικῶν Ἀρτεμιδώραν τὰν βασιλικὰν παιδίσκαν τῶι Ἀπόλλωνι τῶι Πυθίωι for freedom. On νόμος βασιλικός in Jas 2⁸ Deissmann refers to a heading probably added in the time of Trajan to an inscription at Pergamum containing the law of astynomy—τὸν βασιλικὸν νόμον ἐκ τῶν ἰδίων ἀνέθηκεν, "he set up the royal law out of his own means." This designation of the law as "royal," because made by one of the kings of Pergamum, points, he thinks, to a similar reference in the first place to the *origin* of the law in the James passage (see *LAE*, p. 367, n.³). Grimm notes that the phrase is applied to τὸ ὀρθόν in Plato.

βασίλισσα.

This characteristic Κοινή form was borrowed by Attic from B.C. 307 down: see Meisterhans *Gr.* p. 101, and cf. Thumb *Dial.* p. 380. The suffix was probably of Macedonian origin, and therefore not Greek at all (Brugmann-Thumb *Gr.* p. 214, where references are given to literature on the subject : add Glaser, *De ratione*, p. 18). It was the regular term for the wife of the ruling sovereign : see, e.g. P Petr I. 19²⁵ (B.C. 225) βασιλέα Πτολεμαῖον . . . καὶ βασίλισσαν Βερενίκην, P Eleph 23¹⁰ (B.C. 223) ὀμνύω βασιλέα Πτολεμαῖον . . . καὶ βασίλισσαν Βερενίκην. P Par 38¹ (B.C. 160) βασιλεῖ Πτολεμαίῳ καὶ βασιλίσσῃ [Κλεο]πάτρᾳ τῇ ἀδελφῇ, and P Grenf II. 15ⁱⁱ (B.C. 139). In *Syll* we find it in 183⁴ (end of iv/B.C.) of the wife of Demetrius Poliorcetes, and in five inscrr. of iii/B.C. In *OGIS* 35¹ (B.C. 285-47) βασίλισσαν Φιλωτέραν, the title is given to the unmarried sister of King Ptolemy II, a proof, according to Wilcken (*Archiv* ii. p. 541), that amongst the Ptolemies the title was from the beginning purely titular. A similar inscription from Schedia (east of Alexandria), belonging to the reign of Ptolemy III., has the further interest that it contains the earliest known reference to a Jewish proseucha in Upper Egypt—ὑ[πὲρ βασιλέως Πτολεμαίου καὶ βασιλίσσης Βερενίκης ἀδελφῆς καὶ γυναικὸς καὶ τῶν τέκνων τὴν προσευχὴν οἱ Ἰουδαῖοι : see *Archiv* ii. p. 541 with Wilcken's note. It should be noted, however, that προσευχήν here may simply = "prayer," answering to the heathen τὸ προσκύνημα

βάσις.

The word is common in the inscriptions for the "base" of a statue, e.g. *OGIS* 705[6] (ii/A.D.) τὸν ἀνδριάντα σὺν τῆι βάσει ἀνέθηκε, *Magn* 92[b. 17] τὸ] δὲ ψήφισμα τόδε ἀναγραφῆναι εἰς τὴμ βάσιν τῆς εἰκόνος τῆς Ἀ[πο]λλοφάνου. See also P Lond 755 *verso*[6] (iv/A.D.) (= III. p. 222) β]άσις καὶ κεφαλίδες, "base mouldings and capitals" of pillars. P Grenf I. 14[15] B.C. 150 or 139) βάσιν λυχνί(ου), *Syll* 540[103] (B.C. 175–1) ἐργᾶται (*sc.* a builder contracting for a temple) τῶν λίθων πάντων τὰς βάσεις ὀρθάς, ἀστραβεῖς, ἀρραγεῖς κτλ, *ib*[161] τῶν λίθων πάντων τοὺς ἁρμοὺς καὶ τ[ὰς βά]σεις, 588[167] (*c.* B.C. 180) λαμπὰς χαλκῆ ἐπὶ βάσεως, etc. The medical use of **β.** = "foot" in Ac 3[7] is illustrated by Hobart, *Medical Language of St Luke*, p. 34 f. It may have this meaning in the great magical papyrus, P Lond 121[518] (iii/A.D.) (= I. p. 101) παρέστω σοι τοῖς δυσὶ βάσεσιν σκιαθι. Its geometrical meaning, as the "base" of a triangle, appears with fragmentary context in P Brit Mus 372[50] (ii/A.D.), printed in P Tebt II. p. 339 ff., a land survey.

βασκαίνω.

The popular belief in the power of the evil eye (cf. Deut 28[54], Sir 14[6, 8]), underlying the Pauline metaphor in Gal 3[1], is well illustrated by the common formulas in closing greetings, e.g. P Oxy II. 292[12] (*c.* A.D. 25) (= *Selections*, p. 38) πρὸ δὲ πάντων ὑγιάνειν (= -αίνειν) σε εὔχ[ο]μαι ἀβασκάντως τὰ ἄριστα πράττων, "but above all I pray that you may be in health unharmed by the evil eye and faring prosperously," *ib.* VI. 930[23] (ii/iii A.D.) ἀσπάζονταί σε πολλὰ αἱ ἀδελφαί σου καὶ τὰ ἀβάσκαντα παιδία Θεωνίδος, and similarly P Fay 126[10], P Lips I. 108[9] (both ii/iii A.D.). Cf. the opening salutation in BGU III. 811[4] (between A.D. 98 and 103) πρὼ (*i. e.* πρὸ) μὲν πάντων ἀναγκαῖον δι' ἐπιστολῆ[ς] σε ἀσπάσεσθαι καὶ τὰ ἀβάσκαντα [δ]οῦ[ν]αι. For the subst. **βασκανία** (as Wisd 4[12]) cf. the new compound **προβασκανία** in the vi/A.D. Christian amulet edited by Wilcken *Archiv* i. p. 431 ff. (= *Selections*, p. 132 ff.)—7 ff. ὅπως διώξῃς ἀπ' ἐμοῦ τοῦ δούλου σου τὸν δαίμονα προβασκανίας, "that thou mayst drive from me thy servant the demon of witchcraft." The adj. **βάσκανος** is found in Vettius Valens, pp. 2[2], 358[5], and in *IosPE* i. 22[31] (Minns, p. 644) ὑπὸ τοῦ βασκάνου δαίμονος ἀφῃρέθη. The relation of the word to the certainly identical Lat. *fascinum* is accounted for by the consideration that a word of magic was likely to be borrowed by Greek from Thracian or Illyrian, where original *bh* (Lat. *f*) passed into *b*: see Walde *Lat. etym. Wörterbuch, s.v.*

βαστάζω.

The meaning *lift* occurs in P Ryl II. 81[5] (*c.* A.D. 104), where the θύραι of sluices (apparently) ἐφ'] ὅσον οἱ κατασπορεῖς ἤθελον ἐβαστάχθησαν, "as much as the inspectors of sowing wished" (Edd.). *Carry*, in the figurative sense = *endure*, appears in a formula about taxation, as P Brem [9] (A.D. 117) (= *Chrest.* I. p. 415) ἐπεὶ οὖν αὗται οὐ βαστάζουσι τοσοῦτο τέλεσμα : so in P Ryl II. 96[8] and the other contemporary papers named in the introduction there. Note here Epict. i. 3. 2 οὐδείς σου τὴν ὀφρὺν βαστάσει, "will endure your cheek." (!) (Hort says this is "the only

known passage at all approaching" Rev 2[2].) Nearer the literal sense, and illustrating distantly Ac 9[15], is P Oxy X. 1242[1. 17], an interesting document of early iii/A.D., where Trajan is said to have granted an audience to rival Greek and Jewish emissaries from Alexandria, ἕκαστοι βαστάζοντες τοὺς ἰδίους θεούς. To the same heading may be referred its use in Gal 6[17], for which Deissmann (*BS*, p. 352 ff.) refers to a bilingual (Demotic and Greek) papyrus of iii/A.D. now in the Leiden Museum. The papyrus contains a spell in which the words occur βαστάζω τὴν ταφὴν τοῦ Ὀσίρεως . . . ἐάν μοι ὁ δεῖνα κόπους παράσχῃ, προσ(τ)ρέψω αὐτὴν αὐτῷ, "I carry the corpse of Osiris . . . should so-and-so trouble me, I shall use it against him. Just, that is, as the βαστάζειν of a particular amulet associated with the god acts as a charm against the κόπους παρέχειν of an adversary, so the Apostle finds himself protected against similar attacks by "bearing" the στίγματα Ἰησοῦ. From *carry* is developed *carry away*, which is the commonest meaning. Thus *Cagnat* IV. 446, an inscr. of Roman age, where the Pergamene demos honour C. Julius Maximus σημείωι ἀβαστάκτωι, "ornatus insigni 'quod tolli non poterat,' fortasse purpura perpetua" (Ed.). So very often in papyri. P Fay 122[6] (*c.* A.D. 100) ἐά[σ]ας αὐτὸν βαστάξαι ἀρτάβας εἴκοσι ὀκτώ, "allowing him to carry off 28 artabae." P Ryl II. 168[11] (A.D. 120) βαστάξεις ἐκ τῆς κοινῆς ἅλωι πάντα, "you shall carry it all from the common threshing-floor" (Edd.) : cf. P Thead 5[12] (A.D. 338). Similarly P Oxy III. 507[29] (A.D. 169) ὅνπερ χόρτον οὐκ ἐξέσται μοι βαστάξαι οὐδὲ πωλεῖν οὐδὲ ὑποτίθεσθαι, "it shall not be lawful for me to remove or sell or pledge this hay" (Edd.), *ib.* 522[4] (ii/A.D.) φορέτρο(ν) (πυροῦ) (ἀρταβῶν) ροᾱ βασταχθ εἰσῶν), "carriage of 171 artabae of wheat transported" (Edd.). With personal object, P Amh II. 77[22] (A.D. 139) ἀμφότεροι βίᾳ βασ[τ]άξαντές με εἰσήνεγκαν εἰς τὸ λογ[ι]στήριον τοῦ ἐπιτρόπου τῶν οὐσιῶν, "taking me up by force they together carried me to the counting-house of the superintendent of the domains" (Edd.). This is of course capable of meaning, in contrast to the use named later, a perfectly legitimate action : cf. P Iand 9[13] (ii/A.D.) σ]ὺ οὖν βάσταξε (*sc.* αι) λυπὸν ὁ ἂν ἔτιο[ν ᾖ] τῆς κρίσεως, "tu autem tolle porro, quaecunque causa est iudicii" (Ed.). The firmly established vernacular use determines the meaning of Mt 3[11] as "whose sandals I am not worthy to *take off*": the phrase is an excellent example of Mt's skilful abbreviation, for one word fully expresses all that Mk 1[7] tells us in four. Citations multiply for the meaning "pilfer," as in Jn 12[6], especially in papyri of ii/A.D. P Tebt II. 330[7] (ii/A.D.) εὗρον τὴν οἰκίαν μου σεσυλημένην τε καὶ πάντα τὰ ἔνδον ἀποκείμενα βεβασταγμ[έ]να, *ib.* 331[11] (*c.* A.D. 131) ἐβ]άσταξαν ὅσα κιθῶνα καὶ ἱμ[ά]τιον λευκά : both petitions to the strategus complaining of robbery. Similarly P Oxy I. 69[4] (A.D. 190), BGU I. 46[10] (A.D. 193), *ib.* 157[8] (ii iii A.D.), etc. In MGr the verb has added a new intransitive meaning, "wait, hold out": see Thumb *Handbook*, p. 322, Abbott *Songs*, p. 261. The flexion of the verb differs curiously in the papyri and in NT. In the former the guttural forms, ἐβάσταξα, etc., prevail almost without variant, as will be seen from our quotations, and from the list in the editor's note to P Hamb I. 10[13]. In MGr the aorist is ἐβάσταξα. It will be noticed that our citations are later than NT : the verb does not seem to have entered the vernacular in Egypt during the Ptolemaic period. In that case the late guttural flexion would be an analogy product (cf. the double forms from ἁρπάζω, etc.), confined at first to a limited area. Except in Rev 2² βαστάξαι P I 38 81, ἐβάσταξας Jn 20¹⁵ W, and Lk 11⁴⁶ δυσβάστακτα, the NT has only the dental forms, as in older Greek from Homer down. We can only support these in Egyptian vernacular from BGU I. 195³² (A.D. 161) ἐβάσ[τ]ασεν, P Leid W^i 22 (ii/iii A.D.) βαστάσας, and P Flor I. 59⁷ (iii/A.D.) ἐβάστασεν.

βάτος (1)

in the sense of "bush" is feminine in Lk 20³⁷, Ac 7³⁵, but masculine in Mk 12²⁶ in accordance with the LXX usage (Exod 3²ff., Deut 33¹⁶), which Thackeray (*Gr.* i. p. 145) describes as apparently "vulgar and Hellenistic." See, however, Moeris p. 99, who regards ἡ β. as ἑλληνικῶς, and ὁ β. as ἀττικῶς. The only passage we can cite, P Lond 121⁴⁶⁰ (iii/A.D.) (= I. p. 99) θὲς ὑπὲρ βάτον, throws no light on the gender : since the context is a φίλτρον κάλλιστον, in which kind of literature "meaning is no great matter," βάτον may as well be a Hebrew measure as a bramble-bush. H. A. A. Kennedy (*Sources of NT Greek*, p. 78) includes βάτος in a list of Biblical words for which Aristophanes is practically the only earlier authority. But we must remember Homer (*Od.* 24²³⁹). Kaibel has two epitaphs from Italy of the imperial age : 546⁶ οὐ βάτοι, οὐ τρίβολοι τὸν ἐμὸν τάφον ἀμφὶς ἔχουσιν, and 548² ἄνθεα πολλὰ γένοιτο νεοδμήτῳ ἐπὶ τύμβῳ, μὴ βάτος αὐχμηρή, μὴ κακὸν αἰγίπυρον.

βάτος (2).

This Hebrew loanword (בַּת) is rather strangely transliterated βάδος in Hesychius, who implies that this was commoner than βάτος : perhaps the fact that δ was now generally spirantised (like *th* in *bathe*) made it seem nearer than τ to the Hebrew letter. See Tischendorf on Lk 16⁶ : to אLX, which spell with δ, must now be added W.

βάτραχος.

The γλῶττα βατράχου forms an ingredient in the 4th century magical charm P Lond 46²⁹⁴ (iv/A.D.) (= I. p. 74). The Ionic form βάθρακος appears twice in *ib.* 124²¹ f. (iv/v A.D.) (= I. p. 122), and survives in MGr βάθρακας.

βαττολογέω.

In D this word is βλαττολογέω, the form of which suggests an approximation towards the Latin *blatero*—[query cf. provincial English *blether*, with same meaning, both starting from *°mlatero*]. The Latin text (*d*) has not the word, so that if Latin influence is recognizable here it must lie somewhere in the complex history of the Bezan text itself. Βαττολογέω may be by haplology for βατταλολογέω, in which some connexion may be suspected with Βάτταλος on the one side, the nickname of Demosthenes, and Aramaic *battâl* ("leer, nichtig," says Wellhausen on Mt 6⁷) on the other. Whether Greek or Aramaic, or neither, is the borrower, we must not stay to ask. If the great orator was thus nicknamed because of the torrent of words at his command, which made envious rivals call him "the gabbler, it will fit his case better than the highly im-

probable "stammering" connexion, and will suit the ἐν τῇ πολυλογίᾳ by which the verb is explained in Mt 6⁷. (See Holden on Plutarch's *Demosthenes*, ch. iv.)

βδέλλιον.

which figures twice in the Pentateuch according to Aquila, Symmachus and Theodotion, appears doubtfully in P Oxy VIII. 1142³ (late iii/A.D.), where Hunt conjectures it for βρέλλιον because in Galen as in the papyrus it stands next to ὄνυξ : he renders "sweet gum (?) . . . , onyx-shell." The form βδέλλη occurs in P Lond 121¹³¹ (iii/A.D.) (= I. p. 98) ζμύρνα βδέλλης.

βδέλυγμα

is "a bibl. and eccl. word" in Grimm, and we are not able to challenge its right to a place in this greatly reduced category. But it is almost as much a part of the verb as βδελυκτός, which likewise has independent status on Grimm's page. The verb having appealed to the LXX translators as an excellent rendering of שִׁקֵּץ and other Hebrew verbs, it was inevitable that when a derived noun was wanted the regular formation should have been adopted or coined. Probably any Greek writer who wanted to express the idea of τὸ ἐβδελυγμένον would have done the same without hesitation.

βδελύσσομαι.

Phrynichus (ed. Lobeck), p. 226, extols this word as Attic as compared with the vulgar σικχαίνομαι (MGr σιχαίνομαι), but it is by no means confined to Attic writers, as Nageli (p. 15) has pointed out : cf. Thumb *Hellen.* p. 80. *Pelagia-Legenden*, p. 6⁹ μὴ βδελύξῃ με τὴν ῥερυπωμένην ἀλλὰ κάθαρόν με ἐν τῇ κολυμβήθρᾳ τοῦ ἁγιάσματος.

βέβαιος.

Deissmann (*BS*, p. 104 ff.) has shown very fully how much force the technical use of this word and its cognates to denote legally guaranteed security adds to their occurrence in the NT. Thus with the use of this adjective in Rom 4¹⁶, 2 Cor 1⁷, we may compare P Amh II. 85²¹ (A.D. 78) where, in an application for a lease, provision is made that if no objection is raised "the lease may remain guaranteed to us for the period of five years without change "—μένηι ἡμῖν ἡ μίσθωσις βεβαία ἐπὶ τὸν πενταετ[ῆ] χρόνον ἀμεθεστάτους (*l.* -οις). P Strass I. 22²³ (iii/A.D.) ἔχειν τ[ὸ] βέβαιον τοὺς κατασχόντας, "that those who have obtained possession may be secured in it," P Oxy IX. 1200²⁹ (A.D. 266) ἔτι τε καὶ παρέξομαί σοι βέβαια διὰ παντὸς ἀπὸ πάντων πάσῃ βεβαιώσει, "and I will further guarantee the property always against all claims with every guarantee" (Ed.), BGU IV. 1116³¹ (B.C. 13) ποιοῦντος δὲ αὐτοῦ ἕκαστα ἀκολ(ούθως) καὶ τὴ(ν) Ἀντω(νίαν) Φιλη(μάτιον) βεβαίαν αὐτῷ παρέχεσθαι τὴ(ν) μίσθω(σιν), *ib.* 1127¹⁶ (B.C. 18) παρέχεσθαι τὴν παραχώρησιν βεβαίαν. So from inscr. *OGIS* 669²⁵ (i/A.D.) ὧν βεβαίαν δεῖ τὴν πρωτοπραξίαν φυλάσσειν. It will be noticed that ἔχω and παρέχομαι tend to associate with the adjective : cf. Heb 5¹⁴, 6¹⁹, 2 Pet 1¹⁹. We need not multiply citations for a common word, unless we should give an instance with the negative : P Tor I. 1^viii. 10 (B.C. 116) (= *Chrest.* II. p. 32) αἰσθομένη ὡς οὐθὲν εἶχεν βέβαιον.

βεβαιόω.

The verb is very common in the juristic sense noted under βέβαιος : see e.g. P Petr III. 74(*a*)⁸ βεβαιώσω σοι, " I shall give you a guarantee," P Amh II. 95¹⁰ (A.D. 109) ἐὰν δὲ ἐ]πελθ[ω ἢ μὴ β]εβα[ιώσω, ἥ τ' ἔφο]δος [ἄκυρος ἔ]στ[ω, " if I make a claim or fail to guarantee the sale, the claim shall be invalid " (Edd.), P Fay 92¹⁹ (A.D. 126) βεβαιώσιν πά[σ]η βεβαιώσι, " will guarantee the sale with every guarantee." Note also the recurrent formula in which a vendor promises βεβαιοῦν καὶ πάντα τὸν ἐπελευσόμενον ἀποστήσειν παραχρῆμα τοῖς ἰδίοις δαπανήμασιν : so BGU IV. 1131²⁵ (B.C. 13) etc. Hence it is that Paul, associating β. with another legal term ἀρραβών (see *s.v.*), the guaranteeing the delivery of something of which the earnest has already been paid, can describe the relation of God to believers in 2 Cor 1²¹ ᶠ : Deissmann *BS*, p. 230, quotes BGU II. 446¹⁸ (A.D. 158-9) (= *Chrest.* II. p. 295) στερίκεθαι (*i.e.* στερίσκεσθαι) αὐτὸν τοῦ ἀραβῶνος, ἔτι δὲ καὶ βεβαιώσιν (fut. inf.) αὐτὴν Σωτηρίαν τὰ κατὰ τ[αύτην τὴν ὁμολογίαν πάση βεβαιώσει. For the possibly weaker sense of " accomplish," " fulfil " in Rom 15⁸ Rouffiac (p. 48) cites *Priene* 123⁹, where a magistrate, having promised on entering on office to make a distribution of beef, ἐβεβαίωσεν δὲ τὴν ἐπαγγελίαν παραστή[σ]ας μὲν τοῖς ἐντεμενίοις θεοῖς τὴν θυσίαν, " fulfilled his promise by making a sacrifice to the gods (and distributing the flesh to those entered on the list)." Cf. BGU IV. 1073¹³ (A.D. 275) (= *Chrest.* II. p. 219) καὶ κατὰ τὰ εἰθισμένα προσκυνήσαντες τὰ θεῖα (*l.* θεῖα) ἔτι μᾶλλον ταῦτα αὐτῷ ἐβεβαιώσαμεν. Another instance of a less technical use is in P Oxy VIII. 1119¹⁷ (A.D. 254) διαδεξάμ]ενοι τὴν βασιλείαν τὴν ὑπάρχου[σ]αν ἡμεῖν καὶ ἐν τούτου ἄδιαν ἐ[βεβ]αίωσαν πολλάκις, " [Hadrian's] successors on the throne often confirmed our immunity in this respect " (Edd.).

βεβαίωσις.

To the use of this word in P Fay 92¹⁹ already cited *s.v.* βεβαιόω we may add P Giss I. 51¹⁰ (A.D. 202) βέβαιον διὰ [παντὸς ἀπὸ πάντων πάσ]η βεβαιώσει, PSI I. 79¹⁷ (A.D. 216-7) βεβαιώσω σοι τὴν πρᾶσιν πάση βεβαιώσει. For πάση βεβαιώσι καὶ ἀπὸ δημοσίων as denoting that the object sold is guaranteed as owing nothing to the fiscal authorities, see BGU I. 153²³ (A.D. 152). Deissmann *BS*, p. 104 ff., has an interesting exposition showing how the technical term εἰς βεβαίωσιν, the antithesis of εἰς ἀθέτησιν, was adopted by the LXX from legal phraseology in Lev 25²³, not to render לִצְמִתֻת exactly, but to give the general sense, " the ground belongs to Yahweh—therefore it may not be sold *absolutely*," by a legally defined sale. So again in Heb 6¹⁶ " for a legal guarantee." He cites P Par 62 ᵛᶦⁱⁱ (ii/B.C.) . . .]τοι εἰς τὴν βεβαίωσιν ὑποθήκας [. . ., and shows that it survived even till A.D. 600. The forensic flavour of the word is noted as still discernible in Phil 1⁷—" this defence before the court will be at the same time an *erictio* or *convictio* of the Gospel." The papyri discovered since Deissmann's pioneer work was published support with numerous examples his thesis that the word must always be read with the technical sense in mind. It is worth noting that Vettius Valens, p. 2²⁸, has ἀγαθῶν βεβαίωσιν next to εἰσποίησιν and in close company with other legal terms, as well as more general ones. The subst. βεβαιωτής is common in such conjunctions as

P Amh II. 51²⁸ (sale of a house—B.C. 88) προπωλητὴς καὶ βεβαιωτὴ[ς] τῶν κατὰ τὴν ὠνὴν ταύτην πάντων Πετεῆσις ὁ ἀποδόμενος, " the negotiator and guarantor of the sale in all respects is the vendor Peteësis " (Edd.). For the form βεβαιώτρια see Mayser *Gr.* p. 444.

βέβηλος.

Syll 2²⁵ (ii/A.D.) χώραν [σ]καπανεύειν βέβηλον ἐ[πέ]τασσες —the famous ' Gadatas ' inscr., translated from a rescript of Darius I. The derived verb is of late formation, no earlier authority than LXX being quotable. The adj. was an old *term. techn.* of religion, and not a word of the vernacular : the LXX translators needed it, and may well have equipped it with a regularly formed verb.

βελόνη.

This medical term for the needle used in surgical operations (see Hobart, *Medical Language of St Luke*, p. 61) is substituted by Luke for ῥαφίς in Lk 18²⁵, but does not occur elsewhere in Bibl. Grk. See for its more general use the magic papyrus P Lond 121³¹² (iii/A.D.) (= I. p. 98) χαλκῷ βελόνῃ ἀκεφάλῳ. MGr βελόνι.

βέλος.

For this NT ἅπ. εἰρ. Eph 6¹⁶) cf. *IG* VII. 115⁸ βέλος πικρὸν ἐνῆκε πλευραῖς. The word is claimed by van Herwerden as Ionic and poetic : one occurrence in Plato and one in Xenophon (the pioneer of the Κοινή) are the only classical prose citations in LS⁸. From inscr. we may quote *Syll* 221¹⁰ (B.C. 247-23) βέλη καὶ καταπάλτα[ς, *ib.* 522³⁷ (iii/B.C.) καταπάλτην . . . καὶ βέλη τριακόσια, *ib.* 803⁶⁷ (iii B.C.) where it refers to a spear just mentioned. The first two passages suggest a special sense rather than the general : cf. Polybius xi. 11. 3 ζεύγη πλῆθος ὀργάνων καὶ βελῶν κομίζοντα καταπελτικῶν. The catapult would naturally be used if missiles wrapped with blazing tow were to be hurled, and this would suit τὰ βέλη τὰ πεπυρωμένα in Eph *l.c.* A late letter, PSI III. 238⁹ (vi/vii A.D.), mentions one Zenobius as a maker of munitions, βελοποιός.

βελτίων.

For the elative comparative in Acts 10²⁸ D βέλτιον ἐπίστασθε cf. *Magn* 105⁹⁸ (ii/A.D.) βέλτιον ὑπελάβομεν γράψαι ὑμῖν. See also P Tebt I. 27⁸⁰ (B.C. 113) ἀεὶ δέ τινος ἐπὶ τὸ βέλτιον προσεπινοουμένου, " by the continual invention of further improvements " (Edd.), and P Oxy VIII. 1148² (a question to the oracle—i/A.D.) εἰ [? εἰ introducing direct question, as in NT] βέλτιόν ἐστιν κτλ. A locution with β. may be noted from BGU IV. 1086ⁱⁱ ² (A.D. 160 or 183 or 215) τὴν] δὲ πο[λ]ειτίαν ἐπὶ τὸ βέλτιον καὶ εὐτ[υ]χ[έστερον . . . Note also P Leid Wˣˣⁱᵛ·¹⁹ (ii/iii A.D.) βέλτιον δὲ ποιεῖ ἐὰν κτλ.—this is ordinary comparative. For the superlative, which happens not to occur in NT, cf. P Magd 29⁴ (B.C. 117) ἐγλεξάμενος τὸν βέλτιστον τόπον καὶ ἐξώτατον, P Fay 12⁶ (B.C. 103) τῶν . . . οὐ ἀπὸ τοῦ βελτ[ί]στου ἀναστρεφομένων, " of the less reputable class " (Edd.), P Ryl II. 156¹⁹ (i/A.D.) . . .] ἀπὸ τοῦ βελτίστου γεγενημέν[ου, *Syll* 278⁷ (ii/B.C.) οἱ οὐκ ἀπὸ τοῦ βελτίστου εἰωθότες ἀναστρέφεσθαι : the phrase looks like a cant term for the masses current among the classes. Deissmann *BS*, p. 93,

says that (οὐκ ἀπὸ τοῦ β. in 2 Macc]14⁷⁶ ["came not of
good," RV) can be paralleled with "many examples" in
the Inscrr. and in Dionys. Hal. and Plutarch. It may be
noted further that we have ἀγροικότερον ἐσχηκότα in the
preceding clause, which suggests that here Judas Maccabaeus
is observing Nicanor's "boorish" rudeness towards him,
οὐκ ἀ. τ. β. having the same nuance as in the papyri and
inscr. just quoted. The survival of an old use of βέλτιστε
in address may be observed in BGU IV. 1146⁵ (B.C. 4), where
ἡγεμώ(ν) βέλτιστε is corrected into μέγιστε, probably because
the former was too familiar, as its use in Plato would suggest.
The rare form βέλτατα is found P Petr II. 9 5⁷ (B.C. 241–39)
τὰ [β]έλτατα πληρώματα. The verb βελτιόω occurs in the
vi/A.D. P Lond 1044²² (= III. p. 255) φιλοκαλεῖν καὶ
βελτιοῦν: cf. Syll 418⁵ (A.D. 238) ἐν τοῖς εὐτυχεστάτοις
σοῦ καιροῖς κατοικεῖσθαι καὶ βελτιοῦσθαι τὰς κώμας.

Βερνίκη.

This form, for the more usual Βερενίκη, is read by Wilcken
(Add. et Corr. p. xi) in P Petr III. 1⁶·⁷ (B.C. 230) μητρὸς
θεῶν Βερνίκης. Mayser Gr. p. 145 compares also Βερνείκω(νι) in P Tebt I. 120¹² (B.C. 97 or 64). Add P Tebt II.
407¹¹ (A.D. 199) Βερνίκη Διδύμου γυναικί μου χαίρειν, and
for the full form Preisigke 307 (Ptolemaic) βασίλισ[σ]α
Βερενίκη, ib. 438 (do.) Λίβυς Διονυσίου Νειλεὺς καὶ Βερενίκη ἡ γυνή, P Grenf I. 24³ (B.C. 140–17) Βερενείκης
εὐεργετίδος. The shortened form is a good example of a
phonetic principle working in Κοινή Greek, discovered by
Kretschmer, by which an unaccented vowel tends to fall out
after a liquid or nasal if the same vowel occurred in the
neighbouring syllable (σκύρδον for σκόροδον, etc.).

βῆμα.

The collocation βῆμα ποδός (Ac 7⁵, from Dt 2⁵) is found in
Preisigke 4284²¹ (A.D. 207) οὐλὴ βήματι ποδὸς δεξιοῦ: this
of course is not a measure as in Ac lc. but literal. On Syll
763⁵ Ἀπατούριος Διοδώρου Μιλήσιος τὰ βήματα ἀνέθηκεν
Ἴσιδι Δικαιοσύνηι Dittenberger notes that two footprints
are carved in the stone, as in other monuments intended to
commemorate the safe accomplishment of a journey to the
shrine. Most commonly in inscrr. β. == [base], Syll 583
(?ii/B.C.) καὶ ἔστιν αὐτὸς ὁ θεὸς ἐπὶ βήματος μαρμαρίνου καὶ
ἡ παρακειμένη τῷ θεῷ τράπεζα λίθου Λεσβίου, of Apollo:
the image of Artemis is ἐπὶ παραστάδι μυλίνῃ, and that of
Men ἐπὶ βάσει μαρμαρίνῃ. So OGIS 219²⁰ (iii/B.C.) ἐπὶ
βήματος τοῦ λευκοῦ λίθου, ib. 200¹⁵ (ii/B.C.) ἐπιγράψαι ἐπὶ
τοῦ βήματος, Magn 92a¹² (ii/A.D.) εἰς τὸ βῆμα τῆς ἐκκλησίας. In the papyri it is very common in the official sense
"tribunal, judgement-seat," as in NT. P Oxy I. 37¹·³
(A.D. 49) (= Selections, p. 48) ἐπὶ τοῦ βήματος, [Π]εσοῦρι[ς]
πρὸς Σαραεῦν, "in court, Pesouris versus Saraeus," P Tebt
II. 316¹¹ (A.D. 99) τὸν ἀπὸ βήματος χρηματισμόν, "the
deed issued by the court," P Oxy II. 237⁷·¹³ (A.D. 186)
πρὸ βήματος ἐσιώπησεν, and similarly P Amh II. 80⁷
(A.D. 232–3), P Strass I. 5⁷ (A.D. 262) etc. In P Lond
358¹⁹ (c. A.D. 150) (= II. p. 172) we have ἐπὶ τὸ ἱερώτατον
τοῦ ἡγεμόνος βῆμα with reference to the Praefect's court, and
in BGU II. 613¹⁹ (time of Antoninus Pius) ἀξιῶ προσκυνῶν
τὸ ἱερώτατον βῆμα τοῦ [blank follows], and so elsewhere.
A unique phrase in P Grenf II. 15²·⁹ (B.C. 139) ἐφ᾽ ἱερῶν
Πτολεμαίου σωτῆρος . . . καὶ τοῦ βήματος Διονύσου,

"priest of the βῆμα of Dionysos" (Edd.), is noted as
perhaps applicable by translation from demotic, as in other
divergences here from ordinary formulae. In the Christian
fragment P Kyl I. 11² (v/vi A.D.) β. is used of the "terrible
judgement-seat of Christ our God" πρὸς τῷ φοβερῷ βήματι
Χ(ριστο)ῦ τοῦ θ(εο)ῦ ἡμῶν· cf. Pelagia-Legenden (ed.
Usener) p. 6⁸ ἐνώπιον τοῦ φρικτοῦ καὶ φοβεροῦ βήματός σου.

βία.

A few examples will suffice of this common word—P Petr
III. 53 (m)² (iii B.C.) πρὸς βίαν ἔχεται, "he is forcibly detained" (Edd.), P Par 38²² (B.C. 162) περὶ δὲ ἧς πεποίηνται
βίας (cf. P Amh II. 35³¹—B.C. 132), ib. 15¹⁹ (B.C. 120) καὶ
τῇ περὶ ἑαυτοὺς βίᾳ χρώμενοι, P Oxy VIII. 1120¹¹ (early
iii/A.D.) κατὰ τοῦτο μαρτύρομαι τὴν βίαν γυνὴ χήρα καὶ
ἀσθενής, ib.²⁰ ὡς ἐν παντὶ σθένει βίαν με σχεῖν, "so that I
am subjected to unmitigated violence" (Edd.), P Strass I. 5⁹
(A.D. 262) πέπονθεν βίαν πα[ρ]ὰ πάντας τοὺς νόμου[ς], ib.⁶
εἴ τι πρὸ[ς] βίαν ἐλήμφθη, and P Giss I. 34¹⁴ (A.D. 265 or 6)
βίαν οὐ τὴν τυχοῦσαν ἐργάσασθαι. Μετὰ βίας, as in
Ac 5²⁶, occurs in P Tebt I. 5⁵⁷ (B.C. 118), Syll 356³⁴ (B.C. 6),
in the latter case associated with ὕβρεως and applied to
burglars. Note also P Tebt II. 434² (A.D. 104) τῆς βίας
αὐτῶν δεομένης τῆς τοῦ κρατίστου ἡγεμόνος δικαιοδοσίας,
P Amh II. 78¹ (A.D. 184) βίαν πάσχων ἑκάστοτε ὑπὸ
Ἐκύσεως, Chrest. I. 461¹² (iii/A.D.) μετὰ βίαν [π]αθῶν
. . . ὑπὸ Μάρκου κτλ. It is rather curious that in NT
βία is restricted to Ac.

βιάζομαι.

The verb is common, and its compounds ἀπο-, κατα- and
εἰσ- can be quoted; but there seems little that promises
decisive help for the difficult Logion of Mt 11¹² = Lk 16¹⁶.
That in the former βιάζεται can be passive, as all the ancient
versions assume, may be illustrated by such evidence as P
Oxy II. 294¹⁶ (A.D. 22) ἐγὼ δὲ βιάζομαι ὑπὸ φίλων. Cf.
βιάζομαι τάδε in Sophocles (Ant. 66), "I am forced to it."
In the same direction tend the passages quotable for a
transitive use of the middle. So P Giss I. 19¹³ (ii/A.D.), if
rightly supplemented, ἄγ[ε]υστος ἐκοιμώμην ἕως ὁ πατήρ
μου εἰσελθὼν ἐβιάσατό με, "made me take food"; P Amh
II. 35¹⁷ (B.C. 132) βιασάμενος αὐτοὺς ἐπὶ τῆς ἅλω, "compelled them to go to the threshing-floor" (Edd.), P Lond
117¹ recto l.⁹ (A.D. 42) βεβιασμένος τινά, P Magd 27¹ (B.C.
218) βιάζεταί με πλίνθον προσάγων καὶ θεμέλιον σκάπτων
ὥστε οἰκοδομεῖν. The middle can however be used absolutely, = come forward violently or enter by force. Deissmann (BS. p. 258) supports this by Syll 633⁸ (imperial
period), where in the epigraphic regulations for the sanctuary
of Men Tyrannus it is laid down—ἐὰν δέ τις βιάσηται,
ἀπρόσδεκτος ἡ θυσία παρὰ τοῦ θεοῦ. It must be admitted
that Deissmann's second translation above is as preferable for
this inscr. as the first is for Mt l.c. if the verb must be
middle: one who supports either of these renderings
would still have to illustrate the application of the verb
to something abstract or impersonal. There are many
other citations available for the absolute use. Putting
first those where no εἰς follows, we have Syll 418⁴
(A.D. 238) ἐπεὶ δὲ κατὰ καιροὺς εἰς ὕβριν (?) προχωρεῖν τινὲς
καὶ βιάζεσθαι (= use violence) ἤρξαντο, ib. 803¹ (ii/A.D.) εἴ
τις παρὰ τὴν βούλησιν Πυθίδος βιασάμενος (= by force)

ἀνοίξῃ τὴν καμάραν, *JHS* xxxiv. p. 1 ff. (inscrr. from Lycia), no. 43[5] ὁ βιασάμενος of one who has forcibly entered a tomb (cf. 45[6] εἰ δέ τις ἐκβιάσηται). (From literature may be added Demosthenes *Callicl.* 17 (p. 1276) κἂν βιάσηταί ποτε, ἀποφράττειν ἅπαντες καὶ παροικοδομεῖν εἰώθαμεν," when it [the flood water] forces its way.") So in the papyri P Magd 1[17] (B.C. 221) περὶ δὲ τοῦ βεβιασμένους [αὐ]τοὺς κατεσπαρκέναι, "quant à la contrainte imposée par eux pour les semailles" (Edd.), P Tebt I. 6[31] (B.C. 140–30) τινὰς δὲ καὶ βιαζομέν[ου]ς, "some who even take forcible possession" (Edd.), P Flor III. 382[21] (A.D. 222–3) ἐπὶ οὖν ὁ πραγματικὸς ἐπὶ τῶν τόπων εἰσχύει βιάσασθαι, and PSI II. 120[50] (? iv/A.D.) εὐμετάβολος γὰρ ὁ θεός. πεῖσαι ζήτει, μὴ βιάσασθαι· ὁ μὲν γὰρ βιασάμενος ἐχθρός, ὁ δὲ πείσας σοφός. This last, however, implies an object. D. S. Sharp, *Epictetus and the NT*, p. 67, cites a good parallel from Epict. iv. 7. 20 f.: ἀποκλεισμὸς ἐμοὶ οὐ γίνεται, ἀλλὰ τοῖς βιαζομένοις. διὰ τί οὖν οὐ βιάζομαι: "those who (try to) force their way in," as he rightly renders. This meaning of forcible entry is more precisely expressed with εἰς, or by the compound, as is seen from Grimm's illustrations of Lk *l.c.* and by P Tor I. 1[x·2] (B.C. 119) (= *Chrest.* II. p. 39) εἴπαμεν τῶι μὲν Ἑρμίαι μὴ εἰσβιάζεσθαι, τοῖς δὲ περὶ τὸν Ὧρον κρατεῖν, P Leid G[18] (ii/B.C.) μὴ θ[ε]νὶ ἐξεῖναι εἰσβιάζεσθαι εἰς αὐτ[ή]ν, BGU III. 1004[11] (iii/B.C.) ἀφ' οὗ χρόνου εἰσβεβίασται. It is at least clear that Luke's Logion can be naturally rendered "everyone is entering it violently." It may be added that β. in the middle may be followed by an infin. Thus in Arrian's account of Alexander's death we find βιάσασθαι ἰδεῖν. Similarly in P Ryl I. 24[11] (Homeric scholia i/A.D.) ἐὰν τὰ ἑαυτοῦ [ἀπολιπὼν] ἅρματα . . . [ἐφ' ἑτέρων ἐπι]βῆναι βιάζ[ε]ται. With the transitive exx. above will go the *acc. et inf.* constr. in *Michel* 1010[30] (i/B.C. *init.*) βιασαμένων δὲ αὐτὸν τῶν τεχνιτῶν πάλιν τὸ τέταρτον ὑπομεῖναι ἐπιμελητήν.

βίαιος.

BGU I. 45[10] (A.D. 203) ἀνὴρ βίαιος ὑπάρχων μὴ λειτουργῶν, τῇ βίᾳ αὐτοῦ ἐπῆλθεν αὐτῷ. P Leid W[vii·27] (ii/iii A.D.) ἐλεήμων ἐν ὥραις βίαιος (for -αις, or -οις). *Cagnat* IV. 351[31] has ἔργου βιαίου in a fragmentary context, in a rescript of Hadrian at Pergamum. The adj. occurs several times in Vettius Valens, who also has the compound βιαιοθάνατος, and derivatives -τέω and -σία. For the adverb, which is commoner, see P Par 14[22] ἐνοικοῦσιν βιαίως of those who "forcibly" take possession of a house, and cf. BGU II. 467[9] (ii/A.D.) βιαίως ἀπέσπασεν [τ]οὺς καμή[λο]υς *ib.* 648[9] (A.D. 104 or 166) (= *Chrest.* I. p. 423) βιαίως ἀντι[λ]αμβάνονται τ[ο]ῦ πατρικοῦ μου μέρους; and OGIS 669[10] (iii/A.D.) ἐάν τις ὑμῖν ἐπιδημήσῃ βιαίως στρατιώτης. The comparative βιαιότερον is found P Lond 301[18] (B.C. 116–11) (= II. p. 14) βιαιότερον ἐμβατ[εύσ]α]ς εἰς τὸ δη[λούμενο]ν ἔδαφος.

βιβλίον.

This is very much the commonest form in the family, and was the regular word for "book," "writing" in the Κοινή. It never meant a *little* writing: cf. P Ryl II. 382 (early ii/A.D.) μεγάλα βυβλία. The diminutive was supplied by βυβλάριον, as P Lille I. 7[7] (iii/B.C.) ἐπιζητήσαντος αὐτοῦ βυβλάριά τινα, and βιβλίδιον. In *Archiv* v. pp. 262 ff, 441,

Wilcken shows that this latter word was the ordinary term for "petition" till the end of the third century: see e. g. P Oxy VII. 1032[4] (A.D. 162) οὗ ἐπέδομεν Οὐολουσ[ίῳ Μ]αικιανῷ τῷ ἡγεμονεύσαντι βιβλειδίου . . . ἀντίγραφον, "copy of the petition which we presented to Volusius Maecianus, ex-praefect," P Tebt II. 293[8] (c. A.D. 187) πρὸς τὸ ἐπιδοθέν σοι βιβλείδιον ὑπὸ M., "with regard to the petition presented to you by M.," P Oxy I. 79[11] (a notice of death–A.D. 181–92) (= *Selections*, p. 89) διὸ ἐπιδίδωμι [τὸ] βιβλείδιον ἀξιῶν ταγῆναι αὐτὸν ἐν τῇ τῶν τετελευτηκότων τάξει, "I therefore present this petition and ask that he be enrolled in the roll of the dead," and P Grenf II. 61[19] (A.D. 194–8) ὅθεν ἐπιδί[δω]μι κ[α]ὶ ἀξιῶ ἐν καταχωρισμῷ γενέσθαι τοῦτο βιβλίδιον. From the beginning of the fourth century βιβλίον or λίβελλος as a rule displaced βιβλίδιον in this connexion, e. g. P Oxy I. 86[6] (A.D. 338) τούτου χάριν τὸ βιβλί[ον ἐπι]δίδωμι ἀξιῶν τοῦτον μετ[α]πεμφθ[ῆ]ναι, a petition that a certain man who had failed in a public duty should be sent for, *ib.* VI. 900[14] (A.D. 322) ἐκ τούτου ἠπίχθην τὰ βιβλία ἐπιδοῦναι, "I therefore hasten to present this petition" (Edd.). Naturally the bulk of our citations refer to state papers of various kinds, or petitions sent in to a public official. The distinction between *book* and *paper* easily vanishes when it is only a question of a single roll of greater or smaller length: the βιβλίον ἀποστασίου of Mt 19[7] (see *s.v.* ἀποστάσιον) is a document comparable with the petitions. For *papers* cf. P Petr II. 19 (2)[9] (iii/B.C.) θεὶς τὰ βυβλία ἐξῆλθον: the writer is a scribe who says he went to the Treasury office to render his account, and it seems natural to assume this to be referred to, though the editor renders "books." P Ryl II. 83[4] (A.D. 138–61) π[ρὸς παράλημψ]ιν καὶ καταγωγὴν βιβλί[ων, "to receive and forward the accounts" (Edd.). P Tebt II. 315[17] (ii/A.D.) ἐὰν μὲν οὖν σχολὴν ἄγῃς γράψας [σ]ου τὰ βιβλία ἄνελθε πρὸς ἐμέ, "so if you have time write up your books and come to me"—a finance inspector, who is a martinet (αὐστηρός), is immediately expected. The word need not be further illustrated, but we may note the combination in P Oxy VIII. 1153[1] (i/A.D.) ἐκομισάμην διὰ Ἡρακλᾶτος τὰς κίστας σὺν] τοῖς βιβλίοις, "the boxes with the books" (Ed.). For the spelling, βυβ. or βιβ., see Moulton *Gram.* II. § 35. The dissimilated form βιβλίον—contrast the converse ἥμυσυ—greatly predominates in papyri: for βυ. cf. P Petr II. 10 (2)[9] and P Ryl II. 382, cited above, also BGU IV. 1096[7] (i/ii A.D.) 1148[35] (B.C. 13), 1152[24] (B.C. 22). In inscrr. naturally there is more variation: for βυ. cf. *Michel* 1001[viii·32] (c. B.C. 200), for βι. *Syll* 653[12] (B.C. 91)—both Doric, and cf. Meisterhans *Gr.* §13.4 (p. 28) for the Attic record. The Ptolemaic papyri show more divergence than those dated A.D. See Mayser *Gr.* p. 102, Cronert *Mem. Herc.* p. 21 f., Dziatzko *Untersuchungen über ausgewählte Kapitel des antiken Buchwesens* (1900), and Maidhof *Zur Begriffsbestimmung der Koine*, p. 303 ff. Amongst interesting compounds found in the papyri may be mentioned βιβλιομαχέω (P Oxy I. 68[31] (A.D. 131) ἐὰν βιβλιομαχήσ[ῃ]η, "if he presents counter-statements"), βιβλιοφύλαξ (P Fay 31[5] (c. A.D. 129) βιβλ(ιοφύλαξι) ἐνκτήσεω(ν), "keepers of the property registers"), and βυβλιαφόρος (P Hal I. 7[6] (B.C. 232) εἴπερ μὴ τὸν βυβλιαφόρον καὶ τὸν ἔφοδον ἐκπέπε[κα]s, "unless you have spoken to the letter-carrier and the control-officer ").

β ί β λ ο ς

111

βιόω

βίβλος.

Nageli (p. 19) well draws attention to the connotation of sacredness and veneration which always attaches to βίβλος in its rare occurrences. He quotes Lucian, and two papyri, the first of these referring to "old, wise, that is Chaldaean books," P Par 19¹ (A.D. 138) σκεψάμενος ἀπὸ πολλῶν βίβλων ὡς παρεδόθη ἡμεῖν ἀπὸ σοφῶν ἀρχαίων, τουτέστι Χαλδαϊκῶν, and the other to a citation in a mathematical treatise from a book of Hermes, P Oxy III. 470⁴ (iii/A.D.) βίβλος λέγει κτλ. According to Thackeray (Arist. p. 55 n.¹) what seems to be the earliest use of ἡ βίβλος for a collection of sacred writings is to be found in Aristeas 316. In the NT β. is either Scripture (Mk 12²⁶), or the Book of Life (Phil 4³), or magical writings regarded as highly potent (Ac 19¹⁹), or again a royal pedigree record (Mt 1¹). In accordance with this is the inscription OGIS 56⁷⁰ (B.C. 239) ὧν καὶ τὰ ἀντίγραφα καταχωρισθήσεται εἰς τὰς ἱερὰς βύβλους : cf P Oxy VI. 886² (iii/A.D.) and P Leid Wⁱⁱ·¹⁹·ᵛⁱⁱⁱ·²² (ii/iii A.D.), both occult or magical. As distinguished from χάρτης, the single sheet of papyrus for writing purposes, βίβλος was the roll, made up of χάρται glued together (Dziatzko Das antike Buchwesen, p. 48), while in contrast to βιβλίον and βιβλίδιον it implies a literary work, see the passages cited above (P Par 19¹, P Oxy III. 470⁴), and the interesting P Tebt II. 291⁴³ (A.D. 162) where a candidate for the priesthood gave proof of his knowledge of hieratic and Egyptian writing by reading from a hieratic book produced by the sacred scribes—τοῦ ἐπίστασθαι [ἱε]ρατικὰ [καὶ] Αἰγύπτια γράμματα ἐξ ἧς οἱ ἱερογραμματεῖς προήνεγκαν βίβλου ἱερατικῆς. It may be added that βίβλος can still mean the papyrus plant, as P Tebt II. 308⁷ (A.D. 174) τιμὴν βίβλου μυριάδων δύο, "the price of 20,000 papyrus stalks," and in the case of the adjective BGU II. 544⁴ (ii A.D.) ζυγείδας βιβλίνας.

For the spelling see the reff. under βιβλίον, the derivative in which dissimilation produced the change of υ to ι. Βύβλος, being a decidedly rarer word, naturally yielded to the influence of βιβλίον, and then reactions between the two produced the variations which affect them both and their derivatives.

βιβρώσκω.

The perfect of this verb, which in the NT is confined to Jn 6¹³ (τοῖς βεβρωκόσιν), occurs in meal receipts P Ryl I. 20 (a)⁴⁹ (ii/A.D.) βεβ[ρω]μένους κανθους. Cf. the verbal adj. in PSI I. 64²¹ (?i B.C.) μήτε ἐν ποτοῖς μήτε ἐν βρωτοῖς, and in OGIS 620¹⁵ᵃ (A.D. 137). For compounds see P Petr II. 4 (8)⁵ (B.C. 255-4) καταβεβρωκέναι, P Grenf II. 36¹⁵ (B.C. 95) ἠκούσαμεν τὸν μῦν καταβεβρωκέναι τὸν σπόρον, "we hear that mice have eaten up the crop" (Edd.), and P Par 6²¹ (i/B.C.) περ]ιβρωθέντα, "devoured in part." On its record in classical Greek and LXX see Anz Subsidia, p. 268. Grimm's grave record of an "unused present βρώσκω whence pf. βέβρωκα" stands among many philological freaks in a fine work.

βῖκος.

For the LXX βῖκος "jar" (Jer 19¹·¹⁰), which is first found in Herodotus, we may quote, in addition to the papyrus examples in Mayser Gr. p. 40, P Hib I. 49⁸ (c. B.C. 257)

ὅπως ἂν ἐμβάληται τὰς ἐλαίας εἰς βίκους, P Hal I. 7⁵ (B.C. 232) εἰς [ξέ]νια φοίνικας καὶ ἐμβαλὼν εἰς βίκους δὸς καὶ ταῦτα παρακομίσαι ἡμῖν, and from a much later date P Lond 239¹² (c. A.D. 346) (= II. p. 298) χεννίω ν) βίκους) β, "two jars of quails." The word had apparently some vogue in Egypt, but it was very rarely found elsewhere.

βίος.

For β. = the period or duration of life, cf. P Petr II. 13(19)¹ (c. B.C. 252) (= Witkowski, Epp.² p. 18) σοῦ προστατήσα[ι τὸν] ἐπ[ί]λοιπον βίον, "to take care of you for the rest of your life," P Magd 18⁷ (B.C. 221) εἰς τὸ [λοι]πὸν τοῦ βίου, P Par 30⁴ (B.C. 161) μετ[ηλλαχότος τοῦ] πατρὸς τὸν βίον, P Tebt I. 45¹² (B.C. 118) τετευχότες [τ]ῆς παρ᾽ ὑμῶν εἰς ἅπαντα τὸν βίον ἀντιλήμψεως, P Oxy III. 473⁷ (A.D. 138-60) τὴν τοῦ λοιποῦ βίου φιλοτιμίαν, CP Herm I. 7ⁱⁱ·⁴ (ii/A.D.?) ἀ[συνε]ξώστου διὰ βίου, "for life," P Ryl I. 28¹⁵³ (iv/A.D.) if the right calf quiver, ἐξ ἀπροσδοκήτου προσλήμψεταί τι κατὰ τὸν βίον, "the person will unexpectedly acquire something in his life" (Ed.—but could it mean "something affecting his livelihood"?), P Fay 19⁴ (the so-called letter of the dying Hadrian) οὔτε ἀπ[ροσ]δοκήτω[ς οὔτε ἀνοή]τως ἀπαλλάσσομαι τοῦ βίο[υ, P Magd 8¹⁰ (B.C. 218) ὅπως ἀπαγγέλλω τὴν . . . κατ]άλυσιν τοῦ βίου (cf. l. 5), and P Oxy VIII. 1121¹² (A.D. 295) πρὸ ὀλίγων τούτων ἡμερῶν τὸν βίον ἀναπαυσαμένης ἀδιαθέτου.

For the common meaning livelihood, cf. Syll 342⁴⁹ (c. B.C. 48) δαπάναις χρώμ[εν]ος ταῖς ἐκ τοῦ βίου, "ex sua re familiari" (Ed.), ib. 325¹³ (i B.C.) τῶν ἰδίων ἀπὸ τοῦ βίου [δ]απαν[η]μάτων, OGIS 194²⁰ (B.C. 51-47) τὸν γὰρ ἑαυτοῦ βίον ὁλοσχ[ερ]ῶς ἀν[έ]θετο τοῖς χρῆσθαι βουλομένοις, P Leid Wˣⁱᵛ·²¹ (ii/iii A.D.) αὔξησόν μου τὸν βίον (καὶ) ἐν πολλοῖς ἀγαθοῖς, P Cairo Preis 2¹² (A.D. 362) ἐμοῦ οὖν ἀποδημήσας (ν. -αντος) εἰς τὸ ἴδιον ἔργον, ὅπως εὕρω ἐξυπερετῆσαι (ν. -υπηρ-) τὸν βίον.

The thought of manner of life, which underlies NT usage in 1 Tim 2², 2 Tim 2⁴, appears in a ii/B.C. inscription from Ægina (OGIS 329⁸), in which a certain Kleon is praised for the εὐταξία which he displayed both in public and private life ἀπόδειξιν πεποιημένον τ[ῆς] πραγματικῆς καὶ τῆς κατὰ τὸν βίον εὐταξίας. So BGU IV. 1098³⁴ (c. B.C. 20), where a wife is bound τηρεῖν τὰ πρὸς τὸν ἄνδρα καὶ τὸν κοινὸν βίον δίκαια. In ib. I. 251⁵ (A.D. 81), another marriage contract, the husband undertakes to provide τὰ δέοντ[α πάντα καὶ τὸν ἱ]ματισμὸν καὶ τὰ ἄλλα, ὅσα καθήκει γυναικὶ γαμετῇ κα[τὰ] δύναμιν τοῦ βί[ο]υ, and ib. II. 372ⁱⁱ·⁸ (A.D. 154) ἀ[νδ]ράσι πονηρ[ὸ]ν κ[αὶ] λησ[τ]ρικὸν β[ίον ποιουμένοις. With this last may be compared IG VII. 395¹⁵ διενέγκας σεμνόν τε καὶ ἡσύχιον βίον παρ᾽ ὅλον τὸν τῆς ζωῆς αὐτοῦ χρόνον, in which, in accordance with classical usage βίος, not ζωή, is the ethical word. For the exchange of the relative position of the two words in the NT and early Christian writings, see s.v. ζωή.

βιόω.

P Lips I. 119 versoⁱⁱ·⁶ (A.D. 274) περὶ τὸ ὀρθῶς καὶ ἀ[ζ]ηλοπραγμόνως τῶν ὑπαρξάντων ἀγαθῶν ἐμφορουμένους βιοῦν, P Flor I. 57³ (A.D. 223-5) (a rescript of Pertinax) τοῖς ἑ[β]δομήκοντα ἔτη βεβιωκόσι γέρας ἀλιτουργησίας [is granted as an old age pension] cf. the contemporary P Flor III. 382⁵⁴ (?), Syll 856¹⁶ (ii/B.C.—a manumission "sale" to

Apollo, in dialect) εἰ γένʼ ἐὰν ποιήσαιτο Δαμαρχὶς Θευδώρας βιούσας, during the lifetime of Th. her mistress). The aor. is abundant in epitaphs, as *Preisigke* 776 (A.D. 250) Ἱερακίαινα . . . βιώσασα ἔτη ᾗ καὶ μηνῶν τριῶν, 1190 (Christian) Ταῆσαι ἐβίωσεν εἴκουσι ὀκτώ, γίνονται ἔτη κη. So in the "letter of Hadrian," P Fay 19[12] τεσσαράκοντα βιώσας ἔτη. For this 1st aor. in -σα see Thackeray *Gr.* i. p. 233 f. An interesting example of this verb is afforded by Musonius (ed. Hense) p. 84[36] ὥστε καὶ τὸν ἄνθρωπον εἰκὸς οὐχ ὅταν ἐν ἡδονῇ βιοῖ, τότε κατὰ φύσιν βιοῦν, ἀλλʼ ὅταν ἐν ἀρετῇ.

βίωσις.

No example of this word in profane sources is as yet forthcoming. With its use in Sirach *Prol.* 10, διὰ τῆς ἐννόμου βιώσεως as a summary of the practical aim of teachers of the law, we may compare a Jewish inscription of A.D. 60–80 in Ramsay *C. and B.* ii. p. 650 οὕστινας κ(αὶ) ἡ συναγωγὴ ἐτείμησεν ὅπλῳ ἐπιχρύσῳ διά τε τὴν ἐνάρετον αὐτῶν [β]ίωσιν καὶ τὴν πρὸς τὴν συναγωγὴν εὔνοιάν τε καὶ σπουδήν. For the poetic βίοτος, see the sepulchral inscription of B.C. 145–40 in *Archiv* i. p. 220[9] ὧι γενόμην εὔνους βίοτον διάγουσʼ ἅμα, 221[20] σαυτὸν μὴ τρύχειν μνησάμενον βιότου.

βιωτικός.

P Tebt I. 52[9] (c. B.C. 114) has ἕτερα βιωτικὰ σύμβολα, "other business documents," a good illustration of the NT passages Lk 21[34], 1 Cor 6[3,4]. Still better is P Ryl II. 125[11] (A.D. 28–9) καὶ ἐμοῦ χωρισθέντος εἰς ἀποδημίαν βιωτι[κ]ῶν χάριν, "when I had left home on business concerning my livelihood" (Edd.). E. Rohde, *Zum griech. Roman,* p. 38 f. (*Kleine Schriften* II.) has a note on the phrase βιωτικαὶ διηγήσεις, "stories of ordinary life," with other phrases from literary Κοινή employing the word. It occurs often in Vettius Valens.

βλαβερός.

P Goodsp Cairo 2[16] (a medical fragment—ii/A.D.) οἱ τῶν ὡραίων ἡμᾶς ἀποξενοῦντες ὡς βλαβερώτερον, "who warn us against ripe fruits as being very harmful" (Edd.). *Syll* 226[14] (iii/B.C.) τὴν πᾶσαν πρόνοιαν ἐποεῖτο τοῦ μηθὲν βλαβερὸν γίνεσθαι περὶ τὴν χώραν. The noun βλάβος may be cited from P Ryl II. 126[19] (A.D. 28–9) ἐξ οὗ βλάβος μοι ἐπηκολούθησεν οὐκ ὀλίγον, P Oxy X. 1282[40] (A.D. 83) τό τε βλάβος καὶ ἐπίτειμον, "the damages and a fine". BGU II. 538[17] (A.D. 100) βλάβος μηδὲν ποιῶν, and in the common formula τά τε βλάβη καὶ δαπανήματα, e.g. BGU III. 1001[13] (B.C. 50–5). Note the uncontracted plur. in P Tor II. 13[14] (B.C. 137), in this formula. Mayser (*Gr.* p. 287) quotes many other instances of the neuter, which he says stands alone in Ptolemaic times, except for P Par 15[37] B.C. 120, εἰς βλάβας; add P Amh II. 33[19] (c. B.C. 157) ἐπὶ βλάβῃ τῶν προσόδων. So from later papyri, P Oxy III. 488[19] (ii/iii A.D.) οὐκ ὀλίγην βλάβην ὑποφέρει με, BGU I. 72[12] (A.D. 191) οὐ χολικὴν βλάβην ἐπεκολούθησεν. Moeris p. 103 makes βλάβος Attic, and βλάβη (which has driven its rival out by the end of iv/A.D.) Hellenistic. A literary quotation for the latter may be

added from PSI II. 120[29] 2iv/A.D.—a collection of maxims) ἀμύνου τὸν ἐ[χ]θρὸν ἄνευ τῆς σεαυτοῦ βλάβη[s. A glance at LS will dispose of the Atticist's contention.

βλάπτω.

For personal injury we may note such passages as P Lips I. 26[6] (A.D. 69) ὀφθαλμὸν δεξιὸν βεβλαμμένος, P Grenf I. 33[13] (c. B.C. 102) ἐζλαμμένος ὀφθαλμοὺς ἀμφοτέρους, P Flor I. 57[63] (A.D. 223–5) τοὺς ὀφθαλμοὺς ἐβλάβην = III. 382, also perhaps *ib.* III. 302 (A.D. 151) βεβλαμμ(ένος)] τὸν ὀφθαλμὸν δεξ[ιόν. It is curious that it should be thus specialised for injury to the eyes. The verb is common for "damage" in a legal sense. Thus P Petr III. 26[3] ἀποτεισάτω ὁ κύριος τῶι βλαφθέντι τὸ βλάβος ὃ ἂν καταβλάψηι, "the owner shall pay to the injured person the amount of damage done," BGU IV. 1057[23] (A.D. 13) = *Chrest.* II. p. 401 ἐκτίνειν αὐτοὺς ὃ ἐὰν πραχθῇ ἢ βλαβῇ, P Oxy II. 286[11] (A.D. 82) ἐκτείσειν ὃ ἐὰν πραχθῶμεν ἢ βλαβῶμεν τούτων χάριν, "paying us in full any loss or damage which we might incur in connexion with the transaction" (Edd.). *ib.* I. 44[8] late (A.D.) ὡς ἱκανὰ βλαπτομένων, "on the plea that they had incurred sufficient loss already" (Edd.). More general sense appears in P Flor II. 151[11] (A.D. 267) μὴ ἐπʼ αὐτοὺς στρατιώτης ἀποσταλῇ, καὶ ἄλλως ἐφόδιον βλαβῶσιν, "lose their wages" (?). It describes the material damage done by a riot in CP Herm I. 119 *recto* [34] (A.D. 266–8), ἀφʼ ὧν οὐδὲν περιγίνεται τῷ πολιτικῷ λόγῳ διὰ τὸ ἐξ ὁλοκλήρου βεβλάφθαι ἐν τοῖς πρόσθεν συμβεβηκότι κατὰ τὴν πόλειν ἀπευκταίοις τὰ ρ̣ άχοις.

βλαστάνω.

For the transitive use of β. (as Jas 5[18]) see Aristeas 230, αἳ (sc. χάριτες) βλαστάνουσιν εὔνοιαν. The subst. βλάστημα as Sir 50[12] is found in P Lond 131 *recto* [195] (A.D. 78–9) (= I. p. 175) τὰ περισσὰ βλαστήματα, and for βλαστολογέω = "pick off young shoots," see *ib.*[397]. See also *IGI* VII. 406[3] βλαστήματα καλῶν τέκνων.

Βλάστος.

For this proper name, as Acts 12[20], cf. *Michel* 1224 (Cyzicus, ii/B.C.) Αἰνείας Βλαστοῦ (so Michel accents).

βλάσφημος.

The more special sense of irreverence towards God which β. and its derivatives have acquired, though not inherent in the word itself (cf. Jas 2[7], 2 Pet 2[11]), may be illustrated from Vettius Valens p. 44[1] εἰς θεοὺς βλασφημοῦσιν ἢ ἐπίορκοι καὶ ἄθεοι καθίστανται, 58[12] εἰς τὰ θεῖα βλασφημοῦντες, 67[20] πολλὰ βλασφημήσει θεούς (for construction cf. 4 Kings 19[6,22]). Thumb (*Hellen.* p. 178) remarks on the word as a genuine piece of "Biblical Greek," that is a word which has acquired a technical meaning in association with Jewish and Christian religion. The etymology which seems to suit best its original meaning of "injurious speaking"—βλάψ, the reduced form of βλάβος, and φη-μί—is not without phonetic difficulties: see Brugmann-Thumb *Gr.*[4] p. 117 f. (where it is accepted with some hesitation), and for an alternative (Brugmann's) Boisacq *Lex. s.v.*

βλέμμα.

For the subjective sense "look" which Mayor finds in this word in 2 Pet 2⁸ cf. P Oxy III. 471⁶⁰ (ii A.D.) ἑόρακε δὲ καὶ βλέμμα ἀναίσχυντον καὶ διαπομπὰς ἀναισχύντου [. . . ους] ἐραστῶν, "each saw the shameless look and shameless goings to and fro of the lovers" (Edd.).

βλέπω.

The papyri have added a perfect to the paradigm of this verb: it proves to have been βέβλοφα (P Lond 42²¹ — B.C. 168) (= Witkowski², p. 63) (see under ἐμβλέπω). It is hard to believe that a form so correct historically, and so distant from any obvious analogy, can be anything but a genuine survival, even if it does meet us only in a woman's letter from Ptolemaic Egypt. If this inference is justifiable, the word has a moral for the argument from silence. Βλέπω has primarily the physical sense, as distinguished from ὁράω (cf. our cognate *watch*): this is well seen in ἀναβλέπω *recover sight*. Usage bears this out. Thus P Par 44⁵ (B.C. 153) = Witkowski², p. 83) has βλέπω Μενέδημον κατατρέχοντά με coming after ἐγὼ γὰρ ἐνύπνια ὁρῶ πονηρά. So in P Hal I. 8⁴ (B.C. 232) a man is incapacitated διὰ τὸ μὴ βλέπειν τὰς νύκτας, and in P Oxy I. 39⁸ (A.D. 52) ὀλίγον βλέπων = "shortsighted." An interesting instance of the word is afforded by P Giss I. 17¹⁶ (time of Hadrian) where a slave writes to her master ἀποθνήσκομεν ὅτι οὐ βλέπομέν σε καθ' ἡμέραν (cf. 1 Cor 15³¹). Closely paralleled with phraseology in Gospel healings of the blind is one of the cases from the Asclepieion, Syll 802²³ (Epidaurus, iii/B.C.): the blind man sleeping in the temple saw a vision (ὄψις) of the god opening his eyelids and pouring in a φάρμακον—whereupon he looked βλέπων ἀμφοῖν ἐξῆλθε. P Oxy II. 258³³ (i A.D.) ὁ Ἀνουβᾶς αὐτὸν οὐχ ἡδέως [β]λέπει "A. looks upon him with no friendly eye," may serve as a transition to the more metaphorical use of βλέπω, as in P Oxy II. 259³² (A.D. 23) βλέπε με πῶς με ἡ μήτηρ ἡμῶν [ἔ]σφαξε χάριν τοῦ χειρογράφου, P Lond 964⁹ (ii/iii A.D.) (= III. p. 212) βλέπε μὴ ἐπιλάθῃ οὐδέν, and P Oxy IX. 1220⁸² (iii/A.D.) οὐδὲν βλέπω φαύλου παρ' ἐμοί. "I see nothing bad in my behaviour" (Edd.). The meaning "beware," implied in some of these passages, is extended to a personal reflexive object in BGU IV. 1079²⁴ (A.D. 41) (= Selections, p. 40) ὡς ἂν πάντες καὶ σὺ βλέπε σατὸν ἀπὸ τῶν Ἰουδαίων, "like everybody else, you too must beware of the Jews," which is a rather neat confutation of those who would detect "Hebraism" in Mk 8¹⁵ and the like. For the geographical sense, the "aspect" of a building, etc. (as Ac 27¹²), cf. P Leid Wˣ·⁶ (ii/iii A.D.) ἔστω δὲ ἡ θύρα πρὸς δυσμὰς βλέπουσα, PSI III. 175¹¹ (A.D. 462) συμπόσιον βλέπον ἐπὶ νότον. Finally, for β. virtually = εὑρίσκω as in Rom 7²³ (cf. v. 21), see P Fay 111¹⁶ (A.D. 95–6) ὡς ἐὰν βλέπῃς [τ]ὴν τιμὴν παντὸς ἀγόρασον, "however you find the price, be sure to buy" (Edd.).

βοάω.

The manifestation of strong *feeling*, which is the distinguishing note of this verb, comes out well in a fragmentary petition written under much excitement, P Oxy IV. 717⁹ (late i B.C.) ἐγὼ οὖν ἐβόων καὶ ἔκραζον, cf. ¹², ¹⁵, ²⁴. See also P Oxy I. 41¹⁹ (iii/iv A.D.) ὁ δῆμος ἐβόησεν—the account of a popular

demonstration. For similar acclamations in the inscriptions we may cite Syll 6 7¹⁵ (iii/iv A.D.) ἐβόησαν οἱ σύνεδροι "Παμφίλῳ καλὴ ἡ [εἰσ]ήγησις. οὕτω γεινέσθω." and the compound ἐξεβόησαν ib. ². 737¹³·⁵⁴ (ii/iii A.D.).

βοήθεια.

The word is perpetually recurring at the end of petitions. P Par 35⁵ (B.C. 163) τούτου δὲ γενομένου ἔσομαι τετευχὼς τῆς παρ' ὑμῶν βοηθείας, BGU I. 22²² (A.D. 114) πρὸς τὸ τυχῖν με τῆς ἀπὸ σοῦ βοηθείας, ib. 38⁴⁷ (A.D. 148–9) ἀναγκαίως ἐπὶ τὴν σὴν βοήθιαν κατέφυγον, P Gen I. 6¹⁶ (A.D. 146) ἵνα δυνηθῶ ἐκ τῆς σῆς βοηθείας κομίσασθαι τὸ ἴδιον, and P Oxy X. 1272²² (A.D. 144) ἵνα δυνηθῶ τῇ σῇ βοηθείᾳ ἀνευρεῖν τὰ ἡμέτερα. A slightly different technical meaning is found in a restoration by Mitteis of P Oxy VII. 1020⁵ (A.D. 198–201) εἰ τὴν ἐκ τῆς ἡλικίας ἔχεις β[οηθίαν, "if you can claim the assistance due to minor's age," = *restitutio in integrum*, for which the verb of *boήthia* is quoted (Edd.). More ordinary, though still in a petition, is BGU IV. 1201¹² (A.D. 2?) καὶ ἡμῶν ἀνακράξαντες τῶν ἑαυτῶν εἰς τὴν κώμην πρὸς βοήθην. On the phrase βοηθείαις ἐχρῶντο in Ac 27¹⁷ see a note by Nestle in ZNTW xix. p. 75 f., where for β. "supports" he quotes Philo *de Jos.* § 33 (cf. Cohn II. 49 M. ὥσπερ γὰρ κυβερνήτης ταῖς τῶν πνευμάτων μεταβολαῖς συμμεταβάλλει τὰς πρὸς εὔπλοιαν βοηθείας "verwendeten Stützen." For the interchange of o and ω in this and similar words, see Meyer Gr. p. 110.

βοηθέω.

Like the noun, the verb is conspicuous in the formula of petitions, e.g. P Par 22¹ (beginning of the Serapeum Twins' petitions) ὅπως ὦμεν δι' ὑμᾶς βεβοηθημέναι, P Fay 11³⁴ (= B.C. 115) τούτων δὲ γενομένων ἔσομαι βεβοηθημένος, P Giss I. 8⁵ (A.D. 119) ἵν' ὦ [β]εβοηθημένος, BGU II. 451² (A.D. 103) καὶ ὦμεν ὑπὸ σ[οῦ βεβοηθημένοι. For its general use cf. P Giss I. 69⁵ (early ii A.D.) ἃ [ἐ]βεβοηθήκεις αὐτῶι, P Tebt II. 286⁴ (A.D. 121–38) κ[α]ὶ πρ[ώην σοι ἀπεφηνάμην ὅτι τὸ ἐ[π]ίκριμά μου βοηθεῖ [σ]οι. "that my edict was of service to you" (Edd.), P Tebt II. 135¹⁰ (A.D. 207 πλείονα [. . . βοίδια ἕξει βοηθεῖν σε . . . (not clear), P Oxy X. 1348 (early A.D.) οὐ γὰρ ἐβοήθησας ἡμῖν ὡς εἰδὼς τὰ [νό]μιμα. Aside from inscr. Syll 320¹³ (B.C. 80), where the Ephesian demos, ἐσχηκὼς καιρὸν πρὸς τὸ βοηθεῖν τοῖς κοινοῖς πράγμασιν, declares war on Mithradates. For divine help cf. P Par 158 Ἀνδρόμαχος Μακεδὼν ἀφίκετο πρὸς Ἀμενώθην χρηστὸν θεὸν μ[ι]σθοῦ ἐργαζόμενος καὶ ἐμαλακίσθη καὶ ὁ θεὸς αὐτῶι ἐβοήθησε αὐθημερῆ, P Leid Wˣ·² (ii/iii A.D.) κλῦθί μοι, ὁ χρηστὸς ἐν βαζάνοις, βοήθησόν με ἐν ἀνάγκαις. These prepare for its use in Christian papyri: P Fay 130 (a letter, iv/A.D.) εἰδότες ὅτι ἔχετέ με ἐς ὅσ' ἂν πάσχετε θεοῦ βοηθοῦντος, P Oxy VII. 1058 (a prayer, iv/v A.D.) ὁ θεὸς τῶν παρακειμένων σταυρῶν, βοήθησον τὸν δοῦλόν σου, . . . VIII. 1152⁴ (annulet, v/vi A.D.) Ἰεσοῦ Χριστέ, βοήθι ἡμῖν καὶ τούτῳ οἴκῳ. Inscriptional instances of βοηθέω are given in G. Meyer Gr.³ p. 63: see Brugmann-Thumb⁴ p. 54. The verb starts from the military sense, so common in Greek historians: Homeric βοηθόος, from which it comes, "succurrit (θοός) ad clamorem (βοή)." Βοηθός was made afresh from the verb.

βοηθός.

The word is very frequent in the ostraca for the "assistants" of the **πράκτορες** or "tax-gatherers," see Wilcken *Ostr.* i. p. 618, and for a similar use in the papyri the editors' note to P Fay 54³ (A.D. 161) **βοηθοῖς γεωργῶν κώμης Πολυδευκείας**, where they translate "assistants in connexion with taxes upon cultivators at the village of Polydeucia." For a description of the Praefect as **ὁ τοῦ νομοῦ βοηθός**, "helper of the district," see P Giss I. 46¹¹ (time of Hadrian) **ἀξιοῦμέν σε τὸν τοῦ νομοῦ βοηθὸν διακοῦσαι ἡμῶν**, and cf. P Oxy III. 488² (ii/iii A.D.) **προσφεύγω σοι τῷ κυρίῳ καὶ πάντων βοηθῷ.** For the word in its widest connotation it is sufficient to cite P Oxy IV. 743²⁰ (B.C. 2) **εἰ καὶ π̣[ρ̣]ὸς ἄλλους εἶχον πρᾶγμα, βοηθὸν αὐτοῦ γ[ε]νέσθαι διὰ ἣν ἔχομε(ν) πρὸς ἑατοὺς φιλίαν**, "for although I (?) have had trouble with others you must assist him for the sake of our friendship" (Edd.), and P Lond 410⁸ (c. A.D. 346) (= II. p. 298) **μετὰ τὸν θεὸν οὐδίναν** (*l.* οὐδένα) **ἔχομεν ἡμῆς βοηθόν**, "after (i.e. except) God, we have none to help us" (Ed.) ; also from ii/B.C., P Leid E⁶ **δεόμεθά σου μεθ᾽ ἱκετείας, καθότι οὐ διαλείπις ἡμῶν ἀντιλαμβανόμενος, καὶ ἐν τούτοις βοιηθὸν γενόμενον προσκαλέσασθαι κτλ.** (For the spelling see on **βοηθέω** *ad fin.*)

βόθυνος.

BGU IV. 1122¹⁷ (B.C. 14) **ἐπὶ τοῦ βοθύνου τὸ φυτόν.** The word is also supplied by the editor in P Hal I. 1⁹⁷ (middle iii B.C.) **ἐὰν δὲ τάφρον ὀρύσσῃ ἢ [βόθυνον ὀρ]ύσσηι.**

βολίζω.

The adj. **βόλιμος** is found *quater* in *Syll* 140 (B.C. 353–2), meaning "leaden": see Dittenberger on l.²⁸ and Boisacq *s.v.* **μόλυβδος.** Thackeray (*Gr.* i. p. 106) notes **μόλιμος** and **βόλιβον** from MSS of LXX, which may illustrate the survival of some of the widely divergent forms current in earlier Greek dialects. The name of "lead" is supposed to have been borrowed very early (before Homer), perhaps from Iberians in Spain: cf. reff. in Walde *Lat. Etym.²* *s.v. plumbum.* It is at least possible that **βολίς** in the sense *plummet* (acc. to Homeric scholia) may be really " the lead," with form affected by **βολή** etc. from **βάλλω.** However this may be, the verb **βολίζω** "sound" is very instructive as a **ἅπ. εἰρ.** in Ac 27²⁸ : eleven centuries later, the Homeric scholar Eustathius uses it as familiar from ancient Greek, and he does not mention Luke or hint that he remembered what for us happens to be the solitary example of the word : see the quotations from Eustathius in Wetstein *ad loc.* It is sufficiently obvious that Luke did not coin the word, and its history may help less obvious cases elsewhere.

βόρβορος.

For this word which is found in Bibl. Grk only in Jerem 45⁶ and 2 Pet 2²², cf. *Apoc. Petr.* 8 **καὶ λίμνη τις ἦν μεγάλη πεπληρωμένη βορβόρου φλεγομένου**, also *Acta Thomae* (ed. Bonnet) 53 **εἶδον βόρβορον . . . καὶ ψυχὰς ἐκεῖ κυλιομένας.** Both the noun and the corresponding verb occur in the *Pelagia-Legenden*, p. 6²¹ᶠ. (ed. Usener) : **ἐλθοῦσα περιστερὰ μελάνη καὶ βεβορβορωμένη περιεπέτατό μοι, καὶ τὴν δυσωδίαν τοῦ βορβόρου αὐτῆς οὐκ ἠδυνάμην φέρειν.** See also Wendland in *Sitz. Berl. Akad.* 1898, p. 788 ff.,

"Ein Wort des Heraklit im Neuen Testament," with reference to 2 Pet 2²².

βορρᾶς.

The contracted form, which is found in the two NT occurrences of this word (Lk 13²⁹, Rev 21¹³), is almost universal in the Ptolemaic papyri, e.g. P Lille I. 1 *recto*⁴ (B.C. 259–8) **ἀπὸ νότου εἰς βορρᾶν**, P Petr I. 2¹¹ and ¹⁸ (B.C. 237) **ἀπὸ δὲ βορρᾶ**, P Par 15¹⁶ (B.C. 120) **ἀπὸ βορρᾶ τοῦ δρόμου τοῦ [ἄ]γοντος ἐπὶ ποταμὸν τῆς μεγίστης θεᾶς Ἥρας**, and other examples in Mayser *Gr.* p. 252 ; but P Hib I. 27⁵⁹ (a calendar, B.C. 301–240) **βορέαι πνείουσιν ὀρνιθίαι**, "the north winds which bring the birds are blowing." P Leid Wxiv. 21 has **βόρεας**, some five centuries later, but it is always rare. Cf. Job 26⁷, Sir 43¹⁷, ²⁰. *Priene* 99¹⁹ (c. B.C. 100) has **τῆς στοᾶς τοῦ βορέου** : cf. *Syll* 552⁷⁹ (latter half of ii/A.D.) **εἰς τὴν παραστάδα τὴν ἀπὸ δυσμῆς τῆς στοᾶς τῆς βορεί[ας**—with corresponding adjective. From inscrr. cf. *OGIS* 176³ (ii/i B.C.) **ἐπὶ βορρᾶν**, *ib.* 178¹⁰ (ii/i B.C.) **ἐπὶ βορᾶν**, *Michel* 1357⁹ (B.C. 300–299) **βορρᾶθεν.** The adj. **βορινός** occurs in P Oxy I. 43 *verso*ⁱ·¹⁹ (after A.D. 295) **ῥ(ύμῃ) τῇ βοριν[ῇ] ἐκκλησία** " North Church St," *ib.* III. 498⁸ (ii/A.D.), *al.* ; but in *ib.* VIII. 1112²³ (A.D. 188) **βορ[ι]νοῖς** implies ρρ. and so P Ryl II. 157¹² (A.D. 135). Thumb, *Hellen.* pp. 56, 65, notes that **βορρᾶς** is a Dorism in the **Κοινή.**

βόσκω.

The verb is used in connexion with **πρόβατα** in P Magd 6¹³ (B.C. 221) **τά τε πρόβα]τα βεβοσκηκότας**, P Tebt II. 298⁵³ (A.D. 107–8) **προβ]άτων βοσκ[ο(μένων)**, P Thead 57² (A.D. 317) **βόσκοντος αὐτοῦ τὰ π[ρό]βατα**, and with a herd of swine, as in Mk 5¹¹, in the illiterate BGU III. 757¹⁰ (A.D. 12) **ἃ βόσκουσιν ὕικα κτήνηι.** Cf. *Syll* 531³⁶ (iii/A.D.) **πρόβατα[δὲ μὴ ἐξ]έστω ἐ[πιβό]σκε[ι]ν ε[ἰς] τὸ τέμενος μηδενί**, on pain of confiscation to the god—see the editor's note. A derived noun occurs in P Lond 219 *recto* (an account for food—ii/B.C.) (= II. p. 2) **ἰδίῳ βοσκῷ.** It is frequently found as a termination, e.g. **ἱερακοβοσκός** (P Petr III. 99⁶, **ἰβιοβοσκός** (*ib.* 58(*e*)) (both iii/B.C.) : see Mayser *Gr.* p. 471.

βοτάνη

is common in the magic papyri, e.g. P Lond 46¹⁹⁹ (iv/A.D.) (= I. p. 71) **κυνοκεφάλ(ιον βοτ(άνην)**—a herb mentioned by Pliny (*N.H.* xxx. 2) as employed for magical purposes (Ed.). In P Amh II. 91¹² (A.D. 159) **κατασπορὰς βοτανισμούς** is rendered by the editors "sowing and weeding." For **βοτανισμός** see also BGU I. 197¹⁷ (A.D. 17), *ib.* II. 526¹⁹·³¹ (A.D. 86).

βότρυς.

BGU IV. 1118¹⁴ (B.C. 22) **σταφυλῆς βότρυας ὀγδοήκοντα.** Similarly P Lips I. 30⁴ (iii/A.D.). A subst. **βοτρεύς**, hitherto unknown to the lexicons, occurs in a list of persons employed by certain village officials, P Lond II. 189⁵³ (ii/A.D.) (= II. p. 157)—was he a "grape-picker"? The note in Moeris (p. 105), **βότρυς, μακρόν, Ἀττικῶς. βραχύ, Ἑλληνικῶς.** makes this word—presumably representing its class—an instance of the tendency to shorten vowels : incidentally it tells us that quantities were not yet levelled as in MGr.

βουλευτής.

Apart from Mk 15[43], Lk 23[50], where both writers had Gentile readers in view, neither **βουλευτής** nor **βουλή** seems to have been used by Jews as a technical term in connexion with their Sanhedrin, although Hicks (*CR* i. p. 43) refers to Josephus *B.J.* ii. 17. 1 οἵ τε ἄρχοντες καὶ οἱ βουλευταί, and *Ant.* xx. 1. 2 (in an edict of Claudius) Ἱεροσολυμιτῶν ἄρχουσι βουλῇ δήμῳ Ἰουδαίων παντὶ ἔθνει. As illustrating the use of **βουλευτής** in Egypt it may be noted that in P Lond 348[4] (c. A.D. 205) (= II. p. 215) a certain Heron is described as βουλευτής of Arsinoe, and an ex-**κοσμητής** (**κεκοσμητευκώς**). A century later a letter is addressed by one Eudaimon γυμ(νασιαρχήσας) βουλ ευτής) of Oxyrhynchus to two colleagues, ἀμφοτέροις συνδίκοις βουλευταῖς τῆς [λαμπρο τ]άτης Ὀξυρυγχ[ιτ]ῶν πόλεος, *Chrest.* II. 196[2ii] (A.D. 307—Mitteis, not here alone, misprints "*v. Chr.*"). An inscr. of A.D. 214 5, *OGIS* 200[4], found at a place beyond Philae, gives the title to a ἱερεὺς γόμου (see *s.v.*). The editor observes that it must refer to some Greek community, and suggests Ptolemais: he quotes *CIG* 5000[a 3], where the brother of the subject of this inscr. is called βουλευτής, ἄρξας Πτολεμαιέων—see the note for other passages. In P Fay 37[2] (iii/A.D.) an order is issued for the arrest of Emes, who has been "accused by Aurelius Nilus councillor" (ἐνκαλούμενον ὑπὸ Αὐρηλίου Νείλου βουλευτοῦ): cf. P Fay 85[2] (A.D. 247) with the editors' note. [The *verso* of P Grenf II. 63[1 8] (? middle iii/A.D.) βουλ ευτὴς σιτολόγων is now solved by the correct reading, βοηθ ὸς) σιτολόγων: see Wilcken *Archiv* iii. p. 124.] In *OGIS* 56 (Canopus Decree of Ptolemy III, B.C. 239) we read of the βουλευταὶ ἱερεῖς ἐν Αἰγύπτῳ, whom Dittenberger (n. 51) describes as "collegium quod de rebus cuiusque delubri administrandis consultabat." See also Hohlwein *L'Égypte Romaine*, p. 133 f., and the index to *OGIS*.

βουλεύω.

For the verb in its general sense followed by an infinitive, as in Ac 5[33] אBD, cf. P Tebt I. 58[45] (B.C. 111) βεβουλεύμεθα ἐκσπάσαι τὸ ἐπιδεδομένον ὑπόμνη[μα, "we have determined to abstract the memorandum" (Edd.). P Fay 116[9] (A.D. 104) ἐπὶ βουλεύομαι [εἰς π]όλιν ἀπελθῖν χάριν [τοῦ μικροῦ, "as I am intending to go to the city on account of the little one" (Edd.). P Leid W[a 11] (ii/iii A.D.) βουλευομένον (= ον) δὲ τὸ τρίτον τρίτον (om.) κακγᾶσε (l. καγχάσαι), "volente vero tertium cachinnari" (Ed.). The active (as in Isai 23[8]) was perhaps obsolete : BGU IV. 1007[2] has been emended—see **συμβουλεύω**. The verb is absolute in the oldest dated Greek papyrus, P Eleph 1[5] (a marriage contract, B.C. 311 0) (= *Selections*, p. 2)—the couple are to live ὅπου ἂν δοκῇ ἄριστον εἶναι βουλευομένοις κοινῇ βουλῇ. It is used of a judge conferring with his assessors in *Chrest.* II. 37[2iii. 19] (ii/A.D.) Εὐδα[ί]μων βουλευσάμενος σὺν τοῖς παρο[ῦ]σι εἶπεν κτλ. Note for the subst. P Fay 20[2] (iii/iv A.D.) ὅθεν μοι παρέστη τὸ βούλευμα τοῦτο, "wherefore I have formed this intention" (Edd.).

βουλή.

The word **βουλή** is always used both in the LXX and the NT = "counsel," and never in its technical sense of "council." For this latter usage in Egypt reference may be made to Hohlwein *L'Égypte Romaine*, p. 134 ff., and to

the editor's note to P Lond 905[13] (c. A.D. 346) (= II. p. 205). The description of a man as θεῶν βουλαῖος, "counsellor of the gods" in *CIG* 4467 (see LS *s.v.* βουλαῖος) may be compared with the reference in Diod. ii. 31 f. to the 30 stars which the Chaldaeans distinguished as θεοὶ βουλαῖοι (*l.c.* i. p. 499). For the ordinary sense of "counsel" it will be enough to quote P Eleph 1[6] (see above, under **βουλεύω**). See Bishop E. L. Hicks's note in *CR* i. p. 43.

βούλημα

is used with reference to the contents of a will in P Lond 171[b 40] (iii/A.D.) (= II. p. 176) τὸ ἐγγεγραμμένον βούλημα : cf. in a similar connexion BGU I. 361[ii 23] (A.D. 184) ἵνα τὸ βούλημα αὐτοῦ φανερὸν γέ[ν]ηται. P Tebt II. 407[9] (A.D. 199) τὸ δ[ὲ] βούλημα τοῦτο ἐὰν μὴ φυλάξῃς the property is to go to the Serapeum at Alexandria if the daughter of the writer does not observe his wish that certain slaves should be set free. *Syll.* 366[12] (c. A.D. 38) ἐκείνου τῆς ἐπιθυμίας βουλήμασιν is a collocation rather like τὴν εὐδοκίαν τοῦ θελήματος αὐτοῦ, Eph 1[5].

For **βούλησις** see P Tebt I. 43[25] (B.C. 118) ὃς ἀκόλουθος ὢν τῇ ἱ[ὑ]μετέρᾳ βουλήσει προνοεῖται κτλ., "who in accordance with your wishes takes care etc.," *OGIS* 383[150] (Antiochus of Commagene—mid i B.C.) οὓς ἐγὼ θεοῖς τε καὶ τιμαῖς ἐμαῖς κατὰ δαιμόνιον βούλησιν ἀνέθηκα, *Syll.* 803[2] (iii/B.C.) as cited under **βιάζομαι**, and the late P Amh II. 144[11] (v/A.D.) θεοῦ βουλήσει, "God willing."

βούλομαι.

The Ptolemaic papyri show this word as freely as the late papyri, and Blass's opinion that the word was "adopted from the literary language" (*Gr.* p. 38, repeated in Blass-Debrunner, p. 40) becomes more and more difficult to support. If the word was literary, the NT writers were not the first to popularize it. The word is common in such recurring phrases as γινώσκειν σε βούλομαι, βούλομαι μισθώσασθαι. The thought of "purpose, intention, not mere will, but will with premeditation" (Hort on Jas 4[4]), which frequently underlies its usage, comes out P Oxy X. 1293[8] (A.D. 128 9) βούλομαι πρώτως . . . χρήσασθαι τῇ τῶν ἐργ[ατῶν] ποταμοῦ τέχ[νῃ, "I wish to begin . . . to practise the trade of a river-worker" (Edd.); cf. *ib.* 1295[10] (A.D. 209). See also the important official decree, P Lond 904[30] (A.D. 104) (= III. p. 125) as revised *Chrest.* I. p. 236, βούλομ αι] πάντα[ς τ]οὺς εὔ[λ]ογον δο[κοῦν]τα[ς] ἔχειν τοῦ ἐνθάδε ἐπιμένιν [αἰ]τίαν ἀπογραφεσ[θ]αι κτλ., and BGU I. 248[11] (ii/A.D.) θεῶν δὲ βουλομένων. In P Oxy II. 244[2] (A.D. 23) a slave named Cerinthus begins a petition with βουλόμενος μεταγαγεῖν. Other instances of **βούλομαι** in phraseology not influenced by formulae, are P Lille I. 10[2] (iii/B.C.) ἔφη . . . σοί τε οὐ βούλεσθαι διαφέρεσθαι περὶ τούτου, "et qu'il ne voulait pas entrer en désaccord là-dessus avec toi" (Edd.); P Flor I. 6[7] (A.D. 210) ἐβουλόμην μὲν οὖν εἰ οἷόν τε ἦν εὐθέως ἐξορμῆσαι, followed by ἀλλά with clause explaining the hindrance—similarly in *ib.* II. 150[2] (iii/A.D.); *ib.* II. 126[5] (A.D. 254) ἐπεὶ αὔριον αὐτοὺς βούλομαι ἀποστεῖλαι εἰς Βερνεικίδα, and PSI III. 230[36] (iii/iv A.D.) ἀντίγραψόν μοι περὶ οὗ βούλει ἡδέως ἔχοντι. In BGU II. 640[7] (A.D. 193) βούλομαι replaces the normal εὔχομαι in the opening greeting, ἐρρῶσθε (= -αι) ὑμᾶς βούλομαι. Two instances of the form **βούλει** may be cited,

P Tebt II. 408[16] (A.D. 3) καὶ σὺ δὲ περὶ ὧν βούλε[ι] γράφε, P Giss I. 47[18] (Hadrian) εἰ δὲ βούλει αὐτὸ ἀγορασθῆναι (δραχμῶν) μ. Reference may be made for the use in classical times to *Syll* 566[5] φηνάτ[ω] ὁ θέλων, on which Dittenberger remarks that ὁ θέλων replaces the Attic ὁ βουλόμενος in Paros (as here), Thasos, Phocis and other districts. But of course the fact that "he who is willing" and "he who is minded" may be used interchangeably in a particular formula, does not prove that the two verbs are synonyms. A literary citation may be added from the collection of maxims in PSI II. 120[38] (?iv/A.D.) μικρὰ βούλου δοῦναι ἢ τὰ ἄλλων ἐγγυήσασθαι.

In P Par 48[10] (B.C. 153) ἥκαμεν εἰς τὸ Σαραπιεῖον βολάμενοι συνμῖξαί σοι, the form βολάμενοι is treated as an aorist by Witkowski (2, p. 92), who compares P Amh II. 63[3] (A.D. 181) βόλομαι μισθώσασθαι παρὰ σοῦ κτλ., and in *Addenda*, p. 141. P Par 63[121] (B.C. 165) κατὰ τῶν δυναμένων μέν, μὴ βολαμένων δέ: see also Mayser *Gr.* p. 369. The instance from P Amh II. 63 is a serious impediment to Witkowski's view. But Ionic had the form in βολ. in v/iv B.C. See the inscr. from the shrine of Amphiaraus at Oropus, *GDI* 5339[31] (= *Syll* 589) θύειν δὲ ἐξεῖν (*i.e.* ἐξεῖναι) ἅπαν ὅτι ἂν βόληται ἕκαστος: for proof see C. D. Buck *Greek Dialects*, p. 173, where an Eretrian inscr. is quoted for βολόμενον. Thumb, *Dial.* p. 273, explains it as a different present stem: the fact that it existed both in Ionic and in Arcadian-Cyprian (*ib.* p. 304) might account for its leaving traces in the Κοινή, and forming a new aorist.

βουνός.

This word, which is quoted in Lk 3[5], 23[30] from the LXX = "hill," "eminence," is thought by Mayser *Gr.* p. 8, to have entered the Κοινή through Doric influence. Hatzidakis (*Einl.* p. 157) quotes Phrynichus (p. 355), who says it was Sicilian, and not intelligible in Athens in the time of Philemon. But could not the Athenians of the late fourth century read Herodotus? (He seems to imply that the word came from Cyrene—see iv. 199 with Blakesley's Excursus. With claimants almost as numerous as those for Homer's birth, we can sympathize with Thumb's scepticism, *Hellen.* p. 224.) But Herodotus, if rightly understood, is a much better witness than Phrynichus.) The literary Κοινή had the word in common use before Polybius, who uses it and βουνώδης. It is found in a Ptolemaic papyrus of ii/B.C. in *Archiv* i. p. 64[15], ἀπηλιώτου βουνοὶ τῆς κώμης, in BGU IV. 1120[14] (B.C. 13) ἀπηλιώ(τη) βουνός, and *bis* in P Amh II. 68[29] (late i/A.D.) again marking locality. A village called Βουνοὶ Κλεοπάτρας appears in P Flor I. 64[7] (iv/A.D. *init.*) and by supplement in 50[32] (A.D. 268). The word is common in inscr., e.g. *Priene* 37[169] (ii B.C.) εἰς τὸν ἀπέναντι βουνὸν τὸν λεπρὸν ἐθήκαμεν ὅρον: cf. *ib.* 168, 42[10,51,65], (after B.C. 133). The diminutive βουνίον occurs *bis* in this last inscr.: cf. *Magn* 122 (*b*)[12] (iv/B.C.). See also P Flor I. 58[12] (iii/A.D.) βουνὸν σείτου presumably a "heap," but context is imperfect. Both βουνός and its diminutive survive in MGr. βουνό and βουνί.

βοῦς.

Except in acc. pl., the inflexions are the same as in Attic, e.g. τὴν βοῦν P Par 58[1] (ii/B.C.) (= Witkowski[2], p. 80).

βοός P Fay 62[1] (A.D. 134), βόες, βοῶν, βουσί in Mayser *Gr.* p. 268. For acc. pl. βόας, as in Jn 2[14f], see P Oxy IV. 729[16] (A.D. 137), P Gen I. 48[32] (A.D. 346); but in Ptolemaic times βοῦς survives in P Petr II. 32 (2*b*)[3] (iii/B.C.). The originally Aeolic dat. βόεσσι is found *OGIS* 200[15] (iv/A.D.) θρέψαντες αὐτοὺς βόεσσι: it may have been kept alive by poetry. In Ptolemaic papyri the word generally means *cow*: Mayser gives "βοῦς (ἡ)" without citing any cases of ὁ β., though some are indeterminate. The word is quite rare in NT, as in post-Ptolemaic papyri, and has lost any differentia it once had. As with other words of irregular flexion, diminutives (such as βούδιον, βοΐδιον) and synonyms encroached upon it. MGr has βούδι (βόδι or βόϊδι). For φόρος βοῶν, the tax levied on those who kept bulls or cows, see Wilcken *Ostr.* i. p. 352, and on βουκόλος as a priestly title, as in P Lond 41[7] (B.C. 161) (= I. p. 27) ὁ βουκόλος τοῦ Ὀσοράπι, see Otto *Priester* i. p. 119. Βουκόλος is found in its ordinary sense of "herdsman" in P Flor III. 321[14f] (iii/A.D.)

βραβεῖον.

For β. = "prize," as in 1 Cor 9[24], Phil 3[14], see *Priene* 118[5] (i/B.C.) τοῖς νικήσασιν ὡς ἀσφαλέστατα πρὸς πάντα τὸν χρόνον γενηθῆναι τὰ βραβεῖα, *CIG* 3674 (A.D. 100) τιμηθεὶς χρυσέῳ βραβείῳ. The word is used by Vettius Valens p. 174[21] κἀκείνοις τὸ βραβεῖον ἀπονέμειν, and similarly p. 288[5]. (An instance of βραβεῖα appears in BGU IV. 1027 xxviii[18] (iv/A.D.) in a fragmentary context: but Wilcken's revision, *Chrest.* I. p. 502, shows that the word is βρέβεια = *brevia*.) Nageli, p. 37, cites Menander and late poets, with some inscr. of ii/iii A.D., and the Paris *Zauberpapyrus* 662.

βραβεύω.

The "applied and general sense" which Field (*Notes*, p. 196) finds in this word is confirmed by P Par 63[10] (B.C. 165) λόγῳ τινὶ ταῦτα βραβευθῆναι, "that these things are *administered* reasonably," *ib.* 161 βραβευθῇ κατὰ τὸ βέλτιστον (*l.* βέλτιον), "be administered in the best way" (Mahaffy), P Leid B[22] (B.C. 164) τὸ θεῖον βραβεύσας, *Michel* 165[11] (B.C. 148-7) πάντα καλῶς καὶ πρεπόντως βραβεύσας. So in a Magnesian inscription (also ii B.C.). *Syll* 929[22] τῶι μὲν ἀκριβεῖ τῆς ψήφου βραβευθῆναι τὴν κρίσιν οὐκ ἠβουλόμεθα, where the law court and not the stadium is the scene of action. In P Oxy VII. 1050[11] however (ii/iii A.D.—an account for games) βραβευταῖς "umpires." Vettius Valens has the verb twice, p. 354[15] and p. 358[2], of the sun or the period of time which "determines" astronomical data. We may endorse accordingly the RV rendering of Wisd 10[12] ἀγῶνα ἰσχυρὸν ἐβράβευσεν αὐτῷ, "over his sore conflict she watched as judge," and Lightfoot's insistence on the element of *award* or *decision* in a conflict between two impulses, in the remarkable phrase of Col 3[15]: whether the figure of the games is present we need not argue. A new literary citation reinforces this, from the Menander fragment in PSI II. 126[5]—

λοιπὸν τοὔνομα
[τὸ] ὑμὸν φράσαι, τίς εἰμι· πάντων κυρία
τούτων βραβεῦσαι καὶ διοικῆσαι, Τύχη.

βραδύνω.

The intrans. use of this verb, which alone is found in the NT, may be illustrated from P Oxy I. 118³⁷ (late iii/A.D.) ἐπὶ οὖν βραδύνουσι, "since they are delaying," and OGIS 515²³ (A.D. 209–11) καὶ διὰ τοῦτο καὶ ἡ εὐ[πορία ἡ πρὸς τοὺς κυρίους αὐ]τοκράτορας τῶν φόρων βραδύνει. So in a papyrus of the second half of ii/A.D., edited by Comparetti in *Mél. Nicole*, p. 59 (col. ii.¹¹) ὡς ἂν βραδύνῃς καὶ ὑστερήσῃ ταῦτα τὰ [κτήνη] τῆς πορείας, οὐκ ἀγνοεῖς οὐδ᾽ αὐτὸς ζημία σε ὑποπ[είπτειν μέλ]λοντα, "if you delay, and these animals are late for the expedition, you yourself know you will get into trouble." (The document is given again in P Flor II. p. 258.) In the Christian letter, P Gen I. 51³¹, ἐβράδυνεν is without clear context, but certainly means "he delayed." In MGr βραδυάζει or βραδύνει == "it is late," "evening draws on."

βραδυπλοέω.

This ἅπ.εἰρ. of Ac 27⁷, cited by Grimm only from Artemidorus (ii/A.D.), is the subject of a note by W. Montgomery in *Exp* VIII. ix. p. 357. He suggests that it is a technical term, "to slow-sail," meaning to work to windward by tacking. Though found earliest in the "iii document," it is quite certainly no coinage of the author. In Artemidorus it is not technical, but only denotes a slow voyage.

βραδύς.

The adverb is common in signatures with reference to those who were unskilled in writing—e.g. BGU II. 543¹¹ (B.C. 27) ἔγραφεν ὑπὲρ αὐτοῦ Ζήνων Ζήνωνος ἀξιωθεὶς διὰ τὸ βραδύτερα αὐτὸν γράφειν, P Fay 97⁷ (A.D. 78) ἔγραψεν ὑπὲρ [αὐτ]οῦ βραδέω[ς] γράφοντος, BGU I. 69¹⁹ (A.D. 120) = *Chrest.* II. 142) ἔγραψα ὑπὲρ αὐτοῦ ἐρωτηθεὶς διὰ τὸ βραδ[ύ]τερα αὐτὸν γράφιν, αὐτοῦ γράφοντος τὸ ὄ[νομα, and P Lond 1164 (?)²⁶ (A.D. 212, = III. p. 167) ἔγραψα ὑπὲρ αὐτοῦ τὸ σῶμα τῆς ὑπογραφῆς, αὐτοῦ ὑστερ[ο]ν ὑπογράφοντος βραδέως—upon which follow the painful uncials of Philantinous Demetrius. So the Ptolemaic Ostr 1027⁹ διὰ τὸ βραδύτερα αὐτὸν γράφειν. Outside this special use, in OGIS 502¹⁷ (ii/A.D.) we have τοῦ] βράδειον ἀπολαῦσαι τὴν πόλιν τῆς [προσηκούσης προσόδου. The positive adv. occurs in P Oxy VIII. 1088⁵⁹ (i/A.D.—a medical receipt) βρα[δέως] πινέται μετὰ γλυκέως ἢ μέλιτο[ς, "to be drunk slowly with raisin wine or honey" (Ed.) It is curious that we cannot illustrate the adj. from our sources, while the adv. is so common. *Syll* 221¹² (latter part of ii/B.C.) has εἰς τε τοὺς μισθοὺς [τοὶς] βραδέσιν, "eis qui non in tempore veniebant" (Ed.). MGr βραδειά and (neut.) βράδυ == "evening"; cf. βραδύνω *ad fin.*

βραδυτής.

For β., which in Bibl. Grk is confined to 2 Pet 3⁹, we can only cite Vettius Valens, p. 289²¹ ἀνακρίσεις καὶ βραδυτῆτες καὶ ἀναλώματα καὶ φθόνοι. Wetstein has good parallels from literary **Κοινή.**

βραχίων.

P Oxy III. 490¹² (a will—A.D. 124) οὐλὴ βραχείονι δεξιῷ: similarly P Amh II. 112⁸ (A.D. 128), P Ryl II. 179⁶ (A.D. 127), etc. In *Syll* 615³² (iii/ii B.C.) τῶι ἱερεῖ τοῦ

ταύρου δίδοται γλῶσσα καὶ βραχίων, it means a "shoulder" of meat, and so of a ram in L.⁸

βραχύς.

The adjective is used of *stature* in P Tebt I. 32²² (B.C. 145) ἔστιν δὲ ὡς (ἐτῶν) κβ βραχὺς μελίχρ ως] κλαστός, "he is about 22 years of age, short, fair, curly-haired" (Edd.); cf. P Petr I. 13 (2)¹⁹, 14²² (both B.C. 237), etc. In P Oxy IV. 705⁷⁷ (A.D. 200–2) we have ἐπίδοσίν τ[ινα] βραχεῖαν, "a trifling benefaction," and in the epigram PSI I. 17¹⁵ (?iii/A.D.) the editor understands οὐ βραχὺν ἄνδρα as a man "not of small account" in view of the ἐπισημ[ό]τατον] which follows. In CPHerm 7⁸·⁶ (? ii/iii A.D.) ἄλλαι ἐσκορπισμέναι ἐν τῷ χωρίῳ βραχεῖαι μύξαι, it is applied to "small plumtrees," and in Vettius Valens, p. 78²⁶ to a "small" army or town. So P Lille I. 1 *verso*⁵⁵ B.C. 259–8 εἰς ὃ ἔσται βραχὺ τὸ ἀνάλωμα. For β. of *time* cf. P Par 51¹⁵ B.C. 160) (= *Sel.* ii n., p. 2) ἔτι βραχὺ ἔχω . . . . "I have still for a little while . . . .," P Fay 204 (ii/iii A.D.) ὁ βίος βραχύ ς, and P Strass I. 22²¹ (iii/A.D.) ἀφορμὴν καν βραχεῖαν δικαίαν κατοχῆς. The phrase διὰ βραχέων, as in Heb 13²², occurs in P Strass I. 41⁵ (A.D. 250) διὰ βραχέων σε διδάξω; cf. also BGU III. 1011¹¹·¹¹ (ii/B.C.) ὡς βραχύτατα γράφειν. That "short," in a document or a sermon, is a relative term, is rather amusingly shown at the end of a very long petition, P Flor III. 296⁶⁰ (vi A.D.) . . . ἡγείσθω δὲ τῶν βραχίων μου γραμμάτων ἡ ἐποφειλομένη ὑμῖν ἐξ [ἐμοῦ] προσκύνησις καὶ ὁ ἀσπασμός μου ὡς οὐ χάρτης χωρεῖ, δέσποτα.

For an example of the irregular comparative, see the astronomical papyrus P Par 1¹²¹, written about ii/B.C., where we have καθ᾽ ὃν ὁ ἥλιος φερόμενος τὴν μὲν ἡμέραν βραχυτέραν ποιεῖ, τὴν δὲ νύκτα μακροτέραν. Doubtless, as Blass assumes, the original author in iv B.C. wrote βραχυτάτην and μακροτάτην, and this makes the scribe's alteration two centuries later all the more significant: see *Proleg.* p. 78. On the "barbarism" βραχήν found in Asia Minor, and its witness to local pronunciation, see Thumb *Hellen.* p. 139.

βρέφος.

BGU IV. 1104²⁴ (time of Augustus) ἐατῆς τὸ βρέφος ἐκτίθεσθαι, P Oxy VII. 1069²² (iii A.D.) ἐὰν γὰρ τέκῃ ἡ Ταμοῦν ἀνάγκασον αὐτὴν τὸ βρέφος φειλοπονῆσε (= φιλοπονῆσαι). *ib.* XI. 1299¹⁶ (A.D. 251 3) ἀρρενικῷ βρέφει, "male nursling child," P Lond 951 *verso*⁶ (late iii/A.D.) (= III. p. 213) εἰ θέλεις, τὸ βρέφος ἐχέτω τροφόν, ἐγὼ γὰρ οὐκ ἐπιτ[ρέ]πω τῇ θυγατρί μου θηλάζειν, a letter from a father-in-law or mother-in-law with reference to the nursing of a new-born child. In the magic papyrus P Lond 122⁵ (iv/A.D.) (= I. p. 116) Hermes is invoked—ἐλθέ] μοι κύριε Ἑρμῆ ὡς τὰ βρέφη εἰς τὰς κοιλίας τῶν γυναι κῶ]ν.

βρέχω.

The verb is very common in connexion with the irrigation of land owing to the inundation of the Nile, e.g. P Lille I. 26³ (iii B.C.) ἡ κώμη ἔρημος διὰ τὸ πλείω χρόνον μὴ βεβρέχθαι, "the village is deserted because for a long time there has been no inundation there," *Chrest.* I. 341⁶ (c. A.D. 120) τῶν . . . βρεχέντων πεδίων καὶ τῶν [δ]υναμένων αὐλακισθῆναι, "irrigated and ready for the plough," P Tebt I. 24³¹ (B.C. 117) κατὰ τὰ προσαγγέλματα τῆς βεβρεγμένης, "in the matter of the reports of the irrigated land," P Lips

I. 105¹⁰ (i/ii A.D.) μόγις τὸν τῆς βεβρεγμένης ἀπήρτισα, "I have with difficulty completed the account of the irrigated land," P Giss I. 60ᵛ ¹² (ii/A.D.) ἐξ ὧν ἐβρέχησαν τῷ β̄ (ἔτει) Ἀδρια[νοῦ κτλ. The old and regular strong aor. pass. was ἐβράχην: this new formation illustrates the extension of the verb's use. Add from inscrr. OGIS 669⁵⁷ (i/A.D.) τῆς οὔσης ἀναβάσεως καὶ τῆς βεβρεγμένης γῆς. From ἄβροχος (cf. below under βροχή) comes a verb ἀβροχέω "to miss irrigation," as BGU I. 139¹⁵ (A.D. 201-2) ἠβροχηκυίας πρὸς τὸ ἐνεστὸς δέκατον ἔτος. MGr βρέχω (ἐβράχηκα, ἐβρέχτηκα —both aor. pass. have survived— "wet, dip, (cause to) rain" (Thumb Handb.).

βροντή.

Of this common Greek word we can quote no instance from the papyri: derivatives like βρονταγωγός and βροντοκεραννοπάτωρ are cited by van Herwerden from the great Paris magic papyrus, as well as the two derived verbs. Βροντάω occurs in the magic papyri P Lond 46¹⁵¹ (iv/A.D.) (= I. p. 70) ἐγώ εἰμι ὁ ἀστράπτω ν̄ καὶ βροντῶν, and 121⁵⁶⁶ (iii/A.D.) (= I. p. 96) ὁ αἰὼν ὁ βροντῶν, and βροντάζω in the last-mentioned papyrus I. 235 (= I. p. 92), and in 122⁹ (iv/A.D.) (= I. p. 119). In Phrygian inscrr. Βροντῶν θεός is a standing title of the sky-god: cf. Iuppiter Tonans at Rome. Βροντῶ is still "to thunder" in MGr. Vettius Valens has βροντοποιός and βροντώδης.

βροχή.

The evidence already adduced under βρέχω is in itself sufficient to throw suspicion on Thayer's (p. 694) classing this amongst "Biblical" words, and as a matter of fact we can now cite many instances of βροχή from profane sources. Thus from Ptolemaic times comes P Petr III. 43 (2) recto(b) ¹³ (B.C. 245) πρὸς τὴν βροχὴν τῆς τῶν κλη[ρο]υχι[κ]ῶν ἱππέων γῆς, and almost contemporary with the NT passage (Mt 7²⁵·²⁷) is P Oxy II. 280⁵ (A.D. 88-9) a lease of land εἰς ἔτη τέσσαρα βροχὰς τέσσαρες. From this it would appear, as the editors point out, that if there was no βροχή, the year was not to count as one of the four years: and they compare the clause frequently found in leases, ἐὰν δέ τις τοῖς ἑξῆς ἔτεσι ἄβροχος γένηται, παραδεχθήσεται τῷ μεμισθωμένῳ (e.g. P Oxy I. 101²⁵, A.D. 142). See also Archiv iv. p. 177, and for a notification of ἀβροχία BGU I. 139 (A.D. 201) (= Chrest. I. 225). For βροχή in another sense see P Tebt II. 401²⁷ (early i/A.D.), where in the accounts of a beer-seller there is an item βροχῆς ἀρτάβαι β̄, which seems to be part of the brewing process. In MGr βροχή is "rain," βροχερός "rainy."

βρόχος.

In P Oxy I. 51¹⁶ (A.D. 173) a public physician, who had been ordered to examine into the cause of a death, reports that he had found the body ἀπηρτημένον βρόχῳ, "hanged by a noose." The verb is found in the iv/A.D. Acts of John, P Oxy VI. 850⁶ ἐννοοῦν[τα] β[ρ]οχίσαι ἑαυτόν, "one who was intending to hang himself."

βρυγμός.

Thayer seems to have overlooked the citation from Eupolis (v/B.C.) given in LS⁸, so that his oldest profane citation is later than LXX, and has moreover a different sense, "biting."

He does not however include it in his list of "Biblical" words, so that no harm is done by the oversight.

βρύω.

To the ordinary citations for this NT ἅπ. εἰρ. (Jas 3¹¹) may be added its occurrence quinquiens in the recently discovered poems of Bacchylides, e.g. III. 15 f. βρύει μὲν ἱερὰ βουθύτοις ἑορταῖς, βρύουσι φιλοξενίας ἀγυιαί, "the temples are rife with festal sacrifice of oxen, the streets with hospitable feasting" (Jebb). Herwerden Lex. s.v. cites also Timotheus Pers. 221 βρύων ἄνθεσιν ἥβας.

βρῶμα

in MGr = "rubbish, stench, dirt" (Thumb. Handb.). Pallis, in his Notes, p. 14, proposes to recognize this word— which would be a variant of βρῶμος, whence we get bromine — in Mk 7¹⁹. His rendering, "which thing (or circumstance) clears away all impurities," ignores the true reading καθαρίζων: it would be better to take the latter as agreeing with ἀφεδρῶνα, by the lapse of concord so common in Rev (Proleg. p. 9). But the RV supplies a much more satisfactory sense, though the new proposal is ingenious.

βρώσιμος

is found in a love-spell, P Lond 124¹ ¹ (iv/v A.D.) (= I. p. 121) καὶ βρώσιμον [λ]αβών. Cf. Syll 289³³ τὰ δὲ κρέα τ[ὰ] βρώσ[ιμα (?).

βρῶσις.

P Lond 1223⁹ (A.D. 121) (= III. p. 139) χόρτο[ν] εἰς μὲν βρῶσ[ιν] προβάτ(ων), "fodder for the pasturing of sheep": so P Lips I. 118¹⁵ (A.D. 160-1).

βυθίζω.

The figurative use in 1 Tim 6⁹ may be illustrated by Syll 324⁷ (ii/B.C.) συνεχέσι πολέμοις καταβυθισθ[ε]ῖσαν τὴν πόλιν. See also Alciphron I. 16, 1 (= Schepers, p. 19) τὸ νῆφον ἐν ἐμοὶ συνεχῶς ὑπὸ τοῦ πάθους βυθίζεται (cited by Dibelius HZNT ad 1 Tim 6⁹).

βυθός.

P Oxy VI. 886¹⁰ (iii/A.D.) (= Selections, p. 111) ἐπικαλοῦ μὲ[ν] (?) τὸν (ἥλιον) κὲ τοὺς ἐν βυθῷ θεοὺς πάντας, "call upon the sun and all the gods in the deep"—in a magic formula. From the same kind of literature we may cite P Leid Wˣ ²² (ii/iii A.D.) ἀναπνεύσας γὰρ πωππύσει ἐκ τοῦ βηθοῦ, "respirans enim poppysmum edit ex profundo," and xxv. ²⁸ ἐν τῷ βυθῷ τὴν δύναμιν ἔχουσαν ἐμοί, "in profundo potentiam habentem mihi" (Ed.). The word was prominent in Valentinian speculation, and it is not surprising that it should figure in magic papyri, which breathe a kindred air.

βυρσεύς.

P Fay 121¹⁵ (c. A.D. 100) τοῦ] κυρτοῦ βυρσέως, "the hunch-backed tanner." From βύρσα, "hide," on the analogy of the gen. βύρσης. we find an acc. βύρσην, as P Petr II. introd. p. 37 (d)⁷ : see Mayser Gr. p. 12, and cf. Proleg. p. 48. P Oxy VII. 1057³ (A.D. 362) has ἀπὸ τιμῆς βύρσας, where analogy has worked the other way. In P Petr II. 32 (1) a βυρσοδέψης, "tanner," is also described as a σκυτεύς, "cobbler": cf. the editor's note and Wilcken Ostr. i. p. 294.

βύσσινος.

The manufacture of this famous material (τὰ βύσσινα, with or without ὀθόνια) seems to have been a Government monopoly in Egypt, and it was carried on under the direction of the priests in the temples, which were hives of industry as well as of devotion. The output of these early ecclesiastics ranged from lawn to beer, as we see from P Eleph 27a[13] (B.C. 225–4) with the editor's note and P Lond 1177[51] (A.D. 113) (= III. p. 182). See also for the linen monopoly Wilcken *Ostr.* i. p. 266 ff. and Dittenberger's note to *OGIS* 90[17] (the Rosetta Stone—B.C. 196) τῶν τ' εἰς τὸ βασιλικὸν συντελουμένων ἐν τοῖς ἱεροῖς βυσσίνων ὀθονίων ἀπέλυσεν τὰ δύο μέρη.

βύσσος.

For this Hellenized Semitic word see P Gen I. 36[19] (A.D. 170) (= *Chrest.* I. 85) βύσσου στολίσματος πήχεις δέκα, and cf. P Tebt II. 313[20] (A.D. 210–1), 598 (A.D. 176–91).

βωμός.

originally "platform," like its kin βῆμα, has been specialized as a ἱερὸς βωμός, "altar," from Homer down. It is common in the papyri and inscriptions. One or two instances must suffice. Thus in the curious P Petr II. p. [28]. Fr. 4[12] (B.C. 241) it appears that the inhabitants of certain houses in Crocodilopolis built up the doors of their houses and set altars against them to avoid having Crown officials billeted on them—ὡσαύτως δὲ καὶ ἐνωικοδομηκότας τὰς θύρας τῶν οἰκιῶν βωμοὺς προσωικοδομήκασιν, τοῦτο δὲ πεποιήκασιν πρὸς τὸ μὴ ἐπισταθμεύεσθαι. Cf. also the phrase ἔξω ἱεροῦ βωμοῦ with reference to being outside the "protection" of a temple and altar, e.g. P Tebt I. 210[5] (B.C. 107) (= *Chrest.* I. 327), P Oxy IV. 785 (c. A.D. 1), *ib.* X. 1258[8] (A.D. 45). In P Grenf II. 111[21] (v/vi A.D.) βωμὸς χαλκ(οῦς) ᾱ is mentioned in an inventory of church property. For the φόρος βωμῶν paid by the priests see Wilcken *Ostr.* i. p. 352 f.

Reference may be made to the inscr. Ζεὺς Βωμός, found on or near an altar erected before a Greek temple in Central Syria. According to L. R. Farnell (*Year's Work in Classical Studies*, 1909, p. 91) this "frank identification of the god with the altar" probably arises from Syrian rather than Hellenic thought. But there was Hellenic thought also: see the account of the whole matter in A. B. Cook, *Zeus*, i. p. 519 f.

Γ

γάζα—Γαλλίων

γάζα.

For this word we may cite the interesting inscription discovered at Adale on the African coast of the Red Sea, in which the conquests of Ptolemy III in the Eastern Provinces, including Babylon and Persia, are recounted—*OGIS* 54[22] (2nd half of iii/B.C.) καὶ ἀναζητήσας ὅσα ὑπὸ τῶν Περσῶν ἱερὰ ἐξ Αἰγύπτου ἐξήχθη καὶ ἀνακομίσας μετὰ τῆς ἄλλης γάζης τῆς ἀπὸ τῶν τόπων εἰς Αἴγυπτον δυνάμεις ἀπέστειλεν. See further Mahaffy *The Empire of the Ptolemies*, p. 199 f. The statement that the noun, borrowed in Greek in iv/B.C., was a Persian word for the King's treasury, depends on Curtius (see Grimm): the Middle Persian *ganj* has the required meaning, and can be shown to descend from the same original, as Dr Louis H. Gray tells us. *Ganj* was the heavenly treasure-house where merits were stored against the Judgement: see Moulton *Early Zoroastrianism*, pp. 162, 382.

Γάζα.

According to Lewy *Fremdwörter* p. 94, in Hellenistic Greek foreign proper names are only found with γ = ע, when this represents the Arabic ‏غ‏: thus Γάζα = עַזָּה ‘*Azzā*.

γαζοφυλάκιον.

In *OGIS* 225[16] (iii/B.C.) provision is made that the price of a certain piece of ground should be paid εἰς τὸ κατὰ στρατείαν γαζοφυλάκ[ι]ον, "into the military treasury."

Γάϊος.

The name was common in the Greek world, but, in connexion with Paul's Macedonian friend Gaius (Ac 19[29]), we may recall that it occurs in the list of politarchs at Thessalonica (*CIG* II. 1967). It is also found in a memorial inscription in the same town—Γάϊος Ἰούλιος Σεκοῦνδος Πρίμῳ τῷ ἰδίῳ τέκνωι μνήμης χάριν (*Duchesne* No. 78)—but here of course we have a Roman, and the name is distinctive as John in English. See further Milligan *Thess.* p. 134: and for the occurrence of the name in a Phrygian inscription at Iconium of A.D. 150–250, cf. Ramsay *Recent Discovery*, p. 72. Since Grimm and many other writers mention a Roman name "Caius," it may be well to refer to the third founder of Gonville's College at Cambridge as probably the earliest person to bear this title. On the late Anatolian stone, *Calder* 436, we find Γανω, which Prof. Calder remarks must be for Γαίῳ, υ being now equivalent to ι: this shows that Γάϊος was trisyllabic. We do not find Γεος in Greek, any more than *Gaeus* in Latin: the *ai* remained a true diphthong. WH are wrong therefore in accenting Γαῖος.

γάλα.

P Oxy IV. 736[13] (c. A.D. 1) γάλακτος παιδ(ῶν) (ἡμιωβέλιον), "milk for the children ½ ob.," in a private account; *ib.* IX. 1211[10] (ii/A.D.) ἔλεον, μέλι, γάλα, articles for a sacrifice; *Syll* 804[15] (? ii/A.D.) γάλα μετὰ μέλιτος προλαβεῖν (= "edere," Dittenberger): BGU IV. 1055[17] (B.C. 13) σταμνὸν ὀκτωκαίδεκα κοτυρὸν (= κοτυλῶν γάλακτος βοήου (= βοείου) ἀρεστοῦ, to be a daily allowance: *ib.* 1109[6] (B.C. 5) συνχωρεῖ . . . παρασχέσθαι τὴν δούλην αὐ[τ]οῦ Χρωτάριο(ν) τροφεύουσαν καὶ θηλάζουσαν τῶι ἰδίῳ αὐτῆς γάλακτι καθαρῷ καὶ ἀφθόρωι—the last a sample of numerous contracts with nurses. In connexion with the use of γάλα in 1 Pet 2[2], it may be mentioned that Reitzenstein (*Die hell. Mysterienreligionen*, pp. 84, 157) shows that milk plays a prominent part in the mystery-cults. He quotes Sallust περὶ θεῶν 4, where milk, the new birth, and crowns are all mentioned together—ἑορτὴν ἄγομεν διὰ ταῦτα . . . ἐπὶ τούτοις γάλακτος τροφή, ὡς ἀναγεννωμένων· ἐφ' οἷς ἱλαρεῖαι καὶ στέφανοι καὶ πρὸς τοὺς θεοὺς οἷον ἐπάνοδος. For the compounds γαλακτοφόρος, -ία, and -έω, see P Lond 3[22] (B.C. 146 or 135) (= I. p. 46), BGU I. 297[11] (A.D. 50), and P Tebt II. 399 (ii/A.D.). The word is MGr.

Γαλατία.

The proximity of Γαλατίαν to Δαλματίαν in 2 Tim 4[10] in itself suggests that by the former we are to understand European Gaul (cf. Γαλλίαν ℵC): and this is confirmed by the famous *Monumentum Ancyranum* (*Res Gestae D. Augusti*, ed.[2] Mommsen, p. lxxxv. 124) ἐξ Ἰσπανίας καὶ Γαλατίας καὶ παρὰ Δαλματῶν: see Zahn *Intr.* ii. p. 25 f. The inscriptional and literary evidence as to the meaning of *Galatia* in other NT passages may be left to the monographs on this burning question.

γαλήνη.

The adj. is found *OGIS* 519[11] (iii/A.D.) πάντων . . . ἥρεμον καὶ γαληνὸν τὸν βίον διαγόντων. In the late papyri γαληνότης is common as an honorific title, e. g. P Oxy VII. 1042[7] (A.D. 578) μετὰ τὴν δευτέραν ὑπατίαν τῆς αὐτῶν γαληνότητ(ος), "after the second consulship of his [? their] serenity." (Ed.)

Γαλλίων.

See Deissmann's *St. Paul*, App. I., where, following Ramsay (*Exp.* VII. vii. p. 467 ff.), it is shown on the evidence of a Delphic inscription, published by Bourguet *De rebus Delphicis*, 1905, p. 63 f., that Gallio entered on his pro-consulship in the summer of A.D. 51, and a fixed point is thus secured for determining the chronology of Paul's life. The name occurs P Ryl II. 155[12] (A.D. 138–61).

γαμβρός.

For this word, which does not occur in the NT, but is common in the LXX, see P Giss I. 13[10] (beginning of ii A.D.), BGU III. 805[9] (ii/A.D.), P Fay 127[11] (ii/iii A.D.) τοῖς γαμροῖς (*l.* γαμβροῖς) τῆς ἀδελφῆς σου, "for the son-in-law of your sister." The fem. γαμβρά is found BGU III. 827[9], and P Lond 403[24] (A.D. 346) (= II. p. 276). On the verbs γαμβρεύομαι and ἐπιγαμβρεύομαι, see Anz, pp. 376, 378. In MGr γαμπρός = "son-in-law," "bridegroom."

γαμέω.

The verb is used in its ordinary classical sense of "take to wife" in a will of B.C. 285-4, P Eleph 2[5], where provision is made in the event of certain of the testator's sons' marrying and being divorced—γημάντων δὲ καὶ καταχωρισθέντων—the property will belong jointly to all his sons. Cf. for the same absolute use a question addressed by a man to the Oracle of Zeus-Helios-Sarapis, P Oxy IX. 1213[4] (ii A.D.) ἀξιοῖ Μένανδρος [εἰ] δέδοταί μοι γαμῆσαι, "M. asks, is it granted me to marry?" (Edd.). So P Flor III. 332[21] (ii A.D.) ἐπεὶ δὲ νῦν Νῖλος ὁ υἱὸς αὐτῆς γαμεῖν μέλλει, and with object, Audollent 78 μήποτ' αὐτὸν γῆμαι ἄλλην γυναῖκα. The use of γαμεῖσθαι to denote the bride's part in a wedding has rather fallen out of use in Hellenistic, but it not infrequently survives in the legal language of marriage-contracts, e.g. P Oxy III. 496[5] (A.D. 127) ἡ [τῆς] γαμουμένης μάμμη Θαὶς κτλ., *ib.* VI. 905[10] (A.D. 170) (= *Selections*, p. 86) καὶ ὁ γαμῶν ἐπιχορηγείτω τῇ γαμουμένῃ τὰ δέοντα, and even P Lips I. 41[11] (about the end of iv/A.D.) where, with reference to the bridal gifts, the bridegroom, after the marriage has been completed, is described as οὐ τὰ ἑαυτοῦ ἐπικομιζόμενος μόνον, ἀλλὰ κα[ὶ] τινα [τ]ῆς γημαμέν[η]ς: see further *Proleg.* p. 159. For the passive, cf. P Oxy X. 1266[16] (A.D. 98) τὴν δὲ τοῦ υἱοῦ μητέρα Θερμούθιον γεγαμῆσθαί μοι τῷ β (ἔτει) Δομιτιανοῦ, P Grenf II. 76[11] (deed of separation—A.D. 305-6) ἀλλ' ἐξεῖναι αὐτῇ ἀποστῆναι καὶ γαμηθῆναι ὡς ἂν βουληθῇ. Γαμετή "wife," is common—P Tebt I. 104[17] (B.C. 92) ὅσα προσήκει γυναικὶ γαμετῆι, PSI I. 64[5] (i B.C.) συνοικ[ήσουσά σοι ὡ]ς γνησί[α] γαμετή, P Oxy IV. 705[4] (A.D. 81-96) γ[αμ]ετὴν φερνὴν προσφερομένην δα[κτύλιον] χρυσοῦν τεταρτῶ[ν, and OGIS 206[9] Ἀκύλα . . . εὐξάμενος ῥῶσιν καὶ τέκνοις καὶ γαμετῇ. This noun and σύμβιος have considerably trenched on the ground of the less explicit γυνή.

γαμίζω.

No instances of this verb have as yet been quoted outside the NT, and it is therefore not possible to determine how far the rule of Apollonius *De Constr.* p. 280, 14 (ed. Bekker) ἐστὶ γὰρ τὸ μέν "γαμῶ," γάμου μεταλαμβάνω· τὸ δὲ "γαμίζω," γάμου τινὶ μεταδίδωμι applies. It may be noted, however, that many verbs in -ίζω are found used in the same way as verbs in -έω (e.g. ἀπολογίζω, ἀπολογέω: cf. Hatzidakis *Gr.* p. 395), and that consequently in 1 Cor 7[38] γαμίζω may = "marry" and not "give in marriage." For this rendering see further *ad l.* Lietzmann in *HZNT*, and J. Weiss in Meyer's *Kommentar*[9].

γάμος.

P Tebt I. 104, a marriage contract of B.C. 92, is docketed on the *verso* -ὁμο(λογία) γάμου. For συγγραφὴ γάμου, see

P Oxy IV. 713[12] (A.D. 97) πεποίηνται πρὸς ἀλλήλους τοῦ γάμου συγγραφήν, and cf. P Amh II. 78[10] (A.D. 184) τῇ συγγενίδι μου . . . πρὸς γάμον συνελθ[ο]ῦν, "being married to my kinswoman" (Edd.). The word is very common in connexion with the wedding festivities, e.g. P Oxy I. 111[2] (iii A.D.) ἐρωτᾷ σε Ἡραὶς δειπνῆσαι εἰς γάμους τέκνων αὐτῆς, *ib.* VI. 927[2] (iii A.D.) καλῖ σαι Ἔρως εἰς γάμους, P Flor III. 332[2] (ii A.D.) τοῖς γάμοις σου, "on the occasion of your marriage." Cf. the use of the singular in Gen 29[22], 1 Macc 10[58], and Mt 22[8] compared with [2], where Field (*Notes*, p. 16) finds no difference between sing. and plur. For the phrase γάμους ποιεῖν (Mt 22[2]) cf. *Michel* 1001[ii 19] (the Will of Epicteta, in the Doric of Thera—c. B.C. 200) μηδὲ χρῆσαι τὸ μουσεῖον μηθενί, εἰ κα μὴ τις τῶν ἐξ Ἐπιτελείας γάμον ποιῇ.

On the distinction between Egyptian, Greek, and Greek-Egyptian marriages in Egypt, and on the γάμος ἄγραφος as a provisional union in contrast to the fully constituted γάμος ἔγγραφος, see Hohlwein, *L'Égypte Romaine*, p. 158 ff. Cf. also *Archiv* iii. pp. 70 f., 507; iv. pp. 264 f., 474 f.

γάρ.

For the *ascensive* force of καὶ γάρ, as in Rom 11[1], cf. P Passalacqua[9] (iii B.C.) (= Witkowski[2], p. 54) φρόντισον οὖν, ὅπως μὴ ἀδικηθῇ ὁ ἄνθρωπος· καὶ γὰρ ὁ πατήρ αὐτοῦ ἐστιν ἐνταῦθα περὶ Π., where Letronne (P Par p. 401) renders, "aie soin qu'il ne soit fait aucun tort à cet homme: car, de plus, son père est employé ici auprès de P." In P Oxy IV. 743[22] (B.C. 2) καὶ γὰρ ἐγὼ ὅλος διαπον[ο]ῦμαι εἰ Ἕλενος χαλκοῦς ἀπόλε[σ]εν, "I am quite upset at Helenos' loss of the money" (Edd.), the same phrase seems to do little more than introduce a new subject. In P Flor III. 367[5] (iii A.D.) καὶ γὰρ καὶ πολλάκις μου ἐπιστείλαντός σοι κτλ., the locution introduces the ground of a complaint just conveyed in the mention of the addressee's ἀπάνθρωποι ἐπιστολαί. The ordinary uses of γάρ need not be illustrated, unless we give one example of the γάρ beginning an exposition of a matter just announced, where our idiom omits: thus P Rein 7[5] (B.C. 141) ἠνάγκασμαι τὴν ἐφ' ὑμᾶς καταφυγὴν π[οι]ήσασθαι ἵνα τύχω βοηθείας. Τοῦ γὰρ κτλ. (the statement of grievance follows).

γαστήρ.

The phrase ἐν γαστρὶ ἔχειν (cf. MGr ἐγγαστρώνομαι), found in Herodotus, and the medical writers from Hippocrates down (see Hobart, p. 92), may be quoted from P Ryl II. 68[13] (B.C. 89), where one woman complains of another who ἐ[πλήξέν] με . . . ἐγ γαστρ[ὶ] ἔχουσαν πεντάμηνον. It is used of a sow, P Magd 4[6] (iii B.C.), and P Flor II. 130[3] (A.D. 257) καταπι[λ]ανθεῖσαν ὗν ἔχουσαν καὶ ἐν γαστρί. Cf. *Syll* 802[3] (iii B.C.) πένθ' ἔτη ὡς ἐκύησε ἐγ γασ[τρ]ὶ Κλεώ βαρος, [ἔγ]κυος δὲ γενομένα ἐγ γαστρὶ ἐφόρει τρία ἔτη. In Vettius Valens, p. 103[33] we have ἐὰν κατὰ γαστρὸς ἔχῃ. For the common compound γαστροκνήμιον ("calf of the leg," see BGU III. 975[11] (A.D. 45) (= *Selections*, p. 42) οὐλὴ καστροκνημίῳ (*l.* γαστρο).

γε.

A good example of the emphasis imparted by this particle is afforded by P Lond 42[13] (B.C. 168) (= I. p. 30, *Selections*, p. 10) εἰς πᾶν τι ἐληλυθυῖα διὰ τὴν τοῦ σίτου τιμήν, καὶ δο[κο]ῦσα ν[ῦ]γ [γ]ε σοῦ παραγενομένου τεύξεσθαί τινος ἀναψυχῆς, "having come to the last extremity because of the high price of corn, and thinking that now at last on your return I should obtain some relief." The same document, l. 23, illustrates the μήτιγε of 1 Cor 6³—μὴ ὅτι γε τοσούτου χρόνου ἐπιγεγονότος, "not to speak of so much time having gone by" (see *Proleg.* p. 240). For the combination εἰ δὲ μή γε cf. P Oxy VIII. 1159⁶ (late iii/A.D.) εἰ δὲ μή γε, σύνταξαι αὐτῷ ὅτι ἐλεύσεται μέχρι ιϛ Φαμενώθ, "otherwise, arrange with him that he shall come by the 13th Phamenoth" (Edd.), *Chrest.* I. 107²⁵ (B.C. 131) προνοήθητι ὡς μάλιστα μὲν συνπληρωθήσεται τὰ τοῦ παρελθόντος ἔτους κεφ[ά]λαια, εἰ δὲ μή γε, οὐκ ἐλάσσω τῶν κζ (ταλάντων), "if possible, . . . but if not, at any rate . . .", *Cagnat* IV. 833 (Hierapolis, after ii/A.D.) οὐδενὶ δὲ ἑτέρῳ ἐξέσται κηδευθῆναι· εἰ δὲ μή γε ὁ ἐπιχειρήσας δώσει τῷ ἱερωτάτῳ ταμείῳ δηνάρια μύρια—the editor needlessly extrudes γε. On εἴ γε, καίτοι γε, μενοῦν γε, etc., see these combinations in their places below.

γέεννα.

This Hellenized form, derived from the Heb. םֹנִּה by dropping the *m*, is one of those "specific Jewish ideas" (Thumb *Hellen.* p. 118) which naturally we cannot illustrate from our sources. We may cite *Orac. Sib.* I. 103 εἰς γέενναν μαλεροῦ λάβρου πυρὸς ἀκαμάτοιο : the spelling here demanded by the metre is found in Mk 9⁴⁷ D, *ib.* 45 B *al.*

γείτων.

BGU III. 830²¹ (i/A.D.) ἐπὶ γὰρ καὶ γείτων αὐτοῦ εἰ[μ]ί, P Oxy X. 1272¹¹ (A.D. 144) ὑπόνοιαν οὖν κατὰ [τ]ῶν γειτόνων μου, "having some suspicion against my neighbours" (Edd.). The adj. is very common in descriptions of locality, e.g. P Par 5¹·⁸ (B.C. 114) τὸν εἰς Τάγην οἶκον . . . οὗ γείτονες· νότου οἰκία Ἁρπαήσιος, βορρᾶ ψιλοὶ τόποι κτλ., P Oxy I. 99⁷ (A.D. 55) γείτονες τῆς ὅλη[ς] οἰκίας, νότου] καὶ ἀπηλιώτο[υ] δημόσιαι ῥύμαι, X. 1276⁸ (A.D. 249) τῆς δὲ ὅλης γείτονες νότου ῥύμη τυφλή, "the adjacent areas of the whole are on the south a blind street" (Edd.). Γειτνία and γειτνιάω are used in a similar way—P Tebt I. 14¹⁰ (B.C. 114) γειτνίας, "adjoining areas," *ib.* 105¹⁹ (B.C. 103) πλὴν τῆς γειτνιώσης τῆι Θοώνιος, "except that which adjoins the land of Thoonis," P Said Khan 2ᵃ⁵ (B.C. 22) ὅρια καὶ γειτνίαι ἀπὸ τῶν ἀνατολῶν κτλ. This noun may = "neighbourhood," as in P Flor III. 319⁵ (A.D. 132 ?) οἱ ἐν γειτνίᾳ μου ὄντες. See also *Syll* 929⁶⁸ (ii/B.C.) for a verb γειτονέω. In MGr γείτονας = "neighbour."

γελάω.

Syll 802⁷⁰ (iii/B.C.) τὸν δὲ θεὸν γελάσαντα φά[μ]εν νιν παυσεῖν (τᾶς νόσου), P Oxy III. 471⁸⁸ (ii/A.D.) γέλωτα πολὺν καὶ ἀνειμένον . . . γελᾶν, "laughed long and freely" (Edd.). If we desiderate proof that the ancients laughed with the same articulation as ourselves, we may refer to P Leid Wˣˡ·²⁰ (ii/iii A.D.) εἰπὼν ἐκρότησε γ. κ(αὶ) ἐγέλασεν ὁ θεὸς ἑπτάκις. χα, χα, χα, χα, χα, χα, χα. γελάσαντος δὲ αὐτοῦ ἐγεννήθησαν θεοὶ ζ, οἵτινες τὰ πάντα περιέχουσιν. A Lycian epitaph may be quoted from Ormerod and Robinson's inscr. in *JHS* xxxiv. p. 1 ff.: no. 20²⁰ παῖζε γέλα παροδεῖτα, βλέπων ὅτι καὶ σὲ θανεῖν δεῖ—it is the analogue of the

commonplace quoted in 1 Cor 15³². For the fut. act., as in Lk 6²¹ (cf. Job 29²⁴, 4 Macc 5²⁸), see *Proleg.* p. 154. MGr has γελῶ.

γέλως.

In the invitation to the celebration of Hadrian's accession the people are summoned to sacrifice γέλωσι καὶ μέθαις ταῖς ἀπὸ κρήνης τὰς ψυχὰς ἀνέντες (P Giss I. 3⁵ ff). In his note the editor suggests that γέλωσι may refer to the "Festzug (πομπή)" which was customary on such occasions, and refers to *Klio* vii. p. 285 ff. In MGr γέλοια (plur.) = "laughter." See another instance cited under γελάω (P Oxy 471) : add BGU IV. 1141¹¹ (B.C. 14) καὶ γράψας αὐτῶι ὑβρίσαι με πρὸς γέλωτά μοι τοῦτο ἔγραψας.

γεμίζω.

The verb is used of loading a ship with grain in P Magd 11¹⁴ (B.C. 221) συντάξαι Εὐφράνορι . . . γεμίσαι τὸ πλοῖον ἐκ (cf. Rev 8³) τῶν καθ' αὐτὸν τόπων τὴν ταχίστην. In l. 11 of the same papyrus we have the pass. γεμίζηται used absolutely, and similarly on the *verso* περὶ τ]οῦ [γεμι]σθῆναι αὐτοῦ τ[ὸ πλοῖ[ο]ν; cf. Mk 4³⁷, Lk 14²³. Other examples of the verb are P Fay 117¹¹ (A.D. 108) πάντα τὰ κτήνη γέμιζε (l. γέμιζε) βάκανον, "load all the animals with cabbage," *ib.* 118²³ (A.D. 110), P Tebt II. 416¹⁷ (iii/A.D.) γέμεισον χόρτου, "load the ass with hay," P Flor II. 184¹⁵ (iii/A.D.) γεμίσας τὰ ἐκκενωθέντα τότε σιτάρια, and ¹⁷ τοὺς τέσσαρες σάκκους γεμίσαι, P Rein 53⁴ (iii/iv A.D.) τὰ ἀποσταλέντα καμήλια γέμωσον (see below) οἴνου. For the constr. with acc. and gen., as in this last instance and others—cf. Mk 15³⁶ etc.), see also *OGIS* 383¹⁴⁶ (i/B.C.) τρ]απέζας μὲν ἱερὰς πρεπούσης θοίνης γεμ[ί]ζων. In MGr γεμίζω is construed with double accusative. The curious form γέμωσον (P Rein 53 *l.c.*) is explained by P Flor II. 184¹⁸ (iii/A.D.) γόμωσον, and other passages where this alternative γομόω occurs : γέμωσον is a compromise. Note the negatived verbal in P Said Khan 1ᵇ³⁴ (B.C. 88) στέμφ[υ]λα ἀγέμιστ[α.

γέμω.

P Lond 122⁹³ (magic, iv/A.D.) (= I. p. 119) πυρὸς γέμι. See also the early Christian inscription *IMAe* I. 1238 ἐπὶ γέμι τὸ θηκίον τοῦτο, "since this tomb is full." For the construction with the acc., as in Rev 17³, cf. the MGr γέμω χρήματα, "I am full of possessions."

γενεά.

The collective sense of this word—involved in its historic relation to γένος—is normal throughout, and survives in MGr γενιά = "race, lineage." Thus it denotes a family, without individual reference : P Oxy I. 104¹¹ (a will—A.D. 96) τῆς τούτου γενεᾶς, "his issue" (should he himself predecease)— similarly PSI III. 240⁶ (ii/A.D.) . . . ἑκά]στου αὐτῶν γενεᾶς, in a will—*ib.* IV. 713¹⁹ (A.D. 97) τῇ ἐξ ἀλλήλων γενεᾷ, "their joint issue," P Hal I. 1²¹⁷ (iii B.C.) ἄλλον δ' ὅρκον μηδένα ἐξέστω ὀμνύναι μη[δ]ὲ ὁρκ[ίζ]ειν μηδὲ γενεὰν παρίστασθαι, "no one may swear by any other oath [than Zeus, Hera and Poseidon], nor offer it, nor may he bring forward his family," *i.e.* to swear by them : see note, p. 121. *Syll* 856¹⁶·¹⁸ (ii B.C.) ὁμοίως δὲ καὶ εἰ γε[ν]εὰν ποιήσαιτο, of a manumitted slave, ἐλευθέρα ἔστ[ω] καὶ ἀνέφαπτος ἁ γ[ε]νεά. *Cagnat* IV.

015⁴ (i/A.D.) καὶ [αὐ]το[ὶ] καὶ γενεαὶ [α]ὐτῶν. The abstract sense appears in P Tebt II. 312⁶ (A.D. 123–4) ἱερεὺς ἀπολύσιμος ἀπὸ τ[ῆς] [.]δ γενεᾶς, "exempted priest of the [.]4th generation."

γενεαλογία.

The plural is found along with μῦθοι (as in 1 Tim 1⁴) in Polyb. ix. 2. 1 περὶ τὰς γενεαλογίας καὶ μύθους, where the reference is to the stories of the births of the demigod founders of states. Hence Hort (*Jud. Christianitr.* p. 135 ff.) understands the word in the Pastorals not of the Gnostic groupings of *aeons* in genealogical relationships, but of "all the early tales adherent, as it were, to the births of founders," etc.

γενέσια.

The distinction between τὰ γενέσια, the commemoration of the dead, and τὰ γενέθλια, the birthday feast of a living man, disappears in late Greek (cf. Lob. *Phryn.* p. 103, Rutherford *NP.* p. 184): and in the papyri τὰ γενέσια is always birthday feast. Thus P Fay 114²⁹ (A.D. 100) τὴν εἰκθύιν (*l.* ἰχθὺν) πέμψις (*l.* πέμψεις) τῆι κδ εἰ (*l.* ἢ) κε εἰς τὰ γενέσια Γεμέλλης, "send the fish on the 24th or 25th for Gemella's birthday feast," for which other dainties are ordered in *ib.* 119²⁰ ⁶. P Fay 115², a year later, says that pigs are going to be sacrificed on the birthday feast (εἰς τὰ γενέσια) of Sabinus. Cf. BGU I. 1⁴ (iii/A.D.) an account of various outlays connected with the γενεσί[οις] τῶν [θεῶ]ν Σεβαστῶν. and *Preisigke* 1525 (A.D. 131—dedication of a statue) γενέσια Ἀδριανοῦ β ἡ πόλις. So for the birthdays of private persons BGU I. 333² (ii/iii A.D.) (= *Chr.* I. 484) π[άντως ποιήσατε, ἐὰν ᾖ δυνατό[ν], κ[α]τελθεῖν ὑμᾶς εἰς τὰ γενέσια τοῦ υἱοῦ ἡμῶ]ν Σαραπίωνος. So in accounts of expenditure, as P Oxy IV. 736⁶ (c. A.D. 1) γενεσίοις Τρυφᾶτος στεφά[νων] (ὀβολοὶ δύο), P Giss I. 31⁶ (ii/A.D.) γενεσίοις Διογενίδ[ος] δ. For γενεθλία used in the same sense we may cite P Oxy III. 494²¹ (A.D. 156) εἰς εὐωχίαν αὐτῶν ἣν ποιήσονται πλησίον τοῦ τάφου μου κατ᾽ ἔτος τῇ γενεθλίᾳ μου, "for a feast which they shall celebrate at my tomb on my birthday every year" (Edd.), BGU I. 149¹⁵ (ii/iii A.D.) γε[νε]θλίο[ι]ς Σοκνοπαίου] θεοῦ μεγάλου μεγάλ[ου], P Oxy I. 112⁴ (iii/iv A.D.) τοῖς γενεθλίοις τοῦ θεο[ῦ. *ib.* VIII. 1144⁴ (i/ii A.D.), etc. From the inscriptions note OGIS 90¹⁶ (the Rosetta Stone – B.C. 196) ἐν ἧι τὰ γενέθλια τοῦ βασιλέως ἄγεται, *ib.* 111⁵⁹ (after B.C. 163) τὴν γενέθλιον ἡμέ[ραν τὴν Βοή]θου, and *Priene* 105¹² (c. B.C. 9) τὴν τοῦ θειοτάτου Καίσαρο[ς γ]ενέθλιον. In the last inscription, l. ⁴⁰, if the restoration can be trusted, we have the remarkable statement ἦρξεν δὲ τῶι κόσμωι τῶν δι᾽ αὐτὸν εὐανγελί[ων ἡ γενέθλιος] τοῦ θεοῦ, "but the birthday of the god [the Emperor Augustus] was for the world the beginning of tidings of joy on his account": cf. Deissmann *LAE.* p. 371.

For ἡ γενέσιος (*sc.* ἡμέρα) see OGIS 583¹³ (i/A.D.) τῆι γενεσίῳ, *Cagnat* IV. 353³·⁴·¹³ (ii/A.D.), of a monthly celebration, γενεσίῳ Σεβαστοῦ, and ἐνμήνῳ γενεσίῳ. Similarly *Michel* 544¹⁰ (B.C. 114) ἐποιήσατο δὲ καὶ γε[νεθ]λίας τοῖς τε παισὶν καὶ παιδευταῖ[ς, of a hospitable Phrygian gymnasiarch. Both these adjectives are replaced by the noun in Gen 40²⁰, where the birthday of Pharaoh is ἡμέρα γενέσεως. We find in P Cairo Preis 31²³ (A.D. 139–40) the compound, παι[δίου πρωτογενεσίοις.

γένεσις.

For γ. = "birth, nativity," as in Lk 1¹⁴, cf. *Priene* 105¹⁵ (c. B.C. 9 – see *s.v.* γενέσια) τὸ ἀπὸ τῆς ἐκείνου γενέσεως ἄρχειν τῷ βίῳ τὸν χρόνον, *Kaibel* 314²¹ οὐδ᾽ οὕτως μοι γένεσις δεινὴ πλησθεῖσ᾽ ἐκορέσθη –the sense appears to be "nativity" (astrological). Other examples are P Lond 98 *recto*⁶⁰ (a horoscope – i/ii A.D.) (= I. p. 130) ὁ [ἐκ]οδεσπότης] τῆς γενέσεως, a common phrase in nativities, and *Ostr* 1601 (a notice of birth or for a horoscope –A.D. 114) γένεσις παιδίου ἀρσενικοῦ ιζ ἔτει) Τραιανοῦ Καίσαρος τοῦ κυρίου. In the pre-Christian inscriptions of the Aegean Sea the phrase κατὰ γένεσιν is frequent in contrast to καθ᾽ υἱοθεσίαν : see e.g. *Syll* 905, and cf. Deissmann *BS* p. 239. In P Oxy I. 120⁵, a philosophic letter of iv/A.D., the word is used in the more general sense of "existence," "life"—μετρίων γὰρ καὶ δυστυχῶν γένεσιν αἴχοντες (*l.* ἔχ-) οὐδὲ οὕτω αἱαυτοῖς προσαίχομεν (*l.* ἑαυτοῖς προσέχομεν), "we fail to realize the inferiority and wretchedness to which we are born" (Edd.). Not very different is P Leid W*xlix*·¹⁰ (ii/iii A.D.) καὶ μηνεύσθω (*l.* -νέσθω) μοι τὰ τῆς γενέσεώς μου, "quae genituram meam spectant" (Ed.).

γενετή.

For ἐκ γενετῆς in Jn 9¹, see the numerous examples, with special references to blindness, in Wetstein *ad l.*, and add Philostratus *Ep.* *l.* 51 μακαρίων τῶν ἐκ γενετῆς τυφλῶν cited by Bauer *HZNT ad l.*). Vettius Valens, p. 292²⁶ ἐπὶ τῶν ἐκ γενετῆς διαστολῶν.

γένημα.

The spelling γένημα, "fruits of the earth," shown in the best MSS in Mt 26²⁹, Mk 14²⁵, etc., is now abundantly attested from the papyri, e.g. P Oxy I. 88⁷ (A.D. 179) πυροῦ γενήματος, *ib.* IV. 729³⁶ (A.D. 137) οἰνικοῦ γενήματος, *ib.* VIII. 1141⁶ (iii/A.D.), X. 1202¹⁶ (A.D. 107) *al.*, and the numerous examples in Deissmann *BS* pp. 110, 184, Mayser *Gr.* p. 214. Add from the inscriptions *CIG* 4757⁵² (Egypt, A.D. 68), 4474⁵⁹ (Syria, iii/A.D.), and OGIS 262⁹ (Syria, iii/A.D.) σὺν τοῖς τοῦ ἐνεστῶτος ἔτους γενήμασιν.

On the phrase on ostraca of the imperial period γενήματος τοῦ δεῖνος ἔτους, referring to the duty payable on the harvest of the preceding year, see Wilcken *Ostr.* i. p. 214: hence the word γενηματογραφεῖν, "confiscate by the government," see *Archiv* i. p. 148. Note also P Kyl II. 154²² (A.D. 66) γενήματα καὶ ἐπιγενήματα, "produce and surplus produce" (Edd.).

The history of this word, unknown to LS, and unsuspected except as a blunder of NT uncials, is peculiarly instructive. Against HR, who regard the totally distinct words γέννημα and γένημα as mere variants of spelling, Thackeray (*Gr.* i. p. 118) shows that γένν. (from γεννάω) is in LXX animal, and γέν. vegetable, as in NT. The hundreds of instances quotable from Egypt must not close our eyes to the apparent absence of attestation elsewhere, except in Syria, which accounts for its appearance in NT. We may however reasonably conjecture that in Polybius when γέννημα = "vegetable produce" we should drop the second ν. This is confirmed by the strictures of Phrynichus (Lobeck, p. 286): γεννήματα· πολλαχοῦ ἀκούω τὴν λέξιν τιθεμένην ἐπὶ τῶν καρπῶν. ἐγὼ δὲ οὐκ οἶδα ἀρχαίαν καὶ

δόκιμον οὖσαν. He would have them say **καρποὺς ξηροὺς
καὶ ὑγρούς**. Polybius then either used **γέννημα**, or adopted
a new meaning for **γέννημα** which was reacted upon by the
other word. In PSI III. 196[2.3], 197[2.3] (both vi/vii A.D.) we
find νν.

γεννάω.

P Fay 28[9] (A.D. 150-1) (= *Selections*, p. 82) ἀπογραφόμεθα
τὸν γεννηθέντα ἡμεῖν . . . υἱόν: the same formula in
BGU I. 111[12] (ii/A.D.). P Gen I. 10[14] (A.D. 148) μηδὲ[π]ω
μου γεννηθ[είσης]. ib. 33[11] (A.D. 156) γεννηθέντα [τ]ῷ ιϛ
[ἔτει] 'Αντω[νίνου] Καίσαρος, Syll 406[9] (A.D. 147) συνησθέντες μοι γεννηθέντος υἱοῦ (of civic congratulations sent to
Antoninus), C. and B. ii. 500 (p. 650) Λούκιος γυν[αι]κὶ
ἰδίᾳ σεμνοτάτῃ, γεννηθείσῃ ἔτους ρξα (= A.D. 77), BGU I.
132[ii] (ii/A.D.) 'Ήρων ἄλλος υἱὸς μη(τρὸς) τῆς α[ὐτῆς] γεν-
νηθείς). The confusion of forms from γίνομαι and forms
from γεννάω, which gave a start to the mixing of γέννημα and
γέννημα, produces in BGU I. 28[16] (A.D. 183) and 110[14]
(A.D. 138-9) the form γενηθέντα: see Deissmann *BS* p. 184.
With Mk 14[21] cf. OGIS 458[10] διὸ ἄν τις δικαίως ὑπολάβοι
τοῦτο ἀτῶι ἀρχὴν τοῦ βίου καὶ τῆς ζωῆς γεγονέναι, ὅ ἐστιν
πέρας καὶ ὅρος τοῦ μεταμέλεσθαι, ὅτι γεγέννηται. In MGr
γεννῶ "beget," "give birth to," and of birds "lay"
(eggs). The derivative ἐπιγέννησις, P Gen I. 33[15] (A.D. 156)
al., means a "birth subsequent to" (a census, etc.). For
the noun γέννα, whence this verb is derived, cf. P Leid
W[xv.47] (ii/iii A.D.) ὃ καλοῦσι Ὥρου γένναν, . . . ἐστιν γὰρ
γέννα κόσμου.

γέννημα.

See s.v. γένημα. So far as we have noticed, the word
with νν does not occur at all in the papyri.

γέννησις

(in Mt 1[18] LW, Lk 1[14] one or two good MSS. incl. 33)
may be quoted from P Leid W[xviii.2] (ii/iii A.D.), where a
magic hand περιέχει γέννησιν πνεύματος, πυρὸς καὶ σκότος
(s..-ους), and Syll 737[130] (ii/A.D.) σπονδὴν ἀξίαν τῆς τάξεως,
γάμων, γεννήσεως, Χοῶν, ἐφηβείας κτλ.: Dittenberger
observes that boys were brought to the Χόες festival before
their coming of age, so that the order of these last three
items is one of time.

γένος

is common in the papyri with reference to a species or
class of things. Thus P Fay 21[10] (A.D. 134) εἴτ' ἐν γένεσιν
εἴτ' ἐν ἀργυρίῳ, "whether in kind or in money," with reference to payments, ib. 90[11] (A.D. 234) χρῆσιν ἐγ γένι
λαχανοσπέρμου ἀρτάβας τρ[ε]ῖς, "a loan in kind of three
artabas of vegetable seed," P Oxy VIII. 1134[13] (A.D. 421)
περὶ ἄλλου τινὸς εἴδους ἢ γένους, "of any other sort or
kind." In P Grenf II. 44[11] (A.D. 101) the word occurs in
connexion with the transport of "goods," and in P Oxy IV.
727[19] (A.D. 154) an agent is authorized γένη διαπωλήσοντα
ἃ ἐὰν δέον ᾖ τῇ αὐτοῦ πίστει, "to sell off produce as may be
needful on his own authority": cf. ib. I. 54[16] (A.D. 201)
εἰς τειμὴν γενῶν, "for the price of materials" for the repair
of public buildings, and ib. 101[16] (A.D. 142) where γένεσι
= "crops." Similarly P Amh II. 91[15] (A.D. 159) οἷς ἐὰν

αἱρῶμαι γένεσι πλὴν κνήκου, "with any crops I choose
except cnecus" (Edd.). In P Oxy IX. 1202[20] (A.D. 217)
κατ' ἀκολουθείαν τῶν ἐτῶν καὶ τοῦ γένους, the word is
used = "parentage": cf. BGU I. 140[26] (B.C. 119) τοῖς
πρὸς [γ]ένους συνγενέσι, "to the legitimate parents." With
γένος "offspring," as in Ac 17[28], cf. IG XIV. 641 (Thurii)
καὶ γὰρ ἐγὼν ὑμῶν γένος ὄλβιον εὔχομαι εἶμεν . . . 'Όλβιε
καὶ μακαριστέ, θεὸς δ'ἔσῃ ἀντὶ βροτοῖο, and 638 γῆς παῖς
εἰμι καὶ οὐρανοῦ ἀστερόεντος, αὐτὰρ ἐμοὶ γένος οὐράνιον
(both cited by Norden *Ignostos Theos*, p. 194). Ac 4[6] has
a close parallel in P Tebt II. 291[36] (A.D. 162) ἀπ[ὸδ]είξας
σεαυτὸν γένους [ὄ]ντα ἱερατικοῦ. In OGIS 470[3] (time of
Augustus) a certain Theophron describes himself as priest
διὰ γένου τῆς 'Αναίτιδος 'Αρτέμιδος, "hereditary" priest.
In ib. 513[10] (iii/A.D.) γένους τῶν 'Επι[λ]αιδῶν, and 635[1]
(Palmyra, A.D. 178-9) οἱ ἐγ γένους Ζαββιβωλείων, it answers
to *gens*, a tribe or clan. For the common τῷ γένει in
descriptions, cf. Syll 852[2] (ii/B.C.) σῶμα ἀνδρεῖον ὧι ὄνομα
Κύπριος τὸ γένος Κύπριον. In Vettius Valens, p. 80[26], εἰς
γένος εἰσελθών is used of a manumitted slave: cf. p. 100[11].

Γερασηνός.

Cagnat IV. 374[11] (A.D. 102-5) 'Αντιοχέων τῶν [ἐπὶ τ[ῷ
Χρυσορόᾳ, τῶν πρότερο]ν Γερασηνῶν. Whether this Gerasa,
which was in Arabia, could put in a claim to be connected
distantly with the Gospel story, we do not discuss here.

γερουσία.

Bishop Hicks has shown (*CR* i. p. 436) the important
place occupied by the γερουσία in Ephesus and other Greek
cities in Roman imperial times, and consequently how the
term, and not βουλή, came to be applied to the Sanhedrin
in Ac 5[21]. In Syll 740[2] (A.D. 212) ἔδοξεν τῇ ἱερᾷ γερουσίᾳ
τοῦ Σωτῆρος ['Α]σκληπιοῦ κτλ, the editor remarks on the
singular use of the word for a private sacred college: on
ib. 882 (Cos, imperial time) τοῦ μνημείου τούτου ἡ γερουσία
κήδεται, he suggests the same connotation, and on ib. 737[132]
(ii/A.D.) he argues an application to the ἱερὰ γερουσία of
Eleusis (see his n. ff). These will suffice to show that a
γερουσία concerned, like the Sanhedrin, with *res sacrae* was
nothing unusual. The use of the word for lay senates of
various kinds is of course abundant, and does not concern us:
see *inter alia* Ramsay *C. and B.* ii. p. 438 ff., and Ferguson
Legal Terms common to the Macedonian Inscrr. and the NT
(Chicago, 1913), p. 39 ff. The two terms of Ac 5[21] appear
together in *Cagnat* IV. 836[7] (Hierapolis? ii/A.D. or after)
ἀποδώσει τῷ [σ]εμνοτάτῳ συνεδρίῳ γερουσίας δηνάρια
χείλια (for violating a tomb).

γέρων.

OGIS 470[11] (ii/A.D. *init.*) ἱερεὺς τῆς τῶν γερόντων
'Ομονοίας. BGU IV. 1141[99] (B.C. 14) εἶπεν ὁ γέρων μ[ὴ]
εἰδέναι αὐτὸν τὸ καθόλον περὶ τούτων μηδέν. P Ryl II. 77[34]
(A.D. 192) μιμοῦ τὸν πα[τ]έρα τὸν φιλότιμον τὸν [γ]έροντα
φῶτα, "imitate your father the lover of office, the brave old
man": note that γέρων here plays the part of adj. to the
poetical word φῶς—see the editors' note. CP Herm 100[7]
(fragment). The word is not very often met with, but its
continued existence in the vernacular is attested by the MGr
γέροντας (also γέρος), as well as derivatives like γερνῶ
(aor. ἐγέρασα) which show mixture with the kindred γῆρας.

γεύομαι.

For γ. with genitive, cf. the standing formula in the *libelli* of the Decian persecution (A.D. 250) τῶν ἱερῶν ἐγευσάμην, e.g. P Oxy IV. 658¹² (= *Selections*, p. 116). With the acc., as in Jn 2⁹ and in the LXX fairly often, it may be cited from *Preisigke* 1106 (Ptolemaic), where sundry officials καὶ οἱ συμπόσιον γενόμενοι join in a complimentary monument to their entertainer. See Abbott, *Joh. Gr.* p. 76 f.; and on the change of construction in Heb 6⁴ᶠ see Milligan *Documents*, p. 68. The verb is used absolutely (as in Ac 10¹⁰) in *Preisigke* 1044 (inscr. on a cup—Roman age) ἐκ τούτου ἐγευσάμην. The verbal occurs, negatived, in P Giss I. 19¹² (ii/A.D.) ἀ[γ]ευστος ἐκοιμώμην, "I was going to bed without bite or sup." The noun from a compound may be observed in a small undated fragment. CPHerm 27 προσγεύσεως τ[. . . : ἀρτοκόπῳ appears just below. MGr has γεύομαι still, = "taste," "eat."

γεωργέω.

Agriculture being the principal industry in Egypt, this word and its cognates are very common in the papyri with reference to the cultivation both of private allotments and of the crown lands, for which rent was paid in kind. A good example of the former class is afforded by the letter in which a father remonstrates with a dilatory son for his neglect of their lot of land—τὸ κτῆμα ἀγεώργητόν ἐστιν· οὐδεὶς τῶν γεωργῶν ἠθέλησεν γεωργεῖν αὐτό, "the whole land is untilled: no tenant was willing to work it" (BGU II. 530²⁰ᶠ (ii/A.D.) (= *Selections*, p. 61). For the latter we may cite P Lond 256 *recto* ²⁶ (A.D. 11-5) (= II. p. 66), an order to deliver seed-corn δημοσίοις γεωργοῖς εἰς ἥν γεωργοῦσι βασιλικὴ[ν] καὶ ἱερὰν καὶ ἑτέρ[α]ν γῆν, and the interesting P Oxy VI. 899⁸ A.D. 200 in which a woman claims on the ground of her sex to be released from the cultivation of various plots of Crown land, which, she states, as long as she had power she cultivated—ἐς ὅσον μὲν οὖν δύναμίς μοι ὑπῆρχεν ταύτας ἐγεώργουν. If an instance of the passive is wanted (for Heb 6⁷), we may cite P Giss I. 4¹⁰ (A.D. 118)—Hadrian has appointed (στήσαντος) τὴ[ν] βασιλ(ικὴν) γῆν καὶ δημοσίαν καὶ οὐσιακὴν γῆν κα[τ] ἀξίαν ἑκάστης καὶ οὐκ ἐκ τοῦ παλαιοῦ π[ρο]στάγματος γεωργεῖσθαι, *Syll* 929⁸⁹ (B.C. 139?) κατὰ χώρας γεγεωργημένης τε καὶ γεωργηθησομένης, etc.

γεώργιον.

For γ. = "cultivated fields," see P Tebt I. 72³⁷⁰ (a land survey—B.C. 114-3) καὶ παραγενομένου αὐτοῦ εἰς τὴν κώμην καὶ ἐπελθόντος ἐπὶ τὰ γεώργια εὑρεθῆναι τὸν σπόρον κακοφυῆ ὄντα καὶ τὰ γενήματα ἀθέριστα. In P Par 63⁴⁶ᶠᶠ (B.C. 165) τὴν ἐκτ[ε]νεστάτην [ποι]ήσασθαι πρόνοιαν ὅπως ἑκάστοις κατὰ δύναμιν μερ[ι]σθῆ τὰ γεώργια, Mahaffy (P Petr III. p. 23) translates, "you should take the most earnest precautions that the field labour be divided to each in accordance with his capacity": cf. P Lond 314¹²ᶠᶠ (A.D. 149) (= II. p. 189) where in a proposal for a sub-lease the lessee undertakes all that is necessary for the proper cultivation of the land—ἐπιτελέσω τὰ γεωργικὰ ἔργα π[άντ]α ὅσα καθήκει, *ib.* 354²¹ (c. B.C. 10) (= II. p. 165) διὰ δὲ τοῦτο τῶν γεωργίων ἀφανιζομένων [. . . . It should be noted that this last document is written in a very graceful literary hand, so that the word here figures in educated language. This

is interesting from the fact that γεώργιον cannot be traced with certainty in literature before Strabo: Dittenberger hesitates as to the supplement in *Syll* 160² (B.C. 323) τὴν ἀτέλει[α]ν . . . τῶν γεωργί[ων], because "reliqua huius vocis testimonia multo inferioris aetatis sunt." LS quote Theagenes (or Theogenes), who in a book on Aegina (Müller *Fragm. Hist. Graec.*, frag. 17) says the Aeginetans dumped εἰς τὰ γεώργια earth dug out of caves. Unfortunately the identity and date of this writer is very uncertain, so that he is not evidence. The abstract γεωργία is also common, e.g. P Oxy VIII. 1124¹⁶ (A.D. 20) τοῦ δ' ἐνκαταλιπεῖν τὴ[ν] γε[ω]ργία(ν) . . . ἐπίτιμον, "the penalty for abandoning the cultivation" (Ed.), P Fay 123¹⁷ (c. A.D. 100) ἤχθην ἰς γεωργίαν, "I have been pressed in as a cultivator" (Edd.), P Lond 1231⁴ (A.D. 144) (= III. p. 108) παραιτούμενοι τὴν εἰς τὸ μ[έ]λλον γεωργείαν ὧν γεωργοῦ[με]ν σὺν Ἀπολλωνίῳ . . . ἀρο[υρῶ]ν δέκα [ἐν]νέα καὶ . . ς, P Flor III. 370² (A.D. 132) ὁμολογῶ ἔσασθαί σοι κοινωνὸς κατὰ τὸ ἥμισυ μέρος γεωργίας τοῦ ἐνεστῶτος ἑπτακαιδεκάτου (ἔτους).

γεωργός.

See *s.v.* γεωργέω for one or two citations of a ubiquitous word, enough to indicate some of the Egyptian farmer's public burdens. We might add reference to a docket of papers in P Eleph, dated B.C. 223-2, relating to the insolvency of tenants who had found their task too heavy: in 15³ οἱ δ' ὑπογεγραμμένοι γεωργοὶ ἐπέδωκαν ἡμῖν (officials who make their report to a bank) ὑπόστασιν, an "undertaking" to take over these liabilities. That γεωργός was common outside Egypt may be illustrated by its appearance in *Syll* 510 (Ephesus, ii/B.C.) *cumptibus*, 531⁹ (Amorgos, iii/B.C.), 632³ (Athens, i/B.C.), 647²⁶ (Eleusis, c. B.C. 320), *OGIS* 519⁷ (Asia, c. A.D. 245). In MGr γιωργός = "peasant."

γῆ.

The rare plural forms of this word which are found in the LXX may be illustrated from the Ptolemaic papyri of ii/B.C., e.g. BGU III. 993ⁱⁱⁱ ¹⁰ (B.C. 128-7) γῶν τε καὶ οἰκιῶν, P Tor I. 1ⁱⁱ ¹⁰ (B.C. 116) ἕνεκεν τοῦ καὶ τῶν γῶν μὴ μετεσχηκέναι αὐτήν, P Tebt I. 6³¹ (B.C. 140-39) γᾶς τε καὶ ἕτερα: see Thackeray *Gr.* i. p. 143. In MGr, beside ἡ γῆ, we have the indeclinable ἡ γῆς, τῆς γῆς, etc.: see Thumb *Handbook*, p. 57. The familiar Biblical ἐπὶ γῆς appears in P Ryl II. 87³ (early iii/A.D.) ὁ αὐτὸς ὁριοδείκτης ἐπέδειξα ἐπὶ γῆς (restored from I.²), "I the said surveyor have verified it on the spot": the editors suggest that ἐπὶ γῆς should be read in P Thead 54⁹ and 55⁶. It may be observed that γῆ in papyri is regularly "land" in small or moderate quantities, a sense never found in NT, where γῆ is always antithetic to sky or sea, or denotes a district or country. The LXX and papyri, in their use which makes a plural possible, can go back to Ionic of v/B.C.: cf. *Syll* 11³ γέας καὶ οἰκίας, *ib.* 154⁴⁰ (a century later) δημόσιοι γέαι. Of course the antithesis of Οὐρανός and Γαῖα is older still, as is that illustrated by the formula κατὰ γῆν καὶ κατὰ θάλασσαν.

γῆρας.

P Magd 18⁶ (B.C. 221) ἔχω [εἰς τὸ] γῆρας τὰ ἀνάγκαια, P Lond 43³ (ii/B.C.) (= I. p. 48) ἕξεις ἐφόδιον εἰς τὸ γῆρας, a mother's optimistic assurance to her son who has just left school for a small post as teacher. P Flor III. 312⁵ (A.D. 92) ἀπολυθῆναι τῶν λειτουργιῶν χχ (? such and such) διὰ γῆρας καὶ ἀσθένιαν. *ib.* 382³⁶ (A.D. 222–3) πρὸ τοῦ γήρως, ⁶⁵ ἡ διὰ τῆς σῆς φιλα|ν̣θρωπίας ἀνάπαυσις τῷ γήρᾳ δεομένη. (The old gen. may be also quoted from a rescript of Nero, *OGIS* 475¹³ ἐπιμελεῖσθαι τοῦ σοῦ] γήρως: so Gen 44²⁹). From iv/A.D. we have P Thead 19¹² ἤδη εἰς γῆρας ἄκρον ἐληλυθ̣ῆ̣ια, and P Oxy VI. 889¹⁸, where a petitioner begs to be let off some municipal burden in view of γῆρας καὶ τὴν τοῦ σώματος ἀσθένειαν. The compound γηρυβοσκία occurs *ib.* ³⁹, and in IX. 1210⁵ (i/ii A.D.) ἐπιλελεγμένων ὑπὸ τῶν γονέων εἰς γηροβοσκίαν ἀφ᾽ ὧν ἔχουσι υἱῶν, "men chosen by the parents from their sons to support them in old age" (Edd.). For the compound εὐγηρία see *OGIS* 168⁵⁵ (B.C. 181–16): the word is defined by Aristotle *Rhet.* I 5. MGr has a derivative noun, γεράματα (plur.), with same meaning as γῆρας.

γηράσκω.

P Oxy VI. 904² (v/A.D.) ἡ τῆς ὑμετέρας δικαιοκρισ[ί]ας καθαρότης πάντως κἀμὲ ἐλεήσει τὸν γεγηρακότα, "the purity of your righteous judgement will surely pity me, an old man" (Edd.). MGr γερνῶ with aor. ἐγέρασα, the η unchanged in pronunciation, attests the verb's continuance.

γίνομαι.

The original meaning "to come into being," "be born," as in Jn 8⁵⁸, Gal 4⁴ *al*, may be illustrated by P Flor III. 382¹⁸ (A.D. 222–3) ὁ ἐξ ἐμ[οῦ] γενόμενος υἱὸς [Μ]έλας ὀνόματι,⁶¹ τοῦ μὴ ὄντος [μ]ηδὲ γενόμενο[ν μ]οι υἱοῦ. *Syll* 802⁹ (iii/B.C.) κόρον ἔτεκε, ὃς εὐ[θ]ὺς γενόμενος αὐτὸς ἀπὸ τᾶς κράνας ἐλοῦτο—this precocious cleanliness is nothing very astonishing among the egregious wonders of the Asclepieum. So P Cattaoui⁴·¹⁶ (ii/A.D.) (= *Chrest.* II. p. 422) ὁ προγενέστερος πού σοι σ[τρα]τ[ε]νομ[έ]νῳ ἐγένετο: This document contains a good instance of the use so common in NT, esp. in Ac, etc. ¹³ ἐὰν γένηταί με ἀποδημεῖν: cf. Mt 18¹³, etc. Cf. P Amh II. 135¹⁰ (early ii/A.D.) ἐὰν γένηται ἡμᾶς μὴ ὑπογίως ἀναπλεῖν, "if it should happen that we do not sail up suddenly" (Edd.). BGU III. 970¹⁵ (A.D. 174) ἐὰν γένηται μὴ εὐτονῆσαι αὐτόν: all these are mentioned in *Proleg.* p. 17. Add P Par 49²⁹ (B.C. 164–58) (= Witkowski², p. 71) γίνεται γὰρ ἐντραπῆναι. Cf. MGr γίνεται νά c. subj. = "it is possible that . . ." For γ. with dat. as in Rom 7³, cf. P Petr II. 40 (*b*)⁷ (B.C. 277) ἐς ἐπακολουθήσει τὴι ἐγχύσει τοῦ γινομένου σοι γλεύκους, "who will see to the pouring out of the must which comes to you" (Edd.). P Lond 21²⁹ (B.C. 162) (= I. p. 13) σοὶ δὲ γίνοιτο εὐημερεῖν, *Ostr* 1530 (B.C. 120) ἀπέχω παρὰ σοῦ τὸ γινόμενόν μοι, "money due to me." With Ac 22¹⁷, 2 Cor 3⁷, we may compare P Petr II. 20ⁱⁱⁱ·¹² (B.C. 252) συνέβη ἐν ἐπισχέσε[ι] γενέσθα[ι, and P Tebt II. 423¹⁴ (early iii/A.D.) ὡς εἰς ἀγωνίαν με γενέσθαι ἐν τῷ παρόντι, "so I am at present very anxious" (Edd.). P Oxy II. 283¹¹ (A.D. 45) καὶ γενόμενος ἐν τῇ Μέμφει τῇ ιε Ἰουλίᾳ [Σ]εβαστῇ τοῦ ἐνεστῶτος μηνὸς Καισαρείου, "I reached Memphis on the day Julia Augusta, the 15ᵗʰ of the present month Caesareus" (Edd.); cf. *ib.* IV. 709⁷ (*c.* A.D. 50) ἐν Μένφει γενόμενος, where the phrase must be translated in the same way (see *Archiv* iv. p. 376). Cf. P Lond 962¹ (A.D. 254 or 261)

(= III. p. 210) γενοῦ πρὸς Ἄταιν τὸν ποιμένα καὶ δέξαι παρ᾽ αὐτοῦ δραχμὰς διακοσίας, P Flor II. 180¹⁵ (A.D. 253) ἐὰν γένηται πρός σε Διόσκορος, *al.* Γίνομαι sometimes supplies an aorist f r εἰμί: ἐγενόμην is normally ingressive (= *became*), but has to serve on occasion for summary ("constative") aorist as well—cf. *Proleg.* p. 109. Thus P Flor III. 382⁶¹ (cited *ad init.*) might be translated "the son whom I neither have nor ever had," as well as "nor was ever born to me." Lk 13² is an instance of this summary use. It appears in a very common technical usage, by which γενόμενος, with the title of an official, etc., denotes "ex-"; where the title forms a verb, the aor. (less often the perf.) partic. of this is used instead. Thus "ex-gymnasiarch" is γυμνασιαρχήσας. For the periphrasis cf. P Oxy I. 38¹¹ (A.D. 49–50) (= *Selections*, p. 53) καθὰ π[α]ρῆλθον ἐπὶ τοῦ γενομένου τοῦ νομοῦ στρατηγοῦ Πασίωνος, "I accordingly brought an action before Pasion, who was ex-strategus of the nome." The idiom has wider applications, as in P Flor I. 99¹ (i/ii A.D.) (= *Selections*, p. 71) τῆς . . . γενομένης γυναικός, "his former wife." In *Cambridge Biblical Essays* ed. Swete, 1909, p. 491, this was applied to the important statement of Papias about Mark, who, "having become the interpreter of Peter, wrote," etc. (Lightfoot): we see now that we should read, "having *been*"—his connexion with Peter was past. See Milligan *Documents*, p. 270. Not quite the same are BGU II. 362ⁱⁱⁱ·²⁴ (A.D. 215) (= *Chrest.* I. p. 126) τοῦ πρὸ ἐμοῦ γε[νο]μένου ἐπιμελητ̣]οῦ, "who was epimeletes before me," and P Oxy VIII. 1119⁷ (A.D. 254) ὁ τότε γενόμενος ἀμφοδογραμματεύς, "the then amphodogrammateus" (Ed.). In P Tebt II. 315²⁹ (ii/A.D.) ἐγένετο γάρ μου φίλος is rendered "as he has become my friend" (Edd.)—aor. of immediate past: in another context it could mean "he was once my friend." For γ. used practically as a passive to ποιῶ, as in Ac 19²⁶, cf. P Ryl II. 231³ (A.D. 40) τ[οὺ]ς ἄρτους καλῶς ποιήσεις εἰπώ[ν γενέσθαι, "kindly order the loaves to be made" (Edd.). There is an extremely common use of γίνεται (generally abbreviated) to denote the total of a column of figures, which "come to" so much: see e.g. the table of abbreviations P Lond III. p. 345, near the end, with reff. Among other special usages there is the Pauline μὴ γένοιτο, common in Epictetus (cf. D. S. Sharp *Epictetus and the NT*, pp. 6, 112), e.g. i. i. 13, τί οὖν; μὴ τι μικρὰ σοι φαίνεται ταῦτα; μὴ γένοιτο. Γέγονεν standing by itself as an answer to a question ("what can you say as to . . .?") in P Strass I. 22¹·¹⁷ (iii/A.D.) looks at first rather like that which occurs in Rev 16¹⁷, 21⁶, but the reference is superficial. On the use of γέγονα aoristically, see *Proleg.* p. 145 f. Add there a typical instance from Diogenes Laert. *Proem.* § 5 παράγουσι καὶ Ὀρφέα τὸν Θρᾷκα, λέγοντες φιλόσοφον γεγονέναι, καὶ εἶναι ἀρχαιότατον, "that he *was* a philosopher, and belongs to the earliest times"; also *Preisigke* 1854, Ἄσελλος ὧδε γέγον[α. This last is one of the 162 sightseers' scribblings on the walls of the tombs of the kings at Thebes: 34 of them add to their name the verb ἱστόρησα, ἀφικόμην, ἐθαύμασα, or other aoristic expression of their feelings, and 9 more use ἥκω. When this one comes to "write him down" Asellus, his unique ὧδε γέγονα may be either compared with ἥκω (perfect) ὧδε, as in no. 1868, or made virtually aoristic like the majority. There is little difference. In *Proleg.* p. 239 a further instance of aoristic **γέγονε** is cited from *C. and B.* ii. p. 477, no. 343.

The loss of γ from the original form, here and in **γινώσκω**, is found in the Ionic from v/B.C., and in Attic inscrr. from c. 300: see Brugmann-Thumb *Gr.* p. 126. It is the only **Κοινή** form—γίνομαι is MGr—but there are a few instances of **γιγν.** in papyri due to the effort to write "correctly": see Mayser *Gr.* p. 164 f. As late as P Thead 13[k.10] (A.D. 322 —a *précis verbal* from a law case) we find **γιγνομένην**. An aorist **ἐγεινάμην** is sometimes found, as in *Ostr* 1616[6] (B.C. 140–8 or 138–7), and it is possible that this (classical) form may be responsible for the rather marked fondness for the spelling **γείνομαι** in pres.: normally we may ignore altogether the difference of ει and ι. For **γέγοναν** Rom 16[7] אAB, cf. BGU II. 597[19] (A.D. 75), *al.* See *Proleg.* p. 52, where however the illiteracy of this form is too confidently expressed. The aor. **ἐγενήθην**, to which the Atticists objected, was common in early **Κοινή**, but fell back after ii/B.C.—see Mayser *Gr.* p. 370.

γινώσκω.

For γ. followed by **ὅτι**, see P Par 47[11] (. B.C. 153) (= *Selections*, p. 22) **γίνωσ** (*l.* γίνωσκε) **ὅτι πιράσεται ὁ δραπέ[τη]ς μὴ ἀφῖναι ἡμᾶς ἐ[πὶ τ]ῶν τόπων ἰναι**, "know that the runaway will try not to allow us to remain on the spot," *ib.* 46[13] (B.C. 164–58) **γίνωσκε σαφῶς ὅτι, ἐὰν ἀναβῶ κἀγὼ προσκυνήσαι, πρός σε οὐ μ[ὴ] ἐπέλθω.** In *ib.* 32[5] (B.C. 162) **γινώσκετε . . . μὴ ἐσχολα[κέν]αι με**, we have the acc. and inf.: so *ib.* 44[1] (B.C. 153) **γίνωσκέ με πεπορεῦσθαι εἰς κτλ.** For the common epistolary phrase **γινώσκειν σε θέλω ὅτι**, see P Oxy IV. 743[27] (B.C. 2) **ὥστ' ἂν τοῦτό σε θέλω γεινώσκειν, ὅτι ἐγὼ αὐτῶι διαστολὰς δεδώκειν,** BGU III. 846[5] (ii/A.D.) **γινώσκειν σαι θέλω, ὅτι οὐχ [ἤλπ]ιζον, ὅτι ἀναβένις εἰς τὴν μητρόπολιν,** "I wish you to know that I had no hope that you would come up to the metropolis," *ib.* I. 27[1] (ii/A.D.) **γινώσκειν σε θέλω ὅτει εἰς γῆν ἐλήλυθα τῇ ϛ̅ τοῦ Ἐπεὶφ μηνός,** "I wish you to know that I arrived at land on the 6th of the month Epeiph," P Grenf II. 73[6] (late iii/A.D.), P Lond 417[5] (. A.D. 346) (= II. p. 299), P Giss I. 11[4] (A.D. 118), P Lond 973[4?] (iii/A.D.) (= III. p. 213), *al.* It will be noticed that the phrase does not come into regular use till early ii/A.D., which accounts for the NT showing a phrase (**οὐ θέλω ὑμᾶς ἀγνοεῖν** in Paul) with the same meaning but with form not yet crystallized.

On the progressive displacement of the old participial object clause after **γινώσκειν** and other verbs of "knowing," see *Proleg.* p. 229. To the instances of **γινώσκειν** with partic. add P Oxy VIII. 1118[7] (i/ii A.D.) **ὅπ]ως . . . γεινώσκωσι ἐμβαδεύσον[τά μ]ε εἰς τα ὑπ[ο]τεθειμένα καὶ καθέξον[τα κτλ.** (other future participles), "that they may know that I shall enter on the mortgaged property," etc. (Ed.).

Grimm's "Hebraistic euphemism" in Mt 1[25] is rather surprising when chronicled in the same breath with "Grk writ. fr. the Alexandrian age down": coincidence of idiom between two entirely different languages is common enough. This use is found earliest in Menander: see this and other references in B. D. Durham, *Vocabulary of Menander* (Princeton, 1913), p. 51.

Some miscellaneous uses may be noted. P Tebt II. 279 (B.C. 231), a contract for the engagement of a nurse,

ends **ἔγνωκεν Σπονησις Ὥρου Φανήσει Νεχθύριος.** The editors translate "made (?) between Sponnesis, daughter of Horus, and Phanesis, son of Nechthuris," but regard **ἔγνωκεν** as "very difficult." In the same collection, 286[5] (A.D. 23), we find a strategus, in demanding from a subordinate a supplementary report of tax-payments, writing **οὕτως γὰρ γνώσομαι πότερον ἐπὶ τόπων σε ἐάσω πράττοντά τι,** "for I shall thus know whether I shall leave you in employment where you are" (Edd.). In the passive we may quote P Oxy X. 1252 *verso*[13] (A.D. 288–95) **γνωσθέντα ὀφείλειν λοιπὸν μῆνα τῆς εὐθη νιαρχείας,** "from whom, it was ascertained, a month more of his superintendence of provision was due" (Edd.), P Giss I. 48[9] (A.D. 202–3) **ἐγνώσθη τὰ κατὰ χρόνους δοθέντα ἐπιθέματα . . . παρεγράφη:** we may suppose the writer was meaning to finish with a participle, and so did not insert **ὅτι** after **ἐγνώσθη.** The perfect passive appears in the (classical) sense "determined" in *Syll* 929[51] (B.C. 139?) **ἐγνωσμένων τῶν καθόλου πραγμάτων ὑπὸ Ῥωμαίων.**

For the forms of the verb, see *Proleg.* pp. 55, 193. The older Attic **γιγνώσκω** occurs fairly often in the new uncial W, and in Atticising documents among papyri and inscrr., as does **γίγνομαι,** cf. P Oxy VI. 932 (late ii/A.D.) **ἵνα ἐπιγνοῖς,** *ib.* VII. 1062[15] (ii A.D.) **ἵνα αὐτὴν ἀναγνοῖς νήφων καὶ σαυτοῦ καταγνοῖς,** P Giss I. 79[iii.8] (. A.D. 117) **ἵν' ἐπιγνοῖ σε σπουδάσαι,** and from new literature, P Oxy III. 413[160] (ii A.D.—a mime) **νῦν τοῦ γέροντ[ος] ἐνκρατὴς θέλω γενέσ[θαι] πρὶν τι τού[των] ἐπιγνοῖ.**

γλεῦκος.

For this NT ἅπ. εἰρ. (Ac 2[13]) cf. P Grenf II. 24[12] (B.C. 105) **οἴνου** and from an earlier date P Petr II. 40(b)[8] (B.C. 277) **ὃς ἐπακολουθήσει τῆι ἐγχύσει τοῦ γινομένου σοι γλεύκους.** "who will see to the pouring out of the must which comes to you" (Ed.). Preuschen (*HZNT ad l.*), cites in illustration of the NT passage Lucian *Philops.* 39 **ἥκω, νὴ τὸν Δία, ὥσπερ οἱ τοῦ γλεύκους πιόντες, ἐμπεφυσημένος τὴν γαστέρα, ἐμέτου δεόμενος.** A late papyrus, Preisigke 4505[22] (A.D. 606), has the combination **οἴνου γλεύκους ἀδόλου,** which occurs a few years earlier in P Flor I. 65[5].

γλυκύς.

The neuter **γλυκύ** could denote some kind of sweet wine. Thus P Oxy II. 234[ii.6] (ii/iii A.D. medical prescriptions) **λεάνας διεὶς γλυκεῖ,** "soften by diluting with raisin wine" (Edd.); cf. *ib.* VIII. 1142[15] (late iii/A.D.) **γλ]ύκιον ῥοιτικόν.** "pomegranate wine" (Ed.), and P Lond 239[13] (. A.D. 346) (= II. p. 298) **γλυκοιδίων ὀμφακηρά** (see note). BGU IV. 1118[16] (B.C. 22) and 1120[15] (B.C. 5) have **πράσον γλυκέως.** *ib.* II. 424[1] (ii/iii A.D.) **ἀλλὰ πάντοτε τὰ τῶν γονέων γλυγύτερά** (= γλυκ.) **ἐστιν.** The rest of our papyrus citations are in superlative, which is very common as a term of affection. Thus P Oxy I. 33[iii.13] (late ii/A.D.) **κλέος σοι ἐστὶν ὑπὲρ τῆς γλυκυτάτης σου πατρίδος τελευτῆσαι,** *ib.* VI. 907[3] (A.D. 276) **τέκνα μου γλυκύτατα,** *ib.* 935[22] (iii/A.D.) **ἄσπασαι πολλὰ τὸν γλυκύτατον ἀδελφὸν Ἁρποκρατίωνα,** P Giss I. 22[5] (early ii/A.D.) **εὔχομαι . . . τὴν [γλυκυ]τάτην σου ὄψιν προσκυ[νῆσαι,** and from the inscriptions OGIS 526[4] **τὴν γλυκυτάτην καὶ σεμνοτάτην σύνβιόν μου.** Ramsay

Luke, p. 374 f. refers to a Lycaonian inscription in which the application of the phrase τὸν γλυκύτατον καὶ πάντων φίλον to a bishop (ὁ μακάριος πάπας) points, he thinks, to an early Christian period when epithets were not so religious and stereotyped as later. He compares a Christian inscription of Rome (A.D. 238) in which a father describes his son who died at the age of seven as γλυκύτερον φωτὸς καὶ ζοῆς, "dearer than light and life." Γλυκύς survives in MGr, partly with change of flexion: see Thumb *Handb.* p. 70. There are also many derivatives noted in his glossary.

γλῶσσα.

Most of the occurrences of this noun, which retains both form and meaning in MGr, need no particular comment. P Oxy I. 138 (A.D. 183 or 215) *saep*, the monthly meat bill of a cook, tells us that "tongue" was a favourite article of diet: so also the numerous passages in inscrr. where in the ritual of sacrifice the victim's tongue is mentioned as a special perquisite. The word figures prominently in magical documents. P Lond 124³¹ (iv/v A.D.) (= I. p. 122) βάλλε εἰς αὐτὸ γλῶσσαν βαθράκου shows the frog's tongue playing the same part as "tongue of dog" in the witches' spell in *Macbeth*: so also *ib.* 46⁴⁹¹ (iv/A.D.) (= I. p. 74). There are many curses which "bind" the tongue of their object: thus *Syll* 808 (Corcyra) Σιλανοῦ τὸν νόον καὶ τὰν γλῶσσαν τουτεὶ καταγράφω—Silanus himself and three witnesses who enabled him to win a suit are cursed with this leaden tablet in mind and tongue. So *ib.* 800 (Piraeus, iv/iii B.C.) begins Μικίωνα ἐγὼ ἔλαβον καὶ κατέδησα τὰς χεῖρας καὶ τοὺς πόδας καὶ τὴν γλῶσσαν καὶ τὴν ψυχήν. καὶ εἴ τι μέλλειε (*l.* μέλλει—a confusion with aor. opt.) ὑπὲρ Φίλωνος ῥῆμα μοχθηρὸν φθέγγεσθαι, ἡ γλῶσσα αὐτοῦ μόλυβδος γένοιτο, καὶ κέντ[η]σον α[ὐτ]οῦ τὴν γλῶσσαν—the changes on these formulae are rung in the rest of the document. Deissmann, *LAE*, p. 306 ff., refers to thirty of Wünsch's Attic *defixiones* where the tongue is "bound" or "cursed." He shows that this was supposed to produce dumbness, and interprets Mk 7³⁵ as release from what was believed to be a daemonic "binding."

Thumb, *Gr. Dial.* p. 22, points out that grammarians used γλῶσσα not only for "language" but also for "local peculiarities of speech": thus Δωρὶς γὰρ διάλεκτος μία ὑφ' ἣν εἰσι γλῶσσαι πολλαί, "sub-dialects." This leaves us free, if we choose, to reduce very considerably the abnormality of the "tongues," which need not always have been foreign languages as in Ac 2⁴ (cf. ⁶ff.). We find it applied to a real foreign language in P Giss I. 99⁹ (B.C. 80-70) ὕμνοι μὲν ᾁ[δονται] γλώττῃ ξενικῇ: the ττ goes with ταῖν στήλαιν and other *recherché* archaisms to show that the piece is not tainted with vernacular!

The tongue of slander appears in P Lond 122³¹ (iv/A.D.) (= I. p. 117) διάσωσόν μου πάντοτε εἰς τὸν αἰῶνα ἀπὸ φαρμάκων καὶ δολίων καὶ βασκοσύνην πάσης καὶ γλωττῶν πονηρῶν—Milton's "evil tongues."

γλωσσόκομον.

This out-of-the-way-looking word proves to be decidedly vernacular, and quite in place in Jn 12⁶, 13²⁹, where it is "money-box" (cf. RV marg.): its original meaning, as "receptacle" (κομίζω) for the "tongues" or mouthpieces of flutes, had been long forgotten, and influenced it only by

stamping on it generally the sense of small size and portability. Phrynichus, who mentions γλώττας αὐλῶν (Rutherford *NP*, p. 308), defines the word thus (*ib.* p. 181) γλωττοκομεῖον· ἐπὶ μόνου τοῦ τῶν αὐλητικῶν γλωττῶν ἀγγείου. ὕστερον δὲ καὶ εἰς ἑτέραν χρῆσιν κατεσκευάζετο, βιβλίων ἢ ἱματίων ἢ ὁτουοῦν ἄλλου· καλοῦσι δ'αὐτὸ οἱ ἀμαθεῖς γλωσσόκομον. This shorter form was perhaps really shortened from the Attic compound: we think of words like ἀγάπη from ἀγάπησις, συνάντη from συνάντησις, and οἰκοδομή from οἰκοδόμημα. In any case it spread while the dialects were still in full vigour, as is proved by its occurring twice in the long Doric inscr. from Thera, Epicteta's Will, *Michel* 1001ᵛⁱⁱⁱ ²⁵,³¹ (c. B.C. 200): τὸ γλωσσόκομον καὶ τὰ ἐν αὐτῶι βυβλία are to be in charge of a γραμματοφύλαξ. From the papyri may be cited P Ryl II. 127²⁵ (A.D. 29) ἀς (*sc.* 120 drachmae) εἶχον ἐν γλοσσοκόμωι, "in a casket" (Edd.). P Grenf I. 14² (B.C. 150 or 139) γλωσσόκομα γ̄. These articles, together with two κίσται and a βῖκος ῥητίνης, etc., were deposited in a temple. Two θίβεις (LXX Exod 2³,⁵,⁶) appear in the list. Grenfell cites Hesychius θίβη· πλεκτόν τι κιβωτοειδὲς ὡς γλωσσοκομεῖον. So P Tebt II. 414²¹ (ii/A.D.) τὸ γλωσόκομον τὸ μέγα, "the big case" (Edd.), P Flor II. 107¹³ (ii/A.D.) γλωσσοκόμων in a rather broken context dealing with irrigation, "(forse le incassature degli assi da far girare (τροπάς) le macchine?)" (Ed.), P Lond 122⁵⁵ (iv/A.D.) (= I. p. 118) ποίησον . . . ἐκ τοῦ νώτου γλοσόκομον καὶ ἐπίγραφε τὸ (ὄνομα) τοῦ Ἑρμοῦ εἰς χάρτην καὶ ἐπίθι εἰς τὸ γλοσόκομον. P Leid Wxxxii.³⁰ (ii/iii A.D.) βάλε αὐτὸ (*sc.* a metal plate inscribed with ineffable words) εἰς κλοσόκομον καθαρόν, P Oxy III. 521¹² (ii/A.D.) where the word has no context to show its meaning. Add also BGU III. 824⁹ (A.D. 55-6) γλοσσοκομίου ἐπιδέδωκα Στοτοήτει, and P Lond 191¹⁴ (A.D. 103-17) (= II. p. 265) γλωσσοκομίον, where the Attic form revives: in neither of them is the nature of the vessel defined. Our instances have illustrated the descriptions of vernacular use in Phrynichus, and have disposed of "bag" as a rendering.

γναφεύς.

P Par 59¹⁰ (B.C. 160) τῷ γναφεῖ, P Oxy IV. 736³⁷ (c. A.D. 1) τὸ περίδ(ε)ιπνο(ν) Ἀθη( ) γναφέω(ς), "the funeral feast of Athe . . . the fuller" (Edd.), *ib.* III. 527³ (ii/iii A.D.) περὶ Σερήνου τοῦ γναφέως, *al.* For the verb (MGr γνάφω) cf. P Oxy X. 1346 (? ii/A.D.) ἐν τῇ(?)] πόλει γέγναπται καὶ κακῶς ἐγνάφη. On the fullers' tax, see Wilcken *Ostr.* i. p. 226 f.

γνήσιος.

The primary sense, "born in wedlock," is overshadowed by derived applications, but it survives in occasional formulae: thus even P Flor III. 294¹² (iv/A.D.) (see p. ix.) has καὶ γνησίων τέκνων σπο[ρ]ᾷ in a marriage contract. In the earliest dated Greek papyrus, P Eleph 1⁴ (B.C. 311-10) (= *Selections*, p. 2), a marriage contract begins λαμβάνει Ἡρακλείδης Δημητρίαν Κώιαν γυναῖκα γνησίαν, "as his lawful wedded wife"; cf. PSI I. 64⁴ (? i/B.C.) where a woman promises a man to live with him as long as he lives, ὡ]ς γνησ[ία] γαμετή, and P Oxy X. 1267¹⁵ (A.D. 209) τοῦ Ζωίλου γνήσιον υἱὸν Ὠρείωνα, "Zoilus' legitimate son Horion." In P Amh II. 86¹⁵ (A.D. 78) we have χωρὶς

γνησίων δημοσίων, "apart from the legal public charges":
cf. P. Oxy VII. 1031² (A.D. 228) γνη[σ]ίοις τελέσμασι,
P Lond 1157⁴ (?.A.D. 197–8) (= III. p. 62) ἐστὶ δὲ ἀριθμή-
σεως Φαῶφι εἰς Ἀθὺρ γνησ(ίων), P Strass I. 2¹³ (A.D. 217)
ἐκτὸς τῶν σιτικῶν γνησίων. From this it is an easy transition to the sense of "suitable," "fitting," as in P Giss I. 47⁴
(Hadrian) ἐπὶ τῶι κατὰ τὰς [ε]ὐχὰς γνησία καὶ λείαν ἄξια
εὑρῆσθαι and ¹⁵ παραξ[ό]νιον γὰρ πρὸς τὸ παρὸν γνήσιον
οὐχ εὑρέθη. Close to this lies its use for "genuine" as an
epithet of φίλος or the like, as in Phil 4²: so BGU I. 86¹⁹
(A.D. 155) τὸν γνήσιον αὐτοῦ φίλον. Thus it becomes an
epithet of affectionate appreciation: so P Oxy I. 48¹²
(A.D. 86) τοῦ μετηλλαχότος αὐτῆς γνησίου ἀδελφοῦ. Cf.
1 Tim. 1² Τιμοθέῳ γνησίῳ τέκνῳ ἐν πίστει: in 2 Tim 1²
ἀγαπητῷ is substituted for γνησίῳ. Cf. the use of the
adverb, as in Phil 2²⁰, = "honestly, sincerely": so P Lond
130³ (i/ii A.D.) (= I. p. 133) γ]νησίως τε περ[ὶ] τὰ οὐράνια
φιλοπονήσαντες, P Tebt II. 326¹¹ (c. A.D. 206) προ[στ]ή-
σεσθαι γνησίως τοῦ παιδίου, "will honourably protect the
child" (Edd.), BGU I. 248²¹ (ii/A.D.) τὰ ἔργα τῶν ἀμπέλων
ἰδίως γνησίως γενέσθαι. Add from the inscriptions Syll
722¹¹ (ii/B.C.) φανερὰ ἦι ἁ εὔνοια τοῖς γνησίως καὶ ἐνδόξως
τῶν καλλίστων ἐπιταδουμάτων προεστακόσι, Michel 544²³
(B.C. 114) γνησίως στοιχῶν ἐν πᾶσιν τῇ ἑαυτοῦ κα[λοκ]ἀγα-
θίαι, and for the adj. OGIS 339⁷ (Sestos, c. B.C. 120) πρὸ
πλείστου θέμενος τὸ πρὸς τὴν πατρίδα γνήσιον καὶ ἐκτενές,
which is a good illustration of 2 Cor 8⁸. Note also Michel
394¹⁵ (middle i/B.C.) γ]νησ[ί]αν ἔχοντι πρὸς πάντας
φιλοστοργίαν, and Syll 365¹³ (A.D. 37) οὐχ ὡς εἰς φίλην
μόνον ἀλλὰ καὶ ὡς εἰς γνησίαν πατρίδα. It seems from the
record that Lightfoot rather overdoes the consciousness of
the word's ultimate origin when he paraphrases (on Phil 2²⁰)
"i.e. as a birth-right, as an instinct derived from his spiritual
parentage." It is by no means clear that γνήσιος was still
felt to be normally the antithesis of νόθος, and most of its
usages are wide of this.

γνόφος.

Vettius Valens, p. 145¹⁹, ἀστασία ἀνέμων γίνεται καὶ
γνόφος. The use of ὁ γνόφος for the earlier and poetic ὁ
δνόφος begins with Aristotle.

γνώμη.

P Lond 17⁴⁷ (B.C. 162) (= I. p. 11) μετὰ τῆς τῶν εἰθι-
σμένων γνώμης. P Oxy X. 1280⁹ (iv/A.D.) ἑκουσίᾳ καὶ
αὐθαιρέτῳ γνώμῃ, "of my own free will." The phrase κατὰ
γνώμην is common in opening greetings, e.g. P Petr II.
11(1)¹ (iii/B.C.) (= Selections, p. 7) καλῶς ποιεῖς εἰ ἔρρωσαι
καὶ τὰ λοιπά σοι κατὰ γνώμην ἐστίν, "I am glad if you are
in good health, and everything else is to your mind": cf.
ib. III. 53(a)⁵, (g)³. The phrase occurs in Wisd 7¹⁵ — εἰπεῖν
κατὰ γνώμην. With Philem¹⁴ χωρὶς δὲ τῆς σῆς γνώμης,
"without your consent," cf. P Grenf II. 14(r)²⁰ (iii/B.C.)
ἄνευ τῆς σῆς γνώμης, and for similar phrases see P Tebt I.
6³⁷ (B.C. 140–39), ib. 104²⁸ (B.C. 92), P Par 62¹⁰ (ii/B.C.),
BGU IV. 1051⁹ (a marriage contract—time of Augustus),
and μετὰ γνώμης in P Oxy IV. 720⁴³ (A.D. 137). It = "consent" in P Flor I. 58⁸ (iii/A.D.), where a complainant declares he has been ousted from a holding δίχα παντὸς
νόμου καὶ δί[χα . . . .] ἐξουσίας καὶ δίχα γνώμης ἐμῆς
καὶ συνκαταθέσε[ω]ς. BGU IV. 1137¹² (B.C. 6) ἔδοξε κοινῇ

γνώμῃ = "carried unanimously." P Gen I. 54¹ (iv/A.D.)
οἴδας τὴν γνώμην μου ὅτι γν[ώ]μη ὁποία ἐστίν: for ὅτι
ὁποία Nicole compares BGU II. 601²⁰ (ii/A.D.) γράψον
μοι . . . ὅτι τί ἔπραξας. For γνώμη = "purpose, decree"
(as in 1 and 2 Esdras, Daniel, Rev 17¹⁷), see P Oxy I. 54¹²
(A.D. 201) γνώμῃ τοῦ κοινοῦ τῶν ἀρχόντων, "in accordance
with the decision of the council of the archons (Edd.),
P Fay 20⁴ (an imperial edict—iii/iv A.D.) ὧν . . . τὴν
γνώμην νῦν ἐμὴν ἐγὼ ποιοῦμαι, "whose policy I now make
my own" (Edd.), and Priene 105³¹ (B.C. 9) ἔδοξεν τοῖς ἐπὶ
τῆς Ἀσίας Ἕλλη[σι]ν, γνώμη] τοῦ ἀρχιερέως Ἀπολ-
λ]ων[ίου κτλ. In MGr γνώμη = "meaning," "opinion."

γνωρίζω.

P Oxy VII. 1024¹⁸ (A.D. 129) ὃν καὶ γνωρίεις ἰδίῳ κινδύνῳ,
"whom you are to recognize at your own risk" (Ed.). P
Hib I. 28⁶ (c. B.C. 265) ἵνα] . . . κ[αὶ] γνωρίζηται ὑπὸ τῶν
φρατόρων" (that he may) . . . be recognized by the members of the phratries" (Edd.). On P Oxy III. 496¹⁶
(A.D. 127), where the noun γνωστήρ occurs, the editors
quote BGU II. 581¹⁴ (A.D. 133), where L. Octavius Longus
γνωρίζει a person. "The γνωστήρ of a person was a witness
of his or her identity." So P Oxy VI. 976 (A.D. 197)
Παυλεῖνος . . γνωρίζω. The verb is found joined with
θαυμάζω in a letter from the Emperor Claudius to a Gymnastic Club in A.D. 47, embodied in P Lond 1178²³ (A.D.
194) (= III. p. 216) τὴν πρὸς ἐμαυτὸν μὲν εὔνοιαν περὶ
δὲ ὑμᾶς φιλανθρωπίαν ἐγνώρισα μᾶλλον ἢ ἐθαύμασα,
and in another London papyrus it has definitely the
meaning "make known," as in all its NT occurrences
even Phil 1²². P Lond 232⁶ c. A.D. 340 (= II. p. 206
γνωρίζω τῇ εὐγενίᾳ σου τὸ πρᾶγμα, P Tor I. 1⁹·¹¹ (B.C. 116)
(= Chrest. II. p. 36) φανερᾶς τῆς κρίσεως γνωρισθείσης
ἑκάστοις. The derived noun occurs in P Tebt II. 288¹⁵
(A.D. 226) μηδεμειᾶς προφάσεως ὑμεῖν ὑπολειπομένης ἐπὶ
τῆς ἀπαιτήσεως ἕνεκεν γνωρισμοῦ, "no pretext with regard
to the collection being left to you touching the identification
(of the crops)" (Edd.). For the mystical use of the verb
see Poimandres 10¹⁴ οὐ γὰρ ἀγνοεῖ τὸν ἄνθρωπον ὁ θεός,
ἀλλὰ καὶ πάνυ γνωρίζει καὶ θέλει γνωρίζεσθαι (Reitzenstein,
p. 58⁴).

For the related adjective see P Fay 12²¹ (c. B.C. 103)
ὑπὸ τῶν γνωρίμων, "by friends," and P Tebt II. 286⁹
(A.D. 121–38) Φιλωτέραν . . . ἐπὶ τῷ ἀ[ρίστῳ] ἐμοὶ
γνωρίμην, "Philotera whose good character is well known
to me" (Edd.), Syll 367¹⁰ (i/A.D.), 373² (i/A.D.).

γνῶσις.

An interesting example of this word in its more general
sense is afforded by P Lond 130¹⁹ (i/ii A.D.) (= I. p. 133),
where a horoscope is prefaced by a letter in which the writer
urges his pupil to be attentive to the laws of the art which
the ancient Egyptians had discovered and handed down—
ἀπέλειπον τὴν περὶ αὐτῶν γνῶσιν. P Hib I. 92¹² (B.C. 263)
ἕως γνώσεως περὶ τῆς δίκης is translated by the editors
"until the decision of the suit." So in P Hal I. 1² (iii B.C.)
ὅταν ἡ γνῶσις ἀναγνωσθῆι παρὰ δικαστῶν ἢ δια[ι]τητῶν
ἢ κριτῶν, and several times in the correspondence of Abinnaeus (iv/A.D.), as P Lond 234¹⁵ (c. B.C. 346) (= II. p. 287)
ἀνενεχθήσεται εἰς γνῶσιν τοῦ αὐτοῦ κυρίου μου [δο]ῦκος.
In P Oxy X. 1253²⁰ (iv A.D.), an official report of certain

military requisitions made at Oxyrhynchus by some officers, they render τῆς γνώσεως τῶν ὑφ᾽ ἑκάστου παρασχεθέντων, "the account of what was provided by each" (Edd.). In a Christian letter of iv/A.D., P Oxy VI. 939[4], the word has the additional connotation of "solicitous" knowledge, when a dependent writes to his master ὡς ἐν ἄλ]λοις πλείστοις νῦν ἔτι μᾶλλον ἡ πρὸς σὲ [τοῦ δεσπό]του θεοῦ γνῶσις ἀνεφάνη ἅπασιν ἡμῖν, "as on many other occasions so now even more plainly than ever has the regard of the Lord God for you been revealed to us all" (Edd.). Dibelius (HZNT ad l.) finds a technical meaning derived from Greek mysticism in the use of γνῶσις in Phil 3[8] διὰ τὸ ὑπερέχον τῆς γνώσεως Χριστοῦ Ἰησοῦ τοῦ κυρίου μου, and quotes the Hermetic prayer from Pap. Mimant (cited by Reitzenstein Hellenist. Mysterienreligionen p. 113 ff.), χάριν σοι οἴδαμεν, ὕψιστε· σῇ γὰρ χάριτι τοῦτο τὸ φῶς τῆς γνώσεως ἐλάβομεν . . . χαίρομεν ὅτι ἐν σώμασιν ἡμᾶς ὄντας ἀπεθέωσας τῇ σεαυτοῦ θέᾳ. Deissmann, on the other hand, thinks that there is here no reference to speculative *knowledge* of Christ, but to personal and pneumatic *acquaintance* with Christ, and illustrates this meaning of the word from a ii/A.D. decree of the Byzantines, *Latyschev* I. 47[6f.], which boasts of a citizen of Olbia that μέχρι τᾶς τῶν Σεβαστῶν γνώσεως προκό[ψ]αντος, "he had advanced to personal acquaintance with the Augusti (Augustus and Tiberius)": see *LAE*, p. 383 n.[5]. It may be added that Dieterich's conclusion, based on the use of γνῶσις in the magic papyri, that "the 'Knowledge,' which also plays so large a part in Christian teaching, is specially due to Greek influence" (*Abraxas*, p. 134) is rejected by Norden *Agnostos Theos*, p. 96 n.[3].

γνώστης.

With the use of this word in Ac 26[3] we may compare Deissmann's restoration in a papyrus letter preserved at Berlin, in which an Egyptian official calls for a procession to to be arranged for the gods—ἐπεὶ γν[ώ]στ[η]ς ἐγενόμην τοῦ εὐανγελ[ίο]υ περὶ τοῦ ἀνηγορεῦσθαι Καίσαρα (—Preisigke 421), "forasmuch as I have become aware of the tidings of joy concerning the proclaiming as Emperor" of C. Julius Verus Maximus: see *LAE*, p. 371. For γνώστης = "a surety" (Lat. *cognitor*), as in Plutarch, we may cite P Lips I. 100[10] (A.D. 98) ἐὰν οὖν ὅ γε γνώστης σὺν τῷ μετόχῳ ἀσφαλίζηταί σε κτλ. For the collateral noun γνωστήρ, which also answers to *cognitor*, see under γνωρίζω, and Wilcken's note in *Archiv* iv. p. 442, where he reads P Flor I 57[80] (A.D. 223–5) γν[ωσ]τευ[όμε]νος ὑπὸ ἀδελφοῦ Πανί σκου, and compares γνωστῆρες in BGU IV. 1032[11 ff.] The document is reprinted in P Flor III. 382. The verb γνωστεύω occurs l.[85] of the same document, and in P Hawara 69 *recto*[5] (ii/i A.D.? (in *Archiv* v. p. 383). The subst. γνωστεία in P Fay 65[4] (ii/A.D.) apparently = "authorisation," "supervision."

γνωστός.

The late P Amh II. 145[9] (v/A.D.) τὸ γνωστὸν τῆς πρὸς ἀλ[λήλο]υς συνηθείας, "the knowledge of our intimacy," may be taken as confirming, so far as it goes, the ordinary LXX and NT usage of γν. = "known" rather than "knowable"—in Rom 1[19]. For the rare use of the word as applied to persons (Lk 2[44], 23[49], Jn 18[15f.]) Abbott (*Fourfold Gospel*,

p. 362 ff.) prefers the strong rendering "familiar friend"; but see *contra* J. B. Mayor *Exp.* VIII. vii. p. 79 ff. W. M. Ramsay (*Athenaeum*, Sept. 7, 1912) cites a (iv/A.D.) inscription, Εὐδαίμων Γνωστοῦ υἱὸς τεκμορεύσας μετὰ τῶν ἰδίων θρεπτῶν Μηνὶ Ἀσκαηνῷ εὐχήν, where Gnostos "the known" might be a reminiscence of 1 Cor 8[2].

γογγύζω.

This familiar LXX and NT word is fairly attested = "murmur" in the vernacular, as in P Petr II. 9(3)[9] (B.C. 241–30) τὸ πλήρωμα γογγύζει φάμενοι ἀδικεῖσθαι, "the gang (of workmen) are murmuring, saying that they are being wronged." In the curious papyrus P Oxy I 33[iii 14] (late ii/A.D.), describing an interview between the Emperor (? Marcus Aurelius) and a rebel, a veteran present interposes with the remark, κύριε, κάθῃ, Ῥωμαῖοι γογγύζο[υσ]ι, "Lord, while you are sitting in judgement, the Romans are murmuring." The verb is MGr. Thumb. *Hellen.* p. 215, discusses this and other alleged Ionic loans to the later Attic and the Κοινή: see under γογγυσμός.

γογγυσμός.

Phrynichus (see Rutherford *NP*, p. 463) says that this noun, like its verb, was not ἀδόκιμον but Ionic: it is quoted from Anaxandrides, a poet of the New Comedy.

γόης.

In P Hib I. 52[18] (c. B.C. 245) we find Ὧρος Πνᾶτος ἱερεὺς γόητος, on which the editors remark that if γόητος is a genitive, then "we must suppose the existence of a deity called 'the Wizard'; if a nominative (of an unknown form), it is a very curious epithet to apply to a priest." A subst. γοητεία is found in Vettius Valens, p. 238[26].

Γόμορρα.

It may be noted that the words Sodoma, Gomorra were found scratched on the wall of a house in Pompeii. They can only be the work of a Jew, or a Christian, and show how fully alive he was to the nature of his surroundings. See Nestle *ZNTW* v. p. 167 f.

γόμος

is common of the cargo or freight of a ship as in Ac 21[3], e.g. P Oxy I. 63[6] (ii/iii A.D.) προνόησον σὺν πάσῃ σπουδῇ ἐνβαλέσθαι αὐτοῦ τὸν γόμον, "please to see that his freight is embarked with all despatch" (Edd), *ib.* IV. 708[3 16] (A.D. 188) τοῦ καταχθέντος γόμου, "the cargo despatched." It may also be a term of quantity, a "load," as in *Ostr* 1258 (A.D. 88) ἀπέχω παρὰ σοῦ γόμου *sc.* ·ον) ἀχύρου α, *ib.* 1010 (Roman) τὴν αὐθεντικὴν ἀποχὴν ἀχύρ[ου] γόμου ἑνός. *Ib.* 1015[1] (ii/iii A.D.) shows the plural: cf. P Fay 102 (A.D. 105), a series of farm accounts, in which we read of γόμοι and δράγμ[ατα] of wheat and barley. Another kind of merchandise figures in P Flor III. 360[48] (A.D. 130 or 140) κ(αὶ) δώσω κατ᾽ ἔτος ξύλων καθάρσεων γόμον ἕνα. An inscr. from Lower Egypt, beyond Philae, dated A.D. 214–5, *OGIS* 200[5], gives the title ἱερεὺς γόμου to a certain Apollonius Soter. Dittenberger's note cites about forty inscrr. for this title, and others where a προστάτης τοῦ γόμου accompanies this priest. He observes that, since γόμος always means a ship's load, these inscriptions must refer to the *navis onerariae*: οἱ ἀπὸ τοῦ γόμου is in several inscrr. a term for the whole of this service. In these the special ref. is to the boats carrying stone from the quarries.

The verb γομόω is mentioned above under γεμίζω: for some instances see P Flor II. 129[5] (A.D. 256) ὅπως γομώσῃ τὰ ξύλα, P Oxy VI. 938[6] (iii/iv A.D.), and P Giss I. 51[11] (iv/v A.D.) πλοῖα παρῆλθαν (*l.* -εν) γομώμενα.

γονεύς.

The following examples from the Oxyrhynchus papyri may serve to illustrate this common word— I. 75[31] (A.D. 129) Διωγενίδαν . . . τετελευτηκέναι ἄτεκνον περιόντων τῶν γονέων, "that D. has died childless in her parents' lifetime," III. 478[11] (A.D. 132) ἐξ ἀμφοτέρων γονέων, VIII. 1121[11] (A.D. 295) οἰκ ἐπαυσάμην τὰ πρέποντα γείνεσθαι ὑπὸ τέκνων γονεῦσι ἀναπληροῦσα, "I was assiduous in performing what is owing from children to parents" (Edd.). From a much earlier period P Eleph 23[12] (B.C. 223–2) will serve as example, θεοὺς Ἀδελφοὺς καὶ θεοὺς Σωτῆρας τοὺς τούτων γονεῖς. The word in the Κοινή is plural only, as predominantly in class. Grk. So with the MGr γονιοί "parents," but there is a γονιός "father," which was perhaps derived from the plural.

γόνυ

is very common in the descriptions attached to persons in official documents, as when in a census return of A.D. 48, P Oxy II. 255[9] (= *Selections* p. 49) a certain Thermoutharion is described as μέση μελίχρως μακροπρόσωπος οὐλὴ(ι) γόνα(τι) δεξι(ῷ) . . . "of medium height, olive-complexioned, long-faced, a scar on the right knee." Cf. P Oxy I. 99[2] (A.D. 55), P Fay 30[22] (A.D. 173?), 28, 68[6] (A.D. 129). For the diminutive see P Oxy I. 52[17] (A.D. 325) δεξιοῦ γονατίου—there is of course no more diminutive force attaching than in ὠτάριον (*s.v.*). MGr ποδάριν, etc. From inscrr. may be noted the phrase μέχρι γονάτων for snow "knee-deep," OGIS 199[9], a monument transcribed in Nubia by the traveller Cosmas (vi A.D.).

γράμμα.

In view of Jn 7[15] it must be remarked that there are hundreds of papyri where someone states that he writes on behalf of the person concerned, who is illiterate: this is most often γράμματα μὴ εἰδότος (εἰδυίης), but also (frequently) ἀγραμμάτου ὄντος (οὔσης). For examples see *s.v.* ἀγράμματος, and add the inscription of the Imperial period *Syll.* 844[6] κελεύουσαν ὑπὲρ αὐ(τὰν) γράψαι, ἐπεὶ ἔλεγεν αὐτὰ γράμματα μὴ εἰδέναι. See Dittenberger's note: he can only quote one parallel from inscrr. With this goes such a phrase as P Tebt II. 316[16] (A.D. 99) τέχνῃ δὲ ὑμῶν (*l.* ἡμ.) γράμματα "we are scribes by profession" (Edd.), and that of P Flor III. 382[59] (A.D. 222–3) μανθ(άνων) γράμμ(ατα), of a child. The exceeding commonness of this phraseology, which never means anything than inability to write, forces us to recognize it in Jn 7[15] and Ac 4[13]. With the biting scorn of the superior person, these learned fools affect to regard Jesus and His disciples as "illiterates."

Under the same heading, with γράμματα = characters formed in writing, comes P Hib I. 29[9] (*c.* B.C. 265), where a notice is to be put on a board μ[ε]γάλοις γράμμασιν. This

may illustrate emphasizes (?) . . . . use of the πηλίκοις γράμμασιν of Gal 6[11]. It is possible, however, that the words may only call attention to the big sprawling letters of the autograph in contrast to the neat scribe's hand of the amanuensis. The contrast may be met in the case of many signatures of legal and other documents, e.g. Rainer Pap. 215 in *Zeitschr. durch die Ausstellung* Taf. 61: see Milligan *Thess.* . . . p. 24, for a discussion of the bearing of this on Gal *l.c.* (so Deissmann *St Paul* p. 51). But it is highly precarious to draw the inference to which Deissmann inclines, namely that . . . are not the only people who may write a big and clumsy hand.

When γράμμα becomes collective, its plural meaning is "a letter," just as Lat. *litterae* produced *lettre*. Thus P Grenf I. 30[5] (B.C. 103) = Witkowski[2] p. 107 διὰ γραμμάτων ἐκρίναμεν σημῆναι, and P Amh II. 145[10] (iv/v) καὶ τούτω . . . τοίτων χάριν ἀπέστιλα Σαᾶν πρὸς σὲ ὅπως μὴ ἐνετρενθῇ τὰ γράμματα "I chose to send Saas to you . . . in order that my letter may not be mislaid" (Edd.). But it may be a paper or document of any kind. Thus it is "bond" in Lk 16[6], with which cf. P Tebt II. 397[17] (A.D. 198) ἀπὸ μηδενὸς ὁρμωμένη δικαίου ἢ γράμματος ἢ ἑτέρου τινὸς συμβολαίου ἐγγράπτου μηδ' ἀγράφου, "on the basis of any claim, bond or other agreement, written or unwritten" (Edd.), P Flor II. 145[3] (A.D. 264) λαμβάνων παρ' αὐτοῦ γράμματα τῆς παραλήμψεως, . . . 226[6] (iii/iv A.D.) καλῶς ποιήσις πέμψας μοι αὐτῶν γράμματα.

With ἱερὰ γράμματα as the name for the OT Scriptures in Greek-speaking Judaism, cf. OGIS 56[70] (B.C. 239) τῇ ἡμέραι ἐν ἧι ἐπιτέλλει τὸ ἄστρον τὸ τῆς Ἴσιος, ἣ νομίζεται διὰ τῶν ἱερῶν γραμμάτων νέον ἔτος εἶναι. Deissmann *BS*, p. 313 has drawn attention to the technical use of the phrase in the LXX and Imperial letters and papyri, e.g. Sb 415 (A.D. 204), which is headed ἱερὰ γράμματα; so P Oxy I. 418[92] (A.D. 238), where certain Imperial orders are described as τὰ θεῖά σου γράμματα. The combination is used in a different sense in OGIS 56[74] ἱεροῖς γράμμασιν καὶ Αἰγυπτίοις, where "hieroglyphs" are intended, as in I. 90[54] (B.C. 196—the Rosetta Stone). This is comparable rather with P Flor I. 43[3] (A.D. 370?) = P Lips 48, where a mother congratulates her son on having learned Αἰγύπτια γράμματα, so as to be qualified to teach Egyptian children. Reference may be added here to the part which the letters of the alphabet played in divination, as in the magical formula P Oxy VI. 886[6] (iii A.D.) = *Selections* p. 112, ὁ δὲ τρόπος ἐστὶν τὰ περὶ τὰ γράμματα κθ δι' ὧν ὁ Ἑρμῆς κὲ ἡ Ἴσις ζητοῦσα ἑαυτῆς τὸν ἀδελφὸν κὲ ἄνδρα Ὄσρεαν "the method is as concerns the 29 letters, which were used by Hermes and by Isis, when she was seeking for her brother and husband Osiris." See further Reitzenstein *Poimandres*, pp. 290, 288 ff.

There only remains to notice the use of γράμμα as a "district" or "quarter" of a town, as when in P Rein 49[2] (A.D. 215–6) certain liturgies are assigned πρὸς τῇ κατ' οἰκίαν ἀπογραφῇ τοῦ β ῆτα γράμματος of Antinoe. Cf. Aristophanes *Eccl.* 683 εἰδὼς ὁ λαχὼν ἀπίῃ χαίρων ἐν ὁποίῳ γράμματι δειπνεῖ, the courts are distinguished by letters A K.

γραμματεύς.

In the LXX γραμματεῖς first occur in connexion with the Egyptian ἐργοδιῶκται, and are rendered "officers" (Ex 5[6],

AV, RV): cf. Deut 20[5], where the word again denotes subordinate military officials, presumably those who kept the register of the army (Driver *ad l.*). Deissmann (*BS*, p. 110 ff.) has shown how readily this technical usage of the word would be adopted by the Alexandrian translators in view of the practice of Egyptian Greek. Thus in P Par 63[15] (B.C. 165) we hear of a certain Eumelus τοῦ γραμματέως τῶν μαχίμων, "the registrar of the μάχιμοι" (Mahaffy, P Petr III. p. 31), and in P Lond 23[95] (= I. p. 41) of a γραμματέα τῶν δ[υ]νάμεων. See also *Archiv* iv. p. 33 f. for the office of γραμματεύς τῶν κατοίκων ἱππέων. The word is very common to denote the official who had to supply returns to the central authority on the number of inhabitants in a village, on their holdings in land, etc. In *Syll* 790[21] (i/B.C.) τὸν γραμματέα τοῦ θεοῦ καὶ τὸν προφήτην we have an example of the word used with reference to a religious office : cf. lines 32, 46, and *Magn* 197[11] (time of Caracalla) οἱ ἀρχιερεῖς καὶ γρ[αμ]ματεῖς ἀνέστησαν (see Nageli, p. 35). In P Petr III. 59 (*b*) we have a census for poll-tax, where in some community numbering 2108 males there are exempted 62 ἱερεῖς and 10 ἱερογραμματεῖς. It is unnecessary to illustrate the large and varied use of γρ. to denote public officials, and especially town clerks : e.g. P Lond 1159[1] (A.D. 145–7) (= III. p. 112) παρὰ γραμματέων Πόλεως (*sc.* Hermopolis) αἰτούμενοι ὑπὸ σοῦ—these officials proceed to furnish a return of well-to-do citizens on the "liturgy" list. The importance of the office at Ephesus, to which Ac 19[35] points, is now abundantly confirmed by the inscrr. : cf. e.g. OGIS 493[11] (Ephesus — ii/A.D.) Λούκιος . . . ἀποδε[δει]γμένος γραμματεύ[ς τοῦ] δήμου, also [28,31], and for a similar use of the verb *ib.* 480[11] (A.D. 104), 510[11] (A.D. 138–61) γραμματεύοντος Ποπλίου Οὐηδίου Ἀντ(ω)νείνου ἀσιάρχου : see further Hicks *Greek Inscr. in the Brit. Museum* iii. p. 154, Ramsay *St Paul*, pp. 281, 305, and art. "Ephesus" in Hastings' *D.B.* i. p. 723. It may be added that the word had as large a range as our "clerk" or "secretary." Thus P Giss I. 45[1] (Hadrian's reign) εἰ δοκ[ε]ῖ, πέμψον ἐνθάδε ἢ τὸν [κω]μογραμματέα ἢ γραμματέα [αὐ]το[ῦ], "the clerk of the village council, or his clerk" : BGU IV. 1090[3] (i/ii A.D.) ἐπεὶ Σαραπίων[α] ἔσχον γραμματέα, ὃν πρότερον εἶχον, ὑπὲρ οὗ [κ]αὶ ἄλλοτέ σοι ἔγραψα, "an official writes to a subordinate to hand over papers to his newly engaged secretary, whom he had employed previously, and not to have dealings with his successor. A new astrological fragment, in PSI III. 158[67] (?iii/A.D.), tells us that there are secretaries and secretaries, the planets differentiating them—ἐὰν δὲ ὁ τοῦ Κρόνου συνπροσγένηται τῷ τοῦ Ἑρμοῦ, αὐτὸς [μ]ὲν ὁ τοῦ Κρόνου προάγων ποιεῖ γραμματεῖς αὐστηροὺς [καὶ] δικογράφους ἢ δικολόγους ἤτοι τούτων παραπλ[η]σίους[. ἐ]ὰν δὲ ὁ τοῦ Ἑρμοῦ αὐτὸς προάγῃ τοῦ Κρόνου, γ[ω]χελεῖς δυσπράξου[ς ά]τυχεῖς ἐν τοῖς πράγμασι. Another configuration (l. [53]) γραμματεῖς μεγά[λ]ους ποιεῖ καὶ κριτηρίων ἄρχοντας.

γραπτός.

In P Oxy II. 292[8] (a letter of commendation—*c.* A.D. 25) (= *Selections*, p. 37) ἠρώτησα δὲ καὶ Ἑρμί[α]ν τὸν ἀδελφὸν διὰ γραπτοῦ ἀνηγεῖ[σθαί] σοι περὶ τούτου, διὰ γραπτοῦ is clearly "in writing" as distinguished from "by word of mouth ;" and that the same meaning is to be given to the phrase in P Oxy II. 293[5] (A.D. 27) οὔτε διὰ γραπτοῦ οὔτε

διὰ σημέου (*l.* σημείου), "neither by letter nor by message" (Edd.), is convincingly shown by Wilcken (*Archiv* iv. p. 259 f.) as against Preisigke's contention that the contrast there is between ordinary and stenographic writing (*Arch. f. Stenographie* NF. I. p. 305 ff.). See also Aristeas 56 ὅσα δ'ἂν ἢ ἄγραφα . . . ὅσα δὲ διὰ γραπτῶν. For the word cf. further P Petr III. 21 (g)[38] (time of Energetes I.) γραπτὸν λόγον, and P Amh II. 78[17] (A.D. 184) ἀσφάλιαν γρ[α]πτήν, "written security." We often find the compound ἔγγραπτος used as antithesis to ἄγραφος. In MGr τὸ γραφτό, like τὸ γραμμένο, makes a phrase for "destiny." That the word included "drawing" is shown by the combination εἰκὼν γραπτή, as in OGIS 571[5] (Lycia—Roman) εἰκόνι γραπτῇ ἐπιχρύσῳ, where Dittenberger gives numerous parallels, and refers it to a gilded shell with a painting of the receiver upon it.

γραφή.

P Hib I. 78[18] (B.C. 244–3) γράψω (*i.e.* -ομ, for -ον) μοι καὶ ὅπως [ἀπο]λήμψει τὴν γραφὴν παρὰ Δωρίωνος ἄνευ ἐμοῦ, "write to me and get the document from Dorion without me" (Edd.), P Amh II. 43[13] (B.C. 173) ἡ πρᾶξις . . . κατὰ τὴν γραφήν, "the right of execution in accordance with the contract," show this word already beginning to have a quasi-official sense. It is common = "list," "register," as in one view of P Lond 911[1] (A.D. 149) (= III. p. 126, *Selections*, p. 80) ἀντίγραφον γραφῆς ἀπόρων : here however see above, *s.v.* ἀπορέω. Other examples are P Tebt I. 88[2] (B.C. 115–4) γραφὴν ἱερῶν καὶ πρ[οφ]ητῶν καὶ ἡμερῶν τῶν ὑπαρχόντων περὶ τὴν κώμην—the edd. wish to add καὶ after ἡμερῶν. Similarly *ib.* II. 298[ⁱⁱ] (A.D. 107–8) γραφῆι ἱερέων, "a return of priests," P Oxy IX. 1189[9] (*c.* A.D. 117) περὶ γραφῆς τῶν τοῖς ['Ι]ουδαίοις ὑπαρξάντων, "a list of property which belonged to the Jews," P Amh II. 124[1] (iii/A.D.) γραφὴ τῶν . . . παλαιστροφυλάκων, "a list of guards of the palaestra," and from the inscriptions OGIS 179[21] (B.C. 95) τὴν κατακειμένην ὑπὸ τοῦ Ἀνικήτου ἐν τῶι ἱερῶι γραφὴν τοῦ κατ' ἄνδρα. In the early OGIS 8[125] (iv/B.C.) ταῖς γράφαις εἰσ[κομίζοισ]ι εἰς τὰν ἐκκλησίαν, Dittenberger understands γραφή = "accusatio," according to the meaning common in Athenian law.

Γραφή is found with reference to Holy Scripture in Aristeas 155, 168. With the NT formulas in Jas 2[8], 1 Cor 15[3 f.], cf. BGU I. 136[10] (A.D. 135) κατὰ γραφάς with reference to the laws. A technical use of γραφή in scholiasts illustrates the Biblical sense : see T. W. Allen's quotations in *CQ* ii. p. 216 f., as οὕτως ἔν τισιν Ἡρωδιανός· ἡ δὲ γραφή "τόνδε τέ μ'ἄνδρα," "so Herodian in some places, but the traditional text reads τόνδε κτλ." In MGr γραφή = "writing, a letter."

γραφικός.

For γραφικός (as 3 Macc 4[21]) cf. P Grenf II. 38[7] (middle i/B.C.) κα]λαμῶν γραφικῶν.

γράφω.

Deissmann (*BS*, pp. 112 ff. 249 f.) has shown the widespread juristic use in the papyri of the "biblical" γέγραπται with reference to the regulative and authoritative character

of the document referred to, e.g. P Par 13[16] (probably B.C.
157) ἐὰν δὲ μὴ ποήσῃ καθότι γέγραπται, ἀποτίνειν αὐτὸν
τὴν φέρνην παραχρῆμα σὺν τῇ ἡμιολίᾳ, in connexion with
a marriage contract, P Leid O[19] (B.C. 89) ἐὰν δὲ μ[ὴ ἀποδῷ
καθ[ότι] γέγραπται, ἀποτεισάτω Πετειμούθης κτλ. To the
examples from the inscriptions we may add *Priene* 105[83]
(c. B.C. 9) ὡς καὶ ἐν τῷ Κορνηλίωι νόμωι γέγραπται, and 12[12]
(soon after B.C. 300) κατὰ τὰ γεγραμμένα of a preceding
decree (cf. 2 Cor 4[13]) : see Rouffiac, p. 49 f.

For the authenticating autographic signatures to the
Pauline letters, as 2 Th 3[17] ὁ ἀσπασμὸς τῇ ἐμῇ χειρὶ Παύλου,
ὅ ἐστιν σημεῖον ἐν πάσῃ ἐπιστολῇ· οὕτως γράφω, see Deissmann *LAE*, p. 153, Milligan *Documents*, p. 24 f., and H.
Erman in *Mélanges Nicole*, p. 130 ff. The perf. γεγράφηκα
occurs in P Hib I. 78[2] (B.C. 244–2), BGU IV. 1205[10] (B.C.
28), both in participle : γέγραφα is exceedingly common.
MGr shows the traces of both passive aorists (ἐγράφτηκα
and ἐγράφηκα). Abbott (*Songs*, p. 200) cites a modern
proverb ὅτι γράφει δὲν ξεγράφει, "what is written cannot
be unwritten" : cf. Jn 19[22].

γρηγορέω.

This new present (Aristotle down), evolved out of the
perf. ἐγρήγορα, is strongly condemned in Lob. *Phryn.*
p. 118 f., cf. Rutherford *NP*, p. 200 f. It is frequent in the
NT and is found in some, mainly late, books of the LXX
(Thackeray *Gr.* i. p. 263). From it was formed the new
verbal noun γρηγόρησις Dan TH. 5[11, 14] : cf. also the proper
name Γρηγόριος. In MGr we have the adv. γλήγορα
(γρήγορα), "quickly."

γυμνάζω.

The metaphorical use of this word, as in 1 Tim 4[7], may
be illustrated from the popular philosophy of the day—
Epict. i. 26. 3 πρῶτον οὖν ἐπὶ τῆς θεωρίας γυμνάζουσιν
ἡμᾶς οἱ φιλόσοφοι, ii. 18. 27 οὗτός ἐστιν ὁ ταῖς ἀληθείαις
ἀσκητὴς ὁ πρὸς τὰς τοιαύτας φαντασίας γυμνάζων ἑαυτόν.
In PSI I. 93[6] (iii/A.D.) πολλὰ συνεγυμνάσθην πρὸς αὐτούς
is presumably, "I had a good bout with" certain ἐπίτροποι. So BGU II. 615[25] (ii/A.D.) συ[ν]γυμνάσθητι ἐ[μ]πί-
ροις, τί δι᾽ ἡμᾶς πράξε. For the literal sense cf. *Syll* 804[8]
(ii/A.D.) δρόμῳ γυμνάζεσθαι, etc. *Ib.* 523[28] (iii/B.C.) ὅπως δὲ
ἐπιμελῶς ἐν τοῖς μαθήμασιν γυμνάζωνται οἵ τε παῖδες καὶ οἱ
ἔφηβοι, τὸν παιδονόμον καὶ τὸν γυμνασίαρχον ἐπιμελεῖσθαι
—τὰ μουσικὰ μανθάνειν has occurred just before—shows the
beginnings of its extension. P Flor III. 338[4] (iii/A.D.) εὐσεβὲς τὸ πρᾶγμα ποιεῖς, ἐὰν ποιήσῃς τὸ βιβλίδιον ἐκεῖνο ὡς
ἐγύμνασα αὐτὸ σύν σοι ἐν τῇ πόλει—the "practising" of
this petition by the two anxious ἀδελφοί is suggestive. The
verb is unchanged in MGr, and still = "practise."

γυμνασία.

Syll 686[19] (Trajan's reign, or early in Hadrian's) τάς τε
γυμνασίας ἐν ὄψει τῶν ἑλληνοδικῶν κατὰ τὸ πάτριον τῶν
ἀγώνων ἔθος ἀπέδωκεν ἐπιμελῶς. There seems no very
special reason why this normal meaning should not be
recognised in 1 Tim 4[8] : the exercises of the games, which
are of service, but only to a limited degree, are contrasted in
Pauline style with the spiritual training which "has promise
of life, here and hereafter."

γυμνός.

The familiar sense of γυμνός = "with only the χιτών"
comes out well in P Magd 6[?] (iii/B.C.) ὡς ἤμην γυμνὸς ὑπ᾽
αὐ[τῶν : the complainant had been stripped of his ἱμάτιον.
On the other hand, the literal sense of "naked" is required
in P Fay 12[20] (c. B.C. 103). Here the complainant reports
a similar robbery of a ἱμάτιον, which he ultimately got back
from the pawnbroker for 2700 drachmae of copper (= 45
silver dr., say 33 s.). The thieves went off with it ἐξέντες
γυμνόν. He meanwhile got away μετ᾽ ἐνδύματος supplied
by his friends (ὑπὸ τῶν γνωρίμων), which at least implies
that he could not have done without the ἔνδυμα. (Note the
substitution of this more general word, that used of the
Wedding Garment in the parable (Mt 22[11f]), where also
it is a ἱμάτιον.) It may be noted that both our citations
illustrate Luke's form of the Logion (6[29]), in which the
assailant snatches the outer garment ; the climax in Mt 5[40]
gets a little emphasis from the high price which our papyrus
shows a ἱμάτιον could fetch. But we are not deterred by
Harnack from pleading out of these documents for the
originality of Luke, whose version obviously describes a common form of robbery. The Matthaean form may possibly
be assimilated to the OT language about taking a man's
garment as a pledge. Another instance where γ. may well
have its literal force is afforded by the well-known letter of
the prodigal son to his mother, BGU III. 846[9] (ii/A.D.)
(= *Selections*, p. 94) αἴγραψά σοι ὅτι γυμνός εἰμει, "I
wrote you that I hadn't any clothes." Cf. for the verb
P Oxy VI. 903[7] (iv/A.D.), where a woman accuses her
husband of applying fire to her daughters—γυμνώσας
αὐ[τὰ]ς παντελῶς, "having stripped them quite naked" :
and for the compound, P Magd 24[7] (B.C. 217) ὥστε καὶ
ἀπογυμνωθῆναί μου τὸ στῆθος, as the result of a certain
woman's ἐπισπασαμένη τῆς ἀ[ναβολῆς τοῦ ἱματίου] according to Wilcken's restoration (*Archiv* vi. p. 274). The verb
is used metaphorically in a difficult papyrus letter printed
from *Mélanges Chatelain* in Preisigke 4317 (c. A.D. 200) :
l. [25] (best taken as beginning a sentence) has γεγύμνωμαι
καὶ ὕβρισμαι (-μαι repeated) παρὰ πάντων τῶν συνπολιτῶν.
The adj. is MGr, and has the corresponding verb γυμνώνω.

γυναικάριον.

For this NT ἅπ. εἰρ. (Vg. *mulierculas*) Sir W. M. Ramsay
(in a letter of Dec. 12, 1910) suggests the analogy of Cicero's
barbatuli juvenes (*ad. Att.* i. 14. 5, and 16. 10), young swells
with neatly and fashionably trimmed beards. The γυναι-
κάρια of 2 Tim 3[8] would then be society ladies, borne by
caprices in various directions and full of idle curiosity. The
word is found in Epictetus iv. 1. 86 τῶν καλῶν γυναικαρίων,
cf. ii. 18. 18, etc. Grimm quotes Diocles, a comedian of
v/B.C.

γυναικεῖος.

An apt parallel to the use of this word in 1 Pet 3[7] is
afforded by P Oxy II. 261[12] (A.D. 55) where a woman
appoints her grandson to act as her representative in a
lawsuit—οὐ δυναμένη προσκαρτερῆσαι τῷ κριτηρίῳ διὰ
γυναικείαν ἀσθένειαν, "since she is unable owing to womanly
weakness to remain at the court" (Edd.). See also P Petr
I. 12[8] (B.C. 238) as completed II. Introd. p. 12 χιτῶνος
ἐρέου γυναικείου, "a woman's woollen *chiton*." PSI I. 64[19]

(?i/B.C.) in which a woman comes under a solemn promise to a man . . . οὐθενὶ ἄλλωι [ἀ]νθρώπων σ[υ]νέσεσθαι κατὰ γυναικεῖον τρόπον πλὴ[ν] σοῦ, P Lond 191⁷ (A.D. 103-17) (= II. p. 264) δίφρος χαλκοῦς γυναικεῖος, P Oxy III. 493¹⁸ (early ii/A.D.) γυνικεῖον (l. γυναικ) κόσμον, P Hamb 1. 10²¹ (ii/A.D.) γυναικείας συνθέσις, "ladies' evening dresses," to which robbers had helped themselves, together with ten πλατύσημο[ι γ]υναικεῖα[ι, "lati clavi." The word is naturally quite common.

γυνή.

This old noun retains from Homer down to MGr—where it has only changed its declension (ἡ γυναῖκα)—the two meanings of "woman" and "wife": it is superfluous to illustrate the one or the other, as we should get no light on the only questions that arise in NT, such as which word to use in rendering Mt 5²⁸. The meeting of two words characteristic of that passage does, however, make it worth while to quote Wunsch AF 5⁴⁵ (iii/A.D.), where Domitiana prays that her lover may be wholly devoted to her, μηδεμίαν ἄλλην γυναῖκα μήτε παρθένον ἐπιθυμοῦντα. That γυναῖκα = "married woman" in Mt l.c. is anyhow probable. The phrase of Mk 12¹⁹ f etc., may be paralleled in the oldest extant Greek papyrus, P Eleph 1³ (B.C. 311) (= Selections, p. 2) λαμβάνει Ἡρακλείδης Δημητρίαν Κώιαν γυναῖκα γνησίαν παρὰ τοῦ πατρός κτλ.

The irregularity of the word's flexion naturally produced some levelling. In general, as MGr shows, the single nom. sing. yielded to the oblique cases ; but sometimes we find the reverse. Thus in Cagnat IV. 833 (Hierapolis. ii/A.D. or later) Αὐρ. Ἀζείου (οὐ)αιτρανοῦ καὶ τῆς γυνῆς αὐτοῦ Σεραπίας.

γωνία.

P Oxy II. 243²¹ (A.D. 79) ἀπὸ τῆς βορινῆ[ς γω]νίας τοῦ προπυλῶνος, "from the northern angle of the gateway," P Lond 122⁸ (magic, iv/A.D.) (= I. p. 116) ἐν ταῖ δ γωνίαις τοῦ οὐρανοῦ (cf. Rev 7¹, 20⁸). P Ryl II. 130⁹ (A.D. 31) εἰς τὸν ὑπάρχοντά μοι περὶ Εὐημερείαν τῆς Θεμίστο(υ) μερίδος ἐλαιῶνα ἐν τῇ γωνίᾳ. "in the area of Euhemeria in the division of Themistes at the corner" (Edd.). Ib. 150¹³ (i/A.D.) ἀπὸ τῆς λιβικῆς γωνίας τοῦ πύργου. The noun was naturally used in architectural documents, like Syll 537 (iv/B.C.) ter. Schlageter, p. 12, gives instances of the adj. γωνιαῖος, "angularis," from the inscriptions, remarking that it seems to be used principally in the Κοινή. In MGr γωνιά = "corner," "angle."

δαιμονίζομαι—δακρύω

δαιμονίζομαι

in its NT sense of being possessed with demons seems to occur only in later Greek. For a form δαιμονιάζω, otherwise unknown, see the Paris Great Magical Papyrus, Leaf 33[007] (c. A.D. 300) πρὸς δαιμονιαζομένους Πιβήχεως δόκιμον, "for those possessed by demons, an approved charm by Pibechis" (cited by Deissmann *LAE*, p. 251). The normal form occurs in P Leid W[xii.30] (ii/iii A.D.) ἐν (*l.* ἐὰν) δαιμονιζομέν(ῳ) εἴπῃς τὸ ὄνομα, προσάγων τῇ ῥεινὶ αὐτοῦ θεῖον καὶ ἄσφαλτον, εὐθέως λαλήσει (*sc.* τὸ δαιμόνιον) κ(αὶ) ἀπελεύσεται. In MGr the act. δαιμονίζω appears, = "drive mad": cf. Abbott *Songs*, p. 224 (no. 47). The derived noun δαιμονισμός occurs in Vettius Valens, p. 2[18].

δαιμόνιον.

The old adj. may be seen in *OGIS* 383[175] (i/B.C.) where Antiochus of Commagene dedicates temple slaves κατὰ δαιμόνιον βούλησιν.

Syll 924[14] (B.C. 210–5) τὰς εἰς τὸ δαιμόνιον εὐσεβείας, and similarly 279[15] (c. B.C. 193) τῆς συναντωμένης ἡμεῖν εὐμενίας διὰ ταῦτα παρὰ τοῦ δαιμονίου (following τῆς πρὸς τοὺς θεοὺς εὐσεβείας, and succeeded by τὴν ἡμετέραν εἰς τὸ θεῖον προτιμίαν) are witnesses to the growing sense in later Hellas of the unity of the Divine. Paul's solitary τὸ θεῖον in Ac 17[29] is the only NT passage which recalls this impersonal conception. The "Septuagint Memorial" from Hadrumetum of iii/A.D., published by Deissmann *BS*, p. 271 ff., opens with an adjuration to the demonic spirit of the tomb on which the spell was laid: ὁρκίζω σε, δαιμόνιον πνεῦμα τὸ ἐνθάδε κείμενον, τῷ ὀνόματι τῷ ἁγίῳ Αωθ κτλ., where the editor refers to the belief of post-biblical Judaism that the δαιμόνια stay beside the grave, and compares the Gospel idea that the demons reside in lonely and desert regions (Mt 12[43]; cf. Mk 5[5] and see Baruch 4[35]). The magic papyrus P Lond 46[12] (iv/A.D. (= I. p. 69 f.) has εἰσάκουσόν μου καὶ ἀπόστρεψο[ν] τὸ δαιμόνιον τοῦτο, and later [164] ὑπόταξόν μοι πάντα τὰ δαιμόνια ἵνα μοι ἦν ὑπήκοος πᾶς δαίμων οὐράνιος καὶ αἰθέριος καὶ ἐπίγειος καὶ χερσαῖο[ς] καὶ ἔνυδρος. That a magic document by a writer who knows Judaism, perhaps even Christianity, should use δαιμόνιον of an evil spirit is, of course, not strange. The noun may be quoted from Vettius Valens: thus p. 67[5] ὑπὸ δαιμονίων καὶ φαντασίας εἰδώλων χρηματισθήσονται, where it is clearly something weird. Elsewhere he uses it much as τὸ θεῖον, as p. 355[15] δυνάμενος τυχεῖν ὧν μὴ ἐβούλετο τὸ δαιμόνιον παρέχειν.

It may be noted that in Lk 4[35] D δαιμόνιον has a masc. predicate—ῥείψας αὐτὸν τὸ δαιμόνιον, and that in 9[1] D it is feminine—ἐπὶ πᾶσαν δαιμόνιον: see Wellhausen *Einleitung*, p. 12.

δαίμων.

The word is used in its old sense in P Leid W[xii.30] (ii/iii A.D.) δαίμων δαιμώνων, in a spell addressed to a divinity. It answers often to the Latin *Genius*. Thus in a notification of the accession of Nero, P Oxy VII. 1021[8] (A.D. 54) the Emperor is described as ἀγαθὸς δαίμων δὲ τῆς οὐκουμένης (*l.* οἰκ—) "the good genius of the world." Similarly *OGIS* 666[2] Νέρων] Κλαύδιος . . . ὁ ἀγαθὸς δαίμων τῆς οἰκουμένης, σὺν ἅπασιν οἷς εὐεργέτησεν ἀγαθοῖς: cf. *ib.* 672[7] (A.D. 80) with reference to the Nile—ὠρύγη Ἀγαθὸς Δαίμων ποταμὸς ἐπὶ τὰ τρία στερεά κτλ. In a private letter of iii/A.D. the combination occurs as a proper name, P Strass I. 73[4] Ἀγαθὸς Δαίμων σὺν σοὶ εἰσελθὼν διεπέμψατο: cf. BGU II. 494[14] (ii/A.D.), *al*. For the word in a bad sense, see the magical incantation, P Par 574[1227] (iii/A.D.) (= *Selections*, p. 113) πρᾶξις γενναία ἐκβάλλουσα δαίμονας, "a notable spell for driving out demons," and the Christian amulet in which the wearer prays, ὅπως διώξῃς ἀπ' ἐμοῦ τοῦ δούλου σου τὸν δαίμονα προβασκανίας, "that Thou mayst drive from me Thy servant the demon of witchcraft" BGU III. 954[9] (c. vi/A.D.) (= *Selections*, p. 133). In P Grenf II. 76[3] (A.D. 305–6) two νεκροτάφοι from Kysis agree to a formal divorce, seeing that "owing to some evil deity" they have renounced their wedded life = ἐπὶ (*l.* ἐπεὶ) ἔκ τινος πονηροῦ δαίμονος συνέβη αὐτοὺς ἀποζεύχθαι ἀλλήλων τὴν κοινὴν αὐτῶν συνβίωσιν. So P Cairo Preis 2[1] (A.D. 362) ὡς τῆς γυναικός μου πῖραν λαβοῦσαν (for λαβούσης) δέμονος, "in the belief that my wife had had experience of a demon."

δάκνω

survives in MGr δαγκάνω, also δάκνω, with noun δάγκαμα "a bite," which puts it among words which have not changed in 3000 years. But we cannot quote from Κοινή documents. Vettius Valens p. 127[23] has the noun, θηρίων δακετῶν αἰτίαις.

δάκρυον.

P Petr II. 1[4] (c. B.C. 260) μετὰ δακρύων, which Mayser, *Gr.* p. 298, notes must not be assigned to δάκρυ, despite the heteroclite δάκρυσιν in NT. BGU IV. 1141[5] (c. B.C. 14) οἵαν γὰρ ὕβριν μοι πεπόηκεν ἐν τῷ κήπῳ καὶ ἐν τῇ οἰκία . . . . . ἣ ἦν δάκρυα σοὶ γράφειν, γεγραφήκειν ἂν ἀπὸ τῶν δακρύων, "wenn Thränen ein Brief wären" (Ed.). The noun survives still.

δακρύω

survives as δακρύζω to-day, with ptc. δακρυσμένος = "red with weeping." It may be quoted from *Preis.* 373, an undated tombstone, Μάγνα (σὲ) θανοῦσ[αν] πᾶσα γῆ δακρυσά[τω].

135

δακτύλιος.

BGU III. 781⁹ ¹⁵ (i/A.D.) ἔχοντα καὶ ὠτάρια δακτύλια, P Oxy III. 497¹⁹ (a marriage-contract—early ii/A.D.) τῆς τοῦ δακτυλίου ἐγλογῆς. A will of ii/A.D., PSI III. 240¹³, concludes a list of γυναικεῖος κόσμος with δ[α]κτύλιον χρυσοῦν. left to the writer's daughter. In the magical papyrus P Lond 46²⁹⁴ (iv/A.D.) (= I. p. 71) a spell is headed Ἑρμοῦ δακτύλιος κανθάρου ποίησις, "The ring of Hermes and the preparation of the beetle." From the inscriptions we may cite OGIS 56²³ (B.C. 239) ἐν τοῖς δακτυλίοις οἷς φοροῦσι (οἱ ἱερεῖς), ib. 229⁸⁸ (iii/B.C.) σφραγισάσθωσαν Σμυρνα[ίων] οἵ τε στρατηγοὶ καὶ οἱ ἐξετασταὶ τῶι τε τῆς πόλεως δακτυλίωι καὶ τοῖς αὐτῶν. There are numerous occurrences in Syll: see Index. For the diminutive δακτυλίδιον, which is rejected by the Atticists, see BGU III. 843⁸ (i/ii A.D.) τό μοι δακτυλίδιον, ib. IV. 1104¹³ (B.C. 8), P Oxy X. 1273¹¹ (A.D. 260) δακτυλίδιον μεικρὸν τετά[ρ]ταις ἥμισυ, "a small ring weighing ¼ quarter." Δακτύλιος occurs with an anatomical sense in P Ryl I. 28⁶³ (iv/A.D.) ἡ ἕδρα, δακτύλιος δὲ ὑπό τινων καλουμένη : see LS. In MGr we have δαχτυλίδι, "finger-ring."

δάκτυλος.

P Amh II. 110⁵ (A.D. 75) οὐλὴ δακτύλῳ μικρῷ χειρὸ[ς] ἀριστερᾶς, so P Fay 92⁷˙¹⁰ (A.D. 126), P Grenf II. 46⁹ (A.D. 137), etc. P Lond 46⁴⁸⁹ (iv/A.D.) (= I. p. 80) τὸν ἴδιον τῆς ἀριστερᾶς σου χειρὸς δάκτυλον is a reference to mythical magicians, the Δάκτυλοι Ἰδαῖοι, whose name is transferred to one of the fingers. With Lk 11²⁰ cf. the ostracon charm of the late Empire, cited by Deissmann LAE, p. 306, . . . ἐξορκίζω κατὰ τοῦ δακτύλου τοῦ θεοῦ, ἵνα μὴ ἀναχάνῃ αὐτῷ, "I adjure . . . by the finger of the god that he open not his mouth to him." The word is found as a measure of length in the new classical fragment P Oxy IV. 669 (iii/A.D.) : cf. the use of δακτυλιστής in P Fay 112¹¹ (A.D. 99), where the editors suggest "measurer" as a possible meaning, and similarly in P Amh II. 126⁷² (early ii/A.D.). MGr is δάχτυλο.

Δαλματία.

The spelling Δελματία (2 Tim 4¹⁰ C 424** and other cursives—cf. Δερματίαν Λ) appears in Preisigke 173 (c. A.D. 200), the tombstone of T. Aurelius Calpurnianus Apollonides, who among other distinctions had been ἐπί(τροπος) Δελματίας. It is supported by the derivative δελματική, the name of a kind of robe, spelt this way in BGU I. 93⁷ (ii/iii A.D.) καλῶς ποιήσεις διαπέμψας αὐτῇ τὴ[ν] δελματικήν, P Oxy VII. 1051¹⁶ (iii/A.D.) δελματικὴ λινᾶ ᾱ, and the diminutive δελματίκιον which occurs twice in the last papyrus, and in ib. 1026¹⁰ (v/A.D.) δελματίκιον ὀνύχινον, "an onyx-coloured Dalmatian vest" (Edd.). See Deissmann BS, p. 182, where against the supposition of Alexandrian spelling (so Hort) is quoted CPR 21¹⁶ (A.D. 230) δαλματική. Dalmatia is the Latin spelling (Souter).

δαμάζω.

Vettius Valens p. 285³⁰. ἐπὶ μὲν τῶν στερεῶν ζῳδίων ἢ μοιρῶν παρόντες ἅπαξ τε καὶ ἀπαραιτήτως δαμάζουσιν, ἐν δὲ τοῖς δισώμοις πλεονάκις.

δάμαλις

is found ter in a Coan inscription Syll 617. See also the Mysteries inscription from Andania, Syll 653³⁴ (B.C. 91) Μεγάλοις θεοῖς δάμαλιν σῦν, so ⁶⁹. A diminutive is found in P Flor II. 150² (A.D. 267) τὰ βούδια ὅσα ἔχεις . . . ἤτε δαμάλια ἤτε μείζονα. Δάμαλις is found as a proper name for Athenian women : see Pape Wört. d. gr. Eigennamen s.v., Renan Saint Paul, p. 209 n³.

Δάμαρις

Renan (Saint Paul, p. 209 n³) suggests that this otherwise unknown proper name in Ac 17³⁴ may really stand for Δάμαλις : see above.

δανείζω.

A few examples will suffice of this very common verb— P Fay 11⁶ (c. B.C. 115) ἐδάνεισα [Θεοτ]ίμῳ . . . πυρῶν ἀρ[τάβας] [ζ (ἥμισυ)], "I lent to Theotimus 7½ artabae of wheat, P Cairo Preis 43¹⁹ (A.D. 59) δρ]αχμὰς . . . [ἃς ἐδ]άνεισεν α[ὐτ]ῷ, P Oxy III. 485¹² (A.D. 178) ἐδάνεισα κατὰ δημόσιον χρηματισμόν, "I lent in accordance with a public deed," ib. 510⁶ (A.D. 101) ἃς ἐδάνεισεν αὐτοῖς κατὰ δανείου συνγραφήν, "which he lent to them in accordance with a contract of loan." For the middle, see P Oxy IV. 830 (i/B.C.) ἀποδότωσαν δὲ οἱ δεδανεισμένοι Θ. τὰς τριάκοντα δύο ἀρτάβας τῶν πυρῶν, "but let the borrowers restore to T. the thirty-two artabae of wheat," ib. X. 1281⁵ (A.D. 21) δεδάνισμαι τὴν τειμήν, "I have borrowed the price," ib. III. 471⁹¹ (ii/A.D.) ὥστε καὶ ἐπίδειξις ἦν αὐτῶι πρὸς τοὺς δανειζομένους ἃ ἔπραττεν, "showed off to the borrowers what he had been doing (Edd.). P Flor I. 1³ (A.D. 153) combines them—δραχμὰς διακοσίας ἃς ἀνείρηται ἡ δεδανισμένη παρὰ τῆς δεδανικυίης. Wackernagel ThLZ 1908, Sp. 637, observes that the new future δανιῶ in LXX proves that itacism goes back to the translators and not merely the scribes. Δανείζω could not make an "Attic future" δανιῶ until the last vestige of difference between ει and ι had gone.

δάνειον.

P Hib. I. 89¹⁰ (loan of money—B.C. 239) Ζηνίων Θεοδό[τ]ηι τὸ δάνειον τὰς Φ (δραχμὰς [διπλοῦν, "Zenion shall forfeit to Theodote twice the amount of the loan of 500 drachmae" (Edd.), P Grenf II. 24¹⁰ (B.C. 105) τὸ δὲ δάνειον τοῦτο ἀποδότω Ψεμμεγχῆς Πετεαρσεμθεῖ, BGU IV. 1095¹² (A.D. 57) τὰ δένηα (l. δάνεια ἐν χερσὶ γέγοναι (l. γέγονε), P Fay 110¹⁵ (c. A.D. 100) τὴν διαγραφὴν τοῦ χόρτου ποῦ τέθικας καὶ τὼ δάνιον αὐτοῦ τῆς μνᾶς ἥ ἐστι γραφή : "where did you put the notice of payment for the hay, and the contract for his loan of a mina?" (Edd.), P Oxy I. 68¹³ (A.D. 131) τοῦ δανείου ἀσφάλ[ε]ιαν, "the security for the loan, ib. X. 1262¹⁶ (A.D. 197) σπέρματα δάνεια, "a loan of seed." For P Petr II. 11 (1)⁶ iii/B.C.) (= Selections, p. 8) τὸ δὲ λοιπὸν εἰς τὸ δάνειον κατέβαλον, Wyse proposes, and Mahaffy adopts (App. p. 4), the rendering "I have paid as an instalment of interest" instead of "I have put out to interest."

δανειστής.

P Petr III. 53 (*ii*[9] (iii/B.C.) φυγαδεύοντας τοὺς δανειστάς, BGU IV. 1079[19] (A.D. 41) (= *Selections*, p. 40) πολλοὺς δανιστὰς ἔχομεν, P Oxy I. 68[25] (A.D. 131) τοῖς τοῦ Σαραπίωνος δανισταῖς, "Serapion's creditors," P. Ryl II. 117[20] (A.D. 260) φάσκων εἶναι αὐτὸν δ[α]νιστὴν ἐκείνου, "professing to be a creditor of his" (Edd.).

δαπανάω.

P Giss I. 21[9] (early ii/A.D.) διὸ δαπανᾶς (*sic leg.*) λίτραν μίαν καὶ ὁλκῆς στατῆρα, P. Oxy VIII. 1143[3] (*c.* A.D. 1) ἐδαπανή(θησαν) εἰς τὸ ἱερὸν ἁλὸς (ἀρτάβαι) β, P Fay 125[6] (ii/A.D.) τὸ δαπανηθ[ὲν] παραδέξομαι, "I will make an allowance for the expense" (Edd.), P Flor III. 334[9] (ii/A.D.) καὶ πάλι τῆι σῆι σφραγῖδι ἀσφαλῶς κλείσας σφράγισον τὸ δαπανηθὲν ἀνάλωμα εἰς τοὺς θησαυρούς, εἰς ἧ (for ἦν) ὅσιόν ἐστιν. In *OGIS* 59[15] (*c.* B.C. 188) Ptolemy V announces a yearly grant of 111 Ptolemaic drachmae to the garrison on the island of Thera—ὅπως ἔχωσιν εἰς τε τὰς θυσίας καὶ τὸ ἄλειμμα δαπανᾶν. With ἐν, as in Jas 4[3], BGU I. 149[5] (ii/iii A.D.) καὶ ἐν πυρῷ κατ᾽ ἔτος δαπανᾶται τὰ ὑπογε-γρ[αμμένα]. Other things than money may be the subject: thus an undated ostracon in *Archiv* v. p. 170, no. 34 τοὺς ἥλους, οὓς ἠγόρασας, ἐπιμελῶς τήρησον, ὅπως Τύραννος ὁ κυβερνήτης μαρτυρήσῃ μοι, ὅτι διὰ αὐτοῦ ὁμοῦ ἐδαπανήθησαν.

δαπάνη

is very common. Thus P Fay 101 *verso*[5] (*c.* B.C. 18) δαπάνης (δραχμαὶ) δ, P Oxy II. 204[27] (A.D. 22) = (*Selections*, p. 36) εἰς δαπάνην οὗ ἔχι μου, "with reference to the expense of what he has belonging to me," *ib.* VIII. 1125[18] (ii/A.D.) ἰδίαις ἑαυτοῦ δαπάναις. In P Lond 356[16] (i/A.D.) (= II. p. 252, *Selections* p. 50) the writer warns his corre-spondent that if he sells him stale drugs—γείνωσκε σαυτὸν ἕξοντα πρὸς ἐμὲ περὶ τῶν δαπανῶν, "understand that you will have to settle with me with regard to the expenses." P Lond III. 1171[24] (accounts—B.C. 8) (= III. p. 178) shows the new word ὑπερδαπάνη, i.e. "debit balance" or "deficit": ὑπερδάπανον(?) and ὑπερδαπάνημα are also found in this sense in the same papyrus. The simple δαπάνημα, which belongs to later Greek, is common, e.g. BGU III. 1001[13] (B.C. 50) τ]ά τε βλάβη καὶ δαπανήματα.

Δανείδ.

On the spelling of this name see J. H. Moulton *Grammar of NT Greek* II. § 45, and cf. below s.v. Σιλουανός.

δέησις.

With δέησις, "supplication," as in Phil 1[4], may be com-pared P Par 69E[11] (A.D. 232) ἔνθα σπονδὰ[ς καὶ δε]ήσεις ποιησάμενος, and the Ptolemaic P Petr II. 19 (1a)[2] where a prisoner supplicates μετὰ δεήσεως καὶ ἱκετείας οὕνεκα τοῦ θεοῦ καὶ τοῦ καλῶς ἔχοντος, "in the name of God and of fair play" (Ed.). In one of the Serapeum documents regarding the Twins, P Lond 21[20] (B.C. 162) (= I. p. 13), Ptolemy petitions Sarapion on their behalf, ἀξιῶ οὖν σε μετὰ δεήσεως νομίσαντα ταῖς διδύμαις ἰδίαι (= ἰδίᾳ) σε ταῦτα διδόναι: cf. the δέησις addressed by a woman to Abinnaeus, P Lond 306 (*c.* A.D. 346) (= II. p. 281), and P Giss I. 41[ii. 10] (time of Hadrian) ἐπινεύσαντος ο[ὖ]ν τῆ[ι]

δεήσει μου, of a petition to the Praefect Apollonius. For petitions addressed to the Emperor cf. CP Herm 6[1] ὑπὲρ τοιούτων ὁποῖα προ[σην]έγκαμεν τὴν δέησιν ποιούμεθα: the statement follows, with θ[ειότατε αὐτοκράτωρ in the next line. So *ib* 110 *verso*[ii. 11], where Gallienus replies κα[λε]ῖ δὲ καὶ ἡ το[ῦ δι]καίου τάξις ὡς καὶ τὰ ἐκ τῆς παρά σου δεήσεως ἑτοίμως [δ]ιδ[ό]ναι τὴν χάριν. It is clear that the word is a strong one, even if the language of exaggeration will sometimes employ it where "request" would express the sense: thus BGU I. 180[15] (A.D. 172) δικαίαν δέ[ησ]ιν ποιούμενος, P Gen I. 16[19] (A.D. 207) δ[έ]ησίν σοι προσφέ-ρομεν, κύριε. The noun and its original verb δέομαι retain connexion with the idea of "need"; and δέησις was thus ready for its special NT use of "entreaty" towards God—we recall Trench's epigram defining prayer as "the mighty utterance of a mighty need."

δεῖ.

For the conjunctive, as in Mt 26[35], cf. P Fay 109[5] (early i/A.D.) ἐάν σε δῆ (for δέη) τὸ εἱμάτιόν σου θεῖναι ἐνέχυρον, "even if you have to pawn your cloak" (Edd.). In P Tebt I. 58[55] (B.C. 111) we have ἐάν followed by the indicative—ἐὰν δεῖ σε συνπεσεῖν τῶι Ἀνικήτωι, σύνπεσαι, "if you must meet Anicetus, meet him" (Edd.; cf. Mayser *Gr.* p. 325. Other examples of the verb are P Par 46[15] (B.C. 153) διὸ καὶ ἡγούμενος δεῖν ἐπ᾽ ἄλλου μὲν μηθενὸς αὐτῶι διακριθῆναι, P Lille I. 26[7] (iii/B.C.) περὶ (corr. from πεερὶ) δὲ τούτου τοῦ μέρους δεήσει ἐπισχεῖν, P Tebt II. 341[4] (A.D. 140-1) δεήσι ἐπισταλῆναι εἰς δάνε[ι]α σπέρματα κατασπ[ο]ρᾶς κτλ., "it will be necessary to send on account of loans of seed-corn for the sowing," etc., *Michel* 1001[iii. 5] (Theran Doric —*c.* B.C. 200) no one may bring forward a proposal ὡς δεείσηι διαλῦσαι τὸ κοινὸν εἴ τᾶς θυσίας, P Flor II. 133[3] (A.D. 257) ἔδι μὲν ὑμᾶς μηδὲ ὑπομνήσεως χρήζειν, "you oughtn't even to have needed a reminder," P Oxy X. 1203[10] (A.D. 117-38) ἔδει αὐτῶι διδόναι οσι [... ὅτι) οὐκ ἔστ᾽ αὐτὸς Σαρᾶς, ἀλλὰ ἄλλος ξένος ἐστὶν οὗ δεῖ με πισθῆναι ὡς ἐσχήκατε, "you ought to have given him a letter, because it is not S. but another stranger whose word I have to take that you have received it" (Edd.). See also s.v. δέον.

δεῖγμα

is found = "Plan," "Planskizze" in P Giss I. 15[3] κόμιζε τῆς Ἰβιῶνο[ς] τὸ δεῖγμα: cf. the fragmentary P Petr II. 8 (2a)[6] (B.C. 246). The word is used of a "sample" in P Hib I. 39[15] (B.C. 265) δεῖγμα σφραγισάσ[θ]ω, "let him seal a sample" of corn, so *ib.* 98[17] (B.C. 251), P Lond 256 *recto*[3] (A.D. 11-5) (= II. p. 97) ἐπεσφραγι[σμέ]νοις δίγμασι, P Oxy IV. 708[5] (A.D. 188) ἐν τῆ[ι τ[ῶ]ν δειγμάτων ἄρσει, "at the weighing of the samples" (Edd.): cf. P Oxy I. 113[3] (ii/A.D.) συνήλλιξα ἐκείνη τῆι ἐπιστολῆ δεῖγμα λευκόινα, "I enclosed in the former packet a pattern of white-violet colour" (Edd.). In P Oxy I. 63[3] (ii/iii A.D.) we have τοὺς δειγματοάρτας, "the inspectors," and in *ib.* X. 1254[5] (A.D. 260) εἰς δειγματοκαταγωγίαν, "for the conveyance of samples" of wheat. MGr δεῖγμα = "proof."

δειγματίζω.

This very rare verb may now be illustrated from P Tebt II. 570 (B.C. 14-3) where a list of lands cultivated by δημόσιοι γεωργοὶ begins ιζ ἔτους σπόρος διγματισθείς?

δημ(οσίων) γεωργ(ῶν). It is also found along with the subst. in the Greek fragment of the Ascension of Isaiah P Amh I. i^viii. 21 ἀπὸ το[ῦ δει]γματισμοῦ ὅτι [ἐ]δειγμάτισεν τὸν [Σ]αμαήλ. The subst. occurs in BGU I. 246^6 (ii/iii A.D.) κινδυνεύω κα[ὶ ταῦ]τα(?) ἀπολέσαι μετὰ καὶ διγματισμοῦ καλῶς ἐτρήκατε (? l. εὑρήκατε) καὶ μονείμως (l. μονίμως), and in P Gizeh 10271^12 (in *Archiv* ii. p. 81) ἕως τοῦ δειγμα[τισμοῦ, and on the Rosetta Stone, *OGIS* 90^39 (B.C. 196) τὰ πρὸς τὸν δειγματισμὸν διάφορα, "the cost of having them verified." The verb takes an infin. in P Ryl I. 28^32 (iv/A.D.), where if the ὑπόταυρος "quivers," δειγματισθήσεται ὁ τοιοῦτ[ο]ς ἀπολέσθαι τι κρυφιμαῖον : in^70 διγματ[ι]σμοὺς καὶ λοιδορίας καὶ κρυφιμαίων πραγμάτων ἐπιφάνιαν seems to mean "exposures."

Since δειγματίζω does not begin to appear till long after παραδειγματίζω, it is quite conceivable that παράδειγμα produced the latter verb, and δειγματίζω was shortened from it by the help of the noun δεῖγμα. The early appearance of δειγματισμός (B.C. 196) is the main difficulty, since that is coeval with παραδειγματίζω.

δείκνυμι.

The verb is not so common as we might have expected, but for the ordinary meaning we may cite P Oxy III. 471^75 (ii/A.D.) σύνβολα δεικνύντα, "showing signs," and for the metaphorical, as Jas 2^18, 3^13, *ib.* II. 237^? (A.D. 186) οὐδεμίαν μὲν οὔτε ὕβριν οὔτε ἄλλο ἀδίκημα εἰς αὐτὸν ἁπλῶς ἐφ' ᾧ μέμφεται δεῖξαι ἔχων, "he could not indeed cite a single insult or any other act of injustice against himself with which he charged me" (Edd.): cf. *ib.* I. 67^19 (A.D. 338) εἴν' οὕτως διχθῇ [αὐ]τῶν ἡ καθ' ἡμῶν [πλεο]νεξία, "in this way their aggression against me will be made clear" (Edd.). A ii/A.D. calculation of the maubion-tax upon catoeci, printed in P Tebt II. p. 339 f., is followed by δέδικ[ται], "proved," written "in a cursive but probably not different hand" (Edd.). *OGIS* 267^16 (ii/B.C.) οἱ μετὰ ταῦτα δεικνύμενοι (στρατηγοί), where the *simplex* takes the place of the commoner ἀποδείκνυμι (see s.v.) in this sense. With the use of the verb in Jn 14^8, etc., we may compare the Christian prayer, P Oxy VIII. 1150^9 (vi/A.D.) δεῖξον τὴν δύναμ[ίν σου. On the Christian sepulchral inscription, P Hamb I. 22^? (iv/A.D.) υἱὲ θεοῦ μεγάλοιο τὸν οὐδέποτε δράκεν ἀνήρ (cf. Jn 1^18), ὃς τυφλοῖσιν ἔδωκας ἰδεῖν φάος ἠελίοιο, δεῖξον ἐν ἀνθρώποισι κτλ., the editor remarks that we may either supply φάος after δεῖξον, cf. Isa 53^11, or possibly take δεῖξον absolutely as in Numb 16^30, Ps 58(59)^10 ὁ θεός μου δείξει μοι ἐν τοῖς ἐχθροῖς μου. For the ordinary meaning "exhibit" we may cite the rescript of Caracalla, P Giss I. 40^ii. 28 (A.D. 215), where the Emperor, from his record an excellent judge of *Kultur*, lays it down that ἔτι τε καὶ ζω[ὴ] δεικνύει ἐναντία ἤθη ἀπὸ ἀναστροφῆς [πο]λειτικῆς εἶναι ἀγροίκους Α[ἰ]γυπτίους. MGr is δείχνω or δείχτω, with meaning unchanged.

δειλία.

For this N.T. ἅπ. εἰρ. (2 Tim 1^7) cf. BGU II. 372^? (A.D. 154) δειλίαν with a gap both before and after, and P Giss I. 40^ii. 11 (A.D. 215) δειλίας αἰτία.

δειλιάω.

In P Par 68^? a person condemned to death writes to the Emperor ἐπὶ τοῦτον δὲ πορευόμενος οὐ δειλιάσω σοι τὴν ἀλήθειαν εἰπεῖν. The form δειλαίνω, found in Aristotle, occurs in P Tebt I. 58^27 (B.C. 111) οὗτος οὖν θεωρήσας με ὡς προσεδρεύοντα καθ' ἡμέραν ὡσεὶ δεδίλανται, "seeing me in daily attendance he has as it were turned coward" (Edd.).

δειλός.

For the neut. plur. used adverbially, see P Iand 11^4 (ii/A.D.) ὀχλεῖ μοι δίλα ὁ Τρωῖλος. MGr δειλός = "timid," "shy."

δεῖνα, ὁ, ἡ, τό.

To the examples of τὸ δεῖνα = "by the way," "by the bye," we may add an instance from the recently recovered Mimes of Herodas, I. 43 τὸ δεῖνα δὲ ἄγριος χειμὼν ἐ[ξ ἐ]ὐ δίης ἐνέπ]εσε. Ὁ δεῖνα in the ordinary sense, = "Mr X.," may be seen in the magic papyri where a formula is given into which any given name may be fitted : thus BGU IV. 1026^xxiii. 20 δό]ς μοι χάριν στ[. . .]ον πρὸς πᾶσαν ἀνθρωπίνην γε[ν]ε[ὰ]ν καὶ πάσας γυναικας, μάλιστα πρὸς τὴν (δεῖνα). It is generally represented by a sign, as here. Cf. P Leid W^xxx. 20 (ii/iii A.D.) γυναικόνορφε (l. -μορφε) θεά, δεσπότι (σελήνη), ποίησον τὸ δ εῖνα) πρᾶγμα. MGr has ὁ δεῖνα(ς), ἡ, τὸ δεῖνα (gen. τοῦ, τῆς δεῖνος) = "So-and-so," unchanged : see Thumb *Handb.* p. 98.

δεινός.

With the use in Mt 8^6 cf. BGU II. 595^14 (c. A.D. 70-80) ὅτι ὁ υἱός μου ἀσθενεῖ δινῶς, P Oxy VIII. 1161^8 (iv/A.D. — Christian) ταῦτα δέ σοι ἔγραψα νοσοῦσα, δ[ιν]ῶς ἔχουσα, πάνυ μὴ δυναμένη ἀναστῆναι ἐκ τῆς κοίτης μου, ὅτι πάνυ δινῶς ἔχω, Syll 802^111 (Epidaurus iii/B.C.) οὗτος τὸ[ν] τοῦ ποδὸς δάκτυλον ὑπὸ τοῦ (Ed. ὑπό του) ἀγρίου ἕλκεος δεινῶς διακείμ[εν]ος. For adj. cf. BGU I. 163^9 (A.D. 108) οὐδὲν δεινὸν ἐγέν[ετο, and from the inscriptions Syll 567^7 (ii/A.D.) μηδὲν αὐτοῖς δεινὸν συνειδότας. *Preisigke* 4282, a dedication in Latin and Greek of an altar in honour of Hadrian, by a general named Serenus, who had annihilated "Agriophagos nequissimos," renders this last word by δει[νοτάτους].

δειπνέω.

Interesting examples of the word occur in invitations to dinner or to a wedding-feast, e.g. P Oxy I. 110 (ii/A.D.) ἐρωτᾷ σε Χαιρήμων δειπνῆσαι εἰς κλείνην τοῦ κυρίου Σαράπιδος ἐν τῷ Σαραπείῳ αὔριον, ἥτις ἐστὶν ιε, ἀπὸ ὥρας θ, "Chaeremon requests your company at dinner at the table of the lord Sarapis in the Serapeum to-morrow, the 15th, at 9 o'clock": similarly *ib.* 111 (iii/A.D.), III. 523 (ii/A.D.), VI. 926 (iii/A.D.), P Fay 132 (ii/A.D.). The hour, which corresponds to our 3 p.m., illustrates the elasticity of a term which will answer to our "lunch" or "supper" on occasion: it relieves some of the difficulty in Lk 14^16 ff., where an ἄριστον seems demanded by the details. In P Oxy VI. 927 (iii/A.D.) we have the same formula, but εἰς γάμους stands in the place of δειπνῆσαι. It is curious to find our phrase "to dine out" paralleled —BGU IV. 1141^36 (c. B.C. 14)] οὐδὲ ἔξω δεδειπνηκέναι. Ξύστον δὲ ἐπιγνοὺς δεδειπνηκέναι ἔσω ἐν τῇ οἰκίᾳ παρὰ Ἔρωτα δὶς προσελαβόμην αὐτὸν εἰς οἶκον παρ' ἐμέ : it is not clear that the parallel is more than verbal. MGr δειπνῶ = "lunch," "dine."

δεῖπνον.

In a lengthy account of private expenses, P Oxy IV. 736³⁶ (c. A.D. 1), we find the entry ἀσπαράγω(ν) [δί]πνῳ Ἀντ(ᾶτος) ὅτ᾽ εἰς τὸ περίδ[ι]πνο(ν) Ἀθη(γναφέω(ς) (ἡμιωβέλιον), "asparagus for the dinner of Antas when (he went) to the funeral feast of Athe . . . the fuller ½ ob." (Edd.) : cf. ib. 735¹ (c. A.D. 1) δίπνωι ε Κανωπικὸν ἧπαρ, "for dinner on the 5th a Canopic liver. For δειπνητήριον = "a civic banqueting-hall" see the inscription of the time of Vespasian (A.D. 69-70) in P Fay p. 33. Another compound, δειπνοκλήτωρ, occurs in the remarkable alternative version of the parable of Lk 14⁷ᶠᶠ found in D Φ al after Mt 20²⁸. Nestle, Text. Criticism, p. 257, remarks that Artemidorus (ap. Athenaeus) called the ἐλέατρος by this name—"a manager of the table, taster" (LS). He equates it to a Syriac phrase = "master of the feast," and claims it as belonging to the later popular language. It may accordingly represent not the entertainer but the nomenclator—the slave who acted as marshal at a dinner-party. Δεῖπνον is not frequent in our documents, but it survives in MGr. We might add P Lond 210(a) verso⁴·² (ii/B.C.) (= II. p. 2), where in accounts concerning ? dinner (περὶ δεῖπνον) the beer (ζῦτον) costs 40 dr. a choa early 6 pints), which the editor observes was a high price.

δεισιδαιμονία.

In OGIS 455¹¹ (B.C. 39) a temp enclosure of the goddess Aphrodite is declared ἄσυλον αὐτῷ δικαίῳ ταύτῃ τε δεισιδαιμονίᾳ, "eodem jure eademque religione" as the temple of Artemis at Ephesus. It is in this general sense of "religion," without any pronouncement as to whether it was right or wrong, that the word is to be understood in Ac 25¹⁹.

δεισιδαίμων.

Beyond the neutral sense attached to the subst. in the passage cited s.v. δεισιδαιμονία, we have no light to throw upon the exact force of the phrase κατὰ πάντα δεισιδαιμονεστέρους in Ac 17²². A convenient summary of the translations given to it with their varying shades of condemnation and commendation will be found in ExpT xviii. p. 485 ff. See also A. W. Verrall's comments, ib. xix. p. 43 : he renders "exceedingly god-fearing," but accepts the view that it is meant to be a neutral term. L. R. Farnell Greece and Babylon, p. 193n, remarks on the prevailing bad sense of the word (as in the Characters of Theophrastus) in connexion with the exclusion of fear and humility from religious virtues. We find the adj. meaning "reverent" in the epitaph of a mimus, Kaibel 607³ (iii/A.D.) πᾶσι φίλος θνητοῖς εἰς τ᾽ἀθανάτους δεισιδαίμων.

The adverb occurs bis in Aristeas 129 with reference to unclean foods—δεισιδαιμόνως γὰρ τὰ πλεῖστα τὴν νομοθεσίαν ἔχειν, ἐν δὲ τούτοις παντελῶς δεισιδαιμόνως, "for the law is scrupulous in most things, but in these matters it is excessively scrupulous" (Thackeray). There is a good list of occurrences in D. B. Durham Menander, p. 53.

δέκα.

The indeterminate use of δέκα to denote simply a period of time, which is found in Biblical Greek (Gen 24⁵⁵, Numb

11¹⁹, Dan 1¹⁴, Rev 2¹⁰), may be illustrated from P Petr III. 36 verso⁵ where a prisoner complains that he has been harshly treated in prison λιμῷ παραπολλύμενος μῆνές εἰσιν δέκα, "perishing from hunger for the last ten months" ; and from a more literary source in the Mimes of Herodas I. 24 — δέκ᾽ εἰσὶ μῆνες, during which a husband, who has gone on a journey to Egypt, does not write to his wife. See further Lumbroso in Archiv iv. p. 316 f. where some parallels are quoted from literary Κοινή. Of course there is no proof that the above is not to be taken literally.

δεκαδύο.

In the Ptolemaic papyri this is the regular form, e.g. P Petr II. 27 (1)⁵ (B.C. 236) ἐκ μετρητῶν δεκαδύο, and so ⁶·⁸, P Amh II. 47⁵ (B.C. 113) πυροῦ ἀρτάβας δέκα δύο ἄτοκα. The only exception which Mayser (Gr. p. 316) has noted is P Vat F³¹ (B.C. 157). Similarly in inscriptions from about ii/B.C. we find δεκαδύο, as well as δώδεκα, e.g. CIA II. 470³¹ (iii/B.C.) δραχμὰς δέκα δύο : see Meisterhans Gr. p. 159. In ostraca δώδεκα greatly predominates over δέκα δύο. In Preis. p. 66 n.² there is an unfortunate mistake, due to trusting Wellhausen : the mistake is copied in Thackeray Gr. i. p. 188 n¹. Wellhausen says (Einleitung in die drei ersten Evangelien¹. p. 14), "Zwölf in D an den beiden Stellen, wo die Zahl ausgeschrieben ist Mt 10⁵, Lk 6¹³, δεκαδύο und nicht δώδεκα heisst." (So far as one can tell, in the absence of an index, he has dropped the statement in ed.²) As a matter of fact, D has δώδεκα in Mt 26²⁰, 11¹, Lk 9¹², Jn 6¹⁰, ⁶⁷, ⁷¹, 11⁹, Ac 19⁷. Not only D but W shows δέκα δύο (ter, according to Sanders, p. 24). P Flor II. 141 (A.D. 264) has instructive differences between three scribes. The first writer mentions οἴνου δίχωρα δωδ[εκ]α γ(ίνεται) οἴ(νου) δίχω(ρα) ιβ ; the second, who endorses it, writes δώδεκα ; the third writes a receipt for δίχωρα [δε]καδύο. The last is a φροντιστής or "superintendent of inland revenue," and unless a big hand is evidence (see under γράμμα) no less educated than Alypius or his correspondent Heroninus. In P Lond 1171⁵ (B.C. 8) (= III. p. 177) we find τῆς ιβμήνου. "the 12 month"; cf. for gender τὰν δευτέραν ἐξάμη[νον, SiB 718⁹ (ii/B.C.). Thackeray remarks (l.c.) that δεκαδύο was a shortlived attempt to displace δώδεκα, much in vogue in the Ptolemaic age, but in LXX only predominant in Chron and Judith. Δώδεκα stands alone in MGr.

δεκαέξ

stands in Rev 13¹⁸ C, and is probably original, in view of Deissmann's convincing exposition in LAE. p. 275 ff. (καισαρ θεος = 616). It is universal in papyri and other Κοινή monuments : the old forms with καί and the unit first disappeared early from all the 'teens—see J. H. Moulton Gram. II. § 71 (1). MGr. δεκάξι and δεκαέξι preserve the original wavering between δεκαέξ and δέκα ἕξ. It may be noticed that here and elsewhere Greek business documents, like our own, often repeat the numeral in letters after writing it in full : hence e.g. Preisigke 1030 (A.D. 68) ἀργ. δραχ. δέκα ἕξ γ(ίνονται) δραχμὰς) ις.

δεκαοκτώ

occurs in Lk 13¹¹ : see J. H. Moulton Gram. l.c. under δεκαέξ. No illustration need be given. MGr. has both δεκοχτώ and δέκα ὀχτώ, which seems evidence that 18 (like 19) could be two words, unlike 13–15. Δέκα καὶ ὀκτώ in Lk 13[16] is abnormal: cf. Thackeray *Gr.* i. p.188.

δεκανός.

whence ultimately our *dean*, is an "eccl." if not a "bibl." word: and it may be interesting to note its earliest appearance. This is apparently in P Tebt I. 27[31] (B.C. 113) δεκανῶν τῶν φ[υ]λακιτῶν. So also *ib.* 25[1] (early i/B.C.) δεκανῶι, and P Oxy II. 387 *verso* (i/A.D.) where among persons receiving (or paying?) certain payments in kind are δεκανοί, and a προφήτης. The editors remark that the date of the first two passages settles the question whether δεκανός is derived from δέκα or from *decem*. Δεκανικός is read by the editors in P Hib I. 30[13] (B.C. 300-271), where see their note. An astronomical use is described by Mahaffy on P Petr III. 134 (p. 323). "The Egyptian year, excluding the intercalary days, was divided into thirty-six parts of ten days each, which were presided over by thirty-six decans; these decans were deities represented by constellations." Cf. Cumont, *Astrology and Religion among the Greeks and Romans*, p. 33. Wilcken, *Ostr.* i. p. 353, remarks that δεκανός, which answers to *de urio*, has the most various meanings. It may be added that the quantity assigned to *decanus* in *Thes. Ling. Lat.* (s. v.) shows that the word is to that extent independent of the older Greek, which can only be δεκανός. The use of the singular is parallel to the Latin *decemvir*, as one of *decem viri*.

δεκάπεντε

for the earlier πεντεκαίδεκα is common—P Tebt I. 111[6] (B.C. 116) πυρῶν ἀρτάβας δέκα πέντε, P Grenf I. 41[4] (ii/B.C.) τάλαντα δεκάπεντε, *ib.* II. 38[8] B.C. 81) κα]λάμων γραφικῶν δεκάπεντε, P Oxy IV. 742[14] (B.C. 2) τὴν χιλίαν δέσμην (δραχμῶν) δ[εκάπ]εντε. See under δεκαέξ.

Δεκάπολις.

Cagnat III. 1057[5] (A.D. 134) Ἀγαθάγγελος Ἀβιληνὸς τῆς Δεκαπόλεος: the editor distinguishes this Abila from A. Lysaniae, near Damascus. See also G. A. Smith (*EBi* 1051). For the formation of the name cf. Τρικωμία (as in P Par 47[21]—c. B.C. 153), Δικωμία (BGU IV. 1208[21]—B.C. 27), and πενταφυλία (*Chrest.* I. 77[9]—A.D. 149).

δεκατέσσαρες.

Ostr 724[7] (Ptol.) (ἀρτάβας) δεκατέσσαρας, *ib.* 735[6] (B.C. 150 or 130) δ]έκα τέσσ(αρας), etc.: see above.

δεκάτη.

The original ἀπόμοιρα paid to the temples on the produce of vineyards, palm-groves, etc. would seem to have been ⅙th, but this was reduced by the Government to ¹⁄₁₀th in the case of certain favoured classes: see P Rev I. 24[4–10] with the editors' notes. An odd inversion of the Jewish conception of tithes comes in P Hib I. 115[1] (c. B.C. 250) where, according to the editors, the μόσχων δεκάτης refers to a 10 per cent. duty levied upon the profits obtained by the priests from calves offered for sacrifice at the temple: see also the introduction to P Tebt II. 307 (A.D. 208) and Wilcken *Ostr.* i. p. 384 f.

For ἐπιδέκατον = an "extra tenth" in connexion with fines, see P Hib I. 32[9] (B.C. 246) note. In *Theb Ostr* 30[6] (? B.C. 87) the word is probably used for a "tithe" simply.

δέκατος.

For the adj. in connexion with time, see P Magd 7[11] (B.C. 217) ἀπόστι(λον) πρὸς ἡμᾶς ἐγ τῆς δεκάτης [τοῦ Χοίαχ. Like other ordinals, it is very frequently represented by the numeral letter: for a rather unusual combination cf. Preisigke 1020 (ostracon, A.D. 64) ὑπὲρ λαογραφ(ίας) δεκάτου (ἔτους) Νέρωνος τοῦ κυρίου.

δεκατόω

cannot be paralleled except in LXX, as far as we can find. Since δεκάτη had become a conspicuous *term. techn.* in Judaism, the coining of a new verb, to express a procedure without any real parallel in profane Greek, was wholly natural in any literature. The coinage was the more encouraged, as δεκατεύω was getting new senses, in addition to "tithe": it was for instance used in astrology = τετραγωνίζω, PSI III. 158[4] note.

δεκτός.

With θυσίαν δεκτήν in Phil 4[18] Nageli (p. 61) compares the sacred inscription of the Lycian Xanthos in ii/A.D. = *Syll* 633[8] ἐὰν δέ τις βιάσηται, ἀπρόσδεκτος ἡ θυσία παρὰ τοῦ θεοῦ. The adj. is very common in the LXX in a sacrificial sense. Grimm can quote nothing outside LXX till c. A.D. 300 (Iamblichus); but such a verbal could hardly be branded as coined, even if there were no parallels. It came into LXX vocabulary just because it was taken to represent a Hebrew term successfully.

δένδρον.

The heteroclite pl. δένδρη occurs in P Hal I. 1[99] (c. B.C. 250), where it is laid down that one who plants an olive or a fig-tree must do it 9 ft from his neighbour's boundary. τ[ὰ δ'] ἄλλα δένδρη πέντε [πό]δας. So in *Syll* 802[121] (iii/B.C.) where a blind man "incubating" in the Asclepieum dreamed that the god pulled his eyes open with his fingers, καὶ ἰδεῖν τὰ δένδρη πρᾶτον τὰ ἐν τῶι ἱαρῶι: the resemblance in language to Mk 8[24] may be noted. The same inscr. tells of a man who fell ἀπὸ τοῦ δένδρεος (l. 91—he had climbed ἐπὶ δένδρεόν τι in l.[90]): Attic preserved the dat. pl. δένδρεσι. Perhaps by fusion of δένδρεον and δένδρος (neut.) the regular δένδρον arose, which is normal in Hellenistic. Thus *Syll* 535[16] (Boeotian—late iv/B.C.) τὰ δένδρα ὅσ' ἂν εἶ ἐν τῶι χωρίωι, *ib.* 532[13] (Ionic—early iv/B.C.) δένδρα ἔμερα μὴ κόπτεν "tame" trees are the opposite of "wild", *ib.* 790[73] (i/B.C.), etc. It is needless to quote papyri for the word. MGr δέντρο, also δεντρί (*i. e.* δενδρίον) and diminutive δεντράκι.

δεξιολάβος.

We have been no more fortunate than our predecessors in tracing earlier appearances of this ἅπ. εἰρ. of Ac 23[23]. It may be a coinage to translate some title used in the Roman army; but obviously it was coined before Luke's time, as its meaning could not be deduced from its form. Preuschen

(*HZNT in loc.*) quotes from Matthaei a scholion which is not in Grimm : δεξιολάβοι λέγονται οἱ παραφύλακες.

δεξιός.

P Magd 24⁶ (B.C. 217) Ψενοβάστις τῆι αὐτῆι δεξιᾶι χειρὶ ἐπισπασαμένη τῆς ἀ[ναβολῆς τοῦ ἱματίου—as completed by Wilcken *Archiv* vi. p. 274. P Tebt I. 30³² (B.C. 114) ἐτραυμάτισαν τὴν γυναῖκά μου εἰς τὴν δεξιὰν χεῖρα, P Oxy X. 1252 *verso*¹⁹ (A.D. 288-95) ἐγὼ . . . χειροτονη[θεὶς διὰ] τῆς εὐτυχοῦς σου δεξιᾶς, "I having been appointed by your propitious right hand " (Edd.). For δεξιά = "pledge" see P Fay 124¹³ (ii/A.D.) πάνυ γάρ μοι δοκεῖς ἄφρων τις εἶ[ν]αι . . . μὴ φυλάσσ[ι]ν σου τὴν δεξιάν, "indeed you appear to me to be quite mad in not keeping your pledge" (Edd.). Cf. P Leid Z⁴ (A.D. 391-2) εἴωθεν ἡ ὑμετέρα φ[ιλ]ανθρωπία πᾶσιν τοῖς δεομένοις χεῖρ[α] δεξιὰν [ὀρέ]γειν. So P Oxy III. 533¹⁸ (ii/iii A.D.) ἵνα τηρήσωσι αὐτῶν τὴν δεξιάν. For the phrase of Mt 20²¹ etc. cf. P Ryl II. 154³⁷ (A.D. 66) οὐλ(ὴ μετώπωι ἐγ δεξιῶν, P Tebt II. 375³ (A.D. 110-1) οὐλὴ στέρ[ν]ῳι ἐγ δεξιῶν. A curious astrological dialogue in P Ryl II. 63⁴ (iii/A.D.) assigns the parts of the body to the planets and zodiac, and begins Ἥλιός [ἐσ]τιν δεξιὸς ὀφθαλμός, Σελήνη ὁ εὐώνυμος. MGr δεξίς is declined like βαθύς. It has a derived meaning, "prosperous, happy," as in the greeting ὁ θεὸς νὰ σοῦ φέρῃ (φέρνῃ) δεξιά.

δέομαι.

Like some others of its class, δέομαι tends in the Κοινή to let its uncontracted forms set the model of its flexion : hence δέεται and the like. See *Proleg.* p. 54 f., Thackeray *Gr.* i. p. 243. Δέομαι is very common both in original and derived meanings, to have a need and to express it. (Cf. on δέησις above). For the former cf. P Giss I. 7¹⁵ (Hadrian) τοιούτου ὄντος τοῦ βάρους καὶ τῆς σῆς χρηστότητος δεομένου, P Flor I. 6¹⁶ (A.D. 210) δ[εό]μεθα πλείονος χρόνου εἰς τὴν συντελείωσιν, *ib.* II. 154⁹ (A.D. 268) καὶ εἴ τι δέονται ἔχειν ὑμῶν, καὶ τοῦτο δήλωσον, *Michel* 200³ (mid. ii/B.C.) τοῖς ἀεὶ δεομένοις χρείας, "those in need." P Oxy VI. 896⁶ (A.D. 316) τὴν σύνοψιν τῶν δεομένων τόπων ζωγραφίας, "an inspection of the places requiring painting " (Edd.). Some of these passages show the verb already half way towards the expression of need. For this cf. P Petr II. 45ᵛ¹⁶ (B.C. 246) δεη[θ]έντων μηθέν, BGU I. 361ⁱⁱ·²⁰ (A.D. 184) ἐδεήθη αὐτοῦ ταύτην [*sc.* διαθήκην] ἔχειν παρ' ἑαυτῷ : as in earlier Greek, there is no passive sense attached to any of the forms. The verb has a regular use in petitions addressed to ruling sovereigns, as distinguished from those addressed to magistrates, to whom ἀξιῶ "claim" (see *s.v.*) was used as appropriately as δέομαι "entreat" to the former. Thus P Par 26³⁸ (B.C. 163-2) (= *Selections*, p. 17) δεόμεθα οὖν ὑμῶν . . . ἀποστεῖλαι ἡμῶν τὴν ἔντευξιν ἐπὶ Διονύσιον, P Lond 45²⁶ (B.C. 160-59) (= I. p. 36) δέομαι ὑμῶν ἀποστεῖλαι μου τὴν ἔντευξιν ἐπὶ Κυδίαν—both petitions addressed to King Ptolemy and Queen Cleopatra. See further Laqueur *Quaestiones*, p. 3 ff. In P Tebt II. 315⁴ (ii/A.D.) ἕτερα γράμ[ματα δι'] ὧν σου ἐδεόμην περὶ [τῶν Πύ]ρρου [ἱ]ματίων ϛ . . ὅπως μοι [πέμψῃς] ὅσον [ἐ]ὰν ἦ, "telling you to send them to me at any cost" (Edd.), entreaty has developed into demand—a still stronger "expression of need." In Wünsch *AF* 5²³ (iii/A.D.) (= Deissmann *BS*, p. 276) ἀγαγεῖν καὶ ζεῦξαι σύμβιον τὸν Οὐρβανὸν

PART II.

. . πρὸς τὴν Δομιτιανὰν . . ἐρῶντα καὶ δεόμενον αὐτῆς, we may fairly render "wooing."

δέον, τό.

P Petr II. 11(1)⁶ (iii/B.C.) (= *Selections*, p. 8) ἀπὸ τούτου τὸ μὲν ἥμυσυ εἰς τὰ δέοντα ὑπελιπόμην, "half of this I have kept by me for necessaries," P Par 38²⁷ (B.C. 162) ὅπως ἔχω τὰ δέοντα, καὶ μὴ διαλύωμαι τῷ λιμῷ, BGU I. 251³ (A.D. 81) τὰ δέοντ[α πάντα, *ib.* IV. 1141⁴ (B.C. 14), where τὰ ἐπείγοντα πράγματα is cancelled and δέοντα substituted for the last two words. Note P Petr II. 25(*a*)² εἰς δέοντα ἅρμασι ε, and so with τοῖς ἡνιόχοις lower, but in (*d*)⁸ δέοντα ὑποζυγίων. For other parts of the participle, cf. P Fay 107¹² (A.D. 133) πρὸς τὴν δέουσαν ἐπέξοδο[ν, "for fitting punishment," P Tebt II. 332²⁰ A.D. 176) ἀξιῶ τὴν δέουσαν ἐξέτασιν [γ]ενέσθαι ἐξ ὧν δέον ἐστίν, "I beg that due inquiry should be made of the proper persons" (Edd.). For δέον ἐστί, see also P Oxy VII. 1061¹³ (B.C. 22) κἂν δέον ἦν Πτολεμαίῳ . . . συντυχεῖν, BGU III. 981ⁱⁱ·⁶ (A.D. 79) ὡς δέον ἐστί σε ἐπιστεῖλαι τῷ μελλήσοντί με γραμματεύειν, PSI III. 235¹⁴ (c. A.D. 175).] θῆναι περὶ ὧν δέον ἐστίν—the context is fragmentary. Cf. 1 Pet 1⁶ S*ACK al*. Δεόντως is found P Oxy IX. 1203⁷ (late i/A.D.) περὶ τοῦ μὴ δεόντως ἠγορακέναι, "concerning his improper purchase" (Ed.). P Tebt II. 287¹⁷ (A.D. 161-9) περὶ ὧν οὐ δ[ε]όντως ἀπα[ι]τοῦνται, CPHerm 52ⁱ·¹⁶ (iii/A.D.) τὰ μ[ὴ] δεόντως ἀπῃτημένα. See also *s.v.* δεῖ.

δέος.

P Lond 405¹⁴ (c. A.D. 346) (= II. p. 295)—we fail to make sense of the line, which ends with a hiatus. An adverb formed from the verb δείδω occurs in Vettius Valens p. 238⁷² βραδέως μὲν καὶ δεδιότως φθέγγεται. As far as we can see, both δέος and δείδω belong to a rather higher literary stratum, and a solitary appearance in Heb is quite what might be expected. A pathetic letter from a wife, PSI III. 177⁶ (ii/iii A.D.), says of their child δ'(έδια] μὴ ἀποθάνῃ σου μὴ ὄν[τος ἐν θάδε : of course δ[είδω] is equally possible—or something else.

δέρμα.

This NT ἅπ. εἰρ. (Heb 11⁷) may be illustrated from P Lond 1171²⁷ (B.C. 8) (= III. p. 178), farm accounts, with προβά των) δέρματα as an item. So in the dream of a visitor who had sought guidance and assistance in the Serapeum, P Par 50¹⁵ (B.C. 160) ᾤετο ἄνθρωπον λέγειν μοι· Φέρε τὸ δέρμα τοῦ ποδός σου καὶ ἐγὼ δώσω σοι τὸ δέρμα τοῦ ποδός μου. See also P Fay 107² (A.D. 133) ὑφείλαντο δέρματα αἰγειὰ corr. from αἰγειὰν τέσσαρα, "they carried off four goatskins," *ib.* 121¹² (c. A.D. 100) τὸ δ[έρ]μα τοῦ μόσχου οὗ ἐθύ[σ]αμεν, "the hide of the calf that we sacrificed," P Grenf II. 51¹² (A.D. 143) ἀ[πέ]χειν αὐτοὺς τιμὴν δερμάτων αἰγικῶν τεσσάρων. From the inscrr., e.g. *Syll* 592¹⁴ (end of ii/B.C.) λαμβάνειν δὲ καὶ γέρα τὸν θυομένων ἱερείων ἐν τῶι ἱερῶι πάντων, σκέλος δεξιὸν καὶ τὰ δέρματα κτλ., and *Cagnat* IV. 1000⁶² (ii/B.C.), ends where at an annual memorial feast in Amorgos it is ordained παρατιθέτωσαν δὲ τἆλλα μὲν θυθέντα, [τ]ὰ δὲ δέρματα ἀποδόμενοι παραχρῆμα καταναλισκέτωσαν παραχρῆμα καὶ ταῦτα ἐν τόπῳ.

δερμάτινος.

BGU III. 814[10] (iii/A.D.) πέμψι]ς μοι ἀβόλλην . . . καὶ ζεῦγος ἱματίω[ν δερμ]ατίνων. In the great Mysteries Inscription of Andania, *Syll* 653[23] (B.C. 91), it is laid down regarding the ἱεραὶ γυναῖκες μὴ ἐχέτω δὲ μηδεμία χρυσία . . . μηδὲ ὑποδήματα εἰ μὴ πίλινα ἢ δερμάτινα ἱερόθυτα. For the form δερματικός, see *Ostr* 1611[6] Rom.) δερματικ ὰ β: or is this for δελματικ(αί) ? (See *s.v.* Δαλματία.

δέρρις.

For this word, which has been transferred from Zech 13[4] into the "Western" text of Mk 1[6], see the Andanian inscription *Syll* 653[9] (B.C. 91) μηδὲ περιτιθέμεν ταῖς σκαναῖς μήτε δέρρεις μήτε αὐλείας where Dittenberger in his note refers to Hesych. δέρρεις· τὸ παχὺ ὕφασμα, ᾧ εἰς παραπέτασμα ἐχρῶντο.

δέρω.

P Oxy III. 653 (*b*) (before A.D. 161) shows us this word in its colloquial sense—first found in Aristophanes—of "beat," "thrash" instead of "flay." In the account of a trial regarding a mortgage upon the property of Voltimus which had been seized by the creditor, Sempronius Orestinus, the Praefect informs the latter that unless he makes restitution —οὐ μόνον κατακριθήσει ἀλλὰ καὶ δαρής[ει. So in *Syll* 737[91] (A.D. 175) ἔστω δὲ τὰ αὐτὰ ἐπιτείμια καὶ τῷ δαρέντι καὶ μὴ ἐπεξελθόντι παρὰ τῷ ἱερεῖ ἢ τῷ ἀρχιβάκχῳ, ἀλλὰ δημοσίᾳ ἐνκαλέσαντι: the δαρείς here has been called ὁ πληγείς a little earlier. It may be noted that for the ordinary rendering of 2 Cor 11[20] εἴ τις εἰς πρόσωπον ὑμᾶς δέρει, "if any one smiteth you on the face," Paspati suggests (see *Exp* III. i. p. 238) "if he upbraideth you to your face," in view of the MGr προσωποδέρει. The ordinary MGr verb δέρνω (aor. ἔδειρα) = "whip," "beat."

δεσμεύω.

For δεσμεύω, "bind together," as in Mt 23[4], cf. P Lond 131 *recto*[426.437] (farm accounts—A.D. 78–9) (= I. p. 182 f.) ἐργάτηι δεσμεύοντι ἀγκάλας . . . δεσμεύων ἀγκάλας ἐν τῷ χωρίῳ ἐργάτης ᾱ, P Oxy VII. 1049[7] (late ii/A.D.) ἄλ(λοις) β ἐργ(άταις) δεσμ(εύουσι) μανδ άκας (δραχμαὶ) γ (τριώβολον), so [12.17.22], and P Flor III. 322[35] (?A.D. 258) δεσμεύοντες τὸν αὐτὸν χόρτον δέσμες . . -αις [22.36]. In this meaning the verb is linked with δέσμη: for that which looks towards δεσμός, as in Lk 8[29], cf. the incantation in the great Paris magical papyrus, P Par 574[1246] (iii/A.D.) (= *Selections*, p. 114) ἔξελθε δαῖμον, ἐπεί σε δεσμεύω δεσμοῖς ἀδαμαντίνοις ἀλύτοις. Cf. P Lond 46[380] (iv/A.D.) (= I. p. 75) δεσμεύων λέγε καταδεσμεύω τὸν (δεῖνα) κτλ.

δέσμη.

is differently accented in our authorities. Mayser *Gr.* pp. 285, 435, cites Herodian (ii/A.D.) in favour of δεσμή, but there are testimonies for δέσμη (see Lobeck *Par.* p. 396), and the oxytone might be a confusion with δεσμός. Δέσμη *bundle* is common in Hellenistic. Thus P Petr II. 25 (*a*)[4] (B.C. 226), *ib.* 30 (*d*)[12] (iii/B.C.) τούτων χόρτου δεσμῶν φη, P Tebt I. 122[8] (B.C. 90 or 63) χόρτον δέσμας σ̅, P Oxy IV. 742[1] (B.C. 2) ἀπόστειλόν μ[οι] πόσας δέσμας παρείληφες, "send me word how many bundles you have received" (Edd.), *ib.*[13] τὴν χιλίαν δέσμην, "the 1000 bundles"

(Edd.). and *ib.* IX. 1212[1] (ii/A.D.) ἀσπαράγου δέσμ(αι) ιθ, *al.* It is curious that the misspelling δύσμη should be found more than once: so the farmer Gemellus in P Fay 119[1.5] (c. A.D. 100), and an equally literate gentleman in P Ryl II. 135[11] (A.D. 34) quoted under διά. Cf. further under δεσμεύω. A diminutive δεσμίδιον is also found, e.g. P Oxy X. 1288[9.15] (iv/A.D.) For the idiomatic and possibly genuine δήσατε αὐτὰ δέσμας δέσμας, Mt 13[30], see *Proleg.* p. 97. Epiphanius, who gives us this, has also ζυγὴ ζυγή.

δέσμιος

in its NT sense of "prisoner" may be illustrated from P Tebt I. 22[18] (B.C. 112) δέσμ[ιο]ν αὐτὸν ἐξαπόστειλον πρὸς ἡμᾶς, P Oxy III. 580 (ii/A.D.) εἰς ἐπιτή]ρ[ησιν] τῶν κατὰ (corr. from παρὰ) φυλακὴν δεσμίων δίδωμι τὸν ὑπογεγραμμένο(ν) ὄντα εὔπορον καὶ [ἐπιτήδ]ειον . . .

δεσμός.

For the full force of ὁ δεσμὸς τῆς γλώσσης, "the bond of the tongue," in Mk 7[35], reference may be made to Deissmann *LAE.* p. 306 ff., where it is shown that the expression has a "technical" meaning derived from the old belief that a man was "bound" by daemonic influences. The man was not merely made to speak, but daemonic fetters were broken, and Satan's work undone. The plur. τὰ δεσμά, which in the NT is characteristic of the Lucan writings, would seem to be more literary than οἱ δεσμοί, the general LXX form: see Thackeray *Gr.* i. p. 154. According to Mayser *Gr.* p. 285 the neuter plur. is never found in the Ptolemaic papyri, nor can we supply any instance from a later period. In the Attic inscriptions both forms are found (see Meisterhans *Gr.* p. 143) with apparently no distinction of meaning, so that Cobet's distinction (*Mnemosyne*, 1858, p. 74 ff.) that the neuter refers to actual bonds, the masculine to the imprisonment, cannot be maintained: cf. Kennedy on Phil 1[13] in *EGT*. By origin, δεσμά should be collective and δεσμοί individualizing, which would be the very opposite of Cobet's dictum: but usage may well have introduced a new differentia. A spell for loosing bonds (δυσμολύτον, *sic*) may be cited from P Leid W[vii.30] (ii/iii A.D.) λυθήτω πᾶς δεσμώς, πᾶσα βία, ραγήτω πᾶς σίτηρω (*i.e.* σίδηρος) κτλ. A curiously close parallel for Heb 11[36] (. . . πεῖραν ἔλαβον, ἔτι δὲ δεσμῶν καὶ φυλακῆς) occurs in Vettius Valens p. 68[17] δεσμῶν πεῖραν ἐπὶ χρόνον ἱκανὸν λαμβάνοντας, ἕως συμπληρώσωσι τοὺς χρόνους τοῦ ἀστέρος.

δεσμοφύλαξ.

P Petr III. 28 (*e*) *verso* (*b*)[5] (iii/B.C.) παρεδόθη δὲ Παῶτι δεσμοφύλακι, "but he was handed over to Paos the gaoler," P Lille I. 7[11] (iii/B.C.) οὗτος δὲ ἀπήγαγέν με εἰς τὸ αὐθι δεσμωτήριον, εἶπεν τωι δεσμοφύ(λακι) δι' ἣν αἰτίαν συνέσχημαι. BGU IV. 1138[12 ff.] (B.C. 19–8) (= *Chrest.* II. p. 123) ἐφάνη τῷ Κασίωι ὄντ(ι) ἐνταῦθα, τὸν τῆ(ς) Σάιεως δεσμοφύλακ(α) Χαιρήμονα καλέσαι, καὶ ἐλεγχο(μένου) αὐτο[ῦ] πρὸς ἔλεγχο(ν) τοῦ Ἰσχυρίω νος, ὃ ἠδίκησεν, ἐμαρτύρησ(εν) ὁ δεσμοφύλαξ Χαιρήμω ν περὶ το[ῦ] παραδεδόσθαι αὐτῷ τὸν Παπία[ν κτλ. Cf. P Flor I. 2[76] (A.D. 265) where a certain person is nominated εἰς δεσμο[φυλακίαν τῆς ἐν τῇ] μητροπόλει εἱρκτῆς: on δεσμοφυλακία as a tax for the support of public prisons, see the editors' introduction to P Fay 53.

δεσμωτήριον.

See the citation from P Lille 7 s.v. δεσμοφύλαξ, and cf. P Hib I. 73[8] (B.C. 243–2) ε[ἰ]ς τὸ ἐν Σινάρυ δεσμω]τήριον, P Tebt II. 567 (A.D. 53–4) ὑπ' ἐμοῦ εἰς δεσμευτήριον βληθήσεται, BGU IV. 1024[v 10] (iv/v A.D.) κ]ελεύει τὸν Διόδημον ἀναλημφθῆναι τῷ δεσμωτηρίῳ, ib.[20] δεσμωτερίῳ.

δεσμώτης.

P Petr II. 13 (3)[9] (B.C. 258–3) εὐθέως γὰρ ἕξομεν ἐξαγόντες καὶ πλέονι τόπ[ω]ι ἀποχρήσασθαι πρὸς τοὺς παραδεδομένους νῦν δεσμώτας (corrected from δια—) [ὑ]π' Ἀπολλωνίου τοῦ διοικητοῦ, "for forthwith, by bringing out these prisoners, we shall have more room at our disposal for the prisoners now being delivered to us by Apollonios the administrator" (Ed.).

δεσπότης.

BGU IV. 1125[7] (B.C. 13) τὰ]ς μελέτας καὶ τὰς ἐπιδίξις ἐγὼι αὐτὸς ὁ δεσπότης χορη[γ]ήσωι αὐτῶι Ναρκίσσωι [. . . N. is the writer's slave. P Giss I. 27[12] (c. A.D. 117) πα[ι]δάρια δύο ἀ[π]ὸ Αὐάσεως (= Ὀάσεως) ἠνέχθη τῷ δεσπό[τ]ῃ, ὧν τὸ] μ[ἐ]ν ἐστιν τετραετές, τὸ δὲ τριετῆ. A derived noun occurs BGU IV. 1187[22] (c. B.C. 1) μενούσης μοι [τῆς] κυρείας καὶ δεσποτήας [τῶ]ν δηλουμένων τόπων [κ]αθότι καὶ ἔστιν (i.e. εἰσίν) ἡμέτεροι. In the same petition, l.[9], we find the kindred verb: καὶ ἐφ' ὃν περιῇ χρό[ν]ον κρατῶν (for -οῦσα?) δεσπόζουσα ἀνεμφ[οδ]ίστω[ς μη]δενὸς ἁπλ[ῶ]ς δια[κωλύοντος διετέλει—referring to the same estate as held by the writer's mother. So P Tor I. 1[viii 26] (B.C. 116) (= Chrest. II. p. 38) ἕκαστον δ' αὐτῶν δεσπόζοντα τῆς ἰδίας κτήσεως. Preisigke 4127[1] ἀκτινοβόλε δέσποτα opens a hymn to the sun. In MGr δεσπότης is a bishop or priest: the voc. δέσποτα survives in eccl. language, "reverend sir." But the fem. δέσποινα (also eccl.) is a title of Mary, descended of course from the classical use of the term in addressing goddesses.

δεῦρο.

For the temporal use of δεῦρο, as in Rom 1[13], cf. P Lond 358[16] (c. A.D. 150) (= II. p. 172) μέχρι τοῦ δεῦρο πέρας οὐδέπω ἐπετέθη τῷ πράγματι, BGU I. 180[9] (ii/iii A.D.) μέχρι τοῦ δευρε[ὶ], P Strass I. 56[12] (ii/iii A.D.), and ib. 73[16] (ii/A.D.) μέχρι δεῦρο, P Gen I. 47[8] (A.D. 346) μέχρι δεύρου. In P Lond 409[26] (c. A.D. 346) (= II. p. 286) ἄχρεις δεῦρο we have a close approach to the Pauline phrase. A form δεῦρε is found in the Attic inscriptions of B.C. 500–450 (see Meisterhans Gr. p. 146): it belongs to the same impulse that produced the plural δεῦτε, through the common imperative use. In P Oxy X. 1297[15] (iv/A.D.) δεῦ μετ' αὐτοῦ καὶ ἔνεγκεν τοὺς ἄμητας, "come here with him and bring the milk cakes," we have an instance of the imperatival δεῦρο, in an apocopated form. See Proleg. p. 172.

δευτερεύω.

This LXX verb (Esth 4[8] Ἀμὰν ὁ δευτερεύων τῷ βασιλεῖ) is found in P Passalacqua[13] (Ptol.) (= Witkowski[2], p. 54) Πετονοῦριν τὸν δευτερεύοντα.

Δευτερονόμιον.

In Exp T xxvi. p. 170 Ramsay publishes the text of an epitaph from a Phrygian gravestone of date equivalent to A.D. 248 o which ends with the words that if any one desecrates the tomb—ἔσται αὐτῷ αἱ ἀραὶ ἡ γεγραμμέναι ἐν τῷ δευτερονόμῳ, "there shall be on him the curses which are written in Deuteronomy." "This," he adds, "is perhaps the earliest writing that has come down to us stating the name of a book in the Old Testament."

δευτερόπρωτος.

It is almost superfluous to say that we have found no support for this famous vox nihili (Lk 6[1]), the only interest of which to-day is the curious problem of its early entrance into the text. (Note that W is now added to the MSS rejecting it.) Grimm's superficially parallel δευτερέσχατος "second last, last but one," is no help: "first but one" is δεύτερος simply. Δεκάπρωτος, "one of ten πρῶτοι," is clearly not parallel. One of the most ingenious explanations is that of F. C. Burkitt (Gosp. Hist. p. 8 ff.) that the βα of σαββάτῳ was repeated at the beginning of a new line, and then βατω expanded as δευτερο- πρώτῳ—cf. ιβμήνου cited above under δεκαδύο.

δεύτερος.

For δεύτερον = "in the second place," as in 1 Cor 12[28], cf. P Tebt I. 58[10] date ii/B.C. καλῶς οὖν ποήσῃς εὐχαριστῆσαι πρῶτον μὲν τοῖς θεοῖς δεύτερον δὲ σῶσαι ψυχὰς πολλάς κτλ., "please therefore in the first place to give thanks (?—see s.v. εὐχαριστέω) to the gods and secondly to save many lives, etc." (Edd.). In P Tebt II. 207[19] (c. A.D. 123) we find ἐγ δευτέρου = "a second time," as in Mk 14[72] al. OGIS 290[17] (c. B.C. 170) τῇ δεύτερον ἡμέραι is defended by Kaibel ap. Dittenberger in loc., appealing to IMAe I. 155[2] τὰι δεύτερον ἁμέραι μετὰ τὰ ἱερά, and the analogy of τῷ ὕστερον ἔτει and ἡ σήμερον ἡμέρα. In MGr δευτέρα is "Monday" (ἡ δεύτερη = 2nd, fem. of δεύτερος and sharing its accent).

δέχομαι.

This common verb hardly needs illustration, but we may note P Hib I. 79 (d)[8] (B.C. 220–8) δέξαι παρὰ Ζωίλου . . . (δραχμὰς) δέκα, P Tebt II. 281[21] (B.C. 125) δέδεγμαι παρὰ σοῦ ἐκ πλήρους ἄνευ παντὸς λοιπήματος, "I have received from you the sum in full without any arrears" (Edd.), ib. 422[11] (iii/A.D.) δέξε παρ' αὐτοῦ τὰς (δραχμὰς) ρ̄, and from the early Christian letter P Heid 6[20] (iv/A.D.) (= Selections, p. 127) καταξίωσον δέξεσθαι τὸ μικρὸν ἐλέου διὰ τοῦ ἀδελφοῦ ἡμῶν Μαγαρίου. It is often used of receiving letters, as P Flor II. 154[2] A.D. 268 ἅμα τῷ δέξασθαί μου τὰ [γράμ]ματα δήλωσόν μοι κτλ., BGU IV. 1208[21] (B.C. 27) αὐτὸ (sc. τὸ πιττάκιον) ἐδεξάμην, where it seems to imply "I accepted it" Abbott (Joh. Voc. p. 220, Fourfold Gospel p. 220) has drawn attention to the fact that δέχομαι occurs only once in the Fourth Gospel, 4[45], where it is used of the Galilaeans' [hospitable] reception of Jesus in His native place. When Jn (13[20]) gives a version of the Logion of Mt 10[40], he substitutes ὁ λαμβάνων for ὁ δεχόμενος, the inferiority of which as Greek is sufficient evidence of its independence. Δέχομαι with a personal object may be quoted from P Leid M⁵·⁷ (ii/B.C.) Ὧρος ὁ ἀποδόμενος, ὃν ἐδέξατο Ὀσορό(ηρις) καὶ οἱ ἀδελφοὶ οἱ πριάμενοι. MGr has the verb unaltered, = "receive," "accept."

δέω.

With Lk 13¹⁶ where demoniac power "binds" the sufferer from curvature of the spine, cf. the use of the verb to describe the "binding" power of curses: *Syll* 809¹⁴ (iv/iii B.C.) ἔδησα τὰς [χε]ῖρας καὶ τοὺς πόδας καὶ [τὴ]ν γλῶσσαν καὶ τὴν ψυχ[ή]ν κτλ. Dittenberger remarks that καταδέω (*ib.*²) is commoner in this cursing formula: he cites another *defixio* in almost the same phrases. Other examples of the verb are P Fay 108¹² (c. A.D. 171) ἔδησαν ἡμᾶς σὺν καὶ τῷ μαγδωλοφύλακι, "bound us along with the guard of the watch-tower," said of thieves, P Oxy X. 1294⁷ (ii/iii A.D.) ἱμάντα δεδεμένον εἰς τὸ πανάριον καλόν, "a good strap tied to the basket" (Edd.).

δή.

P Oxy IV. 705⁶¹ (A.D. 200-2) τ[ὸ] ὅμοιον δὴ καὶ ἐ[π]ὶ τούτου φυλαχθήσεται, "the same rule shall be observed in this case also" (Edd.), *ib.* VI. 899¹⁴ (A.D. 200) οὗ δὴ χάριν, "for which reason," *ib.* 907³⁶ (A.D. 276) λέγω δὴ τῇ Διδύμῃ, "to wit Didyme," P Tebt II. 424⁷ (late iii/A.D.) ὡς ἐὰ (*l.* ἐὰν) μὴ ἀποκαταστασίας [δ]ὴ πέμψῃς [ο]ἶδάς σου τὸ[ν] κίνδυνον, "so unless you now send discharges you know your danger" (Edd.), BGU IV. 1208⁴⁹ (B.C. 27-6) τοῦ σώμα(τος)[ἐπι]με λόμενος· ἵν' ὑγιένῃς, ὃ δὴ μέγιστον ἡγοῦμαι, P Ryl II. 77¹⁶ (A.D. 192) Ὀλυμπιόδωρος εἶπ εν· ἔχομεν δὴ φωνὴν τοῦ Ἀσπιδᾶ ὅτι ἰδίῳ κινδύνῳ αὐτὸν στέφει, "we now have the declaration of Aspidas" (Edd.).

δηλαυγῶς,

the reading of אּ*C (L) Δ in Mk 8²⁵, is found in the *Mithrasliturgie*, p. 18⁸, acc. to the Paris papyrus: ἐὰν δέ ἄλλῳ θέλῃς δεικνύειν, ἔχε τῆς καλουμένης βοτάνης κεντριδίδος χυλὸν περιχρίων τὴν ὄψιν οὗ βούλει μετὰ ῥοδίνου, καὶ ὄψεται δηλαυγῶς ὥστε σε θαυμάζειν. The τηλαυγῶς in Dieterich's text is only an emendation—as it is very probably in אּ ABDNWΘ in Mk *l.c.*, since τηλ. is the commoner word. (Hesychius and Democritus in Grimm should have sufficed to prevent Lagrange from denying the existence of δηλ.)

δῆλος.

CP Herm 6⁵, a petition addressed to an Emperor, has in a fragmentary context]ττ[ω]μένοι καθ' ἕκαστον τῶ[ν λο]γι σ[μ]ῶν δῆλός ἐστιν ἀριθμὸς καὶ λειτουρ[γι]ῶν. P Oxy VIII. 1101¹² (A.D. 367-70) ὅτι δὲ κεκώλυται παρὰ τοῖς νόμοις τοῦτο, δῆλον, "that this is forbidden by the law is clear" (Ed.), *Ib.* X. 1264¹⁷ (A.D. 272) πρὸς τὸ πᾶσι δῆλα εἶναι τὰ ὑπόντα μοι . . . δίκαια. P Thead 19¹⁰ (iv/A.D.) ἕρμαιον δηλονότι ἡ[γη]σαμένη (*i.e.* -η) τὸν θάνατον τοῦ πατρός μου. P Flor I. 36²⁸ (iv/A.D., beginning) ἢ δῆλον ὅτι κιν[δυνεύσ]εις τὸ[ὁρ]ᾶν ἄχραντον δικα[στ]ήριον. *Ib.* III. 367¹¹ (iii/A.D.) ἀλ]λὰ δηλονότι πλούτῳ γαυρωθεὶς κτλ. BGU III. 803³⁹ (ii/iii A.D.) ἐγέν]ετο δὲ δῆλον τότ[ε . . . . *ib.* 902¹⁵ (A.D. 168-9) ἐξ ὧν δῆλ(ον) γ(ίνεται) ὀφείλειν κτλ. The word is by no means common: we have quoted almost all the instances we can find in papyri. The adverb appears in P Oxy III. 474²⁰

(? A.D. 184) εἰ δὲ μὴ δήλως [καὶ ἐμ]προθέσμως τὰ δέοντα . . . MGr has δηλονότι "that is to say, viz.": the combination grows steadily commoner during the Byzantine age.

δηλόω,

unlike δῆλος, is exceedingly common, and needs very few quotations. P Oxy II. 237ⁱⁱ·¹¹ (A.D. 186) ψειλῶς σοι διὰ τῆς ἐπιστολῆς δεδήλωκεν τάδε, "he merely wrote you a letter to the following effect" (Edd.), *ib.* X. 1293⁷ (A.D. 117-38) κομισαμένη οὖν δήλωσόν μοι, "when you have received it, let me know." These are typical of a great many occurrences. P Leid Wˣⁱᵛ·¹⁷ (ii/iii A.D.) ἀπάλιψόν μου τὰ τῆς ἱμαρμένης κακά· μὴ ὑπόστελλε σεαυτόν, κ(αὶ) δῆλου μοι πάντα—addressed to an angel. P Flor I. 86²⁶ (i/A.D., end) ἀκολούθω[ς] ταῖς διὰ τῶν [συν]γραφῶν δηλωθείσαις διαστολαῖς will serve as another type: cf. such papers as P Ryl II. 248² (B.C. 162) ἧς αἱ γειτνίαι δεδήλωνται διὰ τῆς προκειμένης συγγραφῆς, P Tor I. 1ⁱⁱ·¹² (B.C. 116) (= *Chrest.* II. p. 32) συνεισέδωκέ μοι συνχώρησιν, καθ' ἣν ἐδηλοῦτο μήτε πρότερον μήτε νῦν ἀντιποιεῖσθαι τῆς οἰκίας. A legal or quasi-legal tone predominates, but it is also largely used non-technically to denote "informing."

Δημᾶς.

For this proper name, see P Lond 929³⁸ (ii/iii A.D.) (= III. p. 42), BGU I. 10¹² (A.D. 192). The earliest occurrence is P Petr III. 49⁷, where Δημᾶδι follows Φιλίππωι and Τιμοθέωι, but the context has less Biblical suggestion: BGU III. 715ⁱⁱ·¹³ (A.D. 101-2) shows Demas in the company of several Jews, as Ἰωσῆς ὁ καὶ Τεύφιλο(ς), Ἀβράμ[ιος?.....]ς Ἰσάκεως, Σαμβαθ(άων) Ἰακούβου: the paper is a γραφὴ σιτολ(όγων).

Δημήτριος.

The name is common in the inscriptions—*Michel* 835⁷⁷, 867ⁱᵛ·⁹, 1319¹ etc.

δημιουργός.

In BGU III. 937³ (A.D. 250) we hear of the δημιουργοῦ θεᾶς Ῥώμης—one of the few references in the Egyptian papyri to the Roman cultus (see Otto *Priester* i. p. 9). For a Christian use, see the prayer of v/vi A.D., P Oxy VI. 925³ (= *Selections*, p. 131) which begins ὁ θ(εὸ)ς ὁ παντοκράτωρ ὁ ἅγιος ὁ ἀληθινὸς φιλάνθρωπος καὶ δημιουργὸς κτλ. The description of Tarsus in *OGIS* 578¹² (A.D. 222-35) as μόνη τετειμημένη δημ[ι]ουργίαις τε καὶ κιλικαρχί[αις] ἐπαρχικῶν shows that in Tarsus the public magistrates were known as δημιουργοί, as in several towns in Greece during classical times. In Demetrius *Style* § 215 (ed. W. Rhys Roberts, p. 168) Ctesias is said to be ἐναργείας δημιουργός, "an artist in vividness" (Ed.). MGr δημιουργῶ "create."

δῆμος.

E. L. Hicks, in *CR* i. p. 42, draws the moral of the disuse of δῆμος in days when Greek freedom was extinct: where it does occur in NT (Ac 12²², 17⁵, 19³⁰·³³) it suggests merely a rabble. Of course it occurs abundantly in Hellenistic inscr. which record how the people passed complimentary resolutions or voted statues, by way of insisting that their local assembly was still in being. [For a defence of the interpretation of **δῆμος** in Acts as a technical term denoting a political body, see Ferguson, *Legal Terms common to the Macedonian Inscriptions and the NT*, Chicago, p. 38 ff.] But except in the technical sense of "commune," "parish" (still in LXX and MGr), the word was not wanted for practical purposes. Its appearances in the papyri support this account. P Oxy I. 41 *bis* (iii/ivA.D.) gives the acclamations of ὁ δῆμος at Oxyrhynchus, in honour of their prytanis. *Ib.* III. 473² (A.D. 138–60) ἔδοξε τοῖς τῆς λαμπροτάτης πόλεως τῶν Ὀξυρυγχ‌ιτῶν ἄρχουσι καὶ τῷ δήμῳ [καὶ Ῥω‌μαίων καὶ Ἀλεξανδρέων τοῖς παρεπιδημοῦσι to set up a statue of a gymnasiarch whose "unstinted provision of unguents," contribution to the fund for theatrical displays, and his restoration of the baths and the "greater thermae" had earned the popular gratitude : this will serve as a normal specimen of honorific decrees. In P Hib I. 28¹³, ¹⁵, ¹⁷ (c. B.C. 265) δῆμος is the twelfth part of a φυλή, and contains twelve φράτραι, so that the (unnamed) Egyptian town contains sixty of these "demes" or wards. So in P Amh II. 36¹ (c. B.C. 135) παρὰ Δ‌ρ‌ύτωνος τοῦ Πα‌μ‌φίλου Κρητὸς δήμου Φιλωτ‌ε‌ρ‌είου. These, which are the only occurences of δῆμος in the whole series of papyri edited by Dr Grenfell or Dr Hunt up to date, will suffice to illustrate its position, unless we add the "poetry" of P Giss I. 3² in which Phoebus acclaims the accession of Hadrian—ἅρματι λευκοπώλωι Ἄρει Τραιαν‌ῷι συνανατείλας ἥκω σοι, ὦ δῆμ‌ε.

δημόσιος

is exceedingly common as an epithet for "public" officials or property of all kinds : as P Ryl II. 232⁸ (ii/A.D.) καὶ οἱ δημόσιοι προσεφώνησαν αὐτῷ ὅτι μένις ἐν τῇ κώ‌μη, PSI III. 220¹⁶ (ii/A.D.) τοῖς τῆ‌ς κώμης δημοσίοις καὶ πρεσβυτέροις. Δημόσια are public taxes : as P Lond 951⁴ (A.D. 249) (= III. p. 221) τελεῖ τὰ καθήκοντα δ. *Ib.* 1164‌ᵉ‌·¹⁰ (A.D. 212) (= III. p. 160) has ῥύμη δημοσία, which like ὁδὸς δ. is very common. Δημόσιοι γεωργοί in Egypt are constantly mentioned : see *s.v.* **γεωργέω**. A Leipzig papyrus of Hadrian's reign Inv 200⁷ has τὴν βασιλικὴν καὶ τὴν δημοσίαν καὶ οὐσιακὴν γῆν : Wilcken (*Archiv* v. p. 245) would drop the second τήν or add a third. P Flor I. 6⁵ (A.D. 210) βουλομένου μου κατη‌γ‌ορεῖν οὔτε ὄντος corr. from ὡς δημοσίου κατηγόρου. P Strass I. 14²¹ (A.D. 211) καθαρὸν ἀπὸ παντὸς ὀφ‌ειλ‌ήματος δ‌ημο‌σίου τε καὶ ἰδιωτι‌κοῦ illustrates the most normal antithesis. For Ac 5¹⁸ cf. P Lips Inv 244⁵ (A.D. 462) (= *Chrest.* II. p. 80) ἐκλείσθην εἰς τ‌ην δη‌μο‌σ‌ίαν ε‌ἱ‌ρκτ‌ή‌ν.

For the adverb **δημοσίᾳ** cf. *Syll* 807 (after A.D. 138), where three times persons miraculously healed return public thanks—thus⁹ καὶ ἐσώθη καὶ δημοσίᾳ ηὐχαρίστησεν τῷ θεῷ καὶ ὁ δῆμος συνεχάρη αὐτῷ. Dittenberger observes that this meaning, "coram populo," is foreign to antiquity. Vettius Valens p. 71²² ἐὰν δὲ τὰ λοιπὰ συντύχῃ, αἰχμάλωτοι γίνονται καὶ δημοσίᾳ τελευτῶσιν, of public execution. In MGr it makes e.g. the compound δημοσιογραφικός "journalistic." Among its derivatives may be noticed δημοσιεύω "practise" (of a doctor, as in classical Greek. So P Oxy I. 40⁹ (ii/iii A.D.) εἰ ἰατρὸς εἰ δημοσ‌ιεύ‌ων ἐπὶ ταρι‌χείᾳ "if you are a doctor officially practising mummification" (Edd.).

δηνάριον.

Ostr 1265⁵ (A.D. 187) ἔλαβον παρὰ σοῦ ἀπὸ τιμῆς οἴνου [Κο‌λοφωνίου δηνάρια δύο ὀβολοὶ (*l.* ὀβολοὺς) ὀκτώ. In *Syll* 869¹⁴ (Imperial θρέψει δὲ καὶ τοῖς υἱοῖς αὐτοῦ Ἀσφ‌αλη καὶ] Νουμηνίῳ ἑκάστῳ θρέμμα ἄρρεν, ἢ ἑκάστῳ αὐτῶν ἀνὰ δηνάρια ν΄: cf. Mt 20¹⁰ ἔλαβον [τὸ] ἀνὰ δηνάριον καὶ αὐτοί. In his note on P Lond 248⁻¹ (= A.D. 346) (= II. p. 306 the editor remarks "that the term *denarius* replaces that of *drachma*, which was regularly in use before the time of Diocletian ; the Neronian denarius reintroduced by Diocletian being reckoned as equivalent to the drachma, and as $\frac{1}{10000}$ of the talent." In P Gen I. 11¹⁴ (A.D. 350), according to the emended reading Preisigke *Berichtigungs‌liste* i. p. 158), we have ἐπελευ‌σόμενος ἐκτίσ‌‌‌ι τῷ ἑτέρῳ ὑπὲρ στροφῆς καὶ ἐπηρίας λόγου ἀργυρίου δ‌ην‌αρ‌ί‌ων μυριάδας κτλ.

δήποτε.

For **δήποτε**, as in [Jn] 5⁴ whether we read οἵῳ δηποτοῦν with A or ᾧ δήποτε with (ω) cf. P Lond 604²² (A.D. 104 = III. p. 125) καθ' ἥ‌ντινα δήποτε αἰτ‌ίαν, P Tebt II. 381¹⁴ (A.D. 123) καθ' ὃν δήποτε οὖν τρόπον. See also the decree of Ptolemy Philometor found at Delos, published in *Archiv* vi. p. 9—²¹ κ‌ατὰ πρεσβείαν ἢ κατ' ἄλλην δηποτοῦν χρε‌ί‌αν‌ τιμῶν καὶ πολιωρῶν, and Aristeas 104 ὅ τι ἂν δηποτοῦν ἐπιβόληται κακοποιεῖν.

διά.

See Thumb's account of the MGr γιά (pron. *ya*—δ has fallen out before *y*, as is normal), *Handbook* p. 104 f. He shows that the old preposition survives unchanged as far as its use c. acc. is concerned. "The local meaning of διά with gen. has entirely disappeared." But γιὰ τοῦτο "therefore," γιὰ ὄνομα τοῦ θεοῦ "for God's sake," are entirely in the succession of old use. Γιά also = *for* in other senses which had not emerged in our period—Thumb notes it "has acquired the function partly of the old dative and partly those of ἐπί, περί, ὑπέρ, ἀντί." Αὐτὸ εἶναι καλὸ γιὰ σένα, "that is good for you," recalls Phil 1²⁴, Heb 1¹⁴ ; and ὅτι γιὰ μένα δὲν ζητῶ, "what I do not seek for myself," has many parallels in NT. The disappearance of διά c. gen. in MGr is not prepared for in the time of the papyri. According to Rossberg's calculation, out of 714 occurrences of διά in papyri 508 are with genitive, which is a more marked predominance than the NT 382:270 (*Proleg.* p. 105).

Διά c. gen. in the papyri is freely illustrated by Rossberg, p. 37 f. ; his citations need not be repeated. Deissmann's reference in *BS*, p. 289, brings up the "Hebraising periphrases" of which διά takes its share. Wünsch *AF* 5²¹ (iii A.D. = *BS*, p. 270) ὁρκίζω σε τὸν φωστῆρα καὶ ἄστρα ἐν οὐρανῷ ποιήσαντα διὰ φωνῆς προστάγ‌ματος, "by the voice of his command," is based on LXX language, and admitted by Deissmann to be a phrase "which a Greek might feel to be a pleonasm, but which is not altogether un-Greek." The commonest of these locutions is διὰ χειρός, c. gen., with meaning indistinguishable from διά c. gen. alone. This is of course based on בְּיַד, but it is not a literal translation like ἐν χειρί. It is obviously modelled upon the vernacular phrase διὰ χειρός, of money paid "by hand," "directly," ubiquitous in commercial documents : e.g. P Oxy II. 268⁷

(A.D. 58) ἀπεσχηκυῖαι [παρὰ τοῦ Ἀντ]ιφάνους διὰ χειρὸς [ἐ]ξ οἴκου ὃ καὶ ἐπε[ίσθη]σαν κεφάλαιον, "have received from Antiphanes from hand to hand in cash the sum which they severally consented to accept" (Edd.). Among other stereotyped phrases may be mentioned διὰ παντός, common in papyri as in Bibl. Greek in place of the obsolescent ἀεί: thus P Lond 42⁶ (B.C. 168) (= I. p. 30, *Selections* p. 9) σοῦ διὰ παντὸς μνείαν ποιούμενοι, BGU IV. 1078² (A.D. 39) Σαραπίων Σαραπιάδι τῇ ἀδελφῇ πλεῖστα χαίρειν καὶ διὰ παντὸς ὑγιαίνειν. A rather different temporal use appears in διὰ νυκτός, "by night" (Ac 5¹⁹ etc.), as P Ryl II. 138¹⁵ (A.D. 34) κατέλαβα τοῦτον διὰ νυκτὸς ἠλμένον ἐξ ὑπερβατῶν εἰς τὼ τῆς οὐσίας ἐποίκιον Δρομῆως λεγώμενον (*i.e.* -όμενον), "I detected him when under cover of night he had sprung into the farmstead" (Edd.): it is hard to imagine Fritzsche (see Grimm) arguing that here διὰ νυκτός must mean "all night long"! Equally unmistakeable is the spell in P Lond 121⁴⁰⁷ (iii/A.D.) (= I. p. 97) ἐάν τινι ἐθελήσῃς φανῆναι διὰ νυκτὸς ἐν ὀνείροις. Διὰ βίου however = "for life," as P Lond 1178⁵⁰ (A.D. 194) (= III. p. 217) ξυστάρχων διὰ βίου. *Preisigke* 1269⁸ (B.C. 104) ἱερεὺς διὰ βίου, and δι᾽ ἐνιαυτοῦ = "for a year"—P Strass I. 22³⁴ (iii/A.D. *init.*) παρ᾽ ἡμεῖν δ[ὲ ἰ]δοὺ ἡ [δ]ι᾽ ἐνιαυτοῦ νομὴ αὐτάρκης ἐστίν. "der einjährige Besitz" (Ed.). For διά as in Mk 2¹, Ac 24¹⁷, cf. OGIS 56³⁸ (B.C. 239-8) ἐὰν δὲ καὶ συμβαίνηι τὴν ἐπιτολὴν τοῦ ἄστρου μεταβαίνειν εἰς ἑτέραν ἡμέραν διὰ τεσσάρων ἐτῶν, "after four years" (see note). Instrumental διά appears in διὰ γένους, as *Cagnat* IV. 293⁴⁶ (Pergamum, *c.* B.C. 127) τὸν ἀρχιερέα καὶ διὰ γένους ἱερέα τοῦ [Διὸς "hereditary priest," *IHS* xxxiv. p. 5 *ano.* 10³ of Lycian inscrr. λαβὼν τὸ χωρίον διὰ γένους. So διὰ προγόνων, *Cagnat* IV. 293⁴⁷ (see above) καὶ δι[ὰ] προγόνων ὑπάρχοντα τῆς πατρίδος εὐεργέ[την. P Ryl II. 135¹¹ (A.D. 34) ἦραν διὰ ὄνον χόρτου δύσμας τριάκοαν. "carried off on donkeys thirty bundles of hay" (Edd.). The common use of Ac 15²⁷, 2 Cor 10¹¹, may be freely illustrated: thus P Oxy VII. 1066⁷ (iii/A.D.) ἔγραψάς μοι διὰ τῆς [ἐ]πιστολῆς, "you write to me in the letter" (Ed., *ib.* 1070¹⁵ (iii/A.D.) πολλάκις σοι γράψας διὰ ἐπιστολῶν πολλῶν, P Grenf I. 30⁵ (B.C. 103) (= Witkowski², p. 107) διὰ γραμμάτων ἐκρίναμεν σημῆναι. It can hardly be said that there is always insistence on mediate authorship when διά has a personal gen. attached. Thus P Grenf II. 41⁷ (A.D. 46) (= *Chrest.* II. p. 107) πάντος (*l.* -ας) τοῦ (*l.* τοὺς) δι᾽ ἐμοῦ οἰκονομηθησομένους χρηματισμούς : the writer is a principal. P Lond 276⁷ (A.D. 15) (= II. p. 149) ἵν᾽ [εἰδ]ὼς κατακλουθήσας (*l.* κατακολουθῇς) τοῖς δι᾽ αὐτοῦ σημαινο[μέν]οις, P Amh II. 68⁶ (late i/A.D.) τὰς δηλουμένας δι᾽ αὐτοῦ (ἀρούρας (. But this distinction between διά and ὑπό is normally observed. Thus P Amh II. 111¹⁷ (A.D. 132) καθ᾽ ὁμολογείαν τελιωθῖσαν διὰ τοῦ ἐν κώμῃ Σοκνοπαίου Νήσου γραφείου, "executed through the record-office of S.N." (Edd.). BGU I. 136⁴ (A.D. 135) Ταποντὼς δι᾽ ἐκδίκου, his counsel. Note δι᾽ ἑαυτοῦ = *ipse*, as P Oxy II. 273²¹ (A.D. 95) ἀπὸ τῆσδε [τῆς ὁμο]λογίας δι᾽ ἑαυτῆς μεταγράφεσθαι, "to transfer by herself to another" (Edd.). See other instances in Kuhring p. 30 f., also of other uses c. gen. The elliptical locution διὰ κενῆς, P Hib I. 66⁵ (B.C. 228-7) ὥστε σε μὴ διὰ κενῆς εὐχαριστῆσαι ἡμ[ῖν, "so that you shall not oblige me to no purpose" (Edd., presumably arises from the local meaning of διά.

With acc. διά has a recognized use in petitions where the subtle but important difference from gen. may be overlooked—see *Proleg.* p. 105. P Magd 16⁷ (B.C. 222) ἵνα διὰ σέ, βασιλεῦ, τοῦ δικαίου τύ[χω, "grâce à toi" (Ed.), is a good example: διὰ σοῦ would be avoided in addressing a king, and διὰ σέ is more delicate than παρὰ σοῦ. Other instances in Kuhring p. 41, and Rossberg p. 30, whose heading "quo auctore quid fiat" is fairly established. The *acc. rei* sometimes brings the meaning rather near that of διά c. gen. P Fay 110³¹ (. A.D. 100), ἐπὶ κράζει Πᾶσις εἵνα μὴ εἰς ψωμίν γένηται διὰ τὼ ὕδωρ, "for Pasis is crying out that we must not allow it [the manure] to be dissolved by the water" (Edd.). BGU I. 350⁴ (ii/A.D.) πεπρακέ[ναι τὸν ὁμολογοῦντα διὰ τήνδε τὴν] ὁμολογίαν, P Par 17¹¹ (A.D. 154) πριαμένης διὰ χειρόγραφον (Kuhring p. 41). Late and illiterate documents were only anticipating the general development of Greek syntax. Rossberg p. 39 f. has instances of διά c. acc. classified. With Heb 2¹⁰, Rev 4¹¹, cf. P Leid Wxiii. ³³ (ii/iii A.D.), addressing a deity, σοῦ γὰρ φανέντος κ(αὶ) κόσμος ἐγένετο, κ(αὶ) φῶς ἐφάνη κ αὶ) διοικονομήθη τὰ πάντα διὰ σέ. P Oxy I. 41⁸ (*c.* A.D. 300), where a crowd acclaims a magistrate, πολλῶν ἀγαθῶν ἀπολαύομεν διὰ σαί. πρύτανι: the date makes it reasonable to compare this directly with διὰ σοῦ in Ac 24² rather than putting it into the category described above. For διά in composition it will suffice to refer to Moulton *Gr.* II. § 116.

διαβαίνω.

P Eleph 20⁷ ἐὰν δὲ μὴ εὐκαιρῇς τ[ο]ῦ διαβῆναι the river Nile. The verb is construed with εἰς, as Ac 16⁹, in P Lille I. 6³ (iii/B.C.) διαβάντος μου ἐκ Τεβέτνου εἰς Κορφότουν ἐπισκέψασθαι τὴν ἀδελφή[ν, P Fay 110¹⁵ (A.D. 94) διάβα εἰς Διον[υ]σιά[δα] καὶ γνῶθι κτλ, "go over to Dionysias and find out." The special force of δια- seems diluted in some occurrences. Thus cf. the noun in P Tor I. 1 viii. ²⁹ (B.C. 116) (= *Chrest.* II. p. 38) ἐν ταῖς κατ᾽ ἐνιαυτὸν γινομέναις τοῦ Ἄμμωνος διαβάσεσιν εἰς τὰ Μεμνόνεια, of a solemn procession: there δια- only acts as perfective, implying that a goal is reached, without dwelling on the nature of the intervening country. In P Leid W vii. ²⁰ (ii/iii A.D.) a spell is given ἐὰν θέλῃς ἐπάνω κορκοδείλου διαβαίνειν, where the editor renders "sin velis supra crocodilum incedere": if we press the δια-, we must assume that the desire is to "cross" the Nile on top of a crocodile (as distinguished from inside). In P Par 42¹² (B.C. 156 περὶ ἰδίου πράγματος διαβαίνων, we find a more general sense "occupying himself with his own affair": cf. BGU III. 810⁹ (iii/A.D.) ἄξιός ἐστιν πολλῶν, καὶ ἂν διαβῇ τὰ ἐκεῖ πολλά. The verb is apparently "decide," "adjudicate" in *Syll* 210⁷ (B.C. 202) ὃς ἀφικόμ[ενος τ]ῶν δικῶν τὰς μὲν διέλυσεν τὰς δὲ διέβαινεν: so *IG* XII. 5. 125¹¹ (after B.C. 218 (see Schlageter, p. 60).

διαβάλλω.

P Tebt I. 23¹ (*c.* B.C. 119 or 114) ἀπέφαινεν ἠδικῆσθαι ὑπὸ σοῦ καὶ Δημητρίωι ἠναγκάσθαι διαβαλεῖν, "had been compelled to complain to D.", shows that malice need not be assumed in Lk 16¹ any more than falsehood. For the stronger meaning see P Oxy VI. 1158²² (iii/A.D.) ἐὰν οὖν μάθῃς ὅτι μέλλει ζειαβαλεῖν (*l.* διαβαλεῖν) σε Ἀρητίων περὶ τῶν χαλκείων, "if you learn that A. is going to accuse you about the copper" Ed.); cf. *ib.* VI. 906[13] (A.D. 322) ἀλλ' ἐπιδὴ μανθάνω τούτους βουλομένους ἐνεδρεύειν . . . τισὶ μὲν ἀπι[ο]ῦσι, ἐνίους δὲ διαβάλλοντας, "but whereas I learn that these persons are desirous of acting fraudulently, some by absenting themselves, and others by deception" (Edd.). Other examples are P Par 63[8] 70 (B.C. 165) ὡς διαβάλλεται, the Jewish *apologia* in answer to an Imperial rescript, *ib* 68[3] ἅ σοι ἀ[νη]λέως δια[βεβλη]μένοι προτοῦ, and BGU IV. 1040[22] (ii/A.D.) καθαρ[ὰ]ν γὰρ ἔχων τὴν ψυχὴν οὐδενὸς ἐπιστ[. . . .]ν τῶν διαβαλόντων. In *ib.* 1105[14] (B.C. 11) Tryphaena pleading for a divorce calls her husband ὁ| διαβαλλόμενος, "wohl nur ein ungeschickter Ausdruck für der genannte" (Ed.) == "the complained-of person."

διαβεβαιόομαι.

CPR 18[29] (a process for inheritance—A.D. 224) τοῦ δὲ Ἀφροδεισίου διαβεβαιωσαμένου, "Aphrodisios having confirmed," BGU I. 16[7] (A.D. 135) ἐπεὶ δὲ οἱ περὶ τὸν Πετεσ[ο]ῦχον διεβεβαιώσαντο ἐκείνο[υ]ς προτετελευτηκέναι τῆς μητρός κτλ., *ib.* II. 412[3] (iv/A.D.) διεβεβαίωσα τόδε ὡς τρίτας αὐτὴν ἀπαιτῖσθαι τῆς ποσότητος, and the late P Lond 113. 1[21] (vi/A.D.) (== I. p. 201) διεβεβαιώσατο ἑαυτὸν τὸ τηνικαῦτα τέλειον εἶναι. See also Aristeas 99 διαβεβαιοῦμαι πάντα ἄνθρωπον προσελθόντα τῇ θεωρίᾳ τῶν προειρημένων εἰς ἔκπληξιν ἥξειν.

διαβλέπω.

The word is found in an obscure context in P Lond 418[19] (c. A.D. 346) (== II. p. 303).

διαγίνομαι.

P Strass I. 41[12] (A.D. 250) πολὺς χρόνος διαγέγονεν.

διαγινώσκω.

The verb is found == "decide" in P Tebt I. 17[2] (B.C. 114) ἐπεὶ διέγνωσται, and *ib.* 55[2] (private letter—late ii/B.C.) ἐπεὶ διέγνωκα ἐξοδεύσειν ε[ἰ]ς Τεβτῦνιν τῆι η ἔκρινα γράψαι, "since I have decided to travel to T. on the 8th, I have determined to write to you" (Edd.). The phrase ὁ βασιλεὺς διαγνώσεται occurs several times in the long papyrus regarding the affairs of Theodorus, the architect, P Petr III. 43 (B.C. 245): the editors render "the king shall take cognisance." The same formula occurs in P Amh II. 29[18], a contemporary document. It is to be classed with other instances of the technical legal use of διαγινώσκειν, which appears in Ac 24[22]. Cf. CPR 18[23] (A.D. 124) ἰ[πη]γόρευσεν ἀπὸ [ν]όμω[ν δι]ε[γ]νῶσθα[ι] κατὰ λέξιν, "dictirte . . . folgendes Erkenntniss nach dem Wortlaut des Gesetzes" (Ed.), P Hal I. 1[135] (mid. iii/B.C.) ἐὰν δέ [τ]ι[ν]ων φασκόντων (*l.* τινες φάσκωσιν) εἶν[αι] τῆς [ἀ]ποσκευῆς, οἱ δικασταὶ π[ερ]ὶ τούτου δ[ι]αγινωσκέ[τω]σαν, P Oxy VII. 1032[53] (A.D. 162) ἔντυχε οὖν τῷ κρατίσ[τῳ ἐ]πι[στ]ρα[τη]γῷ, ὃς παρόντος αὐτοῦ π[ερὶ τ]οῦ πράγματος δια[γν]ώσετ[α]ι, *ib.* VIII. 1117[3] (c. A.D. 178) ἔναγχος, ἡγεμὼν κύριε, ἐπιδημή[σας ἐν τῇ ἡμετέρᾳ πόλει διέγνως μεταξὺ ἡμῶν καὶ ἀρχόντων.

διάγνωσις.

For the technical use of this word (== *cognitio*) in Wisd 3[18], Ac 25[21], see P Hib I. 93[10] (c. B.C. 250) ἡ διάγ[νωσις περὶ

αὐτοῦ ἔσ[τω πρὸς βασ[ιλικά, "decision about his case shall be made with reference to the royal decrees" (Edd.). This early instance disposes of Deissmann's statement (*LAE*, p. 346 n[2].) that the word is not found in this sense until the end of ii/A.D. *IG* XIV. 1072 ἐπὶ . . . διαγνώσεων τοῦ Σεβαστοῦ, "a . . . *cognitionum Augusti*," P Lond 358[17] (c. A.D. 150) (== II. p. 172) τῆς τοῦ λαμπροτάτου ἡ[γε]μόνος Μουνατίου Φήλικος διαγνώσεως is a little earlier. To the same period belongs PSI I. 103[16] αἱ δηλωθ[εῖσαι] ἐπι[σ]χέσθ(αι) ἄχρι τῆς τοῦ κρατίστου] ἡ[γ]εμόνος διαγνώσεως, which resembles Ac *l.c.* especially.

διαγορεύω.

This LXX word (1 Esdr 5[39], Dan LXX Sus 61) may be illustrated from P Magd 3[4] (B.C. 221) τῆς συγγραφῆς τῆς μισθώσεως διαγορευούσης, P Tebt I. 105[39] (B.C. 103) ἐπὶ τοῖς διηγορευμένοις, BGU II. 473[16] (A.D. 200) τῶν θείων διατάξεω[ν] σαφῶς διαγορευουσῶ[ν.

διαγράφω.

This again is not a NT word, but in view of its occurrence == "pay" in Esther 3[9], 2 Macc 4[9], it may be well to note that this usage is common in the papyri and ostraca, especially in receipts: see Wilcken *Ostr.* i. p. 89 ff., and for the change from the perfect to the aorist in this connexion towards the end of ii/A.D. cf. *Proleg.* p. 247 f. An interesting example of the verb occurs in BGU II. 530[24] (i/A.D.) (== *Selections*, p. 61) where a small farmer points out to his dilatory son the ruin which was falling on their allotment of land owing to his lack of assistance, and adds μόνον διαγράφω τὰ δημόσια μηδὲν συνκομιζόμενος, "only I continue paying the public taxes without getting back anything in return."

διάγω.

A physical use of the verb occurs in the inscr. from the Asclepieum, *Syll* 802[121] (iii/B.C.), where in a blind man's dream ἐδόκει ο[ἱ] ὁ θεὸς ποτελθὼν τοῖς δ[α]κτύλοις διάγειν τὰ ὄμματα, to "draw apart" the closed lids. The normal sense "continue" appears in P Tebt I. 22[16] (B.C. 112) περὶ δὲ τοῦ φυλκίτου (*l.* φυλακίτου) ἐάν τε διάξησθε (*l.* διάξῃ) . . . ἀντ[ι]ποιούμενος περὶ τῶν σπερμάτων δέσμ[ιο]ν αὐτὸν ἐξαπόστειλον πρὸς ἡμᾶς. "as for the inspector, if he still continues to oppose the payment of the seed, send him to us under arrest" (Edd.). For the derived sense with reference to life, conduct, as 1 Tim 2[2], Tit 3[3], cf. *Michel* 352[15] (ii/B.C.) τά τε πρὸς τοὺς θεοὺς εὐσεβῶς δια[γό μενος, P Oxy IX. 1217[6] (iii/A.D.) ὑγιαίνον[τά] σε καὶ εὖ διάγοντα, "in health and prosperity" (Ed.), P Ryl II. 235[9] (ii/A.D.) οὐκ ἐδήλωσάς μοι περὶ τῆς εὐρωστίας σου καὶ πῶς διάγεις ἵν[α] καὶ ἡμεῖς περὶ σου ἀμερ[ί]μνως διάγωμεν. For a similar use of the subst. cf. *OGIS* 308[12] (ii/B.C.) καλὴν καὶ πρέπουσαν πεποίηται τὴν διαγω[γὴν] τοῦ βίου.

διαδέχομαι.

On a special sense of this verb and its correlative διάδοχος (see *s.v.*) in LXX, see Deissmann *BS.* p. 115. The only occurrences of either word in NT are in the normal sense, which can be freely illustrated. On P Ryl II. 84[7] (A.D. 146) ταῦτα γράφω διαδεχόμενος τὴν Πρόκλου τοῦ κρατίστου εἰς Αἴγυπτον ἀποδημίαν, the editors remark that the combination is new, "but there can be little doubt that διαδέχεσθαι here has its usual sense and that the writer's meaning is that he had been deputed to visit the upper country on the praefect's behalf:" they translate "as the deputy of . . Proculus in his visit to Egypt." This is more like Deissmann's "*proximus a rege*" than the ordinary sense "succeed to." This last may be presumed in P Flor III. 308[1] (A.D. 203) βασιλ(ικῷ) γρα(μματεῖ) διαδεχομ(ένῳ) καὶ τὰ κατὰ τὴν [στρα(τηγίαν) τοῦ Ἑρμο-π(ολίτου νομοῦ)]: cf. *ib.* 382[50] (A.D. 222-3) So *OGIS* 210[2] (A.D. 247-8) τοῦ κρατ(ίστου) Μύρωνος διαδεχομέν(ου) τὴν ἀρχιερωσύνην, *Preisigke* 1555[5] (iii/A.D.) διαδεξάμενος τὴν αὐτοῦ τοῦ ἁγιωτάτου Σαράπιδος γυμνασιαρχίαν.

διαδίδωμι.

P Oxy IX. 1194[17] (c. A.D. 265) ἀφ᾽ ὧν διεδόθησ[αν διὰ τῶν ἐπιμελη]τῶν, "of which there were distributed through the superintendents": similarly *ib.* VIII. 1115[6] (A.D. 284) οὗ ἀνηνέγκαμεν καὶ δι[αδεδώ]καμεν ἄρτου, "for the bread which we have delivered and distributed" (Edd.). This last papyrus shows also the subst. διάδοσις —[9] Μίκκαλος ἐπὶ διαδόσεως ἀννώνης, "M. superintendent of the distribution of the annona": so *ib* I. 43[iv. 9] (A.D. 295) εἰς διάδοσιν τῶν στρατιωτῶν. For διαδότης, see Wilcken *Archiv.* iv. p. 557 and P Giss II. p. 88 f.

διάδοχος.

The sense required for LXX. supported by Deissmann (see above *s.v.* διαδέχομαι) from P Tor I. 1[i. 6, 15] (B.C. 116) (= *Chrest.* II. p. 30), can be explained from history, as Peyron showed in a note on P Lond 20[1] (B.C. 162) (= I. p. 9) Σαρα-πίωνι τῶν διαδόχων : see Kenyon's summary *ad loc.* Applied originally to Alexander's "reinforcements," διάδοχοι came to denote a certain rank or privilege in the army of Alexander and his successors, the original meaning having disappeared. The noun not infrequently = *deputy*, that is a *temporary* "successor." So P Tebt II. 293[2] (c. A.D. 187) διαδόχον προφητείας, "deputy prophet" (Edd.), *ib.* 313[4] (A.D. 210-1) ἱερέως καὶ στολ(ιστείας) διαδόχου, "priest and deputy stolistes," and *OGIS* 86[7] (B.C. 221-05) with Dittenberger's note. In Ac 24[27] it has its original meaning : cf. the abstract διαδοχή, "succession," as in P Petr II. 40 (*a*)[15] (iii/B.C.) (= Witkowski[2], p. 41) ἑτοιμάζεται γὰρ ἡ διαδοχή, "the relief is being equipped," P Tebt II. 302[23] (A.D. 71-2) τὴν γῆν τὴν ἀντὶ συ]ντάξεως ἡμεῖν ἐκ διαδοχῆς γονέων τετηρημένην, "by inheritance from our ancestors" (Edd.).

διαζώννυω.

For this word, which is found *ter* in John's Gospel (13[4,5], 21[7]), cf. *IG* II. 730 B[16] (B.C. 307). See also *BCH* x. (1886) p. 405[103] (B.C. 364) κλιμάκιον ξύλινον περικεχρυσω-μένον ὄφεσιν ἀργυροῖς διεζωμένον, and *v.* xiv. (1890) p. 405[55] (B.C. 279). For the subst. διάζωμα cf. BGU IV. 1188[7] (B.C. 15-4) τοῦ κατὰ τὴν κώμην ἀγομένου δημοσίο[υ] διαζώματος, where however the editor notes that the reading is not quite certain.

διαθήκη.

In papyri and inscrr. the word means *testament, will*, with absolute unanimity, and such frequency that illustration is

superfluous. P Petr III. 6 (*b*)[12] (c. B.C. 236) τὴ]ν διαθήκη[ν καταλεί]πω will be about the earliest example : P Grenf I. 17[7] (c. B.C. 147 or 136) and *ib.* 21[4] (B.C. 126) also fall within the LXX period. So do such inscrr. as *OGIS* 338[7] (B.C. 133), of the instrument by which King Attalus of Pergamum devised his country to Rome, *Michel* 1001[v. 8] (c. B.C. 200) κατὰ διαθήκαν (the testament of Epicteta, in Theran Doric), and one of iii/B.C. in Ἀθηνᾶ xx. p. 167 κατὰ τὰς διαθήκας. *Syll* 827[9] (i/B.C.) might also be cited—houses and gardens bequeathed by a woman to Aphrodite Urania, κατὰ τὰς διαθήκας τὰς κειμένας ἐν τῶι ἱερῶι τῆς Ἀφροδίτης καὶ παρ᾽ Εὐνομίδει τῶι ἄρχοντι καὶ παρὰ τῶι θεσμοθέτει Κτησιφῶντι. We may also mention BGU IV. 1151[7] (B.C. 14) καθ᾽ ἥν ἔθετο διαθήκην) διὰ τοῦ τῶν Ἰουδαίων ἀρχείου, if illustration is needed to show that the Jews used the word in this sense. *Cagnat* IV. 804 (= *C. and B.* ii. p. 475, no. 33[3]), a bilingual inscr. from Apamea, has *heredes ex testa-mento* rendered by κληρονόμοι κατὰ διαθήκην. On the verb διατίθεμαι see *s.v.* ; we may mention here that ἀδιάθετος = *intestate*, as in BGU IV. 1185[17] (end of i/B.C.) ἐὰν δέ τινες ἐξ αὐτῶν τελευτήσωσι ἀδιάθετοι, P Oxy IX. 1201[8] (A.D. 258) τῶν κατὰ διαδοχὴν κληρονομηθέντων ὑπ᾽ αὐτοῦ ἀδιαθέτου τετελευτηκότος.

Against this word stands συνθήκη (not in NT), which Aquila substituted in 4 Kings 23[21] for LXX διαθήκη. It is to the last the word for *compact*, just as διαθήκη is always and only the word for *will*. The index to *Syll* will sufficiently prove this for συνθήκη, for which we may add the ostracon in *Chrest.* I. 110.A[10] (B.C. 110) (p. 141) εἰ μὴν ἅτε διενεχθέντες πρὸς ἑαυτοὺς ἐπὶ τοῦ δρόμου τοῦ Ἀπολλωνίηου τῇ β τοῦ αὐτοῦ μηνὸς τὰς συνθήκας ἐδώκαμεν Περιγένη τῶι γραμματεῖ. Any thought of some special "Hebraic" flavour about the use of διαθήκη for *covenant* is excluded by the isolated but absolutely clear passage in Aristophanes (*Birds* 439), where *compact* is the unmistakeable meaning. This passage is enough to prove that διαθήκη is properly *dis-positio*, an "arrangement" made by one party with plenary power, which the other party may accept or reject, but cannot alter. A will is simply the most conspicuous ex-ample of such an instrument, which ultimately monopolized the word just because it suited its differentia so completely. But it is entirely natural to assume that in the period of the LXX this monopoly was not established, and the translators were free to apply the general meaning as a rendering of בְּרִית. For this course there was an obvious motive. A covenant offered by God to man was no "compact" be-tween two parties coming together on equal terms. Δια-θήκη in its primary sense, as described above, was exactly the needed word.

Passing thus to the NT, we ask whether we are bound to keep to one rendering throughout. Westcott and W. F. Moulton in their commentaries on Heb 9[16 f.], and formerly G. Milligan (*Theology of the Epistle to the Hebrews*, p. 166 ff.) held that *covenant* must stand everywhere. Deiss-mann (*St Paul*, p. 152) insists on *testament* everywhere, if we may judge from an express reference to Lk 2.[29] com-pared with [20], and Gal 3[15 ff.], 4[24], 1 Cor 11[25], 2 Cor 3[6], together with "very frequent" appearance in LXX. Now we may fairly put aside the idea that in LXX "testament" is the invariable meaning : it takes some courage to find it there at all. But on the other hand, a Hellenist like the *auctor ad Hebraeos*, or even a Jew like Paul, with Greek language in the very fibre of his thought, could never have used δ. for *covenant* without the slightest consciousness of its ordinary and invariable contemporary meaning. He would use the "Biblical" word—"Biblical" in this case being synonymous with "archaic"—but always with the possibility of a play on the later meaning of the word. This is what comes in Heb 9[15 ff] (probably also in Gal 3[15]), according to the usual view, which is responsible for the RV text in the former: see Milligan *Documents*, p. 75. Deissmann, among other difficulties, would have to prove that in iii/B.C. the older general meaning, established by Aristophanes, was extinct. The view to which we have capitulated, after strongly supporting the Westcott doctrine, is less heroic than consistent holding to one English word, but it can claim to account for its inconsistency. Among recent monographs may be mentioned an article by E. Riggenbach in *Theolog. Studien Th. Zahn . . dargebracht*, and lexical studies by F. O. Norton (1908), J. Behm (1912) and E. Lohmeyer (1913). See also Ferguson *Legal Terms Common to the Macedonian Inscrr. and the NT* (Chicago, 1913), p. 42 ff.

διαίρεσις.

In the long land-survey P Tebt I. 61 (*b*)[54, 68] (B.C. 118 7) we find ἐγ διαιρέσεως *bis* of the "division" of wheat among several cultivators: cf. *ib.* 72 (B.C. 114–3) *quater*. For the same meaning see P Tebt. II. 382[4] (division of land – B.C. 30–A.D. 1) ἐκ κλήρου διαιρέσεως, "in consequence of the division by lot," P Flor I. 5[3] (A.D. 244–5), *ib.* 50[14.6] (A.D. 268), P Strass I. 29[13, 45] (A.D. 289), P Gen I. 11[1] (A.D. 350) *al.* In P Hib I. 110[3] (*c.* B.C. 245) διαίρεσις Μεχὶρ ἕως Ἐπείφ, the word is used of a "period" of time. From the inscriptions we may cite *Syll* 510[21] (ii/B.C.) καὶ κοινὴμ μὲν διαίρεσιν ταύτην εἶναι,—ἂν δέ πως ἄλλως πρὸς αὐτοὺς ὁμολογήσωσιν ὑπὲρ τῆς διαιρέσεως κτλ, with reference to certain μερισμοὺς τῶν ἐγγαίων.

διαιρέω.

Division between two or more parties, as in Lk 15[12], is the ordinary force of the word. Thus in a iii/B.C. inscr. in Ἀθηνᾶ xx. p. 107 ἀγρός . . ὃν ἔλαβεν διαιρούμενος πρὸς τὸν ἀδελφόν, P Magd 29[4] (B.C. 218) διαιρέσεως γενομένης καὶ συγγρα[φ]ῆς τεθείσης διειρῆσθαι ἴσως καὶ ὁμοίως, οὐ διείρηταί μοι δικαίως—of a division of land that had not been carried through justly: cf. BGU IV. 1123[8] (time of Augustus) διαιρεθήσεται εἰς μέ[ρη] ἴσα καὶ ὅμοια τρία, καὶ λήμψεται ἕκαστ[ο]ς ἡμῶν μέρος ἕν. P Oxy X. 1277[19] (A.D. 214) διειρῆσθαι π[ρὸ]ς ἑαυτοὺς τὴν καρπείαν, "have divided among themselves the usufruct," and *OGIS* 573[21] (i/A.D.) διαιρεῖται δ ὁ ἱερεὺς τὰ [ε]ἰσφερόμενα τῶι θεῶι εἰς κατασκευὴν τοῦ τόπου, where the editor remarks that "verbum notionem distribuendae pecuniae in diversas expensas quibus opus sit habere videtur." With the dat. as in Lk *l.c.*, cf. P Lond 880[11] (B.C. 113) (= III. p. 9) ὁμολογεῖ . . διειρῆσθαι τὰ ὑπάρχοντα [αὐ]τῶι ἔγγαια τοῖς ἑαυτοῦ υἱοῖς. The construction with πρός is commoner. The more general sense of "distribute," as in 1 Cor 12[11], may be seen in the Will of Epicteta, *Michel* 1001[3.18] (*c.* B.C. 200) οἱ . . δὲ ἀρτυτῆρ διελεῖ τὰ ἱερὰ τοῖς παροῦσι. For the middle in the same sense cf. *Syll* 229[19] (iii/B.C.) διείλοντο τὸ ἀργύριον

—the meaning is practically = διεῖλον πρὸς ἀλλήλους. In *ib.* 831[7] πάντα ἃ ἔχε[ι] διελόμενος Νικήρατος πρὸς τὸν ἀδελφόν this will not apply.

διακαθαίρω.

For this late form, which WH read in Mt 3[12], Lk 3[15], cf. *BCH* xxvii. (1903) p. 73[79] (B.C. 250) Ὠφελίωνι τοὺς κρουνοὺς διακαθάραντι τοὺς ἐν τῆι σκηνῆι.

διακονέω.

In P Oxy II. 275[10] (A.D. 66) (= *Selections*, p. 55) a lad is apprenticed by his father— διακονοῦ[ν]τα καὶ ποιο[ῦ]ντα πάντα τὰ ἐπιτασσόμενα αὐτῷ, "to serve and to do everything commanded him." For the construction with the dat., see BGU I. 201[5] (? ii/iii A.D.) ἔγραψες Ἡρᾶτι . . ἵνα διακονέσσι (*l.* διακονήσει) ἱμῖν (*l.* ἡμῖν). The pass. is found *OGIS* 383[152] middle of i/B.C. τοῖς τε ἐκπώμασιν οἷς ἐγὼ καθειέρωσα διακονείσθωσαν.

διακονία.

The very interesting parallel in Plutarch for Lk 10[40], given by Field, *Notes*, p. 63, should not be missed. We are unable to quote the word from papyri before vi/A.D.: like διάκονος itself and the verb, it seems to have been somewhat literary except in an almost technical use, which brought it into common speech.

διάκονος.

For the word in its general sense cf. P Flor II. 121[2] (A.D. 253) ἐπεὶ ἔδοξεν τοῖς δεκαπρώτοις[?] τὸν διάκονον Εἰρηναῖον ? ἐπ᾽]ἐνιαυτὸν χρησι[μ]εύειν ἡμῖν[?]. There is now abundant evidence that the way had been prepared for the Christian usage of this word by its technical application to the holders of various offices, as in the i/B.C. *Magn* 217, where the dedicators of a statue to Hermes are described as κομάκτορες, κήρυκες and διάκονοι. A definitely religious connotation belongs to the word in *ib.* 109 (c. B.C. 100) where the remains of a list of temple officials concludes with μάγειρος . . διάκονος. For a similar combination the editor refers to *IG* IX. 1, 486 (ii/i B.C.) and IV. 774[11] (iii/B.C.), and to these examples Thieme (p. 17 f.), from whom the above citations are taken, adds *CIG* II. 1800, where we hear of a "college" of διάκονοι, presided over by a ἱερεύς, in the service of Serapis, Isis etc., and *ib.* 3037 where two διάκονοι and a female διάκονος (cf. Rom 16[1]) are associated with a ἱερεύς and a ἱέρεια τῶν δώδεκα θεῶν.

For the Christian use of the word, see P Oxy VIII. 1162[3] (iv/A.D.) πρεσβυτ[έ]ροις καὶ διακώνοις. P Flor III. 325[22] (A.D. 525), P Giss I. 55[11] (vi/A.D.) etc.

On the form διάκων, see Deissmann *LAE* p. 91, and add BGU IV. 1046[ii.24] (A.D. 158). Prof. W. M. Calder tells us it is common in Anatolian inscrr. It is on the same footing as κατήγωρ (see *s.v.* κατήγορος), which Thumb *Hellen.* p. 126, shows to be a natural Greek development: Radermacher *Gr.* p. 15, gives a number of parallels. It is fairly certain that διάκονος must be associated with ἐγκονέω, ἀκονιτί, and the simplex preserved in the Anthology, also in glosses such as κόνει, σπεῦδε, τρέχε Hesychiust. The difficult ᾱ (Ionic διήκονος) is explained by Brugmann (see Boisacq *Lex. s.v.*) by analogy of διηνεκής etc.

διακούω

is common in the judicial sense, with *gen. person.* as in A. 23[3]. Thus P Grenf I. 11[8] (B.C. 157) διακούσαντα [αὐτῶν] προσανενεγκεῖν ἐπὶ σὲ τ[ὰ συ]γκεκριμένα, so [?], P Fay 110[12] (c. A.D. 100) ἐπιστολὴν τοῦ ἡγεμόνος πρὸς Διονύσιν τὸν στρατηγὸν διακοῦσαι αὐτοῦ. P Giss I. 46[11] (time of Hadrian—petition to the Praefect) ἀξιοῦμέν σε τὸν τοῦ νομοῦ βοηθὸν διακοῦσαι ἡμῶν. BGU I. 1085[23] (ii/iii A.D.) ὅθεν ἀξιῶ . . . διακοῦσαί μου πρὸς αὐτούς, P Lond 924[16] (A.D. 187–8) (= III. p. 135), etc. In *Syll* 929[9] (ii/B.C.) καὶ καθίσαντες ἐν τῷ ἱε[ρ]ῶι τῆς Ἀρτέμιδος τῆς Λευκοφρυηνῆς διηκούσαμεν τῶν διαφερομένων, we have *gen. rei.* Other inscriptional citations are OGIS 335[29] (ii/i B.C.—decree of the Pitanaei) ἄρξονται διακούειν κ[αὶ καθ᾽ ἕκαστον σκοποῦντες ποή]σονται τὴν κρίσιν μεθ᾽ ὅρκου, *Syll* 928[10] (beginning of ii/B.C.), *Magn* 103[49] (2nd half ii/A.D.), *ib.* 93*d*[10] (after A.D. 190) etc.

διακρίνω.

The active = "test," "examine" (cf. Mt 16[3]) in BGU III. 747[i. 20] (A.D. 139) τ]οὺς πράκτορας δ[ι]ακρείνω π[ρ]ὸς τὸν ε[ἰσ[ί]όν[τ]α ὑπὲρ [τ]ῆς ἰδί[α]ς πρακτωρί[α]ς λόγο[ν] αἱ[τ]ούμ[ε]νο[ς. It is "determine," "decide" in OGIS 43[4] (iii/B.C.) ἡ[τ]ήσατο δικαστὰς καὶ διαλ[λακτῆρας τοὺ]ς διακρινοῦντας περὶ τῶν ἀμφ[ισβητουμέν]ων συμβολαίων: *c. acc. pers. ib.*[11] τοὺ]ς δὲ διέκρινεμ μετὰ πάσης δικαιο[σύνης. Similarly in *Syll* 924[13] (B.C. 210–5) τάς τε δίκας μετὰ τῶν συνιερομναμόνων τὰς μὲν διέλυσε τὰς δὲ διέκρινε δικαίως κατὰ τοὺς νό[μ]ους: here we have *acc. rei*, but the same antithesis with διαλύειν as in OGIS 43[11] (above). It appears again in the passive in *Syll* 177[23] (B.C. 303) τὰ δὲ ἐγκλήματα καὶ τὰ συμβόλαια [τὰ ὑπάρχοντα ἑκατέ]ροις, αὐτοὺς πρὸς αὐτοὺς διαλυθῆναι ἢ διακριθῆναι [κατὰ τοὺς ἑκατέρων ν]όμους. The former verb suggests settlement by consent, as against a judicial verdict. Add for the passive P Tor I. 1[vii. 3] (B.C. 110) (= *Chrest.* II. p. 37) προσυποδεικνὺς ὡς εἰ καὶ ἐπὶ λαοκριτῶν διεκρίνοντο καθ᾽ οὓς παρέκειτο νόμους κτλ., P Par 40[15] (B.C. 153) (= Witkowski[2], p. 87) ἡγούμενος δεῖν ἐπ᾽ ἄλλου μὲν μηθενὸς αὐτῶι δ.ακριθῆναι, ἐπὶ σοῦ δ᾽ αὐτοῦ, P Magd 28 *recto*[5] (B.C. 218) ὅπως διακριθῶ αὐτοῖς ἐπὶ Διοφανοῖς, "pour que nous soyons juges par Diophanes" (Edd.). In these last two passages note the *dat. pers.*: διακρίνεσθαί τινι is "to have one's case with so and so decided." The use illustrates Jude[9], where Michael is pleading his case against the devil before God. The verb is absolute in P Magd 1[15] (B.C. 221) γράψαι Μενέλλαι τῶι ἐπιστάτηι ἀποστεῖλαι αὐτοὺς διακριθησομένους, "de les envoyer en justice." For the simple meaning "distinguish" cf. the magic papyrus P Lond 46[103] (iv/A.D.) (= I. p. 68) σὺ (the Deity) διέκρεινας τὸ δίκαιον καὶ τὸ ἄδικον. The distinctive NT sense of διακρίνεσθαι, "to be divided against oneself," "waver," "doubt," as in Mk 11[21], Rom 4[20], Jas 1[6], if not a Christian coinage, seems "to have had its beginning in near proximity to Christianity" (SH *ad* Rom 4[20]). It arises very naturally out of the general sense of "making distinctions."

διάκρισις.

With the use of διακρίνω cited above from BGU III. 747, cf. P Par 69[i. 5] (A.D. 233) διάκρισιν πρακτόρων, the

"revision" of the (books of the) tax-gatherers by the Praefect: see Wilcken *Ostr.* i. p. 600. Other examples of the word are P Lond 276[12] (A.D. 15) (= II. p. 149) ὅπως ἐπὶ τοῦ διαλογισμοῦ [τὴ]ν διάκρισιν δηλώσωσι, P Tebt II. 302[21] (A.D. 71–2) ἱερευ[τι]κῷ λόγῳ πρὸς διάκρισιν, "priestly list for examination," P Strass I. 77[4] (ii/iii A.D.) διακρίσ(εως) Ἀθηναίο(υ), and P Giss I 48[5] (A.D. 202–3) ἐκ τῆς γενομένης ὑπ᾽ ἐμοῦ . . . ἐξετάσεως καὶ διακρίσεως.

διακωλύω.

For this NT ἅπ. εἰρ. (Mt 3[14]) cf. the long land-survey P Tebt I. 72[363] (B.C. 114–3) β[ο]υλομένων ποτίσαι εἰς φύλλον διακωλυθῆναι ὑπὸ τῶν ἐγ Βερενικίδος [Θε]σμοφ[ό]ρου γ]εωργῶν, and the editors' restoration in *ib.* 61 (*b*)[365] (B.C. 118–7). See also *Syll* 929[81] (ii/B.C.) νόμοις γὰρ ἱεροῖς καὶ ἀραῖς καὶ ἐπιτίμοις ἄνωθεν διεκεκώλυντο ἵνα μηθεὶς ἐν τῷ ἱερῶι τοῦ Διὸς τοῦ Δικταίου μήτε ἐννέμηι κτλ.

διαλαλέω.

The corresponding subst. may be illustrated from the late P Lond 77 (viii/A.D.) (= I. p. 231 ff.), the last will and testament of Abraham, bishop of Hermonthis. The document is written in Greek, of which language the testator, though a bishop, is ignorant, but he declares his accord with its contents —[69] ἑρμηνευθέντα μοι διὰ τῆς Αἰγυπτιακῆς διαλαλείας, "which have been interpreted to me in the Egyptian tongue." The verb survives in MGr = "announce."

διαλέγομαι.

P Oxy X. 1349 (iv/A.D.) ἐπειδὴ ἐξῆλθα ἀπὸ σοῦ ἐχθὲς μὴ διαλεχθείς σοι περὶ τῆς κυθίδος *i.e.* κυθρ. = χυτρ., P Petr III. 43 (3)[15] (B.C. 240) ἔτι δὲ [οὐ]κ ἀγνοεῖς ὡς σοὶ διελέγην περὶ τοῦ ση[σ]άμου, "you know how I conversed with you about the sesame" (Edd.). BGU IV. 1080[11] (? iii/A.D.) καθὼς οὖν ὁ ἀδελφός σου Ἀμμωνᾶς διελέκταί μοι περὶ ὑμῶν καὶ τῶν ὑμῶν πραγμάτων. P Flor II. 132[3] (A.D. 257) τοῖς κωμάρχαις τῆς Ταυρείνου διελέχθην περὶ τοῦ υἱοῦ τοῦ ὀνηλάτου. These instances will suffice to show that διαλέγεσθαι has in the vernacular the use seen in Mk 9[34]. Elsewhere in the NT, as Bp E. L. Hicks points out in *CR* i. p. 45, "it always is used of addressing, preaching, lecturing," a use which he shows to be predominant in inscriptions.

διαλείπω.

For διαλείπω with the participle, as Lk 7[45], cf. P Par 27[22] (ii/B.C.) καθότι οὐ διαλείπεις ἡμῶν ἀντιλαμβανόμενος (same formula in P Leid E[24]), P Tor I. 1[ii. 18] (B.C. 116) ἐκκλίνοντες οὐ διαλείπουσιν, P Oxy II. 281[16] (complaint against a husband—A.D. 20–5) οὐ διέλειπεν κακουχῶν με. Other examples are BGU III. 747[i. 7] (A.D. 130), P Giss I. 14[4], 85[5] (ii/A.D.), P Flor III. 380[8. 15] (A.D. 203–4).

διάλεκτος.

P Leid W[xx. 29] (ii/iii A.D.) δὲ ὁ [. . .] ἐπὶ τῆς βάρεως φανεὶς . . . ἰδίᾳ διαλέκτῳ ἀσπάζεταί σε, λέγων κτλ.—the speaker is apparently a being with a dog's head, who would naturally use a special dialect. Thumb, *ov. Theol.* p. 224, has an important discussion of the precise differentia of διάλεκτος, which from "Redeweise" came to be "Sprache" in general (as Ac 22²), and was finally specialized to "lokale Sprach-eigentumlichkeit"; see his quotations.

διαλιμπάνω

as in Ac 8²¹ D* and syr[hl mg] can be well supported from vernacular sources for other compounds. See Mayser Gr. pp. 492, 465, Blass-Debrunner, Gr. p. 59, also Thackeray Gr. i. p. 227, and below under ὑπολιμπάνω.

διαλλάσσω

With Mt 5²⁴ may be compared BGU III. 846¹⁰ ii/A.D. (= Selections, p. 94) παρακα[λ]ῶ σαι, μήτηρ, δ[ι]αλάγητί μοι, and P Giss I. 17¹³ (time of Hadrian) ὥστε διαλλάγηθι ἡμεῖν. Belonging perhaps to the same period as this last is the fragmentary letter in P Par p. 422, ⁴ ἡως ὁ θεῖος σ[οι] σοὶ διαλλαγῆ. For the subst. = "reconciliation," see BGU II. 665¹¹ ii/A.D. The verb is found = "change," "exchange," OGIS 484¹⁰ ii/A.D. τοῖς τὸ δηνάριον διαλλάσσειν βουλ[ο]μένοι[ς. Note also the middle in Michel 1001¹¹ ¹⁴ (Theia, c. B.C. 200), where it is forbidden to sell the μουσεῖον or its precinct or appurtenances. μήτε καταθέμεν, μήτε διαλλάξασθαι, μήτε ἐξαλλοτριῶσαι τρόπωι μηθενί.

διαλογίζομαι

The verb and its derivative noun are conspicuous in Egyptian documents to describe the conventus, the judicial "circuit" of the Praefect. The subject has been exhaustively treated by Wilcken, Archiv iv. p. 368 ff. His researches are now supplemented and in one important respect modified by a new document, P Ryl II. 74 (A.D. 133-5), the introduction to which gives a sufficient account of the matter. Hunt shows there that the main object of the Praefect's proposed journey south "was judicial, i.e. that he had meant to hold a conventus somewhere in southern Egypt." Thebes becomes thus, according to the new evidence, a probable assize town, visited not annually, but as business demanded. For the verb in this sense cf. P Ryl l.c. νυνεὶ δὲ διαλογίζομαι τὴν Θηβαΐδ̣α καὶ τοὺς Ἑπτὰ νομοὺς κατὰ τὴν [συνήθειαν, P Oxy III. 484²¹ (A.D. 138) ὅπου ἐὰν ὁ κράτιστος ἡγεμὼν Ἀ[ο]ίδιος Ἡλιόδωρος ἐπ' ἀγαθῷ τὸν νομὸν διαλογίζηται ἢ δικαιοδοτῇ, "wherever his highness the praefect Avidius Heliodorus holds his auspicious court for the nome or administers justice" (Edd.). Cf. ὅπου ἐὰν τὸν τοῦ νομοῦ διαλογισμὸν [ἢ] δικαιοδοσίαν ποιήσῃ, P Lond 358¹⁹ (c. A.D. 150) (= II. p. 172.) Similarly P Oxy IV. 709⁴ (c. A.D. 50), where again the verb takes names of districts judicially visited in the accus. In Vettius Valens p. 245²⁶ ἐκ τούτων δεῖ διαλογίζεσθαι τὰς δὲ [τοιάσ] αἱρέσεις the verb is apparently transitive, with the meaning "discuss," which is not far from the legal sense described. No instance of the verb in this sense can be quoted from the NT, where the reference is always to "inward deliberation or questioning," but see s.v. διαλογισμός.

διαλογισμός

The judicial reference of this word (see s.v. διαλογίζομαι) might perhaps be directly recognized in Jas 2⁴, "judges who give corrupt decisions." It adds point to such NT passages as Phil 2¹⁴ χωρὶς γογγυσμῶν καὶ διαλογισμῶν, 1 Tim 2[⁸]

χωρὶς ὀργῆς καὶ διαλογισμῶν, where the thought of outward disputing and discussion is uppermost. So BGU I. 19[ⁱ] ii/A.D. τῷ διεληλυθότι διαλογισμῷ ἐδικάσατο, ib. 226²² (A.D.) ὅταν ὁ κράτιστος ἡγεμὼν Πομπήιος Πλάντας τὸν τοῦ νομοῦ διαλογισμὸν ποιῆται πρὸς τὸ τυχεῖν με τῆς ὑπὸ σοῦ βοηθείας, P Tebt I. 27³⁵ B.C. 113 ἐπὶ τοῦ συσταθέ[ι]τος πρὸς σὲ διαλογισμοῦ, "at the inquiry instituted against you." And the heading ὁ διαλογι[σ]μός of P Oxy II. 237 (A.D. 22) (= Selections, p. 34) with reference to the heading of a particular case, and P Fay 66² ⁴ (A.D. 185 or 217), where we read of fines imposed as the result of an official inquiry —ὑπὲρ ἐπιτίμου) διαλογισμοῦ: also P Oxy IV. 726¹⁰ (A.D. 135), ib. VII. 1032⁴ (A.D. 162), P Tebt II. 397¹² ? (A.D. 192), etc. In P Leid B ¹¹ (B.C. 164) the Twins at the Serapeum in Memphis make petition to Ptolemy, etc for maintenance ὡς γ̣ραπτόν ἐστιν ἐν τοῖς ἀρχαίοις διαλογισμοῖς, where the noun presumably represents the "original decisions" or "agreements" made when they took office, i.e. P Par 62 ⁴¹ ii/B.C.) ὁ δὲ διαλογισμὸς τῆς ἐγλήψεως συσταθήσεται πρὸς αὐτοὺς κατὰ μῆνα, ἐκ τῶν πιπτόντων ἐπὶ τὴν τράπεζαν, the word = "ratiorum relatio, depositio"; see Witkowski's note, Epp.² p. 52. Similarly in P Rev L. 17¹⁷ τῶν δὲ διαλογισμῶν οἷς ἂ[ν ποιή[σ]ηται ὁ οἰκονό[μ]ος πρὸς τ[ο]ὺς τὰς ὠνὰς ἔχοντας πάντων ἀντίγραφα ἑκάστω[ι] τῶν κοινων[ῶ]ν παραχρῆμα δότω σφραγισάμενος αὐτός: see Mayser's list of reff., Gr. p. 437. We have no citations for the meaning "thought," "cogitation," common in LXX and NT, nor for "dispute," though this lies near to the idea of argument in court. But the former is not "peculiar to Biblical Greek," as is implied by Hatch Essays, p. 7f.: cf. φροντίδες καὶ διαλογισμοί in [Plato] Axiochus (p. 367A) and other citations in LS.

διαλύω

Nearest to its one appearance in NT—Ac 5³⁶, of the dispersal of a horde of rebels—is the use in BGU III. 1012¹² (? B.C. 170) ἵνα οὖν μὴ συμβῆι διαλυθῆναι αὐτά . . . τὰ πρόβατα . Cf. also Michel 1001ᵛᴵᴵᴵ ⁶ , B.C. 200 where it is forbidden to make any proposal ὡς δεεισηι διαλῦσαι τὸ κοινὸν εἴ τὰς θυσίας τὰς προγεγραμμένας, "to break up the society or (intermit) the aforementioned sacrifices"—there is a slight zeugma. Still parallel to ἀπολύω is the frequent use in the Paris papyri in connexion with λιμός 12²³ (B.C. 157) ὅπως μὴ ὑπὸ τῆς λιμοῦ δι'αλύ[ω: here note the intransitive use, as in P Leid E ¹³ ii/B.C. ἡμεῖς δ' ἐν τῷ ἱερῷ μεταξὺ διαλύωμεν καὶ τῷ λειμῷ κινδυνεύομεν τὸ ἱερὸν ἐγλιπεῖν—see Proleg. p. 159. So P Par 22²¹ ii/B.C. ὥστ' ἂν κινδυνεύειν τῷ λιμῷ διαλυθῆναι, 20⁹ petition of the Serapeum Twins— B.C. 163 2 (= Selections, p. 14) ὡς ἂν ὑπὸ τῆς λιμοῦ διαλυόμεναι, and 38²⁸ (B.C. 162) καὶ μὴ διαλύωμαι τῷ λιμῷ. Another kindred use is that in P Strass I. 20¹⁰ iii/A.D. ἔδοξεν ἡμᾶς δίκας μηκέτι λέγειν, ἀλλὰ φιλίᾳ μᾶλλον τὰς . . . 15 letters . .] στάσεις διαλύσασθαι. Not far away is P Hib I. 96² (B.C. 259) ὁμολογοῦσιν διαλελύσθαι πρὸς ἀλλήλους πάντα τὰ ἐγκλήματα, "settled all the claims" (Edd.). Διάλυσις is similarly used with reference to d.bts. P Oxy I. 104²⁰ (A.D. 96), cf. VII. 1034 introd. iii/A.D. In P Hamb I. 25⁵ B.C. 238 αὐτοὺς διαλύσαι, δ. = "reconcile." So P Magd 42¹² B.C. 222 μάλιστα διάλυσον αὐτούς· εἰ δὲ μ[ή], ἀπόστειλον ὅπως ἐπὶ τῶν λαοκριτῶν δι[α]κριθῶσιν—it is the endorsement of the king upon a petition. In P Leid W xxii.²⁷ (ii/iii A.D.) ὡς δὲ ἐν τῷ Νόμῳ διαλύεται 'Αβραϊστί, "uti vero in Lege (Mosis) (sic?) solvitur (nomen) Hebraice" (Ed.), it is used apparently to denote the resolution of the patriarchs' names into magical combinations of letters.

διαμαρτύρομαι.

Nageli, p. 24, gives this among Ionic words in the Κοινή, on the strength of its meaning *bezeugen, versichern*, in Attic, but *ermahnen* in the Hellenist of Paul. But "solemn and emphatic utterance" seems to be the note of NT use throughout; and this is not far from the sufficiently Attic Demosthenes, as *Callicles* 4 (p. 1273) οὐδ' ἀπηγόρευσεν οὐδὲ διεμαρτύρατο, "he neither forbad it nor formally protested" (Sandys & Paley—see their note). The verb occurs in P Petr II. 2 (1)¹² (B.C. 260-50) ἡμῶν διαμαρτυρομένων αὐτόν, *ib.* 37 right col.⁸ (iii/B.C.) with fragmentary context: note that in the former it seems to have *acc. pers.* See Milligan's note, *Thess.* p. 51. From a much later period we may quote BGU III. 836⁷ (time of Justinian) διεμαρτύραντο δὲ ἡμᾶς ἐγγράφως δ[ιὰ] τοῦ λογ]ιωτάτου ἐκδίκου κτλ. For the subst. διαμαρτυρία, see P Lond 483,⁷² (A.D. 616) (= II. p. 328), BGU II. 669 *verso*¹ (Byz.).

διαμένω.

P Tebt I. 27⁴⁰ (B.C. 113) ἐν τῆι αὐτῆι ταλαιπωρίαι διαμένεις οὐδαμῶς τὰ κατὰ τὸ δέον (pap. δειον) κεχειρισμένα διωρθωμένος, "you still continue in the same miserable course with no improvement whatever in your improper procedure" (Edd.). P Oxy II. 237ᵛⁱⁱⁱ·⁴⁰ (A.D. 186) ἵνα] δ' [ο]ὖν β[εβ]αία τε καὶ εἰς ἅπαν διαμένῃ τῶν διαστρωμάτων ἡ χρῆσις, "in order that the use of the abstracts may become secure and permanent" (Edd.). P Fay 135¹⁰ (iv/A.D.) σπούδασον πληρῶσαι ἵνα ἡ φιλία διαμίνῃ μετ' ἀλλήλων, "make haste to pay, in order that we may remain on good terms with each other" (Edd.), and from the inscr. *Syll* 194³¹ (B.C. 280-5) διὰ τοῦ ἔμπροσθεν χρ]όνου διαμεμενηκότας αὐ[τῶι, *ib.* 520⁹ (B.C. 281-0) διέμει[ναν] πάντες εὐτακτ[οῦντες καὶ πε]ιθόμενοι τοῖς τε νόμο[ι]ς κα[ὶ τῶι κοσμητε[ῖ. For the subst. we may cite the common formula of a vow for the Emperor's salvation, as BGU II. 362ⁱⁱ·¹² (A.D. 215) ὑπὲρ σωτηρίων καὶ αἰω[νίου] διαμο[νῆ]ς τοῦ κυρίου ἡμῶν Αὐτοκρά[τορος] Σεουή[ρου 'Α]ντωνίνου, and a corresponding inscr. from Saghir, the religious centre of the Imperial estates near Pisidian Antioch—ὑπὲρ τῆς Κυρίων τύχης καὶ [νί]κης καὶ αἰωνίου διαμονῆς καὶ τοῦ σύνπαντος αὐτοῦ οἴκου σωτηρίας ἀνέστησαν Ξῖνοι Τεκμορεῖοι Τύχην χάλκεον, "for the fortune and victory and eternal continuance of our Lords and the salvation of his whole household the (association of coloni called) 'Guest-friends of the Symbol' dedicated a bronze statue of Fortune" (Ramsay *Studies in the Eastern Roman Provinces*, p. 335 f., and *Recent Discovery*, p. 295 f.).

διαμερίζω.

For διαμερίζω εἰς, as Lk 22¹⁷, cf. P Lond 982¹ (iv/A.D.) (= III. p. 242) διεμερίσα[μεν εἰς ἑαυτούς.

διανέμω.

OGIS 383,¹⁵⁵ (middle of i/B.C.) τοῖς δὲ λοιποῖς χάριν ἐμὴν εἰς ἐλευθέραν ἡδονὴν διανέμων, *ib.* 493³¹ (ii/A.D.) διανέμειν τοῖς πολείταις . . . ἐκ τῶν δημοσίων τ[ῶν εἰς θυσίας

κτλ., and for the subst. *ib.* 335¹³⁷ (ii/i B.C.). The verb is restored in CP Herm 8ⁱⁱ·⁹ καὶ ταῦτα πάν[τα ποιήσαντες διενεί]μαντο τὸ ἀργύριον.

διάνοια.

P Petr II. 13 (19)¹² (B.C. 258-3) τοῦτο ε ἔχε (*l.* τοῦτο δὲ ἔχε) τῆι δια[νοία]ι ὅτι οὐθέν σοι μὴ γενηθῆι λυπηρόν "keep this in mind, that you will never be allowed to have anything to distress you." *Syll* 300⁴³ (B.C. 170) γράμματα ἀποστεῖλαι ἔδοξεν, ὅπως περὶ τούτου τῆι δι[αν]οίαι προσέχηι: Viereck (*SG* p. 15) re-translates this *litteras dari censuerunt ut de ea re animadverteret*. Διάνοια is accordingly a fair equivalent to the Latin *animus*. The word is found on the Rosetta Stone, *OGIS* 90¹⁵ (B.C. 196) βωμοὺς ἱδρύσατο τά τε προσδεόμενα ἐπισκευῆς προσδιωρθώσατο ἔχων θεοῦ εὐεργετικοῦ ἐν τοῖς ἀνήκου[σιν εἰς τὸ θεῖον διάνοιαν. Another interesting inscription shows a curious contact with the LXX. *Syll* 891 (ii/A.D.) mostly consists of curses on any one who may disturb the grave on which they are inscribed. Opening hopefully with ἐπικατάρατος ἔστω, they go on with a quotation of Deut 28²² πατάξαι τὸ ἀνεμοφθορίᾳ, followed by ver. 28 παραπληξίᾳ τὸ διανοίας. The inscr. proves to have been ordered for a pagan, but composed by a proselyte to Judaism. The noun figures in other imprecatory literature. So Wünsch *AF* 1¹⁹ (iii A.D.) ἀναθεματίζομεν σῶμα, πνεῦμα, ψ[υ]χήν, [δι]άνοιαν, φρόνησιν, αἴσθησιν, ζοήν, [καρδ]ίαν λόγοις Ἑκατικίοις ὁρκίσμ[ασ(] τε ἀβραικοῖς *i. e.* "Hebrew"), *ib.* 4²³ (iii/A.D.) ὁρκίζω σε τὸν θεὸν τὸν [τ]ὴν δι[ά]νοιαν παντὶ ἀνθρώπῳ χαρισάμενον, *ib.* ³⁵ βασάνισον αὐτῶν τὴν διάνοιαν τὰς φρένας τὴν αἴσθησιν ἵνα μὴ νοῶσιν τί π[ο]ιῶσιν.

For the neutral sense of διάνοια (as Col 1²¹) we may cite Epict. iii. 22. 20 νῦν ἐμοὶ ὕλη ἐστίν ἡ ἐμὴ διάνοια, ὡς τῷ τέκτονι τὰ ξύλα, ὡς τῷ σκυτεῖ τὰ δέρματα. The subst. is very common in Aristeas, and the verb occurs *ter*, e. g. 56 σεμνῶς ἅπαντα διανοούμενος.

διανυκτερεύω.

A new literary reference for this NT ἅπ. εἰρ. (Lk 6¹²) may be cited from the Greek original of the history of the Trojan War assigned to Dictys Cretensis, P Tebt II. 268⁷³ (early iii/A.D.) διανυκτερεύσ[α]ς after a lacuna, followed by τὰς πάσας ἡμέ[ρας again with a lacuna.

διανύω.

For δ. with the accus., as in Ac 21⁷, cf. Vettius Valens pp. 81⁷, 100⁴, 330⁹ πόνους διήνυσα. In *ib.* p. 58¹⁷ the verb is intransitive = *τείνω*. The simplex appears in CP Herm 119 *verso* ii.⁴ (A.D. 266 8) πάντα ὑμῖν κατ' εὐχὴν ἤνυσται: the passage does not strongly taste of vernacular.

διαπεράω.

P Flor II. 247⁸ (A.D. 256) ἔστ' ἂν διαπεράσῃ τὸ Χθώ. P Leid Wᵛⁱ·²⁴ (ii/iii A.D.) διαπεράσεις τὸ πέρα.

διαπλέω.

Montgomery (*Exp* VIII. ix. p. 357) translates διαπλεύσαντες in Ac 27⁹ "having run across the gulf" between Cilicia and Pamphylia, and notes that the verb "probably implies that at this point a favourable shift of wind enabled them to make a straight course across a stretch of open water (πέλαγος) instead of hugging the shores of the bight." The verb occurs with the same object in *Kaibel* 642¹³ (iii/iv A.D.) καὶ πέλαγος διέπλε[υ]σε : see also LS.

διαπονέω.

For δ., as in Ac 4², 16¹⁸, cf. P Oxy IV. 743²² (B.C. 2) ἐγὼ ὅλος διαπον[ο]ῦμαι, "I am quite upset" (Edd.). For the verb in its more ordinary sense of "work laboriously," see Arist. 92 πάντες γὰρ αὐτοκελεύστως διαπονοῦσι πολλῆς γινομένης κακοπαθείας.

διαπορεύομαι.

Aristeas 322 concludes his letter by assuring Polycrates that if he discovers anything else worthy of narration he will set it forth—ἵνα διαπορευόμενος αὐτὰ κομίζῃ τοῦ βουλήματος τὸ κάλλιστον ἔπαθλον, "in order that in the perusal thereof thou mayst win the fairest reward for thy zealous desire" (Thackeray). BGU IV. 1116¹¹ (B.C. 13) τοῦ δι[απ]ορευ- ομένου μηνός, and so 1136⁹ (c. B.C. 11), "the month now current." P Leid Wˣˣⁱ·³⁹ (ii/iii A.D.) αὐτὸς γὰρ ὁ Αἰὼν Αἰῶνος, ὁ μόνος κ[αὶ] ὑπερέχων, ἀθεώρητος διαπορεύεται τὸν τόπον.

διαπραγματεύομαι.

With the perfective compound διεπραγματεύσαντο in Lk 19¹⁵ = "gained by trading" (see *Proleg.* p. 118) cf. the use of συμπραγματεύομαι in *Syll* 241¹⁷ (ii/B.C.) ἔδωκε δὲ καὶ ἐπιστολὰς τοῖς πρεσβευταῖς εἰς Πολύρηνα πρὸς τοὺς φίλους, ὅπως συνπραγματεύωνται μετ' αὐτῶν περὶ τῶν συμφερόντων, *ib.* 245⁹ (second half iii/B.C.) τοῖς ἀποσταλεῖσι σιτώναις ὑπὸ τῆς πόλεως εἰς Δῆλον συνεπραγματεύθη πάντα προθύμως.

διαπρίω.

The literal sense of this word is seen in *Syll* 587⁷·¹⁶⁰·³⁰⁴ (B.C. 329–8), *Michel* 594¹⁰⁷ (B.C. 279) ξύλον διαπρίσαντι Θεοδήμωι. For the subst. cf. the Delphic inscr. in *BCH* xxxvi. p. 92⁸ ξύλων [Μ]ακεδον[ικῶν με]σόδμᾶν διαπρίσω[ιος : Herwerden compares διαπρίωτος in Hippocrates.

διαρπάζω.

P Lond 35²¹ (B.C. 161) (= I. p. 25) ὁ δὲ βασιλεὺς ἀπο- δέδο[κε τ]ὴν σύνταξιν διαρπάζεται δὲ ὑπὸ τῶν προ[εστη]- κότων τῶν ἱερῶν. *Cagnat* IV. 1029⁵ (c. B.C. 85) διαρπα- σάν[των] δὲ καὶ τὰ [σκεύη τῶν σ]ωμάτ[ων (= slaves) κα]ὶ τῶν ἐν τῶι χωρίωι [καὶ] τοῖς περι[κειμέν]οις τόποις. For the subst., *Syll* 259¹⁰ (B.C. 270) ἐπὶ διαρπαγᾶι τῶ[ν το]ῦ [θ]εοῦ χρημάτων.

διαρρήγνυμι.

P Lips I. 37¹⁹ (A.D. 389) τὴν ἐπικιμένην α[ὐτο]ῦ ἐ[σ]θῆτα διαρ[ρή]ξαντες ἀφ[εί]λαντ[ο.

διασαφέω.

For this verb, common in the earlier papyri, we may cite P Eleph 18³ (B.C. 223–22) κ[α]λῶς ποιήσεις διασαφήσας ἡμῖν, ὅπως ἐπιτελέσωμεν κτλ., P Lond 42⁸ (B.C. 168) (= I. p. 30, *Selections*, p. 9) ἐπιστολὴν . . ἐν ἧι διεσάφεις εἶναι ἐν κατοχῆι ἐν τῶι Σαραπιείωι, P Par 42¹⁰ (B.C. 156)

διασάφησόν μοι, *ib.* 45³ (B.C. 153) ἅ σ[οι] οὐ δεδύνημαι διασαφῆσαι διὰ τοῦ ἐπιστολίου, P Grenf II. 33¹¹ (B.C. 160) περὶ τοῦ διασαφουμένου μέρους γῆς, and from the inscriptions *Syll* 709⁹⁵ (c. B.C.) ἐν τῶι ψηφίσματι διασαφεῖται τῶι κεκ[υ]ρωμένωι περὶ τοῦ [μαν]τε[ίου] ἐφ' ἱερέως Κρίνωνος. If we may judge from the contrast between papyri B.C. and A.D., the verb went out of common vernacular use during the NT period, which would account for the curious fact that only one NT writer (Mt) uses it at all. It occurs however five times in Vettius Valens.

διασείω.

P Tebt I. 41¹⁰ (c. B.C. 119) ἑτέρων γυναικῶν διασείειν gives us an early example of the Hellenistic use—"extort." It takes the (ablative) genitive here, if the cases of a very muddled scribe are to be regarded as deliberate: in Lk 3¹⁴ and many other places it has the accusative, e.g. P Par 15³⁷ (B.C. 120) χάριν τοῦ διασείσαι αὐτοὺς καὶ εἰς βλάβας περιστῆσαι. With the Lukan passage, cf. P Oxy II. 240⁵ (A.D. 37) where we have an oath by a κωμογραμματεὺς that he knows of no villager διασεσεισμέ[νο]ς . . . ὑπό . . . στρατιώτου. This unknown soldier might have come almost fresh from the Baptist's exhortation! For the same com- bination of verbs as in Lk *l.c.*, see P Tebt I. 43⁵⁶ (B.C. 118) συκοφαντηθῶμεν διασεισμῶν (l. διασεσεισμένων ?), "be subject to false accusations and extortions." Other examples of the verb are P Oxy II. 284⁵ (A.D. 50) διασείσθην ὑπὸ Ἀπολλοφάνους, *ib.* 285¹³ (c. A.D. 50) διέσισέν με ἄλλας δραχμὰς τέσσαρας, both referring to extortions by the same tax-collector : cf. also the editor's note to P Giss I. 61¹⁰ (A.D. 119), where a number of references are collected, and P Leid G⁶ σκυλλόμεν[ος δὲ καὶ [δια]σειόμενος παρ' ἕκαστον, where the editor regards σκύλλω as the wider term—"de omni *vexatione* universe," while those are said διασείειν "qui *vani, aliqua ratione illicita* alieni pecuniam vel simile quid *extorquent.*" A rather more general meaning is suggested by P Tor I. 1ᵛⁱⁱ·²¹ (B.C. 116) (= *Chrest.* II. p. 38) ὑπολαμβάνοντα εὐχερῶς διασείειν τοὺς ἀντιδίκους, "consumi se facile concus- surum adversarios," as Peyron renders : but "browbeat, intimidate" seems more appropriate than "blackmail." The combination of Lk 3¹⁴ is repeated with nouns in P Tor I. 1ᵛⁱ·¹⁶ (B.C. 116) ἐπὶ τῆι πάσηι συκοφαντίαι καὶ διασεισμῶι, P Tebt I. 43²⁶ (B.C. 118) συκοφαντίας τε καὶ διασισμοῦ χάριν, "for the sake of calumny and extortion" (Edd.). A form διάσεισις occurs in *ib.* 41²⁰ (c. B.C. 119) πρὸς τῆ[ι] διασε[ί]σει.

διασκορπίζω.

BGU IV. 1049⁷ (a deed of sale—(?) A.D.) ἐν ᾧ φύν[ικες (l. φοίνικες) διεσκορπισμένον κτλ. The verb is found with reference to the broken bread of the Eucharist in *Didache* 9⁴: ὥσπερ ἦν τοῦτο κλάσμα διεσκορπισμένον ἐπάνω τῶν ὀρέων καὶ συναχθὲν ἐγένετο ἕν, οὕτω συναχθήτω σου ἡ ἐκκλησία κτλ. The subst. is found P Tebt I. 24⁵⁵ (B.C. 117) ὑπὸ διασκορπισμὸν τὰ τῆς φορολογίας ἀγάγωσιν, "they might produce the dispersal of this revenue" (Edd.).

διασπάω.

Syll 519¹³ (iii/B.C.) οἱ δὲ λαχόντες διαιρείτωσαν καθ' οὓς ἂν ἕκαστοι τόπους λάχωσιν μὴ διασπῶντες μήτε τὰ τοῦ τοκιστοῦ μέρη μήτε τὰ τοῦ γεωργοῦ, ἀλλὰ τὰ μέρη τέμνοντες συνεχῆ ἀλλήλοις.

διασπείρω.

The verb is found in a list of persons subject to the poll-tax, P Lond 259⁷⁻ (Roman) (= II. p. 38) διεσπαρμένα διὰ τῶν τοῦ ιγ̄ ἔτους ἐνκεφαλαιω(μάτων). We have no citations for the noun διασπορά, but it occurs in Plutarch.

διαστέλλω.

The verb is common = "enjoin, give instructions to," e.g. P Hal I. 7⁶ (B.C. 232) Π]τολεμαίωι δὲ διά[σ]τειλαι, εἴπερ μὴ τὸν βυβλιαφόρον καὶ τὸν ἔφοδον ἐκπέπει[κα]ς, "give instructions to Ptolemaeus, in case you have not persuaded the letter-carrier and the post-controller." P Par 26·³ (B.C. 163–2) (= Selections, p. 16) ἡμῶν δὲ τοῖς δέουσι θλιβομένων καὶ Ἀχομάρρῃ μὲν τῷ ἐπιστάτῃ τοῦ ἱεροῦ πλεονάκι διεστάλμεθα ἀποδιδόναι ἡμῖν, "when we were being crushed by our wants, we often made representations even to Achomarres the supervisor of the temple to give us (our rights)," ib. 63ᵛⁱⁱ·¹⁹ (B.C. 165) διεστάλμεθα τοῖς ἄλλοις ἐπιμεληταῖς καὶ ὑποδιοικηταῖς ταῦτά, etc. In P Rein 7²⁰ (?B.C. 141) διασταλέντος, "it having been ordered" in the contract (συμβολαίωι), is followed by the acc. and the infin.: in the NT we have the equivalent ἵνα construction. P Lond 44¹⁷ (B.C. 161) (= I. p. 34) καὶ τὴν μὲν θύραν τοῦ ἱεροῦ προσφθάσαντός μου καὶ κλείσαντος, μετὰ κραυγῆς τε διαστελλομένου μεθ'ἡσυχίας ἀναλύειν οὐδ' ὡς ἀπεχώρουν, "I shouted to them to go away quietly." The same petitioner uses the active in ib. 45²·⁹ (p. 36) a year later, ὅπως ἀνακαλεσάμενος τοὺς προειρημένους διαστελῇ ταύτοις μηκέτι εἰσβιάζεσθαι εἰς κτλ. We might further quote P Ryl II. 113¹¹ (A.D. 133), where διέστειλαντό μοι is rendered "served a summons upon me" (Edd.). Quite distinct is the meaning in P Amh II. 40⁵ (ii/B.C.), showing how the best land in a glebe had been "separated" by a Greek for the use of some compatriots—διεσταλμένας ἀπὸ τῆς γῆς τὰς κρατίστας (ἀρούρας) κ̄ᾱ καὶ μεμισθωμένας τισὶ τῶν Ἑλλήνων: this agrees with the use of the noun διαστολή in the NT, see s.v. Cf. also Aristeas 152 ἡμεῖς δ'ἀπὸ τούτων διεστάλμεθα, where Thackeray (Transl. p. 52) remarks that διαστέλλειν "seems here to combine the two senses of 'to distinguish' and 'to command,' with a reference to Lev 10¹⁰, 11⁴⁷." Finally we find διαστέλλειν almost a term. tech. in orders for payment in kind, P Oxy I. 88⁵ (A.D. 179) διαστείλατε ἀφ'ὧν ἔχετε τῶν γυμνασιάρχων ἐνθέμα[τι] πυροῦ γενήματος τ[ο]ῦ δ[υ̣ἐ̣λ̣]θόν[τ]ος ιθ ἔτους ἀρτάβας ἑξήκοντα, "pay from the past 19th year's store of wheat belonging to the gymnasiarchs and deposited with you sixty artabae" (Edd.), so ib. III. 516⁵ (A.D. 160), P Laps I. 112² (A.D. 123), 113³ (A.D. 127 or 128) etc. Ostr 1164 (ii/iii A.D.) shows it in the formula of a cheque, διάστειλον ἐκ τοῦ ἐμοῦ θέματος ἐς ὄνομ(α) Λουκιλλάτος.

διάστημα.

The word is found in the astronomical papyrus P Par 1⁸⁴ (ii/B.C.) ὁ τῶν ἐπιτολῶν καὶ δυσμῶν χρόνος ἔνεστιν ἐν τῷ τῆς ἡμέρας καὶ νυκτὸς διαστήματι, cf. 453, 491. See also P Oxy VI. 918ᵛ·¹³ (a land survey—ii/A.D.) ἀνὰ μ(έσον)

οὔσης διώρυχο(ς) καὶ ἱκανοῦ διαστήματ(ος), P Giss I. 40ⁱ·¹⁵ (edict of Caracalla) μετὰ τ[ὸ] π[λ]ηρωθῆναι τὸ τοῦ χρ̣όνου διάστημα, P Ryl II. 207 (a)²⁷·³¹ (ii/A.D.) μετὰ διάστεμα, of space: on the shortening of η to ε, irrespective of etymology (which would have produced α) see Proleg. p. 46.

διαστολή.

We are unable to illustrate the NT use of this word (cf. also Exod 8²⁰ = "distinction," "difference" (see under διαστέλλω), but the subst., like the verb, can be freely quoted in the sense of "injunction," "notification," "memorandum." P Tebt I. 24¹⁵ (B.C. 117) ἀκολούθως ταῖς δεδομέναι (l.—αις) δι' α[ὑ]τῶν διαστολὰς (l.—αῖς), "in accordance with the memoranda given by them" (Edd.). ib. 34¹³ (c. B.C. 100) γράφω σοι δὲ διαστολὰς αὐτοῖς δοῦναι, "I am therefore writing to you to give their instructions" (Edd.). P Oxy IV. 745²⁵ (B.C. 2) διαστολὰς δεδώκειν, "praecepi" (Witkowski², p. 130), ib. I. 68³¹ (A.D. 131) ἀρκουμένου μου τῇδε τῇ διαστολῇ ὡς καθήκει, "since I am ready to abide by the present memorandum, as is right (?)" (Edd.). Cf. also the corresponding use of τὸ διαστολικόν of an official "notification" or "writ," in this last papyrus ³⁴, et saepe. The noun, like διαστέλλω, is also frequent with reference to payments, e.g. P Tebt II. 363¹ (early ii/A.D.) διαστολῆς μετρήματος Τεβτύνεως, "statement of a payment in kind at Tebtunis," ib. 395²³ (A.D. 150) ἀντί[γρα(φον)] διαστολ(ῆς?), with reference to the copy of a banker's receipt: cf. the use of the rare word διαστολεύς in P Rein 53⁵ (iii/iv A.D.). See also Wilcken Ostr i. p. 638.

διαστρέφω.

For the use of δ. in Phil 2¹⁵ Lightfoot cites Epict. iii. 6. 8 οἱ μὴ παντάπασι διεστραμμένοι τῶν ἀνθρώπων (cf. i. 29. 3). Kennedy (EGT ad l.) aptly compares the Scotch expression "thrawn," "having a twist" in the inner nature. The subst. occurs in the vi/A.D. P Oxy VIII. 1165⁷ where one advocate writes to another expostulating— διὰ τοὺς γεωργούς μου τοὺς ἐν τῷ Ἀμούλῃ ἐν τοιαύτῃ διαστροφῇ γενέσθαι, "because my cultivators at Amoules have been put to such straits" (Ed.).

διασώζω.

P Lille I. 17¹³ (iii/B.C.) ἀ]πόστιλον αὐτῶι τινά, ἵνα διασωθῇ ὁ σῖτος ὁ παρ' ὑμᾶς, P Vat A⁶ (B.C. 168) (= Witkowski², p. 65) κομισάμενος τὴν παρὰ σοῦ ἐπιστολήν, ἐν ᾗ διεσάφεις διασεσῶσθαι ἐγ μεγάλων κινδύνων, P Par 29¹ (B.C. 161–0) διασωθεὶς κατὰ τὸ δίκαιον ἐκ τῶν ἔξωθεν τόπων, BGU I. 332⁷ (ii/iii A.D.) ἐχάρην κομισαμένη γράμματα, ὅτι καλῶς διεσώθητε, ib. 341¹³ (ii/A.D.) (as restored in Preisigke p. 40) ὅσοι μὲν τελέω]ς δ[ι]σ̣ρωθησόμενοι πρὸς τοὺς ἰδί(ους) κατέφυγον. See also the iv/A.D. Christian letter, P Oxy VI. 939⁸ ἡμῖν ἵλεως ἐγένετο [καὶ ταῖς εὐ]χαῖς ἡμῶν ἐπένευσεν διασώσας ἡμῖν [τὴν τ̣ἡμῶν] κυρίαν, "He was gracious to us and inclined His ear to our prayers by preserving for us our mistress." Add from inscr. Syll 490¹⁵ (ii/B.C.) ἀλλ' ὁμοίως περὶ πάντα[ς τὸ]ς πολεί[τ]ας [σπουδ]άζων διέσωσε πολλούς. In connexion with 1 Pet 3²⁰, where it describes Noah's being "safely brought into" the Ark, it is worth noting that Josephus uses the verb about Noah, in c. Apion. i. 130 περὶ τῆς λάρνακος, ἐν ᾗ Νῶχος . . διεσώθη.

διαταγή.

Deissmann (*LAE*, p. 86 ff.) has shown how completely the new evidence sets aside the statement by Grimm (but cf. Thayer, p. 094) that this is "purely" a biblical and ecclesiastical word used for the Greek διάταξις. Thus P Oxy I. 92³ (an order for a payment of wine—? A.D. 335) Ἀμεσύστῳ ἱπποιάτρῳ ἐκ διαταγῆς οἴνου κεράμιον ἓν νέον, *ib.* 93² (A.D. 302), and P Tav 133⁴ (iv/A.D.) ἀπέστειλα τὸν οἰκ[ον]όμον . . . ἵνα τὴν διαταγὴν τῆς τρύγης ποιήσηται, "I have sent to you the steward to make arrangements about the vintage" (Edd.). From inscrr. we may quote *Cagnat* IV. 661¹⁷ (A.D. 85), where the διαταγή of T. Praxias of Acmonia appears in his will; *ib.* 734¹², providing that no one shall be buried in the tomb παρὰ γνώμην τοῦ Ῥούφου ἢ διαταγήν, and similarly *ib.* 840⁴ εἴ τις παρὰ τὴν διαταγὴν τὴν ἐμὴν ποιήσι, which the editor glosses as "excerptum testamenti, relati in tabularium civitatis." For this specialized meaning of "testamentary disposition," Deissmann, *LAE*, p. 87, cites this last inscr. (from Hierapolis), and refers to the Pauline use of ἐπιδιατάσσεσθαι in Gal 3¹⁵.

For the difficult εἰς διαταγὰς ἀγγέλων in Ac 7⁵³ Nestle (*Exp T* xx. p. 93) cites the Heb. בְּיַד or בְּיָדוֹ "through the hand" or "hands" (*i.e.* the mediation) of angels, and compares the LXX διὰ χειρὸς Δαυείδ = Heb. עַל־יְדֵי דָוִיד in 2 Chron. 23¹⁸ (Vg. "juxta *dispositionem* David"—a view confirmed, he adds, by the Syriac version which has בְּיַד with the addition of פֻּקְדָּנָא "the command."

διάταγμα

was in Imperial times the technical term for an "edict," see e.g. P Giss I. 40ⁱ·⁸ (A.D. 212) where Caracalla refers to the words προτέρου διατάγματος, in which his χάρις had been displayed: cf. also P Oxy VIII. 1102¹ (A.D. 206), 1101² (A.D. 367–70) of the edicts of Praefects, and numerous exx. in *OGIS*, as 458·¹ (c. B.C. 9) κατά τε τὸ Παύλου Φαβίου Μαξίμου τοῦ ἀνθυπάτου διάταγμα. The word is used of a "testamentary disposition" in P Oxy X. 1282²⁷ (A.D. 83) καθ' ὃ ἔθετο ὁ Παποντῶς ὁπότε περιῆν διάταγμα, "in accordance with the disposition made by Papontos in his lifetime" (Edd.)—the constr. is mixed. Cf. BGU I. 140²⁵ (A.D. 119—so Mitteis *Chrest.* II. p. 424) ἐξ ἐκείνου τοῦ μέρ[ο]υς τοῦ διατάγματος, and see above under διαταγή.

For διάταξις, which is not found in the NT but ten times in the LXX, we may cite BGU I. 180⁶ (ii/A.D.) παρὰ δὴ ταύτην τὴν δ[ι]άτ[α]ξιν ἐγὼ] ἐπηρεάσθην μ[ε]τὰ διετίαν τῆς [ἀπο]λύσεως κτλ., P Par 60¹·²⁸ (acts of Alexander Severus—A.D. 233) αἱ γὰρ θεῖαι διατάξεις, and similarly of Imperial decrees in BGU IV. 1022⁹ (Hadrian), P Flor III. 382⁴⁵·⁵⁰ (A.D. 222–3), P Strass I. 22¹⁸ (iii A.D.), etc.

διατάσσω.

The technical use of the verb in connexion with wills (see above under διαταγή, διάταγμα) is seen in P Fay 97¹³ (A.D. 78) ἀργυρίου δραχμὰς εἴκοσι . . . αἵ εἰσιν δ[ι]αταγεῖσαι ἀ[πὸ] τοῦ τετελευτηκότος αὐ[το]ῦ π[α]τρός, "twenty drachmae of silver, being the sum bequeathed by his deceased father" (Edd.), so²², P Oxy I. 75·⁹ (A.D. 129) δηλῶ δὲ τὴν ἀδελφήν μου Διογενίδαν διαταγεῖσαν διὰ τῆς διαθήκης προικὸς δραχμὰς χειλίας κτλ.: *ib.* 105⁷ (A.D. 117–37) μὴ ἐξέστω ἐνχιρεῖν τοῖς ὑπ' ἐμοῦ διατεταγμένοις,

al. For the more general sense, cf. P Oxy IV. 718²⁵ (A.D. 180–92) κατὰ τὰ διατεταγμένα, "in accordance with the decrees," *ib.* VI. 899²² (A.D. 200) διετάσσετο γῆν βασιλικήν τε καὶ δη[μοσ]ίαν, "was appointed to cultivate Crown and public land" (Edd.), P Tebt II. 423⁵ (early iii/A.D.) ἤδη οὖν ὡς δι[ε]τάγη χωρησάτω, "so now as was ordered let it go" (Edd.), P Flor II. 127¹⁷ (A.D. 256) ἐπεὶ καὶ τὰ ὑπόλοιπα χωρ[ί]δια ἐπιθεωρεῖν μέλλομεν καὶ τὰ παρὰ σοὶ διατάξαι. In the curious Pergamene inscr., *Cagnat* IV. 504⁸ διαταγεῖσα ἰδίᾳ γνώμῃ, indicating "infra expressam esse sententiam Nicodeni," the subject is conditioned in its phraseology by the necessity of making the letters of each line add up to 1461 (Ed.).

διατελέω.

P Hib I. 35⁵ (c. B.C. 250) διατελο[ῦ]μεν τοὺς φόρους εὐτακτοῦντες εἰς τὸ ἱερὸν διὰ τὴν παρ' ὑμῶν σκέ[π]ην, "we have long administered with regularity the revenues of the temple on account of your protection" (Edd.), P Lond 42⁴ (B.C. 168) (= I. p. 30, *Selections*, p. 9) εἴην ἂν τοῖς θεοῖς εὐχομένη διατελῶ, "it would be as I am continually praying to the gods," BGU I. 287⁷ (a libellus—A.D. 250) (= *Selections*, p. 115) καὶ ἀεὶ θύων τοῖς θεοῖς διετέλεσα, P Oxy IX. 1204¹⁶ (A.D. 299) διετέλεσεν γοῦν ὑπηρετούμενος τῇ σῇ τοῦ ἐμοῦ κυρίου τάξει. In P Oxy I. 120 *verso*¹⁰ (iv/A.D.) we have μὴ ἄρα αἱ ἡμέραι τὰ πάντα διατελοῦσι; "Can time accomplish everything after all?" (Edd.). From the inscrr. it is sufficient to quote *Syll* 393⁴ (Roman) which also shows the adj. διατελοῦς ἀρετῆς ἕνεκεν [ἧς ἔχων] διατελεῖ . . . The standing intransitive use with participle, recognisable in all but one of the instances quoted above, can be illustrated to any extent.

διατηρέω.

P Petr II. 20 (*ii*)² (Ptol.) διατήρει ἐπιμελῶς καὶ ἐπιμέλου αὐτῶν, P Grenf II. 14 (a)¹⁶ (B.C. 270 or 233) δ[ι]ὰ τὸ διατετηρηκέναι ἐμαυτὸν μηδένα τρόπον ἐνοχλεῖν, *Syll* 246⁷ (B.C. 220–16) ὅπως ἂν παρ' ἑκατέρων τῶι [δ]ήμωι ἥ τε φιλί[α κ]αὶ ἡ εἰρήνη διατηρῆται, *ib.* 521⁷⁶ (B.C. 100) διετήρησεν δὲ αὐτῶν καὶ τὴν πρὸς ἀλλ[ή]λ[ο]υς ὁμόνοιαν καὶ φιλίαν δι' ὅλου τοῦ ἐνια[υ]τοῦ. In the magic papyrus P Lond 46⁴¹ (iv/A.D.) (= I. p. 69) we have διατήρησόν με καὶ τὸν παῖδα τοῦτον ἀπημάντους ἐν ὀνόματι τοῦ ὑψίστου θεοῦ· cf. *ib.* 121⁴⁵³ (iii/A.D.) (= I. p. 99). On the "perfective" force in the compound see P Leid W^viii·²¹ (ii/iii·) the dream of Nectonebus, the last Egyptian King of the old dynasties, where we have a striking parallel to 2 Tim 4⁷— διατετήρηκα τὴν χώραν ἀμέμπτως. The perfective in the King's words emphasises the fact that the watchful care has been successful: the simplex in Paul lays the stress on the speaker's own action, "I have *guarded* my trust" (*Proleg.* p. 237, cf. p. 119).

διατίθημι.

As noted under διαθήκη, the regular formula in a will is τάδε διέθετο (νοῶν καὶ φρονῶν κτλ.): see e.g. P Eleph 2² (B.C. 285–4 τάδε διέθετο Διονύσιος κτλ., P Lips I. 29⁸ (A.D. 295) νοῦσα καὶ φρονοῦσα διεθέμην τόδε μου τὸ βούλημα, P Lond 171²³³ (iii/A.D.) (= II. p. 176) δι[έ]θετό μοι διαθήκην α[ὐ]τοῦ ἐσφραγισμένην. The use of the verb accords more closely with LXX and NT than that of the noun,

Thus *Syll.* 342²⁶,³⁸ (c. B.C. 48), of an envoy from a king to Pompey, οὐ μόνον τοὺς ὑπὲρ τοῦ βα[σιλ]έως χρηματισμοὺς διέθετο τὴν εὔνοιαν τὴν Ῥωμαίων πα[ρ]αγόμενος τῷ βασιλεῖ, ἀ[λ]λὰ καὶ περὶ τῆς πατρίδος τοὺς καλλίστου[ς δ]ιέθετο χρηματισμοῖς, "he not only *negotiated* terms on behalf of the King, winning the King the Romans' good will, but also *negotiated* the most honourable terms for his country." The selection of διαθήκη in the LXX for "covenant" may well have followed this still current use of the verb, perhaps with the feeling that the δια- compound was more suitable than the συν- for a covenant with God—συνθ. might suggest an agreement on equal terms. As showing, however, how closely the usage of the two verbs approached, see Polyb. xxxii. 8. 13 ὁ γὰρ πατὴρ συνέθετο μὲν ἑκατέρᾳ τῶν θυγατέρων πεντήκοντα τάλαντα δώσειν. In P Ryl II. 116⁹ (A.D. 104) ἀκολούθως ᾗ ἔθετο διαθήκῃ, we have a sporadic appearance of the simplex. In P Par 63ᵛⁱⁱⁱ·⁶ (B.C. 164) we have πρὸς δὲ τοὺς ὁπωσδηποτοῦν (*par.* ὁπωσ-) ἠγνωμονηκέναι φάσκοντας, εὐδιαλύ[τ]ως καὶ πραέως διατίθεσθαι, and in P Lille I. 3⁵⁸ (after B.C. 241) the verb is used of the vendors of oil—ἐά[ν] τι[ν]ας καταλαμβάνηι διατιθεμένους [π]λείονων τι[μ]ῶν τῶν συντεταγμένων, "if he detect any disposing of it for larger sums than those agreed upon." P Oxy I. 99⁹ (A.D. 55) οἰκία τῆς τοῦ διατιθεμένου Πνεφερῶτος ἀδελφῆς, "sister of P. the seller": Wilcken (*Archiv* i. p. 128) quotes Herodotus i. 1. In BGU IV. 1202¹⁰ (B.C. 18) ἐφ' ᾧ διαθ[ήσ]ε[ι] κα[ὶ] τὰ νουμηνίαν ἑκάστην τῶι τοπογραμματεῖ . . . κύλλησιν εἰς τὸν ἀεὶ χρόνον. "on condition that (the temple) supplies *cyllestis* (a kind of fancy bread)," we have—if the reading is sound—another development from the central idea of "making a disposition." The passive in BGU IV. 1109¹¹ (B.C. 5) τῆς Καλλιτύχης ἐν ἀσθενείᾳ διατεθείσης shows yet another natural development.

διατρίβω

is common = "live," "sojourn," e.g. P Hal I. 1¹⁸² (middle iii/B.C.) ἀλλὰ καὶ ἐν Ἀπόλλωνος πό[λ]ει διατρίβωσιν, P Lille I. 7⁴ (iii/B.C.) διατρίβοντος γάρ μου μετὰ Ἀπολλωνίου ἐμοῦ οἰκείου, BGU I. 267¹¹ (A.D. 199) πρὸς μὲν τοὺς ἐν ἀλλοτρίᾳ πόλει διατρείβοντας ἐτῶν εἴκοσι ἀριθμῷ βεβαιοῦται (cf. P Strass I. 22⁶, *ib.* IV. 1140⁴ (B.C. 5) διατρείψας ἐνταῦθα (in Alexandria) τὸν πάντα χρόνον—the complaint of a Jew named Helenus, son of Tryphon an Alexandrian, *Preisigke* 1002⁹ (? iii/A.D. ἐν τῇ βασιλ[εν]ο[ύ]σῃ Ῥώμῃ χρόνῳ πολλῷ διατρίψας, P Oxy III. 486³¹ (A.D. 131) ἐνθάδ[ε] μοι διατριβούσῃ ἀπηνγέλη τὰ ἐμὰ πάν[τα] . . . ἀπολωλένα[ι, *ib.* IX. 1204¹⁸ (A.D. 299) ἐπειδὴ κατὰ τὴν Ὄασιν τὴν Μεικρὰν διέτρειψεν, etc. So from the inscrr. *Michel* 332⁴ (ii/B.C.) διατρίβων παρὰ βασιλεῖ Σκυθῶν, "living at the court of the King of the Scythians." These exx. make against the constr. suggested by Field (*Notes* p. 121) for Ac 14³, by which χρόνον is the object of διέτριψαν instead of the acc. of time. For the subst. see *OGIS* 505⁷ (A.D. 150) ὡς ἐν πατρίδι ταῖς Ἀθήναις τὴν διατριβὴν ποιησάμενος (= ἐν ταῖς Ἀ. ὡς ἐν π., as Dittenberger notes).

In connection with the frequent use of this verb in Ac, Hobart (p. 221 f.) adduces exx. of its varied employment in medical writings. Διατριβή in MGr = "dissertation," as in technical phraseology of ancient times, from which it apparently descends.

διατροφή

is found, as in 1 Tim 6³, in P Oxy II. 275¹⁹ (a contract of apprenticeship—A.D. 66) εἰς λόγον διατροφῆς δραχμὰς πέντε, "on account of his keep five drachmas," III. 494¹⁶ (a will—A.D. 156) ἡ δ' αὐτὴ γυνή μου χορηγήσει τῷ υἱῷ μου Δείῳ εἰς δ[ια]τρο[φὴ]ν αὐτοῦ καὶ τὴν ἄλλην δαπάνην κτλ., "my said wife shall supply to my son Dius for his sustenance and other expenses" etc. (Edd.), *ib.* 497⁸ (a marriage contract—early ii/A.D.) χορηγείτω ὁ αὐτὸς Θέων τοῖς τέκνοις τὰ πρὸς τὴν διατροφήν, BGU I. 321⁷ (A.D. 216) τὰ εἰς διατροφὴν ἀποκείμενα σειτάρια, etc. For the verb, as in Judith 5¹⁰, cf. P Oxy III. 638 (A.D. 112) ἐπὶ τὸν τῆς ζωῆς αὐτῆς χρόνον ἐφ' ὃν καὶ διατρέφειν ἡμᾶς αὐτήν.

διαυγάζω

P Lond 130⁷⁰ (a horoscope—i/ii A.D.) (= I. p. 135) οὐ τὸ δωδεκατημόριον διηύγαζεν σκορπίου περὶ τὸν πρῶτον σφόνδυλον. P Leid Wⁱᵛ·³⁹ (ii/iii A.D.) καχάσαντος (i.e. καγχ—) πρῶτον πρῶτον (om.) αὐτοῦ ἐφάνη φῶς αὐτή. κ[αὶ] διηύγασεν τὰ πάντα. In BGU IV. 1143¹⁵ f. [υ κεκοπημ[ένα] καὶ διευγασ[μένα] καὶ ἐπιδιευγασμένα καὶ κε[καυμένα τῇ καθηκούσῃ ὀπτήσι, of pottery. The editor, W. Schubart, after glossing the first participle as "mit Griffen versehen," confesses that the next word is unintelligible to him—it might begin with διευτ. A perf. partic. from διαυγάζω is possible: could it mean "(semi) transparent," like διαυγής?

διαυγής

found in the Receptus at Rev 21²¹ for διαυγής, on no known authority, survives in the MGr διάφανος.

διαφέρω

It may be well to illustrate at length the varying shades of meaning which this common verb exhibits. In P Lond 45⁹ (B.C. 160–59) (= I. p. 36) a certain Ptolemy addresses a petition to King Ptolemy Philometor stating that his house had been sacked, and goods valued at twenty talents had been "carried off"—τῶν ἀπ' αὐτῆς φορτίων διενηνεγμένων. For δ. = "differ" cf. P Tor I. 1ᵛⁱᵇ·¹⁵ (B.C. 116) μηδὲ τὴν αὐτὴν ἐργασίαν ἐπιτελεῖν, διαφέρειν δὲ τὴν τούτων λειτουργίαν. From this is naturally developed the meaning "surpass, excel," common in NT. For this see P Tebt I. 27⁶ (B.C. 113) τῶν οὖν ἐν τοῖς καθ' ἡμᾶ[ς ὑ[μᾶ]ς) τόποις πίστει καὶ ἀσφαλείαι δι[α]φ[ε]ρόντων . . . τὰς κατ' ἄνδρα γραφάς, "the lists of individuals in your district who are conspicuous for honesty and steadiness" (Edd.), so again⁵¹, P Oxy VII. 1061¹² (B.C. 22) διαφέρετε γὰρ τοῦ Πτολεμαίου ἐμπειρίᾳ, "for you are superior to Ptolemaeus in experience" (Edd.), *Syll.* 305⁹ (A.D. 37) θεῶν δὲ χάριτες τούτῳ διαφέρουσιν ἀνθρωπίνων διαδοχῶν, ᾧ ἡ νυκτὸς ἥλιος κτλ. Out of "differing" comes also the meaning "be at variance." So P Lille I. 16⁹ (iii/B.C.) σοί τε οὐ βούλεσθαι διαφέρεσθαι περὶ τούτου, "qu'il ne voulait pas entrer en désaccord là-dessus avec toi" (Ed.), P Oxy III. 496⁸ (a marriage contract—A.D. 127) ἐ[ὰ]ν δέ τι διαφέρωντα[ι] πρὸς ἀλλήλους, of a husband and wife, P Par 69ᴮ·¹⁰ (A.D. 233) ὁ στρατηγὸς πρὸς τῷ λογιστ[ηρί]ῳ τοῖς] διαφέρουσι ἐσχόλασεν, of granting an audience to "litigants," P Lond 237⁷ (c. A.D. 346) (= II. p. 290) διαφέρι μοι διαφέρι δὲ καὶ . . . Παύλῳ, "has a difference with me and has a

difference also with Paul," and from the inscr. *Syll.* 929²⁹
(? B.C. 130) δικηκούσαμεν τῶν διαφερομένων. For the subst.
in the same sense, cf. the marriage-contract BGU I. 251⁵
(A.D. 81) where certain provisions are made—ἐὰν δὲ
διαφορᾶς [γενομένης χωρίζωνται ἀπ' ἀλλή]λων, so *ib.* 252⁷
(A.D. 98), and P Ryl II. 154²¹ (A.D. 66). There remains
the well attested meaning "belongs to," as of property, for
which LS quote only Philo—P Lond 946²⁴ (A.D. 226)
(= III. p. 118) ἀδήλου ὄντος εἰ ὑμῖν διαφέρει ἡ κληρονομία
αὐτοῦ, P Strass I. 22²² (iii/A.D.) τοῦ νομίζοντος αὐτῷ
διαφέρειν, "since he thinks that it belongs to himself,"
ib. 29⁵ (iv/A.D.) σπούδασον παρασχεῖν Ἑρμῆτι τῷ ἐμοὶ
διαφέροντι τὰ δύο νομίσματα, ἃ χρεωστεῖς μοι, "pay as
soon as possible to Hermes, who belongs to my household,
the two coins, which you are owing to me." With this
may be compared P Tebt II. 288¹¹ (A.D. 226) ὡς τοῦ
κινδύνου καὶ ὑμεῖν [αὐ]τοῖς ἅμα ἐκείνοις διοίσοντος ἐάν
τι φανῆ [κε]κακουργημέ[νο]ν ἢ οὐ δεόντως πεπρ[α]γμένον,
"since you not less than they will incur the risk if any
misdemeanour or irregularity be proved to have occurred"
(Edd.). So P Thead 8²¹ (A.D. 306), P Gen I. 62⁶ (iii/A.D.),
Chrest. II. 88i ³¹ (ii/A.D.), BGU IV. 1062²¹ (A.D. 237), etc.
See also *CR* xxiv. p. 12. The editor's rendering of P Oxy
IX. 1204¹¹ (A.D. 299) ὧν τὸ διαφέρον μέρος καὶ τῶν
ἀποφάσεων οὕτως ἔχει, "the essential part of the proceedings and the judgement being as follows," with reference
to certain legal proceedings, may be taken as supporting
Moffatt's translation of Rom 2¹⁸ καὶ δοκιμάζεις τὰ διαφέροντα,
"and with a sense of what is vital in religion" (cf. Phil 1¹⁰):
τὰ διαφέροντα would thus offer a positive counterpart in
popular usage to the negative τὰ ἀδιάφορα. We set with
this passages where διαφέρει = Lat. *interest*, as P Thead 15¹⁷
(A.D. 280–1) τὰ ἀναγκαιότερα τὰ τῷ ταμιείῳ διαφέροντα,
"most vital interests of the Treasury."

διαφεύγω.

The "perfective" sense in διαφυγεῖν "escape through
fleeing" (see *Proleg.* p. 112) comes out well in P Tebt I.
44²⁸ (B.C. 114) μή ποτε ἐξ ὑστέρου παθόντος τί μου ἀθῶιος
διαφύγηι, "so that if anything happens to me subsequently
he may not escape unpunished" (Edd.); cf. P Amh II. 131⁶
(early ii/A.D.) ἐλπίζω δὲ θεῶν θελόντων ἐκ τῶν λαλουμένων
διαφεύξεσθαι καὶ μετὰ τὴν πεντεκαιδεκάτην ἀναπλεύσειν,
"but I hope, if the gods will, to yet escape from the
talking and after the fifteenth to return home" (Edd.).

διαφημίζω

occurs thrice in Vettius Valens, as p. 250⁵ ἀλλ' ὅμως ἐπὶ
ταῖς καλοκαγαθίαις διαφημίζονται. The simplex (*q.v.*)
occurs in P Giss I. 19⁴ (ii/A.D.).

διαφθείρω,

as befits a perfective compound, denotes usually a completed process of damage. It is used for the death of
animals, as P Strass I. 24³¹ (A.D. 118) καὶ διεφ[θά]ρησ(αν)
μετὰ Φαῶ(φι) αἴγ(ες) ᾱ, P Oxy I. 74¹⁴ (A.D. 116—registration
of sheep) ἐξ ὧν διεφθάρη πρ(όβατα) ἑξ, ἄρνας δύο, and so
P Amh II. 73⁶ (A.D. 129–130); P Lond 309⁸ (A.D. 146)
(= II. p. 73) διεφθάρη μετὰ τὴν ἐξαρίθ(μησιν) κάμηλος [α],
P Oxy VI. 938⁴ (iii/iv A.D.) ὡς ἐκ τούτου κινδυνεύειν τὰ
κτήνη διαφθαρῆναι, "with the result that the oxen are in

PART II.

danger of destruction" (Edd.). BGU IV. 1109¹¹ (B.C. 5),
a contract with a wet-nurse, is made διὰ τὸ τῆς Καλλιτύχης
ἐν ἀσθενείᾳ διατεθείσης διεφθάρθαι τὸ ταύτης γάλα. Vettius
Valens uses it thrice of abortion. Passing to inanimate
things, we find the verb used in a British Museum papyrus,
P Lond Inv No. 1885¹⁰ (A.D. 114–5), with reference to
public records, and strikingly illustrating the carelessness
with which these were sometimes kept συνέβη . . . . α
μὲν . . . (*i.e.* τῶν βιβλίων) μὴ σῴζεσθαι πο[λλὸ] χρόνο
διαφθαρέντα, ἃ [δὲ] καὶ ἀπ[ὸ] μέρους διεφθάρθα[ι], ἔνια δὲ
κεφαλόβρωτα γεγονέναι διὰ τὸ τοὺς τό[π]ους καυσώδεις
εἶναι: see H. I. Bell in *Archiv* vi. p. 101. In P Oxy I.
95³ (A.D. 129) it is used in connexion with the failure of a
contract, ἣν ἐὰν συμβῇ παραπεσεῖν ἢ ἄλλως πῶς διαφθαρ[ῆ]-
ναι, "if the terms of it should be broken or if in any other
way be rendered invalid" (Edd.). *Syll.* 540³⁵ (B.C. 175–1),
the "breaking" of a stone—ἐάν τινα ὑγιῆ λίθον διαφθείρηι
κατὰ τὴν ἐργασίαν ὁ τῆς θέσεως ἐργώνης.

διάφορος.

For its simplest sense, as in Rom 12⁶, Heb 9¹⁰, cf. P Oxy
VII. 1033⁸⁵ (A.D. 392) ἀναγκαζόμεθα δὲ συνεχῶς ἕνεκεν τῆς
παραστάσεως διαφόρων προσώπων, "we are often called
upon for the production of various persons" (Edd.), P
Grenf II. 62⁸ (vi/vii A.D.) σπέρματα λαχάνων διαφόρων.
Hence, as in the verb, the derived sense of "superiority,"
as *Preisigke* 1005 διαφόρους πράξεις . . . ἱστορήσας ἐθαύμασα: this in Heb 1⁴, 8⁶ is expressed by the comparative
διαφορώτερος. NT use is now completely described, but in
inscrr. and papyri the development goes much further.
First τὸ διάφορον = "difference," as P Tebt I. 61 ᵇ ³³³ (a
land survey—B.C. 118–7) διάφορον) σχοινισμοῦ (see the
editors' notes, and P Petr II. 20¹⁰ ¹⁵ (B.C. 252) διάφορον ἀν-
ε[σεσθαι] παρὰ τὰς ρ ἀρτ[άβας] ε δραχμάς, which is translated III. p. 77), "the difference will amount to five
drachmae for every hundred artabae." Out of this develops
an exceedingly common meaning, "payment, money,"
which survives in MGr διάφορο[ς] neut. = "interest,
gain." It figures in Polybius (Kalker, p. 301): inscriptional exx. may be seen in the indices to *Syll.* and *OGIS.*
Thus in the great "Mysteries Inscr." from Andania, *Syll.*
653 (B.C. 91) there is a section headed περὶ τῶν διαφόρων
dealing with finance. From papyri may be selected P Oxy
VIII. 1118⁷ (i/ii A.D.) ὅπως ἔτι καὶ νῦν ἀποδῷ μοι τὰ
ὀφειλόμε[να] καὶ τοὺς προσοφειλομένους τόκους καὶ τὰ
[διά]φορα, "in order that he may yet pay to me the debt
and the interest due in addition and extras," so Hunt, who
compares for [διά]φορα P Eleph I. 80² (ii A.D.) τόκους καὶ τὰ
τέλη καὶ δαπάνας, and notes that διάφορον is sometimes
practically synonymous with τόκος, e.g. P Oxy VII. 143
(A.D. 225), an acknowledgement of a loan of four artabae
of wheat to be repaid ἐπὶ διαφόρῳ ἡμιολίας, "at the interest
of one-half" (Edd.).

The subst. διαφορά may be illustrated by P Par 63⁹⁶
(B.C. 165) = P Petr III. p. 291 τίς γὰρ οὕτως ἐστὶν
ἀνάλητος ἐν τῷ λογίζεσθαι κ[αὶ] πράγματος διαφορὰν
εὑρεῖν ὃς οὐδ' αὐτὸ τοῦτό γε δυνήσεται συννοεῖν κτλ, which
Mahaffy renders, "for who is so utterly wanting in reason
and the capacity for making distinctions, that he cannot
understand this" etc., P Magd 11³⁰ (B.C. 221) where the
word has the unusual sense of "delay," ὅπως ἂν μή . . . .

24

διαφορὰ τῇι καταγωγῆι τοῦ σίτου γίνηται, "qu'il ne se produise pas de retard dans la descente des transports de blé" (Ed.), and *ib.* 26 *verso*[4] (B.C. 217) περὶ διαφόρου οἴνου, "au sujet de vin livré en moins" (Ed.), cf. *ib. recto*[12] τὸ διάφορον τῶν ἐλαττονούντων ιδ κεραμίων.

διαφυλάσσω.

Winer (*ap.* Grimm *s.v.*) remarks that the LXX used this word specially of God's providential care, as in the passage quoted in Lk 4[10], its one NT occurrence (= Ps 90 (91)[11]). It is interesting to compare P Giss I. 17[7] (time of Hadrian) χάρις τοῖς θεοῖς πᾶσι ὅτι σε διαφυλάσσουσι ἀπρόσκοπον, BGU IV. 1081[4] (ii/iii A.D.) εὔχομαι τοῖς θεοῖς ὑπὲρ] σοῦ, ἵνα σὲ διαφυλά[ξ]ωσι, *ib.* III. 984[27] (as emended—iv/A.D.) ἐρρωμένον σε [ὁ θεὸς κ]αθ' ὑπόνοια (*l.* ὑπόνοιαν) διαφυλάξι ἐν ἀφθο[νητ.] κτλ., and the late *ib.* II. 547[8] (Byz.) ὁ κύριος τῶν αἰώνων διαφυλάξῃ τὴν ὑμῶν περίβλε(πτον) μεγαλοπρέπειαν). Two letters addressed by Apammus to Abinnaeus, P Lond 243. 413 (*c.* A.D. 346) (= II. pp. 301, 302) end—ὁ θε]ὸ]ς δὲ διαφυλάξῃ σε. The verb is also found in the magical P Lond 121[497] (iii/A.D.) (= I. p. 100) διαφυλάξατέ με τὰ μεγάλα καὶ θαυμαστὰ (ὀνόματα) τοῦ θ[εοῦ, P Leid W[xiv. 36] (ii/iii A.D.) addressed to a god, διαφύλαξόν με ἀπὸ πάσης τῆς ἰδίας μου ἀστρικῆς. "guard me from all stellar malignity personal to myself (?)" (*i.e.* due to my own horoscope). *ib.*[xxv. 4] διαφύλαξόν με ἀπὸ παντὸς φόβου κτλ. It seems fair to claim that quite outside Biblical language the verb was already specialized for divine guardianship. It was capable however of a general meaning. A Doric inscr. from Carpathos in *CR* iii. p. 333 has κ]αὶ τὰ φρούρια ἀ[κέραια π]άντα διαφυλάξας τῷ [δάμῳ. Add *OGIS* 117[5] (ii/B.C.) ἐπαγγέλλε[τ]αι δὲ καὶ εἰς τὸ λοιπὸν [τὴ]ν αὐτὴν αἵρεσιν διαφυλάξειν, also *Michel* 477[33] (middle ii/B.C.) εἰδότας ὅτι καὶ Στρατονικεῖς τὴν πρὸς Ἀσσίους εὔνοια[ν] διαφυλάξουσιν, *ib.* 508[19] (beginning ii/B.C.) προαιρούμενος διαφυλάσσειν τὴν πρὸς τὸ πλῆθος ἡμῶν εὔνοιαν, *Syll* 401[23] (iv/iii B.C.), 643[10] (end iii/B.C.), 918[5] (iv/iii B.C.), 526[4] (i/B.C.) διεφύλαξαν τ[ὴν πόλιν under arms, and so [44] φιλοτιμότεροι . . εἰς τὸ διαφυλάσσειν τὴν πατρίδα.

διαφωνέω.

The curious meaning "fail, perish," appearing in LXX, supported by LS with citations from Diodorus and Agatharchides, appears in P Petr II. 13 (3)[4] (middle iii/B.C.): a prison wall has partly fallen, and the rest is going, ὥστε κινδυνεύει πεσόντος αὐτοῦ διαφωνῆσαί τι τῶν σωμάτων, "so that there is a risk, if it comes down, of killing some of the people" (Ed.). It might also mean "escaping." Mahaffy's note is very instructive :—"But διαφωνῆσαι, for *to die*, would be a complete puzzle did it not occur in Agatharchides, a writer of this very century, as well as in Diodoros, in the sense of *to perish*." Some day, perhaps, doctors of divinity may discover the LXX, and classical experts purchase E. A. Sophocles' Lexicon !

διαχειρίζω.

For this word in its original sense of "have in hand," "administer," see P Tebt I. 112 introd. (B.C. 112) ἀφ' ὧν (*c.* 4885 dr.) προφέρεται Ἑρμίας διαχειρίσθαι (*l.* διακεχειρίσθαι) ἐπὶ τῆι τρα[πέζηι χ, and from the inscr. *OGIS*

218[74] (iii/B.C.) ὅσ'ἂν διαχειρίσηι χ[ρή]ματα, *Michel* 976[13] (B.C. 300) ὅσοι τι τῶν κοινῶν διεχείρισαν, *ib.* 977[5] (B.C. 298-7) τὰ κοινὰ καλῶς καὶ δικαίως διεχείρισεν. For the derived sense of "kill," "slay" in Ac 5[30], 26[21], cf. the medical usage with reference to surgical operations, in Hobart, p. 202.

διαχωρίζω

can be quoted from the literary "LXX Memorial" from Adrumetum (iii/A.D.)—[11] ὁρκίζω σε τὸν διαχωρίσαντα τοὺς εὐσεβεῖς, "I adjure thee by him who separates the devout ones from the godless"; see Deissmann *BS.* p. 275. Add from the iv/A.D. Leyden magic papyrus (ed. Dieterich, p. 817)—xv. [26] ποίησον τὸν (δεῖνα) διαχωρισθῆναι ἀπὸ τοῦ δεῖνος).

διδακτικός.

Grimm's citation from Philo is the more welcome in that even Vettius Valens (p. 150[29]—adverb pp. 158[4], 304[24]) still uses διδασκαλικός, which Grimm notes as the classical form : see under διδάσκαλος. MGr keeps δασκαλικός, "of a school master."

διδακτός.

To the classical reff. for this not very common word we may add Pss. Sol. 17[35] in the description of Israel's King, καὶ αὐτὸς βασιλεὺς δίκαιος καὶ διδακτὸς ὑπὸ θεοῦ ἐπ' αὐτούς (cf. LXX Isai 54[13]).

διδασκαλία

In P Oxy VIII 1101[4] (A.D. 367-70) a Praefect states that certain orders he was issuing were based not on information gained from a few first-comers (π[αρ' ὀ]λίγων τῶν πρώτων [πυθόμενο]ς, ἀλλὰ πρὸς διδασκαλίαν τρόπον τινὰ λαμβάνον (*l.* — ων) [ἐκ τῶν εἰ]ς ἑκάστ[η]ν πόλιν τε καὶ ἐνορίαν γιγνομένων, "but on instruction in a way derived from what occurs in every city and district" (Ed.). Cf. from the inscrr. *Syll* 306[9] (ii/B.C.) ὑπὲρ τὰς τῶν παίδων διδασκαλίας, *ib.* 423[6], 603[10]. A new literary citation may be given from P Ryl II. 62[23] (iii/A.D.—translated from an unknown Latin writer by one Isidorianus) καὶ τὴν τῶν φαρμά[κων δι[δ]ασκαλίαν ποιεῖ : the edd. are not satisfied with the reading, but see no alternative. An interesting Christian example of δ. occurs in the prayer of the end of iv/A.D. published by C. Schmidt in *Neutestamentliche Studien für G. Heinrici* (1914) p. 71[26] φώτισον ἐν τῇ [σῇ πα]ρακλήσει ὅπως καταξιωθῶμεν . . . τῆς μεγαλοφυοῦς διδασκαλίας τῶν εὐαγγελίων τοῦ σ(ωτῆ)ρ ο)ς ἡμῶν Ἰ ησο ῦ Χ ριστο ῦ.

διδάσκαλος

occurs *ter* in the contract of apprenticeship P Oxy IV. 725 (A.D. 183) : cf. BGU IV. 1021[32 al.] (iii/A.D.). *OGIS* 146[5] (ii/B.C.) διδάσ[καλος μαθημάτων] τακτικῶν. For διδασκαλεῖον cf. the dream from the Serapeum P Par 51[9] (B.C. 160) (= *Selections*, p. 19) ἐξαί[φνης] ἀνύγω τοὺς ὀφθαλμούς μου, καὶ ὁρῶ [τὰς] Διδύμας ἐν τῷ διδασκαλήῳ τοῦ Τοθῆ[τος, "in the school of Tothes," and the adj. διδασκαλικός in P Par 63[94] (B.C. 165) (P Petr III. p. 22) τρόπον τινὰ διδασκα[λι]κή]ν ἡμῶν πεποιημένον τὴν [ὑ]φήγησιν, "we made our explanation such as almost to teach you, like schoolboys" (Mahaffy) : cf. P Oxy II. 275³¹ (A.D. 66) κυρία ἡ διδασκαλική, "the contract of apprenticeship is valid." MGr δάσκαλος, "teacher, schoolmaster." with derivative δασκαλεύω "censure, teach one his lesson," keeps the old word without its reduplication.

διδάσκω.

Like διδάσκαλος, διδάσκω is by no means so common as we might have expected ; but from the instances we have noted we may select the following— P Lond 43⁶ (ii/B.C.) (= I. p. 48), where a mother congratulates her son on having finished his education and being now in a position to earn his livelihood as a teacher— νῦν γε παραγενόμενος εἰς τὴν πόλιν διδάξεις . . . τὰ παιδάρια καὶ ἕξεις ἐφόδιον εἰς τὸ γῆρας, P Oxy I. 40⁸ (ii/iii A.D.), where a doctor practising mummification is asked— δίδαξον τ[ὸ κατα]ττήκον, "tell me what is the solvent" (Edd.), P Strass I. 41⁸ (A.D. 250) περὶ δὲ οὗ δικάζομαι, διὰ βραχέων σε διδάξω, CP Herm 23ⁱⁱ ⁵ (a law report) ἡμεῖς ἃ ἐδειδά[χ]θ[η]μεν ὑπὸ τῆς λα[μπρ . . .] ταῦτά σοι παρεθέμεθα, and ib. 25ⁱⁱ·⁵ ἵνα πάλιν σε διδάξωμεν· εἰ οὖν σοι δοκ[εῖ] ἀκοῦσαι τ[. . .

διδαχή.

The word is used of military instruction or training in an Imperial letter, which Wilcken (cf. Archiv ii. p. 170) dates in the time of Hadrian— BGU I. 140¹⁶ (A.D. 119) καὶ τ]οῦτο οὐκ ἐδόκει σκληρὸν [εἶ]ναι [τοὐν]αντίον αὐτῶν τῆ[ς] στρατιω[τ]ικῆ[ς διδα]χῆς πεποιηκότων. An interesting parallel to Mk 1²⁷ occurs in the new uncanonical gospel, P Oxy X. 1224 Fr. 2 verso³ π[ο]ίαν σέ [φασιν διδα]χὴν καιν[ὴν] δι[δάσκειν, ἢ τί β]ά[πτισμ]α καινὸν [κηρύσσειν; "what is the new doctrine that they say thou teachest, or what the new baptism that thou dost preach?" (Edd.)

δίδραχμον.

With the Jewish Temple tax of τὸ δίδραχμον (Mt 17²⁴) may be compared a tax for a similar amount for the temple of Suchus : cf. e.g. the receipt for this tax in P Tebt II. 281 (B.C. 125) and BGU III. 748ⁱⁱⁱ· ⁶ (A.D. 48) where it is paid upon a sale of house property— διαγέγραφ(ας) τὴν διδραχμία(ν) τοῦ Σούχου θεοῦ μεγάλο(υ) μεγάλο(υ) ἧς ἐώνησαι οἰκί(ας) κτλ. See further Wilcken Ostr. i. p. 369, Otto Priester i. p. 356 f., ii. p. 334. Can we recognize it in P Tebt II. 404¹² (late iii/A.D.) λόγος τῶν διδράχμων στατῆρες ξζ, "on account of the didrachms 67 staters" (Edd.)? If so, it is a very close parallel to τὰ δίδραχμα in Mt l.c., with the same use of the article and absence of further definition. In P Amh II. 50²⁰ (B.C. 106—a loan of money) provision is made for τοῦ ὑπερπεσόντος χρόνου τόκους διδράχμους τῆς μνᾶς τὸν μῆνα ἕκαστον, "the overtime interest at the rate of two drachmae on the mina each month" (Edd., who remark that this is 24 % a year, "the ordinary rate required upon loans not paid back at the specified date"). For δίδραγμον in late MSS. of the LXX. see Thackeray Gr. i. p. 103.

δίδυμος.

This word has become very familiar to students of the papyri owing to the lengthy correspondence regarding the grievances of the Serapeum Twins, Thaues and Thaus or Taous, that has come to light. Their story has been reconstructed by Kenyon, P Lond I. p. 2 ff. For a specimen of their petitions see P Par 26 (B.C. 163-2), reproduced in Selections, p. 12 ff. It opens— Βασιλεῖ Πτολεμαίῳ καὶ Βασιλίσσῃ Κλεοπάτρᾳ τῇ ἀδελφῇ, θεοῖς Φιλομήτορσι, χαίρειν. Θαυὴς καὶ Ταοῦς δίδυμαι, αἱ λειτουργοῦσαι ἐν τῷ πρὸς Μέμφει μεγάλῳ Σαραπιείῳ κτλ. From ib.¹²⁴ καὶ ἐκ τούτων καὶ τῶν προτοῦ γενηθεισῶν δ[ι]δύμων κομισαμένων τὰ ἑαυτῶν καθ' ἡμέραν δέοντα, we learn that the Twins were there ex officio as twins, in connexion with some Dioscuric-cultus : see Rendel Harris Boanerges, p. 272. From later documents it will be enough to quote P Oxy III. 533¹⁶ (ii/iii A.D.) εἴπατε καὶ τοῖς διδύμοις ὅτι προνοήσ[α]τε τοῦ κερματίου, "tell the twins also to be careful about the small change" (Edd.). The frequency of Didymus as a proper name is curious : we compare the Latin Geminus and Gemellus (cf. for the latter the turner whose correspondence at end of i/A.D. is preserved in P Fay), but it is much less prominent than Δίδυμος becomes in Hellenistic Egypt—after iii B.C., if we may judge from the almost complete absence of Dioscuric names from the indices of P Petr and P Hib. There is a diminutive Διδυμάριον in P Lond 604¹⁶ (ii/iii A.D.) (= III. p. 24), the name of a woman. In P Lond 604 B³⁷ (c. A.D. 47) (= III. p. 80) we find two brothers named Castor and Didymus, which suggests that Didymus is a surrogate for Polydeuces. The index of proper names in this volume is suggestive as to the prevalence of Dioscuric worship in Egypt. There are 28 Castors, 9 (or 11) with the name Polydeuces, 28 with Didymus (Didyme and Didymarion once each), 40 with Dioscorus or Dioscurides. It is also noteworthy that names of this class tend to recur in families, and that six of them are linked with an Isidotus, Isidorus or Ision. One Didymus is the son of Amphion, which takes us into another Greek twin-cultus. Since Ἀμφίων is short for ἀμφιγενής, as Dr Harris points out, the classical pair Zethus and Amphion are named exactly on the same principle as our Castor and Didymus above. One of a pair had a name of his own, and his brother was nothing but "Twin." The Apostle Thomas no doubt was "Judas the Twin ;" but if the well attested "Judas" were rejected, the name by which we always know him was entirely capable of standing alone. Whether every Didymus really was a twin may be questioned. Like Dioscorus and the rest, it might often only imply a cult relation : Pollux was the "patron saint"—to describe the practice in terms of its medieval derivative.

In BGU I. 115¹² (A.D. 189) (= Chrest. I. p. 238) Wilcken conjectures a hitherto unknown compound δ[ι]δυμαγεν εἰς, which is confirmed by ib. II. 447¹⁰ (A.D. 173-4) (= I. 2).

δίδωμι.

P Oxy X. 1292⁹ (c. A.D. 30) ἔδωκα Ἑρμᾶτι δοῦναί σοι (δραχμὰς) ιβ, ib. VII. 1002¹⁵ (ii/A.D.) τὸ ἀργύριον δὸς Ζωίλωι τωι φίλωι, ib. 1068²⁴ (iii A.D.) ἵνα δῶς αὐτοῖς γράμματα should serve as exx. of the ordinary usage of this common verb. For διδόναι λόγον cf. P Oxy X. 1281⁹ (a loan—A.D. 21) ἐφ' ὧι κομιζομένου [τοῦ] Ἰωσήπου ταῦτα πρότερον δώσει λόγο[ν] τούτων, "on condition that when Joseph receives it he shall first render an account of it" (Edd.), P Strass I. 32⁹ (A.D. 261) δότω λόγον, τί αὐτῷ ὀφείλ[ε]ται καὶ ποῦ παρέσχεν, ἵνα οὕτως αὐτῷ ἐνλογηθῇ. Lest Ac 13²⁹ should be supposed a Hebraism, after e.g.

Numb 14[1], we may quote P Lille I. 28[11] (iii/B.C.) αὐτοῖς ἐδώκαμεν μεσίτην Δωρ[ί]ωνα, "nous leur avons donné pour arbitre Dorion" (Edd.), P Flor I. 2[52] (A.D. 265) δίδομεν καὶ προσαγγέλλομεν τὸν ὑπογεγραμμένον εἰς δεσμοφυλακείαν: cf. ib. 91[3] (ii/A.D.) ἐδόθην εἰς ἑ[τέραν αὖ λιτουργία]ν, and P Oxy IX. 1195[1] (A.D. 135) Ἀπολλωνίωι κριτῆι δοθέντι ὑπὸ Πετρωνίου Μαμερτείνου τοῦ κρατίστου ἡγεμόνος. Similarly Deissmann (L.AE. p. 117) disposes of the "Latinism" in Lk 12[58] by reference to a letter of B.C. 2 written in vulgar Greek, P Oxy IV. 742[4], δὸς ἐργασία[ν], "give your attention to it," and to the occurrence of the same phrase in the unpublished P Bremen 18 (c. A.D. 118). He also cites OGIS 441[109] (B.C. 81) φροντίζωσιν διδῶσίν τε ἐργασίαν, "may they take heed and give diligence" (but see Dittenberger's note). Herwerden (Lex. s.v.) illustrates the elliptical use (e.g. Rev 2[23]) from Rev. pap. Lips. 13[ii.3] ὁ ἄλλος λίθω δέδωκεν τῷ υἱῷ μου, sc. πληγήν: cf. our "he gave it him with a stick." For δίδωμι ἐμαυτόν τινι or ὑπέρ τινος (as 2 Cor 8[5], Tit 2[14]) cf. P Par 47[26] (c. B.C. 153) (= Witkowski[2], p. 90) ἵ καὶ αὐτοὺς δεδώκαμεν καὶ ἀποπεπτώκαμεν ὑπὸ τῶν θεῶν καὶ πιστεύοντες τὰ ἐνύπνια, and see Nageli, p. 50. There is a suggestive use of δ. in the question addressed to an oracle, P Oxy IX. 1213[1] (ii/A.D.) ἀξιοῖ Μένανδρος [εἰ] δέδοταί μοι γαμῆσαι: [τοῦ]τό μοι δὸς "M. asks, is it granted me to marry? Answer me this" (Ed.), so Wessely Spec. gr. 12. 26 εἰ οὐ [δέ]δοταί μοι συμβιῶσαι Ταπεθεῦτι: cf. Archiv v. p. 232). There is the same collocation of verbs in Mt 19[11], where it is implied that there are those οἷς οὐ δέδοται. For δός at the end of the first oracle cf. P Oxy VIII. 1149[9] (ii/A.D.): it answers to τοῦτό μοι σύμφωνον ἔνενκε in ib. 1148[9], and κύρωσ[όν] μοι τοῦτο τὸ γραπτόν in Wessely's oracle. Δὸς πεῖν (as in Jn 4[7]) may be cited from P Leid W[viii.9] (ii/iii A.D.).

On the forms of this verb, which was rapidly coming over into the -ω class, like other -μι verbs in the Hellenistic age—cf. MGr δίδω, δίνω or δώνω—see BS. p. 192, CR xv. pp. 37 f., 436, xviii. pp. 111 f., and the editor's note on P Oxy VII. 1053[13]. On ib. 1066[12] (iii/A.D.) ἔλεγέν μοι Ἀπόλλων ὅτι οὐδέν μοι ἔδωσεν, attention is drawn to ἔδωσεν as "a rather early instance of the sigmatic form which is occasionally found in writers of the decadence."

διεγείρω.

P Leid W[viii.16] (ii/iii A.D.) ὀρκίζω σε, πνεῦμα ἐν ἀέρι φοιτώμενον, εἴσελθε, ἐνπνευμάτωσον, δυνάμωσον, διαέγειρον τῇ δυνάμει τοῦ αἰωνίου θεοῦς (om. -s) ὅδε (l. τόδε) τὸ σῶμα— a spell for the ἔγερσις σώματος νεκροῦ.

διεξέρχομαι.

For this compound, which is used by ℵAEC 61 in Ac 28[3], cf. Syll 846[1] (B.C. 177 ?) διεξέλθοντι τὰ ἓξ ἔτη. P Oxy VII. 1069[21] (illiterate—iii/A.D.) ἀγόρασον τῷ Νεικήτη ὄνον ἕνα δυνασθῇ σου τὰ πράγματα διεξερτεῖν (l. διεξελθεῖν), "that he may be able to accomplish your business." P Lond 977[15] (A.D. 330) (= III. p. 232) διεξελθούσης τὸν βίον. See also Aristeas 168 ὅσον ἐπὶ βραχὺ διεξελθεῖν.

διέξοδος.

In P Magd 12[11] (B.C. 217) διέξοδος is used for the "conclusion" of a trial: it is prayed that men who have wrongfully taken possession of land should not be allowed

to get in the harvest ἕως δὲ τοῦ διέξοδον λαβεῖν τὴν κρίσιν μὴ θερίζειν αὐτούς. This rather supports Grimm's view of Mt 22[9], "the issues of the streets," i.e. where they lead out from the city into the country. Cf. Aristeas 105, where, as Thackeray (Trans. p. 23 n.[2]) points out, the διέξοδοι, the main streets leading out of the city, and the δίοδοι, cross-streets, seem to be distinguished. In Vettius Valens, p. 334[16], we have ἐγὼ δὲ τούτου φρουρίου ἐκκόψας τινὰ μέρη πυλῶν τοῖς βουλομένοις τὴν διέξοδον ἐμήνυσα πλέον. There is a curious derivative in P Brem 73[1] (ap. Chrest. I. p. 277) (c. A.D. 117) περισσὸν ἡγοῦμαι διεξωδέστερον ὑμεῖν γράφειν, which Wilcken notes = διεξοδικώτερον, "ausführlicher."

διερμηνευτής.

According to Nageli (p. 50) this word, which in NT occurs in 1 Cor 14[28] only (with the significant dissent of B and DFG), reappears first in the Byzantine grammarians, e.g. Eust. ad Il. p. 106, 14.

διερμηνεύω.

With this verb, which is found six times in the NT practically = the simplex, we may compare P Tor I. 1[v.4] (B.C. 116) (= Chrest. II. p. 35) καθ'ἃ παρέκειτο ἀντίγραφα συγγραφῶν Αἰγυπτίων διηρμηνευμένων δ'Ἑλληνιστί. See Aristeas 15 ἣν (sc. νομοθεσίαν) ἡμεῖς οὐ μόνον μεταγράψαι ἐπινοοῦμεν ἀλλὰ καὶ διερμηνεῦσαι: also 308, 310. A phrase almost identical with that cited from P Tor may be seen in P Tebt I. 164[3.2]—see s.v. μεθερμηνεύω.

διέρχομαι.

OGIS 665[26] (A.D. 49) καὶ τούτους δὲ στέγῃ μόνον δέχεσθαι τοὺς διερχομένους. Field (Notes, p. 88) points out that the preposition must not be pressed, as in Jn 4[15] RV: all that it implies is merely that a certain distance is to be traversed, whether long or short, cf. Lk 2[15], Ac 9[32]. But this does not involve ignoring the difference between the compound and the AV simplex: the RV exaggeration is slight, and very effective. Ramsay Exp V. i. p. 385 ff. argues that δ. in Ac implies missionary travel. The verb is very common in connexion with past time, e.g. Rev I. 18[19] (iii/B.C.) ὅταν δὲ ὁ πεπραμένος χρόνος ἅπας διελθῇι, P Oxy II. 238[5] (A.D. 72) ἐν τῶι διεληλυθότι τετάρτωι ἔτει, ib. IX. 1198[12] (A.D. 150) τῶι διελθόντι δωδεκάτῳ ἔτι, ib. III. 475[16] (A.D. 182) ἐψ[ί]ας τῆς διελθούσ[η]ς, etc.

διετής.

P Amh II. 87[28] (lease of land—A.D. 125) ἀμεθέστατόν σε φυλάξω [ἐ]ὶ[ς] τὸν διετῆ χρόνον, "I will guarantee your tenancy for the period of two years (Edd.): cf. P Lond 856[7] (late i/A.D.) (= III. p. 92) διετο[ῦ]ς and OGIS 513[13] (iii/A.D.) Αὐ[ρ]ηλίαν . . . ἱερασαμένην ἐνδόξως καὶ μεγαλοπρεπῶς διετεῖ χρόνω, JHS xxxiv. p. 116, inscr. no. 13[19] (Lycia) θύσει δὲ κ[τήτ]ωρ τῆς ο[ἰ]κίας [κα]τ'ἐνιαυτὸν ἐν τῇ ιβ [το]ῦ Ξανδικοῦ ἔριφον [δ]ιτ[ῆ] (l. διετῆ), P Cairo Preis 31[20] (A.D. 130-40) ἐπὶ διετῆ χρόνον ἀπὸ τοῦ εἰσιόντος μηνό[s].

διετία.

This subst., for which Grimm cites only Philo, can now be freely authenticated—e.g. P Oxy IV. 707[24] (c. A.D. 136) τῇ δὲ λοιπῇ διετίᾳ τελέσαι τὰ διὰ τῆς μισθώσεως ὑπὲρ φόρου ἀνειλημμένα, "that for the remaining two years he should pay the rent set forth in the lease" (Edd.), *ib.* VI. 910⁵¹ (A.D. 107) τῆς μὲν ἐν π[υ]ρῷ διετίας, BGU I. 180⁷ (ii/iii A.D.) μ[ε]τὰ διετίαν τῆς [ἀπο]λύσεως, P Strass I. 2¹⁰ (A.D. 217) τὴ[ν] λοιπὴ[ν] δι[ε]τίαν, and from the inscrr. *Syll* 805¹ (?i/A.D.) ἐκ διετίας βήσσοντά με ἀδ[ι]αλεί[π]τως, *OGIS* 485¹² (Roman) γενόμενον δὲ καὶ ἐπὶ τῶν ἐπιπηγῶν διετίαν. The word δεκαετία is found P Strass I. 22²³ (iii A.D.).

διηγέομαι.

A good ex. of this word is found in the prodigal's letter, BGU III. 846¹⁴ (ii/A.D.) ἤκουσα παρὰ το[ῦ] Ποστ[ο]ύμον τὸν εὑρόντα σαι ἐν τῷ Ἀρσαινοείτῃ καὶ ἀκαίρως πάντα σοι διήγηται, "and unseasonably related all to you." Cf. P Rein 48⁵ (ii/A.D.) φθάσας ἀπέστειλα πρός σε τὸν ἀγροφύλακα διηγησάμενός σοι ("pour te raconter") τὴν οὖσαν διάθεσιν ἐνθάδε, P Lond 470⁷ (? iii/A.D.) (= II. p. 250) διηγήσομαι τὰ συνβάντα μοι περὶ τῶν καμήλω(ν). MGr δι(η)γοῦμαι = "relate," "narrate," as of old.

διήγησις

is used *ter* in the letter of Aristeas to Polycrates (1. 8. 322) to describe the "narrative" he has to unfold—one thinks of the first and last lines of *Sordello*. The noun occurs twice in PSI I. 85 (iii/A.D.), from a rhetorical treatise, defining what was technically known as ἡ χρεία : see above *s.v.* ἀπομνημόνευμα. The χρεία is to be "concise" :—⁸ Διὰ τί σύντομον; ὅτι πολλάκις ἐκταθὲν ἡ διήγησις γίνεται ἢ ἄλλο τι. Δ. therefore implies some fullness of narrative, which suits the use of the word in the Preface of Lk. MGr keeps the -μα noun—διήγημα "narrative" with dimin. διηγηματάκι.

διηνεκής.

In NT peculiar to Heb, and there only in the locution εἰς τὸ διηνεκές = *in perpetuum*. This occurs twice in P Ryl II. 427 (end of ii/A.D.), once without context and once following μισθώσασθαι. Deissmann (*BS*, p. 251) cites *IMAe* 785¹⁶ (Imperial) τετειμημένος ἐς τὸ διενεκές. The adj. was in use, as may be seen from BGU II. 646²² (A.D. 193) εὐχομένους ὑπέρ τε τοῦ διηνεκοῦς αὐτοκρατοῦς, *Syll* 540¹⁰³ (B.C. 175–1) ποιῶν ὀρθὰ πάντα πρὸς κανόνα διηνεκῆ μὴ ἐλάττω τοῦ ἐνεργουμένου λίθου, *OGIS* 669⁶⁵ (i/A.D.) οὗ (*sc.* τοῦ Σεβαστοῦ) [καὶ π]ε[ρ]ὶ τῆς πάντων [ἡ̣μ̣]ῶ̣[ν] σωτηρίας ἣι (*l.* ἡ) δ[ι]ην̣εκὴς [εὐ]εργεσίαι (*l.* —ία) καὶ πρόνοιά [ἐσ]τιν. In P Lips I. 20⁵ (beginning of iv/A.D.) we have ἐπὶ τὸ διηνε[κ]ές. For the adv. διηνεκῶς see *OGIS* 194¹² (B.C. 42) ἀνενλιπεῖς μὲν διηνεκῶς [παρὰ τοῦτον τὸν χρόν]ον πάντας πάντων ἐτήρησεν. The η, where ἁ *purum* would be expected in Attic, suggests that the word generally came into Attic literature from Ionic poetry—it is found in Homer. See Mayser *Gr.* p. 13.

διάστημα.

P Tebt I. 22⁴ (B.C. 112) περὶ ὧν σοι διεστάμην, "about the matters on which we had a dispute" (Edd.). So BGU IV. 1099⁵ (Augustus) περὶ] ὧν διεστάμεθα συνχωροῦμεν—a marriage contract, which is apparently the happy ending to a difference. *Ib.* 1100⁵, of same period, shows the parents

drawing up the contract. In *ib.* 1115¹, (B.C. 13) περὶ τῶν διεστα[μένων] συνχωρεῖ, and 1100¹ (same date and form), we have loans negotiated. Schubart has an elaborate paper on these συγχωρήσεις in *Archiv* v., esp. p. 484. Is it possible to take δ. in a weaker sense, "discuss," rather than "dispute"? That would reconcile these formulae with the one in P Rein 18¹³ (B.C. 108) ὁ ἐγκαλούμενος ἐγκρατὴς γενόμενος τῶν συναλλαξ[έ]ων οὐθὲν τῶν διασταθέντων μοι πρὸς αὐτ[ὸ]ν ἐπὶ τέλος ἤγαγεν, "mon adversaire, une fois en possession desdits actes, n'a exécuté aucun des engagements convenus entre nous" (Ed.), and so *ib.* 16¹¹. It would be literally "the things I discussed with him." See also *OGIS* 315¹⁵ (B.C. 164–3) ὀρθῶς οὖν καθ' ὑπερβολὴν διίστω, a difficult passage where Dittenberger's note balances two very different renderings. In the NT δ. is confined to the Lucan writings : Hobart (p. 170) characteristically adduces a number of medical parallels. There is a parallel for the weak aorist active (Ac 27²⁸) in P Leid W³⁰ ᵇ (ii/iii A.D.) διέστησεν τὰ πάντα, "separavit omnia" (Ed.). The verb is similarly transitive in Ac *l.c.*, βραχύ being the object—Blass (*Comm. ad loc.*) paraphrases βραχὺ διάστημα ποιήσαντες.

διϊζω.

This verb, which is read *bis* by B in Lk 6³⁷, may be illustrated. P Hib I. 30¹⁹ (B.C. 300–271) διὸ δικάζομαί σοι τοῦ ἀρχαίου [καὶ τόκο]υ, "I therefore am taking legal proceedings against you for principal and interest" (Edd.), P Oxy II. 237ᵛⁱⁱ ³² (A.D. 186) δεδικάσθαι ὑπογίως πρὸς αὐτόν, "had recently brought an action against him" (Edd.), P Lond 973ᵃᵇ (iii/A.D.) (= III. p. 213) δικάζομαι χάριν τῶν τοῦ ἀδελφοῦ μου καὶ οὐ δύναμαι ἄρτι ἐλθεῖν πρός σ[ε, P Strass I. 41⁸ (A.D. 250) περὶ δὲ οὗ δικάζομαι, διὰ βραχέων σε διδάξω, and CPHerm I. 25ᵢᵢ ⁹ σίνδικος εἶ(πε)· σήμερον μόγις ἐδυνήθης καὶ σὺ δικάσαι.

δικαιοκρισία.

The emphasis which this compound lays on the character of the Judge rather than on the character of the judgement in Rom 2⁵ (see SH *l.c.*), receives support from two passages in the Oxyrhynchus papyri—the first in I. 71ⁱ ⁴ (A.D. 303) where a petitioner appeals confidently to the Praefect εὔελπις ὢν τῆς ἀπὸ τοῦ σοῦ μεγέθους δικαιοκρισίας τυχεῖν, "being of good hope to obtain righteous judgement from thy Magnificence" (cf. Nageli, p. 48, *LAE*, p. 89 f.). The second is in VI. 904² (v/A.D.) where a certain Flavius, who has been subjected to indignity in the discharge of certain official duties, addresses the Praeses ἡ τῆς ὑμετέρας δικαιοκρισ[ί]ας καθαρότης πάντως κἀμὲ ἐλεήσει τὸν γεγηρακότα καὶ ἀσυνθηκεὶ διαπεπονθότα καὶ χλεύην παρὰ Φιλοξένου, "the purity of your righteous judgement will surely pity me, an old man who has suffered a breach of covenant and mockery at the hands of Philoxenus" (Edd.). The word occurs again in the very fragmentary P Flor I. 88²⁶ (? A.D. 215) σου δικαιοκρι[σ]ίας τυχεῖν?

δικαιολογία.

For δ., as in 2 Macc 4³³, we may cite P Hawara 60 *verso* ⁸ (ii/A.D.) (= *Archiv* v. p. 383) ἐπὶ ταύτης εἰμὶ τῆς δικαιολογίας π[. . . . P Flor I. 6¹³ (A.D. 210) πρὸς δὲ τούτοις μ[εί]ζο̣να δικαιολογίαν παρατίθεμαι, P Lips I. 38ⁱⁱ ⁴

(A.D. 390) αἱ ἐκ νόμων ἁρμό[ζ]ουσαι δικαιο[λ]ογίαι καὶ π[αρ]αγραφαὶ κτλ. The verb occurs P Tor I. 1^iii. 1^s (B.C. 117) καὶ δικαιολογηθέντων τῶν συνκαταστάντων αὐτοῖς: see Peyron's note, p. 100.

δίκαιος.

Our sources have naturally little light to throw upon the deeper Christian significance of this important word, but we may give a few examples showing its general usage. The adjective is applied to a "just measure" (μετρήσει δ.) P Tebt I. 11^13 (B.C. 119), 105^41 (B.C. 103) etc., and a "just rule" (σκυτάλη δ.) P Rein 20^21 (B.C. 108). Then it would seem to have become a *vox propria* in connexion with the rise of the Nile, e.g. *OGIS* 666^11 (i/A.D.) νῦν μᾶλλον ἀπέλαυσε (*sc.* ἡ Αἴγυπτος) τῆς δικαίας ἀναβάσεως τοῦ θεοῦ: see Dittenberger's note and cf. Deissmann *BS*, p. 116. In P Petr II. 28^viii. 6 (taxing account—iii/B.C.) we hear of a δικαίου νήσου. The neuter is very largely used substantially, for "duty," "rights" or "claims." Thus in P Petr II. 10^27 the royal gooseherds make petition that certain grievances be set right, ἵνα δυνώμεθα τὰ δίκαια ποιεῖν τῶι βασιλεῖ, "in order that we may be able to do our duty to the king": cf. the neuter plural of the "duties" of marriage, e.g. P Oxy VI. 905^9 (marriage contract—A.D. 170) συμβιούτωσαν [οὖν ἀλλήλοις οἱ γ]αμοῦντες φυλάσσοντες τὰ τοῦ γάμου δίκαια, *ib.* X. 1273^23 (A.D. 260), BGU IV. 1098^34 (*c.* B.C. 18) τηρεῖν τὰ πρὸς τὴν ἄνδρα καὶ τὸν κοινὸν βίον δίκαια. The meaning of "right," "justice," to which this leads, figures in the concluding formula of numerous petitions: cf. also Col 4^1. Thus P Magd 2^1 (iii/B.C.) where a widow petitions Ptolemy III ἵνα ἐ[πὶ] σὲ καταφυγοῦσα, βασιλεῦ, τοῦ δικαίου τύχω, and P Oxy III. 486^35 (A.D. 131) ἵνα τὰ ἐ[μα]υτῆς δίκαια λάβω. Cf. P Oxy IV. 746^6 (a letter of recommendation—A.D. 16) τοῦτο οὖν ἐάν σοι φα[ί]νηται σπουδάσεις κατὰ τὸ δίκαιον, "please therefore further him in this matter, as is just" (Edd.). So with the negative in a complaint, as BGU IV. 1187^20 (*c.* B.C. 1) μη[δ]ενὸς δικα[ίο]υ ἀντεχόμενος. "Claim" or the like will render it in P Ryl II. 68^27 (B.C. 89) ἵν' . . . ἐὰν δὲ περιγένωμαι, λάβω παρ' αὐτῆς τὸ δίκαιον ὡς καθήκει, "if I survive, I may obtain satisfaction from her as is right" (Edd.). P Tor 1^viii.27 (B.C. 116) καὶ ταύτην μηδ' ὁλοσχερῶς πᾶσιν, ἀλλὰ τοῖς ἔχουσίν τι δίκαιον, P Tebt II. 320^10 (A.D. 181) ὑπετάξαμ[εν [ἡ]μῶν τὰ δίκαια, "we append our claims" (Edd.). Δ. often answers to the Latin *ius*, as P Lond 1164(*h*)^6 (A.D. 212) (= III. p. 160) τὰ ὑπάρχοντα αὐτῷ μέρη οἰκιῶν δύο οὐσῶν ἐν τῇ Ἀντινοουπόλει ἐλθόντα εἰς αὐτὸν ἀπὸ [δι]καίου [π]αρα χωρήσεως γενομένης κτλ, and often for the *ius liberorum*, which qualified a woman to appear in legal transactions without a guardian. Thus so in the same formula P Thead 1^5 (A.D. 306), P Oxy IX. 1199^7 (iii/A.D.), *ib.* X. 1276^4 (A.D. 249) ἡ δὲ Μεῖλοῦς χωρὶς κυρίου χρηματίζουσα κατὰ τὰ Ῥωμα[ίω]ν ἔθη τέκνων δικαίῳ, so ^21 and *ib.* 1277^3 (A.D. 255), and cf. *Archiv* i. p. 310 f. The difficult phrase ὑπέχειν καὶ λαμβάνειν τὸ δίκαιον ἐπὶ τῶν χρηματιστῶν, P Tebt I. 5^24 (B.C. 118), is translated "they shall give and receive satisfaction before the chrematistae" by the editors, who note that it is "apparently another way of saying διδόναι καὶ δέχεσθαι δίκην, according as the verdict was against or for them"; but see Wenger in *Archiv* ii. p. 493, who renders

"Recht zu geben und zu nehmen, d. i. sich beklagen zu lassen und zu klagen." **Δικαία** appears as a fem. subst. in *OGIS* 829 (iv/B.C.) βαθόεντι τᾶ πόλε[ι] καὶ τᾶ δικαία, "helping the state and justice." In the late P Lond 483^5 (A.D. 616) (= II. p. 325) τὸ δίκαιον is applied to a monastery, evidently with reference to its "corporate unity as distinct from the individual who happens at any given time to represent it as prior" (see the editor's note).

For the adverb, cf. P Magd 20^5 (B.C. 218) οὐ διείρηταί μοι δικαίως a complaint that the division of a piece of land has not been made "fairly." For the combination ὁσίως καὶ δικαίως, as in 1 Thess 2^10, see P Par 63^viii. 12 ff. where a letter-writer claims that he has acted "in a holy and just way" before the gods—ἐγὼ γὰρ πιστεύσας σοί τε καὶ τοῖς θεοῖς, πρὸς οὓς ὁσίως καὶ δίκ . . . δικαίως [πολι]τευσάμενος κτλ. MGr is δίκιος: the phrase ἔχω δίκιο, "I am right," recalls the old substantival use. It should be added that Δίκαιος appears as a proper name: cf. the Latin *Iustus*, as in Ac 1^23, 18^7, Col 4^11.

δικαιοσύνη.

So far as we have noticed, this word is rare in the papyri, though it occurs very frequently in the inscriptions. From the papyri we can quote P Rein 10^9 (B.C. 111), where it is used as a name or title of Cleopatra: cf. *Syll* 763 Ἴσιδι Δικαιοσύνηι with the editor's note, BGU IV. 1138^1 (B.C. 10), in a cancelled line, ἐπὶ τὸ[ν τῆς δικαιοσύνη(ς) σου [χ]ρηματισ[μόν), in a petition to an epistrategus. P Leid W xvii. 39 (ii/iii A.D.) is addressed to a deity οὗ ἡ δικ(αιο)σύνη οὐκ ἀποκινῖται, οὗ αἱ μοῦσαι ὑμνοῦσι τὸ ἔνδοξον (ὄνομα). In the magic P Lond 46^401 (iv/A.D.) (= I, p. 78) it is found in a hymn addressed to Hermes. In P Thead 23^9 (A.D. 342) a man petitions Flavius Abinnaeus with reference to his neighbour who has attacked his sheep ληστρικῷ τρόπ[ῳ] . . . παρὰ τὴν [δικα]ιοσύνην, "after the manner of a brigand, contrary to justice." From the inscr. it is sufficient to add *OGIS* 339^15 (*c.* B.C. 120) διὰ τὴν τῶν ἀνδρῶν δικαιοσύνην τε καὶ φιλοτιμίαν, *ib.* 438^9 (i/B.C.) ἄνδρα ἀγαθὸν γενόμενον καὶ διενένκαντα πίστει καὶ ἀρετῇ καὶ δ[ικ]αιοσύνῃ καὶ εὐσεβείᾳ (cf. 2 Pet 1^5 ff.), *Cagnat* IV. 247^5 (*c.* B.C. 150), where the Demos of Assos, having been asked by that of Stratonicea to appoint an arbitrator for them, gives itself a testimonial as διὰ παντὸς πρόνοιαν ποιούμενος περὶ δικαιοσύνης. The Index in *Syll* III. contains about thirty references for the word.

δικαιόω

is used in a general sense "think or deem right" in P Giss I. 47^16 (time of Hadrian) with reference to a girdle (παραζώνιον) of which a man reports—ἀλλ' οὐδὲ ἐδικαίωσα ἀγοράσαι ἀποδοκιμασθῆναι δυνάμενον, "I did not think it right to purchase it, seeing that it is liable to be rejected." In P Ryl II. 119^11 (A.D. 54–67) the reference is to awarding a verdict in the courts: ἐδικαίωσεν ἀποδοῦναι ἡμᾶς τὸ κεφάλαιον καὶ ἀνακομίσασθαι τὴν ὑποθήκην, "he decided that we should repay the capital sum and recover the mortgage," etc. The case was before a δικαιοδότης, and the verb gives an interesting contemporary illustration of Paul's usage. From the same century comes P Tebt II. 444 τὰ δ[ιὰ] τῆς συνγραφῆς δετακιομένα κεφάλαι (*l.* δεδικαιωμένα κεφάλαια), "the sums *taxed* [declared just] by the contract." The spelling may be taken as evidence that the word was good vernacular. Add the fragmentary P Oxy III. 653 (A.D. 162–3), where the Praefect refers to a trial before the Chiliarch—ὃν μεταπέμπειν δικα[ιο]ῦμεν. For the force of ἐδικαιώθη in 1 Tim 3[16] Dibelius (*HZNT ad l.*) compares the use of the verb in the mystery-religions, e. g. Reitzenstein *Poimandres* 13[9] (p. 343) ὁ βαθμὸς οὗτος, ὦ τέκνον, δικαιοσύνης ἐστὶν ἕδρασμα. χωρὶς γὰρ κρίσεως ἰδὲ πῶς τὴν ἀδικίαν ἐξήλασεν. ἐδικαιώθημεν, ὦ τέκνον, ἀδικίας ἀπούσης, where δικαιοῦσθαι refers to "die Wesensänderung, die im Mysterium mit dem Mysten vergeht (nahezu = ἐθεώθημεν)." So "Christus ward der Sphäre der ἀδικία entrückt, in die Himmelswelt emporgehoben, erhöht und vergottet."

δικαίωμα.

In P Tor I. 1[iii.21] (B.C. 117) δικαιώματα means apparently "arguments of counsel"—παραγινωσκομένων αὐτοῖς ἐξ ὧν παρέκειντο δικαιωμάτων ὧν ἑκάτερος ᾑρεῖτο: so[25] and [25] ἐπελθὼν δὲ καὶ ἐπὶ τὰ τοῦ ἀντιδίκου δικαιώματα. Similarly in OGIS 13[14] (early iii/B.C.) when the people of Priene proved their immemorial possession of certain territory ἔκ τε τῶν ἱστοριῶν κ[αὶ ἐκ τῶν ἄλ]λων μαρτυριῶν καὶ δικαιωμάτων [με]τὰ τῶν ἐξετῶν [σπονδῶν, the meaning "awards" would seem to be possible, but "arguments" suits μαρτυριῶν better. Bishop Hicks's note (*Historical Ins rr.*[1] p. 206) will show the stages in this centuries-old dispute. P Lille 1. 26[25] (from a code—iii/B.C.) prescribes examination of slaves by torture ἐὰμ μὴ ἐκ τῶν τιθέντων δικαιωμάτων δύνωνται κρίνειν, "si les pièces du procès ne leur permettent pas de juger" (Ed.). Cf. P Petr II. 38 (c)[52] (iii/B.C.) (= III. p. 55), where a man is sent to Alexandria ἔχοντα καὶ τὰ πρὸ[ς] τὴν κατάστασιν δικαιώματα, "having with him the papers justifying his case," the *pièces justificatives* as the editors describe them. The same phrase occurs in Preisigke 3925[5] (B.C. 149–8 or 137–6). There is also P Petr III. 21 (g)[43] (iii/B.C.) ὃ καὶ παρέδοτο ἐν τοῖς δικαιώμασι, which follows ἅμα τε γραπτὸν λόγον [καὶ δικαιώ]ματα θεμένης with the same meaning. In BGU I. 113[10] (A.D. 143) ἃ δὲ παρέθεντο δικαιώμ ατα) the word = "credentials"; so ib. 265[17] (A.D. 148), and IV. 1033[7, 19] (Trajan). Cf. the combination here with that in P Tor 1 above (*ad init.*). In P Lond 360[8] (? ii/A.D.) (= II. p. 216) a certain Stotoetis surrenders to his sisters his "claim" on a slave-girl belonging to their mother—οὗ ἔχει δικαιώματος τῆς ὑπ[αρχ]ούσης τῇ μητρὶ αὐτῶν παιδίσκης δούλης. Similarly P Oxy VIII. 1119[15] (A.D. 254) τῶν ἐξαιρέτων τῆς ἡμετέρας πατρίδος δικαιωμάτων, "the exceptional rights claimed by our native city" (Ed.). MGr δικαίωμα = "justice."

δικαστής.

The word is found *quater* in P Petr I. 27, 28, fragmentary legal records of iii/B.C. In P Oxy III. 653 (time of Antoninus Pius), the account of a trial, the Praefect declares—εἴτε οὖν πάρεισιν οἱ ἀντίδικ[οι] εἴτε μὴ πάρεισι, δικαστὴν λήμψονται ὃς παρακολουθῶν τῇ Ὀνοράτου κρίσει τὴν Κανωπῖτιν ἐξετάσει κτλ.: cf. ib. I. 67[17] (A.D. 338) καταλα[μ]βάνοντες τὴν σὴν ἀρετὴν δ[εό]μεθα συ[ν]χωρηθῆναι δικα[στ]ὴν ἡ[μ]εῖν εἶναι Ἀέτιον τὸν προπολιτευόμενον, "knowing your goodness, I beg you to allow Aetius, ex-magistrate, to be judge in this matter" (Edd.), P Lond 971[19] (iii/iv A.D.) (= III. p. 129). The importance of the office

comes out in OGIS 499[3] (ii/A.D.) τῶν ἐκλέκτων ἐν Ῥώμῃ δικαστῶν, 528[7] δικαστὴν ἐν Ῥώμ η. On the ἀρχιδικαστής, who seems to have occupied the position of a permanent judge at Alexandria, before whom parties in civil cases could elect to have their disputes tried, see Milne, *Roman Egypt*, p. 100 ff. P Lond 196[b] (A.D. 130) (= III. p. 132) mentions an ἀ., and also (l.[19]) Εὐδαί[μονος διέπ]οντος τὰ κατὰ τὴν ἀρχιδικαστείαν. The abstract figures without ἀρχι- in Michel 477[10] (mid. ii/B.C.) ἀπ[ολυθεὶ]ς τε ἀπὸ τῆς δικαστείας ἐπεδήμησεν κτλ. For the δικαστήριον, as the Praefect's tribunal or court, see P Strass I. 5[7, 19] (A.D. 202), P Oxy I. 59[11] (A.D. 292), P Amh II. 82[4, 19] (iii/iv A.D.), etc. MGr δικαστής survives unchanged.

δίκη.

This word in Homer may = "custom," "usage"; hence "right" as established usage, extended farther to a "process of law" or "judicial hearing," e.g. P Hib I. 30[4] (B.C. 300–271) ἡ δίκη σοι ἀναγραφήσετ[α]ι ἐν [τῶι ἐν Ἡρ]ακλέους πόλει δικαστηρίωι, "the case will be drawn up against you in the court at Heracleopolis" (Edd.), P Rein 15[21] (B.C. 109) ἄνευ δίκης καὶ κρίσεως καὶ πάσης εὑρεσιλογίας, "sans procès, contestation ni chicane d'aucune sorte" (Ed.), similarly P Lond 208[b] (A.D. 124) (= II. p. 206), P Oxy III. 486[28] (A.D. 131) τὴν μὲν μητέρα μου συνέβη ἀποθανεῖ[ν] πρὸ τῆς δίκης, "it happened that my mother died before the trial" (Edd.), etc. From this it is a natural transition to the result of the law-suit, "execution of a sentence," "penalty," as P Fay 21[24] (A.D. 134) ὅπ[ως] τῆς ἀποθίας (= ἀπειθ.) ἐκείνοι τὴν προσήκουσαν δίκη[ν ὑ]πόσχωσι, "in order that they may pay the fitting penalty for their disobedience"; cf. 2 Thess 1[9], Jude [7], Wisd 18[11], 2 Macc 8[11]. From P Eleph 1[12] (B.C. 311–10) (= *Selections*, p. 3) onwards, the phrase καθάπερ ἐγ δίκης is very common = "as if a formal decree of the court had been obtained." In partial illustration of the personification of Δίκη in Ac 28[4] we may quote in addition to the exx. in Wetstein and Field (*Notes*, p. 148 f.) *Syll* 810 εἰ δέ τι (ἐ)ὼν ἐξαμαρτ[ήσει], οὐκ ἐμὸν ἐπαράσ ασθαι, δίκη δὲ ἐπικρέματα[ι] τιμωρὸς ἀπελθόν[τι] ἀπειθὴς Νεμέσε[ως]. A fairly early Christian inser. from Attica, *Kaibel* 173[17], has δίκης μετὰ λοίσθιον ἦμα[ρ, of the Day of Judgement.

δίκτυον.

A Christian epitaph from Aegina, *Kaibel* 421 (? v A.D.) makes the departed rejoice because
δίκτυα λυγρὰ
καὶ γοερὰς παγίδας προὔφυγον ἀμπλακίης.
This is of course purely literary, but between Epictetus and the Gospels we may be sure of vernacular warranty. Moreover it survives in MGr δίχτυ.

δίλογος

must be recorded as one of the small class that cannot be illustrated. Διλογία "repetition" and διλογεῖν "repeat" are quoted from Xenophon and later writers, δίλογος itself in the same sense from Pollux. But the Pauline sense is still unsupported: see Nägeli, p. 52.

διό.

P Oxy III. 485[4] (A.D. 178) διὸ ἐπιτελεῖτε ὡς καθήκ(ει), "execute the deed therefore, as is fitting" (Edd.), ib. IX.

1198[15] (notification of death—A.D. 150), διὸ ἀξιῶ τούτους ἀναγραφῆναι τῇ τῶν τετελευτηκότων τάξει. For διὸ καί see P Par 46[14] (B.C. 153) διὸ καὶ ἡγούμενος δεῖν ἐπ' ἄλλου μὲν μηθενὸς αὑτῶι διακριθῆναι.

διοδεύω.

In P Amh II. 36[15] (c. B.C. 135) a cavalry officer petitions the Strategus concerning some danger which he experienced in "passing through" certain districts on his way to Thebes —λείπω τε τὴν ὑπερβολήν, διοδεύων κινδυν[εύω π]αρ' ἕκαστον διὸ ἀξιῶ . . . Cf. OGIS 613[2] (A.D. 392) τοὺς διοδεύοντας καὶ τὸ ἔθνος διὰ παντὸς εἰρηνεύεσθαι ἠσφαλίσατο, 665[2] (A.D. 49) τοὺς διοδεύοντας διὰ τῶν νομῶν στρατιώτας. See Anz Subsidia, p. 344.

Διονύσιος.

The extreme frequency of this name in the Hellenistic period is seen at a glance in the indices personarum. It is to be taken into account in estimates of the religion of the world in which Paul worked. On survivals of the Dionysus cult, evidenced by the posthumous importance of Dionysius the Areopagite, see Rendel Harris Annotators of Codex Bezae, p. 77 ff.

διόπερ.

P Flor III. 382[18] (A.D. 222–3) διόπερ θαυμάσας αὐτο[ῦ τὴ]ν ἀνυπέρβλητον τόλμ[αν καὶ] ἐπήρειαν καὶ ἀνομίαν, οὐκ ἡσύχασα κτλ, P Fay 20[11] (imperial edict —iii/iv A.D.) διόπερ ἴστωσαν ἅπαντες ἐν ταῖς πόλεσιν ἁπάσαις κτλ.

διοπετής.

The marginal rendering of the word in the RV "fallen from heaven" rather than "from Jupiter" is supported by Field (Notes, p. 130), who cites Dion. Hal. Ant. ii. 71 ἐν δὲ ταῖς πέλταις ἃς οἱ Σάλιοι φοροῦσι, πολλαῖς πάνυ οὔσαις, μίαν εἶναι λέγουσι διοπετῆ (afterwards explained by θεόπεμπτον). Of course the two amount to the same thing, since Zeus is the primeval sky-god; see A. B. Cook's great monograph, Zeus.

διόρθωμα.

Rev L. 57[1] (iii/B.C.) δ]ιόρθωμα το[ῦ νόμου ἐπὶ τῆ]ι ἐλ'αικῆι, "revision of the law concerning the oil-contract"; cf. P Par 62[7] (ii/B.C.) κατὰ τοὺς νόμους καὶ τὰ δια[γράμματα καὶ τὰ πρ]οστάγματα καὶ τὰ διορθώμεθα (l. διορθώματα), Michel 466[17] (ii/B.C.) κατὰ τὸ Θαλιεύκτου διόρθωμα. The verb is common, e.g. P Tebt I. 25[12] (c. B.C. 119 or 114) διὸ καὶ ἔτι καὶ νῦν καλῶς ποιήσεις φιλοτιμότερον προθυμηθεὶς ἵνα τὰ πρὸς αὐτὸν [. . .] διορθώσηι, "I shall therefore be glad if you will even now endeavour more earnestly to correct your behaviour towards him" (Edd.), ib. 27[9] (B.C. 113) οὐδαμῶς τὰ παρὰ τὸ δέον (pap. δειον) κεχειρισμένα διωρθωμένος, "with no improvement whatever in your improper procedure" (Edd.), P Petr III. 53[b][9] . . .]ατην ἀπόστειλον πρός με ὅπως διορθωθῆι, P Giss I. 41[ii][10] (time of Hadrian) μετὰ τοῦ (l. τὸ) διορθώσ[αι] κατὰ τὸ δυνατὸν τὰ ἡμέτερα. It is used in connexion with "payments" in P Oxy III. 485[16] (A.D. 108 τόκου) . . . ὃν καὶ διορ[θώσω ἐ]π[ὶ] συνκλ[εισ]μῶ ἑκάστης δωδεκα-μήνου, BGU III. 620[18] (A.D. 180) ὅνπερ φόρον διορθώσομαί

σοι ἐνενιαῦτα κατ' ἔτος. It acquired a technical sense in book-production, where the διορθωτής was what we call a printer's reader. Vettius Valens (p. 276) tells a story of an audacious youth who offered Euripides to "correct" his poems, observing γράφειν ποιήματα οὐκ ἐπίσταμαι, τὰ δὲ κακῶς γραφέντα διορθοῦσθαι. The poet replied: τοιγαροῦν κακῶς γράψας . . τὰ σαυτοῦ καλῶς διόρθωσον. (Note the juxtaposition of middle and active.)

διόρθωσις.

Like the verb (see above), διόρθωσις is used of "payments," as P Tebt I. 61[a][33] (B.C. 118 7) διὰ τὸ μὴ εὐσυνθετηκέναι ἐν τῆι διορθώσ[ε]ι τοῦ ἐπιβληθέντ[ος α]ὑτῶι στεφάνου, ib. 646[a][114] (B.C. 140–5). A better parallel to the NT usage (Heb 9[10]) is P Leid W[xvi. 12] (ii/iii A.D.) ἀλλὰ κατηξιώθης τῶν πρὸς διάρθωσιν (l. διόρ—) βίου μελλόντων.

διορύσσω.

The exact phrase of Mt 24[43], Lk 12[39], is found in P Petr III. 28 verso (b[2] (B.C. 260) ὅτι διώρυξεν οἰκίαν, "because he broke into a house." Cf. OGIS 483[18] (ii/B.C.) μὴ ἐξουσία δὲ ἔστω ἐπὶ τοὺς κοινοὺς τοίχους μήτε ἐποικοδομεῖν μήτε διορύσσειν μήτε ἄλλο καταβλάπτειν μηθέν, and an interesting inscription from a tomb published in ZNTW i. p. 100, where mention is made of certain persons βουλομένο[υ]ς διορύττιν.

Διόσκουροι.

On the form see Mayser Gr. p. 10 f., where it is shown that the divine name was regularly Διόσκοροι, the Attic form: Διοσκούριον occurs once, in P Petr III. 117(d)[24] (iii/B.C.) τοῦ [περὶ] τὸ Διοσκούριον. The Ionic form with ου appears in Ac 28[11] practically without variant. It is noteworthy that the extremely common personal names derived from the Dioscuri—see above, s.v. Δίδυμος—take the forms Διόσκορος and Διοσκουρίδης, and the latter figures even in Attica (Meisterhans Gr. p. 27). Schweizer, Perg. p. 67, discusses the relation of the forms, which may be confidently assigned to dialect mixture. The suggestion is that Dioscorus and Dioscurides as personal names came in by different channels. See also Pauly-Wissowa v. col. 1141.

διότι.

For διότι with its full causal force, see P Tebt I. 24[34] (B.C. 117) καὶ διότι δι' ἄλλων προσανενηνόχαμεν, "owing to my giving information through the officials" (Edd.), P Giss I. 82[22] (A.D. 117), P Lond 243[14] (c. A.D. 346) (= II. p. 300) ἵνα . . . ἀπολύσῃς αὐτοὺς διότι οἶδας καὶ αὐ[τὸς ὅτ]ι ἑορτή ἐστι ν, etc. In the papyri, however, as in the LXX and late Grk generally, the word is often used practically = ὅτι, "that," e.g. P Petr II. 40[a][8] (B.C. 255 4) οἶδας δὲ διότι [ὁ] τόπος ἔρημός ἐστιν, P Tebt I. 12[29] (B.C. 118) ἐπὶ οὐ καὶ σὺ οὐκ ἀγνοεῖς ἐν ἧι ἐσμὲν ἀσχολί (l. -ίαι) καὶ διότι ἐν τῆι τ[ο]ῦ στρα[τηγοῦ] ἐσμὲν φ]υλακῆι ?), "for you know how busy I am, and that I am in attendance upon the strategus" (Edd.), and from the inscr. OGIS 90[8] (Rosetta Stone—B.C. 196) ὅπως γνώριμον ἦι διότι οἱ ἐν Αἰγύπτωι αὔξουσι καὶ τιμῶσι τὸν θεὸν Ἐπιφανῆ Εὐχάριστον βασιλέα, Syll 654 ter (? ii/B.C.—in Messenian Doric). For the corresponding NT usage, see Blass Gr. p. 274, where

Rom 1[19,21], 3[20], 8[7], are quoted for **διότι** = "for," and add 1 Pet 1[16,24], 2[6], as compared with 3[10]. 1 Th 2[8] and Gal 2[16] may be quoted as illustrating the ease of the colloquial transition: see Jebb in Vincent and Dickson *Mod. Greek*[2] App. p. 338. Mayser *Gr.* p. 161 has shown that the use of of **διότι** for **ὅτι** is by no means confined to occurrences after vowe's: cf. Thackeray *Gr.* i. p. 138 f. and Kaelker *Quaest.* pp. 243 f., 300. It may be added that, according to Meisterhans *Gr.* p. 252 f. **διότι** is never used with a causal force in the Attic inscrr. from iii/B.C. onwards.

Διοτρεφής.

For this proper name, as 3 Jn[9], cf. *OGIS* 219[1] (iii/B.C.) ἐπιμηνιεύοντος Νυμφίου τοῦ Διοτρεφοῦς.

διπλοῦς.

For this common word we may quote P Amh II. 33 (c. B.C. 157), where reference is made to the severe penalties incurred by advocates who had assisted persons charged with defrauding the Treasury. No longer were they allowed to practise, and had to pay to the Crown (εἰς τὸ βασιλικόν) "twice the sum (of the damage) increased by one tenth"—διπλοῦν τὸ ἐπιδέκατον. Other exx. are P Tebt I. 11[16] B.C. 110) τὰ προκείμενα διπλᾶ, "twice the aforesaid amount," P Oxy VIII. 1124[15] (A.D. 26) ἐκφόρ[ιο]ν διπλοῦν, "double the rent," P Fay 110[30] (A.D. 94) τὰς δὲ ὠλένας τοῦ ἐλαιουργίου δ[ι]πλᾶς ποίησον, "make the hinges (?) of the oil-press double" (Edd.), P Oxy IV. 741[3] (ii/A.D.) σφυρὶς διπλῆ καρύων α, "1 double basket of nuts" (Edd.), P Hamb I. 21[10] (A.D. 314-5) ἐκτίσιν σοι τοῦ ὑπερπεσόντος χρόνου τιμὴν ἐπὶ τοῦ τότε καιροῦ ἐσομένην τιμὴν διπλὴν ὡς ἔσσεται, etc. In *Ostr* 1291[3] (A.D. 148) ἔσχ(ομεν) ὑπὲρ διπλῶν so much, διπλοῦν seems to be a tax. Wilcken (*Archiv* i. p. 126) refers to P Oxy I. 141 of date A.D. 503 as the earliest ex. of διπλοῦν as a wine measure known to him. In P Petr II. 13 (17)[4] (B.C. 258-3) we find a form δίπλειον — δίπλεον — καὶ δίπλειον εἰληφέναι τοῦ διαγεγραμμένου ὀψωνίου ἐν τῷ κθ̅ ἔτει, "and that I received double the allowance of provision money in the 29th year" (Ed.). In BGU I. 213[1] (A.D. 112) διπλώματος ὄνων may a "licence" to own donkeys: cf. P Tebt II. 360[3] (A.D. 146) διπ λώματος ?) λαχα νοπώλου ?) with the editors' note.

δίς.

BGU III. 913[2] (A.D. 206) δὶς μηνός: the document is of special interest as having been written in Myra in Lycia, and hence being one of the very few known papyri from Asia Minor, see *Archiv* ii. p. 138. For the phrase εἰς δίς, cf. P Flor II. 184[9] iii/A.D.) ἔπεμψα οὖν εἰς δὶς πρός σε τὸν ὀνηλάτην. With δὶς ἀποθανόντα in Jude[12] we may compare P Oxy I. 33[iv. 3-4] where a man condemned to death salutes the Emperor (? Marcus Aurelius), τίς ἤδη τὸν δεύτερόν μου ᾅδη προσκυνοῦντα . . . μετεκαλέσατο: "who has recalled me when I was now saluting my second death?" Edd.

διστάζω.

P Par 63[ii. 57] (B.C. 165) τὸν πάντων ἀπειρότατον . . . τὰ τῆς χρίας σ[υ]νπληροῦν, ἐπαν[άγ]οντα τὸ διστ[α]ζόμενον ἐπὶ τὸν ἐγκείμενον κανόνα, "that even the most inexperienced

person in the world might be able to accomplish what was required, if he applied the doubtful cases to the rule provided for him" (Mahaffy), and for the corresponding substantive see *ib.*[iii. 83] παραχρῆμα προσαναφέρειν ὑπὲρ τῶν δοκούντων τινὰ διστασ[μό]ν, "to refer to us at once concerning any points which seemed to be open to doubt." *ib.* P Giss I. 18[9] (time of Hadrian) δηλῶ οὖν σοι, ἵνα μὴ διστάζῃς· ἐπο[ρ]εύθη γὰρ εἰς Ἑρμοῦ πόλιν.

δίστομος

is found in a fragmentary context in an inscr. from Delos, c. B.C. 230, published in *BCH* xxix (1905), p. 598, no. 107 B[35]. See also P Lond W[10] (ii/iii A.D. ἔχε . . . μαχαίριν ὁλοσίδηρον δίστομον.

διχάζω.

We are unable to cite any vernacular instances of this verb (found in Plato): but δίχα is common, e.g. P Oxy II. 237[viii. 37] (A.D. 186) δίχα ἐπιστάλματος τοῦ βιβλιοφυλακ[ίου, "without an order from the record-office," P Giss I. 60[i] (early ii/A.D.) δίχα τῆς ἡμετέρας ἐπιστολ[ῆς, BGU III. 908[ii. 2] (time of Trajan) δίχα πάσης ἐξουσίας ἐπελθόντες etc.

διχοστασία.

Michel 448[35] (end ii/B.C.) τᾶν τε κτησίων καὶ τῶν ποτ' ἀλλάλος συναλλαγμάτων πάντων ἐν ταραχᾶι τε καὶ διχοστασίαι τᾶι μεγίσται κειμένων. To Wetstein's examples of this word (*ad* Rom 16[17]) Field (*N tes.* p. 100) adds two from Dionysius of Halicarnassus and one in Ionic from the *Florilegium* of Stobaeus.

διχοτομέω.

The word is found in a very touching sepulchral inscription from Lycaonia (iii/iv A.D.), published in *JHS* xxii. (1902), p. 369 f., which on account of its simplicity and pathos may be given entire, as freshly read by Prof. W. M. Calder:— Γορδιανὸς τῇ γλυκυτάτῃ μου συμβίῳ Γαεάνῃ, ὑπὲρ τοῦ μέλιτος γλυκυτάτῃ, τῇ συνζησάσῃ μοι χρόνους ὀλίγους ἐπι[τ]ίμως, κὲ τῷ νείῷ μου τῷ πρωτοτόκ[ῳ] Ἀμβροσίῳ τῷ διχοτομήσαντί με τοῦ πολοέτιον ζῆν. εὐθίως γὰρ πεντήκοντα ἡμέρας πληρώσας ἐξηκολούθησεν τῇ μητρὶ τῇ πανμακαρίτῃ. ἐλεύσομε δὲ κάτω πρὸς ὑμᾶς πληρώσας τὸ χρέος τ[ο]ῦ βίου, "Gordianus to my sweetest wife Gaiana, sweetest beyond honey, who lived with me honorably for a little time, and to my firstborn son Ambrosius, who cut me off from living through many years. For as soon as he had fulfilled fifty days he followed his sainted mother. But I shall come down to you when I have fulfilled my appointed portion of life." The verb may be quoted from 3 Baruch 16 (*Texts and Studies* v. 1. p. 94) διχοτομήσατε αὐτοὺς ἐν μαχαίρᾳ καὶ ἐν θανάτῳ καὶ τὰ τέκνα αὐτῶν ἐν δαιμονίοις.

διψάω.

The verb is found in no. 5 of the first discovered collection of Λόγια Ἰησοῦ, P Oxy I. p. 3.—λέγει Ἰησοῦ;ς Ἔ[σ]την ἐν μέσῳ τοῦ κόσμου καὶ ἐν σάρκι ὤφθην αὐτοῖς καὶ εὗρον πάντας μεθύοντας καὶ οὐδένα εὗρον διψῶντα ἐν αὐτοῖς κτλ. See also the late metrical epitaph from Rome, *Cagnat* I. 317[11] (= *IGSI* 1890) ψυχὴ διψώσῃ ψυχρὸν ὕδωρ μετάδες (*l.* -δος).

δίψος.

Nägeli (p. 14) draws attention to the fact that the word **δίψος**, which is praised by the Schol. on *Il.* 19[166] as Attic, in contrast to the Ionic **δίψα**, is found also in the LXX and Epictetus. In the LXX the two words are used interchangeably, e.g. Wisd 11[4] **δίψης**, [8] **δίψους**: Am 8[11] **δίψαν**, [13] **δίψει**: see Thackeray *Gr.* i. p. 157. In a medical fragment, P Tebt II. 272[17] (late ii/A.D.), we have, **κριθήσεται δὲ [ο]ὕτως ἔχον ἐὰν τοῦ κατὰ τὸν [π]υρετὸν μεγέθους μᾶλλον [π]αραύξηται τὸ δίψος**, "such will be judged to be the case if the increase of thirst is out of proportion to the height of the fever" (Edd.), cf. [20] (cited above under **ἀνεξίκακος**) **μὴ ὑπομένοι τὸ δίψ[ο]ς**. In P Flor II. 176[12] (iii/A.D.) **δίψα** is used in connexion with the "dryness" of figs—**ἐκ τῆς τῶν σύκων κακίας καὶ ξηρότητος καὶ δίψης**. MGr has **δίψα**.

δίψυχος

is first found apparently in Jas 1[8], 4[8], and may be regarded as a parallel case to **διακρίνεσθαι** = "waver," see *s.v.* **διακρίνω** *ad finem*. The verb is found in Didache 4[4] **οὐ διψυχήσεις, πότερον ἔσται ἢ οὔ**. J. B. Mayor's note (*Comm.* on Jas 1[8]) shows how rapidly the word "caught on" with the sub-apostolic writers—Clement of Rome, "Barnabas" and especially Hermas. If James really coined it—and the manner of its appearance in both passages is quite in keeping with such a supposition—its occurrence in i/A.D. writers reinforces many arguments for the early date of Jas. Analogous words are well provided by Mayor. Among them is **διχόνους** in Philo, in the fragment from the heading of which Thayer cites **δίψυχος** itself. But can we be assured that Philo himself entitled the paragraph **περὶ Δειλῶν καὶ Διψύχων**? Mayor's silence suggests that he thinks otherwise. Cf. the MGr **δίγνωμος**, "fickle."

διώκτης.

The LXX compound **ἐργοδιώκτης** (Exod 3[7] al) is found in the same sense in the correspondence of the "architect" Kleon, P Petr II. 4 (1)[5] (B.C. 255-4), where certain quarrymen complain that they are being ill-treated by the "ganger" Apollonius, by being kept at work at quarries of hard stone—**ἀδικούμεθα ὑπὸ Ἀπολλωνίου τοῦ ἐργοδιώκτου ἐμβαλὼν ἡμᾶς εἰς τὴν στερεὰν πέτραν**.

διώκω.

P Fay 111[20] (A.D. 95-6)—*Selections*, p. 67—**τὸν λ[ι]μνασμ[ὸν] δ[ί]οξον τῶν [ἐ]λα[ι]ών[ω]ν τ[ῶ]ν πάντον**, "hasten with the flooding of all the olive-yards" (Edd.), *ib.* 112[2] (A.D. 99) **εὖ πυήσις διῶξαι τοὺς σκαφήτρους τῶν ἐλαιώνον**, "please carry forward the digging of the olive-yards" (Edd.). For **διώκω** = "pursue," cf. *OGIS* 532[25] (B.C. 3) **ὅπλο[ις τε] καὶ σιδήρωι διώξειν**, and the moral tale in P Grenf II. 84[5] (v/vi A.D.) where a patricide, fleeing into the desert, **ἐδιόκαιτο** (*l.* ἐδιώκετο) **ὑπὸ λέοντος**, "was pursued by a lion." The phrase **δίωκε τὸν λόγον** = "pursue the recital of the formula" is common in the magic papyri: see the editor's note on P Lond 46[25] (iv/A.D.) I. p. 78. We may add two exx. of the verb from Christian amulets. The first, P Oxy VIII. 1151 (v/A.D.) opens, **Φεῦγε πν(εῦ)μ(α) μεμισ(ε)μένον, Χριστό[ς] σε διώκει**, "Fly, hateful spirit! Christ pursues thee." In the second, BGU III. 954[2] (vi/A.D.)

(= *Selections*, p. 133), the Lord God is invoked—**ὅπως διώξης ἀπ' ἐμοῦ τοῦ δούλου σου τὸν δαίμονα προβασκανίας**, "that Thou mayst drive from me Thy servant the demon of witchcraft." MGr. **διώχνω, διώχτω**, "hunt."

δόγμα.

Bishop Hicks (*CR* i. p. 44 f.) has shown that **δόγμα** was not the regular word in republican Greece for a decree of the **βουλή** and the **δῆμος**, but was specially used for a decree of the Roman Senate. So, e.g., *Syll* 930[60] (B.C. 112) **ἐξυγκλήτου δόγματος** = *e senatusconsulto*. See the index *s.v.* in *Cagnat* I. p. 947. It came also to be applied to the *placita philosophorum*, and in general conveyed the idea of "a positive ordinance, emanating from a distant and unquestionable authority." With its use by Luke for the decrees of the Emperor (Lk 2[1], Ac 17[7]) we may compare P Fay 20[22] (iii/iv A.D.), an important Edict, apparently of Severus Alexander, regarding the *Aurum Coronarium*, which ends—**τούτου τοῦ ἐμοῦ δόγματος ἀντίγραφα τοῖς καθ' ἑκάστην πόλιν ἄρχουσιν γενέσθω ἐπιμελὲς εἰς τὸ δημόσιον μάλιστα ἐστάν[αι] σύνοπτα τοῖς ἀναγιγνώσκουσιν**, "let the rulers of the several cities see that copies of this my edict are set up in the most public places in full view of those who wish to read" (Edd.). As showing the different uses to which the word came to be put, it must be sufficient to add *Syll* III. Index p. 173, where references are given to 150[16] (B.C. 333) **κατὰ τὸ δόγμα τῶν Ἑλλήνων**, 412[2] (Roman period) **δόγματι τῆς Ὀλυμπικῆς βουλῆς**, 557[24] **παρὰ τὸ δόγμα τῶν Ἀμφικτυόνων**, etc. An interesting example of the later ecclesiastical use of the word is found in the Christian prayer (end of iv/A.D.) published by Schmidt in *Neutliche Studien für G. Heinrici*, p. 71[24] **ὅπως καταξιωθῶμεν τῶ[ν] εὐαγγελιζομένων δογμάτων τῶν ἁγίων σου ἀποστόλων**.

δογματίζω.

In the art. by Bishop Hicks cited *s.v.* **δόγμα**, three instances of this verb are cited from the inscrr.,—*CIG* 2485[17] (B.C. 105) **τὰ] πε[ρὶ τῶν συνθηκῶν?] δογματισθέντα** of *Senatus consulta*, *CIG* 3524[4] (time of Augustus) **πὰρ ταῖς δεδογματισμέναις αὐτῳ τείμαις**, and *CIG* 5785[13] **ἐὰν δόξη τῆ ἀγάρρει [οὕτως], καθὼς καὶ ὑπὲρ φρητάρχου καὶ χαλκολόγων δογματί[ζε]ται**. In the LXX **δογματίζω** is used several times of issuing a decree, and twice at least (2 Macc 10[8], 15[4]) of religious enactments. As against AV and RV, the verb may possibly be passive in Col 2[20]—"Why do you allow yourselves to be overridden by Jewish enactments?" The Polybian compound **δογματοποιέω** (i. 81. 4) is found in *Syll* 653[7] (B.C. 91) **οἱ ἄρχοντες καὶ οἱ σύνεδροι δογματοποιείσθωσαν ὅτι κτλ.**

δοκέω.

The verb is naturally common, e.g. P Par 49[16] (B.C. 164-58) **εἶπα αὐτῷ μὴ ἐμὲ ἀξιοῦν, ἀλλά, δόξαντα ἀδελφὸν αὐτοῦ ἐν τῇ αὐλῇ εἶναι, παραγίνεσθαι**, P Oxy VII. 1027[9] (i/A.D.) **ὑπόμνημα ἀφ' οὗ ἔδοξεν δυνήσασθαι ἐμποδισθῆναί μου τὴν πρᾶξιν**, "a memorandum by means of which he hoped that my execution might be prevented" (Edd.), *ib.* 1032[8] (A.D. 162) **ἐάν σου τῇ τύχῃ δόξῃ**, "if your fortune sees fit." For other exx. of this last phrase we may cite P Petr I. 29[7] (B.C. 241) **ἐάν σοι δοκεῖ**, P Oxy IV. 718[24] (A.D. 180-92) **ἐάν σοι δόξῃ**, and *ib.* IX. 1220[5] (iii/A.D.) **ἢ δοκί σοι, κύριέ μου, πέμψε μοι** κέρμα; "would you be pleased, sir, to send me some money?" (Ed.). In P Oxy IX. 1218[1] (iii/A.D. δοκῶ is used absolutely, as in 1 Cor 4[9] ἡ μήτηρ μου Θαῆσις εἰς Ἀντινόου, δοκῶ, ἐπὶ κηδίαν ἀπῆλθεν, "my mother Thaesis went, I think, to Antinoopolis for a funeral" (Ed.); cf. P Amh II. 64[6] A.D. 108 δοκῶ μοι. For the more official usage of δοκέω = "censeo," see OGIS 233[30] (B.C. 220-3) ἔδοξε τῆι ἐκκλησίαι πρυτάνεων εἰπάντων κτλ., Priene 105[28] (c.B.C.?) ἔδοξεν τοῖς ἐπὶ τῆς Ἀσίας Ἕλλησιν γνώμῃ κτλ.: cf. P Tebt II. 335[15] (a petition to the Praefect (?)—middle of iii/A.D.) εἰ δέ τι τοιοῦτον ἔδοξας κελεύειν, "if you really did vouchsafe to give such orders" (Edd.). For δοκέω followed by the acc and inf, as in 2 Cor 11[16], cf. P Tebt II. 413[6] (ii/iii/A.D.) μὴ δόξῃς με, κυρί[α], ἠμεληκέναι σου τῶν ἐντολῶν, "do not think, mistress, that I am negligent of your commands" (Edd.). In P Ryl II. 229[15] (A.D. 38) we find it with partic. - δοκῶ γὰρ συναιρόμενος πρὸς σὲ λογάριον, "for I expect to make up an account without you" (Edd.). The personal constr. c. inf. predominates: note BGU IV. 1141[9] (c. B.C. 14) οὐδὲ σὲ γὰρ δοκῶι εἰς ἐνφα[ν]ιστοῦ τόπον με ἔχειν, ib.[10] ἐγὼ μέν οὐ δοκῶι ἄξιος εἶναι ὑβρίζεσθαι—per contra add P Oxy VI. 937[17] (iii/A.D.) παρατηρεῖσθαι αὐτὴν μὴ δόξῃ αὐτῷ τῷ Ἀ. λαβῆ[σ]αι τὴν φιάλην, "to keep a watch on it, lest A. should determine to take the bowl" (Edd.), CP Herm 26[3] (a prayer verba?) ὃ ἐὰν αὐτοῦ δόξῃ τῷ μεγέθι, "whatever his highness shall determine."

δοκιμάζω

is not uncommon in its primary sense of "testing." Syll 522[14] (iii/B.C.) δοκιμάζειν δὲ τὰ ἱερεῖα τοὺς προβούλους, with other officials. P Ryl II. 114[5] (c. A.D. 280) . . .] κατὰ τὸ δικαιότατον δοκιμάσει ὁ κράτιστος [ἐπιστράτηγο]ς, "his excellency the epistrategus shall sit the matter with the utmost equity." So still in vi/vii A.D., P Oxy I. 128 verso[2] ἵνα τὸ παριστάμενον ἐπ' αὐτῷ δοκιμάσῃ, "in order that you may judge of his present condition (Edd.). P Flor II. 119[4] (A.D. 254) ὅπως δοκι[μάσας γρά]ψῃς μοι εἰ οὕτως ἔχ[ει, "that after inquiry you may write to me whether it is so." P Gen I. 32[2] (A.D. 148), of an inspector of calves for sacrifice—καὶ δοκιμάσας ἐσφράγ[ισα ὡς] ἔστιν καθαρός. From "proving" to "approving" was a step taken long before these documents were written, so that the ambiguity which meets us in Rom 2[18] and Phil 1[10] is based on the normally coexisting uses. So in the earliest known marriage-contract, P Eleph 1[9] (B.C. 311-0) (= Selections, p. 3) differences between husband and wife are to be settled by three men οὓς ἂν δοκιμάζωσιν ἀμφότεροι, "whom both shall approve," and in P Fay 106[23] (c. A.D. 140) a plea for exemption from certain public services is put forward on behalf of physicians, and especially of those who have "passed the examination"—the petitioner—μάλ[ιστα [δὲ οἱ δε]δοκιμασμένοι ὥσπερ κἀγώ: cf. Syll 371[9] (time of Nero) ἀνὴ[ρ] δεδοκιμασμένος τοῖς θείοις κριτηρίοις τῶν Σεβαστῶν ἐπί τε τῇ τέχνῃ τῆς ἰατρικῆς καὶ τῇ κοσμιότητι τῶν ἠθῶν—a character certificate and an examination, to qualify for M.B. In the inscr. indeed the verb is almost a term. techn. for passing as fit for a public office, see Milligan Thess. p. 18. So OGIS 90[3] (the Rosetta Stone—B.C. 196) ὅν (sc. Πτολεμαῖον Ἐπιφανῆ) ὁ Ἥφαιστος ἐδοκίμασεν, i.e. "examinatum probavit ideoque regem constituit" (Dittenberger): the same phrase meets us in a Munich papyrus, Chrest. I. 109[19] (end of iii/B.C.,

of Ptolemy Philopator, ὃν ὁ Ἥφαιστος ἐδοκ[ίμασεν, ὧι ὁ Ἥλιος ἔδωκεν τὸ κρ[άτος. Hence comes a meaning hardly distinguishable from δοκεῖν, as in P Petr III. 41 verso[10] ὁ]ποτέρως οὖν καὶ σὺ δοκιμάζεις, οὕτως [ἔσ]ται, "whichever way, then, you also approve of, so it shall be" (Edd.). P Oxy VI. 928[7] (ii/iii A.D.) φανερόν σοι ποιῶ ἵνα ἐὰν δοκιμάσῃς ποιήσῃς πρὶν προλημφθῆναι, "I therefore inform you, in order that if you think fit you may act before she is entrapped" (Edd.) with reference to a plot against a girl. P Giss I. 40[ii 30] (A.D. 215) δηλωταιον (=δηλοποιεῖν) [ἐ]δοκίμασα, P Tebt II. 326[10] (c. A.D. 266) τὸν ἴδιον ἐμαυτῆς ἀδελφὸν . . . δοκιμάσασα προ[στ]ήσεσθαι γνησίως τοῦ παιδίου, "having found that my own brother will honourably protect the child" (Edd.). P Oxy I. 71[i 5] (A.D. 303) κελεῦσαι εἴ σοι δοκοῖ ἢ τῷ στρατηγῷ ἢ ᾧ ἐὰν δοκιμάσῃς, "to instruct, if you will, the strategus or any other magistrate whom you may sanction" (Edd.). For a verb δοκιμάω, unknown to LS, see P Tebt I. 24[75] (B.C. 117) καθότι [ἂ]ν δοκιμήσῃς, P Oxy III. 533[24] (ii/iii A.D.) ὃν ἐὰν δ]οκιμᾷς, and cf. Mayser Gr. p. 459, also below s.v. δοκιμή. Note that δοκιμόω is odd, at any rate in its Aeolic form δοκίμωμι, found in Sappho, and in the learned Aeolic of Julia Balbilla, in the suite of Hadrian, Kaibel 991[5].

δοκιμασία.

Syll 540[29] (B.C. 175-1) περὶ δὲ τῶν προπεποιημένων οἱ ἐξ ἀρχῆς ἔγγυοι ἔστωσαν ἕως τῆς ἐσχάτης δοκιμασίας (. τοῦ ἔργου). In a papyrus containing various chemical formulae, P Leid X[VII B 20, 30 etc. 12] (iii/iv A.D.) we hear of χρυσοῦ and ἀσήμου δοκιμασία. In another papyrus of the same collection, Q[4] (B.C. 50—acc. to Mayser B.C. 260-50) we read of a certain Orsenouphis who occupied the position of δοκιμαστής at Syene, apparently with reference to the inspection of the food returns (see the editor's note), and cf. P Petr II. 4 (8)[6] (a report regarding a quarry—B.C. 255-4) παραδεικνύοντος ἔργα δοκι[μαστοῦ, by whom Lumbroso (see p. 28) understands the officer in quarries called Petanu by the Romans. Note also Syll 388[12] (A.D. 129), where Hadrian commends to the archons and senate of Ephesus Lucius Erastus, a sea-captain, who wishes to become a senator: κἀγὼ τ[ὴ]ν μὲν [δοκι]μασία[ν ἐφ']ὑμεῖν ποιοῦμαι, but if he is approved the Emperor will himself pay the fee.

δοκιμή

is cited by Grimm from Dioscorides, who flourished under Hadrian (acc. to W. Christ): Paul is accordingly the earliest authority, but certainly not the coiner, unless we are to make the medical writer dependent on him. If δοκιμάω really existed as a by-form of δοκιμάζω, δοκίμησις might produce δοκιμή as ἀγάπησις produced ἀγάπη and ἀπάντησις ἀπάντη. In any case δοκιμή is a new formation of the Hellenistic age.

δόκιμος.

Since Deissmann (BS p. 259 ff.) drew this unsuspected adjective from the papyri to interpret Jas 1[3] and 1 Pet 1[7]—a good example with which to meet those who assert that the papyri have not given us any new meanings for NT words—examples have been further accumulating, e.g. BGU IV. 1065[6] (A.D. 97) ἀπέχειν αὐτὸν τιμὴν χρυσίου δοκιμεί[ο]υ μναιαίων ὀκτώ, and so[20], ib. 1045[ii 12] (A.D. 154) τὴν φερνὴν

χ[ρ]υσίου δοκιμίου τετάρτας τέσσαρες, *ib.* III. 717[8] (A.D.
149) χρυσίου δοκιμείου σταθμῷ Ἀλεξανδρείνῳ, P Tebt II.
302[22] (A.D. 134 5) χρυσίου [δ]οκιμίου, "standard gold"
(Edd.). Hort's divination (1 *Pet.* p. 42) detected that the
needed meaning in the NT passages was "what is genuine
in your faith": the papyri have given a welcome endorsement to the master's instinct, and have at the same time
rendered unnecessary his preference for the less well attested
reading τὸ δόκιμον (*Notes on Select Readings*, p. 102, in *The
NT in Grk*[2] ii. Appendix). For the noun δοκιμεῖον =
"crucible," which is found in the LXX, cf. *OGIS* 308[15]
(ii/B.C.) καὶ τῆ(ς) πρὸς θεοὺς εὐσεβείας ἔ[ργ]ωι καλλί[στω]ι
οὐ μεικρὸν δοκιμεῖον ἀπέλιπεν, *Syll* 588[9] (*c.* B.C. 180)
δοκιμεῖα. The editor in his note on the last passage compares *IGSI* 303[28] ἐγδότω δὲ ἡ ἀρχὴ [κ]αὶ ἐξ οὗ ἂν παραλάβῃ
χρυσίου ἀσήμου καὶ ἐπισήμου κατασκευάσαι τῷ θεῷ φιάλην
χρυσῆν, καταλιπομένη δοκιμεῖον.

δόκιμος.

P Hamb I. 2[15] (A.D. 59) ἀργύριον ἐπίσημον δόκιμον
ἀρεστὸν ἀνυπόλογον παντὸς ὑπ[ο]λόγου. P Amh II. 86[9]
(A.D. 121) τὸ (*l.* τὸν) δὲ ἀργυρικὸν φόρον δόκιμον ἄριστον
(οι ἀριστόν for ἀρεστόν), P Oxy II. 265[25] (A.D. 81–95)
τὰ τοῦ χρυσίου δοκίμου μναιαῖα τέσσαρα. P Flor I. 41[16]
(A.D. 140) τὸ μὲν ἀργύριον δόκιμον, τὸν δὲ πυρὸν νέον
καθ(αρὸν) ἄδολ(ον), so *ib.* 72[11] (A.D. 128–9), etc. The combination with ἀρεστός in the first (and probably the second)
citation may partly illustrate the combination of Rom 14[18]
(cf. 12[2]). In another combination we have the adj. in
the Will of Epicteta, *Michel* 1001[b] [31] (Theran Doric—
c. B.C. 200) παρεξοῦντι δὲ οἱ δωρεὰν ἐπιμηνιεύοντες οἶνον
ξενικὸν ἱκανὸν δόκιμον ἕως τριῶν πινόντων.

δοκός.

In P Petr II. 33[b] [24] (a steward's account) we have mention of δοκοί in a fragmentary context, but following τὰ
ξύλα. Cf. P Lond 280[11] (A.D. 55) (= II. p. 194, *Chrest.* I.
p. 371) ἐκ τῶν ἐμῶν δαπανῶ[ν μ]ηχανὴν ἐλαιου[ργικὴν καὶ
τ]ῆς αὐτῆς θυίαν καὶ τὰ ἀνήκοντα ξυλικά[α] καὶ
δοκὸν τὴν ὑπὲρ τ[ὴ]ν μηχανὴν προσαγγέλλω, τοῦτο κτλ.,
Chrest. I. 176[15] (middle i/A.D.) ἐπεὶ οὖν καὶ αὐτὸ τὸ
ἐλαιουργῖον συνεχυτρώθη καὶ ἠναγκάσθην δοκοὺς καὶ ἐρείσματα παρατιθένα[ι, "props" for the repair of an oil-press,
P Flor II. 127[5] (A.D. 256) τὸ βαλανεῖον παντὶ τρόπῳ ποίησον
ὑποκαυθῆναι καὶ δοκοὺς εἰς αὐτὸ παρενεχθῆναι ποιήσας,
"logs" for the heating of a bath. *Syll* 587[62] (B.C. 329–8)
mentions δοκοί and στρωτῆρες together in the accounts for
the building of a temple τοῖν θεοῖν: Dittenberger shows that
the prices indicate the former to be heavy beams on which
the latter were laid transversely. It is obvious that the
Oriental hyperbole in Mt 7[3ff] will admit of no tempering
from the usage of the word. A new verb δοκόω, "furnish
with beams," occurs in the P Grenf II. 35[6] (B.C. 98),
P Amh II. 51[13, 23] (B.C. 88), P Ryl II. 240[3] (B.C. 118).

δόλιος.

We can quote the derived abstract from Vettius Valens,
p. 2[3] τυφώδεις, ἀποκρύπτοντας τὴν δολιότητα, αὐστήρους
κτλ. The verb δολιόω (LXX and NT), "not found in
prof. writ.," was easily formed when wanted, but whether the
translator of Num 25[18] was the first to coin it no one can say.

δόλος.

For δόλος in the forensic sense, as Deut 27[24], cf. the
Jewish prayer for vengeance from Rheneia, *Syll* 816[3]
(ii/i B.C.) ἐπὶ τοὺς δόλωι φονεύσαντας: see Deissmann
LAE. p. 423ff. Cf. the compound δολοφονέω, BGU II.
388[i 23] (ii/iii A.D.), *Syll* 324[19] (i/B.C.). In BGU I. 326[ii 3]
(a will—A.D. 189) we find ταύτῃ τῇ διαθήκῃ δόλος πονηρὸς
ἀπέστη (= ἀπέστω). Mommsen (*Sitzungsberichte der
Akad. zu Berlin*, phil.-hist. Klasse, 18 Jan. 1894, p. 50)
states that he has not met the phrase elsewhere in this
connexion, and compares the common formula on graves,
ab hoc monumento dolus malus abesto. A much earlier
instance of δόλος πονηρός is *Syll* 319[9] (ii/B.C.) μήτε να[υσὶν
βοηθείτωσαν δημοσ]ίαι βουλῇ μετὰ δόλου πονηροῦ: cf. *OGIS*
629[112] (A.D. 137) χωρὶ[ς] δόλου πο[νηροῦ, PSI III. 158[17]
(astrological ?iii/A.D.) διὰ μετεωρισμῶν καὶ κακῶν [δόλ]ων.
The first of these inscriptions is about contemporaneous with
the famous Oscan *Tabula Bantina*, where *perum dolom
mallom* recurs (with other parts of the noun), representing
sine dolo malo. In view of the fixity of the formula in Italy
from the beginning of our records, we can hardly doubt that
it was transferred to Greek from Italic: it is noteworthy
that *Syll* 319 was obviously Latin in phrase before it took
Greek form. The meaning "taint," of material things,
which gives us ἄδολος as described *sub voce.*, appears in the
formula for χρυσοῦ δόλος in the chemical papyrus P Leid
X [iii. 10] (iii/A.D.). So *ib.* [iv 13 f] in a test (δοκιμασία) for
unstamped silver (see under ἄσημος): ἄσημον ἐπιγνῶναι εἰ
δόλον ἔχει· κατάθου εἰς ἅλμην, θέρμην (*l.* θέρμαινε), ἐὰν δόλον
ἔχῃ μέλαν γείνεται. Add Vettius Valens, p. 73[11] ἐξ ὀνειδισμῶν
καὶ ἐνέδρας καὶ δόλου καὶ ἐπιθέσεως ἀναγομένους. The word
is MGr.

δολόω.

Like δόλος, the verb is found in P Leid X[37] and [vii.3]
(iii/iv A.D.)—κασσίτερον γνῶναι εἰ δεδόλωται· χωνεύσας
αὐτὸν κτλ., and δολοῦται χρυσὸς εἰς αὔξησιν μισύει καὶ γῇ
Σινωπίδι κτλ. See also *Syll* 802[102] (ii/B.C.) δολωθεὶς ὑπὸ
ματρυιᾶς, and Vettius Valens p. 248[2] ὁπόταν δὲ κακωθῇ,
δολουμένη ἀδιανόητος γίνεται. Our first instance reinforces
Grimm's quotation from Lucian and Thayer's from Dioscurides to make clear the metaphor of 2 Cor 4[2].

δόμα.

P Petr III. 42 C[1] [4] (B.C. 255) οὐδενὶ τρόπῳ ἐργάζονται
διὰ τὸ μ[ὴ ἔχειν τὰ δέ]οντα, τὸ γὰρ προδοθὲν αὐτοῖς δόμ[α
ἀνενηνόχασιν] ἡμῖν καταβεβρωκέναι, σχολάζοντ[ες ἐξ διατελοῦσι—with reference to the idleness of certain quarrymen,
owing to some defective supply. For the preference for the
short radical vowel in nouns of this class in Hellen. Grk see
Thackeray *Gr.* i. p. 79, Mayser *Gr.* p. 65.

δόξα.

In the account of a popular demonstration at Oxyrhynchus,
P Oxy I. 41[4] (iii/iv A.D.), the prytanis is hailed as δόξα
πόλεω[ς. Deissmann (*Hellenisierung d. Semitischen Monotheismus*, p. 165 f.) throws out the suggestion that the word
may originally have had a "realistic" meaning in the
ordinary Grk of the day, and cites as a partial parallel its use
as a name for women and ships (cf. F. Bechtel, *Die attischen
Frauennamen* (1902), p. 132). The plur. δόξαι occurs in the

astrological papyrus PSI III. 158[24, 41] (? iii/A.D.). For the Biblical history of the word, see Milligan *Thess.* p. 27 and Kennedy *St Paul's Conceptions of the Last Things*, p. 209 ff. In an early Christian prayer *NL. Stud.* as cited *s.v.* δόγμα p. 69 we have [21] α[ἰ]νέσεις καὶ δοξολογείας [ἀνα]φ[έρ]ομέν σοι. A familiar NT phrase is applied to the sun in P Leid W[si. 7] (ii/iii A.D.) Ἀχεβυχρωμ, ὃ ὃ (om.) μηνύει τοῦ δίσκου τὴν φλόγα κ αἰ τὴν ἀκτῖνα, οὗ ἡ δόξα · ααα, ηηη, ωωω, ὅτι διά σ' ἐνεδοξάσθη ἀέρας (? a new nom., anticipating MGr): see also below *s.v.* δύναμις.

δοξάζω.

The verb is found in the sepulchral epitaph of a *mimus*, already cited *s.v.* δεισιδαίμων, *Kaibel* 607[7] (iii/A.D.) εὐφρανθεὶς ἐφ' ὅσον μοῖραι χρόνου ὥρισαν αὐτῷ, εὐσεβίης ἕνεκεν δοξασθεὶς καὶ μετὰ λήθην. As illustrating the NT usage of this word, the following invocation from the magical papyrus P Lond 121[502 ff] (iii/A.D.) (= I. p. 100) is noteworthy—κυρία Ἶσις . . . δόξασόν μοι (for με), ὡς ἐδόξασα τὸ (ὄνομα) τοῦ υἱοῦ (pap. υἱοῦς) σου Ὥρου: cf. Reitzenstein *Poimandres*, p. 22 n[5]. See Anz *Subsidia*, p. 350. A further magical quotation was given above under δόξα. Grimm's "use not found in prof. writ." viz. "to make glorious, adorn with lustre" etc., disappears from that category, as we might expect: cf. also *OGIS* 168[5] (B.C. 115) ἐν Ἐλ[ε]φαντίνηι ἱεροῦ δεδοξασμένου ἐξ ἀρχαίων καὶ [. . . The verb survives in MGr, with partic. δοξασμένος as an adj., "celebrated."

Δορκάς

is found as a feminine name among both Greeks and Jews (see Knowling *ad* Ac 9[36] in *EGT*). An interesting example is afforded by a Delphic inscription of ii/B.C., *Syll* 854[11, 2], where a certain Alexon entrusts the care of a manumitted slave of this name to one Thracidas—τρεφ[έ]τω Θραικίδας Δορκάδα, εἴ κα θέλῃ [ο]ἰκεῖν ἐν τα[ὐ]τῶι · εἰ δὲ μή, ἐνβαλ-λέτω Θραικίδας Δορκάδι τροφὰν τοῦ μηνὸς ἑκάστου πυρῶν τέσσαρα ἡμίεκτα κτλ. See also Deissmann *BS*, p. 189, *ZNTW* i. p. 88. The diminutive, which is found in LXX Isai 13[14], occurs in a papyrus letter P Lond 413[14] (c. A.D. 346) (= II. p. 302), complaining of the gazelles which are spoiling the writer's crops—ἐπιδὴ τὰ δορκάδι[α] ἀφανίζουσειν τὸ (l. τὰ σπόριμα.

δόσις.

The word is very common in financial transactions. Thus it is = "instalment" in P Petr III. 41[8, 19] τὴν β δόσιν, "the second instalment," so *ib.* 46 1)[27] τὴν δευτέραν δόσιν, P Oxy IV. 724[7] (A.D. 155) ἐξ ὧν ἔσχες τὴν πρώτην δόσιν ἐν δραχμαῖς τεσσαράκοντα, "of which sum you have received the first instalment amounting to 40 drachmae" (Edd.), *ib.* VIII. 1127[19] (A.D. 183) ἀποδότω τῷ μεμισθωκότι τὸ ἐνοίκιον κατ' ἔτος ἐν δόσεσι δυσὶ διὰ ἑξαμήνου τὰς αἱρούσας δραχμὰς τριάκοντα, "shall pay the rent annually in two half-yearly instalments of 30 drachmae" (Ed.). Similarly *ib.* VI. 912[30] (A.D. 235). For δόσις in connexion with the payment of a rate or tax, see P Flor II. 133[5] A.D. 257) ἔδι μὲν ὑμᾶς μηδὲ ὑπομνήσεως χρήζειν ἰδόντων ὑμῶν τὰς τακτὰς ἡμέρας τῆς δόσεως—a delicately worded reminder with reference to the dyke-tax: cf. *Ostr* 6[1] (ii/A.D.) in Fayûm Papyri p. 322, δόσις βαλ ανευτικῶν?). In a proposed lease of a vineyard,

P Lond 163[32] (A.D. 88 = II. p. 185) we find provision εἰς μισθῶν δόσιν, and in BGU II. 473[9] (A.D. 200) ἕνεκεν χρηματικῆς δόσεως. Add P Oxy III. 474[21] (? A.D. 184) ἐπέσχεν ἂν τὴν δόσιν τοῦ φθάσαντος αὐτῷ ὑπὸ σοῦ ἐξοδιασθῆναι ἀργυρίου, and *SyII* 540[11] (B.C. 175–1) ἐργάται δὲ συνεχῶς μετὰ τὸ τὴν δόσιν λαβεῖν ἐντὸς ἡμερῶν δέκα, with the editor's note where δόσις is explained as "pensio pretii qua redemptor opus licitus est." *ib.* 505[12] (early iii/B.C.) περὶ τὴν τοῦ σ[ίτου δόσιν illustrates the use with other than money objects; while *ib.* 858[11] (ii B.C. Delphi) εἰ δέ τινι ζῶων δόσιν ποέοιτο τῶν ἰδίων Σῶσος, shows it as a pure *nomen actionis*. So also BGU IV. 1151[23] (B.C. 13) οὐδεμί αν δόσιν κοιλῆ ν ποιούμενοι, *ib.* 1150[16] B.C. 13) ἐὰν δέ τινα τῶν καθ' ἡ[μέραν δ]όσεων κοιλάνωσι. The combination with λῆμψις, as in Phil 4[15], is of the same character: with this cf. the astrological fragment, P Tebt II. 277[16] iii/A.D.) δόσις καὶ λήμψις plur.). The distinction from δόμα is observed throughout the documents: we have not noticed any instances of the purely concrete use generally recognised in Jas 1[17]. A form δόσιμος (MGr δόσιμο) is found in the long list of royal ordinances, P Tebt I. 5[176] (B.C. 118) τῶν δ' ἄλλων τῶν δοσίμων μὴ πλεῖον ἐπισταθμεύεσθαι τοῦ ἡμίσους, where the editors render, "and in the case of their other buildings which may be used for quarters, not more than half shall be occupied for that purpose."

δότης.

For this rare form, which in 2 Cor 9[7] Paul borrows from LXX of Prov 22[8], Nageli (p. 62 n[1]) compares ἐκδότης ("Verdinger") in *CIG* 2347c[61] (pre-Christian).

δουλαγωγέω.

For δ. used in a moral sense, as in 1 Cor 9[27], we may cite Epict. iii. 24. 76 τί λέγεις πρὸς τοῦτον τὸν δουλαγωγοῦντά σε; "what sayest thou to this man who is treating thee as a slave?" cf. *ib.* iv. 7. 17 (Sharp *Epictetus and the NT*, p. 71). For the subst. used literally cf. P Oxy I. 38[10] (A.D. 49–50) (= *Selections*, p. 53) τοῦ Σύρ[ου] ἐπικεχειρη-κότος ἀποσπάσαι εἰς δουλαγωγία[ν] τὸν ἀφήλικά μου υἱὸν Ἀπίωνα, "Syrus having endeavoured to carry off into slavery my young son Apion," *ib.* IX. 1206[11] (A.D. 335) εἰς δουλαγωγείαν ἄγειν, and the dialect inscription, apparently of Roman times, *Syll* 841[11] εἰ δέ τις ἐπιλανβάνοιτο αὐτῶν ἢ καταδουλίζοιτο, ἅ τε γενηθῖσα δουλαγωγία αὐτῶν ἄκυρος καὶ ἀρεμένα (l. ἀρμένα = ἡρμένη) ἔστω.

δουλεία.

P Ryl II. 153[32] ἔξι[. . ἐφ' ὃν αὐτὴ περίεστιν χρόνον τὴν τῶν αὐτῶν δούλων δουλ[ίαν, "shall retain for so long as she survives the services of the said slaves" (Edd.). P Grenf II. 75[4] (A.D. 305) ὁμολογῶ τετροφευκέν[αι] σοι τὸ τέταρτον μέρος τῆς δουλίας, where, according to the editors, "the sense seems to require that δουλεία should be taken in its abstract meaning, and τὸ τέταρτον μέρος as an indirect accusative." The document is an acknowledgement by Tapaous, a νεκροτάφη of the city of Month, that she had received payment for food and clothing as one of four nurses in a certain household. In MGr δουλειά is used generally of any work or task, especially of a menial character.

δουλεύω.

We can cite no example of δ. used in a religious sense from pagan literature, but the syncretistic occult P Leid W xiii.38 (ii/iii A.D.) shows it : ὅτι δουλεύω ὑπὸ τὸν σὸν κόσμον τῷ σῷ ἀγγέλῳ. Note also the mention of the ἱερόδουλοι in connexion with the Serapeum in P Leid D i.22 (B.C. 162) σοὶ δὲ γίνοιτο, ἀνθ' ὧν πρὸς τὸ θεῖον ὁσίως διάκ[ει]σαι καὶ τῶν ἱεροδούλων καὶ τῶν ἐν τῷ ἱερῷ π[ά]ντων ἀντιλαμβάνῃ, ἐπαφροδισία, χάρις κτλ., and in P Tebt I. 6²⁵ (B.C. 140–39) where reference is made to the revenues accruing to the priests from various sources including the ἱερόδουλοι. The mention immediately afterwards of "the so-called ἀφροδίσια" leads the editors to believe that these ἱερόδουλοι were ἑταῖραι, like the votaries of Aphrodite at Corinth : but cf. Otto (Priester i. p. 118), who understands simply a "lower" order of priests in contrast to the titled priests. See Grenfell-Hunt's note on P Tebt l.c. Δουλεύω in MGr = "work," "serve."

δοῦλος.

In Wilcken Ostr. i. p. 681 ff. there is a valuable account of the occupations which in the Graeco-Roman world were monopolized by slave labour. Among those that were not, the following classes, which are represented in the NT, are mentioned—ἁλιεύς, ἀμπελουργός, γεωργός, γραμματεύς, διδάσκαλος, ἔμπορος, ἐργάτης, ἰατρός, ναύκληρος, ποιμήν, τέκτων, τραπεζίτης, χαλκεύς. For the Pauline δοῦλος Χριστοῦ it is sufficient to refer to Deissmann's well-known discussion (LAE, p. 323 ff.), in which the phrase is set in the light of old Greek custom, and especially of the right of manumission as evidenced by the Delphic inscriptions.

A further contrast is drawn later (p. 381) with the familiar title a "slave of the Emperor," as in the Phrygian inscription, BCH xxviii. (1904) p. 195. Ἀγαθόποδι δούλῳ τοῦ κυρίου αὐτοκράτορος. Reference may also be made to Thackeray Gr. i. p. 8, where the growing tendency in the LXX renderings to emphasize the distance between God and man is shown by θεράπων giving place to οἰκέτης, this to παῖς, and this again to δοῦλος. The phrase of Mt 25³⁰ is found in P Par 68E.54 (Imperial) ἀχρείους δούλους. (See under ἀχρεῖος, where however Mt l.c. is accidentally overlooked). On Δοῦλα as a proper name, see Proleg. p. 48 n¹.

The adj. δουλικός, which is not found in the NT, is very common—BGU IV. 1058¹² (B.C. 13) δουλικὸν παιδίον, ib. I. 193¹² (A.D. 136) δουλικὸν ἔγγονον, P Tebt II. 407⁵ (?A.D. 199) δουλικὰ σώμ[ατ]α, etc. Δοῦλος, fem. δούλα, remains in MGr.

δουλόω.

The negatived verbal may be quoted from OGIS 449⁶, an honorific decree of the Pergamenes to P. Servilius Isauricus, proconsul of Asia B.C. 46, whom they describe as ἀποδεδωκότα τῆι πόλει τοὺς πατρίους νόμους καὶ τὴν δημοκρατίαν ἀδούλωτον.

δοχή.

This word in its NT sense of "entertainment" is read by Schubart (see Berichtigungen, p. 5) in BGU III. 815¹⁵ ὁ Σωκρά[τ]ης ὁ προ[κου]ράτωρ μου κόπους [τινὰ]ς πα[ρ]έχῃ περὶ τῆς [δο]χῆς (pap. [. . .] λης). The derivative δοχικός may be quoted as adj. from P Ryl II. 85¹⁴ (A.D. 185) [μέτρῳ

δημο]σίῳ δοχικῷ, "measured by the official standard," and as a neuter noun ib. 200⁵ ff. (A.D. 111–2) (πυροῦ) δοχ(ικῷ) "by receiving measure" (Edd.). See the long note, P Hib I. p. 228 f., on the ratio of an artaba ἀνηλωτικῷ, "by spending measure," to one δοχικῷ, the former being 2½ larger. In ib. 87¹³ (B.C. 256–5) the same is called μέτροις παραδ[ο]χικοῖς. Δοχή itself is common in accounts : see e.g. index to P Tebt I.

δράκων

is common in the magic papyri, e.g. P Leid W ii.5 (ii/iii A.D.) δράκοντα δάκνοντα τῇ (l. τὴν) οὐράν, so x.28, ib. V iii.16 (iii/iv A.D.) δράκων εἶ πτεροειδής, P Lond 121⁵⁸⁶ (iii/A.D.) (= I. p. 102) ὁ δράκων οὐροβόρος, ib. ⁷⁸¹, and PSI I. 28⁴ (?iii/iv A.D.), 29⁹ (?iv/A.D.). In P Oxy III. 490¹² (A.D. 124) one of the witnesses to a will records that ἔστιν μου ἡ σφ[ραγὶς] δρακόμορφος : the edd. correct to δρακοντόμορφος, but in view of the common MGr δράκος, the bogey of many a folk-story, it seems better to assume the short form as genuine. It is one of many anticipations of MGr in a simplified word-formation.

In a Christian amulet, Kaibel 1140 b 3, Satan is addressed as μί[α]σμα, δράκων, θη[ρῶν λ]όχε, κτλ.

δράσσομαι.

For this verb, which is found in the NT only in 1 Cor 3¹⁹, where it is substituted for the less vivid καταλαμβάνων of the LXX Job 5¹³, cf. P Oxy X. 1298¹⁰ (iv/A.D.) σὲ γὰρ μόνον ἔχω μάρτυρα πῶς ὁ Γοῦνθος δραξάμενός μου — "laid hands on me." An otherwise unknown active is doubtfully restored in P Lond 1170 verso¹¹³ (A.D. 258–9) (= III. p. 196) ὁμοί[ως] δ[ρά]ττοντες χόρτον ἐν τῷ ἀ κλήρῳ). For the constr. with the acc. in the NT passage see Proleg. p. 65. For the subst. δράγμα = "handful," then "sheaf," as Gen 37⁷, Ruth 2⁷, cf. P Fay 120⁹ (c. A.D. 100) θέρισον τὸν ὤ[γ]μον τῆς Ἀπιάδος καὶ λύσις εὐθέω εἰς Ἀ. [. .] τὰ δράγματα, "reap the field at Apias and let the sheaves go off immediately to A. ." (Edd.). From a series of farm-accounts, P Fay 102 (c. A.D. 105), it appears that the wages paid to workmen were coupled with accounts of γόμοι and δράγμ(ατα) of wheat and barley : see the editors' introduction, and cf. P Cairo Preis 44⁸ (ii/iii A.D.), where a payment is made εἰς δράγμα χόρτου. The compounds δραγματηγία and δραγματηγέω are found P Flor II. 185³.17 (A.D. 254), and in P Petr III. 28 verso (d)⁶ (B.C. 260?) we have ἐδραγματοκλέπτει, "stole sheaves in gleaning."

δραχμή.

This coin, which is only mentioned in the NT in Lk 15⁸ f., was of the same value as the denarius in ordinary calculations or about 9½d. : see Kennedy in Hastings' D.B. iii. p. 428. Raphael when he accepted service with Tobit did so for δραχμὴν τῆς ἡμέρας καὶ τὰ δέοντά σοι (Tobit 5¹⁵) : cf. Mt 20² ff. In BGU I. 183 (a will—A.D. 85) we read of a bequest Στοτοῆτι καὶ Ὥρωι ἑκάστῳ [ἀ]νὰ ἀργυ[ρίου δρα]χμὰς ὀκτώ. The same sum is mentioned in the will of Thaesis, P Tebt II. 381¹⁵ (A.D. 123) (= Selections, p. 79) where the editors conjecture that it may have been "a conventional legacy where a serious bequest was not intended": cf. our "cut off with a shilling." According to Thackeray Gr. i. p. 103 the form δραγμή, which is found in late MSS

of the LXX (2 Macc 4[19], 10[50] etc.), does not occur in the
Ptolemaic papyri. As against the ordinary derivation of
δραχμή from **δράσσομαι**, Lewy (*Fremdwörter*, p. 18) makes
it of Eastern origin, connecting it with the Phoenician
דרכמין : see also BDB *Heb. Lex.* under this word, and
Boisacq *Etym. Lex. s.v.* **δράσσομαι** and **δραχμή**. **Δραχμή**
is of course still in use as the name of a coin, worth about a
franc.

δρέπανον.

P Magd 8[6] (B.C. 218) **δρέπανον θεριστικὸν οὗ τιμὴ
(δραχμαὶ) β̄**, "a sickle for reaping worth 2 drachmae."
P Petr II. 33[a].[16] **καὶ φελίου καὶ δρεπάνου**. In two (apparently Jewish or Jewish Christian) inscrr. from Phrygia we
find **δρέπανον** used in connexion with an imprecation—
C. and B. ii. p. 565, no. 466, **ἐὰν δέ τις αὐτῶν μὴ φοβηθῇ
τούτων τῶν καταρῶν, τὸ ἀρᾶς δρέπανον εἰσέλθοιτο εἰς τὰς
οἰκήσις αὐτῶν καὶ μηδίναν ἐνκαταλείψετο**: cf. *ib.* p. 652,
no. 563. MGr **δρεπάνι**.

δρόμος

in NT keeps the older sense as *nomen actionis*, = **τὸ δραμεῖν**.
For this cf. Wünsch *AF* 3[13] (Carthage, imperial), where
rivals in a race are vigorously cursed—**κατάδησον αὐτῶν τὰ
σκέλη καὶ τὴν ὁρμὴν καὶ τὸ πήδημα καὶ τὸν δρόμον**. So of
the sun and moon, P Leid W[xiii] 29 (ii/iii A.D.) **δρόμους
ἔχειν τακτούς**. In Egypt it had become specialized to
denote a place where running might no doubt take place,
though the possibility is no more remembered than in some of
our modern *-drome* compounds. See Wilcken *Ostr.* i. p. 771.
Dittenberger on *OGIS* 178[11], and Otto *Priester* i. p. 284. It
was the area in front of the entrance to a temple, paved with
stones—cf. P Flor I. 50[97] (A.D. 268) **ἐπὶ τοῦ λιθοστρώτου
δρόμου Ἑρμοῦ**—and often adorned with Sphinxes: it often
became a central point in the business life of the city:
see Strabo 17, p. 805, 28 cited *al* P Hamb I. 5[18]. BGU
IV. 1130[10] (B.C. 4) **ὧν γείτον]ες νότωι δρόμος τοῦ ἱεροῦ
Χ[νο]ύβεως θεοῦ μεγίστου** will serve as an example. Hence
the **μέτρον δρόμων** came to denote such a measure as
was customary on the **δρόμος**. In their note on P Fay 19[8]
(i/B.C.) GH describe **δρό(μῳ)** as "the artaba of the largest
capacity": see further the introd. to *ib.* 101 (B.C. 18) where
we have in l.3 the full formula. **πυροῦ δρό(μῳ) (ἀρτάβαι) γ
(ἥμισυ) ἔ**, "3½ large artabae of wheat." See also the note
on P Tebt I. 61 (*b*)[350], and *Archiv* ii. p. 202f. In MGr
δρόμος = "way," "street," and this is practically what we
have in P Par 15[16] (B.C. 120), where we read of a house
**ἥ ἐστιν ἐκ τοῦ ἀπὸ νότου καὶ λιβὸς τῆς Διοσπόλεως, ἀπὸ
βορρᾶ τοῦ δρόμου τοῦ ἄγοντος ἐπὶ ποταμὸν τῆς μεγίστης
θεᾶς Ἥρας**, and in P Oxy VI. 911[12] (A.D. 233 or 265) of
property situated **ἐπ' ἀμφόδου Δρόμου Θοήριδος**, "in the
quarter of the Square of Thoeris" (Edd.). For **δρόμος** in
connexion with racing contests see Vettius Valens p. 2[31]
ὅθεν καὶ δρόμον ταῖς ἀθλήσεσι παρέχεται. In P Oxy VI.
900[6] (A.D. 322) **τοῦ ὀξέος δρόμου** the editors, following
Wilcken, find a reference to the express postal service, and
so probably in P Flor I. 36[7] (A.D. 300) etc. For Ps 18(19)[5],
where **δρόμος** might have been very fitly used, we may
compare the portentous "impromptu" **καίριον**) which Q.
Sulpicius Maximus perpetrated for his tomb, *Kaibel* 618[9]:
μούνῳ σοὶ πυρόεντος ἐπειγομένῳ κύκλοιο ἀντολίη καὶ πᾶσα

καλὸς δρόμος ἔπλετο δυσμή. The "poet" may well have
borrowed his phrase from some predecessor less unworthy
of being named with the Hebrew singer.

δύναμαι.

The following exx. of this common verb may be cited—
P Par 47[10] (c. B.C. 153) (= *Selections*, p. 22) **ἐνβέβληκαν** (*sc.*
οἱ θεοὶ) **ὑμᾶς εἰς ὕλην μεγάλην καὶ οὐ δυνάμεθα ἀποθανεῖν**,
"they have cast us into a great forest, where we may possibly die." P Oxy IV. 743[29] (B.C. 2) **οὐκ ἠδυνάσθην συντυχεῖν Ἀ.**, "I was unable to meet A.," *ib.* 744[12] (B.C. 1) (=
Selections, p. 33) **πῶς δύναμαί σε ἐπιλαθεῖν**: "how can I
forget you?". P Lond 144[11] (?i/A.D.) (= II. p. 253) **ἵνα
δυνηθῇ τὸ παιδάριόν μου ἐλθεῖν πρό[ς μ]ε**, P Oxy III. 472[10]
(c. A.D. 130) **οὐ δύναται γὰρ κεκλέφθαι τὸ μηδ' ἀρχὴν
γενόμενον μὴ δυνατὸν δ' εἶναι**, "for it is impossible for that
to have been stolen which neither ever existed at all nor
could exist" (Edd.). It takes an *aor. ref* as in I.l. 12[6] in
P Ryl II. 77[38] (A.D. 192) **οὐ γὰρ δύναμαι κοσμητείαν**. In
P Leid Uiv[30] (ii/B.C.) **ἔφη δύνασθαι τὰ ἔργα πάντα ἐπιτε
λέσαι ἐν ηλι** (= was ὀλίγαις meant?) **ἡμέραι** (*l.* αις) we
have **δ.** construed with the fut. inf. as a substitute for the
aor. For the form **δύνομαι**, which is read by B in Mt 19[12],
26[54] etc. cf. BGU II. 388[ii] (ii/iii A.D.) **ἐγώ, ἃ δύναμαι
ἐνθάδε εὑρίσκειν, ζητῶ**, *ib.* I. 159[5] (A.D. 216) **ἀπέστη]ν τῆς
κώμης οὐ δυνόμενος ὑποστῆναι τὸ βάρος τῆς λειτουργίας**,
P Catt[iii] 22 (ii/B.C.) (= *Chrest.* II. p. 421): (see further
Deissmann *BS*, p. 193). In P Par 45[2] (B.C. 153) we have
ἅ σ'οὐ δεδύνησμαι διασαφῆσαι διὰ τοῦ ἐπιστολίου, and in
P Oxy VI. 939[15] (iv/A.D.) **εἴ πως ἐκ παντὸς τρόπου δυνηθείης
[πρὸς ἡμᾶς] ἀφικέσθαι**. According to Meisterhans *Gr.*
p. 169, **δύναμαι** first begins to augment with η in the Attic
inscrr. after B.C. 300. It occurs in some of the earliest
papyri, as P Hib I. 27[34] (iii/B.C. *init.*), 34[b] (B.C. 243-2). The
future **δυνηθήσομαι** is found in P Lond 897[15] (A.D. 84)
(= III. p. 207), and the aorist **ἠδυνάσθην** in P Petr III.
42 C (14)[1] (B.C. 255 : see Mayser *Gr.* p. 393 for other
forms. MGr has **δύνομαι**.

δύναμις

For the more ordinary meanings of **δύναμις** we may cite
such passages as P Oxy II. 292[5] (c. A.D. 25) (= *Selections*,
p. 37) **διὸ παρακαλῶ σε μετὰ πάσης δυνάμεως ἔχειν
αὐτὸν συνεσταμένον**, "wherefore I beg you with all my
power to hold him as one recommended to you," *ib.* VI.
809[8] (A.D. 200) **ἐς ὅσον μὲν οὖν δύναμίς μοι ὑπῆρχεν**, "as
long as I had the power," *ib.* 940[4] (v/A.D.) **τὴν τῶν ἄλλων
μερίδων δύναμιν**, "the capacity of the other holdings" (Edd.),
and, for a Christian example, *ib.* VIII. 1150[9] a prayer—
vi/A.D. **ὁ θεὸς . . . δείξον τὴν δύναμ[ίν σου**. In P Petr II.
3 (*b*)[2] we have **παρὰ δύναμιν**, and **κατὰ δύναμιν**, "according
to one's means," as in 2 Cor 8[3], is very common, especially in
marriage contracts, as when in BGU IV. 1050[14] (time of Augustus) a certain Dionysius undertakes **τρέφειν καὶ ἱματίζειν
τὴν Ἰσιδώραν ὡς γυναῖκα γα[μετὴν] κατὰ δύναμιν**. In *ib.*
1051[17] (same date) we have the fuller phrase **κατὰ δύναμιν
τῶν ὑπαρχόντων**, and in *ib.* III. 717[19] (A.D. 149) **κ]ατὰ
δύναμιν [το]ῦ βί[ου**. P Oxy IV. 282[8] (A.D. 30-5) shows
the contrasting phrase, again as in 2 Cor 8[3], when a man
makes a complaint against his wife, notwithstanding the
fact that he had provided for her in a manner "beyond his

means" –ἐ]γὼ μὲν οὖν ἐπεχορήγησα αὐτῇ τὰ ἑξῆς καὶ ὑπὲρ δύναμιν. The combination of Mt 6¹³ LW@ is found in P Leid W¹ⁱⁱ ²⁹ (ii/iii A.D.) σὺ γὰρ ἔδωκας ἡλίῳ τὴν δόξαν καὶ τὴν δύναμιν ἅπασαν. Ramsay (*Recent Discovery*, p. 118) has drawn pointed attention to the technical use of δύναμις "in the language of religion, superstition, and magic," and describes it as "one of the most common and characteristic terms in the language of pagan devotion. 'Power' was what the devotees respected and worshipped; any exhibition of 'power' must have its cause in something that was divine." He quotes by way of illustration from Lydia a dedication to the goddess, εὐ)λογῶν σου τὰς δυνάμις (Buresch, *Aus Lydien*, p. 113), and also (p. 117), in illustration of Ac 8¹⁰, another Lydian inscription, "There is one God in the heavens, great Mēn the Heavenly, the great power of the ever-living God"—μεγάλη δύναμις τοῦ ἀθανάτου θεοῦ (Keil and Premerstein, II *Reise in Lydien*, p. 110). Another parallel to the same passage in Acts is cited by Deissmann (*BS*, p. 336) from the great Paris magical papyrus, 1275 ff. (Wessely i. 76) ἐπικαλοῦμαί σε τὴν μεγίστην δύναμιν τὴν ἐν τῷ οὐρανῷ (ἄλλοι : τὴν ἐν τῇ ἄρκτῳ) ὑπὸ κυρίου θεοῦ τεταγμένην. In Vettius Valens δύναμις is used as a synonym for ἀγωγή (p. 172²⁵ etc.). For "forces" i.e. "troops," cf. OGIS 139⁸ (B.C. 140-16) αἱ ἀκολουθοῦσαι δυνάμεις. MGr has ἡ δύναμι (decl. like nouns in -η).

δυναμόω.

For this new verb, which is found in a few late LXX books and twice in the NT (Col 1¹¹, Heb 11³⁴) we may cite the early Christian prayer (referred to *s.v.* δόγμα) p. 7¹²¹ δυνάμωσον ἡμᾶς ἐ[ν τῇ σῇ] ἀντιλήμψει · καὶ φώτισον ἐν τῇ[σῇ πα]ρακλήσει, also P Leid W¹ⁱⁱⁱ ¹⁶ (ii/iii A.D.) ὁρκ[ίζω σε, πνεῦμα ἐν ἀέρι φοιτώμενον, εἴσελθε, ἐνπνευμάτωσον, δυνάμωσον. διέγειρον τῇ δυνάμει τοῦ αἰωνίου θεοῦ ο δε (*l.* θεοῦ τόδε) τὸ σῶμα. MGr has δυναμώνω "strengthen," a further corroboration of the hold the verb had in the Κοινή.

δυνάστης.

In OGIS 573²² (i/A.D.) the title of δυνάστης is applied to the son of Archelaus who succeeded his father in the government of Cilicia without the title of King. It describes the chief of a Thracian clan in *Syll* 318²² (B.C. 118) συνεπελθόντος μετ' αὐτῶν Τίπα τοῦ τῶν Μαίδων δυνάστου μετ' ὄχλ[ου π]λείονος. The Commagene rescript, OGIS 383²⁹ (middle of i/B.C.) has ὅστις ἂν βασιλεὺς ἢ δυνάστης ἐν μακρῷ χρόνωι ταύτην ἀρχὴν παραλάβῃ, and *ib.* 441¹³² (B.C. 81) αἵδε ἀπεδέξαντο τῶν πόλεων καὶ βασιλέ[ων] καὶ δυναστῶν τήν τε ἀσυλίαν τοῦ ἱεροῦ καὶ τὸ[ν] ἀγῶνα τὸν τιθέμενον κατὰ πενταετηρίδα Ἑκάτηι Σωτείραι Ἐπιφανεῖ κτλ. For δυναστεύω see the Canopic decree, OGIS 56²² (B.C. 237) τήν τε χώραν ἐν εἰρήνηι διατετήρηκεν προπολεμῶν ὑπὲρ αὐτῆς πρὸς πολλὰ ἔθνη καὶ τοὺς ἐν αὐτοῖς δυναστεύοντας, and for δυναστεία. BGU II. 428⁷ (ii/A.D.). This last word is applied to the Divine soverainty in Aristeas 194 καὶ γὰρ ὁ θεὸς διδοὺς ἀνοχὰς καὶ ἐνδεικνύμενος τὸ τῆς δυναστείας φόβον ἐγκατασκευάζει πάσῃ διανοίᾳ, "for God also by granting a reprieve and making but a display of His soveranty instils terror into every breast."

δυνατός.

For δ. with a "complementary" infinitive, as in 2 Tim 1¹², cf. P Magd 3⁵ (B.C. 221), where in a lease it is laid down with reference to certain land –ἡ δυνατὴ σπαρῆναι ἕως Χοίαχ ι, τὴν δὲ μὴ δυνατὴν σπαρῆναι ἕως ι τοῦ Χοίαχ. For other exx. of the infin. construction cf P Eleph 8¹⁸ (iii B.C.) οὗτος δὲ δυνατός ἐστιν εἰσενέγκαι καὶ ἔν[γυο]ν [ὑ]κ[ανό]ν, P Hib I. 78¹⁵ (B.C. 244-3) ἐὰν δὲ μὴ δυνατὸς ἦσθα ἀπολῦσαι, P Giss I. 79ⁱⁱ ⁴ (ii/A.D.) εἰ δυνατόν μ[οι] ἦν διατρ[έ]χ[ει]ν πρὸς τὴν οἰκονομίαν τῶν ἡμετέρων, οὐκ ἂν ὤ[κ]νήκειν, P Leid W¹ⁱ ¹³ (ii/iii A.D.) ὅτι δυνατός εἰ (sc. ποιῆσαι κτλ.), *Syll* 721¹⁸ (iv/B.C.) promising to render help καθ' ὅτι ἂν ἦι δυνατός, etc. For the neuter δυνατόν see further P Petr II. 11(1)³ (c. B.C. 252) εἰ δυνατόν ἐστιν καὶ μηθὲν σὲ τῶν ἔργων κωλύει, πειράθητι ἐλθεῖν εἰς τὰ Ἀρσινόεια, and cf. *ib.* 39 (e)¹⁶ (middle iii/B.C.) διότι ὑπάρχει ἐν τῇι δωρεᾶι χόρτος ἱκανὸς ἀφ' οὗ ἐὰν ἐν δυνατῶι ἦι εἰς τὰς ἐν τῶι νομῶι ἀβχ^ρ, OGIS 771⁴⁹ (B.C. 172-1) ἐὰν ἐν δυνατῶι εἶ. For κατὰ τὸ δυνατόν, see P Giss I. 36⁹ (B.C. 161), *ib.* 41ⁱⁱ ⁴ (ii/A.D.), and for ὅσον δυνατόν σοι ἐστιν see P Flor II. 178³ (A.D. 258). It forms a masc. noun in plur. = "troops" in P Revill Mél p. 295⁹ (= Witkowski², p. 96) (B.C. 131-0), where a man is heard of as coming μετὰ δυνατῶν ἱκανῶν to suppress riotous crowds : perhaps there is an additional suggestion of competence—"mighty men of valour." The adverb occurs in *Michel* 1001ⁱⁱⁱ ²⁷ (Theran Doric—c. B.C. 200) ὅπως δὲ πάντα διοικεῖται κατά τε τὰν διαθήκαν καὶ τὸν νόμον καὶ τὰ δόξαντα τῶι κοινῶι δυνατῶς ἐς πάντα τὸν χρόνον. MGr δυνατός = "able," "possible," "strong," "loud" (Thumb).

δύο.

P Hib I. 27⁵² (calendar—B.C. 301-240) ἄγουσιν κατ' ἐνιαυτὸν] τῆι αὐτῆι ἡμέραι τ[ὰς] πλείστας οὐθὲν πα[ραλ]-λάσσοντες ἐπ' ἄστρω[ι] ἢ δύνοντι ἢ ἀνατ[έλ]λοντι, " they (sc. the astronomers and sacred scribes) keep most of the festivals annually on the same day, without alterations owing to the setting or rising of a star " (Edd.), P Oxy II. 235¹⁵ (horoscope—A.D. 20-50) δύνει Σκορπίος οἶκος Ἄρεως. In the Eudoxus papyrus, P Par 1¹¹⁵ (c. B.C. 165) we have ἀεὶ δὲ φανερὸς ὁ μηδέποτε δύνων, ᾧ εἰσὶν αἱ ἄρκτοι, and ¹⁷³ εἰ μὲν γὰρ ὁ πόλος ἀνανεύσει ἢ κατανεύσει. αἱ ἄρκτοι δύσονται καὶ ἐπιτελοῦσιν. P Hal I. 1²⁴⁰ (c. B.C. 250) ὡς δὲ ἂν ἥλιος] δύηι, μηδὲ εἰς ἐνεχυραζ[έ]τω μηδὲ πρὶν ἥλιον ἀνατέλλειν has the strong aorist, as the sense shows. We might also quote an application to the sunset of life, from *Kaibel* 508⁴ (Rome, iii/A.D.?) : ἥτις ἐνὶ ζωοῖσιν ὅκως ἀνέτελλεν Ἕως, νῦν δύνει δ' ὑπὸ γῆν Ἕσπερος ἐν φθιμένοις. The daring versifier is adapting Plato's gem, the epitaph of Aster.

δύο.

The disappearance of the dual flexion of δύο is in line with the whole tendency of Hellenistic : see *Proleg.* p. 77 ff. The gen. and dat. δυοῖν appears occasionally in a document where the writer desires to make broad his Attic phylacteries : thus P Giss I. 99¹⁵ (B.C. 80) ἐ]ν στή[λαι]ν δυοῖν [ἔ]μπροσθεν ἱδρυμέ[ν]αιν τοῦ[ν]εῴ, P Strass I. 52³³ (A.D. 151) ἀρουρῶν δυοῖν ἡμίσους τρίτου (or was this δυεῖν?), P Oxy VIII. 1119²⁰ (A.D. 254) δυοῖν θάτερον. The literary Hellenistic δυεῖν (late Attic), which arose phonetically out of δυοῖν (Brugmann-Thumb *Gr.* p. 78), appears in several papyri, as P Par 1²⁹³ (the Eudoxus astronomical treatise—c. B.C. 165) δυεῖν μηνῶν χρόνος, P Ryl II. 109⁵ (A.D. 235) πατὴρ τῶ[ν] δυεῖν—the document has υἱέας later ¹, *ib.* 266⁵ (ii/A.D.) ἐκ δυεῖν οἰκ[ῶ]ν —this document also betrays artificial dialect by the "registering" historic present τελευτᾷ (*Proleg.* p. 120), *ib.* 357 (A.D. 201-11) ἀρουρῶν δυεῖν, P Oxy VIII. 1117¹⁶ (c. A.D. 178) ἐκ δυεῖν ταλάντων—here again there is some fine writing in the context, a petition to a Praefect, who would no doubt be impressed by it. Greek dialects pluralized the flexion in different ways—see Brugmann-Thumb *Gr.* p. 249 f. In Hellenistic we have dat. δυσί, *passim* in all our documents, and to a very limited extent gen. δυῶν: see Mayser, *Gr.* p. 314, who can only quote OGIS 56⁶² (B.C. 239-8 – the Canopus decree) ἐκ σταχύων δυῶν (in copy A), and BGU I. 287²⁵ (ii/A.D.) ἀρουρῶν δυῶν – it is ancient Ionic (Herod. and Hippocrates) and Cretan Doric (Gortyn Inscr.). That in MGr δυῶν(ε) occurs occasionally (Thumb *Handb.* p. 81) may show that the form ran underground to emerge in a few places, but it might be independent analogy. Δυσίν is Ionic (first in Hippocrates), as we might expect from that dialect's early sacrifice of the dual. With the indeclinable δύο for nom., acc. and gen., it forms the whole of the Κοινή flexion. (The pre-classical δύω, which lived on in δ(ὑ)ώδεκα, is cited by Mayser p. 313 from P Leid T ¹·²⁴ (B.C. 164-0) and P Grenf II. 38¹² (B.C. 81) – but there are other cases of ω for o in this last document by sheer miswriting.) Mayser makes *Syll* 177²⁶ (Teos, B.C. 304) the oldest inscriptional warrant for δυσί, which appears in literature before Aristotle. In Attic inscr. (Meisterhans, p. 157) δυεῖν supplants δυοῖν in Alexander's time, and lasts a century, δυσί beginning in iii/B.C.

On δύο δύο see *Proleg.* p. 97 : add to illustrate ἀνὰ δύο δύο P Oxy VI. 886¹⁹ (magical—iii/A.D.) ἔρε κατὰ δύο δύο, "lift them up two by two" (Edd.). It may be noted that οἱ δύο supplants ἄμφω, as in Mk 1⁸ etc., P Giss I. 2^{ii·5·14} (B.C. 173) μάρτυρες Φίλιος Μακεδών, Δημοκρατίων Θέσσαλος, οἱ δύο τῶν Κινέου, and οἱ δύο τῆς ἐπιγονῆς—the document has also οἱ τρεῖς. MGr has κ'οἱ δυό, "both," οἱ δυό μας, "both of us."

δυσβάστακτος.

See for the guttural under βαστάζω above. It would seem that the compound was coined LXX. Philo and Plutarch) when the guttural forms were coming in, so that the older alternative in -στος never took its place.

δυσεντέριον.

Moeris, p. 120. δυσεντερία, θηλυκῶς, Ἀττικῶς. δυσεντέριον, Ἑλληνικῶς, settles the form in Ac 28⁸, where all the uncials have the neuter. If Hobart's long list of citations (p. 52 f.) can be trusted for this detail, Luke's medical books all presented him with δυσεντερία (in Hippocrates), and his faithfulness to the spoken Hellenistic form is the more noteworthy. We have not noticed the word in the medical documents among the papyri : it would be a fortunate chance if any of these scattered papers dealt with this particular subject.

δύσις.

In the Eudoxus papyrus as under δύνω *sub fin.*, we have ⁴⁷⁸ ἀνα[τολαὶ τοῦ] ἡλίου τροπικαὶ τρεῖς [καὶ δ]ύσεις τρεῖς. See also P Hib I. 27¹⁵ (B.C. 301-240) πρὸς τὰς δόσεις (*l.* δύσεις) καὶ ἀ[να]τολὰς τῶν ἄστρω[ν, P Oxy IV. 725¹² (A.D. 183) ἀπὸ ἀν[ατολῆς] ἡ[λίου] μέχρι δύσεως, and so BGU IV. 1021¹³ (iii/A.D.). In OGIS 199³³ (i A.D.) ἀπὸ δὲ δύσεως μέχρι τῶν τῆς Αἰθιοπίας καὶ Σάσου τόπων, the word is used of "the west" as in the "Shorter Conclusion" of Mark. So *Preisigke* 358², as cited under ἀνατολή : the same document (1.²¹) has πλειάδος δύσιν, "setting of the Pleiad"—the inscr. is on a sundial. In *Syll* 740¹³ (after A.D. 212) we find ἀπὸ δύσεως correlated with ἀπὸ ἠοῦς, ἀπὸ μεσημβρίας and ἀπὸ ἄρκτου—terms which suggest learning on the part of the ἱερὰ γερουσία τοῦ Σωτῆρος [Ἀ]σκληπιοῦ who inscribe this tablet. MGr has δύσι "sunset," "west."

δύσκολος.

In a letter to a father from his son, P Oxy IX. 1218⁵ (iii/A.D.), giving him some domestic news, the phrase occurs οὐδὲν δύσκολον ἔνι ἐπὶ τῆς οἰκίας σου, which the editors render, "there is nothing unpleasant at your house." For the ordinary meaning "difficult" we may cite the important Calendar inscription from Priene, OGIS 458¹⁶ (c. B.C. 9) ἐπειδὴ δύσκολον μέν ἐστιν τοῖς τοσούτοις αὐτοῦ εὐεργετήμασιν κατ' ἴσον ε[ὐχαρισ]τεῖν. Add *ib.* 339⁵¹ (c. B.C. 120) ἐν καιροῖς δυσκόλοις, and *Syll* 213²³ (iii/B.C.) περιστάντων τεῖ πόλει καιρῶν δυσκόλων, which the editor refers to the war waged between Demetrius and the Aetolians. For the adverb we may cite P Oxy X. 1294³¹ (ii/iii A.D.) ἐὰν δὲ σὺ μὴ δυνηθῇς ἀνοῖξαι τὸ πανάριον, δυσκό[λ]ως γὰρ ἀνοί[γ]εται, δὸς τῷ κλειδοποιῷ καὶ ἀνοίξει σοι, "if you cannot open the basket yourself, for it opens with difficulty, give it to the key-maker, and he will open it for you" (Edd.). MGr has δυσκολία, and δυσκολεύω, "make difficult."

δυσμή.

In P Tebt 54¹⁵ (A.D. 200) and BGU IV. 1049⁶ (A.D. 342) we find ἀπὸ μὲν ἀνατολῶν and ἀπὸ δὲ δυσμῶν contrasted : cf. Mt 8¹¹ etc. *Syll* 552⁷⁰ (late ii/B.C.) εἰς τὴν παραστάδα τὴν ἀπὸ δυσμῆς τῆς στοᾶς τῆς βορεί[ας shows the sing., as does *Chrest.* I. 341²⁸ (reign of Hadrian) ἀρχό[μενον] ἀπὸ δυσ[μῆς] τῆς κώμης, as printed : but Wilcken remarks "oder δύσεως)," and presumably δυσμῶν is equally possible. For another prepositional combination see P Leid W^{vi·5} (ii/iii A.D.) πρὸς δυσμὰς βλέπουσα, of a door.

δυσφημία.

Syll 366¹⁵ (c. A.D. 38) ὅπως μὴ τὸ πολυδάπανον αὐτῆς τῶν κατασκευαζομένων ἔργων [αἰ] περὶ τὴν ἀγορὰν ἐνποδίσωσι δυσφημίαι.

δώδεκα.

See under δεκαδύο. It is MGr.

δωδέκατος.

For this word, which in the NT is confined to Rev 21²⁰, cf. P Flor I. 20¹² (A.D. 127) εἰς τὸ εἰσιὸν δωδέκατον ἔτος Ἀδριανοῦ Καίσαρος τοῦ κυρίου, *ib.* 35¹³·¹⁵ (A.D. 107), and the ostraca PSI III. 255⁴ (B.C. 104-3), 256⁶ (B.C. 103-2),

δωδεκάφυλον.

To the reff. to this word in Grimm-Thayer we may add (from Hort *James*, p. 2) Joseph. *Hypomnesticum* (Fabricius *Cod. Pseud. V. T.* ii. p. 3) τοὺς δώδεκα φυλάρχους ἐξ ὧν τὸ δωδεκάφυλον τοῦ Ἰσραὴλ συνίσταται. For the formation cf. τὸ δωδεκάμηνον "twelvemonth," common in papyri. We should not expect to find δωδεκάφυλον itself outside Jewish circles.

δῶμα.

In P Oxy III. 475[22] (A.D. 182) βουληθεὶς ἀπὸ τοῦ δώματος τῆς αὐτῆς οἰκίας παρακύψαι καὶ θεάσασθαι τὰς [κρο]ταλιστρίδας—of a young slave who was killed in trying to see a performance of castanet players in the street below—δῶμα is clearly to be understood as "the top of the house," whether a top room or the flat roof as in Mk 13[15] etc. Cf. P Strass I. 14[12] (A.D. 211) ἐ]ν ἀπρ[ά]τω δώματι ἐν τῇ λαύρᾳ τῶν Ποιμένων, where the editor renders "auf einem unverkäuflichen flachen Dache in der Hirtenstrasse," and the late P Flor I. 13[b] (vi/vii A.D.) τῆ[ς] αὐλῆς καὶ το (*l.* τοῦ) δώματο[ς, "della terrazza sul tetto della casa" (Vitelli). The note on this last passage quotes Babrius 5[5], of a cock which εἰς τὸ δῶμα πηδήσας ἐπικροτῶν τε τοῖς πτεροῖς ἐκεκράγει. Add P Tebt I. 123[12,14] (early i/B.C.), 241 *verso* (B.C. 74) ἔχωι ἐπὶ τοῦ δώματος. In P Petr I. 20[19] (B.C. 241) ἐπὶ τῶν δωμάτων, the context is fragmentary, but the editor understands it of difficulties attending the arrangements of new "homesteads" in the Fayûm. We have the word twice in a Petrograd ostracon, no. 34[6 f.] published by Zereteli in *Archiv* v. p. 170. τὸ ξύλον τὸ [μυρί]κινον τὸ ἐν τῇ αὐλῇ, ἄν χρῄζῃς, [εἰς τὰ δ]ώματα λαβὲ καὶ ἐν.υλια, ἄν χρῄζῃς ἐκ τοῦ δώματο[ς] λαβέ : the editor prints χ ?]ώματα, but Wilcken emends. In P Ryl II 233[7] (ii/A.D.) ὅταν δὲ ἐπ' ἀγαθῷ ἐκβῶμεν καὶ τὸ δῶμα ἀσφαλισθήσεται is rendered by the edd. "but when we reach a fortunate issue and the house is established." A rather striking epitaph, *Kaibel* 720, reminding us distantly of the great passage in Lucretius (iii. 894 ff.) which Gray imitated in the *Elegy*, has the lines οὐκέτι σοι φάος ἠελίοιο, οὐδὲ τὰ κλεινὰ δὲ δώματα Ῥώμης, οὔδ' ἄλοχος (= husband), οὔτε φίλη κασιγνήτη. Here again the meaning is *house*, which has only shrunk into *room* in MGr.

δωρεά.

For δωρεά "gift," "largess," cf. BGU I. 140[8] (A.D. 119), a copy of an Imperial letter of the time of Hadrian, where reference is made to the Emperor's *beneficium* to the soldiers—ταύτην μου τὴν δωρεὰν καὶ τοῖς στρατιώταις ἐμοῦ καὶ τοῖς οὐετρανοῖς εὔγνωστόν σε ποιῆσαι δεήσει : cf. P Oxy IX. 1202[7] (A.D. 217) ἐκ τῆς τῶν [κυρί]ων Σεουήρου καὶ μεγάλου Ἀντωνίνου [δω]ρεάς, and from the inscr. OGIS 335 (ii/B.C.) ἐν τῆι . δωρεᾷ ταύτηι, "per hanc munificentiam" (Edd.), *Syll* 300[14] (mid. ii/B.C.) δωρεὰν εἰς πάντα τὸν χρόνον ἀΐδιος. P Lille I. 10[9] (mid. iii/B.C.) π]αρὰ Σαραπίωνος τοῦ προεστηκότος τῆς Καλλιξε[ίνους] δωρεᾶς, "ancien régisseur du bénéfice de K." (Edd.). *Syll* 740[6] ἔδωκε δωρεάν, and P Lond 1171 *verso* [c][3] (A.D. 42) (= III. p. 107) μηδὲ ἐφόδια ἢ ἄλλο τι δωρεὰν αἰτεῖν ἄτερ ἐμο[ῦ] διπλώματος, afford a link with the special use of the acc. = "freely," "gratis" as in Rom 3[24], 2 Cor 11[7], 2 Thess 3[8]. This is common, e.g. *Syll* 480[15] (B.C. 304-3) ἐπιδεδω[κε]ν ἑαυτὸν

δημοσιεύειν δωρε[ά]ν, "has offered his services as an honorary physician," *Michel* 1001[iv. 28] (*c.* B.C. 200) λειτουργεῖν ἅπαξ ἀνὰ πρεσβύτατα, δωρεὰν πάντας, with which cf. [v. 11] εἰ δέ κα ἐγ δωρεᾶς ἐπιμήνιοι μηκέτ' ὦντι, making provision for the roll of compulsory free service being exhausted. So *Priene* 4[17] (B.C. 332-20) λελειτούρκηκε δ., *Cagnat* IV. 783[7] πρεσβεύσαντα πρὸς τοὺς Σεβαστοὺς δωρεά, *ib.* 914[2] (i/A.D.) similarly. From the papyri, e.g. P Tebt I. 5[197] (B.C. 118) μηδὲ συναναγκάζειν ἔργα δωρεὰν συντελεῖν παρευρέσει μηδεμιᾷ, "nor oblige them to work without payment on any pretext whatever" (Edd.), [250] δωρεὰν μηδὲ μισθῶν ὑφειμένων, "gratis or at reduced wages" (Edd.). For the tax δωρεά, which suggests a "benevolence," and that on γῆ ἐν δωρεᾷ, see the editors' note on P Hib I. 66[1] and P Lille I. 10[9]. In two tablets of B.C. 252, quoted by Wilcken *Ostr.* i. p. 66 f., we find the adj.—τῆς δωρεαίας γῆς. The slightly developed meaning of δωρεάν "for nothing," "in vain," which Grimm notes as unparalleled in Greek writers, seems to be regarded by Nägeli, p. 35 f., as sufficiently accounted for by the instances where it means "gratis" : Grimm's own parallel with uses of *gratuitus* in Latin shows how easily it would arise. For the form, see Mayser *Gr.* p. 68 : the older δωρειά (Meisterhans *Gr.* p. 40) does not occur in our documents.

δωρέομαι.

The active may be neglected, having disappeared after early classical times. The passive sense (as 1 cv 7[5]) may be quoted from OGIS 435[1] (ii/B.C.) ὅσα ἐν Ἀσίαι ἕω]ς τῆς Ἀττάλου τελευτῆς ὑπὸ τῶν [βασιλέων δι]ωρθώθη ἐδωρήθη ἀφέθη ἐξ]τιμιώθη]. CP Herm 121[13] (iii/A.D.) τοῦ δωρηθέντος ἡμῖν ὑπὸ τῆς θείας μεγαλοδωρ[εί]ας of Gallienus. For the ordinary deponent use cf. P Oxy VIII. 1153[b] (i/A.D.) ἃ (*sc.* καρποδέσμια, "wrist-bands") ἐδωρήσατό σοι Παυσανίας ὁ ἀδελφός σου, Preisigke 4284[7] (A.D. 207) μεθ' ὧν πλείσων (*l.* στων) ἀγαθῶν ἐδωρήσαντο, "among the multitude of gifts they (the Emperors) bestowed." P Lond 130[151] (i/ii A.D.) (= I. p. 138) ὅν τινες ζυγῷ δωρήσονται ἀγνοίᾳ, P Gen I. 11[12] (A.D. 350) δωρῦμέ σοι. From the inscr. it is sufficient to cite the Rosetta Stone, OGIS 90[31] (B.C. 196) τῶι τε Ἀπει καὶ τῶι Μνεύει πολλὰ ἐδωρήσατο, and the leaden tablet of a *defixio*, Wünsch *AF* 4[30] (iii/A.D.) ὀρκίζω σε τὸν θεὸν τὸν τὴν κοίμησίν σοι δεδωρημένον καὶ ἀπολύσαντά σε ἀπὸ δ[εσμῶ]ν τοῦ βίου Νεθμομαω.

δώρημα.

PSI I. 29[23] (magic—? iv/A.D.) δότε καὶ μοι χάριτα καὶ τιμὴν ἔπροσθεν (*l.* ἔμπ—) πάντω[ν] καὶ τἀγαθὰ δορήματα. P Oxy V. 841, p. 37, has a scholion (mid. ii/A.D.) by which Pindar's βιόδωρον ἀμαχανίας ἄκος is glossed as δώρημα τῷ βίῳ. The same use of the dat. appears in the new fragment of the *Oeneus* (?) of Euripides, P Hib I. 4[5] ἀδ[ελφ[ῷ]ι Μελ[εάγρωι δ[ωρ]ήματα. An acrostic oracle, *Kaibel* 1039[13] Lycia], has the line Νεικηφόρον δώρημα τὸν χρησμὸν τε]λεῖ, which the ed. explains as telling him who draws this line "ubi largitus eris, quod cupis consequeris."

δῶρον.

In P Lond 429 (*c.* A.D. 350) (= I. p. 314 f.) we have a long account of δῶρα made on the occasion of various festivals, which the editor thinks are to be regarded as temple-offerings. If so, we may compare the similar use in the inscrr., e.g. *OGIS* 407 βασιλεὺς Ἰούλιος Ἐπιφάνης Φιλόπαππος Δεσποίν[αι] καὶ Σωτίρα[ι] δῶρον . ἐπὶ ἱερέος Σωτηρίχου, *Sic.* 774 σ]τρατία ὑπὲρ τῆς ὁράσεως θεᾷ Δήμητρι δῶρον, *ib.* 787 (iv/iii B.C.) Διὶ δῶρον. This illustrates the common Biblical use of δῶρον for a sacrifice, or an offering to the Temple treasury. For the ordinary sense of δῶρον it will suffice to quote BGU IV. 1114⁷ (B.C. 8–7) ἀποκαταστῆσαι ἐνταῦθα τῶι Ἱμέρωι δῶρον δούλους (names follow), *ib.* I. 248 (ii/A.D.) κατὰ δῶρον, PSI III. 236³ (iii/iv A.D.) οὐκ ὀκνῶ γὰρ οὐδὲ περὶ δώρων οὐδὲ περὶ κέρματος, εἰδώς σου τὴν ἀγαθὴν προαίρεσιν, and the boy's letter, P Oxy I. 119¹¹ (ii/iii A.D.) (= *Selections*, p. 103) καλῶς δὲ ἐποίησες, δῶρά μοι ἔπεμψε[ς] μεγάλα, ἀράκια, "it was good of you, you sent me a present, such a beauty – just

husks!" One interesting literary use may be quoted, *Kaibel* 815¹ (ii/A.D. Crete), where Salvius Menas offers a libation and a sacrifice to Hermes in memory of his wife, ψυχικὰ δῶρα διδούς: the ed. explains this as gifts "quae pro defunctae uxoris anima Mercurio animarum duci comitique obferuntur."

δωροφορία.

So Ph G Ambst in Rom 15¹⁶ witness good enough to bring it into the circle of Biblical words. We may mention it only to note that Alciphron and Pollux (ap. Grimm) albeit a good century later, are sufficient warrant that the word, if Paul did use it, came out of ordinary "profane" vocabulary.

ἐάν.

The difference between ἐάν and εἰ is considerably lessened in Hellenistic Greek, with the result that the former is found fairly frequently with the ind. (as in Lk 16⁴⁰, Ac 8³¹, 1 Thess 3⁸, 1 Jn 5¹⁵, e.g. P Par 62ᵛⁱⁱⁱ·⁸ (c. B.C. 170) ἐὰν δ' ὑπερβόλιον ἐνέστη, ib. 18¹⁰ (Imperial period?) ἐὰν μάχουσιν (or -οῦσιν) μετ' ἐσοῦ οἱ ἀδελφοί σου, P Tebt I. 58⁵⁵ (B.C. 111) ἐὰν δεῖ σε συνπεσῖν τῶι Ἀνικήτωι σύνπεσαι, "if you must meet Anicetus, meet him," P Amh II. 93²⁴ (A.D. 181) ἐὰν φαίνεται μισθῶσαι, and P Oxy VIII. 1157¹⁵ (late iii/A.D.) ἐὰν δὲ ἦσαν. See further Deissmann *BS* p. 201 f. and *Proleg.* p. 168, where attention is also drawn to the ambiguous ἐὰν ἦν, which is normally to be read ᾖ, cf. Moulton *CR* xv. pp. 38, 436. The following exx. of conditional ἐάν may be cited from P Ryl II.—153²¹ (A.D. 138-61) ὡς ἐὰν αὐτοὶ δο[κ]ῶσι χορηγοῦντα ς, 154²⁸ (A.D. 66) οἷα ἐὰν . . ἐγβῇι, 155²¹ (A.D. 138-61) ὥστε ἐὰν αἱρῆται, 163¹³ (A.D. 139) ὁπηνίκα ἐὰν αἱρῇ. See also *s.v.* ἄν.

ἐάνπερ.

For this intensive particle which in Bibl. Greek is confined to Heb 3¹⁴ (contrast v. 6), 6³, cf. BGU IV. 1141³⁰ (B.C. 14) διασαφήσουσιν οὓς ἀπέσταλκες, ἐάνπερ μὴ θελήσωσιν προσχαρίσασθαι συνδούλωι, P Fay 124⁹ (ii A.D.) ἐάνπερ μὴ εὐ[γ]νομωῆς (*l.* εὐγνωμονῇς) τὰ πρὸς τὴν μητέρα, "if so be you are unfair in your conduct towards your mother."

ἑαυτοῦ.

There is no decisive instance in the NT of ἑαυτοῦ in the sing. for the 1st or 2nd person: in 1 Cor 10⁵⁹ ἑαυτοῦ is indef. "one's own," not "thine own," as AV, RV: and in Jn 18³⁴ σεαυτοῦ, and in Rom 13⁹, Gal 5¹⁴ σεαυτόν, are the better readings. But the usage can be illustrated from the illiterate papyri: *1st pers.*—BGU I. 86⁹ (A.D. 155) συγχωρῶ μετὰ τὴν ἑαυτοῦ τελευτὴν τοῖς γεγονόσι α[ὐτ]ῷ ἐκ τῆς συνούσης αὐτοῦ γυναικός, *2nd pers.* P Tebt I. 18⁵ (B.C. 114) φρόντισον ὡς πάντα [τ]ὰ ἐνοφειλόμενα ἑαυτῶι . . ἐμ μέτρωι ἔσται τῆι αὐτῆι. "see that all the debts due to you are in order on that day" (Edd.), P Oxy II. 295⁵ (c. A.D. 35) μὴ σκύλλε (*l.* σκύλλε) ἑατὴν ἐνπῆναι (*l.* ἐμφῆναι?), "don't trouble yourself to explain (?)" (Edd.). For the ordinary use with the *3rd pers.* there may be cited P Tebt I. 49³ (B.C. 113) τ[ὰ] ἐν τῆι ἑαυτοῦ γῆι ὕδατα κατακέκλυκεν, "let out the water on his own land," as distinguished from Crown land cultivated by a neighbour, BGU I. 45¹² (a complaint of violence—A.D. 203) Στοτόητις . . ἀνὴρ βίαιος . . ἐπῆλθεν αὐτῷ (*sc.* the complainant's son), ἐπαγαγὼν σὺν α[ὐ]τῷ τὸν ἑαυτοῦ υἱόν. Other exx. show a somewhat faded use of the reflexive as in the common phrase in legal papyri, μετὰ κυρίου τοῦ ἑαυτῆς ἀνδρός (ἀδελφοῦ, etc.),

where a woman is the principal, or in the interchangeable use of ὁ πατήρ, ὁ ἴδιος πατήρ, and ὁ ἑαυτοῦ πατήρ in sepulchral inscr., when a son is speaking of his father: see *Proleg.* p. 87 f., and add the contract where Tryphon arranges to apprentice τὸν ἑαυτοῦ υἱὸν Θοῶνιν to another weaver (P Oxy II. 275⁷—A.D. 66) and the reference in a magical formula to Isis as seeking ἑαυτῆς τὸν ἀδελφὸν κὲ ἄνδρα Ὄσιρειν (ib. VI. 886⁶—iii/A.D.).

From ii/B.C. the plural ἑαυτῶν is regularly extended to the 1st and 2nd persons, as frequently in the NT: thus P Par 47²⁶ (c. B.C. 153 = *Selections*, p. 23) ἱ καὶ αὐτοὺς δεδώκαμεν, P Lond 401⁶ (B.C. 116-11) (= II. p. 13) ἡμῖν τε καὶ ταῖς ἑαυτῶν (= "our") ἀδελφαῖς, P Tebt I. 47³⁰ (B.C. 113) ἵν' ἡμεῖς μὲν κομισώμεθα τὰ ἑαυτῶν, P Par 63¹²⁸ (B.C. 165) (= P Petr III. p. 28) περ[ὶ] ἑαυτῶν κήδεσθε, P Grenf I. 30⁹ (B.C. 103) ἐπιμελό[μενο]ι δὲ καὶ ἑαυτῶν ἵν' ὑγιαίνητε, and the other exx. in Mayser (*Gr.* p. 303).

For ἑαυτῶν = ἀλλήλων we may quote P Grenf II. 25⁴ (B.C. 103) ὁμολογία ἣν ἑκόντες συνχωρήσαντες ἔθεντο πρὸς ἑαυτούς, BGU IV. 1157¹⁴ (B.C. 10) τανῦν συνχωροῦμε ν πρὸς ἑαυτοὺς ἐπὶ τοῖσδε, P Oxy II. 260¹⁵ (A.D. 59) μέχρι οὗ ἃ ἔχωμεν πρὸς ἑαυτοὺς ἐγ[β]ιβασθῆι, ib. I. 115¹¹ (ii/A.D.) (= *Selections*, p. 96) παρηγορεῖτε οὖν ἑαυτούς. On the *a fortiori* argument underlying the use of ἑαυτοῖς for ἀλλήλοις in some of its NT occurrences, see Lightfoot on Gal 5¹³.

The simple ὑμᾶς is substituted for ὑμᾶς αὐτούς (or perhaps rather σεαυτήν) in P Oxy II. 293¹⁶ (A.D. 27) ἐπ[ι]σκοπ[οῦ] δ[ὲ] ὑμᾶς καὶ [πά]ντας του[ς] ἐν οἴκῳ: cf. P Amh II. 131¹⁴ (early ii/A.D.) ὡς . . ἔχόντων (*sc.* ἡμῶν) ἐκ τούτου εἰς ἡμᾶς δαπανῆσαι, and see *CR* xv. p. 441. Sharp (*Epist.* p. 6) cites an interesting parallel to Lk 15¹⁷ from Epict. iii. i. 15—ὅταν εἰς σαυτὸν ἔλθῃς. For the shortened forms σαυτοῦ (cf. Jas 2⁸ B) and αὑτοῦ, see *s.v.* αὐτοῦ, and Moulton *Gr.* ii. § 70.

ἐάω.

For ἐάω followed by the inf., cf. P Grad 8¹⁶ (c. B.C. 223-22) καλῶς ποιήσεις γράψας τοῖς φυλακίταις ἐὰν αὐτοῖς κατανέμειν, "to allow them to use the pastures," P Fay 122⁶ (c. A.D. 100) ἐά[σ]ας αὐτὸν βαστάξαι ἀρτάβας εἴκοσι ὀκτώ, τὰς δὲ λοιπὰς ὑπὸ τὴν ἀμφοτέρ[ω]ν σφραγεῖδα ἐάσας, "allowing him to carry off 28 artabae and leaving the rest under the seals of you both" (Edd.): see also *Proleg.* p. 205. In P Tebt II. 289⁶ (A.D. 23) we have the participle, οὕτως γὰρ γνώσομαι πότερον ἐπὶ τόπων σε ἐάσω πράττοντά τι. "for I shall thus know whether I shall leave you in employment where you are" (Edd.). In P Oxy X. 1293¹⁹ ᶠᶠ (A.D. 117-38), as in Ac 16⁷, 19³⁰, an inf. has to be supplied—λέγει μοι Σαρᾶς Ἔασον τοὺς ἄλλους πέντε μετρητὰς περὶ ὧν γράφεις εἰς τὸ ἄλλο ἀγώγιον· ἐὰν δὲ μὴ εὕρω τὸν βαστάζοντα.

ἐάσω αὐτό, "Saras says to me, 'Let the other five metretae about which you write wait for the other load, and if I cannot find a carrier, I shall do so'" (Edd.): see also P Flor II. 213[7] (A.D. 255) ἔασον παρά σοι, "keep by you" certain memphitia of wine. For ἐάω = "leave," as on its second occurrence in P Fay l.c. above, see also P Tebt II. 319[24] (A.D. 248) εἰακέναι δὲ αὐτοὺς κοινὰς τὰς ὑπαρχούσας (ἀρούρας) β οὔσας περὶ κώμην Τεπτῦνιν, "they have left as common property the two arourae belonging to them near the village of Tebtunis." In P Par 63[102] (B.C. 165) (= P Petr III. p. 32) καὶ μηθεὶς ἐαθῆι στρατεύσασθαι, Mahaffy translates, as required by the context, "and if no one be let off to serve in the army."

ἐβδομήκοντα.

In P Flor III. 382[i.3] (A.D. 222–3) exemption from public services is granted τοῖς ἐ[β]δομήκοντα ἔτη βεβιωκόσι, an equivalent to our old-age pensions: cf. ib.[ii.55] ἐ]γὼ κατὰ τὰς προκειμένας θείας διατάξεις ἤδη ὑπὲρ ἐβδομήκοντα [ἔτ]η βεβιωκὼς καὶ αὐτὸς τῆς ἀναπαύσεως διά σου τοῦ κυρίου τυχεῖν . . . On the number "seventy" bearing "not infrequently an approximate sense," see König in Hastings' DB iii. p. 563. MGr ἐβδομήντα.

ἐβδομηκοντάκις.

If LXX Gen 4[24] is to be taken as determining the meaning of the phrase ἑ. ἑπτά in Mt 18[22] (see Proleg. p. 98 and cf. Moulton Gr. ii. § 72 D), the omission of the connecting "and" in the LXX as compared with the Heb שִׁבְעִים וְשִׁבְעָה still leaves it uncertain whether we are to understand 70 + 7 or 70 × 7: see McNeile al Mt l. c. The phrase is found with the latter meaning in Test. xii. patr. Benj. vii. 4.

ἔβδομος.

P Tor I. 1[vi.17] (B.C. 117) τὸ ἑαυτῆς μέρος ἔβδομον, with reference to the "seventh" share of a house belonging to a certain woman. PSI I. 30[7] (A.D. 82) μεχρὶ ἐβδόμου ἔτους.

Ἑβραῖος.

While Ἑ. (on the breathing, see WH Intr.[2] § 408) came to be applied to a Greek-speaking Jew with little or no knowledge of Hebrew, such as Philo (Eus. HE ii. 4. 2) or Aristobulus (Praep. Evang. xiii. 11. 2), the word strictly denotes a Hebrew- or Aramaic-speaking Jew, and is used by Paul in Phil 3[5] Ἑ. ἐξ Ἑβραίων to emphasize the purity of his descent: see Kennedy EGT ad l., and as further elucidating the full force of the ἐκ cf. OGIS 90[10] the Rosetta stone—B.C. 196) where Ptolemy V. is described as ὑπάρχων θεὸς ἐκ θεοῦ καὶ θεᾶς. As illustrating Ac 18[4] Deissmann (LAE p. 13 f.) refers to an interesting inscription found in Corinth — συνα]γωγὴ Ἑβρ[αίων, and compares a similar Roman inscr. — συναγωγὴ Αἰβρέων (Schürer Gesch.[3] iii. p. 46): he does not, however, think that Ἑβραῖοι means Hebrew-speaking Jews. Wünsch (AF p. 6) cites an invocation against evil spirits from the great Paris magical papyrus which begins—[30]19 ὀρκίζω σε κατὰ τοῦ θεοῦ τῶν Ἑβραίων Ἰησοῦ Ιαβα Ιαη Αβραωθ, and ends—[308]1 ὁ γὰρ λόγος ἐστὶν ἑβραϊκὸς καὶ φυλασσόμενος παρὰ καθαροῖς ἀνδράσιν.

Ἑβραϊστί.

In P Leid W[ii. 38] (ii/iii A.D.) we have an invocation to a god — ἱερογλυφιστί, Λαιλαμ· Ἀβραϊστί, Ανοχ, "hieroglyphice Laulam; Hebraice Anoch": cf. ib.[iv. 24].

ἐγγίζω.

This verb is not so common as we might have expected, but see P Oxy IX. 1202[8] (A.D. 217) ἐνγίζοντος τοῦ ἑκάστου ἔτους ἀγῶνος, "as the contest of each year approaches," and P Gen I. 74[17] (probably iii/A.D.) εἶπ]εν αὐτῷ μὴ ἐγ[γ]ίζειν τῷ γρ . . τει. For the constr. with the gen., as in 1 Macc 11[1], 13[21], cf. P Thead 17[12] (A.D. 322) οὐκ ἐπε[τρέ]ψαντο οὔτε τῆς [θύ]ρας τοῦ ἐποικίου ἐνγίσαι μεθ' ὕβρεων.

ἔγγιστα.

This superlative, which is substituted for κύκλῳ in the Western text of Mk 6[36], is used of place in BGU III. 759[9] (A.D. 125) ἔνγιστα τῆς κώμης. In ib. I. 69[8] (A.D. 120) ἃς (sc. δραχμὰς) καὶ ἀποδώσω σοι τῷ ἔνγιστα δοθησομένῳ ὀψωνίῳ, the word = "next," and the dat. marks accompaniment (as in Rev 8[4] ταῖς προσευχαῖς, "with the prayers"). For the class. οἱ ἔγγιστα, "the next of kin," cf. ib. IV. 1185[18] (end of Ptol. or beginning of Aug. period) ἔρχεσθαι τοὺς κλήρους τούτων εἰς τοὺς ἔγγιστα γένους. Note further the letter of the Emperor Claudius of A.D. 47, incorporated in the diploma of an Athletic Club, where a certain Διογένης is described as ὁ ἔγγιστα τῆς συνόδου ἀρχιερεὺς γενόμενος — P Lond 1178[29] (A.D. 194) (= III. p. 216), and Syll 306[24] (B.C. 170) ὅπως οὗτοι ἔτη δέκα τ[ὰ] ἔγγιστα κυριεύωσιν.

ἐγγράφω

is used as practically equivalent to the simple γράφω in P Lond 358[15] (c. A.D. 150) (= II. p. 172) ἐνέτυχ[ον τῷ] ἡγεμονεύσαντι Ὀναράτ[ῳ] ὃς ἐνέγραψέ μοι ἐντυχ[ε]ῖν κρατίστῳ τῷ ἐπιστρατ[ηγή]σαντι. For the meaning "record" see P Cairo Preis 1[16] (ii/A.D.) ἐὰν γὰρ μηδὲν ἐπερώτημα ἢ ἐνγεγρα[μμένον . . . ., and for "inscribe" see PSI I. 28[19] (iii/iv A.D. ?) συντέλεσον τὰ [ἐγγ]εγραμμένα τῷ πεδάλῳ τούτου (l. πετάλῳ τούτῳ). The verbal ἔγγραπτος is common, e.g. P Rein 18[31] (B.C. 108) δοῦναι δέ μοι τὰς πίστεις δι' ἐγγράπτων, "des sûretés écrites" (Ed.), P Tebt II. 434 (A.D. 104) ἔχοντες ἔνγραπτον [ἐπι]στολήν, and, in contrast with ἄγραφος, P Oxy II. 268[16] (A.D. 58) περὶ ἄλλου μηδενὸς ἁπλῶς ἐνγράπτου ἢ ἀγράφου πράγματος, and similarly P Ryl II. 174[20,32] (A.D. 112) al. A good example of ἔγγραφος is afforded by P Oxy I. 70[1] (iii/A.D.) πᾶσα κυρ[ί]α ἔγγραφος συναλλαγὴ πίστιν καὶ ἀλήθ[ειαν ἔ]χει, "every valid written contract is credited and accepted" (Edd.). On the ἔγγραφος as distinguished from the ἄγραφος γάμος see Chrest. II. i. p. 209 ff. Ἐγγράφως = "in writing," P Oxy I. 53[8] (A.D. 316), ib III. 475[8] (A.D. 182), ib. VI. 902[10,37] (c. A.D. 465) al.

Ἐγγράμματος occurs in a woman's petition to a prefect: she claims the right to act without a guardian, in view of the fact, amongst other conditions, that she is ἐνγράμματος δὲ κα[ὶ ἐ]ς τὰ μάλιστα γράφειν εὐκόπως δυναμένη, "literate and able to write with the greatest ease" (P Oxy XII. 1467[13 ff.]—A.D. 263).

ἔγγυος.

This NT ἅπ. εἰρ. (Heb 7²²) is common in legal and other documents, e.g. P Petr III. 41 *recto*² εἰ οἱ πρότερον ὑπάρχου[σιν] ἔγγυοι, χρημάτισον Ἀ. κτλ., "if there are the former sureties, pay to A.," etc., P Grenf I. 18²³ (B.C. 132) ἔγγυοι ἀλ[λ]ήλων εἰς ἔκτεισιν τῶν διὰ τοῦ δανείου πάντων οἱ δεδανεισμένοι, and so 20¹⁵ (B.C. 127), P Oxy I. 38⁸ (A.D. 49-50) (= *Selections*, p. 52) δι' ἐγγύου ἐμοῦ, "on my security." P Gen I. 24⁸ (A.D. 96) ὁμολογοῦσι Πετεσοῦχις . . καὶ Σαταβοῦς . . ἀλλήλων ἔγγυοι [εἰς ἔ]κτ[ισιν. An early example of the fem. noun may be seen in P Eleph 27⁹ (B.C. 223-2) πρὸς ἐγγύην, ἣν ἐνεγυησάμεθα εἰς ἔκτισιν. For instances of the verb cf. P Oxy II. 259⁷ (A.D. 23) ὃν ἐγγεγύημαι . . . ἐκ [τ]ῆς πολιτικῆς φυλα[κ]ῆς, "whom I bailed out of the common prison" (Edd.), *ib.* VI. 905¹⁷ (A.D. 170) (= *Selections*, p. 87) ὁ πατὴρ . . . εὐδοκεῖ τῷ [τε] γάμῳ καὶ ἐγγυᾶται εἰς ἔκτισιν τὴν προκειμένην φερνήν, "the father assents to the marriage, and is surety for the payment of the aforesaid dowry," and for ἐγγυητής such a passage as P Oxy XII. 1483⁸ (ii/iii A.D.) τὸν ἐγγυητήν σου κατέχω ἕως ἂν τ[ε]λῇς μοι τὴν τιμὴν τῶν ζητουμένων, "I hold your surety, until you pay me the value of the claims." On "Pfandrechtliches" in ancient Egypt, see Manigk in *Archiv* vi. p. 114 ff. Ἔγγυος is probably derived from an old word for "hand" (cf. γύαλον, Lat. *vola*, Av. *gava*), like ἀμφίγυος and ὑπόγυος, so = "what is put in the hand."

ἐγγύς.

BGU III. 608¹⁷ (ii/A.D.) ἐγγὺς τῆς ἅλω, *ib.* 814³⁰ (iii/A.D.) ἐνγὺς τοῦ ἀδελφοῦ. For the form see Moulton *Gr.* ii. § 130.

ἐγείρω.

OGIS 677³ (early ii/A.D.) οἱ ἐγείραντες τὴν οἰκοδομὴν τοῦ πυλῶνος. With the use of the verb in Mk 13⁸ and parallels, Boll (*Offenbarung*, p. 131) compares Catal. VII. p. 51 f. 72 ἐγερθήσονται κατὰ τῆς βασιλείας, but notes that it is "von zweiter Hand." An interesting example of the word is found in the much-discussed Logion of Jesus No. 5 (P Oxy I. 1) ἔγει[ρ]ον τὸν λίθο(ν) κἀκεῖ εὑρήσεις με. For possible references to this saying in the Glossaries, see a note by Reitzenstein in *ZNTW* vi. p. 203.

ἔγερσις.

With Mt 27⁵³, the only occurrence of this word in the NT, may be compared the heading of a magic spell in P Leid Wˣⁱ ¹⁴ (ii/iii A.D.) ἔγερσις σώματος νεκροῦ. Nägeli (p. 49) refers to a use of the word in the same sense in Apollod. II. § 124 Wagn. See also Aristeas 160 where τὴν ἔγερσιν is contrasted with ὅταν εἰς ὕπνον ἔρχωνται.

ἐγκ.

See also ἐνκ.

ἐγκαλέω.

For ἐ. which was early specialized *in malam partem*, calling in a man to accuse him, and hence "bring a charge against," cf. P Eleph 1⁷ (B.C. 311-10) (= *Selections*, p. 3) ἐπιδειξάτω δὲ Ἡρακλείδης ὅ τι ἂν ἐγκαλῆι Δημητρίαι ἐναντίον ἀνδρῶν τριῶν, "and let Herakleides state whatever charge he makes against Demetria in the presence

of three men," and for the passive see BGU I. 22²⁵ (A.D. 114) (= *Selections*, p. 76) διὸ ἀξιῶ ἀκθῆναι (*l.* ἀχθῆναι) τοὺς ἐνκαλουμένους ἐπί σε πρὸς δέουσ(αν) ἐπέξοδον, "I require therefore that you will cause the accused to be brought before you for fitting punishment," and from the inscr. *OGIS* 90¹⁴ (Rosetta stone—B.C. 196) τοὺς ἐν αἰτίαις ὄντας ἐκ πολλοῦ χρόνου ἀπέλυσε τῶν ἐνκεκλη[μ]ένων. Another ex. from the papyri is P Hamb I. 25³ (B.C. 238-7) γράφ[ε]ις μοι ἐπισκεψάμενον περὶ ὧν ἐγκαλεῖ Διομέδων Κάλαι. The verb is very common in the sense of "make a claim." Thus in P Petr III. 61⁸, after a long list of supplies, we have the statement ὁμολογεῖ Ἀπολλώνιος ἔχειν κατὰ τὰ προγεγραμμένα καὶ μηθὲν ἐγκαλεῖν, "Apollonius admits that he has received the above mentioned supplies and makes no further claim": cf. PSI I. 30⁸ (A.D. 82) πλήρης εἰμὶ καὶ οὐδέν σοι ἐνκαλῶ περὶ οὐδενὸς ἁπλῶς, P Ryl II. 174 (*a*)¹⁶ (repayment of a loan— (A.D. 139) καὶ μηδὲν τὸν ὁμολογοῦντα ἐνκαλεῖν περὶ ὧν ἀπέχι καθότι πρόκειται μηδὲ περὶ ἄλλου τινὸς ἁπλῶς πρ[ά]γματος, "and that he, the acknowledging party, makes no further claim either concerning this money as received aforesaid or concerning any other matter at all" (Edd.). In P Oxy IX. 1204³ (A.D. 299) we have ἔκκλητον πεποίημαι, "I brought an action of appeal" (Ed.): cf.⁹ ποιήσας τὰ ἐπὶ τῇ ἐκκλήτῳ δέοντα, "having taken the proper steps for the appeal" (*ib.*). *Ostr.* 1154 ὅπου θέλεις ἀναβαλεῖν τὰ ἱμάτιά σου, οὐκ ἐνκαλῶ σε shows the acc. constr. See also Anz *Subsidia*, p. 377.

ἐγκαταλείπω.

P Par 46³ (B.C. 153) (= Witkowski², p. 86) ὁ ἀδελφός σου . . . λῃστῶν ἐπικειμένων ἐνκατελοίπει με ἀποδημήσας is a good ex. of the prevailing NT sense of this verb —to "leave in the lurch" one who is in straits: cf. P Oxy II. 281²¹ (A.D. 20-50) κατελίπέ με λειτὴν καθεστῶσαν, "he deserted me, leaving me in a state of destitution" (Edd.). With a place as object, see P Ryl II. 128¹¹ (c. A.D. 30) ἀλλότρια φρονήσασα ἐνκαταλιποῦσα τὸ ἐλαιούργιον ἀπηλάγη, "changed her mind, left the mill, and departed" (Edd.). So P Oxy VIII. 1124¹⁵ (A.D. 26) τοῦ δ' ἐνκαταλιπεῖν τὴ[ν γε]ωργία(ν) . . . ἐπίτιμον, "the penalty of abandoning the cultivation" (Ed.), *Chrest.* I. 72⁹ (A.D. 234) μηδένα δὲ τῶν ἱερέω[ν ἢ] ἱερωμένων ἐνκαταλελοιπέναι τὰς [θρ]ησκείας: cf. Heb 10²⁵. For the subst., which is found in the LXX, see P Petr II. 4 (11)² (B.C. 255-4) ἐγκατάλειμμα γέγονεν, "a silting up has taken place" (Ed.).

ἔγκλημα.

P Tebt I. 5³ (a royal decree—B.C. 118) proclaims an amnesty ἀγνοημάτων ἁμαρτημ[άτ]ων [ἐν]κλημάτων "for errors, crimes, accusations," (Edd.). Cf. also BGU IV. 1030³¹ (A.D. 108) τεσσάρις ἐπιδέδωκε τὸ ἔνκλημα καθὼς πρόκειται, P Oxy II. 237ⁱⁱⁱ ¹⁶ (A.D. 186) ἐπὶ προφάσει ἑτέρων ἐνκλημάτων, "on the pretence of counter-accusations," *ib.* viii. 20 οὐκ ἀπέχεται τὰ χρηματικὰ διὰ τούτων τῶν ἐνκλημάτων, P Ryl II. 116¹ (A.D. 194) ἀντίγραφον ἐγκλήματος Σ., "copy of a complaint by S.", P Tebt II. 616 (ii/A.D.) τῶν τεθέντων ἐνκλημάτων. For ἔγκλησις we may cite P Ryl II. 65¹⁵ (B.C. 67?) τοὺς δὲ τ[ὴ]ν ἔγκλησιν πεποιημένους, "those who brought the accusation" (Edd.), and for ἔγκλητος P Tebt I. 27⁴² (B.C. 113) πλὴ[ν] ἴσθι μὲν ἔγκλητος ὑπάρχων, "but be sure that you are liable to accusation" (Edd.).

ἐγκομβόομαι.

We have found no instance of this rare verb (1 Pet 5⁵) in our sources. Suidas (*Lex. s.v.*) cites a passage from Apollodorus of Carystus, a comic poet of iv/B.C., where the meaning apparently is "gird something on oneself": cf. MGr κομβόω = "button." For an interesting, though, it seems to us, doubtful interpretation of the Petrine passage, see Bigg *ICC ad l.*

ἐγκοπή, ἐγκόπτω.

See ἐκκοπή, ἐκκόπτω.

ἐγκράτεια.

In the important Imperial edict, P Fay 20, which is probably to be assigned to Julian (see *Archiv* ii. p. 169) rather than to Alexander Severus, the Emperor claims to be an example to all governors, in view of the fact that he administers the affairs of the Empire—²¹ μετὰ τοσαύτης κοσμιότητος καὶ σωφροσύνης καὶ ἐγκρατείας. See also Vett. Valens p. 355²⁹ διὰ τῆς ἰδίας ἐγκρατείας ἀκηρύκτως καὶ κοσμίως τὸ τέλος τοῦ βίου ὑποίσει. Ramsay *Luke*, p. 360 ff. cites an interesting iv/A.D. Lycaonian inscription in honour of a presbyter, who is described as ⁶ ἐν]κρατὴς ὁ διάκονος, "the minister of continence," while his wife is ¹⁶ πιστὴν ἐνκρατίης οἰκόνομον, "a trusty dispenser of continence."

ἐγκρατεύομαι.

With the Christian inscription cited *s.v.* ἐγκράτεια *sub fin.* may be compared another inscription erected in honour of a certain Orestina "who lived in continence"—ἐνκρατευσαμένη (*Ath. Mitth*., 1888, p. 272): see Ramsay *Luke*, p. 399 f. where "no extravagant asceticism" is thought to be implied in any of these terms.

ἐγκρατής.

For ἐ. in its more literal sense of "having power over" cf. P Tebt I. 30⁹ (B.C. 114) where certain assailants are described as ἡμῶν ἐγκρατεῖς γενόμενοι, and so *ib.* 230 (late ii/B.C.). The weaker sense, "possessed of," as in Wisd 8²¹, appears in P Rein 18¹² (B.C. 108) ὁ ἐγκαλούμενος ἐγκρατὴς γενόμενος τῶν συναλλάξ[ε]ων, P Oxy VI. 808¹⁹ (A.D. 123) ταύτης ἐνκρατὴς γενομένη, with reference to a deed, and BGU I. 168⁶ (A.D. 169) ἐ[ν]κρ[α]τ[ὴς] ἐγένετο π[ά]ντων τῶν [ἀ]νηκόντων τοῖ[ς ἀφ]ήλιξι. From the new literature we may cite P Oxy III. 413¹⁶⁰ (a mime—ii/A.D.) νῦν τοῦ γέροντ(ος) ἐνκρατὴς θέλω γενέσ(θαι) πρίν τι τούτ(ων) ἐπιγνοῖ, *Menandrea* p. 54²²⁸ τοῦ παιδίου ἐγκρατῆ. On the composition of the word see Moulton *Gr.* ii. § 118 (c), where it is shown that since κράτος suggests the possession of strength, as βία the using of it, ἐν κράτει ὤν, = "self-controlled," involves only the specializing reference to *moral* κράτος.

ἐγχρίω,

which in the NT is confined to Rev 3¹⁸, occurs twice in magical papyri—P Lond 46⁶⁴ (iv/A.D.) (= I. p. 67) (ἐν)χριε δὲ τὸν δεξιὸν ὀφθαλμ(ὸν) μεθ' ὕδατος πλοίου νεναυαγηκότος, *ib.* 121³¹⁶ (iii/A.D.) (= I. p. 95) ἔνχρειε τοὺς ὀφθαλμούς σου.

ἐγώ.

Deissmann (*LAE* p. 134 ff.) has drawn attention to the parallels to the solemn use of the first personal pronoun in the Fourth Gospel that may be adduced from inscriptions and magical texts. Thus in an inscr. in honour of Isis from Ios, written in ii/iii A.D., the contents of which are pre-Christian, we find—Εἶσις ἐγώ εἰμι ἡ τ[ύρανν]ος πάσης χόρας . . ἐγὼ νόμους ἀνθρώποις ἐθέμην . . ἐγώ εἰμι Κρόνου θυγάτηρ πρεσβυτάτη *al.* And similarly in the magical papyrus P Lond 46¹⁴⁵ ff. (iv/A.D.) (= I. p. 69) ἐγώ εἰμι ὁ ἀκέφαλος δαίμων . . ἐγώ εἰμι ἡ ἀλήθεια ὁ μεισῶν ἀδικήματα γείνεσθαι ἐν τῷ κόσμῳ *al.* With the construction of the phrase τί ἐμοὶ καὶ σοί; in Jn 2⁴ we may compare BGU IV. 1141³⁸ (B.C. 14) ἐδίδουν αὐτῷ διαστολὰς μηδὲν αὐτῶι καὶ ἐκείνωι εἶναι: for its meaning see F. C. Burkitt in *JTS* xiii. p. 594 f., where it is rendered, "What have I and thou to do with that?"

On the difficult question of the substitution of ἡμεῖς for ἐγώ see *Proleg.* p. 86 f., and the Appended Note on "Did St. Paul use the Epistolary Plural?" in Milligan *Thess.* p. 131 f., where the following passages are cited in support of the view that the two numbers can be used interchangeably—P Hib I. 44 ¹·⁴· (B.C. 253) ἐγράψαμεν . . ὁρῶντες . . ὤιμην, P Tebt I. 58 ⁶·¹⁵ (B.C. 111) εὑρήκαμεν . . εὗρον, P Par 43 ¹ ᶠ· (B.C. 154) (= Witkowski², p. 79) εἰ ἔρρωσθαι, ἔρρωμαι δὲ καὐτοί, P Flor I. 34⁷ (A.D. 342) ὁμολογῶ ὄμνυντες.

ἐδαφίζω.

In support of the RV rendering in Lk 19⁴⁴ "and shall dash thee to the ground," see Field *Notes*, p. 74. We have not come across any example of the verb in the papyri or the inscrr. though the subst. (see *s.v.*) is common.

ἔδαφος.

P Oxy 1262 (Ptol.) ἔχω παρὰ σοῦ τὸ ἐκφόριον καὶ τὸ ἐμβαδικὸν τοῦ ἐδάφους μου ἀμπελῶνος, and similarly P Grenf I. 21⁸ (B.C. 126) ἔδα(φος) ἀμπελῶ(νος), P Lond 401¹¹ (B.C. 116–11) (= II. p. 14) ἀπὸ ἐδάφους ἀμπελῶνος. For the plur. = "lands," see P Tebt II. 302¹⁰ (A.D. 71–2) where certain priests petition against an increase of rent τοῖς προκιμέν]ο[ι]ς ἐδάφεσι ἡμῶν, "on our aforesaid lands," and P Oxy XII. 1409¹⁹ (A.D. 278) πρὸς ἀρδείαν τῶν ἐδαφῶν, "for the irrigation of the fields." The derived sense of "buildings" appears in P Oxy II. 286²² (A.D. 82) σειτικῶν ἐδαφῶν καὶ ἑτέρων, "granaries and other possessions." In *Michel* 594⁵⁷ (B.C. 279) τὸ ἔδαφος ὁμαλίσασι the reference is to levelling the floor, and in the late Preisigke 5114⁹ (A.D. 613–40) a house is purchased ἀπὸ ἐδάφο(υ) ἄχρι ἀέρος. Note the gen. in -ου: Boisacq, p. 215, points out that ἐ. was originally a masc. stem in -ο which became a neut. in -ε ς through the influence of ἔδος.

ἑδραῖος.

In P Strass I. 40²⁴ (A.D. 569) a certain Colluthus is described as φαμιλιάριος ἑδραῖος κατάδουλος παῖς, "Hausbediensteter in fester Stellung eines Haussklaven" (Ed.). Cf. Vett. Valens p. 9¹⁵.

ἑδραίωμα.

For this word, which is found in the NT only in 1 Tim 3¹⁵, Hort (*Christian Ecclesia*, p. 174) strongly advocates the translation "stay" or "bulwark," in accordance with the almost universal Latin rendering *firmamentum*. Cf. the use of ἕδρασμα in Reitzenstein *Poimandres*, p. 343[1] ὁ βαθμὸς οὗτος, ὦ τέκνον, δικαιοσύνης ἐστὶν ἕδρασμα.

θελοθρησκεία.

Apparently a Pauline coinage (Col 2[23]) on the analogy of ἐθελοδουλεία; see Nageli, p. 51 for other examples of new Christian word-formations, and cf. ἐθελοταπεινοφροσύνη, which Hort would restore in Col 2[18] for the almost unintelligible θέλων ἐν ταπεινοφροσύνῃ. See Moulton *Gr*. ii. § 108 B.

ἐθέλω.

See θέλω

ἐθίζω.

P Petr III. 104[9] (B.C. 243?) τὸν εἰθισμένον ὅρκον, P Fay 12[3] (c. B.C. 103) τὰς εἰθισμένας προσαγγελίας, *ib*. 124[5] (ii/A.D.) μὴ εἰθισμένου μου τοῖς [γ]ρ[άμ]μασι, Meyer *Ostr* 73[1] (ii/B.C.) ὡς εἴθισμα[ι. Cf. also the conventional phrase τοῖς ἐξ ἀρχῆς ἐθισμοῖς, "the ancient traditions," as P Tebt I. 40[20] (B.C. 117) (= *Selections*, p. 29), etc., and P Magd 11[8] (B.C. 221) ἐθισμοῦ ὄντος, "habituellement."

ἐθνάρχης.

For the technical uses of this title, which in 2 Cor 11[32] occurs in the more general sense of a deputy governor or subordinate ruler, see Hohlwein *L'Égypte Romaine*, p. 207; also Lumbroso in *Archiv* i. p. 66 f.

ἐθνικός.

In the late P Oxy I. 126[13] (A.D. 572) ἐθνικός is used of a "collector" of taxes, a sense not found elsewhere. In MGr the adj. means "national."

ἔθνος.

Hicks in *CR* i. p. 42 f. has shown that "Hellenic life found its normal type in the πόλις, and barbarians who lived κατὰ κώμας or in some less organised form were ἔθνη," and that similarly in the LXX and NT ἔθνος "describes the pagan world, outside the Jewish Church," but occasionally stands for the λαός itself, as in Ac 10[22], 24[17] *al*. In an Imperial rescript of A.D. 198–201 we have a good example of the word = "province"—P Oxy VII. 1020[5] ὁ ἡγού-μ[ενος] τοῦ ἔθνους τὸν ἀγῶνα τῆς ἀφέσεως ἐκδικ[ήσει, "the praefect of the province shall decide the suit for release" (Ed.); cf. P Strass I. 22[19] (iii/A.D.) διατάξεις εἰσὶν τῶν κυρίων περὶ τῶν ἐν τοῖς ἔθνεσιν οἰκούντων, where the editor understands by ἔθνη "*provinciae populi Romani*," and the exx. from Greek writers of this usage in Magie p. 59. *Archiv* i. p. 66; see also Deissmann *Paul*, p. 100. In the edict regarding the *aurum coronarium*, P Fay 20[11] (iv/A.D.) ἅπαντες ἐν ταῖς πόλεσιν ἁπάσαις ταῖς τε κατ᾽ Ἰταλίαν κα[ὶ] ταῖς ἐν τοῖς ἄλλοις ἔθνεσιν, we may render "all persons in all the cities throughout Italy and in the provinces besides," cf. [19,20]. In P Petr III. 59 (*b*)[4] ἱερὰ ἔθνη are "priestly associations or corporations": cf. P Tebt I. 6[24] (B.C. 140–39) τῶν κατὰ μέρος ἐθνῶν where the reference is to the different classes of priests as contrasted with the πλῆθος of them, P Tor I. 1[ii. 24] (B.C. 116) τὸ ἔθνος ("hoc Collegium") μεταγαγεῖν εἰς

τὰ Μεμνονεῖα, and *OGIS* 90[17] (Rosetta stone—B.C. 196) ἐκ τῶν ἱερῶν ἐθνῶν, where Dittenberger defines ἔθνος as "genus hominum communione victus, officii, condicionis civilis definitum," but cf. Otto *Priester* i. p. 77. See also P Ryl II. 65[3] (B.C. 67?) οἱ ἐκ τοῦ ἔθνους νεκροτ[άφοι, "the grave-diggers belonging to the association," and for a wider use of the term P Petr III. 32 (*f*)[2], where for ἐθνῶν the editor proposes to read ἐθνῶν (cf. *verso* 11) with reference to "associations" for trade purposes. MGr ἔθνος = "nation," "people."

ἔθος.

For ἔθος = "usage," "custom," as in the Lukan writings, cf. P Oxy II. 370 (late i/A.D.) ἃς (*sc*. δραχμὰς) καὶ διαγράψομεν ἐπὶ τὴν δημοσίαν τράπεζαν ταῖς ὡρισμέναις προθεσμίαις κατὰ τὸ ἔθος, and similarly P Ryl II. 78[17] (A.D. 157). P Grenf I. 48[15] (A.D. 191), P Lond II. 171 *b*[19] (iii/A.D.) (= II. p. 176) Other prepositional phrases are ἐν ἔθει (e.g. P Oxy III. 471[78] (ii/A.D.) ἅπαξ γὰρ ἐν ἔθει τῆς α[ἰσ]χύνης γενόμενον, "for when once accustomed to his shame"), and ἐξ ἔθους (e.g. P Oxy VI. 900[7] (A.D. 322) τοὺς ἐξ ἔθους ταύτην τὴν χώραν ἀποπληροῦντας, "those who customarily fill this post"). See also P Fay 125[5] (ii/A.D.) ὡς ἔθος ἐστί σοι, "as is your custom," P Ryl II. 258[6] (A.D. 262) ὅσα ἔθος ἔχουσι λαμβάνειν, "whatever they are accustomed to receive," and the other exx. in Deissmann *BS* p. 251 f. From the inscrr. we may cite *Syll* 316[11] κατὰ τὸ τῶν προγόνων ἔθος, and *Magn* 100 b.[12] (ii B.C.) κατὰ τὸ πά[τριον ἔθος with reference to a day when children are freed from lessons and slaves from work. For the narrower sense of "law," "rite," Thieme (p. 22) refers to such a passage as *Magn* 179[10] (ii/A.D.) an inscr. in honour of one—δόντα τὰ ἐξ ἔθους καὶ ὡρισμένα ὑπὲρ τῆς καύσεως τῆς βαίτης (δηνάρια) ͞χ: cf. [19] τὸ ἐξ ἔθους ἐπὶ ἡμέρᾳ διδόμενον ἔλαιον.

For the adj. ἔθιμος, see BGU II. 581[5] (A.D. 133) ὀμνύω τὸν ἔθιμον Ῥωμαίων ὅρκον, P Oxy IV. 729[7] (lease of a vineyard—A.D. 137) τὴν δὲ ἀν[α]βολὴν ποιήσονται ἀπὸ τῶν ἐθίμων ἀναβολῶν.

ἔθω.

P Hib I. 77[5] (B.C. 249) καὶ πρότερον εἰώθει, P Oxy VII. 1024[31] (A.D. 129) ἣν καταθήσεται εἰς τὴν γῆν ὑγιῶς ἐπακολουθούντων τῶν εἰωθότων, "he shall sow it on the land in good faith under the observance of the usual officers" (Ed.), P Giss I. 80[6] (ii/A.D.) τὰ [π]εριστερίδι[α καὶ ὀ]ρνυθάρια, ἃ οὐκ ἤωθα ἐσθεῖν (*l.* ἐσθίειν), πέμψον, P Thead 19[5] (iv/A.D.) τοὺς ἀδικουμένους ὀρφανο[ύς], ἡγέμων δέσποτα, ἐκδικεῖν εἴωθεν τὸ μεγαλεῖον τὸ σόν.

εἰ.

The weakening of the distinction between εἰ and ἐάν in Hellenistic Greek is seen not only in the use of ἐάν with the indicative (see *s.v.* ἐάν), but in the occasional use of εἰ with the subjunctive, as P Ryl II. 234[12] (ii/A.D.) λέγοντος μὴ δύνασθαι ἀπο[χ]ωρῆσαι, εἰ μὴ ἀντιφωνηθῇ, "I stated that I could not leave without an answer" (Edd.), and the inscr. of Mopsuestia in Cilicia in Waddington *Inscriptions* iii. 2, No. 1490 (Imperial) ἐκτὸς εἰ μὴ (cf. 1 Cor 14[5]) [ἐ]ὰν Μάγνα μόνη θε[λή]σῃ (cited by Deissmann *BS* p. 118). See further *Proleg*. p. 187 and for εἰ . . ἄν, as in 1 Cor 7[5] (om. ἄν B),

see the exx. collected in *ib.* pp. 160, 230, e.g. P Tebt II.
391²³ (A.D. 99) ἴ τις δὲ ἡμῶν τῶν τεσσάρων ἐὰν παραβῇ
πρὸς τὰ προγεγραμμένα ἐκτίσι κτλ., BGU I. 326⁰·¹⁰ (ii/A.D.)
εἴ τι ἐὰν ἀν[θ]ρώπιν[ο]ν πά[θῃ] Μαρκέλλ[α, *ib.*⁰·² εἴ τι ἐὰν
ἐγὼ μετὰ ταῦτα γεγραμμένον καταλίπω, P Fay 130¹³ (iii/A.D.)
εἴ τινος ἦαν χρία σοί ἐστιν, and from the inscrr. *C. and B.*
ii. p. 380, No. 210 εἰ δέ τις ἂν φανείη μετὰ τὸ ἐμὲ τεθῆναι,
JHS xxv. p.63 ἴ τις δ' ἂν τολμήσι, μετέλθῃ αὐτὸν ὁ θεός. For
εἴ γε μή see the Imperial edict, P Fay 20⁵, where the Emperor,
now identified with Julian (*Archiv* ii. p. 169), states—εἴ γε μὴ
τὸ τῆς π[α]ρὰ τοῖς καὶ τοῖς δημοσίας ἀπορίας ἐμποδὼν ἦν,
"if the fact of the public embarrassment existing in various
parts had not stood in my way" (Edd.), I would have made
a more conspicuous display of magnanimity, etc. Εἰ μὴ—
ἀλλά, as in Gal 1⁷, may be illustrated from the vi/A.D. *OGIS*
201²⁰ οὐκ ἀφῶ αὐτοὺς καθεσθῆναι εἰς τὴν σκιάν, εἰ μὴ ὑπὸ
ἡλίου ἔξω (where see Dittenberger's note): for the more regular usage cf. P Tebt II. 414⁹ (ii/A.D.) ἰ μὴ ὅτι ἠσθένηκα, πάλαι
πεπόνφην σοι, "had it not been for the fact that I was ill,
I should have sent them to you long ago" (Edd.), and P
Ryl II. 165⁵⁰ (A.D. 139) πλὴν εἰ μὴ . . . [ἀφισ]τάνειν με
αὐτὸν παραχρῆμα ἰδίοις μου ἀναλώμασι, "otherwise I will
repel him forthwith at my own expense" (Edd.): see also
Proleg. p. 171. Instances of εἰ δὲ μή γε will be found *s.v.*
γε. In the illiterate P Oxy I. 119⁸ (ii/iii A.D.) (= *Selections*,
p. 103) ἂμ μὴ θέλῃς ἀπενέκαι μ[ε], ταῦτα γε[ί]νετε, ἂμ μή =
εἰ οὐ (see Blass *Hermes* xxiv. p. 312).

For the emphatic εἴπερ, "if indeed," cf. P Hal I. 7⁶ (B.C.
232) Π[τ]ολεμαίωι δὲ διά[σ]τειλαι, εἴπερ μὴ τὸν βυβλιαφόρον
καὶ τὸν ἔφοδον ἐκπέπει[κα]ς, P Lond 42³⁰ (B.C. 168) (= I.
p. 31, *Selections*, p. 11) κα[λῶ]ς ποιήσεις . . . παρα[γεν]ό-
μενος εἰς τὴν πόλιν, εἴπερ μὴ ἀναγκαιότερον σ[ε] περισπᾷ,
"please return to the city, unless indeed something most
pressing occupies you," P Fay 124¹⁴ (ii/A.D.) εἴπερ εἰ καὶ
γράμματα μὴ ἦν, ἀλλὰ τοῖ[ς] θ[εο]ῖ[ς] ἐστ[ι]ν χάρις ὅτι
οὐδεμία ἐστιν πρόλημψις ἡμεῖν γεγενημένη κτλ., "even if
there were no documents, still, thank heaven, there is no
preconceived principle on our part," etc. (Edd.) See also
the late P Oxy VI. 942³ (vi/vii A.D.) καὶ ὁ θεὸς οἶδεν εἴπερ
μὴ ἤμεθα ἀπολύσαντες τὰ ζῷα, εἰ δ' αὐτὰ εἴχαμεν ἐπανα-
λῦσαι, "God knows whether we had not released the animals, and whether we had any more to unloose" (Edd.).

With the construction in Lk 22⁴² where εἰ βούλει forms
the protasis followed by an apodosis introduced by the inf.
= imperative προσένεγκαι, may be compared a iv/B.C. letter,
reprinted by Deissmann *LAE* p. 149, στέγασμα εἴ τι βό-
λεσθε ἀποπέμψαι, "if ye be willing, send me some covering":
see the translator's note.

εἰ μήν,

which is well attested in Heb 6¹⁴, is best understood as an
orthographical variation of ἦ μήν. The spelling is fully
established after iii/B.C.: cf. e.g. *Syll* 578²⁰ (iii/B.C.) εἰ
μὰν μηθὲν νοσφίζεσθαι, *ib.* 653²⁷ (a "Mysteries" inscr.—
B.C. 91) ὁρκιζόντω τὸν γυναικονόμον ἐπὶ τῶν αὐτῶν ἱερῶν,
εἰ μὰν ἕξειν ἐπιμέλειαν κτλ., P Tebt I. 22¹³ (B.C. 112)
ὀμν[ύ]ομεν τοὺς θεοὺς εἰ μὴν μετρῆσ[αι] Κό[τ]υος τὰ ἐκφόρια
σου ἀπολέγοντος αὐτόν, *ib.* 78¹⁵ (B.C. 110-8) ὀμνύω]ι . .
εἰ μὴν [ἐπιδ]εδωκέναι τὸ προκείμενον προσάγγελμα, BGU II.
543³ (B.C. 28-7) ὄμνυμι Καίσαρα Αὐτοκράτορα Θεοῦ υἱὸν εἰ
μὴν παραχωρήσειν ἐπάναγκον Σωχάρμωι . . τὸν ὑπάρχοντά

μοι κλῆρον. See further Deissmann *BS* p. 205 ff., *Proleg.*
p. 46.

εἰδέα.

This poetic form, which in the NT is confined to Mt 28³,
is found in P Gen I. 16¹⁷ (A.D. 207) (= *Chrest* I. p. 417)
καὶ διὰ αὐτὸ τ[ο]ῦτο τὸ (om.) μέρος πάντα τὰ ὑποστέλλοντα
τῇ κώμῃ πάμπολλα ὄντα ἀποδ[ί]δοται ἕνεκ[α] τοῦ μὴ ἔχιν
τὴν κώμην μήτε ἰδι[ω]τικὴν γῆν μήτε βασ[ιλ]ικὴν μηδὲ
ἄλλην εἰδέαν.

εἶδον, (-δα).

P Tebt II. 417⁵ (iii/A.D.) ὕπαγε πρὸς τὸν Μῶρον καὶ εἰδὲ
τί λέγει περὶ τῆς Ἀντινόου, "go to Morus and see what he
says about Antinoe" (Edd.). For the form εἶδα (as in Mk 2¹²
al., cf. Blass *Gr.* p. 45), see e.g. the *libellus* P Meyer 15¹⁸
(A.D. 250) εἴδαμέν σε θυσιάζοντα, and on εἶδον written ἴδον,
see *Proleg.* p. 47. The verb is used without an obj. in such
wall-scratchings as *Preisigke* 1822 Κύριλλος εἶδεν, 1828
Ἀνδ]ρόνικος [. . .]νος ἴδον καὶ ἐθαύμασα. See also *s.v.*
ὁράω.

εἶδος.

The RV rendering of 1 Th 5²² ἀπὸ παντὸς εἴδους πονηροῦ
ἀπέχεσθε, "abstain from every form of evil," is confirmed by
the recurrent formula in the papyri παντὸς εἴδους = "of every
kind," found in business documents *passim*, e.g. in P Tebt I.
58²¹ (B.C. 111) a tax-farmer undertakes προσάξιν ἀπὸ παντὸς
εἴδους (πυροῦ) υ, "to collect from every class 400 artabae
of wheat more" (Edd.): see further Milligan *Thess.* p. 76 f.
Cf. P Tebt II. 289⁵ (A.D. 23) where the strategus writes to
a toparch—πέμπε μοι πρόσγραφον τῶν μέχρι τῆς σήμερον
διαγεγρ[αμμένων] κατ' εἶδος, "send me a supplementary
classified statement of payments made up to date" (Edd.),
and P Oxy II. 237ᵛⁱⁱⁱ·⁴² (A.D. 186) τῆς τελευταίας ἑκάστου
ὀνόματος ὑποστάσεως κατὰ κώμην καὶ κατ' εἶδος, "the last
statement of property of each person arranged under villages
and classes" (Edd.): but see *Chrest.* II. i. p. 103. In
P Tebt I. 60¹¹⁷ (B.C. 118) a detailed account of land is
headed -ῶν ἐστιν τὸ κατ' ἔτος καὶ τὸ κατ' εἶδος, *i.e.* the
land is regarded both under temporal and material conditions, and in P Lond 847¹¹ (A.D. 170) (= III. p. 54)
μονοδεσ[μία] χόρτ(ου) κ(αὶ) ἄλλ(ων) εἰδ(ῶν) the editors suggest the rendering "harvesting of hay and other miscellaneous
crops." A list of personal property, P Oxy I. 100¹ (iii/iv
A.D.), is headed Λόγ(ος) εἰδῶν, "List of effects." P Tebt
II. 287¹²·²⁹ (A.D. 161-9) shows εἶδος = a "report" furnished
to the prefect: the editors compare BGU I. 16⁵ (A.D. 159-
60) (= *Selections*, p. 84) πρὸς τὸ μεταδοθὲν εἰς ἐξέτασιν
εἶδος, "with regard to the report handed over to us for
examination"; see also P Amh II. 65¹¹ (early ii/A.D.) ἀναγνωσθέντος εἴδους ἵνα μὴ παιδαγωγὸν ἔχωι, P Oxy VII.
1032¹⁷ (A.D. 162) ἔγνωμεν . . [ἤ]χθαι εἶδος δι' [ο]ῦ δηλ[οῦ]ται
κτλ., "we have discovered that a report was made whereby
it is declared" etc. The word is very fully discussed in
P Meyer, p. 13 f. In MGr εἶδος still means "kind,"
"species," and from it comes (ἐ)δικός, "one's own."

εἰδωλεῖον,

or εἰδώλιον as the word is read in the best MSS., occurs
several times in the LXX, but in the NT only in 1 Cor 8¹⁰.

No instance has been found as yet in profane Greek, but we may compare such analogous forms as Ἰσιεῖον and Ἀνουβιεῖον, shrines dedicated to Isis and Anubis: see e.g. P Tebt I. 5[70f.] (B.C. 118). The invitation in P Oxy I. 110 (ii/A.D.) δειπνῆσαι εἰς κλείνην τοῦ κυρίου Σαράπιδος ἐν τῷ Σαραπείῳ, "to sup at the table (couch) of the lord Serapis in the Serapeum" is also an excellent illustration of 1 Cor 8[10], 10[21, 27]: cf. P Oxy III. 523 (ii/A.D.) (= *Selections*, p. 97) and Wilcken *Archiv* iv. p. 211.

εἰδωλολάτρης

and εἰδωλολατρία are regarded by Nägeli (p. 51) as Christian formations: cf. the Acts of the martyrdom of Christina PSI I. 27[21] (v/A.D.) ἐξῆλθεν τὸ πῦρ ἀάφν[ω (*l.* ἄφνω) καὶ ἀπέκτ]εινεν ψυχὰς [εἰδωλολατ]ρῶν. A compound εἰδωλοποιητής is found in Vett. Valens p. 112[34]. Εἰδωλομανία, a stronger formation than εἰδωλολατρία, appears *quater* in *Barlaam and Ioasaph* (viii/A.D.), e.g. ch. i. § 3 τῷ τῆς εἰδωλομανίας ἐμελαίνετο ζόφῳ, "(Persia) was darkened with the gloom of idolatry."

εἴδωλον

In P Leid W[xx. 6] (ii/iii A.D.) εἴδωλα θ̄ are the "nine constellations," but in the astrological P Ryl II. 63[3] (iii/A.D.) the word is used in the more general sense of "image," "phenomenon," when Plato asks an Egyptian, τίς δὲ ἡ αἰτία τούτων [τ]ῶ[ν εἰ]δώλων; "what is the cause of these phenomena?" (Edd.), and receives a reply connecting various parts of the body with the sun, moon, etc. Cf. also the horoscope, P Lond 130[136] (i/ii A.D.) (= I. p. 137) ἀστέρα τὸν ἐν τῆι χλαμύδι καλούμενον Γανυμήδην ὁμωνύμως τῶι ὅλωι εἰδώλωι, and *ib.* 122[38] (iv/A.D.) (= I. p. 117) ἐγὼ γάρ εἰμι τὸ εἴδωλόν σου. The word is used of the images of heathen gods in the vi/A.D. Silco inscr. *OGIS* 201[5] ἐποίησα εἰρήνην μετ᾽ αὐτῶν καὶ ὤμοσάν μοι τὰ εἴδωλα αὐτῶν καὶ ἐπίστευσα τὸν ὅρκον αὐτῶν. Vett. Val. pp. 67[5] ὑπὸ δαιμονίων καὶ φαντασίας εἰδώλων χρηματισθήσονται, 113[17] τοῦ δὲ Κρόνου ἐν τῷ ὑπογείῳ εὑρεθέντος θεῶν καὶ νεκρῶν εἴδωλα ἐφαντάσθη.

εἰκῆ

is found in P Lips I. 104[29] (B.C. 96–5) (= Witkowski[2], p. 118) εἰκῆ ἐφ᾽ ἀλλαχῆ βαδίζετε. Witkowski notes that the meaning may be either "audacter" or "frustra": cf. P Leid G[15] (B.C. 181–145) εἰκῆ καὶ ὡς ἔτυχεν, where the editor translates "temere et forte." For εἰκαῖος see P Ryl II. 235[12] (ii/A.D.) ἀλλὰ οὐ πρώτως σου τὸ εἰκαῖον μανθάνομεν, "but it is not the first time that we learn your heedlessness" (Edd.). Since εἰκῆ is an adverbial dat. like ἰδίᾳ, δημοσίᾳ, and the ancient inscriptional evidence shows some confusion, we cannot be certain whether to write εἰκῆ or εἰκῇ: see Moulton *Gr.* ii. § 66.

εἴκοσι,

and not εἴκοσιν, is the regular form in the papyri even before a vowel, as in the best MSS. of Ac 1[15], e.g. BGU II. 644[19] (A.D. 69) εἴκοσι ἤ, *ib.* I. 207[11] (A.D. 199) εἴκοσι ἀριθμῷ, P Grenf II. 59[11] (A.D. 189) εἴκοσι ἀπό. Cronert *Mem. Herc.* p. 141 n.[2] notes only one exception, P Grenf II. 75[7] (A.D. 305) τάλαντα εἴκοσι, ἃ πλήρωσέν (*l.* ἐπλήρωσέν) μοι: see also Mayser *Gr.* p. 239.

In *Preisigke* 1931 (ostracon—A.D. 69) the word is written ἴκοσι: so 1932. For ἡ εἰκοστή as a tax of 5 per cent. on the rent of an οἰκόπεδον cf. P Petr II. 11 (2)[4] (mid. iii/B.C.) (= III. p. 112) ἀπογέγραμμαι δὲ ἐπὶ τελώνιον τὸ οἰκόπεδον φέρον ἐν[οίκιο]ν (δραχμῶν) ιζ (ἡμισείας), ἵνα ἐκ τοσούτου φέρωμεν τὴν εἰκοστήν: see further Wilcken *Ostr* i. p. 393 f., and for a similar succession duty see Hunt in P Oxy VIII. p. 192.

εἰκών

is the term used for the *description* of individuals in official documents, e.g. BGU IV. 1050[7] (bill of sale of a female slave—i/B.C.) ἧς τὰ ἔτη καὶ αἱ εἰκόνες ὑπόκεινται: cf. P Tebt I 32[21] (B.C. 145?) ὑποτετάχ[α]μεν δὲ κα[ὶ] τὴν εἰκόνα αὐ[τοῦ] καὶ τοῦ υἱοῦ τὸ ὄνομα, "we have, further, appended the description of him and the name of his son," P Strass I. 70[10] (B.C. 16) ἐν ᾧ αἱ εἰκόνες αὐτῆς δηλοῦν[ται. For a similar use of εἰκονισμός see P Ryl II. 156[33] (i/A.D.) where the heading εἰκ ονισμοί) is followed by the names and descriptions of various individuals. If Wilcken's restoration can be accepted we have an interesting instance of the diminutive εἰκόνιον in BGU II. 423[21] (ii/A.D.) (= *Chrest.* I. p. 566, *Selections*, p. 92), where a soldier-son writing home to his father from Italy adds — ἔπεμψά σο[ι ε]ἰκόνιν μ[ου] διὰ Εὐκτήμονος, "I send you a little portrait of myself at the hands of Euctemon." A further diminutive εἰκονίδιον occurs several times in a Return of Temple Property, P Oxy XII. 1449 (A.D. 213–17). With the Pauline phrase of the believer's being renewed κατ᾽ εἰκόνα τοῦ κτίσαντος αὐτόν (Col 3[10]) and the descriptions of Christ as εἰκὼν τοῦ θεοῦ (e.g. 2 Cor 4[4]) we may compare *OGIS* 90[3] (the Rosetta stone — B.C. 196) εἰκόνος ζώσης τοῦ Διός, with reference to Ptolemy Epiphanes. Later in the same inscr.[38] we hear of a statue (εἰκόνα) of Ptolemy being erected ἐν ἑκάστωι ἱερῶι ἐν τῶι ἐπιφα[νεστάτωι τόπωι, and for this common usage cf. further *ib.* 332[22] (B.C. 138–2), 383[27] (mid. i/B.C.) In *Syll* 888[5] (ii/A.D.) τὰς τούτων τῶν ἀγαλμάτων εἰκόνας is explained by Dittenberger on the assumption that the ἀγάλματα comprise the sculptor's whole work, of which the actual *bust* is a part. Thieme (p. 26 f.) has well pointed out how the ancient practice of erecting εἰκόνες of their gods would give a concrete force to such Bibl. passages as are cited above, and instances as of special interest *Magn* 101 (2nd half of ii/B.C.), where not only do three ambassadors receive each his εἰκών at the hands of the grateful Larbeni, but it is also decided to erect εἰκόνα χαλκῆν in honour of the "Magnesian people" (τὸν δῆμον τὸν Μαγνήτων) themselves. In P Fay 36[23] (A.D. 111–2) the verb is used = "draw up," "write" — Κάστωρ νομογράφος εἰκόνικα φαμένου μὴ εἰδέναι γράμματα, "I, Castor, scribe of the nome, have drawn up this deed, since (Sanesneus) stated that he could not write": cf. P Meyer 4[21] (A.D. 101) with the editor's note, and Preisigke *Fachwörter*, p. 60. See the intr. to P Oxy I. 34 on the εἰκονισταί. In P Ryl II. 161[15] (A.D. 71) μεχρὶ τοῦ ἐσομένου ἑτεροῦ ἰκονισμοῦ ἀπογραφῆς, the reference is to the next census.

εἰλικρίνεια

or —ία (WH *Notes*[2] p. 160 f., and for breathing *ib.* p. 151), not found in class. Greek, may be illustrated from P Oxy X. 1252 *verso*[38] (A.D. 288–95) προσφεύγω ἐπὶ τὴν σὴν ἱλεικρινείαν, "I have recourse to your probity" (Edd.). The etymology is doubtful (cf. Moulton *Gr.* ii. § 105), but Boisacq *Dict. Etym.* *s.v.* **εἰλικρινής** inclines to the old derivation (rejected by LS) from **εἴλη** (cf. Skr. *s(ú)var* "light," "sun," and **κρίνω**, as if = "examined by the light of the sun" and found pure, sincere : cf. T. H. Green's definition of **εἰλ.** as "perfect openness towards God" (*Two Sermons*, p. 41.).

εἰλικρινής

is attached as a qualitative adj. to **εὔνοια** in *OGIS* 763[40] (ii/B.C.) ἐξηγο[ύμενοι σύμπαν]τος τοῦ πλήθους πρὸς ἡμᾶς ἐκτενε[στάτην τε καὶ] εἰλικρινῆ τὴν εὔνοιαν, and to **ἀπόδειξις** in *ib.* 227[12] (B.C. 246–26) εἰλικρινῆ καὶ βεβαίαν ποιουμένους ὑμᾶς πρὸς τοὺς φίλους ἀπόδειξιν. The adv. is found *ib.* 441[5] (B.C. 81) τὴν πρὸς ἡ[μᾶς πί[σ]τιν εἰλικρινῶς τετηρηκότας : cf. *Michel* 394[18] (mid. i/B.C.) ὁ δῆμος [ζ]ηλοῖ αὐτὸν . . . . . κα[ὶ] εἰλ[ικρινῶ]ς [γ]νησ[ί]αν ἔχοντι πρὸς πάντας φιλοστοργίαν εὐχαρισ[τ]εῖ.

εἰλίσσω.

See **ἑλίσσω**.

εἰμί.

Middle forms in the flexion of **εἰμί** other than the present tense (cf. however MGr **εἶμαι**, **-σαι**, etc.) begin to appear very early in the dialects and are well established in the papyri. Thus the 1st sing. impf. **ἤμην**, which always takes the place of the class. **ἦ** in the NT (but see Ac 20[18] D) may be illustrated from PSI IV. 362[21] (B.C. 251–0) ἤμην δὲ πρὸς τῶι λαμβάνειν τὸν χαλκόν, P Magd 6[6] (B.C. 221) ἤμην γυμνός, P Par 8[7] (B.C. 129) ὧν ἤμην δι᾽ αὐτῶν [π]αραμε-[μετ]ρηκ[υῖα, P Oxy III. 526[3] (ii/A.D.) οὐκ ἤμην ἀπαθὴς ἀλόγως σε καταλείπιν. For 1st plur. **ἤμεθα** see P Petr II. 4 (7)[3] (B.C. 255–4) τεθλιμμένοι ἤμεθα : cf. Ac 27[37], Eph 2[3], as contrasted with the act. **ἦμεν** in Ac 11[11] (NB), 16[12], Rom 7[5] *al.* : the two forms are found together in Gal 4[3] (NDFG). The non-classical **ἦς** (Lob. *Phryn.* p. 149) is found *septies* in the NT as compared with **ἦσθα** (from an old perf. form **ἤησθα**), which is confined to Mk 14[67] with its parallel Mt 26[69]. For **ἤμην**, **ἦς** in Epictetus, see Sharp *Epict.* p. 83. On the other hand **ἦσθα** is the commoner form in the LXX (Thackeray *Gr.* i. p. 256), and Moulton (*Gr.* ii. § 86) throws out the conjecture that this **ἦσθα** in Mt may have started under LXX influence, and that the text of Mk was harmonized. In P Hib I. 78[16] (B.C. 244–3) ἐὰν δὲ μὴ δυνατὸς ἦσθα ἀπολῦσαι γράψμ [*l.* γράψον] μοι, **ἦσθα** must be treated as subj., like **ἦσαν** in P Tebt II. 333[13] (A.D. 216) ἐὰν ἦσάν τι παθόντες ἀνθρώπ[ι]νον and P Oxy VIII. 1157[15] (late iii/A.D.) ἐὰν δὲ ἦσαν . . ἐπείγον τες ἀπαιτῆσαι τὸ ἐπικεφάλαιον, "and if they are [hurrying on with] the collection of the poll-tax" (Ed.), where a past tense is excluded by the context. The forms may probably be regarded as extensions of the curious but common substitution of **ἤν** for **ἦ**, the iota being lost and the parasitic **ν** being added after the long vowel, in such passages as P Oxy IV. 744[6] (B.C. 1) (= *Selections*, p. 33) ἐὰν ἦν ἄρσενον, ἄφες, ἐὰν ἦν θήλεα, ἔκβαλε, BGU III. 821[6] (ii/A.D.) ὅταν ἦν τι καινότερον, εὐθέως σοι δηλ[ώ]σω, P Fay 124[15] (ii/A.D.) εἴπερ εἰ καὶ γράμματα μὴ ἦν, P Oxy I. 63[18] (ii/iii A.D.) ἵνα μη[δ]ὲν ἐνπόδιον ἦν, "in order that there may be no delay." The same phenomenon is found in NT uncials,

e.g. Mt 10[13] C ἐὰν μὲν ἦν ἡ οἰκία ἀξία, Mk 5[18] B*D ἵνα μετ᾽ αὐτοῦ ἦν, Lk 20[28] N° ἐὰν . . οὗτος ἄτεκνος ἦν, 1 Cor 16[4] A ἐὰν δὲ ἄξιον ἦν. See further Moulton *Gr.* ii. § 86 *n.* 2 (ε) and for additional papyrus exx. *CR* xv. pp. 38, 436, xviii. p. 108. In certain cases we may have instances of **ἐάν** construed with the indicative (cf. Deissmann *BS* p. 201 f.) : the context alone can decide.

For 3rd sing. **εἴη(ι)**, the only form of the opt. which occurs in the NT (*undecies*), we may cite P Vat A[3] (B.C. 168) (= Witkowski[2], p. 64) εἴηι ἄν, ὡς βούλομαι, P Grenf I. 21[2] (B.C. 126) εἴ[ι]ηι μέμ μοι ὑγιαίνοντι τῶν ἐμαυτοῦ κύριον εἶναι, and the frequently recurring phrase εὐορκοῦντι μέν μοι εὖ εἴη, ἐφιορκοῦντι δὲ τὰ ἐναντία, as in P Tebt I. 79[17f.] (B.C. 110–8). In P Hib I. 79[5] (*c.* B.C. 260) we have **εἴ** (for εἴη) ἄν, ὡς ἐγὼ θέλω, a form apparently not found elsewhere in Ptolemaic papyri (cf. Witkowski[2], p. 25), and in P Par 44[2] (B.C. 153) εἴε (for εἴη) ἄν, ὡς βούλομαι. The 3rd plur. is seen in P Par 35[29] (B.C. 163) πυνθανομένων δ᾽ ἡμῶν τοῦ χάριν εἴησαν εἰσπορευσάμενοι.

The 2nd sing. imperf. **ἴσθι**, as in Mt 5[25], Mk 5[34], occurs in such passages as P Tebt I. 58[31] (B.C. 111) καὶ σὺ ἀναγωνίατος ἴσθει (*l.* ἴσθι), P Leid W[iii. 10] (ii/iii A.D.) σὺ δὲ ἐν ἐλίνοις ἴσθοι (*l.* λίνοις ἴσθι. According to Mayser (*Gr.* p. 327) the ending -θι is found in the Ptolemaic papyri only in **ἴσθει** = **ἴσθι** from **εἶναι**, and **ἴσθι** from **οἶδα**. "Εστω hardly needs illustration, but its frequency may be noted in such formulas as P Petr I. 16 (2)[14] (B.C. 230) ἡ πρᾶξις ἔστω ὡς πρὸς βασιλικά, P Oxy II. 270[43] (A.D. 94) ἄκυρον [ἔ]στω, "**κυρία ἔστω** *al.* For **ἤτω**, which in the NT is found only in 1 Cor 16[22] (contrast Gal 1[8]), Jas 5[12], see BGU I. 276[24] (ii/iii A.D.) παρά σοι ἤτω, P Oxy III. 533[9] (ii/iii A.D.) ἐν ἀσφαλεῖ [ἤ]τω, P Lond 948 *verso*[8] (A.D. 257) (= III. p. 210) ἤτω οὖν ὁ Σύρος πρ[ὸ]ς τοὺς ποιμένας, BGU II. 419[13] (A.D. 276–7) ζημίωμα [π]ρὸς σὲ ἤτω, and P Lond 46[825] (iv/A.D.) (= I. p. 75) ὑποτεταγμένος δέ μοι ἤτω. None of these exx., it will be noticed, carries us back to i/A.D., and the inscriptional evidence is also late (Schweizer *Gr.* p. 177, Meisterhans *Gr.* p. 191). For **ἔστωσαν**, which is found in Attic inscrr. from B.C. 200 onwards (Meisterhans, *ut s.*) and occurs twice in the NT (Lk 12[35], 1 Tim 3[12]), we may cite P Petr III. 2[22] (B.C. 237) ἔστωσαν ἐλεύθεροι. CPR I. 1[22] (A.D. 83–4) αἱ γεγονυῖαι διὰ τῶν καταλοχισμῶν οἰκονομίαι κυρίαι ἔστωσαν ἐπὶ τὸν ἅπαντα χρόνον, and for **ἤτωσαν** P Leid W[iii. 40] (ii/iii A.D.) ἤτωσαν δὲ οἱ λύχνοι τεταρτημόριοι.

The periphrastic use of **εἰμί** with the participle (the so-called σχῆμα Χαλκιδικόν), which is common both in the LXX and the NT (see a useful list of exx. in Conybeare and Stock *Selections*, p. 68 ff.) may be illustrated in somewhat fuller detail :—(a) *present* : BGU I. 183[25] (A.D. 85) ἐφ᾽ ὃν χρόνον ζῶσα ἡ Σαταβοῦς : cf. P Giss I. 19[7] (ii/A.D.) μεγάλως ἀγωνιῶσα περί σου διὰ τὰ ὄν[τα τ]οῦ καιροῦ φημιζόμενα. (b) *perfect* : P Petr II. 13 (3)[3] (B.C. 258–3) τεῖχος . . πεπτωκός ἐστιν, and often in such a phrase as ἵν᾽ ὦ εὐεργετημένη, e.g. P Oxy III. 486[16] (A.D. 131) : cf. Jn 16[24], 17[19, 23]. See also Radermacher *Gr.* p. 83 for exx. from Vett. Valens, Diodorus, Herondas, and others. (c) *future perfect* : PSI IV. 424[8] (iii/B.C.) ἔσει ἐμέ τε σεσωικώς, P Par 35[38] (B.C. 163) ἔσομαι τετευχώς, P Tebt I. 56[16] (*c.* B.C. 130–121) τοῦτο δὲ ποήσας ἔσηι μοι κεχαρισμένος εἰς τὸν ἅπαντα χρόν[ον], BGU II. 596[12] (A.D. 84) (= *Selections*, p. 64) ἔση μοι μεγάλην χάριταν κατατιθειμ[έ]νο ς), P Leid W[b. 35] (ii/iii

A.D.) καὶ ἔσῃ τελεσμένος (*l.* τετελ) αὐτός: other exx. in Mayser *Gr.* p. 377. Three papyri of iii/A.D. have an aor. part. with εἰμί in a future perfect sense—P Tebt II. 333[13] (A.D. 216) ἐὰν ἦσάν τι παθόντες ἀνθρώπ[ι]νον, *ib.* 423[18] (early iii/A.D.) ἐὰν οὖν μὴ ἧς λαβὼν τὰ πρόβατα πρὸς κοιτασμός (*l.* -όν) ("folding"), P Lond 948 *verso*[3] (A.D. 257) (= III. p. 210) ἀνερχέστω ἐὰν ἦν παυσάμενος τοῦ ἀχύρου. The wholly exceptional Lk 23[19] B ἦν . . βληθείς may be compared, but there the sense is aoristic: cf. Robertson *Gr.* p. 860. (d) *imperfect:* P Oxy I. 115[5] (ii/A.D.) (= *Selections*, p. 96) ὅσα ἦν καθήκοντα ἐποίησα, *Syll* 929[81] ὅπερ οὐκ ἦν ἐνδεχόμενον: cf. also *ib.* 927[22] (ii/B.C.) ὡς ἁρμόζον ἦν, and *Pelagia-Legenden*, p. 18[7] ἦν . . . ἀκούσασα. (e) *pluperfect:* P Par 8[7] (B.C. 129) ὧν ἤμην δι' αὐτῶν [π]αραμε[μετ]ρηκ[υ]ῖα, P Oxy II. 285[10] (*c.* A.D. 50) ἀφήρπασεν ὃν ἤμην ἐνδεδυμένος (*l.* -ος) χιτῶνα λεινοῦν. On how far all these periphrastic constructions are due to Semitic influence, see *Proleg.* p. 226 f.

For οὐκ ἔστι = "it is impossible," as in 1 Cor 11[20], Heb 9[5], cf. P Par 47[23] (*c.* B.C. 153) (= *Selections*, p. 23) οὐκ ἔστι ἀνακύψα< >ι με> πόποτε ἐν τῇ Τρικομίαι ὑπὸ τῆς αἰσχύνης, "it is impossible ever to show my face in Tricomia for very shame": for πρέπον ἐστί, as in Mt 3[15], cf. P Oxy I. 120[24] (iv/A.D.) τὰ κατὰ σὲ διοίκησον ὡς πρέπον ἐστίν, "see that matters are properly conducted on your own part," (Edd.), and for δέον ἐστί, as in Ac 19[36], cf. P Oxy IV. 727[19f.] (A.D. 154) ἃ ἐὰν [δ]έον ἦν followed by πρὸς οὓς ἐὰν δέῃ, and the exx. cited *s.v.* δέον. In P Oxy VI. 899[40] (A.D. 200) δέον οὖν τὴν μεταδιαταγὴν ἑτέροις γενέσθαι κατὰ τὰ γραφέντα ὑπὸ σοῦ, "the change in appointment of other cultivators ought accordingly to take place in conformity with your letter" (Edd.), ἐστί is omitted in 1 Pet 1[6] ℵ*B.

With the idiomatic use of ὁ ὢν in Ac 13[1] κατὰ τὴν οὖσαν ἐκκλησίαν, "in the local church," and *ib.* 14[13] D τοῦ ὄντος Διὸς πρὸ πόλεως where τοῦ ὄντος is almost equivalent to τοῦ ὀνομαζομένου (see Ramsay *CRE*, p. 52), cf. P Lond 1168[5] (A.D. 18) (= III. p. 136) ἐπὶ ταῖς οὔσαις γειτνίαις, also such phrases as PSI III. 229[11] (ii/A.D.) τοῦ ὄντος μηνὸς Τῦβι, "the current month Tubi," P Oxy XII. 1583[11] (ii/A.D.) γράψον μοι περὶ τῶν ὄντων ὄντων (omit) καὶ τὰ γενόμενα. With 1 Cor 1[28] we may compare P Leid W[viii. 9] (ii/iii A.D.) σὲ μόνον ἐπικαλοῦμαι . . . τὸν ἑαυτὸν (omit) ἀλλάξαντα σεαυτὸν μορφαῖς ἁγίαις καὶ ἐκ μὴ ὄντων εἶναι ποιήσαντα, καὶ ἐξ ὄντων μὴ εἶναι.

For Rom 13[1] see P Par 5[2] (B.C. 114) ἐφ' ἱερέων καὶ ἱερειῶν καὶ κανηφόρου τῶν ὄντων καὶ οὐσῶν, and note P Petr III. 42 F (a)[1] (mid. iii/B.C.) ἐφ' ἱερέως τοῦ ὄντος Ἀλεξάνδρου καὶ τῶν θεῶν, "in the time of the priest who is (priest) of Alexander and the gods," the form of expression implying ignorance of the name of the priest of a new year: the editors remark on this very early occurrence of a usage which afterwards became common.

Ἐστὶ δέ is found at the head of lists, as in PSI III. 160[13] (A.D. 149), P Flor III. 321[5] (iii/A.D.), P Grenf II. 77[16] (iii/iv A.D.) (= *Selections*, p. 121), *al.* For τουτέστιν, which is always written τοῦτ' ἔστιν by WH in the NT, see P Flor II. 157[4] (iii/A.D.) εἰς [τ]ὸ ἔργον ἐκεῖνο τὸ τῆς Θεο[ξ]ένιδος τουτέστιν τὸ τῆς ἄμμου, PSI IV. 298[9] (iv/A.D. *init.*) οὐκ ἴασέν με τὸν τεταγμένον χρόνο(ν) [ἐκεῖσε διαμεῖναι?,] τουτέστιν τοὺς ἓξ μῆνας πληρῶσαι. Cf. also P Meyer 6[21] (A.D. 125) τούτου ὄντος, "this being the case." Εἰμί with the

PART III.

---

gen. of time, as in Mk 5[42], is seen in P Oxy II. 275[9] (A.D. 66) (= *Selections*, p. 55) οὐδέπω ὄντα τῶν ἐτῶν. "not yet of age." The present ἔστι is used in a futuristic sense in P Oxy III. 531[22] (ii/A.D.) ἔστι δὲ τοῦ Τῦβι μηνός σοὶ ὃ θέλεις, where a father promises his son that in the forthcoming month Tubi he will receive whatever he wishes.

The use of εἰς with a predicate (as in Ac 8[23], 1 Cor 4[3]) can hardly be regarded as "after a Hebrew model" (Blass *Gr.* p. 85, cf. Radermacher *Gr.* p. 16 f.) in view of the vernacular usage of εἰς to denote destination, e.g. P Hib I. 99[10] (B.C. 270) ὁμ[ολο]γεῖ . . ἔχε[ιν] . . ἐς τὰ ἐκφόρια . . ἀρτ(ά)βας) ῡ, "agrees that he has received for the rent 400 artabae": cf. *Proleg.* p. 71 f. Deissmann (*LAE* p. 123) gives a similar instance from an official text of about ii/B.C.—*Priene* 50[39] τ]αῦτα δὲ εἶναι εἰς φυλακὴν τῆς πόλεως. Other instances of εἰμί with prepositions are P Petr II. 11 (1)[8] (iii/B.C.) (= *Selections*, p. 8) γράφε . . . ἵνα εἰδῶμεν ἐν οἷς εἰ, P Eleph 1[5] (B.C. 311–10) (= *Selections*, p. 2) εἶναι δὲ ἡμᾶς κατὰ ταὐτό, P Par 70[11] (Ptol.) καὶ γὰρ ὁ πατήρ αὐτοῦ ἐστιν ἐνταῦθα περὶ Πετόνουριν, P Petr II. 42 (b)[5] (mid. iii/B.C.) εἰμὶ γὰρ πρὸς τῶι ἀποδημεῖν, BGU I. 87[20] (A.D. 144) καὶ πάντων [τῶν] δ[ημο]σίων πρὸ[s] αὐτ[ὸ]ν ὄντων.

εἵνεκεν.

See ἕνεκα.

εἴπερ.

See εἰ.

εἶπον, (—πα).

In Witkowski's collection of Ptolemaic letters the form εἶπον does not occur, but see εἶπα before a vowel in P Par 49[15] (B.C. 164–158) (= Witkowski[2], p. 70) εἶπα αὐτῶι μὴ ἐμὲ ἀξιοῦν, and the participle εἴπας in *ib.*[20] ἀπέλυσα εἴπας αὐτῶι ὀρθρίτερον ἐλθεῖν. In P Par 45[7] (B.C. 153) (= Witkowski[2], p. 85) we have—μὴ εὕρη τι κατὰ σοῦ ἰπῖν. For the judicial use of the verb cf. P Tor I. 1[8.1] (B.C. 117–6) εἴπαμεν τῶι μὲν Ἑρμίαι μὴ εἰσβιάζεσθαι, "edicimus Hermiae, ne vim inferat" (Ed.): cf. *Archiv* iv. p. 30. See also *s.v.* λέγω, and for the weak aor. terminations, which did not become common till i/A.D., see Moulton *G.* ii. § 88. A "unique" fut εἰπόσει is found in BGU II. 597[6] (A.D. 75): see Radermacher *Gr.* p. 77.

εἰρηνεύω.

For εἰρηνεύω = "be at peace," as in all its occurrences in the NT, cf. the inscr. from Halicarnassus, *Brit. Mus. Inscr.* 894S (time of Augustus) εἰρηνεύο[υσ]ι μὲν γὰρ γῆ καὶ θάλαττα, a vivid picture of the *Pax Romana*, and OGIS 613[1] (A.D. 302) καὶ τοὺς διοδεύοντας καὶ τὸ ἔθνος διὰ παντὸς εἰρηνεύεσθαι ἠσφαλίσατο.

εἰρήνη.

P Strass I. 5[8] (A.D. 262) ἀνάξια [τ]ῆς ὑπὸ σοῦ πᾶσιν ἡμῖν πρυτανευομένης εἰρή[ν]ης ὁ πρεσβύτης παθών, P Goodsp Cairo 15[4] (A.D. 362) τὰ τετολμημένα εἰς ἐμὲ ἐν τοιαύτῃ πρ[υ]τα[ν]ευομένῃ εἰρήνῃ τοῦ δεσπότου [ἡ]μῶν βασιλέως Φλαουίου Ἰουλιανοῦ αἰωνίου Α[γο]ύστου, "the things perpetrated against me in the tranquillity enjoyed under our lord king Flavius Julianus, eternal Augustus" (Ed.). P Oxy I. 64[2] (iii/iv A.D.) shows an order for arrest addressed ἐπιστάτῃ

25

εἰρήνης κώμης Τῆεως : cf. *ib.* XII. 1507³ (iii/A.D.), *ib.* 1559³ (A.D. 341) ἐπόπτη εἰρήνης Ὀξυρυγχίτου, and Preisigke 4636 (iii/A.D.) a list of police officials including εἰρηνοφύλακες. P Oxy I. 41²⁷ (iii/iv A.D.) εἰρήνη πόλεως (voc.), addressed to a strategus, is worth quoting in connexion with Eph 2¹⁴. From Christian sources we may quote Ramsay *C. and B.* ii. p. 720 No. 655 (prob. iii/A.D.) εἰρήν[η] πάσῃ τῇ ἀδελ[φότητ]ι from the dedication of a καιμητήριον, and the commendatory letter P Oxy VIII. 1162⁹ (iv/A.D.) συνδέξασθαι αὐτὸν ἐν ἰρήνῃ. For Εἰρήνη as a proper name see P Petr III. 30⁴, BGU I. 115⁸ (A.D. 189), and the letter of consolation P Oxy I. 115¹ (ii/A.D.) (= *Selections*, p. 96).

εἰρηνικός.

P Oxy VII. 1033⁵ (A.D. 392) a petition from two νυκτοστράτηγοι, who describe themselves as τῶν εἰρηνικῶν τὴν φροντίδα ἀναδεδοιημένοι, "entrusted with the care of the peace" (Ed.). For the adv. see Aristeas 273 ἐπηρώτα . . πῶς ἂν κατὰ ψυχὴν καὶ ἐν τοῖς πολέμοις εἰρηνικῶς ἔχοι.

εἰς.

For this common preposition following verbs of *motion*, it is sufficient to quote P Par 63¹¹¹ (B.C. 164) τὰ σπέρματα κατενεγκεῖν εἰς τοὺς ἀγρούς, P Tebt I. 59⁴ (B.C. 99) καταντήσαντος γὰρ εἰς τὴν πόλιν Σ. κτλ., BGU I. 27⁶ ff. (ii/A.D.) (= *Selections*, p. 101) ὅτει εἰς γῆν ἐλήλυθα . . ἀνέβην δὲ εἰς Ῥώμην, and Meyer *Ostr* 66² (iii/A.D.) ἀπῆλθεν εἰς μακράν (cf. Ac 2³⁹). When Polycrates writes to his father—γίνωσκέ με . . . εἰς γεωμέτρων πορευόμενον (P Petr II. 11 2³—mid. iii/B.C.), Witkowski (*Epp.*² p. 2) understands the meaning to be that "apud agrimensores regios artem agros metiendi discebat": cf. P Oxy IX. 1215⁴ (ii/iii A.D.) μὴ ἀπέλθῃς εἰς τὸ Σατύρου, "do not go to the house of S.," P Iand 14⁶ (iv/A.D.) ἀπελθὲ εἰς Λύκ[ου]. The usage survives in MGr : see Thumb *Handbook*, § 46. A metaphorical usage underlies such passages as P Vat A¹² (B.C. 168) (= Witkowski², p. 65) τοῦ παιδίου σου εἰς τὰ ἔσχατα ἐληλυθότος, P Lond 42¹⁶ (B.C. 168) (= I. p. 30, *Selections*, p. 10) εἰς πᾶν τι ἐληλυθυῖα διὰ τὴν τοῦ σίτου τιμήν, "having come to the last extremity because of the high price of corn," and P Meyer 19⁴ (ii/A.D.) ὕπνωσα εἰς λύσιν, where the editor, following Wilcken, renders "ich habe bis zur Lösung (der Glieder) geschlafen." The idea of *direction* may still be traced in P Tebt I. 39³² (B.C. 114) ἐτραυμάτισαν τὴν γυναῖκά μου εἰς τὴν δεξιὰν χεῖρα, P Ryl II. 145¹³ (A.D. 38) ἔδωκεν πληγὰς πλείους εἰς πᾶν μέρος τοῦ σώματος, and the way is thus prepared for εἰς following verbs of *rest*, etc., e. g. P Par 49³⁵ (B.C. 164–158) εἰς . . . τὰ Πρωτάρχου καταλύσω, "I shall stay at the inn of Protarchus," P Fay 111¹² (A.D. 95–6) εἰς Διο[νυσι]άδα μῖναι (*l.* μεῖναι), BGU II. 423⁷ (ii A.D.) μου κινδυνεύσαντος εἰς θάλασσαν, "when I encountered danger at sea," *ib.* III. 845²⁰ (ii/A.D.) οἱ δαῦλοί σου εἰς τὴν κέλλαν α(ὐ)τῶν ἔχουσιν ἐλαίας, P Oxy III. 523² (ii/A.D.) δειπνῆσαι . . εἰς κλείνην τοῦ κυρίου Σαράπιδος, "to dine at the table of the lord Sarapis," and the Christian letter P Heid 6¹⁶ (iv/A.D.) (= *Selections*, p. 126) παρακαλῶ . . . ἵνα μνημον[ε]ύῃς μοι εἰς τὰς ἁγίας σου εὐχάς, "I beseech you to remember me in your holy prayers." The interchange of εἰς and ἐν in late Greek is well illustrated by a letter from Alexandria of A.D. 22, where the writer states —ἐπὶ τῷ γεγονέναι ἐν Ἀλεξανδρίᾳ . . . ἔμ[αθον παρά τινων]

ἁλιέων εἰς Ἀλεξάνδρι[αν (P Oxy II. 294² ff. = *Selections*, p. 34) : see further *Proleg.* pp. 234 f., 245.

For εἰς in the wide sense in which we use "for" we may cite such passages as P Lille I. 26¹ (iii/B.C.) ἔγραψάς μοι περὶ τῆς εἰς τὴν σησαμείαν γῆς, *ib.*⁸ ἕως ἂν μάθωμεν περὶ τῶν κ[εχρ]ηματισμένων εἰς τὸν νομόν, P Petr II. 11 (1)⁶ (mid. iii/B.C.) (= Witkowski², p. 8) ἀπὸ τούτου τὸ μὲν ἥμυσυ εἰς τὰ δέοντα ὑπελιπάμην, τὸ δὲ λοιπὸν εἰς τὸ δάνειον κατέβαλον, P Lond 43⁹ (ii/B.C.) (= I. p. 48, Witkowski², p. 110) ἕξεις ἐφόδιαν εἰς τὸ γῆρας, P Tebt I. 5⁷⁷ (B.C. 118) προστε]τάχασι δὲ καὶ τὰ εἰς τὴν ταφὴν τοῦ Ἄπιος, P Oxy I. 37ⁱ·⁹ (A.D. 149) (= *Selections*, p. 49) ἐγένετο ἐνθάδε ἡ τροφεῖτις εἰς υἱὸν τοῦ Πεσούριος, "there was concluded here the nursing-contract for the son of Pesouris" ; and the recurring formulae in a private account of *c.* A.D. 1, *ib.* IV. 736⁹ θρύων εἰς τοὺς ἄρτους (ὀβολοὶ δύο), "omelette for the bread 2 ob.," ¹¹ εἰς κατανθρωπισμὸν γυναικ(ὸς) Γεμέλλου (τετρώβολον ?), "for treating (?) the wife of Gemellus 4 ob." (Edd.), etc. This extension in the vernacular of εἰς expressing destination makes it unnecessary to think of Semitism in εἶναι εἰς, ἐγείρειν εἰς (Ac 8²³, 13²²) : cf. *Proleg.* p. 71 f. The meaning "to the extent of," "amounting to," is found in P Par 47¹⁸ (*c.* B.C. 153) χάριν γὰρ ἡμῶν ἠζημίαται εἰς χαλκοῦ τ(άλαντα) ιε̄, P Tebt I. 50¹⁶ (B.C. 112–1) βλάβος γενηθῆναι εἰς (πυροῦ) (ἀρτάβας) λ̄. The thought of resulting *advantage* appears in P Lond 42²¹ (B.C. 168) (= I. p. 30, *Selections*, p. 10) μηδ᾽ ἐνβεβλοφέναι εἰς τὴν ἡμετέραν περί<στασιν>, "nor spared a look for our helpless state," P Par 30¹⁰ (B.C. 161) ἐμβλέψαντες εἴς τε ἐμὲ . . . καὶ εἰς τὴν ἐκείνων ὀρφάνειαν, P Meyer 1²⁷ (B.C. 144) τούτου δὲ γενομένου [τευξόμεθα τ]ῆς παρ᾽ ὑμῶν εἰς τὸν βίον βοηθείας, and of resulting *disadvantage* in P Eleph 1⁹ (B.C. 311–0) κακατεχνεῖν μηδὲν . . . εἰς Δημητρίαν, P Par 14⁴⁷ (ii/B.C. περὶ μὲν γὰρ τῆς ὕβρεως καὶ πληγῶν καὶ ὧν συντετελεσμένοι εἰσὶν εἴς με, P Fay 12⁷ (*c.* B.C. 103) Διοκλείους . . . ἀδικήματα εἴς μ[ε] σὺν ἄλλοις συντελεσαμένου. A good example of εἰς followed by the acc. of the person = "in the name of" is afforded by P Tebt I. 30¹⁹ (B.C. 115) ἔτι ἀναγράφουσι τὸν κλῆρον εἰς τὸν Πέτρωνα, "they continue to register the holding under the name of Petron" (Edd.). The full phrase occurs in P Hib I. 74³ (*c.* B.C. 250) σύμβολα δὲ ποιῆσαι πρ[ὸ]ς αὐτο[ὺς] β, τὸ μὲν ἕν εἰς τὸ Κλεομάχου ὄνομα κτλ., P Petr II. 2(1)³ δόντων ἡμῶν [τὴν ἐν]τευξιν εἰς τὸ τοῦ βασιλέως ὄνομα, P Meyer 8¹³ (A.D. 151) πάντα [καταγραφῆναι] συνέταξεν εἰς τὸ τῆς γυναικὸς αὐτοῦ ὄνομα : see further *s.v.* ὄνομα, and cf. P Giss I. 66⁹ (early ii/A.D.) ἐρωτᾷ [σ]ε εἰς τὴν τῶν θεῶν εὐσέβειαν, "*per pietatem oro.*"

For εἰς in connexion with payments cf. e. g. P Amh II. 55⁴ (B.C. 176 or 165) ὁμολογῶ ἔχειν παρ᾽ ὑμῶν εἰς τὰ ἐκφόρια τοῦ ε (ἔτους) Παῦνι ιγ̄ (πυροῦ) (ἀρτάβας) πεντήκοντα ἑπτά, "I acknowledge that I have received from you for the rent of the fifth year on Pauni 13 fifty-seven artabae of wheat," P Petr II. 275¹⁹ (A.D. 66) ἐφ᾽ ᾧ δώσει αὐτῷ κατὰ μῆνα ὁ Πτολεμαῖος εἰς λόγον . . . Phil 4¹⁵) διατροφῆς δραχμὰς πέντε, "on condition that Ptolemaeus shall give him monthly five drachmae on account of victuals," *ib.* III. 400¹⁰ (A.D. 127) ἐὰν δὲ ἔνκυο[ς] οὖσα ἡ γα[μου]μένη ἀπαλλαγῇ δώσει αὐτῇ ὁ γαμῶν ἄλλας εἰς λόγον λοχείας δραχμὰς ἑξήκοντ[α, "and if the bride is at the time of separation in a state of pregnancy the husband shall give her on account of the birth 60 drachmae more" (Edd.), *ib.* 530¹⁵ (ii/A.D.) **εἰς λ[ό]γον τόκου δραχμὰς ὀκτώ**, "8 drachmae on account of interest," BGU I. 171¹ (A.D. 156) **ἔσχον παρ' ὑμῶν εἰς δάνιον σπέρ(ματα) κτλ.**, *ib.* III. 927⁴ (iii/A.D.) **παρ]εσχήκαμέν σοι εἰς λόγον συντελείας κτλ.** With this usage of **εἰς** to specify the various purposes of the items of an account, Deissmann (*BS,* p. 117 f.) compares such passages as 1 Cor 16¹, 2 Cor 8⁴, 9¹·¹³, Rom 15²⁶, also Ac 24¹⁷, and perhaps Mk 8³⁹⁴. Elsewhere (*ib.* p. 194 f.) he cites CPR I. 1¹¹ (A.D. 83–4) **τὰς εἰς τὸν Μάρωνα . . . οἰκονομίας**, which the editor translates as *the endorsement of Maron's account,* and *ib.* 18¹² (A.D. 124) **εἰς ἄλλον τινὰ γράφειν διαθήκην**, *to draw up a will in favour of any other person :* see also P Fay 83⁶ (A.D. 163), an acknowledgment by the sitologi of a payment of 4⅔ artabae of wheat which have been placed **εἰς Σαραπιάδα**, "to the account of Sarapias," similarly *ib.* 84⁸ (A.D. 163), 162 (A.D. 172) and the editors' introduction to 81.

The *temporal* use of **εἰς** to denote the end of a period is seen in P Hib I. 27¹²¹ (calendar—B.C. 301–240) **κδ̄ ἡλίου τροπαὶ εἰς θέρος**, P Par 51² (B.C. 160) **Τῦβι ῑβ̄ εἰς τὴν ῑγ̄**, P Tebt I. 5⁹⁶ (B.C. 118) **ἀπ[ὸ το]ῦ ξ̄ (ἔτους) εἰς ἄλλα τρία**, P Oxy II. 277⁵ (lease of land—B.C. 19) **ὥστε σπεῖραι εἰς τὸ δωδέκατον ἔτος πυρῶι.** With Mt 28¹ cf. more particularly P Petr III. 28(*e*)⁵ (B.C. 260) **νυκτὸς τῆι κ̄ζ̄ εἰς τὴ[ν κη]** τοῦ **Πάχων**, P Ryl II. 127⁶ (A.D. 29) **νυκτὶ τῇ φερούσῃ εἰς τὴν ῑζ̄ τοῦ ἐνεστῶτο(ς) μηνό(ς).** See also BGU III. 916¹⁵ (i/A.D.) **ἡ μίσθωσις ἥδ' ἥ εἰς ἐνιαυτὸν [ἕ]να**, and such temporal phrases as P Petr III. 42 G (9)⁸ (mid. iii/B.C.) **εἰς τὸ λοιπόν**, P Tebt I. 56¹⁶ (*c.* B.C. 130–121) **εἰς τὸν ἄπαντα χρόν[ον**, and P Oxy X. 1294¹⁴ (ii/iii A.D.) **εἰσάπαξ γὰρ αὐτὸ λήμψῃ**, "for you will get it once for all" (Edd.).

As showing the growth in the use of **εἰς**, two instances may be cited where, with the acc. of a person, it takes the place of a possessive genitive—P Tebt I. 16⁹ (B.C. 114) **οὐ λήγοντες τῆι [εἰς] αὐτοὺς αὐθαδίᾳ χρώμενοι**, "persisting in *their* violent behaviour," P Par 5ⁱⁱ·² (B.C. 114) **χωρὶς τοῦ εἰς αὐτὴν οἶκον** (*l.* οἴκου) : cf. *ib.* 5ⁱ·⁷ (B.C. 114) **τὸν εἰς Τάγην οἶκον ᾠκοδομημένον**, where **εἰς Τάγην** has the force of a *dat. commodi.* For further particulars reference must be made to the useful Dissertations by Kuhring and Rossberg : see Abbreviations I.

On **εἰς**, "into," for **ἐνς** which survived in Cretan before vowels, see Moulton *Gr.* ii. § 117. In MGr the forms **εἰς**, **'ς**, **εἰσέ**, and **σέ** are used.

εἷς.

P Oxy VIII. 1153¹⁴ (i/A.D.) **καρποδέσμια μικτὰ δύο, ἐν μὲν σανδύκινον καὶ ἓν πορφυροῦν**, "two variegated (?) wristbands, one scarlet and one purple" (Ed.). For **εἷς** as an ordinal see BGU II. 623⁴ (ii/iii A.D.) **τῇ μιᾷ καὶ εἰκάιδι** (*l.* εἰκάδι) **τοῦ Ἐπίφ**, and the full discussion of this vernacular Greek usage in *Proleg.* p. 95 f. In P Giss I. 19¹⁰ (ii/A.D.) **τῆι α [ἡμέρα] τοῦ νέου ἔτους** : does the **ᾱ** help the substitution of **μιᾷ** for **πρώτη**? **Εἷς** with a partit. gen. may be illustrated from the iv/A.D. Christian letter P Heid 6¹⁵ (= *Selections,* p. 126) **εἷς γὰρ ἰμὶ** (*l.* εἰμὶ) **τῶν ἁμαρτουλὸν.** The usage of **εἷς** = **τις**, as in Mt 8¹⁹, Lk 5¹²·¹⁷ *al.,* is well established, without any necessity of postulating Semitic influence (as Blass *Gr.* p. 144, WSchm. p. 243), e.g. P Amh II. 30²⁸ (ii/B.C.) **Κονδύλου ἑνὸς τῶν ἁλιέων** (*sc.* **προσκληθέντος**, BGU IV. 1044⁶ (iv/A.D.) **ἑνὸς** (*l.* εἷς) **λεγόμενον**

(*l.*—ος) **Φαῆσις** : cf. *Proleg.* p. 97, where the use of **ὁ εἷς** in Mk 14¹⁰ is also paralleled from early papyri, as P Par 15⁵⁰ (B.C. 120) **τὸν ἕνα αὐτῶν °Ωρον**, ⁵⁴ **τοῦ ἑνὸς τῶν ἐγκαλουμένων Νεχουθοῦ**, P Tebt II. 357¹⁰ (A.D. 197) **τοῦ το[ῦ] ἑνὸς αὐτῶν Κρονίω[ν]ος πατρός.** Add *ib.* I. 138 (late ii/B.C.) **ὁ εἷς τῶν προγεγραμμένων Ὀννῶφρις**, P Oxy VII. 1032⁵⁶ (A.D. 162) **διὰ τοῦ ἑνὸς ἡμῶν Ἀμμωνίου ἐπιδεδώκαμεν.** In P Oxy VI. 940⁶ (v/A.D.) **τὸν δὲ Φοιβάμμωνα τὸν φροντιστὴν μεταστειλάμενος ἔχε ἐγγύς σου μίαν μίαν**, we seem at first sight to have an instance of the distributive use of **εἷς**, but, as the editors point out in their note, the context shows clearly that **μίαν μίαν** is here = "together." We may have a Semitism in the curious repetition **εἷς καὶ εἷ[ς] καὶ εἷς ἐν τόποις καὶ τόποις** in P Amh I. 1 ˣⁱⁱ·¹⁴ f.—the Greek fragment of the *Ascension of Isaiah.* With Jn 11⁵² cf. P Oxy XII. 1411³ (A.D. 260) **τῶν δημοσίων εἰς ἓν συναχθέντων.** For the phrase **τὸ καθ' ἕν**, cf. P Lille I. 11⁸ (mid. iii/B.C.) where certain particulars regarding grain used by *pastophori* are headed—**ἔστιν δὲ τὸ καθ' ἕν**, "this is the list in detail," and similarly P Ryl II. 65⁹ (B.C. 67 ?) **ὧν τὸ καθ' ἕν ἐπὶ τῆς [ἐ]σομένης [διεξα]γωγῆς σημανθήσεται**, "the details of which will appear in the forthcoming inquiry" (Edd.), *ib.* 127¹⁵ (A.D. 29) **ᾔρησαν τῶν ἐμῶν ὧν τὸ καθ' ἕν ὑπόκειται**, "they carried off property of mine of which a list is appended" (Edd.). In *ib.* 233¹⁰ (ii/A.D.) **ὑφ' ἕν γεγραμμένον** = "written continuously" of an account. We may also note P Amh II. 87²¹ (A.D. 125) **ἐποίσεις μοι μέτρησιν μίαν Ἀθηναίῳ ἀντὶ μιᾶς δοχικῷ** with reference to the measurement of artabae of wheat, the meaning of the phrase apparently being that half the artabae were to be on the standard of Athens and half on the **δοχικόν** standard : see the editors' note, and cf. P Oxy IV. 740¹⁷ (*c.* A.D. 200), P Strass I. 26¹³ (iii/A.D.) *al.* Amongst the inscrr. in the Graeco-Roman Museum at Alexandria one, *Preisigke* 2685, bears the words—**Εἷς θεός.** See also P Leid W ⱽⁱ·³⁶ (ii/iii A.D.) **αὐθέντα ἥλιε, ὁ ὑπ' αὐτὸν τὸν ἕνα καὶ μόνον τεταγμένος.** MGr has **ἕνας, μιά, ἕνα(ν).**

εἰσάγω.

For **εἰσάγω** = "bring in," without mention of place, as in Lk 2²⁷, Ac 7⁴⁵, see the legal usage in P Amh II. 33¹⁴ (*c.* B.C. 157) **ἤδη τῶν καθ' ἡμᾶς εἰσαγομένων πυνθανόμεθα τὸν ἐγκαλούμενον Τεσενοῦφιν μετὰ συνηγόρων συνκαθίστασθαι**, "just as our side is already coming into court we hear that the defendant T. is pleading with the assistance of advocates" (Edd.): cf. also P Oxy II. 259¹⁰ (A.D. 23) where a man who had been "arrested" for debt is described as **τὸν εἰσηγμένον.** In P Par 43² (B.C. 154) (= Witkowski², p. 79) **συγγέγραμμαι τῆι Ἑσπέρου θυγατρί. μέλλω δὲ ἰσάγειν ἐν τῷ Μεσορὴ μηνί**, the verb is used absolutely = "marry"; similarly in P Grenf II. 78³ (A.D. 307) **εἰσαγόμην ἐμαυτῷ γυναῖκα**, where the dropped augment may be noted. In P Tebt II. 285⁶ (A.D. 239) **οὔτε τοὺς ἀλλοτρίους . . . εἰς τὴν οἰκετείαν εἰσάγουσιν**, "nor can they introduce outsiders into the family," we have the construction with **εἰς**, as in Ac 9⁸ etc. P Tebt I. 20⁷ (B.C. 113) **χαριεῖ σὺν σοὶ αὐτὸν εἰσαγαγών** shows us the meaning "introducing." **Εἰσάγω** is also common = "import" contrasted with **ἐξάγω**, "export," e.g. P Lond 929⁵ (ii/iii A.D.) (= III. p. 41) **Μέλας ἐξ(άγων) ἐλέου καμ(ήλους) ῡ̄, Σώτας ἐξ(άγων) πυροῦ καμ(ήλους) δ̄, Πόσις ἰσά(γων) οἴνου κεράμ(ια) ῑβ̄**, P Ryl II. 197¹⁰·¹⁴ (custom-house receipts—

late ii/A.D.) ἐξάγων ὀρόβου ἐπὶ ὄνῳ ἑνὶ . . . . . εἰ(σάγων) ἐπὶ ὄνοις δυσὶ [. .] . [. .] . . ἕξ, "exporting pulse on one donkey, importing six . . . on two donkeys." See also BGU IV. 1207[11] (B.C. 28) σὺ οὖν καὶ ['Αραμώτης] ἀνδραγαθεῖτε καὶ εἰσάγεσθε τ[ιμὴν φ]ακῷ ὀλυρίῳ. For εἰσαγωγή it must be enough to cite P Tebt I. 41[26] (c. B.C. 119) αὐτ[οὶ] τε ἀπαρενόχλητοι ὄντες δυν[ώ]μεθα ἀντέχεσθαι τῆς εἰσαγωγῆς, "we being undisturbed may be able to attend to the collection of the revenues" (Edd.); for the office of εἰσαγωγεύς see *Archiv* iii. p. 23 ff.

εἰσακούω.

With 1 Cor 14[21] (cf. Exod 6[12] but not [9]) cf. PSI IV. 377[20] (B.C. 250–49) ἔγραψα οὖν σοι ἵνα εἰδῇς, ἐπειδὴ οὐ βούλει μου εἰσακοῦσαι.

εἰσδέχομαι.

Syll 330[21] (Roman Age) εἰσδεδεγμένοι τέ εἰσιν εἰς τὰν τᾶς πόλεως χάριν, *OGIS* 515[36] (iii/A.D.) τὰς δὲ τοιαύτας προσαγγελίας εἰσδέ[χ]εσθαι τὸν γραμματέα. The verb was used technically in connexion with the "receiving" or "storing" of wheat in the θησαυρός, e.g. P Lille I. 13[3] (B.C. 244–3) : for the corresponding subst. εἰσδοχή see P Tebt I. 123[l.al.] (early i/B.C.), *ib.* 159 (B.C. 112), P Fay 86[1] (ii/A.D.).

εἴσειμι.

P Petr II. 16[6] (mid. iii/B.C.) Φιλωνίδης δε[. . . . .]ωι εἰσιέναι ἔστιν [πρὸς τὸ]ν βασιλέα, P Tor I. 1[viii. 19] (B.C. 117–6) καὶ εἰς τὸ Ἡραῖον εἰσιόντας τὸ ὅμοιον ἐπιτελεῖν. The verb is very common in notices of time, e.g. P Oxy II. 243[41] (A.D. 79) ἀπὸ τοῦ εἰσιόντος μηνὸς Φαρμοῦθι, *ib.* IX. 1187[5] (A.D. 254) τῷ εἰσιόντι ἔτει, *ib.* X. 1278[17] (A.D. 214) τοῦ ἰσι[ό]ντος κδ (ἔτους), "of the coming 24th year."

εἰσέρχομαι.

With the use of εἰσέρχομαι in Lk 17[7] we may compare P Eleph 13[6] (B.C. 223–2) οὔπω εἰσελήλυθεν ἐξ ἀγροῦ. For other examples of this common verb, cf. P Ryl II. 151[8] (A.D. 40) εἰσελθὼν εἰς τὴν ὑ[πάρ]χο(υσαν) ἐν τῇ κώμῃ οἰκ[ίαν, P Oxy II. 237[viii. 17] (A.D. 186) τὸν μείζονα ἀγῶνα ε[ἰ]σελεύσεται, "he shall enter upon the more serious lawsuit" (Edd.), and P Tebt II. 418[8ff.] (iii/A.D.) καλῶς ποιήσεις, ἄδελφέ, [ἐ]ὰν εἰσέρχη ἐνεγκὼν μετὰ σεαυτοῦ τὴν γυναῖκά μου, ἔγραψα [γ]ὰρ αὐτῇ σὺν σοὶ εἰσελθεῖν, "you will do well, brother, to come up and bring my wife with you, for I have written to her to come with you" (Edd.). See also P Leid Wᵛ·⁴⁹ (ii/iii A.D.) Κύριε . . . εἴσελθε καὶ ἐπάκουσόν μοι. On the use of the mid. εἰσέλθοιτο for the active in Phrygian sepulchral inscrr. see W. M. Ramsay *Exp T* xxvi. p. 174.

εἰσκαλέομαι.

This NT ἅπ. εἰρ. (Ac 10[23]) is found in a petition of B.C. 241, P Petr II. 12(3)[10] οὖ[ν?] σε εἰσκαλέσασθαι ἡμᾶς καὶ ἐπισκεψάμενον ἃ διὰ τῆς ἐντεύξεως αὐτῶι ἐγκεκλήκαμεν, ἐπαναγκάσαι αὐτὸν τὸ δίκαιον ἡμῖν ὑποσχεῖν, "(we ask you), therefore, to summon us and, having inquired into our charges against him, to force him to do us justice" (Ed.); cf. *ib.* III. 29(4)[5] ἀξι[ῶ σ]ε εἰσκα[λε]σάμενός [με] ἐπισκέ-

ψασθαι περὶ ὧν κτλ. Like ἀνακαλέομαι, the verb seems to denote summoning by word of mouth, as distinguished from formal citation (παραγγέλλω) : see P Hamb I. p. 109 n.[5], and for medical usage cf. Hobart, p. 219.

εἴσοδος.

In the NT εἴσοδος is generally used of "the act of entering," though possibly it may refer to "the place of entering" in Heb 10[19] (cf. ver. 20) and 2 Pet 1[11]. In any case, this latter is the predominant use in the papyri where the word is constantly found of "the entrance" of a temple or a house, e.g. P Oxy II. 241[19] (c. A.D. 98) ὑποθήκης τρίτον μέρους οἰκίας, ἐν ᾗ αἴθριον, καὶ αὐλῆς καὶ εἰσώδων (*l.* -ό-) καὶ ἐξόδων καὶ τῶν συνκυρόντων τῶν ὄντων, "on the security of the third part of a house, in which there is a hall, with the court and entrances and exits and appurtenances" (Edd.), and the interesting ii/A.D. letter, P Ryl II. 233[1], regarding the building and fitting up of a house, where it is stated διὰ τῆς πλαγίας ἡ εἴσοδός ἐστι καὶ ἡ ἔξοδος τῶν ἐργαζομένων πάντων, "the entrance and exit for all the work-folk is at the side" (Edd.). For the more metaphorical meaning, as in 1 Th 1[9], cf. the Latin papyrus letter of ii/A.D., P Oxy I. 32[14], in which a military tribune commends a certain Theon to the good offices of Domitius, "et ideo peto a te ut habeat intr[o]itum ut te." See also M. Anton. v. 19, τὰ πράγματα αὐτὰ οὐδ' ὁπωστιοῦν ψυχῆς ἅπτεται· οὐδ' ἔχει εἴσοδον πρὸς ψυχήν.

εἰσπηδάω.

This strong verb, which is found in the NT only in Ac 16[29], may be illustrated by P Oxy I. 37[i. 16] (A.D. 49) (= *Selections*, p. 50) εἰσεπήδησεν εἰς τὴν τοῦ ἡμετέρου [ο]ἰκίαν καὶ τὸ σωμάτιον ἀφήρπασεν, "burst into my client's house and carried off the foundling," *ib.* VIII. 1120[13] (early iii/A.D.) εἰσεπήδησεν εἰς τὴν οἰκίαν μου καὶ ἐτόλμησεν ἀποσπάσαι δούλην μου, and P Tebt II. 304[10] (A.D. 167–8) μετὰ ξύλων ἰσπηδῆσαι, "rush in with staves." See also *Syll* 190[9] (B.C. 306–281) εἰσ]πηδήσαντας νύκτωρ ἐπ' ἀδικίαι [καὶ] ἀσεβείαι τοῦ ἱεροῦ. A new literary citation (*Menandrea*, p. 54[2·9]) shows a close parallel to the absolute use in Ac 16[29], and well illustrates the "violent" connotation of the verb— οὑτοσὶ μελαγχολᾷ. εἰσπεπήδηκεν.

εἰσπορεύομαι.

P Par 35[30] (B.C. 163) πυνθανομένων δ' ἡμῶν τοῦ χάριν εἴησαν εἰσπορευσάμενοι, P Oxy IV. 717[7] (late i/B.C.) εἰσπορεύομαι πρὸς τὸν στρατηγόν, *ib.* 744[4] (B.C. 1) (= *Selections*, p. 32) μὴ ἀγωνιᾷς ἐὰν ὅλως εἰσπορεύονται, ἐγὼ ἐν Ἀλεξανδρέᾳ (*l.* -είᾳ) μένω, "do not worry if when all the others enter (*sc.* their homes), I remain at Alexandria."

εἰσφέρω.

As illustrating the varied uses of this common verb we may cite P Eleph 8[19] (i/B.C.) οὗτος δὲ δύνατός ἐστιν εἰσενέγκαι καὶ ἔν[γυο]ν [ἱ]κ[ανό]ν, P Ryl II. 154[22] (A.D. 66) ε[ἰ]σφέρον]τος εἰς τὸν κοινὸν τῆς [σ]υμβιώσεως οἶκον, "carrying it (*sc.* the produce of his work) to the home of their common wedded life" (Edd.), P Amh II. 77[22] (A.D. 139) ἀμφότεροι βίᾳ βασ[τ]άξαντές με εἰσήνεγκαν εἰς τὸ λογ[ι]στήριον τοῦ ἐπιτρόπου, "taking me up by force they together carried me to the counting-house of the superintendent" (Edd.), P Oxy

II, 237⁵⁻²⁴ (A.D. 186) ἃ αὐτὸς εἰσήνεγκεν εἰς τὸ βιβλιοφυλάκιον, P Fay 124²ᵃ (ii/A.D.) καὶ μετάμελόν σ[ο]ι πάλειν εἰσο[ίσ]ει ἡ πλεονεξ[ί]α σου, "and your cupidity will again cause you regret," *Michel* 472²² (end of ii/B.C.) πᾶσαν κακοπαθίαν εἰσενεγκάμενος, "having brought forward every grievance." With the usage in Ac 17²⁰ cf. *Syll* 660⁴ (iv/B.C.) καθότι Σκιρ[ίδα]ι ἐξηγούμενοι εἰσφέρουσι (*sc.* εἰς τὸν δῆμον). For the verb = "pay," see P Ryl II. 84⁵ (A.D. 146) ἐὰν τὰ ὀφιλόμενα εἰ[σ]ηνηνχθῇ, "if the debts are paid," and cf. the common use of the subst. in connexion with taxation, e.g. P Tebt I. 36⁹ (late ii B.C.), etc. See also *Michel* 473⁹ (ii/B.C.) εἰσφερόμενος εἰς τὰ κοινά, "contributing to the common fund."

εἶτα

is praised by Phrynichus (ed. Lobeck, p. 124) as against the "barbarous" εἶτεν, but it occurs frequently alike in the New Menander and in vernacular documents : see e.g. P Fay 12²⁰ (c. B.C. 103) ἐξέδυσαν ὃ περ[ιε]βεβλήμην ἱμάτιον καὶ τοῦτο ἀπηλλάγησαν ἔχοντ[ες] ἐ[ξ]έντες γυμνόν. εἶθ' οὕτως μετ' ἐνδύματος . . . ὑπὸ τῶν γνωρίμων κτλ. "they stripped me of the garment I was wearing, and went off with it, sending me forth naked. Afterwards, a garment having been (supplied) by my friends," etc. (Edd.). BGU II. 665¹⁰ (i A.D.) ἐγ[ὼ] τῷ πατρί μου γράψω τὸ μὲν πρῶτον περὶ τοῦ τοκετοῦ αὐτῆς τὸ ἀνανκαιότερον, εἶτα καὶ περὶ τῆς διαλλαγῆς, *ib.* IV. 1010⁴ (mid. ii/A.D.) πολλὰς καταστάσεις πρὸς αὐτὸν πεποίηται. Ε[ἶ]τα καὶ ἐπὶ Νεοκύδην τὸν γενόμενον δικαιοδότην ἥκεν, and P Lond 1173⁵ (A.D. 125) (= III. p. 208) ἐπ[έτρε]ψάς [μ]οι διὰ λόγον μηκέτι κατερ[γάζεσθαι] εἶτα τὸ ἐμὲ δαπανῆσαι ἀπὸ τῆ[ς] συμ[φ]ωνίας ἧς ἐποίησας πρὸς τοὺς [ἐργά]τας. These exx. confirm Hort's comment on Jas 1¹⁵ that "εἶτα, when historical . . . marks a fresh and distinct incident." This force is considerably weakened in the boy's letter to his father, P Oxy I. 119⁶ (ii/iii A.D.) (= *Selections*, p. 103), where the word hardly admits of translation—οὐ μὴ γράψω σε ἐπιστολήν, οὔτε λαλῶ σε, οὔτε ὑίγένω σε εἶτα, "I won't write you a letter, or speak to you, or wish you health no more."

εἶτεν.

To the exx. of this dialectic form, which in the NT is found only in Mk 4²⁸ אB*L, add a Messenian inscr. of B.C. 91, dealing with the Mysteries, *Michel* 694³⁰ ff. μετὰ δὲ ταῦτα αἱ παρθένοι αἱ ἱεραί . . . εἶτεν ἁ θοιναρμόστρια ("the lady president of the feast") ἁ εἰς Δάματρος . . . εἶτεν ἁ ἱέρεα τᾶς Δάματρος κτλ., and from the papyri P Leid Wˣ·⁹ (ii/iii A.D.) εἶτεν κατὰ πρόσθεσιν τῶν φωτῶν ὑψωθέντων κτλ. Dittenberger supplies the word in *OGIS* 237¹³ (end of iii/B.C.) corresponding to a preceding ¹³ πρῶτομ μέν, and cites *Syll* 540¹⁵⁰ (B.C. 175-4), 653³¹ (B.C. 91). The word therefore can hardly now be described as "very rare" (Grimm-Thayer).

εἴωθα.

See ἔθω.

ἐκ.

It is unnecessary to illustrate at length the commoner uses of this preposition, but for the sense "out of" a place see P Par 26²⁹ (B.C. 163-2) (= *Selections*, p. 16) τοῦ δὲ τοῦ Ψιν-

ταέους υἱοῦ ἐκ τῆς Μέμφεως χωρισθέντος, "but no sooner had the son of Psintaes departed from Memphis," followed a few lines further down by ³²ⁱ ἄλλοι τῶν ἐκ τοῦ Σαραπιείου καὶ ἕτεροι τῶν ἐκ τοῦ Ἀσκληπιείου, where the meaning is somewhat weakened, "connected with," "belonging to" the Serapeum and Asclepieum respectively. With this last usage cf. P Tebt I. 40¹¹ (B.C. 117) (= *Selections*, p. 28) αὐτὸς προθυμούμενος εἶναι ἐκ τῆς οἰκίας, "being myself eager to be a member of your house," *ib.* 59⁵ (B.C. 99) Σοκονώφεως καὶ Ὤπεως τῶν ἐξ ὑμῶν, "Sokonophis and Opis, members of your body" (Edd.). For ἐκ used instead of the more common ἀπό to denote the inhabitants of a village or community cf. P Tebt I. 40¹⁹ (B.C. 117) (= *Selections*, p. 28) ἐπαναγκάσαι τοὺς ἐκ τῆς κώμης κατακολουθεῖν τοῖς ἐξ ἀρχῆς ἐθισμοῖς, "to compel the inhabitants of the village to follow the ancient customs": see also *ib.* 26¹⁶ (B.C. 114) τοὺς ἐκ τῆς κώμης [β]ασιλικοὺς γεωργούς, *ib.* 56² (late ii/B.C.) Πετεσοῦχος . . . γ[εωρ]γὸς τῶν ἐκ Κερκεσήφεως.

Other miscellaneous exx. of a somewhat similar use of the preposition are—P Vat A⁷ (B.C. 168) (= Witkowski², p. 65) διασεσῶσθαι ἐγ μεγάλων κινδύνων (cf. Ac 28⁴, Heb 5⁷), P Lond 42¹⁴ (B.C. 168) (= I. p. 30, *Selections*, p. 10) ἐκ τοῦ το[ιού]του καιροῦ ἐμαυτὴ[ν] . . . διακεκυβερνηκυῖα "having piloted myself out of such a crisis," *ib.*²⁵ ὑπὲρ τοῦ ἀπολελύσθαι σε ἐκ τῆς κατοχῆς, "concerning your having been released from your retreat," P Tebt I. 5⁷⁷ (B.C. 118) τὰ εἰς τὴν ταφὴν τοῦ Ἄπιος . . ζητεῖν ἐκ τοῦ βα[σιλικοῦ], and BGU III. 075¹¹·¹⁵ (A.D. 45) (= *Selections*, p. 42 f.) οὐλὴ καστροκνημίῳ κξ ἀριστεροῦ(ν) (*l.* γαστροκνημίῳ ἐξ ἀριστερῶ(ν)) . . . οὐλὴ κασ[τ]ροκ[νη]μιο ἐκ δεξιό(ν), "a scar on the calf of the leg on the left side" and "a scar on the calf of the leg on the right side"; cf. *a sinistra, a dextra.*

The thought of *origin* comes out very clearly in the early marriage-contract P Eleph 1⁹ (B.C. 311-0) (= *Selections*, p. 3) where it is laid down—μὴ ἐξέστω δὲ Ἡρακλείδηι . . . τεκνοποιεῖσθαι ἐξ ἄλλης γυναικός : cf. also the notice of birth P Fay 28⁹ (A.D. 150-1) (= *Selections*, p. 82) ἀπογραφόμεθα τὸν γεννηθέντα ἡμεῖν ἐξ ἀλλήλων υἱὸν Ἰσχυρᾶ[ν], and such passages as BGU II. 447⁷ (A.D. 173-4) τὴν ἐξ ἀμφοτ(έρων) ἡμῶν θυγατέρα Οὐεττί[αν, P Gen I. 19¹ (A.D. 323) Δίδυμος οὐετρανὸς ἐκ πατρὸς Ἰσχυρίωνος, *Michel* 1001ⁱⁱⁱ·³² (c. B.C. 200) τὰ ἐκ ταυτᾶν τέκνα, and *OGIS* 90¹⁰ (Rosetta stone—B.C. 196) where Ptolemy Epiphanes is described as ὑπάρχων θεὸς ἐκ θεοῦ καὶ θεᾶς : cf. Phil 3⁵ and the language of the Nicene Creed, of which the oldest copy, belonging to vi/A.D., has been published in P Ryl I. 6. See also the Christian amulet BGU III. 954²⁸ (vi/A.D.) (= *Selections*, p. 134) ὁ φῶς ἐκ φωτός, θ(εὸ)ς ἀληθινὸς χάρισον ἐμὲ τὸν δοῦλόν σου τὸ φῶς.

Origin leads easily to *cause*, as in P Oxy VII. 1020³ (A.D. 198-201) τὴν ἐκ τῆς ἡλικίας . . β[οήθιαν, "the assistance due to immature age" (Ed.) : cf. P Grenf II. 76³ (A.D. 305-6) where a wedded couple agree to a formal divorce, having separated ἐκ τινὸς πονηροῦ δαίμονος, "owing to some evil deity". The phrase ἐκ τούτου, as in Jn 6⁶⁶, 19¹², is naturally common, e.g. BGU II. 423¹⁷ (ii/A.D.) (= *Selections*, p. 91) ἐκ τούτου ἐλπίζω ταχὺ προκόσαι (*l.* προκόψαι) τῶν θε[ῶ]ν θελόντων, "on this account (viz. my having been brought up well) I hope to be quickly promoted, if the gods will"; cf. *OGIS* 139¹⁰ (ii/B.C.) ἐκ τοῦ τοιούτου συμβαίνει ἐλαττοῦσθαι τὸ ἱερόν. See also such passages as P Tebt I. 23⁵ (c. B.C. 119 or 114) οὐκ ὀρθῶς κρίνομεν πέπρακταί σοι μὴ ἐκ τῆς ἡμῶν προεδρίας πεφροντικέναι ἀπροσδέητον ἑτέρων γενέσθαι, "I consider that you have acted badly in not having been careful that he should be independent of others owing to my superior rank" (Edd.), ib. 24³⁹ (B.C. 117) ἔκ τε τῆς πλείστης προσεδρείας, "on account of the prolonged attendance" (Edd.), and P Fay 12¹⁶ (c. B.C. 103) ἐκ κοινολογ[ί]α[ς] τ[ῆ]ς συνσταθείσης πρὸς αὐτούς, "as the result of the colloquy which took place between us" (Edd.).

From this it is an easy transition to the meaning "according to" or "in accordance with," as in the common legal phrase καθάπερ ἐγ δίκης, "as if in accordance with a legal decision," i. e. "as if a formal decree of the court had been obtained," as in P Eleph 1¹³ (B.C. 311–0) (= Selections. p. 3). P Ryl II. 154⁵⁰ (A.D. 66): cf. P Petr III. 26⁹ ἐκ κρίσεως. OGIS 48¹² (iii/B.C.) κολάζοντ[ε]ς τοῖς] ἐκ τῶν νόμων ἐπιτίμοις. So in the land-survey P Tebt I. 60⁸⁵ (B.C. 118) we hear of land let at a certain sum—ἐκ τῆς ἀξίας, "in proportion to its value": cf. the similar document ib. 61 (b)⁹⁰ (B.C. 118) ἐξ ἐπισκέψεως, "as the result of inspection." In the interesting report of a lawsuit, which resembles so much the judgment of Solomon, the parentage of the child is decided—ἐκ τῆς ὄψεως, "from its features" (P Oxy I. 37ⁱⁱ·³—A.D. 49 = Selections. p. 51): cf. Jn 7²⁴ μὴ κρίνετε κατ' ὄψιν. See also P Tebt II. 284¹⁰ (i B.C.) ἐξ εὐτυχίας "by good fortune," ib. 298⁴⁵ (A.D. 107–8) ἀπὸ τῶν ἐξ εὐ[σεβ]είας δι]δομέν[ω]ν ἡμῖν], "from pious gifts to us" (Edd.).

The preposition is used of material, as in Mt 27²⁹, Rev 18¹², in P Magd 42⁵ (B.C. 221) περιτραχηλίδιον ἐκ καθορμίων λιθίνων, "a necklace made of strings of stones," P Oxy IV. 707²⁸ (c. A.D. 136) τροχὸν ἐκ καινῆς ἐξ ὀ[πτῆς] πλίνθου, "a new wheel of baked brick," and OGIS 194²⁸ (B.C. 42) where reference is made to a statue ἐκ σκληροῦ λίθου.

For measure see P Oxy I. 43ⁱⁱⁱ·²⁷ (A.D. 295) ἔσχον παρὰ σοῦ κοφίνους δέκα δύο ἐκ λιτρῶν τεσσαράκοντα.

A certain instrumental force underlies the use of ἐκ in such a passage as P Oxy III. 486²⁵ (A.D. 131) ἐγὼ δὲ ἔκτοτε ἐκ τῆς τοῦ ἐπιστρατήγου ἐπιστολῆ[ς] . . . ἐνθάδε κατήντησα, "I thereupon in consequence of the letter of the epistrategus presented myself here," and ib.³² τὰ ἐμὰ πάν[τα] ἐκ τῆς ὑπερβαροῦς ἀνα[βάσ]εως τοῦ ἱερωτάτου Νίλου ἀπολωλένα[ι, "that all my property has been lost through the excessive rise of the most sacred Nile" (Edd.). See also Rossberg's exx. (p. 25 f.) of the preposition with verbs of buying and selling, as P Tebt I. 5⁵⁰ (B.C. 118) τὰς ἠγορασμένας προφητείας . . εἰς τὰ ἱερὰ ἐκ τῶν ἱερῶν προσόδων = "with money from the temple revenues": cf. Lk 16⁹.

For ἐκ to denote price, as in Mt 20² (cf. the simple gen. in ¹³), Ac 1¹⁸, we may cite P Oxy IV. 745² (c. A.D. 1) τ[ὸ]ν δὲ οἶνον ἠγόρασας ἐκ (δραχμῶν) ἕξ, "you bought the wine at six drachmae," P Fay 111¹⁶ (A.D. 95–6) λέγουσι εἶναι τὼ λώτινον ἐν τῇ Διονυσιά[δι] ἐγ (δραχμῶν) ιη, so ib. 110⁵ (c. A.D. 100), ib. 131⁵ (iii/iv A.D.) ποίησον αὐτὰς πραθῆναι ἐκ (δραχμῶν) ιδ, and BGU III. 916¹⁹ (i/A.D.) τὸν φόρον ἀπὸ μὲν μην[ὸ]ς Φαῶφι ἕω[ς] μηνὸς Μεχεὶρ μηνῶν] πέντε ἐγ δραχμῶν τριάκοντα. See also P Petr II. 11 (2)⁴ where Polycrates informs his father that he has just had his garden valued at 17½, instead of 30, drachmae, in order that he

may pay the 5 per cent. tax (due to the State) on the smaller valuation—ἵνα ἐκ τοσούτου φέρωμεν τὴν εἰκοστήν, and P Lond 277⁹ (A.D. 23) (= II. p. 217) the record of a loan on which interest is charged at the rate of a drachma per mina per month—τόκου ὡς ἐκ δραχμῆ (l. —ῆς) μιᾶς τῇ μνᾷ τὸν μῆνα ἕκαστον, and P Gen I. 42²³ (A.D. 224) ἐ]πὶ τοῦ πάντες διδόντος (l. διδόναι) ἕκαστος ἐκ δραχμῶν εἴκοσι τοῖς [γ]εναμένοις πραισβοίτεροι (l. πρεσβυτέροις), where the editor notes that ἐκ δραχμῶν is distributive.

Partitive ἐκ may be illustrated from P Tor I. 1ⁱᵛ·²⁰ (B.C. 117–6) μέρος ἐγ νόμου, and P Oxy I. 117¹⁵ (ii/iii A.D.) ῥάκη δύο . . . ἐξ ὧν δώσεις τοῖς παιδίοις σου ἓν ἐξ αὐτῶν, "two strips of cloth, one of which please give to your children" (Edd.). Cf. also P Grenf II. 73¹³ (late iii/A.D.) (= Selections, p. 118) καὶ [τ]αύτην παραδέδωκα τοῖς καλοῖς καὶ πιστοῖς ἐξ αὐτῶν τῶν νεκροτάφων εἰς τήρησιν.

For the preposition in connexion with time, see PSI IV. 403²⁰ (iii/B.C.) παρέσομαι δὲ κἀγὼ εὐθὺς ἐξ ἑορτῆς, where the editor renders the last words "subito finita che sia la festa."

The preposition is common in adverbial phrases of time, as P Tebt I. 40²⁰ (B.C. 117) κατακολουθεῖν τοῖς ἐξ ἀρχῆς ἐθισμοῖς "to follow the ancient customs." With 2 Pet 2⁸ ἡμέραν ἐξ ἡμέρας (cf. LXX Ps 96²) cf. P Oxy I. 86¹⁵ (A.D. 338) οὗτο]ς δὲ μίαν ἐκ μιᾶς ὑπερτιθέμεν[ο]ς, putting it off "day after day." For other adverbial phrases with ἐκ see P Grenf II. 36¹² (B.C. 95) οὐθὲν ἡμῖν κακὸν ἐποίησεν ἀλλ' ἐκ τῶν ἐναντίων ἐπιμεμέληται, where ἐκ τῶν ἐναντίων equals ἐναντίον, "contra," P Ryl II. 233⁶ (ii/A.D.) τὰ μέλαθρα τῶν θυρίδων . . ἐκ μέρους . . ἡρμολόγηται, "the beams of the windows have been partly fixed" (Edd.), cf. 1 Cor 12²⁷, 13⁹, P Hib I. 73¹⁴ (B.C. 243–2) ἐγ μέσου ἀ[φήρηκεν αὐτόν, "has removed it (sc. a donkey) from my reach" (Edd.), P Lond 1178⁴³ (A.D. 194) (= III. p. 217, Selections, p. 100) ἐν]τάγιον πᾶν ἐκ πλήρους δηνάρια ἑκατόν, "a fee amounting altogether to a hundred denarii," CPR I 11¹⁴ (A.D. 108) καθὼς ἐκ συμφώνου (as in 1 Cor 7⁵) ὑπηγόρευον, P Hib I. 54³ (c. B.C. 245) ἀπό[σ]τειλον ἡμῖν ἐκ παντὸς τρόπου τὸν αὐλητήν, "make every effort to send me the flute-player," P Tebt I. 27⁶⁰ (B.C. 113) ὅπως καὶ τἄλ[λα γένηται κατὰ θερείαν ἐξ ὑγιοῦς, "that all else is rightly done in the summer" (Edd.), P Hib I. 52¹⁰ (c. B.C. 245) ὅπως μηθὲν δι[ά]πτωμα ἐξ ὑστέρου γίνη[ται, "in order that there may be no subsequent loss" (Edd.), and P Oxy IV. 707²⁷ (c. A.D. 136) ἐκ καινῆς (sc. ἀρχῆς).

In MGr ἐκ has been supplanted by ἀπό and ἔξω, though it lives an obscure life as a prefix in such words as βγαίνω, γδέρνω, ξεγράφω, ξέσκεπος.

ἕκαστος.

P Fay 91⁴² (A.D. 99) ἕκαστα ποιήσω καθὼς πρόκιται, ib. 100⁶ (A.D. 99) μετὰ κυρίων ἑκάστ[η]ς τοῦ ἀνδρός, "with their respective guardians their husbands" (Edd.), P Oxy X. 1278²⁴ (A.D. 214) ἕκαστον δὲ μέρος π[α]ραδοῦν[αι ἑ]κατέρῳ, "each party is to deliver to the other" (Edd.), ib. VI. 886¹⁶ (a magical formula—iii/A.D.) ἐπίγρ(αψον) ἐν ἑκάστῳ τῶν φύλλων τὰ τῶν θεῶν ὀνόματα. The phrase καθ' ἑκάστην ἡμέραν, as in Heb 3¹³, is common, e.g. P Fay 130⁵ (iii/A.D.), and similarly καθ' ἕκαστον μῆνα, καθ' ἕκαστον ἔτος. For εἷς ἕκαστος, see P Tebt II. 307¹ (A.D. 198) ἐ ἐξεδό(θησαν) ἐνὶ ἑκάστῳ, "5 copies were issued, one to each one" (Edd.).

ἑκάοτοτε

is unknown to the LXX, and appears in the NT only in 2 Pet 1[15]; but its place in the vernacular is confirmed by P Gen I. 31[3] (A.D. 145–6) ἑκάστοτέ σοι κατ' ἐπιδημίαν παρενοχλῶν, P Amh II. 78[4] (A.D. 184) βίαν πάσχων ἑκάστοτε ὑπὸ Ἐκύσεως, P Flor III. 367[20] (iii/A.D.) ἑκάστ[ο]τε [πε]ρὶ τῆ[ς ὑγ]είας σου πυνθάνομαι. Also Michel 543[24] (c. B.C. 200) τοὺς πρυτάνεις τοὺς ἑκάστοτε γινομένους, "who from time to time are in office": cf. the frequent use of ἀεί in class. Greek, e.g. Herod. ix. 116 ὁ ἀεὶ βασιλεύων, "the king for the time being."

ἑκατόν.

P Lond 1178[43] (A.D. 194) (= III. p. 217, Selections, p. 100) ἐν]τάγιον πᾶν ἐκ πλήρους δηνάρια ἑκατόν, "a fee amounting altogether to a hundred denarii." Other citations are needless. MGr has ἑκατό(ν).

ἑκατοντάρχης (–ος).

The variations between 1st and 2nd decl. forms of this word in the papyri may be illustrated by P Ryl II. 141[2] (A.D. 37) a petition addressed Γαίωι Τρεβίωι Ἰούστωι ἑκατοντάρχη and ib. 81[12] (c. A.D. 104) διὰ τοῦ [. . . . . . .] ἑ[κατον]τάρχου Ἰουλίου. See for the Biblical usage Thackeray Gr. i. p. 156. For a reference to a soldier λεγεῶνος δευτέρας ἑκατονταρχίας Βραβιρίου who accompanied apparently as a guard a cargo-boat of grain belonging to the government, see P Oxy II. 276[a] (A.D. 77). The form ἑκατόνταρχος along with πεντηκόνταρχος (cf. Exod 18[21] al.) is found in Preisigke 599 (Ptol.). The τ in ἑκατόνταρχος is due to false analogy with πεντηκόνταρχος, as in English "tobacconist" has borrowed its "n" from such a word as "pianist." See Boisacq Dict. Étym. p. 233 n.[1], where ἑκατοντακάρανος is cited from Pindar.

ἐκβαίνω.

For this verb = "disembark," cf. P Lille I. 1 verso[30] (B.C. 259–8) συνέπλευσα αὐτῶι ἕως Φυλακῆς κἀκεῖ ἐξέβην. It is used of "issue," "result," in BGU IV. 1206[9] (B.C. 28), οὔπωι σεσήμαγκε τί ἐκβέβη[κ]ε, ib. III. 717[22] (A.D. 149) οἵα ἐὰν ἐκβῇ ἐκ τῆς χρείας, P Ryl II. 233[2] (ii/A.D.) ὅταν δὲ ἐπ' ἀγαθῷ ἐκβῶμεν, and in P Tebt II. 300[11] (A.D. 116–7) = "abandon," "give up," βούλομαι ἑκουσίως . . . ἐγβεβηκέναι τῆς . . . [γεωργίας τῶ]ν . . [σι]τικῶν ἐδ[α]φῶν. For the meaning "produce," "yield," see P Fay 122[15] (c. A.D. 100) δήλωσόν μοι πόσαι (s. ἀρτάβαι) ἐξέβησ[αν], P Lips I. 23[20] (iv/A.D.) π[αρ]έξω σοι τὴν ἡμί[σεια]ν πάντω[ν] τῶν ἐκβησομένων καρπῶν, and cf. P Ryl II. 122[21] (A.D. 127) ἐξέβησαν μόναι πυροῦ ἀρτάβαι δύο κτλ., P Tebt II. 555 (ii/A.D.) κόφιν[οι] . . . ὧν ἐξέβ[η] οἴνου κεράμ[ια] νβ, and for the meaning "project" of a piece of ground, see P Tebt I. 84[91] (B.C. 118): see further s.v. ἔκβασις. Other miscellaneous exx. are P Ryl II. 154[29] (A.D. 66) τὰ παράφερνα οἷα ἐὰν ἐκ τῆς τρίψεως ἐγβῆι, "the parapherna as they emerge from wear and tear" (Edd.), and BGU I. 183[8] (A.D. 85) ἐὰν ἐγβ[ῇ ἀποδότ]ω ὁ ὁμο[λ]ογῶ[ν ῞Ω]ρος τῇ Ἑριέᾳ τὴν φέρνην, where provision is made that if Horus "fails" in certain duties, he is to repay his wife's dowry. In MGr the verb assumes the form βγαίνω.

ἐκβάλλω.

In P Ryl II. 80[1] (i/A.D.), in view of danger threatening the Nile banks, the village elders are ordered—ἐκβάλετε εἰς τὰ χώματα [τοῦ Πατεμίτου]῎Ανωι ὑδροφύλακας, "send out irrigation-guards on to the banks of the Upper Patemite district" (Edd.). With its use, no fewer than 11 times in Mk, in connexion with the driving out of demons may be compared the heading of the magical incantation in P Par 574[1227] (iii/A.D.) (= Selections, p. 113) πρᾶξις γενναία ἐκβάλλουσα δαίμονας, and for the literal usage, as in Mt 21[12], cf. the early P Lond 887[6] (iii/B.C.) (= III. p. 1) ἐγβέβληκέ με ἐκ τῶν ἐμῶν μερῶν τῆς αὐλῆς τῆι βίαι χρώμενος, P Magd 12[11] (B.C. 217) ἐγβαλεῖν με ἐκ τῶν κλήρων, and P Flor III. 319[5] (A.D. 132–7) ὧν (sc. ἀρουρῶν) ἐξέβαλόν με οἱ ἐν γιτνίᾳ μου ὄντες. The sense of banishment from a family or society, as in Gal 4[30] (from Gen 21[10]), 3 Jn[10], may be paralleled from BGU IV. 1050[15], a marriage-contract of the time of Augustus, where a man is bound over not to ill-treat his wife, μηδ' ἐγβάλλειν μηδ' ἄλλην γυναῖκα ἐπεισάγειν, "nor to put her away, nor to marry another woman in addition to her": cf. P Tebt I. 104[22] (B.C. 92) and ib. 105[1] (B.C. 103) where in a lease of land provision is made that it shall not be in the power of the lessee to let the land to others μηδ' ἐγβάλλειν τὸν Πτολεμαῖον πρὸ τοῦ χρόνου, "nor to expel P. before the proper period," also P Sa'id Khan I. A[216] (B.C. 88) (= JHS xxxv. p. 28). In P Oxy IV. 744[10] (B.C. 1) (= Selections, p. 33) a man writes to his wife with reference to the expected birth of a child—ἐὰν ἦν θήλεα, ἔκβαλε, "if it is a female, expose it": cf. Syll 737[95] (c. A.D. 175) ἐπιτείμια δὲ ἔστω τὰ αὐτὰ τῷ εὐκόσμῳ μὴ ἐκβαλόντι τοὺς μαχομένους. For the meaning "bring forth," "produce," as in Mt 12[35], we may point to BGU I. 197[12] (A.D. 17) "de agrorum proventu," τῶν ἐγβαλ[λομένων] καθ' ἔτος ἐκ τοῦ κλήρου γενημάτων καὶ ἐπιγενημάτω[ν. A similar weakened force of the verb is found in such NT passages as Mt 13[52], Lk 10[35], Jn 10[4], Jas 2[25]. MGr βγάλλω.

ἔκβασις.

For ἐ. = "end," "completion," cf. P Fay 91[21] (A.D. 99) μέχρει ἐγβάσεως πάσης ἐλαιουργίας, "until the completion of the entire oil-manufacture" (Edd.): cf. Heb 13[7]. In P Ryl II. 122[5] (A.D. 127) τὰ πλεῖσ[τα μ]έρη τῆς ἐκβάσεως τῶν ἐδαφῶν the word = "produce," and in ib. 157[9] (A.D. 135) it is used like ἐκβαίνω (see s.v.) of land "projecting."

ἐκβολή.

With the use of ἐκβολὴν ποιεῖσθαι = "jettison" in Ac 27[18], cf. the directions on the back of a mummy-ticket, Preisigke 2052, ἐκβολὴν ποιῆσαι ἰς ὅρμον κώμης Ἐμμαυ: so ib. 1207. In P Hib I. 110 recto[9] (c. B.C. 270) the word is found in a very broken context, and in BGU IV. 1116[3] (B.C. 13) we have ἐπ[β]ολῆς καὶ ἐγβολῆς. See also CP Herm I. 127[10 11] (p. 79), and for medical usage cf. Hobart, p. 143.

ἐκγαμίζω,—ίσκω.

Both these verbs now disappear from the true text of the NT, nor does there seem to be evidence for them elsewhere, except for the former in Pandect. Byz. (LS).

ἔκγονος.

In *OGIS* 90³ (Rosetta stone – B.C. 196) ἐκγόνου θεῶν Φιλοπατόρων, Dittenberger renders ἐ. by "*filii*," and compares the restoration in *ib.* 91², but Wilcken (*Archiv* iii. p. 321) does not think ἐ. suitable in a pure Greek inscr. and prefers τοῦ ἐ[κ βασιλέως] Πτολ. κτλ. In *ib.* 197³ Wilcken (*l.c.*) renders ἔκγονον by "Urenkel," "great-grandchild": cf. 1 Tim 5⁴ where AV renders "nephews" = "grandchildren," according to the original, but now antiquated sense of the word. The plur. is common in the general sense of "descendants," e.g. P Lille I. 4²⁷ (B.C. 218–7) ὧι ὑπῆρχεν αὐτῶι ἡ γῆ καὶ ἐκγόνοις, CPR I. 1⁴ (A.D. 83–4), P Oxy IX. 1206²⁵ (A.D. 206) κρατεῖν σε καὶ κυριεύειν σὺν ἐκγόνοις καὶ τοῖς παρὰ σοῦ μεταλημψομένοις τοῦ προκειμένου ψειλοῦ τόπου, and so *ib.* 1208¹⁷ (A.D. 291). Down to about B.C. 300 the form ἔγγονος is found in Attic inscrr.: see Meisterhans *Gr.* p. 107 and cf. Mayser *Gr.* p. 228. Ἔγγονος survives in MGr = "grandchild."

ἐκδέχομαι.

For the primary meaning "receive" cf. P Lille I. 16⁷ (iii/B.C.) ἀξιοῖ δὲ γράψαι αὐτῶι Κόμωνα ἐγδεχόμενον τὰς μ̄ (δραχμάς), P Tebt I. 33⁷ (B.C. 112) (= *Selections*, p. 30) μεγαλοπρεπέστερον ἐγδεχθῆτωι, "let him be received with the utmost magnificence," BGU IV. 1024ⁿ·¹⁶ (iv/v A.D.) ἐκδέξι το[ίνυν] τὴν (*l.* τὴν) ἕως κεφ[αλῆ]ς τ[ι]μωρίαν. In P Par 63²⁶ (B.C. 164) (= P Petr III. p. 21) τῶν πρὸς ταῖς πραγματείαις οὐ κατὰ τὸ βέλτιστον ἐγδεχομένων τὸν τοῦ περὶ τῆς γεωργίας προστάγματος νοῦν, Mahaffy translates "because the officials do not put the best interpretation on the meaning of the decree concerning agriculture," and in P Petr III. 64 (*b*)⁶ ἃς ἐξεδέξατο Ἡράκλειτ[ος . . . . he renders "which (drachmas) Heracleitus undertook to pay (?)": cf. Gen 43⁹ where Conybeare and Stock (*LXX Selections*, p. 132) propose the rendering "I undertake him." In P Alex 4¹¹ (iii/B.C.) ἐγδέδεκται γὰρ Στοτοῆτις ἔχειν σε εἰς τὴν διαλογήν . . . Witkowski (*Epp.*², p. 52) regards ἐκδέχομαι as = "comperio." The derived sense of "wait for," "expect," as in Jas 5⁷, is well illustrated by P Flor III. 332⁵ (ii/A.D.) οὐ λανθάνει σε ὅτι δίμηνος σήμερον ἐστάλην τὸν ἄτακτον Λισκᾶν μὴ ἐκδεχόμενόν σου τὴν παρουσίαν: cf. P Oxy IV. 724¹² (A.D. 155) ἐὰν δὲ ἐντὸς τοῦ χ[ρ]όνου αὐτὸν ἀπαρτίσῃς οὐκ ἐκδέξομαι τὴν προκειμένην προθεσμ[ί]αν, "if you make him perfect within the period, I will not wait for the aforesaid limit" (Edd.), with reference to a contract of apprenticeship, BGU III. 892⁶ (iii A.D.) προσ[ἐ]δρευσα ἐφ' ἡμέρας δύο ἐκδεχό[μ]ενός σε, P Oxy VI. 930²⁷ (iv A.D.) (= *Selections*, p. 130) παραμυθούμ[ε]θα δὲ αὐτὴν ἑκάστης ὥρας ἐκδεχόμενοι τὴν [σ]ὴν ἄφιξιν. See also Moulton *Gr.* ii. § 119 (*a*).

ἔκδηλος.

For this NT ἅπ. εἰρ. (2 Tim 3⁹, cf. 3 Macc 3¹⁹, 6⁵) see CP Herm I. 6³ παρεῖχεν ἑκάσ[το]υ ἔτους ἔκδηλόν τινα σίτου μοῖραν, *Syll* 552⁶³ (late ii/B.C.) χάριν τοῦ [τοῖς πολλοῖς μᾶλ]λον ἔκδηλον ὑπάρχειν τὴν τοῦ δήμου σπουδήν, *OGIS* 665¹¹ (A.D. 49) ἵνα [παν]τὶ [ἔκ]δηλα γένηται τὰ ὑπ' ἐμοῦ [σταθέντα, and Vett. Val. p. 92¹⁰ ἔκδηλα γὰρ οὕτως καὶ ἐκφανῆ τὰ κακὰ γίνεται τοῖς γεννωμένοις.

ἐκδημέω.

PSI IV. 410³ (iii/B.C.) ἐξεδημήσατε οὐκ ἀναγγείλαντές μοι ἃ εἶπεν Ἀμμώνιος περί μου. BGU IV. 1197⁷ (B.C. 4) ἐκδημήσαντος δὲ σοῦ εἰς τοὺς ἐκ[τὸ]ς [τόπους. P Tebt II. 316²⁰ (A.D. 99) ἐὰν δὲ μεταβαίνωμεν ἢ ἐγδημῶμεν [μ]εταδώσωμεν κτλ., "but if we change our residence, or go abroad, we shall give notice," etc.—a declaration required of *ephebi* in view of their enrolment in the Alexandrian demes. P Oxy I. 59¹⁶ (A.D. 292) ἵνα . . ἦ τάχος ἐκδημῆσαι, "that no time be lost in his departure" (Edd.). For the subst. see *Syll* 276¹³ (c. B.C. 195) οὐδ[ὲν φροντίσας τῶν] κατὰ τὴν ἐκδημίαν κινδύνων, Vett. Val. p. 16³³ εὔθετοι ταῖς εἰς στρατιὰν καὶ ἐκδημίαν γενέσεσιν, and for the form ἐγδημία BGU III. 1011ⁱⁱⁱ·¹ (ii/B.C.) τὸν [τῆ]ς ἐγδημίας τοῦ Μεννέου χρόνον, PSI IV. 330⁵ (B.C. 258–7) οὐ γὰρ [ἐδοκί]μασα ἄνευ σου τὴν ἐγδημίαν ποιήσασθαι.

ἐκδίδωμι.

With ἐκδίδομαι = "let out for my advantage" may be compared the sense of "apprentice" found in the papyri, e.g. P Oxy II. 275⁶ (A.D. 66) (= *Selections*, p. 55) ὁ μὲν Τρύφων ἐγδεδόσθαι τῷ Πτολεμαίῳ τὸν ἑαυτοῦ υἱὸν Θοῶνιν, "T. (agrees) that he has apprenticed to P. his son Th.," P Tebt II. 385³ (A.D. 117) ἐξέδοτο Τεφερσάεις . . . τὸν ἑαυτῆς υἱὸν Κρονίωνα, "T. has apprenticed her son C." Similarly the fragment of a marriage-contract, dated A.D. 74–5, P Oxy II. 372, begins ἐξέδοτο Ταοννῶφρις (the mother of the bride): so P Giss I. 2¹·⁸ (B.C. 173), BGU IV. 1100⁵ (time of Augustus). P Oxy X. 1273¹ (A.D. 260), and often. Cf. P Oxy II. 237ᵛⁱⁱ·²⁸ (A.D. 186) τῆς παιδὸς τῆς ἐκδεδομένης, "a daughter given in marriage." For the form ἐξέδετο, as in Mk 12¹ and parallels (cf. Exod 2²¹ A), see PSI IV. 288⁸ (ii/A.D.) ἀποχὴν ἡμ[ε]ῖν ἐξέδετο. The general sense "issue," "give out," appears in P Petr III. 43(2)ᵛᵉʳˢᵒⁱⁱ·⁶ ἐξεδόθη, and P Tebt II. 397¹ (A.D. 198) ἐξεδό(θησαν), both of the giving out of certain contracts: so P Ryl II. 163¹⁶ (A.D. 130) ἡ π[ρᾶσις κυρία . . . ἣν καὶ ἐξεδό[μην σοι δισσήν (?), "this deed of sale is valid, and I have issued it to you in duplicate" (Edd.), PSI III. 204¹⁶ (A.D. 140) διὰ τραπέζης ἐγδώσω of a receipt, P Fay 34⁵ (A.D. 161) ἐκδῶναι σύμβολα, "to issue receipts." For the use of the subst. ἔκδοσις in marriage-contracts, see *Chrest.* II. i. p. 216, and on ἐκδόσιμα = official copies, see the editors' note on P Oxy III. 494²⁵. An unexplained term ἀπέγδοσις is found in P Petr II. 13 (4)² (B.C. 258–3). The corresponding εἰσδίδωμι, hitherto almost unknown, is now well attested: see exx. in Mayser *Gr.* p. 480, and similarly *ib.* p. 438 for εἴσδοσις (not in LS). See ἔκδοτος, *infra*.

ἐκδικέω.

In P Ryl II. 94¹² (A.D. 14–37) the head and the secretary of a guild of weavers become sureties for five of their number, undertaking to produce them whenever required—ἐκδικοῦντες τὰ διὰ τοῦ ὑπομνήματος Πανινούτιος τοῦ Ἀφροδισίου ἐρι(ουργοῦ?), "to answer the claims stated in the petition of Paninoutis son of Aphrodisius, wool-worker" (Edd.). For the meaning "vindicate" cf. P Amh II. 134¹⁰ (early ii/A.D.) where Heliodorus is urged to take action on behalf of Peteus, whom certain πρεσβύτεροι had attempted to carry off—ἐκδικῆσαι αὐτὸν "to vindicate him," and ἐντυχεῖν κατά, "to draw up a petition against," the persons concerned : cf. P Strass I. 41⁹ (A.D. 250). In P Oxy VII. 1020⁵ (A.D. 198-201) the word is used of a judicial decision—εἰ τὴν ἐκ τῆς ἡλικίας ἔχεις β[οήθιαν,] ὁ ἡγούμ[ενος] τοῦ ἔθνους τὸν ἀγῶνα τῆς ἀφέσεως ἐκδικ[ήσει, "if you can claim the assistance due to immature age, the praefect of the province shall decide the suit for release" (Ed.) : so P Lond 245¹⁹ (A.D. 343) (= II. p. 272) αὐτοῦ γάρ ἐστιν τὰ τοια[ῦτ]α τολμῶντες ἐκδικῖν αὐ. It would appear therefore that the thought of "avenge" (AV, RV) is not necessarily primary in Lk 18³ᶠᶠ., but rather of "do right to" and so "protect" the wronged party (cf. Exp T xxv. p. 70 f.). The context, however, suggests the stronger sense in the striking Jewish prayer for vengeance for a murdered girl, Syll 816¹¹, which Deissmann (LAE p. 434) carries back as far as the end of the second or beginning of the first century B.C. where "the most high God" is implored—ἵνα ἐγδικήσῃς τὸ αἷμα τὸ ἀναίτιον ζητήσῃς καὶ τὴν ταχίστην, "that Thou mayst avenge the innocent blood and require it again right speedily" : cf. Joel 3 4)²¹Α ἐκδικήσω τὸ αἷμα αὐτῶν. See also P Oxy VI. 937⁷ (iii/A.D.) where a brother writes to his sister regarding some wrong that had been done to him—ἐὰν οὖν ζήσω χρόνον καὶ ἔλθω εἰς τὴν πατρίδα μου ἐκδικήσω ἐμαυτόν, "well, if I live and come to my native land I will have my revenge" (Edd.) : cf. Rom 12¹⁹.

ἐκδίκησις.

A striking curse from Phrius may be cited from Syll 810 to illustrate Rom 12¹⁹. The fragment runs—καὶ ὅτι ἂν ποιῇς, το[ῦτο] εἰς σεαυτὸν τρεπέ[σθω·] ταῦτά σοι εὐχόμε[θα.] εἰ δέ τι ἑκὼν ἐξαμαρτ[ήσει], οὐκ ἐμὸν ἐπαράσ[ασθαι], δίκη δὲ ἐπικρέματα[ι] τιμωρὸς ἀπελθόν[τι] ἀπειθὴς Νεμέσε[ως], "it is not mine to invoke curses, but the inexorable vengeance of Nemesis hangs over you as you go." Ἐκδικία is found in P Oxy VIII. 1121³¹ (A.D. 295) ἐκδικίαν αἰτεῖν, "demand satisfaction," ib. XII. 1550⁸ (A.D. 247) ἄχρι τῆς παρὰ τῷ μείζονι ἐκδικίας.

ἔκδικος

is the regular term in the papyri for a legal representative, e.g. P Oxy II. 237ᵛⁱⁱ ⁵⁰ (A.D. 186) Διδύμη ἧς ἔκδικος ὁ ἀνὴρ Ἀπολλώνιος πρὸς Σαβεῖνον, "Didyme, defended by her husband Apollonius, against Sabinus," ib. 261¹⁴ (A.D. 55) συνεστακέναι αὐτὴν τὸν προγεγραμμένον υἱωνὸν Χα[ιρ]-ήμονα ἔγδικον ἐπὶ πάσης ἐξουσίας, "that she has appointed her said grandson Chaeremon to appear for her before every authority" (Edd.), and for a similar use in the inscrr. = "advocatus," Michel 459²⁰ (ii/B.C. ad init.) ὑπέμεινεν ἑκουσίως [ἔκ]δικος : see further Gradenwitz Einführung i. p. 160, Nageli p. 33, and for the Bibl. usage Milligan on 1 Thess 4⁶. Ὁ ἔκδικος τῆς πόλεως, defensor civitatis, appears in Egypt early in iv/A.D. : see the notes on P Oxy XII. 1413¹⁷, 1426⁴. Moulton (Gr. ii. § 119 (c)) suggests that in ἔκδικος = "avenger" we may see the same force of ἐκ as in the recurrent legal phrase καθάπερ ἐγ δίκης, "just as after a legal decision"; the ἔκδικος would thus be the man who carries out a sentence. Alternatively the classical compositum ἐκδικάζω, "avenge," may have influenced the meaning of ἔκδικος with its derivatives.

PART III.

ἐκδιώκω.

This NT ἅπ. εἰρ. (1 Th 2¹⁵) is found in the late BGU III. 836⁵ (time of Justinian) κατεστασιασάντων κατὰ τῶν ἀπελθόντων (l. — όντων) ἐκεῖσε στρατιωτῶν ἐξεδίωξ[αν αὐτ]οὺς μὴ βουλόμενοι αὐτῶν ἀπόκρισιν ποιῆσαι. The simplex occurs in the sense of "drive out," "persecute," in Lk 11⁴⁹ אBC, where the compound is found as a v.l. in AD al.

ἔκδοτος.

This adj., as in Ac 2²³ (cf. Field Notes, p. 111 f., is found in Syll 190¹³ (B.C. 306 281) παραγενόμενος ὁ βασιλ[εὺς εἰ]ς τοὺς τόπους δέδωκεν ἐγδότου[ς τ]ῆι πόλει καὶ ἀφέσταλκε πρὸς τὸ[ν δῆμον : cf. Vett. Val. p. 106²⁴ ἑαυτοὺς ἐκδότους ὑποταγαῖς παραδώσουσιν. For ἔκδοτος = "bride" (see s.v. ἐκδίδωμι) cf. P Oxy VI. 905⁵ (A.D. 170 (= Selections, p 85) as restored ἡ δ' ἔκδοτ]ος φέρει τῷ ἀνδρὶ [εἰς φε]ρνήν κτλ, "the bride brings to her husband for dowry" etc. In P Oxy X. 1273²⁶ (A.D. 260) ἔκδοτις is used in an active sense = "bride's mother "—ἀπ[οδότω] ὁ γαμῶν τῇ ἐκδοτιδι.

ἐκδοχή

is used = "interpretation" in P Par 63⁸⁶ (B.C. 164) (= P Petr III. p. 24) παιδαριώδη τὴν τοῦ προστάγματος ἐγδοκὴν ποιησαμένους, "after having made the interpretation of the decree puerile," Syll 250¹⁸ (c. B.C. 200) τὴν ἐκδοχὴν τοῦ χρησμοῦ ταύτην λαβόντες. We have no light to throw upon the use of ἐ. = προσδοκία in Heb 10²⁷, the only place where it occurs in the NT, but see s.v. ἐκδέχομαι and cf. Field Notes, p. 231. For the title ἐκδοχεύς see OGIS 140⁸ with the editor's note.

ἐκδύω

is frequent in the sense of "strip one of his garments," as Mt 27²⁸, Lk 10³⁰, e.g. P Lille I. 6⁸ (iii/B.C.) ἐξέδυσαν χιτῶνα, P Magd 6¹³ (B.C. 221) τά τε πρόβα]τα βεβοσκηκότας κάμε ὑβρικότες καὶ ἐγδεδυκότες, P Fay 12¹⁸ (c. B.C. 103) ἐξέδυσαν ὁ περ[ιε]βεβλήμην ἱμάτιον, BGU IV. 1061¹⁶ (B.C. 14) ἐξέδυσαν (sc. ἔμπορον) καὶ περιείλοντο αὐτοῦ πόκους ἐρίων, and from the inscrr. Syll 803⁴⁷ (iii/B.C.) ἐδ[όκ]ει αὐτόν νιν ὁ θε[ὸ]ς ἐγδύσας καὶ γυμνὸν καταστάσας ὀρθὸν κτλ. In the new fragment of a lost Gospel, P Oxy IV. 655²², in answer to the disciples' question πότε σε ὀψόμεθα ; the Lord is described as replying : ὅταν ἐκδύσησθε καὶ μὴ αἰσχυνθῆτε . . . . Ἐκδύω is an ex. of a verb which, though perfective already, forms a further perfective ἀπεκδύομαι which, like ἀπέκδυσις (see s.v.), connotes complete stripping of oneself or another in one's own interest Col 2¹¹·¹⁵, 3⁹) : see Moulton Gr. ii. § 119 (a). MGr γδύνω, "doff," "pillage."

ἐκεῖ.

P Eleph 1¹⁴ (B.C. 311-10) (= Selections, p. 4) ὡς ἐκεῖ τοῦ συναλλάγματος γεγενημένου, "on the ground that the agreement had been come to there," P Fay 110¹³ (A.D. 94) ἵ[ν]α τὰ πρόβατα ἐκεῖ κοιμηθῇι, ib. 118³⁴ (A.D. 110) ἔχ' ἐκὶ ἕ[ως] ποτίσῃς τῷ ἐπτάρουρον τοῦ ἐλαιῶνο[ς, "stay there till you have watered the seven-acre at the olive-yard," P Ryl II. 239⁹ (mid. iii/A.D.) ἐπίμινον τοῖς ἐκεῖ, "stay on for the men there." In the boy's letter P Oxy I. 119¹² (ii/iii A.D.)

20

(= *Selections*, p. 103) the word is used somewhat pleon-
astically—πεπλάνηκαν ἡμῶς (*l.* ἡμᾶς) ἐκεῖ, τῇ ἡμέρᾳ ιβ ὅτι
(*l.* ὅτε) ἔπλευσες, "they deceived us there on the 12th, the
day you sailed." For the laxer use = ἐκεῖσε, as in Rom 15⁴,
cf. P Meyer 20⁴⁶ (1st half iii/A.D.) ἵνα ἐκεῖ πέμπω τὰς
ἐπιστολάς. For a contrast with ἐνταῦθα, see *Preisigke*
1002¹⁰ f. (time of Diocletian?) τὰ ἐκεῖ θαύματ[α] εἶδον καὶ τὰ
ἐνταῦθα. The word is MGr.

ἐκεῖθεν.

For a causal force of this adverb = "wherefore," "hence,"
see the editor's note to the early Christian letter P Heid 6⁹
(iv/A.D.) (= *Selections*, p. 126) πιστεύομεν γὰρ τὴν πολιτία[ν σ]ου ἐνν οὐρανῷ. ἐγῖθεν (*l.* ἐκεῖθεν) θεωροῦμέν σε τὸν
δεσπότην καὶ κενὸν (π ά[τ]ρω[να, "we believe that your
citizenship is in heaven. Wherefore we regard you as master
and new patron." In MGr the word = "whence,"
"yonder," "beyond."

ἐκεῖνος.

See *s.v.* αὐτός, and cf. *Proleg.* p. 91.

ἐκεῖσε.

P Thead 21⁸ (A.D. 318) τίνες κακοῦργοι ἐπιστάντες ἐκεῖσε
διὰ νυκτός κτλ., and a Cairo papyrus, *Chrest.* I. 240⁹ (A.D.
322) γενό[μ]ενοι ἐκεῖσε. For ἐκεῖσε = ἐκεῖ, cf. PSI III. 162¹¹
(A.D. 286) παραμεῖναι ἐν τῷ ἐκῖσαι (*l.* ἐκεῖσε) κατασκευα-
ζομένῳ βαλανίῳ, *ib.* IV. 298⁸ (iv/A.D. *ad init.*) μόνον μῆνα
ἕνα ἐκεῖσε διαμείναντος, P Oxy IX. 1204⁶ (A.D. 299) πρὸς
ἐκσφούνγευσιν (cf. Lat. *expungere*) τῶν ἐκεῖσε διακειμένων
στρατιωτῶν, "for the discharge of the soldiers stationed
there." This "pregnant" construction (Ac 22⁵ τοὺς ἐκεῖσε
ὄντας, "those who were (collected) there") is illustrated
by P Petr II. 45ⁱⁱ·⁴ (B.C. 246) where, if we may trust the
restoration, the writer—probably Ptolemy III. himself (cf.
P Petr III. p. 336)—describes how certain ships, acting in
his interest, sailed along the coast of Cilicia to Soli and took
on board τὰ ἐ[κεῖ ?]σε κατασκεθέντ[α χρή]ματα, "the money
that had been seized (and carried) there."

ἐκζητέω.

To the single instance of this verb from profane sources
(Aristid. I. 488) cited by Thayer and LS, we can now add
BGU IV. 1141⁴¹ (B.C. 14) περὶ δὲ τῆς σκιᾶς φανερόν μοι
ἐγενήθη ἐκζητήσαντι ἠλλάχθαι μὲν τὴν πορφυρᾶν ὑπὸ τοῦ
Διοδώρου καὶ μὴ δεδωκέναι σοί, P Oxy XII. 1465¹¹ (i/B.C.)
ἀξιῶ συντ[ά]ξαι ἐ[κ]ζητήσαντας τοὺς α[ἰτίο]υς, "I request
you to give orders (to your subordinates) to search out the
guilty persons" (Edd.), and the inscr. from Hierapolis
Cagnat IV. 834⁵ δώσει . . τῷ ἐκζητήσαντι δηνάρια δισχίλια.
With Lk 11⁵⁰ ἵνα ἐκζητηθῇ τὸ αἷμα πάντων τῶν προφητῶν,
cf. the use of the simplex in the Jewish prayer for vengeance
Syll 816¹² (ii/B.C.) ἵνα ἐγδικήσῃς τὸ αἷμα τὸ ἀναίτιον
ζητήσῃς καὶ τὴν ταχίστην : for the text and the date, see
Deissmann *LAE* p. 423 ff.

ἐκθαμβέω.

P Grenf I. 53¹⁸ (iv/A.D.) (= *Chrest.* I. p. 158) γράφ[ει] δὲ
ἡμῖν ὡς ἐχθαμβῶν (*l.* ἐκθαμβῶν) ἡμᾶς.

ἔκθαμβος.

For this rare adj. (Ac 3¹¹) which hitherto has been
attested in profane Greek only from Polybius (xx. 10. 9), we
may cite the imprecatory tablet of iii/A.D. discovered in the
necropolis of Hadrumetum, Wünsch *AF* 5²⁰ καὶ οἱ δαίμονες
ἐξεγερθῶσιν ἔκθαμβοι καὶ περίφοβοι [γ]ενόμενοι.

ἐκθαυμάζω.

Aristeas 312 λίαν ἐξεθαύμασε τὴν τοῦ νομοθέτου διάνοιαν.

ἔκθετος.

For this NT ἅπ. εἰρ. (Ac 7¹⁹) we may compare Vett. Val.
p. 106¹⁴ ἔκθετοι ἢ αἰχμάλωτοι γενόμενοι ὑποταγῆς πεῖραν
λήψονται, where ἔκθετοι is apparently = "exiles." The
subst. ἔκθεσις is common = "list," "schedule," e.g. P Oxy
II. 291³ (A.D. 25–26) τ[ὴν] ἔκθεσιν τοῦ ιβ (ἔτους) Τιβερίου
Καί[σαρ]ος Σεβαστοῦ σειτικὴν καὶ ἀρ[γ]υρικὴν εὐθέως
γράψον, "write out immediately the list of arrears both of
corn and money for the twelfth year of Tiberius Caesar
Augustus" (Edd.) : on the verso of P Tebt II. 410 (A.D.
16) is a short account, with the heading ἔκθεσις τιμ(ῆς)
προβά(των). *Syll* 929³⁷ (ii/B.C.) περὶ ἧς καὶ τὴν καθήκουσαν
ἔκθεσιν πεποιήμεθα, has the same spelling as in Wisd 11¹⁴
ℵAC. In calling attention to the needless margin at RV
here (where the ἐχθ. spelling seems to have been taken as a
form of ἔχθος) Thackeray (*Gr.* i. p. 103) has achieved the
rare feat of catching Hort and his colleagues tripping. For
ἔκθεμα see *s.v.* ἐκτίθημι.

ἐκκαθαίρω

is found *quater* with the acc. of the person or object cleansed
(as in 2 Tim 2²¹) in OGIS 483 (ii/B.C.), e.g. ¹⁵⁸ ἀναγ]καζέτωσαν
ἐκκαθαίρειν τοὺς ὑπονόμους. See also the Delos inscr.
BCH xxvii. p. 73⁷⁸ (B.C. 250) Ὠμανέαι καὶ τοῖς μεθ' αὑτοῦ
τὸ [στά]διον ἐκκαθάρασιν, and ⁷⁵ ἐργάταις τὸν ἠθμὸν
ἐκκαθάρασιν τοῦ Ἰνωποῦ. Vett. Val. p. 242¹⁵ τὸν τρόπον
μου ἐκκαθᾶραι πάσης κακίας καὶ παντὸς μολυσμοῦ. The
verb is supplied in *Kaibel* 1082¹⁶ Φολόην Κεντ[αύρων
ἐξεκάθηρεν, of one of the labours of Hercules. On the form
ἐκκαθάρατε in 1 Cor 5⁷, see Moulton *Gr.* ii. § 89, Note 2.

ἐκκαίω.

For the metaphorical use of this verb in Rom 1²⁷ we may
cite the new Menander fragment, *Menandrea* p. 64⁴² πάντα
δ' ἐξεκάετο ταῦθ' ἕνεκα τοῦ μέλλοντος, "all the feelings
were fanned into flame for the sake of the plot." See also
Herodas iv. 49 where a slave is rebuked for her slowness—
ὡς ἔκ με κάεις οὐ θέλουσαν οἰδῆσαι, "how you set me on
fire with fury, though I do not wish to rage."

ἐκκακέω.

See ἐνκακέω.

ἐκκλείω.

Cf. the Ionic inscr. OGIS 8⁷ (iv/B.C.) τοῖς μὲν πολίταις
παρελόμενος τὰ ὅπλα ἐξεκλάισε ἐκ τᾶς πόλιος [πα]νδάμι.
Also *Menandrea* p. 53²⁰¹.

ἐκκλησία.

For the Biblical history of the word ἐκκλησία, which meant originally any public assembly of citizens summoned by a herald, it is sufficient to refer to Hort, *The Christian Ecclesia*, p. 1 ff. It is the LXX term for the community of Israel, whether assembled or no. In the Gospels the word is confined to Mt 16[18], 18[17], where it denotes Christ's new ἐκκλησία, as distinguished from the old. Deissmann (*LAE* p. 112 ff.) has emphasized the significance of the fact that the Latin-speaking people of the West, to whom Christianity came, did not translate the word, but simply borrowed it, and cites an interesting bilingual inscr. of A.D. 103-4, found in the theatre of Ephesus, which refers to the gift by a Roman official of a silver image of Artemis (cf. Ac 19[24]) and other statues—ἵνα τιθηνται κατ᾽ ἐκκλησίαν (cf. Ac 14[23]) ἐν τῷ θεάτρῳ ἐπὶ τῶν βάσεων, or, in the parallel text, *ita ut [om]n[i e]cclesia supra bases ponerentur*. Other reff. to ἐκκλησίαι in the theatre at Ephesus will be found *s.v.* θέατρον. For the "inclusive" as distinguished from the "exclusive" character of the Greek ἐκκλησία (cf. Hicks *CR* i. p. 43), we may cite the case of an ἐκκλησία summoned at Apamea—ἀγομένης πανδήμου ἐκκλησίας, which the editor Cagnat (note on IV. 791[7]) describes as "concilium totius populi Apamensis, civium cum Graecorum, tum Romanorum": see also Ramsay *C. and B.* ii. p. 465, where the inscr. is dated as perhaps of the time of Vespasian and Titus. MGr ἐκκλησ(ι)ά.

ἐκκλίνω.

In a decree of Ptolemy Philometor (B.C. 181-145) published in *Archiv* vi. p. 9 we find [12] οὔτε κίνδυνον οὔτε κακοπαθίαν οὐδεμίαν ἐκκέκ[λ]ικεν: cf. *OGIS* 339[9] (*c.* B.C. 120), 443[14] (i/B.C.), and *Cagnat* IV. 134[14] (ii/B.C.). The verb is taken as = "faire défaut" by the editor (see Index p. 476) in P Par 15[22] (B.C. 120), συνιστοροῦντες ἑαυτοῖς οὐδὲν βέβαιον ἔχουσι ἐξέκλιναν. Similarly P Tor I. 2[33], and *cf. ib.* 1[ii. 17] (B.C. 117) καὶ μετὰ ταῦτα πολλάκις ἐπιβεβληκότος εἰς τὴν Διόσπολιν, ἐκκλίνοντες οὐ διαλείπουσιν, "semper occursum meum devitant" (Ed.).

ἐκκομίζω

is used of carrying out for burial, as in Lk 7[12], in BGU I. 326[ii. 1] (ii/A.D.) ἐκκο[μι]σθῆναι περιστ[αλ]ῆναί τε ἐμαυτό[ν] θέλω τῇ φροντίδι καὶ εὐσεβείᾳ τῶν [κ]ληρονόμων μου. For a more general sense cf. PSI IV. 436[5] (B.C. 248-7) ἐκκομίζεσθαι τὰ ὀψώνια, P Lille I. 3[7] (after B.C. 241) λόγους ἐκκομίζεσθαι, P Lond 21[23] (B.C. 162) (= I. p. 13) ἐκκ[ο]μίσασθαι σύνταξιν, P Fay 12[24] (*c.* B.C. 103) ἐξεκομισάμην α[ὑτ]ό, "I recovered it"—of a pawned garment which had been redeemed. The verb is contrasted with εἰσκομίζω in *OGIS* 629[28 al.] (A.D. 137).

ἐκκοπή (ἐνκοπή).

This somewhat rare word is found in its literal sense of "cutting" or "cutting down" in BGU IV. 1121[27] (B.C. 5) ξυλείας] ἐκκοπήν, P Lond 214[24] (A.D. 270-5) (= II. p. 162) where with reference to the cutting down of two acacia trees an official is sent to inspect τῆς ἐκ[κοπ]ῆς τὴν διάθεσιν, and P Gen I. 62[7] (mid. iv/A.D.) τεχνίτας πρὸς τὴν ἐκκοπὴν τῶν ξύλων, cf. [11]. The derived meaning of "hindrance" in

the only occurrence of the word in the NT (1 Cor 9[12]) may be illustrated from Vett. Valens p. 2[7] ἐγκοπὰς τῶν πρασσομένων : the adj. ἐγκοπτικός, also occurs *ter*, e.g. p. 182[12] κωλυτικοὶ καὶ ἐγκοπτικοὶ δόξης καὶ ὠφελείας.

ἐκκόπτω (ἐνκόπτω).

For the literal usage, as in Mt 3[10] etc., cf. P Fay 113[10] (A.D. 100) ἐξ αὐτὸν ἐκκόψαι θέλι φυτά, "he wishes to cut down some of the trees" (Edd.), and similarly 114[14], P Oxy VI. 802[19] (A.D. 338) ἵνα . . . διὰ ταχέων ταῦτα ἐκκόψας παρενεχθῆναι ποιήσης, "to get the timber cut and delivered" (Edd.). See also BGU I. 72[9] (A.D. 191) ἐξέκοψαν πλεῖστον τόπον ἐν ἀρούραις πέντε. A good parallel to the NT usage, as in 1 Th 2[18] (where see Milligan's note), is afforded by P Alex 4[1] (iii/B.C.) (= Witkowski [2], p. 51) ἡμῖν ἐνκόπτεις καλά : cf. Vett. Val. p. 268[6] ἐὰν μή πως ἀκτὶς ἀγαθοποιῶν συνδραμοῦσα τὰ πόλλα τῶν φαύλων ἐκκόψῃ. The verb is intrans. in *ib.* p. 260[24] ὥσπερ γὰρ τροχὸς κυλιόμενος ἐνέκοψεν (*sc.* ἡ Σελήνη) ἐπὶ τὴν ἰδίαν ἐλθοῦσα ἐποχήν.

ἐκλαλέω.

For a suggestion that we should read this verb in Mk 8[32] see Burkitt *JTS* ii. p. 111 ff.

ἐκλάμπω.

This verb, which in the NT is confined to Mt 13[43], is found in P Lond 130[95] (a horoscope—i ii A.D.) (= I. p. 135) ἐξέλαμπεν.

ἐκλανθάνω.

P Oxy IX. 1203[8] (late i/A.D.) ἐγλαθόμενος τῆς ἐξακολ[ο]υθούσης αὐτῷ εὐθύνης, "heedless of the reckoning that would follow" (Ed.).

ἐκλέγω.

The middle of this verb, which is used in all its NT occurrences, may be illustrated by PSI IV. 422[14] (iii/B.C.) ταῦτα τὰ ἀσθενέστερα ἐγλεξάμενος, P Meyer 8[12] (A.D. 151) μέχρι τοῦ . . . τῶν σωμάτων τὰς ἀποφορὰς ἐγλεγομένον, P Oxy II. 237[iv. 8] (A.D. 186) δούλο]υς καὶ ἀπελευ[θέρου]ς χορηγίας ἐκλεγομένων, and P Flor II. 228[22] (iii/A.D.) κάλλ[ιστ]όν ἐστιν ἐγλέξασθαι αὐτά : also *Syll* 653[15] (B.C. 91) τὰ δὲ πίπτοντα διάφορα ἐκ τῶν μυστηρίων ἐγλεγόντω οἱ κατασταθέντες ὑπὸ τοῦ δάμου πέντε. On the use of the middle in Lk 14[7] ἐξελέγοντο, "they picked out for themselves," and so "chose," see *Proleg.* p. 157.

ἐκλείπω.

Notwithstanding Field (*Notes*, p. 79) and Moffatt, it seems more than doubtful that in Lk 23[45] any reference is intended to an *eclipse*. To find such a reference is to involve the Evangelist in a needless blunder, as an *eclipse* is impossible at full moon, and to run counter to his general usage of the verb = "fail" (16[9], 22[32], cp. Heb 1[12]. For this meaning cf. P Hamb I. 27[14] (B.C. 250) ἐάν τι αὐτῶν ἐγλιμπάνηι, P Leid B[ii. 7] (B.C. 164) εἰς τὸ μηθὲν ἡμᾶς τῶν δεόντων ἐγλιπεῖν, and even *ib.* W[ix. 6] (ii/iii A.D.) τὴν ὥραν ἐν ἧ μέλλι (*l.* μέλλει) ἡ σελήνη ἐκλιπεῖν (*l.* ἐκλείπειν), "horam in qua luna deficiet (in ariete)." P Par 27[14] (B.C. 160) ἡμεῖς δὲ ἐν τῷ μεταξὺ διαλυόμεναι τῷ λιμῷ κινδυνεύομεν τὸ ἱερὸν ἐγλείπειν shows ἐ. followed by the acc. of place. In P Tebt I. 105⁴¹ (B.C. 103) and 106²³ (B.C. 101) it is used of "renouncing" a lease—ἐγλιπεῖν τὴν μίσθωσιν: for a similar use of the subst. cf. P Lond 1166⁶ (A.D. 42) (= III. p. 104) μεχρὶ ἐκλείψεως τῶν λουομένω(ν). From the inscrr. may be cited *Syll* 226¹¹⁰ (iii/B.C.) ἐγλείπειν τὴν πόλιν, and *OGIS* 90¹⁶ (the Rosetta stone—B.C. 196) τά τε ἐγλελειμμένα πάντα ἐν τοῖς πρότερον χρόνοις ἀποκατέστησεν εἰς τὴν καθήκουσαν τάξιν. On the form ἐγλείπειν see Mayser *Gr.* p. 227.

ἐκλεκτός.

In P Rein 43⁹ (A.D. 102) a "choice" or "beautiful" lodging which is being let is described as ἐκλεκτὸν ἀντρῶνα (*l.* ἀνδρῶνα). For the distinctive Biblical use of the word, cf. farm-accounts—P Fay 102³·*ᵃˡ* (*c.* A.D. 105) where ἐγλεκ(τοί) is applied to baskets "'selected,' i.e. of a better quality than the rest" (Edd.), and *OGIS* 409³ (ii/A.D.) τῶν ἐκλεκτῶν ἐν Ῥώμῃ δικαστῶν, with which Dittenberger compares *ib.* 567¹⁰ (ii/A.D.) ἐπίλεκτον κριτήν, the *iudex selectus* of the Latin inscriptions. The Avircius epitaph—late ii/A.D.—from MS. of *Acta Sanctorum* has ἐκλεκτῆς πόλεως ὁ πολείτης τοῦτ' ἐποίησα. See also BGU II. 603¹⁸ (*c.* A.D. 167) ἐλαίας ἐγλεκτῆς.

ἐκλογή.

In the Royal Ordinances issued by Euergetes II. and the two Cleopatras, P Tebt I. 5¹⁶⁶ (B.C. 118), it is enacted that officials are not to take the richest Crown land from the cultivators by fraud μηδὲ ἐπὶ ἐγλογῆι γεωργεῖν, "nor to cultivate it at choice," i.e. select the best land for themselves. Similarly in the marriage contract, P Oxy III. 496¹⁵ (A.D. 127), provision is made that in certain eventualities the "choice" shall rest with the bride—ἐκλογῆς οὔσης περὶ τὴν γαμουμένην: so *ib.* 497¹⁹ (early ii/A.D.), *ib.* IV. 729⁴¹ (A.D. 137), CPR I. 22²³ (ii/A.D.). Cf. BGU IV. 1158¹³ (B.C. 9) where two contracting parties retain τὴν ἐξουσία(ν) καὶ ἐγλογή(ν) . . . πράσσειν τὸ κεφά[λ]αιο(ν), "the power and choice to call in the principal." In P Flor I. 47¹⁴ (A.D. 213–17) (= *Chrest.* II. p. 158) ἀπέσχεν . . . ὑπὲρ ἐκλογῆς ἀργ(υρίου) (δραχμὰς) διακοσίας, the reference is to an "additional payment" made to equalize an exchange of property: cf. BGU IV. 1013¹⁶ (time of Claudius or Nero), P Ryl II. 157⁶ (A.D. 135). [Cf. ἡ ἔγλογος = "the surplus," Wilcken *Ostr* i. p. 733.] The word occurs in an interesting connexion in the epitaph of M. Julius Eugenius, Bishop of Laodicea, composed about A.D. 340–2, where Ramsay (*Exp* VII. ix. p. 53) reads ε[ἰς τύμβον ἐ]μὸν τῆς τε ἐκλ[ογῆς ἀπ]ὸ τοῦ γένους μου, "to be my grave and that of the Elect from my race": cf. Rom 11⁷. "He belonged to a family some of whose members were still pagan; and he restricted the right of sharing this sepulchre to those members who were Christian." In the sepulchral inscr. *Preisigke* 4315³ Ἐκλογὴ καλουμένη, the word is a proper name.

ἐκλύω.

For this verb in its literal sense cf. P Tebt I. 49⁶ (B.C. 113) Νίκωνος . . . ἐγλύοντος τ[ὰ] ἐν τῆι ἑαυτοῦ γῆι ὕδατα, "when Nicon let out the water on his own land," *ib.* 54¹⁶ (B.C. 86) ἐπὶ τὸν δ[ια]σαφούμενόν μου κλῆρον ἐγλέλυκαν

τὰ ἐκ τῆς γῆς αὐτῶν ὕδατα. The metaph. meaning, which alone is found in the NT, may be illustrated by Vett. Val. p. 18³³ πονηρῶν ἀνθρώπων ἀδρανῶν καὶ ἐκλελυμένων. For the corresponding subst., see *ib.* p. 166² ἔκλυσιν ψυχῆς μεγίστην ἕξει. Cf. MGr γλυτώνω, "rescue," "escape," and ξεγλυτώνω, "finish a work," "am freed from work."

ἐκμάσσω.

Kaibel *Epigr.* 1003³ᶠ·:—

> ἔθραυσε Καμβίσης με τόνδε τὸν λίθον
> βασιλέος ἑῷον εἰκόνα ἐκμεμαγμένον.

We may add a literary reference from Herodas vi. 9 νῦν αὐτὸν ἐκμάσσεις τε καὶ ποεῖς λαμπρόν, ὅτ' ἐστὶ χρ[είη], λῃστρί, where Nairn renders "wipe dry."

ἐκνεύω.

For a transitive use of this NT ἅπ. εἰρ. (Jn 5¹³) see BGU IV. 1189⁷ (*c.* B.C. 1) τῶν προκειμένων ἀνδρῶν ἐγγενευκότων τὴν ἐνφανήαν ἠναγκάσθην κτλ. In the Jn passage the verb is best rendered intransitively "had turned aside," "had retired": cf. Field *Notes*, p. 88.

ἐκνήφω.

Nageli (p. 33) reckons this strong non-classical word as belonging to the higher Κοινή and pointing to Paul's true Hellenism. In 1 Cor 15³⁴, the only place where it occurs in the NT, ἐκνήψατε should have its full force, "get sober out of your drunken condition."

ἑκούσιος

is found in what appears to be a legal formula in P Oxy X. 1280⁶ (iv/A.D.) ὁμολογῶ ἑκουσίᾳ καὶ αὐθαιρέτῳ γνώμῃ συντεθίσθαί με πρὸς σέ, "I acknowledge that I have of my own free will covenanted with you" (Edd.): cf. *ib.* XII. 1426¹⁴ (A.D. 332), and P Lips I. 26⁶ cited *s.v.* ἀμετανόητος. See also P Ryl II. 174²³ (A.D. 112) ἐκ[ο]ύσιον κατ[ο]χήν, "voluntary notification" of a personal claim with reference to the repayment of a loan, and P Oxy III. 473³ (A.D. 138–160) the decree in honour of a gymnasiarch, who had devoted himself εἰς ἑκούσιον γυμν[ασ]ιαρχίαν.

ἑκουσίως.

For a legal formula similar to that cited *s.v.* ἑκούσιος, cf. P Strass I. 29³¹ (A.D. 289) ὁμολογοῦμεν καὶ νῦν διῃρῆσθαι πρὸς ἀλλήλους χωρεῦτ[ι]κῶς ἑκουσίως καὶ αὐθαιρέ[τ]ως καὶ ἀμετανοήτως. Other exx. are P Fay 11²¹ (*c.* B.C. 115) ὁ ἐνκαλούμενος πλεονάκις ἀπῃτημένος [ο]ὐχ ὑπομένει ἑκουσίως ἀποδιδόναι, "the accused, though frequent demands have been made, persistently refuses to pay voluntarily" (Edd.), P Ryl II. 154²⁵ (A.D. 66) a contract of marriage in which certain provisions are made in the event of the bride "voluntarily" withdrawing from her husband—αὐτῆς ἑκουσίω[ς ἀ]παλλασσομέν[η]ς [ἀ]π' αὐτοῦ, and *ib.* 169¹ (A.D. 196–7) βουλόμεθα ἑκουσίως μισθώσασθαι παρὰ σοῦ . . . τὰς ὑπαρχούσας σοι . . (ἀρούρας), *Michel* 459⁷ (an honorary decree—beginning of ii/B.C.) μετά τε ταῦτα ἀνεδέξατο ἑκου[σ]ίω[ς] τὴν αὐτὴν πάλιν λειτουργίαν δαπάνας μὲν οὐδενὶ [ἐν] λόγ[ωι] ποιούμενος.

ἔκπαλαι.

This late word (for the form, see *Proleg.* p. 99), which in the NT is confined to 2 Pet 2³, 3⁵, occurs in P Oxy VI. 938³ (iii/iv A.D.) ἔκπαλαι ἐπισταλεὶς δώδεκα σαργάνας χόρτου ἐκεῖ ἀποστεῖλαι, "although you had been long ago instructed to send twelve baskets of hay thither" (Edd.): cf. the fragmentary *OGIS* 584⁵ (ii/A.D.) δι' ὧν ἔκπαλαι αὐτὴν (*sc.* τὴν πατρίδα) εὐεργέ[τησεν]. Ἔκτοτε is found in P Oxy VIII. 1119²⁸ (A.D. 254) ἔκτοτε μαθ[ὼν ὑπέστ]ην τὴν ὑπὲρ αὐτῶν λειτουργίαν, "thereafter on learning this I undertook the burden on their behalf": cf. *ib.* III. 486⁹ (A.D. 131).

ἐκπέμπω.

P Leid W*.* ¹¹ (ii/iii A.D.) τῶν (*l.* τὸν ἦχον δυναμικώτερον ἐκπέμπει. The verb is common in judicial proceedings of "sending up" to trial, e. g. P Ryl II. 132¹⁹ (A.D. 32) ἀρχεφό(δῳ) ἐκέμψω(ν), *ib.* 148²⁸ (A.D. 40) ὅπως . . . ἐκπέμψῃ σοι τοὺς αἰτίους, P Tebt II. 290¹ (an order for arrest—i/ii A.D.) ἐκπέμψον Γαλάτην καὶ τὴν τούτου γυναῖκα, P Oxy II. 237ᵛⁱⁱ·²⁵ (A.D. 186) ἵνα οἱ ἀντίδικοι ἐκπεμφθῶσι. For a weakened sense, practically = the simple verb, see P Tebt I. 55⁶ (late ii/B.C.) χαριεῖ οὖν ἐκπέμψας ἡμῖν φακοῦ (ἀρτάβας) β, "you will therefore confer a favour on me by sending me two artabae of lentils" (Edd.), and P Oxy IX. 1223¹¹ (late iv/A.D.) σπούδασον πάραντα τὸν ναύτην ἐπὶ τὴν πόλιν ἅμα τῷ πεμφθέντι συμμάχῳ ἐκπέμψαι, "make haste to send the sailor to the city at once with the attendant whom I have sent" (Ed.). The double compound συνεκπέμπω, used by Plato and Xenophon, is found in BGU IV. 1127³⁸ (B.C. 8).

ἐκπετάννυμι.

For this NT ἅπ. εἰρ. (Rom 10²¹ from Isai 65²) = "spread out," the ἐκ showing the action of the verb carried as far as it will go (cf. ἐκτείνω), cf. *Kaibel* 779²—

Οὔριον ἐκ πρύμνης τις ὁδηγητῆρα καλείτω
Ζῆνα κατὰ προτόνων ἱστίον ἐκπετάσας.

See Anz *Subsidia*, p. 286.

ἐκπηδάω.

A good example of this expressive compound (Ac 14¹⁴, cf. Judith 14¹⁷) is P Par 14²⁸ (ii/B.C.) ἀφορήτῳ δὲ ἀνομίᾳ ἐξενεχθέντες καὶ ἐκπηδήσαντές μοι καὶ μιάναντες—a petition: cf. *ib.* 11¹¹ (B.C. 157) ἔτι δὲ καὶ ἐκπη]δηκέναι, and the astonishing account of Sarapion's daughters, P Grenf I. 53²⁵ (iv/A.D.) ἐξεπήδησαν αἴδε λέγουσαι ὅτι ἄνδρες θέλομεν. In the important historical narrative P Petr II. 45ⁱⁱ·¹³ (B.C. 246) τοῦ Ἀριβάζου δὲ ἐκπεπεδηκότος καὶ πρὸς τὴν ὑπερβολὴν τοῦ Ταύρου συνάπτοντος, Mahaffy translates, "but Aribazos having escaped and reached the passes of Tauros." The verb is also found twice in the magic PSI I. 28¹⁷·³⁸ (iii/iv A.D.?).

ἐκπίπτω.

For the literal meaning "fall out of," "leave," we can cite P Rein 11¹⁰ (B.C. 111) διὰ τὸ τοῦτον ἐκπεπτωκέναι καὶ μὴ εὑρίσκεσθαι, "attendu que mon mari a quitté le pays et a disparu" (Ed.). The idea of ending in failure or nothingness, as in Jas 1¹¹, is seen in Vett. Val. p. 70²⁷ καθαιρεῖται

γὰρ τὸ ἀγαθὸν τοῦ ἀστέρος καὶ εἰς τὸ ἐναντίον ἐκπίπτει. See also *Michel* 827 A¹⁴ (mid. iii/B.C.) τό τε νόμισμα τὸ ἐκπεπτωκὸς ἀριθμῶι, of coins that have fallen out of use. The verb is not infrequent with reference to crops that "fall to be included" in the produce of a particular year, e. g. BGU II. 591⁹ (A.D. 56-7) βουλόμεθα μισθώσασθαι τοὺς ἐκπεπτωκότας εἰς τὸ τρίτον ἔτος Νέρωνος . . . φοινεικίνους καρπούς, P Fay 91¹⁸ (A.D. 99) ἐ]λαϊκοὺς καρποὺς ἐκπεπτωκότας (*l.* ἐκπεπτωκ—) εἰς τὸ ἐνεστὸ(ς) τρίτον ἔτος. Cf. P Hib I. 78¹⁰ (B.C. 244-3) a letter requesting that two persons should be released from some public service—διὰ τὸ μὴ ἐκπεσ[εῖ]ν αὐτοῖς τὸ νῦν λειτουργῆσαι, "because it is not at present their turn to serve," where the editors point out that ἐκπεσ[εῖ]ν, which has been corrected in the papyrus, is practically equivalent to προσπέσηι in l. ⁴ of the same document. For the compd. ὑπερεκπίπτω, see P Thead 10¹⁴ (A.D. 307) ὑπὲρ τ]οῦ ὑπερεκπίπτ[οντ]ο[ς] χρόνου, "pour le temps supplémentaire" (Ed.).

ἐκπλέω.

PSI IV. 444¹ (iii/B.C.) μετὰ τὸ ἐκπλεῦσαι εἰσήγαγον κτλ., *Syll* 220¹³ (iii/B.C.) πειρατικῶν ἐκπλεόντων ἐκ τοῦ Ἐπιλιμνίου, and the memorial tablet, *OGIS* 69 (Ptol., erected by one who had been saved ἐγ μεγάλων κινδύνων ἐκπλεύσας ἐκ τῆς Ἐρυθρᾶς θαλάσσης. For the corresponding subst. cf. ἔκπλωι in P Petr III. 21 (*e*)⁵ and P Hib I. 30²⁶ (B.C. 300-271), in both cases after an hiatus.

ἐκπληρόω.

For the meaning "make good" in Ac 13³³, cf. an interesting letter from Petenephies, apparently a priest, requesting the release of certain persons that they may be able to furnish the supplies of food for the sacred crocodiles, P Tebt I. 57¹⁵ (B.C. 114) τὰς τῶν ἱερῶν ζώιων σειταγωγίας ἐκπληρῶσαι, cf. *ib.* 48¹² (c. B.C. 113) μεχρὶ τοῦ τὸ προκείμενον ἐκπληρῶσαι, "until we make up the aforesaid amount," and P Ryl II. 66⁸ (late ii/B.C.) ἵνα καὶ αὐτὸς ἀπροφασίστως ἐκπληρῶ τὰ πρόσλοιπα, "so that I also may make up the residues in full without excuse for failure" (Edd.). Other examples of the verb are P Par 62ˣ·⁴ (ii/B.C.) (cited *s.v.* ἀναπληρόω), BGU IV. 1053ⁱⁱ·¹⁵ and 1055¹⁵ (both B.C. 13). P Oxy I. 104¹⁸ (A.D. 96) ᾧ χορηγήσει ὁ αὐτὸς υἱὸς Ἀ. κατ' ἔτος ἀργυρίου δρ[α]χμὰς τεσσαράκοντα ὀκτὼ ἄχρι οὗ ἐκπληρώσωσι ἀργυρίου δραχμαὶ τριακόσιαι, where the verb is used intransitively, unless it is a mistake for ἐκπληρωθῶσι (see Herwerden *Lex. s.v.*), cf. P Tebt I. 10⁷ (B.C. 119) φρόντισον ὡς τὰ τῆς ὑποσχέσεως ἐκπληρωθήσεται, "take care that the terms of his agreement are fulfilled" (Edd.). From the inscrr. we may cite the honorary decree of Epaminondas *Syll* 376⁵⁴ (i/A.D.) ἵνα τούτων οὕτως τελεσθέντων καὶ ἡ ἡμετέρα πόλις φαίνηται πᾶσαν τειμὴν καὶ εὐσέβειαν ἐκπεπληρωκυῖα εἰς τὸν τοῦ κυρίου Σεβαστοῦ [Νέρωνος οἶκον.

ἐκπλήσσω.

Are we to find this verb in BGU I. 246⁷ (ii/iii A.D.) ὅτι σὺ αὐτὰ ἐκπλέξ[ει]ν ὡς ἐργαζομ[έ]νου μου, cf.¹⁰? In the magic P Lond 121⁹²³ (iii/A.D.) (= I. p. 113) for ἐκπλαγήσει the editor proposes (see Index *s.v.*) ἐκπλαγὴς εἶ. The passive is found in its usual NT sense in the dialect inscr.

Syll 802[48] (iii/B.C.) where with reference to the healing of a dumb boy we read—ὁ δὲ πατὴρ ἐκπλαγεὶς πάλιν [ἐκέλετο αὐ]τὸν εἰπεῖν· ὁ δ᾽ ἔλεγε πάλιν καὶ ἐκ τούτου ὑ(γ)ιὴς ἐγέ[νετο. See also Aristeas 190 τοῖς ἐγγόνοις παρακελευόμενος μὴ ἐκπλήττεσθαι τῇ δόξῃ μηδὲ τῷ πλούτῳ, "by warning thy descendants not to be dazzled by fame or wealth" (Thackeray).

ἐκπορεύομαι.

BGU IV. 1078[4] (A.D. 39) οὐ καλῶς δὲ ἐπόησας ἐκπορευομένων πολλῶν φίλων μὴ σημᾶναί μοι. The verb is similarly used of the messengers by whom a letter was carried in P Iand 10[3] (iii/A.D.) ἐπένσαμέν σοι ταύτην τὴν ἐπ]ιστολὴν διὰ τῶν φυλάκων ἐκπορευομένων. Cf. also P Leid W[viii. 17] (ii/iii A.D.) ἄνοιγε, ἄνοιγε τὰ δ̄ μέρη τοῦ κόσμου, ὅτι ὁ κύριος τῆς οἰγουμένης ἐκπορεύεται. The act. is found in P Par 37[11] (ii/B.C.) ἐκπορ[ευ]όντων δὲ τῶν φυλακιτῶν. See *Archiv* Subsidia, p. 286 f.

ἐκπτύω

occurs in the NT only in Gal 4[14], where Clemen (*Primitive Christianity*, p. 342) thinks it is to be understood literally, and alludes to spitting as a prophylactic custom observed at the sight of invalids and especially of epileptics: cf. Krenkel *Beiträge zur Aufhellung der Geschichte u. der Briefe des Paulus*, 1890, p. 47 ff. On the other hand for the metaphorical sense usually found in the passage, cf. Plut. *Mor.* p. 328 C ὥσπερ χαλινὸν τὸν λόγον ἐκπτύσαντες. For an exposition of the whole verse with the aid of MGr see de Zwaan in *ZNTW* x. p. 246 ff., where reference is made to a corresponding "shaking out the lap" as a kind of curse in Nehem 5[13].

ἐκριζόω.

For this late word cf. *Syll* 890[16] (ii/A.D.) ἀλλὰ ἐκρειζωθήσετ(αι) πανγενε[ί. For the formation of the compound cf. ἐκτοπίζω (transitive in 2 Macc 8[13]) in P Tor I. 1[ii. 30] (B.C. 117-6) οἱ δ᾽ ἐκτοπίσαντες οὐκ ἀπήντησαν. MGr ξεριζώνω.

ἔκστασις

is used = "cessio bonorum" in CPR I. 20[ii. 9] (A.D. 250) τὰ ἀντιγραφέντα μοι . . . [ἐ]ξ ἀξιώσεώς μου μ[ε]τ᾽ ἐκστάσεως πάντων τῶν ὑπαρχόντων μου: see the editor's note p. 106 and cf. *Chrest.* II. i. p. 287 f. For τέλος ἐκστάσεως i.e. an ἐγκύκλιον or tax on sales, see the editors' introduction to P Tebt II. 350, and cf. BGU III. 914[6] (A.D. 113). The curse of Deut 28[28] is repeated in *Syll* 891[14] (ii/A.D.) τοῦτόν τε θεὸς πατάξαι ἀπορίᾳ . . . καὶ παραπληξίᾳ καὶ ἀορασίᾳ καὶ ἐκστάσει διανοίας. A good illustration of the NT usage is afforded by the new Menander fragment, *Menandrea* p. 35[472] βρυχηθμὸς ἔνδον, τιλμός, ἔκστασις συχνή. "in the house there followed a bellowing, a tearing of hair, and frequent outbursts of frenzy." See also Hobart, p. 41.

ἐκταράσσω.

For this NT ἅπ. εἰρ. (Ac 16[20]) = "*graviter turbare*" rather than perfective "*conturbare*" (Vg.), see P Gen I. 1[12] (A.D. 213) as amended (*Add.* p. 35) μηδὲ ἐκταράσσειν τοὺς γεωργούς. The verb is suggested by Mahaffy (*Empire of the*

Ptolemies, p. 322) in *OGIS* 90[27] (Rosetta stone—B.C. 196) καὶ τὴν χώραν ἐ[κταράξ ?]αντας καὶ τὰ ἱερὰ ἀδικήσαντας.

ἐκτείνω.

In a curious temple-oath of B.C. 110, *Chrest.* I. 110A[21], provision is made that if one of two contracting parties takes the oath, it shall fall to the other ἐκτείνειν . . . τῷ κοινῷ οἴνου κε(ράμιον) ἃ παραχρῆμα, cf. [25]. See *Syll* 540[128] (B.C. 175-1) ἐκτείνας τὴν λινέην κατὰ κεφαλή[ν, and somewhat differently *ib.* 802[28] (iii/B.C.): also the inscr. on the wall of a sepulchral chamber *Preisigke* 2134[5] (time of the Antonines) σὺ μὲν τέθνηκας καὶ ἐξέτεινας τὰ σκέλη. For the force of the ἐκ see *s.v.* ἐκπετάννυμι.

ἐκτελέω.

This word, which in the NT occurs only in Lk 14[29 f.], is well attested, especially with reference to the performance of religious duties, e.g. P Tebt II. 302[30] (A.D. 71-2) ἐκτελοῦντες τὰς τῶν θεῶν λειτουργίας, and *ib.* 293[21] (c. A.D. 187), a report regarding the circumcision of an aspirant to the priesthood, as otherwise he cannot perform the sacred offices—διὰ [τ]ὸ μὴ δύνασθαι τὰς ἱε[ρου]ργίας ἐκτελεῖν. Other exx. of the verb are P Oxy VIII. 1121[15] (A.D. 295) τὰ καθήκοντα ἐπὶ τῷ θ[α]νάτῳ ἐξετέλεσα, "I did all that was fitting on the occasion of her death," *ib.* XII. 1426[15] (A.D. 332) ἐκτελοῦντα τὴν χρείαν εἰς τὸ ἐν μηδενὶ μεμφθῆναι, "for his performance of the duties to complete satisfaction," BGU IV. 1021[15] (iii/A.D.) ἐκτελοῦντα πάντα τὰ ἐπιτραπησόμενα αὐτῷ ὑπὸ τοῦ διδασκάλου—of a slave apprenticed to a trade, P Oxy I. 71[i. 15] (A.D. 303) ἧς ἐξετέλεσα ἐπιμελίας ἀννώνης, "the duty which I have performed as superintendent of the corn-supply" (Edd.). P Cairo Preis 2[8] (A.D. 362) ἐξετέλεσα καὶ τὸ συνῆθες τῶν γάμων, and *Cagnat* IV. 844[9] (= C. and B. i. p. 182) ἀνδρὸς . . πάσας ἀρχὰς κὲ λειτουργίας λαμπρῶς κὲ ἐπιφανῶς ἐκτετ[ε]λεκότος. MGr ξετελεύω, "finish completely."

ἐκτένεια.

This subst., which is unknown to Attic Greek (cf. Lob. *Phryn.* p. 311), is found in its ethical meaning, as in Ac 26[7] (cf. 2 Macc 14[38] *al.*), in P Par 63[i. 12] (B.C. 164) (= P Petr III. p. 18) καλῶς ποιήσεις τὴν πᾶσαν προσενεγκάμενος ἐκτένειαν καὶ π[ρο]νοηθείς, "you will do well in using every effort and taking every precaution" (Mahaffy): cf. from the inscrr. *Priene* 108[382] (after B.C. 129) ἢ τοῦ δήμου πρὸς τοὺς εὐεργετοῦντας [αὐτὸν ἐ]κτένεια δι᾽ αἰῶνος ἐπίσημον ἔχῃ τὴν χά[ριν, *IMAe* 1032[10] (ii/B.C.) τὰν πᾶσαν ἐκτένειαν καὶ κακοπαθίαν παρεχόμενος. *Syll* 732[28] (i/B.C.) ἡ σύνοδος ἀποδεξαμένη τὴν ἐκτένειαν καὶ φιλοτιμίαν αὐτοῦ, and *Cagnat* IV. 984[6] μετὰ πάσης ἐκτενείας καὶ λαμπρότητος.

ἐκτένης.

P Par 63[46] (B.C. 164) (= P Petr III. p. 22) ἀλλὰ [με]τὰ πάσης ἀκριβείας τὴν ἐκτ[ε]νεστάτην [ποι]ήσασθαι πρόνοιαν, "but (acting) with the greatest strictness, you should take the most earnest precautions" (Mahaffy). Cf. *Syll* 225[9] (iii/B.C.) ἐκτενεῖς κα[ὶ προθύ]μους αὑτοὺς παρέσχοντο πρὸς τὴν τῆς πόλεως φυλακ[ήν, *ib.* 722[40] (ii/B.C.) ἃ τᾶς πόλεος ἐκτενὴς προαιρέσεις, and for the comp. *Cagnat* IV. 293[ii. 38] (c. B.C. 130) ὅπως . . . ἐκτενέστερος γίνηται τῇ προθυμίᾳ.

ἐκτενῶς.

Syll 491³ (ii/B.C.) ἐκτενῶς τε καὶ φιλο[τί]μως θεραπεύων διατετελέκει: cf. *ib.* 284¹⁴ (ii/B.C.) e *suppl.* συναγωνιζόμε[νος ἐκτε]νῶς διατελεῖ.

ἐκτίθημι

is used = "expose" an infant, as in Ac 7²¹ (cf. ¹⁹ ἔκθετα), in BGU IV. 1104²¹ (B.C. 8) τὸ βρέφος ἐκτίθεσθαι. The verb is common = "post up" a notice etc., e.g. P Hib I. 29⁹ (*c.* B.C. 265) ὁ δὲ τελώνης τὸ[ῦτο τὸ] γραμματ[εῖον] γράψας εἰς λεύκωμα μ[ε]γάλοις γράμμασιν (cf. Gal 6¹¹) ἐκτιθέτ[ω πρὸ] τοῦ ἀγοραν[ομ[]ου ἑκάστης ἡ[μ]έρας. "and the tax-farmer shall write this document upon a notice board in large letters and expose it in front of the agoranomus-office every day" (Edd.), P Par 63⁶⁵ (B.C. 164) (= P Petr III. p. 24) ὅπως τοῦτο μὲν ἔν τε ταῖς μητροπόλεσιν ἐκ[τ]εθῆι, "that this be posted up in the chief towns": cf. *ib.* 49³ (B.C. 164-158) (= Witkowski,² p. 69) τοσ[αύ]την ἐμαυτοῦ ἐλευθερ[ιότητ]α [ο]ὐ βαναυσίαν ἐκτέθει[κ]α πᾶσιν ἀνθρώποις, and with the corresponding subst. (as in Esther 8¹⁴, ¹⁷ A) P Petr II. 13 (18*b*)¹⁰ (B.C. 258-3) ἔκθες οὖν ἔκθεμα καὶ προκήρυξον, "issue a public notice and have it cried." The subst. is also found in P Flor I. 99¹ (i/ii A.D.) (= *Selections*, p. 71). See also Wilcken *Ostr* i. p. 527 f. For the metaphorical usage (as in Ac 11⁴) cf. P Hib I. 27²⁴ (B.C. 301-240) πᾶσαν οὖν τὴν ἀλήθει[αν] ἡμῖν ἐξετίθι, "he expounded to me the whole truth" (Edd.). See also *s.v.* ἔκθετος.

ἐκτινάσσω.

In BGU III. 827²² we have ἔπεχε τῇ οἰκίᾳ μου, ἐκτίνασσε τὰ ἔρια καὶ τὰ ἱμά[τ]ια, apparently as part of a "spring cleaning": cf. P Fay 117²¹ (A.D. 108) ἐκτίναξον τὸ διειρον εἵνα ἀμέριμνος ᾖς. The verb is used of "making an upturn" in connexion with a domiciliary visit to the Serapeum, P Par 35¹¹ (B.C. 163) τῶν τε φυλακιτῶν ἐκτε[νῶς] ἐκτιναξάν[τω]ν καὶ μηθὲν ἄτοπον π[αραλαβόντων: so *ib.* 37¹². A weaker sense appears in P Lond 1170 *verso*⁸ (A.D. 258-9) (= III. p. 193) ἐκτινάσσοντες ἐπὶ μὲν τῷ ἐλαιῶνι, so ¹¹ and cf. Preisigke 4369 I²⁰ᶠ· (iii/B.C.). For the subst. see P Fay 114²² (A.D. 100) μὴ ὂν (*l.* οὖν) ληρήσῃς τὸν ἐκτιναγμόν σου, "don't talk nonsense about your threshing" (Edd.). It is used metaphorically in Nahum 2¹¹ ἐκτιναγμὸς καὶ ἀνατιναγμός, καὶ ἐκβρασμὸς καὶ καρδίας θραυσμός.

ἕκτος.

For a ἕκτη παραδείσων, or a tax of ⅙ levied upon gardens, see the editors' note to P Tebt II. 343⁶⁹ (ii/A.D.), and cf. the introduction to P Oxy VI. 917 (ii/iii A.D.). Also *Preisigke* 1924² (A.D. 73-4) ἕκτου ἔτους Οὐεσπασιανοῦ τοῦ κυρίου.

ἐκτός

is found in the substantival phrase τὸ ἐκτός, as in Mt 23²⁶, in P Tebt II. 316⁹⁵ (A.D. 99) οἰκῶ δὲ ἐν τῷ ἐκτὸς τῇ (*l.* τῆς) ξυληρᾷ (?*l.*—ᾶς), "on the outskirts of the wood-market (?)." Cf. P Oxy X.1258⁸ (A.D. 45) where the writer declares that he will appear before the strategus—ὄντα ἐκτ[ὸ]ς ἱεροῦ βω[μοῦ κτλ., "unprotected by any temple, altar," etc., *ib.* 1295¹¹ (ii/iii A.D.) δέο οὖν, μὴ ἀνάπειθε αὐτὸν τοῦ ἐκτός μου ε[ἶ]ναι,

"I therefore beg that you will not persuade him to desert me" (Edd.), and P Amh II. 143¹⁶ (iv/A.D.) μὴ θελήσῃς οὖν, κύριε, μίνε (*l.* μείναι) ἐκτὸς ἡμῶν αὔριον, "so please, sir, do not stay away from us to-morrow" (Edd.). In the long astronomical papyrus P Par 1³⁹⁸ (ii/B.C.) we have ἐκτὸς ἡμέραν μίαν καὶ νύκτα, "except for a single day and night." Ἐκτός is used absolutely in P Tebt II. 380⁹ (A.D. 67) οὐλὴ χιρεὶ δεξιᾷ ἐκτό(ς): cf. OGIS 762¹² (ii/B.C.) ἃ δ[ὲ] ἂν προστιθῶσιν ἐν ταῖς συνθήκαις, ἐνέστ[ω] ἐν ταῖς συνθήκαις, ἃ δὲ ἂν ἀφέλ[ω]σιν τῶν συνθ[η]κῶν, ἐκτὸς ἔστω, and *Syll* 567 (ii/A.D.) where the external purifications required in drawing near to a temple are headed—καὶ τὰ ἐκτός. See also Kuhring, p. 50 f. For the pleonastic negation ἐκτὸς εἰ μή (as in 1 Cor 14⁵, 15², 1 Tim 5¹⁹) Deissmann (*BS* p. 118) cites an inscription of Mopsuestia in Cilicia, belonging to the Imperial period—ἐκτὸς εἰ μὴ [ἐ]ὰν Μάγνα μόνη θε[λή]σῃ (Waddington *Inscriptions*, iii. 2, No. 1499). See also the Lycian inscr. in *JHS* xxxiv. (1914), p. 31, No. 44⁶ ὦν ὁ ἐλέν[ξ]ας λήνψετε τὸ τρίτον, ἐκτὸς εἰ μή τινι ἐγὼ ἐν[γραφ]ῶς ἐπιτρέψω. On the form of the word as a derivative of ἐξ, see Moulton *Gr.* ii. § 130.

ἐκτρέπω.

In P Ryl II. 133²² (A.D. 33) the mention of the danger of fields being "left unsown"—εἰς ἄσπορον ἐκτραπῆν[α]ι—shows the verb in a more general sense than in the possible medical reference in Heb 12¹³ ἵνα μὴ τὸ χωλὸν ἐκτραπῇ, "be put out of joint" (RV mg.). For the meaning "turn aside," as in 1 Tim 1⁶, we may compare Epict. i. 6. 42 οἱ δ' ὑπ' ἀγεννείας εἰς μέμψεις καὶ [τὰ] ἐγκλήματα τῷ θεῷ ἐκτρεπόμενοι, and for the acc. constr., as in 1 Tim 6²⁰, see Oenoanda col. 29, 7 ἑ. δεῖ τοὺς σοφιστικοὺς λόγους (cited by Nageli, p. 19), and Musonius p. 26⁸ τὰ μὲν ἀληθῶς κακὰ πάσῃ μηχανῇ ἐκτρέπεσθαι.

ἐκτρέφω.

With the use of this verb in Eph 6⁴ we may compare P Ryl II. 178¹⁴ (early i/A.D.), an agreement with a nurse, in which she states—τέθειμαι τὴν ὁμολογίαν καὶ ἐκθρέψωι τὸ δουλικὸν σωμάτιον Θερμουθάριον ἐπὶ τὰ δύο ἔτηι, "I have made the agreement and I will nurse the infant slave Thermoutharion for the two years" (Edd.), and the interesting inscr. from the southern cemetery at Karabunar (Calder, No. 8) in which a son commemorates his mother—τὴν τε [οἰκί]αν κυβερνήσασα ἀνενκλήτως καὶ τὸ παιδίον ἐκθρέψασα. See also *Syll* 326³⁴ (i/A.D.) τὸν μὲν ἐκθρέψαντα αὐτόν, and *Menandrea* p. 41⁵⁷⁷ παιδία ἐκτρέφομεν.

ἔκτρομος.

For this form, which is read in Heb 12²¹ ℵ D₂*, we may compare the Hadrumetum inscription of iii/A.D., reproduced by Deissmann *BS* p. 273 ff., ²⁵ ff· ὁρκίζω σε τὸν συνσείσαν[τ]α πᾶσαν τὴν οἰκουμένην καὶ τὰ ὄρη ἐκτραχηλίζοντα καὶ ἐκβρά[ζ]οντα, τὸν ποιοῦντα ἔκτρομον τὴν [γ]ῆν ἄπασ(αν), "causeth the whole earth to quake." See also the great magical Paris papyrus ³⁰⁷⁶ (= Deissmann *LAE* p. 254) ὁρκίζω σε, πᾶν πνεῦμα δαιμόνιον, τὸν ἐφορῶντα ἐπὶ γῆς καὶ ποιοῦντα ἔκτρομα τὰ θεμίλια αὐτῆς, and Wünsch *AF* 5²⁶ ὁρκίζω σε . . . τὸν ποιοῦντα ἔκτρομον τὴν [γ]ῆν ἄπασ(αν): cf. Ps 103 (104)²².

ἔκτρωμα.

This NT ἅπ. εἰρ. (1 Cor 15⁸, cf. Numb 12¹²) may be illustrated from the verb in P Goodsp Cairo 15¹⁵ (A.D. 362) where a complaint is made with reference to certain persons—τὴν μὲν Τάησιν βαρέαν οὖσαν ἐκ τῶν πληγῶν αὐτῶν ἐξέτρωσεν (*l.* —αν) τὸ βρέφος, "to Taesis who was pregnant they occasioned by their violence the miscarriage of her child" (Ed.). Cf. also Apoc. Petr. 11 αὗται δὲ ἦσαν α[ἱ τὰ βρέφη φθείρο]υσαι καὶ ἐκτρώσασαι. Ἐκτρωσμός is found *Preisigke* 3451⁵·¹⁰. Hesych.: ἔκτρωμα· παιδίον νεκρὸν ἄωρον. ἐκβολὴ γυναικός. For the form see Moulton *Gr.* ii. § 119 (*b*).

ἐκφέρω

is by no means so common as we might have expected. In P Par 26²¹ (B.C. 163–2) (= *Selections*, p. 15) the Serapeum Twins petition Ptolemy and Cleopatra against those who had maltreated them and "were appropriating the privileges conferred on us by you"—τῶν . . . τὰ ὑφ' ὑμῶν ἡμῖν χρηματιζόμενα ἐκφερομένων: cf. *Michel* 1001 ⁱⁱ·²² (*c.* B.C. 200) μὴ ἐχέτω δὲ ἐξουσίαν μηδὲ ἐξενέγκαι τῶν ἐν τῶι μουσείωι ὄντων μηθέν. In another papyrus in the Paris collection the verb occurs in the passive in connexion with an assault, P Par 14²⁸ (ii/B.C.) ἀφορήτω δὲ ἀνομίᾳ ἐξενεχθέντες καὶ ἐκπηδήσαντές μοι . . . πληγὰς ἔδωκαν: cf. also P Tebt I. 5ⁱⁱⁱ ⁶⁸ (B.C. 118) ὁμοίως δὲ καὶ τοὺς πλείονας καρπείας (*l.* καρπείας) ἐξενηνεγμένους ἕως τοῦ αὐτ[οῦ χ]ρόνου τῶν ἐπιτίμων, "likewise (they remit) the penalties incurred by those who have appropriated more (than their due) emoluments up to the same period." An interesting use is found in a Question to the Oracle, P Fay 138³ (i/ii A.D.) Κύριοι Διόσκουροι, ἦ κρείνεται αὐτὸν ἀπελθεῖν ἰς πόλειν ; τοῦτο ἐκξένειγκον καὶ συμφονήσατο πρὸς τὸν ἀδελφόν σου, "O lords Dioscuri, is it fated for him to depart to the city? Bring this to pass, and let him come to an agreement with thy brother" (Edd.): cf. BGU I. 229³ (ii/iii A.D.) cited *s.v.* ἀσθένεια. In *Syll* 152¹⁸ (B.C. 330–25) τὴν βουλὴν προβουλεύσασαν ἐξενεγκεῖν εἰς τὴν πρώτην ἐκκλησίαν περὶ Ἡρακλείδου, the meaning is to "produce" or "make public" a προβούλευμα, a "preliminary decree" which became a βούλευμα, when passed by the Ecclesia. The subst. ἐκφόριον is used of "rent in kind" as distinguished from φόρος "rent in money" as in P Tebt II. 377²³ ff. (A.D. 210): see the editors' note *ad l.c.*, and cf. Modica *Introduzione*, p. 163 f.

ἐκφεύγω.

P Oxy VI. 898²⁵ (A.D. 123) οἰομένη ἐκ τούτου δύνασθαι ἐκφυγεῖν ἃ διέπραξεν, "thinking by this means to escape the consequences of her misdeeds" (Edd.). In the curious P Ryl I. 28 (iv/A.D.), in which prognostications are drawn from the involuntary quivering of various parts of the body, we have ¹⁶⁴ ff. σφυρὸν εὐώνυμον ἐὰν ἄληται, ἐν κρίσει βαρη[θ]ὶς ἔσται καὶ ἐκφεύξεται, "if the left ankle quiver, he will be burdened with a trial, and will be acquitted" (Ed.): cf. Rom 2³. In the iv/A.D. Christian letter, P Heid 6¹³ (= *Selections*, p. 126), the writer, citing loosely from Prov 10¹⁹, has—ἐν γὰρ [πο]λλῇ λαλιᾳ οὐκ ἐκφεύξοντ[αι](τ)ὴ(ν)ἁμαρτίη. MGr ξεφεύγω.

ἐκφοβέω.

P Lond 342⁹ (A.D. 185) (= II. p. 174) καὶ ἐκφοβηθέντες ἀφανεῖς ἐγένοντο, Preisigke 4284¹⁰ (A.D. 207) ἐκφοβῶν ἡμᾶς.

ἐκφύω

survives in MGr ξεφυτρώνω, "shoot up," "flourish." The adj. ἐκφυής is found in Vett. Val. p. 110¹⁵ ἐκφυεῖς τοῖς ὀδοῦσιν ἢ τοῖς ὀφθαλμοῖς ὑπόστραβοι, "with prominent teeth or squinting eyes."

ἐκχέω.

With Mt 23³⁵ cf. *Syll* 816⁵ (ii/B.C.) (= Deissmann *LAE* p. 424) ἐγχέαντας αὐτῆς τὸ ἀναίτιον αἷμα ἀδικῶς. For the subst. see P Tebt I. 86⁹ (late ii/B.C.) ἐκχύ(σεως) Ἵππωνος βαλα(νείου), P Lond 1177⁸⁴ (A.D. 113) (= III. p. 183) ἐκχύσεων, and for a previously unknown adj. see P Oxy IX. 1220¹⁶ (iii/A.D.) πέμψις μοι τοὺς ἐκχυσιαίους ἥλους, "you will send me the nails for emptying (?)" (Ed.). For other compound forms cf. P Ryl II. 154¹⁴ (A.D. 66) λιβὸς διῶρυξ λεγομένηι Ἀρχείου δι' οὗ (*l.* ἧς) ἀποχεῖεται (*l.* ἀποχεῖται) ὁ κλῆρ[ο]ς, "on the west the dyke called that of Archias by which the holding is drained," and ¹⁸ διῶρυξ εἰς ὃν (*l.* ἣν) εἰσχεῖτα[ι] ὁ κλῆρ[ος, "the dyke into which the holding drains."

ἐκχωρέω

is used absolutely, as in Lk 21²¹, in P Lond 106¹⁰ (B.C. 261 or 223) (= I. p. 61) ἐμοῦ δὲ οὐκ ἐκχωροῦντος. Other exx. of the verb are P Magd 20⁷ (B.C. 221) δέομαι . . . ἐπαναγκάσαι αὐτοὺς ἐκχωρῆσαι τῆς οἰκίας, P Amh II. 30⁴² (ii/B.C.) παρηγγείλαμεν τῆι Θεμβῶτος ἐκχωρεῖν ἐκ τῆς οἰκίας, and P Tebt II. 310³ (A.D. 186) ὁμολοκῶ ἐκχωρῆσε (*l.* ὁμολογῶ ἐκχωρῆσαι) τῷ πλήθει τῶν ἱερέων ὥσα (*l.* ὅσα) ἔχω ἔτη τῆς μιᾶς ἡμίσους ἀρούρης ἱερευτικῆς, "I acknowledge that I have surrendered to the corporation of priests for my term of years the 1½ arourae of temple land" (Edd.). The verb is used transitively in BGU I. 96¹³ (2ⁿᵈ half iii/A.D.) ἐκκεχωρηκ[έ]ναι αὐτοὺς αὐτὸν τῷ Μάρωνι κυριευτικῶς. Cf. MGr ξεχωρίζω "separate," "pick out."

ἐκψύχω.

To Hobart's (p. 37) medical instances of this rare verb, which is confined in the NT to Lk (Ac 5⁵·¹⁰, 12²³), we may now add Herodas iv. 29 οὐκ ἐρεῖς αὐτήν, ἢν μὴ λάβῃ τὸ μῆλον, ἐκ τάχα ψύξει, where the tmesis gives a gasping effect that suits the sense admirably. MGr ξεψύχω.

ἑκών.

In a deed of gift BGU III. 993¹⁰ (B.C. 127) the signatories are introduced by ἑκόντες συνεγράψαντο. From the inscrr. we may cite *Syll* 810⁴ εἰ δέ τι ἑκὼν ἐξαμαρτ[ήσει], οὐκ ἐμὸν ἐπαράσ[ασθαι], δίκη δὲ ἐπικρέματα[ι] τιμωρὸς ἀπελθόν[τι] ἀπειθὴς Νεμέσε[ως : cf. Rom 12¹⁹. In OGIS 139¹⁰ (ii/B.C.) the priests of Isis complain that they are obliged παρουσίας αὐτοῖς ποιεῖσθαι οὐχ ἑκόντας, evidently with reference to the preparations which the παρουσίαι or "visits" of high officials entailed.

ἐλαία.

In the magical spell for casting out demons, P Par 574[1229] (iii/A.D.) (= *Selections*, p. 113), the instruction is given—βάλε ἔμπροσθεν αὐτοῦ κλῶνας ἐλαίας, "place before him (i.e. the possessed one) branches of the olive-tree." See also Cf Herm I. 28[14] ἐλαῖα[ι] ἐσκορπισμέναι ζωφυτοῶσαι ζ. The word refers to the fruit, as in Jas 3[12], in P Hib I. 49[8] (c. B.C. 257) ὅπως ἂν ἐμβάληται τὰς ἐλαίας εἰς βίκους, P Fay 130[16] (iii/A.D.) κεράμιν ἐλεῶν (*l.* ἐλαιῶν), P Oxy XII. 1494[16] (early iv/A.D.) ἀγοράσω ἐλέας κνίδια παλεά, "I will buy some old jars of olives" (Edd.), where the sense is collective as in the next exx. For contracted forms from a nom. ἐλάα, see P Ryl II. 97[7] (A.D. 139) τὸν δὲ κατασπασμὸν τῆς ἐλᾶς ποιησόμεθα, "we will perform the gathering of the olives," *ib.* 130[11] (A.D. 31) ἐτρύγησαν ἐκ τῶν καρπῶν οὐκ ὀλίγην ἐλᾶν, "they gathered of the fruits a quantity of olives," and *ib.* 231[3] (A.D. 40) τὴν ἐλᾶν. In PSI IV. 438[8] (iii/B.C.) νυνεὶ δ᾽ ἐλαία γέγονεν τῆι κϛ, ἐλαία seems = "gathering of olives." The adj. ἐλάϊνος is found e.g. in P Ryl II. 138[11] (A.D. 34) φυτὰ ἐλάϊνα διακώσια, and ἐλαϊκός e.g. in P Fay 91[15] (A.D. 99) ἐλαϊκοὺς καρπούς. MGr ἐλιά.

ἔλαιον.

For ἔ. = "olive-oil," it is sufficient to cite P Par 43[4] (B.C. 154) καλῶς ποιήσεις ἀποστείλαί μοι ἡμίχουν ἐλαίου, P Oxy I. 91[16] (receipt of wages for nursing—A.D. 187) ὑπὲρ τροφείων καὶ ἐλαίου καὶ ἱματισμοῦ, P Grenf II. 77[36] (iii/iv A.D.) (= *Selections*, p. 122) where arrangements are made that a man conveying a dead body should be entertained ἐν ψωμίοις καὶ [οἴ]γαρίῳ καὶ ἐλαίῳ, and the Christian letter P Heid 6[21] (iv/A.D.) (= *Selections*, p. 127) καταξίωσον δέξεσθαι τὸ μικρὸν ἔλεον διὰ τοῦ ἀδελφοῦ ἡμῶν Μαγαρίου. The word is used = "olive-tree" in P Petr I. 29[7] (iii/B.C.) τὸ δὲ ἔλαιον δέδωκεν χοῦς ϛ. For ἐλαιοκάπηλος, see PSI IV. 372[5] (B.C. 250-49), and for ἐλαιουργεῖον, *ib.* 438[6] (iii/B.C.).

ἐλαιών.

Deissmann (*BS* p. 208 ff.) has sufficiently demonstrated against Blass (*Gr* pp. 32, 64, 85) the reality of this word: see also *Proleg.* pp. 49, 69, 235, and add from the recently published P Ryl II. 130[9] (A.D. 31) εἰς τὸν ὑπάρχοντά μοι . . . . ἐλαιῶνα, 138[9] (A.D. 34) εἰς τὰ νεώφυτα τῶν ἐλαιώνων, "into the young plantations in the olive-yards" (Edd.), 152[11] (A.D. 42) ἐν ἐλαιῶ νι Θερμουθαρίου, also P Lond 214[10] (A.D. 270-5) (= II. p. 161, *Chrest.* I. p. 209) εἰς ἀμπελικὸν χωρίον καλούμενον Ἐλαιῶνα. The formation is a favourite one, as φοινικών, "palmgrove" (P Amh II. 31[5] al.—B.C. 112, P Gen I. 38[5]—A.D. 207-8), καμηλών, "camel-shed" (P Oxy III. 507[26]—A.D. 169, 533[22] ii/iii A.D.). The specializing of the —ών suffix ("place of . . .", as in ἀνδρών, γυναικών, κοιτών, etc.) for *groves* is found in δαφνών, ἀμπελών, φηγών, πιτυών, μηλών, κυπαρισσών, συκών, Ἑλικών ("willow mountain")—the last a specially good parallel for Ἐλαιών, if the etymology is sound. Cf. Brugmann *Kurze Vergl. Gramm.* § 414, and Moulton *Gr.* ii. § 61 (*b*).

PART III.

ἐλάσσων.

In P Petr III. 32(f[10] a complaint is brought against a tax-collector that he makes agreements "at too low a rate" with certain persons who are liable to the police tax· ἐξ ἐλάττ[ονο]ς συγχωρήσεις ποιεῖται: cf. P Par 63[28] (B.C. 165) (= P Petr III. p. 20) ἕκαστον αὐτῶν γεω[ργ]ήσειν ἐπὶ τὸ ἔλασσον, "that each man is personally liable for field labour on the smaller assessment" (Mahaffy), *ib.*[120] (= *ib.* p. 28) τοῖς δυναμένοις οὐκ ἔλασσον τούτου μεριστέον, "not less than this (assessment) is to be allotted to those who are capable" (*id.*), and P Oxy II. 237[viii 11] (A.D. 186) ἐπ᾽ ἐλάττονι συμβήσεσθαι, "to accept less than the full amount" (Edd.). So P Giss I. 61[16] (A.D. 119) ἀξιοῦμε[ν] . . . τὴν ἐξέτασιν ποιήσασθαι πρὸς τὸ μηδὲν ἔλασσον τῷ φίσ[κωι] ἐπακολουθῆσαι, with which the editor contrasts P Oxy II. 270[3] (A.D. 44-5) πλεῖον περιποιήσαι τοῖς δη[μοσί]οις. For a direct antithesis with πλείων, see PSI III. 187[10] (iv/A.D.) μισθώσασθ[αι] . . . [ἀρ]ούρας δέκα ἢ ὅσας ἐὰν ὦσ[ι] ἐπὶ τὸ πλεῖον ἢ ἔλασσον, and for a similar antithesis with μείζων see P Ryl II. 77[39] (A.D. 192) Ὀ. εἶπ[εν] ἀναδεξάμενος τὴν μείζονα ἀρχὴν οὐκ ὀφείλει τὴν ἐλάττον᾽ ἀποφεύγειν, "O. said :—'A person who has offered to undertake the greater office ought not to shun the lesser'" (Edd.). For the corresponding subst. cf. e.g. P Tebt I. 97[1] (B.C. 118) where an account of payments in kind is headed—list of payments εἰς τὴν μί[σ(θωσιν) τοῦ] αὐτ[οῦ] (ἔτους) εἰς τὸ ἐλάσσωμα, "on account of leases of the said year to meet the deficiency," and BGU IV. 1060[26] (time of Augustus) ἀξιοῦμεν ἐν μηδενὶ ἐλαττώματι ἡμᾶς πρόνοιαν γενέσθαι. On the interchange of -σσ- and -ττ- see Mayser *Gr.* p. 223, and Moulton *Gr.* ii. § 43.

ἐλαττονέω.

Grimm's statement that this NT ἅπ. εἰρ. (2 Cor 8[15] from LXX Exod 16[18]) is "not found in prof. auth." requires correction, in view not only of Aristot. *de plant.* 2, 3 p. 825[3], 23 (as Thayer), but of P Magd 26[12] (B.C. 217) ἐπαναγκάσαι αὐτὸν ἀποδοῦναι . . . . τὸ διάφορον τῶν ἐλαττονούντων ιδ κεραμίων, cf. [9], and the illiterate BGU IV. 1105[18] (c. B.C. 10) ἐλατωνῖ, apparently = ἐλαττονεῖ.

ἐλαττόω.

For this, the more ordinary equivalent of the foregoing verb, we may cite P Tebt I. 19[11] (B.C. 114) σὺ δὲ ὀρθῶς ποιήσεις τὸ προσάγγελμα μὴ ἐλαττώσας παρὰ τὸ πρῶτον, "you will be right in not diminishing the report compared with the first one" (Edd.), *ib.* II. 382[12] (B.C. 30–A.D. 1) ἐμ μηδενὶ ἐλαττουμένου τοῦ Ἀκουσιλάου ἐν ᾗ ἔχει μ[ό]υ μίσθωσιν, "Acusilaus shall incur no loss in the lease which he holds of me" (Edd.), P Lond 897[1] (A.D. 84) (= III. p. 206) λαογραφίας τότε γὰρ ἐλασσωθεὶς ὑπὸ τοῦ προόντος κωμογραμμάτεως, and P Hamb I. 8[12] (A.D. 136) μὴ ἐλαττουμένων ἡμῶν ὑπὲρ ὧν ὀφίλεται λοιπῶν φόρων τοῦ αὐτοῦ ιδ ἔτους), "ohne dass wir beeintrachtigt werden in Bezug auf die übrigen Abgaben desselben Jahres, die Ihr uns noch schuldet" (Ed., who refers to Gradenwitz *Einführung* i. p. 31).

ἐλαύνω

is found in the illiterate P Fay 111[10] (A.D. 95-6) λέγον (*l.* —ων) ὅτι (*l.* ὅτι) σὺ εἴρηκας πεζῶι [τὰ χ]υρίδια ἐλάσαι,

27

"saying that you had told him to drive the pigs on foot." For ships "driven" by the wind, as Jas 3[4], cf. *Preisigke* 997 (iv/A.D.) ἥκω εἰς τὸν τόπον ἀπὸ Συένης καταπλέων ὑπὸ χειμῶνος ἐλασθείς, where note the late form of the aor. pass. The verb is used in connexion with horses in Wünsch *AF* 4[60] (iii/A.D.) οἱ ἵπποι οὓς μέλλουσιν ἐλαύνειν.

ἐλαφρός

occurs literally in P Giss I. 47[7] (time of Hadrian) ὁ μὲν γὰρ θῶραξ . . . τὸ μεῖζον ἐλα[φ]ρότατος ὡς μὴ κάμνειν τὸν φοροῦντα αὐτὸν [ἢ]γοράσθη κτλ., and *Preisigke* 315 (a sepulchral inser.) ἐλαφρά σοι γῆ γένοιτο, "*sit tibi terra levis.*" For the verb ἐλαφρίζω see *Syll* 330[26] (Roman age) ἵνα μὴ δῷ ἃ ἀμέτερα πόλις, ἀλλὰ ἐλαφρισθῇ, and for ἐλαφρύνω the Christian P Gen I. 14[22] (Byz.) ἐ]λαφρυνθῆναι τῶν χρεῶν. See also *Cagnat* IV. 292[3] (Pergamon—B.C. 130) περὶ ἐλαφροτοκίας, "as regards lowering of interest." The adj. ἐλαφρός (—ύς) survives in MGr beside ἀλαφρός.

ἐλάχιστος

For this form as a true superlative, as in 1 Cor 15[9] (cf. *Proleg.* p. 79), we may cite P Tebt I. 24[67] (B.C. 117) ἐπὶ τὸ ἐλάχιστον, "at least": the document is official, though written in very bad Greek. It survives even as late as viii/A.D. in P Lond 77[32] (= I. p. 233) ἀπὸ μικροῦ εἴδους ἕως ἐλαχίστου. The phrase ἐν ἐλαχίστῳ, as in Lk 16[10], cf. Josh 6[26], occurs in P Catt[x, 26] (ii/A.D.) (= *Chrest.* II. p. 422), and the plur. in P Hib I. 27[35] (B.C. 301-240) ὡς οὖν ἠδυνάμην ἀκριβέστατα ἐν ἐλαχίστοις συναγαγεῖν. With reference to persons, as in Mt 5[19], see *Syll* 418[58] (A.D. 238) καὶ γὰρ ὡς ἀληθῶς ἀπὸ πολλῶν οἰκοδεσποτῶν εἰς ἐλαχίστους κατεληλύθαμεν.

ἐλαχιστότερος

With this form (Eph 3[8]) we may compare the double superlative μεγιστότατος in the horoscope P Lond 130[49] (i/ii A.D.) (= I. p. 134) ὅθεν ὁ μὲν μεγιστότατος ἥλιος καὶ τῶν ὅλων δυνάστης. See further *Proleg.* p. 236.

Ἐλεάζαρ

For this proper name cf. BGU III. 715[3] (as amended—A.D. 101-2) Ἐλεά[ζαρος] Πτ[ολεμ]αίου, and the sepulchral inser. *Preisigke* 719 (i/A.D.) Ἐλεάζαρε ἄωρε χρηστὲ πασίφιλε: see also *ib.* 1163 (B.C. 28) Ἐλάζαρος χρηστός κτλ.

ἐλεάω

See *s.v.* ἐλεέω.

ἔλεγχος

occurs = "proof," "evidence," as in Heb 11[1], in P Oxy II. 237[viii. 17] (A.D. 186) τότ' ἐὰν θαρρῇ τοῖς τῆς κατηγορίας ἐλέγχοις, τὸν μείζονα ἀγῶνα ε[ἰ]σελεύσεται, "then if he has confidence in the proofs of his accusation, he shall enter upon the more serious law-suit" (Edd.), P Strass I. 41[6] (A.D. 250) "I don't require papers for this case," ὁ γὰρ ἔλεγχος δεικνύ[σει . . . .] [ἔ]κ τε μαρτύρων καὶ τῶν πεπραγμένων αὐτῶν ὑπὸ τῆς ἀντιδίκου. In BGU IV. 1138[13] (B.C. 19-18) (= *Chrest.* II. p. 123) the meaning is rather "conviction," as in the received text of 2 Tim 3[16]. ἐφάνη τῷ Κασίωι ὄντ[ι] ἐνταῦθα, τὸν τῆ(ς) Σάεως δεσμοφύλακ(α)

Χαιρήμονα καλέσαι, καὶ ἐλενχο(μένου) αὐτο.ῦ) πρὸς ἔλενχο ν) τοῦ Ἰσχυρίω(νος), ὃ ἠδίκησεν, ἐμαρτύρησ εν) ὁ δεσμόφυλαξ Χαιρήμω(ν) περὶ το(ῦ) παραδεδόσθαι αὐτῷ τὸν Παπία(ν) κτλ. See also *Kaibel* 814 Ἑρμῆς δίκαιός εἰμι καὶ με Σ[ώστρατο]ς ἔστησ' ἔλεγχον τῶν δικαίων καὶ ἀδίκων.

ἐλέγχω

For the meaning "convict," i.e. bring to light the true character of a man and his conduct, as in the Fourth Gospel (3[20], 8[46], 16[8]), see the citation from BGU IV. 1138 *s.v.* ἔλεγχος, and cf. P Amh II. 33[34] (c. B.C. 157) ἐὰν δέ τις τῶν καταβλαπτόντων τὰς προσόδους ἐλεγχθῆι συνηγορήσας περὶ πράγματός τινος, αὐτόν τε πρὸς ἡμᾶς μετὰ φυλακῆς ἐπιστείλατε, "if any of these who are injuring the revenues is in the future convicted of having acted as advocate in any case, send him to us under arrest" (Edd.), P Strass I. 41[51] (A.D. 250) οἵτινες δύνανται ἐκείνους ἐλέγξαι. In a Lycian inscr. *JHS* xxxiv. p. 14, No. 18[20] we find ὁ ἐλένξας = "the prosecutor." For the milder sense "expose," "set forth," which best suits this word in 1 Cor 14[21], Eph 5[11] (where see Robinson's note), cf. such a passage from the vernacular as P Hib I. 55[1] (B.C. 250) παραγενοῦ εἰς Ταλαῶν ἤδη ἄγων καὶ τὸν ποιμένα τὸν ἐλέγξοντα περὶ ὧν μοι εἶπας, "come to Talao at once, and bring with you the shepherd in order that he may give evidence in the matter about which you told me" (Edd.); see also P Oxy II. 237[viii. 40] (A.D. 186) ἵν' εἴ τις γένοιτο ζήτησις εἰς ὕστερον περὶ τῶν μὴ δεόντως ἀπογραψαμένων ἐξ ἐκείνων ἐλεγχθῶσι, "may supply the proofs." In *ib.*[vii. 38] we have καὶ ἐκέλευ[σε]ν δι' [ἑρ]μηνέως αὐτὴν ἐνεχθῆν[α], τί βούλεται, where the editors understand ἐνεχθῆναι as a corruption of ἐλεγχθῆναι and translate "and he ordered that she should be asked through an interpreter what was her choice": cf. P Tebt II. 297[17] (c. A.D. 123) ἔγραψας τῷ στρατηγῷ ἐλ[έγξαν]τα δηλῶσαί σοι, "you wrote to the strategus to make an inquiry, and state the facts to you" (Edd.).

ἐλεεινός

See the late P Oxy I. 130[3] (vi/A.D.) π(αρὰ) Ἀνοῦπ ἐλεεινοῦ ὑμετέρου δούλου: cf. [7] and *ib.* 131[2] (vi/vii A.D.). The form ἐλεινός read by WH in Rev 3[17] (see *Notes*[2], p. 152) is explained by Blass-Debrunner (p. 20) as ἐλεινός = ἐλεεινός.

ἐλεέω (—άω)

is found in the interesting but obscure letter written to a man in money difficulties BGU IV. 1079[23] (A.D. 41) (= *Selections*, p. 40) ἐρῶτα αὐτὸν καθ' ἡμέραν· τάχα δύναταί σε ἐλεῆσαι, "ask him daily: perhaps he can have pity on you": cf. P Fay 106[16] (c. A.D. 140) ἐξησθένησα[. . . .] κύριε, ὅθεν ἀξιῶ σαὶ τὸν σω[τῆρα] ἐλεῆσαί με, "I became very weak, my lord: wherefore I entreat you my preserver to have pity on me," P Oxy VI. 904[2] (v/A.D.) (cited *s.v.* γηράσκω), and from the inscr. *Syll* 418[83] (A.D. 238) ἵνα ἐλεηθέντες διὰ τὴν θείαν σου πρόνοιαν κτλ. For a Christian use, see the prayer P Oxy III. 407[3] (iii/iv A.D.) βοήθησόν μοι ἐλέησόν με ἐξαλιψόν μοι τὰς ἁμαρτίας. For a suggestion that "*Kyrie eleison* was a common Jewish prayer formula, which was adopted by Christians," see *JTS* xvi. p. 548 f. Sharp (*Epict.* p. 4) cites in illustration of Mt 20[30] f. Epict. ii. 7. 12 τὸν θεὸν ἐπικαλούμενοι δεόμεθα αὐτοῦ· κύριε, ἐλέησον· ἐπίτρεψόν μοι ἐξελθεῖν—a passage dealing with divination. In MGr the verb is used with the acc. = "give alms to."

WH read forms derived from ἐλεάω in Rom 9[16], Jude [22f.] For other exx. of the mixing of —άω and —έω in the NT cf. Blass-Debrunner *Gr.* p. 50, and on the similar tendency in "vulgar" writers and in MGr see Maidhof *Begriffsbestimmung,* p. 361 f.

ἐλεημοσύνη.

In the Christian P Gen I. 51[26] the writer, after petitioning a certain Ammninaeus to use his influence in preventing a widow's only son from being taken on military service, continues—καὶ ὁ θ ἐὸ)ς ἀποδιδῖ (*l.* ἀποδιδοῖ) σ[ο]ι πρὸς τὴν ἐ[λ]εημοσύνην σου. McNeile's statement (*ad* Mt 6[2]) that the word is not used specifically for "almsgiving" earlier than B. Sira will require modification if the early date ascribed to Tobit, in which the word is very frequent, is accepted (cf. *Oxford Apocrypha* i. p. 183 ff.). The word survives in this sense in MGr.

ἐλεήμων.

P Leid W[vii. 27] (ii/iii A.D.) ἐλεήμων ἐν ὥραις βιαίος (*l.* —αις). In the NT the adj. is confined to Mt 5[7], Heb 2[17]: in the LXX it is frequent of God, but of men only in Ps 111 (112)[4] and *ter* in Prov.

ἔλεος.

The masc. form of this word, which in the NT is wholly rejected by WH, and in the LXX is comparatively rare (e.g. Ps 83 (84)[12]: see further Thackeray *Gr.* i. p. 158) is found in *Syll* 376[21] καὶ νῦν δὲ οὐ δι' ἔλεον ὑμᾶς, ἀλλὰ δι' εὔνοιαν εὐεργετῶ, Nero's address to the Greeks at Corinth: the Emperor's composition master took care that he atticized properly in this great oration. For the word see also P Magd 18[6] (a petition—B.C. 221) ἵνα ὦ, βασιλεῦ, διὰ σοῦ τοῦ δικαίου καὶ ἐλέου τετευχὼς εἰς τὸ [λοι]πὸν τοῦ βίου. The subst. remains neuter in MGr, cf. Hatzidakis *Gr.* p. 357, and see further Moulton *Gr.* ii. § 54.

ἐλευθερία.

The historical background which lends so much significance to the Pauline descriptions of the ἐλευθερία which His people enjoy in Christ, has been vividly presented by Deissmann *LAE* p. 324 ff. Here, in illustration of the phrase ἐπ' ἐλευθερίᾳ in Gal 5[13], it must be enough to recall the interesting Delphi inscription of B.C. 200–199, *Syll* 845[4 ff.] ἐπρίατο ὁ Ἀπόλλων ὁ Πύθιος παρὰ Σωσιβίου Ἀμφισσέος ἐπ' ἐλευθερίαι σῶμ[α] γυναικεῖον, ἇι ὄνομα Νίκαια, τὸ γένος Ῥωμαίαν, τιμᾶς (cf. 1 Cor 6[20], 7[23]) ἀργυρίου μνᾶν τριῶν καὶ ἡμιμναίου . . . τὰν δὲ ὠνὰν ἐπίστευσε Νίκαια τῶι Ἀπόλλωνι ἐπ' ἐλευθερίαι, "the Pythian Apollo bought from Sosibius of Amphissa, for freedom, a female slave, whose name is Nicaea, by race a Roman, with a price of three minae and a half of silver. . . . The purchase, however, Nicaea hath committed unto Apollo, for freedom." The same phrase is found in BGU IV. 1141[24] (B.C. 14) ὡς δοῦλος ἐπ' ἐλευθερίᾳ θέλει ἀρέσαι, οὕτω κἀγὼ τὴν φιλίαν σου θέλων ἄμεμπτ[ον] ἐμ ατὸν ἐτήρησα.

ἐλεύθερος.

For the spiritual significance of this term in the Pauline writings cf. the preceding article, and what is said *s.v.* ἀπελεύθερος. In the oldest Greek marriage contract we possess, P Eleph 1 (B.C. 311–0) (= *Selections,* p. 1 ff.), the contracting parties are described as ἐλεύθερος ἐλευθέρα, and in the curious law-suit, P Oxy I. 37[i. 18] (A.D. 49) (= *Selections,* p. 50), which recalls in various particulars the Judgment of Solomon, the nurse, who is charged with carrying off a foundling, defends herself on the ground that she did so ὀν[ό]ματι ἐλευθέρου, "in virtue of its being freeborn." Other exx. of the adj. are P Ryl II. 117[26] (A.D. 269) πρὸς τὸ ἔχειν με τ[ὰ ἐ]μὰ ἐλεύθερον, "so that I may keep my property in freedom," and P Oxy IX. 1186[6] (iv/A.D.), the edict of a Preses in which it is declared that for slaves punishment by scourging (διὰ τῶν ἱμάντων) is lamentable (ἀνιαρόν), but "for free men to be submitted to such an outrage is contrary to the laws and an injustice"—ἐλευθέρους δὲ ἄνδρας τοιαύτην ὕβριν ὑπομένειν οὔτε τοῖς [νόμοις] ἀκόλ[ου]θον ἀδικείαν τε [ἔ]χον ἐστίν.

For the adverb see P Tebt II. 284[7] (i/B.C.) where the writer informs his sister that in obedience to an oracular response from the god Soknebtunis—καταβήσομαι ἐλευθέρως, "I will go with boldness" (Edd.).

ἐλευθερόω.

For this verb, which is found "in innumerable documents of manumission," see again Deissmann as cited *s.v.* ἐλευθερία. Cf. from the papyri P Oxy III. 494[18] (A.D. 156) ἐλευθερουμένων δούλων σωμάτων with reference to certain slaves whom the testator had set free κατ' εὔνοιαν καὶ φιλοστοργίαν, "in consequence of their goodwill and affection" The verb appears to be always punctiliar in the NT: see *Proleg.* p. 149. For subst. ἐλευθέρωσις see BGU II. 388[i. 16] (ii/iii A.D.) ἐπηνέχθ[ησ]αν ταβέλλαι δύ[ο] ἐλευθερώσεων τοῦ αὐτοῦ ὀνόματος διαφόροις χρόνοις (note dat. of point of time, as in Mk 6[21] τοῖς γενεσίοις). MGr (ἐ)λευτερώνω.

ἐλεφάντινος.

The adj. (Rev 18[12]) is found *quater* in *Syll* 586 (iv/B.C.). For the subst. = "elephant," see *Preisigke* 174 (iii/B.C.) ἀποσταλεὶς ἐπὶ τὴν θήραν τῶν ἐλεφάντων, and = "ivory" *Syll* 588[165, 170] (*c.* B.C. 180).

ἐλίσσω.

In the directions for a love-philtre, P Lond 121[463] (iii A.D.) (= I. p. 99) we have ἕλιξον κ[αὶ] β[ά]λε εἰς θάλασσαν: cf. further the magic papyri *ib.* 122[67] (iv/A.D.) (= I. p. 118) ἐλλίξας τὸ ὑπόλοιπον τοῦ ῥάκους περὶ τὸν τράχηλόν σου and *ib.* 46[405] (iv/A.D.) (= I. p. 78) αἰθέριον δρόμο(ν) εἰλίσσων. The compound συνελίσσω is found P Oxy I. 113[4] (ii/A.D.) συνήλλιξα ἐκείνη τῆι ἐπιστολῆ δεῖγμα λευκόϊνα, "I enclosed in the former packet a pattern of white-violet colour" (Edd.), P Giss I. 25[7] συνήλιξα οὖν τὴν ἐπιστολὴν Ἀπολλωτᾶτος τῇ Ἑρμοφίλου. The subst. ἕλιγμα is read by WH in Jn 19[39], following א*B.

ἕλκος.

Syll 802[114] (iii/B.C.) ὑπὸ τοῦ ἀγρίου ἕλκεος δεινῶς διακεί μ[εν]ος, 803[38] (iii/B.C.) ἀνὴρ ἐ[ντὸ]ς τᾶς κοιλίας ἕλκος ἔχων. For ἕλκωσις, "ulceration," see Vett. Val. pp. 3[4], 236[5].

ἑλκύω.

P Petr III. 46 (1)[22] οἱ ἐξειληφότες ἑλκύσαι π[λίνθου] Μ ὥστε εἰς τὴν συντελουμένην ἐν Πτολεμαίδι βασιλ[ικὴν] κατάλυσιν, "who have contracted to draw 20,000 bricks to the Royal quarters which are being completed at Ptolemais" (Edd.), P Oxy I. 121[20] (iii/A.D.) τοὺς κλάδους ἔνικον (*l.* ἔνεγκον) εἰς τὴν ὁδὸν πάντα εἴνα δήσῃ τρία τρία κὲ ἑλκύσῃ, "carry all the branches into the road and have them tied together by threes and dragged along" (Edd.): cf. BGU III. 822[9] (iii/A.D.) μὴ μελησάτω σοι περὶ τῶν σιτικῶν· εὗρον γεοργόν, τίς αὐτὰ ἑλκύσῃ, ἀλλὰ τὰ σπέρματα τίς διδοῖ; With Jas 2[6] cf. P Tor I. 1[vi. 11] (B.C. 117) ἑλκυσθέντων ἀπάντων εἰς τὸ κριτήριον. A metaphorical usage is found in P Hib I. 83[9] (c. B.C. 258–7) καὶ τοῦτο μὴ ἑλκύσῃς, "and do not let this be delayed" (Edd.): see also PSI IV. 333[2] (B.C. 257–6) ἑλκ[υσ]θῆναί σε ἐν ἀρρωστίαι.

ἕλκω.

For the literal sense "draw," cf. PSI IV. 365[11] (B.C. 251–0) τῶν τὴν ὀπτὴν πλίνθον ἑλκόντων, OGIS 483[82] (ii/B.C.) ἐάν τινες ἐν ταῖς ὁδοῖς χοῦν ὀρύσσωσιν . . . ἢ πλίνθους ἕλκωσιν. In P Magd 11[6] (B.C. 221) it is used of "towing" a ship—μόγις ἕλκοντες τὸ πλοῖον ἠγάγομεν ἐπὶ τὸν ὅρμον τοῦ Ἀρσινοΐτου, and in P Tebt II. 383[33] (A.D. 46) of an exit "leading" to the north and east—δ[ι]ὰ τῆς ἑλκο[ύσης] εἰς τὸν βορρᾶ (*l.* βορρᾶν) καὶ ἀπηλιώτ[ην] ἐξόδου: cf. P Oxy II. 259[23] (A.D. 23). See also for meaning "compel," "impress," P Tebt I. 5[179] (B.C. 118) προστετάχασι δὲ μηδὲ τοὺς στρα(τηγοὺς) καὶ τοὺς ἄλλους τοὺς πρὸς ταῖς πραγματείαις ἕλκειν τινὰς τῶν κατοικούντων ἐν τῆι χώρᾳ εἰς λειτουργίας ἰδίας, "and they have decreed that the strategi and the other officials may not compel any of the inhabitants of the country to work for their private service" (Edd.), P Par 63[203] (B.C. 164) (= P Petr III. p. 30) ὑπὲρ ὧν δεῖ ἕλκεσθαι εἰς τὴν γεωργίαν, "concerning the persons who should be impressed for labour in the fields" (Edd.). The exact force to be assigned to the verb in the second of the New Oxyrhynchus Logia, P Oxy IV. 654[10] τίνες οἱ ἕλκοντες ἡμᾶς (εἰς τὴν βασιλείαν εἰ) ἡ βασιλεία ἐν οὐρα[νῷ] ἐστιν; is disputed: see Deissmann *LAE*, p. 437 ff., and Evelyn-White *JTS* xvi. p. 246 ff.

Ἑλλάς.

A Delphic inscr., *Syll* 383 (A.D. 125–9), is inscribed to Hadrian σωτῆρι, ῥυσαμένῳ καὶ θρέψαντι τὴν ἑαυτοῦ Ἑλλάδα, "the saviour who rescued and nurtured his own Hellas."

Ἕλλην.

In the ordinance of Euergetes II. P Tebt I. 5[168] (B.C. 118) Ἕλληνας = "probably . . . all non-Egyptian soldiers, whether Macedonians, Cretans, Persians, etc." The editors compare the opposition between Greeks and Egyptians later in the same decree. This illustrates excellently the familiar antithesis between Jews and "Greeks," so pronounced in Mk 7[26], to which an exact parallel is quoted below.

Ἑλληνίς.

P Giss I. 36[10] (B.C. 161) τάδε λέγει γυνὴ Ἑλληνὶς Ἀμμωνία Πτο(λεμαίου) ἡ καὶ Σενμῖνις κτλ.

Ἑλληνιστί.

P Giss I. 36[6] (B.C. 161) ἀ(ντίγραφον) [συγχωρήσεως Αἰγυπτ]ί[ας με]θη[ρ]μην[ευ]μένης Ἑλληνιστὶ κατὰ τὸ δυνατόν, P Tor I. 1[v. 4] (B.C. 117) ἀντίγραφα συγγραφῶν Αἰγυπτίων διηρμηνευμένων δ᾽ Ἑλληνιστί. For this form of the word see Mayser *Gr.* p. 457, and for the elliptical usage in Ac 21[37] see Field *Notes*, p. 135 f.

ἐλλογάω (—έω).

To Lightfoot's examples of this word from the inscriptions in his note on Philem [18] τοῦτο ἐμοὶ ἐλλόγα, may now be added several occurrences in the papyri in its general Hellenistic form ἐλλογέω. Thus the technical sense of "set to one's account," as in the Philemon passage, comes out well in P Ryl II. 243[11] (ii/A.D.) where two women write to their steward—ὅσα ποτὲ οὖν ἐὰν ἀναλώσῃς (*l.* ἀναλώσῃς) ἰς τὴν τοῦ κλήρου κατεργασίαν, ἡμεῖν ἐνλόγησον ἐπὶ λόγου, "put down to our account everything you expend on the cultivation of the holding" (Edd.), and in P Grenf II. 67[18] (A.D. 237) (= *Selections*, p. 109) ἐντεῦθε[ν] δὲ ἐσχή(καμεν) ὑπὲρ ἀραβῶνος (τῇ τ]ιμῇ ἐλλογουμέν[ο]υ σ[ο]ι (δραχμὰς) [.] β, "earnest money to be reckoned in the price": cf. P Strass I. 32[10] (A.D. 261) καὶ δότω λόγον, τί αὐτῷ ὀφείλ[ε]ται καὶ ποῦ παρέσχεν, ἵνα οὕτως αὐτῷ ἐνλογηθῇ, and so P Flor II. 134 * #[10] (A.D. 2[6]1), PSI I. 92[27] (iii/A.D.). The more metaphorical usage of Rom 5[13] may be paralleled from an interesting rescript of the Emperor Hadrian in which he authorizes the announcement of certain privileges to his soldiers: BGU I. 140[12] (A.D. 119) οὐχ ἕνεκα τοῦ δοκεῖν με αὐτοῖς ἐνλογεῖν, "not however that I may appear to be making a reckoning against them." The form ἐνελογήθ(ησαν) is found *septies* in BGU IV. 1028 (ii/A.D.).

On the mixing of —άω and —έω, see *s.v.* ἐλεέω *ad fin.*

The verb is = ἐν λόγῳ τίθημι, according to the common use of λόγος, "accounts." There is no connexion with ἔλλογος, "rational," which is derived from ἐν λόγῳ in the other sense.

ἐλπίζω.

In a soldier's letter to his father the writer announces— ἐλπίζω ταχὺ προκόσαι (*l.* προκόψαι) τῶν θε[ῶ]ν θελόντων, "I hope to be quickly promoted, if the gods will" (BGU II. 423[17] (ii/A.D.) = *Selections*, p. 91). Nero is described as ὁ δὲ τῆς οἰκουμένης καὶ προσδοκηθεὶς καὶ ἐλπισθεὶς in P Oxy VII. 1021[6] (A.D. 54): cf. *Syll* 364[5] (A.D. 37) ἐπεὶ ἡ κατ᾽ εὐχὴν πᾶσιν ἀνθρώποις ἐλπισθεῖσα Γαίου Καίσαρος Γερμανικοῦ Σεβαστοῦ ἡγεμονία κατήγγελται, οὐδὲν δὲ μέτρον χαρᾶς εὕρηκ(ε)ν ὁ κόσμος κτλ. When in P Ryl II. 243[8] (ii/A.D.) two women write to their steward ἐλπίζοντες σὺν θεῷ τὸ πεδείον σπαρῆναι, the use of θεός alone does not, as the editors note, imply that the writer was a Christian (cf. *Archiv* i. p. 436), but P Iand 11[2] (iii/A.D.) ἐλπίδω γὰρ εἰς θεὸν ὅτι παρακληθῆναι [βούλεται ὁ κύριός] μου ὁ Ἐ[πίμα]χος seems to point to Christian (or Jewish) authorship, cf. 1 Pet 3[5] and see the editor's note. See also PSI IV. 301[9] (v/A.D.) ἐλπίζωμεν (*l.* —ομεν) γὰρ εἰς τὸν θεὸν τὸν παντοκράτορα. MGr ἐλπίζω, ἐρπίζω.

ἐλπίς.

BGU II. 486[6] (ii/A.D.) ὅτε καὶ οἱ νέοι καρ[ποὶ τὰς βελτίσ]τας παρέχουσιν ἡμεῖν ἐλπίδας. P Oxy VII. 1070[10] (iii/A.D.) a pompous letter from a man to his wife in which he beseeches Serapis τῶν χρηστῶν ἐλπίδων τῶν ἐν ἀνθρώποισι νεονομισμένων (*l.* νενομ—), "for the good hopes that are held by mankind." *Syll* 529[35] (i/B.C.) καὶ ἐφοδεύοντες διεφύλαξαν τ[ὴν πόλιν ἕω]ς τοῦ ἀποκατασταθῆνα[ι] τὸν δῆμον εἰς βελτίονας ἐλ[π]ίδας. For a disk with the inscr. ἔχω ἐλπίδας καλάς, see *JHS* xxxiii. p. 84 ff., *BCH* xxxviii. (1914), p. 94 ff. Christian uses of the word are P Oxy VI. 939[9] (iv/A.D.) (= *Selections*, p. 128) an affectionate letter regarding a sick mistress ἐν γὰρ αὐτῇ πάντες τὰς ἐλπίδας [ἔχ]ομεν, and *ib.* VII. 1059[1] (v/A.D.) a prayer commencing Κύ ρι ε) θ(ε)έ μου καὶ ὑ ἐρπίς (*l.* ἡ ἐλπίς) μου. The word is a proper name in BGU II. 632[9] (ii/A.D.) (= *LAE*, p. 174) Ἐλπὶς καὶ Φορτου[νᾶτα (cf. 1 Cor 16[17]), and in *Syll* 865[10] of a slave, see also *Cagnat* IV. 889[15], 1069[2], 1071[2]: cf. Ac 23[6] περὶ ἐλπίδος καὶ ἀναστάσεως νεκρῶν κρίνομαι, where Lake (*Earlier Epp. of St. Paul*, p. 16) translates "for 'Hope' and a resurrection of the dead am I being judged." For the aspirated form ἐφ' ἐλπίδι which WH read in Rom 8[20] cf. *Proleg.* p. 44, and see *s.v.* ἀπελπίζω. In Lat. inscrr. we find Helpis, Helpidius. MGr ἐλπίδα, ἐρπίδα, ὀρπί(δ)α.

Ἐλύμας.

For this proper name (Ac 13[8]) which cannot be regarded as an interpretation of Bar-Jesus, Blass (*Comm. ad l.*) proposes to read Ἑτοιμᾶς, "Son of the Ready," in accordance with D*. But Burkitt (*JTS* iv. p 127 ff.) has pointed out that "no variation in spelling can make *Bar-Jesus* mean 'ready'," and ingeniously conjectures that the reading should be ὁ λοιμός, "the pestilent fellow," Bar-Jesus being then popularly interpreted as *Bar Yeshá* (בר ישׁוע).

ἐλωΐ.

A Christian amulet of v/vi A.D., P Oxy VIII. 1152, containing magical, Jewish, and Christian elements, invokes the help of Ωρωρ φωρ ἐλωεί, ἀδωναεί, Ἰαω σαβαώθ, Μιχαήλ, Ἰεσοῦ Χριστέ.

ἐμαυτοῦ.

P Petr I. 12[10] (iii/B.C.) τῆι ἐμαυτοῦ γυναικί, *ib.* III. 1[iii. 4] (iii/B.C.) τῶν ἐμαυτοῦ ὑπαρχόν[των κύ]ριον εἶναι, "to be master of my property," P Oxy II. 281[13] (A.D. 20–50) ἀνέγκλητον ἐματὴν ἐν ἁπάσει παρειχόμην, "conducted myself blamelessly in all respects" (Edd.), *ib.* VI. 937[7] (iii/A.D.) ἐὰν . . ἔλθω εἰς τὴν πατρίδα μου ἐκδικήσω ἐμαυτόν, BGU II. 846[11] (ii/A.D.) (= *Selections*, p. 94) οἶδα τί [ποτ'] αἱμαυτῷ παρέσχημαι, "I know what I have brought upon myself," and the Christian letter P Oxy VI. 939[14] (iv/A.D.) (= *Selections*, p. 129) οὐκ ὢν ἐν ἐμαυτῷ, "not being master of myself" (cf. the classical ἐν ἐμαυτοῦ). For a weakened sense cf. P Ryl II. 77[34] (A.D. 192) πειθόμενος τῇ ἐμαυτοῦ πατρίδι, "obedient to my native city," *ib.* 98(*a*)[16] (A.D. 154–5) ἔξω δὲ σὺν ἐμαυτῷ ἐργάτας δύο, *ib.* 117[9] (A.D. 269) συνε[σ]τῶ[τός μοι τ]οῦ ἐμαυτῆς ἀνδρός, "with the concurrence of my husband."

ἐμβαίνω.

P Petr III. 26[5] ἐ]ὰν ἐμβῆι βοῦς . . . εἰς ἀλλότριον κλῆρον, "if an ox trespass on another man's allotment" (Edd.), P Oxy II. 259[31] (A.D. 23) εἰ δὲ [μ]ὴ ἐμβέβηκ(εν)—on a ship,

BGU II. 665[ii. 12] (i/A.D.) διὸ παρακαλῶ σε, πάτερ, τὸ μὲμ πρῶτον ἐμβῆναι σὺν αὐτῇ τὰ περὶ ἔσχατα τοῦ Μ[ε]χείρ, and P Ryl I. 28[19] (iv/A.D.) ἐν πολλοῖς [ἐ]μβήσεται, "will engage upon many things" (Ed.). See also *Syll* 895[1] ἐτελεύτησα ἐμβὰς (εἰς ἔτη πέντε. It may be noted that in *ExpT* xxvi. p. 248 ff. Rendel Harris quotes Syriac evidence to show that ἐμβάντα καθῆσθαι in Mk 4[1] is an "Aramaism" for "to go aboard."

ἐμβάλλω.

With the solitary occurrence of this verb in the NT, Lk 12[5] ἐμβαλεῖν εἰς τὴν γέενναν, may be compared P Par 47[8] (*c.* B.C. 153) (= *Selections*, p. 22) ἐνέβληκαν (*s.* οἱ θεοί) ὑμᾶς εἰς ὕλην μεγάλην, where apparently ὕλην must be understood metaphorically like Dante's "selva oscura," and the Christian letter P Oxy VI. 939[12] (iv/A.D.) (= *Selections*, p. 129) ἐς τηλικαύτην σε [ἀγωνία]ν ἄκων ἐνέβαλον, "unwittingly I cast you into such distress." For a similar literal usage cf. *Michel* 247[7] (end iii/B.C.) ἐνέβαλον εἰς τὸ κιβώτιον, "cast into the chest." The verb is common with πληγάς, e.g. P Magd 38[6] (B.C. 221) πληγάς τέ μοι ἐνέβαλον, P Tebt I. 39[29] (B.C. 114), etc. In P Tebt I. 37[7] (B.C. 73) περὶ ὧν ἐὰν ὁμόσωσι ἔργων ἐμβεβλῆσθαι εἰς τὴν γῆν, the editors render "concerning the works which they swear have been imposed upon their land"; cf. P Hib I. 63[5] (*c.* B.C. 265) τὴν τιμὴν τοῦ σπέρμα[το]ς οὗ ἔφη ἐμβεβληκέν[α]ι εἰς τὸν Πρωταγόρου κ[λ]ῆρον. Another usage of the verb and the corresponding subst. (ἐμβολή), which has come to be almost technical, is in connexion with the "lading" of a ship, e.g. P Hib I. 54[30] (*c.* B.C. 245) ἐμβαλοῦ δὲ αὐτὰ καὶ φυλακίτας, "put them (i. e. various provisions) on board with the guards," P Oxy X. 1292[3] (*c.* A.D. 30) εὖ [π]οήσεις ἐμβαλόμενός μοι κενώματα διακ[ό]σια, "please put on board for me two hundred empty jars." P Giss I. 69[11] (A.D. 118–9) ἵν[α δι]ὰ σπ[ο]υδῆς ἐμβαλόμενος πᾶσαν τὴν [κρειθὴν τα]χέως εἰς τὴν Καινὴν παρακομίσῃ, and P Oxy I. 62[11] (iii/A.D.) a letter of a centurion with reference to the embarkation of corn— ἵνα μὴ ἐκ τῆς σῆς ἀμελείας ἐνέδρα περὶ τὴν ἐμβολὴν γένηται, "in order that there may be no fraud in the lading through any neglect of yours," where the editors note that ἐμβολή "was the technical term for the annual contribution of corn supplied to Rome and afterwards to Constantinople" (cf. Wilcken *Ostr* i. p. 364 f.). See for other exx. of the verb *s.v.* βῖκος and *Archiv* v. p. 50 n.[2], and for ἔμβλημα apparently = "embankment" or "dam" see P Tebt II. 378[20] note and P Ryl II. 133[12] note.

ἐμβατεύω.

For ἐ. = "take possession of," as in Josh 19[51] ἐπορεύθησαν ἐμβατεῦσαι τὴν γῆν, cf. a will of iii/B.C., P Eleph 2[14], where in the event of their parents leaving debts, right is reserved to the sons not to "enter on" the inheritance— ἐξέστω τοῖς υἱοῖς μὴ ἐμβατεύειν, ἐὰμ μὴ βούλωνται. See also BGU IV. 1167[64] (B.C. 12) ἐξέστω . . . ἐμβαδεύειν εἰς τὰς τρεῖς (ἀρού[ρας], P Oxy VIII. 1118[7] (i/ii A.D.) ὅπ]ως . . . γεινώσκωσι ἐμβαδεύσον[τά μ]ε εἰς τὰ ὑπ[ο]τεθειμένα, "that they may know that I shall enter on the mortgaged property" (Ed.), BGU I. 101[16] (A.D. 114–5) μὴ ἐξεῖναι δὲ μοὶ λυτρῶσαι μηδὲ ἐνβαδεύειν αγ . . υ . . . μ . . . . The verb and the corresponding noun ἐμβαδεία are also used technically of a creditor's entry into possession of property, e.g. P Lond 1164(d)⁸·¹¹ (A.D. 212) (= III. p. 159) τὰ ἑξῆς νόμιμα πάντα ἐτελείωσεν μεχρὶ ἐμβαδείας . . . . ἀνακομιδῆς τοῦ ἐμβατευθέντος τρίτου μέρους: see also Modica *Introduzione*, p. 286. The idea of forcible entry (1 Macc 12²⁵ *al.*) is well brought out in P Par 14¹⁹ (ii/B.C.) οἱ ἐγκαλούμενοι δ' ἐμβατεύσαντες εἰς τὴν σημαινομένην οἰκίαν καὶ περιοικοδομήσαντες ἑαυτοῖς οἰκητήρια ἐνοικοῦσιν βιαίως, P Lond 401¹⁹ (B.C. 116–111) (= II. p. 14) βιαιότερον ἐμβατ[εύ]σ[α]ς εἰς τὸ δη[λούμενο]ν ἔδαφος τοῦ ἀμπελῶ[νος]. More significant however than any of the above citations for the meaning of the verb in its only occurrence in the NT (Col 2¹⁸) is its use in the mystery religions to denote the climax of initiation, when the mystès "sets foot on" the entrance to the new life which he is now to share with the god. The point has been fully examined by Ramsay *Teaching of Paul*, p. 287 ff., where reference is made to inscrr. from Klaros, according to which the inquirer, after being initiated, ἐνεβάτευσεν, "set foot on—," and performed the entire series of rites. From this, according to Ramsay, it would appear that in Col *l.c.* ἐμβατεύων is to be taken as a quoted word, containing a sarcastic reference to the man of the mysteries with his false worship and fleshly mind. "Let no one cozen you of the prize of your life-race, finding satisfaction in self-humiliation and worshipping of angels, 'taking his stand on' what he has seen (in the Mysteries), vainly puffed up by his unspiritual mind, and not keeping firm hold on [Christ] the Head." It will be further noted that this interpretation has the advantage of rendering unnecessary the conjectural emendations of the text proposed by Bishop Lightfoot and Dr. C. Taylor: see also Field *Notes*, p. 197 f. On the form of the word in which δ and τ are freely interchanged, see Mayser *Gr.* p. 176, and for the technical use of τὸ ἐμβαδικόν as "the tax paid by tenants to the owners of the land" see Wilcken *Ostr* i. p. 190 f. See also Moulton *Gr.* ii. § 118(b).

ἐμβιβάζω.

P Flor I. 56¹⁷ (A.D. 234) ἐμβιβάσαι με εἰς τὰ [κ]αταγρα(φέντα): cf. *ib.* 55³¹ (A.D. 88–96), PSI IV. 282¹⁶ (A.D. 183). See also *Syll* 266¹⁴ (B.C. 200–100) ἐθελοντὴς [ν]αύτας δώδεκα ἐνεβίβασεν. For ἐκβιβάζω cf. P Oxy XII. 1483¹⁶ (ii/iii A.D.) ἐὰν μή . . . ἐγβιβάσῃς τὰ [πρ]ὸς σὲ ζητούμενα, "unless you discharge the claims made against you" (Edd.), and see *Michel* 883³⁵ (beginning ii/B.C.), where in a list of victors at the Panathenaea mention is made of a chariot-driver—ἡνίοχος ἐγβιβάζων. MGr μπάζω, "bring in."

ἐμβλέπω.

P Lond 42²¹ (B.C. 168) (= I. p. 30, *Selections*, p. 10) μηδ' ἐνβεβλοφέναι (for form, see *s.v.* βλέπω) εἰς τὴν ἡμετέραν περί·στασιν·, "nor spared a look for our helpless state." The figurative meaning, as in Mt 6²⁶, is seen in P Tor I. 1ⁱⁱⁱ·⁷ (B.C. 117) διὸ ἀξιῶ ἐμβλέψαντα εἰς τὴν γεγενημένην μοι καταφθορὰν ὑπὸ ἀσεβῶν ἀνθρώπων κτλ., "*mente reputans damnum*" etc., P Tebt I. 28¹⁵ (*c.* B.C. 114) ἀξιοῦμεν ἐμβλέψαντα εἰς τὰ ὑποδεδειγμένα, "we beg you to look into the matters indicated" (Edd.).

ἐμβριμάομαι.

We can produce no fresh evidence to throw light on the meaning of this difficult verb in the NT, but the LXX

usage (Dan 11³⁰, cf. Ps 7¹² Aq, Isai 17¹³ Sm) is in favour of the meaning "am angry," "express violent displeasure," perhaps with the added idea of "within oneself." See Allen on Mk 1⁴³, and Souter *Lex. s.v.*

ἐμέω.

Syll 803¹²⁶ (iii/B.C.) μετὰ δὲ τοῦτο φιάλαν οἱ δό[μεν φάρμακον ἔχουσαν] καὶ κέλεσθαι ἐκπιεῖν, ἔπειτα ἐμεῖν κέλεσ[θαι· αὐτὰ δὲ ἐμέσαι, πᾶν] δὲ ἐμπλῆσαι τὸ λῶπιον τὸ αὐτᾶς. Cf. Cic. *Att.* xiii. 52. 1 ἐμετικὴν agebat.

ἐμμαίνομαι.

For this NT ἅπ. εἰρ. (Ac 26¹¹) we may cite the adj. in *Menandrea* p. 53²⁰⁰ ὥσπερ ἐμμανὴς ἐπεισπεσ[ών], "rushing in like a madman."

ἐμμένω.

For the legal formula ἐμμένω with or without ἐν followed by the dat. of a participle, of which apparently we have a reminiscence in Gal 3¹⁰, cf. P Tor II. 8³¹ (ii/B.C.) ἐμμένειν δὲ ἀμφοτέρους ἐν τοῖς πρὸς ἑαυτοὺς διωμολογημένοις, P Oxy I. 38¹⁶ (A.D. 49–50) (= *Selections*, p. 53) τοῦ δὲ Σύρου μὴ βουλομένου ἐνμεῖναι τοῖς κεκριμένοις, "Syrus, however, refuses to comply with the judgment," BGU II. 600⁶ (ii/iii A.D.) ἐνμένω πᾶσι ταῖς προγεγραμμέν[α]ις [ἐν]τολαῖς, and, as showing its persistence, the late P Flor I. 93²⁹ (a deed of divorce—A.D. 569) ἄκοντα ἐμμεῖναι πᾶσι τοῖς προγεγραμμένοις. The dat., as in Ac 14²², is found also in *Syll* 879²⁰ (end of iii/B.C.) ἐπεύχεσθαι τοῖς ἐμμένουσιν καὶ ταῖς πειθομέναις τῶιδε τῶι νόμωι εὖ εἶναι, and in the much later P Oxy I. 138³⁶ (A.D. 610–1) τούτοις ἐμμένειν, ταῦτα διαφυλάττειν, "abide by these conditions and observe them." See also P Tebt II. 382²² (B.C. 30—A.D. 1) ὀμνύω Καίσαραν θεοῦ υἱὸν Αὐτοκράτορα εἶ μὴν ἐμμενεῖν καὶ ποιήσειν πάντ[α κτλ., "will truly abide by and perform all etc.," P Oxy III. 494²⁸ (A.D. 156) τὸν δὲ παραβησόμενον ἐκτίνειν τῷ ἐμμένοντι τό τε βλάβος καὶ ἐπίτειμον ἀργυρίου τάλαντα δύο, "and that he who shall transgress [the terms of a will] shall forfeit to the party abiding by it the damages and a fine of two talents of silver," and so P Flor I. 51²³ (A.D. 138–61). Cf. Deissmann *BS*, p. 248 f., Berger *Strafklauseln*, p. 3.

ἐμμέσῳ.

For this form read, instead of ἐν μέσῳ, by AC in Rev 1¹³, 2¹, etc., see P Petr I. 23⁽³⁾ ² (iii B.C.) χῶμα καινὸν ἐμμέσωι τοῦ ἃ εἰς ῑ ναυβία χξή (608). See further Robertson *Gr.* p. 1210 for the NT usage.

ἐμός.

Commenting on P Petr I. 12¹⁰ cited *s.v.* ἐμαυτοῦ *ad init.*, Mahaffy draws attention to the substitution of cases of ἐμαυτοῦ for ἐμός in the Ptolemaic papyri. The only exception he notes is P Petr I. 14¹³ (B.C. 237) (= III. p. 12) τ]ῆι ἐμῆ[ι γ]υναικί. A later example (A.D. 192) is found on an ostracon published in *LAE*, p. 186 δὸς τῇ ἐμῇ παιδίσκη, where Deissmann remarks that ἐμή is unemphatic, as, for example, in Rom 10¹: cf. also P Oxy VIII. 1159¹⁵ (late iii A.D.) περὶ δὲ καὶ τῶν ἐμῶν συνέργων, "with regard to my tools." PSI III. 225⁶ (A.D. 580) ὁλόγραφον χειρὶ ἐμῇ shows us the Pauline phrase (1 Cor 16²¹ *al.*). In *ib.* 213⁵ (iii/A D.) we have ἐμὰ γάρ ἐστιν, while the masculine = "the members of my family" is found in P Par 70¹⁶ (Ptol.) τὸ σύμβολον τῶν ἐμῶν, P Oxy I. 115⁷ (ii/A.D.) πάντες οἱ ἐμοί: cf. *Preisigke* 1768 (Thebes) τ]ὸ προ‒σ‒κύνη[μα] τῶν [ἐ]μ[ῶν] πάντων. The use of ἐμός is very characteristic of the Johannine writings (cf. *Proleg.* p. 40 n.²), and Thumb (*ThLZ.* 1903, p. 421) regards this as a sign of their connexion with Asia Minor, in view of the fact that ἐμός survives in modern Pontic—Cappadocian Greek, as against μου elsewhere: but see *Proleg.* p. 211.

ἐμπαιγμός.

We are unable to cite from our sources any instance of this word (Heb 11⁶) which Grimm pronounces to be "unknown to prof. auth.", but a related form συμπαιγμός = "collusion" is found in P Tor I. 1ⁱⁱⁱ⁻¹⁵ (B.C. 117-6) ἀγνοούντων τῶν ἀντιδίκων, εἴ τινα συνπαιγμὸν ποιεῖται τῆι Λοβαίτι μόνηι, "nam adversarii haud liquido compertum habent, utrum colluserit cum una Lobaite" (Ed.).

ἐμπαίζω

is used = "delude," as in Mt 2¹⁶ (cf. Jer 10¹⁵), in *Anth. Pal.* x. 56. 2 τοῖς ἐμπαιζομένοις ἄνδρασι ταῦτα λέγω. Cf. Vett. Valens p. 10¹¹ ἐμπαιζομένων ἀνθρώπων.

ἐμπί(μ)πλημι.

PSI IV. 413²⁰ (iii/B.C.) ταρίχου τὸ σταμνίον σύνταξ[ο]ν ἡμῖν ἐμπλῆσαι. *Syll* 803⁵⁷ (iii/B.C.) ὥστε ἑπτὰ καὶ ἑξ[ή]κοντα λεκάνας ἐνέπλησε πύους, ¹²⁷ πᾶν δὲ ἐμπλῆσαι τὸ λώπιον τὸ αὐτᾶς. See also *Kaibel* 241¹⁰ (ii/i B.C.)—

ἐρημωθεῖσα δὲ τέκνων
γηραιομβιοτᾶς τέρμα ἐνέπλησε κακ[ῶ]ν.

ἐμπί(μ)πρημι, ἐμπρήθω.

P Tebt I. 61 (b)²⁸⁹ (B.C. 118-7) ἐμπρήσαντο πυ[ρ]οῦ γενήματα, "burned the stores of wheat," BGU II. 651⁴ (A.D. 192) ἐνεπρήσθη μοι ἅλων, *ib.* III. 909¹⁶ (A.D. 359) ἐνέπρησαν αὐτὴν (*sc.* οἰκίαν) ἐκ θεματίου ("on purpose"), and *ib.* IV. 1047ⁱⁱ·¹⁰ (time of Hadrian) ἀ]πὸ συνοικιῶν ἐμπε[πρ]ησμένων. See also *OGIS* 8¹¹ (iv/B.C.) τὰν δὲ πόλιν καὶ τὰ ἱρ[α] . . . ἐνέπρησε, *Syll* 350¹⁹ (B.C. 31) ὑπέδ(ε)ιξαν δέ μοι καὶ περὶ . . . τῶν ἐπαύλεων τῶν ἐμπεπρησμένων.

ἐμπίπτω.

P Lille I. 16⁶ (iii/B.C.) εἰς τὸν Ε. λόγον ἐμπεσεῖν, "to be paid into the account of H.": cf. P Tebt I. 17⁹ (B.C. 114) ὅπως μὴ ἐπικατασχὼν αὐτὸν εἰς δαπάνας ἐμπέσης οὐκ ὀλίας, "so that you may not detain him and thus incur no little expense" (Edd.). In *ib.* 39²⁰ (B.C. 114) the verb is construed with the dat.—ἐμ]πεσόντος μου τῶι Σισόϊτ[ι, "I fell in with Sisois," and in P Ryl II. 68⁹ (B.C. 89) it has the stronger sense of "attack"—ἐμπεσοῦσα ἐξ ἀντιλο[γ]ίας ἔ[πλη]ξέν με ταῖς αὐτῆς χερσὶν [πλη]γαῖς πλεί[στα]ις, "attacking me in consequence of a dispute gave me many blows with her hands" (Edd.). Cf. P Oxy II. 243²⁶ (A.D. 79) σὺν τ[ο]ῖς ἐμπεσουμένοις εἰς τούτοις (*l.* τούτους) [φ]ορτίοις πᾶσι, "together with all fixtures which may be included in them" (Edd.), and similarly *ib.* III. 494²¹ (A.D. 156) καὶ καταχρᾶσθαι εἰς τὸ ἴδιον χ . [.] . ς τοῖς ἐμπεσουμένοις

ἤτοι ἐκ πράσεως καὶ ἐξ ὑποθήκης ἀργυρίοις, "to use for her personal requirements the money accruing from the sale or mortgage" (Edd.). With the use in Heb 10³¹ we may now compare Ev. Petr. 10 μὴ ἐμπεσεῖν εἰς χεῖρας τοῦ λαοῦ τῶν Ἰουδαίων.

ἐμπλέκω

is used of a hostile attack in P Tebt I. 39¹⁷ (B.C. 114) καὶ ἐπελθὼν οὕτως ὁ προγεγραμμένος καὶ ἡ τού[το]υ γυνὴ Ταυσῖρις ἐμπλεκέντες μοι καὶ δόντες πληγὰς πλείους, "thereupon the aforesaid and his wife T. closed with me and gave me many blows." Vett. Val. p. 118¹ προσέτι δὲ καὶ εἰς δουλικὰ πρόσωπα καὶ παῖδας ἐμπλέκονται, *de re venerea.* With 2 Tim 2⁴ cf. Epict. iii. 22. 69 μή ποτ' ἀπερίσπαστον εἶναι δεῖ τὸν Κυνικὸν . . . οὐ προσδεδεμένον καθήκουσιν ἰδιωτικοῖς οὐδ' ἐμπεπλεγμένον σχέσεσιν, ἃς παραβαίνων κτλ.: (see Sharp *Epict.* p. 72), Polyb. xxv. 9. 3 τοῖς Ἑλληνικοῖς πράγμασιν ἐμπλεκόμενος. The compound παρεμπλέκω occurs in P Tor I. 1ᵛⁱⁱⁱ·²⁵ (B.C. 117) τὸν δὲ Ἑρμίαν παρεμπλέκοντα τὰ μηδαμῶς ἀνήκοντα πρὸς τὴν ἐνεστῶσαν κρίσιν, "Hermias vero interserens ea, quae nullo modo cum praesenti causa cohaerent" (Ed.), and for ἐκπλέκω see P Tebt II. 315²⁹ (ii/A.D.) πρὶν γὰρ [α]ὐτὸ[ν] π[ρό]ς σε ἐλθεῖν ἐγὼ αὐτὸν ποι[ήσ]ω ἐκπλέξαι σε, "for I will make him let you through before he comes to you" (Edd.), with reference to an official scrutiny of certain temple books, and P Oxy XII. 1493⁶ (late iii/A.D.) εἰ οὖν πάλιν δύνη ἐκπλέξαι παρὰ σεαυτῷ, τύχῃ τῇ ἀγαθῇ, "if then you can again get him off by yourself (?), good luck to you" (Edd.).

ἐμπλοκή

in the sense of "struggle," "scuffle," occurs P Ryl II. 124²⁸ (i/A.D.) καὶ ἐν τῇ ἐνπλοκῇ ἀπολέσσθαι (*l.* -έσθαι) αὐτῆς ἐγώδιον χρυσοῦν, "in the struggle she lost a golden earring" (Edd.); cf. *ib.* 150¹² (A.D. 40) καὶ ἐν τῇ ἐμπλοκῇ ἀπώλοντό μο(υ) ἀργ(υρίου) μ. With the use in 1 Pet 3³ cf. *Syll* 653²² (B.C. 91) μὴ ἐχέτω δὲ μηδεμία χρυσία . . . μηδὲ τὰς τρίχας ἀνπεπλεγμένας, regulations regarding the ἱεραί in the celebration of the mysteries of Demeter and Kore: cf. *ib.* 939¹⁹. For the *simplex* πλοκή cf. P Giss I. 47⁷ (time of Hadrian) where a θώραξ is described as τ]ὴν πλοκὴν λεπτότατος. In P Ryl II. 154³¹ (A.D. 66) ἀποπλοκή is used of the "separation" of divorce, as the verb occurs elsewhere, and the editors note γενόμενος καὶ ἀποπεπλεγμένος as a euphemism for death in BGU I. 118ⁱⁱ·¹¹ (ii/A.D.).

ἐμπνέω.

Kaibel 562ᵐ·⁴ (ii/iii A.D.)—

ἐς δ' ὅσον ἐνπνείει βίοτόν τε ἐπὶ ἦμαρ ἐρύκει
δύσμορος ἀντλήσει πένθος ἀεξίβιον.

ἐμπορεύομαι.

For ἐ. of travelling on business, as in Jas 4¹³, see the question addressed to the oracle of Zeus at Dodona, *Syll* 800 (iii/B.C. ?) ἦ τυγχάνοιμί κα ἐμπορευόμενος κτλ. The verb has nothing to do with πορεύομαι: its meaning is entirely determined by ἔμπορος (see below), but, had there been no πορεύομαι, the verb would more probably have been ἐμπορέω, cf. Moulton *Gr.* ii. § 118(a).

ἐμπορία.

For this NT ἅπ. εἰρ. (Mt 22⁵) see P Giss I. 9³ ἀποστάντ[ο]ς εἰς Ὄασιν ἐνπορίας χάριν, "for the sake of business." In P Oxy I. 76¹⁰ (A.D. 179) the words κατά τινα ἐμπορίαν have been erased in the original. Cf. also *Syll* 118³² (mid. iv/B.C.) ἐπιδημῶσιν κατ' ἐμπορίαν Ἀθήνησι, *OGIS* 629¹⁶⁴ (A.D. 137) ὅσα εἰς ἐμπορείαν φέρεται. Aristeas 114 ἐργάσιμος γὰρ καὶ πρὸς τὴν ἐμπορίαν ἐστὶν ἡ χώρα κατεσκευασμένη.

ἐμπόριον.

P Petr II. 45ⁱⁱⁱ ⁵ (B.C. 246) τὰς τιμὰς ἐν τῶι ἐμπορίωι, P Tebt I. 5³³ (B.C. 118) περ[ὶ] τῶν εἰσαγό[ντων] διὰ τοῦ ξενικοῦ ἐμπορίου, "in the case of persons importing goods through the foreign mart" (Edd.), *ib.* 6³⁵ (B.C. 140–39) ἱεροδούλων ἀπὸ ἐμπορίων καὶ ἐργασιῶν καὶ μισθῶν τασσομένων, "sacred slaves from trades and manufactures and salaries" (Edd.). In *Syll* 932²¹ (beginning of iii/A.D.) τὰ ὄντα ἐνπόρια is used simply of inhabited places : see Dittenberger's note. On the form of the word, cf. Mayser *Gr.* p. 93.

ἔμπορος.

In BGU III. 1012³ (ii/B.C.) we have a letter addressed to Antaeus παρὰ Μαρρέου[ς τ]οῦ Πετ[ο]σείριος ἐμπόρου, and in *ib.* IV. 1061¹⁵ (B.C. 14) an attack is made λῃστρικῶι τρόπωι ἐπί τινα ἔμπορον τῶν ἐκ τοῦ Ὀξυρυγχ[ίτου]. P Oxy I. 36ⁱⁱ ⁹ (ii/iii A.D.) provides that if the tax-farmer desires that a ship be unloaded—¹³ ᶠᶠ ὁ ἔμπορος ἐκφορτιζέ[τ]ω, "the merchant shall unload it," but that if the ship's "manifest" be found correct—ὁ τελώνης τ[ὴ]ν δαπάνην τῷ ἐμπό[ρ]ῳ τοῦ ἐκφορτισμοῦ ἀποδ[ότ]ω, "the tax farmer shall repay to the merchant the cost of unloading." Add *Preisigke* 1070 τὸ προσκύνημα Ἡρακλεί[δ]ου Μενεμεν.αλιτος ἐμπόρου παρὰ τῷ θ[ε]ῷ κυρί[ῳ Βησᾷ. For ἔμπορος in its primitive sense of *viator* Herwerden (*Lex. s.v.*) cites Bacchyl. xvii. 36 ἔμπορον οἷ' ἀλάταν ἐπ' ἀλλοδαμίαν, "like a wayfarer who wanders forth to a strange folk" (Jebb) : cf. *Cagnat* IV. 144¹⁰ (Cyzicus, i/A.D.) τῶν ἀπὸ τῆς [Ἀσίας . . .]ν ἐνπόρων καὶ ξένων τῶν ἐληλυθότων εἰς τὴν πανήγυριν. For the "classic" distinction between ἔμπορος and κάπηλος see Plato *de Rep.* ii. 371D.

ἔμπροσθεν.

For ἔ. of *place*, as in all its NT occurrences, cf. P Tebt II. 316ⁱⁱ ²² (A.D. 99) οἰκοῦμεν δὲ ἐν τῷ ἐμπροσθι̣ς (*l.* ἔμπροσθε) ναυάρχου, "we live opposite the admiralty" (Edd.), P Giss I. 99¹⁶ (ii/iii A.D.) τὰ γράμματα ἐ̣]ν στή[λαι̣]ν δυοῖν [ἔ]μπροσθεν ἱδρυμέ[ν]αιν τοῦ [ν]εώ, and the magical P Par 574¹²²⁹ (iii/A.D.) (= *Selections*, p. 113) βάλε ἔμπροσθεν αὐτοῦ κλῶνας ἐλαίας. The word is very common in the papyri with reference to *time*, e.g. P Petr II. 8 (1)ᴬ ⁷ (c. B.C. 250) ἐν τοῖς ἔνπροσθεν χρόνοις, *ib.* 13 (1)⁸ (B.C. 258–3) καθὰ καὶ ἔνπροσθεν ἐγένετο, P Ryl II. 157²² (A.D. 135) τῶν ἔμπροσθεν καὶ τῶν ἐπεσομένων χρόνων. Cf. *Michel* 978³ (B.C. 281–0) ἔν τε τῶι ἔμπροσ[θε]ν χρόνωι. MGr ἐμπρός, (ἐ)μπροστά.

ἐμπτύω.

With ἐ. used in the NT in the sense of the Attic καταπτύω, "spit upon," as in Mk 10³⁴, cf. P Magd 24⁷ (B.C. 218),

where the words καὶ ἐνέπτυσεν εἰς τὸ πρόσω[πον have been inserted above the line : cf. Plut. *Mor.* 189A ἐνέπτυσεν . . εἰς τὸ πρόσωπον, and Herodas v. 76 καὶ τίς οὐκ ἀπαντῶσα ἔς μευ δικαίως τὸ πρόσωπον ἐμπτύοι : and see Rutherford *NP* p. 66. In Ev. Petr. 3 the verb is construed with the dat.—ἐνέπτυον αὐτοῦ ταῖς ὄψεσι.

ἐμφανής.

The phrase ἐν τῷ ἐμφανεῖ is found in P Hib I. 93⁴ (c. B.C. 250) where a man, acting as surety, undertakes to produce his friend ἐν] τῶι ἐμφανεῖ ἔξω ἱεροῦ κα[ὶ πάσης] σκέπης, "openly, outside of a temple or any other shelter," and similarly P Oxy IV. 785 (c. A.D. 1) and the other citations in P Hamb I. p. 121 n⁴. The quasi-legal use of the adj. may be further illustrated from BGU IV. 1145⁴⁰ (B.C. 5) ἐὰν δὲ καὶ ἡ Διδύμη μὴ π[αρ]έχηται τ[ὴ]ν Λύκαν καὶ Διονύσιον τῷ Ἀχιλ(λεῖ) ἐνφανεῖς, εἶναι καὶ αὐ(τὴ)ν ἀγωγίμη(ν), P Oxy II. 260¹¹ (A.D. 59) ἔσασθα[ι ἐμ]φανῆ τῷ Σαραπίωνο[ς] ἀρχιδικαστοῦ [β]ήματι, "I will appear at the court of the chief justice Sarapion," and so *ib.* X. 1258⁸ (A.D. 45), P Gen I. 28²⁴ (A.D. 136) *al.* In P Oxy VII. 1021² (A.D. 54) the deceased Emperor Claudius is described as ἐνφανὴς θεός, "god manifest" : see further *s.v.* ἐπιφανής. For a Christian use see the fragment of a lost Gospel, P Oxy IV. 655¹⁹, where the disciples ask the Lord—πότε ἡμῖν ἐμφανὴς ἔσει καὶ πότε σε ὀψόμεθα ; and receive the answer ὅταν ἐκδύσησθε καὶ μὴ αἰσχυνθῆτε.

The corr. subst. ἐμφανεία may be illustrated from P Grenf II. 62¹⁰ (A.D. 211) where Demetrius agrees to act as surety μονῆς καὶ ἐμφανίας, "for the non-removal and appearance" of Pasis : cf. P Oxy VIII. 1121²², ²⁵ (A.D. 295).

ἐμφανίζω.

The quasi-technical sense of this word = "make an official report," as in Ac 23¹⁵, ²² (cf. 2 Macc 3⁷), may be illustrated from P Magd 11⁹ (B.C. 221) ἐθισμοῦ ὄντος, ἐάν τισιν τῶν ναυκλήρων τοιοῦτό τι συμβῇ, ἐμφανίζειν τοῖς ἐπὶ τῶν τόπων στρατηγοῖς, *ib.* 17² (B.C. 221) ἀποδόντος γάρ μου] ἔντευξιν Διοφάνει τῶι στρατηγῶι, δι' ἧς ἐνεφάν[ισα κτλ., *ib.* 26¹¹ (B.C. 217) ὡς δ[ι]ὰ τῆ[ς] ἐντεύξεως ἐμφανίζομεν, P Par 26¹⁸ (petition from the Serapeum Twins—B.C. 163–2) (= *Selections*, p. 15) ὑμῖν, καθ' ἃς ἐποείσθ' ἐν Μέμφει παρουσίας, ἐνεφανίζομεν ὑπὲρ τούτων, "we laid information on these matters before you, on the occasion of your visits to Memphis," PSI IV. 442²³ (iii/B.C.) ταῦτα δὲ ἐνεφάνισά σοι, ὅπως ἂν μηθείς σε παρακρούηται. Cf. the use of ἐμφανισμός in P Amh II. 33¹² (c. B.C. 157) ἀφ' ὧν ἐπιδ[ε]δώκειμεν αὐτοῖς ἐνφανισμῶν περὶ τινων ἀδικημάτω[ν] καὶ παραλογειῶν σίτου τε καὶ χαλκοῦ, "by written declarations previously handed in to them of certain misdeeds and peculations of both corn and money" (Edd.), and of ἐμφανιστής in P Tor I. 1 ᵛⁱⁱⁱ· ¹² (B.C. 117) ἐμφανιστοῦ καὶ κατηγόρου, where Peyron translates ἐ. by "delator," and refers (p. 178) to Ac 24¹, 25². ¹⁵. See also Ev. Petr. 10 συνεσκέπτοντο οὖν ἀλλήλοις ἐκεῖνοι ἀπελθεῖν καὶ ἐνφανίσαι ταῦτα τῷ Πειλάτῳ.

ἔμφοβος.

P Leid Wˣⁱˣ ²⁵ (ii/iii A.D.) ἐπικαλοῦμαί σου τὸ (ὄνομα) . . . ἔσται σισμός (*l.* σεισμός). ὁ (ἥλιος) στήσεται, καὶ ἡ σελήνη ἐνφωβος (*l.* ἔμφοβος) ἔσται, καὶ ἡ (*l.* αἱ) πέτραι, καὶ

τὰ ὄρη . . . . ὑποπετρωθήσεται κτλ. See also Vett. Val.
p. 59[7] εἰς στασιώδεις καὶ ἐμφόβους, where however the
reading is doubtful. The verb is found BGU II. 613[18] (time
of Anton. Pius) ἐμφοβοῦντες.

ἐμφυσάω.

The use of this word in Jn 20[22], the only place where it
occurs in the NT, though it is found eleven times in the
LXX, is well illustrated by P Leid W[xvii. 15] (ii/iii A.D.) ὁ
ἐνφυσήσας πνεῦμα ἀνθρώποις εἰς ζωήν. For a new literary
reference see the medical receipt to stop sneezing, P Oxy
VIII. 1088[25] (early i/A.D.) ἐλλεβόρου λευκοῦ προσφατώτερον
τρίψας ἐμφύσας (l. ἐμφύσα) εἰς τοὺς μυκτῆρας, "pound
fresh some white hellebore and blow it into the nostrils"
(Ed.).

ἔμφυτος.

The meaning of "inborn," "natural," which Hort
advocates for Jas 1[21], as distinguished from "implanted"
from without, is supported by BGU II. 613[10] (time of Anton.
Pius) κ]ατὰ τὴν ἔμφυτόν σου εὐμένειαν, "in accordance with
your natural kindness": cf. P Oxy VI. 899[19] (A.D. 200) διὰ τὴν
ἔμφυτόν σου εὐεργεσίαν, CP Herm I. 52 [17] (iii/A.D.) κατὰ
τὴν ἔμφυτον αὐτοῦ πρὸς το[ὺς ὑπ]ηκόους φιλανθρωπίαν,
Cagnat IV. 144[7] (Cyzicus, i/A.D.) τῆι δὲ ἐμφύτωι φιλανθρωπίᾳ πρός τε τοὺς ἐγχωρίους καὶ τοὺς ξένους ἐχρήσατο, Syll
326[15] (i/A.D.) τῶν δὲ Σκυθᾶν τὰν ἔμφυτον [αὐ]τοῖς ἀθεσίαν
ἐκφανῆ καταστασάντων. The late P Hamb I. 23[16] (A.D.
569) ἀμπελικὸν χωρίον ἔμφυτον may be compared with
P Giss I. 56[7] (vi/A.D.) χωρίον ἀμπελικὸν ζωόφ[υ]τ[ον,
where the editor (see Intr. p. 96 n.[1]) understands ζωόφυτον
as = ζώφυτον / pflanzenernährend," "fruchtbar." For
the verb = "graft," see Syll 531[34] (iii/A.D.) ἐὰν δὲ μὴ
ἐμφυτε[ύηι] τὰ φυτά, ἀποτεισάτω ἑκάστου δραχμήν: cf. [46]
συκᾶς [ἐμφυ]τ[εύειν.

ἐν.

It is impossible in our limits to deal exhaustively with the
extended uses in late Greek of this "maid-of-all-work"
among the prepositions. Most of these uses, so far as they
touch upon points of interpretation in the NT, are referred to
in Moulton's *Prolegomena* (see Index *s.v.*), and the evidence
there adduced from the Κοινή may be supplemented from
the Dissertations by Kuhring and Rossberg (for full titles
see "Abbreviations"). As however these Dissertations are
not readily accessible, it may be well with their aid to
illustrate the developments of ἐν here, as far as our space
permits.

We may begin with its encroachment in Hellenistic upon
the use of the simple cases. Thus P Par 63[xiii. 3] (B.C. 165)
ἐνεσχημένους ἔν τισιν ἀγνοήμασιν may be compared with the
Pauline Gal 5[1] μὴ πάλιν ζυγῷ δουλείας ἐνέχεσθε, and in
P Oxy III. 488[17] (ii/iii A.D.) παρέγραψεν . . πλέον τῆς
ὑποστάσεώς μου ἐν ὅλῃ ἀρούρῃ μιᾷ καὶ πρὸς κατ᾽ ἔτος,
"registered more than my actual substance by one whole
aroura and more each year," ἐν is added without materially
altering the sense. For this "usurping" ἐν Kuhring (p. 12)
also quotes P Oxy III. 487[17] (A.D. 156) τὰ ἐκκ (l. ἐκ) τῆς
χρίας ἐν οἷς ὀφλήματα ἀποδοῦναι, "*officia mea efficere*."
In *OGIS* 56[7] (B.C. 237) ἐν τῶι ἐν Κανώπωι ἱερῶι, the pre-

positional phrase represents subj. gen., and in P Petr II.
2 (3)[1] (B.C. 260) (= *ib.* III. 28 (*a*)[1]) εἰ ἔρρωσαι καὶ ἐν τοῖς
ἄ]λλοις ἀλύπως ἀπαλλάσσεις, it takes the place of the acc.
of respect, if the restoration is to be trusted. On ἐν used in
the LXX instead of an acc. after αἱρετίζω, εὐδοκῶ, etc., see
Thackeray *Gr.* i. p. 47.

The question to the oracle P Fay 137[3] (i/A.D. (= *Selections*, p. 69) χρημάτισόν μοι, ἦ μείνω ἐν Βακχιάδι:
"Answer me, Shall I remain in Bacchias?" may serve to
illustrate the ordinary *local* use of ἐν, within the limits of some
space, while the closely related idea of proximity is seen in
P Tebt I. 60[3] (B.C. 118) παραδεί σων) τῶν ἐν περιμέτρῳ τῆς
κώ(μης). Interesting confirmation of the RV rendering of
Lk 2[49] is afforded by P Oxy III. 523[3] (ii/A.D.) where a
certain Antonius invites a friend to dine with him ἐν τοῖς
Κλαυδ(ίου) Σαραπίω(νος), "in the house of Claudius
Serapion": cf. Rev L[xxxviii. 1] (iii/B.C.) ἐν τοῖς Ἀπολλωνίου
τοῦ διοικητοῦ, P Tebt I. 12[3] (B.C. 118) ἐν τοῖς Ἀμεννέως,
"in A.'s office," and *ib.* 27[27] (B.C. 113) ἐν τῶι Ὡρ[ου]
βασιλικοῦ γραμματέως.

For ἐν denoting *condition, state,* we may cite Polycrates'
letter to his father P Petr II. 11 (1)[8] (iii/B.C.) γράφε . .ἵνα
εἰδῶμεν ἐν οἷς εἶ, and such passages as P Par 63[175] (B.C. 164)
(= P Petr III. p. 34) ἕτερός τις ἐμ βαρυ[τέ]ραι κείμενος
ἐξουσίαι, "any other persons in high office." P Tebt I. 33[4]
(B.C. 112) (= *Selections*, p. 30) ἐν μίζονι ἀξιώματι κα[ὶ] τιμῆι
κείμενος, of a Roman senator, *ib.* 5[37] (B.C. 118) τὴν ἐν
ἀφέσει γῆν, [165] τὴν ἐν ἀρετῆι κειμένην βα(σιλικὴν) γῆν.
See also P Petr II. 39(*g*)[16] ἐὰν ἐν δυνατῶι ἦι. The preposition is used with the verb ἀνδραγαθέω to denote perseverance
in a certain course of action in BGU IV. 1205[14] (B.C. 28)
ἀνδραγάθι (= -ει) ἐν τῆι ἀριθμήσ[ι] καὶ ἐν [τ]ῆι εἰσαγωγῆι,
and similarly *ib.* 1206[13].

P Tebt I. 58[41] (B.C. 111) shows ἐν = "in the number
of"—ἐν οἷς εἰσιν οἱ διὰ τοῦ νομοῦ κω(μο)γρ(αμματεῖς): cf.
P Par 63[99] (B.C. 164) (= P Petr III. p. 26) ἐν τοῖς "συμ-
πᾶσιν ἀνθρώποις" καταριθμεῖσθαι κτλ., "in the expression
'all men' are included," etc., and P Petr II. 4 (6)[16] (B.C.
255-4) δινὸν γάρ ἐστιν ἐν ὄχλωι ἀτιμάζεσθαι, where the
meaning is "in the presence of"—"for it is a dreadful
thing to be insulted before a crowd." From this it is
a natural transition to a usage which helps with several
NT passages. Thus in P Tebt I. 5[227] (B.C. 118) we have
τὰς δὲ πράξεις τῶν ἐν αὐτοῖς, where the editors translate
"but the executions in cases which come before the collectors," and in support of this rendering compare *ib.* 27[9]
(B.C. 113) τὸ ἐν αὐτῶι ὀφειλόμενον πρὸς τὴν ἐπιγραφήν,
"the amount owing to the epigraphe in his department,"
ib. 72[330] (B.C. 114-3) ἃς (*sc.* ἀρούρας) ἐν Μαρρεῖ τοπογραμματεῖ, *ib.* 120[129] (B.C. 97 or 64): cf. Lk 6[2], 14[1],
perhaps Jude 1. All are cases where παρά c. dat. might
equally have been expected in a classical writer: cf. the
variant reading in Mt 21[25]. A good parallel to Ac 17[31] is
afforded by Syll 850[6] (B.C. 173-2) κριθέντω ἐν ἄνδροις τρίοις
οὓς συνείλοντο.

Another abnormal use of ἐν = "amounting to," as in Ac
7[14] (LXX), is seen in BGU III. 970[14] (ii/A.D.) προσηνέγκα-
μεν αὐτῷ προοῖκα ἐν δραχμαῖς ἐνακοσίαις—a passage
which also resembles, in its use with a numeral, the difficult
ἐν (*bis*) of Mk 4[8] (WH). [Cannot there be "at all
rates *up to*" thirty-fold?] Cf. also BGU IV. 1050[6] (marriage-

28

contract—time of Augustus) ἱμάτια γυναικεῖα ἐν ἀργυ(ρίου) δραχμαῖς ἑκατόν, P Oxy IV. 724⁷ (A.D. 155) ἐξ ὧν ἔσχες τὴν πρώτην δόσιν ἐν δραχμαῖς τεσσαράκοντα, ib. I. 56⁸ (A.D. 211) δανειζομένη . . . ἀργύριον ἔντοκον ἐν δραχμαῖς ἑξακισχειλίαις, and P Grenf II. 77⁶ (iii/iv A.D.) (=Selections, p. 120) το]ὺς μισθοὺς . . ὄντας ἐν δραχμαῖς τριακοσίαις τεσσαράκοντα. Similar are P Oxy IV. 708⁴ (A.D. 188) γόμου . . ἐν (πυροῦ)(ἀρτάβαις) ʼΒ, BGU I. 72¹¹ (A.D. 191) ἐξέκοψαν πλεῖστον τόπον ἐν ἀρούραις πέντε: with which may be compared Eph 2¹⁵ τὸν νόμον τῶν ἐντολῶν ἐν δόγμασιν, "consisting in." In P Lond 921⁹ (ii/iii A.D.) (=III. p. 134) γεγονέναι ἐν ἀμπέλῳ = "to be planted with vines."

A *predicative* use of ἐν is seen in P Hib I. 42¹⁰ (B.C. 262) δώσομεν Λευκίωι ἐν ὀφειλήματι, "as a debt," P Petr I. 12¹⁴ (cf. II. p. 22) ὅσα δὲ Ἀξιοθέα προσενήνεγκται ἐμ φερνῆι, "as dowry," and P Tebt I. 120¹²⁵ (B.C. 97 or 64) ὧν ἔχωι ἐν θέματι, "as a pledge."

The *instrumental* use of ἐν, as in Lk 22⁴⁹, 1 Cor 4²¹, is now rescued from the list of Hebraisms (cf. Deissmann *BS*, p. 120) by "its use in an original Greek document, free from all suspicion of Semitic influence," P Tebt I. 16¹⁴ (B.C. 114) ἐν μαχαίρῃ, "armed with a sword": see the editors' note where the following additional passages are cited, ib. 41⁵ (c. B.C. 119) Μαρρείους . . σὺν ἄλλοις πλείοσι ἐν μαχαίραις παρ[α]γινομένου, 45¹⁷ (B.C. 113), 46¹⁵ (B.C. 113), P Par 11⁴ (B.C. 157): add P Tebt I. 48¹⁹ (c. B.C. 113) Λύκος σὺν ἄλλοις ἐν ὅπλοις. See also *Proleg.* pp. 11 f., 61, and the Preface to the 3rd Edit. p. xvii. It should however be noted that Kuhring (p. 43 f.) thinks that ἐν in the above passages is sufficiently explained as ἐν of accompanying circumstances. A good ex. of *causal* ἐν is afforded by P Par 28¹³ (c. B.C. 160) where the Twins describe themselves as διαλυόμεναι ἐν τῷ λιμῷ as compared with ib. 27¹⁴ διαλυόμεναι τῷ λιμῷ, and ib. 26⁹ ὑπὸ τῆς λιμοῦ διαλυόμεναι in similar documents. On the other hand, *Syll* 891¹¹ (ii/A.D.) quoting the LXX Deut 28²² πατάξαι σε Κύριος ἐν ἀπορίᾳ drops the preposition, and cf. *C. and B.* ii. p. 609, No. 500 (i/B.C.) where φεισάμενον ἐν ἐπιδώσεσιν is followed by μὴ φεισάμενον ἀναλώμασιν. In *Exp T* xxviii. p. 322 f. Prof. H. A. A. Kennedy has collected a number of instances of this use of ἐν = "because of," "on account of," from the LXX and from the Pauline Epp., e.g. Ps 30 (31)¹¹ ἠσθένησεν ἐν πτωχίᾳ ἡ ἰσχύς μου, "my strength failed because of my wretchedness," Rom 1²⁴ ἐν ταῖς ἐπιθυμίαις τῶν καρδιῶν, "because of the lusts of their hearts," and 1 Cor 7¹⁴ ἡγίασται γὰρ ὁ ἀνὴρ ὁ ἄπιστος ἐν τῇ γυναικί, "for the unbelieving husband is sanctified on account of his wife." See also Schmid *Atticismus*, iv. p. 449.

We have seen already (s.v. εἰς) that εἰς and ἐν can be transposed in late Greek, as when ἐν follows a verb of motion in P Par 10³ (B.C. 145) ἀνακεχώρηκεν ἐν Ἀλεξανδρείᾳ: cf. the late gloss at Jn 5⁴, and for LXX instances see Thackeray *Gr.* i. p. 25. As paving the way for this usage we may note such a passage as *OGIS* 90¹³ (Rosetta stone—B.C. 196) τοὺς ἐν ταῖς φυλακαῖς ἀπηγμένους . . . ἀπέλυσε τῶν ἐνκεκλ[η]μένων, where the motion implied by the verb is accompanied by the thought of the rest following on that motion—the men were "led off" to prison and remained there until freed from the charges of which they had been convicted. See further Hatzidakis *Einl.* p. 210 f., and note that Thumb (*Neue Jahrb.* 1906, p. 253) commenting on

Heitmüller's proof (*Im Namen Jesu*, Göttingen 1903) that εἰς (τὸ) ὄνομα belonged, in various *nuances*, to Greek mercantile phraseology, while ἐν (τῷ) ὀνόματι was almost exclusively Jewish, though not foreign to the genius of Greek, observes that the promiscuity of εἰς and ἐν in Hellenistic explains the survival of the more literary archaizing ἐν by the side of the common εἰς.

The *temporal* use of ἐν to denote the period within which anything is done is naturally very common, e. g. *Syll* 177¹⁵ (B.C. 303) ἐ[ν] ἔτεσιν τρίσιν, P Eleph 20²⁷ (iii/B.C.) ἐν τοῖς καθήκουσιν χρόνοις, P Tebt II. 386²¹ (B.C. 12) ἐκτίσω ἐν ἡμέραις τριάκοντα, P Oxy II. 275⁴⁰ (A.D. 66) ἕκαστα ποιήσω ἐν τῷ ἐνιαυτῷ ἑνί, and P Tebt II. 591 (ii/iii A.D.) ἐγὼ γὰρ ἡ (l. εἰ) μὴ συνκομίσω τὸν χόρτον ἐν τρίσι ἡμέραις (cf. Jn 2²¹) οὐ δύναμε (l. -μαι) αὐτὰ καταλίψαι.

For ἐν in adverbial phrases, see P Eleph 10⁷ (B.C. 223-2) τῶν λοιπῶν ἐν ἑτοίμῳ ὄντων, P Hib I. 47³⁵ (B.C. 256) ἀπόστειλον . . ἐν τάχει (cf. Lk 18⁸, Rom 16²⁰, Rev 1⁴, 22⁶).

The characteristically Lukan usage of ἐν τῷ followed by an inf. can no longer be ranked as a pure Hebraism, but belongs rather to the category of "possible but unidiomatic" Greek (see *Proleg.* pp. 14, 215, 249), though it should be noted that as yet no parallel has been found for it with the sense "daring": see P Par 63⁹⁵ (B.C. 164) (= P Petr III. p. 26) τίς γὰρ οὕτως ἐστὶν ἀνάλητος (?) ἐν τῶι λογίζεσθαι: "for who is so utterly wanting in reason?" and P Oxy IV. 743³⁵ (B.C. 2) where it is = διὰ τό: ἐν τῷ δέ με περισπᾶσθαι οὐκ ἠδυνάσθην συντυχεῖν Ἀπολλω(νίῳ), "owing to my worries I was unable to meet A." (Edd.).

In his monograph *Die neutestamentliche Formel "in Christo Jesu"* (Marburg, 1892) Deissmann has conclusively shown the originality of Paul's use, though the idea of the mystic indwelling may rightly be traced to the Lord's own teaching, see SH on Rom 6¹¹. The Psenosiris letter, P Grenf II. 73³ (late iii/A.D.) (= Selections, p. 117), is addressed Ἀπόλλωνι . . ἀγαπητῷ ἀδελφῷ ἐν Κ(υρί)ῳ, and concludes with the prayer ²¹ f. ἐρρῶσθαί σε εὔχομαι ἐν Κ(υρί)ῳ Θ(ε)ῷ.

We may conclude with a few miscellaneous examples— P Petr I. 22 (1)⁴ τοῦ ἐν ταῖς προσόδοις, "who controls the revenues" (Ed.), P Lille I. 7⁷⁷ (iii/B.C.) ἃ ἐδεδώκειν ἐν φυ(λακῆι), "had given me to keep," P Hib I. 113¹⁵ (c. B.C. 260) ἐν Τοτόηι Πάσιτος λογευτῆι ὧι μηθὲν ὑπάρχει, "owed by Totoes son of Pasis, tax-collector, who has no property" (Edd.), P Par 66⁷¹ (iii/B.C.) λ[οι]πά, ἀφ' ὧν ἐν τοῖς γεωργο[ῖ]ς κτλ., a curious usage which Smyly (P Petr III. p. 344) understands as = "of this remainder (so much) is due from the cultivators," P Lond 1171⁴⁵ (B.C. 8) (= III. p. 179) ἀνθ' ὧν τῶν ἐπάνωι ἐν ὑπερδαπανήμασι, "under the head of deficits," and from the inscr. *Syll* 178¹¹ (iv/B.C.) καθάπερ καὶ Φίλιππος ἔδωκεν ἐμ πατρικοῖς καὶ αὐτοῖς καὶ ἐκγόνοις, where Dittenberger notes, "eodem iure ac si a patre hereditatem accepisset."

In MGr ἐν has been supplanted by εἰς, though it survives as a prefix in such disguised forms as μπαίνω, μπάζω, ντρέπομαι.

ἐναγκαλίζομαι.

IG XII. 7. 395²⁵ ὧν τέκ[ν]α ἐνηνκαλίσατο (cited by Herwerden *Lex. s.v.*).

ἔναντι.

That ἔναντι with the gen., as in the phrase ἔναντι τοῦ θεοῦ (Ac 8[21], can no longer be confined to bibl. Greek (Grimm) is proved by its occurrence in the translation of a Roman senator's "Consultum," *Syll* 300[52] (B.C. 170) περὶ τούτου τοῦ πράγ[ματο]ς ὕστερον ἔναντι Γαΐου Λοκρετίου βουλεύσασθαι ἔδοξεν: cf. also for imperial times P Oxy III. 495[5] (A.D. 181–9) ἔναντι Πέλα. Wackernagel *Hellenistica*, pp. 1 ff. shows that the word came into the Κοινή about B.C. 300 from Cretan, Delphian, or a like dialect, helped by the fact that the Attic ἐναντίον had this sense : see further *s.v.* ἀπέναντι.

ἐναντίος

is common in the adjuration εὐορκοῦντι μέν μοι εὖ εἴη, ἐπιορκοῦντι δὲ τὰ ἐναντία, "if I observe the oath may it be well with me, but if I swear falsely, the reverse." as e. g. P Oxy X. 1258[10 f.] (A.D. 45). The adj. is followed by dat., as in Ac 28[17], in PSI IV. 282[13] (A.D. 183) μηδὲ ποιῆσαι τ[ι] ἐναντίον τι τῇ αὐτῇ ὑπογραφῇ. For ἐκ τῶν ἐναντίων = "on the contrary," see P Par 63[49] (B.C. 165), P Grenf II. 36[13] (B.C. 95). Ὁ δι' ἐναντίας is found = "the opponent" in a lawsuit, as *Chrest.* I. 461[6] (beg. iii A.D.) δέομαί σου ἀκοῦσαί μο]υ πρὸς τὸν ἐξ ἐναντίας ἀ[ντίδικον, P Flor I. 58[15] (iii A.D.) πρὸς τοὺς δι' [ἐ]ναντίας, P Strass I. 41[8] (A.D. 250) ἔδει μὲν γὰρ τὴν δι' ἐναντίας . . . ἔτι μᾶλλον δ[ι]αγωνίσασθαι καὶ ἐκδικῆσαι τὰ τῆς παιδός. In P Ryl II. 144[15] (A.D. 38) we have ὃς δὲ ἐκ τοῦ ἐναντίου ἄλογον ἀηδίαν μοι ἐπιχειρήσας παρεχρήσατό μοι πολλὰ καὶ ἄσχημα, "whereupon he opposing me made a brutal and odious attack upon me and subjected me to much shameful mishandling" (Edd.). For ἐναντίον "in the presence of," cf. P Eleph 1[7] (B.C. 311–0) (= *Selections*, p. 3) ἐπιδειξάτω δὲ Ἡ. ὅτι ἂν ἐγκαλῆι Δ. ἐναντίον ἀνδρῶν τριῶν, "and let H. prove his charge against D. in the presence of three men," P Hib I. 89[ii] (B.C. 239) ἐναντί[ον τῶν ὑπογε]γραμμένων μαρτύρων, P Lille I. 29[i 31] (iii/B.C.) λέγων τὸ ἀδίκημα τῶι κυρίωι ἐναντίον μὴ ἔλασσον ἢ δύο μαρτύρων, *ib.*[ii. 31] ἐναντί[ον τῶν νομο]φυλάκων. In this sense the word is peculiar to the Lukan writings in the NT. MGr ξάγναντος (= ἐξ ἐναντίας), "against," "opposite."

ἐνάρχομαι.

The ritual sense, which underlies this word in classical Greek, may perhaps still be latent in its two NT occurrences Gal 3[3], Phil 1[6] (cf. 2 Cor 8[6] B), but how completely the simple sense "begin" prevailed in late Greek may be seen from P Tebt I. 24[34] (B.C. 117) διαλαμβάνοντες εἰς ἀπραξίαν ἡμᾶς περιστήσειν ὁπότε δὴ ἐνάρξασθαι, ἀνεχώρησαν κτλ., "supposing that they would bring me to a standstill at the commencement, they retired etc." (Edd.): cf.[36] ἐναρχομένου τ[οῦ Με]χείρ, "at the beginning of Mecheir." See also Vett. Val. p. 212[26] ἐὰν δέ πως καὶ ἕτερόν τινα ἐναρξάμενον πράγματος εὕρῃς κτλ.

ἔνατος

for ἔννατος is read by WH in all the occurrences of this word in the NT : cf. P Grenf II. 24[1] (B.C. 105) ἔτους ιβ̄ τοῦ καὶ ἐνάτου Τῦβι, *Ostr* 714[4] (Ptol.) τοῦ ἐνάτου ἔτους, BGU I. 174[2 f.] (A.D. 7) ἐνάτου καὶ εἰκοστοῦ (*bis*), *Preisigke* 1925[2]

(A.D. 77) ἐνάτου (ἔτους) Οὐεσπασιανοῦ, but *ib.* 2104[1] (Ptol.) μηνὸς Δαισίου ἐννάτῃ, and the late PSI IV. 283[4] (A.D. 550) ἔτους ἐννάτου.

ἐνδεής.

PSI IV. 418[11] (iii B.C.) ὅπως μὴ ἐνδεεῖς ὦμεν καὶ ἐλαιδίου, P Tebt I. 52[12] (c. B.C. 114) ἐνδεὴς οὖσα τῶν ἀναγ[καίων, "being in want of the necessaries (of life)," P Oxy II. 281[20] (complaint against a husband—A.D. 20–50) τῶν ἀναγκαίων ἐνδεῆ καθιστάς: cf. P Magd 13[5] (B.C. 217) ἐνδεεῖς δὲ γενόμενοι εἰς τὴν ταφὴν τοῦ Φιλίππου (δραχμὰς) κε̄ ἐδώκαμεν τὰ κατάφρακτα κτλ., "being in want of 25 drachmas for the funeral of Philip we have given his cuirass etc." For ἔνδεια (as in LXX) cf. P Par 62[b. 11] (ii. B.C.) τὰς ἐνδείας πραχθ[ήσεσθαι . . ., and for ἐνδέημα P Ryl II. 214[23] (ii/A.D.) τὰς ἀπὸ μερισμοῦ ἐνδημάτος τελωνικῶν, "the amount of the assessment of the deficiency of farmed taxes" (Edd.), so[43,63], P Oxy I. 71[i. 15] (A.D. 303) ἀπὸ λόγου ἐνδημάτων, "on account of the deficit." The verb is found *IG* XII. 7, 409[9] ὥστε μ]ηδὲν ἐν μηδενὶ τῇ πατρίδι ἐνδεδεηκέ[ναι.

ἐνδείκνυμι.

P Magd 3[10] (B.C. 221) ἐὰν ἐνδειξώμεθα τὰ διὰ τῆς ἐντεύξεως ὄντα ἀληθῆ, "if we prove that what we set forth in the petition is true," *ib.* 28[8] (B.C. 217) ἐὰν ἐνδείξωμαι αὐτοὺς κατακεκλυκότας μου τὸν σπόρον, "if I prove that they have flooded my sown field." With the construction of ἐ. in 2 Tim 4[14] πολλά μοι κακὰ ἐνεδείξατο (cf. Gen 50[15, 17]) cf. P Oxy III. 494[9] (A.D. 156) εὐνοούσῃ μοι καὶ πᾶσαν πίστιν μοι ἐνδεικνυμένῃ (a passage which also helps to confirm the meaning of "faithfulness" for πίστις in such passages as Mt 23[23], Gal 5[22]): see also *Syll* 211[7] (iii B.C. ?) διατε[λ]εῖ εἰς τὸν δῆμον τὸν Ἐρυθραίων [π]ᾶσαν προθυμίαν ἐνδεικνύμενο[ς (cf. Heb 6[11]), and P Oxy IV. 705[72] (A.D. 200–2). For the act. which is not found in the NT, see P Grenf II. 70[8] (A.D. 200) εὐνοίας ἕνεκεν [κ]αὶ ἧς ἐνέ[δειξᾱ]ς εἰς ἐμ[έ. The subst. ἐνδείκτης = "informer," "complainant," occurs P Par 45[8] (B.C. 153) διὰ τὸν ἐφελκόμενόν σοι ἐνδίκτην, *ib.*[7] εὐλαβοῦμαι τὸν ἐνδίκτην τὰ πλεῖστα.

ἔνδειξις.

Cagnat IV. 40[14] (Lesbian dialect) κατ' αὐτῶν καὶ ἐνδείξιος κατ̄τὰ διατεταγμένα.

ἕνδεκα.

Preisigke 1926 (an ostracon-receipt—A.D. 79) διέγραψ(εν) Ἑρμογ(ένης). Βάσσου ὑπ(ὲρ) λαογραφίας ια ἔτους Οὐεσπασιανοῦ τοῦ κυρίου κτλ.: the numeral is *written* in earlier ostraca of this series. The semi-literary P Eud 15[7] (before B.C. 167) shows however ἕνδεκα, and also a tessera in the Louvre, Revillout *Mélanges* 4, 7, 9 (ii/B.C.): see Mayser *Gr.* p. 316. MGr ἕντεκα.

ἑνδέκατος.

P Leid D[i. 3] (B.C. 162) ἔτος τοῦτο ἑνδέκατον, P Tebt I. 104[7] (B.C. 92) μηνὸς Ξανδικ[ο]ῦ ἑνδεκάτῃ Μ[εχεὶ]ρ ἑνδεκάτῃ, "the eleventh of the month Xandicus which is the eleventh of Mecheir." *Preisigke* 19[10] (A.D. 25) ὅρᾳ ἑνδεκάτῃ τῆς ἡμέρας.

ἐνδέχομαι.

For the impersonal use in Lk 13³³ cf. P Petr II. 45 ⁱⁱⁱ ˣ (B.C. 246) ὡς ἐνδέχεται, "as far as it is possible," and similarly P Giss I. 48⁶ (A.D. 202–3); also P Oxy II. 237 ᵛⁱⁱⁱ·³¹ (A.D. 186) ὅπερ οὐ καλῶς ἐνδέχεται εἰ μὴ ἄνωθεν γένοιτο ἀντίγραφα, "this cannot be done adequately unless copies are made from the beginning" (Edd.). Cf. also such a phrase as ὡς ἐνδεχομένως in P Petr II. 15 (3)⁴ (B.C. 241–39). [The meaning of the adv. in Aristeas 41 πρὸς ταύτην τὴν ἐπιστολὴν ἀντέγραψεν ἐνδεχομένως ὁ Ἐλεάζαρος ταῦτα is not clear. Thackeray translates "to this letter E. replied appropriately as follows"; Wendland suggests "so far as he could write Greek," the writer excusing the imperfect use of this language by a Jew of Palestine.] Other examples of the verb are P Par 63⁴¹ (B.C. 165) (= P Petr III. p. 20) μετὰ τῆς ἐνδεχομένης προσοχῆς, "with fitting care" (Mahaffy), PSI III. 168⁴⁰ (B.C. 118) τὴν ἐνδεχομένην ἔμσκεψιν (l. ἐν-), P Flor II. 173⁹ (A.D. 256) καὶ εἴ τι ἄλλο ἐνδέχεται, "if anything else suits him," and from the inscrr. *Michel* 482⁷ (iii/B.C.) τὴν ἐ[ν]δεχομένην ἐπιμέλειαν ἐποιήσα[ντο κατὰ] τοὺς νόμους, *Syll* 929⁵³ (ii/B.C.) ὅπερ ἐπὶ τῆς ἱερᾶς χώρας οὐκ ἦν ἐνδεχόμενον.

ἐνδημέω.

For the antithesis with ἀποδημέω see the exx. cited under that word. Cf. further P Petr III. 53 (*q*)⁵ (iii/B.C.) ἐνεδήμει (in an imperfect context), P Oxy I. 59¹⁵ (A.D. 211) βασιλικὸν γραμματέα μὴ ἐνδημεῖν, and from the inscrr. *Syll* 925⁶ (B.C. 207) καὶ τούτοι συνδιεφύλαξαν τό τε ἱερὸν καὶ τὰν πόλιν καλῶς καὶ ἀσφαλῶς καὶ ἐνεδάμησαν εὐτάκτως, and similarly ¹⁷, also *ib.* 790⁸⁰ (i/B.C.) μηθενὶ ἐξεῖναι τῶν π[ολιτῶν μηδὲ τῶν παρ]οικούντων μηδὲ τῶν ἐνδημούντων ξείνω[ν δένδρα κόπτειν ἐν τῶ]ι διασαφουμένωι τόπωι. For the subst. see *OGIS* 764⁸⁵ (ii/B.C.) ποιησα]μένων τὴν ἐνδημίαν, and on the derivation of ἔνδημος from ἐν δήμῳ (ὤν), ἐν being used distributively, see *Proleg.* p. 105.

ἐνδιδύσκω.

The range of this somewhat rare verb is extended by the dialect inscr. *Syll* 857¹³ (ii/B.C.) ἐνδυδισκόμενος, clearly a hewer's error for ἐνδιδυσκόμενος : see *LAE* p. 78.

ἔνδικος.

The only occurrences we can quote of this adj. (Rom 3⁸, Heb 2²) are from the laws of Gortyna (v/B.C.) edited in *Michel* 1333, e.g. ⁱⁱⁱ·²³ αἰ δέ τι τὸν τέκνον πέροι, ἔνδικον ἔμεν.

ἐνδό(-ώ-)μησις.

The spelling ἐνδώμησις which WH adopt in Rev 21¹⁸ is confirmed by *Syll* 583³¹ (i/A.D. ?) τὴν ἐνδώμησιν τοῦ τεμένους, where the editor pronounces this orthography "nova." The form ἐνδόμησις occurs in Jos. *Antt.* xv. 335 = a "mole" or "breakwater." Neither of the above reff. supports Souter's suggestion (*Lex. s.v.*) that the word is probably = "roofing" (from δῶμα, "roof") rather than "building."

ἐνδοξάζω.

For this verb, found in the NT only in 2 Th 1¹⁰·¹², but common in the LXX (e.g. Exod 14⁴, Ps 88 (89)⁸), cf. P Leid

Wˣⁱ ⁷ (ii/iii A.D.), an invocation to the Sun—οὗ ἡ δόξα . . ὅτι διά σ' (l. σε) ἐνεδοξάσθη (l. – θην).

ἔνδοξος.

An interesting example of this adj. is found in a letter from the Emperor Vespasian confirming certain privileges bestowed on an athletic club by the Emperor Claudius, P Lond 1178³⁴ (A.D. 194) (= III. p. 216) εἰδ]ὡς ὑμῶν τῶν ἀθλητῶν τὸ ἔνδοξον καὶ φιλότειμον πάντα ὅσα [καὶ] ὁ Κλαύδιος αἰτησαμένοις ὑμεῖν συνεχώρησε καὶ αὐτὸς φυλάττειν [π]ροαιρούμαι. In P Leid Wˣⁱᵛ·⁹ (ii/iii A.D.) we have an invocation which runs—βασιλεῦ βασιλέων . . . ἔνδοξο (l. – ε) ἐνδοξοτάτων, and in the curious mantic text P Ryl I. 28¹⁰⁸ (iv/A.D.) the twitching of the right leg is said to portend that the man will "become illustrious"—γενέσθαι ἔνδοξον. In P Oxy VI. 943⁴ (vi/A.D.) an agreement is reached τῷ ἐνδόξῳ οἴκῳ regarding the payment of certain dues. For the adverb we may cite *OGIS* 513¹¹ (iii/A.D.) where a priestess is described— ἱερασαμένην ἐνδόξως καὶ μεγαλοπρεπῶς : cf. *Kaibel* 358³ ζήσασα ἐνδόξως.

ἔνδυμα.

In P Fay 12²⁰ (c. B.C. 103) a man who is stripped of his ἱμάτιον and sent forth γυμνός, is supplied by his friends μετ' ἐνδύματος, evidently an outer cloak. Cf. *Syll* 813⁷ τὰ ὑπ' ἐμοῦ καταλιφθέντα ἱμάτια καὶ ἔνδυμα, and *ib.* 877³ (v/B.C.), where it is laid down that the dead are to be buried ἐν ἐμ[ατ]ίο[ις τρι]σὶ λευκοῖς, στρώματι καὶ ἐνδύματι [καὶ ἐ]πιβλέματι. In the new fragment of a lost Gospel, P Oxy IV. 655¹¹ ᶠ, to the question "Having one garment (ἐν ἔχοντ[ες ἔ]νδυμα) what do ye (lack ?)?" the answer is given, αὐτὸ]ς δ]ώσει ὑμῖν τὸ ἔνδυμα ὑμῶν. With *Menandrea* p. 80²⁶⁹ ἐνδύμαθ' οἷα, —"what dresses!" of a woman's finery, cf. the "wedding garment" of Mt 22¹¹ ᶠ. The word survives in literary MGr. The simple δύμα, which is unknown to the lexicons, is found in P Oxy VI. 929⁸ (ii/iii A.D.).

ἐνδυναμόω.

The adj. ἐνδύναμος is found in Byz. Greek : see Sophocles *Lex. s.v.*

ἐνδύνω.

P Lond 121²⁷¹ (magic—iii/A.D.) (= I. p. 93) ἔ]νδυνε. See further *s.v.* ἐνδύω.

ἔνδυσις.

In Aristeas 96 amazement is caused by the appearance of the high priest Eleazar—διὰ τὴν ἔνδυσιν ὧν φορεῖ χιτῶνος καὶ τῶν περὶ αὐτὸν λίθων, "by the wearing of the coat wherewith he is clad and the precious stones about his person" (Thackeray). Cf. MGr ντύσιμο, "dressing."

ἐνδύω.

P Oxy II. 285¹¹ (c. A.D. 50) πολλῇ βίᾳ χρώμενος ἀφήρπασεν ὃν ἤμην ἐνδεδυμένο (l. – ἐνος) χιτῶνα λεινοῦν, P Giss I. 77⁸ τότε ἔγνων, ὅτι ἔπεμ[ψ]άς μοι τὸν κιθῶναν. λείαν δέ σοι εὐχαριστ[ή]σω π[α]ρὰ πᾶσι τοῖς θεοῖς, ὅτι σύ με ἐνδέδυκ[ας] με (om.). See also the interesting v/A.D. magic spell in which a goddess is transformed into an old woman, and then, when her service is accomplished—**πάλιν θεὸς ἐνδεδύ[σετ]ε** (*l.* **ἐνδύσεται**) **τὸ ἑαυτῆς κάλλος ὅ[περ] ἐξεδύσατο**, "the god will again clothe her with her own beauty, which she has doffed" (P Lond 125 *verso*[19] = I. p. 124). *Kaibel* 610[5] **ἐνδεδύμην δὲ τὸ σῶ[μ' ἐσθήμα]σι χρώμασι θείοις.** Cf. MGr **ντύνω,** "put on," **ντύνομαι,** "dress."

ἐνέδρα.

The derived meaning of "treachery," "fraud," is illustrated by P Oxy I. 62[10] (iii/A.D.) **ἵνα μὴ ἐκ τῆς σῆς ἀμελείας ἐνέδρα περὶ τὴν ἐμβολὴν γένηται,** "in order that there may be no fraud in the lading through any neglect of yours" (Edd.): cf. *ib.* XII. 1428[5] (iv/A.D.) **ὑπ]ὲρ τοῦ τοίνυν μὴ ἐνέδραν ἐπακολουθῆσαι,** "so as to prevent any deception from ensuing," *ib.* 1455[12] (A.D. 275) **εἰς τὸ μηδεμί[α]ν ἐνέδρ[αν] ἐπακολ[ουθε]ῖ]ν.** For the form **ἐνεδρεία** cf. the endorsement of a petition to the logistes—**ἐνεδρείας γεγενημένης,** "concerning a case of fraud" (P Oxy VI. 900[19] —A.D. 322).

ἐνεδρεύω.

The NT usage of this Lukan verb is well illustrated by P Rein 7[26] (B.C. 141?) **δέομαι οὖν ὑμῶν τῶν μεγίστων θεῶν μή με ὑπερίδ[ε]ιν ἐνεδρευόμεν[ο]ν ὑπὸ ἀνθρώπου [ἀγ]νώμονος,** "I beseech you, therefore, most high gods, not to show yourselves indifferent to the trap laid for me by this unfeeling man," and P Oxy VI. 898[17] (A.D. 123) where a minor complains that his mother, in her capacity as guardian, **ἐνήδρευσεν,** "laid a trap" against him, by gaining possession of a certain deed : cf. *ib.* 938[2] (iii/iv A.D.) **οὐκ ἀκόλουθον πρᾶγμα ἐποίησας ἐνεδρεύσας τὰς τροφὰς τῶν κτηνῶν τῆς Σεναώ,** "it was an unfitting act of yours to intercept the fodder of the oxen at Senao" (Edd.), P Giss I. 105[14] (v A.D.) **ἵνα μὴ ἐν** (om.) **ἐνεδρε[ύ]σῃς τὴν διάπρασιν,** "that you may not place difficulties in the way of the sale," and from the inscr. *Syll* 324[19] (i/B.C.) **ἐνεδρεύσαντες δὲ αὐτὸν νύκτωρ ἐδο[λοφ]όνη[σαν.** For the meaning "defraud," see P Oxy II. 237[viii. 36] (A.D. 186) cited *s.v.* **ἄγνοια,** *ib.* III. 484[10] (A.D. 138) **ὡς ἐνεδρεύσαντι Δ..** "with defrauding D.", and P Ryl II. 239[16] (mid. iii/A.D.) **πέμψο[ν] δὲ πάντως αὐ[τῶν] τὸ σύμβολον . . . πολλάκις Σ. . . [ἐ]νέδρευσεν ἡμᾶς,** "by all means send the receipt ; S. has often defrauded us" (Edd.).

ἔνεδρον

is found in the TR of Ac 23[16] = "treacherous ambush," as *ter* in the LXX (cf. Thackeray *Gr.* i. p. 156 f.). For the more general sense of "fraud," see P Oxy VI. 892[11] (A.D. 338) **εἰς τὸ μηδὲν ἔνεδρον γενέσθαι περὶ τὸ δημόσιον λουτρόν,** "that there may be no fraud in connexion with the public bath."

ἐνειλέω.

For the *bad* sense in which this forcible NT **ἅπ. εἰρ.** (Mk 15[46]) is generally used, see Abbott as cited *s.v.* **ἐντυλίσσω**: cf. P Tebt I. 24[62] (B.C. 117) **ἐνίων μὲν αὐτοὺς ἐνειληκότων οἰκονομ[ίαις κτλ,** "some have wormed themselves into the positions of oeconomus," etc., and P Ryl II. 144[18] (A.D. 38) **ἐνειλούμενός μοι,** of a violent struggle. On the other hand, the verb is colourless in P Oxy VIII. 1153[23] (i/A.D.) **τῆς**

γινομέ(νης) συνθέσεως τὸ πρόσχρωμον ἐνείλικται τῇδε τῇ ἐπιστολῇ, "a pattern of the colour of the dress that is being made is enclosed in this letter" (Ed.).

ἔνειμι.

The interpretation of Lk 11[41] **πλὴν τὰ ἐνόντα δότε ἐλεημοσύνην,** "the contents of your cup and platter give in alms," may be supported by P Tebt II. 414[20] (ii/A.D.) **τὸ σφυρίδιν μετὰ τῶν ἐνόντων κάτω,** "the little basket with its contents at the bottom": cf. P Magd 13[7] (B.C. 217) **τὴν ἐφαπτίδα, σὺν τῇ σακκοπήραι ἐν ἧι ἐνῆν,** "the mantle, with the bag which contained it." P Oxy II. 242[16] (A.D. 77) **σὺν τοῖς ἐνοῦσι φορτίοις,** "with the fixtures they contain," *ib.* III. 506[7] (A.D. 143) **σὺν τ]οῖς ἐνοῦσι πᾶσι,** "with all their contents," *ib.* VI. 912[12] (A.D. 235) **τὸ ἐνὸν κατάγειον,** "the cellar within it" (*sc.* a house). See also P Oxy II. 268[16] (A.D. 58) **ἐν δὲ τοῖς προκειμένοις οὐκ ἔνεστι σωματ(ισμός),** "in the above agreement there is no **σωματισμός**" (a word of uncertain meaning), and PSI III. 184[6] (A.D. 292 **καύματος ἐνόντος,** where the context leads us to think of something in the nature of spontaneous combustion. See also *s.v.* **ἔνι.**

ἕνεκα, ἕνεκεν, εἵνεκεν.

For **ἕνεκα** which is found only *quater* in the NT (Mt 19[5], Lk 6[22], Ac 19[32], 26[21]), cf. P Lond 42[14] (B.C. 168) (= I. p. 30, *Selections,* p. 10) **ἕ]νεκα τοῦ ἐκ τοῦ το[ιού]του καιροῦ ἐμαυτή[ν] τε καὶ τὸ παιδ[ίον σ]ου διακεκυβερνηκυῖα,** P Oxy X. 1293[16 f.] (A.D. 117–38) **τοῦτο οὐχ ἕνεκα ἡμῶν ποιῶ ἀλλὰ ἕνεκα τῶν καμηλειτῶν,** *ib.* III. 533[25] (ii/iii A.D.) **ἕνεκα τῆς προσόδου,** "about the revenue." The form **ἕνεκεν,** which prevails from iii/B.C. onwards, and is probably Ionic in origin (cf. Thumb *Hellen.* p. 57), may be illustrated from P Petr III. 36(*a*) *verso*[27] (iii/B.C.) **τῆς Διοφάνου[ς οὖν ἀ]κριβείας ἕνεκεν ἀπήχθην,** P Flor II. 158[3] (iii/A.D.) **ἕνεκεν [ἀνα]γκαίας χρείας,** *ib.* 163[5] (iii/A.D.) **ἕνεκεν ὑμῶν φρόντισον,** P Meyer 23[6] (end iv/A.D.) **ἕνεκεν ἀργυρίου,** and before a consonant in the late P Oxy VI. 902[12] (*c.* A.D. 465) **εἰς τελείαν γὰρ ἀνατροπὴν . . . περιέστην ἕνεκεν τοῦ προειρημένου πολιτευομένου,** "I have been reduced to complete ruin through the aforesaid member of the council" (Edd.), *ib.* 943[3] (vi/A.D.) **ἀπελθεῖν εἰς δίαιταν ἕνεκεν τοῦ λουτροῦ,** "to come to arbitration with respect to the bath." In all these instances **ἕνεκεν** precedes the subst., as generally in the NT: cf. Blass-Debrunner *Gr.* § 216. 1. On a corresponding usage in the Attic inscrr. see Meisterhans *Gr.* p. 217 where it is stated that in ii/B.C. the relation of **ἕνεκα : ἕνεκεν = 4 : 22 :** cf. also Thieme p. 8, and Rouffiac *Recherches,* p. 22. For the forms **οὕνεκα, –εν,** see P Petr II. 19 (1*a*)[2] **οὕνεκα τοῦ θεοῦ καὶ τοῦ καλῶς ἔχοντος,** "in the name of God and of fair play" (Ed.), P Hib I. 170 (B.C. 247) **τούτου γὰρ οὕνεκεν πρὸ πολλοῦ σοι γράφω,** and for **εἵνεκεν,** as in Lk 4[18], Ac 28[20], cf. *Preisigke* 1568 (time of Euergetes II., B.C. 145–116) **εὐνοίας εἵνεκεν τῆς πρὸς αὐτούς,** P Giss I. 40[ii. 21] (A.D. 212–5) **κατάγειν θυσίας εἵνεκεν ταύρους καὶ ἄλλα τινὰ ἐνψ[υ]χα :** the form **εἵνεκα** occurs in an epigram regarding Homer's birthplace, *Ostr* 1148[6] (ii/B.C.)—

Εἵνεκ' ἐμῆς δόξης φ[ασὶ] τεκεῖν με πόλεις.

ἐνενήκοντα.

For the form see WH *Notes*[2] p. 155, and cf. PSI IV. 432[3] (iii/B.C.) **ἀρούρας ἐνενήκοντα,** *Ostr* 1508[5] (B.C. 144–3), 1511[4 ff.]

(B.C. 143–2) *al.* See also *Preisigke* 3534 ἐβίωσεν ἐτὸν ἐνήκοντα πλείου ἔλατον. MGr ἐνενήντα.

ἐνεός.

Brugmann discusses this word in V. Thomsen *Festschrift* (1912) p. 1 ff.

ἐνέργεια.

With the limitation of this word in the NT to superhuman activity (see Milligan *Thess.* p. 104), cf. *OGIS* 262⁴ (iii/A.D.) προσενεχθέντος μοι περὶ τῆς ἐνεργείας θεοῦ Διὸς Βαιτοκαίκης: also Aristeas 266 θεοῦ δὲ ἐνεργείᾳ κατευθύνεται πειθώ, and for demonic influence (as in 2 Thess 2⁹) Reitzenstein *Poimandres*, p. 352²³ δαίμονος γὰρ οὐσία ἐνέργεια. The generally strong sense of the word comes out in a fragmentary letter from Cronion, a προφήτης, P Tebt II. 616 (ii/A.D.) ἐκ π[άσης ?] ἐνεργίας καὶ σπουδῆς καὶ φιλείας.

ἐνεργέω

seems always to have the idea of *effective* working: see *s.v.* ἐνέργεια, and cf. Robinson *Eph.* p. 241 ff. The verb has begun in later Greek to be followed by a direct obj. in the acc. (cf. *Proleg.* p. 65), as in P Oxy XII. 1567 (iv/A.D.) according to the editors' alternative reading—εἰ Θαεὶς εὖρεν τοῦτο τὸ τετράποδων (*l.*—δον), ἐνεργήτω (*l.*—είτω) τοῦτό μοι ἔξω. For the intrans. use see P Giss I. 78⁴ (ii/A.D.) καλῶς δὲ ποιήσεις καὶ περὶ τὰ λοιπὰ ἐνεργήσασα, Vett. Val. p. 226² ἐνεργήσει πρὸς τὸ ἀγαθὸν ἢ φαῦλον: cf. Gal 2⁸, where, however, the trans. of Πέτρῳ is uncertain, either "for Peter" (RV), or perhaps better "by Peter" (Hort *Christian Ecclesia*, p. 85). On the possibility that in 1 Th 2¹³ ἐνεργεῖται is pass. = "is set in operation," see Milligan *Thess. ad l.*, and for a similar usage of ἐνεργουμένη in Jas 5¹⁶ see *Proleg.* p. 156, *ExpT* xxvi. p. 381 ff. From the inscrr. we may cite *Syll* 540¹⁴ (B.C. 175–1) ἐνεργῶν τεχνίταις ἱκανοῖς κατὰ τὴν τέχνην, and ¹⁰⁸ ποιῶν ὀρθὰ πάντα πρὸς κανόνα διηνεκῆ μὴ ἐλάττω τοῦ ἐνεργουμένου λίθου.

ἐνέργημα.

Vett. Val. p. 264¹³ ἀγαθὸς πρὸς τοὺς ζωτικοὺς χρόνους καὶ πρὸς τὰ τῆς ψυχῆς ἐνεργήματα.

ἐνεργής.

This adj. in the form ἐνεργός is applied to a mill "in working order"—μυλαῖον ἐνεργόν—in P Ryl II. 167¹⁰ (A.D. 39), cf. *ib.* 321⁵ (ii/A.D.), BGU IV. 1067⁴ (A.D. 101–2), and P Oxy XII. 1401⁶ (A.D. 222). In P Oxy I. 84¹⁴ (A.D. 316) it is used of "wrought" iron—σιδή[ρο]υ ἐνεργοῦ, and in *Syll* 929⁷² (ii/B.C.) of "tilled" land—ὑπάρχουσαν τὴν διαμφισβητουμένην χώραν ἐνεργόν. In PSI IV. 341⁵ (B.C. 256–5 the reference is to persons—ἵνα οὖν ἐνεργοὶ ὦμεν: cf. *ib.* 407⁹ (iii/B.C.). For the NT form ἐνεργής, cf. Vett. Val. p. 276¹¹ ἐν τούτοις γὰρ τὰ ἀποτελέσματα ἐνεργῆ τὴν δύναμιν κέκτηνται, and the new literary text P Oxy VIII. 1088⁵⁶ (early i/A.D.), where a medical receipt is described as ἐνεργὲς ἱκανῶς, "tolerably strong."

ἐνέχω.

Numerous instances of this verb in the passive with the simple dative, as in Gal 5¹ (cf. 2 Thess 1⁶ B) are forthcoming, e.g. P Tebt I. 5⁵ (B.C. 118), an amnesty granted by Euergetes II. and the two Cleopatras, the "sister" and the "wife," to all their subjects π]λὴν τ[ῶν φόν]ους (*l.*—οις) ἑκουσίοις καὶ ἱεροσυλίαις ἐνεχομ[ένων, "except to persons guilty of wilful murder or sacrilege," BGU IV. 1051³⁴ (time of Augustus) χορὶς (*l.* χωρὶς) τοῦ τὸν παραπαίνοντα (*l.* παραβαίνοντα) ἐνέχισθαι τῷ ὡρισμίνῳ προστίμῳ, "apart from the transgressor's being involved in the appointed penalty," P Oxy II. 237 viii. 18 (A.D. 186) τοῖς τεταγμένοις ἐπιτίμοις ἐνεχόμενος, "subject to the legal penalties," P Giss I. 48¹⁴ (A.D. 202–3) ἐπὶ τῷ μὴ ἐνέχεσθαι ἐπιθέμασι προτέρων ἐτῶν. Cf. also *Syll* 154²⁶ (end of iv/B.C.) ἐνεχέσθων τῶι ψηφί[σ]ματι. For *ἐ.* construed with ἐν, see P Par 63 xiii. 5 (ii/B.C.) ἐνεσχημένους ἐν τισιν ἀγνοήμασιν ἢ ἁμαρτήμασιν. On Mk 6¹⁹, Lk 11⁵³, see Field *Notes*, pp. 28 f., 64, and note that the Sahidic translates respectively "was angry with," and "to provoke him": cf. class. ἐπέχω = "attack."

ἐνθάδε.

P Oxy I. 37 i. 9 (A.D. 49) (= *Selections*, p. 49) ἐγένετο ἐνθάδε ἡ τροφεῖτις εἰς υἱὸν τοῦ Πεσούριος, *ib.* VIII. 1154¹⁰ (late i/A.D.) αὐτόπτης γὰρ εἰμι τῶν τόπων καὶ οὐκ εἰμὶ ξέν[ο]ς τῶν ἐνθάδε, "for I am personally acquainted with these places and am not a stranger here" (Ed.), *ib.* X. 1296⁵ (iii/A.D.) τὸ προσκύνημά σου ποιῶ καθ' ἑκάστην ἡμέραν παρὰ τοῖς ἐνθάδε θεοῖς, "before the gods of this place," and so often, P Ryl II. 234¹⁷ (ii/A.D.) εἰ βούλει παραμεῖναί με ἐνθάδε μετὰ τῶν ἀνθρώπων, *ib.* 244¹¹ (iii/A.D.) τὰ σωμάτια πολλοῦ ἐστιν ἐνθά[δ]ε καὶ οὐ συμφέρει ἀγοράσαι, "slaves are very dear here and it is inexpedient to buy." In PSI III. 177⁷ ff. (ii/iii A.D.) *ἐ.* is interchanged with ὧδε—δ[έδια] μὴ ἀποθάνῃ σου μὴ ὄν[τος ἐν]θάδε. μάθε δὲ ὅτι, ἐὰν ἀ[ποθάνῃ] σου μὴ ὄντος ὧδε κτλ. For ἐ. = "hither," as in Jn 4¹⁵ f., Ac 25¹⁷, see P Oxy VI. 967 (ii/A.D.) φασὶ τὸν κράτιστον ἡγεμόνα ἐλεύσεσθαι ἐνθάδε περὶ τὴν τριακάδα, ὅ ἵν' εἰδῇς γράφω σοι, and the early Christian letter P Grenf II. 73³ (late iii/A.D.) (= *Selections*, p. 118) οἱ νεκροτάφοι ἐνηνόχασιν ἐνθάδε εἰς τὸ ἔγω (*l.* ἔσω) τὴν Πολιτικήν. Contrast Preisigke 1810 Παρθ]ενίων . . . ἴκετο ἔνθα. For the meaning "at this point" cf. P Ryl II. 215⁴⁷ (ii/A.D.) where after a list of official accounts we find—καὶ ἐνθάδε κατ' ἀκολουθίαν τοῦ προτέρου ἔτ[ου]ς ἀναλαμβάνεται κτλ., "here are introduced according to the precedent of the previous year" certain additional sums; cf. P Oxy XII. 1434⁸ (A.D. 107–8).

ἐνθυμέομαι.

For this verb, which is common in the LXX, but in the NT is confined to Mt 1²⁰, 9⁴, see PSI IV. 436⁹ (B.C. 248–7) ἐνθυμηθεὶς ἵνα μηθείς [με] . . . ἀδικῆι, P Tebt I. 27⁷⁷ (B.C. 113) καθόλου δ' ἐνθυμηθεὶς ἡλίκην συμβάλλεται ἡ περὶ τὰ ὑποδεικνύμεν[α] προσοχὴν τοῖς πράγμασι ῥοπήν, "in general consider how great an impulse attention to the matters indicated contributes to business," P Oxy XII. 1477¹³ (iii iv A.D.) εἰ δύναμαι ὃ ἐνθυμοῦμαι ἆρα[ι; "Am I able to carry off what I am thinking of?" (Edd.). For the gen. constr. see P Lond 42²⁰ (B.C. 168) (= I. p. 30, *Selections*, p. 10), σὲ δὲ μηδ' ἐντεθυμῆσθαι τοῦ παραγενέσθαι, "and that you have never even thought of returning," P Par 63²⁰¹ (B.C. 164) φαίνεσθε οὖν μηδὲ κατὰ μικρὸν ἐντεθυμῆσθαι τῶν ἐξηριθμημένων ὑμῖν, "you appear therefore not to have understood in the smallest degree the points enumerated to you" (Mahaffy). The late compd. παρενθυμέομαι, "disregard," "neglect," occurs in a Lycian inscr., *JHS* xxxiv. p. 5. No. 10¹³ ἐὰν δέ τις παρενθυμηθεὶς μὴ θύσῃ, ἔσται αὐτῷ ἐπιβλαβῆ. MGr θυμοῦμαι (c. acc.), "remember," a meaning which gives good sense in Wisd 7¹⁵, if with אA we read ἐνθυμηθῆναι ἀξίως τῶν λεγομένων (cf. Goodrick *Oxf. Ch. Bibl. Comm. ad l.*).

ἐνθύμησις.

P Lond 46³²⁸ (iv/A.D.) (= I. p. 75) καταδεσμεύω δὲ αὐτοῦ τὸν νοῦν καὶ τὰς φρένας τὴν ἐνθύμησιν τὰς πράξεις ὅπως κτλ.—a magic charm; BGU IV. 1024ⁱᵛ·¹² (iv/v A.D.) ποίας δὲ ἔσχεν ἐνθυμήσεις τὸν ἤδη κληθέντα καὶ τῆς ἐσχάτης ἐλπίδος (*l.* —ος) ἀποστε[ρ]ῆσαι: Vett. Val. p. 301⁸ τὸ ἐξελέγξαι ἀλλοτρίας ἐνθυμήσεις μυστικῶς κατακεχωσμένας.

ἔνι.

BGU IV. 1141⁸ (B.C. 14) ὅτι δὲ ἐν τῇ πρώτῃ μου ἐπιστολῇ οὐθὲν ἁμάρτημα ἔνει (*l.* ἔνι), P Oxy IX. 1218⁵ (iii/A.D.) οὐδὲν δύσκολον ἔνι ἐπὶ τῆς οἰκίας σου. In P Iand 118 (iii/A.D.) ὅτι ἀπ[ρ]επία ἐστιν καὶ οὐκ ἔνι, the editor renders οὐκ ἔνι *"fieri non potest,"* and compares P Strass 1. 35¹⁹ (iv/v A.D.) φρόντ[ι]σόν μου δὲ περὶ τῶν ἐλεῶ[ν] . . . , ἐπιδὴ ἐν Ἀλεξανδρίᾳ οὐκ ἔνει. The above exx. show ἔνι = ἔνεστι, and practically equivalent in meaning to the simple ἐστί, cf. Sir 37², 4 Macc 4²², and see Thackeray *Gr.* i. p. 257. The form ἔνι is regarded as the prep. ἐνί, the Ionic form of ἐν, "strengthened by a more vigorous accent, like ἔπι, πάρα, and used with an ellipsis of the substantive verb" (Lightfoot on Gal 3²⁸; cf. Hort on Jas 1¹⁷). See also Boisacq, p. 247 n.², Dieterich *Untersuch.* p. 225.

ἐνιαυτός.

For ἐ. as a definite period of time, cf. P Hib I. 28²⁰ (c. B.C. 265) ὑπαρχουσῶν [δὲ εἰ]ς [τὸν] ἐν[ι]αυτὸν [ἡ]μερῶ[ν τρια]κοσίων ἑξήκοντα, P Tor I. 1ᵛⁱⁱ·²³ (B.C. 117–6) μὴ συνχωρητέον εἶναι πλείονα ἐνιαυτοῦ ἢ καὶ ἐτῶν δύο ἢ τριῶν, "a longer period must not be granted than a year or two years or three years," P Oxy I. 37¹⁰ (law-suit with reference to a nursing contract—A.D. 49) (= *Selections*, p. 49) τοῦ πρώτου ἐνιαυτοῦ ἀπέλαβεν τὰ τροφεῖα· ἐνέστη ἡ προθεσμία τοῦ δευτέρου ἐνιαυτοῦ, "for the first year she [the nurse] received her wages for nursing: there arrived the appointed day in the second year." The word is frequently found with εἷς as in P Flor I. 2²¹² (A.D. 205) ἐπ' ἐνιαυτὸν ἕνα, and (with the aspirate) P Oxy VIII. 1116¹¹ (A.D. 363) ἐφ' ἐνιαυτὸν ἕνα: cf. also *ib.* II. 275⁹ (A.D. 66) (== *Selections*, p. 55) ἐπὶ χρόνον ἐνιαυτὸν ἕνα. For other prepositional phrases, cf. P Strass I. 22²² (iii/A.D.) ἡ [δ]' ἐνιαυτοῦ νομὴ αὐτάρκης ἐστίν, P Hib I. 27²·⁰ (B.C. 301–240) ἐν τῶι ἐνιαυτῶι, *ib.* ⁴⁸ κατ' ἐνιαυτόν, P Ryl II. 110⁸ (A.D. 259) καθ' ἕκαστο[ν] ἐνιαυτόν, P Thead 16⁴ (after A.D. 307) κατὰ τὸν προπέρυσι ἐνιαυτὸν καὶ πέρυσι, "depuis l'avant-dernière et la dernière année," P Flor I. 50¹⁰⁸ (A.D. 268) ἐνιαυτῷ παρ'

ἐνιαυτόν, *ib.* 64²¹ (iv/A.D. *al init.*?) ἐ]νιαυτὸν παρ' ἐνιαυτόν. In *Syll* 438¹⁶² (c. B.C. 400) μηδ' ἐν ταῖς δεκάτ[α]ις, μηδ' ἐν τοῖς ἐνιαυτοῖ[ς, the reference is to "anniversaries." *Syll* 802³ (iii/B.C.) shows the word along with ἔτος, the heading of a cure effected by Apollo and Asclepios—Κλ]εὼ πένθ' ἔτη ἐκύησε, being immediately followed by—Αὔτα πέντ' ἐνιαυτοὺς ἤδη κυοῦσα κτλ. For the adj. ἐνιαύσιος see P Ryl II. 98⁹ (A.D. 172) φόρου ἐνιαυσίου σύνπαντι, "at a total yearly rent," and for ἐξενίαντα "annual sum" see P Amh II. 86¹¹ (A.D. 78) ἃς (*sc.* δραχμὰς) καὶ ἀπ[οδ]ώσω κατ' ἔτος ἐξενίαντα ἐν μηνὶ Φαῶφι, "I will pay every year the annual sum in the month of Phaophi" (Edd.).

ἐνίστημι.

Contemporary usage makes it clear that in 2 Th 2² ὡς ὅτι ἐνέστηκεν ἡ ἡμέρα τοῦ Κυρίου, ἐνέστηκεν should be rendered as pointing to strictly *present* time, "as that the day of the Lord is *now* present" (RV) and not "is at hand" (AV): see, e.g., the references to the *current* month and year in such passages as BGU I. 22⁶ (A.D. 114) (= *Selections*, p. 74) τῇ δ τοῦ ἐνεστῶτος μηνὸς Φαρμοῦθι, P Fay 28¹⁰ (A.D. 150–1) (= *Selections*, p. 82) εἰς τὸ ἐνεστὸς ἰδ (ἔτος): cf. Milligan *Thess.* p. 97, Zahn *Intr.* i. p. 235. Add such passages as P Tebt II. 383³⁷ (A.D. 46) where certain shares are assigned to contracting parties ἀπὸ τῆς ἐνεστώσης ἡμέρας ἐπὶ τὸν ἅπαντα χρόνον, P Lond 1164(*h*)⁶ (A.D. 212) (= III p. 164) ἀπὸ τῆς ἐνεστώσης καὶ ὑποκειμένης ἡμέρας, P Oxy I. 37¹·¹¹ (A.D. 49) ἐνέστη ἡ προθεσμία τοῦ δευτέρου ἐνιαυτοῦ. κα[ὶ] πάλιν ἀπέλαβεν, "the appointed day in the second year came, and again she received (her wages)," and P Flor I. 1⁶ (A.D. 153) τῆς προθεσμίας ἐνστάσης, so *ib.* 81¹⁰ (A.D. 103). Mayser *Gr.* p. 371 collects many instances illustrating various forms of the verb.

ἐνισχύω.

For the transitive use of this verb, as in Lk (Ac 9¹⁹): cf. Lk 22⁴³ D) cf. Hippocrates *Lex.* p. 2, 26 ὁ δὲ χρόνος ταῦτα ἐνισχύει πάντα, ὡς τραφῆναι τελέως (see Hobart, p. 80 f.). In Theophr. *Fragm.* i. 65 τοῦτ' ἐνισχύειν ἑκάστῳ, "this, in each thing, is strong," we have the usual intrans. sense: see Abbott *Fourfold Gospel*, p. 177 n².

ἐνκαινίζω.

If we can trust the restoration in P Par 16²⁴ (B.C. 127) εἴπαμεν κα[τα]κολουθεῖν τοῖς ἐξ ἀρχῆς ἐθισμοῖς καὶ μηθὲν ἐνκαινί[ζ]ειν, this verb can no longer be regarded as "exclusively bibl. and eccl." (Grimm-Thayer). In the above passage, it will be noticed, it has the meaning of "make no innovation" as compared with "initiate," "inaugurate," in Heb 9¹⁸, 10²⁰. LS cite ἐγκαινιάζομαι from *CIG* IV. 8606.

ἐνκακέω.

BGU IV. 1043³ (iii/A.D.) contains the word ἐνκακήσα[ντος (?), but in an uncertain context: it is, however, worth recording in view of the poverty of the "profane" attestation of this verb. See also Polyb. iv. 19. 10 τὸ μὲν πέμπειν τὰς βοηθείας . . . ἐνεκάκησαν, "they omitted through cowardice to send assistance," and Vett. Valens. p. 201¹³ ἐκκακοῦντες. On the form cf. WH *Notes*², p. 150 f.

ἐνκαυχάομαι.

Though we have no profane evidence for this word other than Æsop's Fables (230, ed. Halm), its occurrence in the LXX (Pss 51³, 96⁷ *al.*) and in 2 Thess 1⁴ indicates that it was already then in common use: see Nägeli, p. 44. For the form cf. WH *Notes* ², p. 156 f.

ἐνκεντρίζω

belongs to the higher **Κοινή**: see the citations in Grimm-Thayer, and cf. Nägeli, p. 33. As against the view that the process described by Paul in Rom 11¹⁷ is "wholly unnatural," and that the strength of his argument depends on this fact (SH *ad l.*), see W. M. Ramsay *Pauline Studies*, p. 219 ff.

ἐνκοπή.

See *s.v.* ἐκκοπή.

ἐνκρίνω.

With this verb in 2 Cor 10¹² Nägeli (p. 56) compares the use in the inscr. ἐ. εἰς τοὺς ἐφήβους, "enroll," as *CIG* II. 2715ᵃ·¹¹ (*c.* A.D. 20), *IG* VII. 29⁶ (iii/ii B.C.). The Alexandrian critics of the third and second centuries B.C. employed it to mark out or select the best writers, as when the orator Deinarchus is described by Suidas as τῶν μετὰ Δημοσθένους ἐγκριθέντων εἰς: see *Companion to Greek Studies*, p. 147. For the subst. cf. *Syll* 278¹⁶ (ii/B.C.) στοχαζομένων ὑμῶν ἐκ τῶν ὑπ' ἐμοῦ γεγραμμένων ἐγκρίσεων.

ἔνκυος.

For this NT ἅπ. εἰρ. (Lk 2⁵) cf. BGU IV. 1104²¹ (B.C. 8) ἐπεὶ δὲ καὶ ἔνκυος καθέστηκεν ἡ Διονυσάριον, P Oxy II. 267²⁰ (A.D. 36) ἐνκύου σ[ο]ῦ οὔση[s, *ib.* X. 1273³³ (A.D. 260) ἐὰ]ν·[δὲ] καὶ ἐπὶ τῆς ἀπαλλαγῆς ἔγκυος ἦν (*l.* ᾖ) ἡ γαμουμένη, "if at the time of the separation the bride should be pregnant." See also *Syll* 802¹⁴ (iii/B.C.) ἔγκυος δὲ γενομένα ἐγ γαστρὶ ἐφόρει τρία ἔτη, and ¹²·¹⁷.

ἔννατος.

See *s.v.* ἔνατος.

ἐννεός.

See *s.v.* ἐνεός.

ἔννοια.

P Par 63³² (B.C. 165) (= P Petr III. p. 20) ἐπὶ τῆς αὐτῆς ἐννοίας [γενομέν]ους, "having come to the same conclusion" (Mahaffy), P Rein 7¹⁵ (B.C. 141 ?) ὑποσχόμενός τε [ἀποδοῦναι ? διὰ πάση]ς ἡσυχίας εἶχον τῶι μηδεμίαν ἔννοιαν [κ]ακίας ἔχειν, "comme il promit de me le rendre, je restai complètement tranquille, n'ayant aucun soupçon qu'il me cherchât malice" (Ed.). For the verb, as in Judith 9⁵, cf. Aristeas 133 κἂν ἐννοηθῇ τις κακίαν ἐπιτελεῖν. MGr ἔννοια (ἔγνοια), "care," "worry."

ἔννομος.

Sir William Ramsay's contention (*Pauline Studies*, p. 203 ff.) that Ac 19³⁹ ἐν τῇ ἐννόμῳ ἐκκλησίᾳ = "in a lawful assembly" (AV), rather than "in the regular assembly"

(RV), is supported by the use of the adj. in our documents. Thus P Oxy II. 247¹² (A.D. 90) of the registration of a man—προστρέχοντι τῇ ἐννόμῳ ἡλικίᾳ, "who is approaching the legal age" (cf. *ib.* III. 651 (A.D. 126–7) τῆς κατὰ νόμους ἡλικίας, P Ryl II. 153¹⁹ (A.D. 138–61) ἄχ]ρι οὗ γένη[ται τῆ]ς ἐννό[μο]υ [ἡ]λικίας, P Thead 18⁹ (iii/iv A.D.) ἡγεμὼν δεσπ]ότα τὴν ἔννομον ἀξίωσιν προσφέρω ὑπὲρ τῶν ἀφηλίκων παί[δων, P Oxy I. 41¹⁶ (iii/iv A.D.) τὰς δὲ τοιαύτα[ς] μαρτυρίας ἀξιῶ εἰς καιρὸν ἔννομον ὑπερτεθῆναι, "but I beg that these demonstrations be reserved for a legitimate occasion" (Edd.), *ib.* 67¹¹ (A.D. 338) ποιῆσαι ἔνν[ο]μόν τε τυπωθῆν[αι] τὴν [το]ῦ δικαστηρίου προκάταρξιν (*l.* -ιν), "to have the preliminary proceedings of the court conducted under legal forms" (Edd.). In *Syll* 922⁵ (iii/B.C.) we read of a decision reached in the city of Delphi—ἐν ἀγορᾶι τελείωι σὺν ψάφοις ταῖς ἐννόμοις, and similarly *OGIS* 241¹³ (ii/B.C.): cf. also *Michel* 468²⁹ (mid. ii/B.C.) προγράψ[ασ]θαι τοῖς προστάτας ἐν τοῖς ἐννόμοις χρόνο(ι)s.

ἔννυχος.

For this poetic adj. (but see 3 Macc 5⁵ and Æsop. 110 ed. Halm), which is used adverbially in its only occurrence in the NT (Mk 1³⁵ ἔννυχα ℵBCD *al.*), Herwerden (*Lex. s.v.*) cites a metrical inscr. of v/A.D., *IG* VII. 584⁵ ὅταν σε λάβῃ ἔννυχος ἠώς.

ἐνοικέω.

In P Par 14²² (ii/B.C.) ἐνοικοῦσιν βιαίως is used of taking forcible possession of a house: cf. P Tor I. 1¹⁴·⁵ (B.C. 117) καὶ τῶν περὶ τὸν Ὧρον ἐνοικούντων καὶ κρατούντων τῆς οἰκίας. Other exx. are P Oxy II. 638 (A.D. 112) καὶ] ἐνοικεῖν τὴν μητέρα ἡμῶν ἐφ' ἡμεῖ ἐν μιᾷ τῶν προγεγραμμένων οἰκιῶν οἰκίᾳ, BGU III. 895²³ (ii/A.D.) ἐνοικεῖν ἀμίσθῳ ἐν οἴκῳ. For ἐνοικέω along with ἐνοικίζω see P Hamb I. 30²¹ (A.D. 89) μηδὲ τοὺς παρ' αὐ[τῆ]s ἐνοικοῦντας καὶ ἑτέρους ἐνοικίζοντας οὓς ἐὰν βούληται ἐν τοῖς σημειουμένοις μέρεσι δυσὶ . . τῆς οἰκίας, P Tebt II. 372¹² (A.D. 141) ἐφ' ᾧ ἐξέσται] τῷ Ἀρείῳ ἐνοικῖν καὶ ἐνοικίζιν, "on condition that Arius shall have the right of domicile whether for himself or others" (Edd.). For ἔνοικος see BGU I. 119⁴ (A.D. 175) κ]ατ' οἰκ(ίαν) ἀπογρ(αφὴν) ἐνοίκ(ων), and for ἐνοίκησις and ἐνοίκιον see P Oxy I. 104¹⁵ (a will—A.D. 96) Ἀ. ἕξει τὴν ἐνοίκησιν καὶ τὰ πε[ρ]ιεσόμενα ἐνοίκια ("rents") τῆς σημαινομένης οἰκίας. This document shows also ²¹ a subst. ἐνοικισμός (not in LS). See also Modica *Introduzione*, pp. 172, 272 f.

ἐνορκίζω,

confined in the Bibl. writings to 1 Th 5²⁷, except as a variant in 2 Esdr 23 (13)²⁵, is a strengthened form of ὁρκίζω (cf. Rutherford *NP* p. 466 f.), and, like it (Mk 5⁷, Ac 19¹³), is construed with two accusatives. Thus in *CIG* IV. 9288⁶, which Ramsay (*C. and B.* ii. p. 499) assigns to the first half of iv/A.D., we have an adjuration to the public not to intrude any corpse into the tomb, as well as a reference to the Angel standing on the tomb as guardian—ἐνορκίζω ὑμᾶς τὸν ὧδε ἐφεστῶτα ἄγγελον, μή τίς ποτε τολμῇ ἐνθάδε τινὰ καταθέσθε. Cf. also the Jewish Chr. epitaph *CIG* IV. 9270⁴ ἔνθα κεῖντε ὀστέα τοῦ σώφρονος Παύλου διακόνου. ἐνορκιζόμ[ε]θ[α] τὸν παντ[ο]κράτο[ρ]α θ(εὸ)ν . . . . For ἐξορκίζω see P Leid

V. iv. 31 (iii/A.D.) ἐξορκίζω σε, τὴν δύναμίν σου, τὸν μέγαν θε(ὸν) κτλ., and the magical incantation P Par 574[1239] (iii/A.D.) (= Selections, p. 113) ἐξορκίζω σε δαῖμον, ὅστις ποτ' οὖν εἶ, κατὰ τούτου τοῦ θεοῦ κτλ. A late form ἐνορκέω, unknown to LS, is found in BGU III. 836⁹ (time of Justinian) ἐνορκο[ῦ]μεν κατὰ τοῦ δεσπότου Χριστοῦ. For the adj. ἔνορκος see OGIS 5⁵³ (B.C. 311) ἐνόρκων γενομένων τῶν τε Ἑλλήνων πάντων καὶ τῶν ἐν τοῖς [π]ράγμασιν ὄντων.

ἐνότης.

With the use of this subst. in Eph 4³,¹³ cf. Usener Epic. p. 13¹⁴ ὁμοιομερεῖς ὄγκους (corpuscula) . . τινὰ διασώζοντας συμπάθειαν πρὸς ἀλλήλους καὶ ἑνότητα ἰδιότροπον . . (cited by Linde Epic. p. 34).

ἐνοχλέω.

This common verb, as in Greek writers generally, is construed both with the acc. and the dat. As exx. of the former constr. we may cite P Hib I. 56⁷ (B.C. 249) σὺ οὖν μὴ ἐνόχλει [α]ὐτόν, P Leid W ᶦᶦᶦ·³⁴ (ii/iii A.D.) μαθὼν δὲ τὸν κύριον τῆς ἡμέρα (l.—ας), ἐκεῖνον ἐνόχλει λέγων· Κύριε κτλ., and P Oxy VI. 899⁴⁴ (A.D. 200) where a woman petitions that the collectors of certain dues should not be allowed ἐνοχλεῖσθαί με γυναῖκα οὖσ[α]ν ἄνανδρον καὶ ἀβοήθητον, "to harass me, a woman without a husband or helper" (Edd.): cf. from the inscr. Syll 253¹⁶ (iii/B.C.) γέγρα[φ]α τῶι Ἡρακλείδηι μὴ ἐνο[χ]λεῖν ὑμᾶς. For the dat. constr. see P Tebt II. 286⁸ (A.D. 121–38) σὺ δὲ περὶ τῶν οὐ ζη[τ]ουμένων ἐνοχλεῖ (l.—εῖν) μοι θέλεις, "but you still wish to trouble me about points which are not at issue" (Edd.), P Oxy VII. 1068¹¹ (iii/A.D.) ἐφ' ᾧ μηδὶς ἐνοχλήσι αὐτῷ, ib. IX. 1221⁹ (iii/iv A.D.) τῷ οὖν Ζωιλᾷ μὴ ἐνόχλει περὶ τούτου. and from the inscr. Syll 418⁶² (A.D. 238) οὐδεὶς ἡμεῖν ἐνόχλησεν. P Tebt II. 335¹³ᶠ (mid. iii/A.D.) παύεσθαί μου τὸν ὀφφικιάλιον τῆς τάξεως ἐνο[χ]λοῦντα. ἐνοχλεῖ γάρ μοι κτλ., "that the magistrates' subordinate may give up troubling me. For he troubles me" etc.—shows an unusual construction with the gen. due to the influence of παύεσθαι. For the pass. we may cite P Petr II. 16¹⁰ (mid. iii/B.C.) = Witkowski ², p. 12) ἵνα μη]θὲν ἐνοχλῆται τὸ οἰκόπεδον, OGIS 669⁶⁰ (i/A.D.) μὴι (l. μὴ) μάτην ἐνοχλείσθωσαν. In P Hamb I. 27² (B.C. 250) συνέβη οὖμ μοι ἐνοχληθῆναι ἐμ Φιλαδελφείαι [ὥστε ἀσχολί]αν με ἔχειν τῆι ἡμέραι ἐκείνηι, the verb does not seem to mean much more than "be engaged." In P Petr II. 25 (a)¹² εἰς ἵππον ἐνοχλούμενον = "for a sick horse." For διενοχλέω see BGU III. 830⁸ (i/A.D.) διενοχλ[ο]ύμενος ὁ αὐτοῦ καρπώνης.

ἔνοχος.

Wellhausen's assertion (Einl. p. 33 f.) that ἔ. τῇ κρίσει in Mt 5²² is "ungriechisch" is sufficiently ruled out by Grimm's apt parallel ἔ. τῇ γραφῇ, "liable to be indicted," from Xenophon (Mem. i. 2. 64): Blass Gr. p. 106 makes the dative in Mt l.c. "the commoner classical construction." The dat. of the crime, also classical, is found in Hellenistic, as P Eleph 23¹⁹ (B.C. 223–2) ἔ. τῆι ἀσεβείαι τοῦ ὅρκου, and other exx. cited under ἀσέβεια: the phrase ἡ ἔνοχος εἴην τῷ ὅρκῳ recurs very frequently, e.g. P Oxy I. 82⁷(mid. iii/A.D.), P Ryl II. 82¹¹ (A.D. 113), ib. 88²⁵ (A.D. 156), P Fay 24¹⁷ (A.D. 158). In an edict of the Prefect Aulus Avillius Flaccus (i/A.D.) we find θανάτωι ἔνοχος

PART III.

ἐσ[τωι, which prompts Wilcken (Archiv. i. p. 170, n.³) to observe on Mt 26⁶⁶ that the Prefect writes better Greek than the Evangelist. "Or is the illogical genitive θανάτου only a MS. corruption due to the fusion of u and o vowels in the later vernacular?" The gen. in 1 Cor 11²⁷ is claimed by Deissmann (LAE p. 116) as a Cilician provincialism of Paul. For an ex. of ἔ. with the dat. of the penalty. contemporary with the NT writings, see P Oxy II. 275² (a contract of apprenticeship—A.D. 66) (= Selections, p. 57) ἐὰν δὲ καὶ αὐτὸ[ς ὁ] Πτολεμαῖος μὴ ἐγδιδάξῃ τὸν παῖ[δ]α, ἔνοχος ἔστω τοῖς ἴσοις ἐπιτε[ί]μοις, "but if Ptolemaeus himself does not teach the boy thoroughly, let him be liable to like penalties": cf. Ach. Tat. viii. 10 δυσὶ θανάτοις ἔνοχ. From the inscr. we have Michel 827 ᴬ·⁵⁰ (mid. iii/B.C.) ἔνοχοι ἔστωσαν τῶι κατὰ τὸν τῆς οἰκονομίας νόμωι. Vett. Val. p. 117¹⁰ κατάμοιχοι γίνονται ἢ ἔνοχοι μοιχείας shows the gen. of the crime, as in Mk 3²⁹, Gen 26¹¹, 2 Macc 13⁶.

For the subst. ἐνοχή = "obligatio," see P Iand 48¹¹ (A.D. 582) with the editor's note, and Wenger Stellvertretung, p. 262.

ἐνταφιάζω.

On the use of the corresponding subst. ἐνταφιαστής in LXX Gen 50² to describe the Egyptian physicians who embalmed the body of Jacob, see Deissmann BS p. 120 f., where the professional designation is illustrated from P Par 7⁸ (B.C. 99). It occurs again in P Oxy III. 476⁸ (ii/A.D), the report of two ἐνταφιασταί who had been commissioned to examine a dead body—an indication, as Lumbroso has pointed out (Archiv iii. p. 163 f.), that the ἐνταφιασταί were trained physicians, and able to conduct the work not only of embalming but of autopsy: cf. also Archiv v. p. 26 f. and Otto Priester ii. p. 195 n¹. The mummy-tablet Preisigke 25 is inscribed τῷ Πανεχάτῃ ἐνταφιαστῇ, similarly ib. 3442. The verb is found in Test. xii. patr. Jud. xxvi. 3 (ed. Charles) μηδείς με ἐνταφιάσει ἐν πολυτελεῖ ἐσθῆτι.

ἐνταφιασμός.

With Jn 12⁷ we may compare a striking passage from Philodemus de morte ed. Meckler, p. 49, 17 : vir sapiens εὐθὺς ἤδη τὸ λοιπὸν ἐνταφιασάμενος (quasi) περιπατεῖ καὶ τὴν μίαν ἡμέραν ὡς αἰῶνα κερδαίνει (cited Herwerden Lex. s.v. ἐνταφιάζειν). In Jn l.c. the word should be translated not "burying" (as AV, RV), but "laying out" or "preparation for burial": see further on the passage Field Notes, p. 98.

ἐντέλλομαι.

For this common verb = "give orders," "charge," it is sufficient to cite P Grenf I. 30³ (B.C. 103) οἷς καὶ ἐντετάλμεθ[α] ἀσπάσεσθαι ὑμᾶς παρ' ἡμῶν φιλοφρόνως, P Tebt I. 37¹¹ (B.C. 73) ἐντέταλταί μοι παραλαβὼν στρατιώτας ἐκπορθῆσαι αὐτούς, P Ryl II. 229⁵ (A.D. 38) Ὠφελίωνι ἐνετειλάμην ἵνα καὶ αὐτὸς δοῖ ἑτέραν (sc. ὄνον), ib. 241³⁶ (iii/A.D.) περὶ ὧν σοι ἐνετίλατο Σ. The later juristic usage = "invest one with legal powers," is discussed by Mitteis Papyruskunde, p. 201, and Wenger Stellvertretung, p. 105.

ἐντεῦθεν.

For ἐντεῦθεν = "from this time" cf. P Lond 1164(f)¹⁸ (A.D. 212) (= III. p. 161) ἃς καὶ ἐντεῦθεν χαρίζεται τοῖς

29

αὐτοῖς τέκνοις, *ib.* (*h*)[16] (= p. 164) ἐντεῦθεν δὲ παρέλαβεν ὁ αὐτὸς παρὰ τοῦ Πβήκιος τὸ προκείμενον [π]λοῖον, *ib.* (*k*)[16] (p. 167), and *ib.* 948[6] (A.D. 236) (= III. p. 220) ἀφ' ὧν ἐντεῦθεν ἔσχεν ἀργ(υρίου) δραχμὰς τεσσεράκοντα. In P Oxy X. 1277[11] (A.D. 255) we have ἃς (*sc.* δραχμὰς) καὶ ἐντεῦθεν ἀπέσχον, "which I thereupon received": cf. P Tebt II. 378[11] (A.D. 265) ἐντεῦθεν δὲ ἔσχον παρ' ὑμῶν εἰς ἀνάκτ[ησιν] ἔργων τῶν ἀρουρῶν, "and I have received forthwith from you for the restoration of the operations upon the land" (Edd.), P Ryl II. 96[9] (A.D. 117-8) ἐντεῦθεν ὑπεχόμεθα, "we henceforth undertake," and so P Giss I. 6[ii] ㎏[1] (A.D. 117). In P Oxy VI. 930[3] (ii/iii A.D.) μὴ ὄκνι μοι [γ]ράφειν καὶ περὶ ὧν ἐ[ὰ]ν χρείαν ἔχῃς. ἐντεῦθεν ἐλοιπήθην (*l.* ἐλυπήθην) κτλ, ἐντεῦθεν may = "forthwith" or "therefore": see the editors' note. Ἐντεῦθεν ἤδη in Byzantine documents (e.g. P Iand 48[17]—A.D. 582) = "now."

ἔντευξις.

The usage of this word in 1 Tim 2[1], 4[5], is readily explained by its constant recurrence in the papyri and inscriptions as a kind of "vox sollemnis" for a "petition" of any kind: cf. Deissmann *BS* pp. 121, 146, Laqueur *Quaestiones*, p. 8. Thus in the Ptolemaic papyri it is constantly used of any writing addressed to the King, e.g. in P Par 26[5] (B.C. 163-2) (= *Selections*, p. 13) the Serapeum Twins remind Ptolemy Philometor and Cleopatra II.—ἐνετύχομεν, καὶ ἐπεδώκαμεν ἔντευξιν: cf. P Amh II. 33[21] (*c.* B.C. 157), a petition from five cultivators of domain lands to the same Royalties—δεόμεθ' ὑμῶν τῶν μεγίστων θεῶν εἰ ὑμῖν δοκεῖ ἀποστεῖλαι ἡμῶν τὴν ἔντευξιν ἐπὶ τοὺς αὐτοὺς χρηματιστάς, P Fay 12[26] (to Cleopatra III. and Ptolemy Alexander—B.C. 103) δέομαι ἐπιστεῖλαί μου τὴν ἔντευξιν ἐπὶ τοὺς ἀποτεταγμένους τῆι κατοικίᾳ χρηματιστάς. In Roman times the word occurs, but rarely, of petitions addressed to the Strategus, e.g. P Flor I. 55[18] (A.D. 88) τὰ διὰ τῆς ἐντεύξεως δεδηλωμένα, *ib.* 56[8] (A.D. 234): see further Mitteis *Papyruskunde,* p. 13 ff., and the editor's note to P Hamb I. 29[16]. For ἐντυχία = "intercession," "petition," as in 3 Macc 6[40], cf. P Lond 44[26] (B.C. 161) (= I. p. 34) τὸν τὴν ἐντυχίαν ποιησόμενον, and for a new subst. παράτευξις see P Amh I. 3(*a*)[iii. 22] quoted under παρατυγχάνω.

ἔντιμος.

In P Hamb I. 31[16] (ii/A.D.) a certificate is granted to a retired soldier who had served for 26 years, and been discharged ἐντείμῳ ἀπολύσσει, "with honourable release": cf. for a similar use of the adv. with ἀπολελυμένος of an "honourably discharged" veteran, P Oxy XII. 1471[6] (A.D. 81), *ib.* 1459[4] (A.D. 226), P Lond 906[4] (A.D. 128) (= III. p. 108), BGU IV. 1021[2] (iii/A.D.), *Preisigke* 424, while the magical BGU IV. 1026[4] (p. 25), ἔντιμος (*l.* -ον) ὡς Μιχαήλ, ἔνδοξας (*l.* -ον) [ὡς] Γαβριήλ, "suggests," as Dr. E. A. Abbott (*CR* xxxi. p. 153) has pointed out, "a connection between ἔντιμος and the military distinction of Michael, as contrasted with the peaceful glory of Gabriel." These and similar exx. have led Abbott (*ut s.*) to the conclusion that in Lk 7[2] the epithet ἔντιμος is almost certainly misplaced, and should be attached not to the "servant" but to the "centurion" in the sense of "honourable." This meaning suits all the other NT passages, where the

word occurs—Lk 14[8], Phil 2[29], 1 Pet 2[4,6] (see Hort's note on [4]). *Syll* 837 records the freeing of a female slave μηδε[νὶ μη]δὲν προσήκουσαν κατὰ τοὺς Αἰτωλῶ[ν] νόμους ἰσοτελῆ καὶ ἔντειμον, and in the iii/A.D. Hadrumetum imprecatory tablet (*BS*, p. 274 ff.) after the invocation we have—[3] ἄκουσον τοῦ ὀνόματος ἐντίμου καὶ [φοβ]εροῦ καὶ μεγάλου καὶ ἄπελθε κτλ.

ἐντολή

is used of a royal "ordinance" of Euergetes II. in P Tebt I. 6[10] (B.C. 140) ὑποτετάχα]μεν δὲ καὶ τῆς παρὰ τοῦ βασιλέως[καὶ τῶν βασιλισσῶν παραδεδο]μένης περὶ τῶν ἀνηκόντων [τοῖς ἱεροῖς κομίζεσθαι ἐ]ντολῆς τὸ ἀντίγραφον, and in Par 65[18] (B.C. 146), the writer, after informing Ptolemy Philometor that he had executed certain instructions regarding Egyptian contracts, adds—ἡ μὲν ἐντολὴ ἐγδέδοται ἡμῖν εἰς τὴν Λ τοῦ Ἀθύρ: cf. P Lille I. 3[55] (*c.* B.C. 240) ἐν(τολὴ) τοῖς ἐλαιοκαπήλοις, "circulaire aux revendeurs" (Ed.). From Roman times we may cite the reference to Imperial ordinances —ταῖς θείαις ἐντολαῖς in an inscr. from Bulgaria, *Syll* 418[21] (A.D. 238): cf. 1 Cor 7[16] *al.* Other more general exx. are P Ryl II. 81[22] (the letter of an official—*c.* A.D. 104) μεμνῆσ[θαί μ]ου τῆς γενομένη[ς] αὐτῷ ἐντολῆς, BGU II. 600[6] (ii/iii A.D.) ἐνμένω πᾶσι ταῖς προγεγραμμέν[α]ις [ἐν]τολαῖς [κ]αθὼς πρό[κι]ται, and P Tebt II. 413[7] (ii/iii A.D.) μὴ δόξῃς με, κυρί[α], ἠμεληκέναι σου τῶν ἐντολῶν —the letter perhaps of a slave to her mistress. For κατὰ τ. ἐ. cf. PSI III. 236[6] (iii/iv A.D.) κατὰ τὰς ἐντολὰς ἃς εἶχο[ν, BGU III. 941[11] (A.D. 376) ταῦτα δὲ παρέσχες τῷ [. . .]Ἀπολλωνί[ῳ] κατ' ἐντολήν.

ἐντόπιος.

In P Lond 192[64] (early i/A.D.) (= II. p. 225) a list of "local"—ἐντοπίων—names is opposed to a list of "Alexandrian"—Ἀλεξανδρέων—names. Cf. P Oxy VIII. 1153[26] (i/A.D.) ἐντοπίᾳ δὲ πορφύρᾳ χρήσασθ(αι) μέλλομεν, "we are going to use local purple" (Ed.), CPR I. 12[7] (A.D. 93) χρυσοῦ δοκιμίου σταθμῷ ἐντοπίῳ, "standard gold according to the local weight," P Lond 755 *verso* [10] (iv/A.D.) (= III. p. 222) ἀπ[ὸ] ἐντοπίου λίθου, "from native stone." For the form ἔντοπος see *OGIS* 629[70] with Dittenberger's note.

ἐντός.

We have no citation which throws any light on the much disputed meaning of ἐντὸς ὑμῶν in Lk 17[21], but it may be noted that the same phrase occurs in a similar connexion in the second of the new sayings of Jesus, P Oxy IV. 654[16], ἡ βασ[ιλεία τῶν οὐρανῶν] ἐντὸς ὑμῶν [ἐ]στι [καὶ ὅστις ἂν ἑαυτὸν] γνῷ ταύτην εὑρή[σει . . . , where the context favours the translation "within you": for a different restoration of the latter part [καὶ ὃς ἐὰν τὰ ἐντὸς ὑμῶν] γνῷ, see Deissmann *LAE* p. 438. The word is used of *time* in such passages as P Oxy IV. 724[11] (A.D. 155) ἐὰν δὲ ἐντὸς τοῦ χ[ρ]όνου αὐτὸν ἀπαρτίσῃς, "if you make him (the pupil) perfect within the period," in a contract of apprenticeship, and *ib.* X. 1278[26] (A.D. 214) ἐντὸς τοῦ προκειμένου αὐτοῦ χρόνου, and of *place* in P Ryl II. 161[8] (A.D. 71) ἐντὸς περιβό[λου ἱε]ροῦ θεοῦ Σοκνοπαίου, *ib.* 157[7] (A.D. 135) ἐντὸς τείχου τοῦ κτήματος, and P Oxy VIII. 1128[14] (A.D. 173) τὸ συμπόσιον καὶ τὴν ἐντὸς αὐτοῦ κέλλαν, "a dining-room and the storechamber within it": see also the famous temple inscr. cited *s.v.* ἀλλογενής. In P Oxy X. 1274¹³ (iii/A.D.) a minor is described—ἔτι ὄντος ἐντὸς τοῦ Λαιτωρίου νόμου, "being still subject to the Laetorian law"—a law protecting persons under the age of twenty-five from fraud: see the editors' note, where reference is made to BGU II. 378²¹ (ii/iii A.D.) and 611⁶·⁶ (i/A.D.). In the medical receipt P Oxy VIII. 1088³³ (early i/A.D.) the remedy to stop nose-bleeding is—μάνναν φύρασον χυλῶι πράσου καὶ ἐνάλιψον τὸν χυλὸν ἐνδόθεν, "mix frankincense with onion-juice and apply the juice inside" (Ed.).

ἐντρέπω.

The late metaphorical sense of ἐντρέπομαι "am ashamed," which is found in the NT in 2 Th 3¹⁴, Tit 2⁸, and survives in MGr, may be illustrated by such passages from the Κοινή as P Par 49³⁰ (B.C. 164–58) παρακαλέσας αὐτὸν ἀπόστειλον πρὸς ἐμέ, γίνεται γὰρ ἐντραπῆναι, *ib.* 47⁴ (*c.* B.C. 153) (= *Selections*, p. 22) ἱ μὴ μικρόν τι ἐντρέπομαι, οὐκ ἄν με ἴδες τὸ πρόσωπόν μου πόποτε, "but for the fact that I am a little ashamed, you would never have seen my face," and *ib.* 37²⁴ (ii/B.C.) ἐντρεπέντος (for form, see Mayser *Gr.* p. 19) δὲ τοῦ Ἀμώσιος. On ἐ. in its middle sense of "have respect to" construed with the acc., as in Mk 12⁶, see *Proleg.* p. 65, Anz *Subsidia*, p. 269.

ἐντρέφομαι.

For ἐ. c. dat., as in 1 Tim 4⁶, Dibelius (*HZNT ad l.*) aptly cites Epict. iv. 4. 48 τούτοις τοῖς διαλογισμοῖς ἐντρεφόμενος.

ἔντρομος.

For ἔντρομος *ter* in the NT cf. ἔκτρομος, not found in the lexicons, but apparently used in the same sense in the great Paris magical papyrus of about A.D. 300— ³⁰⁷⁶ ὁρκίζω σε . . . τὸν ἐφορῶντα ἐπὶ γῆς καὶ ποιοῦντα ἔκτρομα τὰ θεμέλια αὐτῆς, "and maketh tremble the foundations thereof": see Heb 12²¹ ℵD₂, and cf. Deissmann *LAE* p. 254 and *BS* p. 290.

ἐντροπή.

We are unable to illustrate the meaning of "shame" which this word has in its two NT occurrences (1 Cor 6⁵, 15³⁴, cf. Ps 34(35)²⁶, 43(44)¹³ *al.*), and which survives in MGr; but for the derived sense of "respect," "reverence," cf. *OGIS* 323⁷ (B.C. 159–38) πολὺ δὲ τῶν καθ' ἑαυτὸν συνέσει καὶ παιδείαι προάγων [παρὰ μὲ]ν τοῖς ἄλλοις ἐντροπῆς καὶ δόξης δικαίως ἐτύγχαμεν, and the late magical papyrus P Lond 46¹⁷ (iv/A.D.) (= I. p. 65) δὸς ἐντροπὴν τῷ φανέντι πρὸ πυρός.

ἐντρυφάω.

For this verb = "take delight in" with dat. of person cf. Plat. *Pelopidas* 30 Πελοπίδα δὲ οὕτω μὲν οὐκ ἐνετρύφησε. The verb construed with ἐν is found with a somewhat stronger meaning in its only NT occurrence, 2 Pet 2¹³.

ἐντυγχάνω.

For the technical use of this verb = "petition," "appeal," (see *s.v.* ἔντευξις) it is enough to cite P Tebt I. 58⁶³ (B.C. 111)

ἔντευχαν (*l.* ἐνέτευχαν) οἱ ιγ κωμογρ(αμματεῖς) . . τῶι διοικη(τῆι), "the 13 komogrammateis appealed to the dioecetes," *ib.* 183 (late ii/B.C.) ὑπὲρ ὧν καὶ ἐνέτυχον [Ἀπολ]λωνίωι, *ib.* II. 297⁹ (*c.* A.D. 123) τοῦτο ἐπιγνοὺς ὁ συνηγορούμενος ἐνέτυχε Τε[ι]μοκράτει, "on learning this my client appealed to T." (Edd.), *ib.* 335² (mid. iii/A.D.) Φιηνοῦς . . . ἐντυγχάνει, "petition of Phienous," P Oxy XII. 1502⁹ (*c.* A.D. 260–1) Θαῒς Σερήνου ἐντυγχάνει. For the more directly religious use (as in Rom 8²⁶, Heb 7²⁵), see BGU I. 246¹² (ii/iii A.D.) ἰδότες ὅτι νυκτὸς καὶ ἡμέρας ἐντυγχάνω τῷ θεῷ ὑπὲρ ὑμῶν. In the question to an oracle, P Fay 137³ (i/A.D.) we have the simple, classical sense ἢ μέλω (*l.* μέλλω) ἐντυγχάνιν: "shall I meet him?" Cf. *Michel* 308¹⁸ (1st half ii/B.C.) τοῖς ἐντυγχάνουσιν αὐτῶι τῶν πολιτῶν ἴσον αὐτὸν παρεχόμενος διατετέλεκεν, "has continued dealing fairly with any of the citizens who came across him." For ἐντυγχάνω κατά, as in Rom 11², cf. P Giss I. 36¹⁶ (B.C. 161) ἐνετύχομεν καθ' ὑμῶν περὶ τῶν λε [ἀρ]ου(ρῶν), P Amh II. 134¹⁰ (early ii/A.D.) ἐντυχεῖν κατὰ Π., and for ἐ. περί see PSI IV. 340⁵ (B.C. 257–6) ἀποκέκριται γὰρ τοῖς ἐντ[υ]γχάνουσι περὶ Πτολεμαίου, *ib.* 410¹⁴ (iii/B.C.) περὶ Ὥρου ἐντυχεῖν Ἀμμωνίωι, and P Amh II. 142¹⁰ (iv/A.D.) ἐνέτυχα τῷ σῷ ἀδε[λ]φῷ Φιλαγρίῳ περὶ τούτ[ω]ν. In P Oxy III. 533²⁵ (ii/iii A.D.) we have ἐνέτυχον τῷ διοικητῇ ἕνεκα τῆς προσόδου. In the Petition of Dionysia, P Oxy II. 237 (A.D. 186), the editors note that the verb is used both of presenting and of answering a petition: see their note on ⱽ·²¹, and cf. Laqueur *Quaestiones*, p. 15 ff. where ἐντυγχάνειν = "*legere*" is fully illustrated.

ἐντυλίσσω

is found in the magic P Lond 121⁸³⁹ (iii/A.D.) (= I. p. 110) ἐντύλισσε τὰ φύλ(λα) ἐν σουδαρίῳ κενῷ (*l.* καινῷ), a passage which strangely recalls Jn 20⁷: cf. also Mt 27⁵⁹, Lk 23⁵³, where ἐντυλίσσω is substituted for the Markan ἐνειλέω (Mk 15⁴⁶). Abbott (*Joh. Voc.* p. 346) suggests that "Matthew and Luke may have objected to the word (especially when applied, as by Mark, not to 'body' but to 'him') as being unseemly, because it is used of fettering prisoners, swathing children hand and foot, holding people fast in a net, entangling them in evil or in debt, and generally in a bad sense." See *s.v.* ἐνειλέω. In P Lond 402 *verso*¹⁶ (ii/B.C.) (= II. p. 11) we find mention of an ἐριᾶ (ἐρεᾶ) ἐντύλη, by which the editor understands a woollen wrapper or rug: the word is new to LS.

ἐντυπόω.

Aristeas 67 ἐφ' ᾗ κρυστάλλου λίθος καὶ τὸ λεγόμενον ἤλεκτρον ἐνετετύπωτο, "into this were inlaid crystal and the so-called electron"—in the description of the table sent by Ptolemy Philadelphus to Jerusalem. MGr ἐντύπωσι, "impression."

ἐνυβρίζω.

P Oxy II. 237ᵛⁱ ¹⁷ (A.D. 186) ἐπιμένει τῇ αὐτῇ ἀπονοίᾳ ἐνυβρίζων μοι, "she continues her outrageous behaviour and insulting conduct towards me" (Edd.).

ἐνυπνιάζομαι.

The importance attached to temple visions and dreams in Egypt (cf. Milligan *Selections*, p. 18 ff.) is shown by the mention in P Par 54⁷⁹ of an ἐνυπνιοκριτής in the Serapeum : see also *s.v.* ἐνύπνιον. Boll *Offenbarung*, p. 135 cites Lyd. *de ost.* p. 76, 21 αἰσίους ὀνείρους οἱ ἄνθρωποι ἐνυπνιασθήσονται, οἳ κακὸν πέρας ἕξουσιν.

ἐνύπνιον.

This common LXX word (cf. Ac 2¹⁷) may be illustrated by two passages from the Paris Papyri, both belonging to ii/B.C., P Par 44⁵ (B.C. 153) (= Witkowski², p. 82) ἐγὼ γὰρ ἐνύπνια ὁρῶ πονηρά, 47³⁰ (*c.* B.C. 153) (= *Selections*, p. 23) ἀποπεπτώκαμεν πλανόμενοι ὑπὸ τῶν θεῶν καὶ πιστεύοντες τὰ ἐνύπνια, " we have fallen from hope, being deceived by the gods and trusting in dreams " : cf. the heading of P Leid C (B.C. 163–2) τὸ ἐνύπ[ν]ειον ὃ [εἶ]δεν Τάγης. From the inscrr. we may cite *Syll* 802⁵⁶ (iii/B.C.) where the lame and the blind became whole—ἐνύπνιον ἰδόν[τα]ς μό]νον (ἐνύπνιον = ὄψις), and *Preisigke* 685 (ii/B.C.) ἐνύπνια κρίνω, τοῦ θεοῦ πρόσταγμα ἔχων, τύχ᾽ ἀγαθᾶι.

ἐνώπιον.

To Deissmann's proof (*BS* p. 213) that this word belongs to the vernacular, and is not to be treated as a new formation of " biblical " Greek, much additional evidence can now be added from iii/B.C. onwards. The earliest ex. of the word known to us, P Hib I. 30²⁵ (before B.C. 271), is unfortunately followed by a lacuna—ἡ δίκη σου ἀναγραφήσετ[α]ι ἐν [τῶι ἐν Ἡρ]ακλέους πόλει δικαστηρίωι [ἐ]νώπιον [. . . . , " the case will be drawn up against you in the court at Heracleopolis in the presence of . . ." (Edd.). Wilcken's translation of BGU II. 578¹ (A.D. 189) μετάδ(ος) ἐνώπιον, " deliver personally " (cited by Deissmann *ut supra*) finds an exact parallel in P Tebt I. 14¹³ (B.C. 114) παρηγγελκότες ἐνώπι[ον, " I gave notice in person " (Edd.), P Flor I. 56²⁹ (A.D. 234) μετέδωκ(α) Αὐρηλ(ίω) . . ἐνώπιον ὡς καθήκει. For the prepositional use with the gen. see P Lond 35⁶ (B.C. 161) (= I. p. 25) εἰπάς μοι ἐ[νώπ]ι τοῦ Σάραπι, P Grenf I. 38¹¹ (ii/i B.C.) ὁ ἐνκεκλη[μ]ένος προσπηδήσας μοι ἐ[ν]ωπιό[ν] τινων ἔτυπτεν κτλ., P Oxy IV. 658⁹ (A.D. 250) ἐνώπιον ὑμῶν . . ἔσπεισα, and *Syll* 843⁷ (time of Trajan) ἐνώπιον τῶν προγεγραμμένων θεῶν. In P Grenf II. 71ⁱⁱ ²⁶ (A.D. 244–8) we have ἐνόπιν αὐτοῖς, for which the editors read ἐνώπιον αὐτῶν. In *Syll* 588²⁴⁵ (*c.* B.C. 180) the word is used as a substantive—ποι]ῆσαι κεφαλὴν ἑκατέρωι ἐνωπίωι τῶν στοῶν.

A new adj. ἐνόπιος occurs in P Par 63³⁶ (B.C. 164) (= P Petr III. p. 20) τοσούτω[ν κ]αὶ τηλικούτων διαστολῶν γεγονυίω[ν ὑμῖ]ν καὶ ἐνοπίοις καὶ διὰ γραμμάτων, " though so many and so extensive explanations have been given to you both face to face and in writing" (Mahaffy), Preisigke 3925⁶ (B.C. 149–8 or 137–6) παρηγγελκότε[ς] Ταγῶτι μὲν ἐνωπίωι, Ἐσοροήρει δὲ ἀπ᾽ οἰκίας δι᾽ Ἐπωνύχου φυλακίτου : see Preisigke *Fachwörter*, p. 78.

ἐνωτίζομαι.

Vorstius *de Hebraismis NT*, p. 10 ff. questions the coinage of this word by the LXX translators in order to render the Heb. הֶאֱזִין, and thinks that it was already in use in common speech (" non noviter et a Graecis Interpretibus, aut a scriptoribus N.T., est fabricata ; sed in vulgari sermone obtinuerat iam ante "). Anz, however, regards (p. 378) the

constr. with the dat. found in Exod 15²⁶ BAF as due to Hebraistic influence (וְהַאֲזַנְתָּ לְמִצְוֹתָיו). We are unable to cite any ex. of the verb from vernacular sources, but ἐνώτιον " earring," as in Exod 35²², Isai 3²⁰, is fairly common, e.g. BGU IV. 1101⁷ (B.C. 13) ἐνωτίω(ν) χρυσ(ῶν), P Ryl II. 124³⁰ (i/A.D.) ἐνώδιον χρυσοῦν, *al.* : in P Petr I. 12²⁴ we find the form ἐνώιδιον, as in Attic inscrr. from B.C. 398 onwards, cf. Meisterhans *Gr.* pp. 65, 79.

ἕξ.

PSI IV. 320¹² (A.D. 18) ἀρούρας ἕξ. The adv. ἑξάκις is found in one of the wall scribblings on the royal graves at Thebes, *Preisigke* 1838 Θεόφιλος Κλεοβού[λου] ἑξάκις. MGr ἕξι, ἕξε.

ἐξαγγέλλω.

For this word, found in the NT only in 1 Pet 2⁹, cf. the magic P Lond 46²⁸³ (iv/A.D.) (= I. p. 74) ὅπως αὐτοῖς ἐξαγγείλω τὰ προγεγονότα αὐτοῖς, and from the inscrr. *OGIS* 266³¹ (iii/B.C.) ἐξαγγελῶ . . . τὸν τούτων τι ποιοῦντα [Εὐμέν]ει with the passages cited by Dittenberger *ad l.*, and *ib.* 383¹²¹ (mid. i/B.C.) νόμον δὲ τοῦτον φωνὴ μὲν ἐξήγγειλεν ἐμή, νοῦς δὲ θεῶν ἐκύρωσεν.

ἐξαγοράζω.

For the use of the *simplex* in connexion with the purchase or redemption of slaves, see *s.v.* ἀγοράζω. The similar use of the compound in Gal 3¹³, 4⁵ suggests that in Eph 5¹⁶, Col 4⁵, the meaning is not so much " buying up," " making market to the full of " the opportunity, as " buying back (at the expense of personal watchfulness and self-denial) the present time, which is now being used for evil and godless purposes " (Williams *ad* Col *l. c.* in *CGT*).

ἐξάγω.

For this verb in connexion with leading out from prison, as in Ac 16³⁹, cf. P Tebt I. 15¹³ (B.C. 114) ἔφησαν . . . τὸν μὲν Ἀπολλόδωρον ἐξηγμένον, τοῦ δὲ Μάρωνος ἐν ἔρκτει (*l.* εἱρκτῆι) γεγονότων (*l.*—ος), " they informed us that Apollodorus had escaped, but Maron had been put in prison," so *ib.*²² ὡς ἦν ἐξηγμένος : the pf. part. act. ἐξαγηγοχότα (for form, see *s.v.* ἄγω) is found in P Hib I. 34¹⁰ (B.C. 243–2). The meaning " conduct," " carry out " to the end appears in *Michel* 409¹⁸ (beg. iii/B.C.) τὰ ἐπιτραπέντα αὐτοῖ]ς ἐξα[γ]αγόντας με[χρὶ τέλους. The verb is very common in custom-house receipts = " export," e.g. P Ryl II. 197² (late ii/A.D.) Σαραπίων ἐξάγ(ων) ἐπὶ καμήλ(ῳ) ᾱ μιᾷ λαχανοσπέρμ(ου) ἀρτάβ(ας) ἕξ, " S. exporting on one camel six artabae of vegetable-seed " : cf. PSI IV. 406¹³ (iii/B.C.) ἄλλην (παιδίσκην) ἐξήγοσαν ἐξ Ἀμμώνων, and the use of the subst. in P Lille I. 29¹⁴ (iii/B.C.) μηθενὶ ἐξέστω σώματα πωλεῖν [ἐπ᾽] ἐξαγωγῆι, " that no one be permitted to sell slaves for exportation," P Oxy XII. 1440³ (A.D. 120) receipt for tax on articles exported—ἐξακοκῆς (*l.* ἐξαγωγῆς). It may be noted that Ἐξαγωγή was used by Philo as the title for the second book of the Law, instead of Ἔξοδος : see Nestle in Hastings' *DB* iv. p. 442. In the Rainer Gospel Fragment, which contains a narrative somewhat similar to Mk 14²⁶⁻³⁰, Bickell's later reading is—μετὰ δὲ τὸ φαγεῖν, ὡς ἐξ ἔθους, instead of ὡς ἐξῆγον : see *Mittheilungen aus der Sammlung der Papyrus Erzherzog Rainer* i. p. 53 ff., ii. p. 41 f.

ἐξαιρέω.

PSI IV. 426[17] (iii/B.C.) πρὶν τὸ δεύτερον μέλι ἐξελεῖν, ib. 444[2] (iii/B.C.) τοὺς (δορκαδέους) ἐκ κρεῶν ὠμῶν ἐξειρῆσθαι (l. ἐξῃρῆσθαι). In P Petr III. 36 (a) recto [21] ἀξιῶ οὖν σε ἐξελοῦ με ἐκ τῆς ἀνάγκης, the verb is = "rescue," "deliver," as in Ac 7[10] al. The meaning "pick out," "regard with favour," is found in the Christian amulet P Oxy VIII. 1151[9] (v/A.D.) ἐξελοῦ τὴν δούλην σου 'Ιωαννίαν : cf. ἐξαίρετος as quoted below. For a contrast with προστίθημι see OGIS 762[8] (ii/B.C.) ἐάν τι πρὸς ταύτας τὰς συνθήκας ὁ δῆμος ὁ 'Ρωμαίων καὶ ὁ δῆμος ὁ Κιβυρατῶν κοινῇ βουλῇ προσθεῖναι ἢ ἐξελεῖν βούλωνται. Cf. also P Par 64[58] (B.C. 164-0) καὶ τὸν πύργον ὑμῶν ἐμαυτὸν ἐνσταθμευόμενον ἐξειρῆσθαι, and BGU I. 176[4] (time of Hadrian) ἐξειρέθημεν τῆς ἀπεργασ[ίας. For the verbal ἐξαίρετος = "eximius," "egregius," cf. P Oxy I. 73[26] (A.D. 94) ἐ[ξ]αίρετον δούλην, and P Ryl II. 172[11] (A.D. 208) where after the rental of a palm-garden mention is made of certain "special items"—ἐξερέτων (l. ἐξαιρέτων), and for the subst. ἐξαίρημα cf. Syll 734[78]. On the subst. ἐξαίρεσις = "wharf" at the harbours of Alexandria see P Tebt I. 5[26] (B.C. 118), and cf. Archiv v. p. 306 f.

ἐξαίρω.

For this strong verb (1 Cor 5[13]), cf. P Ryl II. 133[19] (A.D. 33) where in view of an attack upon a dam (?) it is stated that there is a danger τῷ ὅλωι ἐξαρθῆνα[ι], "of its being entirely carried away." It also occurs in the magical papyrus P Lond 121[367] (iii/A.D.) (= I. p. 96) ὁ . . . καθ' ὥραν ἐξαίρων τὸν κύκλον τοῦ οὐρανοῦ : cf. ib. 131 * [73] (A.D. 78) (= I. p. 191), and from the inscrr. Syll 802[87] (iii/B.C.) ἀνῷξε τὸγ γυλιὸν ("wallet") καὶ ἐξαῖρεν ὑγιῆ τὸγ κώθωνα ("cup") γεγενημένον. See also Anz Subsidia, p. 270 f.

ἐξαιτέω.

Field (Notes, p. 76) takes the aor. mid. ἐξῃτήσατο in Lk 22[31] as indicating the success of the requisition, and paraphrases, "Satan hath procured you (" obtained you by asking," RV marg.) to be given up to him"; cf. Syll 330[15] (i/B.C.) ὅτε ἰδίαν χάριν ἐξαιτησάμενοι Πόπλιόν τε Αὐτρώνιον καὶ Λεύκιον Μαρκίλιον. See for the act. ib. 168[29] (iv/B.C.) δι' ὅπερ ἐξαιτή[σαντος αὐτὸν (Λυκοῦργον) 'Αλεξάνδρου ὁ δ]ῆμος ἀπέγνω μὴ συνχωρῆ[σαι μηδὲ λόγον ποιεῖσθαι τῆς] ἐξαιτήσεως, and BGU III. 944[5] (iv/v A.D.) ἐξήτησας τὴν μισθαποχήν ("receipt for pay"). The verb is fully illustrated by Wetstein ad Lk l.c.

ἐξαίφνης.

For the form ἐξαίφνης, which is read by WH only in Ac 22[6] (cf. Notes.[2] p. 158), see P Par 51[8] (B.C. 160) (= Selections, p. 19) καὶ ἐξαί[φνης] ἀνύγω τοὺς ὀφθαλμούς μου, and PSI III. 184[5] (A.D. 292) περὶ ἕκτην ὥραν ἐξαίφνης καύματος ἐνόντος πῦρ κτλ. The very fragmentary letter P Giss I. 86 (ii/A.D.) shows ὅτι ἐξαίφνης ἀπέστιλας : so P Flor II. 175[7] (A.D. 255). In Cagnat III. 1145[5] we have ἐξεφάνης. On the ease with which αι and ε would be interchanged by the scribes, see Proleg. p. 35. MGr ἔξαφνα, ἄξαφνα, ξάφνω, with ξαφνίζω, "frighten," "surprise."

ἐξακολουθέω.

This compound (2 Pet 1[16], 2[2.15]) is often used with reference to "merited" punishment, e.g. P Par 62[v.10] (ii/B.C.) τοῖς δ' ἐγλαβοῦσι ἐξακολουθήσεται τὰ ὑποκείμενα πρόστιμα, and ib. 63[130] (B.C. 165), P Tebt I. 5[132] (B.C. 118) ἀπολύεσθαι τῶν ἐξακολουθο[ύντων αὐ]τ[οῖς προσ]τίμων, "be released from the penalties which they have incurred," PSI III. 168[33] (B.C. 118) ἵν', ἐὰν ἐνσχεθῶσι, τύχωσι τῶν ἐξακολουθούντων (sc. προστίμων). P Rein 17[15] (B.C. 109) οἱ [δὲ] αἴτιοι τύχωσι τῶν ἐξακολουθούντων. Cf. BGU IV. 1208[47] (B.C. 27) τὴν δὲ μετὰ ταῦτα ἐξηκολουθηκυῖαν ὕβριν, P Oxy IX. 1203[9] (late i/A.D.) ἐγλαθόμενος τῆς ἐξακολ[ο]υθούσης αὐτῷ εὐθύνης, "heedless of the reckoning that would follow" (Ed.). From the inscriptions we may cite the notice on the marble barrier of the Temple at Jerusalem, threatening death to any Gentile who was caught penetrating into the inner court—ὃς δ' ἂν ληφθῇ, ἑαυτῶι αἴτιος ἔσται διὰ τὸ ἐξακολουθεῖν θάνατον (OGIS 598[5]—i/A.D.). For the meaning "devolve," "rest upon," see P Ryl II. 163[10] (A.D. 139) τῆς βεβαιώσεως διὰ παντός μοι ἐξ[ακολουθούσης, "the duty of guaranteeing the sale perpetually resting upon me" (Edd.), ib. 323[8] (A.D. 124-5), P Tebt II. 376[16] (A.D. 162) ἀντὶ τῶν ἐξακολουθούντων τῇ μιᾷ τετάρτῳ ἀρού[ρᾳ] ἐκφορίων, "at the rent devolving upon the 1¼ arourae" (Ed.).

ἐξαλείφω.

Syll 439[20] (iv/B.C.) ὃς δ' ἂν δόξηι μὴ ὢν φράτηρ ἐσαχθῆναι, ἐξαλειψάτω τὸ ὄνομα αὐτὸ ὁ ἱερεύς, OGIS 218[129] (iii/B.C.) ἐξαλείψαντας τ[ὸ ὀνομ]α τὸ ἐκείνου—passages which at once recall Rev 3[5]. Cf. also the προσκύνημα Preisigke 4116[9] καὶ μ' ἐξαλείψας ἐπὶ σ' ἐξαλείψας ἐξαλειφθῆναι αὐτῷ τὸ ζῆν, and the Christian prayer P Oxy III. 407[3] (iii/iv A.D.) ἐξαλίψον μου τὰς ἁμαρτίας. For the meaning "deface," "obliterate," see PSI IV. 403[5] (iii/B.C.) τὴμ μὲν ἐπιστολὴν ἣν ἀπέστειλας οὐκ ἠδυνάμην ἀναγνῶναι διὰ τὸ ἐξηλεῖφθαι. The practice of "washing out" the writing on papyrus, so that the sheet might be used for other purposes, is discussed by Erman Mélanges Nicole p. 119 ff.; for the added force thus given to the figure in Col 2[14], see Milligan Documents, p. 16. For a new literary reference see Menandrea, p. 83[210] ὑπόνοιαν . . . [ἀκοσμίας], | ἣν ἐξαλείψαιτ' οὐκέτ' οὐδ' αἰσχ[ύνομαι.

ἐξάλλομαι.

On this medical term, peculiar to Luke in the NT (Ac 3[8]), see Hobart, p. 36 f.

ἐξανάστασις.

This late word, which is not found in the LXX, and in the NT is confined to Phil 3[11], occurs in BGU III. 717[11] (A.D. 149) as amended, unfortunately in a broken context, 'Α]φροδείτην σὺν θήκῃ, ἐξανάστασις, σκάφιον Αἰγύπτιν (l. —τιον) βαθ[. . . κτλ.

ἐξανίστημι.

The verb is used in a juristic sense in P Petr III. 21 (g)[10] (B.C. 226-225) (= Chrest. II. p. 17) πάντας δικαστὰς πλὴν οὗ ἂν ἑκάτερος αὐτῶν ἐξανασ[τήσηι κατὰ τὸ] διάγραμμα, "all judges with the exception of those whom both parties reject," literally "cause to stand down" from the places they occupy: see further P Hal I. p. 205 ff. Cf. *Syll* 879[14] (end of iii/B.C.) ἐξανίστασθαι ἐκ τῆς κηδείας ("mourning") . . . τὰς γυναῖκας.

ἐξαπατάω.

Syll 510[37] (ii/B.C.) ἐξαπατήσαντες τοὺς ὑστέρους δανειστάς, *ib.* 533[47] (beginning of iii/A.D.) εἰ δέ τις ἐξαπατήσα[ς τῶν] ὀφειλόν[των ξένῳ ὑποθείη τι τῶν χωρίων τῶ]ν δημοσίων καὶ τοῦτο ἐλενχθείη, "and if any of the debtors should fraudulently mortgage" etc. For the pass., as in 1 Tim 2[14], cf. P Oxy III. 471[42] (ii/A.D.) ἐξαπατηθ[ῆναι] ἢ καὶ δωρεὰ[ς λαβεῖν] φήσεις; "will you say that you were deceived or that you took bribes?" (Edd.).

ἐξάπινα.

For this rare form (Mk 9[8]) cf. P Giss I. 68[6] (ii/A.D.) ἐξάπινα ἐγένετο τὸ ἀτύχημα καὶ δεῖ αὐτὸν δευτέρᾳ ταφῇ ταφῆναι.

ἐξαπορέω.

Moulton (*Proleg.* p. 237) claims the use of this verb in 2 Cor 4[8] as a good ex. of the "perfectivising" of an imperfective verb, the perfective ἐξ showing "the ἀπορία in its final result of despair." The verb is used in a weaker sense in P Eleph 2[10] (B.C. 285–4) where, amongst other testamentary dispositions, provision is made that if the parents are in want of anything—ἐὰν δέ τι ἐξαπορῶνται—they are to be provided for by their sons. In *Syll* 226[12] (iii/B.C.) it is used of the exhaustion of the public resources of Olbia— τῶν δὲ κοινῶν ἐξηπορημένων.

ἐξαποστέλλω.

For the common Bibl. meaning "commission," "send forth," cf. OGIS 90[20] (Rosetta stone—B.C. 196) προενοήθη δὲ καὶ ὅπως ἐξαποσταλῶσιν δυνάμεις ἱππικαί τε καὶ πεζικαί, *Syll* 276[19] (a plebiscite of the Lampsacenes—B.C. 196) ὁ δῆμος τοῦ Ῥωμαίων δήμου ἐξαπέσ[τει]λεν αὐτούς, *ib.* 295[8] (a decree found at Delphi—*c.* B.C. 175) ἐξαπ[ε]σταλκὼς θεωρούς. We may also cite PSI IV. 384[4] (B.C. 248–7) ἐξαπέσταλκεν αὐτὸν . . . εἰς Φιλαδέλφειαν, and for the verb in the judicial sense of "sending" before a ruler or tribunal, cf. P Tor I. 1[iii. 13] (B.C. 117–6) ἐξαποσταλῶσι πρός σε, ὅπως τύχωσι τῆς ἁρμοζούσης ἐπιπλήξεως, P Tebt I. 22[15] (B.C. 112) δέσμ[ιο]ν αὐτὸν ἐξαπόστειλον πρὸς ἡμᾶς, P Ryl II. 127[22] (A.D. 29) καὶ τοὺς αἰτίους ἐξαποστεῖλαι ἐπὶ σὲ πρὸς τὴν ἐσομένην ἐπέξοδ(ον), and so P Par 38[20] (B.C. 162), P Rein 17[13] (B.C. 109), P Grenf I. 38[18] (ii/i B.C.): see Semeka *Prozessrecht* i. p. 247. For the frequency of the double compd. in late Greek, see Glaser *De ratione*, p. 33 f.

ἐξαρτίζω.

As this verb is said to be "rare in prof. auth." (Grimm-Thayer), it may be well to illustrate it pretty fully from the Κοινή. P Oxy II. 296[7] (i/A.D.) πέμψον ἡμεῖν περὶ τῶν βιβλίον (*l.* —ίων) ᾗ ἐξήρτισας, "send me word about the documents, how you have completed them," where the editors remark that ἐξήρτισας probably = ἐτελείωσας: cf. Ac 21[5]. In *Chrest.* I. 176[10] (mid. i/A.D.) αὐτὸς ἠναγκάσθην ἐκ τοῦ ἰδίου ἀγοράσας ἐξαρτίσαι καὶ μηχανή[ν, the verb =

"supply," "furnish": with 2 Tim 3[17], cf. P Amh II. 93[8] (A.D. 181) ἐλαιουργῖον . . . ἐνεργὸν ἐξηρτισμένον ἄπασι, "an oil-press in working order and completely furnished," P Tebt II. 342[17] (late ii/A.D.) κεραμεῖον . . . ἐξηρτισμ(ένον) πᾶσι, P Lond 1164(*h*)[11] (A.D. 212) (= III. p. 164) of a boat σὺν κώποις δυσὶ ἐξηρτισμένον, "supplied with two oars." For the subst. see P Ryl II. 233[13] (ii/A.D.) τὰς τιμὰς ὧν ἀγοράζει ἐξαρτισμῶν, "the prices of the fittings which he buys," and cf. Aristeas 144 πρὸς . . . τρόπων ἐξαρτισμὸν δικαιοσύνης ἕνεκεν σεμνῶς ταῦτα ἀνατέτακται, "for the perfecting of character." See also *s.v.* καταρτίζω.

ἐξαστράπτω.

See *s.v.* ἀστράπτω. The compound, which occurs in the NT only in Lk 9[29] (cf. LXX Ezek 1[4, 7], Nah 3[3]) may convey the idea of "flashing forth" as from an *inward* source (cf. Farrar *CGT ad l.*), but is perhaps simply intensive, "dazzling" (RV).

ἐξαυτῆς.

For this late Greek word (= ἐξ αὐτῆς τῆς ὥρας) found six times in the NT, we can supply an almost contemporary instance from P Lond 893[6] (A.D. 40) (published in P Ryl II. p. 381) καλῶς π[οιή]σεις ἐξαυτῆ(ς) πέμψας μοι τὸν μεικρόν. See also P Ryl II. 236[22] (A.D. 256) ποίησον δὲ ἐξαυτῆς ὤμους δύο ἐλαιουργικοὺς κοπῆναι, "have two beams (?) cut at once for oil-presses" (Edd.), P Tebt II. 421[2] (iii/A.D.) (= *Selections*, p. 106) ἐξαυτῆς ἅμα τῷ λαβεῖν σε ταῦτά μου τὰ γράμματα γενοῦ πρὸς ἐμέ, P Oxy I. 64[3] (iii/iv A.D.) ἐξαυτῆς παράδοτε, "deliver at once." The word is fully illustrated by Wetstein *ad* Mk 6[25].

ἐξεγείρω.

With the use in 1 Cor 6[14] cf. *Syll* 802[118] (iii/B.C.), where, in connexion with the healing of a man in the Asclepieum, we read—ἐξεγερθεὶς δὲ ὡς ἦν ὑγιής, ἔφα ὄψιν ἰδεῖν. See also Wünsch *AF* 5[21] (iii/A.D.) ἐν τῷ ἰσα[ρίθμ]ῳ ὀνομάσω αὐτὸ καὶ οἱ δαίμονες ἐξεγερθῶσιν ἔκθαμβοι, of the arousing of the spirits of the dead by means of the divine name.

ἔξειμι.

P Oxy VI. 934[3] (iii/A.D.) ἐξιόντος μου εἰς Ἀλεξάνδριαν, "as I was setting forth for A.," P Lips I. 110[5] (iii/iv A.D.) μέλλων ἐξειέναι ἐπὶ τὴν Καπαδοκίαν.

ἔξειμι

from εἰμί, see *s.v.* ἔξεστι.

ἐξελέγχω.

This verb which is read in the TR of Jude 15 occurs in an official letter of B.C. 117, P Tebt I. 25[14] καὶ ὡς ἔν τι παραδώσιν ὑπαρχόντων τῶν ἐξελεγξέντων (*l.* —όντων) ὑμᾶς. See also *Syll* 237[8] (Delphi—end of iii/B.C.) ἐξήλεγξαν τοὺς ἱεροσυληκότας, OGIS 669[58] (i/A.D.) ἐὰν δέ τις ἐξελεγχθῆι ψευσά[μενος.

ἐξέλκω

is found in its literal sense of "draw out" (cf. Gen 37[23]) in connexion with the account of the healing in the Asclepieum of a man who had been blinded by a spear, *Syll* 803[87] (iii/B.C.) ἐδ[όκει οἱ τὸν θεὸν] ἐξελκύσαντα τὸ βέλος εἰς τὰ β[λέφα]ρα τὰς καλουμ[ένας οἱ κόρας πά]λιν ἐναρμόξαι.

ἐξέραμα.

With the use of this noun in 2 Pet 2²² (cf. Prov 26¹¹ ἔμετον) we may compare the verb ἐξεμέω in the account of a cure in the Asclepieum, *Syll* 803¹²⁸ (iii/B.C.) ὅλον] τὸ λώπιον ("cloak") μεστὸν ὢν ἐξήμεσε κακῶν. MGr ξερνῶ "vomit."

ἐξεραυνάω.

For the idea of careful, minute search, as in 1 Pet 1¹⁰, cf., in addition to the LXX passages (1 Macc 9²⁶ *al.*), Pss Sol 17¹¹ ἐξηρεύνησε (ὁ θεὸς) τὸ σπέρμα αὐτῶν καὶ οὐκ ἀφῆκεν αὐτούς: also Vett. Val. p. 267⁵ διαίρεσιν ἐκ πείρας καὶ πόνου ἐξηρεννημένην. On the spelling see *s.v.* ἐραυνάω.

ἐξέρχομαι.

For this verb in its ordinary sense it is sufficient to cite P Oxy II. 282¹¹ (a complaint against a wife—A.D. 30–35) κατὰ πέρ[α]ς ἐξῆ[λθε] καὶ ἀπηνέκαντο (*l.* —ἔγκαντο) τὰ ἡμέτερα, "finally she left the house and they carried off my belongings," *ib.* III. 472¹ (*c.* A.D. 130) ἀπὸ τῆς ἐκείνου οἰκίας ἐξεληλύθει, *ib.* 528⁷ (ii/A.D.) ἀφ' ὡς ἐξῆλθες (*l.* ἐξ—) ἀπ' ἐμοῦ πένθος ἡγούμην, "ever since you left me I have been in mourning" (Edd.): cf. for the constr. with ἀπό, Lk 5⁸. P Oxy I. 112⁵ (iii/iv A.D.) δήλωσόν μοι ἣ πλοίῳ ἐξέρχ[ει] ἢ ὄνῳ shows the verb followed by the instrumental dat.: cf. Jn 21⁸. For ἐξέρχομαι of the driving forth of demons, as in Mk 1²⁹ *al.*, cf. the magical P Par 574¹²⁴³ (iii/A.D.) (= *Selections*, p. 114) ἔξελθε, δαῖμον, . . . καὶ ἀπόστηθι ἀπὸ τοῦ δ.ε)ῖ(να), and for the verb followed by ἐπί cf. P Tebt II. 283³ (B.C. 93 or 60) ἐξελήλυθεν ἐπὶ τὴν . . μητέρα μου, "made an attack upon my mother." For a technical usage to denote the going out of a court attendant to carry out a magistrate's instructions cf. *Chrest.* II. 89³⁸ (time of Antoninus Pius) ἐξῆλθεν Δ[ι]όσ[κ]ορ[ος] Ἁρποκρατ-(ίωνος) ὑπη[ρ]έτης (with Mitteis's note), and *ib.* 372ᵛ·⁴ (ii/A.D.): see also Wilcken *Archiv* vi. p. 294.

ἔξεστι.

BGU IV. 1127¹⁰ (B.C. 18) μὴι ἐξῖναι τῶι Ἀ. λέγιν, PSI III. 203⁷ (A.D. 87) μὴ ἐξέστω δὲ τῇ Φιλωτέρᾳ προσρείπτειν τῷ Παποντῶτι τὸ σωμά[τιον ἐντὸς τοῦ χρόνου(?), *ib.* 218² (A.D. 250) οὐκ ἐξόντος οὐδενὶ τῶν ὁμολογούντων παραβαίνειν τὰ προκείμενα. With the inf. omitted, as in 1 Cor 10²³, cf. P Ryl II. 77⁴³ (A.D. 192) τοῦτο δὲ οὐκ ἐξῆν, "this was not permissible," and *ib.* 62¹⁶ (translation of an unknown Latin work—iii/A.D.) πάντα τὰ ἄλλα ἔξεστί μοι, a passage which recalls 1 Cor 6¹²: see also Epict. ii. i. 23 νῦν ἄλλο τί ἐστιν ἐλευθερία ἢ τὸ ἐξεῖναι ὡς βουλόμεθα διεξάγειν; In PSI III. 218² *ut s.* and P Oxy II. 275²² (A.D. 66) (= *Selections*, p. 56) οὐκ ἐξόντος τῷ Τρύφωνι ἀποσπᾶν τὸν παῖδα, gen. abs. stands for the older acc. abs., which has not kept its place in the Κοινή except in τυχόν, "perhaps" (1 Cor 16⁶): cf. Blass *Gr.* p. 252, *Proleg.* p. 74.

ἐξετάζω

is found along with ἀκριβῶς. as in Mt 2⁸, in P Oxy II. 237ᵛⁱ·³¹ (A.D. 186) καὶ ὅτι φθάνει τὸ πρᾶγμα ἀκρειβῶς [ἐξ]η-τασμένον, "and the fact that a searching inquiry into the affair had already been held" (Edd.). Other examples of

this common verb are P Gen I. 54³⁰ ἐξέτασον περὶ τοῦ πράγματος τούτου ὅτι οὐδεμία διαφορὰ οὔκ ἐστιν, P Oxy III. 582 (ii/A.D.) ἐξήτασα ἕνεκα τοῦ ἄλλου χαλκοῦ καὶ τοῦ συμβόλου, BGU II. 380⁵ (iii/A.D.) (= *Selections*. p. 104) ἐξέτασε (*l.* ἐξήτασα) περὶ τῆς σωτηρίας σου καὶ τῆς πεδίων (*l.* παιδίων) σου, and P Grenf I. 53²² (iv/A.D.) μὴ ἐμὲν ἐξέταξε ἀλλὰ τ[ο]ὺ[ς] πρεσβυτέρους τῆς ἐκκλησίας where, as the editor points out, the meaning is "if you do not be-lieve me, ask the elders of the church." In P Amh II. 79⁹⁰ (*c.* A.D. 186) the verb is construed with the gen.—ὅταν γὰρ ἐξεστάσῃς (*l.* ἐξετάσῃς) ἑνὸς ἑκάστου [τῶ]ν ἀρχόντων. For the pass. see P Petr III. 20ⁱⁱⁱ·⁶ Δημήτριος δὲ ἐξητάσ[θη] τοῦ μὴ γνῶσιν εἰστεθ[ῆ]ναι, P Tebt II. 335¹¹ (mid. iii/A.D.) Ἑρμα[ίσκος δὲ] εὕρηται καὶ ἐξήτασται. From the inscrr. we may add *OGIS* 773⁵ (iv/iii B.C.) ἀνακαλεσάμενος τοὺς τριηρ-άρχους καὶ ἐξετάσας ἀνέσωισε τὰ ἀνδράποδα μετὰ πάσης φιλοτιμίας, and *Syll* 356¹² (B.C. 6) ἐξετάσαι προστάξας . . . διὰ βασάνων = *quaerere tormentis*, of slaves after the murder of their master. The subst. is used forensically, as in Wisd 1⁹, 3 Macc 7⁵, in P Oxy X. 1272²¹ (a complaint of theft—A.D. 144) ἀξιῶ . . ἀχθῆναι ἐπί σε τὸν Ἡρᾶν . . . καὶ τὴν δέουσαν ἐξέ[τ]ασιν γενέσθαι, "I ask that Heras should be brought before you and that the proper inquiry should be made," and so *saepe*. For the derivation of the verb see *s.v.* ἀνετάζω. MGr (ἐ)ξετάζω, ζητῶ, "prove," "try."

ἐξηγέομαι.

BGU IV. 1208⁴⁸ (B.C. 27) μεταπε[μ]φθεὶς ὑπὸ σοῦ ὁ [Καλατ]ύτις ἐξηγή[σατό μ]οι ἀκεραίως ("afresh"), *OGIS* 763⁷⁸ (ii/B.C.) μετὰ πλεί[σ]ονος σπουδῆς διελέχθησαν ἐξηγο[ύ-μενοι σύμπαν]τος τοῦ πλήθους πρὸς ἡμᾶς ἐκτενε[στάτην τε καὶ] εἰλικρινῆ τὴν εὔνοιαν: cf. *Syll* 600⁴ (iv/B.C.) καθότι Σκιρ[ίδα]ι ἐξηγούμενοι εἰσφέρουσι (*sc.* εἰς τὸν δῆμον), where the editor notes "Sciridarum gens ins habet de iure sacro respondendi (ἐξηγεῖσθαι), ut apud Athenienses Eumolpidae." Numerous exx. of the technical use of the verb, and of its corresponding subst. to denote the communication of divine and other secrets are given by Wetstein *ad* Jn 1¹⁸, e.g. Pollux VIII. 124 ἐξηγηταὶ δὲ ἐκαλοῦντο οἱ τὰ περὶ τῶν διοσημείων καὶ τὰ τῶν ἄλλων ἱερῶν διδάσκοντες. See also the combination of the offices of ἱερεύς and ἐξηγητής in P Oxy III. 477⁴ (A.D. 132–3) and the discussion on the varied duties of the ἐξηγητής in Hohlwein *L'Égypte Romaine*, p. 224 ff., and in *Archiv* iii. p. 351 f. Ἐξήγησις, at first written ἐξέτησις (*i.e.* ἐξαίτησις), occurs in the magic P Lond 122⁷³ (iv/A.D.) (= I. p. 118). MGr ἐξηγῶ, "explain."

ἐξήκοντα.

In a marriage-contract of A.D. 170 provision is made that in the event of a separation taking place the dowry shall be repaid ἐν ἡμέραις ἑξήκοντα ἀ[φ' ἡ]ς ἐ[ὰν ἡ ἀ]παλλαγὴ γένηται (P Oxy VI. 905¹³ = *Selections*, p. 87). The editors note that "in Roman marriage-contracts thirty days is a commoner limit." According to Thumb (*Handbook*, p. 328) ἑξήντα δυό, "sixty-two," in MGr denotes an indefinitely large number.

ἐξηλόω

is not found in the NT, but in view of Justin's use (*Dial.* 108) of ἀφηλωθείς to denote that Christ was "unnailed" from the cross (cf. Stanton *Gospels* i. p. 100), we may give one or two exx. of its use in the **Κοινή**—P Oxy X. 1272[8] (A.D. 144) εὗρον . . . [π]ανάριον ἐξηλωμένον, "I found a box unfastened" (Edd.), P Tebt II. 332[15] (A.D. 176) where complaint is made of robbers who τὰς θύρ[α]ς ἐξηλώσαν[τ]ες ἐβάσταξαν, "extracting the nails from the doors carried off" what was within, and P Flor I. 69[21, 24] (iii/A.D.) ἐξήλουσι σανίδες (= —ας). See also Sophocles *Lexicon s.v.*: the verb is not in LS.

ἑξῆς.

For this word in reference to *time*, as in all its NT occurrences, cf. P Oxy II. 257[27] (A.D. 94-5) τοῦ ἑξῆς ἤ (ἔτους), "of the following 8th year," *ib.* VII. 1035[8] (A.D. 143) τοῦ ἑξῆς μηνὸς Φαμενώθ, "of the next month Phamenoth," and the elliptical usage, as in Ac 21[1] *al.*, in *ib.* 1003[6] (ii/iii A.D.) τῇ ἑξῆς (*sc.* ἡμέρᾳ) following a preceding σήμερον. With the *v.l.* ἐν τῷ ἑξῆς (probably = ἐν τῷ ἑξῆς χρόνῳ) "soon afterwards" (RV), in Lk 7[11] cf. the MGr στὸ ἑξῆς, "for the future," which Thumb (*Handbook*, p. 328) quotes from Aegina. In P Hamb I. 12[1] (A.D. 209-10) the heading ἡ ἐπίσκεψις ἑξῆς δηλοῦται = "the revision is carried on further in this column," and in [21] the same words = "the revision is carried on further in the following column": see p. 46. The thought of "in order," "suitably," appears in such passages as P Par 26[48] (B.C. 163-2) (= *Selections*, p. 18) ἵνα, πᾶν τὸ ἑξῆς ἔχουσαι, πολλῷ μᾶλλον τὰ νομιζόμενα . . . ἐπιτελῶμεν, "that, when we have everything in order, we may be much better able to perform our regular duties," P Oxy II. 282[7] (A.D. 30-35) ἐγὼ μὲν οὖν ἐπεχορήγησα αὐτῇ τὰ ἑξῆς καὶ ὑπὲρ δύναμιν, "I for my part provided for her what was suitable and indeed beyond my resources": cf. P Tebt II. 319[34] (A.D. 248) where an agreement regarding the division of property after the enumeration of certain particulars concludes—καὶ τὰ ἑξῆς, "and so on," indicating, as the editors point out, that the document is a copy of the original, breaking off at the immediately preceding word, and omitting the concluding formula.

ἐξίστημι, ἐξιστάω, ἐξιστάνω.

The verb is common in the sense of "resign" property, etc., e.g. P Oxy II. 268[11] (A.D. 58) ἡ δὲ Ὠφελοῦς καὶ αὐ[τὴ]ς ἐξέσταται τῶι Ἀντιφάνει τοῦ κατ᾽ αὐτὴν μ[έ]ρους τῶν ὑπὸ τοῦ μετηλλαχότος αὐτῆς πατρὸς Ἡρακλᾶτος ἀπολελιμμένων πάντων, "and Ophelous on her part resigns to Antiphanes her share of all the property left by her late father Heraclas" (Edd.), P Tebt II. 380[19] (A.D. 67), P Ryl II. 75[6, 10, 16] (late ii/A.D.), *ib.* 117[22] (A.D. 269) *al.* Ἐξέστην occurs in BGU IV. 1208[37] (B.C. 27): cf. also *ib.* II. 530[13] (i A.D.) (= *Selections*, p. 61) κινδυνεύω ἐκστῆναι οὗ ἔχω [κλή]ρου, "I run the risk of losing the allotment which I now possess." See further for the usage of Mk 3[21], 2 Cor 5[13], *Menandrea* p. 47[84] ἐξέστηχ᾽ ὅλως, and *ib.* p. 57[275] ἐξέ[στηκα] νῦν τελέως ἐμαυτοῦ καὶ παρώξυμ[μαι σ]φόδρα, and Vett. Val. p. 70[25] πρὸς γὰρ καὶ ταῖς διανοίαις ἐκστήσονται. The trans. use "bewilder," "confound," as in Lk 24[22], Ac 8[9], is illustrated by Musonius p. 35[12] ταῦτα γὰρ δὴ τὰ ἐξιστάντα καὶ φοβοῦντα τοὺς ἀνθρώπους ἐστίν, ὅ τε θάνατος καὶ ὁ πόνος.

ἐξισχύω.

BGU I. 275[11] (A.D. 215) καὶ ἐπείρασαν αὐτὴν (*sc.* μηχανὴν) ἐπανοῖξαι καὶ οὐκ ἐξείσχυσαν, P Oxy VIII. 1120[7] (early iii/A.D.) ἀλλὰ οὗτος ἐξείσχυσεν τὰ βιβλείδια ἀθετηθῆναι, "but his influence procured the failure of the petition" (Ed.). See also Vett. Val. p. 288[12] πολλάκις γὰρ ὑπ᾽ ὄψιν προδείξαντες τὸ ἀποτέλεσμα ἠτόνησαν διὰ τὸ ἐπὶ δυναστικοῦ τόπου ἕτερον τετευχότα ἐξισχῦσαι. These examples make it at least doubtful whether it is possible to give the verb the intensive meaning "be fully able," "be strong" (RV), often assigned to it in Eph 3[18].

ἔξοδος.

For ἔξοδος in contrast with εἴσοδος see *s.v.* εἴσοδος, and note further P Leid R[4] where ε]ἰσόδου κ[αὶ] ἐξόδου refer to "income" and "expenditure": so *Michel* 1001[vi. 34] (*c.* B.C. 200). Similarly ἐξοδιάζω and ἐξοδιασμός are common = "pay" and "payment." Cf. MGr ἔξοδα, "expenses," ἐξοδεύω, ξοδεύω, ξοδιάζω, "spend." In BGU IV. 1105[24] (*c.* B.C. 10) ἔξοδος = "divorce," in *ib.* I. 168[15, 16] (A.D. 169) = "judicial decision," and in P Oxy XII. 1417[9] (early iv/A.D.) apparently = "voyage." For the word = "death," as in Lk 9[31], 2 Pet 1[15], see the Will of Abraham, Bishop of Hermonthis, about the end of vi/A.D.—P Lond 77[57] (= I. p. 234, *Chrest.* II. p. 372) κελεύω μετὰ τὴν ἐμὴν ἔξοδον τοῦ βίου τὴν περιστολὴν τοῦ ἐμοῦ σώματος κτλ., and cf. Epict. iv. 4. 38 ὅρα ὅτι δεῖ σε δουλεύειν ἀεὶ τῷ δυναμένῳ σοι διαπράξασθαι τὴν ἔξοδον, τῷ πάντως ἐμποδίσαι δυναμένῳ κἀκεῖνον θεραπεύειν ὡς Κακοδαίμονα: see further *ExpT* xviii. p. 237.

ἐξολοθρεύω.

In Ac 3[23], from LXX Deut 18[19], WH read ἐξολεθρευθήσεται in accordance with the preponderant evidence of the LXX uncials. The other spelling has survived in MGr ξολοθρεύω: see Thackeray *Gr.* i. p. 87 f. As showing the strength of the verb we may cite *Pelagia-Legenden*, pp. 23[15] εἰσαγαγεῖν σε ἐν τῷ οἴκῳ μου οὐ τολμῶ, μή πως ἀκούσῃ ὁ ὁρμαστός σου καὶ παγγενῆ με ἐξολοθρεύσῃ, 24[18] ἄγγελον ἐξαποστελεῖ καὶ ἐξολοθρεύσει πᾶσαν τὴν στρατιάν.

ἐξομολογέω.

For the ordinary meaning "acknowledge," "avow openly," cf. P Hib I. 30[18] (B.C. 300-271) οὔτε τῷ πράκτορι ἠβούλου ἐξομο[λογήσ]ασθαι, "nor were willing to acknowledge the debt to the collector" (Edd.), P Oxy XII. 1473[9] (A.D. 201) ἀμφότεροι δὲ ἥ τε Ἀπολλωνάριον καὶ ὁ Ὡρείων ἐξομολογοῦνται τὸν καὶ διὰ τῆς περιλύσεως ἐξομολογηθέντα γεγονότα αἱαυτοῖς ἐξ ἀλλήλων υἱόν, "both Apollonarion and Horion acknowledge the son born to them, who was also acknowledged in the deed of divorce" (Edd.): see also the Median parchment P Sa'id Khan [i 7] (B.C. 22-1) (= *JHS* xxxv. (1915) p. 28) ἐξωμολογήσατο καὶ συνεγράψατο Βαράκης καὶ Σωβήνης . . . εἰληφέναι παρὰ Γαθάκου τοῦ Οἰπάτου ἀργυρίου ἐπισήμου δραχμὰς τριάκοντα. MGr ξομολογῶ = "hear one's confession" (c. acc.) = "shrive": ἐξομολόγησι, "confession." How readily this may pass into the sense of "consent," "agree," as in Lk 22[6], may be seen from such passages as P Tebt I. 183 (late ii/B.C.) τοῦ κω[μάρχ]ου ἐξωμολογησαμένου ἕκαστα, P Flor I. 80[11] (i/A.D.) ἐξομολογουμένην (*l.* —μένη) τὴν πίστιν (*l.* —ιν), *Syll* 925[85] (B.C. 139?) ἐξωμολογημένας εἶχεν τὰς ἀποδ(ε)[ί](ξ)[εις. In the LXX the idea of "give thanks," "praise," is prominent: cf. in the NT Mt 11[25], Lk 10[21], and perhaps Phil 2[11] (see Lightfoot *ad l.*).

ἐξόν.

See s.v. ἔξεστι.

ἐξορκίζω.

With Mt 26⁶³ may be compared the heathen amulet BGU III. 956⁶ (iii/A.D.) ἐξορκίζω ὑμᾶς κατὰ τοῦ ἁγίου ὀνόματος θεραπεῦσαι τὸν Διονύσιον, and the magical papyri P Par 574¹²⁰ (iii/A.D.) (= Selections, p. 113) ἐξορκίζω σε δαῖμον . . . κατὰ τούτου τοῦ θεοῦ κτλ., P Lond 46⁵⁰ (iv/A.D.) (= I. p. 67) ἐξορκίζω σε κατὰ τῶν ἁγίων ὀνομάτων . . . καὶ κατὰ τῶν φρικτῶν ὀνομάτων . . . παράδος τὸν κλέπτην κτλ. See also BGU IV. 1141¹⁰ (B.C. 14) ἐρωτῶ σε οὖν καὶ παρακαλῶι καὶ τὴν Καίσαρος τύ[χη]ν σε ἐξορκίζωι, P Leid Wᵛⁱ·²¹ (ii/iii A.D.) ὡς ἐξώρκισά σε, τέκνον, ἐν τῷ ἱερῷ, "veluti obtestatus sum te, fili, in templo" (Ed.), and the love-spell Preisigke 4947⁷ (iii/A.D.) ἐξορκίζω τὸν πάντα συνέχοντα κύριον θεόν . . ποίησον Α . . . . φιλεῖν με. See also Wünsch AF 3²⁵ cited s.v. ἀποδιορίζω.

ἐξορύσσω.

In BGU IV. 1024ⁱᵛ·⁴ (iv/v A.D.) the editor supplies ἐξο-ρώρυχαις γὰρ [ὃν ἔθαψε δημοσία [νεκρὸ]ν ἡ πόλις (καὶ) ἠλέησεν, understanding by the first word ἐξορώρυχας instead of ἐξορωρυχώς which would have suited the construction better. See also Syll 801⁵ (ii/A.D.) ἀλλὰ ἀτειμάσει ἢ μετα-θήσει ὅρους ἐξορ[υσσ ων, amended by Dittenberger from ἐξορῶν on the stone.

ἐξουδενέω, ἐξουθενέω.

For this strong compound = "set at nought" (Suidas: ἀντ' οὐδενὸς λογίζομαι), as in Mk 9¹², cf. BGU IV. 1117³¹ (B.C. 13) μέχρι τοῦ ἐξ̣ο̣υδ̣ε̣νη̣σ̣αι καὶ ἐκτελέσαι καὶ ἐκτεῖ-σαι τῷ Εἰρηναίωι [ὃ ἐ]ὰν ἐνοφιλήσωσιν κτλ. The form ἐξουθενέω is found in Mk.¹, Lk³, and Paul⁸, and in the more literary LXX writers. The later LXX books show ἐξουδενόω coined when οὐδείς was reasserting itself against οὐθείς: see Thackeray Gr. i. p. 105, and cf. Lob. Phryn. p. 182. Ἐξουδενίζω, which is used by Plutarch, occurs in Lk 23¹¹ W.

ἐξουσία.

For the primary meaning of this important word "power of choice," "liberty of action," cf. BGU IV. 1158¹³ (B.C. 9), where it is joined with ἐγλογή--μένε(ιν) περὶ ἑατ[ὴν Κορ-ν(ηλίαν) τὴν ἐξουσία(ν) καὶ ἐγλογή(ν) ἑαυτὸν πράσσειν τὸ κεφά[λ]αιο ν). Hence the common usage in wills, contracts, and other legal documents, to denote the "claim," or "right," or "control," one has over anything, e.g. P Oxy II. 272²⁹ (A.D. 66) ὁμολογ[ο]ῦμεν ἔχειν σε ἐξουσίαν σε]αυτῆ τὴν ἀπ[αί]τη[σ]ιν ποιεῖσθαι παρὰ τοῦ Ἡρακλέου τῶν προ-κειμένων ἀργ(υρίου) δραχμῶν, BGU I. 183²³ (A.D. 85) ἔχειν αὐτὴν τὴν ἐξουσίαν τῶν ἰδίων πάντων, P Tebt II. 319²¹ (A.D. 248) ἐξουσίαν ἔχειν τῶν ἑαυτοῦ ὑπαρχόντων: see also Milligan ad 2 Thess 3⁹. For the definite idea of right given by law, see P Oxy II. 237ᵛⁱⁱ·¹⁷ (A.D. 186) ἀξιῶ τοῦ νόμου διδόντος μοι ἐξουσίαν κτλ. and ib. ᵛⁱⁱ·²⁷,ᵛⁱⁱⁱ·⁴: cf. also ib. 259¹³ (A.D. 23) where a man undertakes to produce a prisoner within a month—μὴ ἔχοντός μου ἐκξουσίαν (l. ἐξ—) χρόνον ἕτερον [κ]τή[σ]εσθαι, "as I have no power to obtain a further period of time." In Syll 328⁶ (B.C. 84) π]ρὸς ἐμὲ ἦλθ[εν ἐ]ν Ἀπαμήᾳ ἠρώτησέν τε [ὅπως ἂν] ἐξου-

σίαν αὐ[τ]ῷ [π]οιήσω ἐπὶ τοῦ συν[βο]υλίο[υ, where we seem at first to have the same construction as in Rev 14¹³, the editor understands the last words as " . . . . " The meaning "power of rule," "authority," appears in BGU IV. 1200²⁰ (B.C. 2) Ἡρακλείδης καὶ Διονύσιος . . . . . . ἐξουσίαν ἔχοντες τῶν Ἀσκληπιάδου ἀνόμως ἀποδέ-δωκαν κτλ., P Kal II. 81² (. A.D. 194) τὴν γὰρ ὅλου τοῦ πράγματος ἐξουσίαν τοῖς κατασ[π]ορεῦσι ἐπέθεμην, P Giss I. 11¹⁰ (A.D. 118) (= Chrest. I. p. 524) οὐκ ἀγνοεῖς ὅτι ἄλλας ὀκτὼ μυριάδες ἔχω πλοίων ὧν ἐξουσίαν ἔχω, and Wünsch AF 4²¹ (iii A.D.) ὁρκίζω σε τὸν θεὸν τὸν ἔχοντα τὴ[ν ἐξουσίαν τῆς ὥρας ταύτης. For the general sense of exhibiting weight and authority, as in Mk 1²², cf. P Fay 125⁶ (ii/A.D.) ἀντι-λαβὼν ἣν ἐξουσίαν ἔχεις, "using all the influence you have" (Edd.), and on the bearing of this meaning in the difficult 1 Cor 11¹⁰, see Ramsay Cities, p. 202 ff., where it is shown that, in accordance with the Oriental view, "a woman's authority and dignity vanish along with the all-covering veil that she discards." In P Par 63¹¹⁰ (B.C. 164) (= P Petr III. p. 34) we have ἕτερός τις ἐμ βαρυ[τέ]ραι κειμενος ἐξουσίαι. "any other persons in high office" (Mahaffy), and for the reference of the word to civil magistracy or rule, as in Rom 13¹. see P Lond 1178⁹ (A.D. 194 (= III. p. 215. Selections, p. 68) δημαρχικῆς ἐξουσίας, the tribunicia potestas of Claudius, and cf. P Oxy VI. 904²⁰ (petition to a praeses—v/A.D.) ὅθεν τὰς ἱκεσίας προσφέρω τῇ ὑμετέρᾳ ἐξουσίᾳ . . . ἵνα κἀγὼ τούτου τυχὼν εὐχαριστήσω ταῖς ἀκλεινεῖς (l. ἀκλινέσι) ἀκοαῖς τῆς ὑμετέρας ἐξουσίας, "accordingly I make my en-treaties to your highness . . . in order that having gained my request I may bless the impartial ears of your highness." (Edd.). In an interesting note in his Poimandres, p. 48 n.², Reitzenstein claims that in the NT, as in the Hermes dialogue, the idea of "knowledge" is mingled with that of "power."

ἐξουσιάζω.

In the sepulchral inscr. CIG III. 4584, after the statement that the monument had been provided by certain persons ἐξ ἰδίων καμάτων, it is added—θυγατέρα αὐτῶν μὴ ἐξουσιά-ζειν τοῦ μνήματος: cf. the inscr. from the catacombs of Syracuse IG XIV. 70² Ἀφροδισίας καὶ Εὐφροσύνου ἀγορασία τόπος· μηδὶς ἐξουσιάσῃ ἄλλος.

ἐξοχή.

For the metaph. phrase κατ' ἐξοχήν (Ac 25²³) see Syll 373¹⁶ (i/A.D.) ἐπιτελέσαι τῷ κατ' ἐξοχὴν παρ' ἡμεῖν τειμω-μένῳ θεῷ Διὶ Καπετωλίῳ, OGIS 764⁶² (ii/B.C.) ἔπαθλα κατ' ἐξοχὴν καλά: cf. Vett. Val. p. 17² καθόλου ἐξοχὰς ἐχόντων περὶ ἐπιστήμην, and the use of the word in our slang sense of "a lead" in Cic. Att. iv. 15. 6. A corresponding use of the adj. is found in Vett. Val. p. 101 ἐν παντὶ δὲ τὸ ἔξοχον μάλιστα προδώσουσιν ἐν τῷ παιδευτικῷ: cf. OGIS 645⁶ (iii/A.D.) τοῦ ἐξοχωτάτου ἐπάρχου and P Oxy XII. 1469¹ (A.D. 298) Αἰμιλίῳ . . . διαδεχο μένῳ τὰ μέρη τῶν ἐξοχω-τάτων ἐπάρχων, where the editors note that ἐξοχώτατος (eminentissimus) occurs frequently in inscr. with reference to prefects of the Praetorian Guard or of Syria, but is very rare in Egypt. See also the fragmentary dinner-menu P Giss I. 93 καυλίων ἔξοχα ϛ[. . . .] λοπὰς ἰχθύος μ[. . . . For the verb in the mid. = "cling to," like προσέχομαι, cf.

P Oxy VII. 1027⁶ (i/A.D.) ἐξ οὗ καὶ ἐξεχομένου μου τῆς τῶ[ν] ἠνεχυρασμένων προσβολῆς, "when I therefore pursued my right of entry upon the transferred property" (Edd.). In MGr ἐξοχή has developed a new meaning "country."

ἐξυπνίζω.

"I wake out of sleep," as in Jn 11¹¹ (cf. 3 Kings 3¹⁵, Job 14¹²) is Hellenistic for ἀφυπνίζω (see Lob. *Phryn.* p. 224); cf. also ἐξυπνόω in Ps 120(121)⁴ and apparently Vett. Val. p. 344² where for ἐξ ὕπνου μέγεθος Kroll reads ἐξυπνουμένη. MGr ξυπνῶ.

ἔξυπνος.

The adverb is found P Giss I. 19⁴ (ii/A.D.) ὅτι ἐξ[ύπ]νως ἐ[ξ]ῆλθες ἀπ' ἐμοῦ. MGr ἔξυπνος, "wide-awake," hence "sharp," "clever."

ἔξω.

For this common adverb we may refer to the numerous nursing-contracts in BGU IV. where a very general provision is that the child shall be cared for ἔξω κατὰ πόλιν, that is "outside" the house of the person who gives it in charge, but "in the town": thus in 1108⁶ (B.C. 5) the nurse promises τροφεύσειν καὶ θηλάσειν ἔξω παρ' ἑατῇ κατὰ πόλ(ιν): see further *Archiv* v. p. 38. In PSI IV. 340¹⁰ (B.C. 257–6) Ἀμύνταν δὲ ἔξω τε σκηνοῦντα, ἔξω is opposed to ἐν τῇ χώρᾳ, and for a similar contrast with ἔσω cf. BGU IV. 1141³¹ ˡ. (B.C. 14) περὶ δὲ Ξύστου μοι γράφεις, ὅτι ἔξωι καχεκτεύεται, ἤ (= εἰ) τι μὲν ὁ σύνδουλος αὐτὸν δυνήσεται συστῆσαι, ἐγὼ οὐκ ἐπίσταμαι, οὐδὲ γὰρ καθεύδωι ἔσωι ἵνα εἰδῶι. Exx. of the adv. equivalent to an adj., as in Ac 26¹¹, are BGU IV. 1114⁵ (B.C. 4) ἐν τοῖς ἔξω τόποις, and P Oxy VI. 903²⁰ (iv/A.D.) τὰς ἔξω θύρας. For the word as a prep. c. gen., as in 2 Cor 4¹⁶, cf. P Oxy III. 489¹⁴ (A.D. 132), a declaration in a census-return that no one dwells in a certain house—ἔξω τῶν προγ(εγραμμένων), "except the aforesaid," and the phrase ἔξω ἱεροῦ βωμοῦ, with reference to the being "outside" the protection of a temple and altar, as discussed s.v. βωμός.

The collocation δεῦρ' ἔξω (Jn 11⁴³) is found in *Menandrea* p. 35⁴⁸ ˡ διόπερ ὑπεκδέδυκα δεῦρ' ἔξω λάθρᾳ, and for the comp. cf. P Oxy III. 498¹² (ii/A.D.) τῶν μὲν ἐξωτέρω λίθων κύβων καμηλικῶν, "the outer squared camel stones." In P Rev Lᵃᵇ·¹⁵ (iii B.C.) ἔξω ὅρα "at the end of the line, 'look outside,' calls attention to the fact that a note on the *verso* is to be inserted at this point" (Edd.). A quaint parallel to οἱ ἔξω (e.g. in Col 4⁵) is seen in the MGr ὁ ἔξω ἀπ' ἐδῶ, "he who is far from this place," meaning "the devil." The word is also found in MGr under the forms ὄξω, ὄξου.

ἔξωθεν.

P Fay 110⁸ (A.D. 94) κ[α]ὶ τὰ κύκλωι τοῦ ἐλαιουργίου ἔξωθεν σκάψον ἐπὶ βάθος, "and dig a deep trench round the oil-press outside" (Edd.).

ἐξωθέω.

In PSI I. 41¹⁶ (iv/A.D.) a woman complains regarding her husband—ἐξώσε[μ]ε ἄνευ αἰτίας πρὸ δέκα τούτω[ν ἐνι]αυτῶν εἰς τὴ[ν πα]ροῦσαν [ἀπορίαν(?)—cf. the stronger force

of the *v.l.* in Acts 27³⁹. Cf. also P Flor I. 58⁹ (iii/A.D.) ἐξέωσαν followed by a lacuna, and perhaps P Leid Wⁱ·¹⁰ (ii/iii A.D.) εἰσηλθόντος γὰρ τοῦ θεοῦ περισσότερον ἔξα (*l.* ἔξω) ὠθήσονται, where the editor suggests that we should perhaps read ἐξωσθήσονται.

ἐξώτερος.

An adj. ἐξωτικός, which survives in MGr, is found in the vi/A.D. PSI IV. 284² τῶν ὑπὸ σε ἐξω[τ]ικῶν ἀρουρ(ῶν). Cf. also MGr ξωτικό, "ghost."

ἔοικα.

P Oxy VI. 899¹⁸ (A.D. 200) ἀνδράσι γὰρ ἔοικεν τὰ τῆς γεωργίας, "for men are the persons suitable for undertaking the cultivation" (Edd.). For εἰκός cf. BGU IV. 1208¹⁸ (B.C. 27–6) εἰκός σε μετειληφέναι κτλ.

ἑορτάζω.

For this verb which in the NT is confined to 1 Cor 5⁸, but is frequent in the LXX, cf. BGU II. 646⁶ (A.D. 193), an order issued by a prefect during the short reign of the Emperor Pertinax—ἵνα πάντες ἰδιῆτα[ι] (*l.* εἰδῆτε) καὶ ταῖς ἴσαις ἡμέραις ἑορτάσητ[α]ι (*l.* ἑορτάσητε). See also *OGIS* 493²⁵ (ii A.D.) κ[αθ'] ἕκαστον ἐνιαυτὸν] ἑορτάζειν τὴν γενέθλιον αὐ[τοῦ καὶ πᾶσιν] ἀνθρώποις αἰτίαν ἀγαθῶν ἡμέ[ραν, with reference to a birthday celebration.

ἑορτή.

For this common word it is sufficient to cite BGU II. 596⁷ (A.D. 84) (= *Selections*, p. 64) ὅπως εἰς τὴν ἑωρτὴν (cf. Jn 13²⁹) περιστερίδια ἡμεῖν ἀγοράσηι, P Fay 118¹⁶ (A.D. 110) ἀγόρασον τὰ ὀρνιθάρια τῆς εἰορτῆς, P Oxy III. 475¹⁷ (A.D. 182) ἑορτῆς οὔσης ἐν τῇ Σενέ[πτα, *ib.* IV. 725³ⁱ (contract of apprenticeship—A.D. 183) ἀργήσει δὲ ὁ παῖς εἰς λόγον ἑορτῶν κατ' ἔτος ἡμέρας εἴκοσι, "the boy shall have 20 holidays in the year on account of festivals" (Edd.), *ib.* IX. 1185²⁹ (c. A.D. 200) τὴν τοῦ βασιλέως ἑορτὴν ἐπιτελείτωσαν, "let them celebrate the festival of the sovereign"—perhaps his birthday: cf. τὴν ἑορτὴν . . ποιῆσαι, Ac 18²¹ D. With ἑόρτασμα, LXX Wisd 19¹⁶, cf. the adj. ἑορτάσιμος. P Giss I. 40ⁱⁱ·²⁰ (A.D. 212) ἑτέραις τισὶν ἑορτασί[μοις ἡ]μέραις, *OGIS* 524⁷ ἐν ταῖς ἑορτασίμοις τῶν Σεβαστῶν ἡμέραις. A form ἑορτικός occurs P Strass I. 42¹⁹ (A.D. 509). In P Tebt II. 417²⁴ ᶠᶠ (iii/A.D.) μάθε τοῦ Μώρου ὅτι τί θέλις ἀγοράσωμεν εἰς Ἀντινόυ (*l.* -όου), we may perhaps supply ἑορτήν, as in Jn *l.c.*

ἐπαγγελία.

For this word in its original sense of "announcement" we may cite *Syll* 605⁷ (iii/B.C.) καὶ τοῖς ἀποδημοῦσιν ἐπὶ τὰς σπονδοφορίας διατελεῖ μετ' εὐνοίας ἀπογράφων τὴν ἐπαγγελίαν, *ib.* 260⁹ (not after B.C. 199) οἱ ᾑρημένοι ὑπὸ Μαγνήτων περὶ τῆς ἐπαγγελίας τοῦ ἀγῶνος. In *Michel* 473¹⁰ (ii/B.C.) καὶ αὐτὸς ἐπαγγελίαν ποιησάμενος ἐκ τῶν ἰδίων ἔδωκεν εἰς τὴν [κατασκευὴν τῆς] στοᾶς, the word is seen with the meaning of "promise," which apparently it always has in the NT: cf. further *Priene* 123⁹ with reference to a magistrate who on taking office had promised a distribution of food—ἐβεβαίωσεν δὲ τὴν ἐπαγγελίαν παραστή[σ]ας μὲν τοῖς ἐντεμενίοις θεοῖς τὴν θυσίαν. In PSI IV. 281³⁸ (ii/A.D.)

κατὰ τὰς ἐπαγγελίας αὐτοῦ, the "promises" are almost = "threats": see the editor's note.

ἐπαγγέλλομαι,

= "promise," as in Heb 10²³, 11¹¹, may be illustrated by P Petr I. 29¹² (iii B.C.) (= Witkowski², p. 31) ἐχρησάμην δὲ καὶ παρὰ Δύνεως ἀρτάβας ὃ κριθοπύρων αὐτοῦ ἐπαγγελομένου καὶ φιλοτίμου ὄντος, P Tebt II. 411⁹ (ii/A.D.) εἰ μὴ ἐπηγγειλάμην σήμερόν σε παρέσασθαι, "had I not promised that you would be present to-day," P Oxy I. 71⁶·⁸ (A.D. 303) ἅπερ διὰ τῶν αὐτῶν γραμματίων ἐπηγγίλατο ἀποδώσειν ἄνευ δίκης κτλ. Ramsay (Exp VII. viii. p. 19) draws attention to the use of the verb in 1 Tim 6²¹ where it is applied to "volunteers, who set up as teachers with the intention to make a business and a means of livelihood out of the Word of God," and notes its application "to candidates for municipal favours and votes in the Greek cities, who publicly announced what they intended to do for the general benefit, if they gained popular support"—cf. Cagnat IV. 766 (Mossyna in Phrygia—A.D. 80–100) (= C. and B. i. p. 146) τὰ δὲ λοιπὰ οἱ ἐπαγγειλάμενοι καθὼς ὑπογέγραπται — the names of the promisers being appended. The verb is also a kind of term. tech. in the inscr. for the announcement of public sacrifices, e.g. Syll 258⁹ (iii/B.C.) τοῖς ἐπαγγέλλοσι τὰν θυσίαν καὶ ἐκεχηρίαν τᾶς Ἀρτέμιδος : cf. 1 Tim 2¹⁰ and Philo de Human. 1 (= II. p. 384 ed. Mangey) ἐπαγγέλλεται θεοῦ θεραπείαν.

ἐπάγω.

With 2 Pet 2¹·⁵ cf. P Ryl II. 144²¹ (A.D. 38) ἔτι δὲ καὶ ἐτόλμησεν πθόνους (l. φθόνου) μοι ἐπαγαγεῖν αἰτίας τοῦ μὴ ὄντος, "moreover he had the audacity to bring baseless accusations of malice against me" (Edd.). In the early marriage contract P Tebt I. 104¹⁹ (B.C. 92) we have μὴ ἐξέστω Φιλίσκωι γυναῖκα ἄλλην ἐπ[α]γ[α]γέσθαι ἀλλὰ Ἀπολλωνίαν, "it shall not be lawful for P. to bring in any other wife but A." (cf. the t.t. ἐπεισάγω), and in P Oxy VIII. 1121²¹ (A.D. 295) the verb is = "induce," when a petitioner complaining of certain persons who had carried off valuables adds — τίνι ἐπαγόμενοι οὐκ ἐπίσταμαι, "on what inducement I cannot tell" (Ed.). A new formula with reference to enrolment is found in P Hib I. 32⁴ (B.C. 246) Ἡράκλειτος Ἡρ[ακλεί]του Καστόρειος τῶν οὔπω [ἐ]πηγμένων, "H. son of H., of the Castorian deme but not yet enrolled," and more fully in P Petr I. 27(3)⁵ τῆς ἐπιγονῆς τῶν οὔπω ἐπηγμ[ένων, and so ib. III. 11²⁷, 132²⁰. In the Egyptian calendar ἐπαγόμεναι ἡμέραι = Aug. 24–28, with a sixth ἐπαγομένη ἡμέρα (= Aug. 29), were "inserted" once in four years.

ἐπαγωνίζομαι.

Syll 732¹⁶ (B.C. 36–5) ἀδιαλίπτως δὲ ἐπαγωνιζόμενος, Michel 394¹⁹ (mid. i/B.C.) διαδεξάμενός τ' αὐτὸς ἐπηγωνίσατο τῇ πρὸς τὴν πόλιν ε[ὐ]νοίᾳ, "vied in good will towards the city."

Ἐπαίνετος.

This proper name (Rom 16⁵) is found in an imprecatory tablet from Corcyra, Syll 808⁴: cf. the list of names from Hermopolis Magna Preisigke 599¹⁵⁰ (Ptol.) Ἐπαίνετος Θόαντος, and the fem. in Michel 1503ᴰ·ⁱ·²⁹ (ii/i B.C.)

Ἐ]παινέτη Ἀριστοβούλου. For the adj., apparently in an active sense, cf. the rhetorical fragment PSI I. 85⁴ (iii/A.D.) ἀπομνημόνευμα σύντομον ἐπὶ προσώπου τινὸς ἐπενετόν (l. ἐπαινετόν), "a concise laudatory memoir regarding some person": see further s.v. ἀπομνημόνευμα.

ἐπαινέω.

Syll 192⁶² (B.C. 290–87) καὶ ἐπὶ πᾶσι τούτοις ἐπείνεκε (for form see Meisterhans Gr. p. 171) καὶ ἐστεφάνωκεν αὐτὸν ὁ δῆμος [οὔθεν ἐλλείποντα] σπουδῆς πρὸς τὴν πόλιν, Magn 115ᵃ·¹³ (ii/A.D.) ὅτι μὲν γὰρ τ]ὴν ἐμὴν ἐκπονεῖς [γ]ῆν . . . ἐπαι[ν]ῶ σὴν πρόθεσιν. According to Meisterhans Gr. p. 211 the construction with the acc. prevails from B.C. 350: previous to that the verb is found also with the dative. For the constr. in Lk 16⁸ with the acc. of the person and the gen. of the thing we may compare IMAe iii. 910 Θ. τὴν ἑαυτοῦ γυναῖκα . . . στοργῆς καὶ καλοκάγαθίας ἧς ἔσχεν ἰς ἐμὲ ἀφηρόϊσεν ("canonized as a hero"). In P Eleph 13⁴ (B.C. 223–21) ἐγὼ οὖν ἐπυνθανόμην τοῦ Σανῶτος, εἴ τι βούλοιτο ἐν τοῖς καθ' ἡμᾶς τόποις, ὁ δὲ ἐπῄνει μόνον, ἐπέταξεν δ' οὐθέν, ἐπῄνει is = "approbat," "assentiebatur," almost = "thanked me," "said he was obliged" (cf. the classical formula, κάλλιστ' ἐπαινῶ, a sense which apparently does not occur elsewhere in the papyri : see Witkowski's note, Epp.², p. 43. MGr παινῶ retains the meaning "praise."

ἔπαινος.

Rouffiac (Recherches, p. 46) aptly illustrates the use of this common noun in Phil 1¹¹ from Priene 109⁹ (beginning of i/B.C.) μεγίστου τέ]τευχεν ἐπαίνου καὶ δόξης ἀτα[ράκτου, and in 1 Pet 1⁷ from ib. 53¹⁵ (ii/B.C.) ἀξίως ἐπαίνου καὶ τιμῶν ποιεῖσθαι τὰς κρίσεις. The word is MGr.

ἐπαίρω.

P Petr III. 46(3)¹¹ εἰς τοὺς ἐπαρθέντας τοίχους (corrected from τὸν ἐπαρθέντα), "walls built to a greater height" (Edd.). P Oxy X. 1272¹² (A.D. 144) καὶ τὴν τοῦ πεσσοῦ θύραν ἐπηρ[μ]ένην "and that the door of the terrace had been lifted" (Edd.). Syll 737²¹ (ii/A.D.) "whoever wishes the resolutions just read to be passed and inscribed on a pillar—ἀράτω τὴν χεῖρα. πάντες ἐπῆραν," where the compound following the simplex has the stronger perfective force (Proleg. p. 113). As illustrating the Jewish (Ps 28²) and Christian (1 Tim 2⁸) as well as Pagan (Virg. Aen. i. 93) practice of "lifting up" hands in prayer, reference may be made to the two uplifted hands shown on the stele inscribed with the Jewish prayer for vengeance found at Rheneia : see Deissmann LAE, Fig. 64, p. 424. MGr παίρ(ν)ω, "take," "fetch."

ἐπαιτέω.

In P Lond 24⁴ (B.C. 163) (= I. p. 32) a recluse at the Serapeum describes himself as living—ἀφ' ὧν ἐπαιτῶ ἐν τῶι ἱερῶι, "from what I beg in the temple": cf. Lk 16³ ἐπαιτεῖν αἰσχύνομαι. That temples generally were a promising haunt for the profession Luke reminds us elsewhere. Ἐπήτρια, the Greek for a "beggaress"—to parallel it with an equal novelty—appears as a ἅπ. εἰρ. in P Par 59¹⁰ (B.C. 160) (= Witkowski,² p. 76, where see note): cf. ἀγύρτρια

(Aesch. *Ag.* 1273), δέκτρια (Archil. 8). The pass. of the verb is found in P Tebt I. 26¹³ (B.C. 114) πρὸς πῆι (*l.* τῆι) ἐπιδόσει τῶν ἐπαιτουμένων λόγων, "for the delivery of the accounts which were required" (Edd.).

ἐπακολουθέω.

From its original meaning "follow," "follow after," this verb came to be used in a number of closely related senses from iii/B.C. onwards. Thus it means "am personally present at," "see to," in P Petr II. 40(*b*)⁶ (iii/B.C.) καλῶς οὖν ποιήσεις ἀποστείλας τινά τῆι ῗ, ὃς ἐπακολουθήσει τῆι ἐγχύσει τοῦ γινομένου σου γλεύκους, "it were well for you, then, to send some one on the 8th who will see to the pouring out of the must which comes to you" (Ed.): cf. P Oxy VII. 1024³³ (A.D. 129) ἣν καταθήσεται εἰς τὴν γῆν ὑγιῶς ἐπακολουθούντων τῶν εἰωθότων, "under the observance of the usual officers" (Ed.), and *ib.* 1031¹⁸ (A.D. 228). Hence the meaning develops to "conform to," "concur with," as P Lille I. 4⁰² (B.C. 218–7) τῆς πρὸς Θ. ἐπιστολῆς ὑπογέγραφα ὑμῖν τὸ ἀντίγραφον, ὅπως ἐπακολουθοῦντες ποιῆτε κατὰ [τα]ῦτα, "pour que vous vous y conformiez" (Ed.), P Fay 24 ⁹ (A.D. 158) ἐγρ(άφη) δ(ιὰ) Σα . . . . ς νομο-[γ]ρ άφου) ἐπακολουθοῦντος Διοδώρου ὑπηρέτου, "written by S . . . . , scribe of the nome, with the concurrence of Diodorus, clerk," and similarly P Greuf II. 62¹¹ (A.D. 211). The derived meaning "ensue," "result," is common, as P Ryl II. 126¹⁹ (A.D. 28–9) ἐξ οὗ βλάβος μοι ἐπηκολούθησεν (*l.* ἐπηκολ—) οὐκ ὀλίγον, "by which no small loss resulted to me," BGU I. 72¹² (A.D. 191) οὗ χολικὴν βλάβην ἐπεκολούθησεν, *ib.* 2¹¹ (A.D. 209) ὡς ἐκ τούτου οὐκ ὀλίγη μοι ζημία ἐπηκολούθησεν, P Oxy X. 1255¹⁰ (A.D. 292) τῶν μετρημάτων γ[ι]νομένω[ν] εἰς τὸ μηδεμίαν μέμψιν ἐπακολουθῆσαι, and from the inscrr. *Syll* 325²⁶ (i/B.C.). Another development of meaning is "ratify," as in P Gen I. 22¹ (A.D. 37–8) Ἐπίμαχος Ζωπύρου ἐ[π]ηκολούθηκα τῇ [πρ]οκειμένῃ διαγραφῇ, P Oxy II. 260²⁰ (A.D. 59), P Ryl II. 122²⁰ (A.D. 127), P Flor I. 1²⁶ (A.D. 153), and more particularly "verify," "check" an account, as in the signatures to a series of tax receipts P Tebt I. 100²⁰ᶠ. (B.C. 117–6) Δρεῦος ἐπηκολούθηκα (*l.* ἐπηκολ—), Ἀκουσίλαος ἐπηκολούθηκα. This last usage throws an interesting side-light on [Mk] 16²⁰ τοῦ κυρίου . . . τὸν λόγον βεβαιοῦντος διὰ τῶν ἐπακολουθούντων σημείων: the signs did not merely follow, they acted as a kind of authenticating signature to the word (cf. Milligan *Documents*, p. 78 f.). We need only cite further the usage in registration documents, e. g. P Oxy II. 244⁹ (A.D. 23) τοὺς ἐπακολουθ(οῦντας) ἄρνας [κ]αὶ ἐρίφους, "the lambs and kids that may be produced" (Edd.), *ib.* 245¹¹ (A.D. 26). See also the important discussion on the verb in Wilcken *Ostr* i. pp. 76 f., 640, and cf. *Archiv* ii. p. 103, iii. p. 14. In P Oxy VI. 909⁴ (A.D. 225) the mother of certain minors is described as ἐπακολουθήτρια, "a concurring party": cf. P Lips I. 9⁶ (A.D. 233) and see *Chrest.* II. i. p. 250 f. For the subst. ἐπακολούθησις cf. P Ryl II. 233¹⁴ (ii/A.D.) μηδὲν χωρὶς ἐπακολουθήσεως αὐτοῦ ἀγοράζεται, "nothing is being bought without his cognizance" (Edd.), P Oxy XII. 1473⁸ (A.D. 201) γ]ράμματα ἐκδιδομένη τῆς ἐπακολουθήσεως τῷ Ὡρείωνι, "delivering to Horion the documents of settlement" (Edd.). Note the syncopated form which persists in MGr ἀκλουθῶ, and cf. P Tebt I. 100²⁰ (quoted above) for its early date, B.C. 117–16.

ἐπακούω.

With ἐπακούω in 2 Cor 6² (fr. LXX Isai 49⁸) cf. the invocation to Isis by a dreamer in the Serapeum P Par 51²⁴ (B.C. 160) (= *Selections*, p. 20) ἐλθέ μοι, θεὰ θεῶν, εἵλεως γινομένη, ἐπάκουσόν μου, ἐλέησον τὰς διδύμας. So also P Leid Wᵛ·⁴¹ (ii/iii A.D.) κύριε . . . εἴσελθε καὶ ἐπάκουσόν με (note the late acc. of person as after the MGr ἀκούω), *ib.* x. ³⁶ ἄτερ γὰρ τούτων ὁ θεὸς οὐκ ἐπακούσεται, BGU IV. 1080⁶ (iii/A.D. ?) κατὰ τὰς κοινὰς ἡμῶν εὐχὰς καὶ προσευχάς, ἐφ' αἷς οἱ θεοὶ τέλιον (*l.* —ειον) ἐπακούσαντες παρέσχον, and the Christian P Oxy XII. 1494⁷ (early iv/A.D.) εἴν' οὕτως ἐπακούσῃ ὁ θαιὸς τῶν εὐχῶν ὑμῶν. In a ii/B.C. Delphic inscr. a certain Bacchius is described as having bestowed benefactions on the city—ἐπακούσας προθ[ύ]μως τὰ ἀξιούμενα (*Syll* 306¹¹). The adj. is found in a iii/A.D. love-spell, *Preisigke* 4947⁶ ἵνα με φιλῇ καὶ ὃ ἐὰν αὐτὴν αἰτῶ, ἐπήκοός μοι ἦν (*l.* ᾖ).

ἐπακροάομαι.

For the medical usage of this verb, which in the NT is peculiar to Lk (Ac 16²⁵), see Hobart, p. 234.

ἐπάν.

See for this word P Tebt I. 27⁶² (B.C. 113) ἐπὰν καὶ περὶ (om.) τὸ περὶ τῆς [ἀφέσε]ως πρόγραμμα ἐκτεθῇ, P Ryl II. 153²³ (A.D. 138–61) ἐπὰν δὲ γένηται τῆς ἐννόμου ἡλικίας, "when he attains the legal age," *ib.* 172²⁹ (offer to lease a palm-garden —A.D. 208) ἐπὰν δὲ μή τις προσθῇ σοι, "as long as there is no higher offer" (Edd.), P Oxy VIII. 1102²⁰ (c. A.D. 146) ἐπὰν τὰ ὑπ' ἐμοῦ κελευσθέν[τ]α γένηται, "as soon as my orders have been carried out" (Ed.), *ib.* XII. 1473³⁶ (A.D. 201) ἐπ[ά]ν, ὃ μὴ εἴη, ἀπαλλ[αγῶμεν, "whenever, which heaven forbid, we are divorced" (Edd.), PSI IV. 299¹⁸ (iii/A.D.) ἐπὰν πλοίου εὐπορηθῶ.

ἐπάναγκες.

This word, which in the NT occurs only in Ac 15²⁸, and is described by Blass (*ad l.*) as a "doctum vocabulum" which Luke might naturally be expected to use, may be illustrated by P Ryl II. 65⁵ (B.C. 67?) δι' ἧς ἐπάναγκες τὸν παραβησόμενον . . . ἀποτεῖσαι τῶι ἔθνει ἐπίτιμον, "whereby it was provided that any person breaking the agreement should be compelled to pay to the association a fine," P Flor I. 50¹⁰⁷ (A.D. 268) ὥστε ἑκάστην μερίδα ἐπάναγκες χορηγεῖν, P Oxy I. 102¹⁸ (A.D. 306) βεβαιουμένης δέ μοι τῆς ἐπιδ[ο]χῆς ἐπάναγκες ἀποδώσω τὰ λυπὰ (*l.* λοιπὰ) τοῦ φόρου, and from the inscrr. *Syll* 737⁸⁶ (c. A.D. 175) ὁ δὲ ἐπάνανκες ἀγορὰν ἀγέτω, *ib.* 871⁹ (with reference to a Trust) ὅπως ἐπάναγκες αὐτοῖς οἱ δ[εό]μενοι τῆς πορθμείας χρῶνται. See also Menander *Fragm.* p. 176 οὐδὲν διαβολῆς ἐστιν ἐπιπονώτερον· τὴν ἐν ἑτέρῳ γὰρ κειμένην ἁμαρτίαν εἰς μέμψιν ἰδίαν αὐτὸν ἐπάναγκες λαβεῖν. For ἐπάναγκον, see P Fay 91¹⁵ (A.D. 99) ἐπάνα[γ]κον οὖν παρεμβαλεῖν τὴν Θ. ἐν [τ]ῶι . . . ἐλαιουργίωι . . . [ἐ]λαϊκοὺς καρποὺς ἐκπεπτωκότας (*l.* ἐκπεπτ—) εἰς τὸ ἐνεστὸ(ς) τρίτον ἔτος, "Th. is accordingly obliged to feed the olive-press with the olive produce included in the present third year," and for ἐπαναγκάζω, see P Oxy II. 281²⁵ (A.D. 20–50) ὅπως ἐπαναγκασθῇ συνεχόμενος ἀποδοῦναί μ (om.) μοι τὴν [φ]ερνὴν σὺν ἡμιολίᾳ, "that he may be compelled perforce to pay back my dowry increased by half its amount" (Edd.), and *ib.* XII. 1470¹⁶ (A.D. 336) ἐπαναγκασθῆναι τὸν αὐτὸν Δημητριαγὸν κτλ.

ἐπανάγω.

P Par 63⁶ (B.C. 164) (= P Petr III. p. 18) τῶι Δὶ ἱκανῶς ἐπανήγομεν, "we give ample acknowledgments to Zeus" (Mahaffy): cf. *ib.* ⁵⁷ ἐπανάγοντα τὸ διστ[α]ζόμενον ἐπὶ τὸν ἐκκείμενον κανόνα, "if he applied the doubtful cases to the rule provided for him" *id.*'. See also P Vat A¹⁵ (B.C. 168) (= Witkowski², p. 65) οὐ γὰρ πάντως δεῖ στενῶς ἐπανάγοντά σε (omit) προσμένειν ἕως τοῦ πορίσαι τι καὶ κατενεγκεῖν.

ἐπαναπαύομαι.

A new citation for this verb, which is found only twice (Lk 10⁶, Rom 2¹⁷) in the NT, may be given from Didache 4² ἐκζητήσεις δὲ καθ' ἡμέραν τὰ πρόσωπα τῶν ἁγίων, ἵνα ἐπαναπαῇς τοῖς λόγοις αὐτῶν, "that you may be refreshed by their words," where the form of the 2nd aor. pass. ἐπαναπαῇς recalls the fut. ἐπαναπαήσεται read by אB in Lk *l.c.* (cf. also ἀναπαήσονται in Rev 14¹³).

ἐπανέρχομαι.

For this verb (Lk 10³⁵, 19¹⁵) we may cite the interesting rescript P Lond 904²³ (A.D. 104) (= III. p. 125, *Selections* p. 73) ordering all persons who happen to be residing out of their homes ἐπα[νελ]θεῖν εἰς τὰ ἑαυ[τῶν] ἐ]φέστια in view of the approaching census: cf. Lk 2¹ᶠᶠ. For other exx. see P Flor I. 61⁸⁴ (A.D. 85) (= *Chrest.* II. p. 89) μ]ετὰ εἴκοσι ἔτη ἐπανελεύσῃ πρὸς ἐμέ, P Oxy VI. 933¹⁷ (late ii/A.D.) ὥστε ἐπανελθόντα σε μαρτυρήθῃ (*l.* μαρτυρήσειν), "so that when you come back you will bear me witness," so *ib.* VII. 1064¹¹ (iii/A.D.), P Tebt II. 333¹⁰ (A.D. 216) μέχρι τούτ[ο]υ οὐκ ἐπανῆλθαν, "up to this time they have not returned," BGU I. 260¹² (iii/A.D.) δ[η]λῶ . . . ἐπανεληλυθέναι [τοὺ]ς πρ[ο]-κειμ[έν]ους καμήλ[ους] δύο, and from the inscrr. *Syll* 276⁷ (*c.* B.C. 105) ὅταν ἐπανέλθωσιν οἱ πρεσ[β]ευταί.

ἐπανίστημι.

Syll 136¹⁰ ἀπὸ] . . . τῶν ἐπαν[αστ]ά ν τ[ων τῶι δήμωι τ]ῶι Κερκυραίων. For the subst. Boll (*Offenbarung* p. 132) cites *Catalogus codd. astr. gr.* VIII. 3, 174, 3 ἐχθρῶν ἐπανά-στασιν, 169, 26 μεγάλου προσώπου ἐπανάστασιν ἑτέρου πρὸς ἕτερον. MGr ἐπανάστασι, "insurrection," "revolution."

ἐπανόρθωσις.

For the literal meaning of this subst. see *Michel* 830⁴ (end ii/B.C.) εἰς τὴν ἐπανόρθωσιν τοῦ ἱεροῦ τῆς Ἀρτέμιδος. With the metaph. usage in 2 Tim 3¹⁶, cf. P Oxy II. 237ᵛⁱⁱⁱ· ³⁹ (A.D. 186) καίτοι πολλάκις κριθὲν ὑπὸ τῶν πρὸ ἐμοῦ ἐπάρχων τῆς δεούσης αὐτὰ τυχεῖν ἐπανορθώσεως, "although my predecessors often ordered that these (abstracts) should receive the necessary correction," *ib.* I. 78²⁹ (iii/A.D.) ὃ προσῆκόν ἐστι πρᾶξαι περὶ τῆς τούτων ἐπανορθώσεως, and *ib.* 67¹⁴ (A.D. 338) πάντα μέν, ὡς ἔπος ἐστὶν εἰπεῖν, ὅσα εἰσχύειν τι δύν[α]-τ[αι] παρὰ τὴν τῶν νόμων [ἰσχὺ]ν πρὸς ὀλίγον εἰσχύει, ἐπανορθοῦτε (*l.*—αι) δὲ ὕστερον ὑπὸ τῆς τῶν νόμων ἐπεξε-λεύσεως, "everything, it may be said, that is able to withstand the power of the law withstands but for a short time

and then submits to the law's correcting vengeance " (Edd.). For an additional ex. of the verb, see P Gen I. 1³⁷ (A.D. 158) εἰ μάθοιμι παρὰ τὰ κεκελευσμένα πρά[σ]σοντας ἐπι-στρεφ[ή]στερον ὑμᾶς ἐπανορθώ[σω]μαι. P Ryl II. 302 (iii/A.D.) is addressed to an official—ἐπανορθωτῇ τῆς ἱερᾶς . . ., and in OGIS 711⁴ this noun is used with a political reference (" vocabulum sollenne iuris publici est, expressum ex Latino *corrector*," Dittenberger).

ἐπάνω

is common with reference to something already mentioned, e.g. P Oxy III. 502⁵⁴ (A.D. 164) μεμίσθωκα σὺν τοῖς ἐπάνω τὰς ἐν τῇ αὐλῇ κέλλας, "I have leased together with the above-mentioned premises the chambers in the court" (Edd.), BGU IV. 1046ⁱⁱ· ⁷ (ii/A.D.) ὁ αὐτὸς ἐπάνω γενόμενος καὶ σιτολ(όγος), P Hamb I. 12¹⁷ (A.D. 209–10) ὑπὸ τῶν ἐπάνω πρεσβ υτέρων): cf. P Oxy VII. 1032³⁴ (A.D. 162) ὡς ἐπάνω δηλοῦται, "as stated above." In connexion with time the phrase οἱ ἐπάνω χρόνοι, "the former times," is often met: e.g. in P Hib I. 66⁶· ²³ (B.C. 250), P Oxy II. 268¹⁷ (A.D. 58) *ib.* 237ᵛⁱⁱⁱ· ³⁸ (A.D. 186), P Tebt II. 307¹⁷ (A.D. 198). For the use of ἐπάνω as an "improper" preposition (= "above," "over," cf. P Oxy III. 405⁵ (A.D. 181–9) ἐ]ν . . . κέλλῃ τῇ ἐπάνω τοῦ πυλῶνος, P Leid Wᵛⁱⁱ· ⁶ (ii/iii A.D.) ἐὰν θέλῃς ἐπάνω κορκοδείλου (*l.* κροκο- by metathesis) διαβαίνειν, P Ihr I. 56³² (B.C. 208) ἐπάνω λίμνης, and see Thumb in *ThLZ* xxviii. p. 422 for the survival of this usage in MGr ἐπάνω, ἐπάνω's, ἀπάνω. It may be added that ἐπάνω charged out of ἐπάνου is found in an ancient "curse" strongly tinged with Jewish influences—Wünsch *AF* 3²⁴ (Carthage—Imperial time) (ἔ)τι ἐξορκίζω ὑμᾶς κατὰ τοῦ ἐπάν ω τοῦ οὐρανοῦ θεοῦ: cf Isai 14¹³. For ἐπάνωθεν, not found in the NT, but frequent in the LXX, see BGU IV. 1198⁷ (B.C. 4).

ἐπάρατος.

For this NT ἅπ. εἰρ. (Jn 7⁴⁹) cf. *Syll* 356²³ (c. A.D. 38) τὸν δὲ κακουργοῦντ[α πε]ρ[ὶ τ]ὴν κοινὴν τῆς πόλεως εὐ-ετηρίαν . . . ὡ ς κοινὸν τῆς πόλεως λυμεῶνα ἐπάρατον εἶναι ζημιοῦσθαί τε ὑπὸ τῶν [ἀρχόν]των. For the verb see OGIS 532²³ (B.C. 3 ἐὰν δέ τι ὑπεναντίον τούτωι τ[ῶι ὅρκωι] ποήσω . . . ἐπαρῶμαι αὐτός τε κατ' ἐμοῦ κτλ., and *Syll* 810 εἰ δέ τι ἑκὼν ἐξαμαρτ[ήσει], οὐκ ἐμὸν ἐπαράσ[ασθαι], δίκη δὲ ἐπικρέματα[ι] τιμωρὸς ἀπελθόν[τι] ἀπειθὴς Νεμέσε[ως—an inscr. which recalls the teaching of Rom 12¹⁹.

ἐπαρκέω.

P Par 46⁵ (B.C. 153) εἰ ἔρρωσαι καὶ τὰ παρὰ τῶν θεῶν κατὰ λόγον σοι χρηματίζεται, εἴη ἄν, ὡς βούλομαι, καὶ αὐτὸς δὲ μετρίως ἐπ[αρ]κῶ—where however the reading is far from certain: see Witkowski², p. 86. See also *Cagnat* IV. 743 (Eumeneia—time of Alexander Severus = C. and B. ii. No. 232¹³) τοῦτο γὰρ ἦν μοι τερπνὸν ἐπαρκεῖν εἴ τις ἐχρῆζε—a Jew speaks. In Polyb. i. 51. 10 the verb is used as nearly synonymous with ἐπιβοηθέω: cf. 1 Tim 5¹⁶· ¹⁶.

ἐπαρχεία,

which is used, like the Lat. *provincia*, in Ac 23³⁴, 25¹, to denote "province," "sphere of duty," is restored by the editors in P Par 17² (B.C. 154) ἐπαρχίας Θηβαίδος, τοῦ περὶ Ἐλεφαντίνην νομοῦ. They also remark in connexion with this document on the interest of finding a contract of sale drawn in official form and in the Greek language in this remote province at such an early date. See also P Oxy III. 471²² (ii/A.D.) ἀπαλ[λ]αγῆι τῆς ἐ[π]αρχείας, and ib. XII. 1410³ (early iv/A.D.) ἐξ αὐθεντείας Μαγ[νί]ο[υ] Ῥούφου τοῦ διασημ(οτάτου) καθολ(ικοῦ) ἐπαρχείας Αἰγύπτου καὶ Λιβύης, where "the addition of Libya to Egypt in the title of the catholicus is new" (Edd.).

The title ἔπαρχος is found in the interesting order to return home for the approaching census—P Lond 904¹ (A.D. 104) (= III. p. 125. Selections, p. 73) Γ[άιος Οὐί]-βιο[ς Μάξιμος ἔπα]ρχ[ος] Αἰγύπτ[ου λέγει κτλ. : cf. P Oxy X. 1271¹ (A.D. 246), a petition addressed Οὐαλερίῳ Φίρμῳ ἐπάρχῳ Αἰγύπτου. In P Lond 904²³ (as above) the enrolment is to be made by a certain Festus who is described as ἐπάρχω[ι] εἴλης (l. ἴλης) : cf. P Gen I. 47¹ (A.D. 346) Φλαουΐω Ἀβιννέῳ ἐπάρχω εἴλης στρατιωτῶν κάστρων Διο[ν]υσιάδος. A number of exx. of the title are classified in P Oxy XII. Index VIII. s.v.

ἔπαυλις.

This NT ἅπ. εἰρ. (Ac 1²⁰ from Ps 68(69)²⁶) may be illustrated from a property-return, P Oxy II. 248²⁸ (A.D. 80), where mention is made of δίμοιρον μέρος τετάρτου μέρου[ς] κοινωνικῆς ἐπαύλεως συνπεπ[τω]κυίας, "a common homestead that is in a state of ruin": cf. P Ryl II. 177²⁰ (A.D. 246) λιβὸς ἔπαυλ[ις Φοι]βάμμωνος Τρύφωνος, "on the west the homestead of Phoebammon son of Tryphon," and P Hamb I. 23¹⁸ (A.D. 569) καὶ οἰκία καὶ ἐπαύλιδι (contrast ἐπαύλεως supra), with the editor's note, where other instances are collected. From the inscrr. we may add Syll 510¹³. ⁶⁸ (ii/B.C.), and for the diminutive OGIS 765¹³ (iii/B.C.) τά τε ἐ]παύλια ἐνέπ[ρη]σαν.

ἐπαύριον.

For this LXX and NT word, for which LS have no profane citations, cf. P Hamb I. 27⁴ (B.C. 250) τῆι δὲ ἐφαύριον αὐτὸν ἐπεζήτουν, P Lille I. 15² (B.C. 242) τῆι δ' ἐπαύριον ἡμέραι, P Tebt I. 119¹⁷ (B.C. 105–4) τὸ ἐφαύρι[ο]ν. For the aspirate see s.v. αὔριον.

Ἐπαφρᾶς.

The name, a pet form of Ἐπαφρόδιτος, is common in the inscrr., e.g. Syll 893³¹ (ii/A.D.), Dessau 7843, 7864, etc. Preisigke 1206 shows Ἐπαφρῦς. Contrast with the gen. Ἐπαφρᾶ in Col 1⁷ the form Ἐπαφράδος in the Papers of the American School of Classical Studies at Athens, iii. 375 (Phrygia)—cited by Hatch JBL xxvii. p. 145.

Ἐπαφρόδιτος.

In OGIS 441 (B.C. 81) Ἐπαφρόδιτος appears as a surname of Sulla (= Felix). In the papyri the spelling of the name, which is common, is generally Ἐπαφρόδειτος, e.g. P Oxy IV. 743²⁵ (B.C. 2) ἤλθαμεν ἐπὶ Ἐπαφρόδειτον. For the adj. see P Ryl II. 77³⁶ (A.D. 192) ἐπὶ τῇ ἐπαφροδείτῳ ἡγεμονίᾳ Λαρκίου Μέμορος, "during the delightful prae-fecture of Larcius Memor" (Edd.).

ἐπεγείρω.

Syll 324¹⁰ (i/B.C.) τούς τε διὰ παντὸς ἐπεγει[ρ]ομένους ἐπὶ τ[ὴ]ν [π]όλιν πολεμίους [ἀμυνόμενος : cf. Ac 13⁵⁰, 14², and see Hobart, p. 225 f.

ἐπεί.

Citations of this very common word are hardly necessary, but we may quote PSI IV. 435¹² (B.C. 258–7) ἐπεὶ δὲ τάχιστα ὑγιάσθην, παρεγένετό τις ἐκ Κνίδου, P Lond 42²³ (B.C. 168) (= I. p. 31) ἐπεὶ καὶ ἡ μήτηρ σου τυγχάνει βαρέως ἔχουσα, "since your mother is much annoyed about it," and P Meyer 20⁴⁶ (1st half iii/A.D.) εἰπὲ τῇ ἱερίσσᾳ (l. -ίσσῃ) τοῦ ἱεροῦ τῶν Ἑρμωνθιτῶν, ἵνα ἐκεῖ πέμπω τὰς ἐπιστολάς, ἐπὶ (l. ἐπεὶ) εὐσήμαντά ἐστιν, "tell the priestess of the sanctuary of Hermonthitis that I am sending my letters thither, since she is well known." For ἐπεὶ μή see BGU II. 530⁷⁵ (i/A.D.) ἡ μήτηρ σου μέμφεταί σε, ἐπὶ μὴ ἀντέγραψας αὐτῇ—a letter from a father to his son : cf. the similar use of ὅτι μή in Jn 3¹⁸ and see Proleg. p. 239 f. and Abbott Joh. Gr. p. 534 ff. Ἐπεί = alioquin, as in Rom 11⁶, is illustrated by Wetstein ad l., and by Field Notes, p. 162.

ἐπειδή.

For the causal reference of this word, as in Phil 2²⁶, cf. P Tebt II. 382³⁰ (B.C. 30—A.D. 1) ἐπειδ[ὴ] Κάστωρ . . παρακεχώρη(κεν) ἀπὸ τῶν λοιπῶν τοῦ κλήρου . . . Ἀκου-σιλάωι γράφ[ομεν ὑμῖν ἵν' ἦ ἐπιμε]λὲς κτλ, "whereas Castor has ceded the remainder of his holding to Acusilaus, we write to you in order that you may be careful," etc., P Oxy VII. 1061² (B.C. 22) ἐπειδὴι καὶ ἄλλοτέ σοι ἐγρά-ψαμεν. MGr ἐπειδή(ς), "because," "since."

ἐπειδήπερ

appears with its usual meaning "since" in P Flor II. 118⁵ (A.D. 254) ἐπέστειλα ὅπως χόρτου μοι ἡμιξηροῦ φροντίδα ποιήσῃσθαι ἐπειδήπερ μετὰ τὴν αὔριον γίνομαι εἰς τὸν νομὸν ἐποψόμενος τὰ παρ' ὑμῖν ἔργα, P Ryl II. 238¹⁰ (A.D. 262) κτηνύδριον δὲ αὐτοῖς ἓν γοργὸν τῶν ὑπὸ σὲ παράσχες, ἐπειδή-περ τὸ αὐτῶν ὃ εἶχαν βουρδωνάριον εἰς ἐμὴν ὑπηρεσίαν κατέσχον, "give them one spirited donkey from those in your charge, since I have kept for my own use the mule which they had" (Edd.), P Strass I. 5¹⁰ (A.D. 262) ὅμως αὐτός, ἐπειδήπερ ἐκ παλαιοῦ χρόνου τὴν γεωργίαν ἐνπιστευ-θεὶς ἐτύγχανεν, τοὺς φόρους καταβέβληκεν.

ἐπεῖδον.

P Tebt II. 286²⁰ (A.D. 121–38) ἐκ τῆς α[ὐ]τοψ[ί]ας ἣν ἐγὼ ἐπεῖδον, "of my own personal observation" (Edd.), P Flor II. 118⁶ (A.D. 254) γίνομαι εἰς τὸν νομὸν ἐποψόμενος τὰ παρ' ὑμῖν ἔργα, Preisigke 1817 (a wall scribble) Ν. ὁ ἐπιδὼν καὶ ὁ γράψας [ ]. For the aspirated form (see s.v. ἀφοράω) cf. P Oxy I. 44¹² (late i/A.D.) ἀντιγράψαντος οὖν αὐτοῦ μοι περὶ τοῦ ἐφιδόντα τὰς π[ρο]τέρας μισθώσεις, "he replied requesting me to examine the terms under which the taxes had previously been farmed" (Edd.), ib. 51⁷ (A.D. 173) ἐφιδεῖν σῶμα νεκρὸν ἀπηρτημένον, "to inspect the body of a man who had been found hanged" (Edd.), and BGU II. 647⁶ (A.D. 130) παρηγγέλη ἡμεῖν . . ἐφιδεῖν τὴν ὑπὸ Μυσθαρίωνα Καμείους διάθεσιν.

ἔπειμι.

P Petr III. 56 (*b*)[12] αὐθήμερον ἢ τῆι ἐπι[ού]σηι, P Ryl II. 157[22] (A.D. 135) τῶν ἔμπροσθεν καὶ τῶν ἐπεσομένων χρόνων, "for the past and future." *Syll* 481[19] (iii/ii B.C.) εἰς τὴν ἐπιοῦσαν ἐκκλησίαν. In P Lond 948 *verso*[2] (A.D. 257) (= III. p. 209) we have τούπιὸν (= τὸ ἐπιὸν) ξύλων, " what remains over of the wood."

ἐπείπερ.

For ἐπείπερ, which is read in the TR of Rom 3[20], cf. P Par 63[186] (B.C. 165) (= P Petr III. p. 34) ἐπείπερ ὑμᾶς δεῖ συνεχέστερον ὑπὲρ τῶν α[ὐτ]ῶν ὑπομιμνήσκειν, "since it is necessary to keep reminding you continuously about the same things" (Mahaffy), and P Oxy XII. 1469[4] (A.D. 298) ἐπείπερ ἐὰν πλεονεξία τις προχωρήσῃ καθ' [ἡ]μῶν δι' ἀδυναμείαν ἀναπρόστατοι καταστη[σ]όμεθα, "since, if any advantage of us is taken, our weakness will leave us no escape" (Edd.).

ἐπεισαγωγή.

We have found no instance as yet of this interesting subst. (Heb 7[19]), but the verb is used as a *term. techn.* in marriage-contracts, forbidding a man to "introduce" another woman into his house. e.g. P Eleph 1[8] (B.C. 311–0) (= *Selections*, p. 3) μὴ ἐξέστω δὲ Ἡρακλείδηι γυναῖκα ἄλλην ἐπεισάγεσθαι ἐφ' ὕβρει Δημητρίας, P Giss I. 2[i. 20] (B.C. 173), BGU IV. 1050[16] (time of Augustus). This would seem to justify the RV translation of Heb *l.c.* "a bringing in thereupon " or " besides," as against Field *Notes*, p. 227. See also the verbal ἐπείσακτος in *Osb* 757[4] (B.C. 106–5) σὺν τῷ ἐπισάκτῳ with reference apparently to "imported" wine: cf. the use of παρείσακτος in Gal 2[4]. Musonius (p. 6[12]) has—εἰ ὅλον ἐπείσακτον τὸ τῆς ἀρετῆς ἦν, καὶ μηδὲν αὐτοῦ φύσει ἡμῖν μετῆν . . .

ἐπεισέρχομαι.

For this verb cf. P Oxy VI. 902[5] (c. A.D. 465) μετὰ δὲ τὴν τούτου τελευτὴν ὁ [τούτ]ου ἀδελφὸς Θεόδωρος ἐπισῆλθεν εἰς τὴν φροντίδα τῶν τούτου πραγμάτων, where the verb is practically = ἐπῆλθεν, as perhaps in Lk 21[35]: see Field *Notes*, p. 75. The stronger force, which is seen in 1 Macc 16[16], is well illustrated by P Par 41[19] (B.C. 160) ἐπισελθόντες Τεεβήστιος υἱοὶ . . . ἐπέπεσόν τε καρτερῶς [ἐμοί. For the subst. ἐπεξέλευσις see PSI IV. 313[13] (iii/iv. A.D.), and P Oxy I. 67 cited *s.v.* ἐπανόρθωσις.

ἔπειτα

is used of *time* in *OGIS* 90[43] (the Rosetta stone—B.C. 196) νῦν τε καὶ εἰς τὸν ἔπειτα χρόνον. For a reference to *order* see P Giss I. 23[11] where, after referring to her prayers on behalf of her daughter, the writer proceeds—ἔπειτα δὲ χάρι (*l.* χάρις) τῷ θεῷ κτλ. Similarly the word is contrasted with πρῶτον (cf. Heb 7[2]) in P Oxy IX. 1217[5] (iii/A.D.) πρῶτον μὲν ἀσπαζομένη σ[ε], ἔπιτα εὐχομένη παρὰ πᾶσι θεοῖς κτλ. The form and meaning persist in MGr.

ἐπεκτείνω.

Vett. Val. p. 362[20] εἶθ' οὕτως τὴν ἑτέραν ἐπεκτείνειν ἕως τῆς ζητουμένης ὥρας.

ἐπέρχομαι

is common in the sense " proceed against," "make a claim against," e.g. P Eleph 3[3] (B.C. 284–3) μὴ ἐξέστω δὲ Ἀντιπάτρωι ἐπελθεῖν ἐπ' Ἐλάφιον εἰσπράττοντι τροφεῖα, P Ryl II. 174[16] (A.D. 112) καὶ μὴ] ἐπελεύσ[εσθ]αι μήτε αὐτὴν Ἡρακλοῦν μηδὲ τοὺς παρ' αὐτῆς [ἐπὶ τὴν] Τασουχάρ[ιον, "and that neither Heraclous herself nor her assigns will proceed against Tasoucharion," and especially the phrase μηδὲν ἐνκαλεῖν μηδ' ἐνκαλέσειν μηδ' ἐπελεύσεσθαι, as P Oxy X. 1282[29] (A.D. 83) *ib.* II. 266[16, 21] (A.D. 96), *ib.* I. 91[22] (A.D. 187), P Fay 94[7] (A.D. 222–35) *al.* For the meaning "come upon" with the idea of violence, as in Lk 11[22] (cf. 1[35], "an illapse sudden and irresistible," Swete *Holy Spirit in NT*, p. 26), see P Ryl II. 116[12] (A.D. 194) ἐπῆλθέ μοι μετὰ Σερήνου, "assaulted me with the aid of Serenus," and cf. BGU I. 22[13] (A.D. 114) (= *Selections*, p. 75) Ταορσενοῦφις . . . ἐπελθοῦσα ἐν τὴν οἰκία (*l.* οἰκίαν) μου ἄλογόν μοι ἀηδίαν συνεστήσατο, "T. having burst into my house picked a brutal quarrel with me." In P Oxy I. 69[15] (A.D. 190) ἐπέλευσις = "raid," "robbery '—ἐξέτασιν ποιήσασθαι περὶ τῆς γενομένης ἐπελεύσεως, "to make due inquiry about the robbery" (Edd.), and in P Fay 26[14] (A.D. 150) τῶν ἐκ τῆς ἐπελεύσεως φανέν[των the editors suggest as an alternative translation "review." "examination." See also P Oxy XII. 1502[22] (A.D. 276–82) ὁμολογῶ μηδεμίαν ἔφοδον ἢ ἐπέλευσιν ἔχ[ειν πρὸς τὸν Δ., and for ἐπελευστικός, cf. P Oxy VIII. 1120[10] (early iii/A.D.) ἵνα μὴ φανῇ ἐπελευστικός, "so that he should not seem indictable " (Ed.).

ἐπερωτάω.

For this verb in its ordinary NT sense of " ask," see P Hib I. 72[15] (B.C. 241) ἀποσταλεὶς Ἀ· πρὸς τὸν [ἐν τῶι] ἀδύτωι Χ. ἐπηρώτα εἰ ὑπάρχει ἐν τῶι ἱερῶι . . . ἡ σφραγίς, "A. having been sent to Ch. in the sanctuary asked him if the seal was in the temple"; P Flor III. 331[3] (ii/A.D.) ἐπερωτώμενος ὑπ[ὸ] σου περὶ τῶν ἐντὸς περιχώμα[τος ἀν]αγραφομένων . . . προσφωνῶ ὡς ὑπόκειται. For a "remarkably early example" of the stipulatory formula ἐπερωτηθεὶς ὡμολόγησα cf. P Oxy VI. 905[30] (A.D. 170) (= *Selections*, p. 87) κυρία ἡ συγγραφὴ δισσὴ γραφεῖσα πρὸς τὸ ἑκάτερον μέρος ἔχειν μοναχόν, καὶ ἐπερωτη[θέν]τες ἑαυτοῖς ὡμολόγησαν, "the contract is valid, being written in duplicate in order that each party may have one : and in answer to the formal question they declared to each other their consent." Other examples of the same formula (cf. Modica *Introduzione*, p. 128) are P Gen I. 42[31] (A.D. 224–5), P Fay 90[22] (A.D. 234), P Tebt II. 378[30] (A.D. 265): in P Oxy X. 1273[41] (A.D. 260) we have—περὶ δὲ τοῦ ταῦτα ὀρθῶς καλῶς γείνεσθαι ἀλλήλους ἐπερωτήσαντ[ε]ς ὡμολόγησαν, "and to each other's questions whether this is done rightly and fairly they have given their assent" (Edd.). Cf. the technical use of the verb in P Oxy X. 1277[14] (A.D. 255) βεβαιώσω καὶ ἐπερώτημε (*l.*—μαι) ὡς πρόκειται, "I will guarantee (the sale) and have been asked the formal question as aforesaid," and in the late P Iand 48[9] (A.D. 582) διὰ Μηνᾶ οἰκέτου τοῦ ἐπερωτῶντος καὶ προσπορίζ οντος) . . . τὴν ἀγωγὴν καὶ ἐνοχήν with the editor's note.

ἐπερώτημα

is used in the same technical way as the verb (see *s.v.* ἐπερωτάω) in P Cairo Preis 1[16] (ii/A.D.) ἐὰν γὰρ μηδὲν ἐπερώτημα ἢ ἐνγεγρα[μμένον . . . , with Wilcken's note "ἐπερώ-τημα = stipulatio (d. i. ἐπερωτηθεὶς ὡμολόγησα)." This would seem to help the meaning of the word in the difficult passage 1 Pet 3²¹: cf. Blenkin's note in *CGT ad l.* For the word = "inquiry of" and hence "sanction," cf. *Syll* 397⁶ (Roman age) κατὰ τὸ ἐπερώτημα τῶν κρατίστων Ἀρεοπαγειτῶν, *ib.* 593⁴ (after middle of iii/A.D.) καθ' ὑπομνηματισμὸν τῆς ἐξ Ἀρείου πάγου βουλῆς καὶ ἐπερώτημα τῆς βουλῆς τῶν Φ. For the form ἐπερώτησις, see P Oxy IV. 718¹³ (A.D. 180–92) ὡς ἐξ ἐπερω[τήσεως κτήτ]ορος, "in answer to an inquiry concerning the landlord" (Edd.), *ib.* IX. 1205⁹ (A.D. 291) ἐπερωτήσεώς τε γενομένης [ὡμολογή-σαμεν, *Syll* 555² (about A.D. 1) τὰς] δ'ἐπερωτάσ[ε]ως καὶ τοῦ χρησμοῦ ἀντίγραφά ἐστι τάδε.

ἐπέχω.

For ἐπέχω, "fix attention on," "pay heed," as in Ac 3⁵, 1 Tim 4¹⁶, cf. P Fay 112¹¹ (A.D. 99) ἐπέχον τῷ δακτυλιστῇ Ζωίλωι καὶ εἵνα αὐτὸν μὴ δυσωπήσῃς, "give heed to the measurer (?) Zoilus ; don't look askance at him," BGU IV. 1040²⁶ (ii/A.D.) οἱ γὰρ γ[ε]ωργοὶ ἡμεῖν ἐπέχουσιν [καὶ] κα[θ' ἡ]μῶν μέλλουσιν ἐντυν[χ]άνει[ν. Cf. P Oxy I. 67⁵ (A.D. 338) παρα[νόμω]ς ἐπέχοντάς μου τῶν οἰκοπέδων, "making illegal encroachments on my estates" (Edd.). The sense of "delay," "hinder," is found in the legal phrase μηδενὸς ἐπεχομένου, "if no one objects," or "if there is no hindrance," as in P Tebt II. 327³⁷ (late ii/A.D.), P Oxy III. 488⁴³ (ii/iii A.D.). For the use of the verb in connexion with the "suspension" of payments, see P Tebt II. 337⁴ (ii/iii A.D.) μετὰ τὰς ἀπὸ ἐποχίμων συστ[αλ(είσας)?] διὰ τὸ εἰσπραχ-θῆναι) πρὸ τοῦ ἐπισχεθῆναι, "after deducting the sums which were withdrawn from the category of suspended payments because they were collected before they were suspended" (Edd.), and P Giss I. 48¹¹ (A.D. 202–3) with the editor's note : cf. also P Tebt II. 336¹³ (c. A.D. 190) of lands ἐν ἐποχῇ, *i.e.* lands on which the collection of rents had been suspended, owing to their having been flooded and rendered useless. So P Giss I. 8¹³ (A.D. 119) ἀξιῶν ἐπι-σχεθῆναι τὴν πρᾶσιν μέχρι ἂν περὶ τούτου κριθῶμεν, "asking that the sale should be stopped until a decision had been given in this matter." The meaning of "wait," as in Ac 19²², may be illustrated from P Lille I. 26⁷ (iii/B.C.) πεερὶ (*l.* περὶ) δὲ τούτου τοῦ μέρους δεήσει ἐπισχεῖν [ἕως ἂν] μάθωμεν, "wait until we learn," and the curious love-charm, *Preisigke* 4947¹⁵ (iii/A.D.), where the petitioner prays that the lady of his affections should be led to love him—καὶ μὴ ἐπεχέτω μίαν ὥραν, ἕως ἔλθη πρὸς ἐμὲ . . . εἰς τὸν ἅπαντα χρόνον, "and let her not wait one hour, until she come to me for all time": cf. also P Petr II. 20ⁱ ¹⁵ (B.C. 252) ἐπεὶ καὶ αὐτὸς ἐπεσχον τοῦ ἐντυχεῖν, "wherefore I also refrained from meeting him" (see *ib.* III. p. 77), P Flor II. 151¹³ (A.D. 267) μέλλων γὰρ στρατιώτης πέμπεσθαι ἐπ' αὐτοὺς ἐγὼ ἐπεσχον. None of the above citations can be said to throw any fresh light on the use of the verb in Phil 2¹⁶, but it may be noted that against the translation "holding forth" (AV, RV: cf. Hom. *Od.* xvi. 444 cited by Moule *CGT ad l.*), Field (*Notes*, p. 193 f.) brings forward a number of exx. from late Greek in support of rendering λόγον ἐπέχω τινός = "correspond," "play the part of," and hence translates "being in the stead of life to it (*sc.* the world)." On the other hand, evidence can be quoted for ἐπέχω = a strength-

ened ἔχω, as Plut. *Oth.* 17 τὴν πόλιν ἐπεῖχε κλαυθμός (see Haupt in Meyer ⁸ *ad l.*), and hence the translation "holding fast the word of life." It may be added that in *Att.* xiii. 21. 3 Cicero objects to *inhibere* as a rendering of ἐπέχειν, on the ground that *inhibere*, as a term used in rowing, = "to back water," whereas ἐπέχειν = "to hold oneself balanced between two opinions": see Tyrrell *Cicero in his Letters*, p. 242.

ἐπηρεάζω.

The verb is common = "insult," "treat wrongfully." Thus in P Flor I. 99¹⁰ (i/ii A.D.) (= *Selections*, p. 72) we find the parents of a youth, who had squandered his and their property, announcing—οὗ χάριν προορώμεθα μήποτε ἐ[π]ηρεάσηι ἡμεῖν ἢ ἑτερο[ν] ἢ (omit.) ἄτοπόν τι πράξῃ[ι, "on that account we are taking precautions lest he should deal despitefully with us, or do anything else amiss": cf. P Fay 123⁷ (c. A.D. 100) διὰ τὸ ἐπηρεάσθαι οὐκ ἠδυνήθην κατελθεῖν, "owing to my having been molested I was unable to come down," P Gen I. 31¹⁶ (A.D. 145–6) πρὸς τὸ μὴ ἔτι ὕστερόν με ἐπηρεάζεσθαι, BGU I. 15¹² (A.D. 194) ὅτι νῦν κωμογραμματεὺς ἐπηρεάζει τῷ συνηγορουμ[έ]νῳ, PSI I. 92⁴ (iii/A.D.) ὁ ἄνθρωπος ἐπηρέασεν ἡμῖν, and OGIS 484²⁶ (ii/A.D.) δι' ὧν ἐπηρέαζον μάλιστα τοὺς τὸν ἰχθῦν πιπρά-σκοντας. The middle is found in an interesting document in which a weaver petitions on the ground of poverty against his name being inserted in the list of those eligible for the office of πρεσβύτερος τῆς κώμης, or village elder, P Lond 846⁶ (A.D. 140) (= III. p. 131) οἱ δὲ τῆς κώμης πρεσβύτεροι ἐπηρεάζοντ[ό μοι ὅπως] ἀναδώσω καί μου τὸ κτῆμα εἰς πρεσ-βυτερείαν τῆς κώμης ἀπ[όρου] μου ὄ[ν]τος. For the subst. ἐπηρεασμός, see P Tebt I. 28⁴ (c. B.C. 114) διὰ τὸν . . . ἐ[πηρ]εασμόν, "on account of the insolent conduct," and for ἐπηρεία, BGU I. 340²¹ (A.D. 148–9) ἐπὶ οὖν οὗτοι οὐκ ἀφί[στα]ντε (*l.*—νται) τῆς κατ' ἐμοῦ ἐπηρίας, and the curious mantic P Ryl I. 28¹⁵⁹ (iv/A.D.) where the quivering of the right leg-bone is taken as a sign that the person will be involved ἐν ἐπηρίᾳ, "in ill-treatment."

ἐπί.

The uses of ἐπί in Hellenistic Greek are hardly less varied than those of ἐν. From one point of view, indeed, they are even more varied, as ἐπί is the only preposition which continues to be largely represented with all three cases. According to Moulton (*Proleg.* p. 107) the figures in the NT are—gen. 216, dat. 176, acc. 464. In accordance with the general development of the use of the acc., the instances with this case are far the most numerous, and often occur where we might have expected the gen. or dat., while the constructions with these two cases are frequently interchanged, as will be seen from some of the exx. cited below. It will be kept in view that, as with the other prepositions, the treatment of ἐπί here makes no attempt at being exhaustive, but must be supplemented by the special dissertations of Kuhring and Rossberg. It is hoped, however, that sufficient evidence has been adduced to throw light on the main usages of the preposition in the NT.

(1) c. gen.—For the common *local* sense "at," "on," "upon," see P Par 47¹⁶ (c. B.C. 153) (= *Selections*, p. 23) ἐ[πὶ τ]ῶν τόπων ἴναι, P Tebt I. 33⁷ (B.C. 112) (= *Selections*, p. 30) ἐπὶ τῶν καθηκόντων τόπων, *ib.* II. 397²⁵ (A.D. 198)

ἐπὶ ξένης εἶναι, and P Giss I. 21[13] μένε ἐπὶ ἑαυτοῦ, "stay at home." The sense of "near," "in the vicinity of" appears in P Ryl II. 127[2] (A.D. 29) κοιμωμένου μου ἐπὶ τῆς θύρας: cf. Ac 5[23] and see Jn 6[19], 21[1] ἐπὶ τῆς θαλάσσης, where the rendering "near the sea," or, as we should say, "on the shore," is to be preferred (cf. Abbott *Joh. Gr.* p. 261). In P Lond 1168[5] (A.D. 18) (= III. p. 136) ἐν τοῖς ἀπὸ λίβος μέρεσι ἐπὶ ταῖς οὔσαις γειτνίαις, ἐπί is almost = "with." The local force still underlies the meaning of such a phrase as ἐπ᾽ ἀληθείας (cf. Mk 12[14]) in the census paper P Oxy II. 255[16] (A.D. 48) (= *Selections*, p. 47), where it is stated that the return is "sound" and res's "on a true basis"—ἐξ [ὑ]γιοῦς καὶ ἐπ᾽ ἀληθείας. Cf. also P Lille I. 20[4] (iii B.C.) τὴν δὲ λοιπὴν γῆν ἑτοιμάζω, εἰ μὴ ἀκολουθεῖς ἅπαντα καθὼς ἐπὶ τῆς διαγραφῆς τ[ο]ῦ [εἰς τὸ] ιε̄ ἔτος σπόρου μεμισθῶσθαι τοῖς γεωργοῖς, where ἐπὶ τῆς διαγραφῆς refers to the conditions laid down in the agreement, and P Grenf II. 77[9] (iii/iv A.D.) (= *Selections*, p. 121) (γίνεται) ἐπὶ τοῦ λ[όγο]υ τῆς ὅλης δα[πά]νης = "total of the account for the whole outlay." An even more elliptical usage is found in Mk 12[26] ἐπὶ τοῦ βάτου, "in *the place concerning* the Bush" (RV).

The preposition is used of "oversight," "authority," as in Mt 24[45], Ac 8[27], Rom 9[5], in such passages as P Tebt I. 5[85] (B.C. 118) ὁ ἐπὶ τῶν προσόδων, BGU IV. 1122[1] (B.C. 5) πρωτάρχωι ἐπὶ τοῦ κριτηρίου, P Oxy I. 60[1] (A.D. 55) τραπέζης ἐφ᾽ ἧς Σαρα[π]ίων καὶ μέτοχοι, P Lond 1159[49] (A.D. 145-47) (= III p. 113) ἐπὶ οἴνου καὶ ὄξου οἱ πρόοντες, and the *libellus* BGU I. 287[1] (A.D. 250) (= *Selections*, p. 115) where the magistrates who presided over the sacrifices are referred to—τοῖς ἐπὶ [τ]ῶν θυσιῶν ᾑρημένοις. In P Leid W[20] (ii/iii A.D.) ἔσεθε (*l.* ἔσεσθε) ἀμφότεροι ἐπὶ πάσης ἀνάγκης, the editor translates "*supra omnem necessitatem.*"

From this we may pass to the *judicial* reference, as in Mt 28[14] (ὑπό βD), in P Par 46[15] (B.C. 153) διὸ καὶ ἡγούμενος δεῖν ἐπ᾽ ἄλλου μὲν μηθενὸς αὐτῶι διακριθῆναι, ἐπὶ σοῦ δ᾽ αὐτοῦ, γέγραφά σοι κτλ., P Oxy I. 38[11] (A.D. 49-50) (= *Selections*, p. 53) καθὰ π[α]ρῆλθον ἐπὶ τοῦ γενομένου τοῦ νομοῦ στρατηγοῦ Πασίωνος, "I accordingly brought an action before Pasion, who was ex-strategus of the nome," and BGU III. 909[23] (A.D. 359) ἀχθῆναι ἐπὶ σοῦ τοὺς προειρημένους Ἄριον καὶ ... Ἀγάμμωνα. See also P Oxy I. 37[1.3] (A.D. 49) (= *Selections*, p. 48) ἐπὶ τοῦ βήματος, [Π]ε-σοῦρι[ς] πρὸς Σαραεῦν, "in court, P. *versus* S": cf. Ac 25[10]. Akin to this is the usage in an oath, as P Petr III. 56(d)[12] (iii/B.C.) ὤμοσά σοι τὸν πάτριον ὅρκον ἐπὶ τοῦ ποταμοῦ. In P Par 63[9] (B.C. 164) (= P Petr III. p. 20) ὅρκους παρ᾽ ὑμῶν λαβεῖν μὴ μόνον ἐπὶ τῶ[ν] θεῶν ἀλλὰ καὶ κατὰ τῶν βασιλέων, Mahaffy is unable (p. 38 f.) to discover any distinction between the prepositions, and translates "to exact oaths from you not only by the gods, but also by the kings." In BGU I. 153[27] (A.D. 152) ἀπογράψασθαι ἐν τῇ τῶν καμήλων ἀπογραφῇ . . . ἐπ᾽ ὀνόματος αὐτῶν, the reference is to "the entering on the list of a camel *under the name* of its new owner" (Deissmann *BS*, p. 197 n.[2]).

A good parallel to ἐπί = "concerning," "in the case of," as in Gal 3[16], is afforded by P Tebt I. 5[75] (B.C. 118) προστε-τάχασι δὲ καὶ τὰ εἰς τὴν ταφὴν τοῦ Ἄπιος καὶ Μνήσιος ζητεῖν ἐκ τοῦ βα[σιλικοῦ [ὥ]ς καὶ ἐπὶ τῶν ἀποτεθεωμένων, "and they have decreed that the expenses for the burial of

PART III.

Apis and Mnesis should be demanded from the Crown revenues, as in the case of the deified personages" (Edd.): cf. *ib.* 7[6] (B.C. 114) τὰ ἐπ᾽ αὐτῶν ἐνεστηκότα, "the state of the matter concerning them" (Edd.), and Menander *Fragm.* p. 188 οὐδεὶς ἐφ᾽ αὑτοῦ τὰ κακὰ συνορᾷ, Πάμφιλε, σαφῶς, ἑτέρου δ᾽ ἀσχημονοῦντος ὄψεται, "no one clearly sees evil in his own case, but when another misbehaves, he'll see it." See also such phrases as P Tebt I. 27[4] (B.C. 113) ἐπὶ τοῦ βελτίστου, "in the best possible manner" (but cf. ἐπ᾽ ἀληθείας above), P Strass I. 70[16] (A.D. 138) ὡς ἐπὶ τῶν ὁμοίω[ν, "as in similar cases," and BGU IV. 1098[44] (c. B.C. 20) ὡς ἂν ἐπὶ το[ῦ κα]ιροῦ κοινῶς κρίνωσι, "under the circumstances."

This last ex. leads naturally to the temporal use of ἐπί: cf. e.g. P Meyer 6[14] (A.D. 125) ἐπὶ τῆς τριακάδ[ο]ς το[ῦ] Παῦνι μηνός: also P Petr II. 11(1)[2] (iii/B.C.) (= *Selections*, p. 7) ὅπως τῆς ἐπὶ τοῦ παρόντος σχολῆς ἀπολυθῶ, "that I may be relieved from my present occupation," where ἐπὶ τοῦ παρόντος is practically = ἐν τῷ παρόντι. With such passages as Mk 2[26], Ac 11[28], where ἐπί = "in the time of," cf. P Amh II. 43[2] (B.C. 173) ἔτους ὀγδόου ἐφ᾽ ἱερέως Ἡρακλείδου, P Tebt I. 61(b)[70] (B.C. 118-7) ἐν τῶι κθ ἔτει ἐπὶ τοῦ ἀ[δε]λφοῦ, P Tor I. 1[v.8] B.C. 116 τοῦ κη ἔτους Παχὼν ἐπὶ τοῦ Φιλομήτορος, and OGIS 90[10] (Rosetta stone—B.C. 196 προσέταξεν δὲ [Ptolemy V. Epiphanes] καὶ περὶ τῶν ἱερέων, ὅπως μηθὲν πλεῖον διδῶσιν εἰς τὸ τελεστικὸν οὗ ἐτάσσοντο ἕως τοῦ πρώτου ἔτους ἐπὶ τοῦ πατρὸς αὐτοῦ [Ptolemy IV. Philopator], where, as against Dittenberger *ad l.*, Wilcken *Archiv* iii. p. 320 f.) is shown that this use of ἐπί c. gen. carries back the dating to the beginning of the previous reign, i.e. "until the first year of his father's reign." On the importance of this in connexion with the chronological statement in the Prologue to Ecclesiasticus, see Wilcken *ut s.* and Deissmann *LS*, p. 339 ff. For the temporal use of ἐπί with an abstract noun, as in Rom 1[10], etc., see P Tebt I. 58[21] (B.C. 111) μή ποτε ἐπὶ τοῦ διαλόγου χειμασθῶμεν, "in order that we may not come to grief at the audit" (Edd.).

(2) c. dat.—The idea of "in" or "at" (as in Mt 24[33]) and "on" or "upon" (as in Mk 6[25, 39]) may be illustrated by P Tebt I. 6[27] (B.C. 140-39) ἐν Ἀλεξανδρείαι καὶ ἐπὶ χώρας, "at Alexandria and in the country," P Petr III. 1[ii.3] (B.C. 235) οὐλὴ . . . ἐπ᾽ ὀφρύι δεξιᾶι. See also P Oxy I. 115[2] (ii/A.D.) (= *Selections*, p. 96) ἔκλαυσα ἐπὶ τῶι εὐμοίρωι ὡς ἐπὶ Διδύματος ἔκλαυσα, where the dat. and gen. are interchanged in the same sentence. Ἐπί is common with the dat. = "with a view to," as in Gal 5[13], e.g. P Tebt I. 44[6] (B.C. 114) ὄντος μου ἐπὶ θεραπείαι ἐν τῷ αὐτόθι μεγάλωι Ἰσιείωι, "while I was in the great temple of Isis here for medical treatment" (see the editor's note), P Oxy IX. 1203[30] (late i/A.D.) πάντα τὰ . . . ἐπὶ τῇ ἡμῶν ἀδικίᾳ πραχθέντα, "all the things done to our hurt," P Oxy I. 71[i.4] (A.D. 303) κακουργίαν ἐπὶ ἀποστερέσει τῇ ἡμετέρᾳ "a fraud to my detriment."

Similarly with abstract nouns denoting *manner*, as in Rom 4[18]—P Tor I. 1[vi.3] (B.C. 116) περιεσπακέναι . . . ἐπὶ τῆι πάσῃ συκοφαντίαι καὶ διασεισμῶι, *ib.* I.[13] κακοτρόπως καὶ ἐπὶ ῥαιδιουργίαι, P Oxy II. 237[vi.21] (A.D. 186) ἐπὶ φθόνῳ δὲ μόνον λοιδορούμενος. In P Eleph 1[8] (B.C. 311-0) (= *Selections*, p. 2 f.) the irregularity in elision between ἐπὶ αἰσχύνῃι and ἐφ᾽ ὕβρει may be noted, its avoidance in the first instance being due to the tendency in the **Κοινή** to isolate words for the sake of greater clearness : see Helbing *Gramm.* p. 124, and cf. Mayser *Gr.* p. 155 ff. In P Oxy III. 531⁶ (ii/A.D.) ὡς ἐπ' ἀγαθῷ πρὸς σὲ παραγένομαι (*l.* ωμαι), the meaning is "until I come to you auspiciously," much like the Latin "*quod bonum faustumque sit.*" See also ἐφ' ἡμισείᾳ = "equally," cited *s.v.* ἥμισυς.

The thought of "on account of" underlies such passages as BGU I. 200³ (A.D. 90) ἀπέχωι παρά σου ἃς ὤφιλές μοι ἐπ' ἐνυκήσει (*l.* ἐνοικήσει) κατὰ δημόσ[ιον] χρη[μ]α[τ]ισμὸν ἀργυρίου δραχμὰς ἑξακοσίας, Wilcken *Ostr* 1131 (A.D. 212) ἔλαβον ἐπὶ προ[χρείᾳ] πυροῦ ἀρτ[άβην] μίαν ὑπ(ὲρ) μηνὸς Χὔακ. An interesting ex. occurs in the letter of the Emperor Claudius in which he acknowledges the gift of a "golden crown"—ἐπὶ τῇ κατὰ Βρετάννων νείκῃ, "on the occasion of his victory over the Britons" (P Lond 1178¹² = III. p. 216, *Selections*, p. 99) : cf. Lk 5⁵. This construction is common after verbs of feeling, as in P Eleph 13³ (B.C. 223-2) ἣν (*sc.* ἐπιστολὴν) ἀναγνοὺς ἐχάρην ἐπὶ τῶι με αἰσθέσθαι τὰ κατὰ σέ, and P Lond 42¹⁹ (B.C. 168) (= I. p. 30, *Selections*, p. 10) ἐπὶ μὲν τῶι ἐρρῶσθα[ί] σε εὐθέως τοῖς θεοῖς εὐχαρίστουν.

Another usage which deserves notice is afforded by such a passage as P Meyer 6² (A.D. 125) μετηλλαχότος δὲ τοῦ Φιλίππου ἐπὶ κληρονόμωι υἱῷ Ἀφροδεισίῳ, where the meaning is that when Philip died he left as heir his son Aphrodisius : cf. P Ryl II. 76³ (late ii/A.D.) Ἑρμιόνης . . τελευτησάσης . . ἐπί τε ἐμοὶ καὶ τοῖς ὁμομητρίοις ἀδελφοῖς κληρονόμοις, *ib.* 121⁷ (ii/A.D.) ἐτελεύτησεν Ἡρᾶς . . ἐπ' ἀφήλικι υἱῷ, "leaving his son a minor."

For ἐφ' ᾧ = "on condition that" see P Tebt I. 108⁴ (B.C. 93 or 60) where the owner leases certain arourae—ἐφ' ᾧ δώ[σει] σπέρμα (ἀρτάβας) ιε, "on condition that he (the owner) shall supply 15 artabæ for seed," and P Tebt II. 381¹⁶ (A.D. 123) where a mother bequeaths her property to her daughter—ἐφ' ᾧ ι . . ποιήσεται τὴν τῆς μητρὸς κηδίαν καὶ περιστολὴν ὡς καθήκει, "on condition that she shall perform the obsequies and laying out of her mother as is fitting." In P Hib I. 77⁶ (B.C. 249) the meaning is rather "to the effect that"—συντετάγμεθα γὰρ περὶ τῶν τελωνικῶν ἐφ' ὡι [τοῖς θε]οῖς [τὰ] ἱερὰ σωθήσεσθαι καθὰ καὶ πρότερον, "for we have received instructions with regard to the collection of taxes that the sacred revenues (?) are to be preserved for the gods as in former times" (Edd.).

Examples of ἐπί construed with the inf. are P Ryl II. 153²¹ (A.D. 138-61) where a father in his will nominates certain guardians—ἐπὶ τῷ αὐτ[ο]ὺς τρέφειν κ[αὶ] ἱματίζειν τὸν προγεγραμμένον μου υἱὸν καὶ κληρονόμον, "on condition that they shall provide my aforesaid son and heir with food and clothing," and P Lond 932¹⁹ (A.D. 211) (= III. p. 149) ἐπὶ τῷ καὶ αὐτοὺς ὅσα ὀφείλει ὁ πατὴρ δάνεια . . ἀποδιδόναι : and with reference to time P Oxy II. 294³ (A.D. 22) (= *Selections*, p. 34) ἐπὶ τῷ γεγονέναι ἐν Ἀλεξανδρίᾳ, "on my arrival in Alexandria."

Ἐπί c. dat. marks a point of time in P Tebt I. 5⁶⁸ (B.C. 118) πρὸς τὰς ἐπὶ ἐνίοις καιροῖς ἀπητημέν[α]ς [καρ]πείας, "for the emoluments demanded on certain occasions," P Oxy II. 275²⁰ (A.D. 66) (= *Selections*, p. 56) ἐπὶ συνκλεισμῷ τοῦ ὅλου χρόνου, "at the expiry of the whole period," P Lond III. 954¹⁸ (A.D. 260) (= III. p. 154) ἐπὶ τέλει δ[ὲ]

τοῦ πενταετοῦς χρόνου παραδ[ώσω] σο[ι, and the late P Amh II. 157 (A.D. 612) τοῦ χρυσίου τῆς καταβολῆς ἐπὶ μη(νὶ) Φαῶφι. Cf. also P Tebt I. 60²⁷ (B.C. 114) ἐπ' ἐσχάτῳ. The idea of "in addition to," as in Lk 3²⁰, 2 Cor 7¹³, Col 3¹⁴, appears in such a construction as P Eleph 5¹⁷ (B.C. 284-3) μη(νὸς) Τῦβι τρίτηι ἐπ' εἰκάδι.

The manner in which the gen. and dat. alternate is seen in P Lond 171 (*b*)¹⁸ (iii/A.D.) (= II. p. 176) ἀξιῶ λυθῆναι ἐπὶ σοῦ κατὰ τὸ ἔθος, a request by a widow that the will of her late husband may be opened "in your presence according to custom," as compared with P Ryl II. 109¹⁹ (A.D. 235) ἐπὶ παρόντι σοι διὰ βοηθοῦ, "you being represented by an assistant," and in ἐπὶ παρόντων ὑμῶν of the *libellus* P Meyer 15⁸ (A.D. 250), which appears as ἐπὶ παροῦσιν ὑμεῖν in the similar document BGU I. 287⁸ (A.D. 250) (= *Selections*, p. 115).

(3) c. acc.—The usage after verbs of motion hardly needs illustration, but see *OGIS* 90²⁰ (Rosetta stone—B.C. 196) προενοήθη δὲ καὶ ὅπως ἐξαποσταλῶσιν δυνάμεις . . . ἐπὶ τοὺς ἐπελθόντας ἐπὶ τὴν Αἴγυπτον κατά τε τὴν θάλασσαν καὶ τὴν ἤπειρον, where, as the editor points out, the use of ἐπί, not εἰς, Αἴγυπτον shows that the invading army had not yet entered the country. For other exx. of ἐπί followed by the acc. of a person see P Par 20⁸¹ (B.C. 163-2) (= *Selections*, p. 17) δεόμεθα οὖν ὑμῶν . . ἀποστεῖλαι ἡμῶν τὴν ἔντευξιν ἐπὶ Διονύσιον τῶν φίλων καὶ στρατηγόν, P Oxy IV. 743³⁵ (B.C. 2) παραγενομ(ένου) γὰρ Δαμᾶτος εἰς Ἀλεξάνδρειαν ἤλθαμεν ἐπὶ Ἐπαφρόδειτον, and P Meyer 3¹⁶ (A.D. 148) ἵν' οὖν τὸ κελευσθ(ὲν) εἰδῇς καὶ εὐθέως ἐπὶ τὸν κρά(τιστον) ἐπίτροπ(ον) καταντήσῃς [ἐ]πέστειλά σοι. This last ex. brings us to the more distinctively *judicial* usage, as BGU I. 22⁶ (A.D. 114) (= *Selections*, p. 76) διὸ ἀξιῶ ἀκθῆναι (*l.* ἀχθῆναι, and cf. Mt 10¹⁸, Ac 18¹²) τοὺς ἐνκαλουμένους ἐπὶ σὲ πρὸς δέουσ(αν) ἐπέξοδον, "I beg therefore that you will cause the accused to be brought before you for fitting punishment," and, before an abstract noun, P Oxy II. 294¹⁸ (A.D. 22) (= *Selections*, p. 35) ἵνα σὺν αὐτῷ ἐπὶ διαλογισμὸν ἔλ[θ]ω, "in order that I may come along with him to the inquiry" : cf. Mt 3⁷, Lk 23⁴⁸.

The phrase ἐπὶ τὸ αὐτό, as in Ac 1¹⁵, 2⁴⁷, is perpetually recurring, especially in accounts, where it represents an addition sum, "together," "in all," e.g. P Tebt I. 14⁴⁰ (B.C. 114) ἀξίας ἐπὶ τὸ αὐτὸ χα(λκοῦ) (ταλάντου) α, "of which the total value is one talent of copper" (Edd.), P Fay 102⁶ (c. A.D. 105) γί(νονται) ἐπὶ τὸ αὐτὸ (ὀβολοὶ) ππα, and P Oxy IV. 716¹⁴ (A.D. 186) where one-sixth of a slave owned by one man and a half owned by two others are reckoned as τὸ ἐπὶ τὸ αὐτὸ δίμοι[ρ]ον μέρος, "together two-thirds" ; also the Messenian inscr. *Syll* 653⁶⁶ (B.C. 91) ἐγδιδόντες ἄν τε δοκεῖ συνφέρον εἶμεν ἐπὶ τὸ αὐτὸ πάντα τὰ θύματα. For the possibility that in Ac 2⁴⁷ the phrase = "greatly" in accordance with another meaning of the Aramaic word which lay behind Luke's translation, see Torrey's Harvard study on *The Composition and Date of Acts* (Milford, 1916), p. 10 ff.

The thought of *degree* attained, as in 2 Tim 2¹⁶, may be seen in P Par 63¹²¹ (B.C. 164) (= P Petr III. p. 28) τοῖς μὲν ἐπὶ τὸ χεῖρον διαλαμβάνουσι, "to those who put a less favourable interpretation upon it," P Tebt I. 27⁸⁰ (B.C. 113) αἰεὶ δέ τινος ἐπὶ τὸ βέλτιον προσεπινοουμένου, "by the continual invention of further improvements" (Edd.), *Cagnat*

IV. 247³⁵ (c. B.C. 150) ἐπὶ πλεῖον αὔξειν. In P Tebt I. 33⁶ (B.C. 112) (= *Selections*, p. 30) we find *purpose* implied—ἀνάπλουν . . . ἐπὶ θεωρίαν ποιούμενος, "making the voyage to see the sights" (cf. Lk 23⁴⁸), and similarly with the inf. construction in BGU IV. 1124²¹ (B.C. 18) the apprenticeship of a boy—ἐπὶ τὸ μανθάνειν τὴν ἡλοκοπικὴ(ν) τέχνην. Cf. P Petr II. 11(2)³ (mid. iii/B.C.) (= Witkowski², p. 6) ἀπογέγραμμαι δὲ ἐπὶ τελώνιον, "I am enrolled for the purpose of taxation" in certain particulars which are stated—contrast Mt 9⁹ ἐπὶ τὸ τελώνιον of place.

The *temporal* use = "for," "during," as in Lk 4²⁵, Ac 13³², 1 Cor 7³⁹, may be seen in BGU IV. 1058⁹ (B.C. 13) ἐπὶ χρόνον ἔτη δύο ἀπὸ Φαρμοῦθι [τοῦ ἐνεσ]τῶτος ιε ἔτους Καίσαρος, P Oxy II. 275⁹ (A.D. 66) (= *Selections*, p. 55) ἐπὶ χρόνον ἐνιαυτὸν ἕνα ἀπὸ τῆς ἐνεστώσης ἡμέρας, *ib.* ¹⁵ ἐπὶ τὸν ὅλον χρόνον, P Tebt II. 381¹⁹ (A.D. 123) (= *Selections*, p. 79) ἐφ' ὃν δὲ χρόνον περίεστιν ἡ μήτηρ Θαῆσις, "as long as her mother Thaesis lives," and P Heid 6²⁷ (iv A.D.) (= *Selections*, p. 127) ἐπὶ μέγιστον χρόνον.

On the survival of ἐπί in MGr in adverbial expressions, see Thumb *Handbook* p. 98.

ἐπιβαίνω.

P Oxy VIII. 1155³ (A.D. 104) ὅτι (*l.* ὅτι) εὐθὺς ἐπιβέβηκα εἰς Ἀλεξάνδρειαν, "as soon as I arrived at Alexandria" (Ed.), P Flor II. 275²² (iii/A.D.) ὅτι οὐκ ἐξὸν ἄλλον ἐπιβῆναι εἰς Σα . . . . . In P Tebt I. 58¹⁰ (B.C. 111) ἐπιβεβή(κασιν) ἡμῖν (πυροῦ) ογβ, the verb = "have been assigned"; in *ib.* 5³⁵ (B.C. 118) τοὺς ἐπιβεβηκότας ἐπὶ τὴν βα(σιλικήν) the editors render "those who have encroached on the Crown land": cf. P Oxy I. 67²¹ (A.D. 338). The verb is used of hostile intent in P Hamb I. 10⁶ (ii/A.D.) ἐπέβη μου ταῖς οἰκίαις . . . λῃστήριον ("a band of robbers"): cf. P Oxy X. 1278²⁷ (A.D. 214) οὐκ οὔσης ἐξουσί[α]ς ὁποτέρῳ μέρει ἐπιβαίνειν ο[ὐ]δετέρῳ ἐντὸς τοῦ προκειμένου αὐτοῦ χρόνου, "none of the parties having the right to molest another during his aforesaid period" (Edd.). In *Syll* 364¹⁶ (A.D. 37) the verb, as in Ac 25¹, is construed with the dat. of entrance on an office—ἐπιβὰς πρώτως τῇ ἐπαρχείᾳ τῆς ἡμετέρας πόλεως (see Dittenberger's note), and for the subst. ἐπίβασις in the same sense see P Lond 1170⁸ (iii/A.D.) (= III. p. 93).

ἐπιβάλλω.

For the transitive use of this verb, cf. P Leid Wⁱⁱⁱ ⁴¹ (ii/iii A.D.) οἷς (*sc.* τοῖς λύχνοις) οὐκέτι ἐπιβαλεῖς ἔλαιον, so ˣᵛ·³⁷. In P Ryl II. 69⁶ (B.C. 34) we have a complaint against a man—ἐπιβαλό ντος . . . τὰ ἑαυτοῦ πρόβατα ἐφ' ὃν ἔχομεν ἐν τῶι ψυγμῶι . . κνῆκον, "having let his sheep loose on the cnecus which we have in the drying-place" (Edd.), while in P Leid G¹⁸ (B.C. 181–145) the phrase ἐπιβάλλει [ἐπ' ἐμὲ] τὰς χεῖρας is used with the idea of violence, as in Mt 26⁵⁹ *al.* For the intrans. use meaning "attack," cf. P Ryl II. 127¹⁰ (A.D. 29) ἐπιβαλόντες τινὲς λῃστρικῶι τρόπωι ὑπώρυξαν . . τὸ ἀπὸ βορρᾶ τεῖχος τοῦ οἴκου, "certain individuals making a thievish incursion undermined the northern wall of the house" (Edd.), *ib.* 133⁸ (A.D. 33) ἐπιβαλὼν Ὀ. εἰς τὸ λεγόμενον Τ. ἔμβλημ α), "O. making an attack upon the dam (?) called that

of T." (Edd.). A late usage by which the verb = "arrive at," "reach to" may be illustrated by P Par 6³ (B.C. 129) Λόχον τοῦ συγγενοῦς [ἐπι]βεβληκότ[ος] εἰς Διόσπολιν [τὴν] μεγάλην, P Amh II. 31⁵ (B.C. 112) ἐπιβάλλοντες εἰς τὸν Παθυρίτην διεπεμψάμεθα κτλ., and the almost technical phrase ἐπιβάλλειν ἐπὶ τοὺς τόπους in P Hal I. 8⁴ (B.C. 232), P Grenf I. 49⁷ (ii B.C.). The sense of "endeavour" underlies the use of the mid. followed by the inf. in P Par 63¹³⁶ (B.C. 164) (= P Petr III. p. 30) ἐπιγράφει[ν τοῖς] μὴ δυναμένοις ἐπιβεβλημένους, "endeavouring to impose the corvée on those who cannot perform it" (Mahaffy), *ib.* 20²⁶ (B.C. 161–0) ὑμῖν δὲ γίνοιτο πᾶν ὃ ἂν ἐπιβάλλησθ' ἐπιτυγχάνειν. The legal phrase τὸ ἐπιβάλλον μέρος, as in Lk 15¹², is very common: in addition to exx. in Deissmann *BS* p. 230 cf. P Grenf I. 33³¹ (c. B.C. 103–2) τὰς ἐπιβαλούσας αὐτῇ μερίδας γῆς, P Oxy IV. 715¹⁸ᶠ (A.D. 131) τὸ ἐπιβάλλ[ον] αὐτῶι . . τρίτον μέρος οἰκίας καὶ τὸ ἐπιβάλλον αὐτῶι μέρος ψιλοῦ τόπου, P Fay 93⁸ (A.D. 161) ἀπὸ τοῦ ἐπιβάλλοντός σοι [ἡμί]σους μέρους. See also P Hib I. 115⁵·²² (c. B.C. 250) ἐπιβάλλει of instalments of money falling due, P Lond 3²¹ (B.C. 146 or 135) (= P. 46) καρπείων ἐπιβαλλόντων μοι, P Fay 100²⁰ (A.D. 99) τὰς ἐπιβαλούσας μοι ἀργ(υρίου) δραχμὰς τριακοσίας, BGU I. 104¹² (A.D. 177) τὰς λειτουργείας ἐπιβαλλούσας αὐτοῖς. Other impersonal exx. are P Par 63¹⁰ (B.C. 164) (= P Petr III. p. 18) κοινῇ πᾶσιν ἐπιβάλλει, "is a common duty incumbent on all" (Mahaffy, P Tebt I. 40¹² (B.C. 117) (= *Selections*, p. 28) διὰ τὸ μάλιστα ἐπιβάλλειν προνοεῖσθαι τῶν βασιλικῶν, "because it chiefly falls to you to look after the interests of the Crown." Another passage from the Tebtunis papyri throws a welcome light on the *crux* of Mk 14⁷². In I. 50¹² (B.C. 112–1) ἐπιβαλὼν συνέχωσεν τὰ ἐν τῆι ἑαυτοῦ γῆι μέρη τοῦ σημαινομένου ὑδραγωγοῦ, we translate "set to and dammed up" the part of the water-course in question: see further in *Proleg.* p. 131, and cf. Allen *ad* Mk *l.c.* where this rendering of ἐπιβαλών in the Markan passage is accepted as probable, and the use of the word by the Evangelist's favourite ἤρξατο is explained as due to a misreading of the Aramaic original. Note that ἐπιβαλών occurs also in Syr. *S* aeth = 505 at Mk 16⁵⁰ (see Burkitt *Ev. Da-Mepharreshe* ii. p. 259).

For ἐπιβολή = ἐπιβάλλον μέρος, see P Tebt II. 391¹⁹ (A.D. 99) τὸ λοιπὸν τῆς ἐπιβολῆς τῆς λαογραφίας with the editor's note. It is common = "embankment" as in P Petr I. 23¹ εἰς ἐπιβολὴν παλαιοῦ χώματος. In P Lond 1157¹¹¹ (A.D. 197–8?) (= III. p. 66) the editors suggest that in the phrase ἐπιβολ(ῆς) πηχισμοῦ the reference is to an "additional charge" for certain measurements, or to an "allotment" of such a charge.

ἐπιβαρέω.

The use of this verb in 1 Th 2⁹, 2 Th 3⁸, is well illustrated in *Syll* 371¹⁶ (time of Nero) where a certain physician is said to have behaved—ὡς μηδένα ὑφ' αὑτοῦ παρὰ τὴν ἀξίαν τοῦ καθ' ἑαυτὸν μεγέθους ἐπιβεβαρῆσθαι: cf. P Oxy XII. 1481¹² (early ii/A.D.) where a soldier writing to his mother adds as a postscript μὴ ἐπιβαροῦ πέμπειν τι ἡμῖν, "do not burden yourself to send me anything." Add *Michel* 394¹¹ (mid. i/B.C.) εἰς π[αρά]τασιν καθ[ίστησιν] ὅσον ἐπ' αὐτῷ τοὺς ἐπιβαροῦντας, καὶ τοῖς ἀδίκως ἐπι[βαρη]θ[εῖ]σι δικαίαν παρέχεται βοήθειαν, and see further *s.v.* βαρέω.

ἐπιβλέπω.

P Leid W xiv. 23 (ii/iii A.D.) ἐπίβλεψόν μου τῇ γεννέσει (*l.* γεννήσει or γενέσει)—an appeal for divine regard and help: cf. Lk 1⁴⁸, 9³⁸, and see Hobart p. 18f.

ἐπίβλημα.

For this word in connexion with dress, as in Mt 9¹⁶ (cf. Isai 3³², Josh 9⁶¹¹⁾ Symm.), cf. the early inscr. *Syll* 877⁴ (*c.* B.C. 420) στρώματι καὶ ἐνδύματι [καὶ ἐ]πιβλέματι.

ἐπιβοάω.

This verb, which is read for the *simplex* in the TR of Ac 25²¹, may be illustrated by P Leid W xi. 27 (ii/iii A.D.) ὁ δ' ἐπὶ τοῦ ἑτέρου μέρους ἱέραξ ἰδίᾳ φωνῇ ἀσπάζεταί σε καὶ ἐπιβοᾶται, ἵνα λάβῃ τροφήν.

ἐπιβουλή.

For ἐ. = "plot" as *quater* in Ac, cf. P Oxy II. 237 vi. 21 (A.D. 186) πρόφασις δέ ἐστιν ἐπιβουλῆς, "a pretext for plotting against me" (Edd.), and *ib.⁶* ἑτέρῳ ἐπέτρεψεν τὴν κατ' ἐμοῦ ἐπιβουλήν. The verb is found in P Oxy III. 472⁸ (*c.* A.D. 130) εἰ δ' ἄρα τις καὶ ἐπεβούλευσεν αὐτῷ, ὁ υἱὸς ἐπιτηδειότατος, "but if any one really plotted against him, his son is the most likely person" (Edd.), BGU IV. 1024 iv. 10 (iv/v A.D.) σὺ δὲ ἐπεβούλευσας σῶμα (*l.* σώματι) ἀλλοτρ[ι]ωθέντι ὑπὸ τοῦ [γ]ένους τῶν ἀνθρώπων, and from the inscrr. *Syll* 510³² (ii/B.C.) ὡς ἀπειθοῦντα καὶ ἐπιβουλεύοντα τοῖς συ(μ)φέρουσι τῆς πόλεως.

ἐπιγαμβρεύω.

For this *terminus technicus* which is used c. acc. in sense of "take to wife after" in Mt 22²⁴, under the influence of Gen 38⁸, see Anz *Subsidia*, p. 378. Elsewhere in the LXX (e.g. 1 Kings 18²²) it represents the Heb. הִתְחַתֵּן = "become son-in-law."

ἐπίγειος.

In striking resemblance to Phil 2¹⁰ is the use of this word in the magic P Par 574⁴³ (iii/A.D.) (= Deissmann *LAE*, p. 252 f.) καὶ σὺ λάλησον ὁποῖον ἐὰν ᾖς ἐπεουράνιον ἢ ἀέριον εἴτε ἐπίγειον εἴτε ὑπόγειον ἢ καταχθόνιον κτλ. The passage "is not a quotation from St. Paul," but "the papyrus and St. Paul are both using familiar Jewish categories" (*ib.* p. 257 n.¹¹). See also P Lond 46¹⁶⁷ (iv/A.D.) (= I. p. 70) ἵνα μοι ἦν ὑπήκοος πᾶς δαίμων οὐράνιος καὶ αἰθέριος καὶ ἐπίγειος καὶ ὑπόγειος κτλ., and Wunsch *AF* 4¹¹ (iii/A.D.) where ἐπίγειος is found in combination with οὐράνιος and χθόνιος. In P Petr II. 8²¹⁰ (B.C. 246) ἐπίγεια, "ground-floor buildings," are contrasted with πύργος διώροφος, "a tower of two stories" (see the Editor's note). On the form see Mayser *Gr.* p. 448.

ἐπιγίνομαι

is common of *time*, e.g. P Lond 42²³ (B.C. 168) (= I. p. 30, *Selections*, p. 10) μὴ ὅτι γε τοσοῦτον χρόνον ἐπιγεγονότος, P Fay 11¹⁹ (*c.* B.C. 115) τῶν τῆς ἀποδόσεως χρόνων διεληλυθότων καὶ ἄλλων ἐπιγεγονότων πλεόνων, "the periods fixed for the repayment have passed, and still further periods elapsed" (Edd.). In P Oxy II. 246¹³ (A.D. 66) the verb is used of lambs "born after" a first registration —καὶ νῦ[ν]

ἀπογράφομαι τοὺς ἐπ[ιγε]γονότας εἰς τὴν ἐνεστ[ῶσαν] δευτέραν ἀπογραφήν: cf. P Ryl II. 111¹² (census-return—A.D. 161) ἀν]αγεγρα(μμένον) ἐν ἐπιγεγενημ(ένοις), *OGIS* 56¹⁹ (B.C. 237) ὑπόμνημα καταλείποντες τοῖς τε νῦν οὖσιν καὶ τοῖς ἐπιγινομένοις. See further P Par 45⁸ (B.C. 153) εὐλαβοῦμαι τὸν ἐνδίκτην τὰ πλεῖστα, τὰ (= ἃ) πράσεις, μὴ ἐπιγέν[οι]το, where Witkowski (*Epp.²*, p. 85) understands ἐπιγίνομαι as = "de improviso appareo, aggredior": cf. Ac 28¹³, and see Hobart, p. 290. The double compound ἐπιπαραγίνομαι is found P Petr III. 31⁷ (B.C. 240). The subst. ἐπιγονή = "offspring," "descendants," as in 2 Chron 31¹⁶, is common, e.g. P Par 63¹⁵⁶ (B.C. 164) τὴν τούτων ἐπιγονήν. See also the editors' note in P Tebt I. p. 556 ff. on the meaning of the phrase τῆς ἐπιγονῆς.

ἐπιγινώσκω.

Dean Robinson's careful study of this verb in *Eph.* p. 248 ff., in which he comes to the conclusion that the verb denotes not so much fuller or more perfect knowing, as knowing arrived at by the attention being directed to (ἐπί) a particular person or object, is on the whole borne out by the evidence of the papyri. Thus one of the letters in the Gemellus correspondence, P Fay 112¹⁴ (A.D. 99), has—ἐπίγνωθι εἰ ἐσκάφη ὁ τῆς Διονυσιάδος ἐλαιών, "find out whether the olive-yard at Dionysias was dug," while another letter in the same collection in a similar context has the *simplex*—*ib.* 110¹⁶ (A.D. 94) γνῶθι εἰ πεπότισται ὁ [ἐ]λαιὼν δυσὶ ὕδασι: cf. Mt 11²⁷ with Lk 10²². See also P Tebt II. 297⁹ (*c.* A.D. 123) where, in the account of legal proceedings concerning the purchase of a priestly office, the advocate, after recalling a report that the office ought to be sold, proceeds—τοῦτο ἐπιγνοὺς ὁ συνηγορούμενος ἐνέτυχε Τε[ι]μοκράτει, "on learning this my client appealed to Timocrates"; and an application for division of property in the same volume, 319¹¹ (A.D. 248) ἔδοξεν δὲ νῦν αὐτοῖς ταύτας δι[αιρή]σασθαι ἐπὶ τῷ ἕκαστον αὐτῶν ἐπιγεινώσκειν τ[ὸ] ἴδιον μ[έρος, "they have now decided to divide these (*c.* arourae) on the understanding that each should distinguish his own share" (Edd.). Other examples where no intensive force can be claimed for the ἐπι- are P Oxy IX. 1188¹⁶ (A.D. 13) ἐπιγνοὺς τὴν διάθε(σιν) καὶ ἐπιθεὶς τὴν ἐπ' ἀληθείας ἀξίαν προσφώνη σον, "after learning their condition and adding the true value furnish a report" (Ed.), with reference to the purchase of logs, *ib.* VI. 930¹⁴ (ii/iii A.D.) ἐμέλησε δέ μοι πέμψαι καὶ πυθέσθαι περὶ τῆς ὑγίας σου καὶ ἐπιγνῶναι τί ἀναγεινώσκεις, "I took care to send and ask about your health and learn what you are reading" (Edd.), *ib.* 932⁸ (late ii/A.D.) ἐὰν δύνῃ ἀναβῆναι ἵνα ἐπιγνοῖς τὸν ὄνον, "if you can go up to find out the ass, do so" (Edd.) (for this omitted apodosis cf. Lk 19⁴², 2 Th 2⁶), P Cairo Preis 48³ (ii/A.D.) ἐπιγνοὺς ἐξ ἧς μοι ἔγραψας ἐπιστολῆς, ὅτι ἔρρωσαι, ἥσθην, ἀδελφέ, and Preisigke 4630¹² (ii/A.D.) καὶ γὰρ λείαν δακνόμεθα ἕως ἄν ἐπιγνῶμεν πῶς τὸν πόδα ἔχεις. In BGU IV. 1139¹³ (B.C. 5) the writer has deleted ἐπιγνοὺς and inserted συνιδών above the line. P Lond 354²³ (*c.* B.C. 10) (= II. p. 165) ἐπιγνόντα ἀκρειβῶς ἕκαστα shows the force of the verb strengthened by means of an adverb: cf. Ac 25¹⁰.

It may be added that the vernacular is rich in ἐπι- compounds of the kind Dean Robinson describes: cf. e.g. P Lips I. 37²³ (A.D. 389) ἡμιθανῆ αὐτὸν [πο]ιήσαντες ὡς κα[ὶ] φανε[ρ]ά ἐστιν τὰ προσφωνηθέντα ὑπὸ τῶν ἐπιθεωρησάντων τὰ πλήγματα, "by those who inspected the blows," and P Tebt II. 406²⁴ (inventory of property—c. A.D. 266) καὶ ὧν ἐπικρατῖ δούλων, "and the slaves he owns."

ἐπίγνωσις

is found in P Tebt I. 28¹¹ (c. B.C. 114) πρὸς τὸ μὴ ἕκαστα ἐπ᾽ ἐπίγνωσιν ἀχθῆναι, where the editors render "in order to prevent the details being accurately known": it is doubtful, however, whether the addition of "accurately" is required. The term, as in Phil 1⁹, Heb 10²⁶, may well have been borrowed from the popular philosophy of the day: cf. Epict. ii. xx. 21 λαβὼν . . . κανόνας εἰς ἐπίγνωσιν τῆς ἀληθείας.

ἐπιγραφή

in the literal sense of an "insertion" is found in P Lond II. 178¹⁴ (A.D. 145) (= II. p. 207) τὸ δὲ χειρόγραφον . . καθαρὸν ἀπὸ ἐπιγραφῆς καὶ ἀλίφαδος κύριον ἔστω: see *Archiv* i. p. 125. Cf. also P Ryl II. 316² (ii/A.D.) ἀ̣πὸ δὲ ἐπιγραφῶν καὶ παραγραφῶν from a much mutilated sale of land. In PSI IV. 424⁹ (iii/B.C.) τοῦτο δὲ ποιήσας ἔσει ἐμέ τε σεσωικὼς . . καὶ τὴν ἐπιγραφὴν ταύτην ἕξεις, the word is used of a mark or title of honour. It is common as a special term in connexion with a tax whose precise nature remains uncertain. Grenfell and Hunt describe it as in any case "an extra burden" as distinguished from the ordinary land taxes (*Tebtunis Papyri*, I. p. 58 ff.); see also their note on P Oxy XII. 1445⁵ (ii/A.D.), where the word is said to be used in papyri of the Roman period "in the wide sense of 'assessment' in connexion with many kinds of taxes upon land," and cf. P Par 63⁷¹ (B.C. 164) (= P Petr III. p. 24) καὶ μήτ᾽ ἐνίοις καταδεεστέραν τοῦ μετρίου τὴν ἐπιγραφὴν γενηθῆναι μήτε πάλιν ὑπερτείνουσαν αὐτὴν τυχοῦσαν, "if the corvée were not unduly relaxed in some cases, nor, on the other hand, excessive in amount" (Mahaffy).

ἐπιγράφω.

The use of the subst. for a "special impost" (see s.v. ἐπιγραφή) is supported by the verb in P Tebt I. 48¹² (c. B.C. 113) where reference is made to certain supplies of wheat "imposed" in view of the approaching visit of King Soter II.—τὴν ἐπιγεγραμμένην πρὸς τὴν τοῦ βασιλέως παρουσίαν ἀγορὰν (πυροῦ) (ἀρταβῶν) π̅: cf. P Hib I. 44³ (B.C. 253) of compulsory labour. The verb is also used of any one "appointed to" or "set apart for" an office, as P Oxy II. 251³² (A.D. 44) ἐπιγέγραμμαι αὐτῆς κύριος, P Tebt II. 380³¹ (A.D. 67) ὑπογραφεὶς τῆς <Θ>ομμοῦτο(ς) <καὶ τοῦ> ἐπιγραψ<αμ>ένου αὐτῆς κυρίου Λυσᾶς κτλ., "the signatories for Thommous and her appointed guardian are Lysas, etc."; so *ib.* 397²⁰⋅ ²⁵ (A.D. 198). Similarly of the witnesses entered in an act, as e.g. Petr II. 21(a)⁵ ἐπε]ὶ ἐπεγράφην μάρτυς ἐπὶ συγγραφῆ[ι. For the general sense "direct" see P Ryl II. 153⁴³ (A.D. 138–61) ἐπέγραψα δὲ Εὐδαίμονι . . . γράψαι ὑπὲρ ἐμο̣ῦ̣ τῆς ὑπογραφῆς τὸ σῶμα διὰ τὴν περὶ ἐμὲ ἀσθενίαν, "I have directed Eudaemon . . . to write for me the body of the subscription on account of my illness" (Edd.). The meaning "inscribe," as in Ac 17²³, is found P Oxy VI. 886¹⁶ (a magical formula—iii A.D.) (= *Selections*, p. 111) ἐπίγρ(αψον) ἐν ἑκάστῳ τῶν φύλλων τὰ τῶν θεῶν ὀνόματα.

ἐπιδείκνυμι.

For this verb in its primary sense of "show," cf. P Flor II. 125⁸ (A.D. 254) ἐπιδέξω(ν) τοὺς τόπους ἔνθα ἀπετέθη, P Fay 20⁸ (iii/iv A.D.) πολὺ ἂν φανερωτέραν τὴν ἐμαυτοῦ μεγαλοψυχίαν ἐπιδεικ[ν]ύμενος, "making a much more conspicuous display of my magnanimity," P Oxy I. 42⁵ (A.D. 325) ὅτι προθυμότατα τοὺς ἐφήβους [τ]ὰ γυμνι̣κ̣ὰ̣ ἐπιδείκνυσθαι προσήκει. In P Ryl II. 175¹⁴ (A.D. 168) ἐπιδεδιγμένος ἐξηγητ[ής is "exegetes-elect." See also P Petr III. 53(n)⁸ (iii B.C.) ἀ[λ]λ᾽ οὐ τυχὼν ἐπιδείξ(αι?)(?or- δεῖξαι) π[ρ]ὸς βίαν ἔχεται, "but since he did not succeed in clearing himself he is forcibly detained;" and for the meaning "prove," as in Ac 18²⁸, Heb 6¹⁷, cf. P Eleph 1² (marriage contract—B.C. 311–10) (= *Selection*, p. 3) ἐπιδειξάτω δὲ Ἡρακλείδης ὅ τι ἂν ἐγκαλῆι Δημητρίαι ἐναντίον ἀνδρῶν τριῶν, "and let H. prove his charge against D. in the presence of three men," P Giss I. 2¹⋅ ²⁴ (marriage-contract—B.C. 173) ἐὰν δέ τι τούτων ἐπιδει[χθῆι] ποιῶν, P Tor I. 1¹ⁱⁱ⋅⁴ (B.C. 117–6) προσυποδεικνὺς . . . πρότερον εἶναι ἐπιδεικνύειν αὐτόν, ὡς ἐστιν υἱὸς τοῦ τε Πτολεμαίου καὶ . . . μητρός, and P Ryl II. 87 (early iii/A.D.) where ἐπέδειξα is used *ter* of a surveyor who has "verified" the condition of certain arourae of land. For the subst. see P Tor I. 1ᵛⁱⁱⁱ⋅⁷ (B.C. 119) μετὰ τὰς ἐπιδείξεις ταύτας "three demonstrations" (Ed.). P Oxy III. 471⁹ (ii/A.D.) ὥστε καὶ ἐπίδειξις ἦν αὐτῷ πρὸς τοὺς δανειζομένους ἃ ἔπραττεν, "and even showed off to the borrowers what he had been doing" (Edd.).

ἐπιδέχομαι.

With the use of this verb in 3 Jn⁹ we may compare P Par 63¹⁶¹ (B.C. 165) (= P Petr III. p. 32) ἀσμένως ἐπιδέξασθαι τὸ προτεινόμενον, "to receive cheerfully what is proposed," and for the slightly different sense in the following verse (3 Jn¹⁰) cf. P Oxy II. 281⁹ (A.D. 20–50) ἐγὼ μὲν οὖν ἐπιδεξαμένη αὐτὸν εἰς τὰ τῶν γονέων μου οἰκητήρια λειτὸν παντελῶς ὄντα, "as he was destitute of means I received him into my parents' house" (Edd.). For the general sense "accept" cf. P Oxy I. 44⁹ (late i A.D.) τῶν ὤνων μὴ ἐπιδεδεγμένων ὑπὸ τῶν τελωνῶν, "the taxes not having been accepted by the tax-farmers": the verb is also common with μισθώσασθαι of "accepting" the terms of a lease, e.g. P Oxy X. 1270⁵ (A.D. 159). A derived sense "undertake" appears in P Par 63⁹ (B.C. 165) (= P Petr III. p. 20) ἐπιδέχεσθαι τὰ τῆς γεωργίας, "to undertake field labour," P Oxy III. 498⁶ (ii A.D.) ἐπιδεχόμεθα λαξείαν τῶν οἰκοδομουμένων λίθων κύβων, "we undertake to cut the squared building stones": cf. *ib.* XII. 1412² (c. A.D. 284) οὐδὲ βραχεῖαν ἀναθέσ(ι̣)ν ἐπιδέχεται, "does not admit even a brief delay" (Edd.).

The subst. is found in PSI IV. 316¹⁶ (iv/A.D. ?) βεβαι̣ου̣μένης δέ μο̣ι̣ τῆς ἐπιδοχῆς.

ἐπιδημέω.

The meaning of this word (see Ac 2¹⁰, 17²¹) is well brought out in P Par 69 (A.D. 233), extracts from the day-book of a strategus, where it is used of his arrival and temporary sojourn in a place, as ἀποδημέω is of his departure: see further Wilcken *Archiv* iv. p. 374, cf. p. 422. The actual Lukan phrase οἱ ἐπιδημοῦντες ξένοι (Ac 17²¹) may be paralleled from the inscrr., e.g. *Priene* 108²⁶⁶ (after B.C. 129) παρὰ

τοῖς ἐπιδεδ[ημηκόσι τῶν ξένων, 111¹⁶⁷ (i/B.C.) τοὺς ἐπιδεδ[ημηκότας ξένους: see Rouffiac, p. 44. Other exx. of
the verb are P Par 26³·⁴ (B.C. 163–2) (= *Selections*, p. 13)
where the Serapeum Twins refer to a petition which they
had addressed to Ptolemy and Cleopatra—ἐπιδημήσα[σι]ν
ἐν Μέμφει, "when they were in residence at Memphis,"
P Oxy IV. 705³⁶ ἐπιδημήσ[αν]τες τῷ ἔθνει of the visit of
Severus and Caracalla to Egypt in A.D. 202, and CP Herm
I. 8¹¹·² μέχρις ἂν ἐπιδημήσῃ ἐπ᾽ ἀγαθοῖς ὁ λαμπρότ[ατος
ἡγεμών. For the corresponding subst. see P Gen I. 31⁴
(A.D. 145–6) Διόσκορος . . . ἑκάστοτέ σοι κατ᾽ ἐπιδημίαν
παρενοχλῶν, "Dioscurus who is always troubling you (the
strategus) on the occasion of your visitation." OGIS 517⁷
(iii/A.D.) κατὰ τὴν . . . [Αὐ]τοκράτορος Ἀντωνίνου [ἐ]πι-
δημίαν: the word is thus practically synonymous with the
more technical παρουσία; see Milligan *Thess.*, p. 145 ff.

ἐπιδιατάσσομαι.

The Pauline use of this verb in connexion with a will in
Gal 3¹⁵ may be illustrated from the occurrence of διατάσ-
σεσθαι, διάταξις, etc., in inscrr. from Asia Minor with the
specialized meaning of "determine by testamentary disposition": see W. Judeich *Altertümer von Hierapolis*, p. 110,
cited by Deissmann *LAE*, p. 87 n⁵.

ἐπιδίδωμι

is the ordinary formula for sending in a report to a magistrate or official body, e.g. P Oxy II. 255¹⁶ (A.D. 48) (=
Selections, p. 47) ὀμνύω . . . εἰ μὴν [ἐ]ξ [ὑ]γιοῦς καὶ ἐπ᾽
ἀληθείας ἐπιδεδωκέναι τὴ[ν π]ροκειμένην [γρα]φὴν τῶν παρ᾽
ἐμοὶ [ο]ἰκούν[των, "I swear that assuredly the preceding
document makes a sound and true return of those living with
me"—a census-return; P Fay 28¹¹ (A.D. 150–1) (= *Selections*, p. 82) διὸ ἐπιδίδωμ[ι] τὸ τῆς ἐπιγενήσεως ὑπόμνημα—
a notice of birth; P Oxy I. 79¹⁰ (A.D. 181–92) (= *Selections*,
p. 80) διὸ ἐπιδίδωμι [τὸ] βιβλίδιον ἀξιῶν ταγῆναι αὐτὸν ἐν
τῇ τῶν τετελευτηκότων τάξει—a notice of death; BGU I.
287¹⁶ (A.D. 250) (= *Selections*, p. 116) Αὐρήλ(ιος) [Δι]ο-
γένης ἐπιδέ[δωκα—a certificate of pagan sacrifice. Cf. also
P Oxy III. 487⁵ (A.D. 156) Σερῆνος ἐπέ[δ]ωκέ με εἰς ἐπιτροπὴν ἀφηλίκ[ω]ν υ[ἱ]ῶν, "Serenus appointed me guardian of
(two) minors." For other exx. see *s.v.* βιβλίον, and the
editor's note on OGIS 515³⁸ (iii/A.D.).

With the use of the verb in Ac 27¹⁵ we may compare P
Par 49⁹ (B.C. 164–158) εἰς πᾶν τό σοι χρήσιμον ἐμαυτὸν
ἐπιδιδόναι. In P Lille I. 5³⁹ (after B.C. 241–0) συνχρημά-
τιζε ὅ[σα]ς ἂν ἡμέρας ἐπιδώῃ, the editors treat the verb as
an opt.; but see *Proleg.* p. 55, where similar forms are
treated as subjunctives. For the subst. see P Ryl II. 119²⁹
(A.D. 54–67) καθ᾽ οὗ καὶ πλείστας ἐντυχίας καὶ ἐπιδόσεις
ἀναφορῶν ἐποιησάμεθα, "against whom we made numerous
petitions and presented reports" (Edd.), and for the adj. *ib.*
233¹¹ (ii/A.D.) λόγον . . . ὑφ᾽ ἓν γεγραμμένον κεχωρισμένον
δὲ εἰς ὃ ἐπιδοσίμους, "an account written under one head,
but divided into 4 sections."

ἐπιδιορθόω.

For this verb, which in the NT is confined to Tit 1⁵,
Grimm-Thayer refer to CIG II. 2555⁹ αἰ δέ τί κα δόξῃ βωλευο-
μέ[νοις] ἐπὶ τῷ κοινῷ συμφέροντι ἐπιδιορθῶσαι ἢ ἐξελεῖν ἢ
ἐνβαλέν. Cf. Field *Notes*, p. 219.

ἐπιείκεια.

An interesting ex. of this word occurs in the Abinnaeus
correspondence, when an official writes urging him in his
character of πραιπόσιτος to keep a look-out for any natron
that might be smuggled into Arsinoe, and to arrest those
engaged in the attempt—P Lond 231¹⁹ (c. A.D. 346) (= II.
p. 285, *Chrest.* I. p. 379) τὰ αὐτὰ δηλῶ. ἵνα μετὰ πάσης
ἐπιεικείας τὴν φρουρὰν τῶν ταμειακῶν νίτρων ποιήσῃ καὶ
πάντας ὅσους καταλαμβάνεις ἐπισχῇς μετὰ καὶ τῶν κτηνῶν
αὐτῶν. Cf. from the inscrr. OGIS 504⁹ (time of Hadrian)
where a certain Οὔλπιος Εὐρυκλῆς is praised ὡς . . . ἐν
τῶι κοινῶι ἐπὶ παιδείαι τε καὶ τῆι ἄλληι ἀρετῆι καὶ ἐπιει-
κείαι διάδηλον ἑαυτὸν πεποιηκέν[αι, *ib.* 507⁸ (time of
Hadrian) αὐτῶι τὰ αὐτὰ ἐπιεικείᾳ τε καὶ αἰδοῖ πάσηι κεχρη-
μένωι, and *Syll* 932³⁵ (iii/A.D. *ad init.*) ἐντειλ]ας μὴ ὕβρει
μηδὲ βίᾳ, δικαιοσύνῃ δὲ καὶ ἐπιεικείᾳ [κρατ]εῖν τοὺς ἐνοικοῦντας. In P Oxy I. 67⁶ (A.D. 338) ἅπερ ἀντέγραψεν πρὸς
τὴν σὴν ἐπιείκιάν τε καὶ καθαρότητα, "which in reply he
wrote to your clemency and impartiality" (Edd.), the abstract honorific periphrasis: cf. CPR I. 19¹⁵·²⁴ (A.D. 350).
The word is used by Proclus in his description (*Epistologr.
Gr.* p. 8 6) of an ironical epistle—λίαν ἄγαμαι τὴν σὴν
ἐπιείκειαν, ὅτι οὕτω ταχέως μεταβάλλῃ ἀπ᾽ εὐνομίας εἰς τὸ
ἐναντίον (cited by Dibelius *HZNT ad* Phil 4⁵). From the
above instances it will be seen that ἐπιείκεια is a very elusive
term, and is by no means always = "sweet reasonableness."

ἐπιεικής

is found in the fragmentary P Petr II. 3(c) —*hiat cont.*
Cf. P Oxy IX. 1218⁶ (iii/A.D.) οἶδα γάρ σου τὸ σπουδεῖον
καὶ ἐπικές (*l.* τὸ σπουδαῖον καὶ ἐπιεικές), "for I know your
goodness and reasonableness" (Ed.). With 1 Tim 3³ cf. the
use of the adverb in *Priene* 119¹³ (i/B.C. *ad init.*) where a
man who has been elected ἀντιγραφεύς is said to have discharged his duties in an equitable manner—ἦρξεν ἐπιεικῶς:
also P Tebt II. 484 (*c.* A.D. 14) where writing to certain
πράκτορες who were deficient in their reckoning the strategus (?) says—καὶ ἐπικέστερον (*l.* ἐπιεικέστερον) ὑμῖν
ἐχρησάμη(ν), and P Oxy XII. 1414²³ (A.D. 270–5) οἱ
βουλευταὶ εἶπ ον· ἐπιεικῶς ὁ πρύτανις, "the senators said,
'The Prytanis has done right'" (Edd.). According to
Radermacher *Gr.* p. 39 n.¹ ἐπεικής is the form found in
the inscrr. and ἐπιεικής in the papyri: but cf.
Priene 119 *ut s.* On the relation of the two forms, see
Moulton *Gr.* ii. § 38.

ἐπιζητέω.

A few exx. may be quoted to illustrate the varying shades
of meaning of this verb in the NT. Thus for the sense
"seek for," as in Lk 4¹², cf. P Hamb I. 27⁴ (B.C. 250) τὴι δὲ
ἐφαύριον αὐτὸν ἐπεζήτουν καὶ οὐχ ηὕρισ[κον ἐμ Φιλαδελ-
φείᾳ, and for "inquire," cf. P Fay 36¹⁴ (A.D. 185) ἐπιζητ-
οῦντί σοι, "in answer to your inquiry," and so P Oxy I. 77⁶
(A.D. 223): the directive rather than the intensive force of
the compound is well seen in P Tebt II. 411⁷ (ii/A.D.) ὁ γὰρ
κράτιστος ἐπιστράτηγος ἱκανῶς σε ἐπεζήτησε, "has made
several inquiries about you." Similarly for "desire," cf. P
Tebt II. 314⁶ (ii/A.D.) ἐπιζητοῦντος τοῦ [ἀ]ρχιερέως τὸν
παῖδα ε[ἰ]δῖν, and for the stronger "demand," P Lille I. 7⁶
(iii/B.C.) καὶ ἐπιζητήσαντος αὐτοῦ βυβλάρια τινα, ἃ ἐδεδώ-

κειν ἐν φυλακῆι), P Tebt II. 416[20] (iii/A.D.) μηδὲν ἐπιζητείτω, "let her want for nothing" (Edd.). The passive appears in P Oxy I. 80[15] (A.D. 238–44) τοὺς ἐπιζητουμένους, of criminals who are "wanted," P Oxy IX. 1194[2] (c. A.D. 205) πρὸς τὰ ἐπιζητηθέντα ὥστε μεταδοθῆναι τὰ λοιπαζόμενα, "in answer to the requisition for a report of the arrears" (Ed.), ib. 1190[15] A.D. 211–12) ἐμφανὴς ὢν ὁπόταν ἐπιζητηθῶ, "appearing whenever I may be required" (Ed.), and in the interesting P Oxy I. 36[6, 5] (ii/iii A.D.) from which we learn that if a tax-gatherer had any suspicion that a merchant had more goods on his ship than he had declared (ἀπεγράψατο) he had the right of requiring the cargo to be unloaded—ἐ[ὰν] δὲ τελώνης ἐκφορ[τισ]θῆναι τὸ πλοῖον ἐπιζητήσῃ, ὁ ἔμπορος ἐκφορτιζέ[τ]ω.

ἐπίθεσις.

The only exx. we have found of this word are in the hostile sense of "setting upon," "attack," "machination," e.g. P Rein 17[8] (B.C. 109) ἐπε̣ὶ οὖν ὑπο[λα]μβάνω [δ]ιὰ τῆς ἐπιθέσεως γεγονέναι Κωννῶτος, "comme j'ai lieu d'attribuer ce coup à une machination de Konnos" (Ed.), P Oxy II. 283[15] (A.D. 45) ὃν καὶ ἀγήοχα (l. ἀγήοχα) ἐπὶ σὲ μεθ' ἱκανῆς τῆς γεγονυίας μοι ἐπιθέσεως καὶ πληγῶν ἐπιφορᾶς, "I have brought him to you at the expense of a severe and violent attack upon myself" (Edd.), ib. VIII. 1121[7] (A.D. 295) καὶ αὐτὴ γὰρ ἀνυπέρβλητον ἐπίθεσιν καὶ ἁρπαγὴν πάσχουσα πρόσειμι μαρτυρο[μέν]η τὰ εἴς με ἐπιχειρηθέντα. "I therefore, being the victim of a most outrageous attack and robbery, approach you to testify to the assault upon me" (Ed.). Cf. Vett. Val. p. 73[11] ἐξ ὀνειδισμῶν καὶ ἐνέδρας καὶ δόλου καὶ ἐπιθέσεως ἀναγομένους κτλ., and for ἐπιθέτης ib. p. 161[1]. Ἐπίθεμα = "addition" is found in P Oxy III. 509[14] (A.D. 130), and according to the editors' note ad l. it should be rendered "higher bid" in P Amh II. 85[21] (A.D. 78) : see further for the word the note on P Giss I. 48[10] and for the phrase ἱλαστήριον ἐπίθεμα in Exod 25[16, 17] see Deissmann, BS, p. 124 ff.

ἐπιθυμέω.

For the late acc. constr. with this verb, as in Mt 5[28] BD, cf. the Hadrumetum Memorial of iii/A.D. reproduced in BS, p. 274 ff. [45] μηδεμίαν ἄλλη[ν] γυναῖκα μήτε παρθένον ἐπιθυμοῦντα. In P Lond 897 (A.D. 84) (= III. p. 207) after the closing word of l. 28 the following words have been written and struck out— . . με . . σε οὐκ ἐπιθυμῶι εἰς Ἀρσινοΐτην π. Other exx. of the verb are BGU II. 248[4] (ii/A.D.) ὧν κοινῆισε βούλεθαι (l. κοινῆσαι βούλεται) καὶ αὐτὸν ἐ[.] ε . [.] . . ἐπιθυμεῖν τῶν ἠθῶν σου ἀπολαῦσαι, P Oxy VI. 963 (ii/iii A.D.) ἀσπάζομαί σε, μῆτερ, διὰ τῶν γραμμάτων τούτων ἐπιθυμοῦσα ἤδη θεάσασθαι, and from the inscrr. Syll 226[108] (iii B.C.) πρὸς δὲ τούτοις Θισαμάτας καὶ Σκύθας καὶ Σαυδαράτας ἐπιθυμεῖν τοῦ ὀχυρώματος ("fortress"). OGIS 764[19] (ii B.C.) τοῖς ἄλλοις ἄρχουσιν πᾶσιν καὶ Ῥωμαίων τοῖς ἐπιθυμοῦσιν καὶ τοῖς ἐλευθέροις παισίν.

ἐπιθυμητής.

For ἐ. used in a bad sense as in 1 Cor 10[6], Deissmann (BS, p. 224) compares BGU II. 531[ii. 22] (ii/A.D.) ὡς οὔτε εἰμὶ ἄδικος οὔτε ἀ[λ]λοτρίων ἐπιθυμητής. On the other hand cf. an inscr. from about the beginning of the Christian era, Syll 935[40] ἵνα οὖν καὶ ὁ δῆμος φαίνηται εὐχάριστος καὶ

τιμῶν τοὺς ἀρετῆι διαφέροντας πολλοί τε δόξης ἐπιθυμηταὶ γένωνται.

ἐπιθυμία

in the widest sense of "desire," which Hort finds even in Jas 1[14], may be illustrated from P Giss I. 79[iii, 10] (c. A.D. 117) δι' ἣν ἕξομεν εὐω[νεῖν κατ' ἐπ]ιθυμίαν σου, "and then we shall be able to buy cheaply in accordance with your desire" (ἀθυμέω = "draw back," "hesitate," occurs in the same document : see s.v.). BGU III. 970[25] (ii A.D.) μεταδῶναί μοι ἀντίρρησιν . . . πρὸς τὴν ἰδίαν ἐπιθυμίαν, and Syll 366[12] (A.D. 38) ἀ λείπτοις ("steadfast") ἐκείνου τῆς ἐπιθυμίας βουλήμασιν. See also the iii A.D. love-spell from Hadrumetum edited by Deissmann BS, p. 273 ff. where the forsaken husband is described as[34] ἐρῶντα μαινόμενον ἀγρυπνο[ῦν]τα ἐπὶ τῇ φιλίᾳ αὐτῆς καὶ ἐπιθυμίᾳ, "loving, frantic, sleepless with love and desire for her."

ἐπικαθίζω

is found in the NT only in Mt 21[7]. Cf. ἐπικάθημαι in P Tebt II. 391[11] (A.D. 99) τοὺς ἐν τῇ κώμῃ καταγινομένους καὶ ἐπικαθημένους ἄνδρες (l. -ας, "the inhabitants of and settlers in the village" (Edd.).

ἐπικαλέω.

The various NT usages of this common verb can all be illustrated from our documents. Thus for the meaning "surname" : see P Fay 12[1] (c. B.C. 103) βασιλεῖ Πτολεμαίωι ἐπικαλ(ουμένω) Ἀλ[ε]ξάνδρωι . . . χαίρειν, P Tebt II. 399[15] (ii A.D.) ὑπὲρ ἐγγό[νου] Εὐδαίμονος ἐπικεκλημένου [Μυ . . . , BGU II. 447[25] (ii A.D.), etc. ; and for the simple "call," see P Tebt II. 585[7] (B.C. 30—A.D. 1) ἀρού(ρας) 5 ἐπεικαλουμένας Βασιλ(ικοῦ) Γρ(αμμάτεως), "ὁ arourae called those of the Basilico-grammateus." ib. 319[8] (A.D. 248) ἐν τόπῳ ἐπικαλουμένῳ Καρίωνι, P Ryl II. 172[9] (A.D. 208) Φοινικῶνα περὶ κώμ(ην) Ἡφ(αιστιάδα) ἐπικαλούμενον Ἑρεννίου, "the palm-garden called that of Herennius in the area of the village Hephaestias." For ἐ. = "accuse," see P Hib I. 62[5] (B.C. 245) κακοῦργον τὸν τ[ὴν] λείαν ποιήσαντα ἐπικαλεῖ Τνᾶς Ἀρνούφιος, "the criminal who did the pillage is accused by Tnas son of Harnouphis" (Edd.), P Fay 97[29] (A.D. 78) ἐνκαλεῖν μηδ' ἐπικ[αλεῖν. "make any claim or charge," so BGU I. 350[34] (time of Trajan). The middle usage "invoke," "call upon," as in A 7[59], is frequent in the magic papyri, as P Leid Wxx[25] (ii/iii A.D.) ἐπικαλοῦ τὸν τῆς ὥρας καὶ τὸν τῆς ἡμέρας θεόν, P Oxy VI. 886[19] (iii A.D.) (= selections, p. 111) ἐπικαλοῦ με [ν (?)] τὸν (ἥλιον) κὲ τοὺς ἐν βυθῷ θεοὺς πάντας : cf. Syll 810[1] (ii B.C.) (= LAE, p. 424) ἐπικαλοῦμαι καὶ ἀξιῶ τὸν θεὸν τὸν ὕψιστον . . . ἐπὶ τοὺς δόλωι φονεύσαντας κτλ. (for constr. with ἐπί, see 2 Cor 1[23]). For ἐπίκλησις = "spell," see P Lond 121[259] (iii A.D.) (= I. p. 93) : in P Lille I. 29[27] (iii B.C.) δούλων ἐπίκλησις καὶ τοῖς καταδικασαμένοις πρᾶξις is rendered "recours contre les esclaves et moyens d'exécution pour ceux qui les ont fait condamner," the editor noting that this usage of ἐ. is unknown to the Attic vocabulary.

ἐπικατάρατος

is described by Grimm-Thayer as "only in bibl. and eccl. use," but Deissmann (LAE, p. 93 f.) quotes it from Syll

891² (ii/A.D.) ἐπικατάρατος ὅστις μὴ φείδοιτο κατὰ τόνδε τὸν χῶρον τοῦδε τοῦ ἔργου, " cursed whoever doth not spare this work in this place " (viz. a monument on a tomb), and also from an undoubtedly pagan inscr. from Halicarnassus of ii/iii A.D., *CIG* 2664 εἴ τις δὲ ἐπιχειρήσι λίθον ἆραι ἢ λῦσαι αὐτό, ἤτω ἐπικατάρατος ταῖς προγεγραμμέναις ἀραῖς.

ἐπίκειμαι.

For the meaning "lie upon," "cover," see P Tebt I. 47²⁵ (B.C. 113) τοῦ ὕδατος ἐπικειμένου, of the water covering the land at the annual rising of the Nile, P Grenf II. 57⁹ A.D. 168) τὴν ἐπικει[μέν]ην σποράν : cf. also P Ryl II. 121¹¹ (ii/A.D.) τ[ὰς] σφραγεῖδας ἃς ἐπέθηκ[ε ἐπ]ικεῖνται, "the seals which he affixed are still in their place" (Edd.), P Oxy VIII. 1127²⁴ (A.D. 183) καὶ τὰς ἐπικειμένας θύρας δύο κλεῖν μίαν, "and the two doors and one key attached" (Ed.). The sepulchral inscr. *Kaibel* 622⁸ has φθίμενος τήνδ' ἐπίκειμαι κόνιν, "in death I have this dust laid upon me." The stronger sense of "attack" occurs in P Par 46⁸ (B.C. 153) (== Witkowski², p. 86) λῃστῶν ἐπικειμένων : cf. P Rein 48⁸ (ii/A.D.) ὁρῶ σὲ ἐπικείμενόν μοι, "très irrité contre moi" (Ed.), P Oxy III. 488²¹ (ii/iii A.D.) τοῦ ἀνθρώπου ἐπικειμένοι μοι, "since the man oppresses me" (Edd.). The verb is used much as in Lk 5¹ in P Ryl II. 243⁷ (ii A.D.) καὶ νῦν ἐπιστάμεθά σου τὸ σπουδαῖον καὶ ὡς ἐπίκεισαι τοῖς ἔργοις τοῦ κλήρου, "we now know your zeal and attentiveness to the work of the holding" (Edd.). See also the late P Lips I. 66¹ (Byz.) σὺν θ(ε)ῷ ἐπικείμ[ενος τῆς χειρογραφείας, and P Lond 24¹ (vi/vii A.D.) ὁ ἐπικείμενος τῶν ἀγγαρευτῶν with the editor's note.

ἐπικέλλω.

Blass (*Philology of the Gospels*, p. 186) finds in the phrase ἐπέκειλαν τὴν ναῦν of Ac 27¹¹ evidence that Luke was acquainted with Homer (cf. *Od.* ix. 148, 546) on the grounds that the form ἐπικέλλω is altogether poetical, and that the obsolete ἡ ναῦς is not used anywhere else in the NT. On the other hand, poetical phrases often live on in common speech.

ἐπικεφάλαιον.

That ἐ., which is read for κῆνσον in Mk 12¹⁴ by D Θ *al.*, normally refers to the poll-tax rather than to a tax on trades (as Milne *Theb. Ostr.* p. 155 f.) is shown by the editors in their note on P Ryl II. 191⁷ (A.D. 115-7) ἐπικεφαλαίου ιθ (ἔτους) δραχμὰς δεκαὲξ (ὀβολοὺς) β [ἡμιωβέλιον], "for the poll-tax of the 16th year sixteen dr. 2½ ob." On the more general ἐπικεφάλιον, as applied to taxes other than the poll-tax, but levied *per capita*, see P Oxy XII. p. 110 f.

Ἐπικούρειος.

Cagnat IV. 997, an inscr. in honour of a certain man -Ἀμυνίαν . . . φιλόσοφον Ἐπικούρηον, πλεῖ[σ]τα τὴν πόλιν ὠφελήσαν[τα.

ἐπικουρία.

For this word which in the NT is peculiar to Luke (cf. Hobart, p. 207), see *Syll* 601²⁴ (ii/B.C.) ποιείσθω δὲ ἡ ἱέρεια καθ ἑκάστην νουμηνίαν ἐπικουρίαν ὑπὲρ πόλεως. The adj.

with reference to auxiliary or mercenary troops is found in *OGIS* 338¹⁷ (B.C. 133) δεδόσθαι πολιτείαν . . παραφυλακίταις καὶ τοῖς ἄλλοις ἐ[πικού]ροις τοῖς κατοικοῦσιν ἢ ἐνεκτημένοις ἐν τ[ῆι πόλει] ἢ τῆι χώραι. An Imperial rescript of late iii/A.D. shows the verb—P Oxy XII. 1407⁶ ἡμεῖς σοι ἐπικουροῦ[μεν.

ἐπικρίνω.

This verb, along with the corresponding subst. ἐπίκρισις, is very common of the "examination" of persons liable to military service, as e.g. in P Oxy I. 39¹¹ (A.D. 52) where, with reference to a man who had been released owing to defective eyesight, it is stated—ἐπεκρίθ(η) ἐν Ἀλεξανδ(ρεία) : cf. BGU I. 142¹ (A.D. 159) ἐπεκρίθη Ἰσίδωρος . . . ἱππεύ[s] τύρμης Ἀπο[λ]λιναρίου ὑ[πὸ] Ἰσιδώρου. Both ἐπικρίνω and ἐπίκρισις are also used in connexion with the "selection" of boys aged 11-14 for admission to the list of privileged persons who were exempt from the poll-tax : see P Lond II. p. 42 ff., P Oxy II. p. 217 ff., and Wilcken *Papyruskunde* I. i. p. 142. For the ἐπικριτής, or magistrate who made the ἐπίκρισις, see P Fay 27³ (A.D. 151-2), P Tebt II. 320² (A.D. 181 *al.* A wider use of the verb is seen in *ib.* II. 284² (i B.C.) where, in obedience to an oracular response from the god Soknebtunis, Lysimachas informs his sister—ἐπικέκριταί μοι μὴ καταβῆναι ἕως τῆς κε, "it has been decided for me that I should not go down till the 25ᵗʰ" (Edd.) : cf. Lk 23²⁴, and for ἐπίκριμα = "edict," see P Tebt II. 286⁴ (A.D. 121-138). In MGr the verb = "judge," "criticize."

ἐπιλαμβάνομαι.

For the active of this verb see P Par 26⁴³ (B.C. 163-2) (== *Selections*, p. 17) ἐπιλαβόντα παρ' ἡμῶν τὴν γραφὴν τῶν ὀφειλομένων ἡμῖν δεόντων, "having received from us the written list of the necessaries due to us," BGU IV. 1138²⁰ (B.C. 19) ἐπιλαβόντ[α παρ' αὐτ[οῦ τὸν κεχωρηκ(ότα) : in a Magdola papyrus re-edited by Reinach in *Mél. Nicole*, p. 451 ff., we have ὁ ἐπιλαβ[ὼν] μάρτυρας. In *OGIS* 257⁹ (B.C. 109) the verb is used without an accus. "de rebus subito ingruentibus"—ἐν τοῖς ἐπε[ιλ]ηφόσιν ἀναγκαι[ο]τάτοις καιροῖς. The mid., which alone is found in the NT (cf. Prov 4¹³), may be illustrated from P Hal I. 1¹⁰·³ (iii/B.C.) ὁ μαρτυρίας ἐπιλαμβανόμενος, PSI IV. 366⁴ (B.C. 250-49) ἐὰν ἐπιλαμβάνηται τῶν ἀνθρώπων καὶ τῆς βοός, and P Tebt II. 417¹⁰ (iii/A.D.) ἐπὶ γὰρ ἐ[ὰν] φθάσωμεν ἐπιλαβέσθαι τοῦ ἔργον δυνόμεθα αὐτ[ὸ ἀ]φῖναι (= ἀφεῖναι), "for as soon as we make haste to set ourselves to the work we can finish it" (note the late constr. of φθάνω c. inf.). The subst. occurs in P Tebt II. 335⁹ (mid. iii/A.D.) φοβούμενος μὴ ἄρα εὑρεθείη ἐν αὐτοῖς ἐπίλημψι[s], "from fear that they might disclose a claim by seizure" (Edd.), and see Preuschen *Mönchtum*, p. 65 for ἐπίλημπτος.

ἐπιλανθάνομαι.

The construction with the acc. in Phil 3¹³, while not unknown in classical, is amply attested in later Greek, e.g. P Oxy IV. 744¹² (B.C. 1) (= *Selections*, p. 33) εἴρηκας δὲ Ἀφροδισιᾶτι ὅτι μή με ἐπιλάθῃς· πῶς δύναμαί σε ἐπιλαθεῖν ; The correct middle also has the acc. in P Lond 964⁹ (late ii/iii A.D.) (= III. p. 212) βλέπε μὴ ἐπιλάθῃ μηδὲν τοὺς στεφάνους κτλ.: cf. also P Par 32[11] (B.C. 162) ἐπιλελῆσθαι τὰ μέτρα τῶν ὀθονίων, and P Oxy XII. 1480[3] (late iii/A.D.) τὸ κιθῶνιν ἐπιλέλισμε (l. ἐπιλέλησμαι), "I have left my cloak behind." These passages, of which at least the first and the two last occur in illiterate documents, are further of interest as against Harnack's contention (*Sayings of Jesus*, p. 84) that the use of the compound in Lk 12[6] οὐκ ἔστιν ἐπιλελησμένον marks "the language of literature": see Moulton *Camb. Bibl. Essays*, p. 404. For ἐ. with the gen., as in Heb 6[10], cf. PSI IV. 353[16] B.C. 254-3) μὴ ἐπιλανθάνου ἡμῶν, OGIS 116[15] (B.C. 181-146) μὴ ἐπιλανθανόμενοι δὲ [καὶ τ]ῶν εὐεργεσιῶν τῶν γεγενημέ[νων εἰς τ]ὰς ἑαυτῶν πατρίδας, and the passage from the Hermetic writings in Reitzenstein *Hellen. Mysterienrelig.* p. 116—πασῶν γὰρ τῶν σωματικῶν αἰσθήσεών τε καὶ κινήσεων ἐπιλαθόμενος (*v.l.* ἐπιλαβόμενος) ἀτρεμεῖ.

ἐπιλέγω.

For this verb in its original meaning cf. P Leid W[vi. 25] (ii/iii A.D.) ἐπιλέγων τὸ ὄνομα, "insuper pronuntians nomen." The sense of "choose," as in Ac 15[40], appears in P Petr II. 40(*a*)[16] (iii/B.C.) (= Witkowski[2], p. 41) καὶ οἱ [κ]υνηγοὶ ἐπιλελεγμένοι εἰ[σὶν οἱ] μέλ[λο]ντες παραγενέσθ[αι με]τὰ τοῦ στρατηγοῦ, P Hib I. 78[12] (B.C. 244-3) ἐὰν ἐκ τοῦ Ὀξυρυγ[χ]ίτου ἐπιλέγωνται, "if people are being chosen from the Oxyrhynchite nome," P Oxy IX. 1210[4] (i/B.C.—i A.D.) ἐπιλελεγμένων ὑπὸ τῶν γονέων εἰς γηροβοσκίαν ἀφ' ὧν ἔχουσι υἱῶν, "men chosen by the parents from their sons to support them in old age" (Ed.). See also OGIS 383[70] (mid. i/B.C.) θεραπείαν τε ἀνέγλειπτον καὶ ἱερεῖς ἐπιλέξας σὺν πρεπούσαις ἐσθῆσι Περσικῶι γένει κατέστησα, and for ἐπίλεκτος, which is fairly frequent in the LXX, cf. *ib.* 48[14] (iii/B.C.) εἶτα] καὶ ἐψηφ[ίσαν|το] ἐξ ἐπιλέκτων ἀνδρῶν τὴν βουλὴν [καὶ τὰ] δικαστή[ρια αἱρεῖσ]θαι, and P Par 63[21. 196] (B.C. 165) with reference to "picked" troops.

ἐπιλείπω.

Michel 332[9] (ii/B.C.) σπουδῆς οὐθὲν ἐπιλείπων ἐν πᾶσι τοῖς ἀξιουμένοις. On the verb c. acc., as in Heb 11[32], see Schmidt *de Flavii Josephi elocutione*, p. 385, and on the literary character of the phrase in Heb *l.c.* Wendland *Urchristlichen Literaturformen*, p. 307 n[1]. Ἐπιλείπομαι = "fail," "come short in," is found with the dat. in the recently recovered *Constitution of Athens* (ed. Sandys) xx. 2 ὁ δὲ Ἰσαγόρας ἐπιλειπόμενος τῇ δυνάμει, xxvii. 4 πρὸς δὴ ταύτην τὴν χορηγίαν ἐπιλειπόμενος ὁ Περικλῆς τῇ οὐσίᾳ. See also *CQ* ii. (1908), p. 209.

ἐπιλείχω.

A curious illustration of Lk 16[21] is afforded by *Syll* 805[36] (iii/B.C.), where an inscription found in the Asclepieum of Epidaurus records how a dog healed a boy— τ]ᾶι γλώσσαι ἐθεράπευσε καὶ ὑγιῆ ἐπόη]σε. Upon the presence of dogs in the Asclepieum see Dittenberger *Syll* 651 n[4].

ἐπίλοιπος.

With ἐ. in 1 Pet 4[2] cf. P Petr II. 13 (19)[4] (c. B.C. 252) (= Witkowski[2], p. 18) σοῦ προστατῆσα[ι τὸν ἐ[π]ίλοιπον βίον, "to take care of you for the rest of your life." In P Ryl II. 154[33] (A.D. 66) provision is made that in the event PART III.

of divorce taking place between two contracting parties, Sisois (the father-in-law) is to receive "the remainder"— τὸ ἐπίλοιπον—of the dowry, after the claims of the bridegroom have been met. The *recto* of the papyrus letter P Tebt I. 58[36] (B.C. 111) ends τἀπίλοιπα ὀπείσωι "the Greek equivalent of our 'P.T.O.'" (Edd.).

ἐπίλυσις.

For the metaphorical sense which this word has in 2 Pet 1[20] see Vett. Val. p. 221[9] τὰς δὲ αἰτίας ἢ τὰς λοιπὰς ἐπιλύσεις μὴ ἐπιγνῷ. p. 330[10] οὐ μὴν κατὰ τὴν δόκησιν τινῶν ἀμφιβόλως ἐπιλίσεις καὶ γραφὰς ἀναρίθμους περιττῶν συντάξεων. In the papyri the word is used for the "discharge" of an account, etc., as in P Eleph 27[23] (B.C. 223-2) ἐπειδὴ . . . τετάγμεθα τὸ ἀργύριον καὶ τοὺς τόκους ἐπὶ τὴν βασιλικὴν τράπεζαν, καλῶς ποιήσεις δοὺς ἡμῖν τὴν ἐπίλυσιν, P Grenf II. 26[27] (B.C. 103), *ib.* 30[21] (B.C. 102), etc.: see further *s.v.* ἐπιλύω.

ἐπιλύω.

Like ἐπίλυσις, the verb is used in monetary transactions, e.g. P Grenf I. 26[2] (B.C. 113) ἐπελύσατ[ο] Ψενενοῦπις Ὀννώφριος δάνειον πυροῦ ἀρ νς, a usage hitherto unknown: see further *Philologus N.F.* xvii. pp. 564 f. 577. For the metaphorical meaning as in the NT, cf. Vett. Val. p. 173[8] τὸ τῆς ἀληθείας μέρος ὡς ὑπὸ οὐδενὸς ἀνδρὸς ἐπιλελυμένον αὐτὸς ἐφώτισα, p. 259[4] προεῖπον γὰρ ἐν τοῖς ἔμπροσθεν, ὅτι ἃ μὲν ἐκ τῶν παλαιῶν σκοτεινῶς συντεταγμένα ἐπελυσάμην.

ἐπιμαρτυρέω.

For this verb = "bear witness to," which is found in the NT only in 1 Pet 5[12], cf. P Leid W[xxvi] (ii/iii A.D.) ἐπιμαρτυροῦντος μηδενὸς κακοποιοῦ Κρόνου. The stronger form ἐπιμαρτύρομαι (cf. 1 Macc 2[56]) occurs e.g. in P Petr II. 17 (3)[11] οὐδ' ἐπεμαρτύρατό με Ἀ., "neither did A. appeal to me," P Grenf I. 38[15] (ii/i B.C.) περὶ ὧν (particulars of an assault) τοὺς παρόντας ἐπεμαρτυράμην, "I called those present to witness."

ἐπιμέλεια.

P Hib I. 41[20] (c. B.C. 261) ἐπιμέλειαν δὲ ποίησαι, "be careful," BGU IV. 1106[28] (B.C. 13) ποιεῖσθαι . . . [τοῦ] παιδίου προσηκούσαν ἐπιμέλειαν, of a nurse, P Amh II. 64[12] (A.D. 107) ἀ]θέτους . . κ[αὶ] μὴ ἀναλογοῦντας τὴν ἐ[π]ιμέλειαν, "inefficient and incapable of doing their duties" (Edd.), P Oxy I. 58[12] (A.D. 288) αἱ ταμιακαὶ οὐσίαι τῆς προσηκούσης ἐπιμελείας τεύξονται, "the estates of the treasury will receive proper attention" (Edd.). Note also the common usage in such an address as P Oxy II. 281[2] (A.D. 20-50) Ἡρακλείδῃ ἱερεῖ καὶ ἀρχιδικαστῆι καὶ πρὸς τῇ ἐπιμελείᾳ τῶν χρηματιστῶν, "to H., priest, chief justice, superintendent of the chrematistae." In the Christian letter P Oxy XII. 1495[10] (iii/iv A.D.) we have—τούτου οὖν τὴν ἐπιμέλειαν ποιήσω ὡς ἰδίου υἱοῦ, "I shall take care of him as if he were my own son" (Edd.). On the "excellent Greek phrase" ἐπιμελείας τυχεῖν, "to receive attention" (kV mg. in Ac 27[3]) cf. the citations from Wetstein in Field *Notes* p. 143, and see further Hobart pp. 29, 200 f. where it is shown that both the noun and the corresponding verb are common in medical language for the "care" bestowed upon the sick, a meaning which may underlie its usage here. In the inscrr. the phrase τὴν ἐπιμέλειαν ποιησαμένων is very common with reference to the persons charged with putting up the inscr. : see Rouffiac *Recherches*, p. 56.

Ἐπιμελητής is the regular term for a "curator" or "supervisor." Thus we hear of ἐπιμεληταὶ ἀννώνης, ἀχύρου, βαλανείου, γυμνασίου, ἱεροῦ, etc. : for citations see Hohlwein *L'Égypte Romaine*, p. 232 ff.

ἐπιμελέομαι, ἐπιμέλομαι.

For the constr. with the gen., as in Lk 10³¹ᶠ, 1 Tim 3⁵, cf. P Petr II. 11 (1)⁸ (iii/B.C.) (= *Selections*, p. 8) ἐπιμέλου δὲ καὶ σαυτοῦ, "take care also of yourself," P Lond 42¹² (B.C. 168) (= I. p. 31, *Selections*, p. 11) χαριεῖ δὲ καὶ τοῦ σώματος ἐπιμελ[ό]μενος, ἵν᾽ ὑγιαίνῃς, BGU IV. 1078¹¹ (A.D. 39) τὰ δ᾽ ἄλλα ἐπιμελῶ — εἶ σ᾽ε ἀτῶν (= ὑμῶν αὐτῶν), P Oxy VIII. 1154³ (late i/A.D.) ἐπιμελοῦ σεαυτῆς ἵνα μοι ὑγιαίνῃς, "take care of yourself so that I may have you well " (Ed.). The verb is construed with the dat. in P Tebt I. 58⁶² (B.C. 111) ἐπιμέλου τοῖς ἐν οἴκωι, P Oxy IV. 744⁶ (B.C. 1) (= *Selections*, p. 32) παρακαλῶ σε ἐπιμεληθῆ[ι] ᾱ. —ήθητι τῷ παιδίῳ. From the inscrr we may cite *Cagnat* IV. 684¹⁴ (A.D. 88-9) ἐπιμελησαμένου Ἡρακλείτου with reference to the undertaking to set up a χαριστήριον, and *ib*. 685¹³ ἐπιμεληθέντος in the same sense.

ἐπιμελῶς.

P Fay 121⁷ (c. A.D. 100) ζυγόδεσμον καινὸν στερεόν, ὃ καὶ ἀλείψεις ἐπιμελῶς, "a new strong yoke-band, which you will carefully grease " (Edd.). P Oxy XII. 1581¹⁴ (ii/A.D.) διὰ π[αντ]ὸς ἔχε τ[ὸ]ν Σαραπίωνα ἐπι[μ]ελῶς. PSI IV. 405²⁷ (iii/B.C.) ἐπιμελέστερον σύνταξον Θεοπόμπωι διδόναι ταῦτα τῶι υἱῶι μου. P Hamb I. 35¹² (c. A.D. 160) ἵνα καὶ ἡ εἴσπραξις ἐπιμελέστερον γίν[η]ται. For the adj., which does not occur in the NT, see P Oxy XII. 1412¹¹ (c. A.D. 284) εἰς ἐπιμελῆ τόπον, "at a suitable place."

ἐπιμένω.

For ἐ. "remain" in a place, as in Ac 10⁴⁸, 1 Cor 16⁷ᶠ, cf. P Lond 897¹² (A.D. 84) (= III. p. 207) κέκρικα γὰρ νὴ τοὺς θεοὺς ἐν Ἀλεξανδρείᾳ ἐπιμένειν, P Fay 206 (A.D. 113) πρὸς τὸ δύνασθαί με ἐπιμένιν ἐν τῇ ἰδίᾳ διευθύνων τὰ δημόσια. The construction with the dative is found in P Ryl II. 153³ (A.D. 138-61) τῷ αὐτῷ ἀπελευθέ[ρω] . . . ᾧ ἐπιμ[έ]νοντι ὡς προγέγραπται τῇ πατρίδι μου : cf. *ib.* 239⁹ (mid. iii/A.D.) ἐπίμινον τοῖς ἐκεῖ, "stay on for the men there," PSI III. 158²⁴ (iii/A.D.?) a planetary configuration makes men ἐπιψόγους μὴ ἐπιμένοντας μιᾷ γυναικί (the opposite of "love one only and cleave to her). For the tropical use, as in Rom 6¹, cf. P Oxy II. 237ᵛⁱ·¹⁸ (A.D. 186) ἐπιμένει τῇ αὐτῇ ἀπονοίᾳ ἐνυβρίζων μοι, P Tebt II. 424⁴ (late iii/A.D.) εἰ μὲν ἐπιμένις σου τῇ ἀπονοίᾳ, συγχέρω σοι, "if you persist in your folly, I congratulate you " (Edd.), and with [ἐπ]ι 8⁷ ἐπέμενον ἐρωτῶντες cf. the late P Oxy I. 128⁷ (vi/vii A.D.) ἐπιμένει γὰρ λέγων μὴ δύνασθαι ἐπὶ τοσοῦτον κοπωθῆναι, "he insists that he is unable to bear such a strain " (Edd.). See also *Menandrea* p. 39 ἐπιμένει τὸ χρέος ἀπεργαζόμενος, "he stays on to work out the debt."

ἐπινεύω.

P Petr II. 32 (1)²⁸ κώιδια ἃ ἐπένευσεν ὁ Φίλιππος πᾶσιν ἡμῖν ἐργάζεσθαι, "hides which Philip permitted all of us to prepare," P Ryl II. 119²¹ (A.D. 54-67) οὐκ ἐπένευσεν, "he refused," P Giss I. 41ⁱⁱ·⁹ (Hadrian) ἐπινεύσαντος ο[ὖ]ν τῇ[ι] δεήσει μου, CP Herm I. 52ⁱ·¹⁹ (iii/A.D.) ἐπινεύσειν τῇ δεήσει τοῦ κοινοῦ ἡμῶν συνεδρίου, *Syll* 418¹³ (A.D. 238) εὐχόμενοι ἵλεως ἐπινεῦσαι ἡμεῖν δεομένοις τὸν τρόπον τοῦτον. In the Christian letter P Oxy VI. 939⁵ (iv/A.D.) (= *Selections*, p. 128) we have ταῖς εὐ]χαῖς ἡμῶν ἐπένευσεν, "He inclined His ear to our prayers."

ἐπίνοια.

For this NT ἅπ. εἰρ. (Ac 8²²), cf. P Oxy II. 237ᵛⁱ·³⁵ (A.D. 186) μὴ ἠκολουθηκέναι τῇ τοῦ νόμου ἀπανθρωπίᾳ ἀλλὰ τ[ῇ] ἐπι[νοί]ᾳ τῆς παιδός, *ib.* XII. 1468⁵ (c. A.D. 258) οὐ δικαίας ἐπινοίας, OGIS 580⁷ (A.D. 367-75) ἐξ οἰκ(ε)ίων ἐπινοιῶν. For the corresponding verb, see P Tebt II. 382³⁸ (B.C. 30—A.D. 1) τἄλλ᾽ ἐπινο[εῖ]ν [ὡς καθήκει, "to manage the other formalities, as is fitting " (Edd.), and from the inscrr the important *Priene* 105¹⁸ (B.C. 9) (= Rouffiac *Recherches*, p. 71) εἰ μὴ παρ᾽ ἕκ[ασ]τα [ἐ]πινοήσαιμεν τρόπον τινὰ τῆς ἀμείψ[εω]ς καινόν. See also P Lond V. 1674²² (c. A.D. 570) καθ᾽ ἑκάστην (*sc.* ὥραν) ἐπινοούμενοι, "being plotted against each hour " (Ed.).

ἐπ[ιϝ-]ιορκέω.

The aspirated form, banned by WH as "Western," and explained by Thumb (*Spiritus asper*, p. 72) as due to a "contamination " of ἐφορκέω and ἐπιορκέω, is common in papyri and inscrr. in the legal formula εὐορκοῦντι μέν μοι εὖ εἴη, ἐφιορκοῦντι δὲ τὰ ἐναντία, "if my oath is kept, may it be well with me, but if false, the reverse ": e.g. P Tebt I. 78¹⁷ (B.C. 110-8), P Oxy II. 253²³ (A.D. 19), *ib.* 255²⁴ (A.D. 48), OGIS 229⁶⁹ (iii/B.C.). See also Moulton *Gr.* ii. § 40.

ἐπιούσιος.

The papyri have as yet shed no clear light upon this difficult word (Mt 6¹¹, Lk 11³), which was in all probability a new coinage by the author of the Greek Q to render his Aramaic original. The unlikely derivation from ἐπί and οὐσία is not supported by the papyri where οὐσία generally means "property," "estate," the abstract sense being confined to certain magical documents (see *s.v.*) : and it is much more probable that ἐπιούσιος should be connected with ἡ ἐπιοῦσα [ἡμέρα], "the *immediately* following day," in accordance with the sense of ἐπιέναι "to come close after," *instare* (cf. Ac 16¹¹ and P Petr III. 56 (*b*)¹² αὐθήμερον ἢ τῆι ἐπι[οὐ]σηι, cited *s.v.* ἔπειμι. That ἡ ἐπιοῦσα is not always equivalent to ἡ αὔριον is clearly shown by the opening scene of Plato's *Crito* (44 A), where τῆς ἐπιούσης ἡμέρας refers to the same day as σήμερον (43 D). The desire to emphasize *immediacy* made the translator dissatisfied with τὸν τῆς αὔριον or the like as a rendering of the Aramaic before him : he followed a right instinct in coining a new adjective from the common term for "the coming day." Lightfoot supports this derivation in his well-known discussion (*On a Fresh Revision*³, p. 217 ff.), and it is adopted as certain by Schmiedel (Winer-Schmiedel *Gr.* i. p. 130 ff.), Deissmann

(*NT'liche Studien Heinrici dargebracht*, 1914, p. 115 ff.), and Robertson *Gr.* p. 159.

On the other hand Debrunner (*Glotta* iv. (1912) p. 249 ff.: cf. Blass-Debrunner p. 75) prefers to regard ἐπιούσιος as a substantivising of ἐπὶ τὴν οὖσαν [ἡμέραν], "for the current day," comparing ἐπιμήνιος (Polybius), "for the current month," ἐφημέριος, etc. ; and in spite of the valid objection that ἡ οὖσα, unlike ἡ ἐπιοῦσα, has not been found with ἡμέρα understood, he has obtained the weighty support of Thumb (Brugmann-Thumb, p. 675). Moulton, from whose Grammar (II. § 120 *b*) the above brief account has been epitomized, gives his vote for ἡ ἐπιοῦσα as being on the whole the most probable etymology. See also Klostermann *ad* Mt 6[11] (in *HZNT*), and cf. *ZNTW* i. p. 250 ff., vii. p. 206 ff.

ἐπιπίπτω.

The idea of "hostility" appears in P Petr II. 18(2*b*)[14] (B.C. 246) καὶ ἐπιπεσὼν ἔτυπτεν [αὐ]τ[ὸ]ν κατὰ τοῦ τραχ-ήλου : cf. P Flor II. 168[4] (iii/A.D.). In illustration of Mk 3[10] Field *Notes*, p. 25, aptly cites Thuc. vii. 84 ἄθροοι γὰρ ἀναγκαζόμενοι χωρεῖν ἐπέπιπτόν τε ἀλλήλοις καὶ κατεπά-τουν. The subst. ἐπίπτωμα is found in PSI III. 252[28] (iii/A.D. ?) as a medical term : cf. Hobart. p. 44, on the use of the verb in the TR of Ac 13[11].

ἐπιπλήσσω.

This NT ἅπ. εἰρ. = "rebuke," "reprove" (1 Tim 5[1]), may be illustrated by BGU IV. 1138[22] (B.C. 19) καὶ αὐτὸ(ν) ἐπιπλῆξαι καταξίως, and P Flor II. 241[2] (A.D. 254) . . . απιτ . . ν ἢ τοὺς σὺν αὐτῷ ἐπιπλήσσιν, where the editor translates "punish." The same strong sense appears in the use of the subst. (cf. 2 Macc 7[33]) in P Tebt I. 41[33] (*c.* B.C. 119) τύχηι τῆς ἁρμοζούσης ἐπιπλήξεως, "may receive suitable punishment" (Edd.), and so P Tor I. 1[iii. 14] (B.C. 117-0). A good parallel to the NT passage is afforded by Epict. *Ench.* xxxiii. 16 with reference to approaches to indecent speech—ἂν μὲν εὔκαιρον ᾖ, καὶ ἐπίπληξον τῷ προελθόντι, "rebuke him who makes the approach" (see Sharp *Epict.* p. 72 f.), and for the sense of *severity* in the word cf. Eustath. on Hom. *Il.* x. 500 τὸ ἐπιπλ. καὶ κόπτειν λέγεται —ἔτι δὲ καὶ μαστίζειν—ἀφ' οὗ καὶ τὸ λόγοις ἐπιπλήσ-σειν εἴρηται (cited by Wetstein *ad* 1 Tim 5[1]). See also Field *Notes*, p. 209.

ἐπιπορεύομαι.

In P Petr II. 10(1)[11] (*c.* B.C. 240) ἐ. is used of the "visit" of an administrator who makes extortionate demands on the hospitality of the natives—ἐπιπορεύεται ἡμῖν συντάσσων διδόναι εἰς τὰ ξένια χῆνας ιβ, ἡμῶν οὐ δυναμένων, "comes to see us, and orders us to give him for his entertainment twelve geese, this being out of our power" (Ed.). The verb is fairly common in legal documents = "proceed against," e.g. P Tebt II. 383[38] (A.D. 46) καὶ μὴ ἐπιπορεύεσθαι ἑκάτερον τῷ ἑτέρῳ [ἐ]φ' ἃ ὁ ἕτ[ερος αὐτῶν κεκλή]ρωται τρόπῳ μηθενί, "and neither shall proceed against the other on any account in respect of the shares which each of them has received" (Edd.) : see also Modica *Introduzione*, p. 120 f. For the simple meaning "journey to" cf. P Lille I. 3[78] (after B.C. 241) συντετάχαμεν Μιύσει τῶι τοπ[ογρ(αμματεῖ) ἐπὶ] τού-

τους ἐπιπορεύεσθαι τοὺς τόπο[υς, *Chrest.* I. 116[7] (ii/iii A.D.) θύε πᾶσι τοῖς θεοῖς. ἐφ' ἕκαστον ἱερὸν ἐπιπορεύου προσκυ-νῶν, and cf. such an expression as P Tor I. 1[viii. 13] (B.C. 117) καὶ μὴ ἐξεῖναι ἐπὶ τὰ τῶν τετελευτηκότων ἐπιπορεύεσθαι, where it is forbidden to "approach" the affairs of the dead, with the view of administering the inheritance, until certain conditions have been fulfilled : see the editor's note p. 166. We may add Heraclitus *Fragm.* 71 ψυχῆς πείρατα οὐκ ἂν ἐξεύροιο πᾶσαν ἐπιπορευόμενος ὁδόν· οὕτω βαθὺν λόγον ἔχει, "travelling over the whole road."

ἐπιρίπτω.

For this verb (for form see Moulton *Gr.* ii. § 41 (*b*)) "used apparently as a stronger form" of ἐπιβάλλω, see P Tebt I. 5[183] (B.C. 118) μηδὲ τοὺς στρα(τηγοὺς) . . . ἐπιρίπτειν μόσχους μηδὲ ἱερεῖα τρέφειν, "nor that the strategi force them (the inhabitants of the land) to feed calves and other animals for sacrifice" (Edd.), so [185] μηδὲ οἰνικὰ ἢ σιτικὰ γενή(ματα) ἐπιρίπτειν τιμῆς, and [249] μηδὲ . . . ἐπιρίπτειν τοῖς λινύφοις καὶ βυσσουργοῖς. Ἐκρίπτω occurs in P Lond 106[13] (iii/B.C.) (= I. p. 61) τά τε σκεύη μου ἐξέρριψεν εἰς τὴν ὁδόν.

ἐπίσημος.

In P Petr III. 73[8] we hear of a ship—οὗ [ἐ]πίσημον N̄, "on which is the number 50" (Edd.) : cf. BGU IV. 1132[10] (B.C. 16) γύου ς ἐπισήμου, "a district with the number 6," and *Syll.* 588[3] (*c.* B.C. 180) δακτύλιον . . ἔχοντα ἐπίσημον Ἀπόλλωνα. The adj. is common in connexion with money, e.g. P Ryl II. 160(*c*)[ii. 18] (A.D. 32) ἔχο (*l.* ἔχω) τὰς τοῦ ἀργυρίου ἐπισήμον καιφαλέον (*l.* — αίου) νομίσματος δρα-χμᾶς ἑκατόν, "I have received the capital sum of 100 drachmae of coined silver" (Edd.), *ib.* 154[2] (A.D. 66), P Hamb I. 2[14] (A.D. 59) ἀργύριον ἐπίσημον δόκιμον ἀρεστὸν ἀνυπόλογον παντὸς ὑπ[ο]λόγου, P Tebt II. 392[23] (A.D. 134-5). For the metaphorical use, which alone is found in the NT, cf. *Michel* 544[26] (B.C. 114) ἐπίσημον τὴν ἑαυτοῦ [ἀρετ]ὴν κατέστησεν, BGU IV. 1086[ii. 4] (A.D. 160 or 183 or 215) ταύτης μου [τῆς ἐπιστ]ολῆς τὸ ἀντίγραφον δημοσίᾳ ἔν τε [ταῖς μητροπόλεσι καὶ ἐν τοῖς] ἐπισήμοις τ[ῶν νο]μῶν τόποις προθεῖναι φροντίσατε, and P Ryl II. 153[5] (A.D. 138-61), a will in which the testator makes provision for a ceremony to be performed at his grave—ἐν ταῖς ἐπ[ισ]ήμοις τοῦ ὅρους ἡμέραις, "on the high days of the cemeteries" (Edd.) ; similarly the Will of Abraham, Bishop of Her-monthis, about the end of vi/A.D., P Lond 77[68] (= I. p. 234, *Chrest.* II. p. 372), where reference is made to τὰς τοῦ θανάτου ἐπισήμους ἡμέρας in connexion with the rites accompanying mummification and interment, see P Lips I. 30 Intr., and cf. LXX Esther 5[4], 8[13]. In MGr ἐπίσημος = "official."

ἐπισιτισμός.

OGIS 200[15] (iv/A.D.) θρέψαντες αὐτοὺς βόεσίν τε καὶ ἐπισιτ[ισ]μῷ ἀννών(ης).

ἐπισκέπτομαι

is common = "inspect," "examine." "inquire into," e.g. P Lond 887[8] (iii/B.C.) (= III. p. 1) καὶ ἀνακαλεσ[ά]-μενον αὐτὸ[ν] ἐπισκέψασθαι περὶ τούτων, P Hamb I. 25[2]

(B.C. 238) γράφ[ε]ις μοι ἐπισκεψάμενον περὶ ὧν ἐγκαλεῖ Διομέδων Κάλαι, P Petr II. 10(1)²³ (a complaint from the Royal Gooseherds) ἀποστεῖλαι ἡμῶν τὸ ὑπόμνημα εἰς τὸ λογιστήριον ἐπισκέψασθαι, "that you should send our minute to the Treasury Office to be examined" (Ed.), and P Tebt I. 58¹⁴ (B.C. 111) where a tax-farmer describes how by means of a bribe he had "obtained a view of" (ἐπεσκεψάμην) the document containing his rival's offer. For the passive see BGU I. 73¹⁵ (A.D. 135) (= Chrest. II. p. 228) ἐπιλαβοῦσι τὸν χρ[η]ματισμὸ]ν ἐπε[σ]κε[μ]μένον, and P Ryl II. 426 Fr. 4 (ii/iii A.D.) fragments of a report on land, where, at the end of each section, the result of the ἐπίσκεψις is noted, as ⁹ ἐπ(εσκέφθησαν) ἀβρ(όχου) (ἀρ.) εἴκοσι ὀ[κτώ (cf. Archiv i. p. 151). The meaning "visit," as in Ac 7²³, is found in P Lille I. 6⁵ (iii/B.C.) διαβάντος μου . . . ἐπεσκέψασθαι τὴν ἀδελφή[ν : cf. the Christian amulet P Oxy VIII. 1151²⁸ (v/A.D. ?) ἴασαι καὶ ἐπίσκεψαι καὶ τὴν δούλην σου Ἰωαννίαν. With the use of the verb in Ac 6³ we may compare P Petr II. 37 2b verso¹ (iii/B.C.) ἐπισκεψάμενος ἐν ἀρχῆι ἃ δεῖ γενέσθαι ἔργα, P Oxy III. 533²⁰ (ii/iii A.D.) ἐπισκέψασθε ἐκ τοῦ λογιστηρίου τοῦ στρα(τηγοῦ) ἐπιστολ(ὴν) τοῦ διοικητοῦ, "look out at the office of the strategus a letter of the dioecetes" (Edd.). The simplex is found P Cairo Preis 48⁵ (ii/A.D.) τὸ μὲν πλοῖόν σοι, ὡς ἠθέλησας, σκέψομαι, and for ἐνσκέπτομαι see P Lond 106²⁸ (iii/B.C.) (= I. p. 61). For the title ἐπισκέπτης see P Lond 1171⁵³ (B.C. 8) (= III. p. 179) τιμῆς οἴνου τοῖς ἐπισκέπτ[αι]ς (δραχμὰς) κ, P Oxy III. 589 (ii/A.D.) ἐπισκέπτηι τῶν παρὰ ποταμῶν ἐδαφῶν, P Flor I. 6¹⁴ (A.D. 210) ἐπισκέπτης γ[ὰ]ρ ἐχειροτονήθην, and the exx. in P Strass I. 78 Introd., and for ἐπίσκεψις, P Par 6²⁷ (B.C. 129) τὴν προσήκουσ[αν] ἐξ ἐπισκέψεως διάληψ[ιν] ποιήσασθαι, P Oxy XII. 1446³⁵, ⁸² (A.D. 161–210), al.

ἐπισκευάζω

is common = "repair," e.g. P Petr II. 13 (2)¹² (B.C. 258–3) of bridges—ἵνα ἐπισκευασθῶσι πρὸ τῆς τοῦ ὕδατος ἀφέσεως, ib. 20ⁱⁱ·⁷ (B.C. 252) πλοίων μὴ ἐπισ[κε]υαζομένων ὑπὸ χέρα, P Tor I. 1ⁱⁱ·¹ (B.C. 117) ἐπισκευάσαντες τὰ καθειρημένα μέρη, P Ryl II. 161¹⁷ (A.D. 71), P Oxy IX. 1220¹³ (iii/A.D.), ib. I. 53⁵ (A.D. 316), al. For a fut. ἐπισκευῶ see PSI IV. 382³ (B.C. 248–7) γινώσκεις ὅτι συνειπάμεθά σοι τὴν πρώιραν ἐπισκευᾶν τοῦ πλοίου : cf. Meisterhans Gr. p. 180. We have no parallel for the use of the mid. in Ac 21¹⁵, where the meaning seems to be "having furnished ourselves for the journey" (see Field Notes, p. 135) : Ramsay (Hastings' DB V. p. 398) prefers to think of the getting ready or saddling of horses, in view of such passages as Xen. Hell. v. 3. 1. etc. For the subst. ἐπισκευή = "repairs," see P Lond 1177¹⁷⁵ (A.D. 113) (= III. p. 186) τιμῆς ξύλων εἰς ἐπισκευὰς μηχ(ανῆς), P Oxy XII. 1450¹⁰ (A.D. 249–50) τοπικῶν εἰδῶν τῆς ἐπισκευῆς, al.

ἐπισκηνόω.

On the force of this rare verb in 2 Cor 12⁹ see an interesting note in ExpT xxii. p. 312 f.

ἐπισκιάζω

is found in the mid. in Vett. Val. p. 111¹ γίνονται δὲ ἑτερόχροες συγγενήματα ἔχοντες φαλακροὶ ἐπισκιαζόμενοι

ἢ ὀφθαλμοπόνοι κτλ., and for the subst. see ib. pp. 3⁹, 109³⁰, etc. The LXX usage is discussed by Anz Subsidia, p. 289, and Hatch Essays, p. 4.

ἐπισκοπέω.

The NT (Heb 12¹⁵) connotation of this word "exercise oversight or care" may be illustrated by its common use as an epistolary formula in the closing salutations of letters, e.g. P Revill Mel p. 295¹² (B.C. 131–0) (= Witkowski Epp.² p. 96) ἐπισκοποῦ - δ[ὲ] > καὶ τὰς ἀδελφὰς . . καὶ Πέλοπα κτλ., P Lips I. 104¹⁸ (c. B.C. 96–5) ἐπισκοπεῖτ[α]ι ὑμᾶς Ἀλμέντις, Ψενοσῖρις κτλ., P Oxy IV. 743¹³ (B.C. 2) ἐπισκοπ(οῦ) τοὺς σοὺς πάντε(ς), ib. II. 294³¹ (A.D. 22) ἐπισκωποῦ Δημητροῦ[ν] καὶ Δωρίωνα [τὸν πατ]έρα, P Giss I. 12⁷ ἐπισκοποῦμαι τὴν σὴν σύνβιον καὶ τοὺς φιλοῦντάς σε πάντας. For the verb = "inspect" see P Lille I. 1 verso²⁷ (B.C. 259–8) ὕστερον δὲ ἐπισκοπούμενος τὸ περίχωμα συνέκρινεν τὰ χώματα ποῆσαι, P Tebt I. 30²⁵ (B.C. 115) ἐπισκοποῦντες διὰ τοῦ ἀπολογισμοῦ τοῦ ἐδάφους, "on examining the land-register" (Edd.). From the inscrr. we may cite Syll 802³² (iii/B.C.) ἀνῶιξε τὸγ γυλιὸ[ν] κα[ὶ ἐ]πεσκόπει τὰ συντετριμμένα σ[κε]ύη.

ἐπισκοπή.

A iv/A.D. Lycaonian inscr. describes a bishop as—εἴκοσι πέντε ὅλοις ἔτεσιν τὴν ἐπισκοπὴν μετὰ πολ[λ]ῆς ἐπιτειμίας διοι[κ]ήσας (Exp VII. vi. p. 387 : C. and B. ii. p. 543).

The subst. ἐπισκοπεία is found in the Royal Ordinances P Tebt I. 5¹⁸⁹ (B.C. 118), where reference is made to penalties incurred for making false returns "in connexion with the government inspections"—πρὸς τὰς βα̣ σιλικὰς) ἐπισκοπείας.

ἐπίσκοπος.

The use of this word as an official title in pre-Christian times has been fully illustrated by Deissmann (BS, p. 230 f.) from the inscrr. From his exx. it is enough to recall the application of the word to communal officials in Rhodes, as IMAe 49⁴³ᶠᶠ (ii/i B.C.) where we hear of a council of five ἐπίσκοποι, and, more significant still in view of its later usage, the mention of an ἐπίσκοπος amongst the officials of the temple of Apollo at Rhodes in ib. 731⁸. To these instances we may add P Petr III. 36(a) verso¹⁷ where in a petition to the epimeletes the words occur—ἐπ[ὶ] τῶν ἀποδεδειγμένων ἐπισκόπων, "in the presence of the appointed supervisors" (Edd.), and the curious religious letter, P Par 63ⁱˣ·⁴⁷ᶠᶠ. (B.C. 165) ἀπόκειται γὰρ παρὰ θ[εοῦ] μῆνις τοῖς μὴ κατὰ τὸ βέλτιστον [προαι]ρουμένοις ζῆν, καὶ τῶν ἀνθρόπων . . . ἐπίσκοπός ἐστιν τὸ δαιμ[όν]ιον καὶ νέμε[σις] ἀπὸ Δι[ὸς] τοῖς ὑπερηφάνοις (cf. Jas 4⁶, 1 Pet 5⁵ from Prov 3³⁴). With this last may be compared the curse against any one who injures a sepulchral monument, Syll 891 (ii/A.D.), which concludes with the words ἐπισκόπους δὲ ἔχοι Ἐρεινύας, "let him have the Erinyes as his guardians," while the prayer for the man who respects it is—ἐπισκοποίη δὲ Χάρις καὶ Ὑγεία, "may Grace and Health attend him." See also Boll Offenbarung, p. 143 where, with reference to the "eyes" of the four living creatures, the description of heaven with its thousands of star-eyes as ἐπίσκοπος is cited from Sextus Emp. ix. 54. In P Oxy VI. 903¹⁵ (iv/A.D.), an accusation against a husband, the accused is said to have made a certain statement on oath ἐπὶ παρουσίᾳ τῶν ἐπισκόπων καὶ τῶν ἀδελφῶν, "in the presence of the bishops and of his own brothers," with which the editors compare P Lips I. 43 (iv/A.D.) where a bishop acts as judge. See also P Lond 981⁷ (iv/A.D.) (= III. p. 242), as restored by Wilcken *Chrest.* I. p. 157, where a deacon writes "to his beloved and most reverend father"—καθὼς γέγραπται ἐν τῇ γραφῇ ὅτι Μακάριοί εἰσιν οἱ ἔχοντες σπέρμα ἐν Σιών, τὰ νῦν ἡμεῖς ἔσμεν, ὅτι ἔχομέν σε <ἐπί>σκοπον καὶ ἀγαθότατον πατέρ<α ..

For the distinctive NT use of ἐπίσκοπος it must be sufficient to refer to Hort's *Christian Ecclesia*, where it is shown that the word is descriptive of function, not of office, thus Phil 1¹ σὺν ἐπισκόποις καὶ διακόνοις, "with them that have oversight, and them that do service [minister]" (p. 212).

ἐπισπάω.

For this strong verb cf. P Magd 24⁶ (B.C. 218) (as completed *Archiv* vi. p. 274) of an assault—ψενοβάστις τῆι αὐτῆι δεξιᾶι χειρὶ ἐπισπασαμένη τῆς ἀ[ναβολῆς τοῦ ἱματίου. Cf. P Tebt I. 27⁴ (B.C. 113) περὶ τῶν ἐπισπασθησομ[ένων] εἰς τὰς γενημ[α]τοφυλακίας, "concerning the persons to be made to undertake the custody of the crops" (Edd.), so ¹³, and *Syll* 929⁴⁰ (ii/B.C.) where the mid. ἐπεσπάσαντο = "brought in to help." In P Par 46¹⁰ (B.C. 153) (= Witkowski², p. 86) ἀλλὰ σὲ αὐτὸν μάρτυρα ἐπισπάσω, the verb = "to subpoena": cf. P Lond 1164 (*f*)⁶ (A.D. 212) (= III. p. 161) μετὰ κυρίου οὗ ἑκοῦσα ἐπεσπάσατο πρὸς μόνην ταύτην τὴν οἰκονομίαν κτλ. For the meaning "persuade" cf. *OGIS* 225¹⁸ (iii/B.C.) καὶ νῦν πολύ τι μᾶλλον ἐπεσπάσμεθα, κατανοοῦντες τὸ εὐγενὲς ὑμῶν. The compound προσεπισπάω occurs in P Tor I. 1ᵛⁱⁱⁱ·³⁹ (B.C. 117) πολυπραγμόνως δὲ προσεπισπώμενον τὴν τῶι στρατηγῶι καθήκουσαν ἐξουσίαν, "tum totis viribus distendens auctoritatem, quae Stratego competit" (Ed.).

ἐπισπείρω.

With the usage in Mt 13²⁵ cf. the subst. in P Tebt II. 375¹⁴ (A.D. 140) ε[ἰς σπορὰν κ[αὶ] ἐπισποράν, "to be sown and resown" (Edd.), and the adj. in *ib.* I. 27³⁷ (B.C. 113) τῶν χλωρῶν καὶ τ[ῶ]ν ἄλλων ἐπισπόρων, "the green stuffs and the other second crops" (Edd.).

ἐπίσταμαι.

For this verb, which is common in Ac. it is sufficient to cite P Hib I. 40⁶ (B.C. 261) ἐπίστασο μέντον (*l.* -οι) ἀκριβῶς, "you must clearly understand," P Tebt II. 408³ (A.D. 3) ἐπιστάμενος πῶς σε τίθεμαι κὲ φιλῶ, "since you know how I esteem and love you" (Edd.), P Ryl II. 243⁶ (ii/A.D.) καὶ νῦν ἐπιστάμεθά σου τὸ σπουδαῖον. P Leid Wˣⁱˣ·⁹ (ii/iii A.D.) ἐπικαλοῦμαί σε (a god), ὃν οἱ (θεοί or ἄγγελοι) προσκυνοῦσιν, P Oxy VIII. 1121² (A.D. 295) τίνι ἐπαγόμενοι οὐκ ἐπίσταμαι, "on what inducement I cannot tell" (Ed.), and the common phrase regarding an illiterate person διὰ τὸ μὴ ἐπίστασθαι γράμματα, as in P Ryl II. 73¹⁹ (B.C. 33–30): cf. P Tebt II. 291⁴¹ (A.D. 162) ἀπ[ό]δειξιν δοὺς τοῦ ἐπίστασθαι [ἱε]ρατικὰ [καὶ] Αἰγύπτια γράμ[ματ]α. See also *Syll* 726⁵⁴ (B.C. 301–0) εἰδότες ὅτι ἐπίστανται χάριτας ἀποδιδόναι οἱ θιασῶται. The acc. of the person (as in Ac 19¹⁵), which LS (*s.v.* II. 3) describe

as rare, is used by Musonius p. 12⁵, where he characterizes τὴν φιλοσοφοῦσαν as παράδειγμα .. χρηστὸν ταῖς ἐπισταμέναις αὐτήν: see also P Leid cited *supra*.

ἐπίστασις.

P Amh II. 134⁹ (early ii/A.D.) ἐρῶ (*l.* ἐρωτῶ) οὖν σὲ πρὸς ἐπίστασιν τῶν ἄλλων ἐκδικῆσαι αὐτόν, "I ask you therefore, in order to check the other elders (?), to vindicate him" (Edd.), similarly P Oxy XII. 1465¹⁵ (i/B.C.). For the meaning "attention," which some commentators find in 2 Cor 11²⁸, we may add to the Polybian passages referred to by Grimm-Thayer, Aristeas 256 ἵνα δ' ἐπίστασιν τούτων λαμβάνωμεν, θεραπεύειν δεῖ τὸν θεόν, "but we must pray to God for the gift of a regard for these things" (Thackeray) But both in 2 Cor *l.c.* and Ac 24¹² (cf. 2 Macc 6²) the word is best understood = "onset," or "caballing (conspiring) against" (Souter). For the obscure phrase ἐν ἐπιστάσει καὶ ἐν ἀπολογισμῷ applied to land, see P Tebt I. p. 576 ff.

ἐπιστάτης.

in its original sense of "superintendent," "overseer," found in a number of different connexions, e.g. ἐ. εἰρήνης κώμης (P Oxy I. 64²—iii/iv A.D.), ἐ. τοῦ ἱεροῦ (P Par 26²²—B.C. 163) and τῶν ἱερῶν (P Leid G⁴—end of ii/B.C.), ἐ. τῆς πόλεως (BGU III. 1006⁸—iii B.C.), ἐ. τῶν φυλακιτῶν (P Tebt I. 5¹⁸⁹—B.C. 118). For further particulars regarding ἐ. τῆς κώμης, a local justice, see *Archiv* iv. p. 35 ff., and for ἐ. τοῦ ἱεροῦ Preisigke *Prinz-Joachim-Ostr* p. 60 ff., and for the word generally Preisigke *Fachwörter*, p. 89 f. The verb ἐπιστατέω is found in P Oxy XII. 1413²⁰ (A.D. 270–5). In connexion with the Lukan use of the subst. applied to Jesus instead of the Hebrew Ῥαββί in the sense of "Master," Rouffiac (*Recherches*, p. 56f.) refers to an ἐπιστάταν τῶν παίδων (*IG* XII. 1, 43), apparently a sort of headmaster, and to τὸν ἐπιστά[την τὸ]ν τῶν ἐφήβων, whose duty it was τ[ὰς ψυχ]ὰς πρὸς ἀρετὴν καὶ πάθος ἀνθρώπινον προάγεσθαι (*Priene* 112⁷⁸ᶠᶠ·—after B.C. 84). He adds that the vocative was often used in the Greek gymnasia when the ephebi addressed their masters. See also Dalman *Words of Jesus*, p. 336.

ἐπιστέλλω.

For the meaning "send," "send to," cf. P Amh II. 33³⁵ (*c.* B.C. 157) αὐτόν τε πρὸς ἡμᾶς μετὰ φυλακῆς ἐπιστείλατε, P Oxy II. 276¹³ (A.D. 77) παρειληφέναι πα[ρ]' αὐτῶν τὰς ἐπισ[τ]αλείσας (*sc.* ἀρτάβας) α[ὐτ]οῖς. The general use of the verb, however, is in connexion with sending a letter or other written communication, as in P Par 61² (B.C. 156) τῆς πρὸς Δωρίωνα ἐπιστολῆς τὸ ἀντίγραφον ὑπόκειται· νομίσαντες οὖν καὶ πρὸς ὑμᾶς τὰ αὐτὰ ἐπεστάλθαι, σκοπεῖτε ἵνα μηδὲν παρὰ ταῦτα γίνηται, *ib.* 63¹⁵⁵ (B.C. 164) (= P Petr III. p. 34) ἐν τοῖς περὶ τούτων [ἐπ]εσταλμένοις χρηματισμοῖς, "in the communications we have sent to you dealing with these matters" (Mahaffy), P Fay 20⁴ (A.D. 150) πρὸς [τὸ] ἐπισταλὲν ἡμεῖν ὑπὸ σοῦ ἐπίσταλμα, BGU IV. 1081⁶ (ii/iii A.D.) εὖ ποιήσ[ει]ς ἐπιστείλας ἡμεῖν περὶ τῆς σῆς ὑγίας, P Fay 133¹³ (a letter—iv/A.D.) μοι ἐπίστειλον, "send me word." From the usage of the word in official documents the meaning readily passed over into "instruct," "enjoin," as in Ac 15²⁰ (RV marg.), Heb 13²² : cf. e.g. P Ryl II. 121¹³ (ii/A.D.) ἀξιῶ [ἐ]πισταλῆ[ν]αι τοῖς τῆς [π]όλεως γραμματεῦσι [ἐ]πίτροπον αὐτῷ καταστα[θῆ]ναι, " I request that an order be sent to the scribes of the city for the appointment of a guardian for him " (Edd.), P Fay 31²⁰ (c. A.D. 129) διὸ προσαγγέλλωι ὅπως ἐπισταλῆι τῷ τὸ γραφεῖον Θεαδελφείας συνχρημα[τίζ]ειν μοι ὡς καθήκει, " I therefore give notice, in order that instructions may be sent to the director of the record office of Theadelphia, duly to join me in the transaction of the business " (Edd.), P Strass I. 5¹⁸ (a decision of the prefect—A.D. 262) ἐπ]ισ[τ]ελῶ τῷ στρατηγ[ῷ. P Oxy IX. 1194³ (c. A.D. 265) δύναται ἐπισταλῆναι τῷ στρατηγῷ τ]ὰ δέοντα, " the proper measures can be communicated to the strategus," and hence in BGU I. 144ⁱⁱ·³ (iii/A.D.) ἐπεστάλ(η) ὑπὸ ἐμοῦ, virtually = " he was confirmed by me " in a certain office. See further Laqueur Quaestiones, p. 16 f. where it is shown that in letters written by Roman Emperors or Magistrates ἐπιστέλλω is always = " write " rather than " send," e.g. CIG III. 3835⁴ ἐπέστειλα αὐτῷ δηλῶν τὸ πρᾶγμα ὅλον. ἐπέστειλα δὲ Ἑσπέρῳ τῷ ἐπιτρόπῳ, and cf. P Hamb I. p. 77 for the ending of ἐπιστάλματα, official acts or decisions in letter form, with ἐπιστέλλω, or ἐπέστειλα, or ἐπιστέλλεταί σοι. With this the NT usage cited supra corresponds : cf. also Ac 21²⁵ ℵ.

ἐπιστήμων.

For this adj. (Jas 3¹³, cf. Deut 1¹³, 4⁶), which carries with it a certain idea of " expert " knowledge, see P Oxy XII. 1469¹² (A.D. 298) ἀεὶ γὰρ ὁ δημόσιος γ[εω]μέτρης ἐπιστήμων ὢν τῶν τόπω[ν] αὐτῶν κτλ., and cf. the use of the subst. in P Fay 106²² (c. A.D. 140) οἱ τὴν ἰατρικὴν ἐπιστή[μην] μεταχειριζόμενοι, " those practising the profession of physician," P Oxy VI. 896⁶ (A.D. 316) ζωγράφου τὴν ἐπιστήμην, " a painter by profession." In Vett. Val. p. 211¹⁸ τὸ γὰρ θεῖον βουληθὲν προγινώσκειν ἀνθρώπους τὰ μέλλοντα εἰς φῶς προήγαγε τὴν ἐπιστήμην, δι᾽ ἧς τὸ καθ᾽ αὑτὸν ἕκαστος προγινώσκων εὐθυμότερος μὲν πρὸς τὸ ἀγαθόν, the editor defines ἐπιστήμη as "mathesis." The noun survives in MGr = " knowledge," " science."

ἐπιστολή.

Preisigke in his Fachwörter, p. 90, has classified various more or less technical usages of this common word. Thus in P Amh II. 64¹⁰ (A.D. 107) the copy of an official letter addressed to the strategus with reference to the public baths of Hermopolis is headed—ἀντίγραφον ἐπιστολῆς, and in P Hamb I. 18ⁱⁱ·⁶ (A.D. 222) a συνκολ(λήσιμον) is mentioned αὐθ(εντικῶν) ἐπιστολ(ῶν) καὶ βιβλ(ιδίων) ὑποκεκολ(λημένων). In BGU IV. 1046ⁱⁱ·⁵ (not before A.D. 166) (= Chrest. I. p. 315) we learn that the persons selected for certain public duties were appointed by the epistrategus—δι᾽ ἐπιστολῆς) κομισθ(είσης) καὶ προγρα(φείσης) (" openly placarded up ") ; while in Chrest. I. 26¹⁶ (A.D. 135) a petition, instead of being lodged in the usual way as a ὑπόμνημα, takes the form of an ἐπιστολή : see Wilcken's note ad l. In BGU IV. 1135⁷ (prob. B.C. 10) κατὰ] νομογραφικὴν ἐπιστ[ολήν, the word is = " despatch," and in the business letter P Giss I. 105·⁹ (v/A.D.) λήμψῃς ἐπιστολάς it is = " receipt." The range of the word was thus wide, and its official usage in the above-noted instances may serve as a needed corrective to the over-emphasis which Deissmann (BS, p. 3 ff., LAE,

p. 217 ff.) is inclined to lay upon the " popular " character of the Pauline ἐπιστολαί : see Milligan Documents, p. 94 f.

We may further cite BGU III. 827²⁰ (undated) ἰδοὺ δ[ὴ] τρίτην ἐπιστολήν σοι γράφω, which recalls 2 Pet 3¹ with an opening like 2 Cor 12¹⁴, and P Oxy XII. 1409² (A.D. 278) τῆς γραφείσης ἐπιστολῆς εἰς κοινὸν ἡμῖν στρατη[γοῖς καὶ δε]καπρώτοις, with reference to a " circular letter " addressed to the strategi and δεκάπρωτοι of the Heptanomia and Arsinoite nome by the dioecetes. For the diminutive it is enough to refer to the soldier's letter to his mother, ib. 1481³ (early ii/A.D.), in which he explains the reason why he has been so long in sending her an ἐπιστόλιον—διότι ἐν παρεμβολῇ ἤμι καὶ οὐ δι᾽ ἀσθένε[ι]αν, ὥστε μὴ λοιποῦ, " that I am in camp, and not that I am ill ; so do not grieve about me " (Edd.), and P Par 45⁴ (B.C. 153) ἀπόντος μου πεφρόντικα ὑπέρ σου χρήσιμα τῶν σῶν πραγμάτων ἃ σ[οι] δεδύνημαι διασαφῆσαι διὰ τοῦ ἐπιστολίου, cf. 2 Cor 10¹¹.

ἐπιστομίζω.

To the exx. of this rare verb (Tit 1¹¹), we may add Philostr. Opera ii. p. 122⁵ (ed. Kayser) ἐπεστόμιζεν αὐτόν, and ib. p. 376²⁴. Cf. also the use of ἐνστομίζω in the magical papyrus P Par 574²·¹⁷⁴.

ἐπιστρέφω

is used literally = " turn " or " turn back " in P Tebt I. 138 (late ii/B.C.) ἐπιστρέψας καὶ σπασάμενος ταύτην (sc. τὴν μάχαιραν). The word has a certain ethical significance in P Oxy III. 486³⁰ (A.D. 131) τ[οῦ Σ]αραπίωνος μὴ ἐπιστραφέντος ὥστε κ[ατα]πλεῦσαι, " but S. has paid no attention to the instruction to sail down " (Edd.), BGU I. 36⁷ (ii/A.D.) οἱ ἀδελφοὶ Ἀ. καὶ Ὦ. ὀφείλοντές μοι κατ᾽ οὐδὲν ἐπιστρέφονται ἀποδῶναί μοι, " the brothers H. and II., although they owe me (money), do not show the smallest inclination to repay me," P Fay 128³ (iii/A.D.) οὐκ ἐπέστρεπται ὁ Ποντικὸς λαβεῖν τὴν οἰκίαν παρ᾽ ἡμῶν, " Ponticus has not shown any inclination to take the house from us " (Edd.). On the misleading translation of the verb by " am converted " in the AV see Field Notes, p. 8 f., and especially p. 246 ff. The absolute use of the verb in certain portions of the LXX is discussed in Thackeray Gr. I. p. 53 : see also Anz Subsidia, p. 289 f. For the moral sense of " conversion," as in Ac 3¹⁹, Sharp (Epict. p. 73) cites Epict. ii. 20. 22 ἵν᾽ οἱ πολῖται ἡμῶν ἐπιστραφέντες τιμῶσι τὸ θεῖον.

ἐπιστροφή

occurs = " attention," " regard " in a prisoner's petition P Petr II. 19 (2)² (iii B.C.) καλῶς οὖν ποιήσεις ἐ[πι]στροφήν [μου π]οιησάμενος, ἔρρειμαι γὰρ κακῶς διακείμενος ἀπ᾽ ἐκείνου : cf. PSI IV. 380⁸ (B.C. 249-8), and Michel 543³ (c. B.C. 200) ὁ δῆμος ἐπι[στροφ]ῆς ἀξίαν πρόσευξιν . . ποιούμενος. In Chrest. I. 176¹² (probably time of Nero) the lessee of an olive-yard complains of certain outlays that he had been obliged to make—μηδεμίαν μου ἐπιστρ[ο]φὴν ποιησαμένων αὐτῶν (sc. τῶν προεστώτων) : cf. Syll 790⁷⁶ (i/B.C.) ὑπολαμβάνομεν δὲ ἀναγκαῖ[ον] εἶναι καὶ συμφέρον γενέσθαι τινὰ περὶ τούτων ἐπιστροφήν with reference to the renewal of trees that had been destroyed. On the deepened meaning which this and similar words assumed in the language of Christianity, see Milligan Documents, p. 58 f., and cf. Hobart, p. 172 f.

ἐπισυνάγω.

For this verb cf. *OGIS* 90²³ (Rosetta stone—B.C. 196) ὡς ἂν ἐκ πολλοῦ χρόνου συνεστηκυίας τῆς ἀλλοτριότητος τοῖς ἐπισυναχθεῖσιν εἰς αὐτήν *sc.* Λύκων πόλιν ἀσεβέσιν, *Syll* 318²³ (B.C. 118) ἐπισυναχθέντων τῶν Γαλατῶν ἱππέων ἔτι πλειόνων. It is used of "accumulated" interest in P Grenf II. 72³ (A.D. 290–304) with reference to a loan of 2 talents—ἅπερ σοι ἀποδώσω σὺν τοῖς ἐπισυναχθεῖσι τόκοις ἄχρι ἀποδόσεως, and so P Flor I. 46¹⁴ (iii/A.D. *al init.* . See also Milligan *Thess.* p. 96.

ἐπισυναγωγή,

which in Bibl. Greek is confined to 2 Macc 2⁷, 2 Thess 2¹, Heb 10²⁵, has been pronounced by Cremer "unknown in profane Greek," but Deissmann (*LAE*, p. 101 ff.) cites it from an inscr. from the island of Syme not later than B.C. 100, *IG* XII. 3 Suppl. No. 1270¹¹ τὰς δὲ ἐπισυναγωγὰς τοῦ διαφόρου γινομένας πολυχρονίου, "the collection, however, of the sum (to defray expenses) taking a long time."

ἐπισυντρέχω.

We have no citation for this NT ἅπ. εἰρ. (Mk 9²⁵), but ἐπιτρέχω is used in the curious title of a minor village official in P Fay 107⁷ (A.D. 133) ὧν χάριν ἀξιῶ συντάξαι τῶι τῆς κώμης ἐπιτρέχοντι ποιήσασθαι τὴν καθήκουσαν ἀναζήτησιν, "wherefore I entreat you to give instructions to the village inspector to hold the due enquiry" (Edd.): cf. *ib.* 23² (ii/A.D.) Σαραπίων . . . δοθεὶς εἰς ἐπιδρομ(ὴν) τῆς μητροπ(όλεως) and see Jouguet *La Vie Municipale*, p. 207.

ἐπισύστασις.

This word which is found in the LXX Numb 16⁴⁰, 20⁹, and 1 Esdr 5¹³ A) and in the received text of Ac 24¹², 2 Cor 11²⁸, may be illustrated from *Syll* 325²⁷ (i/B.C. διὰ τὰς τῶν κρατούντων τῆς χώρας βαρβάρων ἐπισυνστάσεις, where the thought of "hostile" combination is prominent: see further Field *Notes*, p. 185 f. On the other hand the verb is sometimes used practically = "appoint," as when certain πρεσβύτεροι of the village of Karanis grant one of their number a certificate stating that they had appointed him their deputy in the collection of the beer-tax—P Lond 255¹⁰ (A.D. 139) (= II. p. 117) ἐπισυνεστάκαμέν σοι ἀνθ' ὑμῶν *l.* ἡμῶν πρακτορεύιν (*l.* -ειν κ αὶ χιρίζιν (*l.* χειρίζειν) τὴν δὲ ζυτηρὰν κτλ.: cf. *ib.* 309⁸ (A.D. 145) (= II. p. 118) τὸν [ὁ]μολογοῦντα συνεστακέναι τὸν Σα[το]ρνῖλον πρακτορεύοντα.

ἐπισφαλής.

This adj., which is peculiar to Lk in the NT (Ac 27⁹: cf. Hobart, p. 201) appears *ter* in *Alexandrea*, e.g. p. 14¹²⁶ ὄντ' ἐπισφαλῆ φύσει ‖ τὸν βίον ἁπάντων τῆι προνοίαι δεῖ, πάτερ, τηρεῖν. For the adv., as in Sap 4⁴, cf. P Oxy I. 76²⁰ (A.D. 179) νοσήσας ἐπισφαλῶς ἔχει, "has fallen ill and is in a precarious condition" (Edd.).

ἐπισχύω.

An interesting parallel to Lk 23⁵ is afforded by Vett. Val. p. 48⁶ τῶν δὲ τοιούτων καὶ ὁ λόγος ἐπισχύσει πρὸς συμβουλίαν ἢ διδαχήν. For the compound συνεπισχύω see BGU IV. 1189¹⁴ (B.C. 1) ἀξιῶ ἐὰν φαίνηται ἐπιτάξαι τῷ α(ὐτῷ) τοπάρχηι συνεπισχύε[ι]ν μοι κτλ.

ἐπισωρεύω.

Vett. Val. p. 332²⁴ ἐκ τούτων γὰρ συνορᾶται καὶ εὐκατάληπτα γίνεται τὰ πολλῷ χρόνῳ καὶ καμάτῳ ἐπισωρεύοντα τοῖς ἀνθρώποις τὴν παρὰ τούτων ἐνέργειαν: cf. p. 344²⁹. Epict. i. 10. 5 λοιπὸν ἐν ἐξ ἑνὸς ἐπισεσώρευκεν, "has gone on adding to his heap ever since" (Matheson).

ἐπιταγή.

The ordinary meaning appears in a fragmentary letter P Flor II. 119⁵ (A.D. 254) ὅπως . . ἐπιταγὴν λάβωσιν, with reference to an "order" or "instruction" given to certain fishermen. The use of the word in Paul to denote a *divine* command (Rom 10²⁶, 1 Tim 1¹, Tit 1³) is in accord with its technical use in dedicatory inscriptions. Thus in *Syll* 786⁴ Isias dedicates an altar to the Mother of the gods κατ' ἐπιταγήν. "by command" of Cybele herself conveyed in dream or oracle, as Dittenberger remarks. He compares other formulae like κατὰ μαντείαν, κατ' ὄναρ, καθ' ὅραμα. See also *Syll* 805³ (Rom.), *IG* XII. 1. 785. It is at least possible that this connotation may be present in 1 Cor 7⁶, 2 Cor 8⁸. Add the Phrygian inscr. Ἀγαθῇ τύχῃ Σόλων ἱερὸς κατὰ ἐπιταγὴν Δ[ι]ὶ Δίῳ εὐχὴν καὶ ἑαυτῷ ζῶν, which Sir William Ramsay (*Stud. in the East. Rom. Prov.* p. 275) cites in illustration of the old Phrygian custom of consecrating any sacred place by a grave. "Here Solon, in service at an Anatolian hieron, was ordered by the god to fulfil a vow, and in the same act of dedication he made the grave for himself." Cf. also the stele inscr. in *JHS* xxvi. (1906), p. 28 Οὐάρι(ο)s . . . Πωλλίων κατ' ἐπιταγὴν τοῦ θεοῦ ἀνέθηκα εἰκετεύων.

For ἐπίταγμα, see P Oxy XII. 1469³ (A.D. 298) ἐν τοῖ[ς] καθ' ἡμᾶς ἐπιτάγμασιν, "in commands concerning us." According to the editor's note ἐπίταγμα is used in P Grenf I. 18⁶ (B.C. 132) τοῦ ἐπιτάγματος ἱππάρχου of a "reserve" of cavalry, but see *contra* Schubart in *Archiv* ii. p. 149.

ἐπιτάσσω.

P Eleph 13¹ (B.C. 223) ὁ δὲ ἐπῄνει μόνον, ἐπέταξεν δ' οὐθέν, P Tebt I. 59⁶ (B.C. 99) ἐπιτάσσοντές μοι προθυμότερον διὰ τὸ ἄνωθεν φοβεῖσθαι καὶ σέβεσθαι τὸ ἱερόν, P Oxy II. 294²¹ (A.D. 22) (= *Selections*, p. 35) ὡς ἐπέταξεν ὁ ἡγεμών, *ib.* 275¹¹ (A.D. 66) (= *Selections*, p. 55) ποιο[ῦ]ντα πάντα τὰ ἐπιτασσόμενα αὐτῷ—of an apprentice, *ib.* XII. 1486⁶ (A.D. 32) οὐκ ἠμέλησα περὶ οὗ μοι ἐπιτέταχας, "I did not neglect your instructions" (Edd.).

ἐπιτελέω.

For this verb in connexion with the performance of religious duties cf. P Leid G²¹ (B.C. 181–145) ἵνα τυχὼν τῆς παρ' ὑ[μ]ῶν φιλαν[θρ]ωπίας. [ἐ]πιτελῶ τὰς τῶν θεῶν λε[ι]τουργίας, P Tebt I. 6⁸ (B.C. 140–30) ἐπιτ]ελεῖν τὰ νομιζόμενα τοῖς θεοῖς ὑπὲρ ἡμῶν καὶ τῶν τ[έκ]νων, *ib.* II. 294⁷ (A.D. 146) τὰ τῇ προφητείᾳ προ[σ]ήκοντα ἐ[πιτ]ε[λε]ῖ]ν, *ib.* 292¹ (A.D. 189–90) τὰς ἐπιβαλλ[ούσας ἱερουρ]γίας ἐπιτελεῖν, and from the inscrr. *Priene* 108²⁷ (after B.C. 129) τάς τε θυσίας ἐπετέλεσεν, *al.* (cf. Rouffiac *Recherches*, p. 66). The word is very common = "accomplish," "complete" any work or duty. Thus P Tor I. 1ᵛⁱⁱⁱ·¹⁵ (B.C. 117) μηδὲ τὴν αὐτὴν ἐργασίαν ἐπιτελεῖν, P Par 63¹⁶ (B.C. 164) (= P Petr III p. 18) ἕκαστα δ' ἐπιτελεσθῆι κατὰ τὸν ὑποδεδειγμένον ἐν τῶι πεμφθέντι σοι παρ' ἡμῶν ὑπομνήματι τρόπον, "that everything be performed in the manner laid down in the minute sent to you by us" (Mahaffy), *ib.* 26²⁸ (B.C. 163–2) ἡμῖν μὲν ὑπέσχετο τὸ προκείμενον ἐπιτελέσειν (for form see Mayser *Gr.* p. 357), "promised us that he would perform what he had been directed to do." So in connexion with building P Grenf I. 21¹⁷ (B.C. 126) ἕως ἂν ἐπιτελέσωσι—of a dove-cote, P Ryl II. 161¹⁶ (A.D. 71) ἀν[ο]ικοδομοῦντος καὶ ἐπιτελοῦντος [καὶ ἐπισκ]ενάζοντος— of a priest's chamber, or with agricultural operations *ib.* 166⁹ (A.D. 26) τὰ δὲ γεωργι[κ]ὰ ἔργα πάντα ἄ[ξ]ω καὶ ἐπι-τελέσω καθ᾽ ἔτ[ος], PSI I. 57²³ (A.D. 52) προήγμ[ε]θα ἐγβῆναι τῆς τοῦ κλή(ρου) γεωργ(ίας) τὸ καθῆκον ἐπιτελέσας, and with the execution of a deed in P Oxy III. 483³¹ (A.D. 108) διὸ ἐπιτελεῖτε ὡς καθήκ(ει). In BGU IV. 1062¹⁹ (A.D. 236–7) the verb is used of a payment—πάντα ἐπιτελέσαι ὅσα τῇ αὐτῇ ὠνῇ ἀνήκει, and in P Giss I. 39¹¹ (B.C. 204–181) ὃ γέγ[ραφά σοι διὰ? τῆς συγγραφῆς], ὥστε ἐμὲ ἐπιτε-λέσαι, ἐγὼ ἐπ[ιτελέσω ἄνευ λόγου παντὸς ὁτ]ινοσοῦν τοῦ πρός σε, the editor notes that ὥστε ἐμὲ ἐπιτελέσαι is dependent on the foregoing ὃ γέγραφά σοι. For a weakened sense corresponding to our "do," cf. P Oxy VIII. 1118¹⁰ (i–ii A.D.) ἐξαλλοτριώσοντα καὶ ἐπιτελέσοντα ὃ ἐὰν αἱρῶμαι, "alienate it (mortgaged property) and do with it whatever I choose" (Ed.), P Ryl II. 105²⁷ (A.D. 136) ἐπιτελ(έσον) ὡς καθ(ήκει) "do what is proper" (Edd.). For the adj. see *Michel* 1001⁴·¹⁸ (c. B.C. 200) ἐντειλαμένου ἐπιτελῆ με ποιῆσαι τὰν τοῦ πατρὸς αὐτοῦ Φοίνικος ἐντολάν. In the same inscr. the daughter's name is seen to be Ἐπιτέλεια.

ἐπιτήδειος.

For τὰ ἐπιτήδεια, "the necessaries of life," as in Jas 2¹⁶, cf. P Hib I. 110¹⁰ (c. B.C. 270) where payments are made εἰς τὰ ἐπιτήδ[ε]ια, and P Lond 1159³ (A.D. 145–7) (= III. p. 112) ἐπὶ παροχῆς τῶν ἑτοιμαζομένων ἐπιτηδείων with reference to furnishing provisions and other supplies in view of an impending official visit. See also P Ryl II. 238⁶ (A.D. 262) παρασχεῖν τὰ ἐπιτήδια πάντα "to provide all that is necessary" for certain huntsmen, P Giss I. 85¹³ τὰ ἐπιτήδια τῇ σχολῆς (*l.* σχολῇ), and for the superlative P Oxy III. 472⁶ (c. A.D. 130) ὁ υἱὸς ἐπιτηδειότατος. P Strass I. 32¹³ (A.D. 261) ζυγὸν δὲ ἐνάγων παρά σοι τὸν ἐπιτηδει-ότερον αὐτῷ παράσχες shows the comparative where the context demands a superlative: see *Proleg.* p. 78. In P Fay 22²⁴ (ii/A.D.) a husband undertakes to provide for his divorced wife τὰ ἐπιτήδεια, in a manner befitting her rank. The adj. is common along with εὔπορος, e.g. BGU I. 235¹² (ii/A.D.?) εὐπόρους καὶ ἐπιδηδίο[υς] (*l.* ἐπιτηδείους) γνώμῃ καὶ κινδύ[ν]ων (*l.* –ύνῳ), P Oxy IX. 1187¹¹ (A.D. 254) ὅ[ν]τα εὔπορον καὶ ἐπιτήδειον, "being a person of means and suited for the post" (Ed.), of a phylarch. For the meaning "convenient" cf. P Hib I. 83¹⁰ (c. B.C. 258–7) οὐ γὰρ ἐπιτήδειός (*l.* –όν?) ἐστιν, P Tebt II. 409¹¹ (A.D. 5) εἰδὼς ὅτι ἐπιτ[ή-διό]ν [σο]ι. The adv. may be illustrated by P Oxy VI. 938⁶ (iii/iv A.D.) ἠπείχθην καὶ νῦν σοι γράψαι ὅπως αὐτῆς ὥρας γομωσασθῆναι (*l.* γομωθῆναι) ἐπιτηδείως τὰς σαργάνας ποι-ήσας ἀποστείλῃς, "I hasten to write to you now once more and beg you instantly to get the baskets properly laden and send them off" (Edd.), and the subst. ἐπιτήδευμα (common in the LXX) by Vett. Val. p. 73⁵⁰ τοὺς δὲ ἐκ τῶν ἐπιτηδευμάτων καρποὺς οὐ λαμβάνουσι.

ἐπιτίθημι

is construed with the acc. and dat., as in Ac 28¹⁰, in BGU IV. 1208¹·⁴ (B.C. 27) ὃ ἐπιτέθ[εισα]ι τοῖς παρ᾽ αὐτοῦ [πιττάκ]ιον, *ib.* 1139⁷ (B.C. 5) Πάρθος . . . αὐτῇ ἐπέθηκεν πρίμα (cf. Mk 3¹⁶ ff.), P Ryl II. 81⁹ (c. A.D. 104) τὴν γὰρ ὅλην τοῦ πράγματος ἐξουσίαν τοῖς κατασ[π]ορεῦσι ἐπεθέμην, "for I gave the inspectors of sowing the conduct of the whole matter" (Edd.), and with the acc. alone in *ib.* 121¹⁰ (ii/A.D.) τ[ὰς] σφραγεῖδας ἃς ἐπέθηκ[ε, "the seals which he affixed" (Edd.). In BGU IV. 1019⁷ (mid. ii/A.D.) we have ὃς ἔδωκεν τὸν στρατηγὸν τοῦ νομοῦ εἰς τ[ὸ] πέρας ἐπιθεῖναι τ[ῇ] λογοθεσίᾳ. For the meaning "persuade," "enjoin," cf. P Oxy X. 1255⁶ (A.D. 292) ἐπειθεμένου σου ἡμῖν, *ib.* 1265¹¹ (A.D. 336) ἐπέθετό μοι ἡ σὴ ἐμμέλε[ια ἐγγρά]φως δηλῶσαι, "your grace enjoined me to state in writing" (Edd.), and for the meaning "attack," "assault," as in Ac 18¹⁰, cf. P Tebt I. 15¹¹ (B.C. 114) καὶ τὸν τούτου υἱὸν Μάρωνα ἐπιτεθεῖσθαι τῶι Πολέμωνι, *ib.* 53¹⁰ (B.C. 110) ἐπιθέμενοι λῃστρικῶι τρόπωι, and so BGU IV. 1061¹⁴ (B.C. 14): cf. P Flor III. 332² (ii/A.D.) ἀλλ᾽ ἐπιζητεῖ νῦν μετὰ καὶ ἄλλων γυμναστικῶν φίλων πῶς ἐπιθῆταί μοι ἀπόντος σου, and see *s.v.* ἐπίθεσις. With the use of the verb = "add to" in Rev 22¹⁸ as opposed to ἀφαιρέω, cf. προστίθημι in *Cagnat* IV. 1028¹·²⁰ ἐὰν δέ τις] πρὸς ταύτας τὰς συνθήκας κοινῇ(ι) βουλῇ ι) προσθεῖναι ἢ ἀφελεῖν βούλ[ω]νται ὁ δῆμος καὶ ἡ βουλὴ κτλ.

ἐπιτιμάω

= "censure," "lay under a penalty," as notably in Mk (see Allen *ad* Mk 8³⁰), may be illustrated from P Magd 24⁵ (B.C. 218) ἀγανακτήσαντος δέ μου καὶ ἐπιτιμῶντος αὐτ[ῆι, P Par 42⁷ (B.C. 156) μεταπεμψάμενος οὖν αὐτὸν καὶ τὸν φυλακίτην ἐπετίμων αὐτῷ, P Oxy X. 1295⁵ (ii/iii A.D.) ἐὰν δὲ μέλλῃς οὕτω αὐτῷ ἐπιτιμᾶν, and *Syll* 177⁵⁵ (B.C. 303) ὅπω]ς, ἐάν τινες φαίνωνται μὴ τὰ βέλτιστα νομογραφοῦντες, ἀλλ᾽ [ἀνεπιτήδεια, αὐτοῖς] ἐπιτιμῶμεν καὶ ζημιῶμεν. In PSI IV. 356⁷ (B.C. 253–2) ἐπιτετίμηται is used of χόρτος that has been "augmented" in price. For ἐπιτιμή = "penalty," "fine," see P Petr III. 20 *verso*⁵ (B.C. 246) τὰς ἐπιτιμὰς εἰς τὸ βασιλικ[ό]ν, and for the corresponding use of τὸ ἐπίτιμον, see P Gen I. 20¹⁵ (ii/B.C.) προσαποτισάτω ἐπίτιμον παραχρῆμα, P Oxy II. 275²⁹ (A.D. 66) (= *Selections,* p. 57) ἐπίτιμον δραχμὰς ἑκατόν, *ib.* X. 1282⁴⁰ (A.D. 83) τό τε βλάβος καὶ ἐπίτιμον, "the damages and a fine," and the large number of exx. from iii/B.C. to iv/A.D. in Berger *Strafklauseln,* p. 5. Berger (p. 14) also recalls the rare use of ἐπίτιμον = contraband goods, as P Tebt I. 30¹⁹ (B.C. 114) ἐλαϊκὸν ἐπίτιμον, "contraband oil" (Edd.): cf. P Petr II. 30(f)³ ἀπέφαινεν παῖς ὑπάρχειν ἐπίτιμον ἐν τῶι Μητροδώρου ἐποικίωι δραχμὰς ρν, where Mahaffy translates "the slave showed that there was an assessable value (?) in the dwelling of Metrodorus worth 150 drachmae."

ἐπιτιμία.

For this NT ἅπ. εἰρ. (2 Cor 2⁶, cf Wisd 3¹⁰) = "punishment," "penalty," cf. the use of ἐπιτίμιον in P Hal I. 1²⁰⁸ (iii/B.C.) τριπλάσια τὰ ἐ[πι]τίμια ἀποτεισάτ[ω, ἐὰν δίκηι] νικηθῆι, P Oxy XII. 1408⁷ (c. A.D. 258) τοῖς ἐκ τῶν νόμων ὡρισμένοις ἐπιτειμίοις, "the decreed penalties of the laws," and see what is said of τὸ ἐπίτιμον *s.v.* ἐπιτιμάω *sub fin.*

The subst. in its sense of "franchise," "citizenship," occurs in a rescript of Severus, P Oxy XII. 1405[10] (iii/A.D.) ἡ δὲ ἐπιτειμία σου ἐκ τούτου οὐδὲν βλαβήσεται, "your citizenship, however, will in no way be injured thereby."

ἐπὶ τὸ αὐτό.

For this phrase, as in Ac 1[15], 2[1], see s.v. ἐπί.

ἐπιτρέπω.

For the distinctive NT sense of this verb "permit," "allow," cf. P Magd 2[7] (B.C. 221) δέομαι οὖν σου, βασιλεῦ, . . . μὴ ἐπιτρέπειν τῶι Ποώρει κωλύειν ἡμᾶς οἰκοδομεῖν, ib. 12[11] (B.C. 217) μὴ ἐπιτρέπειν αὐτοῖς ἐγβαλεῖν με ἐκ τῶν κλήρων, BGU II. 451[10] (i/ii A.D.) θεῶν ἐπιτρεπόν[τ]ων, P Ryl II. 120[16] (A.D. 167) διὸ ἀξιῶ ἐπιτρέψαι μ[ο]ι χρήσασθαι αὐτῷ τῷ Ἑρμείνῳ, P Lond 951 verso[4] (late iii/A.D.) (= III. p. 213) τ[ὸ] βρέφος ἐχέτω τροφόν, ἐγὼ γὰρ οὐκ ἐπιτ[ρέ]πω τῇ θυγατρί μου θηλάζειν, and for the pass., P Oxy III. 474[40] (A.D. 184?) δεύτερον τοῦτο προσαγορεύω ἄνευ τοῦ ἐπιτραπῆναι μὴ ἐφάπτεσθαι τοῦ κυριακοῦ χρήματος, "I now make this second order that the imperial moneys are not to be touched without leave" (Edd.). For the use of the inf. after ἐπιτρέπω in the NT, as in the Pontic dialect of MGr, see Proleg. p. 205. For the verb = "entrust," "commission," "instruct," we may cite a letter from a farm-bailiff to his employer, P Lond 1173[3 ff.] (A.D. 125) (= III. p. 208) ὡς ἐ]πέτρεψάς μοι κατεργά[ζεσθ]αι τὴν χερσάμπελον ἐποίησα, ὕστερον ἐπ[έτρε]ψάς [μ]οι διὰ λόγου μήκετι κατερ[γά]ζεσθαι, and the report of a public physician to the strategus, P Oxy I. 51[5] (A.D. 173) ἐπετράπην ὑπὸ σοῦ διὰ Ἡρακλείδου ὑπηρέτου ἐφιδεῖν σῶμα νεκρὸν ἀπηρτημένον ("found hanged"), and similarly ib. III. 476[10] (ii/A.D.). For the more strictly legal usage, cf. further P Lips I. 8[6] (A.D. 220) (= Chrest. II. 210) μετὰ κυρίου . . . [τοῦ αἰτηθέν]το[ς ὑπ᾿ αὐτῆ]ς καὶ ἐπιτραπέντ(ος) ὑπὸ Αὐρηλίου Κάστορος . . . ἐν[ά]ρ[χ]ου ἐξη]γη[τοῦ, of a guardian for whom a woman had asked, and who "had been installed" by the exegete Aurelius Kastor.

ἐπιτροπεύω.

For this verb which is read by D al. in Lk 3[1] for the more general ἡγεμονεύοντος to mark that Pilate was "procurator" of Judæa cf. the use of the subst. ἐπίτροπος in Syll 404[15] (ii/A.D.), al. The more general sense of "act as trustee or guardian" is seen in BGU IV. 1113[9] (B.C. 14) ἐπετρόπευσεν τοῦ Λουκίου, P Oxy IV. 727[15] (A.D. 154) ἐπιμελησόμενον ὧν καὶ αὐτοὶ ἐπιτροπεύουσιν ἀφηλίκων ἑαυτῶν ἀδελφιδῶν, "to take charge of their brother's children who are minors and their wards" (Edd.), OGIS 141[5] (B.C. 146–116) ἐπιτροπεύσαντα τῶν τέκνων ἡμῶν. For the corresponding subst. cf. P Oxy VI. 907[20] (A.D. 276) πᾶσι τοῖς τῇ ἐπιτροπείᾳ διαφέρ]ουσι, "in all that pertains to the guardianship" (Edd.), and more generally P Fay 20[17] an imperial edict by Julian (cf. Archiv ii. p. 169) addressed—τοῖς ἡγεμόσιν τοῖς κατ᾿ ἐπιτροπείας παρ᾿ ἐμοῦ ἀπεσταλμένοις, "the governors dispatched by me to posts of rule" (Edd.).

ἐπιτροπή.

For ἐ., as in Ac 26[12], cf. P Par 45[4] (B.C. 153) (= Witkowski[2], p. 84) ἀλ᾿ ὅμως τοῖς θεοῖς τὴν ἐπιτροπὴν δίδομει,

P Oxy IV. 743[32] (B.C. 2) περὶ πάντων αὐτῷ τὴν ἐπιτροπὴν δέδωκα. It is = "the office of guardian" in P Oxy VI. 898[24] (A.D. 123) αἰτοῦσά μ[ε] ἀντὶ ταύτης ἀποχὴν τῆς ἐπιτροπῆς, "demanding from me in return a receipt for her guardianship." P Ryl II. 153[20] (A.D. 138–61) οὓς [οἶδα ἐπιτηδείου]ς καὶ ἀξίου[ς τ]ῆς ἐπιτροπῆ[ς, "whom I know to be suitable and worthy of the office of guardian," and = "the office of procurator" in BGU I. 108 (A.D. 159–60) (= Selections, p. 84) τῆς τοῦ ἰδίου λόγου ἐπιτροπῆς. In MGr ἐπιτροπή = "committee."

ἐπίτροπος

is very common in connexion with the guardianship of minors (cf. Gal 4[2], e.g. P Ryl II. 109[15] (A.D. 235) Α(ὐρήλιος) Ἑρμόδ[ωρ]ος . . ἐπίτροπ[ος] τῶν ἀφηλ(ίκων) . . . ὤμοσα ὑπὲρ αὐτῶν, "I, Aurelius Hermodorus, guardian of the minors, have taken the oath on their behalf," ib. 121[15] (ii/A.D.) ἀξιῶ . . . [ἐ]πίτροπον αὐτῷ κατασταθῆ]ναι, and a Will, ib. 153[15] (A.D. 138–61) οὓς καὶ καθίστημι ἐπιτρόπους [ἄχ]ρι οὗ γένη[ται τῆ]ς ἐννό[μο]υ [ἡ]λικίας. Preisigke Fachwörter, p. 93, has classified the uses of the word in connexion with the office of "procurator": cf. Magie, p. 162 f., and Rouffiac Recherches, p. 46, where we are reminded of the Imperial procurator at Priene—ὁ τῶν κυρίων ἐπίτροπος (Priene 230[5] A.D. 196–212). The agreement with Mt 20[8] λέγει ὁ κύριος . . . τῷ ἐπιτρόπῳ αὐτοῦ is of course, as Rouffiac remarks, purely verbal.

ἐπιτυγχάνω.

Hort on Jas 4[2] states that "ἐπιτυγχάνω does not properly mean to 'obtain,' i.e. get possession, but to 'attain,' i.e. either fall in with or hit the mark, and is specially used absolutely of being successful." Of this meaning we have a good ex. in P Tebt II. 314[10] (ii/A.D.) τῆς δὲ τῶν φίλων σπουδῆς τυχόντος ἐπετύχαμεν, "by means of the good offices of our friends we achieved it" (Edd.; cf. BGU I. 332[8] (ii/iii A.D.) εὐχομένη ἡμᾶς ὑγιαίνοντες (. —τας) ἀπολαβεῖν, ὡς εὔχομαι ἐπιτετευχότας (cf. Heb 8[6] אᶜB, Deissmann BS p. 190). For the absolute use see also P Oxy I. 72[7] (A.D. 90) ἀπογράφομαι Μάρκῳ Πουρκίῳ ἐπιτυγχάνοντι ἀπόντι, "I register for M. P. who happens to be away." For the constr. with the gen., as in Heb 6[15], 11[33], cf. BGU I. 113[3] (A.D. 143) ἐπιτυχόντες . . . τῆς Ῥωμαίων πολειτίας, ib. II. 522[3] (ii/A.D.) αὐτὴ οὖσα, γυν[ὴ] χήρα καὶ ἀβοήθητος (l. ἀβοή)η), ἐπιτ[υχε]ῖν τῆς αὐτῆς φιλανθρωπίας. With the acc., as in Rom 11[7], cf. P Par 26[28] (B.C. 161 o) ὑμῖν δὲ γίνοιτο πᾶν ὃ ἂν ἐπιβάλλησθ᾿ ἐπιτυγχάνειν, and with the dat., cf. P Oxy III. 474[35] (A.D. 184?) ἐπιτυγχάνων τοῖς ἀργυρικοῖς λόγοις, where the editors translate "on examining the accounts of the money revenue." The subst. = "success" appears in OGIS 678[2] (time of Hadrian) ὑπὲρ . . τῆς τῶν ὑπὸ αὐτοῦ ἐπιταγέντων ἔργων ἐπιτυχίας: cf. the adv. ib. 556[6] πρεσβεύσαντα ἐπιτυχῶς ὑπὲρ τῆς ἐλευθερίας. MGr ἐπιτυχαίνω, "succeed," "attain."

ἐπιφαίνω

is used of the "epiphany" of the goddess Artemis Leukophryene in a Magnesian inscr. not before B.C. 200, Syll 256[6] ἐπιφαινομένης αὐτοῖς Ἀρτέμι[δο]ς Λευκοφρυηνῆς: cf. Tit 2[11], 3[4]. See also Syll 802[26] (iii/B.C.) ἐπιφανέντα [τ]ὸν θεὸν ἐφαλέσθαι ἐπὶ τὰν χῆρα καὶ ἐκτεῖναί οὐ τοὺς δακτύ[λ]ους, of a temple-vision by which a man with powerless fingers was healed.

ἐπιφάνεια.

The NT usage of this word to denote "manifestation," more particularly in connexion with the παρουσία of the Lord (2 Thess 2[8], 1 Tim 6[14], 2 Tim 4[1, 8], Tit 2[13]), is prepared for by the occurrence of the word in late Greek to denote any conspicuous intervention on the part of higher powers. Thus from the inscr. we may cite *OGIS* 233[35] (iii/B.C.) ἀπελογίσαντο διὰ πλειόνων τήν τε τῆς θεᾶς ἐπιφάνειαν, *ib.* 331[52] (mid. ii/B.C.) διὰ τὰς ἐξ αὐτοῦ (τοῦ Διὸς τοῦ Σαβαζίου) ἐπιφανείας, *ib.* 383[85] (mid. i/B.C.) μεγάλων δαιμόνων ἐπιφανείαις, *Syll* 650[13] (ii/A.D.) διὰ τὰς ὑπ' αὐτῆς (τῆς Ἀρτέμιδος) γενομένας ἐναργεῖς ἐπι[φανείας. In *Cos* 391 the accession of Caligula is described as an "epiphany"—ἐ]νιαυτοῦ πρώτου τὰς [Γαί]ου Καίσαρος . . . . ἐπιφανείας, and in *OGIS* 763[19] (ii/B.C.) it is united with δόξα—πολλὰ τῶν πρὸς ἐπιφάνειαν καὶ δόξαν ἀνηκόντων: cf. Tit *l.c.* and see Epict. iii. 22. 29. For a medical use of the word in describing symptoms, see the papyrus fragment of ii/A.D. published by Goodspeed in *AJP* xxiv. p. 327[1].—[5] τὴν ἐπειφάνεια[ν?

ἐπιφανής.

For this adj. = "manifest," "illustrious," as in Ac 2[20], cf. *OGIS* 90[47] (Rosetta stone—B.C. 196), where it is said of King Ptolemy V.—ἐπιφανῆ ποιήσαντος τήν τε ἄνω χώραν καὶ τὴν κάτω. The same inscr. shows the word frequently as a title of the King when it can only be regarded as = "Avatar," see Dittenberger's note on *ib.* 5 Πτολεμαίου . . . Θεοῦ Ἐπιφανοῦς Εὐχαρίστου, and cf. what has already been said *s.v.* ἐπιφάνεια. We may also refer to E. R. Bevan's discussion of this title of Antiochus IV. in *JHS* xx. p. 28 f. He shows that Seleucus I. was worshipped as Zeus Olympius: Antiochus replaced Zeus on his coins, the intervening kings having substituted Apollo. His title meant a claim to be worshipped as "Zeus incarnate."

The wider sense of the word may be further illustrated from P Oxy XII. 1425[2] (A.D. 318), where an official return is headed—ὑπατίας τῶν δεσποτῶν ἡμῶν Λικ[ι]ννίο[υ] Σεβαστοῦ τὸ ε καὶ Κρίσπου τοῦ ἐπιφανεστάτ[ου] Καίσαρος τὸ α, "in the consulship of our lords Licinius Augustus for the fifth time and Crispus the most illustrious Caesar for the first time" (Edd.). For the adv. see a Phrygian inscr. *C. and B.* i. p. 182, No. 70, Διονοισίου ἀνδρὸς βουλευτοῦ καὶ πάσας ἀρχὰς κὲ λειτουργίας λαμπρῶς κὲ ἐπιφανῶς ἐκτετελεκότος.

ἐπιφέρω

is common = "produce," "bring forward." Thus P Eleph 2[16] (B.C. 285–4) ἡ δὲ συγγραφὴ ἥδε κυρία ἔστω πάντηι πάντως, ὅπου ἂν ἐπιφέρηται ὡς ἐκεῖ τοῦ συναλλάγματος γεγενημένου, similarly P Grenf I. 10[19] (B.C. 174). P Oxy II. 257[19] (A.D. 94–5) καθ' [ἃς] ἐπήνεγκεν ἀποδείξεις, "in accordance with the proofs he produced," P Tebt II. 297[15] (*c.* A.D. 123) τὴν ἐπ[ε]νεχθεῖσαν ὑπὸ τοῦ Μαρσισο[ύχου κύ]ρωσιν, "the certificate of appointment produced by Marsisuchus" (Edd.), P Ryl II. 163[14] (A.D. 139) ἐποίσω τὸ τῆς ἐνκτήσεως ἐπίσταλμα, "I will submit the authorization of

the land registry office" (Edd.), and for a new future see P Fay 64[7] (ii/A.D.) ἐπενεγκούμέ (*l.*—μέν) σοι τὸ δημόσιον σύμβολον, "we will hand over to you the treasury receipt" (Edd.), P Hamb I. 44[7] (A.D. 215) ἐπενεγκῶ σοι τὸ δημόσιον σύμβολον. The verb is used of "recording" votes in *Michel* 487[19] (ii/B.C.) ψῆφοι ἐπηνέχθησαν δισχίλιαι ἑκατὸν δεκατρεῖς. For the meaning "bring forward" an accusation (cf. the simplex in Ac 25[18]), see P Oxy III. 472[9] (*c.* A.D. 130) διὰ τί δ' ἐπήνενκεν τὸ ἔνκλημα ταύτη δῆλον, "why he brought the accusation is now clear" (Edd.), and for the meaning "inflict," as in Rom 3[5], see P Tebt II. 331[10] (*c.* A.D. 131) ἐ]πήνεγκά[ν μο]ι πληγὰς εἰς πᾶν μέλ[ο]ς το[ῦ σ]ώματος: cf. the subst. in P Oxy II. 283[16] (A.D. 45) πληγῶν ἐπιφορᾶς. The adj. = "appropriate," "relative," is found in *ib.* 266[14] (A.D. 96) ἣ]ς τὴν ἐπίφορον (*sc.* ὁμολογίαν) αὐτόθεν ἀναδεδωκέναι αὐτῷ [κεχιασμένην εἰ]ς ἀκύρωσιν, "this bond she has thereupon returned to him cancelled" (Edd.), and similarly *ib.* X. 1282[33] (A.D. 83).

ἐπιφωνέω

is followed by direct discourse, as in Lk 23[21], in P Ryl II. 77[33] (A.D. 192) τῶν π[αρ]εστώτων ἀπὸ τῆς πόλεως ἐπιφωνη[σ]άντων· στεφέσθω Ἀχιλλεὺς κοσμητείαν, "the citizens standing by cried out, 'Let Achilles be crowned as cosmetes'" (Edd.): so *OGIS* 595[15] (ii/A.D.) ἐπεφώνησαν· καλῶς εἶπεν Φιλοκλῆς, *al.*

ἐπιφώσκω.

A horoscope P Lond 130[39] (= I. p. 134) is dated—ἔτους τρίτου θεοῦ Τίτου Φαρμουθὶ τῇ ἐπιφωσκούσῃ, *i.e.* April 1st, A.D. 81, though the use of the title θεός = "*divus*," shows, as the editor points out, that the document itself was not drawn up until after the Emperor's death : cf. also the late P Grenf II. 112[15] (a Festal Epistle by the Patriarch of Alexandria with reference to the date of Easter—A.D. 577 ?) τῇ ἑξῆς ἐπιφωσκούσῃ κυριακῇ. We cannot discuss here the *crux* of Mt 28[1] (see Allen's note in *ICC ad l.*), but two instances of the verb may be cited from the Gosp. of Peter —2 ἐπεὶ καὶ σάββατον ἐπιφώσκει (cf. Lk 23[54]), 9 τῇ δὲ νυκτὶ ᾗ ἐπέφωσκεν ἡ κυριακή. On the meaning see Notes by C. H. Turner in *JTS* xiv. p. 188 ff., and by F. C. Burkitt in *ib.* p. 538 ff. The latter claims the verb as apparently "a real example of that 'Jewish Greek' which the discoveries of Egyptian papyri have reduced to such restricted compass," but see the first citation *supra*, in which no direct trace of Semitic influence can be predicated.

ἐπιχειρέω.

For this verb, which in the NT is confined to the Lukan writings (Lk 1[1], Ac 9[29], 19[13]), it is sufficient to cite P Par 63[112] (B.C. 164) (= P Petr III. p. 28) εἰ συναναγκάζειν ἐπιχειροίη προσδέχεσθαι, "if one were to endeavour to compel them to accept (the work)" (Mahaffy), *ib.* 61[15] (B.C. 156) μάλιστα δὲ τῶν συκοφαντεῖν ἐπιχειρούντων [τελωνῶν, P Tebt I. 6[38] (B.C. 140–39) ἄλλους δὲ ἐπιχειρεῖν ἐπ[ιπλ]έκειν ἑα[υ]τοὺς ταῖς προσόδοις, "and others try to mix themselves up with the revenues" (Edd.), P Ryl II. 144[16] (A.D. 38) ὃς δὲ ἐκ τοῦ ἐναντίου ἄλογον ἀηδίαν μοι ἐπιχειρήσας παρεχρήσατό μοι πολλὰ καὶ ἄσχημα, "whereupon he opposing me made a brutal and odious attack upon me and subjected me to much shameful mishandling" (Edd.), P Oxy I. 38⁹ (A.D. 49–50) (= *Selections*, p. 53) τοῦ Σύρ[ου] ἐπικεχειρηκότος ἀποσπάσαι εἰς δουλαγωγία[ν] τὸν ἀφήλικά μου υἱόν Ἀπίωνα, "S. having endeavoured to carry off into slavery my young son A.," P Oxy III. 492⁹ (A.D. 130) ἐκτείσι ὁ ἐπιχειρ[ῶ]ν πρὸς ἀθέτησίν τι τούτων ἄγειν ἐπιτείμου δρα[χμὰς] χειλίας, "the person attempting to set aside aught of them (viz. certain dispositions) shall forfeit a fine of 1000 drachmae" (Edd.), and *ib.* VIII. 1119¹⁸ (A.D. 254) τῆς παρανομίας παρὰ τῶν πλημ[μελ]εῖν ἐπιχειρούντων εἰς τε τὰς θείας νομοθεσίας, "the lawlessness of those who attempt to offend against the Imperial legislation" (Ed.). These examples show that any idea of failure, though often suggested by the context, does not lie in the verb itself. For the construction with the inf. see *Proleg.* p. 205. In *Chrest.* II. 372ᵛ·²⁴ (ii/A.D.) the verb is followed by the dat.—ἐπιδὴ τοίνυν ἐπιχειρεῖς τοῖς ἀδυνάτοις, οὔτε οὗτος οὔτε οἱ ἄλλοι υἱοί σου Ἀ[λε]ξανδρέων πολεῖταί εἰ[σι]ν.

ἐπιχέω.

P Leid W i ₁₀ (ii/iii A.D.) καὶ μηκέτι ἐπιχέῃς (the vessel being already full) : cf. the late form in *ib.* ᶦˣ·²⁶ καὶ κεμείσας (*l.* γεμίσας) τοὺς λύχνους μηκέτι ἐπίχυννε (*l.* ἐπίχυε). We may cite from the inscr. *Michel* 1001 ⁱᵛ·²² (B.C. 200) καὶ ποιείσθαι τὰν τὰν (om.) συναγωγὰν ἀπὸ τοῦ πράτου ἀλείμματος καὶ ἐπιχείσθαι πάντας ἀπὸ δείπνου. For the subst. = "a surplus" see P Ryl II. 97⁵ (A.D. 139) καὶ ἐπιχύματος ἑκάστῳ μετρητῇ κοτυλῶν δύο, "and an extra amount of 2 cotylae for each metretes" (Edd.).

ἐπιχορηγέω.

Though the simple χορηγέω is more common, the compound verb is also well attested in the papyri: see e.g. P Oxy II. 282⁶ (A.D. 30–5) where a man in lodging a complaint against his wife states—ἐ]γὼ μὲν οὖν ἐπεχορήγησα αὐτῇ τὰ ἑξῆς καὶ ὑπὲρ δύναμιν, "I for my part provided for my wife in a manner that exceeded my resources" (Edd.). The passage may perhaps be taken as illustrating the "generous" connotation underlying the corresponding subst., as in Phil 1¹⁹ (see Kennedy *ad l.* in *EGT*). Examples of the verb from marriage-contracts are BGU I. 183⁶ (A.D. 85) ἐπιχορη[γοῦντος Ὥρου δέοντα] πάντα, P Oxy VI. 905¹⁰ (A.D. 170) (= *Selections*, p. 86) καὶ ὁ γαμῶν ἐπι]χορηγείτω τῇ γαμουμένῃ τὰ δέοντα κατὰ δύναμιν [τοῦ βίου, CPR I. 27¹² (A.D. 190) τοῦ Ἰσιδώρου [ἐ]πιχορηγοῦ[ντος] αὐτῇ τὰ δέοντα, *al.*

ἐπιχορηγία.

Syll 378⁹ (A.D. 79–81) τῆς ἐπιχορηγίας γενομένης ἐκ τῶν [ἱερῶ]ν προσόδων.

ἐπιχρίω.

A very striking parallel to the healing of the blind man in Jn 9⁶ is afforded by an inscription probably from the temple of Asclepios at Rome after A.D. 138 : *Syll* 807 ¹⁵ᶠᶠ· Οὐαλερίῳ Ἄπρῳ στρατιώτῃ τυφλῷ ἐχρημάτισεν ὁ θεὸς ἐλθεῖν καὶ λαβεῖν αἷμα ἐξ ἀλεκτρυῶνος λευκοῦ μετὰ μέλιτος καὶ κολλυρίου συντρῖψαι καὶ ἐπὶ τρεῖς ἡμέρας ἐπιχρεῖσαι ἐπὶ τοὺς ὀφθαλμούς· καὶ ἀνέβλεψεν καὶ ἐλήλυθεν καὶ ηὐχαρίστησεν δημοσίᾳ τῷ θεῷ, "Valerius Aper, a blind soldier, was

warned of the god to come and take the blood of a white cock along with honey, and to mix together an eye-salve, and for three days to anoint the eyes with it. And he received his sight, and came, and gave thanks publicly to the god." (For the tenses here note an exact parallel in Jas 1²⁴, and cf. *Proleg.* p. 144 n¹.) See also P Leid X ⁷ᵛ· ⁵⁵ (iii/iv A.D.) ὅμοιον γὰρ εἶδος ἔχει τὸ ἐπιχρισθὲν ἢ γραφέν, which the editor explains "aes totum illinitum, aut literae, figuraeve in eo sculptae eandem auri speciem offerunt."

ἐποικοδομέω.

In connexion with the sale of a piece of land, power is given to the purchaser καὶ ἐμβατεύειν [καὶ ἐποι]κοδομεῖν καὶ ἐγμισθοῦν [καὶ] ἑτέροις παραχωρεῖν (BGU IV. 1130¹⁴ – B.C. 5) : cf. P Giss I. 67¹² (ii/A.D.) οὐ[κ] ἐπῳκοδομήσαμεν ταῖς κέλλαις, "wir haben nicht an den Magazinen (Kellern) weiter gebaut" (Ed.), and Epict. ii. 15. 8 ἐποικοδομεῖν αὐτῷ τὴν εὐτονίαν, τὴν ἀσφάλειαν, "build on it (a sound foundation) your firmness and unshaken resolve" (Matheson). For the constr. with ἐπί, as in 1 Cor 3¹², see *OGIS* 483¹¹⁷ (ii/B.C.) μὴ ἐξουσία δὲ ἔστω ἐπὶ τοὺς κοινοὺς τοίχους μήτε ἐποικοδομεῖν μήτε διορύσσειν μήτε ἄλλο καταβλάπτειν μηθέν : cf *Syll* 531³² (iii/B.C.) ἐποικοδομήσει τειχίον ὑπὲρ γῆς, and for the subst. *ib.* 543¹ τῆς ἐποικοδομίας τῶν προκειμένων χωμάτων.

ἐπονομάζω.

This NT ἅπ. εἰρ. is found in the Median parchment P Sa'id Khan 1 ᴬ·¹¹ (B.C. 88) (= *JHS* xxxv. p. 28) τειμὴν ἀμπέλου τῆς οὔσης ἐν κώμῃ Κωπάνει τὴν ἐπονομαζομένην Δαδβακανράς, and so ᴮ·¹¹.

ἐποπτεύω

occurs in an inscr. of Imperial times erected in memory of their daughter by a man and his wife, who describe themselves as Καίσαρος δοῦλ[οι), *Cagnat* IV. 235⁵ –

η γὰρ ἐμοὺς αἰῶνας ἐποπτεύουσα χελιδὼν
τὸ τρίτον ἡ ξείνη μύρατ' ἀποιχομένην.

In the astrological PSI III. 157³³ (iii/A.D. ?) the verb is used of the sun.

ἐπόπτης.

With the application of ἐπόπτης to God in the Greek Bible (e.g. Esth 5¹, 2 Macc 7³⁵) may be compared the corresponding use in the inscrr. Thus an inscr. from Cyzicus describes Pompey the Great as ἐπόπτης γῆς τε καὶ θαλάσσης (*JHS* xxvii. p. 64), and in Pergamene inscrr. the Emperor Augustus is similarly described, e.g. *Cagnat* IV. 309² (B.C. 29) θ]εοῦ υἱὸν θεὸν Σεβαστὸ[ν, πάσης] γῆ[ς κ]αὶ θ[α]λάσσης [ἐ]π[όπ]τ[ην: cf. *OGIS* 666²⁰ (time of Nero) τὸν Ἥλιον Ἁρμαχιν ἐπόπτην καὶ σωτῆρα with reference to an Egyptian Sun-god, *Preisigke* 1323 (ii/A.D.) Θεῷ ὑψίστῳ καὶ πάντων ἐπόπτῃ καὶ Ἡλίῳ καὶ Νεμέσει, and the magic P Lond 121³⁵¹·⁵⁷² (iii/A.D.) (= I. pp. 95, 102). In P Oxy VI. 991 (A.D. 341) a petition (?) is addressed to a police official as ἐπόπτῃ ἰρήνης : cf. *ib.* XII. 1559³ (A.D. 341). With the usage in 2 Pet 1¹⁶ we may compare more particularly *Michel* 1141¹ (ii/B.C.) ἱεροποιοὶ καὶ μυστηρίων ἐπόπται, *Syll* 657⁴ Ῥοδίων ἱεροποιοὶ μύσται καὶ [ἐ]πόπται εὐσεβεῖς, and *ib.* 658³ ἐφόπται εὐσεβεῖς, all with reference to those initiated into the mysteries and hence "eye-witnesses." In the last passage the editor explains the aspirated form as due to the influence of ἐφοράω.

ἔπος.

The phrase ὡς ἔπος ἐστὶν εἰπεῖν occurs in P Oxy I. 67¹⁴ (a dispute concerning property—A.D. 338) qualifying a preceding πάντα: it is a literary reminiscence as in Heb 7⁹, the only place where ἔπος occurs in the NT. In the early *Syll* 17²³ (v/B.C.) we have οὐδ' ἐπεὶ οὐδὲ ἔργοι, cf. 55⁷, and in *OGIS* 51³⁷ (iii/B.C.) ἐπῶν ποιηταί are contrasted with τραγωδιῶν π. and κωμωδιῶν π., cf. Sir 44⁵: see also *Syll* 693²¹ (iii/B.C.), 722⁶ (ii/B.C.). As distinguished from λόγος, speech in progress, (F)έπος, *vox*, Sanskrit vāc, etc., describes a single utterance: see *Proleg.* p. 111.

ἐπουράνιος.

That this classical word (Homer, Plato) had survived in Hellenistic Greek outside the NT is shown by its occurrence in the Jewish text of the great Paris magical papyrus, P Par 574³⁰⁴² (iii/A.D.) (= Deissmann *LAE*, p. 252) καὶ σὺ λάλησον ὁποῖον ἐὰν ᾖς ἐπεουράνιον ἢ ἀέριον εἴτε ἐπίγειον εἴτε ὑπόγειον ἢ καταχθόνιον—a passage which at once recalls the Pauline usage (Phil 2¹⁰, Eph 2², *al.*), but is not a quotation from the Apostle. "The papyrus and St. Paul are both using familiar Jewish categories" (Deissmann *ut s.* p. 257 n.¹¹). See also *Kaibel* 261⁹⁴ (ii/A.D.)—

κεῖται μὲν γαίῃ φθίμενον δέμας, ἡ δὲ δοθεῖσα
ψυχή μοι ναίει δώματ' ἐπουράνια.

ἑπτά.

As we have no fresh light from our sources, it lies outside our sphere to discuss the uses of this number in the NT, but reference may be made to the notes by Allen on Mk 16³, and by Moffatt (in *EGT*) on Rev 5¹. Note also Ac 12¹⁰ D κατέβησαν τοὺς ζ βαθμούς and Ev. Petr. 8 ἐπέχρισαν ἑπτὰ σφραγῖδας. MGr ἐφτά shows the aspirate in compensation for the loss (in pronunciation) of the rough breathing.

ἑπτάκις.

See *s.v.* ἑβδομηκοντάκις, and with reference to W. C. Allen's contention that in Mt 18²² we are to understand 70 7, add (from *Proleg.* p. 107) a further parallel for cardinal in place of adverb from BGU IV. 1074 (p. 119—late iii/A.D.) τρισπυθιονείκης, but δεκαολυμπιονείκης, etc.

Ἔραστος.

For this common name it is sufficient to refer to *Syll* 388 (A.D. 129) where we hear of an Ἔραστος, a shipowner of Ephesus.

ἐραυνάω, ἐρευνάω.

The spelling ἐρευνάω is found *ter* in the fragmentary P Petr III. 65(*b*)⁶, ¹⁰, ¹¹ (Ptol.), apparently part of a professional searcher's report, but ἐραυνάω, which is adopted throughout by WH, is certain from i/A.D. onwards, e.g. P Oxy II. 294⁹⁶ (A.D. 22) (= *Selections*, p. 35) ὁ ο[ἶκος . . . . .] Σεκόνδας ἡραύνηται κ[αὶ . . . . .] ὁ ἐμ[ὸς] οἶκος ἡραύνητ[αι: see *Proleg.* p. 46, where the spelling of the subst. is also discussed. As illustrating the two forms it is

enough to cite here P Tebt I. 38¹⁹ (B.C. 113) ἔρ]ευναν δὲ τούτου σὺν αὐτοῖς ποιησάμενος, P Oxy I. 67¹⁸ (A.D. 338) ἐπὶ δυσὶ κεφαλαίοις τὴν ἔρ. αυναν ποιούμενον, "making the inquiry concerning two points." MGr ἔρευνα. In P Fay 104 (late iii/A.D.) reference is made *ter* to ἐραυνηταί, "searchers," apparently Customs officials (see the editors' note *ad* ¹⁴).

ἐργάζομαι.

P Petr II. 4 S)³ (B.C. 255-4) οὐδενὶ τρόπωι ἐργάζονται, P Tebt II. 384¹ (contract of apprenticeship—A.D. 10) παρε[ξόμεθά σοι τὸν] ἀδελφὸν . . . . ἐργαζ[όμενον κατὰ τὴν] γερδ[ιακὴν τέ]χνην, "we will produce our brother to work at the weaver's trade" (Edd.), P Ryl II. 233² (ii/A.D.) ἡ ἔξοδος τῶν ἐργαζομένων πάντων, "the exit for all the work-folk" (Edd.), P Lond 1177⁷⁰ (A.D. 113) (= III. p. 183) τῶν διὰ νυκτὸς ἐργασαμένων, P Meyer 20²¹ (1st half iii/A.D.) ἐργαζέσθω Λουκιᾶς καὶ ζώτω ἐκ τοῦ μισθάρου (*l.*—ίου) αὐτῆς (cf. 2 Th 3¹²). Εἴργασται, "work has been done," is very common in certificates granted for work done on embankments, as P Ryl II. 210³ (A.D. 131) εἴργ(ασται) ὑπὲρ χωματικῶν ἔργων, so *ib.* 211⁵, 212⁵ (both ii/A.D.), and P Fay 79³ (A.D. 197). With the use of the verb = "perform" sacred rites, as in 1 Cor 9¹³, cf. the related ὀργιάζω = "celebrate mysteries"; see Boisacq *Dict. Etym.* p. 272. For the fut. ἐργῶμαι, which is found in the LXX, but not in the NT, cf. *Syll* 540¹⁰ (Eleusis—B.C. 175-171) ἐργᾶται δὲ συνεχῶς μετὰ τὸ τὴν δόσιν λαβεῖν. The compound ἀπεργάζομαι occurs in P Lille I. 10⁷ (iii/B.C.) ἐπειδὴ καὶ ἀπεργάζονται οἱ λαοὶ τὸ κέρμα τοῦτο εἰς ἄριστον, "puisque précisément les indigènes acquittent (?) au mieux cette petite taxe" (Ed.), and P Oxy XII. 1409¹⁰ (A.D. 278) ταῦτα ἀπεργάζεσθαι ἤδη μετὰ πάσης προθυμίας, "to build these up now with all zeal"; and the compound συνεργάζομαι in BGU II. 530¹⁵ (i/A.D.) ὁ κοινωνὸς ἡμῶν οὐ συνηργάσατο. On the augment see Moulton *CR* xv. p. 35 f., and on the constative ἐργάσασθαι in Mt 25¹⁶, 3 Jn⁵, and Heb 11³³, see *Proleg.* p. 116.

ἐργασία.

P Tebt II. 286¹¹ (A.D. 121-138) τὰ σώματα καὶ τὰς ἐργασίας ἀπολήμψεται Ἀπολλ[ω]νίδης παρὰ τοῦ Ἀντωνίνου τοῦ κληρονόμου, "Apollonides shall receive back the slaves and their labour from Antoninus, the heir" (Edd.), P Fay 21¹¹ (A.D. 134) εἴτ' ἐν γένεσι εἴτ' ἐν ἀργυρίῳ εἴτ' ἐν σωματικαῖς ἐργασίαις, "whether in kind or in money or in bodily labour" (Edd.), P Oxy XII. 1581⁶ (ii/A.D.) Σαραπίωνα μὴ ἀφῇς ἀργεῖν καὶ ῥέμβεσθαι, ἀλλὰ εἰς ἐργασίαν αὐτὸν βάλε. For the word = "business," "trade," see P Lond 906⁶ (A.D. 128) (= III. p. 108) βουλόμεθα ἐπιχωρηθῆναι π[αρ'] ὑμῶν τὴν χρυσοχ[οϊ]κὴν ἐργασίαν, "we wish that a grant should be made by you of your gold-smith's business," P Fay 93⁷ (A.D. 161) βούλομαι μισθώσασθαι παρὰ σοῦ τὴν μυροπωλαϊκὴν καὶ ἀρωματικὴν ἐργασίαν, "I wish to lease from you your business of perfume-selling and unguent-making" (Edd.), P Tebt II. 287³ (A.D. 161-9) οἱ μὲ]ν εἰ[σὶ] γναφεῖς ο[ἱ δὲ] βαφεῖς τὴν ἐργασίαν, "some are fullers and others dyers by trade" (Edd.). MGr ἐργασία, "activity." How thoroughly the Latinism of Lk 12⁵⁸ had become acclimatized is shown by its occurrence in the colloquial P Oxy IV. 742¹¹ (B.C. 2) ἐάν τι δύνῃ σὺ ἐ[. . . .]ναι μοι δὸς ἐργασία[ν . . . ., "if you can . . . give your attention to it" (Edd.). For the word = "guild" of workmen, see *Alterthümer von Hierapolis* iv. p. 87, No. 42[5] ἡ σεμνοτάτη ἐργασία τῶν πορφυροβάφων, p. 92. No. 50 τοῦτο τὸ ἡρῶον στεφανοῖ ἡ ἐργασία τῶν βαφέων, cited by Dittenberger *ad Syll* 873[1] where we have the compound—ἡ συνεργασία τῶν ἀργυροκόπων καὶ χρυσοχόων.

For ἐργαστήριον, see P Oxy XII. 1455[9] (A.D. 275) ἐν ᾧ ἔχω ἐργαστηρίῳ, "in the factory which I possess."

ἐργάτης.

P Fay 331 (A.D. 125–6) contains payments to ἐργ(άται) at the rate of 9 obols per man : cf. P Oxy X. 1263[13] (A.D. 128–9) βούλομαι . . . χρήσασθαι τῇ τῶν ἐργ[ατῶν] ποταμοῦ τέχ[νη, "I wish to practise the trade of a river-worker" (Edd.), P Ryl II. 98(a)[16] (A.D. 154–5) ἔξω δὲ σὺν ἐμαυτῷ ἐργάτας δύο, *Chrest.* I. 96[vii. 17] (accounts of the Temple of Jupiter Capitolinus—A.D. 215) ἐργάταις κ[ωμ-ά]σασι τὸ ξόανον τοῦ θεοῦ πρὸς [ἀ]πάντη[σιν τοῦ] ἡγεμόνος. P Flor I. 3[6] (A.D. 301) ἐργάτας . . . ὄντ[α]ς εὐθέτους καὶ ἐπιτηδείους. One of the columns of P Lond 1170 *verso* (A.D. 258–9) (= III. p. 193 ff.), an account of receipts and expenditure by a steward at Theadelphia, is headed—[45] λόγος ἐργατῶν ἀργησάντων. An interesting inscr. dedicated to Αἰών as a deity, *Syll* 757 (i/A.D.), ends by describing Αἰών as θείας φύσεως ἐργάτης αἰωνίου πάντα, where the editor thinks that the difficult acc. πάντα is best explained by the accidental omission of a preceding κατά. For the subst. ἐργατεία, used in a concrete sense, see BGU IV. 1159[9] (time of Augustus) πᾶσαν] ἐργατήαν παρεσσκευακώς (*l.* παρεσκευακώς), and P Oxy XII. 1450[6] (A.D. 249–50), and for ἐργατεύω, as in Tobit 5[5]. cf. P Par 63[102] (B.C. 165) (= P Petr III. p. 26) οἱ διὰ τὴν τῶν δεόντων σπάνιν ἐργατεύοντες πορίζονται τὰ πρὸς τὸ ζῆν, "who, through lack of necessaries, supply themselves with the means of life by hard labour" (Mahaffy). The adj. is seen in P Fay 111[6] (A.D. 95–6) ἔχων ἐν τῇ [κ]όμῃ ἐργατικὰ κτήνη δέκα : PSI I. 38[5] (A.D. 101) ὁμολογῶ πεπρακέναι σοι ὃν ἔχω ἐργατικὸν ὄνον recalls the μύλος ὀνικός of Mk 9[42]. Ἐργάτης is a unique formation for * ἐργότης through the influence of ἐργάζομαι, cf. Boeot. Ϝεργοτίων (Boisacq *Dict. Etym.* p. 272 n.[1]). It persists in MGr.

ἔργον.

A few miscellaneous exx. of this common word (MGr ἔργο) will suffice : P Petr II. 11 (1)[3] (mid. iii/B.C.) εἰ δυνατόν ἐστιν καὶ μηθέν σε τῶν ἔργων κωλύει, πειράθητι ἐλθεῖν εἰς τὰ Ἀρσινόεια, P Par 66[71] (i/B.C.) ὧν τὰ ἔργα ἀναβάλουσιν (*l.* —λλ—), "whose work is postponed," P Oxy XII. 1457[13] (B.C. 4–3) ὅ[νους] θηλάς δύο . . ἐργαζομένας μου τὰ ἴδια ἔργα, P Ryl II. 154[20] (A.D. 66) τὰ κατ' ἔ[το]ς γεωργικὰ ἔργα πάντα, and P Tebt II. 423[3] (early iii/A.D.) ἄλλοτέ σοι ἔγραψα ὑπομιμνήσκων περὶ τῶν ἔργων. In P Giss I. 20[16] (ii/A.D.) the word is almost = "sample"—ἐργά[ζο]μαι τὰ ἔρια[. . . . ἃ] ἔγρα[ψ]ας . ὁποῖον δέ σοι χρῶ[μ]α ἀρέσκει, [δήλω]σον δι' ἐπι[σ]τολῆς ἡ μεικρὸν ἔρ[γο]ν (or ἔρ[ιο]ν, see *s.v.* ἀρέσκω) αὐτοῦ π[έμψο]ν.

ἐρεθίζω.

The subst. is used physically in *Syll* 891[12] (ii/A.D.) τοῦτόν τε θεὸς πατάξαι ἀπορίᾳ καὶ πυρετῷ καὶ ῥίγει καὶ ἐρεθισμῷ

καὶ ἀνεμοφθορίᾳ κτλ.—a passage borrowed apparently from Deut 28[22]. The verb is cognate with ὄρνυμι and *orior* : cf. the Epic ὀροθύνω (Boisacq *Dict. Etym.* p. 273 f.). It is used (*in malam partem*) in Epict. *Enchir.* 20.

ἐρείδω

is found in a petition of village-representatives against carrying out certain repairs on an embankment—P Oxy XII. 1469[8] (A.D. 298) οὐ ταῦτα μὲν οὖν μόνα ἤρισto τ[ῇ κ]ώμῃ ἡμῶν, "nor was this all that was imposed upon our village" (Edd.). The compound ἀπερείδω, as in LXX Dan 1[2], occurs in P Tor I. 1[ii. 19] (B.C. 117–6) of "depositing" dead bodies in a house—ἀλλὰ καὶ νεκροὺς ἀπηρεισμένοι τυγχάνουσιν ἐνταῦθα, cf. *ib.* iii. 13. Hunt restores the subst. in P Hawara 17[4] (i/A.D.) (= *Archiv* v. p. 380) ἐνέδωκα[ν . . . ἐρ]είσματα, and cites Polyb. v. 100. 5 τῶν δ'ἐρεισμάτων οὐ δυναμένων ὑποφέρειν τὸ βάρος ἀλλ' ἐνδόντων : cf. *Syll* 588[171] (*i.* B.C. 180) ἐρείσματα σιδηρᾶ, and Vett. Val. pp. 333[20], 334[10]. See also Anz *Subsidia*, p. 271, and for the medical usage Hobart p. 280 f.

ἐρεύγομαι.

A new literary reference for this word, corresponding to the usage in Mt 13[35] (cf. LXX Ps 78 (77)[2]), may be cited from P Oxy VII. 1011, fol. 1 *verso* [7], a fragment of Callimachus—

    ὤναο κάρ' (*l.* κάρθ') ἔνεκ' οὔ τι θεῆς ἴδες ἱερὰ φρικτῆς,
    ἐξενέπειν καὶ τῶν ἤρυγες ἱστορίην.

"Lucky indeed for thee that thou hast never seen the mysteries of the dread goddess, or thou hadst e'en begun to blurt out the tale of them" (Ed.). In his note Hunt says "ἐξενέπειν ἤρυγες is perhaps a just possible expression for 'began to tell.'"

ἐρημία.

BGU III. 888[15] (A.D. 160) ἐν ἐκτελ[. . .] . μέγη τάξει αἰρημία (*l.* ἐρ—), P Thead 16[17] (after A.D. 307) περὶ τῆς ἐρη[μί]ας τῆς κώμης, and the schoolboy's exercise containing the tale of a parricide who, to escape justice, fled into the desert, P Grenf II. 84[4] (v/vi A.D.) υἱὸς τὸν εἴδιον πατέραν φωνεύσας καὶ τοὺς νομοὺς φοβηθεὶς ἔφυγεν εἰς ἐρημίαν. The word is MGr.

ἔρημος.

P Lille I. 26[3] (iii/B.C.) ἡ κώμη ἔρημος διὰ τὸ πλείω χρόνον μὴ βεβρέχθαι, "the village deserted because for long there has been no inundation," P Tebt II. 308[4] (A.D. 174) ἐρήμου αἰγιαλοῦ, "desert shore," OGIS 586[7] (A.D. 367–75) τὸν τόπον . . . πρότερον ἀγνοούμενον καὶ ἔρημον. For the legal use of the adj. to denote judgment going "by default" owing to the non-appearance of the accused party, cf. P Hib I. 32[3] (B.C. 246) Νεοπτολέμου Μακεδόνος ἰδι[ώ]του τ[ῶν] Ἀντιόχου πρὸς καταδίκην ἔρημον ὕβρεως πρὸς (δραχμὰς) ͞σ, "(property of) Neoptolemus, Macedonian, a private in Antiochus' troop, who had been condemned by default for violence to a fine of 200 drachmae" (Edd.) : cf. *Chrest.* II. i. p. 18 n.[3] On the accent of ἔρημος see Brugmann-Thumb *Gr.* p. 185. The adj. survives in MGr = "lonely," "forsaken" : cf. also the Klepht ballad, Abbott *Songs*, p. 18[19], where τάρημα τ' ἄρματα τάρημα τὰ τσαπράξια = "the wretched arms, the wretched knee-plates." The form ἕρμος (by stress of accent) is also found.

ἐρημόω.

For the use of this verb in Rev 18[19], Boll (*Offenbarung*, p. 133) cites from Hellenistic astrology Catal. VII. 170, 16 and 21, ναοὶ (μεγάλοι) ἐρημωθήσονται, 171, 14 ναὸς μέγας ἐρημωθήσεται. See also *OGIS* 519[32] (*c.* A.D. 245) συνέβη . . . τὰ χωρία ἐρημοῦσθαι. The noun (as in Mt 24[15]) survives in the MGr ἐρήμωσι, "isolation."

ἐρίζω.

P Leid W[v. 36] (ii/iii A.D.) ἤρισεν αὐτῷ ὁ πρότερος λέγων, ἐγὼ τούτου ἰσχυρότερός εἰμι. BGU IV. 1043[5] (iii/A.D.) ὥστε ἔτι μοι ἐρίζις.

ἐριθεία (—ία).

For the spelling see WH *Notes*[2], p. 160. The original meaning of the verb ἐριθεύομαι, "work for hire," as in LXX Tob 2[11], may be illustrated from ἔριθος in P Hib I. 121[34] (B.C. 251–0) ἐρίθοις ἐρίων, "wool-weavers," and from the compound συνέριθος, "fellow-worker," in a Magdola papyrus of B.C. 216 re-edited by Reinach in *Mél. Nicole*, p. 451 ff.—[3] τῆι συνερίθωι μου προσνοήσας, "s'étant concerté avec ma compagne d'atelier," while the derived sense of intriguing for office appears in ἀνερίθευτος, "unmoved by party spirit," in *Syll* 177[46] (B.C. 303) if the restoration is correct—(ἀ)[πο]δεῖξαι δὲ ἑκατέρους νομογράφους τρεῖς μὴ νεωτέρους ἐτῶν τεσσεράκοντα [ὄντας ἀνεριθεύτ]ους. The meaning of "selfish" rather than "factious" ambition perhaps suits best all the NT occurrences of ἐριθεία : cf. Kennedy's note *ad* Phil 1[16] in *EGT*.

ἔριον.

PSI IV. 368[43] (B.C. 250–49) τὰ ἔρια . . ἄστατα, "wool not weighed," P Par 59[8] (B.C. 160) (= Witkowski[2], p. 76) ἐρείου (ἥμυσυ) (δραχμῶν) σ̄, P Ryl II. 138[22] (A.D. 34) ἐρίων σταθμία ῑε̄, "fifteen measures of wool," similarly *ib.* 146[15] (A.D. 39), P Oxy VI. 929[11] (ii/iii A.D.) λέντιον τριβακόν, καὶ ἔρια, "a worn towel, and some wool" (Edd.). In P Lond 402 *verso*[15] (an inventory—ii/B.C.) (= II. p. 11) ἐριᾶ (for ἐρεᾶ) ἐντυλή is apparently = "a woollen wrapper or rug." For the diminutive ἐρίδιον see P Meyer 20[36] (1st half iii/A.D.) χαλκὸν αὐτῷ οὐκ ἔδωκα τοῦ πόκου τῶν ἐρειδίω(ν), BGU III. 948[19] (iv/v A.D.) θέλησον [ο]ὖν υἱέ μου Θεόδουλε ἀγοράσιν μοι ϛ λι(τρὰς) ἐριδίου μελα̣νο̣]ς, and for a possible occurrence of ἐριουργός = "wool-worker," see P Ryl II. 94[14] (A.D. 14–37).

ἔρις.

As a new literary reference we may cite the Alexandrian Erotic Fragment P Grenf I. 1[21] (ii/B.C.) γίνωσκε (pap. γινωσχ΄) ὅτι θυμὸν ἀνίκητον ἔχω ὅταν ἔρις λάβῃ με, "know that I have a heart unconquerable when hate takes hold upon me." The word is used *in bonam partem* in *Kaibel* 142[4]—

    ἣ κάλλει ψ[υχῆς πᾶσιν ἔβαλ]λεν ἔριν

where the editor renders "*animi pulcritudine illa omnibus aemulandi studium iniecit.*"

ἐρίφιον.

This diminutive is found several times in P Thead 8[11 *al.*] (A.D. 306). For a good parallel to the usage in Lk 15[29], cf. P Hib I. 54[16] (*c.* B.C. 245), where in view of a coming festival, the recipient of the letter is asked—κόμισαι δὲ καὶ τὸν ἔριφον παρὰ Ἀριστίωνος καὶ πέμψον ἡμῖν. See also P Oxy II. 244[10] (A.D. 23) τοὺς ἐπακολουθοῦντας ἄρνας [κ]αὶ ἐρίφους, and P Strass I. 24[49] (a list of cattle—A.D. 118) πρόβ(ατα) χλᾱ καὶ αἶγες ὁ[μ]οίως τέλ(ειαι) ι ἔριφος ᾱ.

Ἑρμᾶς.

For the wide use of this proper name (cf. Rom 16[14]), see Rouffiac *Recherches*, p. 91, and add P Lond 1178[14] (A.D. 194) (= III. p. 216). Cf. Milligan *Documents*, p. 183 n[1].

ἑρμηνεία.

The Greek translation of a will originally written in Latin is headed—Ἑρμηνί[α διαθήκης (BGU I. 326[i. 1]—ii/A.D.). Attached to it is—Ἑρμηνία κωδικίλλων διπτύχων (*ib.* [ii. 19]). Cf. P Oxy XII. 1466[8] (A.D. 245) and P Thead 13[iii. 1] (A.D. 322 or 323), and see P Fay 23[11] (ii/A.D.) for an ἐπιτ(ηρητὴς) ἑρμηνίας. Vett. Val. p. 4[5] <ὃ> δὲ τοῦ Ἑρμοῦ σημαίνει παιδείαν, γράμματα, ἔλεγχον, λόγον, ἀδελφότητα, ἑρμηνείαν, κηρυκείαν κτλ. In the MGr Velvendos dialect ὁρμήνεια = "counsel," "advice."

ἑρμηνευτής.

We are unable to cite any instance of this word (as in 1 Cor 14[28] B) from the Κοινή, but for ἑρμηνεύς see P Oxy II. 237[vii. 37] (A.D. 186) where the presiding magistrate directs that a woman be asked "through an interpreter" what is her choice—ἐκέλευ[σε]ν δι' [ἑρ]μηνέως αὐτὴν ἐνεχθῆν[α]ι τί βούλεται : cf. BGU III. 985[10] (A.D. 124–5) μ[έ]τ[ρ]ῳ [ἐξα]-χοινίκῳ ἑρμηνέως Καρανίδος, similarly P Tebt II. 450 (A.D. 140–1 or 150–1), P Strass I. 41[36] (A.D. 250) δ[ι'] ἑρμηνέως, and P Oxy XII. 1517[6] (A.D. 272 or 278) where Θέων ἑρμηνεύς makes a payment for oil.

ἑρμηνεύω.

To the legal BGU I. 326, cited *s.v.* ἑρμηνεία, there is added the following official docket—[ii. 22] Γάϊος Λούκκιος Γεμινι(ανὸ)ς νομικὸς Ῥωμαϊκὸς ἡρμήνευσα τὸ προκείμενον ἀντίγραφον καί ἐστιν σύμφωνον τῇ αὐθεντικῇ διαθήκῃ. Cf. the fragment of an unknown Latin work, P Ryl II. 62 (iii/A.D.), which ends—Ὀλύμπ[ιος Ἰσ[ι]δωριανὸς [. . . . . .] ἑρμήνευσα ἀπὸ Ῥω[μα]ϊκῶν. The verb is used in a wider sense in BGU I. 140[20] (A.D. 201–2) τὸ αὐστηρότερον ὑπὸ τῶν πρὸ ἐμοῦ αὐτοκρατόρων σταθὲν φιλανθρωπότερ[ο]ν ἑρμηνεύω : cf. Lk 24[27] D. MGr = "explain," "comment upon."

Ἑρμῆς.

P Oxy VI. 886 (iii/A.D.) (= *Selections*, p. 110 f.) contains a magical formula, purporting to be derived from a sacred book ἐν τοῖς τοῦ Ἑρμοῦ ταμίοις, while the method employed is concerned with the 29 letters, which were used by Hermes and by Isis, when she was seeking her brother and husband Osiris—δι' ὧν ὁ Ἑρμῆς κὲ ἡ Ἴσις ζητοῦσα ἑαυτῆς τὸν ἀδελφὸν κὲ ἄνδρα Ὄσιρειν. In the curious astrological dialogue, P Ryl II. 63[5] (iii/A.D.), in which various parts of the body are connected with the sun, moon, planets, etc., the tongue, smell, and hearing belong to Hermes—Ἑρ]μοῦ γλῶσσα ὄσφρησις ἀκοή. For Ἑρμῆς as the name of a man, as in Rom 16[15], see *OGIS* 507[4] Διὶ Ἡλιοπολίτῃ παρὰ Ἑρμοῦ with the editor's note; also *Syll* 753[2] (not older than A.D. 213) and the other exx. in Rouffiac *Recherches*, p. 91.

Ἑρμογένης.

For this proper name, as in 2 Tim 1[15], see *Michel* 307[1,29] (1st half ii/B.C.) and *ib.* 1211[1,5] (i/B.C. ?). The latter inscr. may be recorded in full—Μηνὶ Ἀξιοττηνῷ. Ἐπεὶ Ἑρμογένης Γλύκωνος καὶ Νιτωνὶς Φιλοξένου ἐλοιδόρησαν Ἀρτεμίδωρον περὶ οἴνου· Ἀρτεμί(δ)ωρος πιττάκιον ἔδωκεν· Ὁ θεὸς ἐκολάσετο τὸν Ἑρμογένην· καὶ ἐλάσετο τὸν θεόν, καὶ ἀπὸ νῦν· εὐδοξεῖ.

ἑρπετόν.

In the vi/A.D. Gnostic amulet, P Oxy VII. 1060[7], we have the petition—ἀπάλλαξον τὸν οἶκον τούτου ἀπὸ παντὸς κακοῦ ἑρπετοῦ καὶ πράγματος ταχὺ ταχύ, "free this house with all speed from every evil reptile and thing." See also *Kaibel* 1033[17] (iii/B.C.)—

> ἑρπέθ' ἅμ' αὐτῶι
> ...... τὰ] θεοὶ στυγέουσι βροτοί τε.

ἐρυθρός.

OGIS 69 is a dedicatory tablet erected θεοῖς μεγάλοις Σαμοθρᾳξι by a certain Apollonius—σωθεὶς ἐγ μεγάλων κινδύνων ἐκπλεύσας ἐκ τῆς Ἐρυθρᾶς θαλάσσης, where the editor considers that the Arabian Gulf is referred to; cf. *ib.* 186[6] (B.C. 62) στρατηγὸς τῆς Ἰνδικῆς καὶ Ἐρυθρᾶς θαλάσσης, 199[25] (vi/A.D.) πέραν δὲ τῆς Ἐρυθρᾶς θαλάσσης οἰκοῦντας Ἀρραβίτας, and P Ryl II. 66 (late ii/B.C.) a petition addressed στρατη]γῷ Ἐρυθρᾶ[ς θαλάσσης. For the adj. ἐρυθρίας, "of ruddy complexion," cf. the description of a certain Euphronius in P Petr III. 13(a)[26] (B.C. 235) (as amended p. ix.)—εὐμεγέθ]ης ἐρυθρία[ς ἐ]πίγρυπος, and for the verb in its derived sense, as in Tob 2[14], cf. P Tebt I. 37[19] (B.C. 73) μεγάλως ἠρυθρίακε, "he has become much ashamed" (Edd.).

ἔρχομαι.

P Fay 123[15] (c. A.D. 100) ἐλήλυθεν γὰρ Τεύφιλος Ἰουδαῖος λέγων [ὅ]τι ἤχθην ἰς γεωργίαν, "Teuphilus the Jew has come saying, 'I have been pressed in as a cultivator'" (Edd.) will serve as an instance of the ordinary use of this very common verb; the mention of the Jew Teuphilus (or Theophilus) is interesting. A few miscellaneous exx. may be added which illustrate NT constructions or phrases—with Jn 5[24] cf. P Lond 42[17] (B.C. 168) (= I. p. 30, *Selections*, p. 10) εἰς πᾶν τι ἐληλυθυῖα διὰ τὴν τοῦ σίτου τιμήν, "having come to the last extremity because of the high price of corn," P Vat A[12] (B.C. 168) (= Witkowski[2], p. 65) τοῦ παιδίου σου εἰς τὰ ἔσχατα ἐληλυθότος, P Flor II. 212[3] (A.D. 254) εἰς τοσαύτην ἀτυχίαν ἦλθες ... ὡς μὴ ἔχειν σε ἀρτά[β]ην μίαν λωτίνου: with Jn 9[39] cf. P Tor I. 1[ii,29] (B.C. 116) ἔρχεσθαι ἐπὶ τὸ κριτήριον: with Jn 18[4] cf. the late P Iand I. 21[2] (vi/vii A.D.) ἡμῶν τὰ ἐρχόμεν[α ο]ὐκ οἴδ[α: with Rev 2[5,16] cf. BGU IV. 1041[16] (ii/A.D.) ὅτι

ἔρχομαί σοι, unfortunately in a somewhat obscure context (Aesch. *Prom. Vinct.* 358 ἀλλ' ἦλθεν αὐτῷ Ζηνὸς ἄγρυπνον βέλος is a classical parallel to the construction); and with 1 Cor 11[23] cf. P Tebt II. 416[20] (iii/A.D.) ποίησον αὐτῆς τὴν χρίαν ἕως ἔλθω, "supply her needs until I come." *Preisigke* 1142 Μηνόφιλος ἐλθών (a wall-scratching from El-Amarna) shows ἐλθών used like ἥκω (cf. *ib.* 1143) of a worshipper (cf. Jn 6[37]).

The intermediate form in which 1st aor. terminations are attached to the 2nd aor. appears in BGU II. 530[11] (i/A.D.) οὔτε ἀντέγραψας οὔτε ἦλθας (other exx. in Deissmann *BS*, p. 191). For the perf. and aor. used together (see *Proleg.* p. 142 f.) cf. BGU I. 27[6] (ii/A.D.) εἰς γῆν ἐλήλυθα τῇ ϛ τοῦ Ἐπεὶφ μηνός, καὶ ἐξε[κ]ένωσα μὲν τῇ ιη τοῦ αὐτοῦ μηνός.

ἐρῶ.

For this fut. we may cite from P Oxy VI.—920[22] ii/iii A.D. ἐρεῖς δέ μοι ἐν τάχει περὶ τούτου, 932[3] (late ii A.D.) ἐρῖ σοι δὲ Ἀπολινάρις πῶς τὰ θέματα καὶ τὰ δημόσια· τὸ ὄνομα ὃ ἂν αὐτός σοι εἴπῃ. "Apolinarius will tell you how the deposits and public dues stand; the name will be that which he will tell you himself" (Edd.); and for the perf. *ib.* 940[3] (v/A.D.) ὡς ἀνωτέρω εἴρηται, "as stated above" (Edd.). Cf. εἶπον and λέγω.

ἐρωτάω

in the sense of "ask," "entreat," is so amply vouched for in the Κοινή that it is quite unnecessary to bring in the influence of the Heb. שָׁאַל (Grimm): cf. e.g. P Oxy II. 292[7] (c. A.D. 25 ἠρώτησα δὲ καὶ Ἑρμί[α]ν τὸν ἀδελφὸν διὰ γραπτοῦ ἀνηγεί[σθαι] σοι περὶ τούτου, P Ryl II. 229[5] (A.D. 38) ἐρωτῶ σε ἐκ παντὸς τρόπου εὐθέως μοι πέ[μ]ψαι τὰς ἄλλας ἀρτάβας] γ, and from the inscr. *Syll* 328[5] (B.C. 84) π]ρὸς ἐμὲ ἦλθ]εν ἐν Ἀπαμήᾳ ἠρώτησέν τε [ὅπως ἂν] ἐξουσίαν αὐ[τ]ῷ [π]οιήσω ἐπὶ τοῦ συν[βο]υλίο[υ (where see Dittenberger's note). Ἐρωτηθείς = "being asked what your pleasure is" comes to mean "please," e.g. P Oxy II. 269[1] (A.D. 57) ἐὰν δύνῃ ἐρωτηθεὶς ὄχλησον Διόσκορον, "if you can, please worry Dioscorus" (Edd.): cf. Abbott *Joh. Gr.* p. 468. For the conjunction with παρακαλῶ, as in 1 Th 4[1], cf. P Oxy II. 294[28] (A.D. 22) ἐρωτῶ δέ σε καὶ παρακαλ[ῶ γρά]ψει μοι ἀντιφώνησιν περὶ τῶν γενομέν[ων: see further Milligan *Thess.* p. 46. On the relation of ἐρωτάω and αἰτέω in Jn 16[24], see *Proleg.* p. 66 n.[1], and cf. Field *Notes*, p. 101 f., and for an apparently exceptional (cf. Abbott *Joh. Gr.* p. 469 f.) instance of ἐρωτάω in the sense of Christian prayer for Christians see the inscr. from the Roman catacombs ΖΗCΗC ΕΝ ΚΩ ΚΑΙ ΕΡΩΤΑ ΥΠΕΡ ΗΜΩΝ (Northcote and Brownlow *Roma Sotterranea*, ii. p. 159) cited by Westcott *ad* 1 Jn 5[16]. In MGr ἐρωτῶ may expand to ἐρωτάγω or contract to ῥωτῶ: a form ἀρωτῶ is also found.

ἐσθής.

P Oxy III. 471[131] (ii/A.D.) ἐν λευκαῖς ἐσθῆσιν, P Ryl II. 116[15] (A.D. 104) τὴν ἐσθῆτά μου περιέσχισαν, P Thead 40[4] (A.D. 307-324?) ἐσθῆτα στρατιωτικήν, BGU I. 21[iii,6] (iv/A.D.) ἐσθῆτος, P Oxy XII. 1428[9] (iv/A.D.) τὴν ἐσθῆτα ἀνεπι[κλή]τοις τοῖς ὑφάσμασιν κατασκευάσαι, "to manufacture the clothing in irreproachable (?) materials" (Edd.),

OGIS 383¹³⁵ (inscr. of Antiochus I. of Commagene—i/B.C.) κόσμον Περσικῆς ἐσθῆτος ἀ[ν]αλαμβάνων (see *s.v.* ἀναλαμβάνω). In *Syll* 817⁷ we have ἐσθ[ῆ]ν τετιμημένην διακοσίων δραχμῶν, where Dittenberger remarks that this form of the acc. is not found elsewhere, but refers to Meyer *Gr.*³ p. 427: for the ordinary form, in addition to the exx. cited above, see *Michel* 833⁶² (B.C. 279) ὁ κόσμος ὁ τοῦ ἀγάλματος τοῦ τὴν ἔρειαν ἐσθῆτα ἔχοντος.

ἔσθησις.

An interesting ex. of this somewhat rare word is found in BGU I. 16¹² (A.D. 159–160) (= *Selections*, p. 84) where a priest is informed against—ὡς κομῶντος [κ]αὶ χρω[μ]ένου ἐρεαῖς ἐσθήσεσι, "on the charge of letting his hair grow too long, and of wearing woollen garments": cf. Ac 1¹⁰.

ἐσθίω.

P Giss I. 80⁸ (ii/A.D.) τὰ [π]εριστερίδι[α καὶ ὁ]ρνυθάρια, ἃ οὐκ ἤωθα ἐσθεῖν (*l.* ἐσθίειν), πέμ[ψον . . . , *ib.*¹⁰ ὅσα ποτὲ οὐκ ἔφαγον παρὰ σοῦ ἀφοσεστια (*l.* ἀφέστια ?), P Oxy IX. 1185¹⁰ (*c.* A.D. 200) παῖδα τὸν μεικρὸν δεῖ ἄρτον ἐσθίειν, and *ib.* X. 1297¹⁹ (iv/A.D.) προ. εινάριον ἐλαίου, ἀνικαλύψαι (*l.* ἀνα-) αὐτὸν καὶ φάγαι, "a . . . of oil for you to uncover and eat"—so the editors, who for the form φάγαι compare P Tor I. 1 ᵛˑ²⁷ (B.C. 117) μετῆλθαι, BGU I. 250⁸ (time of Hadrian) ἐπενέγκαι. See also *Syll* 807¹³ (after A.D. 138) ἆραι κόκκους στροβίλου καὶ φαγεῖν μετὰ μέλιτος ἐπὶ τρεῖς ἡμέρας. On the constative force of φαγεῖν as distinguished from the durative ἐσθίειν cf. *Proleg.* p. 111, and for φάγομαι as an Hellenistic mixture of ἔδομαι and ἔφαγον cf. *ib.* p. 184 n³. MGr φαγί, "eating," "repast." Thumb (*Hellenismus*, p. 128 n.²) doubts the necessity of finding a Hebraism in ἐσθίειν ἀπό (Mk 7²⁸).

ἔσοπτρον.

CPR I. 27¹⁰ (A.D. 190) ἔσοπτρον δίπτυχον: cf. the restoration in *ib.* 21²⁰ (A.D. 230). In a list of articles of furniture in the fragmentary P Oxy VI. 978 (iii/A.D.) we find mention of an ὅσοπτρον (*l.* ἔσοπτρον), and in a return of temple property, P Oxy XII. 1449¹⁹ (A.D. 213–7), of ὅσυπτρον (*l.* ἔσοπτρον) ἀργ(υροῦν) π[αιδικ όν), "a silver mirror for a child."

ἑσπέρα.

With Lk 24²⁹ cf. P Par 69ᶜˑ⁴ (A.D. 233) πράξας περὶ ἑσπέραν. The word is found in the fragment of a lost Gospel P Oxy IV. 655² ἀφ' ἑσπ[έρας ἕως π]ρωί. In *ib.* VIII. 1163² (v/A.D.) it refers to locality—τῇ τετράδι καταλαβὼν εἰς ἑσπέραν τὴν Δαρνιτῶν, "I arrived on the 4th at the western border of Darne" (Ed.): cf. *Preisigke* 4651¹¹ (A.D. 250–1) καθ' [ἑ]σπέ[ρ]αν οἰκίας. For the rough, instead of the smooth, breathing taking the place of an original simple *F* see Brugmann-Thumb, p. 52. MGr σπέρα.

ἑσπερινός.

For this adj., as in Lk 12³⁸ D, cf. P Oxy VI. 901⁵ A.D. 336 ἑσπερινὲς ὥρες (*l.* ἑσπεριναῖς ὥραις) τῇ χθὲς ἡμέρᾳ, "in the evening time of yesterday," BGU IV. 1024 ᵛⁱˑ⁶ (iv/v A.D.) κατὰ τὰς [ἑ]σπερινὰς ὥρας.

ἔσχατος.

For ἔ. with reference to *time* cf. P Oxy II. 280¹⁴ (A.D. 88–9) ἐν δὲ τῷ ἐσχάτῳ ἐνιαυτῷ, P Tebt II. 375²⁰ (A.D. 140) τῷ δὲ πέμπτο (*l.*—τῳ) ἔτι (*l.* ἔτει) ὅ ἐστιν ἔσχατον ἔτος τῆς μισθώσεως. See also BGU IV. 1024ⁱᵛˑ¹³ (iv/v A.D.) τῆς ἐσχάτης ἐλπίδας (*l.*—ος) ἀποστε[ρ]ῆσαι, and from the inscr. *Michel* 326² (ii/B.C.) τῆς ἐσχάτης τοῦ βίου τε[λ]ευτῆς. With τὰ ἔσχατα in Mt 12⁴⁵ *al.*, cf. P Vat A¹² (B.C. 168) (= Witkowski³, p. 65) τοῦ παιδίου σου εἰς τὰ ἔσχατα ἐληλυθότος. *Michel* 394³⁴ (mid. i/B.C.) τῆς πόλ[ε]ως ἐν τοῖς ἐσχάτοις ὑπαρχούσης κινδύνοις supports Hort's rendering of ἐν καιρῷ ἐσχάτῳ in 1 Pet 1⁵ "in a season of extremity," "when things are at their worst," for which he adduces various classical exx. For the adverbial ἔσχατον, as in 1 Cor 15⁸, see P Oxy VI. 886²¹ (iii/A.D.) (= *Selections*, p. 112) τὸ δὲ ὑπολιπό[μ]ενον ἔσχατον ἀνάγνωτι (*l.*—θι), *Syll* 879¹¹ (end of iii/B.C.) ἐπιτελεῖν δὲ τὰ νόμιμα τοῖς ἀποιχομένοις ἔσχατον ἐν τρισὶ μησίν.

ἐσχάτως.

The phrase ἐσχάτως ἔχειν, which in the NT occurs only in Mk 5²³, is censured by the Atticists, see Lobeck *Phryn.* p. 389, Rutherford *NP* p. 481. For other exx. of the intrans. use of ἔχω with an adv., see *s.v.* ἔχω.

ἔσω.

P Par 41¹⁷ (B.C. 160) ἐμοῦ δὲ καθημένου ἔσω ἐν τῷ παστοφορίῳ, BGU IV. 1127⁹ (B.C. 18) ἐν τῷ ἔσῳ κύκλωι, *Syll* 574² (ii/B.C.) τὸ τέμενος τῆς ['Αρτέμιδος ἀσυλον] πᾶν, ὅσον ἔσω π[εριβόλου, and the early Christian letter P Grenf II. 73⁹ (late iii/A.D.) (= *Selections*, p. 118) where the gravediggers bring the banished Politike—εἰς τὸ ἐγώ, evidently a mistake for εἰς τὸ ἔσω, "into the interior." The form εἴσω is found in the grave-inscription, *Archiv* i. p. 220 No. 2⁶ (B.C. 145–116)—

> εὔνοια γάρ μιν
> βαῖνε καὶ εἴσω γᾶς ἄχρι καὶ ὠκεανόν.

See also P Giss *Inv.* 137⁶ (= *Archiv* v. p. 137) εἴσω ἡμερῶν εἴκοσι.

ἔσωθεν.

P Oxy XII. 1449¹⁴ (Return of Temple Property—A.D. 213–7) λαμπ(ὰς) σὺν ζῳδίῳ Κόρης ἀργυρῷ ἀσήμ ῳ) ὁλκ ῆς) λί(τρας ᾱ ἔσωθ(εν) ξυλ(ίνη), "a lamp with a small figure of Core in unstamped silver weighing 1 lb., the interior being of wood" (Edd.). With the use in Mt 7¹⁵ cf. Epict. ii. S. 14 αὐτοῦ δὲ τοῦ θεοῦ παρόντος ἔσωθεν.

ἐσώτερος.

See the quotation from P Magd 29 *s.v.* ἀπορρίπτω.

ἕταιρος.

We are unable to quote any instance of this word, which in the NT is confined to the First Gospel (cf. Ev. Petr. 7), from the papyri, but it is by no means infrequent in the inscrr., e.g. *Syll* 365¹ (*c.* A.D. 37) συντρόφους καὶ ἑταίρους ἑαυτῶι γεγονότας, *OGIS* 573¹ (i/A.D.) ἔδοξε τοῖς ἑταίροις καὶ Σαββατισταῖς θεοῦ [εὐν]οίαι Σαββατιστοῦ συνηγμένοις. Cf. Vett. Val. p. 331¹³ ὅπως διὰ τούτων οἱ ἀμαθεῖς καὶ θεομάχοι πίστιν ἐνεγκάμενοι καὶ ἑταῖροί γε τῆς ἀληθείας γενόμενοι

ὑπαρκτὴν καὶ σεβάσμιον τὴν ἐπιστήμην καταλάβωσιν.
Aphaeresis is seen in MGr ταίρι, "pair," "mate."

ἑτερόγλωσσος.

With this compound (I Cor 14²¹) cf. the similarly formed ἑτερογνώμων, e.g. Vett. Val. p. 79¹³ οὗτοι γάρ εἰσι ἑτερογνώμονες τόποι αἰτίας ἐπάγοντες καὶ καθαιρέσεις.

ἑτεροζυγέω.

For the use of the corr. adj. in the LXX (Lev 19¹⁹) Herwerden *Lex. s.v.* compares Philo *Princ.* II *init.* (= II. p. 369 ed. Mangey) κτήνη ἑτερόζυγα.

ἕτερος

and ἀμφότεροι are claimed by Blass (*Gr.* pp. 36, 179 f.) as the only surviving words in the Hellenistic age which denote *duality* as distinct from plurality, and abundant evidence can be cited from the Κοινή of the correct use of ἕτερος in this sense. See e.g. P Ryl II. 229⁶ (A.D. 38) ἵνα δοῖ σοι ὄνον . . ἵνα καὶ αὐτὸς δοῖ ἑτέραν (a *second* ass), P Amh II. 65⁸ᶠᶠ. (early ii/A.D.) δίκαιον τὸν ἕτερον ἀπολυθῆναι ἐὰν ἄλλος ἀντ' αὐτοῦ κατασταθῇ, "it is just that one of them (*sc.* two brothers) should be released, if some one else is appointed in his stead" (Edd.), BGU I. 5ⁱⁱ ⁵ (A.D. 79–80) ἕτερον εἶναι ὁμώνυμο(ν), "another of the same name," P Fay 100⁸ (A.D. 99) τ[ῇ] μὲν Χαριτίῳ . . [τ]ῇ δὲ ἑτέρᾳ Χαριτίῳ, with reference to two women, both named Charition, CPR I. 11⁸ (A.D. 108) ἑτέρας . . οἰκίας, *ib.* 223¹⁹ (ii/A.D.) μέχρι [ἑ]τέρας ἀπογραφῆς, "until the next (lit. "another") census," P Tebt II. 381⁹ (A.D. 123) ἑτέρας θυγατρός, "her other daughter," P Amh II. 88⁹ᶠᶠ. (A.D. 128) ἐν δυσὶ κοίταις (here = σφραγῖσι, "parcels") . . ὧν μιᾶς μὲν . . ἑτέρας δὲ . ., BGU I. 194¹⁵ᶠ (A.D. 177) ἐπιστολῶν δύο, μειᾶς μὲν . . τὴν δὲ ἑτέραν . . P Fay 164 (ii/A.D.) ἐπὶ ὄνῳ ἑνὶ φοι(νίκων) ἀρτάβας τρεῖς καὶ ἐφ' ἑτ(έρῳ) . . (ἀρτάβας) δύο, and similarly *ib.* 165. On the other hand, ἕτερος is incorrectly used for ἄλλος in such passages as P Leid Bⁱⁱ·ⁱⁱ (B.C. 164) ὑπὲρ ὧν ἂν προσδεώμεθα ἑτέρων, P Par 45⁵ (B.C. 153) (= Witkowski,² p. 82) ἡ (= εἰ) ἕτερον θέλις λέγειν, λέγε, *ib.* 46⁹ (B.C. 153) (= Witkowski², p. 86) οὐ]χ ἕτερόν τινα, ἀλλὰ σὲ αὐτὸν μάρτυρα ἐπισπάσῳ, P Fay 12¹⁴ (*c.* B.C. 103) ἑτέρους συμπαρόντας ὑπό τε τῶν α[ὐτῶν, "others besides themselves being present" (Edd.), *ib.* 36¹¹ (A.D. 111–2) ἑτέροις ἐπιχωρηθεὶς διδόναι, "with power to pass on the right (of making and selling bricks) to others" (Edd.), P Flor I. 99⁷ (i/ii A.D.) (= *Selections*, p. 71) ὁ υἱὸς ἡμῶν Κάστωρ μεθ' ἑτέρων ἀσωτευόμενος ἐσπάνισε τὰ αὐτοῦ πάντα, "my son Castor along with others has squandered all his own property in riotous living," and BGU I. 86²⁵ (i²/A.D.) ὑποτίθεσθα[ι] ἑτέροις παρασ[υ]νχωρούντω[ν, a formula allowing liberty to alienate. Cf. Lk 8⁶ᶠᶠ. where even the stylist Luke substitutes ἕτερος for the correct ἄλλος of his (presumed) source-narrative (Mk 4⁵ᶠᶠ.: cf. Mt 13⁵ᶠᶠ.): see *Proleg.* p. 79. The opposite error of using ἄλλος for ἕτερος in Lk 6²⁹ (so Mt 5³⁹) may be paralleled from P Grenf II. 23ᵃ·ᶠ· (B.C. 107) τῆς μὲν μιᾶς . . τῆς δ' ἄλλης . ., P Tor II. 8⁴⁴ᶠ· (ii/B.C.) υἱῶν δύο, ἑνὸς μὲν . . ἄλλου, BGU II. 456¹⁰ᶠᶠ (A.D. 348) φοίνικας δύο, τὸν μὲν ἕνα . . καὶ τὸν

ἄλλον . ., and the Andanian inscr. *Syll* 653,⁹¹ (B.C. 91) τὸν μὲν ἕνα . . τὸν δ' ἄλλον of *two*. The readiness with which the two words could be interchanged is shown by P Oxy II. 276¹¹ (A.D. 77) Φρίβι Ἡρακλήου τῷ σὺν ἄλλοις σιτολόγοις compared with P Gen I. 36¹⁰ (A.D. 170) παρὰ Πεκύσιος Σαταβοῦτος ἱερέως σὺν ἑτέροις ἱερεῦ[σ]ι. Nor is it easy to differentiate them in such passages as CPR I. 103²¹ ἀπό τε ἄλλων πρασέων ἢ ἑτέρων [οἰκονομιῶν : cf. *ib.* 3¹⁹ (ii/iii A.D.), 6¹⁷ (A.D. 238). That however the original difference between them was often observed with great nicety even in vernacular documents is shown by the Twins' petition P Par 26³²ᶠ· (B.C. 163–2) (= *Selections*, p. 16 f.; the note on l. 33 requires correction) where ἄλλοι τῶν ἐκ τοῦ Σαραπιείου (to which the Twins themselves belonged) are distinguished from ἕτεροι τῶν ἐκ τοῦ Ἀσκληπιείου, and P Ryl II. 102ⁱ·¹⁰·¹⁴ (2nd half ii/A.D.) μετ' ἄλ(λων) . . μεθ' ἕτερα, where, as the editors point out, the former phrase introduces extracts from the original census-lists, while the second points to details that had been omitted. Other exx. showing how readily ἕτερος from meaning "the other class (of two)" came to imply "different" in quality or kind are *OGIS* 458⁸ (*c.* B.C. 9) ἑτέραν τε ἔδωκεν παντὶ τῶι κόσμωι ὄψιν, and P Oxy VI. 939¹⁸ (iv/A.D.) ἕτερα . . γράμματα, where the reference is not only to "another," a second letter, but to a letter containing very "different" news from that previously despatched. Ἕτερος is used without a subst. in P Tebt II. 381¹⁴ (A.D. 123) (= *Selections*, p. 78) ἕτερα καθ' ὃν δήποτε οὖν τρόπον, "other things of whatsoever kind," following a list of articles bequeathed in a will, P Flor I. 99¹⁰ (i/ii A.D.) (= *Selections*, p. 72) ἕτερο[ν] ἄτοπόν τι, "anything else amiss," and CPR I. 32¹⁵ (A.D. 218) οὐδὲν δὲ ἕτερον πραχθησόμεθα (cf. Ac 17²¹). An interesting confirmation of the RV rendering of Lk 23³² ἕτεροι κακοῦργοι δύο, "two others, malefactors" is afforded by P Tebt I. 41⁹ (a petition—*c.* B.C. 119) καὶ [μ]ετὰ τοῦ παντὸς σκυλμοῦ συνεχεῖς ἐπιλήψεις ποιουμένων τινῶν ἡμῶν καὶ ἑτέρων γυναικῶν διασείειν, "to extort from some of us and from others, viz. women"—the petitioners are men.

According to Lightfoot (*Gal.*¹⁰, p. 76) the primary distinction between ἄλλος and ἕτερος is that the former is another "as one besides," and the latter another as "one of two." But Ramsay in an important discussion on Gal 1⁶·ᶠ· (*Comm.* p. 260 ff.) contends that this reverses the facts regarding the force of the two words when they are pointedly contrasted. In Gal *l.c.* he has now definitely adopted the construction given by the American Revisers in the margin ("a different gospel, which is nothing else save that there are some that trouble you"), and agrees with the opinion expressed by Professor A. W. Mair who has supplied a long list of passages from Demosthenes and others, showing that any distinction in usage between the two words results naturally from the fact that one is a positive, or absolute, word (ἄλλος), while the other is a comparative, or relative (ἕτερος), and further that, where this is not essential, they are used indifferently: see e.g. Demosthenes xxiii. 71 (ed. Butcher) οὔτ' ἄλλος οὐδείς, but xxv. 17 ἕτερος δ' οὐδὲ εἷς.

ἑτέρως.

Syll 406¹⁰ (A.D. 147) εἰ καὶ ἑτέρως τοῦτο ἀπέβη.

ἔτι.

P Lond 42²² (B.C. 168) (= I. p. 30, *Selections*, p. 10) ὡς ἔτ[ι] σοῦ παρ[όν]τος πάντων ἐπεδεόμην, "while you were still at home, I went short altogether." In *ib.* ²⁵ we have—ἔτι δὲ καὶ Ὥρου τοῦ τὴν ἐπιστολὴν παρακεκομικό[το]ς ἀπηγγελκότος κτλ., "and now that Horus who brought the letter has told" etc.: cf. P Ryl II. 145⁹ (A.D. 38) ἔτι καὶ μὴ ἀρκ[εσ]θείς. P Oxy IV. 744³ (B.C. 1) (= *Selections*, p. 32) shows a common phrase γίνωσκε ὡς ἔτι καὶ νῦν ἐν Ἀλεξανδρεία (*l.* -δρείᾳ) σμὲν (*l.* ἐσμέν): cf. P Hib I. 46¹⁶ (B.C. 258) ἔτι οὖν καὶ νῦν ἢ τὸ ἀργύριον εἰσάγετε ἢ κτλ, "now therefore at length either collect the money, or," etc., Revillout *Mél.* p. 295⁶ (B.C. 131-0) (= Witkowski², p. 96) ἔτι καὶ νῦν καλῶς ποιήσεις παρακαλῶν σαυτὸν καὶ τοὺς παρ' ἡμῶν. P Oxy VIII. 1111 ⁱⁱ ¹³ (A.D. 203) ὃν δηλ(ῶ) τετελ(ευτηκέναι) ἔτι πάλα[ι]. "whom I declare to have died long ago." For the adv. used of *degree*, as in Phil 1⁹, see the Christian letter *ib.* VI. 939³ (iv/A.D.) (= *Selections*, p. 128) νῦν ἔτι μᾶλλον ἡ πρὸς σὲ [τοῦ δεσπό]του θεοῦ γνῶσις ἀνεφάνη ἅπασιν ἡμῖν.

ἑτοιμάζω.

P Petr II. 40(a)¹⁵ (iii/B.C.) (= Witkowski², p. 41) ἑτοιμάζεται γὰρ ἡ διαδοχή. "the relief is being equipped," P Lille I. 20⁴ (iii/B.C.) τὴν δὲ λοιπὴν γ[ῆ]ν ἑτο[ι]μάζω, of preparing land by cultivation, PSI IV. 434¹⁷ (B.C. 261-0) ἑτοιμάζονται θηρεύειν, P Hib I. 47²³ (B.C. 256) καὶ ὄλυραν δὲ κ[αὶ κρ]ιθὴν ἑτοίμαζε ἵνα [παραμ]ετρήσωμεν εἰς τὸ βασιλικόν, "prepare both olyra and barley in order that we may measure it to the State" (Edd.). The verb is almost a *t.t.* for preparations in view of an approaching visit, e.g. P Tebt II. 592 (iii/A.D.) ἐπισ[τολ]ήν σοι ἔπεμψα ὡς σοῦ ταχὺ ἐρχομέν[ο]υ καὶ ἑτοιμάκιν (*l.* ἡτοιμάκειν) σοι πάντα, P Oxy X. 1299⁹ (iv/A.D.) ἑτυμάσο αὐτῶ (*l.* ἑτοιμάσω αὐτὸ) ἕως ἔρχῃ, "I will prepare it for your coming" (Edd.), *ib.* XII. 1490⁷ (late iii/A.D.) ἐπίστειλον τί θέλεις ἑτοιμασθῆναι, "give instructions as to what preparations you wish to be made" (Edd.): cf. Philem 22. We have an instance of dropped augment in P Grenf II. 14(b)¹ (B.C. 264 or 227) ἑτοιμάκαμεν ἐπὶ τὴν παρουσίαν τὴν Χρυσίππου: in BGU III. 830¹⁸ (i/A.D.) χρ]ὴ οὖν ἑτοιμάσ[ε]ιν καὶ προαιρ[εῖ]ν, we should have expected either the pres. or aor. inf. for the future. The verb is current in MGr.

ἑτοιμασία.

BGU II. 625¹⁷ (ii/iii A.D.) ἕως ὅτου ἡ ἑτυμασί[α] (*l.* ἑτοιμασία) γένηται μετὰ τὴν κατασπορὰν καὶ εὐσκοληθῆς (*l.* εὐσχοληθῆς), CP Herm I. 95²⁰ πρὸ ἑτοιμασίας. With the Pauline passage Eph 6¹⁵ cf. M. Anton. iv. 12 δύο ταύτας ἑτοιμότητας ἔχειν ἀεὶ δεῖ, where Crossley, comparing *ib.* iii. 13, regards ἑτοιμότητας as meaning δόγματα ἕτοιμα or πρόχειρα, and translates "have these two principles always at hand." In MGr the noun = "preparation," "equipment."

ἕτοιμος.

For ἕτοιμος applied to *things* cf. P Oxy II. 201¹¹ (A.D. 25-26) ἕτο[ι]μα ποίησον . . . σιτικὰ καὶ [ἀργυρικά], "prepare the statements of corn and money" (Edd.), P Flor III.

326¹⁰ (A.D. 117-8) τὰ ὑπογεγραμμένα ἐδάφη πάντα ποιῆσιν αὐλακίσεσθαι, ὥστε ἕτοιμα εἶναι πρὸς κατασποράν, and *ib.* II. 123⁴ (A.D. 254) ἐκ τῶν ἑτοιμοτέρων οἴνου μονόχωρα ἑκατόν, of wine ripe or ready for drinking. For the adj. applied to *persons* cf. P Hib I. 44⁷ (B.C. 253) τοὺς δὲ θεριστὰς ὡς ἂν ἑτοίμους ποιήσῃς ἐπίστειλον ἡμῖν, "as soon as you can get the harvesters ready let me know" (Edd.), BGU IV. 1209¹⁷ (B.C. 23) ἵνα πρὸς μὲν κατάπληξιν τῶν τολμησάντων ἔχωμεν α[ὐτο]ὺς ἑτοίμους πρὸς ἐντυχίαν, and P Tebt II. 410¹⁰ (iii A.D.) ἐὰν μὲν ἑτοίμη ἦν ἡ θυγάτηρ μου, ἀνερχέσθω διὰ τῆς ὄνου. For the phrase ἐν ἑτοίμῳ, as in 2 Cor 10⁶, see P Gen I. 76⁴ (iii/iv A.D.) τοὺς ἐργάτας ἐν ἑτοίμῳ ἐποίησα: cf. *Michel* 394¹³ (mid. i/B.C.) προθυμότατα ἔδωκεν ἐξ ἑτοίμου, "he gave most readily without hesitation." The word is MGr.

ἑτοίμως.

For the phrase ἑτοίμως ἔχω followed by the inf., as in Ac 21¹³, 2 Cor 12¹⁴, 1 Pet 4⁵, cf. P Amh II. 32⁸ (ii/B.C.) ἑτοίμως ἐχόντω[ν χειρο]γραφε[ῖ]ν τὸν βασιλικὸν ὅρκον, "being ready to subscribe the royal oath." BGU I. 86¹⁷ (A.D. 158-9) ἡ Σωτηρία ἑτοίμως ἔχουσα καταγράψαι, P Oxy XII. 1469²¹ (A.D. 298) ἡμῶν ἑτοίμ[ως] ἐχόντων ὅσαπερ ἄλλα ἡμῖν αἱρεῖ ἀπεργάσασθαι, and the late PSI I. 46⁴ (v/vi A.D.) ἑτύμως (*l.* ἑτοίμως) ἔχω λογίσασθαι. See also *Michel* 884²⁴ (B.C. 164-3) τῶν . . ἑτοίμως διδόντων, "those who give willingly."

ἔτος.

P Tebt II. 412³ (late ii/A.D.) ἄνελθε εἰς τὴν μητρόπολιν τοῦ νέου ἔτους, "come up to the metropolis at the New Year." For κατ' ἔτος, "yearly," as in Lk 2⁴¹, cf. P Amh II. 86¹¹ (A.D. 78) ἃς (*sc.* δραχμὰς) καὶ ἀπ[οδ]ώσω κατ' ἔτος ἐξενίαντα, the yearly charge was to be paid annually, P Oxy IV. 725³⁶ (a contract of apprenticeship—A.D. 183) ἀργήσει δὲ ὁ παῖς εἰς λόγον ἑορτῶν κατ' ἔτος ἡμέρας εἴκοσι, "the boy shall have 20 holidays in the year on account of festivals" (Edd.): for καθ' ἔτος see P Tebt II. 311²⁵ (A.D. 134), 373¹⁰·¹⁴ (A.D. 110-1), *al.* The aspirated form καθ' ἔτος is also fairly common, e.g. P Petr III. 19(e)³⁶ (B.C. 224) where the words καθ' ἔτος have been added above the line, and the editor explains the form as due to false analogy with καθ' ἡμέραν: see further Meyer *Gr.* p. 326 f., *Proleg.* p. 44. Καθ' ἔτος is read *quater* in P Ryl II. 166 (A.D. 26), and ἐφ' ἔτος in P Oxy X. 1299⁵ (iv/A.D.): cf. MGr (ἐ)φέτο(ς), "this year." In P Oxy III. 477⁵ (A.D. 132-3) τὸ [π]έμπτον ἔτ[ο]ς Δομιτιανοῦ, "in the fifth year of Domitian," we have a good ex. of the acc. denoting a point of time, as occasionally in the NT (Jn 4⁵², Ac 20¹⁶, Rev 3³): cf. *Proleg.* p. 63, *CR* xviii. p. 152. On the other hand, the instrumental dat. of extension of time (see *Proleg.* p. 75) may be illustrated by *Syll* 607²⁸ (iii/iv A.D.) ἐβ[ί]ωσεν) ὁ δ[ῆμος]· "πολλοῖς ἔτεσι τοὺς νεωκόρους," "Long live the temple-wardens," and by the iv/A.D. inscr. regarding a Lycaonian Bishop—¹² εἴκοσι πέντε ὅλοις ἔτεσιν τὴν ἐπισκοπὴν . . διοι[κ]ήσας (see *Exp.* VII. vi. p. 387).

A new adv. ἀνετεύτως is found joined with ζῆν, "to live for countless years," in an imprecatory tablet published by Wünsch in *Excavations in Palestine*, edd. Bliss and Macalister 1902, p. 176, No. 35².

εὖ

is rare in the papyri, having given place to **καλῶς**: cf. Mayser *Gr.* p. 459. It must, however, be kept in view that εὖ continues to recur in certain epistolary phrases, as in P Oxy X. 1292³ (c. A.D. 30) εὖ [π]οήσεις ἐμβαλόμενός μοι κενώματα διακ[ό]σια, "please put on board for me two hundred empty jars" (Edd.), *ib.* I. 115¹² (ii/A.D.) εὖ πράττετε, *ib.* III. 527⁹ (ii/iii A.D.) ἐρρῶσθ(αι) εὔχομ(αι) εὖ πράττοντ(α), "I pray for your health and prosperity" (Edd.), and in such closing adjurations as P Eleph 23¹⁶ (B.C. 223–2) ἐ[ὑ]ορκοῦ[ντι! μέμ μ[ο]ι [ε]ῦ εἴη, ἐφιορκοῦντι δὲ ἔνοχον εἶναι τῆι ἀσεβείαι τοῦ ὅρκου, P Ryl II. 108¹⁹ (A.D. 110–11) εὐορκοῦ[σι] μὲν ἡμεῖν εὖ ε[ἴ]η, [ἐπ]ι[ο]ρκοῦσι δὲ τ]ὰ ἐν[αν]τία, *et alibi.* The classical phrase εὖ γὰρ ἴσθι (cf. the simple ἴστε in Eph 5⁵, Heb 12¹⁷) is found in the touching letter of Epicurus to a child—εὖ γὰρ ἴσθι, ἡ αἰτία ὅτι καὶ ἐγὼ καὶ ο[ἱ] λοιποὶ πάντες σε μέγα φιλοῦμεν κτλ., "for be sure, the reason why I and all the others love you greatly," etc.: see *Selections*, p. 6.

εὐαγγελίζω.

For the rare use of the active of this verb, as in Rev 10⁷, 14⁶, we can now appeal not only to Dion Cass. lxi. 13. 4 where the reading is doubtful, but to P Giss I. 27⁶ (end of Trajan's reign or beginning of Hadrian's) (= *Chrest.* I. 17) where reference is made to the arrival from Memphis of a slave of the strategus Apollonius, announcing a victory he had gained—ἐρχομένῳ εὐαγγελίζοντι τὰ τῆς νείκης αὐτοῦ καὶ προκοπῆς. See also the Christian hymn of iv/A.D. P Amh I. 2¹⁶ παισὶν δ' [ε]ὐηγγέλιζε λέγων, Πτωχοὶ βασιλείαν . . . The literary and Biblical usage of the mid. is fully illustrated by Milligan *Thess.* p. 141 ff.: add for the former *Menandrea* p. 105⁶³ εὐ]αγγελίσασθαι πρ[ὸς] σὲ ταῦτ' ἐβουλόμην, and Longus *Daphnis and Chloe* iii. 33 τὸν γάμον εὐηγγελίζετο, "full of joy brings her the annunciation of the marriage" (Thornley).

εὐαγγέλιον.

For the very rare use of this word in the singular outside the NT and early Christian literature, see the iii/A.D. pap. letter cited *s.v.* γνῶστης *ad init.*, and cf. *Archiv* v. p. 406 f. The plur. is found = "good tidings" in the striking calendar inscr. from Priene of date about B.C. 9 with reference to the birthday of the Emperor Augustus—ἦρξεν δὲ τῶι κόσμωι τῶν δι' αὐτὸν εὐαγγελί[ων] ἡ γενέθλιος, "but the birthday of the god was for the world the beginning of tidings of joy on his account" (*OGIS* 458⁴⁰, Deissmann *LAE*, p. 370 f.) For the more ordinary usage = "sacrifices," "thank-offerings," cf. *OGIS* 4⁴² (iv/B.C.) εὐαγγέλια καὶ σωτήρια ἔ[θ]υσε, *Michel* 1325⁷ εὐαγγέλια θύσω, and the new literary instance in *Menandrea* p. 90⁴¹⁵. On the history of the word and its cognates, see Harnack *Constitution and Law*, p. 278 f., and Milligan *Thess.* p. 141 ff. MGr βαγγέλιο, "gospel."

Εὐάγγελος is found in the magical P Hawara 312 (possibly ii/A.D.) (= *Archiv* v. p. 393) which begins—'Εξορκείζ[ω] σε Εὐάγγελε κατὰ τοῦ 'Ανούβι<δο>ς κτλ., where Wünsch (p. 397) notes that "Εὐάγγελος muss ein übermenschliches, aber dem Anubis untergeordnetes Wesen sein." For the word as a proper name see also BGU II. 583¹ (before

A.D. 76), *ib.* III. 816⁶ (iii/A.D.), *al.*, and for a similar use of **Εὐαγγέλιος** see the vi/A.D. P Iand 51⁵ and P Oxy VI. 998.

εὐαγγελιστής.

H. Achelis (*ZNTW* i. p. 87 f.) finds a trace of early Christianity in the use of this word in an inscr. from the Greek islands edited by H. von Gaertringen (*IGInr* I. 1, No. 675⁶ (Rhodes) Δάφνας καὶ θεοῦ ἀρχιερεὺς . . . ΟΗΡΟΣ (= ὁ [ἱε]ρός, Kaibel) εὐαγγελιστής, but see, on the other hand, A. Dieterich (*ib.* p. 336 ff.) who reads ὁ ἥρως εὐαγγελιστής, and thinks that "the chief priest of Daphne and the god" is so described as the proclaimer of the oracular announcements. The word occurs in the Christian amulet P Oxy VIII. 1151¹⁵ (v/A.D. ?) with reference to the evangelist John—τοῦ ἁγίου καὶ ἐνδόξου ἀποστόλου κ[αὶ] εὐαγγελιστοῦ κ[αὶ] θεολόγου 'Ιωάννου: cf. CPR I. 30⁴ (vi/A.D.) τοῦ ἁγίου 'Ιωάννου τοῦ εὐλόγου καὶ εὐαγγελιστοῦ.

εὐαρεστέω.

This verb, which in the NT is confined to Heb, is found, if we can trust the restoration, in the marriage contract P Oxy II. 265¹³ (A.D. 81–95) καὶ εὐαρ[εστοῦμαι ?] τοῦ προγεγρα]μμέν[ο]υ μου ἀνδρός. Cf. the double compound in *Michel* 1001⁴ (c. B.C. 200) συνευαρεστούσας καὶ τὰς θυγατρὸς 'Επιτελείας τᾶς Φοίνικος.

εὐάρεστος.

To Deissmann's citation (*BS*, p. 215) of this word from an inscr. of Nisyros (pre-Christian ?) γενόμενον εὐάρεστον πᾶσι (*Mittheilungen des athen. Institute* 15, p. 134 D.5.) to dispose of Cremer's claim that it belongs only to Bibl. and eccles. Greek, we may add *Priene* 114¹⁸ (after B.C. 84) γενηθεὶς δὲ εὐάρεσ[τος] ἐν τοῖς τῆς γυμνασιαρχίας ἀναλώμασιν: cf. Rouffiac *Recherches*, p. 32 f. See also such passages as P Fay 90¹⁷ (A.D. 234) τὸ λ[α]χανόσπ(ερμον) λαμβάνιν εὐάρεστον, P Flor I. 30³⁰ (A.D. 362) τὰς τοῦ πύρου εὐαρέστου ἀρταβά]ς, P Strass I. 1⁹ (A.D. 510) ἐν οἴνω καλλίστω καὶ εὐαρέστω, and P Gen I. 15² (Byz.) τὴν τιμὴν σίτου εὐαρέστου ἀρταβῶν τεσσάρων, where the adj. has the meaning "choice," "in good condition." See also *s.v.* ἀρεστός.

εὐαρέστως.

CIG II. 2885²⁰ (pre-Christian) τελέσασα τὴν ὑδροφορίαν εὐαρέστως τοῖς πολείταις, *Syll* 325²⁰ (i/B.C.) ἱερησάμενος εὐαρέστως ὑπὸ πάντων ἐπηνήθη τῶν πολειτῶν.

εὐγενής.

For this adj. = "well born," "noble," see the striking interview with an Emperor described *s.v.* ἀγενής, where a certain Appianus appeals to his εὐγένεια, stating further that he is εὐγ[ενὴς καὶ γυμνασί]αρχος (P Oxy I. 33 iv.13.v.3—late ii/A.D.). So P Oxy IX. 1206¹¹ (A.D. 335) where stipulations are made regarding a son to be adopted that he is not to be disavowed or reduced to slavery—διὰ τὸ εὐγενῆ αὐτὸν εἶν[α]ι κ[αὶ] ἐξ εὐγενῶν γονέων ἐλευθέρων, "because he is well born and the son of well born and free parents" (Ed.), and PSI I. 41¹³ (iv/A.D.) where certain acts are described as ἃ μὴ τοῖς ε]ὐγενέσι πρέπι. For the comparative (as in Ac 17¹¹) see P Grenf I. 53³³ (iv/A.D.) (as revised *Chrest.* I. p. 155) ἐὰν ἦν δὲ ὀνομάζειν περὶ γένου (l. γένους), καὶ ταῦτα πάλιν φθάνομεν ἀποδείξειν, τίνος εὐγενό(= έ)στερός ἐστι. The adv. is found in P Lips I. 28¹⁸ (A.D. 381) where, again with reference to a case of adoption, we find—ὅνπερ θρέψω καὶ ἱματίζω (/. —ίσω) εὐγενῶς καὶ γνησίως ὡς υἱὸν γνήσιον καὶ φυσικὸν ὡς ἐξ ἐ[μ]οῦ γενόμενον: cf. ¹². For the subst. as a title of address, see P Gen. I. 50¹⁴ (iv/A.D.) γράφ[ω οὖν] τῇ εὐγ[ενε]ίᾳ σου ἵν[α κτλ., so ib. 55¹⁰. This usage survives in MGr— ἡ εὐγενεία σου, "your lordship" (Thumb Handbook § 130). Note also that in MGr vernacular εὐγενικός, "polite," has been formed beside the literary εὐγενής (ib. § 115).

εὐδία.

This originally poetical word (Thumb Dial. p. 373), which is rejected in the best texts of Mt 16², occurs on the Rosetta stone OGIS 90¹¹ (B.C. 196) καὶ δαπάνας πολλὰς ὑπομεμένηκεν ἕνεκα τοῦ τὴν Αἴγυπτον εἰς εὐδίαν ἀγαγεῖν, where Dittenberger notes that it is used metaphorically "de beato et tranquillo rerum publicarum statu": cf. Herodas i. 28, where amongst the glories of Egypt are mentioned— δύναμις, εὐδ[ί]η, δ]όξα, "power, peace, fame." For the literal sense cf. P Oxy IX. 1223¹² (late iv/A.D.) ἡ (/. εἰ) καὶ εὐδία ἐστὶ καὶ τὸ πλοῖον ἀνενέγκε οὐ δύναται ἐν τῇ σήμερον, "if it is calm weather and he cannot bring back the boat to-day" (Ed.).

εὐδοκέω.

It may be well to illustrate somewhat at length the different constructions of this characteristically Jewish Greek verb. In P Lond 3⁶ (B.C. 146 or 135) (= I. p. 46) ηὐδόκησάς με τῆς τιμ[ῆς τ]οῦ ἡμίσους τοῦ [τρί]του λογείας τῶν κειμένων νεκρῶν, the meaning apparently is, "you have granted me the honour of the half of the third offering collected for the dead (mummies)." The construction with the inf. to denote determination, as in Lk 12³², comes out in P Tebt II. 591 (ii/iii A.D.) ὅτι οὐκ εὐδόνηκα (/. ηὐδόκηκα) οὐδένα πέμψαι ἐκθὲς οὐδὲ σήμερον, and to denote readiness, as in 1 Th 2⁸, in P Grenf I. 1¹⁷ (ii/B.C.) εὐδοκῶ ζήλῳ δουλεύειν, "I have goodwill to serve thee zealously." For the constr. with the dat., which is found in the best texts of 2 Th 2¹², cf. the common legal phrase εὐδοκῶ πᾶσι τοῖς προγεγραμμένοις as in P Lond 1168¹⁵ (A.D. 18) (= III. p. 136), and such passages as P Oxy II. 261¹⁷ (A.D. 55) εὐδοκεῖ γὰρ τῇδε τῇ συστάσει, "for she gives her consent to this appointment," ib. IV. 725¹⁷ (A.D. 183) ὁ [δ]ὲ Ἡρακλᾶς εὐδοκῶν τούτοις πᾶσι, and ib. X. 1273⁴⁰ (A.D. 260) διὰ τὸ ἐντεῦθεν εὐδοκεῖν τῇ ἐσομένῃ δημοσιώσει, "because both sides now agree to the future publication" (Edd.), and for the constr. with ἐπί cf. P Oxy I. 94⁵ (A.D. 83) εὐδοκεῖν γὰρ αὐτὸν ἐπὶ τούτο[ι]ς, so ib. 97¹⁸ (A.D. 115–6), ib. IV. 726²² (A.D. 135), and P Tebt II. 317²³ (A.D. 174–5) εὐδοκῶ γὰρ ἐπὶ τούτοις ἵν[α] ᾖ, "for I consent to these provisions" (Edd.). We are unable to illustrate the Bibl. constr. with ἐν from our documents, but see Polyb. ii. 12. 3. The verb is used absolutely in P Ryl II. 155¹⁷ (A.D. 138–61) ε]ὐδοκῖν τὴν μητέρα Θασῆν, "her mother Thases approves": cf. such an attesting signature as ib. 120²⁴ (A.D. 167) Ἑρμεῖνος] Ἑρμέου εὐδοκῶ, and the phrase ἐξ εὐδοκούντων, "by consent" in P Tebt II. 382³ (B.C. 30–A.D. 1), al. See also the marriage-contract P Oxy III. 496⁸ (A.D. 127) where the husband is not allowed to dispose of certain property χωρὶς εὐδοκούσης

τῆς γαμουμένης, "without the consent of the bride": cf. Gradenwitz Einführung i. p. 160 ff. As showing the difficulty of getting an adequate translation for the verb, it may be mentioned that Plummer (2 Cor. p. 153) has pointed out that the Vg renders it in ten different ways in its fifteen occurrences in the Epp., and five different ways in the six occurrences in the Gospels, three of which differ from all the renderings in the Epp. On the derivation of εὐδοκέω straight from εὖ δοκεῖ, "it pleases me well," fused into a closer union by usage, see Moulton Gr. ii. § 109.

εὐδοκία

is apparently confined to Jewish and Christian literature (to the usual reff. add Pss Sol 3⁴, 8³⁹), but we can cite from our documents instances of the cognate noun εὐδόκησις, e.g. P Lond 289⁸⁵ (A.D. 91) (= II. p. 185) γεγωνεισμαι (/. γέγονε εἴς με) ἡ εὐδόκησις καθὼς προκῖται, P Oxy IX. 1200³⁵ (A.D. 266) οὐ προσδεόμενος ἑτέρας μου εὐδοκήσεως ἢ μεταλήμψεως, "without requiring any further consent or concurrence from me" (Ed.), and similarly ib. X. 1273³⁹ (A.D. 260). From the inscr. we may cite Syll 929¹⁰⁸ (B.C. 139?) ἔλαβον εὐδόκησιν, and OGIS 335¹²² (ii/B.C.) κατὰ τὴ[ν τοῦ δήμου ἐπιταγὴν καὶ τὴν βασιλέω]ς εὐδόκησιν. All these passages confirm the meaning "good pleasure," "good will," which εὐδοκία seems to have in all its NT occurrences, even in Rom 10¹. On the important Lk 2¹⁴ see Field Notes, p. 48 f., and for a defence of the reading of the TR and on εὐδοκία ἔμπροσθέν σου as "a common periphrasis to avoid the anthropomorphism involved in God's volition" see McNeile on Mt 11²⁶.

εὐεργεσία.

P Flor I. 61¹⁴ (A.D. 85) (= Chrest. II. p. 88) τῆς σῆς εὐεργεσίας δεόμενος ἐντυγχάνει σοι—an advocate addresses the prefect on behalf of his client, P Ryl II. 96¹⁰ (A.D. 117–18) κατὰ τὴν εὐεργεσίαν τοῦ κυρίου ἡμῶν Ἀδριανοῦ Καίσαρος, P Oxy VI. 899¹⁹ (A.D. 200) διὰ τὴν ἔμφυτόν σου εὐεργεσίαν, P Fay 20¹⁶ (iii/iv A.D.) πλὴν μᾶλλον φιλανθρωπίᾳ τε καὶ εὐεργεσίαις συναύξειν ταύτην τὴν ἀρχήν, "but rather by liberality and the conferring of benefits to increase the welfare of this empire" (Edd.), and BGU III. 970⁹ (ii/A.D.) τῆς εἰς ἅπαντας εὐεργεσίας . . ἀβοήθητος, where note the gen. after a negative adj. (cf. Proleg. p. 74). Add from the inscrr. Michel 383¹⁵ (ii/B C.) ἀρετῆ[ς ἕν]εκεν καὶ εὐνοίας καὶ εὐεργεσίας τῆς εἰς [τὸ]ν δῆμον, ib. 965² (ii/B.C. ad init.) διὰ ταῦτα καὶ τὰς ἄλλας εὐεργεσίας ἃς πο[ιῶν διατελεῖ τὸν δῆμον, et alibi.

εὐεργετέω.

Michel 468¹⁴ (mid. ii/B.C.) ἵνα οὖν καὶ ὁ δῆμος φαίνηται χάριν ἀποδιδοὺς τοῖς εὐεργετοῦσιν αὐτόν, Priene 105⁴⁶ (c. B.C. 9) εὑ[ρήμασιν ἰδί]οις εὐεργέτησεν (for form, cf. Wisd 11⁵) τὴν ἐπαρχήαν. In OGIS 666² (A.D. 54–68) an Egyptian inscr. records how the Emperor Nero—ὁ ἀγαθὸς δαίμων τῆς οἰκουμένης, σὺν ἅπασιν οἷς εὐεργέτησεν ἀγαθοῖς τὴν Αἴγυπτον . . . ἔπεμψεν ἡμεῖν Τιβέριον Κλαύδιον Βάλβιλλον ἡγεμόνα, after which the inscr. mentions this man's χάριτας καὶ εὐεργεσίας: cf. also Cagnat IV. 852 Ἀνίκιον Ἄσπρον, τὸν ὑπατικὸν καὶ κτίστην, ἀνθ᾽ ὧν εὐεργέτηται ἀνέθ.ηκαν). From the papyri cf. such a passage as P Ryl II. 119⁶ (A.D. 54–67) ὧν χάριν ἀξιοῦμεν περὶ πάντων τούτων διαλαβεῖν ὅπως τύχωμεν τῶν παρὰ σοῦ δικαίων καὶ ὦμεν εὐεργετημένοι, "therefore we beg you to give a decision on all these points, so that we may obtain our rights from you and be relieved" (Edd.). The phrase ἵν' ὦμεν εὐεργετημένοι is very common at the close of petitions, as in P Tebt II. 302³¹ (A.D. 71–2), 326¹⁶ (c. A.D. 266) ἠυεργετημένοι, al. See also P Thead 20¹⁵ (iv/A.D.) ἀξιοῦμεν τὸ νῦν τὴν σὴν ἀνδρίαν εὐεργε[τῆσαι ἡ]μᾶς κα[τ]ὰ τοὺς νόμους.

εὐεργέτης.

In a petition to the prefect of A.D. 49–50 a woman asks that her son should be restored to her—ἀκολούθως τοῖς ὑπὸ σοῦ τοῦ εὐεργέτου προστεταγμένοις, "in accordance with what had been enacted by you, my benefactor" (P Oxy I. 38¹³ = Selections, p. 53): cf. P Lond 177²¹ (A.D. 40–1) (= II. p. 169) ἀξιῶ σὲ τὸν πάντων σωτῆρα καὶ εὐεργέτην. The word is a regular title in P Oxy III. 486²⁷ (A.D. 131) τὴν ὅλην ὑπόθεσιν ὑπερθεμένου τοῦ ἐπιστρ[ατήγο]υ ἐπὶ σὲ τὸν εὐεργέτην, "the epistrategus referred the whole case to your beneficence" (Edd.). This honorific use of εὐεργέτης with reference to Emperors and distinguished men is very common in the inscrr. Thus as early as B.C. 334 the Prienians describe King Antigonus as εὐ]εργέτηι γενομένωι καὶ προθύμωι ἐόντ[ι εἰ]ς τὴμ πόλιν (2⁶): in a Spartan inscr., Ann. Brit. School at Athens xii. 458, Hadrian is described as σωτῆρος καὶ εὐεργέτου τῆς Λακεδαίμονος, and similarly Trajan is ὁ παντὸς κόσμου σωτὴρ καὶ εὐεργέτης (IG XII. I, 978): other exx. in Magie, p. 67 f. Deissmann (LAE, p. 248 f.) cites a fragmentary inscr. from Cos, of date c. A.D. 53, with reference to Gaius Stertinius Xenophon, body-physician to the Emperor Claudius—τοῦ εὐεργέτ[α Γ. Στε]ρτινίου Ξενοφῶντ[ος] ἀνιερωθεῖσαν τ[αι] πόλει, and in view of this widespread usage suggests that in such a passage as Lk 22²⁵ Jesus "mentioned the title not without contempt, and forbade His disciples to allow themselves to be so called: the name contradicted the idea of service in brotherhood." To show the Egyptian "religiosity" at the time of the Imperial worship, Wilcken (Chrest. I. p. 147) reproduces an inscr. from ii/iii A.D. (CIG III. 5041) which ends—σέ[β]ου Ἶσιν Σαράπιν το[ὺς με]γίστους τῶν [θεῶν σω]τῆρας ἀγα[θ]ο[ὺς εὐμε]νεῖς εὐεργέτα[ς. For the subst. εὐεργέτημα see Priene 105¹⁷ (c. B.C. 9) τοῖς τοσούτοις αὐτοῦ εὐεργετήμασιν.

εὔθετος.

For εὔθετος = "adapted," "suitable" for a place or office, as in Lk 9⁶², cf. P Tebt I. 27⁴¹ (B.C. 113) ἵνα μὲν πρὸς ταῖς προειρημέναις χρείαις εὔθετοι κατασταθῶσιν, "see that suitable persons are appointed to the aforesaid offices" (Edd.), P Flor I. 3⁶ (A.D. 301) ἐργάτας . . . ὄντ[α]ς εὐθέτους καὶ ἐπιτηδείους (contrast P Amh II. 64¹² (A.D. 107) λέγων τοὺς σὺν αὐτῶι κατασταθέντας ἐ[π]ιμελητὰς βαλανείου [ἀ]θέτους, "inefficient"), Syll 653⁷⁶ (Mysteries inscr. from Andania—B.C. 91) αὐλητὰς καὶ κιθαριστάς, ὅσους κα εὑρίσκωντι εὐθέτους ὑπάρχοντας, so ¹⁴⁸ ῥαβδοφόρους τοὺς εὐθετωτάτους. For a similar reference to persons see Polyb. xxvi. 5. 6 πρὸς πᾶσαν σωματικὴν χρείαν . . εὔθετος. The meaning "seasonable," as in Ps 31 (32)⁶, is found in Diod. v. 57. 4 οἱ

Αἰγύπτιοι καιρὸν εὔθετον λαβόντες. See also s.vv. ἀνεύθετος and ἀθετέω. Hobart p. 75 gives exx. from medical authors.

εὐθέως,

the more common Hellenistic form for εὐθύς and εὐθύ, is found before both vowels and consonants: cf. Schmid Atticismus iii. p. 126 and Mayser Gr. p. 245. The following may serve as exx. of its use—P Par 63ˣⁱ·⁶⁵ (B.C. 165) ἠβου-[λόμ]ην μὲν εὐθέως καταπλεύσας ὀφθῆ[ν]αί σοι κατὰ τὸ ἐπιβάλλον, P Tebt I. 30¹⁹ (B.C. 114) εὐθέως παραλαβὼν Τρύχαμβον, P Ryl II. 229⁹ (A.D. 38) ἐρωτῶ σε ἐκ παντὸς τρόπου εὐθέως μοι πέ[μ]ψαι τὰς ἄλλας (ἀρτάβας) γ, ib. 230¹⁰ (A.D. 40) μὴ [ο]ὖν ἄλλως ποιή[σ]ῃ s) μὴ ἵνα δόξωμέν σε εὐθέως ἠλλάχθαι τὰ πρὸς ἡμᾶς, "do not neglect this, lest we think you to have become all at once estranged towards us" (Edd.), P Fay 110⁴ (c. A.D. 100) εὐθέος πέμσις τὰ κτήνη, "send the animals at once," and BGU II. 423⁸ (ii/A.D.) (= Selections, p. 91) εὐθέως ὅτε εἰσῆλθον εἰς Μησηνούς, ἔλαβα βιάτικον παρὰ Καίσαρος χρυσοῦς τρεῖς, "straightway when I entered Misenum, I received my travelling money from Caesar, three gold pieces."

εὐθυμέω.

P Amh II. 133⁴ (early ii/A.D.) περὶ τῆς κρειθ(ῆς) τῆς ἐνθάλλου εὐθύμει, πέπρακα γάρ, "don't be anxious about the young barley, for I have sold it" (Edd.), P Iand 13¹⁸ (iv/A.D.) ἵνα μετὰ χαρᾶς σε ἀπολάβωμεν καὶ εὐθυμήσ[αι δυνώμεθά] σε. The verb is common with ὑγιαίνω as an epistolary phrase, e.g. P Lips I. 111⁵ (iv/A.D.) πρὸ μὲν [πά]ντων εὔχομαι τῷ ὑψίστῳ Θε[ῷ] περὶ τῆς σῆς ὑγίας καὶ ὁλοκληρίας, ἵνα ὑγιαίνοντά σε καὶ εὐθυμοῦντα ἀπολάβῃ τὰ παρ' ἐμοῦ γραμματί[δ]ια : cf. P Lond 1244⁷ (iv/A.D.) (= III. p. 244) παρακαλῶν τὸν θεὸν ἵνα σαι ἀπολάβω εὐθυμοῦντα καὶ εὐπυγ'μοῦντα καὶ ὁλοκληροῦντα, P Oxy XII. 1593² (iv/A.D.) εὐθυ]μοῦντί σαι (l. σοι) καὶ εὐδαιμονοῦντι.

εὔθυμος.

P Oxy VI. 939¹⁹ (iv/A.D.) ἵνα σε εὐθυμότερον καταστήσω, "that I may make you more cheerful": cf. OGIS 669⁷ (i/A.D.) ἵνα δὲ εὐθυμότεροι πάντα ἐλπίζητε κτλ. For the subst. see the fragmentary P Ryl II. 439 (iii/A.D.) where the desire is expressed—αὖθις μετ' εὐθυμίας τὸ θεοφιλέστατόν σου πρόσωπον ἀπολαβεῖν.

εὐθύμως.

OGIS 669⁴ (i/A.D.) πᾶσαν πρόνοιαν ποιούμενος . . . τοῦ τὴν Αἴγυπτον ἐν εὐσταθείᾳ διάγουσαν εὐθύμως ὑπηρετεῖν τῇ τε εὐθηνίᾳ καὶ τῇ μεγίστῃ τῶν νῦν καιρῶν εὐδαιμονίᾳ. The comparative of the adverb may be seen, as in the "received" text of Ac 24¹⁰, in P Giss I. 41ⁱⁱ·¹² (beginning of Hadrian's reign) ἐπινεύσαντος ο[ὖ]ν σου τῇ[ι] δεήσει μου . . . δυνή[σο]μαι εὐθυμότερον προσέρχεσθαι [τῇ] τῆς [σ]τρατηγ[ίας] ἐπιμελείαι.

εὐθύνω

is used of a magistrate who calls others to account: hence in the Pass. οἱ εὐθυνόμενοι = "the culprits," e.g. P Tor I. 1ⁱⁱⁱ·²⁰ (B.C. 117) μεταπεμψάμενον τοὺς εὐθυνομένους ἐπισκέψασθαι περὶ τούτων, P Tebt I. 14⁶ (B.C. 114) εὐθυνομένωι δὲ φόνωι, "arraigned for murder" where note the dat. for the usual *gen. criminis*), *ib.* 53[22] (B.C. 110) οἱ εὐθυνόμενοι ἀναζητηθ[έ]ντες, "the culprits having been searched for." The metaph. application of the ordinary meaning "guide straight" may be illustrated from Vett. Val. p. 340[9] ἀγαπητὸν γὰρ εἰ . . . ἄρξαιτό τις ἑρμηνεύειν μὴ διὰ πλήθους λόγων, ἀλλὰ διὰ βραχέων εἰς ἀλήθειαν εὐθυνόντων.

εὐθύς.

as an adj., is found in an early iv/A.D. Christian letter, where the writer asks for prayers—P Oxy XII. 1494[9] εἴν οὕτως ἐπακούσῃ ὁ θαιὸς τῶν εὐχῶν ὑμῶν καὶ γένηται ἡμεῖν ὁδὸς εὐθεῖα, "in order that God may thus hear your prayers, and a straight way be made for us" (Edd.) ; cf. 2 Pet 2[15].

εὐθύς.

instead of εὐθέως, is now read in almost all the occurrences in Mk. and, though not so common as εὐθέως, can also be illustrated from the Κοινή. Thus in P Petr II. 13(9)[5] (B.C. 258–253)—a document already cited under εὐθέως—we have εὐθὺς τἀντίγραφα ἔπεμψα : cf. PSI IV. 403[20] (iii/B.C.) παρέσομαι δὲ κἀγὼ εὐθὺς ἐξ ἑορτῆς, P Oxy IV. 744[7] (B.C. 1) (= *Selections*, p. 33) ἐὰν εὐθὺς ὀψώνιον λάβωμεν ἀποστελῶ σε ἄνω, P Fay 109[2] (early i/A.D.) εὐθύς σε οὐ κρατῶι, "I at once give in to you" (Edd.), P Ryl II. 234[4] (ii/A.D.) ἀνέδωκα τῶι κρατ[ίστ]ῳ ἐπιστρ]ατήγῳ τὰς ἐπιστολὰς καὶ [ε]ὐθὺς μὲ[ν τ]ῷ γραμμάτει αὐτοῦ ἔδωκεν. For the form εὐθύ see P Leid C[i. 2?] (B.C. 162) (= I. p. 119) ε]ὐθὺ μέλαινα ἐγένετο—an account of a dream, and the Alexandrian Erotic Fragment P Grenf I. 1[i. 24] (ii/B.C.) νῦν ἀνοργισθῶμεν· εὐθὺ δεῖ καὶ διαλύεσθαι, "let us now cease from anger: yes, for we must quickly be reconciled" (Loeb trans.). The Markan use of εὐθύς is discussed by J. Weiss in *ZNTW* xi. p. 124 ff. In MGr an unaspirated form εὔτύς is also found.

εὐκαιρέω.

The idea of "favourable opportunity" underlying the word comes out well in P Eleph 29[7] ἐὰν δὲ μὴ εὐκαιρῇς τ[ο]ῦ διαβῆναι, P Par 46[13] (B.C. 153) (= Witkowski[2], p. 87) αὐτὸς δέ, ὡς ἂν (cf. Rom 15[24], 1 Cor 11[34], Phil 2[23]) εὐκαιρήσω, παραχρῆμα παρέσομαι πρὸς σέ, P Giss I. 67[14] (ii/A.D.) ἐὰν εὐκαιρήσῃ Ἡράκλειος καὶ ἀρετήσηται αὐτοῦ, BGU IV. 1035[12] (1st half v/A.D.) Θεὸς οἶδεν ὁ μόνος [ἐ]ὰν οὐκ εὐκέρημε (*l.* ηὐκαίρημαι) εἰς Ὀξυρύγχων κακὸν εἰχι (*l.* ἄγχι) γενέσθαι, and *Michel* 1499[B. 4] (B.C. 171) τ[οῖς πρεσβευτα]ῖς ἐλθοῦσιν συνέθηκεν, καίπερ οὐκ εὐκαίρων. For the meaning "have time or leisure," as in Mk 6[31] and MGr εὐκαιρέζω, see PSI IV. 425[29] (iii/B.C.) εἰ δὲ μὴ εὐκαιρεῖ τις τῶν παρά σοι γραμματέων, ἀπόστειλόν μοι κτλ. : a different meaning is found in *ib.* 392[9] (B.C. 242–1) δοὺς Ἀμμωνίωι τῶι κεκομικότι σοι τὴν ἐπιστολὴν ὅσον ἂν ποτε εὐκαιρῇς, where the editor renders "quanto puoi senza disturbo."

εὐκαιρία

is found, as in Mt 26[16], Lk 22[6], in BGU II. 665[ii. 4] (i/A.D.) εὐκαι[ρί]αν δὲ οὐκ ἔχει, *ib.* I. 46[18] (A.D. 193) ἐὰν εὐκαιρίας τύχω τοῦ εὑρεῖν, ἀποσπάσω, P Oxy I. 125[3] iii/iv. A.D.) εὐκαιρη (*l.* – ία) τις καὶ νῦν τοῦ ἀνερχομένου πρὸς ὑμᾶς, *ib.* X. 1300[2] (v/A.D.) εὐκερίαν εὑρὼν διὰ τοῦτον (*l.* εὐκαιρίαν εὗρον διὰ τούτων) μου τῶν γραμμάτων τὰ πολλὰ προσαγορεῦσαί σε. The word is MGr.

εὔκαιρος.

OGIS 762[4] (ii/B.C.) βοηθείτω κατὰ τὸ εὔκαιρον, *Michel* 164[25] (*c.* B.C. 140) μερίσαι Ἀπολλωνίωι ξένιον ὅσον ἂν αὐτοῖς εὔκαιρον εἶ[ν]αι φαίνηται. The superlative is found in P Petr II. 12 (1)[15] (B.C. 241) μεταθεῖναι τοὺς βωμοὺς ἐπὶ τοὺς εὐκαιροτάτους τόπους καὶ ἐπιφανεστάτους ἐπὶ τῶν δωμάτων, "to remove the altars to the most convenient and conspicuous place on the houses" (Ed.). It may be mentioned that Pallis *A Few Notes*, p. 11 regards the adj. in Mk 6[21] γενομένης ἡμέρας εὐκαίρου. as = an "empty" day, a day without work, a festival; the meaning is supported from Byzantine (see Sophocles *Lex. s.v.*) and modern Greek.

εὐκαίρως.

P Hal I. 17[8] (iii/B.C.) ἐὰν εὐκαίρως ἔχῃς, P Lond 33[23] (B.C. 161) (= I. p. 20) ὑπομνήσαντά σε εὐκαίρως. A form εὐκαιρεῖ, unknown to the lexicons, is found in P Grenf I. 64[5] (vi/vii A.D.) (as amended *Archiv* iii. p. 121) καὶ σὺν θεῷ εὑρίσκω εὐκαιρεῖ ὃν προσαναφέρω: cf. also the new εὐχαιροτέρως (*l.* εὐκ–) in P Lond 1349[11] (A.D. 710) (= IV. p. 23).

εὔκοπος.

For the corresponding verb cf. the closing greeting of a letter PSI IV. 286[38] (iii/iv A.D.) ἐρρῶσθαί σε εὔχομ[αι] εὐκοποῦντα διὰ ὅλου βίου. The editor states that he has not found the formula elsewhere, and compares the Homeric ῥεῖα ζώοντες.

εὐλάβεια.

In P Par 26[21] (B.C. 163–2) (= *Selections*, p. 15) the Twins describe the Serapeum officials as—οὐδεμίαν εὐλάβειαν προορωμένων, "paying no regard to religious scruple," where εὐλάβειαν has the same religious connotation as in Prov 28[14]. (MGr = "piety.") For the use of the subst. as a title of respect, like our "Your reverence," see P Flor I. 73[7] (A.D. 505) ὁμολογῶ ἑκουσίως καὶ αὐθαιρέτως μεμισθῶσθαι παρὰ τῆς σῆς εὐλαβε[ί]ας κτλ.

εὐλαβέομαι.

P Par 45[7] (B.C. 153) εὐλαβοῦμαι τὸν ἐνδίκτην τὰ πλῖστα, BGU IV. 1116[42] (B.C. 13) καὶ μηδὲν τὴν Ἀντωνίαν Φιλημάτιο ν) εὐλαβ(εῖσθαι), and the Christian P Fay 136[4] (iv/A.D.) ὅθεν μηδένα εὐλαβούμενοι μᾶλλον ἀπαντήσατε ἀπ' ἑαυτῶν πρὸ τοῦ τις ὑμᾶς ἐνέγκῃ. "therefore heed no one rather than me and return from where you are before some one fetches you" (Edd.). See also the letter Preisigke 4650[13] εὐλαβήθητι μήπως μὴ καταλάβουσίν σε ἐν [Ἀ]λεξανδρείᾳ, where the construction may be compared with Ac 23[10]HLP. The active, which does not occur in the NT, is found in BGU II. 665 (i/A.D.) ὅπως σε παρακαλέσῃ [ε]ὐλαβεῖν αὐτήν.

εὐλαβής.

After the close of the fifth century εὐλαβέστατος is very common as a designation for various orders of the clergy (see *s.v.* εὐλάβεια), as in BGU I. 305[10] (A.D. 556) τοῦ εὐλαβεστάτου διακόνο(υ), and in P Giss I. 57[1] (vi/vii A.D.) ὁ εὐλαβέστατος Ἄπα Κόλλουθος ὁ πρεσβύτερος, where see the editor's note. For the adv. we may cite P Par 12[10] (B.C. 157) εὐλαβῶς μου σχόντος, BGU IV. 1141[38] (B.C. 14) εὐλαβῶς ἔχων διὰ τὸ

προεγνωκέναι με περὶ τῶν δακτυλιδίων, P Tebt II. 304[14]
(A.D. 167–8) εὐλαβῶς ἔχων τὸν περὶ τοῦ θαναθανάτου *l.*
θανάτου) αὐτοῦ κιντυνων (*l.* κίνδυνον), "being careful for
the danger to his life" (Edd.). The adj. in MGr retains
the NT meaning "pious."

εὐλογέω.

We can illustrate this verb only from the Christian papyri,
as P Amh II. 145[1] (iv/v A.D.) τῷ ἀγαπητῷ ἀδελφῷ καὶ
ηὐλ[ο]γημένῳ, and the late P Grenf II. 113[7] (vii/ix A.D.)
τῶν εὐλογημένων τριῶν συνόδων, [11] μετὰ τῶν σὺν αὐτοῖς καὶ
εὐλογημένων ὁμονόων. It occurs, however, in inscr. in such
a formula as *OGIS* 73 εὐλογεῖ τὸν θεὸν Πτολεμαῖος Διονυσίου
Ἰουδαῖος, and was by no means confined to the Jews as
Dittenberger shows from *CIG* 4705[*b*2] (of Pan) ε[ὐ]λογ[ῶ]
τὸν εὔο[δο]ν θεόν, *ib.* 4705[*c*2] εὐλογῶ [τ]ὴν Εἶσιν. See also
Syll 801[24] (ii/A.D.) where the prayer is uttered that a protector of a tomb—τῶν λῴων ἀπολαύοι εὐλογοῖτό τε ἐν παντὶ
δήμῳ, and the exx. of the verb in votive inscriptions given
by Ramsay *ExpT* x. p. 54, as when a person who has been
chastised for his sin by the god dedicates a stele— εὐλογῶν
σου τὰς δυνάμ[ει]ς: he adds that the stele which is dedicated is in one case called εὐλογία. In MGr εὐλογῶ =
"praise," "bless": a form βλογῶ is also found.

εὐλογία.

With the use of the verb in *OGIS* 73 (see *s.v.* εὐλογέω), cf.
ib. 74 (from the Thebaid—B.C. 247–221) Θεοῦ εὐλογία·
Θεύδοτος Δωρίωνος Ἰουδαῖος σωθεὶς ἐκ πελ(άγ)ους. See
also *Preisigke* 317 Εὐλογία Κυρίου, and from Christian
times the vase inscr. *ib.* 1117 Εὐλογία τοῦ ἁγίου Μηνᾶ.
The subst. is used as a Christian title of address in P Lond
891[16] (iv/A.D.) (= III. p. 242, *Chrest.* I. p. 157) a letter to
a Bishop—γινώσκει(ν) σε βούλομαι, ὦ ἀγαπητὲ πάτερ, ὅτι
ὅτε ἀπήντησα τῷ δουκὶ μετὰ τῆς Εὐλογία[ς] σου, ἐ]δέξατο
αὐτήν κτλ. For εὐλογία in the sense of a "good report"
cf. P Oxy I. 65[4] (iii/iv A.D.) εἰ δὲ ἔχετε εὐλογίαν τινὰ πρὸς
αὐτὸν ἀνέρχεσθε ἅμα αὐτῷ καὶ λέγετε, "if you have anything to say in his favour, come with him and tell me"
(Edd.): cf. Aristeas 161. The adj. is found = "reasonable," "probable," in P Tor I. 1[v. 2] (B.C. 117) οὐθενὸς
εὐλόγου ἀντεχόμενοι: cf. *OGIS* 504[9] (A.D. 128–9), 666[10]
(i/A.D.), and for the adverb P Oxy IV. 718[23] (A.D. 180–192).

εὐμετάδοτος.

This NT ἅπ. εἰρ. (1 Tim 6[18]), which is best rendered
"ready to impart" (see Field *Notes*, p. 113 f.), occurs
eight times in Vettius Valens, e.g. p. 46[24] γίνονται δὲ
συνετοί, ἁπλοῖ, εὐμετάδοτοι, ἡδεῖς, φιλοσυμβίωτοι κτλ.

εὐνοέω.

For this verb, which is rare in Bibl. Greek and in the
NT is confined to Mt 5[25], we may cite PSI I. 64[5] (i/B.C. ?)
where a woman comes under a solemn promise εὐνοεῖν, "to
be well-disposed" towards her husband: cf. P Ryl II. 153[10]
(A.D. 138–61) κα[ὶ] αὐτὸς εὐνοήσας ἐμα[υτῷ κ]αὶ τῷ πατρί
μου, P Oxy III. 494[9] (A.D. 156) εὐνοούσῃ μοι καὶ πᾶσαν
πίστιν μοι ἐνδεικνυμένῃ. "being well-disposed and showing
entire faithfulness towards me" (Edd.). So from the inscrr.
OGIS 532[9] (B.C. 3) ὀμνύω Δία, Γῆν, Ἥλιον . . . εὐνοή[σειν

Κα[ὶ]σαρι Σεβαστῶι, similarly *Syll* 364[29] (A.D. 37). There
seems no good warrant for the transl. "agree with" in Mt
l.c. AV, RV: see Abbott *Joh. Voc.* p. 207.

εὔνοια.

With the use of εὔνοια in Eph 6[7], cf. P Oxy III. 494[8]
(A.D. 156) where a testator sets free certain slaves κατ'
εὔνοιαν καὶ φιλοστοργίαν. Other examples are *ib.* 642
(ii/A.D.) πεφροντίκαμεν τῆς πρὸς ὑμᾶς . . . εὐνοίας καὶ
ἀρετῆς. P Tebt II. 326[10] (c. A.D. 266) εὐνοίᾳ καὶ πίστι καὶ
τῇ τοῦ γένους οἰκειότητι, "owing to his kindness, fidelity,
and ties of kinship" (Edd.), *Syll* 722[13] (Cretan—ii/B.C.)
ὁμοίως δὲ καὶ τὰν εὔνοιαν ἃν ἔχει ποτὶ τὰν πόλιν, and so
frequently in the inscrr. In P Par 63[160] (B.C. 164) (= P Petr
III. p. 32) οἷς ὀφειλόμενόν ἐστι διὰ [τὴν] πρὸς τὰ [πρ]άγματ'
εὔνοιαν ἀσμένως ἐπιδεξάσθαι τὸ προτεινόμενον, Mahaffy
renders "whose duty it is, on account of their loyalty to the
existing state of affairs, to receive what is proposed cheerfully." A different turn is given to the word in BGU IV.
1121[19] (B.C. 5) ἐργάζεσθαι δὲ τὰ μεμισθωμένα . . . τῇ καθηκούσῃ εὐνοίᾳ: cf. P Giss I. 56[14] (vi/A.D.) πᾶσα]ν [σπου]δὴν
κα[ὶ] εὔνοιαν ποιεῖσθαι, and the Jewish inscr. in *C. and B.*
ii. p. 650 (c. A.D. 60–80) διά τε τὴν ἐνάρετον ("virtuous")
αὐτῶν [β]ίωσιν καὶ τὴν π[ρ]ὸς τὴν συναγωγὴν εὔνοιάν τε
καὶ σπουδήν. For the adj. εὔνους (as in 4 Macc 4[3]) cf. *Syll*
649[19] (B.C. 282–1) ὅσ]οι εἰσὶν εὔνους καὶ φίλοι τοῦ δήμου
(on the heterocl. plur. see Meisterhans *Gr.* p. 149): it
occurs as a proper name in BGU III. 999[*b* 4] (B.C. 69) *al.*
(cf. Mayser *Gr.* p. 258).

εὐνοῦχος.

Vett. Val. p. 86[31] ὁ τοιοῦτος γέγονεν εὐνοῦχος ἱερεὺς θεᾶς
ἐπίσημος: cf. also p. 18[19]. The word occurs in the address
of the late BGU III. 725 (A.D. 615 εἰς τὸν εὐδοκιμ ὥτατον)
ἅπα Ὀλ εὐνοῦχον. It survives in MGr.

Εὐοδία.

This proper name is common in inscrr., as *CIG* 3002,
5711, and the other references in Zahn *Introd.* i. p. 533.
See also *OGIS* 77 (B.C. 217) a memorial tablet—Εὐοδίαι,
and the late BGU II. 550[1] (Arab.) ἔχει Εὐοδία εἰς λόγ(ον)
καμισί(ων) λιναρ(ίων) λίτρ(ας) δύο κτλ. The masc. Εὐώδιος
is found in BGU III. 793[2] (iii/A.D.), but the commoner
man's name is Εὔοδος: see Zahn *ut supra*, and cf. the use
of the adj. in *Preisigke* 4056 Πανὶ εὐόδωι καὶ ἐπηκόωι
Λυκίσκος ὑπὲρ αὐτοῦ, and *CIG* 4705 [*l* 2] (cited *s.v.* εὐλογέω).

εὐοδόω.

For the literal use of this verb of a successful journey cf.
PSI IV. 299[11] (iii/A.D.) μακροψ[ύ]χ[ει] οὖν, ἀδελφή, ἄχρεις
οὗ ἄν με θεὸς εὐοδώσῃ [πρὸς] ὑμᾶς, and so [14], also P Iand
62[3] (vi/A.D.) ἢ ο[ἴκο]θε[ν] εὐοδ[ω]θῶ, in a much mutilated context. On the pres. subj. εὐοδῶται in 1 Cor 16[2], see *Proleg.*
p. 54. The LXX use of the verb is fully illustrated by Anz
Subsidia, p. 290.

εὐπειθής.

The force of this adj. in Jas 3[17] (cf. 4 Macc 12[6]) "willing
to yield," "compliant," may be illustrated from a contract
in which a woman Ammonarion and her daughter Ophelous
agree to accept from Antiphanes a certain sum of money in

lieu of Ammonarion's dowry—P Oxy II. 268⁶ (A.D. 58)
συνχωροῦμεν [πρὸς ἀλλήλο]υς ἐπὶ τοῖσδε, ὥστε ἡ ['Aμ-
μωνάριο]ν [καὶ] ἡ Ὠφελοῦς εὐπιθεῖς γεγοννῦαι καὶ ἀπεσχηκυῖαι [παρὰ τοῦ 'Ἀντ]ιφάνους κτλ., "we agree with each
other as follows :—A. and O. have given their consent and
have received from A. etc." (Edd.). Other instances of the
word from legal documents of the Augustan age are BGU
IV. 1104²³ (B.C. 10) διὰ τοῦ ὑπὲρ τούτων εὐπειθῆ γεγονέναι,
ib. 1155¹⁷ (B.C. 10) νυνὶ δὲ εὐπ[ε]ιθῆς γεγονὼς ὑπὸ [τῆς]
Μάρθας, ib. 1163⁷ (B.C. 17). The verb is supplied by the
editor in OGIS 665⁵ (A.D. 49) ἵν' εἰδό[τες] αὐτὰ καὶ [εὐπ]-
ειθῆτε, where he explains εὐπειθεῖν as = εὐπειθῆ εἶναι.

εὐπερίστατος.

Deissmann's reference (BS. p. 150) to the use of the
subst. περίστασις in the evil sense of "distress," "calamity,"
as in 2 Macc 4¹⁶, in the vernacular P Lond 42²¹ (B.C. 168)
(= I. p. 30, Selections, p. 10) μηδ' ἐνβεβλοφέναι εἰς τὴν
ἡμετέραν περίστασιν, "nor spared a look for our miserable
state," may perhaps be taken as supporting Theophylact's
explanation of the compound adj. in Heb 12¹, "because of
which one easily falls into distresses (περιστάσεις)." As
against Westcott (Comm. ad loc.), Moulton [Gr. ii. § 106 (c)]
has shown that there is nothing in the form of the verbal to
forbid this interpretation, and he enumerates the various
meanings as follows—(1) "easily avoided," (2) "admired"
(lit. "well-surrounded"), (3) "easily surrounding," "besetting," or (4) "dangerous" (lit. "having easy distress").

εὐποιΐα.

P Lond 1244⁸ (iv/A.D.) (= III. p. 244) περὶ τῶν εὐποιειῶν
σου. The subst. survives in MGr, as does the verb εὐποιῶ,
which may accordingly be accepted as a proper form for the
Hellenistic period : see ExpT xxiii. p. 379 f.

εὐπορέω.

P Oxy VII. 1068³ (iii/A.D.) μὴ εὐπορήσας πλοῖον ἐν τῷ
'Ἀρσενοεΐδῃ ἔγραψα τῷ κυρίῳ μου Κλημάτίῳ κτλ., "finding
no boat available in the Arsinoite nome I wrote to my
lord Clematius etc." (Ed.). PSI IV. 299¹⁸ (iii/A.D.) ἐπὰν
πλοίου εὐπορηθῶ, P Flor III. 367³ (iii/A.D.) πολλάκις μου
. . . χάρτας ἐπιστολικο[ὺς ἀπο]στείλαντος, ἵν' εὐπορῇς τοῦ
γρά[φειν] μοι, ¹⁷ἵν]α καὶ διὰ τῶν γραμ[μάτων ὁ φίλος
εὐ]πορῇ μανθάνων [τὰ σοῦ? See also the curious mantic
document where prognostications are derived from involuntary twitchings, P Ryl I. 28¹⁵ (iv/A.D.) ὀσφύος δεξιὸν μέρος
ἐὰν ἄλληται μεγάλως εὐπορήσει κα[ὶ] δοῦλος καὶ πένης ἐκ
κόπων, "if the right part of the loin quiver, a slave or poor
man will prosper greatly after distress" (Edd.), cf ¹²⁵, and
from the inserr. Michel 984⁹ (ii/B.C. ad init.) εὐπορῶν πλεονάκις ἐκ τῶν ἰδίων. A somewhat unusual use of the verb is
found in P Ryl II. 162²⁷ (A.D. 159) where a woman who
has bought a half share of a house is described as— εὐπορ-
[οῦσα σὺν τοῖς] νῦν δικαί[ο]ις πᾶσι καὶ πωλοῦσα καὶ
ὑποτιθοῦσα κτλ., "enjoying it with all present rights,
having the power of sale, mortgage," etc. (Edd.).

εὐπορία.

With the last citation s.v. εὐπορέω cf. P Grenf II. 72¹⁰
(A.D. 290-304) εἰ δὲ μὴ ἀποδῶ, ἐξέσται σοι χρήσασθαι κατὰ

παντοίας μου εὐπορείας, and see P Oxy I. 71 i. 17 (A.D. 303)
οὐδεμία δέ μοι ἑτέρα εὐπορία ἐστὶν ἢ τὰ χρήματα ταῦτα,
"I have no other resources than this money in question"
(Edd.). The adj. is common especially along with ἐπι-
τήδειος to denote a person "rich and capable" of undertaking
some duty laid upon him, as in P Oxy IX. 1187¹¹ (A.D. 254)
ὃν ἐὰν αἱρῶνται φύλαρχον ὄ[ν]τα εὔπορον καὶ ἐπιτήδειον, P
Cairo Preis 18⁹ (A.D. 339) ὄντ[α]ς εὐπόρους κ[αὶ] ἐπιτηδίους
δυναμένους ἐκτελέσαι τὴν τὴν (om.) ἐνχειρισθεῖσαν αὐτ[οῖς]
λειτουργείαν, al.

εὐπρέπεια.

The idea of "majesty," "stateliness," which Hort (James,
p. 17) finds in the OT use of this word and in Jas 1¹¹, its
only occurrence in the NT, comes out well in Syll 932¹⁷
(iii/A.D. init.) ο[ἱ κ]ύ[ρι]οι ἡμῶν μέγιστοι καὶ θειότατοι
αὐτοκράτορες διὰ παντός τε τοῦ ἑαυτῶν αἰῶνος βουληθέντες
ἐν τῇ αὐτῇ εὐπρεπείᾳ διαμεῖναι τὴν αὐτῶν ἐπαρχείαν, προσ-
έταξαν κτλ. 'Ἀπρέπια is read by the editor in P Iand 11⁸
(iii/A.D.). In MGr εὐπρεπής has given place to πρεπός,
"proper," "becoming" : similarly ἄπρεπος (Thumb
Handbook § 115).

εὐπρόσδεκτος.

Cf. Syll 633⁸ (ii/A.D.) cited s.v. δεκτός, and see Field
Notes, p. 184.

εὐπροσωπέω.

P Tebt I. 19¹² (B.C. 114) ὅπως εὐπροσωπῶμεν, "that we
may make a good show," is some three centuries older than
the earliest citation hitherto given for this Pauline word
(Gal 6¹²).

Εὐρακύλων.

For the formation of this word, which is not found except
in Ac 27¹⁴, the lexicographers compare Εὐρόνοτος. According to Blass (ad l.), it is a "vox hybrida" made up of εὖρος
and aquilo (qui Lat. = κῦ as in 'Ἀκύλας 18²) : cf. Goodspeed
Exp VI. viii. p. 140, "the Greek east wind combined with
the Latin north-east (more exactly east-north-east) wind."

εὑρίσκω.

P Hib I. 48⁶ (B.C. 255) οὐ γὰρ εὑρίσκω ἐν τοῖς βιβλίοις,
"for I cannot find the entry in the books" (Edd.), P Tebt
I. 58⁵ (B.C. 111) εὑρήκαμεν δὲ τὸν ἐπιδεδωκότα τὸ ὑπόμνη μα, P Oxy III. 532¹⁸ (ii/A.D.) καὶ γὰρ ἐν Παώμει τότε
σε εὗρον, P Iand 8¹¹ (ii/A.D.) ἐὰν τὸ χυτρί]ον εὗρωι (for form
cf. Mayser Gr. p. 134 f.), διαπέμψ[ομαι διὰ το]ῦ ὀνολάτου
ἀμερίμνω[ς : cf. for the passive P Rein 11¹¹ (B.C. 111) διὰ τὸ
τοῦτον ἐκπεπτωκέναι καὶ μὴ εὑρίσκεσθαι, "because this man
has left the country and is not to be found," P Oxy IV.
743²⁵ (B.C. 2) καὶ εὑρέθη μήτε εἰληφὼς μήτε δεδωκώ(ς), "it
was discovered that he had neither received nor paid anything," and P Giss I. 47⁴ (Hadrian) λείαν ἄξια εὑρῆσθαι.
For a weaker sense, as in Mt 27³² al., see P Tebt II. 330⁶
(ii/A.D.) παραγενομένου εἰς τὴν κώμην εὗρον τὴν οἰκίαν μου
σεσυλημένην, P Gen I. 54³¹ (iv/A.D.) ἀπελθόντων ἡμῶν
ἐκεῖσαι εὑρήκαμεν τὸν πραιπόσιτον τοῦ σάγου ἐκῖσαι. Cf.
also Ev. Petr. 6 εὑρέθη ὥρα ἐνάτη. The verb is used absolutely in the curious acrostic P Tebt II. 278³⁰ (early i/A.D.)

ζητῶι καὶ οὐχ εὑρίσκωι : cf. P Leid Wᵛⁱ·³ (ii/iii A.D.) ἐλθὼν εἰς τὴν ἑπτάζωνον, μέτρει ἀποκάτωθεν, καὶ εὑρήσεις. With Lk 6⁷, 11⁵⁴ D, we may compare the use of εὑρίσκω in P Par 45⁷ (B.C. 153) προσέχων μὴ εὕρῃ τι κατὰ σοῦ ἰπῖν. In *Syll* 535³⁷ (ii/B.C.) τοῦ δὲ εὑρόντος ἀργυρίου λογισάμενοι ἐπὶ δραχμεῖ τὸν τόκον, it is = "fetch" (by sale), and in PSI IV. 403¹⁹ (iii/B.C.) τοῦ εὑρίσκοντος καὶ ἔτι ἐλάττονός σοι ὑπάρξει, it is used of the "current" price (see the editors' notes). For the form εὑρήκειμεν see P Fleph 13⁵ (B.C. 223 2), and for εὕροσαν, as often in LXX, see BGU IV. 1201¹⁶ (A.D. 2) εὕροσαν τὸν στροφέα τοῦ ἑνὸς μέρους [τ]ῆς θύρας ἠρμένον χ[ε]ρσεῖν. The verb occurs in the Christian prayer P Oxy VI. 925⁶ (v/vi A.D.) (= *Selections*, p. 131) φανέρωσον . . εἰ . . εὑρίσκω σε σὺν ἐμοὶ πράττοντα (καὶ) εὐμενήν, "reveal whether I shall find Thee aiding me and gracious," and in the new Logion, P Oxy IV. 654¹⁷, ἡ βασ[ίλεια τῶν οὐρανῶν] ἐντὸς ὑμῶν [ἐ]στι [καὶ ὅστις ἂν ἑαυτὸν] γνῶ ταύτην εὑρή[σει . . . . . It is perhaps worth noting that in P Ryl II. 125²⁷ (a charge of robbery—A.D. 28-9) ὡμολ[ό]γησεν τὴν πυξίδα ὡς προφέρεται κενήν, "he acknowledges (having found) the box but alleges that it was empty" (Edd.), the omission of εὑρηκέναι is oddly like Rom 4¹ B. In P Grenf I. 1⁴ (ii/B.C.) the faithless lover is called ἀκαταστασίης εὑρέτης, while for εὕρημα we may compare P Oxy III. 472³³ (c. A.D. 130) εἰς συκοφαντίαν εὕρημα, "an excuse for calumnies" (Edd). For exx. of the unaspirated εὑρίσκω, see Crönert *Mem. Herc.* p. 146 f. MGr εὑρίσκω, βρίσκω, βρίστω, εὑρήκω : ξεύρω, "I know."

εὐρύχωρος.

For the subst. see P Tebt II. 383¹⁷ (A.D. 46) βορρᾶ εὐρυχωρ[ία, "on the north an open space," and cf. *Syll* 431¹² (mid. iv/B.C.) ὅπως ἂν ἦι εὐρυχωρία Σουνιεῦσιν ἀγοράζεν καὶ ἄλλωι τῶι βουλομένωι. In the OT the adj. connotes freedom and prosperity, as in Ps 30 (31)⁹, Hos 4¹⁶, Isai 30²³ : see McNeile on Mt 7¹³.

εὐσέβεια.

As emphasizing the place of this word and its cognates in religious phraseology, see P Par 29¹⁰ (B.C. 161-0) δι᾿ ἣν ἔχετε πρὸς τὸ θεῖον εὐσέβειαν, and the payments made ἐξ εὐ[σεβ(είας) to the temple of Soenopaeus in P Tebt II. 298¹⁵ (A.D. 107-8) ; cf. P Leid Wˣᵛⁱ·²¹ (ii/iii A.D.) οὕτω τούτῳ (sc. τῷ θεῷ) πάντοτε θυσίαζε, καὶ τὰς εὐσεβίας πρόσφερε. The word = "loyalty" occurs in the copy of a letter of date A.D. 46 in which the Emperor Claudius thanks an athletic club for a golden crown sent to him on the occasion of his victorious campaign in Britain—ἐπὶ τῇ κατὰ Βρεταννῶν νεικῇ χρυσοῦν σ[τέ]φανον ἡδέως ἔλαβον σύμβολον περιέχοντα τῆς ὑμετέρας πρός με εὐσεβείας (P Lond 1178¹⁴ = III. p. 216, *Selections*, p. 99) : cf. BGU I. 326² (ii/A.D.) τῇ φρόντιδι καὶ εὐσεβείᾳ τῶν [κ]ληρονόμων μου, and CP Herm I. 52¹⁹ (A.D. 266-7) (= *Chrest.* I. p. 57) κατὰ τὴν ἔμφυτον αὐτοῦ πρὸς το[ὺς ὑπ]ηκόους φιλανθρωπίαν καὶ πρὸς τὰ θεῖ[α] εὐσέβε[ιαν. In BGU IV. 1197¹⁶ (time of Augustus) a petition to a high state-official Asclepiades, who is addressed—τῷ θεῶι καὶ κυρίωι,—runs δ]εόμενοι οὖ (*l.* οὖν) τῆς παρὰ σοῦ εὐσεβήας [μεταλαβεῖν . . . . .]ειτου ἀξιοῦμεν κτλ. The religious connotation of the word denoting "operative, cultive piety" (Alford on Ac 3¹²) comes out well in the inscrr., as when the

inhabitants of Priene are praised ἐπὶ τῇ πρὸς] τὸ θεῖον εὐσεβείᾳ (*Priene* 117⁶³-i B.C.) ; cf. *ib.* 118³³, and Rouffiac *Recherches*, p. 80 f.), or when a certain Posidcus is described as—τῆς τε πρὸς τὸ θεῖον εὐσεβείας καὶ τῆς πρὸς τὸ κοινὸν φιλοστοργίας τὴν μεγίστην πρόνοιαν ποιούμενο[ς (*Michel* 459⁹-ii/B.C. *ad init.*) : see also the Commagene rescript of Antiochus I. OGIS 383¹⁴ (mid. i/B.C.) ἐγὼ πάντων ἀγαθῶν οὐ μόνον κτῆσιν βεβαιοτάτην, ἀλλὰ καὶ ἀπόλαυσιν ἡδίστην ἀνθρώποις ἐνόμισα τὴν εὐσέβειαν, and the pompous decree in which Nero invites the presence of the Greeks at Corinth in A.D. 67—τῆς εἴς με εὐνοίας τε καὶ εὐσεβείας ἀμειψασθαι θέλων τὴν εὐγενεστάτην Ἑλλάδα, "desiring to requite most noble Hellas for her good-will and piety towards me" (*Syll* 376²). With the list of virtues in 2 Pet 1⁵ᶠ Deissmann (*LAE* p. 322) compares an inscr. from Asia Minor, iᵇ.C., in honour of one Herostratus, OGIS 438⁸ ἄνδρα ἀγαθὸν γενόμενον καὶ διενένκαντα πίστει καὶ ἀρετῇ καὶ δ[ικ]αιοσύνῃ καὶ εὐσεβείᾳ καὶ . . . τὴν πλείστ[η]ν εἰσενηνεγμένον σπουδήν. See also Aristeas 229, Philo *Quod Deus sit immutabilis* 14 (ed. Cohn ii. p. 72). As showing the true Hellenistic character of this word, it may be noted that in the NT it is confined to 2 Pet, Acts, and the Pastorals, and that of 59 occurrences in the LXX 47 belong to 4 Macc : see Dibelius on 1 Tim 2² (in *HZNT*).

εὐσεβέω.

For the religious connotation of this verb, cf. two of the recently discovered *libelli*, P Ryl II. 112 (a)⁵ (A.D. 250) καὶ ἀεὶ μὲν θύουσα καὶ εὐσεβοῦσα τοῖς θεοῖς διετέλεσα, *ib.* (c)⁶ ἀεὶ μὲν τοῖς θεοῖς θύω καὶ εὐσεβῶ διατελοῦσα, where the dat. is due to θύειν. For the constr. with the acc., as in Ac 17²³, see a decree by Epaminondas attached to Nero's decree cited *s.v.* εὐσέβεια, where the Emperor is belauded as προειρημένος εὐεργετεῖν τὴν Ἑλ(λ)άδα, ἀμειβόμενος δὲ καὶ εὐσεβῶν τοὺς θεοὺς ἡμῶν παριστανομένους αὐτῷ πάντοτε ἐπὶ προνοίᾳ καὶ σωτηρίᾳ (*Syll* 376³⁶) : see also *s.v.* ἀσεβέω. The verb is followed by the more regular πρός in *Michel* 1558²² (iii/B.C.) πρὸς τοὺς θεοὺς εὐσεβεῖν.

εὐσεβής

occurs in a somewhat general sense in P Flor III. 338² (iii/A.D.) εὐσεβὲς τὸ πρᾶγμα ποιεῖς, ἐὰν ποιήσῃς τὸ βιβλίδιον ἐκεῖνο ὡς ἐγύμνασα αὐτὸ σύν σοι ἐν τῇ πόλει : it is applied to taxes in P Cairo Preis 4⁹ (A.D. 320) ἐγεώργησα πλεῖστα ἀναλώματα ποιησάμενος ὑπὲρ τοῦ εὐμαρῶς δύνασθαί με διαλύσασθαι τὰς εὐσεβεῖς εἰσφοράς. For its use as an Imperial designation (= *Pius*), from the close of ii/A.D., see P Hamb I. 15² (A.D. 210) ἔτους τῇ Λουκίου Σεπτιμίου Σεουήρου Εὐσεβοῖς Περτίνακος κτλ., with the editor's note. In the Commagene rescript (see *s.v.* εὐσέβεια) we find—στεφανούτω πάντας τοῖς χρυσοῖς στεφάνοις, οὓς ἐγὼ καθιέρωσα δαιμόνων εὐσεβέσι τιμαῖς (OGIS 383¹³⁹). Interesting too are the occurrences in Egyptian sepulchral inscrr., as *Preisigke* 2048 (ii/B.C.) Πτολεμαῖε χρηστέ. χαῖρε, καὶ εὐσεβῶν ἵκοιο χῶρον, and the poetical inscr. edited by Rubensohn in *Archiv* v. p. 164, where one of the lines runs—

Μίνω σύνθωκος δ᾿ εἰμὶ παρ᾿ εὐσεβέσιν.

εὐσεβῶς.

P Oxy VIII. 1119[17] (A.D. 254) οἷς ἐπόμενοι εὐσεβῶς καὶ οἱ κατὰ καιρ[ὸ]ν ἡγησάμενοι τοῦ ἔθνους, "they have been scrupulously followed by the praefects appointed from time to time" (Ed.). From the inscrr. cf. OGIS 51[7] (iii/B.C.) πρὸς τὸν Διόνυσον καὶ τοὺς ἄλλους θεοὺς εὐσεβῶς καὶ ὁσίως διακείμενος τυγχάνει, ib. 322[9] (B.C. 157–6) ἱέρειαν . . . ἀναστρ[αφεῖσα]ν καλ[ῶς] καὶ εὐσεβῶς καὶ ἀ[ξίως τῆς θεᾶς, al.

εὔσημος,

like ἄσημος (q.v.), is used in personal descriptions with reference to any "distinguishing" marks, as in P Petr I. 19[14] (B.C. 225) ο[ὐ]λὴ εὔσημος μετώπωι μέσ[ωι, P Flor III. 316[8] (ii/A.D.) Πασίωνι . . . εὐσήμωι ὀ[φθαλ]μῷ δεξιῷ. From the inscrr. we may cite OGIS 90[43] (the Rosetta stone —B.C. 195) ὅπως δ᾽ εὔσημος ἦι νῦν τε καὶ εἰς τὸν ἔπειτα χρόνον, and ib. 665[13] (A.D. 49) βούλομαι οὖν [σ]ε . . . καθ᾽ ἕ[καστον τόπο]ν αὐτὸ (a decree) προθεῖναι σαφέσι καὶ εὐσήμοις [γράμμασιν. For the adv. = "legibly" see P Par 62[ii 7] (c. B.C. 170) and cf. P Oxy IX. 1188[5] (A.D. 13) προσανένε[γκε] εὐσή[μως), "report clearly." In P Tebt I. 14[11] (B.C. 114) the editors render εὐσήμως "in detail" with reference to various items in a report on certain property.

εὐσχημόνως.

Syll 521[14] (B.C. 100) καὶ ἤραντο ταῖς θυσίαις τοὺς βοῦς εὐσχημόνως, ib. 653[42] (B.C. 91) ῥαβδοφόροι δὲ ἔστωσαν . . . . ὅπως εὐσχημόνως καὶ εὐτάκτως ὑπὸ τῶν παραγεγενημένων πάντα γίνηται, ib. 604[11] (B.C. 98–7) πεπομπευ[κέναι κα]τὰ τὰ προστεταγμένα ὡς ὅ τι κ[άλλισ]τα καὶ εὐσχημονέ[στατα.

εὐσχημοσύνη.

Syll 246[36] (B.C. 220–16) προδιδοὺς ἀργύριον εἰς ἐσθῆτα, ἀεὶ προνοούμενο[ς τ]ῶν ὑφ᾽ αὑτὸν τεταγμένων τῆς εὐσχημοσύνης, OGIS 339[32] (c. B.C. 120) τῆς τε ἄλλης εὐσχημοσύνης τῆς κατὰ τὸ γυμνάσιον ἀντελάβετο καλῶς καὶ φιλοτίμως, Michel 545[8] (ii/B.C.) τό τε ἦθος κοσμιότητι καὶ εὐσ[χη]μοσύνῃ, Cagnat IV. 1029[35] (i/B.C.) τὴν τοῦ σώμ]ατος εὐσχημοσύνην.

εὐσχήμων.

With 1 Cor 7[35] πρὸς τὸ εὔσχημον, "for that which is seemly," "to promote decorum," cf. the office of the εὐσχήμων or guardian of public morals in Egypt, e.g. BGU III 026[3] (A.D. 188) ἵνα παραγενομένων τ[ῶν] κρατίστων εὐσχημόν[ων] μη δε]μία μέμψις γένη[ται, ib. I. 147[1] (ii/iii A.D.) ἀρχεφόδοις καὶ εὐσχήμοσι κώμης, P Ryl II. 230[15] (A.D. 259) εἰς τὴν οἰκίαν τοῦ εὐσχήμονος, "to the house of the magistrate," and Ostr 1153 (Rom.) πέμψατε τοὺς εὐ[σ]χήμονας τοὺς ἐπὶ τῶν παρολκημ[άτων. The adj. is used in the weaker sense of "fitting," "suitable," in Michel 1516[5] (B.C. 167–146) with reference to erecting a statue—ὅπου ἂν δόξηι εὔσχημον εἶναι. For the meaning "of honourable position" (in society), as in Mk 15[43], which is cond mned by Phrynichus (ed. Lobeck, p. 333), and described by Rutherford (NP p. 417) as apparently "confined to Christian writers," we can now add to the exx. cited by Wetstein from Plutarch and Josephus such passages as P Hamb I. 37[2] (ii/A.D.) σὺ γὰρ ἀληθινὸς φιλόσοφος καὶ εὐσχήμων γεγένη[σαι, and P Flor I. 16[20] (A.D. 239) ἐντεῦθεν δὲ παρέλαβον παρὰ τῆς εὐσχήμονος, "from the noble lady"

—an interesting parallel to Ac 13[50], 17[12], and 17[34] D (see Ramsay CRE, p. 161). In a trial before the prefect, P Flor I. 61[61] (A.D. 85), the sentence is pronounced—ἄξιος μ[ὲ]ν ἧς μαστιγωθῆναι, διὰ σεαυτοῦ [κ]ατασχὼν ἄνθρωπον εὐσχήμονα καὶ γυν[αῖ]καν. See also Syll 717[13] (ii/B.C.) τὴν παρεπιδημίαν ἐποιήσατο εὐσχήμονα καὶ ἀξίαν τειμῆς, Kaibel 352[2] (a physician's epitaph) σπουδαῖον, εὐ[προσήγορον] καὶ εὐσχή[μονα, and the passages in Vettius Valens, where the word is defined in the Index as = "illustris."

εὐτόνως.

For the comparative of this adverb which in the NT is confined to Lk, cf. P Lille I. 3[i 14] (B.C. 241–0) ἐπ]ιστείλαι εὐτονώτερον, P Petr II. 9 (1)[3] (B.C. 241–39) καλῶς ποιήσεις εὐτονώτερον γράψας Ἀνδροσθένει, ib. 14 (2)[8] γράψον οὖν εὐτονώτερον Θερῶνι. For the adj. cf. P Oxy XII. 1468[7] (c. A.D. 258) ἡ σὴ εὔτονος καὶ περὶ πάντα ἀκοίμητος πρόνοια, "your active and in all cases unresting vigilance" (Edd.), OGIS 315[53] (mid. ii/B.C.) Χλῶρος δ᾽ εὐτονώτατος ἦν τὰ Ῥωμαϊκὰ προτείνων: for the subst., BGU III. 786[ii. 1] (ii/A.D.) διὰ τῆς [σ]ῆς ε[ὐ]τονίας: and for the verb, ib. 970[15] (A.D. 177) ἐὰν γένηται μὴ εὐτονῆσαι αὐτὸν [ἀ]ποδοῦναί μοι τὴν προῖκα, Michel 1504[30] (A.D. 175) εὐτονήσουσι γὰρ οἱ προεστῶτες τοῦ μηδὲν αὐτῶν λυθῆναι, and ib. [49].

εὐτραπελία.

For this word in a good sense we may cite Demetr. de Eloct. 177 (ed. Roberts) ἡ γὰρ Ἀττικὴ γλῶσσα συνεστραμμένον τι ἔχει καὶ δημοτικὸν καὶ ταῖς τοιαύταις εὐτραπελίαις πρέπον, "the Attic dialect has about it something terse, and popular, and so lends itself naturally to the pleasantries of the stage": cf. the adj. ib. 172 ἡ γὰρ ἀντίθεσις εὐτράπελος, "there being wit in a play on words." The simplex *τράπελος is not found, but is vouched for by the Lat. torculus also = "turning," but applied in a different way: see Brugmann-Thumb, p. 231.

Εὔτυχος.

This proper name is common in the inscrr.: see also P Petr I. 12[8], where it is the name of a Syrian slave—παῖ[δας] Διονύσιον καὶ Εὔτυχον Σύρους. The form Εὐτύχης is found in Perg 568[3] (Imperial times), and the fem. Εὐτυχίς in Michel 1560[il 15] (c. B.C. 135).

For the subst. εὐτυχία, as in 4 Macc 6[11] A, cf. P Tebt II. 284[10] (i/B.C.) ἐξ εὐτυχίας.

εὐφημία,

which by derivation is = "good φήμη," "auspicious sound," came to be applied in a wider sense to "reputation," as presumably in 2 Cor 6[8], its only NT occurrence: cf. the letter addressed to a bishop, P Lond 891[9] (iv/A.D.) (= III. p. 242, Chrest. I. p. 157) ἡ γὰρ εὐφημία σου, πάτερ, περιεκύκλωσεν τὸν κ[όσ]μον ὅλον ὡς ἀγαθὸν πατέρα (l. ἀγαθοῦ πατρός), and from the inscrr. Michel 394[39] (mid. i/B.C.) εἶναι θ᾽ ἑαυτ[ῷ] . . τὴν πα[ρὰ] πᾶσιν ἀγαθὴν εὐφημίαν, OGIS 339[30] (c. B.C. 120) περιτιθεὶς τὴν ἐκ τῶν ξένων εὐφημίαν τῆι πάτριδι, and for the verb Syll 653[38] (B.C. 91) ὅταν δὲ αἱ θυσίαι καὶ τὰ μυστήρια συντελεῖται, εὐφαμεῖν πάντας καὶ ἀκούειν τῶν παραγγελλομένων. From Menander we may cite Fragm. p. 194 τοὺς εὖ γεγονότας καὶ τεθραμμένους καλῶς | κἂν τοῖς κακοῖς δεῖ λόγον ἔχειν εὐφημίας. "the well born and nicely nurtured must carefully abstain from evil speech even in misfortune," and *ib.* p. 80 εὐφημείσθω | τέμενος περὶ Λευκάδος ἀκτῆς. "let the shrine be held in good repute along the Leucadian shore."

εὔφημος.

A suggestion of the earlier associations of this word (see *s.v.* εὐφημία) may perhaps be found in Phil 4⁸, where it recalls Greek ethical teaching, and "signifies the delicacy which guards the lips, that nothing may be expressed in public worship that could disturb devotion or give rise to scandal" (E. Curtius *Gesch. Abhandl.* ii. p. 532, *Exp.* VII. iv. p. 442).

εὐφορέω.

With this verb in Lk 12¹⁶ cf. the use of the subst. in the dialect inscr. of Nisyros *Eph. Arch.* 1913, p. 7, No. 1⁷ (iii/B.C.) ὅπως σίτου τε [εὐφ]ορία γίνηται. See also Hobart, p. 144.

εὐφραίνω.

The thought of merrymaking at a feast, as in Lk 16¹² (cf. Field *Notes*, p. 69 f.), comes out in a ii/A.D. letter from the Fayûm, where the writer asks—χρῆσόν μοι ὀνάριον ὑπὸ τρίχωρο[ν] οἴνου καὶ τὸ ἀντίφορτον, ἵνα σχῶμεν αὐτὸ εἰς τὰ Σουχεῖα (the festival of Souchos, a Fayûm deity), ἵνα καὶ ἐν τούτῳ διὰ σὲ δόξωμεν εὐφραίνεσθαι (BGU I. 248²⁸). In BGU IV. 1080⁷ (iii/A.D.) (= *Chrest.* I. p. 564) a father, congratulating his son on his marriage, writes—καὶ ἡμεῖς δὲ ἀκοῇ ἀπόντες ὡς παρόντες διαθέσι ηὐφράνθημεν κατευχόμενοι ἐπὶ τοῖς μέλλουσι. From the inscr. we may cite *OGIS* 504¹⁰ (A.D. 128–9) καὶ εὐφρᾶναι ὑμᾶς ἐνδειξάμενοι ἣν πρὸς αὐτὸν εὔνοιαν ἔχομεν, and *C. and B.* ii. p. 386, No. 232¹⁹ (time of Caracalla or Alex. Severus) σπεύδετε, τὴν ψυχὴν εὐφραίνετε πάντοτε, [θ]νη[τοί—a Jew speaks. See also *Kaibel* 929¹¹·⁶ (time of Severus) εὐφραίνεσθαι (*l.*—εσθε), φίλοι, εἰς λαβύρινθον ἀεί.

εὐφροσύνη.

P Lips I. 119ⁱⁱ·¹ (A.D. 274) εὐφροσύνην ἂν παρέσχεν τὴν τελιοτάτην. The word occurs as a proper name in *Preisigke* 457 (iii/B.C.): Ἰωάννα Εὐφροσύνη: cf. the Christian letter P Oxy VI. 939¹⁹ iv/A.D.) (= *Selections*, p. 129) διὰ Εὐφροσύνου. For the adj. see *Preisigke* 411 (iii/iv A.D.) where in a sepulchral inscr. a certain Serapion is eulogized as φιλότεκνε φιλόγυναιε φιλόφιλε εὐφρόσυνε ἄλυπε χρηστέ, and P Lond V. 1684³ (mid. vi/A.D.) ἐν εὐφροσύνῳ εἰμι, where the editor notes that the meaning may be "I have a good opportunity," or merely "I am glad."

εὐχαριστέω

was originally = "do a good turn to," "oblige," as in P Petr II. 2(4)⁶ (c. B.C. 260) (= Witkowski², p. 24) εὐχαριστήσεις μοι, "gratiam meam merebis, gratiam tibi habebo," *ib.* 15 (3)⁷ (B.C. 241–39) τοῦτο δὲ ποιήσας εὐχαριστήσεις ἡμῖν, "by doing this you will oblige us" (Edd.), P Hib I. 66⁵ (B.C. 228) ὥστε σε μὴ διὰ κενῆς εὐχαριστῆσαι ἡμ[ῖν, "so that you shall not oblige me to no purpose" (Edd.), P Eleph 13⁷ (B.C. 223–2) εὐχαριστήσεις οὖμ μοι σαυτοῦ τε

ἐπιμελόμενος, "oblige me by taking care of yourself" (on the use of the fut. see *Proleg.* p. 177). In late Greek this passed readily into the meaning "be grateful," "give thanks": cf. Lob. *Phryn.* p. 18 "pro gratias agere ante Polybium usurpavit nemo." Thus we have P Amh II. 133² (early ii/A.D.) πρὸ τῶν ὅλων ἀσπάζομαί σε καὶ εὐχαριστῶ σοι ὅτι ἐδήλωσάς μοι στὴν (*l.* τὴν) ὑγείαν σου, P Oxy I. 71ⁱ·²² (A.D. 303) πρὸς τὸ δυνηθῆναί με τὰ ἴδια ἀπολαβεῖν καὶ τὴ[ν] τύχην σου εὐχαρειστῖν, "so I shall be enabled to recover my property and acknowledge my gratitude to your excellency" (Edd.), and more particularly with a religious reference, P Lond I. 42¹¹ (B.C. 168) (= I. p. 30, *Selections*, p. 10) ἐπὶ (cf. 1 Cor 1⁴) μὲν τῶι ἐρρῶσθα[ί] σε εὐθέως τοῖς θεοῖς εὐχαρίστουν, "I immediately gave thanks to the gods that you were well," P Tebt I. 56³ (late ii/B.C.) καλῶς οὖν ποήσης εὐχαριστῆσαι πρῶτον μὲν τοῖς θεοῖς, δεύτερον δὲ σῶσαι ψυχὰς πολλάς, BGU II. 423⁶ (ii/A.D.) (= *Selections*, p. 90) εὐχαριστῶ τῷ κυρίῳ Σεράπιδι, ὅτι μου κινδυνεύσαντος εἰς θάλασσαν ἔσωσε, and from the inscr. *Syll* 807 as cited *s.v.* ἀναβλέπω (cf. Lk 17¹⁸). See also Ramsay *Exp T* x. p. 54 for the prevalence of the formula εὐχαριστῶ τῇ θεῷ in votive inscr., recalling at once the Pauline εὐχαριστῶ τῷ θεῷ μου. [On the place of "thanksgiving" in early letters, and the correspondence suggested with the outward form of the Pauline Epistles, cf. Deissmann *LAE*, p. 168 n.³, Milligan *Documents*, p. 93.] With the use of the passive in 2 Cor 1¹¹, Deissmann (*BS*, p. 122) compares the mutilated P Petr II. 2 (4)⁸ (B.C. 260–59) εὐχαριστηθεῖς μοι. In still another set of passages εὐχαριστέω passes into the meaning "pray," as P Lond 413³ (*c.* A.D. 346) ε[ὐ]χ[αρ]ειστῶ (εὐχαριστῶ GH) τῷ θεῷ περὶ [τῆ]ς σ[ωτ]ηρίας, *ib.* 418³ (*c.* A.D. 346) (= II. p. 303) εὐχαρι[σ]τ[ο]ῦμε τ[ῷ] θεῷ περὶ [τ]ῆς ὁλοκληρα σε (? *l.* ὁλοκληρίας σου) both as amended P Lond III. p. 387), and the vi/A.D. Christian amulet BGU III. 954⁴ (= *Selections*, p. 132) εὐχαριστῶ ἐγὼ Σιλουανὸς υἱὸς Σαραπίωνος καὶ κλίνω τὴν κεφαλὴν [μο]υ καενώπιόν (*l.* κατεν- -) σου. MGr εὐκαριστῶ, "thank," "satisfy."

εὐχαριστία.

For this subst. we can cite only one ex. from the papyri, P Lond 1178²⁵ (A.D. 194) (= III. p. 216) τῆς πρὸς αὐτοὺς εὐχαριστίας, in the copy of a letter written by the Emperor Claudius to a Gymnastic Club expressing his gratification at games performed in his honour. It is, however, common in the inscr., e.g. *OGIS* 227⁶ (iii/B.C.) διὰ τὴν τοῦ δήμου εὐχαριστίαν, *Syll* 365⁵ (*c.* A.D. 37) εἰς εὐχαριστίαν τηλικούτου θεοῦ εὑρεῖν ἴσας ἀμοιβάς, and *OGIS* 199³¹ (i/A.D.) δι᾽ ἣν ἔχω πρὸς τὸν μέγιστον θεόν μου Ἄρην εὐχαριστίαν, where the editor notes that εὐχαριστία = τὸ εὐχάριστον εἶναι, and that as the adj. denotes "non modo grati animi hominem . . . sed etiam gratiosum, acceptam," the meaning almost amounts to "quia deus mihi favet." On the Christian use of εὐχαριστία with the corresponding verb see a note by Hort in *JTS* iii. p. 594 ff. In *JHS* xxvii. p. 65 we hear of a εὐχαριστήριον to Dionysus. MGr εὐκαρίστησι, "contentment," "pleasure."

εὐχάριστος

is applied to the "beneficent" gods in P Par 29¹³ (B.C. 161–0) δι᾽ ὑμᾶς τοὺς εὐχαρίστους θεούς, and in P Lond

879[11] (B.C. 123) (= III. p. 7) is an epithet of Ptolemy Euergetes II.—Πτολεμαίου θεοῦ Εὐεργέτου καὶ Σωτῆρος ἑαυτῶν Εὐχαρίστου: similarly of Ptolemy V. in *OGIS* 90[5] (the Rosetta stone—B.C. 196), where see the editor's note. Like the subst., it is very common in the inscrr. to denote the "gratitude" of the people to their benefactors, as *Priene* 103[8] (c. B.C. 100) γεν[όμενος ὁ δῆμος εὐχάριστος. The way was thus prepared for the Christian use as in Col 3[15]: see further s.v. εὐχαριστία.

εὐχή.

For εὐχή = "prayer" (as in Jas 5[15]) cf. P Strass I. 41[32] (A.D. 250) τῆς μὲν παιδὸς ἤδ[η γ]εγαμημένης κατὰ τὰς εὐχὰς τοῦ πάππου, BGU IV. 1080[5] (iii/A.D.?) συνχαίρων ἐπὶ τῇ ὑπαρχθείσῃ σοι ἀγαθῇ [ἐ]σευβεῖ (*l.* εὐσεβεῖ) καὶ εὐτυχῇ (*l.* εὐτυχεῖ) [σ]υμβιώσι κατὰ τὰς κοινὰς ἡμῶν εὐχὰς καὶ προσευχάς, and P Giss I. 22, where a father writes to his son, rejoicing that he is ἀπρόσ[κοπ]ον καὶ ἱλαρώτατον, and adds [10] ταῦ[τά μ]οι ἡ πᾶσα εὐχή ἐστι [καὶ μ]έριμνα. In *ib.* 23 the same father writing to his daughter speaks of his prayer for his children as [5] πάντων (πασῶν?) τῶν εὐχῶν μου ἀναγκαιοτάτη. The Christian usage is seen in P Oxy VI. 930[5] (iv/A.D.) ταῖς εὐ]χαῖς ἡμῶν ἐπένευσεν διασώσας ἡμῖν [τὴν ἡμῶν] κυρίαν, "He inclined His ear to our prayers by preserving for us our mistress" (Edd.), BGU III. 954[15] (vi/A.D.) τὴν εὐαγγελικὴν εὐχήν, *i.e.* the Lord's Prayer. According to *Priene* 174[18] (ii/B.C.) one of the duties of the priest of Dionysus is prayer—καὶ τὰς εὐχὰς εὔξεται ὑπὲρ τῆς πόλεως τῆς Πριηνέων: cf. the inscr. (probably i/B.C.) found on the lintel of the Temple of Pnepheros and Petesuchos in the Fayûm—Πνεφερῶτι καὶ Πετεσούχῳ καὶ τοῖς συννάοις θεοῖς μεγάλοις μεγάλοις ὑπὲρ αὐτοῦ καὶ τῆς γυναικὸς καὶ τῶν τέκνων εὐχήν (P Fay p. 32), and the fragmentary Jewish inscr. over a seven-branched candlestick from Akmonia— ὑπὲρ εὐχὴ (*l.* εὐχῆς) πάσῃ (*l.* πάσης) τῇ πατρίδι (*C. and B* ii. p. 651). In this latter connexion it is interesting to notice in a series of accounts of the four commissioners for the waterworks of the "metropolis" (? Hermopolis) the mention not only of the water-rate (128 drachmae a month) for the *proseucha* of Theban Jews, but also of a similar water-rate for the εὐχεῖον, apparently "a place for prayer" (P Lond 1177[60]—A.D. 113) (= III. p. 183, *Chrest.* I. p. 227): see further *Exp T* xix. p. 41. For εὐχήν (with ἀνέθηκεν or ἀνέστησεν understood) at the end of Anatolian inscrr. see Ramsay in *Exp T* x. p. 13, where it is noted that the word indicates both "prayer" and "vow," sometimes the one thought being more prominent, sometimes the other. MGr εὐχή, "blessing," "prayer."

εὔχομαι.

With 3 Jn [2] cf. P Oxy II. 292[11] (c. A.D. 25) (= *Selections,* p. 38) πρὸ δὲ πάντων ὑγιάνειν (*l.* ὑγιαίνειν) σε εὔχ[ο]μαι ἀβασκάντως τὰ ἄριστα πράττων, "but above all I pray that you may have good health, faring prosperously unharmed by the evil eye." The verb is very common in similar epistolary phrases in the opening or closing greetings of letters, e.g. P Fay 117[7] (A.D. 108) ἐρρῶσθαί σαι εὔχομαι εἰς τὸν ἀεὶ χρόνον, P Ryl II. 233[15] (letter of a retainer— ii/A.D.) εὔχομαί σε τὸν κύριον ἰδεῖν ἐν μείζοσι προκοπαῖς, ἐν ἀδραῖς εὐημερίαις. ἔρρωσο, κύριε, "I pray, my lord, that I may see your further advancement and ripe

prosperity. Farewell, my lord" (Edd.), *ib.* 244[3] (iii/A.D.) πρὸ μὲν πάντων εὔχομαι θεοῖς πᾶσιν [ὅ]πως ὑγιαίνοντας ὑμᾶς ἀπο[λ]άβω, [27] ἐρρῶσθαι ὑμᾶς εὔχομαι πολλοῖς χρόνοις, and the Christian P Oxy X. 1298[4] (iv/A.D.) πρὸ παντὸς εὔχομε (*l.* εὔχομαι) τῷ κυρίῳ θεῷ περὶ τῆς ὁλοκληρίας σου καὶ τῶν φιλτάτων σου. From the inscrr. we may cite *OGIS* 378 (A.D. 18-9) θεῷ ἁγίῳ ὑψίστῳ ὑπὲρ τῆς Ῥοιμητάλκου καὶ Πυθοδωρίδος ἐκ τοῦ κατὰ τὸν Κοιλα- (λ)ητικὸν πόλεμον κινδύνου σωτηρίας εὐξάμενος καὶ ἐπι- τυχὼν Γάϊος Ἰούλιος Πρόκ(λ)ος χαριστ(ήρι)ον, and the address to a deceased person in an Alexandrian *graffito* (Imperial period?) cited by U. von Wilamowitz-Moellen- dorf *Berlin. Sitzungsberichte* 1902, p. 1098—εὔχομαι κἀγὼ ἐν τάχυ σὺν σοὶ εἶναι: cf. Phil 1[23] and see Deissmann *LAE,* p. 305.

The verb is by no means so common in the NT as we might have expected, having given place to the compound προσεύχομαι, perhaps because, like εὐχή, it had come to be "too much connected with the idea of a vow and a gift promised to God" (Ramsay *Exp T* x. p. 13). MGr εὐκοῦμαι, "bless," "wish well."

εὔχρηστος.

For εὔχρηστος with the dat. of pers. (2 Tim 2[21]), cf. P Petr III. 53 (*n*)[5] Πέτωυς, ἐν οὐδὲ σὺ ἀγνοεῖς εὔχρηστον ὄντα τοῖς ἐν τῶι νομῶι, ἀπέσταλται εἰς Ἀλεξανδρείαν, "Petous, who, as you know very well, is of great value to those in the nome, was sent to Alexandria" (Ed.), *Priene* 102[5] (c. B.C. 100) προ[γ]όν[ων] δὲ ὄντα γεγ[ε]νημένων εὐχρή- στων κοινῇ [τ]ε τῶι δήμωι καὶ κατ' ἰδίαν ἑκάστωι τῶν π[ολιτῶν, and for the comp. see PSI IV. 361[21] (B.C. 251-0) προθυμότερος ἔσται καί σοι εὐχρηστότερος. The constr. with εἰς is found in *Cagnat* IV. 818[23] where a certain C. Ageleius is honoured at Hierapolis for fiscal services he had rendered—εἰς χρείας κυρ[ια]κὰς εὔχρηστο[ν] γενόμενον. For the subst. see P Par 63[101] (B.C. 164) (= P Petr III. p. 35) ὅταν ὁρῶσιν ἀντικαταλλασσομένην αὐτοῖς τὴν εὐχρηστίαν, "as soon as they see that the benefit will accrue to them- selves also" (Mahaffy), and for the verb = "lend" (cf. Lob. *Phryn.* p. 402) see P Oxy II. 241[30] (c. A.D. 98) πρός ται (*l.* τε) ἃς εὐχρήστησαν αὐτῷ κατὰ χιρόγραφον, "in return for an accommodation in accordance with a note of hand" (Edd.), *ib.* XII. 1473[26] (A.D. 201).

εὐψυχέω.

The force of this rare verb, as in Phil 2[19], comes out well in a letter from a wife to her husband, BGU IV. 1097[15] (time of Claudius or Nero) ἐγὼ γὰρ οὐ[ο] ὀλιγωρῶ, ἀλλὰ εὐψυχοῦσα πα[ρα]μένω. It is found, instead of the usual χαίρειν, in the salutation of a letter of condolence, P Oxy I. 115[1] (ii/A.D.) (= *Selections,* p. 96) Εἰρήνη Ταοννώφρει καὶ Φίλωνι εὐψυχεῖν. See also Hermas *Vis.* i. iii 2 σὺ μόνον μὴ ῥαθυμήσῃς, ἀλλὰ εὐψύχει καὶ ἰσχυροποίει σου τὸν οἶκον. Εὐψύχει is very common in sepulchral inscrr., as *Preisigke* 46 Νίγερ μαχαιροφόρος, εὐψύχι, (ἐτῶν) ξ. For the subst. see *Syll* 686[30] (ii/A.D.) ἐπὶ τοσοῦτον δὲ καὶ ἀρετῆς καὶ εὐψυχίας ἦλθεν.

εὐωδία.

For the adj. cf. P Amh II. 133[7] (early ii/A.D.) ἠγορ- ά[κ]αμέν σοι εὐώδη κεράμια ἑκατόν, "I have bought for you

a hundred sweet-smelling jars" (Edd.), P Oxy IX. 1211[4]
(ii/A.D.) οἴνου εὐώδη κεράμ(ια) β̄, P Leid W[i. 15] (ii/iii A.D.)
στύραξ, ἐστὶν γὰρ βαρὶς (l. βαρὺς) καὶ εὐώδης. Nestle contributes two interesting notes on the NT use of the subst. in
ZNTW iv. p. 272, vii. p. 95 f.

εὐώνυμος.

It is curious that, while δεξιός is common, εὐώνυμος does
not occur at all in the indices to P Oxy I.—XII. and BGU
I.—IV. For an interesting usage see the astrological P Ryl
II. 63 cited s.v. δεξιός, and cf. Syll 801, a v/B.C. inscr.
from Ephesus dealing with augury, where it is laid down
that if a bird flying from right to left concealed its wing, it
was a good omen (δεξιός), but if it raised its left wing (ἢν δὲ
ἐπάρει τὴ[ν ε]ὐώνυμον πτέρυγα), then, whether it raised or
concealed the wing, it was of ill omen (εὐώνυμος).

ἐφάλλομαι.

Ostr 1220[7] (ii/iii A.D.) καὶ ἐνθάδε ἐφάλλομαι μὴ ἔχων
[. . . ., Syll 802[27] (iii/B.C.) ἐδόκει . . . . [τ]ὸν θεὸν ἐφαλέσθαι ἐπὶ τὰν χῆρα, with reference to the healing of
a powerless hand in the Asclepieum of Epidaurus.

ἐφάπαξ

occurs in the late P Lond 483[58] (A.D. 616) (= II. p. 328).
A new form ἀφάπαξ is found in P Flor II. 158[10] (iii/A.D.)
in a context which suggests the meaning "at one time" or
"all at once"—ἐπέστειλα δὲ καὶ εἰς Ταυρείνου ἵνα κἀκεῖνο
ἔλθῃ τὸ ταυρικὸν καὶ ἀφάπαξ τὰ ξ[ύ]λα παρενέχθη εἰς
τη . . . .: but note that Vitelli (Berichtigungsliste i.
p. 150) now describes ἀφάπαξ as an error in writing for
ἐφ' ἄπαξ.

ἐφευρετής.

For the verb see Syll 366[5] (c. A.D. 38) πᾶσαν ἀεὶ ὁσίαν
τῆς εἰς τὸν Σεβαστὸν εὐσεβείας ἐφευρίσκουσα ἐπίνοιαν.

ἐφημερία.

A hitherto unknown derivative of this word is found in P
Petr II. 10(2)[13] (iii/B.C.) ἐν τῶι ἐφημερευτηρίωι, with reference apparently to the "guardroom, where soldiers remain
all day on duty" (Ed.). For the verb ἐφημερέω see OGIS
595[20] (ii/A.D.) ἐφημερ οῦντος Γ(αίου) Οὐαλερίου Καλλι-
κράτους. The subst. ἐφημερίς = "daybook" occurs in official documents e.g. P Oxy II. 268[10] (A.D. 58), 271[8] (A.D.
56), ib. XII. 1497[6] (c. A.D. 279). In MGr ἐφημερία is an
eccles. term = "parish," "cure," and ἐφημερίδα = "news-
paper."

ἐφήμερος.

To the exx. usually cited for this NT ἅπ. εἰρ. (Jas 2[15])
add Vett. Val. p. 62[17] ἀτυχεῖς καὶ ἀσχήμονας ποιοῦσι καὶ
ἐνδεεῖς τῆς ἐφημέρου τροφῆς. The phrase implies "food for
the day" or "the day's supply of food" rather than "daily
food": cf. Field Notes, p. 236 f.

ἐφίστημι

occurs = "delay," "check," in P Petr II. 20 [ii. 6] (B.C.
252) ἵνα οὖν μὴ ἡ ἐξαγωγὴ τοῦ σίτου ἐπισταθῇ, "that the
transport of the wheat may not be delayed," and in the

medical receipt P Oxy VIII. 1088[20] (early i/A.D.) ἴσχαιμον·
χαλκίτιδει λήᾳ χρῶι καὶ εὐθέως ἐπιστήσει, "styptic: use
pounded rock-alum, and it will stop (the blood) at once"
(Ed.). It is also common = "put up," "fix," of doors, as in
PSI IV. 300[8] (B.C. 241-0) θύραν τὴν ἐφεστηκυῖα[ν ἐ]πὶ τῆς
προστάδος ("vestibule"), P Fay 110[27] (A.D. 94) τὰς θύρας
ἐπιστησάτωσαν οἱ τέκτονες: cf. P Oxy VI. 912[27] (A.D. 235)
τὰς ἐφεστώσας τοῖς τόποις θύρας καὶ κλεῖδας, "the existing
doors and keys" (Edd.). In the late P Hamb I. 23[9] (A.D.
569) ἀμπελουργῶν ὁρμωμένων μὲν ἀπὸ κώμης . . . , ἐφεστ-
ώτων δὲ ἐνταῦθα ἐπὶ τῆς α[ὐ]τῆς Ἀντινοέων πόλεως) the
reference is to domicile: "ihre ἰδία (origo) ist das Dorf
. . . , ihr Domizil Antinoupolis" (Edd.). The idea of
hostile intent, as in 1 Th 5[3] (on form ἐπ—, see WH Notes[2],
p. 151), appears in P Thead 21[7] (A.D. 318) τινές κακοῦργοι
ἐπιστάντες ἐκεῖσε διὰ νυκτὸς ἔνθα τὰ θρέμματα ἐβόσκετο καὶ
ἀπεσύλησαν : cf., on the other hand, P Fay 20[20] (iii/iv A.D.)
προορᾶσθαι τῶν ἐθνῶν οἷς ἐφεστήκασι, "providing for the
interests of the peoples over whom they are placed" (Edd.).
See also P Flor II. 236[1] (A.D. 267) ἔπεμψα Ἀπολλώνιον καὶ
Κλαύδιον ἐπιστησομένους τῇ τρύγῃ τοῦ Χρυσοχόου, and
P Oxy IX. 1220[22] (iii/A.D.) οὐδὲν ἠφάνισεν ὁ ἱπποπόταμις,
ἤ τι γάρ ἐστιν περίεργον, ἐφίσταμε αὐτῶν, "the hippopotamus has destroyed nothing, for if there is any superfluity, I
watch over the place" (Ed.).

ἐχθές.

For this form, which alone is found in the NT, and is predominant in the LXX (cf. Thackeray Gr. i. p. 97), we can
cite numerous exx. from our documents from Ptolemaic times
onwards, e.g. P Eleph 29[6] (iii/B.C.) περὶ ὧν σοι συνελάλησα
σοι (omit) ἐχθές, PSI IV. 442[1] (iii/B.C.) ἤμελλεν ἂν ἀναχωρῆσαι ἐχθές, P Fay 108[1] (c. A.D. 171) ἐχθὲς ἥτις ἦν ιη̄ τοῦ
[ὄ]ντος μηνὸς Θώθ, P Lips I. 105[1] (i/ii A.D.) ἐχθὲς κατέσχον
τὸν φύλακα νομίζων σοι δύνασθαι πέμψαι ὃν ἐπεζήτησας
λόγον, P Oxy X. 1349 (iv/A.D.) ἐπειδὴ ἐξῆλθα ἀπὸ σοῦ
ἐχθὲς μὴ διαλεχθείς σοι περὶ τῆς κυθίδος (l. κυθρίδος). For
ἐκθές cf. P Fay 123[3] (c. A.D. 100) ἐκθές σοι ἔγραψα διὰ
Μάρδωνος, and for ἐκχθές, as in LXX Ps 89[4] A, see Cronert
Mem. Herc. p. 89 n[3]. Χθές is found in P Lond 214[4] (A.D.
270 275) (= II. p. 161) Παταλᾶς ναυπηγὸς χθὲς ἀλόγως
γενόμενος εἰς ἀμπελικὸν χωρίον.

The above evidence, it will be seen, strongly supports the
use of the form ἐχθές in the Κοινή, notwithstanding the
conflicting views of the older grammarians (cf. Lob. Phryn.,
p. 323, Maidhof Begriffsbestimmung, p. 362). Even Rutherford (NP, p. 370 ff.), who claims ἐχθές as the regular Attic
form as compared with the old Ionic χθές, draws his evidence
almost entirely from the comic poets, who borrowed freely
from the vernacular. MGr (ἐ)χτές, (ἐ)ψές.

ἔχθρα.

P Hib I. 170 (B.C. 247) ἵνα μὴ ἀντὶ φιλίας ἔχθραν [ποιώ]-
μεθα, P Oxy XII. 1588[1] (early iv/A.D.) ἡ φιλικὴ σχέσις
πρὸς σὲ καὶ τὸν υἱόν σου ἐλπίζε[ι] μεγάλη[ν] ἔχθραν γενέσθαι. For the form ἔκθρα cf. the royal ordinance P Tebt
I. 5[259] (B.C. 118) where it is enacted that no one shall be
arrested πρὸς ἴδιον ὀφείλημα ἢ ἀδίκημα μηδὲ ἰδίας ἔκθρας
ἕνεκεν, "for a private debt or offence or owing to a private
quarrel" (Edd.), and BGU II. 389[8] (iii/A.D.) (as amended
p. 356) τὴν ἔκθραν καὶ παρανο[μίαν : see also s.v. ἐχθρός.

ἐχθρός.

The Commagene rescript of Antiochus I. ends—παρανό-μωι δὲ γνώμηι κατὰ δαιμόνων τιμῆς καὶ χωρὶς ἡμετέρας ἀρᾶς παρὰ θεῶν ἐχθρὰ πάντα (*OGIS* 383²³⁷—mid. i/B.C.). On the forms ἐκθρός, which occurs several times in Cod. Bezae, and ἐκχθρός, see Crönert *Mem. Herc.* p. 89. MGr ἐχτρός, ὀχτρός.

ἔχιδνα.

Ramsay (*Luke*, p. 63 ff.) has shown that by the ἔχιδνα of Ac 28³ we are probably to understand a constrictor snake, closely resembling a viper, without poison-fangs, which fixes its teeth firmly into the human skin so as to hang on, with-out, however, doing any real injury to the skin. The verb καθῆψεν in the sense of "fastened upon" rather than "bit" ("momordit," Blass) is therefore correctly applied to it, as against Harnack *Lukas der Arzt*, p. 123 f. (E. Tr., p. 177 f.). On γεννήματα ἐχιδνῶν as equivalent to the simple ἔχιδναι in Mt 3⁷ see McNeile *ad l.*, following Nestle in *ZNTW* xiv. p. 267 f.

ἔχω.

It may be well to illustrate some of the less usual forms of this common verb. The future σχήσω (cf. Kühner-Blass *Gr.* I. ii. p. 112 n.³) is restored by the editor in *OGIS* 751⁸ (ii/B.C. ἐπεὶ θλιβέντες ἐμ πλείοσιν ἀσθενῶς [σχή]σετε. For the 2 aor. with 1 aor. termination (cf. Ac 7⁵⁷ D συν-έσχαν) see BGU II. 451⁸ (i/ii A.D.) ἀναγκαίως ἔσχαμεν δ[ι] ἐπιστολῆς σε ἀσπάσεσθαι, and for ἔσχοσαν cf. *OGIS* 315⁶⁹ (B.C. 164–159) ὑφοψίαν μοχθηράν, ἣν καὶ περὶ τοῦ ἀδελφοῦ ἔσχοσαν. In *ib.* 223⁷ (iii/B.C.) we have αὐτοὶ ἀπολογισ-άμενοι περί τε τῆς εὐνοίας ἣν διὰ παντὸς ἐσχήκατε εἰς τὴν ἡμετέραν οἰκίαν, and for similar forms see the editor's note³ to *ib.* 323.

For the trans. use of the verb see such passages as P Oxy IV. 743¹⁹ (B.C. 2) εἰ καὶ π[ρ]ὸς ἄλλους εἶχον πρᾶγμα, βοηθὸν αὐτοῦ γ[ε]νέσθαι διὰ ἣν ἔχομε(ν) πρὸς ἑαυτοὺς φιλίαν, BGU I. 22⁸ (A.D. 114) (= *Selections*, p. 74), which illustrate 1 Cor 6¹ : P Leid U 3²⁰ (1st half ii/B.C.) τέλος ἔχει πάντα παρὲξ τῆς ἐπιγραφῆς, as in Lk 22³⁷ : and P Petr III. 42 G 9⁷ (mid. iii/B.C. ἐάν τινος χρείαν ἔχηις, as in Mt 6¹². With the metaphorical usage in Mk 16⁸, cf. P Giss I. 65a⁴ πα]ρακαλῶ σε, κύριέ μου, εἰδότα τ[ὴ]ν [ἔ]χουσάν με συμφορὰν ἀπολῦσαί μοι κτλ., and BGU II. 380¹⁵ (iii/A.D.) (= *Selections*, p. 105) οὐδὲν περισσότε[ρ]ον ἔχι σε, "there is nothing so much the matter with you," followed by—εἰ δὲ οἶδες σατῶ, ὅτι ἔχεις ἔτι, γράψον μοι, "but if you yourself know that matters are still not going well with you, write to me." In BGU I. 33⁶ (ii/iii A.D.) ἐγὼ γὰρ ἐμαυτὸν οὐκ ἔχω εἰ μὴ περαιωθῇ τὸ πρᾶγμα τοῦτο, the verb has the force of "have rightly or really" : cf. P Oxy VII. 1020⁵ (A.D. 198–201) εἰ τὴν ἐκ τῆς ἡ[λ]ικίας ἔχεις βοήθιαν, where the editor translates "if you can claim the assistance due to immature age," and notes that ἔχεις implies "is rightly yours." In P Lond 962³ (A.D. 254 or 261) (= III. p. 210) δέξαι παρ' αὐτοῦ δραχμὰς δια-κοσίας καὶ ἔχε αὐτὰς εἴς τε περιχωματισμὸν ἢ καὶ λόγον ὀψωνίων, ἔχε = "spend." This might give some support to the imper. (as RV marg.) in Mt 27⁶⁵, against which the durative tense is a serious objection. For the phrase γυναῖ-κα ἔχειν (1 Cor 7²·¹²) see *Syll* 794 περὶ γε<ι>νεῆς, ἣ (not

ἢ as Dittenberger) ἔσται[ι] ἐκ τῆς γυναικὸς Α[ἴ]γλης, τῆς νῦν ἔχει, and cf. P Leid Wᵛⁱⁱⁱ·⁹ (ii/iii A.D.) ἐὰν θέλῃς γυνὲ-κας οὐ μὴ σχεθῆναι ὑπὸ ἄλλου ἀνδρός. The Latinism of Lk 14¹⁸ f is well illustrated by P Oxy II. 292⁶ (c. A.D. 25) (= *Selections*, p. 37) παρακαλῶ σε . . . ἔχειν αὐτὸν συνεστ-αμένον, and similarly *ib.* IV. 787 (A.D. 16). P Giss I. 71⁴ (time of Hadrian). For the verb in receipts we may cite Meyer *Ostr* 10⁷ (Ptol.) ἔχουμεν (*l.* ἔχομεν) παρὰ σοῦ τοῦ (*l.* τὸ) τέλος, and the much more common aor. in *ib.* 26³ (A.D. 118) ἔσχ ον) ὑπ(ὲρ) λαο(γραφίας) . . . β͞ς ῥυπ(αρὰς) δραχ(μάς) : see further Wilcken *Ostr* i. p. 86, and *Archiv* i. p. 76 ff. The pres. part. mid. = "next," "following," of time, is seen in P Rev Lˣˣⁱᵛ·²⁹ (iii/B.C.) ἐν τ[ῶι ἐχο]μένωι ἐνιαυτῶι, and is = "adjoining" of place in P Par 51⁵ (B.C. 160) (= *Selections*, p. 19) ἄν]θρωπ[ος] . . . ἐχόμενός μου, P Tebt I. 86 (late ii/B.C.) where the land of Demetrius is βορρᾶ ἐχομένη to that of Apollonius and νότου ἐχομένη to that of Hermione : see the editors' Introd. p. 381. For ἐχόμενα used adverbially = "hard by," "near," as in Judg 9³⁷, see *PSI* V. 514² (B.C. 252–1) εὐθέως δὲ τούτων ἐχόμενα κατάπεμψον τὰ ἐπισταλέντα εἰς τὰ γενέθλια τοῦ βασιλέως.

For the verb used intransitively with an adverb, as in Ac 21¹⁸, 2 Cor 12¹⁴, cf. P Lond 42²⁹ (B.C. 168) (= I. p. 31) ἡ μήτηρ σου τυγχάνει βαρέως ἔχουσα, BGU I. 80¹⁷ (A.D. 158–9) ἡ Σωτηρία ἑτοίμως ἔχουσα καταγράψαι, P Cairo Preis 45⁶ (ii/A.D.) καλῶς δ' ἔχει σε ἐνθάδε ἐλθόντα μετ' ἐμοῦ μένειν, the Christian letter P Oxy VI. 939²¹ (iv/A.D.) (= *Selections*, p. 129) εἰ μὴ ἐπινόσως ἐσχήκει τὸ σωμάτιον τότε ὁ υἱὸς 'Αθανάσιος, "unless my son Athanasius had then been in a sickly state of health," and from the inscrr. *Michel* 543¹² (c. B.C. 200) καλῶς ἔχον ἐσ[τὶ] τιμᾶσθαι τοὺς εὔνους ἄνδρας, *ib.* 687⁴⁴ (end iii/B.C.) ὅπως ἂν τούτων γενομένων ἔχει καλῶς καὶ εὐσεβῶς τῶ[ι] δήμωι τὰ πρὸς τοὺς θεούς. MGr ἔχω : note ἔχει (c. acc.), "there is," "there are."

ἕως.

For ἕως as a conjunction followed by ἄν and the aor. subj., as in Mt 2¹³ *al.*, cf. P Petr II. 40 (*a* ²⁸ (iii/B.C.) ἕως ἂν ὑγιαίνοντας ὑμᾶς ἴδωμεν, P Oxy VIII. 1124⁷ (A.D. 26) ἔ]ω[ς ἂν τὸ ἀ]πότακτο[ν] κομίσηται. 'Αν is omitted in such passages as P Grenf II. 35¹⁶ (mid. i/B.C.) γράψον μοι περὶ τοῦ μὴ λογεύιν, ἕως καταβῆις, P Oxy III. 531⁶ (ii/A.D.) ἕως ἐπ' ἀγαθῷ πρὸς σὲ παραγένομαι (*l.* —ωμαι), *ib.* VIII. 1125¹⁵ (ii/A.D.) ἕως τὰ ὀφειλόμενα κομίσωνται : cf. Mk 14³² *al.*, and on the NT usage generally see further Blass *Gr.* p. 219, also *Proleg.* p. 168 f. In P Oxy VIII. 1159²¹ (late iii/A.D.) ἐασ[ο]ν δὲ παρ' αὐτοῖς τὰ σύν[ερ]γα ἕως πέμψω τὰ ἀναλώματα, "leave the tools with them until I send the expenses" (Ed.), we may perhaps have the fut. ind., as in Lk 13³⁵AD, but the aor. subj. is more probable. In P Fay 118¹² (A.D. 110) πορεύου εἰς Διονυσιάδα . . ἕως τὸν ἐκεῖ ἐλαιῶνα ποτίσῃς, ἕως appears to have a final force (= ὡς).

For the later prepositional usage of ἕως with gen. of place, see P Tebt I. 33⁶ (B.C. 112) (= *Selections*, p. 30) ἀνάπλουν ἕως τοῦ 'Αρσι(νοΐτου) νο(μοῦ) ἐπὶ θεωρίαν ποιούμενος, "making the voyage as far as the Arsinoïte nome to see the sights," and with gen. of time see BGU IV. 1128⁸ (B.C. 14) ἕως τοῦ προκ(ειμένου) χρό νου) and *OGIS* 90¹⁶ (Rosetta stone—B.C. 196) ἕως τοῦ πρώτου ἔτους ἐπὶ τοῦ πατρὸς αὐτοῦ

= "usque ad primum Ptolemaei Philopatoris annum" (Ed.): cf. also *ib.* 226²⁰ (iii/B.C.) μαχοῦμαι [ὑπὲρ α]ὑτοῦ καὶ – [ν] πραγμάτων τῶν ἐκείνου ἕως ζωῆς καὶ θανά[του (cf. Mk 14³¹), with the editor's note. With ἕως τούτου in Lk 22⁵¹, cf. P Tebt I. 56⁷ (late ii B.C.) οὐκ ἔχομεν ἕως τῆς τροφῆς τῶν κτηνῶν ἡμῶν, "we have not so much as food for our cattle" (Edd.), and with ἕως τοῦ νῦν in Mt 24²¹, cf. BGU IV. 1197⁵ (B.C. 4) οἱ σοι] προς[τ]άται ἕως τοῦ νῦν ἀ[πὸ] τοῦ ἐννεακαιδεκ[άτου] ἔτους [Κα]ίσαρος οὐκ ἔδωκαν ἡμῖν. The supposed "Hebraism" in ἕως πότε Mk 9¹⁹) is discussed by Moulton in *Cambridge Biblical Essays*, p. 473 f.

Z

Ζακχαῖος—ζῆλος

Ζακχαῖος.

This proper name is restored by Wilcken (*Archiv* ii. p. 174 n.³) in one of Crum's *Coptic Ostraca*—435⁷ Ζα]κχαῖος.

ζάω.

For this common verb = "live" it is enough to cite such passages as P Petr II. 13 (19)⁷ (B.C. 258-253) καὶ ζῶντός σου καὶ εἰς θεοὺς ἀπελθόντος, *ib.* III. 2²¹ (B.C. 236) ἕ]ως ἂν ἐγὼ ζῶι, P Oxy III. 472⁷ (c. A.D. 130) ἄλλοι πολλοὶ τὸν θάνατον τοῦ ζῆν προκρείναντες, *ib.* VI. 937⁵ (iii/A.D.) ἐὰν οὖν ζήσω χρόνον καὶ ἔλθω εἰς τὴν πατρίδα μου ἐκδικήσω ἐμαυτόν, *ib.* XII. 1477⁹ (question to an oracle—iii/iv A.D.) εἰ ζῇ ὁ ἀπόδημος : As might be expected, the word is constantly found in sepulchral epitaphs. e.g. *Preisigke* 173⁶ (c. A.D. 200) Τ. Αὐρήλιος . . . ζήσας ἔτη νε. For the phrase ἔτι ζῶν, as in Mt 27⁶³, cf. *C. and B.* ii. p. 660 No. 618 (A.D. 193-4) Ζώσιμος [— τοῖς τ]έκνοις . . . καὶ ἑαυτῷ ἔτι ζῶν κατεσκεύασεν. The articular inf. is very common in the vernacular—P Par 63¹⁰³ (B.C. 165) τὰ πρὸς τὸ ζῆν, "the means of living," P Tebt II. 283¹⁵ (B.C. 93 or 60) κινδυνῶι (*l.* κινδυνεύει) τῶι ζῆν, "her life is in danger," *ib.* 304¹³ (A.D. 167-8) ὡς ἐκ τούτου τῷ ζῆν κινδυνεύειν, "so that his life is endangered in consequence," P Lond 846¹¹ (a poor weaver's petition—A.D. 140) (= III. p. 131) μισθοῦ πορίζοντος τὸ ζῆν, *OGIS* 515²⁷ (iii/A.D.) τὸ ζῆν οὐκ ἔχομεν : cf. Heb 2¹⁵, and see *Proleg.* p. 215. With ζῆν ἐκ, "get a living from," as in 1 Cor 9¹⁴, cf. P Oxy VIII. 1117¹⁹ (c. A.D. 178) μέτρια κεκτήμεθα ἐξ ὧν καὶ μόλις ζῶμεν, *ib.* XII. 1557¹² (A.D. 255) ἐξ αὐτῶν τὸ ζῆν αὐτῇ πορίζομένης, P Meyer 20²¹ (1st half iii/A.D.) ἐργαζέσθω Λουκιᾶς καὶ ζῶτω ἐκ τοῦ μισθαρου (*l.* μισθαρίου) αὐτῆς (cf. 2 Th 3¹²). In BGU I. 246⁹ (ii/iii A.D.) the verb is construed with the dat.—ἄρτῳ καὶ ὕδατι ζῶν. For the deeper meaning of the verb we may refer to an inscr. which Sir W. M. Ramsay formerly placed among Christian inscrr., but now assigns to mystic paganism (see his *Recent Discovery*, p. 176), *C. and B.* ii. p. 565 No. 463 ζῶσιν μ]έγαν κίνδυ[ν]ον ἐκπεφευ[γ]ότες, "they live, having escaped great danger," In P Oxy VI. 924¹¹, a Gnostic charm of iv/A.D., a certain Ἀρεία is described as δούλη . . τοῦ θ(εο)ῦ τοῦ ζῶντος, and in *ib.* 943⁷, a Christian letter of vi/A.D., we have the common LXX phrase ζῇ Κύριος, "as the Lord lives." See also the magical P Par 574¹⁰³⁶ (iii/A.D.) ἐπιτάσσει σοι ὁ μέγας ζῶν θεός. In *Syll* 852⁴ (ii/B.C.) μέχρι κα Ἀρχέλαος ζώῃ, the verb would seem to be opt., for *ib.* 850¹² (ii/B.C.) shows subj. ζῇ ἕως κα ζῇ Θευδώρα. A familiar fairy-tale phrase occurs in Musonius, p. 30⁹, τὸ εὐδαιμονεῖν καὶ ζῆν μακαρίως εἰς τὸ λοιπόν.

According to Boisacq (p. 309) this verb is "une invention des grammairiens" : the Attic ζῶ represents *ζηιω. The

connexion between this form and the aor. ἐβίων, and their relation to δίαιτα and ὑγιής are revealed in the base gu̯ei̯ē = "live." MGr ζῶ and ζῶ.

ζβέννυμι.

For ζβέννυμι as a graphic variety of σβέννυμι, see P Lond 121³⁶⁴ (iii/A.D.) (= I. p. 96) ζβέσας αὐτόν, and cf. Jannaris *Gr.* § 68.

ζεῦγος

is very common = "a pair," as in Lk 2²⁴. It is sufficient to cite by way of example—P Petr III. 31⁵ (B.C. 240) τοῦ ζεύγους τῶν βοῶν, P Ryl II. 127³⁵ (A.D. 29) σφυρὶς ἐν ᾗ ἄρτο(ι) ν̄, ζεύγ(η) κ̄ε̄, "a basket in which were 50 loaves, 25 pairs," P Oxy II. 267⁶ (A.D. 36) ἐνωτίων χρυσῶν ζεύγους ἑνός, BGU I. 22³¹ (A.D. 114) (= *Selections*, p. 76) ζεῦγος ψελλίω(ν) ἀργυρῶν. According to the editors' note on P Oxy XII. 1438²¹ (late ii/A.D.) the commonest application of the word in the papyri is to a pair of loaves. For ζευγηλάτης = "driver" cf. e.g. P Fay 112⁶ (A.D. 99) ἐ]πιτίνας τὸν ζευγηλάτην εἵνα ἑκάσ[της] ἡμέρας τῷ ἔργον ἀποδῦ (*l.* ἀποδοῖ), "urge the driver to do his proper work every day" (Edd.), BGU II. 624²² (time of Diocletian) παρὰ ζευγηλάτο(υ) ταυρικ(οῦ). In MGr ζευγάρι == "pair," "couple."

ζευκτηρία,

which occurs in Ac 27⁴⁰ and according to Grimm is "found nowhere else," may now be illustrated from the neut. plur. of the adj. in P Oxy VI. 934⁵ (iii/A.D.) εἰς τιμὴν ζευκτηρίων δραχμὰς ἑξήκοντα, "as the price of yokes 60 drachmae": cf. PSI IV. 280²⁰ (iii/iv A.D.), CP Herm I. 95¹⁸. In P Lond 1177¹⁶⁷ (A.D. 113) (= III. p. 185) σχοινίων καὶ ζευκτηρίων, and in P Flor I. 16²⁶ (A.D. 239) τοῦ τε φορέτρου [κ]αὶ μηχανῆς καὶ ζευκτηρίω(ν) the word is used in connexion with the mechanism of a water-wheel.

ζέω

is found in its literal sense in a iii/A.D. recipe, P Lond 121¹⁷⁰ (= I. p. 80) ᾠὸν ὅμοιον μῆλον (*l.* μήλῳ) γενέσθαι ζέσας τὸ ᾠὸν χρείε κρόκῳ μείξας μετ' οἴνου : cf. the medical recipe P Oxy XI. 1384³⁶ (v/A.D.) λαβὸν (*l.* -ὼν) μῆλα κυπαρίσου ζέσας κλοίζου, "take the fruit of a cypress, boil it and apply" (Edd.). MGr ζέσι, ζέστη, "heat," and ζεσταίνω, "make warm."

ζῆλος

occurs twice in the Alexandrian erotic fragment P Grenf I. 1¹³ (ii/B.C.) μέλλω μαίνεσθαι, ζῆλος γάρ με ἔχει καὶ κατακαίομαι καταλελειμμένη, and ¹⁷ εὐδοκῶ ζήλῳ δουλεύειν ἐπιμανοῦσα ὁρᾶν—passages which support "fervour" rather than "emulation" as the primary idea (ζέω) of the word: cf. Ellicott on 1 Cor 14¹. In 2 Cor 9², Phil 3⁶ the word is neuter (as in MGr), but elsewhere in the NT it is masculine, as always in the LXX. In the Psalms of Solomon both genders are found: cf. WH *Notes*², p. 165.

ζηλόω.

For ζηλόω c. acc., as in Ac 7⁹ according to the RV rendering (cf. Gal 4¹⁷), see PSI I. 94⁹ (ii/A.D.) ζηλοῖ γὰρ τὴν μάθησιν, and from the inscrr. *Michel* 394⁴⁷ (mid. i/B.C.) ἐφ' οἷς οὐχ ἧττον ὁ δῆμος [ζ]ηλοῖ αὐτόν, and *ib.* 1007²⁹ (ii/B.C.) καὶ ζηλῶσιν αὐτοὺς οἱ ἐπιγινόμενοι Ἐχιναδῶν. The compound ζηλοτυπέω may be illustrated from P Oxy III. 472¹¹ (c. A.D. 130) ἐζηλοτύπει αὐτὴν μὴ ἐπισταμένην, "he was jealous of her without her knowledge" (Edd.): cf. for the subst. Numb 5¹⁵ θυσία ζηλοτυπίας.

ζηλωτής.

With the use of ζηλωτής in such passages as 1 Cor 14¹², cf. from the inscrr. *Syll* 308²⁸ (ii/B.C.) γίνωνται δὲ καὶ ἄλλοι ζηλ]ωταὶ τῆς αὐτῆς αἱρέσεως, *ib.* 521³³ (B.C. 100) γινόμενοι δὲ καὶ ζηλωταὶ τῶν καλλίστων ἐκ τῆς πρώτης ἡλικίας, and *OGIS* 339⁹⁰ (c. B.C. 120) ζηλωταὶ μὲν τῶν καλλίστων γίνωνται. A close parallel to Ac 22³ may be found in Musonius p. 37³, where the ideal king is styled ζηλωτὴς . . τοῦ Διός: cf. Sthenidas of Locris (Stob. *Flor.* ii. p. 265¹¹) ἀντίμιμος καὶ ζαλωτὰς τῶ πράτω θεῶ.

ζημία.

For ζημία = "loss" as in all its NT occurrences (Ac 27¹⁰·²¹, Phil 3⁷·⁸), cf. BGU I. 2¹⁴ (A.D. 209) ὡς ἐκ τούτου οὐκ ὀλίγη μοι ζημία ἐπηκολούθησεν, *ib.* 146¹⁰ (ii/iii A.D.) καὶ οὐχ [ὀ]λ[ί]γην ζη[μ]είαν μοι ἐζημιωσάμην, where note the not very common cognate acc. In *Chrest.* I. 176¹⁸ (mid. i/A.D.) the lessee of a vineyard petitions that as he has spent so much on repairs he is entitled to abatement in rent—ἀξιῶ οὐκέτι εὐ[τον]ῶν ὑπομέν[ειν] τὰς ζημίας ἐπαναγκάσαι τοὺς πρ[ο]εστῶτας ἀπαρενόχλητόν με ποιῆσαι ὑπὲρ τ[ῶ]ν φόρων, and in P Flor II. 142⁸ (iii/A.D.) where 2 asses are to be sold at such a price—ὥστε μήτε τὸν πιπράσκοντα ζημιοῦσθαι μήτε ἡμᾶς ζημίαν πλείονα ὑπομένειν τῆς τιμῆς. Cf. *Syll* 418⁸⁶ (A.D. 238) μεγίστην ζημίαν ("soloece pro dativo," Dittenberger) τὸ ταμεῖον περιβληθήσεται, *OGIS* 484¹⁹ (ii/A.D.) συνέβαινεν δὲ πᾶσιν αἰσθητὴν γείνεσθαι τοῖς ὠνουμένοις τὴν ἄδικον τῶν πιπρασκόντων ζημίαν. The word is united with αἰτία in BGU IV. 1118²² (B.C. 22) αἰτίαις καὶ ζημίαις. and *ib.* 1185¹⁹ (c. B.C. 30): cf. P Tebt II. 420⁴ (iii/A.D.) οἴδατε ὅτι ἀπὸ ζημίας ἡμί, "you know that I am blameless" (Edd.). For the meaning "penalty," "fine," cf. P Hal I. 1¹⁹³ (iii/B.C.) διπλασία[ν] τὴν ζημίαν ἀποτεισάτω τῆς γεγραμμένης, P Tebt I. 105⁷ (B.C. 103) ἀνυπεύθυνοι ἔστωσαν παντὸς ἐπι[τί]μου καὶ πάσης ζημίας, "shall be liable to no fine or penalty of any kind" (Edd.): cf. from the inscrr. *OGIS* 218¹⁰⁵ (iii/B.C.) ἔνοχον εἶναι τῆι α[ὐτ]ῆι ζημίαι, 483⁵ (ii/B.C.) οἱ μὲν] στρατηγοὶ ζημιώσαντες αὐτοὺς [τῆι] ἐκ τοῦ νόμου ζημίαι παραδότωσαν τῶι πράκτορι πράσσειν, ¹⁹ καὶ ἐκτὸς ἀποτεινέτωσαν ζημία(ν) δραχμὰς ἑκατόν. An interesting use of the word is found in the Gnostic fragment P Oxy I. 4⁶ (early iv/A.D.) οὐδὲν ἄλλο

PART III.

ἦν ὁ θάνατος τῷ θ(ε)ῷ ἢ ζημία ὅπερ ἀδύνατον, which Harnack (*Chron.* ii. p. 181) renders, "so wäre der Tod nichts anderes für Gott als Strafe, was unmöglich ist." adding in a note that the meaning may be, "Wäre Gott der, welcher den Tod verhängt, so wäre er ein strafender Gott, was unmöglich ist."

The subst. ζημίωμα is found in P Flor II. 150⁷ (A.D. 267) οὐχ ὀλίγον ζημίωμα εἰς τοῦτο γειν[ό]μενον ἡμῖν, BGU II. 410¹³ (A.D. 276-7) τὰ περιγινόμενα λήμματα καὶ ζημιώμα [π]ρὸς σὲ ἤτω.

ζημιόω.

To the exx. of this verb cited *s.v.* ζημία we may add P Tebt I. 5⁸² (B.C. 118) τοὺς δὲ παρὰ ταῦτα ποιοῦντας θαν[άτωι ζ]ημιοῦσθαι, and for the more special sense of "fine" P Par 47¹⁸ (c. B.C. 153) (= *Selections*, p. 23) χάριν γὰρ ἡμῶν ἠζημίοται εἰς χαλκοῦ τ(άλαντα) ιε, "for on our account he has been fined to the amount of 15 bronze talents," BGU IV. 1044¹³ (iv/A.D.) ποιήσω ὑμῖς ζημιᾶσθαι (*l.* ὑμᾶς ζημιοῦσθαι) δέκα ἀντὶ τούτου. For the verb in the inscrr. see *Michel* 1342⁴ (i/B.C.) ἐζημιωμένον ὑπὸ τῶν πρυτάνεων . . ὀφίλοντα τοὺς κατὰ τὸν νόμον στατῆρας δύο, and *OGIS* 669⁴⁰ (i/A.D.) ὁ τοῦτο ποιήσας ἀπαραιτήτως ζημιωθήσεται. In accordance with the primary meaning of the word "suffer loss," "receive damage" (see e.g. the citation from P Flor II. 142⁸ *s.v.* ζημία) Field (*Notes*, p. 61) translates Lk 9²⁵ "and lose, or receive damage in, his own self." A new verb ζημιοπρακτέω, "exact punishment from," is found in P Tor II. 7⁷.

Ζηνᾶς.

This proper name (Tit 3¹³), probably a contraction for Ζηνόδωρος (Lightfoot on Col 4¹⁵), appears in a late Roman wall-scribbling at Magnesia, *Magn* 323. Cf. Ἀρτεμᾶς, Ὀλυμπᾶς—pet-names for the longer forms in -δωρος.

ζητέω.

PSI IV. 382⁵ (B.C. 248-7) ξύλα ἐζητήκαμεν πανταχοῦ. The verb is found along with εὑρίσκω in the curious nursery acrostic P Tebt II. 278³⁰ (early i/A.D.) ζητῶι καὶ οὐχ εὑρίσκωι: cf. P Giss I. 21⁵ (Rom.) ἐζήτησα τὸ λακώνιον καὶ οὐχ εὗρον ἀλλὰ ἀτταλιανὸν σαπρόν, where both λακώνιον and ἀτταλιανόν are to be understood as articles of dress. In their note on P Ryl II. 220⁷⁴, an official list of names belonging to ii/A.D., the editors state that the note ζη(τητέον) δίπ(λωμα) is found frequently in the margin of similar fragments, and that in one case οὐχ εὑρέθ(η) . . . occurs. With Mt 7⁷ cf. especially the new Logion P Oxy IV. 654⁵ μὴ παυσάσθω ὁ ζη[τῶν . . . . . . ἕως ἂν] εὕρῃ: see also Epict. i. 28. 19 ζήτει καὶ εὑρήσεις. Other examples of this common verb are P Oxy I. 34ⁱⁱⁱ·¹³ (A.D. 127) τοὺ[ς] διὰ ἀπειθίαν κ[αὶ] ὡς (or κ[ακ]ῶς, see *s.v.*) ἀφορμὴν ζητοῦντας (cf. Lk 11⁵⁴ D) ἁμαρτημάτω[ν] τειμωρήσομαι, and *ib.* II. 237ⁿⁱ⁴¹ (A.D. 186) ἐ[ζ]ήτησεν ἀκρειβ[ῶ]ς [τὸ πρ]ᾶγμα ἐκ τῶν βιβλιοφ[υ]λάκ[ω]ν, "made a searching inquiry into the matter on the evidence of the keepers of the archives." A similar judicial reference is found in P Oxy IV. 726¹⁶ (A.D. 135) περὶ τῶν πρὸς αὐτὸν ζητηθησομέ[ν]ων ἐπί τε τοῦ κρατίστου ἡγεμ[ό]νος, "in the inquiry to be held against him before his highness the praefect" (Edd.), and *Theb Ostr* 134⁴ (i/ii A.D.) οὐδὲν γὰρ

39

ζητεῖται πρὸς αὐτόν, "for there is no question against him" (Edd.). In *Kaibel* 215[3] (i/A.D.) ἤλυθες εἰς Ἀίδην ζητούμενος οἷς ἀπέλειπες, the verb is = ποθέω (see Herwerden *Lex. s.v.*). MGr ζητῶ, "request," "ask."

ζήτημα.

For ζήτημα, which in the NT is confined to Ac, cf. P Oxy IX. 1188[5] (A.D. 13) ὡς πρὸς σὲ τοῦ περὶ τῶν ἀγνοη-(θέντων) ζη(τήματος) ἐσο(μένου), "knowing that you will be held accountable in any inquiry concerning facts that remain unknown" (Edd.), *ib.* l. 9[14] (A.D. 115-6) περὶ ἧς τὸ ζήτημα ὑπερετέθη ἐπὶ τὸν κράτιστον ἡγεμόνα. The word = "claim" in P Ryl II. 117[14] (A.D. 269) τοὺς μηδὲν [τ]ῶν κατοιχομένων κεκληρονομηκότας μὴ κατέχεσθαι τοῖς ἐκείνων ὀφε[ιλήμασι]ν ἢ καὶ ζητήμασιν, "that those who have inherited nothing from deceased persons cannot be held responsible for their debts or the claims made against them" (Edd.). In MGr ζήτημα = "controversy."

ζήτησις.

The more technical use of this word, as in Ac 25[20], may be illustrated from the long petition of Dionysia P Oxy II. 237[vii. 7] (A.D. 186) περὶ ἰδιωτικῶν ζητήσεων, "concerning private suits," *ib.* εἴ τις γένοιτο ζήτησις εἰς ὕστερον περὶ τῶν μὴ δεόντως ἀπογραψαμένων, "if any inquiry is made hereafter concerning false returns" (Edd.): cf. *ib.* III. 513[9] (A.D. 184) ἐάν τις ζήτησις περὶ τούτου πρὸς σὲ γένηται, and from the inscr. OGIS 629[9] (A.D. 137) συνέβαινεν δὲ πλει-στάκις περὶ τούτου ζητήσεις γείνεσθ[αι με]ταξὺ τῶν ἐνπόρων πρὸς τοὺς τελώνας. For the ordinary meaning "search" see a proclamation by the prefect in A.D. 154-5 promising all who had fled from public burdens that, if they returned within three months—μ[ηδ]εμίαν πρὸς α[ὐ]τοὺς ζήτησιν ἔσεσθαι (BGU II. 372[ii. 19]). The subst. occurs in a difficult phrase in an Imperial edict, probably to be assigned to Julian (see *Archiv* ii. p. 169), P Fay 20[14] ἐπεὶ Καῖσάρ εἰμι καὶ περικέκμηκα τὸ κλῖνον ἀναλήμψεσθαι οὐχ ὅρων ζητή-σεσιν ἀλλὰ σωφρο[σύνη, "ever since I became Caesar, I have earnestly striven to restore vigour to what was in decline, not by acquisitions of territory (?) but by economy" (Edd.). The word survives in literary MGr = "search," "seeking."

ζιζάνιον.

For this Semitic word, see Lewy *Fremdwörter*, p. 52.

Ζμύρνα.

The wavering of the inscriptional testimony (see Deissmann *BS*, p. 185) makes it impossible to decide between Ζμύρνα which is read by ℵ vg[some indication] *al.* in Rev 1[11] and the commoner Σμύρνα, but the fact that the reading Ζμύρνα is supported by Smyrnaean coins down to Trajan's reign (Waddington, *Ver. arch* 804) makes it difficult to reject the witness of ℵ, on suspicion of "Western" taint: see WH *Notes*[2], p. 155, *Prolog.* p. 45. For Ζμύρνα (-η) in the papyri see P Ryl II. 155[13] (A.D. 138-161) ὃν κατέλιψα ἐν Ζμύρνῃ τῆς Ἀσίας, and for the same spelling of the common noun cf. PSI IV. 328[2] (B.C. 258-7) ζμύρνης τάλαντα ἑκατόν. P Tebt I. 35[16] (B.C. 111) ζμύρναν, and see Mayser *Gr.* pp. 41, 204. An adj. ζμύρνινος is found in P Oxy XII. 1584[18] (ii/A.D.) παλλίον ζμύρνιν[ον.

ζόφος.

For the corresponding adj. see Vett. Val. p. 312[32] διὰ τὸ ζοφῶδες τοῦ ἀέρος. The subst. is cited by Thumb (*Hellen.* pp. 218, 225) as amongst the "poetic" words, which have passed into general use in the Κοινή. MGr ζοφός, "dark."

ζυγός.

For this word, which survives in MGr. in its literal sense cf. P Rein 17[20] (B.C. 109) ἄροτρον ἃ ζυ[γὸ]ν α, P Fay 121[4] (c. A.D. 100) εὖ ποιήσεις δοὺς Οὐηστείνῳ εἰς τὸν ζυγὸν αὐτοῦ ζυγόδεσμον καινὸν στερεόν, "kindly give Vestinus for his yoke a new strong yoke-band" (Edd.), P Strass I. 32[12] (A.D. 261) ζυγὸν δὲ ἐνάγων παρά σοι τὸν ἐπιτηδειότερον αὐτῷ παράσχες. The neuter form of the subst. = "balance," as in Rev 6[5], occurs in *Michel* 1222[4] (ii/B.C.) τὸ ζυγὸν καὶ τὰ σταθμία.

ζύμη.

In a proposal to lease 10½ arourae of catoecic land, P Tebt II. 375[7] (A.D. 140), a certain Psion amongst other conditions says—δ]ώσω σοι καθ' ἔτος ζύμης ἠρτυμένης ἀρτάβης δίδυρον, "I will pay you annually ⅔ artaba of prepared leaven" (Edd.): cf. *ib.* 401[35] (early i/A.D.). The word represents *ζύσμα or *ζύμα, cf. ζωμός, "broth," Lat. ius (Boisacq. p. 311).

ζωγρέω.

With the thought of capture *alive* (Suid. ζωγρεῖ ζῶντας λαμβάνει) in Luke 5[10] ἀνθρώπους ἔσῃ ζωγρῶν (Beza, *vivos capies homines*) cf. the use of the subst. in *Syll* 318[20] (B.C. 118) καὶ πολλοὺς μὲν αὐτῶν ἐν χειρῶν νομαῖς ἀπέκτεινεν, οὓς δὲ ζωγρίαι συνέλαβεν, and Polyb. iii. 84. 10 where δεόμενοι ζωγρεῖν is contrasted with διαφθείρειν. *Kaibel* 841[7] (A.D. 149) ζώγρε[ι], δέσποτ' ἄναξ, τὸν σὸν ναετῆρα μεθ' ἡμῶν | Κλαυδιανόν is a good example of the LXX usage = "preserve alive," as in Numb 31[15], Josh 6[25].

ζωή.

P Lond 177[11] (A.D. 40-1) (= II. p. 168) ἐπὶ τὸν τῆς ζωῆς αὐτῆς χρόνον, and so often. P Oxy VII. 1070[9] (iii/A.D.) τὸν μέγαν θεὸν Σαράπιν παρακαλῶ περί τε τῆς ζωῆς ὑμῶν καὶ τῶν ἡμῶν πάν[τ]ων, P Leid W[xvii. 16] (ii-iii A.D.) ὁ ἐνφυσήσας πνεῦμα ἀνθρώποις εἰς ζωήν. For OGIS 266[29] (iii/B.C.) ἕως ζωῆς καὶ θανά[του = ἐν ζωῇ ἕως θανάτου see Dittenberger's note *ad loc*. We may also refer to the touching inscr. cited *s.v.* γλυκύς *sub fin*. In contrast to the classical usage in which βίος is the ethical term (see further *s.v.*), the "nobler" connotation is attached in Biblical Greek to ζωή, which is generally used as equivalent to "the very highest blessedness": see Trench *Syn.* p. 86 ff., and cf. Hort *Hulsean Lectures*, pp. 98 ff., 189 ff., for an important discussion on the Biblical doctrine of Life. In *ZNTW* xii. p. 228 ff. Burkitt treats the relation of ζωή to hayyim. The noun survives in MGr.

ζώνη.

P Petr I. 14[12] (B.C. 237) τὴν ζώνην θωρακίτ[ου, "the girdle of a coslet-armed soldier" (Edd.). In P Oxy III. 496[4], a marriage contract of A.D. 127, the dowry of the bride includes ζώνας δύο σανδυκίνην ῥοδίνην, " 2 girdles, one red, the other rose-coloured " (Edd.) : cf. *ib.* I 109[11] (iii/iv A.D.) ζῶναι β̄, in a list of personal property. With the use of the ζώνη for carrying money, as in Mk 6[8], cf. P Ryl II. 127[32] (A.D. 29) ζώνη ἐν ᾗ κέρματ[ος] (δραχμαὶ) δ, and *ib.* 141[22] (A.D. 37), where a man states that he has been robbed of ἀργ(υρίου) δραχμὰς ᾱ καὶ ζώνην. In the Leucadian epigram, *Kaibel* 482[9] it is said of a man whom a storm prevented from setting out on a voyage—ἀπέδησε τὴν ζώνην ἑαυτοῦ. *i.e.* "he loosed his girdle," he did not set out. MGr ζουναριά.

ζωογονέω.

With this verb == "preserve alive," as in 1 Tim 6[13] (cf. Exod 1[17], Judg 8[19]), see the invocation addressed to the sun in the magic P Lond 121[529] (iii/A.D.) (= I. p. 101) κύριε θεὲ μέγιστε ὁ τὰ ὅλα συνέχων καὶ ζωογονῶν καὶ συνκρατῶν τὸν κόσμον. Hobart (p. 155) has shown that the verb is used to signify "producing alive," "enduing with life" in medical writers : cf. Lk 17[33], Ac 7[19], where, however, the meaning is probably "preserve alive," *ut s.* A form ζωγονέω is found in P Oxy IX. 1188[4] (A.D. 13) ἀπ[ὸ] ζωγονούση[ς] περσ(έας) κλάδους ξηρο[ὺς] δύο, "two dry branches of a living persea-tree" (Ed.) : cf. [21.23].

ζῷον.

With the use of ζῷον (for form, see Blass-Debrunner § 26) in Rev to denote "a *living* creature," the symbol of the Divine immanence in Nature, as distinguished from θηρίον, "a brute beast," we may compare the frequent reff. to ἱερὰ ζῷα in the papyri, e.g. P Tebt I. 57[8] (B.C. 118), where it is laid down that the expenses of the burial of Apis and Mnevis and τῶν ἄλλων ἱερῶν ζῳν (*l.* ζώων) shall be defrayed by the Crown, and *ib.* 57[12] (B.C. 114), where reference is made to furnishing τὰς τῶν ἱερῶν ζώιων σειταγωγίας, "the supplies of food for the sacred animals." Cf. also P Oxy IX. 1188[4] (A.D. 13) ἐπὶ τῆς ς τῶν ἱερῶν ζώων θήκης, and from the inscrr. *OGIS* 90[31] (the Rosetta stone—B.C. 196) τῶι τε Ἄπει καὶ τῶι Μνεύει πολλὰ ἐδωρήσατο καὶ τοῖς ἄλλοις ἱεροῖς ζώιοις τοῖς ἐν Αἰγύπτωι. In Aristeas 147 the reference is to "tame birds."—τὰ τῶν προειρημένων πτηνῶν ἥμερα ζῷα. MGr ζῷο.

ζωοποιέω.

The adj. ζωοποιός is a frequent attribute of the Trinity in late papyri, e.g. P Flor I. 38[1] (vi/A.D.) ἐν ὀνόματι] τῆς ἁγίας καὶ ζωοποιοῦ καὶ ὁμοουσίου [τριάδος πατ]ρὸς καὶ υἱ[ο]ῦ καὶ ἁγίου πνεύματος. For the verb see Aristeas 16 δι᾽ ὅν (*sc.* θεὸν) ζωοποιοῦντα τὰ πάντα καὶ γίνεται.

H

ἤ—ἡγεμονία

ἤ.

For this particle in interrogative sentences, where we should accent ἦ, and for which from ii/B.C. εἰ is a graphic equivalent, cf. the questions to the oracle, P Fay 137²⁴ (i/A.D.) (= *Selections*, p. 69) χρημάτισόν μοι, ἦ μείνωι ἐν Βακχιάδι; ἦ μέλω (*l.* μέλλω) ἐντυγχάνιν; "answer me, Shall I remain in Bacchias? Shall I meet (him)?", BGU I. 229³ (ii/iii A.D.) (see *Berichtigungen* i. p. 27) ἤ μὲν σοθήσωμαι (*l.* εἰ μὲν σωθήσομαι) ταύτης, ἧς ἐν ἐμοὶ ἀσθενίας. τοῦτόν μοι ἐξένικον (*l.* τοῦτό μοι ἐξένεγκον). For ἤ = "or," see BGU IV. 1141⁶ (B.C. 14) ἔπεμψας . . . ἵνα ἐπιγνῶσιν πρὸς ἃ ἔγραψά σοι ἤ (= εἰ) ἔστιν ἤ οὔ, and for ἤ . . . ἤ PSI IV. 324² (B.C. 261–0) ἐάν τινες . . . διαγράφωσιν ὑμῖν ἤ τὰς τιμὰς ἤ τὸ παραβόλιον, παραλαμβάνετε κτλ.: the alternative is emphasized by the addition of τε . . . καί in *IG* XII. 2, 562⁵ (Rom. time) εἰ δέ τις τολμήσ[η ἐπι]βαλέσθαι πτῶμα ἤτε ἀπὸ τοῦ γένους μου ἤ καὶ ἕτερός τις, δώσει κτλ. (cited by Radermacher *Gr.* p. 27). Ἤτοι . . ἤ, while found in classical Greek, is characteristic of Hellenistic speech (Radermacher *ut s.*), see e.g. P Tebt I. 5⁵⁹ (B.C. 118) ἤτοι κώ(μας) ἤι γᾶς ἤ ἄλλας ἱερὰς πρ(οσόδους), P Ryl II. 154²⁵ (a contract of marriage—A.D. 66) ἤτοι τοῦ Χαιρήμονος ἀποπέμποντος τ[ὴ]ν Θαισάριον ἤ καὶ αὐτῆς ἑκουσίω[ς ἀ]παλλασσομέν[η]ς [ἀ]π᾽ αὐτοῦ: cf. Rom 6¹⁶. The combination is common in Vett. Val. (e.g. p. 58²⁰), who also uses ἤπερ (p. 141⁴⁹) and ἤγουν (p. 138¹²) for simple ἤ. Ἤτοι stands alone in PSI IV. 314¹² (A.D. 195) δραχμὰς ἑξακισχευλί[α]ς ἤ[τ]οι τάλαντον, P Oxy VI. 888⁵ (iii/iv A.D.) διὰ τὸ μὴ παρεῖναι τοῖς ὀρφανοῖς ἐπιτρόπους ἤτοι κου[ράτορας. In PSI III. 158⁶⁸ (iii/A.D.?) the place of the particles is reversed—δικογράφους ἤ δικολόγους ἤτοι τούτων παραπλ[η]σίους. For ἤ καί suggesting an afterthought, see P Lond 962⁵ (A.D. 254 or 261) (= III. p. 210) δέξαι παρ᾽ αὐτοῦ δραχμὰς διακοσίας καὶ ἔχε αὐτὰς εἴς τε περιχωματισμὸν ἤ καὶ λόγον ὀψωνίων ὡς ἐὰν θέλης, "receive from him two hundred drachmas and employ them for banking-up or (for that matter) for the payment of supplies, as you may wish," and for ἀλλ᾽ ἤ, as in 2 Cor 1¹³, see *s.v.* ἀλλά, and cf. Blass-Debrunner *Gr.* § 448. 8.

A good parallel to θέλω . . . ἤ in 1 Cor 14¹⁹ (cf. 2 Macc 14⁴²) is found in BGU III. 846¹⁶ (ii/A.D.) (= *Selections*, p. 95) οὐκ οἶδες, ὅτι θέλω πηρὸς γενέσται (*l.* γενέσθαι), εἰ (= ἤ) γνῶναι, ὅπως ἀνθρόπω [ἔ]τ[ι] ὀφείλω ὀβολόν; "do you not know that I would rather be a cripple than be conscious that I am still owing any one an obolus?"

On the Semitic use of the positive of an adj. followed by ἤ, as in Mk 9⁴³ ff., see Wellhausen *Einl.*² p. 21, where reference is also made to the corresponding use of ἤ after a verb with μᾶλλον implied in Mk 3⁴, Lk 15⁷: in Mt 18¹³ μᾶλλον is expressed.

Πρὶν ἤ with inf., as in Mt 1¹⁸ *al.* (cf. Blass-Debrunner *Gr.* § 395) may be illustrated by PSI III. 171²⁵ (ii/B.C.) πρὶν ἤ τὰ λοι[π]ὰ τῆ[ς οἰ]κοδομῆς τοῦ ὅρμου συντελεσθῆναι.

For πρότερον ἤ see PSI IV. 330² (B.C. 258–7) ὤ[ι]μην οὖν σοὶ μὲν γράφειν πρότερον ἤ ἀντιτεῖναι, and cf. *ib.* 343³ (B.C. 256–5) μὴ θαυμάσηις ἐπὶ τῶι Νικόλαον ἀπελθεῖν προτοῦ ἤ τὸν λόγον συνθεῖναι, where the editor points out that προτοῦ = πρὸ τοῦ, and compares *Syll* 300²² (B.C. 170) πρὸ τοῦ ἤ Γάιος Λοκρέτιος τὸ στρατόπεδον πρὸς τὴν πόλιν Θίσβας προσήγαγεν = "*antequam . . . admovit.*"

ἦ μήν.

This spelling which is found in the TR of Heb 6¹⁴, and is common in the LXX, occurs in iii/B.C. papyri, e.g. P Petr III. 56(*a*)⁶ (*c.* B.C. 260) ἦ μὴν ἀποδώσω ὑμῖ[ν, P Rev L¹ᵛⁱ· ⁸ (B.C. 259) ὁρκίσαι ἐν ἱερῶι ἦ μὴν μηθενὸς ἄλλου ἕνεκεν τὴν ζήτησιν ποιεῖσθαι, "to swear that the search is made for absolutely no other purpose." See further *s.v.* εἰ μήν, and cf. Thackeray *Gr.* i. p. 83 f.

ἡγεμονεύω

is applied to the rule of a prefect in P Tebt II. 302⁷ (A.D. 7) ἐπὶ Πετρωνίου) τοῦ ἡγεμονεύσαντος, "in the prefecture of P.", P Ryl II. 113²⁰ (A.D. 133) of a case—δεομέ[ν]ου τῆς διαγνώσεως Φλαυίου Τιτιανοῦ τότε τοῦ ἡγεμονεύσαντ(ος), "which required the decision of the late praefect Flavius Titianus" (Edd.), and P Strass I. 41¹⁷ (A.D. 250) Ἀννιανῷ τῷ ἡγεμονεύσαντι ἡ ἡμετέρα βιβλίδ[ι]ον ἐπέδωκεν, "my client gave in her petition to the late prefect Annianus." It may be noted that in Lk 3¹ Cod. Bezae reads ἐπιτροπεύοντος for ἡγεμονεύοντος.

ἡγεμονία.

Like the preceding verb, ἡγεμονία is used for the office or rule of the prefect, e.g. P Oxy I. 59¹⁰ (A.D. 292) ἀπαντῆσαι ἐπὶ τὴν ἡγεμονίαν καὶ προσεδρεῦσαι τῷ ἀχράντῳ αὐτοῦ δικαστηρί[ω, "to proceed to his highness the praefect and attend his immaculate court" (Edd.), *ib.* II. 237ᵛ· ⁶ ᵃˡ· (A.D. 186) γράφειν τῇ ἡγεμονίᾳ, P Ryl II. 77³⁶ (A.D. 192) ἐπὶ τῇ ἐπαφροδείτῳ ἡγεμονίᾳ Λαρκίου Μέμορος, "during the delightful praefecture of Larcius Memor" (Edd.), P Oxy X. 1252 *recto* ¹⁹ (A.D. 288–95) ἐκ προστάξεως τῆς ἡγεμονίας, "in accordance with the order of the prefect." The word is also used in a military sense (as in Plut. *Camill.* 23) of a "battalion," or division of an army, under its ἡγεμών or officer: cf. P Rein 9¹³ (B.C. 112) Διονύσιος Ἀπολλω]νίου [Πέρσ]ης τῆς Ἀρτεμιδώρου ἡγεμονίας, "Dionysios fils d'Apollonios, Perse, du commandement d'Artémidôros" (Ed.) and the discussion on p. 32 f., and *Syll* 197²³ (B.C. 284–3) τοὺς μὲν βουλομέν[ους στρατ]εύεσθαι διώικησεν ὅπως ἂν καταχωρισθῶσιν [ἐν] ἡγεμονίαις, with the editor's note where ἡγεμονίαι are defined as "partes exercitus ex quibus suum quaeque ἡγεμόνα habuit." As illustrating the elastic nature of this group of words (see *infra* and cf. Sir 10¹·²), we may cite from the astrological fragment P Tebt II. 276¹⁴ (ii/iii A.D.) ὁ δὲ τοῦ Διὸς τῷ τοῦ Ἄρεως τρίγωνος [ὑπάρχων] ἢ καὶ συνπαρὼν μεγάλας [βασιλεία]ς καὶ ἡγεμονίας ἀποτελεῖ, "Jupiter in triangular relation to Mars or in conjunction makes great kingdoms and empires" (Edd.), cf. ³⁵, and the Christian letter P Grenf II. 73¹¹ (late iii/A.D.) (= *Selections*, p. 118) where a certain Politike is described as sent into the Oasis ὑπὸ τῆς ἡγεμονίας, "by the Government."

ἡγεμών.

The breadth of this word and its derivatives, which in a single verse (Lk 3¹) can be applied to the Emperor and to the *chargé d'affaires* of a tiny district like Judaea, is well seen in the papyri. Thus in P Lille I. 4¹⁷ (B.C. 218–7) the editor notes that it means "officier en général, et plus particulièrement, dans certains cas, officier d'infanterie." He compares P Rev L^xxxvii. 3, where Dr. Grenfell points out that "the hegemones are thus subordinate to the strategi; nevertheless the Romans chose this title as an equivalent for the praefectus." See also the notes on P Tor I. 1^i. 15 (B.C. 117–6) and on *OGIS* 69³, and the Index to *OGIS*, where four different connotations are distinguished. The word is used in a general sense of the "captain" of a chosen band of youths in P Amh II. 39¹ (B.C. 103) (= Witkowski², p. 106) Πόρτεις ἡ[γ]εμὼν τῶν ἐν προχειρισμῶι. For its common use with reference to the prefect of Egypt it is sufficient to cite BGU IV. 1079³⁰ (A.D. 41) (= *Selections*, p. 40), where according to Wilcken's reading (*Chrest.* I. p. 85) ἡ (= εἰ) δύναται διὰ Διοδώρου ὑπογραφῆναι ἡ τάβλα διὰ τῆς γυναικὸς τοῦ ἡγεμόνος, the last clause may be an Alexandrian witticism implying backdoor influence. In the iv/A.D. letter P Grenf I. 53¹⁸ ὁ ἡγεμὼν δὲ τὰς ἀπονοίας ταχὺ ταπεινοῖ, and ¹⁹ ὁ ἡγεμὼν οὐ θέλει οἰκοφθέρους, Cronert (*Stud. Pal.* i. p. 84 f.) thinks that the reference is to God: but for this usage Wilcken (*Chrest.* I. p. 158) can find no support, and understands the word in its ordinary sense of "praeses."

ἡγέομαι.

Apart from the use of the participle as a noun (see below) this verb in general is not very common, but the following may serve as exx. of its use—P Ryl II. 65⁸ (B.C. 67?) παρ' οὐδὲν ἡγησαμένους τὰ διωρισ[μένα, "taking no heed whatever of the fixed rules" (Edd.), *ib.* 119³⁰ (A.D. 54–67) ἐν οὐδενὶ ἡγήσατο καθὸ ὑπερισχύων ἡμᾶς ἐπὶ τῶν τόπων, "(reports which) he scorned in virtue of his superior local power" (Edd.), P Giss I. 48²⁰ (A.D. 202–3) (= *Chrest.* I. p. 205) ἐν πραξί[μ]οις ἡγηθῆναι, "es soll unter die gleich einzutreibenden Posten gerechnet werden" (Ed.). For ἀναγκαῖον ἡγ. followed by an inf., as in 2 Cor 9⁵, see BGU III. 824⁴ (A.D. 55–6) πρὸ μὲν πάντων ἀναγκαίω[ν] (*l.* -αῖον) ἡγησάμην διὰ ἐπιστολῆς σε ἀσπάσασθαι, P Ryl II. 235⁴ (ii/A.D.) ἀναγκαῖον ἡγησάμην ἀσπάσασθαί σε καὶ πάντας τοὺς φιλοῦντάς σε, and cf. P Lond 908²⁹ (A.D. 139) (= III. p. 133) δέον ἡγοῦμαι συντάξαι, and P Oxy VII. 1070¹⁷ (iii/A.D.) τὸ μὲν οὖν γράφειν σοι περὶ τῶν πραγμάτων ἡμῶν . . . περιττὸν νῦν ἡγησάμην, "I think it superfluous to

write to you about our business" (Ed.): cf. the use of a perf. with a pres. sense in Ac 26⁵ (but not Phil 3⁷). The unusually strong sense of "esteem" required by the verb in 1 Thess 5¹³ finds a parallel in *Chrest.* I. 116⁴ (ii/iii A.D.) ἡγοῦ μάλιστα τοὺς πατρῴους καὶ σέ[β]ου Ἶσιν Σαράπιν κτλ. The original sense of *leading* may still be seen, even as late as P Oxy I. 128 *verso* ¹² (vi/vii A.D.) ἡγείσθω τῆς ἐπιστ[ο]λῆς, "let it stand in the forefront of the letter." But the would-be-literary taint is on this document: *ib.* I. 55⁹ (A.D. 283) ἀπὸ ἡκουμένου (*l.* ἡγουμένου) πυλῶνος γυμνασίου ἐπὶ ν[ότ]ον, "leading southwards," is at least free from this reproach.

The "ambiguous title" ἡγούμενος (cf. Ac 15²²), occurs, as GH note on P Fay 110²⁶ (A.D. 94), in very different senses. Thus it is used absolutely in P Fay 110 *l.c.* and in P Oxy I. 43 *recto* vi. 14 (A.D. 295). It may denote a superior, as P Grenf II. 43⁹ (A.D. 92) ἡγούμενος γερδίων, a kind of "sheikh" of the weavers (Edd.), *ib.* 67³ (A.D. 237) (= *Selections*, p. 108) ἡγούμενος συνόδου κώ[μη]ς Βακχιάδος, "president of the village council of Bacchias," P Oxy VII. 1020⁵ (A.D. 198–201) ὁ ἡγούμεν[ος] τοῦ ἔθνους, "the praefect of the province" (Ed.); or a subordinate, as P Oxy II. 294¹⁹ (A.D. 22) (= *Selections*, p. 35) ὁ μὲν ἡγούμενος τοῦ στρα[τ]-ηγοῦ, "the marshal of the strategus."

For the religious use of the title (cf. Heb 13⁷) cf. P Tebt II. 525 (c. A.D. 1) a fragment which commences—Παεῦς ἡγ(ούμενος) ἱερέων κτλ., P Lond 281² (A.D. 66) (= II. p. 66) where the death of a priest is notified—ἡγουμένοις ἱε[ρέων, and the epitaph from Laodicea, belonging to the latter part of iv/A.D., in which a woman Doudousa is described (regardless of gender) as ἱ(γού)μενος τῆς ἁγίας [κὲ] καθαρᾶς τοῦ θ(εο)ῦ ἐκλησείας, "Hegoumenos of the holy pure Church of God" (see Ramsay *Luke*, p. 400). As an ecclesiastical title it passed into Arabic in later times (*Studia Sinaitica*, xii. p. 52). MGr (ἡ)γούμενος, "abbot."

Since Grimm assumes that ἡγέομαι is akin to ἄγω, it may be worth while to observe that the harmless necessary *h* really does matter in etymology. It would have been more to the point to compare the English *seek* and the Latin *sāgio*, originally "follow the track" in hunting, hence "perceive"; cf. Boisacq *s.v.*

ἡδέως.

An interesting example of this adverb is found in the letter in which the Emperor Claudius thanked a Gymnastic Club for the golden crown they had sent him to commemorate his victory over the Britons—τὸν πεμ[φ]θέντ[α μο]ι ὑφ' ὑμῶν ἐπὶ τῇ κατὰ Βρεττάννων νείκῃ χρυσοῦν σ[τέ]φ[α]νον ἡδέως ἔλαβον (P Lond 1178¹³ (= III. p. 216, *Selections*, p. 99). Other examples are P Oxy II. 298³³ (ii/A.D.) ὁ Ἀνουβᾶς αὐ[τὸ]ν οὐχ ἡδέως [β]λέπει, *ib.* I. 113³⁰ (ii/A.D.) περὶ δὲ καὶ σὺ ὧν θέλεις δῆλόν μοι ἡδέως ποιήσοντι, *ib.* III. 531³ (ii/A.D.) ἡδέως σε ἀσπαζόμεθα πάντες οἱ ἐν οἴκωι, *ib.* IX. 1218¹² (iii/A.D.) καὶ οὓς ἡδέως ἔχομεν κατ' ὄνομα, PSI III. 236¹⁸ (iii/iv A.D.) ἀντίγραψόν μοι περὶ οὗ βούλει ἡδέως ἔχοντι. See also *Preisigke* 4317¹⁰ (c. A.D. 200) ἐκ σοῦ ἡδέως ἔχω παρ' ἐμοί, which Haussoullier (*Mélanges Chatelain*, p. 283) renders "j'en ai de l'agrément avec toi." We may quote further the letter of Psenosiris for the same phrase as in P Oxy I. 113 (*ut supra*), P Grenf II. 73²⁰ (late iii/A.D.) (= *Selections*, p. 119) δ[ή]λω[σ]ον [δὲ] μοι κ[αὶ σὺ] περὶ ὧν θέλεις ἐνταῦθα ἡδέως ποιοῦντι, and another Christian letter P Oxy VIII. 1162¹¹ (iv/A.D.) δι' οὖ ὑμᾶς καὶ τοὺς σὺν ὑμῖν ἐγὼ δὲ καὶ οἱ σὺν ἐμοὶ ἡδέως ὑμᾶς προσαγορεύεσθαι κ(υρί)ῳ.

ἤδη.

For the idea of "logical proximity and immediateness" (cf. Baumlein *Griech. Partikeln*, p. 138 ff.) which underlies this word and is perhaps to be seen in 1 Cor 6⁷ (cf. Ellicott *ad l.*), we may cite the common use of the adverb in magical incantations. e.g. P Par 574¹²⁴⁵ (iii/A.D.) (= *Selections*, p. 114) ἔξελθε, δαῖμον, . . . καὶ ἀπόστηθι ἀπὸ τοῦ δ⟨ε⟩ῖ(να) ἄρτι ἄρτι ἤδη, P Lond 121³⁷⁵ (iii/A.D.) (= I. p. 96) ἐν (τ)ῇ ἄρτι ὥρᾳ ἤδη ἤδη ταχὺ ταχύ: see also Deissmann *BS*, p. 280, *Archiv* i. p. 426. Other examples of the word are P Fay 109¹ (early i/A.D.) τοὺς τρεῖς στατῆρες (l. -as) οὒς εἴρηκέ σοι Σέλευκος δῶναί μοι ἤδη δὸς Κλέωνι, "the three staters which S. told you to give me, now give to C.," P Ryl II. 77⁴⁶ (A.D. 192) κα[ὶ] ὀφείλει στεφῆναι, ἤδη γὰρ ἡ ἀρχὴ ἀδιάπτωτός ἐστιν τῇ πόλ(ει), "and he ought to be crowned, for the office is now secured to the city" (Edd.). For ἤδη οὖν see P Tebt II. 423¹ (early iii/A.D.) ἔμαθον εἰληφότα παρ' Ἀματί[ο]υ τὸν ἄρακα. ἤδη οὖν ὡς δι(ε)τάγη χωρησάτω εἰς τὴν Τβεκλῦτιν χορτάρακός τε καὶ ἄρακος μ[ο]ναχὸς εἰς σπέρματα, "I have learned that you have received the aracus from Amatius. Now therefore, as was ordered, let the grass-aracus and the aracus go alone to Tbeklutis for seed," and for ἤδη ποτέ, "now at length," as in Rom 1¹⁰ ("some near day at last," SH), Phil 4¹⁰, see the ostrakon from Thebes of A.D. 192 published in *LAE*, p. 186 (= Meyer *Ostr* 57⁶) καὶ ἤδη ποτὲ δὸς τῇ ἐμῇ παιδίσκῃ τὰς τοῦ πυ(ροῦ), "and now at length give my maid the (artabae) of wheat": cf. also Epict. iii. 24. 9 οὐκ ἀπογαλακτίσομεν ἤδη ποθ' ἑαυτούς;

ἥδιστα.

P Oxy VII. 1061²¹ (B.C. 22) σὺ δὲ γράφε ὑπὲρ ὧν ἐὰν θέλῃς καὶ ἥδιστα ποιήσω, P Lond 897⁸ (A.D. 84) (= III. p. 207) ἥδιστα πάντας καταλείψω εἶνα μὴ τὴν πρός σε φιλείαν καταλείψω, P Oxy VI. 933⁵ (late ii/A.D.) ἥδιστά σε ἀσπάζομ[αι. For a good ex. of the elative ἥδιστα see the Bezan addition in Ac 13⁸ ἐπειδὴ ἥδιστα ἤκουεν αὐτῶν: cf. 2 Cor 12⁹·¹⁵.

The adj. is found in a medical prescription of ii/iii A.D., P Oxy II. 234³⁹ λιβ]ανωτὸν οἴνῳ [διέι]ς ἡδίστῳ κλύζε [τὸ ο]ὖς, "dilute frankincense with very sweet wine and syringe the ear."

For the comp. ἥδιον (as in Sir 22¹¹) see BGU II. 372¹·¹⁵ (A.D. 154) (as amended *Chrest.* I. p. 33) ἵνα δὲ τοῦτο προθυμ[ότ]ερο[ν] κα[ὶ] ἥδιο[ν π]ο[ιή]σω[σιν, and *Priene* 105¹⁹ (c. B.C. 9) ἥδειον δ' ἂν ἀνθρώποι[ς] ἣν κοινὴν πᾶσιν ἡμέραν γενέθλιον ἀγαγ[εῖν, ε]ὰν προσγένηται αὐτοῖς καὶ ἰδία τις διὰ τὴν ἀρχὴν ἡδονή[ή—the important Calendar inscr. of the proconsul Paullus Fabius Maximus proposing to the Greeks in Asia to commence the year with the birth-day of the Emperor Augustus (see Deissmann *LAE*, p. 370 f., Routhac *Recherches*, p. 67 ff.).

ἡδονή.

See the quotation from *Priene* 105²⁰ *s.v.* ἥδιστα *sub fine*. and cf. *Cagnat* IV. 566¹² (rescript of Sept. Severus) τὴν

ἡδονὴν ἣν ἐπὶ τοῖς κατωρθωμένοις ἔχετε. The baser signification which is found in the five occurrences of the word in the NT may be illustrated from Vett. Val. p. 76¹ πάθεσιν ἀκαθάρτοις καὶ παρὰ φύσιν ἡδοναῖς χρήσονται, and Musonius p. 89¹⁰¹ as cited *s.v.* βιόω *sub fine*. The word survives in MGr.

For the verb see P Petr III. 144ⁱᵛ·¹⁶ (B.C. 246) οὕτως ἡδόμεθα, P Cairo Preis 48¹ (ii/A.D.) ἐπιγνοὺς . . . ὅτι ἔρρωσαι, ἥσθην, ἄδελφε, P Giss I. 72·⁹ (ii/A.D.) ἵνα γε κατὰ τοῦτο ἐν Χάκοις ὄντες ἡσθῶμεν ἐπὶ σοί. The compound ἡδονοκρασία = "self-indulgence" occurs in Aristeas 278: cf. P Tor II. 8⁹⁷ (ii/B.C.) αὐτοκρασίαι τινὶ ἐκφερόμ[ενος].

ἡδύοσμος.

Τὸ ἡδύοσμον, the popular name for μίνθη, "mint" (Vg. *mentha*), in Mt 23²³, Lk 11⁴² survives in MGr in the form δυόσμος, "jasmine."

ἦθος.

For this word, which in the NT is found only in a quotation (1 Cor 15³³), generally believed to be taken from Menander, but assigned to Euripides in the new anthology P Hib I. 7⁹¹ (c. B.C. 250–210), we may compare BGU I. 248¹⁴ (ii/A.D.) ἐπιθυμεῖν τῶν ἠθῶν σου ἀπολαῦσαι, P Hamb I. 37⁵ (ii/A.D.) ἀναγκαῖον γάρ ἐστι μνημίσκεσθαι (l. μιμνήσκεσθαι) τῆς καλοκαγαθίας σου καὶ τοῦ ἤθους σου τοῦ ἀληθινοῦς (l. -οῦ) φιλοσόφου. P Giss I. 67⁵ (ii/A.D.) δι' ἧς (*sc.* ἐπιστολῆς) τὰ πρέποντά σου τῇ ἀξίᾳ καὶ [τῷ] ἤθει ἁρμόζοντα δηλοῖς, P Oxy III. 642 (ii/A.D.) ἡμεῖς γ[ὔ]ν ἀπολαύσωμεν τῷ χρηστῷ ὑμῶν ἤθει, *ib.* VI. 963 (ii/iii A.D.) οὐκ ἀλλότριο[ν γὰρ] τοῦ ἤθους ποιεῖς, φιλ[τάτη μῆτερ, σ]πουδάζουσα . . . , and from the inscr. *Michel* 545⁸ (ii/B.C.) τό τε ἦθος κοσμιότητι καὶ εὐσ[χη]μοσύνῃ, *Magn* 164³ (i/ii A.D.) ἤθει καὶ ἀγωγῇ κόσμιον. See also Aristeas 290 ἦθος χρηστὸν καὶ παιδείας κεκοινωνηκὸς δυνατὸν ἄρχειν ἐστι, "a good disposition which has had the advantage of culture is fitted to bear rule" (Thackeray).

ἥκω.

Preisigke 1046 (i/A.D.) Σεραπίων ἥκω πρὸς Σέραπι(ν) πατέρ(α) illustrates a common formula. Of greater importance is the use of the verb in relation to worship, as in Jn 9³⁷, in such a passage as *OGIS* 186⁷ (B.C. 62) ἥκω πρὸς τὴν κ[υ]ρίαν Ἴσιν: see Deissmann *LAE*, p. 356 n⁶. The aor. ἦξα, as in Rev 2²⁵, may be cited from P Oxy VI. 933¹³ (late ii/A.D.) . . . μεγ[ά]λην ἑορτὴν ἦξα, "I came to the great festival," and for the use of the perf. form owing to the perf. meaning, as ἥκασιν in Mk 8³ אADN, cf. P Par 48⁹ B.C. 153) (= Witkowski,² p. 91) ἥκαμεν εἰς τὸ Σεραπιεῖον βολάμενοι συνμῖξαί σοι, P Grenf II. 36¹⁸ (B.C. 95) καλῶς ἡμῖν ὧδε ἣ ἐν Διοσπόλει ἐὰν αἴρησθε πυρὸν ἀγοράσαι ἥκατε, also P Par 35³⁰ (B.C. 163) ἀπεκρίθησαν ἡμῖν φήσαντες ἐπ' ἐνεχυρασίαν ἡκένα[ι: see further Mayser *Gr.* p. 372. For other instances of the verb it is sufficient to quote *ib.* 40²⁷ (B.C. 164–158) διὰ τοῦτο οὐκέτι ἥκει πρὸς ἐμὲ αἰσχυνθείς, P Oxy III. 531⁸ (ii/A.D.) ἐὰν γὰρ θεοὶ θέλωσι τάχιον πρὸς σὲ ἥξω μετὰ τὸν Μεχεὶρ μῆνα, *ib.* VII. 1025¹⁰ (late iii/A.D.) ἐξαυτῆς ἥκετε, "come at once," and *ib.* X. 1252 recto³⁰ (A.D. 288–95) προσέταξεν . . . ἥκειν μετὰ τῶν ἀποδείξεων, "gave orders to come with the proofs." See also the striking invitation to celebrate the accession of Hadrian, P Giss I. 3² (A.D. 117) (= *Chrest.* I. p. *571*), where the god Phoebus is represented as saying—

ἥκω σοι, ὦ δῆμ[ε,
οὐκ ἄγνωστος Φοῖβος θεὸς ἄνακτα καινὸν Ἀδριανὸν ἀγγελῶ[ν.

'Ηλεί.

With this Aramaic form of the Heb. ἐλωί as read by DE a*l.* in Mt 27⁴⁶, cf. the opening words of the imprecatory tablet Wunsch *AF* 2¹ (ii/iii A.D.).—Ἰάω ᾿Ηλ Μιχαὴλ Νέφθω. The editor quotes from the *Etym. Magnum*, p. 477, 4 τὸ ἠλ ὃ σημαίνει τὸν θεόν, and refers to a passage from Philo Byblius (*Fragm. Histtric. Graec.* iii. p. 570 fr. 4) in which Κρόνος and ᾿Ηλ are identified.—Κρόνος τοίνυν ὃν οἱ Φοίνικες ᾿Ηλ προσαγορεύουσιν. The description of God as אל = δύναμις is supported by a striking variation of the cry of Mt *l.c.* in Ev. Petr. 5—῾Η δύναμίς μου, ἡ δύναμις, κατέλειψάς με.

ἡλικία.

Lk 19³ is the only NT passage where the word *must* mean "stature": apart from it (and the rather different Eph 4¹³) the NT represents the general *usus loquendi* of our vernacular sources. We are indeed unable to quote any example from these (for the word in a theological fragment see below) in which "stature" is the natural meaning, and hardly any in which it is possible : while for "age" we can present a long list. Thus the word is very common in connexion with being "under age" or coming "of age," which in Egypt took place at the age of 14 years : see e.g. P Ryl II. 250⁴ (late i/B.C.) νυὶ (*l.* νυνὶ) δ᾽ ἐμοῦ ἐν ἡλικίᾳ γεγονότος, P Oxy II. 247¹³ (A.D. 90) ἀπογράφομ[αι τῷ ὁμογν]ησίῳ μου ἀδελ[φῷ] . . . προστρέχοντι τῇ ἐννόμῳ ἡλικίᾳ, "approaching the legal age," *ib.* 273¹³ (A.D. 95) συνκεχωρηκέναι τῇ ἑαυτῆς θυγατρὶ . . . οὐδέπω οὔσῃ ἐν ἡλικίᾳ, *ib.* III. 496¹² (A.D. 127) τέκνων παρὰ τῇ μητρὶ διαιτ[ο]υμένων ἕως ἡλικίας γέ[ν]ωντ[α]ι, P Ryl II. 153¹⁹ (A.D. 138-61) ἄχ]ρι οὗ γένη[ται τῆ]ς ἐννό[μο]υ [ἡ]λικίας, BGU I. 80¹⁹ (A.D. 155) μέχρι ἐὰν ἐν τῇ νόμῳ ἡλικίᾳ γένο[νται, and P Flor III. 382¹¹ (A.D. 222-3) where a man who has reached the age of 70 petitions to be freed from certain public duties ἀπὸ τῶν λειτουργιῶν ἐλευθερωθῆναι διὰ τὴν ἡλικίαν. Other miscellaneous examples of the word are BGU I. 168⁹ (ii/iii A.D.) τοῖς ἀτελέσι ἔχουσι τὴν ἡλικίαν, P Oxy VII. 1020⁵ (A.D. 198-201) εἰ τὴν ἐκ τῆς ἡλικίας ἔχεις β[οήθιαν,] ὁ ἡγούμ[ενος] τοῦ ἔθνους τὸν ἀγῶνα τῆς ἀφέσεως ἐκδικ[ήσει, "if you can claim the assistance due to immature age, the praefect of the province shall decide the suit for release" (Ed.), P Tebt II. 326³ (c. A.D. 266) ὑπὲρ θυγατρὸς ὀρφανῆς καὶ καταδεοῦς τὴν ἡλικίαν . . . ἱκετηρίαν τιθεμένη, "making supplication for my orphan daughter who is under age." The list of citations might be almost indefinitely increased, but it must be sufficient to summarize by stating that no one who reads the papyri can have any doubt that the word meant "age" in ordinary parlance. In the fragment of a lost Gospel referred to above, P Oxy IV. 655¹⁴ (not later than A.D. 250) τίς ἂν προσθῆ (*l.* προσθείη) ἐπὶ τὴν ἡλικίαν ὑμῶν; αὐτο[ς δ]ώσει ὑμῖν τὸ ἔνδυμα ὑμῶν, the editors translate "who could add to your stature? He himself will give you your garment."

We must not yield to the temptation of discussing the meaning of the word in "Q"; but we cannot resist expressing amazement that anyone could call it ἐλάχιστον Lk 12²⁶ to add half a yard to one's height ! The *Twentieth Century* translators boldly render, "Which of you, by being anxious, can prolong his life a moment?"—and we cannot but applaud them. That worry *shortens* life is the fact which adds point to the irony. The desire to turn a six-footer into a Goliath is rather a bizarre ambition. See the admirable argument and citations in Wetstein *ad* Mt 6⁷.

A quotation from an inscription in honour of a wealthy young citizen of Istropolis, near the mouth of the Danube, should be given, as a most interesting parallel to Lk 2⁵² : *Syll* 325¹³ (i/B.C.) ὑπεστήσατό τε ἡλικίᾳ προκόπτων καὶ προαγόμενος εἰς τὸ θεοσεβεῖν ὡς ἔπρεπεν αὐτῷ πρῶτον μὲν ἐτείμησεν τοὺς θεούς κτλ.

ἡλίκος.

P Tebt I. 27⁷⁸ (B.C. 113) (= *Chrest.* I. p. 390) καθόλου δ᾽ ἐνθυμηθεὶς ἡλίκην συμβάλλεται ἡ περὶ τὰ ὑποδεικνύμεν[α] προσοχὴι τοῖς πράγμασι ῥοπήν, "in general consider how great an impulse attention to the matters indicated gives to business" (Edd.), *Syll* 405¹¹ (A.D. 145) ἐδήλ[ωσεν ὅσα κα]ὶ ἡλίκα οἰκοδομήματα προστίθησιν τῇ πόλ[ει. In the medical prescriptions P Oxy VIII. 1088⁴² (early i/A.D.) κολλύρια πόει ἡλίκον Αἰγύπ(τιον) κύαμον, "make pastilles of the size of an Egyptian bean " (Ed.), and *ib.* II. 234¹¹ ²⁰ (ii/iii A.D.) ἡλίκον (ὀ)ρόβῳ, "of the size of a pea" (Edd.), the context suggests that, as in the case of the Lat. *quantus* sometimes = *quantulus*, ἡλίκος from meaning "how great" has come to mean also "how small" : cf. Jas 3⁵.

ἧλιος.

P Hib I. 27³⁰ (a calendar—B.C. 301-240) ἔλεγεν δὲ [δύο] τὰς πορείας εἶναι τοῦ ἡλίου μία (*l.* μίαν) μὲν τὴν διορίζουσαν νύκτα καὶ ἡμέραν μία (*l.* μίαν) δὲ τὴν διορίζουσαν χιμῶνα καὶ θέρος, "he said that the courses of the sun were two, one dividing night and day and one dividing winter and summer" (Edd.), P Petr III. 144ᴵⱽ ²⁰ (B.C. 246) ἡλίου περὶ καταφορὰν ὄντος, "at sunset," P Oxy IV. 725¹² (A.D. 183) ἀπὸ ἀν[ατ-ολῆς] ἡ[λίου] μέχρι δύσεως, and an astronomical dialogue of iii/A.D., P Ryl II. 63⁴, where in answer to a question regarding certain εἴδωλα, it is replied—"Ηλιός [ἐσ]τιν δεξιὸς ὀφθαλμός, Σελήνη ὁ εὐώνυμος : see also the ii/B.C. papyrus of the astronomer E doxus, καθ᾽ ὃν ὁ ἥλιος φερόμενος τὴν μὲν ἡμέραν βραχυτέραν ποιεῖ τὴν δὲ νύκτα μακροτέραν. Two instances may be added from the inscrr., *Michel* 466¹⁰ (iii/B.C.) ἅμα τῶι ἡλίωι [ἀν]ατέλλοντι, *ib.* 1357¹⁰ (B.C. 300-299) ἡλίου ἀνιόντος ὁδός. For the late ἡλιαστήριον, "a place for sunning oneself," cf. P Ryl II. 206⁴⁸ (late ii/A.D.), and the introduction to P Oxy VII. 1014 : also for a literary ex. *ib.* VI. 985. In MGr ἥλιος is found also in the form νήλιος, the ν having been carried over from a preceding word owing to a mistaken separation of words : see Thumb *Handbook*, p. 25, and cf. "newt," "nickname," also Fr. *lierre* (Lat. *hedera*).

ἧλος.

P Lond 1177⁶³¹ accounts—A.D. 113) (= III p. 187) τι[μ]ῆς ἥλων καὶ ἄλλων, P Strass I. 32⁴ (A.D. 261) ἔπεμψα δὲ καὶ ἥλους τέσσαρας εἰς τὴν τούτου πῆξιν, P Oxy IX.

1220[16] (iii/A.D.) πέμψις μοι τοὺς ἐκχυσιαίους ἥλους καὶ γλυοῦ (l. γλοιοῦ) κεράμιον, " you will send me the nails for emptying (?) and a jar of gum " (Ed.), and the citation from *Archiv* v. p. 179 *s.v.* δαπανάω *sub fine*. The mention of the nails in the hands of the crucified Lord, as in Jn 20[25], is found in Ev. Petr. 6 καὶ τότε ἀπέσπασαν τοὺς ἥλους ἀπὸ τῶν χειρῶν τοῦ κυρίου.

For a subst. ἡλοκόπος = "nail-smith" cf. BGU IV. 1028[19] (ii/A.D.) τοῖς σὺν αὐτῷ ἡλοκόπ(οις), and for the corresponding adj. *ib.* 1124[11] (B.C. 18) τὴν ἡλοκοπικὴν τέχνην.

ἡμέρα.

P Par I[34] (B.C. 117) ἡμέρας, "during the day," *ib.* 27[21] (B.C. 160) τῆς ἡμέρας, "every day," *ib.* 49[26] (B.C. 164–158) τὴν ἡμέραν ἐκείνην ἀσχοληθείς, P Tebt I. 17[3] (B.C. 114) ἅμ' ἡμέραι, "at daybreak," P Giss I. 17[10] (time of Hadrian) καθ' ἡμέραν, P Oxy VII. 1029[26] (A.D. 107) εἰς τὴν ἐνεστῶσαν ἡμέραν, *ib.* 1068[14] (iii/A.D.) ἡμερῶν ἀνοχὴν ἔχω, *ib.* X. 1275[13] (iii/A.D.) ἐφ' ἡμέρας ἑορτῶν πέντε. In P Giss I. 19[7] (ii/A.D.) a wife writes to her husband—συν]εχῶς ἀγρυπνοῦσα νυκτὸς ἡ[μέρας μ]ίαν μέριμναν ἔχω τὴν περὶ [τῆς σωτ]ηρίας σου. The noun is used of *time* generally, as in Jn 14[20], Ac 9[23] *al.*, in P Amh II. 30[43] (ii/B.C.) where a woman, who has been ordered to vacate a house, asks "for time"—ἡμέρας αἰτοῦσα, promising that she will quit—ἐν ἡ[μ]έραις ι, "within ten days." For the parenthetic nominative of time, as Mt 15[32], Mk 8[2], Lk 9[28], we may perhaps cite P Lond 417[10] (c. A.D. 346) (= II. p. 299) ἐπειδὴ ἀσχολῶ ἐλθῖν πρὸ[ς] σὲν αὐτὲ (= —αἱ) ἡμέρε, "his diebus," according to Crönert's reading (*CR* xvii. p. 197), but see *Chrest.* I. 129 where Wilcken reads αὐτεημερε = αὐθημερόν : see *Proleg.* p. 69 f. The phrase πάσας τὰς ἡμέρας (Mt 28[20]) may be illustrated from an important Ephesian inscr. of ii/A.D., *Syll* 656[49] διὸ [δεδόχθαι ἱερ]ὸν τὸν μῆνα τὸν Ἀρτεμισιῶνα εἶ[ναι πάσας τ]ὰς ἡμέρας. It is accordingly a vernacular Greek expression like the Homeric ἤματα πάντα = "perpetually," though one does not willingly drop the suggestiveness of the literal translation in the Great Commission, the aid from heaven given day by day. To the same effect Rouffiac (*Recherches*, p. 49) quotes *Priene* 174[8] (ii/B.C.) where it is stated that the priest of Dionysus has, amongst other advantages, that of being supplied with "daily" food—εἶναι δὲ αὐτῶι . . σίτησιν πάσας τὰς ἡμέρας. For ἡμέραν ἐξ ἡμέρας, as in 2 Pet 2[8], see *s.v.* ἐκ. In the account of the excavations at Didyma (*Abh. der Berl. Akad. d. W.* 1911, *Anhang*, p. 54) mention is made of an inscr. found in the Temple, in which the day of Hadrian's visit is described as ἱερὰ ἡμέρα, and see *Archiv* v. p. 342, where it is shown that in all probability from B.C. 30 to the time of Trajan the 24th day of every month was observed as a ἡμέρα Σεβαστή in memory of the birth of Augustus on 24 Thoth B.C. 30. For an invocation to the god of the day see Wünsch *AF* 4[19] (iii/A.D.) ὁρ[κίζω σε τὸν θεὸν τὸν τῆς ἡμέρας ταύτης ἧς σε ὁρκίζω Αωαβαωθ. MGr ἡμέρα may suffer aphaeresis and become μέρα.

For the adj. ἡμερινός, cf. P Lond 1177[1-3] (A.D. 113) (=III. p. 185) βοηλάτας ἡμερινοὺς δ, and the same document for ἡμερεύω and ἡμερήσιος. See also εὐημερέω, "bene me habeo," in P Amh II. 39[5] (B.C. 103) δι' ἃ παντὸς εὐημερεῖν, and the subst. in P Leid D[24] (B.C. 162) εὐημερία, καὶ ἐν τοῖς [πράγμασιν εὐ]τυχία.

ἡμέτερος.

For the ordinary use of ἡμ. with a subst. cf. P Tebt I. 27[81] (B.C. 113) κατὰ τὴν ἡμετέραν πρόθεσιν, *ib.* II. 326[4] (c. A.D. 266) ὁ γὰρ ἡμέτερος ἀνὴρ . . ἀδιάθετος ἐτελεύτα τὸν βίον, "for my husband died intestate," P Oxy VII. 1056[3] (A.D. 360) τῷ ἡμετέρῳ ὀνόματι, "on my account." In P Flor III. 309[2]f (iv/A.D.) ἡμ. is used interchangeably with μου—τῇ ἡμετέρα [συμ]βίῳ καὶ τῇ παρθένῳ μου θυγατρί. A letter of introduction, P Oxy IV. 787 (A.D. 16), runs—ὡς ἔστιν ἡμέτερος (cf. Tit 3[14]). ἐρωτῶ σε οὖν ἔχειν αὐτὸν συνεσταμένον κτλ. In P Oxy I. 37[i 16] (A.D. 49) (=*Selections*, p. 50) εἰς τὴν τοῦ ἡμετέρου [ο]ἰκίαν = "into the house of our client," and in P Ryl II. 114[18] (c. A.D. 280) we have τὰ ἡμέτερα = " my property," cf. Lk 16[12]. A good parallel to the use of οἱ ἡμέτεροι in Tit 3[14] is afforded by *Chrest.* I. 16[7] (time of Trajan) where the writer complains that in a Jewish uprising οἱ ἡμέ[τ]ερο[ι ἡττ[ή]θησαν.

ἡμιθανής.

A good parallel to the use of this rare word (for class. ἡμιθνής) in Lk 10[30] is afforded by P Amh II. 141[13] (A.D. 350) where a woman lodges a complaint regarding an assault committed on her by her brother and his wife—πληγαῖς ἱκαναῖς με κατέκτι[να]ν . . . . ἡμιθανὴ καταστήσαντες, "they nearly killed me by numbers of blows and left me half dead " (Edd.).

ἥμισυς.

P Petr II. 11 (1)[5] (iii/B.C.) (=*Selections*, p. 7) ἀπὸ τούτου (a sum of 70 drachmae) τὸ μὲν ἥμισυ εἰς τὰ δέοντα ὑπελιπόμην : the word is almost always so written in papyri of iii/B.C., while in the two following centuries ἥμυσυ and ἥμισυ occur with almost equal frequency, see Mayser *Gr.* p. 100 f. Deissmann (*BS*, p. 186) gives a number of exx. of the gen. ἡμίσους from Imperial times, and cites ἥμισον μέρος from BGU I. 183[11] (A.D. 85) as probably from a vulgar form ἥμισος common in Egypt (cf. Jannaris *Gr.* § 401[b]). For neut. plur. ἡμίση see P Lond 265[23] (i/A.D.) (= II. p. 261) εἰς ἡμίση. Other exx. of the word from Imperial times are P Ryl II. 76[6] (late ii/A.D.) τὸ κατ' ἐμὲ ἥμισυ μέρος τῶν ὑπαρχόντων αὐτῆς, *ib.* 168[12] (A.D. 120) κατὰ τὸ ἥμισυ, "by halves," and Meyer *Ostr* 19[7] (A.D. 170) Μιῦις σεση-(μείωμαι) γόμ(ον) ἕνα ἥμισυ τρίτον, where ἥμισυ is indeclinable as in the variant τὰ ἥμισυ of Lk 19[8] (cf. LXX Tob 10[10], and see WH *Notes*[2], p. 165). Add P Tebt I. 110[5] (B.C. 92 or 59) πυρῶν ἀρτάβας εἴκοσι τέσσαρες ἥμισυ, "24½ artabae of wheat," BGU I. 290[13] (A.D. 150) πυροῦ . . ἀδόλου ἀρτάβην μίαν ἥμισυ, and *ib.* III. 920[11] (A.D. 180-1) τῶν ἐπὶ τὸ αὐτὸ ἀρουρῶν τ[ρ]ιῶν ἥμισυ τετάρτου καθαρῶν. Also P Oxy II. 277[4f.] (B.C. 19), a lease of 30¾ arourae—ἀροὺρ(ας) τριάκοντα ἓξ ἥμισυ τέταρτον, the produce of which was to be shared "equally"—ἐφ' ἡμεσίᾳ (l. ἡμισείᾳ)—between landlord and tenant. Aphaeresis of the initial vowel produces the MGr μισός, μιση, μισό, but in connexion with other numbers (ἥμισυ is used, as in P Tebt I. 110 (*v. supra*).

ἡμίωρον.

For the form ἡμιώριον which is read in Rev 8[1] by AC *al.*, add to the similar formations cited by Grimm-Thayer P Giss

I. 47[13] (time of Hadrian) (= *Chrest.* I. p. 383) τὸ ἡμιλεί-[τρ]ιον τῆς πορφύρας.

ἡνίκα.

It may be well to illustrate some of the different constructions of this word. Thus it is construed with the ind. in P Goodspeed 3[9] (iii/B.C.) (= Witkowski[2], p. 47) ἡνίκα ἤμελλον κοιμηθῆναι, P Ryl II. 119[6] (A.D. 54–67) ἡνίκα ἦν δικαιοδότης, *ib.* 181[5] (c. A.D. 203–4) ἡνίκα περιῆν, P Oxy VI. 939[23] (iv/A.D.) (= *Selections*, p. 130) ἡνίκα ἐβαρεῖτο τῇ νόσῳ: with the conj. without ἄν in P Oxy I. 68[21] (A.D. 131) ἡνίκα περιῇ," in her lifetime" (Edd.) : and with the conj. with ἄν or ἐάν in *ib.* 104[26] (A.D. 96) ἡνίκα ἐὰν ἀπαλλαγῇ τοῦ ἀνδρός, P Tebt II. 317[18] (A.D. 174–5) ἡνίκα ἐὰν εἰς τὸν νομὸν παραγένηται, " whenever he visits the nome" (Edd.).

ἤπιος.

In *Archiv* v. p. 166 No. 17 Rubensohn publishes a sepulchral inscr. (late Rom.) stating that μοῖρ' ὀλοὴ θανάτοιο had brought Sarapion down εἰς Ἀΐδαο, and describing him as— μειλείχιον πάντ[εσσ]ι καὶ ἤπιον ἀνθρώποισι. This illustrates well the idea of outward mildness or mildness towards others which Tittmann finds in the adj. (*Synon.* i. p. 140, " qui hanc lenitatem in aliis ferendis monstrat "), and which appears in both its NT occurrences (1 Th 2[7] Nc ACb Dc, 2 Tim 2[24]). The adj. is found *ter* in the semi-literary invocation to Isis, P Oxy XI. 1380[11, 86, 155] (early ii/A.D.).

ἤρεμος.

The Pauline phrase in 1 Tim 2[2] finds a striking parallel in *OGIS* 519[10] (c. A.D. 245) ἤρεμον καὶ γαληνὸν τὸν βίον δια-[γόντων]. Lest Paul should be credited with a literary word we may cite the use of the verb in BGU IV. 1019[2] (mid. ii/A.D.) σω]φροσύνῃ [ἱ]κ[α]νὸν χρόνο[ν] ἠρεμήσας μετῆλθεν.

Ἡρώδης

is to be written with an iota subscript in view of its derivation—Ἡρω–ίδης (Blass *ad* Ac 4[27]). The full form is seen in P Petr III. 32(e)[2] Ἀριστοκρίτωι οἰκονό[μωι παρὰ] Ἡρώί-δου τοῦ ἐξειληφότος τ[ὴν] ζυτηρὰν (" beer-tax ") Ἀπίαδος κτλ.: but cf. Ἡρώδης with reference to a ship-master in P Lille I. 23[5] (B.C. 221) and a weaver in BGU I. 115[6] (ii/A.D.). From Cos comes an inscr. in honour of Herod Antipas— *Cos* 75 (= *OGIS* 416) Ἡρώδην Ἡρώδου τοῦ βασιλέως υἱόν, τετράρχην, Φίλων Ἀγλαοῦ φύσει δὲ Νίκωνος τὸν αὐτοῦ ξένον καὶ φίλον. For a fem. Ἡρωδίαινα see BGU II. 542[4] (ii/A.D.) ἀπ[ηλιώτου Ἡρω]διαίνης. The original sense of " protector" underlying ἥρως appears in Lat. *servāre* " preserve intact ": cf. Ἥρα, " protectress." That ἥρως became simply " the dead" is well seen in the testamentary disposition of Epicteta, *Michel* 1001 (c. B.C. 200).

ἥσσων.

Mayser (*Gr.* p. 223) gives only one example from the Ptolemaic papyri of the Attic ἥττων, viz. P Petr II. 47[26] (B.C. 208) where Wilcken (see P Petr III. p. xviii.) now reads—καὶ μηθὲν ἧττον ἡ [συγγραφὴ κυρία : elsewhere, in accordance with the general preference in the Κοινή for –σσ– rather than –ττ– we have ἥσσων, e.g. P Par 61[12] (B.C. 156) πάντα ἐστὶν ἀλλότρια τῆς τε ἡμῶν ἀγωγῆς, οὐχ

PART III.

ἧσσον δὲ καὶ τῆς ὑμετέρας σωτηρίας, P Tebt I. 105[26] (B.C. 103) μηθὲν ἧσσον ἡ μίσθωσις κυρία ἔσ[τω, " while the validity of the lease shall not be affected " (Edd.), *ib.* 150 (B.C. 91) καὶ μηδὲν ἧσσον ἡ χεὶρ ἥδε κυρία ἔσται πανταχῆ ἐπιφερομένη. In Roman times we find a mixture of the forms: thus for ἥσσων see P Oxy II. 271[27] (A.D. 56) καὶ μ[ηδ]ὲν ἧσσον κυρία [ἡ] συνγραφήι. *ib.* 270[16] (A.D. 94), *ib.* III. 492[11] (A.D. 130), and for ἥττων see P Tebt II. 329[29] (A.D. 139) οὐδὲν δὲ ἧττον ὑπέταξα τῆς ἡ[μετέρας συγγρα-φῆς (?), P Ryl II. 77[37] (A.D. 192) εἰ δὲ μὴ οὐχ (pap. omits) ἧττον ἑαυτὸν ἐχειροτόνησεν, " otherwise he none the less nominated himself" (Edd.), P Oxy VII. 1070[16] (iii/A.D.) διὰ ἐπιστολῶν πολλῶν οὐχ ἧττον δὲ καὶ κατ' ὄψιν, " by many letters not less than in person." On the form see further Maidhof *Begriffsbestimmung*, p. 316 ff.

ἡσυχάζω.

For this favourite Lukan word (see also 1 Th 4[11]) cf. P Tebt II. 330[8] (ii/A.D.) ὅθεν οὐ δυνάμ[ε]νος ἡσυχάζειν ἐπιδί-δωμι, " wherefore, being unable to submit to this, I apply to you" (Edd.)—a petition to the strategus, and BGU II. 372[ii. 14] (A.D. 154) ἄλλοις δὲ τῶν ποτε προγραφ[έ]ντων ἡσυ-χάζουσι καὶ ἐν τῇ οἰκείᾳ τῇ γεω[ργ]ίᾳ προσκατέχουσι *l.* προσκατέχουσι μὴ ἐνοχλεῖν—a good example of the force of the verb in 1 Th *l.c.*: cf. also PSI I. 41[23] (iv/A.D.) σ]ωφρονεῖν καὶ ἡσυχάζειν, and the late P Oxy I. 128 *verso*[2] (vi/vii A.D.) Παμούθιος . . ἐβουλήθη ἐπαναχωρῆσαι τῶν πραγμάτων καὶ ἡσυχάσαι, " Pamouthius has expressed the desire to retire from his duties and take rest " (Edd.). In the illiterate P Fay 117[23] (A.D. 108) we have ὦ ἔγραφός μυ μὴ ἡσυχάσαι τῷ κτιστῷ περιτὸν γέγραπτα[ι, " what you write to me about not neglecting the building you have said more than enough " (Edd.). For the compound ἀφησυχάζω, see P Goodsp Cairo 15[24] (A.D. 362) ὅθεν μὴ δυναμένη ἀφησυχάζειν, and for καθησυχάζω, see BGU I. 36[14] (ii/A.D.).

ἡσυχία.

P Lond 44[17] (B.C. 161) (= I. p. 34) μετὰ κραυγῆς τε διαστελλομένου μεθ' ἡσυχίας ἀναλύειν, P Rein 7[15] (B.C. 141?) διὰ πάση]ς ἡσυχίας εἶχον, " I was completely at rest (in mind)," P Oxy II. 237[vii. 3] (A.D. 186) τὴν ἡσυχίαν ἄγειν καὶ μήτε τῷ κυρίῳ ἐνοχλεῖν, BGU II. 614[21] (iii/A.D.) τὰς ἡσυχίας με ἄξοντα, and similarly P Thead 19[13] (iv/A.D.). See also *Cagnat* IV. 33[31] καθ' ἡ[συχίαν.

ἡσύχιος.

For this adj. (MGr ἥσυχος), as in 1 Tim 2[2], cf. *CIG* III. 5361[13 f.] (Jew. inscr. of Berenice) ἔν τε τῆι ἀναστροφῆι ἡσύχιον ἦθος ἐνδικνύμενος, *IG* VII. 300[15] διενέγκας σεμνόν τε καὶ ἡσύχιον βίον παρ' ὅλον τὸν τῆς ζωῆς αὐτοῦ χρόνον, and the late P Oxy I. 129[5] (vi/A.D.) where a father repudiates a betrothal because he wishes that his daughter " should lead a peaceful and quiet life "—εἰρηνικὸν καὶ ἡσύχιον βίον διάξαι. For the adverb ἡσυχίᾳ (or form, see Mayser *Gr.* p. 122 f.) = " quietly," cf. P Hib I. 73[9] (B.C. 243–2) ἡσυχῆι . . . ἀπήγαγον τὸν Κ. εἰς τὸ ἐν Σινάρυ δεσμω]τήριον: it is used = " slightly " in personal descriptions, such as P Petr I. 16[1. 4] (B.C. 237) σύνοφρυς ἡσυχῆι, " with slightly meeting eyebrows," *ib.* 19[3] (B.C. 225) ἀνα-φάλανθος ἡσυχῆι, " slightly bald in the forehead," P Grenf

I. 33³ (c. B.C. 103–2) προκέφαλος ἡσυχῇ, "with a slightly sugar-loafed head," P Leid N[m. 7] (ii/B.C.) (= I. p. 69) ἔνσιμος ἡσυχῇ, "slightly snub-nosed."

ἤτοι.

See s.v. ἤ.

ἡττάομαι.

For this form in –ττ–, which is read in the NT in 2 Pet 2[19 f.] (for the LXX see Thackeray Gr. i. p. 121 f.), cf. PSI IV. 340⁷¹ (B.C. 257–6) οὐκ ἐττηθήσεσθε (l. ἡττ–) ὑπὸ ἀνθρώπου ἀνελευθέρου, and the interesting report of a Jewish uprising in an Egyptian village during the reign of Hadrian, Chrest. I. 16⁷, when the writer admits—οἱ ἡμέ[τ]ερο[ι] ἡττ[ή]θησαν καὶ πολλοὶ [α]ὐτῶν συνεκόπ[η]σαν. In P Hal I. 1⁵⁴, ¹¹⁵ (mid. iii/B.C.) we have ἡσσηθῆι twice: cf. 2 Cor 12¹³ where ἡσσώθητε (from Ionic ἑσσοῦσθαι) is read in ℵ* BD*. See further Wackernagel Hellenistica, p. 12 ff., where it is shown that Hellenistic writers have retained –ττ– in certain words which were taken over directly from Attic and were not current in another form in the Κοινή.

ἥττημα.

The use of the verb in the passage from Chrest. I. 16 cited s.v. ἡττάομαι may help to strengthen Field's contention (Notes, pp. 160 f., 171 f.) that both in Rom 11¹² and in 1 Cor 6⁷, the thought of "defeat" is present without any special ethical tinge. The subst. is found elsewhere in Bibl. Greek only in Isai 31⁸.

ἦχος.

For the masc. ὁ ἦχος (as in Heb 12¹⁹) cf. P Leid W[x. 3] (ii/iii A.D.) ἵνα ἐκ τοῦ ἤχους (om.) ὕδατος ὁ ἦχος ἀναβῇ, and ib.[x. 9] ἦχον ἐκπέμπει. The gen. ἠχοῦς from the fem. ἡ ἠχώ is, however, read by the editor in ib.[v. 38] σὺ μὲν ἀπὸ ποππυσμοῦ τυγχάνεις, οὗτος δὲ ἐξ ἠχοῦς, [xi. 39] καὶ ἡ γῆ ἀκούσασα ἠχοῦς, καὶ ἰδοῦσα αὐτήν, ἐθαμβήθη, and [xii. 51] σὺ μὲν ἐξ ἠχοῦς εἶ, οὗτος δὲ ἐκ φθόγγου: cf. Lk 21²⁵, where WH similarly accent ἠχοῦς, stating (Notes², p. 165) that the direct Bibl. evidence for the neut. τὸ ἦχος is confined to Jer 28 (51)¹⁶ ℵAB, where ἦχος is apparently an accusative. For masc. nouns passing into the neut., in accordance with a not uncommon practice in Hellenistic, see Hatzidakis Einl. p. 356 ff., Proleg. p. 60.

Θ

θάλασσα—θάπτω

θάλασσα.

BGU II. 423[7] (ii/A.D.) (= *Selections*, p. 99) εὐχαριστῶ τῷ κυρίῳ Σεράπιδι, ὅτι μου κινδυνεύσαντος εἰς θάλασσαν (cf. 2 Cor 11[26]) ἔσωσε, P Oxy VII. 1007[21] (iii/A.D.) ἀγόρασόν μοι ὀψαρίδιον ἐκ τῆς θαλάσσης (cf. Jn 21[10]), and from the inscr. *Michel* 372[11] (ii/B.C.) ἐργα[ζ]όμενός τε κατὰ θάλασσαν ἐργασίαν, *ib.* 521[13] (ii/B.C.) κατὰ γῆς καὶ κατὰ θαλάσσας. For references to ἡ ἐρυθρὰ θάλασσα, as in Ac 7[36], Heb 11[29], cf. P Grenf I. 9[3] (ii/B.C.) ἐρ]υθρᾶι θαλάσσηι, *OGIS* 186[3] (B.C. 62) ὁ συγγενὴς καὶ ἐπιστράτηγος καὶ στρατηγὸς τῆς Ἰνδικῆς καὶ Ἐρυθρᾶς θαλάσσης, *ib.* 190[9] (B.C. 51) ἐπὶ τῆς Ἰνδικῆς καὶ Ἐρυθρᾶς θαλάσσης : cf. also the intr. to P Ryl II. 66 (late ii/B.C.). For the adj. θαλάττ[ι]σσ[ι]ος, see P Oxy I. 87[7] (A.D. 342) θαλαττίου ναυκλήρου, "a sea-going vessel," *ib.* X. 1288[9] (iv/A.D.) εἰς διαγραφὴν πλόου θαλασσίας τιτέσματος (. πλοίου θαλασσίου τελέσματος ?)) (τάλ.) θ. "in payment for a sea-vessel, for charges 9 tal." (Edd.), and for ἐπιθαλάσσιος, P Rev L[xviii. 5] (B.C. 258) ἐπιθαλασσίαν. In 3 Kings 18[32. 35. 38] θάλασσα is used = "channel," doubtless because of its similarity in sound to the Heb. תְּעָלָה : see Thackeray *Gr.* i. p. 37.

θάλπω.

For this poetic verb (in NT only 1 Th 2[7], Eph 5[29]) cf. the vi/A.D. marriage-contract, CPR I. 30[20], where a husband undertakes ἀγαπᾶν καὶ θάλπειν καὶ θεραπεύειν his wife, and for a similar metaphorical usage see *OGIS* 194[5] (B.C. 42) τὴν πόλιν ἔθαλψε. The verb occurs several times in the *Mimes* of Herodas : cf. also Bacchylides *Frag.* iv. 16[2] (ed. Jebb, p. 417) θάλπησι θυμόν, and the Christian epigram *Kaibel* 725[3]—

θάλπεο ψυχὴν
ὕδασιν ἀενάοις πλουτοδότου σοφίης.

θαμβέω.

See P Leid W[v. 39] (ii/iii A.D.) ἰδὼν τὸν δράκοντα ὁ θεὸς ἐθαμβήθη καὶ ἐπόππυσε, and *ib.*[xi. 29] καὶ ἡ γῆ ἀκούσασα ἠχοῦς, καὶ ἰδοῦσα αὐτήν, ἐθαμβήθη, where the aor. has its full pass. force as in Mk 1[27] (cf. Blass-Debrunner § 78). The verb is restored in the new Logion, P Oxy IV. 654[1] μὴ παυσάσθω ὁ ζη[τῶν . . . . ἕως ἂν] εὕρῃ [θαμβηθήσεται καὶ θαμ]βηθεὶς βασιλεύσει. In MGr we have θαμπαίνω and θαμπώνω = "blind," "dazzle."

θάμβος.

This originally poetic word (Thumb *Dial.* p. 373) is confined in the NT to the Lukan writings, where, to judge from Ac 3[10], it is to be regarded as neuter : cf. gen. sing. θάμβους in Cant 3[8] (Thackeray *Gr.* i. p. 158). On the other hand in Lk 4[36] the Bezan text has θ. μέγας : cf. Eccles 12[5] θάμβοι.

θανάσιμος.

The phrase in [Mk] 16[18] may be paralleled from a *defixio* from Cnidus, *Syll* 815[2], where a woman devotes to Demeter and Kore τὸν κατ' ἐμοῦ [ἐ]ίπ[α]ντα ὅτι ἐγὼ τῶι ἐμῶι ἀνδ[ρὶ] φάρμακα ποιῶ θανά[σι]μα—if the restoration is sound.

θανατηφόρος.

This NT ἅπ. εἰρ. (Jas 3[8]) occurs *repeatedly* in Vett. Val., e.g. p. 225[7] κινδυνώδεις καὶ θανατηφόροι περιστάσεις, and p. 237[7] χαλεπὸς καὶ θανατηφόρος.

θάνατος.

For this common noun we may cite such passages as P Petr III. 36[a. verso 7] τ]ὸν θάνατον ὑποκείμενον [ἐν] τῆι φυλακῆι διὰ τὴν ἔνδειαν, P Tebt I 5[92] (B.C. 118) τοὺς δὲ παρὰ ταῦτα ποιοῦντας θανάτωι ζ]ημιοῦσθαι, P Oxy III. 472[7] (c. A.D. 130) ἄλλοι πολλοὶ τὸν θάνατον τοῦ ζῆν προκρείναντες, *ib.* II. 237[viii. 36] (A.D. 186) ἡ δὲ κτῆσις μετὰ θάνατον τοῖς τέκνοις κεκράτηται, "but the right of ownership after their death has been settled upon the children" (Edd.). The well-known inscr. at the entrance of the inner court of the Temple at Jerusalem, threatening all who were not Jews with the penalty of death for entering, ends—ὃς δ' ἂν ληφθῇ, ἑαυτῶι αἴτιος ἔσται διὰ τὸ ἐξακολουθεῖν θάνατον (*OGIS* 598[7], i/A.D.). In a Latin papyrus containing military accounts, P Fay 105[iii. 24] (c. A.D. 180), opposite the name Turbo a letter θ has been inserted, implying, according to the editors, that he has died. The letter, they add, has the same signification on Roman gravestones, and as in a Latin list of soldiers in the Rainer Collection, where the name itself is crossed through : cf. Persius *Sat.* iv. 13 ("nigrum . . . theta"), Mart. vii. 37, and the line of Lucilius (?)—"O multum ante alias infelix littera Theta." It was used by critics and grammarians to mark a *locus conclamatus*. In MGr the subst. survives, while θανατικό = "plague," "disease."

θάπτω.

P Par 22[17] (ii/B.C.) μέχρι τοῦ νῦν οὐ τετόλμηκεν αὐτὸν ἡ Νέφορις θάψαι, BGU IV. 1131[5] (B.C. 13) ἐπεὶ ἡ ἐμὴ μήτηρ . . μετήλ[λ]αχε καὶ . . χι . . . . . . οὐδέπω τετάφθαι, ὁμολογῶι κτλ., *ib.* 1024[iv. 2] (iv/v A.D.) νεκροῦ [μετ' εὐσε]βείας ταφθέντος. In P Giss I. 68[7] (ii/A.D.) δεῖ αὐτὸν δευτέρᾳ ταφῇ ταφῆναι, the meaning seems to be that the body must be buried in a second mummy-wrapping : see further *s.v.* ταφή. On the mummy-ticket *Preisigke* 3580 we read, Ἀπολλώνιος . . . Ἀθὺρ ιγ ἐτάφη : cf. Meyer *Ostr* 68[1] (ii/A.D.) ἐτάφησεν Θὼτ ιδ. The verb appears in MGr as θάβω, θάφτω, with a subst. θαφτό = "grave," and a *nomen actionis* θάψιμο = "burial."

θαρρέω.

For the later Attic form θαρρέω, which in the Κοινή, as in the more literary portions of the LXX (Thackeray *Gr.* i. p. 123) and in the NT (Paul, Heb), is interchanged with θαρσέω (see *s.v.*), cf. Thumb *Hellen.* p. 77. The verb = "have confidence in," as in 2 Cor 7[16], 10[1f], in P Oxy II. 237[viii.17] (A.D. 186) ἐὰν θαρρῇ τοῖς τῆς κατηγορίας ἐλέγχοις, τὸν μείζονα ἀγῶνα ε[ἰ]σελεύσεται, "if he has confidence in the proofs of his accusation, he shall enter upon the more serious law-suit" (Edd.): cf. P Oxy XII. 1468[9] (c. A.D. 258) ἐπὶ τὴν σὴν ἀνδρείαν καταφεύγω θαρρῶν τεύξεσθαι τῶν προσόντων μοι δικαίων, "I appeal to your nobility with the full confidence that I shall obtain the rights due to me" (Edd.), P Cairo Goodsp 15[18] (A.D. 362) θαρρῶν ὁ αὐτὸς Ἰσακις τοῖς χρήμασι αὐτοῦ καὶ τοῦ πλούτου βούλεταί μ[α]ι ἐξελάσαι ἀπὸ τῆς κώμης, "the aforesaid Isakis, relying on his means and wealth, wishes to drive me from the village" (Ed.). The sense of *audere*, rather than *confidere*, appears in P Oxy I. 68[19] (A.D. 131) μὴ τεθαρρηκαίναι (*l.* τεθαρρηκέναι) τ[ὸν] Θέωνα προελθεῖν, "without Theon having ventured to bring forward his claim" (Edd.). In MGr θαρρῶ = "believe," "think."

θαρσέω,

which in the NT is found only in the imper., may be illustrated by P Par 51[10] (B.C. 160) (= *Selections*, p. 19) ὄμμα . . ψυχῆς θάρσ[ει, "eye . . of my soul, take courage." See also P Petr II. 1[8] (iii/B.C.) θαρσήσας ᾠκονόμησα, P Lond 354[9] (c. B.C. 10) (= II. p. 164) ἐθάρσησαν ἐπιδόντες, BGU IV. 1080[14] (iii/A.D.?) περὶ τούτου θαρσῶν ἀμέλι (*l.* ἀμέλει). For the form θαρσύνω, cf. Aristeas 272 θαρσύνας δὲ τοῦτον ἕτερον ἐπηρώτα κτλ., "he spoke encouragingly to him, and asked another" etc. (Thackeray).

θαῦμα.

For this subst. (MGr θάμα), which in the NT is confined to 2 Cor 11[14], Rev 17[6], we may cite *Preisigke* 1002 (time of Diocletian?) where a certain Antonius Theodorus states that he had stayed for a considerable time ἐν τῇ βασιλ[ευ]ο[ύ]σῃ Ῥώμῃ . . . καὶ τὰ ἐκεῖ θαύματ[α] εἶδον καὶ τὰ ἐνταῦθα, and *ib.* 1099 Καθολικὸς Θεόδμος [. .]ν ἤγαγεν ἐς τόδε θαῦ[μα, and the poetical inscr. describing the foundation of Magnesia in which the words occur—καὶ θαῦμα καταθνητοῖσιν ἐφάνθη (*Magn* 17[18]). See also the sepulchral inscr. *Kaibel* 591[2] (ii/iii A.D.) where a certain Nilus is described as—

ῥητορικός, μέγα θαῦμα, φέρων σημεῖον ἐφ' αὑτῷ,

and *ib.* 909[5] (iv/A.D.)

Πάντη Πλουτάρχοιο κλέος, πάντη δέ τε θαῦμα,
πάντη δ' εὐνομίης εὖχος ἀπειρέσιον.

θαυμάζω.

For exx. of this verb denoting incredulous surprise, as in Jn 3[7] *al.*, see P Oxy III. 471[17] (ii/A.D.) π]ροσθήσω τι κύριε περ[ὶ οὗ] (cf. Lk 2[18]) θαυμάσεις οἶμαι καὶ ἀπι[στήσ]εις, "I will add a fact, my lord, which will, I expect, excite your wonder and disbelief" (Edd.), *ib.* I. 123[5] (iii/iv A.D.) πάνυ θαυμάζω, υἱέ μου, μέχρις σήμερον γράμματά σου οὐκ ἔλαβον, "I have been much surprised, my son, at not receiving hitherto a letter from you" (Edd.). For the astonishment of admiratio cf. P Giss I. 47[5] (time of Hadrian) ὡς καὶ [ὑ]πὸ πάντων τῶν ἰδόντων θαυμασθῆναι, with reference to certain goods that had been purchased, and from the inscrr. *Preisigke* 1799 (from the walls of the Kings' graves at Thebes) Βησᾶς ἰδὼν ἐθαύμασα, *ib.* 1802 Πύρος ἐθαύμασα, *al.* For θαυμάζω followed by εἰ, as in Mk 15[44] (cf. 1 Jn 3[13]), see P Hib I. 159 (c. B.C. 265) θαυμάζω οὖν εἰ πιστεύεις (so after ἀπιστεύσας in P Oxy II. 237[v.5]—A.D. 186), and by πῶς, P Oxy I. 113[20] (ii/A.D.) θαυμάζω πῶς οὐκ ἐδικαίωσας, "I wonder that you did not see your way" (Edd.), P Ryl II. 235[6] (ii/A.D.) ἐθ[αύ]μασε (*l.* -ασα) δὲ πῶς . . οὐκ ἐδήλωσάς μοι περὶ τῆς εὐρωστίας σου, "I was surprised that you did not inform me of your good health" (Edd.), BGU IV. 1041[12] (ii/A.D.) θαυμάζω [οὖν] πῶς οὐκ ἔγραψάς μ[οι ἐπι]στολήν. MGr θαυμάζω, θαυμάζομαι, θαμάζω, θαμαστῶ.

θαυμάσιος.

The comparative of this adj., which in the NT is confined to Mt 21[15], appears in *Syll* 365[11] (c. A.D. 37) μεγάλων . . μείζονες καὶ λαμπρῶν θαυμασιώτεροι. See for the superlative *OGIS* 504[12] (A.D. 128–9) πρὸς τὸν θαυμασιώτατον ἡμῶν ἄρχοντα, and so frequently in addresses in late papyri, e.g. P Oxy VI. 940 *verso* (v/A.D.) ἐπίδο(ς) τῷ θαυμασ[ιω(τάτῳ) Ἰωσὴφ νοταρίῳ, P Giss I. 57 *verso* (vi/vii A.D.) ἐπίδ(ος) τῷ δεσπότῃ μου τῷ τὰ πάντα θαυμασιωτάτῳ καὶ [ἐ]ναρέτῳ ἀδελφῷ Φοιβάμμωνι.

θαυμαστός.

occurs in the important soldier's narrative regarding the Syrian campaign during the reign of Ptolemy III., P Petr II. 45[iii.15] ἦ]σαν γὰρ θαυμαστοί—the immediately preceding words are unfortunately lost. See also the Christian amulet P Oxy VIII. 1151[53] (v/A.D.?) ὅτι τὸ ὄνομά σου, κ(ύρι)ε ὁ θ(εό)ς, ἐπικαλεσά[μ]ην τὸ θαυμαστὸν καὶ ὑπερένδοξον καὶ φοβερὸν τοῖς ὑπεναντίοις, "upon thy name, O Lord God, have I called, the wonderful and exceeding glorious name, the terror of thy foes" (Ed.). From the inscrr. we may note *Preisigke* 1008 θαυμαστὰς σύριγγας.

θεά.

Ἡ θεά (Ac 19[27]), and not ἡ θεός as generally in Attic prose (cf. Ac 19[37]), is the usual form in Ptolemaic papyri, e.g. P Par 37[27] (B.C. 163) εἰσέλθοντες εἰς τὸ τῆς θεᾶς ἄδυτον, *ib.* 51[28] (B.C. 160) (= *Selections*, p. 20) θεὰ θεῶν (of Isis), P Grenf II. 15[10] (B.C. 139) Κλεοπάτρας τῆς μητρὸς θεᾶς ἐπιφανοῦς, and other exx. in Mayser *Gr.* p. 254 f.: cf. from Imperial times P Oxy VIII. 1117[2] (c. A.D. 178) Ἀθη[νᾶς τῆς καὶ Θοήριδος θεᾶς μεγίστης. The same form is also common in the inscrr., e.g. *Magn* 47[13] (a decree of Chalcis—not after B.C. 199) τήν τε τῆς θεᾶς (*sc.* Ἀρτέμιδος Λευκοφρυηνῆς) ἐπιφάνειαν. On the other hand it is noteworthy that the classical ἡ θεός is frequently found in Magnesian inscrr. proper as a kind of technical term to describe this goddess as the great goddess of the city, e.g. *ib.* 100 a[28] τὴν ἐπιβάλλουσαν τιμὴν καὶ παρεδρείαν ποιούμενοι τῆς θεοῦ. Accordingly it is rightly put by Luke into the mouth of the town clerk in Ac 19[37] (cf. ver. 27): see further Thieme, p. 10 f., Nachmanson, p. 126, and cf. *Proleg.* pp. 60, 244.

θεάομαι.

The deeper meaning, involving moral and spiritual perception, which underlies the use of this verb in such a passage as Jn 1¹⁴, may be illustrated from P Par 51³⁸ (B.C. 160), where the recipient of a "vision" in the temple of Serapis at Memphis writes—τὸ ὅραμα τοῦτο τεθήαμαι : cf. *Syll* 324²⁰ (i/B.C.) αἰφνίδιον σ(υ)μφορὰν θεασάμενος. The thought of attentive, careful regard, as in Mt 11⁷, appears in the account of the death of a slave from leaning out of a bed-chamber (?) θεάσασθαι τὰς [κρο]ταλιστρίδας, "to behold the castanet-players" (P Oxy III. 475²¹—A.D. 182). But in other passages the verb cannot denote more than ordinary seeing with the eyes, as when a woman writes to her mother — ἀσπάζομαί σε, μῆτερ, διὰ τῶν γραμμάτων τούτων ἐπιθυμοῦσα ἤδη θεάσθαι (P Oxy VI. 963—ii/iii A.D.), or as when a woman who has quarrelled with her husband and has appealed to the tribunal, regrets that she has had anything to do with him from the first—εἴθε μὴ τεθέαμαι αὐτόν, εἴθε μὴ συνήφθ[ην α]ὐτῷ ἐξ ἀρχῆς (PSI I. 41¹⁹—iv/A.D.). So in one of the scribblings on the walls of the royal tombs at Thebes a visitor writes . . . θεασαμένη . . . (*Preisigke* 1800). It may be noted that the Attic θεάομαι is modelled upon θέα, "sight" : the Ionic θηέομαι points to an original *θᾱϝέομαι.

θέατρον.

The use of the θέατρον as a place for public assemblies, as in Ac 19²⁹, can be readily illustrated from the inscrr., e.g. *Brit. Mus. Inscr.* III. 481³²⁵ (A.D. 104) φερέτωσαν . . . κατὰ πᾶσαν ἐκκλησίαν εἰς τὸ θέατρον (at Ephesus), *Syll* 314⁴⁶ ἐκκλησία συνήχθη κυρία ἐν [τῶι θεά]τρωι (see Preuschen *HZNT ad loc.*). See also the "neat confirmation" of Ac 19³², ⁴¹ in the inscr. cited from Deissmann *LAE*, p. 114 *s.v.* ἐκκλησία. Miscellaneous exx. of the word from the papyri are P Flor I. 61²⁹ (A.D. 85) (as amended *Chrest.* II. p. 89) ἄνθρωπον στα[τέον] εἰς τὰ θέατρ[α, P Oxy III. 471¹⁶⁶ (ii/A.D.) καὶ τὸν οὐκ ἐν λευκαῖς ἐσθῆσιν [ἐ]ν θεάτρῳ καθί-σα[ντα] παρέδωκας εἰς θ[ά]ν[ατον, "and the man who took his seat at the theatre without wearing white garments you delivered to death" (Edd.), *ib.* VI. 937¹¹ (iii/A.D.) παραγ-γέλλω σοι . . . ἵνα παραβάλῃς πρὸς τῇ πλατείᾳ τοῦ θεάτρου, "I bid you go to the street of the theatre," *ib.* VII. 1050¹⁶ (ii/iii A.D.) φύλ(αξι) θεάτ[ρου. The adj. occurs in an inscr. from the theatre at Ephesus, OGIS 510⁷ (A.D. 138–61) τὴν λοιπὴν παρασκευὴν τῶν θεατρικῶν. MGr θέατρο(ν).

θεῖος.

With θείας κοινωνοὶ φύσεως in 2 Pet 1⁴ may be compared the remarkable inscription *Syll* 757 (not later than Augustus). It is in honour of Αἰών, and strongly suggests Mithraism, though Dittenberger dissents from the connexion. Vv.⁷⁻ᵉⁿᵈ must be quoted entire : Αἰὼν ὁ αὐτὸς ἐν τοῖς αὐτοῖς αἰεὶ φύσει θείαι μένων κόσμος τε εἰς κατὰ τὰ αὐτά, ὁποῖος ἔστι καὶ ἦν καὶ ἔσται, ἀρχὴν μεσότητα τέλος οὐκ ἔχων, μεταβολῆς ἀμέτοχος, θείας φύσεως ἐργάτης αἰωνίου κατὰ? πάντα. See also the decree of Stratonicea in honour of Zeus Panhemerios and of Hekate, cited by Deissmann (*BS*, p. 360 ff.) for its remarkable linguistic parallels to 2 Pet—καθίδρυται δὲ ἀγάλματα ἐν τῷ σεβαστῷ βουλευτηρίῳ τῶν προειρημέν[ω]ν θεῶν ἐπιφαν]εστάτας παρέχοντα τῆς θείας δυνάμεως ἀρετάς (*CIG* II. 2715 a, b).

The word is very common with an "imperial" connotation both in the papyri and the inscriptions. Thus in *Priene* 105²² (c. B.C. 9) the birthday of Augustus is described as—τὴν τοῦ θειοτάτου Καίσαρο[ς γ]ενέθλιον, and the use of the superlative is continued down even into the 6th and 7th centuries. e.g. P Lond 1007(c)¹ (A.D. 558) (= III. p. 264) βασιλε[ί]ας τοῦ θειοτάτου ἡμῶν δεσπότου Φλαυίου Ἰουστινι-ανοῦ τοῦ αἰωνίου Αὐγούστου [καὶ αὐτοκρά]τορος, and 1012² (A.D. 633) (= III. p. 266) βασιλείας τῶν θειοτάτων καὶ γαληνοτάτων καὶ θεοστεφῶν ἡμῶν δεσποτων Φλαυίων Ἡρακλείου καὶ Ἡρακλείου Νέου Κωνσταντίνου τῶν αἰωνίων Αὐγούστων αὐτοκρατόρων καὶ μεγίστων εὐεργετῶν. This last citation is taken from a deed which is prefaced with the full Christian trinitarian formula. Other exx. of the adj. imperially used in the papyri are BGU II. 473¹⁵ (A.D. 200) τῶν θείων διατάξεω[ν, with reference to an immediately preceding rescript of the Emperor Septimius Severus, P Ryl II. 117⁹⁷ (A.D. 269) κατὰ τὰς θείας διατάξεις, similar ordinances of the Emperor Claudius, and P Lips I. 62¹⁴ (A.D. 385) (= *Chrest.* I. p. 220) ἀπ[ε]στάλησαν εἰς τοὺς θείους θησαυρούς. An interesting instance of the adj. is BGU II. 655⁶ (A.D. 215) Αὐρήλιος Ζώσιμος πρὸ μὲν τῆς θίας δωρεᾶς καλούμενος Ζώσιμος, where the "imperial gift" refers to the so-called *Constitutio Antoniniana* of A.D. 212, by which Caracalla bestowed the rights of citizenship on all the inhabitants of the Roman Empire : in consequence many Egyptians thereafter prefixed Aurelius to their former name (see Erman and Krebs, p. 174 n.³). The phrase θεῖος ὅρκος is very common, as in P Oxy I. 83⁵ (A.D. 327) ὁμολογῶ ὀμνὺς τὸν σεβάσμιον θεῖον ὅρκον τῶν δεσποτῶν ἡμῶν Αὐτοκρατόρός τε καὶ Καισάρων : in *ib.* 125²⁰ (A.D. 560) we hear of an oath "by Heaven and the Emperor," τ]ὸν θεῖον καὶ σεβάσμιον ὅρκον, which is given in full in *ib.* 138¹³ᶠᶠ (A.D. 610–11) ἐπωμο-σάμην πρὸς τοῦ θεοῦ τοῦ παντοκράτορος, καὶ νίκης καὶ σωτηρίας καὶ διαμονῆς τῶν εὐσεβ(εστάτων) ἡμῶν δεσποτων Φλαουίου Ἡρακλείου καὶ Αἰλίας Φλαβίας. In late papyri θεῖος ὅρκος was practically a solemn affidavit, in which per-jury would have serious consequences, e.g. P Oxy VI. 893⁶ (vi/vii A.D.) ζητῆσαι τοῦ θεου (l. θείου) ὅρκου διὰ Σοφία, "to make inquiry by means of the divine oath through Sophia" (Edd.). From the inscrr. we may cite *Magn* 113⁹ ἀνὴ[ρ] δεδοκιμασμένος τοῖς θείοις κριτηρίοις τῶν Σεβαστῶν, with reference to Claudius, and *ib.* 201² τ]ὸν θειότατον καὶ μέ[γ]ιστον καὶ φιλανθρωπότατον βασιλέα, with reference to Julian : see also *Syll* 418⁹⁵ (A.D. 238) τὰ θεῖά σου γράμματα, a good parallel to 2 Tim 3¹⁶. We are also able to illustrate the striking use of τὸ θεῖον in Ac 17²⁹ (cf. Menander *Fragm.* p. 215, No. 766 φοβούμενοι τὸ θεῖον ἐπὶ τοῦ σοῦ πάθους, Epict. ii. 20. 22 ἵν' οἱ πολῖται ἡμῶν ἐπιστραφέντες τιμῶσι τὸ θεῖον), showing how Paul, in addressing an audience of heathen philosophers, adapts his language to them. Thus in P Leid Bⁱⁱ·⁸ (B.C. 164) we have συντετηρημένως πρὸς τὸ θεῖον ἑκουσίως ποεῖ (l. ποιεῖ), which the editor renders "divino numini obsecutus sponte gerit" : cf. *ib.* Dⁱ·¹⁵ (B.C. 162) δι' ἧς (*i.e.* τῆς βασιλίσσης) ἔχεις πρὸς τὸ θεῖον ὁσιό-τητα, *ib.*ⁱ·²² ἀνθ' ὧν πρὸς τὸ θεῖον ὁσίως διάκ[ει]σαι, P Lond 21¹¹ (B.C. 162) (= I. p. 13) σὺ δὲ ὦν πρὸς τὸ θεῖον ὁσίως διακείμενος, *ib.* 35⁵ (B.C. 161) (= I. p. 19) δι' ἣν ἔχεις εἰς τὸ θ[εῖο]ν εὐσέβειαν, and *ib.* 41 *verso* ⁴ (B.C. 161) (= I. p. 29) πρὸς τὸ θῆον (l. θεῖον) εὐσέβειαν : see also the editor's intr. to P Meyer 20 (beginning of iii/A.D.). Similarly with two inscrr. in *Chrest.* I.—70[14] (B.C. 57–6) δεόμεθα καθ' ἥν ἔχεις πρὸς τὸ θεῖον εὐσέβειαν προστάξαι τὸ σημαινόμενον ἱερόν κτλ., [21] τούτου δὲ γενομένου ἔσται τὸ θεῖον μὴ παρατεθεωρημένον, *ib.* 116[2] (ii/iii A.D.)—Σανσνῶς γράφει ὁ υἱὸς Ψενο-[σοράπιος] Σέβου τὸ θεῖον. θύε πᾶσι τοῖς θεοῖς, and *Magn* 62[19] εὐσεβὼ]ς διακείμενος πρὸς τὸ θεῖ[ον διατελεῖ.

This long note may conclude with a citation from the early Christian letter, P Heid 6[25] (iv/A.D.) (= *Selections*, p. 127), where the writer ends with the prayer—ἐρρωμένον σε ἡ θία πρόνοια φυλάξα[ι] ἐπὶ μέγιστον χρόνον ἐν κῶ Χω, κύριε ἀγαπητέ[: cf. PSI I. 71[9] (vi/A.D.). MGr has both θεῖος and θεϊκός = "godly."

θειότης.

This subst., which in the NT is confined to Rom 1[20], is used in P Lond 233[8] (A.D. 345) (= II. p. 273, *Chrest.* I. p. 68) with reference to a visit which Abinnaeus had paid to the Imperial court to obtain an appointment as tax-collector παρὰ τῆς θιότητος τῶν δεσποτῶν ἡμῶν αἰωνίων Αὐγούστων. It is also restored by Dittenberger in *OGIS* 519[14] (c. A.D. 245) ὅπως περὶ τούτων ἐκειν(ή)θη σου ἡ θειότης, and in *Syll* 420[23] we read of the θειότης of Jovius Maximinus Daza (A.D. 305–13). *Syll* 656[31] (ii/A.D.) declares that Artemis has made Ephesus ἀ[πασῶν τῶν πόλεων] ἐνδοξοτέραν διὰ τῆς ἰδίας θειότητος, where the context is an expansion of the last clause in Ac 19[37]. With the Bibl. usage cf. Aristeas 95 with reference to the priests' ministration in the Temple—φόβῳ καὶ καταξίως μεγάλης θειότητος ἅπαντ' ἐπιτελεῖται, "everything is performed with reverence and in a manner worthy of the divine majesty."

θέλημα.

This word, which is almost unknown outside Bibl. and eccles. writings, occurs in P Oxy VI. 924, a Christian charm of Gnostic character, belonging to iv/A.D. After a prayer to the Deity to protect the petitioner from ague etc., the charm continues—[8] ταῦτα εὐ[μενῶ]ς [π]ρά[ξ]εις ὅλως κατὰ τὸ θέλημά σου πρῶτον καὶ τὴν πίστιν αὐτῆς, "all this thou wilt graciously do in accordance with thy will first and with her faith" (Edd.). Cf. also P Lond 418[9] (c. A.D. 346) (= II. p. 303) τὸ θέλημα τῆς ψυχῆς σου. The Pauline usage of the word is discussed by Slaten *Qualitative Nouns*, p. 52 ff.

θέλω.

For the form ἐθέλω, which is wanting in the NT as in the LXX, Nageli (p. 57) refers to the magic papyri and to the poetic *Il.Ae* III. 1004: it is common in the Attic inscrr. up to the end of iv/B.C., but from B.C. 250 θέλω occurs, and eventually takes its place as the regular form in the Κοινή (cf. Meisterhans *Gr.* p. 178).

For the verb denoting a personal wish or desire we may cite P Petr I. 11[2] (a Will) τὰ [ἐμαυτοῦ διοικεῖν ὡς ἐ]γὼ θέλω, P Oxy VII. 1061[21] (B.C. 22) σὺ δὲ γράφε ὑπὲρ ὧν ἐὰν θέλῃς (cf. Mt 8[2]), *ib.* III. 531[28] (ii/A.D.) περὶ ὧν θέλεις δήλωσόν μοι, P Cairo Preis 48[5] (ii/A.D.) τὸ μὲν πλοῖόν σοι, ὡς ἠθέλησας, σκέψομαι, and the constant epistolary phrase γινώσκειν σε θέλω, as in P Oxy IV. 743[27] (B.C. 2) ὥστ' ἂν τοῦτό σε θέλω γεινώσκειν ὅτι ἐγὼ αὐτῷ διαστολὰς δεδώκειν τὸ βαδίσαι εἰς Τακόνα, "I wish you therefore to know this

that I had given him orders to go to Takona" (Edd.), BGU I. 27[5] (ii/A.D.) (= *Selections*, p. 101) γινώσκειν σε θέλω ὅτι εἰς γῆν ἐλήλυθα τῇ ξ τοῦ Ἐπείφ μηνός, "I wish you to know that I came to land on the 6th of the month Epeiph": cf. the Pauline formula οὐ θέλω δὲ ὑμᾶς ἀγνοεῖν, Rom 1[13] etc. With τοῦ θεοῦ θέλοντος in Ac 18[21], we may compare P Amh II. 131[6] (early ii/A.D.) ἐλπίζω δὲ θεῶν θελόντων ἐκ τῶν λαλουμένων διαφεύξεσθαι, "but I hope, if the gods will, to escape altogether from the talking," P Giss I. 18[10] (time of Hadrian) θε[ῶν δὲ θ]ελόντων εἰς τὰ Δημήτρια ἐλεύσεται καὶ ἀσπάσεταί σε, and the other exx. in Deissmann *BS*, p. 252: with 1 Cor 12[18], 15[38], cf. BGU I. 27[11] (ii/iii A.D.) (= *Selections*, p. 101) ὡς ὁ θεὸς ἤθελεν. With the construction in Lk 18[41] cf. *Chrest.* I. 14[iii 6] (not before A.D. 200) καί σοι, λέγε τίνος θέλεις, [κα]τηγορήσω, and with Rom 13[3] cf. P Tebt II. 421[3 f.] (iii/A.D.) with reference to a tunic—ἀλλὰ θέλις αὐτὸ πωλῆσα[ι], πώλησον· θέλις αὐτὸ ἀφεῖναι τῇ θυγατρί σ[ου], ἄφες, "but if you wish to sell it, sell it; if you wish to let your daughter have it, let her have it."

One or two miscellaneous exx. may be added—P Oxy III. 653 (A.D. 162–3) θέ[λ]ων καὶ μὴ θέλων ἀποκαταστήσεις αὐτῷ, BGU III. 846[10] (ii/A.D.) (= *Selections*, p. 94) οὐκ οἶδες, ὅτι θέλω πηρὸς γενέσται εἰ γνοῦναι κτλ., "do you not know that I would rather be a cripple than . . ?" where θέλω is followed by ἤ (pap. εἰ) as in 1 Cor 14[19], and for the remarkable perf. τεθέληκα (as in LXX Ps 40[12]: cf. Rutherford *NP*, p. 415), see P Amh II. 130[10] (A.D. 70) οὐ τεθελήκουσι, and P Oxy VII. 1070[54] (iii/A.D.) οὐ τεθελήκατε α]ὐτῷ διδόναι ἐπιστολάς, as restored by the editor. See also *s.v.* βούλομαι.

θεμέλιος.

The neut. τὸ θεμέλιον can be seen in P Petr II. 14(3)[2] (as completed Introd. p. 30—iii/B.C.) εἰς? τὸ θεμέλιον ψύξαι, "for drying the foundation," *ib.* III. 46(4)[4] τοῖς τὸ θεμέλιον ὀρύξασι ε, "to those who dug the foundation, 5 (drachmae)," and the plur., as in Ac 16[26] (cf. Prov 8[29]), in P Strass I. 9[8] (c. A.D. 307 or 352) πηχισμοῖς καὶ θεμελίοις καὶ τίχεσιν, and P Lond 121[619] (iii/A.D.) (= I. p. 101) καὶ ἐκεινήθη τῆς γῆς τὰ δ θεμέλια. In P Magd 27[4] (B.C. 218) βιάζεταί με πλίνθον προσ[ά]γων καὶ θεμέλιον σκάπτων ὥστε οἰκοδομεῖν, the gender is indeterminable, as in a number of the NT passages. So *Chrest.* II. 68[11] (A.D. 14) οὓς καὶ ἀνοικοδόμησα ἐπὶ τῶι [ἀρχ]α[ί]ωι θεμελίωι, P Lond 991[10] (vi/A.D.) (= III. p. 258) ἀπὸ θεμελίου ἕως ἀέρως, *Michel* 1185[3] (ii/B.C.) ἐκ θεμελίω. For the LXX usage, see Thackeray *Gr.* i. p. 154 f., and cf. Moeris p. 185: θεμέλιον καὶ θεμέλια, οὐδετέρως, Ἀττικῶς.

θεμελιόω.

Syll 732[15] (B.C. 36–5) προεστάτησεν τοῦ θεμελιωθῆναι τὴν σύνοδον. In MGr the verb survives as θεμελιώνω.

θεοδίδακτος.

With this verbal adj. (1 Th 4[9]) we may compare the Homeric αὐτοδίδακτος in *Cagnat* IV. 176 εἰμὶ μὲν ἐκ Παρίου Ὀρτὴξ σοφὸς αὐτοδίδακτος. See *Proleg.* p. 221 f. on the varied meanings of verbals in—τος.

For the similarly formed Christian θεόγνωστος we can

now cite a pagan parallel from P Oxy II. 237 $^{vi. 2}$ (A.D. 186) ἀλλὰ σὺ ὁ κύριος τῇ θεογνώστῳ σου μνήμῃ καὶ τῇ ἀπλανήτᾳ προαιρέσει ἀνενεγκὼν τὴ[ν γραφεῖσ]άν σοι ὑπὸ τοῦ στρατηγοῦ ἐπιστολήν, "but your lordship exercising your divine memory and unerring judgement took into consideration the letter written to you by the strategus" (Edd.).

θεολόγος.

As this adj. is applied to John in the title of the Apocalypse in certain MSS., it may be well to draw attention to the interesting note which Deissmann (*BS*, p. 231 f.) cites from Frankel, showing on the evidence of inscrr. that in Pergamus and Ephesus the same individual is described as θεολόγος and ὑμνῳδός: cf. Rev 5⁹. 14³, and Deissmann's consequent preference of "herald of God" as a rendering of θεολόγος (*LAE*, p. 353 n.¹). At Heraclea in the Pontus, as Frankel goes on to point out, there is a theologian for the mysteries, *CIG* 3803 [ὑ]πατικὸν καὶ θεο[λόγο]ν τ[ῶ]ν τῆδ[ε] μυ[σ]τηρίων, and in Smyrna female theologians, αἱ θεολόγοι, who, with the male, are engaged in the mysteries of Demeter Thesmophoros (*CIG* 3199, 3200). See further the exx. collected by Dittenberger in note⁴ to *OGIS* 513. In P Leid W ˣˣⁱ ²¹ (ii/iii A.D.) we hear of ὁ θεόλογος (*l.* θεολόγος) Ὀρφεύς, and in *Syll* 737¹¹⁶ (*c.* A.D. 175) τιθέτω τὴν τῶν καταγωγίων σπονδὴν στιβάδι μίαν καὶ θεολογίαν, the editor defines the last word as "orationem sollennem, qua per ferias dei laudes praedicantur et exornantur," a custom, he adds, arising "sine dubio ex antiquiore hymnos cantandi usu." A iii/A.D. epigram, *Kaibel* 882, commences—

Θεολόγου Λαίτοιο μετάρσιον ὕμνον ἀκούσας
οὐρανὸν ἀνθρώποις εἶδον ἀνοιγόμενον,

where θεολόγου is rendered "*divina loquentis*," and Wilamowitz is cited as uncertain whether to understand by μετάρσιον ὕμνον "*carmina*" or "*philosophiam*" or "*declamationes*."

It may be added that a Christian amulet P Oxy VIII. 1151⁴⁵ (v/A.D. ?) invokes the intercession τοῦ ἁγίου καὶ ἐνδόξου ἀποστόλου κ(αὶ) εὐαγγελιστοῦ κ(αὶ) θεολόγου Ἰωάννου.

θεομαχέω.

For this verb (which is read in the TR of Ac 23⁹, cf. 2 Macc 7¹⁹) along with its corresponding subst. see Epict. iii. 24. 24 εἰ δὲ μή, θεομαχήσω, ἀντιθήσω πρὸς τὸν Δία, ἀντιδιατάξομαι αὐτῷ πρὸς τὰ ὅλα. καὶ τἀπίχειρα τῆς θεομαχίας ταύτης καὶ ἀπειθείας οὐ παῖδες παίδων ἐκτίσουσιν κτλ., and Menander *Fragm.* p. 54, No. 187—

μὴ θεομάχει, μηδὲ προσάγου τῷ πράγματι
χειμῶνας ἑτέρους, τοὺς δ' ἀναγκαίους φέρε.

θεομάχος.

This NT ἅπ. εἰρ. (Ac 5³⁹) occurs in Vett. Val. p. 331¹² ὅπως διὰ τούτων οἱ ἀμαθεῖς καὶ θεομάχοι πίστιν ἐνεγκάμενοι καὶ ἑταῖροί γε τῆς ἀληθείας γενόμενοι ὑπαρκτὴν καὶ σεβάσμιον τὴν ἐπιστήμην καταλάβωσιν.

θεόπνευστος.

Syll 552¹² (ii/B.C.) opens a decree in connexion with the Parthenon at Magnesia with the words θείας ἐπιπνοίας καὶ παραστάσεως γενομένης τῶι σύνπαντι πλήθει τοῦ πολιτεύματος εἰς τὴν ἀποκατάστασιν τοῦ ναοῦ a divine "inspiration and desire" which has impelled the people to arise and build to the glory of Artemis. Cf. also Vett. Val. p. 330¹⁹ ἔστι δέ τι καὶ θεῖον ἐν ἡμῖν θεόπνευστον δημιούργημα.

θεός.

For the application of the title θεός to the Ptolemaic kings it is sufficient to recall *Brit. Mus. Inscr.* IV. 1 No. 006³ (B.C. 284-273) where a votive offering is dedicated in honour of Πτολεμαίου τοῦ σωτῆρος καὶ θεοῦ, and the description of Ptolemy V. (Epiphanes) on the Rosetta stone *OGIS* 90¹⁹ (B.C. 196) ὑπάρχων θεὸς ἐκ θεοῦ καὶ θεᾶς: cf. Deissmann *LAE*, p. 348 and the full discussion by E. Kornemann "Zur Geschichte der antiken Herrscherkulte" in *Beiträge zur alten Geschichte* [Klio] i., p. 51 ff. (Leipzig, 1602).

The same practice is still more strikingly illustrated in the Imperial period, as when in an inscr. from the Fayum district, dated March 17th, B.C. 24, Augustus is described as θεὸς ἐκ θεοῦ (*OGIS* 655²), or as when a votive inscr. is addressed to Nero—ἀγαθῷ θεῷ (*Cos* 92⁷): see Deissmann *ut s.* p. 349. With this may be compared the frequent use for Augustus of the title υἱὸς θεοῦ, corresponding to the *divi filius* of the Latin inscrr., e.g. BGU I. 174¹ (A.D. 7) ἔτους ἐ[κ]του καὶ τριακοστοῦ [τῆς] Καίσαρος κρατήσεως θεοῦ υἱ[ὸ]ν (*l.* υἱοῦ), and, interesting as coming from the Emperor himself, the letter, *LMAe* III. 174 (A.D. 5), which begins—Καῖσαρ θεοῦ υἱὸς Σεβαστός. Other examples will be found in Deissmann *BS*, p. 166 f., *LAE*, p. 350 f., where the bearing of this usage upon the early Christian title of Christ is discussed: cf. also Harnack *History of Dogma* i. p. 118 ff. Mention should also be made of the Imperial oath, in which, following Ptolemaic practice, the person of the Emperor is directly invoked. A very early example is BGU II. 543¹ (B.C. 27) ὄμνυμι Καίσαρα Αὐτοκράτορα θεοῦ υἱόν: cf. *Chrest.* I. 111² A.D. ὀ' ὄμνυ[μι] [Καίσαρα] Αὐτοκράτορα θεοῦ υ[ἱὸ]ν Δία Ἐλευθέριον [Σεβαστόν] with Wilcken's important note. It gives one a thrill to find the very combination of Jn 20²⁸ applied in BGU IV. 1197¹ (B.C. 4) to Asclepiades, apparently a high official—τῷ θεῷ καὶ κυρίῳ: the same designation recurs in *ib.* 1201¹ (A.D. 2) with reference to a priest, but the editor knows of no other exx. of this use of θεός.

From pagan letters we may cite a few instances of constantly recurring expressions—P Hib I. 79⁶ (c. B.C. 260) τοῖς θεοῖς πολλὴ χά[ρι]ς. P Giss I. 17⁶ (time of Hadrian) (= *Chrest.* I. p. 566) χάρις τοῖς θεοῖς πᾶσι ὅτι σε διαφυλάσσουσι ἀπρόσκοπον, P Lond 42³ (B.C. 168) (= I. p. 30, *Selections*, p. 9) ὡς τοῖς θεοῖς εὐχομένη διατελῶ, BGU I. 248¹¹ (ii/A.D.) θεῶν δὲ βουλομένων, *ib.* I. 27¹¹ (ii A.D.) (= *Selections*, p. 101) ὡς ὁ θεὸς ἤθελεν, *ib.* II. 451¹⁰ (i/ii A.D.) θεῶν ἐπιτρεπόν[τ]ων, and P Oxy VI. 935³ (iii A.D.) θεῶν συλλαμβανόντων, cf. ¹⁰ συνλαμβ[ά]νο[υ]σι γὰρ ἡμεῖν ἀεὶ ο[ἱ] π[άτ]ριοι θεοὶ ἡμῶν δ[ιδό]ντες ἡμεῖν ὑγία[ν] καὶ σω[τ]ηρίαν. With this last may be compared the soldier's letter to his sister, BGU II. 632⁶ (ii/A.D.), in which he assures her that he is μνίαν σου ποιούμενος (cf. Rom 1⁹ *l.*) παρὰ τοῖς [ἐν]θάδε θεοῖς, showing that for the time being he has transferred his allegiance to the gods of the place where he is garrisoned (cf. Deissmann *LAE*, p. 173).

For prepositional phrases see P Petr II. 13(19)[7] (mid. iii/
B.C.) (= Witkowski[2], p. 19) καὶ ζῶντός σου καὶ εἰς θεοὺς
ἀπελθόντος, P Tebt I. 58 recto[25] (B.C. 111) σὺν τοῖς θεοῖς,
"by the grace of the gods," P Ryl II. 243[5] (ii/A.D.) ἐλπίζοντες σὺν θεῷ τὸ πεδίον σπαρῆναι, "hoping that with
God's help the field will be sown," where, as the editors
point out, the use of θεῷ alone does not imply that the writer
was a Christian (cf. Archiv i. p. 436), and, for an undoubtedly Christian ex., the letter of the presbyter Psenosiris, P
Grenf II. 73[16] (late iii/A.D.) (= Selections, p. 118) ὅταν ἔλθῃ
σὺν Θεῷ, with the corresponding use of ἐν Θ.εῷ in [6]. In
P Iand 11[2] (iii/A.D.) ἐλπίδω γὰρ εἰς θεόν, the writer may well
be a Christian (or a Jew), cf. Ac 24[15], 1 Pet 3[5]; and the
same may perhaps be said regarding BGU I. 246[1] (ii/iii A.D.)
νυκτὸς καὶ ἡμέρας ἐντυνχάνω τῷ θεῷ ὑπὲρ ὑμῶν, cf. 1 Th 3[10].
A iv/A.D. letter of a Christian servant to his master, which
abounds in echoes of NT language, has—ὡς ἐν ἄλ]λοις
πλείστοις νῦν ἔτι μᾶλλον ἡ πρὸς σὲ [τοῦ δεσπό]του θεοῦ
γνῶσις ἀνεφάνη (cf. Lk 19[11]) ἅπασιν ἡμῖν, "as on many
other occasions so now still more plainly the favour of the
Lord God towards you has been revealed to all of us" (P
Oxy VI. 939[4] = Selections, p. 128): cf. also P Oxy I. 120[16]
(iv/A.D.) μὴ ἄρα παρέλκομαι ἡ καὶ εἴργομαι ἔστ' ἂν ὁ θεὸς
ἡμᾶς αἰλαιήσῃ (l. ἐλεήσῃ), "am I to be distracted and
oppressed until Heaven takes pity on me?" For the voc.
θεέ, which is found in Mt 27[46], cf. the magical P Lond 121[829]
(iii/A.D.) (= I. p. 101) κύριε θεὲ μέγιστε, which is reinforced
by a Pisidian inscr., unfortunately undated, JHS 1902, p. 355,
θέ. See also s.v. ἄγνωστος, ἄξιος, κύριος, παντοκράτωρ,
σωτήρ, ὕψιστος, and for the Pauline usage Slaten Qualitative Nouns, p. 64 ff.

θεοσέβεια.

This word, which is found in the NT only in 1 Tim 2[10],
where it is practically equivalent to εὐσέβεια (ver. 2), came
early to be used as a quasi-technical term for the worship of
the only true God, and hence was adopted as an ecclesiastical title in Christian circles, e.g. P Amh II. 145[5] (iv/v A.D.)
where Apa Johannes writes to Paul—βούλο]μαι μὲν καταξιωθῆναι ἀεὶ γράφειν [τῇ σῇ] θεοσεβείᾳ κτλ., "though I wish
to be found worthy of writing continually to your holiness,"
etc. (Edd.), P Meyer 24[3] (vi/A.D.) καταξιώσῃ οὖν ἡ σὴ
θεοσέβεια εὔξασθαι ὑπὲρ ἐμοῦ, and P Giss I. 55[8] (vi/A.D.)
with reference to a Bishop, etc.: see also Ramsay Luke,
p. 384.

θεοσεβής.

Like the preceding subst., the adj. is found in addresses,
e.g. the already cited P Giss I. 55[1] (vi/A.D.) τῷ ἀγ[απ]ητῷ
καὶ θεοσεβεστάτῳ ἀδελφῷ . . . For its pagan use we may
cite P Lond 23 (a)[20] (B.C. 158-7) (= I. p. 38) where
the assistance of Ptolemy Philometor is appealed to on
behalf of a certain Apollonius—ἧς ἔχετε πρὸς πάντας τοὺς
τοιούτους θεοσεβουάς. A remarkable form of the word
appears in the interesting inscr., cited by Deissmann LAE,
p. 446 f., which marked the place of the seats of the Jews
in the theatre at Miletus:—Τόπος Ειουδέων τῶν καὶ
Θεοσεβίο (= ω)ν, "Place of the Jews, who are also called
God-fearing." Deissmann assigns the inscr. to the Imperial
age, and remarks that Θεοσέβιοι "must already have been

felt to be a proper name," comparing the use of Θεοσε-
βεῖς for the Hypsistarians (Schürer[3], iii. p. 124). See
also Vett. Val. pp. 17[1, 19], 18[16], and the sepulchral inscr.,
Kaibel 729[2]—

> Ἐνθάδε ἐν εἰρήνῃ κεῖτε Ῥουφεῖνος ἀμύμων,
> θεοσεβής.

For the verb see the citation from Syll 325 s.v. ἡλικία
sub fin.

Θεόφιλος

is found as a proper name as early as iii/B.C. both in
the papyri and inscr., e.g. P Hib I. 103[1] (B.C. 231-0)
Ἀπολλοφάνης Θεοφίλωι χαίρειν, P Ryl II. 72[90] (B.C. 99-8)
Θεόφιλος Νικάνορος, Michel 594[80] (B.C. 279) ὑπὲρ Θεοφίλου
τοῦ ἐργολαβήσαντος τὰς παραετίδας ἐργάσασθαι τῶι νεῶι
τῆς Ἀρτέμιδος κτλ., and similarly 685[2], 1260[5] (both iii/B.C.):
see also Preisigke 3780 Θεόφιλος ἰατρός. Θεόφιλος, as a
Jewish name, occurs in P Petr II. 28 il. 9 (iii/B.C.) Σαμαρείας
Θεόφιλος, "Theophilus of Samaria," but the previous exx.
seem to render unnecessary Mahaffy's suggestion (p. [97])
that the name may have been of Jewish origin: cf. however
P Fay 123[15] (c. A.D. 100) where a certain Τεύφιλος (for the
form, see Mayser Gr. pp. 10, 179 f.) Ἰουδαῖος desires release
from the service of cultivating the domain-lands, and Meyer
Ostr 30[1] (A.D. 111) Τεύφιλος Τευφίλου, where a Jew is
again referred to, see p. 150. For the use of the word as an
adj. see BGU III. 924[1] (iii/A.D.) where it is applied to the
city of Herakleopolis Magna—Ἡρακλέους πόλεως ἀρχαίας
καὶ θεοφίλου ἡ [κρατίστη βου]λή, cf. ib. 937[4] (A.D. 250).
The classical θεοφιλής is found in OGIS 383[42] (mid. i/B.C.)
θεοφιλῆ ψυχήν, and its superlative in the fragment of a
iii/A.D. private letter, P Ryl II. 439, where the desire is
expressed—αὖθις μετ' εὐθυμίας τὸ θεοφιλέστατόν σου πρόσωπον ἀπολαβεῖν.

θεραπεία.

An interesting example of this subst. = "medical treatment," a "cure" in the sense in which we often use that
term, as in Lk 9[11], is found in P Tebt I. 44[6] (B.C. 114)
where the writer states that he had been staying in the great
temple of Isis ἐπὶ θεραπείαι . . . χάριν τῆς περιεχούσης με
ἀρρωστίας, i.e. not "for devotional purposes," but, as the
editors alternatively render the phrase in their note, "for
medical treatment on account of the sickness from which I
am suffering": cf. Wilcken Chrest. I. p. 148 "zur Kur."
The word is found in the same sense in the new Logion,
P Oxy I. 1 recto[18] λέγει Ἰησοῦς, οὐκ ἔστιν δεκτὸς προφήτης
ἐν τῇ πατρίδι αὐτ[ο]ῦ, οὐδὲ ἰατρὸς ποιεῖ θεραπείας εἰς τοὺς
γεινώσκοντας αὐτόν. For a similar association with "healing," "health," cf. Preisigke 159 τὸ προσκύνημα Εὐγράφιος
παρὰ τῷ κυρίῳ θεῷ Ἀσκληπιῷ καὶ Ἀμενώθῃ καὶ Ὑγιείᾳ.
Μνήσθητι ὑμῶν καὶ παράδος ὑμῖν θεραπείαν, and ib. 1537 b
Ἀλέ[ξαν]δ[ρ]ος ὁ καὶ Ἀγαθὸς Δαίμων θεραπίας ἐπιτυχὼν
ὅλου σώματος χαρίον (l. χαριστήριον) ἀνέθηκεν, ἐπ' ἀγαθῶι.
In P Par 31[7] (ii/B.C.) the word is used with reference to the
religious service which the Twins render in the Serapeum—
πρὸς τῇ θεραπείᾳ τοῦ Σαράπιος καὶ τῆς Ἴσιος. Cf. OGIS
383[70] (mid. i/B.C.) θεραπείαν τε ἀνέγλειπτον καὶ ἱερεῖς
ἐπιλέξας σὺν πρεπούσαις ἐσθῆσι Περσικῶι γένει κατέστησα,
and ib. [131] προνοούμενος θεραπείας τε καὶ κόσμου πρέποντος

ἱερῶν ἀγαλμάτων : also *Michel* 829[18] (1st half i/B.C.) ἐπεσκεύασα δὲ καὶ τὸ προσκήνιον [καὶ εἰς] τὴν τῶν ἀγαλμάτων ἐπαγάνωσιν καὶ θ᾽ε]ραπείαν ἔδωκα τῇ κατασταθείσῃ ἀρχῇ δραχμὰς διακοσίας ἐνενήκοντα τέττ[α]ρας.

θεραπεύω.

The most effective point which Harnack (*Luke the Physician*, p. 15 f.) has gleaned after Hobart is his proof that Luke practised in Melita (Ac 28[10] "honoured us with many honours"). To this Ramsay (*Luke*, p. 16 f.) has added the note that θεραπεύω, used as a medical term, means strictly "treat medically" rather than "heal" (cf. what is said *s.v.* θεραπεία *ad init.*), and it may be well to illustrate this somewhat fully both from the papyri and the inscriptions. Thus in a medical receipt of early i/A.D. for sores in the nose, P Oxy VIII. 1088[30], it is enjoined— ἀρσενικὸν τρίψον λῆον, ὕπτιον κατακλίνας τὸν ἄνθρωπον θεράπευε, "rub yellow orpiment smooth, then lay the man on his back and treat him" (Edd.). From a somewhat later date, ii/iii A.D., *ib.* I. 40, we have a petitioner asking immunity from some form of public service on the ground that he was a doctor—[5]ᵢₐ ἰατρὸς ὑπάρχων τὴ[ν τέ]χνην τούτους αὐτοὺς οἵτινές με εἰς λειτο[υ]ρ[γ]ίαν δεδώκασι ἐθεράπευσα, "I am a doctor by profession and I have treated these very persons who have assigned me a public burden": to which the prefect replies—[7]ᵢ τάχα κακῶς αὐτοὺς ἐθεράπευσας, "perhaps your treatment was wrong" (Edd.). Similarly in P Flor II. 222[14] (A.D. 259) a man writes asking that a certain medicine should be sent, ἵνα καὶ ὁ ταῦρος θεραπεύθῃ, "in order that my bull may be treated," and in P Oxy IX. 1222[3] (iv/A.D.) a request is made that along with a colt various drugs may be forwarded, εἵνα θεραπεύσω αὐτὸν ὧδε ἔξω, "that I may doctor him away here" (Ed.). To these exx. we may add a heathen amulet of iii/A.D., where the meaning passes into actual healing, BGU III. 956 ἐξορκίζω ὑμᾶς κατὰ τοῦ ἁγίου ὀνόματος θεραπεῦσαι τὸν Διονύσιον . . . ἀπὸ πα[ν]τὸς ῥίγου (*l.* ῥίγους) καὶ πυρετοῦ: with the constr. cf. Lk 5[15] *al.* Turning to the inscrr. a good example of the stricter meaning of the verb occurs at the end of the great inscr. from the Asclepieum at Epidaurus, *Syll* 802[136] (iii/B.C.) where of a παῖς ἀιδής it is said οὕ[τος] ὕπαρ ὑπὸ κυνὸς τῶν κατὰ τὸ ἱαρὸν θε[ραπ]ευόμενος τοὺς ὀπ[τί]λλους (Dor. for ὀφθαλμούς) ὑ[γιὴ]ς ἀπῆλθε. Four or five centuries later a similar inscription from the same place, *ib.* 804[20], has τεθεράπευσαι, χρὴ δὲ ἀποδιδόναι τὰ ἴατρα, "treatment has been prescribed for you, and you must pay the physician's fee": the actual treatment is to follow. Cf. also *OGIS* 220[4] (iii/B.C.) ἐπειδὴ ὁ βασιλεὺς Ἀντίοχος ἐπέσταλκεν ὅτι τραυματίας γενόμενος ἐν τῆι μάχηι εἰς τὸν τράχηλον θεραπευθ[είη] ὑπὸ Μητροδώρου τοῦ ἰατροῦ ἀκινδύν[ω]ς κτλ. For the verb used of religious service (as in Ac 17[25], and Is 54[17] its only occurrence in the LXX : see Thackeray *Gr.* i. p. 8) we may cite P Lond 22[5] (B.C. 164–3) (= I. p. 7) ἡμῶν θεραπευουσῶν ὑπὲρ τοῦ βασίλεως—of the Twins in the Serapeum, and P Giss I. 20[30] (ii/A.D.) (= *Chrest.* I. p. 124) where, with reference to a private shrine of the Dioscuri, the owner Apollonius is informed that a certain Areius, is ready to undertake the needful service—Ἄρειος ὁ κωλοπλάστης ("modeller") θεραπεύει αὐτοὺς καὶ ἔλεγεν ὅτι ἐὰ[ν] Ἀπολλώνιός μοι γράψῃ περὶ αὐτῶν, θεραπε[ύ]σω προῖκα. So

PART III.

Michel 982[14] (B.C. 217–16) καλῶς καὶ εὐσεβῶς διετέλεσεν θεραπεύουσα τὰς θεάς, *OGIS* 90[40] (the Rosetta stone, B.C. 196) τοὺς ἱερεῖς θεραπεύειν τὰς εἰκόνας τρὶς τῆς ἡμέρας, *Syll* 583[30] (i/A.D.) τῶν ἱεροδούλων καὶ τὸν θεὸν θεραπευόντων, and *ib.* 653[11] (ii A.D.) καὶ εὐείλατος γένοι τ]ο ὁ θεὸς τοῖς θεραπεύουσιν ἁπλῇ τῇ ψυχῇ. In P Tor I. 1[22] (B.C. 117–6) the verb is used with reference to those who "care for" dead bodies—αἷς [οἱ θεαῖς ἀθέμιτά ἐστιν νεκρὰ σώματα, καὶ οἱ ταῦτα θεραπεύοντες, and in P Giss I. 79[iii 3] (*c.* A.D. 117) of cloaks that had been repaired—τοὺς φαινο[ύ]λας σου τεθεραπευμένους ἤνεγκεν ἀπ᾽ Ἀλεξανδρείας Ἀπολλώνιος ὁ ἀδελφός σου. See also the early P Magd 15[3] (B.C. 221) where a barber claims that he has served his patron in an irreproachable manner—τεθεραπευκὼς ἀνεγκλή[τως.

For the subst. θεραπευτής, see P Lond 44[19] (B.C. 161) (= I. p. 34) ὑπὸ τοῦ Σαράπιος θεραπευτῶν, and *OGIS* 251[4] (B.C. 175–164), where the editor states that the word connotes both "deorum cultores" and "hominum ministri."

θεράπων.

For this word, which in the NT is confined to the OT quot. in Heb 3[5]. cf. BGU I. 301[iii 11] (A.D. 184) ἐὰν μεταπέμψῃ Κρονοῦν θεράπ[οντα] αὐτοῦ, μαρτυρήσει κτλ. In connexion with its LXX usage, Thackeray (*Gr.* i. p. 7 f.) has pointed out the interesting fact that it is gradually superseded in the later books by the less intimate and confidential terms οἰκέτης, παῖς, and δοῦλος, in keeping with the growing tendency to emphasize the distance between God and man.

The fem. θεράπαινα (cf. Rutherford *NP*, p. 22) occurs in P Giss I. 34[6] (A.D. 265–6) τὴν τούτου θε[ρ]άπαιναν, P Oxy XII. 1468[13] (*c.* A.D. 258) θεράπαινα Θαῆσις.

θερίζω.

An interesting example of this verb is found in P Magd 12[12] (B.C. 217), where a farmer, finding himself expelled by the proprietors from his holding on the approach of harvest, on the ground that his contract had not been properly sealed, petitions that they should not be allowed to reap the crops until the case had been decided—ἕως δὲ τοῦ διεξόδον λαβεῖν τὴν κρίσιν μὴ θερίζειν αὐτούς. See also P Fay 112[2] (A.D. 99) where the considerable, but illiterate, landowner Gemellus writes to his nephew—τῶν ὠγμ[ον] (*l.* τὸν ὄγμ[ον]) τῆς Ἀπιάδος ἕως σήμερον οὐ ἐθέρ[ι]σας ἀλλ᾽ ἠμέληκας αὐτοῦ καὶ μέχρι τούτου τῶ ἥμυσυ αὐτοῦ ἐθέρισας, "up to to-day you have not harvested the field at Apias, but have neglected it, and so far have only harvested the half" (Edd.): cf. *ib.* 120[7] (*c.* A.D. 100). Other exx. are P Flor I. 80[7] (i/ii A.D.) ὁμολογοῦμ᾽ε ν παρέξειν ἡμᾶς θερίζοντες (*l.* —τας) οὓς ἔχεις [π]υρίνους σπόρους, BGU I. 349[10] (A.D. 313) ἐμοῦ δαὶ (*l.* δὲ) τοῦ μισθωσαμένου θερίζοντος τῶ μισθῶ, and *Ostr* 1302[5] ἐξ ὧν ἀνδ[ρες] ἃ θερίζ οντες θρύα ("rushes"). See also the alphabetical acrostic, *Kaibel* 1039[10] where under O we have—

Οὐκ ἔστι μ[ὴ] σπείραντα θερίσαι κάρπιμα.

θερισμός.

P Lille I. 1 *verso*[9] (B.C. 250–8) ἐὰν δὲ μὴ πρὸ τοῦ θερισμοῦ συντελῆται, P Hib I. 90[5] (B.C. 222) ἐμίσθωσεν εἰς ἐνιαυτὸν [ἕνα σ]πόρον ἕνα (deleted in pap.) καὶ θερισμόν, a lease "for one year, for one seed-time and harvest," BGU II. 594[5] (A.D. 70-80) μετὰ τὸν θερισμὸ[ν ἐργολ]αβήσομα[ι, and P Flor I. 80[13] (i/ii A.D.) ἀρξόμεθα δὲ τ[οῦ] θερισμ[ο]ῦ ὁ[πό]τε ἐὰν κελευσθῶμεν ὑπό σου. See also τὰ θέριστρα with reference to harvesting operations in P Oxy II. 277[8] (B.C. 19).

θεριστής.

P Hib I. 44[1] (B.C. 253-2) ὡσαύτως δὲ καὶ τοὺς ἐπιγεγραμμένους θεριστὰς κατὰ τὴν δοθεῖσάν σοι γραφήν, "and likewise the harvesters who have been levied in accordance with the list given to you," P Flor I. 80[6] (i/ii A.D.) ἓξ θερισταί. For the adj. θεριστικός see P Magd 1 8[6] (B.C. 218) δρέπανον θεριστικόν. The word survives in MGr.

θέρμη.

We have no ex. of this subst. = "heat," as in Ac 28[3] (see Hobart, p. 287 f. for medical exx.), but it is common in connexion with public "baths," e.g. P Oxy I. 54[14] (A.D. 201) εἰς ἐπιμέλειαν ἐπισκευῆς καὶ κατασκευῆς Ἀδριανῶν θερμῶν, "to superintend the repairs and fixtures of the baths of Hadrian" (Edd.), ib. III. 473[5] (A.D. 138-160) τῆ[ς] τῶν μειζόνων θερμῶν ἐπιμελείας, ib. VI. 896[3] (A.D. 316), τοῦ εὐτυχῶς ἐπισκευαζομένου Τραιανῶν Ἀδριαγῶν θερμῶν δημοσίου τῆς αὐτῆς πόλεως βαλανίου. With the rare form θέρμη Rutherford (NP, p. 198) compares κάκη and λεύκη, λεύκα being applied to a form of leprosy (like the English term "the blues"): so in MGr ζέστη = "heat," ψύχρα = "cold weather."

θέρος.

P Hib I. 27[33] (a calendar—B.C. 301-240) ἔλεγεν δὲ [δύο] τὰς πορείας εἶναι τοῦ ἡλίου μία μὲν τὴν διορίζουσαν νύκτα καὶ ἡμέραν μία δὲ τὴν διορίζουσαν χιμῶνα καὶ θέρος, "he said that the courses of the sun were two, one dividing night and day and one dividing winter and summer" (Edd.). OGIS 56[41] (B.C. 237) ἐν τῶι χειμῶνι ... ἐν τῶι θέρει. In P Flor II. 150[5] (A.D. 267) ὥστε .. πατῆσαι τὰ ἐν τῷ αἰγιαλῷ θέρη, the word is = "crop." For the adj. see BGU IV. 1188[9] (B.C. 15-4) τὰ θερινὰ ἔργα, and P Oxy IV. 810 (A.D. 134-5) where land is to be cultivated χόρτῳ εἰς κοπὴν καὶ θερινὴν ἐπινομήν. Θέριστρον apparently = "a summer garment" (as in LXX Gen 24[65] al.) occurs in P Petr I. 12[18] (iii/B.C.) (= III. p. 18). MGr θέρος, "summer."

Θευδᾶς.

The name occurs in a sepulchral inscr. from Hierapolis, Syll 872, where Flavius Zeuxis, ἐργαστής (? a frumentarius: he speaks of his seventy-two voyages past Cape Malea to Italy. His name suggests a late date in i/A.D., or not far on in ii/A.D.), has two sons, Flavius Theodorus and Flavius Theudas. On the ordinary assumption (Blass-Debrunner Gr. § 125, 2) this would be like having a Theodore and a Teddy as baptismal names of brothers. Are we to infer that Theudas is short for something else, say Theodotus? To judge without an exhaustive study, the abbreviated names were used together with the full forms much as they are with us: thus Acusilaus in P Tebt II. 409 (A.D. 5) is Acûs on the back of the letter, and in P Oxy I. 119 (ii/iii A.D.) (= Selections, p. 102 f.) young Theon calls himself Theonas in the address.

In P Oxy X. 1242[i. 14] (early iii/A.D.) we hear of Θεύδης as one of the members of a Jewish embassy to Trajan.

θεωρέω.

A tendency to use θεωρέω more lightly might be deduced from such passages as P Tebt I. 58[25] (B.C. 111) οὗτος οὖν θεωρήσας με ὡς προσεδρεύοντα καθ' ἡμέραν ὡσεὶ δεδίλανται, "seeing me in daily attendance he has as it were turned coward " (Edd.), though "watched " will translate it here; ib. 61 (b)[33] (B.C. 118-7) ἠξίου[ν] . . . συνθεωρεῖσθαι, "conquiri," and again [373] θεωρῆσ[θαι (l. τεθεωρῆσ[θαι) ἐκ τῆς γε[γεν]ημένης εἰκασίας μετὰ ταῦτα, "it was perceived from the subsequent estimate." But whether the verb belonged to the Volkssprache (Blass N.T. Grammatik[2], p. 59, s.v. ὁρᾶν) or not, it was hardly a synonym of ὁράω: cf. the use of the two verbs in Jn 16[16] (Abbott Joh. Voc., p. 104 ff.). See P Oxy I. 33 verso [iii. 9] (ii/A.D.) θεωρήσατε ἕνα ἀπ' αἰῶνος ἀπαγόμ[ενο]ν, "behold one led off to death " (lit. "from life "), P Giss I. 9[10] (ii/A.D.) ὡς δὲ οὐτὲ ἴχνος ἐθεώρο[υν, of a woman searching for her husband, and the Christian P Heid 6[9] (iv/A.D.) (= Selections, p. 126) ἐγῖθεν (l. ἐκεῖθεν) θεωρούμέν σε τὸν δεσπότην καὶ κενὸν (l. καινὸν) (π)ά[τ]ρω[να, "wherefore we regard you as master and new patron." Similarly from the inscr. OGIS 751[9] (ii/B.C.) θεωρῶν οὖν ὑμᾶς μετανενοηκότας τε ἐπὶ τοῖ[s] προημαρτημένοις, Priene 113[72] (i/B.C.) τελειῶν δ' ὁ μετὰ ταῦτα χρόνος ἐθεωρεῖτο πρὸς τὴν εἰς τὸ πλῆ[θος] ἀρέσκειαν, and OGIS 666[10] (c. A.D. 55) ἡ Αἴγυπτος, τὰς τοῦ Νείλου δωρεὰς ἐπαυξομένας κατ' ἔτος θεωροῦσα, νῦν μᾶλλον ἀπέλαυσε τῆς δικαίας ἀναβάσεως τοῦ θεοῦ. Boisacq (p. 343) derives the word from θέα and ὁράω. MGr θωρῶ = θεωρῶ (see Thumb Hellen., p. 17).

θεωρία.

With the use of this subst. in Lk 23[48] we may compare P Tebt I. 33[6] (B.C. 112) (= Selections, p. 30), where arrangements are made for the reception of a Roman senator who is making the voyage to Egypt "to see the sights "—ἀνάπλουν . . . ἐπὶ θεωρίαν ποιούμενος: cf. P Oxy VII. 1025[16] (late iii/A.D.) τῶν θεωριῶν, " the spectacles " at a village festival. It refers to a judicial "investigation " in P Tor I. 1[viii. 5] (B.C. 117-6) καὶ μὴ προσεκτέον αὐτῶι ἐφ' ἑτέραν θεωρίαν μεταφέροντι τὴν γεγονυῖαν αὐτῶι πρὸς ἄλλους περὶ οὐδη(π)οτοῦν πράγματος ἀμφιζβήτησιν, and to an agricultural "survey" in P Amh II. 68[57] (late i/A.D.) ἐκ τῆς νυνεὶ κατ' ἀγρὸν θεωρίαι. In Michel 509[3] (B.C. 241) ἐκδεξάμενος τάς τε παρούσας θεωρίας πρ[επ]όντως, it = "embassy," "mission." MGr θωρία, "look," "glance," θεωρία, "theory."

For θεώρημα see P Lond 121[473] (magic—iii/A.D.) (= I. p. 99), for θεώρησις CP Herm I. 7[ii. 23] (ii/A.D.?), and for θεωρός OGIS 232[8] (ii/B.C.). P Oxy III. 473[4] (A.D. 138-60) τά τε [θε]ωρικὰ χρήματα are the funds provided for theatrical displays: see also Wilcken Ostr. i. p. 373 f.

θήκη.

With the use of this word = "scabbard," "sheath," in Jn 18[11] cf. P Petr III. 140 (a)[4] (accounts) περικεφαλαίας καὶ θήκης ν̄. For the more ordinary meaning "box," "chest," see P Ryl II. 148[15] (A.D. 40) θήκην ἀννήσου, "a store of anise," BGU III. 781[v. 16] (i/A.D.) πίναξ μέγας ἐν θήκῃ, P Giss I. 47[24] (time of Hadrian) (= Chrest. I. p. 583) ξυλίνης θήκης, and the mutilated inventory of a temple, BGU II. 387 ¹¹·¹³ (A.D. 177–181) θῆκαι χαλκᾶ[ι. In P Oxy IX. 1188¹ (A.D. 13) it is used of the "tomb" of the sacred animals—ἐπὶ τῆ(ς) τῶν ἱερῶν ζῴων θήκης. so ²¹: cf. P Oxy I. 79 verso ¹³ κ]ηδίας ἡ βασιλ[ικ(ῶν)] θηκῶν. The diminutive is similarly used in the early Christian inscr. cited s.v. γέμω. For the verb θηκοποιέω = "store," see BGU III. 757¹⁵ (A.D. 12), P Ryl II. 142¹⁶ (A.D. 37).

θηλάζω

is common in the series of nursing contracts in BGU IV., e.g. 1107⁶ (B.C. 13) συνχωρεῖ ἡ Διδύ]μη τροφεύσειν καὶ θηλάσειν ἔξω [πα]ρ' ἑα[τῆι κατὰ πόλιν τῶι ἰδίωι] αὐτῆς γάλακτι καθαρῶι καὶ ἀφθόρωι. For a similar transitive usage, as in Mt 24¹⁹, cf. the family-letter of late iii/A.D., P Lond 951 verso ²ff. (=III. p. 213), where the writer urges the getting of a nurse for a newly arrived infant, rather than that the mother should be compelled to "nurse" herself—ἤκουσ[α] ὅ[τ]ι θηλάζειν αὐτὴν ἀναγκάζεις, εἰ θέλεις τ]ὸ βρέφος ἐχέτω τροφόν, ἐγὼ γὰρ οὐκ ἐπιτ[ρέ]πω τῇ θυγατρί μου θηλάζειν. The verb is intransitive, as in Mt 21¹⁶, in P Ryl II. 153¹³ (A.D. 138–161) ὃν κατέλιψα ἐν Ζμύρνῃ τῆς Ἀσίας παρὰ τροφῷ θηλάζοντα, "whom I have left at Smyrna in Asia being yet a foster-child" (Edd.). For a form θελάσζω see PSI IV. 369¹⁹ (B.C. 250–49) with the editor's note.

θῆλυς

A striking ex. of this adj. occurs in P Oxy IV. 744¹⁰ (B.C. 1) (= Selections, p. 33) where a husband writes to his wife with reference to an unborn child—ἐὰν ἦν ἄρσενον, ἄφες, ἐὰν ἦν θήλεα, ἔκβαλε, "if it is a male, let it live; if it is a female, expose it." The word is common with reference to animals, e.g. P Ryl II. 145¹⁶ (A.D. 38) ὄνον θήλειαν, PSI I. 39⁵ (A.D. 148) ἴπον (l. ἵππον) θήλειαν, and P Strass I. 30⁵ (A.D. 276) αἶγας θηλείας τε[λ]είας ἀθανάτους. already cited s.v. ἀθανασία, but recalled to correct the unfortunate blunder by which ἀθανάτους is there referred to the goats' "constitution" instead of to their "number": they were "immortal" in the same sense as the Persian Guard, in that the stock was to be kept up at its full strength ("eiserner Bestand"). For the form θηλυκός, as in MGr, see P Oxy XII. 1458¹⁰ (A.D. 216–17) πρ[όβ(ατα) ξ, ἄ]ρρ(ενα) ζ, θηλ(υκὰ) λ[., "60 sheep, 7 male, 3[.] female" (Edd.).

θήρα

PSI IV. 350⁴ (B.C. 254–3) ἐμοὶ δὲ τῶι ὄντι πρὸς τῆι θήραι εὐτάκτως ἐφέλκεται τὰ ὀψώνια, P Tebt II. 612 (c) (i/ii A.D.) θήρας ἀγρίων Τεβ[τ]ύνεως: in P Hamb I. 6¹¹ (A.D. 129) μηδὲν ἀπὸ θή[ρ]ας ἰχθύας περιγεγονέναι μεχρὶ νῦν, the reference is to the tax paid on fish caught in Lake Moeris, cf. PSI II. 160⁶ (A.D. 149). See also OGIS 82⁶ (end of iii/B.C.) στρατηγὸς ἀποσταλεὶς ἐπὶ τὴν θήραν τῶν ἐλεφάντων τὸ δεύτερον, Preisigke 285³ (Ptol.) οἱ ὑπογεγραμμένοι κυνηγοὶ ἐπὶ τὴν θήραν τῶν τράγων.

θηρεύω

is found in its literal sense in PSI IV. 434¹⁷ (B.C. 261–0) ἀλλ' οὐδὲ τὸμ μῦν ἑτοιμάζοντα θηρεύειν (cf. μυοθηρεύω and –της in P Oxy II. 299 cited s.v. ἀρραβών), P Ryl II. 98 (a)

(A.D. 154–5) βούλομαι ἐπιχωρηθῆναι παρ' ὑμῶν θηρεύειν, αἱ ἀγριεύειν ἐν τῷ προκειμένῳ] δρυμῷ πᾶν ὄρν[εο]ν ἐπὶ γῆς, "I desire to be granted a permit by you for hunting and catching in the aforesaid mere every bird therein" (Edd.): cf. OGIS 54¹¹ (c. B.C. 247) οὓς (ἐλέφαντας) ὅ τε πατὴρ αὐτοῦ (Πτολεμαίου τοῦ Εὐεργέτου) καὶ αὐτὸς πρῶτοι) ἐκ τῶν χωρῶν τούτων ἐθήρευσαν.

θηριομαχέω.

The subst. θηρομαχία is found OGIS 533¹⁸ (i/B.C.) θηρομαχίαν ἔδωκεν. For the verb, see Vett. Val. p. 129³³ ὁ τοιοῦτος ἐθηριομάχησεν, and similarly p. 130²¹. A close parallel to the Pauline usage (1 Cor 15³²) occurs in Ignat. Rom. 5 ἀπὸ Συρίας μέχρι Ῥώμης θηριομαχῶ. Though the verb used is different, we may compare the maiden's lament in P Ryl I. 15⁷ (ii/A.D.)—

            κακοῖς
[θηρίοις νιν] μονομαχήσειν ἀνέπεισαν.

"They have persuaded him to fight alone with evil beasts" (Ed.).

θήριον.

In P Tebt II. 355⁶ (c. A.D. 145) we read of a tax of 1 obol—θηρ(ίων), and in ib. 638 (A.D. 180–192) 2 obols are charged for the same purpose: cf. also the reference to a μερισμὸς θηρίων in P Lond 844⁸ (A.D. 174) (= III. p. 55), where the editors note that the nature of the tax must remain doubtful. A letter to a prefect of date iii/iv A.D. contains an apology, because the writer had not been able to procure some wild animals which were required—P Oxy I. 122⁹ ἡμεῖ[ς] δὲ ἀγριεύειν τῶν θηρίων δυνά[με]θα οὐδὲ ἕν, "we cannot catch a single animal" (Edd.), and BGU IV. 1024ⁱᵛ·⁵ff. (iv/v A.D.) conveys a stern rebuke by the prefect to one who had dug up a dead man whom the city had buried publicly—σύ μοι δοκεῖς [ψυχὴν ἔ]χειν θηρίου καὶ [ο]ὐκ ἀνθρώπου, [μᾶλλον δ]ὲ οὐδὲ θηρίου. καὶ γὰρ τὰ θηρία [τ]οῖς μὲν ἀνθρώποις πρόσειν, τῶν δὲ [ἀ]ποθνησκόντων φίδοντα[ι]. σὺ δὲ ἐπεβούλευσας σῶμα (l. σώματι) ἀλλοτρ[ι]ωθέντι ὑπὸ τοῦ [γ]ένους τῶν ἀνθρώπων: cf. Vett. Val. p. 78⁹ γίνονται γὰρ οἱ τοιοῦτοι θηρίου παντὸς χείρονες. For the adj. θηριώδης see s.v. ἀνήμερος, and cf. OGIS 424³ (1st half i/A.D.) θηριώδους καταστάσεω[ς. In MGr the subst. appears as θηρίο, θερί.

θησαυρίζω.

Syll 515⁸ᵛ (i/B.C.) σιτωνίωι Φρύνιος ἔσοδος χίλια τάλαντα τὸ θησαυρισθέν.

θησαυρός,

which survives in MGr, is very common = "granary" or "storehouse" for all kinds of agricultural produce, e.g. corn (P Ryl II. 231³—A.D. 40) and wine (P Flor II. 194⁶—A.D. 259): cf. P Oxy I. 101⁹ (A.D. 142) εἰς δημόσιον θησαυρόν, and Ostr 503 (A.D. 109–110) a receipt for a payment ὑπ(ὲρ) θησ(αυροῦ) ἱερῶ·ν. In P Tebt I. 6²⁷ (B.C. 140–39) in connexion with an Egyptian temple sums are collected—εἰς θησαυροὺς καὶ φιάλας καὶ ποτήρια: the meaning of θησαυρούς has caused the editors difficulty, but Otto (Priester i. p. 396) thinks that the "collection-box" is meant. A θησαυροφύλαξ is mentioned in P Fay 225 (ii/iii A.D.).

θιγγάνω.

For this verb, which is classed as un-Attic by Rutherford *NP*, pp. 169 f., 391, cf. P Oxy IX. 1185¹¹ (*c.* A.D. 200) ὀψαρίου μὴ θιγγάνειν, "do not touch the sauce." For the gen. constr., as in Heb 11²⁸, 12²⁰, and LXX, cf. also Aristeas 106 ὅπως μηδενὸς θιγγάνωσιν ὧν οὐ δέον ἐστιν.

θλίβω.

The varied usage of this common verb may be illustrated by the following passages—P Petr II. 4 (1)⁷ (B.C. 255–4) ἵνα μὴ ἡμεῖς θλιβώμεθα, P Par 26³² (B.C. 163–2) (= *Selections*, p. 15) ἡμῶν δὲ τοῖς δέουσι θλιβομένων, P Oxy VI. 898³³ (A.D. 123) ἐκ παντὸς θλείβουσά με εἰς τὸ μὴ δύνασθαι κατ' αὐτῆς προελθεῖν, "using every means of oppressing me so as to render me incapable of proceeding against her" (Edd.), P Ryl II. 116⁹ (A.D. 104) θλειβομένη τῇ συνειδήσει περὶ ὧν ἐνοσφίσατο κτλ., of a woman "oppressed by the consciousness" that she had wrongfully appropriated certain articles, P Tebt II. 423⁸ (early iii/A.D.) περὶ τῶν βοῶν μὴ ἀμελὴς (*l.* ἀμελήσῃς) μηδὲ θλείβε αὐτά, "do not neglect the oxen or work them hard" (Edd.), P Oxy I. 123⁸ (iii/iv A.D.) πάνυ γὰρ θλείβομαι διότι οὐκ ἐδεξάμην σου γράμματα, *ib.* 120 *verso*⁷ (iv/A.D.) ἀλ' (*l.* ἀλλ') ὅρα μὴ καταλίψῃς μαι (*l.* με) θλιβόμενον, and *ib.* VI. 903³ (iv/A.D.) where a wife complains of her husband—καὶ περὶ Ἀνίλλας τῆς δούλης αὐτοῦ ἔμεινεν θλίβων τὴν ψυχήν μου, "he also persisted in vexing my soul about his slave Anilla" (Edd.). Cf. MGr θλιβερός, "sad," "perplexed." The literal sense of the verb in Mt 7¹⁴ may be illustrated from Apoc. Petr. 10 καὶ τοὺς φονεῖς ἔβλεπον καὶ τοὺς συνειδότας αὐτοῖς βεβλημένους ἔν τινι τόπῳ τεθλιμμένῳ καὶ πεπληρωμένῳ ἑρπετῶν πονηρῶν.

θλῖψις.

The metaphorical meaning of θλῖψις (for accent, see W.-Schm. *Gr.* p. 68) is generally thought to be confined to Bibl. and eccles. Greek (cf. Milligan on 1 Th 1⁶), but the beginning of the later usage may be traced in *OGIS* 444¹⁵ (B.C. 125 or 77) διὰ τὰς τῶν πόλεων θλίψεις, apparently = "because of the straits of the cities," and perhaps in BGU IV. 1139⁴ (B.C. 5) χάρν (*l.* χάριν) τῆς ἐσχηκυίας ἡμᾶς [κοινκη] βι . . . ης θλε[ίψ]εως, where, however, the meaning is not clear. See also the exx. which Boll (*Offenbarung*, p. 134 f.) quotes from Hellenistic astrology in illustration of Mt 24²¹, Mk 13¹⁹, e.g. Catal. VIII. 3. 175. 5 ἔννοιαι <ἔσονται> καὶ θλῖψις, VII. 169, 12 λύπαι καὶ πένθη καὶ κλαυθμοὶ ἔσονται ἐν ἐκείνῳ τῷ τόπῳ καὶ στοναχαὶ καὶ θλίψεις. The NT usage may be further illustrated from two Christian papyrus letters—P Oxy VI. 939¹³ (iv/A.D.) (= *Selections*, p. 129) τὰ μὲν γὰρ πρῶτα ἐν θλίψει αὐτῆς [πολλῇ οὔ]σης οὐκ ὦν ἐν ἐμαυτῷ ἀπέστειλα, "for my first messages I despatched when she was in great affliction, not being master of myself," P Amh II. 144¹³ (v/A.D.) καὶ γὰρ ἐγὼ ἐν πολλῇ μέριμνα (*l.* μερίμνῃ) καὶ θλείψει ὑπάρχω, "for I am in much anxiety and trouble" (Edd.). MGr θλῖψι (χλῖψι), "affliction."

θνητός.

Syll 365¹⁰ (*c.* A.D. 37) θεῶν δὲ χάριτες τούτῳ διαφέρουσιν ἀνθρωπίνων διαδοχῶν, ᾧ ἡ νυκτὸς ἥλιος καὶ τὸ ἄφθαρτον θνητῆς φύσεως.

θορυβέω.

P Tebt II. 411¹² (ii/A.D.) μηδὲν μέντοι θορυβηθῇς, παραγενόμενος γὰρ εἴσῃ ὅ τι ποτέ ἐστιν, "do not be disturbed however, for when you come you will know what it means" (Edd.), P Oxy XII. 1587¹³ (late iii/A.D.) ἐπεὶ θορυβούμεθα, *Syll* 737⁶¹ (*c.* A.D. 175) οὐδενὶ δὲ ἐξέσται ἐν τῇ στιβάδι οὔτε ᾆσαι οὔτε θορυβῆσαι οὔτε κροτῆσαι.

θόρυβος.

For the stronger sense of this word "riot," "disturbance," as in Mk 14² (Vg. *tumultus*), Ac 20¹, 24¹⁸, cf. P Tebt I. 15³ (B.C. 114) θορύβου γενομένου ἐν τῆι κώ(μῃ) with reference to a village riot and an attack upon the epistates by two persons. See also *OGIS* 48⁹ (iii/B.C.) ὁρῶντές τινας τῶν πολιτῶν [μ]ὴ ὀρθῶς ἀνα[στρ]ε[φ]ομένους καὶ θόρυβον οὐ τὸν τυχόντα παρ[έχ]οντας ἐν τ[αῖς] βουλαῖς [καὶ] ἐν ταῖς ἐκκλησίαις . . . [μέχρι βίας καὶ ἀσ[ε]βείας, *Magn* 114³ ἴς ταραχὴν καὶ θορύβους ἐνπίπτειν.

θραύω.

For the perf. part. pass. of this verb, which is found in Lk 4¹⁸ (from LXX), cf. *Syll* 226¹⁶⁸ (iii/B.C.) τ]εθραυσμένος : in *ib.* 588²⁷ (*c.* B.C. 180) we have ποτήρια παντοδαπὰ τεθραυμένα. See also for the verb *ib.* 891⁸ (ii/A.D.) ἢ αἰκίσεται ἢ θραύσει ἤ τι μέρος ἢ σύμπαν, and *Kaibel* 1003, an inscr. on the left leg of Memnon, referring to the breaking of the stone by Cambyses—

ἔθραυσε Καμβύσης με τόνδε τὸν λίθον.

The verb is common in Vett. Val. with reference to the "crushing" of the power of evil etc., e.g. p. 276⁷ θραύεται δὲ τὸ φαῦλον ὑπὸ τοῦ ἀγαθοῦ παρηγορούμενον, cf. Judith 9¹⁰, and the subst. θραῦσις in *ib.* 7⁹. The verbal θραυστός occurs in an epigram of early i/B.C., P Tebt I. 3⁴ θαυστά (*l.* θραυστά) unfortunately in a broken context.

θρέμμα.

For this NT ἅπ. εἰρ. (Jn 4¹²) = "cattle" (AV, RV) we may cite P Oxy II. 246¹⁶ (A.D. 66) ἀπεγραψάμην . . ἀπὸ γ[ο]νῆς ὧν ἔχω θρεμμάτω[ν] ἄρνας δέκα δύο, "I registered twelve lambs which were born from sheep in my possession" (Edd.), BGU III. 759¹¹ (A.D. 125) ἐπελθόντες μοι . . ποιμαίνοντι θρέμματα Ἀνουβίωνος, P Amh II. 134⁵ (early ii/A.D.) Πετέα ὄντα ἐν ἀγρῷ μετὰ τῶν θρεμμάτων νυκτὸς ἀποσπάσαι, "to seize Peteus by night while he was in the fields with the cattle" (Edd.), and from the inscrr. *Syll* 293²⁶ (B.C. 178–7) ποτάγειν τὰ ἰδιωτικὰ θρέμματα, *OGIS* 200¹¹ (iv/A.D.) αὐτοὺς ἤγαγον πρὸς ἡμᾶς μετὰ καὶ τῶν θρεμμάτων αὐτῶν. With θρέμμα in its literal sense of "nursling" we may compare the use of θρεπτάριον in a Paris papyrus, p. 422¹³ τὰ ἀβάσκαντά σου θρεπτάρια, "tes charmants petits nourrissons," and θρεπτός = "foster-child" in P Oxy II. 298⁵·⁴⁶ (i/A.D.), or "foundling" as in C. and B. i. p. 147 No. 37 (cf. p. 350), where it is noted that θρέμμα has the same meaning.

θρηνέω.

A new reference for this verb occurs in the much mutilated classical fragment, P Petr I. 9⁶; cf. *Archiv* iii. p. 165. For the subst. θρηνητής see BGU I. 34 *recto*ⁱᵛ·⁴ εἰς πεῖν τοῖς παιδίοις ᾱ, θρηνητῇ ᾱ, where the numerals probably refer to jars of wine: and cf. the use of θρήνωμα (= θρήνημα) in P Tebt I. 140 (B.C. 72) θρηνώματα εἰς τὸν Ὄσιριν β̄. MGr θρῆνος, "a dirge."

θρησκεία.

As against the common idea that θρησκεία means only ritual, Hort (on Jas 1[26]) has shown that the underlying idea is simply "reverence of the gods or worship of the gods, two sides of the same feeling"—a feeling which, however, frequently finds expression in θρησκείαι or ritual acts. Of this use of the plur. a good example occurs in a ii/A.D. Rainer papyrus published by Wessely (*Karanis*, p. 56) where precautions are taken πρὸς τῷ ἰδίῳ λόγῳ . . . ἵνα μήκετι αἱ τῶν θεῶν θρησκεῖαι ἐμποδίζο(= ω)νται (cf. 1 Macc 9[58]): see also another Rainer papyrus, *Chrest.* I. 72[10] (A.D. 234), where it is reported—μηδένα δὲ τῶν ἱερέω[ν ἢ] ἱερωμένων ἐνκαταλελοιπέναι τὰς [θρ]ησκείας, and cf. the curious inscr. from Talmis in Nubia, *ib.* 73[10] (A.D. 247-8), where the strategus gives orders that all "swine" should be driven out of the village—πρὸς τὸ δύνασθαι τὰ περὶ τὰ ἱερὰ θρήσκια κατὰ τὰ νενομισμένα γείνεσθαι In the Delphic inscr., first published by Bourguet *De rebus Delphicis*, 1905, p. 63 f., which has proved of such importance in dating Gallio's proconsulship, and consequently in fixing a point in the Pauline chronology (see *s.v.* Γαλλίων), the words ἐπετήρη[σα δὲ τὴ]ν θρησκεί[αν τ]οῦ Ἀπό[λλωνος] τοῦ Πυθίου are put into the mouth of the Emperor Tiberius, to which Deissmann (*St. Paul*, p. 251) furnishes a parallel from the same source in a letter of Hadrian's to Delphi: καὶ εἰς τὴν ἀρ[χαιότητα τῆ]ς πόλεως καὶ εἰς τὴν τοῦ κατέχοντος α[ὐτὴν θεοῦ θρησ]κείαν ἀφορῶν (Bourguet, p. 78). We may add *Syll* 656[18] (Ephesus—ii/A.D.) which describes as θρησκεία the keeping of the month Artemision as sacred to the tutelary goddess, *OGIS* 513[13] (beginning of iii/A.D.) in honour of a priestess— εὐσεβῶς πᾶσαν θρησκείαν ἐκτελέσασαν τῇ θεῷ, and the interesting passage quoted by C. Taylor (*Exp T* xvi. p. 334) in illustration of Jas 1[26] from the end of c. 12 of the Ποιμάνδρης of Hermes Trismegistos—καὶ τοῦτό ἐστιν ὁ θεός, τὸ πᾶν . . . τοῦτον τὸν λόγον, ὦ τέκνον, προσκύνει καὶ θρήσκευε. θρησκεία δὲ τοῦ θεοῦ μία ἐστί, μὴ εἶναι κακόν, "et hoc deus est, universum . . . hoc verbum, o fili, adora et cole. Cultus autem dei unus est, malum non esse" (ed. Parthey, Berlin, 1854). For the verb see *Preisigke* 991 (A.D. 200) where an inscr. on a temple-pillar is dated—ἐπὶ Διδύμου ἱερέως θρησκεύοντος. Boisacq (p. 340) derives the Ionic word from the root of θεράπων, θεραπεύω: cf. θρόνος.

θριαμβεύω.

A cognate verb appears in BGU IV. 1061[19] (B.C. 14) περὶ ὧν καὶ ἐν αὐτῆι τῆι Σιναρὺ παρεδόθησαν καὶ πρὸς τὸ μὴ ἐκθριαμβισθῆναι τὸ πρᾶγμα ἀπε[λύθησαν, "for which crimes they were delivered up in Sinary itself, and were released in order that the affair should not be noised abroad." (So Dr. A. S. Hunt, who kindly notes for us Basil *De Spir. Sanct.* xxvii. ἐκθριαμβεύειν, and Photius, who glosses θριαμβεύσας with δημοσιεύσας). This meaning is obviously allied to 2 Cor 2[14] "make a show of," and contributes additional evidence against the impossible rendering of the AV (cf.

Field *Notes*, p. 181). Lietzmann (*HZNT ad l.*) prefers to take the verb in the further weakened sense of περιάγειν, "herumführen": Ramsay (*Luke*, p. 297 f.), on the other hand, keeps to the military metaphor and translates: "Thanks be to God, who always leads us (His soldiers) in the train of His triumph": cf. also Pope in *Exp T* xxi. p. 19 ff., and Menzies *Comm. ad l.*

θρίξ.

With Mk 1[6] we may compare the reference to τρίχες εἰς τοὺς σάκκους in P Petr II. 33(*t*)(1[9] (as completed *ib.* III. p. 333). The word is naturally common in the personal descriptions of parties to a will or deed, e.g. P Petr III. 2[6] (B.C. 236) οὐλὴ μετώπωι ὑπὸ τρίχα: cf. *ib.* 12[14] and 14[18] (both B.C. 234), P Lond 882[13] (B.C. 101) (= III. p. 13). *ib.* 142[6] (A.D. 95) (= II. p. 203). In P Fay 58[7] (A.D. 155-6) we have the receipt for a tax κοπ(ῆς) καὶ τριχ(ὸς) καὶ χιρωναξίου, "on cutting and hair and trade." The same tax is referred to in P Grenf II. 60[4] (A.D. 193-4) and BGU II. 617[2] (A.D. 215), and as in both these cases the payers of the tax were weavers, Wilcken thinks that the words κοπή and θρίξ had to do with the terminology of their trade (see the editors' introd. to P Fay 58). *Michel* 1170[4] (i/A.D.) Ἐπαφρόδιτο[s] Ἐπαφροδίτου ὑπὲρ τοῦ παιδίου Ἐπαφροδίτου τὴν παιδικὴν τρίχα Ὑγίᾳ καὶ Ἀσκληπιῷ: cf. the similar dedication of a girl's ringlets to Isis, *Anth. Pal.* vi. 60.

θρόμβος.

Hobart (p. 82 f.) has shown that the expression θρόμβοι αἵματος, which is strongly supported by "Western" authority in Lk 22[44], was very common in medical language.

θρόνος.

For this word, which in the NT, and notably in the Apocalypse, is always an official seat or chair of state, we may compare *OGIS* 383[25] (rescript of Commagene—mid. i/B.C.) ἐγὼ πατρῷαν [ἀ]ρχὴν [π]αρ[αλ]α[β]ὼν βασιλείαν [μ]ὲν ἐμο[ῖ]ς ὑπήκοον θρόνοις, *ib.* [42] πρὸς οὐρανίους Διὸς Ὠρομάσδου θρόνους, and *Preisigke* 082[7] (B.C. 4) ὑπὲρ Αὐτοκράτορος Καίσαρος θεοῦ υἱοῦ Σεβαστοῦ . . . τ[ὸ]ν θρόνον καὶ τὸν βωμὸν ἀνέθηκε, *ib.* 1164[8] (B.C. 181-45) ὑπὲρ βασιλέως Πτολεμαίο[υ καὶ βασιλίσσης Κλεοπάτρας . . . τὸ Πτολεμαῖον καὶ τὸν θρόνον Ἑρμεῖ Ἡρακλεῖ. In connexion with the above it may be noticed that Deissmann (*LAE*, p. 280 n 2) from personal observation thinks that ὁ θρόνος τοῦ Σατανᾶ (Rev 2[13]) at Pergamum can only have been the altar of Zeus, which there dominated the whole district, and was thus a typical representative of satanic heathendom. The word in its original sense of "seat," "chair," is found in P Oxy VII. 1050[4] (ii/iii A.D.) θρόνῳ (δραχμαὶ) κ̄, "for a chair 20 dr."

Θυάτειρα.

For the guild of purple dyers at Thyatira (Ac 16[14]) see *CIG* 3496-8, and the inscr. on a tomb at Thessalonica which the guild of purple dyers erected to the memory of a certain Menippus from Thyatira—ἡ συνήθεια τῶν πορφυροβάφων τῆς ὀκτωκαιδεκάτης Μένιππον Ἀμ[μ]ίου τὸν καὶ Σεβῆρον Θυατειρηνόν, μνήμης χάριν (Duchesne et Bayet *Mission au Mont Athos*, p. 52, No. 83; cf. Zahn *Introd.* i. p. 535 f.).

θυγάτηρ.

This common word (MGr θυγατέρα) hardly needs illustration, but we may refer to the formula κατὰ θυγατροποιίαν δέ, which is found in the inscrr. for the adoption of females, corresponding to καθ᾽ υἱοθεσίαν δέ, for males: see Deissmann *BS*, p. 239.

θυγάτριον.

P Petr III. 53(*r*)³ τὸ θυγάτριον, P Lond 24⁶ (B.C. 163) (= I. p. 32) θυγ[α]τρίου. For θυγατριδῆ, "granddaughter," see BGU I. 300¹⁷ (A.D. 148), and for θυγατριδοῦς, "grandson," see P Oxy I. 45⁶ (A.D. 95), BGU I. 300¹⁷ (A.D. 148).

θύϊνος.

We seem to have an instance of this adj., unfortunately in a very imperfect context, in P Lond 928²⁰ (ii/A.D.) (= III. p. 191) θυίνων. For the subst. see *Chrest.* I. 176¹¹ (mid. i/A.D.) ὁμοίως καὶ θυίας καὶ τὰ ἄλλα τὰ ἐνχρῆζοντα, and P Amh II. 118⁵ (A.D. 185) τέλους θυιῶν, "for the tax on thyia-wood," *al.*: on the use of thyia-wood for oil-presses, see Otto *Priester*, i. p. 295 ff.

θυμίαμα.

The subst. is found several times in the Ptolemaic papyri, e.g. P Leid C^{iii. 13} (= I. p. 93), T^{i. 14} (= I. p. 112) *al.*, P Tebt I. 112²² (B.C. 112) θυμιάματος ε. In BGU I. 1¹⁰ (iii/A.D.) the editor reads εἰς θυσίας καὶ [ἐπι]θυμ[ιάμ(ατα)?, but Wilcken *Chrest.* I. p. *122* has [?]θυμ[ιάματα]. The word also occurs in the Arcadian inscr. *Syll.* 939¹⁵ ff along with words of similar reference—ἀγάλμα[τι], μάκων[σ]ι λευκαῖς, λυχνίοις, θυμιάμασιν, [ζ]μύρναι, ἀρώμασιν.

θυμιατήριον.

Some quotations may be given from *Syll.* Thus in 804¹⁹ (? ii/A.D.) the patient in the Asclepieum sees παιδάριον ἡγεῖσθαι θυμιατήριον ἔχον ἀτμίζο[ν: it is "censer" here, obviously. The same seems to be the case in 5*S*3¹² (i/A.D.)—so Dittenberger—and 588²⁸ (ii/B.C.), though there is nothing decisive: naturally in many contexts we cannot say whether the censer was fixed or movable. So also 734¹²⁴. In P Oxy III. 521¹⁹ (ii/A.D.) a θυμιατήριον is mentioned in a list of articles, perhaps belonging to some temple, and a θυμιατήριον is also found along with a φιάλη ἀργυρῆ καὶ σπον[δ]εῖ[ο]ν lying ἐπὶ τρίποδι in a *triclinium* (BGU II. 388^{ii. 22}.—ii/A.D.): cf. BGU II. 387^{ii. 8. 21}, 488¹¹ (both ii/A.D.).

θυμιάω.

For this NT ἅπ. εἰρ. (Lk 1⁹) see OGIS 352³⁷ (ii/B.C.) καὶ σ[τε]φα[νοῦν τὸ ἄγαλμα τὸ τοῦ βασιλέως] καὶ θυμιᾶν κ[αὶ] δᾶιδα ἱστάνειν. Hobart (p. 90 f.) has shown that the verb, which survives in MGr as θυμιάζω, was the medical term for fumigating with herbs, spices, etc.

θυμός

is not so common as might have been expected, but it is found in the curious alphabetical acrostic of early i/A.D., P Tebt II. 278³² where, with reference to the loss of a garment, it is said of the thief—θυμοῦ περιπεσῖτε *l.* -εῖται), "he will meet with anger" (Edd.): cf. BGU IV. 1141³¹

(B.C. 14) ἐπὶ θυμῶι. So in the new Alexandrian erotic fragment P Grenf I. 1²¹ (ii/B.C.) γίνωσκε ὅτι θυμὸν ἀνίκητον ἔχω ὅταν ἔρις λάβη με. Add from the inscrr. the early *Syll* 2²¹ (the "Gadatas" inscr. translated from a rescript of Darius I.) δώσω σοι μὴ μεταβαλομένωι πεῖραν ἠδικ[ημέ]νου θ[υ]μοῦ, *Michel* 1322 A⁴ Δ]ιονύσιον κατα[δ]ῶ καὶ τὴν γλῶτ(τ)αν τὴν κακὴν καὶ τὸν θυμὸν τὸν κακὸν καὶ τὴν ψυχὴν τὴν κακή[ν, and *Magn* 115(a)²¹ (letter of Darius Hystaspes) δώσω σοι . . πεῖραν ἠδικη[μέ]νου θυμοῦ. [In P Lond 42²⁸ (B.C. 168) (= I. p. 31) for the editor's θυμήν, from an apparently new form θυμή, we should read οὐ μήν, see *Chrest.* I. p. *132*.] MGr θυμώνω, "enrage."

θύρα.

For this common noun see P Petr II. 10(2)¹¹ (*c.* mid. iii/B.C.) γενομένου μου πρὸς τῆι θύραι τοῦ στρατηγίου, "when I had reached the door of the strategus' office" (Ed.), P Ryl II. 127⁹ (A.D. 29) κοιμωμένου μου ἐπὶ τῆς θύρας οὗ καταγείνομαι οἴκου, "as I was sleeping at the door of the house which I inhabit" (Edd.), BGU II. 507²⁶ (A.D. 75) μὴ ἀφέτωσαν τὴν θύραν, ἡνίκα κλιστὴ (*l.* κλειστὴ) ἦν. In P Petr II. 13(16)¹³ (B.C. 258–3) ἀρθήτωσαν αἱ θύραι, the reference is to the raising of the sluice-gates of the canals: cf. *ib.* III. 44(3)³ ἀνοιχθήτω οὖν ἡ θύρα. In leases the restoration of existing doors and keys is frequently laid down as a condition, perhaps because doors were often detachable and might readily come to harm, e.g. P Oxy III. 502³³ (A.D. 164) where the tenant is to deliver up certain buildings—καθαρὰ ἀπὸ κοπρίων καὶ ἃς παρείληφεν θύρας καὶ κλεῖς πάντων τῶν τόπων, "free from filth and with the doors and keys received by her of all the premises" (Edd.): so *ib.* IV. 729²³ (A.D. 137), VIII. 1127²⁴ (A.D. 183), 1128²⁶ (A.D. 173) and P Strass I. 4²¹ (A.D. 550) with the editor's note. Other exx. of the word are P Tebt I. 45¹² (B.C. 113) τὴν παρόδιον θύραν, "the street door," P Oxy X. 1272¹² (A.D. 144) τὴν τοῦ πεσσοῦ θύραν, "the door of the terrace," and *ib.* VI. 903²⁰ (iv/A.D.) τὰς ἔξω θύρας, "the outside doors." On the θύρα of Ac 3²·¹⁰, see *ZNTW* vii. p. 51 ff. For the ethnic use of θύρα on tombs see Ramsay in *C. and B.* ii. p. 395 where reference is made to an inscr. on an altar found near the hot springs of Myrikion in Galatia, where a man erected to his wife τὸν βωμὸν καὶ τὴν θύραν, the word θύρα being added because "according to Phrygian ideas there were two necessary elements in the sepulchral monument; and when there was no real door, the word at least was engraved on the altar to represent the actual entrance. The door was the passage of communication between the world of life and the world of death: on the altar the living placed the offerings due to the dead": cf. *JHS* v. (1884), p. 254. For the diminutive θύριον, see P Lond 1177²⁴³ (A.D. 113) (= III. p. 187) θύριον and P Tebt II. 414⁵⁶ (ii/A.D.) τὸν ξύλινον δίφρον καὶ τὸ θύριν (*l.* -ιον), "the wooden stool and the little door." The verb θυρόω (cf. 1 Macc 4⁵⁷) is common, e.g. P Amh II. 51¹⁴ (B.C. 88) οἰκίαν . . . τεθυρωμένην: for θύρωμα (as in 2 Macc 14⁴³ *al.*) see BGU IV. 1028²⁰ (ii/A.D.).

θυρεός.

For the late usage of this word for the long oblong shield of Roman equipment (cf. Polyb. vi. 23. 2), as in Eph 6¹⁶, see PSI IV. 428³⁶ (iii/B.C.) ὅπλα ἀσπὶς φαρέτρα θυρεός

θυρίς.

In P Petr III. 48[15] we hear of θυρίδας κοιλοστάθμους, where for the last word the editors refer to LXX Hagg 1[4], and for the corresponding verb to 3 Kings 6[9], and understand the meaning to be to put a sheath of wood over the door-posts or the sides of the windows. BGU IV. 1116[23] (B.C. 13) describes a house θύραις καὶ θυρίσι καὶ κλεισί : see ib.[15] for the verbs—τὴν οἰκίαν τεθυρωμένην καὶ τεθυριδωμένην καὶ κεκλεισμένην. [Θυριδόω is not in LS, but cf. θυριδωτός.] Cf. also P Ryl II. 233[5] (ii A.D.) τὰ μέλαθρα τῶν θυρίδων τοῦ μεγάλου συμποσίου, "the beams of the windows in the great dining-hall" (Edd.), and P Oxy I. 69[7] (A.D. 190) where stolen barley is removed from a house διὰ τῆς αὐτῆς θυρίδος, "by the said door," according to the editors, but any opening may be intended. In P Lond 35[5] (B.C. 161) (= I. p. 25) τὴν παρὰ [τοῦ βα]σιλέως διὰ τῆς θυρίδος ἐ[σφρα]γισμένην, the reference, as Kenyon notes, is to "the opening of a folded papyrus sheet, which would be sealed up to hold it all together and to hide the contents." An interesting inscr. in C. and B. ii. p. 650 tells of the honour paid by the Synagogue to certain Jews who ἐποίησαν τὴν τῶν θυρίδων ἀσφάλειαν καὶ τὸν λυπὸν πάντα κόσμον. MGr παραθύρι, "window."

θυρωρός.

For this word, as in Mk 13[34], Jn 10[3], see P Par 35[32] (B.C. 163) παρέθεντο δὲ τὰ ποτή[ρια] Κεφα[λᾶτ]ι τῷ θυρωρῷ (cf. ib. 37[46]), P Tebt I. 112 intr. (4) (B.C. 112) Θεῶνι θυρω[ρῶι], BGU IV. 1141[34] (B.C. 14) καθ' ἡμέραν δὲ τὸν θυλωρὸν (l. θυρ–) ἐξερωτῶι μή τις ἔξω ὕπνωκε, P Lond 604[14] (A.D. 47) (= III. p. 71) Πτολεμαίο[υ] θυρουρο(ῦ), P Flor I. 71[380] (iv/A.D.) Μουσῆς θυρουρὸς ἴ πάγ(ου). For the form θυρουρός in the last two exx., as in Mk 13[34] D*, see Mayser Gr. p. 15, and Moulton Gr. ii. p. 75. The interesting reference to a woman door-keeper in Jn 18[16,17] (cf. 2 Kings 4[6]) may be illustrated by BGU IV. 1061[10] (B.C. 14) τὴν ἀποτεταγμένην πρὸς τῆι τηρήσει θυρωρὸν Μαλήφιος γυναῖκα παραχρῆμα ἐφόνευσαν, P Ryl II. 36[b] (A.D. 34) λογοποιουμένου μου πρὸς Ἀγχερίμφ[ι]ν κα[ὶ] τὴν τούτου γυναῖκα Θεναπύγχιν θυλουρὸν (l. θυρ–) τῶν ἀπὸ Ἀνχεμίας τῆς Θεμίστου μερίδος, "as I was talking to Ancherimphis and his wife Thenapunchis, a door-keeper of Euhemeria in the division of Themistes" (Edd.), and P Strass I. 24[17] (A.D. 118) Θατρῆτι θυλουρῶι (l. θυρ–). See further for the interpretation of Jn l.c. ExpT xxvii. pp. 217 f., 314 ff., and 424 f.

θυσία.

P Hib I. 54[15] (c. B.C. 245) χρεία γάρ ἐστι ταῖς γυναιξὶν πρὸς τὴν θυσίαν, P Tebt I. 33[16] (B.C. 112) (= Selections, p. 31) τὰ . [. .] . [. . σ]ταθησόμενα θύματα καὶ τῆς θυσί[α]ς, BGU IV. 1198[12] (beginning of i/B.C.) ποιούμενοι ἁγνήας καὶ θυσίας, ib. 1201[8] (A.D. 2) πρὸς τὰς λιτουργείας καὶ θυσείας τῶν θεῶν, P Oxy IX. 1211[1] (ii/A.D.) τὰ πρὸς τὴν θυσίαν τοῦ ἱερωτάτου Νείλου, P Giss I. 40[ii. 21] (A.D. 212)

κατάγειν θυσίας εἵνεκεν ταύρους. The libelli of the Decian persecution are regularly addressed—τοῖς ἐπὶ τῶν θυσιῶν ᾑρημένοις, "to those chosen to superintend the sacrifices," or some similar phrase : see e.g. BGU I. 287[1] (A.D. 250) (= Selections, p. 115), and cf. the similar use of θυσιάζω in P Ryl II. 112 (a)[10], (b)[15], (c)[14] (A.D. 250). From the inscr. we may cite OGIS 59[15] (B.C. 188) ὅπως ἔχωσιν εἴς τε τὰς θυσίας καὶ τὸ ἄλειμμα δαπανᾶν, Syll 633[9] (ii/A.D.) ἐὰν δέ τις βιάσηται, ἀπρόσδεκτος ἡ θυσία παρὰ τοῦ θεοῦ (cf. Phil 4[18], Sirach 32[9]).

θύω.

An early instance of this verb occurs in the interesting, but fragmentary, papyrus containing a royal edict regarding the constitution of one of the Greek cities in Egypt, P Hib I. 28[7] (c. B.C. 265), where it is laid down with reference to the incorporation of the demes in the phratries— κ[αὶ] γνωρίζηται ὑπὸ τῶν φρατόρων θυέτωσαν, "(in order that they may) be recognized by the members of the phratries, let them sacrifice" (Edd.). Other examples are P Fay 121[13] (c. A.D. 100) καὶ τὸ δ[έρ]μα τοῦ μόσχου οὗ ἐθύ[σ]αμεν αἴτησον πα[ρὰ τοῦ] κυρτοῦ βυρσέως. "ask the hunch-backed tanner for the hide of the calf that we sacrificed" (Edd.), P Giss I. 3[7] (invitation to the festival on Hadrian's accession—A.D. 117) τοιγαροῦν θύοντες τὰς ἑστίας ἀνάπτωμεν, BGU I. 250[5] (time of Hadrian) μόσχους τεθύκασι, ib. II. 463[6] (A.D. 148) τέλος μόσχ(ου) θυομέ(νου), Chrest. I. 110[2] (Sayings of Sansnōs—ii/iii A.D.) σέβου τὸ θεῖον. θύε πᾶσι τοῖς θεοῖς, and from the libelli (see s.v. θυσία) BGU I. 287[7] (A.D. 250) (= Selections, p. 115) καὶ ἀεὶ θύων τοῖς θεοῖς διετέλεσα.

Θῶμας.

On the relation of this proper name to the Heb. אֹם = "twin" see Nestle in Enc. Bibl. 5057 ff., where reference is made to the use of אֹם as a name in the Phoenician inscrr., e.g. Corpus Inscriptionum Semiticarum i. No. 46 בן אֹם רבבא, cf. Θαμὸς Ἀβδουσίρου (Insor. Mission de Phénicie, p. 241). See also Herzog Philologus, 56 (1897), p. 54, and the note in the present work on δίδυμος.

θώραξ.

Amongst the bequests in the will of Demetrius (P Petr III. 6 (a)[29] (B.C. 237), we find τὸν [θ]ώρακα and [τὴ]ν ζώνην θωράκιτ[ιν]. The word is similarly used = "breastplate" in P Giss I. 47[6] (time of Hadrian) ὁ[μὲν γὰρ θ]ώραξ ἐκ καλοῦ ὠροχάλκου ὢν καὶ [τ]ὴν πλοκὴν λεπτότατος καὶ τὸ μεῖζον ἐλα[φ]ρότατος ὡς μὴ κάμνειν τὸν φοροῦντα αὐτὸν [ἠ]γοράσθη κτλ. For the verb, as in 1 Macc 4[7], cf. OGIS 332[42] (B.C. 138–133) ἄγαλμα πεντάπηχυ τεθωρακισμένον, while in the list of traders, which makes up the alphabetical acrostic P Tebt II. 278[5] (early i/A.D.), we find a θωρακοποίς (l. θωρακοποιός), "a breastplate-maker," between an ἡπητής, "a cobbler," and an ἰατρός, "a physician."

I

Ἰάειρος — ἰατρός

Ἰάειρος.

Apart from the Gospels (Mk 5²², Lk 8⁴¹) this name is found in the Greek Bible in Esth 2⁵ Μαρδοχαῖος ὁ τοῦ Ἰαείρου. A similar form occurs in Wilcken *Ostr* 1231 (Thebes—Ptol.) Θεόδωρος καὶ Ἀβαιοῦς καὶ Σκύμνος Ἰαείρη χα(ίρειν).

Ἰακώβ.

The appeal to the *God of Abraham, of Isaac, and of Jacob* (cf. Mk 12²⁶) is very common in the magic papyri, e.g. P Par 574¹²⁸¹ᶠ (iii/A.D.) (= *Selections*, p. 113 f.) χαῖρε φνουθι ν Ἀβραάμ· χαῖρε πνουτε ν Ἰσάκ· χαῖρε πνουτε ν Ἰακώβ, "hail, spirit of Abraham": see further Deissmann *BS* p. 282, where Orig. *c. Cels.* v. 45 is quoted to the effect that these Hebrew names had to be left untranslated in the adjurations if the *power* of the incantation was not to be lost, and *ib.* p. 316 on the tendency of the early Christians to prefer the "Biblical" form Ἰακώβ to the Graecized Ἰάκωβος. Cf. also the sepulchral inscr. *Preisigke* 2034¹³ ἀνάπαυσον τὴν ψυχὴν τοῖς δούλοις σου πιστὰ ἐν κόλποις Ἀβράμ καὶ Ἰσάκ καὶ Ἰακώβ. For the spelling Ἰακούβ see Wünsch *AF* 3² (Imperial age).

Ἰάκωβος.

This Graecized form of the Hebr. Ἰακώβ (see *supra*) with the spelling Ἰάκουβος is found in P Oxy II. 276⁵ (A.D. 77), where we hear of a Jew, son of Jacob (Ἰακούβου), as steersman on a cargo-boat: cf. BGU III. 715ⁱⁱ·¹¹ (A.D. 101–2) Σαμβαθ(ίων) Ἰακούβου, and 1 Esdr 9⁴⁸ A.

ἴαμα.

Syll 802 (iii/B.C.) Ἰά]ματα τοῦ Ἀπόλλωνος καὶ τοῦ Ἀσκλαπίου—the heading of a list of cures worked in the Asclepieum at Epidaurus: cf. *ib.*²⁴·³⁵. See also the sepulchral epitaph *Kaibel* 314¹³ᶠ (Smyrna)—ἀλλ' ὁ ταλαίφρων γεννήσας εἰάσατό μου νόσον αἰνήν, τοῦτο δοκῶν ὅτι μοῖραν ἐμὴν εἰάμασι σώσει.

ἰάομαι.

As distinguished from θεραπεύω "treat medically" (see *s.v.* and cf. Ac 28⁸ᶠ·) ἰάομαι denotes "heal," as in *Syll* 802¹¹³ (referred to *s.v.* ἴαμα) ἀνὴρ δάκτυλον ἰάθη ὑπὸ ὄφιος, and the similar 803⁷ τοῦτο]ν τυφλὸν ἐόντα ἰάσατο: cf. also the magic text BGU IV. 1026ˣˣⁱⁱ·¹⁵ αἱμαροῦαν ἰάται. On the Lukan usage of the verb see Hobart, p. 8 ff., and on the "aoristic present" in Ac 9³⁴ see *Proleg.* p. 119. Thayer's hint of a connexion with ἰός is not supported by modern philologists, see Boisacq, p. 362.

ἴασις.

For a metaphorical use of this Lukan word cf. Vett. Val. p. 190³⁰ εἴθ' οὕτως ἀπόροις κατόρθωσιν τῶν πραγμάτων καὶ τῶν φαύλων ἴασιν ἀποτελεῖ. Lk 13³² shows the same collocation—ἰάσεις ἀποτελῶ. See also Hobart, p. 23 f.

ἴασπις.

Syll 587⁸⁷ᶠ· (iv/B.C.) σφραγὶς ἴασπις χρυσὸν δακτύλ[ιον ἔχοσα,] σφραγὶς ἴασπις περικεχρυσωμένη. The word is Phoenician (Boisacq, p. 364).

Ἰάσων.

For this proper name cf. P Petr I. 19² (B.C. 225) (as read *ib.* III. p. 32) Ἰάσω[ν] Ἀχαιός, *ib.* III. 21 (*h*)² (B.C. 225) ἐπὶ προέδρου Ἰάσονος. *ib.* (.)¹ Ἰάσων Διονύσιος, *Michel* 1203² (ii/B.C.) Ἱεροκλῆς Ἰάσονος, *al.* The name is widely spread, e.g. it is found several times amongst the graffiti at Priene, as in *Priene* 313¹³³: for the bearing of this on Rom 16²¹ cf. Milligan *Thess.* p. 183. On the use of Ἰάσων by the Jews as a substitute for Ἰησοῦς, see Deissmann *BS* p. 315 n².

ἰατρός.

This common noun is found in the curious alphabet acrostic P Tebt II. 278⁹ (early i/A.D.), where ἰατρός is inserted between θωρωκοποῖς ("breast-plate maker") and κλειτοποῖς ("locksmith"). The existence of public physicians in Egypt is well illustrated by P Oxy I. 51⁴ (A.D. 173), the report δημοσίου ἰατροῦ, who had been instructed by the strategus ἐφιδεῖν σῶμα νεκρὸν ἀπηρτημένον, "to inspect the body of a man who had been found hanged": cf. *ib.* 52⁷ (A.D. 325), *ib.* III. 475⁵ (A.D. 182), and BGU II. 647² (A.D. 130) where C. Minucius Valerianus ἔχων ἰατρεῖον ἐπὶ κωμὴν Καράνιδι is charged (παρηγγέλη) by the strategus to inspect the wound of a certain Mystharion. In P Oxy I. 40³ (ii/iii A.D.) we find a man, in view of the fact that he is ἰατρός . . δημοσ[ιεύ]ων ἐπὶ ταρι[χεία, "a doctor officially practising mummification" (Edd.), getting exemption from some form of public service, and similarly P Fay 106 (*c.* A.D. 140) is a petition addressed to the prefect by a physician ὅπως] τέλεον ἀπολύονται τῶν [λειτουρ]γιῶν οἱ τὴν ἰατρικὴν ἐπιστή[μην] μεταχειριζόμενοι, "that those practising the profession of physician be completely exempted from public services." Physicians were thus apparently State officials (cf. *OGIS* 104 n.⁵) and consequently a tax was levied for their maintenance: cf. P Hib I. 102 (B.C. 248), an undertaking to a physician by a military settler to pay by way of ἰατρικόν, ὀλυρ(ῶν) (ἀρτάβας) ι ἢ δραχμὰς τέσσαρας, "10 artabae of wheat or 4 drachmae": see further Wilcken

Ostr. i. p. 375 ff. One of the wall-scratchings at Thebes, *Preisigke* 1852, commemorates a certain Ἱπποκράτης ἰατρός, and a dialect inscr. from Delphi, of the middle of ii/B.C., *Syll* 857¹² is a deed of sale to Apollo Pythius, by which Dionysius manumits Damon, a slave physician, who has apparently been practising in partnership with his master, to judge from the concluding provision—εἰ δὲ χρείαν ἔχοι Διονύσιος, συνιατρευέτω Δάμων μετ' αὐτοῦ ἔτη πέντε, receiving board and lodging and clothes.

As illustrating Mk 5²⁶ we may cite *Preisigke* 1934, an inscr. in the Serapeum at Memphis, recording that Aristullus has set up a votive-offering fearing that the god is not well-disposed towards him—ἐπεὶ καὶ ἰατ]ρείαις χρώμενος τοῖς πε[ρὶ ναὸν ὀνείροις ο]ὐκ ἠδυνάμην ὑγιείας [τυχεῖν παρ' αὐτο]ῦ. For Mt 9¹² Wendland (*HZNT* I. ii p. 44) recalls Diogenes in Stobaeus *Florileg.* III. p. 462¹¹, ed. Hense: οὐδὲ γὰρ ἰατρὸς ὑγιείας ὢν ποιητικὸς ἐν τοῖς ὑγιαίνουσι τὴν διατριβὴν ποιεῖται. P Oxy I. 1 *recto* ¹² contains a new *Logion* ascribed to Jesus—οὐκ ἔστιν δεκτὸς προφήτης ἐν τῇ πατρίδι αὐτ[ο]ῦ, οὐδὲ ἰατρὸς ποιεῖ θεραπείας εἰς τοὺς γινώσκοντας αὐτόν. For Θεόφιλος ἰατρός see *Preisigke* 3780. In *CR* xxxii. p. 2 Sir W. M. Ramsay publishes an interesting Christian inscr. of *c.* A.D. 350 regarding a certain ἀρχιατρός, who in words and deeds acted according to the precepts of Hippocrates. In another inscr. from the same district and period (p. 5) a mother commemorates her son as τ]ὸν σοφὸν ἰητρὸν εἰκοστὸν ἄγοντα ἔτος, "the skilful physician who was in his twentieth year." The art. contains some interesting reff. to the honour in which the profession of medicine was held by Christians of the third and fourth centuries. The verb ἰατρεύω occurs in *Michel* 1250 (ii/B.C.) Μελά[ν]θιος Ἐπιτέλευ ἰατρευθεὶς Ἀσκληπιῶι χαριστήρια. For ἰατρίνη, "midwife," see P Oxy XII. 1586¹² (early iii/A.D.). MGr γιατρός, "physician," γιατρικό[ν], "medicine," γιατρεύω, "I heal."

ἴδε.

For ἴδε = "look out for," see P Ryl II. 239²¹ (mid. iii/A.D.) πανταχόθεν ἴδε αὐτῷ μικρὸν ὀναρίδιον, "look out everywhere for a small donkey for him" (Edd.). The word, as the imper. of εἶδον, was originally accented ἰδέ: cf. Moeris, p. 193 ἰδέ . . Ἀττικῶς . . ὡς τὸ εἰπέ, λαβέ, εὑρέ· MGr [ἰ]δές, δέ[σ]τε.

ἰδέα.

See *s.v.* εἰδέα, and add P Oxy X. 1277³⁰ (A.D. 255) προσκεφάλαια . . λινᾶ τῆς αὐτῆς εἰδαίας (*l.* ἰδέας), "of the same quality" (Edd.), and the magical papyrus P Lond 121⁷⁶⁰ (iii/A.D.) (= I. p. 108) ἵνα πᾶσαν εἰδέαν ἀποτελέσῃς. Note εἰ- for ἰ-, as in Mt 28³, and cf. the cognate forms εἶδος and εἴδωλον. Ἰδέα comes from *Ϝιδεσα (Boisacq, p. 220): see also *s.v.* ἴσος. On the AV translation "countenance" in Mt *l.c.* see Field *Notes*, p. 22. The word in MGr = "thought," "idea."

ἴδιος.

For an "exhausted" ἴδιος in Hellenistic Greek, equivalent to little more than the possessive pronoun, Kuhring (p. 13) cites such passages as BGU IV. 1061²⁵ (B.C. 14) ἐν τῶι ἰδίωι αὐτοῦ κλήρωι, P Oxy III. 483²⁵ (A.D. 108) ὀ]μνύω . . . εἶναι τὰς προκ[ειμ]ένας ἀρούρας εἰδίας μου, *ib.* 494³³

(A.D. 156) ἐγνώρισα τὴν ἰδίαν μου σφραγῖδα, *ib.* 495¹⁵ (A.D. 181-9) γράψω τῇ ἰδίᾳ μου χειρί, BGU III. 865² (ii/A.D.) ἀκολούθω[ς τῇ ἰδ]ίᾳ σοι (*l.* σου) ἐπιστολῇ, *ib.* I. 13¹⁸ (A.D. 289) ἐκδικήσωμεν . . τοῖς ἰδίοις ἑαυτῶν δαπανήμασιν, P Grenf II. 80¹¹ (A.D. 402) ὑπὲρ ἰδίας σου κεφαλῆς. It will hardly be denied, however, that in all these passages ἴδιος adds a certain emphasis, and this undoubtedly holds good of the general NT usage, as e.g. Jn 1¹¹, 1 Cor 3⁸, Gal 6⁵, Heb 7²⁷, etc.: see more particularly *Proleg.* p. 87 ff. (as against Deissmann *BS* p. 123 f.), and cf. Souter (*Lex. s.v.*) where the word is rendered "one's own," "belonging to one," "private," "personal," without any mention of a weaker meaning. Winer-Schmiedel *Gr.* § 22, 17, on the other hand, claims for the word both senses in the NT, and illustrates these in detail. It is probably impossible to draw the line strictly, so much depends on the special *nuance* of the context. Thus in the interesting papyrus in which proceedings are instituted for the recovery of a foundling child that had been put out to nurse, the defendant asserts that the foundling had died, and that the child now claimed was her own child—τὸ] ἴ[δι]όν μου τέκνον (P Oxy I. 37ⁱⁱ·¹—A.D. 49) (= *Selections*, p. 51). But when in P Goodsp Cairo 4⁸ (ii/B.C.) (= *Selections*, p. 25) Polycrates writes to a friend introducing one Glaucias—ἀπεστάλκαμεν πρὸς σὲ Γλαυκίαν, ὄντα ἡμῶν ἴδιον, κοινολογησόμενόν σοι, the meaning can be little more than "who is one of ourselves": cf. P Par 41¹¹ (B.C. 158) οὗ <ἐν> κατοχῇ ἰμὶ μετὰ τοῦ πρεσβυτέρου ἀδελφοῦ ἰδίου (= ἐμοῦ) Πτολεμαίου, P Tor I. 8²⁷ (B.C. 119) εἰς τὰς ἰδίας αὐτῶν (= εἰς τὰς ἑαυτῶν) μετοικισθῆναι (both cited by Mayser *Gr.* p. 308). This last ex. illustrates the absolute use of ὁ ἴδιος as in Jn 1¹¹, 13¹, etc.: cf. also P Oxy XIV. 1680⁵ (iii/iv A.D.), where a son prays for his father—ὑγιαίνοντί (*l.*—τά) σε ἀπολαβεῖν ἐν τοῖς ἰδίοις, "that we may receive you home in good health" (Edd.). On the principle of the ἰδία, involving a man's personal attachment to the house and soil of his birth, see Zulueta in Vinogradoff's *Oxford Studies in Social and Legal History* i. (1909), p. 42 ff., and cf. *Exp* VIII. iv. p. 487 ff., where Ramsay applies this principle in connexion with Lk 2³. In *Proleg.* p. 90 f. special attention is drawn to the use of ὁ ἴδιος in addressing near relations at the beginning of a letter. Thus in P Fay 110² (A.D. 94) Gemellus sends greeting Ἐπαγαθῶι τῶι ἰδίωι, Epagathus being probably a nephew, and similarly in other letters of the same correspondence: when the son Sabinus is addressed, the words τῷ οιείῶι (= τῷ υἱῷ) are always used, as *ib.* 113² (A.D. 100). If this were at all a normal use of ὁ ἴδιος it might add something to the case for translating Ac 20²⁸ τοῦ αἵματος τοῦ ἰδίου, "the blood of one who was His own" (Weiss, etc.).

For the adv. ἰδίᾳ (for form cf. Moulton *Gr.* ii. p. 84) = "privately," see PSI IV. 434¹² (B.C. 261-0) ἰδίαι συμφωνήσας πρὸς αὐτούς, and cf. *Michel* 392⁷ (ii B.C.) καὶ κοινῆι τῆι πόλ[ει] καὶ καθ' ἰδίαν τοῖς ἐντυγχάνουσ[ιν] αὐτῶι. The phrase ἐκ τοῦ ἰδίου, "at one's own expense," is found in BGU IV. 1118³¹ (B.C. 22), and similarly ἐξ ἰδίων in *ib.* 1209¹¹ (B.C. 23).

Brugmann derives from *Ϝίδιος: cf. skr. *vi*, "en séparant" (Boisacq, p. 221). The adj. therefore implies "sequestrated from the common stock." MGr ἴδιος and γίδιος: ὁ ἴδιος, "the same," "self": cf. ἰδιότητα, "identity."

ἰδιώτης.

In *Syll* 847[16] (Delphi— B.C. 185) the witnesses to a manumission are the priest, two representatives of the ἄρχοντες, and five ἰδιῶται, "private citizens": cf. *ib*. 846[8] (B.C. 197) and *OGIS* 90[52] (B.C. 196) where again a distinction is drawn between ἱερεῖς and οἱ ἄλλοι ἰδιῶται. In connexion with the difficult 1 Cor 14[16. 23], Thieme (p. 32) cites *Magn* 99[26] (beg. ii/B.C.) φερόμενον ὑπὸ τῶν [ἰ]διωτῶν, where the word may have some reference to worship at the founding of a sanctuary in honour of Serapis, but the context is far from clear. In P Fay 19[12] (ii/A.D.) the Emperor Hadrian refers to his father's having died at the age of forty—ἰδιώτης, "a private person," and in P Oxy XII. 1409[14] (A.D. 278) we read of overseers chosen—ἐξ ἀρχόντων ἢ καὶ ἰδιωτῶν, "from magistrates or private persons": cf. P Ryl II. 111(a)[17] (census-return—c. A.D. 161) ἰδιώ(της) λαογραφούμενο⟨ς⟩, "a private person paying poll-tax." The adj. ἰδιωτικός is similarly used with reference to a private bank—ἰδιωτικὴ τράπεζα—in P Lond 1168[21] (A.D. 18) (= III. p. 137), and in *ib*. 932[8] (A.D. 211) (= III. p. 149) with reference to δάνεια ἤτοι ἰδιωτικὰ ἢ δημόσια: cf. the Will, P Tebt II. 381[15] (A.D. 123) (= *Selections*, p. 79), where Thaesis bequeaths her property to her daughter on condition that she discharges her private debts—διευλυτώσει ὧν ἐὰν φανῆι ἡ Θαῆσις ὀφίλουσα ἰδιοτικῶν χρεῶν, and BGU V. 1210[196] (c. A.D. 150) Παστοφόρο[ις] ἐξὸν ἰδιωτικῶν ἐφίεσθαι τάξεων, "Pastophoren ist es erlaubt, nach Laienstellungen zu streben" (Ed.). See further Preisigke *Fachworter*, p. 101. To the rare use of ἰδιώτης to denote absence of military rank, a private, in P Hib I. 30[21] (B.C. 300-271) and *ib*. 89[7] (B.C. 239), we can now add P Hamb I. 26[11] (B.C. 215). In contrast to rhetoricians and philosophers, Epictetus describes himself as ἰδιώτης (iii. 7. 1, *al*.): cf. 2 Cor 11[6], and see Epict. iii. 9. 14 οὐδὲν ἦν ὁ Ἐπίκτητος, ἐσολοίκιζεν, ἐβαρβάριζεν (cited by Heinrici *Litt. Char.* p. 2).

ἰδού.

Moulton (*Proleg.* p. 11) has shown that the frequency with which ἰδού (originally the imper. of εἰδόμην and accented ἰδοῦ) is used by certain NT writers is due to the fact that they were accustomed to the constant use of an equivalent interjection in their own tongue: cf. Wellhausen *Einl.*[2] p. 22. As showing, however, that the interjection was used in the Κοινή where no Hebraistic influence is predicable, we may cite P Oxy VII. 1066[5] (iii/A.D.) εἰδ[ο]ὺ οὖν ἀπέστιλά σοι αὐτήν, with reference to the return of a file, *ib*. 1069[11] (very illiterate—iii/A.D.) εἰδοὺ γὰρ καὶ τὸ πορφύρειν μετὰ τῶν συ[ν]έργων κεῖντε, "see, the purple is put with the tools" (cf. l.[6]), *ib*. X. 1291[7] (A.D. 30) οὐδ[εὶ]ς μοι ἤνεγκεν ἐπιστολὴν περὶ ἄρτων, ἀλλ' εὐθέως, ἡ (= εἰ) ἔπεμψας διὰ Κολλούθου ἐπιστολή, εἰδοὺ ἀρτάβηι σοι γίνεται, "no one has brought me a letter about the bread, but if you send a letter by Colluthus, an artaba will come to you immediately" (Edd.), *ib*. 1295[3] (ii/iii A.D.) ἰδοὺ μὲν ἐγὼ οὐκ ἐμιμησάμην σε τοῦ ἀπ(οσπ)ᾶν τὸν υἱόν μου, "see, I have not imitated you by taking away my son" (Edd.). A curious verbal parallel to Lk 13[16] occurs in the Christian letter BGU III. 948[6] (iv/v A.D.) γινώσκιν ἐ[θ]έλω ὅτι εἰπέν σοι ὁ πραγματευτ[ὴς ὅ]τι . . ἡ μήτηρ σου Κοφαηνα ἀσθενῖ, εἰδού, δέκα τρῖς μῆνες: cf. P Oxy I. 131[12] (vi/vii A.D.) καὶ ἰδοὺ

τρία ἔτη σήμερον ἀπ' ὅτε ἀπέθανεν. For ἰδού followed by a noun in the nom. without a finite verb, as in Lk 22[38], cf. an old Attic inser. ἰδοὺ χελίδων, cited by Meisterhans *Gr.* p. 203, § 84, 2. See also Epict. iv. 11. 35 ἰδοὺ νέος ἀξιέραστος, ἰδοὺ πρεσβύτης ἄξιος τοῦ ἐρᾶν καὶ ἀντερᾶσθαι (cited by Sharp *Epict.* p. 109). MGr ἐδῶ, "here": cf. the French *ici* from the popular Lat. *ecce hic*.

ἱδρώς.

This word, which in the NT is confined to Lk 22[11] ℵ* D (cf. Hobart, p. 82), may be illustrated from the magic P Lond 46[162] (iv/A.D.) (= I. p. 70) ἐγώ εἰμι οὗ ἐστιν ὁ ἰδρὼς ὄμβρος ἐπιπείπτων ἐπὶ τὴν γήν. In *ib*. 402 *verso*[15] (ii/B.C.) (= II. p. 11) we read of ἱδρώια παλ(αιά), perhaps, as the editor suggests, "old sweaters": the same word may be lurking in P Tebt I. 116[34] (late ii/B.C.) τι(μῆς) ἱδροίων β ὦμ, and in P Goodsp Cairo 30[iii 22] (A.D. 191-2) ἱδρώων ϛ, cf. Mayser *Gr.* p. 137. For the derived meaning see P Amh II. 40[17] (ii/B.C.) μετὰ πολλοῦ ἱδρῶτος, "by great exertions" (Edd.): cf. Lat. *multo sudore*. The verb, as in 4 Macc 3[8], 6[11], Didache i. 6, occurs in P Oxy X. 1242[52] (early iii/A.D.) ἡ τοῦ Σαράπιδος προτομὴ . . αἰφνίδιον ἱδρωσεν, "the bust of Sarapis suddenly sweated": cf. Verg. *Georg.* i. 480 et maestum inlacrimat templis ebur aeraque sudant. MGr ἵδρος, ἱδρῶτας, with the verb ἱδρώνω or δρώνω.

Ἰεζάβελ.

Schürer's suggestion (*Theol. Abhandlungen Weizsacker gewidmet*, p. 39 ff.) that the Jezebel or Isabel of Rev 2[20] was the local prophetess of the shrine of Sambethe the Chaldean Sibyl at Thyatira (cf. *CIG* 3509), which led to Nestle's highly doubtful identification of the names Isabel and Sibyl (*Berl. Phil. Woch.* 1904, p. 764 ff.), has not been received with much favour (see e.g. Bousset and Moffatt *ad l.*). On the proposed etymologies of the Heb. name see *EB* 2457, and for form Zezabel see Souter *ad* Rev 2[20].

Ἱεράπολις.

Schürer in Hastings *DB* v. p. 94 cites three Jewish inscrr. from *Alterthumer von Hierapolis* (in *Jahrbuch des deutschen Archäol. Instituts*, Ergänzungsheft iv.), pointing to the presence of a considerable Jewish community in Hierapolis —(1) No. 69 a tomb-inser. closing with the threat: εἰ δὲ μή, ἀποτείσει τῷ λαῷ τὸν Ἰουδα⟨ί⟩ω]ν προστε(ί)μου ὀν[όμ]ατι δηνάρια χείλια, (2) No. 212 (= *Cagnat* IV. 834) another tomb-inser. ending: εἰ δὲ ἔτι ἕτερος κηδεύσει, δώσει τῇ κατοικίᾳ τῶν ἐν Ἱεραπόλει κατοικούντων Ἰουδαίων προστείμου (δηνάρια) . . καὶ τῷ ἐκζητήσαντι (δηνάρια) (δισχίλια) ἀντίγραφον ἀπετέθη ἐν τῷ ἀρχίῳ τῶν Ἰουδαίων, and (3) No. 342 (= *C. and B.* ii. p. 545) an inscr. in memory of a certain Publius Aelius Glykon, who bequeathed to the managing body of purple-dyers (τῇ σεμνοτάτῃ προεδρίᾳ τῶν πορφυραβάφων) a capital sum, the interest of which was to be applied yearly ἐν τῇ ἑορτῇ τῶν Ἀζύμων to decorate his tomb. Cf. Ramsay *Exp* VI. v. p. 95 ff., and see the same writer's *C. and B.* ii. p. 679 ff. for Hieropolis as the local form of the city's name. On the separation into Ἱερᾷ Πόλει in Col 4[13] (cf. Ac 16[11]), see Moulton *Gr.* ii. § 61 (b).

ἱερατεία(-τία)

of the actual service of a priest (Lk 1⁹, Heb 7⁵) as distinguished from the more abstract ἱερωσύνη (Heb 7¹¹ ᵃˡ.), may be illustrated from *Priene* 139⁷ (before B.C. 335) περὶ τῆς δίκης τῆς γενομένης περὶ τῆς ἱερατείης τοῦ Διός. The distinction, however, frequently disappears : cf. e.g. P Tebt II. 298¹¹ (A.D. 107–8) where certain priests pay 52 drachmae ὑπὲρ . . τῆς ἱερατεία[ς, *Syll* 601⁵ (iii/B.C.) ὁ] πριάμε[νο]ς [τὴ]ν ἱερητείαν τῆς Ἀρτέμιδος τῆς Περγαίας πα[ρέξ]εται ἱέρειαν ἀστὴν κτλ., and *OGIS* 90⁵² (Rosetta stone—B.C. 196) καὶ καταχωρίσαι εἰς πάντας τοὺς χρηματισμοὺς . . . [τὴν] ἱερατείαν αὐτοῦ, "and that his priesthood shall be entered upon all formal documents" (Mahaffy). See further *s.v.* ἱερωσύνη.

The adj. ἱερατικός is used of "priestly" descent in P Tebt II. 293¹³ (*c.* A.D. 187) ἐ]πιζητοῦντί σοι εἰ ἔστιν ἱ[ερα]τικοῦ [γέ]νους, and in *ib.* 291⁴⁸ (A.D. 162) where a priest claims to be γένους ἱερατικ[ο]ῦ on the ground of his knowledge of hieratic and Egyptian writing ⁴¹ ᶠᶠ· ἀπ]όδειξιν δοὺς τοῦ ἐπίστασθαι [ἱε]ρατικὰ [καὶ] Αἰγύπτια γράμ[ματ]α ἐξ ἧς οἱ ἱερογραμματεῖς προήνεγκαν βίβλον ἱερατικῆς.

ἱεράτευμα.

No ex. of this subst. has yet been found outside Biblical and ecclesiastical Greek, but cf. *OGIS* 51¹¹ (iii/B.C.) ἐκτενῶς ἑαυτὸν συνεπιδιδοὺς εἰς τὸ συναύξεσθαι τὸ τεχνίτευμα, where τεχνίτευμα seems to be used in the same collective sense of a "body" of artificers, as ἱεράτευμα of a "body" of priests in 1 Pet 2⁹ : in *ib.*⁵ Hort *ad l.* gives good reason for preferring the meaning "act or office of priesthood." His whole note on this group of words should be consulted.

ἱερατεύω.

Early evidence for this word from the inscrr. is afforded by *OGIS* 90⁶¹ (Rosetta stone—B.C. 196) τῶν θεῶν ὧν ἱερατεύσουσιν, *Magn* 178⁶ (ii/B.C.) ἱέραιαν Ἀρτέμιδος Λευκοφρυηνῆς ἱερατεύσασαν, *Priene* 177 (ii/B.C.) Ἀθηνόπολις Κυδίμου ἱερητεύων (for the form cf. Thumb *Hellen.* p. 68) Διονύσωι, etc. The writers of the LXX and Luke (1⁸) were, therefore, only applying to the rites of the Jewish religion a term already current in the pagan world : see further Deissmann *BS* p. 215 f., *Anz Subsidia*, p. 370 f., Thieme, p. 15, Rouffiac *Recherches*, p. 66 f., and Poland *Vereinswesen*, p. 347 n². The only example we can cite from the papyri is P Giss I. 11¹⁰ (A.D. 118) ὥστε εἱερατεύειν τοῦ χειρεισμοῦ τῶν κυβερνητ(ῶν), where see the editor's note : the gen., which is similar to that after ἐπιμελοῦμαι, κήδομαι, ἐπισταῶ, etc., is sometimes varied by the *dat. commodi* as in *Priene* 177 (*supra*).

ἱερεύς.

It is unnecessary to illustrate at length this very common word, but reference may be made to the complaint in BGU I. 16 (A.D. 159–60) (= *Selections*, p. 83 f.) which five presbyter-priests (οἱ ε πρεσβύτεροι ἱερεῖς) lodge against a brother-priest (συνιερεύς) "of letting his hair grow too long and of wearing woollen garments"—ὡς κομῶντος [κ]αὶ χρω[μ]ένου ἐρεαῖς ἐσθήσεσι. On the popular use of ἱερεύς to designate a bishop or presbyter in Christian inscrr. of iv/A.D.

see Ramsay *Luke*, p. 387, and for the fem. ἱέρεια = "wife of a *hiereus*" see *ib.* p. 365. This last is found joined with ἱέρισσα in P Lond 880⁷ (B.C. 113) (= III. p. 8), *al.* For the verb ἱεράω cf. *Chrest.* I. 72⁹ (A.D. 234) μηδένα δὲ τῶν ἱερέω[ν ἢ] ἱερωμένων ἐνκαταλελοιπέναι τὰς [θρ]ησκείας, where, however, the meaning is far from clear : see Wilcken's note. See also the interesting libellus of a heathen ἱέρεια in *Chrest.* I. 125 (A.D. 250).

ἱερόθυτος.

For this late word (for the class. ἱερεῖα θεόθυτα) see the citation from *Syll* 653 *s.v.* δερμάτινος. We hear of ἱεροθύται, "sacrificing priests," in connexion with the ceremonial at marriages, e.g. in P Fay 22³ (i/A.D.) : see further Schubart *Archiv* v. p. 77 ff. For ἱεροποιός, "a sacrificial magistrate," cf. P Oxy XIV. 1664²⁰ (iii/A.D.) with the editors' note.

ἱερόν.

In P Tebt I. 59¹¹ (B.C. 99) a certain Posidonius writes to the priests at Tebtunis assuring them of his good will—διὰ τὸ ἄνωθεν φοβεῖσθαι καὶ σέβεσθαι τὸ ἱερόν, "because of old I have revered and worshipped the temple." The reference, as the editors point out, is to the temple of Soknebtunis, the principal temple at Tebtunis ; on other ἐλάσσονα or δεύτερα ἱερά, see their introduction to *ib.* 88 (B.C. 115–4) (= *Chrest.* I. 67), a list of no fewer than thirteen shrines belonging to the village of Kerkeosiris. Many shrines in Egypt were privately owned, cf. *ib.* 14¹⁸ note. For a convenient list of epithets applied to ἱερά, see Otto *Priester* ii. p. 373, and for a ἱερὸς οἶκος at Priene, used for mystic rites, see Rouffiac *Recherches*, p. 62 : at the entrance was the inscr.—

Εἰσίναι εἰς [τὸ]
ἱερὸν ἁγνὸν ἐ[ν]
ἐσθῆτι λευκ[ῆι].

It may be convenient to reproduce here in full the famous inscr., discovered in 1871, warning Gentiles against penetrating into the inner courts of the Temple at Jerusalem :— *OGIS* 598 (i/A.D.) μηθένα ἀλλογενῆ εἰσπορεύεσθαι ἐντὸς τοῦ περὶ τὸ ἱερὸν τρυφάκτου καὶ περιβόλου ("within the screen and enclosure surrounding the sanctuary") ὃς δ᾽ ἂν ληφθῇ, ἑαυτῶι αἴτιος ἔσται διὰ τὸ ἐξακολουθεῖν θάνατον : see also *s.v.* ἀλλογενής and Deissmann *LAE* p. 74 ff.

ἱεροπρεπής.

The meaning which Souter (*Lex. s.v.*) gives to this adj. (not found in Attic writers) in its only occurrence in the NT (Tit 2³ : cf. 4 Macc 9²⁵, 11²⁰) "like those employed in sacred service," is supported by Dibelius (*HZNT ad l.*), who cites an inscr. from Foucart *Associations religieuses*, p. 240, No. 66³· ¹³ ἱεροπρεπῶς καὶ φιλοδόξως of certain religious functions : cf. also *Michel* 163²¹ (Delos—B.C. 148–7) τὰς θυσίας . . . καλῶς καὶ ἱεροπρεπῶ[ς] συνετέλεσεν, *Priene* 109²¹⁶ (*c.* B.C. 120) προεπόμπευσεν . . ἱεροπρεπῶς. For the adj. see Dio Cass. lvi. 46, and for ἱερόδουλος see *s.v.* δουλεύω, and cf. P Hib I. 35⁵ (*c.* B.C. 250) οἱ λοιποὶ ἱερόδουλοι διατελο[ῦ]μεν τοὺς φόρους εὐτακτοῦντες εἰς τὸ ἱερόν, with the editors' note.

ἱερός.

This adj., which remains unchanged in MGr, is very common in the inscrr. with reference to heathen temples, sacred revenues, and sacrificial and other rites. With the use in 2 Tim 3[15] we may compare the νόμοι ἱεροὶ καὶ ἀραί by which the temple of Jupiter at Magnesia was protected against harm : see *Magn* 105[53] (ii/A.D.) as cited by Thieme p. 36. See also *s.vv.* βίβλος and γράμμα, and for the protection afforded by the "sacred" area see *s.v.* βωμός, and the note on PSI V. 515[15]. The βῆμα of the Prefect of Egypt is described in P Hamb I. 4[3] (A.D. 87) as ἱερώτατον : cf. P Lond 358[19] (c. A.D. 150) (= II. p. 172), and BGU II. 613[19] (time of Anton. Pius). See also P Oxy IX. 1211[1] (ii/A.D.) τὰ πρὸς τὴν θυσίαν τοῦ ἱερωτάτου Νείλου. The adj. is found in the title of an athletic club in P Lond 1178[16] (A.D. 194) (= III. p. 217, *Selections*, p. 99) ἡ ἱερὰ ξυστικὴ περιπολιστικὴ . . . σύνοδος, "the Worshipful Gymnastic Club of Nomads." For ἱερὰ νόσος = "epilepsy" cf. P Oxy I. 91[11] (A.D. 83). 95[19] (A.D. 129) and the other passages collected by Modica *Introduzione*, p. 146. The word is used in the address of a Christian letter, P Oxy XII. 1492[1] (iii/iv A.D.) χα[ῖ]ρε, ἱερ[ὲ υἱέ, also *ib. verso* and 1592[7].

Ἱεροσόλυμα.

This Greek neut. plur. form of the Hebraic Ἰερουσαλήμ is found in the important P Leid W[xxiii.18] (ii/iii A.D.) τὸ μέγα (ὄνομα) τὸ ἐν Ἱεροσολύμοις. It lies outside our purpose to discuss the usage of the two forms in the NT, but, as showing that a real distinction was present to the minds of Lk and Paul, reference may be made to Harnack *Acts*, p. 76 ff., Ramsay, *Exp* VII. iii. pp. 110 ff., 414 f., and Bartlet, *ExpT* xiii. p. 157 f. But see *contra* the elaborate paper by Schütz in *ZNTW* xi. (1910) p. 169 ff. WH (*Intr.*[2] p. 13) refuse the rough breathing as due to a "false association with ἱερός," but cf. Moulton *Gr.* ii. p. 101. The fem. πᾶσα Ἱεροσόλυμα, as in Mt 2[3], cf. Tobit 14[4] B, is found in *Pelagia-Legenden*, p. 14[14]. Have we here an anticipation of the MGr indeclinable πᾶσα? queries Blass-Debrunner, § 56, 3.

ἱεροσυλέω

is used in its literal sense of robbing temples in *Syll* 237[8,19] (end of iii/B.C.) ἐξήλεγξαν τοὺς ἱεροσυληκότας . . . καὶ τὰ ἄλλα ἃ αὐτοὶ ἐκτημέν[οι] ἦσαν οἱ ἱεροσυλήσαντες ἱερὰ ἐγένοντο τῶι θεῶι, with reference to those who had stolen part of the Phocians' ἀνάθεμα at Delphi. Cf. also Pseudo-Heracleitus *Ep.* 7, p. 64 (Bernays) φίλους φαρμακεύσαντες. ἱεροσυλήσαντες. It is probable, however, that the word, which is here used with special reference to Ephesus, should be understood in the wider sense of "doing sacrilege," as in the RV margin of Rom 2[22], the only place where it occurs in the NT : see, in addition to the commentators on this passage, *ZNTW* ix. p. 167 and *s.v.* ἱερόσυλος.

ἱερόσυλος.

The wider sense, which we have seen the corresponding verb has in Rom 2[22] (see *s.v.* ἱεροσυλέω), also attaches to ἱερόσυλος in Ac 19[37] (cf. 2 Macc 4[42]), where Ramsay (Hastings' *DB* i. p. 441) understands οὔτε ἱεροσύλους οὔτε βλασφημοῦντας τὴν θεάν as implying "guilty neither in act

nor in language of disrespect to the established religion of our city" : see further *CRE*[5] p. 260, and Lightfoot *Essays on Supernatural Religion*, p. 299 f., who cites an inscr. found in this very temple of Ephesus, though of a later date than the passage in Acts,—ἔστω ἱεροσυλία καὶ ἀσέβεια, "let it be regarded as sacrilege and impiety" (Wood *Inscr.* vi. I, p. 14). Other exx. of the adj. from the inscrr. are *Syll* 523[19] (iii/B.C.) ὁ δὲ εἴ]πας ἢ [πρήξ]ας τι παρὰ τόνδε τὸν νόμον . . . ἔστω ἱερόσυλος, *ib.* 602[8] (iv/iii B.C.) ἢν δέ τις [τὴν στήλην] ἀφαν[ίζηι ἢ τὰ γράμματα], πασχέτω ὡς ἱερόσυλος, and *ib.* 680[19] (Rom.). The new Menander shows several exx. of ἱερόσυλε used in abuse with a general sense (cf. "horse-thief") : e.g. *Menandrea*, p. 60[333] ἱερ[ό]συλε παῖ, p. 38[21] ἱερόσυλε γραῦ.

ἱερουργέω

should receive the full force of "sacrifice" in Rom 15[16], the only place where it occurs in the NT : cf. Field *Notes*, p. 165 and SH *ad l.* The subst. is used in the wider sense of "a sacred function" in P Tebt II. 203[29] (c. A.D. 187) a report on an application for circumcision—διὰ [τ]ὸ μὴ δύνασθαι τὰς ἱε[ρου]ργίας ἐκτελεῖν εἰ μὴ τοῦτ[ο γενήσετα]ι, *ib.* 294[4] (A.D. 146) ἵνα καὶ αἱ ὀφίλ[ο]υσαι ἱερουργίαι τῶν σε φιλούντων θεῶν ἐπιτελῶνται : cf. also P Par 69[E.14] (A.D. 233) συ]νηθῶν ἱερουργιῶν Δι[ὶ . . . . γει]νομένων. In *Syll* 644[3] (end of iii/B.C.) reference is made τοῖς ἱερουργοῖς τῆς Ἀθηνᾶς τῆς Ἰτωνίας, who are described by Dittenberger as "collegium eorum qui sacris Minervae Itoniae intererant."

Ἱερουσαλήμ.

See *s.v.* Ἱεροσόλυμα.

ἱερωσύνη.

The older form of this word was ἱερεωσύνη (from ἱερεύς), e.g. *OGIS* 56[23] (B.C. 237) τὴν ἱερεωσύνην τῶν Εὐεργετῶν θεῶν, see Dittenberger's note and cf. Mayser *Gr.* pp. 15, 154. For ἱερωσύνη = "the priestly office," as in Heb 7[11 al.] cf. *Priene* 174[2] (ii/B.C.) ἐπὶ τοῖσδε πωλοῦμεν τὴν ἱερωσύνην τοῦ Διονυσίου τοῦ Φλέου, *ib.* 205[2] (iii/A.D.) ἔλαχε τὴν ἱερωσύν[ην] Ἀναξίδημος Ἀπολλων[ίου, *Michel* 704[15] (ii/B.C.) ἐπρίατο τὴν ἱερωσύνην Τίμ[αιος, *ib.* 977[13] (B.C. 298-7) τὴν ἱερωσύνην ἀξίως ἱερεώσατο τοῦ θεοῦ. *ib.* 981[7] (B.C. 219-8) καλῶς καὶ εὐσεβῶς τὴν ἱερωσύνην ἐξήγαγεν. See also *s.v.* ἱερατεία, and for the abstract suffix—σύνη see *s.v.* ἀγαθωσύνη.

Ἰησοῦς.

As showing that the name Ἰησοῦς, the Greek form of the Hebrew Joshua, was widely spread amongst the Jews both before and after the beginning of the Christian era, we may cite such passages as P Oxy IV. 816, the fragment of an account written before the end of i/B.C., where]s Ἰσιδώρου καὶ Ἰησοῦς occurs ; P Lond 1119a[2] (a census-return—A.D. 105) (= III. p. 25) τῆς Ἰησοῦτος μητ(ρὸς) Τα[; and an ostrakon of A.D. 103-4 registering the poll-tax of a Jew described as Σαμβαθίω(ν) ὁ καὶ Ἰησοῦς Παπίου *Archiv* vi. p. 220 : cf. Meyer *Ostr.* p. 150 with Deissmann's note). In the magical P Par 574[1233] (iii/A.D.) (= *Selections*, p. 113) Ἰησοῦς πι Χριστὸς πι ἅγιος ν πνεῦμα, "Jesus the Christ, the holy one, the spirit," is invoked to drive the demon out f a man ; and later in the same papyrus, ³⁰¹⁹ ᶠ·, an exorcism begins—ὁρκίζω σε κατὰ τοῦ θυ τῶν Ἑβραίων Ἰησοῦ · Ιαβα · Ιαη · Αβραωθ, where Deissmann thinks that the name *Jesu* can hardly be part of the original formula. "It was probably inserted by some pagan : no Christian, still less a Jew, would have called Jesus 'the god of the Hebrews'" (*LAE* p. 256, n.⁴). On the declension of Ἰησοῦς, see Moulton *Proleg.*, p. 49, and on the use of the art. before Ἰησοῦς, see von Soden *Schriften des NT* I. 2, p. 1406 f. The omission by so many scribes of the name Ἰησοῦν before Βαραββᾶν in Mt 27¹⁶ᶠ· can doubtless be explained on the ground brought forward by Origen, "ut ne nomen Jesu conveniat alicui iniquorum." And the same reason probably lies at the root of the variants for Βαρισοῦς in Ac 13⁶ (see Wendt in Meyer's *Kommentar*⁸ *ad l.* as cited by Deissmann *Urgeschichte*, p. 24). On the possibility that in Ac 17¹⁸ the Athenians thought that Paul was proclaiming a new god of healing, Ἰησοῦς, see an interesting note by Mr. A. B. Cook in Chase *Credibility of the Acts*, p. 205, where it is suggested that there may have been some confusion with Isis, whose name was later derived from Hebr. *iasa* = "salvavit" (Roscher, *Lex. d. Mythologie*, II. i. 522. 42). "She bore the title σώτειρα (*ibid.* 46), and was credited with the discovery of the drug ἀθανασία (Diod. i. 25)." It should be noted, however, that the explanatory clause in Ac 17¹⁸ is omitted by D : cf. Ramsay *Paul*, p. 242. On the contractions IC, IHC, in MSS., as a sign of sanctity, see Traube *Nomina Sacra*, p. 113 ff., and on the Lat. forms Hiesus–Ihesus, see a note by Nestle in *ZNTW* ix. (1908), p. 248 ff. Reference may also be made to Deissmann's monograph *Die neutestamentliche Formel "in Christo Jesu,"* Marburg, 1892.

ἱκανός.

P Petr II. 20 ⁱⁱ·⁷ (B.C. 252) καὶ ταῦτα ἱκανοῦ τινος πλήθους [ἐπ]ιπεπτωκότος ἀπό τε τοῦ ἀγοραστοῦ καὶ τοῦ φορικοῦ, "and this when a large quantity of market and tax wheat has come in" (Ed.), P Lille I. 3⁷⁶ (after B.C. 241) ἱκανὰ πλήθη, "des sommes considérables" (Ed.), P Tebt I. 24³ (B.C. 117) ἱκανὰ κεφάλαια, *ib.* 20¹² (*c.* B.C. 110) ἱκανῆς φορολογίας, and *Michel* 308¹⁶ (first half ii/B.C.) ἱκανά τινα λυσιτελῆ περιπεπόηκεν, *Cagnat* IV. 914⁵ (A.D. 74) ἱ]κανὸν ἀ[ρ]γύριον. With reference to *time* cf. P Par 15²⁹ (B.C. 120) ἐφ' ἱκανὸν χρόνον, P Tor I. 1ⁱⁱ·¹⁵ (B.C. 117) ἐφ' ἱκανὰς ἡμέρας. For the word of persons see P Oxy XIV. 1672¹⁵ (i/A.D.) ἐπιγνοὺς [οὗ]ν τὸν παρὰ σοὶ ἀέρα ἱκανὸς ἔσῃ περὶ πάντων, and for its absolute use, as in Ac 12¹², 1 Cor 11³⁰, see *Chrest.* I. 11B Fr. (a)¹⁰ (B.C. 123) εἰς τ[ὴ]ν πόλιν ἐπιβαλόντες μ[ετὰ τ]ῶν ἱκανῶν καὶ ἱ[ππ]έων [these two words are inserted above the line] περιεκάθισαν ἡμῶν τὸ φρούριον : cf. P Tebt I. 41¹³ (*c.* B.C. 119) ἱκανῶν ἡμῶν, "many of us" (Edd.), and P Oxy I. 44⁸ (late i/A.D.) ὡς ἱκανὰ βλαπτομένων, "on the plea that they had incurred sufficient loss already" (Edd.). The neut. ἱκανόν is common = "bail," "security," e.g. P Oxy II. 294²³ (A.D. 22) ἐὰν μή τι πίσωσι τὸν ἀρχιστάτορα δο[ῦν]αι ἱκανὸν ἕως ἐπὶ διαλογισμόν, "unless indeed they persuade the chief usher to give security for them until the session" (Edd.), BGU II. 530²⁸ (i/A.D.) (= *Selections*, p. 62) ἀπαιτεῖται ὑπὸ τῶν πρακτόρων ἱκανόν "security is demanded by the tax-gatherers," P Ryl II. 77³⁰ (A.D. 192) κελεύσατε ὃ ἔδωκα ἱκανὸν ἀνεθῆναι, "order the bail which I provided to be released" (Edd.), P Strass I.

41⁵¹ (A.D. 250) Ἀντ[ω]νῖ[νος] ῥήτωρ εἶπεν · 'Ἱκανὸν διδόασιν.' Ἑρμανοῦβις εἶπεν · 'Ἱκανὰ [παρ]ασχέτωσαν' : cf. also the new verb ἱκανοδοτέω = *satis do* in P Oxy II. 259²⁹ (A.D. 23) and ἱκανοδότης in BGU IV. 1189³ (about the end of i/B.C.). For τὸ ἱκανὸν ποιεῖν, as in Mk 15¹⁵, cf. BGU IV. 1141¹³ (B.C. 14) ἐάν σοι Ἔρως τὸ ἱκανὸν ποήσῃ γράψον μοι, P Giss I. 40ⁱ·⁵ (A.D. 212) τὸ ἱκανὸν ποι[εῖν, and for τὸ ἱκανὸν λαμβάνειν, as in Ac 17⁹, cf. *OGIS* 484⁵⁰ (ii/A.D.) τὸ ἱκαν[ὸν πρὸ κρίσ]εως λ[α]μβάνεσθαι, *ib.* 629¹⁰¹ (ii/A.D.) οὗ[τος τ]ὸ ἱκανὸν λαμβανέτω. On the Latinisms involved in these phrases see *Proleg.* p. 20 f. The thought of "sufficient in ability," as in 2 Cor 2¹⁶, is seen in P Tebt I. 37¹⁸ (B.C. 73) ἐγὼ οὖν περισπώμενος (cf. Lk 10⁴⁰) περὶ ἀναγκαίων γέγραφά σοι ἵνα ἱκανὸς γένῃ, "therefore, as I am occupied with urgent business, I have written to you so that you may undertake the matter" (Edd.). MGr ἱκανός, "ready," "able." For the adverb see P Petr III. 53(n)³ (iii/B.C.) κἀγὼ δ' ἱκανῶς εἶχον, "I am myself well enough," P Oxy VIII. 1088⁵⁶ (medical prescription—early i/A.D.) ἄλλο ἐνεργὲς ἱκανῶς, "another, tolerably strong," P Tebt II. 411⁶ (ii/A.D.) ὁ γὰρ κράτιστος ἐπιστράτηγος ἱκανῶς σε ἐπεζήτησε, "for his highness the epistrategus has made several inquiries for you" (Edd.).

ἱκανόω.

P Tebt I. 20⁸ (B.C. 113) ἐὰν λογάρια ἀπαιτῶνται ἱκανωθῆναί σε μέχρι τοῦ με παραγενέ[σθαι, "if accounts are demanded consider that you have full powers until my arrival" (Edd.). See also Anz *Subsidia*, p. 353.

ἱκετηρία.

With the use of this word in Heb 5⁷ cf. P Tebt II. 326³ (*c.* A.D. 266) ὑπὲρ θυγατρὸς ὀρφανῆς καὶ καταδεοῦς τὴν ἡλικίαν, δέσποτα ἡγεμών, ἱκετηρίαν τιθεμένη ἐπὶ τὸ σὸν μέγεθος καταφεύγω, "on behalf of my orphan daughter who is under age, my lord praefect, I make this supplication and take refuge in your power" (Edd.), P Oxy I. 71ⁱ·³ (A.D. 303) τὴν ἱκ[ετ]ηρίαν προσάγω εὔελπις ὢν τῆς ἀπὸ τοῦ σοῦ μεγέθους δικαιοκρισίας τυχεῖν, "I make my petition to you with full confidence that I shall obtain justice from your highness" (Edd.), *Syll* 666³ (ii/B.C.) ὑπὲρ ὧν ὁ ἱερεὺς τῆς Ἴσιος ἔθετο τὴν ἱκετηρίαν ἐν τῆι βουλῆι κτλ. For a similar use of ἱκετεία (cf. Sir 32¹⁴ ᵃˡ·) cf. P Petr II. 19 (1a)² (iii/B.C.) μετὰ δεήσεως καὶ ἱκετείας, P Par 39⁹ (B.C. 161) δέομαι ὑμῶν μεθ' ἱκετείας : see also *ib.* 68ᶜ·²⁰ (ii/A.D.) ἱκεσίους σοι χεῖρας.

ἰκμάς.

For the medical usage of this word, which in the NT is confined to Lk 8⁶, see Hobart p. 57 f., but contrast Cadbury *Diction.* p. 43, where it is shown that the word occurs in LXX, Joseph, Plut., Luc., and is, therefore, in no way the sole property of medical writers.

Ἰκόνιον.

The old controversy as to whether during the Roman period Iconium belonged to Phrygia or Lycaonia may now be said to have been settled by the discovery of inscriptional evidence showing that during ii-iii/A.D. the inhabitants used the old non-literary Phrygian tongue : see especially Ramsay

Recent Discovery, p. 65 ff. According to Ramsay (p. 75) the Phrygian form of the city name was probably Καοανια. This was hellenized to Κονιον and modified to Ἰκόνιον or Εἰκόνιον "to suggest a connexion with εἰκών, an image, giving rise to a legend about a sacred statue in the city." See also Blass *Gr.* p. 8.

ἱλαρός.

BGU I. 332[12] (ii/iii A.D.) ἱλαρά εἰμι περὶ τῆς σωτηρίας ἡμῶν, P Giss I. 22[9] (time of Trajan) τῆς εὐσεβείας μου ἀ[ναλ]αμβανούσης σε ἀπρός[κοπ]ον καὶ ἱλαρώτατον. Nageli (p. 65 f.) has shown that in the magic papyri ἱλαρός is used practically = the cognate ἵλεως, which appears in Homer as ἱλα[F]ος, e.g. P Lond 46[416] (iv/A.D.) (= I. p. 78) δεῦρο μάκαρ μνήμης τελεσίφρονος υἱὲ μέγιστε σῇ μορφῇ ἱλαρός τε φάνηθι ἱλαρός τ' ἐπιτειλον ἀνθρώπῳ ὁσίῳ μορφήν τ' ἱλαρὸν ἐπιτειλον ἐμοὶ τῷ δεῖνα ὄφρα τε μαντοσύναις ταῖς σαῖς ἀρεταῖσι λάβοιμι, P Leid W[xiv. 10] (ii/iii A.D.) ἔλθε μοι πρόθυμος, ἱλαρός, ἀπήμαντος, and, in accordance further with LXX usage, he finds a similar meaning in 2 Cor 9[7], where the adj. seems to have the force of "gracious," "friendly." In P Leid X[iii. 12] (iii/iv A.D.) it is used of the bright colour of gold which has been cast into a furnace. A new literary reference is provided by P Oxy XI. 1380[127] (early ii/A.D.), where a ἱλαρὰ ὄψις is ascribed to Isis. In *Preisigke* 5510 Ἱλαρά is a proper name.

ἱλαρότης.

For the form ἱλαρία see *Preisigke* 991[6] (A.D. 200) μετὰ πάσης χαρᾶς καὶ ἱλαρίας: cf. Vett. Val. p. 3[27] γέλωτα, ἱλαρίαν, κόσμον.

ἱλάσκομαι.

For this verb = "render propitious to oneself" c. acc. of the person, as in classical Greek, see *Syll* 641[5 ff.] (end of iii/B.C.) ἔχρησεν ὁ θεὸς ἔσεσθαι λώϊον καὶ ἄμεινον αὐτοῖς ἱλασκομένοις καὶ τιμῶσιν . . . Δία Πατρώϊον καὶ Ἀπόλλωνα . . . τιμᾶν δὲ καὶ ἱλάσκεσθαι καὶ Ἀγαθὸν Δαίμωνα Ποσειδωνίου καὶ Γοργίδος, and *Michel* 1211[5] (i/B.C.?) ὁ θεὸς ἐκολάσετο τὸν Ἑρμογένην καὶ εἱλάσετο τὸν θεόν, καὶ ἀπὸ νῦν εὐδοξεῖ: cf. Menander Ἐπιτρέποντες 558 τοῦτον (θεὸν) ἱλάσκου ποῶν | μηδὲν ἄτοπον μηδ' ἀμαθές. A similar use of the compound ἐξιλάσκομαι, which extends to the LXX (Gen 32[20] (Jacob and Esau), Zech 7[2] (God) : cf. Thackeray *Gr.* i. p. 270), is seen in Menander *Fragm.* p. 164, No. 544[6] καὶ τὴν θεὸν | ἐξιλάσαντο τῷ ταπεινοῦσθαι σφόδρα. Both in the LXX (e.g. Ps 78(79)[9]) and NT (Lk 18[13]) ἱλάσκομαι is found in the pass. c. dat. = "be propitious," "be merciful," while the striking use of the verb c. acc. of the thing for which propitiation is made in Heb 2[17] ἱλάσκεσθαι τὰς ἁμαρτίας can be illustrated from the use of the compound not only in such LXX passages as Sir 3[3] al., but in an inscr. belonging to the Imperial period found near Sunium, where in the directions for a sanctuary in honour of the god Mēn Tyrannus, the words occur :— ὃς ἂν δὲ πολυπραγμονήσῃ τὰ τοῦ θεοῦ ἢ περιεργάσηται, ἁμαρτίαν ὀφ(ε)ιλέτω Μηνὶ Τυράννῳ, ἣν οὐ μὴ δύναται ἐξειλάσασθαι (*Syll* 633[14 ff.] : cf. Deissmann *BS*, p. 225). This last ex. from a profane source should perhaps make us careful in not pressing too far the theological implications which are sometimes found in the

grammatical constructions of the verb in Biblical Greek (cf. e.g. Westcott *Epp. of St. John*, p. 83 ff.). According to Boisacq (p. 373) ἱλάσκομαι derives from a reduplicated form *σι–σλα–σκομαι, as ἵλεως represents *σι–σλα–Fος.

ἱλασμός.

On the formation of this and similar substantives in –μός, see Hatzidakis *Einl.* p. 179 f.

ἱλαστήριος.

The meaning of ἱλαστήριον in the important passage Rom 3[25] has been recently fully discussed by Deissmann in *BS* p. 124 ff. and *ZNTW* iv. (1903) p. 193 ff., where he comes to the conclusion that the word must be understood not as a *term. techn.* for the כפֹּרֶת or cover (of the ark of the covenant), but as an adj. = "of use for propitiation," on the analogy of such word-formations as σωτήριον or χαριστήριον with reference to votive offerings. And in support of this view, he is able to appeal, not only as Lightfoot had already done (*Notes on Epistles of St. Paul*, p. 271), to such a passage as Dion Chrys. *Or.* xi. p. 355 ed. Reiske : καταλείψειν γὰρ αὐτοὺς ἀνάθημα κάλλιστον καὶ μέγιστον τῇ Ἀθηνᾷ καὶ ἐπιγράψειν: ἱλαστήριον Ἀχαιὸν τῇ Ἀθηνᾷ τῇ Ἰλιάδι, but to two interesting exx. of the word from the inscrr. of Cos. The first, *Cos* 81, is found on a votive-gift which the people of Cos erected as a ἱλαστήριον for the welfare of the Emperor Augustus — ὁ δᾶμος ὑπὲρ (τ)ᾶς Αὐτοκράτορος Καίσαρος, θεοῦ υἱοῦ, Σεβαστοῦ σωτηρίας θεοῖς ἱλαστήριον. The second, *Cos* 347, which also belongs to the Imperial period, runs—ὁ δᾶμος ὁ Ἀλεντίων . . . . . . Σεβασ[τ]ῷ Διὶ Σ[τ]ρατίῳ ἱλαστήριον, δαμαρχεῦντος Γαΐου Νωρβανοῦ Μοσχίωνο[ς φι]λοκαίσαρος. Nor is this all, but, as he points out, the adjectival use of ἱλαστήριος is now definitely established by the fragment of a philosophical work concerning the gods, P Fay 337[i. 3 ff.] (ii/A.D.) τοῖς θεοῖς εἱλαστη[ρίο]υς (for form cf. εἱλαστήριον Rom 3[25]B*D*)*) θυσίας ἀξιω[θέ ?]ντες ἐπιτελεῖσθαι: cf. 4 Macc 17[22] διὰ . . . τοῦ ἱλαστηρίου θανάτου, where, however, some MSS. read διὰ τοῦ ἱλαστηρίου τοῦ θανάτου αὐτῶν (see SH, p. 88). The theological consequences of the above interpretation cannot be discussed here, but reference may be made, in addition to the commentators, to an art. by C. Bruston in *ZNTW* vii. (1906), p. 77 ff. It should be added, however, that, whatever view is taken of Rom 3[25], in Heb 9[5], the only other place where the word occurs in the NT, ἱλαστήριον must mean "place of propitiation" or "mercy-seat," as in the LXX of the Pentateuch.

ἵλεως.

With Heb 8[12] cf. P Par 51[24] (B.C. 160) (= *Selections*, p. 20) ἐλθέ μοι, θεὰ θεῶν, εἵλεως γινομένη, ἐπάκουσόν μου, ἐλέησον τὰς Διδύμας, and similarly Leid U[vii. 19] (ii/B.C.). See also *OGIS* 383[226] (mid i/B.C.) ἐγὼ πατρῴους ἅπαντας θεοὺς . . . εἵλεως εἰς πᾶσαν χάριν εὔχομαι διαμένειν,[203] παρὰ τῆς ἐμῆς εὐχῆς ἵλεως δαίμονας καὶ θεοὺς πάντας ἔχέτω. For the phrase in Mt 16[22] (cf. LXX Gen 43[23], 2 Kings 20[20], 1 Chr 11[19]) see *Cagnat* I. 107[10] Ἵλεως σοι, ἀλύπι, and *OGIS* 721[10] (iv/A.D.) (= *Letronne* 221) ἵλεως ἡμῖν Πλάτων καὶ ἐνταῦθα, with the other exx. in *Proleg.* p. 240, where the deprecatory meaning is compared with our vernacular expression, "Mercy on us!"

Ἰλλυρικόν.

For what was understood by "Illyricum" in the Imperial age see SH on Rom 15¹⁹, and cf. W. Weber *Untersuchungen zur Geschichte des Kaisers Hadrianus*, Leipzig, 1907, p. 55.

ἱμάς.

P Petr II. 25 (*l*)² (iii/B.C.) εἰς ἱμάντας ἐλαίου, a receipt for oil for greasing straps. P Oxy X. 1204⁷ (ii/iii A.D.) ἱμάντα δεδεμένον εἰς τὸ πανάριον καλόν, "a good strap tied to the basket" (Edd.). An edict of iv/A.D., P Oxy IX. 1186³, directed against the use of the whip (ἱμάντες) in the punishment of free men, has—τὸ τὴν διὰ τῶν ἱμάντων ληταρι[.]ων ἐπιχωρίως οὕτω καλουμένων αἰκείαν ὑπομένειν ἐστὶν μὲν καὶ ἐπὶ τῶν δουλικὴν τύχην εἰληχότων ἀνιαρόν, "subjection to the punishment of scourging, called in the native speech . . ., is even for those of servile estate lamentable" (Ed.): cf. Ac 22²⁵ (RV marg. "for the thongs"). In *Syll* 537⁶⁵ (2nd half iv/B.C.) ἐπιθεὶς ἱμάντας πλάτος ἡμιποδίου the reference is to "asseres horizontali positura canteriis imposti" (Ed.): cf. *ib*. 587⁶⁴ (B.C. 329–8). A good illustration of Mk 1⁷ is afforded by Menander *Fragm* p. 33, No.109² ὑποδούμενος τὸν ἱμάντα γὰρ τῆς δεξιᾶς | ἐμβάδος ἀπέρρηξ(α).

ἱματίζω.

"Found neither in LXX nor in prof. auth.", says Grimm. But P Lond 24¹¹ (B.C. 163) (= I. p. 32) τοῦτ[ο] ἐπιτελέσασα ἱματιεῖ αὐτήν, BGU IV. 1125⁸ (B.C. 13) ἐ]μοῦ τρέφοντος καὶ ἱματίζοντος αὐτόν, P Tebt II. 385¹⁵ (A.D. 117)"Ἥρωνος ἱματίζοντος τὸν παῖδα, P Ryl II. 153²¹ (A.D. 138–61) ἱματίζειν τὸν προγεγραμμένον μου υἱόν, and many exx. of the active = "to provide clothing for," will dispel any idea that Mark (5¹⁵) coined this word. Cf. also P Oxy II. 275¹¹ (A.D. 66) (= *Selections*, p. 56) τοῦ παιδὸς τρεφομένου καὶ ἱματισζομένου (*l*. ἱματιζ-) ἐπὶ τὸν ὅλον χρόνον ὑπὸ τοῦ πατρός, in a contract of apprenticeship, and similarly *ib*. III. 489⁹·¹⁷ (A.D. 117), P Lips Inv. No. 598¹⁸ (deed of adoption—A.D. 381) (= *Archiv* iii. p. 174) ὅνπερ θρέψω καὶ ἱματίζω (*l*.-ίσω) εὐγενῶς καὶ γνησίως ὡς υἱὸν γνήσιον.

ἱμάτιον.

The plural is used = "garments" generally, as in Mk 5³⁰, in the marriage contract P Ryl II. 154⁸ (A.D. 66) ἱμα[τίω]ν σ[τ]ολὰ[ς] δύο, λευκὴι μία [ναρ]κ[ι]σσίνη μία, καὶ πάλλ[ι]α πέντε, "in raiment two robes, one white, one narcissus, and five mantles" (Edd.): cf. PSI I. 94¹⁶ (ii/A.D.) μὴ ἀγωνία δὲ περὶ τῶν ἱματίων. In P Lille I. 6⁹ (iii/B.C.) the ἱμάτιον is distinguished from the inner χιτών in the account of a robbery—ἐξέδυσαν χιτῶνα ἄξιον (δραχμὰς) ϛ, ἱμάτιον τριβακὸν ("smooth," "fine") ἄξιον (δραχμὰς) ϛ: cf. P Par 59⁴ (B.C.160) πέπρακα τὸ ὀθόνιον (δραχμῶν) φ καὶ τὸ εἱμάτιον (δραχμῶν) ͅτπ. The weaving of the χιτώνιον and ἱμάτιον is mentioned in P Lond 429⁸·⁴¹ (*c.* A.D. 350) (= II. p. 315) "probably a religious ceremony," "according to the editor, "like the weaving of the peplos at Athens." Other exx. of the word are P Petr II. 32 (1)¹⁸ ἱμάτια Αἰγύπτια, P Fay 12¹⁹ (*c.* B.C. 103) ἐξέδυσαν ὁ περ[ιε]βεβλήμην ἱμάτιον, "they stripped me of the garment I was wearing," *ib*. 109⁵ (early i/A.D.) ἐάν σε δῃ (*l*. δέῃ) τὸ εἱμάτιόν σου θεῖναι ἐνέχυρον, "even if you have to pawn your cloak" (Edd.), and of the diminutive, P Par 10²² (B.C. 145) ἱμάτιον καὶ ἱματί-

δίον παιδαρίου. In P Amh II. 76¹⁴ (ii/iii A.D.) we hear of a ἱματιοπώλης: cf. *Preisigke* 756 (ii/iii A.D.). Εἱμάτιον, quoted twice above, is the (Ionic) diminutive of εἷμα: the Attic ἱμάτιον is due to itacism and perpetuates a vulgarism (Boisacq, p. 375).

ἱματισμός.

For the Hellenistic usage of this word = "clothing' generally, as in Lk 7²⁵, Ac 20³³ see P Hib I. 54¹⁶ (*c.* B.C. 245) ἐχέτω δὲ καὶ ἱματισμὸν ὡς ἀστειότατον, "and let him wear as fine clothes as possible" (Edd), the contract P Tebt II. 384¹⁹ (A.D. 10) τρο[φ]ῆς καὶ] ἱματισμοῦ καὶ λαογραφίας, "keep and clothing and poll-tax," and the will *ib*. 381¹³ (A.D. 123) (= *Selections*, p. 78) σκεύηι καὶ ἐνδομενίαν καὶ ἱματισμόν, "utensils and household-stock and clothing." P Ryl II. 189² (A.D. 128) is a receipt issued by the "receivers of public clothing" to certain weavers for the delivery of tunics and cloaks for the guards—δημοσίο(υ) ἱματισμοῦ κουστωδιῶν. The word is used of a bride's "trousseau," "dowry," as in Tobit 10¹⁰ ℵ, in P Eleph 1⁴ (B.C. 311–0) (= *Selections*, p. 2) προσφερομένην εἱματισμὸν καὶ κόσμον (δραχμὰς) ͅα, "the bride bringing clothing and adornment to the value of 1000 drachmae": cf. BGU IV. 1101¹⁰ (B.C. 13) χορηγ(εῖν) αὐτὸ(ν) τῇ Διονυσί(αι) τὰ δέοντα πάντα καὶ τὸν εἱματισ(μόν). This spelling with εἱμ- is frequent in the inscrr. e.g. *Syll* 939⁶ πορφύρε[ο]ν εἱματισμόν: it is, as Dittenberger remarks *ad l.*, "origini vocis accommodatior." See also *s.v.* ἱμάτιον *ad fin.*

ἱμείρω.

For this verb which is read in the TR of 1 Th 2⁸ (but see Milligan *ad l.*) we may cite Bacchylides i. 62 ἴσον ὅ τ' ἀφνεὸς ἱμείρει μεγάλων ὅ τε μείων παυρότέρων, "the rich man yearns for great things, as the poorer for less" (Jebb).

ἵνα.

The use of this conjunction is very widely extended in the Κοινή, nor is it always easy to determine the exact shade of meaning to be attached to it, but the following exx. may give an idea of its varied uses. (1) For the original meaning of *purpose*, "in order that," we may cite P Petr II. 11 (1)⁷ (iii/B.C.) (= *Selections*, p. 8) γράφε δ' ἡμῖν καὶ σύ, ἵνα εἰδῶμεν ἐν οἷς εἶ, καὶ μὴ ἀγωνιῶμεν, "write to us yourself that we may know how you are circumstanced, and not be anxious," P Oxy IV. 742⁸ (B.C. 2) θ[έ]ς αὐτὰς εἰς τόπον ἀσφαλῶς ἵνα τῇ ἀναβάσει αὐτὰς ἄξωμεν, "put them (bundles of reeds) in a safe place in order that we may take them on the journey up" (Edd), and *ib*. VI.939¹⁹ (Christian letter—iv/A.D.) ἕτερά σε γράμματα ἐπικαταλαβεῖν ἐσπούδασα διὰ Εὐφροσύνου ἵνα σε εὐθυμότερον καταστήσω, "I am anxious that you should receive another letter by Euphrosynus, in order that I may make you more cheerful" (Edd.). Interesting exx. in this same sense are afforded by *ib*. II. 237ⁱᵛ·¹² (A.D. 186) ἵνα τῷ Ἀσκληπιάδῃ ἀποδιδόναι δυνηθείην, and somewhat later by P Leid Wˣˣˣ·²⁹ (ii/iii A.D.) ἵν' εὔοδον ἄρτι μοι εἴη, "ut facilis via iam mihi sit" (Ed.). Ἵνα c. fut. ind., as not infrequently in the NT (Jn 7³, 1 Cor 9¹⁸, 1 Pet 3¹, Rev 22¹⁴ *al.*), is illustrated by P Oxy VII. 1068⁵ (iii/A.D.) ἔγραψα τῷ κυρίῳ μου Κληματίῳ τῷ ἀρχερεῖ (*l*. ἀρχιερεῖ) εἵνα μοι πλοῖον διαπέμψεται, followed, however, by εἵνα δυνηθῶ τὸ σωμάτιν κατενενκῖν ἐν Ἀλεξανδρίαν : cf. also ib.[19] παρακαλῶ οὖν, κύριέ μου, ὑπάρξε (l. ὑπάρξαι) αὐτοῖς καὶ τὰ τῆς σῆς σπουδῆς, εἵνα μοι μαρτυρήσουσιν ἀνελθόντες, "I urge you, my lord, to supply them with the marks of your good will, that on their return they may testify of it to me " (Ed.). It is possible that we have an instance of ἵνα with the pres. ind., as in Gal 4[17], in P Lond 971[12] (iii/iv A.D.) (= III. p. 129) ἵν' . . βοηθοῦσιν, but the reading is uncertain. See also BGU IV. 1081[3] cited below. (2) After verbs of saying, wishing, commanding, ἵνα frequently denotes *purport* rather than *purpose*: see e.g. P Lond 42[32] (B.C. 168) (= l. p. 31, *Selections*, p. 11) χαριεῖ δὲ καὶ τοῦ σώματος ἐπιμε[λό]μενος, ἵν' ὑγιαίνῃς, "pray take care of yourself that you may be in health," P Fay 112[6] (A.D. 99) ἐ]πιτίνας τὸν ζευγηλάτην εἵνα ἑκάσ[της] ἡμέρας τῷ ἔργον ἀποδῦ (l.-οῖ), "urge the driver to do his proper work every day" (Edd.), BGU III. 843[11] (illiterate—i/ii A.D.) ἴρηκα τῷ υ[ἱῷ] σου, εἵνα σοι πέμψ (l. πέμψῃ) κιθών[ιο]ν, and as showing how readily transition is made from one usage to another, the soldier's letter P Meyer 20[44 ff.] (1st half iii/A.D.) εἰπὲ τῇ ἱερίσσᾳ (l.-η) τοῦ ἱεροῦ τῶν Ἑρμωνθιτῶν, ἵνα ἐκεῖ πέμπω τὰς ἐπιστολάς, ἐπὶ (l. ἐπεὶ) εὐσήμαντά ἐστιν, "tell the priestess of the temple of the Hermonthites, that I am sending my letters there, since she is well known," which is immediately followed by—δήλωσόν μοι οὖν, εἰ ἐνετείλω αὐτῇ, ἵνα σοι ἐκεῖ πέμψω τὰς ἐπιστολάς, "let me know, therefore, if you have so charged her, in order that I may send my letters to you there." Attempts have been made to trace this construction to Latin influence, but, as Moulton (*Proleg.* 208 f.) has shown, "the usage was deeply rooted in the vernacular, in fields which Latin cannot have touched to the extent which so far-reaching a change involves." Amongst other passages he cites P Oxy IV. 744[13] (B.C. 1) (= *Selections*, p. 33) ἐρωτῶ σε οὖν ἵνα μὴ ἀγωνιάσῃς, "I urge you therefore not to worry" (Edd.), P Gen I. 7[16] (i/A.D.) ἔ]γραψα . . ἵνα [σ]οι μὲν αἱ προσήκουσαι τάξ[εις] φυλαχθῶσι, BGU II. 625[9] (ii/iii A.D.) ἐδήλωσα Λονγείνῳ, εἵνα ἑτυμ[άσ]η (l. ἑτοιμάσῃ) πάντα, and P Oxy I. 121[4] (iii/A.D.) εἰπά σοι περεὶ τῶν δύο ἀκάνθων εἵνα δώσωσιν ἡμῖν αὐτά. (3) Related to this is ἵνα c. subj. with "I pray," or some such phrase understood—P Tebt II. 408[17] (A.D. 3) καὶ σὺ δὲ περὶ ὧν βούλε[ι] γράφε, τὰ δ' ἄλλα ἵν' ὑ(γιαίνῃς), "and do you too write about anything you wish for, and for the rest take care of your health" (Edd.), P Ryl II. 230[9] (A.D. 40) μὴ [ο]ὖν ἄλλως ποιή[σ]η[ς] μὴ ἵνα δόξωμέν σε εὐθέως ἠλλάχθαι τὰ πρὸς ἡμᾶς, "do not neglect this, lest we think you to have become all at once estranged towards us" (Edd.), BGU IV. 1079[20] (A.D. 41) (= *Selections*, p. 40) πολλοὺς δανιστὰς ἔχομεν· μὴ ἵνα ἀναστατώσῃς ἡμᾶς, "we have many creditors : do not drive us out," P Fay 112[12] (A.D. 99) ἐπέχον τῷ δακτυλιστῇ Ζωίλωι καὶ εἵνα αὐτὸν μὴ δυσωπήσῃς, "give heed to the measurer (?) Zoilus : don't look askance at him" (Edd.), and BGU I. 48[13] (ii/iii A.D.) ἐὰν ἀναβῇς τῇ ἑορτῇ, ἵνα ὁμόσε γενώμεθα : cf. Mk 5[23], 1 Cor 7[29], 2 Cor 8[7], Eph 5[33], al., and MGr νὰ 'πῇς, "say !" (4) For ἵνα to express a *consequence*, as in Rom 11[11] (where see the note by SH), Gal 5[17] al., cf. P Lond 964[13] (ii/iii A.D.) (= III. p. 212) λαβὼν κοτύλας τ[ό]σας φακῶν ἵνα ἀρκέσ[η] ἡμῖν, and such a passage as Epict. iv. 8. 21 εἰ δ' οὕτω κωφὸς εἶ καὶ τυφλός, ἵνα μηδὲ τὸν Ἥφαιστον ὑπολαμβάνῃς καλὸν χαλκέα, "but if thou art so deaf and blind that thou dost

not suppose even Hephaestus to be a good smith " (Sharp *Epict.* p. 95). See also the long list of exx. in Jannaris *Gr.* §§ 1758, 1951. (5) With Jn 8[56] al., where the ἵνα clause is practically equivalent to a complementary inf., cf. BGU IV. 1081[3] (ii/iii A.D.) εὐκαίρου εὑρὼν τοῦ πρὸς σὲ ἐρχομένου (gen. for acc. and part. for inf. ἐχάρην, ἵνα σὲ ἀσπάζομαι, " I was glad to have the opportunity of greeting you." (6) For ἵνα τί ; (*ut quid*?), "why ?" "wherefore ?" as in Mt 9[4] al., we may again cite Epictetus i. 29. 31 ἵνα τί ; οὐ γὰρ ἀρκεῖ . . . ; " why ? is it not sufficient ?" (Sharp *Epict.* p. 8). "Ἵνα, not followed by a verb, is found = " where " in the Attic inscrr., e.g. *IG* II. 667[4] (B.C. 385) ἵνα ἡ Νίκη, ἵνα [τ]ὰ καμπύλα φύλλα κτλ. : see Meisterhans *Gr.* p. 251. Useful tables by Mr. Scott showing the different constructions of ἵνα in the NT will be found in Robertson *Gr.*[3] pp. 1388, 1400, 1402 f., 1413.

Ἰόππη.

According to Winer-Schmiedel *Gr.* p. 56 f. the spelling Ἰόππη of the NT MSS. and of 1 Macc is supported only by a few coins. The grammarians and others declare for Ἰόπη : cf. *IG* III. 2498 Ἰοπίτης.

ἰός.

Syll 587[3,10] (B.C. 329) σίδηρος καταβεβρωμένος ὑπὸ τοῦ ἰοῦ illustrates the special sense of " rust," found in Jas 5[3] : cf. ib. 139[15] (iii/B.C.) ὅπως δὲ καθαρὸς [ἰ]οῦ ἔσται ὁ ἀνδρίας . . . ἐπιμελεῖσθαι τοὺς ἀγορανόμους. The more general sense is seen in P Tebt II. 273[18] (ii/iii A.D.) ἰοῦ Κυπρί[ου] (δραχμὴ) α, similarly [27], in medical prescriptions for the eyes.

As against Grimm's "very uncert. deriv." the word is obviously cognate with the Latin *virus* (Zend vis-, viša-, skr. *viṣam* : see Boisacq, p. 379).

Ἰουδαία.

In P Ryl II. 189[5], a badly spelled receipt for " public clothing " of A.D. 128, we read of five cloaks ἰς τρατιωτικὰς (l. στρατ-) χρείας τῶν ἐν τῇ Ἰουδαίᾳ (l. Ἰουδ) στρατευομένων, " for the needs of the soldiers serving in Judaea." For Judaea in its wider sense = " all Palestine," see Abbott *Fourfold Gospel*, p. 210 n.[3]

Ἰουδαϊκός.

Durham (*Menander*, p. 27) cites an interesting passage from Cleomedes, a mathematician of ii/A.D., criticizing Epicurus for his frequent use of nouns formed with the suffix —μα. After giving exx. he continues—ὧν τὰ μὲν ἐκ χαμαιτυπείων ἄν τις εἶναι φήσειε, . . . τὰ δὲ ἀπὸ μέσης τῆς προσευχῆς καὶ τῶν ἐπ' αὐλαῖς (αὐταῖς M, edd. ; coni. Ziegler) προσαιτούντων, Ἰουδαϊκά τινα καὶ παρακεχαραγμένα καὶ κατὰ πολὺ τῶν ἑρπετῶν ταπεινότερα.

Ἰουδαϊκῶς.

On the irregular aspiration οὐχ Ἰουδαϊκῶς in Gal 2[14] (א* ACP 17 37) see *Proleg.* p. 244, and add WH *App.*[2] p. 313 f. as supporting Lightfoot's view ad l. Cf. also Moulton *Gr.* ii. p. 100.

Ἰουδαῖος.

There is abundant evidence from our sources of the large part which Jews played in Egypt, a special district (ἄμφοδος) or Ghetto being assigned to them in such towns as Alexandria, Oxyrhynchus, and Apollinopolis Magna. Many questions are thereby raised into which we cannot enter here, but one or two citations of a general kind may be of interest. Thus from Apollinopolis Magna from late Ptolemaic times we have the two following dedicatory inscrr.: Εὐλογεῖ τὸν θεὸν Πτολεμαῖος Διονυσίου Ἰουδαῖος, and Θεοῦ εὐλογία. Θεόδοτος Δωρίωνος Ἰουδαῖος σωθεὶς ἐκ [Τρω]γο[δ]υ[τῶν] (Lepsius *Denkmäler*, XII. Taf. 11 Nr. 136, 144 cited in Meyer *Ostraca*, p. 149). On the other hand, *CIG* 3418 οἱ ποτὲ Ἰουδαῖοι seems to point to Jews converted from Judaism to heathenism. The earliest known reference to the Jews as money-lenders (cf. Wilcken *Archiv* iv. p. 567) occurs in a private letter to a man in money difficulties. BGU IV. 1079²⁸ (A.D. 41) (= *Selections*, p. 40) ὡς ἂν πάντες καὶ σὺ βλέπε σατὸν ἀπὸ τῶν Ἰουδαίων, "like everybody else, you too must beware of the Jews." P Oxy IX. 1189⁹ (c. A.D. 117) is a letter of a strategus relating to a schedule of "property which belonged to the Jews"—τῶν τοῖς ['Ι]ουδαίοις ὑπαρξάντων. The editor thinks that "it is highly probable that the papyrus belongs to the period of the great Jewish outbreak which occurred in the previous year, and was not ended until after the accession of Hadrian." With this may be compared the interesting fragments of an Alexandrian papyrus, edited by Wilcken under the title "Ein Aktenstück zum jüdischen Kriege" (*Hermes* xxvii. (1892). p. 464 ff.), in which, in an audience before the Emperor Trajan, the Jews complain that the Egyptian Prefect, M. Rutilius Lupus, has mockingly ordered their "king" of the carnival to be brought before him—¹·⁵ ᶠᶠ· προάγειν αὐ[τ]οὺς [ἐ]κέλευε χλευάζων τὸν [ἀ]πὸ |σ]κηνῆς καὶ ἐκ μείμου (*l.* μίμου) βασιλέα : cf. Jn 19³, and for a somewhat different explanation of the circumstances see Reinach *Revue des Études Juives* xxvii. (1893). p. 70 ff., and *Textes relatifs au Judaïsme* (1895). p. 218 ff.

Ἰούδας

is found with a gen. Ἰούδου in a sepulchral inscr. of i/A.D.—*Preisigke* 722 Ἰούδας Ἰούδου, ὡς ἐτῶν τρίκοντα. For the NT usage, see Moulton *Gr.* ii. § 60 (6).

Ἰουλία

is a very common name amongst the slaves of the Imperial household, e.g. *CIL* VI. 20416 D.M. | IVLIAE NEREI · F · | CLAVDIAE. See SH p. 427 on the bearing of this on Rom 16¹⁵, and cf. Milligan *Documents*, p. 183.

Ἰουνιᾶς.

The name has not yet been found elsewhere than in Rom 16⁷, but is probably a contracted form of *Iunianus*, which is common in the inscrr., e.g. *CIL* III. 4020 : see Lietzmann *ad Rom l.c.* (*HZNT*). Souter (*Lex. s.v.*) treats the name as feminine, Ἰουνία, as in AV ; similarly, Moulton *Gr.* ii. § 63.

ἱππεύς

denoting one of a body of "mercenary cavalry" in the Ptolemaic army occurs in P Lille I. 10¹ (iii/B.C.) τῶν μισθοφόρων ἱππέ[ων, and cf. *ib.* 14⁴ (B.C. 243–2) γέγραφεν . . . τετελευτηκέναι τῶν περὶ Φαρβαῖθα καταμεμετρημένων μισθοφόρων ἱππέων ἐπιλ(άρχην) Θεόδωρον, P Hal 1. 15⁵ (iii/B.C.) *al.* See also P Tebt II. 382¹⁸ (B.C. 30—A.D. 1) Ἡρακλῆς Ἀκουσιλάου Μα[κε]δὼν τῶν κατοίκ[ω(ν)] ἱππέω(ν), "Herakles son of Acusilaus, a Macedonian belonging to the catoecic cavalry," P Oxy I. 43 *recto*ⁱᵛ·¹⁵ (military accounts—A.D. 295) διαδέδωκάς μοι τοῖς γεννεοτάτοις ἱππεῦσι ἐκ διαφόρου κοφίνους ἀννώνας εἴκοσι.

ἱππικός.

In BGU II. 447¹³ (A.D. 173–4) there is a reference to a certain Valerius Aphrodisius — στρ(ατιώτου) σπείρης ᾱ [ἱπ]πι[κῆς, "soldier in the first cavalry regiment." The words τὴ]ν ἱππικήν, inserted above the line in P Petr III. 34(a)⁵, may, according to the editor, mean "the stable." Other exx. of the adj. are P Oxy III. 482¹⁸ (A.D. 109) ἐν ἱππικῷ σταθμῷ, "in cavalry barracks," *ib.* 506²⁴ (A.D. 143) ἱππικοῦ κλήρου, "a horseman's holding," and *ib.* IV. 741¹¹ (ii/A.D.) ἱππικὸν ᾱ, apparently with reference to a σανδάλιον, "strap," "belt."

ἵππος.

In P Petr I. 11¹⁰ a cavalry officer bequeaths to a friend— τὸν ἵππον καὶ τὰ ὅπλα : cf. *ib.* 12¹⁰. See also P Tebt I. 208 (B.C. 95) πορείοις καὶ ἵππου]ς εἰς Τ]εβτῦνιν, and BGU II. 665ⁱⁱⁱ·¹¹ (i/A.D.) ἀηδὸς δὲ ἔσχον περὶ τοῦ ἵππου. A horse is included in the salutations of P Oxy XIV. 1772² (late iii/A.D.) ἄσπ]ασαι πολλὰ τὴν ἀγαθήν σου σύμβιον καὶ Ἰουλίαν καὶ τὸν ἵππον καὶ [Τίβ]εριν. For the fem. = "mare" see P Grenf I. 43⁵ (ii/B.C.) τὴν ἵππον, PSI IV. 377³ (B.C. 250–49) τὰς ἵππους ῆ ἐπιτόκους παρέξω : but cf. *ib.* I. 39⁵ (A.D. 148) τυγχάνω ἠγορακέναι ἵπον (*l.* ἵππον) θήλειαν παρὰ Διοσκύρου, and P Fay 301 (A.D. 167), a contract for the sale of two horses—θηλείας σιτοχρόους ("of the colour of ripe wheat"). See Mayser *Gr.* p. 261, and on the use of horses in Egypt see P Hamb I. p. 31.

ἶρις.

This subst. in its derived sense of the white iris plant, from whose aromatic root the orris-root of commerce is produced, occurs in P Tebt II. 414¹¹ (ii/A.D.) ἐὰν κομψῶς σχῶ (cf. Jn 4⁵²) πέμψω [τ]ῇ θυγατρί σου κοτύλην ἴρις (*l.* ἴρεως), "if my health is good I will send a cotyle of orris-root for your daughter" (Edd.).

Ἰσάκ.

See s.v. Ἰακώβ, and cf. the sepulchral inscr. *Preisigke* 2034¹¹ ἀνάπαυσον τὴν ψυχὴν τοῖς δούλοις σου πιστὰ ἐν κόλποις Ἀβράμ καὶ Ἰσὰκ καὶ Ἰακώβ, similarly *ib.* 3901¹². In P Amh II. 143⁶ (iv/A.D.) the writer exclaims—εἶπον γὰρ τῷ Ἰσάκ, δῖ κέρμα, καὶ λέγι, οὐκ ἔχω, "I said to Isaac, 'I want money,' and he said 'I have none'" (Edd.). For other exx. of the spelling Ἰσάκ (as frequently in Cod. Sin.) see *BS* p. 189, and add gen. Ἰσακέως in BGU III. 715⁴·⁹ (A.D. 101–2). For a form Εἰσάκ, see *Preisigke* 1156 εὐχὴ Ἰουλιανοῦ, Εἰσάκ, Ἀββιβοῦ εὐλογητοῦ.

ἰσάγγελος,

which in Biblical Greek is confined to Lk 20³⁶, is found in the Christian epitaph *Kaibel* 542⁶ ᶠ·—

ὡς νῦν ἔμοιγε τῆς ἰσαγ[γέλου τύχης
ἐχθρῶν ποτ᾽ εἴ τις ἐπ[ιγελῶν ἁβρύνεται.

For the formation of the compound we may compare ἰσόθεος from *Syll* 202[28], 289[1], ἰσοβασιλεύς from P Ryl II. 62[15] (iii/A.D.), and ἰσουράνιος (not in LS) from a metrical epitaph of the Ptolemaic age in the Gizeh Museum *BCH* xx. (1896), p. 191[10] συγγενική(ν) τε φορῶν δόξαν ἰσουρανίαν (written ἰσουρ- in *BCH*). See also s.v. ἰσότιμος, and cf. MGr ἰσόβαρος.

Ἰσκαριώτης.

a Graecized form of the Markan Ἰσκαριώθ, which Dalman (*Words*. p. 51 f.) regards as equivalent to the Heb. אִישׁ קְרִיּוֹת, though he thinks it surprising that it should not have been translated. For the form cf. Ἴστοβος = אִישׁ טוֹב (Jos. *Antt*. vii. 6. 1).

ἴσος.

In BGU II. 646[9] (A.D. 193) ἵνα πάντες ἰδιῆτα[ι (*l*. εἰδῆτε) καὶ ταῖς ἴσαις ἡμέραις ἑορτάση[τα]ι (*l*. ἑορτάσητε) Wilcken (*Chrest*. I. p. 570) understands the reference to be not to the same calendar-days, but to the same length of time, viz. 15 days as stated later in the document. For the meaning "equal" in quality, cf. P Strass I. 32[14] (A.D. 261) ζυγὸν δὲ ἐνάγων παρά σοι τὸν ἐπιτηδειότερον αὐτῷ παράσχες, τὸν ἴσον σεαυτῷ ποιήσας εἰς τὰ παρά σοι ἔργα. The neut. is common as a subst. = "copy," e.g. P Lond 1222[5] (A.D. 138) (= III. p. 126), a letter enclosing a copy of a rescript, and requesting that another copy should be given to a certain woman—τὸ ἴσον δι᾽ ὑπηρέτου μεταδοθῆναι τ[ῇ] διὰ [σ]ου δηλ[ουμέ]νῃ Θερμουθαρίωι, and similarly P Tebt II. 301[21] (A.D. 190) ἔσχον τούτου [τὸ ἴ]σον ἄχρι ἐξετάσεως, "I have received a copy of this [a notice of death] for investigation." For τὰ ἴσα, as in Lk 6[34], cf. P Ryl II. 65[7] (B.C. 67 ?) εἰς τὸ βασιλικὸν τὰ ἴσα, "the same sum to the Treasury," and for ἴσα used adverbially (as in Phil 2[6], cf. Job 11[12], 30[19]), see the curious nursery alphabet P Tebt II. 278[33] (early i/A.D.)—

ἴσα οὕτωι ἦρκε.
κάλλιστον ἱμάτιν,

"just so he stole it, my lovely garment." This usage survives in MGr ἴσ(ι)α μέ (*i.e*. μετά), "till," "up to" (Thumb *Handb*. p. 111). Cf. also the adverbial phrase ἐξ ἴσου, as in P Fay 34[14] (A.D. 161) κατὰ μῆνα τὸ αἱροῦν ἐξ ἴσου, "in equal monthly instalments" (Edd.), *ib*. 93[17] (A.D. 161), *al*., and ἐπ᾽ ἴσηι καὶ ὁμοίηι, "upon equal and similar terms," as in *Syll* 162[27] (end of iv/B.C.). The difficult phrase ἴσος πλήρης in P Goodsp Cairo 28[3] (ii/A.D.) with reference to a boat's lading is discussed by Wilcken *Archiv* iii. p. 116. As regards derivation ἴσος < *Fιτσο-Fος, from the root of εἶδος (Boisacq, p. 383). On ἴσος see Thumb *Hellen*. p. 64. MGr ἴσιος.

ἰσότης.

The sense of "fairness," "fair dealing," into which this word passes in Col 4[1], may be illustrated by Menander Μονοστ. 259 ἰσότητα τίμα καὶ πλεονέκτει μηδένα. See also Vett. Val. p. 332[34] ἰσότητας ποιεῖν, and for the verb ἰσόω in its literal sense cf. P Oxy XIV. 1674[7] (iii/A.D.) καὶ ἰσοθήτω τὸ πᾶν τοῦ κεχωσμένον, "and let the whole of the bank be levelled."

ἰσότιμος.

Field (*Notes*, p. 240) has shown that the emphatic idea in this word is *equality*, and hence that in 2 Pet 1[1], the only place where it occurs in the NT, it means "equal," "equally privileged," a faith which puts the readers of the letter on an equality with the Apostles. In support of this rendering we may refer to *OGIS* 234[55] (B.C. 225-187) Ἀπόλλωνος Ἰσοτίμου, where the unusual epithet brings out, as the editor remarks, that this god was not of less honour than Zeus Chrysaoreus, mentioned just before, and to *ib*. 544[33] (ii/A.D.), where a man is described as ζῶντά τε δικα-[ί]ως καὶ ἰσοτείμως, the adverb showing "merita hominis virtutesque non minores esse honoribus quibus afficiatur": cf. also P Ryl II. 253 (B.C. 143-2) Ἀπο[λ]λοδώρω]ι τῶν ἰσ[οτίμ]ων τοῖς π[ρ]ώτοις φίλοις, *Chrest*. I. 13[10] (A.D. 34-5), and for the force of compounds with ἰσο—such expressions as P Lond 1200[10] (B.C. 102 or 108) (= I. p. 3) χαλκοῦ ἰσονόμου, "copper at par," and P Hawara 65[12] (= *Archiv* v. p. 382) ἀρρωστίαν ἰσοθάνατο[ν] [ἐξ]ήντλησα. "I have endured a sickness like death."

ἰσόψυχος.

For the form of this very rare word, found in the NT only in Phil 2[20], where it is perhaps a play upon words with the preceding εὐψυχῶ Dibelius *HZNT ad l.*, cf. ἰσόψηφος as discussed s.v. ἀριθμός *ad fin.*, and the note on ἰσότιμος.

Ἰσραηλείτης.

Prof. Kirsopp Lake in his monumental edition of the *Codex Sinaiticus Petropolitanus* (Oxford, 1911) has pointed out (p. xi.) that in eight of the nine places where Ἰσραηλείτης occurs in the NT the Cod. Sinaiticus spells ΙϹΔΡΑΗΛΕΙΤΗϹ, while in the Cod. Vaticanus it appears in the form ΙϹΤΡΑΗΛΕΙΤΗϹ. WH have used this fact to support their theory of a Western provenance for one or both of these MSS., but, as Lake goes on to show, their argument has lost its force through the discovery of the same spelling in Egypt. He cites by way of example for Ἰσραήλ the great magical P Par 574, and for Ἰσδραήλ a Jewish inscr. published in *Bull. Soc. Alex*. xi. (1909), p. 326 (= *Preisigke* 617 Ἰσ[δ]ραήλ): add P Lond 46[11] (iv/A.D.) (= I. p. 68) Ἰστραήλ.

ἴστημι (ἱστάνω)

= "fix," "agree upon," is common in financial transactions, as in BGU IV. 1131[44] (B.C. 13) ἐφ᾽ ᾗ ἐστάμεθα τιμῇ, *ib*. II. 456[13] (A.D. 348) τιμῆς τῆς [ἑσ]ταμένης καὶ συμπεφωνημένης, P Tebt II. 385[17] (A.D. 117) ἀπὸ τῶν ἑσταμένων . . . δραχμῶν τεσσαρά[κ]ο[ν]τα ἕξ, "out of the 46 dr. agreed upon," PSI IV. 287[17] (A.D. 377) μηδὲ κοιλένιν (*l*. κοιλαίνειν), "to be deficient in") τὸν σταθέντα μισθόν. In Mt 26[15] the 1st aor. act. denotes actual weighing or paying, (cf. Field *Notes*, p. 19 f., as in *ib*. 442[12] (iii/B.C.) ὅτε ἤμελλον στῆσαι τοὺς ἀμφιτάπους (cf. Prov 7[16], "when I was about to weigh the rugs," and the late P Iand 20[5] (vii/ vii A.D.) Σ[ε]ρῆνε, στῆσον τὸ χρυσίον Ποσόμπους. For the meaning "set up," as in [Jn] 8[3], Ac 12[8], *al*., see P Fay 20[12] τούτου τοῦ ἐμοῦ δόγματος ἀντίγραφα τοῖς καθ᾽ ἑκάστην πόλιν ἄρχουσιν γενέσθω ἐπιμελὲς εἰς τὸ δημόσιον μάλιστα ἑστάν[αι] σύνοπτα τοῖς ἀναγινώσκουσιν, "let the rulers of the several cities see that copies of this my edict are set up in the most public places in full view of those who wish to read" (Edd.): cf. P Leid Wxi. 9 ff. (ii/iii A.D.) τοὺς ἀστέρας ἱστάς, καὶ τῷ φωτὶ τῷ ἐνθέῳ κτίζων τῶν κόσμον· ἐν ᾧ δὲ ἔστησας τὰ πάντα. The verb is used metaphorically in P Rein 44³⁸ (A.D. 104) περὶ μὲν γὰρ τῶν τῆς μητρῴας οὐσίας προσόδων . . οὐδὲν ἠδυνήθην στῆσαι, "regarding the revenues of the maternal fortune I was unable to establish anything," and in the passive in BGU I. 140¹⁹ (time of Hadrian) δι' ὧν τὸ αὐστηρότερον ὑπὸ τῶν πρὸ ἐμοῦ αὐτοκρατόρων σταθὲν φιλανθρωπότερ[ο]ν ἑρμηνεύω: cf. P Gen I. 7⁸ (i/A.D.) (= Chrest. I. p. 108) αἱ μὲν οὖν πρ[οσ]ήκουσαι αὐτῷ τάξεις φυλαχ[θ]ήτωσαν ὥσπερ οἱ πρ[ὸ ἐ]μοῦ ἔστησαν κατὰ τὸ ἐξ ἀρχῆς ἔθος, P Lips Inv. 266⁶ (ii/A.D.) (= Archiv v. p. 245) τοῦ κυρ[ίο]υ ἡμῶν Ἀδριανοῦ Καί[σ]αρος ὁμόσε ταῖς ἄλλαις εὐεργεσίαις στήσαντος τὴν βασιλικὴν . . γῆν . . γεωργεῖσθαι, and Syll 426²³ (ii/B.C. ad init.) μ]ετὰ τῶν ἀρχόντων τῶν στα[θ]έντων ἐν Στίρι (cf. Mt 12²⁵). The verb passes into the meaning "stop" in P Oxy VIII. 1088²¹ (early i/A.D.), a medical receipt—αἷμα ἀπὸ μυκτήρων στῆσαι, "to stop nose-bleeding." For the form ἱστάνω (Rom 3³), which is found from i/B.C., cf. Syll 732²⁵ (B.C. 36-5) ἀφιλαργύρως ἱστανόμενος ἡστίασεν τοὺς ἐρανιστάς: see also s.v. παριστάνω. MGr σταίνω, στήνω (trans.): στένω (trans.): στέκω (intrans.), cf. perf. ἔστηκα.

ἱστορέω.

The only NT sense of this word = "visit" (Gal 1¹⁸) is paralleled in the interesting scrap of a traveller's letter P Lond 854⁵ (i/ii A.D.) (= III. p. 206, Selections, p. 70) ἵνα τὰς χε[ι]ροπ[οι]ή[τους τέ]χνας ἱστορήσωσι: cf. ¹⁰ εὔτομα (l. εὔστομα) ἱστόρ[η]σα. It is used often thus (= inspicio) in the inscrr. e.g. OGIS 694 (Rom.) Ἑρμογένης Ἀμασ[εὺ]ς [τὰ]ς μὲν ἄλλας σύριγγας ἰδὼν ἐθαύμασα, τὴν δὲ τοῦ Μέμνονος ταύτην εἱστορήσας ὑπερεθαύμασα, and in the wall-scratchings of visitors to the royal tombs at Thebes, e.g. Preisigke 1004 (Rom.) Ἰούλιος Δημήτριος χειλίαρχος ἱστορήσας ἐθαύμασα: cf. also the Theban inscr., Kaibel 1020—

Τατιανὸς ἡγεμὼν Θηβάιδος ἱστορήσα[ς] ἐθαύμασεν
τὸ θαῦ[μα ξ]υνὸν τῶν σοφῶν Αἰγυπ[τί]ων.

For the verb = "relate," see BGU IV. 1208⁵ (B.C. 27-6) πιττάκ]ιον, δι' οὗ [μοι] ἱστορεῖς τὴν [Καλατύ]τεως πλ[άν]ην, P Oxy VII. 1027¹¹ (i/A.D.) ὑπόμνημα . . . δι' οὗ ματαίως εἰστορεῖ περί τε τοῦ ἀγνοεῖν α[ὐ]τὸν τὴν τῶν ἐμοὶ γενη[μένων] (l. γεγενη[μένων]) ἀσφαλιῶν θέσιν, "a memorandum wherein he vainly relates that he was ignorant of the securities which had been given to me" (Ed.): cf. the use of the compound συνιστορέω in BGU IV. 1141⁴⁹ (B.C. 14), PSI I. 64⁴ (i/B.C. ?) al. The subst. ἱστορία, which survives in MGr = "narrative," "history," may be illustrated from OGIS 13¹³ (c. B.C. 300-299), where the Prienians are represented as establishing their possession of a certain district—ἔκ τε τῶν ἱστοριῶν κ[αὶ ἐκ τῶν ἄλ]λων μαρτυριῶν. For its use in Byzantine literature = "painting," owing to the development of picture histories, see Birt Buchrolle, p. 307 f.

ἰσχυρός.

With Mt 3¹¹ cf. P Leid Wv. 33 (ii/iii A.D.) ἰδὼν ὁ θεὸς πάλιν ἐπτοήθη, ὡς ἰσχυρότερον θεωρήσας (viz. ἔνοπλόν τινα, who appears suddenly on his πόππυσμα) μήποτε ἡ γῆ ἐξέ-

βρασε θεόν. In P Ryl II. 165¹² (A.D. 266) we have a reference to the legio Traiana Fortis Germanica—λεγιῶνος Τραιανῆς Ἰσχυρᾶς Γερμ[ανικῆς. Syll 226⁶⁹ (iii/B.C.) σιτοδείας γενομένης ἰσχυρᾶς, is a good parallel to the usage in Lk 15¹⁴. Cf. also ib. 929⁸⁴ (ii/B.C.) τὸ δὲ πάντων μέγιστον καὶ ἰσχυρότατον τεκμήριον, Chrest. I. 27⁵ (ii/A.D.) ε[ἰ γὰ]ρ ὑπεναντίον ἐστὶν τὸ πα[ρά]δειγμα οὐκ ἰσχυρόν κτλ., and Menandrea p. 14¹³⁰ τοῦτο γὰρ | ἰσχυρὸν οἴεταί τι πρὸς τὸ πρᾶγμ' ἔχειν, "un argument décisif" (Croiset).

ἰσχύς.

The only exx. of this subst. from our sources are late, e.g. P Lond 1319⁵ (A.D. 544 or 545) (= III. p. 272) τὴν ἰδίαν ἰσχὺν καὶ δύναμιν, and BGU II. 371²¹ (Arab.) πράσεως τῆς . . . ἐχούσης τὴν ἰδίαν πίστειν (l. -ιν) καὶ ἰσχὺν εἰς πλήρης καὶ εἰς ὁλόκληρον, with reference to the validity of a receipt.

ἰσχύω.

The special sense in Gal 5⁶, Heb 9¹⁷, occurs in P Tebt II. 286⁷ (A.D. 121-138) νομὴ ἄδικος [οὐ]δὲν εἰσχύει, "unjust possession is invalid ": cf. the use of the verb with reference to money like the Lat. valeo, Cagnat IV. 915a¹² ἡ Ῥοδία δραχμὴ τούτου τοῦ δηναρίου ἰσχύει ἐν Κιβύρᾳ ἀσσάρια δέκα. For the meaning "have power" cf. P Petr II. 18(1)¹³ (B.C. 246) διὰ τὸ μ[ὴ] ἰσχύειν αὐτόν με κωλύειν, "because I was not strong enough to hinder him," and P Oxy I. 67¹⁴ (A.D. 338) πάντα μέν, ὡς ἔπος ἐστὶν εἰπεῖν, ὅσα εἰσχύειν τι δύν[α]τ[αι] παρὰ τὴν τῶν νόμων [ἰσχὺ]ν πρὸς ὀλίγον εἰσχύει, "everything, it may be said, that is able to withstand the power of the law withstands but for a short time" (Edd.). The ordinary sense "to be able," without the connotation of strength, may be seen early in P Eleph 17²³ (B.C. 223) διὰ τὸ μὴ εἰσχύειν αὐτοὺς καταβαλεῖν τὰς λοιπὰς ἀναφοράς, "because they were not able to pay the remaining imposts ": cf. P Oxy X. 1345 (ii/iii A.D.) οὐκ ἴσχυσα ἐλθεῖν σήμερον, P Leid Wviii. 31 (ii/iii A.D.) βίβλον ἣν οὐδεὶς ἴσχυσε μεθερμηνεῦσας (l. —σαι), P Ryl II. 237⁸ (mid. iii/A.D.) ἵνα κἀγὼ εἰς [. . . . ἐκεῖνον] εἰσχύσω συνπεριενεχθῆναι (l. συμπεριενεχθῆναι) εὐχρόμως, "that I may be able to keep up appearances in my relations with him" (Edd.). The expressive compd. ὑπερισχύω, which is fairly frequent in the LXX, may be illustrated from P Ryl II. 119⁵⁹ (A.D. 54-67) ἐν οὐδενὶ ἡγήσατο καθὸ ὑπερισχύων ἡμᾶς ἐπὶ τῶν τόπων, "he scorned (petitions and reports) in virtue of his superior local power" (Edd.).

ἴσως.

P Magd 29⁵·⁸ (B.C. 218) ἴσως καὶ ὁμοίως, P Giss I. 76⁶ (ii/A.D.) ἀσπάζομαί σε πολλά, ἴσως καὶ Χαιρᾶς καὶ Ἡρώδης. With the usage in Lk 20¹³ cf. P Amh II. 135¹⁶ (early ii/A.D.) τί δὲ ἡμεῖν συνέβη μετὰ τῶν ἀρχόντων ἴσως ἐγνώκατε ἢ κνώσσεσθε (l. γνώσεσθε), "what befell us in connexion with the magistrates you have probably heard or will hear" (Edd.), P Tebt II. 424³ (late iii/A.D.) ἔπεμψά σοι ἐπιστολὴν διὰ τοῦ ἀρτοκόπου καὶ εἴσως οἶδας τί σοι ἔγραψα, P Oxy IX. 1204²¹ (A.D. 299) μὴ ἐπιγνοὺς ὡς ἀξιώματος μείζονος μετελήφεν, ὃ ἀπαλλάττει ἴσως αὐτὸν τῶν λειτουργιῶν τῶν πολειτικῶν, "ignoring his acquisition of a superior rank, which presumably releases him from municipal offices" (Ed.), ib. XIV. 1681⁴ (iii/A.D.) ἴσως με νομίζετε, ἀδελφ[ο]ί, βάρβαρόν τινα ἢ Αἰγύπτιον ἀνάνθρωπον εἶναι, "you are, my brothers, perhaps thinking me a barbarian or an inhuman Egyptian" (Edd.).　MGr ἴσως, "perhaps."

Ἰταλικός.

On the σπεῖρα Ἰταλική in Ac 10¹ see Ramsay *Was Christ born in Bethlehem?* p. 260 ff.　From Delos at the end of ii/B.C. comes the inscr.—Γάϊον Ὀφέλλιον Μαάρκου υἱὸν Φέρον Ἰταλικοὶ δικαιοσύνης ἕνεκα καὶ φιλαγαθίας τῆς εἰς ἑαυτούς (*Michel* 1163).

Ἰτουραῖος.

For Ituraeans in Mount Lebanon about A.D. 6 see *Ephemeris Epigraphica*, 1881, p. 537 ff.

ἰχθύδιον.

P Flor II. 119⁷ (A.D. 254) ἰχθύδ.α.

ἰχθύς.

P Petr III. 107(e)⁶·⁹ (iii/B.C.) ἰχθύος, BGU IV. 1123⁹ (time of Augustus) ἢ ἰχθύας ἢ ἀγρίας, P Fay 113¹³ (A.D. 100) τῇ πόλι πέμψις εἰκθύας (*l.* ἰχθύας) (δραχμῶν) ιβ, P Hamb I. 6¹¹ (A.D. 128) μηδὲν ἀπὸ θήρ̣ας ἰχθύας περιγεγονέναι μέχρι νῦν, OGIS 484²⁶ (ii/A.D.) δι᾽ ὧν ἐπηρέαζον μάλιστα τοὺς τὸν ἰχθὺν πιπράσκοντας.　The noun is used collectively in P Flor II. 201⁹ (A.D. 259) τοὺς παρά σοι ἁλιέας ἀποστεῖλαι ἔχοντας ἰχθὺν κάλλιστον, "spedire i tuoi pescatori con assai quantità di pesce" (Ed.).　For the adj. ἰχθυϊκός (2 Chron 33¹¹ A) see *Ostr* 331⁴ (Ptol.) ἰχθυϊκῶν ἁλιέων, and for ἰχθηρός (2 Esdr 13³) see P Par 63⁹⁸ (B.C. 165) τοὺς ὑποτελεῖς τῇ τε ἰχθηρᾷ καὶ ζυτηρᾷ, "those subject to the fish tax and the beer tax."　The Christian epigram *Kaibel* 725 (iii–v/A.D.) is partly acrostic, the initial letters of the first five lines making up the word ἰχθύς.

ἴχνος.

Syll 325⁶ (i/B.C.) has a good parallel for Rom 4¹² and 1 Pet 2²¹ : the excellent young man who is the hero of the laudation comes of a patriotic and pious stock, καὶ αὐτὸς στοιχεῖν βουλόμενος καὶ τοῖς ἐκείνων ἴχνεσιν ἐπιβαίνειν. The literal use of ἴχνος is seen in P Giss I. 9¹⁰ (Rom.) ὡς

δὲ οὐτὲ ἴχνος ἐθεώρο[υν κτλ., P Oxy XII. 1449²¹ (A.D. 213-7) μηδὲ ἴχνη, and in the tax ἴχνους ἐρημοφυλακία, for the desert police who protected the caravan "route," e.g. P Fay 75² (ii/iii A.D.) : cf. p. 106 and the introduction to P Ryl II. 197.　For the metaph. use of ἰχνεύω = "search out," as in Sir 51¹⁵, cf. *Kaibel* 227¹ ἰχνεύεις, ὦ ξεῖνε, τίς εἴμ᾽ ἐγώ.

Ἰωάννης, Ἰωάνης.

On the uncertainty in the spelling of this Semitic proper name, see Moulton *Gr.* ii. p. 102, Winer-Schmiedel *Gr.* p. 57, Blass *Philology*, pp. 75 f., 81.

Ἰωνάθας.

This name, found in the exceedingly plausible reading of D at Ac 4⁶ (cf. Blass, pp. 35 f., 72 f.), occurs in P Petr III. 7¹⁵ (B.C. 236) with reference to the will of a Jewish παρεπίδημος in the Fayûm—Ἀπολλ(ώνιον) παρεπίδημον, ὃς καὶ Συριστὶ Ἰωνάθας καλεῖται.　Cf. *Preisigke* 2137¹¹ (ostracon —vi/vii A.D.) Ἰωνάθαν Ἰωά(ννου).

Ἰωσῆς.

In *Preisigke* 1742, a Cyrenaic inscr., Ἰωσῆς Κρίσπου is mentioned along with Λύκα Γαΐου and Σάρρα προσήλυτος. IGU III. 715ᵇ·⁴ (A.D. 101-2) Ἰωσῆς ὁ καὶ Τεύφιλο(s) : cf. Ac 13⁹.

Ἰωσήφ.

For the form Ἰώσηπος see BGU IV. 1068 (A.D. 101), where a certain Σωτέλης Ἰωσήπου makes official notification of the death of his son, who bore his grandfather's name—ἔ̣ff ὁ υἱός μου Ἰ[ώσ]ηπος μητρὸς Σάρρας ἀφῆλιξ μήπω καταλήξας εἰς λαογραφίαν ἐτελεύτησε τῷ Τῦβι μηνὶ τοῦ ἐνεστῶτος τετάρτου ἔτους Τραιανοῦ Καίσαρος τ[ο]ῦ κυρίου.

ἰῶτα.

This word, borrowed from the Phoenician, is written in full in *Preisigke* 358¹² (iii/B.C.).　See also the horological inscr. of iii/B.C. quoted by Herwerden *Lex. s.v.* γνώμων— ἐπὶ τῶν ἰῶτα (*sc.* γραμμῶν) φερόμενον σημαίνει ζεφύρου πνοήν.　Cf. Moulton *Gr.* ii. § 70.

K

κἀγώ.

For this common crasis in the NT (cf. WH *Notes*[2] p. 152) we may cite PSI V. 540[17] (iii/B.C.) καλῶς ποιήσεις?] γράψασά μοι [περὶ τούτου? ἵ]να καὶγὼ εἰδῶ. The editor compares P Tebt II. 412[1] (late ii/A.D.) καλῶς ποιήσις ἄνελθε εἰς τὴν μητρόπολιν . . ἐπὶ καὶγὼ ἀνέρχομε (*l.* -μαι) εἰς τὴν πόλιν, "please come up to the metropolis, since I also am coming up to the city" (Edd.), and the amended reading (*Archiv* vi. p. 204) of P Par 51[15] (B.C. 160) (= *Selections*, p. 20) ὁρῶ σοι αὐτὸν καθιστῶντα αὐτὰς κἀαγὼ ἔμπροσθεν αὐτῶν ἐπορευόμην. See also Meisterhans *Gr.* p. 72, Moulton *Gr.* ii. p. 63, and for the LXX usage Thackeray *Gr.* i. p. 137 f.

καθά.

This late form for καθάπερ is first used in literature by Polybius, and is frequently found in the papyri, e.g. P Petr II. 13(1)[5] (B.C. 258–3) καθὰ ἐξειλήφαμεν, "according as we have received," P Ryl II. 160(d)[ii. 18] (A.D. 42) καθὰ καίγραπται (*l.* γέγραπται), "as aforesaid," P Oxy XII. 1473[10] (A.D. 201) συμβιούτωσαν οὖν ἀλλήλοις οἱ γαμοῦντες ἀμέμπτως καθὰ καὶ πρότερον συνεβίουν. Cf. from the inscr. *Michel* 1009 B[81] (*c.* B.C. 129) εἰς] τὸν ἀεὶ χρόνον καθὰ ἐξ ἀρχῆς ὑπῆρχεν, and the reff. in Kälker *Quaest.* p. 300. See also Meisterhans *Gr.* p. 257.

καθαίρεσις.

P Magd 9 (iii/B.C.), containing a request by a certain ἱσιονόμος or possessor of a shrine of Isis, that the sanctuary should be repaired, is entitled on the *verso*—Ἐποῆρις Πανῆτος περὶ καθαιρέσεως Ἰσιείου, "Époëris, femme de Panès, au sujet d'un sanctuaire d'Isis qui menace ruine." See also *Syll* 587[76] (B.C. 329–8) μισθωτε[ῖ] . . . οἰκοῦ(ν)τι τῆς καθαιρέσεως τῶν οἰκοπέδων τῆς ἱερᾶς οἰκίας, *Michel* 823[2] (B.C. 220) λόγος τῶν αἱρεθέντων ὑπὸ τοῦ δήμου ἐπὶ τὴν καθαίρεσιν καὶ τὴν ἐπισκευὴν τῶν ἐν τῶι Ἀσκληπιείωι.

καθαιρέω

is used apparently in the full sense of "pull down," "demolish," in P Petr I. 26[6] (B.C. 241) καθειρηκότος τὰς στέγας, and *ib.* III. 46(1)[15] χρημάτισον Διονυσίωι Ἀπολλωνίου τ[ῷ]ι ἐξειληφότι (corr. -ότι) τὴν βασιλεικὴν (corr. -ικὴν) κατάλυσιν προυπαρχοῦσαν ἐν Πτολεμαίδει (corr. -δι) καθελεῖν διὰ τὸ πεπονηκέναι, "pay Dionysios, son of Apollonios, who has contracted to take down the Royal quarters previously existing at Ptolemais, owing to their dilapidation" (Edd.). A somewhat weaker meaning is found in P Amh II. 54[3] (B.C. 112) οἶκος καθειρημένος ἧς οἱ τῦχοι (*l.* οἴκου καθῃρημένου οὗ οἱ τοῖχοι) περίεισιν καὶ εἴσοδος καὶ ἔξοδος,

"a dismantled house of which the walls are standing and the entrance and the exit": cf. P Tor I. 1[ii. 1] (B.C. 117), P Leid M[15] (ii/B.C.). See Field *Notes*, p. 129, on the translation of Ac 19[27], and cf. further Aristeas 263 ὁ θεὸς τοὺς ὑπερηφάνους καθαιρεῖ, τοὺς δὲ ἐπιεικεῖς καὶ ταπεινοὺς ὑψοῖ. In P Oxy XII. 1408[23] (*c.* A.D. 210–4) [τὸ? τοὺς λῃστὰς κα]θαι[ρ]εῖν χωρὶς τῶν ὑποδεχομένων μὴ δύνασθαι πᾶ[σι φανερόν, the editors render "that it is impossible to exterminate robbers apart from those who shelter them is evident to all."

καθαίρω.

With the use of this verb in Jn 15[2] we may compare P Lille I. 5[21] (B.C. 260–59) ἐκ τοῦ ἰδίου ξυλοκοπήσει καὶ τὴν γῆν καθαρεῖ. Cf. P Tebt II. 373[10] (A.D. 110–1) ἐφ' ᾧ ὁ Ἥρων μετρήσι καὶ καθαρεῖ καθ' ἔτος εἰς τὸ δημόσιον . . . [τ]ὰ . . . ἐκφόρια, "on condition that Heron shall measure out and winnow the produce (cf. 2 Kings 4[8]) annually for the State." The verb is common in the inscrr. of ceremonial cleansing, e.g. *Michel* 694[68] (B.C. 91) ἔστι δὲ ἃ δεῖ παρέχειν πρὸ τοῦ ἄρχεσθαι τῶν μυστηρίων· ἄρνας δύο λευκούς, . . . καὶ ὅταν ἐν τῶι θεάτρωι καθαίρει, χοιρίσκους τρεῖς: cf. *Kaibel* 104[1 f.]—

> Ἐνθάδε Διάλογος καθαρῶι πυρὶ γυῖα καθήρας
> ἀσκητὴς σοφίης ᾤχετ᾽ ἐς ἀθανάτους.

The compound ἀνακαθαίρω is found in P Lond 1177[332] (A.D. 113) (= III. p. 190).

καθάπερ

is very common in the legal phrase καθάπερ ἐκ δίκης. Thus our earliest Greek marriage contract, P Eleph 1[12] (B.C. 311–0) (= *Selections*, p. 3), concludes—ἡ δὲ πρᾶξις ἔστω καθάπερ ἐγ δίκης, "and let the right of execution be as if a formal decree of the Court had been obtained": cf. P Amh II. 46[13] (ii/B.C.), P Fay 22[14] (i/A.D.), *ib.* 91[33] (A.D. 99), etc. Other exx. of the word are P Hib I. 49[6] (*c.* B.C. 257) ε[ἶπ]ον δὲ αὐτῶι καθάπερ ἔγραψα [α]ὐτῶι ὅπως ἂν ἐμβάληται τὰς ἐλαίας εἰς βίκους, "tell him that, as I wrote to him, he is to put the olives into jars" (Edd.), P Eleph 12[1] (B.C. 223–2) καθάπερ ᾤου δεῖν, "nach deinem Antrag," P Vat A[10] (B.C. 168) (= Witkowski *Epp.*[2], p. 65) ἠβουλόμην δὲ καὶ σὲ παραγεγονέναι εἰς τὴν πόλ[ι]ν, καθάπερ καὶ Κόνων καὶ οἱ ἄλλοι οἱ ἀπειλη[μμένοι] π[ά]ντες, ὅ[πως] καὶ κτλ. In the decrees τὰ μὲν ἄλλα καθάπερ ὁ δεῖνα "was the usual introduction to an amendment proposed in the Ecclesia to a probouleuma," e.g. *CIG* 84[6 f.] Κέφαλος εἶπε· τὰ μὲν ἄλλα καθάπερ τῇ βουλεῖ· ἀναγράψαι δὲ . . . : see *Roberts-Gardner*, p. 18, and cf. Milligan *Thess.* p. 25.

καθάπτω.

See *s.v.* ἔχιδνα and add Epict. iii. 20. 10 ὁ μὲν τοῦ τραχ-ήλου καθάπτων.

καθαρίζω.

The ceremonial usage of this Hellenistic verb is illustrated by Deissmann *BS* p. 216 f., where reference is made to the Mystery inscription of Andania, *Syll* 653[37] (B.C. 93 or 91) ἀναγραψάντω δὲ καὶ ἀφ' ὧν δεῖ καθαρίζειν καὶ ἃ μὴ δεῖ ἔχον-τας εἰσπορεύεσθαι, and to *ib* 633[3] (ii/A.D.) already cited *s.v.* ἀκάθαρτος *sub fin.*, both of which show the construction with ἀπό as e.g. in 2 Cor 7[1], Heb 9[14]. The word is used in con-nexion with plants in P Lond 131 *recto*[102] (accounts—A.D. 78-9) (= I. p. 175) καθαρίζ(ων) [τῶν] νεοφύτ(ων) τοῦ χω(ρίου) τὰ περισσ(ὰ) βλαστήματα, and *ib.* 131*[83] (A.D. 78) (= I. p. 191): see also P Strass I. 2[11] (A.D. 217) τοῦ σοῦ καθαρίζοντος καὶ μετροῦντος with reference to the "cleansing" of wheat, and P Lips I. 111[12] (iv/A.D.) καθαρί-σομεν τὸ γεώργι[ο]ν. In the iv/v A.D. BGU IV. 1024[iv. 16] we have νὴ γὰρ Δία, ἢν τὰ κοσμήματα τὰ τῶν νόμων, ἢν ὑπὸ τῆς πόλ[ε]ως ἢν δεδομένα τῶι νεκρῷ, ἢν κεκ[αθα]ρισμένα. On the forms of the verb see Reinhold, p. 38 f., Moulton *Gr.* ii. §§ 33, 95.

καθαρισμός

occurs in the lease of an oliveyard, P Lond 168[11] (A.D. 162) (= II. p. 190) ἡμῶν ποιο[ύν]των τὰ καθήκον[τ]α ἔργα π[ερὶ] τοὺς καθαρισμούς.

καθαρός.

The word and its derivatives have a wide range of use, being applied physically to animals, land, grain, bread, milk, etc., e.g. *Chrest.* I. 89[5] (A.D. 149) κ]αὶ δοκιμάσας (μόσχον) ἐσφράγισα ὡς ἔστιν καθαρός, BGU IV. 1018[25] (iii/A.D.) παραδώσω (*l.*-ώσω) τὰς ἀρούρας καθαρὰς ὡς παρέλαβον, P Oxy VIII. 1124[11] (A.D. 26) πυρὸν νέο[ν] καθαρὸν ἄδολον, *ib.* IV. 736[26] (c. A.D. 1) ἄρτου καθαροῦ παιδ[ῶν], BGU IV. 1109[6] (B.C. 5) θηλάζουσαν τῶι ἰδίῳ αὐτῆς γάλακτι καθαρῷ, and metaphorically to "freedom" from disadvantages of various kinds, as in *ib.* 1040[21] (ii/A.D.) καθαρ[ὰ]ν γὰρ ἔχων τὴν ψυχὴν οὐδενὸς ἐπισ τ[. . . .]ν τῶν διαβαλόντων, or in the epitaphs *Kaibel* 516[13] (c. A.D. 1) καθα[ρ]ὰν δὲ φυλάξας [σωφροσύνης ἀρετὴν τόν]δε λέλονχε τάφον, 653[4] (iii/A.D.) ὡς ἀνίη καθαρή, of a mind freed from care : cf. also P Lond 178[13] (A.D. 145) (= II. p. 207) τὸ δὲ χειρόγραφον τοῦτο δισσὸν γραφὲν καθαρὸν ἀπὸ ἐπιγραφῆς καὶ ἀλίφαδος, P Oxy X. 1277[13] (A.D. 255) κυρία ἡ πρᾶσις ἁπλῆ γραφεῖσα καθαρά ("free from mistake"). The old idea that καθαρὸς ἀπό is "Hebraistic" has been completely exploded by Deissmann *BS* p. 196, where the formula *free of a money-debt* is illus-trated by passages scattered over a period of nearly three hundred years. e.g. BGU I. 197[14] (A.D. 17) καθαρῷ ἀπὸ δημοσίων καὶ παντὸς εἴδους, *ib.* 94[19] (A.D. 289) καθαρὰς ἀπὸ . . δημοσίων τελεσμάτων : cf. also *BS* p. 221 *s.v.* ὀφειλή. P Hib I. 84(*a*)[6] σῖτον καθαρὸν ἀπὸ πάντων is an interesting new ex. coming as it does from B.C. 285-4 (not B.C. 301 as formerly believed : see Egypt Exploration Fund—*Archaeo-logical Report*, 1907-8, p. 50). In P Lond 1157 *verso*[16f.] (A.D. 246) (= III. p. 110) ψιλῆ γῆ ἀπὸ [ἀ]μπέλου there seems to be a similar use with ψιλός. For καθαρὰ ποίηση =

"acquit" see *JHS* xxxv. p. 54, and for (τὰ) καθαρά used as a subst. see P Lond 429[6, 12, al.](c. A.D. 350) (II. p. 314 f.). In P Par 51[28] (B.C. 160) (= *Selections*, p. 21), a dream from the Serapeum, we find the words—αὗται δὲ γυναῖκές εἰσιν. ἐὰν μιανθῶσιν, [οὐ μ]ὴ γένονται καθαραὶ πώποτε. For the higher pagan developments see what is said *s.v.* ἁγνός, and add the interesting *Syll* 567[3 ff.] (ii/A.D.) prescribing the con-ditions of entrance to a temple—πρῶτον μὲν καὶ τὸ μέ[γ]ισ-τον, χεῖρας καὶ (γ)νώμην καθαροὺς καὶ ὑγιε[ῖς] ὑπάρχοντας καὶ μηδὲν αὑτοῖς δεινὸν συνειδότας. Then follow τὰ ἐκτός —one thinks of Mt 23[26] : after eating pease-pudding (ἀπὸ φακῆς) an interval of three days is prescribed, after goat's flesh three, after cheese one, after practising abortion (ἀπὸ φθορείων) forty, after the death of a relative forty, after lawful sexual intercourse they may come the same day when sprinkled and anointed with oil. For the beginnings of the same distinction between lawful and illicit intercourse we may compare *Syll* 566, a Pergamene inscr. of ii/B.C.—[3 ff.] ἁγνευέτωσαν δὲ κ[α]ὶ εἰσίτωσαν εἰς τὸν τῆς θεο[ῦ] ναὸν οἵ τε πολῖται καὶ οἱ ἄλλοι πάντες ἀπὸ μὲν τῆς ἰδίας [γυναι]κὸς καὶ τοῦ ἰδίου ἀνδρὸς αὐθημερόν, ἀπὸ τὲ ἀλλοτρίας κ[αὶ] ἀλλοτρίου δευτεραῖοι λουσάμενοι· ὡσαύτως δὲ καὶ ἀπὸ κήδους καὶ τεκούσης γυναικὸς δευτεραῖος· ἀπὸ δὲ τάφου καὶ ἐκφορ[ᾶς] περιρασάμενοι (*i.e.* ραν-) καὶ διελθόντες τὴν πύλην, καθ' ἣν τὰ ἁγιστήρια τίθεται, καθαροὶ αὐθημερόν. The whole is an illustration of the four prohibitions in the Apostolic decree. As showing the Christian use of the adj. we may also cite the new fragment of an uncanonical gospel where the Saviour, who has taken His disciples with Him inside the Temple to the ἁγνευτήριον, is reproached by the chief priest for having failed to perform the necessary cere-monies before entering the holy place—ἀλλὰ μεμολυ[μμένος] ἐπάτησας τοῦτο τὸ ἱερὸν τ[όπον ὄν]τα καθαρόν, ὃν οὐδεὶς ἄ[λλος εἰ μὴ] λουσάμενος καὶ ἀλλά[ξας τὰ ἐνδύ]ματα πατεῖ (P Oxy V. 840[16 ff.]). For the subst. cf. P Lond 604B[112] (c. A.D. 47) (= III. p. 81) εἰς κάθαρσιν. Καθάρσιος = "purging draught" is found in the medical recipe P Oxy XI. 1384[1] (v/A.D.), and in the same document [(27)] the compd. adj. πανκάθαρος is applied to angels.

καθαρότης.

A v A.D. petition, addressed to an unknown preses, P Oxy VI. 904[2], begins—ἡ τῆς ἡμετέρας δικαιοκρισ[ί]ας καθαρότης κἀμὲ ἐλεήσει τὸν γεγηρακότα, "the purity of your righteous judgement will surely pity me, an old man" (Edd.). In *ib.* I. 67[6] (A.D. 338) the word is used in a complimentary periphrasis—ἅπερ ἀντέγραψεν πρὸς τὴν σὴν ἐπιείκιάν τε καὶ καθαρότητα, "which in reply he wrote to your clemency and impartiality" (Edd.). See also *Michel* 545[18] (ii/B.C.) τὴν . . πίστιν τε καὶ καθα[ρ]ότητα, and cf. Aristeas 234 where it is shown that God is truly honoured οὐ δώροις οὐδὲ θυσίαις. ἀλλὰ ψυχῆς καθαρότητι καὶ δια-λήψεως ὁσίας. For the form καθαρειότης cf. *OGIS* 339[14] (c. B.C. 120) διὰ τὴν ἐν τοῖς πιστευομένοις καθαρειότητα.

καθέδρα

is used instead of βῆμα in Ev. Petr. 3, perhaps, as Swete (*ad l.*) suggests, because of its Jewish associations (Ps 100 (107)[32], Mt 23[2]. From the Κοινή we may cite BGU III. 717[14] (A.D. 149) κόφιν[ος], καθέδρα, μυροθήκη πάντα ξύλινα, and the astrological P Ryl II. 63[10] (iii/A.D.) Σκορπείου **καθέδρα**, where the word is used = "the posterior." For the diminutive **καθεδράριον**, "stool," cf. P Oxy VI. 963 (ii/iii A.D.) χάριν δέ σοι οἶδα, μῆτερ, ἐπὶ τῇ σπουδῇ τοῦ **καθεδραρίου**, ἐκομισάμην γὰρ αὐτό. **Καθέδρα** occurs with reference to the sophistical chair occupied by Nicagoras in mid. iii/A.D. in *Syll* 382[2] instead of the usual θρόνος (cf. Philostratus *Vit. Soph.* 618 τὸν Ἀθήνησι τῶν σοφιστῶν θρόνον κατασχών, of Nicagoras). The holder of this chair seems to have ranked above the other professors, cf. Walden *Universities of Ancient Greece*, p. 94.

καθέζομαι.

For this verb, which is always purely durative in the NT "sit," not "sit down" (*Proleg.* p. 118), we may cite *Syll* 737[55] (c. A.D. 175) ἐὰν δὲ ἱερὸς παῖς ἐξωτικὸς καθεσθεὶς ἀναλώσῃ τὰ πρὸς τοὺς θεοὺς καὶ τὸ Βακχεῖον, ἔστω μετὰ τοῦ πατρὸς ἰόβακχος ἐπὶ μιᾷ σπονδῇ τοῦ πατρός. In the v/A.D. Acts of the martyr Paphnutius we read—Ἄπα Παπνούτιος δὲ ἐκαθέσθη ἐπὶ τὴν γῆν, ἐκ[αθέσθησαν δὲ αὐ]ταὶ παρὰ τοὺς πόδας αὐτοῦ (PSI I. 26[2]): cf. the Sileo rescript *OGIS* 201[13] (vi/A.D.) οὐκ ἀφῶ αὐτοὺς καθεζόμενοι (for **καθε**ζομένους) εἰς χώραν αὐτῶν, [20]οὐκ ἀφῶ αὐτοὺς καθεσθῆναι εἰς τὴν σκιάν. Vett. Val. p. 78[24] ποιοῦσι γὰρ ἄρχοντας πόλεων καὶ ἐπὶ δικαστηρίου **καθεζομένους**.

καθεξῆς

is confined in the NT to Lk 1[3], where Blass (*Philology of the Gospels*, p. 18 f.) understands it as "referring to the *uninterrupted* series of a complex narrative."

καθεύδω.

BGU IV. 1141[32] (B.C. 14) οὐδὲ γὰρ καθεύδωι ἔσωι ἵνα εἰδῶι, PSI I. 94[17] (ii/A.D.) **καθεύδει** τῇ νυκτί. In the rules regulating visitors to a sacred shrine, *Syll* 589[44] (iv/B.C.), it is provided—ἐν δὲ τοῖ κοιμητηρίοι καθεύδειν χωρὶς μὲν τὸς ἄνδρας, χωρὶς δὲ τὰς γυναῖκας. The compound ἐγκαθεύδω occurs several times in the same document. We may add Epict. ii. 20. 10 βαλὼν κάθευδε καὶ τὰ τοῦ σκώληκος ποίει, "lie down and sleep and play the part of the worm." On the irregular construction in Mk 4[27] see *Proleg.* p. 185 f.

καθηγητής.

For this word, which in the NT is confined to Mt 23[10], cf. P Giss I. 80[11] (ii/A.D.) πέμψον τῷ καθηγητῇ τῆς θυγ[ατρό]ς μου, ἵνα φιλοπονήσῃ εἰς αὐτήν, "send to my daughter's teacher that he may bestir himself about her," P Oxy VI. 930[6] (ii/iii A.D.) ἐλοιπήθην ἐπιγνοῦσα παρὰ τῆς θυγατρὸς τοῦ **καθηγητοῦ** ἡμῶν, "I was grieved to learn from our teacher's daughter." In the fragmentary P Tebt II. 591 (ii/iii A.D.) the editors suggest that **καθηγητής** may denote a priestly office. MGr **καθηγητής** = "professor."

καθήκω.

There is no need to look to the influence of Stoic philosophy, in which τὰ **καθήκοντα** was a *term. tech.* (cf. Cic. *de Off.* i. 3), to explain the use of this word in Rom 1[28] (cf. Ac 22[2], 2 Macc 6[4]): the verb in the sense of "is becoming," "is fit," is abundantly attested from the Κοινή in both papyr and inscrr. See, e.g., P Lille I. 3[42] (after B.C. 241)

τὸ **καθῆκον** ἡμῖν ὀψώνιον, P Fay 91[20] (A.D. 99) where a woman named Thenetkoueis is engaged to serve for the season in an oil-press—ποιούσαν πάντα ὅσα **καθήκει**, *ib.* 10,[8] (A.D. 133) ποήσασθαι τὴν **καθήκουσαν** ἀναζήτησιν, "to hold the due inquiry," P Oxy I. 115[5] (ii/A.D.) (= *Selections*, p. 96) πάντα ὅσα ἦν **καθήκοντα** ἐποίησα, and from the inscrr. the honorific decree *Priene* 114[32] (after B.C. 84) **καθῆκον** δ' ἐστὶν αὐτὸν . . . ἐπαινεῖσθαί τε καὶ τῆς καθη-[κ]ούσης ἀξιῶσαι τιμῆς (see Rouffiac *Recherches*, p. 40 f.). With Rom 1[28] we may also compare Menander *Fragm.* p. 175 ἐμὲ δὲ ποιεῖν τὸ **καθῆκον** οὐχ ὁ σὸς λόγος, | εὖ ἴσθ' ἀκριβῶς, ὁ δ' ἴδιος πείθει τρόπος.

κάθημαι.

P Petr III. 42 H (8) f [21] (mid. iii/B.C.) ἡμέρας κ ἐκάθητο, P Par 18[11] κάτισον ἕς (*l.* κάθισον ἕως) ἴδωμεν τί μέλλομεν ποιεῖν, BGU IV. 1141[33] (B.C. 14) εὑρίσφωι αὐτὸν **καθήμενο**(ν), *ib.* 1078[6] (A.D. 39) οὐ γὰρ ἀργὸν δεῖ με **καθῆσθαι**. With the use of **κάθημαι** in Ac 23[3], cf. the curious interview between an Emperor (? Commodus) and a certain Appianus, who has been condemned to death, where, in view of an impending riot, a soldier is represented as saying to the Emperor—κύριε, **κάθῃ**, Ρωμαῖοι γογγύζο[υσ]ι, "Lord, while you are sitting in judgement, the Romans are murmuring" (Edd.) (P Oxy I. 33 *verso* iii. 13, late ii/A.D.). For the form **κάθου** (Mk 12[36], Ac 2[34], from Ps 110[1]), see Maidhof, p. 300 : cf. Menander *Fragm.* p. 254, where Kock quotes other three passages from comic poets. With *Pelagia-Legenden*, p. 4[1] **καθημένη** εἰς βαδιστήν, "seated on an ass," Musonius p. 43[18] **καθῆσθαι** εἰς Σινώπην, "to settle in S.," cf. Mk 13[3], Ac 8[40]. Musonius p. 59[7], uses the word of an idle, sedentary life. For the Aramaism in Mk 4[1] see *s.v.* ἐμβαίνω. MGr **κάθομαι**.

καθημερινός

is found in various iii/A.D. magical texts, e.g. P Lond 121[218] (= I. p. 91) φυλακτήριον πρὸς ῥιγοπυρέτιον **καθημε**ρινόν, P Tebt II. 275[1] ἀπὸ παντὸς ῥίγους . . τριταίου ἢ τεταρταίου ἢ **καθημερινοῦ** ἢ παρημερινοὺς (*l.*—οῦ) ἢ νυκτο-πυρετ[ο]ῦ, " from every fever, whether it be tertian or quartan or daily or on alternate days, or by night " (Edd.) : cf. Hobart, p. 134 f. The phrase **καθημερινῆς** προαιρέσεως is found in a London papyrus, Inv. 1885[iii] of A.D. 124 : see *Archiv* vi. p. 101. In *Syll* 612[22] (Olympia—B.C. 24) the title **καθημεροθύτης** is given to the priest who sacrifices daily : see the editor's note. MGr **καθημερνός**.

καθίζω.

A good ex. of the trans. use of this verb, as in 1 Cor 6[4], Eph 1[20], Ev. Petr. 3, is afforded by P Oxy XII. 1469[7] (A.D. 298) ὁ τῇ ἐπίζει (*l.* ἐπείξει) τῶν χωμάτων ἐπικείμενος **καθείζων** ἡμᾶς τοὺ[ς ο]ἰκίζοντας τοῖς τόπο[ι]ς ἠνάγκασεν ἀ[ν]αβαλεῖν ναύβια σν, "the overseer of labour on dykes set us, the local inhabitants, to work, and made us bank up 250 naubia " (Edd.). For the intrans. usage, as probably in Jn 19[13] (see P. Corssen *ZNTW*, 1914, p. 338 ff.), with reference to "judicial" sitting, see *Syll* 929[28] (ii/B.C.) cited *s.v.* διακονέω, and cf. PSI V. 502[21] (B.C. 257-6) **καθίσαντες** εἰς τὸ ἱερόν, P Meyer 19[5] (ii/A.D.) τῇ ια **ἐκάθισα** εἰς πλ[ο]ιόν [μου, *Preisigke* 4117[5] (A.D. 117) τὸ προσκύνημα ἀνδρὸς ἀγαθοῦ καὶ ἀγνοτάτου ὧδε καθίσαντος τρίς, also Aristeas 94. The verb survives in MGr. For καθιζάνω used intransitively as in early poetry, cf. P Par 51²⁰ (B.C. 160) (= *Selections*, p. 20).

καθίημι.

P Petr III. 42 C (14)⁵ (B.C. 255) καθεῖκα. For the post-classical use of the verb, which in the NT is confined to the Lukan writings, see the exx. in Schmid *Atticismus* iv. p. 360.

καθίστημι

in the sense of "appoint" may be illustrated from P Hib I. 82¹·³⁴ (B.C. 239-8) καθεστήκαμεν γραμματέα Ἰσοκράτην τῶν ἀπεσταλμέν[ω]ν εἰς τὸν ['Αρσι]νοίτην κληρούχων, "I have appointed Isocrates as scribe of the cleruchs sent to the Arsinoite nome " (Edd.), P Ryl II. 153²¹ (A.D. 138-161) οὗ καὶ καθίστημι ἐπιτρόπους [ἄχ]ρι οὗ γένη[ται τῆ]ς ἐννό-[μο]υ [ἡ]λικίας . . . οὓς [οἶδα ἐπιτηδείου]ς, "I appoint as his guardians until he attains the legal age. . . . (the afore-said persons) whom I know to be suitable " (Edd.), and P Amh II. 65² (early ii A.D.) where, in answer to a petition that one of two brothers should be released from public service to attend to the cultivation of their own land, the Prefect decides—δίκαιον τὸν ἕτερον ἀπολυθῆναι ἐὰν ἄλλος ἀντ' αὐτοῦ κατασταθῇ, "it is just that one of them should be released, if some one else is appointed in his stead " (Edd.). The verb is also used technically of presenting oneself before judges, e.g. P Petr III. 30ⁱⁱ·² (Ptol.) κατα-στάντος μου ἐπὶ [σοῦ πρὸς] Εἰρήνην, "when I appeared in your court in my suit against Eirene " (Edd.), P Oxy II. 281²¹ (A.D. 20-50) διὸ ἀξιῶ συντάξαι καταστῆσαι αὐτὸν ἐπὶ σέ, "I therefore beg you to order him to be brought before you," P Ryl II. 65¹⁰ (B.C. 67?) ἠξίουν συντάξαι καταστῆσαι τοὺς ἐγκαλουμένους, " they asked that the accused should be ordered to be brought forward " (Edd., *ib.* 136¹⁴ (A.D. 34) καταστῆσαι ἐπὶ σὲ πρὸς τὴν ἐσομένην ἐπέξοδον, "to bring them before you for the ensuing punishment " (Edd.). The simpler meaning of "conduct " or "bring," as in Ac 17¹⁵, occurs in P Par 51²³ᶠ (B.C. 160) (= *Selections*, p. 20) ἐγὼ καταστήσ[ας] Διδύμας ἐπὶ σέ, ὁρῶ σοι αὐτὸν καθιστῶντα αὐτάς, "I have conducted the Twins to you: I see him con-ducting them to you," BGU I. 93²² (ii/iii A.D.) κατάστησον αὐτοὺς εἰς Μέμφιν. For the verb = "come into a certain state," as in Jas 3⁶, 4⁴, we may compare P Ryl II. 281²¹ (A.D. 54-67) οὐκ ἐπένευσεν ἐξόφθαλμος αὐτῆς καθεστὼς διὰ τὸ πλῆθος τῶν κατ' ἔτος γεννημάτων, "he refused, having grown covetous of it owing to its great yearly productivity " (Edd.); see also Aristeas 289 καὶ γὰρ ἐκ βασιλέων βασιλεῖς γινόμενοι πρὸς τοὺς ὑποτεταγμένους ἀνήμεροί τε καὶ σκληροὶ καθίστανται, "for *some* kings of royal lineage are inhuman and harsh towards their subjects " (Thackeray), and Menander *Fragm.* p. 215 ἅπαντα δοῦλα τοῦ φρονεῖν καθίσταται, "everything is found to be the servant of good sense." For the pass., as in Rom 5¹⁹, cf. P Rein 18⁴³ (B.C. 108) προ-νοηθῆναι ὡς ἀπερίσπ[αστο]ς κατασταθήσεται, "veiller à ce qu'il soit laissé en repos " (Ed.). In P Revill Mél 295¹⁴ (B.C. 131-0) (= Witkowski *Epp.*² p. 26) προσπέπτωκεν < γὰρ > Παῶν ἀναπλεῖν ἐν τῶι Τῦβι < μ ηνὶ > μετὰ δυνα-τῶν ἱκανῶν πρὸς τὸ καταστεῖσαι τοὺς ἐν Ἑρμώνθει ὄχλους, Witkowski understands the verb as = "reprimere," "com-primere." For the subst. κατάστασις used legally (see

supra) cf. P Fay 11²⁷ (c. B.C. 115) διαλέξαντες αὐτὴν εἰς κα[τά]στασιν, "having selected it a petition) for trial "; see also *Archiv* ii. p. 576.

καθό.

P Ryl II. 119³⁰ (A.D. 54-67) ἐν οὐδενὶ ἡγήσατο καθὸ ὑπερισχύων ἡμᾶς ἐπὶ τῶν τόπων, "he scorned (petitions and reports) in virtue of his superior local power " (Edd.). *Michel* 731²² (ii B.C.) τὰ δὲ περὶ τὴν πομπὴν ἐπιτελέσαι καθὸ πάτριόν ἐστιν, "according to traditional custom." With the use in 2 Cor 8¹² cf. Aristeas 11 χαρακτῆρσι γὰρ ἰδίοις κατὰ τὴν Ἰουδαίων χρῶνται, καθάπερ Αἰγύπτιοι τῇ τῶν γραμμάτων θέσει, καθὸ καὶ φωνὴν ἰδίαν ἔχουσιν.

καθολικός.

For this adj. = "general," "universal," as in the titles of the "Catholic " Epistles, see *Syll* 355¹ (B.C. 6) κατακο-λουθῶν τῇ καθολικῇ μου [προ]θέ[σ]ει τοῦ [τ](η)[ρ]εῖν τὰ ὑπὸ τῶν πρὸ ἐμοῦ ἀνθυπάτων γραφέντ[α. Cf. also *OGIS* 669⁴⁷ (i/A.D.) οὐκ ἔξον τοῖς βουλομένοις εὐχερῶς καθολικόν τι καινίζειν, and the decision of a judge in a case of inherit-ance, BGU I. 19¹·⁵ (A.D. 135) which begins—ὑπερεθέμην τὸ νῦν π[ρᾶγ]μα, ἐπεὶ καθολικὸν ἦν, "I have delayed the present matter, since it was of general interest." In late Roman and Byzantine times the title καθολικός was given to the chief of the general department of finance, e.g. P Oxy IX. 1204⁹ (A.D. 299) ποιήσας τὰ ἐπὶ τῇ ἐκκλήτῳ δέοντα κατέ-φυγον πρὸς τὸν κύριόν μου τὸν διασημότατον καθολικὸν Πομπώνιον Δόμνον, "having taken the proper steps for the appeal I had recourse to my lord the most honourable catholicus Pomponius Domnus " (Edd.), cf. P Lond 1157 *verso*¹¹ (A.D. 246) (= III. p. 110), P Rein 56² (iv/A.D.), and *OGIS* 686² (end of iii/A.D.), and see Wilcken *Grundzüge* I. i, pp. 157, 162. Amongst the acclamations at a popular demonstration in honour of the prytanis, P Oxy I. 41³ (iii/iv A.D.), we find εὐτυχῶ[ς], τῷ καθολικῷ, "prosperity to our ruler," where, as the editors remark, the word is used in a wider sense, as a title of the ἡγεμών; cf. Wilcken *Ostr.* I. p. 69. In P Oxy XIV. 1663¹⁵ (ii/iii A.D.) the term is applied to a subordinate official. For the adv. see *OGIS* 669⁴⁹ (i/A.D.) καθολικῶς ἦι πληθικῶς.

καθόλου.

P Tebt I. 27⁷⁷ (B.C. 113) καθόλου δ' ἐνθυμηθεὶς ἡλίκην συμβάλλεται ἡ περὶ τὰ ὑποδεικνύμεν[α] προσοχὴν τοῖς πράγμασι ῥοπήν, "in general consider how great an impulse attention to the matters indicated gives to business " (Edd.), P Oxy II. 239¹⁰ (A.D. 66), εἰς μηδένα λόγον τῷ καθόλου, "for no purpose whatever," *ib.* 207⁹ (A.D. 36) αἷς (*sc.* δραχμαῖς) οὐδὲν τῶι καθόλου προσῆκται, "to which nothing at all has been added " (Edd.). In P Ryl II. 174²⁰ (A.D. 112) in connexion with the repayment of a loan provision is made that certain parties will not proceed against others— περὶ ἄλλου μηδενὸς ἁπλῶς πράγματος μηδὲ ὀφειλήματος μηδὲ [μηδενὸς τῷ καθόλου ἐνγράπτου μηδὲ ἀγράφου ἀπὸ τῶν ἔμπροσθεν χρόνω ν) [μέχρι] τῆς ἐνεστώσης ἡμέρας τρόπῳ μηδενί, "on any matter at all or debt or count of any kind whatsoever, written or unwritten, in the past down to the present day, in any manner " (Edd.). Cf. *OGIS* 715³ where the highest financial official in Egypt is described as placed ἐπὶ τῶν καθ' ὅλου λόγων : see also *s.v.* καθολικός.

καθοπλίζω.

P Leid Wxiii. 34 (ii/iii A.D.) ἐφάνη διὰ τοῦ ποππυσμοῦ Φόβος καθωπλισμένος: cf. Aristeas 14 ἐπιλέξας τοὺς ἀρίστους ταῖς ἡλικίαις καὶ ῥώμῃ διαφέροντας καθώπλισε.

καθοράω.

For the aor. of this NT ἅπ. εἰρ. (Rom 1²⁰: cf. *Proleg.* p. 117) cf. P Lond 342¹³ (A.D. 185) (= II. p. 174), where the production of certain offenders is demanded—ὅτι κα[τ]ίδωμεν τ[ίς ἔ]σται ὁ καρπιζόμενός σε. In the well-known epitaph of Abercius, Bishop of Hierapolis towards the close of ii/A.D., Christ is described as the pure Shepherd—

ὃς βόσκει προβάτων ἀγέλας οὔρεσι πεδίοις τε,
ὀφθαλμοὺς ὃς ἔχει μεγάλους πάντα καθορόωντας.

See Lightfoot *Apost. Fathers²* II. i. p. 496.

καθότι.

For this word, which is peculiar to Luke in the NT, we may cite P Hib I. 66³ (B.C. 228) καθότι ὑμῖν καὶ Ἀσκληπιάδης γέγραφεν, P Amh II. 49³ (B.C. 108) καθότι πρόκειται, P Tebt II. 386²³ (B.C. 12) καθότι προγέγραπται, *etc.* The meaning "as," "just as," is seen in P Eleph 24⁵ (iii/B.C.) καθότι ἂν ἡμῖν ἐπιδείξωσιν οἱ βασιλικοὶ γραμματεῖς, P Ryl II. 154¹⁹ (contract of marriage—A.D. 66) καθότι π[ρότ]ερον [συ]νεβίουν, P Oxy XII. 1473¹⁶ (A.D. 201) καθότι πρὸς ἀλλήλους συνεχώρησαν, *Michel* 534²⁸ (iii/B.C. ad init.) καθότι ἂν δοκεῖ αὐτοῖς. For the iterative force of ἄν in this last ex. cf. Ac 2⁴⁵: practically the same phrase, though now with the subjunctive, is found in PSI IV. 415⁹ (iii/B.C.) καθ' ὅ τι ἄν σου τυγχάνηι [χρ]εία[ν] ἔχων.

καθώς.

P Oxy X. 1299⁹ (iv/A.D.) καθὼς ἐνετιλάμην (*l.* -άμην) σ[ο]ι [περ]ὶ λωβιν μαχερῶν καὶ περὶ πιπεράδιον, "do as I told you about the . . . of knives and the pepper " (Edd.) is a good parallel to the construction in 1 Tim 1³. Other exx. of the particle, which is condemned by the Atticists (Lob. *Phryn.* p. 426), are P Eleph 18⁶ (B.C. 223-2) καθὼ[ς συντέτα]χεν Μνήσαρχο[ς, P Lille I. 26⁴ (iii/B.C.) τὴν δὲ λοιπὴν γ[ῆ]ν ἑτοιμάζω, εἰ μὴ ἀκολουθεῖ ἅπαντα καθώς ἐστιν ἐπὶ τῆς διαγραφῆς, P Oxy XII. 1453¹⁶ (B.C. 30-29) εἰ μὴν προστατήσ[ειν] τοῦ λύχνου τῶν προδεδηλωμέν[ων] ἱερῶν καθὼς πρόκειται, "that we will superintend the lamps of the above mentioned temples, as aforesaid " (Edd.), and from the inscr. *Michel* 230⁵ (ii/B.C. ad fin.) καθὼς καὶ πρότερον. MGr καθώς.

καί.

In *LAE* p. 129 ff. Deissmann discusses the thoroughly *popular* character of the Johannine style with its short paratactic sentences, introduced by καὶ . . . καί. To illustrate this, he cites amongst other exx. a Dream from the Serapeum, P Par 51 (B.C. 160) (= *Selections*, p. 18 ff.: see especially the amended readings in *Archiv* vi. p. 204), which runs—²ff. ὤμ[ην] βατ(   ) δίζειν με [ἀπ]ὸ λειβὸς ἕως ἀ[πηλι]ώτου, καὶ ἀναπίπτομαι ἐπ' ἄχυρον· καὶ [ἄν]θρωπ[ος] ἀπὸ λιβός μου, ἐχόμενός μου· ἀναπίπτει καὶ αὐτός, καὶ ὥσπερ κεκλειμμ[ένοι] μου ἦσαν οἱ ὀφθαλμοί μου, καὶ ἐξαί[φνης] ἀνύγω τοὺς ὀφθαλμούς μου, καὶ ὁρῶ κτλ., " I dreamed that I was going from West to East, and I lie down upon chaff. And there

is a man west of me, near to me. He also lies down, and my eyes were as if they were closed. And suddenly I open my eyes, and I see etc." Cf. also the letter of consolation P Oxy I. 115³ff. (ii/A.D.) (= *Selections*, p. 96) οὕτως ἐλυπήθην καὶ ἔκλαυσα ἐπὶ τῶι εὐμοίρωι ("the blessed one ") ὡς ἐπὶ Διδύματος ἔκλαυσα, καὶ πάντα ὅσα ἦν καθήκοντα ἐποίησα καὶ πάντες οἱ ἐμοί, and the inser. *Syll* 807 ¹⁵ff. cited *s.v.* ἐπιχρίω, on which Deissmann (*op. cit.* p. 132) remarks: " this text is, if possible, even more paratactic ('Semitic,' people would say, if it were a quotation from the New Testament) than the corresponding passage in St. John [9⁷,¹¹]." So also the simple parataxis of Jn 4³⁵ *al.* is illustrated by the illiterate P Par 18¹⁴ ἔτι δύο ἡμέρας ἔχομεν καὶ φθάσομεν εἰς Πηλ[οῦσι, and by the dedicatory inser. at El-Kab, *Preisigke* 158 Ἀνδρόμαχος Μακεδὼν ἀφίκετο πρὸς Ἀμενώθην χρηστὸν θεὸν μ[ι]σθοῦ ἐργαζόμενος καὶ ἐμαλακίσθη (" he was weakly ") καὶ ὁ θεὸς αὐτῶι ἐβοήθησε αὐθημερή: cf. Thumb *Hellen.* p. 129. Notwithstanding, however, this use of καί in later Greek idiom, it is impossible to deny that the use of καί in the LXX for the Heb.) influenced the Johannine usage.

For δέ after καί, as in Mt 10¹⁸, Jn 6⁵¹, 1 Jn 1³, cf. P Hib I. 54²⁰ (c. B.C. 245) καὶ τὸ σῶμα δὲ εἰ συνείληφας παράδος αὐτὸ (deleted in the original) Σεμφθεῖ. For καί after μετά in Phil 4³ Deissmann (*BS,* p. 265) can quote only BGU II. 412⁶ (iv/A.D.) Λαννοῦς χήρα οὖσα μετὰ καὶ τοῦ υἱοῦ ἑαυτῆς, but he gives (p. 266) several instances of σὺν καί, e.g. *ib.* 515¹⁷ (A.D. 193) Πτολεμαῖος σὺν καὶ ὑπη[ρ]έ[τ]η Ἀμμων[ί]ῳ: add from the inser. *PAS* 612 (Imperial) σὺν καὶ τῷ ἀνδρὶ αὐτῆς. For καὶ γάρ see *s.v.* γάρ, and add P Giss I. 69⁴ (A.D. 118-9) καὶ γὰρ πέρυσι ἐπὶ τὴν παράλημψιν τῶν ἱματίων αὐτὸν παρὰ σοὶ κατέλειψα: and for ὁ καί see *s.v.* ὁ. The strange form κά for καί occurs seven times in Codex Washington (W).

Καϊάφας (or Καϊφας).

See F. C. Burkitt *Syriac Forms*, pp. 5, 9.

καινός.

Papyrus usage hardly tends to sharpen the distinction between καινός and νέος. In P Petr III.80⁴·⁵ (Ptol.) a town named Ptolemais is Πτ. ἡ καινή, while in *ib.* 72(b)¹⁶ it is Πτ. ἡ νέα. P Petr III. 37(a)ⁱ ¹⁸ (Ptol.) has χῶμα καινόν contrasted with ²¹ χῶμα παλαιόν: *ib.* 46(1)¹⁷ has πρὸς τὰ θεμέλια τῆς καινῆς καταλύσεως, " new quarters." *Ostr* 1142⁴ (beginning iii/A.D.) gives us οἶνος καινός to contrast with οἶνος νέος in Mk 2²². P Amh II. 64² (A.D. 107) περὶ δαπάνης εἰς τὸ ἐκ καινῆς κατασκευαζόμενον βαλανεῖον, " concerning expenditure on the baths which were being refitted " (Edd.): so P Oxy IV. 707⁴·⁷ (c. A.D. 136) οἰκοδομή]σω τροχὸν ἐκ καινῆς, " a new wheel," P Tebt II. 342¹⁶ (late ii/A.D.) τὸ κατασκευασθ(ὲν) ἐκ καινῆς ἐν Σομολ(ῷ) κεραμεῖον. Two inventories P Tebt II. 405⁸ (iii/A.D.), 406¹⁷ (c. A.D. 266) have κόβ(= φ)ινος καινός, " a new basket," and κολόβιον λινοῦν δ[ί]σημον καινόν, " a new linen shirt with two stripes ": it may be doubted whether stress is to be laid on their being hitherto unused, though perhaps they were of ancient manufacture. See also P Hib I. 54²⁶ (c. B.C. 245) κέραμον κα[ι]νόν, P Lond 402 *verso*¹² (B.C. 152 or 141) (= II. p. 11) ὀθόνια καινά, P Fay 121⁵ (c. A.D. 100) ζυγόδεσμον καινόν, and

CPHerm I. 86[10] καινοῦ νομίσματο[ς : cf. [18]. In P Heid 6[10] (iv/A.D.) (= *Selections*, p. 126) the writer addresses a Christian "brother" as δεσπότην καὶ κενὸν (*l.* καινὸν) (π)ά[τ]ρω[να. Τὰ καινότερον (like τὰ πάλαι, etc.), unless it is a mere mistake for τι, is the phrase for "news" in BGU III. 821[4] (ii/A.D.) ἀνέβη εἰ[ς τ]ὴν πόλιν, ἵνα εἰδ[ῶ] τὰ καινότερον, followed by [6] ὅταν ἦν (= ᾖ, as often) τι καινότερον, εὐθέως σοι δηλ[ώ]σω: cf. Ac 17[21]. For the subst. καινισμός see P Lond 354[16] (*c.* B.C. 10) (= II. p. 165) ἀποστάσεως καινισμὸν παραλογιεῖσθαι, and for the verb καινίζω see P Tor II. 7[19] μὴ προσέχειν τοῖς ἐπὶ χρειῶν τεταγμένοις καὶ(νί)ζειν τι, and Wünsch *AF* 5[87] (iii/A.D.) ὁρκίζω σε . . τὸν ποιοῦντα ἔκτρομον τὴν [γ]ῆν ἅπασ[αν καὶ] καινίζοντα πάντας τοὺς κατοικοῦντας (cf. Wisd 7[27]).

In MGr καινός is "literary": the New Testament in Pallis' edition is ἡ νέα διαθήκη, which shows how νέος has gained ground at the expense of its rival.

καίπερ.

P Giss I. 47[22] (time of Hadrian) ἃς μέντοι δεδώκεις εἰς τρ̅ο̅υ̅τ̅ο̅ (δραχμὰς) κ̅δ̅ ἔπεμψά σοι, καίπερ Διονυσ[ί]ου τοῦ ἀργυροκόπου κατασχόντος μου ὅλας (δραχμὰς) μ̅, PSI IV. 298[17] (iv/A.D.) καίπερ αὐτοῦ τὸ σύνολον μὴ ἐπιστα[μένου.

καιρός.

For the idea of "fitting season," "opportunity," which is specially associated with this word, we may cite such passages as PSI IV. 375[8] (B.C. 250-49) ὡς ἄν σοι καιρὸς γένηται, P Oxy I. 37[i. 15] (A.D. 49) (= *Selections*, p. 50) καιρὸν εὑροῦσ[α] εἰσεπήδησεν εἰς τὴν τοῦ ἡμετέρου [ο]ἰκίαν καὶ τὸ σωμάτιον ἀφήρπασεν, "seizing a favourable opportunity, she burst into my client's house, and carried off the foundling"—an advocate speaks, P Amh II. 130[10] (A.D. 70) οὔτε κερὸν (*l.* καιρὸν) γνούς, "and perceived no opportunity," P Meyer 20[20] (1st half ii/A.D.) συνπεριφέρου τῷ καιρῷ ἕως σε καταλάβω, "adapt yourself to circumstances until I join you," *ib.* [22] βλέπετε καὶ ὑμεῖς τὸν καιρόν, P Tebt II. 332[9] (A.D. 176) ἐπῆλθάν τινες ληστρικῷ τρόπῳ οἰκίαν μου . . . καιρὸν λαβόμενοι τῆς ἐκκυτ(= οιτ)είας μου, "certain persons broke into my house in a thievish manner taking advantage of my absence." Cf. also such phrases as P Par 46[7] (B.C. 157) ἐν τοῖς ἀναγκαιοτάτοις καιροῖς, BGU IV. 1185[4] (end i/B.C.) ἐν τοῖς . . ἐπείγουσι κα[ιρ]οῖς, P Amh II. 87[20] (A.D. 125) τῷ δήοντι καιρῷ, "at the due time," and in plur. *ib.* 91[13] (A.D. 159) τοῖς δεοῦσι καιροῖς, P Giss I. 19[4] (ii/A.D.) διὰ τὰ ὄν[τα τῷ καιρῷ φημιζόμενα. The word passes into the meaning "crisis" in the interesting letter P Lond 42[15] (B.C. 168) (= I. p. 30. *Selections*, p. 10) which a wife addresses to her husband "in retreat" in the Serapeum telling him of her difficulties, and of having piloted herself and child "out of such a crisis"—ἐκ τοῦ το[ιού]του καιροῦ ἐμαυτή[ν] τε καὶ τὸ παιδί[ον σ]ου διακεκυβερνηκυῖα, and *ib.* [24] ὡς ἔτ[ι] σοῦ παρ[όν]τος πάντων ἐπεδεόμην, μὴ ὅτι γε τοσούτου χρόνου ἐπιγεγονότος καὶ τοιούτων καιρῶν, "while you were still at home, I went short altogether, not to mention how long a time has passed since with such disasters." In P Tebt II. 272[14] (late ii/A.D.) οἱ καιροί are used of "the stages" of a fever. For a happier connotation see the mantic P Ryl I. 28[153] (iv/A.D.) γαστροκνημία δεξιὰ ἐὰν ἅλληται ἐξ ἀπροσδοκήτου προσλήμψεταί τι κατὰ τὸν βίον καὶ ἕξει τοῦ καιροῦ, "if the right calf quiver, the person will

unexpectedly acquire something in his life and will have prosperity" (Edd.). Adverbial phrases are seen in P Fay 90[17] (A.D. 234) τὴν ἐπὶ τοῦ καιροῦ ἔσο μένην πλίστην τει(μην), "the highest price current," P Ryl II. 70[9] (late ii/A.D.) τῶν κατὰ καιρὸν ἐπιτρόπων τε καὶ ἡγεμόνων, "successive procurators and praefects" (Edd.), *ib.* 104[6] (A.D. 167) ταῖς κατὰ καιρὸν κατ' οἰκ ίαν [ἀ]πογρα(φαῖς), "the successive household censuses," P Lond 974[5] (A.D. 305-6) (= III. p. 116) τῶν κατὰ καιρὸν εἴδων ὀπωριμείων, "fruits in season." As showing the transition to the meaning "weather," which the word has in MGr, cf. PSI V. 486[10] (B.C. 258-7) ὁ γὰρ καιρὸς ὁ βέ[λ]τιστος ἐνέστηκε, P Oxy X. 1257[3] (iii/A.D.) τοῦ καιροῦ λήξαντος τῆς παραδόσεως σίτου, "the time for the delivery of corn had passed" (Edd.), P Fay 133[9] (iv/A.D.) ὁ καιρὸς νῦν ἐστιν ὀψιμώτερος, "the season is now rather late," *ib.* 135[2] (iv/A.D.) τοῦ καιροῦ καλέσαντος τῆς συνκομιδῆς ὀφ[. . . , "as the season requires the gathering . . ." (Edd.). The adj. καίριμος is applied to "seasoned" wine in P Flor II. 139[*2] (A.D. 264), cf. *ib.* 143[2], 266[3], P Rein 53[2] (iii/iv A.D.) (where, however, the editor translates doubtfully " au moment le plus opportun (?) "), and the compd. verb καιροτηρέω, "wait for a favourable opportunity," occurs in P Amh II. 35[3] (B.C. 132), BGU III. 909[6] (A.D. 350). See also P Lond 379[3] (iii/A.D.?) (= II. p. 162) ἀκαιρί, "at inconvenient seasons." For the relation of καιρός to χρόνος see Trench *Syn.* §lvii., *Rhein. Mus.* N.F. lix. (1904), p. 233 ff., and for a discussion of the Greek idea of καιρός see Butcher *Harvard Lectures on Greek Subjects*, p. 117 ff. In MGr χρόνος = "year," and καιρός = "weather."

Καῖσαρ.

Lightfoot (*Phil.*[2] p. 169 ff.) has shown that by the phrase οἱ ἐκ τῆς Καίσαρος οἰκίας in Phil 4[22] we are probably to understand slaves and freedmen attached to the palace, and has appealed to inscriptional evidence to prove that the designation embraced a large number of persons both in Rome and elsewhere (e.g. Ephesus), filling every description of more or less domestic office: see further SH p. 418 ff. In BGU I. 156[3] (A.D. 201) χρηματίσατε Σατουρνείνῳ Καισάρων οἰκονόμῳ, Wilcken (*Ostr.* i. p. 409 n.[4]) holds that Καισάρων stands for Καισάρων δούλῳ; similarly in P Lond 256 *recto*[1] (A.D. 11-15) (= II. p. 96) Φαῦστος Πρίσκου Καίσαρος = Φ. Π. Καίσαρος δούλου (*ib.* p. 602); cf. the simple gen. Χριστοῦ, "belonging to Christ" Gal 3[29] *al.*: Deissmann *LAE* p. 382). On the other hand Καισάρειοι = "Imperial freedmen," e.g. in P Oxy III. 477[1] (A.D. 132-3), though their exact position is far from clear: see *Chrest.* I. i. p. 47, and cf. Schubart *Archiv* v. p. 116 ff. For Καισαριανοί, "Caesar's officials," see Epict. i. 19. 19, and for καισάριον, "palace," see an inscr. of the time of the Emperor Maurice referred to in *Archiv* ii. p. 403.

καίτοι.

P Petr II. 3(*b*)[2] (iii/B.C.) παρὰ δύναμιν δὲ καίτοι πάλαι ἐκ[. . . . .] ἀντέχομαι, BGU III. 850[4] (A.D. 76) θαυμάζω(ι) ἐπὶ τῆι[. . .]νταξίᾳ σου, καίτοι ἐμοῦ σε πολλὰ ἐρωτήσαντος, P Giss I. 84[ii. 10] (beg. ii/A.D.) μέχρι τούτ'ο]υ σοι οὐ πα[ρ]εστάθη καίτοι πρόγραμμά σου π[ροετέθη κελεῦον κτλ., PSI IV. 298[12] (iv/A.D.) τοὺς τοῦ μηνὸς [μισθοὺς οὐ παρ]έσχεν μοι καίτοι αὐτὸς ἐκδεξάμενος κτλ.

καίτοιγε.

Syll 929[82] (ii/B.C.) διεκεκώλυτο ἵνα μηθεὶς ἐν τῷ ἱερῶι τοῦ Διὸς τοῦ Δικταίου μήτε ἐννέμηι μήτε ἐναυλοστατῆι . . . καίτοιγε Ῥωμαίων.

καίω.

P Oxy XII. 1453[18] (B.C. 30–29) τὸ καθῆκον ἔλαιον εἰς τοὺς καθ᾽ ἡμέραν λύχνους καομένους ἐν τοῖς σημαινομένοις ἱεροῖς, "the proper oil for the daily lamps burning in the temples signified" (Edd.), P Tebt II. 273[15] (medical prescription—ii/iii A.D.) χαλκοῦ κεκαυμένου (δραχμὴ) ā, the magic P Lond 46[154] (iv/A.D.) (= I. p. 70) ἐγώ εἰμι οὗ τὸ στόμα καίεται δι᾽ ὅλου, and PSI I. 28[60] (iii/iv A.D. ?) καομένη πυρουμένη βασανιζομένη γοργονία. With the usage in Lk 24[82] we may compare the new erotic fragment P Grenf I. 1[1 9] (ii/B.C.) συνοδηγὸν ἔχω τὸ πολὺ πῦρ τὸ ἐν τῆι ψυχῆι μου καιόμενον, and the citation from the same papyrus *s.v.* κατακαίω. On the possibility of explaining the different renderings in this Lukan passage as due to a single Syriac original in three stages of corruption cf. W. C. Allen in *JTS* ii. p. 299. For flexions (e.g. 2 Pet 3[10]) see Moulton *Gr.* ii. § 95. MGr καίω, καίγω, κάβω : for the metaphorical sense cf. καγμός, "longing," "desire," "pain."

κακία

is used in P Petr II. 23(1)[3] (Ptol.) ἰδ[ό]ντες τὴν κακίαν τῶν ἡμῶν, apparently of the damage done to a crop of rye and barley by hail (?) : cf. P Flor II. 170[11] (A.D. 250) ἐκ τῆς τῶν σύκων κακίας. In P Petr II. 19(2)[5] (Ptol.) διὰ τὴν ἐν[εστ]ῶσαν κακίαν, the reference is to the "idleness" of certain workmen. For the stronger meaning "malice," "wickedness," see P Rein 7[15] (B.C. 141 ?) διὰ πάση]ς ἡσυχίας εἴχον τῶι μηδεμίαν ἔννοιαν [κ]ακίας ἔχειν, "je restai complètement tranquille, n'ayant aucun soupçon qu'il me cherchât malice" (Ed.), P Oxy VIII. 1101[7] (A.D. 367–70) εἴτε ὑπὸ κακίας ἢ καὶ ὑπὸ κακο[βουλεία]ς τῆς πρ[ο]αιρέσεως, "whether from malice or from perversity of judgment" (Ed.) : also *Preisigke* 4127[6] ἀλότριον ἐμαυτὸν ἐποιησάμην πάσης κακείας καὶ πάσ[ης . . .]ατος καὶ ἁγνείας ἐς πολὺν χρόν[ον. The special usage in Mt 6[34] is supported by the LXX, where κακία frequently translates Heb. רָעָה in the sense of "trouble," "evil circumstances" : cf. Kennedy *Sources*, p. 100.

κακοήθεια.

For this NT ἅπ. εἰρ. (Rom 1[29]) see the late P Grenf I. 60[13] (A.D. 581) where the word is found with a number of others of a similar character ἄνευ παντὸς δόλου καὶ φόβου . . . [καὶ οἱ]ασδήποτε κακονοίας καὶ κακοηθείας καὶ παντὸς ἐλαττώματος κτλ. The adj. is found in P Giss I. 40[ii. 11] (A.D. 212–5) παρὰ το[ῖ]ς κακοήθεσιν.

κακολογέω.

For this verb, which in the NT seems always to be used in the weaker sense of "speak evil of," cf. P Fay 12[15] (c. B.C. 103) ο[ὐ] τυχόντως πλεῖστα κακολογηθείς, "abused . . . in the most unmeasured terms" (Edd.), P Ryl II. 150[5] (A.D. 40) ὕβρισεν οὐ μετρίως καὶ ἐκακολόγησεν πολλὰ καὶ ἀ[σ]χήμονα, "insulted me immoderately with much shameful abuse" (Edd.). The subst. occurs in P Tebt I. 24[77] (B.C. 117) τῆς προσεσχηκυίας αὐτ[οῖ]ς κακολογίας.

κακοπαθέω.

The only exx. we can quote from our sources of this verb, whose formation Thumb (*Dial.* p. 373) ascribes to Ionic influence, are P Lond 98 *recto*[73] (i/ii A.D.) (= I. p. 130) κακοπαθήσεται καὶ ξενιτεύει, and the mantic P Ryl I. 28[54] (iv/A.D.) ἐὰν ἄλληται (μηρὸς εὐώνυμος) σκυλμοὺς καὶ πόνους δηλοῖ κακοπαθήσαντα δὲ εὐφρανθῆναι. See also Teles (ed. Hense) p. 61[6] κακοπαθῶν καὶ δαπανῶν, Musonius p. 28[9] πόσα δ᾽ αὖ κακοπαθοῦσιν ἔνιοι θηρώμενοι δόξαν.

κακοπαθία.

For this form which is adopted by WH instead of the itacistic κακοπάθεια in Jas 5[10], and supported by the evidence given below, see Deissmann *BS* p. 263 f. Whether the word is to be understood actively or passively is not so clear, but the probability is that the two meanings pass into each other, as Deissmann (*ut s.*) practically admits : cf. Thieme (p. 29) who quotes *Magn* 105[3] (B.C. 138) (= *Syll* 929[30]) πᾶσα]ν ἀναδεχόμενοι κακοπαθίαν χάριν τοῦ μ[η]θενὸς ὑσ[τ]ερῆσαι [δικ]αίου μηθένα τῶν κρ[ινομένων, and points out that both "Bemuhung" and "Beschwerde" give good sense. Dittenberger in his note on *OGIS* 244[12] (iii/B.C.) τὴν περὶ τὸ σῶμα [γε]γενημένην ἀσθένειαν διὰ τὰς συνεχεῖς κακο[π]αθίας warns against treating τ. γεγ. ἀσθένειαν διὰ τ. κακοπαθίας as tautological in view of the tendency in late Greek to use κακοπαθία "non tam de malis, quibus quis afflictatur, quam de negotiis laboriosis et molestis, quae in se suscipit," and compares *ib.* 339[23] (c. B.C. 120) πάντα κατωικονόμησατο διὰ τῆς τῶν πρεσβευόντων κακοπαθίας = "omne bene et ex voluntate composuit populus usus labore legatorum." See also *Syll* 255[23] (iii/B.C.) ἐν ἀνάγκαις καὶ κακοπαθίαις γένηται, 246[9] (B.C. 220–16) οὔτε κακοπα[θί]αν οὐδεμίαν οὔτε κί[ν]δυνον ὑποστελλόμενος. For the word passing over almost into the sense of "endurance," see BGU IV. 1209[7] (B.C. 23) οὐδὲν σπουδῆς οὐδὲ κακοπαθίας παρέλιπον.

κακοποιέω.

The wider sense of evil-doing from a moral point of view, as in 1 Pet 3[17], 3 Jn[11], may be illustrated by P Hib I. 59[10] (c. B.C. 245) εἰ μὴ παύσει κ[α]κοποῶν ἐν τῆι κώμη[ι] μεταμελή[σ]ει σοι, "if you do not stop your malpractices in the village you will repent it" (Edd.). P Ryl II. 437[7] (i/A.D.) ἐὰν κακοποιο[—] καὶ ἄπρακτα τ[—] εἰς πλοῖον ἐλ[is too fragmentary to enable us to determine the exact force, but it seems to point to a more restricted sense "injure," "do harm to," as in the few occurrences of the verb in class. literature, and in *Syll* 653[103] (B.C. 91) ἐχέτω δὲ ἐπιμέλειαν ὁ ἀγορανόμος καὶ περὶ τοῦ ὕδατος, ὅπως . . . . μηθεὶς κακοποιεῖ μήτε [τὸ] πλῆμα μήτε τοὺς ὀχετούς, *ib.* 893[15] (ii/A.D.) εἰ δέ τις τὴν ἐπιγραφὴν ἐκκόψῃ ἐκ τῆς παραστά[δο]ς ἢ αὐτὴν ἄρῃ ἢ κακο[ποι]ήσῃ, δώσ(ε)ι κτλ. See also Aristeas 164 πάντα γὰρ λυμαίνονται καὶ κακοποιοῦσι μύες οὐ μόνον πρὸς τὴν ἑαυτῶν τροφήν, ἀλλὰ καὶ εἰς τὸ παντελῶς ἄχρηστον γίνεσθαι ἀνθρώπῳ, ὅ τι ἂν δηποτοῦν ἐπιβάληται κακοποιεῖν, and Musonius p. 32[17] εὐεργετοῦνται μὲν οἱ ἀξιούμενοι τῶν ὠφελίμων καὶ συμφερόντων, κακοποιοῦνται δὲ οἱ ἐμβαλλόμενοι τοῖς ἀσυμφόροις καὶ βλαβεροῖς.

κακοποιός.

An interesting instance of this Petrine adj. is afforded by PSI I. 64²¹ (i/B.C.?), where a woman promises her husband (?)—μηδὲ ποι[ή]σειν εἴς σε φάρμακα φίλτρα μηδὲ κακοποιὰ μήτε ἐν ποτοῖς μήτε ἐν βρωτοῖς: cf. especially 1 Pet 4¹⁵ where the word probably means "a sorcerer, magician, or poisoner" (Souter *Lex. s.v.*). See also P Leid Wxxiv.¹⁸ (ii/iii A.D.) ἐπιμαρτυροῦντος μηδενὸς κακοποιοῦ Κρόνου, ἢ Ἄρεως.

κακός.

This familiar adj. is by no means so common in our sources as we might have expected, but the following may serve as exx. of its varied uses—PSI IV. 340⁴ (B.C. 257–6) ἐστὶ δέ σοι πάντων μὲν τῶν κακῶν αἴτιος Μητρόδωρος. P Oxy III. 532²² (ii/A.D.) οὐκ ἀνέμεινας ὑπὸ κακοῦ συνειδότος κατεχόμενος, "you would not stay, being oppressed by an evil conscience" (Edd.), *ib.* 488¹⁰ (ii/iii A.D.) κακῆς παραγραφῆς, "a false entry," *ib.* VII. 1060⁷ (a Gnostic amulet—vi/A.D.) ἀπάλλαξον τὸν οἶκον τοῦτον ἀπὸ παντὸς κακοῦ ἑρπετοῦ καὶ πράγματος, "free this house from every evil reptile and thing," and, by way of contrast, the imprecatory tablet *Michel* 1322 A Ἀνδροκλείδη καταδῶ καὶ τὴν γλῶτ(τ)αν τὴν κακὴν καὶ τὸν θυμὸν τὸν κακὸν καὶ τὴν ψυχὴν τὴν κακὴν καὶ τὸ ἐργαστήριον καταδῶ καὶ τοὺς παῖδας. For the neut. τὸ κακόν cf. P Amh II. 77³¹ (A.D. 139) Ἁρπα[γάθην τὸ]ν κράτιστον τοῦ κακοῦ καὶ προσεπίτροπο[ν, "Harpagathes, the chief cause and prime mover in the mischief" (Edd.). The word in its wide sense of "troublesome," "distressing," to mind or body, is seen in P Oxy IX. 1215⁶ (ii/iii A.D.) μὴ ἀπέλθῃς εἰς τὸ Σατύρου, αἰπεῖ (. ἐπεὶ) γὰρ ἀκούομεν ὅτι κακά μέλλι πράσι (l. πράσσειν), "do not go to the house of Satyrus, for we hear that he is going to get into trouble" (Edd.), and P Lond 653¹² (early iv/A.D.) (= III. p. 241) ἐν κακοῖς εἰμι. For the collocation κακὸς κακῶς see *s.v.* κακῶς.

κακοῦργος.

P Lille I. 7²⁰ (iii B.C.) ἀνενήνοχέν με εἰς τὸ . . . δεσμωτήριον, φάσκων εἶναί με κακοῦργον, P Hib I. 62³ (B.C. 245) κακοῦργον τὸν τ[ὴν] λείαν ποιήσαντα ἐπικαλεῖ Τνᾶς Ἀρνούφιος, P Fay 108¹¹ (c. A.D. 171) ἐπῆλθαν ἡμεῖν κακοῦργοί τινες, and P Amh II. 83⁴ (iii/iv A.D.) where in connexion with a census certain irregularities are alleged οὐχ ὑπὸ τοῦ κηνσίτορος ἀλλ' ὑπό τινων κακούργων. This last document shows also the verb—¹⁰ κακουργῆσαι καὶ τολμῆσαι: cf. P Oxy XII. 1468⁴ (c. A.D. 258) τοῖς κακουργεῖν προχείρως ἔχουσιν, "those who are designing to commit crime," and ¹⁹ εὑρέν τι κακουργηθέν, "she discovered that a crime had been committed." For the subst. see *ib.* 1469¹⁸ (A.D. 298) τῆς τοῦ βοηθοῦ τοῦ στρατηγοῦ κακουργίας καταφανοῦς οὔσης, "the unfairness of the assistant of the strategus is evident" (Edd.), P Oxy I. 71ⁱ·¹⁰ (A.D. 303) ἐπειράθη μέν τινα κακουργίαν ἐπὶ ἀποστερέσι τῇ ἡμετέρᾳ ποιήσασθαι διὰ τὸ ἀγράμματόν με εἶναι, "he attempted, owing to my being illiterate, to commit a fraud to my detriment" (Edd.). In P Gen I. 31¹⁷ (A.D. 145–6) the editor supplies κακούργημα—ἐάν σοι δόξῃ . . . πέρας ἐπιθεῖναι τοῖς κ[ακουργήμασι, remarking that the word is strong, but that it is a step-mother who speaks! The adj.

ἀκακούργητος is used with reference to the delivery of cargo "safe and sound" in P Lond 948⁸ (A.D. 236) (= III. 220) φορτία . . . σῶα καὶ ἀκακούργητα.

κακουχέω

is common in marriage-contracts, where the husband undertakes as regards his wife—μὴ κακουχεῖν αὐτὴν μηδ' ὑβρίζειν μηδ' ἐγβάλλειν μηδ' ἄλλην γυναῖκα ἐπεισάγειν, see BGU IV. 1050¹⁴ (time of Augustus) *al.*: cf. the complaint against a husband, P Oxy II. 281¹⁷ (A.D. 20–50) οὐ διελείπεν κακουχῶν με καὶ ὑβρί[ζ]ων, and for the corr. subst. see the deed of divorce, BGU IV. 1105¹⁸ (time of Augustus) τοῖς προκειμένοις κακουχίας (l. -αις) με καὶ καθυβρίζει.

κακόω.

Michel 1001ᵛⁱⁱⁱ·⁵ (c. B.C. 200) εἴ τῶν τοῦ κοινοῦ τι κακῶσαι ἢ διελέσθαι ἢ τοῦ ἀρχαίου τι καταχρήσασθαι. The verb is used intransitively in P Tebt II. 407⁹ (A.D. 199?) εὖ ποιήσεις] μὴ κακώσασα, "you will do well not to interfere" (Edd.).

κακῶς.

For the phrase κακῶς ἔχειν, as in Mt 4²⁴ etc., cf. P Oxy VI. 935¹⁵ (iii/A.D.) ἔμελλον . . ἀναβῆναι . . ἐπεὶ οἱ παρὰ] Σαραπίω[νος] εἶπον [κακ]ῶς ἔχειν α[ὐ]τ[όν, "I intended to come up since Sarapion's friends said that he was ill" (Edd.), *ib.* 938⁵ (iii/iv A.D.) τῶν οὖν κτηνῶν κακῶς ἐχόντων, "since, then, the oxen are in a bad way." The combination κακοὺς κακῶς ἀπολέσει αὐτούς in Mt 21⁴¹ sounds rather literary, but cf. ὁ τούτων τι ποιῶν κακὸς κακῇ ἐξωλείᾳ ἀπόλοιτο in *Syll* 584⁵⁴, which Michel doubtfully assigns to i B.C. The inscr. is from Smyrna, apparently from a temple of Atargatis, whose sacred fishes are protected by this portentous curse: he who injures them is to die, ἰχθυόβρωτος γενόμενος (cf. the formation of the adj. σκωληκόβρωτος, Ac 12²³). It seems clear that the collocation κακοὺς κακῶς ἀπολέσθαι, starting as a literary phrase, had been perpetuated in common parlance, like our stock quotations from Shakespeare. Cf. also the inscr. from the Roman catacomb of Priscilla, *Kaibel* 734⁷ᶠ·—

ὁ ποτε πλούσιος περὶ τέκνα νῦν κακὸν κακῶς
τηρῶν ὡς Τάνταλος κολάζομαι.

For other exx. of the adverb see P Petr II. 19 2)³ (Ptol.) ἔρρειμαι γὰρ κακῶς διακείμενος ἀπ' ἐκείνου, P Oxy X. 1349 (ii/A.D. ?) ἐν τῇ (?)] πόλει γέγραπται καὶ κακῶς ἐγγράφη. *ib.* I. 34 *verso* ii.¹² (A.D. 127) διὰ ἀπειθίαν κ[ακ]ῶς ἀφορμὴν ζητοῦντας ἁμαρτημάτω[ν] τειμωρήσομαι, where Brinkmann (see Kuhring *Praef.* p. 41 n.³) suggests κ[ακ]ῶς for the editors' κ[αὶ] ὥς, and *ib.* 40³ ii (iii A.D.) τάχα κακῶς αὐτοὺς ἐθεράπευσας, of possible wrong medical treatment.

κάκωσις.

In PSI III. 158¹³ (iii A.D. ?) a certain astrological conjunction is said to signify ἀτεκνίαν . . . καὶ κάκωσιν [σ]ώματο[ς.

καλάμη.

P Hib I. 90¹⁷ (B.C. 222) ἡ δὲ καλάμη ἔστω Διοδώρου, "the straw shall belong to Diodorus" (Edd.), P Amh II. 89⁵ (A.D. 121) τ[ὰ] ἀπο καλάμ[η]ς ἀνὰ ἀργ[υρίου δραχ[μὰς)

εἴκοσι, BGU II. 661[22] (A.D. 140–1) μετὰ τὸν χρόνον παραδώσω τὸ τρίτον μέρος ἀπὸ ἀναπαύσεως καὶ τὸ λοιπὸν
δίμοιρον μέρο[s] ἀπὸ καλάμης πυροῦ, CPR I. 38[21] (A.D. 263)
παραδώσω τὰς ἀρούρας ἀπὸ καλάμης ἀπὸ θρύου καλάμου,
ἀγρώσ[τεω]ς καὶ δείσης πάσης, where Wessely, supplying
καθαρὰς after ἀρούρας, translates "frei von Schilf und
Binsengewachs, von Queckgras und jeglichem Schlamm,"
and is supported in this translation, as against Wilcken
(*Archiv* i. p. 158), by P Tebt II. 375[30] cited *s.v.* κάλαμος.
For a new word καλαμεία, "reed-land," see e.g. *ib.* 457
(ii/A.D.) καλαμείας (ἄρουρα). MGr καλαμιά, καλαμνιά,
"reed."

κάλαμος.

P Tebt II. 375[30] (A.D. 140) παραδώσω πάσας τὰς ἀρούρας
καθαρὰ (*l.* – ὰς) ἀπὸ θρύου καλάμου δί[σ]ης πάσης, "I
will deliver up the arourae free from rushes, reeds, and dirt
of all sorts" (Edd.) : and so P Fay 345 (A.D. 139-40), P
Amh II. 90[22] (A.D. 159), 91[23] (A.D. 159). In place of
ἄχυρον, κάλαμος is used for heating purposes according to
P Giss I. 40[ii 12] (A.D. 212) κάλαμον πρ[ὸ]s τὸ ὑποκαίειν τὰ
βαλα[νεῖ]α καταφέρουσι. From the close connexion between
the cultivation of κάλαμος and vine-growing, to which the
papyri witness, GH in their note on P Oxy IV. 729[3] (A.D.
137) have shown the probability that a crop of reeds was
planted between or under the vines. The collective use of
κάλαμος in the above citations and in P Oxy IV. 742[2] (B.C.
2) παράλαβε παρὰ Πόθου τὸν κάλαμ[ο]ν πανα[ρ]ιθμῶι καὶ
ἀπόστειλόν μ[ο]ι πόσας δέσμας παρείληφες, "take over
from Pothus the reeds all together, and send me word how
many bundles you have received" (Edd.), points to a similar
sense in Mt 11[7]. The reference is to "the very ordinary
sight of cane grass shaken by wind," and "there is no
contrast intended between the moral strength of the Baptist
and the weak pliability of the reed" (McNeile *ad l.*). With
Ezekiel's "reed" of six cubits *i.e.* about 9 feet (see David-
son *ad* Ezek 40[5]), which underlies the imagery of Rev 11[1],
we may compare the κάλαμος of similar length in P Ryl II.
64[2] (iv/v A.D.) : see the editors' note and cf. *Archiv* iii. p.
440. In a list of articles sent by one woman to another, P
Tebt II. 413[21] (ii/iii A.D.), ε καλάμ[ους] στημίων, "five
reeds of thread," are included, and with 3 Jn[13] cf. P Grenf
II. 38[7] (B.C. 81) κα]λάμων γραφικῶν δεκάπεντε. We may
note the contrast between the καλάμο(υ) Ἑλλη(νικοῦ) of P
Lond 105[b 11] (A.D. 14-37) (= II. p. 128) and *ib.* 191[11]
(A.D. 103-117) (= II. p. 265) καλαμοῦ Ἰνδικοῦ : see *Archiv*
i. p. 150. A new subst. καλαμουργία is found in P Lond
163[24] (A.D. 88) (= II. p. 183), and for the corresponding
verb see PSI IV. 317[8] (A.D. 95) ἐὰν μ[έ]λλῃς καλαμουργεῖν,
γρά[ψ]ον μοι.

καλέω.

For this verb = "summon," "invite," as in Mt 22[3] *al.*,
see P Oxy XII. 1487[1] (iv/A.D.) καλῖ σε Θέων υἱὸς Ὡριγένους
εἰς τοὺς γάμους τῆς ἀδελφῆς ἑαυτοῦ ἐν τῇ αὔριον, and similarly *ib.* 1486[1] (iv/A.D.). In both instances it is noticeable
that καλῖ takes the place of the earlier ἐρωτᾷ, cf. *ib.* 1484,
1485. See also P Hamb I. 29[3] (A.D. 89) κληθέντων τινῶν
. . καὶ μὴ ὑπακουσάντων. The participle is common =
"called," "named," as in Lk 7[11] *al.*, e.g. P Petr II. 45[ii. 20]
(B.C. 246) εἰς φρούριον τὸ καλούμενον [Π]οσιδέον, Ostr

1210[4] (Roman) Πασῆμι(s) Πικῶτο(s) καλ(ούμενος), BGU I.
349[2] (A.D. 313) ἐν κλήρῳ καλουμένου (*l.* – ένῳ) Ἀφρικιανός
and P Oxy X. 1273[7] (A.D. 260) περιτραχήλιον μανιάκην,
καλούμενον, "a necklace of the kind called *maniaces*"
(Edd.). With the usage in Gal 1[15] we may compare CP
Herm I. 25[ii. 7] Ἀντωνῖνος κληθήσεται and *ib.* 26[14] εἰ δοκεῖ
σ[οι] κληθῆναι . . . αὐτούς, where the reference is to summoning or calling as a witness : cf. BGU IV. 1138[13] (B.C.
19). In P Leid W[ix. 36] (ii/iii A.D.) the worshipper is exhorted
to invoke the gods of hours and days—εἰ μὴ γὰρ αὐτοὺς
καλέσῃς, . . οὐκ ἐπακούουσι : cf. also *Kaibel* 481[2 f.] τὴν
σὴν εὔνοιαν καὶ πίστιν, Φαῖδρε, καλοῦντες [ἐν βιοτῆς
μέτροις οὔποτε παυσόμεθα, where the verb is practically =
κλείω. See also P Fay 135[2] (iv/A.D.) cited *s.v.* καιρός.
MGr καλνῶ, καλῶ.

καλλιέλαιος.

This NT ἅπ. εἰρ. (Rom 11[24]) is fully discussed by Plasberg
in *Archiv* ii. p. 219 ff. in connexion with a Strassburg papyrus containing certain fragmentary Sayings. In one of these,
C[2], the phrase εἰς καλλιελαίαν occurs, and, though the
context is far from clear, the editor thinks there is evidence
that the word forms part of a Saying current in Jewish-
Christian circles, and may therefore have been derived from
the Pauline passage. If not, both the unknown writer and
Paul must have found the word in current usage.

καλοποιέω.

This verb, "do the fair (honourable) thing," is confined
in the NT to 2 Thess 3[13] : cf. the late Aphrodito papyrus P
Lond IV. 1338[28] (A.D. 709) (= *Chrest.* I. 255) μέλλομεν
γὰρ κελεύσει θεοῦ καλοποιῆσαι τῷ καλῶς διαπραττωμένῳ.
For a list of similar compounds see Lob. *Phryn.* p. 199 f.

καλός.

Hort in his note on 1 Pet 2[12] has pointed out that while
ἀγαθός "denotes what is good in virtue of its results," καλός
"denotes that kind of goodness which is at once seen to be
good." It may not be possible always to press the distinction, but what we may call this self-evidencing power of
καλός, a goodness as it appears to, and is realized by, others
comes out generally speaking in the citations that follow.
Thus in its application to persons the adj. is united with
πιστός in the well-known early Christian letter of Psenosiris,
where Psenosiris writes regarding Politike—τ]αύτην
παραδέδωκα τοῖς καλοῖς καὶ πιστοῖς ἐξ αὐτῶν τῶν νεκροτάφων ("grave-diggers") εἰς τήρησιν (P Grenf II. 73[12] (late
iii/A.D.) (= *Selections*, p. 118). And so in the Silco inscr.,
OGIS 201[9] (vi/A.D.), the King announces—ἐπίστευσα τὸν
ὅρκον αὐτῶν, ὡς καλοί εἰσιν ἄνθρωποι, "quia honesti homines
sunt" (Lepsius). With Heb 13[18] we may compare P Rein
52[5] (iii/iv A.D.) οὐ καλῷ συνειδότι χρώμενοι. Similarly with
reference to animals we read of μόσχους καλούς in PSI IV.
409[31] (iii/B.C.), and in P Tebt II. 409[12] (A.D. 5) of certain
he-asses(?) as—καλοὺς . . καὶ τελήους καὶ εὐνοικούς, "fine
animals without blemish and good-tempered" (Edd.). The
varied usage with reference to things is seen in such
passages as : P Lond 356[4] (i/A.D.) (= II. p. 252, *Selections*,
p. 59) καλῶς ποιήσεις ἰδίῳ κινδύνῳ τὸ καλὸν πωλήσας ἐξ
ὧν ἐάν σοι εἴπῃ φαρμάκων ἔχειν χρείαν Σώτας ὁ φίλος μου,

"be so good as to sell at your own risk good quality of those drugs of which my friend Sotas says that he has need," where **καλόν** is contrasted with **σαπρόν** a few lines further on, just as in Mt 12³³, 13⁴⁸: P Oxy I. 116¹⁹ᶠ (ii/A.D.) (as amended II. p. 319) κ[ί]στην σταφυλῆς λείαν **καλῆς καὶ σφυρίδα φοίνικος καλοῦ**, "a box of very good grapes, and a basket of good dates": P Fay 133⁸ (iv/A.D.) ὑ]**περθοῦ δὲ ἡμερῶν δ[ύο] καὶ τριῶν ἵνα . . . ὁ οἶνος . . καλὸς γένηται**, "wait for two or three days in order that the wine may become good": and with reference to clothing, P Tebt II. 278³¹ (early i/A.D.) **κάλλιστον ἱμάτιν**, ib. 423³¹ (early iii/A.D.) **καλὸν χιτῶνα**, P Oxy VII. 1069⁵ᶠ (iii/A.D.) **σπούδασον γὰρ τὸ κειθώνειν μου γενέσθε** (l. γενέσθαι) **πρὸ λόγον, καὶ κ[α]λὰ μέτρα αὐτῷ βαλέτωσαν**, "be careful to have my tunic made properly, and let them put good measure into it" (Ed.). An unusual compar. form is seen in P Oxy XIV. 1672⁶ᶠᶠ (A.D. 37–41) **αἱ πράσεις ἡμῶν καλλιότεραι γεγό]νασι λείαν, καὶ ἐλπίζομεν ὅτι καλλιότεραι τούτων γενήσονται**, "our sales have become much more favourable and we hope that they will become more favourable than this" (Edd.). The word is used more generally in P Petr II. 13(19)⁶ (B.C. 255–59), where, writing to his father, Philonides expresses the hope **καὶ ἐάν τι τῶν κατ' ἀνθρώπινον γίνηται, τυχεῖν σε πάντων τῶν καλῶν**, "and should any mortal chance befall you, that you should receive all attention" (Ed.), and P Tebt II. 418⁷ (iii/A.D.) **εὐχόμενός σοι τὰ ἐν βίῳ κάλλιστα ὑπαρχθήσεσθαι**, "praying that you may have life's greatest blessings" (Edd.), and P Oxy XIV. 1070⁴ (iii/A.D.) **πολλά σε ἀσπάζομαι, κυρία, εὐχομένη σοι τὰ κάλλιστα**, "I send you many salutations, my lady, and best wishes" (Edd.). For *time* we may cite P Goodsp Cairo 3³⁹ (iii/B.C.) (as completed in Witkowski², p. 48) **ἐπίχεον, ὃν τρόπον κἀγὼ ἡμέραν καλὴν ἤγαγον**, while the phrase **καλὴ ὥρα** = "a la bonne heure" is found in a Paris papyrus (see P Par p. 422). With this last cf. P Tebt II. 418¹⁴ (iii/A.D.) **καλῇ πίστει**, "in good faith." To the instances of the superlative given above we may add P Oxy II. 237ᵛⁱⁱⁱ·⁵ (A.D. 186) a proclamation beginning—**παραδείγματι τῷ καλλίστῳ χρώμενος**, "following a most illustrious precedent" (Edd.), and P Flor II. 201¹⁹ (A.D. 259) **ἰχθὺν κάλλιστον**, "a sufficient quantity of fish." MGr **πάαινε στὸ καλό**, or simply **στὸ καλό**, "farewell."

κάλυμμα.

The plur. is used of "tabulae ligneae" in *Syll* 537⁵⁷ (2nd half iv/B.C.) **ἐπιθεὶς καλύμματα, πάχος δακτύλου, πλάτος ἐξ δακτύλων.**

καλύπτω.

The use in the **Κοινή** of the simplex, which is rare in prose as compared with the compound **κατακαλύπτω**, is traced by Nägeli (p. 27) to Ionic influence, see e.g. the Ionic inscr. of B.C. 420, *Syll* 877⁶ **ἐχφέρεν δὲ ἐγ κλίνηι σφ[ε]νό-[ποδι κ]αὶ μὲ καλύπτεν.** Other exx. of the verb from the inscrr. are *Syll* 438¹⁴⁵ (Delphi—c. B.C. 400) **τὸν δὲ νεκρὸν κεκαλυμμένον φερέτω σιγᾶι**, and ib. 939¹⁰ **μηδὲ (παρέρπην τὰς γυναῖκας) τὰς [τρί]χας ἀμπεπλεγμένας μηδὲ (τοὺς ἄνδρας) κεκαλυμμένος.** See also Aristeas 87 **τῶν λειτουργούντων ἱερέων κεκαλυμμένων μέχρι τῶν σφυρῶν βυσσίνοις χιτῶσιν** (cf. Exod 36³⁵), "the ministering priests were clad in 'coats of fine linen' reaching to the ankles" (Thackeray).

καλῶς.

Michel 163⁶ (B.C. 148-7) **καλῶς καὶ ἐνδόξως ἀναστραφείς,** . . . ¹¹**πάντα καλῶς καὶ πρεπόντως βραβεύσας** may serve as exx. of the ordinary usage of this adverb. The epistolary formula **καλῶς ποιήσεις**, which is practically = "please," is very common, and is generally construed with a paratactic participle (cf. 3 Jn⁶, and in the past Ac 10³³, Phil 4¹⁴: see also 2 Pet 1¹⁹, e.g. P Hib I. 82¹⁷ (B.C. 239-8) **καλῶς οὖν [π]οιήσεις συναν[τι]λ[α]μβανόμενος προθύμως περὶ τῶν εἰς ταῦτα συγκυρόντων**, "please therefore to give your zealous co-operation in all that concerns this" (Edd.), P Amh II. 41¹⁰ (ii/B.C.) **καλῶς οὖν ποιήσεις συνπαραστάντες αὐτῶι ἕως ἂν π[ο]ήσητ[α]ι τὸν σφραγ[ισμό]ν**, "please therefore assist him until he carries out the sealing" (Edd.), BGU II. 596¹ (A.D. 84) **καλῶς ποιήσεις συνελθὼν [Ἁ]ϊλου-ρίωνι τῶι κομίζοντί σοι τὸ ἐπ[ι]στ[ό]λιον**, P Fay 125³ (ii/A.D.) **καλῶς [ποιή]σεις, ἄδελφε, μὴ ἀμελήσας το[ῦ] κλήρου τοῦ στρατηγικοῦ**, "you will do well, brother, not to neglect the ballot for strategus" (Edd.), and the early Christian letter P Amh I. 3(a)ᶦᶦᶦ·¹ (A.D. 250–285) **καλῶς οὖν ποιήσαντ[ες] ὠνησάμενο[ι] τὰ ὀθόν[ια**, "you will do well, therefore, to purchase the linen cloth." The construction with the inf. is found in BGU IV. 1203⁷ (B.C. 20) **καλῶς ποιήσεις γράψαι**: cf. ib. 1078³ (A.D. 39) **οὐ καλῶς δὲ ἐπόησας . . μὴ σημᾶναί μοι**, P Oxy VII. 1097³ (very illiterate—iii/A.D.) **οὐ καλῶς ἔπραξας μὴ ἐλθεῖν**, and with εἰ in P Petr II. 11(1)¹ (iii/B.C.) (= *Selections.* p. 7) **καλῶς ποιεῖς εἰ ἔρρωσαι καὶ τὰ λοιπά σοι κατὰ γνώμην ἐστίν.** One or two miscellaneous exx. of the adverb with ἔχω (cf. [Mk] 16¹⁸) may be added—P Petr II. 19(1a)³ (Ptol.) **οὕνεκα τοῦ θεοῦ καὶ τοῦ καλῶς ἔχοντος**, "in the name of God and of fair play" (Ed.), ib. III. 53(l)¹⁰ (Ptol.) **αὐτῶν ὑμῶν ἕνεκα καὶ ἡμῶν καὶ τοῦ καλῶς ἔχοντος**, "for your own sake and for ours, and in the name of propriety," PSI IV. 361¹⁹ (B.C. 251-0) **ἐάν σοι [φ]αίνηται καλῶς ἔχειν, γράψον Ἀρι-στάνδρωι περί μου**, P Par 40⁴⁷ (B.C. 156) **οὔτε τοῦ ἱεροῦ στοχασάμενοι, οὔτε τοῦ καλῶς ἔχοντος**, and P Gen I. 54⁸ (iv/A.D.) **θέλο σου πάντοτε καλῶς ἔχειν.** See also P Oxy II. 237ᵛⁱⁱⁱ·²¹ (A.D. 186) **ὅπερ οὐ καλῶς ἐνδέχεται εἰ μὴ ἄνωθεν γένοιτο ἀντίγραφα**, "this cannot be done adequately unless copies are made from the beginning" (Edd.). The very rare **ἀκάλως** is found in P Oxy XIV. 1676²² (iii/A.D.) **ἐὰν δὲ ἐκτός μου οὐκ ἀκάλως ἔχῃς, χαίρω ὅτι καλῶ[ς] ἔχεις μέν**, "if you are not unhappy away from me, I rejoice for your happiness" (Edd.). MGr **καλῶς τον**, "he is welcome."

κάμηλος.

In P Tebt I. 252 (B.C. 95-4 or 62-1) 1 talent is paid for]. ρης **καμή(λων?)**, but, as will be observed, the editors regard the completion of the word as doubtful, and the doubt is increased when we note that this is the only reference to camels as beasts of burden that we can produce from Ptolemaic times. In Imperial times, on the other hand, they are constantly referred to, as in the custom-house receipt P Ryl II. 197²ᶠᶠ (late ii/A.D.) **τετελ(ώνηται) διὰ πύλης Σοκνο(παίου) Νήσου ρ´ ν´ Σαραπίων ἐξάγ(ων) ἐπὶ καμήλ(ῳ) α μιᾷ λαχανοσπέρμ(ου) ἀρτάβ(ας) ἐξ τελ(ούσας) (δραχμὰς) πέντε**, "paid at the custom-house of Socnopaei Nesus for the tax of 1/100 and 1/50 by Sarapion, exporting on one camel six artabae of vegetable-seed paying five drachmae" (Edd.), and in the illiterate P Oxy VII. 1069[17] (iii/A.D.) τάχα γὰρ δυνασθῶμεν φο[ρ]υτρεῖσε (ί. φο[ρ]ετρίσαι) σοι δύο καμήλους [πυ]ροῦ καὶ πέμψε πρὸ σέν, "for we may be able to load two camels with wheat for you and to send them to you" (Ed.). BGU I. 352[11] (A.D. 135-6) mentions as registered— καμήλους τελείους τρεῖς, and similarly in P Lond 328[7] (A.D. 163) (= II. p. 75) the writer announces that of the two camels and a foal (καμήλων δύο καὶ πώλου) which he possessed in the previous year, one has been requisitioned εἰς κυριακὰς χρείας, "for Imperial service": he therefore returns two camels for the current year—[15] τοὺς δὲ λοιποὺς καμήλους β ἀπογρ(άφομαι) εἰς τὸ ἐνεστὸς (ἔτος). For the diminutive see P Hamb 1. 54[7] (ii/iii A.D.) ἕτερα β καμήλια. In P Oxy III. 498[8] (ii/A.D.) we read of "squared building-stones transportable by camel"— λίθων κύβων καμηλικῶν, though too heavy for other beasts: this is remarkably like μύλος ὀνικός in Mk 9[12]. Cf. also OGIS 629[18] (A.D. 137) τεσσάρων γόμων καμηλικῶν τέλος ἐπράχθη: so [35,88]. On the τέλεσμα καμήλων see Wilcken Ostr. i. p. 378.

κάμινος.

Ostr 1168 (Ptol.) λό[γος] ἀχύρου. εἰς τὰς καμείνους ἀγω(γαὶ) κζ, P Petr III. 46(4)[1] (Ptol.) εἰς κάμινον τὴν οἰκοδομηθεῖσαν πρὸς τὴν διάληψιν τῆς εἰς τὴν τροφὴν τῶν μόσχων ὀλύρας, "for the oven built to receive the rye intended for the food of the calves" (Edd.), BGU III. 669[3] (ii/A.D.) πλινθοφόρους ἀπὸ καμείνου ἰς οἰκοδομὴν ἰσαγωγοῦ.

καμμύω.

This syncopated form (= καταμύω), which is found in Mt 13[15], Ac 28[27], both from LXX Isai 6[10], is warranted good Κοινή by the ban of Phrynichus (ed. Lobeck p. 339 f., Rutherford NT p. 426 f.): see also Thumb Hellen. p. 63 f. As a matter of fact, it occurs in the magic P Lond 121[855] (iii/A.D.) (= I. p. 111) καμμύσας ἀναβλέψ[α]ς ὀψῇ ἔ[μ]προσθεν σοῦ σκίαν ἑστῶσαν.

κάμνω.

P Giss 1. 47[8] (time of Hadrian) ὡς μὴ κάμνειν τὸν φοροῦντα αὐτόν, BGU III. 884[i] (ii/iii A.D.) καὶ μὴ λίαν οὕτωι κάμω, P Flor III. 382[29] (A.D. 222-3) τοῖς ἑβδομήκοντα ἔτη βεβιω]κόσιν καὶ ἐν ταῖς λειτουργ]ίαις κεκμηκόσιν αἱ προτε[τα]γμέναι θεῖαι διατάξεις, P Oxy XII. 1414[27] (A.D. 270-5) κάμε ἄξια τοῦ ἐπάν[ω χρόνου, "labour in a manner worthy of the past" (Edd.). Note the compound in PSI I. 47[2] (vi/A.D.?) ἀπέκαμον τὸ λοιπὸν κεκτημένων ἐν τῇ ὑμῶν πεδιάδει. The subst. occurs in P Tebt II. 314[4] (ii/A.D.) ὅσον κάμ[α]τον ἤνεγκα, "how much trouble I had," P Fay 106[19] (c. A.D. 140) ὅπ[ως δυ]νηθῶ ἐμαυτὸν ἀνακτήσα[σθαι ἀ]πὸ τῶν καμάτων, "so that I may be able to recover from the effects of my labours" (Edd.), OGIS 717[11] (building of a temple—A.D. 261-208) ταῦτα πάντα ἐκ τῶν ἐμῶν καμάτων εὐχαριστήσας τῷ Σαράπιδι τῷ Μινιεῖ. For the derived sense "am ill," as in Jas 5[15], cf. Musonius p. 20[8] θεραπείαν τῶν καμνόντων. In MGr κάμνω, κάμω, κάνω, = "make," "do," generally with the added idea of "toil."

κάμπτω.

P Tebt II. 307[6] (A.D. 198) κεκαμμένον δάκτυλον μικρὸν χειρὸς ἀριστερᾶς, "a bent little finger on the left hand."

similarly CPR I. 170[3] (A.D. 97-117), P Oxy X. 1287[4] (early iii/A.D.) καμψάντων (gen. abs.) ἐπὶ βορ(ρᾶν), ib.[15] καμψάντων ἐπ' ἀπηλ(ιώτην).

κἄν.

For this crasis, as in Mk 5[28], 6[56], Ac 5[15], cf. PSI IV. 286[9] (iii/iv A.D.) ἵνα κἂν ἐγὼ εἰδῶ, P Oxy XII. 1593[6 ff.] (iv/A.D.) οὐκ [ἐ]δήλωσάς μοι κἂν περὶ τῆς ὁλοκληρίας ὑμῶν . . . κἂν νῦν, ἄδελφε, πάντα ὑπερθέμενος ἀντίγραψόν μοι κτλ. See also P Rein 52[6] (iii/iv A.D.) ὑμεῖς δὲ ἠμελήσατε ἴσως οὐ καλῷ συνειδότι χρώμενοι· ὃ κἂν νῦν ποιήσατε κτλ, "but you have neglected to do it perhaps because you have not a good conscience: do it now at least," etc. (cf. Archiv iii. p. 527 f.). On the intensive force of κἄν, as distinguished from the simple καί, cf. Jannaris Gr. § 598.

Κανά.

See F. C. Burkitt Syriac Forms, pp. 18 f., 22.

Καναναῖος.

Dalman (Words, p. 50) thinks that the original Greek form of this surname (Mt 10[4], Mk 3[18]) was Κανναῖος = קַנָּא, "a zealot" (cf. Lk 6[15]). On the form see also Moulton Gr. ii. p. 109, Burkitt Syriac Forms of NT Proper Names (Brit. Acad. 1912), p. 5.

Κανδάκη.

An interesting inscription belonging to B.C. 13 comes to us from the ancient Pselkis on the borders of Ethiopia in which an embassy on its homeward journey πρὸς] τὴν κυρίαν βασίλισσαν records its "adoration." Wilcken (Hermes xxviii. (1893) p. 154 ff.) has shown good grounds for believing that in this βασίλισσα we are to see the famous Κανδάκη of Ac 8[27]. The whole inscr. is in consequence worth recording here—Ἁρποκρᾶς ἥκω ἀναβαίνων μετὰ Ἐ[μάτου) πρεσβευτοῦ καὶ Ταμίου γραμματέως [πρὸς] τὴν κυρίαν βασίλισσαν καὶ τὸ προσ[κύνημα] ἐπόησα ὧδε παρ[ὰ] τῷ κυρίῳ Ἑρμ[ῇ θεῷ μεγίστῳ] καὶ Ἐμάτου καὶ Ἀνθούσης καὶ [Ἀλε]ξανδρήας, ἔτους ιζ Καί[σα](ρος) Μεχ[εὶρ (Cagnat 1. 1359). In itself the name Κανδάκη, like Ptolemy, was a dynastic title ("quod nomen multis iam annis ad reginas transiit," Pliny H.N. vi. 35). See also Laurent NT Studien, p. 140 ff.

κανών.

One or two citations for this difficult word may be useful. Syll 540[18] (B.C. 175-1) ποιῶν ὀρθὰ πάντα πρὸς κανόνα διηνεκῆ shows κ. in its original use as "a straight rod," "a level," with reference to the building of a temple: cf. Job 38[5] (Aq.) of a measuring line. For the metaphorical use derived from this, as in Gal 6[16], cf. P Par 63[58] (B.C. 165) (= P Petr III. p. 22) ἐπαγαγόντα τὸ δισταζόμενον ἐπὶ τὸν ἐκκείμενον κανόνα, "if he applied the doubtful cases to the rule provided for him" (Mahaffy), and P Lond 130[12] (i/ii A.D.) (= I. p. 133) διὰ κανόνων αἰωνίων, of the ancient rules of astrology. An interesting ex. of the word as applied to the model or ideal man is afforded by Epict. iii. 4. 5 εἰδέναι σε οὖν δεῖ, ὅταν εἰσέρχῃ εἰς τὸ θέατρον, ὅτι κανὼν εἰσέρχῃ καὶ παράδειγμα τοῖς ἄλλοις. We can cite no passages from our sources in support of the meaning "a measured area" or "province" (RV), which κανών apparently has in 2 Cor

10¹³, ¹⁵, but after the time of Diocletian (cf. Wilcken *Ost.* i. p. 387 f.) the word is common with reference to a regular contribution or charge for public purposes. Thus in P Amh II. 138¹² (A.D. 326) a pilot declares that he has embarked two hundred centenaria of charcoal for transport to Alexandria on account of "taxes"—κ]ανόνος, and in P Lond 99⁵ ᵃˡ· (iv/A.D.) (= I. p. 158) a distinction is drawn between the normal charge (κανών) and a special addition to it (πρόσθεμα) : cf. *ib.* 234⁹ (*c.* A.D. 346) (= II. p. 287) εἰς τὴν ἀπαίτησιν τῶν δεσποτικῶν κανόνων, "the Imperial dues." See also P Grenf II. 80¹⁴ (A.D. 402) and the late *ib.* 95² (vi/vii A.D.) where κ. is applied to the contributions of the laity for the support of the clergy. The dim. κανόνιον occurs in connexion with a supplementary list of persons liable to the poll-tax in P Lond 25¹²⁶ (A.D. 94-5) (= II. p. 40). In the Christian BGU I. 310¹⁷ (Byz.) we have a reference to ἱερῷ κανόνι, but unfortunately the context is very mutilated. For the history of the word with special relation to its ecclesiastical meaning, see Sophocles *Lex. s.v.*, Westcott *On the Canon*, App. A, and Souter *Text and Canon*, p. 154 ff. Dr. Rouse tells us he attended a sale of some leases of Church property in the island of Astypalaea in 1905. "Bills of sale describing each plot were on the wall ; and when I asked what these were, I was told εἶνε ὁ κανονισμός." He suggests that κανών may have meant the "official description" of anything : he would apply this in 2 Cor 10¹³. Boisacq, p. 406 f., favours the connexion with κάννα, "a reed," a word which may be of Semitic origin.

καπηλεύω.

This verb is confined in Biblical Greek to 2 Cor 2¹⁷, where the meaning "deal in for purposes of gain" rather than "adulterate" may be illustrated from BGU IV. 1024ᵛⁱⁱ ²³ (end of iv/A.D. : *Archiv* iii. p. 302) with reference to a harlot—ὅτι [τὸν μ]ὲν βίον ἀσεμνῶς διῆγεν, τὸ δὲ τέ[λος . .]μως γυπεριον ἐκαπήλευσεν. See also the rebuke addressed by Apollonius of Tyana to Euphrates *Vita Apoll.* i. 13 ἀπῆγε τοῦ χρηματίζεσθαί τε καὶ τὴν σοφίαν καπηλεύειν, "tried to wean him of his love of filthy lucre and of huckstering his wisdom" (Conybeare). and the use of καπηλικός = "mercenary" in M. Anton. iv. 28. The verb is used = "trade," "sell," in *Michel* 594¹⁶ (B.C. 279) τῶν οἰκημάτων ἐν οἷς Ἔφεσος καπηλεύει, and for the subst. κάπηλος, "dealer," "huckster" (cf. Isai 1²², Sir 26²⁹), especially with reference to a retailer of wine, cf. P Tebt II. 612 (i/ii A.D.) καπήλων Τεβτύνεως διὰ τῶν οἰνοπρατῶν ἕκαστ(ου) (δραχμαὶ) η. For the fem. καπηλίς, see P Fay 12³ (*c.* B.C. 103), and for καπηλεῖον, "inn," "tavern," see P Tebt I. 43¹⁸ (B.C. 118). Cf. MGr καπηλειό, "retail shop."

καπνός.

BGU IV. 1026ˣˣⁱⁱ· ¹⁷ (magic) λαβὲ παρ' αὐτοῦ τὰ περιάμματα ("amulets") πρόσβαλε ῥίζαν καὶ θὲς ὑπὲρ [κ]απν[ό]ν. For the verb, which is found in the LXX, cf. P Lond 121¹⁷⁶ (iii/A.D.) (= I. p. 89) κάπνισον λαγοῦ κεφαλ(ήν). Καπνός, which survives in MGr, stands for *κϝαπνός, Lat. *vapor*.

καρδία.

In the magic P Lond 46¹⁵⁷ (iv/A.D.) (= I. p. 70) we read of—καρδία περιεζωσμένη ὄφιν. With Lk 24³² we may compare *ib.* 121⁴⁷¹ (iii/A.D.) (= I. p. 99) καιομένην τὴν ψυχὴν

καὶ τὴν καρδίαν. The same conjunction of ψυχή and καρδία (cf. Mt 22³⁷ *al.*) is seen in the imprecatory tablet Wünsch *AF* 3¹⁵ (Imperial age) στρέβλωσον (cf. 2 Pet 3¹⁶) αὐτῶν τὴν ψυχὴν καὶ τὴν καρδίαν. The new Logion 3 (P Oxy I. p. 3) πονεῖ ἡ ψυχή μου ἐπὶ τοῖς υἱοῖς τῶν ἀνθρώπων, ὅτι τυφλοί εἰσιν τῇ καρδίᾳ αὐτῶ[ν offers an interesting parallel to Eph 1¹⁸.

καρδιογνώστης.

This word, which is first found in Ac 1²⁴, is traced by Preuschen (*HZNT al l.*) to the Christian-liturgical usage of the time. It occurs again in *ib.* 15⁸ : for the thought cf. Jer 17¹⁰ ἐτάζων καρδίας.

καρπός

is common in the sense of "fruit," "produce" of the land generally, e.g. P Eleph 14¹⁵ (Ptol.) τῆς δὲ γῆς κυριεύσει καὶ τῶν καρπῶν (A.D. 54-67), or, more particularly, of an olive-yard, P Ryl II. 130¹⁰ (A.D. 31) ἐτρύγησαν ἐκ τῶν καρπῶν οὐκ ὀλίγην ἐλᾶν, or of a vineyard, P Fay 127⁶ (ii/iii A.D.) τοῦ καρποῦ τοῦ ἀμπελῶνος. The phrase ξυλί[νων κ]αρπῶν is used in *OGIS* 55¹⁴ (iii/B.C.) with reference to tree-fruits, such as apples, etc. : see Dittenberger's note *ad l.* and cf. PSI V. 528¹⁸ (iii/B.C.) περὶ τοῦ καρποῦ τοῦ ξυλικοῦ, apparently the tax ξυλίνων καρπῶν. Another ex. of the sing. is P Oxy XIV. 1632¹⁰ (A.D. 353) καρπὸν φύ(= οἴ)νικος χωρίων σου δύο, "the date-crop of your two estates" (Edd.). For the metaphorical usage Rouffiac (p. 51) cites *Priene* 112¹⁴ (after B.C. 84) συνιδὼν δὲ ὅτι μόνη μεγίστους ἀποδίδωσιν ἡ ἀρετὴ καρποὺς καὶ χάριτας : cf. Jas 3¹⁷ ᶠ·, *al.* We have no example of καρπός = "profit," "credit," as in Phil 4¹⁷ ("the interest which is accruing to your credit," Moule *CGT ad l.*), but, as showing how easily this sense might arise, we may quote the corresponding use of καρπεία in P Petr III. 53 (*p*)⁵ (iii/B.C.) π]ρὸς τὰς καρπείας ἃς . . . . ἡμᾶς κομίζεσθαι ἐκ τοῦ [ἱ]εροῦ, "with respect to the profits which we should obtain from the temple" (Edd.) : cf. also καρπίζομαι in P Ryl II. 119²⁶ (A.D. 54-67) μέχρι νῦν καρπίζεται τὴν αὐτὴν ὑποθήκην ἀφ' ἧς ἀπηνέγκατο εἰς λόγον ἀργυ(ρίου) (ταλάντων) ε, "he continues up to the present to enjoy the mortgage aforesaid by which he has profited to the extent of 5 talents" (Edd.). For the adj. κάρπιμος see *Kaibel* 1039¹⁵ *s.v.* θερίζω.

Κάρπος.

According to Thieme (p. 40) this proper name (2 Tim 4¹³) is found on a Magnesian coin of A.D. 230, Μ. Αὐρ. Κάρπος.

καρποφορέω.

The corresponding subst. is found in P Oxy IX. 1220⁸ (iii/A.D.) ἢ δοκῖ σοι, κύριέ μου, πέμψε (*l.*-αι) μοι κέρμα εἰς τὰ γινόμενα παρ' ἐμοὶ ἔργα τῆς κοφορίας (*l.* καρποφορίας) ; "would you be pleased, sir, to send me some money for the business of harvesting going on here ?" (Edd.).

καρποφόρος.

In the Median parchment P Sa'îd Khan 1 A¹³ (B.C. 88) a vineyard is provided μετὰ ὕδατος καὶ ἀκροδρύοις καρποφόροις τε καὶ ἀκάρποις, "with water and vine-stocks, both those in bearing and those not." Cf. also *Preisigke* 991⁵ (A.D. 290) τὸ ἐπ[ἀγαθ]ον γόνιμ[ον] νέον ὕδωρ σὺν τῇ καρπ[οφό]ρ[ῳ γ]αίη.   For the adj. as an epithet of Demeter cf. the Ephesian inscr. *Syll* 655[5] (A.D. 83) Δήμητρι Καρποφόρῳ καὶ Θεσμοφόρῳ.

καρτερέω.

The meaning "persevere," "endure," usually given to this verb in Heb 11[27], is supported by the new Alexandrian erotic fragment, P Grenf I. 1[19] (ii/B.C.) μέγαν ἔχει πόνον, ζηλοτυπεῖν γὰρ δεῖ, στέγειν, καρτερεῖν. See also Arist. *Magn. Mor.* ii. 6. 34 ὁ γὰρ καρτερῶν καὶ ὑπομένων τὰς λύπας, οὗτος καρτερικός ἐστιν (cited by Mayor on 2 Pet 1[6]). A somewhat different usage occurs in P Amh II. 130[6] (A.D. 70), where a certain Gloutas excuses himself for not having sold some barley, on the ground that others had vainly offered to sell — τούτου χάριν καρτερῶ, "this is why I am holding on" (Edd.). If we assume that τὴν κριθήν is understood here after καρτερῶ, we might find support for Luther's rendering of Heb *l.c.* "denn er hielt sich an den, den er nicht sahe, als sähe er ihn." For an interesting suggestion that the verb in this verse may mean "kept his eyes upon," on the analogy of certain passages in Plutarch, see *ExpT* xxvii. p. 186. The adv. καρτερῶς = "strongly" occurs in P Par 41[22] (B.C. 100) ἐπέπεσόν(?) τε καρτερῶς [ἐμοί. MGr (ἀ)καρτερῶ, "expect," "wait for."

κάρφος.

is found in a sepulchral epitaph *Kaibel* 086[9] where it is said of the pious man (ὁ εὐσεβής) — οὐδὲ κάρφος ἐβλάβη, "he was not a whit injured" (cf. LS *s.v.*): see Mt 7[3], where all our English versions from Wycliffe down to RV adopt the translation "mote" = "a very small particle." The Old Lat. has *stipula*, and the Vulg. *festuca*: cf. Hesych. κάρφος· ἄχυρον, χόρτος. κεραία ξύλου λεπτή.

κατά,

the favourite preposition of Polybius, by whom it is often used in place of ἐν, εἰς, and περί (Krebs *Präp.* p. 4), is also found with considerable variety of application in the NT, where it occurs 73 times c. gen., and 391 times c. acc. (cf. *Proleg.* p. 105). Brugmann (*Kurze Vergleichende Grammatik*, p. 479) considers that the earliest use of the word was "along" something, so as to remain in connexion and contact with the object, and from this most of the senses found in the NT can be derived.

I. (1) Turning to the construction c. gen. we find that the meaning "along" has passed into "down," a usage not found in MGr, in such passages as P Petr II. 18(2*b*)[10] (B.C. 246) ἐπιπεσὼν ἔτυπτεν [αὐ]τ[ο]ν κατὰ τοῦ τραχήλου, *Chrest.* I. 499[8] (ii/iii A.D.) the body of a mummy ἔχων τάβλαν κατὰ τοῦ τραχήλου : cf. Mt 8[32], 1 Cor 11[4], 2 Cor 8[2].

(2) This in turn becomes "against," as in Mt 10[35], Mk 14[56], e.g. P Eleph 1[14] (B.C. 311–0) (= *Selections*, p. 4) ὅπου ἂν ἐπιφέρηι Ἡρακλείδης κατὰ Δημητρίας ἢ Δημητρία τε καὶ τοὶ μετὰ Δημητρίας πράσσοντες ἐπεγφέρωσιν κατὰ Ἡρακλείδου, "wheresoever Heraclides brings the charge against Demetria, or Demetria and those acting with Demetria bring the charge against Heraclides," P Petr II. 2 (2)[2] (B.C. 260) ἐκόμισέν μοι Δωρίμαχος ἐντευξιν κεχρηματισμένη[ν] κατὰ Διονυσίου, "Dorimachus brought me an official (or certified) petition against Dionysius" (Edd.), P

Par 45[7] (B.C. 153) προσέχων, μὴ εὕρῃ τι κατὰ σου ἰπῖν, P Tebt I. 7[3] (B.C. 114) ἐγκλήματα κατὰ τῶν ὑποτεταγμένων τῆι διοικήσει, "complaints against subordinates of the finance administration," P Fay 12[8] (*c.* B.C. 103) ἐπέδωκα κατ' αὐτοῦ περὶ τούτω[ν] τὰς εἰθισμένας προσαγγελίας, "I made the customary charges against him on these counts" (Edd.), P Oxy VI. 898[14] (A.D. 123) κατ' αὐτῆς προελθεῖν, "to proceed against her." This usage, which is only figurative in good Attic writers, is common in the Κοινή throughout the Ptolemaic and Roman periods, as the above exx. show : it is, however, lost in MGr (Thumb *Handbook*, p. 106).

(3) By a usage which in the NT is confined to Lk (4[14] *al.*), and is always associated with ὅλος, κατά has also the force of "throughout" as in P Giss I. 48[8] (A.D. 202–3) κατὰ κυριακῆς γῆς : cf. Polyb. iii. 19. 7 κατὰ τῆς νήσου διεσπάρησαν. The phrase καθ' ὕδατος is frequent with reference to land "under water," e.g. BGU II. 571[11] (ii/A.D.) (as amended *Archiv* i. p. 151 n.[8]) ἀβρόχου καὶ καθ' ὕδ(ατος), P Oxy VI. 918[xi. 13 *al.*] (ii/A.D.) αἱ οὖσ(αι) καθ' ὕδ(ατος), of certain flooded arourae.

(4) Good exx. of the prep. in asseverations, oaths, as in Mt 26[63], 1 Cor 15[15], Heb 6[13, 16], are afforded by P Par 63[9] (B.C. 164) (= P Petr III. p. 20) λαβεῖν μὴ μόνον ἐπὶ τῶ[ν] θεῶν ἀλλὰ καὶ κατὰ τῶν βασιλέων, "to exact oaths from you not only by the gods, but also by the kings" (Mahaffy), P Par 574[1240] (iii/A.D.) (= *Selections*, p. 113) ἐξορκίζω σε δαίμον, ὅστις ποτ' οὖν εἶ, κατὰ τούτου τοῦ θεοῦ σαβαρβαρβαθιωθ, "I adjure thee, O demon, whoever thou art, by the God Sabarbarbathioth."

II. (1) When we pass to κατά c. acc., we are at once met with a number of instances of the κατά phrase forming a mere periphrasis (a) for the possessive pronoun, or (b) for the gen. of a subst., or even (c) for an adj.

(a) The following are examples of the first class of these periphrases—P Eleph 13[1] (B.C. 223–2) ἐχάρην ἐπὶ τῶι με αἰσθέσθαι τὰ κατὰ σέ, "I was glad when I had learned your affairs," P Leid B[9] (B.C. 164) ἐπὶ τῆς καθ' ἡμᾶς λειτουργίας, P Tebt I. 24[64] (B.C. 117) τῆς καθ' ἑαυτοὺς ἀσχολία(= -ας), P Tor I. 1[ii. 32] (B.C. 116) ὑπόμνημα ὑπὲρ τῶν κατ' αὑτούς, P Tebt I. 7[5] (B.C. 114) μηδ' ἄλλοις ἐπιτρέπειν κατ' αὐτοὺς διεξάγειν, "nor allow others to decide their case" (Edd.), and OGIS 168[17] (B.C. 115) παραγεγονότες εἰς τοὺς καθ' ὑμᾶς τόπους, as in Phil 1[12] *al.*, we may add the illiterate P Oxy I. 129[14] (iv/A.D.) ἄχρις ἂν γνῶ πῶς τὰ κατ' αἰμαὶ ἀποτίθαιται (*l.* ἐμὲ ἀποτίθεται). For further exx. of this usage in late Greek see Schmidt *Jos.* p. 360, Kaelker *Quaest.* p. 282 f.

(b) The periphrasis for the gen. of a subst. is seen in P Hib I. 82[19] (B.C. 239–8) τὰ κατὰ τὴν γραμματείαν, "the duties of the scribe's office," P Tebt I. 5[25] (B.C. 118) ἐπὶ τῶν κατ' Ἀλεξά(νδρειαν) ὁρ[μων], "at the harbours of Alexandria," *ib.* 13[17] (B.C. 114) τὰ κατ[ὰ τ]ὴν ἐπισ(τατείαν) τ[ῆς κ]ώ μης], "the duties of epistates of the village," *ib.* 16[5] (B.C. 114) περὶ τῶν κατὰ Πολέμωνα, "regarding the case of Polemon," *ib.* 105[17] (B.C. 103) τὰ κατὰ τὴ[ν μ]ίσθωσιν, "the provisions of the lease," P Lond 1164(*k*)[20] (A.D. 212) (= III. p. 167) ὑπὸ [το]ῦ κατὰ πατέρα μου ἀνεψειοῦ, and Polyb. iii. 113. 1 ἡ κατὰ τὸν ἥλιον ἀνατολή.

(c) This usage went even the length of a κατά phrase taking the place of an adj., as in P Hib I. 27[42] (B.C. 301–240) ταῖς κατὰ σελήνη[ν] ἡμέραις, "the lunar days."

(2) For **κατά**, "according to," of standard, law, rule, as in Rom 10[2], 1 Cor 7[6], 2 Cor 8[3], Heb 11[14], cf. P Petr II. 11(1)[1] (iii/B.C.) (= *Selections*, p. 7), τὰ λοιπά σοι κατὰ γνώμην ἐστίν, P Tebt I. 40[25] (B.C. 117) κατὰ τοὺς τῆς κώμης ἐθισμούς, P Oxy I. 37[ii.5] (A.D. 49) (= *Selections*, p. 51) κατὰ τὰ ὑπὸ τοῦ κυρίου ἡγεμόνος κριθέντα, *Chrest.* I. 352[11] (A.D. 117) κατὰ <τὰ> κελευσθέντα, *ib.* [17] κατὰ τὸ ἔθος (cf. Lk 1[8]), and from the inscr. *OGIS* 56[33] (B.C. 237) κατὰ τὸ πρότερον γραφὲν ψήφισμα. Similarly κατὰ λόγον, as in Ac 18[14], "in accordance with what is right, befitting," is common in epistolary phrases, e.g. P Eleph 13[1] (B.C. 223–2) εἰ ἔρρω[σ]αι καὶ τὰ λοιπά σοι κατὰ λόγον ἐστίν, εἴη ἂν ὡς ἐγὼ θέλω, "if you are well, and other things are going rightly, it would be as I wish," P Lond 42[2] (B.C. 168) (= I. p. 30, *Selections*, p. 9) εἰ ἐρρωμένωι τἄλλα κατὰ λόγον ἀπαντᾶι, εἴη ἂν ὡς τοῖς θεοῖς εὐχομένη διατελῶ, P Goodsp Cairo 4[3] (ii/B.C.) (= *Selections*, p. 24), P Par 63[5] (B.C. 165).

We may note here the use of **κατά** in the titles of the Gospels, where it practically points to authorship (cf. Zahn *Introd.* ii. pp. 387 f., 396 f.). MGr κατὰ τὸ νόμο, "according to the law," κατὰ τὸν καιρό, "according to the weather" (Thumb *Handbook*, p. 106). **Κατά** has a local sense in P Oxy VI. 904[6] (v/A.D.) πληγαῖς κατακοπτόμενον κατὰ τὸ σῶμα, "belaboured with blows on my body": cf. Rom 7[22], Eph 6[5].

(3) This brings us to the idea of "throughout" with reference to place, as in P Hib I. 82[19] (B.C. 239–8) κατὰ τόπον, "throughout the district," P Tebt I. 8[8] (c. B.C. 201) ἐν τοῖς κατὰ Λέσβον καὶ Θραίκην τόποις, *ib.* 5[184] (B.C. 118) τοὺς κατὰ τὴν χώραν φυ(λακίτας), *OGIS* 90[7] (Rosetta stone—B.C. 196) ἐκ τῶν κατὰ τὴν χώραν ἱερῶν, and the contracted κατὴν (= κατὰ τὴν) χώραν in P Par 63[9] (B.C. 165) (= P Petr III. p. 26). An interesting memorial inscr. from Egypt, published in *Archiv* v. p. 168 f., commemorates one who has been laid between his mother and brother—ὧν καὶ ἡ σωφροσύνη κατὰ τὸν κόσμον λελάληται.

(4) The meaning "during," "about," with reference to time is common—P Lille I. 1 *recto*[14] (B.C. 259–8) κατὰ χειμῶνα, "pendant l'hiver," P Tebt I. 28[9] (c. B.C. 114) κατὰ τὸ παρόν, "at the present time," *ib.* 27[60] (B.C. 113) κατὰ θερείαν, "in summer," P Oxy XIV. 1635[11] (B.C. 44–37) κατὰ τὸν βίον, "for his lifetime," and *OGIS* 90[27] (Rosetta stone—B.C. 196) καθ' ὃν καιρόν. Cf. MGr κατὰ τὰ μεσάνυκτα, "about midnight," and the common usage to indicate direction towards something, e.g. ἔρχεται κατὰ τὸ χωριό, "he is coming towards the village" (see Thumb *Handbook*, p. 105 f.).

(5) The distributive force of **κατά** is well seen in the contract of apprenticeship P Oxy IV. 725[36] (A.D. 183) ἀργήσει δὲ ὁ παῖς εἰς λόγον ἑορτῶν κατ' ἔτος (cf. Lk 2[41]) ἡμέρας εἴκοσι, "the boy shall have 20 holidays in the year on account of festivals" (Edd.): see further s.v. ἔτος, where the form καθ' ἔτος is also illustrated, and cf. *Michel* 1001[vi. 21] (c. B.C. 200) καθ' ἐνιαυτόν (cf. Heb 9[25]). Other exx. of distributive **κατά** are P Oxy II. 275[13] (B.C. 66) κατὰ μῆνα, P Par 26[13] (B.C. 163–2) (= *Selections*, p. 14) τὰ ἑαυτῶν καθ' ἡμέραν δέοντα, "their daily necessities," P Giss I. 17[10] (time of Hadrian) οὐ βλέπομέν σε καθ' ἡμέραν, and P Tebt II. 412[2] (late ii/A.D.) τὸ προσκύνημά σου κατ' ἑκάστην ἡμέραν ποιῶ, "I make supplications for you every day." For the Lukan phrase τὸ καθ' ἡμέραν (Lk 11[3], 19[47], Ac 17[11]) we may com-

pare the reference in a bailiff's letter to his "diary" or journal—P Oxy IX. 1220[4] (iii/A.D.) ἀνέπεμψά σοι διὰ σημι[ώ]σεως τὸ καθ' ἡμέρα (= αν) τοῦ ἀναλώματος ἵν (*l.* ἵν') εἰδῇς, "I send in some notes the daily account of our expenditure for your information." Cf. also P Lond 904[29] (A.D. 104) (= III. p. 125, *Selections*, p. 73) τῆς κατ' οἰκίαν ἀπογραφῆς, "the house-to-house census" (cf. Ac 2[46], 5[42]), and the magical formula P Oxy VI. 886[19] (iii/A.D.) (= *Selections*, p. 111) ἔρε (*l.* αἶρε) κατὰ δύο δύο, "lift them (viz. palm leaves on which were written the names of the gods) two by two," which may illustrate Lk 10[1] ᴮᴷ (cf. *Proleg.* p. 97, Thackeray *Gr.* i. p. 54 f.). For the phrase τὸ δὲ καθ' εἷς in Rom 12[5] (cf. Mk 14[19], [Jn] 8[9]) cf. τὸ καθ' ἕν as the heading of a list of articles etc.—P Tebt I. 47[34] (B.C. 113) ἔστιν δὲ τὸ καθ' ἕν· θύραν μυρικὶ νην, σκαφεῖα β, *al.*, "the list is: a door of tamarisk-wood, two hoes" etc., also P Rein 17[8] (B.C. 109) where, after the mention of certain agricultural implements and other objects, it is added—ὧν τὸ καθ' ἓν ὑπόκειται, "of which the list is given below," P Ryl II. 65[8] (B.C. 67) πλείονα σώματα ὧν τὸ καθ' ἓν ἐπὶ τῆς ἐ[σο]μένης [διεξα]γωγῆς σημανθήσεται, "a number of corpses, the details of which will appear in the forthcoming inquiry" (Edd.), *ib.* 127[35.24] (A.D. 29). The phrase κατ' ὄνομα, "individually," "one by one," occurs frequently in closing greetings, as in 3 Jn[15], e.g. BGU I. 27[18] (ii/A.D.) (= *Selections*, p. 102) ἀσπάζομαι . . . πάντες (= -ας τοὺς φιλοῦντάς σε κατ' ὄνομα, P Tebt II. 422[16] (iii/A.D.) ἀσπάζομαι . . τοὺς ἐνοίκους πάντες (= -ας) κα[τ'] ὄνομα, P Meyer 23[13] (end of iv/A.D.) ἀσπάζομαι ὑμᾶς πάντας κατ' ὄνομα. For the similar use of κατ' ἄνδρα see P Amh II. 69[8] (A.D. 154) καταχω(ρίζομεν) ὑμεῖν μέτρημ[α] κατ' ἄνδρα ἰσδοχῆς ἀπὸ Παῦνι ἕως Μ[εσ]ορή, "we report to you the individual amounts received by us from Pauni to Mesore" (Edd.), *ib.* [13] κατ' ἄνδρα καταγωγῆς, "individual deliveries," and P Lond 259[73] (A.D. 94–5) (= II. p. 35) διὰ τῶν . . κατ' ἄνδρα λόγων. In *ib.* 604[3] (A.D. 47) (= III. p. 71) we have κάτανδρα for κατ' ἄνδρα, and in P Tebt I. 72[17] (B.C. 114) the phrase is contracted into κάνδρα according to Mayser *Gr.* p. 145. With the distributive κατά cf. in MGr καθείς, καθένας, καθέτις (κάθα εἷς, "every one," and such a phrase as ὀλίγο κατ' ὀλίγο, "little by little."

III. A few miscellaneous phrases may conclude this long note. Thus c. gen. we have P Tor II. 12[7] (Ptol.) οὐ γεγόνεν (*l.* γέγονεν) ἐφ' ἡμῶν ὠνὴ κατὰ τῆς σῆς οἰκείας, "emptio tuae domus"—"Graecitas vere barbara" (Edd.), and P Fay 32[14] (A.D. 131) ἐὰν δέ τι κατὰ τούτου ου) ἐξοικονομῶ πρότερον ἀποδίξω ὑπάρχειν, "if I alienate any of my rights over it, I will first establish my title to the ownership" (Edd.). With the acc. we have P Tebt I. 104[18] (B.C. 92) κατὰ δύναμιν τῶν ὑπαρχόντων αὐτοῖς, "so far as their property shall admit," *ib.* 27[iii. 83] (B.C. 113) ἡ δ' εἴσπραξις τῶν προεθησομένων παρὰ σοῦ κατὰ κράτος ἔσται, "and any losses will be rigorously exacted from you" (Edd.), *OGIS* 90[26] (Rosetta stone—B.C. 196) τὴν τε πόλιν κατὰ κράτος εἷλεν, P Tebt I. 6[31] (B.C. 140–39) τῶν κατὰ μέρος ἐθνῶν, "the several associations," *ib.* II. 382[24] (B.C. 30–A.D. 1) πάντ[α] τὰ [κ]ατὰ δύο μέρη, "all that pertains to the two shares," P Petr II. 11 (1)[7] (iii/B.C.) (= *Selections*, p. 8) τοῦτο δὲ γίνεται διὰ τὸ μὴ ἀθροῦν ἡμᾶς, ἀλλὰ κατὰ μικρὸν λαμβάνειν, "this happens because we do not get our money in a lump sum, but in small instalments." P Tebt I. 5[253]

(B.C. 118) κατὰ μηδεμίαν παρεύρεσι (= -σιν), "on no pretext whatsoever," *ib.*[87] (B.C. 118) κατὰ τοῦτο, "on this account," "in consequence," *ib.* II. 381[14] (A.D. 123) (= *Selections*, p. 78) ἕτερα καθ' ὃν δήποτε οὖν τρόπον, "other things of whatsoever kind," P Lond 904[21] (A.D. 104) (= III. p. 125, *Selections*, p. 73) καθ' ἥ[ντινα] δήποτε αἰτ[ίαν (cf. 2 Macc 14³, 3 Macc 7⁷), and P Tebt I. 42⁵ (*c.* B.C. 114) ἠδικημένος καθ' ὑπερβολὴν ὑπ[ὸ] Ἁρμιύσιος, "having been excessively wronged by Harmiusis." The marriage contract P Eleph 1⁶ (B.C. 311–10) (= *Selections*, p. 2) εἶναι δὲ ἡμᾶς κατὰ ταὐτὸ ὅπου ἂν δοκῇ ἄριστον εἶναι, "and that we should live together wherever it may seem best" supports the rendering of κατὰ τὸ αὐτό in Ac 14¹ AV, RV. On the other hand, the meaning *similiter*, "after the same manner," preferred by Blass *ad l.*, and adopted for κατὰ τὰ αὐτά in Lk 17³⁰ RV, is found in the Will P Eleph 2⁶ (B.C. 285–4) ἐὰν δέ τι πάσχηι Διονύσιος, καταλειπέτω τὰ ὑπάρχοντα πᾶσιν τοῖς υἱοῖς τοῖς αὐτοῦ, κατὰ ταὐτὰ δὲ καὶ Καλλίστα ἐάν τι πάσχηι, καταλειπέτω τὰ ὑπάρχοντα κτλ.: cf. OGIS 56⁶⁶ (B.C. 237) ἐξεῖναι δὲ κατὰ ταὐτὰ καὶ ταῖς ἄλλαις παρθένοις ταῖς βουλομέναις συντελεῖν τὰ νόμιμα τῆι θεῶι.

On the derivation of κατά, and its use in composition, see Moulton *Gr.* ii. § 121.

κατάβαινω.

See *s.v.* ἀναβαίνω, and add P Grenf II. 38¹⁶ (B.C. 81) γράψον μοι περὶ τοῦ μὴ λογεύιν ἕως καταβῆς, P Tebt I. 37²² (B.C. 73) ἔχε ἀπὸ τοῦ χαλκοῦ (τάλαντον) ᾱ ἕως καταβῶ καὶ λάβωι, *ib.* II. 284³ (i/B.C.) ἐπικέκριταί μοι μὴ καταβῆναι ἕως τῆς κε̄, "it has been decided for me (by an oracular response from the god Soknebtunis) that I should not go down till the 25th" (Edd.). In P Par 42¹⁰ (B.C. 156) the verb is used with reference to the possibility that certain malefactors might escape from the right of asylum in an Egyptian temple—ἐὰν τολμήσωσι καὶ καταβῶσι ἐκτὸς τοῦ ἀσύλου, διασάφησόν μοι. See also P Oxy IX. 1223¹³ (late iv/A.D.) of "depreciated" coin—ὁ ὁλοκόττινος νῦν μυ(ριάδων) βκ ἐστίν· κατέβη γάρ, "the solidus now stands at 2,020 myriads; it has come down" (Edd.). MGr κατεβαίνω: the aor. may take the augment, (ἐ)κατέβηκα.

κατάβαλλω

is used of a woman "stricken" with sickness in P Oxy VIII. 1121⁹ (A.D. 295) νόσῳ κατα[β]λ[η]θεῖσα. The classical meaning "pay" is common in the papyri of all periods, and especially so in Byzantine documents (cf. *Ostr.* i. p. 89): see e.g. P Hib I. 29⁶ (*c.* B.C. 265) καταβαλ[ὼν] τὰ γινόμενα τέλη, "on payment of the usual taxes," P Fay 12²² (*c.* B.C. 103) καταβαλὼν διὰ Πτολεμαίου τραπαιζίτ[ου, "paying through Ptolemaeus the banker," *ib.* 63¹ (A.D. 240) κατέβαλ[εν εἰς τ]ὸν Ἀντωνίου Φιλοξένου . . . λόγον "he paid into the account of Antonius Philoxenus," and so P Strass I. 6² (A.D. 255–61): also P Eleph 3² (B.C. 284–3), *ib.* 17²¹ (B.C. 223–2), BGU IV. 1158²¹ (B.C. 9), and P Petr II. 11(1)⁶ (iii/B.C.) cited *s.v.* δάνειον, and *Syll* 936⁶ cited *s.v.* ἀνάγω.

καταβαρέω.

P Oxy III. 487¹⁰ (A.D. 156) ἐμοῦ τε καταβαρηθέ[ν]τος ἐν ταῖς λιτουργίαις, "since I am weighed down by my official duties" (Edd.), shows this Pauline word (2 Cor 12¹⁶) in a

very uneducated document : cf. the similar use of the simplex construed with ἐν in Lk 21³⁴.

κατάβασις.

In P Grenf II. 67¹⁵ (A.D. 237) in connexion with a village festival three asses are provided for the conveyance of certain dancing girls "down and back again"—ὑπὲρ καταβάσεως καὶ ἀναβάσεως.

καταβιβάζω.

P Lond 130¹⁰⁵ (a horoscope—i/ii A.D.) (= I. p. 136) ἐπὶ τοῦ χελειδονιαίου ἰχθύος καταβιβάζων.

καταβολή.

Like its verb (see *s.v.* καταβάλλω) this noun is frequently found in the sense of "payment," e.g. P Par 62ᵛ·¹² (*c.* B.C. 170) τῶν δὲ καταβολῶν σύμβολα λαμβανέτωσαν παρὰ τοῦ τραπεζίτου, BGU IV. 1135⁸ (prob. B.C. 10) τῇ μην[ιαία κ]αταβολῇ, P Lond 1171 *verso*ᶦ·⁷ (A.D. 42) (= III. p. 106) ἰς καταβολὴν τῷ ἐγλήμπτορι τοῦ μέλιτος καὶ κηροῦ, P Strass I. 26¹¹ (iv/A.D.) ἡ γὰρ προθεσμία τῆς καταβολῆς συνέστηκεν. See also P Eleph 23¹³ (B.C. 223–2) with reference to land ἔ]χειν με ταύτης προσβολὴν καὶ κατ[α]βολήν, ἃ καὶ ἐπιδέδειχά σοι. With the noun in Heb 11¹¹ cf. καταβολαῖος used of a "store-place," P Fay 110⁶·³⁰ (A.D. 94).

καταβραβεύω.

This rare verb (Col 2¹⁸) is found in a Ptolemaic dispute regarding succession, *Preisigke* 4512ᴮ·⁵⁷ (B.C. 167–134) ὅθεν καταβεβραβευμένοι [. . . . .]ήρου συνερι[ο]υ ἀξιοῦμεν, ἐὰν φαίν[η]ται, συντάξαι κτλ. See also *s.v.* βραβεύω, and cf. Vett. Val. p. 344²⁹ δοκεῖ δὲ καθὼς ὁρῶμεν ἡ γῆ καταβραβεύειν τῶν λοιπῶν ἐπέχουσα αὐτὴ τὰ πάντα ὡς πρόγονος. A certain sense of "assumption" and "officialism" connected with the word may have led Paul to prefer it to κατακρίνω in Col *l.c.*: see Field *Notes*, p. 196 f.

καταγγελεύς.

The occurrence of this NT ἅπ. εἰρ. (Ac 17¹⁸) in a decree of the Mytilenians in honour of the Emperor Augustus, OGIS 456¹⁰ (B.C. 27–11) καταγγελεῖς τῶν πρώτων ἀ(γ)θησο-[μένων ἀγώνων, "heralds of the first games that shall be held," is, as Deissmann points out (*LAE* p. 97), sufficient to prevent its relegation to "eccles. writ." (Thayer).

For καταγγελία see OGIS 319¹³ (after B.C. 159) τὴν καταγγ[ε]λίαν ἐποιήσαντο πρεπόντως.

καταγγέλλω.

In P Oxy X. 1274⁸ (iii/A.D.) a widow announces the appointment of a representative to act for her—ἐπεὶ ἀπευκταίας μ[ο]ι καταγγελείσης φάσ[ε]ως περὶ τελευτῆς τοῦ μακαρείτου μου ἀνδ[ρός, "in consequence of the lamentable news announced to me concerning the death of my blessed husband" (Edd.). The official sense of the word "make proclamation with authority," which appears in its NT occurrences (see Westcott on 1 Jn 1⁵), is very evident in such a psephisma as *Syll* 364⁵ (A.D. 37) ἐπεὶ ἡ κατ' εὐχὴν πᾶσιν ἀνθρώποις ἐλπισθεῖσα Γαΐου Καίσαρος Γερμανικοῦ Σεβαστοῦ ἡγεμονία κατήνγελται . . . ἔδοξεν τῇ βουλῇ κτλ.

καταγελάω.

BGU III. 814²¹ (iii/A.D.) πάντες καταγελῶσί μοι—so a soldier writes complainingly to his mother, because his father had visited him, but given him no gifts. *Syll* 802¹²² (iii/B.C.) αἰσχυνόμενος δ[ὲ ἅτε] καταγελάμενος ὑπ[ὸ] τῶν ἄλλων ἐνε[κάθε]υδε—with reference to a man who, having no hair on his head, sought healing in the temple of Aesculapius at Epidaurus : cf. *ib.*³⁵ διεγέλα, which is perfective like κατεγέλων in Mk 5⁴⁰.

καταγινώσκω.

The RV rendering in Gal 2¹¹ ὅτι κατεγνωσμένος ἦν, "because he (Peter) stood condemned," *i.e.* either by his own contradictory actions, as Paul proceeds to explain, or by his own conscience, gains a certain amount of support from such passages as P Oxy VII. 1062¹⁴ (ii/A.D.) αὐ[τ]ὴν δέ σοι τὴν ἐπιστολὴν πέμψω διὰ Σύρου ἵνα αὐτὴν ἀναγνοῖς νήφων καὶ σαυτοῦ καταγνοῖς, "I will send you the very letter by Syrus in order that you may read it in a sober mood and be self-condemned" (Ed.), P Flor II. 175¹⁶ (A.D. 255) εἰδὼς ὅτι ἐὰν [ἐν ? τ]οῦτο καταγνωσθῇς [συ?] αὐτοῦ αἴτιος γείνῃ, "knowing that if in this you are condemned, the blame will fall upon yourself": cf. also BGU III. 1004¹·⁵ (iii/B.C.), and *OGIS* 691² ἱστορήσας κατέγνων ἐμαυτοῦ διὰ τὸ μὴ ἐγνωκέναι τὸν λόγον. It should be noted, however, that Field (*Notes*, p. 188 f.) still prefers the AV rendering "because he was to be blamed," following the Vg *quia reprehensibilis erat*; so Souter *Lex. s.v.*, and apparently F. W. Mozley (*Exp* VIII. iv. p. 143 f.) who thinks that the passage runs easier if we get rid of the idea of condemnation, and quotes a paraphrase by Farrar "manifestly and flagrantly in the wrong." A weaker sense, as in Polyb. v. 27. ὁ παρολιγωρεῖσθαι καὶ καταγινώσκεσθαι, is seen in P Magd 42⁴ (B.C. 221) ἐμοῦ δὲ οὐκ ἐκχωρούσης καταγνοῦσά μου ὅτι ξένη εἰμ[ί, πλ]ηγάς μοι ἐνέβαλεν, "mais comme je n'en sortais pas, me méprisant parce que je suis étrangère au pays, elle me donna des coups" (Ed.).

The verbal εὐκατάγνωστος, which LS describe as "Eccl.", is found = "evident" in P Tor I. 1ᵛⁱⁱⁱ·¹¹ (B.C. 117–6). For the subst. κατάγνωσμα see the citations *s.v.* ἀγνόημα, and for κατάγνωσις the late P Strass I. 46²⁹ (A.D. 569) δίχα παντοίας μέμψεως καὶ καταγνώσεως καὶ ῥᾳδιουργίας.

κατάγνυμι.

The curious forms κατεάξω, etc. (Blass *Gr.* p. 52, Radermacher *Gr.* p. 69 f.) can now be illustrated from BGU III. 908²⁵ (time of Trajan) κατέαξαν ἐνίων οἰκιῶν τὰς θύρας. P Flor II. 185⁷ (A.D. 254) τὰ δὲ κανθήλια ("pack-saddles") . . κατεαγμένα καὶ ἄχρηστα : cf. *ib.* 175⁷ (A.D. 255) and *Syll* 588¹⁰ (*c.* B.C. 180) κατεαγότες. The subst. occurs *bis* in connexion with a wound in the head, BGU II. 647¹·²ᶠ· (A.D. 130) ὑπὲρ τὸν ἀριστερὸν κρόταφον τῆς κεφαλῆς τραῦμα κάταγμα ἐπὶ βάθους, ἐν ᾧ εὗρον μι[κρ]ὰ κατάγματα λ[ί̈θ[ο]υ : cf. P Amh II. 93¹⁹ (A.D. 181) ἐὰν δέ τις ἐπισκευῆς ἢ ἀνοικοδομῆς ἢ καταιάγματος ξυλικῶν ἢ ἀργαλίων ὁμοίως ὄντων πρὸ (*l.* πρὸς) σὲ τὸν Στοτοῆτιν, "if any repairs or rebuilding or breakage of wood-work or tools occur you, Stotoetis, shall be responsible" (Edd.). See also Moulton *Gr.* ii. § 83. 1.

καταγράφω.

This verb, which is found in [Jn] 8⁶, like the corresponding subst., generally occurs in our sources in a more or less technical sense, e.g. P Petr II. 23(4)¹ (Ptol.) καλῶς ἂν ποιήσαις καταγράψας τὴν οἰκίαν τοῦ Ὥρου, with reference to which the editors note (P Petr III. p. 148) that "καταγραφή means a register of sales, and καταγράφειν to enter upon a register." See however Mitteis in *Chrest.* II. i. p. 177, and especially GH on P Oxy XIV. 1636¹²·³ (A.D. 249), where it is shown that both subst. and verb refer not to the contract by which the cession is conveyed, but to the actual cession itself. Thus in P Ryl II. 164¹¹ (A.D. 171) καταγρά[ψω ὁπηνίκα ἐὰ]ν αἱρῇ, the meaning is "I will make the conveyance whensoever you please" (Edd.). The verb is used in curses with reference to the consignment of the victim to the lower regions, e.g. *Audollent* 47⁶·⁶ καταγράφω Εὐαγόραν χεῖρας πόδας ψυχὴν γλῶταν ἔργα ἐργασ[ί]ας καὶ τὰ ἐ[κ]είνης ἅ[παντα. On the significance of the act. in [Jn] 8⁶, see the exx. quoted by Wetstein *ad l.*, and add the note in *ExpT* xxx. p. 475 f.

κατάγω

is frequently used of "bringing down" corn etc. to the sea coast or a harbour, e.g. P Grenf II. 44¹¹ (A.D. 101) ὡς εἰς φόρετρα ὧν κατήγαν γένων ἐπὶ κώμη(ς) Βακχιάδος, of goods "brought down" the canal which at one time ran past Philadelphia to Bacchias and the lake, P Oxy IV. 708² (A.D. 188) τοῦ] καταχθέντος γόμου ἐκ τοῦ ὑπὸ σοὶ νομοῦ, BGU I. 81²⁰ (A.D. 189) ἃς καὶ κατήξαμεν εἰς ὅρμον ἄλσους μητρο(πόλεως). For a similar use of the subst. καταγωγή see P Magd 11¹⁰ (B.C. 221) τῇ καταγωγῇ τοῦ σίτου, and cf. *Archiv* iii. p. 219 f. On τὸ καταγώγιον = "the sum paid for this transport," see Wilcken *Ostr.* i. p. 379.

καταγωνίζομαι.

OGIS 553⁷ καταγωνισάμενος τοὺς ὑπεναντίους. On the perfective καταγωνίσασθαι in Heb 11³³ see *Proleg.* p. 116.

καταδέω.

See the magic P Lond 46³¹³ (iv/A.D.) (= I. p. 75) καταδεθήτω αὐτοῦ ἡ φρόνησις, *ib.* ³⁴⁴ (= I. p. 76) κατάδησον δεσμοῖς, and *ib.* 121⁸⁷⁷ (iii/A.D.) (= I. p. 112) καταδήσεις. In this last papyrus ²⁹⁹ (= I. p. 94) we seem to have the plur. of a new subst.—καταδέσματ(α). The verb occurs in cursing formulae e.g. *Syll* 809² (iv/iii B.C.) κα(τ)έδησα τὰς χεῖρας καὶ τοὺς πόδας καὶ τὴν γλῶσσαν καὶ τὴν ψυχήν : cf. Wünsch *AF* p. 16⁸ (a leaden tablet found in a grave) ἐξορκίζω ὑμᾶς κατὰ τῶν μεγάλων ὀνομάτων ἵνα καταδήσητε πᾶν μέλος καὶ πᾶν νεῦρον Βικτωρικοῦ. See also *s.v.* δέω.

κατάδηλος.

This adj., which in Biblical Greek is confined to Heb 7¹⁵, in the sense of "quite clear," "certain," occurs *ter* in P Lips I. 64 (A.D. 368–9) (as amended *Chrest.* I. p. 331 ff.), e.g.²⁵ κατάδηλον ποίησον ἔχειν παρ' αὐτοῖς τὸ μέτρον.

καταδικάζω.

A good example of this legal term, which preserves the same form and meaning in MGr, is afforded by the fragment of a legal code of iii/B.C., which begins—ἐὰν δέ τις περὶ

ἀδικήματος ἑ[τέ]ρο[υ] οἰκέτηι ὄντι δίκην γραψάμενος, ὡς
ἐλευθέρωι, καταδικάσηται, ἐξέστω τῶι κυρίωι ἀναδικῆσαι
ἐν ἡμέραις ε̅, ἀφ' ἧς ἂν ἡ εἴσπραξις γίνηται, καὶ ἂν κατα-
δικασθῆι ἡ δίκη, τότε ἐπιδεκάτων ἢ ἐπιπεντεκαιδεκάτων
ἀποτινέτω ὁ κύριος κτλ. (P Lille I. 29¹ ﬀ.). Cf. P Hal I. 1⁴⁴
(iii/B.C.) ἐὰν δέ τις καταδικασθείσης αὐτοῦ δίκης ἐπιλαβόμενος τῶν μαρτύρων γράψηται δίκην κατὰ τὸ διάγραμμα,
and so ⁶⁵. For κατεδικάσθη see P Petr II. 28(1)⁵ (B.C. 225),
and *ib.* 27(2)³˒⁸, and for ἀπεδικάσθη, *ib.* III. 21(a)³˒⁹ (time
of Euergetes I.). [In P Par 51²⁵ (B.C. 160) (= *Selections*,
p. 21) Wilcken (*Archiv* vi. p. 205) now reads σὺ κατέδιξας
(= κατέδειξας) for κατεδίκας (= κατεδίκασας) διδύμας.] We
may also cite a papyrus letter of A.D. 209 with reference to
the release of a man who had been condemned to work in
the alabaster quarries, *Preisigke* 4639² Νιγέραν Παπειρίου
καταδικασθέντα εἰς ἀλαβαστρῶνα ἐπὶ πενταετίαν . . . πληρώσαντα τὸν τῆς καταδίκης χρόνον ἀπέλυσα. See further
Artem. v. 49 καταδικασθεὶς τὴν ἐπὶ θανάτῳ καὶ προσδεθεὶς
ξύλῳ ἐβρώθη ὑπὸ ἄρκτου.

καταδίκη.

For καταδίκη, as in Ac 25¹⁵, see *Preisigke* 4639 cited *s.v.*
καταδικάζω, and P Hib I. 32⁷ (B.C. 246) where we hear
of a certain Neoptolemus—πρὸς καταδίκην ἔρημον ὕβρεως
πρὸς δραχμὰς σ, "who had been condemned by default
for violence to a fine of 200 drachmae" (Edd.). In P Hal
I. 1⁵² (iii/B.C.) ἀφείσθω τῆς καταδίκη[ς, the word is itself =
"fine." See also *OGIS* 483²¹³ (ii/B.C.) ἐάν τινες διὰ ταῦτα
γείνωνται καταδίκ[αι.

καταδιώκω.

This perfective verb is confined in the NT to Mk 1³⁶,
where it should be translated "pursue after," "hunt down,"
and not simply "follow after" (AV, RV): see *Proleg.* p.
116 and cf. the LXX usage in Ps 17(18)³⁸, 34(35)⁶ *al.*, and
in Pss Sol 15⁹. The same idea of "force" underlies Gen
33¹³, where the verb == "overdrive."

καταδουλόω.

An interesting instance of this verb (Gal 2⁴, 2 Cor 11²⁰)
occurs in an invocation of iv/v A.D., where the invoker summons the Gnostic deity βαινχωωωχ to subdue all the race of
men before him—P Lond 123⁴ (= I. p. 120) καθυπόταξον
φίμωσον καταδούλωσον πᾶν γένος ἀνθρώπων, cf. ⁹ καταδούλωσον φίμωσον τὴν ψυχὴν τὸν θυμόν etc. See also
Menander *Fragm.* p. 98 παιδισκάριόν με καταδεδούλωκ'
εὐτελές, | ὃν οὐδεὶς τῶν πολεμίων - οὐ - πώποτε, "a silly
little wench has hopelessly entangled me--me, whom no
enemy has yet enslaved." The mid. καταδουλούμενον is similarly used of an hetaera in P Eleph 3³, 4⁴ (B.C. 284-3).
According to the law of Antiochus, *OGIS* 383¹⁸² (mid.
i/B.C.), no one is allowed—μήτε αὐτῶι καταδουλώσασθαι
μήτε εἰς ἕτερον ἀπαλλοτριῶσαι certain ἱεροδούλους and their
descendants. The form καταδουλίζω occurs in *Syll* 836⁴
(1st half of iii/B.C.), and in *ib.* 841⁶ (Roman) in a deed of
enfranchisement with reference to certain slaves—μὴ κατα-
δουλιξάσθω δὲ αὐτοὺς μηθεὶς μηδὲ καθ' ὁποῖον τρόπον. See
also *LAE* p. 329 f., and for the subst. *Michel* 1417 A⁸
(Delphi-i/A.D.) ἐπὶ καταδουλισμῶι, "with a view to making
[him] a slave."

καταδυναστεύω.

The rather generalized use of this verb in Ac 10³⁸ is illustrated by P Petr III. 36 (a) *verso*² (Ptol.) πολλάκ[ις] σοι γέγραφα διότι καταδεδυνάστευμαι (*sic*—the writer wished to
change the tense) ἐν τῆι φυλ[α]κῆι λιμῶι παραπολλύμενος, "I
have often explained to you in writing why I am being harshly
treated in the prison, perishing from hunger": though the
agent in Acts *l.c.* is the devil, the reference is to the physical
sufferings attributed to possession.

For the verb of men in authority misusing their power, as
in Jas 2⁶ (cf. Wisd 2¹⁰, 15¹⁴, 17²), see also P Oxy I. 67¹⁵ (A.D.
338) where, in a dispute concerning property, the petitioner
complains—καταδυναστεύοντες ἐπέχουσιν τῶν ἡμῖν διαφε-
ρόντων οἰκοπέ[δω]ν, "certain persons are oppressing me and
occupying my own estates."

κατάθεμα

is confined in Biblical Greek to Rev 22³, but cf. the difficult Didache xvi. 5 οἱ δὲ ὑπομείναντες ἐν τῇ πίστει αὐτῶν
σωθήσονται ὑπ' αὐτοῦ τοῦ καταθέματος. It is apparently a
stronger form of ἀνάθεμα (cf. Zech 14¹¹ and for the form SH
on Rom 9³), and in Rev *l.c.* refers to the object on which a
ban is laid, "an accursed thing." No instance of the word
has yet been cited from profane writings, but see what is
stated *s.v.* ἀνάθεμα.

καταθεματίζω,

like κατάθεμα (*q.v.*), is ἅπ. εἰρ. in Biblical Greek (Mt 26⁷⁴).
Ἀναθεματίζω, which occurs in Mark (14⁷¹) and *ter* in Ac, is
frequent in the LXX.

καταισχύνω.

For the usage of this verb in 1 Cor 11⁴ᵉ we may perhaps
cite Babrius lxxxii. 8 χαίτην ("hair") δ' ἔμελλε τὴν ἐμὴν
καταισχύνειν.

κατακαίω.

This verb is found *ter* in the Calendar of B.C. 301-240. P
Hib I. 27⁷³˒⁷⁹˒⁸⁷, with reference to the parching power of a
strong south wind—τὰ ἐκ τῆς γῆς κατακάει: cf. *aduri* in
Pliny xvii. 24. 37. § 216 of trees being "blasted" *feruore
aut flatu frigidiore*. See also P Amh II. 30³⁶ (ii/B.C.)
ἠναγκάσθην . . . ἐνέγκαι τὰς συνγραφὰς καὶ ταύτας κατακαῦσαι, BGU IV. 1201¹⁶ (A.D. 2) εὕροσαν ἀπὸ μέρους τὰς
θύρας κατακεκαυμέν[ας, and for the metaphorical usage, like
the simplex in Lk 24³², the new erotic fragment, P Grenf I. 1¹³
(ii/B.C.) μέλλω μαίνεσθαι, ζῆλος γάρ με ἔχει καὶ κατακάομαι
καταλελειμμένη.

κατακαλύπτομαι.

Syll 877¹¹ (c. B.C. 420) τὸν θανό[ν]τα [δὲ φέρεν κ]ατακε-
καλυμμένον σιωπῆι μέ[χ]ρι [ἐπὶ τὸ σ]ῆμα.

κατάκειμαι.

For this verb used of one ill, as in Mk 1³⁰ *al.*, cf. P Ryl II.
68¹⁶ (B.C. 89) ὥ[στε] διὰ τὰς πληγὰς ἀρρωστήσασα (*l.* -σαν)
κατακεῖσαι (*l.* -κεῖσθαι) κινδυνεύουσα (*l.* -σαν) τῶι βίωι,
"the blows caused me to be laid up with sickness and my
life is endangered" (Edd.), P Tebt II. 422¹⁸ (iii/A.D.) κατά-
κιται, "she is laid up," and see Field *Notes*, p. 25. The

word has a technical significance in P Oxy VII. 1040³² (A.D. 225) κύρια [τὰ γ]ράμματα δισσὰ γραφέντα ὡς ἐν [δ]ημοσίῳ κατακείμενα, "this bond, which is written in duplicate, is valid as if publicly registered" (Ed.), *ib.* X. 1257¹ (iii/A.D.) τῷ κατ' ἄνδρα τῷ ἐν δ[η]μοσ[ίῳ κατα]κειμένῳ, "to the individual list lodged in the archives" (Edd.). See also P Strass I. 41²⁹ (A.D. 250) δύο ταλάντ]ων παρ' ἐκείνῳ κ[ατ]ακειμένων, "indem die zwei Talente bei ihm beruhten" (Ed.), and the contracted κατακ in Meyer *Ostr* 70³ (A.D. 68) which the editor resolves into κατακ(ειμένου) and understands as referring to "verfallenen (?)" wheat. In *Kaibel* 702⁷ κατάκειμε λιπῶν πένθος γονέ[εσ]σι, the compound takes the place of the simplex κεῖμε in ¹.

κατακλάω

is used metaphorically in Aristeas 149 πῶς οὐ φυλακτέον παντάπασι τοῖς τρόποις εἰς τοῦτο κατακλασθῆναι; "what strict precautions must we not take to prevent the character from degenerating to a like condition?" (Thackeray).

κατακλείω.

The construction of this verb with the simple dat. (Ac 26¹⁰ TR) and with ἐν (Lk 3²⁰) in similar connexions may be illustrated from P Amh II. 80¹ (A.D. 232–3) λογιστηρίῳ κατακλεισθείς and P Tebt II. 420²⁶ (iii/A.D.) ἐπὶ γὰρ κατάκλειστός ἠμι μέχρι σήμερο (*l.* -ον) ἐν τῷ λογιστηρίῳ, "for I have been shut up in the finance-office until to-day" (Edd.). See also *Syll* 540¹⁵⁸ (B.C. 175–1) αὐτῷ λί[θος οὐδεὶς] κατακλεισθήσεται and OGIS 669¹⁷ (i/A.D.) μηδ' (*l.* μηδ') ὅλως κατακλείεσθαί τινας ἐλευθέρους εἰς φυλακὴν ἡντινοῦν. The act. aor. is found in an obscure context in P Lond 429⁵¹ (c. A.D. 350) (= II. p. 315) and the pass. in CP Herm I. 6¹ κατεκλεί[σθ]η. The subst. κατακλείς is used of canal-locks in P Petr II. 13(18a)¹ (B.C. 258–3) περὶ τοῦ πρὸς ταῖς κατακλείσιν τόπον, "concerning the place at the locks" (Ed.).

κατακληροδοτέω.

For this rare verb, which is found in the TR of Ac 13¹⁹ and *ter* in the LXX (always with the variant κατακληρονομέω), Herwerden *Lex. s.v.* cites Theophyl. Sim. *Hist.* vi. 7. 12 τῷ στρατηγῷ τῇ πόλει . . . κατακληροδοτοῦντι ἀριστείας καὶ τρόπαια—a passage hitherto unnoticed by the lexicons.

κατακλίνω.

This medical term (Hobart, p. 69 f.), which in the NT is found only in the Lukan writings, occurs in a medical receipt of early i/A.D., P Oxy VIII. 1088²⁹ ὕπτιον κατακλίνας τὸν ἄνθρωπον θεράπευε, "lay the man on his back and treat him" (Ed.): cf. the use of the adj. in P Ryl II. 124⁶ (i/A.D.) ὥστε αὐτὴν κατακρινῇ (*l.* κατακλινῆ) εἶναι, "so that she is laid up in bed" (Edd.). The verb is found in *Cagnat* IV. 661²¹ (a will—A.D. 85) ἵνα μόνοι οἱ παρόντες καὶ κατακλεινόμενοι βουλευταὶ λαμβάνωσι τὴν διανομὴν [τα]ύτην: for the subst. cf. *ib.*⁵ γείν[εσ]θαι δὲ τὴν κατάκλισιν μηνὸς Πανήμου ἡμέρᾳ εὐδαιμοσύνης.

κατακλύζω

is common of land that has been "flooded," e.g. P Magd 28¹⁰ (B.C. 218) (= *Chrest.* I. p. 399) ἀπὸ δὲ τῆς αὐτοὶ γεωρ-

γοῦσιν γῆς ἀντιδοθῆναί μοι τὸ ἴσον πλῆθος ἀνθ' ἧς κ[ατα]κ[ε]κλύκασιν, P Tebt I. 56⁹ (late ii/B.C.) γείγ[ωσ]κε δὲ περὶ τοῦ κατακεκλῦσθαι τὸ πεδίον ὑμῶν (*l.* ἡμῶν), "you must hear about our plain having been inundated" (Edd.), BGU IV. 1132¹¹ (B.C. 16) γῆν χέρσον κατακεκλυσμένην, and P Lond 131 *recto*¹⁶³ (A.D. 78–9) (= I. p. 174) πρὸς τὸ κατακλυσ(θῆναι) ὑπὸ τοῦ ὕδατο(ς). Cf. also the Rosetta stone, OGIS 90²¹ (B.C. 196) τοῦ τε Νείλου τὴν ἀνάβασιν μεγάλην ποιησαμένου ἐν τῶι ὀγδόωι ἔτει καὶ εἰθισμένου κατακλύζειν τὰ πεδία κατέσχεν κτλ.

κατακλυσμός

is supplied by the editor in BGU IV. 1121²⁷ (B.C. 5) ἐὰν δὲ συμβῇ αὐτοῖς πρ . . . . ἔφοδον γενέσθαι ἢ κατακλυσμὸν ἢ ξυλείας] ἐκκοπήν. The word survives in MGr = "inundation," "flood."

κατακολουθέω

is found in the NT (Lk 23⁵⁵, Ac 16¹⁷) only in its literal sense, but for the derived meaning, as in LXX Dan 9¹⁰, we may compare P Tor I. 1ⁱˣ·²⁶ (B.C. 117) καὶ αὐτοὶ κατακολουθήσαντες ταῖς ἐπενηνεγμέναις ὑπ' αὐτῶν συγγραφαῖς, P Tebt I. 30¹ (B.C. 115) ὅπως εἰδὼς κατακολουθῇς τοῖς ἐπισταλμένοις, *ib.* 49¹⁹ (B.C. 117) (= *Selections*, p. 28) κατακολουθεῖν τοῖς ἐξ ἀρχῆς ἐθισμοῖς, P Grenf II. 23³ (B.C. 108?) κατακολουθήσας οὖν τοῖς διὰ τούτου σημαινομένοις, OGIS 329³ (ii/B.C.) κατηκ[ο]λουθηκότος ταῖς ἑκάστων αὐτῶν βουλήσεσιν. In P Lond 256⁵¹ (B.C. 158–7) (= II. p. 30) a docket instructs the clerks to "carry out" a certain order—τοῖς γραμματεῦσιν κατακολουθεῖν: cf. P Meyer 1⁵⁰ (B.C. 144). See also Laqueur *Quaestiones*, p. 25 f.

κατακόπτω.

For this verb in the derived sense of "beat," "bruise," as in Mk 5⁵ (cf. Wycliffe "betynge hym-silf," and see Field *Notes*, p. 27), we may cite P Lips I. 37²⁰ (A.D. 389) ἔπειτα κατέκοψα[ν] π[ληγ]αῖς αὐτὸν κατὰ τ[ε] τῶν σκελῶν καὶ κατὰ τῶν ἄλλων μελῶ[ν] τοῦ σώματος, and the illiterate PSI IV. 313¹⁰ (iii/iv A.D.) πληγές μαι κατέκοψεν καθ' ὅλου τοῦ σώματος. See also *Kaibel* 316³ ᶠ·—

μάμμη] δ' Εὐτοχία μασ[τοὺ]ς κατεκόψατο, οἷς ἔτρεφέν σε Μοίραις, [κ]αὶ φθιμένους ὀκταέτης ἔμ'ολες.

The editor suggests a new word κατακοπτικόν in the magic P Lond 121¹⁹⁰ (iii/A.D.) (= I. p. 98), but the line in which it occurs has been intentionally obliterated, and the context is wholly wanting.

κατάκριμα.

Deissmann (*BS* p. 264 f.) quotes several passages from CPR I. where he thinks the word must be understood technically to denote "a burden ensuing from a judicial pronouncement—a servitude," as in 1¹⁰ (A.D. 83–4) where a piece of land is transferred to the purchaser καθαρὰ ἀπὸ παντὸς ὀφειλήματος ἀπὸ μὲν δημοσίων τελεσμάτων πάντων καὶ [ἑτέρων εἰ]δῶν καὶ ἀρταβίων καὶ ναυβίων καὶ ἀριθμητικῶν καὶ ἐπιβολῆς κώμης καὶ κατακριμάτων πάντων καὶ παντὸς εἴδους, and 188¹⁴ ᶠ (A.D. 105–6) where in a deed of sale similar expressions occur. To these exx. we may add P

Oxy II. 298⁴ (i/A.D.) τοῦ κατακρίματος (δραχμῶν) Σ, where though unfortunately the phrase follows an hiatus, the word is apparently = "a judgment" for a sum of money to be paid as a fine or damages. Cf. P Tebt II. 298⁶⁵ (A.D. 107-8) κατακ[ρ]ι[μ(άτων)], where the editors point out that the reference is to "fines," and compare *ib.* 363¹⁵ (early ii/A.D.), P Fay 66¹ (A.D. 185 or 217), and P Amh II. 114⁸ (A.D. 130); these fines were normally collected by πράκτορες, cf. Lk 12⁵⁸. It follows that this word does not mean *condemnation*, but the punishment following sentence, so that the "earlier lexicographers" mentioned by Deissmann were right. This not only suits Rom 8¹ admirably, as Deissmann points out, but it materially helps the exegesis of Rom 5 ¹⁶. ¹⁸. There is no adequate antithesis between κρίμα and κατάκριμα, for the former never suggests a trial ending in acquittal. If κατάκριμα means the *result* of the κρίμα, the "penal servitude" from which οἱ ἐν Χριστῷ Ἰησοῦ are delivered (8¹), δικαίωμα represents the "restoration" of the criminal, the fresh chance given him. The antithesis is seen better in ver. 18, for δικαίωσις is "a process of absolution, carrying with it life" (SH), which exactly answers to κατάκριμα, the permanent imprisonment for a debt we cannot pay: Mt 18³⁴ paints the picture of this hopeless state.

κατακρίνω.

P Petr I. 16¹² (B.C. 230) ἀλλὰ κατακριθῆι μου, "but if the case be decided against me," and P Oxy III. 653 (*b*) (before A.D. 101) where in the account of a trial regarding a mortgage upon the property of Voltinus which had been seized by the creditor, Sempronius Orestinus, the Prefect informs the latter that unless he makes restitution—οὐ μόνον κατακριθήσει ἀλλὰ καὶ δαρήσ[ει]. The verb occurs several times in the i/A.D. edict *OGIS* 669, e.g. ²⁷ ἐνετέχθην δὲ καὶ περὶ τῶν ἀτελειῶν καὶ κουφοτελειῶν . . . λεγόντων ὕστερον κατακεκρίσθαι τὰ ὑπὸ ἰδιωτῶν πραχθέντα ἐν τῶι μέσωι χρόνωι μετὰ τὸ Φλάκκον κατακρεῖναι καὶ πρὸ τοῦ τὸν θεὸν Κλαύδιον ἀπολῦσαι: cf. also *ib.* 437⁸² (i/B.C.) τὸ κατακριθὲν πρασσέτωσαν παραχρῆμα. The distinction between κατακρίνω, "condemn," and ἀνακρίνω, "examine judicially," is well seen in Sus Th. 48 οὐκ ἀνακρίναντες οὐδὲ τὸ σαφὲς ἐπιγνόντες κατεκρίνατε θυγατέρα Ἰσραήλ;

κατάκρισις.

Grimm's statement "Not found in prof. auth." must be corrected in view of the occurrence of the word in Vett. Val. pp. 108¹ τουτέστιν ἡ δύσις περὶ δεσμῶν καὶ συνοχῶν καὶ ἀποκρύφων πραγμάτων καὶ κατακρίσεως καὶ ἀτιμίας, 117³⁵ φθονικαὶ κατακρίσεις, "condemnations for envy": see Deissmann *LAE* p. 91 f.

κατακύπτω.

With the usage in [Jn] 8³ = "stoop down," Sharp (p. 75) compares Epict. ii. 16. 22 εὐθὺς ἐγὼ ὅταν πλέω, κατακύψας εἰς τὸν βυθὸν ἢ τὸ πέλαγος περιβλεψάμενος . . . "for instance, whenever I am on a voyage, stooping and looking into the deep or glancing around upon the sea . . . ": cf. also Aristeas 91 ἐκέλευσαν κατακύψαντα συνακοῦσαι, "bade me stoop down and listen." See also *s.vv.* κύπτω and παρακύπτω.

καταλαλέω.

See the fragmentary P Hib I. 151 (*c.* B.C. 250) εἰ οὖν τιν' ἐπιχώρησιν ποιεῖ ἔντυχε ἐκείνωι καταλάλησον, συντετάχαμεν γὰρ . . ., and cf. *Syll* 278⁶ (ii/B.C.) ἵνα μηδ' ἐν τούταις ἔχωσιν ἡμᾶς καταλαλεῖν αἱ οὐκ ἀπὸ τοῦ βελτίστου εἰωθότες ἀναστρέφεσθαι.

καταλαμβάνω.

Many of the NT meanings of this common verb can be paralleled from our sources. Thus P Oxy XII. 1413¹⁴ (A.D. 270-5) κατείληφα πόρον, τουτέστιν γενήματα ἀποκείμενα ἐν τῷ Μονίμου, "I have impounded the property, that is to say produce deposited at the farmstead of Monimus" (Edd.), *Syll* 933⁶⁰ (iv/B.C.) οὐδὲ κατέλαβον τὰν χώρ[αν καὶ ἐτεί]χιξ]αν τὰν πόλιν—then follow the names of colonists who "appropriated" the land : this is Paul's regular use of the verb in active and passive. In the letter of Epicurus to a child, discovered at Herculaneum, 176⁴ (= *Selections*, p. 5), the philosopher writes—ἀ]φείγμεθα εἰς Λάμψακον . . . καὶ ἐκεῖ κατειλήφαμεν ὑγ[ι]αίνοντας Θεμίσταν καὶ τοὺς λοιποὺς [φί]λο[υ]s, "we have arrived at Lampsacus, and there we have found Themistas and the rest of our friends in good health": cf. P Tebt I. 15⁵ (B.C. 114) ἡμῶν συνεκπηδησάντων κατέλαβον (*l.* κατέλαβον) ὄχλον τῶν ἐκ τῆς κώ(μης), "on running out we found a crowd of the villagers" (Edd.). For a weaker meaning "meet with" a person or thing, cf. P Fay 130⁸ (iii/A.D.) ἕως ἂν καταλαμβάνω σε πρὸς τὴν ἑαρτήν, "until I meet you at the festival" (Edd.), P Meyer 20²⁰ (1st half iii/A.D.) συνπεριφέρου τῷ καιρῷ ἕως σε καταλάβω, "adapt yourself to circumstances until I join you," *ib.* 23³ (end iv/A.D.) ἤδη γὰρ ὑμᾶς καταλάβω, P Oxy IX. 1223⁵ (late iv/A.D.) τὸ πλοῖον . . . καταλαμβάνει, *ib.* X. 1297¹⁴ (iv/A.D.) ἐὰν καταλάβῃ Θεόδωρος ἐκεῖ, "if Theodorus reaches you there" (Edd.). Hence in late papyri the verb comes to mean "visit" as in *Chrest.* I. 297⁶ (vi/A.D.) ἅμα] δὲ Ἀπολλῶτι κατάλαβε, ἐπειδὴ ἀναγκαίως θέλω σοι λαλῆσαι, where Wilcken renders κατάλαβε "komm," "besuche mich." To "overtake," of evils, as in Jn 12³⁵, and probably in 1⁵, is the meaning in *Syll* 214¹⁴ (iii/B.C.) καὶ νῦν δὲ καιρῶν ("crises") κατειληφότων ὁμοίων τὴν Ἑλλάδα πᾶσαν : see also the Christian letter P Oxy VI. 939⁵ (iv/A.D.) (= *Selections*, p. 128) ὥστε τὴν] κυρίαν ἀνασφῆλαι ἐκ τῆς καταλαβούσης [αὐτὴν νόσ]ου, "in that my mistress has recovered from the illness that struck her down." 1 Th 5⁴ may be illustrated by *Syll* 803¹⁴ (Epidaurus, iii/B.C.) μεταξὺ δὲ ἁμέρα ἐπικαταλαμβάνει.

For καταλαμβάνω = "detect," "catch," in a crime, cf. P Lille I. 3⁵⁸ (after B.C. 241-0) ἀπεστάλκαμεν Ἡρακλείδην, συντάξαντες [α]ὐτῶι, ἐά[ν τι]νας καταλαμβάνηι διατιθεμένους [π]λειόνων τι[μ]ῶν συντεταγμένων, παραδιδ[ό]ναι αὐ[τα]ὺς τοῖς φ[υ]λακίταις, P Ryl II. 138¹⁵ (A.D. 34) κατέλαβα ταῦτον διὰ νυκτὸς ἡλμένον . . εἰς τῶι (*l.* τὸ) . . ἐποίκιον, "I detected him when under cover of night he had sprung into the farmstead" (Edd.), and especially BGU IV. 1024ᵛⁱⁱ ¹¹ (iv/v A.D.) γυναῖκα καταλημφθεῖσαν ὑπὸ τοῦ ἐδι[κ]η[μέ]νος (*l.* ἠδικημένου) μετὰ μοίχου, which offers an almost exact parallel to [Jn] 8³ᶠ. The mid. = "perceive," "comprehend," as in Ac 4¹³ *al*, may be illustrated from Vett. Val. p. 225⁸ ἅπερ ἐκ τῆς τῶν ἀστέρων ἀφέσεως κατελαβόμην, and so frequently. See Dittenberger's note on *OGIS* 8²⁰ for the verb = "condemn" in the Ionic and Aeolic dialects. MGr καταλαβαίνω, "comprehend," "understand."

καταλέγομαι.

The technical use in 1 Tim 5⁹ = "enroll," occurs in BGU IV. 1073¹⁰ (A.D. 274) περὶ τοῦ καταλ[ε]λέχθαι αὐτὸν εἰς τὸν σύλλογον τῆς ἱερᾶς συνόδου, *Michel* 165² (ii/B.C.) τῆς καταλεγείσης κανηφόρου, "enrolled as basket-bearer." For καταλογεῖον = "bureau," see *Chrest.* II. i. p. 67. Καταλογή in the derived sense of "respect," "reverence," is found in *Syll* 328⁸ (B.C. 84) : see the editor's note.

καταλείπω.

For the 1st aor. formation κατέλειψα, as in Ac 6², cf. P Giss I. 69⁶ (A.D. 118–9) αὐτὸν παρὰ σοὶ κατέλειψα, P Ryl II. 153¹⁸ (A.D. 138–61) ὃν κατέλιψα ἐν Σμύρνῃ τῆς Ἀσίας παρὰ τροφῷ θηλάζοντα, and the exx. in Deissmann *BS* p. 190. The verb is very common of property "left" or bequeathed, as in P Eleph 2³ (B.C. 285–4) ἐὰν δέ τι πάσχηι Διονύσιος, καταλείπειν τὰ ὑπάρχοντα αὐτοῦ πάντα Καλλίσται, P Magd 13¹ (B.C. 217) ἐπιζητοῦντές τινα μέρη τῶν καταλειφθέντων ὑπαρχόντων ὑπὸ Φιλίππου, P Tebt II. 380²² (A.D. 67) καταλιφθησωμένων ὑπαρχόντων ἀπάντων, *ib.* 327¹⁴ (late ii/A.D.) τετελευτηκότος ἀπ[όρου] μηδὲ ἓν καταλείπ[οντο]ς, "he died without means, leaving nothing at all" (Edd.), *ib.* 406⁸ (c. A.D. 266) λόγος ὧν κατάλειψεν (*l.* κατέλ–) Παῦλος γενόμ[εν]ός μου ἀ[ν]ήρ, "account of effects left by Paulus, my late husband" (Edd.). With the usage in Mk 10⁷ we may compare P Oxy III. 526¹ (ii/A.D.) οὐκ ἤμην ἀπαθὴς ἀλόγως σε καταλείπιν, "to leave you in the lurch without reason" : see also P Lond 897⁵ (A.D. 84) (= III. p. 207) ἥδιστα πάντας καταλείψωι εἶνα μὴ τὴν πρός σε φιλείαν καταλείψωι, and P Oxy I. 120 *verso* ⁶ (iv/A.D.) ἀλ' (*l.* ἀλλ') ὅρα μὴ καταλίψῃς μαι θλιβόμενον, "whatever you do, do not fail me in my trouble" (Edd.). Similarly for Heb 4¹ we may cite P Lond 1171⁴³ (B.C. 8) (= III. p. 179), accounts with reference to ἄρακος as fodder for flocks—

γίνονται ἀρ(άκου)   ō σκ
καταλείπονται ἀριάκου)   ο υλγ

For καταλιμπάνω (cf. Gen 39¹⁶) see P Petr I. 14³ (a will —B.C. 237) καταλιμπάνω τὰ ὑπ[άρχοντα κτλ., *ib.* 15¹⁷ (B.C. 237), and P Grenf I. 1³ (ii/B.C.) ὀδύνη μ' ἔχει ὅταν ἀναμνησθῶ ὥς με κατεφίλει ἐπιβούλως μέλλων με καταλιμπάν[ει]ν.

καταλλαγή

seems to be found in the same sense as ἐπαλλαγή, "exchange," in P Hib I. 100⁴ (an account—B.C. 267) εἰς] τοῦτο κομίζει [πα]ρὰ τῶν τὰ ἀφίλια ε̄, [κ]αὶ παρὰ τὴν καταλ[λα]γὴν γ̄ : see the editor's note.

καταλλάσσω.

For this characteristic Pauline verb cf. the question to an oracle, P Oxy XII. 1477⁶ (iii/iv A.D.) εἰ καταλλάσσομαι εἰς τὸν γόνον ; where the editors translate, "am I to be reconciled (?) with my offspring (?)" but in their note state that they regard the reading γόνον as "not very satisfactory." See also OGIS 218¹⁰⁵ (iii/B.C.) φόνον δὲ ἐπιγαμία(ι)ς μὴ καταλλάσ[σεσ]θαι μηδὲ χρήμασιν. For ἀντικαταλλάσσω see P Par 63¹⁹¹, cited *s.v.* εὔχρηστος.

PART IV.

κατάλοιπος.

For this NT ἅπ. εἰρ. (Ac 15¹⁷) cf. P Leid Sᵃ ³¹ (ii/B.C.) (= I. p. 69) τὸ κατάλοιπον τοῦ ὕδωρ (*l.* ὕδατος). P Oxy VII. 1061⁸ (B.C. 22) καὶ τὸ κατάλοιπον ἀποδοθῆι τῶι Πτολεμαίωι, "and the remainder paid over to Ptolemaeus" (Ed.), *Michel* 829²³ (1st half i/B.C.) τ[ὸ] δὲ κατάλοιπον παρέδωκα τῷ ἐπιστήσοντι ἀγωνοθέτῃ.

κατάλυμα.

For this noun (the Hellenistic equivalent of καταγωγεῖον), as in Lk 2⁷ (cf. Exod 4²⁴), see P Par 34⁵ (ii/B.C.) εἰς τὸ κατάλυμα τῶν Ἀρσινοϊτῶν, where the reference is to the "lodging-place" provided for the inhabitants of Arsinoe in the Serapeum. Elsewhere in Biblical Greek, e.g. 1 Kings 1¹⁸, Mk 14¹⁴, it has rather the sense of "guest-room." Κατάλυσις is similarly used in P Petr II. 14(1²)² τὴν βασιλεικὴν κατάλυσιν, where Mahaffy notes that the Royal quarters served as an "inn" for the convenience of officials who visited the place. In P Magd 8¹⁰ (B.C. 218) we have κατ]άλυσιν τοῦ βίου, "the dissolution of life." MGr κατάλυμα, "lodging."

καταλύω.

Corresponding to the use of κατάλυσις in the last citation *s.v.* κατάλυμα, we may note the occurrence of the verb in the same papyrus, P Magd 8⁵ (B.C. 218) τῆς γυναικός μου τὸν β[ί]ον καταλυσάσης. On the other hand the meaning "lodge," as in Lk 9¹², 19⁷, may be illustrated from P Par 49³⁶ (B.C. 164–158) (= Witkowski², p. 72) πρός σε οὐ μ[ὴ] ἐπέλθω, εἰς δὲ τὰ Πρωτάρχου καταλύσω, BGU IV. 1097⁵ (time of Claudius or Nero) περὶ δὲ Σαραπᾶτος τοῦ υἱοῦ οὐ καταλέλυκε παρ' ἐμὲ ὅλως, ἀλλὰ ἀπῆλθεν εἰς παρεμβολὴν στρατεύσασθαι, and the dialect inscr. *Syll* 561⁹ (mid. iii/B.C.) μὴ ἐ[ξῆμ]εν καταλύε[ν ἐν τῷ] ἱαρῷ τῶμ [Βάκχων μ]ηδένα, where the editor notes "vocem intransitive usurpatam divertendi vel commorandi vi apparet." On the other hand, in *Michel* 725²⁰ᶠ (end of ii/B.C.) the verb has the meaning "set at naught," "annul," as in Mt 5¹⁷ —καὶ μηθενὶ ἐξέστω κατα[λ]ῦσαι τόδε [τὸ ψήφι]σμα, εἰ δὲ μή, [ὁ κα[ταλ]ύσας ἀποτεισάτω δίκ[ην εἰς τὸ]ν [ναὸν τοῦ Διός. See also *Kaibel* 1005⁴ νὺξ αὐτοὺς καταλύει—with reference to the departed glories of Homeric heroes.

καταμανθάνω.

With this verb, as in Mt 6²⁸ (Sir 9⁵) cf. P Oxy VIII. 1153²⁰ (i/A.D.) ὁ δώσεις τῷ Νικάνορι [κατα]μαθεῖν, "give it (viz. a pattern of a dress) to Nicanor to look at" (Ed.), P Fay 114¹¹ (A.D. 100) ἐπὶ ἐρώτησέ με Ἑρμόναξ . . . καταμαθιν τὸν ἐλαιῶνα αὐτοῦ ἐπὶ πυκνός ἐστιν, "for Hermonax has asked me to look to his olive-yard, as it is overgrown" (Edd.). BGU IV. 1041⁵ (ii/A.D.) κατέμαθον αὐτὰ εἰς ἀπόδοσιν, P Tebt II. 449 (ii/iii A.D.) κατέμαθον τὰ δύο λ[ί]να τὰ ἰσχνά. See also *Proleg.* p. 117 f.

καταμαρτυρέω.

P Tor I. 1ᵛ·²³ (B.C. 117) ὥστε ὁμολογουμένως ἑαυτοῦ καταμαρτυροῦντα συμφανὲς καθεστακέναι.

καταμένω.

Various passages from our sources show that this verb has not necessarily the meaning of "remain permanently,"

43

"abide," ascribed to it by Grimm-Thayer. Thus P Fay 24 (A.D. 158) is a declaration by a police officer that he had set up in a certain farmstead the copy of an edict ordering all strangers who were (temporarily) staying there to return to their own homes—¹⁵ ff. περὶ τῶν ἐπιξένων καταμενόντων ἐν τῷ ἐποικίῳ ὥστε αὐτοὺς εἰς τὴν ἰδίαν ἀνέρχεσθαι. And similarly one of the libelli of the Decian persecution is lodged on behalf of a man belonging to the village, but at the moment residing in another—P Ryl II. 112(b)⁵ (A.D. 250) π̣αρὰ Αὐρηλίου Ἀούτεως ἀπὸ κώμης Δίννεως καταμένων ἐν κώμη Θεαδελφείᾳ : cf. P Meyer 15¹⁷ (A.D. 250). On the other hand in P Oxy VIII. 1121¹⁷ (A.D. 295) Σωτᾶς τις καὶ Παποντῶς καταμένοντες ἐν τῇ αὐτῇ οἰκίᾳ ἔνθα ἡ μήτηρ μου ᾤκει, "a certain Sotas and Papontos, who are my neighbours in the same house where my mother lived" (Ed.) the verb may point to more settled residence : cf. the complaint in Syll 418³¹ (A.D. 238) οἱ ἐκεῖσε τῆς πανηγύρεως ἕνεκεν ἐπιδημοῦντες ἡμέρας πεντεκαίδεκα ἐν τῷ τόπῳ τῆς πανηγύρεως οὐ καταμένουσιν, ἀλλ' ἀπολιμπάνοντες ἐπέρχονται εἰς τὴν ἡμετέραν κώμην καὶ ἀναγκάζουσιν ἡμᾶς ξενίας αὐτοῖς παρέχειν.

καταναλίσκω.

This expressive compound (Heb 12²⁹) is found in a woman's complaint against her husband—PSI I. 41²⁰ (iv/A.D.) εἴθε μὴ τεθέαμαι αὐτόν, . . . κατηνάλωσεν γὰρ τὰ ἡμέτερα. Cf. also Syll 306³⁹ (mid. ii/B.C.) καταναλισκέσθω ὁ τόκος εἰς παιδευτάς.

καταναρκάω,

which in the NT is confined to 2 Cor 11⁹, 12¹³ ff., is classed by Jerome (Ep. ad Alga. qu. 10) among Paul's cilicisms. It may, however, have been a medical term in regular use, as it is found in Hippocrates (Art. 816 C) : cf. the simplex ναρκάω in Gen 32²⁵, ²², Job 33¹⁹, and ἀποναρκάω in Plut. De Liber. Educ. p. 8. The subst. νάρκα (Lob. Phryn. p. 331) = "torpor" is found in Menander Fragm. p. 143 : cf. M. Anton. x. 9 πτοία, νάρκα, δουλεία.

κατανεύω.

See BGU IV. 1119²⁴ (B.C. 6–5), 1120³⁰ (B.C. 5), where however the reading and the meaning are far from clear.

κατανοέω.

The characteristic force of this verb, "perceive," "understand," "take note of," is seen in P Hib I. 27³⁸ (B.C. 301–240) if we accept the editors' restoration—μακ[ρὸν] καὶ ξένον σοι κατα̣νοεῖν?, "a long and unfamiliar thing to understand (?)" (Edd.) : cf. P Par 63⁹² (B.C. 165) (= P Petr III. p. 35) ὅταν . . τὸ συμφέρον κατανοῶσι κοινὸν νομιζόμενον, "as soon as they perceive that the advantage is regarded as common to all" (Mahaffy), BGU III. 1011ii. 37 (ii B.C.) διότι γὰρ πολλὰ λ̣ηρω̣[δη] καὶ ψευδῆ προσαγ-(γ ελ λε]ται κατανοεῖς καὶ αὐτός, Syll 928⁷³ (ii B.C. ad init.) πολὺ μᾶλλον [ἀδύνατον ἦν] κατανοεῖν [τὰ ἐμ]ρη[σθέν]τα. See also Aristeas 3 τὴν προαίρεσιν ἔχοντες ἡμεῖς πρὸς τὸ περιεργως τὰ θεῖα κατανοεῖν ἑαυτοὺς ἐπεδώκαμεν κτλ., "it was my devotion to the careful study of religion which led me to offer my services" etc. (Thackeray).

καταντάω.

Κατανταν εἰς in the legal sense of property "descending to" an heir is very common, e.g. BGU IV. 1169²¹ (B.C. 10) ἥσπερ μετηλλαχυίας κατήντηκεν ἰς αὐτοὺς τὰ ταύτης, P Oxy II. 274¹⁹ (A.D. 89–97) τὰ δὲ προκείμενα αὐτοῦ πατρικ[ὰ] . . κατήντ(ησεν) εἰς α(ὐτὸν) μετὰ τὴν τ[ο]ῦ πατρὸς τελευ[τήν, BGU III. 969¹⁶ (ii/A.D.) εἰς τὸν συνηγορούμενον κατήντηκεν ἡ κτηνοτ[ρ]οφία. In BGU I. 326ii. 12, 13 (A.D. 194) καταντῆσαι πρός τινα occurs twice in the same sense. This technical meaning seems very appropriate in 1 Cor 10¹¹ ἡμῶν, εἰς οὓς τὰ τέλη τῶν αἰώνων κατήντηκεν, on which Prof. Findlay's unconscious comment is—"The Church is the heir of the spiritual training of mankind" (EGT ad l.). [Dr. Rendel Harris suggests that in this case τὰ τέλη means "the revenues" of the ages]. The Tennysonian parallel "I, the heir of all the ages" suggests itself at once. In 1 Cor 14³⁶ ἢ εἰς ὑμᾶς μόνους κατήντησεν (ὁ λόγος τοῦ θεοῦ); the same sense is probable—"was the gospel your exclusive inheritance?"

Like our descent, the word keeps its ordinary meaning elsewhere. Thus in illustration of its nine-fold occurrence in Acts with reference to travellers reaching their destination we may cite P Tebt I. 50³ (B.C. 99) καταντήσαντος . . εἰς τὴν πόλιν Σοκονώφεως, P Oxy III. 486³⁰ (A.D. 131) ἐνθάδε κατήντησα, and Priene 112⁹⁷ (after B.C. 84) κατανταν εἰς τὸ γυμνάσιον, while P Meyer 3¹⁶ (A.D. 148) ἵν' οὖν . . εὐθέως ἐπὶ τὸν κρά[τιστον] ἐπίτροπ(ον) καταντήσῃς (ἐ)πέστειλά σοι shows the verb of "presenting oneself before" a person. In PSI I. 101¹³ (end of ii/A.D.) εἰς μόνους κατηντηκέναι ἄνδρας γ̄, the reference is to certain taxation which has "fallen upon" three men : cf. ib. 102¹⁰, 105⁹. The verb is found in MGr = "come to," "end in," as in Abbott Songs xvi. 5 (p. 140) τρελλὸς θὰ καταντήσω, "I shall end in madness"—a lover's serenade : cf. κατάντημα, "end," "goal," in LXX Ps 18⁷. The subst. κατάντησις = "entrance" occurs in P Hamb I. 4⁷ (A.D. 87) κατάντησιν εἰς Ἀλεξ-άνδριαν.

κατάνυξις.

This NT ἅπ. εἰρ. (Rom 11⁸) occurs in Pelagia-Legenden, p. 3⁷ πάσης γὰρ ὠφελείας καὶ κατανύξεως πεπλήρωται τὸ διήγημα, where it seems to have the unusual meaning of "incitement," "stimulus."

κατανύσσω.

An interesting illustration of the use of this verb in Ac 2³⁷ is afforded by Pelagia-Legenden, p. 7¹⁶ καὶ οὕτως κατενύγη πᾶς ὁ λαὸς ἐπὶ τοῖς λόγοις οἷς ἐλάλει τὸ πνεῦμα τὸ ἅγιον δι' αὐτοῦ, ὥστε ὅλον τὸ ἔδαφος τῆς ἐκκλησίας καταρρανθῆναι ὑπὸ τῶν δακρύων τοῦ λαοῦ. MGr κατανύσσομαι, "I am seized with compunction," "I become contrite."

καταξιόω.

Like the simplex, καταξιόω denotes not "make" but "count worthy": cf. BGU IV. 1080¹⁵ (iii/A.D. ?) σπούδασον ἡμᾶς καταξιῶσαι τῶν ἴσ[ω]ν γραμμάτων, OGIS 201²⁴ (vi/A.D.) εἰ μὴ κατηξίωσάν με καὶ παρακαλοῦσιν. For the pass., as in Lk 20³⁵, Ac 5⁴¹, cf. P Leid Wxvi. 11 (ii/iii A.D.) κατηξιώθης τῶν πρὸς διά (= ό)ρθωσιν βίου μελλ̣ό̣(ν)των σοι λέγεσθαι, P Amh II. 145⁴ (iv/v A.D.) βούλο]μαι μὲν καταξιωθῆναι ἀεὶ γράφειν [τῇ σῇ] θεοσεβείᾳ, *CIA* III. 690⁹¹ ἀνατροφῆς τῆς αὐτῆς καταξιωθείς. In late Greek the verb is common = "be so good as," "vouchsafe," e.g. P Heid 6²⁰ (iv/A.D.) (= *Selections*, p. 127) παρακαλῶ καταξίωσον δέξεσθαι τὸ μικρὸν ἐλέου, P Meyer 24⁴ (vi/A.D.) καταξιώσῃ οὖν ἡ σὴ θεοσέβεια εὔξασθαι ὑπὲρ ἐμοῦ. It is condemned by the Atticists, cf. Thom. Mag. 9, 7 ἀξιῶ τὸ ἄξιον κρίνω οὐ καταξιῶ.

For the adj. see *OGIS* 763²⁴ (ii/B.C.) τὰς καταξίας τιμὰς τοῖς εὐεργέταις ἀπονέμοντες, and for the adv. BGU IV. 1138²² (B.C. 19) καταξίως.

καταπατέω

occurs in the late PSI I. 76³ (A.D. 574-578) ἡ πίστις . . . τἀναντία καταπατουμένη σαφῶς ἀπεργάζεται. Cf. *Syll* 803¹¹⁵ (iii/B.C.) καταπατεῖν νιν τοῖς ἵπποις. For the noun see CP Herm I. 7ⁱⁱ ⁷ (ii/A.D. ?) καταπάτησιν ποιήσασθαι χωρίων.

καταπαύω.

See Anz *Subsidia*, p. 294 f. Herwerden (*Lex.*) cites καταπαυστικός of a musical pause from Philodemus *De Musica* (ed. Kemke) p. 29³³ ταραχῶν εἶναι κ]ατα[πα]-υστικὸν (. τὸ μέλος).

καταπέτασμα

can no longer be regarded as a wholly "Biblical," or even "Alexandrian" (Grimm-Thayer) word, if only in view of an inscr. from Samos of B.C. 346-5, cataloguing the furniture of the temple of Hera (cited by Deissmann *LAE* p. 101 from Hoffmann *Die Griechischen Dialekte* III. p. 72) κατα-πέτασμα τῆς τραπέζης, "table cover."

καταπίνω.

For this verb in its literal sense see the magic P Lond 46³⁰² (iv/A.D.) (= I. p. 74) ἐὰν δέ τις αὐτῶν μὴ καταπίῃ τὸ δοθὲν αὐτῷ κτλ., 121⁶⁶ (iii/A.D.) (= I. p. 96) ὁ καταπεπωκὼς τον (*l.* τὸν) ὄφιν, and *Syll* 802¹⁰² (iii/B.C.) κατέπιε δ' αὐτὰ . . ἐγ κυκᾶνι. With the use in 1 Cor 15⁵⁴ we may compare P Leid Vⁱⁱ·⁵ (iii/iv A.D.) ἐφ]θασε τὸ πῦρ ἐπὶ τὰ εἴδωλα τὰ μέγιστα, καὶ κ[α]τεπειέτω (*l.* κατεπίετο ὁ) οὐρανός.

καταπίπτω.

P Oxy VIII. 1112²³ (A.D. 188) καταπεπτω(κυίας) of acacia trees, P Strass I. 31⁹ (ii/iii A.D.) οἰκίας καταπεπτω-κ(υίας), BGU III. 735ⁱ·⁹ (A.D. 235) οἰκ(ία) νυνεὶ κατα-π(επτωκυῖα) καὶ ψειλ(ός), and *ib.* 889²² (A.D. 151). *OGIS* 483¹⁰¹ (ii/B.C.) τῶν δὲ δεομένων ἐπισκευῆς κοινῶ[ν τ]οιχῶν ἢ καταπεσόντων. The verb is used metaphorically of the accidents of fortune in Vett. Val. p. 40¹⁵ γενναίως τὰ κατα-πίπτοντα φέρειν.

καταπλέω

is the word regularly used for "sailing down" the Nile to Alexandria: cf. e.g. P Lille I. 17⁷ (iii/B.C.) καταπλεῖ γὰρ εἰς Ἀλεξάνδρειαν Φίλων, P Magd 22⁶ (B.C. 221) πρὶν τοῦ] καταπλεῦσαί με εἰς τὴν πόλιν : cf. also P Giss I. 25¹⁰ (Rom.) συνέστησα γὰρ αὐτὸν διὰ τό σε τότε καταπεπλευκέναι, *OGIS* 344² (i/B.C.) οἱ καταπλέοντες εἰς Βιθυνίαν ἔμποροι καὶ ναύ-κληροι. For the subst. see P Flor I. 6¹⁴ (A.D. 210) εἰς τὸν

κατάπλουν (to Alexandria). *OGIS* 90¹⁷ (Rosetta stone—B.C. 196) τοῦ κατ' ἐνιαυτὸν εἰς Ἀλεξάνδρειαν καταπλου.

καταπονέω.

BGU IV. 1188¹⁷ (time of Augustus) αὐτός τε καταπονού-μενος ὑπὸ τῶν τελωνῶν ἀναφορὰν ἡμεῖν [ἀνήνεγκεν, P Oxy VIII. 1101⁹ (A.D. 307-70) βουλόμενοι τοὺς διαδικοῦν̣τας πάνυ κ̣αταπονῖν, "in their desire thoroughly to worst their adversaries at law" (Ed.). In BGU IV. 1060²⁴ (B.C. 14) ὅθεν καταπεπονημένοι προήγμεθα πρὸς ἀπειλαῖς, the peti-tioners seem to complain of definite ill-treatment. This is the meaning in Ac 7²⁴. Can we not recognise it in 2 Pet 2⁷? It is not mental distress that is referred to here—that comes in ver. 8—but the threatened violence of Gen 19⁹. The conative present shows that the angels' rescue (ἐρύσατο) was in time.

καταποντίζω.

For the literal use of this verb, as in Mt 14³⁰, 18⁶, cf. P Petr II. 40(a)²⁷ (iii/B.C.) (= Witkowski², p. 42) with refer-ence to the sinking of an elephant-transport ship—ἀφ' οὗ ἡ ἐλεφαντηγὸς κατεποντίσθη.

κατάρα.

In C. and B. ii. p. 653, No. 504, Sir W. M. Ramsay publishes a striking epitaph of A.D. 243-4 from Ushak in Phrygia, in which the following curse occurs: εἴ τις ἀνύξῃ τὸ μνημῖον, ἔσονται αὐτῷ κατάραι ὅσε ἀγεγραμμένα̣ι ἰσὶν εἰς ὅρασιν καὶ εἰς ὅλον τὸ σῶμα αὐτῷ καὶ εἰς τέκνα καὶ εἰς βίον, "if any one shall open the tomb, there shall be upon him the curses as many as are written in (the book), on his sight and his whole body and his children and his life." In the curses here, and in similar epitaphs found in a number of towns scattered throughout central Phrygia, Ramsay finds distinct traces of "Jewish influence," cf. especially Deut 27-29, and see further *Exp T* xxvi. p. 171 f. The subst. is also found in *Syll* 889¹ ἐπάρα κατάρα κακὴ τῷ ἀσεβήσαντι τοὺς δαίμονας.

καταράομαι.

For κατάρατος cf. *OGIS* 8²² (iv/B.C.) κατάρατον ἔμμεναι καὶ αὐτὸν καὶ γένος τὸ κήνω, *Syll* 479⁴² (iii/B.C.) ἐὰν δέ τις τούτων τι λύῃ, κατάρατος ἔστω. See also *s.v.* ἐπικατά-ρατος.

καταργέω.

This favourite Pauline verb (see Milligan on 2 Th 2⁸) is found in the weakened sense of "hinder" in P Oxy I. 38¹⁷ (A.D. 49-50) (= *Selections*, p. 54) καταργοῦντός με χειρό-τεχνον ὄντα, "hinders me in my handicraft," and not infre-quently = "render idle or inactive," as in P Flor II. 176⁷ (A.D. 256) ὥστε καὶ ἄνθρωπον καὶ ὄνον καταργηθῆναι, *ib.* 218¹⁸ (A.D. 257) ἵνα τὸ κάρνον μὴ καταργηθῇ, P Strass I. 32⁷ (A.D. 261) ἵνα . . τὸ ταυρικὸν μὴ καταργῆται. W. H. D. Rouse writes (4/11/08): "Καταργεῖν = darken. Mod. Gr. ἀργά = late. Can the word have got its sense by association with night?" [when no man can work].

καταριθμέω.

A good parallel to the use of this verb in Ac 1¹⁷ is afforded by P Par 63⁹⁹ (B.C. 164) (= P Petr III. p. 26) τοὺς ὑποτελεῖς τῆι τε ἰχθυηρᾶι καὶ ζυτηρᾶι καὶ ταῖς ἄλλαις ὠναῖς ἐν τοῖς 'σύνπασιν ἀνθρώποις' καταριθμεῖσθαι, "that in the expression 'all men' are included both those who are subject to the fish tax and the beer tax and the other imposts" (Mahaffy).

καταρτίζω

occurs in P Tebt I. 6⁷ (B.C. 140–39) καταρτισθῶσι and *ib.* 24¹⁸ (B.C. 117) καταρτισόμεθα—both times in broken contexts. A good ex. of the original meaning "prepare," "perfect" a thing for its full destination or use is afforded by P Oxy VIII. 1153¹⁶ (i/A.D.) where the recipient of the letter is informed that he will receive certain garments ἃ ἐδωρήσατό σοι Παυσανίας ὁ ἀδελφός σου πρὸ πολλοῦ ἐκ φιλοτιμίας αὐτοῦ κατηρτισμένα, "which your brother Pausanias went to the expense of having made some time ago and presented to you" (Ed.). Cf. from the inscrr. OGIS 177¹⁶ (B.C. 96–5) κατηρτίσατο δίδοσθαι . . πυροῦ ἀρτάβας, and similarly 17.,⁹ (B.C. 95). Wynne in *Exp* VII. viii. p. 282 ff. understands the verb in Mk 1¹⁹ not of "mending" but of "folding" the nets to be ready for use, quoting an old Scholion where the Vg "componentes" is explained as "vel farcientes, vel complicantes," "either stowing or folding": cf. Wycliffe "makinge nettis." The various NT usages are fully discussed by Lightfoot on 1 Th 3¹⁰. For ἀπαρτίζω see the citations *s.v.* ἀπαρτισμός, and add P Giss I. 62¹² (ii/A.D.) εἰς τὸ ἤδη ποτὲ ἀκολ[ούθ]ως [ταῖς ἐ]ντολαῖς τοῦ κρατίστου ἡγεμόνος τὴν ἐπίσκεψιν ἀπαρτισθῆναι.

καταρτισμός.

For the literal sense of this subst., which is used metaphorically in Eph 4¹², see P Tebt I. 33¹² (B.C. 112) (= *Selections*, p. 31) τ[ὰ] εἰς τὸν τῆς αὐλῆς καταρτισμόν, "the things for the furnishing of the guest-chamber," P Ryl II. 127²⁸ (A.D. 29) ἱματίου καταρτισμὸν κρόκη(s) καὶ στήμονο(s) ἄξι(ον) ἀργ(υρίου) (δραχμῶν) ιη, "a preparation of woof and warp for a cloak worth 18 silver dr." (Edd.).

κατασείω.

For this verb with the dat., as in Ac 12¹⁷ *al.*, cf. the magical invocation P Lond 46¹⁵³ (iv/A.D.) (= I. p. 80) κατασείων τῷ λύχνῳ ἅμα λέγων τὸν λόγον κτλ. See also Hobart p. 103.

κατασκάπτω

occurs *ter* in *Syll* 177 (Teos—B.C. 303), e.g. ⁷ ἐὰν δὲ δεῖ κατασκάπτειν τὴν ὑπάρχουσαν πόλιν, [καταλειφθῆναι μὲ]ν τῶν ὑπαρχουσῶν τὰς ἡμισείας. For the subst. cf. *ib.* 211⁹ (iii/B.C.?) εἰς τὴν ἔκπεμψι[ν τ]ῶν στρατιωτ[ῶν] καὶ τῆς ἀκροπόλεως τὴν κατα[σκα]φήν.

κατασκευάζω

occurs in the more general sense of "furnish," "provide," in BGU IV. 1065⁷ (A.D. 97) with reference to the purchase of a pair of bracelets which the goldsmith κατεσκεύασε αὐτῷ: cf. P Oxy XII. 1428¹⁰ (iv/A.D.) τοὺς ὑπευθύνους τὴν ἐσθῆτα ἀνεπι(κλή)τοις τοῖς ὑφάσμασιν κατασκευάσαι, "that the persons responsible provide (or manufacture) the clothing in irreproachable(?) materials." For the use of the verb in the sense of building, or equipping a building, as in

Heb 3³, see P Tebt I. 33⁸ (B.C. 112) (= *Selections*, p. 30) where, with reference to the visit of a Roman senator to the Fayûm, directions are given—φρόντισον ὡς ἐπὶ τῶν καθηκόντων τόπων αἵ τε αὐλαὶ κατασκευασ[θ]ήσ[ο]νται, "take care that at the proper places the guest-chambers be got ready," and cf. *ib.* II. 342¹⁶ (late ii/A.D.) τὸ κατασκευασθ(ὲν) ἐκ καινῆς ἐν Σομολ(ῷ) κεραμεῖον σὺν πᾶσι χρηστ(ηρίοις), "the newly fitted pottery at Somolo together with all furniture" (Edd.), P Amh II. 64² (A.D. 107) περὶ δαπάνης εἰς τὸ ἐκ καινῆς κατασκευαζόμενον βαλανεῖον, and P Oxy VI. 892⁸ (A.D. 338) εἰς . . . [τ]ὴν κατασκευαζ[ο]μένην βορρινὴν πύλην τῆς πόλεως, "for the construction of the north gate of the city" (Edd.). From the inscrr. it is sufficient to cite *Syll* 500²² (B.C. 320) where, with reference to the ὁδοί (cf. Mt 11¹⁰ *al.*) by which the procession was to reach the temple of Zeas Soter, it is provided—ὅπως ἂν ὁμαλισθῶσιν καὶ κατασκευασθῶσιν ὡς βέλτιστα.

For the subst. κατασκευή, see P Ryl II. 157¹⁶ (A.D. 135) τῆς δαπάνης τῆς τε ἐπισκευῆς καὶ κατασκευῆς τοῦ ξυλικοῦ [ὀργάνου], "the cost of keeping and repairing the wooden water-wheel" (Edd.), P Oxy XII. 1461¹² (A.D. 222) ἐ[ὶ]ς κατασκευὴν ἅλ(ας) (δραχμὰς) ϙ, "for repairs 20 drachmae more" (Edd.), *Michel* 487¹¹ (ii/B.C. *ad init.*) εἰς τὴν κατασκευὴν τοῦ θεάτρου. For κατασκεύασμα, cf. *Syll* 169¹ (*c.* B.C. 306) εἴς τε τὰ κατασκευάσμα[τα τοῦ ἱεροῦ καὶ τῆ]ς πανηγύρεως, and Aristeas 52 προεθυμεῖτο μὲν οὖν ὁ βασιλεὺς ὑπερβολόν τι ποιῆσαι τοῖς μέτροις τὸ κατασκεύασμα, "now, the king's intention was to make this piece of work of gigantic dimensions" (Thackeray).

κατασκηνόω.

For the form κατασκηνοῖν (= κατασκηνοῦν) in Mt 13³², Mk 4³², cf. δηλοῖν in P Lond 231¹³ (*c.* A.D. 346) (= II. p. 285) and see the other exx. in Hatzidakis *Gr.* p. 193: see also Moulton *Proleg.* p. 53, *Gr.* ii. § 84. To the transitive instances of the verb in the LXX (Ps 22², 2 Chron 6²), add Didache x. 2.

κατασκήνωσις.

The use of this subst. in Mt 8²⁰ = "lodging-place," "roost," is well illustrated by OGIS 229⁵⁷ (iii/B.C.) where in an agreement between the inhabitants of Smyrna and of Magnesia, the former undertake to provide κατασκήνωσιν, "shelter," for those who are about to migrate to Smyrna, in order that they may have a place to live in while they are building new houses for themselves.

κατασκιάζω.

Kaibel 405 (Rom.)—

Τοὔνομα μὲ[ν] Χαρίας, Θήβη πατρίς, ἀλλὰ θανόντα
Ποιμάνδρου χυδανὴ γαῖα κατεσκίασεν.

κατασκοπέω.

P Oxy XII. 1414⁴ (A.D. 270–5) ὁ πρύτανις εἶπ(εν)· τὴ]ν τοῦ ἱεροῦ γραφ[ὴ]ν κ[ατ]εσκέψασθαι καὶ ὅρον δεδώκατε, "the prytanis said, 'You examined the list of the temple and fixed a limit.'" It may be added that W. Schubart (see Deissmann *LAE* p. 178 n.¹¹) proposes to read κατ[ε]σκοπούμην for Deissmann's restoration αἰδ[υ]σοπο[ύ]μην in

BGU III. 846⁹ (ii/A.D.) (= *Selections*, p. 94), but the meaning is then far from clear. For the form κατασκοπεύω, as in the LXX (Exod 2⁴ *al.*), cf. P Tebt I. 230 (late ii/B.C.), and see Anz *Subsidia* p. 379.

κατάσκοπος.

Menander Περικειρ. 105 τῶν ὅλων κατάσκοπος | πραγμάτων γενοῦ.

κατασοφίζομαι.

For this NT ἅπ. εἰρ. (Ac 7¹⁹ from LXX Ex 1¹⁰), see Anz *Subsidia*, p. 366.

καταστέλλω.

P Tebt I. 41²¹ (c. B.C. 119) ἵνα τοῦ Μαρρείους κατασταλέντος καὶ εἰσπραχθέντος τὰ σείσματα τύχηι τῆς ἁρμοζούσης ἐπιπλήξεως, "so that Marres may be sent for and made to refund his extortions and may receive suitable punishment" (Edd.). In BGU IV. 1192⁵ (late Ptol. or time of Aug.) τῶν Ἀράβων κατεσταλμένων καὶ πάντων ἐν τῆι μεγίστη[ι] εἰρήνηι γεγονότων, the verb is perhaps used, as in Ac 19³⁵ᶠ, = "quieten," "restrain": see also *s.v.* καταστολή, and cf. its medical usage as contrasted with παροξύνω in Hobart, p. 247 f.

κατάστημα.

With the use of this subst. in Tit 2³ we may compare Aristeas 122 τὸ μέσον ἐξηλωκότες κατάστημα—τοῦτο γὰρ κάλλιστόν ἐστιν, "they cultivated the due mean, the best of courses": see also *ib.* 210 τὸ τῆς εὐσεβείας . . κατάστημα, 278 τὸ δὲ τῆς ἀρετῆς κατάστημα. Cf. further *OGIS* 669³ (i/A.D.) πᾶσαν πρόνοιαν ποιούμενος τοῦ διαμένειν τῷ προσήκοντι καταστήματι τὴν πόλιν.

καταστολή

is confined in Bibl. Greek to Isai 61³, 1 Tim 2⁹. In both these passages it is usually understood of "clothing": but in view of the word's being used also with an inner reference, as in *Priene* 109¹⁸⁶ (c. B.C. 120) τῆι δὲ καταστολῆ καὶ τῆι εὐσχημ[οσύνῃ, it is probable that it should be understood in the wider sense of "demeanour," "deportment" (like κατάστημα *q.v.*) in 1 Tim *l.c.*: see Dibelius' note *HZNT ad l.*, and cf. Aristeas 284 μετ᾽ εὐσχημοσύνης καὶ καταστολῆς, "with decency and restraint," and *ib.* 285 σὺ δὲ πᾶσαν ἠσκηκὼς καταστολήν, "but thou hast practised all restraint." For κ. = "overthrow," "subjugation," see *Chrest.* I. 12¹⁵ (B.C. 88) Ἱέρακα δὲ προκεχειρίσθαι μετὰ δυνάμεων μυρίων ἐπὶ καταστολὴν τῆς Θηβαΐδος.

καταστρέφω.

Syll 168²⁴ (iv/B.C.) Ἀλε[ξάνδρωι Θηβῶν ἐπικρατήσα]ντι . . κ[αὶ ἄλλα δὲ τῆς οἰκουμένης μ]έρη καταστρεψαμένωι διετέλει ἐναντιούμενος ὑπὲ]ρ τοῦ δήμου. The verb is used metaphorically in Vett. Val. pp. 66³ ποιεῖ δὲ καὶ γυμνῆτας ἐπαίτας κακῶς τὸν βίον καταστρέφοντας, 87¹⁷ κακῶς δὲ τὸν βίον καταστρέφουσιν.

καταστρηνιάω.

For this compound, which is found in the NT only in 1 Tim 5¹¹, see *s.v.* στρηνιάω.

καταστροφή.

in the sense of death, has been ingeniously read in *C. and B.* ii. p. 473, No. 322, an inscr. commemorating a woman who died suddenly in the third year of her married life—κατ[α]στραφ[ῆ]ς τυχοῦσα, συντόμως ἔλυσε τὸν | γ]άμον. In Menander Περικειρ. 12 death is described as τοῦ ζῆν καταστροφή τις. For καταστροφεύς (not in LS) Herwerden (*Lex. s.v.*) cites the new classical farce, P Oxy III. 403¹¹² πάλι λαλεῖς, καταστροφεῦ: "are you talking again, you bungler?" (Edd.).

καταστρώννυμι

is used of "spreading" or "laying" dust in P Tor I. 1ᵛᶦᶦ ¹⁸ (B.C. 117–6) μεταφέροντας αὐτοὺς κονίαν καταστρωννύειν ἐπὶ τοῦ δρόμου τοῦ Ἄμμωνος: cf. Aristeas 319 τρικλίνου πᾶσαν κατάστρωσιν. For the derived sense of "overthrow," "prostrate," as in 1 Cor 10⁵, see P Leid Cⁱ·²⁸ (B.C. 163–2) (= I. p. 119) καταστρωννύει (*l.*—ωννύει) αὐτή[ν, "prosternit ipsam" (Ed.).

κατασφάζω.

The only citation we can furnish for this NT ἅπ. εἰρ. (Lk 19²⁷) is P Giss I. 82¹¹ (A.D. 117) κατ[έ]σφαξα[ν in a much mutilated context, but apparently with the meaning "zum Opfer fielen" (Ed.).

κατασφραγίζω

is found *bis* in the unfortunately very fragmentary report of a professional searcher for stolen goods, P Petr III. 65 (*b*)⁶·¹³. Cf. P Par 35⁵¹ (B.C. 163) κ]αὶ τοῦτον (*sc.* σταμνὸν) κατασφραγισάμενος: the verb παρασφραγίζω occurs *bis* in the same document. See also PSI IV. 358⁸ (B.C. 252–1) ὃ κατεσφράγισται ἐν κυψάληι ("chest") ἐν τῷ σιτοβολῶνι ("storehouse," cf. Gen 41⁵⁶) ἀρτάβαι δέκα. With the use in Rev 5¹ cf. *OGIS* 266⁴² (iii/B.C.) τά τε γράμματ᾽ ἀνοίσω κατεσφραγισμένα, and *Syll* 790⁴³ (i/B.C.), cited *s.v.* ἀγγεῖον.

κατάσχεσις.

On the translation of this word in Ac 7⁵·⁴⁵ see Field *Notes*, pp. 114, 116.

κατατίθημι.

With the use of this verb in the TR of Mk 15⁴⁶ cf. P Lond 256 *recto*⁷ (A.D. 11–5) (= II. p. 97, *Chrest.* I. p. 408) τὰ δὲ σπέρματα . . . ὑγιῶς καταθήσεσθαι εἰς τὴν γ[ῆν, and the similar use of the act. καταθήσω in P Oxy VII. 1031¹⁷ (A.D. 228). In P Tebt II. 329⁷ (A.D. 139) the verb is used of "paying into" the bank—κατ]εθέμην ἐπὶ τὴν δημοσία[ν τράπεζαν: cf. 2 Macc 4¹⁹, Aristeas 321. For the classical phrase χάριν κατατίθεσθαι found *bis* in Acts (24²⁷, 25⁹) see BGU II. 596¹³ (A.D. 84) (= *Selections*, p. 64) τοῦτ[ο] οὖν ποιήσας ἔσῃ μοι μεγάλην χάριταν κατ[α]τεθειμ[έ]νο(ς), "if you do this, you will have laid up for yourself a great store of gratitude at my hands," and Menander *Fragm.* p. 187 ὦ τρὶς κακοδαίμων, ὅστις ἐκ φειδωλίας | κατέθετο μῖσος διπλάσιον τῆς οὐσίας, "laid up for himself a dislike twice as big as his property."

κατατομή

in its literal sense of "cutting," "incision," as in Jer 48 (31)[37] (Symm.) occurs in *CIG* I. 160[27] ἄνευ κατατομῆς. For the verb cf. *Syll* 537[7] (2nd half iv/B.C.) κατατεμών τοῦ χωρίου βάθος ἀπὸ τοῦ μετεωροτάτου τρεῖς πόδας.

κατατρέχω.

A good ex. of this verb, which in the NT is confined to Ac 21[32] (cf. Hobart, p. 193), occurs in P Par 44[6] (B.C. 153) (= Witkowski *Epp.*[2] p. 83) βλέπω Μενέδημον κατατρέχοντά με, where Witkowski renders κατατρέχω, "persequor fugientem, impetum facio, aggredior, impugno." Cf. also P Tebt I. 41[30] (c. B.C. 119) ὁ ἐγκαλούμενος Μαρρῆς πρὸς τῆι διασείσει κατατρέχει τοὺς γεωργούς, "Marres the accused besides his extortions oppresses the cultivators." For the more literal sense see BGU III. 935[5] (iii/iv A.D.) οἱ καταδραμόντες τοὺς τόπους, and the ii/B.C. inscr. *Syll* 241[5] καθ' ὃν καιρὸν συνέβη Βούκριν καταδραμόντα τὴν χώραν καταγαγεῖν εἰς Κρήτην τῶν τε πολιτῶν πλείους κτλ.

καταφέρω

is used with reference to an assault in P Tebt I. 138 (late ii/B.C.) σπασάμενος ταύτην (*sc.* μάχαιραν) βουλόμενός με ἀλογῆσαι κατήνεγκε [πλ]ηγαῖς τρισὶ καὶ τὴν κεφαλὴν καὶ τὸν τράχηλον. For the meaning "bring down," "carry down," cf. P Giss I. 40[ii. 19] (A.D. 215) οἵτινες κάλαμον πρ[ὸ]ς τὸ ὑποκαίειν τὰ βαλα[νεῖ]α καταφέρουσι. P Oxy X. 1292[13] (c. A.D. 30) ἐὰν δὲ χρέαν ἔχῃ (*l.* -ῃς) μάλιστ[α] ξυλαρίων δύο ἵνα μοι τὸν τροχὸν τῆς μηχανῆς κατενέγκῃς, "if you specially require two pieces of wood to bring down to me the wheel of the machine" (Edd.), and of "bringing down" corn to Alexandria *ib.* 1260[28] (A.D. 286) κατενεγκῶ καὶ παραδώσω ὡς πρόκειται. Similarly of a dead body, *ib.* VII. 1068[8] (iii/A.D.) εἵνα δυνηθῶ τὸ σωμάτιν κατενενκίν ἐν Ἀλεξάνδριαν: cf. *OGIS* 674[31] ταφῆς ἀναφερομένης καὶ καταφερομένης, with Dittenberger's note. The special usage in Ac 20[9] is well illustrated by Ps 75(76)[7] (Aq.): see also Hobart p. 48 ff.

For the subst. see P Petr III. 144[iv. 29] ἡλίου περὶ καταφορὰν ὄντος, BGU IV. 1133[11] (B.C. 18) ἔν τισι ὡρισμέναις καταφορα(ῖς).

καταφεύγω

is a kind of technical expression for suppliants "fleeing" or "resorting" to any one for help, e.g. P Magd 2[8] (B.C. 221) ἵνα ἐ[πὶ] σὲ καταφυγοῦσα, βασιλεῦ, τοῦ δικαίου τύχω, P Oxy XII. 1468[9] (c. A.D. 258) ἐπὶ τὴν σὴν ἀνδρείαν καταφεύγω θαρρῶν τεύξεσθαι τῶν προσόντων μοι δικαίων, ἡγεμὼν κύριε, P Tebt II. 326[4] (c. A.D. 266) ἱκετηρίαν τιθεμένη ἐπὶ τὸ σὸν μέγεθος καταφεύγω: cf. Ac 14[6]. In P Fay p. 49[9] (B.C. 69-8) it is used in connexion with the right of asylum at a temple at Kasr el Banát for all manner of fugitives— τοὺς κατ[αφ]εύγοντας καθ' ὁνδηποτοῦν τρόπον: cf. Heb 6[18]. For a similar use of the subst. see P Tebt I. 43[27] (B.C. 118) προήγμεθα τὴν ἐφ' ὑμᾶς καταφ . υγὴν (*l.* καταφυγὴν) ποιήσασθαι, "we have been impelled to take refuge with you" (Edd.), *Preisigke* 6[24] (A.D. 216) ἀναγκαίως τὴν ἐπί σε καταφυγὴν ποιοῦμαι.

καταφθείρω

occurs in connexion with an accident to a corn-ship, where steps are taken ὅπως ἂν μὴ καταφθείρηται τὰ πλοῖα ἐπὶ τῶν τόπων (P Magd 11[9]—B.C. 221). For injury to persons, see P Petr II. 12(2)[13] (B.C. 241) where a petitioner demands investigation into certain charges against her adversary—ἵνα μὴ τὸν πλείω χρόνον καταφθείρωμα[ι: cf. *ib.* 19(1*b*)[2], a petition from a prisoner. συμ]βῆι μοι καταφθαρῆναι ἐν [τῆι φυλακῆ]ι, and PSI IV. 377[11] (B.C. 250-49) ἵνα μὴ ἐνταῦθα καταφθείρωμαι. From the inscr. we may cite *Syll* 790[74] (i/B.C.) ἐπεὶ τὰ ὑπάρχοντα [δ]ένδρα . . . εἰσὶν κατεφθαρμένα, ὑπολαμβάνομεν δὲ ἀναγκαῖ[ον] εἶναι κτλ. For the subst. see P Par 63[126] (B.C. 164) (= P Petr III. p. 28) τοὺς ἀνθρώπους ἐκ τηλικαύτης καταφθ(ο)ρᾶ[ς] ἀρτ[ί]ως ἀνακτωμένους, "the population just recovering from so great a distress" (Mahaffy), P Tor I. 1[iii. 8] (B.C. 117) διὸ ἀξιῶ ἐμβλέψαντα εἰς τὴν γεγενημένην μοι καταφθορὰν ὑπὸ ἀσεβῶν ἀνθρώπων . . συντάξαι κτλ., *OGIS* 339[5] (c. B.C. 120) τὴν ἀπαντωμένην καταφθορὰν τῶν ἰδίων τοῖς ὑπὲρ τῆς πόλεως πρεσβεύουσιν ὑπολογιζόμενος.

καταφιλέω.

A new ex. of this compound occurs in the Alexandrian Erotic Fragment P Grenf I. 1[3] (ii/B.C.) quoted *s.v.* καταλείπω *ad fin.* Both this passage and more particularly Epict. iv. 10. 20 ἀγρυπνῆσαί σε δεῖ, περιδραμεῖν, τὰς χεῖρας καταφιλῆσαι, "thou must watch, run about, kiss hands," where, as Sharp (*Epict.* p. 104) says, stress is laid "not on kissing fervently, but on the very fact of kissing at all," make the RV marg. of Mt 26[49], *al.*, very doubtful: cf. also *Mithrasliturgie* (ed. Dieterich) p. 14[23] καταφιλῶν πάλιν τὰ φυλακτήρια καὶ λέγων κτλ., with reference to a spell. On the other hand *Menandrea* p. 11[56] λαμβάνων μου κατεφίλει | τὰς χεῖρας, "he caught and kissed my hands"—of one in a passion of gratitude. See Anz *Subsidia*, p. 334.

καταφρονέω.

P Gen I. 6[13] (A.D. 146) τ[ὸ]ν Πεκῦσιν καταφρονεῖν μου τῆς ἡλικίας, is much like 1 Tim 4[12], even to the position of the pronoun. So *ib.* 31[10] (A.D. 145-6) καταφρονῶν μου τῆς χηρείας, and similarly P Magd 2[6] (B.C. 221) καταφρονῶν ὅτι ὁ ἀνήρ μου τετελεύτηκεν, and P Petr II. 4(6)[17] (B.C. 255-4), where an official who has been disturbed in the discharge of his duty adds—δινὸν (*l.* δεινὸν) γάρ ἐστιν ἐν ὄχλωι ἀτιμάζεσθαι, ἐὰν γὰρ εἰδῶσιν ὅτι οὗτοι καταπεφρονήκασιν, οὐθὲν τῶν ἔργων συντελεσθήσεται, "for it is a dreadful thing to be insulted before a crowd, and if the rest see that these have despised me, none of the work will be completed" (Ed.). The formula is accordingly associated with petitions from defenceless people wronged by those who presumed on their defencelessness; the word does not denote a mere feeling of contempt—it is *active*. We may infer that Timothy is told not to let men *push him aside* as a stripling ; and in all the NT passages the action encouraged by contempt seems implied, rather than the mental state. Add BGU I. 340[21] (A.D. 148-9) καταφρονοῦν[τ]ες τῆς [π]ερὶ ἐμὲ ἀπωγμοσύνη[ς (*l.* ἀπραγ—), *ib.* 291[9] (time of Severus) καταφρονή[σ]ας μου ὡς γυναικὸς ἀβοηθήτου, P Oxy XII. 1470[15] (A.D. 336) τῆς δὲ ἡ]μετέρας ὀρφανίας καταφρονῶν, and from the inserr. *Syll* 930[36] (B.C. 112) **καταφρονήσαντες** the decree of the Senate and the Praetor and the congress of workmen (**τεχνῖται**, as in Ac 19[24]), they went off to Pella and entered into negotiations, etc. Cf. also what is said *s.v.* **ἀνέχω**. For the subst., as in 2 Macc 3[18], see P Lond 44[27] (B.C. 161) (= I. p. 34) **εἰς μείζονα καταφρόνησιν ἐλθεῖν**, and cf. Aristeas 249 **ἡ δὲ ξενιτεία τοῖς μὲν πένησι καταφρόνησιν ἐργάζεται**, "residence in a foreign country brings contempt upon the poor man" (Thackeray).

καταφρονητής.

This NT ἅπ. εἰρ. (Ac 13[41]) occurs in Vett. Val. p. 47[33] **ἀδρεπιβόλους** ("attaining great things"), **καταφρονητάς, πλανήτας.**

καταχέω

is construed with the gen., as in Mk 14[3] אBC, in P Magd 24[9] (B.C. 218) **ἐσ[έρχεται ἡ Ψενόβαστις εἰς τὸ ὑπερῷον]**, **ὅθεν τὸ οὖρον κατέχεέν μου**: see Rutherford *NP* p. 66 f. Cf. also *Syll* 356[24] (B.C. 6) **σὺν τοῖς καταχεομένοις . . . ἀφεῖναι τὴν γάστραν** ("jar"), and the cognate vb. **καταχώννυμι** (*abscondo*) in Vett. Val. p. 301[9] **τὸ ἐξελέγξαι ἀλλοτρίας ἐνθυμήσεις μυστικῶς κατακεχωσμένας.**

καταχθόνιος.

OGIS 382[1] (ii/A.D.)—an inscr. in which Aurelius Pacorus, King of Armenia, announces **θ(εοῖς) κ(αταχθονίοις)** that he has purchased a sarcophagus for his brother. Cf. such common formulae as *CIG* III. 4252[67] **ἁμαρτ]ωλὸς ἔστ[ω θεοῖς κατα]χθονίοις**, 4253[22] **ἔστω ἱερόσυλος [θ]εοῖς οὐ[ρ]ανίοις καὶ καταχθονίοις**, and the mention of **ἄγγελοι καταχθόνιοι** for the older **ἀμφίπολοι χθόνιοι** in *Audollent* 74[1] *al.*

καταχράομαι.

The intensive force of this compound "use up," "use to the full," which is found in 1 Cor 7[31], may be illustrated from P Oxy II. 281[11] (A.D. 20–50) where a woman lodges a complaint against her husband—**ὁ δὲ Σαραπίων καταχρησάμενος τῆι φερνῆι εἰς ὃν ἠβούλετο λόγον οὐ διέλειπεν κακουχῶν με καὶ ὑβρί[ζ]ων**, "but Sarapion, having squandered my dowry as he pleased, continually ill-treated and insulted me" (Edd.): and similarly P Tebt II. 334[12] (A.D. 200–1) where a woman complains that, after the death of her parents, her husband carried off all that they had left her to his house—**κ[αὶ αὐ]τὸς κατα[χρῆται**, "and is using it up" (Edd.). Cf. also BGU IV. 1105[17] (c. B.C. 10) **ὁ δὲ] διαβαλλόμενος Ἀσκληπιάδης ἐπε[ὶ ἐ]νέαινε διὰ τῆς συμβιώσεως [ἀ'π]ὸ μηδενὸς καταχρησάμενος τοῖς προκειμένοις κακουχίας [sic] με καὶ καθυβρίζει καὶ τὰς χεῖρας ἐπιφέρων χρῆται ὡς οὐδὲ ἀργυρωνήτωι**, *ib.* 1133[10] (B.C. 18) **αὐτο(ὺ)ς δὲ τῷ παντ ἰ) [εἰς τ]ὸ ἴδιο(ν) κατακεχρῆσθαι.**

On the other hand the verb is practically = the *simplex* in P Petr III. 39[ii. 15] **τοῦ προσηγμ[ένου καὶ] κατακεχρημένου [θ]ρύου** with reference to rushes used in irrigation works, *ib.* 46(3)[3] **πλίνθου καταχρησθείσης εἰς τοὺς οἰκοδομηθέντας τοίχους**, P Oxy III. 494[20] (A.D. 156), a will in which the testator leaves to his wife certain monies—**καταχρᾶσθαι εἰς τὸ ἴδιον**, "to use for her personal requirements," and Preisigke 4630[15] (ii/A.D.) **ἐκ τῶν παρασκευασθέντων ἡμῖν πρὸς τὸ δ[ε]ῖπνον καταχρῆσαι.** From the inserr. we may

cite *Syll* 653[62] (B.C. 91) **μηδὲ γραψάτω μηθεὶς δόγμα, ὅτι δεῖ ταῦτα τὰ διάφορα εἰς ἄλλο τι καταχρήσασθαι**, *OGIS* 669[19] (i/A.D.) **οἱ τῆι πρωτοπραξίᾳ πρὸς ἃ μὴ ι · δεῖ καταχρώμενοι.**

καταψύχω

is peculiar in the NT to Luke (16[24]): cf. Hobart, p. 32. Jos. *BJ* i. 66 **τὴν ὁρμὴν οὐ κατέψυξαν**, "they did not suffer their zeal to cool."

κατείδωλος,

found only in Ac 17[16], is regularly formed on the analogy of such words as **καταβελής, κατάγελος** etc., with the meaning *simulacris referta* [*urbs*] (cf. Vigerus *de Idiotismis* (ed. Hermann) p. 638): cf. Liv. xlv. 27 *Athenas . . habentes . . simulacra deorum hominumque omni genere et materiae et artium insignia.*

κατέναντι.

The usage of **κατέναντι** (for form see *Proleg.* p. 99) c. gen. = "opposite," "over against," as in Mk 12[41], 13[3] *al.*, 1 Macc 2[31], is not so unknown to "profane" Greek, as Grimm-Thayer (*s.v.*) would lead us to suppose. Thus Rouffiac (*Recherches*, p. 34) quotes from *Priene* 37[170] (ii B.C.) with reference to a treaty made—**κατέναντι τοῦ ὄρευς**, and in P Par 50[11] (B.C. 160) we read of a woman seated on the sand with a child—**κατέναντι αὐτῆς**: cf. also P Flor III. 370[7] (A.D. 132) **κ[άταν]τα Σαραπίωνος.** According to Wackernagel *Hellenistica*, p. 3 ff. (as quoted *s.v.* **ἀπέναντι**) the usage is due to Doric influence, and passed into the **Κοινή** about B.C. 300. The word survives in MGr.

κατενώπιον,

like **κατέναντι**, is to be removed from the category of Hebraistic constructions : see further *s.v.* **ἐνώπιον**. With its usage in Eph 1[4], Col 1[22], Jude [24] (cf. 2 Cor 2[17] A, 12[19] A) we may compare the sixth century Christian amulet BGU III. 954[6] (= *Selections*, p. 133) **κλίνω τὴν κεφαλήν [μο]υ κα · τ ἐνώπιόν σου.**

κατεξουσιάζω.

For the subst. **κατεξουσία** cf. *IG* XIV. 1047[5] **τὴν κατεξουσίαν καὶ τὸ βασίλειον τῶν νερτέρων θεῶ[ν.**

κατεργάζομαι.

This perfective compound, which lays stress on the result, as distinguished from the process, of the action (cf. 2 Cor 7[10 f.], Phil 2[12]), is very common with reference to the "cultivation" of allotments, e.g. P Tebt I. 16[2] (B.C. 119) **ἐφ'ὧι κατεργάται τοῖς ἰδίοις ἀνηλώμασιν . . γῆς (ἀρούρας) δέκα**, "on condition that he shall cultivate at his own expense 10 arourae of land," PSI I. 32[10] (A.D. 208) **ἐπὶ τῷ σε τοῦτο κατεργάσασθ[αι] πάσ[η] ἐργασ[ία] καὶ ἐπιμελεία** : cf. also BGU IV. 1121[16] (B.C. 5) **μὴ ἐξόντο[ς] αὐτοῖς διδόναι τοῖς κατεργαζομένοις τὴν μίσθωσιν ἐ[ργάτ]αις π[λ]είον τῶν [διδο]μένων ἐν τῶι Κόλπωι [κατ]έργων.** In *Syll* 342 (c. B.C. 48) it is used with reference to public services—[26] **τὰ βέλτιστα κατεργάζεται τῇ πατρίδι**, [21] **κινδύνους ἐπι[δ]εχόμενος [ἀό]κνως πρὸς τὸ πάντως τι κατεργάζεσθ[αι] τῇ πατρίδι συμφέρον** : in *ib.* 504[5] (iii/A.D.) we find the soloecism **πάντας**

τοὺς κατεργαζομένους τὴν πόλιν (*sc. publicanos*) for ἐργα-
ζομένους κατὰ τὴν πόλιν (see the editor's note). Cf. also
Aristeas 225 ἠσκηκὼς πρὸς πάντας ἀνθρώπους εὔνοιαν καὶ
κατεργασάμενος φιλίας λόγον οὐθενὸς ἄν ἔχοις, "if thou hast
studiously practised goodwill towards all men and formed
friendships, thou needest fear no man" (Thackeray). For
κατεργασία see P Ryl II. 171[15] (A.D. 56-7) εἰς κατεργασίαν,
"for the purpose of tillage," and for κάτεργον in the sense
of "work," "service," as twice in the LXX (Exod 30[16],
35[21]) we may perhaps cite P Petr II. 4 (2)[8] (B.C. 255-4)
ἔγραψά σοι ὅ δεῖ δοθῆναι εἰς ἕκαστον ἀργοῦ καὶ τὸ κάτεργον,
where Mahaffy translates, "I have written to you what
should be given to each of idle and the working (time?),"
but the meaning is far from clear : see also the editor's note
on Rev L [xlvi. 2], and cf. BGU 1121 *ut s.*

κατέρχομαι.

This favourite Lukan word (cf. Hobart, p. 212) hardly
needs illustration, but we may cite P Ryl II. 119[32] (A.D. 54-
67) κατελθεῖν εἰ[ς] τὸν διαλογισμόν, "to go down to the
assize," P Fay 123[8] (*c.* A.D. 100) οὐκ ἠδυνήθην κατελθεῖν,
"I was unable to come down," *ib.* 131[10] (iii/iv A.D.) ἐ[ὰ]ν
τὸ ὕδωρ κατέλθῃ πάσῃ προθυμίᾳ χρῆσαι ἔστ' ἄν τὸ ὑδρο-
στάσιον γεμισθῇ, "if the water comes down, make every
exertion until the basin is filled" (Edd.). In P Flor II.
236[8] (A.D. 267) ἕπονται δὲ καὶ τούτοις ἄλλοι καὶ ἀπὸ νυκτὸς
κατέρχονται, the verb means little more than "arrive."

κατεσθίω.

The perfective force of this verb (cf. *Proleg.* pp. 111, 115)
is well seen in P Ryl II. 152[13] (A.D. 42), a complaint of
damage to pasturage by sheep which κατενέμησαν καὶ κατέφαγαν καὶ τοῖς ὅλοις ἠφάνισαν, "overran, cropped, and
utterly destroyed it" (Edd.) : cf. P Flor II. 150[6] (A.D. 267)
of crops ἀπὸ τῶν μυῶν κατεσθιόμενα, and P Oxy I. 58[8, 19]
(A.D. 288) with reference to the multitude of officials who
were "swallowing up" the estates of the treasury along with
its surplus—βουλόμενοι τὰς ταμιακὰς οὐσίας κατεστείειν (*l.*
κατεσθίειν) . . τὰ δὲ περιγεινόμενα κατεστείουσιν (*l.* κατε-
σθίουσιν). For the fut. καταφάγομαι, as in Jn 2[17] from
the LXX, cf. P Iand 20[23] (A.D. 98) ἐφ' ᾧ καταφάγονται (*sc.*
τὰ πρόβατα), and with the shorter form of the part. κατέ-
σθοντες in Mk 12[40] cf. the magic P Lond 46[268] (iv/A.D.)
(= I. p. 73) ὑπὸ τῶν ἰχθύων σου ἡ κοιλία κατέσθεται.

κατευθύνω.

For the metaphorical usage of this verb in its NT occurrences, we may add to the usual citations from the LXX
Aristeas 18 κατευθύνει τὰς πράξεις καὶ τὰς ἐπιβολὰς ὁ
κυριεύων ἁπάντων θεός.

κατέχω.

(1) In enumerating the varied meanings of this interesting
verb, it may be well to begin with it as the perfective of ἔχω
= "possess," as in 1 Cor 7[30], 2 Cor 6[10] ὡς μηδὲν ἔχοντες
καὶ πάντα κατέχοντες. To this last passage a good parallel
is afforded by *Magn* 105[51] (ii/B.C.) ἵνα ἔχωσιν κατέχωσίν τε
καρπί[ζ]ωνταί τε, with reference to the right of possessing
certain territory. The citation also prepares us for some of
the more technical uses of the verb, as in P Tebt I. 5[47] (a

royal ordinance—B.C. 118) κρατεῖ]ν ὧν κατεσχήκασι κλή-
(ρων), "shall have the legal ownership of the lands which
they have possessed" (Edd.), P Oxy II. 237 [viii. 22] (A.D. 186)
διαζητοῦντί μοι μαθεῖν ἐκ τίνος ὑποθέσεως ἐτελεῖτο τὰς
Αἰγυπτιακὰς γυναῖκας κατὰ ἐνχώριον νόμιμα (*l.* νόμισμα)
κατέχειν τὰ ὑπάρχοντα τῶν ἀνδρῶν διὰ τῶν γαμικῶν συν-
γραφῶν κτλ., "when I wished to know on what pretext it
came about that Egyptian wives have by native Egyptian
law a claim upon their husbands' property through their
marriage contracts" etc. (Edd.). Cf. also P Oxy IV. 713[15]
(A.D. 97) where the parents κατέσχον τῇ ἐξ ἀλλήλων γενεᾷ
τὰ ἑαυτῶν πάντα, "settled upon their joint issue the whole
of their property" (Edd.). (2) From this it is an easy
transition to the meaning "lay hold of," "take possession
of," as in Lk 14[9]: see e.g. P Amh II. 30[26] (ii/B.C.) where
an official report regarding the ownership of a house, proofs
were adduced to establish that a certain Marres κατεσχηκέναι τὴν οἰκίαν, "had become owner of the house," P Oxy
I. 118 *verso*[11] (late iii/A.D.) ἐπέμψαμέν σοι ἐπίσταλμα ἵνα
. . . [κα]τάσχῃς ἃ δεῖ, "we accordingly send you this message, in order that you may procure what is necessary"
(Edd.), and for the subst. κατοχή = *bonorum possessio*, BGU
I. 140[24] (time of Hadrian) ὅμως κατ[ο]χὴ[ν] ὑ[πα]ρχόντων
ἐξ ἐκείνου τοῦ μέ[ρ]ους τοῦ διατάγματος. In the same way
the κάτοχοι of the Serapeum are often regarded as those
"possessed" by the spirit of the god, see especially Preuschen *Mönchtum und Serapiskult*[2] (Giessen, 1903), and cf. in
support of this view *Priene* 195[29] (*c.* B.C. 200) ἀπὸ δὲ τῶν
τραπεζῶν ὧν ἄν δημ[ος κοσμῇ, δεδόσθω τ]οῖς κατεχομένοις
ὑπὸ τοῦ θεοῦ (cited by Wilcken *Archiv* iv. p. 207). If, on
the other hand, they are to be thought of as a species of
monks living for the time being ἐν κατοχῇ within the temple-
precincts (cf. P Lond 42[27] (B.C. 168) (= I. p. 31, *Selections*,
p. 11) ὑπὲρ τοῦ ἀπολελύσθαι σε ἐκ τῆς κατοχῆς), this prepares us for a further modification in the meaning of κατέχω
viz. "arrest," "seize." (3) Of this meaning (cf. Gen 39[20])
a good ex. is afforded by P Flor I. 61[60] (A.D. 85) (= *Chrest.*
II. p. 89) ἄξιος μ[ὲ]ν ἦς μαστιγωθῆναι, διὰ σεαυτοῦ [κ]ατα-
σχὼν ἄνθρωπον εὐσχήμονα καὶ γυν[αῖ]καν. Similarly in
BGU II. 372[i. 16] (A.D. 154) we read of a man κατεχόμενον
"arrested," as a tramp, and in the fragmentary P Lond 422
(*c.* A.D. 350) (= II. p. 318) of directions to arrest another
and "put him in irons" (σιδηρῶσαι αὐτόν) for selling stolen
camels : it is added that his wife is already arrested—[3] κατέχεται ἡ γυνή. Cf. the use of the subst. in P Amh II. 80[9]
(A.D. 232-3) ἵν[α] . . . [ἐ]γλύσωσίν με [τῆς κα]τοχῆς. The
verb is common in this connexion in respect of arrest for
non-payment of debts, as in the late P Amh II 144[4] (v/A.D.)
where a man writes to his wife that a creditor finding him at
Alexandria κατέσχεν με καὶ οὐδὲν εὗρον δοῦναι αὐτῷ, and
suggests that she might raise money to help him by a mortgage on a young slave. For the closely related meaning
"seize" cf. the important rescript regarding the Third
Syrian War, in which Ptolemy III. relates how certain ships
sailed along the coast of Cilicia to Soli, and took on board
τὰ ἐ[κεῖ?]σε κατασκεθέντ[α χρή]ματα, "the money that had
been seized there" (P Petr II 45[ii. 4], cf. III. p. 335 f.), and
P Oxy XII. 1483[18] (ii/iii A.D.) ἐὰν μὴ διὰ τάχους πᾶν τελῇς
. . . τὸν ἐγγυητήν σου κατέχω, "unless you pay all quickly,
I shall seize your security" (Edd.). Hence too the metaphorical usage that appears in such passages as P Amh II

97¹⁷ (A.D. 180–192) οὐ κατασχε[θ]ήσομαι τῇ [ὑ]ποσχέσει, "I will not be bound by my promise" (Edd.), P Oxy III. 532²³ (ii/A.D.) ὑπὸ κακοῦ συνειδότος κατεχόμενος, "being oppressed by an evil conscience" (Edd.), P Ryl II. 117¹³ (A.D. 269) μὴ κατέχεσθαι τοῖς ἐκείνων ὀφε[ιλήμασι]ν, "not be held responsible for their debts" (Edd.), and PSI IV. 299³ (iii/A.D.) κατεσχέθην νόσῳ, "I was held fast by disease" (cf. [Jn] 5⁴). In *Michel* 1325¹ (iv–ii/B.C.) the verb is used of binding by a curse—Μανῆν καταδῶ καὶ κατέχω. (4) The verb is also = "lay hands on," "impress" for some public duty, as in P Giss I. 11⁹ (A.D. 118) κατεσχέτ(= θ)ην ὑπὸ τοῦ ἐπιτρόπου ὥστε εἰρατεύειν τοῦ χειρεισμοῦ τῶν κυβερνητ(ῶν), and P Lond 342⁷ (A.D. 185) (= II. p. 174) where a charge is laid against one Sempronius of attempting to lay hands on the relatives of the petitioner as boat-overseers—προφάσι τοῦ κατέχειν ἐπιπλόους τοὺς συνγενεῖς μου. (5) There still remains the common NT meaning "hold back," "detain," "restrain," as e.g. in Lk 4⁴², Rom 1¹⁸, 2 Thess 2⁶ᶠ, Philem ¹³. The following may serve as illustrations—PSI V. 525⁹ (iii/B.C.) where a man complains that having been "detained" (κατασχεθείς) in town, he has spent his money, BGU IV. 1205²⁷ (B.C. 28) μὴι κατάσχῃς Ἀχειλλέα ἀλλὰ δὸς αὐτῶι τὰ δύο πλοῖα διὰ τὸ πορεύεισθαι εἰς Ἑρμοῦ πόλιν, *ib.* I. 37⁶ (A.D. 50) (as amended p. 353) ὅρα οὖν μὴ αὐτὸν κατάσχῃς· οἶδας γὰρ πῶς αὐτοῦ ἑκάστης ὥρας χρῄζωι, P Fay 109¹¹ (early i/A.D.) μὴ κατάσχῃς Κλέωνα καὶ συνπροσ[γενοῦ Κ]λέωνι, "don't keep Cleon waiting, but go and meet him" (Edd.), P Giss I. 70³ (ii/A.D.) ἡ ἀναγραφὴ Τετραγώνου κατέσχεν ἡμ[ᾶς] μέχρι ὥρας ἕκτης, P Oxy III. 527⁷ (ii/iii A.D.) where a man writes to his brother telling him to send and fetch a certain fuller if he requires his services—ὅρα μὴ ἀμελήσῃς, ἐπεὶ γὰρ ἐγὼ αὐτὸν κατέχω, "do not neglect this, as I am keeping him" (Edd.), and P Leid Wxviii ¹⁰ (ii/iii A.D.) κατάσχες τὰ ὄμματα τῶν ἀντιδικούντων ἐμοὶ πάντων. Reference may also be made, in view of its intrinsic interest, to the heathen (*Archiv* ii. p. 173) charm which Crum prints in his *Coptic Ostraca* p. 4, No. 522 : it begins—Κρόνος ὁ κατέχων τὸν θυμὸν ὅλον τῶν ἀνθρώπων, κάτεχε τὸν θυμὸν Ὥρι κτλ. In some of the southern islands of Greece κατέχω is still used, as in Plato, = καταλαμβάνω, in the sense of "know."

κατηγορέω.

For this verb, which has generally a judicial connotation in the NT, cf. P Lond 41¹⁰ (B.C. 161) (= I. p. 28) ὁ δὲ βουκόλος ἐλθὼν κ[α]τηγόρησεν αὐτὰς λέγων κτλ., *ib.* 893¹² (A.D. 40) (as published in P Ryl II. p. 381) Ζηνόβ. [ο]το(ς) [π]ολλὰ κατηγόρησεν ἐπὶ Φόλω, "Zenodotus made many charges before Pholus," P Oxy II. 237ᵛⁱⁱⁱ ²¹ (A.D. 186) εἰ δὲ μή, πάντες ἐροῦσιν ὅτι κατηγορῶ, "otherwise every one will say that I am your accuser" (Edd.), and from the inscrr. OGIS 218⁹⁵ (iii/B.C.) ἐὰν δὲ χρήματα ἐ[κ]τείσηι, διπλάσια ἀποτινέ[τ]ω ὁ κατηγορήσ[ας], *Syll* 356⁵ (c. B.C. 6) τὸ ψήφισμα ἀποδόντες κατηγόρησαν Εὐβούλου . . τεθνεῶτος ἤδη. For the verbal ἀκατηγόρητος see the sepulchral inscr. *Preisigke* 343 Ἀντωνεῖνε συνεξούσιε . . . ἀκατηγόρητε ὁλόκαλε φιλάνθρωπε κτλ.

κατηγορία.

P Oxy II. 237ᵛⁱⁱⁱ ⁷ (A.D. 186) τότ' ἐὰν θαρρῇ τοῖς τῆς κατηγορίας ἐλέγχοις, τὸν μείζονα ἀγῶνα ἐ[ἰ]σελεύσεται, "if

he has confidence in the proofs of his accusation, he shall enter upon the more serious law-suit" (Edd.), *Michel* 458³¹ (c. B.C. 165) πολλὰς καὶ ψευδεῖς κατηγορίας πο[ιησαμένων τινῶν.

κατήγορος.

P Tor I. 1ᵛⁱⁱⁱ ¹² (B.C. 116) ἐμφανιστοῦ καὶ κατηγόρου, "delatore ac accusatore" (Ed.), P Lond 359⁹ (i/ii A.D.) (= II. p. 150) ἐν μὲν οὖν τῷ κατηγόρῳ, "one word to the prosecutor," P Oxy III. 472³² (c. A.D. 130) φαμὲν τοῦτο [πᾶ]ν μηδὲν εἶναι πρὸς τὸν κατήγορον, "we assert that all this has nothing to do with the plaintiff" (Edd.), P Flor I. 6⁶ (A.D. 210) δημοσίου κατηγόρου, *Syll* 316¹⁷ (ii/B.C.) πα]ρασχομένων τῶν κατηγόρων ἀληθινὰς ἀποδείξεις, OGIS 669³⁹ (i/A.D.) μηκέτι ἐξεῖναι τούτωι εἰσαγγέλλειν κατηγόρωι μηδὲ εἰς κρίσιν ἄγεσθαι.

κατήγωρ,

which in the NT is confined to Rev 12¹⁰, occurs in the magical papyrus P Lond 124²⁵ (iv/v A.D.) (= I. p. 122) a charm effective against all ills — ποιεῖ γὰρ πρὸς ἐχθροὺς καὶ κατηγόρας καὶ λῃστῶν καὶ φόβους καὶ φαντασμοὺς ὀνείρων, "for it works against enemies and accusers and robbers and terrors and dream-spectres" : see Deissmann *LAE* p. 90 f., where it is argued that the word is not a Heb. adaptation of κατήγορος (so W Schm *Gr.* p. 85), but a Greek "vulgarism," formed in the same way as ῥήτωρ. Cf. also Thumb *Hellen.* p. 126, Radermacher *Gr.* p. 15, Moulton *Gr.* ii. § 54.

κατήφεια.

In P Oxy III. 471⁹² (ii/A.D.) τί οὖν ὁ κατηφὴς σὺ καὶ ὑπεραύ[σ]τηρος οὐκ ἐκώλυες ; the context suggests that κατηφής = "with eyes cast down for shame," and the same reference to the *outward* expression of the countenance underlies the only occurrence of the subst. in the NT, Jas 4⁹, where it should be rendered "gloominess" rather than "heaviness" (AV, RV). See also the citations in Field *Notes*, p. 238, e.g. Charit. Aphrod. vi. 8 : πρὸς δὲ τὴν φήμην κατήφεια πᾶσαν ἔσχε Βαβυλῶνα (these tidings cast a gloom over the whole city).

κατηχέω

is used of legal "instruction" in P Strass I. 41³⁷ (A.D. 250) ἐμὲ οὐδέποτε κατήχησεν ("mich hat. sie in keiner Weise überzeugt" Ed.)—an advocate speaks. Cf. the use of περιηχέω in P Oxy VIII. 1110⁷ (A.D. 254) αὐτοί τε εὐθέως περιηχηθέντες, "and we immediately on receiving information of it" (Ed.). With reference to the application of κατηχημένος to Apollos in Ac 18²⁵, Blass (*Philology of the Gospels*, p. 31) argues that this does not necessarily imply that Apollos was wholly dependent upon oral instruction. Even as early as A.D. 50 he may have been in possession in Egypt of a written Gospel, not improbably that of Mark— "let κατηχεῖσθαι be employed of hearing even in the passage of the Acts : the book will still be there."

κατισχύω.

This verb, which is very common in the LXX and occurs *ter* in the NT (Mt 16¹⁸, Lk 21³⁶, 23²³), is construed with the acc. in P Leid Wxviii (ii/iii A.D.) οὐ κατισχύσει με ἅπας δρὰξ κινουμένη, "non valebit adversus me omnis pugillus motus" (Ed.), much in the same sense as with the gen. in Mt *l.c.*: cf. also Aristeas 21 τοῦ θεοῦ κατισχύοντος αὐτόν, 230. See Anz *Subsidia*, p. 295 f., and Durham *Menander*, p. 70. The verb survives in MGr in the sense "prevail," "gain the mastery over."

κατοικέω,

in the general sense of "dwell in," "inhabit," is found in such passages as P Fay 98[14] (A.D. 123) τὰ ἐνοίκια . . ἧς κατοικεῖ αὐτῶν κοινωνικῆς ο[ἰκίας] ἐν κώμῃ Εὐημερείᾳ, "the rent of the house at Euhemeria jointly owned by them at which she lives" (Edd.), P Oxy VIII. 1102[12] (c. A.D. 146) ὁ τοῦ νομοῦ στρατηγὸς ἀκριβέστερον ἐξετάσει ᾗ κατοικ̣εῖ, "the strategus of the nome shall hold a more exact inquiry in the place where he lives" (Ed.). More technically used, the verb refers to the permanent "residents" of a town or village, as distinguished from those "dwelling as strangers" or "sojourners" (παροικοῦντες): cf. Gen 37[1]. See further Hohlwein *L'Égypte Romaine*, p. 351 f., Jouguet *Vie municipale*, p. 57 f.

κατοικία.

For this NT ἅπ. εἰρ. (Ac 17[26]) it is sufficient to cite P Tor 1. 1[1 20] (B.C. 116) οἱ ἐγκαλούμενοι τὴν κατοικίαν ἔχοντες ἐν τοῖς Μεμνονείοις, "citati domicilium habentes in Memnonis" (Ed.), P Fay 12[27] (c. B.C. 103) δέομαι ἀποστεῖλαί μου τὴν ἔντευξιν ἐπὶ τοὺς ἀποτεταγμένους τῆι κατοικίᾳ χρηματιστάς, "I entreat you to send my petition to the assize-judges appointed for the settlement" (Edd.), P Ryl II. 165[17] (A.D. 200) the sale of four arourae of catoecic land (γῆς κατοικικῆς)—τῷ τῆς κατοικίας δικαίῳ σχοινίῳ, "measured by the just measure of the settlement" (Edd.), and from the inscr. *Cagnat* IV. 834[4] (Hierapolis) εἰ δὲ ἔτι ἕτερος κηδεύσει, δώσει τῇ κατοικίᾳ τῶν ἐν Ἱεραπόλει κατοικούντων Ἰουδαίων προστείμου δηνάρια . . This last inser. is discussed by Ramsay in *Exp* VI v. p. 96 f., where it is shown that the technical term κατοικία points to a "settlement" of Jews in the city with definite rights and a legalized position, so that there was little distinction between them and the old population.

κατοικίζω.

This verb, which is read in the best MSS. of Jas 4[5], is properly transitive, as in Aristeas 13 κατῴκισεν ἐν τοῖς φρουρίοις, "settled them in the fortresses": see further Mayor *ad* Jas *l.c.* for the transitive rendering there, which renders unnecessary Souter's suggestion (*Lex. s.v.*) that κατῴκισεν is an itacistic error for κατῴκησεν. In BGU IV. 1116[18] (B.C. 13) we find ἐνοικίζω and ἐξοικίζω contrasted: cf. also P Tebt II. 372[12] (A.D. 141) ἐνοικεῖν καὶ ἐνοικίζιν . . ἐν τῇ προκε[ι]μένῃ οἰκίᾳ, "to have the right of domicile in the aforesaid house."

κατοπτρίζω.

Syll 802[64] (iii/B.C.) ἀπονίψασθαι τὸ πρόσωπον ἀπὸ τᾶς κράνας κα[ὶ] ἐγκατοπτρίξασθαι εἰς τὸ ὕδωρ means of course "to look at his reflection in the water." It would perhaps be too fanciful to apply this prevailing sense of the middle in 2 Cor 3[18], making the glory of the Lord the mirror which reveals our own darkness and then floods that darkness with

light, but for this thought we may compare the opening words of the thirteenth Ode of Solomon: "Behold! the Lord is our mirror: open the eyes and see them in Him: and learn the manner of your face" (Harris). The pass. is found in the new metrological fragment (Eudorus?) P Oxy XIII. 1609[19] (ii/A.D.) ἀπορροὰς . . ἀπὸ ἑκάστου τῶν κ[α]τοπτριζομένων, "emanations from each of the objects shown in the mirror" (Edd.). For the subst. see *ib.* [10], BGU III. 717[12] (A.D. 149) κάτοπτ[ρ]ον δίπτυχον, and Aristeas 76 where the smoothness of certain silver bowls is described as such that anything brought close to them was reflected more clearly than in mirrors—ἢ ἐν τοῖς κατόπτροις.

κατόρθωμα.

With the TR of Ac 24[2] cf. CP Herm 1. 125[ii. 4] (A.D. 260-8) where a certain Aurelius Ploution is praised—τὰ μέγιστα κ[α]τορθώματα κ[α]τωρθώσας τῇ πατρί[δ]ι, and cf. *Syll* 324[25] (i/B.C.) εὐερ[γέτη]ν ὄντα καὶ πλεῖστα τ]ῆι πόλει κατορθωσάμενον ἀγαθά. For the verb see further P Lond 130[31] (i./ii A.D.) (= 1. p. 134) κατορθοῦται, Aristeas 251 κατορθοῦται γὰρ βίος, ὅταν ὁ κυβερνῶν εἰδῇ, πρὸς τίνα σκοπὸν δεῖ τὴν διέξοδον ποιεῖσθαι, and Menander Ἐπιτρέπ. 339 π[ό]ει κατορθοῦν τοὺς λόγους οὓς ἂν λέγω. On the medical usage, see Hobart, p. 261 f.

κάτω

used of place "down," "downwards," is found 8 times in the NT, and may be illustrated by P Hal 1. 11[11] (B.C. 238) οὐλὴ τ]ραχήλωι κάτωι (for form, see Mayser *Gr.* p. 136), P Magd 11[14] (B.C. 221) τῆς κάτω μερίδος, and P Tebt II. 414[29] (ii/A.D.) τὸ σφυρίδιν μετὰ τῶν ἐνόντων κάτω, "the little basket with its contents at the bottom" (Edd.). An ostracon receipt of iii/A.D. published by GH in *Egypt. Archaeol. Report* 1904-05 p. 16, No. 12, runs—λί(τρας) δ (ἥμισυ) ὀκτασοῦφα καὶ τρισοῦφα ἄνω καὶ κάτω δικόντυλα (l.-δυλα) δωδεκάκυκλα.

κατώτερος

is found as an astrological term contrasted with ἀνώτερος in Vett. Val. p. 34[21]. Cf. *IG* XIV. 2476 (Arles) ἐνθάδε κῖτη Ἰωσῆς ἀπὸ κώ[μης] Ἐπικίου(?) ἀνοτέρου κατοτέρου with the editor's note: "extrema non intellego; Ἐποίκιον ἀνώτερον κατώτερον vici nomen fuisse putat Mommsenus."

Καῦδα.

In *Exp* T xxi. p. 17 ff. Dr. Rendel Harris has shown good cause for believing that Καῦδα should be read in the original text of Ac 27[16] with אc B as against Κλαῦδα in א A, but see WSchm *Gr.* p. 65. MGr Γαυδονῆσι.

καῦμα.

P Lond 1166[6] (A.D. 42) (= III. p. 104) τὰ αὐτάρκη καύματα—adequate heat for the baths attached to a gymnasium, PSI II. 184[6] (A.D. 292) καύματος ἐνόντος. See also *Kaibel* 649[5] (Rome—iii./A.D.)—

οὐ χειμὼν λυπεῖ σ', οὐ καῦμα, οὐ νοῦσος ἐνοχλεῖ.

καῦσις.

P Lond 1166[14] (A.D. 42) (= III. p. 105) χωρὶς τοῦ παρασχέσθαι τοὺς ὁμολοῦντας (l. ὁμολογοῦντας) τὴν καῦσιν καθὼς πρόκειται, *ib.* 1177[74] (A.D. 113) (= III. p. 183) κα[ύ]σεως λύχνων. Cf. from the inserr. *Chrest.* I. 70[10] (B.C. 57–6) τάς τε θυσίας καὶ σπονδὰς καὶ καύσεις λύχνων . . . ἐπιτελοῦντες. *Magn* 179[11] (ii/A.D.) τὰ ἐξ ἔθους καὶ ὡρισμένα ὑπὲρ τῆς καύσεως τῆς βαίτης ("bath") δηνάρια χ. For καυσμός cf. Wilcken *Ostr* 1014 (ii iii A.D.) ἀχύρου καυσμοῦ γόμο(ν) ἕκτον, and for the adj. καύσιμος cf. P Fay p. 325 *Ostr* 21[3] (A.D. 306) ἀχύρου καυσίμου σάκ κον) α, "a sack of chaff for fuel."

καυστηριάζω.

Wilcken suggests as a possible restoration of BGU III. 952[4] (ii/iii A.D.) καυστηριά]ζουσι τὴν γύψον. The subst. καύστης is found in *ib.*[5]

καύσων.

This late word means "burning heat" in Mt 20[12], Lk 12[55], and probably Jas 1[11]: cf. Gen 31[40] and Athenaeus iii. p. 73[a] μελιλώτινοι στέφανοι πάνυ εὐώδεις καὶ καύσωνος ὥρᾳ ψυκτικώτατοι. In the LXX it is more frequent of a "scorching wind," or "sirocco," and Hort prefers this meaning in Jas *l.c.* In Dioscor. i. 21. 149 it is used as a medical term, "heat in the stomach," and survives in MGr = "heat" (see Kennedy *Sources*, p. 154).

καυχάομαι.

The 2nd sing. pres. midd. καυχᾶσαι, as in Rom 2[17. 23], 1 Cor 4[7] (cf. Sir 6[7] κτᾶσαι, and see Thackeray *Gr.* i. p. 218) which has been formed afresh in the Κοινή with the help of the—σαι that answers to 3rd sing.—ται in the perf., is paralleled by χαριέσαι = χαριεῖ in P Grenf II. 14 (*c.*)[7] (B.C. 264 or 227): cf. P Oxy II. 292[9] (*c.* A.D. 25) χαριέσαι δέ μου τὰ μέγιστα, "you will confer upon me a very great favour," and see *Proleg.* p. 53 f., Mayser *Gr.* p. 328, Radermacher *Gr.* p. 73, and Wackernagel *ThLZ* xxxiii. (1908) p. 639. For the verb cf. P Oxy VIII. 1160[7 ff.] (iii/iv A.D.) ἔγραψάς μοι . . . ὅτι καυχώμενος ἔχ (*l.* ἔχω) ὄνομα Διοδώρου ὅτι ἔπεμψά σοι ἀργύρια· ἐγὼ γὰρ οὐ καυχόμαι (*l.* καυχῶμαι) ἐμαυτὸν ‹ἃ› ἔπεμψά σοι, "you wrote me that my boastfulness earns me the name of 'Gift of Zeus' because I sent you money; but I do not boast about what I sent you" (Ed.), PSI I. 26[16] (v/A.D.) καυχᾶσθαι γὰρ [εἰς ἐ]λπίδας μ[αταίας. For Harnack's defence of the reading καυχήσωμαι in 1 Cor 13[3] see *Berliner Sitzungsberichte*, 1911, p. 139 ff. (E. Tr. *Exp.* VIII. iii. p. 395 ff.), and for the constructions of καυχάομαι in the NT see Deissmann *In Christo*, p. 64 f.

Καφαρναούμ.

On this form of the proper name, which is found in all the critical editions, see F. C. Burkitt *Syriac Forms*, p. 27 f.

κέδρος.

We appear to have the gen. plur. of this word in the generally accepted reading of Jn 18[1] πέραν τοῦ χειμάρρου τῶν Κέδρων, but it is probable that this is due to a popular misunderstanding of the real reading τοῦ Κεδρών, where Κεδρών is the indeclinable Hellenized form of a Semitic word קִדְרוֹן, "dark," and indicates that the stream was

---

so called from the turbid character of its waters: see especially Lightfoot *Biblical Essays*, p. 172 ff., Moulton *Gr.* ii. § 60 (12).

κεῖμαι

is used with reference to a dead body (as in Mt 28[6]) in P Ryl II. 114[17] (*c.* A.D. 280), the petition of a woman against a certain Syrian who had endeavoured - ἀφαρπάζειν τὰ των [νηπίων μου τέ]κνων . . . παρὰ [αὐτῆς τῆς κοί]της τοῦ ἀνδρός μου καὶ τοῦ σώματος κειμένου, "to tear the property of my young children from the very bed of my husband where his body was lying" (Edd.). Cf. the A.D. sepulchral inscr. from Alexandria, *Preisigke* 1397 Ξηνόφιλος κεῖμαι πατρὸς Ξηνοφίλου. Hence, more generally, of things "lying" or "set" in a place (cf. 1 Cor 3[11]), e.g. PSI IV. 365[20] (B.C. 251–0) ὁ γ]ὰρ σεῖτος ἐπὶ τῆς ἅλῳ κείμενος οὐθὲν ὠφελεῖ ἡμᾶς (cf. Lk 12[9]), P Oxy XII. 1470[4] (late i/B.C.) διὸ τὰ βυβλία οὔπω εἴληφ α], ἀλλὰ κεῖται ἀντιβεβλημένα, "I have not yet obtained the documents, but they are lying collated" (Edd.), *ib.* 1488[18] (ii A.D.) ἡ ἐν τῷ αἰθρίῳ κειμένη μεγάλη θυία, "the large mortar placed in the portico" (Edd.). So of vessels in pledge or pawn, as in PSI V. 525[5] (iii/B.C.) ἅ ποτε σκεύη εἶχον ἐνέχυρα κεῖται, P Oxy I. 114[3] (ii/iii A.D.) κεῖται πρὸς β μνᾶς, "it is pledged for two minae," and of persons "living" in a district, as in P Tebt I. 27[7] (B.C. 113) ἐν π[ερι]στάσει κειμένων : cf. 1 Jn 5[19], and in further illustration of this passage Menander *Fragm.* p. 176 τὴν ἐν ἑτέρῳ γὰρ κειμένην ἁμαρτίαν, where the phrase seems to mean "depends upon." The common metaphorical usage "laid down," "established," as in 1 Tim 1[9], may be illustrated from BGU III. 1002[14] (B.C. 55) πᾶσαι αἱ κατ' αὐτῶν κείμεναι συνγραφαί, and P Tebt II. 334[7] (A.D. 200–1) κατ]ὰ τὴν κιμ[έ]νην ἡμῖν συνγραφήν, with reference to a marriage-contract. See also P Par 63[176] and P Tebt I. 33[4] cited *s.v.* ἐν (denoting *condition*, *state*), and *Magn* 115[15] cited *s.v.* ἀπόκειμαι. P Oxy II. 293[7] (A.D. 27) ἔτι καὶ νῦν κεῖται μέχρι οὗ ἀποστείλῃς μοι φάσιν of clothes "laid past," "they are still waiting until you send me word." In *Michel* 542[18] (beg. ii/B.C.) καὶ μετὰ τὸ δικάσαι ἐπικρινάσης [τ]ῆς βουλῆς τὰς κειμένας δίκας καὶ ὀφειλούσας τελεσθῆναι ἐπὶ τοῦ μετὰ ταῦτα δικαστηρίου, can the reference be to cases which were "held over"?

κειρία.

This vernacular word (cf. Kennedy *Sources*, p. 40) is found in the NT only in Jn 11[44]. The form κηρία, which is read in this passage by A X Δ Λ *al.*, occurs several times in the fragments of a medical papyrus, P Lond 155 (i/ii A.D.) (= II. p. xiv.), edited by Kalbfleisch *ad Scholas* (Rostock, 1892), p. 5[ii. 24 *al.*]. Field (*Notes*, p. 96) quotes Moschopulus' definition : κειρία· ὁ τῶν νηπίων δεσμός, ἤγουν ἡ κοινῶς φασκία (fascia), καὶ ᾗ δεσμοῦσι τοὺς νεκρούς.

κείρω

is used of shearing sheep in PSI IV. 368[45] (B.C. 250–49) ἐκάρη πρόβατα ριε, cf. [61] ἔκειρε ζ. For the derived meaning "ravage" (cf. Lat. *tondeo* and our "fleece") see *OGIS* 765[10] (iii/B.C.) κείρο[ντ]ες τ[ὰ] τεμένη, and the corresponding use of the subst. = "plunder," "theft," in P Lond 403[12] (A.D. 346) (= II. p. 276) τὴ[ν τ]ῶν προβάτων κορρὰν καὶ ἀπελασίαν. A new literary citation is supplied by Herondas iii. 40 τὴν μάμμην . . κείρει, "he fleeces his grandmother."

κέλευσμα.

The form κέλευσμα for the more ancient κέλευμα (cf. Cronert *Mem. Herc.* p. 227 n.⁵) is found in 1 Th 4¹⁶, the only occurrence of the word in the NT (in LXX only Prov 24⁶²(30²⁷)): see further for the usage of the word Milligan *Thess. ad l.*, where reference is made to a passage cited by Reitzenstein (*Poimandres* p. 5 n.³) from the *Descensus Mariae* in which the Archangel Michael is described as τὸ κέλευσμα τοῦ ἁγίου πνεύματος. The nouns κέλευσις and ἐγκέλευσις are common, e.g. BGU I. 286⁹ (A.D. 306) κατὰ κέλευσιν τῆς ἡγεμονίας, P Tebt II. 338¹¹ (A.D. 194-6) ἐ]ξ ἐν[κε]λεύσεως τοῦ κρα[τίστο]υ ἐπιστρατήγου: for κελευστής, see P Lond 977³⁶ (A.D. 330) (= III. p. 232).

κελεύω.

PSI IV. 420⁹ (iii/B.C.) ἐκελεύοσαν (for form cf. Mayser *Gr.* p. 322 f.) δέ με καταβαίνοντα συγχωνεύειν, P Par 44⁴ (B.C. 153) τί κελεύεις ὑπὲρ τούτων; P Meyer 3¹⁵ (A.D. 148) ἵν' οὖν τὸ κελευσθ(ὲν) εἰδῇς, P Tebt II. 327²¹ (late ii/A.D.) κε]κελευσμένου οὖν, κύριε, γ[υ]ναῖκας ἀφεῖσθαι τῶν τ[οιο]ύτων χρειῶν, "wherefore, my lord, since it has been decreed that women should be exempt from such burdens" (Edd.). For the gen. abs. without noun or pronoun in agreement in this last instance cf. Mt 17¹¹, Ac 21³¹ (*Proleg.* p. 74), and with the constr. in Ac 25²³ cf. *Michel* 594⁵³ (B.C. 279) τούτοις ἐδώκαμεν, ἀρχιτέκτονος καὶ ἐπιμελητῶν κελευόντων, τὴμ πρώτην δόσιν δραχμὰς κτλ. The somewhat rare constr. of κελεύω with a dat., as in the "received" text of Mt 15³⁵, is seen in Menander Περικειρ. 224 τί δ' ἐστιν ὁ κελεύεις ἐμοί; Note also that in a school-book of iii/A.D., published by Kenyon in *JHS* xxix. (1909), p. 34¹·⁹, we find—κελεύω τούτῳ.

κενοδοξία.

To the usual late Greek citations for this word (Phil 2³) we may add Vett. Val. p. 358³¹ ἀλλά τινες σφαλέντες καὶ θρυληθέντες ἐδυστύχησαν, ματαίαν τὴν ἐγχειρισθεῖσαν κτησάμενοι κενοδοξίαν. The Latins adopted this word.

κενόδοξος.

Like the subst., κενόδοξος is an ἅπ. εἰρ. in the NT (Gal 5²⁶). It is found once in Epictetus with the same meaning "vainglorious," iii. 24. 43 ὁ προσποιούμενος τὰ μηδὲν πρὸς αὐτὸν ἔστω ἀλαζών, ἔστω κενόδοξος. Cf. also Vett. Val. p. 271² αἱροῦνται . . τῆς κενοδόξου κληρονομίας ἀπαλλαγῆναι.

κενός

is found in the literal sense "empty" in P Magd 11¹⁵ (B.C. 221) μηδὲ κενὸν τὸ π[λοῖ]ον . . . [κατα]κομισθῆναι πρὸς τὴν πόλιν, P Ryl II. 125²⁶ (A.D. 28-9) ἐκκενώσας τὰ προκείμενα ἔριψεν ἐν τῇ οἰκίᾳ μου τὴν πυξίδα κενήν, "having rifled the contents aforesaid he threw the box empty into my house" (Edd.). In *OGIS* 629¹⁶⁶ (A.D. 137) a distinction is drawn between κεναί ("unladen") and ἔνγομοι ("laden") camels. With the metaph. usage in Eph 5⁶ cf. P Par 15⁶⁸ (B.C. 120) φάσει κενῇ: see also Didache ii. 5. For the rare

use of κενός applied to men as in Jas 2²⁰, in the sense of "pretentious," "hollow," Hort (*ad l.*) compares Epict. ii. 19. 8 ἀλλ' ἂν ᾧ κενός, μάλιστα ἐπὶ συμποσίῳ, καταπλήσσομαι τοὺς παρόντας ἐξαριθμούμενος τοὺς γεγραφότας, "but if I am κενός, especially at a banquet, I astonish the visitors by enumerating the writers (on a particular subject)," and *ib.* iv. 4. 35 κενόν, ἐφ' οἷς οὐ δεῖ ἐπαιρόμενον. For the phrase εἰς κενόν, which in the NT is used only by Paul, cf. P Petr II. 37 1*b* recto¹² (iii/B.C.) ἵνα μὴ τοῦ ὕδατος ἀφεθέντος διὰ τοῦ σωλῆνος ("pipe") εἰς κενὸν φέρηται, of water running to waste, *Kaibel* 646¹⁰ (iii/iv A.D.) ἰς κενὸν ἡ δαπάνη: for διὰ κενῆς cf. P Hib I. 66² (B.C. 228) ὥστε σε μὴ διὰ κενῆς εὐχαριστῆσαι ἡμῖν, "so that you shall not oblige me to no purpose" (Edd.), and, as one word, PSI IV. 434⁹ (B.C. 261-0) οὐκ ἂν νῦν διακενῆς ἐφλυάρει: and for κατὰ κενόν cf. P Tor 1. 1ⁱᵛ·³⁶ (B.C. 116) προηνέγκατο τὸν Ἑρμίαν κατὰ κενὸν περιεσπακέναι.

κενοφωνία.

A good parallel to the use of this subst. (for form see Moulton *Gr.* ii. p. 69) in 1 Tim 6²⁰ is afforded by Epict. ii. 17. 8 ἢ κενῶς τὰς γραφὰς ταύτας ἀπηχοῦμεν;

κενόω.

A new literary example of this word from ii/A.D. occurs in the *Meliambi* of Cercidas, P Oxy VIII. 1082 Fr. 1ⁱⁱ·⁵ᶠᶠ· ῥεῖα γάρ ἐστι θεῷ πᾶν ἐκτελέσαι χρῆμ' ὅκκ' ἐπὶ νοῦν ἴῃ, ἢ τὸν ῥυποκιβδοτόκωνα καὶ τεθνακοχαλκίδαν ἢ τ[ὸ]ν παλινεκχυμενίταν τῶν κτεάνων ὄλεθρον τοῦτον κενῶσαι τὰς συοπλουτοσύνας, "for it is easy for a god to accomplish everything whenever it comes into his mind, and to empty of his swinish wealth the dirty usurer and hoarder or this outpourer and ruin of his substance" (Ed.). So far as it goes this would seem to support the RV rendering "emptied Himself" in Phil 2⁷. [For a note on this passage see *JTS* xii. p. 461 ff.] Cf. further the use of the compound ἐκκενόω in BGU I. 27⁷ (ii/iii A.D.) where a man in the corn service writes to say—ἐξε[κ]ένωσα μὲν τῷ ιη τοῦ αὐτοῦ μηνός, "I finished unloading on the 18th of the same month," P Ryl II. 125²¹ (A.D. 28-9), cited *s.v.* κενός, and *Preisigke* 4368 Λατομίας τὸ πρῶτον ἀνέρετο, αὐτὰρ ἔπειτα τάσδ' ὁ Μενιππείδης ἐξεκένωσε πέτρας—a building inscription. On the other hand, the simplex appears to have the meaning "make void" in Vett. Val. p. 90⁷ ὁ τῆς περιποιήσεως κύριος ἐναντιούμενος τῷ περιποιήματι κενοῖ τὰς ὑπάρξεις. In *ib.* p. 190³⁰ we have the phrase κένωσιν βίου, and in BGU III. 904¹³ (A.D. 161-2) ἐ]κ τῆς κενώσεως is found in a broken context. An epigram from Smyrna of iii/B.C. speaks of—οἱ κένωμα τάφου ποθέοντες, and κενώματα, "empty jars," is found in P Oxy X. 1292¹ (*c.* A.D. 30) *al.*

κέντρον

is used metaphorically = "desire" in a sepulchral inscr. from Byzantium of iii/iv A.D. *Kaibel* 534⁹·—

σῆς γλυκερῆς ψυχῆς κέντρον ἄπαυστον ἔχων.

κεντυρίων.

This Markan Latinism (15³⁹·⁴⁴ᶠ·: cf also Ev. Petr. 8 ff.) for the familiar ἑκατόνταρχος may be illustrated from *OGIS*

106 (B.C. 32) where a Roman official records his visit to the temple of Isis at Phylae σὺν κεντορίωσι Ῥούφωι, Δημητρίωι κτλ. The soldier Apion writing to his father from Italy to announce his safe arrival signs himself as enrolled in the Κεντυρί(α) Ἀθηνονίκη (BGU II. 423[4] (ii/A.D.) = *Selections*, p. 92).

κενῶς.

P Lond 908[28] (A.D. 139) (= III. p. 133) κενῶς καὶ [ἀ]νωφελῶς.

κεραία.

See s.v. κερέα.

κεραμεύς

is found *passim* in the papyri, e.g. P Tebt I. 120[1] (accounts —B.C. 97 or 64) τῶι κεραμί εἰς τι μὴν πίσσης ("pitch") ἀργυ(ρίου) (δραχμαὶ) ιβ, *ib.* II. 414 *verso* (ii A.D.) ἀπό[δο]ς Θεναπύνχι τῇ γυναικὶ τοῦ κεραμέως, and P Oxy XII. 1407[9] (c. A.D. 279) ὑπὸ Θέωνος κεραμέως. In P Lond 113. 8(*b*)[3] (vii/A.D.) (= I. p. 220) we hear of κεραμουργοί.

κεραμικός.

P Lond 121[667] (iii/A.D.) (= I. p. 112) ἀπὸ τρόχου [κε]ραμικοῦ.

κεράμιον.

Ostr 757[3] (B.C. 106–5) ἀπέχω παρὰ σοῦ οἴνου κεράμια δέκα ἕξ, P Oxy IX. 1211[5] (ii/A.D.) οἴνου εὐώδη κεράμ(ια) β, *ib.* 1220[17] (iii/A.D.) γλυνοῦ ("gum") κεράμιον ᾱ. According to Wilcken *Ostr.* i. p. 758 ff. the κεράμιον contained a fixed quantity of fluid, but in their note on P Petr III. 70 (*a*), the editors show that the amount was variable, as the papyrus refers to κεράμια of 5, 6, 7 and 8 χόες : cf. also *Archiv* iii. p. 435. For κεραμίς in the same sense see P Lond 1177[158] (A.D. 113) (= III. p. 185) an account for κεραμείδων, the number required each month proving, as the editor points out, that "jars" for water and not "tiles" must be meant, and further explaining the countless number of ostraca found in Egypt. On the other hand in P Iand 12[3] (iii/iv A.D.) γινώσκιν σε θέλω περὶ τῶν κεραμίδων ὧν ἔγραψές μοι, the reference appears to be to "tiles."

κέραμος

is found = "jar" in P Hib I. 54[26] (c. B.C. 245) where amongst various articles wanted reference is made to κέραμον κα[ι]νόν. For the collective meaning "tiling," as in Lk 5[19], see the accounts dealing with the building of a temple at Delos, *Michel* 594[52] (B.C. 279) ξύλων καὶ κεράμου, [73] κεράμου ζεύγη : cf. *ib.* 1387[123] (iii/B.C.) κ]έραμον τὸν ἐπόντα καὶ θύρας τὰς ἐπούσας.

κεράννυμι.

For the commoner form κεκραμένος as distinguished from the κεκερασμένος of Rev 14[10], we may cite *Syll* 616[30] (iii/B.C.) κύλικα οἴνου κεκραμένου, and P Oxy VIII. 1088[55], a medical receipt of early i/A.D., to which the instruction is appended—μετὰ γλυκέως καὶ μέλιτος καὶ στροβίλων κ[ρ]α-μένων (l. κεκραμένων) δὸς πεῖν, "give to drink with raisin

wine and honey and pine-cones mixed" (Ed.). An interesting ex. of the subst. is found in the famous inscr. of Abercius, in which a παρθένος ἁγνή (the Virgin Mary or the Church) is described as—[16] οἶνον χρηστὸν ἔχουσα, κέρασμα διδοῦσα μετ' ἄρτου, "having good wine and giving the mixed cup with bread": see Lightfoot *Apost. Fathers* Part II. i. p. 496 f., Ramsay *C. and B.* ii. p. 722 ff. MGr κερνῶ, "pour in," "treat," "regale."

κέρας.

For κέρας (MGr κέρατο) in its literal sense cf. P Giss I. 93[5] κέρα[ς] ὀπτοῦ δέλφακος, OGIS 764[23] (ii/B.C.) κριὸν ὡς κάλλιστον κεχρυσω]μένον τὰ κέρατα. It is used of the "horn" of an altar, as in Rev 9[13], in P Leid V[x] (iii/iv A.D.) ποίησον κέρατα δ, and of a "sail-yard" in P Lond 1164 (*h*)[7] (A.D. 212) (= III. p. 164) and similarly in the famous tariff-stele of Koptos, OGIS 674[9] (A.D. 90). For the adj. κεράτινος, see BGU I. 40[3].

κεράτιον.

In P Lond 131[*recto* 147] (A.D. 78) (= I. p. 189) κεράτ(ια) is used of the fruit of the carob, as in Lk 15[16]; cf. P Leid X[xvi. 51] (medical prescription— iii/iv A.D.) (= p. 237) ἀκάνθης κεράτια. From v/A.D. onwards the word is used in Egypt, like the Latin *siliqua*, of a money-measure, the "carat": see e.g. P Oxy I. 154 *verso* (vii/A.D.) with the editor's notes, and *Chrest.* I. i. p. lxvii.

κερδαίνω

is used absolutely, as in Jas 4[13], in P Oxy XII. 1477[10] (question to an oracle—iii/iv A.D.) εἰ κερδαίνω ἀπὸ τοῦ πράγματ[ος] ; "am I to profit by the transaction?" (Edd.). Cf. Aristeas 270 ἐπανάγουσι πάντα πρὸς τὸ κερδαίνειν. For the translation "and so have been spared this injury and loss" in Ac 27[21] κερδῆσαί τε τὴν ὕβριν ταύτην καὶ τὴν ζημίαν, see Field *Notes*, p. 145.

κέρδος.

An interesting ex. of this word, which in the plur. usually has reference to money, is afforded by P Giss I. 54[15] (iv/v A.D.) (= *Chrest.* I. p. 498) σπούδασον οὖν μετὰ τῶν ἑ[τ]έρων σου καταλαβεῖν, ἵνα μὴ οἱ ἀπὸ διαδοτῶν λάβοιντο τὸ κέρδος ὑμῶν, where the editor (p. 89) suggests that the meaning may be "bakshish," "a bribe."

κερέα.

For κερέα (for form cf. Moulton *Gr.* ii. p. 81) = "extremity," see P Leid W[viii. 4] (ii/iii A.D.) ἔστιν γὰρ ἡ πρώτη κερέα τοῦ (ὀνόματος) ὁ ποππυσμός, δεύτερον συριγμός, where the editor (II. p. 168) remarks : "Nomen sacrum dei constat septem vocalibus, et duobus sonis, poppysmo et sibilo expressis, quorum hic in fine, poppysmus in initio ponitur quique hic κερέαι nominis, *extremitates*, vocantur": cf. also *ib.*[xiii. 19] ἐκλήθη δὲ τῶν θ θεῶν ἀποσπάσας σὺν τῇ δυνάμει, καὶ τὰς κερέας τῶν (ὀνομάτων) ἀποσπάσας, Βοσβεαδι. For a similar use see *Orac. Sib.* v. 21, al. In P Magd 11[4] (B.C. 221) τὴν κεραίαν = "sail-yard," and similarly in *Syll* 197[14] (B.C. 284–3) ὑπὲρ κεραίας καὶ ἱστοῦ : cf. s.v. κέρας.

κέρμα

is frequently used of "small money." "change," as in Jn 2¹⁵, e.g. PSI V. 512¹³ (B.C. 253–2) ἐμοὶ δὲ οὔπω παράκιται κ[έ]ρμα ἀπὸ τοῦ οἴνου, P Ryl II. 127³² (A.D. 29) ζώνη ἐν ᾗ κέρματ(ος) (δραχμαὶ) δ, "a belt in which were 4 drachmae in copper" (Edd.), P Oxy I. 114¹¹ (ii/iii A.D.) ἐὰν μὴ ἀρκεσθῇ τὸ κέρμα . . . πώλησον τὰ ψέλια εἰς συμπρωπλήρωσιν (l. συμπλήρωσιν) τοῦ κέρματος, "if the cash is insufficient, sell the bracelets to make up the money" (Edd.), ib. IX. 1220⁷ (iii/A.D.) πέμψ̣ε μοι κέρμα, P Meyer 23⁵ (not before end of iv/A.D.) ποίησον τὸν ἀδελφόν μου ἑτοιμάσαι τὸ κέρμα αὐτοῦ ἕως ἔλθω. In P Gen I. 77⁵ (ii/iii A.D.) a distinction is drawn between "silver" and "copper" money —ἀργυρίου δραχμαὶ διακόσιαι τεσσαράκοντα τέσσαρες. κέρματος δραχμαὶ πεντήκοντα δύο. For the dim. κερμάτιον see P Hib I. 45⁸ (B.C. 257) εἴ τι κερμάτιον λελογεύκατε φέρετε εὐθέως, "if you have collected any money bring it at once" (Edd.), P Oxy III. 533¹⁶ (ii/iii A.D.) εἴπατε καὶ τοῖς διδύμοις ὅτι προνοήσ[α]τε τοῦ κερματίου, "tell the twins also to be careful about the small change" (Edd.).

κερματιστής

appears to be practically confined to the NT and the literature dependent upon it. The verb is found in the pass. in P Ryl II. 224(a)⁵ (ii/A.D.) ἐκερματίσθη: and in P Oxy XII. 1411¹² (A.D. 60) we find the compd. κατακ[ερμα]τίζειν = "exchange" money.

κεφάλαιον.

With Ac 22²⁸ cf. BGU IV. 1200¹⁷ (B.C. 1) οὐ μίκρωι κεφαλαίωι, and for the plur. see P Ryl II. 133¹⁵ (A.D 33) οἰκοδομημένον μετὰ δαπάνης οὐκ ὀλίγων κεφαλαίων ἀργυρικῶν, "built at the expense of no small sums of money" (Edd.). Other exx. of the word with the same meaning are P Oxy II. 268⁷ (A.D. 58) ὃ καὶ ἐπε[ίσθη]σαν κεφάλαιον, "the sum which they severally consented to accept" (Edd.), ib. X. 1281⁷ (A.D. 21) τὰς τοῦ ἀργυ(ρίου) (δραχμὰς) τ κεφαλαίου, "the capital sum of 300 drachmae of silver," ib. 1273¹⁹ (A.D. 260) πάντα κεφαλαί[ο]υ, "a sum total," and P Tebt II. 339⁶ (a revenue return—A.D. 224) μ]ηνιαῖος (sc. λόγος) ἐν κεφαλαίῳ τοῦ [Θ]ωθ, "monthly summary for the month Thoth," as distinguished from individual (κατ᾿ ἄνδρα) returns (cf. Wilcken Ostr. i. p. 662 f.). In OGIS 509¹⁸ (ii/A.D.) the added interest (τόκος) produces a total amount (κεφάλαιον) of so much. For κεφάλαιον = "the chief or main point," as in Heb 8¹, cf. P Oxy I. 67¹⁸ (A.D. 338) ἐπὶ δυσὶ κεφαλαίοις τὴν ἔρανναν ποιούμενον, "let his inquiry concern two points" (Edd.), and the more technical usage in such late passages as P Lond 1008¹⁰ (A.D. 561) (= III. p. 265) ἐγγυωμένου καὶ ἀναδεχομένο(υ) τὸ [π]ρόσωπ[ον αὐτ]ῆς σὺν πᾶσι τοῖς ἐμφερομένοις αὐτῇ κεφαλαίοις τε καὶ ὁμολογήμασι, and the subscription to Bishop Abraham's will ib. 77⁷⁸ (end of vi/A.D.) (= I. p. 235, Chrest. II. 319) ἐφ᾿ οἷς πᾶσι περιέχει (i.e. διαθηκιμαίου γράμμα) κεφαλαίοις τε καὶ ὁμολογήμασι. To the literary exx. of κεφάλαιον in this sense (cf. Field Notes, p. 227 f.) we may add Menandrea p. 74¹⁷³ καὶ τὸ κεφάλαιον οὐδέπω λογίζομαι, "and the most important point I have not thought yet," ib. p. 106⁷⁵ κ]εφάλαιόν ἐστι τοῦτο τοῦ παντὸς λόγου. According to Quintil. Inst. iii. 11. 27 Menander used κεφάλαιον = caput

rei. Cf. also Eus. H.E. iii. 23(114) ἀπέβη γὰρ πονηρὸς καὶ ἐξώλης, καὶ τὸ κεφάλαιον, λῃστής, "he has turned out a villain and a desperado, and worst of all, a brigand."

κεφαλαιόω.

The natural meaning of ἐκεφαλαίωσαν which is read in TR of Mk 12⁴, and is retained by von Soden, would be "summed up," "stated summarily" (see s.v. κεφάλαιον and cf. κεφαλαιωτής, "collector," in P Oxy X. 1253¹⁹ (iv/A.D.) with the editor's note), but the context clearly requires some such rendering as "smote on the head." The explanation may be either that Mk "adopted a known word in an unknown sense in preference to ἐκεφάλωσαν, of which both sound and sense were unknown" (Field Notes, p. 35 f.), or that "something in the Aramaic original suggested it" (Allen Mark, ad l., cf. JTS ii. p. 298 ff.). The reading of NBL ἐκεφαλίωσαν, from an otherwise unknown κεφαλιόω (cf. Lob. Phryn. p. 95), may be, according to Burkitt (AJT, 1911, p. 173 ff.), a palaeographical blunder for ἐκολάφισαν.

κεφαλή.

For the literal sense of κεφαλή it is sufficient to quote PSI V. 455¹² (A.D. 178) ἐφῖδον τοῦτον . . . ἔχοντα ἐπὶ τῆς κεφαλῆς τραύματα τρία, and P Lond 47⁵ (ii/A.D.) (= I. p. 81) κεφαλὴν κομώσαν ἐθείραις. Cf. also P Par 574¹²²⁸ (iii/A.D.) (= Selections, p. 113) λόγος λεγόμενος ἐπὶ τῆς κεφαλῆς αὐτοῦ, "an invocation to be uttered over the head (of the possessed one)," and the Christian amulet BGU III. 954⁹ (vi/A.D.) (= Selections, p. 133) κλίνω τὴν κεφαλήν [μο]υ κα<τ>ενώπιόν σου. With Ac 18⁶ we may compare BGU IV. 1024ⁱᵛ·¹⁷ (end of iv/A.D.) ἐκδέξι το[ίννν] τὴν (l. τὴν) ἕως κεφ[αλῆ]ς τ[ι]μωρίαν, and to McNeile's rendering of Mt 21⁴² κεφαλὴν γωνίας, "the furthest extremity (not 'the top') of the corner," a certain support is given by P Flor I. 50⁶³ (A.D. 268) ἐπ᾿ ἀπηλιωτικῆ[ς κε]φαλῆς πρώτης μερίδος, apparently = "at the eastern extremity of the first division." In P Oxy II. 273¹⁸ (A.D. 95) κεφαλή is used of the "whole amount" of land that was being ceded; in Michel 588¹⁶ (2nd half ii/B.C.) of "the total expenditure"; and in Vett. Val. pp. 74⁷, 292¹¹·¹³, κεφαλὴ μεγάλη = πρόσωπον. The late P Lond 1075⁹ (vii/A.D.) (= III. p. 82) gives us ἀνεγκέφαλος used figuratively like our "brainless," and an imprecatory tablet from Palestine (Bliss and Macalister Excavations in Palestine, 1902, p. 174, No. 34⁸) shows a man calling down punishment on another —διὰ τὸ κεφαιλαλγεῖν με, "because I am suffering from headache."

κεφαλιόω.

See s.v. κεφαλαιόω.

κεφαλίς.

From meaning the "little head" or "capital" of a column (cf. P Lond 755 cited s.v. βάσις) it is said that κεφαλίς came to be used of the "knob" (cornu) at the end of the stick round which a papyrus roll was wound, but no instance of this sense has been found. For the usage in Heb 10⁷ (from Ps 39(40))⁸, in addition to the LXX passages (Ezek 2⁹, 3¹ ff., 2 Esdr 6²), we may appeal to Ephrem 2 (Migne 65. 168): ἔχοντα ἐπὶ χεῖρας κεφαλίδα, τούτεστι τόμον γεγραμμένον ἔσωθεν καὶ ἔξωθεν, where Birt (Rhein. Mus. N.F.

lxii. (1907), p. 488) understands **κεφαλίς** as = "roll": cf
Gardthausen *Griech. Palaeographie*² i. p. 141.

κῆνσος.

An early example of this Latinism = "capitation-tax"
(Mk 12¹⁴ *al.*) occurs in what is probably a i/B.C. inscr. from
Bizye—β]ασιλέα Κό[τυ](ν) βασιλέως Ῥησκουπορέως υἱ[ὸν]
Ῥωμαῖοι οἱ πρώ(τ)ως κατακληθέντες εἰς κῆνσον ἑατῶν θεόν
(*Annual of Brit. School of Athens* xii. p. 178). For the
meaning "census," see BGU III. 917⁶ (A.D. 348) ἐκ τοῦ
ἱερ[οῦ] κήνσου ἐπὶ Σαβίνῳ κηνσίτορι, P Amh II. 83²
(iii/iv A.D.) ἐν τῷ κήνσῳ τῷ [γενομένῳ ὑπὸ] Σαβείνου τοῦ
κην[σ]ίτορος.

κῆπος.

This homely word, substituted by Lk (13¹⁹) for ἀγρός in
Mt (13³¹) and γῆ in Mk (4³¹), is well attested in the vernacular, e.g. P Petr III. 26⁷ (Ptol.) ἡ παράδεισον ἢ κῆπον,
where Grenfell (*Rev. Laws*, p. 95) thinks that the παράδεισος
may have contained palms and fruit trees and the κῆπος
vegetables and flowers, and *ib.* 39¹⁴·¹⁵ (Ptol.), an account
for a χῶμα between the κῆποι of two men. See also PSI
V. 488¹² (B.C. 258-7) πρὸς λίβα τοῦ βασιλικοῦ κήπου (in
Memphis). BGU IV. 1141²⁶ (B.C. 14) οἵαν γὰρ ὕβριν μοι
πεπόηκεν ἐν τῷ κήπῳ, P Flor I. 16³ (A.D. 239) βούλομαι
μισθώσασθαι κήπου λαχανευομένου (ἄρουραν) α, and from
the inscr. *Syll* 590⁵ (iii/B.C.) ἀνέθηκε] καὶ τὴν οἰκίαν καὶ
τὸν κῆπον. The dim. κήπιον may be illustrated from a
receipt for a rope—εἰς τὴν μηχ(ανὴν) τοῦ κηπίου τῆς ἁγί(ας)
Μαρίας ἐπὶ τῷ ἀντλῆσαι ὕδωρ εἰς τὴν ἁγί(αν) κολυμβήθραν,
"for the machine in the garden of the Holy Mary for raising
water to fill the holy font" (P Oxy I. 147—A.D. 556).
Κηποτάφιον = "a tomb in the garden" (cf. Jn 19¹¹) occurs
in BGU IV. 1120⁷ (B.C. 5).

κηπουρός.

A ἅπ. εἰρ. in the NT (Jn 20¹⁵), but common elsewhere—
PSI IV. 330⁶·¹³ (B.C. 257-6), P Petr III. 59(a)⁵ (Ptol.), P
Ryl II. 152³ (A.D. 42), P Oxy XII. 1483⁷ (ii/iii A.D.), *al.*
In P Tebt II. 401⁹·¹⁵ (early i/A.D.) the word is spelt κηπορός
for κηπωρός.

κηρίον

disappears from the true text of Lk 24⁴², but for the word
itself see PSI V. 535¹⁹ (iii/B.C.) κηρίον ά. Cf. also P Lond
1171 verso(col.)⁸ (A.D. 42) (= III. p. 106) where we read of
an ἐγλήμπτωρ μέλιτος καὶ κηροῦ, and P Leid Wⁿⁱⁱ·⁴⁶ (ii/iii
A.D.) ποίσον (*l.* ποίησον) ἱπποπόταμων (*l.* -ον) ἐκ κηροῦ
πυρροῦ.

κήρυγμα.

P Petr III.125⁹ (Ptol.) ἔχθεμα [ἐ]χθεῖναι . . καὶ κήρυγμα
ποιήσασθαι, of a public announcement: similarly, *Michel*
390³⁶ (c. B.C. 200). In an Egyptian sepulchral inscr., reproduced in *Archiv* v. p. 169, a certain Seratus, who has
been laid between his mother and brother, announces—καὶ
ἀδελφοῦ εἰμι κήρυγμα μέγιστον, ὧν καὶ ἡ σωφροσύνη κατὰ
τὸν κόσμον λελάληται.

κῆρυξ

is common as the designation of a subordinate official in
connexion with public and other gatherings, as when at the
games at Oxyrhynchus, P Oxy III. 519¹⁵ (ii/A.D.), eight
drachmae were paid κήρυκι: cf. *ib.* VII. 1050⁶ (ii/iii A.D.).
In P Hib I. 29²¹ (c. B.C. 265), the farming of a tax upon
slaves, we read—κήρυκας δὲ καὶ ὑπη[ρ]έτα[ς] καθίστω ὁ
τε[λώ]νης, and in BGU III. 992ⁱⁱ·⁴ (ii/B.C.) διὰ κήρυκος
Ἀρχελάου τῶ[ν σ]τρατοκηρύκων, the reference is again
apparently financial. In *Syll* 226¹³² (Olbia—iii/B.C.) ἀπεδότω
πάντα τὰ ἔργα ὑπὸ κήρυκα, the word points to a public sale.
Cf. also OGIS 505¹ (A.D. 156) ἡ ἐξ Ἀρείου πάγου βουλὴ
καὶ ὁ κῆρυξ αὐτῆς καὶ ἀγωνοθέτης τῶν τῆς Σεβαστῆς ἀγώνων
. . . δήμωι χαίρειν, and for the κῆρυξ in connexion with the
mystery cult associations see Poland *Vereinswesen*, p. 395.
Amongst the seats set apart for the priests in the temple of
Dionysus at Athens we hear of seats Στρατηγοῦ—Κήρυκος—
Ἱερομνήμονος κτλ. (*Michel* 86,9ⁱᶠ—ii/B.C.-ii/A.D.). The
dedicatory inscr. of a certain choragus Eutyches, *Kaibel*
*603¹ (ii/iii A.D.), begins—κῆρυξ καὶ τάφος εἰμὶ βροτοῦ πάρος
ἀρχεχόροιο Εὐτύχους, and *ib.* 772¹ is a dedication—κήρυκι
ἀθανάτων Ἑρμῆι. In an Eleusinian inscr., *Syll* 382¹ (mid.
iii/A.D.), Nicagoras is described as—ὁ τῶν ἱερῶν κῆρυξ καὶ
ἐπὶ τῆς καθέδρας σοφιστής: Dittenberger cites Philostratus
Vit. Soph. II. 33. 4 p. 628—καὶ περὶ Νικαγόρου τοῦ
Ἀθηναίου, ὃς καὶ τοῦ Ἐλευσινίου ἱεροῦ κῆρυξ ἐστέφθη.
These last exx. prepare us for the "strange dignity and
world-wide importance" which, as Hicks has pointed out
(*CR* i. p. 44), the Gospel gave to the old title and office:
cf. 1 Tim 2⁷, 2 Tim 1¹¹, 2 Pet 2⁵, and Dibelius' note in
HZNT ad 1 Tim *l.c.*

κηρύσσω.

In BGU IV. 1024, a curious papyrus codex of the end of
iv/A.D. made up of various widely differing documents, we
find in the account of a legal process ⁱⁱᶦˣ καιρύσδετε δὲ ἡ
γυναικί, which apparently stands for κηρύττετε οἱ κήρυττε
δὲ τῇ γυναικί. On the form κηρύττω see Thumb *Hellen.*
p. 79, and on the use of the verb in 1 Cor 9²⁷ see Field
Notes, p. 174, where any allusion to the office of the κῆρυξ
in the public games is set aside in favour of a direct reference
to the *preaching* of the Gospel. A new compound ἐνεκηρύξ-
αμεν in the sense of "we applied for tenders" is found in
P Petr III. 41 verso² (Ptol.).

Κηφᾶς.

See F. C. Burkitt *Syriac Forms*, p. 5.

κιβωτός.

In P Tebt II. 270¹ (B.C. 231) we find the phrase πέπτωκεν εἰς κιβωτόν, which is confined to iii B.C. papyri, with
reference to the depositing of documents, here a nursing contract, in the "official" chest: see the editors' introd. and
cf. *Archiv* v. p. 230 f. Other instances of the word are P
Fay 121⁸ (c. A.D. 100) ἐν τῆι (for gender, Mayser *Gr.* p. 261)
κειβωτῶι τῶν ἄσκων ἣι ἔχεις παρὰ σοί, P Oxy X. 1269²¹
(early ii/A.D.) κιβωτὸς κειμένου παρακλειδίου, "a coffer
supplied with a false key" (Edd.), and BGU III. 717¹³ (A.D.
149) together with κόφινος. The word is apparently of
Semitic origin (cf. Lewy *Fremdwörter*, p. 99 f.). It may be

noted that Jos. *c. Apion.* i. 130 improves it into **λάρναξ**. For **κιβωτός** and **κιβώτιον** = "book-chest," see Birt *Buchrolle*, p. 248. MGr **ἐν κιβώτιον**, "a box."

κιθαρίζω.

In a law of Teos regulating the employment of a sum of money devoted to the instruction of children, provision is made that boys, before they are enrolled among the ephebi, shall learn **τὰ μουσικὰ καὶ κιθαρίζειν ἢ ψάλλειν** (*Michel* 498[18]—iii/B.C. = *Syll* 523[18]).

κιθαρῳδός.

With this word, as in Rev 14[2], 18[22], cf. *Priene* 113[80] (i/B.C.), where a **κιθαρῳδός** is mentioned among the musicians hired to amuse the crowd : cf. also *OGIS* 51[41] (iii/B.C.), 352[87] (ii/B.C.).

Κιλικία.

Two reff. which have a certain relation to this district may be recorded here. The first introduces us to a Cilician physician who, on visiting the tombs of the Kings at Thebes, records his impression in the words—**Θεόκριτος Κίλιξ ἰατρὸς ἰδὼν [ἐθαύμασα]** (*Preisigke* 1911). The second mentions in a boat's equipment **κιλίκιον**, evidently an article of the "coarse cloth" or *cilicium*, woven from the hair of Cilician goats (P Lond 1164(*h*)[10] (A.D. 212) (= III. p. 164). The ingeniously minded, in search of links of connexion with the NT, may be reminded by the former that Luke, even if an Antiochene by birth, may have acquired some of his medical knowledge at Tarsus, while the second points to the trade of tent-making from this very material, which Paul may first have learned in his native city (cf. Ac 18[3]).

κινδυνεύω.

In BGU II. 423[7] (ii/A.D.) (= *Selections*, p. 90) the soldier Apion after a stormy passage to Italy writes to his father—**εὐχαριστῶ τῷ κυρίῳ Σεράπιδι, ὅτι μου κινδυνεύσαντος εἰς θάλασσαν ἔσωσε**. The verb is common with an instrum. dat. in the sense of endangering one's life, e.g. P Lond 44[6] (B.C. 161) (= I. p. 34) **τῶι ζῆν πλεονάκις κεκινδυνευκώς**, P Tebt II. 283[15] (B.C. 93 or 60) **κινδυνωι** (*l.*—εύει) **τῶι ζῆν**, *ib.* 304[13] (A.D. 167–8), and P Ryl II. 68[16] cited *s.v.* **κατάκειμαι** *ad init.* For the constr. with the inf., as in Ac 19[27, 40], cf. P Par 15[10] (B.C. 120) **κινδυνεύων τῶν ἰδίων στερηθῆναι**, BGU II. 530[12] (= *Selections*, p. 61) **κινδυνεύω ἐκστῆναι οὗ ἔχω [κλη]ροῦ**, "I run the risk of losing the lot (of land) which I possess," *ib.*[30] **ἐπὶ κινδυνεύει τὰ φυτὰ διαφωνῆσαι**, "since there is a risk that the plants perish," and P Oxy I. 44[9] (late i/A.D.) **κινδυνευόντων μεταναστῆναι**, "in danger of absconding."

κίνδυνος.

In P Petr II. 13 (19)[19] (B.C. 258–3) Kleon writes to his father begging him to come and visit him at the time of the falling of the river, **καθ' ὃν χρόνον οὐθείς ἐστιν κίνδυνος**. Another pleasing family illustration is afforded by the letter of Dionysius to his brother Hephaestion, P Vat A (B.C. 168) (= Witkowski[2], p. 64 ff.), congratulating him on the news that he had been saved [7] **ἐγ μεγάλων κινδύνων**, and reminding him (Hephaestion was **ἐν κατοχῆι** at the time in the

Serapeum) that every one when he has been so saved—[17f.] **ὁπηνίκ' ἂν ἐκ κινδύνων διασωθῆι**, endeavours to come quickly and greet his wife and children and friends. We may contrast the menacing letter to a creditor, P Tebt II. 424 (late iii/A.D.), which ends—[7ff.] **ὡς ἐὰ** (*l.* ἐὰν) **μὴ ἀποκαταστασίας [δ]ὴ πέμψῃς [ο]ἶδάς σου τὸ[ν] κίνδυνον**, "so unless you now send discharges you know your danger" (Edd.). For the phrase **ἰδίῳ κινδύνῳ**, "at one's own risk," see P Lond 356[4] (i/A.D.) (= II. p. 252, *Selections*, p. 50), P Oxy VII. 1024[19] (A.D. 129), and P Ryl II. 90[32] (early iii/A.D.) **τῶν ἡμῶν κινδύνων** (*l.* τῷ ἡμῶν κινδύνῳ), where the superfluous **ν** **ἐφελκυστικόν** should be noted (Moulton *Gr.* ii. p. 113). And see P Tebt I. 105[18] (B.C. 103), P Hamb I. 5[13] (A.D. 89) for **ἀκίνδυνος παντὸς κινδύνου**, "warranted against all risks," a good example of the gen. of definition (*Proleg.* pp. 74, 235). MGr **κίντυνος, κίδυνος**.

κινέω

is used in the sense of moving away from a place in PSI V. 534[8] (iii/B.C.) **οὐ δύναμαι οὖν ἐντεῦθεν κινηθῆναι ἕως ἂν τ[οὺ]ς λοιποὺς ἀποστείλωι** (for form cf. Mayser *Gr.* p. 134 f.), and similarly of articles in P Oxy VIII. 1121[18] (A.D. 295) **ἐπιστάντες τοῖς καταλιφθεῖσι ὑπ' αὐτῆς κεινουμένοις τε πλείστοις**, "possessing themselves of the extensive movables left by her" (Ed.). Two lines earlier in this last papyrus the verb is used metaphorically—**τίνι λόγῳ ἢ πόθεν κεινηθέντες**, "on what ground or with what impulse" (Ed.): cf. the very illiterate *ib.* III. 528[13] (ii/A.D.) **οὕτως ὑ λόγῳ σου καικίνηκάν με**, "so much have your words moved me," also BGU I. 8[ii] (A.D. 247) **ἐν [τε] κεινητοῖς καὶ ἀκεινητοῖς**, and P Gen I. 54[2] (iv/A.D.) **οὐκ ἠθελήσαμεν τὸ πρᾶγμα κινῆσαι**. This last ex. leads to the stronger sense of "stir," "excite," as in the account of a Jewish revolt at Alexandria, P Par 68A[6] (Rom.) **θορυβ]ὸς ἐκινήθη** (cf. Ac 24[5]), and in P Oxy II. 237[vii. 26] (A.D. 186) where an advocate states that his client had had good reason for being provoked—**μὴ χωρὶς λόγου . . κεκεινῆσθαι**. With the usage in Ac 17[28] Sharp (p. 76) compares Epict. ii. 20. 18 **πῶς γὰρ δύναται ἄμπελος μὴ ἀμπελικῶς κινεῖσθαι, ἀλλ' ἐλαϊκῶς ;**

κίνησις

occurs with reference to the Jewish sedition in Syria (A.D. 132–5) in *OGIS* 543[15] **διὰ τὴν κίνησιν τὴν Ἰουδαϊκήν**. Cf. also Wünsch *AF* 4[28] (iii/A.D.) **ὁρκίζω σε τὸν θεὸν τὸν χαρισάμενον τοῖς ἀνθρώποις τὴν διὰ τῶν ἄρθρων κείνησιν**, and see the late P Mon I. 6[41] (A.D. 583).

κιννάμωμον.

With the spelling **κινάμωμον** adopted by WH in Rev 18[13], cf. *OGIS* 214[9] (mid. iii/B.C.) **κινναμώμου μναῖ δύο**, and P Leid W[ox. 15] (ii/iii A.D.) **φόρει δὲ κιννάμωμον**. According to Herodotus iii. 111) the word is of Phoenician origin : see further Swete on Rev *l.c.*

κίχρημι or *χράω.*

For this verb, which in the NT is confined to Lk 11[5], c.. PSI V. 510[2] (B.C. 251–0) **χρῆσαί μοι**, P Par 44[3] (B.C. 153) (= Witkowski[2], p. 82) **τοὺς χαλκοῦς, οὓς κέχρηκας Πετοσίριος**, P Oxy II. 299[1] (late i/A.D.) **Διονυσίῳ . . . κέκρηκα** (*l.* κέχ—) **(δραχμὰς) η̅**, P Tebt II. 414[23] (ii/A.D.) **δώσι Κότος** τὴν κίστην Τεφερσάιτι ἣν κέχρηκα αὐτῷ, BGU III. 814²⁷ (iii/A.D.) κέχρημαι χαλκὸν π[α]ρὰ συστρατιώτου.

κλάδος.

P Oxy IX. 1188³ (A.D. 13) ἀπὸ περσέας ζωφυτο(ύσης) κλάδον ἕνα, *ib.* I. 121¹⁷ (iii/A.D.) τοὺς κλάδους ἔνικον (*l.* ἔνεγκον) εἰς τὴν ὁδόν. In the sepulchral epitaph *Kaibel* 368⁷ a girl is described as "a branch of olive"—

Θεοδώρα, κλάδος ἐλέας, τάχυ πῶς ἐμαράνθης ;

MGr κλαδί (κλαρί).

κλαίω.

P Oxy I. 115³ᶠᶠ (letter of consolation—ii/A.D.) (= *Selections*, p. 96) ἔκλαυσα ἐπὶ τῶι εὐμοίρωι ("blessed one") ὡς ἐπὶ Διδύματος ἔκλαυσα. In P Oxy III. 528⁸ (ii/A.D.) a husband writes to his wife, who had left him, urging her return—γινώσκειν σε θέλω ἀφ' ὡς ἐκεξῆλθες (*l.* ἐξ-) ἀπ' ἐμοῦ πένθος ἡγούμην νυκτὸς κλέ(= αἰ ων ἡμέρας δὲ πενθῶ (*l.* θῶν), "I assure you that ever since you left me I have been in mourning, weeping by night and lamenting by day" (Edd.). For the form κλάω (cf. ἔκλαεν 3 Kings 18⁴⁵) see P Par 34⁷ (ii/B.C.) γυναῖκας κλαούσας, and for κλάγω see *ib.* 51¹⁵ (B.C. 160) (= *Selections*, p. 20) κλάγω ἔμπροσθεν αὐτῶν ; see further Mayser *Gr.* p. 104 f., Moulton *Gr.* ii. p. 81. MGr κλαί(γ)ω.

κλάσμα.

This late Greek word occurs frequently in two temple inventories found at Delos—*Michel* 833 (B.C. 279) and *Syll* 588 (*c.* B.C. 180). Thus in the latter we read of ¹⁸² στεφάνον κισσίνου κλάσματα, ¹⁹³ κλάσματα παντοδαπά, *al.* See also Vett. Val. p. 110³¹⁻³⁴. In Didache ix. 3f. κλάσμα is used of the broken bread of the Agape and Eucharist.

Κλαῦδα.

See *s.v.* Καῦδα.

Κλαυδία.

Notwithstanding the inscriptional evidence that is sometimes appealed to. Lightfoot (*Apost. Fathers* I. i. p. 76 ff.) has shown conclusively that there is no valid ground for the romances which have woven themselves round the names of Claudia and (her supposed husband) Pudens in 2 Tim 4²¹. It may be of interest, however, to some to recall a Lat. inscr., which he cites, mentioning a married couple bearing the same combination of names, *CIL* VI. 15066 : TI. CL. TI. LIB. PVDENS ET . CL . QVINTILLA FILIO DVLCISSIMO. See also Bernard *CGT ad l.*

κλαυθμός.

The reduction of αυ to α, which can be freely illustrated from the less educated papyri after i/B.C. (cf. Mayser *Gr.* p. 114 f.), is seen in the form κλαθμός, read six times in the *Washington Manuscript* according to Sanders (p. 21 n.: see Moulton *Gr.* ii. p. 87). The MGr κλάματα (pl.) shows the same phonetic change from the classical form κλαύματα. MGr also κλάψα (cf. the MGr aor. ἔκλαψα).

κλάω.

P Lips I. 39¹² (A.D. 390) τύψας με [ἀν]ελεῶς κλά[σα]ς καὶ χεῖράν μου ὡς καὶ τὰ ὑπώπια (cf. I Cor 9²⁷) ἔχω ἀφ' ὅλων

PART IV.

τῶν ὤ.[. . . See also the bitter epigram on a son, *Kaibel* 538⁵ᶠ (ii/A.D.)—

ματέρι πένθος ἔφυς, λύπα πατρί· [οἵ]α δὲ δένδρου κλῶν [νῦ]ν ἐκλάσθης ἔ[κτ]ομος εἰς Ἀΐδαν.

The verbal κλαστός, "curly-haired," is common in personal descriptions, e.g. P Petr I. 19⁷ (B.C. 225) (cf. *ib.* ²³ κλαστόθριξ), P Tebt I. 32²³ (B.C. 145), P Leid N⁰ 6 (B.C. 103) (= I. p. 69) (as against *auribus fractis* Reuvensius), and P Lond 1209¹² (B.C. 89) (= III. p. 20). See also the exx. of ὑπόκλαστος, "slightly curly-haired," cited by Mayser *Gr.* p. 482.

κλείς.

P Petr II. 39 (*d*)¹⁶ (accounts—iii/B.C.) κλειδοποιῷ τιμὴν κλειδῶν. For acc. sing. κλεῖδα, as in Lk 11⁵², cf. P Oxy I. 113³ (ii/A.D.) ἔπεμψά σοι διὰ Ὠρ[ίων]ο[ς] τὴν κλεῖδα (cf. *ib.*¹⁶ μὴ δόξῃς με ἡμελήκοτα τῆς κλειδός), and for acc. plur. κλεῖδας, as in Mt 16¹⁹, cf. CP Herm I. 8⁵·⁶ λαβόντες τὰς κλίδας τῶν θησ[α]υρῶν, BGU I. 253¹⁵ (iii/A.D.) κλείδας ἐπιστήσομαι. On the other hand, for κλεῖν, as in Rev 3⁷, 20¹, cf. P Oxy VIII. 1127²⁵ (A.D. 183) κλεῖν μίαν, and for κλεῖς, as in Rev 1¹⁸, cf. *ib.* IV. 729²³ (A.D. 137) ἃς ἂν παραλάβωσι θύρας καὶ κλεῖς, "any doors and keys they may have received," a common phrase in leases: cf. P Lond 216·⁹ (A.D. 94) (= II. p. 187) παραδόσθαι τὸν θ[η]σαυρὸν . . σὺν ταῖς ἐφεστώισαι[ς] θυραῖσι κ[αὶ] κλ[εῖ]σι. See further Mayser *Gr.* p. 272, Reinhold, p. 51. We can supply no good parallel to the figurative use of κλείς in the NT, but the κλειδὸς πομπὴ or ἀγωγὴ in honour of the goddess Hecate is perhaps worth recalling, when a priestess, known as the κλειδοφόρος, carried a golden key, the symbol of Hecate, in the solemn procession at Stratonicea : see *Syll* 420¹⁴ with the editor's note, and *BCH* xi. (1887) p. 36 f. A curious verbal correspondence to our phrase "having the power of the keys" may be seen in *OGIS* 229¹⁶ (iii/B.C.) καὶ ἄρχοντα δὲ ὃν ἂν ἀποστέλληι ὁ δῆμος κυριεύσοντά τε τῶγ κλειδῶν καὶ ἐσόμενον ἐπὶ τῆς φυλακῆς τῆς πόλεως, with reference to the protection of the city of Smyrna. With Lk 11⁵² cf. the new fragment of a lost gospel, P Oxy IV. 655⁴¹ᶠᶠ τὴν κλεῖδα τῆς [γνώσεως ἐ]κρύψ[ατε· αὐτοὶ οὐκ] εἰσῆλ[θατε, καὶ τοῖς] εἰσερ[χομένοις οὐ]κ ἀν[εῴξατε . . . . For the Ionic form κληΐς see *Michel* 594⁹¹·ᵈ (Delos—B.C. 279), and for the dim. κλειδίον see BGU III. 775⁸·¹ᵇ (ii/A.D.). The adj. κλειδοποιός occurs in P Oxy XII. 1518²¹ (ii/A.D.). MGr κλειδί, "key."

κλείω.

P Lond 44¹⁶ (B.C. 161) (= I. p. 34) τὴν μὲν θύραν τοῦ ἱεροῦ προφθάσαντός μου καὶ κλείσαντος, P 51⁶ (B.C. 100) (= *Selections*, p. 19) ὥσπερ κεκαλυμ[ένοι] μου ἦσαν οἱ ὀφθαλμοί μου, BGU IV. 1116¹⁵ (B.C. 13) τὴν οἰκίαν τεθυρωμένην καὶ τεθυριδωμένην καὶ κεκλεισμένην, P Flor III. 334⁸ (ii/A.D.) καὶ πάλι τῆι σῆι σφραγῖδι ἀσφαλῶς κλείσας σφράγισον τὸ δαπανηθὲν ἀνάλωμα εἰς τοὺς θησαυρούς, *Syll* 324²³ (i/B.C.) κλεισθῆναι [δὲ τὰ ἐν τῆι πόλει ἐργαστ]ήρια. For κλειστός see BGU II. 507²·⁶ (A.D. 75) μὴ ἀφέτωσαν τὴν θύραν, ἡνίκα κλειστὴ ἦν, and for κλειδόω (MGr κλειδώνω) see *Syll* 583¹⁹ (not before ii/A.D.) ναὸς . . τεθυρωμένος καὶ κεκλειδωμένος. An abstract verbal subst. κλεισμός, as in P Oxy XII. 1578⁷ (ii/A.D.), survives in

45

MGr κλείσιμο (for form cf. Thumb *Handbook* § 104), "locking."

κλέμμα

of "the object stolen" is found in *Syll* 653[75 ff.] (Mystery inscr. from Andania—B.C. 91), where an interesting distinction is made between the fate of the "free man" and the "slave"—ἂν δέ τις . . . ἁλῷ εἴτε κεκλεβὼς εἴτε ἄλλο τι ἀδίκημα πεποιηκώς, ἀγέσθω ἐπὶ τοὺς ἱερούς, καὶ ὁ μὲν ἐλεύθερος ἂν κατακριθεῖ ἀποτινέτω διπλοῦν, ὁ δὲ δοῦλος μαστιγούσθω καὶ ἀποτεισάτω διπλοῦν τὸ κλέμμα. For κλεψιμαῖος (Tob 2[13], see P Lond 422[3] (*c.* A.D. 350) (= II. p. 318) πωλήσας καμήλια κλεψιμεα (*l.*-αῖα), "having sold stolen camels."

Κλεόπας.

On the possibility of identifying Κλεόπας (for Κλεόπατρος) and Κλωπᾶς, see Moulton *Gr.* ii. p. 88. The name Κλεόπας occurs *ter* in Wilcken's *Ostraka*—1438, 1442, and 1448—(all ii/A.D.).

κλέος.

For the derived sense of "glory," "fame," which this word has in its only NT occurrence (1 Pet 2[20]: cf. Job 28[22]), see PSI IV. 341[3] (B.C. 256-5) ἀκούοντες γὰρ τὸ κλέος τῆς πόλεως, P Oxy I. 33 *verso*[12] (late ii/A.D.) κλέος σοί ἐστιν ὑπὲρ τῆς γλυκυτάτης σου πατρίδος τελευτῆσαι.

κλέπτης.

PSI IV. 395[13] (B.C. 242-1) νυκτὸς παραγενόμενοι κλέπται recalls 1 Thess 5[2]. In P Lond 46[372 ff.] (iv/A.D.) (= I. p. 70) we have a charm—[372] κλέπτην πιάσαι, "to catch a thief," in which there occurs an invocation to Hermes—[388] κλέπτην εὑρέτην. With Paul's list of vices in 1 Cor 6[9 f.] Deissmann (*LAE* p. 320 f.) compares the popular names of vices in Latin on the backs of *tesserae* or counters, which were used in an ancient game resembling draughts : thus corresponding to κλέπται we have *fur*, and to ἄρπαγες *arpax*. With the use of κλέπται for "false teachers" in Jn 10[8] we may perhaps compare the mention of φῶρες in a census-paper containing a list of professions, P Petr III. 59 (*a* ii.[9]) (Ptol.). These, as the editors point out, can hardly be "thieves" in the ordinary sense of the word : they were more likely "searchers for stolen property" on the principle "set a thief to catch a thief."

The Klefts of modern Greece have made the MGr form κλέφτης familiar to every one : to propitiate the brigands a capital letter is generally used.

κλέπτω.

P Ryl II. 134[12] (A.D. 34) ἐκλέπη μο(υ) ἐν τῇ κώμῃ ὗς illustrates a late form of the aor. pass. : cf. *ib.* 137[21] (A.D. 34). 140[11] (A.D. 36). P Oxy III. 472[14 ff.] (*c.* A.D. 130) is worth recording, as showing three different parts of the verb —ἐὰν λέγωσιν δοῦλον Σμάραγδον ἀνεύρετον γε[γ]ονέναι αὐτὸν αἰτίαν ἔχοντα τοῦ τὴν πίστιν κεκλοφέναι, φη[σ]ὶν δ οὖν καὶ πίστιν γεγονέναι ἵνα κλέπῃ, οὐ δύναται γὰρ κεκλέφθαι τὸ μηδ᾽ ἀρχὴν γενόμενον μὴ δύνατον δ᾽εἶναι, "if they say that the slave Smaragdus has disappeared being himself accused of having stolen the mortgage—he only

asserts that a mortgage was made in order that it might be stolen ; for it is impossible for that to have been stolen which neither ever existed at all, nor could exist" (Edd.). In BGU I. 322[27] (A.D. 216) (= *Chrest.* II. p. *140*) we have a petition that certain petitioners should be brought to justice —π]ρὸς τὸ . . . δυνηθῆναί με ἀντὶ πλειόνων τῶν κλεπέντων τὰ[ς σ]ταθείσ[ας] μου πυροῦ ἀρτάβας ἑπτὰ ἀπολαβ[εῖ]ν. With the perf. act. κέκλεβα, as in *Syll* 653[75] (cited *s.v.* κλέμμα), cf. MGr κλέβω, found alongside κλέφω and κλέφτω.

κλῆμα.

In P Flor II. 148[9] (A.D. 266-7) in connexion with the operations in a vineyard we have—συλλέξατε δὲ κλήματα Θηβαϊκὰ καὶ λευκά.

Κλήμης.

This Lat. name *Clēmēns* appears in the nom. (not in NT) as Κλήμης with a gen. Κλήμεντος (Phil 4[3]) : cf. P Oxy II. 241[1] (*c.* A.D. 98) Καικιλλίς (*l.*-ιος) Κλήμης τῷ ἀγρανόμῳ (*l.* ἀγορ.) χ(αί)ρειν with reference to the registration of a mortgage, also *ib.* 340 (A.D. 98-9), and *Preisigke* 4613 τὸ προσκύνημα Ἀντ[ω]νίου Κλήμεντος.

κληρονομέω.

For this verb in the original sense of "inherit" we may cite BGU I. 19[ii.1] (a petition—A.D. 135) τὰ μαμμῷα (not in LS) κληρονομεῖν, "to inherit her grandmother's belongings," P Ryl II. 117[13] (A.D. 269) τοὺς μηδὲν [τ]ῶν κατοιχομένων κεκληρονομηκότας μὴ κατέχεσθαι τοῖς ἐκείνων ὀφε[ιλήμασ-ι]ν ἢ καὶ ζητήμασιν σαφῶς τοῖς θείοις νόμοις διώρισται, "it is clearly stated in the Imperial laws that those who have inherited nothing from deceased persons cannot be held responsible for their debts or the claims made against them" (Edd.), BGU IV. 1024[viii. 16] (end of iv/A.D.) κληρονομήσι (*l.*-σει) δέκατον μέρος τῶν ὑπαρχόντων Διοδήμῳ. In all these cases the verb is construed with the acc. of the thing as generally in later writers and in the NT (cf. Schmidt *Jos.* p. 374 f.). For the acc. of a person (cf. LXX Prov 13[22]) see P Oxy VII. 1067[8] (iii/A.D.) μάθε οὖν ὅτι ἀλλοτρίαν γυναῖκαν (*l.* ἀλλοτρία γυνὴ) ἐκληρονόμησεν αὐτόν, "know then that another man's wife is made his heir," P Ryl I. 28[226] (iv/A.D.) δοῦλος δὲ αὐ[τὸν κληρ]ονομήσει, "a slave will be his heir," and for the absolute use, as in Gal 4[30], see *Syll* 386[3] (A.D. 120) where certain persons are described as— οὐσίας τῶν δεδαν(ε ισ[μέ]νω[ν κ]ατέχοντας, οὐ φάσκοντας δὲ κληρονομεῖν. The special Biblical use of the word and its cognates, in which "heirship" passes over into the sense of "sanctioned and settled possession" (Hort *ad* 1 Pet 1[4]), is fully illustrated by Westcott *Heb.* p. 167 ff. : cf. also SH p. 203 f., Dalman *Words*, p. 125 ff.

κληρονομία.

A registration of property of the year A.D. 110-111, P Ryl II. 108[9], runs—ἀπογραφόμεθα ἐπὶ τοῦ παρόντος εἰς τὸ ἐνεστὸς ιδ (ἔτος Τραιανοῦ Καίσαρος τοῦ κυρίου ἀπὸ κληρον[ο]μίας τῆς μετηλλαχυίης ἡμῶν μη(τρὸς) Εὐδαιμον-ίδ(ος) . . . κατοικικὰς ἀρούρας δύο, "we register now for the current 14th year of Trajanus Caesar the lord two arurae of catoecic land forming part of the inheritance of our deceased mother Eudaemonis" (Edd.) : cf. P Oxy I. 76 (A.D. 179), where a certain Apia writes to the strategus with reference to property that would come to her from her father who was dangerously ill—[21 ff.] οὐκ οὖσα δὲ προαιρέσεως προέρχεσθαι τῇ τούτου κληρονομίᾳ ἀναγκαίως ἐντεῦθέν δηλῶ σοι ὅπως κελεύσῃ τὸ ἀκόλουθον γενέσθαι, πρὸς τὸ μετὰ τελευτὴν αὐτοῦ ἀνεύθυνόν με εἶναι, "as I have no intention of entering on his inheritance, I am obliged to send you notice, that you may give instructions about the next step to be taken, in order to free me from responsibility after his death" (Edd.), and P Tebt II. 319 (A.D. 248) which, after describing how the property jointly held by two men is to be divided, proceeds—[24 ff.] μένοντος δὲ αὐτοῖς λόγου περὶ ὧν ἂν ἑτέρων εὑρίσκωσιν τῆς κλ[η]ρονομίας ὑπαρχόντων, "and further settlement shall be made by them about whatever other property they find to appertain to the estate" (Edd.). See also from the inscrr. *Michel* 546[19] (i/B.C.) περιεποίησεν τῶι δήμωι κατὰ ἀπόφασιν τὴν κληρονομίαν.

κληρονόμος.

For κληρονόμος in its ordinary sense of "heir," which is found in the NT in such passages as Mt 21[38], Gal 4[1], we may cite P Oxy I. 105[3] (A.D. 117–137) ἐὰν δὲ ἐπὶ ταύτῃ τελευτήσω τῇ διαθήκῃ, κληρονόμον ἀπολείπω τὴν θυγατέραν (corrected to -έρα) μου Ἀμμωνοῦν . . . , "if I die with this will unchanged, I leave my daughter Ammonous heir . . . ," P Meyer 6[:2] (A.D. 125) μετηλλαχότος δὲ τοῦ Φιλίππου ἐπὶ κληρονόμῳ υἱῷ Ἀφροδεισίῳ, "Philip has died and his son Aphrodisius is heir," and *ib.* 8[5] (A.D. 151) ἡ ἀμφοτέρων μήτηρ Διδυμάριον ἐτελεύτησεν . . . ἐπὶ κληρονόμοις ἡμεῖν. The word as involving the responsibilities of heirship is illustrated from the Macedonian inscrr. by Ferguson *Legal Terms*, p. 56 ff., e.g. No. 180—

Εἰ δὲ ὁ κληρονόμος ὁ ἐμὸς
παραπέμψῃ τι, δώσει
τῷ ταμιείῳ δηνάρια ψν.

"But if my heir neglect anything he shall pay to the treasurer a fine of 750 denarii." Attention is also drawn to the "conditions" attaching to heirship as an element common to the inscrr. and to the NT. "In the latter every man might become an heir by complying with the conditions of the promise given to Abraham. In the inscriptions the one thing most often emphasized is the obligation of the κληρονόμος to fulfil certain conditions devolving upon him as heir. When Paul insists that only those who fulfil the conditions of heirship are truly heirs, he is making use of a well-known principle" (p. 58).

κλῆρος

in its primary sense of "a lot" (cf. Mt 27[35], Ac 1[26]) is found in P Fay 125[3] (ii/A.D.) καλῶς [ποιή]σεις, ἄδελφε, μὴ ἀμελήσας το[ῦ] κλήρου τοῦ στρατηγικοῦ, "you will do well, brother, not to neglect the ballot for the strategus" (Edd.—see their note *ad l.*): see also P Lond 1220 (A.D. 202–7) (= III. p. 114 f.), a document endorsed κλῆρος πράκτ(ορος), which contains the names of two persons suitable for the post of πράκτωρ ἀργυρικῶν, to be submitted to the Prefect in order that one of them may be selected by lot—[11 ff.] πεμφθησομένους εἰς κλῆρον τῷ λαμπροτάτῳ ἡγεμόνι, and P Oxy III. 533[21] (ii/iii A.D.) ἐπισκέψασθε . . ἐπιστολ(ὴν) . .

γραφεῖσαν περὶ τοῦ ὀνόματα πεμφθῆναι ἀντ' ἐμοῦ εἰς κλῆρον τῆς πρακτορείας. "look out a letter written about the substitution of other names for mine in drawing lots for the post of collector" (Edd.). From this the transition is easy to an "office" or "post" assigned by lot (cf. Ac 1[17]), as when an incoming official, who has been elected to the office of local registrar, certifies that he has received a copy of a census-return in the words—Αὐρήλιος Ὡριγένης ἐν κλήρῳ ἔσχον ἴσον. Cf. Wilcken *Ostr.* i. p. 603 f. The word is very common with reference to the "allotments" or "parcels of land" assigned to the κάτοικοι (see *s.v.*), which were usually called after the names of their first occupiers, as in P Oxy I. 45[10] (A.D. 95) ἐκ τοῦ Μενοιτίου κλήρου κατοικικῆς γῆς σειτοφόρου σπορίμου ἐξ ὀρθογωνίου, "a square piece of allotment corn land ready for sowing, forming part of the lot of Menoetius," *ib.* 46[19] (A.D. 100) ἐκ τοῦ Ἀνδρονείκου κλήρου. In P Tebt II. 376[7] (A.D. 162) the word is used with reference to βασιλικὴ γῆ. One or two miscellaneous exx. may be added—P Lille I. 14[5] (B.C. 243–2) ἀνάλαβε ("confiscate") δ' [οὖν α]ὐτοῦ τὸν κλῆρον εἰς τὸ βασιλικόν, P Magd 1[7] (B.C. 221) a complaint against a man who, having a right only to half an allotment, ὅλον τὸν κλῆρον κατέσπειρεν, and P Petr III. 20[6] (Ptol.), where provision is made that if an ox, or any other animal, ἐμβῇ . . εἰς ἀλλότριον κλῆρον, "trespass on another man's allotment," the owner shall be responsible for any damage done. In P Par 63[105] (B.C. 164) (= P Petr III. p. 26) reference is made to the μάχιμοι or native troops who are unable to work even their own farms—οὐδὲ τοὺς ἰδίου (: ἰδίους) κλήρους αὐτουργεῖν δυναμένους—and consequently in the winter time borrow money on their rents—κατὰ τὸ ν̣. χειμῶνα δανειζομένους ἐπὶ τοῖς ἐκφορίοι[ς, in P Ryl II. 243[10] (ii/A.D.) two women write to their steward—ὅσα ποτὲ οὖν ἐὰν ἀναλώσῃς (: ἀναλώσῃς) ἰς τὴν τοῦ κλήρου κατεργασίαν, ἡμεῖν ἐνλόγησον ἐπὶ λόγου, "put down to our account everything you expend on the cultivation of the holding" (Edd.), and in P Meyer 3[20] (A.D. 148) an official order is witnessed in the words—Ἀρρε[ιο]ς . . ἐν κλήρῳ ὑπηρέτ(ης) μεταδέδοκ(α). The difficult κλήρων of 1 Pet 5[3] is probably best understood of the "portions" or "congregations" ("parisshes," Tind. Cranmer) of God's people assigned or allotted to the presbyters (cf. Deut 9[29]), while an ex. of the later ecclesiastical use of the term may be found in a Macedonian inscr., not earlier than ii/A.D.—

ὁρκίζω οὖν
τὴν εὐλογημένην τῆς Ἀμφιπολιτῶν
ἁγίας ἐκκλησίας ἐπισκοπὴν
καὶ τὸν ταύτης θεοφιλῆ κλῆρον,

where Ferguson (*Legal Terms*, p. 65) thinks that κλῆρον is best understood of "the clergy," considered collectively. Κλῆρος is apparently = "will" (see the editor's note) in the late P Lond V. 1733[35] (A.D. 594). In BGU IV. 1209[5] (B.C. 23) a man who has died is described as ὁ εὔκληρος, "the fortunate one."

κληρόω

is common in the pass. = "am assigned" or "chosen," e.g. P Iand 27[4] (A.D. 100–1) ἐκληρ[ώ]θημεν εἰς [γε]ωργίαν, BGU II. 625[5] (ii/iii A.D.) γείνωσκε, ἄδελφε, ἐκληρώθην εἰς τὰ βουκόλια : cf. Eph 1[11] ἐν ᾧ καὶ ἐκληρώθημεν, "in whom also we were made a heritage" (RV). The AV rendering "in whom also we have obtained an inheritance" seems at first sight to gain support from such passages as P Tebt II. 391[10] (agreement concerning tax-collecting—A.D. 99) τὸν μὲν Ἀθηνόδωρον) καὶ Ἡρακλῆν κεκληρῶσθαι τοὺς ἐν τῇ κώμῃ καταγινομένους καὶ ἐπικαθημένους ἄνδρες, "that Athenodorus and Heracles have been allotted the inhabitants of and settlers in the village" (Edd.) and BGU II. 405[3] (A.D. 348) ἐπιδὴ λίθον σιτοκόπτην καὶ σιταλετικὴν μηχανήν, πατρῷα ἡμῶν ὄντα, ἐκληρώθημεν κτλ., but, as Armitage Robinson (ad Eph l.c.) points out, this meaning "am assigned a thing" seems to be justified only when the acc. of the object assigned is expressed.

κλῆσις.

A section of the long legal P Hal I. 1 (mid. iii/B.C.) is headed—[222] Εἰς μαρτ[υρί]αν κλῆσις, "a call to witness": then follows a description of the process. The word is used in the same restricted sense in Epict. i. 29. 49 ταῦτα μέλλεις μαρτυρεῖν καὶ καταισχύνειν τὴν κλῆσιν ἣν κέκληκεν [ὁ θεός]; cf. ib. l.c. 46 ὡς μαρτὺς ὑπὸ τοῦ θεοῦ κεκλημένος, and see further Bonhöffer Epict. pp. 37 ff., 207 f. The meaning is raised to a higher power in such passages as Eph 4[1], where, as always in the NT, κλῆσις is the divine call to salvation. In the sepulchral epitaph of a young child, Kaibel 571[4] (i/ii A.D.), the word is used = "name"——

Φιλησίη τὴν κλῆσιν, Αὐσονὶς γένος.

And in the magical P Leid V ix.[30] (iii/iv A.D.) (= II. p. 33) τελοῦντος δέ σου, καθ' ἑκάστην κλῆσιν ἐπίσπενδε τὰ προκείμενα, the editor (p. 68) understands by καθ' ἑκ. κλ. "ad singulas invocationes, i.e. quotiescumque haec invocatio pronuntiabitur."

κλητός

is found in P Amh II. 79[5] (c. A.D. 186), but unfortunately in a much mutilated context. The way is prepared for the NT usage (see Lightfoot on Col 3[12]) by the mention of the "guests" (οἱ κλητοί) of Adonijah in 1 Kings 1[41, 49]. Slaten (Qualitative Nouns, p. 57) throws out the conjecture that κλητός was a cult term adopted by the Christians from the terminology of the Greek mysteries, but he offers no evidence. As bringing out that οἱ κλητοί, as distinguished from οἱ κεκλημένοι, denotes that the call has been obeyed, we may cite Cl. Alex. Strom. I. 89. 3 (p. 57, ed. Stählin) πάντων τοίνυν ἀνθρώπων κεκλημένων οἱ ὑπακοῦσαι βουληθέντες 'κλητοὶ' ὠνομάσθησαν.

κλίβανος.

This Ionic form, which is found in Mt 6[30], Lk 12[28] (and always in the LXX) for the Attic κρίβανος, is supported by P Petr III. 140 (a)[3] (Ptol.) ξύλα κλιβάνωι, of a furnace fed with logs of wood, the word κλιβάνωι being inserted above the line, P Grenf I. 21[11] (B.C. 126) εἰς κλιβάνου τόπον, and BGU IV. 1117[10] (B.C. 13) κτήσεως σὺν τοῖς ἐν αὐτῷ κλιβάν[οις δυσί]ν τε καὶ κλιβανικοῖς σκέυεσσιν. This last document also shows [8, 24] κλιβάνιον, and an adj. κλιβανικός. See also Crönert Mem. Herc. p. 77 n[4]. The word is probably of Semitic origin (Lewy Fremdwörter, p. 105 f.).

κλίμα.

For κλίμα, "region," as in Rom 15[23] al., cf. OGIS 519[18] (c. A.D. 245) οἱ πεμφθέντες εἰς τὸ Ἀππιανῶν κλίμα, and the magic P Lond 121[481] (iii/A.D.) (= I. p. 99) ἐξορκίζω σε κατὰ τῶν τεσσάρων κλιμάτων τοῦ κόσμου. Cf. Ramsay Galatians, p. 278 ff. For κλίμα, "slope," cf. Aristeas 59 τὸ . . ἐκτὸς κλίμα, "the side which sloped outwards (of a table)." See also Archiv i. p. 422, and cf. Kaibel 579[2] (ii/A.D.) ἑπταετε[ῖ] κλίματι, where the reference is to death occasioned by a "fall" at seven years of age.

κλινάριον.

With this rare word (Ac 5[15]) we may compare the adj. κλινήρης, "bed-ridden," in P Oxy VI. 896[33] (A.D. 316) ὁρῶμε[ν αὐτὸ]ν το[ῦτ]ον κλε[ινή]ρην ὄντα πυραιτίοις . . . συνεχ[όμενον], "we saw the man himself lying on a bed seized with a slight fever" (Edd.). The same phrase occurs in the corresponding passage of ib. 983: cf. BGU I. 45[14] (A.D. 203) πληγαῖς πλείσταις αὐτὸν ᾔκιζον καὶ ἐκ τούτου κλεινήρη γεγονέναι.

κλίνη.

An interesting parallel to 1 Cor 8[10], 10[21], is afforded by P Oxy I. 110[2] (ii/A.D.) ἐρωτᾷ σε Χαιρήμων δειπνῆσαι εἰς κλείνην τοῦ κυρίου Σαράπιδος ἐν τῷ Σαραπείῳ αὔριον, ἥτις ἐστὶν ιε, ἀπὸ ὥρας θ, where the nature of the invitation points to a ceremonial rather than to a private feast: cf. ib. XII. 1484 (ii/iii A.D.), and see Wilcken Archiv iv. p. 211, Otto Priester ii. p. 16. See also the temple-account P Oxy VIII. 1144[6] (i/ii A.D.) δαπάνης ἱερᾶς κλεί[νης] ἕως ιϛ (δραχμαὶ) ιδ, where the editors note that ἱερ. κλ. = lectisternii. In ib. III. 523 (ii/A.D.) (= Selections, p. 97) the meal takes place not in a temple, but in the house of Claudius Serapion—ἐν τοῖς (cf. Lk 2[49]) Κλαυδ(ίου) Σαραπί(ω(νος), where the difficulty of avoiding the εἰδωλόθυτον must have been specially great if the Christian was not to shun all social intercourse with heathen neighbours. In Syll 877[21] (c. B.C. 420) the word occurs (ex suppl.) meaning "bier," as in Thucydides and Plato. Had we later authority, it would be tempting to apply this in Rev 2[22]. [Charles (Studies in the Apocalypse, p. 98 ff.) understands κλίνη here = "bed of illness or suffering" in accordance with Heb. idiom: cf. Judith 8[3].]

In a will of B.C. 123 preserved in the Gizeh-Museum (Inv. Nr. 10388), and published by GH in Archiv i. p. 63 ff., the testator leaves practically the whole of his property to his wife, while his two sons receive nothing but a bed apiece (or perhaps a mattress and bed jointly) -[6] πλὴν στρώματος ἑνὸς καὶ κλείνης τορνευτῆς α. The inequality of the disposition leads the editors to remark that "the bequest of a bed may well have been the Egyptian method of cutting off with a shilling."

κλινίδιον.

Like κλινάριον (Ac 5[15]) κλινίδιον (Lk 5[19, 24]) is peculiar to Luke in the NT, and Hobart, in support of his thesis of common authorship based on the medical language of the Gospel and Acts, has collected instances of its use to denote "a litter for carrying the sick" (p. 116); but see further Cadbury Diction. p. 50 n[32].

κλίνω.

To illustrate the varied uses of this verb, we may cite P Hib I. 38[8] (B.C. 252–1) συνέβη κλεῖναι τὸν δεξιὸν τοῖχον τοῦ πλοίου καὶ καταδῦναι τὸ πλοῖον διὰ [τ]οῦτο, "it came about that the right side of the ship listed and the ship thereby sank" (Edd.), P Fay 20[14] (Imperial edict—iii/iv A.D.) ἀεὶ [ἐ]πεὶ Καῖσάρ εἰμι καὶ περικέκμηκα τὸ κλῖνον ἀναλήμψεσθαι, "ever since I became Caesar, I have earnestly striven to restore vigour to what was in decline" (Edd.), BGU IV. 1024[iv.12] (end of iv/A.D.) ποίας δὲ ἔσχεν ἐνθυμήσεις τὸν ἤδη κληθέντα (l. κλιθέντα, sc. νεκρόν) καὶ τῆς ἐσχάτης ἐλπίδας (l.—ος) ἀποστε[ρ]ῆσαι; and ib. III. 954[5] (Christian amulet—vi/A.D.) (= Selections, p. 133) εὐχαριστῶ ἐγὼ Σιλουανὸς υἱὸς Σαραπίωνος καὶ κλίνω τὴν κεφαλήν [μο]υ κα‹τ›ενώπιόν σου κτλ., "I Silvanus, the son of Sarapion, pray and bow my head before Thee" etc. See also the love-spell Preisigke 4947[1] (iii/A.D.) ἀγριανθήτω ἡ ψυχὴ αὐτῆς, εἰς τὸ παραλλαγῆναι τὴν ψυχὴν αὐτῆς καὶ κλιθῆναι εἰς τὴν ἐμὴν ψυχήν, ἵνα με φιλῇ.

κλισία.

Syll 737[74] (c. A.D. 175) ἐπ' ἀλλοτρίαν κλισίαν ἐρχόμενος. The same meaning of "couch" with reference to a banquet occurs bis in Aristeas 183. See also Kaibel 810[7 f.]—

Βάκχου γὰρ κλισίαις με συνέστιον ἐστεφάνωσεν,
εἰς ἐμὲ τὸν κυλίκων ὄγκον ἐφελκομένη.

"Bacchi sedibus me vicinam posuit eoque effecit, ut iam potatores gravia pocula mihi offerant et propinent" (Ed.). For the plur. = "companies," as in Lk 9[14], cf. 3 Macc 6[31].

κλοπή.

BGU I. 242[23] (time of Commodus) ἐξ οὗ φαίνεται ἡ κλοπή, ib. 321[12] (A.D. 216) ἡ δὲ αἰτία τῆς κλοπῆς ἐφάνη τοῦ τόπου ὑπερῴου ὄντος ἐκ τοῦ ποδώματος διατηρηθέντος τὴν κακουργίαν γεγονέναι. Cf. Syll 584[5] (Smyrna—i/B.C.?) ἰχθῦς ἱερούς μὴ ἀδικεῖ(ν) μηδὲ σκεῦος τῶν τῆς θεοῦ (sc. Atargatis) λυμαίνεσθαι, μηδὲ [ἐ]κφέρειν ἐκ τοῦ ἱεροῦ ἐπ[ὶ] κλοπῇ. The adj. κλόπιμος is found in P Hib I. 59[7] (c. B.C. 245) (= Chrest. I. p. 362) τὸ κλέ(= ό)πιμον ἔλαιον, "the contraband oil": cf. P Rev L[iv. 20] (B.C. 259–8) (= Chrest. I. p. 558).

κλύδων.

Hort (on Jas 1[6]) has pointed out that the proper sense of κλύδων is always "rough water" rather than "wave": cf. Lk 8[24], I Macc 6[11], and to the passages from profane sources cited by Armitage Robinson on Eph 4[14] add M. Anton. xii. 14. The plur. = "waves" is found in Vett. Val. p. 344[15] with reference to a ship exposed τοῖς . . μυρίοις κλύδωσιν.

κλυδωνίζομαι.

Vett. Val. p. 354[26] τὸν κυβερνήτην κλυδωνίζεσθαι καὶ ἀστοχεῖν θαλασσομαχοῦντα. The verb κλύζω, "syringe," occurs in the medical prescriptions P Oxy II. 234[ii. 39, 48] (ii/iii A.D.): cf. the subst. ib.[34] κλυσμοὶ ὠτὸς [πρὸς] πόνους, "clysters for the ear against earache" (Edd.).

Κλωπᾶς.

See Deissmann BS, p. 315, and cf. s.v. Κλεόπας.

κνήθω.

The use of this rare Hellenistic verb in 2 Tim 4[3] is well illustrated by Clem. Al. Strom. I. iii. 22. 5 (p. 15, ed. Stahlin) κνήθοντες καὶ γαργαλίζοντες οὐκ ἀνδρικῶς, ἐμοὶ δοκεῖν, τὰς ἀκοὰς τῶν κνήσασθαι γλιχομένων, "scratching and tickling, in what I consider an unmanly way, the ears of those who wish to be tickled," with reference to the "jargon" of the Sophists. For a new literary reference see Herodas iv. 51 ἔσσετ' ἡμέρη κείνη, ἐν ῇ τὸ βρέγμα τοῦτο τὠσυρὲς κνήσῃ, "the day will come when you will scratch your dirty poll": cf. for the Attic κνάω ib. viii. 8 τὸν θρύζε καὶ κνῶ, "grumble and scratch your head."

κοδράντης,

a Hellenized form of quadrans (Mt 5[26]), for which Luke (12[59]) with his characteristic avoidance of Aramaic and Latin words (see Thumb Hellen. p. 184) substitutes λεπτόν, which was ½ quadrans (cf. Mk 12[42]).

κοιλία.

For κοιλία (MGr κοιλιά) "belly," "abdomen," it is sufficient to cite P Magd 33[1] (B.C. 221) κατέκαυσεν τήν τε κοιλίαν καὶ τὸν ἀριστερὸν μηρόν, P Leid U[ii. 16] (ii/B.C.) (= I. p. 124) πεσόντα ἐπὶ κοιλίαν, P Par 18 bis[13] (Rom.) ἐπιγεγραμμένον ἐπὶ τῆς κοιλίας τὸ ὄνομα αὐτῆς - of a dead body, P Ryl II. 63[8] (astrological—iii/A.D.) Λέοντος κοιλία, and from the inscr. Syll 803[8] (iii/B.C.) ἀνήρ ἐ[ντὸ]ς τὰς κοιλίας ἕλκος ἔχων. For the usage in Phil 3[19] it is customary to quote Eupolis Κόλακ. Fr. 172 (Kock I.) κοιλιοδαίμων, "a devotee of the belly," and for the deeper, inner sense, which the word has in Jn 7[38], see the passages from the LXX cited in Grimm-Thayer. An interesting ex. of κοίλωμα = "hollow," as in the LXX, occurs in P Petr II. 13 (18a)[13] (B.C. 258–3) where preparations are made—ἵνα ἀναχωσθῇ καὶ ὁμαλισθῇ τὰ κοιλώμα[τα] πρὸ [τοῦ] τὸν βασιλέα παραγενέσθαι, "that the excavation may be filled up and levelled before the king arrives" (Ed.): cf. Lk 3[5].

κοιμάομαι.

Κοιμάομαι, "sleep," is common, e.g. P Ryl II. 127[3] (A.D. 29) κοιμωμένου μου ἐπὶ τῆς θύρας, "as I was sleeping at the door," P Oxy VI. 633[25] (late ii/A.D.) ἐποίησα δὲ καὶ τὸν νυκτοστράτηγον φ[ύ]λακα κοιμᾶσθαι πρὸς τῇ οἰκίᾳ, "I made the night-strategus sleep on guard at the house" (Edd.). In P Giss I. 19[12] (ii/A.D.) a wife writes to an absent husband that she had gone to bed without food—ἄ[γ]ευστος ἐκοιμώμην—so great was her anxiety regarding him. We may also cite the curious ostrakon-letter, O tr 1157 (Thebes—ii/iii A.D.), in which certain taxgatherers give permission to an hetaera—τῇ ὑπογεγραμμέν(ῃ) ἡμέρᾳ μεθ' οὗ ἐὰν θέλῃς ἐνθάδε κοιμᾶσθαι (cf. Archiv vi. p. 220 n.[1]). A purely middle use of κοιμηθῆναι is found in P Goodsp Cairo 3[19] (iii B.C.) ἡνίκα ἤμελλον κοιμηθῆναι ἔγραψα ἐπιστόλια β̄: on the other hand P Fay 110[13] (A.D. 94) ἵ[ν]α τὰ πρόβατα ἐκεῖ κοιμηθῆι ("may be folded") is a clear instance of the passive, as possibly in 1 Th 4[14], 1 Cor 15[18]. In Mél. Nicole p. 181 Goodspeed gives a wooden tablet "probably for school use," in which this distich is repeated several times—

ᾧ μὴ δέδωκεν ἡ τύχη κοιμωμένῳ
μάτην δραμεῖται κἂν ὑπὲρ Λάδαν δράμῃ.

The thought is parallel with that of Ps 127² when read as in RV marg., "so he giveth unto his beloved *in sleep*." See also *OGIS* 383⁴³ (mid. i/B.C.) ἱεροθεσίου τοῦδε . . . ἐν ὧι . . . σῶμα μορφῆς ἐμῆς . . . εἰς τὸν ἄπειρον αἰῶνα κοιμήσεται, and such Christian inscrr. as *IGSI* 549¹ σὺν θεῷ . . ἐκοιμ[ήθη] ἡ δουλὴ τοῦ [θεοῦ] Σαβεῖνα, *ib.* 68¹ ἐκοιμήθη ἡ θεοκοίμητος Αἰγεία, and the striking inscr. of v/vi A.D. found on the Mount of Olives (*Revue archéologique* iv. 3 (1904), p. 141—cited by Radermacher *Gr.* p. 88)—

> ἐνθάδε κεῖται ἡ δουλη καὶ νύμφη τοῦ Χριστοῦ
> Σοφία ἡ διάκονος ἡ δευτέρα Φοίβη, κοιμηθεῖσα
> ἐν εἰρήνῃ τῇ κᾱ τοῦ Μαρτίου μηνός κτλ.

In contrast to this, for the general hopelessness of the pagan world in the presence of death, see such an inscr. as *IGSI* 929¹³ κοιμᾶται τὸν αἰώνιον ὕπν(ον), *ib.* 1879¹¹ εὐψυχῶ . . ὅστις οὐκ ἤμην καὶ ἐγενόμην, οὐκ εἰμὶ καὶ οὐ λυποῦμαι, and the other citations in *Thess.* p. 56. The active is found in the illiterate BGU III. 775⁸ (ii/A.D.) πρὸς δύο ἡμέρας ἐκύ(= οἴ)μησα ἐκεῖ: cf. Gen 24¹¹, and for the form κοιμίζω, "cause to rest," which is read here in א, and which survives in MGr, cf. a fragment of an Anthology, P Tebt I. 1¹³ᶠ (*c.* B.C. 100)—

> ἐρῶντος ψυχὴ καὶ λαμπάδιον ὑπ' ἀνέμου
> ποτὲ μὲν ἀνήφθη ποτὲ δὲ πάλι κοιμίζεται.

"A lover's spirit, as a torch fanned by the wind, is now ablaze, and now again dies away" (Edd.).

κοίμησις.

This NT ἅπ. εἰρ. (Jn 11¹³) is used of "rest in death" in Wünsch *AF* 4³⁰ (iii/A.D.) ὁρκίζω σε τὸν θεὸν τὸν τὴν κοίμησίν σοι δεδωρημένον καὶ ἀπολύσαντά σε ἀπὸ δ[εσμῶ]ν τοῦ βίου. See also the inscr. to a Roman Jew, cited by Schürer *Geschichte* ii. p. 441, ἐν εἰρήνῃ ἡ κοίμησίς σου, and *Pelagia-Legenden* p. 15¹⁶ τὴν κοίμησιν τοῦ ἁγίου Πελαγίου. For κοιμητήριον, "sleeping-place," we may cite the early *Syll* 580⁴³ (1st half iv/B.C.) ἐν δὲ τοῖ κοιμητηρίοι καθεύδειν χωρὶς μὲν τὸς ἄνδρας. . . . The word in the sense of "grave" is often thought to be exclusively Christian, but Roberts-Gardner (p. 513) quote two Attic inscrr. where the accompanying figures of a seven-branched candelabrum seem to indicate Jewish origin. The first of these, *CIG* IV. 9313 (= *IG* III. 2, 3545) runs—Κοιμητήριον Εὐτυχίας τῆς μητρὸς Ἀθηναίου κὲ Θεοκτίστου. The Christian formula of dedicating τὸ κοιμητήριον ἕως ἀναστάσεως is seen at Thessalonica in *ib.* 9430, which Ramsay (*C. and B.* ii. p. 495) dates about mid. iv/A.D.

κοινός.

We may begin by citing a few miscellaneous exx. showing the varied uses of this adj.—P Petr I. 21¹⁷ (B.C. 237) αὐλὴ κοινή, P Eleph 1⁵ (B.C. 311-0) (= *Selections*, p. 2) κοινῆι βουλῆι, "in consultation together," BGU IV. 1137¹² (B.C. 6) ἔδοξε κοινῇ γνώμῃ κτλ., P Oxy II. 282¹⁰ (A.D. 30-35) τῆς κοινῆς συμβιώ[σεως, of husband and wife, P Lond 932⁴ (A.D. 211) (= III. p. 148) ὁ κοινὸς αὐτῶν πατὴρ Ἑρμαῖο[ς, P Tebt II. 319²⁴ (A.D. 248) κοινὰς τὰς ὑπαρχούσας (ἀρού-ρας), and BGU IV. 1080⁴ (iii/A.D.?) κατὰ τὰς κοινὰς ἡμῶν εὐχὰς καὶ προσευχάς. Similarly from the inscr.—*Syll* 213³³

(iii/B.C.) διετέλεσεν ἀγωνιζόμενος ὑπὲρ τῆς κοινῆς σωτηρίας, *ib.* 226¹² (iii/B.C.) τῶν δὲ κοινῶν ἐξηπορημένων, "the resources being exhausted," and *ib.* 347⁸ (B.C. 48) an Ephesian decree in honour of Julius Caesar—τὸν ἀπὸ Ἄρεως καὶ Ἀφροδε[ί]της θεὸν ἐπιφανῆ καὶ κοινὸν τοῦ ἀνθρωπίνου βίου σωτῆρα. In *Brit. Mus. Inscr.* III. 413⁴ (Priene) κοινὴν ἐπο[ίησαντ]ο τὴν ἀρχήν, κ. = "impartial." Τὰ κοινά is frequently used in the sense of "the customary formula" in such phrases as μετὰ τὰ κοινά (P Leid M¹·² —B.C. 135) (= I. p. 59) and τὰ δ'] ἄλλα τῶν κοινῶν (P Oxy II. 236 (*b*)³ — B.C. 64 : see note). This last is a common periphrasis to avoid the trouble of writing the long lists of priest-hoods at Alexandria which generally occur in protocols of ii/B.C. (see the editors' note *ad l.*, and for a further list of exx. the note on P Giss I. 36³). For τὰ πάντα κοινά = "the world," "the universe," cf. P Leid B¹¹ ¹⁸ (B.C. 164) (= I. p. 10). The technical τὸ κοινόν, "society," "guild," may be illustrated by the references to τὸ κοινὸν τῶν τεκτό-νων in P Oxy I. 53² and τὸ κοινὸν τῶν σιδηροχαλκέων ("ironworkers") in *ib.* 84¹³, both of A.D. 316 : cf. *ib.* 54¹² (A.D. 201) γνώμη τοῦ κοινοῦ τῶν ἀρχόντων, "in accordance with the decision of the council of magistrates," and P Thead 17² (A.D. 332) παρὰ τοῦ κοινοῦ τῶν ἀπὸ κώμης Φιλαδελφίας. See also Jouguet *Vie municipale*, p. 309 f., San Nicolò *Aeg. Vercin wesen*, i. p. 204 ff. In P Lond 1178⁸⁷ (A.D. 194) (= III. p. 218) κοινὰ τῆς Ἀσίας are the great games of Asia. Κοινός, "profane," as in Ac 10¹⁴ *al.*, appears to be a specifically Jewish usage, but as leading up to this meaning Lietzmann (*ad* Rom 14¹⁴ in *HZNT*) cites Plutarch *Eroticus* 4 p. 751ᵇ καλὸν γὰρ ἡ φιλία καὶ ἀστεῖον, ἡ δὲ ἡδονὴ κοινὸν καὶ ἀνελεύθερον. For the adv. κοινῶς see P Ryl II. 108¹⁴ (A.D. 110-111) κοινῶς ἐξ ἴσου, "jointly in equal shares," and for κοινῆι see P Magd 29² (B.C. 218) *al.* Marcus Antoninus (i. 16) coins the expressive compound κοινονοημοσύνη to denote "public spirit."

κοινόω.

The classical use of this verb may be illustrated by Aristeas 290 ἦθος χρηστὸν καὶ παιδείας κεκοινωνηκὸς δυνατὸν ἄρχειν ἐστί, "a good disposition which has had the advantage of culture is fitted to bear rule" (Thackeray).

κοινωνέω.

Ellicott's contention (*ad* 1 Cor 10¹⁷) that the difference sometimes drawn between κοινωνέω (partake with others in one undivided thing) and μετέχω (share with those who also have their shares) in 1 Cor 10¹⁶ ff. "cannot be substantiated" is borne out by the evidence of the inscrr. where the words are practically synonymous : cf. *Magn* 33²³ (iii/B.C.) τοὺς κοινωνήσοντας τῆς θυσίας with *ib.* 44¹² ff. (end iii/B.C.) μετέχειν τάς τε θυσίας καὶ τοῦ ἀγῶνος, καὶ ἀποστέλλειν θιαρούς, . . . τοὺς κοινωνησοῦντας τάς τε θυσίας καὶ τῶν λοιπῶν τιμίων παρ' αὐτοῖς (cf. Thieme, p. 29 f.). See also the proclamation by a Prefect, P Oxy XII. 1408²⁵ᶠ (A.D. 210-14), where reference is made to the different methods of sheltering robbers—οἱ μὲν γὰρ κοινων[οῦντες τῶν ἀδικη]μάτων ὑποδέχονται, οἱ δὲ οὐ μετέχοντες μὲν κα[. . ., "some do so because they are partners in their misdeeds, others without sharing in these yet . . ." (Edd.). This

last ex. bears out Ellicott's further remark that of the two
verbs κοινωνέω "implies more distinctly the idea of a community with others": cf. Brooke *ad* 1 Jn 1³: "κοινωνεῖν is
always used of active participation, where the result depends
on the co-operation of the receiver as well as on the action
of the giver." The editors of the Commagenian Inscriptions
(in Humann and Puchstein's *Reisen in Kleinasien und
Nordsyrien*, Textband p. 371) note the resemblance between
a religious inscr. of King Antiochus I. (mid. i. B.C.) πᾶσιν
ὅσοι φύσεως κοινωνοῦντες ἀνθρω[π[ί]νης and 2 Pet 1⁴ ἵνα . .
γένησθε θείας κοινωνοὶ φύσεως : see Deissmann *BS*, p. 368
n². Cf. also the phrase τ[οὶ τῶ]ν ἱερῶν κοινωνεῦντες with
reference to the hereditary priesthood of Heracles in Cos
(*Syll* 734⁷ ᵃⁱ): Dittenberger's Index (*Syll* III. p. 347) gives
several exx. of the verb with temples, rites, or mysteries as
the object. For the constr. with dat. of person, as in Phil
4¹⁵, cf. BGU III. 969ⁱ·²³ (A.D. 142?) ἀπηλλάγησαν μὲν
οὖν οἱ ἀντίδικοι τῆς κτηνοτροφία[ς] ἧς ἐκοινώνουν τῷ
τετελευτηκότι, P Flor I. 36⁶ (iv/A.D.) ἑτέρᾳ γυναικὶ κοινω-
νήσαν[το]ς, and the touching inscr. which a doctor puts up
to his wife (who had herself studied medicine), *Cagnat* IV.
507 ⁹¹⁹ ὡ[ς ζωῆ]ς μον[αχῇ] σοι ἐκοινώνησα, "as with you
alone I shared my life."

κοινωνία.

It is worth noting that the subst. like the verb (*s.v.*
κοινωνέω *ad fin.*) is used specially of the closest of all human
relationships, e.g. BGU IV. 1051⁹ (marriage contract of
time of Augustus) συνχωρ[οῦσι Λύ]καινα καὶ Ἱέραξ συνεληλ-
λυθέναι ἀλλ[ήλοις] πρὸς βίου κοινωνίαν, the coeval 1052⁷,
and P Oxy XII. 1473³³ (A.D. 201) συνῆλθ[ο]ν τῷ . .
Ὠρείωνι πρὸς γάμου κοινωνία (*l.*-ίαν). We have the phrase
κατὰ κοινωνίαν with gen., "belonging in common to," in
P Flor I. 41⁵ (A.D. 140), *al.* For κοινωνία="partnership"
see P Ryl II. 117⁸ (A.D. 269) ὁ ὁμ]οπάτριός μου ἀδελφὸς
. . πρὸς ὃν οὐδεμία[ν κοι]νωνίαν ἔχ[ω, "my brother on my
father's side, with whom I have no partnership," and the
commercial association of *Syll* 300⁸⁸ (B.C. 170) (where see
the editor's note). Cf. the active relationship underlying
the word in such passages as Ac 2⁴², 2 Cor 13¹³, Phil 2¹,
and the full discussion of the NT usage by Armitage Robinson in Hastings' *DB* i. p. 460 ff. With 1 Jn 1⁶ Sharp
(p. 111) compares the use of the term in Epict. ii. 19. 27
περὶ τῆς πρὸς τὸν Δία κοινωνίας βουλευόμενον, "aiming to
have fellowship with Zeus."

κοινωνικός

is used in the more primary sense of "common" in BGU
IV. 1037¹⁴ (A.D. 47) ἴσοδος καὶ ἔξοδος τοῦ κοινωνικοῦ ἐλαι-
[ῶνος, the vineyard being "common" to two properties :
cf. also P Giss I. 30⁵·³²·³⁴ (A.D. 140-161). For evidence in
support of the derived meaning "willing to communicate"
(RV) rather than "ready to sympathise" (RV marg.) in
1 Tim 6¹⁸, see Field *Notes*, p. 213 f.

κοινωνός,

as in Lk 5¹⁰, is illustrated by the fisher-compact in P
Amh II. 100⁴ (A.D. 198-211), where Hermes takes Cor-
nelius as his "partner" to the extent of a sixth share in
the yearly rent of a lake—προσελάβετο τὸν Κορνήλιον

κοινωνὸν τῆς αὐτῆς λίμνης κατὰ τὸ ἔκτον μέρος ἐπὶ φόρῳ :
cf. BGU IV. 1123⁴ (a lease—time of Augustus) ὁμολογοῦμεν
εἶναι τοὺς τρεῖς με[τό]χους καὶ κοινωνοὺς καὶ κυρίους
ἕκαστον κατὰ τὸ τρίτον μέρος, *ib.* II. 530¹⁴ (i/A.D.) (=
Selections, p. 61), where in connexion with the care of an
allotment a father writes to his son—ὁ κοινωνὸς ἡμῶν οὐ
συνηργάσατο, "our partner has taken no share in the
work." P Amh II. 92¹⁸ (A.D. 162-163) οὐχ ἕξω δὲ κ[ο]ινωνὸν
οὐδὲ μίσθιον γεν[ό]μενον τῆς ὠνῆς ὑποτελῆ, "I will have
no partner or servant who is liable on account of the contract" (Edd.), PSI IV. 306³ (contract—ii/iii A.D.) προσειλη-
φέναι Τ[. . .]ορην κοινωνὸν ἐξ ἴσου, and P Oxy XIV.
1626² (A.D. 325) οἱ κοινωνοί, "their associates" (Edd.).
With 1 Cor 10¹⁸ we may compare BGU I. 287¹⁹ (A.D. 250)
(= *Selections*, p. 116), a certificate of pagan sacrifice, where
the presiding magistrate certifies a certain Diogenes as "par-
ticipant" in the sacrifice—Αὐρή[λ]ιος] Σῦρος Δι[ογένη]
θύοντα ἅμα ἡ[μῖν?] κοινωνὸς σεσ[ημείωμαι: it should be
noted, however, that the reading is doubtful, see *Chrest.* I.
p. 152, *Archiv* v. p. 277 f. Sharp (p. 22) compares Epict.
i. 22. 10 γονεῖς, ἀδελφοί, τέκνα. πατρίς, ἁπλῶς οἱ κοινωνοί
with 2 Cor 8²³.

κοίτη

in the sense of "bed" occurs in the Serapeum dream P
Par 51¹¹ (B.C. 160) (= *Selections*, p. 19) μεταβέβλ[ηκα] τὴν
κοίτην μου, "I have changed my bed": cf. also the Christian
letter written by a sick woman, P Oxy VIII. 1161¹⁰ (iv A.D.)
—πάνυ μὴ δυναμένη ἀναστῆναι ἐκ τῆς κοίτης μου, "quite
unable to rise from my bed." The word seems to have the
general meaning of "resting-place" in P Lips I. 118¹⁵ (A.D.
160-1), where ground is set aside εἰς βρῶσιν προβάτων καὶ
κοίτην. In this way κοίτη is frequently used of a "parcel"
of land (cf. σφραγίς) as in P Ryl II. 168⁹ (A.D. 120) κοίτην
ἣν ἐγεώργει Φιβίων, "a parcel cultivated by Phibion." P
Amh II. 85⁹ (A.D. 128) ἐν δυσὶ κοίταις ἀρούρας ἑπτά,
"seven arourae in two parcels," etc. The derived meaning
"box," "chest," is seen in P Petr II. 4 (6)³ (B.C. 255-4)
διὰ τὸ μὴ εἶναι ἄρτους ἐν τῇ κοίτῃ. P Tebt I. 180 (B.C. 62 or
59) εἰσὶν οἱ δεδωκ[ότες] χαλκὸν εἰς τὴν κοίτην Εἰρήμονος.
For the verb κοιτάζω, which is found in the LXX, cf. P
Oxy XII. 1495⁹ (i/B.C.) τοὺς ἄλλους τοὺς ἐκεῖ κοιταζο[μέ-
νους, "the others who sleep there" (Edd.), for the subst.
κοιτασμός cf. P Tebt II. 423¹⁹ (early iii/A.D.) ἐὰν οὖν μὴ
ᾖς λαβὼν τὰ πρόβατα πρὸς κοιτασμός (*l.* όν), "so if you
have not received the sheep for folding" (Edd.), for ἀπό-
κοιτος cf. *ib.* 384⁶ (A.D. 10) οὐ γεινόμενος (*l.* -ον) ἀπόκοιτον
οὐδ' ἀφ[ήμερον ἀπ]ὸ τῆς [Πασώνιος] οἰκίας, "he shall not
sleep away or absent himself by day from Pasonis' house"
(Edd.), and for ἐκκοιτεία see P Tebt II. 332⁹ (*s.v.* καιρός).
With the use of κοίτη for "sexual intercourse" in Rom 13¹³
we may compare the verb ἀνδροκοιτέω in BGU IV. 1100⁹
(B.C. 13), P Cairo Preis 31²⁴ (A.D. 139-140).

κοιτών.

This late word = "bed-chamber," which is condemned
by Phrynichus (ed. Lobeck, p. 252), may be illustrated from
P Tebt I. 120¹⁴ (B.C. 97 or 64) ἐν τῶι κοιτῶ νι., P Oxy I.
76²⁰ (A.D. 179) συμπόσιον καὶ κοιτῶνα, *ib.* III. 471²⁹ (ii/A.D.)
ἐκ τ[οῦ] κοιτῶνος ἐξιόντα τὸν παῖδα. This last papyrus
shows also (²⁸) κοιτωνείτης, "chamberlain": κοιτονική μία,

"a bed-cover" or "mattress," is mentioned on an ostracon containing an inventory of clothing and furniture, *Mél. Nicole* p. 184, No. 10² (prob. Ptol.). In the inscrr. we frequently meet with ὁ ἐπὶ τοῦ κοιτῶνος = "*cubicularius*," e.g. *OGIS* 256⁶ (*c.* B.C. 130) ἐπὶ τοῦ κοιτῶνος τῆς βασιλίσσης (other exx. in Magie, p. 73) : cf. Ac 12²⁰.

κόκκινος.

To the quotations for this adj. from Plutarch and Epictetus given by Grimm-Thayer, Deissmann (*LAE* p. 77) adds a reference to Herodas vi. 19 τὸν κόκκινον βαυβῶνα. From a later date we have such occurrences in the papyri as P Hamb I. 10²⁴ (ii/A.D.) κοκκίνην, P Tebt II. 405⁵ (iii/A.D.) φορφυροῦ[ν] καὶ κόκκινον, "purple and scarlet" (cf. Rev 17⁴), and P Lond 193 *verso*³² (ii/A.D.) (= II. p. 246), the accounts of a pawnshop, which show that a "scarlet shirt" —κιτῶν κόκκινος—realized an advance of 20 drachmae as against 11 drachmae for a "new white shirt" (χιτῶν ἄγναφος λευκός). On Heb 9¹⁹ we may refer to Abt (*Die Apologie des Apul.*, p. 148), who quotes Theocr. ii. 2 φοινικέω οἰὸς ἀώτω, and P Lond 46⁸⁸⁸ (iv/A.D.) (= I. p. 77) ἅμματι φοινικίνω, pointing out "der lustrative Charakter des Purpur." MGr κόκκινος, "red" : κοκκινίζω, "blush."

κόκκος.

Ostr 1218⁴ (Rom.) κόκκου μάτας δ̄, P Lond 121⁶³⁸ (iii/A.D.) (= I. p. 104) θῦσον λιβ(άνου) κόκκους γ̄, *Syll* 807¹³ (after A.D. 138) κόκκους στροβίλου, "pine-cones." The verb κοκκολογέω is found in P Oxy VII. 1031¹⁶ (A.D. 228) ἅσπερ κοκκολογήσας ἀπὸ κριθῆς καὶ αἵρης καταθήσω εἰς τὴν γῆν ὑγιῶς, "which (arourae) I will clear of barley and darnel and plant upon the land honestly" (Ed.) : see also P Hamb I. 19¹⁶ (A.D. 225) with the editor's note.

κολάζω.

In P Fay 120⁵ (*c.* A.D. 100) εὖ πυήσις π[έ]μσ[ις] μυ θρ[ί]νακες δύωι καὶ λικμητρίδες δύωι καὶ πτύν (*l.* πτύον) ἕν, ἐπὶ κ[ο]λάζωμαι (*l.*-ομαι) αὐτῶν, the editors translate "please send me two forks and two shovels and a winnowing-fan, as I am feeling the want of them," and so in *ib.* 115¹⁹ (A.D. 101), a letter by the same illiterate writer, where the object is not expressed. The word occurs with the same meaning in BGU I. 249⁷ (ii/A.D.) ἔγραψά σοι, ἵνα δύο ἀρτάβαι σει[ταρίου] ἰδιασθῶσί μοι (*l.* ἰδιασθῶσί μοι) ἐπεὶ λείαν ἐκολάσθημεν, which gives us independent authority. The meaning "cut short," which the presumable connexion with κόλος and κολούω would suggest, seems to be the original sense of the word. In the Paris *Thesaurus* we find quotations for the meaning "prune" (κόλασις τῶν δένδρων), and a number of late passages where the verb denotes "correcting," "cutting down" a superfluity. Thus Galen *ad Gl.* 1 τὰ γὰρ ἐναντία τῶν ἐναντίων ἰάματά ἐστι, κολάζοντα μὲν τὸ ὑπερβάλλον. Of course this may be a derived sense, like that of *castigo* and of our "correct," but in any case it is clearly a familiar sense during the NT period, and we cannot leave it out of consideration when we examine this very important word. For the meaning "punish," as in Ac 4²¹, 2 Pet 2⁹, 3 Macc 7³, we may cite a Prefect's decree of A.D. 133-7, PSI V. 446¹⁴, in which he threatens to punish sharply soldiers making illegal requisitions—ὡς [ἐμ]οῦ κο[λ]άσοντος ἐρρω-

μένως ἐάν τις ἁλῷ κτλ. : cf. BGU I. 341¹⁴ (ii/A.D.) π]αρεστάθησαν καὶ ἐκολάσθησα[ν, P Ryl II. 62⁸ (iii/A.D.), the translation of an unknown Latin work, ἀγρυπνεῖται καὶ κολάζεται [καὶ τι]μωρεῖται καὶ παρηγορεῖται, and from the inscrr. *OGIS* 90²⁸ (Rosetta stone—B.C. 196) πάντας ἐκόλασεν καθηκόντως. See also Aristeas 208 ὅθεν οὔτε εὐκόπως δεῖ κολάζειν οὔτε αἰκίαις περιβάλλειν, "thou must not therefore on slight provocation punish or subject men to injuries" (Thackeray).

κολακία.

For the form of this NT ἅπ.εἰρ. (1 Th 2⁵), see WH *Notes*², p. 160. The word carries with it the idea of the tortuous methods by which one man seeks to gain influence over another, generally for his own ends, and when we keep in view the selfish conduct of too many of the heathen rhetoricians of the day (see e.g. Dion Cass. *Hist. Rom.* lxxi. 35, Dion Chrys. *Orat.* xxxii. p. 403) we can easily understand how such a charge might come to be laid against the Apostles. For a new work περὶ κολακείας by Philodenus the Epicurean (B.C. 50) see *Rhein. Mus. NF* lvi. p 623.

κόλασις.

For κόλασις = "punishment," cf. *Syll* 680¹³ (Rom.) καὶ πρὸς τὴν κόλασιν ἀγέτωσαν τοὺς αἰτίους οἱ [ἄρχ]οντες. In 1 Jn 4¹⁸ the idea of "deprivation," a kind of *poena damni* (see above *s.v.* κολάζω), is decidedly helpful : fear checks development, and is the antithesis of τελείωσις which love works. For κόλασις, with reference to the next world as in Mt 25⁴⁶, cf. the fragment of an uncanonical gospel P Oxy V. 840⁶ οὐ γὰρ ἐν τοῖς ζωοῖς μόνοις ἀπολαμβάνουσιν οἱ κακοῦργοι τῶν ἀν[θρώπ]ων ἀλλὰ [κ]αὶ κόλασιν ὑπομένουσιν καὶ πολ[λ]ὴν βάσανον, "for the evil-doers among men receive their reward not among the living only, but also await punishment and much torment" (Edd.). In the Apoc. of Peter τόπος κολάσεως = "hell," and in MGr κόλασις is used alone in the same sense.

κολλάω.

P Fay 112⁸ (A.D. 99) καὶ μὴ τὺς (*l.* τοῖς) κει[.]ασι ἀριθμὸν ταυρικὸν (*l.*-ῶν) κόλλα, "and do not unite a number of bulls . . ." The lacuna prevents our defining κολλάω exactly, and the same difficulty recurs in connexion with its four-fold occurrence in a return of temple property, P Oxy XII. 1449¹⁶,²⁰,²³,²⁴ (A.D. 213-17). The verb is found in its literal sense in P Lond 46⁴⁵⁷ (iv/A.D.) (= I. p. 80) οὕτε) κολλήσας τὸν λίθον τῷ ἀριστερῷ σου ὠτίῳ : cf. *Michel* 594¹⁰² (B.C. 270), a payment to a certain Aristarchus who had "stuck on"—κολλήσαντι—the handle of a cup. The figurative use in the NT is clearly traceable to the influence of the LXX, where the verb is nearly always = דבק. For the frequency of the verb and its derivatives in medical language see Hobart p. 128, where it is pointed out that Luke uses κολλᾶσθαι *seven* times as against *four* other occurrences in the rest of the NT. MGr κολλῶ, "glue," "fasten to," "adhere."

For κόλλημα as the technical term for a "sheet" formed of two layers of papyrus fastened or glued together, see P Leid Wᵛⁱ ⁴¹ (ii/iii A.D.) ἱς ἱερατικὸν κόλλημα γράψας τὸ (ὄνομα), for κόλλησις, "soldering," see P Oxy VI. 915[1] (A.D. 572) εἰς κόλλησιν τῶν σωλήνων ("pipes") τοῦ λου-τρ(οῦ), and for κολλητής, see *Preisigke* 805 (iii/A.D.).

κολλούριον

is common in medical receipts, e.g. P Oxy VIII. 1088[1] (early i/A.D.) τὸ μήλινον κολλ(ύριον) πρὸς ῥεῦμα καὶ ἑλκώματα καὶ πληγὰς καὶ αἱμάλωπας, "the yellow salve for discharges, wounds, bruises, and weals" (Ed.), *ib.*[12] καὶ χωρὶς ἕκαστον ἀναπλάσας μεθ' ὕδατος κολλύρια πόει ἡλίκον Αἰγύπ(τιον) κύαμον, "work them up separately with water and make pastilles of the size of an Egyptian bean" (Ed.), P Flor II. 177[20] (A.D. 257) χρήζουσι γὰρ αὐτοῦ οἱ ἰατροὶ καὶ εἰς κολλούρια καὶ εἰς ἑτέρας ἰατρικὰς χρείας (*sc.* λαγωδίων). The word is used with reference to eye-salve (cf. Rev 3[18]) in *Syll* 807[16] (after A.D. 138) where a receipt for anointing the eyes of a blind soldier is made up μετὰ μέλιτος καὶ κολλυρίου. In Rev *l.c.* there may be an allusion to the "Phrygian powder" used by oculists of the famous medical school at Laodicea: see *C. and B.* i. p. 52 (cited by Moffatt *EGT ad l.*). Cf. also Epict. ii. 21. 20 τὰ γὰρ κολλύρια οὐκ ἄχρηστα τοῖς ὅτε δεῖ καὶ ὡς δεῖ ἐγχριομένοις, *ib.* iii. 21. 21. In P Ryl I. 29 (*a*)[16] (ii/A.D.) either κ[ολ]λούριον or κ[ο]λ-λύριον could be read. On the form of the word see Moulton *Gr.* ii. p. 78 f., Dieterich *Untersuch.* p. 23.

κολλυβιστής.

This late word (Mt 21[12], Mk 11[15], Jn 2[15]), which is con-demned by the Atticists (cf. Rutherford *NP* p. 499) occurs in the census-paper P Petr III. 59 (*a*)[i. 7] (Ptol.), where mention is made of κολλ]υβισταὶ ς. Its meaning "money-changer" is determined by κόλλυβος, which from denoting "a small coin" had come to be applied to the "rate or premium of exchange": cf. the long papyrus roll of accounts P Goodsp Cairo 30[v. 12] (A.D. 191-2), the payment of a tax—κο[λ]ούβου, "on exchange," P Fay 41[i. 15, ii. 14] (A.D. 186), 56[7] (A.D. 106), and P Lond 372[7] (ii/A.D.) as published in P Tebt II. p. 339 (with the editors' note): see also Wilcken *Ostr.* i. p. 381. The subst. κολλυβιστήριον is found in the fragmentary P Tebt II. 485 (ii/B.C.) and the adj. κολλυβι-στικός in BGU IV. 1118[23] (B.C. 22) διὰ τῆς Κάστορος κολλυβιστικῆς τραπέζης, *al.* (see further Preisigke *Giro-wesen*, p. 32). The word is of Semitic origin (Lewy *Fremdwörter*, p. 119 f.).

κολοβόω,

properly = "amputate" (Swete on Mk 13[20]: cf. 2 Kings 4[12]). For a form κολοβίζω (not in LS) of this late verb, cf. *IMA* iii. 323 (Thera i/B.C. or i/A.D.) τὰ πλείωι κεκολοβισμέ-[νων] καὶ ἀφιρημένων. The subst. κολόβιον, an under-vest with shortened sleeves, occurs in an inventory of property, P Tebt II. 406[17] (*c.* A.D. 266) κολόβιον λινοῦν δ[ί]σημον καινόν, "a new linen shirt with two stripes" (Edd.) *al.*, and the adj. κολοβός, "maimed," "mutilated," in the descrip-tion of an ass—μυόχρουν κολοβόν—in P Gen I. 23[5] (A.D. 70) *al.*: cf. P Petr III. 19 (*g*)[2] (Ptol.), P Oxy I. 43 *verso*[v. 9] (iii/A.D.). The epithet ὁ κολοβοδάκτυλος, "the stump-fingered," applied to Mark in iii/A.D. (Hippolytus *Philos.* vii. 30), has been traced to a desire on the part of the philosophers to ridicule the shortness of his Gospel, but is

more probably due to some natural defect of the evangelist himself : see a curious note by Nestle, *ZNTW* iv. p. 347.

κόλπος.

With the figurative use of κόλπος in the NT (Lk 16[22], *al.*) we may compare its occurrence in sepulchral epitaphs, e.g. *Preisigke* 2034[11] ἀνάπαυσον τὴν ψυχὴν τοῖς δούλοις σου πιστὰ ἐν κόλποις Ἀβρὰμ καὶ Ἰσὰκ καὶ Ἰακώβ, and *Kaibel* 202[1] Τύ[μ]βος μὲν κρύ[πτ]ει με τὸν ἐν κόλπ[οισι] τραφέντα, where the editor draws attention to the "frigidum acumen" with which τύμβος and κόλποι are contrasted. On the other hand κόλπος is used of a sepulchre in *ib.* 1135[2], and in *ib.* 237[3] (ii/B.C.) we have—Ἀΐδεω νυχίοιο μέλας κόλπος: cf. *ib.* 50[1] Σῶμα σὸν ἐν κόλποις, Καλλιστοῖ, γαῖα καλύπτει, with reference to the "bosom" of mother Earth. See also Herondas vi. 101 f. οὐ γὰρ ἀλλὰ πορθεῦ[σι] ὤρν[ι]θο[κ]λέ[π]ται, κἢν τρέφη τις ἐν κόλπῳ. "for the bird-stealers will plunder out of one's very lap" (Nairn). For the meaning "bay," "gulf," as in Ac 27[39], cf. *OGIS* 441[213] (B.C. 81) Σελεύκεια [ἡ π]ρὸς τῶι Ἰσσικῶ[ι κ]όλπωι.

κολυμβάω.

For this verb which properly means "dive," but is used = "swim" in Ac 27[43], Hobart (p. 283) refers to the medical writer Galen, by whom it is used of invalids taking exercise in a swimming-bath (κολυμβήθρα). With ἐκκολυμβάω in Ac 27[42] we may compare *Syll* 803[20] (iii/B.C.) οὗτος [ἀ]ποκο-λυμ[βήσ]ας εἰς τὰν θ[άλασσ]αν ἔπειτα δενδρύων ("lurking in the wood") εἰς τόπον ἀφίκετο ξηρόν. The subst. κολυμ-βητής is found in *Preisigke* 3747 (i/B.C.). MGr κολυμπῶ, "dive," "swim."

κολυμβήθρα.

For the later ecclesiastical usage of κ., "font," see P Oxy I. 147[2] (A.D. 556), cited *s.v.* κῆπος *sub fin.*

κολωνία.

This designation is given to a settlement of veteran soldiers, established by Severus and Caracalla in the neighbourhood of the village Kerkesoucha in the Fayûm, *Chrest.* I. 401 (beginning of iii/A.D.): cf. also P Oxy III. 653 (A.D. 160-2) (κολωνεία *bis*) and *ib.* XII. 1508 (ii/A.D.), which throws light on the manner in which the land was obtained. On the whole position of these *coloniae*, see Wilcken *Archiv* v. p. 433 f., and the introd. to P Giss I. 60, p. 29. A fourth century inscr. from Eaccaea, *Kaibel* 908[6], ends—εὐτυχίτω ἡ κολωνία.

κομάω.

An interesting illustration of this verb, which in Bibl. Greek is confined to 1 Cor 11[14 f.], is afforded by BGU I. 16[11] (A.D. 159-160) (= *Selections*, p. 84), where a charge is brought against a priest of "letting his hair grow too long and of wearing woollen garments"—ὡς κομῶντος [κ]αὶ χρω[μ]ένου ἐρεαῖς ἐσθήσεσι: cf. Herod. ii. 36 f.

κόμη.

With 1 Cor 11[15] we may compare *Cagnat* IV. 1019[8] κοματροφήσαν[τος] τοῦ υἱοῦ μου Αὐρ. with the editor's note —"comam pascere, ut deo postea consecraretur, crebrior religio fuit " : see also *Syll* 420 n². For κ. = "foliage," see P Petr III. 43(2) *verso*[iv. 10] (B.C. 246) π[αρ]αφρυγανίσαι τὸ χῶμα τ[ῆ]ι μυρικίνηι κόμηι.

κομίζω

in the sense of "bring," "carry," as in Lk 7³⁷, may be illustrated from P Petr III. 53(*k*)⁵ (iii/B.C.) κομιοῦμεν γάρ σοι ταύτην τε καὶ τὴμ πρὸς Παγκράτην ἐπιστολήν, P Tebt I. 55⁴ (late ii/B.C.) κεκόμικε δέ μοι ὁ παρὰ σοῦ ἅμιος (ἀρτάβην) ᾶ, "your agent has brought me one artaba of ami" (Edd.), P Oxy II. 296³ (i/A.D.) δὸς τῷ κομίζοντί σου τὴν ἐπιστολὴν τὴν λαογραφίαν Μνησιθέου, "give the bearer of this letter the poll-tax of Mnesitheus," and BGU III. 417³² (ii/iii A.D.) τὰ ὀξείδιά μοι κόμισον. The middle is very common with the meaning "receive," e.g. BGU IV. 1206⁴ (B.C. 28) κεκόμισμαι ἃ ἐγέγραφις (on pluperf. see *Proleg.* p. 148), P Fay 114³ (A.D. 100) κομισάμενός μου τὴν ἐπιστολήν, "on receipt of my letter," P Oxy VIII. 1153³ (i/A.D.) ἐ]κομισάμην διὰ Ἡρακλᾶτος τὰς κίστας [σὺν] τοῖς βιβλίοις, "I have received through Heraclas the boxes with the books," *ib.* III. 530¹⁰ (ii/A.D.) κόμισ[αι] παρὰ Χ[αιρ]ήμονος τ[ο]ῦ κομίζοντός σο[ι] τὸ [ἐπι]στόλιον ἀργυρίου δραχμὰς ἑκατὸν δέκ[α] δύο, "receive from Chaeremon the bearer of this letter 112 drachmae of silver," *ib.* VI. 963 (ii/iii A.D.) χάριν δέ σοι οἶδα, μῆτερ, ἐπὶ τῇ σπουδῇ τοῦ καθεδραρίου ("stool"), ἐκομισάμην γὰρ αὐτό, and *ib.* XII. 1493⁷ (Christian—iii/iv A.D.) ἐκομισάμην σου τὸν υἱὸν εὐρωστοῦντα ὁλοκληροῦντα διὰ παντός, "I received your son safe and sound in every respect" (Edd.). For the further meaning "receive back," "recover," which the middle apparently has in all its NT occurrences (cf. Hort on 1 Pet 1⁹) we can cite such passages as P Hib I. 54⁹ (*c.* B.C. 245) (= *Chrest.* I. p. 563) ἐάν τι δέῃ ἀνηλῶσαι δός, παρὰ δὲ ἡμ[ῶ]ν κομι(εῖ), "if any expense is necessary, pay it, and you shall recover it from us" (Edd.), and P Tebt I. 45³³ (B.C. 113) διὸ ἐπιδίδωμί σοι . . ἵνα τῶν ἐγκαλουμένων κατασταθέντων ἐγὼ μὲν κομίσωμαι τὰ ἐμαυτοῦ, "I therefore present this complaint to you in order that the accused having been produced I may recover my property" (Edd.). Hence the use of the verb in connexion with recovering a debt, getting it paid—P Hamb I. 27⁵ (B.C. 250) τὴν δὲ τιμὴν οὔπω ἐκεκόμιστο, P Eleph 13⁵ (B.C. 223-2) περὶ δὲ τῶν εἴκοσι δραχμῶν οὔπω ἐκεκόμιστο Φίλων, Πιστοκλῆς (*l.* -κλέα) [γ]ὰρ οὐχ εὑρήκειμεν, P Oxy I. 101²³ (A.D. 142) ἕως τὰ κατ' ἔτος ὀφειλόμενα κομίσηται, "until the yearly rent is paid."

κομψός.

With the adverbial phrase Jn 4⁵² κομψότερον ἔσχεν, "got better" (rather than "began to amend" AV, RV), cf. P Fay 18⁵ κομψῶς ἔχω, P Tebt II. 414¹⁰ (ii/A.D.) ἐὰν κομψῶς σχῶ πέμψω [τ]ῇ θυγατρί σου κοτύλην ἴρις ("a cotyle of orris-root"), P Oxy VI. 935⁵ (iii/A.D.) θεῶν συνλαμβανόντων ἡ ἀδελφὴ ἐπὶ τ[ὸ] κομψότερον ἐτράπη, "with the assistance of heaven our sister has taken a turn for the better" (Edd.). See also Epict. iii. 10. 13 ὅταν ὁ ἰατρὸς εἰσέρχηται, μὴ φοβεῖσθαι τί εἴπῃ, μηδ' ἂν εἴπῃ ʽκομψῶς ἔχεις,ʼ ὑπερχαίρειν : *ib.* ii. 18. 14 γίγνωσκε ὅτι κομψῶς σοί ἐστι. Κόμψη is found as a woman's name in *Preisigke* 4119.

κονιάω,

"whitewash," is found in a series of temple accounts, *Michel* 594⁹¹ (Delos—B.C. 279) τὴν θυμέλην τοῦ βωμοῦ τοῦ ἐν τῇ νήσωι κονιάσαντι Φιλοκράτει. The pass., as in Mt 23²⁷, occurs in *CIG* I. 1625¹⁶. For κονία, "plaster," and κονιατής, "plasterer," see P Oxy XII. 1450 ⁴,⁶ (A.D. 249-50), and for κονίασις, "plastering," P Flor III. 384⁷³ (v/A.D.) τὴν τῶν δωμάτων κονίασιν, and for κονίαμα PSI V. 547¹⁹ (iii/B.C.) τὴν κρύπτην ὁμοίαν τῶι κονιάματι. In the private account P Oxy IV. 739⁷ (*c.* A.D. 1) κονίου εἰς πρ[ο]σφαγίου (ὀβολός), the meaning may be "powder (?) for a relish 1 ob." (Edd.).

κονιορτός.

Chrest. I. 198¹⁶ (B.C. 240) κ.[. . . . .]ματα ἀπὸ τῆς ἅλω σὺν τῶι κονιορτῶι ἀ(ρτάβαι) ιε̄—a declaration for purposes of taxation. For κόνις, "dust," see *Kaibel* 622³ φθίμενος τῇνδ' ἐπίκειμαι κόνιν, "in death I have this dust laid upon me."

κοπάζω.

On the Ionic origin of this word = "cease," "sink to rest," which survives in MGr, see Thumb *Hellen.* pp. 209, 211, 214. Cf. Hesychius κόπασον· ἡσύχασον.

κοπετός.

For this familiar LXX word, which in the NT is confined to Ac 8², we may compare *Kaibel* 345³⁴—

μῆτερ ἐμή, θρῆν[ων ἀ]ποπαύεο, λ[ῆ]ξον ὀδυρμῶν
κ[αὶ] κοπετῶν· Ἀίδης οἶκ[τ]ον ἀποστ[ρέφ]εται.

κοπή

is common in the papyri = "cutting," e.g. P Oxy II. 280¹⁷ (A.D. 88-9) τὸ μὲν ἥμισυ εἰς ἄρωσιν τὸ δὲ ἕτερον ἥμισυ εἰς κοπήν, "the half for ploughing, the other half for cutting," *ib.* III. 499¹⁵ (A.D. 121) χόρτον εἰς κοπὴν καὶ ἐπινομήν, "grass for cutting and grazing." In P Rev L[Mᵛ.⁵] (B.C. 259) οἱ κοπεῖς are the men who cut the crop in an oil-factory—a new sense of the word. See also *s.v.* θρίξ, and for the impost called κοπὴ τριχός cf. P Tebt II. p. 66. In a curious medical questionnaire, certainly later than ii/A.D., we find—τί ἐστιν κ[οπή] ; [ἡ τῶν] σωμάτων τομή (see *Archiv* ii. p. 1 ff.).

κοπιάω.

The special Biblical sense of this verb, "work hard," "toil," may perhaps be seen in Vett. Val. p. 266⁸ ἱλαροὺς περὶ τὰς πράξεις καὶ μεθ' ἡδονῆς κοπιῶντας. Lightfoot on Ignat. *ad Polyc.* vi. thinks that the notion of "toilsome training" for an athletic contest underlies the word, and cites Phil 2¹⁶, Col 1²⁹, 1 Tim 4¹⁰, in illustration; but it should be noted that the word can also be used without any such metaphorical reference, as in LXX 2 Kings (Sam) 17², Isai 49⁴, Sir 51²⁷: see also Field *Notes*, p. 7. An uncommon usage is found in P Leid Xᵛ·²⁷ (iii/iv A.D.), where in a recipe for making silver the direction occurs—καὶ ἔμβαλε τὴν πίσσαν τὴν ξηράν, ἕως κοπιάσῃ, "et inicito picem siccam, donec saturatum sit" (Ed.). For the form κεκοπίακες in Rev 2³ see W Schm *Gr.* p. 113, n¹⁶.

κόπος.

For the phrase κόπους παρέχειν τινί, which occurs four times in the NT (also once with sing. κόπον) = "to give trouble to one," see P Tebt I. 21[10] (B.C. 115) ἐὰν δέ σοι κόπους παρέχηι συναναβαίνε αὐτῷ. "if he gives you trouble, go up with him" (Edd.), BGU III. 844[12] (A.D. 83) κόπους γάρ μο[ι] παρέχει ἀσθενοῦντι. For the word, which survives in MGr, see also P Amh II. 133[11] (early ii/A.D.) μετὰ πολλῶν κόπων ἀνηκάσαμεν αὐτῶν ἀντασχέσθαι (l. ἠναγκάσαμεν αὐτοὺς ἀντισχέσθαι) τῆς τούτων ἐνεργγίας ἐπὶ τῷ προτέρῳ ἐκφορίῳ (l. -ίῳ), "with great difficulty I made them set to work at the former rent" (Edd.), P Oxy XII. 1482[6] (ii/A.D.) οὐ οὕτως αὐτὴν λελικμήκαμεν μετὰ κόπου "we never had so much trouble in winnowing it (sc. barley)" (Edd.).

κοπρία.

This NT ἅπ. εἰρ. (Lk 14[35]) may be illustrated from P Oxy I. 37[i. 6] (A.D. 49) (= Selections, p. 49) Πεσοῦρις . . . ἀνεῖλεν ἀπὸ κοπρίας ἀρρενικὸν σωμάτιον ὄνομα Ἡρακ[λᾶν, "Pesouris picked up from the dung-heap a male foundling named Heraclas," P Ryl II. 162[17] (A.D. 159) βορρᾶ κοπρία, "on the north a dung-heap." On this word as common to the NT and the comic poets, see Kennedy Sources, p. 72 ff.: it survives in MGr. The wider usage of κοπρία to denote the spot where all kinds of rubbish are gathered together is discussed by Wilcken Archiv ii. p. 311 f.

κόπριον.

For this diminutive = "dung," "manure," which in the NT occurs only in Lk 13[8] in the plural, it is sufficient to refer to P Fay 110[5] (A.D. 94) ἀναγκάσας ἐκχωσθῆναι τὸ ἐν αὐτῶι κόπριον, "have the manure there banked up" (Edd.), ib.[10] χώρισον τὸ κόπριον εἰς τὴν κοπρηγίαν, "take away the manure to the manure heap," P Oxy III. 502[32] (A.D. 164) premises καθαρὰ ἀπὸ κοπρίων, "free from filth," and OGIS 483[81] (ii/B.C.) ἐὰν τινες μὴ ἀποδιδῶσιν τῶν κοινῆι ἀνακαθαρθ(έ)ντων ἀμφόδων τὸ γεινόμενον μέρος τῆς ἐκδόσεως τῶν κοπρίων ἤ τῶν ἐπιτίμων, λαμβανέτωσαν αὐτῶν οἱ ἀμφοδάρχαι κτλ. Ἡ κόπρος (cf. Exod 29[14]) occurs in P Oxy IV. 729[10] (A.D. 137) τὴν δὲ αὐτάρκιαν κόπρον περιστερῶν πρὸς κοπρισμὸν τοῦ κτή[μ]ατος, "the necessary amount of pigeon's dung for manuring the vineyard," ib. VI. 934[10] (iii/A.D.) μὴ οὖν ἀμελήσης τοῦ βαλεῖν τὴν κόπρον, "do not fail therefore to throw the manure on the land," Michel 594[43] (B.C. 279) τῶμ περιστερῶν τῆς κόπρου, al. See also P Fay 119[33] (c. A.D. 100) πέμψις τὰ κτήνη κοπρηγεῖν εἰς τὸ λάχανον τῆς Ψινάχεως καὶ τὰ κοπρηγά, "send the animals to carry manure at the vegetable-ground at Psinachis and the manure-carts" (Edd.).

κόπτω

in its original sense of "cut" may be illustrated by PSI II. 171[39] (ii/B.C.) κόψας τοὺς ἐν αὐτῶι φ[οίνι]κας, P Tebt I. 5[205] (B.C. 118) τοὺς κεκοφότας τῶν ἰδίων ξύλα, "those who have cut down wood on their own property" (Edd.), P Ryl II. 228[12] (i/A.D.) ὄργανο(ν) τροχ(οῦ) τὸ εἰς κόπτειν, "machinery of the wheel for cutting" (Edd.), ib. 236[24] (A.D. 256) ποίησον δὲ ἐξαυτῆς ὤμους δύο ἐλαιουργικοὺς κοπῆναι, "have two beams (?) cut at once for oil-presses"

(Edd.), P Oxy XII. 1421[4] (iii/A.D.) τὸ ξ[ύ]λον τὸ ἀκάνθινον τὸ κεκομμένον ἐν τῇ Εἰόνθει, "the acacia-wood which has been cut at Ionthis." For the simplex κόπτω as an equivalent of the immediately preceding compd. ἐκκόπτω, see P Fay 114[14 ff.] (A.D. 100) θέλι ἐξ αὐτοῦ ἐκκόψαι φυτά, εἴνα ἐνπίρος κοπῇ τὰ μέλλοντα ἐκκόπτεσθαι, "he wishes to cut down some trees, so that those which are to be cut down may be cut skilfully" (Edd.): cf. Proleg. p. 115 for exx. of the survival in NT Greek of this classical idiom. A new noun κόπτρον is found in P Lond 1171[62] (B.C. 8) (= III. p. 179) κόπτρα ἀράκου : for κοπτός, "a cake," see P Oxy I. 113[31] (ii/A.D.). MGr κόβ[γ]ω, κόφτω.

κόραξ.

P Magd 21[5] (B.C. 221) ὕστερον δὲ αὐτὴν εὕρομεν ὑπὸ τῶν [κυνῶν καὶ τ]ῶν κοράκω[ν διαβεβρωμένην, "but afterwards we found it (sc. a sheep) devoured by the dogs and the ravens." MGr κόρακας.

κοράσιον.

P Strass I. 79[2] (a deed of sale—B.C. 16-15) κοράσιον δουλικόν, BGU III. 887[9] (A.D. 151) πέπρ[ακα τὸ] κ[ορ-[ά]σ[ι]ον δηναρίων τριακοσίων πεντή[κοντα, ib. 913[7] (A.D. 206) δουλικὸ[ν] αὐτῆς κοράσιον—a female slave, and P Lond 331[5] (A.D. 165) (= II. p. 154) where a certain Cosmas is hired σὺν ἐπιστή(μοσι) . . . τρισὶ καὶ κορασίοις τέσσαρασι (l. τέσσαρσι), "with three . . . and four girls" (not "lads" as Ed.) to assist at a village-festival (see Wilcken Archiv i. p. 153, iii. p. 241). The word, which survives in MGr, is late and colloquial (cf. Sturz Dialect. p. 42 f.), and the idea of disparagement which old grammarians noticed (cf. Lob. Phryn. p. 73 ff., Rutherford NP, p. 148) reappears to some extent in the above papyri, though it is wanting in LXX and NT ("cum nulla εὐτελισμοῦ significatione") : see Kennedy Sources, p. 154.

κορέννυμι.

Kaibel 314[21 f.] (iii/A.D.)—

οὐδ' οὕτως μου γένεσις δεινὴ πλησθεῖσ' ἐκορέσθη,
ἀλλ' ἑτέραν πάλι μοι νόσον ἤγαγε γαστρὸς μοῖρα.

κόρος.

This Hellenized Semitic word denoting a measure, cor or homer = 10 ephahs, is fairly common in the LXX, but in the NT is confined to Lk 16[7]. See Lewy Fremdwörter, p. 116.

κοσμέω.

In P Oxy XII. 1467[5] (A.D. 263) reference is made to certain laws which entitle women "who are honoured with the right of three children"—ταῖς γυναιξὶν ταῖς τῶν τριῶν τέκνων δικαίῳ κεκοσμημένα[ι]ς—to act without a guardian. The metaphorical use of the verb, as in Tit 2[10], is seen in Cagnat IV. 288[9] (ii/B.C.) κ[εκ]όσμηκε τὸν αὐτοῦ [β]ίον τῆι καλλίστηι παρρησίαι, and in the important Priene 105[6] (B.C. 9), where Augustus is described as "having made war to cease, and established order everywhere"—τὸν παύσαντα μὲν πόλεμον, κοσμήσοντα [δὲ πάντα. Epict. iii. 1. 26 τὸ λογικὸν ἔχεις ἐξαίρετον· τοῦτο κόσμει καὶ καλλώπιζε· τὴν κόμην δ'ἄφες τῷ πλάσαντι ὡς αὐτὸς ἠθέλησεν, "your reasoning faculty is the distinctive one : this you must adorn and make beautiful. Leave your hair to Him that formed it in accordance with His will " (Matheson), may be cited in illustration of 1 Pet 3³⁶.

κόσμιος.

"orderly," "virtuous," which in the NT is confined to 1 Tim 2⁹, 3², is common as an epithet of honour in the inscrr., e.g., Magn 165⁶ διὰ τὴν τοῦ ἤθους κόσμιον (for form see Blass Gr., p. 33) ἀναστροφήν, ib. 179¹ (ii/A.D.) διὰ . . τὴν ἰς τὴν πόλιν αὐτοῦ κόσμιον ἀναστροφήν, and OGIS 485³ (Roman) ἄνδρα . . . ἤθει καὶ ἀγωγῇ κόσμιον. Sharp (p. 52) quotes Epict. Ench. 40 κόσμιαι . . καὶ αἰδήμονες of women, as in 1 Tim 2⁹ : cf. also the late PSI I. 97¹ (vi/A.D.) τὴν ἐμὴν κοσμι(ίαν) [γυναῖκα. For the subst. κοσμιότης, see Syll 371¹¹ (time of Nero), where a physician is praised ἐπὶ . . τῇ κοσμιότητι τῶν ἠθῶν, and an honorific inscr. BCH xi. (1887). p. 348 διά τε τὴν ἰδίαν αὐτοῦ κοσμιότητα καὶ διὰ τὰς τῶν προγόνων εὐεργεσία[ς.

κοσμίως.

This adverb, which is read in 1 Tim 2⁹ אD₂*G (WH marg.), occurs, like the adj. κόσμιος (q.v.), as a descriptive epithet in the inscrr., e.g. Cagnat IV. 255⁹ ἄνδρα . . . ἐζηκότα τε καλῶς καὶ κοσμίως, πάσης ἀρετῆς ἕνεκεν, ib. 785¹⁴ (early iii/A.D.) (= C. and B. ii. p. 466) ἄνδρα . . . στρατηγήσαντα γ̄ ἁγνῶς, ἀγωνοθετήσαντα φιλοτείμως, εἰρηναρχήσαντα κοσμίως, and Magn 162⁸ ζήσαντα σωφρόνως καὶ κοσμίως (cf. 1 Tim 3²). See also Vett. Val. p. 355⁷⁰ διὰ τῆς ἰδίας ἐγκρατείας ἀκηρύκτως καὶ κοσμίως τὸ τέλος τοῦ βίου ὑποίσει.

κοσμοκράτωρ.

The Emperor Caracalla receives this title in an Egyptian inscr. Archiv ii. p. 449, No. 83.

κόσμος.

Interesting exx. of ὁ κόσμος, "the world," are afforded by OGIS 458¹⁰ (c. B.C. 9) (= Priene 105), where the birthday of the divine Augustus is referred to as the beginning of good news to the world—ἦρξεν δὲ τῶι κόσμωι τῶν δι' αὐτὸν εὐανγελί[ων ἡ γενέθλιος] τοῦ θεοῦ, and Syll 376³¹ where, on the occasion of the proclamation of the freedom of all the Greeks at the Isthmian games in A.D. 67, the Emperor Nero is described as ὁ τοῦ παντὸς κόσμου κύριος Νέρων. With the hyperbolical usage in Rom 1⁸ we may compare a sepulchral inscr. from Egypt, in which a certain Seratus states that he lies between mother and brother—ὧν καὶ ἡ σωφροσύνη κατὰ τὸν κόσμον λελάληται (Archiv v. p. 169, No. 24⁸): see also P Lond 981¹⁰ (iv/A.D.) (= III p. 242, Chrest. I. p. 157) ἡ γὰρ εὐφημία σου, πάτερ, περιεκύκλωσεν τὸν κ[όσ]μον ὅλον ὡς ἀγαθὸν πατέρα—a letter to a bishop. Other exx. of the word are OGIS 56¹⁵ (iii/B.C.) μετελθεῖν εἰς τὸν ἀέναον κόσμον, and PSI III. 157³⁶ (an astrological song —iii/A.D.) where κόσμος = οὐρανός (cf. Gen 2¹, Deut 4¹⁹). For the plur. = "magistrates," see OGIS 270¹⁰ (mid. ii/B.C.) ἐπιμ[ε]λὲς γενέσθω τοῖς κόσμοις, ὅπως καρυχθῇ, and for the collective sing. in the same sense see the exx. collected by Dittenberger Syll 427 n.¹: cf. also the use of the compd. εὔκοσμος in ib. 737⁹¹ (c. A.D. 175) of "magistratus collegii

constitutus ad ordinem et decorem in conventibus sodalium conservandum" (Dittenberger).

For the word = "adornment," as in 1 Pet 3³, see P Eleph 1⁴ (B.C. 311–10) (= Selections, p. 2) εἱματισμὸν καὶ κόσμον (δραχμὰς) ‿α, with reference to a bride's trousseau, PSI III. 240¹² (ii/A.D.) γυνα[ι]κεῖον κόσμον, OGIS 531¹³ (A.D. 215) κατασκευάσας τὸν ναὸν μετὰ παντὸς τοῦ κόσμου, and the good parallel to the Petrine passage in Menander Γνῶμαι 92 γυναικὶ κόσμος ὁ τρόπος, οὐ τὰ χρύσια. Add, as arising from this usage, such instances as P Tebt I. 45²⁰ (B.C. 113) a complaint against certain persons who— οὐδενὶ κόσμωι χρησάμενοι συντρίψαντες τὴν παρόδιον θύραν, "throwing off all restraint knocked down the street door," similarly ib. 47¹² (B.C. 113), P Oxy VI. 909²⁹ (A.D. 225) τὸν [κ]όσμον τῶν τόπων, of setting a vineyard in order, and ib. 1467¹¹ (A.D. 263) καὶ αὐτὴ τοίνυν τῷ μὲν κόσμῳ τῆς εὐπαιδείας εὐτυχήσασα, "accordingly I too, fortunately possessing the honour of being blessed with children" (Edd.)—a petition from a woman claiming the right to act without a guardian in virtue of her possession of three children and ability to write. See also the compd. κοσμοποίησις in P Oxy III. 498³⁰ (a contract with stone-cutters— ii/A.D.) οὐδεμίας πρὸς ἡμ[ᾶς οὔσης κ[ο]σμοπ[ο]ιήσεως, "no ornamentation being required of us." On the "evil" sense of κόσμος, which must be Jewish in origin, see Hort's notes on Jas 1²⁷, 3⁶: in the latter passage, it should be noted, Carr (Exp VII. viii. p. 318 ff.) prefers to understand by ὁ κόσμος, "the ornament" or "the embellishment" of unrighteousness. For the curious phrase πρὸ (or ἀπὸ) καταβολῆς κόσμου, which is employed by six writers in the NT, Hort (ad 1 Pet 1²⁰) can find no nearer parallel from profane sources than Plutarch Moralia ii. 956 A τὸ ἐξ ἀρχῆς καὶ ἅμα τῇ πρώτῃ καταβολῇ τῶν ἀνθρώπων.

κουστωδία.

P Oxy II. 294²⁰ (A.D. 22) (= Selections, p. 35) ἐν κοσ[τ]ωδε[ία εἰσί is, so far as we know, the earliest ex. of this borrowed word. For the spelling κουστωδία, as in Mt 27⁶⁵ f., 28¹¹, cf P Ryl II. 189² (A.D. 128) δημοσίο(υ) ἱματισμοῦ κουστωδιῶν, "public clothing for the guards": see also Hatzidakis Gr. p. 109. In a fragmentary report referring to the Jewish War of Trajan, P Par 68^A ⁹, we find κωστωδία —ταῦτα ἐγένετο ὅτι τινὰς ἐπὶ κωστωδίαν ἥρπασαν καὶ [τοὺς ἁρπασθέντ]ας ἐτραυμάτισαν : the word is similarly restored in BGU I. 341³ (ii/A.D.).

κουφίζω.

This verb, which in the NT is confined to Ac 27³⁸, is found in the general sense of "lighten" in P Giss I. 7¹² (time of Hadrian) ἐκούφισεν τῶν ἐγχωρίων τὰ βάρη καθολικῶς διὰ προγράμματος: cf. further with reference to taxation BGU II. 619⁶ (A.D. 155) τὴν παραγ[ρ]αφεῖσαν [πρ]όσοδον ὀφείλειν κουφισθῆναι το(ῦ) συναγομ(ένου) ἄχρι ἂν ἐξετασθῇ, PSI I. 103²¹ (end of ii/A.D.) τὸ] συναγόμενον αὐτῶν ἐκού[φισαν] ἐπὶ τῷ τοὺς ἐπ' αὐτῶν ἀναγρ[αφομέ]νους ἄνδρας, OGIS 90¹² (B.C. 196) ἀπὸ τῶν ὑπαρχουσῶν ἐν Αἰγύπτῳ προσόδων καὶ φορολογιῶν τινὰς μὲν εἰς τέλος ἀφῆκεν, ἄλλας δὲ κεκούφικεν, and see P Petr II. 13(18b)⁹ (B.C. 258–253) where the words κουφίζων τὸν βασιλέα, "lightening the king's burden," are written over the line in connexion with a notice inviting tenders at a lower rate for some public work. For κουφίζω, "*levo*," "*absolvo*," see P Iand 62[11] note. In BGU I. 321[11] (A.D. 216) ἐφευρέθη τὰ σειτάρια κεκουφισμένα, the reference is to a robbery, and in PSI IV. 299[5] (iii/A.D.) ὡς δ᾽ ἐκουφίσθη μοι ἡ νόσος, to illness (cf. Hobart, p. 281). In the curious mantic P Ryl I. 28[133] (iv/A.D.) we have apparently an instance of the verb used intransitively—τὰ ἐν δουλίᾳ κουφίσιν (*l.* -ειν) ἐκ τῆς δουλίας, "for a slave in servitude it means an alleviation of his servitude" (Edd.—see their note). For a similar metaphorical use of the subst. see *Kaibel* 406[8] πένθους [κ]ουφι[σ]μὸς ἐγένετο, and for the adj. see P Oxy XIV. 1627[11] (A.D. 342) ἠξιώσαμεν δέ σαι εἰσαγγεῖλαι ἡμᾶς εἰς κουφοτάτην χρίαν, "we requested you to assign to us a very light duty" (Edd.). The wish is frequent on grave-stones—ἀλλὰ κόνιν σοι . . . κουφὴν καὶ δοίη ψυχρὸν Ὄσειρος ὕδωρ (see Schubart *Einführung*, p. 370). Κοῦφα is often used in the papyri substantivally, e.g. P Strass I. 1[10] (A.D. 510) σοῦ παρέχοντ]ος τὰ κοῦφα : see further GH on P Oxy XIV. 1631[16] (A.D. 280).

κόφινος.

In an interesting note in *JTS* x. p. 567 ff. Dr. Hort has shown that the distinction between κόφινος and σπυρίς is one of material rather than of size, for either basket might be of different sizes, to judge by the uses mentioned in classical and patristic writers. This conclusion can now be confirmed from the Κοινή, as when in certain military accounts, P Oxy I. 43 (A.D. 295) we hear of κόφινοι holding 40 λίτραι—iⁱⁱ. 27 ἔσχον παρὰ σοῦ κοφίνους δέκα δύο ἐκ λιτρῶν τεσσαράκοντα, and a little later iv. 16 of—κοφίνους ἀννώνας, which contained only 20 λίτραι. For the contrast between the two words in Mk 8[19 f.] we may quote an ostrakon-letter from the middle of iii/B.C.—Φίλωνι Νίκωνος κόφινοι β̄ Πτολεμαίωι Ἀσκληπιάδου σφυρίδιον (*Archiv* vi. p. 220, No. 84 f.). Other exx. of κόφινος are—P Petr II. 39(*h*)[6, 14] (taxing accounts) εἰς κοφίνους, where the editor thinks the reference is to a box or basket set on wheels to form a cart, PSI IV. 428[52] (iii/B.C.) ἐν κοφίνωι με[γά]λωι, P Oxy IV. 739[8] (*c.* A.D. 1) κοφίνων γ̄, P Tebt II. 405[8] (iii/A.D.) κόβ(= φ)ινος καινός, BGU II. 417[12] (ii/iii A.D.) περὶ τοῦ κοφίνου τῆς σταφυλῆς, and P Flor II. 269[10] (A.D. 257) ἐντολὰς λαβέτωσαν οἱ ὀνηλάται κομίσαι σοι τοὺς κοφίνους. The word, which is of Semitic origin (cf. Lewy *Fremdwörter*, p. 115), was used specially by Jews (cf. Juvenal iii. 14, vi. 542), and Hort (*l.c.*) thinks that it was equivalent to the κάρταλ(λ)ος in which Jews carried first-fruits to Jerusalem. See further *s.vv.* σαργάνη and σπυρίς. For a form κόφος, which Dr. Hunt suggests may be equivalent to κόφινος, see the *verso* of a i/A.D. Hawara papyrus reproduced in *Archiv* v. p. 381, No. 42, and for the dim. κοφίνιον see P Petr III. 53(*m*)[6] (B.C. 224). The widespread use of κόφινος in the Κοινή is fully illustrated by Maidhof p. 308 ff. The word still survives in MGr along with such forms as * κόφα, * κοφούνι.

κράββατος,

the poor man's bed or mattress, and therefore better suited to the narrative in Mk 2[4] than κλίνη which Mt (9[2]) and Lk (5[18]) substitute. In Ac 5[15] κράββατος is distinguished

from κλινάριον : cf. 9[33] where Lk may have kept the original word of his informant. The word is late (Lob. *Phryn.* p. 62 σκίμπους λέγε, ἀλλὰ μὴ κράββατος), and is probably rightly traced to Macedonian origin (Sturzius *Dial. Mac.* p. 175 f.). With Mk 2[12] Norden (*Ant. Kunstprosa* ii. p. 532 n.[1]) contrasts Lucian *Philops.* 16 ἀράμενος τὸν σκίμποδα, ἐφ᾽ οὗ ἐκεκόμιστο, ᾤχετο ἐς τὸν ἀγρὸν ἀπιών. The spelling varies, but the form given above is found in the best NT MSS. (WSchm p. 56), though ℵ on 10 out of 11 occurrences prefers κράβακτος, for which we can now cite P Tebt II. 406[19] (inventory of property—*c.* A.D. 260) κράβακτος ξύλινος τέλειος, "a wooden bedstead in good order," P Gen I. 68[10] (A.D. 382) ἑρματικῶν χράβακτων (*l.* ἑρματικὸν κράβακτον) : see also the late P Grenf II. 111[32] (v/vi A.D.) (= *Chrest.* I. 135) κραβάκτ ιον, where the editors note that κράββατος is used of a bier by Cedrenus. *Justinian.* an. 31 τοὺς κ. τῶν ἐκκλησιῶν (Migne, *P.G.* cxxi. 736 c), and compare κραβαττάρια in the same sense in *Chron. Paschal.* an. 605 *ib.* xcii. 970 a). *al.* Κράββατος is found in an inventory of Trajan's reign, P Lond 191[16] (A.D. 103–117) (= II. p. 265) : cf. Epict. i. 24. 14 and κραββάτιον in *ib.* iii. 22. 74. In an ostracon, probably Ptolemaic, published in *Mél. Nicole* p. 184 we find κράβατος as in Mk 2[4] B* : cf. Lat. *grabattus*, showing that in the West the form with one β prevailed. WSchm p. 56 cites κραββάτριος from *CIG* II. 2114[d1] in the sense of ἀρχικοιτω[ε]ίτης *ib.* add. 2132[f6] : cf. Ac 12[20]). In the German edition of his *Prolegomena* (*Einleitung*, p. 60) Moulton has a note on the significance of the orthographical peculiarities of the NT uncials in connexion with such a word as κράββατος in helping to fix the *provenance* of the MSS. : the note is reproduced in Luke's Introduction to his edition of the *Cod. Sinaiticus*, p. xi. Add that Codex Washington (W) regularly spells the word κράβαττον. According to Thumb (*Indog. Forsch.* ii. p. 85) κρεββάτι is the normal form in MGr.

κράζω

occurs *quater* in the general sense of "cry out" in a late i/B.C. petition, P Oxy IV. 717, e.g. [1] ἐκβοῶντος δέ μου καὶ κράζοντος τὰ τοσαῦτα : cf. P Fay 119[33] (*c.* A.D. 100) ἐπὶ κράζει Πᾶσις εἴνα μὴ εἰς ψωμὶν (for ψωμίον) γένηται διὰ τῶ ὕδωρ, "for Pasis is crying out that we must not allow it (*sc.* manure) to be dissolved by the water" (Edd.), BGU III. 816[18] (iii/A.D.) ἐπὶ κράσι (*l.* ἐπεὶ κράζει) Ἀπᾶς Εὐάγγελος (*l.* -ου) περὶ τοῦ χαλκοῦ. For κέκραγα as a perfect with present force in Jn 1[15] see *Proleg.* p. 147, and to the LXX exx. there adduced add *Menandrea* p. 44[11] τὸ παιδίον κέκραγός, "the baby screaming," and so *ib.* 45[24]. The verb, which survives in MGr, is discussed by Abbott *Joh. Gr.* p. 348.

κραιπάλη.

Lat. *crapula*, "surfeiting" (AV, RV). On the form κρεπάλη, which is read by WH in Lk 21[34], the only place where the word occurs in the NT, see Moulton *Gr.* ii. p. 81, and for the medical usage = "drunken nausea," see Hobart p. 167.

κρανίον

is found *bis* in the magic P Lond 125 *verso* (v/A.D.) (= I. pp. 123, 125)—[2] ἴβιος κρανίον, [47] τὸ κρανίον τοῦ ὄνου. P

Ryl II. 152¹⁷ (A.D. 42) ἐκρανοκόπησαν πλῖστα φυτ(ά), "they cut the heads off very many young trees" (Edd.), shows a new equivalent of καρατομέω.

κράσπεδον,

the "fringe" or "tassel," which the Law required every Jew to attach to the corners of his outer garment (Numb 15³⁸ ᶠ, Deut 22¹²). The word is found in the magic P Lond 121³⁷¹ (iii/A.D.) (= I. p. 96) ἐξάψας κράσπετον (l. -δον) τοῦ ἱματίου σου.

κραταιός.

That this "poetic" word also formed part of the common stock of the Κοινή is shown by its occurrence not only in the LXX and NT, but in the magic papyri, e.g. P Lond 121⁴⁸² (iii/A.D.) (= I. p. 98) θεοὶ κραταιοί, ib. ⁵⁶³ (= p. 102) ἐν φωτὶ κραταιῷ καὶ ἀφθάρτῳ, ib. ⁷⁸⁹ (= p. 109) ἐπεύχομαι τῇ δεσποίνῃ τοῦ παντὸς κόσμου, ἐπάκουσόν μου ἡ μόνη (= ι)-μος ἡ κρατει (= αι)ά.

κρατέω.

For κρατέω in its primary sense of "become master of," "rule," "conquer," we may cite P Oxy I. 33 verso ᵛ·¹² (late ii/A.D.) π[ρῶτον μὲν Καῖσαρ ἔ]σωσε Κλεοπάτρ[αν] ἐκράτησεν βασι[λείας], "in the first place Caesar saved Cleopatra's life when he conquered her kingdom" (Edd.). The gen. construction, which is here supplied, is comparatively rare in the NT (cf. Proleg. pp. 65, 235), but may be further illustrated by P Par 26⁵² (B.C. 163–2) (= Selections, p. 18) ὑμῖν δὲ γίνοιτο κρατεῖν πάσης ἧς ἂν αἱρῆσθε χώρας, and by the magic P Lond 121⁶⁸⁹ (iii/A.D.) (= I. p. 106) ἄρκτε . . . κρατοῦσα [τοῦ ὅ]λου συστήματος—an invocation to the constellation of the Bear. [See also the interesting parallels to Ac 27¹³ in Field Notes, p. 144.] Another magic papyrus ib. 46⁴⁵¹ (iv/A.D.) (= I. p. 80) κράτει τῇ ἀριστερᾷ σου τὸν δάκτυλ ιον) shows the more common accusative; see also the curious theological fragment P Oxy XI. 1384²⁵ (v/A.D.) where certain angels are represented as having gone up to heaven to seek a remedy for their eyes—σφόγγον κρατοῦντες, "holding a sponge," cf. Rev 2¹. For the meaning "continue to hold," "retain," as in Ac 2²⁴, see P Tebt I. 61 (b)²²⁰ (a land survey—B.C. 118–7) γραφή-τωι λαβε[ῖν] ἑνὸ[ς ἐνιαυ]τοῦ ἐκφόριον, ἐὰν κ[ρ]ατεῖν, "let it be noted that one year's rent shall be exacted from them, and they shall be allowed to keep the land" (Edd.): cf. also P Fay 109² (early i/A.D.) ὅταν πρὸς ἀνάνκαιν (= ἀνάγκην) θέλῃς παρ' ἐμοῦ χρήσασθαί τι, εὐθύς σε οὐ κρατῶι, "whenever you from necessity want to borrow anything from me, I at once give in to you" (Edd.). In P Oxy II. 237ᵛⁱⁱⁱ·²⁴ (A.D. 186) παρατιθέτωσαν δὲ καὶ αἱ γυναῖκες ταῖς ὑποστάσεσι τῶν ἀνδρῶν ἐὰν κατά τινα ἐπιχώριον νόμον κρατεῖται τὰ ὑπάρχοντα, "wives shall also insert copies in the property-statements of their husbands, if in accordance with any native Egyptian law they have a claim over their husbands' property" (Edd.), κρατεῖσθαι is used as equivalent to κατέχειν in ib. ²² (see further Mitteis in Archiv i. p. 188): cf. ib. ²⁶ ἡ δὲ κτῆσις μετὰ θάνατον τοῖς τέκνοις κεκράτηται, "but the right of ownership after their death has been settled upon the children" (Edd.), and P Amh II. 51²⁶ (B.C. 88), a contract for the sale of a house—

ἧς κρ[α]τεῖ Τοτοῆς, "over which Totoes has rights," and the similar use of the compound ἐπικρατέω of rights acquired or exercised over the property of others in P Tebt II. 343¹⁴ (ii/A.D.), where see the editors' note. As further bringing out this strong sense of κρατέω, we may notice that it is joined with κυριεύω in BGU I. 71¹⁸ (A.D. 179), ib. 282³³ (after A.D. 175), and with δεσπόζω in P Tebt II. 383³⁵ (A.D. 46). At Delos a dedicatory inscr. has been found—Διὶ τῷ πάντων κρατοῦντι καὶ Μητρὶ Μεγάληι τῆι πάντων κρατούσῃ (BCH vi. (1882), p. 502 No. 25): cf. the use of παντοκράτωρ in the LXX, and see Cumont Relig. Orient. p. 267. In the vi/A.D. P Lond V. 1663⁸ the Emperor is described as ἡ κρατοῦσα τυχή.

κράτιστος

(egregius) is very common as an honorific title in addressing persons of exalted rank, much as we use "Your Excellency," e.g. P Fay 117⁵ (A.D. 108)—a prefect, P Tebt II. 411⁵ (ii/A.D.)—an epistrategus, P Oxy X. 1274¹⁰ (iii/A.D.) —a procurator, al. [By the end of the third century the title was applied to persons of less importance, e.g. a ducenarius in P Oxy XIV. 1711⁴: see the editors' note on ib. 1643².] This corresponds with the usage in Ac 23²⁶, 24³, 26²⁵, and possibly Lk 1³, though in this last case the word may be simply a form of courteous address. If, however, it is regarded here also as official, it is very unlikely that Theophilus was at the time a Christian, "since," as Zahn (Introd. iii. p. 42) has pointed out, "there is no instance in the Christian literature of the first two centuries where a Christian uses a secular title in addressing another Christian, to say nothing of a title of this character." On the title as applied to the βουλή of Antinoë in BGU IV. 1022¹ (A.D. 196) see Wilcken in Archiv iii. p. 301, and cf. the introd. to P Strass I. 43. The adj. is never found as a true superlative in the NT, but is so found in literary books of the LXX (cf. Thackeray Gr. i. p. 185): cf. BGU IV. 1118¹¹ (B.C. 22) τῶν ὄντων ἐν τῶι κήπωι τὰ κράτιστα καὶ βέλτιστα.

κράτος.

An interesting ex. of this word is found in P Leid G¹⁴ (B.C. 181–145) (= I. p. 42), a petition to Ptolemy Philometer and Berenice, in which the petitioner states that he is offering prayers and sacrifices to the gods, in order that they may give the Sovereigns—ὑγίειαν, [ν]ίκην, κράτος, σθένος, κυριείαν τῶν [ὑ]πὸ τὸν οὐρανὸν χώρω[ν: cf. the invocation to Isis, ib. ᴵᴵ·¹⁷ (2nd half ii/B.C.) ἐλθέ μοι θεὰ θεῶν, κράτος ἔχουσα μέγιστον. From the time of Augustus comes a dedication—εἰς κράτος Ῥώμης καὶ διαμονὴν μυστηρίων (Syll 756⁵), with which may be compared the acclamation at a popular demonstration at Oxyrhynchus on the occasion of a visit from the Prefect, P Oxy I. 41ⁱ·² (iii/iv A.D.) εἰς [ἐ]ῶνα τὸ κράτος τ[ῶ]ν ['Ρ]ωμαίων, "the Roman power for ever!" (Edd.). This and similar usages find a parallel in the language of Christian worship, as in the prayer P Oxy III. 407⁹ (iii/iv A.D.) which is offered—διὰ . . . Ἰησοῦ Χριστοῦ, δι' οὗ ἡ δόξα καὶ τὸ κράτος εἰς τοὺς αἰῶνας τῶν αἰωνῶ[ν: cf. especially the doxology in 1 Pet 4¹¹. See also the magic PSI I. 29²¹ (iv/A.D. ?) τὸ κράτος τοῦ Ἀδωναὶ καὶ τὸν στέφανον τοῦ Ἀδωναὶ δότε, and the late BGU I. 314¹³ (A.D. 630) ἔργῳ δυνάμει κράτ(ει) (cf. Archiv iv. p. 214). For the phrase **κατὰ κράτος**, as in Ac 19[20], cf. P Tebt I. 27[83] (B.C. 113) ἡ δ' εἴσπραξις τῶν προεθησομένων παρὰ σοῦ κατὰ κράτος ἔσται, "any losses will be rigorously exacted from you" (Edd.). In MGr **κράτο(ς)** is used = "kingdom, kingdom of Greece."

The late form **κράτησις** = "dominion," as in Wisd 6[3], is found in P Fay 89[2] (A.D. 9) ἔτους ὀγδόου καὶ τριακοστοῦ τῆς Καίσαρος κρατήσεως θεοῦ υἱοῦ, "the 38th year of the dominion of Caesar, son of the god": see also *Hermes* xxx. (1895), p. 151 ff. For the meaning "possession," see P Tor I. 1[iii. 32] (B.C. 116) τῆς κρατήσεως τῆς οἰκίας, *ib.*[v. 36] μηδεμίας κρατήσεως μηδὲ κυριείας τινὸς ἐγγαίου περιγενομένης αὐτῶι, where the editor (p. 117) distinguishes **κράτησις**, "possessio facti," from **κυριεία**, "dominium, ius, quod a possessione disiunctum esse potest": cf. P Tebt II. 294[19] (A.D. 146) μενεῖν (*l.* μενεῖ) δέ μοι καὶ ἐγγόνοις καὶ τοῖς παρ' ἐμοῦ μεταλημψομένοις ἡ τούτων κυρεί[α] καὶ κράτησ[ις ἐπὶ τ]ὸν ἀεὶ χρόνο[ν, "and I and my descendants and assigns shall have the permanent ownership and possession of the office for ever" (Edd.).

κραυγή.

In P Petr II. 45[iii. 25] (B.C. 246) (cf. III. p. 334) Ptolemy III. describes his triumphal reception— καὶ οἱ μὲν ἐδεξιοῦ[ντ'ο, οἱ δὲ [. . . .] μετὰ κρότου καὶ κραυγῆς [. . ., where the word has the "joyful" association that we find in Lk 1[42]. On the other hand, in P Tebt I. 15[i. 3] (B.C. 114) τῆι ᾱ τοῦ ὑποκειμένου μηνὸς ὡσεὶ περὶ ὥραν ιᾱ [[κραυγῆς]] θορύβου γενομένου ἐν τῆι κώμηι, "on the first of the current month at about the eleventh hour a disturbance occurred in the village" (Edd.), we are reminded of the usage in Ac 23[9]. The plur. is found in the interesting literary text, P Oxy X. 1242[iii. 34] (early iii/A.D.), describing an audience between the Emperor Trajan and certain rival Greek and Jewish emissaries from Alexandria, where it is stated that sweat broke out on the image of Sarapis carried by the Alexandrians— θεασάμενος δὲ Τραιανὸς ἀπεθαύμασ[εν], καὶ μεθ' ὀλίγον συνδρομαὶ ἐγένοντο εἰς [τὴ]ν Ῥώμην κραυγαί τε παμπληθεῖς ἐξεβοῶντ[ο κ]αὶ πά[ν]τες ἔφευγαν εἰς τὰ ὑψηλὰ μέρη τῶν λό[φ]ων, "and Trajan seeing it marvelled; and presently there were tumults in Rome and many shouts were raised, and all fled to the high parts of the hills" (Edd.): cf. Vett. Val. p. 235 πολέμοις, ἁρπαγάς, κραυγάς, ὕβρεις. For the word see also P Lond 44[17] cited *s.v.* ἀναλύω.

κρέας.

In P Petr III. 58(a)[2] (iii/B.C.) a mother gives security of 20 dr. on behalf of her son who had undertaken to supply the village of Philoteris with salt meat and cheese—κρεῶν ταλ(= ρ ιχηρῶν καὶ τυροῦ. Cf. P Oxy XIV. 1674[2] (iii/A.D.) ἐπειδὴ οὐχ εὕρ[ο]ν κρέας σοι πέμψαι, ἔπεμψα ᾠὰ κ̄ καὶ λάχανα—a father to his son, *ib.* VII. 1056[2] (A.D. 360) ὑπὲρ τιμῆς κρέως λιτρῶν πεντακοσίων, "for the price of 500 pounds of meat." Frequent mention is made of κρέας χοίρειον, "swine-flesh," which was evidently a staple article of diet, see e.g. P Giss I. 49[15] (iii/A.D.) with the editor's note. The different forms the word takes are fully illustrated by Mayser *Gr.* p. 276. According to Meisterhans *Gr.* p. 143 the gen. sing. κρέατος is found once in an Attic inscr. of B.C. 338, but Thumb (*Hellen.* p. 96) thinks that the

declension κρέας κρέατος must have prevailed in the Κοινή in view of the MGr κρέατο, κριάτο.

For the diminutive **κρεάδιον** see the soldier's begging letter, BGU III. 814[25] (iii/A.D.), in which the writer complains that his mother had sent him nothing, while a friend's mother had sent her son κεραμεῖον ἐλαίου κ[αὶ] σφυρίδαν κρεδίων (*l.* κρεαδίων).

κρείσσων, κρείττων,

is always strictly comparative in the NT, cf. P Oxy XIV. 1676[15] (iii/A.D.) ἀλλὰ πάντως κρείττονα εἶχες· διὰ τοῦτο ὑπερηφάνηκας ἡμᾶς, "but you doubtless had better things to do; that was why you neglected us" (Ed.). It is found with a superlative force in such a passage as P Oxy VII. 1062[5] (ii/A.D.) προσθεὶς ὅτι τὰ θερειά ἐστιν τὰ κρείσσονα, "adding that the summer ones were the best" (Ed.)—a letter referring to the purchase of some fleeces. On the relative proportion of the two forms in the LXX, see Thackeray *Gr.* i. p. 122.

κρεμάννυμι.

Syll 803[3] (dialect inscr. from Epidaurus—iii B.C.) τὸ σῶμα κραμάσαι κάτω τὸν τράχαλον ἔχον, *Michel* 833[107] (B.C. 279) τῶν κρεμαμένων στεφάνων. For the shortened pass. **κρέμαμαι** cf. *Syll* 588[34] (*c.* B.C. 180) στέφανος χρυσοῦς καὶ στρεπτόν, κρεμάμενα πρὸς τῶι τοίχωι, [201] ἐκ τῆς σει[ρας κρεμαμένων. A new compd. **εἰσκρεμάννυμι** is found in P Lond 964[18] (ii/iii A.D.) (= III. p. 212) ἄλλα μέτρια ἰσκρέμασε ἐς τὸν νυμφῶνα. In P Tebt II. 527 (A.D. 101) mention is made of a κρεμαστὴ ποτίστρεα used for irrigation: for the subst. **κρεμαστήρ** see P Leps I. 42[19] (end of iv/A.D.). MGr κρεμ(ν)ῶ, κρεμάζω (trans.), κρέμομαι (intrans.). See also Radermacher *Gr.* pp. 35 n.[2], 81.

κρημνός.

This word, which in the NT is confined to Mk 5[13] and parallels, is found in an account of rushes used in irrigation works, P Petr III. 39[ii. 8], where mention is made of those employed— εἰς τοὺς κρημνούς, for the steep banks or edges of the trench. See also the epitaph on one who had hurled himself from the cliffs, *Kaibel*, 225[1]—

Ὀστέα μὲν καὶ σάρκας ἐμὰς σπιλάδες διέχευαν
ἐξεῖαι, κρημνῶν ἅλμα ὑποδεξάμεναι.

κριθή.

For this common word, which in the NT is found only once and in the plur. (Rev 6[6]), it is sufficient to cite P Hib I. 47[22] (B.C. 256) καὶ ὄλυραν δὲ κ[αὶ κρ]θὴν ἑτοίμαξε, "prepare both olyra and barley," P Petr II. 23(1)[2] (Ptol.) ἡ ζεὴ (= ζειὰ) ἡ δὲ κριθὴ ἐπλήγη, "the rye and the barley had been smitten" with hail (?. Ed.), P Giss I. 69[3] (A.D. 118-9) νῦν δὲ πρὸς παράλημψιν κρειθῆς ἔπεμψα αὐτόν, P Oxy I. 69[3] (A.D. 190) κριθῆς ἀρτόβας δέκα.

κρίθινος.

P Eleph 5[5] (B.C. 284-3) καὶ τοῦ σίτου τοῦ κριθίνου καὶ πυρίνου ἀπέχω τοὺς λόγους, BGU IV. 1062[8] (A.D. 372) παρ[αδώσ]ω δὲ σοὶ κριθίνου ἀχύρου γύργαθα ("wicker-baskets") δύ[ο.

κρίμα.

Κρίμα (on the accent, see *Proleg.* p. 46) = "legal decision" is found in P Petr III. 26² (iii/B.C.) το]ὺς τοπάρχ[ους] κρίματα καθήκει εἰς τοὺς φόρους, "it is (not) the duty of the Toparchs to give decisions regarding the taxes" (Edd.), *ib.* 36 (a) *verso*²⁰ (iii/B.C.) δεήσει συντελεῖσθαι τὰ κατὰ τὸ [κρίμα] ἐὰν δέηι κρίμα, "(the dioiketes) shall require the legal decision to be carried out, if such a decision be necessary" (Edd.). Cf. also the restoration in *OGIS* 335¹⁰⁰ (ii/i B.C.), where αὐτ[οὶ ἐ]πιδεξάμενοι τὴν κρίσιν π[is followed after an hiatus by ἐφε]ῖναι τὰ κρί[ματα ἑαυτοῖς. From denoting "judgment," "sentence," the word came to denote the "offence" for which one is sentenced, and hence in MGr is frequently used = "sin," as in the song entitled "The Confessor," where the penitent asks—'ξομολόγα με, τὰ κρίματά μου 'ρώτα με, "confess me : ask me about my sins," and receives the answer—τὰ κρίματά σου 'ναι πολλά, καὶ ἀγάπη νὰ μὴ κάνῃς πλεία, "thy sins are many ; thou must make love no more" (Abbott *Songs*, p. 122, cf. p. 272). Cf. τί κρῖμα, "what a pity !"

κρίνον

is used in the plur. of an architectural device in *Michel* 594⁷² (B.C. 279). The adj. κρίνινος, "made of lilies," is applied to myrrh in P Lond 46²¹² (iv/A.D.) (= I. p. 72) μύρον κρίνινον, and to oil in *ib.* 121⁶³¹ (iii/A.D.)(= I. p. 104) κρίνινον ἔλαιον : in P Leid W*ix.* ¹² (ii/iii A.D.) κρίνινον is one of the seven flowers of the seven stars. A i/A.D. sepulchral epitaph, *Kaibel* 547, begins—Εἰς ἵα σου . . [κ]αὶ [εἰ]s κρίνα βλα[σ]τείσειεν ὀστέα, "may thy bones bourgeon into violets and lilies." MGr κρίνο, κρίνος.

κρίνω.

For κρίνω c. inf., "decide to . . ," as in Ac 20¹⁶, 1 Cor 2², Tit 3¹², see P Par 26³⁷ (B.C. 163-2) (= *Selections.* p. 17) οὐκ ἐκρίναμεν καταχωρίσαι (cf. 1 Chron 27²⁴), "we have decided not to record," and cf. P Tebt I. 55⁴ (late ii/B.C.) ἔκρινα γράψαι, P Lond 897¹¹ (A.D. 84) (= p. 207) κέκρικα ("I have decided once and for all" : cf. Jn 19²² γέγραφα) γὰρ νὴ τοὺς θεοὺς ἐν Ἀλεξανδρείᾳ ἐπιμένειν, P Oxy XII. 1402⁸ (iii/iv A.D.) εἰ οὖν ἔκρεινας κατὰ τὸ παλ[αιὸν] ἔθος δοῦναι τὴν ἀρ[ο]υραν τῷ τόπῳ, "if then you have decided in accordance with ancient custom to give the arura to the place" (Edd.). [LS quote Menander Φιλ. 5 ζῆν μεθ' ὧν κρίνῃ τις (*sc.* ζῆν), but this is rather for ζῆν μετ' ἐκείνων οὓς κρίνῃ τις (κρίνω c. acc. "choose " or "prefer," a classical use).] The verb is also used as a kind of *term. techn.* for the response of an oracle, e.g. P Fay 138¹ (i/ii A.D.) Κύριοι Διόσκουροι, ἢ κρείνεται αὐτὸν ἀπελθεῖν ἰς πόλειν ; "O lords Dioscuri, is it fated for him to depart to the city?" Cf. the use of the compound in P Tebt II. 284² (i/B.C.) ἐπικέκριται μοι μὴ καταβῆναι ἕως τῆς κε̄, "it has been decided for me (by the local oracle) that I should not go down till the 25th " (Edd.). The *forensic* sense is very common, e.g. P Petr III. 26¹ (iii/B.C.) ἐὰν δέ τις παρὰ ταῦτα κρίνῃ ἢ κριθῇ ἄκυρα ἔστω, "and if any one judge or be judged contrary to these regulations, the decisions shall be invalid," *ib.* I. 16 (2)¹¹ (B.C. 230) κριθήσομαι ἐπ' Ἀσκληπιάδου, "I shall submit to the judgement of A." P Oxy I. 37ⁱⁱ·⁸ (A.D. 49) (= *Selections.* p. 51) κατὰ τὰ ὑπὸ τοῦ κυρίου ἡγεμόνος κριθέντα, "in accordance

with the judgement of our lord the Prefect," *ib.* 38¹⁶ (A.D. 49-50) (= *Selections*, p. 53) ἐνμεῖναι τοῖς κεκριμένοις, "to comply with the judgement" (Edd.)—a legal formula, P Ryl II. 119³ (A.D. 54-67) τυγχάνωι κεκριμένος ὑπὸ τοῦ κρατίστου ἡγεμόνος. "I happen to have had a case decided by his highness the Prefect," and *ib.* 75⁸ (judicial proceedings—late ii/A.D.) ἤδη μέντοι τύπος ἐστὶν καθ' ὃν ἔκρεινα πολλάκις καὶ τοῦτο δίκαιον εἶναί μοι φαίνεται, "only there is a principle according to which I have often judged and which seems to me fair" (Edd.). Deissmann (*LAE* p. 118) has shown that help is given to the difficult phrase κρίνω τὸ δίκαιον in Lk 12⁵⁷ by a prayer for vengeance addressed to Demeter on a leaden tablet found at Amorgos, *BCH* xxv. (1901) p. 416 ἐπάκουσον, θεά, καὶ κρῖναι τὸ δίκαιον, "prononce la juste sentence" (Ed.). A good parallel to 1 Cor 6² occurs in *Syll* 850⁸ (B.C. 173-2) κριθέντω ἐν ἄνδροις τρίοις οὓς συνείλοντο. On the weakened use of κρίνω in Ac 15¹⁹ (cf. 13¹⁸, 16¹⁵, 26⁸), where it is practically = νομίζω, see Hort *Christian Ecclesia*, p. 80.

κρίσις

in the sense of "judging," "trial," is found in such passages as PSI II. 173¹⁷ (ii/B.C.) κα[τὰ προε]νεστῶσαν . . ἐπὶ σοῦ κρίσιν, P Oxy IX. 1203²⁹ (late i/A.D.) where certain petitioners ask that no step be taken against them μέχρι κρίσεως, "before the trial of the case," the curious mantic P Ryl I. 28 ¹⁶⁵ (iv/A.D.) σφυρὸν εὐώνυμον ἐὰν ἄληται ἐν κρίσει βαρη[θ]εὶς ἔσται καὶ ἐκφεύξεται, "if the left ankle quiver, he will be burdened with a trial, and will be acquitted " (Edd.), and *OGIS* 669²⁹ (i/A.D.) εἰς κρίσιν ἄγεσθαι. From this it is an easy transition to the result of the judging, "judgement," "decision," e.g. P Petr III. 26⁹ (iii/B.C.) ἐκ κρίσεως, "in accordance with a legal decision," P Oxy I. 68³·¹ (A.D. 131) οὖσαν δ ἐμοὶ τὴν πρὸς αὐτὸν κρίσιν, "judgement against him being entered in my favour" (Edd.), P Ryl II. 78³⁵ (A.D. 157) περὶ ἀπολογισμοῦ κρίσεων, "concerning the report of judgements," P Oxy XII. 1464⁶ (*libellus*—A.D. 250) κατ]ὰ τὰ κελευσθέντα ὑπὸ τῆς θείας κρίσεως, "in accordance with the orders of the divine decree," and such legal phrases as ἄνευ κρίσεως καὶ πάσης ἀντιλογίας (BGU IV. 1140¹⁶—B.C. 18) and ἄνευ δίκης καὶ κρίσεως καὶ πάσης εὑρησιλογίας (P Tebt II. 444—i/A.D.).

An approach to the moral and ethical sense which, following the general usage of the LXX, κρίσις has in such passages as Mt 23²³ Lk 11⁴², may be traced in *Michel* 542⁶ (ii/B.C. *ad init.*) πίστιν ἔχοντα καὶ κρίσιν ὑγιῆ, *OGIS* 383²⁰⁷ (mid. i/B.C.) ἦν ἀθάνατος κρίσις ἐκύρωσεν—with reference to a certain ordinance, and *ib.* 502⁸ (ii/A.D.) μείξας τῷ φιλανθρώπῳ τὸ δίκαιον ἀκολούθως τῇ περὶ τὰς κρίσεις ἐπιμελείᾳ. For κρίσις, "accusation," in Jude⁹, see Field *Notes*, p. 244. For an adj. κρίσιμος with reference to the day of judgement, see a Christian inscr. from Eumeneia in *C. and B.* ii. p. 514—ὃς δὲ ἂν ἐπιτηδεύσει, ἔσται αὐτῷ πρὸς τὸν ζῶντα θεὸν καὶ νῦν καὶ ἐν τῇ κρισίμῳ ἡμέρᾳ. Ramsay (p. 518) remarks that "the term κρίσιμος ἡμέρα seems to be used elsewhere only in the medical sense, 'the critical day determining the issue of the disease '": cf. also Durham *Menander*, p. 72. MGr κρίσι, "judgement "; ἔρχομαι στὴ κρίσι, "appear before court of judgement " (Thumb, *Handbook*, p. 337).

Κρίσπος

is mentioned Ac 18⁸, 1 Cor 1¹⁴. For other instances of a Jew bearing this Roman cognomen (= "curly"), see Lightfoot's citations from the Talmudists (*Hor. Hebr. ad* 1 Cor *l.c.*).

κριτήριον

in the sense of "tribunal," "court of justice," as in 1 Cor 6²·⁴ (RV marg.), Jas 2⁶ (cf. Judg 5¹⁰ *al.*), is frequent in the papyri, e.g. P Hib I. 29 Fr. (*a*) *recto*⁵ (*c.* B.C. 265) (= *Chrest.* I. p. 506) ἐὰν δὲ ἀν]τιλέγηι, κριθήτωσα[ν ἐ]π[ὶ] τοῦ ἀ[ποδε]δειγμένου κ[ρι]τηρίου, "if he dispute the decision, they shall be tried before the appointed tribunal" (Edd.), P Grenf I. 15⁷ (B.C. 146 or 135) ὅπ]ως μὴ περισπώμεθα ἐπὶ τὰ [. . . . .]-τα κριτήρια, BGU IV. 1054¹ (time of Augustus) Π]ρωτάρχωι τῶι ἐπὶ τοῦ κριτηρίου παρὰ Ἀπολλωνίου, P Oxy X. 1270¹⁶ (A.D. 159) πρὸς τῇ ἐπιμελείᾳ τ[ῶν χρηματιστῶν] καὶ τῶν ἄλλων κριτηρί[ων, and similarly P Tebt II. 319² (A.D. 248). See also *s.vv.* ἀγοραῖος and ἑλκύω, and cf. *Archiv* iv. p. 81, v. pp. 40, 50 f. In *Syll* 371⁸ (time of Nero) ἀνὴ[ρ] δεδοκιμασμένος τοῖς θείοις κριτηρίοις τῶν Σεβαστῶν ἐπί τε τῇ τέχνῃ τῆς ἰατρικῆς, the word has its original sense of "standard," "test."

κριτής

is used of one designated by the Prefect to the office of "judge," as in P Oxy IX. 1195¹ (A.D. 135) Ἀπολλωνίωι κριτῇ δοθέντι ὑπὸ Πετρωνίου Μαμερτείνου τοῦ κρατίστου ἡγεμόνος: it is also applied to this same Prefect himself in *ib.* IV. 726²⁰ (A.D. 135). Cf. also *ib.* I. 97³ (A.D. 115 6) ἐπί τε πάσης ἐξουσίας καὶ παντὸς κριτοῦ. For the "technical-political" sense of the word, as frequently in the LXX, Wackernagel (*Hellenistica*, p. 11) cites *OGIS* 467¹⁰ ἐπίλεκτον κριτὴν ἐκ τῶν ἐν Ῥώμῃ δεκουριῶν, compared with *ib.* 499³ τῶν ἐκλέκτων ἐν Ῥώμῃ δικαστῶν, both ii/A.D. inscr. from Asia Minor.

κρούω.

For this verb of "knocking" at the door, as in Lk 13²⁵, Ac 12¹³, where the Purists would have preferred κόπτω (cf. Lob. *Phryn.* p. 177 f.), see P Par 50⁷ (B.C. 160) εἶδον Πτολεμαῖον . . . κρού[οντα] θύραν. Other exx. of this usage in late Greek are given in Field *Notes*, p. 120. In the magic P Lond 46⁷⁰ (iv/A.D.) (= I. p. 67) we have—κρούε εἰς τὸ οὖς λέγων κτλ. For the subst. κροῦμα see BGU IV. 1125⁴·³¹ (B.C. 13), and for the compd. ἐκκρούω in the sense of "put off," "evade," cf. P Fay 109⁹ (early i/A.D.) Σέλευκος γάρ μου αὐτοὺς ὧδε ἐκκ[έκ]ρουκε λέγων ὅτι συνέστακας ἑαυτῶι, "Seleucus has evaded paying the money by saying that you have made an arrangement with him (to pay instead)" (Edd.).

κρύπτη (κρυπτή)

in the sense of "vault," "cellar," as in Lk 11³³ (RV), occurs in PSI V. 547¹⁸ (iii/B.C.), where in a list of parts of a building (doors, windows etc.) we read οἱ τὴν κρύπτην ὁμοίαν τῶι κονιάματι, "the cellar similarly plastered": cf. γρύτης, perhaps a vulgar Egyptian form of κρύπτης, in *ib.* 546³ (iii B.C.), where see the editor's note.

κρυπτός.

P Leid Wˣᵛⁱⁱ·¹⁶ (ii iii A.D.) ὁ παντοκράτωρ, ὁ ἐνφυσήσας πνεῦμα ἀνθρώποις εἰς ζωήν· οὗ ἐστιν τὸ κρυπτὸν (ὄνομα) καὶ ἄρρητον ἐν ἀνθρώπους (*l.* -οις). In BGU I. 316²³ (A.D. 359) the seller assumes responsibility with reference to any κρυπτὸν πάθος ("*latens vitium*") in the case of a slave whom he has sold: cf. Modica *Introduzione*, p. 145.

κρύπτω.

P Tor I. 1ᵛⁱ·¹⁴ (B.C. 116) διὰ κεκρυμμένης σκευωρίας, "by means of hidden endeavour." In an elaborate accusation, P Oxy VI. 903 (iv/A.D.), a young wife mentions among other insults that had been heaped upon her, that though her husband had sworn in the presence of the bishops and of his own brothers—¹⁶ ἀπεντεῦθεν οὐ μὴ κρύψω αὐτῇ (*l.* -τὴν) πάσας μου τὰς κλεῖς, "henceforward I will not hide all my keys from her," nevertheless—¹⁵ ἔκρυψεν πάλιν ἐμὲ τὰς κλεῖς εἰς ἐμέ, "he again hid the keys from me." With the formally pass. ἐκρύβη in Jn 8⁵⁹ (cf. Gen 3¹⁰) Moulton (*Proleg.* p. 161) compares BGU IV. 1055¹ (B.C. 13) τὸ ἐν ὀφιλῇ θησόμενον, "the amount that shall be charged as due," a middle in a pass. sense. The familiar saying of Mt 5¹⁴ is expanded in the New Logion 7, P Oxy I. 1 *recto* ¹⁵ᶠ·, into—λέγει Ἰ(ησοῦ)ς, πόλις οἰκοδομημένη ἐπ᾽ ἄκρον [ὄ]ρους ὑψηλοῦς καὶ ἐστηριγμένη οὔτε πε[σ]εῖν δύναται οὔτε κρυ[β]ῆναι.

κρύσταλλος.

P Lond 130¹⁵⁰ (horoscope—i ii A.D.) (= I. p. 137) ὁμοία κρυστάλλῳ, P Leid Wˣᵛⁱⁱⁱ·²⁹ (ii/iv A.D.) κρυστάλλου ῥεινήματος (*l.* ῥινήματος, "filings") στατῆρες δ. With Wisd 19²¹ κρυσταλλοειδὲς γένος ἀμβροσίας τροφῆς, cf. Usener *Epic.* p. 45, 2 πῆξιν . . . κρυσταλλοειδῆ. In MGr κρυσταλλένιος, "of crystal," is used as an endearing address to a girl.

κρυφῆ

or κρυφῇ (Moulton *Gr.* ii. p. 84) "secretly," as in Eph 5¹², is found in a iii/B.C. ostrakon-letter published in *Archiv* vi. p. 220, No. 8³ ἀπόστειλον τοῖς ὑπογεγραμμένοις τὰς πεταλίας κρυφῇ καὶ μηθεὶς αἰσθανέσθω. The form κρυβῇ (cf. 2 Kings 12¹²) occurs in a declaration by an egg-seller that he will sell only in the open market—P Oxy I. 83¹⁴ (A.D. 327) ὁμολογῶ . . . μὴ ἐξῖναί μοι εἰς τὸ ὑπιὸν κρυβῇ ἢ καὶ ἐν τῇ ἡμετέρᾳ οἰκίᾳ πωλῖν, "I acknowledge that it shall not be lawful for me in the future to sell secretly or in my house" (Edd.). MGr κρυφά, "secretly," κρυφὰ ἀπό, "without the knowledge of."

κτάομαι.

Occurrences of pres. and aor. may help some difficult NT passages—P Petr II. 8(3)⁷ (B.C. 246) ἐὰν δέ τινες [κ?]τήσωντ[αι, "but if any shall acquire them," P Tebt II. 281¹¹ (B.C. 125) παρὰ τῶν κτωμένων οἰκίας ἢ τόπους, "from acquirers of houses or spaces," *ib.* I. 5⁴·¹² (B.C. 118) μηδ᾽ ἄλλους κτᾶσθαι μηδὲ χρῆσθαι τοῖς τε λινυφαντικοῖς κα[ὶ] βυσσουργικοῖς ἐργαλείοις, "nor shall any other persons take possession of or use the tools required for cloth-weaving or

47

byssus-manufacture" (Edd.), P Oxy II. 259⁶ (A.D. 23) ὀμνύω . . . εἰ μὴν κτήσεσθαι ἡμ[έ]ρας τριάκοντα ἐν αἷ (l. αἷς) ἀ[πο]καταστήσω ὃν ἐνγεγύη/μαι παρά σου ἐκ [τ]ῆς πολιτικῆς φυλα[κ]ῆς, "I swear that I have thirty days in which to restore to you the man whom I bailed out of the public prison" (Edd.), where we seem to have the rather common confusion of aor. and fut. inf., cf. *ib.*¹⁸ μὴ ἔχοντός μου ἐκξ (= ἐξ)ουσίαν χρόνον ἕτερον [κ]τή[σ]εσθαι, "and I have no power to obtain a further period of time" (Edd.), *ib.* 237ᵛⁱⁱ ⁴² (A.D. 186) ὧν ἐὰν καὶ ἴδια κτήσωνται μεθέτερα "of whatever they may acquire themselves besides" (Edd.). A good illustration for Lk 21¹⁹ "you shall win your own selves," as opposed to "forfeiting self" in 9²⁴, may be found in P Par 63ᵢ²⁷ (B.C. 164) (= P Petr III. p. 28) τοὺς ἀνθρώπους ἐκ τηλικαύτης καταφθ(ο)ρᾶ[ς] ἀρτ[ί]ως ἀνακτωμένους, "the population recovering from so great a distress" (Mahaffy). So we say of a sick man, "He isn't himself yet." This same meaning of "acquire," "gradually obtain the complete mastery of the body," is probably to be preferred in 1 Th 4¹ (as against *Thess.* p. 49). For the perf. κέκτημαι (not found in the NT) with its present force "possess" (cf. *Proleg.* p. 147) we may cite P Tebt I. 5⁹⁷ (B.C. 118) οἷ τὴν [σπό]ριμον κεκτημένοι, P Oxy IV. 705⁷⁰ (A.D. 200–2) χωρία κεκτήμεθα, "own estates," *ib.* VI. 903²⁴ (iv/A.D.) ὅσα κέκτηται, "how much she has possessed herself of," and from the inscr. *Syll* 178¹¹ (end of iv/B.C.) ἔδωκεν . . . καὶ αὐτοῖς καὶ ἐκγόνοις, κυρίοις οὖσι κεκτῆσθαι καὶ ἀλλάσσεσθαι καὶ ἀποδόσθαι. See also P Eleph 14²³ (Ptol.) κυριεύσουσιν δὲ καθ᾽ ἃ καὶ οἱ πρῶτον κύριοι ἐκέκτηντο, and the contracted ἐκτῶντο in BGU III. 992 ⁱⁱ· ⁶ (B.C. 167). Other reff. to the inscriptional evidence will be found in Mayser *Gr.* p. 340.

κτῆμα

may mean "a piece of landed property" of any kind, "a field," as in Ac 5¹ (cf. ³ χωρίον). Thus BGU II. 530²¹ (i/A.D.) (= *Selections*, p. 61) τὸ κτῆμα ἀγεώργητόν ἐστιν refers to an allotment that was lying neglected and untilled, while the word is frequently applied to a "vineyard," e.g. P Giss I. 79ⁱⁱⁱ ¹¹ (c. A.D. 117)οὖ χ[άρι]ν οὐδ[εὶ]ς ἄθυμ.ῖ πωλεῖν κτῆμα, P Oxy IV. 707²⁵ (c. A.D. 136) τὰς τοῦ κτήματος καὶ πωμαρίου πλάτας, "the walls (?) of the vineyard and orchard" (Edd.), and with the adj. P Ryl II. 157⁴ (A.D. 135) οὐσιακ[ὸ]ν ἀμπελικὸν κτῆμα, "the domain-land vineyard" (Edd.). For the plur., as in Mk 10²², see *ib.* 76¹¹ (late ii A.D.) a deposition regarding the division of certain property—τὴν διαίρεσιν τῶν κτημάτων—"according to households and not individuals" (κατ᾽ οἶκον καὶ μὴ κατὰ πρόσωπον), and *ib.* I. 28¹⁸² (iv/A.D.) δεσπότης ἔσται πολλῶν ἀγαθῶν καὶ κτημάτων, "he will be master of many blessings and possessions." The dim. κτημάτιον may be illustrated from P Tebt II. 616 (ii/A.D.) ἐπιμέλεσθαι τ[οῦ] κτηματίου τῶν καθηκόντων ἔργων, and the collective κτῆσις from P Ryl II. 145⁷ (A.D. 38) ζυτοποιὸς τῆς κτήσεως, "a brewer on the estate." For the adj. κτηματικός cf. P Oxy I. 136¹⁸ (A.D. 583) γεωργῶν κτηματικῶν τε καὶ κωμητικῶν καὶ ἐξωτικῶν, "labourers both on the estate and in the villages and adjacent property" (Edd.), and for the word κτηματώνης, "the purchaser of an article," which is confined to the inscrr., see Deissmann *BS* p. 147.

κτῆνος,

mostly in plur. "flocks and herds," is common, e.g. P Tebt I. 56⁸ (late ii/B.C.) οὐκ ἔχομεν ἕως τῆς τροφῆς τῶν κτηνῶν ἡμῶν, "we have not so much as food for our cattle" (Edd.), P Ryl II. 126¹⁵ (A.D. 28–9) τὰ ἑατοῦ πρόβατα καὶ βοικὰ κτήνη. For the more specialized sense "beast of burden," (as in Lk 10³⁴, Ac 23²⁴) cf. BGU III. 912²¹ (A.D. 33) τὰ ὀνικὰ κτήνη, P Fay 111⁶ (A.D. 95–6) (= *Selections*, p. 66) ἐργατικὰ κτήνη δέκα, P Oxy XIV. 1756¹⁰ (c. i/A.D.) ἐὰν τὰ κτήνη ἐξέρχηται ἐπὶ γράστιν ("green fodder") πέμψω σοι ἐλαίαν: cf. also M. Anton. v. 11 where κτῆνος, "a domestic animal," is contrasted with θηρίον, "a wild beast." The adj. κτηνοτρόφος occurs several times in the Fayûm papyri and ostraca, e.g. 18(*b*)² (i/B.C.): cf. LXX Numb 32⁴ where it is applied to land.

κτήτωρ.

For this word = "possessor," "owner," as in Ac 4³⁴, cf. P Oxy II. 237ᵛⁱⁱⁱ· ³¹ (A.D. 186) κελεύω οὖν πάντας τοὺς κτήτορας ἐντὸς μηνῶν ἓξ ἀπογράψασθαι τὴν ἰδίαν κτῆσιν εἰς τὴν τῶν ἐνκτήσεων βιβλιοθήκην, "I command all owners to register their property at the property record-office within six months" (Edd.), P Tebt II. 378²¹ (a lease of land—A.D. 265) τ[ῶν δ]ημοσίων πάντων ὄντων πρὸς ὑμ[ᾶς τοὺ]ς κτήτορας, "all the State dues being paid by you the landlords" (Edd.). See also *Archiv* v. p. 374 f. For the later sense of "founder" Preuschen (*HZNT* ad Ac *l.c.*) refers to Krumbacher *Indogerm. Forsch.* xxv. p. 393 ff. The adj. κτητορικός occurs in the fragmentary P Giss I. 124⁷ (vi/A.D.).

κτίζω

in the sense of "found" a city or colony, as in 1 Esdr 4⁵³, may be illustrated from an inscr., probably to be assigned to B.C. 60–8, which is reproduced in P Fay p. 48¹ κτ[ι]σθέντος τοῦ σημαινομένου ἱεροῦ: cf. also the Alexandrian erotic fragment P Grenf I. 1⁴ (ii/B.C.) ὁ τὴν φιλίαν ἐκτικὼς λαβέ με ἔρως, "love the stablisher of friendship overcame me." The usage in this last passage approximates more nearly to the distinctive Biblical usage of the word, "create," "form," which occurs again in the imprecatory tablet Wunsch *AF* 4¹ (iii/A.D.) ἐξορκίζω σε ὅστ[ι]ς ποτ᾽ εἶ, νεκυδαῖμον, τὸν θεὸν τὸν κτίσαντα γῆν κ[α]ὶ οὐρανὸν Ἰωνα.

κτίσις.

Syll 608⁴ (i/B.C.) τοὺς γεγ[ενημένους] ἀπὸ τῆς κτίσεως κατὰ γένος ἱερεῖς τοῦ Ποσειδῶ]νος, *ib.* 301² (A.D. 133) ἔτους γ̄ τῆς καθιερώσεως τοῦδε τοῦ Ὀλυμπίου καὶ τῆς κτίσεος τοῦ Πανελληνίου. In connexion with the NT usage for the Creation (Mk 10⁶ *al.*), Hicks (*CR* i. p. 7) draws attention to κτίσις as the regular term for the founding of a city, e.g. Polyb. ix. 1. 4.

κτίσμα.

In the NT (1 Tim 4⁴ *al.*, cf. Wisd 9²) κτίσμα seems to be always used in a concrete sense = "created thing," "creature," but for the meaning "foundation" we may cite P Lond 121¹⁸³ (iii/A.D.) (= I. p. 99) ἐπάνω τῶν τεσσάρων κτισμάτων τοῦ κόσμου, BGU I. 3¹⁹ (A.D. 605) τὰ ἀναλωθέντα παρά σου εἰς τὸ κτίσμα τῆς ἐκεῖσε ἐπαύλεως.

κτίστης.

This NT ἅπ. εἰρ. (1 Pet 4¹⁹ of God) is applied *quinquies* to the prytanis of Oxyrhynchus as κτίστης τῆς πόλεως in the account of a popular demonstration made in his honour—P Oxy I. 41⁶·⁴⁷ (iii/iv A.D.). The same title is given to Domitian in *Priene* 229¹, and similarly to Trajan (*CIG* II. 2572 τῷ τῆς οἰκουμένης κτίστῃ): cf. Magie p. 68, and see *CR* i. p. 7. Other exx. of the word, which is not found in Attic writers, are the magic P Lond 46²³⁷ (iv/A.D.) (= I. p. 72) where the invoker assumes the name of the god Thoth—ἐγώ εἰμι θωῦθ φαρμάκων καὶ γραμμάτων εὑρέτης καὶ κτίστης, and *ib.* 121⁹⁶³ (iii/A.D.) (= I. p. 114) δεῦρό μοι ὁ ἐν τῷ στερεῷ πνεύματι ἀόρατος παντοκράτωρ κτίστης τῶν θεῶν. A subst. (or verbal adj.) κτιστόν is found in one of the Gemellus letters, P Fay 117²³ (A.D. 108) ᾧ ἔγραφος μυ (*l.* ὃ ἔγραφές μοι) μὴ ἡσυχάσαι τῷ κτιστῷ περιτὸν (*l.*—ιττὸν) γέγραπτα[ι, "what you write to me about not neglecting the building you have said more than enough" (Edd.). On a κοινὸν τῶν κτιστῶν ("soldiers"), see *Archiv* i. p. 208.

κυβεία.

The corresponding verb is used in its literal sense of playing with dice or gaming in the magic P Lond 121⁴²⁴ (iii A.D.) (= I. p. 98) ποίησόν μοι κυβεύοντα νικῆσαι. For the derived meaning "cheat" see Epict. ii. 19. 28, iii. 21. 22. The subst. κυβευτής is found in Vett. Val. p. 202⁶ πλαστο-γράφοι ἅρπαγες θυρεπανοῖκται κυβευταί.

κυβέρνησις.

The verb, which is used of Divine "guiding" in Wisd 14⁶, is applied to the management of a household in the inscr. quoted *s.v.* ἀνέγκλητος *ad fin.*: cf. 1 Cor 12²⁸. The compd. διακυβερνάω is used of a woman "piloting" herself and her child out of a time of crisis—ἐκ τοῦ το[ιού]του καιροῦ ἐμαυτή[ν] τε καὶ τὸ παιδί[ον σ]ου διακεκυβερνηκυῖα (P Lond 42¹⁶ (B.C. 168) (= I. p. 30, *Selections*, p. 10)). For a new literary citation for κυβερνάω see Herodas ii. 99 f. ταῦτα σκοπεῦντες πάντα τὴν δίκην ὀρθῇ γνώμῃ κυβερνᾶτε.

κυβερνήτης

in the sense of "steersman," "pilot," is common, e.g. P Oxy II. 276⁶ (A.D. 77) κυβερνήται π[λ]οίο[υ] ναυλωσίμου, *ib.* III. 522¹⁵ (ii/A.D.) ναυτικ(οῦ) Ὠρίωνος κυβε(ρνήτου), P Tebt II. 370³ (ii/iii A.D.) κυβερνήτου πλοίου. In *OGIS* 676³ (A.D. 106-7) (= *Archiv* ii. p. 439, No. 43) we hear of an official described as—κυβερνήτου Νείλου. In Ac 27¹¹ τῷ κυβερνήτῃ καὶ τῷ ναυκλήρῳ is rendered by Ramsay (*Paul.* p. 322) "the sailing-master and the captain."

Isis is described as κυβερνῆτις in the literary papyrus P Oxy XI. 1380⁶⁹ (early ii/A.D.).

κυκλεύω

is used in connexion with working the water-wheel in P Lond 131 *recto* ³⁰⁶ (A.D. 78-9) (I. p. 185) κυκλευτῇ κυκλεύ-οντι τὸ ὄργ(ανον) (cf *Archiv* i. p. 131), and in a lease of land P Grenf I. 58⁷ (c. A.D. 561) ἑτοίμως ἔχω κυκλεῦσαι τὸ αὐτὸ γεώργιον. For κυκλευτής see P Ryl II. 157¹⁵ (A.D. 135), and for κυκλευτήριον (not in LS) P Lond 1012³³ (A.D. 633) (= III. p. 266), P Giss I. 56⁸ (vi/A.D.).

κυκλόθεν.

Kaibel 546⁷·⁴ (Imperial)—a sepulchral epitaph—

ἀλλά με πᾶν δένδρος χαρίεν περὶ ῥίσκον ἀνέρπει,
κυκλόθεν εὐκάρποις κλωσὶν ἀγαλλόμενον.

Cf. also BGU IV. 1117²⁵ (B.C. 13), and the late P Lond V. 1686¹⁶ (A.D. 565) κύκλωθεν (see Lob. *Phryn.* p. 9).

κύκλος.

For the dat. κύκλῳ used adverbially "round about," as in Rev 4⁶, see CPR I. 42¹⁰ κύκλῳ τοῦ χωρίου: cf. P Fay 110⁷ (A.D. 94) τὰ κύκλωι τοῦ ἐλαιουργίου ἔξωθεν σκάψων ἐπὶ βαθός, "dig a deep trench round the oil-press outside" (Edd.), P Tebt II. 342²⁶ (late ii/A.D.) τοῦ κεραμ(είου) ἐν κύκλῳ αὐτ οῦ ψ[ι]λοῦ τόπου, "the vacant space surround-ing the pottery" (Edd.), and from the inscr. *OGIS* 455¹² (i/B.C.) κύκλῳ τε ἐκείνου τοῦ ἱεροῦ . . . [οὗτος ὁ] τόπος ἄσυλος ἔστω. The adj. κύκλιος is found in *ib.* 213³⁸ (iv/iii B.C.) ἐν] τοῖς κυκλίοις ἀγῶσιν.

κυλισμός.

The form κυλισμός, "rolling," which is read in the best texts of 2 Pet 2²², is found in Prov 2¹⁸ (Theod.). For κύλισμα, as in the TR, cf. Ezek 10¹³ (Symm.), where, how-ever, the word has its proper meaning, "something rolled round," rather than a "rolling-place" as in the Petrine passage. In P Hib I. 110 (iii B.C.) certain documents are described as κυλιστοί "rolls." According to the editors the difference from ἐπιστολαί, which are also mentioned, was "perhaps one of size rather than of contents": cf. also *Preisigke* 1¹⁷ (iii/A.D.) κυλιστοὺς ἱματίων δέκα.

κυλίω.

For this form which replaces the older pres. in –ίνδω, see the citations *s.v.* βόρβορος.

κυλλός.

In P Lond 776¹⁰ (A.D. 552) (= III. p. 278) we read of a κυλλὴ κυκλάς ("crooked wheel"?) used for purposes of irrigation: the exact character of the machine is unknown. In Herodas *Procem.* 4 (ed. Nairn p. 101) τ]ὰ κυλλὰ ἀείδειν refers to the "limping" verse, the "choliambic": cf. the use of χωλός in *ib.* i. 71 χωλὴν δ' ἀείδειν χωλ' ἂν ἐξεπαίδευσα, "I'd have taught her for her lame (vicious) advice to go limping away" (Ed.), and the juxtaposition of the two adjectives in Mt 15³⁰.

κῦμα.

P Lond 46²⁶³ (iv/A.D.) (= I. p. 73) ὑπὸ τῶν τῆς θαλάσσης κυμάτων: cf. *ib.* ²⁴ (= I. p. 66) κυματούμ(ενον), "rolled like a wave" (Ed.).

κύμβαλον.

With 1 Cor 13¹ cf. P Hib I. 54¹³ (c. B.C. 245) (= Wit-kowski², p. 34), where in preparation for a domestic festival Demophon sends for a certain Zenobius—ἔχοντα τύμπανον καὶ κύμβαλα καὶ κρόταλα, "with tabret, and cymbals, and rattles": cf. Deissmann *LAE* p. 150 ff. The word is frequent in the LXX, e.g. 1 Kings 18⁶: for the verb κυμβαλίζω see Neh 12²⁷.

κύμινον.

"cummin," a word of Phoenician origin (Heb. כַּמֹּן—Isai 28²⁵․²⁷). Cf. P Tebt I. 112¹³ (an account—B.C. 112) λόγος . . . κυμίνου ε̄, ἐλ(αίου) νε̄, ib. II. 314¹⁰ (ii/A.D.) κυμ[ί]νου μέτρον ᾱ, P Fay 101ⁱ·⁹ (c. B.C. 18) et saepe.

κυνάριον.

This dim. of κύων, which occurs quater in the NT, is used at least once by Epictetus—iv. 1. 111 εἶθ᾽ οὕτως . . προσελθε ἐπὶ κυνάριον, ἐπὶ ἱππάριον, ἐπὶ ἀγρίδιον, "then proceed thus . . to a dog, a horse, an estate" (Sharp, p. 23). For the more classical κυνίδιον (Lob. Phryn. p. 180) see M. Antoninus vii. 13 κυνιδίοις ὀστάριον ἐρριμένον, "a bone thrown to lap-dogs."

κύπτω.

See s.vv. ἀνακύπτω, κατακύπτω, παρακύπτω. Ἐκκύπτω is found several times in the LXX, e.g. Ps 101 (102)¹⁹ ἐξέκυψεν ἐξ ὕψους ἁγίου αὐτοῦ.

Κυρηναῖος

is found in P Petr I. 16 (1)³ (B.C. 237) the will of a certain Menippus—Κ[υρ]ηναῖος τῆς ἐπιγονῆς, "a Cyrenean by descent": cf. ib. 22(1)³ (B.C. 249) Θεάρίστιος Κυρηναῖος τῶν περὶ Λυσίμαχον, and Michel 897²⁶ (i/B.C. ad init.).

Κυρήνη.

For the presence of a Jewish population in Cyrenaica see the decree set up at Berenice by the Jewish community in honour of the Roman governor, M. Tittius—CIG III. 5361 ἔδοξε τοῖς ἄρχουσι τῷ πολιτεύματι τῶν ἐν Βερενίκη Ἰουδαίων κτλ.

Κυρήνιος.

Upon the different forms of this proper name in the MSS. of Lk 2², see Robertson Gr. p. 192, and for the bearing of certain recently discovered inscrr. on Quirinius' Governorship of Syria, and the date of the Nativity (now to be placed in all probability in B.C. 8), see W. M. Ramsay Recent Discovery, pp. 222–300, Journal of Roman Studies vii. p. 273 ff. There is also a convenient summary of the new evidence by W. M. Calder in Discovery i. (1920), p. 100 ff.

κυρία.

The use of κυρία as a courteous, and even affectionate, form of address in the ordinary correspondence of the time, may be said to have settled what Westcott (Epp. of S. John, p. 214) regarded as the "insoluble" problem of 2 Jn⁵ by showing that κυρία there must be understood not of a church, nor of any dignified "lady," but of a "dear" friend of the writer. Thus in P Oxy IV. 744² (B.C. 1) we find a man writing—Βερούτι τῇ κυρίᾳ μου, "to my dear Berous," and similarly in an invitation to a festival, ib. I. 112¹·³·⁷ (iii/iv. A.D.), the appellative occurs thrice in the same sense—χαίροις. κυρία μου Σερηνία . . π(αρὰ) Πετοσείριος. πᾶν ποίησον, κυρία, ἐξελθεῖ[ν τῇ] ̄κ τοῖς γενεθλίοις τοῦ θεο[ῦ] . . . ὅρα [μὴ] ἀμελήσῃς, κυρία, "greeting, dear Serenia, from Petosiris. Be sure, dear, to come up on the 20ᵗʰ for the birthday festival of the god. See that you do not forget, dear." Cf Exp VI. iii., p. 194 ff., where

Rendel Harris with his accustomed ingenuity further discovers that John's "dear" friend was a Gentile proselyte of the tribe of Ruth, and like Ruth a widow! The word is also used with more formality by a slave addressing her "mistress" in P Tebt II. 413¹·⁶·²⁰ (ii/iii A.D.) Ἀφ(= Ἀφρ)οδίτη Ἀρσινόητι τῇ κυρίᾳ πολλὰ χαίρειν . . μὴ δόξῃς με, κυρί[α], ἡμελημένᾱι σου τῶν ἐντολῶν . . . ἀπόδος παρ᾽ Ἀπ- (= Ἀφρ)οδίτης κυρία, and in the Christian P Oxy VI. 939⁵⁹ (iv/A.D.) (= Selections, p. 128), where a servant writes to his master that the favour of the Lord God had been shown—ὥστε τὴν] κυρίαν ἀνασφῆλαι ἐκ τῆς καταλαβούσης [αὐτὴν νός]ου, "by the recovery of my mistress from the sickness which overtook her" (Edd.), and by saving her life in answer to her prayers—ταῖς εὐ]χαῖς ἡμῶν ἐπένευσεν διασώσας ἡμῖν [τὴν ἡμῶν] κυρίαν. See also s.v. κύριος.

κυριακός,

which occurs in 1 Cor 11²⁰, Rev 1¹⁰, is described by Grimm-Thayer as "a bibl. and eccles. word," but exx. of it from the inscrr. = "Imperial" are given by LS, and the same usage is amply supported by our documents. The following instances may suffice—P Lond 328¹⁰ (A.D. 163) (= II. p. 75) a camel is provided εἰς κυριακὰς χρείας τῶν ἀπὸ Βερνείκης γεινο(μένων) πορίων (l. πορειῶν), "for Imperial service on the caravans that travel from Bernice," P Oxy III. 474⁴¹ (A.D. 184 ?) τοῦ κυριακοῦ χρήματος, "the Imperial revenue," P Giss I. 48⁸ (A.D. 202–3) κατὰ κυριακῆς γῆς (see the editor's note), P Oxy XII. 1461³⁰ (A.D. 222) ἐν κτήσει κυριακῇ, "in Imperial ownership," BGU I. 15¹⁵ (iii/A.D.) εἰς τὸν κυριακὸν λόγον, "into the Imperial treasury," and ib. 266¹⁸ (A.D. 216–7) εἰς τὰς ἐν Συρίᾳ κυρι[α]κὰς ὑπηρεσίας, "for the Imperial service in Syria." The earliest known ex. of this official use of the word is apparently OGIS 669¹³ (A.D. 68) εἰδὼς τοῦτο συμφέρειν καὶ ταῖς κυριακαῖς ψήφοις ("the Imperial finances"),¹⁸ ἔξω < ι.> τῶν ὀφειλόντων εἰς τὸν κυριακὸν λόγον ("the Imperial treasury"): see Deissmann LAE p. 362 ff., where attention is also drawn to the significant use of Σεβαστή, as denoting "Emperor's Day" in this same inscr., and the conjecture is thrown out "that the distinctive title 'Lord's Day' may have been connected with conscious feelings of protest against the cult of the Emperor with its 'Emperor's Day'" (p. 364); cf. also Encycl. Brit. 2813 ff., and Wilcken Ostr. i., p. 812. The word κυριακός had been previously discussed by Deissmann in BS p. 217 ff., and to his citations from the inscrr. we may add PAS ii. 14 (Makuf, ancient Heraclea, in Caria) ἀποτίσει τῷ κυριακῷ [φ]ίσκῳ, ib. 21 (same place) ἀπο[τ]είσει [τ]ῷ κυριακῷ φίσκῳ (cited by Hatch JBL xxvii. 2, p. 138 f.). The word is used of a church-building in the iv/A.D. P Oxy VI. 903¹⁹ ἀπελθοῦσα [εἰ]ς τὸ κυριακὸν ἐν Σαμβαθώ, "when I had gone out to the church at Sambatho" (Edd.), cf. ²¹. A Syracusan inscr., Kaibel 737—no date, runs—

Ἡμέρα κυριακῇ δεσμευθεῖσα ἀλύτοις καμάτοις ἐπὶ κοίτης,
ἧς καὶ τοὔνομα Κυριακή, ἡμέρα κυριακῇ παντὸς βίου λύσιν ἔσχε.

MGr κυριακή, "Sunday."

κυριεύω

is construed with gen. of obj., as in Lk 22²⁵ etc., in such passages as P Par 15¹³ (B.C. 120) οἰκιῶν, ὧν καὶ τῶν προγό-

νων μου κεκυριευκότων ἐφ' ὅσον περιῆσαν χρόνον, οr P Tebt
I. 104[15] (B.C. 92), a marriage contract in which provision is
made that the wife is to own their property in common with
her husband—κυρεύουσαν (l. κυριεύουσαν—but cf. Mayser
p. 147) μετ' αὐτοῦ κοινῇ τῶν ὑπαρχόντων αὐτοῖς: cf. also
Michel 976[11] (B.C. 300) ὧν τε αὐτὸς ἐκυρίευσεν, "those
things for which he was personally responsible." P Lond
154[14] (A.D. 68) (= II. p. 179) μηδὲ τοὺς παρ' αὐτοῦ κυριεύ-
οντα[ς αὐτῶν] . . κ αὶ] κατασπῶντες shows part. acc. plur.
in -ας followed by one in -ες (Thackeray Gr. i. p. 149). In
the magic P Lond 121[838] (iii/A.D.) (= I. p. 111) the verb is
followed by the acc.—τοῦ κυριεύοντος τὴ ν] ὅλην οἰκουμένην,
and in P Eleph 14[14] (Ptol.) the usual constr. with the gen.—
τῆς δὲ γῆς κυριεύσει καὶ τῶν καρπῶν—is accompanied by an
absol. constr.—[22] κυριεύσουσιν δὲ καθ' ἃ καὶ οἱ πρῶτον
κύριοι ἐκέκτηντο. For the same two constructions we may
compare the verb with the gen. in Rom 6,9,14 al. and its
absol. occurrence in 2 Cor 3[17] οὗ δὲ τὸ πνεῦμα κυριεύει, ἐλευθερία according to Bishop Chase's happy conjectural reading:
see JTS xvii. p. 60 ff. On ὁ κυριεύων as the colloquial name
for the "master" argument, see Epict. ii. 19. 1. The subst.
κυριεία is found in P Tor I. 1[x. 37] (B.C. 110) μηδεμιᾶς κρατήσεως μηδὲ κυριείας τινὸς ἐγγαίου περιγενομένης αὐτῶι, where
the editor (p. 152) distinguishes between κράτησις, occupatio,
possessio, or ius in re, and κυριεία, dominium, or ius ad rem:
for the form κυρεία, as in Dan 4[15] (Theod.) al., cf. P Amh
II. 95[1.6] (A.D. 109) τὴν τούτων κυρ[εί]αν καὶ κράτησιν, P
Tebt II. 294[19] (A.D. 146). See also Mayser Gr. pp. 92,
417.

κύριος.

(1) κύριος is used in the wide sense of "possessor,"
"owner," as in Mk 13[35], in P Tebt I. 5[147] (B.C. 118) τοὺς
κυρίους τῶν . . οἰκιῶν, "the owners of the houses," and
hence the meaning "master," as in P Amh II. 135[11] (early
ii/A.D.) ὁ κύριος τῆ γ] προέγραψεν ἡμᾶς, "the master wrote
us on the 3rd"—with reference to certain instructions which
the writer of the letter had received.

(2) From this the transition is easy to κύριος either as a
title of honour addressed by subordinates to their superiors,
or as a courteous appellative in the case of persons nearly
related. (a) As exx. of the first class we may cite P Fay
106[15] (c. A.D. 140) ἐξησθένησα . . . κύριε, "I became very
weak, my lord"—a petition to a Prefect, and, more generally,
ib. 129[1] (iii/A.D.) χαῖρε, κύριε τ[ι]μιώτατ[ε, ib. 134[2] (early
iv/A.D.) παρακληθεὶς κύριε σκύλον σεαυτὸν πρὸς ἡμᾶς,
"I entreat you, sir, to hasten to me" (Edd.), P Lond 417[5]
(c. A.D 346) (II. p. 299, Selections, p. 124) γινώσκιν σε
θέλω, κύριε, π[ερὶ] Παύλω τοῦ στρατιότη περὶ τῆς φυγῆς—
the village priest of Hermopolis to a military official with
reference to a deserter named Paulus, and the Christian
P Heid 6[6] (iv/A.D.) (= Selections, p. 125) κύριέ μου ἀγαπιτέ
—a certain Justinus to a Christian "brother" Papnuthius.
See also s.v. κυρία, and cf. Preisigke 1114[2.5] (A.D. 147–8)
ἐκόψαμεν τοὺς μεγάλους λίθους . . εἰς τὴν πύλην τοῦ κυρίου
Ἀπόλλω[νος καὶ] τῆς κυρίας [. (b) The designation is
applied to near relatives, e.g. a father—BGU II. 423[2]
(ii/A.D.) (= Selections, p. 90) Ἀπίων Ἐπιμάχῳ τῷ πατρὶ
καὶ κυρίῳ πλεῖστα χαίρειν, a mother—P Lips I. 110[1] (iii/iv
A.D.) Σαραπίω]ν . τῇ κ[υ]ρίᾳ μου μητρὶ . . . , a brother—

BGU III. 949[1] (. A.D. 300) κυρίῳ μου ἀδελφῷ Ἡρᾷ, a
sister (and probably wife)—P Oxy IV. 744[1] (B.C. 1) (Selections, p. 32) Ἱλαρίωνα [. ων] Ἄλιτι τῆι ἀδελφῆι πλεῖστα
χαίρειν, and even a son—ib. I. 123[1] (iii/iv A.D.) κυρίῳ μου
υἱῷ Διονυσοθέωνι.

(3) It is, however, with the religious use of κύριος that
we are specially concerned, and in keeping with the conception of "lordship," which was so characteristic of Oriental
religions, we may begin by noticing its common use in connexion with the cult of the Egyptian God Sarapis. Letters
frequently begin with some such formula as—πρὸ μὲν πάντων
εὔχομαί σε ὑιαίνειν (l. ὑγ—) καὶ τὸ προσκύνημά σου ποιῶ
παρὰ τῷ κυρίῳ Σαράπιδι, "before all else I pray for your
health, and I supplicate the lord Sarapis on your behalf"
(P Fay 127[5]—ii/iii A.D.), and we may add, owing to the
striking resemblance of phraseology to 1 Cor 10[21] such
invitations to a ceremonial feast in the Serapeum as P Oxy I.
110[2] (ii/A.D.) ἐρωτᾷ σε Χαιρήμων δειπνῆσαι εἰς κλείνην τοῦ
κυρίου Σαράπιδος ἐν τῷ Σαραπείῳ αὔριον, ἥτις ἐστὶν ιε, ἀπὸ
ὥρας θ, "Chaeremon requests your company at dinner at the
table of the lord Sarapis in the Serapeum to-morrow, the
15th, at 9 o'clock" (Edd.), cf. ib. III. 523 (ii/A.D.)
(= Selections, p. 97).

(4) From this it is easy to see how the title came to be
applied to sovereigns or rulers in the East. Thus, to confine
ourselves to the period immediately preceding the Christian
era, Deissmann (LAE, p. 356) cites the description of
Ptolemy XIII. as τοῦ κυρίου βασιλ[έ]ος θεοῦ, "the lord king
god," from an inser. of 12th May B.C. 62 (OGIS 186[8]), and
another inser. from Alexandria of B.C. 52 where Ptolemy
XIV. and Cleopatra are called οἱ κύριοι θεοὶ μέγιστοι, "the
lords, the most great gods" (cf. Berl. Sitzungsberichte, 1902,
p. 1096). Similarly, as the same writer points out (LAE,
p. 357) κύριος is applied to Herod the Great (B.C. 37–34)
in OGIS 415[1] Βασιλεῖ Ἡρώδει κυρίῳ, and to Herod
Agrippa I. (A.D. 37–44) in ib. 418[1] ὑπὲρ σωτηρίας κυρίου
βασιλέως Ἀγρίππα, al.

There is no evidence that the title was applied to the
Roman Emperors in the West before the time of Domitian.
Indeed it was specially disclaimed by Augustus and Tiberius
as contrary to the Roman conception of the "Principate"
(see Ovid Fast. ii. 142, Suet. Aug. 53, Tac. Ann. ii. 87,
Suet. Tib. 27, cited by Hatch JBL xxvii. 2, p. 139). In
the East, on the other hand, it was bestowed on Claudius,
and becomes very common in the time of Nero. For
Claudius we may cite the official report of certain events
which had taken place—ζ (ἔτους) Τιβερίου Κλαυδίου Καίσαρος τοῦ κυρίου (P Oxy I. 37[1. 6]—A.D. 49 (= Selections,
p. 49)), and Ostr 1038[6] (A.D. 54) ιδ (ἔτους) (Τιβερίου) Κλαυδίου . . . τοῦ κυρίου. Numerous other ostraca in Wilcken's
collection show the designation as applied to Nero e.g. 16[4]
(A.D. 60) (ἔτους) ζ Νέρωνος τοῦ κυρίου Χοίαχ ε, 17[4], al.:
cf. also for the absence of the art., as in Lk 2[11], Col 3[17],
Meyer Ostr 39[1] (A.D. 62) ἔτος ῆ Νέρονος κυρίου Παῦνι ῆ.
From the papyri it is sufficient to quote P Oxy II. 246[30]
(A.D. 66) in which a registration of cattle is certified as
having taken place—(ἔτους) ιβ Νέρωνος τοῦ κυρου (l. κυρίου),
and from the inser. Syll 376[31] (Boeotia—A.D. 67), where
Nero is hailed as ὁ τοῦ παντὸς κόσμου κύριος Νέρων: cf. [55].
To later dates belong such passages as Meyer Ostr 17[3]
(A.D. 74–5) Οὐεσπασιανοῦ τοῦ κυρίου, Magn 192[8] (time of

Antoninus) τειμηθέ[ντα] ὑπὸ τῶν κυρίων Ἀν[τωνεί]νου καὶ Κομόδου κα[ὶ Λουκί]ου Οὐήρου, and *Priene* 230⁵ (A.D. 196–212), where a proconsul is described as ὁ τῶν κυρίων ἐπίτροπος, the κύριοι being Septimius Severus and Caracalla or Caracalla and Geta. See further the material collected by Roscher *Ausf. Lex. d. griech. u. röm. Mythologie* ii. 1, p. 1755 ff., Kattenbusch *Das apostolische Symbol* ii. p. 605 ff., Lietzmann *HZNT* iii. 1, p. 53 ff., and especially the full investigation in W. Bousset's *Kyrios Christos*, Göttingen, 1913.

(5) It lies outside our immediate purpose to examine the Pauline usage of κύριος in detail (cf. *Thess.* p. 136 ff.) beyond remarking that while that usage was doubtless primarily influenced by the LXX, which employed κύριος to render the tetragrammaton, there is good reason for finding in the Apostle's insistence upon "the name (of κύριος) which is above every name" (Phil 2⁹ a protest against the worship of "the gods many and lords many (θεοὶ πολλοὶ καὶ κύριοι πολλοί)" (1 Cor 8⁵), with which Christianity found itself confronted. See especially Deissmann's illuminating discussion in *LAE* p. 353 ff., which has been freely drawn upon here, and for the Pauline idea of κύριος the art. by Böhlig in *ZNTW* xiv. (1913), p. 23 ff.

(6) One or two miscellaneous exx. of the title may be added. Thus, in view of Lightfoot's statement (*Phil.²* p. 312 n.³) that κύριε is not used in prayer to God before apostolic times, we may quote P Tebt II. 284⁶ (i/B.C.) καὶ ὡς θέλει ὁ Σεκνεβτῦ(νις) ὁ κύριος θεὸς καταβήσομαι ἐλευθέρως—the writer had received an oracular response: cf. *Preisigke* 1068 παρὰ τῷ κυρίῳ θεῷ Βησᾷ. In *OGIS* 655³, an inscr. from Socnopaei Nesus in the Fayum of date March 17 B.C. 24, mention is made of a building dedicated—τῶι θεῶι καὶ κυρίῳ (cf. Jn 20²⁸) Σοκνοπαίωι. And for the Septuagint formula "lord of the spirits" (cf. Numb 16²², 27¹⁶) cf. the Jewish prayer for vengeance *Syll* 816 (ii/i B.C.—see *LAE* p. 423 ff.), which commences—ἐπικαλοῦμαι καὶ ἀξιῶ τὸν θεὸν τὸν ὕψιστον, τὸν κύριον τῶν πνευμάτων καὶ πάσης σαρκός, and the magic P Lond 46⁴⁶⁷ (iv/A.D.) (= I. p. 80) ἐπικαλοῦμαί σε τὸν κτίσαντα γῆν καὶ ὀστᾶ καὶ πᾶσαν σάρκα καὶ πᾶν πνεῦμα . . . θεὸς θε[ῶ]ν ὁ κύριος τῶν πνευμάτων.

(7) There are two other usages of κύριος, which are not found in the NT, but which are so common in our documents that they may be mentioned here for the sake of completeness. (a) The first is the application of ὁ κύριος to the legal "guardian" of a woman, which occurs as early as B.C. 139 in P Grenf II. 15¹·¹³ μετὰ κυρίου τοῦ αὑτῆς ἀνδρὸς Ἑρμίου: cf. from Roman times P Oxy II. 255⁴ (A.D. 48) (= *Selections*, p. 46), a census-return παρὰ Θερ-[μου]θαρίου τῆς Θοώνιος μετὰ κυρίου Ἀπολλω νίου τοῦ Σωτάδου, BGU I. 22⁵ (A.D. 114) (= *Selections*, p. 74), a petition from a woman who states that at the moment she has no guardian—τὸ παρὸν μὴ ἔχοντα κύριον, P Fay 32⁸ (A.D. 131), a property return by Sambous μετὰ κυρίο(υ) τοῦ ὁμοπατρίο(υ) καὶ ὁμομητρίου ἀδελφοῦ Ἀλλόφωνος, "under the wardship of her full brother on both the father's and mother's side, Allothon (?) " (Edd.), and the late P Lond V. 1724⁷⁰ (A.D. 578–82). See further Wenger *Stellvertretung*, p. 173 ff., *Archiv* iv. p. 78 ff., v. p. 471 ff. (b) The second is its usage as an adj. = "valid," e.g. P Eleph 1¹⁴ (B.C. 311–310) (= *Selections*, p. 4) ἡ δὲ συγγραφὴ ἥδε κυρία ἔστω

πάντηι πάντως, "and let this contract be valid under all circumstances," P Tebt I. 104⁴¹ (B.C. 92) Διονύσιος ἔχω κυρίαν, "I, Dionysius, have received the contract, which is valid," P Oxy II. 275³³ (A.D. 66) (= *Selections.* p. 57) κυρία ἡ διδασκαλική, "the contract of apprenticeship is valid," *al.*

κυρόω,

"ratify," "confirm," as in Gal 3¹⁵, is common in legal documents, as when with reference to the sale of property the purchaser undertakes if the sale is confirmed to pay a certain sum into the government bank — P Amh II. 97¹⁴ (A.D. 180–192) ἐφ᾽ ᾧ κυρωθεῖσα διαγράψω ἐπὶ τὴν δ[ημ]οσίαν τράπεζαν, adding that he will remain in undisturbed possession and ownership for ever—¹⁷ ἐὰ]ν φαίν[η]ται κυρῶσαι, "if you consent to confirm the sale": but that if he is not so confirmed, he will not be bound by his promise—¹⁷ ἐὰν δὲ μὴ κυρωθῶ οὐ κατασχε[θ]ήσομαι τῇ [ὑ]ποσχέσει: cf. P Tebt II. 294¹⁶ (A.D. 146) ἃς κ[αὶ] διαγράψω κυρωθεὶς ἐπὶ τὴν ἐπὶ τόπων δημοσίαν τράπεζαν ταῖς συνήθεσι προθεσμίαις, "which sum I will, as soon as my appointment is ratified, pay into the local public bank at the accustomed dates" (Edd.), *Michel* 478⁶ (ii/B.C.) δεδόχθαι οὖν τῶ[ι κοι]νῶι, κυρωθέντος τοῦδε τοῦ ψηφίσμ[ατο]ς, and the interesting Commagene rescript *OGIS* 383¹²² (mid. i/B.C.) νόμον δὲ τοῦτον φωνῇ μὲν ἐξήγγειλεν ἐμή, νοῦς δὲ θεῶν ἐκύρωσεν, ²⁰⁷ διατάξεως ταύτης δύναμιν ἱερὰν ἢ τιμὴν ἡρωΐκήν, ἣν ἀθάνατος κρίσις ἐκύρωσεν. For κύρωσις cf. *ib.* 455¹⁷ (i/B.C.) κατ᾽ οὖσαν μετὰ ταῦτα ἐν ἑαυτοῖς κύρωσιν, P Tebt II. 297¹⁶ (c. A.D. 123) ἀντ[έγραψεν ὁ στρ]ατηγὸς . . . τὴν ἐπ[ε]νεχθεῖσαν ὑπὸ τοῦ Μαρσισο[ύχου κύ]ρωσιν ἐπὶ τῶν τόπων μὴ εἶναι, "the strategus replied . . . that the certificate of appointment produced by Marsisuchus was not to be found on the spot" (Edd.).

κύων.

The metaph. usage of κύων as a term of reproach (cf. Mt 7⁶, Phil 3², Rev 22¹⁵) may be illustrated from the letter of a soldier, who writes to his mother complaining that she has abandoned him "as a dog" — BGU III. 814¹⁹ (iii/A.D.) ἀφῆκές [μοι οὕ]τω[ς] ὡς κύων (*l.* κύνα).

κωλύω.

P Eleph 10⁶ (B.C. 223–2) ἀπόστειλ[ο]ν . ., ὅπως μὴ διὰ ταῦτα κωλυώμεθα . . . τοὺς [λ]όγους εἰς τὴν πόλιν [κα]ταπέμψαι, P Magd 2⁶ (B.C. 221) ἐμοῦ δὲ βουλομένης ἐπισυντελέσαι τὸν τοῖχον, . . . Πώρρης κεκώλυκεν οἰκοδομεῖν, P Petr II. 11(1)³ (iii/B.C.) (= *Selections.* p. 7) μηθέν σε τῶν ἔργων κωλύει, P Oxy III. 471⁹¹ (ii/A.D.) τί οὖν ὁ κατηφὴς σὺ καὶ ὑπεραύ[σ]τηρος οὐκ ἐκώλυες; "why then did not you with your modesty and extreme austerity stop him?" (Edd.), *ib.* VIII. 1101¹² (A.D. 367–70) ὅτι δὲ κεκώλυται παρὰ τοῖς νόμοις τοῦτο, δῆλον, "that this is forbidden by the law is clear" (Ed.). A good ex. of the conative participle is afforded by *Preisigke* 4284⁹ (A.D. 207) Ὀρσεύς τις ἀνὴρ βίαιος καὶ αὐθάδης τυ[γχάν]ων ἐπῆλθεν ἡμῖν . . . κ[ω]λύων τὴν κατεργασίαν: cf. *Chrest.* I. 354²³. For κώλυμα see P Hib I. 90²⁰ (B.C. 222) ἐὰμ μή [τι βα]σιλικὸν κώλυμα γ[ένηται, "if there be no hindrance on the part of the State" (Edd.): for κώλυσις see P Tebt II. 393²² (A.D. 150) ἢ καὶ κώλυσιν ἢ κακοτεχ[νίαν, "or hindrance or fraud"

(Edd.), and for **κωλυτής** see *OGIS* 5⁷ (B.C. 311) εἰ μὴ κωλυταί τι[νες ἐγέ]νοντο, τότε ἂν συνετελέσθη ταῦτα.

κώμη.

This common word hardly needs illustration, but we may note that by the phrase οἱ ἀπὸ τῆς κώμης we are to understand the population of the village in general, and not its functionaries or official representatives, see e.g. the joint responsibility of the **πρεσβύτεροι** and the other members of the community with respect to certain dues in P Ryl II. 219³ (ii/A.D.) δι ἀ) τῶν τοῦ ἔτους πρεσβ[υτέρων [καὶ τῶν λοιπ[ῶν] ἀπὸ τῆ]s κώμης. P Flor I. 2²¹⁴ (A.D. 265) κινδύνῳ ἡμῶν κ[αὶ τῶν] ἀπὸ τῆς [κώ]μης καὶ καταγειν[ομέ]νων πάντων, BGU IV. 1035³ (v/A.D.) οἱ ἀπὸ κώμης Κερκῆσις ἦλθαν εἰ[ί]ς τὸν αἰγιαλὸν τῶν ἀπὸ Ὀξυρύγχων καὶ ἐδίοξαν τοὺς ἁλιεῖς Ὀξυρύγχ(ων). and cf. *Chrest.* I. i. p. 43. See also P Par 63¹⁰¹ (B.C. 165) (= P Petr III. p. 26) τοὺς πλείστους δὲ τῶν ἐν ταῖς κώμαις κατοικούντων λαῶν, P Tebt I. 40⁸ (B.C. 117) σαφέστερον μετειληφὼς τοὺς ἐκ τῆς κώμης ὁμοθυμαδὸν ἀντέχεσθαι τῆς σῆς σκέπης. "having received certain information that the inhabitants of the village are with one accord claiming your protection" (Edd.). For **κωμήτης** see P Ryl II. 219⁹ (ii/A.D.). The difficult **κωμε-** (= η)γέτης of *OGIS* 97¹⁰ (end of ii/B.C.) is discussed by Dittenberger *ad l.* and by *Preisigke Ostr.* p. 35 f.

κῶμος,

"revel," revelling." We are unable to illustrate this word, but reference may be made to the **κωμασία**, or sacred procession of the images of the gods in Egypt, as in P Tor I. 1ᵛⁱⁱ·²¹ (B.C. 110) προάγοντας τῆς κωμασίας, BGU I. 149⁸ (ii/iii A.D.) ταῖς κωμασίαις τῶν θεῶν. P Par 69ᵛ·¹⁴ (A.D. 232) (= *Chrest.* I. 41) παρέτυχεν κωμασίᾳ ἐξ ἔθ[ους ἀγομέ]νῃ Ἴσιδος θεᾶς μεγίστης, and *OGIS* 194²⁵ (B.C. 42) μετήλλαξε διηνεκῶς πο]ηθῆναι τὰς τῶν κυρίων θεῶν κωμασίας. See further Sturzius *Dial. Mac.* p. 193 ff., and the classic passage in Clem. Al. *Strom.* V. vii. p. 354 f. (ed. Stählin). For **κωμαστής** cf. P Oxy X. 1265⁹ A.D. 336) κωμαστοῦ θίων προτομῶν καὶ νίκης αὐτῶν προαγούσης, "celebrant of the divine images and their advancing victory" (Edd.), with the accompanying note, and for **κωμάζω** see Deissmann *BS* p. 237.

Κῶς.

For the history of Cos and of its inscriptions it is sufficient to refer to the important monograph by W. R. Paton and E. L. Hicks *The Inscriptions of Cos*, Oxford, 1891. On the acc. **Κῶ** in Ac 21¹ see Moulton *Gr.* ii. § 53 C (c).

κωφός

is used as a descriptive name in P Tebt II. 283⁵ (B.C. 93 or 60) Πατῦνιν (*l.* -ις) ὁ ἐπικαλούμενον (*l.* -ος) κωφόν (*l.* -ός) : cf. BGU IV. 1196⁴⁵·⁶³ (*c.* B.C. 10). The adj. occurs in several sepulchral epitaphs attached to **τάφοι, δάκρυα,** and **χάρις** (*Kaibel* 208·⁶ (ii/A.D.), 252⁶ (ii/A.D.), 298²). For the adv. **κωφῶς** = Lat. *obscure*, see Vett. Val. pp. 251²⁵, 301²⁸.

Λ

λαγχάνω—λαλιά

λαγχάνω,

"obtain by lot," c. acc., may be illustrated by such passages as P Tebt II. 382⁵ (B.C. 30–A.D. 1) λελονχέναι με εἰς τὸ ἐπιβάλλον μοι μέρος . . ἀρού(ρας) ιβ, "that I have obtained by lot as the share falling to me 12 arourae," and similarly *ib*. 383¹⁴ (A.D. 46). Cf. also P Ryl II. 157¹⁷ (A.D. 135) παρέξει δὲ ἡ λαχοῦσα τὴν ν[ο]τίνην μερίδα τῇ λαχούσῃ [τὴν βορρίνη]ν . . . εἴσ[ο]δον καὶ ἔξοδον, "the recipient of the southern portion shall permit the recipient of the northern portion entrance and exit" (Edd.), P Oxy III. 503²⁰ (A.D. 118) κυριεύειν ὧν λέλοngχεν εἰς τὸν αἰεὶ χρόνον, *ib*. IX. 1186⁵ (iv/A.D.) cited *s.v.* ἱμάς, and from the inscrr. *Syll* 186¹⁰ (end of iv/B.C.) ἔλαχε φυλὴν Ἐφεσεύς, χιλιαστὸν Ἀργαδεύς, *Michel* 978²⁹ (B.C. 281–0) ἱερεὺς λαχών—chosen priest by lot. On the improper use of λαγχάνω, "cast lots," in Jn 19²¹, to which no parallel has been produced, see Field *Notes*, p. 106, and for the phrase λαχὸν βάλλω in the same connexion, see Ev. Petr. 4 with Swete's note. MGr λαχαίνω. Thumb (*Handbook*, p. 338) cites a folksong μὴ λάχῃ καὶ περάσῃ, "let him not by chance pass by," and (p. 198) the phrase μὴ τύχῃ (λάχῃ) καὶ . . . "lest perhaps."

Λάζαρος

is a contracted form of Ἐλεάζαρος: see *s.v.* Ἐλεάζαρ, and cf. Wetstein *ad* Lk 16²⁰. The name survives in MGr: Thumb (*Handbook*, pp. 239–41) gives a Popular Tale of a cobbler called Lazarus—ὁ κὺρ Λάζαρος κ' οἱ δράκοι.

λάθρα,

which Moulton (*Gr.* ii. p. 84) prefers to write instead of λάθρᾳ, occurs in P Par 22²⁸ (B.C. 165) τοῦτον (*sc.* λίνον) λάθρα κομισάμενος: cf. BGU IV. 1141¹³ (B.C. 14). See also Boisacq (p. 549) who treats the form as an instrumental singular.

λαῖλαψ.

This "poetic" word (Thumb *Hellen.* p 218) is found in a strange form as a proper name in *Preisigke* 168 Λαΐλαψς. Cf. P Leid Wᵛⁱⁱⁱ ²¹ (ii/iii A.D.) αὐτὸς γάρ ἐστιν ὁ λαιλαφέτης (for λαλαπαφέτης), "ipse enim est in turbine volans" (Ed.). Boisacq (p. 551) compares the intensive reduplication of this noun with παιφάσσω and μαιμάω.

λακέω.

Ἐλάκησεν, "burst asunder," in Ac 1¹⁸ is best referred to λακέω (not λάσκω): see Blass *ad l.*, who compares διαλακήσασα = διαρραγεῖσα in Aristoph. *Nub.* 410 and Act. Thom. 33 ὁ δὲ δράκων φυσηθεὶς ἐλάκησε καὶ ἀπέθανε, καὶ ἐξεχύθη ὁ ἰὸς αὐτοῦ καὶ ἡ χολή.

λακτίζω.

With the use of this verb in Ac 26¹⁴ cf. BGU III. 1007⁷ (iii/B.C.) τ]ὴν θύραν μου ἐλάκτιζον τοῖς ποσίν. See also Herodas vii 118 βοῦς ὁ λακτίσας ὑμᾶς, "it was an ox that kicked you," with reference to a kick from a clumsy, ill-fitting shoe. The subst. is found in P Amh II. 141¹⁰ (A.D. 350) γρόνθοις τε καὶ λακτί[σ]μασιν, "with their fists and heels" (Edd.): cf. P Gen I. 56²⁷ (A.D. 346) τὴν πλευρὰν πάσχω λάκτιμα λαβών.

λαλέω.

In P Amh II. 131⁶ (early ii/A.D.) a brother writes to his sister with reference to the management of certain family property, stating that he will remain where he is until he learns that all is safely settled, and adding—ἐλπίζω δὲ θεῶν θελόντων ἐκ τῶν λαλουμένων διαφεύξεσθαι καὶ μετὰ τὴν πεντεκαιδεκάτην ἀναπλεύσειν, "but I hope, if the gods will, to escape from the talking and after the fifteenth to return home." See also P Oxy I. 119⁵ (ii/iii A.D.) (= *Selections*, p. 103) where the naughty boy writes to his father—ἢ οὐ θέλις ἀπενέκκειν μετ' ἐσοῦ εἰς Ἀλεξανδρίαν, οὐ μὴ γράψω σε ἐπιστολήν, οὔτε λαλῶ σε, οὔτε νίγένω σε εἶτα, "if you refuse to take me along with you to Alexandria, I won't write you a letter, or speak to you, or wish you health henceforth," P Fay 126⁴ (ii/iii A.D.) ἤκουσα φίλου τοῦ πατρός μου λαλοῦντος περὶ σοῦ ὅτι πεμψεν (*l.* ἔπεμψεν) ἐπὶ τὴν πενθερά (*l.*-ράν) σου χάριν τοῦ κτήματος, "I heard a friend of my father's saying about you that he had sent a message to your mother-in-law about the farm" (Edd.), BGU III. 822¹⁸ (iii/A.D.) ἵνα εὕρωμεν καὶ ἡμῖς εὔλογον λαλῆσαι αὐτῇ. γράψον Κουπανηούτι ἐπιστολήν, and the magic P Lond 121¹⁷⁴ (iii/A.D.) (= I. p. 89) a recipe against old women's garrulity—γραῦν μὴ τὰ πολλὰ λα[λ]εῖν. This last papyrus shows also the subst. λάλημα (LXX), ⁶⁸¹ (= I. p. 105) φίλτρον ἐπὶ λαλήματος κατὰ φίλων. The above exx. all bear out the usual distinction that, while λέγω calls attention to the substance of what is said, the onomatopoetic λαλέω points rather to the outward utterance: cf. McLellan *Gospels*, p. 383 ff. and Milligan's note on 1 Thess 1⁸. With λαλέω, "I make known by speaking" with the further idea of *extolling*, as in Mt 26¹³ *al.*, cf. the inscr. with reference to a mother and brother—ὧν καὶ ἡ σωφροσύνη κατὰ τὸν κόσμον λελάληται (*Archiv* v. p. 169, No. 24⁶). MGr λαλῶ (-έω), "speak."

λαλιά.

From its classical sense "talkativeness," "chatter," λαλιά comes to be used in the NT simply for "speech," "talk": cf. Joseph. *B.J.* ii. 8. 5 οὐδὲ κραυγή ποτε τὸν οἶκον, οὔτε θόρυβος μολύνει, τὰς δὲ λαλιὰς ἐν τάξει παραχωροῦσιν ἀλλήλοις. As showing however the danger accompanying much "talking" we may cite the early Christian letter, P Heid 6[19] (iv/A.D.) (= *Selections*, p. 126) ἵνα οὖν μὴ πολλὰ γράφω καὶ φλυαρήσω (*l.* φλυαρήσω), ἐν γὰρ [πο]λλῇ λαλιᾷ (cf. Sir 20[8]) οὐκ ἐκφεύξοντ[αι] (τ)ὴν ἁμαρτίη (cf. Prov 10[19]), παρακαλ ῶ [ο]ὖν, δέσποτα, ἵνα μνημον[ε]ύῃς μοι εἰς τὰς ἁγίας σου εὐχάς, "in order that I may not by much writing prove myself an idle babbler, for 'in the multitude of words they shall not escape sin,' I beseech you, master, to remember me in your holy prayers." For a new literary reference for the adj. λάλος, see the fragment of an anthology, P Tebt I. 1[9] (*c.* B.C. 100) φιλέρημος δὲ νάπαισιν λάλος ἀνταμείβετ' ἀχώ. "chattering Echo, lover of solitude, answers in the dells" (Edd.).

λαμά.

It may be noted that the Heb. form λαμά in Mk 15[34] is corrected by Mt (27[46]) into the Aram. λεμά. On the variety of spelling in the codd. see WH *Notes*[2], p. 21, and the apparatus in Souter's *Nov. Test. Gr.*

λαμβάνω

in its ordinary sense of "receive," "get," as in Mt 7[8], Jn 3[27], is naturally very common, e.g. P Giss I. 67[3] (ii/A.D.) ἔλαβόν σου ἐπιστολήν, P Ryl II. 122[16] (A.D. 127) λαβόν τὸ πιττάκιον τὸ ἀκόλουθον ποίει, "on receipt of this document, act in accordance with it" (Edd.), P Fay 127[14] (ii/iii A.D.) ἐὰ (= ἐὰν) λάβητε φαγὸν πέμψαι ἐμοὶ διὰ Κατοίτου, "if you get any lentils send them to me by Katoitus" (Edd.), and *ib.* 135[13] (iv/A.D.) τὰ ἀργύρια ἃ ἔλαβες, "money which you received." Similarly in connexion with money receipts, as *ib.* 109[8] (early i/A.D.) ἀποχὴν θέλω λαβεῖν, "I wish to get a receipt," *ib.* 21[13] (A.D. 134) ἀλλήλ[οις] ἀποχὰς τούς τε διδόντας καὶ τοὺς λαμβάν[ο]ντας, "that payer and payee shall mutually give receipts" (Edd.). Wilcken *Ostr.* i. 109 has pointed out that in the case of all ostraca receipts known to him the writers were Romans, but see *Theb Ostr* 105[3] (A.D. 148) ἐλάβαμεν παρὰ σοῦ ἀχύρου δημοσίου γόμου ἑνὸς ἡμίσους, "we have received from you one and a half loads of chaff for public use," where the name of the writer, Paeris, is clearly Egyptian (see the editor's note). For the meaning "take," as in Mt 13[31, 33], cf. P Fay 114[9] (A.D. 100) ἐρώτησέ με Ἑρμῶναξ εἶνα αὐτὸν λάβῃ εἰς Κερκεσούχα, "Hermonax has asked me to let him take him (a certain Pindarus) to Kerkesucha," and for the additional thought "catch," "take captive," cf. the temple-inscr. *OGIS* 508[7] (i/A.D.) ὃς δ' ἂν ληφθῇ, ἑαυτῶι αἴτιος ἔσται διὰ τὸ ἐξακολουθεῖν θάνατον, cf. 2 Cor 11[20] RV, but see Field *Notes*, p. 184 f. The verb is construed with the inf., like the compound παραλαμβάνω in Mk 7[4], in BGU IV. 1114[4] (B.C. 8–7) ἐπεὶ τυ[γ]χάνει ὁ Κόιντος εἰληφὼς παρὰ τοῦ πάτρωνος ἑαυτοῦ ... ἀποκαταστῆσαι ἐνταῦθα τῶι Ἱμέρωι δῶρον κτλ. With the simplex in Mt 13[20] we may compare P Iand 13[16] (iv/A.D.) ἵνα μετὰ χαρᾶς σε ἀπολάβωμεν, and for the dat. of the person, as in LXX 1 Kings 21[9], see the late *ib.* 20[6] (vi/vii A.D.) μὴ θελήσατε λαβεῖν σοι ἐκ τοῦ Ἀμολεῖ[τος . . . The use of the middle in Mk 8[23] D λαβόμενος τὴν χεῖρα τοῦ τυφλοῦ, which Blass-Debrunner § 170. 2 describes as "weder klassisch noch neutestamentlich," may be illustrated from P Flor I. 36[7] (A.D. 312) λ]αβομένου μου τὴ[ν

αὐτὴν παῖδα ἀπὸ τῆς τῆς μητρὸς τελευτῆς. In *OGIS* 8[8] (iv/B.C.) λαβέσθαι δ[ὲ κ]αὶ συναγόροις τὰ[ν] πόλιν, λαβέσθαι is = "eligere" (*Attice* ἑλέσθαι). For the legal phrase λαμβάνειν τὸ δίκαιον, "to receive satisfaction," cf. P Tebt I. 5[213] (B.C. 118) ὑπέχειν καὶ λαμβάνειν τὸ δίκαιον ἐπὶ τῶν χρηματιστῶν, which the editors describe as "apparently another way of saying διδόναι καὶ δέχεσθαι δίκην, according as the verdict was against or for them," but see P Magd. p. 64. See also P Ryl II. 68[26] (B.C. 89) ἐὰν δὲ περιγένωμαι, λάβω παρ' αὐτῆς τὸ δίκαιον ὡς καθήκει, "and if I survive, I may obtain satisfaction from her as is right"—a woman complains to the epistates that she has been beaten by another woman and her life endangered, and *Michel* 394[17] (mid. i/B.C.) λαβὼν πεῖραν, "having made actual proof."

We may add some miscellaneous exx. to illustrate the forms of the verb. For aor. ἔλαβα (as in MGr: see Thumb *Hellen.* p. 250) cf. BGU II. 423[9] (ii/A.D.) (= *Selections*, p. 91) ἔλαβα βιάτικον παρὰ Καίσαρος, "I received my travelling money from Caesar," P Meyer 22[10] (iii/iv A.D.) γράψα (= -ψον) μοι ὅτι ἔλαβας τῶ ἀβίκτωρι ("the handkerchief"?) ἀπὸ τῆς ἀδελφῆ (*l.* -φῆς) μου, *ib.* 21[11] (iii/iv A.D.) ἤδη γὰρ ἔλαβαν [. . . . .] καὶ δραχμὰς τετρακο[σίας. The form ἐλάβοσαν (Thumb, *Hellen.* p. 198 f.) is seen in *Syll* 930[18] (B.C. 112) and *Cagnat* IV. 193[13] (i/B.C.) τὰ χρήματα ἀποδότωσαν ἃ ἐλάβοσαν ἐν τῷ καθήκοντι χρόνῳ: cf. 2 Thess 3[6] ℵ* AD* παρελάβοσαν. Λάβοιντο can be quoted from an illiterate Christian letter of iv/v A.D., P Giss I. 54[13]. For inf. λαβῆσαι, see P Oxy VI. 937[18] (iii/A.D.) λαβ[ῆ]σαι τὴν φιάλην, "to take the bowl" (see the editors' note). For the aor. perf. εἴληφα, as in Rev 5[7], 8[5], cf. the subscription to P Leid B (B.C. 164) (see p. 11 and cf. p. 19), and P Lond 33[6] (B.C. 161) (= I. p. 19) ἡμῶν εἰληφότων, of women (note the breach of concord in gender), and for the pass. (see [Jn] 8[4], cf. P Lond 121[613] (iii/A.D.) (= I. p. 104) εἴλημπται. On Rev 11[17] C εἴληφες see Moulton *Gr.* ii. p. 221. The fut. middle λήμψομαι (perhaps due to a confusion between Ionic λάμψομαι and λήψομαι, H. W. Smyth *Greek Dialects* i. *Ionic*, p. 136) is very common, e.g. P Rev L [lix 29] (B.C. 259–8) λή[μ]ψονται, P Tor II. 3[18] (B.C. 127) (= P Par 14) λήμψομαι παρ' αὐτῶν δι' ἄλλης ἐντεύξεως τὸ δίκαιον, P Oxy XIV. 1664[12] (iii/A.D.) τὰς χρηστὰς ἐντολάς σου ἥδιστα ἔχων ὡς χάριτας λήμψομαι, "for I shall be most pleased to accept your commands as favours" (Edd.), also the Lycian inscr. *CIG* III. 4244[6], 4247[20] (λήνψεται), 4253[15] (λ[ή]νψεται): cf. Reinhold, p. 46 f., and on the fut. middle in act. sense see *Proleg.* p. 154 f. According to Sanders (p. 23) λήμψομαι is regularly used in the *Washington Manuscript*; "no exceptions were noted." Owing to literary influences the intruded μ (from the present stem) frequently disappears in late MSS., cf. also Mt 21[22] C, Jn 5[43] CL *al.* MGr λαβαίνω, "receive," "acquire." Thumb (*Handbook*, p. 134) points out that παίρ(ν)ω is more common than λαβαίνω for the meanings "obtain," "get."

λαμπάς.

In a long list of persons charged with furnishing supplies in view of an official visit from the Prefect to Hermopolis in A.D. 145–47 mention is made of the following: —ἐπὶ ξύλ(ων) καὶ ἀνθράκων καὶ φανῶ ν καὶ λαμπάδ[ων], οἱ προόντες (P Lond 1159[9] = III. p. 113. *Chrest.* I. p. 493). See also

BGU III 717¹² (dowry—A.D. 149) κάτοπτ[ρ]ον δίπτυχον, λαμπάδα, P Oxy XII. 1449¹⁹ (return of temple property—A.D. 213–217) λαμπάδ(ες) ἀργυραῖ καλαί. For the noun = "torch" in connexion with a torch-race cf. OGIS 764⁴³ ᵃˡ. (ii/B.C.), Michel 884⁶ (B.C. 164–3), 893¹² (i/B.C.). MGr λαμπάδα, "lamp," "candlestick."

λαμπρός

is used with reference to shields in Michel 248¹⁴ (2nd half iii/B.C.) ἐπιμελε[ῖ]σθαι . . . ὅπως λαμπρα[ὶ] εἰς τὸν ἀγῶνα παραφέρωνται αἱ ἀσπίδες. An inscr. from Christian times, Preisigke 1190, commemorates the departure of a certain Ταῆσαι to the "shining" land—Ταῆσαι ἐβίωσεν εἴκουσι ὀκτώ, γ(ίνονται) (ἔτη) κη. Εἰς τὴν λαμπρὰν ἀπῆλθεν. A different ellipsis is seen in the MGr λαμπρά (-ή), "Easter." In Preisigke 4127⁹ the adj. is applied to miracles—σημία σού τινα λαμπρὰ θεάμενος. With the usage in Lk 23¹¹, Ac 10³⁰, Jas 2²ᶠ., we may compare Menander Fragm. 669—

ἔξωθέν εἰσιν οἱ δοκοῦντες εὐτυχεῖν
λαμπροί, τὰ δ' ἔνδον πᾶσιν ἀνθρώποις ἴσοι.

The superlative is very common as a title of rank or courtesy, e.g. P Fay 33¹¹ (A.D. 163) τὰ κελευσθέντα ὑπὸ τ[ο]ῦ λαμπροτάτου ἡγεμόνος, P Strass I. 43¹ (A.D. 331) Αὐρηλίᾳ Ῥουφίνᾳ ἡ (l. τῇ) λαμπροτάτῃ, P Oxy I. 87¹³ (A.D. 342) ἀ[παν]τῆσαι ἐπὶ τὴ[ν] λαμπροτ[άτην] Ἀλεξανδρίαν. The positive is similarly used in ib. 158² (vi/vii A.D.) παρακαλῶ τὴν ὑμετέραν λαμπρὰν γνησίαν ἀδελφότητα, "I urge you, my true and illustrious brother" (Edd.). MGr λαμπρός, "brilliant," "shining."

λαμπρότης.

Like the adj., λαμπρότης is used as a title of honour, e.g. P Grenf I. 59⁶ (v/vi A.D.) τὸ κτῆμα τῆς σῆς λαμπρότητος, BGU I. 306⁸ (A.D. 566) ὁμολογῶ [μεμισθῶ]σθαι παρὰ τῆς λ[α]μπρότητος. Cf. also OGIS 470⁸ (time of Augustus) where a certain Theophron is described as—ἐν τῇ ['Α]σίᾳ καὶ πρὸς τὴν πατρίδα [λ]αμπρότητα.

λαμπρῶς.

In C. and B. i. p. 182, No. 70, we hear of ἀνδρὸς βουλευτοῦ καὶ πάσας ἀρχὰς κὲ λειτουργίας λαμπρῶς κὲ ἐπιφανῶς ἐκτετελεκότος. For this epithet = "sumptuously" in connexion with feasting, as in Lk 16¹⁹, see the exx. from late Greek in Field Notes, p. 69f.

λάμπω.

P Leid Wˣᵛⁱⁱ ²² (ii/iii A.D.) ὀφθαλμοί εἰσιν ἀκάματοι, λάμποντες ἐν ταῖς κόραις τῶν ἀνθρώπων—of a god's eyes. Over the door of the Church of St. George at Zorava, erected on the site of a pagan temple, the following inscr. was engraved—θεοῦ γέγονεν οἶκος τὸ τῶν δαιμόνων καταγώγιον, φῶς σωτήριον ἔλαμψεν ὅπου σκότος ἐκάλυπτεν κτλ. (OGIS 610¹ᶠ·—vi/A.D.): cf. 2 Cor 4⁶. The verb survives in MGr λάμπω, "shine," "light."

λανθάνω.

The construction in Ac 26²⁶ may be illustrated by P Oxy I. 34 verso ᶦᶦᶦ·³ (A.D. 127) οὐκ ἔλαθέ με, "it did not escape my notice," ib. III. 530⁵ (ii/A.D.) ἐμὲ δὲ ἐλελήθει διαστέλλ-

[ει]ν τι, "but I had forgotten to make any order for payment" (Edd.), ib. X. 1253⁵² (iv/A.D.) ἵνα μηδέν σου λανθάνῃ τὴν λαμπρότητα μηνύομεν, "we give this information in order that nothing may escape your highness" (Edd.). The verb is used without an obj. in P Strass I. 73⁵ (iii/A.D.) ἐλαθέν γε κεράμια ὀψαρίων εἰς διάπρασιν, "the jars for dainties are lacking for sale." With the usage in Heb 13² cf. P Gen I. 17¹⁶ (iii/A.D.) ὑφορούμε (= ὑφορῶμαι) . . . . . μὴ ἄρ[α ἐ]νθρώσκων [. . . ἐλαθεν ὕ[δατ]ι, "I suspect he may have jumped into the water unnoticed": see also P Hamb I. 27⁹ (B.C. 250) οὐκ ἔτι οὖν παρέλαβέμ με, ἀλλ' ἐλαθέμ με κομισάμενος. MGr λαθαίνω (ἔλαθα).

λαξευτός.

The verb λαξεύω (LXX) is restored by the editors with great probability in a contract with stonecutters P Oxy III. 498²⁰ (ii/A.D.) τὰ δὲ προκείμενα πάντα α[. . . λα]ξ[εύσο]μεν, "all the aforesaid stones we will cut": cf. also P Thead 14²³ (iv/A.D.) τ]ὸ ἐκτὸς ἐλάξευται in a very mutilated context. Λάξος (not in LS), "a stone-mason," is fairly common in the papyri, as e.g. in the early i/A.D. alphabet acrostic P Tebt II. 278¹¹ κλειτοποίς λάξος μυλοκόπος, "locksmith, mason, millstone-maker," and in the census-return P Oxy XII. 1547¹⁶ (A.D. 119) λάξος οὐ λὴ) ποδὶ ἀρισ(τερῷ): cf. also P Amh II. 128⁸⁰ (A.D. 128) with the editors' note. For the subst. λαξεία (not in LS), see P Oxy III. 498⁸ ᵘᵗ ˢ.) ἐπιδεχόμεθα λαξεάν τῶν οἰκοδομουμένων λίθων κύβων, "we undertake to cut the squared building-stones" (Edd.), and for the adj. λαξικός (also unknown to LS), ib. ³⁴ ὑπουργίας λαξικῆς, "services in stone-cutting" (Edd.). In P Fay 44⁸ (B.C. 16?) τὰ λαξικά is the tax paid by a mason on his trade.

Λαοδικεύς.

Michel 164⁴ (c. B.C. 140) Ἀπολλώνιος Δημητρίου Λαοδικεύς. ib. 543¹ (c. B.C. 200) τὸ παρ]ὰ Λαοδικέων, a decree from the Laodiceans.

λαός.

In the papyri λαοί is the regular term for "natives," "fellaheen." Thus in P Petr II. 4(11)¹ (B.C. 255–4) we hear of a salt-tax imposed τοῖς ἐκ Κερκεησίος λαοῖς, where the editor remarks, "an ancient and poetical form for people found both in the LXX and in Papyri": cf. P Lille I. 16⁸ (iii/B.C.) ἐπειδὴ καὶ ἀπεργάζονται οἱ λαοὶ τὸ κέρμα τοῦτο εἰς ἄριστον, "since the natives are working off (?) this small tax as well as they can," P Par 63¹⁰¹ (B.C. 164) (= P Petr III. p. 26) τοὺς πλείστους δὲ τῶν ἐν ταῖς κώμαις κατοικούντων λαῶν οἳ διὰ τὴν τῶν δεόντων σπάνιν ἐργατεύοντες πορίζονται τὰ πρὸς τὸ ζῆν, "also most of the people inhabiting the villages, who, through lack of necessaries, supply themselves with the means of life by hard labour" (Mahaffy), ib. ¹·² τῶν μὲν ταλαιπώρων λαῶν καὶ τῶν μαχίμων καὶ τῶν ἄλλων ἀδυνατούντων φείσεσθε, "you must spare the miserable populace and the μάχιμοι and the others who are incapable" (i.i.), and ib. ¹⁶⁶ προτρεψαμένου τοὺς στρατηγοὺς καὶ τοὺς λαοὺς ἐ[πι]δέξασθαι τὰ τῆς ἀσχολίας, "instigated the strategi and the people to undertake the labour (of seed-sowing)" (ii.). For a similar use in the inscrr. cf. OGIS 90¹² (Rosetta stone—B.C. 196) ὅπως ὅ τε λαὸς καὶ οἱ ἄλλοι πάντες ἐν εὐθηνίαι ὦσιν ἐπὶ τῆς ἑαυτοῦ βασιλείας, where the editor defines λαός as "vulgus Aegyptiorum, praecipue opifices et agricolae, eidem fere qui v. 52 ἰδιῶται appellantur ut distinguantur a sacerdotibus," and *ib.* 225^{8, 99, 34} (iii/B.C.), where it is applied to the native population of Syria. See also *Syll* 897 (Larisa) Θεοφίλα Σελεύκου γυνὴ τῷ λαῷ χα[ί]-ρειν : Dittenberger says the word is often so used in epitaphs. The expression λαϊκὰ (σώματα) occurs *bis* in P Lille I. 10 (iii/B.C.), where it stands with τεθραμμένα between ἀρσενικά and θηλυκά in an enumeration, but the editors are unable to determine the exact meaning. The adj. is also found in BGU IV. 1053^{ii. 10} (B.C. 13) μηδὲ ἐπ' ἄσυλον τόπον μηδὲ ἐπὶ λαϊκὴν βοήθειαν. For λαοκρίτης (not in LS), a native judge, cf. P Tebt I. 5^{219} (B.C. 118) τὰς δὲ τῶν Αἰγυ(πτίων) πρὸς τοὺς αὐτοὺς <Αἰ>γυ(πτίους) κρίσεις μὴ ἐπισπᾶσθαι τοὺς χρημα(τιστὰς) ἀλλ' ἐᾶν κριν (om.) διεξάγεσθαι ἐπὶ τῶν λαοκριτῶν κατὰ τοὺς τῆς χώρας νόμους, "and that suits of Egyptians against Egyptians shall not be dragged by the chrematistae into their own courts, but they shall allow them to be decided before the native judges in accordance with the national laws" (Edd.), and P Tor I. 1^{vii. 3} (B.C. 116) εἰ καὶ ἐπὶ λαοκριτῶν διεκρίνοντο καθ' οὓς παρεκεῖτο νόμους, "si apud Populares Iudices lis instituta esset ad praescriptum legum ab ipso laudatarum " (Ed.) : see further Archiv v. p. 1 ff. For λαογραφία (LXX) in its primary sense of a taxing-list of native Egyptians, cf. P Tebt I. 103 (B.C. 94 or 61) with the editors' introduction, and see *s.v.* ἀπογραφή. On the characteristic use of λαός in the LXX and NT with reference to first the Jews, then the Christians, see Hort on 1 Pet 2^9, and cf. Hicks (*CR* i. p. 42), who, after remarking on the " noble associations " of the word in past Greek life and thought, points out that " it was reserved for Jewish lips to give the word a sacred significance and a world-wide currency." On its application to the "laity" as distinguished from the " clergy " in the Lycaonian inscr. from mid. iv/A.D., see Ramsay *Luke*, p. 387 ff. MGr λαϊκός, "layman."

Mayser thinks the word may originally have been a poetic word used primarily in the plur. : see *Gr.* p. 29, but cf. Thumb *Archiv* iv. p. 490, and Wackernagel *Hellenistica*, p. 10.

Λασέα.

For the spelling of this proper name cf. WH *Notes*^2 p. 167, Moulton *Gr.* ii. p. 81. Though not mentioned by any ancient writer, Lasea is now generally believed to have been situated about the middle of the S. coast of Crete : cf. J. Smith *The Voyage and Shipwreck of St. Paul*^4, 1880, p. 268 f.

λάσκω.

See *s.v.* λακέω. As showing the weakening sense of λάσκω, it may be noted that Thumb (*Handbook*, p. 337) cites λάσκομαι from Pontus with the meaning "seek aimlessly."

λατομέω.

In a letter addressed by the quarrymen (οἱ λατόμοι) in Paston to the architect Kleon, P Petr II. 4 (9)^3 (B.C. 255), they state that they have "quarried out the rocks," and are now idle for want of slaves to clear the sand – λελατόμητ[α]ι ἤδη, νυνὶ δὲ ἀργοῦμεν διὰ τὸ μὴ ἔχειν σώμ[α]τα ὥστε ἀνακαθᾶραι τὴν ἄμμον : cf. *Syll*. 803^{25} (iii/B.C.) (λ ατομήσας τὰ[ν] πέτραν. For λατόμος see P Petr III. 47(a)^2 εἰς λατόμους, *OGIS* 660^3 (A.D. 14–37) λατόμων πάντων τῆς Αἰγύπτου, and for λατομία see P Hib I. 71^7 (B.C. 245) a letter περὶ τ[ῶν] ἀνακεχωρηκότων σωμάτων ἐκ τῆς ἐ[ν] Κεφαλαῖς λατομίας, "about the slaves who have gone on strike from the stone-quarry at Cephalae." Cf. also Wackernagel *Hellenistica*, p. 9 f., Anz *Subsidia*, p. 354 f. MGr λατομῶ.

λατρεία.

The form λατρία, which is not found in the NT, is well attested by the LXX uncials : see Thackeray *Gr.* i. p. 87. The word survives in MGr = " adoration," "worship."

λατρεύω

in Biblical Greek always refers to the service or worship of the true God or of heathen divinities : see SH on Rom 1^9, where the relation of the verb to λειτουργέω is discussed. For its relation to δουλεύω see Thackeray *Gr.* i. p. 8 : cf. also Anz *Subsidia*, p. 296.

λάχανον.

P Hib I. 54^{26} (c. B.C. 245) λάχανα π[αντ]οδαπά, "vegetables of all kinds," BGU I. 22^{22} (A.D. 114) (= *Selections*, p. 75) ἀπὸ τιμῆς ὧν πέπρακον λαχάνων, "from the price of the vegetables I had sold," P Oxy III. 522^{18} (ii A.D.) τιμ(ῆς) λαχ(άνων) τοῖς αὐ(τοῖς) . . . . (τετρώβολον), " price of vegetables for the same, 4 obols." In P Fay 119^{33} (c. A.D. 100) πέμψις τὰ κτήνη κοπρηγεῖν εἰς τὸ λάχανον τῆς Ψινάχεως, the word is = "vegetable ground." For λαχανεία, as in Deut 11^{10}, cf. BGU IV. 1119^{23} (B.C. 5) ποτίζων τοῖς δέουσι ποτισμοῖς καταν ευων(?) τῇ κατὰ καιρὸν λαχανείᾳ, for λαχανοπώλης cf. BGU I. 22^3 (*ut s.*), and for λαχανοσπερμός cf. *ib.* II. 454^{13} (A.D. 193) ἐβάσταξαν ἡμῶν θήκας λαχανοσπέρμ[ο]υ εἰς ἕτερον ψυγμόν (cf. Ezek 26^{34} οὐκ [ἐλα]ττον θηκῶν δέκα δύο. MGr λάχανα, "vegetables," or "herbs generally."

λεγιών.

The spelling λεγιών, which is always found in the NT occurrences of this Latin word (Mt 26^{63}, Mk 5^{9.15}, Lk 8^{30}), is supported by numerous exx. in the papyri, e.g. P Lond 256 *recto* (a)^3 (A.D. 15) (= II. p. 99) λεγιῶνος δευτέρας κίκοστῆς (= καὶ εἰκοστῆς), BGU I. 140^7 (time of Hadrian) λεγιῶνο(ς) [β], *ib.* 156^1 (A.D. 201) Διογένης στρατιώτης λεγιῶνος β, P Oxy XIV. 1666^8 (iii/A.D.) γεγραφηκὼς περὶ τοῦ μεικροῦ Παυσανίου ὡς εἰς λεγιῶνα στρατευσάμενον, "having written you about the little Pausanias becoming a soldier" (Edd.), and BGU III. 899^1 (iv/A.D. ?) στρατιώτης λεγιῶνο[ς] (l. λεγιῶνος) πέμπτης Μακαιδωνικῆς (l. Μακεδονικῆς) : cf. also *ib.* I. 113^{11} (A.D. 143) λ]εγει ῶν]ος. The spelling λεγεών is also found—BGU IV. 1108^3 (B.C. 5) λ[ε]γεῶν[ο]ς, P Oxy II. 276^9 (A.D. 77) λεγεῶνος δευτέρας, BGU I. 21^{iii. 12 f} (A.D. 340) ὑπὸ τοῦ πραιποσίτου τῆς λεγεῶνος τῷ στρατιώτῃ τῆς λεγεῶνος, etc. See further Moulton *Gr.* ii. p. 76.

λέγω.

(1). "I say, speak": see e.g. P Par 47 (= *Selections*, p. 21 ff.), c. B.C. 153, which is addressed on the *verso*—πρὸς τοὺς τὴν ἀλήθειαν λέγοντες (= -as), P Fay 123²³ (c. A.D. 100) γνώσομαι γὰρ εἰ ἀληθῶς λέγι, "I will find out whether he is speaking the truth," P Ryl II. 76¹³ (late ii/A.D.) ᾷ καὶ ἀναγνώσομαι λεγομένου τοῦ [π]ράγματος, "I will read them when the case is argued" (Edd.), P Flor II. 132⁷ (A.D. 257) ἔλε[ξ]αν πεποιηκέναι ταῦτα ἀγνοίᾳ, "they said they had done this in ignorance," and the magical P Par 574¹²²ᵃ (iii/A.D.) (= *Selections*, p. 113) λόγος λεγόμενος ἐπὶ τῆς κεφαλῆς αὐτοῦ, "invocation to be uttered over the head (of the possessed one)." For the phrase τὸ αὐτὸ λέγειν, cf. 1 Cor 1¹⁰, Weiss (Meyer ¹⁰ *ad l.*) cites a sepulchral inscr. of husband and wife from Rhodes, *IMAe* 149 (ii/B.C.) ταῦτα λέγοντες ταῦτα φρονοῦντες ἤλθομεν τὰν ἀμέτρητον ὁδὸν εἰς Ἀίδαν. (2). Closely associated is the meaning "I speak of, mean," as in P Fay 110⁶ (A.D. 94) ὃ λέγεις ταμε[ῖ]ον, "the store-place you speak of," P Oxy VI. 907¹⁶ (A.D. 276) λέγω δὴ τῇ Διδύμῃ, "I mean Didyme." (3). For the verb = "I tell, command," as in Mt 5³⁴·³⁹, Rom 2²², cf. P Fay 109¹ (early i/A.D.) παρακληθεὶς τοὺς τρεῖς στατῆρες οὓς εἴρηκέ σοι Σέλευκος δῶναί μοι ἤδη δὸς Κλέωνι, "please give to Cleon the three staters which Seleucus told you to give me" (Edd.), *ib.* 111⁹ (A.D. 95–6) Ἡρακλίδας ὁ [ὀν]ηλάτης τὼ αἰτίωμα περιεπύησε λέγον ὅτι (*l.* περιεποίησε λέγων ὅτι) σὺ εἴρηκας πεζῷ [τὰ χ]υρίδια ἐλάσαι, "Heraclidas the donkey-driver shifted the blame from himself, saying that you had told him to drive the pigs on foot" (Edd.). Noteworthy for Rev 2¹·⁸ *al.* is the use of λέγει or τάδε λέγει as a formal and solemn phrase to introduce the edicts of Emperors and magistrates, e.g. *Syll* 376¹ (A.D. 67) Αὐτοκράτωρ Καῖσαρ λέγει—Nero's speech at Corinth giving liberty to the Greeks, *OGIS* 584² (ii/A.D.) Τι[β]έριος] Κλαύδιος Ἰοῦνκος ἀνθύπατος λέγει, and the rescript of King Darius I. to a provincial governor in Asia Minor, *Magn* 115⁴ (writing of 1st half ii/A.D.) Βασιλεὺς [βα]σιλέων Δαρεῖος ὁ Ὑστάσπεω Γαδάται δούλωι τάδε λέγε[ι]· πυνθάνομαί σε τῶν ἐμῶν ἐπιταγμάτων οὐ κατὰ πάντα πειθαρχεῖν κτλ. : see also *Exp* VIII. v. p. 286 f. and Lafoscade *De epistulis*, pp. 63, 77. (4). The active = "I call, name," as in Mk 10¹⁸, Phil 3¹⁸ (cf. Kennedy *EGT ad l.*), may be illustrated from P Par 44⁵ (B.C. 163) (= Witkowski ², p. 82) ἦ(= εἰ) ἕτερον θέλις λέγειν, λέγε, ἐγὼ γὰρ ἐνύπνια ὁρῶ πονηρά, and from the usage of the Greek islands, where μὲ λέγει or λέγει με has the meaning "he names me" (see Hatzidakis *Einl.* p. 223). For the passive which is common in the NT in this sense (Mt 1¹⁶, Jn 1⁸, *al.*) cf. BGU IV. 1117⁹ (B.C. 13) ἐν τῇ Εὐδαίμον[ο]ς [λε]γομένῃ ῥύμῃ, P Ryl II. 133¹¹ (A.D. 33) εἰς τὸ λεγό- μενον Ταορβελλείους ἔμβλημ(α), "making an attack upon the dam(?) called that of Taorbelles," (Edd.), *ib.* 137¹⁸ (A.D. 34) πρὸς τῷ ἐποικίῳ Ληνοῦ λεγομένῳ, "near the farmstead called that of the Winepress" (Edd.), *al.*

For λέγων, λέγοντες, used without construction in the LXX, see Thackeray *Gr.* i. p. 23. and with Rev 2²⁴ ὡς λέγουσιν cf. MGr λένε, "they say" (Thumb *Handbook*, p. 180). As usual the intervocalic γ is commonly omitted in the MGr λέω, λέεις or λές, λέει κτλ. : see Thumb *ib.* p. 177. The impf. ἔλεγαν in Jn 9¹⁰ א* *al.* may be illustrated from BGU II. 595⁸ (A.D. 70–80) ἔγραψέ μοι ἐπιστολὴν ὅτι

ἔλεγας κτλ., and for ἐλέγοσαν see *Syll* 928⁷⁵ (after B.C. 190) ὡς ἐλέγοσαν οἱ Πριη[νέων ἔγδι]κοι.

λεῖμμα.

For this NT ἅπ. εἰρ. (Rom 11⁵, WH λίμμα) see P Tebt I. 115²³ (B.C. 115–3) τὸ γεγονὸς (*l.* -ὸς) λίμμα (*l.* λεῖμμα) (πυροῦ): cf. Mayser *Gr.* p. 84.

λεῖος.

BGU III. 781ⁱⁱ·¹⁵ (i/A.D.) ἄλλα λεῖα ("unengraved") πυθμένια, *ib.* I. 162⁵ (ii/iii A.D.) ἄλλο (πλάτυμμα) ἃ ὁμοίως χρυσοῦν μεικρὸν λεῖον χωρὶ[ς θ]εοῦ, *Michel* 833³⁷ (B.C. 279) φιάλαι χρυσαῖ λεῖαι ἑπτά. Λεῖος <* λειϜος shows kinship with the Lat. *lēvis*, which is similarly used of "unchased" silver, e.g. Juv. *Sat.* xiv. 62.

λείπω.

P Amh II. 36¹² (c. B.C. 135) λείπω τε τὴν ὑπερβολήν, "I do not exaggerate" (Edd.), *Preisigke* 276 τάδ' ἔλιπον Ἀτ- ταλάχοις Ἡρακλῆ. As showing that the distinction between the active and the middle of the verb was carefully preserved, it may be noted that "the invariable expression in Anatolian epigraphy, even of the humblest class expressed in the worst Greek, is λείπειν βίον, not λείπεσθαι" (W. M. Ramsay *Exp* VII. vi. p. 548 f.). For the act. in the intrans. sense of "am lacking," as in Lk 18²², we may cite Epict. ii. 14. 19 τί σοι λείπει; and for the middle construed with ἐν, as in Jas 1⁴, cf. *Preisigke* 620⁶ (B.C. 97–96) where a temple that has received other honours is declared to be wanting in the right of asylum—λείπεσθαι δὲ ἐν τῷ μὴ εἶναι ἄσυλον. The verb is a *term. techn.* in accounts to denote a deficiency, e.g. P Par 59¹¹ (B.C. 160) (= Witkowski ², p. 76) λ(είπεται) (δραχμαὶ) ρνε. Examples of λείπομαι with a gen. of the thing wanting, as in Jas 1⁵, 2¹⁵, are to be found only in very late writers, such as Libanius : cf. Field *Notes*, p. 235. The pass. c. dat. is seen in P Tor I. 1ᵛⁱⁱ·⁵⁵ (B.C. 116) λελεῖφθαι τῇ κρίσει, "*causa cecidisse*" (Ed.), P Giss I. 69¹³ (A.D. 118– 119) κρειθῇ λειπόμεθα. The Ionic form -λιμπάνω is found in Attic popular speech in the second half of iv/B.C. (Meist- erhans *Gr.* p. 176) : cf. P Petr I. 14⁹ (a will—B.C. 237) καταλιμπάνω τὰ ὑπ[άρχοντα, similarly *ib.* 15¹⁷, and the late P Grenf I. 60⁴⁶ (A.D. 581) κληρονόμοις κατ]αλιμπάνειν. See also the Alexandrian Erotic Fragment *ib.* I. 1³ (ii/B.C.) με κατεφίλει ἐπιβούλως μέλλων με καταλιμπάνειν, and *OGIS* 519¹⁸·²⁰ (c. A.D. 245) παραλιμπάνοντες . . . καταλιμπά- νοντες. The form occurs sporadically in composition in the LXX (Thackeray *Gr.* i. p. 227), but in the NT only in 1 Pet 2²¹, unless we add three occurences in the "Western" text, Ac 8²¹ D, 17¹³ D, and 2 Cor 4⁹ FG. On the variations in MSS. between ἔλειπον and ἔλιπον, see Moulton *Gr.* ii. § 95. MGr λείπω, "fail," "am wanting," "am absent."

λειτουργέω.

The connotation of public services rendered to the State, which this verb has in classical writers, gives place in the Κοινή to personal services, more particularly in connexion with religious functions, as e.g. with regard to the Twins in the Serapeum, P Par 26⁹·² (B.C. 163–2) Θαυὴς καὶ Ταοῦς δίδυμαι, αἱ λειτουργοῦσαι ἐν τῷ πρὸς Μέμφει μεγάλῳ Σαρα- πιείῳ κτλ., *ib.* 27³ (B.C. 160), *et saepe* : cf. Ac 13², Heb 10¹¹, and see Deissmann *BS* p. 140 f., *Anz Subsidia*, p. 346 f. In P Oxy IV. 731[4] (A.D. 8–9) ἐφ᾽ ᾧ λιτουργήσω ὑμεῖν, "on condition that I give you my services," the reference is to a contract with an *artiste* for the festivals of Isis and Hera. Somewhat similar is the hire of two dancing-girls for an approaching festival in P Grenf II. 67[6] (A.D. 237) (= *Selections*, p. 108) λ]ει[τουρ]γήσιν ἡμῖν, and of a company of musicians in P Oxy X. 1275[12] (iii/A.D.) λειτουργήσοντας τοῖς ἀπὸ τῆς προκιμένης κώμης, "to perform for the inhabitants of the aforesaid village." For more miscellaneous uses of the verb cf. P Hib I. 78[11] (B.C. 244–3) of the release of two persons from some public service—διὰ τὸ μὴ ἐκπεσ[εῖ]ν αὐτοῖς τὸ νῦν λειτουργῆσαι, "because it is not at present their turn to serve" (Edd.), P Oxy VII. 1067[19] (iii/A.D.) εἰπὲ Πετεχῶντι . . . ὅτι εἰ μέλλεις ἐλθεῖν ἐλθέ, Διόσκορος γὰρ λειτουργεῖ ὑπὲρ σοῦ, "say to Petechon, 'Come if you are coming, for Dioscorus is labouring on your behalf'" (Edd.), and *ib.* I. 86[11] (A.D. 338) a complaint that a certain Eustochius τῆς νυνὶ λιτουργούσης φυλῆς, "of the tribe which is at present responsible for this duty," had failed to provide a sailor for a public boat. Exx. of the verb and subst. from Macedonian inscrr. are given by Ferguson *Legal Terms*, p. 62 f. : add also Teles (ed. Hense). p. 61[5] καὶ γὰρ ὑπουργῶν, ἃς αὐτὸς ἐλειτούργεις ζῶντι τῷ τέκνῳ καὶ τῷ φίλῳ καὶ κακοπαθῶν καὶ δαπανῶν, Epict. *Frag. Diss.* 23 τῷ ὄντι θαυμαστόν ἐστι φιλεῖν πρᾶγμα, ᾧ τοσαῦτα λειτουργοῦμεν καθ᾽ ἑκάστην ἡμέραν, and Linde *Epic.* p. 53 where ἀλειτούργητος, *immunis*, is cited. On the form of the verb see Mayser *Gr.* p. 127, Robertson *Gr.* p. 103, and Moulton *Gr.* ii. p. 76 f., and on the whole subject of the liturgical system in Egypt see F. Oertel *Die Liturgie*, Leipzig, 1917. MGr λειτουργῶ, "hold divine service," "serve."

λειτουργία.

The use of λειτουργία for sacerdotal ministration (as in the LXX and Heb 8[6], 9[21]) meets us with reference to the Egyptian priesthood in Diod. Sic. i. 21 τὸ τρίτον μέρος τῆς χώρας αὐτοῖς δοῦναι πρὸς τὰς τῶν θεῶν θεραπείας τὲ καὶ λειτουργίας : cf. the complaint of the Serapeum Twins P Lond 22[17] (B.C. 164–3) (= I. p. 7) οὐδὲν εἰλήφαμεν ποιούμεναι μεγάλας λειτουργίας τῶι θεῶι, and similarly P Par 33[19] (B.C. 160). See also BGU IV. 1201[7] (A.D. 2) πρὸς τὰς λιτουργείας καὶ θυσείας τῶν θεῶν (cf. Phil 2[17] with Lightfoot's note), P Tebt II. 302[20] (A.D. 71–2) ἐκτελοῦντες τὰς τῶν θεῶν λειτουργίας καὶ ὑπηρεσίας—of the priests of Soknebtunis. Other exx. of the word, showing its variety of application, are P Tor I. 1[i.20] (B.C. 116) τῶν τὰς λειτουργίας ἐν ταῖς νεκρίαις παρεχομένων, "publicis in re mortuaria muneribus fungentes" (Ed.), *ib.* viii. 16 μηδὲ τὴν αὐτὴν ἐργασίαν ἐπιτελεῖν, διαφέρειν δὲ τὴν τούτων λειτουργίαν, "neque eodem, ac illi, funguntur officio, sed differunt utrorumque munera" (Ed.), P Strass I. 57[11] (ii/A.D.) οὐκ ἐξαρκῶ δὲ πρὸς τὰς δύο λιτουργίας—proving that two liturgies might be laid on a man if he were able for them, which was not so in this case, P Oxy I. 40[6] (ii/iii A.D.), a claim for immunity from some form of public service (ἀλειτουργησία) on the ground that the petitioner was a doctor—ἰατρὸς ὑπάρχων τὴ[ν τέ]χνην τούτους αὐτοῖς οἵτινές με εἰς λειτο[υ]ρ[γ]ίαν δεδώκασι ἐθεράπευσα, "I am a doctor by profession and I have treated these very persons who have assigned me a

public burden" (Edd.), BGU I. 180[x.6] (ii/iii A.D.) a similar complaint by a veteran that, instead of getting the rest to which he was entitled after his release ἀπόλυσις\, he had been continuously employed for two years in public service —ἀ[ν]εδόθην κατ᾽ ἐτή[σιο]ν εἰς λειτουργίαν καὶ μέχρι τοῦ δευρε[ὶ κα]ς᾽ ἔτος ἐξῆ[ς] ἐν λειτουργίᾳ εἰμ[ὶ] ἀδιαλεί[πτ]ως, P Oxy I. 82[2] (mid. iii/A.D.), a declaration by a strategus that he will distribute the public burdens equitably—ὥστε καὶ τὰς ἀναδόσεις τῶν λειτουργῶν (*l.* -γιῶν) ποιήσασθαι ὑγιῶς καὶ πιστῶς, and from the inscrr. the Commagene rescript of Antiochus I., *OGIS* 383[71] (mid. i/B.C.) κόσμον τε καὶ λιτουργίαν πᾶσαν ἀξίως τύχης ἐμῆς καὶ δαιμόνων ὑπεροχῆς ἀνέθηκα : cf. also Teles (ed. Hense) p. 42[10] νῦν δέ, φησίν, ἀβίωτος ὁ βίος, στρατεία, λειτουργία, πολιτικὰ πράγματα, σχολάσαι [αὐτῷ] οὐκ ἔστι. Reference may also be made to Erman und Krebs p. 148 ff., Wilcken *Chrest.* I. i. p. 339 ff., and Hohlwein *L'Égypte Romaine*, p. 312 ff. For λειτούργημα see P Oxy XII. 1412[11] (c. A.D. 284) with the editors' note, and for λειτουργησία *ib.* 1413[17] (A.D. 270–5).

λειτουργικός

is found in a taxation-roll P Petr II. 39 (e) (1[v] (iii/B.C.)) λειτουργικὸν ϊγ, where it is preceded by φυλακιτικόν (policetax) and followed by ἰατρικόν (medical-tax) : cf. also P Tebt I. 5[41] (B.C. 118) ἀφείᾱσει δὲ πάν[τ]ας καὶ τοῦ ὀφειλομένου λειτουργ[ι]κοῦ, "and they remit to every one the arrears of the work-tax" (Edd.), *ib.* 102[3] (a receipt—B.C. 77 ?) διαγέγρ(αφας) τὸ λει(τουργικὸν) τοῦ δ (ἔτους), "you have paid the work-tax of the 4th year" (Edd.) ; the reference seems to be to a payment instead of personal service cf. Wilcken *Ostr.* i. p. 382). The special sense of *religious* service, as in the LXX and NT (Heb 1[14]), is seen in *ib.* 88[3] (B.C. 115–4) γραφὴν (*l.* γραφὴ) ἱερῶν καὶ πρ[οφ]ητῶν καὶ ἡμερῶν λειτουργικῶν, with reference to "days of service" rendered at the shrines at Kerkeosiris : see the editors' introd., and cf. Wilcken *Chrest.* I. p. 94, Otto *Priester* ii. pp. 33 n.[2], 39 n.[3].

λειτουργός

in the Ptolemaic period is often simply a "workman," as in Polybius, e.g. P Petr III. 46 (3)[5] (iii/B.C.) οἰκοδόμοις καὶ λειτουργοῖς, accounts in connexion with the erection of buildings, but cf. P Hib I. 96[11] (B.C. 259) where it is used of a military settler perhaps, as the editors suggest, because he had some special duties assigned to him. In P Oxy XII. 1412[20] (c. A.D. 284) we hear of a special meeting of the Senate of Oxyrhynchus—ψηφίσασθαί τε τὰς [τ]ῶν λ[ιτ]ουργῶν χειρο[τ]ο[ν]ίας, "to vote upon the election of those who are to serve," in connexion with the transport of corn for the troops : cf. the report of similar proceedings in *ib.* 1415[1 f.] (late iii/A.D.) οἱ βουλευταὶ εἶπ(ον) ᾽Αριστί[ων ὅταν ἔλθῃ ὁλοκληρήσει, λειτουργὸς ἦν ὁλοκληρῶν ᾽Αριστίων. ὁ πρύτανις <εἶπ εν> δότε τοὺς [λειτο]υργούς, ἵνα [μὴ] ἐμποδίζηται, "the senators said, 'Aristion, when he comes, will prosper ; a prosperous public servant was Aristion.' The prytanis said, 'Appoint the persons to office, in order that there may be no delay'" (Edd.), and for the inscrr. see *CIG* II. 2881[13], 2882[5], 2889[1]. With this sense of a public servant cf. LXX Josh 1[1] A, 3 Kings 10[5], and for a religious sense see Neh 10[59], Isai 61[6], Rom 13[6] *al.*

λέντιον.

This Graecized form (Jn 13⁴⁴) = the Lat. *linteum*, which in the second syllable shows the more open form of ι (for ε) before a vowel (cf. Moulton *Gr.* ii. p. 76), is found in *Ostr* 1611¹ ⁿˡ (Rom.) λέν[τ(ια)] β̄, "two linen cloths," and P Oxy VI. 929¹⁶ (ii/iii A.D.) λίνον καὶ λέντιον τριβακόν, "a linen cloth and a worn towel." In *Magn* 116³⁴ (time of Hadrian) we have λειτουργοῦ . . ἐκδόσεως λεντίων ἑκατοστή.

λεπίς.

This subst., which in the NT is confined to Ac 9¹⁸, occurs in *Michel* 833¹¹ (B.C. 279) θυμιατήριον ὑπόχαλκον, λεπίδα ἀργυρᾶν ἔχον : cf. BGU II. 544⁸ (time of Antoninus). For the verb λέπω, see P Par 12¹⁵ (B.C. 157) σπασάμενος λέπει με τῇ μαχαίρᾳ εἰς τὸ σκέλος, and for λεπίζω (Tobit 3¹⁷, 11¹³, *al.*) see P Leid Nˣⁱⁱⁱ·³⁷ (iii/A.D.) λαβὼν ἄγχουσαν (*l.* ἄγχουσαν), λεοντικὴν λέπισον. καὶ λαβὼν τὰ λεπίσματα (Gen 30³⁷) εἰς θυίαν τρίβε.

λεπτόν.

For this coin, the smallest piece of money in circulation (cf. Lk 12⁵⁹), see *OGIS* 484⁹ (ii/A.D.) εἰς τὸν λεπτὸν . . χαλκόν with Dittenberger's note : "distinguitur denarius argenteus, quae est moneta imperialis, ab asse abeneo, i.e. moneta provinciali. Haec adiectivo λεπτός significatur." Cf. *ib.* 485¹² (Roman) κατασταθεὶς δὲ καὶ ἐπὶ τῆς χαράξεως τοῦ λεπτοῦ χαλκοῦ. We may add one or two miscellaneous exx. of the adj.—P Petr III. 42 H (8)ƒ ²ˢ (mid. iii/B.C.) ῥάκος λεπτόν, P Lond 1177¹⁶¹ (A.D. 113) (= III. p. 185) σχοινίων λεπτῶν, P Giss I. 47⁷ (Hadrian) (= *Chrest.* I. 326) θώραξ . . [τ]ὴν πλοκὴν λεπτότατος. PSI II. 177⁵ (ii/iii A.D.) λεπτὸν γέγον[εν, of a sick child, P Flor II. 127¹⁴ (A.D. 256) χοιρίδιον . . λεπτόν, of a thin pig, P Oxy VII. 1066⁵ (iii/A.D.) τὴν ῥίνην . . λεπτοτέραν, of a too fine file. For λεπτόν or λεπτίον, "a jar," see P Oxy VIII. 1153⁴ (i/A.D.) with the editor's note.

λευκαίνω.

We have not noted any instance of this verb in our sources, but for the corresponding λευκόω, "whiten," cf. *Syll* 587¹⁴⁰ (B.C. 329–8) τὸν βωμὸν τοῦ Πλούτωνος . . . λευκῶσαι, *ib.* 306³⁴ (Delphi—ii/B.C.) καὶ τὰ ἐνέχυρα αὐτῶν ἐμ πίνακας λελευκωμένους δύο ἀναγνόντω ἐν ταῖ ἐκκλησίαι. The subst. λεύκωμα, a white board used for public notices, is seen in such a passage as *Syll* 510⁵ (Ephesus—ii/B.C.) ἃ δ' ἂν οἱ δικασταὶ κρίνωσιν, ἀναγράψαντες εἰς λεύκωμα οἱ εἰσαγωγεῖς κτλ.

λευκός.

In a list of soldiers, P Amh II. 62⁵ᶠᶠ (ii/B.C.) three persons called Apollonius are distinguished as μέλας, "the dark," λευκός, "the fair," and σκευοφ(όρος), "the baggage-carrier," respectively. For the more general meaning of λευκός, "white," cf. such passages as P Ryl II. 146¹⁵ (A.D. 39) ἐρίων σταθμία δέκα λευκῶν, "to measures of white wool," P Giss I. 21⁹ (time of Trajan) τὸ συνθεσείδιον τὸ λευκόν, "the white dress"—a loose wrap often worn at meals, P Oxy III. 531¹³ (ii/A.D.) τὰ ἱμάτια τὰ λευκά, and P Hamb I. 38²¹ (A.D. 182) λευκὸν ἐν ὀφθαλμῷ ἀριστερῷ. In P Oxy III. 471²⁴ᶠᶠ (ii/A.D.) the charge is brought against

a high official that if a poor man ἐν] εὐτελέσιν ἱματίοις, "wearing cheap clothes" (cf. Jas 2²), asked a favour, his property was confiscated, and that the man—τὸν οὐκ ἐν λευκαῖς ἐσθῆσιν [ἐ]ν θεάτρῳ καθίσα[ντα, "who took his seat at the theatre in other than white garments" was delivered to death. For the ceremonial use of "white clothing," as in Rev 3⁴, cf. *Priene* 205 εἰσίναι εἰς [τὸ] ἱερὸν ἁγνὸν ἐ[ν] ἐσθῆτι λευκ[ῆι. Constant reference is made to the fact that decrees etc. were written on a pillar of "white stone," e.g. *Michel* 509¹⁷ (B.C. 241) τὰ δεδογμένα ἀναγράψαι εἰς στήλην λευκοῦ λίθου, *Syll* 529⁴¹ (ii/B.C.) ἀν]αγράψαι δὲ [τ]ά τε ψηφίσματα κ[αὶ] τὰ ὀνόματα αὐτῶν εἰ]ς τελαμῶνα λευκοῦ λίθου. The latter citation gives no help to the interpretation of the difficult Rev 2¹⁷, for which we must refer to the commentaries of Swete and Moffatt (in *EGT) ad l.*, where the various associations of "white stones" are fully discussed. See also *s.v.* λίθος.

λέων.

With the figurative use in 2 Tim 4¹⁷ we may compare the early i/A.D. acrostic P Tebt II. 278³⁵, where with reference to a lost garment it is stated—λέων ὁ ἄρας, μωρὸς <ὁ> ἀπολέσας, "a lion he was who took it, a fool who lost it" (Edd.). Cf. also the Silco inscr. *OGIS* 201¹⁵ (vi/A.D.) ἐγὼ γὰρ εἰς κάτω μέρη λέων εἰμι, καὶ εἰς ἄνω μέρη ἄρξ εἰμι : for the conjunction of animals Dittenberger compares 1 Kings 17³⁴ᶠᶠ, Amos 5¹⁹. The word is found in the horoscope BGU III. 957¹ (B.C. 10) ἐν λέοντι, and in the moral tale P Grenf II. 84⁷ (v/vi A.D.), where a patricide, fleeing into the desert, is pursued ὑπὸ λέοντος. MGr λιοντάρι has assumed the diminutive form ; cf. φίδι, "snake."

λήθη.

With 2 Pet 1⁹ we may compare Vett. Val. p. 242⁴ ἡ δὲ διάνοια . . . ἄλλοτε ἀλλαχοῦ πηδῶσα τὴν πρώτην λήθην ἀναλαμβάνει. The word survives in MGr.

λῆ(μ)ψις.

To what is said regarding this word *s.v.* δόσις (*ad fin.*) add such exx. of its use as P Tebt I. 238 (B.C. 116–5) τῆ(ς) λή(ψεως) (πυροῦ), and P Oxy I. 71¹·²⁸ (A.D. 303) μετ' ἐνεχύρων λήμψεως κατὰ τὰ ἔγγραφα αὐτοῦ γραμμάτια, "by seizure of the securities provided in his written bonds" (Edd.).

ληνός.

P Amh II. 48⁷ (B.C. 106) παρὰ ληνόν, "at the wine-press," P Oxy IV. 729¹⁹ (A.D. 137) ἀπ]οδότωσαν τῷ μεμισθ[ω]κότι τὸν μὲν οἶνον παρὰ ληνὸν νέον ἄδολον, "they shall pay to the lessor the wine at the vat, new and unadulterated" (Edd.). *ib.* III. 502³⁶ (A.D. 164) τὰς οὔσας λινοὺς λιθίνας δύο ὑδρίων καὶ ὅλμου, "the two existing stone presses with the water-pitchers and trough" (Edd.). The word is sometimes used to denote generally a receptacle for holding wine, see e.g. P Flor II. 139¹ (mid. iii/A.D.) τὴν δεκάτη[ν] ληνὸν ἀπόλυσον Μαξίμῳ, with the editor's note. In Wünsch *AF* 4¹⁹ (iii/A.D.) τοὺς ληνοὺς ὅλους (for gender cf. Gen 30³⁸· ⁴¹) = "the whole coffins."

λῆρος.

This subst. is read by the editor in PSI V. 534¹⁶ (iii/B.C.) οὔτε λήρων.

For the corresponding verb see P Fay 114³¹ (A.D. 100) **μὴ ον** (*l.* **οὖν**) **ληρήσῃς τὸν ἐκτιναγμόν σου**, "don't talk nonsense about your threshing" (Edd.), cf. P Giss I. 64⁸ (ii/A.D.) **ληρεῖ** : and for the adj. **ληρώδης** see BGU III. 1011ii. 15 (ii/B.C.) **πολ[λὰ] ληρώι[δη] καὶ ψευδῆ προσαγ[γ]έλ[λε]ται.**

λῃστής.

P Petr III. 28 (*e*) *verso* (*a*)¹ (iii/B.C.), memoranda relating to criminals, is headed—**περὶ ἐπ[ιθέσ]εως λῃστῶν** (for form, cf. Mayser *Gr.* p. 122): cf. P Par 46⁷ (B.C. 153) (= Witkowski², p. 86) **ἐν τοῖς ἀναγκαιοτάτοις καιροῖς λῃστῶν ἐπικειμένων**, P Lips I. 37²³ (A.D. 389) **ἑτοιμότατα γὰρ ἔχω ἀπελέγξαι ἐν τῷ ἀχρά[ν]τῳ αὐτοῦ δικαστηρίῳ τούτους λῃστὰς ὁμολό[γ]ους καὶ ζῷα ἀπελακότας** (*l.* **ἀπεληλ**—) **πολλάκις**, and the late P Oxy I. 139²³ (A.D. 612) **ὑποδέξασθαι λιστάς**, "to have harboured robbers." For **λῃστήριον**, "a band of robbers," cf. P Petr III. 28 (*e*)⁶ (iii/B.C.) **ἐπέθετο αὐτοῖς λῃστήρ[ιο]ν**, P Hamb I. 10⁷ (ii/A.D.) **ἐπέβη μου ταῖς οἰκίαις . . λῃστήριον**, and for the meaning "robbers' lairs," cf. *Cagnat* IV. 219⁵ **τὰ ἐν Ἑλλησπόντῳ λῃστήρια.** The adj. **λῃστ(ρ)ικός** is common, e.g. P Tebt I. 53¹¹ (B.C. 110) **ἐπιθέμενοι λῃστικῶι τρόπωι**, *ib.* II. 332⁵ (A.D. 176) **ἐπῆλθάν τινες λῃστρικῷ τρόπῳ οἰκίαν μου.** Other derivatives from the same root are **λῃστεία** (BGU II. 372ii. 13—A.D. 154), **λῃστοπιαστής** (*ib.* I. 325²—*c.* iii/A.D.), an officer detailed for special service in the search for certain criminals, and **λῄσταρχος**, "arch-pirate" (P Oxy I. 33 *verso* iv. 5—late ii/A.D., where the term is used metaphorically).

λίαν.

For the epistolary formula **ἐχάρην λίαν** in 2 Jn ⁴, 3 Jn ³, we may compare BGU II. 632¹⁰ (ii/A.D.) **καὶ ἐπιγνούς σε ἐρρωμένην λίαν ἐχάρην**, "and when I knew that you were in sound health I rejoiced greatly," P Giss I. 21³ (time of Trajan) **λίαν ἐχάρην ἀκούσασα ὅτι ἔρρωσαι**: see also P Par 42³ (B.C. 156) **λίαν σοι χάριν μεγάλην ἐσχήκαμεν.** Otherwise the adv. is common, e.g. P Tebt I. 12²⁴ (B.C. 118) **ἀποδέχομαι δὲ τὰ παρὰ σοῦ λίαν**, "I accept completely your views" (Edd.), P Oxy II. 298²⁶ (i/A.D.) **λίαν αὐτὸν βαρύνομαι**, "I am too severe with him" (Edd.), *ib.* III. 525⁴ (early ii/A.D.) **λείαν τῷ πράγματι καταξύομαι**, "I am extremely worn out with the matter" (Edd.), *ib.* IX. 1216¹³ (ii/iii A.D.) **λείαν γὰρ φιλῶ αὐτόν**, *ib.* XIV. 1676¹⁰ (iii/A.D.) **λείαν ἐλυπήθην ὅτι οὐ παρεγένου ἰς τὰ γενέσια τοῦ παιδίου μου.** The use with an adj., as in Mt 4⁸ *al.*, may be illustrated by P Tebt II. 315¹³ (ii/A.D.) **ὁ γὰρ ἄνθρωπος λείαν ἐστὶ[ν] αὐστηρός.**

λίβανος.

In a list of articles for a sacrifice, P Oxy IX. 1211¹¹ (ii/A.D.), are included **ἔλεον, μέλι, γάλα, πᾶν ἄρωμα χωρὶς λιβάνου**, "oil, honey, milk, every spice except frankincense": cf. P Leid Wix. 11 (ii/iii A.D.) **κασία, λίβανος, ζμύρνα**, the illiterate P Ryl II. 242³ (iii/A.D.) **ἢὰν ἦς ἀδυναατες πέμψ μοι ἀκάνθινος χυλέν, πέμψεν μοι λάβανον.** "if you are unable to send me acacia-juice, please send me incense" (Edd.), and the Pergamum inscr. *Cagnat* IV. 353*b*.¹⁶ **πόπανον** (a round sacrificial cake) **καὶ λίβανον καὶ λύχνους τῶι Σεβαστῶι.** The adj. **λιβάνινος** occurs in P Oxy I. 114⁵ (ii/iii A.D.) **δερματικομαφόρτιν λιβάνινον**, "a casket (?) of

incense-wood" (Edd.), and **λιβανωτικός** in *OGIS* 132¹⁰ (B.C. 130) **τὰ λιβανωτικὰ φορτία.** The word is of Semitic origin. MGr **λιβάνι**, "incense."

λιβανωτός.

= "frankincense" may be illustrated from the ii/iii A.D. medical prescription P Oxy II. 234ii. 5 **λιβ]ανωτὸν οἴνῳ [διεὶ]ς ἡδίστῳ κλύξε [τὸ ο]ὖς**, "dilute frankincense with very sweet wine and syringe the ear" (Edd.) : cf. *ib.* I. 118²⁰ (late iii/A.D.) **λιβανωτόν [τινα σ]υναγοράσας**, "buy some incense," and *OGIS* 383¹⁴² (mid. i/B.C.) **ἐπιθύσεις ἀφειδεῖς λιβανωτοῦ καὶ ἀρωμάτων.** Grimm's note makes Rev 8⁵·⁵ confuse λ. = "frankincense" and **λιβανωτίς** = "censer," but *Syll* 588¹³⁸ (*c.* B.C. 180) **λιβανωτίδος κλάσματα** has the latter word in the former meaning, so that the confusion existed also "in prof. auth.," or at least in profane inscriptions.

Λιβερτῖνος.

For a conjecture that in Ac 6⁹ we should read not **Λιβερτίνων**, but **Λιβυστίνων**, with reference to Jews inhabiting Libya, see Blass *Philology*, p. 69 f.

λιθάζω.

On the *conative* usage of **λιθάζετε** in Jn 10³² see Moulton *Einleitung*, p. 210, and cf. *Proleg.* p. 128 f., Wilcken *Archiv* v. p. 269.

λίθινος.

PSI V. 496³ (B.C. 258-7) **λίθινα καὶ πλίνθινα**, P Magd 42⁵ (B.C. 221) **τό τε περιτραχηλίδιον ἐκ καθορμίων** (LXX Hos 2¹³) **λιθίνων ἀφειλετό μ[οι]**, "he snatched from me my small collar of stone necklets," BGU IV. 1067⁶ (A.D. 101-2) **ὅλμοι λίθινοι**, "stone troughs," P Oxy III. 502³⁷ (A.D. 164) **τὰς οὔσας ληνοὺς λιθίνας δύο**, "the two existing stone presses," *ib.* VI. 937¹³ (iii A.D.) **τῆς φιάλης τῆς λιθίνης**, "the stone bowl." A form **λιθικός** is found in P Leid Uiii. 22 (ii/B.C.) (= I. p. 125) **ἐν τοῖς λιθικοῖς ἔργοις**, where, however, the editor proposes to read **λιθίνοις.**

λιθοβολέω.

With this compound, which is rare outside Biblical Greek (cf. Anz *Subsidia*, p. 366), we may compare **λιθοκοπέω** (not found in LS), for which Mayser (*Gr.* p. 461) cites P Vat F²⁰ (Mai V. 356) (B.C. 157), *ib.* E²⁵ (Mai V. 354), although in both places Mai reads **λιθοκοπετέω.**

λίθος

is always masc. in the NT even when it means a gem (Rev 21¹¹ *al.*, LXX), whereas Attic after B.C. 385 preferred the fem. (Meisterhans *Gr.* p. 129). This is in keeping with the Κοινή usage, e.g. P Petr II. 13 (6)⁶ (B.C. 258-253) **τοὺς λίθους** of stones for building, P Oxy III. 498⁷ (ii/A.D.) **τῶν οἰκοδομουμένων λίθων κύβων καμηλικῶν**, "squared building-stones transportable by camel (?)" (Edd.), *ib.* 528¹² (illit.— ii/A.D.) **ἔπεμψάς μυ ἐπιστολὰς δυναμένου λίθον σαλεῦσε**, "you sent me letters which would have shaken a stone" (Edd.), P Tebt II. 342²⁷ (late ii/A.D.) **κεραμειον . . λίθοις ἀρεστοῖς ἐξηρτισμ(ένον)**, "a pottery fitted with stones in good order" (Edd.), P Oxy X. 1273⁵ (A.D. 260) **περιτραχήλιον . . ἔχον λίθον ὁλκῆς χωρὶς τοῦ [λ[]θ[ο]υ τετάρτων** δεκατριῶν, "a necklace having a stone and weighing apart from the stone 13 quarters" (Edd.), *OGIS* 90[54] (Rosetta stone—B.C. 196) σ]τερεοῦ λίθου, *Priisigke* 1114[3] (A.D. 147-8) ἐκόψαμεν τοὺς μεγάλους λίθους. In connexion with the imprecatory inscr. on limestone found in Palestine, Wünsch remarks that limestone had probably a superstitious significance there, though of what kind we do not know, and compares the "white stone" (ψῆφον λευκήν) with a "new" spell given as an amulet in Rev 2[17]: see Bliss and Macalister *Excavations in Palestine*, 1902, p. 186. Reference should also be made to the striking new saving ascribed to Jesus, P Oxy I. 1 No. 5 ἔγει[ρ]ον τὸν λίθον κἀκεῖ εὑρήσεις με, σχίσον τὸ ξύλον κἀγὼ ἐκεῖ εἰμι, though we cannot enter here upon its interpretation.

λιθόστρωτος.

For this NT ἅπ. εἰρ. (Jn 19[13]) cf. P Flor I. 50[17] (A.D. 268) ἐπὶ τοῦ λιθοστρώτου δρόμου Ἕρμου. See also Aristeas 88 τὸ δὲ πᾶν ἔδαφος λιθόστρωτον καθέστηκε, "the whole floor (of the temple) is paved with stones" (Thackeray). Other exx. in Wetstein.

λικμάω.

For λικμάω in its original sense of "winnow" (as in LXX Ruth 3[2], Sir 5[9]) we may cite PSI V. 522[2] (B.C. 248-7) ὁ δ[ὲ ὅ]ροβος ἄρτι ἐλικμᾶτο, BGU IV. 1040[11] (ii/A.D.) ἐ[πεὶ] ἤμελλεν λικμᾶν, P Ryl II. 442[3] (iii/A.D.) ἐὰν λικμήσωσι τὴν ἁλωνίαν, τὰ ἄχυρα γεμίσονται ... Cf. λικμάζω in P Oxy XII. 1482[3] (ii/A.D.) λελικμήκαμεν τὴν κριθήν. Many find the other LXX usage = "scatter" (Isai 17[13] *al.*) in the two NT passages where the verb occurs (Mt 21[44], Lk 20[18]) : see e.g. Kennedy *Sources*, p. 126 f. On the other hand, Deissmann (*BS*, p. 225 f.) defends the AV translation "crush," "grind to powder" (following the Vulgate *conterere, comminuere*) on the evidence of BGU I. 146[8] (ii/iii A.D.), a complaint against certain men who—ἐλίκμησάν μου τὸ λάχανον, "had stamped, ruined, my λάχανον." Boll (*Offenbarung*, p. 130 n.[1]) supplies further profane evidence in the same direction from Lyd. p. 53, 13 λικμητὸν ἀνθρώποις ἀπειλεῖ, where λικμητός has the meaning of ἀπώλεια.

λιμήν.

P Petr II. 45[ii. 19] (B.C 246) ὁ ἐν Σελευκεί[αι λ]ιμήν, P Amh II. 116[1] (A.D. 178) τετελ[εσται] ... λιμένος Μέμφε[ως, "paid the tax for the harbour of Memphis."

λίμνη.

P Petr III. 37 (a)[9] (B.C. 257) παρὰ τὴν λίμνην, "alongside the lake," P Amh II. 100[3] (A.D. 198-211) an agreement concerning λίμνης [κα]λουμέν[η]s Πάτρω[νο]s, P Flor I. 50[32] (A.D. 268) ἐπάνω λίμνης. In an ostracon letter of A.D. 192, published by Deissmann *LAE* p. 186, instructions are given that certain quantities of wheat are to be delivered to two "husbandmen of the lake"—γεωργοῖς λίμνης, whose homes are in the village of Phmau (ἀπὸ Φμαῦ· cf. Heb 13[24] οἱ ἀπὸ τῆς Ἰταλίας, where Deissmann thinks the reference is to people *in* Italy). See for the same ostracon Meyer *Ostr.* p. 176 f., where the editor identifies this λίμνη with Birket Habu near Thebes, and gives other instances of λίμνη as "Seeland" or "Seegau."

λιμός.

The wavering of gender which is found in the NT (ὁ Lk 4[25]: ἡ Lk 15[14], Ac 11[28]) meets us again in the papyri— P Par 22[21] (B.C. 165) τῷ λιμῷ διαλυθῆναι, but in a document of the same collection *ib.* 26[i. 9] (B.C. 163-2) ὑπὸ τῆς λιμοῦ διαλυόμεναι. Cf. also *ib.* 28[13] (B.C. 160) where, instead of the simple dat., we have διαλυόμεναι ἐν τῷ λιμῷ. Other exx. are P Petr III. 36 (a) *verso* [20] (Ptol.) ἀξιῶ σε δεόμενος μή με ἀπολέσηι τῶι λιμῶι ἐν τῆι φυλακῆι, "I entreat you with prayers not to let me perish of hunger in prison" (Edd.), and P Oxy VI. 902[9] (c. A.D. 465) ἐκ τούτου συνέβη τὸ ὑπόλοιπον τῶν ἐμῶν ζῴων τῇ λιμῷ τεθνάναι, "in consequence of which the remainder of my kine have died of hunger" (Edd.) : see also Crönert, p. 177. The use of the fem. is generally traced to "Doric" influence : cf. Lob. *Phryn.* p. 188 τὴν λιμὸν Δωριεῖς, σὺ δὲ ἀρσενικῶς τὸν λιμὸν φάθι, Rutherford *NP*, p. 274, Thumb *Hellen.* p. 67. The older Attic masc. is usual in the LXX, cf. Thackeray *Gr.* i. p. 146.

For the conjunction λοιμοὶ καὶ λιμοί in Lk 21[11] Boll *Offenbarung*, p. 131, compares Catal. viii. 3, 186, 1 λιμὸς καὶ λοιμὸς καὶ σφαγαὶ κατὰ τόπους : see also *Test. xii. patr.* Jud. xxiii. 3, *Orac. Sib.* viii. 175. The two words are cognate, being connected with the Homeric λοιγός and the Lat. *letum*.

λίνον

is used with reference to "linen" cloths or garments, as in Rev 15[6] PQ (see *contra* WH *Notes*[2], p. 139), in such passages as P Oxy X. 1281[6] (A.D. 21) τὴν τειμὴν τῶν ἑκατὸν λίνων Σινυραιτικῶν, "the price of the hundred cloths of Sinaru," P Tebt II. 314[16] (ii/A.D.) καλῶς π[ο]ιήσεις διαπεμψάμενός μοι τὰ λίνα, "you will oblige me by sending the cloths," *ib.* 406[16] (c. A.D. 266) λίνα λευκὰ ἀριθμῷ ι[β], "white linen cloths twelve in number," P Leid W[viii. 3] (ii/iii A.D.) στώλισον αὐτὸν λίνῳ καθαρῷ, [xv. 4] σὺ δ' ἐν λίνοις ἴσθι καθαροῖς ἐστημμένος, BGU II. 450[17] (ii/iii A.D.) περὶ τῶν λίνων, ὧν χρείαν ἔλεγες ἔχειν, δήλωσόν μοι, *al.* : cf. P Oxy IV. 736[75] (c. A.D. 1) λίνου καὶ ῥαφίδος (ὀβολός), "a needle and thread 1 ob." (Edd.). As illustrating Rev *l.c.* Moffatt (*EGT ad l.*) aptly cites Plutarch *de Iside*, 3, 4, where it is explained that the linen surplice was affected by Egyptian votaries of Isis on religious grounds, e.g. the bright smiling colour of flax etc. In Ev. Petr. 12 τὰ λίνα = "fishing-nets." For the adj. λινοῦς, as in Rev 15[6] ℵ, cf. P Oxy II. 285[11] (c. A.D. 50) ἐνδεδυμένο (l. -ος) χιτῶνα λεινοῦν, *ib.* VII. 1051[15] (iii/A.D.) δελματικὴ λινὰ ᾱ. "1 linen Dalmatian vest," *ib.* X. 1277[7] (A.D. 255) τρίκλιν[ο]ν στρωμάτων λινῶν ποικιλτῶν : in PSI V. 533[5] (iii/B.C.) λινὴ αὐλαία, "a linen curtain," is contrasted with a "woollen" (ἐρεᾷ) one. For λινύφος, "linen-weaver," see P Oxy X. 1281[4] (A.D. 21): cf. λινόυφος in *ib.* 1303 (c. A.D. 336).

λιτανεία.

In view of the occurrence of this word in the LXX (2 Macc 3[20] *al.*) and its subsequent importance in connexion with Christian worship, we may cite an instance of it—the only instance of which we are aware—from the papyri, unfortunately in a broken context, but with reference to consulting the god Soknebtunis, P Tebt II. 284[9] (i/B.C.) σὺ δὲ ἱκανήν μου σὺν τοῖς παιδίος (*l.* -ίοις) περὶ τῆς λιτανήας, "and do you together with the children . . . concerning the supplication" (Edd.).

λίτρα.

For λίτρα, which in the NT is confined to Jn 12³ 19³⁹, cf. P Oxy XII. 1454⁵ (A.D. 116) σταθμοῦ λείτρας δύο. "each weighing 2 pounds." In *ib.* 1513⁷ (iv/A.D.) it is curious to find beer measured by λίτραι—ζυτοῦ λί(τραι) νε̄. See also *ib.* 1543⁵ (*c.* A.D. 299), a receipt for chaff supplied to soldiers on the march—ἐλίτρισεν (a new verb) . . . ἀχύρου . . [λί]τρας τεσσαράκο[ντα. The name of a Sicilian silver coin, λίτρα is an attempt to reproduce a probable form * liprā, which appears in Latin as *libra* (Boisacq, p. 585).

λίψ.

In classical usage λίψ denotes the south-west wind, and hence the quarter from which that wind comes. Consequently in Ac 27¹² the Revisers have translated the words λιμένα τῆς Κρήτης βλέποντα κατὰ λίβα καὶ κατὰ χῶρον, "a haven of Crete looking north-east and south-east," or literally in the margin "down the south-west wind and down the north-west wind." In the LXX, on the other hand, the word denotes almost uniformly simply "south," while in the Egyptian papyri it stands for "west," because, as Deissmann (*BS* p. 141 f.) following Boeckh has pointed out, Libya, with which the word was associated (but cf. Boisacq p. 564), lies directly west from Egypt. One or two exx. of this papyrus usage will suffice. Thus in the will of a Libyan, which was discovered at Gurob in the Fayûm, P Petr III. iᵢᵢ (B.C. 236) we hear of a piece of land bounded—³ ᶠ ἀπηλ[ιώ]το]υ, νότου, [λι]βός, βορρᾶ, and another—¹ᵃ ᶠᶠ ἀπηλιώ[του], νότου, λιβός, βορρᾶ, i.e. "on east, south, west, north." Similarly in the registration of a mortgage, P Oxy II. 243²¹ ᶠᶠ. (A.D. 79), the dimensions of two pieces of land are measured βορρᾶ ἐπὶ νότον, "from north to south," and λιβὸς ἐπ' ἀπηλιότην, "from west to east." See also the account of a dream from the Serapeum P Par 51²ᶠᶠ (B.C. 160) (= *Selections*, p. 19) ὤμ[ην] βατ(=δ)ίζειν με [ἀπ]ὸ λειβὸς ἕως ἀ[πηλι]ώτου, καὶ ἀναπίπτομαι ἐπ' ἄχυρον· καὶ [ἄν]θρωπ[ος] ἀπὸ λιβός μου, ἐχόμενός μου, "I dreamt that I was going from west to east, and sat down upon chaff. And west from me there was someone, who was near to me." In view of this and the pure Latin character of χῶρος (= lat. *caurus, corus*), "north-west wind," in the Lukan passage, Goodspeed in an elaborate note in *Exp* VI. viii. p. 130 ff. thinks that the translation "looking west and north-west" is not "wholly improbable": but see *Archiv* iii. 460 f. For a new adj. λιβικός cf. P Lond 755 *verso* ³⁶ (iv/A.D.) (= III. p. 223) ἐν τῷ λιβικῷ μέρι.

λογ(ε)ία.

Deissmann's confirmation of the meaning "collection" for this word in 1 Cor 16¹ ᶠ has been plentifully supported since the publication of *BS* (pp. 142 ff., 219 f.). See e.g. from Ptolemaic times P Hib I. 51² (B.C. 245) ἐπιστολῆς περὶ τῆς λογείας τῶν χλωρῶν τἀντίγραφ[ον, "the copy of the letter about the collection of (the value of) the green stuffs," P Grenf II. 38¹⁵ (mid. i/B.C.) γράφωμαί σε (*l.* γραφήσομαί σοι) περὶ τῆς λογέας, and P Tebt I. 58⁵⁵ (B.C. 111) προσπαρα-

καλέσαι Νίκωνα περὶ τῆς λογέας, "urge on Nicon concerning the collection." An excellent illustration, almost contemporary with 1 Cor, is afforded by P Oxy II. 239⁸ (A.D. 66) ὀμνύω . . . μηδεμίαν λογείαν γεγονέναι ὑπ' ἐμοῦ ἐν τῇ αὐτῇ κώμῃ, "I swear that I have levied no contributions whatever in the above village," where the editors note that "λογεία is used for irregular local contributions as opposed to regular taxes," and compare BGU II. 515⁷ (A.D. 193) (= *Chrest.* I. 268) where τὰ ὑπὲρ λογίας [ἐ]πιβληθέντα are contrasted with σιτικὰ δημόσια. In this last case the reference may be to a collection for religious purposes, as frequently in the ostraca in connexion with a tax for the priests of Isis, cf. the Theban ostracon of date 4 Aug. A.D. 63, reproduced by Deissmann (*LAE* p. 104 f.), which, after an opening greeting, runs as follows—ἀπέχω παρὰ σοῦ (δραχμὰς) δ ὀβο(λὸν) τὴν λογίαν Ἴσιδος περὶ τῶν δημοσίων, "I have received from thee 4 drachmae 1 obol, being the collection of Isis on behalf of the public works": see further Wilcken *Ostr.* i. p. 253 ff., Otto *Priester* i. p. 359 ff., and from the inscr. the i/A.D. marble tablet from Smyrna, *Syll* 583²⁸ κλεῖν κεχρυσωμένην καὶ ἐμπεφιασμένην πρὸς τὴν λογήαν καὶ πομπὴν τῶν θεῶν, where as Deissmann points out (*LAE* p. 105 n.³⁰), "the reference seems to be to a procession on the occasion of which money contributions were expected from the spectators." Other exx. of the word with varying references are P Lond 3⁷ (B.C. 146 or 135) (= I. p. 46) τῆς τιμ[ῆς το]ῦ ἡμίσους τοῦ [τρί]του λογείας τῶν κειμένων νεκρῶν, P Giss I. 61⁷ (A.D. 119) μηνύοντ[ες] α[ὐ]τὸν λογίαν πε[π]οιηκέναι ἐπὶ τῆς κώμης Ναβόωι, BGU III. 891 *verso* ¹² (A.D. 144) τοὺς δ πρεσβυτ(έρους) [τ]ῆς αὐτῆς κώ(μης) ἐνκαλου[μ]ένους ὑπὸ Χαιρή[μ]ονο[ς] . . περὶ ἧς φησιν πεπο[ι]ῆσθαι λογίας, and P Lond 342¹⁵ (A.D. 185) (= II. p. 174) where complaint is made against a village πρεσβύτερος—παρ' ἕκαστα λογείας ποιεῖται. In view of the above, it is clear that the statement in Grimm-Thayer "Not found in prof. auth." requires modification, and it is instructive to notice that words like this and the adj. δοκίμιος, "genuine," have disappeared so completely from our literary sources, when the vernacular used them with such freedom. Λογεία should probably be read in 2 Macc 12⁴³ ποιησάμενός τε κατ' ἄνδρα λογείαν. On the forms of λογεία see Moulton *Gr.* ii. p. 82.

λογίζομαι

is common in the sense of "reckon," "put down to one's account" as in Rom 4⁶ *al.*, e.g. P Eleph 5¹³ (B.C. 284–3) ἐλογισάμην πρὸς Ἑρμαγόραν ὑπὲρ τοῦ οἴνου . . ., P Par 62ⁱᵛ·¹ (*c.* B.C. 170) ἃ οὐ λογισθήσεται τοῖς τελώναις. P Oxy XII. 1434⁸ (A.D. 107–8) τὰ ἀργυρικὰ καὶ σειτικὰ καθ(ήκοντα) [ἐν]θάδε λογίζεται, "the due amounts in money and corn are reckoned here," *ib.* III. 533⁹ (ii/iii A.D.) αἱ πρόσοδοί μου . . . παρὰ τῷ ταμείῳ ἐ[ν π]αραθέσει λογισθήτωσαν, "let my revenues be placed on deposit at the storehouse" (Edd.), P Flor II. 123⁷ (A.D. 254) λογιζομένου αὐτῷ τοῦ μονοχώρου δραχμῶν δέκα-ἕξ, "reckoning the wine to him at sixteen drachmae the monochore," P Oxy VII. 1056⁵ (A.D. 360) τῆς ἀρτάβης μίας λογιζομένης ἐκ δηναρίων μυριάδων ἑκατὸν ὀγδοήκοντα, "a single artaba being reckoned at one hundred and eighty myriads of denarii," *ib.* X. 1329 (A.D. 309) ἐπὶ τῷ με ταῦτά σοι λογίσασθαι, and *OGIS* 595¹⁵ (ii/A.D.) τὰ

49

γὰρ ἕτερα ἀναλώματα . . . ἑαυτοῖς ἐλογισάμεθα, ἵνα μὴ τὴν πόλιν βαρῶμεν. The verb is construed with εἰς, as in Ac 19[27], Rom 4[3], in P Fay 21[8] (A.D. 134) νυνεὶ δὲ συνλήβδ[ην π]ερ[ὶ πάν]των ὁπωσοῦν διδομένων |[. . .]] ἢ λογιζομένων εἰς τὸ δημόσιον, "I now give orders generally with regard to all payments actually made or credited to the government." From this meaning of the verb comes the λογιστήριον, "finance-office" (see s.v. κατακλείω). The verb has the more general sense of "number," "class amongst," as in Lk 22[37], in a return of camels P Lond 328[8] (A.D. 163) (= II. p. 75) πώλου ἑνὸς λογιζομένου νυνεὶ ἐν τελείοις, "one foal being now numbered among the full-grown (camels)." Cf. also BGU IV. 1028[17] (ii/A.D.) αἱ δὲ λοιπ(αὶ) πρὸς ἡμίσιαν λογίζονται, P Thead 8[16] (A.D. 306) διὰ τὸ τὰ προκίμενα ἐρύφιά τε καὶ αὐτὰ τέλεια λογείζ[εσθ]αι ἐπὶ τῷ μεμισθωμένῳ, "puisque les chevreaux de l'année précédente pourront être comptés comme adultes" (Ed.), and the late P Giss I. 56[4] (vi/A.D.) ἐπὶ δεκαετῆ χρ(όνον) λογιζόμε νον ἀπὸ καρπῶν τῶν νῦν ὄντων ἐν ἀγροῖς. Such a passage as OGIS 665[23] (A.D. 49) ἐὰν δέ τις δῷ ἢ ὡς δεδομένον λογίσηται κτλ. prepares us for the meaning "think," "consider," in ib. 763[67] (ii/B.C.) οἰκειοτάτην ἐλογιζόμην τὴν ἀνάθεσιν (τοῦ ἀνδριάντος) ἔσεσθαι ἐν ταύτηι (τῇ Μιλησίων πόλει): cf. P Par 63[95] (B.C. 164) (= P Petr III. p. 26) τίς γὰρ οὕτως ἐστιν ἀνάλητος ἢ ἄλιτρος ἐν τῶι λογίζεσθαι; "for who is so utterly wanting in reason and the capacity for making distinctions?" (Mahaffy).

On the Pauline metaphorical use of λογίζομαι see Ramsay Luke, p 286 f., and Griffith Thomas, Exp T xvii. p. 211 ff. For the form λογισθείη in 2 Tim 4[16] see Moulton Gr. ii. p. 217. MGr λογιάζω, "consider," "think upon," λο(γ)αριάζω, "reckon," "value."

λογικός.

A good ex. of this adj. is afforded by a i/A.D. inscr. in honour of a certain physician—ἰατρῶι Καισάρων καὶ ἰδίας λογικῆς ἐναργοῦς ἰατρικῆς κτίστηι ἐν βιβλίοις ρ̅ν̅ς̅. (Syll 736[11] f.). With Rom 12[1] we may compare the usage in the hermetic writings where λογικὴ θυσία is contrasted with ceremonial offerings, cf. Reitzenstein Poimandres, p. 338[10] δέξαι λογικὰς θυσίας ἁγνὰς ἀπὸ ψυχῆς καὶ καρδίας πρός σε ἀνατεταμένης, and ib. p. 347[1], and see Lietzmann in HZNT ad l.: also Epict. iii. 1. 26 τὸ λογικὸν ἔχεις ἐξαίρετον· τοῦτο κόσμει καὶ καλλώπιζε, "thy excellence lies in the rational part: this adorn and beautify" (Sharp, p. 126). From the late Greek of the Pelagia legend (ed. Usener, p. 26) we have an admirable illustration of 1 Pet 2[2]. A bishop meets Pelagia and tells her he is "shepherd of Christ's sheep." She takes him literally, and he explains that he means τῶν λογικῶν προβάτων τοῦ Χριστοῦ, τοῦτ᾽ ἔστιν τῶν ἀνθρώπων. So Peter means metaphorical, not literal, "pure milk": see s.v. ἄδολος. MGr λογικό, "understanding," "reason"; ἔρχομαι στὰ λο(γ)ικά μου, "I become conscious of, learn of" (Thumb Handbook, p. 338).

λόγιον.

We are unable from our sources to throw any fresh light upon this word, which is so important in early Christian literature (see reff. in Sophocles Lex. s.v.), but for its Biblical usage see SH on Rom 3[2], and for its application to the recently discovered "Sayings of Jesus" (P Oxy I. 1, IV. 654), see Two Lectures on the "Sayings of Jesus" by Drs. Lock and Sanday (Oxford, 1897) with the literature referred to there, and, more recently, H. G. E. White, The Sayings of Jesus from Oxyrhynchus (Cambridge, 1920).

λόγιος.

On the ground of Phrynichus' statement, supported by Lobeck's citations (Lob. Phryn. p. 198), that the "multitude," as distinguished from Attic writers, use λόγιος of the man who is "skilful and lofty" in speech (ὡς οἱ πολλοὶ λέγουσιν ἐπὶ τοῦ δεινοῦ εἰπεῖν καὶ ὑψηλοῦ), Moulton (Cambridge Essays, p. 498 f.) prefers the AV rendering "eloquent" (V, eloquens) to the RV "learned" (marg. "eloquent") in Ac 18[24], laying it down as "a fair working rule that a meaning condemned by these modistes of literature, Phrynichus and his company, may be accepted as probably intended by the New Testament writer." Field (Notes, p. 129) takes the same line. The papyrus and inscriptional evidence, which is unfortunately for the most part late, does not help us much. Thus P Oxy VI. 902[1] (c. A.D. 465) τῷ λογιωτάτῳ σχολαστικῷ may be either "to the most learned" or "to the most eloquent advocate," and similarly with the same phrase in P Flor III. 377[16] (vi/A.D.) and BGU III. 836[7] (time of Justinian). In P Oxy I. 126[8] (A.D. 572) a woman refers to her father as τ[οῦ σ]οφωτάτου σχολαστικοῦ, and her husband as τοῦ λογιω[τά]του μου συμβίον, where the latter adj. is probably to be taken in a somewhat general sense, as perhaps also in OGIS 408[5] (ii/A.D.) ἐπ᾽ ἀγαθῷ Φιλοπάππου τοῦ βασιλέως καὶ Μαξίμου Στατιλίου ἰδίου λόγου, τῶν λογιωτάτων καὶ φιλτάτων. On the other hand on Cagnat IV. 77 λογίῳ πρυτάνιος, the editor notes: "inter prytanes, qui senatui civitatis quoque anno per vices praeerant, is vocabatur λόγιος cui mandata erat rationum cura." Cf. Michel 1170 (i/A.D.) ἄρχοντος Πυρράκου τοῦ λογίου. Perhaps some such general phrase as "a man of culture" best gives the sense in the Acts passage (cf. Bartlet ad l. in the Century Bible, and Moffatt). For λογιότης as a title of address see P Lips I. 37[24] (A.D. 389) ἐπιδίδωμι τῇ σῇ λογιότητι τούσδε μου τοὺς λιβέλλου[ς· cf. BGU II. 401[12, 21] (A.D. 618). In MGr λόγιος = "learned," "a scholar."

λογισμός

in its primary sense of "reckoning," "computation" is seen in BGU IV. 1074[15] (A.D. 275) in connexion with the payment of a tax—ἀποδεδωκότα κατὰ τὸν λογισμὸν τὸν βασιλικὸν ἐντάγιον πᾶν . . . : cf. P Oxy VI. 940[4] (v/A.D.) καταξιώτων ἐπέχειν τοῦ λογισμοῦ, "please to delay the account-taking" (Edd.). For a more general sense see Michel 976[9] (B.C. 300) καλῶς καὶ δικαίως ἐπεμ[ε]λήθη τῶν κοινῶν πάντων καὶ τοὺς λογισμοὺς ἀπέδωκεν ὀρθ[ῶ]ς καὶ δικαίως, and as showing how the meaning "thought," "reasoning," led to "judgment," "decision," as in Rom 2[15], 2 Cor 10[5] cf. P Oxy XII. 1503[16] (A.D. 288-9) ἕτοιμος λογισμοὺς παρέχει[ν—reports in connexion with a trial, and OGIS 5[50] (B.C. 311) ἀν[θ]ρωπίναι λογισμῶι, "human calculation." See also Test. xii. patr. Gad vi. 2 τὸ πνεῦμα τοῦ μίσους ἐσκότιζέ μου τὸν νοῦν, καὶ ἐτάρασσέ μου τὸν λογισμὸν πρὸς τὸ ἀνελεῖν αὐτόν. The word is used in a bad sense = cupido in Vett. Val. pp. 49[8] πρὸς τὰς τῶν λογισμῶν ἐπιθυμίας, 173[11] καταθύμιος λογισμῶν συντέλεια.

λόγος.

It is hardly necessary to illustrate this common word in its ordinary sense of "word," "saying," but, as showing its developed meaning of "speech in progress" (cf. *Proleg.* p. 111), we may cite P Tor I. 1[iii. 3] (B.C. 116) εἰς λόγους αὐτοῖς ἐλθόντος, "collato cum ipsis sermone" (Ed.), P Ryl II. 229[18] (A.D. 38) παρακάλεσον οὖν τὴν γυναῖκά σου τοῖς ἐμοῖς λόγοις ἵνα ἐπιμέληται τῶν χοιριδίων, "urge your wife from me to look after the pigs" (Edd.): cf. the compound λογοποιοῦμαι in *ib.* 136[4] (A.D. 34) λογοποιουμένου μου πρὸς Ἀγχερίμφ[ι]ν, "as I was talking to Ancherimphis," *ib.* 144[10] (A.D. 38) ἐλ[ογ]οποιησάμην πρὸς Ὀννῶφριν . . . ὑπὲρ οὗ ἔχω πρὸς αὐτὸν ἐνεχύρου, "I entered into conversation with Onnophris concerning a pledge I have against him" (Edd.). The noun is used of a magical "invocation" in P Par 574[1258] (iii/A.D.) (= *Selections*, p. 113) λόγος λεγόμενος ἐπὶ τῆς κεφαλῆς αὐτοῦ, and of a "list" in connexion with the distribution of public burdens in P Cairo Preis 18[12] (A.D. 339) ἔστ[ι] δὲ ὁ λ[όγο]ς· Αὐρήλιος . . . For the legal sense "matter of dispute," "suit at law," as in Ac 19[38], cf. P Tor I. 1[iv. 21] (B.C. 116) καθ' ὃ ἔφη δεῖν τοὺς ἀντιδίκους συνίστασθαι τὸν λόγον πρὸς τοὺς ἀποδομένους αὐτοῖς, "quare aiebat adversarios debere litem instituere contra suos auctores" (Ed.). When we pass to the uses of λόγος with more direct reference to the mind, we may compare with Ac 20[24] (see Field *Notes*, pp. 133, 252 ff.) such passages as P Magd 12[8] (B.C. 217) οὐδένα λόγον ἐποιήσαντο, ἀλλὰ ἐγβεβλήκασίν με ἐκ τῶν κλήρων, "ils n'en ont tenu aucun compte et m'ont au contraire expulsé des tenures" (Ed.), P Par 26[31] (B.C. 163) (= *Selections*, p. 16) τοῦ δὲ τοῦ Ψινταέους υἱοῦ ἐκ τῆς Μέμφεως χωρισθέντος, οὐκέτι οὐδένα λόγον ἐποήσατο, "but no sooner had the son of Psintaes departed from Memphis than he took no further account of the matter," and *Cagnat* IV. 134[15] (after B.C. 133) τῶν κατὰ τὸν βίον ἐλασσωμάτ[ων λ]όγον ποιησάμενος.

See also P Hib I. 53[4] (B.C. 246) πειρῶ οὖν ἀσφαλῶς διεγγυᾶν ὡς πρὸς σὲ τοῦ λό[γ]ου ἐσομένου, "do you therefore endeavour to obtain good security, knowing that you will be held accountable" (Edd.), P Tebt II. 325[22] (c. A.D. 145) τοῦ λόγου ἐσομένου ἐάν τι [παράνομ]ον γένηται, "but you will be held responsible for any violation of the law" (Edd.).

In our documents, which are so often of a monetary character, λόγος = "account" in the sense of "reckoning," "score" (cf. Phil 4[15, 17]) meets us constantly : e.g. the contract of apprenticeship, P Oxy II. 275[18, 24] (A.D. 66) (= *Selections*, p. 56), where so much is paid εἰς λόγον διατροφῆς, "to account of maintenance," and so much εἰς λόγον ἱματισμοῦ, "to account of clothing," P Oxy XII. 1441[7] (A.D. 197–200) βασ[ι]λ(ικῆς) ὁμοίως ἐπὶ λόγ(ου) δραχμὰς δεκαόκτω, "likewise upon State land on account eighteen drachmae" (Edd.), P Fay 103[1] (iii/A.D.) λ[όγος] ἀναλώματος τοῦ νεκροῦ, "account of expenses for the corpse," and P Grenf II. 81 (a)[9] (A.D. 403) οὐδένα λ[όγ]ον ἔχω πρὸς σὲ περὶ τούτου, in connexion with the payment of the wages of a substitute. From this the transition is easy to such an expression as δίκαιον λόγ[ο]ν ἔχει πρὸς σέ, "iusta res est ei tecum," in P Iand 10[3] (v/vi A.D.). For ὁ ἴδιος λόγος, the private account or purse of the sovereign, cf. P Amh II. 31[1] (B.C. 112), and more particularly *Der Gnomon des Idios Logos*, being BGU V. 1.

Λόγον διδόναι with reference to judgment, as in Rom 14[12], occurs in such a passage as BGU I. 164[21] (ii/iii A.D.) ὡς σοῦ μέλλοντος λόγον διδόναι τῷ λαμπροτάτῳ ἡγεμόνι, and λόγον ἀποδιδόναι (cf. Mt 12[6], Lk 16[2], Heb 13[17]) in *ib.* 98[25] (A.D. 211) κελεῦσαι αὐτὸν ἀχθῆναι ἐπὶ σὲ λόγον ἀποδώσοντα περὶ τούτου. See also the Christianized imprecations against violators of tombs cited by Ramsay (*Luke*, p. 306), one probably from Lycaonia and belonging to iv A.D., *JHS* xxii. (1902), p. 354 ὃς δ' ἐὰν ἐπισβιάσητε, δώσει θεῷ λόγον, "whosoever shall force an entrance, shall give account to God," and another from Laodicea, *Athen. Mittheil.* xiii. p. 249 (c. A.D. 400) ἤ τις δ' ἕτερον ἐπενβάλῃ τῷ τάφῳ κριτῇ τῷ ζῶντι λόγον ἔνδικον πο[ι]ή[σει, "and if any one shall lay another in the tomb, he shall render judicial account to the living Judge."

Συναίρειν λόγον, as in Mt 18[23], 25[19], "an expression," according to Grimm-Thayer, "not found in Grk. auth.," can now be cited from BGU III. 775[19] (ii/A.D.) τὰ ἤδη πρόλημα (*l.* -λημμα) ἀφὲς ἄχρης (*l.* -ις) ἂν γένομε ἐκῖ καὶ συνάρωμεν λόγον, and the middle from such passages as P Fay 109[8] (early i/A.D.) συνήρμαι λόγον τῷ πατρί, "I have settled accounts with (his?) father" (Edd.), P Oxy I. 113[27] (ii/A.D.) ὅτι ἔδωκας αὐτῶι δήλωσόν μοι ἵνα συνάρωμαι αὐτῶι λόγον, "let me know what you have given him that I may settle accounts with him" (Edd.).

We may add a few common phrases :—P Oxy XII. 1405[23] (iii/A.D.) οὐκ ἀνὰ λόγον (*l.* -ον) οἶν οὐδὲ πρὸς [τὸ] μέρος τῆς λειτουργίας, "this is unreasonable and contrary to the just apportionment of the liturgy" (Edd.), P Lond 1173[5] (A.D. 125) (= III. p. 208) ἐπ[έτρε]ψάς [μ]οι διὰ λόγου μηκέτι κατερ[γά]ζεσθαι, P Goodsp Cairo 4[3] (ii/B.C.) (= *Selections*, p. 24) εἰ ἔρρωσαι καὶ τἆλλά σοι κατὰ λόγον ἐστίν, εἴη ἂν ὡς αἱρούμεθα, "if you are well and things in general are doing right, it will be as we desire." P Tebt I. 50[4] (B.C. 112–1) δι' ἣν αἰτίαν ἐξησθενηκὼς ἐκ τοῦ μὴ κατὰ λόγον ἀπαντᾶν τὸν σπόρον, "wherefore, because my crops did not meet my expectations I was impoverished" (Edd.), P Rein 28[14] (end ii B.C.) τοῦ ἡμίσους) κατὰ λόγον, where κατὰ λόγον = "in proportion," as in *Syll* 510[46] (ii/B.C.) τὸ πλέον ὀφει[λό]μενον τῆς] τιμῆς ὁ ἔγγυος ἀποτινέτω κατὰ λόγον. P Oxy VIII. 1121[18] (A.D. 295) οὐκ οἶδα τίνι λόγῳ ἢ πόθεν κεινηθέντες, "I know not on what ground or with what impulse" (Ed.) (cf. Ac 10[29]), P Thead 22[5] (A.D. 342) οὐ[κ οἶ]δα τίνι λόγ[ο]ν καὶ ληστρικῷ τρόπῳ, and similarly in the illiterate P Gen I. 47[5] (iv/A.D.).

For the Divine Logos in heathen writers see Sophocles *Lex. s.v.* 10, and cf. Reitzenstein *Zwei religionsgeschichtliche Fragen* (1901), p. 47 ff., and the same writer's *Poimandres* (1904) and *Die Hellenistichen Mysterienreligionen* (1910). Reference may also be made to Rendel Harris *The Prologue to St. John's Gospel* (Cambridge, 1917), where it is argued that the doctrine of Christ as the "Wisdom" of God : cf. the somewhat extended use of λόγος in Heb 4[12] (Nairne *CGT ad l.*), and λόγος = "reason" in Epict. e.g. i. 3. 3 ὁ λόγος δὲ καὶ ἡ γνώμη κοινὸν πρὸς τοὺς θεούς (Sharp *Epict.* p. 127).

MGr λό(γ)ος, pl. λόγια, and note the curious stereotyped circumlocution for the personal pronoun τοῦ λόγου σου = "thou" (Thumb *Handbook*, p. 87).

λόγχη.

P Lond 191[12] (inventory of furniture—A.D. 103–117) (= II. p. 265) λόγχαι ἐννέα. In an account of cures at the Asclepieium at Epidaurus, *Syll* 802[95 ff.] (iii/B.C.), we find the following—Εὔιππος λόγχαν ἔτη ἐφόρησε ἐξ ἐν ταῖ γνάθωι· ἐγκοιτασθέντος δ' (α)ὐτοῦ ἐξελὼν τὰν λ[ό]γχαν ὁ θεὸς εἰς τὰς χῆράς οἱ ἔδωκε. ἀμέρας δὲ γενομένας ὑγιὴς ἐξῆρπε, τὰν λόγχαν ἐν ταῖς χερσὶν ἔχων: cf. *ib.* 803[65] (iii/B.C.) [On *Incubation or the cure of disease in pagan temples and Christian churches*, see Mary Hamilton's essay with that title, London, 1906.]

λοιδορέω.

P Petr III. 21 (*g*)[18] (iii/B.C.) ἐλοιδόρησας φαμένη με ἠρηκέναι, BGU III. 1007[6] (iii/B.C.) ἐλοιδορουν με ἐπὶ πλέο[ν?, P Tebt I. 44[16] (B.C. 114) (= *Chrest.* I. p. *148*) ἐλοιδ[όρησέν με] καὶ ἀσχημό[νει, P Oxy II. 237[vi. 21] (A.D. 186) ἐπὶ φθόνῳ δὲ μόνον [λο]ιδορούμενος καὶ δεινὰ πάσχων ἀπ' ἐμοῦ, and from the inscrr. *Syll* 737[75 ff.] (*c.* A.D. 175) ἐὰν . . εὑρεθῇ τις . . ὑβρίζων ἢ λοιδορῶν τινα, ὁ μὲν λοιδορηθεὶς ἢ ὑβρισθεὶς παραστανέτω δύο ἐκ τῶν ἰοβάκχων ἐνόρκους ὅτι ἤκουσαν ὑβριζόμενον ἢ λοιδορούμενον, καὶ ὁ ὑβρίσας ἢ λοιδορήσας ἀποτιν[νύ]τω τῷ κοινῷ λεπτοῦ δρ(αχμὰς) κε̄. To show the strong character of the word, we may cite Calvin on 1 Cor 4[2]: "Λοιδορία is a harsher railing, which not only rebukes a man, but also sharply bites him, and stamps him with open contumely. Hence λοιδορεῖν is to wound man as with an accursed sting."

λοιδορία.

P Petr II. 18(1)[8] (B.C. 246) λο]ιδορίας, "abusive action," PSI II. 222[14] (iii/A.D.) μεθ' ὕβρεως καὶ λοιδο[ρι]ῶν.

λοίδορος.

For this adj., which in the NT is confined to 1 Cor 5[11], 6[10], we may cite *Cagnat* I. 307[3] (Rome), where a certain Menophilus is described as—οὐδένα λυπήσας, οὐ λοίδορα ῥήματα πέμψας. Cf. also *Test. xii. patr.* Benj. v. 4 ἐὰν γὰρ ὑβρίσει ἄνδρα ὅσιον μετανοεῖ, ἐλεεῖ γὰρ ὁ ὅσιος τὸν λοίδωρον καὶ σιωπᾷ, "for if any one does violence to a holy man, he repenteth: for the holy man is merciful to his reviler, and holdeth his peace" (Charles).

λοιμός,

"pestilence," "plague," as in Lk 21[11], occurs in P Oxy XIV. 1666[20] (iii/A.D.) ἤκουσα . . ὅτι παρ' ὑμεῖν λοιμὸς [ἐγ]ένετο, "I heard that there has been plague in your neighbourhood" (Edd.). For the metaph. use, as in Ac 24[5], where it is used of "a pestilent fellow," (cf. Lat. *pestis*) there is ample support in the LXX (e.g. Ps 1[1], 1 Macc 15[21]). Cf. also Ac 13[8], where for the ordinary reading Ἐλύμας Burkitt (*JTS* iv. p. 127 ff.) conjecturally restores ὁ λοιμός. The passage then runs: ἀνθίστατο δὲ αὐτοῖς ὁ λοιμός, ὁ μάγος, οὕτως γὰρ μεθερμηνεύεται τὸ ὄνομα αὐτοῦ, "now they were withstood by the pestilent fellow, the sorcerer I mean, for 'pestilent fellow' is the interpretation of his name"—an interpretation to which *Bar Yeshu*, changed into ΒΑΡΙΗΣΟΥ א, would readily lend itself.

λοιπός.

For λοιπός with a subst. cf. P Oxy II. 242[18] (A.D. 77) τὰ λυπὰ (*l.* λοιπὰ) μέρη περιτειχίζειν, *ib.* 270[20] (A.D. 94) ταῖς λοιπαῖς ἀρούραις. It is used absolutely in P Ryl II. 229[13] (A.D. 38) τοῦ λοιπ(οῦ) τῆς τιμῆ(ς) τοῦ χόρτου, "the rest of the price for the hay," P Giss I. 78[3] (ii/A.D.) καλῶς δὲ ποιήσεις καὶ περὶ τὰ λοιπὰ ἐνεργήσασα. For τοῖς λοιποῖς πᾶσι in Phil 1[13], "apparently a vague phrase = everywhere else," Kennedy (*EGT ad l.*) compares *CIG* I. 1770 ἐπεὶ καὶ ἐν τοῖς λοιποῖς πᾶσιν φανερὰν πεποήκαμεν τήν τε ἰδίαν καὶ τοῦ δήμου τοῦ Ῥωμαίων προαίρεσιν. The neut. sing. is frequently used adverbially, sometimes with the idea of time "henceforth" (2 Tim 4[8]), as in P Oxy I. 119[8] (ii/iii A.D.) (= *Selections*, p. 103) ἂν δὲ ἔλθῃς εἰς Ἀλεξανδρίαν, οὐ μὴ λάβω χεῖραν παρά [σ]ου, οὔτε πάλι χαίρω σε λυπόν (*l.* λοιπόν), "and if you do go to Alexandria, I won't take your hand, or greet you again henceforth," and sometimes simply to mark transition to a new subject like an emphatic οὖν (1 Thess 4[1]: cf. Milligan *ad l.*), as a few lines further down in the same letter, [13] λυπὸν πέμψον εἴ[s] με, παρακαλῶ σε, "send for me then, I beseech you": cf. BGU III. 846[10] (ii/A.D.) (= *Selections*, p. 94) λοιπὸν οἶδα τί [ποτ'] αἱμαυτῷ παρέσχημαι, "furthermore I know what I have brought upon myself," P Iand 9[13] (ii/A.D.) πάντα γὰρ τὰ νόμιμα πε[ποί]ηκα, καθὼς ἠθέλησας, τοῦ ἦ (ἔτους)· [σ]ὺ οὖν βάσταξε λυπὸν (*l.* βάσταξαι λοιπόν) ὃ ἂν ἔτιο[υ ῇ] (*l.* αἴτιον ῇ) τῆς κρίσεως. For λοιπὸν οὖν, "finally then," cf. BGU IV. 1078[6] (A.D. 39) λοιπὸν οὖν, ἐὰν λάβω τὰ κερμάμια (*l.* κεράμια or κερμάτια), ὄψομαι, τί με δεῖ ποιεῖν, *ib.* 1079[6] (A.D. 41) (= *Selections*, p. 39) λοιπὸν οὖν ἔλαβον παρὰ το(ῦ) Ἄραβος τὴν ἐπιστολὴν καὶ ἀνέγνων καὶ ἐλυπήθην. The transition to λοιπό(ν), τὸ λοιπό(ν), "therefore," "so," the regular meaning in MGr, may be illustrated by such passages from late Greek as Polyb. i. 15. 11 λοιπὸν ἀνάγκη συγχωρεῖν, τὰς ἀρχὰς καὶ τὰς ὑποθέσεις εἶναι ψευδεῖς, Epict. i. 22. 15. 24. 1, ii. 5. 16, *al.*: cf. Schmid *Atticismus* iii. p. 135, and Jannaris *Exp* V. viii. p. 429f. For εἰς τὸ λοιπόν cf. P Petr III. 42 G(9)[6] (mid. iii/B.C.), for τοῦ λοιποῦ (sc. χρόνου), "henceforth," as in Gal 6[17], cf. P Hal I. 1[171] (mid. iii/B.C.) σύνταξον οὖν, ὅπω[s] τοῦ [λ]οιποῦ μὴ γίνηται τοῦτο, P Oxy X. 1293[14] (A.D. 117–38) ὥστε τοῦ λοιποῦ γράφεται (*l.* -ετε), τῶν γὰρ πρώτων τεσσάρων ἡμίσους ἐπιστολὴν οὐκ ἔσχον, "so in future write, for I have had no letter about the first four and a half metretae" (Edd.), and for ὧδε λοιπόν, as in 1 Cor 4[2], cf. Epict. ii. 12. 24.

The subst. λοιπάς, "remainder," "arrear," which is described by LS as "Eccl., Byz.," is found in P Gen I. 57[6] (iv/A.D.) ἐν[ε]κεν τῆς λοιπάδος πυροῦ: cf. P Amh II. 152[3] (v/vi A.D.), and P Oxy I. 136[13] (A.D. 583), and for the verb λοιπάζω see P Oxy IX. 1194[3] (*c.* A.D. 265) τὰ λοιπαζόμενα, "the arrears." Λοίπημα (not in LS) occurs in P Tebt II. 281[21] (B.C. 125) ἄνευ παντὸς λοιπήματος, "without any arrears." On λοιπογραφέω, "allow to remain in arrears," see P Petr III. 53(*h*)[4] (iii/B.C.) ἀνείεται λοιπογραφεῖσθαι, "he is permitted to remain in arrears" (Edd.), and P Hamb I. p. 9, and on the subst. see P Strass I. 77[5] (ii/iii A.D.) with the editor's note.

Λουκᾶς

is generally treated as an abbreviated pet name from Λουκανός (cf. Lightfoot on Col 4[15], Zahn *Introd.* iii. p. 5).

this longer form being actually found in the title of the Third Gospel in various Old Latin texts (*a*, *ff*[2], *s*), and on a v/A.D. sarcophagus at Arles (see *JTS* vi. p. 435). Others prefer the derivation from **Λούκιος**, and Ramsay (*Recent Discovery*, p. 370 ff.) quotes inscrr. showing that in Pisidian Antioch **Λουκᾶς** and **Λούκιος** were interchangeable : cf. *Glotta* iv. (1913), p. 78 ff. and the occurrence of **Σελβεῖνα** and **Σελβεῖνας** in the same letter, P Meyer 20 (1st half iii/A.D.), where see Deissmann's note. Apart from Christian inscrr. the name **Λουκᾶς** is found e.g. in a sepulchral inscr. from Apollonia. *Preisigke* 224 Αὖλου Αὐσφλήνου καὶ Ἐγλογὴ τ[οῦ] Λουκᾶ : cf. also *CIG* III. 4759 and Add. 4700 *k*. On the discovery of Luke's *name* in an early form of the text of the Acts of the Apostles, preserved in a ii/A.D. Armenian catena, see *Exp T* xxiv. p. 530 f., xxv. p. 44.

Λούκιος.

As compared with **Λούκιος** in Ac 13[1], Rom 16[21], we find the transliteration **Λεύκιος** in P Tebt I. 33[3] (B.C. 112) (= *Selections*, p. 30) in connexion with the preparations for the visit of a Roman Senator—**Λεύκιος Μέμμιος Ῥωμαῖος τῶν ἀπὸ** (cf. Ac 12[1]) **συνκλήτου**. Nachmanson (p. 61) gives various exx. of **Λεύκιος** from Magnesian inscrr., and thinks that the spelling may have been affected by a genuine Greek name **Λεύκιος** (from **λευκός**) : cf. Moulton *Gr.* ii. p. 88, and for other exx. see *Michel* 394[2] (mid. i/B.C.), 668[21] (i/B.C.), *al.*

λουτρόν.

In its two NT occurrences Eph 5[26] (where see Robinson's note), Tit 3[5] (cf. Cant 4[2]. Sir 31(34)[30]), **λουτρόν** denotes "the water for washing," or "the washing" itself, as in the Mysteries' inscr. from Andania, *Syll* 653[106] (B.C. 91) where one of the headings is—Ἀλείμματος καὶ λουτροῦ. For **λουτρόν**, like **λουτρών** (*OGIS* 339[33]—*c*. B.C. 120) = "place for bathing," we may cite *Cagnat* IV. 293[i. 22] τὸ παρ' αὐτὴν [λο]υτρὸν ὁμοίως μαρμάρινον : cf. P Oxy X. 1252 *verso* 22 (A.D. 288–95) τὴν διοίκησιν τῶν δημοσίων λουτρῶν, "the management of the public baths," *ib.* VI. 892[11] (A.D. 338), 915[2] (A.D. 572) *al.*, and the dim. **λουτρίδιον** in P Ryl II. 154[9] (A.D. 66). For the LXX **λουτρόν**, "laver," cf. *OGIS* 479[10] (ii/A.D.) γυμνασιαρχήσαντα δρακτοῖς ἐκ λου[τήρ]ων with the editor's note. MGr **λουτρό**, "bath."

λούω,

"bathe," "wash," may be illustrated by P Flor III. 384[30] (v/A.D.?) λούειν τὰ δύο μέρη τοῦ αὐτοῦ βαλανίου : cf P Giss I. 50[15] (A.D. 259) τοῦ λούοντος βαλανείου, where the meaning seems to be "the bath used for the purpose of bathing" (see the editor's intr.). The middle in the sense of "bathe oneself" is very common, e.g. P Magd 33[2] (B.C. 221) λουομένης γάρ μου ἐν τῶι βαλανείωι, P Oxy III. 528[10] (ii/A.D.) where a man writes urging his wife to return home and stating—ιβ Φαῶφι ἀφ' ὅτε ἐλουσάμην μετ' ἐσοῦ οὐκ ἐλουσάμην οὐκ ἤλιμε (*l*. ἤλειμ<μ>αι) μέχρει ιβ Ἀθύρ, "since we bathed together on Phaophi 12, I never bathed nor anointed myself until Athur 12" (Edd.), P Flor II. 127[7] (A.D. 256) ἄχ[υρ]ον πανταχόθεν συλλέξας ἵνα θερμῶς λουσώμεθα χειμῶνος ὄντος. In 2 Pet 2[22] we ought probably to translate "the sow that washes itself by wallowing in the mire," see Clemen *Primitive Christianity*, p. 50 f., and cf. Moulton

Proleg., p. 238 f. For the ceremonial usage of the word, cf. P Flor III. 332[11] (ii/A.D.) οὔτ[ε ἐ]λουσάμην [οὔ]τε προσεκύνησα θεοὺς φοβουμένη σου τὸ μετέωρον, and more particularly from the inscrr. *Perg* 255 (early Roman period) where it is laid down that only [4th] οἱ . . ἀπὸ μὲν τῆς ἰδίας γ[υναι]κὸς καὶ τοῦ ἰδίου ἀνδρὸς αὐθήμερον, ἀπὸ δὲ ἀλλοτρίας κ[αὶ] ἀλλοτρίου δευτεραῖοι λουσάμενοι, ὡσαύτως δὲ καὶ ἀπὸ κήδους κ[α]ὶ τεκούσης γυναικὸς δευτεραῖο(ι) shall enter the temple of Athena at Pergamus, *Syll* 877[30] (B.C. 420) enjoining that those who have become unclean by touching a corpse are purified—λουσαμένο[υς] π[ερὶ] πάντα τὸν χρῶτα ὕδατ[ος] [χ]ύσι, and *Preisigke* 4127[14] (a hymn) ἐν ᾧ καὶ ἁγίῳ τῷ τῆς ἀθανασίας ὕδατι λουσάμενος : see also Deissmann *BS* p. 226 f., and for the custom of washing before prayer in pagan cults cf. Ramsay *Exp* VII. viii. p. 280. An interesting example occurs also in the new fragment of an uncanonical gospel, P Oxy V. 840[14 f.] (iv/A.D.), where a certain Pharisee remonstrates with the Saviour in the temple—μήτε λουσα[μ]έν[ῳ] μ[ή]τε μὴν τῶν μαθητῶν σου τοὺς π[όδας βα]πτισθέντων, "when thou hast not washed nor yet have thy disciples bathed their feet" (Edd.): see also [19, 24, 32] The later Greek form **λελουσμένος** is read in Heb 10[23] ℵ D* P, Jn 13[10] E, and Cant 5[12] B. MGr **λούζω (λούγω), λούνω, λούω.**

Λύδδα.

For gen. **Λύδδας** (—δης FHLP) in Ac 9[38] cf. **Μάρθας** (Jn 11[1]) and from the papyri **Ταμύσθας** from **Τάμυσθα** in BGU III. 981[ii. 25] (A.D. 79) *al.* The LXX usage is illustrated by Thackeray *Gr.* i. p. 161.

Λυδία

in Ac 16[14] is sometimes taken as a cognomen derived from the purple-seller's native place (e.g. Zahn *Intr.* i. p. 533), but the addition of ὀνόματι clearly marks it out as a proper name. In the form **Λύδη** it is found in *CIG* I. 653, III. 6574.

Λυκαονιστί.

For the readiness with which their native Lycaonian would rise to the lips of a common city mob in a moment of excitement (Ac 14[11]), see Ramsay *CRE* p. 57 f., and cf. *Recent Discovery*, p. 42 f. See also a note by C. R. Conder on "The Speech of Lycaonia" in the *Palestine Exploration Fund*, *Quarterly Statement* 1888, p. 250.

λύκος.

P Par 6[19] (B.C. 129) συνέβη δὲ καί, διὰ τὸ ἀχ[ανῆ] τὴν θύραν ἀφεθῆν[αι, ὑπὸ] λύκων λυμανθῆ[ναι] ἀγαθὰ σώματα [περ]ιβρωθέντα, "and it also happened that, owing to the door having been left open, certain bodies in good condition were mangled by wolves, which have partly devoured them." The Latin (or rather Sabine) *lupus* is linked with **λύκος**, and points to an original *luquos*. MGr **λύκος.**

λυμαίνομαι.

For an early example of the late passive use of this verb, see the citation from P Par 6 *s.v.* **λύκος**, and cf. P Petr III. 27 *recto*[3] λελυμάνθαι, in a broken context. For the verb construed with the acc. cf. P Leid W[col.xv. 39] (ii/iii A.D.) οὐ μὴ μου λυμάνῃς σάρκα (of fire), and for the dat. see P Oxy XII. 1409[21] (A.D. 278) λυμαινόμενος τοῖς ἐπὶ τῇ σωτηρίᾳ συνπά-[ση]ς τῆς Αἰγύπτου προῃρ[ημέ]νοις, "injuring measures designed for the safety of the whole of Egypt" (Edd.). The form λοιμαίνομαι, which occurs six times in B. may be illustrated from a ii/B.C. complaint regarding property, P Grenf I. 17[15] (as completed by Gerhard *Erbstreit*) ἕτερα γράμματα λοιμαινάμενοι ἔβλαψαν τὰ δι' αὐτῶν διάφορα : see Mayser *Gr.* p. 111, Moulton *Gr.* ii. p. 83. From the inscrr. we may cite *Syll* 584[3] (ii/B.C. ?) μηδὲ σκεῦος τῶν τῆς θεοῦ λυμαίνεσθαι, *ib.* 653[26] (B.C. 91) ἐξουσίαν ἐχέτω λυμαίνεσθαι, *ib.* 888[11] (ii/A.D.) λυμήνασθαι δὲ μηδὲ λωβήσασθαι μηδέν, *Cagnat* IV. 961[6] τούτ[ω]ν [δέ τι] ὃς ἂν λυμ[ή]νηται, ἐξώλη [εἴναι] καὶ γένος αὐτοῦ.

λυπέω.

A few exx. of this common verb should suffice : P Grenf II. 36[9] (B.C. 95) μὴ λυπεῖσθε ἐπὶ τοῖς χωρισθεῖσι, "do not grieve over the departed." BGU IV. 1079[9] (A.D. 41) = *Selections*, p. 39) λοιπὸν οὖν ἔλαβον παρὰ το ῦ Ἄραβος τὴν ἐπιστολὴν καὶ ἀνέγνων καὶ ἐλυπήθην, "finally then I received the letter from the Arabian, and I read it and was grieved." P Oxy I. 115[3] (letter of condolence—ii/A.D.) (= *Selections*, p. 96) οὕτως ἐλυπήθην καὶ ἔκλαυσα ἐπὶ τῶι εὐμοίρωι ὡς ἐπὶ Διδύματος ἔκλαυσα, "I grieved and wept as much over the blessed one as I wept for Didymas," *ib.* XII. 1481[4] (early ii/A.D.) ὥστε μὴ λοιποῦ. λείαν δ' ἐλοιπήθην ἀκούσας ὅτι ἤκουσας· οὐ γὰρ δεινῶς ἠσθένησα, "so do not grieve about me. I was much grieved to hear that you had heard about me, for I was not seriously ill" (Edd.).—a reassuring letter from a soldier to his mother, BGU I. 246[17 ff.] (ii/iii A.D.) καὶ περὶ Ἑρμιόνης μελησάτω ὑμῖν, πῶς ἄλυπος ἦν· οὐ δίκαιον γὰρ αὐτὴν λυπῖσθαι περὶ οὐδενός· ἤκουσα γάρ, ὅ[τ]ι λυπεῖται. The verb is used in a weaker sense in such passages as P Tebt II. 278[29] (early i/A.D.), εἰ γὰρ ἦν τρίβων οὐκ ἂν ἐλοιπήθην, "if it had been a cloak I should not have minded" (Edd.).—with reference to the loss of a garment, and P Oxy III. 472[10] (c. A.D. 130) δύναται μὲν γὰρ καὶ ἄλλα τινὰ λελοιπῆσθαι παρὰ τὸν τῆς προνοίας χρόνον, "he may indeed have had other troubles during the period of his stewardship" (Edd.)—the speech of an advocate. We may add the inscr. *IGSI* 1879[11] εὐψυχῶ . . . ὅστις οὐκ ἤμην καὶ ἐγενόμην, οὐκ εἰμὶ καὶ οὐ λυποῦμαι, as showing the stoicism with which the pagan world sometimes faced death.

λύπη.

BGU II. 531[ii. 29] (as restored p. 357—ii/A.D.) ἐὰν δὲ ἀστοχήσῃς [αἰω]γίαν μοι λοίπην (= λύπην) [π]αρέχειν μέλλις. See also the curious mantic P Ryl I. 28[211] (iv/A.D.) ἐὰν δὲ ὁ μέγας ἅληται σημαίνει αὐτὸν δοῦλον ὄντα δεσποτεύ-σαι καὶ πάσης λύπης ἀπαλλαγῆναι, "if the great toe quiver, it signifies for a slave that he will become a master and be freed from all pain" (Ed.). An interesting ex. of the adj. occurs in the dutiful letter of Philonides to his father, P Petr II. 13(19)[13] (B.C. 258-3) τοῦτο δ' ἔχε τῆι διανοίαι ὅτι οὐθέν σοι μὴ γενηθῆι λυπηρὸν ἀλλὰ πᾶν ὅτι ἐμοὶ ἔστ αι πεφροντισ-μένον τοῦ σε γενέσθαι ἄλυπον [πάντως], "but hold this fact in your mind, that nothing vexatious may happen to you, but that I have used every forethought to keep you free from trouble" (Ed.).

Λυσανίας.

An inscr., *Cagnat* III. 1086, has been found at Abila, the capital of ancient Abilene, whose author describes himself as Νυμφαῖος . . . . Λυσανίου τετράρχου ἀπελε[ύθερος. There is nothing to show which Lysanias is intended, but as the editor understands by the Σεβαστοί, who are spoken of in the beginning of the inscr., the Emperor Tiberius and his mother Livia (*ob.* A.D. 29), the reference cannot be to Lysanias son of Ptolemy (*regnavit* B.C. 40-34), but to his son or grandson, who may then in turn be identified with the Lysanias of Lk 3[1]. See further the notes to *Cagnat* III. 1085, and an art. in *Revue Biblique*, 1912, p. 533 ff. (cited *Exp* VIII. v. p. 93 f.). For gen. Λυσανίου, see Moulton *Gr.* ii. p. 119.

λύσις,

which in 1 Cor 7[27] is used with reference to the "loosing" of the marriage tie, is common with reference to the "dis-charge" of bonds or debts, e.g. BGU IV. 1149[22] (B.C. 13) λύσιν ποήσασθαι τῶν προκ(ειμένων) δανειστικῶν συγχωρή-(σεων) δύο. P Oxy III. 510[17] (A.D. 101) λύσιν ποιούμενος ὁ Ἀρτεμι[δώρο[ς] τῆς ὑποθήκης, "Artemidorus in release of the mortgage," P Ryl II. 176[3] (A.D. 201-11) λαβεῖν . . . ὑπὲρ λύσεως τῶν τῶν (omit) ὀφιλ(ομένων) αὐτ(ῇ) . . . [δραχμῶν, "to accept in discharge of the drachmae owing to her," P Giss I. 33[1] (A.D. 222) ἀπέσχον . . . ὑπὲρ λύσεως ὧν ὀφ[ε]ί[λ]ει μ[ο]ι ἡ μετηλλαχυῖα αὐτοῦ μήτηρ. See also P Leid W[vii. 41] (ii/iii A.D.) πρὸς λύσιν φαρμάγ(= κ)ων, *Syll* 825[2] (iv/B.C.) ὅρος ἐργαστηρίου καὶ ἀνδραπόδων πεπρα-μένων ἐπὶ λύσει: workshop and slaves attached to it, sold "*à réméré*" (Michel), and for the same phrase *ib.* 831[14] with editor's note.

λυσιτελέω.

For the impersonal λυσιτελεῖ, as in Lk 17[2] (cf. Tobit 3[6]), cf. P Hamb I. 27[17] (B.C. 250) ὥστε λυσιτελεῖ μισθώσασθαι ἢ χορτάσματα ζητεῖν.

The adj. is common—P Petr II. 13(6)[7] (B.C. 258-3) ὅτι εἴη λυσιτελὴς ἡ ἐργολαβία (contract for work), *ib.* III. 41 *verso*[6] λυσιτελέστερον οὖν φαίνεται, P Par 62[iv. 8] (c. B.C. 170) ἐὰν μὴ ἐπί τινων ἄλλο τι λυσιτελέστερον συγχωρηθῇ ἐπὶ τῆς πράσεως.

Λύστρα.

The laxity in the declension of this place-name (Ac 14[6] Λύστραν, [8] Λύστροις; cf. 16[1 f.]) can be readily paralleled from the papyri, cf. e.g. P Grenf II. 46[1] (A.D. 137) ἐν Κερκεσούχῃ and [8] ἀπὸ Κερκεσούχων, and the fem. Τεντύρη in *ib.* 74[3, 6] (A.D. 302) instead of the more usual neut. plur. Τέντυρα : see further Moulton *Proleg.* p. 48, *Gr.* ii. § 60(10), and for similar heteroclisis in the LXX, Thackeray *Gr.* i. p. 167 f.

λύτρον.

Deissmann (*LAE* p. 331 ff.) has shown how readily our Lord's saying regarding "ransom" in Mt 20[28], the only passage where λύτρον occurs in the NT, would be under-stood by all classes in view of the popular usage of the word in connexion with the purchase-money for manumitting slaves. Thus in P Oxy I. 48[6] (A.D. 86) (as amended *ib.* II.

p. 310) we read of a slave Euphrosyne who has been set free ὑπὸ Δία Γῆν Ἥλιον ἐπὶ λύτροι(ς), "under Zeus, Earth, Sun, for a ransom," and similarly *ib.* 49[8] (A.D. 100): cf. also *ib.* IV. 722[30, 40] (A.D. 91 or 107) and *Chrest.* II. 362[19] (A.D. 211) Ἑλένην . . . ἠλευθέρωσα καὶ ἔσχον ὑπὲρ λύτρ[ω]ν αὐτῆς δραχμὰς σεβαστὰς δισκειλίας διακοσία[ς. For the singular, which is not so common as the plural, Deissmann (*ib.* p. 332 n.[2]) cites from Buresch *Aus Lydien,* p. 197 the inscr. on a native relief from Köres near Koula in Asia Minor—Γαλλικῷ Ἀσκληπιάς, κώμη Κερυζέων, παιδίσχη Διογένου λύτρον, "To Gallicus, Asclepias (village of Ceryza), maidservant of Liogenes (Diogenes?) presents this ransom." He thinks that the word here means that Asclepias was releasing herself from a vow. The plural may be further illustrated by *Syll* 325[15] (i/B.C.) τισὶν δὲ τῶν πολειτῶν εἰς] λύτρα προτιθεὶς ἔδειξεν ἑαυτὸν πρὸς πᾶσαν ἀπάντησιν τῶν σωζο[μέ]νων εὐομείλητον, *ib.* 863[4] (Delphi—i/A.D.) ἀπέλυσε Ἀμμία τὰς παραμονὰς Σύνφορον, λαβοῦσα λύτρα ἐκ πολεμίων. It may be noted that in the LXX the word is always used to denote an equivalent.

λυτρόω.

The verb and its kindred are well established in the vernacular. e.g. P Eleph 19[8] (Ptol.) ὑφίστ[αμα]ι τῆς γῆς . . . ἧς λελυτρωμένοι εἰσὶν τῆς πεπραμένης ὑπὸ Μίλωνος, P Par 22[18] (c. B.C. 165) τὰ δ' ἐκείνου ὑπάρχοντα ἀναληφθέντα εἰς τὸ βασιλικὸν ἐλυτρώσατο ἡ Νέφορις ἀποδομένη ἥμισυ οἰκίας τῆς οὔσης κοινῆς ἡμῶν κτλ., P Oxy III. 530[14] (ii/A.D.) ἐξ ὧν δώσεις Σεραπίωνι τῶι φίλω[ι] . . . λυτρώσασά μου τὰ ἱμάτια δραχμὰς ἑκατόν, "of which you will give to my friend Serapion 100 drachmae and redeem my clothes" (on the aor. of identical action see *Proleg.* p. 132 n.[2]), *ib.* I. 114[2] (ii/iii A.D.) νῦν μελησάτω σοι λυτρώσασθαι τὰ ἐμὰ παρὰ Σαραπίωνα, "now please redeem my property from Sarapion," *ib.* VI. 936[19] (iii/A.D.) οὔπω λελύτρωται τὸ φαινόλιν (cf. 2 Tim 4[13]), "the cloak has not yet been redeemed" from pawn. *Syll* 921[11] (iii/B.C.) μήπως συμ[βῆι ἐξαχθ[έ]ντα ἐ[ξ]ανδραποδισθ[ῆναι τὰ σώματα, ὥστε μηκέτι λυ]τρωθῆναι δύνασθαι. In *ib.* 281[5] (B.C. 192-1) καθὼς ἦν λελυτρωμένοι ὑπ' αὐτῶν, the verb has the unusual sense of "pay expenses": see the editor's note. An Akmonian inscr. of A.D. 313-314, reproduced in *C. and B.* ii. p. 566 f., describes a high-priestess Spatale as having ransomed many from the evil torments (of Christianity)—ἐλυτρώσατο γὰρ πολλοὺς ἐκ κακῶν βασάνων: "a parody," as the editor remarks, "of the Chr. zeal for conversion": cf. Tit 2[14] and the Christian prayer from the end of iv/A.D. edited by Schmidt in *Neutest. Stud. Georg. Heinrici dar gebracht* (Leipzig, 1914), p. 69[52] λυτρωσάμ[ε]νος ἀπὸ τῆς ἐξουσίας τοῦ διαβό[λου] εἰς δόξαν ἐλευθερίας. Note that Blass in the β text of Ac 28[19] inserts after κατηγορεῖν the clause—ἀλλ' ἵνα λυτρώσωμαι τὴν ψυχήν μου ἐκ θανάτου. MGr λυτρώνω, "loose," "liberate."

λύτρωσις.

P Tebt I. 120[41] (accounts—B.C. 97 or 64) εἰς λύτρω(σιν) ποτηρί(ω)ν (δραχμαὶ) δ, P Ryl II. 213[161] (late ii/A.D.) λυ]τρώσεως αἰγῶν (δρ.) β . . . : see also P Rein 42[6] (i/ii A.D.) λυτρώσεως, in connexion with a deed of sale, but unfortunately in a broken context. For the meaning "deliverance" "redemption," which the subst. has in the LXX and

NT, cf. Plutarch *Arat.* xi. λύτρωσιν αἰχμαλώτων, cited by Abbott *ad* Eph 1[7] (*ICC*), where the word and its compound ἀπολύτρωσις are fully discussed. Cf. Deissmann *LAE*, p. 331 ff.

λυτρωτής.

To the reff. for this NT ἅπ. εἰρ (Ac 7[35]) add Act. Thom. 60.

λυχνία

is another form of λυχνεῖον, "lamp-stand," which in later Greek passed from the vernacular into the LXX and NT: cf. Lob. *Phryn.* p. 313 f. λυχνίαν ἀντὶ τοῦ λύχνιον (λέγε), ὡς ἡ κωμῳδία. If we may amend the editor's accent in keeping with the context, λυχνία is found as early as B.C. 284-3 in P Eleph 5[7] λυχνία (instead of λύχνια) σιδηρᾶ ᾱ, and Mayser (*Gr.* p. 425) quotes it in Asia Minor before B.C. 243. e.g. *CIG* II. 2852[14, 61] (Didyma.): see also *OGIS* 214[13] (B.C. 240) τήν τε λυχνίαν τὴν μεγάλην, [60] λυχνία χαλκῆ μεγάλη, and cf. *Cos* 36 d.[7] (= *Syll* 734[114]) λυχνίας δύο, κα[ὶ] λύχνους χαλκοῦς ἑπταπύρους δύο, "two stands for lamps, and two bronze lamps with seven wicks" (Edd.). Other exx. from the papyri are P Lond 402[17] (B.C. 152 or 141) (= II. p. 11) λυχνίαν, P Oxy IV. 730[31] (c. A.D. 1) κόλλητρα λυχνίας (ὀβολοὶ δύο) (ἡμιωβέλιον), "cost of tinkering a lamp-stand 2½ ob.," P Tebt II. 414[19] (ii/A.D.) τὸν σκύφον καὶ τὴν λυχνίαν καὶ τὸ σφυρίδιν, "the can, the lamp-stand, the little basket," *ib.* 416[22] (c. A.D. 266) λυχνεῖα τελεία σὺν ἔρωτι καὶ λυχ[νί]ῳ, "a complete lamp-stand with a Cupid and lamp" (Edd.), and P Grenf II. 111[8] f. (inventory of church property—v/vi A.D.) λυχνίαι χαλκα[ῖ] δ, λυχνίαι σιδηρα[ῖ] β. In connexion with the Hebrew tombs in Phrygia, Sir W. M. Ramsay mentions (*Exp T* xxvi. p. 173) that only in one case has he seen the characteristically Hebrew symbol of the seven-branched candlestick, namely *C. and B.* ii. p. 651 f., No. 561, where it is found beneath the inscr. ὑπὲρ εὐχῆ πάσῃ τῇ πατρίδι. We may add the Alexandrian inscr. *Preisigke* 369 Ἰούδα with the same symbol reproduced below.

λύχνος.

P Tebt I. 88[12] (B.C. 115-4) εἴς τε τὰς θυσίας καὶ λύχνων ἁφῶν (l. ἁφάς), "for sacrifices and the lighting of lamps," P Oxy XII. 1453[18] (B.C. 30-29) τὸ καθῆκον ἔλαιον εἰς τοὺς καθ' ἡμέραν λύχνους καομένους ἐν τοῖς σημαινομένοις ἱεροῖς, "the proper oil for the daily lamps burning in the temples signified" (Edd.), P Lond 193 *verso* [9] (ii/A.D.) (= II. p. 246) λύχνον διφανιν όν), "a lamp with a double light" (Ed.), *ib.* 1177[71] (A.D. 113) (= III. p. 183) ἐλαίου κα[ύ]σεως λύχνοις τοῖς διὰ νυκτὸς ἐργαζομένοις, BGU I. 22[28] (A.D. 114) (*=Selections*, p. 70) ἄρας τὸν λύχνον μου ἀνέβη εἰς τὴν οἰκίαν μου, and P Leid W[vii, 6] (ii/iii A.D.) ἐν[ὶ (= ἑλλ)υχνιάσας λύχνον καθαρόν, καινόν, ἔπιθες ἐπὶ τὸν λύχνον τὸν πόδα ἱπποποταμίου (l. -μου).

For λυχναψία, an Egyptian lamp-festival, cf. P Amh II. 70[i, 19] (between A.D. 114 and 117) (= *Chrest.* I. p. 176), and for λυχνάπτης (-τος) cf. P Oxy XII. 1453[4] (B.C. 30-29) with the editors' note: see also Otto *Priester* i. p. 10. The compound ὑπολύχνιον, "lamp-stand," is found in P Oxy XIV. 1645[10] (A.D. 308).

λύω.

With the use of λύω in Rev 5² τίς ἄξιος ἀνοῖξαι τὸ βιβλίον καὶ λῦσαι τὰς σφραγῖδας αὐτοῦ; cf. P Oxy IV. 715¹⁹ (A.D. 131) κατὰ διαθήκην τὴν καὶ λυθεῖσαν τῶι ιβ (ἔτει) Ἀδριανοῦ Καίσαρος τοῦ κυρίου, "in accordance with a will which was opened in the 12th year of Hadrianus Caesar the lord" (Edd.), and similarly BGU I. 326ⁱⁱ·²¹ (A.D. 194) καὶ ἀνεγνώσθησαν τῇ αὐτῇ ἡμέρᾳ ἐν ᾗ καὶ ἡ διαθήκη ἐλύθη. In P Oxy XII. 1473⁸ (A.D. 201) ἥτις συνγραφὴ ἐλύθη τῷ διελθόντι ϛ (ἔτει) μηνὶ Θώθ, the reference is to the "discharge" of a marriage-contract, a usage which lends point to the verb in I Jn 3⁸. For λύω, "set at naught," "break," as in Mt 5¹⁹, Jn 7²³, see Syll 479 (iii/B.C.) where certain regulations are followed by the threat—²¹ἐὰν δέ τις τούτων τι λύηι, κατάρατος ἔστω. With "breaking" the Sabbath we may compare λύειν τὰ πένθη, "to go out of mourning," Syll 879¹² (end of iii/B.C.). In P Fay 119⁷ (c. A.D. 100) rotten hay is described as ὦλον (l. ὅλον) λελυμένον ὡς σκύβαλον, "the whole of it decayed—no better than dung" (Edd.), and in ib. 120⁸ (c. A.D. 100) we have—λύσις εὐθέω (l. εὐθέως) εἰς Ἀ.[. .] τὰ δράγματα, "you will send off the sheaves immediately to A . . . .": cf. also P Oxy XII. 1477¹⁸ (question to an oracle—iii/iv A.D.) εἰ λύεταί μοι ὁ δρασμός; "is my flight to be stopped?" (Edd.). The verb is = "pay" in P Oxy IV. 745⁶ (c. A.D. 1) οὐκ οἶδας γὰρ πῶς μοι ἐχρήσατο ἐν Ὀξυρύγχοις οὐχ ὡς λύσατι (l. λύσαντι) ἀλλ' ὥς τινί ποτε ἀποστερητῆι μὴ ἀποδεδωκότι, "you don't know how he treated me at Oxyrhynchus (?), not like a man who had paid but like a defrauder and a debtor" (Edd.), while in Syll 226¹⁷ (iii/B.C.) the middle is used of "redeeming" property—αὐτὸς ὑπεραποδοὺς τοὺς ἑκατὸν χρυσοῦς ἐλύσατο: cf. P Lond 1179⁵¹ (ii/A.D.) (= III. p. 146) λύ[σασθαι τὴν ὑποθήκην. For the weak aor. stem of this verb see Moulton Gr. ii. p. 215 ff. MGr λυώνω (Pontic λόνω), "dissolve," "melt."

M

μαγεύω—μαίνομαι

μαγεύω.

For this verb, which in the NT is confined to Ac 8[9], we may cite the expanded second table of the Decalogue in Didache ii. 2 οὐ μαγεύσεις, οὐ φαρμακεύσεις, "thou shalt not practise magic, thou shalt not practise sorcery." See also C. Clemen *Myst.* p. 10 (with n.[3]), a Greek-Aramaic inscr. on a στρατηγός—ἐμάγευσε Μίθρῃ. MGr μαγεύω, "bewitch."

μαγία, μαγεία,

found in Ac 8[11], may be illustrated from Wünsch *AF* p. 16[14] (iii/A.D.) ὁρκίζω σε τὸν θεὸν τὸν πάσης μαγείας τὴν ἐωγσιν ἀνθρωπίνην σειυπγ . . . , where the editor understands the last words as equivalent to something like— τὸν πάσης μαγείας τὴν γνῶσιν ἀνθρωπίνην πορίσαντα, and remarks that "magic is originally something divine, holy (ἱερᾶς μαγείας pap. Parth. I 127)."

μάγος.

For μάγος in the sense of "sorcerer," as in Ac 13[6, 8], we may compare *Kaibel* 903a[7] (= p. 537) (iii/iv A.D.) προνοησαμένου τ[ῆς ἀναστάσεως] Ἀπολλωνίου ἀρχιμάγου. See also Vett. Val. p. 74[17] ποιεῖ γὰρ μάγους πλάνους θύτας ἰατροὺς ἀστρολόγους . . . διά τε πανουργίας καὶ ἐπιθέσεως καὶ δόλου τὰς πράξεις διοικοῦντας.

μαζός.

This poetic word = μαστός, "a breast," which is read in Rev 1[13] A, may be illustrated from the epic fragment PSI III. 253[134] (v/A.D.) ἀπὸ μαζῶν. See also *Kaibel* 644[1] (ii/A.D.) Πομπήιον μαζῷ θελγόμενον γλυκερῷ, *ib.* 690[2] (iii/A.D.) παιδὸς ἄφνω μαζῶν μητρὸς ἀποπταμένο[υ]. Swete *ad Rev l.c.* cites Suidas : μαζὸς κυρίως ἐπὶ ἀνδρός . . . μασθὸς καὶ μαστὸς κυρίως ἐπὶ γυναικός, but remarks that "the distinction does not seem to have been commonly observed." See also *s.v.* μαστός.

μαθητεύω.

With the constr. of this late verb in Mt 13[52] D μαθητευθεὶς ἐν τῇ βασιλείᾳ τῶν οὐρανῶν, cf. the iv/A.D. Christian prayer in *Neut. Studien für G. Heinrici* (Leipzig, 1914), p. 69[24 ff.] ὅτι κατηξίωσας ἡμᾶς τῆς ἁγίας κλήσεώς σου καὶ διδασκαλίας καὶ ἀνανήψεως (cf. 2 Tim 2[26]) μαθητευθῆναι ἐν σοφίᾳ καὶ συνέσει.

μαθητής.

In a return of hieroglyphic inscribers, P Oxy VII. 1029[25] (A.D. 107), the ἱερόγλυφοι declare on oath that the list is exhaustive, and that there were no apprentices or strangers versed in their art—ὀμνύομεν . . . μηδὲ ἔχει[ν] μαθητὰς ἢ ἐπιξένους χρωωμένους (*l.* χρωμ-) τῇ τέχνῃ εἰς τὴν ἐνεστῶσαν ἡμέραν. The word is probably to be read in BGU I. 328[i. 34] (ii/A.D.). The distinction between μάθημα and μάθησις is well seen in PSI I. 94[8 f.] (ii/A.D.) προσεδρεύει ἰς τὰ μαθήματα· ζηλοῖ γὰρ τὴν μάθησιν, "he is regular in attendance at his studies, for he is eager in acquiring knowledge": cf. also P Oxy X. 1296[6] (iii/A.D.) ἀμερίμνη οὖν, πάτερ, χάριν τῶν μαθημάτων ἡμῶν, "do not be anxious, father, about my studies" (Edd.), *ib.* IV. 724[3] (A.D. 155) πρὸς μάθησιν σημείων—a contract of apprenticeship to a shorthand-writer, and from the inscr. *IMAe* VII. 440[7] πᾶσαν μάθησιν ὑμνοποιὸν ἐνδιδούς. MGr μαθητής, plur. μαθητές or μαθητάδες.

μαθήτρια.

This feminine form of μαθητής, which in the NT is found only in Ac 9[36], is applied to Mary Magdalene in Ev. Petr. 11, where Swete *ad l.* notes that "in Coptic Gnostic literature (*Pistis Sophia, Second Book of Jeû*), the μαθήτριαι correspond to the μαθηταί = ἀπόστολοι, and are headed by Mary Magdalene (Schmidt, *Gnostische Schriften*, p. 452)."

Ματθαῖος.

On the double aspirate in this proper name see Moulton *Gr.* ii. p. 102, and cf. P Flor III. 297[73] (vi/A.D.), where the editor restores δ(ιὰ) Ματ[θαίο]υ.

Ματθίας.

On the probability that the Old Syriac Version read "Tholomaeus" for "Matthias" in Ac 1[23.26] see Burkitt *Syriac Forms*, p. 22 f.

μαίνομαι.

The proceedings before Festus (Ac 26[24 f.]) find a striking parallel in the curious interview with an Emperor (Marcus Aurelius or Commodus) recorded in P Oxy I. 33, where the Emperor rebukes the violent language of the condemned Appianus in the words— [iv. 9 ff.] ἰ(= εἰ)ώθαμεν καὶ ἡμεῖς μαινομένους καὶ ἀπονενοημένους σωφρι(= ο)νίζειν, "we are accustomed to bring to their senses those who are mad or beside themselves" (Edd.), and receives the answer—[13 f.] νὴ τὴν σὴν τύχην οὔτε μαίνομαι οὔτε ἀπονενόημαι. The verb is also found in CP Herm I. 7[i. 15] (ii/A.D.?) οὐ γὰρ ἐμηνά[μ]ην, and in *Or. Sib.* i. 171 f. οἱ δέ μιν εἰσαίοντες ἐμυκτήριζον ἕκαστος, | ἔκφρονα κικλήσκοντες, ἀτὰρ μεμανημένον ἄνδρα.

μακαρίζω.

For this verb—"deem (account) happy" (Lk 1⁴⁸, Jas 5¹¹) cf. Vett. Val. p. 88²⁵ where it is said of a man born under certain planetary influences—ὑπὸ πολλῶν μακαρισθήσεται.

μακάριος

is used in the LXX for אַשְׁרֵי (Ps 1¹, al.), "Oh, the happiness of . . . !", and in Hebrew thought denotes a state of true well-being : hence Mt 5³, al. In 1 Tim 1¹¹, 6¹⁵, it is applied to God : with the latter passage cf. Philo de Sacrificiis Abelis et Caini, p. 147 περὶ θεοῦ τοῦ ἀγεννήτου καὶ ἀφθάρτου καὶ ἀτρέπτου καὶ ἁγίου καὶ μόνου μακαρίου (cited by White EGT ad l.), and the passages cited by Dibelius HZNT ad 1¹¹. The absence of early exx. of this common prose word is curious, but it is frequent in the New Comedy, and late exx. may be quoted from the papyri, as PSI III. 170¹⁶ (v/A.D.) Φλα(ύιος) Μηνᾶς στρατηλατιανὸς υἱὸς τοῦ μακαρίου Δωροθέου ὑπέγραψα κτλ., and the Christian P Giss I. 55⁶ (vi/A.D.) π]αρὰ τοῦ τῆς μ[α]καρίας μνήμης Φοιβαδίου τοῦ ἐπισκ[όπου. From the inscrr. we may cite Cagnat IV. 808⁵ (Hierapolis) εἰς τὴν εὐτυχῆ καὶ μακαρίαν ὑπατ[OGIS 519⁹ (c. A.D. 245) ἐν τοῖς μακαριωτάτοις ὑμῶν καιροῖς, and the Christian sepulchral inscr. from Akhmim (?) of Byzantine times, Preisigke 1442 ἐτελεύ<τη>σεν ἡ μακαρία Σεμεῦγα ἐπὶ μηνὶ Ἀθὺρ ιθ. For Μακαρία as a proper name cf. the Phrygian epitaph cited by Ramsay Exp T xxvi. p. 170 (cf. p. 172)—ἔτους τλγ (anno 333 of the Phrygian era = A.D. 247-8) Αὐρήλιος Φρουγιανὸς Μηνοκρίτου καὶ Αὐρ. Ἰουλιανὴ γυνὴ αὐτοῦ Μακαρίᾳ μητρὶ καὶ Ἀλεξανδρίᾳ θυγατρὶ γλυκυτάτῃ ζῶντες κατεσκεύασαν μνήμης χάριν.

μακαρισμός.

On the difference between the Biblical "declaration of blessedness" (Rom 4⁶, Gal 4¹⁵) and the ordinary Greek and Latin gratulatory expressions see Norden Agnostos Theos, p. 100 f., the monograph De veterum macarismis by G. L. Dirichlet in Religionsgeschichtliche Versuche und Vorarbeiten xiv. 4 (Giessen, 1914), and W. M. Ramsay CR xxxiii. p. 6, where it is pointed out that μακάριος, as distinguished from μακαρίτης, tended to become characteristically Christian. See also Stob. Flor. T. I. 72 γίνεται δ' ὁ μὲν ἔπαινος ἐπ' ἀρετᾷ, ὁ δὲ μακαρισμὸς ἐπ' εὐτυχίᾳ (cited by Field Notes, p. 154). The verbal μακαριστός occurs ter in the rescript of Antiochus I., OGIS 383¹⁶ ³⁹ ¹⁰⁸ (mid. i/B.C.).

μάκελλον.

For this NT ἅπ. εἰρ. (1 Cor 10²⁵) see Magn 179²¹ (ii/A.D.) παραπράξεις τε ποιήσαντα ἐν τῷ μακέλλῳ παντὸς εἴδους : cf. CP Herm I. 127 3 verso⁵ ἐντὸς μακέλλου, and C. and B. ii. 549 (= p. 646) ἡ γερουσία τὰ ζυγοστάσια πρὸς τῷ μακέλλῳ ἐκ τῶν ἰδίων ποιήσαντα, where the editor notes that "Makellon here evidently denotes the provision market, Latin macellum." [The ζυγοστάσια was the place where weights were officially tested.] The word is Semitic in origin (cf. Heb. מִכְלָה, "enclosure"), and appears in Ionic and Laconian ; cf. Μάκελλα in Sicily. But the Lat. macellum is the most familiar form.

μακράν

is construed with the gen. in P Oxy I. 113¹⁸ (ii/A.D.) ἡ αἰτία αὕτη ἐστίν, διὰ τὸ τὸν χαλκέα μακρὰν ἡμῶν εἶναι, "the reason is that the smith is a long way from us" (Edd.). For εἰς μακράν cf. Meyer Ostr 66² (iii/A.D.) ἐὰν ὁ ἄνθρωπος ἀπῆλθεν εἰς μακράν κτλ., where note also ἐάν c. ind. (cf. Blass-Debrunner § 372).

μακρόθεν.

For this late Greek equivalent of πόρρωθεν (Blass Gr., p. 59) cf. P Tebt I. 230 (late ii/B.C.) μακρόθεν . . . ἀπολύσαντες. On the pleonastic ἀπὸ μακρόθεν (Mk 5⁶ al.) see WM p. 753 f., Dieterich Untersuchungen, p. 183 f.

μακροθυμέω.

A corresponding verb μακροψυχέω, not found in LS, occurs in the (probably Christian) letter PSI IV. 299¹¹ (iii/A.D.) μακροψ[ύ]χ[ει] οὖν, ἀδελφή, ἄχρεις οὗ ἄν με θεὸς εὐοδώσῃ [πρὸς] ὑμᾶς. "have patience, therefore, sister, until God shall give me a successful journey to you." For an interesting note on the translation of μακροθυμεῖ in Lk 18⁷, "is it His way to delay in giving them help ?" see Exp T xxv. p. 71 n.⁶, and cf. Field Notes, p. 72. The verb is found in Plutarch, and belongs to the common vocabulary of late Greek : see Deissmann LAE, p. 72.

μακροθυμία.

In the recently recovered fragment of the Greek text of the Apocalypse of Baruch, P Oxy III. 403, we find—⁸ ff. ἀληθῶς γὰρ ἐν] καιρῷ ἐξυπνισθήσεται [[πρὸς σὲ ἡ ὀργὴ ἡ νῦν ὑπὸ τ]ῆς μακροθυμ[ί]ας ὡς χαλινῷ κατέχεται, "for assuredly in its season the wrath will be awakened against thee which now is restrained by long-suffering as it were by a rein" (Edd.).

μακρός

is used of time in P Giss I. 41ᵢᵢ. ² (beg. of Hadrian's reign) ὑπὸ τῆς μακρᾶς ἀποδημίας τὰ ἡμέτε[ρα] πα[ντ]άπασιν ἀμεληθέντα τυγχ[άνει, "owing to our long absence from home our affairs came to be altogether neglected"; cf. Preisigke 3925⁶ (B.C. 149-8 or 137-6) μακ[ρὸν ἂν εἴη] διασαφῆσαι, and P Strass I. 22³ (iii/A.D.) μακρᾶς νομῆς παραγραφή, "longae possessionis (longi temporis) praescriptio." In a tract on medical training, Berl. Klass. Texte iii. p. 22 ff. Col. 2, 7 ff., it is laid down : δεῖ . . . τοὺς νέους ἐξ ἀρχῆς συνασκεῖν τοῖς ἀνα[γ]καιοτέροις π[ρ]άγμασιν τοῦ βίου βραχέος ὄντ[ο]ς καὶ τῆς τέχνης μακρῆς, ὥς φησιν ὁ Ἱπποκράτης. The reference is to stature in P Lond 1158⁶ (A.D. 226-7) (= III. p. 151) μακρὸς πύκτης, "a tall boxer." The compd. μακροπρόσωπος is common in personal descriptions, e.g. P Ryl II. 153⁴⁶ (A.D. 138-161) μέσος μελίχρως μακροπρόσωπος, "of medium height, with a fair complexion, long-visaged." In MGr the word has changed to μακρύς, "far," "distant."

μακροχρόνιος.

The corresponding verb is found in P Flor III. 296¹⁰ (vi/A.D.) μακροχρονιεῖν (cf. μακροχρονίζω Deut 17²⁰, 32²⁷).

μαλακία.

in the sense of bodily weakness, is found conjoined with νόσος, as in Mt 4²³ *al.* in the Christian amulets P Oxy VIII. 1151²⁷ (v/A.D.?) ὁ ἰασάμενος πᾶσαν νόσον καὶ πᾶσαν μαλακίαν, ἴασαι καὶ ἐπίσκεψαι καὶ τὴν δούλην σου Ἰωαννίαν, BGU III. 954¹² (c. vi A.D.) (= *Selections*, p. 133) πᾶσαν δὲ νόσον καὶ πᾶσαν μαλακίαν ἀφελε ἀπ᾽ ἐμοῦ. Cf. Menander *Fragm.* p. 58 μηκέτ᾽ αἰτιῶ θεόν, ἤδη δὲ τῇ σαυτοῦ ζυγομάχει μαλακίᾳ, and see Hobart, p. 63. For the verb μαλακίζομαι, as in Gen 42³⁸ *al.* cf. *Syll* 850²¹ (B.C. 173-2) εἰ δὲ μαλακισθείη Σωτήριχος, ὃ μὴ γίνοιτο, πλεῖον διμήνου, ἐπαποδότω τοῦ πλείονος χρόνου Σωτήριχος Ἀμύντᾳ, and *Preisigke* 158 ἐμαλακίσθη καὶ ὁ θεὸς αὐτῶι ἐβοήθησε αὐθημερή.

μαλακός.

In P Hib I. 54¹¹ (c. B.C. 245) (= *Chrest.* I. p. 563) a certain musician Zenobius is described as ὁ μαλακός, probably in the same sense in which the word is found in 1 Cor 6⁹, rather than simply with reference to his style of dancing (as GH and Smyly who compares Plaut. *Mil.* 668: *Tum ad saltandum non cinaedus malacus aequest atque ego*). In a Macedonian inser. (*Duchesne and Bayet* p. 46, No. 66) the words ὁ μαλακός have been added in a different style of writing, after the name of the person commemorated, evidently in satirical allusion to his corrupt mode of life. For the adj. = "soft," as in Mt 11⁸, cf. *Syll* 538 (= ³970)⁸ (B.C. 289-8) τιθέναι τοὺς λίθους τῆς μαλακῆς πέτρας, and *Kaibel* 649⁴ ἄνθεσιν ἐν μαλακοῖσι. The epithet is applied to wine in PSI VI. 594²¹ (iii/B.C.). The form persists in MGr.

μάλιστα.

"most of all," "especially," which occurs 12 times in the NT, and is usually elative, may be illustrated by P Lille I. 26² (iii/B.C.) ἔγραψάς μοι περὶ τῆς εἰς τὴν σησαμείαν γῆς, μάλιστα δὲ περὶ τῆς ἐν Πατῶντι, P Goodsp Cairo 4¹³ (mid. ii B.C.) (= Witkowski², p. 95) μάλιστα δὲ σαυτοῦ ἐπιμελόμενος, ἵν᾽ ὑγιαίνῃς, P Tebt I. 40¹¹ (B.C. 117) (= *Selections*, p. 28) διὰ τὸ μάλιστα ἐπιβάλλειν προνοεῖσθαι τῶν βασιλικῶν, "because it devolves upon you before all others to watch over the interests of the Crown" (Edd.), P Amh II. 131¹² (early ii/A.D.) μάλιστα δὲ περὶ τοὺς ἐνυφαντωι (*l.* τῶν ἐνυφαντῶν) ὅπως μὴ δίκας λέγωμεν, "and in particular look after the woven stuffs, so that we may not have any cross-words" (Edd.), P Giss I. 24² (time of Trajan) τ]ῶν θεῶν [οὐ]ν θελόντων καὶ μάλιστα τοῦ ἀνικήτου Ἑρμοῦ, and P Oxy VI. 939²⁰ (iv A.D.) (= *Selections*, p. 129) νὴ γὰρ τὴν σὴν σωτηρίαν, κύριέ μου, ἧς μάλιστά μοι μέλει κτλ., "for by your own safety, my lord, which chiefly concerns me" etc. In MGr μάλιστα = "of course," "quite," "very."

μᾶλλον.

P Oxy III. 474³⁷ (A.D. 184?) ἀβουλίᾳ μᾶλλον ἢ πειθοῖ τῶν παρηγγελμένων, "in defiance of rather than in obedience to the proclamations," *ib.* XIV. 1762¹² (ii/iii A.D.) σοῦ γὰρ μᾶλλον ἢ ἡμῶν (ἀκο)ύσεται, *ib.* VI. 939³ (iv A.D.) (= *Selections*, p. 128) ὡς ἐν ἄλ]λοις πλείστοις νῦν ἔτι μᾶλλον (cf. Phil 1⁹, "as on many other occasions so now still

more," and P Fay 136⁵ (iv/A.D.) ὅθεν μηδένα εὐλαβούμενοι μᾶλλον ἀπαντήσατε ἀπ᾽ ἑαυτῶν, "therefore heed no one rather than me and return from where you are" (Edd.). For the intensive μᾶλλον in the NT see Milligan on 1 Thess 4¹.

Μάλχος.

With this proper name (Jn 18¹⁰) we may compare a certain Ἰρμαῖος Μάλιχος, the only Semite name in a ii A.D. military letter published by Comparetti in *Mél. Nic.* p. 57 ff.: see the editor's note to ³¹ ²⁶, and cf. P Magd 15 *recto* ¹³ (B.C. 221).

μάμμη.

For the later sense of "grandmother," as in 2 Tim 1⁵ (cf. 4 Macc 16⁹), cf. P Rein 40¹¹ (A.D. 215-6) (= *Chrest.* I. p. 245) μου μητρ[ὸς καὶ τῆ]ς μάμμης Αὐ[ρ]ηλία[ς. See also the letter addressed by Epicarus to a child Ex Vol. Hercul. 176⁸ (iii/B.C.) (= *Selections*, p. 5) εὖ δὲ ποιε[ῖ]ς καὶ σὺ ἐ[ὶ ὑ]γιαίνεις καὶ ἡ μ[ά]μμη [σ]ου, "it is well if you also and your grandmother are in good health," P Oxy XIV. 1644¹² (B.C. 63-62) Μοσχίωνος κατὰ μητέρα μάμμη Ἀρσινόη, "Arsinoe maternal grandmother of Moschion," *ib.* III. 496⁵ (A.D. 127) ἡ [τῆς] γαμουμένης μάμμη, "the grandmother of the bride," *ib.* I. 67¹⁶ (A.D. 338) ἀπὸ δικέου (*l.* δικαίου) κληρ[ονομιῶ]ν τῆς ἡμετέρας μάμμης, "by right of inheritance from my grandmother," and from the inscrr. *Syll* 381 (= ³844B)⁶ (iii A.D.) ἡ πρὸς μητρὸς μάμμη Καλλίκλε[ια κα]ὶ οἱ γονεῖς κτλ. The adj. μαμμικός is common, e.g. P Rein 46¹⁹ (A.D. 189) ὑπάρχει τε αὐτοῖς τὸ ἐπιβάλλο[ν] μέρος οἰκ(ίας καὶ αὐλ(ῆς) πατρικὸν καὶ μαμμικόν, "elles possèdent la part qui leur revient, dans la succession de leur père et de leur aïeule, d'une maison et d'une cour" (Ed.), and for the form μαμμῷος (not in LS) see BGU I. 19⁴·⁷ (A.D. 135) where τὰ μαμμικά is corrected into τὰ μαμμῷα, "the grandmother's property": cf. ¹⁵·⁶. MGr μαμμή, "midwife."

μαμωνᾶς.

For the gen. form μαμωνᾶ (Lk 16⁹), see Robertson *Gr.* p. 254 f. According to Dalman (*Gr.*² p. 170 f., Ann. 1) μαμωνᾶς is derived from מַמוֹן, "deposited."

Μαναήν.

This Jewish name (= מְנַחֵם, 2 Kings 15¹⁴) receives a Greek look from the termination -ην: see Deissmann *BS* p. 310, n.⁴. Preuschen (*HZNT ad* Ac 13¹) thinks that the form Μάναιμος, known to Papias (TU v. 2 p. 170) in connexion with a story κατὰ τὴν μητέρα Μαναίμου τὴν ἐκ νεκρῶν ἀναστᾶσαν, may be related.

μανθάνω.

P Lond 43¹ (ii B.C.) (= I. p. 48, *Chrest.* I. p. 162) πυνθανομένη μανθάνειν σε Αἰγύπτια γράμματα συνεχάρην σοι καὶ ἐμαυτῆι, "on hearing that you are learning Egyptian letters I congratulated you and myself," BGU IV. 1125¹⁰ (B.C. 13) μεμαθηκότας τὴν προκιμένη ν τέχνην ἐπιμελῶς, P Ryl II. 235¹² (ii A.D.) ἀλλὰ οὐ πρώτως σου τὸ εἰκαῖον μανθάνομεν, "but it is not the first time we learn your heedlessness" (Edd.). For the punctiliar μαθεῖν, "ascertain," as in Ac 23²⁷, Gal 3², cf. *ib.* 77⁴² (A.D. 192) ἐμάθομεν τὸν Ἀχιλλέα προβαλόμενον ἑαυτὸν εἰς ἐξήγησιν ἀπόντων ἡμῶν, "we have learned that Achilles in our absence put himself forward for the office of exegetes" (Edd.), P Oxy VII. 1067[8] (iii/A.D.) μάθε οὖν ὅτι ἀλλοτρίαν γυναῖκαν ἐκληρονόμησεν αὐτόν, "know then that a strange woman is made his heir" (Ed.), ib. XIV. 1671[20] (iii/A.D.) γράψον οὖν ἵνα τὴν διαταγὴν μάθω, "write therefore, that I may learn the order" (Edd.), P Tebt II. 417[24] (iii/A.D.) μάθε τοῦ Μώρου, "find out from Morus." The form ἐμάθαμεν (cf. Moulton *Proleg.* p. 51) is found in P Oxy VII. 1032[25] (A.D. 162). On the difficult 1 Tim 5[13], where μανθάνω is practically pass. of διδάσκω, see Moulton *Proleg.* p. 229 : cf. Field *Notes*. p. 210. With 2 Tim 3[7] we may compare Epict. i. 29. 35 ἤθελον ἔτι μανθάνειν, "I would fain go on learning." MGr μαθαίνω has lost the nasal : the aor. stem has prevailed over the present, but cf. also the disappearance of the ν from the MGr ἄθρωπος.

μανία.

The somewhat weakened sense of μανία in Ac 26[24], where it is contrasted with σωφροσύνης ῥήματα (25) : cf. *s.v.* μαίνομαι, is seen in an unedited Tebtunis papyrus of ii/B.C.—φαίνῃ εἰς μανίαν ἐμπεπτωκέν[α]ι, διὸ λόγον σαυτοῦ οὐ ποιεῖς καὶ ὑπ[ο]μεμένηκας, "you seem to have gone mad, for you pay no regard to yourself, and have gone off your head" : cf. also PSI IV. 434[6] (B.C. 261–0) εἰδὼς οὖν αὐτοῦ τὴμ μανίαν συναντᾶν ἐκέλευον, ὅταν περιοδεύω, καὶ κωλῦσαί με, and BGU IV. 1024[v. 2] (iv/iv A.D.) φό[νο]ν κατασημαινομένου [αἰτίαν] τὴν ἐπικει[μ]ένην [σ]ου μανίαν [λέγεις] ἔρωτος. For the adj. μανικός see the *florilegium* of apophthegms PSI II. 120[54] (iv/A.D. ?) ἐν ἀγορᾷ μὴ σπεῦδε, μηδὲ χειροτόνει λαλῶν· μανικὸν γάρ.

μάννα.

Natural manna is referred to in a medical recipe to stop nose-bleeding. P Oxy VIII. 1088[21] (early i/A.D.) μάνναν φύρασον χυλῶι πράσωι καὶ ἐνάλιψον τὸν χυλὸν ἐνδόθεν, "mix frankincense with onion-juice and apply the juice inside" (Ed.).

μαντεύομαι.

This word, which in the LXX is always used of lying prophets, or divination contrary to the law (Deut 18[10] al.), has again a sinister reference in its only occurrence in the NT (Ac 16[16]). A more general sense appears in *Michel* 842 (1st half ii/B.C.), a collection of decrees relating to the oracle of Apollo Coropaeus in Thessaly— [41] καθήσθ[ω]σαν δὲ οἱ προγεγ(ρ)αμμένοι ἐν τῶι ἱερῶι . . . . ἁγνεύοντες καὶ νήφοντες καὶ ἀποδεχόμενοι τὰ πινάκια παρὰ τῶν μαντευομένων : cf. also for the act. the magic P Lond 121[547] (iii/A.D.) (= I. p. 101), where divination is resorted to by means of a lamp and a boy— ἐπιδέομαι ὑμῶν ἐν τῇ σήμερον ἡμέρᾳ ἐν τῇ ἄρτι ὥρᾳ φανῆναι τῷ παιδὶ τούτῳ τὸ φῶς καὶ τὸν ἥλιον μαντεύσει. For the subst. μαντεία it is sufficient to cite OGIS 319[10] (ii/B.C.) κατὰ τὰς τοῦ θεοῦ τοῦ ἐν Δελφοῖς μαντείας, P Lond 46[50] (iv/A.D.) (= I. p. 66) ἡ μαντεία εὔτακτος ἀπεργάζεται.

μαραίνω.

Hort (ad Jas 1[11]) has shown that this word, which in the pass. "denoted originally the dying out of a fire" (cf. Arist.

de vita et morte 5. and see P Leid W[vii. 44] (ii/iii A.D.) πῦρ . . καὶ μαραινόμενον, καὶ μὴ μαραίμενον), came to be used of many kinds of enfeeblement and decay. Hence its frequent occurrence in sepulchral epitaphs, e.g. *Kaibel* 201[2] (i/B.C.) ἄ[φν]ως γὰρ | ἁρπάξας σ᾽ Ἀΐδας σὰν ἐμάρανεν ἀκμάν, and the later ib. 368[1] ἄνθεα πάντα φύουσιν, κάλλος δὲ τὸ σὸν μεμάρανται, [7] Θεοδώρα, κλάδος ἐλέας, τάχυ πῶς ἐμαράνθης : cf. also the Senthianic imprecatory tablet 16[61] (Leipzig, 1898, p. 18) μαραίνετε . . : τὴν ψυχὴν . . Καρδήλου . . . εἴσω ἡμερῶν πέντε (quoted by Wünsch in Bliss and Macalister *Excavations in Palestine* (1902), p. 168). For traces of the application of the verb to plants in classical Greek, as in Jas 1[11], see again Hort's note *ad l.*, where reference is also made to Wisd 2[8], Job 24[24].

μαραναθά.

This old Aramaic watchword (1 Cor 16[22]), which is strangely misunderstood in most of our English versions down to the AV, is divided by WH into μαρὰν ἀθά = "our Lord has come," or "cometh." Others prefer to read μαράνα θά = "our Lord, come !" (Dalman *Words* p. 328, Gr.[2] p. 152, n.[3]) : cf. Rev 22[20], and the eucharistic prayer in Didache x. 6 εἴ τις ἅγιός ἐστιν, ἐρχέσθω· εἴ τις οὐκ ἔστι, μετανοείτω· μαραναθά ἀμήν. On the interpretation of the phrase, which lies outside our immediate purpose, see further Schaff *ad Didache l.c.*, Abbott *Joh. Voc.* p. 126 ff., Deissmann *LAE* p. 354 and *Urgeschichte* p. 26 ff., Zahn *Introduction* i. p. 303 ff., and Homme *ZNTW* xv. 4.

Μάρθα.

For this common name it is sufficient to cite BGU IV. 1153[i. 3] (a nursing contract—B.C. 14) ὥσ]τε τιθηνεῖσθαι διὰ τῆς αὐτῆς Μάρθας (cf.[6]), and ib. 1155[4] (payment of a debt—B.C. 10) παρὰ] Μάρθας τῆς Πρωτάρχου.

On the form Μαρθίνη, as an adaptation to Hellenic surroundings, see the prayers for vengeance on the murderers of the Jewish girls Heraclea and Marthine from Rheneia (Magna Delos) c. B.C. 100, discussed by Deissmann *LAE* p. 423 ff.

Μαρία

is the Grecized form of Μαριάμ. For the "singularly intricate and perplexing" variations between the two forms in the NT see WH *Notes*[2], p. 163. Josephus prefers what Deissmann (*Urgeschichte*, p. 22) calls "die kokettere Grazisierung" Μαριάμ(μ)η. Two instances of Μαρία from ostraca are significant in connexion with the Jewish Diaspora in Egypt. The first is Meyer *Ostr* 33 (Edfu—A.D. 116), a receipt for four drachmae which Μαρία Ἀβιήτου, "Mary the daughter of Abietas," has paid by way of Jewish tax—Ἰουδ(αίων τελέσματος). The second, ib. 56 (Thebes—ii/A.D.) is a statement of the payment of certain artabae of wheat in the name of Vestidia Secunda (?), represented by Pollia Maria the younger—διὰ Πολλία (l.—ίας) Μαρία (l. = ίας) νεωτ (l. νεωτέρας) : cf. Deissmann *LAE* p. 113 f.

With ἡ ἄλλη Μαρία in Mt 28[1] we may compare the census paper P Petr III. 59 (c) where various names, *not* duplicated in this document, are followed by ἄλλος or ἄλλη. If only three women are specified in Jn 19[25], then two sisters must have borne the same name "Mary," which Westcott (ad l.) regards as a "most unlikely supposition," but it may be noted that in P Petr III. 117 (g)[ii. 17f] (Ptol.) mention is made of two brothers both called Μάνρης—Μάνρης μικρὸς Τέωτος καὶ Μάνρης ἀδελφὸς ὡσαύτως. The probability, however, is that four women are mentioned, of whom the second is Salome. The rare occurrence of Μαρία and other names of Hebrew origin in early Christian epitaphs may be due to "the dislike for the Jews, and the dread of being taken for Jews" (C. and B. ii. p. 524).

Μᾶρκος.

The spelling Μάαρκος which is found in such inscrr. as Syll 318 (=³ 700)² Macedonia—B.C. 118 Μάαρκος Ἄννιος Ποπλίου υἱός, CIG III. 6155 (Italy) Μάαρκος Κοσσούτιος, Μαάρκου ἀπελεύθερος, is sufficient to justify the accentuation Μᾶρκος, which Blass (Gr. § 4. 2) adopts from the long a in the Lat. Mārcus. For other exx. of the name, showing how widely it was spread, see Swete Mark p. ix f., and add OGIS 170¹ (B.C. 146–116) and ib. 637² (A.D. 196). The Roman praenomen is used alone like a Greek name in Priene 315⁶³⁵ ὁ τ. Μάρκου τοῦ—, Preisigke 4595³ τὸ προσκύνημα Ἀντωνίου . . . καὶ Μάρκου καὶ . . . , and ib. 4949⁸ (sepulchral inscr.—A.D. 753) ἀνάπαυσ[ον τὴν ψ(υχὴν)] Μάρκ(ου) ἐν κόλπ[οις Ἀβραά]μ . . .

μάρμαρος.

This word, which in the NT is confined to Rev 18¹², occurs in P Leid Xˣ·¹² (iii/iv A.D.) (= II. p. 231) ποιεῖ δὲ οὐ μόνον ἐπὶ χάρτου ἢ διφθέρας, ἀλλὰ καὶ ἐπὶ μαρμάρου ἐστιλβωμένου, with reference to χρυσογραφία, "writing in letters of gold." For the adj. μαρμάρινος cf. the Mytilenean decree Cagnat IV. 45¹¹ ἐγχαράχθην ἐς στάλλαν μαρμαρίναν, and for μαρμάριος, "a marble-mason" cf. Kaibel 920 ii. 7 (time of Severus) μαρμαρίων τὸ γένος σῶζε, Σέραπι. Boisacq (p. 611) points out that the primary meaning was "boulder," "block of rock," as in Hom. Il. xii. 380, the meaning "marble" being due to the influence of μαρμαίρω, μαρμάρεος, which are not related to μάρμαρος. He connects with μάρναμαι in its original sense of "break," "crush," and compares the formation of rupes from rumpo.

μαρτυρέω.

The common occurrence of this word after a signature, just as we write "witness," e.g. P Oxy I. 105¹³ (a will—A.D. 117–137) Σαραπίων Σαραπίωνος . . μαρτυρῶ, P Lond 1164 (f)³⁵ (records of sales and receipts—A.D. 212) (= III. p. 162) Ἡλιό[δ]ωρος . . . μαρτυρῶ, P Grenf II. 68²¹ f. (deed of gift—A.D. 247) Αὐρήλιος Φιλοσάραπις . . μαρτ[υρ]ῶ. Αὐρήλιος Ἀμμώνιος . . μαρτυρῶ, may be cited in illustration of the Pauline usage in 2 Cor 8³. The verb has again a judicial sense in P Amh II. 66³⁵ (A.D. 124) Στοτοήτιος λέγοντος . . . παρεῖναι τοὺς μαρτυρῆσαι δυναμένους τὸ[ν] φόν[ο]ν, "Stotoetis stated that there were present persons able to witness to the murder" (Edd.), cf. ³⁸. For the more general meaning, "bear witness to," "report," cf. PSI I. 94³ (ii/A.D.) πρὸς τὸ μαρτυρῆσαι ὑμεῖν τὴν φιλανθρωπίαν μου, P Oxy VII. 1064¹² (iii/A.D.) γράφω σοι . . ὅπως συνλάβῃς τῷ Ἄπει . . ξενίαν δὲ αὐτῷ

ποιήσῃς, πρὸς τὸ ἐπανελθόντα αὐτὸν μαρτυρῆσαί μοι, "I write to you that you may assist Apis, and may show him hospitality, so that on his return he may bear witness of it to me" (Ed.), similarly ib. 1068¹⁹ (iii/A.D.), ib. XII. 1424¹⁷ (c. A.D. 318) ἀλλ' ἵνα μοι μαρτυρήσῃ τὰ ὑπὸ τῆς ἀγαθῆς σου προαιρέσεως αὐτῷ ὑπαρχθέντα, "but let him testify to the benefits gained by your good will" (Edd.) (for the construction cf. Mk 5²³, Eph 5²³, al., and the early Christian letter P Grenf II. 73¹⁶ (late iii/A.D.) (= Selections, p. 118) ὅταν ἔλθῃ σὺν Θεῷ, μαρτυρήσῃ σοι περὶ ὧν αὐτὴν πεποιήκασιν, "when he arrives by the help of God, he will bear you witness of what they have done to her." Another Christian example is P Oxy VIII. 1164¹¹ (vi/vii A.D.) where a minor local magnate writes to a comes—μαρτυρεῖ μοι γὰρ ὁ θεὸς ὅτι σπουδάζω ἐν ἅπασιν τὰ κελευόμενά μοι παρ' ὑμῶν ἀποπληρῶσαι, "God is my witness that I am anxious in everything to perform your orders" (Ed.). For μαρτυρέω, "give a good report," as in Lk 4²², cf. P Oxy VI. 930¹⁶ (ii/iii A.D.), where a mother writes to her son that she had received a good report of his παιδαγωγός from his former teacher—ἐμαρτύρει δὲ πολλὰ περὶ τοῦ παιδαγωγοῦ σου: cf. Syll 107 (= ³374)³⁷ (c. B.C. 287–6) πολλάκις μεμαρτύρηκεν αὐτῷ ὁ βασιλεύς. The corresponding use of the pass. with reference to "the good name" witnessed of a man, as in Ac 6³, 16², 1 Tim 5¹⁰, Heb 11², may be illustrated from BGU IV. 1141¹⁵ (B.C. 14) ὡς καὶ μαρτυρηθήσεταί σοι ὑπὸ τῶν φίλων, ib. 1155¹⁵ (B.C. 10) (= Chrest. II. p. 75) πιττακίου μεμαρτυρημένου δὲ δι' ὧν ἀνήνεγκεν ὁ Πρώταρχος συνχωρήσεων, and from the inscrr. Syll 366 (= ³799)²⁸ (c. A.D. 38) ἀρχιτέκτονας μαρτυρηθέντας ὑπὸ τῆς σεμνοτάτης Τρυφαίν[ης, and Latyschev I. 21²⁶ ff. (Olbia—ii/A.D.), where it is said of a certain Carzoazus—ἀλλὰ καὶ (μέχρι) περάτων γῆς ἐμαρτυρήθη τοὺς ὑπὲρ φιλίας κινδύνους μέχρι Σεβαστῶν συμμαχίᾳ παραβολευσάμενος, "but also to the ends of the world it was witnessed of him that in the interests of friendship he had exposed himself to dangers as an advocate in (legal) strife (by taking his clients' causes even) up to emperors" (Deissmann LAE p. 84 n.⁵); see also the temple inscr. from Abydos Preisigke 1070 δι' ὅλης οἰκουμέν ης) μαρτυρούμενον οὐράνιον θεὸν [Βησᾶν ἐ]δείσα[μεν, and further exx. in Deissmann BS, p. 265, CR i. p. 46. MGr μαρτυρῶ, "acknowledge," "confess"; "inform."

μαρτυρία.

P Hal I. 1²⁴ (mid. iii/B.C.) ὁ μαρτυρίας ἐπιλαμβανόμενος ἐπιλααμβανέσθω (l. ἐπιλαμ)παραχρῆμα κτλ., P Fay 21²² (A.D. 134) μαρτυρίαν ποιήσασθαι, "to give evidence." P Ryl II. 116¹⁵ (A.D. 194) ὅθεν ἐπιδίδωμι τόδε τὸ βιβλείδιον ἀξιῶν εἶναι ἐν καταχωρισμῷ πρὸς μαρτυρίαν, "wherefore I present this petition, requesting that it may be registered as evidence" (Edd.); cf. also Syll 686 (= ³1073)⁴⁷ (after A.D. 117), an inscr. in honour of a pancratiast—ἀνδριάντα αὐτῷ ἐπὶ τῆς Ὀλυμπίας ἀναστῆσαι ἐπιγραφὴν ἔχοντα τήν τε τῶν ἄλλων ἀγώνων μαρτυρίαν καὶ δηλοῦσαν κτλ. In connexion with Rev 1⁹ τὴν μαρτυρίαν Ἰησοῦ Hort (ad l.) refers to Epict. iii. 24. 113 and i. 29. 46. A somewhat different sense appears in P Oxy I. 41¹⁶ (iii/iv A.D.), where, in answer to a popular demonstration in his honour, the prytanis at Oxyrhynchus remonstrates—τὰς δὲ τοιαύτα[ς] μαρτυρίας ἀξιῶ εἰς καιρὸν ἔννομον ὑπερτεθῆναι, "but I beg that these demonstrations be reserved for a statutory occasion."

μαρτύριον.

The words of the sepulchral epitaph *Kaibel* 397[1] μαρτύριον ὀρθοῦ βίου, "the witness of an upright life," have a modern ring about them. In *ib.* 1063[6] (v/vi A.D.) ᾠκοδομήθη τὸ μα[ρ]τύριον Μαίῳ τῇ ε̄, the word refers to a martyr's shrine : cf. P Oxy VI. 941[1] (vi/A.D.) ἀντὶς τοῦ μαρτυρίου, "opposite the martyr's shrine," where the editors draw attention to the remarkable form ἀντίς, employed in a local sense—a usage which survives in MGr. See also *Pelagia-Legenden*, p. 3[16] συνελθόντας οὖν ἐν Ἀντιοχείᾳ ἐκέλευσεν ἡμᾶς ὁ ἐπίσκοπος μεῖναι ἐν τῷ μαρτυρίῳ τοῦ ἁγίου Ἰουλιανοῦ.

μαρτύρομαι.

For this verb in its original sense of "summon to witness" cf P Oxy VIII. 1114[23] (A.D. 237) ἐμαρτύρατο τοὺς τάδε τὸ μαρτυροποίημα σφραγίζειν μέλλοντας, "called to witness the persons about to seal the present affidavit " (Ed.). From this it is an easy transition to the meaning "asseverate," as in *ib.* III. 471[61] (ii/A.D.) μαρτύρονται κύριε τὴν σὴν τύχην, "they swear by your Fortune, my lord," and in Mahaffy's restoration of P Petr II. 46 (a)[1] (B.C. 200) μαρτύρομαι βασιλέα Πτολεμαῖον. This again passes into "solemnly charge," the translation which Hort (*ad* 1 Pet 1[11]) prefers in 1 Thess 2[12], Eph 4[17]. According to Lightfoot (*ad* 1 Thess 2[12] : cf. note on Gal 5[3]) μαρτύρομαι is never "bear witness to " in the NT any more than in class. Greek, but exx. of this usage can be quoted from the Κοινή, e.g. P Oxy VIII. 1120[11] (early iii/A.D.) κατὰ τοῦτο μαρτύρομαι τὴν βίαν γυνὴ χήρα καὶ ἀσθενής, "I accordingly testify to his violence, being a feeble widow woman " (Ed.), P Amh II. 141[17] (A.D. 350) ἐπιδίδωμι τῇ ἐπιεικείᾳ [σο]υ τάδε τὰ βιβλία [μο]υ τοσοῦτο μαρτυραμένη, "I present this my petition to your excellency, bearing witness to the facts" (Edd.), P Strass I. 5[11] (iii/A.D.) βιβλία ἐπιδεδώκαμεν τῷ [σ]τρατηγῷ αὐτὰ ταῦτα μαρτυρόμενοι, and similarly P Thead 21[16] (A.D. 318).

μάρτυς.

The plur. μάρτυρες is naturally very common, introducing the names of "witnesses" to any contract or legal document, e.g. P Eleph 1[16] (B.C. 311-0) (= *Selections*, p. 4), P Hib I. 89[19] (B.C. 239), P Magd 12[3] (B.C. 217) with the editor's note, P Grenf I. 27[iii. 7] (B.C. 109), P Ryl II. 153[45] (A.D. 138-61). Other exx. of the word are P Lille I. 29[i. 31] (iii/B.C.) ἐναντίον μὴ ἔλασσον ἢ δύο μαρτύρων (cf. Mt 18[16]), P Par 46[10] (B.C. 153) (= Witkowski,[2] p. 86) σὲ αὐτὸν μάρτυρα ἐπισπάσω, P Ryl II. 160(a)[6] (A.D. 14-37) ἐπιτε[τάχα]μεν τοῖς μάρτυσι γράφειν, "we have instructed the witnesses to sign," P Oxy X. 1298[19] (iv/A.D.) σὲ γὰρ μόνον ἔχω μάρτυρα, and the Christian *ib.* VIII. 1162[14] (iv/A.D.) Ἐμμ[ανουὴ]λ μάρτ(υς ?), "Emmanuel is my witness." For God as witness, see P Gen I. 54[6] (iv/A.D.) μάρτυρός ἐστιν ὁ θ[ε]ὸς ὅτι οὐ διὰ λῆ[μ]μα μάχομε, ἀλλὰ μάχομε διὰ σέ. In the important calendar of church services at Oxy-

rhynchus. P Oxy XI. 1357 (A.D. 535-6), mention is made of a service to be held—[5]εἰς τὴν μαρτύρ(ων), "at the Martyrs'": see the editors' note *ad l.* On the early use of μάρτυς to denote one who sealed his testimony with his blood see Lightfoot *ad Clem. Rom.* v. In MGr the form has changed to μάρτυρας.

μασάομαι.

The correct spelling of this verb with a single σ, as in Rev 16[10] (cf. Job 30[4], is found in the magic P Lond 46[269] (iv/A.D.) (= I. p. 73) τοὺς ἰχθύας τοῖς στόμασι μασωμένους, "fish gnawing with their mouths." Cf. Artemid. iv. 33 μασήσασθαι ἄρτους. MGr μασσῶ, "chew."

μασθός.

See *s.v.* μαστός.

μαστιγόω.

An interesting ex. of this verb, which is the regular term for punishment by scourging, occurs in P Flor I. 61[59] (A.D. 85) (= *Chrest.* II. p. 89), where the Prefect, while pronouncing the accused deserving of being scourged—ἄξιος μ[ὲ]ν ἧς μαστιγωθῆναι—releases him as a mark of favour to the multitude—[61]χαρίζομαι δέ σε τοῖς ὄχλοις : cf. Mk 15[15]. Other exx. are P Lille I. 29[ii. 54] (iii/B.C.) ὁ δὲ παραλ[αβὼν τὸ ἀνδρά]ποδον μαστιγωσ[άτω μὴ ἔλασσον ἑκατὸν π[ληγῶν καὶ] στιξάτω τὸ μέτω[πον, P Amh II. 77[23] (A.D. 139) ἐποίησάν με . . . μαστιγοῦσθαι, P Oxy XIV. 1643[11] (A.D. 298) where a man appoints a friend to go in search of a fugitive slave, and when he has found him—εὕργιν καὶ μαστιγοῖν, "to imprison and scourge him," *ib.* VI. 903[9] (iv/A.D.) τοῖς δὲ δούλοις μαστιγγομένοι (*l.* μαστιγουμένοις), and from the inscrr. OGIS 483[177] (ii/B.C.) αὐτὸς μαστιγούσθω ἐν τῶι κύφωνι ("in the pillory") πληγαῖς πεντηκόντα.

μαστίζω.

For this NT ἅπ. εἰρ. (Ac 22[25] : cf. Ev. Petr. 3) see P Lille I. 29[i. 15] (fragment of a code—iii/B.C.) μηδὲ στίξειν, μηδ[ὲ] μα[στ]ί[ζε]ι̣ν, "neither to brand nor to flog them"; but the reading is very doubtful, see *Chrest.* II. p. 412. The verb is used figuratively in *Kaibel* 303[5] μαστίξωσι λόγοις.

μάστιξ.

For the literal sense cf. P Leid W[i. 32] (ii/iii A.D.) (= II. p. 85, cf. p. 160) μάστιγας . . . Αἰγυπτίας, "Egyptian whips," such as many of the Egyptian gods are depicted carrying, and the magic tablet PSI I. 28[4] (iii/iv A.D.?) πικραῖς μάστιξιν, borne by the Erinyes. For the metaphorical sense (Mk 3[10] *al.*), which is found as early as Homer, cf. the Phrygian inscr. C. and B. ii. p. 520, No. 361 ὃς δ' ἂν ἐπιχειρήσει ἕτερον ἐπεισενενκεῖν ("to bring in another body"), λήψεται παρὰ τοῦ ἀθανάτου θεοῦ μάστειγα αἰώνιον, where the editor remarks that "the concluding formula is unique, but seems on the whole to be Chr(istian)": see further Diels *Berliner Sitzungsberichte*, 1901, p. 199 f. Μαστιγοφόρος in the sense of "policeman" is found in P Tebt I. 179 (late ii/B.C.).

μαστός.

In *Syll.* 804 (= [3] 1170 [24] (ii/A.D.) M. Julius Apellas telling the story of his cure in the Asclepieum says—ἥψατο δέ μου καὶ τῆς δεξιᾶς χειρὸς καὶ τοῦ μαστοῦ. Cf. also *Kaibel* 316[3] μάμμη δ' Εὐτυχία μασ[τοὺ]ς κατεκόψατο. For the form μασθός in Rev 1[13] ℵ (cf. Lk 11[27], 23[29] DFG), which WH (*Notes*[2], p. 150) regard as "Western," cf. the magic P Lond 121[203] (iii/A.D.) (= I. p. 91) πρὸς μασθῶν σκλήρια .. -ίαν ·). See also *s.v.* μαζός, and cf. Winer-Schmiedel *Gr.* p. 59.

ματαιολογία.

"vain speaking," "empty argument" (Vg *vaniloquium*), belongs to the higher Κοινή, and is found *ter* in Vett. Valens. e.g. p. 257[23] διὰ τὴν φιλονεικίαν διασαφήσω ἐκκόψας τὰς ματαιολογίας: cf. Poimandres 14[1] (ed. Parthey) διὸ τῆς πολυλογίας τε καὶ ματαιολογίας ἀπαλλαγέντας χρὴ νοεῖν κτλ.

ματαιολόγος.

Vett. Val. p. 301[11] οὐκ ἠβουλήθην ὅμοιον ἑαυτὸν ἀποδεῖξαι τοῖς ματαιολόγοις : cf. Tit 1[10].

μάταιος.

P Oxy I. 58[20] (A.D. 288) τὰ μάταια ἀναλώματα, "useless expense." For the adv. see P Oxy VII. 1027[10] (i/A.D.) (= *Chrest.* II. p. 221) δι' οὗ ματαίως εἰστορεῖ περί τε τοῦ ἀγνοεῖν α[ὐ]τὸν τὴν τῶν ἐμοὶ γενη μένων (*l.* γεγενη-) ἀσφαλιῶν θέσιν, "wherein he vainly relates that he was ignorant of the securities which had been given to me" (Ed.), and the sepulchral inscr. *Kaibel* 208[21]—

Τίς τοὔμὸν δύστηνον ἐπ' οὔνομα γράψε τὸ χαῖρε ;
τίς κωφὴν ματέως θήκατό μοι χάριτα ;

The fluctuation between the fem. μάταιος (Tit 3[9], Jas 1[26]) and ματαία (1 Cor 15[17], 1 Pet 1[18]) is found also in classical texts (Moulton *Gr.* ii. § 64). In Vett. Val. p. 350[16] μάταια = "*res viles*," and in *ib.* p. 276[21] μάταιοι == "*inepti*" : see Kroll's Index, p. 404.

ματαιότης.

This subst., which "suggests either absence of purpose or failure to attain any true purpose" Robinson *Eph.*, p. 189), is found *ter* in the NT (Rom 8[20], Eph 4[17], 2 Pet 2[18]) and frequently in the LXX, but rarely in any secular author, cf. Pollux 6. 134 and Sextus Empiricus *adv. Math.* i. 278. The word is restored in *CIG* IV. 8743[6].

μάτην.

For this adverb, "in vain," "to no purpose," cf. the illiterate P Amh II. 130[6] (A.D. 70) ἐξῆλθα (*l.* ἐξῆλθα ?) εὑρὼν ἐκξ (ἐξ ἑπτὰ μάτιαν πωλούτων (*l.* μάτην πωλοῦντας). "I came away after finding six or seven offering in vain to sell (some barley)" (Edd.), and P Oxy XII. 1417[22] (early iv/A.D.) μάτην οὖν θέλω διὰ σοῦ τοῦ στρατηγοῦ, and for the interesting phrase ἐπὶ μάτην cf. *ib.* III. 530[9] (ii/A.D.) ἐπὶ μάτη[ν] δὲ τῶι τοῦ Πανσιρίωνος τοσοῦτον χρόνον προσκαρτερ[ῶ, "and that I have so long been engaged with Pausirion's business to no purpose" (Edd.). Εἰς μάτην is similarly used by Lucian (*Trag.* 28, 241).

μάχαιρα.

In Ptolemaic papyri the usual forms of the gen. and dat. of this common noun are μαχαίρας, μαχαίρᾳ. P Par 12[15] (B.C. 157) σπασάμενος λέπει με τῇ μαχαίρᾳ εἰς τὸ σκέλος, and the same holds generally true of the LXX cf. Thackeray *Gr.* i. p. 141 f., Helbing *Gr.* p. 31 ff. In the NT only μαχαίρης, μαχαίρῃ, are found, and are normal in papyri of the Roman period. For an ex. from an earlier date see P Tebt I. 16[14] (B.C. 114) ἐν μαχαίρῃ "armed with a sword" (for instrumental ἐν cf. 1 Cor 4[21] and the editors' note). See further Moulton *Proleg.* pp. 38, 48, and *Gr.* ii. p. 118. We may add as further illustrating the word P Tebt I. 48[20] f., B.C. 113 σπασαμένων τὰς μαχαίρας, and P Ryl II. 256 (ii/B.C.) where a young man complains that he has been deprived of—πατ]ρικὴν στρατιωτικὴν μάχαιραν, which he had inherited. In Lk 22[36] Field (*Notes*, p. 76 f.) suggests as an alternative rendering "knives," and compares Dion. Hal. *Ant.* xi 37 ὡς ἐγγὺς ἦν ἐργαστηρίου μαγειρικοῦ, μάχαιραν ἐξαρπάσας ἀπὸ τῆς τραπέζης κτλ. For the dim. μαχαίριον see P Eleph 5[13] (B.C. 284–3) and P Oxy XIV. 1658[8] (iv/A.D. μαχαίρια β μει[κ ρά, and for μαχαιρᾶς (not in L.S.), "cutler," see *ib.* 1070[6] (iii/A.D.) δόντος μοι αὐτὴν τοῦ μαχαιρᾶ, "which (letter) was given me by the cutler" (Edd.). On the μαχαιροφόροι, a kind of military police, see P Amh II. 38[5] (ii/B.C.), P Oxy II. 294[20] (A.D. 22) (= *Selections*, p. 35) al., and the editor's note on *OGIS* 737[6] (iii/B.C.); cf. Rom 13[4]. MGr μαχαίρι.

μάχη.

The weaker sense of μάχη, "contention," "quarrel," which alone is found in the NT (except perhaps in Jas 4[1], may be illustrated from the curious mantic P Ryl I. 28[203] (iv/A.D.) ἐὰν ὁ τρίτος ἅληται ἀηδίαν σημαίνι καὶ μάχας ἕξει διὰ θήλυ, ἔχειν δηλοῖ ἔπειτα χαράς· εὔχου Διί, "if the third toe quiver, it signifies trouble, and the man will have strife on account of a female, and afterwards gladness : pray to Dionysus" (Ed.) : cf. from the inscrr. *Syll.* 737 (= [3] 1109) 74 (before A.D. 175) μάχης δὲ ἐάν τις ἄρξηται ἢ εὑρεθῇ τις ἀκοσμῶν, and *Kaibel* 522[9] (Thessalonica) where a claim is made of a man's having lived without quarrelling with his companions—ἑ[τάρ]ο[ι]σιν δίχα μάχης ζήσας. In PSI I. 71[4] (vi/A.D.) the word is used of what was evidently a serious brawl between two men—μάχην κεινήσαντες πρὸς ἑαυτοὺς ἐν μέσῳ τῆς κώμης. On the μάχιμοι, native troops, see *Chrest.* I. i. p. 382, Meyer *Heerwesen*, p. 64 ff. : the term was applied not only to regular soldiers, but to the armed attendants of officials, e.g. P Tebt I. 112[31] (B.C. 112) with the editors' note.

μάχομαι.

The metaph. use of this verb, cf. *s.v.* μάχη, is seen in the sententious letter of a brother to his sister, P Oxy I. 120[6] (iv/A.D.) χρὴ γάρ τινα ὁρῶντα αἱαυτὸν ἐν δυστυχίᾳ κἂν ἀναχωρῖν καὶ μὴ ἁπλῶς μάχαισθαι (*l.* μάχεσθαι τῷ δεδογμένῳ, "when a man finds himself in adversity he ought to give way and not fight stubbornly against fate" (Edd.) : cf. *Kaibel* 1039[10] κύμασι μαχεσθαι χαλεπόν, and *Syll.* 737[93] (c A.D. 175) where, with reference to the magistrates appointed to keep order in assemblies, it is laid down—ἐπιτείμια δὲ ἔστω τὰ αὐτὰ τῷ εὐκόσμῳ μὴ ἐκβαλόντι τοὺς μαχομένους. In P Par 18¹⁰ (Imperial age?) we find ἐάν construed with the ind. act. (present or future according to accentuation) ἐάν μάχουσιν (or μαχοῦσιν) μετ' ἐσοῦ οἱ ἀδελφοί σου, ἔλθε εἰς [τὸν οἶ]κόν μου: see *BS* p. 201 f. The verbal ἀμάχητος is found in P Oxy XII. 1482⁶ (ii/A.D.) ἀμάχητος ἦν ὁ ἄνεμος, "the wind was irresistible."

μεγαλαυχέω.

This compound verb is read in Jas 3⁵ ℵ, but according to BA it should be separated into its component parts μεγάλα αὐχεῖ: a good parallel is thus afforded to the preceding μικρὸν μέλος ἐστίν. The meaning would then seem to be "hath great things whereof to boast," not the mere empty boasting, which is usually associated with μεγαλαυχέω (see s.v. αὐχέω and cf. Hort *ad* Jas *l.c.*). Other exx. of the verb are Vett. Val. pp. 257¹⁹, 202⁴, 358²⁹.

For the adj. μεγάλαυχος see *Kaibel* 208²⁵ f. (ii/A.D.)—

μάτηρ δ' ἁ μεγάλ[αυχος] ἐφ' υἱάσιν, ἁ πάρος εὔπαις,
οὐχὶ τέκη, κω[φοὺς δ'] ἀντὶ δέδορκε τάφους.

Cf. *ib.* 265¹.

μεγαλεῖος.

Syll 365 (= ³ 798)⁴ (A.D. 37) αὐτοῦ τὸ μεγαλεῖον τῆς ἀθανασίας—with reference to Caesar Germanicus. For μεγαλεῖον as a ceremonial title see further P Oxy IX. 1204¹⁰ (A.D. 299) τὸ μεγαλεῖον αὐτοῦ, "his highness," P Amh II. 82¹⁶ (iii/iv A.D.) δι' ὅπερ κ[ατέφυ]γον ἐπὶ τὸ σὸν μεγα[λεῖον —a Prefect, P Oxy I. 71ⁱⁱ·⁵ (A.D. 303) ὅθεν καὶ αὐτὴ πρόσειμ[ι τῷ σῷ] μεγαλείῳ εὐέλπις οἶσα τῆς ἀπὸ σοῦ βοηθείας τυχεῖν, "therefore I myself (a widow whose affairs had been mismanaged by dishonest overseers) make petition to your highness in the full confidence that I shall obtain assistance from you" (Edd.), and P Thead 19⁵ (iv A.D.) τοὺς ἀδικουμένους ὀρφανο[ὺς], ἡγεμὼν δέσποτα, ἐκδικεῖν εἴωθεν τὸ μεγαλεῖον τὸ σόν. In P Lond V. 1708²²⁹ (A.D. 567?) the plur. is used = "gospels"—ἑκάστου τούτων ἐνωμότως ("on oath") θεμένου ὅρκον ἐπάνω τῶν σεπτῶν "august") μεγαλίων. For the adv. see Aristeas 20 μεγαλείως χρησάμενος τῇ προθυμίᾳ.

μεγαλειότης.

This subst., which occurs several times in the LXX and NT in the sense of "majesty," is also found as a ceremonial title, e.g. CP Herm I. 53ⁱⁱ·²³ (= p. 21) ἡ μεγαλειότης τοῦ λαμπροτάτου ἡγεμόνος. With P Giss I. 40ⁱ·¹¹ (A.D. 212) εἰ[ς τὴν] μεγαλειότητα [το]ῦ Ῥωμα[ίων δῆμον, cf. Lat. *maiestas populi Romani*.

μεγαλοπρεπής.

This adj., which occurs several times in the LXX, but in the NT is confined to 2 Pet 1¹⁷, may be illustrated from the use of the adverb in inscrr., where it is frequently found united with such words as ἐνδόξως and κηδεμονικῶς: cf. also *OGIS* 308⁹ ᵐ (ii/B.C.) where Apollonis, wife of Attalus I., is described as having left behind her good proof of her virtue—διὰ τὸ κεχρῆ[σθ]αι καὶ [θε]οῖς εὐσεβῶς καὶ γονεῦσιν ὁσίω[ς ὥ]ς καὶ πρὸς τὸν ἴδιον ἄνδραν συνβεβιωκέναι μεγαλοπρεπῶς, the last two words being translated by Dittenberger *egregie vixit*. Cf. the account of the preparations for the reception of a Roman Senator in Egypt in P Tebt I. 33⁶

(B.C. 112) (= *Selections*, p. 30) μεγαλο[υ]πρεπέστερον ἐγδεχθῆτωι, "let him be received with special magnificence" (Edd.), PSI V. 481⁸ (v/vi A.D.) Ταυρῖνος ὁ μεγαλοπρεπέστ,ατος), and P Amh II. 154⁵ (vi/vii A.D.) τοῦ μεγαλοπρε(πεστάτου) χαρτουλαρίου, "the most magnificent secretary." For the subst. as a title of address cf. P Oxy VIII. 1165¹ (v/A.D.) ἐρωτηθὶς παρὰ τῆς αὐτοῦ μεγαλοπρεπίας ὅσα ἐχρῆν ἀνεδίδαξα αὐ[τ]ὸν περὶ τῆς ὑμετέρας μεγαλοπρεπίας, "on the inquiry of his magnificence I told him what was fitting about your magnificence," *ib.* l. 155⁶ (vi/A.D.) ἐπειδὴ αἱ προσκυνοῦσαι τὴν ὑμετέραν μεγαλοπρ επειαν) καὶ τὰ παιδία ἀρρωστοῦσιν, ὡς ἔθος ἔχει τὸ ὑμῶν μέγεθος χαρίζεσθαί μου τοῦ λογαρίου, "since your magnificence's obedient servants and their children are ill, I hope your highness will excuse my account" (Edd.).

μεγαλύνω.

With the use of this verb in the pass. in Phil 1²⁰ (cf. Pss 30¹⁷, 69⁵) in the sense of "get glory and praise," cf. the Christian letter P Oxy XII. 1592³ (iii/iv A.D.) where a woman writes to her 'father'—αἰδε(= ἐδε)ξά[μ]ην σου τὰ γράμματα, κ ὑρι)έ μου π(άτε)ρ, καὶ πάνυ ἐμεγαλύνθην καὶ ἠγαλλείασα ὅτει τοιοῦτός μου π(ατ)ήρ τὴν μνήμην ποιεῖται. In MGr μεγαλαίνω and μεγαλώνω are both found.

μεγάλως.

P Amh II. 39⁸ (late ii/B.C.) μεγάλως ἐχάρημεν, P Fay 111³ (A.D. 95-6) μένφομαί σαι (*l.* μέμφομαί σε) μεγάλως, P Giss I. 19³ (ii/A.D.) μεγάλως ἀγωνιῶσα περί σου.

μεγαλωσύνη.

To the ordinary citations for this Biblical word we may add Aristeas 192 οὐ κατὰ τὰς ἁμαρτίας οὐδὲ τὴν μεγαλωσύνην τῆς ἰσχύος τύπτοντος αὐτούς, ἀλλ' ἐπιεικείᾳ χρωμένου τοῦ θεοῦ, "God does not smite them according to their sins nor according to the greatness of His might, but uses forbearance" (Thackeray). See s.v. ἀγαθωσύνη, and A. C. Pearson *Verbal Scholarship*, p. 18 f.

μέγας.

The frequency with which μέγας is employed as a predicate of heathen gods and goddesses, e.g. P Strass II. 81¹⁴ (B.C. 115) Ἴσιδος μεγάλης μητρὸς θεῶν, P Oxy VI. 886¹ (a magical formula—iii/A.D.) μεγάλη Ἶσις ἡ κυρία (cf. Ac 19²⁸ μεγάλη ἡ Ἄρτεμις Ἐφεσίων), makes it the more noticeable that only once in the NT is the same epithet applied to the true God (Tit 2¹³) : see Thieme p. 36 f. For the repeated μέγας μέγας = a superlative, imitated from the Egyptian (Wilcken), see the question to the oracle in P Fay 137¹ (i/A.D.) (= *Selections*, p. 69) Σοκωννωκοννὶ θεῶι μελο (*l.* μεγάλωι). χρηματισόν μοι, ἦ μείνωι ἐν Βακχιάδι; "to Sokanobkoneus the great great god. Answer me, Shall I remain in Bacchias?"; cf. BGU III. 748ⁱⁱⁱ·⁶ (A.D. 48), *ib.* II. 590⁷ (A.D. 177-8) *al.* In a Eumeneian inscr. published in *C. and B.* ii. p. 386, No. 232⁵, we hear of Ῥουβῆ μεγάλοιο θ[εο]ῦ θεράποντι, and Ramsay regards the name Roubes as a Grecized form of the Jewish Reuben (Ῥουβήν), and the "great god" as Jehovah. For μέγας used of the Ptolemaic kings, cf. *OGIS* 94² with reference to Ptolemy V. Epiphanes—ὑπὲρ βασιλέως Πτολεμαίου, θεοῦ Ἐπιφανοῦς μεγάλου Εὐχαρίστου, and the other exx. cited by Dittenberger *ad l.*

In P Magd 36[1] (iii/B.C.) (= *Chrest.* I. p. 365) Μαρρῆς μέγας, the epithet is used to distinguish the "older" of two persons bearing the same name, like our own "senior": so in P Petr II. 25 (i)[9] (iii/B.C.) Μάνρης μέγας, not "long Manres," as Mahaffy *ad l.*, cf. also *ib.* pp. 32, 42. Similarly μικρός means "junior."

In P Hib I. 29 (*a*) recto[9] (c. B.C. 265) (= *Chrest.* I. p. 306) provision is made that a proclamation shall be inscribed on a white notice-board—γράψας εἰς λεύκωμα μ[ε]γάλοις γράμμασιν, where the adj. points to "large" distinct letters, in order to draw attention to what was written: cf. P Oxy VIII. 1100[3] (A.D. 206) εὐδήλοις γράμμασι, with the editor's note. [This is probably the meaning to be attached to the πηλίκα γράμματα of Gal 6[11]: cf. Milligan *Documents*, p. 23 f.]. An interesting use of the adj. is also afforded by the illiterate P Oxy VII. 1069[27] (iii/A.D.) σπούδασον γὰρ τὸ κειθώνειν μου γενέστε (*l.* γενέσθαι) πρὸ λόγον, καὶ κ[α]λὰ μέτρα αὐτῷ βαλέτωσαν καὶ μεγάλε (*l.* μεγάλαι?) ἔστωσαν ἐπὶ ῥείδης (*l.* ῥίζης) αὐτοῦ, "be careful to have my tunic made properly, and let them put good measure into it, and be large-handed (i.e. generous, unstinting) in the colouring" (Ed.). See further *s.vv.* μείζων and μέγιστος. In MGr the nom. is altered by the stem to μεγάλος.

μέγεθος,

which in the NT is confined to Eph 1[19] in the general sense of "greatness," is common in our sources as a ceremonial title, e.g. P Oxy I. 71[i. 4] (petition to the Prefect —A.D. 303) τὴν ἱκ[ετ]ηρίαν προσάγω εὔελπις ὢν τῆς ἀπὸ τοῦ σοῦ μεγέθους δικαιοκρισίας τυχεῖν, "I make my petition to you with full confidence that I shall obtain justice from your highness" (Edd.), and *ib.* XII. 1467[18] (A.D. 263) where a woman, "being blessed with children" and "able to write with the greatest ease," claims from the Prefect the right to act without a guardian—διὰ τούτων μου τῷ[ν] βιβλειδίων προσφω (*l.* προσφωνῶ) τῷ σῷ μεγέθι πρὸς τὸ δύνασθαι ἀνεμποδίστως ἃς ἐντεύθεν ποιοῦμαι οἰκ[ον]ομία[ς] διαπράσσεσθαι, "I appeal to your highness by this my application with the object of being enabled to carry out without hindrance all the business which I henceforth transact" (Edd.). The transition to this usage is seen in such a passage as P Tebt II. 326[4] (c. A.D. 266) ἐπὶ τὸ σὸν μέγεθος καταφεύγω, "I take refuge in your power"—a widow's petition to the Prefect asking that her brother might be appointed guardian of her daughter: cf. P Strass I. 5[6] (A.D. 262) κατέφυγον ἐπὶ τὸ μέγεθος τοῦ λαμπροτάτου Θεοδότου ἡγεμόνος. We may cite from the inscr. OGIS 519[24] (c. A.D. 245) περὶ ὧν ἀπά[ντων] ἐγράφη πρὸς τὸ σόν,] Σεβαστέ, μέγεθος, and *C. and B.* ii. p. 700, No. 635[4] ἐνορκιζόμεθα δὲ τὸ μέγεθος τοῦ θεοῦ καὶ τοὺς καταχθονίους δαίμονας μηδένα ἀδικῆσαι τὸ μνημίον, where Ramsay notes that the expression τ. μέγεθος τ. θεοῦ is not native Phrygian, and is probably due to Christian feeling or Jewish thought.

μεγιστάν.

This late Greek word = "a great one," "a courtier," (Lob. *Phryn.* p. 196 f., Sturz *Dial. Mac.* p. 180 ff.), is

found, generally in the plur. μεγιστᾶνες, in the later books of the LXX (e.g. Dan 5[23]), and *ter* in the NT (Mk 6[21], Rev 6[15], 18[23]): cf. also Pss. Sol. ii. 36 οἱ μεγιστᾶνες τῆς γῆς, perhaps the leading men of Palestine, but more probably the victorious party of Caesar (Ryle and James). From the papyri we may cite P Leid W[vi. 39] (ii/iii A.D.) (= II. p. 101) θυμοκάτοχον πρὸς βασ[ιλεῖς] ἢ μεγιστάναις (*l.* μεγιστάνας), "(formula) for restraining anger against kings or great men."

μέγιστος.

The occurrence of the superlative of μέγας only once in the NT, 2 Pet 1[4], where it is elative, is in keeping with its comparatively rare use in Hellenistic Greek. It survives principally as an elative epithet of gods, e.g. P Par 15[i. 17] (B.C. 120) τῆς μεγίστης θεᾶς Ἥρας: cf. *Syll* 342 (= [3]762,[23] (c. B.C. 48) νεωστ]εί τε τοῦ βασιλέως Βυρεβίστα πρώτου καὶ μεγίστου γεγ]ονότος τῶν ἐπὶ Θράκης βασιλέων, and *ib.*[25] ἐν τῇ πρώτῃ καὶ με γίσ[τῃ βασι]λία. The adj. is also found in such idiomatic phrases as P Petr II. 13 (19)[6] (B.C. 258–253) ὃ ἐμοὶ [μ]έγιστόν ἐσται, "which will be my main object," BGU IV. 1204[8] (B.C. 28) σεατοῦ [ἐπιμέλου ἵν'] ὑγιαίνῃς ὃ δὴ μέγιστόν ἐστι, *ib.* 1208[50] (B.C. 27–6) ὃ δὴ μέγιστον ἡγοῦμαι, *al.* Cf. also P Tebt I. 33[17] (B.C. 112) (= *Selections*, p. 31) ἐπὶ πάν[των] τὴν μεγίστην φροντίδα ποιουμένου, "taking the greatest care on all points," P Oxy II. 292[9] (c. A.D. 25) (= *Selections*, p. 38) χαριεῖσαι δέ μοι τὰ μέγιστα, "you will do me the greatest favour," and P Heid 6[27] (iv/A.D.) (= *Selections*, p. 127) ἐπὶ μέγιστον χρόνον, "for many years." On μεγάλη in the sense of μεγίστη in Mt 22[36] see Field *Notes*, p. 16 f. The double superlative μεγιστότατος is seen in the horoscope P Lond 130[49] (i/ii A.D.) (= I. p. 134) ὅθεν ὁ μὲν μεγιστότατος ἥλιος καὶ τῶν ὅλων δυνάστης.

μεθερμηνεύω,

"translate" (from one language into another), is found in P Tebt I. 164[i. 1] (late ii/B.C.) ἀντί[γραφον] συγγραφῆς Αἰγυπτίας . . . μεθη[ρ]μηνευμένης, translation of a demotic document regarding the sale or cession of land: cf. P Giss I. 36[6] (B.C. 161) (cited *s.vv.* Ἑλληνιστί), BGU III. 1002[6] (B.C. 55) ἀντίγραφον συγγραφῆς πράσεως Αἰγυπτίας μεθηρμηνευμένης κατὰ τὸ δυνατόν, *Preisigke* 5275[23] (A.D. 11) ἀντίγραφον ἀπ' ἀντιγράφου ὑπογραφῆς Αἰγυπτίας Ἑλληνιστὶ μεθερμηνευμένης κατὰ τὸ δυνατόν, BGU I. 140[1] (imperial letter written at Alexandria(?) in the time of Hadrian, cf. Wilcken *Hermes* xxxvii. (1902), p. 84 ff.) ἀν'τί]γρ[αφον] ἐπιστ[ολ(ῆς) τοῦ κυρίου μεθ]ηρ[μηνευ]μένης, and P Leid W[viii. 21] (ii/iii A.D.) βίβλον, ἢν οὐδεὶς ἴσχυσε μεθερμηνεῦσαι (*l.* -σαι) ἢ πρᾶξαι, *ib.*[x. 42] ἐκλήθη Ἑρμῆς, δι' οὗ τὰ πάντα μεθερμηνευσται (*l.* μεθερμ-) (*paronom.*). See also Aristeas 38 προῃρήμεθα τὸν νόμον ὑμῶν μεθερμηνευθῆναι γράμμασιν Ἑλληνικοῖς ἐκ τῶν παρ' ὑμῖν λεγομένων Ἑβραϊκῶν γραμμάτων.

μέθη,

"drunkenness," is found in the plur., as in Rom 13[13], Gal 5[21], in the invitation to the celebration of Hadrian's accession P Giss I. 3[8] (A.D. 117) (= *Chrest.* I. p. 575) γέλωσι καὶ μέθαις ταῖς ἀπὸ κρήνης τὰς ψυχὰς ἀνέντες. See also Vett. Val. p. 90[13] εἰς ἡδονὰς καὶ μέθας ἀναλίσκουσι τὰ περικτηθέντα, and cf. *Poimandres* § 27 (ed. Reitzenstein, p. 337) ὦ λαοί, ἄνδρες γηγενεῖς, οἱ μέθη καὶ ὕπνῳ ἑαυτοὺς ἐκδεδωκότες καὶ τῇ ἀγνωσίᾳ τοῦ θεοῦ, νήψατε, παύσασθε δὲ κραιπαλῶντες, θελγόμενοι ὕπνῳ ἀλόγῳ.

μεθιστάνω, μεθίστημι.

in the sense of "remove from," is seen in a contract regarding letting a house, BGU IV. 1116³² (B.C. 13) μεθισταμέ(νη) τῆ(ς) μισθώσεως ἐντὸς τοῦ χρό(νου) καὶ ἑτέρο(ις) μεταμισθο(ῦν): cf. *ib.* 1117⁴³, 1159¹⁵, and the late P Oxy I. 135²¹ (A.D. 579) μεθ[[ε]]ίστασθαι εἰς ἕτερον τόπον. For the verb, "depart from life," "die," see P Lond 354¹⁰ (*c.* B.C. 10) (= II. p. 164) φάσκοντες τὸν πατέρα αὐτῶν ἐκ τοῦ ζῆν μεθεστακέναι, and for a causal sense, see BGU I. 36¹³ (ii/A.D.) τοῦ ζῆν με[τ|α[σ]τῆσαι, and without τοῦ ζῆν (cf. Ac 13²²) OGIS 308⁴ (ii/B.C.) μεθέστηκεν εἰς θεούς, which the editor describes as "usitata formula de regum regiaeque familiae hominum mortibus," and compares *ib.* 338⁴ (ii/B.C.) μεθισ]τάμενος ἐξ ἀνθρώπων ἀπολέλοιπεν τῆ[μ πατρί]δα ἡμῶν ἐλευθέραν (of Attalus III.), and 339¹⁶ (*c.* B.C. 125) τῶν τε βασιλέων εἰς θεοὺς μεταστάντων. Cf. also Vett. Val. p. 94⁹ ἔκπτωτος ἐγένετο καὶ ἑκὼν μετέστη (*mortem sibi conscivit*).

μεθοδία.

This noun, which in the NT occurs only in Eph 4¹⁴, 6¹¹, in the sense of "scheming," "craftiness," is said by Grimm-Thayer to occur "neither in the O.T. nor in prof. auth." It is found, however, in late papyri in the more primary sense of "method," e.g. P Oxy VIII. 1134⁹ (A.D. 421) where certain rents are said to have been collected πρὸς τὴν μεθοδίαν ἀκολούθως τῷ δοθέντι ὑπὸ σοῦ λόγῳ τοῦ τε λήμματος καὶ τοῦ ἐξωδιασμοῦ, "in method corresponding to the account given by you of receipt and expenditure" (Ed.), *ib.* I. 130¹⁸ (A.D. 583) τὴν μεθοδίαν τρέψαι, "to conduct my dealings." *ib.*²⁴ ἣν ἐ|ν]δείκνυμι μεθοδίαν περὶ τὴν εἴσπραξιν, "the method of collection adopted by me" (Edd.), and P Amh II. 140¹⁵ (vi/A.D.) τῷ κυρίως ὑπὲρ αὐτῆς τὴν μεθοδίαν κατ᾽ ἐμοῦ ποιουμένῳ, with reference to a loan to be repaid to the person lawfully demanding it. For the verb see P Leid W XVI.¹⁷ (ii/iii A.D.) (= II. p. 137) ἐρώτα, ἵνα αὐτὸς ἀπολί(= εἴ)ψῃ ἢ μεθοδεύσῃ (*altera ratione iterum tractet*): δύναται γὰρ πάντα ὁ θεὸς οὗτος. Cf. MGr ἡ μέθοδο, "method." According to Thumb (*Handbook*, p. 58) "the pl. is rarely used, yet a pl. οἱ μέθοδες may be formed for the word ἡ μέθοδο taken from the literary language."

μεθόριον.

On the formation of this word, which is read in Mk 7³¹ ANX *al.*, see Robertson *Gr.* p. 156 f.

μεθύσκω.

It seems impossible to draw any clear distinction between μεθύσκω and μεθύω: in 1 Thess 5⁷, e.g., they are virtually synonymous. But the idea of *status* (as distinguished from *actus*), which belongs more naturally to the latter, comes out well in the recipe of the magical papyrus P Lond 121¹⁸⁰ (iii/A.D.) (= I. p. 90) enabling a man πολλὰ πίνειν καὶ

μὴ μεθύειν. For μεθύσκω cf. *Kaibel* 646¹¹ᶠ· (not before iii/iv A.D.)—

    ζῶντί μοι, εἴ τι ἔχεις, μεταδός, τέφραν δὲ μεθύσκων
       πηλὸν ποιήσεις καὶ οὐκ ὁ θανὼν πίεται.

μέθυσος.

Deissmann (*LAE*, p. 321) gives a striking series of parallels to the vices enumerated in 1 Cor 6⁹ᶠ· from counters used in an ancient game: thus to μέθυσοι correspond the counters *ebriose* and *vinose*. For μέθυσος applied to men, as in 1 Cor *l.c.*, 5¹¹ (cf. Lob. *Phryn.* p. 151), see the exx. in Durham *Menander*, p. 77 f., and add P Oxy XV. 1828³ (*c.* iii/A.D.), where πλεονέκτης also occurs (as in 1 Cor *ll.c.*).

μεθύω.

See *s.v.* μεθύσκω, and add P Hal 1¹⁹⁴ᶠᶠ· (mid. iii/B.C.) μεθύοντος ἀδικιῶν. ὅταν τις τῶν εἰς τὸ σῶ[μ]α ἀδικημάτ[ων] μεθύων ἢ νύκτωρ ἢ ἐν ἱερῶι ἢ ἐν ἀγορᾶι ἀδικήσηι, διπλασί[αν] τὴν ζημίαν ἀποτεισάτω τῆς γεγραμμένης, and the temple scribbling at Abydos *Preisigke* 1079 Νικάνωρ ἥκω μεθ᾽ Ἡρακλέας [Δ]ρυγχίτιδος μεθύων, where, however, we ought perhaps to read μεθ᾽ ὑῶν. See also the new Logion P Oxy I. 1¹¹ᶠᶠ· λέγει Ἰ(ησοῦ)ς ἔ[σ]την ἐν μέσῳ τοῦ κόσμου . . καὶ εὗρον πάντας μεθύοντας καὶ οὐδένα εὗρον δειψῶντα ἐν αὐτοῖς, and cf. Reitzenstein *Poimandres*, p. 240 f. and the passage quoted *s.v.* μέθη. Hesychius understands μεθύει in 1 Cor 11²¹ as = πεπλήρωται, in view of the contrast with πεινᾷ: for this use of the verb cf. Hos 14⁸.

μείζων.

Like μέγας (see *s.v.*) μείζων is used in the sense of "senior" in ostracon receipts, e.g. *Ostr* 144³ (A.D. 128) διέγραψεν Πετορζμῆθ(ις) μείζω(ν), 213³ (A.D. 147), and 1199² (Rom.). The word is applied to one in authority, an official, in P Lond 214²² (A.D. 270–275) (= II. p. 162, *Chrest.* I. p. 209) μέλλω [γ]ὰρ περὶ τούτο(υ) ἐντυχεῖν [τ]ῷ μείζονι: cf. P Oxy VI. 900¹⁹ (A.D. 322) μὴ εἰς ἀνάγκην με γενέ[σ]θαι ἐντυ]χεῖν τοῖς μείζοσιν περὶ τούτου, "not be reduced to appeal to the officials upon this matter" (Edd.), with the editors' note. *Ib.* XIV. 1626⁵ (A.D. 325) Πτολεμαίου μείζονος τῆς αὐτῆς κώμης is regarded by GH as the earliest ex. of μείζων "to denote a particular village-official as distinct from a 'higher' official in general": this usage is common from the end of v/A.D. onwards, e.g. P Lond 38¹ (v/vi A.D.). For the more general uses of the adj. cf. P Tebt I. 33⁴ (B.C. 112) (= *Selections*, p. 30) ἐν μείζονι ἀξιώματι κα[ὶ] τιμῆι κείμενος, "occupying a position of highest (cf. *Proleg.* p. 78) rank and honour"—of a Roman senator. BGU V. 1¹⁰¹ (*c.* A.D. 150) τῶν ἐπὶ φόνοις ἢ μίζοσιν ἁμαρτήμασιν κολαζομένων, P Oxy II. 237 viii·¹⁷ (A.D. 186) τότ᾽ ἐὰν θαρρῇ τοῖς τῆς κατηγορίας ἐλέγχοις, τὸν μείζονα ἀγῶνα ἐ[ἰ]σελεύσεται, "if he has confidence in the proofs of his accusation, he shall enter upon the more serious law-suit" (Edd.), and P Fay 20² (iii/iv A.D.) εἰστε[λ]εῖν . . μείζω ἢ δύνανται, "to pay a greater (sum) than they are able." For τὸ μεῖζον as a subst. see P Giss I. 47⁷ (Hadrian) (= *Chrest.* I. p. 382) where a corslet is described as τὸ μεῖζον ἐλα[φ]ρότατος, "very light in view of its size." The double comp. μειζότερος, as in 3 Jn⁴, is found in P Lips Inv. No. 508⁸ (A.D. 381) (= *Archiv* iii. p. 173) ὁ μειζότερος [υ]ἱ[ὸς] ἐμοῦ, "my elder son," P Oxy I. 131²⁵ (vi/vii A.D.) ταῦτα δέδωκεν Ἐλισάβετ τῇ μειζοτέρᾳ ἀδελφῇ, and BGU II. 368⁹ (A.D. 615) Φλ(αουίῳ) . . τῷ μεγαλοπρεπεστάτῳ κόμετι καὶ μειζοτέρῳ Στρατηγίου τοῦ πανευφήμου: cf. Jannaris *Gr.* § 506.

μέλας

is used in the neut. "ink," as in 2 Cor 3³, 2 Jn¹², 3 Jn¹³, in P Grenf II. 38⁸ (B.C. 81) μ[έ]λαν στατῆρου ὀκτώ, P Oxy II. 326 τὸ βροχίον τοῦ μέλανος, "the ink-pot," and P Leid X⁸·¹ff· (iii/iv A.D.) (= II. p. 229 f.) where a recipe for making ink is found—τρίψας τὸ ἴδιον (*l.* τὸ ἰὸν?), καὶ τὸ θεῖον, καὶ τὴν στυπτηρίαν λείαν, εὖ μάλα μεῖξας (*l.* μίξας) ἐπιμελῶς τρίβε, καὶ χρῶ ὡς μέλανι γραφικῷ, "trita rubiginem (?), et sulphur, et alumen contusum, et probe mixta diligenter terito, et utitor prouti atramento scriptorio" (Ed.), see *s.v.* μετά (1 f.). For other applications of the adj. cf. P Meyer 7⁹ (A.D. 130) κυάμο(υ) μέλανο(s), "black beans," P Oxy XIV. 1631²³ (A.D. 280) ἐλαι[ῶ]ν μελαινῶν, "black olives," P Par 574¹²⁴⁷ (iii A.D.) (= *Selections,* p. 114) παραδίδωμί σε εἰς τὸ μέλαν χάος ἐν ταῖς ἀπωλίαις, and *Kaibel* 274⁸ μέλας θάνατος. Μέλας is used as a distinguishing epithet in P Amh II. 62⁶ (ii B.C.) (cited *s.v.* λευκός, and as a proper name in P Oxy XIV. 1682³ (iv A.D.) ἀπέστειλα [[τινα]] Μέλανα, "I am sending Melas," and in P Grenf II. 77 (iii/iv A.D.). For the form μέλανος,—η,—ον see P Iand 35⁵ (ii/iii A.D.) βοῦν μελ[ά]νην with the editor's note, and for μελάγχρως see Mayser *Gr.* p. 296.

μέλει.

For the impersonal μέλει, "it is a care," c. dat. of the person and περί, as in Mt 22¹⁶ *al.,* cf. P Lond 897²⁷ (A.D. 84) (= III. p. 207) οἶδα γὰρ ἐμαυτῶι (cf. 1 Cor 4⁴) [μὲν ?] ὅτι μέλει σοι πολλὰ περὶ ἐμοῦ, μελήσει σοι δὲ ὡς ὑπὲρ ἰδίου τέκνου, "for I am conscious that you are as much concerned about me as you will be concerned regarding your own child," P Oxy VIII. 1155⁵ (A.D. 104) εὐθέως ἔμελκε ἐμοὶ περὶ τοῦ πραγαματος (*l.* πράγματος) οὗ με ἠρώτηκες, "I immediately attended to the matter about which you asked me" (Ed.), P Ryl II. 241⁵ (iii A.D.) μελησάτσω (*l.*-άτω) σοι περὶ ὧν σοι ἐνετίλατο Σωκ(ράτης), "be careful of the orders which Socrates gave you" (Edd.). Other exx. of the verb are P Amh II. 131⁸ (early ii A.D.) μελησάτω σοι ὅπως ἀγορασθῇ τὰ κενώματα, "see that the empty jars are bought" (Edd.), P Oxy III. 530⁸ (ii A.D.) τὸ δὲ πραγμάτιον περὶ οὗ ἔγραψα Θέωνι μὴ μελέτω σοι εἰ μὴ τετέλεσται, "do not be concerned that the matter about which I wrote to Theon has not been carried out" (Edd.), and *ib.* VI. 930¹¹ (ii/iii A.D.) ἐμέλησε δέ μοι πέμψαι καὶ πυθέσθαι περὶ τῆς ὑγίας σου, "I took care to send and ask about your health" (Edd.), and from the inscrr. *C. and B.* ii. p. 700, No. 635 (iii A.D.) οὐκ ἤμην· ἐγενόμην· οὐκ ἔσομαι· οὐ μέλι μοι· ὁ βίος ταῦτα (note the idiomatic ταῦτα).

μελετάω.

Hesychius defines this verb as = ἀσκέω, ἐπιμελέομαι, γυμνάζομαι, i.e. "exercise oneself in," a meaning which suits admirably both the NT passages Ac 4²⁵, 1 Tim 4¹⁵, in which it occurs; cf. Ps 1² ἐν τῷ νόμῳ αὐτοῦ μελετήσει, "in

His law will he exercise himself" (PBV), and see Field *Notes,* p. 209, adding Vett. Val. p. 330²² ἣν (*sc.* ἀθανασίαν) ἕκαστος ἡμῶν καθ' ἡμέραν μελετᾷ γυμναζόμενος λαμβάνειν. On the other hand P Lond 47²⁸ (ii A.D.) (= I. p. 82) λέγε μελετῶν points rather to the common translation "meditate," "ponder on." The noun is found in BGU IV. 1125⁵ (B.C. 13) τὰ[ς] μελέτας καὶ τὰς ἐπιδίξις . . χορη[γ]ήσωι αὐτῶι Ναρκίσσωι. MGr μελετῶ has the meanings "intend," "study."

μέλι

has a place in all phases of Greek from Homer to MGr: cf. from the Κοινή—P Oxy II. 234ⁱⁱ·¹⁰ (a medical prescription—ii/iii A.D.) πρόσμιξον μέλι καὶ ῥόδινον, "add honey and rose-extract," *ib.* VI. 936ⁱⁱ (iii A.D.) ἡμίχουν μέλιτος, "half a chous of honey." This last papyrus shows also ¹⁰ μελικηρίδα, "honey comb," and ¹¹ μελίτινα στεφάνια γ, which the editors render "3 honey-sweet garlands"; cf. the otherwise unknown adj. μελίσσιος as interpolated in the TR of Lk 24⁴². For acc. μέλιν see P Iand 18¹ (vi/vii A.D.) and for μελίτιν see *Kaibel* 719⁹ γλυκὺν ὡς μελίτιν.

μελίσσιος.

See *s.v.* μέλι.

Μελίτη.

For this proper name in Ac 28¹, WH (cf. RV marg.) read Μελιτήνη with B*, but there can be little doubt that this reading is due to dittography of the following ἡ νῆ(σος). Preuschen (*HZNT ad* Ac *l.c.*) states that the administration of the islands subject to Sicily was in the hands of a governor who bore the title—*municipi Melitensium primus omnium* (CIL X. 7495), and compares *IG* XIV. 601 Λ(ού)κιος Κα[στρί]κιος Κυρ(είνα) Προύδηνς ἱππεὺς Ῥωμ(αίων) πρῶτος Μελιταίων (cf. Ac 28⁷) καὶ πάτρων ἄρξας καὶ ἀμφιπολεύσας θεῷ Αὐγούστῳ . . .

μέλλω.

In the NT μέλλω is construed 84 times with the pres. inf.: cf. P Par 43² (B.C. 154) μέλλω δὲ ἰσάγειν ἐν τῷ μεσορὴ μηνί, *ib.* 48¹⁹ (B.C. 153) καταπλεῖν μέλλομεν πρὸς τὸν βασιλέα, P Meyer 20⁹ (1st half iii A.D.) μέλλι πρὸς ἡμᾶς ἔρχεσθαι, ¹⁸μέλλω σοι ἀεὶ γράφειν, P Tebt II. 416⁵ (iii/ A.D.) μέλλω μένιν εἰς Ἀντινόου, and P Oxy VIII. 1156¹⁰ (iii A.D.) μέλλο[με]ν χόρτου χρίαν ἔχιν. For the constr. with the fut. inf., which is obsolete in the NT (cf. TR Ac 23³⁰), cf. *Syll* 432¹⁰ (B.C. 326–5) ὁμόσασιν . . . [ποιή]σεσθαι τὴν ἐπίτροπὴν καθ' ὅτι ἂν μέλλει ἔσ[ε]σθαι κτλ. Μέλλω followed by the aor. inf. act. is seen in such passages as P Giss I. 12⁵ (ii A.D.) ὁσάκις ἐὰν μέλλῃς πέμψαι, P Oxy XII. 1488²⁰ (ii A.D.) ἔμελλον γὰρ ἀνελθεῖν, and *ib.* VII. 1067¹⁷ (iii A.D.) εἰ μέλλεις ἐλθεῖν ἐλθέ, "come if you are coming," and by the aor. inf. pass. in P Goodsp Cairo 3¹⁰ (iii B.C.) ἡνίκα ἤμελλον κοιμηθῆναι ἔγραψα ἐπιστόλια β, and P Par 47¹² (*c.* B.C. 153) (= Witkowski,² p. 89, *Selections,* p. 22) κἂν ἴδῇς ὅτι μέλλομεν σωθῆναι, τότε βαπτιζώμεθα, "and even if you know that we are about to be saved, just at that time we are immersed in trouble." According to Meisterhans *Gr.* p. 169 the ἠ–augment appears in the Attic inscrr. after B.C. 300. Only one instance of the ἐ–augment is found at Priene, viz. *Priene* 11⁵ (*c.* B.C. 297) ἐμελ[λον τυχεῖν (see Rouffiac *Recherches*, p. 27). For the NT usage see Moulton *Gr.* ii. p. 188. Εἰς τὸ μέλλον in the sense of "next year" is seen in P Lond 1231⁴ (A.D. 144) (= III. p. 108) τὴν εἰς τὸ μ[έ]λλον γεωργείαν—a good parallel to the meaning in Lk 13⁹ as against AV "then after that," RV "thenceforth": cf. Field *Notes*, p. 65.

In Mt 24⁶ μελλήσετε δὲ ἀκούειν πολέμους the meaning may be "you must *then* be prepared to hear of wars," but this use of the fut. tense is out of the question in 2 Pet 1¹² μελλήσω ἀεὶ ὑμᾶς ὑπομιμνήσκειν, as Mayor *ad l.* points out, and accordingly he prefers with Field (*Notes*, p. 240) to read μελήσω instead of μελλήσω with the meaning, "I shall take care to remind you." In MGr μελλούμενο is used for "the future." For compounds, like μελλοπρόεδρος, "a future president," cf. P Giss I. p. 87 f.

μέλος.

P Tebt II. 331¹¹ (*c.* A.D. 131) ἐ]πήνεγκά[ν μο]ι πληγὰς εἰς πᾶν μέλ[ο]ς το[ῦ σ]ώματος, "belaboured me with blows on every limb of my body" (Edd.): cf. P Lips I. 37²¹ (A.D. 389). Cf. also *Kaibel* 547⁷ (i/A.D.) πνεῦμα με[λ]ῶν ἀπέλυε, *ib.* 261²² (ii/A.D.) ψυχῆς ἐκ μελέων ἀπ[ο]πταθείσης.

Μελχισεδέκ.

For the description of Μελχισεδέκ as ἀπάτωρ, ἀμήτωρ, in Heb 7³, see the reff. under these words, and add PSI V. 450⁶⁰ (ii/iii A.D.) (with note), *ib.* 458⁵ (A.D. 155). The name is never spelt in Greek with ζ either in the Old or in the New Testament (Burkitt, *Syriac Forms*, p. 28).

μεμβράνα,

a Grecized form of the Lat. *membrana*, "parchment," said to be so called from Pergamum in Mysia, where it was first manufactured (see Thompson *Greek and Latin Palaeography* (Oxford, 1912), p. 28 ff.). In the NT the word is found only in 2 Tim 4¹³, where the reference is probably to parchment rolls of the OT Scriptures. Dibelius (*HZNT ad l.*) cites Theodosius III. p. 695 Schulze μεμβράνας τὰ εἰλητὰ κέκληκεν· οὕτω γὰρ Ῥωμαῖοι καλοῦσι τὰ δέρματα. ἐν εἰλητοῖς δὲ εἶχον πάλαι τὰς θείας γραφάς. οὕτω δὲ καὶ μέχρι τοῦ παρόντος ἔχουσιν οἱ Ἰουδαῖοι.

μέμφομαι.

The phrase εἰς τὸ ἐν μηδενὶ μεμφθῆναι is common, e.g. BGU I. 18¹⁶ (A.D. 169), P Oxy I. 82⁷ (mid. iii/A.D.), *ib.* XII. 1426¹⁶ (A.D. 332), and PSI I. 86¹³ (A.D. 367-375). For the acc. constr., as in Heb 8⁸ ℵ* AD* (but dat. ℵ° B), cf. P Fay 111³ (A.D. 95-6) μέμφομαί σαι (*l.* μέμφομαί σε) μεγάλως ἀπολέσας χ[υ]ρίδια δύω, "I blame you greatly for the loss of two pigs." P Oxy XII. 1481⁵ (early ii/A.D.) μέμφομαι δὲ τὸν εἴπαντά σοι, "I blame the person who told you," P Ryl II. 230¹³ (mid. iii/A.D.) ἐὰν δέ τις ἀμ[έ]λεια γένηται, οὐκ ἐμ[ὲ ο]ὖν μέμψι ἀλλ[ὰ σεαυτόν, "if any neglect occurs, you will not blame me but yourself" (Edd.). For μεμπτός cf. BGU IV. 1079³² (A.D. 41) (= *Selections*, p. 40) ἐὰν τὰ παρ(ὰ) σατοῦ ποίσῃς (*l.* σαυτοῦ ποιήσῃς) οὐκ εἶ μεμπτός, "if you manage your own affairs, you are not to be blamed," P Oxy XIV. 1772⁵ (late iii/A.D.) ἐγὼ δὲ οὐκ εἰμι μεμπτός, ἀλλὰ σύ . . . In P Amh II. 63⁵ (iii/A.D.) συνκαταθέμενος βραδέως μεμφητά, the editors suggest that μεμφητά, which does not occur elsewhere, may = μεμπτά,

and that the meaning is that the person referred to had taken a long time in producing an unsatisfactory result. Reference may be made to the striking tomb-inscr. *Kaibel* 574⁷ (end of i/A.D.)—

> εἰ δὲ τριήκοντα ζωῆς μόνον ἔσχ' ἐνιαυτούς
> καὶ δύο, τῷ φθονερῷ δαίμονι μεμφόμεθα.

The noun μέμψις is seen in such passages as P Oxy X. 1255¹⁹ (A.D. 292) εἰς τὸ μηδεμίαν μέμψιν ἐπακολουθῆσαι, "so that no complaint may ensue" (Edd.), *ib.* I. 140¹⁶ (A.D. 550) εἰς τὸ μηδεμίαν μέμψιν ἢ ἀμελίαν ἢ κατάγνωσίν τινα περὶ ἐμὲ γενέσθαι.

μεμψίμοιρος.

With μεμψίμοιροι, "complainers," in Jude ¹⁶, cf. the *querulosi* of *Assumption of Moses* vii. 7, occurring in a passage which seems largely to have influenced Jude's language (see James' *Second Peter and Jude* p. xlv. (in *CGT*)). The word is found in the sense of "censorious," in Vett. Val. p. 17¹², where it is joined with κολαστικός. For ἀμεμψιμοίρητος, "blameless," see P Par 63viii. 14 (B.C. 164) δικαίως [πολι]τευσάμενος ἐμαυτὸν ἀμεμψιμοίρητον παρέσχημαι, and *Cagnat* IV. 288⁸ (mid. ii/B.C.?) ἀμεμψιμοίρητ[ος δὲ] ἐν πᾶσιν γεγενημένος, and for the adverb see P Ryl II. 154¹⁹ (a contract of marriage—A.D. 66) ἥ τε Θαισάριον καὶ ὁ Χα[ι]ρήμων ἀμεμψιμοιρήτως καθότι π[ρό]τ[ερο]ν [συ]νεβίουν. Teles p. 56² (ed. Hense) unites ἀπερίεργος and ἀμεμψίμοιρος. The verb μεμψιμοιρέω is found from the time of Polybius, e.g. xviii. 31. 7.

μέν,

an untranslatable particle, was originally a form of μήν (*q.v.*). The correlation μέν . . . δέ, so common in classical Greek, is largely reduced in the NT (cf. Blass *Gr.* p. 266 f.). For μέν *solitarium*, i.e. μέν followed by no contrasting particle, as in Rom 1⁸ πρῶτον μέν, *al.*, cf. BGU II. 423² (ii/A.D.) (= *Selections*, p. 90) πρὸ μὲν πάντων εὔχομαί σε ὑγιαίνειν καὶ διὰ παντὸς ἐρωμένον (*l.* ἐρρωμένον) εὐτυχεῖν,¹³ γράφον μοι ἐπιστόλιον πρῶτον μὲν περὶ τῆς σωτηρίας σου, δεύτερον περὶ τῆς τῶν ἀδελφῶν μου. The combination μὲν οὖν in narrative, summing up what precedes, or introducing what follows (Ac 1⁶, 9³¹, *al.*: cf. Blass *Gr.* p. 273), is seen in such passages as P Petr II. 13 (19)⁸ (mid. iii/B.C.) (= Witkowski², p. 19) μάλιστα μὲν οὖν τὴν πᾶσαν σπουδὴν ποιήσαι [το]ῦ ἀφεθῆναί σε διὰ τέλους, P Lille I. 26² (iii/B.C.) (= Witkowski², p. 40) ἔγραψάς μοι περὶ τῆς εἰς τὴν σησαμείαν γῆς. μάλιστα δὲ περὶ τῆς ἐν Πατῶντι αὐτὴ μὲν οὖν ἐστιν παντελῶς ἀπηρ[γ]μένη, and BGU III. 1009⁴ (ii/B.C.) (= Witkowski², p. 111) περὶ μὲν [ο]ὖν τῶν ἄλλων [οὐ σοι γέγραφα, Μ . . . ο]ς γάρ σοι σημα[ν]εῖ ἕκαστα. See also *s.v.* μενοῦνγε.

μενοῦν.

See *s.v.* μέν.

μενοῦνγε

standing at the beginning of a clause, contrary to classical usage (Lob. *Phryn.* p. 342), as in Rom 10¹⁸ (cf. Lk 11²⁸), may be paralleled by μέντοιγε standing first, e.g. P Lond 807¹³ (A.D. 84) (= III. p. 207) μέντοι γε οὐ θέλω κτλ., P Amh II. 135¹¹ (early ii/A.D.) μέντοιγε ὁ κύριος τῇ γ προέγραψεν κτλ., and P Oxy III. 531¹⁹ (ii/A.D.) μέντοιγε ἕως πρὸς σὲ ἔλθῃ Ἀνουβᾶς ἀπὸ τοῦ σοῦ χαλκοῦ τὸ ὀψώνιόν σου καὶ τῶν σῶν ἐξοδίασον ἕως πέμψω, "until however Anoubas arrives, you must pay for the provisions of yourself and your household out of your own money, until I send you some" (Edd.).

μέντοι.

For this particle of affirmation, which was originally a strengthened μέν, cf. P Tebt II. 411¹² (ii/A.D.) μηδὲν μέντοι θορυβηθῇς, "do not be disturbed however," P Giss I. 47²¹ (time of Hadrian) (= *Chrest.* I. p. 383) ἃς μέντοι δεδώκεις εἰς τοῦτο (δραχμὰς) κδ ἔπεμψά σοι, P Oxy XII. 1420⁸ (c. A.D. 129) ἀλλ[ὰ] μέντοι καὶ τὸ[ν] Ἀγαθεῖνον συν[κατα]χω[ρίσ]αι δεῖ, "Agathinus too, however, must join in presenting them"—certain accounts, and P Ryl II. 75⁸ (late ii/A.D.) μέντοι τύπος ἐστὶν καθ' ὃν ἔκρινα πολλάκις, "only there is a principle according to which I have often judged" (Edd.). Μέντοι stands first in the sentence (see *s.v.* μενοῦνγε) in P Lond 1711³⁴ (A.D. 566–573) μέντοι καὶ αὐτῆς τῆς σῆς κοσμιότητος ὑπακούσης μοι κτλ. Wackernagel (*Hellenistica*, p. 11) draws attention to the Doric form μέντον for μέντοι in P Hib I. 40⁷ (B.C. 261) ἐπίστασο μέντον ἀκριβῶς, "but you must clearly understand," as against the editors' note "that the writer was capable of mistakes." The adversative force of the particle appears in such passages from the NT as Jn 4²⁷, 7¹³, *al.*: cf. also Jas 2⁸, where, however, Hort thinks "that μέντοι retains its original force of a strong affirmation," and translates "indeed," "really": cf. Kühner-Gerth § 503, 3, g.

μένω,

"remain," "abide," is used intransitively with reference to (1) *place*, in P Hib I. 55⁶ (B.C. 250) οὐ γὰρ σχολάζω μένειν πλείονα χρόνον, "for I have no leisure to remain longer," P Oxy IV. 744⁵ (B.C. 1) (= *Selections*, p. 32) ἐγὼ ἐν Ἀλεξανδρέα (= εία) μένω, P Fay 137² (question to an oracle—i/A.D.) χρημάτισόν μοι, ἡ μείνω ἐν Βακχιάδι; P Ryl II. 232¹⁰ (ii/A.D.) οἱ δημόσιοι προσεφώνησαν αὐτῷ ὅτι μένις ἐν τῇ κω (*l.* κώμῃ), and *Preisigke* 2639 ποῦ μένι Θερμοῦθις ἡ γυνὴ Πασοράσιος; (cf. Jn 1³⁸ᶠ·): see also Schulze *Gr. Lat.* p. 22 f.: (2) *time*, in P Ryl II. 172³¹ (A.D. 208) μενεῖς ἐπὶ τῇ προγεγραμμένῃ μισθώσει, "the aforesaid lease shall continue secured to you" (Edd.), and P Oxy VI. 903³⁵ (iv/A.D.) ἔμεινεν λέγων, "he kept saying": and (3) *condition*, in P Flor II. 232¹² (iii/A.D.) ἵνα μὴ λίαν ὁ χόρτος τῆς Θεοξενίδος ἄκοπος μείνῃ, "in order that the hay of Theoxenis may not remain too long uncut," and such a phrase as P Fay 96¹⁹ (A.D. 122) μενούσης κυρίας τῆς μισθώσεως ἐφ' οἷς περιέχει πᾶσι, "the lease in all its provisions remaining valid" (Edd.) contrasted with P Hamb I. 8¹⁹ (A.D. 136) ἀπέλυσα <ὑμᾶς> τῆς μισθώσεως καθὼ(ς) πρόκειται: see further P Ryl II. 157²³ (A.D. 135), P Fay 35¹⁰ (A.D. 150–1). For the verb used transitively = "await," as in Ac 20²³, cf. *Kaibel* 654⁹ (iii/A.D.), κἀμὲ μένει τὸ θανεῖν, and the exx. in Field *Notes*, p. 132. In MGr some dialects form a pres. μείνω from the aor. stem (Thumb, *Handbook* p. 143); μνέσκω and μνήσκω are also found.

μερίζω

in the sense of "distribute," "assign," is seen in such passages as P Tebt II. 302¹² (A.D. 71–2) εἰ ὁ Πετρώνιος ἡμῖν τὰς ἀρούρας ἀντὶ σ]υντάξεως ἐμέρισεν κτλ., "if Petronius had assigned the land to us instead of a subvention" etc., P Oxy IV. 713²⁹ (A.D. 97) ἡ δὲ μήτηρ . . . ἐμέρισε τοῖς προγεγραμμένοις μου ἀδελφο[ῖ]ς ἀπὸ τῶν περὶ Νέσλα ἑκατέρῳ ἀρούρας τέσσαρας, "my mother bestowed upon my brother and sister aforesaid 4 each of the arourae at Nesla" (Edd.), ib. III. 489¹⁰ (a Will—A.D. 117) οἷς τέκνοις ἡμῶν οὐκ ἐξέσται τὰ ἀπ' ἐμοῦ εἰς αὐτοὺς ἐλευσόμενα ἑτέροις μερίζειν εἰ [μὴ μόνῃ ἑκάστῃ αὐτῶ]ν γενεᾷ, "which children shall not have the power to alienate what is inherited by them from me except only to their several families" (Edd.), and P Leid Wˣⁱᵛ·³⁸ (ii/iii A.D.) μερίσόν μοι ἀγαθὰ ἐν τῇ γενέσι (*l.* γενέσει) μου. Cf. also BGU II. 511ⁱⁱ·¹² (time of Claudius) (= *Chrest.* I. p. 36) μερίσω σο[ι ταύτην τὴν] ἡμέραν, Meyer *Ostr* 81¹ (A.D. 23) μέρισον Ὥρωι Ἡρακλ(είδου) ὑπ(ὸ) λαχανὸ σπερμον) ὄνον ἕνα ἀρτά(βης) μιᾶς ἡμίσους.

In the Attic inscrr. the verb is used of paying out money from the public treasury, e.g. *Syll* 74 (= ³ 137)¹⁸ᶠᶠ· (c. B.C. 386) μερίσαι δὲ τὸ ἀργύριον τὸ εἰρημένον τὸς ἀποδέκτας ἐκ τῶν καταβαλλομένων χρημά[τ]ων, ἐπειδὰν τὰ ἐκ τῶν νόμων μερίσωσι. For the pass. see BGU IV. 1053ⁱ·³³ (B.C. 13) τὸν μεμερισμένον αὐτοῖς χρόνον, ib. 1131¹⁶ (B.C. 13) δαπάνης μεριζομένης εἰς μέρη ἴσα δύο.

We may note also the touching inscr. *Kaibel* 675—

   Λείψανα Λουκίλλης διδυματόκου ἐνθάδε κεῖτε,
   ἧς μεμέρισται βρέφη, ζωὸν πατρί, θάτερον αὐτῇ.

μέριμνα.

This strong subst. (see *s.v.* μεριμνάω) occurs in the petition of the Temple Twins P Leid Bⁱⁱ·⁵ (B.C. 164) διὸ τὴν μὲν ἐν τῷ ἱερῷ ἡμῶν ἐπιμέλειαν καὶ τὴν τοῦ βίου μέριμναν, εἰς τὸ μηθὲν ἡμᾶς τῶν δεόντων ἐγλιπεῖν, συντετηρημένως πρὸς τὸ θεῖον ἑκουσίως ποεῖ (*l.* ποιεῖται, ποιεῖ). In P Giss I. 19⁸ (ii/A.D.) a wife writes to her husband—συνεχῶς ἀγρυπνοῦσα νυκτὸς ἡ]μέρας μ]ίαν μέριμναν ἔχω τὴν περὶ [τῆς σωτ]ηρίας σου, and in *ib.* 22¹¹ (ii/A.D.) a mother (not father, as in citation *s.v.* εὐχή), on learning that her son is ἀπρόσ[κοπ]ον καὶ ἱλαρώτατον, exclaims—ταῦ[τά μ]οι ἡ πᾶσα εὐχή ἐστι [καὶ μ]έριμνα. See also the mantic P Ryl I. 28⁴⁹ (iv/A.D.) ἐὰν δ[ὲ] ὁ ἐχόμενος μερίμναις πολλαῖς περιπεσεῖται καὶ κακοπαθίαις, εὔχου Διί, "if the next (toe quiver), he will be involved in much anxiety and distress: pray to Zeus," and *Anacreontea* ed. Bergk *Poetae Lyrici Graeci* III. p. 1066, No. 43¹⁰ ὅταν πίνω τὸν οἶνον, εὕδουσιν αἱ μέριμναι, τί μοι γοῶν, τί μοι πόνων, τί μοι μέλει μεριμνῶν: The connotation of the word comes out in such phrases from Vettius Valens as pp. 131³ μετὰ πόνου καὶ μερίμνης καὶ βίας, 271⁴ διὰ τὸν φθόνον καὶ τὴν μέριμναν: With "uneasy lies the head, etc." cf. Aristeas 271 where to the question, τί βασιλείαν διατηρεῖ; "what preserves a kingdom?" the answer is given, μέριμνα καὶ φροντίς, ὡς οὐδὲν κακουργηθήσεται διὰ τῶν ἀποτεταγμένων εἰς τοὺς ὄχλους ταῖς χρείαις, "care and watchfulness to see that no injury is inflicted by those who are set in positions of authority over the people" (Thackeray).

μεριμνάω.

The idea of "over-anxiety," which readily attaches to this verb, as in Mt 6²², LXX Ps 37¹⁹ *al.*, is well seen in P Tebt II. 315² (ii/A.D.) νῦν δὲ [μετὰ σ]π[ο]υδῆς γράφω ὅπως [μὴ μέρ]ιμνῇς, ἐγὼ γάρ σε ἄσκυλ[τον] πο[ι]ήσω, " I am now writing in haste to prevent your being anxious, for I will see that you are not worried" (Edd.) : see also P Iand 1³ (iv/A.D.) where a father writes to his son—θέλησον οὖν, [τέκνον, δη]λῶσαι ἡμεῖν τὸ τῆς καταστάσεώ[ς σου, καὶ με]ριμνείσεις (*l.* μεριμνήσεις) ἅπαντα τὰ κατὰ σὲ [δηλῶσαι, ἵνα] ἀμεριμνήσωμεν (*l.* ἀμεριμνήσωμεν). See also the citations *s.v.* ἀμέριμνος, and add for the subst. ἀμεριμνία P Oxy XIV. 1627²⁰ (A.D. 342) πρὸς δὲ ἀμεριμνίαν σου τήνδε τὴν ὁμολογίαν σοι ἐξεδόμην, "and for your security I have issued to you this contract." On the force of the participle in Mt 6²⁷, see Moulton *Proleg.* p. 230. The verb sometimes means merely " am occupied with," as in Soph. *Oed. Tyr.* 1124 where Oedipus asks the herdsman—ἔργον μεριμνῶν ποῖον ἢ βίον τίνα ; " employed in what labour, or what way of life? Jebb *ad l.* compares 1 Cor 7³³ μεριμνᾷ τὰ τοῦ κόσμου. In the Phrygian inscr. *C. and B.* ii. p. 565, No. 465, we find the proper name Τιτέδιος Ἀμέριμνος : Ramsay suggests that Amerimnos may be a baptismal name given to Titedios when he became a Christian, marking him as the man who " takes no thought for the morrow" (Mt 6³¹). The verb, connected with μερίζω and μερμηρίζω, denotes " distraction" of mind : cf. Terence *An ir.* i. 5. 25 f. curae animum divorsae trahunt.

μερίς.

The use of this word in Ac 16¹² πρώτη τῆς μερίδος Μακεδονίας πόλις, which Hort objected to on the ground that " μερίς never denotes simply a region, province, or any geographical division" (*Notes*², p. 96), is now amply justified on the evidence of the papyri, as well as of later Greek writers generally (see W. M. Ramsay *Exp* V. vi. p. 320).

An almost contemporary ex. is P Tebt II. 302¹ (A.D. 71–2) τῆς Π[ολ]έμωνος μερίδος, " the division of Polemon" in the Arsinoite nome : cf. *ib.* 315¹³ (ii/A.D.) where a priest connected with temple finance is warned that a government inspector was on the point of coming " to his division"— μ[έ]λλ[ε]ιν καὶ εἰς τὴν με[ρί]δα σου ἔρχ[ε]σθαι. Earlier exx. are P Petr III. 32(e)³ (Ptol.) a memorandum in connexion with the police tax on associations and factories τῆς Θεμίστου μερίδος, " in the division of Themistes," and BGU III. 975⁶ (A.D. 45) (= *Selections*, p. 42) a deed of divorce entered into ἐν τῇ Σοκνοπαίου Νήσου τῆς Ἡρακλίδου μερίδος τοῦ Ἀρσ[ι]νοείτου νομοῦ, " at Socnopaei Nesus of the Heraclides district of the Arsinoite nome." The word is also very common in the sense of " portion," " share," as in Lk 10⁴² *al.*, e.g. P Lond 880¹·¹¹ (B.C. 113) (= III. p. 9) a document in which a man executes a division of his landed property—Πανοβχούνει μὲν τῶι πρεσβυτέρωι υἱῶι αὐτοῦ μερίδας δύο . . . ταῖς ἑαυτοῦ θυγατράσιν μερίδα μίαν, and P Oxy XII. 1482²¹ (ii/A.D.) ἐν τῷ δὲ τόπῳ τοῦ πατρός σου ἀποτέθεικα τὴν μερίδαν μου, " I have stored my share (of barley) in the room belonging to your father" (Edd.). For μερίς as a portion of food, cf. Gen 43³³ *al.*, and the classical exx. in Wetstein *ai* Lk 10⁴² : see also Field *Notes*, p. 64, and add Vett. Val. p. 345¹⁶ εἰ δέ τις τῶν κεκλημένων ἐθέλοι

ἀβλαβὴς διαμένειν, μιᾷ μερίδι ἢ καὶ δευτέρᾳ χρησάμενος εὐφρανθήσεται. We may have an ex. of the adj. μερικός in P Oxy XIV. 1655⁷ (iii/A.D.) μερικῶν μ̄, " forty divisible (?) (loaves)," but see the editors' note. Geldart (*Mod. Greek Language*, p. 97) traces the invention of the adj. to the Cyrenaics, who used it in the philosophical sense of " particular" (as in the phrase μερικαὶ ἡδοναί). In MGr it does not mean more than " some," " several."

μερισμός.

For μερισμός, " division," " share," cf. P Tebt I. 5⁵⁸ (B.C. 111) (= Witkowski², p. 104) γέγραπται ὁ μερισμὸς, " the division (of artabae) has been drawn up," P Fay 125⁷ (ii/A.D.) δύνασα[ι] τὸν μερισμὸν τῆς Φιλ[ο]πά[το]ρος ἔχειν, " take care to secure the share of Philopator." For the meaning " a distributing," cf. *Syll* 603 (= ³ 1017 ¹⁷ iii B.C.) πωλήσει δὲ καὶ τὰ συν[ειλε]γμέν[α] ἐκ τοῦ [μ]ερισμοῦ, " ex distributione victimarum deo oblatarum" (Ed.). Wilcken (*Ostr* i. p. 256 ff.) has shown that in the ostraca μερισμός (= τὸ μεμερισμένον) denotes a personal tax assessed at the same rate for all, e.g. *Ostr* 613³ (A.D. 141–142) ὑπ(ὲρ) μερισμ(οῦ) ἀπόρω(ν), perhaps a kind of poor-rate (*Ostr* i. p. 161), or more likely an extra levy to make up deficiencies caused by ἄποροι, who were unable to pay taxes (see *Archiv* iv. p. 545) : cf. also P Tebt I. 29¹⁶ (*c.* B.C. 110) πυρίνου μερισμοῦ, " items of the corn-dues," BGU I. 20³ (A.D. 141–2) μερισμὸς [σπ]ερμάτων, *ib.* 21¹·¹¹ (A.D. 340) μεμερίσθαι καὶ ἀπαιτῆσθαι (*l.* ἀπῃτῆσθαι) ἐπὶ τῆς ἡμετέρας κώμης εἰς τοὺς ἑξῆς ἐγγεγραμμένους ἄνδρας τοὺς ἑξῆς ἐγγεγραμμένους μερισμοὺς ἐφ᾽ ἑκάστου μέρους. For a possible ex. of the rare μερίσμα see P Strass II. 107⁶ (iii/B.C.) εἰς πάντας τοὺς λόγους τὰ μερίσ[ματα (?) . . . .

μεριστής.

In P Leid W^xiv. 42 (ii iii A.D.) (= II. p. 131) μεριστής is used as a title of Sarapis : Dieterich compares Lk 12¹⁴. See also Vett. Val. p. 62¹ ὁ κύριος τοῦ ὡροσκόπου ἐπιτόπως κείμενος ἢ ἰδίας αἱρέσεως μεριστὴς χρόνων ζωῆς γίνεται.

μέρος.

The varied applications of μέρος, which we find in the NT, can all be illustrated from the vernacular. (1) The meaning of a " part" assigned to one, as in Rev 22¹⁹, is seen in P Strass I. 19⁵ (A.D. 105) τοῦ ὑπάρχοντος αὐτῶι μέρο[ο]υς ἑνὸς ἀπὸ μερῶν ἐννέα, and the Christian P Heid 6¹⁷ (iv/A.D.) (= *Selections*, p. 126) παρακαλῶ [ο]ὖν, δέσποτα, ἵνα μνημον[ε]ύῃς μοι εἰς τὰς ἁγίας σου εὐχάς, ἵνα δυνηθῶμεν μέρος τῶν (ἁμ)αρτιῶν καθαρίσεως, " I beseech you, master, to remember me in your holy prayers, that I may be able (to receive) my part in the cleansing of sins." (2) For μέρος = the constituent " part" of a whole, as in Lk 11³⁶, cf. P Petr II. 13 (3)² (B.C. 258–3) τὸ πρὸς νότον [τ]οῦ ὀχυρώματος τεῖχος, μέρος μέν τι αὐτοῦ πεπτωκός ἐστιν, " the wall to the south of the prison, part of it has fallen" (Ed.), BGU IV. 1123⁸ (time of Augustus) διαιρεθήσεται εἰς μέ[ρη] ἴσα καὶ ὅμοια τρία, P Ryl II. 145¹⁴ (A.D. 38) ἔδωκεν πληγὰς πλείους εἰς πᾶν μέρος τοῦ σώματος, and P Hamb I. 54¹·¹⁴ (ii/iii A.D.) ἰς τὰ ἄνω μέρη—with reference to the upper reaches of the Nile. Similarly with Mt 15²⁴ cf. P Leid M⁴ (ii B.C.) (= I. p. 59) οἰκίας . . . τῆς οὔσης ἐν ἀπὸ νότου μέρει Διοσπόλεως τῆς μεγάλης, and with Ac 23⁶, where the word has the force of "party," cf. P Oxy X. 1278²¹ (A.D. 214) ἕκαστον δὲ μέρος π[α]ραδοῦν[αι ἑ]κατέρῳ τὸν αὐ[τ]ὸν περιστερεῶνα, "each party is to deliver to the other the said pigeon-house," P Flor I. 47¹⁷ (A.D. 213–17) where an ἀντικαταλλαγή is written out in four copies—εἰς τὸ παρ᾽ ἑκατέρῳ μέρει εἶναι δισσήν, and the late P Lond 1028¹⁸ (vii/A.D.) (= III. p. 277) τοῦ πρασίνου μέρ(ους), "the green faction." (3) Μέρος in the sense of "branch or line of business," as in Ac 19²⁷ (cf. ²⁵), is seen in P Flor I. 89² (iii A.D.) (as amended *Berichtigungen*, p. 147) δικαιοδό[τ]ης διέ[π]ων τὰ μέρη τῆς διοικήσεως. (4) For the derived sense of "matter" (2 Cor 3¹⁰, 9³) cf. P Ryl II. 127²¹ (A.D. 29) διὸ ἀξιῶ συντάξαι τῷ τῆ(ς) Εὐημερείας ἀρχεφόδωι ἀναζητῆσαι ὑπὲρ τοῦ μέρους, "wherefore I request you to order the archephodus of Euhemeria to inquire into the matter," and similarly *ib.* 140¹⁷ (A.D. 36): see also *Menandrea*, p. 69¹⁰⁷ τὸ τοιουτὶ μέρος ("all this kind of thing") οὐκ ἀκριβῶς δεῖ φρ[άσαι] σοι, and p. 10¹⁷. (5) From this again we have the meaning "nature," as in P Tor II. 8¹⁵ (ii B.C.) καθ᾽ ὃ ἂν μέρος ἢ εἶδος παρασυνγραφῆς, "quaecumque demum fuerit natura aut species infractionis" (Ed.), see the note on p. 58, "apud Polybium τοῦτο τὸ μέρος saepe est *hoc*, *hac res*; rei ergo intimam substantiam ac rationem significat." (6) Adverbial phrases are very common, e.g. (a) ἀπὸ μέρους (2 Cor 2⁵) in BGU IV. 1201¹⁵ (A.D. 2) εὕροσαν ἀπὸ μέρους τὰς θύρας κατακεκαυμέν[ας], "they found the doors partly burnt down," P Tebt II. 402² (A.D. 172) λόγος ἔργου ἀπὸ μέρ[ο]υς γενομένου πρὸς τῷ πλινθουργίῳ, "account of the work partially done at the brick-factory" (Edd.), and P Oxy XIV. 1681⁹ (iii/A.D.) ἀπὸ μέρους πεῖραν, "partial proof"; (b) ἐκ μέρους (1 Cor 12²⁷) in P Lond 1166¹⁴ (A.D. 42) (= III. p. 105) ἕν τι[νι ἡμέ]ρᾳ ἢ ἐγ μέρους ἐν τῷ ἐνιαυτῷ, BGU II. 538¹⁵ (A.D. 100–101) παραδό(= ω)σομεν τὸν κλῆρον ὡς καὶ ἐγ μέρους παρειλήφαμεν, and P Ryl II. 233⁶ (ii A.D.) τὰ μέλαθρα . . . ἐκ μέρους σήμερον ἡρμολόγηται, "the beams have to-day been partly fixed": (c) κατὰ μέρος (Heb 9⁵) in P Tebt I. 6²⁴ (B.C. 140–139) τῶν κατὰ μέρος ἐθνῶν, "the several associations," *ib.* II. 382²⁴ (B.C. 30–A.D. 1) ὀμνύω . . . ποιήσειν πάντ[α] τὰ [κ]ατὰ δύο μέρηι ἀπὸ μερῶν πέντε ἐπειμερείζειν δὲ . . . , "I swear that I will perform all that pertains to the two shares out of five shares and will divide . . .": cf. Cic. *ad Att.* xiii. 22. 2 τὰ κατὰ μέρος, of a detailed account. MGr μέρος, "part," "side," "region," "locality."

μεσημβρία.

For μεσημβρία in its literal sense of "midday," as in Ac 22⁶ (cf. Gen 18¹ al.), cf. the astronomical P Ryl I. 27⁸⁶ (iii/A.D.) ἐαρινὴ ἰσημερία Παχὼν ζ μετὰ ὥρ(αν) α ἔγγιστα τῆς μεσημβρίας, "the vernal equinox is Pachon 7, one hour approximately after noon" (Ed.), and P Lond 121¹⁵⁷ (iii/A.D.) (= I. p. 89) where the time of day most favourable for divinations on the second day of the month is stated to be μεσημβρίας, "at noon." The derived meaning of "south," as probably in Ac 8²⁶, appears in *Syll* 540 (= ³972)⁹⁸ (B.C. 175–2) τοῦ < τοῦ > τόπου τοῦ πρὸς μεσημβρίαν βλέποντος. For the poetic adj. μεσημβρινός, see P Lond 130¹⁷⁴ (i/ii A.D.) (= I. p. 135), a horoscope, and the Christian amulet P Iand 6¹¹ (v/vi A.D.) μεσημβρινὸν δαιμόν[ι]ον with the editor's note. MGr μεσημέρι, "midday."

μεσιτεύω.

To the literary exx. of this verb (from Aristotle downwards) we may add such occurrences in the Κοινή as BGU III. 906⁷ (A.D. 34–5) μεσιτεύοντας ἑτέροις καὶ παραχωροῦντας, *ib.* 709¹⁸ (time of Antoninus Pius) τὰ ἐξ αὐτῶν περιγινόμενα ἀποφερομένους καὶ μεσιτεύοντας, CPR I. 1¹⁹ (A.D. 83–4) μεσειτεύοντας καὶ παραχωροῦντας ἑτέροις, and *ib.* 206¹². Cf. from the inscr. *OGIS* 437⁷⁶ (i B.C.) γενομένου κλήρου ἀπὸ [τῆς μεσ]ιτευούσης τὰς συνθήκας πόλεως, *ib.* ⁷⁹ πρὸς τὸν μεσιτεύοντα δῆμον. For the verb μεσιδιόω see P Rein 7²² (B.C. 141?) ἐμεσιδίωσαν τὸ προειρημένον χειρόγραφον Πετεχῶντι, cf. ³² τὸ μεμεσιδιωμένον χειρόγρ(αφον).

μεσίτης

= "arbiter" is common in connexion with legal transactions, e.g. P Lille 28¹¹ (iii/B.C.) αὐτοῖς ἐδώκαμεν μεσίτην Δωρ[ί]ων[α, P Cattaoui ¹ ³ (before B.C. 87) (= *Chrest.* II. p. 98) ὁ κράτιστος διοικητὴς Ἰουλιανὸς ὁ διέπων τὰ κατὰ τὴν δικαι[ο]δοσίαν ἠθέλησεν σὲ μεσείτην ἡμῶν καὶ κριτὴν γενέσθαι περὶ ὧν ἔχομεν πρὸς τοὺς ἀντιτεταγμέν[ο]υς, P Rein 44⁸ (A.D. 104) Ἄκυλος ὁ κατασταθεὶς κριτὴς μεσίτ(ης) Ἀπολλω(νίου), P Goodsp Cairo 20ⁱⁱⁱ·⁵ (c. A.D. 150) ἐάν σοι δόξῃ μεσείτην ἡμεῖν δὸς ἵνα ὁ ἀντίδικος ἀποκαταστήσῃ τῇ συνηγορουμένῃ τὸ . . . , "if it seems good to you, give us an arbiter in order that the defendant may restore to the plaintiff the . . ." (Ed.). In P Lond 370 (ii/iii A.D.) (= II. p. 251) mention is made several times of a μεσίτης, who may be the "surety" for a debt. The reference is to business transactions in P Strass I. 41¹⁴ (A.D. 250) παρακαταθε[σθα]ι τὰ δύο τάλ[α]ντα παρὰ κοινῷ μεσείτῃ Κολλούθῳ, BGU II. 419⁸ (A.D. 276–7) (= *Chrest.* I. p. 457) παρόντων μεσιτῶν, CPR I. 19²³ (A.D. 330) ὁ μεταξὺ μεσίτης, and P Oxy X. 1298¹⁹ (iv/A.D.) σὺ τούτου μεσίτης, "you being intermediary in this." For the subst. μεσιτεία cf. BGU II. 445² (A.D. 148–9) ἐπὶ μεσιτίᾳ τῶν ὑπαρχόντων . . ἀρουρῶν, *ib.* I. 98²³ (A.D. 211) οὐκ ἔμεινεν τῇ γενομένῃ μεσιτίᾳ—of a man who did not discharge his duties as trustee, the late P Lond 113²⁷ (vi/A.D.) (= I. p. 201) συνβέβηκεν μεσητίαν γε[νέ]σθαι μέσων εἰρηνικῶν ἀνδρῶν, and Vett. Val. p. 2²⁷ μεσιτείας κρίσεων.

μεσονύκτιον.

For this poetical word (cf. Lob. *Phryn.* p. 53) see P Leid Wⁱⁱⁱ ²⁷ (ii/iii A.D.) (= II. p. 91) τὸ μεσανύκτιον (for acc. cf. Mk 13³⁵), ὥρᾳ πέπτῃ (*l.* πέμπτῃ), ὅταν ἡσυχία γένηται, ἀνάψας τὸν βωμὸν κτλ., and similarly *ib.* ˣᵛ ³⁴ (= p. 135). The form μεσανύκτιον, as in Mk *l.c.* B, Lk 11⁵ D, occurs also in P Oxy XIV. 1768⁶ (iii/A.D.) γ[ρ]άφω ἐλθὼν εἰς Σχεδίαν τῇ κ̄ᾱ κατὰ τὸ μεσανύκτιον (cf. Ac 16²⁵). With the interchange of cases in Mk 13³⁵, cf. P Oxy XII. 1489⁶·⁸ (late iii/A.D.) τοῦ ἄλλο (*l.* ἄλλου) μηνὸς . . . τῷ ἄλλο (*l.* ἄλλῳ) μηνί. MGr μεσονύχτι, pl. μεσάνυχτα.

μέσος

is common as an adj. in personal descriptions, e.g. P Ryl II. 128³⁰ (c. A.D. 30) Ἀτρῆ(ς) (ἐτῶν) λε οὐ(λὴ) μετώπ(ῳ) μέσῳ, "Hatres, aged 35, with a scar on the middle of the forehead," *ib.* 154³ (A.D. 66) Χαιρήμων . . . οὐλὴι ῥινὶ μ[έ]σηι, "Chaeremon with a scar on the middle of the nose," similarly of height, as in P Oxy I. 73¹⁸ (A.D. 94)

Θαμούνιον . . μέση μελίχρως. "Thamounion of middle height, fair": cf. also *ib.* X. 1260¹⁰ (A.D. 286) μέσης τοπ αρχίας), "the middle toparchy." In P Petr I. 12³ (iii/B.C.) μέσος is followed by the dat.—Λύκιος . . μέσος μεγέθει. The neut. μέσον is frequently found in adverbial expressions: e.g. ἀνὰ μέσον—P Kyl II. 166¹¹ (A.D. 26) γύης δημόσιs ἀνὰ μέσον οὔσης δ[ιώ]ρυγος, "a plot of state land separated by a dyke" (Edd.), P Oxy IX. 1200¹⁸ (A.D. 266) ἐν τοῖς ἀνὰ μέσον μέρεσι τῆς κώμης, "in the middle part of the village": εἰς τὸ μέσον—P Gen I. 11⁷ (A.D. 350) τὸ στάβλον τῶν ὄνων, τὸ εἰς τὸ μέσον καὶ ἐκ νότου τῆς οἰκία[s] ἀστέγαστον ὄν, cf. P Mon 1⁸⁶ (A.D. 574) ἐλθόντος εἰς μέσον: ἐκ μέσου—P Hib I. 73¹⁴ (B.C. 243–2) ἐγ μέσου ἀ[φ]ήρηκεν αὐτόν (*s.* ὄνον), "has removed it from my reach" (Edd.), BGU II. 388ʰ ²³ (ii/iii A.D.) ἆρον ταῦτα ἐκ τοῦ μ[έ]σ[ου (cf. Col 2¹⁴ and Epict. iii. 3. 15 αἶρε ἐκ τοῦ μέσου). Several good exx. of the "improper preposition" ἀνὰ μέσον will be found *s.v.* ἀνά. On ἐμ μέσῳ for ἐν μέσῳ in certain good MSS. of the NT, but never in אBDD₂, see WH *Notes*², p. 157, and on μέσον c. gen. with the force of a preposition, as in Mt 14²⁴ א, Phil 2¹⁵, Lk 8⁷ D, and in LXX Exod 14²⁷ *al.*, see Hatzidakis *Einl.* p. 214, where the usage is traced to Semitic influence, but cf. the classical exx. in LS V. 1, and Epict. ii. 22. 10 βάλε καὶ σοῦ καὶ τοῦ παιδίον μέσον ἀγρίδιον, "throw an estate between thyself and the child" (Sharp, p. 94). The MGr μέσα('s) is similarly used: see Thumb *Handbook*, p. 108. For μεσίδιον = "in consegna" (Ed.), cf. PSI VI. 551¹⁹ (B.C. 272–1).

μεσότοιχον.

A parallel to this ἅπ. εἰρ. = "partition-wall" (Eph 2¹⁴) may be found perhaps in a fragmentary list of abstracts of contracts regarding sales of house property at Hermopolis, P Amh II. 98⁹ (ii/iii A.D.) (ἥμισυ) μέρ ος) [τῶν] μεσοτύχ-(ων?), where the editors propose to read μεσοτοίχων from μεσότοιχος (see LS). For ὁ μεσότοιχος see also an inser. from Argos, *BCH* xxxiii. (1909) p. 452, No. 22¹⁶.

μεσουράνημα,

"mid-heaven," as in Rev 8¹³ *al.*, is found in the horoscope P Oxy II. 235¹³ (A.D. 20–50) μεσουρά νημα Ὑδροχόῳ ζῴδιον ἀρσενικὸν οἰκητη[. . Κρόνου: see the editors' note, where it is suggested that possibly a verb should be substituted for μεσουρά νημα), and cf. the use of μεσουρανέω in P Leid Vⁱⁱ·⁶ (iii/iv A.D.) (= II. p. 13) with the accompanying note.

Μεσσίας.

On the spelling and use of this distinctive name, which in the NT is confined to Jn 1⁴¹, 4²⁵, see Winer-Schmiedel *Gr.* p. 57.

μεστός.

For this adj. in its literal sense of "full," as in Jn 19²⁹ *al.*, cf. P Oxy VII. 1070³² (iii/A.D.) τραγη[μ]άτων σφυρίδαν μεστὴν μίαν, "one basket full of sweetmeats," *ib.* XII. 1449¹⁶ (A.D. 213–217) ἄλ(λος) λύχ νος) χρ υσοῦς) μεικ ρὸς) μεστ(ός), "another gold lamp, small, full," and for its metaphorical application, as in Jas 3¹⁷ *al.*, cf. CPR I. 19¹⁶ (A.D. 330) ἀντεπιστάλματα . . μεστὰ ψευδολογίας, "replies

full of falsehood," and the late P Oxy I. 130⁶ (vi/A.D.), where a debtor appeals for indulgence on the following ground—οὐδὲν ἄδικον ἢ ἀσεβὲς κέκτηται ὁ ἔνδοξος οἶκος τοῦ ἐμοῦ ἀγαθοῦ δεσπότου, ἀλλ' ἀεὶ μεστός ἐστι ἐλεημοσύνης ἐπιρέον (*l.* ἐπιρρέων) τοῖς ἐδεέσιν (*l.* ἐνδε-) τὰ χρειώδη, "no injustice or wickedness has ever attached to the glorious house of my kind lord, but it is ever full of mercy and overflowing to supply the needs of others" (Edd.). MGr μεστός, "full," "exuberant."

μεστόω.

With the metaphorical use of μεστός (see above) cf. Didache ii. 5 οὐκ ἔσται ὁ λόγος σου ψευδής, οὐ κενός, ἀλλὰ μεμεστωμένος πράξει, "thy speech shall not be false, nor vain, but fulfilled by deed." On the use of the verb (and adj.) by medical writers, see Hobart, p. 189. Cf. MGr μέστωμα, "development," "maturity."

μετά.

In the NT (as in classical prose) μετά is construed only with the gen. and the acc., and the various shades of meaning connected with these two usages can be readily illustrated from our sources.

(1) c. gen.—(a) For the ordinary meaning "with," "in company with," we may cite P Eleph 1¹⁵ (B.C. 311–10) (= *Selections*, p. 4) τοῦ μετὰ Δημητρίας, "those acting with Demetria," P Tebt I. 35¹⁰ (B.C. 111) ὃς κ[α]ὶ μεθ' ὑμῶν ὑπὸ τὴν ἐντολὴν ε(om.) ὑπογράφει, "who shall append his signature to the edict together with yours" (Edd.), P Amh II. 135²¹ (early ii/A.D.) ἐρρῶσθαί σε εὔχ(ομαι μετὰ τῶν τέκν[ω(ν)], "I pray for your health and for that of your children" (Edd.), P Oxy III. 531⁴ (ii/A.D.) ἡδέως σε ἀσπαζόμεθα πάντες οἱ ἐν οἴκωι καὶ τοὺς μετ' ἐσοῦ πάντας, and *ib.* I. 119² (ii/iii A.D.) (= *Selections*, p. 102) καλῶς ἐποίησες οὐκ ἀπένηχές (*l.* ἀπήνεγκες) με μετ' ἐσοῦ εἰς πόλιν, "so kind of you not to have taken me along with you to the city!"—a schoolboy to his father. For the collocation μετὰ καί, as in Phil 4³, cf. BGU II. 412⁶ (iv/A.D.) προσῆλθέν μοι Λαννοῦς χήρα οὖσα μετὰ καὶ τοῦ υἱοῦ ἑαυτῆς: see Deissmann *BS* p. 265 f.

(b) Closely associated with this is the meaning "in the employment of," e.g. P Passalacqua 5 (iii/B.C.) (= Witkowski², p. 53) Φίλωνος ἀδελφὸς τοῦ μετὰ Λύσιδος ἐπιστολογράφου, "brother of Philon, the employé of Lysis the epistolographer": cf. BGU I. 27¹⁵ (ii/iii A.D.) (cf. p. 353) ὥστε ἕως σήμερον μηδένα<ν> ἀπολελύσθαι τῶν μετὰ σίτου, "so that up till to-day no one of us in the corn-service has been let go."

(c) For μετά indicating *manner*, cf. P Petr II. 19 (1a)² (petition of a prisoner—iii/B.C.) ἀξιῶ σε μετὰ δεήσεως καὶ ἱκετείας οὔνεκα τοῦ θεοῦ καὶ τοῦ καλῶς ἔχοντος, "I beseech you with prayer and supplication in the name of God and of fair play," P Lond 44¹⁷ (B.C. 161) (= I. p. 34) μεθ' ἡσυχίας (2 Thess 3¹²) ἀναλύειν, P Oxy II. 292⁵ (*c.* A.D. 25) παρακαλῶ σε μετὰ πάσης δυνάμεως ἔχειν αὐτὸν συνεσταμένον (cf. Lk 14¹⁸ f.), and *OGIS* 56¹⁰ (B.C. 237) τὴν ἐπιμέλειαν διὰ παντὸς ποιοῦνται μετὰ μεγάλης δαπάνης καὶ χορηγίας.

(d) With this may be compared the gen. of *equipment* (as in Mt 26⁴⁷ *al.*) in the instructions to wear a befitting costume for an official function, P Oxy I. 123¹⁵ (iii/iv A.D.) εἰσβαίνων οὖν μετὰ τῆς αἰσθήτος (*l.* ἐσθῆτος γνώτω ὁ ἐρχόμενος ἵνα ἕτοιμος εἰσβῇ, "let him remember when he enters that he must wear the proper dress, that he may enter prepared" (Edd.), ¹⁰ ἐκ[ε]λεύσθημεν γὰρ μετὰ τῶν χλαμύδων εἰσβῆναι, "for the orders which we received were to wear cloaks when we entered" (Edd.).

(e) This prepares us for a corresponding usage in connexion with mental states or feelings, e.g. P Amh II. 133¹¹ (early ii/A.D.) μετὰ πολλῶν κόπων ἀνηκάσαμεν αὐτῶν ἀντάσχεσθαι (l. ἠναγκάσαμεν αὐτοὺς ἀντίσχεσθαι) τῆς τούτων ἐνεργίας ἐπὶ τῷ προτέρῳ ἐκφορίου (l. -ίῳ), "with great difficulty I made them set to work at the former rent" (Edd.), P Lond 358⁸ (c. A.D. 150) (= II. p. 172) ἐπανανκάσαι με μετὰ ὕβρεων καὶ πληγῶν. Allied to this is the meaning "according to," as in P Tebt I. 27³² (B.C. 113) μετὰ τῆς ἑαυτοῦ γνώμης.

(f) The instrumental usage "by means of" is specially noticeable in the magic papyri, e.g. P Lond 121²²⁶ (iii/A.D.) (= I. p. 91) γράφε μ[ε]τὰ μέλανος γραφικοῦ, ib. 46⁶⁵ (iv A.D.) (= I. p. 67) ἔνχριε δὲ τὸν δεξιὸν ὀφθαλμὸν μεθ' ὕδατος. Cf. also BGU III. 909⁸ (A.D. 359) ἐβουλήθη ἐπέλευσίν μοι ποιήσασθαι μετὰ ξίφους, although this may be classed with (d) supra. In Acta S. Marinae, p. 30⁸ ἔτυπτεν τὴν κεφαλὴν μετὰ τῆς σφύρας may be contrasted with the classical dative ib. p. 31 τύπτουσα τῇ σφύρᾳ. This leads to the common MGr use of μέ with the acc. to denote the instrument (cf. Evans CQ xv. p. 28).

(g) In Lk 1⁵⁸ (cf. Ac 14²⁷, 15⁴) it is customary to see a usage influenced by literal translation from the Semitic (see Proleg. p. 106, but cf. p. 246), but the usage is not unknown to vernacular Greek, e.g. P Amh II. 135¹⁶ (early ii/A.D.) τί δὲ ἡμεῖν συνέβη μετὰ τῶν ἀρχόντων ἴσως ἐγνώκατε ἢ κνώσεσθε (l. γνώσεσθε), "what befell us in connexion with the magistrates you have probably heard or will hear" (Edd.), and the Byzantine BGU III. 798⁸ εὐχαριστοῦμεν . . . τῇ ἡμῶν δεσποίνῃ εἰς πάντα τὰ καλὰ ἃ ἐποίησεν μετὰ τῶν δούλων αὐτῆς. Thumb Hellen. p. 125 shows that MGr disproves Semitism in πολεμεῖν μετά τινος (cf. Rev 12³ al.), comparing a MGr folksong τρεῖς ὦρες ἐπολέμαεμε (= μετά) δεκόχτω χιλιάδες. We may also cite the Nubian inscr. of Silco I. OGIS 201³ ἐπολέμησα μετὰ τῶν Βλεμύων, ¹⁰ οἱ φιλονεικοῦσιν μετ' ἐμοῦ.

(h) Under the gen. construction we need only add μεθ' ὧν, "wherewith," an epistolary formula introducing the closing greeting, e.g. BGU IV. 1080⁴³ (iii/A.D.) (as amended Chrest. I. p. 564) προσα[γ]όρευε ἀπ' ἐμοῦ πολλὰ τὴν σοι φιλτάτην σύνευνον, μεθ' ὧν ἐρρῶσθαί σε καὶ εὐανθοῦντα εὔχομαι, κύριέ μου υἱέ — the words from ἐρρῶσθαι to the end are added in a different hand, and similarly P Lips I. 110²⁷ (iii/iv A.D.).

(2) c. acc.—(a) with persons, meaning "besides," "in addition to": P Lond 260⁸⁷ (a list relating to the poll-tax— A.D. 72-3) (= II. p. 50) μετ[ὰ τοὺ]ς τετ[ε]λ(ευτηκότας), "including those who have since died" (Ed.), P Flor III. 338 (iii A.D.) ἄλλον γὰρ σπουδαῖον οὐκ ἔχω(=ο)μεν μετὰ τοῦτον. Cf. P Giss I. 50¹³ (A.D. 259) μετὰ τὰ κριθέντα, "besides what has been determined."

(b) "after," of time: P Petr III. 104⁴ (B.C. 244-3) μετὰ τὸν σπόρον τοῦ δ (ἔτους), "after the sowing of the 4th year," P Tebt I. 72³⁶⁷ (B.C. 114-3) μετὰ τὸν διαλογισμόν, "after the inquiry," P Oxy II. 278¹⁶ (hire of a mill—A.D. 17) μετὰ τὸν χρόνον ἀπ[οκα]ταστησάτωι ὁ μάνης τὸν μύλον ὑγιῆι καὶ ἀσινῆι, "at the end of the time the servant shall restore

the mill safe and uninjured" (Edd.), ib. 76¹⁵ (A.D. 179) πρὸς τὸ μετὰ τελευτὴν αὐτοῦ ἀνεύθυνόν με εἶναι, "in order to free me from responsibility after his death" (Edd.), ib. VI. 903³⁶ (iv/A.D.) ἔμεινεν λέγων ὅτι μετὰ μῆναν λαμβάνω πολιτικὴν ἐμαυτῷ, "he kept saying 'A month hence I will take a mistress'" (Edd.); cf. Ac 1⁵ and see further Schulze Gr. Lat. p. 17. Similarly ib. XIV. 1637²⁸ (A.D. 257-9) μετ' ἄλλα, "etc.," P Tebt II. 286³ (report of a trial—A.D. 121-138) μεθ' ἕτερα, "after other evidence," and P Ryl II. 77⁴¹ (A.D. 192) μετ' ὀλίγον. A curious usage, as yet unexplained, is found in a few tax-receipts, where μετὰ λόγον is inserted between the name of the month and the day, e.g. P Fay 53² (A.D. 110-1) Φαῶφι μετὰ [λόγο]ν κϛ: see the editors' note.

(c) For μετὰ τό c. inf. cf. P Par 63¹⁹³ (B.C. 164) (= P Petr III. p. 36) μετὰ τὸ γράψαι τὴν πρὸ ταύτης ἐπιστολήν, "after writing the former letter."

For further exx. of the different uses of μετά the monographs of Kuhring and Rossberg (see Abbreviations I.) should be consulted. The form μετά still occurs in MGr dialects (e.g. in Pontus): also with 1st and 2nd personal pronouns (e.g. μετὰ σένα, μετὰ ἐσένα), and in a few stereotyped formulae (e.g. μετὰ βίας, "with effort"). The common form, however, is μέ (Thumb, Handbook, p. 103 f.).

μεταβαίνω.

The ordinary meaning "remove," "depart," as in Lk 10⁷, is well brought out in P Tebt II. 316²⁰ (A.D. 99) ἐὰν δὲ μεταβαίνωμεν ἢ ἐγδημῶμεν [μ]εταδώσωμεν ἀμφ[ότ]εροι τῷ συνμοριάρχῃ, "if we change our abode or go abroad, we will both give notice to the president of the symmory" (Edd.); cf. ib. I. 61 (b)²⁶² (B.C. 118-7). With the metaphorical usage in Jn 5²⁴, 1 Jn 3¹⁴, cf. OGIS 458⁷ (c. B.C. 9) εἰς ἀτυχὲς μεταβεβηκὸς σχῆμα. For the subst. it is sufficient to quote BGU I. 137⁶ (ii/A.D.) where, in connexion with a census return, reference is made to one who had been enrolled ἐπ' ἀμφόδου Λινυφεῶν (= είων) νυνεὶ δὲ μετάβασιν ποιουμένου ἐ[πὶ] τῶν Χην[ο]βοσκῶν Πρώτων.

μεταβάλλομαι.

For the metaphorical usage, as in the only ex. of the verb in the NT (Ac 28⁶), see the letter addressed by Darius I. to a provincial governor, Gadatas, in Asia Minor, Priene 115²⁰ the writing of the copy is of the 1st half of ii/A.D.) ὅτι δὲ τὴν ὑπὲρ θεῶν μου διάθεσιν ἀφανίζεις, δώσω σοι μὴ μεταβαλομένωι πεῖραν ἠδικη[μ]ένου θυμοῦ: cf. the oracular Kaibel 1039¹² μοχθεῖν ἀνάγκη· μετα[β]ολὴ δ'ἔσται καλή. The verb in the sense of "move," "transfer," "change," is common, e.g. P Hib I. 42³ (B.C. 262) τὸν σῖτον ὃν ἔφης μεταβαλεῖσθα[ι] τοῖς παρὰ τῶν σιτολόγων, "with regard to the corn which you said you would transfer to the agents of the sitologi" (Edd.), ib. 45⁶ (B.C. 257) παραγίνεσθε [ἵν]α [τ]ὸν ἐν Σέφθαι σῖτον μεταβάλη[ησ]θε πρὸ τοῦ τὸ . . . τῷ ἐμβαλεῖν, "come here in order to transfer the corn at Sephtha before lading . . ." (Edd.), P Par 51¹¹ (dream from the Serapeum—B.C. 160) (= Selections, p. 19 θάρσ[ει] . . . ὅτι μεταβέβλ[ηκα] τὴν κοίτην μου, "take courage, for I have changed my bed," P Ryl II. 231⁸ (A.D. 40) τὸν πυρὸν τὸν ἐν τῷ θησαυρῶι μεταβαλοῦ δι[ὰ] τὴν βροχήν, "get the corn in the granary removed because of the inundation" (Edd.), P Fay 122² (c. A.D. 100) εὖ ποιήσεις

μεταβαλόμενος τὸ παρά σοι σί[ν]απι . . . τῶι κομίζοντί
σοι τὸ ἐπιστόλιον, "please transfer the mustard that is with
you to the bearer of this letter" (Edd.), and P Tebt II.
402⁶ (A.D. 172) μετεβλήθ(η) ἀπὸ τοῦ πλινθουργίου, "transported from the factory"—of bricks. For the meaning
"hand over," "credit," "pay," see P Oxy VIII. 1153⁶
(i/A.D.) τὰς [δ]ρ[α]χμὰς ἐξακοσίας μεταβαλέσθαι ἡμε(ῖν),
"to pay us the 600 drachmae," ib. XII. 1419⁵ (A.D. 265)
ἃς μετεβάλου δι(ὰ) δημοσίας τραπέζ(ης), "which you credited
through the public bank" (Edd.), and ib. XIV. 1665²²
(iii/A.D.) τῆς τιμῆς ἐξαυτῆς μεταβαλλομένης ὑπ' ἐμοῦ ᾧ ἐὰν
δοκιμάσῃς, "the value to be handed over by me at once to
any one approved by you" (Edd.). Μεταβόλος "retailer"
(as in Isai 23²⁴) is seen in P Rev L^xlviii. ³ (B.C. 258) οἱ
κάπηλοι καὶ οἱ μεταβόλοι, "the dealers and retailers," P
Oxy XIV. 1675³ (iii/A.D.) κ[ό]μι[σα]ι διὰ τῶν . . . περὶ
Ἡρακλέωνα μεταβόλων (δραχμὰς?) μ̄, "receive through the
traders with Heracleon 40 drachmae (?)," and Ostr 1449¹
(Thebes—A.D. 164–5) ἐπιτ(ηρητὴς) τελ ους) μεταβόλ(ων)
ἁλιεῶν (l. ἁλιεῶν) (see Chrest. I. i. p. 136).

μετάγω,

"transfer," "transport," is seen in P Oxy II. 244³ (A.D.
23) βουλόμενος μεταγαγεῖν . . . πρόβατα τριακόσια εἴκοσι,
with reference to the transference of sheep from one district
to another, and ib. 259¹⁹ (A.D. 23) μὴ ἔχοντός μου ἐκξουσίαν
(l. ἐξ-) . . . μετάγει (l. -γειν) ἐμαυτὸν εἰς ἑ[τ]έραν φυλακ[ή]ν,
"I have no power to transfer myself to another prison":
cf. also P Tor I. 1^ii. 24 (B.C. 116) τὸ ἔθνος μεταγαγεῖν εἰς
τὰ Μεμνόνεια, P Leid M^ii. 3 (B.C. 114) (= I. p. 60) τῶν
μεταγομένων εἰς τοὺς τάφους, of dead bodies, and the
fragmentary P Ryl II. 67⁵ (late ii/B.C.) μεταγειοχότω[ν,
again apparently of removal from one place to another.
For the meaning of "translate," see Sir prol. ὅταν μεταχθῇ
εἰς ἑτέραν γλῶσσαν. Hort ad Jas 3³ cites Plut. ii. 225 F
and Epict. Ench. xxxiii. 3, where the verb is used of turning
men to a better mind, but can find no clear authority for the
sense of "leading not from one place to another but from
one direction to another," which the Jas passage requires.

μεταδίδωμι

is used in the general sense of "inform" in such passages
as P Oxy VIII. 1153⁶ (i/A.D.) μετάδος Νικάνορι ὅτι . . . ,
"tell Nicanor that . . . ," P Giss I. 91 (fragment of a
letter—ii/A.D.) τοῦ ἀδ[ελ]φοῦ μετα[δ]όντος ὅτι μιμνή[σκει]
ἡμῶν συνεχῶς, P Lond 1231¹⁴ (A.D. 144) (= III. p. 109)
ἀξιοῦμεν δὲ τοῦ διαστολικοῦ ἀντίγραφον αὐτῷ μεταδοθῆναι,
and P Oxy XIV. 1667⁶ (iii/A.D.) μετέδωκεν ὁ [Θε]όχρηστος
ὅσα ἔπραξας, "Theochrestus informed me of your doings"
(Edd.). A quasi-legal meaning appears in P Par 26¹· ²⁶ (B.C.
163 2) (= Selections, p. 16) τῷ υἱῷ δὲ Ψιντάεους . . .
προσήλθομεν, καὶ περὶ ἑκάστων μετεδώκαμεν, "we (the
Serapeum Twins) approached the son of Psintaes, and gave
him detailed information," BGU I. 16⁷ (A.D. 159–160)
(= Selections, p. 83) πρὸς τὸ μεταδοθὲν εἰς ἐξέτασιν εἶδος,
"with regard to the report handed over to us for information," the report of five presbyter-priests regarding a brother
priest, and more particularly in such passages as P Ryl II.
119³¹ (A.D. 54–67) μεταδόντες αὐτῶι καὶ τοῖς αὐτοῦ υἱοῖς
Ἑρμοφίλωι καὶ Κάστορι διαστολικὸν ὑπόμνημα κατελθεῖν

εἰ[ς] τὸν διαλογισμόν, "we served a summons upon him
and his sons Hermophilus and Castor to go down to the
assize" (Edd.), P Oxy XII. 1472⁶ (A.D. 136) τοῦ δεδομέν[ο]υ
ὑπομνήματος ἀντίγρα(φον) σύνταξον μεταδοθῆναι ὡς ὑπό-
κει[τ(αι), "give instructions that a copy of the memorandum
which has been presented be served, as follows" (Edd.), ib. X.
1270⁴⁸ (A.D. 159) ἀξιῶ συντάξαι γράψαι τῷ τοῦ Ὀξυ[ρυγχίτου
στρα(τηγῷ) μετα]δοῦναι τούτου τὸ ἴσον [τῇ Ἀμμων . . . .,
"I beg you to give orders that instructions should be sent
to the strategus of the Oxyrhynchite nome to serve a copy
of this application upon Ammon . . ." (Edd.), and, with
ἐνώπιον, in BGU II. 578¹ (A.D. 189) μετάδ(ος) ἐνώπι(ον)
ὡς καθήκ(ει) τοῖς προστεταγμ(ένοις) ἀκολού[θως, where
Deissmann (BS p. 213) treats μεταδιδόναι ἐνώπιον as an
"official formula," and cites Wilcken to the effect that it
means to deliver personally: "the demand for payment
shall be made to the debtor, face to face, for the greater
security of the creditor." See also P Flor I. 50²⁹ (A.D. 234)
cited s.v. ἐνώπιον, and Preisigke's elaborate note in the
introduction to P Strass I. 41, where the sense of "responsibility" conveyed by the verb in legal phraseology is fully
discussed. The subst. μετάδοσις occurs in P Oxy XII.
1473⁴³ (application concerning a remarriage—A.D. 201)
τούτου ὄντος ἀξιῶ τὴν μετ[άδοσιν] γε[νέσθα]ι [τῇ] Ἀπολλων[α]ρίῳ [ὡς καθ]ήκει, "this being so, I request that the
notification be made to Apollonarion in the proper way,"
ib. X. 1276¹⁹ (A.D. 249) κυρία ἡ πρᾶσις . . ἥνπερ . .
δημοσιώσεις . . οὐ προσδεόμενος με[τ]αδόσεως οὐδὲ ἑτέρας
συνευδοκήσεως ἡμῶν, "the sale is valid, and you shall make
it public without requiring a notification or any further concurrence on our part" (Edd.). For τὸ μεταδόσιμον, "the
certificate," cf. P Tebt II. 316¹² (A.D. 99) (= Chrest. I. p.
174) ὀμνύω . . . ἔχειν τὸ μεταδόσιμον ("ein den abgehenden
Epheben überreichtes Zeugnis," Wilcken).

μετάθεσις.

PSI V. 546³ (mid. iii/B.C.) τοῦ ἀναβαθμοῦ τὴν μετάθεσιν,
"the removal of the stair"—in connexion with repairs on a
house. In Aristeas 160 the subst. is used of the divine and
incomprehensible "interchange" of the states of sleeping
and waking : ὡς θεία τίς ἐστι καὶ ἀκατάληπτος τούτων ἡ
μετάθεσις.

μεταίρω

is intrans. "change my position," "depart," in its two
occurrences in the NT (Mt 13⁵³, 19¹), but for the trans.
usage "remove," "transfer," as in the LXX, we may cite
a Cilician rock inscr. found in the neighbourhood of a temple
OGIS 573¹⁵ (i/A.D.) τῶν δὲ ἀναθεμάτων τῶν ὄντων ἔν τε
τοῖς ναοῖς καὶ τῶν ἐπιγεγραμμένων ἔν τε ταῖς στήλαις καὶ
τοῖς ἀναθέμασιν μηδενὶ ἐξέστω< ι > μήτε ἀπαλεῖψαι μήτε
ἀχρεῶσαι μήτε μεταραι.

μετακαλέω.

The mid. of this verb, which is found quater in Acts in
the sense "summon to myself," "send for" (cf. Hobart,
p. 219 f.), may be illustrated from the curious interview with
an Emperor (Marcus Aurelius or Commodus: P Oxy I. 33
verso^iii. 2 (late ii/A.D.) Αὐτοκράτωρ μετεκ[α]λέσατο αὐτόν,
ib.^iv. 7 τίς ἤδη τὸν δεύτερόν μου ᾄδην προσκυνοῦντα . . .

μετεκαλέσατο : where the meaning apparently is, "who now has sent for me, who am facing death for the second time?", and *ib.* X. 1252 *verso*[26] (A.D. 288–95) ἐπὶ σήμερον ἥτις ἐστὶν ιη μετεκαλέσω ἡμᾶς, "whereas to-day, the 18th, you summoned us" (Edd.). For the act. cf. P Tebt I. 23[12] (B.C. 119 or 114) διὸ καὶ ἔτι νῦν καλῶς ποιήσεις φιλοτιμότερον προθυμηθεὶς ἵνα τὰ πρὸς αὐτὸν [. . . . .] διορθώσηι μετακαλέσας ἐκ τῶν προηγνοημένων, where the editors render, "I shall therefore be glad if you will even now endeavour more earnestly to correct your behaviour towards him, abandoning your previous state of ignorance"; and for the pass. cf. P Par 63[viii. 9] (B.C. 165) ἵνα μετακληθῇς ἔτι πρὸς τὴν ἐμὴν αἵρεσιν.

μετακινέω

occurs in its literal sense of "move away" (transitive) in the Mysteries inscr. from Andania *Syll* 653 (= [3] 736)[186] (B.C. 92) μὴ μετακινοῦντες ἐπὶ καταλ[ύ]σει τῶν μυστηρίων μ[η]θὲν τῶν κατὰ τὸ διάγραμμα : cf. also the inscr. on a stone found amongst the ruins of an ancient temple near Cephisia, *ib.* 888 (= [3] 1238)[3ff.] (*c.* A.D. 160) πρὸς θεῶν καὶ ἡρώων, ὅστις εἰ ὁ ἔχων τὸν χῶρον, μήποτε μετακεινήσῃς τούτων τι. καὶ τὰς τούτων τῶν ἀγαλμάτων εἰκόνας καὶ τιμὰς ὅστις ἢ καθέλοι ἢ μετακεινοίη, τούτῳ μήτε γῆν καρπὸν φέρειν μήτε θάλασσαν πλωτὴν εἶναι, κακῶς τε ἀπολέσθαι αὐτοὺς καὶ γένος.

μεταλαμβάνω

For the gen. construction, as in Ac 2[46], cf. P Ryl II. 77[19] (A.D. 192) τροφῶν μεταλαβεῖν. The acc. (cf. Ac 24[25]) is found in such passages as P Tebt I. 79[19] (*c.* B.C. 148) Θοτορταῖον τὸν μεταλαβόντα τὴν κωμογρ[αμματείαν], "Thotortaeus, who succeeded to the post of komogrammateus" (Edd.). P Amh II. 39[6] (late ii/B.C.) μεταλαβόντες τοὺς συντετελεσμέν[ο]υς πρὸς τοὺς τέβεις Ἑρμων[θ]ίτας ἀγῶνας μεγάλως ἐχάρημεν, P Oxy I. 113[14] (ii/A.D.) χάριν ἔχω θεοῖς πᾶσιν γινώσκων ὅτι ὅτι (omit) μετέλαβον παρατετευχότα Πλουτίωνα εἰς τὸν Ὀξυρυγχείτην, "I thank all the gods to think that I came upon Plution in the Oxyrhynchite nome" (Edd.). The verb is frequent = "obtain information," "learn," e.g. P Tebt I. 40[7] (B.C. 117) σαφέστερον μετειληφὼς τοὺς ἐκ τῆς κώμης ὁμοθυμαδὸν ἀντέχεσθαι τῆς σκέπης, "having received certain information that the inhabitants of the village are with one accord claiming your protection" (Edd.), P Tor I. 1[ii. 2] (B.C. 116) ὑπὲρ ὧν μεταλαβόντος μου παρεγενήθην, εἰς τὴν Διόσπολιν, P Giss I. 27[3] (ii/A.D.) (=*Chrest.* I. p. 29) μετέλαβον πα[ρ]ὰ τινων ἀπὸ Ἰβιῶνος σήμερον ἐλθόντο[ν] συνοδοιπορηκένα[ι] τιν[ὶ] παιδαρίῳ κτλ. For the legal sense of "assign" see P Tebt II. 294[18] (A.D. 146) τοῖς παρ' ἐμοῦ μεταλημψομένοις, "to my assigns," P Ryl II. 162[22] (A.D. 159) ἐνγόνοις αὐτῆς καὶ τοῖς παρ' αὐτῆς μεταληνψομένοις, "to her descendants and assigns," and similarly P Oxy X. 1276[13] (A.D. 249).

μετάλημψις

as read by WH in 1 Tim 4[3] (for the intruded μ see *s.v.* λαμβάνω) is found in the sense of "concurrence" in the marriage-contract P Oxy X. 1273[39] (A.D. 260) οὐ προσδεόμενος τῆς τοῦ ἑτέρου μεταλήμψεως οὐδὲ ἑτέρας εὐδοκήσεως, "without requiring the concurrence of the other side or any further consent" (Edd.); cf. *ib.* IX. 1200[36] (A.D. 266).

μεταλλάσσω

From the meaning "exchange" which this verb has in its only occurrences in the NT (Rom 1[26f.]), the transition is easy to "exchange by leaving," "quit," and hence the common μεταλλάσσω βίον = "I die," e.g. P Par 22[14] (B.C. 165) μετήλλαχεν τὸν βίον, OGIS 326[15] (ii/B.C.) μεταλλάσσων τὸν βίον ἐν Περγάμωι προενοήθη τῆς συνόδου. The use of μεταλλάσσω alone in this sense is perhaps still more common in our sources, e.g. BGU IV. 1148[8] (B.C. 13) τῶι μεταλλαχότι αὐτῆ ς) ἀνδρὶ Ἰσιδώρωι, P Oxy X. 1282[18] (A.D. 83) ὑπὸ τοῦ γενομένου καὶ μετηλλαχότος τῆς Θναῆτος ἀνδρός, "by the former husband, now deceased, of Thnas" (Edd.), P Ryl II. 108[9] (A.D. 110–11) ἀπὸ κληρον[ο]μίας τῆς μεταλλαχυίης ἡμῶν μη(τρὸς) Εὐδαιμονίδ(ος), "from the inheritance of our deceased mother Eudaemonis," P Oxy III. 477[11] (A.D. 132–3) ἡ μ[ε]τήλλαχεν, "who is dead," and *Syll* 731 (= [3] 1109)[10] (*c.* B.C. 200) δέδωκεν δὲ καὶ τοῖς μετα[λλ]άξασιν τὸ ταφικὸν παραχρῆμα.

μεταμέλομαι

A good ex. of the reflexive meaning "repent oneself," as in Mt 21[30] *al.*, is afforded by BGU IV. 1040[20] (ii/A.D.) χα[ίρ]ω ὅτι μο[ὶ τα]ῦτα ἐποίησας ἐμοῦ μ[ετ]αμ[ελομ]ένου π[ερὶ μ]ηδενός. καθαρ[ὰ]ν γὰρ ἔχων τὴν ψυχὴν κτλ. : cf. *ib.* 1208[i] (B.C. 27–6). In the great calendar inscr. *Priene* 105[10] (= OGIS 458[10]) (*c.* B.C. 9), the verb has the somewhat weaker sense of "regret" (cf. 2 Cor 7[8] RV), the birthday of Augustus being described as the beginning of life, the end of a man's regretting that he has been born—πέρας καὶ ὅρος τοῦ μεταμέλεσθαι, ὅτι γεγέννηται. For the impers. act. see P Hib I. 59[11] (*c.* B.C. 245) εἰ μὴ παύσει κ[α]κοποῶν ἐν τῆι κώμη[ι] μεταμελή[σ]ει σοι, "if you do not stop your malpractices in the village you will repent it" (Edd.), and for the pass. form see P Thead 51[15] (iv/A.D.), where a man is warned to give back an artaba of corn he has wrongly taken—εἰ δὲ μὴ μεταμελησθῆναι ἔχεις, "otherwise you will have reason to be sorry for it." The subst. μετάμελος is seen in P Fay 124[23] (ii/A.D.) μετάμελόν σ[ο]ι πάλειν εἰσο[ίσ]ει ἡ πλεονεξ[ί]α σου, "your cupidity will again cause you regret" (Edd.), and for two exx. of the usual form μεταμέλεια cf. Menander *Fragm.* p. 268.

μεταμορφόω

P Leid W[vi. 36] (ii/iii A.D.) (= II. p. 87) σοὶ πάντα ὑποτέτακται, οὗ οὐδεὶς θεῶν δύναται ἰδεῖν τὴν ἀληθινὴν μορφήν. ὁ μεταμορφούμεν(ος) εἰς πάντας, ἀόρατος, ἐφ' αἰῶν' αἰῶνος. "qui transformaris in omnes (i.e. "qui omnium deorum formas assumis," p. 170), invisibilis in seculum seculi," similarly *ib.* XIII 34 (II. p. 127); cf. 2 Cor 3[18] and the parallel expression in Seneca *Ep.* 6. 1—"intellego, Lucili, non emendari me tantum, sed transfigurari" (cited by Clemen *Primitive Christianity*, p. 68). On the translation of Rom 12[2], see Field *Notes*, p. 162.

μετανοέω

A few exx. of this important verb can be quoted from our sources—PSI V. 495[9] (B.C. 258–7) νυνὶ δὲ μετανενόηκεν διὰ τὸ ἐπ[ι]τετιμῆσθαι ὑπὸ κτλ, P Gurob 6[3] (B.C. 212) ἐάμπερ μὴ βούλησθε μετανοῆσαι—in a broken context, OGIS 751[9] (ii/B.C.) θεωρῶν οὖν ὑμᾶς μετανενοηκότας τε ἐπὶ τοῖ[ς] προημαρτημένοις (cf. 2 Cor 12[21]) BGU III. 747[i. 11]

(A.D. 139) οἰό[μ]ενος με[τ]ανοή[σι]ν (*l.* μετανοήσειν) ἡμεῖν
ἐπιχό[ν] (*l.* ἐπεῖχόν) σοι τῷ κυρίῳ δηλῶσαι, P Tebt II. 424[5]
(late iii/A.D.) εἰ μὲν ἐπιμένις σου τῇ ἀπονοίᾳ, συνχέ(= αἴ)ρω
σοι· εἰ δὲ μετανοεῖς, σὺ οἶδας, "if you persist in your folly,
I congratulate you : if you repent, you only know" (Edd.),
BGU IV. 1024[iv. 25] (end of iv/A.D.) ὑπὸ γὰρ τοῦ ἐπι-
κιμέν[ου] αὐτῷ ἔρωτος [παρῆλθεν μ]ετανοῶν. In P Lond
807[22] (A.D. 84) (= III. p. 207) παρακαλῶ δὲ σὲ εἴνα μὴ
μελανήσῃς, the editor suggests that for μελανήσῃς we
may perhaps read μετανήσῃς for μετανοήσῃς. See also
Menandrea p. 12[72] where the verb is used of "change of
mind." Its meaning deepens with Christianity, and in the
NT it is more than "repent," and indicates a complete
change of attitude, spiritual and moral, towards God. MGr
μετανοιώνω, "repent."

μετάνοια.

The transition to the deeper sense of this word (see *supra*)
appears in Aristeas 188, where God is described as by His
gentleness and long suffering—μετατιθεὶς ἐκ τῆς κακίας
[καὶ] εἰς μετάνοιαν ἄξεις, "turning men from their wickedness and leading them to amendment." The interesting
Calendar of Church Services at Oxyrhynchus, P Oxy XI.
1357[4] (A.D. 535-6), mentions a ἡμέρ(α) μεταν(οίας), and we
hear of a μοναστήριον μετανοίας at Alexandria in P Flor
III. 298[54] (vi/A.D.) : cf. P Lond 996[3] (vii/A.D.) (= III.
p. 248), and see Sophocles *Lex. s.v.* The phrase ἐν μετα-
νοίᾳ [γ]ενομένους occurs in PSI V. 452[14] (iv/A.D.), and
similarly in BGU III. 836[5] (time of Justinian). In *ZNTW*
i. p. 66 ff. Wrede discusses the translation of μετάνοια in
the NT ("nicht Sinnesänderung, sondern Busse"). It may
be added that Lactantius (*Div. Inst.* vi. 24. 6) for the
ordinary *paenitentia* of Christian Latinity prefers *resipi-
scentia*, as implying, like μετάνοια, a coming to one's senses,
resulting in a change of conduct.

μεταξύ

is used prepositionally c. gen., as in Mt 18[15], Rom 2[15],
in such passages as P Rein 44[16] (A.D. 104) μετὰ τὸν τῆς
συμφωνίας τῆς γενομένης μεταξὺ αὐτοῦ καὶ Ἰσιδώρας, P
Oxy VIII. 1117[3] (*c.* A.D. 178) μεταξὺ ἡμῶν καὶ ἀρχόντων,
P Gen I. 48[11] (A.D. 346) τὴν συμ[π]εφωνηθεῖσα[ν] μεταξὺ
[ἡ]μῶν ἀλλήλων τιμήν, P Oxy VII. 1026[2] (v/A.D.) μεταξὺ
ἐλάβομεν Γεροντίου κ[α]ὶ Ἰωάννην (*l.* -ης) ὥστε λαβεῖν
Ἰω[ά]ννην τὰ ἱμάτια κτλ., "we have mediated between
Gerontius and John to this effect : John shall take the
cloaks" etc. (Ed.), PSI I. 71[5] (vi/A.D.) μεταξὺ ἐμοῦ τε κ(αὶ)
τῶν λιτουργῶν, and *Kaibel* 418[1] (ii/A.D.) τὸ μεταξὺ βίου
θανάτοιό τε. For the adverbial usage in relation to *time*, as
in Jn 4[31], cf. BGU IV. 1153[7] (B.C. 14) τοῦ μεταξὺ χρόνον,
ib. 1139[8] (B.C. 5) ἐν δὲ τῷ μεταξύ, P Giss I. 30[2] (A.D. 140-
161), *al.* : see also P Oxy X. 1320 (A.D. 497) ὁμολογῶ
ὀφείλειν σοι καὶ χρεωστεῖν ἀπὸ λόγου τιμῆς οἴνου οὗ
ἐώνημαι παρὰ σοῦ καὶ ἐβάσταξα κατὰ τὰ μεταξὺ γενόμενα
[γραμματεῖα (?). The form μετοξύ is found from i/A.D.
onwards in such passages as P Lond 177[11] (A.D. 40-41)
(= II. p. 168) ἐν δὲ τῷ μετοξύ, P Amh II. 64[4] (A.D. 107)
ἄλλα μετοξὺ δεδα[π]ανῆσθαι, "that further expenses had
been incurred meanwhile" (Edd.), P Oxy XIV. 1630[12] (A.D.
222?) μετοξὺ ἡμῶν [καί τιν?]ων ἀνδρ[ῶ]ν, P Tebt II. 433

(iii/A.D.) διαλήμψεται μετοξὺ ἡμῶν ὁ στρατηγός, and, in
relation to space, P Oxy XII. 1475[20] (A.D. 267) τὸ μετοξὺ
πωμάριον, "the intervening orchard" : see also Thackeray
Gr. i. p. 77 for LXX parallels, and Reinhold p. 40 for the
usage in the early Christian Fathers. MGr στὸ μεταξύ,
"in the meantime" : (ἀνα-)μεταξύ of place, "between,"
"among."

μεταπέμπομαι,

"summon," "send for," occurs in such passages as P Petr
II. 19 (1 *a*)[8] (iii/B.C.) ἀξιώσας αὐτὸν [με]ταπέμψασθαί με
καὶ δίεσθαι ("dismiss") [ἀπὸ τῆς] φυ[λα]κῆς, P Tebt II.
289[7] (A.D. 23) μεταπεμψάμε νος) πέμψωι τῶι ἡγεμ[όνι] ὡς
ἀ[με]λοῦντα τῆς εἰσπρά[ξεως. "I shall summon and summon
you to the Prefect for neglecting the collecting," P Ryl II.
77[41] (A.D. 192) μεταπεμφθήσονται δὲ καὶ οἱ κοσμηταὶ ἵνα
ἐπὶ παροῦσι αὐτοῖς αὐτὰ ταῦτα εἴπητε, "but the cosmetae
shall also be summoned in order that you may repeat the
same statements in their presence" (Edd.), and P Oxy I.
118 *verso*[7] (late iii/A.D.) συμβουλευθέντες . . . διὰ τὸ
ἄδηλον τῆς ὁδοιπορίας προθυμεῖον μεταπέμψασθαι (*l.*-
ασθαι), "we have been advised to send for a ferry-boat on
account of the uncertainty of the road" (Edd.).

μεταστρέφω,

which in the NT occurs only in Ac 2[20], Gal 1[7], and as a
v. l. in Jas 4[9], means literally "change from one state to
another" : cf. Deut 23[5], Sir 11[31 (33)]. The verb occurs in
P Par 574[2625] (iv/A.D.) μεταστρέφοντός σου τὸν λόγον ὡς
ἐὰν θέλῃς.

μετασχηματίζω.

For the meaning "refashion," "change the outward
appearance of that which itself remains the same," we may
appeal to *Preisigke* 5174[10] (A.D. 512), where, in connexion
with the purchase of an hermitage, power is given—καθελεῖν,
ἀνοικοδομεῖν, μετασχηματίζειν, ἐν οἷᾳ βούλεται ὄψει καὶ
διαθέσει : similarly *ib.* 5175[12] (A.D. 513) and P Mon 13[46]
(A.D. 594) πωλεῖν καὶ μεταπωλεῖν καὶ μετασχηματίζειν.
The passages, though late, are important in connexion with
the interpretation of Phil 3[21] : see also Field *Notes* p. 169 f.
for the meaning of 1 Cor 4[6]. To the exx. of the verb from
profane sources add Diod. Sic. ii. 57, where it is used in
connexion with the dividing up of the root-forms of the
letters of the alphabet : cf. Gardthausen *Palaeographie*[2], pp.
41, 263. Cf. also Iamblichus *de Myst.* 3, 28, and see further
s.v. σχῆμα.

μετατίθημι.

With the use of this verb in Ac 7[16] we may compare
P Tebt II. 330[12] (*c.* A.D. 190) ἐξ ὧν μ[ε]τατίθ(ενται) εἰς
δη(μοσίαν) γῆν (πυροῦ) (ἀρτάβαι) κτλ., of wheat "transferred" to domain land. See also with reference to persons
P Ryl II. 220[94] (between A.D. 134-5 and 138), an official
list of males, perhaps for military purposes, a certain number
of whom had been transferred to a new heading or a new
village in the 19th year of Hadrian—καὶ ἐνθάδ(ε) μετ]ε(τέ)-
θ ησαν τῷ ιθ (ἔτει) οἱ πλειόνων ("those in excess"), and
P Lond 322[5] (A.D. 214-5?) (= II. p. 159 f., *Chrest.* I.
p. 421), an application for the payment of the porters' hire,

agreed upon for the removal of persons named from the village of Bacchias to that of Socnopaei Nesus—πρὸς ἀπαίτησιν φορέτρου ἀποτάκτου τῶν μετατιθεμένων ἐνθάδε ἀπὸ κώμης Βακχιάδος. In BGU I. 4⁹ (ii/iii A.D.) μετατεθέντος μου εἰς ἄλα (sic) Βουκοντίων, military transference from one *ala* or company to another is indicated : and in P Oxy XII. 1417²⁰ (early iv/A.D.) ἀπὸ τῆς βουλῆς μετατεθῆναι the reference is apparently to change of purpose, though unfortunately the immediate context is wanting : cf. Aristeas 188 μετατιθεὶς ἐκ τῆς κακίας [καὶ] εἰς μετάνοιαν ἄξεις, and *Menandrea* p. 64⁴⁸ ὥστ' εἰ τοῦτ' ἐδυσχέρανέ τις ἀτιμίαν τ' ἐνόμισε, μεταθέσθω πάλιν, "if any one disliked it, and thought it a wicked shame, let him change his mind." The description of Dionysius of Heracleia, who deserted the Stoics for the Epicureans, as ὁ μεταθέμενος, "the Turncoat" (Diog. Laert. vii. 166) may help us with Gal 1⁶ (cf. 2 Macc 7²⁴ μεταθέμενον ἀπὸ τῶν πατρίων) : see also Field *Notes*, p. 188.

μετατρέπω,

which "seems not to have been used in Attic" (LS), is read by WH in Jas 4⁹. The verb occurs *quinquies* in 4 Macc : cf. also **Aq.** Ezek 1⁹, **Sm.** Ezek 1⁹, 10¹¹, and Aristeas 99 where the man, who has been permitted to behold the high-priest's vestments, is described as—μετατραπέντα τῇ διανοίᾳ διὰ τὴν περὶ ἕκαστον ἁγίαν κατασκευήν, "profoundly moved in his mind at the sanctity attaching to every detail" (Thackeray).

μετέπειτα,

"thereafter," occurs in the NT only in Heb 12¹⁷ : cf. *OGIS* 177¹⁴ (B.C. 96-5) εἰς τὸν μετέπειτα χρόνον, and for the form see Mayser *Gr.* p. 242.

μετέχω.

With the use of μετέχω in 1 Cor 10¹⁷ οἱ γὰρ πάντες ἐκ τοῦ ἑνὸς ἄρτου μετέχομεν, cf. *Magn* 44¹⁷ (end of iii/B.C.) μετέχειν τᾶς τε θυσίας καὶ τοῦ ἀγῶνος, where too the immediately following ¹⁹τοὺς κοινωνησοῦντας τᾶς τε θυσίας proves that here, as in the Corinthian passage (¹⁶τὸν ἄρτον ὃν κλῶμεν, οὐχὶ κοινωνία τοῦ σώματος τοῦ χριστοῦ ἐστίν :), μετέχω and κοινωνέω must be regarded as synonymous: see Thieme p. 29 f. For a similar ex. from the papyri, cf. P Oxy XII. 1408²⁶ (c. A.D. 210-14) εἰσὶ δὲ ὑποδεχομένων πολλοὶ τρόποι· οἱ μὲν γὰρ κοινων[οῦντες τῶν ἀδικη]μάτων ὑποδέχονται, οἱ δὲ οὐ μετέχοντες μὲν κα[. . . "there are many methods of giving them (viz. robbers) shelter : some do so because they are partners in their misdeeds, others without sharing in these yet . . ." (Edd.). For the acc. after μετέχω cf. P Petr III. 32 (*f*)⁶ (iii/B.C.) (= *Chrest.* I. p. 310) ἐπέδωκά σοι ἤδη ὑπομνήματα κατὰ Φίλωνος τοῦ μετέχοντός μοι τὴν μερίδα, and for the gen., as in 1 Cor 9¹² *al.*, cf. P Tebt II. 309²⁰ (A.D. 116-7) διὰ τὸ [μὴ δύνασθαι με]τασχέσθαι τῆς γεωργίας, "as I am unable to take part in the cultivation" (Edd.), and *Syll* 213 (= ³ 409)⁶³ (c. B.C. 275-4) ὅσαι ἐπιδόσεις γεγόνασιν ἐν τῶι δήμωι πασῶν μετέσχηκεν.

μετεωρίζομαι.

For this verb in the literal sense of "am lifted up, suspended," cf. P Oxy VI. 904⁶ (v/A.D.) where a certain Flavius complains that he has been maltreated in the per-

formance of his duties—καθ' ἑκάστην ἡμέραν μετεωριζόμενον σχοινίοις καὶ πληγαῖς κατακοπτόμενον κατὰ τὸ σῶμα, "being daily suspended by ropes and having my body belaboured with blows." From this it is a natural transition to the sense of being elated or exalted in mind, seeking high things, as in the LXX (Ps 130¹, 2 Macc 5¹⁷, 7³⁴), and, according to some commentators, in Lk 12²⁹, the only passage where the verb is found in the NT (cf. Vg *n̄ līte in sublime tolli*, Luther *fahret nicht hoch her*, Tind., Cov. "neither clyme ye up on high"). But, in view of the context, the rendering "be not anxious, worried" (cf. "be not ye of doubtful mind," AV, RV) is more likely, and is supported by such a passage from the Κοινή as P Oxy XIV. 1679¹⁶ (iii/A.D.) μὴ μετεωρίζου, καλῶς διάγομεν, "do not be anxious, we are well" (Edd.). The adj. μετέωρος is used technically of an "incompleted" contract, which is therefore still "in suspense" in P Oxy II. 235¹ (A.D. 72) μετεώρους οἰκονομίας : see the editors' introduction, and cf. P Fay 116¹² (A.D. 104), *Chrest.* II. i. p. 99. More general exx. of the same usage are—P Ryl II. 144¹⁹ (A.D. 38) παραγενομένου μου εἰς Εὐημερείαν . . περὶ μετεώρων ἐλ[ογ]οποιησάμην πρὸς Ὀννῶφριν κτλ., "having gone to Euhemeria on some unfinished business, I entered into conversation with Onnophris etc." (Edd.), P Oxy IX. 1219⁵ (iii/A.D.) Θέων ὁ υἱὸς ἡμῶν παραγείνεται πρὸς σὲ πορευόμενος εἰς τὴν Νεικίου ἕνεκα ἀναγκαίου αὐτοῦ μετεώρου, "Theon our son is coming to you on his way to the city of Nikias on account of a pressing incompleted negotiation" (Ed.), *ib.* XIV. 1755¹⁶ (ii/A.D.) μελέτω σοι δὲ καὶ περὶ ὧν ἄλλων ἔχω παρὰ σοὶ μετεώρω[ν] ἐπισχεῖν, and a letter published by Vitelli in *Atene e Roma* vii. p. 124, ll. 11-13 οὔτ[ε ἐλουσάμην [οὔτε προσεκύνησα θεοὺς φοβουμένη σου τὸ μετέωρον, an interesting ex. of the popular idea of reciprocity between gods and men (see the editor's note on P Oxy VII. 1065⁴ᶠ). From the inscrr. we may cite *Syll* 510 (= ³ 364)¹³ (after B.C. 207) ἐκ τῶν [τὰ μετέ]ωρα ἐγγυωμένων, *i.e.* pecunias simpliciter mutuas datas sine pignore aut hypotheca " (Dittenberger): cf. *OGIS* 483⁶² (ii/B.C.) ἐάν τινες . . . μετεώρους ὀχετοὺς ποιῶσιν, κωλυέτωσαν αὐτοὺς οἱ ἀμφοδάρχαι, with Dittenberger's note, "in voce μετεώρους non putaverim editionis loci vim inesse, sed omne genus canalium a superiore parte apertorum intellegi, ut recte eis opponantur tecti (κρυπτοί)." See also Epict. iii. 24. 75 ὅταν θέλω, πάλιν εὐφραίνῃ καὶ μετέωρος πορεύῃ εἰς Ἀθήνας, "when I choose you can put on a glad face again and go off in high spirits to Athens" (Matheson), and for the Ionic μετάρσιος cf. Wackernagel *Hellenistica*, p. 12 f. The subst. μετεωρισμός occurs *quater* in Vett. Valens = *vitae perturbatio*.

μετοικεσία,

"transportation," "deportation." The verb μετοικέω is supplied by A. W. Mair and W. M. Ramsay in a Phrygian epitaph of about the middle of iv/A.D. in honour of C. Calpurnius Collega Macedo—θεοῦ προνοίᾳ καὶ ἱερῶν ἀγγέλων συνοδίᾳ με[τοικήσαντα] εἰς [ο]ὐρανὸν ἐξ ἀνθρώπων (see *CR* xxxiii. p. 2).

μετοικίζω.

With the use of this verb in Ac 7⁴ of "transporting" or "transferring" from one country to another cf. *OGIS* 264⁷ ἐκράτησεν τῶν Περγα[μηνῶν καὶ μ]ετώκισεν αὐτοὺς πάλιν ἐπὶ τὸν κο[λωνὸν εἰς] τὴν πα[λαιὰ]ν πόλιν, *Syll* 932 (= ³889)¹⁰ (A.D. 202) μετῴκισαν εἰς αὐτὸ οἱ ὑποτεταγμένοι, and Aristeas 4 περὶ τῶν μετοικισθέντων εἰς Αἴγυπτον ἐκ τῆς Ἰουδαίας. See also *CR* i. p. 7.

μετοχή.

For this NT ἅπ. εἰρ. (2 Cor 6¹⁴) cf. P Lond 941⁸ (A.D. 227) (= III. p. 119) κατὰ μετοχὴν τοῦ ἄλλου ἡμίσους [τῶ]ν ὅλ[ων οἰκοπ]έδω[ν, *al.* See also Meyer *Jur. Pap.* No. 116⁶³ (c. A.D. 567) εἶ[ν]αί τέ σε μάλιστα . . ἄμοιρον παντελῶς πά[σ]ης μετοχῆς καὶ σχέσεως κληρονομίας μο(υ), cf. ⁷⁸. In MGr μετοχή = "participle," "participation."

μέτοχος.

This adj. in the sense of "sharer," "partner," as in Lk 5⁷ (cf. Heb 3¹⁴), is common in papyri: cf. e.g. P Petr III. 37 (a)⁴⁺⁷ (B.C. 250) διὰ Πασῖτος καὶ τῶν μετόχων, BGU IV. 1123⁴ (time of Augustus) ὁμολογοῦμεν εἶναι τοὺς τρεῖς με[τό]χους καὶ κοινωνοὺς καὶ κυρίους ἕκαστον κατὰ τὸ τρίτον μέρος ἀπὸ τοῦ νῦν εἰς τὸν ἀεὶ χρόνον τῆς προκειμένης μισθώσε[ως . . ., P Ryl II. 189¹ (A.D. 128) Διονύσιος Σωκράτους καὶ οἱ μέτοχοι παραλῆπται δημοσίο(υ) ἱματισμοῦ κονστωδιῶν παρειλ(ήφαμεν) (*l.* παρειλ-) κτλ., "we, Dionysius son of Socrates and the associate collectors of public clothing for the guards, have received etc." (Edd.), *ib.* 192⁵ (A.D. 142) διέγρα(ψε) Σωτᾷ καὶ μετόχ[οις] πράκ(τορσιν) ἀρ[γ]υρικ(ῶν). "paid to Sotas and associates, collectors of money-taxes," and *Theb Ostr* 41¹ (A.D. 64-5) Πικῶς Παμώνθ ου) καὶ μέτοχοι Σενφαήριος χαίρειν, "Pikos son of Pamonthes and his colleagues to Senphaeris, greeting"—receipt for a salt-tax. In P Leid I¹ (ii/B.C.) (= I. p. 34) Ἀλέξανδρος καὶ οἱ μέτοχοι, οἱ πραγμα[τ]ευόμενοι τὸ [ὦ]νητικὸν (*l.* ὠνητικὸν) κα[ὶ τὸ] ἐπιδέκατον ἀπὸ τοῦ . . ., the editor defines μέτοχοι as those who *societatem inierant ad certa quaedam tributa redimenda et exigenda*, or, according to Reuvensius, "co-interesses": in P Lips I. 106¹¹ (A.D. 98) ἐὰν οὖν ὅ γε γνώστης σὺν τῷ μετόχῳ ἀσφαλίζηταί σε διὰ τοῦ γράμματεος (*l.* γράμματος) τῶν γεωργῶ ν), the reference may be either to a second "cognitor," or to the joint-owner of a holding. whose price is under discussion. For μέτοχος c. gen., as in Heb 3¹⁴, cf. *Kaibel* 654⁵ (iii/A.D.) πρόσθεν μὲν θνητή, νῦν δὲ θεῶν μέτοχος. The form μετοχικός is seen in P Strass II. 110¹⁹ (c. A.D. 18) μέρος καὶ ἔχειν μετοχεικ[ὸν . . .

μετρέω.

"measure," is naturally common, e.g. P Petr III. 89² (Ptol.) μετρῆσαι τοῖς ὑπογεγραμμένοις γεωργοῖς . . . δανείον εἰς τὸν σπόρον τοῦ κροτῶνος, P Tebt I. 10⁶ (B.C. 119) τὰ ἀπολείψοντα ἐκ τοῦ ἰδίου μετρήσει, "he shall measure out the deficiency from his private means" (Edd.), *Chrest.* I. 108⁵⁵ (B.C. 95) οἱ δὲ μεταληψόμενοι τὴν χρείαν μετρήσουσι κατ᾽ ἔτος τὸ ἱερόν, P Tebt II. 459⁴ (B.C. 5) ὃ ἐὰν περισσὸν γένηται μέτρη[σ]ον αὐτοῖς, P Ryl II. 168¹¹ (A.D. 120) τὰ δὲ ἐκφόρια μετρήσαι ἐν τῶι Ἐφεὶπ μηνί, "I will measure the rent in the month Epeiph." P Flor II. 154⁴ (A.D. 268) πό[σας] ἀρτάβας ἐμέτρησας τοῖ[ς] δεκαπρώτοις: cf. the compound καταμετρέω LXX Numb 34⁷ *al.*) in connexion with "horsemen," "cavalry," in

P Hal I. 15⁵ (iii/B.C.) ἐπὶ τοὺς καταμεμετρημένους ἱππεῖς, P Lille I. 14³ (B.C. 243-2) τῶν περὶ Φαρβαῖθα καταμεμετρημένων μισθοφόρων ἱππέων. The verb very readily passes into the meaning "pay," as in the ostracon receipt *Theb Ostr* 110¹ (A.D. 61) μεμέτρηκε Ὧρος . . εἰς θησαυροῦ (*l.* ὃν) ἱερατικοῦ Κάτω τοπαρχ(ίας) κτλ. "Horos has paid into the granary of the Lower toparchy etc.": cf. P Oxy XII. 1443⁵ (A.D. 227?) λόγ[ος ἐν κεφαλ αίῳ] τῶν μεμετρημένων ἡμῖν, "summary account of payments to us" (Edd.), *ib.* XIV. 1689³² (A.D. 266) τὸν μὲν πυρὸν ὡς εἰς δημό[σι]ον μετρούμενον.

μετρητής.

For μετρητής, a "measure" of wine, as in Jn 2⁶, cf. P Gurob 8¹¹ (B.C. 210) ἱκάζω δὲ τὰ τετρυγημένα εἰς οἴνου με(τρητὰς) ϛ, "I estimate the grapes gathered at six metretae of wine" (Ed.), and *Syll* 306 (= ³672⁵⁴ (B.C. 102-0) οἴνου μετρητὰς τεσσαράκοντα. See also P Leid D²⁰ (B.C. 162) (= I. p. 25) ἐλαίου μετρητήν, and P Lond 1169ⁿ⁺⁶ (iii/A.D.) (= III. p. 44) Ὅμηρος ἐξάγ[ων] ἐ(πὶ) ὄν(ῳ) ᾱ ἐ(λαίου) μετ(ρητὰς) β̄—an interesting document from which we learn that two metretae of oil were an ass's load, so that the amount of excise duty could be ascertained by counting the number of the animals. The content of the μετρητής amounted to about 39·39 litres or 8⅔ gallons: see also Smyly in P Petr III. p. 197. For μέτρημα cf. P Oxy IX. 1221⁴ (iii/iv A.D.) τὰ μετρήματα τῆς πρὸς λίβα ἐν τῷ Παραιτονίῳ διὰ τῶν ἐκεῖ γεωργῶν κατὰ τὸ ἔθος μετρεῖται, "the deliveries of the western toparchy are being measured in at Paraetonium by the cultivators there according to custom" (Ed.)—with reference to the payment of corn dues, and for μέτρησις cf. P Petr I. 22(2)³ (ii/B.C.) μέτρησις ἔργων τῶν ἐν τῇ Καλλιφάνους μερίδι, "measurement of work done in Calliphanes' division," P Oxy XIV. 1671⁸ (iii/A.D.) τὸν λόγον τῆς μετρήσεως, "the account of the measuring."

μετριοπαθέω.

"feel moderately," does not occur in the LXX, and in the NT is confined to Heb 5², where see Windisch's note in *HZNT*. For the adj. see Aristeas 256, where it is laid down that one of the elements of φιλοσοφία is—τὰ πρὸς τὸν καιρὸν πράσσειν δεόντως μετριοπαθῆ καθεστῶτα, "to do the duty of the moment as it should be done, practising moderation" (Thackeray); cf. the new adj. μετριοφιλής in P Ryl II. 114³ (petition to the Prefect—c. A.D. 280) τὸ μετριοφιλές σου αἰσθομένη. "perceiving your love of equity" (Edd.).

μετρίως.

This NT ἅπ. εἰρ. (Ac 20¹², cf. 2 Macc 15³⁸) may be cited from P Par 46⁵ (B.C. 153) (= Witkowski², p. 86) εἰ ἔρρωσαι . . . εἴη ἄν ὡς βούλομαι, καὶ αὐτὸς δὲ μετρίως ἐπ[α]ρ[κῶ, P Ryl II. 150⁹ (A.D. 40) ὕβρισεν οὐ μετρίως, P Tor I. 2⁴ (ἠ)δικημένος οὐ μετρίως καὶ κινδυνεύων τῶν ἰδίων στερηθῆναι, and the touching letter of a slave to her master, P Giss I. 17⁵ (time of Hadrian) (= *Chrest.* I. p. 566) ἠγωνίασα, κύριε, οὐ μετρίως, ἵνα ἀκούσω ὅτι ἐνωθρεύσας, "I was distressed in no small measure, on hearing that you were sick." For the adj. see P Oxy VIII. 1117¹⁹ (c. A.D. 178) μέτρια κεκτήμεθα ἐξ ὧν καὶ μόλις ζῶμεν, and *ib.* I. 129⁷ (iv A.D.) μετρίων γὰρ καὶ δυστυχῶν γένεσιν αἴχοντες οὐδὲ οὕτω αἱαυτοῖς προσαίχομεν, "we fail to realize the inferiority and wretchedness to which we are born" (Edd.). Ramsay (*Luke*, p. 399) quotes from a iv A.D. Lycaonian inscr. μετρίων χηρῶν, "virtuous widows." The subst. μετριότης is found in P Oxy VIII. 1121⁹ (A.D. 295), where a daughter declares that she has nursed her sick mother—κατὰ τὴν ἐμαυτῆς μετριότητα, "in the goodness of my heart" (Ed.). For a different usage cp. P Beauge 3, 11 (ed. J. Maspero: cited in PSI V. p. 9) κατὰ τὸν δυνατὸν τρόπον τῆς ἐμῆς μετριότητος, "within the possible limits of my modest means."

μέτρον.

The varied uses of μέτρον, "a measure," may be illustrated by P Amh II. 43⁹ (B.C. 173) repayment of a loan in wheat that is "new, pure, free from all adulteration"—μέτρωι δικαίωι τῶι πρὸς τὸ βασιλικὸν χαλκοῦν μετρήσει καὶ σκυτάληι [δ]ικαίαι, "by just measure calculated by the royal bronze standard, and with just measurement and rule" (Edd.). P Par 32¹² (B.C. 162) (= Witkowski², p. 67) ἐπιλελῆσθαι τὰ μέτρα τῶν ὀθονίων, *ib.*²⁴ ἀπόστειλό[ν] μοι τὰ μέτρα τῶν ὀθονίων, P Oxy IV. 717⁸ (late i/B.C.) συμβάλλω] αὐτὸ πρὸς τὸ χαλκοῦν μέτρον ἐν τῶι συνεδρείωι, P Fay 89¹⁵ (A.D. 9) μέτρωι τετάρτωι, "the quarter measure" (cf. *ib.* 90¹⁴ (A.D. 234) ἐνδεκαμέτρῳ, P Ryl II. 156⁶ (i/A.D.) ἐν οἷς καμάρα ὧν μέτρα βορρᾶ ἐπὶ νότον μέχρι . . . , P Tebt II. 417¹⁸ (iii/A.D.) μέτρη[σ]ον τὸν ἐρεγμόν, εἴδε πόσα μέτρα [ἔ]χι, "measure the pulse and see how many measures there are" (Edd.): for further exx. see Preisigke *Fachwörter*, p. 125. With the 1st part of Lk 6³⁸ cf. P Oxy VII. 1069²⁵ (iii/A.D.) κ[α]λὰ μέτρα αὐτῷ βαλέτωσαν, "let them put good measure into it (a tunic)," and P Flor II. 266⁶ (A.D. 255 or 265) καλῶς μετρήσας, and with the second part cf. P Lond 976⁵ (A.D. 315) (= III. p. 231) μετροῦντος (*l.*-ντες) μέτρῳ ᾧ καὶ παρειλήφαμεν. For the phrases ἐν μέτρωι (Ezek 4¹¹, cf. Jn 3³⁴ ἐκ μέτρου) see P Tebt I. 17⁷ (B.C. 114) στόχασαι ὡς πάντα τὰ ἐνοφειλόμενα περὶ τὴν κώμην ἐν μέτρωι ἔσται, "endeavour to have all arrears owing from the neighbourhood in order" (Edd.). From the inscrr. we may cite *Syll* 364 (= ³ 797)⁷ (A.D. 37) οὐδὲν δὲ μέτρον χαρᾶς εὕρηκ[ε]ν ὁ κόσμος.

μέτωπον.

With Rev 13¹⁶, where the allusion is to the habit of marking soldiers and slaves with a distinctive brand (see Moffatt *ad l.* in *EGT*), we may compare P Lille I. 29ⁱⁱ·³⁶ (iii B.C.) ὁ δὲ παραλ[αβ]ὼν τὸ ἀνδρά]ποδον μαστιγωσ[ά]τω μὴ ἔλασσον ἑκατὸν π[λ]ηγῶν καὶ] στίξατο τὸ μέτω[πον—with reference to the punishment of a runaway slave. The word is naturally common in those personal descriptions with which the papyri have made us so familiar, e.g. BGU III. 975⁹ (A.D. 45) (= *Selections*, p. 42) οὐλ]ὴ μετόπο ἀριστερό (*l.* μετώπῳ ἀριστερῷ), "a scar on the left forehead." P Oxy I. 72⁴⁶ (A.D. 90) οὐ λὴ μετώπ(ῳ) μέσῳ, and P Fay 91¹⁰ (A.D. 99) οὐλὴ μετόπωι ἐγ δεξιῶν. MGr μέτωπο.

μέχρι, μέχρις.

Μέχρι is used prepositionally (1) of *time* c. gen.—P Tebt I. 5⁴²⁶ (B.C. 112-1) μέχρι τοῦ νῦν, "up to the present

time," BGU IV. 1148⁴¹ (B.C. 13) μέχρι τῆ[ς] ἐνεστώσης ἡμέρας, P Tebt II. 370¹¹ (A.D. 102) μέχρι τῆς ἐσομένης κοινῆς γεωργῶν διαμισθώσεως, "until the coming joint leasing out among cultivators" (Edd.), *ib.* 390¹¹ (A.D. 188) τοὺς τόκους μέχρι [τῆ]ς ἐνεστώσης ἡμέρας, "the interest to date" (Edd.), P Oxy XIV. 1647²¹ (date iii A.D.) ἀπὸ ἀνατολῆς ἡλίου μέχρι δύσεως, "from sunrise to sun-set": and c. τοῦ and inf.—P Rev Mél p. 295⁴ (B.C. 131-0) (= Witkowski², p. 99) μέχρι τοῦ τὰ πράγματ' ἀποκαταστῆναι, P Tebt I. 29¹⁷ (c. B.C. 110) μέχρι [το]ῦ ἀπὸ τῆς προ[κει]μένης ἀσχολ[ία]ς ἀπολυθῆ[ναι, "until I am free from the labours above mentioned" (Edd.), P Oxy XIV. 1641⁵ (A.D. 68) μέχρι τοῦ τὸν χρόνον πληρωθῆναι: 2) of *place*, as in Rom 15¹⁹—*ib.* 1074⁶ (iii/A.D.) ἐὰν συντελεσθῇ τὸ ἔργον μέχρι τοῦ χώματος, "if the work is finished up to the embankment" (Edd.): and (3) of *degree* —P Tor I. 1⁹·²⁵ (B.C. 116) μέχρι τελευτῆς βίου (cf. Phil 2² μέχρι θανάτου, "to the length of death": Christ did not obey death (as in AV), but obeyed His Father in dying), P Oxy IX. 1203²³ (late ii/A.D.) μέχρι κρίσεως, BGU III. 747ⁱⁱ·¹¹ (A.D. 139) μέχρι αὐθαδίας. For μέχρι with the force of a conjunction "till" c. conj., as in Eph 4¹³, cf. P Cairo Preis 48⁷ (ii A.D.) μέχρι τὸ πλοιαρίδιον εὕρωμεν. On the omission of ἄν in the foregoing exx. see Moulton *Proleg.* p. 168 f. Μέχρις, which is read *ter* by WH in the NT (Mk 13³⁰, Gal 4¹⁹, Heb 12⁴) appears first in the papyri in the Roman period (Mayser *Gr.* p. 244): cf. Vett. Val. p. 357¹⁹ μέχρις ἐκ μηνιαίου ἢ ἐνιαυσιαίου ὑποστασιν ἀναδέξηται ὁ χρόνος, and from the inscrr., as early as the beginning of iii/B.C. *IG* XII. 5, 647 μέχρις ἂν ἥλιος δύῃ. On the LXX usage see Thackeray *Gr.* i. p. 136. See also *s.v.* ἄχρι, which is an *ablaut* variant of μέχρι. The root is an Indo-European *me, which produces μετά and μέσος (Boisacq, p. 631).

μή.

The general distinction between οὐ and μή is that οὐ is *objective*, dealing only with facts, while μή is *subjective*, involving will and thought. But in late Greek μή has encroached very largely upon οὐ, with the result that in the NT οὐ is almost entirely confined to the indicative, while μή monopolizes the other moods (but see I. 5). A few exx. of some of the many uses of μή will make this clear.

I. Μή negatives (1) the *conjunctive* (a) after ἐάν (ἄν)—P Oxy II. 294¹² (A.D. 22) (= *Selections*, p. 36), where certain men are confined to prison, ἐὰν μή τι πίσωσι τὸν ἀρχιστάτορα δο[ῦ]ναι εἰκ(= ἱκανόν), "unless indeed they shall persuade the chief usher to give security," BGU II. 530¹² (i A.D.) (= *Selections*, p. 61) αἰαν (*l.* ἐάν) μὴ ἔλθῃς, κινδυνεύω ἐκστῆναι οὗ ἔχω [κλ]ῆρον, "if you do not come, I run the risk of losing the lot (of land) which I possess"—a father writes to his dilatory son, P Oxy I. 119⁵ (illiterate—ii/iii A.D.) (= *Selections*, p. 103) ἂμ μὴ θέλῃς ἀπενέκαι μ[ε], ταῦτα γε[ί]νετε, "if you refuse to take me, that's what's up!"—a boy to his father: (b) after ἵνα—P Oxy IV. 744¹³ (B.C. 1) (= *Selections*, p. 33) ἐρωτῶ σε οὖν ἵνα μὴ ἀγωνιάσῃς, "I beg you therefore not to worry," P Fay 112¹² (A.D. 99) ἐπέχον τῷ δακτυλιστῇ Ζωίλωι καὶ εἶνα αὐτὸν μὴ δυσωπήσῃς, "give heed to the measurer (?) Zoilus; don't look askance at him" (Edd.), and P Head 6¹¹ (iv/A.D.) (= *Selections* p. 120) ἵνα οὖν μὴ πολλὰ γράφω καὶ φλυαρήσω . . . παρακαλῶ . . . , "in order that I may not by much writing prove myself an idle babbler, I beseech . . . ": μὴ ἵνα is found for ἵνα μή in P Ryl II. 230⁹ (A.D. 40) μὴ [ο]ὖν ἄλλως ποιή[σ]η(ς) μὴ ἵνα δόξωμέν σε εὐθέως ἠλλάχθαι τὰ πρὸς ἡμᾶς, "do not neglect this, lest we think you to have become all at once estranged towards us" (Edd.): (c) in the 2nd pers. aor.—forbidding what is still future (as in Mt 3⁹, 10²⁶, Mk 5⁷, Rom 10⁶ al.) —P Petr II. 40 (a)¹² (iii/B.C.) μὴ οὖν ὀλιγοψυχήσητε. ἀλλ' ἀνδρίζεσθε, P Oxy IV. 744¹¹ (B.C. 1) (= Selections, p. 33) εἴρηκας δὲ Ἀφροδισιᾶτι ὅτι μή με ἐπιλάθῃς· πῶς δύναμαί σε ἐπιλαθεῖν: "You told Aphrodisias, 'Do not forget me.' How can I forget you?", BGU II. 380³⁹ (iii/A.D.) (= Selections, p. 105) μὴ οὖν ἀμελήσῃς, τέχνον, γράψε (l. γράψαι) μοι περὶ τῆς σωτηρίας [σ]ου, "do not then neglect, my child, to write me regarding your health," and P Tebt II. 421⁵ (iii/A.D.) (= Selections, p. 106) τὸ κιτώνιον αὐτῆς τὸ λευκὸν τὸ παρὰ σοὶ ἐνίγκον ἐρχ[ό]μενος τὸ δὲ καλλάϊνον μ[ὴ] ἐνίγκῃς, "her tunic, the white one which you have, bring when you come, but the turquoise one do not bring": for a full discussion of this usage contrasted with the usage immediately following, (2), see Moulton Prolegomena, p. 122 ff.

(2) the present imperative, bidding one desist from what is already begun (as in Mt 7¹, Mk 5³⁶, 1 Thess 5¹⁹, Jas 2¹)— P Hib I. 56⁷ (B.C. 249) σὺ οὖν μὴ ἐνόχλει [α]ὐτόν, "do not molest him (as you are doing)," P Amh II. 37⁷ (B.C. 196 or 172) (as amended Archiv ii. p. 123) μὴ] ἀθύμει, ἀλλ' ἄφες <σ> αὐτὸν χαίρειν, "do not lose heart, but suffer yourself to rejoice," and P Oxy II. 295⁵ (illiterate—c. A.D. 35) μὴ σκλύλλε (l. σκύλλε) ἑατὴν ἐνῆναι (l. ἐμφῆναι), "stop troubling to give information," but, as showing that the distinction must not be pressed too far, note P Oxy VI. 932¹⁰ (late ii/A.D.) where a woman instructs a friend—τὰ χοιρίδια χωρὶς μοῦ μὴ πώλι, "do not sell the young pigs without me," and the natural reference is to the future;

(3) the infinitive (a) after verbs of saying, thinking, commanding etc. (as in Mt 2¹², 5³⁴·³⁹, Mk 12¹⁸, al.)—P Tebt II. 284³ (i B.C.) ἐπικέκριταί μοι μὴ καταβῆναι ἕως τῆς κε, "it has been decided for me that I should not go down till the 25th," P Oxy II. 206²⁰ (A.D. 96) ὁμολογεῖ . . . μὴ [ἐ]νκαλεῖν [μηδὲ ἐνκαλέ]σειν, "acknowledges that he neither makes nor will make any claim," ib. 237ᵛⁱⁱ·²⁵ (A.D. 186) Δίδυμος ῥήτωρ ἀπεκρείνατο μὴ χωρὶς λόγου τὸν Σεμπρώνιον κεκεινῆσθαι, and P Amh II. 135⁵ (ii/A.D.) ἐρωτῶ σε μὴ ἀμελεῖν μου, "I beg you not to forget me"; (b) after a preposition —P Petr II. 11 (1)⁷ (iii/B.C.) (= Selections, p. 8) τοῦτο δὲ γίνεται διὰ τὸ μὴ ἀθροῦν ἡμᾶς, ἀλλὰ κατὰ μικρὸν λαμβάνειν, "this happens because we do not get our money in a slump sum, but in small instalments," P Alex 4³ (iii/B.C.) (= Witkowski², p. 51) πρὸς τὸ μὴ γίνεσθαι τῶι βασιλεῖ τὸ χρήσιμον, and P Lond 42¹² (B.C. 168) (= I. p. 30, Selections, p. 10) ἐπὶ δὲ τῶι μὴ παραγίνεσθαί σε . . . ἀηδίζομαι, "but on account of your not having returned I am distressed"; (c) after ὥστε expressing consequence (as in Mt 8²⁸, Mk 3²⁰, 1 Cor 1⁷)—P Hib I. 66⁵ (B.C. 228) συνλαλήσω σοι ὥστε σε μὴ διὰ κενῆς εὐχαριστῆσαι ἡμῖν, "I will have a conversation with you, so that you shall not oblige me to no purpose" (Edd.);

(4) the participle (as generally in the New Testament)— P Eleph 13⁷ (B.C. 223-2) (= Witkowski², p. 43) μὴ ὀκνῶν (cf. Ac 9³⁸) γράφειν ἡμῖν, "not delaying to write us," P

Grenf II. 38¹ (mid. i/B.C.) καλῶς οὖ]ν ποιήσις μὴ ἀμελή-σ[α]ς α[. . . ἀγο]ράσαι . . . , P Oxy I. 38¹⁶ (A.D. 49-50) (= Selections, p. 53) τοῦ δὲ Σύρου μὴ βουλομένου ἐνμεῖναι τοῖς κεκριμένοις, "as Syrus does not wish to abide by what has been decided," ib. II. 275⁴² (A.D. 66) (= Selections, p. 58) ἔγραψα ὑπὲρ αὐτοῦ μὴ ἰδότος γράμματα, "I wrote for him seeing that he was unlettered," BGU I. 22⁵ (A.D. 114) (= Selections, p. 74) Ταρμοῦθις . . . τὸ παρὸν μὴ ἔχουσα κύριον, "Tarmuthis at present without a guardian," and P Grenf II. 77⁹ (iii/iv A.D.) (= Selections, p. 120) θαυμάζω πάνυ [ὅτι] ἀλόγως ἀπέστητε μὴ ἄραντες [τὸ σ]ῶμα τοῦ ἀδελφοῦ ὑμῶν, "I wonder exceedingly that you went off so unreasonably, without taking the body of your brother": cf. P Tor I. 1ᵛⁱⁱⁱ·²⁴ (B.C. 116) εἰ δὲ καί τις θείηι τὸ μὴ ὄν (cf. 1 Cor 1²⁸)—acc. and inf. follow, P Ryl II. 144²² (A.D. 38) ἐπαγαγεῖν αἰτίας τοῦ μὴ ὄντος, "to bring baseless charges," and see Hort's note ad 1 Pet 1⁸ for the change from οὐ (οὐκ ἰδόντες) to μή (μὴ ὁρῶντες) in that verse:

(5) the indicative (a) in relative clauses as CPR I. 19⁷ (iv/A.D.) ἐντάξας . . . ἃ μὴ συνεφώνησα, BGU I. 114ⁱ·²⁵ (ii/A.D.) προοῖ[κ]α (l. προῖκα) [ἣ]ν ἀπ[ο]δέδωκεν αὐτῷ μήτε δ[ύ]να[τ]αι λαβεῖ[ν, (b) in cautious assertions (as in Lk 11³⁵, Gal 4¹¹, Col 2⁸)—P Tebt II. 333¹¹ (A.D. 216) ὑφορῶμαι οὖν μὴ ἔπαθάν τι ἀνθρώπινον "I therefore suspect that they have met with some accident" (Edd.), P Gen I. 17¹⁵ (iii/A.D.) ὑφωρούμε . . . μὴ ἄρ[α ἐ]νθρώσκων [. . ἔλ]αθεν ὕ[δατ]ι, "I suspect he may have jumped into the water unnoticed"; cf. Moulton Prolegomena p. 193, where it is pointed out that in such cases "the prohibitive force of μή is more or less latent, producing a strong deprecatory tone"; (c) in the volitive future—BGU I. 197¹⁴ (A.D. 17-18) μὴ ἐξέσται [τοῖς μεμισ]-θωμένοις προλιπεῖν τὴν μίσθωσιν ἐ[ν]τὸς τοῦ χρόν[ου, ib. III. 698³² (ii/A.D.) μὴ αὐτοὶ ὄψονται περὶ πάντων . . [ἐν τ]άχει τὴν ἀντιφώνησιν, and ib. 814²⁷ (iii/A.D.) ἐρωτῶ σε οὖν, μήτηρ, μὴ ἀφήσις (l. ἀφήσεις) μοι οὔτος (l. οὕτως): see again Moulton Prolegomena, p. 177.

II. For μή, as a conjunction "that," "lest," "perchance," as in Mt 24¹, Ac 13⁴⁰, Gal 5¹⁵, after verbs of fearing, caution, etc., cf. P Far 45⁷ (B.C. 153) (= Witkowski², p. 85) προσέχων, μὴ εὕρη τι κατὰ σοῦ ἰπεῖν (l. εἰπεῖν). P Lond 964⁸ (ii/iii A.D.) (= III. p. 212) βλέπε μὴ ἐπιλάθῃ οὐδέν, "see to it that he forgets nothing."

III. Μή interrogative occurs 69 times in the NT, and seems to have been a feature of everyday language (see Moulton Prolegomena, p. 239). A good ex. is P Oxy I. 120¹⁴ (iv/A.D.) μὴ ἄρα παρέλκομαι ἢ καὶ εἴργομαι ἔστ' ἂν ὁ θεὸς ἡμᾶς αἰλαίηση (l. ἐλεήσῃ), "am I to be distracted and oppressed until Heaven takes pity on me?" (Edd.): cf. Mt 7⁹·¹⁰, Mk 2¹⁹, Rom 3³, al. With Jn 4²⁹ we may compare Epict. ii. 11. 20 μή τι οὖν βέβαιον ἡ ἡδονή: "can pleasure then be a steady thing?" (cited by Sharp, p. 98). On Jn 21⁵ see Moulton Prolegomena, p. 170 n.¹, and note that in Jas 3¹¹ Hort (Comm. ad l.) finds the stronger sense of impossibility, comparing Mk 4²¹, Lk 6³⁹. See also Exp VIII. xxvi. p. 129 ff.

IV. In BGU IV. 1032¹⁰ (A.D. 173) μή is construed with an adj., ἐκ μὴ νομ[ί]μων γάμων: cf. Rom 12¹¹. For ἐκτὸς εἰ μή see s.v. ἐκτός, and cf. C. and B. ii. p. 391, No. 254, a sepulchral inscr. from the Eumeneian district, where a man provides that his tomb shall not be occupied by any one except his wife and himself—χωρὶς εἰ μή τι πάθῃ ἡ θυγάτηρ

Ἄπφιον πρὸ τῆς ἡλικίας. For εἰ μή see *s.v.* εἰ, and add P Alex 4[7] (iii/B.C.) εἰ μὴ τὴν μήκωνα ("poppy") συνάξεις, οὐδείς σε ἀνθρώπων μὴ ὠφειλήσηι, P Par 47[3] (c. B.C. 153) (= *Selections*, p. 22) ἱ μὴ μικρόν τι ἐντρέπομαι (cf. 2 Thess 3[14]), οὐκ ἄν με ἴδες τὸ π<ό>ρσωπόν μου πό(—ώ)ποτε, "but for the fact that I am a little ashamed, you would never yet have seen my face," and P Oxy VI. 939[21] (iv/A.D.) (= *Selections*, p. 129) εἰ μὴ ἐπινόσως ἐσχήκει τὸ σωμάτιον τότε ὁ υἱός Ἀθανάσιος, αὐτὸν ἄν ἀπέστειλα πρός σε, "unless my son Athanasius had then been in a sickly state of health, I would have sent him to you." For ἐπεὶ μή see *s.v.* ἐπεί, and for οὐ μή see *s.v.* οὐ. Reference may be made to Basil L. Gildersleeve "Encroachments of μή on οὐ in Later Greek" in *AJP* i. (1880), p. 45 ff. and to two important papers dealing with μή in *Studies in Honor of Basil L. Gildersleeve* (Baltimore, 1902) — "Indicative Questions with μή and ἄρα μή" by J. E. Harry, p. 427 ff., and "Μή for οὐ before Lucian" by Edwin L. Green, p. 471 ff.

In MGr a final ν may be added : μήν and μή, like νάν and νά, follow the analogy of δέν and δέ (Thumb *Handbook*, p. 25 n.[2]: also p. 200 where the uses of μή ν) are conveniently summarized).

μήγε.

For εἰ δὲ μήγε see *s.v.* γε.

μηδαμῶς.

P Par 15[64] (B.C. 120) μηδαμῶς δυναμένου ἐπιδεῖξαι καθόλου τινά τῶν ἑαυ[τοῦ] γονέων, P Tor I. 1[viii. 28] (B.C. 116) τὰ μηδαμῶς ἀνήκοντα πρὸς τὴν ἐνεστῶσαν κρίσιν, P Oxy VI. 901[11] (A.D. 336) μηδαμῶς ἀδικηθεὶ[ς] ὑπὸ τῶν χύρ[ων (*l.* χοίρ-), and P Strass I. 40[34] (A.D. 569) μ[η]δαμῶ[ς] ἀποστῆναι τῆς δουλικῆς α[ὐ]τοῦ προσταςί̣ας. On the relation of μηδαμῶς and οὐδαμῶς, see Mayser *Gr.* p. 182.

μηδέ.

P Lond 42[29 f.] (B.C. 168) (= I. p. 30, *Selections*, p. 10) σὲ δὲ μηδ' ἐντεθυμῆσθαι τοῦ παραγενέσθαι μηδ' ἐνβεβλοφέναι εἰς τὴν ἡμετέραν περίστασιν, "that you have neither thought of returning, nor spared a look for our helpless state"—the complaint of a wife to her husband who had shut himself up in the Serapeum, P Grenf I. 43[7 f.] (ii/B.C.) α]ὐτοῦ δὲ μηδ' ἀποδεδωκότος ἡμῖν μ̣ηδ̣[ὲ ἵππον μηδὲ τὴν πορείαν αὐτῆς ἐπ[ιδε]δωκότος ἐγράψαμέν σοι, ὅπως οὖν εἰδῆ[ις.

μηδείς.

According to Thumb (*Hellen.* p. 14) the forms μηθείς and οὐθείς appear in the whole Greek world from iv/B.C., and are in wide use at the beginning of the Christian Era, after which they gradually disappear, without leaving any trace in MGr. We are prepared, therefore, to find that the forms in θ are more frequent in the LXX than in the NT, where there are only a few examples of οὐθείς (principally in the Lucan writings), and only one of μηθείς, namely Ac 27[33] according to ℵBA. A few exx. of μηθείς from the papyri will suffice—P Petr II. 11(1)[3] (mid. iii/B.C.) (= *Selections*, p. 7) εἰ δυνατόν ἐστιν καὶ μηθέν σε τῶν ἔργων κωλύει, "if it is possible and none of your work hinders you,"

P Lond 42[21] (B.C. 168) (= I. p. 30, *Selections*. p. 11) μηθὲν σοῦ ἀπεσταλκότος, P Leid B[v. 7] (B.C. 164) (= I. p. 10) εἰς τὸ μηθὲν ἡμᾶς τῶν δεόντων ἐγλιπεῖν, *ib.*[31] ἄλλως δὲ τῷ (for dat. cf. 2 Cor 2[13]) μηθέν' ἔχειν πλὴν τοῦ Πτολεμαίου, P Ryl II. 66[19] (B.C. 54) πρὸς τὸ μηθὲν τῶν ἐκφορίων διαπεσεῖν, "so that the rents suffer no loss" (Edd.), P Oxy III. 492[19] (A.D. 130) μηθὲν ἦσσον, and similarly *ib.* 495[17] (A.D. 181-9). This last is pronounced by Thackeray (*Gr.* i. p. 59) "the latest date for θ." It should be noted that both in this and the preceding papyrus (and other instances could be cited) the form μηδείς also occurs, and further, as our citations will have shown, "that θ retained its hold more tenaciously in the neut. nom. and acc. than elsewhere" (Thackeray, *Gr.* i. p. 59). For the interchange between μηδείς and μηθείς in Ptolemaic times, see especially Mayser *Gr.* p. 180 ff. See also *s.v.* οὐδείς.

μηδέποτε.

P Tebt I. 57[6] (B.C. 114) μηδέποτε αὐτῶν τοῦτο πεπραχότων, "when they had never made this payment," P Giss I. 59[iv. 1] (A.D. 119-120) Βησαρίων Σιβούλιος μηδέ[ποτε] . . λειτουργήσας.

μηδέπω.

P Oxy III. 471[6] (ii/A.D.) τόκον κατέκρεινεν οὗ μηδέπω χρόνου λαβόντες ἔνιοι τὸ δάνειον ἦσαν. "he condemned people to pay interest for a period at which in some cases they had not yet even received the loan" (Edd.). BGU V. 1210[63] (c. A.D. 150) δούλῳ . . . μηδέπω τριάκοντα ἐτῶν γενομένῳ, "a slave not yet thirty years old."

μηκέτι.

For ἵνα μηκέτι, as in 2 Cor 5[15], Eph 4[14], cf. P Oxy III. 528[23] (ii/A.D.) τούτους τοὺς λόγους λέγεις ἥνα (*l.* ἵνα) μηκέτι [[φ]]πιστευθῶ μου τὴν ἐνβολ[ήν, "you say this to prevent my being believed any longer with regard to my embarkation (?)" (Edd.). As showing that μή with the pres. imper. must not be pressed as necessarily meaning "cease from doing something" (cf. *Proleg.* p. 125 f.), Mr. H. D. Naylor draws our attention to the ἔτι in 1 Tim 5[23] μηκέτι ὑδροπότει. "If Paul thought that there could be no ambiguity in μὴ ὑδροπότει, why should he insert ἔτι at all? Surely it is obvious that μὴ ὑδ. *might* be a warning against an act not begun, and therefore ἔτι is essential (in Paul's Greek) to make the sense 'cease drinking water' obvious at first sight."

μῆκος.

"length," of space, size, is seen in P Ryl II. 224 (a)[5] (ii/A.D.) μῆκο υς πηχῶν [.]: cf. P Lond 755 *verso*[8] (iv/A.D.) (= III. p. 222 f.). The reference is to time in P Leid W[iii. 5] (ii/iii A.D.) (= II. p. 89) σύρισον ἐπὶ μῆκος, and *OGIS* 666[27] (A.D. 54-68) διὰ τὸ μῆκος τοῦ [χρό]νο̣υ.

μηκύνω.

Aristeas 8 ἵνα δὲ μὴ περὶ τῶν προλεγομένων μηκύνοντες ἀδόλεσχόν τι ποιῶμεν, ἐπὶ τὸ συνεχὲς τῆς διηγήσεως ἐπανήξομεν, "but not to weary you with too long an introduction, I will resume the thread of the narrative" (Thackeray).

53

μηλωτή.

For this NT ἅπ. εἰρ. (Heb 11³⁷) = "sheepskin," cf. the list of imposts levied at Palmyra, *OGIS* 629³² (A.D. 137) πορφύρας μηλωτῆ[ς] ἑκά[σ]του δέρμα]τος εἰσκομισθέν[τος πράξει ἀσσάρια ἤ. The word occurs *quinquies* in the LXX always with reference to Elijah.

μήν.

See *s.v.* εἰ μήν. Other exx. of the particle are P Petr II. 16¹³ (mid. iii/B.C.) (= Witkowski², p. 12), ἠκούσ]αμεν ἀριθμὸν ἔσεσθαι ἐκ τῶν Ἀρσινοε[ίω]ν, οὐ μὴ[ν ἀλλ]ὰ πευσόμεθα ἀκριβέστερον, P Lond 42²⁸ (B.C. 168) (= I. p. 30, *Selections*, p. 11) οὐ μὴν ἀλλ' ἐπεὶ καὶ ἡ μήτηρ σου τυγχάνει βαρέως ἔχουσα, κα[λῶ]ς ποιήσεις κτλ., "nor is this all, but since your mother is in great trouble about it, you will do well, etc.," P Oxy III. 471¹²⁶ (ii/A.D.) οὐ μὴν εἰς [τὸ] τοῦ.[. . . . .] ἀγοραίου κριτηρ[ίου βῆμα?] ἑπτακαιδεκαετ[ὴς παῖς ἔσ]πετό σοι; "did not a boy of 17 years accompany you to the judgement-seat in the public court?" (Edd.), and *ib.* 472²⁷ (c. A.D. 130) ἀλλὰ μὴν ντων πίστεως περὶ τούτων οὔσης παρὰ τῷ δοκοῦντι πεπρακέναι, "again, if there had been security given to the supposed seller" (Edd.).

μήν.

For μήν denoting a (lunar) month cf. P Amh II. 50²⁰ (B.C. 106) τόκους διδράχμους τῆς μνᾶς τὸν μῆνα ἕκαστον, "interest at the rate of two drachmae on the mina each month," P Oxy II. 294⁶ (A.D. 22) (= *Selections*, p. 34) ἐπὶ τῷ γεγονέναι ἐν Ἀλεξανδρίᾳ [τῇ . . . τοῦ ὑπογε]γραμμένου μηνός, "on my arrival in Alexandria on the . . of the undernoted month." BGU III. 975¹ (A.D. 45) (= *Selections*, p. 42) μηνὸς Μεχὶρ πέμπτῃ καὶ εἰκάτῃ, "the twenty-fifth day of the month Mechir," and the illiterate P Oxy XII. 1489⁶ (late iii/A.D.) τοῦ ἄλλο (*l.* -ου) μηνὸς ἐλεύσομε (*l.* -μαι), "I shall return in another month," cf. ⁸ εἰ δὲ, ἔρχομε τῷ ἄλλο μηνί (*l.* ἔρχομαι . . ἄλλῳ). In a Ptolemaic ostracon, Mél. Nic. p. 185 No. 12⁷, we find κατὰ μῆναν (for form see *Proleg.* p. 49). The expression εἰς δύο μῆνας ἡμερῶν in P Strass I. 35⁵ (iv/v A.D.) is said to be "peculiar to the Egyptian speech" (see the introd.). The parenthetic nominative in expressions of time (cf. Mt 15³³, Mk 8², Lk 9²⁸; Moulton *Proleg.* p. 69 f.) is well illustrated by P Petr III. 36 (a) *verso*⁴ (Ptol.) λιμῷ παραπολλύμενος μῆνές εἰσιν δέκα, "perishing from hunger for the last ten months" (Edd.); cf. BGU III. 948⁶ (iv/v A.D.) γινώσκιν ἐ[θ]έλω ὅτι εἰπέν σοι ὁ πραγματευτ[ὴ]ς ὅ]τι ἡ μήτηρ σου ἀσθενεῖ, εἰδού, δέκα τρῖς μῆνες—a curious parallel to Lk 13¹⁶. For the adj. μηνιαῖος cf. P Ryl II. 206 (b)⁵ (iii/A.D.) εἰς λόγον διαγραφῆς μηνιαίου Ἀθύρ, "on account of the monthly payments of Hathur," and for ἐπιμήνια, "monthly supplies," see P Oxy III. 531¹⁷ (ii/A.D.). MGr μῆνας, pl. μῆνες, μῆνοι.

μηνύω.

With the forensic use of this verb in Jn 11⁵⁷, Ac 23³⁰, we may compare P Par 10¹⁶ (B.C. 145) where, after the description of a runaway slave, it is added—μηνύειν δὲ τὸν βουλόμενον τοῖς παρὰ τοῦ στρατηγοῦ, "if any one wishes to report him, let him do so to the attendants of the strategus," and the Prefect's proclamation for the protection of the

native population, P Lond 1171 *verso* (c)⁷ (A.D. 42) (= III. p. 107) ἐὰν δέ τις μηνυνθῇ ἢ τῶν στρατευομένων ἢ τῶν μαχαιροφόρων . . βεβιασμένος τινὰ τῶν ἀπὸ τῆς χώρας . . κατὰ τούτου τῇ ἀνωτάτῳ χρήσομαι τειμωρίᾳ. See also P Giss I. 61⁷ (A.D. 110) πολλὰ [αἰ]κι[σθ]έ[ν]τες ὑπὸ Ψάιτος κωμογρ[αμ]ματέως Ναβῶοι ἀναγκαίως μηνύοντ[ες] (*l.* μηνύομεν) α[ὐ]τὸν λογίαν πε[π]οιηκέναι ἐπὶ τῆς κώμης Ναβῶοι, P Tebt II. 297¹² (c. A.D. 123) ἐγράφη Ἀγαθῷ Δαίμονι σ[τρ[α]τηγῷ ἵν' ἐὰν ὁ κ[ωμογ]ραμματεὺς μὴ δεόντως τὴν τάξιν ἢ μεμηνυκὼς πραχθῇ . . . . "a letter was written to Agathodaemon the strategus in order that if the comogrammateus should have made an improper report upon the office he might be mulcted . . ." (Edd.), and P Oxy X. 1253¹² (iv/A.D.) ἵνα μηδέν σου λανθάνῃ τὴν λαμπρότητα μηνύομεν, ἔπαρχε κύριε, "we give this information that nothing may escape your highness, my lord praefect" (Edd.)—an official report concerning certain military requisitions. For the wider sense "make known" cf. *Syll* 237 (= ³ 417)⁷ (B.C. 273-2) χρήματα τῶι θεῶι ἐμάνυσαν ἃ ἦσαν ἐκ τοῦ ἱεροῦ ἀπολω[λό]τα ἀπὸ τοῦ ἀναθέματος τοῦ Φωκέων. See also P Leid Wᵛ ⁱⁱⁱ (ii/iii A.D.) (= II. p. 95) ἐφάνη Μοῖρα κατέχουσα ζυγόν, μηνήουσα (*l.* μηνύουσα) ἐν ἑαυτῇ τὸ δίκαιον, "Fate appeared holding a balance, showing that justice was to be found in her." In MGr the pres. form has changed to μηνῶ, although the aor. ἐμήνυσα retains the old spelling.

μήποτε

(= μή ποτε), in the sense of "lest haply," "lest perchance," as in Mt 4⁶, 5²⁵, *al.*, is seen in P Tebt I. 58³⁰ (B.C. 111) βεβουλεύμεθα ἐκσπάσαι τὸ ἐπιδεδομένον ὑπόμνη(μα) μή ποτε ἐπὶ τοῦ διαλογισμοῦ χειμασθῶμεν, "we have decided to abstract the memorandum lest haply we should come to grief at the audit," and P Oxy I. 118 *verso*⁷⁷ (late iii/A.D.) ἐπὶ (*l.* ἐπεὶ) οὖν βραδύνουσι μήποτε αὐτῶν χρεία γένοιτο εὐθέως αὐτοὺς ἐξέλασον, "since they are delaying, lest haply there might be need of them, send them off immediately." With Lk 21³⁴ cf. P Flor I. 99⁹ (i/ii A.D.) (= *Selections*, p. 72) προορώμεθα μήποτε ἐ[π]ηρεάσηι (cf. Lk 6²⁸) ἡμείν, "we are taking precautions, lest haply he should deal despitefully with us." For the construction with the ind. cf. P Par 49³¹ (B.C. 164-158) (= Witkowski,² p. 71) ἐγὼ γὰρ νὴ τοὺς θεοὺς ἀγωνιῶ, μή ποτε ἀρ[ρ]ωστεῖ τὸ παιδάριον, καὶ οὐκ ἔχω σχολὴν ἀναβῆναι πρὸς ὑμᾶς, "for by the gods I am anxious, lest haply the child is ill, and I have no leisure to come up to you." The constructions of the word in the NT are tabulated by H. Scott in Robertson *Gr.*³ p. 1415. Reference may also be made to Isidore *Epp.* ii. 270.

μήπου.

See *s.v.* μήπω.

μήπω,

"not yet," occurs in P Oxy VII. 1062¹⁵ (ii/A.D.) εἰ δὲ τοῦτό σοι βάρος φέρει καὶ μήπω ἠγόρασας, τὸ ἀργύριον δὸς Ζωίλωι τῷ φίλωι, "if it is troublesome and you have not yet bought them, give the money to my friend Zoilus" (Ed.), with reference to the purchase of some fleeces. In *ib.* 1008¹³ (iii/A.D.) μήπου is for μήπω—εὗρον τὸ σωμάτιν μήπου δυνάμενον κηδευθῆναι, "they found the body not yet ready to be buried" (Ed.).

μήπως

in the sense of "lest perchance" may be illustrated from the interesting letter of a son to his father, expressing anxiety regarding his safety. P Oxy XIV. 1680⁸ (iii/iv A.D.) καὶ γὰρ πρὸ τούτου σοι ἐδήλωσα λυπούμενος ἐπὶ τῇ ἐν ἡμῖν σου ἀπουσίᾳ, μήπως ὃ μὴ εἴοι (l. εἴη σοι γένοιτο καὶ μὴ εὕρωμέν σου τὸ σῶμα, "I have indeed told you before of my grief at your absence from among us, and my fear that something dreadful might happen to you and that we may not find your body" (Edd.). For a similar meaning with the ind. see P Flor II. 104¹¹ (A.D. 259) ὅρα δὲ μήπως οὐκ ἔστιν χρία Λεοντᾶν μαθῖν [π]ερὶ τούτου. In MGr independent μήπως is used in questions expressing doubt or denial, e.g. μήπως σοῦ εἶπα; "have I perhaps told you?" i.e. "I have not, of course, told you" (Thumb, Handbook, p. 181: see also Proleg. p. 248).

μηρός.

"thigh" (Rev 19¹⁶), is common in descriptions, as e.g. of a witness to a will, P Oxy III. 490¹³ (A.D. 124) εἰμὶ ἐτῶν λ οὐλὴ [κατὰ] μηρὸν ἀριστερό[ν, or of a camel that has been sold, P Lond 1132 b⁵ (A.D. 142) (= III. p. 142) κάμηλον θήλιαν φυρὰν κεχαραγμένη (l. πυρρὰν κεχαραγμένην μηρῷ δεξιῷ κάππα.

μήτηρ.

It is not necessary to illustrate at length this common noun, but one or two points may be noted. Thus for its loose use (cf. Rom 16¹³ and see s.vv. ἀδελφός, πατήρ, τέκνον) we may cite P Oxy X. 1296 (iii/A.D.) where the writer greets each of two women as "mother"—⁸ ἀσπάζομαι τὴν μητέραν (for the form cf. Moulton Proleg. p. 49) μου Ταμιέαν, and ¹⁵ τὴν μητέραν μου Τιμπεσοῦρ(ιν): cf. ib. XIV. 1678 (iii A.D.), where the same designation is applied to at least three persons. Similarly in P Giss I. 78¹ (ii/A.D.) Ἀληνὴ Τετῆτι τῆι μητρὶ χαίρειν, the word is used as the pet-name of an old servant. Μήτηρ is used ter as voc. in BGU III. 814 (iii/A.D.). For the adj. μητρικός cf. P Ryl II. 153³³ (A.D. 138–61) ὁ μητρικός μου δοῦλος Μύρων, "my mother's slave Myron." In MGr it has developed the sense "motherly." The MGr noun μητέρα shows its acc. sing. treated as nom. on the analogy of such a noun as χώρα.

μήτι.

On the translation of μήτι in the NT, see Moulton Proleg. p. 170 and Hort ad Jas 3¹¹.

μήτιγε.

With μήτιγε in 1 Cor 6³ μήτιγε βιωτικά, "not to speak of mere affairs of daily life," we may compare the corresponding μὴ ὅτι γε in P Lond 42⁻³ (B.C. 168) (= I. p. 30. Selections, p. 10) ὡς ἔτ[ι] σοῦ παρ[όν]τος πάντων ἐπεδεόμην, μὴ ὅτι γε τοσούτου χρόνου ἐπιγεγονότος, "while you were still at home, I went short altogether, not to mention how long a time has passed since"—the complaint of a wife to her husband. See also Herod. iv. 70.

μήτις

= μή τις, is found in an indirect question in BGU IV. 1141³¹ (B.C. 13) καθ᾽ ἡμέραν δὲ τὸν θυλωρὸν (l. θυρωρὸν) ἐξερωτῶι μή τις ἔξω ὕπνωκε, "and daily I ask the doorkeeper whether any one has slept outside."

μήτρα,

"womb" (Lk 2²³, Rom 4¹⁹), may be illustrated by a magic spell of possibly ii A.D., found among the Hawara papyri, Archiv v. p. 393, No. 312⁹ ff. ἄγε αὐτὴν τὴν Σαραπιάδ[α] ἣν ἔτεκεν εἰδία μήτρα μαει οτε ελβωσατοκ κτλ. Wünsch commenting on this (p. 397) refers to a tablet from Hadrumetum (Audollent 263¹² ⁸) with the words Victoria quem peperit Suavulus: "das letzte ist kaum ein eigentlicher Name, sondern ein Ersatz für den unbekannten Namen der Mutter" (Berl. phil. Wochenschr. 1905, 1080). See also Archiv i. p. 429.

μητρολώας.

For the form (1 Tim 1⁹) see Moulton Gr. ii. p. 68.

μητρόπολις.

This subst., which in the NT is confined to the late subscription of 1 Tim, may be illustrated from P Fay 28² (A.D. 150–1) (= Selections, p. 81), where a notice of birth is addressed to certain men as γραμματεῦσι μητροπόλεως. See also the letter of the prodigal BGU III. 846⁶ (ii/A.D.) (= Selections, p. 93), γεινώσκειν σαι θέλω ὅτι οὐχ [ἤλπ]ιζον ὅτι ἀναβένις εἰς μητρόπολιν, "I wish you to know that I had no hope that you would come up to the metropolis," and the Index to OGIS s.v. Apart from ecclesiastical use, the expression seems to have disappeared in early Byzantine times: see Chrest. I. i. p. 78. For μητροπολίτης cf. the land-survey P Ryl II. 216³⁰ (ii/iii A.D.), where one category is land belonging to citizens and assessed at 3 dr.— τρίδραχμος μητροπολιτῶν.

μιαίνω,

which differs from μολύνω as maculo from inquino, is never found in the NT in good part, but usually represents moral defilement (Tit 1¹⁵, Heb 12¹⁵): cf. the vision in the dream from the Serapeum, P Par 51²⁷ (B.C. 160) (= Selections p. 21, Archiv vi. p. 205) αὗται δὲ γυναῖκές εἰσιν. Ἐὰν μιανθῶσιν, οὐ [μ]ὴ γένονται καθαραὶ πόποτε, "but these are women. If they are defiled, they shall never at all be pure." See also P Leid Wᵛⁱⁱⁱ·⁴ (ii/iii A.D.) ἥκε κύριε, ἀμώμητος καὶ ἀπήμαντος, ὁ μηδὲ ἕνα τόπον μιαίνων, ὅτι τετέλεσμαί σου τὸ (ὄνομα), and for the verb used in a more general sense see P Par 14²¹ (B.C. 127) ἐκπηδήσαντές μοι καὶ μιάναντες, ὑβρίσαντές με, πληγάς ἔδωκαν, and P Flor III. 338³¹ (iii/A.D.) οἶδα γὰρ συνειδήσι (= σει) ("conscientiously") σπουδάζεις ἐμοὶ ἐμιάνθην γὰρ παρὰ πᾶσι. From the inscrr. we may cite OGIS 104¹⁵ (i/B.C.) τοῦ ἀέρος τῆι [νη]νεμίαι μια[ινομένου, where, however, the editor expresses doubts as to the restoration, Syll 891 (= ³ 1240)⁷ (ii A.D.) ὑβρίσει μιάνας, and Kaibel 713³ οὐ χεῖρα φόνοισι μιανας. The sense of legal defilement (טמא), as in the LXX, may be illustrated from Aristeas 166 μιανθέντες αὐτοὶ παντάπασι τῷ τῆς ἀσεβείας μολυσμῷ. For ἀμίαντος, see s.v.

μίασμα.

which in the NT occurs only in 2 Pet 2²⁰, is also found in Apoc. Petr. 9 τῷ μιάσματι τῆς μοιχείας. In the late *Kaibel* 1140 b³ (not before the time of Justinian) it is an epithet of Satan—Βελιὰρ κ[ακό]μορ[φ]ε, . . . μ[ί]ασμα, δράκων κτλ.

μίγμα.

which is read in the TR of Jn 10³⁹, is found in the magic P Lond 121⁸⁶⁷ (iii/A.D.) (= I. p. 112) λαβὼν πηλὸν ἀπὸ τρόχου [κε]ραμικοῦ μῖξον μίγματος τοῦ θίου κτλ.

μίγνυμι.

Chrest. I. 198¹² (B.C. 240) ἀ(ρτάβας) ς βωλοπύρου μεμιγμένοι (*l.* -ου) κριθῇ ἀ(ρτάβας) ιβ̄, BGU II. 372ⁱⁱ ² (A.D. 154) ἀ[νδ]ράσι πονηρὸν κ]αὶ λησ[τ]ρικὸν β[ίον ποιουμέ]νοις μείγνυσθ[αι, P Amh II. 67⁵ (*c.* A.D. 232) τὰ τελευταῖα τοῖς προτέροις μιγνύναι, and *OGIS* 502⁷ (ii/A.D.) μείξας τῷ φιλανθρώπῳ τὸ δίκαιον. The verb is found four times in the NT and six times in the LXX. Amongst the latter we may note the curious use in 4 Kingd 18²³ καὶ νῦν μίχθητε δὴ τῷ κυρίῳ μου βασιλεῖ Ἀσσυρίων, where the sense requires some such translation as "make an agreement or a wager with." For the compd. συμμίγνυμί τινι, *convenio cum aliquo*, cf. P Par 48¹¹ (B.C. 153) ἥκαμεν εἰς τὸ Σαραπιεῖον βολάμενοι συνμῖξαί σοι, and for συμμίσγω cf. P Tebt I. 12¹⁸ (B.C. 118) συμμίσγειν ἅμα ἡμέρᾳ, "to join them at daybreak" (Edd.): see further Mayser *Gr.* pp. 23, 91. MGr σμίγω.

μικρός.

In P Leid Nⁱⁱ ¹² (B.C. 103) (= I. p. 60) we hear of a Νεχούτης μικρός in a context which shows, according to the editor (p. 74), that the reference is to *age* rather than to *stature*: see further Deissmann *BS* p. 144 f. Other exx. are not so clear. P Gen I. 28¹¹ (A.D. 136) ἀγ]οράσαι παρὰ τοῦ πατρὸς αὐτοῦ Στοτοήτιος ἐπικαλουμένου Μικροῦ πυρόν, is not encouraging to the meaning *junior*, though, after all, there is no reason why "Stotoetis junior" should not be the father of a family. In any case the frequent occurrence of the formula makes it probable that it has a constant meaning: see P Eleph 17¹¹ (B.C. 223–222) Πρενέβθιος Ἰστφήνιος καὶ Ψεντῆς μικρός ἀπολέγονται τὴν γῆν κτλ., P Tebt I. 63¹⁵ (B.C. 116–115) γεω(ργὸς) Πετερμοῦθις μι(κρὸς) Ἀμμενέως, and P Goodsp Cairo 30ⁱⁱ·²⁴ (A.D. 191–2) μικρῷ Ἀφροδ(ισίῳ), ⁱⁱⁱ·⁵ Ἀφροδ(ισίῳ) καμηλ(είτῃ) μικ(ρῷ), Ἀφροδ. μικ. *quater* —other persons of the same name figure in this ledger, twice without description, then Ἀφρ. τέκτονι, ποιμένι Ἀφρ., and twice before a lacuna. In P Oxy XIV. 1666⁴ (iii/A.D.) a certain Pausanias writes περὶ τοῦ μεικροῦ Παυσανίου— evidently his son—stating that he desired to be transferred to a cavalry regiment. A similar application of the adj. to children is very common. We may cite, by way of example, P Lond 893⁷ (A.D. 40) (= P Ryl II. p. 381) καλῶς π[οιή]-σεις ἐξαυτῆ(ς) πέμψας μοι τὸν μεικρόν, "please therefore send me the child immediately" (Edd.), P Fay 113¹⁴ (A.D. 100) εἰκθύας (*l.* ἰχθύας) (δραχμῶν) ιβ̄ ἐπὶ τὰ τετρακοσιοστὰ (*l.* -κοστὰ τοῦ μικροῦ, "12 drachmas' worth of fish for the little one's four-hundredth-day festival" (Edd.), P Lond 899⁶ (ii/A.D.) (= III. p. 208) ἔπεμψα τῇ μικρᾷ ᾠὰ ιβ̄, "I sent twelve eggs to the little one," P Giss I. 78⁷ (ii/A.D.) ἡ

μικρά μου Ἡραιδ[ο]ῦς γράφουσα τῶι πατρὶ ἐμὲ οὐκ ἀσπά-ζεται κ[α]ὶ διὰ τί οὐκ οἶδα, P Oxy III. 530²⁶ (ii/A.D.) Θαισοῦν τὴν μικράν (following ²⁴ ἀσπάζου τὰ παιδία . . ., which seems to include Thaisous), and *ib.* 533²⁷ (ii/iii A.D.) ἀσπάσασθε τὸν μεικρὸν Σερῆνον καὶ Κοπρέα καὶ το[ὺ]ς ἡμῶν πάντας κατ' ὄνομα (a grown-up Serenus figures earlier in the letter). Other exx. of the adj. are P Meyer 12¹⁰ (A.D. 115) οὐλὴ δακτύλῳ μικρῷ χειρὸ ς ἀριστερᾶς, P Giss I. 20¹⁶ (ii/A.D.) μεικρὸν ἔρ[γο]ν αὐτοῦ π[έμψω]ν. See also for μικρόν τι, as in 2 Cor 11 ¹·¹⁶, P Par 47³ (*c.* B.C. 153) (= Witkowski², p. 88) ἱ μὴ μικρόν τι ἐντρέπομαι, οὐκ ἄν με ἴδες τὸ πρόσωπον (*l.* πρόσωπον) μου πόποτε, and for κατὰ μικρόν P Petr II. 11 (1)⁷ (iii/B.C.) (= *Selections*, p. 8), where Polycrates writes to his father that he does not get his money ἀθρούν, "in a lump sum," but κατὰ μικρόν, "in small instalments." For the comparative see *Chrest.* II. 372ᵛ ¹⁷ (ii/A.D.), where a soldier is described as— ἕν] χώρτῃ καὶ οὗτος ὁ μεικρότερος.

μίλιον.

For this noun (Mt 5⁴¹), which is a new formation from the Lat. plur. *milia* (*passuum*), cf. P Strass I. 57⁶ (ii/A.D.) μηδὲ μείλιον ἀπεχουσῶν ἀλλήλ[ων, "being less than a mile distant from each other"—of two villages, and *Syll* 418 (= ³ 888)²⁶ (A.D. 238) ἀπό γε μειλίων δύο τῆς κώμης ἡμῶν. For other nouns borrowed from Latin see Moulton *Gr.* ii. § 63.

μιμέομαι.

P Ryl II. 77³⁴ (A.D. 192) μιμοῦ τὸν πα[τ]έρα τὸν φιλότιμον τὸν [γ]έροντα φῶτα, "imitate your father the lover of office, the brave old man" (Edd.). P Oxy X. 1295³ (ii/iii A.D.) ἰδοὺ μὲν ἐγὼ οὐκ ἐμιμησάμην σε τοῦ ἀπᾶν (*l.* ἀποσπᾶν) τὸν υἱόν μου, "see, I have not imitated you by taking away my son" (Edd.), P Flor III. 367³ (iii/A.D.) ἐγὼ δὲ οὐ μειμήσομαί σε : cf. 2 Thess 3⁷·⁹. For μιμέομαί τι, as in Heb 13⁷, 3 Jn¹¹, we may cite *Kaibel* 85³ ἤσκουν μὲν τὸ δίκαιον ἐμιμού[μην τε τὸ καλόν, and Aristeas 188 μιμούμενος τὸ τοῦ θεοῦ διὰ παντὸς ἐπιεικές. For μίμησις cf. P Flor III. 292⁷ (vi/A.D.) κατὰ μ[ί]μησιν τῆς ἄρτι παρελθούσης ἕκτης ἰνδ(ικτίονος), and similarly *ib.* 295⁹ (vi/A.D.), and for μίμημα (Wisd 9⁸), cf. Musonius p. 90⁴ καθόλου δὲ ἄνθρωπος μίμημα . . θεοῦ μόνον τῶν ἐπιγείων ἐστίν.

μιμητής.

The NT usage of this word (1 Cor 4¹⁶ *al.*) is well illus-trated by such a passage as Xen. *Mem.* i. 6. 3 οἱ διδάσκαλοι τοὺς μαθητὰς μιμητὰς ἑαυτῶν ἀποδεικνύουσιν. It is note-worthy that in all its NT occurrences μιμητής is joined with γίνεσθαι, denoting moral effort (cf. Robertson-Plummer *ad* 1 Cor 11¹). For adj. μιμητικός cf. Vett. Val. p. 17²¹.

μιμνήσκομαι.

The act. μιμνήσκω, which is not found in the NT, is seen in P Giss I. 91⁶ (ii/A.D.) μιμνή[σκει] ἡμῶν συνεχῶς, and for pres. mid., as in Heb 2⁶, 13³, cf. P Hamb I. 37⁴ (ii/A.D.) ἀναγκαῖον γάρ ἐστι μνημίσκεσθαι (*l.* μιμνήσκεσθαι) τῆς καλοκαγαθίας σου, and BGU IV. 1024ⱽ·⁶ (iv/v A.D.) μιμνη-σκόμενος ὧν ἔπραξες. The perf. μέμνημαι in the sense of "bear in mind," "hold in remembrance," is common, e.g.

P Ryl II. 81²¹ (c. A.D. 104) τοῦ κατασπορέως . . . ὀφείλοντος . . . μεμνῆσ[θαί μ]ου τῆς γενομένη[ς] αὐτῷ ἐντολῆς παρόν[τος σο]ῦ, "the inspector of sowing ought to have remembered my order given when you were present" (Edd.), P Oxy III. 525⁹ (early ii/A.D.) μέμνη[σ]ο τοῦ νυ[κ]τ[ελίου] "Ισιδος τοῦ ἐν τῶι Σαραπ[ιείωι, "remember the night-festival of Isis at the Serapeum" (Edd.), P Ryl II. 235¹³ (ii/A.D.) διὸ μέμ[νησο] καὶ ἡμῶν κἄν πάνυ τ[ι]νὰ ἄ]λλα πράττῃς, "therefore bear us too in mind even if you are engaged in quite other pursuits" (Edd.), and P Oxy XIV. 1064⁴ (iii/A.D.) ὅτι οὐ μόνοι ἡμεῖς μεμνήμεθά σου ἀλλὰ καὶ αὐτοὶ ἡμῶν οἱ πάτριοι θεοί, τοῦτο δῆλον ἅπασιν, "that not only we but also our ancestral gods themselves hold you in memory is clear to all" (Edd.), ⁷ μεμνημένη τῆς ἀγαθῆς σου προαιρέσεως, "remembering your goodwill" (Edd.). For a similar use of the 1 aor. ἐμνήσθην, cf. P Tebt II. 410⁸ (A.D. 16) μν[ή]σθητι ῷ[s] (cf. Lk 24⁶) ἐν τῷ Τρ[ι]στόμῳ με ἐφιλοτ[ι]μοῦ σὺν ἐμοὶ μεῖναι, "remember how zealous you were at Tristomos to remain with me" (Edd.), ib. 420¹⁷ (iii/A.D.) μνήσθητί μου (cf. Lk 23⁴²) ὄν κἀγὼ πεποίηκά σοι ἀπὸ ἀρχῆς μέχρι τέλους, "remember me and what I also have done for you from beginning to end" (Edd.), P Oxy VIII. 1070³⁸ (iii/A.D.) ὑμεῖς οὐδὲ ὅλως ἐγράψατε οὐδὲ ἐμνήσθητέ μου περὶ τῆς ἀσφαλείας τῆς οἰκίας ἡμῶν, "you have not written at all nor remembered me in regard to the safety of our house" (Edd.), Preisigke 150³ μνήσθητι ἱμῶν καὶ παράδος ἡμῖν θεραπείαν—a temple inscr. to Aesculapius, and ib. 4018 ἱστορήσας ἐμνήσθην τῆς . . . ἀδελφῆς. The verb is also found c. dat. in the sense of "recall" to one in P Lille 8¹¹ (iii/B.C.) καλῶς οὖν ποιή[σε]ις μνησθεὶς Θεοδώρωι, ἵνα . . . "you will do well to recall to Theodorus that . . ." ib. 12¹ (B.C. 250–249) ἐμνήσθην σοι καὶ παρόντι περὶ τῶν ρ (ἀρουρῶν), "I have recalled to you verbally the matter of the 100 arourae." With Lk 1⁵⁴ cf. Pss. Sol. x. 4 καὶ μνησθήσεται (for form see Robertson Gr. p. 357) Κύριος τῶν δούλων αὐτοῦ ἐν ἐλέει (cited by Plummer ad l.), and with Lk 23⁴² cf. the Christian sepulchral inscr. from Antinoopolis Preisigke 1563⁶ Κ[ύρι]ε μ[ν]ήσθητι [τῆς δο]ύλη[s] σου [ἐν τῇ] βασιλεί[ᾳ σου.

μισέω.

which survives in MGr μισῶ, is not so common in our sources as we might have expected, but cf. PSI III. 158³⁷ (iii/A.D.?) βαρυόσμους μεισουμένους ὑπὸ τῶν ἀ[σ]τείων γυναικῶν, "evil-smelling persons hated by refined women," ib. I. 41²² (iv/A.D.) ἅπερ ἡ φύσις μεισῖ, P Oxy VI. 902¹³ (c. A.D. 465) μισοῦσειν γὰρ οἱ νόμοι τοὺς τὰ ἄδικα διαπραττομέν[ο]υς, "for the perpetrators of injustice are hateful to the laws" (Edd.), and the Christian amulet ib. VIII. 1151² (v/A.D.?) φεῦγε πν εὖμα μεμισιμένον (l. μεμισημένον). For the subst. μῖσος cf. Vett. Val. p. 242²⁵ ἡ ἐπιστήμη . . ὑπὸ τῆς ἀληθείας στηριζομένη τὸ . . μῖσος ἀποδιώξει, and the quotation from Menander Fragm. p. 187 s.v. κατατίθημι. With Menandrea p. 18²¹⁶ θεῖον δὲ μισεῖ μῖσος, cf. Is 138 (130 ²²), where the same cogn. acc. occurs.

μισθαποδότης.

With Heb 11⁶ we may compare the Christian P Gen I. 14²⁷ (Byz.) (as corrected p. 36) τῷ μισ[θ]αποδότη θεῷ. For the corresponding verb cf. the sepulchral inscr. from a Coptic cemetery, CIG IV. 9124⁵ μισθαπο[δοτήσας.

μίσθιος.

Deissmann's contention (LAE, p. 72) that this word is not to be regarded as a specifically NT word, but as belonging to the ordinary Greek of the time, receives further confirmation from such a passage as P Amh II. 92¹⁹ (A.D. 162–3) οὐχ ἕξω δὲ κ[ο]ινωνὸν οὐδὲ μίσθιον γεν[ό]μενον τῆς ὠνῆς ὑποτελῆ. The editors translate, "I will have no partner or servant who is liable on account of the contract," but Wilcken (Chrest. I. p. 376) from its association with κοινωνόν prefers to take μίσθιον as "tenant," "sublessee." The adj. is also found in P Flor III. 322²¹ (A.D. 258?) μίσθιοι ξδ.

μισθός.

For the primary sense of this word "wage," "salary," cf. P Tebt II. 384²⁹ (A.D. 10) τέλους γερδίων καὶ τῶν τούτων μισθῶ[ν, "weavers' tax and wages," P Fay 91²³ (A.D. 99) τὸν ἡμερήσιον μισθόν, "daily wage," P Lond 846¹⁰ A.D. 140¹ (= III. p. 131, Chrest. I. p. 242) ἀπ[όρου] μου ὄ[ν]τος καὶ μισθοῦ πορίζοντος τὸ ζῆν ἀπὸ τῆς γερδια[κ]ῆς—petition of a weaver, who works for a wage (μισθοῦ), and has no means (πόρος) for discharging a public liturgy, P Oxy IV. 724⁵ (A.D. 155), where a slave is apprenticed to a shorthand-writer to be taught shorthand μισθοῦ τοῦ συμπεφωνημένου "at a salary agreed upon" of 120 silver drachmae, and P Fay 103³ (iii/A.D.) μ[ισθὸς τοῖς ἠρκάσι αὐτόν, "pay for the bearers" in connexion with funeral expenses. See also the temple inscr. at El-Kab Preisigke 158 Ἀνδρόμαχος Μακεδὼν ἀφίκετο πρὸς Ἀμενώθην χρηστὸν θεὸν μ[ι]σθοῦ ἐργαζόμενος καὶ ἐμαλακίσθη καὶ ὁ θεὸς αὐτῶι ἐβοήθησε αὐθημερή.

The dim. μισθάριον occurs in the illiterate P Tebt II. 413¹³ (ii/iii A.D.) ταῦτά σοι συναλάγη πέμπε[ιν] ἐκ τῶν μισταρίων ἀτῆς, "it was arranged with you that these should be sent from her earnings" (Edd.). A new compd. μισθοπρασία is found in P Lond 1164(f)⁶ (A.D. 212) (= III. p. 164), and is understood by the editors as denoting a sale under the terms of a lease (cf. EEF Arch. Rep. 1907–08, p. 57); for μισθαποχή in the sense of μίσθωσις see P Gen I. 70¹⁰ (A.D. 381) (= Chrest. I. p. 429) ἡ μισθαποχὴ κυρία καὶ ἐπερωτηθεὶς ὡμολόγησα. For μισθοφόροι ἱππεῖς, "mercenary cavalry" cf. P Grenf II. 31² (B.C. 104) (see Intr. ii. p. 155), and for the "requisitioning"—ἐπὶ μισθοφορᾷ—of a camel to assist in transporting a porphyry pillar cf. P Lond 328¹⁹ (A.D. 163) (= II. p. 75).

μισθόω.

The act. of this verb in the sense of "let out for hire" is seen in PSI I. 30² (A.D. 82) μεμίσθωκά σοι εἰς ἔτη ἕξ . . . τὰς ὑπαρχούσας μοι . . ἀρούρας, P Amh II. 92²⁵ application for a lease—A.D. 162–163) ἐξουσίας σοι οὔσης ἑτέρο[ι]ς μεταμ[ι]σθοῦν ὁπότε ἐὰν αἱρῇ, ἐὰν φαίνηται μισθῶσαι, "the right resting with you to make a fresh lease with other persons whenever you choose, if you consent to my proposal" (Edd.). For the mid. "have let out to one," "hire," cf. Meyer Ostr. 59³ ὧν (ἀρουρῶν) ἐμισθωσάμη[ν] τῷ α(ὐτῷ) γ (ἔτει). P Oxy III. 500²⁷ (A.D. 130) μεμε (= μεμι)σθώμεθα τὰς προκιμένας ἀρούρας, and P Fay 93⁵ (A.D. 161) βούλομαι μισθώσασθαι παρά σου τὴν μυροπωλαικὴν καὶ ἀρωματικὴν ἐργασίαν, "I wish to lease from you your business of perfume-selling and unguent-making," to which the vendor replies—[191] **Κάστωρ Ἀντιφίλου μεμίσθωκα κατ**(= θ)**ὼς πρόκιται**, "I, Castor, son of Antiphilus, have made the lease as is above written."

μίσθωμα

is not so common as we might have expected, but for the meaning "rent," "hire," we may cite such a passage as *Syll* 831 (= [3] 1200)[15] (iv/iii B.C.) **ὑποτελεῖ δὲ μίσθωμα Νικήρατος Κτησιφῶντι καθ' ἕκαστον ἐνιαυτὸν ἀργυρίου δραχμὰς πεντα[κ]οσίας ἀτελεῖς**: cf. *ib.* 615 (= [3] 1024)[38] (c. B.C. 200) **μίσθωμα ἀποδιδ[ό]τω αὐτοῦ**. We have the plur. in *ib.* 634 (= [3] 271)[28] (B.C. 335–4) **εἰς δὲ τὰ μι]σθώματα τῆς πόμπης**, *i.e.* "ad apparatum pompae" (Ed.). There seems to be no exact parallel to the usage in Ac 28[30], see Lightfoot *Philippians*,[2] p. 9 n.[3]. For **μίσθωσις**, "a letting for hire," cf. BGU III. 916[15] (time of Vespasian) **ἡ] μίσθωσις ἥδ' ἡ** (cf. *Proleg.* p. 178) **εἰς ἐνιαυτὸν [ἕ]να**, P Fay 96[12] (A.D. 143) (= *Chrest.* I. p. 372) **οὗ ἔχει ὁ Σύρος ἐν μισθώσει ἐλαιουργίου**, "for the oil-press leased by Syrus," *ib.* [20] **μενούσης κυρίας τῆς μισθώσεως ἐφ' οἷς περιέχει πᾶσι**, "the lease in all its provisions remaining valid" (Edd.), and P Oxy XIV. 1673 margin (ii/A.D.) **τῶν ἀμπελουργῶν τὰς μισθώσις πέμψον, [ἵ]να τῆς ξυλοτομίας ἄρξωνται**, "send the leases of the vine-dressers, in order that they may begin the pruning" (Edd.).

μισθωτός.

CPR I. 1[6] (A.D. 83 84) **τοῦ Ἀκουσιλάου γενομένου μισθωτοῦ τινων οὐσίων**, *Syll* 587[29] (B.C. 329–8) **τοῖς ἐπὶ τὸν πύργον καὶ τὸν πυλῶνα πλινθοφοροῦσιν** ("carrying bricks") **καὶ πηλοδευστοῦσιν** ("building with clay"). For **μισθωτής**, "lessee," "tenant," which is not found in the NT (but see 1 Macc 6[29]), cf. P Tebt II. 308[4] (A.D. 174) **μισθωτα[ὶ]ς δρυμῶν**, "lessees of marshes" (Edd.), P Lond 478[2] (ii/iii A.D.) (= II. p. 111) **τοῖς λοι(ποῖς) μισθωταῖς ἱερ(οῦ) χει(ρισμοῦ)** (cf. *Archiv* i. p. 140), and PSI III. 222[4] (iii/A.D.) **μισ]θωτοῦ ἀγρίων θήρας ζῴων [κ]αὶ ὀρνέων** (see the editor's introd.).

Μιτυλήνη.

According to Meisterhans *Gr.* p. 29 the spelling **Μυτιληναῖος** is regularly found in the Attic inscrr. from v–ii/B.C., and it is not till B.C. 100 that **Μιτυληναῖος**, due to dissimilation, takes its place. See however the iii/B.C. papyrus P Petr II. 30(a)[1] **Μιτυλην[αίωι**. So Ac 20[14], except L which reads **Μυτυλίνην** (Moulton *Gr.* ii. p. 79).

Μιχαήλ.

In view of Paul's reference to the **θρησκεία τῶν ἀγγέλων** in Col 2[18], it is interesting to note the existence of the great Church of St. Michael situated close to the walls of Colossai, and continuing as a religious centre long after the name of the town had itself disappeared: see *C. and B.* i. p. 214 ff. Sir W. M. Ramsay also cites various inscrr. showing that the worship of Michael was common in Asia Minor, e.g. *ib.* ii. p. 541, No. 404 where Michael is named along with Gabriel and other angels, and *ib.* p. 741, No. 678 where the words **+ Ἀρχάγγελε Μιχαήλ, ἐλέησον τὴν πόλι σου κ[α]ὶ ῥύση αὐτὴν ἀπὸ τοῦ πονηροῦ +** (cf. Mt 6[13], Lk 11[4] A) ran round the pillar of a very ancient church (now destroyed) at Afion-Kara-Hissar. Other references to Michael are P Leid

W[xxi. 16] (ii/iii A.D.) (= II. p. 153) **διὸ συνίσταμαί σοι διὰ τοῦ μεγάλου ἀρχιστρατήγου Μιχαήλ, κύριε κτλ.**, and the magic P Lond 121[257] (iii/A.D.) (= I. p. 92) **παρεμφαίνων ... τῷ ἀρχαγγέλῳ Μιχαήλ**. On the part Michael played in magic see W. Lueken *Michael: eine Darstellung und Vergleichung der judischen und der morgenländisch-christlichen Tradition vom Erzengel Michael*, Göttingen, 1898, and for Michael, as the angel of peace, guiding the souls of the righteous to the heavenly Jerusalem, see Charles' note on *Test. xii. patr.* Benj. vi. 1.

μνᾶ.

For this Semitic word, used as a Greek money unit for 100 drachmae (about £4), cf. P Lond 277[10] (a loan—A.D. 23) (= II. p. 217) **τόκου ὡς ἐκ δραχμῆ μιᾶς τῇ μνᾷ τὸν μῆνα ἕκαστον**, "at the interest of a drachma per mina per month"—the usual rate of interest: so *ib.* 336[13] (A.D. 167) (= II. p. 221), and P Oxy XIV. 1673[22] (ii/A.D.) **τὸ δὲ πέρας ᾔτησα τὴν μνᾶν, ὡς ἔδοξέν σοι**, "eventually I asked for the mina, as you thought right." The word is used with reference to weight in *ib.* 1739[1] (ii/iii A.D.) **σαππίριν** (*l.* σαπφείριον, "sapphire") **μνᾶν ὅλκην**, *al.* For the form **μναεῖον** cf. *ib.* I. 9 *verso*[15] (iii/iv A.D.) with the editor's note, where it is pointed out that the Attic mina is divided into 16 **τέταρται** (*unciae*) and the Egyptian mina into 18. for **μναιαῖον** cf. *ib.* III. 496[3] (A.D. 127), and for **μναγαῖον** cf. *ib.* VI. 905[6] (A.D. 170) (see Mayser *Gr.* p. 167 f. for the inserted γ).

Μνάσων.

This proper name (Ac 21[16]), which was common among the Greeks, appears e.g. in P Hib I. 41[3] (c. B.C. 261) **ἀπεστ[άλκ]αμεν πρὸς σὲ Μνάσωνα [τὸ]ν δοκιμαστὴν μετὰ φυ[λα]κῆς**, "I have sent to you Mnason the controller under guard" (Edd.). On the reading of Cod. Beza (D) in Ac *l.c.*, which elucidates the narrative, see Knowling *EGT ad l.*

μνεία.

For the epistolary phrase **μνείαν ποιεῖσθαι**, which is used by Paul in 1 Thess 1[2], Rom 1[10], Eph 1[16], Philem[4], cf. the letter of Isias to her husband, who was at the time 'in retreat' in the Serapeum at Memphis, P Lond 42[6] (B.C. 168) (= I. p. 30, *Selections*, p. 9) **οἱ ἐν οἴκωι πάντες <σου διαπαντὸς μνείαν ποιούμενοι >**, and especially, in connexion with prayer, as in the Pauline passages, BGU II. 632[5] (ii/A.D.) **μνίαν σου ποιούμενος παρὰ τοῖς [ἐν]θάδε θεοῖς ἐκομισάμην [ἔ]ν ἐπι[σ]τόλιον κτλ.** and *Kaibel* 983[2 ff.] (B.C. 79)—

> Δημήτριος ἥκω πρὸς μεγάλην Ἰσιν θεάν,
> μνείαν ἐπ' ἀγαθῶι τῶν γονέων ποιούμενος
> καὶ τῶν ἀδελφῶν καὶ φίλων μου κατ' ὄνομα.

Other exx. of the phrase from the inscrr. are *Syll* 929 (= [3] 685)[79] **ὑπ[ὲ]ρ χώρας μόνον ἐφαίνοντο μνείαν πεποιημένοι**, *Priene* 50[10] **ὅπως οὖν καὶ ὁ δῆμος φαίνηται μνείαν ποιούμενος τῶν καλῶν καὶ ἀγαθῶν ἀνδρῶν**, and similarly *Magn* 90[16]—all ii/B.C. On the form **μνεία** for the older **μνηία** see Mayser *Gr.* p. 127.

μνῆμα.

For **μνῆμα**, "tomb," "monument," as in MGr, cf. BGU IV. 1024[iv. 23] (iv/v A.D.) **ἔθα]ψεν εἰς τὸ μνῆμα τ[ῆς φί]λης** αὐτοῦ, and *Kaibel* 82[2] (iv/B.C. εἰκὼν μνῆμα χρόνου (ἐστί) (*c.* "fragile est").

μνημεῖον

is by no means so common in the papyri as we might have expected, but see P Flor I. 9[10] (A.D. 225) φθάσαντός μου πρὸς τοῖς μναμίοις (*l.* μνημείοις) τῆς αὐτῆς κώμης. Vitelli *ad l.* cites also P Casati 10, 5 p. 130. An interesting ex. may be cited from *Syll* 390 (= [3] 858)[1] (after A.D. 104), a stone originally found in Rome, and afterwards transferred to Britain, but now destroyed—Ἡρώδης μνημεῖον καὶ τοῦτο εἶναι τῆς αὐτοῦ συμφορᾶς καὶ τῆς ἀρετῆς τῆς γυναικός· ἔστιν δὲ οὐ τάφος· τὸ γὰρ σῶμα ἐν τῇ Ἑλλάδι καὶ νῦν παρὰ τῷ ἀνδρί ἐστιν: cf. also *Cagnat* IV. 660[2] μη]δενὶ ἐξέσται μήτε πωλῆσα〉ι μήτε ἀγοράσαι μήτ[ε] τὸ μνημεῖον . . . προν[οηθῆναι] ἑαυτοῦ.

μνήμη

For μνήμην ποιεῖσθαι in its ordinary sense of "make mention" as perhaps also in 2 Pet 1[15] : see Mayor *ad l.*), we may cite the letter attributed to the dying Hadrian, P Fay 19[10], in which the Emperor announces his intention of making a simple and accurate statement of certain facts—αὐτῶν τῶν πραγμάτων ἁπλῆν [. . . . . ἀκριβ]εστάτην μνήμην ποιούμενος. Exx. of the subst. = "memory," "remembrance," are *Chrest.* I. 20[30] (A.D. 156) ἐπιστολὴ τοῦ κρατίστης μνήμης Μαμερτείνου, P Ryl II. 233[12] (ii/A.D.) ἔχων ὑπογύως ἐν μνήμηι τὰς τιμὰς ὧν ἀγοράζει ἐξαρτισμῶν, "having fresh in his mind the prices of the fittings which he buys" (Edd.), P Oxy II. 237[vi 30] (A.D. 186) σὺ ὁ κύριος τῇ θεογνώστῳ σου μνήμῃ καὶ τῇ ἀπλανήτῳ προαιρέσει ἀνενεγκὼν τὴ[ν γραφεῖσ]αν σοι ὑπὸ τοῦ στρατηγοῦ ἐπιστολήν, "your lordship exercising your divine memory and unerring judgement took into consideration the letter written to you by the strategus" (Edd.), *ib.* IX. 1219[10] (iii/A.D.) διὰ τὴν μνήμην τ[ο]ῦ πατρὸς αὐτοῦ, *ib.* X. 1320 (A.D. 497) Ἐπιφανίῳ [υἱ]ῷ τοῦ τῆς] μακαρίας μνήμης Ἰωσήφ, and *Syll* 740 (= [3] 1112 [6] (before A.D. 212) ὁ μνήμης ἀρίστης Ἰούλιος Ἀριστέας. For the adj. μνημονικός cf. BGU IV. 1132[2] (B.C. 13) κατὰ μνημονικὴν συγγραφήν, and for μνήμων in the phrase ἀγορανόμωι . . . μνήμονι cf. P Ryl II. 118[13] (B.C. 16–15) with the editors' note.

μνημονεύω

For μνημονεύω, "remember," c. gen., as in 1 Thess 1[3] (see Milligan *ad l.*, cf. PSI VI. 651[2] (iii/B.C.) καλῶς ἂ]ν ποιοῖς cf. Mayser *Gr.* p. 326, μνημονεύων ἡμῶν. We should have expected the same construction in the Christian letter P Heid 6[13] (iv/A.D.) (= *Selections,* p. 126), but the writer substitutes μοι for μου—παρακαλῶ [ο]ὖν, δέσποτα, ἵνα μνημον[ε]ύῃς μοι εἰς τὰς ἁγίας σου εὐχάς. *Syll* 139 (= [3] 284)[5] (iv/B.C.) μνημονεύων (ὁ δῆμος) ἀεὶ τῶν εὐεργετῶν καὶ ζώντων καὶ τετελευτηκότων may recall Heb 13[7]. The verb is followed by the acc., as in 1 Thess 2[9] *al.*, in BGU IV. 1024[v 9] (iv/A.D.) ἀλλὰ τόκον οὐκ ἔν[ι οὐδ]ὲ τὴν σύνπλησιν ἐκείνων μνημονεύε[ι]ν: cf. P Strass I. 41[40] (A.D. 250), where, in a dispute regarding an inheritance, one of the parties exclaims—οὐ μνημ[ο]νεύω δέ, τί ἐν τῇ μεσειτίᾳ ἐγένετο, "I do not remember what took place in the negotiation," and receives the rejoinder—οὐ μέμνησαι οὖν ; "do you not then remember?"

The subst. μνημονεῖον, "record-office," is found in P Oxy X. 1282[22] (A.D. 83) *al.* : cf. *ib. int.* p. 106 f., where it is shown that μνημονεῖον and γραφεῖον are practically identical.

μνημόσυνον

Kaibel 367[11] (iii/A.D.)—

Αἰνέον τόδε σῆμα πατήρ εἱδρισε θυγατρί,
ἀθανάτην μνήμην, μνημόσυνον δάκρυον.

μνηστεύω

For this verb = "promise in marriage," "betroth," cf. P Flor I. 36[1] (iv/A.D.) μνηστευσαμένου μου τοίνυν τῷ ἡμετέρῳ υἱῷ Ζωίλῳ τὴν τῆς θείας μου [. . . . . .]τος θ]υγατέρα Ταε . . τουν [ἅ]μα ἐκ νηπίας ἡλικίας πρὸς γάμου κοινωνίαν.

μογιλάλος

The earliest citation we can give for this NT ἅπ. εἰρ. (Mk 7[32]), except perhaps LXX Isai 35[6], is from a ii/A.D. copy of a probably Ptolemaic astrological calendar, P Oxy III. 465[223] ο]ὗτος ὁ θεὸς ποιεῖ γῆρας πολὺ . . . . οὗτος μὴ ἔχοντα ὀφθαλμούς, οὗτος ὅμοια κτήνι, οὗτος μογιλάλα, οὗτος κωφά, οὗτος νωδά, "this deity causes long old age, and persons with no eyes and like a beast and dumb and deaf and toothless" (Edd.): cf. Vett. Val. p. 73[2] γίνονται δὲ καὶ μογιλάλοι ἢ καὶ ταῖς ἀκοαῖς παραποδιζόμενοι. With the variant μογγιλάλος in Mk *l.c.* (WLNΔ 28 33 *al.*) cf. the word μογγός in P Lond 653[16] early iv A.D. (= III. p. 241) οὐκ εἰμὶ μογγός, "I am not hoarse," and see Moulton, *Gr.* ii. p. 106.

μόγις

Mayser (*Gr.* p. 17) cites only one ex. of μόγις for μόλις (see *s.v.*) from Ptolemaic times, P Magd 11[6] (B.C. 221) (= *Chrest.* I. p. 520) μόγις ἕλκοντες τὸ πλοῖον ἠγάγομεν ἐπὶ τὸν ὅρμον τοῦ Ἀρσινοΐτου, "hauling the vessel with difficulty we brought it to the harbour of Arsinoe." For later exx. see P Oxy II. 298[19] (i/A.D. μόγις (δραχμὰς) χ ἀπαιτήσας, P Lips I. 105[19] (i/ii A.D.) μόγις τὸν τῆς βεβρεγμένης ἀπήρτισα, P Strass I. 41[51] (A.D. 250 μό[γι]ς ἤ[χ]θησαν, and PSI I. 40[2] (vi/A.D.) μόγις μετὰ πολλῶν καμάτων. The adj. μογερός is well illustrated by *Kaibel* 151[1 f.]—

τοῖός τοι θνητῶν μογερὸς βίος. ὧν ἀτέλεστοι
ἐλπίδες. αἷ[ς] μοιρῶν νήματ' ἐπικρέμαται.

μόδιος

a dry measure containing 16 *xestai, i.e.* about a peck : cf. P Thead 32[23] (A.D. 307) κριθῆς μοδίους τεσσε = τεσσ]εράκοντα ἐννέα μοδί[ους] μθ, P Gen I. 62[17] (iv/A.D. νίτρου μοδίους δεκάπεντε, and *OGIS* 533[30] (i/B.C.) σειτομετρίαν ἔδωκεν ἀνὰ πέντε μοδίους.

μοιχαλίς

To the examples of this late word, = "a married woman who commits adultery" (Rom 7[3]), given by Lob. *Phryn.* p. 452, we may add *Test. xii. patr.* Levi xiv. 6, where the high priests are charged with having intercourse both with unmarried and with married women—πόρναις καὶ μοιχαλίσιν συναφθήσεσθε.

In the figurative use of the word in Jas 4[4] Schmiedel (Winer-Schmiedel *Gr.* p. 254) refers μοιχαλίδες both to men and to women (cf. *v.l.* μοιχοὶ καὶ μοιχαλίδες ℵ KLP), but the fem. μοιχαλίς "is alone appropriate in this sense, since God is always thought of as the husband" (Ropes *ICC ad l.*). For the form μοιχαλίς for μοιχάς (Vett. Val. p. 104[11]) Wackernagel (*Hellenistica*, p. 7) compares δορκαλίς for δορκάς, and μαιναλίς for μαινάς. See also Kennedy *Source*, p. 116.

μοιχάομαι.

After the example of the LXX translators of Jeremiah and Ezekiel, this verb, "commit adultery with," is used in the NT with either sex as subject—Mk 10[11] of the man, *ib.*[12] of the woman. According to Wackernagel *Hellenistica* p. 7 ff. the verb would seem to belong to a "more vulgar" layer of Hellenistic Greek than μοιχαλίς. For a verb μοιχαίνω (not in LS) see Vett. Val. p. 118[5] πολυκοιτοῦσι δὲ καὶ μοιχαίνουσι καὶ καταφημίζονται.

μοιχεία.

For the plur. of this subst., as in Mt 15[19], Mk 7[21], cf. the astrological P Tebt II. 276[16] (ii/iii A.D.) ἡ δὲ Ἀφροδίτ]η παρατυγχάνουσα τῷ τοῦ ["Ἄρεως πορ]νίας ‹καὶ› μοιχείας κατίσ[τ]ησιν, "Venus in conjunction with Mars causes fornications and adulteries" (Edd.). On the OT usage of μοιχεία see *s.v.* πορνεία. Wackernagel (*Hellenistica*, p. 9) conjectures a possible Doric form *μοιχά, "adultery."

μοιχεύω.

"commit adultery" on the part of the man, occurs in the astrological PSI III. 158[15] (iii/A.D.?) οἱ δὲ καὶ τὰς ἰδ[ί]ας γυναῖκας μοιχεύουσιν : cf. Mt 5[28]. For a discussion of the verb and its cognates in later classical and in Jewish Greek cf. R. H. Charles, *The Teaching of the New Testament on Divorce* (London, 1921) p. 91 ff., and see *s.v.* πορνεύω, also Wackernagel, *Hellenistica*, p. 9.

μοιχός,

ordinarily "adulterer," is apparently used of sodomy in the illiterate P Oxy VIII. 1160[24] (iii/iv A.D.) ἔγραψές μοι δὲ ὅτι κάθη ἐν Ἀλεξανδρίαν (*l.*-ίᾳ) μετὰ τοῦ μυχο[ῦ] (*l.* μοιχοῦ) σου· γράψον μοι δὲ τίς ἐστιν ὁ μυχός (*l.* μοιχός) μου. "you wrote to me, 'You are staying at Alexandria with your paramour.' Write and tell me, who is my paramour" (Ed.).

μόλις.

P Tebt I. 19[10] (B.C. 114) μόλις ἕως τῆς κε̄ χωρισθήσονται, "they will hardly depart until the 25th" (Edd.), P Ryl II. 113[27] (A.D. 133) μόλις πάντα τὰ ἐμαυτοῦ πωλήσας ἐδυνήθην πληρῶσαι, "I was with difficulty able to complete this by selling all my property" (Edd.), P Oxy VIII. 1117[19] (c. A.D. 178) μέτρια κεκτήμεθα ἐξ ὧν καὶ μόλις ζῶμεν, and *Kaibel* 531[1] μόλις ποτὲ ηὗρον δεσπότ[ην] εὐνούστατον.

In MGr μόλις may have a temporal sense, "just now," "as soon as." The word is perhaps related to μῶλος, Lat. *moles*, just as μόγις comes from μόγος (Boisacq, p. 643).

μολύνω.

The metaphorical use of this word in the NT (1 Cor 8[7], Rev 3[4], 14[4]) is well illustrated by the uncanonical fragment P Oxy V. 840[16] ἀλλὰ μεμολυ[μμένος] ἐπάτησας τοῦτο τὸ ἱερὸν τ[όπον ὄν]τα καθαρόν, "but polluted as thou art thou hast walked in this temple, which is a pure place." Cf. also Epict. ii. 8. 13 ἐν σαυτῷ φέρεις αὐτὸν (*scil.* θεὸν) καὶ μολύνων οὐκ αἰσθάνη ἀκαθάρτοις μὲν διανοήμασι ῥυπαραῖς δὲ πράξεσι.

μολυσμός.

For this NT ἅπ. εἰρ. (2 Cor 7[1]) cf. Aristeas 166 ἀκαθαρσίαν τε οὐ τὴν τυχοῦσαν ἐπετέλεσαν, μιανθέντες αὐτοὶ παντάπασι τῷ τῆς ἀσεβείας μολυσμῷ, "they are guilty of gross uncleanness and are themselves utterly tainted with the pollution of their impiety" (Thackeray), and Vett. Val. p. 242[16] τὸν τρόπον μου ἐκκαθᾶραι πάσης κακίας καὶ παντὸς μολυσμοῦ καὶ τὴν ψυχὴν ἀθάνατον προλεῖψαι.

μονή.

Some exx. of this important Johannine word (Jn 14[2,23]) may be given. In P Hib I. 93[2] (c. B.C. 250) ἐγγύωι μονῆς, *ib.* 111[31] (c. B.C. 250) (= *Chrest.* II. p. 47) μονῆς Καλλιδρόμου, P Grenf II. 79[1,7] (late iii/A.D.) μο[νῆς καὶ ἐμ]φανίας, it is used technically in sureties for the "appearance" of certain persons (cf. *Archiv* i. p. 409 f.): see also P Oxy VIII. 1121[25] (A.D. 295) ἀξιοῦσα δὲ τούτους ἐπαναγκασθῆναι ἱκ[ανὰ] ἔγγραφα παρασχεῖν μονῆς καὶ ἐμφανείας. "requesting that they may be compelled to provide written security that they will stay and appear" (Ed.), P Flor I. 34[9] (A.D. 342) ὁμολογῶ . . . ἐγγυῆ(= ᾶ)-σθαι μονῆς καὶ ἐμφανείας Αὐρ(ήλιον). The meaning is doubtful in P Goodsp Cairo 15[19] (A.D. 362), addressed to the *riparii* of the Hermopolite nome, where the complainant Aurelia states with regard to violences to which she had been subjected—ἐφανέρωσα τῇ μονῇ καὶ τῷ βοηθῷ [το]ῦ πραιποσίτου. The editor translates, "I have made known both to the establishment of the *praepositus* and to his assistant," dismissing as impossible here the later sense of "monastery" which μονή has for example in P Lond 392[2] (vi/vii A.D.) (= II. p. 333) Ἀλεξᾶ(s) καὶ Δανιὴλ οἰκονόμου (*l.* ὅμοι) τῆς μω(= ο)νῆς τοῦ Λευκωτίου, "Alexas and Daniel stewards of the monastery of Leucotius." A similar sense is found by Wilcken in a Munich papyrus, *Chrest.* I. 434[1] (A.D. 390) ἀπὸ τῆς] αὐτῆς Μονῆς Χε[ρ]αίου, where he regards Μονῆς as denoting the "mansio, Station" of Chaireas. In BGU III. 742[ii,A 2] (time of Hadrian) εἰ ταῖς ἀληθ[ι]ναῖς ἀντὶ φερνῆς ἡ παραχώρησις ἐγένετο καὶ εἰ ἡ μ[ο]νὴ προτέρα ἐγένετο τῆς σιτολ(ογίας) κτλ., μονή is apparently the term of residence which was ended by the παραχώρησις. For the adj. μόνιμος, "stable," "enduring," cf. P Amh II. 48[2] (B.C. 106) παρεχέτω τὸν οἶνον μόνιμον ἕως Ἀθὺρ λ, "let him supply wine that will keep until Athur 30," and *Kaibel* 570[1] (ii/A.D.) ὦ μερόπων ἐλπίδες οὐ μόνιμοι.

μονογενής

is literally "one of a kind," "only," "unique" (*unicus*, not "only-begotten," which would be μονογέννητος (*uni-*

... τον μονογενῆ τον ἐξ αὐτοῦ ἀναφανέντα ... εἰσάκουσόν μου ὁ εἰς μονογενής ...

... εὐχαριστῶ σοι κύριε ὅ,τι μοι ἔλυσεν τὸ ἅγιον πνεῦμα τὸ μονογενές, τὸ ζωόν ...

... μονογενῆς πέρ ... ... καὶ πατέρες. φίλος ...

... Φλαβιανὸς ὁ καὶ Μονογενὴς εὐχαριστῶ τῇ ...

Μονογένης Μηνογένης ...

μόνος.

... πρεσβύτης καὶ μόνος τυγχάνων, ... μόνη ἡμεῖς ἐγὼ ...

... μίαν σου ... τόλην ἐκομισάμην μόνην, ... ἐγὼ μόνος ... μόνον, πάνυ ἑαυτὸν παρ' ὑπὲρ τὸν ἀσφαλῆ, ... σὲ γὰρ μόνον ἔχω μάρτυρα. ...

... μόνον ... ... ὁ δὲ ἐπήνει μόνον, ἐπέταξεν ὁ οὐδὲν ...

... τοῖς β.βλίοις σου αὐτὸ μόνον πρόσεχε, ὁμολογῶν καὶ ἀπ' αὐτῶν ουησ.ν ἕξεις. ...

... οὐ μόνον ἀλλὰ καὶ τὴν ἐσθῆτά μου περιέσχισαν. ...

... οὐ μόνον ἐξύβρισαν ἀλλὰ καὶ τὴν ἐσθῆτά μου περιέσχισαν. ...

... οἴδαμεν ὅτι ἁπλῶς ἔχεις διὰ τὴν ἐλευθερίαν, τοῦτο οὐ μόνον ἡμῖν γενόμενον ἀλλὰ καὶ πολλοῖς, ...

... κατὰ μόνας ... ... συνάγουσι κατὰ μόνας, ...

... Μίας μόνος ... μόνος ...

μονόφθαλμος

... ἑτερόφθαλμος· ἑτερόφθαλμος μὲν γὰρ ὁ κατὰ περίπτωσιν πηρωθεὶς τὸν ἕτερον τῶν ὀφθαλμῶν, μονόφθαλμος δὲ ὁ ἕνα μόνον ὀφθαλμὸν ἔχων ὡς ὁ Κύκλωψ ...

μονόω.

... εἰ ὁ ὁμολογήσεις τὴν ἀνθρωπείαν φύσιν μελίσσῃ μάλιστα προσεοικέναι ἢ μὴ δύναται μόνη ζῆν, ἀπόλλυται γὰρ μονωθεῖσα κτλ. ... ... μόνωσις ...

μορφή.

... χάριν καὶ μορφήν, ... περὶ μὲν οὖν τούτων ἐδ. ... δοίη ἐς δοίεν σοι ὁ Σάραπις καὶ ἡ Ἶσις ἐπαφροδισίαν χάριν μορφὴν πρὸς τὸν βασιλέα. ... παρακαλῶ δὲ καὶ αὐτὸς τοὺς θεούς, ὅπως δῶσιν αὐτοῖς χάριν καὶ μορφὴν πρὸς τὸν βασιλέα· ... ... νεανίσκον εὐπρεπῆ τὰμ μορφάν, ... ἥλιος ... σημαίνει ... ἐπὶ γενέσεως βασιλέων ... φρόνησιν μορφὴν κίνησιν, εἶδος τύχης κτλ. ... μορφήν ...

... σὲ μόνον ἐπικαλοῦμαι, τὸν μόνον ἐν κόσμῳ διατάξαντα θεοῖς καὶ ἀνθρώποις, τὸν ἑαυτὸν ἀλλάξαντα σεαυτὸν μορφαῖς ἁγίαις καὶ ἐκ μὴ ὄντων εἶναι ποιήσαντα ... ... ἐπικαλοῦμαι σε κύριε, ἵνα μοι φάνῃ ἡ ἀληθινή σου μορφή ... ... ἔνεγκέ μοι τὸ πνεῦμα τὸ ἀεροπετές, ... καὶ ἐμβῆ. αὐτοῦ εἰς τὴν ψυχήν, ἵνα τυπώσηται τὴν ἀθάνατον μορφὴν ἐν φωτὶ κραταιῷ καὶ ἀφθάρτῳ. ... ... μορφὴ μὲν εἰκόνος παντοία. τέχνῃ ... κοσμήσας. ... μα μορφῆς ἐμῆς ° χαρακτῆρα μορφῆς ἐμῆς ... ... μορφή ... σχῆμα· συγχέει τῆς μορφῆς καὶ τοῦ σχήματος. ...

Μικρὰ μὲν ἡ λίθος ἐστίν, ἔχει δ' ἥλιον ...
ἔνδον τ... ... μορφῶν, ὡς ... ἐν παλάμαις.

... μορφή ...
ἢ ἐκτὸς περιγραφ... σχῆμα ... ...
... ... μορφή ...

peculiar force," but suggests that σχῆμα "would perhaps
be avoided instinctively, as it might imply an illusion or
an imposture." MGr μορφή, μορφιά, ἐμορφιά, ὀμορφιά.
Boisacq (p. 645) notes a possible connexion with Lat.
forma (by dissimilation from *morgᵘhmā or *morgᵘhmā), but
gives also another hypothesis *s.v.* μάρπτω (p. 612).

μορφόω.

The only occurrence of this verb in the Greek Bible is in
Gal 4¹⁹ (but cf. **Aq.** Isai 44¹³), where Burton (*ICC ad l.*)
thinks that "the words not unnaturally suggest a reversal of
the preceding figure [cf. 1 Thess 2⁷], those who were just
spoken of as babes in the womb, now being pictured as
pregnant mothers, awaiting the full development of the
Christ begotten in them." He compares the use of πλάσσω
in Jer 1⁵ πρὸ τοῦ με πλάσαι σε ἐν κοιλίᾳ, Rom 9²⁰,
1 Tim 2¹³.

μόρφωσις.

Pallis *ad* Rom 2²⁰ regards μόρφωσιν as probably a Stoical
term = παίδευσιν, "education," and compares μορφωμένος
in MGr applied to a well-educated person. With 2 Tim 3⁵
cf. Philo *De Plantat.* 70 (ed. Wendland) ἐπεὶ καὶ νῦν εἰσί
τινες τῶν ἐπιμορφαζόντων εὐσέβειαν, οἳ τὸ πρόχειρον τοῦ
λόγου παρασυκοφαντοῦσι φάσκοντες οὔθ᾽ ὅσιον οὔτ᾽
ἀσφαλὲς εἶναι λέγειν ἀνθρώπου θεὸν κλῆρον. The subst.
μόρφωμα is found *quinquies* in Aquila's version of the OT :
see HR *s.v.*

μοσχοποιέω.

This compound verb, which in Ac 7⁴¹ takes the place of
ἐποίησε μόσχον in Ex 32⁴, is claimed by Blass (*ad Ac l.c.*)
as an example of the faculty which the Greek language never
lost of forming new words. No other instance of it occurs
in the LXX or in profane writers, but it follows the model
of the Platonic εἰδωλοποιέω (*Rep.* 605 C) ; cf. εἰδοποιέω
(Plut. *Alex.* 1), ἀγαλματοποιέω, εἰκονοποιέω.

μόσχος.

The invariable Biblical use of μόσχος in the sense of
"calf" is seen in such passages as P Ryl II. 229²⁰ (letter
regarding farm stock—A.D. 38) ἐπιμελοῦ δὲ καὶ τοῦ μόσχου,
"do you also take care of the calf," P Fay 121¹³ (c. A.D.
100) καὶ τὸ δ[έρ]μα τοῦ μόσχου οὗ ἐθύ[σ]αμεν αἴτησον
πα[ρὰ τοῦ] κυρτοῦ βυρσέως, "ask the hunch-backed tanner
for the hide of the calf that we sacrificed" (Edd.), and
P Oxy IX. 1211⁴ (list of objects for a sacrifice "to the most
sacred Nile"—ii/A.D.) μόσχος ᾱ. In BGU V. 1²⁵³ (c. A.D.
150) it is laid down—ἀσφρα[γ]ίστους μόσχους οὐκ ἐξὸν
θύειν, and consequently in P Lond 472⁴ (A.D. 188) (= II.
p. 22) we have a certificate of payment of a tax in respect of
a calf to be sacrificed—διέγραψε τέλος μόσχου θυομένου, and
in P Grenf II. 64³ (ii/iii A.D.) a certificate issued by "a
sealer of sacred calves" that he had examined a sacrificial
calf and found it without blemish—ἱαιρομοσχοσφραγιστὴς
(*l.* ἱερο-) ἐπεθεώρησα μ[ό]σχ[ο]ν θυόμενον (cf. BGU I. 250 =
Chrest. I. 87—after A.D. 130). The dim. μοσχάριον occurs
in PSI VI. 600 (iii/B.C.), which also shows μοσχοτρόφος
(cf. P Gurob 22⁴⁴ iii/B.C.). For μοσχομάγειρος, "a calf-
butcher," see P Oxy XIV. 1764⁶ (iii/A.D.), where the editors

in their note compare BGU I. 3¹¹ (A.D. 605) χοιρομαγείρῳ,
and ἰσικιομάγειρος in a Rainer papyrus *ap.* Wessely *Wien.
Stud.* 1902. 129 (A.D. 590).

μουσικός.

In an action before the Emperor Claudius in which
Isidorus, the Gymnasiarch of Alexandria, raises a complaint
against King Agrippa, the Emperor taunts Isidorus with the
fact that he is the son of a female musician—ἀσφαλῶς [ἐ]κ
μουσικῆς εἶ, Ἰσίδωρε, and receives the answer—ἐγ[ὼ μὲν
οὐκ εἰμι δοῦλος οὐδὲ μουσικῆς [υἱ]ός, ἀλλὰ διασήμου πόλεως
[Ἀ]λεξαν[δρ]εί[α]ς γυμνασίαρχος (*Chrest.* I. 14⁴⁰⁻ˢᶠᶠ). From
P Flor I. 74⁶ (A.D. 181) συμφωνίας πάσης μουσικῶν τε καὶ
ἄλλων, P Oxy X. 1275⁹ (iii/A.D.) συμφωνίας αὐλητῶν καὶ
μουσικῶν (cf. Rev 18²²), T. Grassi (in *SAM* iii. p. 130)
concludes that μουσικοί was not a merely general term, but
denoted a special class of performers. Cf. however P
Oxy III. 519⁶ (account of public games—ii/A.D.) ὑπὲρ
μου[σ]ι[κῆς (δραχμαὶ . . .

μόχθος.

For this expressive subst. = "labour," "hardship" (1 Th
2⁹ *al.*) cf. the mantic P Ryl I. 28¹¹⁷ (iv/A.D.) κνήμη εὐώνυμος
ἐὰν ἄλληται σημαίνι γυναικὶ ψόγον ἐκ μοιχείας δούλοις δὲ
ἀπειλαὶ καὶ μόχθοι (*l.* ἀπειλὰς καὶ μόχθους), "if the left
leg quiver, it signifies for a woman censure in consequence
of adultery, and for slaves, threats and labour" (Edd.), and
Kaibel 851¹ (iii/A.D.) ἐσθ]λοῖς οὐ κενεὰ μόχθων [χ]άρις.
The verb is found in the oracular *ib.* 1039¹² μοχθεῖν ἀνάγκη
μετα[β]ολὴ δ᾽ ἔσται καλή, and the adj. in P Tebt I. 24⁵⁷
(B.C. 117) μ[ο]χθηρὰν ἀγωγήν, "nefarious conduct" (Edd.),
and the epigrammatic PSI I. 17 *recto* ⁱⁱ⁴ (iii/A.D. ?) ἔνθεν
ἐς ἀθανάτους καὶ ἀείζωο[ν] βίον ἦλθεν | τοῦτο τὸ μοχθηρὸν
σῶμ᾽ ἀποδυσάμενος.

μυέω.

For the original technical use of this verb, "initiate" into
the mysteries, which may underlie the Pauline usage in
Phil 4¹² (cf. 3 Macc 2³⁰), it must be enough to refer to such
passages from the inscrr. as *OGIS* 530¹⁵ θεοπρόποι . . .
οἵτινες μυηθέντες ἐνεβάτευσαν, *ib.* 764¹² (ii B.C.) ταῖς
πα[ρα]γεγενημέναις θεωρίαις εἰς τὰ Νικηφόρια καὶ μυηθείσαις,
with the editor's note, "quae legationes ad Nicephoria
venerunt et per eam occasionem mysteriis Cabirorum
initiatae sunt." The subst. μύησις occurs *bis* in the latter
document—⁷ ἡι[περ ἐπιβάλλον τὴ ἡμέραι τὴν τῶν ἐφήβων
μύησιν ἐπιτε[λεῖσθαι, ⁹ τό τε τῆς μυήσεως ἕνεκεν ἀθρο[ισθὲν
πλῆθος ἐδείπνισεν ἐν τῶι . . . In later eccles. Greek ὁ
μυούμενος denotes one who is about to be baptized, a
candidate for baptism : cf. Anrich *Das antike Mysterienwesen* (Göttingen, 1894), p. 158. Inge *Christian Mysticism*,
pp. 4, 349, and for a similar use of μύησις see *SAM* i.
p. 15.

μῦθος.

This subst., which in the NT is confined to the Pastorals
and 2 Pet 1¹⁶ in the sense of "fable," "fanciful story," is
similarly used in *Kaibel* 277¹⁴—

 Ἀψευδεῖς] μούνη καὶ πρώτη [τοὺς πρὶν ἀοιδοὺς
   δεῖξα,] καὶ οὐκέτι μοι μῦθον [ἐρεῖτ᾽ ἀρετήν.

Cf. Epict. iii. 24. 18 σὺ δ' Ὁμήρῳ πάντα προσέχεις καὶ τοῖς μύθοις αὐτοῦ. For the more primary sense of "word," "story" cf. *Syll* 492 (= ³382)⁷ (B.C. 290–280) τοὺς μύθου[ς] τοὺς ἐπιχωρίους γέγραφεν, *Kaibel* 185⁵ (i/B.C.—i/A.D.) καὶ γνῶθι μύθους, οἷς σοφῶς ἐτέρπετο, and 878¹·⁶ ἀλκή καὶ μύθοισι καὶ ἐν βουλαῖσι κρατίστους | ἄνδρας ἀγακλειτοὺς γείνατο Κεκροπίη. A good ex. of the adv. μυθωδῶς is afforded by Aristeas 168 οὐδὲν εἰκῇ κατατέτακται διὰ τῆς γραφῆς οὐδὲ μυθωδῶς, "nothing has been set down in the Scripture heedlessly or in a mythical sense" (Thackeray).

μυκάομαι.

This NT ἅπ. εἰρ. (Rev 10³) is used of the "roar" of the sea in *Kaibel* 1028⁶²—

παντᾶι δὲ μελανθεῖ ῥοίζωι
σπερχόμενος βαρὺ πόντος ἐνὶ σπήλυγξι βαθείαις
μυκᾶτ' ἐξ ἀδύτων.

Cf. P Leid W^xxxvi. 30 (ii/iii A.D.) (= II. p. 155) ἔσω προσβαλόμενος μύκησαι ὀλολυγμός (*l.* -όν), also ³³ μύκησαι ὅσον δύνασαι.

μυκτηρίζω.

This verb, which is rare outside the LXX (cf. 3 Kingd 18²⁷, 4 Kingd 19²¹), and means properly "turn up the nose" as a sign of contempt, "ridicule" (see *Or. Sib.* i. 171 cited *s.v.* μαίνομαι), is found in the NT only in Gal 6⁷ θεὸς οὐ μυκτηρίζεται, where perhaps we may translate "God is not deceived," or "outwitted" by an easy metonymy, he who is outwitted being thereby made ridiculous (Burton *ICC ad l.*): cf. the remark of Pollux (Kock III. p. 257, Fr. 1039) to the effect that Menander used μυκτηρισμός for ἐξαπάτη. Cf. Menander *Fragm.* p. 172, and Durham *Vb.* p. 80.

For μυκτήρ in its literal sense of "nose," "nostril," cf. the medical recipe P Oxy VIII. 1088²¹ (early i/A.D.) αἷμα ἀπὸ μυκτήρων στῆσαι, "to stop nose-bleeding," also²⁶·³²·³⁵.

μυλικός.

For the form cf. ὀνικός, and μυλονικός cited *s.v.* μύλος.

μύλινος.

Syll 583 (= ³906)¹⁶ (c. i/A.D.?) ἄγαλμα μαρμάρινον Ἀρτέμιδος ἐπὶ παραστάδι μυλίνῃ. The editor compares *CIG* II. 3371⁴ σὺν τῇ κειμένῃ σορῷ ἔσω μυλίνῃ, [ἐ]ν ᾗ ἐνεστί μου ἡ γυνή, and quotes Boeckh to the effect that the reference is to the kind of stone of which millstones were made.

μύλος.

"a mill," as in Mt 24¹¹, Rev 18²², occurs in P Oxy II. 278¹⁷ (a lease—A.D. 17), where it is laid down—μετὰ τὸν χρόνον ἀπ[οκα]ταστησάτωι ὁ μάνης τὸν μύλον ὑγιῆι καὶ ἀσινῆι, οἷον καὶ παρείληφεν, "at the end of the time the servant shall restore the mill safe and uninjured in the condition in which he received it" (Edd.). With the μύλος ὀνικός (Mk 9⁴²), cf. P Ryl II. 167¹⁰ (A.D. 39) μυλαῖον ἐνεργὸν ἐν ᾧ μύλοι Θηβαικοὶ τρεῖς σὺν κώπαις καὶ τραπέζαις, "a mill in full working order, containing 3 Theban millstones, with handles and nether-stones" (Edd.), and similarly BGU IV. 1067⁵ (A.D. 101-2). See also the new compound

μυλονικός in P Lond 335⁷ (A.D. 166-7 or 198-9) (= II. p. 191). Μυλοκόπος, "millstone-worker," is found in P Tebt II. 278¹² (early i/A.D.).

Μύρα, Μύρρα.

Μύρρα (neut. plur.) is read in Ac 27⁵ B, but the cursive 81 reads Μύραν, a form which Ramsay (*Paul*, p. 129) supports from the modern name with acc. Μύραν and gen. Μύρων. The single liquid, as in Ac 21¹ D, is also attested in *CIG* III. 4288³ διὰ τῶν ἐν Μύροις ἀρχείων: cf. Winer-Schmiedel *Gr.* p. 58, Moulton *Gr.* ii. p. 101.

μυριάς.

For μυριάς = 10,000, as in Ac 19¹⁹, it is sufficient to cite P Tebt II. 308⁸ (A.D. 174) (= *Chrest.* I. p. 376) τιμὴν βίβλου μυριάδων δύο, "the price of 20,000 papyrus stalks" (Edd.), P Amh II. 107¹⁰ (A.D. 185) κριθῆς ἀρταβῶν μυριάδων δύο, "20,000 artabae of barley," and P Oxy VIII. 1115¹¹ (A.D. 284) μυριάδας τρῖς καὶ ὀκτακισχιλ[ίους, "38,000." The sense of unlimited numbers, like our "myriads," as in Rev 5¹¹ *al.*, is seen in the Christian amulet P Iand 6¹⁰ (v/vi A.D.) ᾧ (*sc.* θεῷ) παραραστκουσιν (*l.* παραστήκουσιν) μύριαι μαιριάτες (*l.* μυριάδες) ἀγγέλω[ν: for other exx. see the editor's note *ad l.*, and cf. Moulton *Egyptian Rubbish-heaps*, p. 31 f.

μυρίζω.

This verb (Mk 14⁸) for "anoint" is restored in the magic P Lond 121¹⁵⁹ (iii/A.D.) (= I. p. 96) after a much mutilated line—δὸς εἰς τὴν ὄψιν μυρ[ίζε]σθαι. In MGr μυρίζω means "smell."

μυρίοι,

which in the NT (Mt 18²⁴ *al.*) denotes a very large, an unlimited number, is used literally = 10,000 before a collective subst. in P Petr III. 41 *verso*⁴ (iii/B.C.) κατὰ μυρίαν δεσμήν, "for 10,000 bundles": cf. *ib.* 7·9.

μύρον.

For this Semitic loan word (cf. Lewy *Fremdwörter*, pp. 42, 44) we may cite a private account of c. A.D. 1, P Oxy IV. 736¹³ μύρου εἰς ἀποστολὴν ταφῆς θυγατρὸς Φνᾶς (τετρώβολον), "perfume for the dispatch of the mummy of the daughter of Phna 4 ob." (Edd.), and the medical prescription *ib.* II. 234¹¹·⁹ (ii/iii A.D.) χαλβάνην σουσίνῳ μύρῳ διεὶς πρόσμιξον μέλι καὶ ῥόδινον, "dilute some gum with balsam of lilies, and add honey and rose-extract" (Edd.). In P Giss I. 93¹¹ μύρον αὐλητήν, the editor suggests that μύρον ought perhaps to be written as a proper name—Μύρον: cf. the name Ἀβρότονον (properly = "southernwood") in Menander's plays. In P Ryl II. 420 (ii/A.D.) we hear of an ἀρτοκόπος, a μυροπώλης, and an ἠπητής ("cobbler"): for the adj. see P Fay 93⁶ (A.D. 161) βούλομαι μισθώσασθαι παρὰ σοῦ τὴν μυροπωλαικὴν καὶ ἀρωματικὴν ἐργασίαν, "I wish to lease from you your business of perfume-selling and unguent-making" (Edd.). We may add that in *Kaibel* 726⁵ (iii-iv A.D.) there is reference to—Χ(ριστο)ῦ μύρον ἄφθιτον. Boisacq (p. 886) refers to σμύρις, connecting with English *smear*.

μυστήριον.

There are many aspects of this important word which lie outside our immediate purpose, but its use as a technical term in pagan religion to denote a "secret" or "secret doctrine" known only to the initiated, which they are not at liberty to disclose, may be briefly illustrated. Thus from the inscr. we have *OGIS* 331⁵⁴ (Pergamon—mid. ii/B.C.) διεταξάμεθα δὲ ἀκολούθως τούτοις καὶ περὶ θυσιῶγ καὶ πομπῶγ καὶ μυστηρίων τῶν ἐπιτελουμένωμ πρὸ πόλεως αὐτῶι ἐν τοῖς καθήκουσι καιροῖς καὶ τόποις, *ib.* 528¹³ τοῦ μεγάλου καὶ κοινοῦ τῆς Βειθυ(νίας να)οῦ τῶν μυστηρίων ἱεροφάντ[ην, *ib.* 540²¹ (end i/A.D.) Ἀτταβοκαοὶ οἱ τῶν τῆς θεοῦ [*Matris Magnae*] μυστηρίων μύστ[αι ἐτε(ί)μησαν τὸν [ἑαυτῶν φίλον καὶ εὐεργέτην, and *ib.* 721² (iv/A.D.) ὁ δᾳδοῦχος τῶν ἁγιωτάτων Ἐλευσῖνι μυστηρίων [Νικαγόρας. In the sepulchral epigram *Kaibel* 588⁴ a priest is described as—ἐκτελέσας μυστήρια πάντοτε σεμνῶς, cf. *ib.*⁷ τὰ βίου συνεχῶς μυστήρια σεμνά, where the adv. συνεχῶς is used for an adj. From the papyri we may cite P Leid Wᵐ·⁴² (ii/iii A.D.) ἄρξαι λέγειν τὴν στήλην καὶ τὸ μυστήριον τοῦ θεοῦ: cf. *ib.*¹² ἄτερ γὰρ τούτων ὁ (θ)εὸς οὐκ ἐπακούσεται, ἄλλως (ἀ)μυστηρίαστον οὐ παραδέξ(ι (= ε)ται, "nam sine his deus non exaudiet, alioqui (non) initiatum non admittet" (Ed.). The word seems to refer to a material object in P Leid Vˣ·¹⁹ (iii/iv A.D.) δότε οὖν πνεῦμα τῷ ὑπ' ἐμοῦ κατασκευασμένῳ μυστ[ηρ]ίῳ. In an interesting love-charm from a Berlin papyrus (P Berol 9909), now edited in *Aegyptus* iv. (1923), pp. 305–8, the unusual formula ⁵⁰κεῖται παρὰ σοὶ τὸ θεῖον μυστήριον occurs, apparently with reference to the fact that some of the hair of the beloved was attached to the papyrus, which had been inserted in the mouth of the mummy (whose νεκυδαίμων was invoked to aid the lover). In an incantation to the Great Deity in P Lond 46¹¹⁰ (iv/A.D.) (=I. p. 68) the words occur—ἐγώ εἰμι Μουσῆς (*l.* Μωυσῆς) ὁ προφήτης σου ᾧ παρέδωκας τὰ μυστήριά σου τὰ συντελούμενα Ἰστραήλ. See also the magical P Par 574²⁴⁷⁷ (iv/A.D.) διέβαλεν γάρ σου τὰ ἱερὰ μυστήρια ἀνθρώποις εἰς γνῶσιν. Another ex. of the word, which we owe to the courtesy of Dr. Victor Martin, is afforded by an unedited Genevan papyrus, unfortunately mutilated at the most interesting point, where the writer assures his readers that if, in priority to extraneous pleasures (ὑπερόρια ἡδέα), they auspiciously perform the mysteries, things will afterwards turn out well for them—εἰ] γὰρ ἐπ' ἀγαθοῖς πρότερον τῶγ.[.ο]υσων τὰ μυστήρια τελέ[σουσι] ὕ(σ)τερ[ο]ν αὐτοῖς συμβαίν[ει . . . . . : a sort of pagan equivalent of Mt 6³³.

The Biblical usage of the word follows different lines and is traced with great fulness by J. A. Robinson *Ephesians*, p. 234 ff., where in particular it is shown that in its NT sense a mystery is "not a thing which *must* be kept secret. On the contrary it is a secret which God wills to make known and has charged His Apostles to declare to those who have ears to hear it" (p. 240). So far then as this word is concerned we are not prepared to find any "intimate" connexion between Paulinism and the mystery-religions: cf. H. A. A. Kennedy *St. Paul and the Mystery-Religions* (London, 1913), C. Clemen *Der Einfluss der Mysterienreligionen auf das älteste Christentum* (Giessen, 1913), and for a different view W. Bousset *Kyrios Christos*, Gottingen, 1913, p. 125 ff., R. Reitzenstein

Die hellenistischen Mysterienreligionen, Leipzig, 1910. Important discussions on the word will be found in E. Hatch *Essays on Biblical Greek*, Oxford, 1889, p. 57 ff., H. von Soden *ZNTW* xii. (1911), p. 188 ff., and T. B. Foster *AJT* xix. (1915), p. 402 ff.: cf. also S. Cheetham's Hulsean Lectures on *The Mysteries Pagan and Christian*, London, 1897. For the μυστήριον κοσμικὸν ἐκκλησίας of Didache xi. 11, explained by Harnack on lines of Eph 5¹², cf. MGr μυστήριον = "sacrament," used of marriage: see G. F. Abbott in *The Nineteenth Century*, 1908, p. 653 ff., who shows that the modern wedding week in Macedonia fits most closely the Eleusinian Mysteries.

μυωπάζω.

For a full discussion of this difficult word in 2 Pet 1⁹ see Mayor *Comm. ad l.*, where it is shown that the meaning is screw up the eyes in order to see, as a short-sighted man does, and consequently that μυωπάζω limits, rather than intensifies, the preceding τυφλός. Apart from the Petrine passage the only known instance of the verb in Greek literature is Ps. Dionys. *Eccl. Hier.* ii. 3, p. 219 (cited by Suicer), where after speaking of the Light which lighteth every man, he proceeds "if a man of his own free will closes his eyes to the light, still the light is there shining upon the soul μυωπαζούσῃ καὶ ἀποστρεφομένῃ (blinking and turning away)."

μώλωψ.

found in the NT only in 1 Pet 2²⁴, is defined by Bengel (*ad l.*) as "*vibex*, frequens in corpore servili": cf. Sir 28¹⁷.

μῶμος.

In 2 Pet 2¹³ this word is used in the "Biblical" sense of "blemish" (cf. Lev 21²¹). For the meaning "blame" "reproach," as in classical Greek (cf. also Sir 11³¹, 18¹⁶) see *Kaibel* 948⁷ f (Rom.)—

οὕνεκ' ἐ[γὼ πι.]νυτ[ᾶ]τα καὶ ἀγλαὸν ἤθεσι κόσμον
δῶ[κ]α καὶ ἐ[γ]μώμου πάντοθεν εἰρυσάμην,

where ἐ[γ]μώμου = ἐκ μώμου (see Index). See *s.v.* ἄμωμος. Boisacq (pp. 57, 637 n.¹, 655) connects μῶμος with the Homeric ἀμύμων and with μιαίνω.

μωρολογία,

"foolish talking" (Eph 5⁴): cf. Plut. *Mor.* 504 B οὕτως οὐ ψέγεται τὸ πίνειν, εἰ προσείη τῷ πίνειν τὸ σιωπᾶν· ἀλλ' ἡ μωρολογία μέθην ποιεῖ τὴν οἴνωσιν.

μωρός.

In the nursery acrostic P Tebt II. 278³⁵ (early i/A.D.) it is said of a lost garment—λέων ὁ ἄρας, μωρὸς ὁ ἀπολέσας, "a lion he was who took it, a fool who lost it": cf. BGU I. 45¹² (A.D. 203) ἐπῆλθεν αὐτῷ, ἐπαγαγὼν σὺν α[ὑ]τῷ τὸν ἑαυτοῦ υἱὸν καὶ μωρ[ό]ν τινα. *Ib.* IV. 1046ⁱⁱ·²² (ii A.D.) Μάρων ἐπικαλ(ούμενος) μωρός shows the word used as a nickname, cf. the cognomen Brutus (Liv. i. 56. 8): so the diploma of club membership in P Lond 1178⁴¹ (A.D. 194) (= III. p. 217) γεινώσκετε] ὄντα [ἡμῶν] συνοδείτην Ἑρμεῖνον, τὸν καὶ Μωρόν, "know that we are adopting as member Herminus, also called Morus." The word is a Greek word, and it is quite unnecessary to identify it in Mt 5[22] with Heb. מוֹרֶה Numb 20[10] (cf. RV marg.). It is found in the Midrashim, and may well have passed into use amongst the Aramaic-speaking population in the time of Christ: see further Field *Notes*, p. 3 ff., Moulton *Gr.* ii. p. 152 f., and Allen *ICC ad Mt l.c.*, MGr μωρέ, "well now!"

Μωϋσῆς.

For this the older form of the proper name, as in the LXX, see Thackeray *Gr.* i. p. 163. The spelling Μουσῆς, Μουσῆ, is found in P Oxy VIII. 1110[21] (A.D. 363), P Grenf II. 102[1] (vii/A.D.), *al.* See further Preisigke *Namenbuch, s.vv.*

N

Ναζαρέτ—ναύκληρος

Ναζαρέτ.

On the form of this proper noun see Burkitt *Syriac Forms*, pp. 16, 28 f., and cf. *JTS* xiv. p. 475 f., Moulton *Gr.* ii. p. 107 f.

Ναζωραῖος.

To Allen's discussion of this word in *ICC* ad Mt 2²³, add *ZNTW* xxi. (1922), p. 122 ff.

ναί.

For this strong particle, responsive and confirmatory of a preceding statement, as in Mt 15²⁷ *al.*, cf. a report of the proceedings of the Senate P Oxy XII. 1413⁷ (A.D. 270-5) γ]ραμματεὺς πολειτικῶν εἶπ[εν]· ναί. See also Ev. Petr. 9 with Swete's note. The word survives in MGr, but is sometimes changed to ναίσκε, and sometimes strengthened with μάλιστα (Thumb *Handbook*, p. 199).

Ναιμάν.

On the different forms of this Semitic name found in the MSS of Lk 4²⁷, see Blass *Gr.* p. 17 n²., Moulton *Gr.* ii. p. 84.

ναός.

which in both LXX and NT is applied to the temple at Jerusalem, occurs in the inscr. on the front of the temple of Athene Polias at Priene—*Priene* 156

βασιλεὺς Ἀλέξανδρος
ἀνέθηκε τὸν ναὸν
Ἀθηναίηι Πολιάδι.

See Fouillac *Recherches*, p. 61, and cf. *Syll* 214¹¹ (c. B.C. 267) παρὰ τὸν νεὼ τῆς Ἀθηνᾶς τῆς Πο[λιάδος with reference to a temple in honour of the same goddess at Athens. In *ib.* 730 (= ³ 1102)²² (B.C. 175-4) the word is apparently to be distinguished from the wider and more general ἱερόν, "the temple precincts"—δοῦναι δὲ αὐτῶι καὶ (ε)ἰκόνος ἀνάθεσιν ἐν τῶι ναῶι. ἀναγράψαι δὲ τόδε τὸ ψήφισμα εἰς στήλην λιθίνην καὶ στῆσαι ἐν τεῖ αὐλεῖ τοῦ ἱεροῦ, and for a still clearer ex. of ναός as the special "shrine" or dwelling-place of the god, cf. P Par 35²² (B.C. 163) (= Wilcken *UPZ* i. p. 130) οὐ μὴν [ἀ]λλὰ καὶ εἰς τὸ ἄδυτον τῆς θεᾶς εἰσελθὼν ἐσκύλη[σε]ν τὸν ναὸν ὥστε κινδυνεῦσαι καὶ συντρῖψαι αὐτόν, where Wilcken notes, "Der ναός in Allerheiligsten ist der Schrein, in dem das Bild der Göttin steht." See also the interesting regulation from the *Gnomen des Idios Logos*, BGU V. 1210¹⁰¹ (c. A.D. 150) ἐν παντὶ ἱερῷ, ὅπου ναός ἐστιν, δέον προφήτην εἶναι καὶ λαμβάνει τῶν προσόδων τὸ π[έμ]πτον: see also *ib.* ²¹¹ τοῖς θάπτουσι τὰ ἱερὰ ζῷ[ια] οὐκ [ἐξ]ὸν προφητεύειν οὐδὲ ναὸν κωμάζειν ο[ὐ]δὲ

τρέφειν ἱερὰ [ζ]ῷ[ι]α, and Epict. i. 22. 16 τί οὖν ναοὺς ποιοῦμεν, τί οὖν ἀγάλματα . . . ; In BGU II. 489⁶ (ii/A.D.) ναοῦ Καίσαρος θ[εοῦ υἱοῦ the context is unfortunately broken. With Ac 19²⁴ we may compare *ib.* I. 162¹² (ii/A.D.) βωμίσκιον ἀργυροῦν. For the compound σύνναος cf. e.g. the temple oath, *Chrest.* I. 110 A⁴ (B.C. 110) νὴ τοῦτον τὸν Ἡρακλῆ καὶ τοὺς συννάους θεούς.

νάρδος.

"spikenard," is found in such passages as PSI VI. 628⁷ (iii/B.C.) νάρδου ξηρᾶς μν(αῖ) β, P Oxy VIII. 1088⁴⁹ (early i/A.D.) νάρδου (ὀβολός). P Leid W⁰ ¹⁷ (ii/iii A.D.) νάρδος Ἰνδικός, and *ib.* ⁱˣ ¹⁰ where νάρδος is included in a list of ἐπιθύματα: cf. Mk 14³, Jn 12³. See also the adj. in Menander *Fragm.* p. 78, No. 274 νάρδινον (μύρον). The word is Semitic, cf. Lewy *Fremdwörter*, p. 40, and is found in Theophr. *HP* ix. 7. 2 ff.

Νάρκισσος.

Thieme (p. 40) quotes instances of this proper name from Magnesia (*Magn* 122 *d*¹¹—not later than iv/A.D.) and Hierapolis (*Hierap.* 80), proving that its occurrence outside Rome was well established, and consequently that the common identification of τοὺς ἐκ τῶν Ναρκίσσου (Rom 16¹¹) with the household of the well-known freedman of that name is by no means certain. Rouffiac (p. 60) cites also an ex. from Thasos *IG* XII. 8. 548, 2; cf. Zahn *Introd.* i. p. 419. The word, as a plant-name, is probably derived from a Mediterranean tongue: for the termination -σσος cf. κυπάρισσος. As the plant is sedative, the influence of νάρκη upon the stem may be traced (Boisacq, p. 657).

ναυαγέω.

With the metaphorical use of this verb, "make shipwreck of," "come to ruin," in 1 Tim 1¹⁹, we may compare the frequent occurrence of the same figure in popular Greek philosophy, e.g. Ps. Kebes 24. 2 ὡς κακῶς διατρίβουσι καὶ ἀθλίως ζῶσι καὶ ὡς ναυαγοῦσιν ἐν τῷ βίῳ, "how wretchedly they live and how miserably they drag out their existence—derelicts, as it were, on life's ocean" (Clark). Other exx. in Dibelius *HZNT ad* 1 Tim *l.c.* The literal sense, as in 2 Cor 11²⁵, is well illustrated in P Oxy IV. 839 (early i/A.D.), where, after describing an accident to a boat, the writer continues—⁶ff ὡς ἐναυάγησεν κατὰ Πτολεμαίδα καὶ ἦλθέ μοι γυμνὸς κεκινδυνευκώς. εὐθέως ἠγόρασα αὐτῶι στολήν.

ναύκληρος.

This word should be translated "captain" rather than "owner" (AV, RV) in its only occurrence in the NT. Ac

27[11], for the vessel belonged to the Alexandrian fleet in the Imperial service: see Ramsay *Paul*, p. 324. In this connexion it is interesting to note that, judging from two ναύκληρος-receipts P Lille I. 22, 23 (both B.C. 221), the Ptolemies were themselves ship-owners and hired out their vessels for corn-transport. The ναύκληρος in both the above cases is described also as μισθωτής or "lessee," though in themselves the two functions were distinct: "die Pacht eines Schiffes für unbestimmte Zwecke schafft einen μισθωτής, die Übernahme eines Staatstransportes einen ναύκληρος" (Rostowzew, *Archiv* v. p. 298). That private persons could also be ship-owners is shown by another receipt P Lille I. 21 (B.C. 221), where a certain Heracleides acts as ναύκληρος for a transport belonging to Heraclitus—Ἡρακλείδης ναύκληρος τῆς Ἡρακλείτου προσαγογείτος (*l.* προσαγωγίδος): see further Wilcken, *Archiv* v. p. 226. Other exx. of the term are P Hib I. 39[5] (B.C. 265) where, as in Ac *l.c.*, Horus is described as ναύκληρος καὶ κυβερνητὴς of a State barge (εἰς κοντω[τὸ]ν βασιλικόν) conveying corn, and as ναύκληρος is instructed to write a receipt and seal a sample of his freight—σύμβολον [δ'ἐ ὑμῖν γραψάσθω . . [κ]αὶ δεῖγμα σφραγισάσ[θ'ω, *ib.* 98[2] (B.C. 251) ὁμολογεῖ [Διονύσιος] ν[αύ]κληρος ἐμ[β]εβ[λ]ῆσθαι . . . κριθ[ῶ]ν ἀρτάβας Δω, "Dionysius, captain, acknowledges that he has embarked 4800 artabae of barley" (Edd.), P Oxy I. 63[1] (ii/iii A.D.) τοῦ ἀναδιδόντος σοι τὸ ἐπιστόλιόν μου ναυκλήρου Πανεμογῶτος, "the bearer of this letter is the captain Panemouotos" (Edd.), and the Delian inscr. *OGIS* 344[1] (i/B.C.) οἱ καταπλέοντες εἰς Βιθυνίαν ἔμποροι καὶ ναύκληροι, where the ἔμποροι, "private-owners," are distinguished from the ναύκληροι, "captains" or "sailing-masters." For the difference between ναύκληρος and πιστικός see the note on P Lond IV. 1341[12] (A.D. 709). Ναυκλήριον, "vessel," is found in P Oxy I. 87[7, 20] (A.D. 342).

ναῦς

is freely found in Aelian, Josephus, and other writers of the literary Κοινή, and, though not common, it occurs also in the vernacular, e.g. in one of the Zeno letters, PSI V. 533[13] (iii/B.C.) εἰς τὴν ναῦν, and in a business document P Lond 1164(*h*)[7] (A.D. 212) (= III. p. 164) διὰ νεὼς σὺν ἱστῷ. Cf. from the inscr. *Cagnat* IV. 33[d. 11] (B.C. 47) μήτε αὐτοῖς ὅπλοις χρῆμα[σι ν]αυσὶ βοηθ[είτω, *Syll* 348(= [3] 763)[7] (B.C. 46) ἐν νηί, *ib.* 499 (= [3] 716) (end of ii/B.C.) ἐν τ[αῖ]ς ἱεραῖς ναυσίν. The nom. plur. νῆες is seen on the Rosetta stone, *OGIS* 90[20] (B.C. 196): for a later use of ναῦς in this same case, cf. Mayser *Gr.* p. 269 n.[1], and see Lob. *Phryn.* p. 170 αἱ νῆες ἐρεῖς, οὐχ αἱ ναῦς, σόλοικον γάρ. Ναῦς is cited twenty times in HR from the LXX, but its solitary occurrence in the NT is in Ac 27[41], where Blass *ad l.* (cf. *Philology*, p. 186) thinks the word is taken from an Homeric phrase. That Luke should use Homer is natural: cf. also the Epic words and forms appearing in late Hellenistic and vulgar epitaphs, especially the metrical ones. For ναῦλον πλοίου the "fare on a boat," see Wilcken *Ostr* i. p. 386 f. and cf. P Goodsp Cairo 30[ii. 13] (A.D. 191–2) with the editor's note.

ναύτης.

To the rare occurrences of this subst. in Greek prose (*ter* in NT) we can now add such exx. as PSI V. 502[24] (B.C.

257–9) πρὸς τῆι τῶν ναυτῶν ἀποστολῆι, P Petr II. 15. 1[7] (B.C. 241–239) τῶν ναυτῶν [ἀπο]πέμπτων οὐκέτι ῥᾳιδιον ἀνακ[?]τήσασθαι, "if the sailors are scattered, it will no longer be easy to collect them again." P Giss I. 40[ii. 15] (A.D. 215) (= *Chrest.* I. p. 38) χοιρεμπο[ρ]οι καὶ ναῦται ποτά[μ]ιοι, P Oxy I. 86[5] (A.D. 338) ναύτην ἕνα, P Gen I. 14[5] (Byz.) τὰ ναῦλα τοῦ μικροῦ πλοιαρίου λαβεῖν παρὰ τοῦ ναύτου, and *OGIS* 674[14] (taxes—A.D. 90) να[ύ]του δραχμὰς πέντε.

The form ναύστης is found on the mummy-label *Preisigke* 1207 ἐκβολὴν ποιῆσαι ναύστην ἰς κώμη. For the adj. ναυτικός cf. P Eleph 1[13] (B.C. 311–10) (= *Selections*, p. 4) τῶν Ἡρακλείδου πάντων καὶ ἐγγαίων καὶ ναυτικῶν, "all Heraclides' possessions both on land and sea," P Oxy VI. 929[1] (ii/iii A.D.) καλῶς ποιήσεις ἀπαιτήσας Τιθόῖν τὸν ναυτικὸν δύμα καροίνου χιτῶνος, "please demand from Tithois the sailor a garment consisting of a brown tunic" (Edd.); and for ναυτεία, "naval affairs," cf. P Rev L[xxv. 6] (B.C. 258), and *OGIS* 90[17] (Rosetta stone—B.C. 196) προσέταξεν δὲ καὶ τὴν σύλληψιν τῶν εἰς τὴν ναυτείαν μὴ ποιεῖσθαι, with Dittenberger's note. Ναύτης survives in MGr.

νεανίας

is restored in P Oxy III. 471[114] (ii A.D.) with reference to a boy of seventeen who had not been sent—ἐπὶ τὰ] διδασκαλε[ῖ]α κα[ὶ] τ[ὰς προ]σηκούσας τοῖς ν[εανί]α[ις] τριβ[ά]ς, "to the schools and the exercises proper for the young" (Edd.): cf. *Syll* 425 (= [3] 546 B[25] (B.C. 216–14) εἰς τὸ ἔλαιον τοῖς νεανίοις (*l.* αις) στατῆρας δέκα. For νεανιεύομαι of acting with youthful recklessness see P Grenf II. 78[9] (A.D. 307). The word is derived from a hypothetical abstract noun *νεϜα, "youth" (Boisacq, p. 659).

νεανίσκος.

In P Amh II. 39[2] (late ii/B.C.) the members of a chosen band of youths are described as—οἱ [ἐκ] τοῦ σημείου νεανίσκοι. Cf. also for the word P Par 60 *bis*[10] (c. B.C. 200) ὥστ[ε φυ]λάττειν καὶ καταστῆ[σαι] τοὺς νεανίσκους, P Oxy III. 533[13] (ii/iii A.D.) where directions are given not to lease a house—νεανίσκοις ἵ[ν]α μὴ ἔχωμεν στομάχου[ς] μηδὲ φθόνον, "to youths that we may not be caused vexation and annoyance" (Edd.), and from the inscr. *Syll* 802 (= [3] 1168)[118] (c. B.C. 320) νεανίσκον εὐπρεπῆ τὰμ μορφάν, *OGIS* 443[9] (i/B.C.) τήν τε τῶν [ὑποτεταγμένων] ἑαυτῶι νεανίσκων ἐνδημίαν εὔτ[ακτ]ον π[αρέχεται καὶ ἄμεμπ]τον. The dim. νεανισκάριον occurs in Epict. ii. 16. 29.

Νεάπολις.

See *s.v.* νέος *ad finem.*

Νεεμάν.

See *s.v.* Ναιμάν.

νεκρός.

Among the numerous passages that might be quoted showing how universally in the ancient world a dead body was regarded as unclean, we may mention P Tor I. 1[ii. 22] (B.C. 116), where it is said of Hera and Demeter—αἷς ἀθέμιτά ἐστιν νεκρὰ σώματα, "quae abhorrent a cadaveribus" (Edd.). Other exx. of the word in this general sense are P Fay 103[1] (iii/A.D.) λ[όγος] ἀναλώματος τοῦ νεκροῦ, "account of expenses for the corpse," P Oxy I. 51⁸ (A.D. 173) the report of a public physician who had been appointed—ἐφιδεῖν σῶμα νεκρὸν ἀπηρτημένον Ἱέρακος, "to inspect the body of a man who had been found hanged, named Hierax" (Edd.) (cf. ib. III. 475⁶—A.D. 182), P Grenf II. 77¹³ (iii/iv A.D.) (= Selections, p. 120), where two men are charged with leaving their brother's body, while carrying off his effects—καὶ ἐκ τούτου ἐμαθον ὅτι οὐ χάριν τοῦ νεκροῦ ἀνήλθατε ἀλλὰ χάριν τῶν σκευῶν αὐτοῦ, "and from this I learned that it was not on account of the dead man you came here, but on account of his goods," and from the inscrr. Syll 438¹¹⁵ (c. B.C. 400) τὸν δὲ νεκρὸν κεκαλυμμένον φερέτω σιγᾶι. In JHS xix. p. 92, a sepulchral inscr. of ii/A.D., we have χαῖρέ μοι μῆτερ γλυκυτάτη καὶ φροντίζετε ἡμῶν ὅσα ἐν νεκροῖς—the correlative of the NT ἐκ νεκρῶν. [Note the alternation of sing. and plur. where the reference is identical (cf. Milligan Thess. p. 131 f.).] With the use of νεκρός in Lk 15²⁴,³², Rev 1¹⁸, 2⁸, 3¹, cf. BGU IV. 1024ᵛⁱⁱ·²⁶ (iv/v A.D.) ἐλέησα τὴν δυσδ[αίμον]α, ὅτι ζῶσα [π]ροσεφέρετο τοῖς βουλ[ομένοις] ὡς νεκρά. In C. and B. ii. 343¹ᶠᶠ· (= p. 477) a certain Menogenes Eustathes expresses his views on life in the spirit of Epicurean philosophy—

τὸ ζῆν ὁ ζήσας καὶ θανὼν ζῇ τοῖς φίλοις·
ὁ κτώμενος δὲ πολλὰ μὴ τρυφῶν σὺν τοῖς φίλοις,
οὗτος τέθνηκε πε[ρι]πατῶν καὶ ζῇ νεκ[ροῦ βίον?

"The Christian spirit which objected to free enjoyment of life for self and friends is stigmatized as 'death in life'" (Ed.). Cf. also Soph. Philoct. 1018 ἄφιλον ἔρημον ἄπολιν ἐν ζῶσιν νεκρόν. Νεκρός is virtually = θνητός in Epict. i. 3. 3, ii. 19. 27 (cited by Sharp, p. 54).

For a subst. νεκρία (not in LS), cf. P Par 22¹⁶ (B.C. 165) τῶν δὲ ἀδελφῶν αὐτοῦ . . . παρακομισάντων αὐτὸν εἰς τὰς κατὰ Μέμφιν νεκρίας, μεχρὶ τοῦ νῦν οὐ τετόλμηκεν αὐτὸν ἡ Νέφορις θάψαι, P Tor I. 1ⁱ·²⁰ (B.C. 116) see note on p. 85, and Preisigke 5216⁵ (i/B.C.), and for νεκροτάφος, "grave-digger," cf. P Grenf II. 73² (late iii/A.D.) (= Selections, p. 118), ib. 77⁸ (iii/iv A.D.) (= Selections, p. 120), and see P Ryl II. 65² note, and Otto Priester i. p. 108 f.

νεκρόω.

To Rom 4¹⁹ κατενόησεν τὸ ἑαυτοῦ σῶμα [ἤδη] νενεκρωμένον, Deissmann (LAE, p. 94) finds a striking parallel in IG III. 2, No. 1355 ἄνθρωπε . . . μή μου παρέλθῃς σῶμα τὸ νεν[ε]κρ[ω]μένον, "O man, pass not by my body, now a corpse."

νέκρωσις.

The use of this word in 2 Cor 4¹⁰ may be illustrated from Photius Bibliotheca, p. 513³⁶, cited by Deissmann (LAE, p. 96 n.¹) from the Thesaurus Graecae Linguae—οἱ γὰρ κόκκοι μετὰ τὴν ἐκ σήψεως νέκρωσιν καὶ φθορὰν ἀναζῶσι, "for the seeds come to life again after death and destruction by decay." See also Vett. Val. p. 53⁸ τὰ ἐκτρώματα γίνονται καὶ δυστοκίαι καὶ νεκρώσεις. In Mk 3⁵ D νέκρωσις is substituted for πώρωσις.

νεομηνία.

For this uncontracted form (Ionic), which is preferred by WH in Col 2¹⁶, we have no evidence earlier than ii/A.D., e.g.

P Tebt II. 318¹² (A.D. 166) μηνὶ Πάχων νεομηνίᾳ, "on the first of the month Pachon." P Goodsp Cairo 30ˣˡ·⁹ (A.D. 191–2) ἐπὶ τῆς νεομ(ηνίας), P Leid Wⁱˣ·⁴⁵ (ii/iii A.D.) ταῖς τῶν θεῶν αὐθεντικαῖς νεομηνίαις, BGU IV. 1021¹⁰ (iii/A.D.) ἀπὸ τῆς οὔσης νεομηνίας τοῦ ὄντος μηνὸς Ἐπείφ: cf. Lob. Phryn. p. 148 "Νεομηνία non contractis primoribus syllabis perrarum est etiam in vulgari Graecitate." It is doubtful, therefore, whether it should be read in the NT passage, especially in view of the occurrence of νουμηνία in most books of the LXX (Thackeray Gr. i. p. 98), and regularly in the Ptolemaic papyri and the inscrr., e.g. P Petr II 4(2)⁶ (B.C. 255–4) ἕως τῆς νουμηνίας, BGU IV. 1053 ²⁰ (B.C. 13) ἐν μησὶν ι ἀπὸ νουμηνίας, Syll 139 (= ³ 284)¹⁶ (c. B.C. 322) στεφανωθήσεται (ὁ ἀνδριὰς) ἀεὶ ταῖς νουμηνίαις καὶ ταῖς ἄλλαις ἑορταῖς, Preisigke 1057 Πέταλος . . . παρεγενέθη πρὸς τὸν Σάραπιν νουμηνίᾳ. Souter draws our attention to the occurrence of numenia in good Lat. MSS.

νέος.

For the relation of νέος to καινός in the papyri see s.v. καινός. The two words are found together, according to the editor's restoration, in P Flor III. 369² (A.D. 139–149) ἐκ [κ(αι)]νῆς καὶ νέας περι[σ]τάσεως. The adj. is applied to the "new" year in P Strass II. 91¹⁸ (B.C. 87?) τοῦ νέου ἔτους, and in the letter of an anxious wife to her husband, P Giss I. 19¹¹ (ii/A.D.) τῆι ἀ [ἡμέρᾳ] τοῦ νέου ἔτους νὴ τὴν σὴν [σωτη]ρίαν ἄ[γ]ευστος ἐκοιμώμην, "on the first day of the new year I swear by your safety I went to bed without tasting food," although, as the editor points out, that day was generally regarded as a laeta dies (Ovid Fasti i. 87). For νέος in relation to crops cf. P Oxy III. 500¹⁹ (A.D. 130) ἐγ νέων [γε]νημάτων, and ib. VII. 1024³⁵ (A.D. 129) ἐκ νέων ἀποδώσει τὰς ἴσας, "he shall repay an equivalent amount out of the new crop" (Ed.). An inscr. from Akoris (Tench) marks the state of the water of the river Nile as—τὸ ἐπ[ἀγαθ]ον γόνιμ[ον] νέον ὕδωρ (Preisigke 991⁹—A.D. 200). On the use of νέος to denote a full-grown man of military age, see Ramsay Teaching, p. 41, and on the Νέοι as a social club of men over twenty (as contrasted with the Ἔφηβοι on the one hand and the Γερουσία on the other), see the same writer in C. and B. i. p. 110 f.: cf. also OGIS 339³¹ (c. B.C. 120) γυμνασίαρχός τε αἱρεθεὶς τῆς τε εὐταξίας τῶν ἐφήβων καὶ τῶν νέων προενοήθη, and Syll 524 (= ³959)⁵ (ii/B.C.) οὔδε ἐνίκων τῶν τε παίδων καὶ τῶν ἐφήβω[ν καὶ τῶν] νέων τοὺς τιθεμένους ἀγῶνας—the νέων being described elsewhere in this document as ἀνδρῶν. The reading Νέαν Πόλιν (for Νεάπολιν), which is adopted by the critical editors in Ac 16¹¹, is supported by inscrr. from B.C. 410 onwards: see Meisterhans Gr. p. 137, Winer-Schmiedel Gr. p. 37.

νεοσσός.

See s.v. νοσσός.

νεότης.

The phrase ἐκ νεότητος, "from youth upwards," as in Mk 10²⁰ al., is found as early as Homer (Il. xiv. 86): cf. P Tebt II. 276³⁵ (astrological—ii/iii A.D.) ἀπὸ νε[ότ]ητος, PSI VI. 685⁷ (iv/A.D.) ἐν τῷ τῆς νεότ?]ητός μου χρόνῳ, and Kaibel 322³ τήνδ ἄρ' ἐμὴν νεότητα πατὴρ Παιδέρως ἐνέγραψεν ("imaginem iuvenilem"). See also Didache iv. 9

ἀπὸ νεότητος διδάξεις τὸν φόβον τοῦ θεοῦ. As showing that νεότης (1 Tim 4¹²) may cover mature age, see Ramsay cited s.v. νέος, and cf. Iren. c. Haer. ii. 22 "triginta annorum aetas prima indolis est iuvenis et extenditur usque ad quadragesimum annum." MGr νιότη "youth."

νεόφυτος.

This word, which in its metaphorical sense of "newly-converted" is confined to Christian literature (cf. 1 Tim 3⁶), is of frequent occurrence in the papyri in the original meaning of "newly-planted" (cf. Ps 127³), e.g. P Ryl II. 138⁹ (A.D. 34) εἰς τὰ νεώ(= ό)φυτα τῶν ἐλαιώνων, "into the young plantations in the olive-yards" (Edd.), BGU II. 563¹·⁹ ⁶ᵗ (ii/A.D.) ἀπὸ νεοφύτ[ων], P Tebt II. 311¹ᵛ (A.D. 134) ἐν τῷ λεγω(= ο)μένῳ Νεω(= ο)φύτῳ γύῳ "in the so-called Newly-planted field" (Edd.), and P Oxy VI. 909¹⁶ (A.D. 225) χώματος ἀμπελ[ι]κοῦ κτήματος νεοφύτου, "the embankment of the newly-planted vineyard." See also Deissmann BS p. 220 f.

νεύω.

As showing how readily this verb, which means literally "nod," "make a sign" (Jn 13²⁴, Ac 24¹⁰), may come to imply words (cf. Field Notes, p. 100), see the letter of a brother to his sister, BGU IV. 1078² (A.D. 39) ἤθελον δὲ ἢ περὶ τῶν ἔργων σεσημάνκαις μοι νεύων ἃ γέγονε ἢ οὔ. For the derived sense "look towards," of countries or places (Lat. vergere, spectare), cf. P Lond 978⁷ (A.D. 331) (= III. p. 233) ἀνδρεῶνα] νεύοντα εἰς νότον, "(a dining-hall) looking to the south," PSI VI. 709¹³ (A.D. 566) οἰκίαν νεύουσαν ἐπ' ἀπηλιώτην, "a house looking towards the east." P Oxy VII. 1038²⁰ (A.D. 568) ἀπὸ οἰκίας νεούσης ἐπὶ νότον, and Preisigke 4127¹⁶ (hymn to Helios) νεύω[ν γὰρ κατ]έδειξάς μοι σεαυτόν.

νεφέλη

is used metaphorically in Kaibel 375² ἔθανον λοιμοῦ [νε]φ[έλη] καταλη[φ]θείς. The editor regards λοιμοῦ νεφέλη as "vox vulgaris . . apud Asianos." For νεφέλαι as the vehicle on which the quick and the dead are wafted to meet the returning Lord, see Milligan on 1 Thess 4¹⁷, and add that the later Jews called the Messiah the Son of the Cloud (Hort Apoc. p. 12). With the constr. in 1 Cor 10¹ cf. P Lond 46²⁶⁶ (iv/A.D.) (= I. p. 73) ὑπὸ τὴν τοῦ ἀέρος νεφέλην.

νέφος.

We are unable to illustrate from our sources the metaphorical use of this NT ἅπ. εἰρ. in Heb 12¹, but cf. Kaibel 1008² πᾶν γὰρ ἀκοσμί[η]ς λέλυται νέφο[ς], and the phrase in the Hymn of Isis ib. 1028⁶⁸ (end of (iii/A.D.) πολέμω(= ου) κρυερὸν νέφος, which recalls Il. xvii. 243.

νεφρός.

In the astrological P Ryl II. 63⁷ (iii/A.D.) we find the "kidneys" assigned to Saturn—Κρόνου νεφροί. For the diminutive cf. P Oxy I. 108¹· ⁹ (A.D. 183 or 215) γλῶσσα μία, νεφρία β, "1 tongue, 2 kidneys"—a cook's monthly meat bill.

νεωκόρος.

In a papyrus of B.C. 217 edited by Th. Reinach in Mél. Nicole, p. 451 ff. (= P Magd 35) we hear of a certain Nicomachus who was νακόρος (Doric form of νεωκόρος) of a Jewish synagogue in an Egyptian village. According to the editor this term, the Greek equivalent of the Hebrew ḥazzān (generally called ὑπηρέτης), was borrowed from the usage of pagan religion, and is still the current title in Greece for the "sacristan" of an orthodox church, as well as of a Jewish synagogue: see also Lumbroso in Archiv iv. p. 317, and cf. Herodas iv. 41, where the νεωκόρος (Lat. aedituus) is sent for to open the temple of Asklepios in Cos. Another early ex. of the word denoting a humble temple-functionary is Priene 231 (iv/B.C.) Μεγάβυζος] Μεγαβύζου νεωκόρος τῆς Ἀρτέμιδος τῆς ἐν Ἐφέσωι, which is interesting as pointing forward to the proud application of the term to Ephesus itself as the "warden" of the temple of Artemis, as in Ac 19³⁵, see e.g. OGIS 481¹ (A.D. 102-6) Ἀρτέμιδι Ἐφεσίᾳ . . . καὶ τῶι νεωκόρωι Ἐφεσίων δήμωι, with Dittenberger's note. The earliest trace of Ephesus as νεωκόρος is said to be on a coin of A.D. 65: see Roumac, p. 65 n.⁴. Later the city came to be known as δίς, τρὶς νεωκόρος: see Ramsay, art. "Ephesus," in Hastings' DB i. p. 722. Instances of the term applied to individuals are P Oxy I. 100² (A.D. 133) Μάρκος Ἀντώνιος Δεῖος . . . νεωκόρος τοῦ μεγάλου Σαρά-πιδος, BGU I. 73¹ (A.D. 135) Κλαύδιος Φιλόξενος νεωκόρος τοῦ μεγάλου Σαράπι[δ]ος, P Tebt II. 286¹³ (A.D. 121-138), 317¹ (A.D. 174-5), al.: cf. also Syll 807 (= ³ 898²⁸ (iii/A.D.) ἐβ(όησεν) ὁ δ(ῆμος)· πολλοῖς ἔτεσι [τοὺς] νεωκόρους. On the form of the word see Thumb Hellen. p. 78, and cf. Otto Priester i. p. 113, Cronert Mem. Herc. p. 165. The subst. νεωκορία is found in BGU I. 14 ii· ¹¹ (A.D. 255), Vett. Val. p. 4²³, and ναοφύλαξ in BGU II. 362 ii· ¹⁰ (A.D. 215) (= p. 4). Boisacq (p. 495) reverts to the traditional derivation from κορέω, "sweep," comparing the Ion. ζάκορος and the Hom. σηκοκόρος.

νεωτερικός.

For this adj., which in the NT is confined to 2 Tim 2²², cf. P Oxy XII. 1449³⁶ (Return of Temple Property—A.D. 213-7) κάτοπ(τρον) νεωτερικ(ὸν) χα λκοῦν) δίπ(τυχον) α, "1 bronze folding mirror in new style" (Edd.).

νεώτερος

in the literal sense of "younger" is seen in P Par 38²² (B.C. 162) παραδεῖξαι Ἀπολλωνίῳ τῷ νεωτέρῳ μου ἀδελφῷ, Syll 790 (= ³ 1157)²⁵ (c. B.C. 100?) ἄνδρας τρεῖς (μὴ) νεωτέ-ρους ἐτῶν τριάκοντα, and P Oxy II. 245¹⁸ (A.D. 26) Στρά-τωνος νεωτέρου, "of Strato the younger." The word is contrasted with πρεσβύτερος in P Strass II. 85¹⁸ (B.C. 113) Πανοβχούνει μὲν τῷ ἑαυτοῦ πρεσβυτέρῳ υἱῶι μερίδα ἃ, Πατῆτι τῶι νεωτέρῳ αὐτοῦ υἱῶι μερίδα μίαν, and in P Par 66²⁴ (Ptol./Rom. period) πρεσβύτεροι καὶ ἀδύνατοι καὶ νεώτεροι: cf. P Tebt II. 317⁸· ¹³ (A.D. 174-5), where we read —Ἡρακλῆου νεωτέρου and Ἡράκλην (l.-ηον) πρεσβύτερον, "Heracleus the younger" and "Heracleus the elder." In a iii/B.C. inscr. from Ptolemais published in Archiv i. p. 202, No. 4¹⁶ a distinction is drawn between οἱ νεώτεροι καὶ οἱ ἄλλοι π[ο]λῖται. It is not very clear whom we are to understand by the former class, but Jouguet (*Vie municipale*, p. 26, cf. Plaumann *Ptolemais*, p. 25) prefers to think of those young in age, rather than of citizens recently introduced into the city, but not yet officially enrolled in the demes. In P Grenf II. 36[12] (B.C. 81) (= Witkowski[2], p. 122) amongst other articles mention is made of—μάρσ[ι]πον μεγάλου α, καὶ τῶν νεωτέρων δύο, "one bag of the large sort, and two of the newer shape," and in P Oxy II. 298[9] (ii/A.D.) the writer, after complaining of the upsetting practices of a certain Hermodorus (πάλι γὰρ πάντα ταράσσει), adds—ἐὰν εὕρῃς παρὰ σοὶ νεώτερον ἐντ[άσ]σειν ἐν τοῖς γράμ-μασ[ι] ἔνεγκον, "if you find where you are a young man to replace him, tell me when you write" (Edd.).

νή.

For this particle, as in 1 Cor 15[31], cf. P Par 49[30] (B.C. 164–158) (= Witkowski[2], p. 71) ἐγὼ γὰρ νὴ τοὺς θεοὺς ἀγωνιῶ, μή ποτε ἀρ[ρ]ωστεῖ τὸ παιδάριον, *Chrest.* I. 110 A[4] (a temple oath—B.C. 110) νὴ τοῦτον τὸν Ἡρακλῆ καὶ τοὺς συννάους θεούς, P Lond 897[11] (A.D. 84) (= III. 207) κέκρικα γὰρ νὴ τοὺς θεοὺς ἐν Ἀλεξανδρείᾳ ἐπιμένειν, P Giss I. 10[11] (ii/A.D.) τῆι ᾱ [ἡμέρᾳ] τοῦ νέου ἔτους νὴ τὴν σὴν [σωτη]ρίαν ἄ[γ]ευστος ἐκοιμώμην, and P Oxy VI. 939[20] (iv/A.D.) (= *Selections*, p. 129) νὴ γὰρ τὴν σὴν σωτηρίαν, κύριέ μου, ἧς μάλιστά μοι μέλει—a Christian letter from a servant to his master. Νή is used incorrectly with negatives in P Oxy I. 33[iv. 13] (interview with an Emperor—late ii/A.D.) νὴ τὴν σὴν τύχην οὔτε μαίνομαι οὔτε ἀπονενόημαι, "I swear by your prosperity, I am neither mad nor beside myself" (Edd.) (cf. Ac 26[25]), and BGU III. 884[3] (ii-iii A.D.) νὴ γὰρ τοὺς θεοὺς [οὐ]κ ἔχωι (*l.* ἔχω) λο[ιπὸ]ν τί σοι γράψωι (*l.* γράψω), cf. [11].

νήθω.

This late form of νέω, "I spin," occurs *bis* in the NT (Mt 6[28], Lk 12[27]): cf. *Kaibel* 501[5] (iv/A.D.) οὕτω μοῖρα βραχὺν ν]ῆσε βίον μερόπων ("mortals"). A verbal ἄνηστος, not in LS, is found in P Oxy X. 1288[34] (iv/A.D.) σιππίου ἀνήστο(υ), of "unspun tow": see the editor's note.

νηπιάζω.

"I am as a babe," which in Bibl. Greek is confined to 1 Cor 14[20], is cited elsewhere only from Hippocrates *Ep.* 1281. 52: cf. the Homeric νηπιαχεύω.

νήπιος.

For this adj. in its ordinary sense of "young," cf. P Tebt II. 326[6] (c. A.D. 266) where a woman notifies the Prefect that her husband had died intestate—τὴν ἐξ ἀμφοῖν γενομένην θυγατέρα κομιδῇ νηπίαν καταλιπὼν ᾗ ὄνομά ἐστι Παυλῖνα, "leaving our daughter, called Paulina, quite young" (Edd.), P Ryl II. 114[31] (c. A.D. 280) a woman's petition for assistance to enable her to recover her property and—μετὰ νηπίων τέκνων ἐν τῇ ἰδίᾳ συν[μένειν, "to live with my young children in my own home" (Edd.), and P Flor I. 36[5] (iv/A.D.) ἅμα ἐκ νηπίας ἡλικίας. An earlier ex. of the word is P Leid B[3.22] (B.C. 164) (= I. p. 9) χρείας ἔτι νηπίας οὔσας, unfortunately after a lacuna. See also

Kaibel 314[1 ff.] (iii/A.D.), a sepulchral epitaph to a child, who had lived only four years, five months, and twenty days—

Νήπιός εἰμι τυχὼν τύμβου τοῦδ᾽, ὦ παροδεῖτα·
ὅσσ᾽ ἔπαθον δ᾽ ἐν βαιῷ τέρματί μου βιοτῆς,
ἐνκύρσας λαϊνέᾳ στήλλῃ τάχα καὶ σὺ δακρύσεις.

Νηρεύς.

To show how little this proper name is confined to Rome (Rom 16[15]) Rouffiac (p. 91) cites exx. of its use not only from Rome (*CIL* VI. 4344), but also from Ancyra in Galatia (*CIL* III. 256), and from Athens (*IG* III. 1053[11], 1160[62], 1177[19]).

νῆσος.

For this fem. subst. in -ος, it is sufficient to cite P Petr II. 28[vii. 9] (iii/B.C.) ἱερᾶς νήσου, BGU IV. 1031[12] (ii/A.D.) ὅρα μὴ ἀμελήσῃς τὸν ἀλοητὸν ("threshing") τῆς νήσου. The word was used (in contrast to ἤπειρος, "high land") of land flooded by the Nile, and was so designated on account of the canals by which it was intersected (see Preisigke *Fachwörter s.v.*). In P Oxy VIII. 1101[24] (A.D. 367–70) a Prefect gives orders that in certain circumstances a man should be deported to an island—τοῦτον νῆσον οἰκῆσαι κελεύ]ω. For the form νήσσον which is read in Ac 13[6] D, see Cronert *Mem. Herc.* p. 93, and for νησιῶτις used as an adj., see P Grenf II. 15[ii. 2] (B.C. 139) γῆς νησιωτίδος. MGr νησί, "island."

νηστεύω.

An interesting ex. of this verb is afforded by the new Logion P Oxy I. 1[5 ff.] λέγει Ἰησοῦς, ἐὰν μὴ νηστεύσητε τὸν κόσμον, οὐ μὴ εὕρητε τὴν βασιλείαν τοῦ θ(εο)ῦ. For the gen. constr. cf. Empedocles (ed. Sturz) 454 νηστεῦσαι κακότητος.

νῆστις.

For the rare form νήστης see the medical receipt P Oxy VIII. 1088[11] (early i/A.D.) ταῦτα νήστηι δίδου πεῖν, "give them to the patient to drink fasting" (Ed.): cf. *Syll* 805 (= [3] 1171)[9] (Rom.) ἔδωκεν εὔζωμον νήστῃ τρώγειν, "he gave rocket to the fasting man to eat." MGr νηστικός, "sober," "hungry."

νηφάλιος.

In *Syll* 631 (= [3] 1040)[20] (beginning of iv/B.C.) νηφάλ[ι]οι τρεῖς βωμοί may refer either to altars at which only wineless offerings were made, or perhaps to cakes made in the form of an altar, free from all infusion of wine: see Dittenberger's note, and cf. *Roberts-Gardner* ii. p. 380. The acc. fem. plur. νηφαλίους in 1 Tim 3[11] is found in Plutarch. For the late νηφάλεος see Moulton *Gr.* ii. p. 76.

νήφω

is found along with ἁγνεύω to mark the proper state of intending worshippers in *Syll* 790 (= [3] 1157)[41] (c. B.C. 100) ἁγνεύοντες καὶ νήφοντες: cf. *ib.* 564[1] (ii/B.C.) ἀπ᾽ οἴνου μὴ προσιέναι. For the metaphorical application, as in 1 Thess 5[6.8] *al.*, see Aristeas 209 where νήφειν τὸ πλεῖον μέρος τοῦ βίου, "to be sober for the greater part of one's life," is laid down as one of the qualities of a ruler, and the exx. in Hort's note *ad* 1 Pet 1¹³. See also BGU III. 1011¹⁰·⁵ (ii/B.C.) νήφ[ει]ν ἀναγκ[α]ζέσθ[ω], and P Oxy VII. 1062¹³ (ii/A.D.) αὖ[τ]ήν δέ σοι τήν ἐπιστολήν πέμψω διὰ Σύρου ἵνα αὐτήν ἀναγνοῖς νήφων καὶ σαυτοῦ καταγνοῖς, "I will send you the very letter by Syrus in order that you may read it in a sober mood and be self-condemned" (Ed.). For the compound ἐννήφω, see M. Anton. i. 16. 0.

Νίγερ.

This Latin surname, as in Ac 13¹, is found in an ostracon tax-receipt of A.D. 174-5, published in *Archiv* vi. p. 213, where one of the πράκτορες ἀργυρικῶν is Αἰβύτιος Νίγερ. It stands alone in a sepulchral inscr. of Roman times, *Preisigke* 46 Νίγερ μαχαιροφόρος, εὐψύχι. On the possibility that Νίγερ (Ac *l.c.*) was a nickname first given to Συμεών at Antioch (cf. Ac 11²⁶), see Kinsey in *Exp T* xxxv. p. 80 f.

Νικάνωρ.

This proper name (Ac 6⁵) is common in the inscrr., e.g. *IG* XIV. 2393³⁷⁵, 2405²⁵ *al.*, and in such wall-scratchings as *Preisigke* 1070 Νικάνωρ ἥκω μεθ' Ἡρακλέας [Δ]ρυγχίτιδος μεθύων (or μεθ' ὑῶν ?), 3736 (i A.D.) Νικάνωρ Ἀπολλώνιος ἥκω. See also P Frankf 5 *recto*²⁰ (B.C. 242-1) and cf. Crönert *Mem. Herc.* p. 170, n.⁴.

νικάω

is found in a legal sense of *winning one's case*, as in Rom 3⁴, in P Hal I. 1⁵⁸ (mid. iii/B.C.) ἐὰν δέ τιν (*l.* τις) . . . γρ[αψ]άμενος δίκην ψευδομαρ[τ]υρίου νικήσηι κτλ., and in relation to games in PSI IV. 364 (B.C. 251-0) γίνωσκε Διονύσιον τὸν ἀδελφὸν νενικηκότα τὸν ἐν Ἱεραι νήσωι ἀγῶνα τῶν Πτολεμαιείων, and P Oxy XIV. 1759⁴ (letter to an athlete—ii A.D.) πρὸ [τ]ῶν ὅλων εὔχομαί σε ὑγιαίνειν [κ]αὶ νικᾶν πάντοτε. It is very common as an epithet of the Emperors, e.g. P Amh II. 140¹² (A.D. 349) τῶ]ν πάντα νικών[των] δεσποτῶν ἡμῶν Ἀγούστων, "of our all-victorious masters the Augusti" (Edd.). A good parallel to Rom 12²¹ is afforded by *Test. xii. patr.* Benj. iv. 3 οὗτος τὸ ἀγαθὸν ποιῶν νικᾷ τὸ κακόν.

νίκη.

An interesting ex. of this word, which in the NT is confined to 1 Jn 5⁴, occurs in the letter of the Emperor Claudius incorporated in the diploma of membership of The Worshipful Gymnastic Society of Nomads, in which he thanks the club for the golden crown sent to him on the occasion of his victorious campaign in Britain in A.D. 43— ἐπὶ τῇ κατὰ Βρετάννων νείκηι (P Lond 1178¹² (A.D. 194)) (= III. p. 216, *Selections*, p. 99). See also P Giss I. 27⁶ (ii/A.D.) ἐρχομένῳ εὐαγγελίζοντι τὰ τῆς νείκης αὐτοῦ καὶ προκοπῆς with reference to the arrival of a slave announcing a victory over the Jews, and the Gnostic charm for victory in the race-course, P Oxy XII. 1478³ (iii/iv A.D.) δὸς νείκην ὁλοκληρίαν σαδίου (*l.* σταδίου), "grant victory and safety in the race-course": the charm begins—νεικητικὸν Σαραπάμμωνι υἱῷ Ἀπολλωνείου, "charm for victory for Sarapammon son of Apollonius," cf. P Lond 121³⁰⁰ (iii/A.D.) (= I. p. 97) νικητικὸν δρομέως. P Strass I. 42¹⁷ (A.D. 310) ὄμνυμει θεοὺς ἅπαντας καὶ τύχην καὶ νίκην τῶν δεσποτων

ἡμῶν τῶν ἀνικήτων βασιλέων μηδένα ἀποκεκρυφέναι shows a common formula. Other exx. of the word are P Leid B¹·⁵ (B.C. 164) (= I. p. 11) ὃς διδοίη σοι μετὰ τῆς Ἴσιος νίκην, *OGIS* 90³ (Rosetta stone—B.C. 196) ὧι ὁ Ἥλιος ἔδωκεν τὴν νίκην, and *ib.* 678¹ (A.D. 117-38) ὑπὲρ σωτηρίας καὶ αἰωνίου νίκης Αὐτοκράτορος Καίσαρος Τραιανοῦ Ἀδριανοῦ Σεβαστοῦ. In BGU IV. 1084·³ (A.D. 222-35) it is the name of a goddess—ἀγυιᾶς Ἀρσινόης Νείκης. For the compound νικηφόρος see P Tebt I. 43²⁵ (B.C. 118) θεοὶ μέγιστοι νικηφόροι, "most great and victorious gods," and the description of Ptolemy IV. (B.C. 221-05), *OGIS* 80 θε[οῦ μ]εγάλου Φιλοπάτορος Σωτῆρος καὶ Νικηφόρου

Νικόδημος.

For this proper name, which is common both to Greeks and Jews, cf. P Hib I. 110 *verso*⁹⁰·⁷⁵·¹⁰⁵ (c. B.C. 255), BGU IV. 1132²·³ (B.C. 13) Νικοδείμου, P Flor I. 6²⁰ (A.D. 201) Νικόδημον βουλευτήν, and the Indexes to *Syll* and Preisigke's *Sammelbuch*.

Νικολαΐτης.

See *s.v.* Νικόλαος.

Νικόλαος.

For this proper name, as in Ac 6⁵, cf. *IG* XIV. 682, 1252, and the many exx. in Preisigke's *Sammelbuch*, see Index. On νικο-λαος in popular etymology a rough Greek equivalent for בלעם‎, leading to the identification of the Nicolaitans with the Balaamites, see Moffatt on Rev 2⁶ in *EGT*. Harnack rejects any allegorical interpretation of the name (*The Journal of Religion* iii. (1923), p. 413 ff.).

νῖκος.

This form, as in Mt 12²⁰, 1 Cor 15⁵⁴·⁵⁵·⁵⁷, 1 Esdr 3⁹, occurs in BGU III. 1002¹¹ (B.C. 55) σαὶ δέ εἰσιν πᾶσαι αἱ κατ' αὐτῶν κείμεναι συνγραφαὶ καὶ ὠναὶ καὶ δίκαια καὶ βέβαια καὶ νῖκος, apparently with reference to victory in a law-suit. According to Wackernagel (*Hellenistica*, p. 26 f.) the word is originally related to the poetic νεῖκος, "strife," but passed into Ionic with the meaning of "victory," through the influence of νίκη: see also Fraenkel *Glotta* iv. (1913) p. 39 ff. Some Lat. MSS. actually translate νῖκος in 1 Cor 15⁵⁵ by *contentio*.

νίπτω.

See Ev. Petr. 1 τῶν δὲ Ἰουδαίων οὐδεὶς ἐνίψατο τὰς χεῖρας: "the callousness of the Jewish leaders is sharply contrasted with the scruples of the Gentile Procurator" (Swete *ad l.*). MGr νίβω (νίβγω).

νοέω.

The phrase νοῶν καὶ φρονῶν is common in wills of both the Ptolemaic and the Roman periods, e.g. P Petr I. 16(1)¹² (B.C. 237) τάδε διέθετο νοῶν καὶ φρονῶν Μένιππος, P Oxy I. 104⁴ (A.D. 96), *ib.* III. 491² (A.D. 126), the testator thus certifying himself as "being sane and in his right mind": contrast the imprecation, Wünsch *AF* p. 20⁵⁹ (iii/A.D.) βασάνισον αὐτῶν τὴν διάνοιαν τὰς φρένας τὴν αἴσθησιν ἵνα μὴ νοῶσιν τί π[ο]ιῶσιν. With 2 Tim 2⁷ we may compare the sepulchral inscr. *Kaibel* 278⁵ καὶ σὺ | ἐρχόμε[ν]ο[ς] π[a]ρ' ὁδῷ τὸ[ν] φίλον ὄντα νόει, "et tu quoque qui praeteris nosce amicum tibi esse." For the meaning "perceive," "understand," cf. further BGU I. 114[i. 9] (A.D. 117) νοοῦμεν ὅτι αἱ παρακαταθῆκαι προῖκές εἰσιν, and for the meaning "purpose," cf. P Par 63[xi. 61] (B.C. 165) τοὺς καθ᾽ ὁντινοῦν τρόπον νοοῦντάς τί σοι ἀντίον, *Preisigke* 5235[7] (A.D. 12) π]λείους μοι πληγὰς ἐνέτεινε[ν] ἐ[ξέλα]σίν μοι νοησάμε[νο]ς. See also P Rein 16[34] (B.C. 109) a legal execution against two men—παρ᾽ οὗ ἂν αὐτῶν νοῆται καὶ ἐκ τῶν ὑ[παρχόντων] αὐτοῖς [πάντων], "tant sur leurs personnes que sur la totalité de leurs biens" (Ed.).

In Rom 1[20] Field (*Notes*, p. 151) understands νοούμενα as "'conceived'—apprehended by the mind." MGr νοιώθω, "perceive," "notice," "feel."

νόημα.

Νοήματα, which is found *sexies* in the NT, is best rendered on each occasion by "thoughts." According to Heinrici *ad* 2 Cor 4[4] (in Meyer[8]) the plur. in the sense of "mind," "reason," which many commentators prefer, can be supported only by Pind. *Ol.* 7. 72. The sing. is seen in *Kaibel* 632 Τραιανοῦ τάφος οὗτος, ὃς εὐσεβὲς εἶχε νόημ[α.

νόθος.

This NT ἅπ. εἰρ. (Heb 12[8]) is found in such passages as P Hib I. 32[15] (return of sheep—B.C. 246) ψιλὰ νόθα ι, "10 are shorn and half-bred," P Petr III. 59 (*b*)[6] (tax-return—iii/ii B.C.) νόθοι ιδ, and P Tebt II. 302[24] (A.D. 71–2) τινῶν ἐκ τοῦ ἱεροῦ νόθων, "certain bastards from the temple," in contrast to the legitimate (νόμιμοι) priests : cf. *Syll* 734 (= ³1106)[144] (Cos—*c.* B.C. 300) ἂν δέ τις νόθος ὢν κρ[ιθ]εὶς γνωσθῆι μετέχειν τῶν ἱερῶ[ν], μὴ ἐξέστω αὐτῶι μετέχειν τῶν [ἱε]ρωσυνῶν, and see also the sepulchral inscr. *Kaibel* 120[7f.]—

ἑξήκοντ᾽ ἔτε[σιν μετ᾽ ἐμῆς ἐβίωσα γυναικός,
ἐ]ξ ἧς ἔσχα τέκνα γνήσια κοὐχὶ νόθα.

The word is of doubtful origin.

νομή.

In P Hib I. 52[7] (*c.* B.C. 245) we read of certain persons who had used up the pastures—ἀποκέχρηνται ταῖς νομαῖς, in circumstances which are far from clear : cf. P Oxy II. 244[5] (A.D. 23) the transference of sheep νο[μῶ]ν χάριν, "for the sake of pasturage," *ib.* X. 1279[15] (A.D. 139) a lease of State and on this condition—ἔχειν με τὰς νομὰς καὶ ἐπινομὰς φόρου τῶν ὁμῶν (*l.* νομῶν) κατ᾽ ἔτος σὺν παντὶ δραχμῶν τεσσάρων, "that I shall have the pastures and secondary pastures at the annual rent for the pastures of four drachmae in all" (Edd.), P Tebt II. 317[28] (A.D. 174–5) π[ε]ρὶ μισθώσεως νομῶν, "concerning a lease of pastures," and P Ryl II. 100[9] (A.D. 238) πρὸς τὴν τῶν προβάτων [βρῶσιν καὶ κοίτη]ν καὶ νομήν, "for the maintenance, folding, and pasturing of sheep." On a tax εἰς τὰς νομάς, see Wilcken *Ostr* i. p. 265 f. For the legal phrase νομὴ ἄδικος, "unjust possession," see P Tebt II. 286[7] (A.D. 121–38) with the editor's note, and cf. *ib.* 355[12] (mid. iii/A.D.), and for μακρᾶς νομῆς παραγραφή, "*longae possessionis praescriptio*," see *Chrest.* II. 374 (iii/A.D.). Νομεύς, "shepherd," appears in P Oxy II. 245[17] (A.D. 26), and the verb in *ib.* [10] ἃ νεμήσεται σὺν τος (*l.* τοῖς) ἐπακολουθοῦσι ἄρνασι περὶ Πέλα, "which (sheep) will pasture, together with the lambs that may be

produced, in the neighbourhood of Pela." The wider sense of "belong to," "hold sway in," is seen in *OGIS* 50[3] (mid. iii/B.C.) τοῖς τὴν σύνοδον νέμουσιν, with reference to the members of an association or club, see Dittenberger's note and cf. Plaumann *Ptolemais*, p. 62.

νομίζω.

For this verb in the pass. with reference to received custom or usage cf. P Hib I. 77[3] (B.C. 249) ἵνα συντελῆται τὰ νομιζόμενα [τοῖς θ]εοῖς, "in order that the customary payments may be made to the gods" (Edd.), P Ryl II. 153[c] (A.D. 138–61) τὰ νενοσμισμένα (*l.* νενομ-) τοῖς κατοιχομένοις, "the accustomed rites for the departed" (Edd.), P Oxy VII. 1070[11] (iii/A.D.) τῶν χρηστῶν ἐλπίδων τῶν ἐν ἀνθρώποισι νενομισμένων (*l.* νενομ-), "the good hopes that are held by mankind" (Ed.), *Syll* 737 (= ³1109)[34] (before A.D. 178) μηδενὶ ἐξέστω ἰόβακχον εἶναι, ἐὰν μὴ πρῶτον ἀπογράψηται παρὰ τῶι ἱερεῖ τὴν νενομισμένην ἀπογραφήν, and *OGIS* 210[10] (A.D. 247–8) (= *Chrest.* I. p. 102) πρὸς τὸ δύνασθαι τὰ περὶ τὰ ἱερὰ θρήσκια κατὰ τὰ νενομισμένα γείνεσθαι. The act. "suppose," "think," is frequent, e.g. P Par 46[19] (B.C. 153) νομίζω γὰρ μάλιστα τῶν ἄλλων παρακολουθήσαντά σε τῇ ἀληθείᾳ, "for I think that you more than the others are a follower of truth," P Tebt I. 50[11] (B.C. 112–1) νομίσας καιρὸν εὐφυῆι ἔχειν, "thinking that he had a favourable opportunity" (Edd.), P Fay 109[4] (early i/A.D.) νομίσας ὅτι κιχρᾷς μοι αὐτούς, "consider that you are lending them (3 staters) to me" (Edd.), P Lips I. 105[2] (i/ii A.D.) ἐχθὲς κατέσχον τὸν φύλακα νομίζων σοι δύνασθαι πέμψαι ὃν ἐπεζήτησας λόγον, BGU II. 450[25] (ii/iii A.D.) ὡς νομ[ί]ζω, οἶδεν ἡ γυνή σου ποῦ ἐστιν Θαῦς, and P Lond IV. 1350[10] (A.D. 710) ὑπὲρ ὃ νομίζεις, "beyond what you expect" (Ed.). The verb survives unchanged in MGr.

νομικός.

Without entering into the discussion as to whether this term when applied to Zenas in Tit 3[13] implies in his case a knowledge of Roman or Hebrew law, it may be noted that exx. of the former sense can be readily produced from the papyri and inscr. : see e.g. BGU I. 326[ii. 22] (ii/A.D.) where a certain Gaius Lucius Geminianus, νομικὸς Ῥωμαϊκός, certifies that he has examined the copy of a will, and finds that it corresponds with the original : cf. Mommsen's commentary *ad l.* in the *Berliner Sitzungsberichte*, 1894, p. 4, n.[1], where a number of instances of νομικός, "lawyer," are cited from Greek inscr. of the Imperial age. See also *Magn* 191[4] (time of Antonines) a decree honouring Ζώβιον Διοσκουρίδου νομικὸν ζήσαντα κοσμίως, and *IAS* ii. p. 137 (Imperial period) Λ. Μαλίῳ Μαξίμῳ νομικῷ. In P Oxy II. 237[viii. 2] (A.D. 186) we have the copy of an answer by a νομικός—ἀντίγραφον προσφων[ή]σεως νομ[ι]κοῦ—to a technical question addressed to him by the presiding magistrate, which prepares ns for the frequent appointment of νομικοί as "assessors," where "the judge was a soldier and therefore not a legal expert": see GH *ad l.* and cf. CPR I. 18[24] (A.D. 124) (= *Chrest.* II. p. 93) Βλαίσιος Μαριανὸς ἔπαρχος . . . συνλαλήσας Ἀρτε[μι]δ[ώ]ρῳ τ]ῷ νομ[ι]κῷ [π]ε[ρὶ το]ῦ πράγματος, ὑ[πη]γόρευσεν ἀπόφασιν ἣ καὶ ἀν]ε[γ]νώσθη, P Cattaoui [iii. 2] (ii A.D.) (= *Archiv* iii. p. 59, *Chrest.* II. p.

.21) Λοῦπ[ος] λαλήσας μετὰ τῶν νομικῶν εἶπεν κτλ. The term is also applied to a private notary, as in BGU I. 361iii.2 (A.D. 184) ὁ νομικὸς ὁ τὴν οἰκονομίαν γράψας : and for the corresponding **νομογράφος** cf. P Fay 28[15] (A.D. 150-1) (= *Selection*, p. 82) ἔγραψ[ε]ν ὑπὲρ αὐτῶν Ἀμμώνιος νομογράφος . On the late variant **νομικάριος** for **νομικός** see P Oxy XII. 1416[21] (. A.D. 290) with the editors' note.

νομίμως.

Epict. iii. 10. 8 ὁ θεός σοι λέγει 'δός μοι ἀπόδειξιν, εἰ νομίμως ἤθλησας' offers a good parallel to 2 Tim 2[5] (see Sharp, p. 2). For the corresponding adj. cf. P Tebt II. 302[26] (A.D. 71-2) ἡμεῖν τοῖς νομίμοις ἱερεῦσι ἐτήρησεν [τὰς ἀρούρας. "he reserved the land for us, the legitimate priests" (Edd. , P Fay 124[15] (ii A.D.) ἄνευ νομίμων, "illegally." BGU IV. 1032[10] (A.D. 173) ἐκ μὴ νομ[ί]μων γάμων. P Oxy IX. 1201[15] (A.D. 258) τοῦ μέρους τοῦ διατάγματος τοῦ τοῖς νομίμοις κληρονόμοις τ`ὴ`ν διακατοχὴν διδόντος, "that portion of the edict which grants succession to the lawful heirs" (Ed.), BGU IV. 1074[2] (A.D. 275) νόμιμα καὶ φιλάνθ[ρ]ωπα, OGIS 56[65] (B.C. 237), συντελεῖν τὰ νόμιμα τῆι θεῶι. and the Christian sepulchral inscr. *Kaibel* 727[5] νομίμοις δὲ θεοῦ παρεγείνατο πᾶσιν.

νόμισμα

In its primary sense of *institution*, anything sanctioned by usage, is in classical Greek almost confined to poetry (cf. Jebb *Antigone* 295). We can however supply an example in the Κοινή from the petition of Dionysia, P Oxy II. 237iii.22 (A.D. 186), where reference is made to the fact τὰς Αἰγυπτιακὰς γυναῖκας κατὰ ἐγχώριον νόμιμα (. νόμισμα) κατέχειν τὰ ὑπάρχοντα τῶν ἀνδρῶν διὰ τῶν γαμικῶν συγγραφῶν, "that Egyptian wives have by native Egyptian law a claim upon their husbands' property through their marriage contracts" (Edd.). It should be noted, however, that the reading is somewhat uncertain. With the more special sense of "coin" in Mt 22[19] (cf. 1 Macc 15[6]) we may compare P Tebt II. 485 (ii B.C.) ὃς δ' ἂν παρὰ ταῦτα ποιῆι τό τε ἀργυρικὸν νόμισμα καὶ τὸν ἀποτ[, P Grenf II. 77[2] (iii/iv A.D.) (= *Selection*, p. 120) ἐν δραχμαῖς τριακοσίαις τεσσαράκοντα παλαιοῦ νομίσματος: see also the introd. to P Thead 33. For the form **νόμιμα** see BGU I. 64[2] (A.D. 120) ἀργυρίου σεβαστοῦ νομίζματος: cf. Deissmann *BS* p. 185.

νομοδιδάσκαλος.

"a teacher of the law," is found *ter* in the NT, but does not seem to occur elsewhere except in eccles. writers: cf., however, **νομοδιδάκτης** in Plut. *Cato Maior* xx. 4.

νομοθεσία.

This classical word (found also in Philo), which in the NT is confined to Rom 9[4], "the giving of the law," occurs in a royal petition of about A.D. 375, P Lips I. 35[5] τῆς θείας ὑμῶν καὶ φιλανθρώπου νομ[ο]θ[εσ]ίας. Cf. Syll 790 (= 31157)[93] (c. B.C. 100) διαπαραδιδόσ[θ]ω δὲ τὸ ψήφισμα τόδε καὶ τοῖς αἱρεθησομένοις μετὰ ταῦτα στρατηγοῖς [καὶ νομοφύ]λαξιν νομοθεσίας τάξιν ἔχον, OGIS 326[26] (time of Attalus II. Philadelphus, B.C. 159-138) καθὼς αὐτὸς ἐν τῆι νομοθεσίαι περὶ ἑκάστων δια`τέ`ταχεν.

νομοθετέω.

An interesting ex. of this verb is found in a letter of remonstrance from the Senate of Antinoopolis to the epistrategus Antonius Alexander, in which they vindicated the privilege bestowed on them by Hadrian to be exempt from public burdens outside their own city, P Oxy VIII. 1119[16] (A.D. 254) θεὸς Ἀδριανὸς . . . . . ἐνομοθέτησεν σαφῶς παρὰ νόμοις μὲν ἡμεῖν ἄρχειν καὶ λειτουργεῖν, πασῶν δὲ ἀπηλλάχθη τῶν παρ' ἄλλοις ἀρχῶν τε καὶ λειτουργιῶν. "the deified Hadrian clearly established the law that we should bear office and burdens nowhere but at home, and we were relieved of all offices and burdens elsewhere" (Ed.) For the pass., which alone occurs in the NT, see OGIS 329[13] (mid. ii/B.C.) τὰ καλῶς καὶ δικαίως νενομοθετημένα ἡμεῖν ὑπὸ τῶ[ν βα]σιλέων, *ib.* 403[56] (ii/A.D.) ταῦτα μὲν ὑμεῖν ὀρθῶς καὶ καλῶς . . νενομοθετήσθω.

νόμος.

For the use of **νόμος** c. gen. obj. to denote a particular ordinance as in Rom 7[2] ἀπὸ τοῦ νόμου τοῦ ἀνδρός ("from that section of the statute-book which is headed 'The Husband,' the section which lays down his rights and duties" SH), cf. Syll 828 (= 31198)[14] (iii/A.D.) κα]τὰ τὸν νόμον τῶν ἐ[ρανισ]τῶν. See also P Rev LXXV.[15] (B.C. 259-8) al. where the various cross-references from one section to another are marked by the phrase **κατὰ τὸν νόμον** (cf. the editors' note, p. 91). Thieme (p. 30) illustrates the quasi-personification of ὁ νόμος in Jn 7[51], Rom 3[19] by Magn 92 a.[11] (ii/B.C. ad init.) πάντων συντελεσθέντων, ὧν ὁ νόμος συντάσσει, cf. b[16] πάντων συντελεσθέντων ὧν ὁ νόμος ἀγορεύει. The phrase **ἐν νόμῳ γέγραπται** is found in legal phraseology from iii B.C. onwards, e.g. Magn 52[85] ὅσα καὶ τοῖς τὰ Πύθια ἐπαγγελλόν[τ]εσσι[ν ἐν ν]όμῳ γέγραπται. For the expression **νόμος βασιλικός** in Jas 2[8] see s.v. βασιλικός ad fin. The inscr. is reproduced in OGIS 483. In a remarkable epitaph from Apameia, *C. and B.* ii. p. 538 No. 399 *bi*, provision is made that the grave shall not be disturbed in the following terms—ἰς ὃ ἕτερος οὐ τεθῇ. εἰ δέ τις ἐπιτηδεύσι, τὸν νόμον οἶδεν [τ]ῶν Εἰουδέων. According to Ramsay, the reference must be not to the law of Moses, but to some agreement made with the city by the resident Jews for the better protection of their graves. For a detailed study of **νόμος** used qualitatively in the Pauline Epistles we may refer to Slaten *Qualitative Nouns*, p. 35 n. Norden (*Agnostos Theos*, p. 11 n.[2]) points out how readily Paul's teaching in Rom 2[14 ff.] ὅταν γὰρ ἔθνη τὰ μὴ νόμον ἔχοντα φύσει τὰ τοῦ νόμου ποιῶσιν, οὗτοι κτλ. would be understood in view of the ἄγραφος νόμος of the Greeks (cf. R. Hirzel *Ἄγραφος Νόμος, Ges. d. Wiss., philol.-hist. Kl.* xx. 1900). See also Ferguson *Legal Terms*, p. 64.

νομός.

Although **νομός** as a *terminus technicus* for a political "department" or "district" of the country does not occur in the NT, we may cite here, owing to the interesting analogy which it presents to Lk 2[1], the rescript of the Prefect Gaius Vibius Maximus commanding all who happened to be out of their own homes to return home in view of the approaching census—τῆς κατ' οἰκίαν ἀπογραφῆς συ[νεστώ]σης or ἐ[νεστώ]σης, see *L.A.E.* p. 268 n.) ἀναγκαῖόν ἐστιν πᾶσιν τοῖ]ς καθ ἥ[ντινα] δήποτε αἰτ[ίαν ἐκστᾶσι τῶν ἑαυτῶν] νομῶν προσα[γγέλλε]σθαι ἐπα[νελ]θεῖν εἰς τὰ ἑαυ[τῶν ἐ]φέστια (P Lond 904²³ ⁰. (A.D. 104) (= III. p. 125, *Selections*, p. 73)). For the word in the LXX see Deissmann *BS* p. 145, and cf. Wackernagel *Hellenistica*, p. 10.

νοσέω

in its literal sense "am sick" occurs in such passages as P Oxy I. 76²⁰ (A.D. 179) νοσήσας ἐπισφαλῶς ἔχει, "has fallen ill and is in a precarious condition" (Edd.), PSI IV. 299¹¹ (iii/A.D.) ἐνόσησαν δὲ πάντες οἱ κατὰ τὴν οἰκίαν. P Oxy VIII. 1161⁸ (Christian—iv/A.D.) ταῦτα δέ σοι ἔγραψα νοσοῦσα, δ[ιν]ῶς ἔχουσα, "I write this to you in sickness, being very ill" (Ed.), *ib.* X. 1299⁵ (iv/A.D.) ἀπὸ τοῦ νέω (= νέου) ἔτους πολλὰ ἐνοσοῦμεν. Cf. also the iii B.C. Coan decree conferring a gold crown on a physician for his services during an epidemic, *Cos* 5⁵ (= *Syll* 490 (= ³943²) παρέχων αὑτοσαυ[τὸ]ν π[ρ]ό[θυμ]ον εἰς τὰν σωτηρίαν τῶν νοσεύντ[ων.

νόσος.

PSI IV. 299³ (ii/A.D.) κατεσχέθην νόσῳ (cf. [Jn] 5¹), P Oxy XII. 1414²⁶ (A.D. 270–5) ἐ (*l.* ἐν) νόσῳ εἰμὶ καὶ τῆς πλευρᾶς [ῥ]έγχομαι, "I have (long) been ill and have a cough from my lung" (Edd.), *ib.* VIII. 1121⁹ (A.D. 295) νόσῳ κατα[β]λ[η]θεῖσα, "stricken with illness" (Ed.), *ib.* VI. 939²³ (iv/A.D.) (= *Selections*, p. 130) ἡνίκα ἐβαρεῖτο τῇ νόσῳ, "when she was oppressed by sickness," *ib.* VIII. 1151²⁶ (Christian—v/A.D.) ὁ ἰασάμενος πᾶσαν νόσον καὶ πᾶσαν μαλακίαν (cf. Mt 4²³) and similarly BGU III. 954¹¹ (vi/A.D.) (= *Selections*, p. 133). For ἱερὰ νόσος, "epilepsy," cf. P Oxy II. 263¹⁰ (A.D. 77) the sale of a slave ἀσυκοφάντητον πλὴν ἱερᾶς νόσου καὶ ἐπαφῆς, "without blemish apart from epilepsy and leprosy," *et saepe*. Cf. also the sepulchral inscr. *Preisigke* 5883⁷ θνήσκω δ' οὐ νούσοισι δαμείς, εὕδων δ' ἐνὶ κοίτῃ | τοῦτον ἔχω μισθὸν δύσθιον (= λοίσθιον "last") εὐσεβίης, and *Kaibel* 314²¹ ᶠ cited *s.v.* κορέννυμι. For the adj. νοσε(η)ρός see Cronert *Mem. Herc.* p. 295 n.². The form νοσηλός is found in the Christian P Oxy VI. 939²⁶ (iv/A.D.) (= *Selections*, p. 130) νοσηλότερον δὲ ὅμως τὸ σωμάτιον ἔχει, "she is still in a somewhat sickly state of body," and ἀνόσητος in P Iand 13¹¹ (iv/A.D.) εἰ ἀνόσειτ[ος εἶ γράψον. The verb νοσηλεύω is found *bis* in the so-called letter of Trajan, P Fay 19⁵·²⁰. Νοσοκομεῖον, "hospital," occurs in the late P Amh II. 154²·⁸ (vi/vii A.D.), and appears in MGr νοσοκομεῖο: but νόσος has dropped out of the vernacular, ἀρρώστια taking its place (Thumb, *Handbook* p. 46).

νοσσιά.

On the form of this collective word = "brood" (Lk 13³⁴) see Dieterich *Untersuchungen*, p. 47. A new ex. of the earlier form may be cited from *Menandrea* p. 81²⁷⁸ νεοττίαν | χελιδόνων. The Ionic form νοσσιή is found in Herodas vii. 72, and hypocoristic proper names Νοσσίς, Νόσσος, Νοσσώ, are quoted by Boisacq, p. 664. See also Hatzidakis *Einl.* p. 268.

νοσσός.

According to Moulton *Gr.* ii. p. 92 this Hellenistic form (for νεοσσός), which is found on the word's only occurrence

in the NT (Lk 2²⁴), arose from the slurring of ε into a *y* sound, just as βορέας much earlier produced (βορρᾶς) βορρᾶς. Νεοσσός is seen in *Kaibel* 1033²⁰ (iii/B.C.) θ]ούροις πτερύγεσσι νεοσσόν, and Herodas vii. 48, and νεοσσοπῶλις, "seller of young birds" in *ib.* vi. 99. For the LXX usage cf. Thackeray *Gr.* i. p. 98. Νεοσσός < *νεϝο-κιός, " * a new occupant of a nest," from κεῖμαι (Boisacq, p. 664).

νοσφίζω.

The absolute use of this verb "purloin," "peculate," in Tit 2¹⁰ is illustrated by P Petr III. 56(b)¹⁰·¹² (later than B.C. 259) where an official swears—οὔτε αὐτὸς νοσφιοῦμαι, "I will neither peculate myself," adding that if he finds any one νοσφιζόμενον, "peculating," he will report him; cf. *ib.* (*c*)² where νοσφίσασθαι occurs in a similar context. See also P Ryl II. 116¹⁰ (A.D. 104) θλειβομένη τῇ συνειδήσει περὶ ὧν ἐνοσφίσατο ἔν τε ἐνδομενείᾳ καὶ ἀποθέτοις, "oppressed by the consciousness of what she had appropriated both of the furniture and stored articles," and *Syll* 578 (= ³993²⁴ (iii/B.C.) εἰ μὰν μηθὲν νοσφίζεσθαι. For the constr. with ἀπό, as in Ac 5²ᶠ, cf. PSI IV. 442¹ (iii/B.C.) ἐφάνη ἐπ' ἀληθείας ὅτι νενόσφισται ἀπὸ τῶν ἀμφιτάπων ("rugs": cf. LXX Prov 7¹⁶), and *Kaibel* 287⁵ (ii/A.D.) ἀλλά με μοῖρ' ἀφ' [ὁμαίμου ἐ]νόσφισεν. Νοσφισμός is found in Vett. Val. pp. 40²⁹, 84³, and νοσφιστής in *ib.* 48²⁶.

νότος.

For νότος, "the southern quarter," "the south," it is sufficient to cite P Oxy II. 255⁷ (census return—A.D. 48) (= *Selections*, p. 46) ἐν τῇ ὑπαρχο[ύσῃ μοι οἰκίᾳ λαύρ]ας νότου, "in the house which belongs to me in the South Lane," P Tebt II. 342⁸ (late ii/A.D.) νότον (see *Proleg.* p. 73) νοτινῆς ῥύμης, "on the south of the southern road." Other exx. of the adj. are P Ryl II. 157⁵ (A.D. 135) τὴν νοτίνην [μερίδα, "the southern portion," and P Oxy IV. 729⁹ (A.D. 137) τοῦ νοτίνου χώματος, "the southern embankment": for the form νότιος cf. *Syll* 538 (= ³970)³ (B.C. 289–8) παρὰ τὸ νότιον τεῖχος τὸ τοῦ ἱεροῦ, and see Cronert *Mem. Herc.* p. 186.

νουθεσία.

This comparatively rare and mostly late word (Lob. *Phryn.* p. 512) is found in BGU II. 613²¹ (time of Anton. Pius?) and P Amh II. 84²¹ (ii/iii A.D.), both times unfortunately in broken contexts. On the form νουθετεία see Cronert *Mem. Herc.* p. 288.

νουθετέω.

For this verb in its derived sense of "admonish," as in all its NT occurrences, cf. the late P Grenf II. 93³ (vi/vii A.D.) παρακαλῶ τὴν ὑμετέραν πατρικὴν θεοφιλίαν νουθετῆσαι αὐτὸ[ν . . . ,—a request to a bishop to put pressure on a presbyter to make him act justly to a letter-carrier.

νουμηνία.

See νεομηνία.

νουνεχῶς.

On the formation of this NT ἅπ. εἰρ. (Mk 12³⁴), which is found from Aristotle downwards, as equivalent to νουνἐχόντως (Lob. *Phryn.* p. 599), see Giles *Manual of Comparative Philology*[2], p. 240, where reference is made to the adj. νουνεχής and the subst. νουνέχεια in the later Greek.

νοῦς.

In P Par 63[27] (B.C. 164) (= P Petrie III. p. 20) a complaint is made that certain people left in their homes are harassed—τῶν πρὸς ταῖς πραγματείαις οὐ κατὰ τὸ βέλτιστον ἐνδεχομένων τὸν τοῦ περὶ τῆς γεωργίας προστάγματος νοῦν, "because the officials do not put the best interpretation on the meaning of the decree concerning agriculture" (Mahaffy). For the wider meaning "thought," "mind," cf. P Tebt II. 334 (A.D. 200–1), a curious petition in which a woman complains that she has been robbed and deserted by her husband, and adds—[8f.] ἐξ οὗ καὶ παι(*l.* ἐπαι)δο-[ποιησάμην πα]ιδία δύο, μ[ὴ] ἔχουσα κατὰ νοῦν ἄλλον, "I have also had two children by him and have no thought of another man (?)" (Edd.). Cf. also P Oxy XIV. 1065[27] (iii/A.D.) ἐρρῶσθαί σε εὔχομαι κατὰ νοῦ (*l.* νοῦν διάγοντα, "I pray for your health and success" (Edd.). The dat. νόῳ is found in BGU II. 385[5] (ii/iii A.D.) ἐν νόῳ ἔχῃς ὅτι ἡ θυγά[τ]ηρ μου ἰς Ἀλεξάνδρειαν ἔσσι (*l.* εἰσι?) and the acc. νόον in *Preisigke* 287[5] ὅταν ἦλθεν ὑπὸ νόον τινός. On the declension of the word see Moulton *Gr.* ii. pp. 127, 142, Winer-Schmiedel *Gr.* p. 84, and cf. Thumb *Handbook.* § 63 n.[2] for the forms in MGr, which also (*ib.* p. 343) shows such phrases as ἔρχεται στὸ νοῦ μου, "it occurs to me," and χάνω τὸ νοῦ μου, "lose my reason." For νοῦς denoting the being of God cf. Epict. ii. 8. 2 τίς οὖν οὐσία θεοῦ; . . . νοῦς, ἐπιστήμη, λόγος ὀρθός.

Νύμφα.

In *Proleg.* p. 48 Moulton suggests that Νύμφαν, which apparently should be read as a woman's name in Col 4[15], is not due to a Doric Νύμφαν, but by a "reverse analogy process" the gen. Νύμφης produced the short nom. Νύμφα, like δόξα, δόξης. He compares Εἰρήνα in a Christian inscr. *C. and B.* ii. p. 497 n.[5]

νύμφη.

Thumb (*Hellen.* p. 123) cites the MGr νύ(φ)φη, "bride," "daughter-in-law," to support the Greek character of the meaning "daughter-in-law" (Mt 10[35], Tob 11[16f.] B, *al.*), as against Grimm's reference to Heb. כלה. The word is used of a little girl five years old in *Kaibel* 570[2] (ii/A.D.). Νύμφη is cognate with Lat. *nubo*, νυός, and νεῦρον (Boisacq, p. 673 f.).

νυμφίος.

For νυμφίος, "bridegroom," see the late CPR I. 30[97] (vi/A.D.), and from the inscr. *Syll* 615 (= [3] 1024)[99f.] (B.C. 200) ὧν οἱ νυμφίοι θύ[ου]σιν τῶν ἀρ[ν]ῶν τῶι ἱερεῖ καὶ τῶι νυμφίωι γλῶσσα ἑκατέρωι, and the sepulchral inscr. *Preisigke* 10 Ἰοάνη Ἰοάνου νύμφιε ἄωρε πασίφιλε καὶ ἄλυπε χρηστὲ χαῖρε, ὡς (ἐτῶν) λ.

νυμφών.

For νυμφών, "bridechamber," rare in profane Greek and in the NT found only *quater* (cf. Tob 6[14. 17]), see P Lond 964[19] (ii/iii A.D.) (= III. p. 212) ἰς τὸν νυμφῶνα—a letter referring to preparations for a wedding-feast.

νῦν.

The classical phrase τὰ νῦν "now," which in the NT is confined to Acts, is found in P Oxy IV. 743[30] (B.C. 2) where the writer states with reference to a certain Damas—καὶ τὰ νῦν ἐπειπέπομφα αὐτὸν πάντα συνλέξαι, "and now I have dispatched him to collect them all (*i.e.* rents)" (Edd.): cf. BGU IV. 1114[17] (B.C. 4) τανῦν συγχωρεῖ ὁ Ἴμερος κεκομίσθαι κτλ., P Oxy IV. 811 (c. A.D. 1) καὶ τὰ νῦν εἴ σοι φαί[νε]ται γράψον αὐτῷ. In PSI VI. 600[19] (iii/B.C.) τό τε παρελ.ον (*l.* παρελθὸν ?) ἐχφόριον καὶ τὸ νῦν ἑτοιμάσας, τὸ νῦν is probably equivalent to τὸ τούτου τοῦ ἔτους ἐχφόριον: see the editor's note. The formula ἀπὸ τοῦ νῦν, "henceforth," as in Lk 1[48] *al.*, 2 Cor 5[16], is common, e.g. P Oxy III. 479[9] (A.D. 157) βούλομαι ἀναγραφῆναι ἀπὸ τοῦ νῦν ἐπὶ τοῦ ὑπάρχοντός μοι μέρους οἰκίας . . . Ὧρον, "I wish that Horus should henceforth be registered at the house of which I own part" (Edd.); other exx. in Deissmann *BS* p. 253. For μέχρι τοῦ νῦν cf. BGU II. 667[5] (A.D. 221–2) κατὰ [τὴ]ν ἐξ ἀρχῆς καὶ μεχρὶ τοῦ νῦν συνήθιαν. See also the emphatic νῦν ἐπὶ τοῦ παρόντος, "now at the present," in P Oxy III. 482[3] (A.D. 109).

νυνί.

The evidence of the papyri, so far as we have remarked it, confirms the equivalence of νυνί to νῦν in the NT (as Grimm notes): cf. e.g. P Petr III. 42 H(8) f.[4] (iii/B.C.) νυνὶ [δὲ ἐν φόβωι εἰ]μὶ οὐ μετρίωι, P Oxy III. 490[5] (A.D. 124) Διονυσίῳ . . . νυνὶ ἀφήλικι, *ib.* 500[2] (A.D. 143) τὸ πρὶν ἀμπελικοῦ κτήματος νυνεὶ δὲ χερσαμπέλ(ου, "what was previously a vineyard but is now dry vine-land" (Edd.), *ib.* VI. 908 (A.D. 199) Σαραπίων . . νυνεὶ εὐθηνιάρχης τῆς αὐτῆς πόλεως, "Sarapion at present eutheniarch of the said city." The adverb is joined to a subst. (cf. Gal 4[25] *al.*) in P Ryl II. 111[4] (A.D. 161) τὴν νυνεὶ γυναῖ[κά μου.

νύξ.

P Oxy II. 235[7] (horoscope—A.D. 20–50) ὥρᾳ τετάρτῃ τῆς νυκτός. For the gen. of time, as in Mt 2[14] *al.*, cf. P Hib I. 36[5] (B.C. 229) ἀπολωλεκέναι ἐκ τῆς αὐλῆς νυκτὸς πρόβατον θῆλυ δασὺ Ἀράβιον, "that he has lost from the pen at night an unshorn ewe of Arabian breed" (Edd.), P Amh II. 134[6] (early ii A.D.) Πετέα . . . νυκτὸς ἀποσπάσαι, "to seize Peteus by night," and P Ryl II. 198[5] (iii/A.D.) κδ νυκτὸς ἰς τὴν κε, "the night of the 24th to the 25th" (Edd.). The phrase νυκτὸς καὶ ἡμέρας, the regular order of the words in Paul (cf. Milligan *Thess.* p. 85), is seen in BGU I. 246[12] (ii/iii A.D.) νυκτὸς καὶ ἡμέρας ἐντυγχάνω τῷ θεῷ ὑπὲρ ὑμῶν—a good parallel to 1 Thess 3[10]. For the other order ἡμ. κ. νυκτός, as in Lk 18[7], Rev 4[8], *al.*, cf. *Magn* 163[8] ἀδιαλείπτως θέντα τὸ ἔλαιον ἡμέρας τε καὶ νυκτός. The dat. occurs in P Tebt I. 54[3] (B.C. 86) τῆι νυκτὶ τῆι φερούσηι εἰς τὴν κε τοῦ Φαῶφι, "on the night before the 25th of Phaophi," where the editors refer to Smyly *Hermathena* xi. p. 87 ff. and note: "the 'day' at this period contained not the whole twenty-four hours, but the period from sunrise to sunset, events which took place at night being described with reference to the 'day' following." Cf. also P Ryl II. 127[4] (A.D. 29) νυκτὶ τῇ φερούσῃ εἰς τὴν ιζ τοῦ ἐνεστῶτο(ς) μηνὸ(ς) Σεβαστοῦ,

" in the night before the 17th of the present month Sebastus" (Edd.). It is interesting to find our common phrase " making day of night " as early as the mid. of iii/B.C. in PSI V. 514[2] νύκτα οὖν ἡμέραν ποιούμενος κατάπεμψον τὰ διαγραφέντα ἐχ Φιλαδελφείας : see the editor's note. We may cite instances of common adverbial phrases—P Flor II. 236[8] (A.D. 267) ἀπὸ νυκτός, P Ryl II. 138[15] (A.D. 34) διὰ νυκτός, "under cover of night" (Edd.), Cagnat IV. 860[10] στρατηγήσαντα διὰ νυκτός, P Mon 6[40] (A.D. 583) ἐν νυκτί, PSI V. 540[11] (B.C. 42–1) κατὰ νύκτα, and P Strass II. 111[5] (iii/B.C.) οἱ δὲ ὑπὸ νύ[κτα ἀνα]στάντες ἀνεχώρησαν εἰς Λεονταμοῦν, P Tebt II. 419[18] (iii/A.D.) ὑπὸ νύκταν, "at dusk." Νύξ is used metaphorically of death in Kaibel 1095[4] νὺξ αὐτοὺς καταλύει, with reference to the departed glories of Homeric heroes. MGr νύχτα.

For the adj. νυκτερινός cf. P Oxy VI. 924[4] (iv/A.D.), a Gnostic charm to protect ἀπὸ τοῦ νυκτερινοῦ φρικός, "from ague by night": similarly BGU III. 956[3] (c. iii/A.D.). The adv. νύκτωρ, said to be the only adv. of this form (LS), is seen in P Hal 1[191] (mid. iii/B.C.) τις . . μεθύων ἢ νύκτωρ ἢ ἐν ἱερῶι. We may note also the compounds νυκτέλιον with reference to the "night-festival" of Isis in P Oxy III. 525[9] (early ii/A.D.), νυκτοστράτηγος in ib. VI. 933[24] (late ii/A.D.), and νυκτοφύλαξ in P Iand 33[8] (time of Commodus).

νύσσω.

For the ἔτυπτον . . καλάμῳ of Mk 15[19], Ev. Petr. 3 substitutes καλάμῳ ἔνυσσον. This may perhaps be taken as supporting the milder sense of "pricked" instead of "pierced" (AV, RV) which Field (Notes, p. 108) prefers in Jn 19[34] πλευρὰν ἔνυξεν, in distinction from ἐξεκέντησαν in ver. 37. Swete ad Ev. Petr. l.c. cites also Orac. Sib. viii. 296 πλευρὰς νύξουσιν καλάμῳ.

νυχθήμερον.

With this NT ἅπ. εἰρ. (2 Cor 11[25]), which is found elsewhere only in late writers (cf. Sturz Dial. Mac. p. 186),

we may compare the new νυκτήμαρ in the Christian letter, addressed perhaps to a Bishop, P Lond 981[12] (iv/A.D.) (= III. p. 242, Chrest. I. p. 157) περιοδεύομεν καὶ περιπατοῦμεν νυκτήμαρ, θαρροῦμεν ταῖς προσευχαῖς σου.

νωθρός.

The sense of "remissness," "slackness," attaching to this adj. in Heb 6[12] ἵνα μὴ νωθροὶ γένησθε, appears in the use of the subst. in P Amh II. 78[15] (A.D. 184) ἐ]ν νωθρίᾳ μου γενομένου, where the editors translate, "moreover as I neglected my rights." Νωθρός is probably cognate with νόσος (Boisacq, p. 672), and the corresponding verb is used of " sickness " in a touching letter addressed by a slave to her master, P Giss I. 17[6] (time of Hadrian) ἠγωνίασα, κύριε, οὐ μετρίως, ἵνα ἀκούσω ὅτι ἐνώθρευσας. Elsewhere, as the editor notes, the verb is found in the papyri only in the middle, see e.g. PSI VI. 717[5] (ii/A.D.) μνήσ[θη]τι πῶς σε νωθρευσάμενον [ὑ]πηρέτησα, BGU II. 449[4] (ii–iii A.D.) ἀκούσας ὅτι νωθρεύῃ ἀγωνιοῦμαι, P Tebt II. 421[5] (iii/A.D.) (= Selections, p. 106) γενοῦ πρὸς ἐμὲ ἐπεὶ ἡ ἀδελφή σου νωθρεύεται, "come to me, since your sister is sick."

νῶτος.

In Rom 11[10] (from LXX Ps 68[24]) νῶτος replaces the classical νῶτον, as generally in the LXX (cf. Thackeray Gr. i. p. 155). In P Tebt I. 21[8] (B.C. 115) σὺ οὖν μὴ δῷς νῶτον μηδενί, "do not therefore run away from anybody" (Edd.), and in P Oxy XIV. 1725[9] (after A.D. 229) ὡς τὰ κατὰ νῶτου ἑξῆς δη(λοῖ), and ib. [17] κατὰ νώτου τοῦ ὅλου ὀνόματος, the gender is indeterminate. The compound νωτοφόρος, as in 2 Chron 2[18] καὶ ἐποίησεν ἐξ αὐτῶν ἑβδομήκοντα χιλιάδας νωτοφόρων, is found in P Petr III. 46 (2)[9] (Ptol.), a contract for the supply and carriage of bricks : cf. P Meyer 61[8,10] (iii/B.C.), P Tebt I. 115[7,22] (B.C. 115–3).

ξενία—ξένος

ξενία.

The vernacular use of ξενία = "hospitality" (cf. Sir 29²⁷) in such passages as P Oxy VI. 931⁷ (ii/A.D.) τὴν οὐγκίαν τῆς πορφύρα[ς] . . . δοθησόμενον (l. δοθησομένην) εἰς τὴν ξενίαν τῆι μεικρᾶ, "the ounce of purple to be presented at the entertainment to the little one" (Edd.), ib. VII. 1064¹⁰ (ii/A.D.) γράφω σοι . . . ὅπως συνλάβῃς τῷ Ἀπει . . ξενίαν δὲ αὐτῷ ποιήσῃς, "I write to you that you may assist Apis, and may show him hospitality" (Ed.), ib. I. 118 verso¹⁸ (late iii/A.D.) εἰδὼς δὲ ὁποία ἐστὶν καὶ ἡ ξενία, "you know what hospitality requires" (Edd.), and Syll 418 (= ³ 888)³² (A.D. 238) ἀπολιμπάνοντες ἐπέρχονται εἰς τὴν ἡμετέραν κώμην καὶ ἀναγκάζουσιν ἡμᾶς ξενίας αὐτοῖς παρέχειν, along with the almost technical sense of τὰ ξένια for the gifts provided on the occasion of the visit of a King or other high official to a district (e.g. P Petr II. 10(1)¹³ (iii/B.C.) εἰς τὰ ξένια χῆνας ιβ, P Tebt I. 33¹¹ (B.C. 112) (= Selections, p. 31); cf. P Grenf II. 14(b) (B.C. 264 or 227) and see Ostr. i. p. 389 f.) seems to make it practically certain that the word is to be understood in the same sense in Ac 28²³, Philem²², rather than of a place of lodging. For this later sense cf. Preisigke 3924⁷ (A.D. 19) καὶ ἐπὶ σκηνώσεις καταλαμβάνεσθαι ξενίας πρὸς βίαν, ib.¹⁷ ἐὰν γὰρ δέῃ, αὐτὸς Βαίβιος ἐκ τοῦ ἴσου καὶ δικαίου τὰς ξενίας διαδώσει, BGU II. 388¹·¹⁵ (ii/iii A.D.) τὸ παιδίον τὸ παραφυλάσσον αὐτοῦ τὴν ξενίαν (l. ξενίαν?) where however the reading is doubtful, and the dim. ξενίδιον in P Tebt II. 335¹⁷ (mid. iii/A.D.) ξενίδιον μεμ[ισθωμένον] μοι εἰς οἴκησιν, "a guest-house rented to me as a dwelling": see also PSI I. 50¹⁶ (iv/v A.D.) καὶ προβῇ τὸ ἔργον τῆς μικρᾶς ξενίας τῆς περὶ τὴν ληνόν, where the editor understands ξενία as "stanzetta," "cella," and cites Hesych. κατάλυμα, καταγώγιον.

ξενίζω

in its ordinary sense of "entertain" as a guest (Ac 10²³ al.) may be illustrated from the Coan sacrificial calendar Syll 616 (= ³ 1025)⁴⁰ (iv/iii B.C.) ἱαροποιοὶ δὲ ξενιζόντω τὰ ἱερῆ καὶ τὸς κάρυκας τ[αύτα]ν τὰν νύκτα: cf. the use of the corresponding subst. (as in Prov 15¹⁷) in OGIS 229³¹ (mid. iii/B.C.) καλεσάτωσαν δὲ οἱ ἐπιμήνιοι τῆς βουλῆς καὶ τοὺς πρεσβευτὰς τοὺς παραγεν[ομένους] ἐγ Μαγνησίας τὸν ξενισμὸν εἰς τὸ πρυτανεῖον. The verb in its derived meaning of "surprise," "astonish," as in Ac 17²⁰, 1 Pet 4⁴·¹², is seen in such passages as P Par 64⁶ (ii/B.C.) ἱκανῶς ἐξενίσθην καὶ τούτῳ ἀντιμεμφομένῳ ὧν χάριν ἐπ' ἐμοὶ ὑπὸ εὐεργεσιῶν ὑπέδειξα, μὴ ἐπὶ βάθος σε τὸ τοιοῦτον πεποιηκέναι, P Strass I. 35⁶ (iv/v A.D.) ξενίζομε μέχρει τῆς σήμερον ἡμέρας πῶς οὐκ . . . , and P Iand 20¹ (vi/vii A.D.): cf. also M. Anton. viii. 15.

ξενοδοχέω.

This form of the verb (cf. 1 Tim 5¹⁰) is condemned by the Atticists, see Lob. Phryn. p. 307. A good ex. of the subst. is afforded by Theophrastus Char. 6 (23) ad fin. where the boastful man declares that he means to sell the house in which he is living—διὰ τὸ ἐλάττω εἶναι αὐτῷ πρὸς τὰς ξενοδοχίας, "as he finds it too small for his entertainments" (Jebb). MGr ξενοδοχεῖον, "hotel."

ξένος,

in the sense of "stranger," is seen in such passages as P Magd 8¹¹ (B.C. 218) καταφρονήσας μου ὅτι ξένος εἰμί (see the editor's note), P Oxy XIV. 1672¹ (A.D. 37–41) πεπράκαμεν χόιας λβ ξένοις προσώποις, "we sold 32 choes to some strangers" (Edd.), and ib. VIII. 1154⁷ ff. (late i/A.D.) μὴ ἀγωνιάσῃς δὲ περὶ ἐμοῦ ὅτι ἐπὶ ξένης εἰμί, αὐτόπτης γὰρ εἰμὶ τῶν τόπων καὶ οὐκ εἰμὶ ξέν[ο]ς τῶν ἐνθάδε (for gen. cf. Eph 2¹²), "do not be anxious about me because I am away from home, for I am personally acquainted with these places and am not a stranger here" (Ed.). In CR i. p. 5 f. Hicks illustrates from the inscrr. ξένοι as a term of Greek public life, denoting temporary sojourners who have not yet secured the rights of πάροικοι or μέτοικοι, e.g. CIG I. 1338 (Amyclae—mid. iv/B.C.) καὶ Μεγαλοπολειτῶν καὶ τῶν ἄλλων ξένων κατοικοῦντες καὶ παρεπιδαμοῦντες ἐν [Ἀμύ]κλ[α]ις, ib. II. 3521 (Pergamon—iii/B.C.) τοὺς παρεπιδημοῦντας ξένους: cf. Ac 17²¹. The phrase ἐπὶ ξένης is common, e.g. BGU I. 22³⁴ (A.D. 114) where a woman complains of an attack and robbery in the absence of her husband—τοῦ ἀνδρός μου ὄντος (l. ὄντος) ἐπὶ ξένης, ib. 159⁷ (A.D. 216) Οὐαλερίου Δάτου κελεύσ[αν]το[ς] ἅπαντας τοὺς ἐπὶ ξένης διατρείβοντας εἰς τὰς ἰδίας κατεισέρχεσθαι, κατεισῆλθον, P Fay 136¹⁰ (Christian letter—iv/A.D.) ἄμινον ὑμᾶς ἐν τοῖς ἰδίοις οἷς ἐὰν τύχοι εἶναι ἢ ἐπὶ ξένης, "it is better for you to be in your homes whatever they may be, than abroad" (Edd.), and Cagnat IV. 293¹¹·¹⁰ κατωι[κονομ]ήσατο [κ]αὶ ἐν τῇ πόλει καὶ ἐπὶ τῆς ξένης. These exx. along with the corresponding phrase εἰς τὴν ξένην in P Oxy II. 251¹¹ (A.D. 44), ib. 253⁷ (A.D. 19) al. show, as the editors remark in their note to ib. 286¹⁵, that the reference may be merely to residence outside the nome in which a person is registered: cf. Jouguet Vie municipale p. 91 ff. In P Tebt I. 118 (late ii/B.C.), the account of a dining-club, a distinction is drawn between the σύνδειπνοι, "members," and the ξένοι, "guests," and in P Hib I. 27³⁵ (a calendar—B.C. 301–240) the adj. has the wide sense of "unfamiliar," ἵνα μὴ δόξω (= ῃ) μακ[ρὸν] καὶ ξένον σοι κατα[νοῆσ] (?) ἡ τῶν μορίων ποικ[ι]λία? "in order that the intricacy of the fractions may not appear to you a long and unfamiliar thing to understand (?)"

(Edd.). For the compound ἐπίξενος, see the receipt for "alien" tax on an ostracon of A.D. 63 reproduced in *LAE* p. 111—ἀπέχων παρὰ σοῦ τέλες (*l.* τέλος) ἐπιξένου Θῶυθ καὶ Φαῶφι (δραχμὰς) β̄, "I have received from you alien tax (for the months) Thoyth and Phaophi 2 drachmae," and for ξενικός cf. P Hal 1¹⁶¹ (mid. iii/B.C.) ἐν [τοῖς] ξεν[ι]κοῖς δικαστη[ρί]οις with the editor's note p. 95 ff. The subst. ξενιτεία, as in Wisd 18³, is found in Aristeas 249 ἡ δὲ ξενιτεία τοῖς μὲν πένησι καταφρόνησιν ἐργάζεται, τοῖς δὲ πλουσίοις ὄνειδος ὡς διὰ κακίαν ἐκπεπτωκόσιν, "residence in a foreign country brings contempt upon the poor man and disgrace on the rich, as though they were in exile for a crime" (Thackeray), and for the verb ξενιτεύω cf. *ib.* 257 πρὸς οὓς ξενιτεύει, "among whom thou sojournest" (*id.*). Both subst. and verb are common in Vett. Valens. The subst. survives in MGr = "foreign land," and the verb = "emigrate." MGr ξένος, "strange," "stranger."

ξέστης,

a Roman dry measure (*sextarius*), rather less than a pint : cf. *Ostr* 1186² (Rom.) οἴνου ξέσται ῑβ̄, and see Wilcken *Ostr.* i. p. 762 f., Hultsch *Archiv* iii. p. 438. In the NT (Mk 7⁴) the word is used rather = "cup" or "pitcher," whether holding a *sextarius* or not : cf. P Oxy VI. 921²³ (iii/A.D.) ξέσται β̄, "two cups," *ib.* 1092¹ (iii/iv A.D.) ξέσται χαλκοῦ γ̄. In an inventory of church property P Grenf II. 111⁶ (v/vi A.D.) ποτήρ[ια] ἀργυρ(ᾶ) ς̄. ξέστ(ης) ἀργυρ(οῦς) ᾱ, ξέστης is apparently = "paten" : see the editors' note. It should be added that Moulton (*Gr.* ii. p. 155) has difficulty in believing that ξέστης is really a Latin word.

ξηραίνω.

With Mt 21¹⁹ ἐξηράνθη παραχρῆμα ἡ συκῆ may be compared the interesting report regarding a persea tree, addressed to the logistes of Oxyrhynchus. The president of the guild of carpenters there states that he found it—ἄκαρπον οὖσαν πολλ[ῶ]ν ἐτῶν διόλου ξηραντῖσαν (*l.* ξηρανθεῖσαν) καὶ μὴ δύνασθαι ἐντε[ῦ]θε[ν καρ]πού[ς] ἀποδιδόναι, "barren for many years, quite dried up and unable to produce any more fruit" (P Oxy I. 53⁹ff.—A.D. 316): cf. P Oxy IX. 1188¹⁹·²⁰·²¹ (A.D. 13), and on the value and associations of the persea tree see Wilcken *Archiv* i. p. 127. Other exx. of the verb are BGU IV. 1040⁴³ (ii/A.D.) τάχα δύνασαι ἀναβιονα[. . .]αι (: ἀναβιώσασθαι) τὴν ποτίστραν ("watering-place"), εἰ δὲ μή, ξηραίν[ετ]αι, P Leid W⁻·²⁶ (ii/iii A.D.) (= II. p. 83) ξήρανον ἐν σκιᾷ (of flowers used in magic), and P Flor II. 148¹¹ (A.D. 266–7) τὰ δὲ τεμνόμενα φυτὰ εὐθέως εἰς ὕδωρ βαλλέσθω ἵνα μὴ ξηρανθῇ. MGr ξεραίνω "I dry."

ξηρός.

P Petr III. 62 (*b*)⁷ (Ptol.) χόρτου ξηροῦ, P Oxy IX. 1188⁴ (A.D. 13) κλάδους ξηρο(ύς), *ib.* IV. 736⁸² (c. A.D. 1) σεμιδάρ(= λ)εως ξηρᾶς (ἡμιωβέλιον), "for dry meal ½ ob.", P Tebt II. 314¹⁸ (ii/A.D.) κορέου ξηρο(ῦ, "dried coriander." and the oracle *Kaibel* 1039¹⁴ ξηρῶν ἀπὸ κλάδων καρπὸν οὐκ ἔσται λα[βεῖν. For the subst. ξηρασία, see P Tebt II. 379⁹ (A.D. 128) χόρτον εἰς κοπὴν καὶ ξηρασ[ί]αν, "grass

for cutting and drying," and for ξηρότης, see P Flor II. 176¹¹ (A.D. 256) ἐκ τῆς τῶν σύκων κακίας καὶ ξηρότητος. The vernacular MGr ξερός reverts to the old Epic and Ionic form (see e.g. Hom. *Od.* v. 402): cf. the MGr θεριό and σίδερο for the short unstressed vowel.

ξύλινος.

For this common adj., which persists in MGr, it is enough to cite P Ryl II. 127³⁰ (A.D. 29), a list of stolen property including—ξύλινον πυξίδιν ἐν ᾧ ἀργ(υρίου) (δραχμαὶ) . . . δ̄, "a small wooden box in which were 4 silver dr.," P Tebt II. 414³⁶ (ii/A.D.) τὸν ξύλινον δίφρον, "the wooden stool," P Oxy VIII. 1127⁸ (A.D. 183) περιστερεῶνα σὺν τῇ τούτου κλείμακι ξυλίνῃ, "a pigeon-house with its wooden ladder," and *ib.* XII. 1449¹¹ (A.D. 213–17) a statue of Demeter— οὗ ἡ προτομ(ὴ) Παρίνη, τὰ δὲ ἄλλα μέρη τοῦ σώματ(ος) ξ(ύλινα, "of which the bust is of Parian marble, and the other parts of the body of wood" (Edd.). In *Syll* 554¹⁷ᶠ· (ii/B.C. *ad init.*) a distinction is drawn between ξύλιναι ὦναι and σιτηραὶ ὦναι. With the remission of the 50% tax on tree-fruits in 1 Macc 10²⁹ cf. *OGIS* 55¹³ (iii/B.C.) ἀφεῖκεν ἀτε[λεῖ]ς τῶν τε ξυλί(νων κ)αρπῶν· see the note. For the form ξυλικός, which cannot be distinguished in meaning, cf. P Ryl II. 157¹⁶ (A.D. 135) τῆς δαπάνης τῆς τε ἐπισκευῆς καὶ κατασκευῆς τοῦ ξυλικοῦ [ὀργάνου, "the cost of keeping and repairing the wooden water-wheel" (Edd.), P Amh II. 93²⁰ (A.D. 181) καταλάγματος (*l.* κατε-) ξυλικῶν ἢ ἀργαλίων (*l.* ἐργ-), "breakage of wood-work or tools" (Edd.), and *OGIS* 510⁷ (Ephesus—A.D. 138–61) τὴν λοιπὴν ξυλικὴν παρασκευὴν τῶν θεατρικῶν. Other exx. in the note to PSI V. 528¹⁵ᶠ·

ξύλον.

For the Hellenistic usage of ξύλον to denote a (living) tree, as in Lk 23³¹, see the Ptolemaic ordinance P Tebt I. 5²⁰⁵ (B.C. 118) remitting penalties on those τοὺς κεκοφότας τῶν ἰδίων ξύλα παρὰ ἐκείμενα (*l.* παρὰ τὰ ἐκκείμενα) προστάγματα, "who have cut down trees on their own property in contravention of the published decrees." The editors find in this regulation a proof that "the king controlled the timber of the country, though whether in the form of a tax upon cutting down trees or of a monopoly is uncertain "; but see Wilcken *Archiv* ii. p. 489. Cf. also P Oxy XII. 1421⁴ (iii/A.D.) τὸ ξ[ύ]λον τὸ ἀκάνθινον τὸ κεκομμένον ἐν τῇ Εἰόνθει ἐξαυτῆς [πέμψατε, "send at once the acacia-wood which has been cut at Ionthis," P Flor II. 152⁴ (A.D. 208) ἀπέστειλα τέκτονα Μαρεῖνον ἵνα κόψῃ ξύλα εἰς τὰ μηχανι[κὰ] τοῦ Πάκι, and for the diminutive ξυλάριον (3 Kingd 17¹³) see P Tebt II. 513 (ii/iii A.D.) τὸ σύκινον ξυλάριον τὸ ἐν τῷ πλινθουργίῳ κοπήτω. The substantives ξυλεία, ξυλολογεία, and ξυλοτομία are found in BGU IV. 1123⁹ (time of Augustus), P Oxy IV. 729³³ (A.D. 137) and *ib.* XIV. 1631⁹ (A.D. 280) respectively. Land planted with trees is called ξυλῖτις in P Lille I. 5⁵⁸ (B.C. 260–59)—it had just been cleared and sown: cf. P Petr II. 39(*a*)⁷ (iii/B.C.). For the more general sense of ξύλον, "wood," "piece of wood," as in Mt 26⁴⁷, cf. P Petr II. 4(11)⁶ (B.C. 255–4) ἀπόστειλον δ' ἡμῖν καὶ ξύλα τὰ λοιπὰ τῶν Σ ὅτι εὐμηκέστατα καὶ παχύτατα, "send us also the remaining 200 beams as long and thick as possible" (Ed.), P Fay 118²³ (A.D. 110) γέμ[ι]σον αὐτὰ (τὰ κτήνη) βάκανον καὶ ξύλον, "load them (the animals) with cabbage and wood," P Giss I. 67[9] (ii/A.D.) ξενικῶν ξύλων, "wood imported from abroad," P Tebt II. 304[10] (A.D. 167–8) μετὰ ξύλων ἰσπηδῆσαι, "to rush in with staves," P Oxy I. 69[3] (A.D. 190) ἴσως προσερείσαντας τῷ τόπῳ ξύλον, "probably using a log of wood as a battering-ram" (Edd.), ib. XIV. 1738[6] (iii/A.D.) ξύλα σώματα, "logs," and P Ryl II. 236[13] (A.D. 256) ἀνερχόμενα δὲ ξύλα ἀνακομισάτω εἰς τὴν οἰκίαν τοῦ εὐσχήμονος. "and when they (a team of four donkeys) come, let them bring up timber to the magistrate's house" (Edd.). Reference may also be made to the law of astynomy at Pergamum, OGIS 483[181] (time of Trajan) μαστειγωθεὶς δὲ ἐν τῶι κύφωνι πληγαῖς ἑκατὸν δεδέσθω ἐν τῶι ξύλωι ἡμέρας δέκα, with the editor's note. For ξύλον, "a measure of length," = 3 cubits cf. P Ryl II. 64[b.3] (iv/v A.D.), the introd. to P Oxy VII. 1053 (vi/vii A.D.), and Archiv iii. p. 430, and for the verb

ξυλομετρέω see BGU I. 12[27] (A.D. 181–2) γ]εωμετροῦντος καὶ ξυλομετροῦντος. Other exx. of the diminutive ξυλάριον are P Oxy X. 1202[12] (. A.D. 50), BGU III. 844[15] (A.D. 83). In P Tebt II. 316[95] (A.D. 99) οἰκῶ δὲ ἐν τῷ ἐκτὸς τῇ (l. τῆς) ξυληρᾷ (l. -ᾶς?) the editors think the reference is probably to the "wood-market." MGr ξύλο, "wood."

ξυράω.

In 1 Cor 11[6] most editors accentuate ξυρᾶσθαι pres. mid. "to go shaven," but in view of the immediately preceding aor. κείρασθαι, it is probably better to read ξύρασθαι, aor. mid. of ξύρω, a form found in Plutarch (see Veitch s.v.): cf. WH Notes[2], p. 172, Moulton Gr. ii. p. 200 f. For ξυρητής (not in LS), "one who shaves," see BGU II. 630[v.10] (c. A.D. 200): ξύρησις, "baldness," is found in Isai 22[12]. MGr ξ(ο)υρίζω.

ὁ, ἡ τό.

(1) Apart from connexion with μέν or δέ (see below) the demonstrative use of the art. in the NT is confined to a poetical quotation Ac 17²⁸, but it is not uncommon in the papyri, e.g. P Par 45⁸ (B.C. 153) (= Witkowski², p. 85) τὰ (for ἃ) πράσεις (l. πράσσεις), P Oxy VIII. 1160¹⁶ (iii/iv A.D.) τὰ (for ἃ) σεσύλληχα (for συνείληχα) δὲ κέρμα ⟨τα⟩ τηρῶ αὐτὰ εἰς τὴν δίκην, "I am keeping for the trial the money that I have collected" (Ed.). For the distributive ὁ μέν . . . ὁ δέ, as in 1 Cor 7⁷, cf. P Lond 33⁶ (B.C. 161) (= I. p. 19, U.P.Z. i. p. 239) καὶ τὰ μὲν ἡμῶν εἰληφότων εἰς τὴν γινομένην ἡμῖν συντάξειν, τὰ δ' ἔτι διὰ τὴν τῶν ὑποτεταγμένων ⟨. . . . .⟩ παρελκομένων.

(2) The use of the art. as a relative, of which there is no trace in the NT, may again be illustrated by the following papyrus citations from c. A.D. 346—P Lond 414⁹ (= II. p. 292) γεινώσκιν σε θέλω περὶ τοῦ βρεονίου (brevium, "memorandum") τό μοι δέδωκες, ib. 413⁹ (= II. p. 301) ἵνα ἀνταποδώσει σοι [τὴν ἀγ]άπην τὴν ποιεῖς δι' αὐτοῦ, and ib. 244¹⁴ (= II. p. 304) τὴν χί(= εῖ)ρα ("certificate") τὴν δέδωκεν. See also P Grenf II. 41¹⁴ (A.D. 46) οἴνου κεράμια δύωι τῶν τε προσδιαγράψο(= ω), P Oxy XIV. 1765¹⁰ (iii/A.D.) τοὺς (= οὓς) γὰρ ἔπεμψάς μοι τρεῖς στατῆρας πάλιν σοι διεπεμψάμην, P Hamb I. 22³ (iv/A.D.) [Υ]ἱὲ θεοῦ μεγάλοιο τὸν οὐδέποτε δρᾶκεν ἀνήρ, and the illiterate BGU III. 948¹² (iv/v A.D.) ποιῶ σοι εἰ = ἱμάτια πρὸς τὸ δύνομε(= αι), "I am making garments for you as far as I can." The usage is rare in the Ptolemaic period (Mayser Gr. p. 310 f.), but see P Magd 28¹⁰ (B.C. 217) ἀπὸ τῆς αὐτοὶ γεωργοῦσιν γῆς.

(3) The RV rendering in Lk 2⁴⁹ ἐν τοῖς τοῦ πατρός μου, "in my Father's house," receives fresh confirmation from passages such as P Oxy III. 523³ (ii/A.D.) (= Selections, p. 97) an invitation to dinner ἐν τοῖς Κλαυδ(ίου) Σαραπίω(νος), P Tebt II. 316ⁱⁱ·²³ (A.D. 99) οἰκοῦμεν δὲ ἐν τῷ ἔνπροσθις (l. ἔμπροσθε) ναυάρχου ἐν τοῖς Ποτάμωνος, "we live opposite the admiralty in the house of Potamon" (Edd.), and in the sing. P Oxy IX. 1215⁴ (ii/iii A.D.) μὴ ἀπέλθῃς εἰς τὸ Σατύρου, αἰπεὶ γὰρ ἀκούομεν ὅτι κακὰ μέλλι(= ει) πράσ⟨σ⟩ι⟨ν⟩, "do not go to the house of Satyrus, for we hear that he is going to get into trouble" (Ed.). From the inscr. we may cite C. and B. ii. p. 655. no. 581 Ἔρως Ἑρμοῦ κατεσκεύασε ἐν τῦς (l. τοῖς) προγονικοῖς ἑαυτῷ καὶ Λουκιανῇ συμβίῳ ζῶντες τὸ μνημίον.

(4) Other prepositional phrases are P Tebt I. 59⁵ (B.C. 99) τῶν ἐξ ὑμῶν, "members of your society," P Amh II. 66³⁰ (A.D. 124) ἐπὶ τῶν κατὰ Στοτοῆτιν Πεκύσεως πρὸς Σαταβοῦν Πεκύσεως, "in the case of Stotoetis son of Pekusis against Satabous son of Pekusis" (Edd.), P Eleph 15³

(B.C. 223–2) ἐχάρην ἐπὶ τῶι με αἰσθέσθαι τὰ κατὰ σέ, "I was glad when I perceived the state of your affairs" (cf. Ac 24²², al.). P Oxy I. 120¹⁴ (iv/A.D.) ἄχρις ἂν γνῶ πῶς τὰ κατ' αἰμαὶ ἀποτίθαιται, "until I know the state of my affairs," and from the inscr. C. and B. i. p. 150, No. 45 ἐπὶ ὅ, "in view of which."

(5) We may notice one or two anarthrous prepositional phrases in the NT which can be paralleled from the papyri—Mt 27⁴⁵ ἀπὸ δὲ ἕκτης ὥρας, cf. P Oxy III. 523⁴ (ii/A.D.) τῆι ις ἀπὸ ὥρας θ, "on the 16th at 9 o'clock"; Ac 2²³, 7²⁵ διὰ χειρός, cf. P Magd 25² (B.C. 221) ὀφείλων γάρ μ[ο]ι διὰ χερὸς κριθῶν (ἀρτάβας) ιε, "il m'a emprunté de la main à la main et me doit quinze artabes d'orge" (Ed.); Ac 7⁻¹, Heb 1⁵ εἰς υἱόν, cf. P Oxy I. 37ⁱ·⁹ (A.D. 49) (= Selections, p. 49) ἐγένετο ἐνθάδε ἡ τροφεῖτις εἰς υἱὸν τοῦ Πεσούριος, "there took place there the contract for the nursing of the son of Pesouris"; Mt 26⁶ ἐν οἰκίᾳ, cf. P Oxy I. 51¹³ (A.D. 173) ἐπὶ παρόντι τῷ αὐτῷ ὑπηρέτῃ ἐν οἰκίᾳ Ἐπαγαθοῦ, "in the presence of the aforesaid assistant at the house of Epagathus"; Rom 5⁶ κατὰ καιρόν, cf. P Lond 974⁵ (A.D. 305–6) (= III. p. 116) τῶν κατὰ καιρὸν εἴδων ὀπωριμείων, "fruits in season"; and Mk 3⁸ περὶ Τύρον καὶ Σιδῶνα, cf. ib. 45⁹ (A.D. 95) περὶ κώμην Κορώβ[ιν ?. Similarly πρὸ προσώπου σου Mt 11¹⁰ may be paralleled by Herodas viii. 50 ἔρρ' ἐκ προσώπου.

In themselves these exx. may not seem of much importance, but they are of interest, as Eakin (AJP xxxvii. (1916), p. 334) has pointed out, as illustrating the liking of the NT writers for "short-cut" phrases in keeping with the common speech of the time, and further as reminding us that, even when the art. is absent, it should frequently be expressed in translation. Ἐν οἰκίᾳ, e.g., in Lk 8²⁷ is not "in any house" (AV, RV), but "in the house," i.e. "at home"; while ἐν συναγωγῇ in Jn 6⁵⁹ is simply "in the synagogue," or, as we would say, "in church," rather than "in time of solemn assembly" (Westcott ad l.).

(6) Deissmann discusses the anaphoric use of the art. with proper names in the Berl. Phil. Woch. xxii. (1902) p. 1467 f., where he shows that, when a name is introduced without an art., the art. is frequently prefixed to each recurrence of the name, much in the sense of our "the aforesaid," e.g. P Grenf I. 40⁹ (ii/B.C.) Νεχθμίνιος, but ⁵ τὸν Νεχθμίνιν, P Oxy I. 37ⁱ·⁵ (A.D. 49) (= Selections, p. 49) Πεσοῦρις, but ⁹ ἡ τροφεῖτις εἰς υἱὸν τοῦ Πεσούριος. But, as showing that the practice was not uniform, cf. BGU I. 276⁶ᶠ· (ii/iii A.D.) λαβὼν τὰ γρ[ά]μματα Σερήνου τοῦ νομεικοῦ, πρὸς Σερῆνον γενέσθαι.

(7) The art. is frequently inserted before the gen. of a father's or mother's name appended to the name of a person, as in P Oxy I. 45⁴ (A.D. 95) Διογένους τοῦ Πτο-

λεμαίου παρακεχωρημένου παρὰ Ταποτάμωνος τῆς Πτολεμαίου τοῦ Κολύλιδ(ος) . . ., "Diogenes, son of Ptolemaeus, has had ceded to him by Tapotamon, the daughter of Ptolemaeus, son of Kolylis . . ."

(8) ὁ καί introducing an alternative name, as in Ac 13⁹, meets us everywhere both in the papyri and in the inscriptions. According to Mayser *Gr.* p. 311 the nom. first appears in Roman times, e.g. BGU I. 22²⁵ (A.D. 114) Ἀμμώνιος ὁ καὶ Φίμων, *ib.* 36¹ (ii A.D.) Στοτόητις ὁ καὶ Φανῆσις. For earlier exx. of the gen., see P Par 15 *bis* ³ (B.C. 143) Σισοῖτος τοῦ καὶ Ἐριέως, P Grenf I. 21¹² (B.C. 126) Ἀπολλωνίας τῆς καὶ Σεμμώνθιος, and of the dat., see P Rein 26⁵ (B.C. 104) Διονυσίωι τῶι καὶ Πλήνει. From the inscrr. we may cite *Priene* 313⁸⁶ (list of place-names from the gymnasium—i B.C.) ὅτ(οπος Ἀπελ[λᾶ τ]οῦ καὶ Ζ[ω]πυρίωνο˙ς, *Magnesia* 122(h)⁴ (iv/A.D.) Εὐτυχίου τοῦ καὶ Ταγηνίου. According to Hatch *JBL* xxvii (1908) p. 141 the phrase has been found as early as B.C. 400 in a fragment of Ctesias. In *Archiv* vi. p. 213 Sir F. G. Kenyon publishes an ostrakon of A.D. 174–5 with the dating ἰε (ἔτους) τοῦ καὶ α (ἔτους), "for the fiftieth year, which is also the first."

(9) With this may be compared the use of the art. in private or familiar letters, showing that the person referred to was well known to the author, as in P Oxy I. 117¹⁷ (ii/iii A.D.) τὴν ἀδελφήν ἀσπάζου καὶ τὴν Κύριλλαν, "salute your sister and Cyrilla."

As regards the names of places, the art. is not used unless it be anaphoric as in P Oxy III. 475¹⁵ (A.D. 182) ἀπὸ Σενέπτα, followed by ¹⁷ ἐν τῇ Σενέ[πτα and ²⁵ εἰς τὴν Σενέπτα: cf. Acts 9²ᶠ, 10⁹·²⁴.

(10) A good ex. of the noun followed by an adj., both with the art. as in Jn 10¹¹, is afforded by P Oxy I. 113²⁰ (ii/A.D.) where a man writes to a business correspondent— ἔσχον παρὰ Κορβόλωνος τοὺς τυροὺς τοὺς μεγάλους, "I received the large cheeses from Corbolon," notwithstanding the fact that it was *small* cheeses he had ordered—οὐκ ἤθελον δὲ μεγάλους ἀλλὰ μεικροὺς ἤθελον.

(11) On the much disputed question whether in Tit 2¹³ τοῦ μεγάλου θεοῦ καὶ σωτῆρος ἡμῶν Χριστοῦ Ἰησοῦ the reference is to one person or to two, we may cite for what it is worth in favour of the former interpretation P Leid G³ (B.C. 181–145) (= I. p. 42) τῷ ἐπὶ [τ]ῶν προσόδ[ω]ν καὶ βασιλ[ικ]ῷ [γρ]αμματεῖ, "redituum Procuratori qui et Regius scriba" (Ed.). As showing that the translation "our great God and Saviour" (one person) was current in vii/A.D. among Greek-speaking Christians reference may also be made to the formula in BGU II. 366¹ ἐν ὀνόματι τοῦ κυρίου καὶ δ[εσπότου] Ἰησοῦ Χριστοῦ τοῦ θεοῦ καὶ σωτῆρος ἡμῶν: cf. *ib.* 367, 368, *al.* See further *Proleg.* p. 84 where a curious parallel is quoted from the Ptolemaic formula applied to deified Kings—P Grenf II. 15¹·⁶ (B.C. 139) τοῦ μεγάλου θεοῦ εὐεργέτου καὶ σωτῆρος [ἐπιφανοῦς] εὐχαρίστο´υ.

We may also note here the use of the art. with the nom. in forms of address, as in Lk 18¹¹ ὁ θεός: see Blass *Gr.* p. 86 f., and Wackernagel *Anredeformen*, pp. 7 ff., 11 ff., where reference is made to the common formula on Christian gravestones—ὁ θεός, ἀνάπαυσον.

(12) The common articular infin. with a preposition (e.g. P Oxy I. 69¹⁵ (A.D. 190) εἰς τὸ καὶ ἐμαὶ (*l.* ἐμὲ) δύνασθαι

τὴν κριθὴν ἀπολαβεῖν, "so that I may be able to recover the barley") need only be referred to here in order to point out that the art. is sometimes omitted in the papyri in the case of family or business accounts, as when provision is made for so much—εἰς πεῖν BGU II. 34⁶·⁷—A.D. 223). Nothing answering to this is found in the NT, another proof of the general "correctness" of its articular usage (*Proleg.* p. 81).

Τοῦ c. inf. (a gen. of reference, Brugmann) occurs in inscrr., e.g. *C. and B.* ii. p. 608, No. 497⁷ τοῦ καὶ τοὺς ἄλλους . . . πειρᾶσ[θαι . . . ἀ]γαθοῦ τινος παραιτίους ἔσ]εσθ[αι? τῷ δήμῳ. With 2 Cor 1⁸ we may perhaps compare the ablatival usage in the Lycaonian inscr. cited *s.v.* διχοτομέω—τῷ διχοτομήσαντί με τοῦ πολοέτιον ζῆν. See further Evans *CQ* xv. (1921), p. 26 ff.

Other exx. will be found in Eakin's paper on "The Greek Article in First and Second Century Papyri" in *AJP* xxxvii. (1916), p. 333 ff., to which we are much indebted, and in the exhaustive study by F. Volker on "Der Artikel" (Munster, 1903) in the *Beilage zu dem Jahresberichte über das Realgymnasium zu Munster i. W. für das Schuljahr* 1902.

ὀγδοήκοντα.

For the form ὀγδοήκοντα see P Petr I. 16²² ὡς ἐτῶν ὀγδοήκοντα, and similarly *ib.* 20(1)⁹, both of B.C. 225: cf. Crönert *Mem. Herc.* p. 121, Nachmanson p. 46. Mayser (*Gr.* p. 15 f.) draws attention to the solitary appearance of ὀδώκοντα on a Theban ostracon of i B.C., *Ostr.* 323⁶, and thinks that it may be Ionic. MGr (ὀγδοήντα), ὀγδόντα.

ὄγδοος,

originally ὄγδοϝος, does not contract in any of its NT occurrences, and this is the general rule in the papyri and inscriptions, e.g. P Grenf I. 10¹ (B.C. 174) ἔτους ὀγδόου, *OGIS* 90²⁰ (Rosetta stone—B.C. 196) ἕως τοῦ ὀγδόου ἔτους. Cf. however P Eud 4¹⁹ (before B.C. 165) ὄγδουν beside ὀγδόης, and *ib.* 14³ ὄγδου (cited in Mayser *Gr.* p. 294), and see also *OGIS* 332¹⁴ (B.C. 138–2) τὴν δὲ ὀγδόην, of the eighth day of the month.

ὄγκος.

For this NT ἅπ. εἰρ. (Heb 12¹) cf. P Lond 130¹⁰⁷ (horoscope—i/ii A.D.) (= I. p. 139) ἐπίτριτος ὄγκωι, and see *Kaibel* 810³ cited *s.v.* κλισία. The meaning "bulk" is seen in Menander *Fragm.* p. 113, No. 394 —

οὐπώποτ' ἐζήλωσα πολυτελῆ νεκρόν·
εἰς τὸν ἴσον ὄγκον τῷ σφόδρ' ἔρχετ' εὐτελεῖ.

"I never envied an expensive corpse: it comes to the same bulk (*i.e.* a handful of ashes) as a very cheap one." For the verb ὀγκόω cf. *Kaibel* 314²³—

ἀλλ' ἑτέραν πάλι μοι νόσον ἤγαγε γαστρὸς μοῖρα,
σπλάγχνα μου ὀγκώσασα καὶ ἐκτήξασα τὰ λοιπά.

Cf. *ib.* 234² (iii/A.D.) ὀγκωτὰ . . κόνις.

ὅδε.

The NT phrase τάδε λέγει (Ac 21¹¹, Rev 2¹ *al.*) may be compared with τάδε διέθετο, the regular formula in wills for introducing the testator's dispositions, e.g. P Petr I. 16(1)¹·

(B.C. 230) τάδε διέθετο νοῶν καὶ φρονῶν Μένιππος κτλ. : cf. P Giss I. 36¹⁰ (B.C. 161) τάδε λέγει γυνὴ Ἑλληνὶς Ἀμμωνία κτλ. (with the editor's note), and P Passalacqua¹¹ (Ptol.) (= Witkowski², p. 54) ἀπεδόθη τάδ' αὐτῶι, where τάδ' = ἤδε ἡ ἐπιστολή. Apart from the phrase cited above, the pronoun occurs only twice (Lk 16³⁹, Jas 4¹³) in the NT (it is commoner in the LXX, Thackeray Gr. i. p. 191), and this corresponds with its rarity in the later **Koινή**: cf. however P Ryl II. 162¹¹ (A.D. 159) κατὰ τήνδε τ[ὴ]ν ὁμολογίαν, "in accordance with this agreement," P Oxy VII. 1033¹⁴ (A.D. 392) τοῦδε τοὺς λιβέλλους ἐπιδίδομεν, and P Grenf I. 53²⁴ (iv/A.D.) αἴδε λέγουσαι. For earlier exx. see Mayser Gr. p. 308, and add P Tor I. 2⁴⁰ (B.C. 241) ἐπὶ τήνδε τὴν οἰκίαν: for the NT usage see Blass-Debrunner § 289. The only survival of the pronoun in MGr is ὁ τάδε(ς) used in the sense of δεῖνα (Jannaris, § 564).

ὁδεύω.

For this verb = "am on a journey," which in the NT is confined to Lk 10³³, cf. P Oxy XIV. 1771¹⁰ (iii–iv A.D.) μετὰ γὰρ τὸ ὁδεῦσε (l. -σαι) ταῦτα ἐκώλυσαν τὸν καμηλείτην κἀμὲ μὴ ἄρε (l. ἄραι), ἀλ' (l. ἀλλ') ἔτι ἐπιμεῖναι τοῖς ἐνθάδε—directions about certain measures of wine. See also the words transcribed by the traveller Cosmas from a monument in Nubia in the first half of vi/A.D., OGIS 199²⁸ ἐκέλευσα καὶ ὁδεύεσθαι μετ' εἰρήνης καὶ πλέεσθαι. It may be worth while to recall the metaphorical use of περιοδεύω in Epicurus (cf. Linde Epic. p. 54) and in Epictetus (e.g. iii. 15. 7) = "investigate thoroughly."

ὁδηγέω.

P Leid Wˣⁱⁱ ³¹ (ii/iii A.D.) (= II. p. 123) ὁ δὲ θεὸς ἔφη πάντα κεινήσεις (l. κινήσεις), καὶ πάντα ἱλαρυνθήσεται, Ἑρμοῦ σε ὁδηγοῦντος. With the use of the verb in Jn 16¹³ we may compare from the hermetic literature Hermes (ed. Parthey) p. 81¹² εἰς δὲ τὴν εὐσεβῆ ψυχὴν ὁ νοῦς ἐμβὰς ὁδηγεῖ αὐτὴν ἐπὶ τὸ τῆς γνώσεως φῶς: cf. the oracular Kaibel 1041¹ νῦν τοι πάντα τελεῖ δαίμων, νῦν ἐς ὀρθ[ὸ]ν ὁδηγεῖ. See also Test. xii. patr. Jud. 19 ἡ φιλαργυρία πρὸς εἰδωλολατρείαν ὁδηγεῖ. For the form ὁδαγέω, which occurs sporadically, see Moulton Gr. ii. p. 71.

ὁδοιπορέω.

For this verb, as in Ac 10⁹, see the prescription in the magic P Lond 121¹⁸¹ (iii/A.D.) (= I. p. 99) ὁδοιποροῦντα μὴ διψᾶν ᾠὸν οἶνον (l. οἴνῳ) ἀνοκόψας (l. ἀνακόψας) ῥόφα, "that you may not be thirsty when on a journey, beat up an egg in wine and gulp it down": the editor compares Mr. Gladstone's similar prescription for support during a long speech. The medical usage is illustrated by Hobart p. 216 f. For the verb cf. also Syll 652 (= ³885)²⁸ (c. A.D. 220) τὴν τοσαύτην ὁδοι[π]ορῆσαι ὁδόν, and for the compound συνοδοιπορέω, cf. P Giss I. 27¹ (ii/A.D.) (= Chrest. I. p. 29) μετέλαβον πα[ρ]ά τινων ἀπὸ Ἰβιῶνος σήμερον ἐλθόντω[ν] συνοδοιπορηκένα[ι] τιν[ὶ] παιδαρίῳ τοῦ κυρίου Ἀπολλωνίου ἀπὸ Μέμφεως [ἐ]ρχομένῳ. The first part of the compound ὁδοιπορέω is the locative ὁδοι- (Boisacq, p. 685).

ὁδοιπορία

is found in a letter of late iii/A.D. containing instructions for the sending of a ferry-boat— διὰ τὸ ἄδηλον τῆς ὁδοιπορίας,

"on account of the uncertainty of the road" (P Oxy I. 118 verse⁶): cf. Epict. iii. 10. 11 μέρος γάρ ἐστι καὶ τοῦτο τοῦ βίου, ὡς περίπατος, ὡς πλοῦς, ὡς ὁδοιπορία, οὕτω καὶ πυρετός, "for fever too is a part of life, like walking, sailing, travelling." For ὁδοιπόρος (Gen 37²⁵) cf. Syll 802 (= ³1168)⁶³ (iv/B.C.) ὁδο[ι]πόρος οὖν τις ἰδὼν αὐτόν, and Kaibel 167¹ μεῖνον, ἄκουσον ἐμοῦ, ὁδοιπόρε, τίς ποτ' ἔφυμε.

ὁδοποιέω.

In Mk 2²³ ἤρξαντο ὁδὸν ποιεῖν [ὁδοποιεῖν BGH] τίλλοντες τοὺς στάχυας, the verb is to be understood in the sense of "journey" (= Lat. iter facio): in more careful Greek it would mean "pave a road" (see Souter Lex. s.v. and Field Notes, p. 25). Cf. OGIS 175¹⁰ (B.C. 108–101) ὁδὸν . . πρὸς εὐχέ[ρειαν] ὡδοποιημένην, and the use of the subst. in a letter announcing the preparations for the visit of an official by repairing the roads, P Grenf II. 14(b)⁶ (B.C. 264 or 227) γινόμ[εθα] δὲ πρὸς τῆι ὁδοποίαι (for form see Mayser Gr. p. 110). "Ὄδια or provisions for his consumption on the journey have also been got ready, amounting to no less than χῆνες πεντήκοντα, ὄρνιθες διακόσιαι, περιστριδεῖς ἑκατόν : cf. Wilcken Ostr. i. p. 390. The late ὁδοιποιέω is modelled on ὁδοιπορέω (Boisacq, p. 685).

ὁδός

in its ordinary sense of "way," "road," is seen in such passages as P Petr I. 21¹¹ (B.C. 237) ὁδὸς δημοσία, ib. 23⁷ (iii/B.C.) (p. [66]) ἀπὸ τῆς βασιλικῆς ὁδοῦ, P Lond 106¹⁴ (iii/B.C.) (= I. p. 61) τά τε σκεύη μου ἐξέρριψεν εἰς τὴν ὁδόν, P Fay 111⁵ (A.D. 95–6) ἀπὸ τοῦ σκυλμοῦ τῆς ὡ( )δοῦ, "owing to the fatigue of the journey" (Edd.), and P Oxy VII. 1068²⁵ (iii/A.D.) καθ' ὁδόν, "on the road" (cf. Lk 10¹, al.). For the metaphorical usage we may cite P Lond 897¹⁰ (A.D. 84) (= III. p. 207) in which a man writes that, in view of the treatment received on his last visit, he will not return to the Arsinoite nome, unless his correspondent can find some "way" of preventing a repetition of the injury—ἐὰν δὲ μὴ ἦσα (l. ἦσθα) εὑρηκώς τινα ὁδὸν γράψον μοι κτλ. In the note on P Strass II. 85²² (B.C. 113) it is suggested that the true reading of P Lond 880²³ (B.C. 119) (= III. p. 9) is πλατεία ὁδὸς τῶν θεῶν. The Christian letter P Oxy XII. 1494⁸ (early iv/A.D.) shows us ὁδὸς εὐθεῖα, as in 2 Pet 2¹⁵. For the difficult ὁδὸν θαλάσσης in Mt 4¹⁵, see McNeile's note ad l.

ὀδούς.

P Grenf II. 32⁵ (B.C. 101) οὐλὴ ὀδόντι—"a curious phrase, meaning presumably that he had a front tooth broken" (Edd.). The nom. of ὀδόντος, which is formed by vocalic assimilation from ἔδοντος, pres. part. of ἔδω (cf. Lat. edo), should really be ὀδών (Boisacq, p. 686). MGr δόντι.

ὀδυνάομαι,

"suffer pain," rare in prose writers, is used in the NT only by Luke: cf. the Alexandrian Erotic Fragment P Grenf I. 1¹⁰ (ii/B.C.) ταῦτά με ἀδικεῖ, ταῦτά με ὀδυνᾷ. It occurs quater in Vett. Val., e.g. p. 240¹⁵ οὗτος ὀδυνώμενος ματαίαν ἡγεῖται τὴν τῆς παιδείας ἐπιβολὴν καὶ εὐδαίμονα προκρίνει τὸν ἀμαθῆ: see also Hobart p. 32 f. For the form ὀδυνᾶσαι (Lk 16²⁵), see Moulton Proleg. p. 53 f. The word may be from the root of ἔδω (cf. *curae edaces* in Horace), or it may be connected with δύη (Boisacq, p. 685).

ὀδύνη.

P Grenf I. 1² (ii B.C.) ὀδύνη με ἔχει ὅταν ἀναμνησθῶ ὥς με κατεφίλει ἐπιβούλως μέλλων με καταλιμπάνειν.

ὀδυρμός.

For the corresponding verb = "lament," "bewail," cf. P Thead 21¹⁵ (A.D. 318) ἀναγκαίως ἀνοσίῳ πρᾶμμα (*l.* ἀνόσιον πρᾶγμα) [ὁ]δυρόμενος, ἐπιδίδωμί σοι τάδε τὰ βιβλία, "driven by necessity and lamenting this impious act, I submit this petition to you," and Ramsay *East. Rom. Prov.* p. 144⁵ ὧν κὲ τὰ τέκνα τὸν ἐμὸν πότμον ὠδύροντο, "their children too bewailed my death." See also *Kaibel* 1003¹ φωνὴ δ' ὀδυ[ρτ]ὸς ἦν πάλαι μοι Μέμνονος.

ὄζω.

With the use of this verb in Jn 11³⁹ (cf. Exod 8¹⁴) cf. PSI IV. 297³ (v/A.D. ?) δριμὺ ὄ[σ]δομένου τοῦ σώματος, "the body emitting a pungent odour": for the form ὀσδομένου see the editor's introduction. When word was brought to Athens of the death of Alexander, Demades denied the report, since, had it been true, the whole earth would long ago have been filled with the stench of the body—πάλαι γὰρ ἂν ὅλην ὄζειν νεκροῦ τὴν οἰκουμένην (Plut. *Phoc.* 22).

ὅθεν,

"whence" of place, as in Mt 12⁴⁴ *al.*, may be illustrated from the interesting letter, P Lond 854⁷ (i/ii A.D.: cf. Deissmann *LAE* p. 162) (= III. p. 206), in which a traveller describes his visit to the spot—ὅθεν τ[υγ]χάνει Νεῖλος ῥέων, "whence the Nile flows out." For the inferential ὅθεν, "wherefore," "on which account," as in Heb 2¹⁷, 1 Jn 2¹⁸, cf. P Tor I. 1⁸·⁴ (B.C. 116) ὅθεν ἐν τῶι αὐτῶι ἔτει τοῖς ἐν τῆι Θηβαίδι χρηματισταῖς ἐνέβαλον ἔντευξιν, BGU III. 731ⁱⁱ·¹² (A.D. 180) ὅθεν ἐπιδίδωμι καὶ [ἀξιῶ] ἐν καταχωρισμῷ [γενέσθαι τάδε τὰ] βιβλείδια : similarly in the inscrr. from i/B.C. (Meisterhans *Gr.* p. 253). The meaning is little more than "when" in P Tebt I. 54⁷ (B.C. 86) κλήρου . . ὡρίμου σπαρῆναι, ὅθεν τῆι νυκτὶ τῆι φερούσηι εἰς τὴν κε τοῦ Φαῶφι, "the holding was ready for sowing, when on the night before the 25th of Phaophi" certain men invaded it, and in P Oxy I. 62 *verso*¹⁶ (iii/A.D.) ὅθεν = "where"—ἵνα δυνηθῶμεν ὅθεν ἐὰν δέω τὴν ἐμβολὴν ποιῆσαι διὰ τάχους, "so that we may be able to do the lading quickly at any point I may require" (Edd.). MGr ὅθε.

ὀθόνη

does not occur in the LXX, and in the NT is confined to Ac 10¹¹, 11⁵: on the possibility that we have here the reminiscence of a medical phrase see Hobart p. 218f. See also *Mart. Polyc.* xv.

ὀθόνιον.

Wilcken *Ostr* i. p. 266 ff. has shown that by ὀθόνιον in Egypt we must understand fine linen stuff, both in its manufactured and in its unmanufactured state. Its manufacture was a government monopoly: cf. P Tebt I. 5⁶⁵ (B.C. 118) ἀφειᾶσ[ι] δὲ καὶ τοὺς ἐπιστάτας τῶν ἱερῶν καὶ τοὺς ἀρχιερεῖς καὶ ἱερ[εῖς τῶν] ὀφε[ι]λομένων πρός τε τὰ ἐπιστατικὰ

καὶ τὰς προστιμή[σεις τῶν] ὀθονίων ἕως τοῦ ν (ἔτους), "and they remit to the overseers of the temples and the chief priests and priests the arrears on account of both the tax for overseers and the values of woven cloths up to the 50th year" (Edd.): see the editors' note *ad l.* and P Rev L xxxvi. with the note on p. 175, also *OGIS* 90¹⁸ (Rosetta stone B.C. 196) τῶν τ' εἰς τὸ βασιλικὸν συντελουμένων ἐν τοῖς ἱεροῖς βυσσίνων ὀθονίων ἀπέλυσεν τὰ δύο μέρη, *ib.*²⁹ τὰς τιμὰς τῶν μὴ συντετελεσμένων εἰς τὸ βασιλικὸν βυσσίνων ὀθονίων. On the manufacture of ὀθόνιον (Suid. λεπτὸν ὕφασμα) see Otto *Priester* i. p. 305f, and cf. the Zeno letter PSI VI. 599 (iii B.C.), where mention is made of 3 slaves and 1 woman as engaged on the manufacture of each ὀθόνιον. The word ὀθονιοπώλης, "a linen-seller," is restored by Wilcken in P Leid K¹³ (B.C. 99) (= I. p. 52): for ὀθονιακός, "a linen-merchant," see P Oxy VI. 933³³ (late ii A.D.). With the use of ὀθόνιον in Jn 19⁴⁰ cf. P Par 53⁸ ὀθώ(= ὁ)νιον ἐγκοιμήτριν (= -ιον), *ib.*⁴² ἔδωκα Δημητρίῳ ὀθόνια β, and P Giss I. 68¹¹ (ii/A.D.) ὀθόνια εὔωνα, fine linen-wrappings for a mummy. Other exx. of the word are P Hib I. 67¹⁰ (B.C. 228) εἰς τιμὰ]ς ὀθονίων τῶν [συντελ]ουμένων εἰς τὸ [βα]σ[ιλικ]όν, P Eleph 27a.¹⁶ (iii/B.C.) βυσσίνων ὀθονίων, P Petr I. 30(1)³ (mid. iii B.C.) (= Witkowski², p. 5) where τὰ ὀθόνια is translated by the editor "sail-cloth " (cf. Ac 10¹¹, 11⁵, and Polyb. v. 80. 2), and the early Christian letter P Amh I. 3(*a*)ⁱⁱⁱ·² (A.D. 250–285) ὠνησάμενο[ς] τὰ ὀθόν[ια. In P Grenf I. 38¹⁴ (ii/i B.C.) ὀθόνιον κατέρηξεν. ὁ. = "outward garment," "cloak": cf. P Par 50⁵ (B.C. 160) (= Witkowski², p. 75) πέπρακα τὸ ὀθόνιον (δραχμῶν) φ καὶ τὸ εἱμάτιον (δραχμῶν) τπ, and a list of clothes classified as ἱμάτια and ὀθόνια in P Oxy XIV. 1741 (early iv A.D.). See also P Strass II. 91¹⁶ (B.C. 87?) ἀφείλοντο τὰ βύσσινα ὀθόνια τῶν θεῶν καὶ ἃ εἶχεν ἱμάτια, and for the dim. ὀθονίδιον see P Oxy XIV. 1679⁵ (iii/A.D.) τὰ κρόκινα ὀθονείδια τῆς θυγατρός σου, "the saffron clothes of your daughter" (Edd.). The word itself is of Semitic origin: Lewy *Fremdwörter*, p. 124 f., Thumb *Hellenismus*, p. 111.

οἶδα.

The distinction between οἶδα, "know" absolutely, and γινώσκω, "come to know" (cf. Lightfoot on Gal 4⁹), cannot be pressed in Hellenistic Greek. For οἶδα in contexts which suggest full, accurate knowledge, we may cite PSI VI. 667⁶ (iii/B.C.) ἐγὼ δέ γε εἰδυῖα τοὺς σου τρόπους [ὅ]τι μισοπόνε(= η)ος εἶ, οὐ ποιῶ αὐτό, P Petr II. 11 (1)⁷ (iii/B.C.) (= *Selections*, p. 8) γράφε δ' ἡμῖν καὶ σύ, ἵνα εἰδῶμεν (1 Cor 2¹²) ἐν οἷς εἶ, καὶ μὴ ἀγωνιῶμεν, P Strass II. 93⁹ (B.C. 120) διασάφησον . . . ὅπως εἰδῶμεν, P Tebt I. 58³⁰ (B.C. 111) (= *Chrest.* I. p. 339) γράψας ὅπως εἰδῆς, καὶ σὺ ἀναγωνίατος ἴσθει, "I write this for your information ; do not have any anxiety" (Edd.), P Oxy IV. 745⁸ (c. A.D. 1) ἐρωτῶ οὖν σε μὴ ἄλλως ποιῆσαι, οἶδα δὲ ὅτι πάντα καλῶς ποιήσεις, "I ask you therefore not to do otherwise : but I know that you will do everything well" (Edd.), and BGU I. 37⁷ (A.D. 50) (= *LAE*, p. 157) ὅρα οὖν μὴ αὐτὸν κατάσχῃς, οἶδας γὰρ πῶς ἑκάστης ὥρας χρῇζωι, "see then that you do not detain him, for you know how I have need of him every hour" : cf. Rev 2² with Swete's note. See also the common asseveration in the Christian papyri οἶδεν γὰρ (ὁ) θεός, e.g. P Iand 11¹⁰ (iii/A.D.), P Strass I. 35¹¹ (iv/v A.D.). P Oxy

VIII. 1165⁸ (vi/A.D.), and *ib.* VI. 942³ (vi/vii A.D.): cf.
2 Cor 12². In *ib.*³ and 1 Cor 1¹⁶ Field (*Notes*, p. 187)
suggests that οἶδα might be rendered "I remember," and
cites Lucian *Dial. Meretr.* i. 1 : οἶσθα αὐτόν, ἢ ἐπιλέλησαι·
τὸν ἄνθρωπον ; οὐκ, ἀλλ' οἶδα, ὦ Γλυκέριον.

The meaning "appreciate," "respect," in 1 Thess 5¹² can
now be paralleled from P Goodspeed 3⁷ (iii/B.C.) (= *Witkowski*², p. 47) ἔδο]ξέ [μο]ι ν[ῦ]ν περὶ τοῦ ὁράματος διασαφῆσαί σοι, ὅπως εἰδῆις, ὃν τρόπον οἱ θεοί σε οἴδασιν, where
the meaning apparently is, "in order that you may know as
clearly as the gods know you." Notice also in the above the
early occurrence of the Hellenistic οἴδασιν. The literary
ἴσασιν is found in the NT only in Ac 26¹: cf. Blass
Philology, p. 9. Eph 5⁵ ἴστε γινώσκοντες is sometimes
treated as a Hebraism ("ye know of a surety" RV: cf.
Gen 15³), but the verbs are different, and the meaning is
rather "ye know by what you observe" (Westcott *ad. l.*).

Οἶδες for οἶδας occurs in BGU III. 923¹¹ (i/ii A.D.) οἶδες
δὲ ὅτι οὐδὲ ἐγὼ μεμ[π]τός εἰμι. *ib.* l. 26¹⁻² (ii/iii A.D.?)
σὺ οἶδες οὖν τῇ ἀδελφῇ σοι ὡς ἔγραψες (cf.¹⁷ ἤρηχες =
εἴρηκας Ἡρᾶτι, *ib.* II. 380¹⁵ (iii/A.D.) εἰ δὲ οἶδες σατῶ, ὅτι
ἔχεις ἔτι, γράψον μοι, P Oxy VII. 1067²⁰ (iii/A.D.) εἰ οἶδες
(cf.⁵ ἀφῆκες) ὅτι οὐ μέλλεις ἐλθεῖν, πέμψον μοι τὸν ἀδελφόν
σου, and *ib.* XII. 1593⁶ (iv/A.D.) περὶ ὄ[ι] οἶδες οὐδεμίαν
ὑπόμνησίν μοι ἐδήλωσας. The form is apparently not so
rare as Mayser (*Gr.* p. 321) would imply, though it seems
generally to occur in the writings of uncultured scribes.
Οἴδαμεν is the usual form in Epict. (e.g. ii. 20. 32) as in the
NT, though ἴσμεν occurs once (ii. 17. 13) : see Sharp *Epict.*
p. 85 f. "Ἴστε is found in the NT in Eph 5³, Heb 12¹⁷, Jas 1¹⁹
(cf. LXX 3 Macc 3¹¹): for ἴστωσαν cf. P Hamb I. 29⁵ (time
of Domitian) οἱ προτεθέντες ἐπ' ἐμὲ καὶ μὴ ὑπακούσαντες
ἴστωσαν, ὅτι . . . . Οἶδα is extinct in MGr, except for the
phrases τίς οἶδε; "who knows?" Κύριος οἶδε, "Heaven
knows": see Jannaris *Gr.* § 976ᵇ.

οἰκεῖος.

"one's own" in contrast to "another's" (ἀλλότριος : cf.
Arist. *Rhet.* i. 5. 7), hence "a member of one's family or
household," is seen in such passages as P Lille I. 7⁵ (iii/B.C.)
διατρίβοντος γάρ μου μετὰ Ἀπολλωνίου ἐμοῦ (αὐτοῦ inserted
above line) οἰκείου, P Magd 13² (B.C. 217) ἀδικούμεθα ὑπὸ
Θευδότου καὶ Ἀγάθωνος, οἳ εἰσιν οἰκεῖοι τῆς μητρὸς Φιλίππου, P Grenf II. 28⁵ (B.C. 103) με[τ]ὰ κυρίου ἑαυτῆς
οἰκήου Θοτούτης, Preisigke 6¹⁹ (A.D. 216) πρώην οὖν εἰς τὸν
τόπον ε[ἰ]σελθόντων τῶν οἰκείων μου . . . οὐχ εὑρέθη τ[ὰ
σ]ειτάρια κεκουφισμένα, and for the neut. cf. P Oxy XIV.
1682⁷ (iv/A.D.) ἡ μὲν τοῦ θεοῦ πρόνοια παρέξει τὸ μετὰ
ὁλοκληρίας σε τὰ οἰκεῖα ἀπολαβεῖν, "may the divine providence grant that you may be restored in security to your
home" (Edd.). For the wider sense of οἰκεῖος, "intimate,"
"spiritually akin with," in its NT occurrences (Gal 6¹⁰,
Eph 2¹⁹, 1 Tim 5⁸), see Whitaker *Exp* VIII. xxiii. p. 76 ff.
The "exhausted" οἰκεῖος, practically equal to a possessive
pronoun, is common in Hellenistic writers such as Josephus
(exx. in Schmidt *Jos.* p. 369). For οἰκεῖος = ἴδιος in Epictetus, see Stob. II ὅπερ οὖν σοι φυσικὸν καὶ συγγενές, ὁ
λόγος, τοῦτο καὶ οἰκεῖον ἡγησάμενος τούτου ἐπιμελοῦ, "that
therefore which is natural and congenial to thee, Reason, think
to be specially thy own and take care of it" (Sharp, p. 127).

For an interesting ex. of the verb οἰκειόω cf. P Ryl II. 114²
(c. A.D. 280), where a widow appeals to the Prefect for protection against the aggression of a certain Syrion—οἰκίωται
δὲ τῷ προκειμένῳ Συρίω[νι ἐμὲ τὴν χήρα]ν μετὰ νηπίων
τέκνων ἀεὶ ἀποστερεῖν, "but it is characteristic of the aforesaid Syrion on all occasions to rob me and my young children" (Edd.). The subst. οἰκειότης is seen in *OGIS* 5⁴¹
(B.C. 311) διὰ τὴν οἰκειότητα τὴν ὑπάρχουσαν ἡμῖν πρὸς
αὐτόν, and οἰκείωσις in Vett. Val. p. 202¹⁷.

οἰκέτεια.

P Tebt II. 285⁶ (A.D. 239), a rescript of the Emperor
Gordian enacting that false insertions in the registers are not
to confer privileges upon any persons not entitled to them by
birth—οὔτε τοὺς ἀλλοτρίους εἰ καὶ ἐγένοντο εἰς τὴν οἰκετείαν
εἰσάγουσιν, "nor, if there actually are registers, can they
introduce outsiders into the family" (Edd.). *Syll* 552
(= ³695)⁶¹ (after A.D. 129) ἀνί]εσθαι . . . τὴν οἰκετείαν
ἀπὸ παντὸς ἔργου, "to release the household from all work."

οἰκέτης.

The use of οἰκέτης to denote "a household or domestic
slave" (Lat. *famulus*) in Lk 16¹³ οὐδεὶς οἰκέτης δύναται δυσὶ
κυρίοις δουλεύειν, "no domestic can be a slave to two
masters," is well illustrated by P Lille I. 29⁵⁻² (iii/B.C.) ἐὰν
δέ τις περὶ ἀδικήματος ἑ[τέ]ρο[υ] οἰκέτῃ ὄντι δίκην γραψάμενος, ὡς ἐλευθέρωι, καταδικάσηται, ἐξέστω τῶι κυρίωι ἀναδικῆσαι ἐν ἡμέραις ἕ, "si quelqu'un en raison d'un dommage
a intenté une action à l'esclave d'un autre, comme a un
homme libre, et l'a fait condamner, qu'il soit permis au
maître de l'esclave d'interjeter appel dans un délai de cinq
jours" (Ed.). For the adj. οἰκετικός, see P Grenf I. 21⁶
(B.C. 126) ἀπὸ τῶν οἰκετικῶν σωμάτων δ. On the different
terms for "slave" in the NT, see Trench *Syn.* § ix., and
cf. Thackeray *Gr.* i. p. 7 f.

οἰκέω.

P Magd 8³ (B.C. 218) οἰκησάντων γὰρ ἡμῶν ἀμφοτέρων
[ἐν τῆι προγεγραμμένηι κώμηι. P Tebt I. 6⁴⁰ (B.C. 140-39)
οἰκεῖν παρὰ τὸν ἐθισμόν. "inhabit (the temple) contrary to
custom," and *ib.* 104²¹ (B.C. 92), a marriage contract, where
it is laid down that the husband shall not reside in a house
over which his wife has no rights—μηδ' ἄλλην [οἰκία]ν οἰκεῖν
ἧς οὐ κυριεύσει Ἀπολλωνία. In P Oxy VIII. 1101²¹
(A.D. 367-70) we have the phrase νῆσον οἰκῆσαι = "to
be deported." For the pass. with an act. significance see
OGIS 8¹²⁴ (iv/B.C.) τῶν τυρ[άν]νων [κα]ὶ τ[ῶν ἐ]μ πό[λει
οἰκη]θέντων, cf. ¹⁴⁷·¹⁴, and for a weakened use of οἰκεῖσθαι
see *Archiv* i. p. 475.

οἴκημα.

In Ac 12⁷, the only place where it occurs in the NT,
οἴκημα is used euphemistically of a "prison chamber": see
Field *Notes*, p. 120. For its more general use cf. *Chrest.*
I. 224ᵇ·¹¹ (iii/B.C.) cited *s.v.* αὐλή, P Lond 887² (iii/B.C.)
(= III. p. 1) where a petitioner complains that a neighbour,
who occupied "apartments" in the same courtyard, had
erected a staircase in the courtyard to the petitioner's injury
—αὐτὸς δὲ εἰσῴκισται εἰς δύο οἰκήματα ἐν τῆι αὐλῆι καὶ
ἀνοικοδόμηκεν ἐν τῆι αὐλῆι κλεῖμα κτλ., P Petr II. 32(1)¹⁷

(Ptol.) εἰσπηδήσας εἰς τὸ οἴκ[ημα] οὗ ᾤκουν, "having rushed into the house where I dwelt," *ib.* 33⁴·¹ ἐνοίκιον τοῦ οἰκήματος, "rent of the house," and *OGIS* 483¹¹⁰ (ii/A.D.) ἐὰν ὁ μὲν ὑπερῷον οἴκημα πρὸς αὐτῶι (τῷ κοινῷ τοίχῳ) ἔχῃ, ὁ [δ]ὲ ἁπλο[ῦ]ν. The dim. οἰκημάτιον occurs in P Ryl II. 77²⁰ (A.D. 192) τὰς κλεῖδας τοῦ οἰκηματίου, and οἴκησις = "right of dwelling" in *ib.* 153⁷·¹⁴ (A.D. 138–61).

οἰκητήριον.

For οἰκητήριον, "dwelling-place," "habitation," as in Jude ⁶, cf. BGU IV. 1167³³ (B.C. 12) ἐν τῇ τετραγώ(νῳ) στοᾷ οἰκητηρίο(υ). P Oxy II. 281¹¹ (A.D. 20–50), complaint against a husband—ἐγὼ μὲν οὖν ἐπιδεξαμένη αὐτὸν εἰς τὰ τῶν γονέων μου οἰκητήρια λειτὸν παντελῶς ὄντα, "as he was destitute of means I received him into my parents' house" (Edd.). In P Tor II. 3³·³ (B.C. 127) οἱ ἐνκαλούμενοι ἐμβατεύσαντες εἰς σημαινομένην οἰκίαν καὶ περιοικοδομήσαντες ἑαυτοῖς οἰκητήρια ἐνοικοῦσιν βιαίως, the editor understands by οἰκητήρια, "apartments," rather than a whole house: cf. the important inscription of B.C. 76–5, cited by Plaumann *Ptolemais*, p. 35, where we read of a shrine of Isis ('Ισιδεῖον), built to the south of Ptolemais— σὺν τοῖς περὶ αὐτὸ κατῳκοδομημένοις οἰκητηρίοις. For οἰκήτωρ, "inhabitant," see P Lond 121⁵⁹¹ (iii/A.D.) (= I. p. 95).

οἰκία.

For οἰκία, "a house," in the ordinary sense of the term, it is sufficient to cite such passages as P Petr II. 12(1)¹² (B.C. 241) ἐνῳκοδομηκότας τὰς θύρας τῶν οἰκιῶν, "built up the doors of the houses," *ib.* I. 14¹⁰ (a Will—B.C. 237) καταλιμπάνω . . [τὴν ἐ]ν 'Αλεξανδρείαι οἰκίαν ἐμοὶ ὑπάρχουσαν, P Ryl II. 125²⁵ (A.D. 28–9) ἔριψεν ἐν τῇ οἰκίᾳ μου τὴν πυξίδα κενήν, "he threw the box empty into my house" (Edd.), P Oxy I. 99⁵ (A.D. 55) μέρος ἥμισυ τῆς ὑπαρχούσης αὐτῷ μητρικῆς οἰκία[ς] τριστέγου, "one half of a three-storied house inherited from his mother," and BGU I. 22²⁹ (A.D. 114) (= *Selections*, p. 76) ἀνέβη εἰς τὴν οἰκίαν μου. In phrases similar to the last, the word οἰκία is sometimes omitted, e.g. P Oxy III. 472⁴ (c. A.D. 130) ἀπὸ δὲ τῆς ἑαυτοῦ τε καὶ τοῦ κληρονομεῖν μέλλοντος υἱοῦ προῆλθε, "but it was from the house of himself and his son and future heir that he came forth" (Edd.), P Iand 14⁵ (iv/A.D.) ἀπελθὲ εἰς Λύκ[ου]. This usage survives in MGr. The difference between οἰκία, the whole house, and οἶκος, an *insula*, or set of rooms, our "flat," is, as the editors point out, well seen in such a document as P Tebt I. 46 (B.C. 113), where a certain Menches complains that a raid had been made on his house—⁹ ἐπὶ τὴν ὑπάρχουσάν μοι οἰκίαν, and that the raiders had burst open the lock of his mother's apartment—¹³ ἐκκρούσαντε[ς] τὸ χελώνιον τοῦ οἴκου τῆς μητρός μου: cf. *ib.* 38¹⁴ᶠ· (B.C. 113), and P Fay 31¹¹ᶠᶠ· (c. A.D. 129). The traces of the distinction are not readily observable in the NT ; but note the appropriateness of the larger word in such passages as Mt 5¹⁵, Lk 15⁸, Jn 12³, 2 Tim 2²⁰. Οἰκοδομέω is not used with οἶκον as object, except in Ac 7⁴⁷·⁴⁹, and the temple is always οἶκος : see the significant contrast ἐν τῇ οἰκίᾳ τοῦ πατρός μου, Jn 14². For οἰκία = "household," as in Jn 4⁵³ *al.*, cf. P Petr II. 23(4 ² καταγράψας τὴν οἰκίαν τοῦ "Ωρου, and for the phrase κατ' οἰκίαν

with reference to the "house to house" census cf. P Tebt II. 301⁹ (A.D. 162) τῇ πρὸς τὸ θ (ἔτος) κ[ατ'] οἰκίαν ἀπ[ο]γραφῇ, and *Selections*, p. 44 f. In the curious contract of service for 99 years, into which a woman enters with another, we find the formula—ἐν τῇ σῇ οἰκίᾳ καὶ τῇ τοῦ ἔργου σου (PSI V. 549¹¹—B.C. 42–1). With Mt 26⁶ cf. P Oxy I. 51¹³ (A.D. 173) ἐν οἰκίᾳ 'Επαγαθοῦ.

οἰκιακός,

"a member of one's household," as in Mt 10³⁶, is seen in such passages as P Oxy II. 294¹⁷ (A.D. 22) (= *Selections*, p. 35) ἐγὼ δὲ βιάζομαι ὑπὸ φίλω[ν] γενέσθαι οἰκιακὸς τοῦ ἀρχιστάτορος 'Απολλωνίου, "I am being pressed by my friends to become a member of the household of the chief usher Apollonius," and P Giss I. 88⁴ (ii/A.D.), the fragment of a letter whose bearer is stated to be—'Απολλωνοῦν τὴν ἀναδιδοῦσάν σοι τὸ ἐπιστόλιον οἰκιακήν μου οὖσαν.

οἰκοδεσποτέω.

This late Greek verb (cf. Lob. *Phryn.* p. 373), which in the NT is confined to 1 Tim 5¹⁴, occurs in the horoscopes P Oxy II. 235¹⁶ (A.D. 20–50) οἰκοδεσποτεῖ 'Αφροδίτη, P Lond 130¹⁶³ (i/ii A.D.) (= I. p. 137) δι' ὃ οἰκοδεσποτήσει τὸ διάθεμα.

οἰκοδεσπότης.

Like the verb, this non-classical subst. is found in horoscopes, e.g. P Lond 98 *recto* ⁶⁹ (i/ii A.D.) (= I. p. 130) ὁ φυ[σικὸς ο]ἰκ[οδεσπότης] τῆς γενέσεως 'Αφροδείτης καὶ 'Ερμοῦς, similarly *ib.* 110 (A.D. 138) (= I. p. 132), and PSI III. 158⁸⁰ (iii/A.D. ?) σκοπεῖν δὲ ἐπὶ παντὸς εἴδους τοὺς οἰκοδεσπότας τῶν φώτων. The word in the sense of "house-steward" (cf. Mt 10²⁵ *al.*) occurs in the late P Meyer 24² (vi/A.D.), where the writer states that he is prevented from receiving the visit of a high dignitary—ὑπὸ κηδίας τοῦ οἰκοδεσπότου, "owing to the death of the house-steward." Hatch (*JBL* xxvii. p. 142) cites the Isaurian inscr. υἱοὺς τοὺς οἰκοδεσπ[ότα]ς from *PAS* iii. p. 150. Epictetus applies the term to God, iii. 22. 4 ἔστι γάρ τις καὶ ἐνθάδ' οἰκοδεσπότης ἕκαστα [ὁ] διατάσσων, "for here too is a master of the house who orders everything" (Sharp, p. 25).

οἰκοδομέω

in the literal sense of "build" is seen in such passages as—P Magd 27¹ (B.C. 218) θεμέλιον σκάπτων ὥστε οἰκοδομεῖν, P Ryl II. 245² (B.C. 162) τῆς ἐν αὐτῆι οἰκίας ᾠκοδομημένης, P Grenf II. 35⁶ (B.C. 98) παστοφόριον (cf. Jerem 42¹ *al.*) ᾠκοδομημένον καὶ δεδοκωμένην, "a priest's chamber built and furnished with beams," P Ryl II. 133¹³ (A.D. 33) ἐμβημ(α) οἰκοδομημένον μετὰ δαπάνης οὐκ ὀλίγων κεφαλαίων ἀργυρικῶν, "a dam (?) built at the expense of no small sums of money" (Edd.), and the interesting P Giss I. 20¹⁹ (beg. ii/A.D.) (= *Chrest.* I. p. 124) with its reference to a private shrine, built in honour of the Dioscuri—ᾠκοδόμηται αὐτῶν ὁ τόπος. See also Logion 7 (= P Oxy I. 1²⁴⁴) λέγει 'Ιησοῦς, πόλις ᾠκοδομημένη ἐπ' ἄκρον [ὄ]ρους ὑψηλοῦ καὶ ἐστηριγμένη οὔτε πε[σ]εῖν δύναται οὔτε κρυ[β]ῆναι. For the augment see Moulton *Gr.* ii. p. 101. The metaphorical use of the verb, with which Paul has familiarized us, is found already in Xen. *Cyr.* viii. 7. 15 οἰκοδομεῖτε ἄλλα φιλικὰ ἔργα : see also Deissmann *Paul*, p. 184 ff.

οἰκοδομή.

This late Greek word, which is condemned by the Atticists (Lob. *Phryn.* pp. 487 ff., 421), but is found in Aristotle (*Eth. Nic.* v. 14. 7), occurs in the literal sense of "building" in the Κοινή, e.g. P Grenf I. 21[17] (B.C. 126) εἰς οἰκ]οδομὴν περιστερῶνος, BGU III. 894[2] (A.D. 109) λόγ(ος) οἰτομῆς (*l.* οἰκοδομῆς) τέκτω(νες) β, P Flor II. 200[1] (A.D. 259) εἰς οἰκοδομὴν κρήνης, and from the inscr. *OGIS* 655[2] (B.C. 25) ἡ οἰκοδομὴ τοῦ περιβόλου τῷ θεῶι καὶ κυρίῳ Σοκνοπαίωι. In Eph 4[29] πρὸς οἰκοδομὴν τῆς χρείας Field (*Notes*, p. 192) suggests that perhaps the meaning is "for the improvement of the occasion." The word is a shortened form of οἰκο-δόμημα : see *s.vv.* ἀγάπη, γλωσσόκομον.

οἰκοδομία.

For οἰκοδομία in its literal sense of "building," cf. *OGIS* 843[104] (ii/B.C.) τὸ ἴσον εἰσφ[ερ]έτωσαν εἰς τὴν οἰκοδομίαν, and *Cagnat* IV. 661[11] (Aemonia—A.D. 85) ὅπως μηδὲν τοῦ μνημείου τούτου ἡ τῶν περὶ [αὐ]τὸ φυτειῶν ἡ οἰκοδομιῶν ἐλασσωθῇ κτλ. The adj. occurs in *Syll* 932 (= [3]880)[65] (A.D. 202) ἐν τοῖς οἰκοδομικοῖς καὶ ἐν τοῖς λειτουργικοῖς καὶ ἐν τοῖς χρηστικοῖς (see the editor's note). In the NT the subst. is read only in 1 Tim 1[4] D[c] (οἰκονομίαν ℵAG *al.*), where it is used metaphorically.

οἰκοδόμος.

P Ryl II. 125[9] (A.D. 28–9) ποιουμέ[ν]ου μου κατασπασμὸν τειχαρίων παλαιῶ[ν) ἐν τοῖς οἰκοπέδο[ι]ς μου διὰ Πετεσούχου τοῦ Πετεσούχου οἰκοδόμ(ου), " I was engaged in demolishing some old walls upon my land through the agency of Petesouchus son of Petesouchus, builder " (Edd.), P Tebt II. 401[10] (early i/A.D.) Ἄγφις οἰκωδόμος εἰς [ο]ἰκων (*l.* οἰκοδόμος εἰς οἰκον) χο[ῦς) α—, P Giss I. 20[13] (ii/A.D.) οἰκοδόμοις καὶ τέκτο[σι, and P Oxy XIV. 1674[9] (iii/A.D.) ἔρχεται ὁ οἰκοδόμος καὶ οἰκοδομεῖ τὴν νοτινὴν πλάτην, "the builder will come to build the south wall" (Edd.).

οἰκονομέω.

The wide sense attaching to this verb with its corresponding subst. in late Greek is fully illustrated from Polybius by Dean Armitage Robinson on Eph 1[10]. We may add a few citations from the papyri. In PSI VI. 584[17] (iii/B.C.) Agesilaus writes to Zeno asking him to " make arrangements " for the transport of certain quantities of barley and wheat in order that he may receive them—εἰ δύνη[ι] οὖν μοι αὐτὰς οἰκονομήσασθαι ἵν[α] αὐτὰς ἀπεγένκωμαι : cf. *ib.* 507[3] (iii/B.C.) καλῶς ποιήσεις . . . οἰκονομησάμενος περὶ τῆς εἰσόδου, and BGU III. 1209[19] (B.C. 23) τοῖς ὑφ' ἡμῶν οἰκονομηθησομένοις. In P Eleph 9[5] (B.C. 223–22) an official summons a subordinate to appear before him bringing with him all his writings and official documents—κομίζων [π]άντα τὰ γράμματα καὶ [εἴ τι ἀλ]λο ὠκονόμηκ[ας] καὶ ὧν πεποίησαι διαγραφῶν τὰ ἀντίγραφα, and in P Oxy IX. 1203[27] (late i/A.D.) certain petitioners ask that their positions should be communicated to the collector of external debts in order that he " may take no step against us . . . before the trial of the case " (Ed.)—μηδὲν καθ' ἡμῶν οἰκονομήσῃ μέχρι κρίσεως. In P Petr II. 11 (2)[2] (mid. iii/B.C.) (= Witkowski[2], p. 6) the verb is used for the administration of a sacred office or priesthood, γίνωσκέ με τὴν ἱεροποίαν ὠκονομημέ[νον, and in *ib.* 38 (c)[60] (iii/B.C.) of the management of the details in some matter relating apparently to cowherds—περὶ βούτων ὃν ἂν [τρό]πον οἰκονομήθ]ηι. See also Preisigke 3925[5] (ii/B.C.) τὰ πρὸς τ[ὴν] κατάστασιν δικαιώματα καὶ ὅ[ν] ἂν τρόπον οἰκονομήσαμεν.

οἰκονομία

describes the office of an οἰκονόμος in P Tebt I. 27[21] (B.C. 114) φρόντι[σον ὅ]πως . . . πρὸς ταῖς οἰκονομίαις καὶ ἀρχιφυλακει[τ]είαις προχειρι[σθῶ]σιν ἀξιόλογοι. "take care that persons of repute are appointed to the posts of oeconomus and archiphylacites" (Edd.).

In P Eleph 11[7] (B.C. 223–22) ὧν δ' ἂν πράξῃς γ' οἰκ[ονο-μιῶν, the word has the general meaning "measures," and as further showing its width of application we may cite BGU III. 1026[3] (A.D. 188) ὅσα δέεται γενέσθαι ἐν τῷ ὑπὸ τὴν οἰκονο-μίαν σου βα[λ]ανείῳ, of the "care" of a bath, and P Ryl II. 78[30] (A.D. 157) περὶ οἰκονομίας, of the conduct of his business by a strategus. The important rescript of the Prefect, P Lond 904[25] (A.D. 104) (= III. p. 124, *Selections* p. 73), which offers such a striking analogy to Lk 2[1 ff.], requires all persons residing out of their own districts to return to their homes—ἵν[α] καὶ τὴν συνήθη [οἰ]κονομίαν τῆ[ς ἀπο]γραφῆς πληρώσωσιν, "that they may carry out the regular order of the census": cf. Col 1[25].

In P Rein 7[34] (B.C. 141?) οἰκονομία is used of a legal transaction—μη]δεμίαν οἰκον[ο]μίαν κατ' ἐμοῦ ποιεῖσθαι: cf. P Magd 32[6] (B.C. 217) μεθ' οὗ τὰς περὶ τούτων οἰκονομίας θήσομεν, "avec l'assistance de qui je puisse passer les actes nécessaires" (Ed.). Other exx. of the word are—P Tebt I. 30[18] (B.C. 115) τῶν δὲ πρὸς ταῖς γραμματείαις ἀγνοούντων τὴν γεγονυῖαν περὶ ἐ[μο]ῦ οἰκονομίαν, "the scribes being ignorant of this transaction affecting me " (Edd.), *ib.* II. 318[19] (notice of a claim—A.D. 166) τὸ εἴς με δίκαι[ον] οἰκονομε[ίας, "my right of procedure " (Edd.), P Oxy I. 56[17] (A.D. 211) ἐπιγραφῆναί μου κύριον πρὸς μόνην ταύτην τὴν οἰκονομίαν Ἀμοιτᾶν, "that I may have assigned to me as my guardian for this transaction only Amoitas " (Edd.), and *ib.* XII. 1467[5] (A.D. 263) where reference is made to the law that women, in virtue of their possession of three children and ability to write, have the right χωρ[ὶς] κυρίου χρηματίζειν ἐν αἷς ποιοῦν[τ]αι οἰκονομίαις, "to act without a guardian in all business which they transact."

Chrest. II. 68[10] (A.D. 14) ἀ]κ[ολού]θ[ω]ς αἷς ἔχωι οἰκ[ο]νο-μίαις shows us the meaning "document," and in the magic P Lond 46[357] (iv/A.D.) (= I. p. 76) οἰκονομία = "incanta-tion." In Cicero's letters the word occurs *bis* in the sense of "arrangement," "order " (*ad Att.* vi. 1. 1, 11), as in Epict. iii. 24. 92. For the derived sense of "utility," "practical expediency," see M. Anton. iv. 19 (with Crossley's note).

οἰκονόμος

in its literal sense of "steward," "manager of an estate" (as in Lk 12[42], 1 Cor 4[2]) is found in P Tebt II. 402[1] (A.D. 172) Μαρτι[. . . .] οἰκονόμῳ Φλαυίας Ἐπιμάχης κα[ὶ] τῶν πρότερον Ἰουλίας Καλλινίδος παρὰ Διδύμου οἰκοδόμου, "to Mart . . ., steward of Flavia Epimache and of the property formerly belonging to Julia Kallinis, from Didymus, builder," P Oxy VI. 929²⁵ (ii/iii A.D.) Νιννάρῳ οἰκονόμῳ Ἀπίωνος στρα τηγοῦ), and P Fay 133² (iv A.D. ἀπέστειλα τὸν οἰκ[ον]όμον ['Ηρα]κλείδην πρὸς σὲ καθὰ ἠξίω[σας] ἵνα τὴν διαταγὴν τῆς τρύγης ποιήσηται. "I have sent to you the steward Heraclides as you requested, to make arrangements about the vintage" (Edd.).

The meaning of "treasurer" which is given to the word in Rom 16²³ RV (cf. 1 Esdr 4¹⁹) is common both in Ptolemaic and in Roman times, though latterly the position sank much in importance: see P Tebt I. 5¹⁵⁹ (B.C. 118) with the editors' note, and for later exx. ib. II. 296¹² (A.D. 123) διέγραψε Σεκούνδῳ τῷ τοῦ κ[υ]ρίου Καίσαρος οἰκονόμῳ ("procurator," G.H.) (δραχμὰς) ⟨Α⟩φ, P Oxy IV. 735⁶ (A.D. 205) Καισάρων οἰκονόμου οὐικαρίου. From the inscrr. we may cite OGIS 50¹³ (mid. iii B.C.) τὸ δὲ ἀνάλωμα τὸ εἰς τὴν στήλην δοῦναι τὸν οἰ[κον]όμο[ν] Σωσίβιον, and Priene 6³⁰ (B.C. 330–29) τὸ δὲ ἀν]άλωμα ὑπηρετῆσαι τὸν οἰκο[νόμον with reference to defraying the expenses of an inscr.

On the difficult usage of οἰκονόμος in Gal 4² to denote one who has charge of the person or estate of a minor, see Burton ICC ad loc.; and against Mahaffy's view on P Petr II. 18 (1) B.C. 246) that the οἰκονόμος "had authority to investigate criminal cases on appeals," see Archiv iv. p. 31 f. The title is discussed by Wilcken Chrest. I. i. p. 150 ff.

οἶκος.

As illustrating the NT conception of the οἶκος πνευματικός and the οἶκος τοῦ θεοῦ Thieme (p. 31) refers not only to the place which "the house of God" had in Jewish religion, but also to the "holy houses" of Greek antiquity, as preparing the way for the Christian usage (1 Tim 3¹⁵, 1 Pet 4¹⁷): see e.g. Magn 94³ (ii/B.C.), where a certain Εὔφημος Παυσανίου νεωκόρος is praised for his liberality—εἰς τ]ὸ[ν οἶκ]ον τ[ὸν ἱερόν, ib. 117⁷ (1st half ii/A.D.) τῷ ἱερῷ οἴκῳ τῶν ἐν Κλίδωνι, and Syll 571 (= ³ 987)⁶·²⁵ (iv/B.C.), where mention is made of an οἶκος τεμένιος ἱερός in Chios. In Herodas i. 26 οἶκος τῆς θεοῦ refers to Aphrodite. From the fact that a tomb was often dedicated to a local deity, and hence became his "temple" or "home," it is natural that οἶκος should be used in inscrr. in the sense of "tomb," as at Cibyra BCH ii. (1878), p. 610 f., and Magnesia ib. xviii. (1894) p. 11 (cited in C. and B. i. p. 100 n.¹): also Kaibel 321⁷ (after A.D. 171) καμάτον οἶκον. For οἶκος used in an astrological sense see P Lond 98 recto (i ii A.D.) (= I. p. 127 ff.). The subst. in its ordinary application to "an inhabited house" is found in such passages as P Oxy II. 294¹⁰ (A.D. 22) (= Selections, p. 35) ὁ ἐμ[ὸς] οἶκος ἠραύνητ[αι, "my house has been searched," P Ryl II. 127⁹ (A.D. 29) ἐπὶ τῆς θύρας οὗ καταγείνομαι οἴκου ἐν τῷ ἐποικίωι, "at the door of the house which I inhabit in the farmstead" (Edd.), and the magical incantation P Oxy VIII. 1152⁵ (v/vi A.D.) βοήθι ἡμῖν καὶ τούτῳ οἴκῳ (for τούτῳ without article cf. Ac 24²¹). See also the prepositional phrases—ἐν οἴκῳ, "at home" (1 Cor 11³⁴), P Lond 42⁵ (B.C. 168) (= I. p. 30) οἱ ἐν οἴκωι πάντες, P Fay 115¹² (A.D. 101): ἐξ οἴκου, "out of the house," P Ryl II. 173 (a)¹¹ (A.D. 99): and ib. 76¹⁰·¹² (late ii A.D.) where κατ' οἶκον, "according to households," is contrasted with κατὰ πρόσωπον, "according to individuals." For a wide sense in

which οἶκος is apparently equivalent to πόλις, see the note on P Oxy I. 126⁴. For οἴκοθεν = "suis impensis," cf. Syll 737 (= ³ 1109)¹⁵¹ (before A.D. 178) παρεχέτω δὲ οἴκοθεν τὸ θερμόλυχνον. See further s.v. οἰκία.

οἰκουμένη.

Ἡ οἰκουμένη (γῆ), "the inhabited world," is a common designation of the Roman Empire, orbis terrarum: cf. e.g. the notification of the accession of Nero, P Oxy VII. 1021²·⁶ (A.D. 54) ὁ δὲ τῆς οἰκουμένης καὶ προσδοκηθεὶς καὶ ἐλπισθεὶς Αὐτοκράτωρ ἀποδέδεικται, ἀγαθὸς δαίμων δὲ τῆς οἰκουμένης [ἀρ]χὴ ὢν [μεγισ·]] τε πάντων ἀγαθῶν Νέρων Καῖσαρ ἀποδέδεικται, "and the expectation and hope of the world has been declared Emperor, the good genius of the world and source of all good things, Nero, has been declared Caesar" (Ed.): cf. OGIS 666³, 668³. Similarly Preisigke 176² (A.D. 161–180) with reference to Marcus Aurelius—τὸν εὐεργέτην καὶ σωτῆρα τῆς ὅλης οἰκου[μένης. In ib. 1070 (Abydos) a god [Besa ?] is invoked as—ἄψευστον καὶ δι' ὅλης οἰκουμέν(ης) μαρτυρούμενον. See also such magic invocations as P Lond 121⁷⁰⁴ (iii/A.D.) (= I. p. 107) σὲ καλῶ τὸν καταλάμποντα τὴν ὅλην οἰκουμένην, P Leid V ⁱⁱ·⁹ (iii/iv A.D.) ἥκε μοι ὁ λ. ὦ) δέσποτα τοῦ οὐρανοῦ, ἐπιλάμπων τῇ οἰκουμένῃ. A very early instance of the phrase occurs in PSI V. 541 ⁷ where a certain Aigyptos supplicates Ptolemy II. or III.—σοῦ τῆς οἰκουμένης πάσης βασιλεύοντος: cf. 1 Esdr 2³. We may add a new ex. from the New Comedy in P Hib I. 5 Fr. (a)¹⁶ τῆς οἰκουμένης | ἱερὰ σαφῶς αὕτη 'στὶν ἡ χώρα μόνη. It is hardly necessary to point out that the pleasant hyperbole of Lk 2¹, Ac 11²⁸ (cf. Ramsay Paul p. 48 f.) al. must not be pressed too far.

οἰκουργός.

This adj. = "house-worker," which is read in Tit 2⁵ ℵ° ACDFG, is pronounced by Grimm-Thayer "not found elsewhere," but Field (Notes, p. 220) refers to Soranus of Ephesus, a medical writer (not earlier than ii/A.D.) "from whose work Περὶ γυναικείων παθῶν (published at Berlin 1838) Boissonade quotes οἰκουργὸν καὶ καθέδριον ("sedentary") διάγειν βίον, where οἰκουρόν would suit at least equally well." For the verb οἰκουργέω see Clem. Rom. 1 with Lightfoot's note. The form οἰκουρός, "keeper at home," read in ℵ° Dᵇ H, occurs in the magic P Lond 125 verso ¹¹ (v/A.D.) (= I. p. 124) ἡ θεὸς ἡ καλο[υμ]ένη οἰκουρός. See further Field ut s. and the citations in Wetstein ad l.

οἰκουρός.

See s.v. οἰκουργός.

οἰκτείρω (Attic οἰκτίρω).

For the form οἰκτίρω in the Attic inscrr. see Meisterhans Gr. p. 170.

The adverb οἰκτρῶς occurs in the interesting school exercise, P Fay 19³ (ii/A.D.), purporting to be the copy of a letter addressed by the Emperor Hadrian to Antoninus regarding his approaching death which, he declares, was neither untimely nor unreasonable nor lamentable nor unexpected—ο]ὔτε ἀώ[ρε]ι οὔ[τ]ε ἀλόγως οὔτε οἰκτρῶς οὔτε ἀπ[ροσ]δοκήτω[ς. For the adj. see Kaibel 50—

σ]ῆς δ' ἀρετῆς καὶ σωφροσύνης μνημεῖον ἅπασιν
λείπ]εις οἰ[κτ]ρὰ παθὼν μοίρας ὕπ[ο] δαίμονος ἐχθροῦ.

οἰκτιρμός.

Preisigke 3923 (graffito) Μέρκη οἰκτειρμῶν. (There is no need for Preisigke's proposed emendation—Μερόη οἰκτείρων (?).)

οἶμαι. οἴομαι.

For this verb construed with the acc. and inf., as in Jn 21²⁵, cf. P Eleph 13⁶ (B.C. 223-2) οὐκ οἶμαι [δ'] αὐτὸν ἔχειν ἐξ ὧν ἡ μήτηρ αὐτοῦ ἀνήγγελλεν, P Petr III. 51⁵ (Ptol.) τὸ ἀργύριον ὃ ᾤοντο ἀπολωλέναι ἐν τῶι μαρσιππίωι, "the money which they thought had been lost in the purse" (Edd.), and P Oxy XIV. 1666² (iii/A.D.) οἴομαι τὸν ἀδελφὸν Σαραπάμμωνα μεταδεδωκέναι ὑμεῖν δι' ἣν αἰτίαν κατῆλθον εἰς Ἀλεξάνδρειαν, "I think that my brother Sarapammon has told you the reason why I went down to Alexandria" (Edd.). It is construed with the inf. alone, as in Phil 1¹⁷, in P Eleph 12¹ (B.C. 223-2) καθάπερ ᾤου δεῖν, P Flor III. 332⁸ (ii/A.D.) οἰόμενος δύνασθαι τυχεῖν ἀδίκως πραγμάτων, and P Oxy VI. 898²⁴ (A.D. 123) οἰομένη ἐκ τούτου δύνασθαι ἐκφυγεῖν ἃ διέπραξεν, "thinking by this means to escape the consequences of her misdeeds" (Edd.). In these passages the underlying idea of the verb seems to be "purpose," as frequently in later Greek: see Kennedy *EGT ad* Phil *l.c.*, and cf. Schmid *Attic.* i. p. 128, Schweighauser *Lex. Polyb. s.v.* Οἴομαι occurs in connexion with dreams in P Leid C⁴ (B.C. 163-2) (= I. p. 118) ᾤετο ἐν τῷ ὕπνῳ καταβαίνον, and P Par 50¹⁵ (B.C. 160) ᾤετο ἄνθρωπον λέγειν μοι· φέρε τὸ δέρμα τοῦ ποδός σου καὶ ἐγὼ δώσω σοι τὸ δέρμα τοῦ ποδός μου, also *ib.*¹⁷ ᾤμην οἰκίαν καθαίρεσθαι, καλλύνοντος αὐτήν. The root is *ὀϝισ–ιο–: cf. Lat. *omen,* old Lat. *osmen* (*ovis–men*) (Boisacq. p. 692).

οἰνοπότης.

This compound subst. (Mt 11¹⁹, Lk 7³⁴) is found in the dream of Nectonabus, P Leid Uiv.²¹ (ii/B.C.) (= I. p. 125), as edited by Wilcken *Mél. Nicole* p. 584, καὶ ἔδοξεν αὐτῷ φύσι ὄντι οἰνοπότῃ ῥαθυμῆσαι πρὶν ἢ ἅψασθαι τοῦ ἔργου, "and it seemed good to him (i.e. Petesius), since by nature he was a wine-drinker, to take a holiday before he began work." Other compounds are οἰνολογία (*Ostr* 711³–Ptol.), οἰνοποιέω (P Rev Lᵪᵪᵛⁱ ¹ – B.C. 258), οἰνοπώλης (P Fay 63⁸– A.D. 240), and οἰνοφόρος (P Lond 402²² (= II. p. 12) –B.C. 152 or 141).

οἶνος.

It is hardly necessary to illustrate this common word, but we may note οἶνος καινός in *Ostr* 1142 (beginning of iii/A.D.) as the antithesis to οἶνος παλαιός in *ib.* 1129, not νέος as in [Lk] 5³⁹. See also P Lond 111¹⁸¹ cited *s.v.* ὁδοιπορέω. For the dim. οἰνάριον cf. P Eleph 13⁵ (B.C. 223-2) (= Witkowski², p. 43) περὶ δὲ τοῦ οἰναρίου Πραξιάδης οὔπω εἰσελήλυθεν ἐξ ἀγροῦ, P Oxy XIV. 1672⁵ (A.D. 37-41) πολλὰ λέα οἰνάρια, "a quantity of quite thin wine," and P Grenf II. 77³⁶ (iii/iv A.D.) (= *Selections,* p. 122), where provision is made that the man who is conveying a dead body for burial shall be entertained—ἐν ψωμίοις καὶ [οἰ]ναρίῳ καὶ ἐλαίῳ, "with delicacies and thin wine and olive-oil." Οἰνηγία, "conveyance of wine," is found in P Oxy XIV. 1651³ (iii/A.D.), and the corresponding adj. οἰνηγός (not in LS) in PSI VI. 568² (B.C. 253-2): cf. οἰνικός in *ib.* 715¹¹ (A.D. 92), with the editor's note.

οἰνοφλυγία.

This NT ἅπ. εἰρ. = "wine-bibbing" (1 Pet 4³) is found in Musonius p. 14¹⁵ καὶ λιχνείαι καὶ οἰνοφλυγίαι καὶ ἄλλα παραπλήσια κακά, Philo *de Vita Mosis,* ed. Mangey II. p. 163¹⁷, οἰνοφλυγίαι καὶ ὀψοφαγίαι καὶ λαγνείαι καὶ ἄλλαι ἀπλήρωτοι ἐπιθυμίαι. Other exx. in Wetstein. For the verb see Deut 21²⁰.

οἷος.

For οἷος without τοιοῦτος in the sense of "such as," "of what kind," as in Mt 24²¹ *al.,* cf. P Oxy II. 278¹⁸ (A.D. 17) ἀπ[οκα]ταστησάτω ὁ μάνης τὸν μύλον ὑγιῆι καὶ ἀσινῆι, οἷον καὶ παρείληφεν, "the servant shall restore the mill safe and uninjured in the condition in which he received it" (Edd.). P Ryl II. 154²⁸ (A.D. 66) τὰ παράφερνα οἷα ἐὰν ἐκ τῆς τρίψεως ἐγβῇ, "the *parapherna* as they emerge from wear and tear" (Edd.). For οἷος used as a relative (cf. *Proleg.* p. 93), cf. P Lond 982⁵ (iv/A.D.) (= III. p. 242) ἀφ' οἵας γὰρ ἡμέρας ἀνήλ[θομεν] ἀπὸ τῆς δοκιμασίας Ἀννιανοῦ, and see also the late P Lond IV. 1343²⁰ (A.D. 709) ὅπως μὴ εὕρωμεν κατ' αὐτῶν ἀφορμὴν τὴν οἵαν οὖν, "in order that we may not find any ground of complaint whatever against them." In P Ryl II. 77²³,²⁵ (A.D. 192) we have the phrases οἷόν τ' ἐστίν (cf. 4 Macc 4⁷) and οὐκ οἷόν τ' ἐστίν, unfortunately both in broken contexts, but see P Tebt II. 411⁷ (ii/A.D.) οἷός τε ἦν καὶ προγράψαι εἰ μὴ ἐπηγγειλάμην σήμερόν σε παρέσασθαι, "he (the epistrategus) might even have proscribed you, had I not promised that you would be present to-day" (Edd.). According to Lob. *Phryn.* p. 372 οὐχ οἷον δὲ ὅτι (Rom 9⁶) is to be understood as a strong negative equivalent to οὐ δήπου, "not of course that," cf. Field *Notes,* p. 158. For οἷος used in an indirect question, as in 1 Thess 1⁶, cf. Epict. iv. 6. 4 καὶ ἡ προσποίησις ὅρα δι' οἵων ἂν γένοιτο, "and consider by what means you would achieve your pretence" (Matheson). Οἷος survives in MGr in ὅ(γ)οιος, which is current in dialects : see Jannaris *Gr.* § 615, Thumb *Handbook,* p. 94.

οἱοσδηποτοῦν.

For this compound, which is read by Lachmann in [Jn] 5⁴ οἱῳδηποτοῦν νοσήματι, we may compare BGU III. 895²⁵ (perhaps from Syria (*Archiv* i. p. 557)—ii/A.D.) οἵῳ δήποτε οὖν τρόπῳ, P Grenf II. 76¹⁵ (A.D. 305-306) ἄλλῳ οἱῳδήποτε τ[ρόπῳ, *ib.* 90¹⁶ (vi/A.D.) οἱασδήποτε εὑρεσιλογίας, and P Oxy VI. 893⁶ (vi/vii A.D.), cited *s.v.* ὅλος.

ὀκνέω.

This verb, followed by an inf. as in Ac 9³⁸, is found in a weakened sense, as an epistolary formula, e.g. P Eleph 13⁷ (B.C. 223-2) (= Witkowski², p. 43) εὐχαριστήσεις οὖμ μοι σαυτοῦ τε ἐπιμελόμενος καὶ μὴ ὀκνῶν γράφειν ἡμῖν, PSI VI. 621⁶ (iii/B.C.) σὺ δὲ καλῶς ποιήσεις μὴ ὀκνῶν γράφειν πρὸς ἡμᾶς· πᾶν γὰρ τὸ δυνατὸν καὶ προθύμως καὶ ἀόκνως ποιήσομεν, P Oxy VI. 930¹ (ii/iii A.D.) μὴ ὄκνι μοι [γ]ράφιν, and *ib.* XIV. 1769⁷ (iii/A.D.) μὴ ὀκνήσις οὖν προσελθὶν αὐτῷ περὶ οὗ ἐὰν χρῄζῃς. See also Field *Notes,* p. 118, and Proclus *de forma epistolari* in Hercher *Epist. Gr.* p. 8ε ὀκνῶ γὰρ εἰπεῖν εἰς μοχθηρίαν. A stronger sense is seen in P Giss I. 79⁴·⁶ (c. A.D. 117) εἰ δυνατόν μ[οι] ἦν διατρ[έ]-

χ[ει]ν πρὸς τὴν οἰκονομίαν τῶν ἡμετέρων, οὐκ ἂν ὤ[κ]νήκειν, and P Oxy XIV. 1775⁸ (iv/A.D.) οὐκ ὤκνησα οὔτε πάλιν ἠμέλησα. A good ex. of the thought of Eph 5¹² is afforded by Menander *Fragm.* p. 186, No. 619—

> χαλεπόν γε τοιαῦτ᾿ ἐστὶν ἐξαμαρτάνειν,
> ἃ καὶ λέγειν ὀκνοῦμεν οἱ πεπραχότες.

ὀκνηρός.

With the use of this adj. in Phil 3¹ we may compare the adverb ἀνόκνως (for Attic ἀόκνως) in P Oxy IV. 743³⁹ (B.C. 2) (= Witkowski², p. 130) καὶ σὺ δὲ ὑπὲρ ὧν ἐὰν θέλῃς γράφε μοι καὶ ἀνόκνως ποήσω, "write to me yourself about anything you want, and I will do it without hesitation" (Edd.), and PSI VI.621⁸ (cited *s.v.* ὀκνέω). Ὀκνηρῶς is found in Menander *Perikeir.* 127 ὡς ὀκνηρῶς μοι προσέρχε[ι], Δᾶε.

ὀκταίμερος,

"eight days old" (Phil 3⁵). On the form of the word see Moulton *Gr.* ii. p. 170.

ὀκτώ.

P Lille I. 17⁵ (iii/B.C.) περὶ σιταρ[ί]ου ὀκτὼ ἀρταβῶν, P Grenf II. 38⁹ (B.C. 81) μ[έ]λαν στατηροῦ ὀκτώ. For the form ὀκτώι cf. P Amh II. 59⁵ (B.C. 151 or 140) ἑξήκοντα ὀκτώι, PSI V. 470⁴ (A.D. 102–103) ἀρτάβας ὀκτώι, and see Mayser *Gr.* p. 136. MGr ὀχτώ shows the regular change : cf. χτίζω, δίχτυ, etc. The combination κτ, like πτ, does not occur in MGr vernacular.

ὄλεθρος.

For a somewhat weakened use of this strong word, which in Biblical usage implies "ruin," the loss of all that gives worth to existence (see Milligan *ad* 1 Thess 5⁹), cf. BGU IV. 1027ˣˣᵛⁱ.¹¹ (iv/A.D.) (as amended *Chrest.* I. p. 501) ἐν ὁποίῳ κιντύνῳ καθεστήκατε, οἵον ὀλέθρου πιρασ[θ]ήσεσθαι οὐκ αὐτοὶ μόνοι, ἀλλὰ καὶ ὁ[λ]όκληρον ὑμῶν τὸ βουλευτήριον—a representation of the great danger that was being incurred at Hermopolis by the withholding of their *annona* from the soldiers for three years. Like Lat. *pernicies* (Ter. *Ad.* 188), ὄλεθρος is used as a comic hyperbole applied to a person ("pest"). For a new ex. see Menander *Samia* 133 χαμαιτύπη δ᾽ ἄνθρωπος, ὄλεθρος. The ordinary force of ὄλεθρος is seen in *Syll* 463 (= ³527)⁸² (c. B.C. 220) κακίστῳ ὀλέθρῳ ἐξόλλυσθαι. For exx. of the adj. ὀλέθριος, which is read by Lachmann in 2 Thess 1⁹, see Crönert *Mem. Herc.* p. 186.

ὀλιγόπιστος

is not found in profane authors, and in Bibl. Greek is confined to four occurrences in Mt: cf. *Act. Thom.* 28.

ὀλίγος.

The following are exx. of the varied uses of this common adj. with reference to (1) *time*, as in Ac 14²⁸, P Petr II. 40(a)¹⁴ (iii/B.C.) (= Witkowski², p. 41) ἀνδρίζεσθε, ὀλίγος γὰρ χρόνος ὑμῖν ἐστιν, P Fay 123¹⁹ (c. A.D. 100) ἡμέρας ὀλίγας, (2) *number*, as in Mt 9³⁷, P Ryl II. 130¹¹ (A.D. 31) οὐκ ὀλίγην ἐλᾶν, "a quantity of olives," and (3) *degree*, as in

Ac 12¹⁸, P Ryl II. 148²² (A.D. 40) ὥστε μοι οὐκ ὀλίγου βλάβους ἐπηκλουθηκότος (= ἐπηκολουθηκότος), "whereby I have suffered no slight damage" (Edd.), P Oxy XIV. 1668¹⁷ (iii/A.D.) ἡ τειμὴ τοῦ σείτου ὀλίγη ἐστίν. For the neut. sing. ὀλίγον, as in Mk 1¹⁹, cf. P Oxy I. 39⁶ (A.D. 52) ὀλίγον βλέπων, "short-sighted," and see *Kaibel* 340¹ (i/A.D.) σπεῖσον ἐμοὶ δακρύων ὀλίγον, 502¹⁶ (iii/iv A.D.) ἐγενήθην εἰς ὀλίγον ἐτῶν ἐναρίθμιος. The phrase δι᾽ ὀλίγων, "briefly," as in 1 Pet 5¹², is well illustrated by P Par 26⁹ (B.C. 163–162) (= *Selections*, p. 14) δι᾽ ὀλίων (for form, see below) τὴν τῶν ἀδικούντων ἡμᾶς φιλαυτίαν ἐχθεῖναι, "in a few words to set before you the selfishness of those who are injuring us." Other phrases are ἀπ᾽ ὀλίγων, as in P Meyer 1¹⁵ (B.C. 144) δεόμεθα ὑμῶν τῶν μεγίστων θεῶν, μὴ ὑπεριδεῖν ἡμᾶς ἀπ᾽ ὀλίγων [διαζῶντας], "bitten wir euch, Ihr grossen Götter, uns, die von geringem unser Leben fristen, nicht zu übersehen" (Ed.) : μετ᾽ ὀλίγον, "after a little," as in P Ryl II. 77⁴¹ (A.D. 192), 234⁵ (ii A.D.), and πρὸς ὀλίγον, "for a little," as in P Oxy I. 67¹¹ (A.D. 338) πρὸς ὀλίγον εἰσχύει, "withstands but for a short time" (Edd.), cf. 1 Tim 4⁸, Jas 4¹¹ (in the latter passage the meaning may be "to a slight degree," Vg *ad modicum*). Thackeray (*Gr.* i. p. 112) has shown that the form ὀλίος, due to the omission of the γ in writing, began about B.C. 300, and spread over a wide area in the Greek-speaking world ; cf. from the papyri P Petr II. 19(2)⁷ (iii/B.C.) χρόνον οὐκ ὀλίον : other exx. in Mayser *Gr.* p. 163 f. The aspirated ὁλίγος does not occur till later, but is not infrequent in papyri of ii iii A.D., e.g. BGU I. 146¹⁰ (ii/iii A.D.) οὐχ [ὁ]λ[ί]γην ζη[μ]είαν μοι ἐξημιωσάμην, *ib.* II. 388¹¹ (ii/A.D.) μεθ᾽ ὁλίγον. According to Moulton (*Gr.* ii. p. 98) "οὐκ ὀλίγος appears 6 8 times in Ac (𝔑⁴. A³. B¹. D¹) as in LXX twice" ; see also Thackeray *Gr.* i. p. 126 f. MGr λίγος as well as ὀλίγος. With ἐν ὀλίγῳ, Ac 26²⁸, cf. MGr σὲ λίγο (καιρό) and μὲ ὀλίγα, "soon," "in a short time." For the derivation from λοιγός, "pestilence," see Boisacq, p. 586.

ὀλιγόψυχος,

"faint-hearted" (1 Thess 5¹⁴). For the corresponding verb cf. P Petr II. 40(a)¹² cited *s.v.* ἀνδρίζομαι, and add P Oxy X. 1294¹³ (ii/iii A.D.) μὴ ὀλιγοψύχει δὲ [π]ερὶ τοῦ ἐνοικίου, εἰσάπαξ γὰρ αὐτὸ λήμψῃ, "do not lose heart about the rent, for you will get it once for all" (Edd.), and the new astragalos inscr. from Pamphylia in *JHS* xxxii. (1912) p. 273 μ]ηδ᾽ [ὀ]λιγοψύχ[ει . . .

ὀλιγωρέω.

For this verb = "make light of," as in Heb 12⁵ (from Prov 3¹¹), cf. PSI VI. 502³⁰ (B.C. 257–6) καλῶς ἂν οὖν ποιήσαις μηδεμίαν ἡμῶν καταγινώσκων ὀλιγωρίαν· οὐ γὰρ ἔστιν σοι ὑπηρετοῦντα ὀλιγωρεῖν. P Tebt I. 27⁴³ (B.C. 113) (= *Chrest.* I. p. 389) διαλαβὼν μηδεμιᾶς τεύξεσθαι συγγνώμης ὀλιγωρηθέντος τινός, "believing that you will receive no pardon for any neglect" (Edd.), BGU IV. 1065⁵ (A.D. 57) μὴ οὖν ὀλιγωρ[ήσῃς] περὶ μηδενός, *ib.* 1007¹⁵ (time of Claudius or Nero) οὐ⁰ (= οὐχ) ὀλιγωρῶ, ἀλλὰ εὐψυχοῦσα πα[ρα]μένω, P Oxy VII. 1065⁶ (iii/A.D.) (= *Chrest.* I. p. 149) ἐὰν δὲ ὀλιγωρήσῃς, ὥσπερ [ο]ἱ θεοὶ οὐκ ἐφίσαντο μ[ο]υ, οὕτως κἀγὼ θεῶ[ν] οὐ φί[σ]ομαι, "if you neglect this, as the gods have not spared me so will

I not spare the gods" (Ed.), P Lips I. 110¹³ (iii/iv A.D.) ὀλιγωρῶ τὰ περὶ σου μὴ κομισάμενός σου γράμματα, and from the inscr. *Syll* 652 (= ³885)²⁴ (*c.* A.D. 220) ὅπως μηδέποτε τοῦτο ἐκλε[ιφθείη μη]δὲ ὀλιγωρηθείη ποτὲ τὰ τῆς εὐσεβείας [τῆς πρὸς τὼ θε]ῶ. See also P Sa'îd Khan I²⁵ (B.C. 88) (= *JHS* xxxv. (1915) p. 28) ἐὰν [δὲ κ]αὶ ὁ Γαθάκης ὀλιγωρήσῃ τὴν [ἄμπε]λον καὶ μὴ ποιήσῃ αὐτὴ[ν] ἔπαφον, ἀποτεινvέτω τὸ α[ὐτὸ ἐπί]τειμον, "but if Gathaces too neglect the vineyard and fail to keep it in good order, let him pay the same fine." For the adv. see P Magd 6¹⁰ (B.C. 221) Ἡρόδ]οτος δέ, ὀλιώρως (for form cf. Mayser *Gr.* p. 163, Meisterhans *Gr.* p. 75) χρησάμενος, παρείλκυσέ με ἕως τοῦ νῦν, "mais Hérodotos, me traitant avec mépris, m'a traîné en longueur jusqu'aujourd'hui" (Ed.). Coming from ὥρα, "care," the word is the opposite of πολυωρέω.

ὀλίγος.

According to Radermacher (*Gr.* p. 54) the extension of forms in –ως belongs essentially to the written language. In this connexion we may notice the appearance of the new adv. ὀλίγως in 2 Pet 2¹⁸ AB (Vg *paululum*) "as characteristic of the writer's bookish style—Aquila and the Anthology appear to be its only supporters" (Moulton *Gr.* ii. p. 163).

ὀλοθρευτής.

For the assimilation of ε to ο in this NT ἅπ. εἰρ. (1 Cor 10¹⁰), cf. Moulton *Gr.* ii. p. 71, and for the same tendency at work in MGr see Dieterich *Untersuchungen*, p. 274 f.

ὀλοθρεύω.

For the form, see Moulton *Gr.* ii. p. 71, Reinhold p. 40. MGr ξολοθρεύω.

ὁλοκαύτωμα.

With the use of ὁλοκαύτωμα to denote a victim the whole of which is burned (Mk 12³³, Heb 10⁶·⁸) cf. *Ostr* 1305⁵ (A.D. 4) ὁλοπυρεῖται ἄρτοι, apparently with reference to loaves of unground wheat, or wheat boiled whole, and the corresponding compound ὁλοκάρπωμα (see Deissmann *BS* p. 138). Phrynichus mentions in his Appendix p. 51 (see Lob. *Phryn.* p. 524) the verbs μηροκαυτέω, ἱεροκαυτέω, ὁλοκαυτέω, also (p. 568) the form ὁλοκαυτίζω.

ὁλοκληρία.

In the NT this word is found only in Ac 3¹⁶, where it is rendered in the Vg *integra sanitas*: cf. P Oxy I. 125⁶ (iii/iv A.D.) πάνυ θαυμάζω, υἱέ μου, μέχρις σήμερον γράμματά σου οὐκ ἔλαβον τὰ δηλοῦντά μοι τὰ περὶ τῆς ὁλοκληρίας ὑμῶν, "I have been much surprised, my son, at not receiving hitherto a letter from you to tell me how you are" (Edd.), *ib.* XII. 1478³ (Gnostic charm for victory —iii/iv. A.D.) δὸς νείκην ὁλοκληρίαν σαδίου (*l.* σταδίου) καὶ ὄχλου τῷ προκειμένῳ Σαραπάμμωνι, "grant victory and safety in the racecourse and the crowd to the aforesaid Sarapammon" (Edd.), *ib.* X. 1298⁵ (iv/A.D.) πρὸ παντὸς εὔχομε, = μαι) τῷ κυρίῳ θεῷ περὶ τῆς ὁλοκληρίας σου καὶ τῶν φιλτάτων σου, "before all else I pray to the Lord God for the prosperity of yourself and those dearest to you" (Edd.), and BGU III. 948⁴ (iv/v A.D.) πρὸ μὲν πάντων εὔχομε (= μαι) τὸν παντοκράτοραν θεὸν τὰ πε[ρὶ τ]ῆς ὑγίας σου

καὶ ὁλοκληρίας σου χαίριν. See also the votive inscr. *Syll* 775 (= ³1142)² (i/ii A.D.) Μελτίνη [ὑ]πὲρ τῆς ὁλοκληρίας [τῶν] ποδῶν εὐχὴν [ἀνέσ]τησεν. The corresponding verb (not in LS) is fairly common in such formulae as the following—P Lips I. 110⁷ (iii/iv A.D.) εὐχόμενος ὅπως ὁλοκληροῦσάν σε καὶ ὑγιαίνουσαν ἀπολάβω, P Oxy X. 1299³ (iv/A.D.) πρὸ μὲν πάντων εὔχομαί σοι ὑγιένειν (*l.* σε ὑγιαίνειν) καὶ ὁλοκληρεῖν παρὰ τῷ κυρίῳ θεῷ, and P Lond 1244⁷ (iv/A.D.) (= III. p. 244) παρακαλῶν τὸν θεὸν ἵνα σαι ἀπολάβω εὐθυμοῦντα καὶ εὐπυγμοῦντα καὶ ὁλοκληροῦντα.

ὁλόκληρος

is common of material or physical soundness and completeness, e.g. P Lond 935⁷ (A.D. 216 or 217) (= III. p. 30) ὁλοκλήρου οἰκίας, P Oxy I. 57¹³ (iii/A.D.) ὑπὲρ τοῦ ὁλόκληρον (ποιῆσαι) τὴν ἐπίσκεψιν τῶν χωμάτων καὶ διωρύχων, "towards the completion of the survey of the dykes and canals" (Edd.), *ib.* XIV. 1772³ (late iii/A.D.) μεθ᾽ ὧν εὔχομαί σε ὁλόκληρον ἀπολαβεῖν, and from the inscr. *OGIS* 519¹⁴ (*c.* A.D. 245) χωρίον ὑμέτερόν ἐσμεν ἱερώτατ[ον καὶ ὥσπερεὶ δῆ]μος ὁλόκληρος. An interesting parallel to 1 Thess 5²³ is afforded by the magic P Lond 121⁵⁹⁰ (iii/A.D.) (= I. p. 103) διαφύλασσέ μου τὸ σῶμα τὴν ψυχὴν ὁλόκληρον: cf. Epict. iv. i. 151 ἔτι τιμῶ τὸ σωμάτιον, ὁλόκληρον αὐτὸ ἔχειν ἀντὶ πολλοῦ ποιοῦμαι, "I still pay regard to my body, I set a great value on keeping it whole" (cited by Sharp, p. 54). The Biblical use is discussed by Milligan, *Thess.* p. 78. MGr ὁλάκερος has lost the second λ through dissimilation (Thumb, *Handbook*, p. 23).

ὀλολύζω.

This NT ἅπ. εἰρ. (Jas 5¹) occurs in the curious spell for transforming a goddess into the appearance of an old woman, P Lond 125 *verso*³⁰ (v/A.D.) (= I. p. 124) ὀλολύξασ᾽ ἡ γραῦς φεύξεται ὅπως μὴ εὐκόλως αὐτὴν ἀπολύσῃς. For the subst. see P Leid W^{xxi 30} (ii/iii A.D.) (= II. p. 155) ἔσω προσβαλόμενος μύκησαι ὀλολυγμός (*l.* -μόν), P Lond 121³²³ (iii/A.D.) (= I. p. 94) μὴ φωνὴ μὴ ὀλολυγμὸς μὴ σιυριγμός (*l.* συριγμός), and ⁷⁶⁹(p. 109). For the adj. ὀλολυγαῖος see *Kaibel* 546⁶ (Imperial) ὀλολυγαία νυκτερίς, "a howling bat," and for ὀλολύκτρια (not in LS) applied to a woman "crying aloud" at a sacrifice see *Syll* 566 (= ³982)²⁵ (ii/B.C.). The words are onomatopoetic: cf. ὑλακτέω, Lat. *ululare*.

ὅλος.

P Grenf II. 77³⁰ (iii/iv A.D.) (= *Selections*, p. 121) τῆς ὅλης δα[πά]νης, "the whole outlay," P Oxy VI. 903⁴ (iv/A.D.) ἐπὶ ὅλας ἕ[πτ]ὰ ἡμέρας, "for seven whole days," and *Priene* 112⁹⁵ (after B.C. 84) διὰ τοῦ χειμῶνος ὅλου, "during the whole winter" (cf. Lk 5⁵). See also P Thead 3³¹ (A.D. 299), where, at the end of a deed of sale, the vendor announces—ἔγραψα τὰ ὅλα. With the use of ὅλος in Jn 9³⁴, 13¹⁰, we may compare P Fay 119⁶ (*c.* A.D. 100) χόρτον σαπρὸν καὶ ὥλον (*l.* ὅλον) λελυμένον, "rotten hay, the whole of it decayed" (Edd.). Other exx. are P Tebt I. 33¹⁶ (B.C. 112) (= *Selections*, p. 31), where the instructions for the entertainment of a Roman visitor are summed up in the words—τὸ δ᾽ ὅλον ἐπὶ πάν[των] τὴν μεγίστην φροντίδα ποιουμένου τοῦ εὐδοκοῦν[τ]α τὸν ἄνδρα κατασταθῆ[ναι, "in general take the greatest pains in everything that the visitor may be satisfied" (Edd.), P Ryl II. 133[19] (A.D. 33) ἐξ οὗ κινδυνεύει τῷ ὅλωι ἐξαρθῆναι, "whereby there is a risk of its (viz. a dam's) being entirely carried away" (Edd.), and *ib.* 152[14] (A.D. 42) τοῖς ὅλοις ἠφάνισαν, "utterly destroyed it," of damage done by an inroad of sheep. In P Oxy VI. 936[20] (iii/A.D.) οὐδὲ Φιλόξενον ὅλ' ἐξ ὅλων οὐχ εὗρον, the editors render, "I have entirely failed to find Philoxenus," and compare *ib.* 893[6] (vi/vii A.D.) οὐδέν[α] λόγον ὑπὲρ οἱασδήποτε ὅλον τὸ σύνολον πράγματος, "no ground of complaint on any matter of any kind whatsoever." For the interchange of ὅλος and πᾶς cf. P Tebt II. 418[4] (iii/A.D.) πρὸ τῶν ὅλων τὸ προσκύνημά σου ποιῶ, for the usual πρὸ πάντων, P Lond 404[15] (c. A.D. 346) (= II. p. 305) ἀσπάζομαι . . . πάντας τοὺς ἐν τῇ οἰκίᾳ ὅλους κατ' ὄνομα, and P Iand 13[20] (iv/A.D.) πάντες οἱ ἀδελφοί σου κατ' ὄνομα ὅλ[οι . . . For δι' ὅλου, as in Jn 19[23], see P Oxy I. 53[10] (A.D. 316) where a persea tree is reported on as διόλου ξηραντίσαν, "quite dried up." Διόλου is found in Cercidas (iii/B.C.), and survives in MGr. In MGr ὅλος in many districts takes the form οὖλος (Thumb *Handbook*, p. 97), which is similar to the Ionic and Epic form οὖλος, from *ὁλϜο-ς : cf. Lat. *salvus, sollus* (Boisacq, p. 699).

We may add that the compound ὁλοσχερής is fully illustrated in Linde *Epic.* p. 13 f.: for the adv. see Cicero *ad Att.* vi. 5. 2.

ὁλοτελής.

For this adj. = "perfect," "complete," which in the NT is confined to 1 Thess 5[23] (but cf. Arist. *Plant.* i. 2. 20, Plut. ii. 909 B), we can now cite the decree of Epaminondas attached to Nero's pompous declaration of the freedom of all Greeks at the Isthmian games of A.D. 67, *Syll* 376 (= [3] 814)[15] ἀνεισφορίαν, ἣν οὐδεὶς τῶν πρότερον Σεβαστῶν ὁλοτελῆ ἔδωκεν, where the adj. has the same adverbial force as in 1 Thess *l.c.* For the adv. ὁλοτελῶς, by which Suidas defines the common ὁλοσχερῶς, cf. Aq. Deut 13[16][17].

Ὀλυμπᾶς.

Rouffiac (*Recherches*, p. 91) has shown that this abbreviated common name (Rom 16[15]) is by no means specially characteristic of Rome, but is common throughout the Empire, e.g. *IG* III. 1080[25] (Athens), *CIL* XIV. 1286 (Ostia), *ib.* III. 4959 (Olympia) : cf. Milligan *Documents*, p. 183.

ὅλως.

For ὅλως = "entirely," "altogether," cf. P Oxy IV. 743[22] (B.C. 2) καὶ γὰρ ἐγὼ ὅλος (*l.* ὅλως) διαπον[ο]ῦμαι εἴ Ἑλενος χαλκοὺς ἀπόλε[σ]εν. "I am quite upset at Helenos' loss of the money" (Edd.), and for the meaning "at all" with a neg. verb, as in Mt 5[34], cf. the letter of a wife to her husband, BGU IV. 1079[6] (time of Claudius or Nero) περὶ δὲ Σαραπᾶτος τοῦ υἱοῦ οὐ καταλέλυκε παρ' ἐμὲ ὅλως, ἀλλὰ ἀπῆλθεν εἰς παρεμβολὴν στρατεύσασθαι, "but as regards our son Sarapas, he has not lodged with me at all, but has departed to the camp on military duty." The meaning of the adv. in 1 Cor 5[1] has caused difficulty, but a certain support is lent to the local sense "everywhere," which Weiss in Meyer[9] *ad l.* prefers (cf. Bachmann in Zahn's *Kommentar*),

by P Oxy IV. 744[1] (B.C. 1) (= *Selections*, p. 32) μὴ ἀγωνιᾷς ἐὰν ὅλως εἰσπορεύονται, ἐγὼ ἐν Ἀλεξανδρε . ᾳ μένω, where ὅλως may perhaps imply all the writer's fellow-workmen. For the meaning "actually," adopted by the Revisers in 1 Cor *l.c.* we may cite *ib.* XIV. 1676[31] (iii/A.D.) καλῶς οὖν ποιήσεις ἐλ[θοῦσ]α τῷ Μεσορὴ πρὸς [ἡμᾶ]ς ἵνα ὅλως ἴδωμέν σε, "you will therefore do well to come to us in Mesore, in order that we may really see you" (Edd.).

ὄμβρος.

This word, which in Lk 12[54] is used of a "rain-storm," appears frequently in our sources as a kind of *term. techn.* in connexion with land which has become waterlogged, e.g. P Tebt I. 61(*b*)[132] (B.C. 118-7) (ἐμβρόχος) διὰ τὸ[ν ὄ]μβρον τῶν παρακειμένων ὑδάτων. See also *Syll* 804 (= [3] 1170)[7] (ii/A.D.). For the adj. ὄμβριμος cf. P Lond 121[221] (iii A.D.) (= I. p. 91) ὕδωρ ὀμβρίμον. Cognate with Lat. *imber*, ὄμβρος retains the nasal which ἀφρός has lost (Boisacq, p. 106).

ὀμείρομαι.

A good example of this rare verb = "long for" (Hesych. ἐπιθυμέω) in 1 Thess 2[8] (cf. Job 3[21] A, Sm. Ps 62(63)[2]) is supplied by the true reading of the Lycaonian sepulchral inscr. *CIG* III. 4000[7] (iv/A.D.), where the sorrowing parents are described as = ὀμειρόμενο[ι] περὶ παιδός, "greatly desiring their son" : see Ramsay in *JHS* xxxviii. (1918), p. 152 ff., as against Boeckh-Franz (in *CIG* and *Kaibel* 406, who unwarrantably change ὀμειρόμενο[ι] to ὀ[δυ]ρόμενοι. The illustration of 1 Thess *l.c.* is peculiarly apt if, with Wohlenberg (in Zahn's *Kommentar ad l.*), we regard ὀμείρομαι there as a term of endearment ("ein edles Kosewort"), borrowed from the language of the nursery. It may be added that WH (*Notes*[2], p. 151) prefer the smooth breathing ὀμειρόμενοι, and that J. H. Moulton finds the root of the verb in *smer*, "remember," as in *memor*, and regards the ὀ- as coming from a derelict preposition ὡ (seen in ὠ-κεανός participle of ὥ-κειμαι, "circumambient") : cf. such parallel formations as δύρομαι and ὀδύρομαι, κέλλω and ὀκέλλω.

ὁμιλέω.

The classical and late Greek meaning of ὁμιλέω, "converse with," which is found in Ac 20[11], 24[26], Dan 1[19], may be illustrated from the vernacular P Oxy VI. 928[5] (ii/iii A.D.) ὠμείλησας δέ μοί ποτε περὶ τούτου, "you once had a conversation with me on this subject" (Edd.). Cf. also the *Pelagia-Legenden* p. 7[10] προτρεψάμενος αὐτὸν ὁμιλῆσαι τῷ λαῷ, and the use in MGr 'δὲν μοῦ 'μιλᾶς; "why dost thou not speak to me?" (Abbott *Songs*, p. 108[6]. The verb is used in the wider sense of "associate with" in PSI II. 120[87] (a collection of apophthegms—iv/A.D.?) πένης ὢν πλουσίοις μὴ ὁμίλει (cf. Hobart, p. 178 f.), and of "busy oneself with" in *OGIS* 282[16] (before B.C. 206) θεωρῶν δὲ] τὸν δῆμον . . . . ὁμιλοῦντα ἐμ Μούσ(αις)[ς δει]νῶς, *ib.* 505[7] (A.D. 156) παιδείᾳ τε ὁμιλῶν, "holding converse with" (metaphorically). Ἡ ὁμιλουμένη is used of vernacular Greek. The word is a reduced form of *ὁμο-μιλέω by haplology. The original meaning is "assemble together": cf. Lat. *milites*, meaning "those who march in a body" (Boisacq, p. 700). MGr μιλῶ, "speak."

ὁμιλία

occurs in the NT only in Paul's citation (1 Cor 15³³) from Menander's *Thais* (*Fragm.* p. 62, No. 218): φθείρουσιν ἤθη χρηστὰ ὁμιλίαι κακαί: cf. Euripides *Fragm.* 1013 (Nauck). Ὁμιλία may mean either "conversation" (Vg *colloquia*) or "companionship" (Beza *commercia*), and the latter is obviously the leading idea here: cf. P Oxy III. 471⁷⁶ (ii/A.D.) σύνβολα δεικνύντα τῆς πρὸς τοῦτον ὁμειλίας. "showing signs of his intercourse (*in malam partem*) with him," and Xen. *Mem.* i. 2. 20 ὁμιλία τῶν χρηστῶν. MGr μιλιά, "conversation," "speech," "gossip": μίλημα, "conversation," "proclamation."

ὅμιλος.

A new literary ex. of this word = "crowd," "throng," which is found in the TR of Rev 18¹⁷, may be cited from the recently recovered fragments of the Ἠοῖαι of Hesiod, PSI II. 130⁷ πολὺς δ' ἀμφίσταθ' ὅμιλος: cf. Hom. *Il.* xviii. 603, xxiv. 712.

ὁμίχλη.

For this NT ἅπ. εἰρ. (2 Pet 2¹⁷) = "mist," cf. the magical P Par 574²⁰²³ f (c. A.D. 300) ὁ ἐν μέσῃ ἀρούρῃς καὶ χιόνος καὶ ὁμίχλης. Herwerden *Lex. s.v.* cites the striking saying Plut. *Mor.* p. 460 A ὡς δι' ὁμίχλης τὰ σώματα, καὶ δι' ὀργῆς τὰ πράγματα μείζονα φαίνεται. The adj. ὁμιχλώδης occurs e.g. in Vett. Val. p. 6²⁶ αἱ δὲ ἑξῆς β μοῖραι πυρώδεις, ὁμιχλώδεις.

ὄμμα.

This common poetic word, which in the NT is found only in the plur. (Mt 20³⁴, Mk 8²³), may be illustrated from the address in the Serapeum-dream P Par 51¹⁰ (B.C. 160) (= *Selections*, p. 19) ὄμμα . . ψυχῆς θάρσ[ει, from the personal descriptions P Leid Mⁱ· ⁶ (ii/B.C.) (= I. p. 59) ἀσ[θενῶν] τοῖς ὄμμασι, P Lond 678⁶ (B.C. 99–8) (= III. p. 18) ἀ]δύνατ[ος ὄμμ]ασι, BGU III. 715⁹ (A.D. 41–2) o]ἰλὴ (*l.* οὐλὴ) ὑπὸ ὄμμα ἀριστερά (*l.* -ρόν), and from the magic P Lond 121³²⁵ (iii/A.D.) (= I. p. 95) ὄμμα φοβερόν. It may also be noted that in an address by the council of Hermopolis to the Imperial Procurator of the time of Gallienus, Eurip. *Ion* 732 is quoted in the form—εἰς ὄμματ' εὔνου ἀνδρὸς ἐμβλέπειν γλυκύ (CPHerm I. 125⁷ = *Chrest.* I. p. 59). The MGr ὄμματι is generally contracted into μάτι, and ματιά μου is used as an endearing term of address "light of my eye," "my darling," see Thumb *Handbook* p. 340 and cf. *ocelle*, Catullus L. 19, *ocelle mi*, Plaut. *Trin.* 245 [ii. 1. 18].

ὄμνυμι, ὀμνύω

with the acc. of the person invoked (cf. Jas 5¹²) is common, e.g. P Eleph 23⁹ (B.C. 223–2) ὀμνύω βασιλέα Πτολεμαῖον, P Par 47² (c. B.C. 153) (= *Selections*, p. 22), ὀμνύω τὸν Σαρᾶπιν, and P Oxy II. 230⁵ (A.D. 60) ὀμνύω Νέρωνα Κλαύδιον Καίσαρα. For the rare form ὄμνυμι cf. BGU II. 543² (B.C. 28–7) ὄμνυμι Καίσαρα Αὐτοκράτορα θεοῦ υἱόν: see Mayser *Gr.* p. 351 f., and for the LXX usage Thackeray *Gr.* i. p. 279. The perf. is seen in PSI I. 64²⁴ (i/B.C. ?) ὀμώμοκα τὸν προγεγραμμένον ὅρκον, and the perf. part. in *ib.* V. 513⁹ (B.C. 252–1) γέγραφεν ἡμῖν Τληπόλεμος προστεταχέναι τὸν βασιλέα τοὺς ἐν ἄλλοις τόποις ὀμω-

μοκ[ό]τας διορθώσασθαι. Cf. P Tebt II. 293²³ (c. A.D. 187) ὤμοσα τὸν προκείμενον ὅρκον κ[α]θὼς πρόκειται, and *ib.* ²⁵ συνομόμεχα (*l.* συνομώμοκα) ὡς [π]ρόκειται: also the legal formula ὀμνύω ἑκουσίως καὶ αὐθαιρέτως ἐγγυᾶσθαι in P Iand 30⁶ᶠᶠ (A.D. 105 or 106) (see the editor's note), P Grenf II. 62⁴ ᶠᶠ (A.D. 211) *al.*, and P Magd 25⁷ (B.C. 211) εἰ δέ τι ἀντιλέγει, μὴ ὀφείλειν ὀμόσας μοι, ἀπολελύσθω, "mais s'il conteste sa dette et jure ne me rien devoir, qu'il soit délié" (Edd.: see the note). MGr ὀμώνω.

ὁμοθυμαδόν.

The sense *unanimiter*, and not merely "together" to which Hatch (*Essays*, p. 63 f.) would limit this word in the NT as in the Greek versions of the OT, is supported by P Tebt I. 40⁹ (B.C. 117) (= *Selections*, p. 28) σαφέστερον μετειληφὼς τοὺς ἐκ τῆς κώμης ὁμοθυμαδὸν ἀντέχεσθαι τῆς σῆς σκέπης, "having received certain information that the inhabitants of the village are with one accord claiming your protection" (Edd.), cf. *Syll* 329 (= ³742)¹³ (c. B.C. 85) ὁμοθυμαδὸν πάντων τῶν πολιτῶν ἐπιδεδωκότων ἑαυτοὺς εἰς τοὺ[ς π]ερὶ τούτων ἀγῶνας, and *ib.* 732 (= ³1104)²⁵ (B.C. 37–6) ἡ σύνοδος ἀποδεξαμένη τὴν ἐκτένειαν καὶ φιλοτιμίαν αὐτοῦ ὁμοθυμαδὸν προεβάλετο τοὺς εἰσοίσοντας αὐτοῖς τὰς καθηκούσας τιμὰς Λεύκιον κτλ.: cf. Ac 15²⁵ ἔδοξεν ἡμῖν γενομένοις ὁμοθυμαδόν,—"the decree is not the manifesto of a cabal or faction, but a decree of the entire Church convened together" (Hicks, *CR* i. p. 45). In P Par 63⁹³ (B.C. 164) (= P Petr III. p. 26) Mahaffy renders ὁμοθυμαδόν "without exception." Mayser (*Gr.* p. 459) points out that the use of the acc. neut. of adjectives to form adverbs is specially characteristic of the Κοινή.

ὁμοιοπαθής,

"of like nature" (Ac 14¹⁵, Jas 5¹⁷, RV marg.) is fully illustrated from late Greek writers by Wetstein *ad* Ac *l.c.*

ὅμοιος.

For ὅμοιος as denoting the same rank or station cf. P Oxy I. 124² (iii A.D.) Ἄδραστος . . . γήμας ἐκ τῶν ὁμοίων ἔσχεν θυγατέρας δύο, "Adrastus married one of his own rank and had two daughters" (Edd.), and the apophthegm in PSI I. 120³³ (iv/A.D. ?) γάμει ἐκ τῶν ὁμοίων· οἱ μὲν γὰρ ἐκ τῶν κρεισσόνων γαμοῦντες δεσπότας κοὐκ οἰκείους κτῶνται. In P Ryl II. 105²⁰ (A.D. 136) ὡς ἐπὶ τῶν ὁμοίω(ν) = "as in similar cases." The adj. is used with ἴσος in *Syll* 162 (= ³312)²⁷ (end iv/B.C.) ἐπ' ἴσῃ καὶ ὁμοίῃ, "upon equal and similar terms," and for a weakened sense see P Tebt II. 300¹³ (A.D. 151) διὸ ἐπιδίδομι ὅπως περιερεθῇ (*l.* διὸ ἐπιδίδωμι ὅπως περιαιρεθῇ) [τ]οῦτο τὸ ὄνομα ταγῆναι ἐν τῇ τῶν ὁμο[ίων] τάξι, "wherefore I present this notice, that this name may be struck off and may be inscribed in the list of such persons" (viz. the dead). On the flexion of the adj. see Moulton *Gr.* ii. p. 157. Hort regards ὅμοιον in Rev 1¹³ as virtually an adverb like οἷον.

ὁμοιότης.

The phrase καθ' ὁμοιότητα, as in Heb 4¹⁵, 7¹⁵, in the somewhat weakened sense of "in the same way as" is found with a gen. dependent upon it in BGU IV. 1028¹⁵ (ii/A.D.) ἐπὶ τῆς ἐξετάσεω[ς] κ[α]θ᾽ ὁμοιότητα ἑτέρας ἐξετάσεως), PSI I. 107² (end of ii/A.D.) καθ᾽ ὁ[μο]ιότητα ἑτέρων δούλων, and P Oxy IX. 1202²⁴ (A.D. 217) κατὰ τὸ ἀναγκαῖον προσφεύγω σοι ἀξιῶν ἐνταγῆναι κἀμοῦ τὸν υἱὸν τῇ τῶν ἐφήβων γραφῇ καθ᾽ ὁμοιότητα τῶν σὺν αὐτῷ, "I perforce have recourse to you, requesting that my son too may be entered in the list of the ephebi in the same way as his companions" (Ed.).

ὁμοίωμα.

According to Souter *Lex. s.v.* ὁμοίωμα, "a thing made like" something else (concrete), differs from ὁμοιότης, "resemblance" (abstract), much as *simulacrum* differs from *similitudo*. As distinguished from εἰκών, which implies an archetype, the "likeness" or "form" in ὁμοίωμα may be accidental, as one egg is like another : cf. Rom 5¹⁴, Phil 2⁷, and see Trench *Syn.* p. 47 ff. The word is found in a difficult context in OGIS 669⁵² (i/A.D.) καὶ νῦν τοῖς αὐτοῖς παραγγέλλω μηδὲν ἐξ ὁμοιώμα[τος ἐπι]γράφειν ἀλ[λ]αχῆι ἄλλο τι τῶν καθόλου χωρὶς τοῦ κρεῖναι τὸν ἔπαρχον.

ὁμοίως.

An interesting parallel to Jn 5¹⁹ where ὁμοίως should not be translated "in like manner" (RV) but "likewise" (AV : cf. 6¹¹, 21¹³) is afforded by P Par 47⁸ (c. B.C. 153) (= *Selections,* p. 22) where the writer bitterly exclaims—ὀμνύω τὸν Σάραπιν . . . ὅτι ψευδῆι πάντα καὶ οἱ παρὰ σὲ θεοὶ ὁμοίως, "I swear by Serapis that all things are false and your gods likewise." Cf. *ib.* 60⁵ᶠ (c. B.C. 154) ὁμοίως καὶ Κότταβος, ὁμοίως καὶ Χεντοσνεύς, BGU IV. 1167²¹ (B.C. 12) ἐφ᾽ ὧι ὁμοίως μὴ (ἐπελεύσε σθαι τὴν Ἰσιδώ ραν) κατὰ μη(δένα) τρόπ(ον), and P Ryl II. 243¹³ (ii/A.D.) δέξαι παρὰ Νιννάρου ἰς λόγον Εἰρήνης τὸ ἐπιβάλλον αὐτῇ μέρος καὶ ἰς τὸ[ν] λόγον Δημαρίου ὁμοίως δέξαι πα[ρ]ὰ [Ἀτ]ρήτος τὸ ἐπιβάλλον αὐτῇ μέρος, "receive from Ninnarus for Irene's account the share belonging to her, and likewise from Hattes for Demarion's account the share belonging to her." The adv. is common = "ditto," e.g. CP Herm I. 127ⁱⁱⁱ·¹⁴ᵃˡ. (= p. 73). See also *s.v.* ὡσαύτως.

ὁμοίωσις.

On the distinction between ὁμοίωσις and εἰκών, the latter "image belonging to fundamental nature," the former "likeness to progressive character," see Hort's note on Jas 3⁹, the only place in the NT where ὁμοίωσις occurs.

ὁμολογέω.

The root meaning of this verb "agree with" is seen in the contract P Oxy II. 275¹ (A.D. 66) ὁ[μ]ο[λ]ογοῦσιν ἀλλή-[λ]οις Τρύφων . . . καὶ Πτολεμαῖο[ς, "agreement between Tryphon and Ptolemaeus" : cf. the legal formula ἐπερωτη-θεὶς ὡμολόγησα, "in answer to the formal question I have given my consent," as in P Ryl II. 100¹⁵ (A.D. 238). From this the transition is easy to the sense "acknowledge," "publicly declare," e.g. *ib.* 125⁵⁻⁶ (A.D. 28-9) ὡμολ[ό]γησεν τὴν πυξίδα ὡς προφέρεται κενήν, "he acknowledges (having found) the box but alleges that it was empty" (Edd.), *ib.* 180² (A.D. 124) ὁμολογῶ μὴ ἐγκαλεῖν σοι μηδ᾽ ἐγκαλέσειν σοι περὶ μηδενὸς πράγματος ἁπλῶς, "I acknowledge that I neither make nor will make any claim upon you on any

matter whatever" (Edd.), *ib.* 157² (A.D. 135) ὁμολογοῦμεν διῃρῆσθαι πρὸς ἀλλήλας ἐπὶ τοῦ παρόντος [ὃ ἔχομεν ἐ]ν μισθώσει οὐσιακ[ὸ]ν ἀμπελικὸν κτῆμα, "we acknowledge that we have divided between ourselves at the present time the domain-land vineyard which we hold on lease" (Edd.), and the recurring formula in receipts ὁμολογῶ ἀπέχειν, "I acknowledge that I have received," e.g. BGU II. 304²² (A.D. 137) ὁμολογῶι ἀπέχειν [π]αρὰ τοῦ Στοτοήτιος τὰ[ς] προκιμένας [ἀρ]γυρίου [δρα]χ[μὰς] δ[ιακο]σίας τε σ σα-[ρ]ά[κο]ντα ὀκτώ . . . With the usage "praise," "celebrate," in Heb 13¹⁵, which Grimm-Thayer pronounces as "unknown to Grk. writ.," we may compare the somewhat similar phrase ὁμολογῶ χάριτα in petitions, e.g. P Ryl II. 114³² (c. A.D. 280) ὅπως . . . τῇ τύχῃ σου χάριτας ὁμολογεῖν δυνηθῶ, "that I may avow my gratitude to your fortune," P Oxy I. 67² (A.D. 338) ὅπως ταύτ[ης ἡμεῖ]ν τῆς εὐεργεσίας ὑπαρχθείσης εἰσαεί σου τῇ τύχῃ χάριτας ὁμολο-γήσωμεν, and the Christian letter P Oxy VI. 939⁵ (iv A.D.) καὶ εἴη διὰ παντὸς ἡμᾶς χάριτας ὁμο[λογοῦντα]ς διατελεῖν ὅτι ἡμῖν ἵλεως ἐγένετο, "and may it be granted us to continue for ever to acknowledge our thanks to Him because He was gracious to us" (Edd.). A good ex. of the meaning "promise" (class.), as in Mt 14⁷, is afforded by the Phrygian inscr. *Cagnat* IV. 542 θεῷ ὑψίστῳ εὐχὴν Αὐρήλιος Ἀσκλά-πων, ἣν [ὡ]μολό[γ]ησεν ἐ[ν] Ῥώμῃ. On the Semitism in ὁμολογῶ ἐν in Mt 10³², Lk 12⁸) cf. Nestle *ZNTW* vii. p. 279 f., ix. p. 253, Burkitt *Earliest Sources for the Life of Jesus,* p. 19 f., and see *s.v.* ἐξομολογέω. MGr μολογῶ.

ὁμολογία

is very common in our sources in the sense "contract," "agreement," e.g. P Eleph 2² (B.C. 285-4) συγγραφὴ καὶ ὁμολογία—the heading of a Will, P Ryl II. 178¹¹ (early i/A.D.) Τασεῦς Πετεῦτος τέθειμαι τὴν ὁμολογίαν καὶ ἐκθρέψωι τὸ δουλικὸν σωμάτιον Θερμουθάριον ἐπὶ τὰ δύο ἔτηι, "I, Taseus daughter of Peteeus have made the agreement and I will nurse the infant slave Thermoutharion for the two years," *ib.* 101⁵ (A.D. 71) κατὰ τήνδε τὴν ὁμολογίαν, "in accordance with this agreement," P Fay 91² (A.D. 99) ὁμολ ογία Θενετκουεῖς πρὸ[ς] Λούκιο ν, "agreement of Thenetkoueis with Lucius," P Tebt II. 392² (A.D. 134-5) ἕτερα ἐφ᾽ οἷς ἡ ὁμολογεί[α] περιέχει, "other items according to the terms of the agreement" (Edd.), P Oxy XIV. 1627²⁰ (A.D. 342) πρὸς δὲ ἀμεριμνίαν σου τήνδε τὴν ὁμολογίαν σοι ἐξεδόμην, "and for your security I have issued to you this contract" (Edd.), and from the inscr. *Syll* 214¹⁰ (iii/B.C.) τὴν περὶ τῆς συμμαχίας ὁμολογίαν ἤκουσε κομί-ζοντες. For ὁμολόγημα see P Strass I. 40²⁷ (A.D. 569) with the editor's note. Ὁμόλογος is a technical term for a labourer working under a contract, cf. e.g. *O.tr* 413² (A.D. 63) (= *LAE*, p. 105, where Deissmann compares Mt 20¹³, 1 Cor 9⁷), and for ὁμόλογος γῆ, with reference to land of which the liability was "agreed upon," see P Ryl II. p. 286 f.

ὁμολογουμένως.

"admittedly," as in 1 Tim 3¹⁶, is seen in P Par 15⁶⁶ (B.C. 120) ὁμολογουμένως δ᾽ ἐπὶ συκοφαντείᾳ καὶ σεισμῷ ἐπαγειο-χό[τος . . .] ἔγκλημα, and P Tor I. 1ᵛ·²² (B.C. 117) ὥστε ὁμολογουμένως ἑαυτοῦ καταμαρτυροῦντα συμφανὲς καθεστη-κέναι, "ita ut, vel ipso contra se testimonium dicente,

apertissime liqueat" (Ed.).   The word is also found as a
v.l. in Aristeas 24, and see Crönert *Mem. Herc.* p. 241.

ὁμότεχνος.

For the formation of this compound, which occurs in the
NT only in Ac 18³, but was used by medical writers as a
term for physicians (Hobart, p. 239) cf. the common ὁμο-
πάτριος and ὁμομήτριος (e.g. P Fay 32⁷ ⁶, A.D. 131). and
the courtesy title ὁμότιμος (τοῖς συγγενέσι) (e.g. P Tebt I.
254, c. B.C. 113).

ὁμοῦ.

BGU IV. 1022¹² (A.D. 196) γενόμε[νο]ι [ε]ἰς Φειλα[δ]ελ-
φίαν κ[ώ]μην . . ἔνθα ὁμοῦ [ἦ]μεν, of persons gathered
"together," as in Ac 2¹.   The word occurs often in accounts
to denote a total, e.g. P Oxy XIV. 1655¹¹ (iii/A.D.) γίνονται
ὁμοῦ (δην.) μς τέ(ταρτον) α, "total 46 den. 1 quarter," P
Meyer 21⁷ (iii/iv A.D.) ὥστε τὸ πᾶ]ν γί(νεσθαι) ὁμοῦ ἀρτάβας ἑκατὸν [ἐνενήκοντα] ς, "so that the whole amounted to
a total of 196 artabae."

ὁμόφρων.

The likeness of "sentiment or disposition" rather than of
"opinion" which Bigg (*ICC ad l.*) finds in this adj. in its
only occurrence in the NT, 1 Pet 3⁸, may be illustrated from
the use of the corresponding adv. in the sepulchral inscr.
Kaibel 493⁵ᶠ—

τὸν καὶ ἔτ' ἀκμαῖον βίοτον λείποντα καθ' ἥβην
κῆδος ὁμοφρονέως πᾶσ' ἐδάκρυσε πόλις.

ὅμως.

P Par 45⁴ (B.C. 153) ἀλ' (=ἀλλ') ὅμως τοῖς θεοῖς τὴν
ἐπιτροπὴν δίδομει, P Oxy I. 115⁹ (ii/A.D.) (= *Selections*,
p. 9) ἀλλ' ὁμῶς οὐδὲν δύναταί τις πρὸς τὰ τοιαῦτα : cf.
Jn 12¹². See also BGU IV. 1205¹² (B.C. 28) οὐ πεπράκαμεν, ὅμως ὡς θέλετε ποιεῖτε, P Giss I. 99⁷ (ii/iii A.D.)
κατὰ τὸ τῶν αὐτο[χθόνω]ν Αἰγυπτίων ἀλλότρια ταῦ[τα ἦν],
ἐδρᾶτο δὲ ὅμως, and P Oxy VI. 939²⁶ (iv/A.D.) (= *Selections*, p. 30) νοσηλότερον δὲ ὅμως τὸ σωμάτιον ἔχει, "but
nevertheless she is still in a somewhat sickly state of body."
On the supposed trajection of ὅμως from its proper place in
Gal 3¹⁵, 1 Cor 14⁷, see Burton *Gal.* p. 178 f.

ὄναρ.

The phrase κατ' ὄναρ which is found for the Attic ὄναρ
sexies in Mt, is condemned by Photius (*Lex.* p. 149, 25 f.) as
βάρβαρον παντελῶς : cf. Lob. *Phryn.* p. 422 ff. It occurs
not infrequently in votive inscr. but with the meaning "in
consequence of a dream," and not "in a dream," e.g. *Syll*
780 (= ³ 1147)⁶ (ii/iii A.D.) Οὔλπιοι Νείκανδρος καὶ Σωτή-
ριος Ὑγείᾳ Σωτ[εί]ρῃ Συνοδοι[πόρ]ῳ κατ' ὄναρ : see also
Deissmann *BS*, p. 253. A new literary ex. of the word
occurs in Herodas i. 11 οὐδ' ὄναρ : cf. Cic. *al Att.* i. 18. 6.

ὀνάριον.

This conversational diminutive (Jn 12¹⁴) may be illustrated
from P Oxy I. 63¹¹ (ii/iii A.D.) τοὺς δειγματοάρτας καθ'
αὑτὸν ἀναπέμψαι πρὸς ζυγοστα[σ]ίαν λαβόντα παρὰ τῶν
ἀρχεφόδων ὀνάριον, "send up the inspectors yourself to the
examination, getting a donkey from the chiefs of the police"

(Edd.): cf. the double diminutive in P Ryl II. 239²⁴ (mid.
iii/A.D.) πανταχόθεν ἴδε αὐτῷ μικρὸν ὀναρίδιον, "look out
everywhere for a small donkey for him" (Edd.).   The
word appears as a diminutive of ὄνος in its less usual sense
of "wine-cup" in P Giss I. 47¹⁷ (time of Hadrian) τὸ
ὀνάριον τὸ χαλκοῦν, BGU I. 248²⁶ (ii/A.D.) ὀνάριον ὑπὸ
τρίχωρο(ν) οἴνου.

ὀνειδίζω.

For ὀνειδίζω, "reproach," "revile," c. acc. as in Mt 27¹⁴,
cf. BGU IV. 1024ᵛⁱⁱ ²¹ (ii/iii A.D.), where a man is charged
with having basely slain a woman—τὴν ἐπ' ἀ[ν]θρώποις
τύχην ὀνειδίζουσαν. The pass. (cf. 1 Pet 4¹⁴) is seen in P
Giss I. 40ⁱⁱ ⁵ (A.D. 215) οὐκ ὀνειδισθήσεται ἡ τῆς ἀτιμί[α]ς
παρασημεί[ω]σις.

ὀνειδισμός.

To the references for this comparatively rare word (Rom
15³ *al.*) we may add Joseph. *Antt.* xix. 319, and Vett. Val.
pp. 65⁷, 75¹⁰.

ὄνειδος.

This NT ἅπ. εἰρ. (Lk 1²⁵) may be illustrated from Joseph.
c. Apion. i. 285, where it is associated with βλάβη. Cf.
also *Test. xii. patr.* Reub. vi. 3 εἰς ὄλεθρον Βελίαρ καὶ
ὄνειδος αἰώνιον.

Ὀνήσιμος.

This proper name (Col 4⁹, Philem ¹⁰) from the adj.
ὀνήσιμος, "useful," may be illustrated from P Grenf II.
38¹⁷ (B.C. 81) ἡ λογεύσι (*l.* -σει) καὶ ἀνανκάσι (*l.* -σει) με
Ὀνησίμωι (*l.* Ὀνήσιμος) ἀγοράσ[α]ι κριθῆς κτλ., P Gen I.
4¹⁰ (beg. iii A.D.) ὁ] τοῦ τόπου μου ἀμφο[δάρ]χης Ὀνήσιμος
ἀνεγραψάτο με ἐπὶ κώμη[ς] Ἀργεάδος, and from the inscr.
Magn 242 τόπος Ὀν[η]σίμου, *ib.* 300 ἡ σόρος ("grave")
Ὀνησίμου τοῦ Παυσιμάχου. Thieme (p. 40) notes that the
name is specially common in the case of slaves, though not
confined to them, as is shown by the mention of a γραμματεὺς Μ. Ὀνήσιμος on a coin of Caracalla's time: cf. also
Ὀνησίμη in *Syll* 865⁵, a woman whom a manumitted slave
is to serve till her death. Dittenberger's Index (p. 89)
shows other exx.: see also Lightfoot *Col.²* p. 310, Zahn
Introd. i. p. 458, and Hatch in *JBL* xxvii. (1908), p. 146.

Ὀνησίφορος.

On the improbability that Ὀνησίφορος, who, according to
tradition, suffered martyrdom at Parium, a city of Mysia, in
the beginning of ii/A.D., is to be identified with the friend
and disciple of Paul (2 Tim 1¹⁶, 4¹⁹), see W. M. Ramsay
Exp T ix. p. 495 f. The identification, as Ramsay points
out, becomes impossible if we accept the tradition embodied
in the *Acts of Paul and Thekla* (A.D. 150-170), which
makes Onesiphorus, a native of Antioch, converted by Paul
on his first visit, and already a householder at that time,
about A.D. 48.

ὀνικός.

Grimm's statement that this adj. is "not found" outside
its NT occurrences (Mt 18⁶, Mk 9⁴²) requires correction in
the light of the new evidence, e.g. BGU III. 912²⁴ (A.D.

33) τὰ ὀνικὰ κτήνη, P Gen I. 23⁶ (A.D. 70) ἀπὸ τῶν ὑπαρχόντων ἡμῖν ὀνικῶν κτηνῶν ὄνον ἕνα, and OGIS 629³⁰ (A.D. 137) γόμου ὀνικοῦ, a load such as requires an ass to carry it. Cf. for similar formations, P Oxy III. 498³ (ii/A.D.) τῶν οἰκοδομουμένων λίθων κύβων καμηλικῶν, "squared building-stones transportable by camel (?)," and BGU III. 814⁶ (iii A.D.) ἡμιονικὸν ἅρμα, "a chariot drawn by mules." Deissmann (LAE, p. 77) notes that ὀνικός "survives in the Middle Greek τὸ (ὁ νικόν, which is still in dialectal use, for instance in the island of Carpathus."

ὀνίνημι.

Ὀναίμην (Philem²⁰), "may I have satisfaction," is the only opt. form from an unthematic verb in the NT: cf. Audollent 92³ (iii/B.C.) ὄναιντο, Kaibel 502²⁷ (iii/iv A.D.) μήτ᾽ ἐλπίδων ὄναιτο, and see Moulton Gr. ii. p. 213. In C. and B. ii. p. 730 No. 658^{A 59} the gen. has given place to the acc.—τοῖς ὑπὸ ἕνα κερὸν [ὀ]νη[θ]εῖσιν τὸ τῆς ζωῆς μέρος. For the thought of filial offices underlying the word, as in the Philemon passage, see the citations in Lightfoot Comm. ad l. The subst. ὀνή occurs in P Tebt II. 420 (iii A.D.), a letter from Sarapion to his brother, asking for assistance in his pecuniary troubles—²¹δὸς οὖν τὴν ὀνήν σου ἵνα ἀνασπασθῇ ἀναγκαίως, "so give me your help, that (the barley) may of necessity be pulled up (?)" (Edd.). For ὄνησις cf. the good advice of a father to his son, P Oxy III. 531¹¹ (ii A.D.) τοῖς βιβλίοις σου αὐτὸ μόνον πρόσεχ[ε] φιλολογῶν καὶ ἀπ᾽ αὐτῶν ὄνησιν ἕξεις, "give your undivided attention to your books, devoting yourself to learning, and then they will bring you profit" (Edd.).

ὄνομα.

(1) For ὄνομα, the name by which a person or thing is called, we may cite: P Magd 24¹ (B.C. 218) Αἰγυπτία τις, ᾗ λέγεται εἶναι ὄνομα Ψενοβάστι[ς, P Lond 854¹¹ (i/ii A.D.) (= III. p. 206, Selections p. 70) τῶν φίλων [ἐ]μ[ῶν τ]ὰ ὀνόματα ἐνεχάραξα τοῖς ἱ[ε]ροῖς ἀειμνή⟨σ⟩τως, "I carved the names of my friends on the sanctuaries for perpetual remembrance"—a traveller's letter. and BGU II. 423²² (ii/A.D.) (= Selections, p. 92) ἔσ[τ]ι [δέ] μου ὄνομα Ἀντῶνις Μάξιμος. Deissmann (LAE, p. 121) claims the phrase ὧν τὰ ὀνόματα as "a characteristic documentary formula," e.g. P Oxy III. 485³¹ (A.D. 178) ὧν τὰ ὀνόματα ἐπὶ τῶν [τό]πων δηλωθήσεται, "whose names will be ascertained on the spot" (Edd.), BGU II. 432^{ii. 3} (A.D. 190) ὧν τὰ ὀνόματα τῷ βιβλιδίῳ δεδήλωται, "whose names are shown in the little book" (cf. Phil 4³).

(2) By a usage similar to that of the Heb. שֵׁם, ὄνομα comes in the NT to denote the character, fame, authority of the person indicated (cf. Phil 2⁹ᶠ, Heb 1⁴). With this may be compared the use of the word as a title of dignity or rank, as in P Oxy I. 58⁶ (A.D. 288) where complaint is made of the number of officials who have devised "offices" for themselves—ὀνόματα ἑαυτοῖς ἐξευρόντες, and provision is made that, on the appointment of a single trustworthy superintendent, the remaining "offices" shall cease—¹⁴ᶠ τὰ δὲ λοιπὰ ὀνόματα παύσηται. See also the use of the word as a title of address in the sepulchral inscr. Preisigke 343⁹ Ἀντωνεῖνε . . . φιλάνθρωπε καλὸν ὄνομα κύριέ μου κτλ., and the interesting graffito of A.D. 79 (cited by

Deissmann LAE, p. 276), where there is allusion to a certain lady Harmonia—ἧς ὁ ἀριθμὸς με (or αλε) τοῦ καλοῦ ὀνόματος (cf. Jas 2⁷). "the number of her honourable name is 45 (or 1035)." In P Leid Wxix⁷⁰ (ii/iii A.D.) we have an invocation to Γῆ—οὗ τὸ (ὄνομα) οὐδὲ θεοὶ δύναται (: δύνανται) φθέγγεσθαι.

(3) The transition from the foregoing to the meaning "possession," "property," is easy. e.g. P Oxy II. 247¹ (A.D. 90), where a man registers on behalf of his brother certain property which has descended to him ἐξ ὀνόματος τῆς σημαινομένης καὶ μετηλλαχυίας ἀμφοτέρων μητρὸς Τσεναμμωνᾶτος, "from the property of the aforesaid and departed Tsennamonas, the mother of us both" (Edd.), ib. 249⁹ (A.D. 80) τὸ κατηντηκὸς εἴς με ἐξ ὀνόματος τοῦ ὁμογνησίου μου ἀδελφοῦ, and BGU I. 250⁶ (time of Antoninus Pius) τὰ ὑπάρχοντ[α] εἰς ὄνομα δυεῖν, "that which belongs to the property of the two." We may also compare P Ryl II. 174²³ (A.D. 112) συγχωρεῖ ἡ Ἡρακλοῦς [ἄκυρο]ν εἶναι κατὰ πάντα τρόπον ἣν πεποίηται ἡ Τασουχάρι[ο]ν διὰ τῆς [τῶν ἐ]νκτήσ[ε]ων [β]ιβλι[ο]θήκης ἐκ[ο]ύσιον κατ[ο]χὴν τοῦ ὀνόματος [αὐτῆς] εἰς τὸν [τ]ῆ[ς] Ἡρακλοῦτος λόγον, "Heraclous acknowledges that the voluntary notification of the personal claim made by Tasoucharion in favour of Heraclous through the property registration-office is entirely invalid" (Edd.). Sometimes ὄνομα is best left untranslated, as in P Oxy III. 515²² (A.D. 190) (= Chrest. I. p. 216) τὸν τόκον τὸν [ὀ]ν[ό]ματί μου παραγρα[φέ]ντα, "the interest debited to me" (Edd.).

(4) The meaning "person," which is found in Ac 1¹⁵, Rev 3⁴, 11¹³, may be illustrated from P Oxy IX. 1188⁸ (A.D. 13) παρὰ τοῦ ὑπογεγραμμέ(νου) ὀνόματος, "from the person below written," BGU I. 113¹¹ (A.D. 143) ἑκάστῳ ὀνόματι παρα(γενομένῳ), P Thead 41¹⁰ A.D. 300 διέγ ραψεν) Σακάων καὶ οἱ κοι(νωνοὶ) ἀπόρων ὀνομάτων τάλαντα τρία, and the late PSI I. 27²⁷ (Acts of Martyrdom —v/A.D.) ἀπέκτ]εινεν ψυχὰς [εἰδωλολατ]ρῶν ὡς ὀνόματα χείλια πεντακόσια.

(5) The phrase εἰς (τὸ) ὄνομά τινος is frequent in the papyri with reference to payments made "to the account of any one" (cf. Lat. nomen)—P Rein 44²⁷ (A.D. 104) χρησθὲν εἰς τὸ Διονυσίου [ὄ]νομα χρεωστῇ Ἑρμαίῳ νεωτέρῳ, P Meyer 8¹³ (A.D. 151) πάντα [καταγραφῆναι] συνέταξεν εἰς τὸ τῆς γυναικὸς αὐτοῦ ὄνομα, and Osl 1160¹ (ii A.D.) διάγραψον εἰς ὄνομ(α) κληρονόμων Ἀπίδος Νότου (καὶ) Λ(ιβός). The usage is of interest in connexion with Mt 28¹⁹, where the meaning would seem to be "baptized into the possession of the Father, etc." See further Deissmann BS pp. 146 f., 197, and W. Heitmüller's monograph Im Namen Jesu (Göttingen, 1903), where (p. 100 ff.) the phrase is claimed as good vernacular. With εἰς ὄνομα = qua in Mt 10⁴¹ᶠ, cf. P Oxy I. 37^{i. 17} (A.D. 49) (= Selections, p. 50), where in an action against a nurse for the recovery of a male foundling it is stated—βούλεται ὀν[ό]ματι ἐλευθέρου τὸ σωμάτιον ἀπενέγκασθαι, "she wishes (to defend herself on the ground) that the foundling was carried off in virtue of its being freeborn."

The phrase ἐν (τῷ) ὀνόματί τινος, so common in the NT, has not been found outside Biblical Greek, but Deissmann (BS, p. 197 f.) compares the use of the dat. in Syll 304 (=³797)³³ (A.D. 37), where the names of five πρεσβευταί, who had signed the oath of allegiance to Caligula taken by the inhabitants of Assos, are followed by the words—οἵτινες καὶ ὑπὲρ τῆς Γαίου Καίσαρος Σεβαστοῦ Γερμανικοῦ σωτηρίας εὐξάμενοι Διὶ Καπιτωλίωι ἔθυσαν τῶι τῆς πόλεως ὀνόματι. The simple dat. is found in BGU IV. 1205²³ (B.C. 28) δὸς Ἀλεξίωινι τῶι βαφῖ τῶι ἐμῶι ὀνόματι κτλ., P Oxy III. 531²⁵ (ii/A.D.) πέμψον Φρόνιμον πρὸς Ἀσκληπιάδην ἐμῶι ὀνόματι, P Flor II. 226¹³ (iii/A.D.) πέμψον αὐτὰ εἰς Ταλεῖ τῷ ἐμῷ ὀνόμα(α)τι, and from the inscr. IHS xvii. (1897). p. 411 No. 14 προστείμου ὀνόματι, and CIG 3919 στεφανωτικοῦ ὀνόματι, where, as Evans (CQ xv. p. 26) points out, ὀνόματι might be rendered "under the heading of."

(6) Other exx. of ὄνομα with various prepositions are—P Tebt II. 317³² (A.D. 174–5) ἕκαστα ἐπιτελοῦντι ἐκ τοῦ ἐμοῦ ἀπούσης ὀνόματος, "carrying out everything in my name and during my absence" (Edd.), P Oxy VII. 1063³ (ii/iii A.D.) σύμβαλε Ἡρώδη . . . ἐξ ὀνόματός μου καὶ εἰπον αὐτῷ, "go and see Herodes in my name and say to him" (Ed.), P Amh II. 85⁸ (A.D. 78) ὅσα ἄλλα ἐὰν ἀφεύρω ἐπ' ὀνόματος τῶν υἱῶν ὀρφανῶν αὐτοῦ Σαραπίωνος, "whatever else I may find to be owned by the orphan sons of Sarapion" (Edd.), P Rein 44¹³ (A.D. 104) ἐποίησεν τὰς ὠνὰς ἐπὶ τῷ Διονυσίου τοῦ υἱοῦ ὀνόματι, P Tebt II. 407¹⁵ (A.D. 199?) ἀφ' ὧν ἔχω ἐπ' ὀνόματός σου ὑ[π]αρχόντων, "of my property standing in your name" (Edd.), and the slightly different BGU I. 153²⁷ (A.D. 152) ἀπογράψασθαι ἐν τῇ τῶν καμήλων ἀπογραφῇ . . . ἐπ' ὀνόματος αὐτῶν, where, as Deissmann (BS p. 197 n.²) points out, the reference is to the camels' being entered on the list under the name of their new owner: BGU I. 27¹⁸ (ii/A.D.) (= Selections, p. 102) ἀσπάζομαι . . . πάντε(=α)ς τοὺς φιλοῦντάς σε κατ' ὄνομα (cf. 3 Jn¹⁵), P Oxy VII. 1070¹⁶ (iii/A.D.) τοὺς ἡμῶν πάντας κατ' ὄνομα προσαγόρευε καὶ ἄσπασε, and the Christian prayer ib. 1059⁷ (v/A.D.), where, after a prayer to God for various persons, the petition is added ὦψε (l. ὄψαι) κατ' ὄνομα, "look on them severally": and BGU II. 531ⁱⁱ·¹⁰ (ii/A.D.) τὰ περιγεινόμενα ἐνοίκια πρὸς ἕκαστον ὄνομα τῶν τρυγώντων γραφήτωι. In MGr γιὰ ὄνομα τοῦ θεοῦ, "for God's sake!"

ὀνομάζω.

For this verb = "name," cf. P Oxy X. 1272²¹ (A.D. 144) ἐπιδίδωμι τὸ ἀναφόριον καὶ ἀξιῶ . . . ἀχθῆναι ἐπὶ σὲ τὸν Ἡρᾶν καὶ τοὺς σὺν αὐτῷ οὓς αὐτὸς ὀνομάσει, "I present this petition and request that Heras and his associates, whose names he will himself give, should be brought before you" (Edd.), and the following extract from the official record of a judge—BGU III. 969ⁱⁱ·¹² (A.D. 142?) ὀνομάσατε οὓς αἱρεῖ[σθε. Πα]σίων εἶπ(εν)· Ἐγὼ αἱροῦμ[αι Λογ]γεῖνον Κλήμεντα. The pass. is found in BGU IV. 1165³² (B.C. 13) δι' ἧς καὶ ὀνομάζεται ὁ τοῦ Ἡρακλεί[δ(ου) καὶ τῆς Θερμούθιος υἱ(ὸ)ς Ἡρακλ[εί]δη[ς, and ib. II. 388ⁱⁱⁱ·¹² (ii/iii A.D.) ἐν τῇ ἐπιστολῇ ἔγραψας τῷ στρατηγῷ τοῦ Ἀρσινοείτου περὶ τῶν ὀνομασθέντων ὑπὸ τῶν δούλων. οὐ προσεγράφη Σεμπρώνιος Αἰσχίνης ὀνομασθεὶς ὡς πρόβατα ἐκείνου ἀποσπάσας. The verb is not uncommon in the sense of "nominate," e.g. P Oxy X. 1257¹ (iii/A.D.) Ἐπίμαχος ὀνομασθεὶς εἰς δεκαπρωτείαν, "on the nomination of Epimachus to the office of decaprotus" (Edd.), ib. IX. 1204⁴ (A.D. 299) παρὰ πάντας τοὺς νόμους ὀνομασθέντος μου ὡς εἰς δεκαπρωτείαν, and for the corresponding subst. see ib. XIV. 1642³ (A.D. 289)

ἀποσυνίστημί σε κατὰ ταῦτά μου τὰ γράμματα παραστῆναι παρὰ σοὶ ἐν τῷ Ὀξυρυγχείτῃ τῇ ὀνομασίᾳ τῇ ὑπ' ἐμοῦ γενομένῃ παρὰ τῷ διασημοτάτῳ ἡγεμόνι, "I appoint you by this my deed to appear at home in the Oxyrhynchite nome as my representative at the nomination made by me to his excellency the praefect" (Edd.). The verbal ὀνομαστός is found in Kaibel 254³ (iv/iii B.C.) πρόγονοι δ' ὀνομαστοὶ ἀπ' [αἰχμ]ῆς: cf. its use as a proper name in P Ryl II. 88¹³ (A.D. 156) στ]ρατηγῷ Ὀνομάστ ῳ. For the subst. ὀνομαστής cf. BGU I. 96⁹ (2nd half iii/A.D.) Μάρωνος ὀνομ[α]στοῦ τῆς δεκαπρωτίας, and for ὀνομαστεί cf. OGIS 218²⁶ (iii/B.C.) with the exx. cited there, also BGU I. 316³⁸ (A.D. 359).

ὄνος.

The following may serve as exx. of this common word, probably borrowed, like Lat. asinus, from some Asiatic language (Boisacq, p. 705)—P Petr III. 140(a)² (iii/B.C.) ἀπ[οστεί]λόν μοι τὴν ὄνον. P Grenf II. 14(b)⁵·⁶ (B.C. 225) (= Chrest. I. p. 489) συγκεχρήμε[θ]α δὲ ὄνους βαδιστὰς (see s.v. βαδίζω) πέντε . . . ἐτοιμάκαμεν δὲ καὶ τοὺς τεσσαράκοντα ὄνους [τοὺς σ]κ[ε]νοφόρους. P Ryl II. 142²⁰ (A.D. 37) ἤροσαν διὰ ὄνων εἰς λόγο(ν) δεσχ(=μ)ῶν ἑξακοσίων, "they carried off by means of donkeys a matter of six hundred bundles" (Edd.), ib. 145¹⁶ (A.D. 38) ἀφήρπασεν παρ' αὐτοῦ ὄνον θήλειαν, "he robbed him of a female donkey" (Edd.), P Lond II. 331¹⁵f. (A.D. 165) (= II. p. 154, Chrest. I. p. 575) δώσ[ο]μεν ἔτι καταβαίνοντι ὄνους τέσσαρας καὶ ἀναβαίνοντι τοὺς ἴσους, "we shall give him for the down journey four asses, and for the up journey the same number," P Oxy VI. 932⁸ (late ii/A.D.) ἐὰν δύνῃ ἀναβῆναι ἵνα ἐπιγνοῖς (cf. Lk 14ℵ*) τὸν ὄνον. "if you can go up to find out the ass, do so" (Edd.), and ib. I. 112⁶ (iii/iv A.D.) δήλωσόν μοι ἢ πλοίῳ ἐξέρχ[ει] ἢ ὄνῳ, "let me know whether you are coming by boat or by donkey," a good ex. of the instrumental dat. In P Fay 67² (A.D. 80) (πυροῦ) ὄνους τρεῖς. ὄνους = "donkey-loads": cf. BGU II. 362ⁱ·⁶ (A.D. 215) ὄν]ων γ ὑπὸ δένδρα, "three asses laden with trees"—a rare instance of Coptic syntactical influence found in the papyri (cf. s.v. ὀστέον, and see Thackeray Gr. i. p. 20). In Herodas vi. 83 ὁ ὄνος = "the grindstone": cf. μύλος ὀνικός (Mt 18⁶, Mk 9⁴²). On the δίπλωμα ὄνων, see Ostr. i. p. 360 f. For ὀνηλάτης cf. P Fay 119³ (c. A.D. 100), and for ὀνηλάσιον cf. P Ryl II. 183(a)² (A.D. 16). See also s.v. βαδίζω.

ὄντως.

"actually," "indeed," as in Gal 3²¹, is seen in P Giss I. 22⁸ (time of Trajan) πρὸ π]άν[τ]ων εὔχομ[α]ι . . . . τὴν [γλυκυ]τάτην σου ὄψιν προσκυ[νῆσαι] νῦν ὄντως ἀμοιβ[ὴ]ν [. . . .] τῆς εὐσεβείας μου κτλ. For its use, virtually as an adj., preceded by the art. and followed by a noun (1 Tim 5⁴·⁵·¹⁶), we may cite Ep. ad Diogn. x. 7, Arist. Apol. iv. 1. Cf. MGr τόντις, "really"; few adverbs in -ως have survived in MGr.

ὄξος.

For ὄξος, "sour wine" drunk by soldiers, as in Mt 27⁴⁸ al., cf. P Lond 1245⁹ (A.D. 357) (= III. p. 228) a receipt for 4000 ξέσται supplied to soldiers stationed at Hermopolis—ὄξους ξέστας τετρακισχειλίους. Other exx. of the word, where it is distinguished from οἶνος, are *ib.* 856⁵⁷ (tariff of excise duties—late i/A.D.) (= III. p. 92) πλὴν οἴνου κ[αὶ ὄ]ξους, and *ib.* 1159¹⁹ (A.D. 145–7) (= III. p. 113) ἐπὶ οἴνου καὶ ὄξου[ς] οἱ πρόοντες. See also for the word P Flor III. 334³ (ii A.D.) προσένεγκέ μοι εἰς ἕψησιν γάρον ("fish-sauce") καὶ ὄξ[ο]ς ἐκ τοῦ Κώου καὶ ἐλαίαν, P Tebt II. 405¹⁵ (A.D. 212–7) λόγ[ο]ς τοῦ μετρηθέ[ντος] ἡμεῖν ὄξους εἰς τ[ὴν ἐνεσ]τῶσαν ἡμέρα[ν, BGU I. 14ᵘ·¹³ (A.D. 255) ὄξους ὑδρομιγ(οῦς), and P Oxy XIV. 1770⁵ (late iv A.D.) ὅσον χρῇζουσι ἔν τε σίτῳ ἢ ὄξους (*l.* ὄξει) παρασχοῦ αὐτοῖς, "supply them with whatever they require in the way of corn or sour wine." The dim. ὀξείδιον occurs in BGU II. 417³¹ (ii/iii A.D.) ἔρρωσό μοι, γλυκύτατε, καὶ ὀξείδιά μοι κόμισον, cf. ²², and the late P Lond 113. 11(a)³ (vi/vii A.D.) (= I. p. 223) a contract to take the sour wine (τὰ ὀξίδια) of one year's vintage in exchange for the sweet wine (τοῦ οἴνου) of the succeeding year. Ὄξος is to ὀξύς as εὖρος is to εὐρύς: cf. *acetum* and *acies, a er,* etc.

ὀξύς.

P Oxy VI. 900² (A.D. 322) ὑποβληθέντος ἔτι εἰς κονδουκτορίαν τοῦ ὀξέος δρόμου τοῦ εὐτυχῶς εἰσιόντος ἔτους, "I have besides been nominated as contractor for the express-post for the year auspiciously approaching" (Edd.): see the editors' note, and cf. Rom 3¹⁵ ὀξεῖς οἱ πόδες αὐτῶν ἐκχέαι αἷμα. It may be noted that the express postal service (*cursus velox*) with horses was introduced into Egypt after the time of Diocletian, to give way, however, under Justinian to the old service with asses: cf. P Flor I. 39² (A.D. 396), P Oxy I. 140⁷ (A.D. 550), and see the introduction to P Hamb I. 6. On the form ὀξεῖα cf. Moulton *Gr.* ii. p. 118. The comp. ὀξύτερον is contrasted with βαθύτερον in P Lond 899⁵ (ii/A.D.) (= III. p. 208) in connexion with some purple, πορφύριον.

ὄπισθεν.

For the prepositional use of ὄπισθεν c. gen., as in Mt 15²³, Lk 23²⁶, cf. the magic P Par 574¹²³¹ (iii/A.D.) (= *Selections*, p. 113) ὄπισθεν αὐτοῦ σταθείς contrasted with an immediately preceding ¹·²⁹ βάλε ἔμπροσθεν αὐτοῦ κλῶνας ἐλαίας. See also *s.v.* ὀπίσω.

ὀπίσω.

For ὄπισθεν (Rev 5¹—like Juvenal's "scriptus et *in tergo* necdum finitus Orestes"; i. 6), cf. P Tebt I. 58 *recto*³⁷ (B.C. 111) τἀπίλοιπα ὀπείσωι, "continued on the back," and similarly *ib.* 178 (late ii/B.C.). For another form of "P.T.O." we may cite P Rev Lˣᵇ·¹³ (B.C. 259–8) ἔξω ὅρα. See also Meyer *Ostr* 61¹⁵ (ii/B.C.) ὀπίσω, "turn over," at the end of an account, though as a matter of fact nothing is written on the reverse side of the sheet, and BGU III. 1002¹⁰ (B.C. 55), where, at the end of a contract, we find—ἐπεγράφησαν ἐκ τῶν ὀπίσω μαρτύρω⟨ν⟩ (*l.* ἐκ τοῦ ὀπίσω μάρτυρες), with reference to the names of the sixteen witnesses on the back. The superlative ὀπιστωτάτη occurs in Preisigke 4308⁵ (ii/B.C. ?), unfortunately with lacunae before and after. On the Hebraistic influence in such a phrase as ζητεῖν ὀπίσω τινός (Job 39³) see Thackeray *Gr.* i. p. 47, and on the survival of (ὁ)πίσω in MGr cf. Moulton *Proleg.* p. 99.

ὁπλίζομαι.

"arm myself" is found in the NT only in 1 Pet 4¹: for the construction cf. Soph. *Electra* 996 τοιοῦτον θράσος / αὐτή θ' ὁπλίζει, where Jebb also cites *Anthol. Pa.* 5.93 ὥπλισμαι πρὸς Ἔρωτα περὶ στέρνοισι λογισμόν.

ὅπλον.

For ὅπλα in the ordinary sense of "weapons" see P Tebt I. 48⁹ (c. B.C. 113) ἐπελθὼν ἐπὶ τὴν ἅλω Λύκος σὺν ἄλλοις ἐν ὅπλοις, "Lycus proceeded to the threshing-floor with other persons armed" (Edd.). Cf. PSI II. 168¹³ (B.C. 118) ἐπεληλυθέναι τινὰς ἐν ὅπλοις ἐπὶ τὸ σημαινόμενον χῶμα. In a list of artificers, P Tebt II. 278¹⁵ (early i A.D.), we find ὁπλοποίς (*l.* -οιός), "armourer."

ὁποῖος.

though very common in classical Greek, shows a marked tendency to disappear in later Greek. According to Meisterhans (*Gr.* p. 237) it is not found in the Attic inscrr. from B.C. 300 onwards. The word occurs *quinquies* in the NT: cf. P Oxy I. 118 *verso*¹⁷ (late iii/A.D.) εἰδὼς δὲ ὁποῖά ἐστιν καὶ ἡ ξενία, "you know what hospitality requires" (Edd.), and BGU IV. 1027ˣˣᵛⁱ·¹¹ cited *s.v.* ὄλεθρος. Note the curious combination ὅτι ὁποίαν in P Gen I. 54¹⁸ (iv/A.D.) οἶδας τὴν προέ(= αἵρεσίν μοι ὅτι ὁποίαν προέ(—αἵρεσιν ἔχω καὶ οἶδας τὴν γνώμην μου ὅτι γν[ώ]μη ὁποία ἐστιν.

ὁπότε

(in classical Greek "whenever") is freely used for "when" in the papyri, as in the later uncials in Lk 6³, cf. e.g. PSI IV. 432¹ (iii/B.C.) ὁπότε οὖν δοκιμάζεις, συντόμως χορηγείσθω, ἵνα μὴ ὑστερῶμεν τοῖς καιροῖς, P Oxy II. 243¹⁰ (A.D. 79) ὁπότε περιῆν, "when she was alive," and P Ryl II. 245³ (iii/A.D.) περὶ τῶν ἀξόνων ἠμέλησας ὁπότ' ἐδεή[σα]μεν αὐτῶν, "you neglected the matter of the axles when we were in need of them" (Edd.).

ὅπου.

"where," as in Mk 2⁴, is seen in P Oxy I. 76¹³ (A.D. 179) ὅπου σὺν τῷ ἀνδρὶ καταμένω, "where I live with my husband," in P Lond 854⁸ (i/ii A.D.) (= III. p. 206), an interesting account of a journey—εἰς Διβύην ὅπου Ἄμμων πᾶσιν ἀνθρώποις χρησμῳδεῖ, "to Libya, where Ammon sings oracles to all men," and in the question to an oracle P Oxy XII. 1477² (iii/iv A.D.) εἰ μένω ὅπου ὑπάγω; "shall I remain where I am going?" For the meaning "whither" (ὅποι is not found in the NT), as in Jn 7³⁴, see *Ostr* 1102⁵ (Rom.) ὅπου θέλει—with reference to the sending of certain measures of wheat. Ὅπου ἄν (ἐάν) = "wheresoever," as in Mk 6¹⁸, may be illustrated from P Eleph 1⁴ (B.C. 311–10) (= *Selections*, p. 2) εἶναι δὲ ἡμᾶς κατὰ ταὐτὸ (cf. Ac 14¹) ὅπου ἂν δοκῇ ἄριστον εἶναι, "and that we shall live together wherever may seem best," P Oxy XIV. 1636²⁰ (B.C. 73 or 44?) ὅπου ἂν τῶι καθόλου περιπίπτῃς ἡμῖν, "in any place whatsoever where you may encounter us" (Edd.), and *ib.* III. 484²⁰ (A.D. 138) ὅπου ἐὰν ὁ κράτιστος ἡγεμὼν Αὐίδιος Ἡλιόδωρος ἐπ' ἀγαθῷ τὸν νόμον διαλογίζηται, "wherever his highness the praefect Avidius Heliodorus holds his auspicious court for the nome," (Edd.); and = "whithersoever," as in Lk 9⁵⁷, from *ib.* IV. 728¹¹

(A.D. 142) μετενέγκαι ὅ[π]ου ἐὰν αἱρῆται, "transport it to any place that he may choose," with reference to a crop that had been cut. With Jn 14¹ cf. Epict. iv. 7. 14 ὅπου ἂν ἀπέλθω, ἐκεῖ μοι καλῶς ἔσται (cited by Sharp, p. 89), and with 2 Pet 2¹¹ "whereas," cf. Aristeas 149 and see P Flor I. 61⁴⁶ (A.D. 85) (as revised *Chrest.* II. p. 89) οὐχ ὅπου διαλογισμοὶ καὶ ἡγεμόνες παραγενόμενοι. The use of the relative adv. ὅπου (ὁποῦ, ποῦ) for the ordinary relative in MGr is illustrated by Thumb *Handbook* p. 93, e.g. ὁ ἄθρωπος (ὁ)ποῦ ἦρθε, "the man who came."

ὀπτάνομαι

can be definitely removed from the list of so-called "Biblical" words (Grimm-Thayer, p. 695), since to its occurrences in the LXX (3 Kingdoms 8⁸, Tob 12¹⁹: cf. P Oxy XIII. p. 4) and the NT (Ac 1³), we can add such early exx. as P Par 49³³ (B.C. 164–158) (= Witkowski,² p. 72) εἰ δὲ δι' ἄλλο τι οὐκ ὀπτάνεταί μοι, P Tebt I. 24⁵ (B.C. 117) καὶ μηδαμῶς ὀπτανομένων ὑπ[. . . Of a later date we have the great magical papyrus P Par 574³⁰³³ (c. A.D. 300) ὁρκίζω σε τὸν ὀπτανθέντα τῷ Ὀ(= Ἰ)σραὴλ ἐν στύλῳ φωτινῷ καὶ νεφέλῃ ἡμερινῇ, an interesting reference to Exod 13²¹ (see Deissmann *LAE* p. 252). On the implications involved in the use of ὀπτάνομαι in Ac 1³ as denoting actual appearance as distinguished from vision cf. Knowling *EGT ad l.*

ὀπτός.

With the use of this verbal adj. in Lk 24⁴² (cf. Hobart, p. 182 f.) we may compare P Giss I. 93⁶ ὀπτοῦ δέλφακος, "roast pork," in what appears to be a list of goods for a feast. The word = "baked" is common with πλίνθος, e.g. P Ryl II. 164⁷ (A.D. 171) κρηπε[ῖ]ς ἐξ ὀπτοῦ πλίν[θου, "a quay of baked brick," P Oxy XIV. 1674⁸ (iii/A.D.) θὲς τὴν ὀπτὸν πλίνθον π[α]ρὰ τὴν πλάτην, "put the baked bricks alongside the wall(?)" (Edd.), P Flor I. 50⁸·⁶⁵ (A.D. 268), and PSI VI. 712⁵ (A.D. 295).

For the subst. ὄπτησις cf. BGU IV. 1143¹⁷ (B.C. 18) κε[καυμ]ένα τῇ καθηκούσῃ ὀπτήσι. Wilcken (*Ostr.* i. p. 693) cites ὀπτανεύς, "roaster," "keeper of a cook-shop," from an unedited Berlin papyrus of iii/B.C. The verb is seen in P Lond 131 *recto*¹⁵ (A.D. 78–9) (= I. p. 173) περιστερ ὰς ὀπτωμέν ας : if the restoration is right, it is used metaphorically in P Giss I. 24⁸ (time of Trajan) οὐ μή σε ὀπτήσωσισι (*l.* ὀπτήσωσι).

ὀπώρα.

For this class, and vernacular word, which is used metaphorically in Rev 18¹¹, cf. the i/A.D. letter of a tax-gatherer at Oxyrhynchus, P Oxy II. 298, where along with much other miscellaneous matter he informs a friend —³⁸ οὔπω πολλὴ ὑ(= ὀ)πώρα ἐγένετο ἐν Μέμφι ἐπὶ τοῦ παρόντ[ο]ς, "there has not been much fruit in Memphis up to the present": also P Lond 46²²⁰ (iv/A.D.) (= I. p. 72) ὅσα ἀκμάζει τῶν ὀπώρων. For the adj. see *OGIS* 234² (end of iii/B.C.) Πυλαίας ὀπωρινῆς, the autumn meeting of the Amphictyons at Pylae : cf. Jude¹² δένδρα φθινοπωρινὰ ἄκαρπα, "autumn trees without fruit." A form ὀπωριμεῖος (not in LS) should probably be read in P Lond 974³ ᵃⁿᵈ ⁱⁱ·⁵ (A.D. 305–306) (= III. p. 116 f.) (as amended *Addenda*,

p. vii). With ὀπωροφυλάκιον (Ps 78(79)¹, *al.*) cf. the mention of an ὀπωροφύλαξ in P Oxy IV. 729¹¹ (A.D. 137), also the *recto* of P Ryl II. 244 (iii/A.D.). The etymology of ὀπώρα may reveal the meaning, "the season that follows summer" (cf. ὀπ-ἰθεν) (Boisacq, p. 709).

ὅπως.

(1) An interesting use of ὅπως, in which it is virtually a conjunction = "in which case," is seen in such passages as P Tebt II. 414³² (ii/A.D.) ἡ ληνὲ(= ὶ)ς τοῦ Ἀγαθανγέλου ἐστίν, ὅπως τοῖς παιδίο(ι)ς δοθῇ, "the trough belongs to Agathangelus, so let it be given to the children" (Edd.). See further *Proleg.* p. 177 n¹. (2) For ὅπως, like πῶς, used in the sense of ὡς, ὅτι (cf. Blass *Gr.* p. 230 f.), we may recall the letter of the prodigal BGU III. 846¹⁶ (ii/A.D.) (= *Selections*, p. 95) οὐκ οἶδες, ὅτι θέλω πηρὸς γενέσται, εἰ γνοῦναι, ὅπως ἀνθρόπῳ [ἔ]τ[ι] ὀφείλω ὀβολόν; "do you not know that I would rather be a cripple than be conscious that I am still owing anyone an obolus?" Deissmann (*LAE* p. 179 n.²⁸) finds a beginning of this usage in Lk 24²⁰, the only place in the NT where ὅπως is construed with the ind. (but cf. Mt 26⁵⁹ A). A good ex. of ὅπως c. ind. from the papyri is BGU III. 830⁴ (i/A.D.) δ[ιε]πεμψάμην σ[οι τὸ]ν ἐμὸν ἄνθρωπον, ὅπ[ως] καλῶς ποιήσι(= εις), συμβαλὼν χάρ[ακα] περὶ τοῦ ἐ[λαιῶν]ος ἡ(= ἰ)δίου αὐτοῦ τοῦ ἐνθάδε. (3) Ὅπως, "in order that," is seen c. subj. with ἄν in PSI V. 512⁸ (B.C. 253–2) ἐγὼ δὲ πρὸς τοὺς μελισσοργοὺς ἐπορεύθην ὅπως ἂν εἰδήσω ὡς πωλῖται, "I went to the bee-keepers that I might know how it is sold," and without ἄν in such passages as P Par 46¹⁶ (B.C. 153) γέγραφά σοι ὅπω[ς] Ἀπολλωνίῳ παραγγείλῃς, P Ryl II. 130¹⁹ (A.D. 34) διὸ ἀξιῶ γράψαι τῶι τῆς κώμης ἀρχεφόδῳ ὅπως ἀναζήτησιν ποιήσηται, and P Tebt II. 419¹ (iii/A.D.) πέμψον τὴν ὄνον ὅπως σφραγισθῇ. On the relative use of ὅπως and ὅπως ἄν in the Attic inscrr. see Meisterhans *Gr.* § 91. 30. (4) For ὅπως after ἐρωτάω and similar verbs of asking, exhorting, etc. (as in Lk 11³⁷ *al.*) cf. P Tebt II. 409¹⁸ (A.D.) 5) ἐπὶ τῆς πόλεώς σε ἠρώτησα δούς σοι (δραχμὰς) ιβ ὅπως Λυσιμάχῳ δοῖς καὶ ἐρωτήσῃς αὐτὸν οἱ(= ὑ)πὲρ ἐμοῦ ὅπως γ̄ τελήους μοίκλεας (*l.* μύκλους) συντόμως πέμψῃι, "at the metropolis I gave you 12 drachmae and asked you to give them to Lysimachus and ask him on my behalf to send me at once 3 he-asses without blemish" (Edd.), P Amh II. 131⁸ (early ii/A.D.) μελησάτω σοι ὅπως ἀγορασθῇ τὰ κενώματα, "see that the empty jars are bought" (Edd.), and P Oxy I. 67⁶ (A.D. 338) ἐπιδίδωμί σοι ὅπως εἰς ἔργον προαγάγοις τὰ κεκελευσμένα, "I petition you to carry his orders into effect." An apparent ex. of ὅπως c. inf., where we would have expected ὥστε, is to be found in P Tebt II. 315³⁰ (ii/A.D.) ἔχι γὰρ συστατικὰς [ὅ]πως τὸν ἀπιθοῦντα μετὰ φρουρᾶς τῷ ἀρχιερεῖ πέμπιν, "he has instructions to send recalcitrants under guard to the high-priest" (Edd.). MGr ὅπως κι ἄν, "however."

ὅραμα.

In P Goodsp Cairo 3⁵ (iii/B.C.) (= Witkowski,² p. 47) ἔδο]ξέ [μο]ι ν[ῦ]ν περὶ τοῦ ὁράματος διασαφῆσαί σοι, ὅπως εἰδῇς κτλ., ὁράματος refers apparently to a "vision" granted in sleep : cf. P Par 51³⁸ (B.C. 160) τὸ ὅραμα τοῦτο τεθη(= έ)αμαι of a "vision" in the temple of Serapis in Memphis, and *Syll* 760 (= ³ 1128)³ καθ' ὅραμα of a similarly granted vision of the goddess Isis ("quia deam per somnum viderat" Ed.). We may add the fragment of an uncanonical gospel P Oxy X. 1224 Fr. 2 recto[11] καὶ [παρεσταμέ]νου Ἰησοῦ [ἐ]ν ὁράμα[τι λέγει] Τί ἀθ[υμ]εῖς; where there is possibly a reference to a vision of encouragement granted to Peter after his Fall (see the editors' introd.).

ὅρασις.

For ὅρασις = "seeing," "the act of sight," cf. Wünsch AF 4²⁶ (iii/A.D.) ὁρκίζω σε τὸν θεὸν τὸν τὴν ὅρασιν παντὶ ἀνθρώπῳ χαρισάμενον, P Lond 46¹⁴⁷ (iv/A.D.) (= I. p. 70) ἐγώ εἰμι ὁ ἀκέφαλος δαίμων ἐν τοῖς ποσὶν ἔχω[ν] τὴν ὅρασιν, and the dedicatory Syll 774 (= ³ 1141)² (Imperial) ἀγαθῇ τύχῃ. Στρατία ὑπὲρ τῆς ὁράσεως θεᾷ Δήμητρι δῶρον, an offering made by Stratia to the goddess Demeter on account of restored sight. For the meaning "appearance," as in Rev 4³, cf. P Leid Wˣⁱⁱⁱ (ii/iii A.D.) (= II. p. 127) ὁ μεταμορφούμενος ἐν ταῖς ὁράσεσιν. A curious use of the word occurs in OGIS 56⁵⁶ (B.C. 237), where it is employed as a title of the daughter-goddess of the Sun—ὅρασιν αὐτοῦ, i.e. "oculum Solis" (see Dittenberger's note). In an inser. in C. and B. ii. p. 653, No. 564, we find εἰς ὅρασιν καὶ εἰς ὅλον τὸ σῶμα αὐτῷ καὶ εἰς τέκνα καὶ εἰς βίον, "sight, body, children, life," all of which are to feel the κατάραι ὅσε ἀνγεγραμμένα[ι ε]ἰσίν if the tomb is disturbed. Ramsay thinks the curses are Jewish. For ὁρασείας = ὁράσεις in the sense of "visions" (as in Ac 2¹⁷) see P Strass I. 35⁵ (iv/A.D.) with the editor's note. The word, which survives in MGr, was commonly used by the Church Fathers to denote the "visions" of the monks.

ὁρατός.

P Grenf I. 47¹⁴ (A.D. 148) ὁ δὲ Λεοντᾶς ἐπὶ τοῦ παρόντος οὐχ ὁρατός, ἐμφανὴς κατὰ τὸ ἀναγκαῖον προῆλθον. Cf. s.v. ἀόρατος.

ὁράω

(cognate with our beware) is clearly durative wherever it occurs in the NT (Proleg. p. 110 f.). The verb is rare in the popular language, its place being taken by βλέπω and θεωρέω; but it is wrong to say that it is "dead" after i/A.D. See the exx. from late Greek and especially from the papyri cited by Abbott CR xx. p. 232 f., e.g. BGU I. 248⁵ (i/A.D. —cf. Berichtigungen ad l.) ὡς ὁρᾶς, ib. II. 660¹⁶ (ii/A.D.) ὁρᾶται, and the edict of the Emperor Julian P Fay 20²⁰ (iv/A.D.—cf. Archiv ii. p. 169) εἰ ἀποτέτακται τὸν Αὐτοκράτορα ὁρᾶν πᾶσιν αὐτοῖς μετὰ τοσαύτης κοσμιότητος καὶ σωφροσύνης (cf. 1 Tim 2²) καὶ ἐγκρατείας τὰ τῆς βασιλείας διοικοῦντα, "if they have all been commanded to watch the emperor himself acting with so much propriety and discretion and moderation in the affairs of his kingdom" (Edd.).

Ὁράω in its literal sense of bodily vision may be illustrated from P Rev Lˣˡⁱ ¹³ (B.C. 259-8) (= Chrest. I. p. 351) ἔξω ὅρα, "look on the back" of the papyrus sheet.

The verb which is used in the LXX as a t.t. for appearances of the Divinity and similarly by Paul (1 Cor 9¹, 15⁵ ⁸ al.) is found in connexion with dreams in such passages as P Par 51⁸ (account of a dream in the Serapeum—B.C. 160) (= Selections. p. 19) ἐξαί[φνης] ἀνίγω τοὺς ὀφθαλμούς μου, καὶ ὁρῶ [τὰς] Διδύμας ἐν τῷ διδασκαλήῳ τοῦ Τοθῆ[τος,

"suddenly I open my eyes and see the twins in the school of Tothes," ib. 44¹¹ (B.C. 153) ἐγὼ γὰρ ἐνύπνια ὁρῶ πονηρά, followed by βλέπω Μενέδημον κατατρέχοντά με, and ib. 45⁵ (B.C. 153) (= Witkowski², p. 85) ὁρῶ ἐν τῷ ὕπνῳ τὸν δραπέδην Μενέδημον ἀντικείμενον ἡμῖν. See also P Leid Wˣⁱⁱⁱ ²⁶ (ii/iii A.D.) σέ, τὸν αὐτογέννητον θεόν, τὸν πάντα ὁ)ρῶντα καὶ πάντα ἀκούοντα, καὶ μὴ ὁρώμενον, and the iv/A.D. Christian sepulchral inser., P Hamb I. 22³ Υἱὲ θεοῦ μεγάλοιο τὸν οὐδέποτ' ἑδρακεν ἀνήρ: cf. Jn 1¹⁸, 1 Tim 6¹⁶.

The meaning "see" with the mind, "perceive," "discern," may be traced in such exx. as P Hib I. 44⁴ (B.C. 253) ὁρῶντες δέ σε καταραθυμοῦντα ᾠμὴν δεῖν καὶ νῦν ἐπιστειλαί σοι, "but seeing that you are negligent I thought it my duty to send to you instructions again now" (Edd.), BGU IV. 1078⁷ (A.D. 39) λοιπὸν οὖν, ἐὰν λάβω τὰ κερμάμια (l. κεράμια or κερμάτια), ὄψομαι, τί με δεῖ ποιεῖν, P Oxy X. 1293⁴² (A.D. 117–38) ὄψομαι πάλιν τίς σοι βαστάξει, and P Fay 20¹⁰ (Imperial edict—iv/A.D.) ὡς ἐκ τῶν παρόντων ὁρῶ, "so far as I see under present conditions" (Edd.). The sense of "experience," as in Lk 3⁶, may be illustrated by P Oxy I. 129⁵ (iv/A.D.) χρὴ γάρ τινα ὁρῶντα αἱαυτὸν ἐν δυστυχίᾳ κἂν ἀναχωρῖν καὶ μὴ ἁπλῶς μάχαισθαι τῷ δεδογμένῳ, "when a man finds himself in adversity he ought to give way and not fight stubbornly against fate" (Edd.).

For ὅρα μή c. aor. subj. (Burton § 209), as in 1 Thess 5¹⁵, cf. BGU I. 37⁶ (A.D. 50) ὅρα οὖν μὴ αὐτὸν κατάσχῃς, "see then that you do not detain him," P Oxy III. 532¹⁵ (ii/A.D.) ὅρα μὴ ἄλλως πράξῃς. In Mk 1⁴⁴ ὅρα does little more than add emphasis, cf. ib. 531⁹ (ii/A.D.) ὅρα μηδενὶ ἀνθρώπων ἐν τῇ οἰκίᾳ προσκρο[ύ]σῃς, "take care not to offend any of the persons at home" (Edd.), ib. 527⁶ (ii/iii A.D.) ὅρα μὴ ἀμελήσῃς, ἐπεὶ γὰρ ἐγὼ αὐτὸν κατέχω, "do not neglect this, as I am keeping him" (Edd.).

The colloquial σὺ ὄψῃ in Mt 27⁴ (cf.²⁴, Ac 18¹⁵) may not mean more than "you will see to that" (Proleg. p. 177): Gildersleeve, on the other hand, finds in the fut. an imperative conception, "see thou to that" (Syntax i. p. 116 n.). For exx. of the phrase cf. Epict. ii. 5. 29, iv. 6. 11. The perf. ὅπωπα, "I have caught sight of," is found along with ἑώρακα in the same document, P Petr II. 17 (3)⁷ ⁹ (Ptol.). In the late P Lond 113. 3⁷ (vi/A.D.) (= I. p. 208), the lease of a farm, provision is made that the cutting and the carrying away of the hay are to "look to" the landlord (ὁρώντων πρὸς σέ, ad te spectantium) for their accomplishment: cf. Jn 19³⁷ ὄψονται εἰς . . . where Abbott (Joh. Gr. p. 245) finds the idea of reverence. See further s.vv. βλέπω, εἶδον, and θεωρέω.

ὀργή.

For ὀργή in the sense of natural "anger," "passion," cf. P Leid Wˣˣⁱᵛ ³¹ (ii/iii A.D.) (= II. p. 161) ὅταν ὑποτάσῃς (l. ὑποτάσσῃς) φόβον ἢ ὀργήν, BGU IV. 1024¹⁵ ²⁹ (end iv/A.D.) μὴ [κατέχ]ων τῆ[ν ὀ]ργὴν ἐφόνευσεν αὐτὴν ξ[ίφει. The common Biblical use with reference to divine wrath may be illustrated by such passages from the inscr. as OGIS 383²¹⁰ (mid. i/B.C.) τούτωι δαιμόνων ὀργὴ καὶ θεῶν ἁπάντων αὐτῶι καὶ γένει πρὸς ἅπασαν τιμωρίαν ἀνείλατος ἔστω, and Syll 887 (= ³ 1237)⁶ where any one disturbing a tomb is warned—ἕξει δὲ κ(αὶ) ὀργὴν μεγάλην τοῦ μεγάλου Διός.

See also Aristeas 254 γινώσκειν δὲ δεῖ, διότι θεὸς τὸν πάντα κόσμον διοικεῖ μετ' εὐμενείας καὶ χωρὶς ὀργῆς ἁπάσης. In Rom 12¹⁹ the subst. should be personified, "Make room for the Wrath (the Divine Retribution which alone can do justice on wrong)": cf. 5⁹, 1 Thess 2¹⁶.

ὀργίζομαι,

"am angry," is seen in P Par 63 viii. ³ (B.C. 165) ἐγὼ τὰ μέγιστα ἠγνωμονημένος ὑπό σου καὶ μεμαθευκὼς ἔτι πρότερον τοῖς μὲν ἀδικήμασιν ἀπαρακαλύπτως [ὀ]ργίζεσθαι καὶ δυσχεραίνειν κτλ., and Syll 804 (= ³ 1170)⁵ (ii/A.D.) κατὰ δὴ τὸν πλοῦν ἐν Αἰγείνῃ ἐκέλευσέν με μὴ πολλὰ ὀργίζεσθαι: cf. also the restoration in P Iand 16² (v/vi A.D.) ὁ λαμπρ-(ότατος) κύριος [ὑμῶν] ὀρ[γίζ]ει. On the 'Western' reading ὀργισθείς Mk 1⁴¹ see Nestle Philologia Sacra (Berlin 1896), p. 26, but cf. Deissmann Sprachliche Erforschung, p. 30 f. MGr ὀργισμένος, "angry," "furious."

ὀργίλος.

This NT ἅπ. εἰρ. (Tit 1⁷) = "prone to anger" (iracundus) occurs in Didache iii. 2 μὴ γίνου ὀργίλος· ὁδηγεῖ γὰρ ἡ ὀργὴ πρὸς τὸν φόνον.

ὀργυιά.

On the accent of ὀργυιά, "fathom" (Ac 27²⁸), see Winer-Schmiedel Gr. p. 72. The word is found in the fragment of a metrological work, P Oxy IV. 669³⁹ (later than A.D. 287) οἱ δ (πήχεις) ὀργυιά, ὀ[ργυιά]δέ ἐστιν ἡ διάστασις τῶν χιρῶ[ν, "4 cubits an ὀργυιά, which is the distance of the outstretched hands" (Edd.): cf. Archiv iii. p. 440.

ὀρέγομαι

is found ter in the NT (1 Tim 3¹, 6¹⁰, Heb 11¹⁶) in the sense "seek for," "long for," but in Kaibel 448⁴ οὗ τινος [αὐ]τῷ αὐτοκασιγνήτων χεῖρας ὀρέξα[μέ]νου, the concluding phrase is βοηθήσαντος, "having come to the assistance of," rather than "having sought assistance from": see Herwerden Lex. s.v., and cf. P Oxy VI. 902¹¹ (c. A.D. 465) ἐπὶ τοίνυν οἱ ἔκδικοι ἐπενοήθησαν ἐν ταῖς πόλεσιν πρὸ[ς] τῷ βοήθειαν ὀρέξαι τοῖς ἀδικουμένοις κτλ., "therefore, since advocates have been devised in the cities for the purpose of lending assistance to the oppressed," etc. In 1 Tim 3¹ Field (Notes, p. 204) prefers the translation "aspires to" rather than "seeketh" (RV), to bring out that the idea of ambitious seeking does not necessarily belong to the word itself or to its connexion: see his exx. from late Greek, and add Polyb. v. 104. 7 πραγμάτων (= imperii) ὀρέγεται (cited by Parry ad 1 Tim 3¹). MGr ρέγομαι.

ὀρεινός.

The itacistic form ὀρινός, which is read by WH in Lk 1³⁹, ⁶⁵ is amply attested in the papyri, where the word is regularly used to describe all canals on the border of the desert, e.g. P Strass I. 17⁴ (A.D. 124) ἐν ὀρινῇ (v. διώρυχι Πατσώντ(εως) Βακχ(ιάδος), "on the desert canal of Patsontis at Bacchias" (see the editor's Introd.). See also Aristeas 107, 118, and cf. s.v. ὄρος.

ὄρεξις.

"strong desire," has a bad sense in the only passage (Rom 1²⁷) in which it is found in the NT, but Matheson (Epictetus i. p. 31 f.) has shown that in Stoic philosophy the word is neutral, and that if in certain passages (e.g. i. 4. 1, iii. 22. 13) Epictetus speaks of the necessity of removing or postponing it altogether, that is because he is addressing those who are still under discipline, learning how to avoid what is evil, but not yet fully attracted towards what is good. See also Epict. ii. 13. 7, iii. 9. 18 and 22; and CR xxxi. (1917), p. 172 f.

ὀρθοποδέω.

This verb used metaphorically "make a straight course" is found only in Gal 2¹⁴ and in later eccles. writers, who have borrowed its use from that passage. Westcott (St. Paul and Justification, p. 27) thinks that the verb may have been a word of Antioch, or of Tarsus, and that it has a kind of "sporting" ring about it. Burton ad Gal l.c. cites ὀρθόποδες βαίνοντες from Nicander Al. 419.

ὀρθός

is used of "standing" hay in P Lond 1165² (ii/A.D.) (= III. p. 191) [χόρτ] χλωροῦ ὀρθοῦ: cf. ib. 755 verso ² (iv/A.D.) (= III. p. 221) where "standing" columns (ἑστῶτες corrected from ὀρθοί) are contrasted with those that have fallen (χαμαὶ κείμενοι). In Syll 540¹⁸ (B.C. 175-1) ποιῶν ὀρθὰ πάντα πρὸς κανόνα διηνεκῆ, we have the meaning "straight." The metaphorical use of the adj. is seen in PSI V. 549³ (B.C. 42-1) ὀρθὴ στήσομαι ἀπέναντί σου, with reference to the attitude of a servant to her mistress, and BGU I. 248⁹ (i/A.D.: see ib. II. 594 note) διὰ γὰρ τὴν [σ]ὴ[ν] πρόν[ο]ια[ν] ἐν ὀρθῶι μέλλει γείνεσθαι (l. γίνεσθαι): cf. P Oxy III. 490¹⁶ (A.D. 124) καὶ ἔστιν μου ἡ σφραγὶς Ἁρποχράτου ὀρθοῦ, the signature of a witness, Kaibel 307¹ μαρτύριον ὀρθοῦ βίου, and OGIS 320¹⁰ (mid. ii/B.C.) ἀπ' ὀρθῆς, "from the right" (way): Heb 12¹³. MGr ὀρθός (ὀρτός in Eastern dialects: Thumb Handbook p. 18), "straight," "correct": "steep." The last meaning recalls the cognate Lat. arduus: ὀρθός, however, had originally an initial, and probably also a medial, digamma (*Ϝορθός, *ϜορθϜός) (Boisacq, p. 711).

ὀρθοτομέω.

The meaning of this NT ἅπ. εἰρ. (2 Tim 2¹⁵: cf. Prov 3⁶, 11⁵) is by no means clear, but on the analogy of the similarly formed καινοτομέω, "make a new or strange assertion," it seems best to lay the main stress on the adj. and to understand by ὀρθοτομέω τὸν λόγον, "teach the word aright." Sophocles (Lex. s.v.) renders "expound soundly"; cf. the use of ὀρθοτομία = "orthodoxy" in eccles. writers. Parry (ad 2 Tim l.c.) adopts the suggestion that the metaphor may be derived not from road making (τέμνειν ὁδόν), but from the mason's cutting stones fair and straight to fit into their places in a building, and compares the use of their simplex subst. in Syll 587¹⁷ (B.C. 329-8) μισθωτεῖ τῆς τομῆς τῶν λίθων, and ²² τομὴ καὶ κομιδὴ καὶ θέσις τοῦ λίθου. A different turn is given to the verb by Paspati, who translates "preach fearlessly" on the ground that in MGr ὀρθὰ κοπτά is used to denote "clearly and fearlessly": see *Exp* III. i. p. 238.

ὀρθρίζω,

"rise early," takes the place of the classical ὀρθρεύω in Biblical Greek (except in Tob 9⁶ B): see Lk 21³⁸ and the LXX *saepe*. According to Thumb (*Hellen.* p. 123) the dependence of the verb on the Heb. הִשְׁכִּים in the sense of "rise early" is very improbable, and reference is made to such analogous verbs in MGr as νυχτορεύω, "work throughout the night," and μεσημεριάζω, "do something at midday."

ὀρθρινός.

This late form for ὄρθριος (see *s.v.*), is condemned by the Atticists (Lob. *Phryn.* p. 51). In the NT it is confined to Lk 24²² (cf. Rev 22¹⁶ TR), but is found *quater* in the LXX.

ὄρθριος.

For this adj. = "belonging to the morning," "early," which is read in the TR of Lk 24²², cf. BGU IV. 1208²⁵ (B.C. 27–6) ἵνα δὲ ἰδῆς τὸ ὄρθριον τοῦ ἀνθρώ(που), πέπομφά σοι ἣν τέθειται μίσθωσιν, where the editor suggests that τὸ ὄρθριον = "his morning greeting," "his first deed." The comparative is seen in P Par 49²⁹ (B.C. 164–158) (= Witkowski², p. 70) καὶ ἀπέλυσα εἴπας αὐτῶι ὀρθρίτερον ἐλθεῖν, BGU IV. 1204⁴ (A.D. 2) ὀρθρίτερον τῆς . . . [το]ῦ ἐν[ε]στῶτος μηνὸς Παῦνι, and P Strass I. 37¹⁴ (iii/A.D.) ὀρθρέτερον οὖν [. . .], "recht bald nun . . ." (Ed.).

ὄρθρος.

P Fay 108¹⁰ (*c.* A.D. 171) ὑπὸ τὸν ὄρθρον, "about dawn," the same phrase as in Ac 5²¹: cf. P Flor III. 305¹¹ (iv/A.D.) ὄρθρου, "di buon mattino" (Ed.).

ὀρθῶς.

In P Petr III. 56 (*b.*)¹⁰ (B.C. 269–258) an official swears that he will manage affairs in connexion with the dykes uprightly and justly—τὰ χωματικὰ πραγματεύσεσθαι ὀρθῶς καὶ δικαίως. Cf. P Eleph 9³ (B.C. 223–222) οὐκ ὀρθῶς οὖν ποιεῖς ἀ[ναβαλόμενος τὰ π]ράγματα, and P Ryl II. 177¹⁴ (A.D. 246) περὶ δὲ τοῦ ὀρθῶς καλῶς [γεγενῆσθαι, "but as to whether this has been rightly and fairly done."

ὁρίζω

in its primary sense of "divide," "separate from," is well seen in OGIS 335¹¹² (ii/i B.C.) εἰ]ς τὴν ὁδὸν τὴν ὁρίζουσαν [τ]ήν τε Πιταναίαν καὶ [τὴν . . . . . . : cf. P Fay 126⁶ (ii/iii A.D.) ἐπὶ μέλι (*l.* μέλλει ὁρίζεσθαι, "since the boundaries (of a piece of land) are to be fixed" (Edd.). From this it is an easy transition to "fix a limit to," "set apart," as in Ac 11²⁹ (cf. Field *Notes*, p. 119). The verb is construed with an acc. of time, as in Heb 4⁷, in P Flor I. 61⁴⁵ (A.D. 85) (as amended *Chrest.* II. p. 59) ἡγεμόνες πεν[τ]αετίαν ὥρισαν περὶ τοῦ πολυχρον[ί]ων: cf. Aristeas 157. For the pass. of what has been *appointed*, *decreed*, as in Lk 22²², cf. P Par 63¹² (B.C. 164) (= P Petr III. p. 26) τοῦ διὰ τοῦ προστάγματος ὡρισμένου κε[φ]αλαίου. "the assessment defined in the decree" (Mahaffy), P Lond 1108¹³ (A.D. 18) (= III. p. 136) μετὰ τὴν ὡρισμένην

ἀπόδοσιν. Similarly of time, P Fay 11¹⁶ (*c.* B.C. 115) ἐν τοῖς διὰ τῶν συμβολαίω[ν] ὁρισθεῖσιν χρόνοις, "within the periods fixed by the contracts" (Edd.), P Amh II. 50¹⁵ (B.C. 106) ἐν τῶι ὡρισμένωι χρόνωι, P Tebt II. 327¹² (late ii/A.D.) μετὰ τὸν [ὡ]ρισμένον χρόνον τῆς [ἐ]πιτηρήσεως, "after the appointed term of his office" (Edd.). For the subst. ὁρισμός, "boundary," cf. BGU II. 599² (ii/A.D.) ἕως ὁρισμοῦ καρπῶν. *ib.* IV. 1001²⁵ (A.D. 212–3) (φόρου) τ[ο]ῦ δι' ἐπισ[κέ]ψεως ὁρισμοῦ φα[ι]νομένου, P Amh II. 97¹¹ (A.D. 180–192), where certain properties are set forth as— γίτονες καθὼς διὰ τῆς τοῦ ὁρισμοῦ πορείας δηλοῦ[τ]αι νότου καὶ λιβὸς οἰκόπ[εδα] Εὐνοίδια λεγόμ[ενα]. "adjoined, as is set forth in the survey. on the south and west by the plots called Eunoidia" (Edd.), and the introd. to P Strass I. 31. Note the curious use of the word in Exod 8¹² περὶ τοῦ ὁρισμοῦ τῶν βατράχων. "about the limitation of the frogs (to the river)." In MGr ὁρισμός = "order," "command," cf. ὁρισμός σου φιρμάνι, "thy order is an imperial decree (firman)."

ὅριον.

For this word, which in the NT is always found in the plur. = "boundaries." *i.e.* "territory," "district" (Lat. *fines*), cf. P Grenf II. 15ⁱⁱ ³ (B.C. 139) ὅρια καὶ γείτονε[ς τ]ῆς ὅλης γῆς νότου καὶ ἀπηλιώτου νήσος Ἀφροδίτης . . . καὶ νήσος Λητοῦς, P Tebt II. 277¹⁶ (astrological—iii A.D.) ἐν μὲν Κρόνου ὁρίοις, P Fay 38⁸ (iii/iv A.D.) ἕως τῶν ὁρίων ἐποικίου, "as far as the boundaries of the farmstead," and BGU IV. 1049⁹ (iv/A.D.) ἐπὶ τοῖς οὖσι τῶν ὅλων ἐνγεγραμμένων ἀρ[ουρῶ]ν ὁρίοις. For ὁριοδείκτης, "one who marks out boundaries," see BGU II. 616⁸ (ii/iii A.D.).

ὁρκίζω.

For ὁρκίζω, "adjure," with a double acc., as in Mk 5⁷, Ac 19¹³, we may cite the imprecatory tablet from Hadrumetum, written in iii/A.D. but composed not later than ii/A.D., which Deissmann reproduces in *BS* p. 274 ff., e.g. ὁρκίζω σε, δαιμόνιον πνεῦμα τὸ ἐνθάδε κείμενον, . . . τὸν θεὸν τοῦ Ἀβρααν κτλ., "I adjure thee, demonic spirit, who dost rest here, by the God of Abraan," etc.: cf. OGIS 229²⁷ (B.C. 246–220) ὁρκισάτωσαν αὐτοὺς οἱ ἀποδειχθησόμενοι πρεσβευταὶ τὸν ὅρκον τὸν ἐν τῆι ὁμολογίαι γεγραμμένον. For ὁρκίζω τινά followed by κατά with gen., as in 3 Kingd 2¹², cf. the magic papyrus P Lond 121²⁴² (iii/A.D.) (= I. p. 92) ὁρκίζω σε δαίμων κατὰ τῶν βοηθημάτων σου, *al.* See also *s.vv.* ἐνορκίζω, ἐξορκίζω. Ὁρκίζω is still used in MGr.

ὅρκος.

P Petr III. 56 (*a*)¹² (iii/B.C.) ὤμοσά σοι τὸν πάτριον ὅρκον ἐπὶ τοῦ ποταμοῦ. *ib.* 104¹⁰ (B.C. 244–3) κε[χει]ρογράφηκασι τὸν εἰθισμένον ὅρκον τοσούτου μεμισθῶσθαι, "they have written under their hands the usual oath that it was let for this amount" (Edd.)—with reference to a farm holding. BGU III. 1002¹⁵ (B.C. 55) ἐὰν δέ τίς σοι ὅρκος ἢ ἐπίδειξις ἐπιβληθῆι περὶ αὐτῶν, ἐγὼ αὐτὸς ἐπιτελέσωι κτλ.—a deed of sale, and P Ryl II. 88²⁶ (A.D. 156) ἢ ἔνοχος εἴην τῷ ὅρκ[ῳ, "otherwise may I be liable to the consequences of the oath"—a common formula. Cf. also the unusual formula P Eleph 23²⁰ (B.C. 223–2) ε[ὑ]ορκοῦ[ντι] μέμ μ[ο]ι [ε]ὖ εἴη, ἐφιορκοῦντι δὲ ἔνοχον εἶναι τῆι ἀσεβείαι τοῦ ὅρκον. With Lk 1⁷³ cf. *Pelagia-Legenden* p. 13⁹ ἐν ὅρκῳ εἶχεν τοῦ μὴ γεύσασθαί τι.

For an oath sworn on the Gospels see P Lond V. 1708²²⁸ (A.D. 567?) ἐκάστου τούτων ἐνωμότως θεμένου ὅρκον ἐπάνω τῶν σεπτῶν μεγαλί(= εἰ)ων, and cf. P Mon I. 1²⁶ (A.D. 574) τὸν ἐνώμοτον καὶ φρικτὸν ὅρκον ἐπὶ τῶν θείων καὶ ἀχράντων καὶ σεπτῶν κειμηλίων ("relics"). On various forms of oaths from the inscr. see Herwerden *Lex. s.v.* ὅρκος, and for the idea of "fence," "something that shuts you in" (cf. the cognate ἕρκος), underlying the word cf. Murray *Rise of the Greek Epic*, p. 265 f. The dim. ὅρκιον is found in *OGIS* 453²⁶ (B.C. 39–35).

ὀρκωμοσία.

This rare word = "taking of an oath" with reference to the whole action is confined in the NT to Heb 7²⁰, ²¹, ²⁸. For the neut. ὀρκωμόσιον see *Syll* 592 (= ³1007)²⁹ (B.C. 130–100), and for the plur. *OGIS* 229⁶² (iii/B.C.) τὰ δὲ ἱερεῖα τὰ εἰς τὰ [ὀρ]κωμόσια ἐν Σμύρνηι [δότω ὁ ταμίας Καλ]λῖνος. The easy transference to 1st decl. is suggested by such analogies as ἀντωμοσία. For ὀρκωμότης see P Grenf I. 11ⁱⁱ·¹⁷ (B.C. 157), and cf. Preisigke *Fachwörter s.v.*

ὁρμάω,

used intransitively as in all its NT occurrences = "rush," is seen in P Strass II. 100¹⁷ (ii/B.C.) εἰς φυγὴν ὥρμησαν, "took to flight," and similarly P Tebt I. 48²⁴ (c. B.C. 113). For a somewhat weakened sense cf. P Oxy I. 118 *verso*²⁹ (late iii/A.D.) ἔχων ὧν χάριν ὥρμι(= η)σας, "when you have obtained what you went for" (Edd.). The verb is construed with the dat. in P Oxy IX. 1204²⁰ (A.D. 299), when a certain Oxyrhynchite "made a design upon him (one Plutarchus) and ventured to nominate him for the decemprimate"—αὐτῷ ὁρμώμενος τετόλμηκεν αὐτὸν ὀνομάζειν εἰς δεκαπρωτείαν. For the mid. in the sense of origin, "starting from," cf. P Tebt II. 397¹⁷ (A.D. 198) ἀπὸ μηδενὸς ὁρμωμένη, "not on the basis of any claim," and such late exx. as P Hamb I. 23⁹ (A.D. 569) ἀμπελουργῶν ὁρμωμένων μὲν ἀπὸ κώμης Ἰβιῶνος . . ., ἐφεστῶτες δὲ ἐνταῦθα ἐπὶ τῆς α[ὐ]τῆς Ἀντινοέων πόλ(εως), PSI VI. 686⁴ (vi/A.D.?) ὁρ]μώμενος ἐκ τῆσδε τῆς κώμης, and P Mon I. 1⁷ (A.D. 574). For the metaph. usage of the verb we may cite Epict. ii. 6. 10 εἰ δέ γε ᾔδειν ὅτι νοσεῖν μοι καθείμαρται νῦν, καὶ ὥρμων ἂν ἐπ᾿ αὐτό, "nay, if I really knew that it was ordained for me now to be ill, I should wish ("direct my impulse") to be ill" (Matheson), and Aristeas 270 ὃς γὰρ ἐπὶ τὸ πλεονεκτεῖν ὁρμᾶται, προδότης πέφυκε. The compd. ἐξορμάω (LXX) is seen in P Oxy IX. 1216²⁰ (ii/iii A.D.) θεῶν γὰρ θελόντων σπεύδω ἐξορμῆσαι πρὸς ὑμᾶς, "for with the help of the gods I am hastening to set out to you" (Ed.).

ὁρμή

in its literal sense of "onset," "rush," is seen in such passages as *Syll* 318 (= ³700)²⁴ (B.C. 117) ἔστεξεν ("repressed") τὴν ἐπιφερομένην τῶν βαρβάρων ὁρμήν, P Oxy VI. 901⁶ (A.D. 336) ἡμέτεροι χῦροι δύο τὴν ὁρμὴν ποιούμενοι ἐπὶ ἡμέτερον ἔδαφος, "our two pigs making a rush into our piece of land": cf. Ac 14⁵ and see Field *Notes*,

p. 122. The metaph. sense, "impulse to act," as probably in Jas 3⁴, may be illustrated by the petition P Grenf II. 78¹⁶ (A.D. 307) ἀναγκαίως περὶ πο[λλοῦ] τὴν ὁρμὴν ποιούμενος πρὸς τὸν σὸν μεγαλεῖ[ον, ἡγε]μὼν δέσποτα, τάδε μαρτύρομαι: cf. M. Anton. iv. 40 πῶς ὁρμῇ μιᾷ πάντα πράσσει, with relation to the world ; and see *s.v.* ὁρμάω. Thackeray (*Gr.* i p. 38) cites ὁρμή = חֵמָה, "fury," in Ezek 3¹⁴, Dan Θ 8⁶, as an instance of the tendency on the part of the translators to use Greek words of similar sound to the Hebrew.

ὅρμημα.

The meaning of this NT ἅπ. εἰρ. in Rev 18²¹ is doubtful. It is often rendered "a rush," "a mighty onset," as in Deut 28³⁹, but Charles (*ICC ad l.* = II. p. 107 f.) suggests that the meaning is rather "indignation," as in Hos 5¹⁰ *al.* See *s.v.* ὁρμή *ad fin.*

ὄρνεον.

This dim. form, which is, however, to be translated simply "bird" in Rev 18², 19¹⁷·²¹ (cf. Mk 4⁴W), occurs uncontracted on the *verso* of P Petr III. 71 (iii/B.C.) οἱ θηρευταὶ τῶν ἀγρίων ὀρνέων : cf. also P Ryl II. 98(a)⁹ (A.D. 154–5) πᾶν ὄργ[εο]ν, and P Lond 1259¹⁶ (iv/A.D.) (= III. p. 240) ὄρνεα ῑγ. For other dim. forms see P Oxy XIV. 1729⁴ (iv/A.D.) ὀρνιθίων, and P Fay 118¹⁶ (A.D. 110) ἀγόρασον τὰ ὀρνιθάρια τῆς ἑορτῆς, "buy the birds for the feast" (Edd.).

ὄρνιξ.

This Doric form, which is read in Lk 13³¹ NDW, is attested in the papyri, e.g. P Lond 131 *recto*¹²⁵ (accounts—A.D. 78–9) (= I. p. 173) ὄρνιξι καὶ περιστ(εραῖς). The word survives in the MGr (Cappadocian) ὄρνιχ: cf. Thumb *Hellen.* p. 90 f., *Archiv* iv. p. 490.

ὄρνις

was specialized at an early date to mean "cock" or "hen," just as ἄλογον was restricted to the meaning "horse" as early as iv/A.D. (Hatzidakis *Einl.* p. 34 f.): cf. the use of "fowl" in English. The word is naturally common in food accounts, e.g. P Tebt II. 468 (late ii/B.C.) ὄρνιθας β, P Oxy IV. 738⁸ (c. A.D. 1) ὄρνις σιδυτὴ ἐξ ὕδα(τος) ᾱ, "1 bird . . . from the water": note also the provisions prepared in expectation of a visit (παρουσία) from the διοικητής Chrysippus, P Grenf II. 14(b)³ᶠ. (B.C. 264 or 227) ἑτοιμάκαμεν . . . ὄρνιθας πεντήκοντα, [ὅ]δια χῆνες πεντήκοντα, ὄρνιθες διακόσια[ι], περ[ι]στριδεῖς ἑκατόν : cf. 3 Kingd 4²³ ὀρνίθων ἐκλεκτῶν among Solomon's delicacies—the only occurrence of the form ὄρνις in the LXX (Thackeray *Gr.* i. p. 152 f.). In a i/B.C. memorandum of rent, P Goodsp Cairo 9, Pates acknowledges leasing an island for the sixteenth year for forty-five artabae of wheat and ten birds— ⁶ ὄρνιθας ῑ. Α φόρος ὀρνίθων, "a tax on fowls," is coupled with a φόρος προβάτων, "a tax on sheep," in P Strass I. 67 (A.D. 228). From the inscrr. we may cite a Lycian inscr., *JHS* xxxiv. (1914) p. 5. No. 10⁸ βούλομαι καθ᾿ ἔτος θύεσθαι [ἡμ]εῖν ἀλέκτορα καὶ ὄρνειθα τελέα[ν] καὶ καλ[ήν. For ὀρν(ε)ιθών, "fowl-house," see P Oxy IX. 1207⁴ (A.D. 175–6?). The same document refers to "8 laying hens in

perfect condition " (Ed.)—⁹ ὀρνείθων τελείων τοκάδων ὀκτώ:
cf. P Oxy XII. 1508 (A.D. 265) order to a poultry-dealer
(ὀρνιθᾶς) to supply two hens and twenty eggs for a birthday festival—εἰς γενέσια Πανάρους τοκάδες δύο . . . ᾠὰ
εἴκοσι. MGr ὄρνιθα, ὀρνίθι, "hen."

ὁροθεσία.

Ac 17²⁶ has hitherto been regarded as the only instance
from Biblical or profane Greek of this compound = "boundary" (cf. Winer-Schmiedel Gr. p. 22), but it is now found in
a closely allied sense in *Priene* 42³¹ ᵇ (after B.C. 133) δικαίαν
εἶναι ἔκριναν τὴν] Ῥωδίων κρίσιν τε καὶ ὁροθεσίαν, "ils
décidèrent que le jugement des Rhodiens et leur délimitation
étaient équitables " (Fouillac *Recherches*, p. 37).

ὄρος.

That ὄρος is used in the papyri to denote the "desert" is
seen in the reference in P Tebt II. 383⁶¹ (A.D. 46) to the
keepers of the registry-offices of Tebtunis and Kerkesucha-
on-desert—τῶν πρὸς γρ(αφείῳ) Τεβτ(ύνεως) καὶ Κερκεσού-
χ(ων) Ὄρους. Cf. also the following passages showing that
the "desert" was the regular place of burial—P Oxy II.
274²⁷ (A.D. 89–97) ὑπάρχει δὲ αὐτῶι ἐπὶ τοῦ ἀπὸ λιβὸς
μ[. . . . . .] ὄρους ἥμισυ μέρος τάφου, P Ryl II. 153⁵
(A.D. 138–161) ἐν ταῖς ἐπ[ισ]ήμοις τοῦ ὄρους ἡμέραις, "on
the high days of the cemeteries" (Edd.), and P Grenf II.
77²² (iii/iv A.D.) (= *Selections*, p. 121), a letter regarding
funeral expenses, which include a *pourboire* to a νεκροτάφος
for conveying a body εἰς τὸ ὄρος for burial. According to
Bell (P Lond IV. p. xvii.) ὄρος came to be used as a
synonym of μοναστήριον (= "desert-monastery"). The
ordinary meaning "mountain," which survives in MGr, is
seen in P Leid Wˣⁱˣ·³⁶ (ii/iii A.D.) (= II. p. 149) ἡ (l. αἱ)
πέτραι, κ(αὶ) τὰ ὄρη, κ(αὶ) ἡ θάλασσα κτλ. For the uncontracted gen. pl. ὀρέων, as in Rev 6¹⁵, cf. Aristeas 119
ἐκ τῶν παρακειμένων ὀρέων τῆς Ἀραβίας, and see Schweizer
Perg. p. 153. Cf. ὀρινός s.v. ὀρεινός.

ὀρύσσω.

P Petr III. 46(4)⁴ (Ptol.) τοῖς τὸ θεμέλιον ὀρύξασι ε, "to
those who dug the foundation, 5 (drachmae)." BGU IV.
1121²⁵ (B.C. 5) τὰς πλαγίους δι]ώρυγας παρα[θάψειν καὶ]
ὀρύξειν, P Lond 46³³³ (a spell—iv/A.D.) (= I. p.75) ὄρυξον
ἐπὶ δ δακτύλους, and P Oxy I. 121⁸ (iii/A.D.) αὐτὸς ὁ Φανείας
ἀνανκασέτω (l. ἀναγκασάτω) αὐτὰς ὀρυγῆνε (l. ὀρυγῆναι, the
late 2nd aor. pass.), "let Phanias himself have them (acanthus trees) dug round." This last document shows also the
compd. περιορύσσω—⁶ ἤδη ἐν τῇ σήμερον περειορυγήτωσαν,
"let them be dug round to-day." From the inscrr. we may
cite *OGIS* 483⁶² (ii/A.D.) ἐάν τινες ἐν ταῖς ὁδοῖς χοῦν ὀρύσσωσιν . . . κωλυέτωσαν αὐτοὺς οἱ ἀμφοδάρχαι.

ὀρφανός.

In P Petr II. 39(c) (Ptol.) we have what appears to be a
list of taxes paid by orphans, and beside one of the names
the note has been scribbled—(7)¹³ οὐκ ἔστιν ὀρφανὸς ἀλλὰ
υἱὸς Δαιφάντου, "he is not an orphan, but the son of Dai-
phantos." The word (= Lat. *orbus*) is common in petitions,
e.g. P Flor III. 319⁷ (A.D. 132–7) τοῦ δὲ [ἀ]δελφιδοῦ μου
ὀρφανοῦ ὄντος, P Tebt II. 326² (c. A.D. 266) ὑπὲρ θυγατρὸς

ὀρφανῆς καὶ καταδεοῦς τὴν ἡλικίαν δέσποτα ἡγεμών, ἱκετηρίαν τιθεμένη ἐπὶ τὸ σὸν μέγεθος καταφεύγω, "on behalf
of my orphan daughter who is under age, my lord praefect,
I make this supplication and take refuge in your power "
(Edd.), P Thead 19⁴ᶠᶠ (iv/A.D.) τοὺς ἀδικουμένους ὀρφανο[ύς],
ἡγεμὼν δέσποτα, ἐκδικεῖν εἴωθεν τὸ μεγαλεῖον τὸ σόν· ἑαυ-
τὸς το[ί]νυν ὀρφανὸς καταλελιμμένης (l. -ένος) στερηθεὶς
ἑκατέρων τῶν γονέων οὐκ ὀλίγ[ον] ἀδικοῦμαι κτλ., and P
Lips I. 41² (end iv/A.D.) ἀμφοῖν τοῖν γονέοιν ὀρφανή. See
also P Magd 13¹⁵ (B.C. 217) with the editor's note, and
BGU IV. 1209¹⁴ (B.C. 23) ὡς ἂν λάβῃς τὸ γράμμα ἐμβαλοῦ
(sc. εἰς πλοῖον) τόν τε ὀρφανὸν καὶ τὴν τούτου μητέρα. The
more general sense of the word may be illustrated from MGr
as in the distich, Abbott *Songs*, p. 226 No. 50, where a lover
mourns that his mistress is going away leaving him friendless
—καί μ' ἀφίνει ὀρφανό', the same combination as in Jn 14¹⁸:
see also Epict. iii. 24. 14 ὡς ὀρφανοὺς ἀφιείς, and *ib.* 15
οὐδείς ἐστιν ἄνθρωπος ὀρφανός, ἀλλὰ πάντων ἀεὶ καὶ διηνεκῶς ὁ πατήρ ἐστιν ὁ κηδόμενος (cited by Bauer *HZNT* ad
Jn 16³²). For the form ὀρφανικός see P Grenf I. 17¹⁷ (c. B.C.
147 or 136), P Oxy VI. 888⁴ (iii/iv A.D.), and for the subst.
ὀρφάνεια cf. P Par 39¹¹ (B.C. 161) ἐμβλέψαντες . . . εἰς τὴν
ἐκείνων ὀρφάνειαν, and P Fay 94⁵ (A.D. 222–235) a formal
release given by an orphan girl to her late guardian—τῷ
γε]νομένῳ τῆς ὀρφανείας αὐτῆς ἐπιτρόπῳ.

ὀρχέομαι.

For the subst. ὀρχηστής cf. P Strass II. 92⁶ (B.C. 244–3)
Ὀνόρις [ὀρ]χηστής, P Oxy III. 526⁹ (ii/A.D.) ἀναβῆ(=αἴ)-
νω σὺν [τῷ ὀρ]χηστῆ, and for ὀρχήστρια, "dancing-girl,"
cf. P Grenf II. 67 (A.D. 237) (= *Selections*, p. 108), a contract for the services of two dancing-girls for an approaching
festival—⁴ᶠᶠ βούλομαι [ἐ]κλαβεῖν παρά σου Τ[.]σαῖν [ὀρ]χή-
στριαν σὺν ἑτέρᾳ μιᾷ [λ]ει[τουρ]γήσειν ἡμῖν κτλ. (cf. Mt 14⁶).
For references to music and dancing in the papyri see a paper
in *SAM* iii. p. 117 ff.

ὅς

is found as a demonstrative pronoun in P Ryl II. 144¹⁴
(complaint of assault—A.D. 38) ὃς δὲ ἐκ τοῦ ἐναντίου ἄλογον
ἀηδίαν μοι ἐπιχειρήσας παρεχρήσατό μοι πολλὰ καὶ ἄσχημα,
"whereupon he opposing me made a brutal and odious
attack upon me and subjected me to much shameful mishandling" (Edd.): cf. Mk 15²³, Jn 5¹¹. For ὃς μέν . . .
ὃς δέ, "the one . . the other," as in Mt 21³⁵ *al.*, see P Oxy
IX. 1189⁷ (c. A.D. 117) ἐπιστολὰς δύο ἃς ἔγραψα ἣν μὲν σοὶ
ἣν δὲ Σαβείνῳ, and for ὃς δέ *solitarium* see PSI IV. 313³
(iii/iv A.D.) with the editor's note.

"Ὃς ἄν (ἐάν) c. conj. = "whosoever" may be illustrated
by P Par 46²² (B.C. 153) (= Witkowski², p. 87) περὶ ὧν ἂ̣ν
βούληι γράφε, P Grenf I. 30⁶ (B.C. 103) ἐ[φ]' οἷς ἂν οὖν
ὑμῶν προσδέωνται, P Oxy IV. 743²³ (B.C. 2) ἐν οἷς ἐὰν σου
προσδέηται, ²⁹ ὑπὲρ ὧν ἐὰν θέλῃς. For the comparative
usage of ὃς ἄν and ὃς ἐάν, see Thackeray *Gr.* i. p. 68, cited
s.v. ἄν. The relative preceding its "antecedent" is common, e.g. P Amh II. 35¹⁶ (B.C. 132) τῶν ἐκφορίων ἧς γεωργοῦσι ἱερᾶς γῆς Σοκνοπαίου θεοῦ μεγάλου, "the rents of the
land sacred to the great god Soknopaeus which they cultivate" (Edd.).

Pleonastic ὅς is seen in P Ryl II. 160³ (A.D. 28–9) ὃν

(l. ὧν) τὰ μέτρα ὅλης τῆς οἰκίας καὶ αὐλῆς ἃ πρόγειται, "of which the measurements and adjacent areas of the whole house and court are as aforesaid" (Edd.). Cf. also P Oxy I. 117[13] (ii/iii A.D.) ἐξ ὧν δώσεις τοῖς παιδίοις σου ἐν ἐξ αὐτῶν, "one of which please give to your children" (Edd.).

A few exx. may be cited of ὅς with prepositions—P Petr II. 40 (a)[26] (iii/B.C.) (= III. p. 149, Witkowski[2], p. 42) ἀφ' οὗ (cf. Lk 13[25]) ἡ ἐλεφαντηγὸς κατεποντίσθη, BGU I. 252[9] (A.D. 98) ἀφ' ἧς (sc. ἡμέρας, cf. the ellipsis of ὥρας in Lk 7[45]) [ἐὰ]ν ἀπα[ι]τ[η]θῇ: P Petr II. 11 (1)[8] (iii/B.C.) (= Selections, p. 8) γράφε δ' ἡμῖν καὶ σύ, ἵνα εἰδῶμεν ἐν οἷς εἶ, P Tebt I. 58[11] (B.C. 111) (= Witkowski[2], p. 104) ἐν οἷς εἰσιν ("in quo numero comprehenduntur") οἱ διὰ τοῦ νομοῦ κω(μο)γρ(αμ)ματεῖς: P Oxy VII. 1027[6] (i/A.D.) ἐξ οὗ καὶ ἐξεχομένου μου τῆς τῶ[ν] ἠνεχυρασμένων προσβολῆς, "when I therefore pursued my right of entry upon the transferred property" (Ed.): P Amh II. 31[16] (B.C. 112) ἐφ' ᾧι (cf. Rom 5[12]) ταξαμένη ἕξει ἐν φυτείαι τὸν τόπον φοίνιξι, "on the understanding that, having paid this sum, she shall retain the plot planted with palms" (Edd.), P Oxy II. 286[12] (A.D. 82) ἐφ' οἷς ἄλλοις ἡ ἀσφάλεια περιέχει, "with the other guarantees contained in the agreement" (Edd.): BGU III. 846[12] (ii/A.D.) (= Selections, p. 94) παιπαίδδευμαι, καθ' ὃν δι (= δεῖ, Wilcken) τρόπον, "punished I have been, as I deserve": and P Ryl II. 144[13] (A.D. 38) ὑπὲρ οὗ ἔχω πρὸς αὐτὸν ἐνεχύρον, "concerning a pledge I have against him" (Edd.).

Τίς is used for ὅς in BGU III. 822[5] (iii/A.D.) εὗρον γεο(= ω)ργόν, τίς αὐτὰ ἐλκύσῃ. ἀλλὰ τὰ σπέρματα τίς διδοῖ :—a usage of which there is no instance in the NT. On the other hand Radermacher (Gr. p. 63 note) finds in Mt 26[50] ἑταῖρε, ἐφ' ὃ πάρει the earliest ex. of ὅς in place of the interrogative τίς, and refers to Usener Der hl. Tychon, p. 50. He thus supports the AV rendering of Mt l.c.: cf. Sharp Epict. p. 41 f. For another suggestion see Rendel Harris, Exp T xxxv. p. 523 f.

In MGr ὅς is rarely used even in writing, and has disappeared in common speech: "so simple a form ceased to satisfy the desire for emphasis" (Jebb in Vincent and Dickson, Handbook to Modern Greek, p. 302). It survives in the compound ἐνῷ, "during," "while" (cf. ἐν ᾧ Mk 2[19], Lk 5[34], Jn 5[7]).

ὁσάκις,

"as often as," with ἐάν and subj., as in 1 Cor 11[25f], Rev 11[6], is seen in BGU IV. 1115[22] (B.C. 13) ὁσάκις ἐὰν δέῃ, P Hamb I. 37[3] (ii/A.D.) ὁσάκις ἐὰν εὕρω ἀφορμήν, γράφω σοι, and P Giss I. 12[5] (ii/A.D.) παρακαλῶ σε οὖν, τέκνον, ὁσάκις ἐὰν μέλλῃς πέμψαι, ἐντύπην (something to do with weaving?) μοι τοιαύτην πέμψον. For the construction with the ind. cf. P Oxy III. 471[52] (ii/A.D.) ὁσάκις ἠξιώθη μεταλαβεῖν ἱστιάσεως, "whenever he was invited to join the banquet" (Edd.).

ὅς γε.

For the emphasis imparted by this combination, as in Rom 8[32], cf. P Flor III. 370[9] (A.D. 132) ἔξω ἀρουρῶν ἓξ ἃς γε ἐμίσθωσας ἑτ[έ]ροις πρὸς ἃς οὐχ ἕξω πρᾶγμα. "apart from the six arourae, which as a matter of fact you let to others, and with which I shall have nothing to do"

ὅσιος,

"holy," "pious," is of course common in inscrr. dealing with religion. Note Syll 814 (= [3] 1199)[7], a leaden plate from Cnidus containing an invocation of ὅσ[ι]α on certain persons if they restore a trust (παραθήκη) and ἀν[όσια] if they do not. The meaning seems to help us for ὅσια Δαυείδ in Ac 13[34] (from LXX: Field Notes, p. 121), as does the combination ὅσια καὶ ἐλεύθερα in other inscrr., such as Syll 815 (= [a] 1180)[6] ἐμοὶ δ' ε(ἴ)η ὅσια καὶ ἐλεύθερα ὁμοστεγησάσηι ἦ ὧι πο[τε] τρόπωι ἐπιπλεκομένηι. For the adj. see also a iii/B.C. law regulating mourning for the dead, Syll 879 (= [3] 1219)[25] where it is laid down regarding women who do not conform—μὴ ὅσιον αὐταῖς εἶναι, ὡς ἀσεβούσαις, θύειν μηθενὶ θεῶν ἐπὶ δέκα ἔτη, and notice P Flor III. 354[11] (ii/A.D.) σφράγισον τὸ δαπανηθὲν ἀνάλωμα εἰς τοὺς θησαυρούς, εἰς η ("a vulgarism for a simple ἤ" (Ed.)) ὅσιόν ἐστι. The acc. fem. pl. ὁσίους in 1 Tim 2[8] is best explained as "an isolated slip, affected by the analogy of other adj. in—ιος fem." (Moulton Gr. ii. p. 157). On the ὅσιοι Ἰουδαῖοι of P Par 68 c.[14] as the successors of the Ἀσιδαῖοι of the Maccabean period see the introd. p. 348. Deissmann, however, prefers to regard it as a general title of honour self-applied by the Alexandrian Jews (BS p. 68 n.[2]). In Aristeas 234 "to honour the gods" is said to consist—οὐ δώροις οὐδὲ θυσίαις, ἀλλὰ ψυχῆς καθαρότητι καὶ διαλήψεως ὁσίας (cf. 2 Macc 12[45]).

ὁσιότης.

This subst., which in the NT is confined to Lk 1[75], Eph 4[24], may be illustrated by P Leid D[1. 15] (B.C. 162) (= I. p. 25, cf. P Par p. 282) περὶ μὲν οὖν τούτων δοί (l. δοίη or rather δοῖεν) σοι ὁ Σάραπις καὶ ἡ Ἶσις ἐπαφροδισί[α]ν, χάριν, μορφὴν πρὸς τὸν βασιλέα καὶ τὴν βασίλισσαν, δι' ἧς ἔχεις πρὸς τὸ θεῖον ὁσιότητα, Syll 521 (= [3] 717)[83] (B.C. 100–99) ἐφρόντισεν δ[ὲ] καὶ ἐν ἄλλοις πλείοσιν μετὰ πάσης ὁσιότητος καὶ δι[ε]τήρησεν πάντας ὑγιαίνοντας καὶ σωζομένους, and OGIS 383[19] (the proclamation of Antiochus I.—mid. i/B.C.) παρ' ὅλον τε τὸν βίον ὤφθην ἅπασι βασιλείας ἐμῆς καὶ φύλακα πιστοτάτην καὶ τέρψιν ἀμίμητον ἡγούμενος τὴν ὁσιότητα, where it no doubt represents the Zoroastrian asha, "right." The word is used in a similar wide sense of what is just and benevolent towards men in Priene 61[12] (before B.C. 200) ἐποιήσαντο δὲ καὶ τὴν ἀ[ναστροφὴν τήμ] παρ' ἡμῖν μετὰ πάσης εὐκοσμίας καὶ ὁσιότητος, and more particularly of piety towards the gods in ib. 108[30] (after B.C. 129) καλὸν ἀπόδειγμα τῆς τε πρὸς θεοὺς ὁσιότητος καὶ τῆς πρὸς τὴν πόλιν ἀρέσεως (cf. Rouffiac, p. 81). With ὁσιότης as an honorific title cf. s.v. ἁγιότης.

ὁσίως.

P Lond 21[11] (B.C. 162) (= I. p. 13) σὺ δὲ ὢν πρὸς τὸ θεῖον ὁσίως διακείμενος καὶ οὐ βουλόμενος παραβῆναί τι τῶν ἐν τῶι ἱερῶι ἐπηγγελμένων. The combination with δικαίως, as in 1 Thess 2[10], is common, e.g. P Par 63[viii. 13] (B.C. 164) where the writer claims—ἐγὼ γὰρ πιστεύσας σοί τε καὶ τοῖς θεοῖς, πρὸς οὓς ὁσίως καὶ . . δικαίως [πολι]τευσάμενος ἐμαυτὸν ἀμεμψιμοίρητον παρέσχημαι, and, from the inscrr., Priene 46[12] (i/B.C.) εὐσ[ε]β[ῶ]ς μὲν πρὸς τοὺς πατρίους θεούς, ὁσίως δὲ καὶ δικαίως π[ρὸς τοὺς ἀνθρώπους.

See further *Apol. Arist.* xv. *sub finem*, and for the combination with ἀμέμπτως Clem. R. *Cor.* xliv. 4.

ὀσμή

is used of the "sense of smell" in P Rein 54[10] (iii/iv A.D.) where, with reference to certain consignments of wine, the writer instructs his correspondent—ἀπὸ ὀσμῆς σὺ αὐτὸς χορ[ήγησον]?, "tu feras le choix toi-même d' apres ton flair" (Ed.). In P Leid W[ix. 22] (ii/iii A.D.) (= II. p. 111) provision is made—ἵνα κ(αὶ) χωρὶς τῶν θυμιαμάτων ἡ θυσία ὀσμὴν παρέχῃ: cf. 2 Cor 2[14 ff.], Eph 5[2], and see Nestle *ZNTW* iv. p. 272, vii. p. 95 f., on a "sweet smell," as a sign of the presence of deity, also Field *Notes*, p. 181 f.

ὅσος.

The varied uses of ὅσος in the NT can be readily illustrated from our sources. Thus for the meaning "as great as," "how great," "how much," as in Mk 5[19], cf. P Tebt II. 310[4] (A.D. 186) ὅσα (*l.* ὅσα ἔχω ἔτη, "for my term of years" (Edd.), *ib.* 314[4] (ii/A.D.) ὅσον κάμ[α]τον ἤνεγκα, "how much trouble I had," *ib.* 378[22] (A.D. 265) τὰ ἄλλα ὅσα καθήκει, "all else that is fitting," and P Oxy VI. 903[34] (iv/A.D.) αὐτὴ οἶδεν ὅσα κέκτηται, "she knows how much she has possessed herself of" (Edd.). From this it is an easy transition to practically the meaning "all," as in *ib.* 898[13] (A.D. 123) ὑποθέσθαι ὅσα ἔχω ἐν τῇ Ὀάσε[ι] κτήματα, "to mortgage all my property in the Oasis" (Edd.). The combination πάντα ὅσα, as in Mt 7[12] *al.*, is very common, e.g. BGU IV. 1113[19] (B.C. 14) πά]ντα ὅσα ποτ' ἔσχεν [ὁ πατὴ]ρ, P Oxy I. 115[5] (ii/A.D.) (= *Selections*, p. 96) πάντα ὅσα ἦν καθήκοντα ἐποίησα, "everything that was fitting I did": cf. also the rhetorical πολλῶν ὅσων λεχθέντων καὶ ἀντιλεχθέντων (with its curious attraction) in the late P Mon I. 14[31] A.D. 594. Ὅσος ἐάν (ἄν) generalizes, "how great soever," and in the plur. "as many soever as" (Mt 18[18], 22[9] *al.*). Thus in P Amh II. 85[6 ff.] (A.D. 78) an application for a five years' lease of land belonging to orphan children, the writer states that he desires to lease τὰ καταλελειμμένα πάντα καθ' ὁνδηποτοῦν τρόπον τοῖς αὐτοῦ υἱοῖς ὀρφανοῖς ὑπὸ Σαραπίωνος, "all the property of every kind bequeathed by Sarapion to his orphan sons," and adds—καὶ ὅσα ἄλλα ἐὰν ἀφεύρω ἐπ' ὀνόματος τῶν υἱῶν ὀρφανῶν αὐτοῦ Σαραπίωνος, "and whatever else I may find to be owned by the orphan sons of Sarapion" (Edd.). For other exx. see P Tebt II. 441 (A.D. 91–2) ἀρούρας δύο ἥμισυ ἢ ὅσαι ἐὰν ὦσι, "two and a half arourae or as many as there may be." P Ryl II. 81[10] (c. A.D. 104) ὅσον ἐὰν χρείαν ἔχωσι ὕδατος, "as much water as they may have need of." P Tebt II. 315[7] (ii/A.D.) ὅπως μοι [πέμψῃς] ὅσου [ἐ]ὰν ᾖ, "that you may send them (*sc.* garments) to me at any cost," and P Ryl II. 243[3] (ii/A.D.) ὅσα ποτὲ οὖν ἐὰν ἀναναλώσῃς (*l.* ἀναλώσῃς) ἰς τὴν τοῦ κλήρου κατεργασίαν, ἡμεῖν ἐνλόγησον ἐπὶ λόγον, "put down to our account everything you expend on the cultivation of the holding" (Edd.). For εἰς ὅσον, "as long as," see *ib.* 899[2] (A.D. 200) ἐς ὅσον μὲν οὖν δύναμίς μοι ὑπῆρχεν, "as long as I had the power": cf. Mk 2[19] ὅσον χρόνον. The commoner phrase ἐφ' ὅσον, as in Mt 9[15], *al.*, is seen in P Tor I. 1[4. 23] (B.C. 116) ὧν οἱ πρόγονοί μου κεκυρίευκαν ἐφ' ὅσον περιῆσαν, "over which my ancestors exercised lordship as long as they lived," and

Preisigke 4317[12] (c. A.D. 200) οὐ[δ]ὲν θέλω παρα<σχεῖν> σοι ἐφ' ὅσον ἐν Ἀλεξανδρίαν εἰμί, "I do not wish to provide you with anything as long as I am in Alexandria." For the same phrase meaning "as much as" see the restoration in P Ryl II. 81[6] (c. A.D. 104) ἐφ'] ὅσον οἱ κατασπορεῖς ἤθελον, "as much as the inspectors of sowing wished" (Edd.). The MGr ἐνόσῳ may mean "in so far as" or "so long as." Καθ' ὅσον, "in proportion as," is found in Heb 3[3], 7[20], 9[27]. Wellhausen (*Einl.* p. 11) pronounces ὅσον ὅσον in Lk 5[2] D (= ὀλίγον of other MSS.: cf. English *so so*) "mehr volkstümlich als literarisch," and compares Isai 26[20] (hence Heb 10[37]). The phrase is thus "not an essential Hebraism, but a vernacular idiom in harmony with the Hebrew" (Robertson *Gr.* p. 733: cf. *Proleg.* p. 97). Radermacher (*Gr.* p. 57 n.[2]) cites Acta Philippi 142 βάδιζε ἀνὰ δύο δύο in illustration of the Lucan passage. See also Wackernagel in *Glotta* iv. (1913). p. 244 f., who quotes Aristophanes *Vesp.* 213 τί οὐκ ἀπεκοιμήθημεν ὅσον ὅσον στίλην: here the last words may = τοσοῦτον ὅσον (or ὥστε) στίλην εἶναι, a usage preparing the way for the wider meaning "just," as in Diphilus 43. 14 οὐδὲν ἡδέως ποεῖ γὰρ οὗτος ἀλλ' ὅσον νόμου χάριν, "just for form's sake." The Latin employs *tantum quod* in this sense, e.g. Suet. *Aug.* 98 *navis Alexandrina quae tantum quod adpulerat*, "an Alexandrian ship which had only just come to land": cf. also Petron. 37 *et modo modo quid fuit?* "and what was she a little while ago?"

ὅσπερ

is supported by ℵ[c]B[3]CN as an alternative reading in Mk 15[6], where it is also defended on general grounds by Field *Notes*. p. 43. The word is common in the papyri, e.g. P Tor II. 8[24] (ii/B.C.) οὗπερ καὶ τὴν κατοικί[α]ν εἶχ[ε]ν, "where also he had his domicile," BGU IV. 1149[9] (B.C. 13) Ποπιλλίωι Σαραπίωνι ὅσπερ μετήλλαχεν δάνεια δύο, P Oxy IV. 729[6] (A.D. 137) ὅνπερ χοῦν εἰσοίσουσι εἰς τὸ κτῆμα κατ' ἔτος κοινῶς, *ib.* [11] ἅπερ κτήνη ἐπάναγκον θρέψομεν τῆς κατ' ἔτος γο[γήσ . . ., and P Ryl II. 176[5] (A.D. 210–11) ἅσπερ (ἀρούρας) η παρεδίξ(ατο) εἰς ἐνεχυρασίαν, "which 8 arourae she had assigned to herself for the purposes of execution."

ὀστέον.

The open forms of this word in the NT are discussed by Moulton *Gr.* ii. p. 121, Robertson *Gr.* pp. 203, 260. For the contracted acc. plur. ὀστᾶ, as in Lk 24[39] DN, cf. P Lond 1170 *verso*[466] (A.D. 258–259) (= III. p. 204) (ὄνοι) β ὑπὸ ὀστᾶ, "2 (asses) laden with bones," *ib.* 40[160] (iv/A.D.) (= I. p. 80) ἐπικαλοῦμαί σε τὸν κτίσαντα γῆν καὶ ὀστᾶ καὶ πᾶσαν σάρκα, and the sepulchral inscr. found near Jerusalem, *OGIS* 599 ὀστᾶ τῶν τοῦ Νεικάνορος Ἀλεξανδρέως. ποιήσαντος τὰς θύρας. The LXX usage is discussed by Thackeray *Gr.* i. p. 144.

ὅστις.

The classical distinction between ὅστις and ὅς which in the NT is maintained on the whole in Paul, but not in Luke (nor in the LXX, Thackeray *Gr.* i. p. 192), has worn very thin in the papyri. Thus with Mt 27[62] *al.* we may compare P Oxy I. 110[4] (an invitation to dinner = ii/A.D.) αὔριον, ἥτις ἐστιν ιε̄, ἀπὸ ὥρας θ, "to-morrow, which is the 15th, at nine o'clock," P Fay 108⁷ (c. A.D. 171) ἐχθὲς ἥτις ἦν ιθ τοῦ [δ]ντος μηνὸς Θώθ, "yesterday which was the 19th of the present month Thoth," and many similar exx. See also P Oxy I. 40⁶ (a doctor's claim for immunity from some form of public service—ii/iii A.D.) ἰατρὸς ὑπάρχων τὴ[ν τέ]χνην τούτους αὐτοὺς οἵτινές με εἰς λειτο[υ]ρ[γ]ίαν δεδώκασι ἐθεράπευσα, "I am a doctor by profession and I have treated these very persons who have assigned me a public burden" (Edd.).

With the indefinite use of ὅστις = "whosoever" in Mt 5³⁹ cf. P Par 574¹²⁴⁰ (iii/A.D.) (= *Selections*, p. 113) ἐξορκίζω σε δαῖμον, ὅστις ποτ᾽ οὖν εἶ, "I adjure thee, O demon, whoever thou art," and similarly Wünsch *AF* 4¹ (iii/A.D.). For the neut. ὅ τι see P Tebt II. 411¹⁴ (ii/A.D.) παραγενόμενος γὰρ εἴσῃ ὅ τι ποτέ ἐστιν, "for when you come you will know what it means" (Edd.); and note the curious combination in P Gen I. 54³ ff. (iv/A.D.) οἶδας τὴν προέρεσίν μου ὅ τι ὁποίαν προέρεσιν ἔχω καὶ οἶδας τὴν γνώμην μου ὅ τι γν[ώ]μη ὁποία ἐστιν, and in BGU II. 601¹⁰ (ii/A.D.) γράψον μοι περὶ τῆς οἰκίας, ὅ τι τί ἔπραξας.

Other exx. are P Eleph 1⁷ (B.C. 311–10) (= *Selections*, p. 3 amended), ἐπιδειξάτω δὲ Ἡρακλείδης ὅ τι ἂν ἐγκαλῆι Δημητρίαι, "but let Heraclides state whatever charge he brings against Demetria," P Rev L^xliv. 11 (B.C. 258) ὅ τι ἂ[ν ἡ ω̣]νὴ διὰ τούτους καταβλάβηι διπλοῦν, "twice the amount of the loss which they may have incurred on account of these (workmen)" (Edd.), PSI IV. 415³ (iii/B.C.) καθ᾽ ὅ τι ἂν σου τυγχάνηι [χρ]εία[ν] ἔχων, ib. VI. 623¹³ (iii/B.C.) σὺ καλῶς ποιήσεις δοὺς τῆι παιδίσκηι ὅ τι ἂν σοι δόξηι, and P Tebt II. 383³⁹ (A.D. 46) ὅ τι δ᾽ ἂν τῶν προγεγραμμένω[ν παρασυν-γρα]φῆι τις τῶν ὁμολογούντων, "whichever of the aforesaid provisions any one may violate." Cf. PSI V. 533⁸ (iii/B.C.) λόφους τριχίνους ὅ τι βελτίστους γ.

On the whole ὅστις is comparatively rare in the papyri, and where found is generally in the nom. as in the NT, rarely acc. as P Lond 77⁶⁵ (end of vi/A.D.) (= I. 235, *Chrest.* II. p. 372) ἥντινα (διαθήκην) πεποίημαί σοι εἰς ἀσφάλειαν. Ἐξ ὅτου is found in P Lond 190¹⁴ (iii/A.D. ?) (= II. p. 254), and ἕως ὅτου (NT *quinquies*) in P Gen I. 56¹⁹ (A.D. 346) ἕως ὅτου ἀποδῶ τὸ χρέως.

Reference may be made to an art. in *JBL* xlii. (1923), p. 150 ff. on "The Relative Pronouns in Acts and Elsewhere," in which H. J. Cadbury comes to the conclusion "that the indefinite relative is merely a synonymous substitute for the simpler form in many **Koινή** writings" including most New Testament writings. A good ex. of the interchange of ὅστις and ὅς is to be found in Diodor. xiv. 101. 1 ἥτις ἂν ὑπὸ τῶν Λευκανῶν λεηλατηθῇ—ἧς δ᾽ ἂν πόλεως (cited by Radermacher *Gr.* p. 185).

ὀστράκινος,

"of earthenware," occurs in a list of abstracts of contracts, P Oxy XIV. 1648⁶³ (late ii/A.D.) χαλκεῖον μολυβοῦν καὶ πίθον ὀστράκ(ινον), "leaden pot and cask of earthenware." The adj. is joined with σκεῦος as in 2 Cor 4⁷, 2 Tim 2²⁰, in the Will of Abraham of Hermonthis, P Lond 77²² (end of vi/A.D., see *Chrest.* II. p. 370) (= I. p. 233) τοῦ τυχόντος ὀστρακίνου καὶ ξυλίνου καὶ λιθίνου σκεύους. Cf. Epict. iii. 9. 18 σὺ χρυσᾶ σκεύη, ὀστράκινον τὸν λόγον

κτλ. (sc. ἔχεις): *ib.* i. 18. 15, iii. 22. 106. For the subst. ὄστρακον (LXX Ps 21¹⁶ al.) "a potsherd," see *Ostr* 1152⁹ (end of Ptol. and beg. of Rom. times) διδόντι σοι τὸ ὄστρακ(ον), P Oxy II. 234 ii.3 (a medical prescription—ii/iii A.D.) καστορήου καὶ μηκωνίου ἴσον φώσας ἐπ᾽ [ὀ]στράκου μάλιστα [μὲ]ν Ἀττικοῦ, "heat an equal quantity of beaver-musk and poppy-juice upon a potsherd, if possible one of Attic make" (Edd.), and *ib.* XII. 1450⁴ (A.D. 249–50) τῶν ὀστράκων διὰ πηλοῦ, where the editors in their note refer to the use of potsherds in making mortar as an ancient Egyptian custom.

ὄσφρησις.

This NT ἅπ. εἰρ. (1 Cor 12¹⁷) is found in the astrological P Ryl II. 63⁵ (iii/A.D.) Ἑρ]μοῦ γλῶσσα ὄσφρησις ἀκοή, "the tongue, smell, and hearing belong to Mercury."

ὀσφύς,

"loin" (cognate with ὀστέον), is found in the fragment of a iii/B.C. treatise on physiology, P Ryl I. 21 Fr. 3^ii. 11 εἰ[ς] τρόπον τῆς ὀσφύος, and in the mantic *ib.* 28¹¹ (iv/A.D.) ὀσφύος δεξιὸν μέρος ἐὰν ἅλληται μεγάλως εὐπορήσει κα[ὶ] δοῦλος καὶ πένης ἐκ κόπων, "if the right part of the loin quiver, a slave or poor man will prosper greatly after distress" (Edd.): cf. also the astronomical *ib.* II. 63⁸ (iii/A.D.) Π]αρθένου σιαγὼν ὀσφύες, "the cheek and loins to Virgo."

ὅταν,

"whenever," is construed (1) c. subj. pres. in such passages as P Fay 109¹ (early i/A.D.) ὅταν πρὸς ἀνάνκαιν (l. ἀνάγκην) θέλῃς παρ᾽ ἐμοῦ χρήσασθαί τι, εὐθύς σε οὐ κρατῶι, "whenever you from necessity want to borrow anything from me, I at once give in to you" (Edd.), P Oxy XIV. 1676²⁶ (iii/A.D.) τὸ σύνφορόν σου ποίει· ὅταν γὰρ θέλῃς ἡμᾶς πάντοτε ἰδεῖν, ἥδιστά σε παραδεξόμεθα, "do what suits you; for when you wish to see us always, we shall receive you with the greatest pleasure" (Edd.), and (2) c. subj. aor. in such passages as P Lips I. 104¹⁶ (c. B.C. 96–5) (= Witkowski². p. 110) ὅταν ἡμῖν γ[ρ]άψῃς, ἐνψυχόν τι λαμβάνω, P Ryl II. 233² (ii/A.D.) ὅταν δὲ ἐπ᾽ ἀγαθῷ ἐκβῶμεν καὶ τὸ δῶμα ἀσφαλισθήσεται ἡ διαβάθρα καγγελωτὴ (l. καγκελλωτὴ) καὶ τὰ προσκήνια γενήσεται, "but when we reach a fortunate issue and the house is established, then a balustrade will be added to the stairway and the porch" (Edd.), and P Grenf II. 73¹⁶ (late iii/A.D.) (= *Selections*, p. 118) καὶ ὅταν ἔλθῃ σὺν Θεῷ, μαρτυρήσι (= ει) περὶ ὧν αὐτὴν πεποιήκασιν, "and when he arrives by the help of God, he will bear you witness of what they have done to her."

Of ὅταν c. ind., which occurs *quinquies* in the NT, we can quote P Hamb I. 70¹⁹ (soon after A.D. 144–5) ὅταν τὸν λόγον δίδομεν τῷ ἀφήλικι. In PSI IV. 434⁶ (B.C. 261–0) ὅταν περιοδεύω, the verb is probably in the subj., and in P Par 26^i.14 (B.C. 162) (= *Selections*, p. 14) Wilcken (UPZ i. p. 247) now reads ὅτ᾽ ἀνέβημεν for ὅταν ἔβημεν. See however P Ryl 233 *ut s.*, where, with reference to ἀσφαλισθήσεται, the editors remark that "the writer apparently forgot that ὅταν had preceded."

For ὅταν c. imperf. (Mk 3¹¹, cf. Burton § 315) we may quote the curious anti-Christian inscr. in *C. and B.* 343⁵

(= ii. p. 477) οὗτος ὁ βίος μοι γέγονεν (aoristic !) ὅταν ἔζων ἐγώ. In Mk 11¹³ we may perhaps translate " when evening fell," i.e. the evening before the πρωί of ²⁰: in this way an awkward sequence is avoided, cf. *Proleg.* p. 248.

ὅτε.

This common word is almost invariably construed in the NT with the indicative and generally with the aorist : cf. PSI IV. 322¹ (B.C. 266–5) ὅτ' ἔγραψ[άς μοι], ἐπιστολὴν ἀπεστάλκειμεν ἐξ Ἀλεξα[νδρείας, *ib.* V. 447¹² (A.D. 167) ὅτε αὐτοῖς ἡ πολιτεία ἐδόθη. 'Ἀφ' ὅτε occurs in an amusing letter which a man writes to his wife who had left him, but whom he wishes to return—P Oxy III. 528⁹ (ii/A.D.) ιβ Φαῶφι ἀφ' ὅτε ἐλουσάμην μετ' ἐσοῦ οὐκ ἐλουσάμην οὐκ ἤλιμ⟨μ⟩ε (*l.* ἤλειμ⟨μ⟩αι) μεχρεὶ ιβ Ἀθύρ, " since we bathed together on Phaophi 12 I never bathed nor anointed myself until Athur 12 " (Edd.). For ὅτε μὲν . . . ὅτε δέ, see the *Gnomon des Idios Logos* § 67 (= BGU V. p. 27) ὅτε μὲν ἐξ ὅλων ὅτε δὲ ἐξ ἡμίσους ὅτ]ε ἐκ τετάρτ[ο]υ ἀνελήμ[φ]θησαν. Vett. Val. p. 106³⁶ ἔστι δὲ αὐτῆς καὶ ἄλλο σχῆμα, ὅτε ἄρξεται πρῶτον μειοῦσθαι is an ex. of ὅτε c. conj. According to the best attested reading the words ἥξει ὅτε form no part of the true text in Lk 13³⁵.

ὅτι.

(1) For ὅτι, "that," introducing an objective clause after verbs of knowing, saying, etc., cf. P Tebt II. 409³ (A.D. 5) εἰδὼ[ς ὅ]τι ἐξ⟨ι⟩ουσίαν αὐτῶν ἔχει καὶ Λυσίμαχος καὶ σύ, "I knew that both you and Lysimachus had plenty of them" (Edd.), P Fay 109⁵ (early i/A.D.) νομίσας ὅτι (cf. Mt 5¹⁷) κιχρᾷς μοι αὐτούς, "consider that you are lending them (*sc.* staters) to me" (Edd.), BGU III. 846⁴ᶠ (ii/A.D.) (= *Selections*, p. 93) γεινώσκειν σαι θέλω, ὅτι οὐχ [ἤλπ]ιζον, ὅτι ἀναβένις (*l.* ἀναβαίνεις) εἰς τὴν μητρόπολιν, "I wish you to know that I had no hope that you were coming up to the metropolis," *ib.*⁹ αὔγραψά σοι, ὅτι γυμνός εἰμει. "I wrote you that I am naked," and P Tebt II. 420⁴ (iii/A.D.) οἴδατε ὅτι ἀπὸ ζημίας ἡμί, "You know that I am blameless." Ὅτι, however, is frequently omitted, e.g. BGU III. 815³ (ii/A.D.) γεινόσκιν σε θέλω [τὴ]ν ἐπιστολήν σου λάβε (corrected by another hand into ἔλαβα): similarly in the NT. The periphrasis with ὅτι has superseded acc. c. inf. in nearly all NT writers, but the two constructions have been mixed in P Oxy II. 237ᵛ ⁵ (A.D. 186) δηλῶν ὅτι εἰ τὰ ἀληθῆ φανείη μηδὲ κρίσεως δεῖσθαι τὸ πρᾶγμα : cf. Ac 27¹⁰ and Aristeas 125. In Mk 9¹¹·²⁸ the AV rightly takes ὅτι = τί, "why" : for this use of ὅτι in *indirect* interrogation, see the exx. in Field *Notes*, p. 33.

(2) Ὅτι *recitativum*, when it is practically equivalent to our quotation-marks. is seen, as in Mt 7²³ *al.*, in P Oxy IV. 744¹¹ (B.C. 1) (= *Selections*, p. 33) εἴρηκας δὲ Ἀφροδισιάτι ὅτι μή με ἐπιλάθῃς. "you told Aphrodisias ' Do not forget me,' " P Oxy I. 119¹⁰ (ii/iii A.D.) (= *Selections*, p. 103) ἡ μήτηρ μου εἶπε Ἀρχελάῳ, ὅτι ἀναστατοῖ με, "my mother said to Archelaus, ' He upsets me,' " and *ib.* VII. 1064⁵ (iii/A.D.) γενόμενος πρὸς Ἀχιλλᾶν πυνθανόμενος περὶ σοῦ ἔφη ὅτι ἐν τῇ Ψώβθει ἐστίν, "I went to Achillas and inquired about you and he said ' He is at Psobthis.' " Cf. the construction in such passages as P Oxy III. 533¹⁶ (ii/iii A.D.) εἴπατε Ζωίλῳ τῷ ἀπὸ Σεντὼ γεωργῷ ὅτ[ι] κατὰ

τὰς συνθήκας φρόντισον τοῦ χαλκοῦ, "tell Zoilus the cultivator from Sento that in accordance with the agreements he must look after the money" (Edd.), and P Tebt II. 410¹⁷ (iii/A.D.) μετάδ⟨ο⟩ς = οἷς καὶ Ἀκουτᾶτι τῷ ἀδελφῷ ὅτι ἐὰν χρίαν τινὸς ἔχῃ ἡ γυνή μου ποίησον αὐτῆς τὴν χρίαν ἕως ἔλθω. "tell my brother Akoutas also to do anything that my wife requires until I come" (Edd.). For the redundant ὅτι, cf. further P Oxy XIV. 1668⁵ (iii/A.D.) πρότερον μὲν ἔλεγεν ὅτι ἢ δός μοι (ἀρτάβας) ιβ, ἢ λαβὲ (ἀρτ.) ιβ, "formerly he said ' Either give me 12 artabae or take 12 art.' " (Edd.), *ib.* 1682⁹ (iv/A.D.) ἀναγκαίως δὲ καὶ ἡμεῖν ἐπίστειλον ὅτι εἰ ἦς ἐπιδημήσασα, "do you by all means send word to us whether you have arrived " (Edd.).

(3) ὅτι, as a causal particle. "because," may be illustrated by P Par 48¹⁹ (B.C. 153) καλῶς οὖν ποιήσεις παραγίνεσθαι ἡμῖν εἰς Ποεὶ, ὅτι καταπλεῖν μέλλομεν πρὸς τὸν βασιλέα, BGU II. 423¹⁶ (a soldier to his father—ii/A.D.) (= *Selections*, p. 91) ἵνα σου προσκυνήσω τὴν χεῖραν, ὅτι με ἐπαίδευσας καλῶς, "that I may kiss your hand, because you have brought me up well," and *ib.* III. 846⁹ (ii/A.D.) (= *Selections*, p. 94) αἰδ[υ]σοπο[ύ]μην (*l.* ἐδυσωπούμην) δὲ ἐλθεῖν εἰς Καρανίδαν ὅτι σαπρῶς παιριπατῶ (*l.* περιπατῶ), "but I was ashamed to come to Karanis, because I am going about in rags."

(4) A few miscellaneous exx. may be added. P Oxy I. 37¹·¹² (report of a lawsuit—A.D. 49) (= *Selections*, p. 49) ὅτι δὲ ταῦτα ἀληθῆι λέγωι, ἔστιν γράμματα αὐτῆς δι' ὧν ὁμολογεῖ εἰληφέναι, "and in proof that I am telling the truth, there are the documents in which she admits that she has received them (wages)." For the consecutive ὅτι in Jn 7³⁵ Bauer (*HZNT ad l.*) cites *Pelagia-Legenden*, p. 20, τί διδοῖς τοῖς ἀμνοῖς σου, ὅτι ζωὴν αἰώνιον ἔχουσιν ; A similar ex. is cited by Radermacher (*Gr.* p. 160) from the *Acta Christophori*, ed. Usener 68, 18 : τοιοῦτοί γάρ εἰσιν οἱ θεοὶ ὑμῶν, ὅτι ὑπὸ γυναικὸς ἐκινήθησαν. With the NT οὐχ ὅτι (2 Thess 3⁹ *al.*) cf. μὴ ὅτι in P Lond 42²³ (B.C. 168) (= I. p. 30, *Selections.* p. 10), μὴ ὅτι γε τοσούτου χρόνου ἐπιγεγονότος. "not to speak of so much time having gone by." In the difficult 1 Tim 6⁷ Parry reads οὐδ' ὅτι (= *nedum*) with a similar meaning : see his note *ad l.*, and for a different view Field *Notes*, pp. 212, 243. In 2 Cor 5¹⁹ *al.* ὡς ὅτι is taken by Blass *Gr.*² 321 f. as = Attic ὡς c. gen. abs. (Vg *quasi*), but in papyri of late date ὡς ὅτι often means merely "that," e.g. CPR I. 19³ (A.D. 330) πρώην βίβλια ἐπιδέδωκα τῇ σῇ ἐπιμελείᾳ ὡς ὅτι ἐβουλήθην τινὰ ὑπάρχοντά μου ἀποδόσθαι, where Wessely (p. 58) notes "ὡς ὅτι seem combined, where the single word would be adequate," and cites as a further ex. Papyrus No. 6085 ὡς ὅτι χρεοστεῖται ἐξ αὐτοῦ ὁ κύρις Ἰανός.

A superfluous ὅτι in ὡς ὅτι c. superlat. is seen in Roberts-Gardner 65¹⁷ (B.C. 101–100 or 100–99) (β)οῦν ὡς ὅτι κάλλιστον παρήγαγον. The editors compare *CIA* ii. 482⁴⁸ (B.C. 41–30) παραστήσαντες ὦ]ς ὅτι κάλλιστα θύματα.

οὐ.

In addition to its regular use with the ind., οὐ is frequently found in the papyri with the participle, due apparently to the fact that it is the proper negative for a statement of fact. Exx. are P Oxy IV. 726¹⁰ (A.D. 135) οὐ δυνάμενος δι' ἀ[σ]θενείαν πλεῦσαι, " since he is unable through sickness to make the voyage" (Edd.), and P Amh II. 78²¹ (A.D. 184) τοιαύτης ο[ὖ]ν αὐθαδίας ἐν αὐτῷ οὔσης οὐ δυνάμενος [ἐν]καρτερεῖν ἐπιδίδωμι, "his audacity having reached this pitch I can endure no longer and present this petition." See further *Proleg.* p. 231 f.

In support of the translation "I determined not to know" in 1 Cor 2², we may cite P Par 26³⁷ (B.C. 163) (= UPZ i. p. 248) οὐκ ἐκρίναμεν καταχωρῆσαι, "we determined not to record," P Tebt I. 124⁵ (c. B.C. 118) οὐκ ⟨ἐκ⟩ρίναμεν ἐξαρ[ιθ]μεῖ[σθαι, "we determined not to be counted," and the classical formula in P Hamb I. 27⁵ (B.C. 250 (249)) οὐκ ἔφη εἰδέναι, "he said that he did not know."

The origin of the double negative οὐ μή is fully discussed by Moulton *Proleg.* p. 187 ff. When we pass to its actual occurrences in the NT, we find that these for the most part are found in passages derived from the OT and in the Sayings of our Lord, which, therefore, have Semitic originals. This corresponds with the rarity of οὐ μή in the papyri. See, however, the following passages—P Par 49³⁵ (B.C. 164–158) (= Witkowski², p. 72) γίνωσκε σαφῶς ὅτι . . ⟨πρὸς σὲ οὐ μὴ εἰσέλθω⟩, P Oxy I. 119⁵˙¹⁴ᶠ. (ii/iii A.D.) (= *Selections*, p. 103) ἢ οὐ θέλις ἀπενέκκειν (*l.* ἀπενέγκαι) μετ' ἐσοῦ εἰς Ἀλεξανδρίαν, οὐ μὴ γράψω σε ἐπιστολήν . . . ἂμ μὴ πέμψῃς, οὐ μὴ φάγω, οὐ μὴ πείνω, "if you refuse to take me along with you to Alexandria, I won't write you a letter . . . If you do not send, I won't eat, I won't drink," P Leid W^vni. 9 (ii/iii A.D.) (= II. p. 107) ἐὰν θέλῃς γυνή(= αἶ)κας οὐ μὴ σχεθῆναι ὑπὸ ἄλλου ἀνδρός, P Oxy VI. 903¹⁶ (iv/A.D.) a man declares regarding his wife ἀπεντεῦθεν οὐ μὴ κρύψω αὐτῆ⟨ν⟩ πάσας μου τὰς κλεῖς, "henceforward I shall not hide all my keys from her," and the magic P Lond 46²⁷⁵ (iv/A.D.) (= I. p. 73) οὐ μὴ ἐάσω.

For the still stronger negative οὐδ' οὐ μή Radermacher (*Gr.* p. 172) cites Wessely *Papyrorum scripturae Graecae specimina* XXVI.: τῷ μεγίστῳ κραταιῷ θεῷ Σοκνοπαίῳ παρὰ Ἀσκληπιάδου τοῦ Ἀρείου. εἰ οὐ δίδοταί μοι συμβιῶσαι Ταπεθευτι Μαρρειους οὐδ' οὐ μὴ γένηταί μοι γυνή, ὑπόδειξόν μοι καὶ κύρωσόν μοι τοῦτο τὸ γραπτόν. πρώην δ' ἦν Ταπεθευς Ὡρίωνος γυνή. Cf. also P Petr II. 13(19)¹³ (B.C. 258–253) τοῦτο ⟨δ'⟩ ἔχε τῆι δια[νοία]ι, ὅτι οὐθέν σοι μὴ γένηθῆι λυπηρόν, P Alex 4¹⁰ (iii/B.C.) (= Witkowski², p. 52) οὐδείς σε ἀνθρώπων μὴ ὠφειλήσῃ, and P Oxy XII. 1483¹⁹ (ii/iii A.D.) ἐξωδίασας τοῖς αὐτοῖς ὧν οὐδὲ ἷς μὴ παρεδέξατο τιμήν, "you have spent upon them things of which absolutely no one has received the value" (Edd.).

In a legal process of the 2ⁿᵈ half of iv/A.D. published in *Archiv* i. p. 293 ff. we have ⁶˙⁹ ὁ δὲ ἀδελφὸς Φιλάδελφος ὃς καὶ ἐν τῇ Αἰγύπτῳ ἐστὶν καὶ οὐ μετ' οὐ πολὺ ἥξει, where the phrase οὐ μετ' οὐ πολύ can only mean "after no long time": cf. BGU II. 614¹¹ (A.D. 216), and Gradenwitz *Einführung* i. p. 40 n.¹ In MGr (Pontic) 'κί is used for "not."

οὗ.

For this relative adverb = "where," cf. PSI VI. 620¹⁷ (iii/B.C.) τὸ ταμεῖον οὗ ἔκειτο ὁ . . οἶνος, "the store-house where the wine was placed," P Tebt I. 105¹¹ (B.C. 103) οὗ ἂν συντάσσῃ ἐ[ν] τῆι αὐτῆι κώμῃ, "at whatever place he may fix in the said village," P Par 47¹⁰ (c. B.C. 153)

(= *Selections*, p. 22) ἐνβέβληκαν ὑμᾶς (*l.* ἡμᾶς) εἰς ὕλην μεγάλην καὶ οὐ δυνάμεθα ἀποθανεῖν, "they have cast us into a great forest, where we may possibly die," and P Ryl II. 145¹⁹ (A.D. 38) οὗ καὶ κα(ταγείνονται), "where they live."

οὐά.

For this interjection denoting wonder real or ironical (Mk 15²⁹), not commiseration, as οὐαί (*q.v.*), cf. Epict. iii. 23. 24 ἐπαίνεσόν με . . . εἰπέ μοι ' οὐά ' καὶ ' θαυμαστῶς.'

οὐαί.

This word, which is not found in class. Greek, but is common in the LXX and NT, occurs in a farce of date rather earlier than the Roman period, P Oxy III. 413¹⁸⁴ᶠ οὐαί σοι, ταλαίπωρε, ἄκληρε, ἀ[λγ]εινέ, ἀναφρόδιτε· οὐαί σοι· οὐαί μοι, "Woe to thee wretched, hapless, miserable, loveless one! Woe to you, woe to me!" (Edd.). Cf. also Epict. iii. 19. 1, 22. 32 οὐαί μοι.

οὐδαμῶς.

P Tebt I. 24⁵³ (B.C. 117) τὰς δὲ κατ' ἄνδρα γραφὰς οὐδαμῶς προέμενοι, "but failing to issue the lists of individual items" (Edd.), *ib.* 27⁴¹ (B.C. 113) ἐν τῆι αὐτῆι ταλαιπωρίαι διαμένεις οὐδαμῶς τὰ παρὰ τὸ δέιον (*l.* δέον) κεχειρισμένα διωρθωμένος, "You still continue in the same miserable course with no improvement whatever in your improper procedure" (Edd.), and *ib.* 58⁴ (B.C. 111) οὐδαμῶς προσκεκλήμεθα, "we have not yet been summoned" (Edd.). In P Meyer 23² (not before end of iv/A.D.) οὐδαμὶ γὰρ ἀνέμινα τοσοῦτον χρόνον ἐνταῦθα, "for never have I waited here for so long a time," the editor regards οὐδαμί as written for οὐδαμῆ = οὐδαμᾶ = οὐδαμοῦ, οὐδαμόθι, not for οὐδαμῶς. For οὐθαμόθεν cf. P Lond 23¹⁶ (B.C. 158–7) (= I. p. 38). See further *s.v.* μηδαμῶς.

οὐδέ

is used adverbially = "not even," as in Mk 6³¹, 1 Cor 5¹. in P Oxy XIV. 1666⁷ (iii/A.D.) τοὺς ἐγδοχεῖς οὐκ ἔπεμψας ὡς ἐνετειλάμην σοι, ἀλλ' οὐδὲ ἔγραψας εἰ ἀπετάξαντο, "you have not sent the middlemen as I bade you, and you have not even written whether they departed" (Edd.), *ib.* 1765⁴ (iii/A.D.) οὐδὲ ἅπαξ ἠξίωσάς μοι γράφειν, "not even once have you deigned to write me." For οὐδὲ εἷς, as in Ac 4³², cf. *ib.* 1668¹⁹ (iii/A.D.) καὶ οὐκέτι φόβος οὐδὲ εἷς ἔνει, "and there is no longer any fear at all" (Edd.), *ib.* I. 122¹⁰ (iii/iv A.D.) ἡμεῖ[s] δὲ ἀγρεύειν τῶν θηρίων δυνά[με]θα οὐδὲ ἕν, "and we cannot catch a single animal" (Edd.).

οὐδείς.

P Alex 4² (iii/B.C.) (= Witkowski², p. 52). οὐδείς σε ἀνθρώπων μὴ ὠφειλήσῃ. For a similar use of οὐδείς, cf. P Petr II. 13(19)¹³ (B.C. 258–3) (= Witkowski², p. 20) τοῦτο ⟨δ'⟩ ἔχε τῆι δια[νοία]ι, ὅτι οὐθέν σοι μὴ γενηθῆι λυπηρόν, ἀλλὰ πᾶν ἐ[μοὶ ἔστ]αι πεφροντισμένον τοῦ σε γενέσθαι ἄλυπον, "but hold this fact in your mind, that nothing vexatious may happen to you, but that I have used every forethought to keep you free from trouble" (Ed.). Another ex. of the neut. οὐδέν is the illiterate BGU II. 380¹¹ (iii/A.D.) (= *Selections*, p. 105) οὐδὲν περισσότε[ρ]ον ἔχι σε.

"there is nothing so much the matter with you." The stronger οὐδέν is sometimes used for οὐ : see Epict. iv. 10. 36 οὐδὲν κωλύονται ἀθλιώτατοι εἶναι καὶ δυστυχέστατοι (cited by Radermacher *Gr.* p. 26), and possible NT exx. in Ac 18[17] (but cf. Blass *Gr.* p. 104), Rev 3[17]. The usual accumulation of negatives may be noted in P Oxy VIII. 1118[11] (i/ii A.D.) οὐδεν[ὸ]ς αὐτοῖς οὐδὲ ἄλλῳ οὐδενὶ ἐξ ὑστέρου [κατ]αλειπομένου λόγου [περ]ὶ οὐδε[νὸς ἁπλῶς . . . "without any claim being left to them [debtors] or to any one else for the future in any respect. . ." Cf. also for οὐδέν strengthening the negative, as in Mk 15[4f], P Oxy II. 294[15] (A.D. 22) (= *Selections*, p. 35) where a man, whose house has been searched in his absence, writes to his brother—ἐγὼ δὲ αὐτὸς οὔπω οὐδὲ ἐνήλεπα (*l.* ἐναλήλιφα) ἕως ἀκούσω φάσιν παρὰ σοῦ περὶ ἁπάντων, "but I am not so much as anointing myself, until I hear a report from you on all points."

οὐδέποτε.

P Hib I. 78[5] (B.C. 244–3 (243–2)) οὐδέποτε ὑ[πα]κήκοας ἡμῶν, "you have never listened to me" (Edd.) : cf. P Oxy VII. 1062[11] (ii/A.D.). The word appears to be rare in our sources.

οὐδέπω,

"not yet," as in the contract of apprenticeship P Oxy II. 275[4] (A.D. 66), where a boy is described as—οὐδέπω ὄντα τῶν ἐτῶν, "not yet being of age," i.e. not yet having reached the legal age of fourteen years, when men become liable to the poll-tax : cf. *ib.* 273[13] (A.D. 95), the cession by a woman of certain arourae of land to her daughter—οὐδέπω οὔσῃ ἐν ἡλικίᾳ. In P Ryl II. 178[7] (early i/A.D.) it is laid down in an agreement with a nurse that she shall give back the sum she is found to owe for the period of nursing not completed—πρὸς ὃν οὐδέπωι τετρόφευκεν χρόνον.

οὐθείς.

This late form of οὐδείς is usually said to occur first early in iv/B.C., but if the dating is correct, a wooden tablet, P Strass II. 125[4] κούθέν σοι ἐνκαλῶ, carries it back to v/iv B.C. It is predominant throughout the Ptolemaic period, but during i/A.D. οὐδείς reasserts itself, and before iii/A.D. has driven out οὐθείς. It is therefore a proof of the accuracy of our great NT Uncials that οὐθείς, by this time obsolete in general usage, should have survived in such passages as Lk 22[35], Ac 19[27], *al.* Cf. *Proleg.* p. 56 and the full details in Mayser *Gr.* p. 180 ff., and Thackeray *Gr.* i. p. 58 ff. See also for the inscrr. Thieme, p. 9. It may be added that in Cicero's Greek quotations the form οὐθείς does not occur. It is found in Epict. *Ench.* xxxii. 2 καὶ τοῦτο οὐθεὶς κωλύσει. Both forms appear in Musonius— p. 30[15] οὐθενός, *ib.*[13] οὐδείς.

One or two sporadic exx. of the form from different centuries must suffice here—P Eleph 13[4] (B.C. 223–2) (= Witkowski[2], p. 43) ὁ δὲ ἐπῄνει μόνον, ἐπέταξεν δ᾽ οὐθέν, P Par 45[5] (B.C. 153) (= Witkowski[2], p. 84) ἄνευ τῶν θεῶν οὐθὲν γίνεται, P Grenf II. 36[11] (B.C. 95) οὐθὲν ἡμῖν κακὸν ἐποίησεν, and P Tebt II. 278[39] (acrostics—early i/A.D.) οὐθὲν τηλικούτωι, "it was nothing to one like him" (Edd.).

PART V.

οὐκέτι.

For οὐκέτι, "no longer," "no more," cf. P Par 49[17] (B.C. 164–158) (= Witkowski[2], p. 71) εἴπερ οὖν ἐστιν αὕτη ἡ αἰτία καὶ διὰ τοῦτο οὐκέτι ἥκει πρὸς ἐμὲ αἰσχυνθείς, P Oxy XIV. 1658[13 ff.] (iii/A.D.) καὶ οὐκέτι φόβος οὐδὲ εἷς ἔνι· ἐὰν οὖν θέλεις, ἴσελθε καταφρονῶν, [ἐπὶ] ἡμεῖς γὰρ οὐκέτι δυνόμεθα ἔσω μεῖναι, "and there is no longer any fear at all ; so if you will, come boldly ; for we are no longer able to stay indoors" (Edd.), and P Ryl II. 244[2] (iii/A.D.) οὐκέτι περὶ τούτο γέγονα, "I have done nothing further in the matter" (Edd.).

οὐκοῦν.

In the NT only in Jn 18[37] οὐκοῦν βασιλεὺς εἶ σύ; "so then you are a king?" The word expects an affirmative answer : cf. German "nicht wahr ?"

οὖν.

This common particle, which occurs in the NT nearly 500 times, is used in our sources in a variety of connexions, the exact shade of meaning being determined by the context.

(1) For the causal meaning "therefore" we may cite BGU II. 423[11] (ii/A.D.) (= *Selections*, p. 91) καὶ καλῶς μοι ἐστίν. ἐρωτῶ σε οὖν, κύριέ μου πατήρ, γράψον μοι ἐπιστόλιον πρῶτον μὲν περὶ τῆς σωτηρίας σου . . . , "it is well with me. I beg you, therefore, my lord father, write me a letter, first regarding your health . . . ," and P Oxy XIV. 1665[15] (iii/A.D.), where a son in urgent need of oil writes to his father—ἀναγκαίως οὖν, ἐὰν ἔτι παρὰ σεαυτῷ χρ[ῖ]ον ἔχῃς, δήλωσον ἢ τῷ υἱῷ σου ἢ ᾧ ἐὰν σὺ βούλῃ τούτους μοι ἐν τάχει παρα[σ]χεῖν, "perforce, therefore, if you have still with you any unguent, instruct your son or any one else you wish to supply me with them speedily" (Edd.).

(2) Οὖν is very common in a looser temporal sense, resuming or continuing a narrative, as in P Oxy X. 1293[7] (A.D. 117–38) κόμισαι παρὰ Σαράτος Μάρκου ἐλαίου ἀφροδ(ισιακοῦ) καλοῦ μετρητὰς τέσσαρας ἥμισυ· κομισαμένη οὖν δήλωσόν μοι, "receive from Saras son of Marcus four and a half metretae of fine aphrodisiac oil ; and having done so let me know" (Edd.). For the combination μὲν οὖν in the same connexion (as in Ac 16[18], 2[41], *al.*), cf. P Oxy II. 281[9] (complaint against a husband—A.D. 20–50) συνεβίωσα Σαραπίωνι . . . ἐγὼ μὲν οὖν ἐπιδεξαμένη αὐτὸν εἰς τὰ τῶν γονέων μου οἰκητήρια λειτὸν παντελῶς ὄντα, ἀνέγκλητον ἐματὴν ἐν ἅπασι παρειχόμην. "I married Sarapion . . . as he was destitute of means I received him into my parents' house, and I for my part conducted myself blamelessly in all respects" (Edd.), *ib.* 282[3] (complaint against a wife—A.D. 30–35) συνεβίω[σα] Δημ[η]τροῦτι Ἡρακλείδου, κα[ὶ] ἐγὼ μὲν οὖν ἐπεχορήγησα αὐτῇ τὰ ἑξῆς καὶ ὑπὲρ δύναμιν, "I married Demetrous, daughter of Heraclides, and I for my part provided for my wife in a manner that exceeded my resources" (Edd.).

(3) Οὖν is also used with an intensive force in exhortations, etc.—P Lond 28[4] (*b.* B.C. 162 =) (= I. p. 43) καλῶς οὖν ποιήσῃς φροτίσαι (*l.* φροντίσαι) μοι σιτάριον, "please be sure to look after the grain for me," P Tebt I. 33[2] (B.C. 112) (= *Selections*, p. 30) φρόν[τι]σον οὖν ἵνα

γένη(ται) ἀκολούθως, "take care that action is taken in accordance with it (a letter)." P Ryl II. 229[17] (A.D. 38) παρεδεξάμην σοι πάντα.–παρακάλεσον οὖν τὴν γυναῖκά σου τοῖς ἐμοῖς λόγοις ἵνα ἐπιμελῆται τῶν χοιριδίων, "I have given you every allowance. Urge your wife from me to look after the pigs" (Edd.), BGU I. 37[5] (A.D. 50) ὅρα οὖν μὴ αὐτὸν κατάσχῃς, "see then that you do not detain him," and P Oxy I. 115[11] (letter of consolation=ii/A.D.) (= *Selections*, p. 96) ἀλλ' ὅμως οὐδὲν δύναταί τις πρὸς τὰ τοιαῦτα. παρηγορεῖτε οὖν ἑαυτούς, "but still there is nothing one can do in the face of such trouble. So I leave you to comfort yourselves" (Edd). In drawing attention to this usage, Mantey (*Exp.* VIII. xxii. p. 210f.) thinks that this emphatic sense might be given to οὖν in about 65 places in the NT, e.g. Mt 3[8, 10] "*By all means* produce fruit worthy of acceptance. . . . Every tree, *rest assured* that does not produce good fruit . . ."

(4) From this is developed a slightly adversative sense in such a passage as P Tebt I. 37[16] (B.C. 73) ἐγὼ οὖν περισπώμενος περὶ ἀναγκαίων γέγραφά σοι ἵνα ἱκανὸς γένῃ, "howbeit as I am occupied with urgent affairs, I have written to you, in order that you may undertake the matter"; cf. Ac 25[4], 28[5], and Mantey *ut s.* p. 207 f.

(5) Οὖν intensifies the indefiniteness of a preceding pronoun in P Lond 1171 *verso* (c)[9] (A.D. 42) (= III. p. 107) ἢ ὅστις οὖν τῶν ὑπηρετῶν, P Amh II. 86[9] (A.D. 78) καθ' ὁνδήποτε οὖν τρόπον, "of whatever description," P Ryl II. 243[9] (ii/A.D.) ὅσα ποτὲ οὖν ἐὰν ἀνα(να)λώσῃς ἰς τὴν τοῦ κλήρου κατεργασίαν, ἡμεῖν ἐνλόγησον ἐπὶ λόγου, "put down to our account everything you expend on the cultivation of the holding" (Edd.), and P Par 574[1210] (iii/A.D.) (= *Selections*, p. 113) ὅστις ποτ' οὖν εἶ.

Λοιπὸν οὖν, which is read in 1 Thess 4[1] ℵ AD, is found in the private letter BGU IV. 1079[6] (A.D. 41) ἔπεμψά σοι ἄλλας δύο ἐπιστολάς, διὰ Νηδύμου μίαν, διὰ Κρονίου μαχαιροφόρου μίαν. λοιπὸν οὖν ("then at last") ἔλαβον παρὰ το(ῦ) Ἄραβος τὴν ἐπιστολὴν καὶ ἀνέγνων καὶ ἐλυπήθην. See further s.v. λοιπός. Οὖν has not survived in MGr.

οὔπω.

An interesting ex. of this strong negative is afforded by P Oxy II. 294[15] (A.D. 22) (= *Selections*, p. 35), where a man, who is anxious regarding certain news, writes to his brother–ἐγὼ δὲ αὐτὸς οὔπω οὐδὲ ἐνήλεπα (= ἐναλήλιφα ἐμαυτὸν) ἕως ἀκούσω φάσιν παρὰ σοῦ περὶ ἁπάντων, "I am not so much as anointing myself until I hear word from you on each point" (Edd.). Other exx. are P Hamb I. 27[5] (B.C. 250) τὴν δὲ τιμὴν οὔπω ἐκεκόμιστο, "but he has not yet received the price," P Tebt II. 423[12] (early iii/A.D.) οὔπου (*l.* οὔπω) μοι ἐδήλωσας περὶ τ(ο)ύτου, "you have not yet told me about it," and P Oxy XIV. 1763[3] (after A.D. 222) οὔπω μέχρι σήμερον τὰ πλοῖα τῆς ἀνώνας ἐξῆλθεν. In PSI IV. 423[13] (iii/B.C.) the two parts of the word are separated–οὐ γάρ πω εἰργασμένοι εἰσὶν κτλ.

οὐρά,

"tail" (Rev 9[10, 19], 12[4]), occurs in P Leid W[x 29] (ii/iii A.D.) (= II. p. 115) δράκοντα δακόνοντα κονοντα τὴ (*l.* δάκνοντα τὴν) οὐράν, and in the magical P Lond 121[857] (iii/A.D.) (= I. p. 111) φυλακτήριον ἡ οὐρὰ κτλ. MGr οὐρά, νουρά (see Thumb *Handbook*, p. 25).

οὐράνιος,

"heavenly," is seen in P Eud 24[3] (before B.C. 165) οὐράνια διδασκαλέα, and in P Thead 40[3] (A.D. 307–324?) ἰς γνῶσιν τῆς οὐρανίου αὐτοῦ πρ[ο]μηθείας [ἀ]φίκται. In both these instances it is an adj. of two terminations as in Lk 2[13] στρατιᾶς οὐρανίου (but subst. οὐρανοῦ in B* D*), and Ac 26[19] τῇ οὐρανίῳ ὀπτασίᾳ. The fem. in -α, as in class. Greek, is restored by the editor in PSI I. 86[3] (A.D. 307–375) ὁμολ[ογῶ ὀμνὺς τὴν θεί]αν καὶ οὐρανί[αν τύ]χην κτλ. The adj. is naturally common in the magic papyri, e.g. P Lond 46[168] (iv/A.D.) (= I. p. 70) πᾶς δαίμων οὐράνιος καὶ αἰθέριος καὶ ἐπίγειος καὶ ὑπόγειος: cf. also the horoscope *ib.* 130[4] (i/ii A.D.) (= I. p. 133), where a master of astrology urges his pupil to be very exact in the application of the rules which the ancient Egyptians had discovered and handed down with such care–τ]ῶν Αἰγυπτίων οἱ τὸ παλαιὸν ἄ[νδρ]ες γενόμενοι [γ]νησίως τὰ περ[ὶ] τὰ οὐράνια φιλοπονήσαντες . . . ἀπέλειπον τὴν περὶ αὐτῶν γνῶσιν, and the imprecation Wünsch *AF* p. 17[22] (iii/A.D.) ὁρκίζω σε τὸν θεὸν τὸν τῶν οὐρανίων στερεωμάτων (cf. Gen 1[8]) δεσπόζοντα Ἰάω ιβοηα.

οὐρανόθεν.

See Lob. *Phryn.* p. 93 f.

οὐρανός.

For οὐρανός in the wide sense of "sky," "heaven," as opposed to γῆ, "earth," cf. P Leid G[14] (B.C. 181–145) (= I. p. 42), a prayer to the gods that they would grant to Ptolemy Philometor and Berenice–κυρίαν τῶν [ὑ]πὸ τὸν οὐρανὸν χώρω[ν, "dominationem terrestrium regionum" (Fd.), and the magic P Lond 121[261] (iii/A.D.) (= I. p. 93) πρὶν γενέσθε (*l.* γενέσθαι) οὐρανὸν ἢ γῆν ἢ θάλασσαν κτλ. The thought of a series of heavens, as in 2 Cor 12[2], may be illustrated from PSI I. 29[2 ff.] (iv/A.D. ?) ἐπικαλοῦμέ(= αἱ) σε τὸν καθήμενον ἐν τῷ πρώτῳ οὐρανῷ . . . ἐν τῷ β οὐρανῷ . . . ἐν τῷ γ οὐρανῷ κτλ. P Leid 6[6] (iv/A.D.) (= *Selections*, p. 126) πιστεύομεν γὰρ τὴν πολιτία[ν σ]ου ἐνν οὐρανῷ is evidently a reminiscence of Phil 3[20]. On the use of the plur. οὐρανοί in the NT, see Blass *Gr.* p. 83, and the statistics in Hawkins *Hor. Syn.*[2] p. 52 f. A new subst. οὐρανουσία occurs in P Lond 121[881] (iii/A.D.) (= I. p. 110).

Οὐρβανός.

This proper name of a συνεργός of Paul (Rom 16[9]) in Rome or Ephesus (cf. Milligan *Documents*, p. 182 ff.) is found in the Septuagint Memorial from Hadrumetum (iii/A.D.) reproduced by Deissmann *BS* p. 274 ff., along with other persons who were probably slaves or had been emancipated–e.g. [41] ἄπελθε πρὸς τὸν Οὐρβανόν, ὃν ἔτεκ(ε)ν Οὐρβανά. Both Urbanus and Urbana are found in the Latin inscrr. (Dessau 7566, 7986 *al.*): see further Lightfoot *Philippians*[2], p. 172.

οὖς.

P Oxy II. 237[vi. 22] (A.D. 186) ὦτα παρέχω ἄνοα αὐτῷ, "I turned a deaf ear to him" (Edd.): cf. Ac 7[57] συνέσχον τὰ ὦτα αὐτῶν. In a magic spell for procuring the public appearance of a deity P Lond 121[329] (iii/A.D.) (= I. p. 95) ἄνοιξόν μου τὰ ὦτα ἵνα μοι χρηματίσῃς περὶ ὧν σε ἀξιῶ ἵνα ἀποκριθῇς μοι. See further s.v. ὠτίον.

οὐσία.

"property in land," "estate" (cf. Lk 15[12 f.]) can be illustrated from Ptolemaic times by P Tebt I. 6[31] (B.C. 140–139) ἀπ' οὐσιῶν, with reference to the proceeds derived "from properties." In Roman times the word is very common, e.g. P Ryl II. 126[7] (A.D. 28–9) γεωρ]γοῦ τῆς Ἰουλίας Σεβ[αστῆς] οὐσίας, "farmer on the estate of Julia Augus a," ib. 138[10] (A.D. 34) τῶν ἐλαιώνων τῆς αὐτῆς οὐσίας, "the olive-yards of the aforesaid estate," P Oxy III. 471[37] (ii/A.D.) τὴν οὐσίαν αὐτοῦ καὶ τῆς γυναικὸς καὶ τῶν περὶ αὐτὸν ἀναλη[μ]-φθῆναι κελεύεις, "you order his property and that of his wife and friends to be confiscated" (Edd.), al. The word is used of Imperial estate in such a passage as P Ryl II. 134[6] (A.D. 34) γεωργοῦ τῆ[ς] Τιβερίου Καίσαρος Σεβαστοῦ οὐσία[ς] Γερμανικιανῆς, "farmer on the Germanician estate of Tiberius Caesar Augustus." For the corresponding use of the adj. οὐσιακός, cf. P Tebt II. 317[17] (A.D. 174–5) ἐπὶ τοῦ κρατίστου οὐσιακοῦ ἐπιτ[ρό]που Οὐλπίου Ἡρακλείδου, "before his highness the procurator of the Imperial estates" (Edd.), al., and on the οὐσιακὴ γῆ as the patrimonial possession of the Emperor, see Chrest. I. i. p. 298 ff.

For οὐσία in the sense of "essence," "being," cf. P Leid W[vii. 8] (ii/iii A.D.) (= II. p. 105) ἀποσκεδασθήτω μου πᾶσα φλόξ (l. φλόξ), πᾶσα δύναμις οὐσίας (cf. MGr πάνω στὴν οὐ., "in the prime of life"), and on the general use of οὐσία and οὐσιάζω in the magic papyri see Wiener Studien xl. (1918), p. 5 ff. For the ὁμοούσιος of the Creeds Sharp (Epict. p. 128) compares Epict. ii. 8. 2 τίς οὖν οὐσία θεοῦ; σάρξ; μὴ γένοιτο κτλ.

οὔτε.

P Petr III. 53 (η)[6] (iii B.C.) (= Witkowski[2], p. 45) οὐκ οἶμαί σε ἀγνοεῖν οὔτ[ε . . . . ἀ]πεσχίσθην ἀπὸ σοῦ . . . . . P Oxy XIV. 1641[6] (a loan with right of habitation—A.D. 68) οὐκ οὔσης με οὔτ' ἄλλῳ οὐδενὶ ἐξουσίας ἐκβάλλιν σε οὐδὲ τοῖς παρὰ σοῦ ἐκ τοῦ ἐνοικισμοῦ, "neither I nor any one else having the right to expel you or your agents from the habitation" (Edd.), ib. 1775[5] (iv/A.D.) οὐχ ᾤκησα οὔτε πάλιν ἠμέλησα. A good ex. of οὔτε . . . οὔτε is afforded by the well-known boy's letter, P Oxy I. 119[6] (ii/iii A.D.) (= Selections, p. 103), where the boy threatens his father that if he does not take him to Alexandria—οὐ μὴ γράψω σε ἐπιστολήν, οὔτε λαλῶ σε, οὔτε νἰγένω σε εἶτα, "I won't write you a letter, or speak to you, or wish you health": cf. also BGU II. 530[9 f.] (i/A.D.) (= Selections, p. 60 f.) οὔτε ἀντέγραψας οὔτε ἦλθας, "you neither answered nor came."

οὗτος.

A few of the prepositional phrases with this common demonstrative pron. may be illustrated—διὰ τοῦτο, "on this account," cf. P Ryl II. 84[5] (A.D. 146) τὴν ἄνεσιν τὴν διὰ τοῦτο γενομένην τῶν ὑπαρχόντων, "the ensuing remission

of the lands" (Edd.): ἐκ τούτου, "for this reason." In 6[66] cf. ib. 81[34] (c. A.D. 104) ἐκ τούτου δὲ [φανε]ρὸν ἐστιν [καὶ] μηδένα χρῆζειν, "it is evident from this that nobody wants it" (Edd.), BGU II. 423[17] (a son to his father—ii/A.D.) (= Selections, p. 91) με ἐπαίδευσας καλῶς, καὶ ἐκ τούτου ἐλπίζω ταχὺ προκόσ(= ψαι) τῶν θε[ῶ]ν θελόντων, "you have brought me up well, and for this reason I hope to be quickly promoted, if the gods will": τούτου ἕνεκα, "for this purpose," cf. P Oxy I. 113[28] (ii/A.D.) ἐὰν δ' ἄρα μὴ ἅμα τῷ υἱῷ μου ἐξέρχομαι τούτου ἕνεκα, "otherwise I and my son will come for this purpose" (Edd.): ἐπὶ τούτων, "upon this," "in the meanwhile," cf. PSI VI. 598[21] (iii/B.C.) περὶ ὧν γράψω Ἑρμαφίλωι καὶ Ἵππωνι καὶ Ἡρακλείτωι· διωμολογήθη γὰρ ἐπὶ τούτων, where, however, the editor prefers the meaning "in their presence": and κατὰ ταῦτα, "in the same way," Lk 6[23] v.l. cf. ib. III. 235[25] (ii/A.D.) κατὰ ταῦτα δὲ ἀξιῶ, "and in the same way I ask."

The abrupt ταῦτα (sc. γίνεται) of the boy's letter P Oxy I. 119[18] (ii/iii A.D.) (= Selections, p. 103) ἂμ μὴ πέμψῃς, οὐ μὴ φάγω, οὐ μὴ πείνω. ταῦτα, "if you don't send, I won't eat, I won't drink. There now," may be paralleled from the inscrr., as C. and B. ii. p. 386, No. 232[21], where a certain Gaius sums up his principles with the words—ταῦτα, φίλοι, and ib. p. 700, No. 635, where a protest is uttered against Christian teaching in the words—οὐκ ἤμην· ἐγενόμην· οὐκ ἔσομαι· οὐ μέλι μοι ὁ βίος· ταῦτα. See Evans CQ xv. (1921), p. 24, and add the long metrical epitaph and curse, BCH iii. p. 144, which ends with ταῦτα, "so much," in a line by itself: see Ramsay Luke, p. 274. For the expressive αἱ χεῖρες αὗται in Ac 20[34], "these hands" (stretching them out), Field (Notes, p. 133) compares Philost. Her. p. 162 (ed. Boiss.): εἰπόντος γοῦν ποτε πρὸς αὐτὸν Ἀχιλλέως, Ὦ Παλάμηδες, ἀγροικότερος φαίνῃ τοῖς πολλοῖς, ὅτι μὴ πέπασαι τὸν θεραπεύσοντα, Τί οὖν ΤΑΥΤΑ, ἔφη, ὦ Ἀχιλλεῦ; τὼ χεῖρε ἄμφω προτείνας.

The combination αὐτὰ ταῦτα is found in P Oxy IV. 743[38] (B.C. 2) ἵνα αὐτῷ αὐτὰ ταῦτα ὑποδίξω, "in order that I may inform him of these very things," similarly PSI III. 235[25] (ii/A.D.), cf. ib. IV. 343[7] (B.C. 256–5) ἠσχολήμεθα πρὸς αὐτοῖς τούτοις. In P Meyer 13[11] (A.D. 141) an ass is sold—τοῦτον τοιοῦτον ἀναπόριφον, "such as it is, without the possibility of its being returned": cf. P Ryl II. 158[13] (A.D. 138?), P Oxy I. 95[18] (A.D. 129). A fem. form ταύτων, explained by Mayser Gr. p. 113 as due to false analogy with the sing., was formerly found in P Lond 24[53] (B.C. 162) (= I. p. 33) περὶ ταύτων, but Wilcken (UPZ i. p. 213) now reads περὶ ταῦτ' ὧν: see, however, P Tebt I. 24[98] (B.C. 117). There are traces in the inscrr. and papyri of a vulgar form τοῦτος, which survives in MGr: see Dieterich Untersuchungen, p. 197.

οὕτως, οὕτω.

Οὕτως is the general form both before vowels and consonants in the best MSS. of the NT (and of the LXX), and this usage is on the whole confirmed by the papyri. See e.g. (1) before vowels—PSI III. 171[22] (ii B.C.) τούτων δὲ οὕτως ἐχόντων, "this being so." P Oxy IV. 743[35] (B.C. 2) ὑπέρ σου οὕτως ὡς ὑπ(ὲρ) μου, "for you just as for me," ib. II. 294[11] (A.D. 22) (= Selections, p. 35) εἰ ταῦτα οὕτως ἔχι, ib. I. 115[3] (ii/A.D.) (= Selections, p. 96) οὕτως ἐλυπήθην καὶ ἔκλαυσα ἐπὶ τῶι εὐμοίρωι ὡς ἐπὶ Διδυμᾶτος ἔκλαυσα, "I grieved and wept as much over the blessed one, as I wept over Didymas," P Grenf II. 77[11] (iii/iv A.D.) (= *Selections*, p. 120) σ[υ]νλέξαντες ὅσα εἶχεν καὶ οὕτως ἀπέστητε, "having collected what he had you then went off"; (2) before consonants—P Petr II. 16[14] (mid. iii/B.C.) οὕτως δὲ ὑπολάμβανε, P Lond 44[7] (B.C. 161) (= I. p. 34) νομίζων μάλισθ' οὕτως τεύξεσθαι τῶν δικαίων, P Tebt I. 24[32] (B.C. 117) οὕτως λήγοντες τῆς ἀγνοίας, and the striking P Oxy VII. 1065[7] (iii/A D.), with its doctrine of strict reciprocity between gods and men, ἐὰν δὲ ὀλιγωρήσῃς. ὥσπερ [ο]ἱ θεοὶ οὐκ ἐφίσαντό μ[ο]υ οὕτως κἀγὼ θεῶ[ν] οὐ φί[σ]ομαι, "if you neglect this, as the gods have not spared me, so will I not spare the gods" (Ed.). Examples are, however, forthcoming of οὕτω (1) before consonants, e.g. P Petr II. 13 (19)[2] (B.C. 258-3) οὕτω γὰρ [ἔστα]ι τυχεῖν κτλ., PSI IV. 346[6] (B.C. 255-4) ἐπίστειλόν μοι, ὅπως οὕτω ποιῶ, P Par 63[iii. 84] (B.C. 164) (= P Petr III. p. 24) τάχα γὰρ οὕτω πρέπει ῥηθέν, "for that is perhaps the proper expression" (Mahaffy), *Magn* 92 (b)[16] (ii/B.C.) οὕτω κύρια εἶνα[ι τὰ] ἐψηφισμένα, and even (2) before a vowel, e.g. P Lond 41[14] (B.C. 161) (= I. p. 28) ἐγένετο ἡ κρίσις οὕτω· ἀφίλεσαν κτλ., and from a late date *ib*. 483[78] (A.D. 616) (= II. p. 328) διὰ τὸ οὕτω ὀρθῶς καὶ δικαίως δεδόχθαι. See further Mayser *Gr*. p. 242 f., Crönert *Mem. Herc*. p. 142 n.[1], Nachmanson, p. 112. Field *Notes*, p. 87 f. discusses the translation of Jn 4[6] ἐκαθέζετο οὕτως.

οὐχί.

For this strong form of οὐ (οὐκ, οὐχ), which is found 54 times in the NT and generally in questions (cf. Robertson *Gr*. p. 1406), we may compare the Alexandrian Erotic Fragment P Grenf I. 1[1.25] (ii/B.C.) εὐθὺ δεῖ καὶ διαλύεσθαι· οὐχὶ διὰ τοῦτο φίλους ἔχομεν οἳ κρινοῦσι τίς ἀδικεῖ; "for we must soon be reconciled; to what end else have we friends, who shall judge which of us two is in the wrong?" (Ed.). For the non-interrogative use, cf. PSI V. 499[4] (B.C. 257-6) where a farm-steward asks that money be sent him—ἐγλέλοιπε γὰρ ἡμᾶς, καὶ οὐχὶ ἔχομεν χορηγεῖν οὔτε εἰ[ς τ]ὴν φυτε[ί]αν τοῦ κρότωνος . . οὔτε εἰς τὴν ξυλοκοπίαν κτλ.

ὀφειλέτης.

In a Christian amulet of *c*. vi/A.D., BGU III. 954[20 ff] (= *Selections*, p. 133 f.) the petition of the Lord's Prayer is found in the form—ἄφες ἡμῖν τὰ ὀφειλ[ή]ματα ἡμῶν [κα]θὰ καὶ ἡμεῖς ἀφεί<ο>[μεν] τοῖς ὀφει[λέται]ς ἡμῶν. On the frequency of the metaphor in Rom, see Ramsay *Luke*, p 286.

ὀφειλή.

This word (*ter* in NT), which, according to Grimm-Thayer, is "found neither in the Grk. OT nor in prof. auth.", occurs frequently in the papyri in the literal sense of "debt." To Deissmann's exx. in *BS* p. 221 we may add such passages as BGU IV. 1155[18] (B.C. 9) μενεῖ δὲ ἡ ὀφιλὴ ἀ[κ]ίνδυνο(ς) παντὸ[ς] κινδύν(ου), P Oxy II. 286[18] (A.D. 82) ὑπὲρ τῆς προκειμένης ὀφειλῆς, P Fay 247 (*c*. A.D. 100) an account headed ἔχθεσις Εὐημερ[εί]ας ὀ[φ]ειλῆς, P Tebt II. 323[15] (A.D. 127) οἰ]κίαν . . . καθαρὰ[ν] ἀπὸ ὀφιλῆς, P Oxy IV. 719[24] (A.D. 193) ἀπό τε δημοσίας κα[ὶ ἰδιωτικῆ]ς ὀφιλῆς,

al. It may be noted that BGU IV. 1055[31] (B.C. 13) τὸ ἐν ὀφιλῇ θησόμενον, cited by Moulton *Proleg*. p. 161 n.[1], should be read τὸ ἐνοφιληθησόμενον, and similarly *ib*. 1053[.35]: cf. P Tebt I. 17[8] (B.C. 114) πάντα τὰ ἐνοφειλόμενα περὶ τὴν κώμην, "all arrears owing from the neighbourhood" (Edd.).

ὀφείλημα.

For ὀφείλημα in its literal sense of a money "debt," cf. P Hib I. 42[10] (B.C. 262) τὸν δὲ λοιπὸν . . δώσομεν Λευκίωι ἐν ὀφειλήματι, "but the rest we shall give to Leucius as a debt" (Edd.), P Lond 1203[4] (B.C. 113) (= III. p. 10) τὸ δὲ ὀφείλημα τοῦτο ἀποδότω Τοτόης Παν[ο]β[χού]νει, "but let T. pay this debt to P.", P Oxy III. 494[10] (A.D. 156) ὀφειλήματα ἔγγραφα καὶ ἄγραφα, "debts recorded and unrecorded," and P Ryl II. 117[14] (A.D. 269), where it is laid down that those who had inherited nothing from deceased persons "should not be held responsible for their debts or the claims made against them"—μὴ κατέχεσθαι τοῖς ἐκείνων ὀφειλήμασι[ν] ἢ καὶ ζητήμασιν. See also *Syll* 736 (= [3]1108)[10] (iii/ii B.C.) τοῦ κατὰ τὸν νόμον ὀφειλήματ[ο]ς ἀπολυθείς (with the editor's note).

ὀφείλω.

For ὀφείλω in its ordinary sense "owe" money, see P Eleph 2[10] (a Will—B.C. 285-3) (= *Chrest*. II. p. 356), where provision is made that their sons are to be responsible for any debts that their parents may contract during their lifetime—ἐὰν δέ τι ἐξαπορῶνται ἢ χρέος ὀφείλωσιν Διονύσιος ἢ Κάλλιστα ζῶντες τρεφέτωσαν αὐτοὺς οἱ υἱεῖς πάντες κοινῆι καὶ συναποτινέτωσαν τὰ χρέα πάντες: cf. P Magd 25 *recto*[7] (B.C. 221) εἰ δέ τι ἀντιλέγει, μὴ ὀφείλειν ὀμόσας μοι, ἀπολελύσθω, "if he denies the debt, and swears that he owes me nothing, let him be released," BGU III. 846[16] (ii/A.D.) (= *Selections*, p. 95) ὀφείλω ὀβολόν, P Oxy VII. 1067[12] (iii/A.D.) εἰπὲ αὐτῷ περὶ τῆς κέλλας ὅτι ἐσφραγίσθη τὴν κέλλαν αὐτοῦ μηδὲν ὀφείλων (*l*. ὀφείλοντος), "tell him about his cellar, that it has been sealed up although he owes nothing" (Ed.), *ib*. XII. 1489[4] (late iii/A.D.) ἐνοχλεῖς μοι ὅτι ὀφείλεις Ἀγαθὸς (= ῷ) Δαίμονι χαλκόν· πεπλήρωσ(=κ)α αὐτόν, "you worry me about the money which you owe to Agathodaemon: I have paid him in full" (Edd.), and P Tebt II. 424[6] (late iii/A.D.) ἴσθι δὲ ὅτι ὀφίλις φόρους καὶ ἀποφορὰς ἑπτὰ ἐτῶν, "let me tell you that you owe seven years' rents and dues" (Edd.). An interesting ex. of the verb used metaphorically is afforded by P Oxy VII. 1021[1] (A.D. 54) with reference to the decease of the Emperor Claudius—ὁ μὲν ὀφειλόμενος τοῖς προγόνοις καὶ ἐνφανὴς θεὸς Καῖσαρ εἰς αὐτοὺς κεχώρηκε, "the Caesar who had to pay his debt to his ancestors, god manifest, has joined them" (Ed.). Cf. P Tebt II. 294[21] (A.D. 146) ἵνα καὶ αἱ ὀφίλ[ο]υσαι ἱερουργίαι τῶν σε φιλούντων θεῶν ἐπιτελῶνται, "in order that the due services of the gods who love you may be performed" (Edd.), and the important inscr. *Syll* 633 (= [3]1042)[15] (ii/iii A.D.) cited *s.v.* ἱλάσκομαι.

For ὀφείλω c. inf. = "ought," cf. P Oxy VII. 1021[2] (A.D. 54) διὸ πάντες ὀφείλομεν . . θεοῖς πᾶσι εἰδέναι χάριτας, "therefore we all ought to give thanks to all the gods," P Ryl II. 77[20] (A.D. 192) ἀναδεξάμενος τὴν μείζονα ἀρχὴν οὐκ ὀφείλει τὴν ἐλάττον' ἀποφεύγειν, "a person who has offered to undertake the greater office ought not to shun the lesser" (Edd.), and P Giss I. 40ⁱⁱ ²³ (A.D. 215) ἐ[κεῖνοι] κωλ[ύ]εσθαι ὀφε[ί]λουσιν, οἵτινες φεύγουσι τὰς χώρας τὰς ἰδίας. See also s.v. προσοφείλω.

ὄφελον.

This form = "I would that," which is found in the NT (1 Cor 4⁸ al.) for ὤφελον (cf. Moulton *Proleg.* p. 201), may be illustrated from OGIS 315¹⁶ (B.C. 164–3) ὄφελομ μὲν ἡ θεὸς . . . στερῆσαι τὸν ταῦτα πο[ήσαντα ὧν] μάλιστα ἐπιθυμεῖ, where it will be noted the editor reads στερῆσαι (inf.) rather than στερήσαι (opt.). In P Giss I. 17¹⁰ (time of Hadrian), a slave writes to her sick master—ὤφελον εἰ ἐδυνάμεθα πέτασθαι καὶ ἐλθεῖν καὶ προσκυνῆσαί σε, "would that I could fly and come and pay my respects to you." Ὤφελον is common with the 1st pers. in Epictetus (but does not occur in the NT), e.g. ii. 21. 1 ὤφελον ὡς φρένας ἔχω οὕτω καὶ τύχην εἶχον : for the 3rd pers. following, as in Gal 5¹², cf. *ib.* ii. 18. 15 ὤφελόν (ὄφελόν S) τις μετὰ ταύτης ἐκοιμήθη.

ὄφελος,

which in the NT is confined to 1 Cor 15³², Jas 2¹⁴·¹⁶ (cf. Job 15⁵, the only occurrence in the LXX), is seen in P Oxy I. 118 *verso* ³⁰ (late iii/A.D.) οὐδὲν γὰρ ὄφελος ὑστερησάντων τῶν χρειωδῶν τῇ παρουσίᾳ αὐτοῦ, "it is of no use if a person comes too late for what required his presence" (Edd.) : cf. *ib.* XII. 1468⁸ (c. A.D. 258) τοῖς κακουργεῖν προχείρως ἔχουσιν τέχνη οὐ δικαίας ἐπινοίας πρὸς τῷ μηδὲν ὄφελος ἔχειν ἔτι καὶ κτλ., "the wicked designs of those who are ready to commit crimes by artifice are not only made to be of no avail, but" etc. (Edd.), and from the inscrr. OGIS 519⁸ (A.D. 244–7) οὐδὲν ὄφελο[ς ἡ]μεῖν ἐκ ταύτης τῆ[ς ἀντιγραφῆς ἐγένετο.

ὀφθαλμός

is naturally common in personal descriptions, e.g. P Ryl II. 159⁶⁵ (A.D. 31–2) οὐ(λὴ) ὑπ' ὀφθ(αλμὸν) δεξιόν, P Leid Wˣᵛⁱⁱ. ²² (ii/iii A.D.) (= II. p. 141) ὀφθαλμοί εἰσιν ἀκάματοι, λάμποντες ἐν ταῖς κόραις τῶν ἀνθρώπων, of a god's eyes. The phrase *peto, domine, ut eum ant<e> oculos habeas tanquam me*, in a Latin letter of recommendation on papyrus, P Oxy I. 32⁶ ᶠᶠ (ii/A.D.), may be paralleled from such passages as P Par 63⁴³ (B.C. 164) (= P Petr III. p. 22) ἀντ' ὀφθαλμῶν [θεμένου]ς, "keeping it before your eyes" (Mahaffy), P Tebt I. 28¹⁸ (c. B.C. 114) ὅπως καὶ οἱ λοιποὶ προοφθάλμως λαβόντες τὴ[ν] ἐσομένην ὑπὸ σοῦ μισοπόνηρον ἐπίστα[σιν, "in order that the rest may obtain a conspicuous illustration to show how you will suppress wrongdoing" (Edd.), BGU II. 362ᵛ ⁸ (A.D. 215) πρὸ ὀφθαλμῶν θέμενος [τ]ὰ κελευσθέντα ὑπὸ Αὐρη[λίου] Ἰταλικοῦ, and from the inscrr. *Syll* 226 (= ³405 ¹²⁰) (c. B.C. 230) τὰ δεινὰ πρὸ ὀφθαλμῶν ποιούμενος παρεκάλει πάντας τοὺς ἰσχύοντας βοηθῆσαι, OGIS 210⁵ (A.D. 247–8) πρὸ ὀφθαλμῶν ἔχουσι τὰ περὶ τούτου κελευσθέντα. There is no need, therefore, to scent a Hebraism in the expression, as Deissmann (*LAE* p. 184) points out. The phrase ἐν ὀφθαλμοῖς occurs only in the later historical books of the LXX, and is not found in the NT : see Thackeray *Gr.* i. p. 43. A fragmentary official letter, belonging to Ptolemaic times, published in P Par

p. 411, shows us Ἀμ]μώνιον ἀκολουθοῦντά σοι ὀφθαλ[μοῖς —to which the editor can provide no parallel. For ὀφθαλμὸς πονηρός (Mk 7²² al.) see s.v. βασκαίνω, and cf. Burton *Gal.* p. 143 f. The verb ἐποφθαλμιάω is restored by the editors in P Oxy XIV. 1630⁶ (A.D. 222?) ἐπ]οφθαλμ[ιῶν]τες τοῖς ἔργοις μου, "through envy of my operations" : cf. P Lond V. 1674¹⁷ (c. A.D. 570) with the editor's note : for the other form ἐποφθαλμέω, see s.v. ἀντοφθαλμέω. The compound adj. ὀφθαλμοφανής is found in P Hib I. 89⁸ (B.C. 239) ἀργυρίου ὀφθαλμοφα[νο]ῦς ἐναντ[ίο]ν τῶν ὑπογε]γραμμένων μαρτύρων (δραχμὰς) φ, "500 drachmae of silver produced to view in the presence of the witnesses below written" (Edd.) : cf. P Strass II. 92⁵ (B.C. 244–3), P Hamb I. 28⁴ (1st half ii/B.C.), and for the corresponding adverb see LXX Esth 8¹³ and Cleomedes (ed. Ziegler) p. 212²⁵. Another compound ὑψηλόφθαλμος, "one who casts lewd eyes" (cf. 2 Pet 2¹⁴) may be cited from Didache iii. 3.

ὄφις.

In P Leid Wᵛⁱⁱ ⁴⁰ (ii/iii A.D.) (= II. p. 101) we have a spell—ὄφιν ἀποκτεῖναι, "to kill a serpent." In P Lond 122 (iv/A.D.) (= I. p. 116) Hermes is invoked under his various shapes and titles, e.g. ⁱⁱἐν τῷ βορεᾷ μορφὴν ἔχεις ὄφεως. For the name ascribed to Satan cf. a Christian amulet not later than Justinian, *Kaibel* 1140 L² —

φεῦγ' ἀπ' ἐμῶν μελέων, ὄφ[ι], πῦρ, Βελιὰρ κ[ακό]μορ[φ]ε.

The MGr φίδι has assumed the diminutive suffix and become neuter.

ὀφρῦς

(for accent see Moulton *Gr.* ii. p. 141 f.) in its literal sense of the cognate word "brow," "eyebrow," is naturally common in the personal descriptions in which papyrus documents abound, e.g. P Petr I. 11¹² (B.C. 220) οὐλὴ ἐπ' ὀφρύος ἀριστερᾶς, "a scar on his left eyebrow," P Fay 107¹⁵ (A.D. 133) οὐλ(ὴ) ὀφρύι δεξιᾷ, and similarly BGU I. 287⁶ (A.D. 250) (= *Selections*, p. 115). We may add the famous description of Paul in the *Acta Pauli* 3, where the apostle is described as σύνοφρυς, "with eyebrows meeting." In Epict. i. 3. 1 ὀφρῦς has the metaphorical sense "pride" ; cf. Lat. *supercilium*.

ὀχετός.

This subst. is substituted for ἀφεδρών in Mk 7¹⁹ D. It is found in its ordinary sense of "water-pipe," "conduit" (cf. ὄχος and Lat. *veho*) in P Petr II. 6⁹ (c. B.C. 250) (= P Petr III. p. 104) δεῖ δὲ καὶ ὀχετὸν ποι[ῆσαι, and BGU IV. 1116¹³ (B.C. 13) τῆς (corr. from τῶν) τῶν δημοσίων ὀχετῶν ἐπιβολῆς : see also *Archiv* v. p. 37 n.¹. For the verb cf. P Petr I. 29 *verso* (ii/B.C.) ὀχετεύομεν καὶ ποτίζομεν, "we are making conduits and watering."

ὀχλέω.

While there may be traces of a technical medical use of this word in Ac 5¹⁶ (see Knowling in *EGT al l.*, and cf. Tob 6⁸), there is ample evidence that the word had come to be used quite generally in the vernacular, cf. e.g. P Fay Ostr 45 (i A.D.) (= *Fayûm Towns*, p. 331) μὴ ὤχλει (*l.* ὄχλει) τοὺς Σαμβᾶτος, "don't worry the people (or 'sons'?) of

Sambas" (Edd.), P Oxy II. 269ⁱⁱ ⁴ (A.D. 57) ἐὰν δύνῃ ἐρωτηθεὶς ὄχλησον Διόσκορον καὶ ἔκπραξον αὐτὸν τὸ χειρόγραφον, "if you can, please worry Dioscorus and exact from him his bond" (Edd.), ib. XII. 1481⁶ (early ii/A.D.) μὴ ὄχλου δὲ πέμπειν τι ἡμῖν, "do not trouble to send me anything," ib. I. 121²⁷ (iii/A.D.) τοὺς τέκτονες (= —ας) μὴ ἄφῃς ὅλως ἀργῆσε· ὄχλει αὐτοῖς, "don't allow the carpenters to be altogether idle; worry them" (Edd.), BGU III. 820²⁴ (ii/A.D.) ἐὰν ὀχληθῶ ὑπὸ τῶν πρα[κτόρων?. P Iand 11⁴⁴ (iii/A.D.) ὀχλεῖ μοι δῖλα ὁ Τρωῖλος . . . ἵνα μὴ οὕτως ὀχληθῶ, the late P Gren II. 92⁷ (vi/vii A.D.) ὅπως καὶ ἡμεῖς εὕρωμεν μετὰ παρρησίας ὀχλῆσαι ὑμῖν περὶ ὧν χρεία, and from the inscr. OGIS 262²² (Syria–iii/A.D.) μηδὲ ἐπιχειροῦντος ἢ ὀχλοῦντος προφάσει παροχῆς καὶ τέλους. For the subst. ὄχλησις see P Oxy XII. 1491⁶ (early iv/A.D.) θαρρῶ . . . . ὅτι ὄχλησις ἐὰν ᾖ προΐστασαι ἡμῶν, "I am confident that if there is any trouble you are supporting me" (Edd.), for the adj. ὀχληρός see P Oxy III. 525² (early ii/A.D.) ὁ παράπλους τοῦ Ἀνταιοπολίτου ὀχληρότατός ἐστιν, "the voyage past the Antaeopolite nome is most troublesome," ib. XIV. 1760¹⁷ (ii/A.D.) ἐὰν δὲ σοι ὀχληρὸν ἦν τοῦτο, and for the adv. ὀχληρῶς see BGU I. 340¹⁵ (A.D. 148–9) συνεχῶς καὶ ὀχληρῶς. Cf. s.v. ἐνοχλέω.

ὀχλοποιέω.

For this word, which is not found elsewhere than in Ac 17⁵, Hobart (p. 230) compares the phrase ὄχλον ποιέει from Hippocrates (*Morb. Mul.* 597).

ὄχλος.

In P Petr II. 4 (6)²⁶ (B.C. 255–4) an official complains that on his way to work he had been hustled, and that, if care is not taken, he will be assaulted—δινὸν γάρ ἐστιν ἐν ὄχλωι ἀτιμάζεσθαι, "for it is a dreadful thing to be insulted before a crowd" (Ed.), and in ib. 45ⁱⁱⁱ ²³ (B.C. 246) ἄλλος ὄχλ[ος ἐστεφ]ανωμένος is distinguished from various officials. A striking parallel to Mk 15¹⁵ (noted by the editor) is afforded by P Flor I. 61⁶¹ (A.D. 85) (= *Chrest.* II. p. 89), where the Egyptian Governor addresses a certain Phibion, who had been tried before him, in the words—ἄξιος μ[ὲ]ν ἦς μαστιγωθῆναι . . . χαρίζομαι δέ σε τοῖς ὄχλοις, "you deserved to be scourged, but I hand you over to the multitude." [Note the use of ὄχλος in the plur., as frequently in Mt (e.g. 4²⁵), with apparently the same meaning as the sing.] A Gnostic charm of iii/iv A.D., P Oxy XII. 1478⁴, contains the invocation—δὸς νείκην ὁλοκληρίαν σ<τ>αδίου καὶ ὄχλου τῷ προκειμένῳ Σαραπάμμωνι, "grant victory and safety in the race-course and the crowd to the aforesaid Sarapammon" (Edd.). We hear of συναγωγαὶ ὄχλων in OGIS 383²⁵⁴ (mid. i/B.C.), and the sing. is used of a "mass" of soldiers in Syll 318 (= ³700)²³ (B.C. 117) συνεπελθόντος μετ' αὐτῶν Τίπα τῶν Μαίδων δυνάστου μετ' ὄχλ[ου π]λείονος, cf. OGIS 544¹⁹ (ii/A.D.) ἐν τῆι τῶν ὄχλων παρόδωι (with Dittenberger's note).

ὀχύρωμα.

We are unable to illustrate from our sources the metaphorical meaning which this word has on its only occurrence in the NT (2 Cor 10⁴), but for the original force of "stronghold," "prison" (as in Gen 39²⁰), cf. P Petr II. 13(3)²

(B.C. 258–53) τὸ πρὸς νότον [τ]οῦ ὀχυρώματος, "the wall to the south of the prison," P Strass II. 85²³ (B.C. 113) ἀπὸ τῆς ἐντὸς τοῦ ὀχυρώματος οἰκίας ᾠκοδομημένης, and OGIS 455¹⁴ (B.C. 39). For ὀχύρωσις see P Lille I. 3²¹ (after B.C. 241–0) εἰς ὀχύρωσιν. The verb is found in the Petrie papyri of strengthening the dykes in view of the rise of the Nile, e.g. II. 9(1)⁸ (B.C. 241–39) τοῦ γὰρ ποταμοῦ πρὸς πόντα τὰ χώματα προσβαίνοντ[ος τὰ π]άντα ὀχ[υρῶσ]αι δεῖ: cf. OGIS 90²³ (the Rosetta stone—B.C. 196) τὰ πεδία κατέσχεν ἐκ πολλῶν τόπων ὀχυρώσας τὰ στόματα τῶν ποταμῶν ("canals").

ὀψάριον.

With the use of ὀψάριον to denote fish eaten as a titbit along with bread in Jn 6⁹·¹¹, 21⁹ ᵈ (cf. Tob 2² S), cf. BGU IV. 1095¹⁷ (A.D. 57), where after the mention of bread and pigeons we read of a λαγύνιον ταριχηροῦ (= ὦν) ὀψαρίων, "a jar of pickled fish": see further P Oxy IV. 736⁵² (a private account—c. A.D. 1) ὀψαρί[ο]υ (ὀβολός), "sauce 1 ob.", P Ryl II. 229²¹ (A.D. 38) τοὺς ἄρτους μοι πέμψον καὶ τὸ ὀψάριον, "send me the loaves and the relish," P Fay 119³¹ (c. A.D. 100) εἰς τὰ γενέσια Γεμέλλ[ης] πέμψις ὡψάρι[α καὶ . . . . . καὶ ἄρτον (πυροῦ ἀρτάβην) α̅, "for Gemella's birthday feast send some delicacies . . . and an artaba of wheaten bread," and the late P Lond 483⁷⁷ (A.D. 616) (= II. p. 328) ὀψάρια ἐκ τῶν παντοίων ὑδάτων. For the word in a more general sense cf. P Oxy III. 531¹⁸ (ii/A.D.), where a father, after bestowing good advice on his son, adds τοῖς ὀψαρίοις ἐξήλλαξας ἡμᾶς, "you won me over by the dainties" (Edd.). From the inscr. we may cite OGIS 484¹⁸ (ii/A.D.) τῶν λεπτῶν ὀψαρίων, and the mention in the same document l.21 of an ὀψαριοπώλης. The simple ὄψον (Tob 2², 7⁸) occurs in P Hib I. 54³⁸ (c. B.C. 245) λάχανα π[αντ]οδαπὰ καὶ ἐὰν ὄψον τι ἔχη[ι]ς. "vegetables of all kinds, and some delicacies if you have any" (Edd.), P Tebt II. 563 (account—early i/A.D.) ἄρτων κ̅, ὄψου κε̅, and the double diminutive ὀψαρίδιον in P Oxy VII. 1067²³ (iii/A.D.) ἀγόρασόν μοι ὀψαρίδιον ἐκ τῆς θαλάσσης (cf. Numb 11²² πᾶν τὸ ὄψος τῆς θαλάσσης). The MGr ψάρι, "fish," shows aphaeresis, which reveals the derivation from ψωμός, "morsel," and ψάω (Boisacq, pp. 737, 1076).

ὀψέ.

For ὀψέ, "late," cf. P Oxy XIV. 1679¹² (iii/A.D.) λείαν γὰρ ὀψαί (l. ὀψέ) σοι ταῦτα ἔγραψα, "for I am writing this to you very late" (Edd.). The word is construed with a partitive gen. in such phrases as P Par 35¹⁵ (B.C. 163) ὀψὲ τῆς ὥρας: cf. Philostratus (ap. Kayser II. p. 171⁴) ὀψὲ τῶν Τρωικῶν, "at a late stage in the Trojan war." This would support the RV rendering of Mt 28¹ ὀψὲ [δὲ] σαββάτων, "late on the sabbath day"; but Blass now prefers "after the sabbath day," in accordance with ὀψὲ τούτων, "after these things," again from Philostratus (ap. Kayser I. p. 213³¹), and other similar passages from late Greek: see Blass-Debrunner § 164. 4 and the discussion in Moulton *Proleg.* p. 72 f. In P Hamb I. 27¹³ (B.C. 250) the writer states that he has received the yokes of oxen "late yesterday, so as to be ready to work to-day"—ἐχθὲς ὀψέ, ὥστε εἰς τὴν σήμερον ἐργάζεσθαι. Ὀψέ is used practically as an indeclinable noun in P Lond 1177⁶⁸ (A.D. 113) (= III. p. 183) ἀπὸ πρωίας ἕως ὀψέ. Among other items in an account, P Tebt I. 121 (B.C. 94 or 61), we find—ὀψὲ οἴνου κε(ράμια) β ʹΓ.

ὀψία.

For ὀψία as a subst. = "evening," see s.v. ὄψιος.

ὄψιμος.

"late," as in Jas 5[7] (cf. Exod 9[32]: also Xen. Oec. xvii. 4), occurs in PSI IV. 433[3] (B.C. 261–0) τὰ μὲν οὖν παρ᾽ ἐμοὶ ὄψιμα ὄντα ὑπάρξει εἰς φυτείαν. For the comparative cf. P Flor II. 131*[9] (A.D. 269) ὁ καιρὸς νῦν ἐστιν ὀψιμώτερος, "the season is now rather late," similarly P Fay 133[8] (iv A.D.) and for the adverb cf. P Tebt I. 72[361] (B.C. 114–3) διὰ τ[ὸ] ὀψίμως σπαρῆν[αι, and P Oxy III. 474[26] (A.D. 184?) οὐδέν ἐστιν τὸ καλούμενον ὀψίμως ὑπ᾽ αὐτοῦ περιγεγραμμένον.

ὄψιος.

P Tebt II. 304[5] (A.D. 167–8) ὀψίας τῆς ὥρας γενομένης, "when the hour was late" (cf. Mk 11[11]), P Oxy III. 475[16] (A.D. 182) ὀψ[ί]ας τῆς διελθούσ[ης] ἕκης (l. ἕκτης), "at a late hour of yesterday the 6th" (Edd.), ib. 528[3] (ii/A.D.) καθ᾽ ἑκάστης [ἡμέρα]ς κα[ὶ] ὄψας (l. ὀψίας), "every day and evening" (Edd.), and BGU II. 380[3] (iii/A.D.) (= Selections, p. 104) ὀψείας τῆς ὥρας. For the comparative ὀψίτερος (so written instead of the classical ὀψιαίτερος in MSS. of Plutarch and Pollux), see P Tebt I. 230 (late ii/B.C.) τῆι προκειμένηι ια ὀψίτερον τῆς ὥρας, BGU I. 181[7] (A.D. 57), al. Cf. MGr ἀπόψε, "this evening."

ὄψις.

In certain proceedings before the Prefect regarding the custody of a child, which strikingly recall 3 Kingd 3[16 ff.], judgment was given that as the child in question ἐκ τῆς ὄψεως, "from its features," appeared to be that of Saraeus, it should be restored to her, P Oxy I. 37[ii. 3] (A.D. 49) (= Selections, p. 51), with which may be compared the use of κατ᾽ ὄψιν in Jn 7[24]. The latter phrase, = "in person," is common. e.g. P Oxy VIII. 1154[4] (late i/A.D.) πρὸ πάντων ὡς ἐνετειλάμην σοι κατ᾽ ὄψιν ἐπιμελοῦ σεαυτῆς, "above all else, as I enjoined you when with you, take care of yourself" (Edd.), P Oxy I. 117[9] (ii/iii A.D.) κατ᾽ ὄψιν σε παρακέκληκα, ib. XIV. 1665[3] (iii/A.D.) παρόν[τ]ι σοι (l. παρόντα σε) κατ᾽ ὄψιν ἠτησάμην, and PSI III. 210[10] (iv/v A.D.) ὅπως . . αὐτὸν κατ᾽ ὄψιν ἀπολάβωμεν. For a similar use of εἰς ὄψιν cf. Preisigke 4317[13] (c. A.D. 200) πολεμεῖ με διότι εἰπόν σοι εἰς ὄψιν. See also the fourth of the so-called Sayings of Jesus, P Oxy IV. 654[27 ff.] λέγει Ἰη(σοῦ)ς [πᾶν τὸ μὴ ἔμπροσθεν τῆς ὄψεώς σου καὶ [τὸ κεκρυμμένον] ἀπό σου ἀποκαλυφ<θ>ήσεται, "Jesus saith, Everything that is not before thy face and that which is hidden from thee shall be revealed to thee." P Fay 133[11] (iv/A.D.) shows the phrase καθ᾽ αὑτὴν οὖν τὴν ὄψιν, "as soon therefore as you see this" (Edd.), and for the meaning "face," "countenance," as in Jn 11[44], Rev 1[16], cf. P Giss I. 22[5] (time of Trajan) τὴν [γλυκυ]τάτην σου ὄψιν προσκυ[νῆσαι, and the literary P Oxy XI. 1380[127] (early ii A.D.) τὴν ἐν Λ[ή]θῃ ἱλαρὰν ὄψιν, with reference to Isis. The plur. is similarly used in P Amh II. 141[12] (A.D. 350) ὡς καὶ ἐπὶ τῶν ὄψεών μοι τὰ οἰδήματα φαίνεται, "so that the swellings

are apparent even on my face" (Edd.)—the result of an accident. Αἱ ὄψεις, "the eyes," is found in P Oxy VI. 911[6] (A.D. 233 or 265) ἀσθενεῖ τὰς ὄψεις, "he has weak sight"; cf. Ev. Petr. 5 ἐνέπτυον αὐτοῦ ταῖς ὄψεσι (with Swete's note), Musonius p. 106[8], and Vogeser Heidigenlegenden, p. 43. In the remarkable Calendar inscr. Priene 105[5] (c. B.C. 9) (= OGIS 458) the birthday of Augustus is described as having given another "aspect" to the world—ἑτέραν τε ἔδω[κεν παντὶ τῷ κόσ]μῳ ὄψιν: cf. what is said of Gaius Caesar Germanicus Augustus in a decree of Assos of the year A.D. 37, Syll 364 (= [3]797)[8] πᾶν ἔθνος ἐπὶ τὴν τοῦ θεοῦ ὄψιν ("presence") ἐσ[π]ευκεν. The editor understands ὄψις as = "dignity" or "position" in P Lond 77[59] (end of vi/A.D., see Chrest. II. 319) (= I. p. 234) κατὰ τὴν ἐμὴν ὄψιν καὶ ὑπόλημψιν. The compound κάκοψις (not in LS) occurs in P Lips I. 1[9] (B.C. 104) and P Grenf II. 28[4] (B.C. 103), and for a new adj. ἐνόπιος see P Par 63[38] B.C. 164 (= P Petr III. p. 20) τηλικούτων διαστολῶν γεγονυιω[ν ὑμῖ]ν καὶ ἐνοπίοις καὶ διὰ γραμμάτων, "extensive explanations having been given to you both face to face and in writing." A Hebraism ἡ ὄψις τῆς γῆς, "the eye of the earth," is found in Ex 10[5, 15], Numb 22[5, 11]. MGr ὄψι, "countenance."

ὀψώνιον.

This interesting word (derived from the classical ὀψωνέω), which is banned by the Atticists (Lob. Phryn. p. 420, is said to have entered the Greek language with Menander (Fr. 1051: cf. Sturz Dial. Mac. p. 187), and is freely used by Polybius (vi. 39.12 ὀψώνιον δ᾽ οἱ πεζοὶ λαμβάνουσι τῆς ἡμέρας δύο ὀβολούς: cf. Kalker, p. 204) and other late writers (see Wetstein ad Lk 3[14] and Durham Menander, p. 83). It is very common in the papyri and inscrr., and its various uses may be illustrated as follows:—(1) For the meaning "provisions" see P Oxy III. 531 (ii/A.D.) where, after various pieces of good advice, a father writes to his son: [20 ff.] ἕως πρὸς σὲ ἔλθῃ Ἀνουβᾶς ἀπὸ τοῦ σοῦ χαλκοῦ τὸ ὀψώνιόν σου καὶ τῶν σῶν ἐξοδίασον ἕως πέμψω, "until however Anoubas arrives, you must pay for the provisions of yourself and your household out of your own money, until I send you some" (Edd.). (2) The reference is particularly to a soldier's "pay," "ration-money," "allowance" (as in Lk 3[14], cf. 1 Cor 9[7]) in P Lond 23 (a)[26] (B.C. 158–157 (= I. p. 38), where a certain Ptolemy petitions King Ptolemy Philometer that his brother may obtain a place in a company stationed at Memphis, and receive the usual allowance—ὅσον καὶ αὐτοὶ λαμβάνουσιν μετρήματα καὶ ὀψ[ό](= ώ)νια: cf. ib. 15(8)[8, 10] (B.C. 131–130) (= I. pp. 55, 59). Similarly in BGU I. 69[2] (A.D. 120) (= Chrest. II. p. 155) a soldier writes promising the repayment of a loan of 140 drachmae τῷ ἔγγιστα δοθησομένῳ ὀψωνίῳ, "with my next pay," and in OGIS 266[7] (iii/B.C.) provision is made for mercenary soldiers—ὅπως τὸ ὀψώνιον λαμβάνωσι τοῦ προειργασμένου χρόνου. (3) From this the transition is easy to "pay," "wages," "salary" in general. Thus for the sing. ὀψώνιον may be cited the early P Petr II. 13 (7)[3] (B.C. 258–253) τοῦ χρηματισθέντος σοι ὀψωνίου, ib. (17)[5] διπλεῖον εἰληφέναι τοῦ διαγεγραμμένου ὀψωνίου, "that I received double the allowance of provision-money," and Ostr 1538[2] (ii/B.C.) δοθήτω Μέμνονι . . ρ τὸ καθῆ(κον) μέτρη(μα) καὶ ὀψώνιον. Cf. also P Oxy IV. 744⁷ (B.C. 1) (= *Selections*, p. 33) ἐὰν εὐθὺς ὀψώνιον λάβωμεν (cf. 2 Cor 11⁸) ἀποστελῶ σε ἄνω, "as soon as we receive wages I will send them to you," P Grenf II. 43¹³ (A.D. 92) the payment of an ὀψό(= ώ)νιον of 80 drachmae to a watchman, P Tebt II. 391²⁰ (A.D. 99) τὸ δὲ ὀψό(= ώ)νιον τοῦ μαχαιροφόρου, "the salary of the sword-bearer," P Oxy VI. 898³¹ (A.D. 123) οὐδὲ ὀψώνιόν μοι ἐχορήγησεν ἔτι πρὸ μηνῶν τριῶν, "she has failed to supply my allowance for the last three months"—the complaint of a minor regarding his mother, and from the inscrr. *Syll* 790 (= ³ 1157)²⁷ (c. B.C. 100 ?) διδόσθω δὲ τῷ ῥαβδούχωι ἐκ τῶν λογευθησομένων χρημάτων ὀψώνιον ἡμερῶν δύο, and *Magn* 116⁵⁴ (time of Hadrian) ὀψωνίου, "wages" for the cultivation of arable land. The plur. ὀψώνια is seen in P Petr II. 33 (*a*)ᴬ ²⁷

(Ptol.) τὰ ὀψώνια τοῖς κατὰ τὴν οἰκίαν, P Par 62ᵛ³ (c. B.C. 170) τοῖς δ' ἀναπληρώσουσιν τὰς ὠνὰς δοθήσεται ὀψώνια, P Ryl II. 153²⁵ (A.D. 138–161) ὀψώνια, "allowances," to crowned athletes, P Tebt II. 420²⁴ (iii/A.D.) ἵνα καὶ αὐτὸς δῦ (*l.* δοῖ) ἀρτάβην κριθῆς εἰς λόγον ὀψωνίων, "that he also may give an artaba of barley on account of wages," and for a wider sense *Priene* 121³⁴ (i/B.C.), where certain citizens are described as having rendered public services χωρὶς ὀψωνίων, "without recompense": cf. *ib.* 109³⁴⋅¹⁰⁶ (c. B.C. 120) ἄτερ ὀψωνίου, and the question to an oracle, P Oxy XII. 1477¹ (iii/iv A.D.) εἰ λήμψομαι τὸ ὀψώνιον; "shall I receive the present?" (Edd.): see Rom 6²³. (4) In P Grenf II. 63⁴ (iii/A.D.) ἔσχον παρὰ σοῦ εἰς λόγον ὀψωνίου ἐπὶ λόγου ὑπ(ὲρ) [. . .] δραχμὰς εἴκοσι τέσσαρες, the editors suggest that ὀψωνίου is perhaps = "interest."

Π

παγιδείω—παιδαριον

παγιδεύω,

"ensnare," "entrap," is found in the NT only in Mt 22[15]: cf. 1 Kingd 28[9], Eccles 9[12], and *Test. xii. patr.* Jos. vii. 1 περιεβλέπετο ποίῳ τρόπῳ με παγιδεῦσαι.

παγίς,

a late form of πάγη (from πήγνυμι), "snare," "trap" (Lk 21[34] *al.*) occurs in a v/A.D. Christian epitaph, *Kaibel* 421[5]—

δίκτυα λυγρά
καὶ γοεράς παγίδας προϋφυγον ἀμπλακίης.

For the form πακίς in the LXX, see Thackeray, *Gr.* i. p. 102.

Πάγος.

Ramsay has shown (*Paul,* p. 260 f., *Recent Discovery,* p. 102 ff.) that ὁ Ἄρειος Πάγος had come to denote in colloquial use (as in Ac 17[19, 22]) "the Council of the Areopagus" as distinguished from "the Hill of Ares," where in early times the Council had met: see e.g. Cavvadias, *Fouilles d'Épidaure* i. p. 68, No 206 (A.D. 50-100) Ἄρειος Πάγος ἐν Ἐλευσῖνι λόγους ἐποιήσατο. For the full expression cf. *Syll* 593 (=³ 1008)[3] (iii/A.D.) τῆς ἐξ Ἀρείου πάγου βουλῆς.

πάθημα.

For the properly colourless character of this word, "disposition" "propensity," see Burton's note *ICC ad Gal* 5[24]. From this it comes naturally to be used *in malam partem* = "evil experience," "suffering," as 14 times in Paul.

παθητός,

the only verbal in —τός in the NT (cf. Jannaris *Gr.* § 1052[1], is used in the weakened sense of "capable of suffering," *patibilis*, in Ac 26[23]: see *Proleg.* p. 222.

πάθος,

which in the NT has always a bad connotation "passion," "lust" (see Trench, *Syn.* § lxxxvii), may be illustrated from *Preisigke* 3451[3] (i/B.C.) ἀπὸ πάθους ἰδίου, *Syll* 373 (=³ 810)[20] (A.D. 55) σπουδαίῳ πάθει τοὺς ὑπὲρ ὑμῶν ἐπ' ἐμοῦ ποιησαμένων λόγους, and *ib.* 890 (=³ 1239)[20] (ii/A.D.), where ὅσα κακὰ κ[αὶ πά]θη ἀνθρώπο[ς] γ[ί]νεται are invoked as a curse on the man who disturbs a tomb. BGU II. 588[1] (i/A.D.) shows the noun, unfortunately in a broken context: in *ib.* 1. 316[28] (A.D. 359) κρυπτὸν πάθος, the reference is to bodily sickness. See also Epict iii. 2. 3. MGr πάθος, "suffering," "passion"; pl. πάθη, πάθια.

παιδαγωγός.

In P Oxy VI. 930 (ii/iii A.D.) a mother writes to her son regarding his education,[13 ff.] μελησάτω σοί τε καὶ τῷ παιδαγωγῷ σου καθήκοντι καθηγητῇ σε παραβάλλειν, "let it be the care both of you and your attendant that you go to a suitable teacher," and concludes,[26 ff.] ἄσπασαι τὸν τειμιώτατον παιδαγωγόν σου Ἔρωτα, "salute your highly esteemed attendant Eros." The passage is of importance as showing the position which the παιδαγωγός frequently occupied. He did not merely conduct the boy to school, but had a general charge of him as a tutor in the old sense of the word, until he reached maturity: cf. Gal 3[24] with Burton's note in *ICC ad l.,* and Clem. *Paed.* i. 1 where the "ethical" aspect of the παιδαγωγός is specially affirmed. In Artem. p. 74[19] the word is associated with τροφός. The verb παιδαγωγέω occurs in P Oxy III. 471[117] (ii/A.D.).

For a subst. παιδικωρός, "keeper of children," cf. BGU II. 594[3] (A.D. 70-80), where it appears under the form πατικουρας: cf. the note in Olsson, *Papyrusbriefe,* p. 134.

παιδάριον.

The latitude of this word, formerly a diminutive, is well seen in its record. In *Syll* 797 (=³ 1163)[5] (ii/B.C.) τὸ παιδάριον ὃ Ἀννύλα κύει is of course an unborn child, while in Tob 6[2 f.] παιδάριον describes a young man who can drag on shore the magic fish that is to supply the safeguard for his marriage. In P Lond 43[8] (ii/B.C.) (= I. p. 48. *Chrest.* I. p. 162) a mother congratulates her son and herself because he is learning Αἰγύπτια γράμματα and will soon be able to teach τὰ παιδάρια in a school: cf. P Par 49[21] (B.C. 161-0) (= *UPZ* i. p. 309) ἀγωνιῶ, μήποτε ἀ[ρ]ρωστεῖ τὸ παιδάριον, and P Lond 1171[5] (B.C. 8) (= III. p. 177), where 12 drachmae are entered as paid παιδαρίωι ὑπαίνω ἀγέλη, implies a boy old enough to look after sheep.

Παιδάριον is very common = "slave," as in BGU IV. 1079[15] (A.D. 41) (= *Chrest.* I. p. 84) ἐγὼ παιδάριν (*l.* παιδάριον) εἰμί, in an appeal to a Jewish money-lender: cf. P Amh II. 88[27] (A.D. 128) (= *Chrest.* II. p. 162) δώσω . . . παιδαρίοις τῷ μὲν ἐνεστῶτι (ἔτει) πυροῦ (ἀρτάβης) ἥμισυ, P Oxy IX. 1207[10] (A.D. 175-6?) σπονδ[ῆς] παιδαρίοις δραχμῶν ὀκτώ, *ib.* 1. 117[6] (ii/iii A.D.) τὴν πρᾶσιν [[καταγραφὴν]] τῶν παιδαρίων τῶν παιδίων, "the sale of the slaves' children," and P Strass I. 6[8] (A.D. 255-261) διὰ Κάστορος παιδ(αρίου) with the editor's note. This may be the meaning of the word in Jn 6[9] (cf. Bauer *HZNT ad l.*). See also Rostovtzeff, *Large Estate,* p. 177. For παιδαριώδης, "childish," see *s.v.* ἐκδοχή.

παιδεία.

The idea of "discipline" is uppermost in the NT occurrences of this word (Eph 6⁴, 2 Tim 3¹⁶, Heb 12⁵˙⁷˙⁸˙¹¹), but also for the more general sense of "training," "education," both on the intellectual and moral sides, exx. can be freely quoted from the papyri, as BGU IV. 1140⁶ (B.C. 4) τῷ πατρὶ [τῆ]ς ἀρεσκούσης παιδείας, P Oxy II. 265²⁴ (A.D. 81–95) τὴν πρέ]πουσαν ἐλευθέροις παισὶ παιδείαν, and from the inss.rr., as Syll 523 (=³ 578)⁶¹ (ii/B.C.) τὸ ἀργύριον τὸ ἐπιδοθὲν . . . εἰς τὴν παιδείαν τῶν ἐλευθέρων παίδων, and ib.³ 836⁵ (A.D. 125–7) ἀνὴρ ἤθει καὶ παιδείᾳ διαφέρων. A Laconian inscr. in Ann. Br. Sch. at Athens xii. p. 460 honours a boy κ[οσμι]ότατος καὶ παιδείας ἕνεκα (sedulitatis causa (Ed.)): cf. CIG I. 1376² ἤθει τε φιλοσόφῳ καὶ παιδ[ε]ίᾳ καὶ τοῖς λόγοις διαφέροντα τῶν ἡλίκων, and ib. 1375 where παιδεία is joined with σωφροσύνη. See also Kaibel 152⁹ᶠ. (ii/B.C.) ὥς τε μάλιστα παιδείᾳ πινυτῇ καὶ σοφίῃ μελόμην.

παιδευτής,

"a teacher"; used of God in LXX Hos 5² and of man in Rom 2²⁰: cf. Syll 306¹⁵ (=³ 672¹⁰) (B.C. 162–0) ὅπως . . . οἱ μισθοὶ τοῖς παιδευταῖς εὐτακτέωνται κτλ. and Preisigke 5941² (A.D. 509) παιδευτῇ Ἑλληνικῶν λόγων ἐλευθερίων. In late papyri παίδευσις came to be used as a title, e.g. P Oxy VIII. 1165¹ (vi/A.D.) ἔδει τὴν ὑμετέραν ἀδελφικὴν λ[α]μπρὰν παίδευσιν ἀντιποιηθῆναι τῆς εὐτελείας μου, "your fraternal, illustrious learnedness ought to have helped my insignificance" (Ed.).

παιδεύω.

For the meaning "discipline," "chasten," which this verb frequently has in Paul, cf. the abject appeal of a prodigal to his mother, BGU III. 846¹¹ (ii/A.D.) (= Selections, p. 94) παιπαίδδευμαι καθ' ὃν δὶ (l. δεῖ) τρόπον, "chastened I have been as I deserve." The meaning is more general "instruct," "bring up," in PSI IV. 424¹⁵ (iii/B.C.) ἐστὶν δὲ πεπαιδευμένος πᾶσαν παιδείαν, and BGU II. 423¹⁶ (a soldier to his father—ii/A.D.) (= Selections, p. 91) με ἐπαίδευσας καλῶς. See also Syll 518 (=³ 956)⁶ (2nd half v/B.C.) ὅπως ἂν οἱ παῖδες παιδεύωνται οἱ ἐν τῶι δήμωι, and the striking epitaph Kaibel 615⁷ (ii/iii A.D.) παιδεύθην, παίδευσα. Kennedy (Sources, p. 102) cites Polyb. ii. 9. 6 παιδεύεσθαι πρὸς τὸ μέλλον, "recevoir une bonne leçon pour l'avenir" (Schweighauser). For the stronger meaning of actual blows in Lk 23¹⁶, see Wetstein ad l., and cf. the use of νουθετέω in Plat. Sertor. 19 πληγαῖς νουθετήσας, and Headlam's note on Herodas VII. 11.

παιδιόθεν.

For this word preceded by ἐκ in Mk 9²¹ = "from childhood" (classic, ἐκ παιδός), cf. Chrest. I. 176¹⁷ (mid. i/A.D.) ἐξ [οἴ]κόθεν.

παιδίον,

a "child" from birth onwards: P Giss I. 2¹³ (B.C. 173) τὸ ταύτης παιδίον ὑποτίτθιον (cf. LXX Hos 14¹) ἧι ὄνομα

. . . "her child at the breast whose name . . .," BGU IV. 1109¹⁰ (B.C. 5) παιδίον θῆλυ ᾧ ὄνομα Πωλλαροῦς, P Oxy IV. 744⁷ (B.C. 1) (= Selections, p. 33) ἐρωτῶ σε καὶ παρακαλῶ σε ἐπιμελήθ<ητ>ι τῷ παιδίῳ—a husband to his wife, ib. I. 37ⁱⁱ·⁴ (A.D. 49) (= Selections, p. 51) ἐκ τῆς ὄψεως φαίνεται τῆς Σαραεῦτος εἶναι τὸ παιδίον, "from its features the child appears to be the child of Saraeus," ib. II. 298²¹ (i/A.D.) παιδίωι Σαραπίωνι ἱμάτ[ι]α πεποίηκεν, ib. I 117¹⁶ (ii/iii A.D.) ῥάκη δύο . . . ἐξ ὧν δώσεις τοῖς παιδίοις σου ἓν ἐξ αὐτῶν, "two strips of cloth, one of which you will give to your children," and PSI IV. 299¹⁵ (probably Christian—iii/A.D.) ἐνόσησαν δὲ πάντες οἱ κατὰ τὴν οἰκίαν, ἥ τε μήτηρ καὶ τὰ παιδία πάντα.

The word is naturally common in greetings—e.g. P Ryl II. 230¹² (A.D. 40) ἀσπάζου Θέρμιο(ν) τὴ(ν) ἀδελφὴν καὶ τὰ παιδία σο(υ), P Fay 126¹¹ (ii/iii A.D.) ἀσπάζομ[α]ι . . . Τεψό[ι]ν καὶ τὸ ἀβάσκαντον αὐτῆς παιδίον, "I salute Tepsois and her child, whom the evil eye shall not harm." The address παιδία, "Lads!" in Jn 21⁵ may be paralleled from the Klepht ballad, Abbott Songs p. 42, where τὰ παιδία is used of soldiers: cf. the colloquial use of "lads" in English, and the Irish "boys."

For παιδίον = "slave" we may cite BGU IV. 1153⁷ (B.C. 14) ἐπὶ τὸ δουλικ(ὸν) σω(μάτιον), where πα ιδίο(ν) has been written over σωμάτιον as if it were less offensive. See also P Amh II. 131⁹ (early ii/A.D.) μελησάτω σοι . . . ὅπως τὰ παιδία περὶ τὴν ἰδιοσπορίαν ἡμῶν καὶ τοὺς γεωργοὺς ἐπιμελῶς ἀναστραφῶσιν, "see that the slaves give attention to the sowing of our private land and to the cultivators" (Edd.), ib. 144⁸ (v/A.D.) σπούδασον οὖν τὸ μικρὸ(ν) παιδίον ἡμῶν Ἀρτεμίδωρον[.]] θεῖναι ἐν ὑποθήκῃ, "make haste therefore and put our little slave Artemidorus under pledge" (Edd.), and Syll 868⁹ (deed of manumission) ἠλευθέρωσεν παιδίον Ἀγαθόποδα. For adj. παιδικός see P Hamb I. 10¹⁶ (ii/A.D.), P Oxy VII. 1066¹⁰ (iii/A.D.), and cf. MGr dim. παιδάκι.

παιδίσκη

from meaning originally "a young woman" came in later Greek to denote "a female slave": see Rutherford NP, p. 312 f., Kennedy, Sources. p. 40 f. Exx. of this meaning, as in LXX and NT, are—PSI IV. 406²⁵ (iii/B.C.) Δριμύλος παιδίσκην ἠγόραζεν (δραχμὰς) τ, P Giss I. 2ⁱⁱ·¹³ (B.C. 173) παιδίσκην δο[ύλην αὐτῆς] ἧι ὄνομα Στολίς, P Grenf I. 43³ (ii/B C.) Ἀφροδισία καὶ ἡ θυγάτηρ καὶ ἡ παιδίσκη, BGU I. 95¹⁹ (ii/A.D.) ὑπάρχι δὲ τ[ῇ θυγατρὶ] παιδίσκη δούλη Τασου[χάρ]ιον, and the illiterate P Oxy VII. 1069¹⁹ (iii/A.D.) τὴν πεδεσκην μου δὲ πρὸ λόγον ἀνάγκασον φειλοπονεῖστε (= φιλοπονεῖσθαι), "make my slave-girl be properly industrious" (Ed.). Other reff. in Rostovtzeff, Large Estate, p. 115 f. In PSI VI. 667 (iii/B.C.) a παιδίσκη writes to her employer that she is "tired of dragging wood" (κεκ[μηκυῖ?]α ξυλοφορούσα), but "does not wish to go on strike" (οὐ θέλουσα ἀναχωρῆσαι). On the honoured place which female slaves frequently occupied in the family see Wilcken Ostr. i. p. 686, and cf. Milligan Here and There, p. 98 f.

The masc. ὁ παιδίσκος is not found in the Ptolemaic papyri, but see P Strass I. 50²³ (ii/iii A.D.).

παίζω.

For this NT ἅπ. εἰρ. (1 Cor 10⁷) cf. the sepulchral inscr. *Kaibel* 362⁵ (ii/iii A.D.)—

παῖσον, τρύφησον, ζῆσον· ἀποθανεῖν σε δεῖ.

The verb is found in the magic P Lond 121⁴²⁸ (iii/A.D.) (= I. p. 98 ; cf. the compounds ἐμπαίζω *s.v.*, προσπαίζω in P Par 50²¹ (B.C. 159) (= *UPZ* i. p. 365) προσπαίζουσι αὐτ<ῷ>, and συμπαίζω in BGU IV. 1027ˣˣᵛⁱ ²⁰ (end iv/A.D.) συμπέ(= αί)ζοντες τῇ ἡγεμονικῇ [τάξει, and in P Cairo Preis 2¹¹ (*s.v.* πεῖρα). See also Aristeas 284 θεωρεῖν ὅσα παίζεται μετὰ περιστολῆς, "to watch plays which are played with propriety" (Thackeray), and the subst. παίστης in P Gen I. 73⁵ (ii/iii A.D.) (= *Chrest.* I. p. 575), where a woman makes a contract for herself σὺν ἄλλοις παισταῖς τρισί, "with three other dancers."

For the tense formation of παίζω cf. Thackeray *Gr.* i. p. 222, and note MGr ἔπαιξα, ἐπαίχτηκα: see also Hatzidakis, *Einl.* p. 135 f.

παῖς.

In Gnomon 41 (*c.* A.D. 150) it is laid down—ἐὰν Αἰγύπτιος ἐκ κοπρίας [ἀν]έληται παῖδα καὶ τοῦτον υἱοποιήσηται, μετὰ θάνατον τεταρτολο[γεῖτ]αι, "if an Egyptian shall take up a child from the dungheap, and adopt him as a son, he shall be mulcted after his death to the extent of one fourth of his property." For παῖς applied to a female child see P Strass I. 41⁹ (A.D. 250) ἐκδικῆσαι τὰ τῆς παιδός, and P Oxy I 52¹⁵ (A.D. 325) ε[ἴ]δαμεν τὴν παῖδα ἔχουσαν κατὰ τῶν ἰσχίων ἀμυχὰς μετὰ πελιωμάτων (see *ib.* II. p. 310), "we saw that the girl had wounds on her hips with livid spots": cf. Lk 8⁵⁴ (for voc. of address see *Proleg.* pp. 70, 235).

The word is commonly applied to slaves, as in Lk 7⁷ *al.*, e.g. P Lille 27 (iii/B.C.), where 11 male slaves are enumerated under the heading παῖδες, then 2 female slaves, and then again 3 male slaves: cf. P Strass I. 40²⁴ (A.D. 569) Κολλοῦθος Βίκτορος φαμιλιάριος ἑδραῖος κατάδουλος παῖς, and P Iand 20⁷ (vi/vii A.D.) ἔασον τὸν Μηνᾶν καὶ τὸν παῖδαν λαβεῖν, where the editor cites Usener, *Epic.* p. 168¹⁰ ἀφίημι δὲ τῶν παίδων ἐλεύθερον Μῦν Νικίαν Λύκωνα. See also *s.v.* θεράπων.

παίω.

For παίω, "strike," "smite," as in Lk 22⁶⁴ (see Streeter, *Four Gospels*, p. 325 ff.), cf PSI III. 168¹⁵ (B.C. 118) οἱ] ἐπιθέμενοι ἐπαισάν με [ῥάβ]δωι εἰς τὸν δεξιὸν [ἀ]ρ[μό]ν, "who attacking smote me with a rod on the right shoulder-joint." See also Artem. p. 149¹⁸ ff.

πάλαι.

"long ago": P Eleph I. 46¹⁴ (B.C. 258) ἔδει δὲ πάλαι τὰ ἐνέχυρα αὐτῶν ὧδε εἶναι, "their securities ought to have been here long ago" (Edd.), P Oxy IX. 1219⁶ (iii/A.D.) ὃ καὶ σὺ ἐπίστασαι ἔτι πάλαι ἀπὸ τοῦ πατρὸς αὐτοῦ, "which also you know long since from his father," P Lond 113.1²² (vi/A.D.) (= I. p. 201) πρὸς τοῖς ἤδη πάλαι δοθεῖσιν, "in addition to those (*sc.* monies) already given long ago." In 2 Cor 12¹⁹ πάλαι with durative present = "all this time." For the comp. παλαίτερον, see PSI IV. 349⁶ (B.C. 254–3) ἀπεστάλκαμεν δὲ περὶ τούτου παλαίτερον εἰς Ἀλεξάνδρειαν πρὸς Ἀπολλώνιον.

παλαιός,

"old," is naturally very common in our sources. A few exx. will suffice—P Ryl II. 125⁷ (A.D. 28–9) τειχαρίων παλαιῶ(ν), "old walls," BGU IV. 1095¹⁰ (A.D. 57) περὶ δὲ τοῦ φοίνικος παλαιὸν οὐχ εὕραμεν . . . τὰ δὲ νήα (*l.* νέα) ἐν χερσὶ γέγοναι, where dates which had been gathered for some time are contrasted with new, freshly gathered ones, P Oxy VIII. 1159²⁵ (late iii/A.D.) τὸ τυλάριον τ[ὸ] παλαιὸν τὸ ἐν τῷ συμποσίῳ ἄνω, "the old cushion that is up in the dining-room," *ib.* XII. 1494¹⁷ (early iv/A.D.) ἐλέ(= αἴ)ας κνίδια παλε(= αι)ά, "old jars of olives," and *Ostr* 1129⁴ (A.D. 207) οἴνου π(αλαιοῦ?), "old wine," cf. 1 Cor 5⁷ᶠ. See also P Ryl II. 186² (late ii/A.D.) παλαιῶν ὀφλη[μάτων), "ancient fines," i.e. arrears of fines incurred in lawsuits, and P Grenf II. 77⁷ (iii/iv A.D.) (= *Selections*, p. 120) παλαιοῦ νομίσματος, "old coinage," i.e. prior to the new coinage of Diocletian. The adj. is used with reference to time in BGU III. 993⁹ (ii/A.D.) τοῖς παλαιοῖς χρόνοις. With 1 Jn 2⁷ cf. P Giss I. 4⁹ (A.D. 118) (= *Chrest.* I. p. 414) of land οὐκ ἐκ τοῦ παλαιοῦ π[ρο]στάγματος γεωργεῖσθαι, and the Christian letter P Oxy XII. 1492⁹ (iii/iv A.D.) κατὰ τὸ παλ[αιὸν] ἔθος.

The compar. occurs in P Ryl II. 236¹¹ (A.D. 256) ἐχέτω δὲ τὰ παλαιότερα μανδάκια, "let them have the older bundles," and adverbially in PSI IV. 349⁶ (B.C. 254–3) ἀπεστάλκαμεν δὲ περὶ τούτου παλαίτερον ("a long time ago").

παλαιόω,

in pass. = "become old," as in Heb 8¹³: cf. *Preisigke* 5827¹¹ (B.C. 60) πεπαλαιῶσθαι with reference to a temple building. Preisigke *Wörterbuch s.v.* also cites *Archiv* ii. p. 441, No. 55⁴ (ii/A.D.) τείχη β περιβόλου παλαιωθέντα. In Heb *l.c.* the verb on its two occurrences is sometimes understood transitively = "abrogate": so Tindale "he hath abrogat."

πάλη,

"wrestling": Artem. p. 255¹⁶ ἀνδρῶν πάλη: cf. *Preisigke* 678⁵ (*c.* A.D. 100) π[α]λαισταὶ κρίσεως πα πάλης. For the metaph. usage, as in Eph 6¹², cf. a iv/v A.D. homily P Oxy XIII. 1601⁹ πνευματικ[ή ἐστιν ἡμῖν] ἡ πάλη. See also M. Anton. vii. 61 ἡ βιωτικὴ τῇ παλαιστικῇ ὁμοιοτέρα ἤπερ τῇ ὀρχηστικῇ. Παλαίστης in the literal sense of "wrestler" occurs in P Lond 1178⁵⁶, ⁷⁹ (A.D. 194) (= III. p. 217 f.). MGr παλεύω, "wrestle."

πάλιν,

an adverbial acc. like δίκην, μάτην, χάριν, originally meaning "back," return to a previous position, in later Greek came to be used rather in the sense of "again," repetition of a previous action. Exx. are P Tebt I. 58⁵² (B.C. 111) πάλιν προσεντελλομαί σοι προσεδρεῦσαι, "I again bid you be in attendance" (Edd.), P Fay 122¹⁰ (*c.* A.D. 100) ἕως ἀπολαβὼν τὸ λοιπὸν τῆς τιμ[ῆ]ς πάλιν σοι γράψω, "until I get the remainder of the price and write to you again" (Edd.), PSI IV. 299¹⁸ (iii/A.D.) ε[ὔχομαι τ]ῷ θεῷ ἕως οὗ ἄν με πάλιν πρὸς ὑμᾶς εὐοδώσῃ, "I pray God until he again gives me a prosperous return to you," P Oxy

XII 1490[6] (late iii/A.D.) εἰ οὖν πάλιν δύνῃ ἐκπλέξαι παρὰ σεαυτῷ, τύχῃ τῇ ἀγαθῇ, "if then you can again get him off by yourself (?), good luck to you" (Edd.), and P Gen I. 53[20] (iv/A.D.) ἐγὼ πάλιν σὸς δοῦλος εἰμεὶ καὶ οὐκ ἀποστατίσωμαί (= ἤσομαί) σου ὡς πρῶτον, "I am again thy slave, and shall not be absent from you as formerly."

For a wider use of πάλιν we may cite P Oxy IV. 742[9] (B.C. 2) (= Witkowski[2], p. 128) παράδος δέ τινι τῶν φίλων ἀριθμῷ αὐτάς, ἵνα πάλιν φ.[ί]λος ἡμεῖν παραδοῖ ἀσφ[αλῶς, "deliver them (sc. bundles of reeds) carefully counted to one of our friends, that a friend may deliver them to me safely," ib. XIV. 1676[21] (iii/A.D.) χαίρω ὅτι καλῶ[ς] ἔχεις μέν, κἀγὼ δὲ πάλι (see below) καταξύομαι μὴ ὁρῶν σε, "I rejoice for your happiness, but still I am vexed at not seeing you" (Edd.), and ib. 1775[9] (iv/A.D.) οὐχ ὤκνησα οὔτε πάλιν ἠμέλησα.

To meet the difficulty of Mk 15[13] where the *first* outcry of the mob is referred to, Souter (*Lex. s.v.*) suggests "an unsuitable mistranslation of an Aramaic word of much wider signification, *further, thereupon*" (cf. Wellhausen, *Einleitung*, p. 28 f.). But for this secondary meaning of πάλιν it is not necessary to go back to Aramaic, as Moffatt has pointed out (*Exp* VIII. xx p. 141), in view of such a passage as P Oxy XIV. 1676[20] (iii/A.D.) ἀλλὰ καὶ λυποῦμαι πάλιν ὅτι ἐκτός μου ε[ἶ, "still I am sorry you are not beside me." Similarly in Gal 5[3] πάλιν is perhaps best rendered by "further," the sequence being logical rather than temporal.

For the byform πάλι, as in Jn 1[35] W, and in MGr, Mayser (*Gr.* p. 241) can only cite from Ptolemaic times the fragment of an anthology, P Tebt I. 1 (*c.* B.C. 100), but it is common in post-Ptolemaic papyri and inscrr., e.g. P Flor III. 334[6] (ii/A.D.) πάλι τῆι σῆι σφραγίδι ἀσφαλῶς κλείσας σφράγισον τὸ δαπανηθὲν ἀνάλωμα εἰς τοὺς θησαυρούς, P Oxy I. 119[7] (ii/iii A.D.) (= *Selections*, p. 103) οὔτε πάλι χαίρω σε λυ(= οι)πόν, "I shall not greet you again henceforth," and the early Christian letter P Amh I. 3 (*a*)[ii 13] (between A.D. 264 and 282) εἰ δὲ ε[. . . .] ἄρτοις (*l.* ἄρτους ?) πάλι πεπράσιν, "but if they have again sold loaves." Further exx. will be found in Cronert, *Mem. Herc.* p. 140 n[3]. It may be noted that the dictum ascribed to Phrynichus (ed. Lob. p. 284) πάλι οὕτω λέγουσιν οἱ νῦν ῥήτορες καὶ ποιηταί, δέον μετὰ τοῦ ν πάλιν, ὡς οἱ ἀρχαῖοι λέγουσιν, is set aside by Rutherford *NP*, p. 347 f.

παλινγενεσία.

It lies outside our object to discuss the meaning of this term in the teaching of the Stoics and Pythagoreans, but as illustrating its reference to the Messianic "rebirth" of the world in Mt 19[28], we may cite its application to the world's renewal after the flood in Philo *Vit. Mos.* (ed. Cohn) II 65 and to the restoration of Judah in Jos. *Antt.* XI. 66 (iii. 9). See also Dalman *Words*, p. 177 ff.

The word occurs in Wünsch *AF* p. 17[17] (iii/A.D.) ὁρκίζω σε τὸν θεὸν τὸν τῆς παλινγενεσίας Θωβαρραβαυ: also in a general sense in the much mutilated P Lond 878 (iii/iv A.D.) (= III. p. xli) δώρ[ον] παλινγενεσίας. For the adj. see the magic P Lond 121[510] (iii/A.D.) (= I p. 100) σὺ εἶ ὁ πατὴρ τῆς παλινγενοῦς αἰῶνος. Dibelius has an elaborate note on παλινγενεσία in the *HZNT ad* Tit 3[5]: for its place in the mystery religions, see also Angus, *Mystery Religions and Christianity*, p. 95 ff.

πάμπολυς,

"very much," "very great," which is read in the TR of Mk 8[1], but not elsewhere in Biblical Greek, is known to classical Greek, and occurs in such passages from the Κοινή as BGU III. 731[ii. 8] (A.D. 180) ξύλα ἐρίκινα πάμπολλα, P Oxy IV. 718[11] (A.D. 186–192) χρόνῳ δὲ παμπόλλῳ ὕστε[ρον, "a very long while afterwards" (Edd.), and P Gen I 16[15] (A.D. 207) (= *Chrest.* I. p. 417) πάντα τὰ ὑποστέλλοντα τῇ κώμῃ πάμπολλα ὄντα.

πανδοχεῖον,

a colloquial word (for form see Lob. *Phryn.* p. 307) found in the comic writers (e.g. PSI I. 99[3]—ii/A.D.: cf. Kennedy *Sources*, p. 74), occurs in Biblical Greek only in Lk 10[34] = "inn." For πανδοκ(ε)ία, "the trade of an innkeeper," cf. P Gen I. 54[26] (iv/A.D.) ἔδωκαν δὲ ὑμῖν ἐν π[α]νδοκίᾳ νομισμάτια δύο καὶ ἀργυρίου τάλ[αν]τα πεντήκοντα.

πανδοχεύς,

"host" (Lk 10[35]): Artem. p. 100[24] *al.* For πανδόκεια, "hostess," cf. *Syll* 901 (= [3]1251)[3] (period of Roman Republic) Δεκομία Συρίσκα πανδόκια χρηστὰ χαῖρε (cf. the Vergilian *Copa Syrisca*), and Herodian I. p. 248[24] (cited by Dittenberger *ad l.*).

πανήγυρις.

The word is common in inscrr. relating to *res sacrae*, but seems to have remained in ordinary use. Thus BGU IV. 1074[9] (official—A.D. 275)]εἶναι οἱ καθ᾽ ἑ[κάστην πα]νήγυριν ἀγωνοθέται πειθαρχήσουσιν, and P Oxy I. 41[1] (iii/iv A.D.) . . .]αρίας πανηγύρεως οὔσης opens (fragmentarily) a very incoherent report of a public meeting. The "festal" idea is prominent in such passages as P Fay 93[11] (A.D. 161) χωρὶς ἀγορῶν σὺν πανηγύρεσιν, "with the exception of markets and festivals"; P Oxy I. 42[3] (proclamation regarding an assault at arms—A.D. 323) τὸ ἔθος ὁμοῦ τε καὶ ἡ πανήγυρις προάγουσα [σ]ημαίνει [ὅτ]ι προθυμότατα τοὺς ἐφήβους [τ]ὰ γυμνι[κὰ] ἐπιδείκνυσθαι προσήκει, "tradition, no less than the distinguished character of the festival, requires that the *ephebi* should do their utmost in the gymnastic display"; and ib. IX. 1214[3] (v/A.D.) φεδρύνων (*l.* φαιδρύνων) τὴν π[α]νήγυριν τῆς γενεθλίου τοῦ υἱοῦ μου Γενναδίου καταξίωσον, "deign to gladden the birthday festival of my son Gennadius." "*Festal* assembly" would apparently render the word best in Heb 12[23], where Moffatt (*ICC ad l.*) aptly cites Philo *in Flacc.* 118 ἱλαρᾶς εὐθυμίας, ἣν πανήγυρις ἐπιζητεῖ: cf. also Trench *Syn* p. 61. For the verb cf. PSI IV. 374[15] (B.C. 250–49) πανηγυριεῖν τοὺς ναύτας, and P Oxy IV. 705[35] (A.D. 200–2) καὶ ἔτι καὶ νῦν τὴν τῶν ἐπινεικίων ἡμέραν ἑκάστου ἔτους πανηγυρίζοντας. MGr πανηγύρι (παναγύρι), πανηγυρίζω.

πανοικεί.

This NT ἅπ. εἰρ. (Ac 16[34]), "with all the household" is common in the closing greetings of private letters, e.g. P Ryl II. 434[12] (ii/A.D.) ἐρρῶσθαί σε, ἄδελφε, εὔχομαι πανοικεὶ εὐτυχοῦντα, and similarly P Iand I. 8[15] (ii/A.D.), P Oxy VI. 935[30] (iii/A.D.), P Fay 129[9] and 130[20] (both iii/A.D.). The adj. πανοίκιος occurs in Nero's letter, *Syll* 373 (= [2]810)[15] (A.D. 55) περὶ τῶν θυσιῶν . . . ἃς ἐνετε[ί]λασθε . . . ὑπὲρ τῆς πανοικίου μου ὑγείας . . . ἐπιτελέσαι. For the subst. **πανοικησία** (cf. Lob. *Phryn.* p. 512 ff.) it is sufficient to cite P Oxy XIV. 1664³ (iii/A.D.) σε προσαγορεύω εὐχόμενός σε σώζεσθαι πανοικησίᾳ: cf. *SAM* i. p. 7.

πανοπλία.

"armour" (Lat. *armatura = omnia arma*). In *Syll* 652 (= ³885)²⁶ (*c.* A.D. 220) the *ephebi* are ordered to be reviewed at a religious festival in Attica—ἔχοντας] τὴν πανοπλίαν: cf. Eph 6¹¹. See also *Priene* 5⁴ (before B.C. 326-5) πομπὴν καὶ πανοπλίαν εἰς Ἀθήνας ἀποστέλλε[ιν. The editor reads π]άνοπλον in a mutilated census-return, P Oxy VIII. 1110⁶ (A.D. 188), but suggests as an alternative ἔνοπλον, with some such word as δρόμον preceding.

πανουργία.

The bad sense of this word, "craftiness," "cunning," which prevails in its NT occurrences (cf. Armitage Robinson on Eph 4¹⁴), is well illustrated by P Oxy II. 237ᵛᵢᵢⁱ ¹² (A.D. 186) παραγγέλλω τῆς τοιαύτης πανουργίας ἀπέ[σ]χεσθαι, "I proclaim that such persons shall abstain from this form of knavery" (Edd.), where the reference is to threatening an action which will make creditors renounce their claims. Note also the conjunction in *OGIS* 515⁴⁷ (iii/A.D.) ἐκ κακουργίας καὶ πανουργίας: cf. Artem. p 240¹⁹ πανουργίαν καὶ κακοτροπίαν. The subst. **πανούργευμα** is found in a good sense in Judith 11⁸.

πανοῦργος.

In *Kaibel* 1103³ **πανοῦργος** is found as an epithet of Eros. The editor renders it *veterator*, "crafty": cf. 2 Cor 12¹⁶, the only occurrence of the adj. in the NT. P Lond 46⁷³ (iv/A.D.) (= I. p. 67) shows πανουργικὸν ξύλον in a spell for discovering a thief. Πανοῦργος is formed on the analogy of κακοῦργος <κακο-Ϝεργος (Boisacq *s.v.* πᾶς, p. 748).

πανπληθεί.

With this adv. = "with the whole crowd" (Lk 23¹⁸). cf. the cognate subst., as in 2 Macc 10²¹, in Aristeas 66 πάντα καθαρίζεσθαι τὰ συναγόμενα παμπληθῆ τῶν θυμάτων αἵματα, "that all the vast accumulation of sacrificial blood is swept away" (Thackeray).

πανταχῇ.

"everywhere" (Ac 21²⁸). For the form with iota subscript, which Moulton prefers (*Gr.* ii. p. 84; cf. Meisterhans *Gr.* p. 145), see P Eleph 3⁶ (B.C. 284-3) ἡ δὲ συγγραφὴ ἥδε κυρία ἔστω πανταχῆι οὗ ἂν ἐπιφέρηι Ἐλάφιον, and similarly *ib.* 4⁶ (B.C. 284-3), and P Oxy XIV. 1036²¹ (B.C. 73 or 44) κυρία [ἡ χ΄εἰρ παντα[χῆ]ι ἐπιφερομένη καὶ παντὶ τῶι ἐπιφέ[ρο]ντι, "this bond is valid wherever and by whomever it is produced" (Edd.). The iota is wanting in P Gen I. 35¹² (A.D. 161) πανταχῆ ἐπιφερόμε[νον, and *ib.* 9¹⁵ (A.D. 251).

πανταχόθεν.

"from all sides," confined in NT to TR of Mk 1⁴⁵, can be readily illustrated from the Κοινή—P Oxy II. 237ᵛⁱ ⁸ (A.D. 186) πανταχόθεν οὖν . . . τοῦ πράγματος πρ[ο]δήλου γενομένου, "on all points, then, the affair being now clear,"

P Tebt II. 423¹³ (early iii/A.D.) ἐὰν καλῶς πράσσῃς [λ]αβὼν πανταχόθεν ἀγόρασον αὐτ[ο]ῦ καλὸν χιτῶνα, "if you fare well, get together all you can and buy there a good tunic" (Edd.), and P Ryl II. 230²¹ (mid. iii/A.D.) πανταχόθεν ἴδε αὐτῷ μικρὸν ὀναρίδιον, "look out everywhere for a small donkey for him" (Edd.). The last document shows ⁶ ἐκ πανταχόθεν, "by all means."

πανταχοῦ.

"everywhere": PSI IV. 382⁶ B.C. 248 7) ξύλα ἐζήτηκαμεν πανταχοῦ, BGU IV. 1125¹² (B.C. 13) κύρια] τὰ διωμολογημένα πανταχοῦ, and *ib.* III. 942⁶ (A.D. 246) κυρία ἡ ἐπὶ λόγου ἀποχὴ πανταχοῦ ἐπιφερομένη ὡς ἐν δημοσίῳ κατακεχωρισμένη.

παντελής.

The NT has this word only in the phrase εἰς τὸ παντελές, Lk 13¹¹, Heb 7²⁵: so in P Lond 1164 (*h*)¹¹ (A.D. 212) (= III. p. 161) a man sells some property ἀπὸ τοῦ νῦν εἰς τὸ παντελές. This would support a temporal meaning in Heb *l.c.* "to save *finally*," which suits well the πάντοτε that follows: so long as our Intercessor lives our σωτηρία is assured. Cf. *Syll* 489⁶¹ (c. B.C. 234) τὸν ἀγῶνα παντελῆ, where the reference is to an interrupted contest, which had been brought to an end, and *OGIS* 642⁴ (end of ii/A.D.) τὸ μνημ[εῖον . . . ἔκτισεν . . . αὐτῷ τε καὶ υἱοῖς αὐτοῦ καὶ υἱωνοῖς εἰς τὸ παντελὲς αἰώνιον τειμήν. See also Preisigke 5357⁷ ὅσα πρὸς ἀνατροπὴν παντελῆ ἄγει τὸν συνηγορούμενον. In Lk *l.c.* the meaning is like that of παντελῶς in P Lille I. 26² (iii/B.C.) (= Witkowski², p. 49) αὐτὴ (*sc.* γῆ) μὲν οὖν ἐστιν παντελῶς ἀπηρ[γ]ημένη ("bare," "uncultivated"), P Lond 42²⁷ (B.C. 168) (= I. p. 31. *Selections*, p. 11) παντελῶς ἀηδίζομαι, "I am utterly distressed," and P Oxy II. 281¹¹ (A.D. 20-50) παντελῶς ὄντα ἀνέγκλητον, "being blameless in all respects": cf. *ib.* XII. 1469¹ (A.D. 298) παντελῶς διανύειν τὰ προσήκοντα, "to accomplish in full our duties," and *ib.* IX. 1186⁶ (iv/A.D.) οὐ μὴν κατὰ τὸ παντελὲς ἀπηγορευμένον, "not entirely forbidden" (Ed.).

πάντη.

This NT ἅπ. εἰρ. (Ac 24³) is seen in P Eleph 1¹⁴ (B.C. 311-10) (= *Selections*, p. 4) with reference to a contract valid πάντηι πάντως, "under all circumstances." Cf. P Fay 113³ (A.D. 100) πάντη πάντο[=ω]ς πέμψις Πίνδαρον, "be very sure to send Pindarus" (Edd.), *ib.* 130⁷ (iii/A.D.) προνοῶ τοῦ χ[α]λκοῦ πά[ντη πάν]τως καθὼς ἐταξάμη[ν, "I am by all means looking after the copper, as I arranged" (Edd.). In the NT occurrences of the word Moulton prefers to read πάντη without ι subscript: see *Gr.* ii. p. 84. An interesting ex. of the word combined with πολλάκις occurs in a iii/A.D. inscr. from Termessos *BCH* xxiii. (1899), p. 180 (as restored by Ramsay, *Cities*, p. 442) Αὐρ Μω[υσ]ῆς Κάρπου, ὁ πάντη πολλάκις γενόμενος καὶ τὸν κόσμον πολλάκις ἱστορήσας, νῦν δὲ κεῖμαι μηκέτι μηδὲν εἰδώς· ταῦτα [δὲ]μ[ό]ν[ο]ν "εὐψύχει, οὐδεὶς ἀθάνατος," "I Aurelius Mo[ses], son of Karpus, having been everywhere often and having often investigated the world, now lie in death no longer knowing anything: but this only (I say) 'be of good courage, no man is immortal'" (Ramsay).

πάντοθεν,

"from all sides," for πανταχόθεν, the prevailing form in Attic prose, cf. P Amh II. 51²⁷ (sale of a house—B.C. 88) οἳ ἂν ὦσι γείτονες πάντοθεν, "whatever may adjoin it on all sides"; similarly P Lond 1164 (*f*)¹⁴ (A.D. 212) (= III. p. 161), and PSI I. 66⁹ (v/A.D.?) πάντῃ πάντοθεν.

παντοκράτωρ

is common in the LXX (cf. Aristeas 185) usually for צְבָאוֹת, and is found in the NT *novies*, always, with one exception (2 Cor 6¹⁸), in the book of Revelation, where Hort (*Comm. ad Rev* 1⁸) understands the title as denoting "not One who can do anything, but One who holds together and controls all things." Outside Jewish or Christian writers, he is able to cite only one occurrence of the word, viz. from a metrical Cretan inscr. παντοκράτωρ Ἑριούνιε (Hermes). We may compare an inscr. from Delos *BCH* vi. (1882), No. 25, p. 502 Διὶ τῷ πάντων κρατοῦντι καὶ Μητρὶ μεγάλῃ τῇ πάντων κρατούσῃ, cited by Cumont *Les Religions Orientales*, p. 267 (Engl. Tr. p. 227), where see the whole note on this attribute of omnipotence assigned to the Syrian and Phrygian deities.

The word is used as an imprecation in the account of a legal process, P Lips I. 40, where one of the parties is represented as saying ii ¹³ εἰ μὴ ἦσαν πρὸς τῇ οἰκίᾳ μου, πάλαι ἂν ὁ Ἀσυγκρίτιος τετελεύτηκεν, μὰ τὸν παντοκράτορα. It is not infrequent in the Christian papyri, e.g. BGU III. 948³ (iv/v A.D.) εὔχομε τὸν παντοκράτοραν θεόν, P Oxy VI. 925¹ (a prayer—v/vi A.D.) (= *Selections*, p. 131) ὁ θ(εὸ)ς ὁ παντοκράτωρ ὁ ἅγιος ὁ ἀληθινὸς . . ., and BGU III. 954¹ (an amulet—vi/A.D.) (= *Selections*, p. 132) δέσποτα θε(ὲ) παντοκράτωρ ὁ πατὴ[ρ] τοῦ κ(υρίο)υ . . . . We may add the interesting letter addressed to Paphnutius by Athanasius (can he be, as Bell suggests, St. Athanasius himself?) which, after the opening address, proceeds—ὁ π[α]ντοκ[ράτωρ] θεὸς καὶ ὁ Χρι[στὸς] αὐτοῦ δοίη τὴν σὴν θεοσέβειαν π[α]ραμένειν ἡ[μῖν] πολὺν [χ]ρό[νον (P Lond 1929³—mid. iv/A.D.). Cf. also *Kaibel* 1007⁶ (not earlier than Justinian) where the word is restored as an epithet of Χριστὸς ἄχραντος.

πάντοτε,

"at all times," "always," used by late writers for διαπαντός (cf. Rutherford *NP*, p. 183 f.), may be illustrated by P Giss I. 17⁴ (a slave to her master—time of Hadrian) (= *Chrest.* I. 481) εὔχομαι πάντοτε περὶ τῆς ὑγιείας σου, and P Oxy XIV. 1759⁴ (letter to an athlete—ii/A.D.) εὔχομαί σε ὑγιαίνειν [κ]αὶ νικᾶν πάντοτε. See also *Syll* 376 (= ³ 814)³⁷ (A.D. 67), where Nero is described as εὐσεβῶν τοὺς θεοὺς ἡμῶν παρισταναμένους αὐτῷ πάντοτε ἐπὶ προνοίᾳ καὶ σωτηρίᾳ. For an earlier ex., from time of Augustus, see BGU IV. 1123⁵.

πάντως.

The strongly affirmative sense of πάντως, "surely," "by all means," is well seen in P Ryl II. 229²⁰ (A.D. 38) πάντω(ς) δέ, Ἀφροδίσιε, τοὺς ἄρτους μοι πέμψον καὶ τὸ ὀψάριον, "be sure, Aphrodisius, to send me the loaves and the relish" (cf. Jn 21⁹), P Fay 129³ (iii/A.D.) ἐτάξατο πάντως καταβῆναι τῇ ἑνδεκάτῃ, "he appointed for certain

the eleventh for his coming down" (Edd.), P Oxy XIV. 1676¹⁵ (iii/A.D.) ἀλλὰ πάντως κρείττονα εἶχες· διὰ τοῦτο ὑπερηφάνηκας ἡμᾶς, "but you doubtless had better things to do; that was why you neglected us" (Edd.), *ib.* 1680¹⁴ (iii/iv A.D.) ὑπονοοῦμαι ὅτι πάντως πάλιν τί ποτε ἔχει πρὸς σέ, "I suspect that he must assuredly have some further claim against you," and P Giss I. 103²² (iv/A.D.) πάντως ταχέως ἡμᾶς κατάλαβε: cf. also Herodas VII. 89.

The word is found in a complete negation in P Vat A¹⁵ (B.C. 168) (= Witkowski², p. 65, *UPZ* i. p. 303) οὐ γὰρ πάντως δεῖ στενῶς ἐπανάγοντά <σε> προσμένειν ἕως κτλ. cf. Rom 3⁹, and for a partial negation see 1 Cor 5¹⁰ (Blass-Debrunner § 433. 2). For a weakened πάντως = "probably," "possibly," see Cadbury *JBL* xliv. p. 223 ff.

παρά

is found in the NT c. gen. (78 times), c. dat. (50 times), and c. acc. (60 times): see *Proleg.* p. 106. All these constructions can be freely illustrated from our sources.

(1) c. gen. indicating source or origin "from the side of," "from," used of persons after verbs of receiving etc. : *Ostr* 1027³ (Ptol.) (= *LAE*, p. 152) ἀπέχω παρὰ σοῦ τὸ ἐπιβάλλον (cf. Lk 15¹²) μοι ἐκφόριον, "I have received from you the fruit that falleth to me," P Petr II. 11 (1)⁵ (mid. iii/B.C.) (= Witkowski², p. 8) γίνωσκε δέ με ἔχοντα παρὰ Φιλωνίδου (δραχμὰς) ο̅, P Eleph 13² (B.C. 223-2) (= Witkowski², p. 42) παραγενόμενος Σανῶτος ἐκομισάμην τὴν παρὰ σοῦ ἐπιστολήν, P Tebt II. 283²² (B.C. 93 or 60) τούτου δὲ γενομ[έ]νου ἔσομαι τετευχὼς [τῆ]ς παρὰ σοῦ ἀντιλήμψεως, "for if this is done I shall have obtained succour from you" (Edd.), P Oxy IV. 742² (B.C. 2) παράλαβε παρὰ Πόθου τὸν κάλαμ[ο]ν πανα[ρ]ιθμῶι, "take over from Pothus the reeds all together" (Edd.), P Fay 121¹³ (c. A.D. 100) καὶ τὸ δ[έρ]μα τοῦ μόσχου . . . αἴτησον πα[ρὰ τοῦ] κυρτοῦ βυρσέως, "ask the hunch-backed tanner for the calf's hide," and *ib.* 93⁶ (A.D. 161) βούλομαι μισθώσασθαι παρὰ σοῦ τὴν μυροπωλαικὴν καὶ ἀρωματικὴν ἐργασίαν, "I wish to lease from you your business of perfume-selling and unguent-making" (Edd.). For παρά c. gen. to denote the agent, as in Mt 18¹⁹, cf. Epict. iv. 10, 20 τὰ ἀλλότρια ὄψεται . . . ὡς ἂν δίδωται παρὰ τοῦ ἔχοντος ἐξουσίαν (see Sharp, *Epict.* p. 92).

For a similar use after pass. verbs (like ὑπό: cf. Ac 22³⁰ TR παρά, but NABC ὑπό), cf. P Tebt I. 12¹⁵ (B.C. 118) ἐκομισάμην τὸ παρὰ σοῦ γρ(αφὲν) ἐπισ(τόλιον), *ib.* 34⁶ (c. B.C. 100) χάριν τοῦ παρ' αὐτοῦ ἀπηγμένου, "about the person arrested by him," and the late P Oxy I. 125¹⁷ (A.D. 560) συγχωρήσω αὐτὴν ὑπομνησθῆναι παρ' οἱουδήποτε προσώπου ὑπὲρ ἐμοῦ, "I should permit you to be reminded of your suretyship for me by any person whatsoever" (Edd.).

Οἱ παρ' αὐτοῦ is common in the sense of a man's "agents" or "representatives," e.g. P Tor II. 4²⁰ (ii/B.C.) μηδένα τῶν παρ' αὐτῶν, "no one of those acting for them," P Tebt I. 5¹⁰⁹ (B.C. 118) οἰκονόμοις) ἢ τοῖς παρ' αὐτῶν, "oeconomi or their agents," P Amh II. 41⁴ (ii/B C.) πέπομφα τὸν παρ' ἐμοῦ, "I have sent my agent" and *ib.* 111²¹ (A.D. 132) καὶ μηδὲν τὸν ὁμολογοῦντα μήτε τοῖς παρ' αὐτοῦ ἐνκαλῖν τοῖς περὶ τὸν Στοτοῆτιν, "and that neither he nor his representatives make any claim on Stotoëtis" (Edd.).

The phrase is also used more generally of a man's "neighbours," "friends," "associates," e.g. P Par 36[16] (B.C. 163–2) (= UPZ i. p. 138) Ἁρμάιν . . τὸν παρ᾽ ἐμοῦ, "Harmais who is closely associated with me," ib. 40[13] (c. B.C. 161) (= UPZ i. p. 308f.) οἱ παρ᾽ ἐμοῦ γραμματεῖς, ib. 51[10] (B.C. 159) (= UPZ i. p. 366) εὐφραίνεσθε, οἱ παρ᾽ ἐμοῦ πάν[τε]ς P Amh II. 35[13] (B.C. 132) τοὺς παρ᾽ ἡμῶν γεωργούς, P Oxy II. 298[37] (i/A.D.) Σαραπίων καὶ πάντες οἱ παρ᾽ ἡμῶν, "all of us," and BGU II. 410[14] (A.D. 277) οὐδεὶς τῶν παρ᾽ ἐμοῦ οὐδὲ τέκνον τ[έ]κνου. Cf. also Herodas I. 2 with Headlam's note.

For a parallel to Mk 3[21], where the context seems to confine οἱ παρ᾽ αὐτοῦ to members of Christ's "family" (see Swete and Field ad l.) we may cite P Revill Mél. p. 295[7] (B.C. 131–0) καλῶς ποιήσεις παρακαλῶν σαυτὸν καὶ τοὺς παρ᾽ ἡμῶν, the reference being to the writer's mother and sisters ; cf.[13] and see Witkowski, Epp.[2] p. 96. This narrower application may also perhaps be found in P Grenf II. 36[9] (B.C. 95) ἔρρωμαι δὲ καὶ αὐτὸς καὶ Ἐσθλῦτις . . . καὶ οἱ παρ᾽ ἡμῶν πάντες, "all our family," and BGU III. 998[ii. 8] (B.C. 101) μήτ᾽ αὐτὸς Ψενμεγχῆς μήδ᾽ ἄλλον μηδένα τῶν παρ᾽ αὐτοῦ.

Τὰ παρ᾽ αὐτῆς πάντα, "all her means," in Mk 5[26] (cf. Lk 10[7], Phil 4[18]), may be illustrated from Priene 111[177] (i B.C.) ἐδαπάνησεν δὲ παρ᾽ ἑαυτοῦ μετὰ τῶν συναγωνοθετῶν, ib. 118[15] (i/B.C.), and C. and B. ii p. 394. No. 277, where a father stated that he has erected τὸν βω[μὸν σὺν τῷ γρά]δῳ to his children πα[ρὰ] ἑαυ[τοῦ], "at his own expense." Ramsay compares the similar use of παρά on coins. See also the exx. from Josephus in Field, Notes, p. 27.

For the neut. art. without a subst. followed by παρά c. gen. cf. P Hib I. 109[9] (B.C. 247–6) τὸ παρ᾽ αὐτῶν καὶ τῶν μετ[όχ]ων, with reference to an amount due "from them and their partners," and PSI VI. 598[2] (iii/B.C.) ἀκούσας τὰ παρ᾽ Ἐτεάρχου.

(2) c. dat. "by," "beside," is used only of persons in the NT except in Jn 19[20], with which we may compare P Oxy I. 120[23] (iv/A.D.) ἐπεὶ (l. ἐπὶ) ξένης καὶ παρὰ τῇ τάξι (= ει) ὄντα (l. ὤν), "being a stranger to the place and engaged at his post." See also Kaibel 703[1] (ii/iii A.D.) ἐννεακαιδεκάμηνος ἐγὼ κεῖμαι παρὰ τύμβῳ. For the ordinary personal use see P Hib I. 147 (early iii/B.C.) σύντασσε [τοὺς] παρὰ σοὶ φ[ύ]λακας φυλάσσειν, P Oxy II 298[23] (i/A.D.) παρὰ σοί, "where you are." P Fay 122[3] (c. A.D. 100) τὸ παρὰ σοὶ σί[ν]απι τὸ ἐν τῶι θησαυρῶι Σοχώτου, "the mustard that is with you in the store of Sochotes," P Oxy IX. 1220[8] (iii/A.D.) πέμψε (= αι) μοι κέρμα εἰς τὰ γινόμενα παρ᾽ ἐμοὶ ἔργα τῆς κ[αρπ>οφορίας, "send me some money for the business of harvesting going on here" (Edd.), ib. XII. 1593[15] (iv/A.D.) περὶ ὧν βούλης παρ᾽ ἐμοὶ ἀντίγραψόν μοι, and ib. VI. 925[5] (Christian prayer—v/vi A.D.) φανέρωσόν μοι τὴν παρὰ σοὶ ἀλήθιαν. Cf. Herodas V. 61.

For the phrase παρὰ τοῖς θεοῖς and its equivalents with verbs of prayer etc. the following exx. may serve—BGU II. 632[6] (ii/A.D.) (= LAE, p. 172) μνίαν σου ποιούμενος (cf. Philem 4) παρὰ τοῖς [ἐν]θάδε θεοῖς, P Oxy XII. 1593[4] (ii/A.D.) τὸ προ[σκ]ύνημά σ[ο]υ ποιῶ παρὰ τῷ κυρίῳ Σ[α]ρά[πι]δι, ib. XIV. 1678[2] (illiterate —iii/A.D.) πρὸ μὲν πάντων εὐχομέ σε ὁλοκληρεῖν καὶ ὑειένειν παρὰ τῷ κυρείῳ θεῷ, ib. XII. 1489[7] (late iii/A.D.) ἄσπα[[ζ]]σον Φίρμον καὶ Τεκοῦσαν καὶ τοὺς ἡμῶν πάντας παρὰ τοῖς θεοῖς τῆς

πόλεως τῶν Ἀντινοαίων, "salute Firmus and Tecusa and all our friends before the gods of Antino-opolis" (Edd.), and ib. 1495[4] (Christian — iv/A.D.) πρὸ μὲν πάντων εὔχομαί σοι τὴν ὁλοκληρίαν παρὰ τῷ κ[υ]ρι[ῷ] θ[ε]ῷ. See also the note by Ghedini in Aegyptus iii. p. 191 f.

(3) c. acc. "by," "beside," "near" : P Eleph 2[17] (B.C. 285–4) τὴν δὲ συγγραφὴν ἑκόντες ἔθεντο παρὰ συγγραφοφύλακα Ἡράκλειτον, P Lille I. 17[19] (iii/B.C.) ὁ σῖτος ὁ παρ᾽ ὑμᾶς, P Petr III. 2[15] (B.C. 236) οὐλὴ ἐπὶ μήλου παρ᾽ ὄφρυν [ἀριστερ]άν, P Par 47[7] (c. B.C. 152–1) (= UPZ i. p. 332, Selections, p. 22) ψευδῆι πάντα καὶ οἱ παρὰ σὲ θεοὶ ὁμοίως, "all things are false and your gods with the rest," P Tebt I. 39[21] (B.C. 114) παρὰ τὸ αὐτόθι Διὸς ἱερόν, "near the temple of Zeus here" (Edd.), and P Oxy XII. 1583[3] (ii/A.D.) γενοῦ παρὰ Ἰσίδωρον χάριν τοῦ [φαι]νόλου, "go to Isidore for the cloak." For a suggestion that in Ac 22[3] ἀνατεθραμμένος δὲ ἐν τῇ πόλει ταύτῃ παρὰ τοὺς πόδας Γαμαλιήλ should be translated "in this city I was brought under the influence of Gamaliel," see Exp T xxx. p. 39 f.

The temporal use of παρά = "during" is seen in P Oxy III. 472[10] (c. A.D. 130) δύναται μὲν γὰρ καὶ ἄλλα τινὰ λελοι[ν]ῆσθαι παρὰ τὸν τῆς προνοίας χρόνον, "he may indeed have had other troubles during the period of his stewardship" (Edd.). In Rom 14[5] ἡμέραν παρ᾽ ἡμέραν, παρά is best understood as = "in preference to," the preceding κρίνει being then taken in the sense of "estimates," "approves of" (see SH ad l.). For the phrase τὸ παρὰ τοῦτο indicating the "difference" between two figures, see P Hib I. 99[10] (c. B.C. 148) with the editors' note.

(4) Some miscellaneous uses of παρά may be illustrated. For the meaning "against," "contrary to," as in Ac 18[13], Rom 1[26] al., cf. P Tebt I. 5[92] (B.C. 118) τοὺς δὲ παρὰ ταῦτα ποιοῦντας θαν[άτωι ζ]ημιοῦσθαι, "those who disobey this decree are punishable with death" (Edd.), ib.[205] τοὺς κεκοφότας τῶν ἰδίων ξύλα παρὰ <τὰ> ἐκ<κ>είμενα προστάγματα, "those who have cut down wood on their own property in contravention of the published decrees" (Edd.), ib. 27[41] (B.C. 113) τὰ παρὰ τὸ δέ[ι]ον κεχειρισμένα, "your improper procedure" (Edd.) ; also the common sepulchral inscr., as in C. and B. ii p. 537, No. 394[9] εἰ δέ τις παρὰ ταῦτα ποιήσει, ἔστε αὐτῷ πρὸς τὸν κρίτην θεόν.

Like the Semitic min, παρά is used of comparison in P Tebt I. 5[85] (B.C. 118) μίζοσι μέ[τ]ροις [πα]ρὰ τὰ εὐσ<ταθμα>, "larger measures than the correct bronze measures," ib. 19[12] (B.C. 114) σὺ δὲ ὀρθῶς ποιήσεις τὸ προσάγγελμα μὴ ἐλατώσας παρὰ τὸ πρῶτον, "you will be right in not diminishing the report compared with the first one" (Edd.) : cf. Lk 13[2,4], 18[14], Rom 1[25], 12[3]. In MGr παρά and ἀπό are used to express comparison.

Παρά "on account of," as in 1 Cor 12[15f.], meets us in P Oxy XII. 1420[2] (c. A.D. 129) οὐ παρ᾽ ἐμὴν δὲ αἰτίαν οὐ κατεχωρίσθησαν, "but it is not on account of my fault that they have not been presented" (Edd.), P Ryl II. 243[5] (ii/A.D.) οὐδὲν παρὰ σὲ γέγονε, "nothing has occurred through any fault of yours" (Edd.). With this may be compared the use of παρὰ τό c. inf. to denote cause or origin, e.g. P Magd 11[1] (B.C. 221) παρὰ τὸ δὲ σύνεγγυς εἶναι τὸ Ἀρσι[ν]οίτην, "because the Arsinoite district was near" : see Mayser Gr. II. i. p. 331.

In BGU IV. 1079[16] (A.D. 41) (= Selections, p. 39) παρὰ

τάλαντόν σοι πέπρακα τὰ φο[ρτ]ία μου, the meaning is perhaps not more than "I have sold my wares for a talent." For an adverbial use cf. P Grenf II. 36³ (B.C. 95) (= Witkowski², p. 110) Παγάνει Πανεβχούνιος καὶ Παθήμει, παρὰ καὶ Πετεαρσεμθεῖ, where παρὰ καί = "una et" (Witkowski). On the force of παρά in composition, see *Proleg.* p. 247.

As in the case of all the prepositions, reference should be made to the important theses by Kuhring and Rossberg, see under Abbreviations I. Full particulars of NT usage are given in Paul F. Regard's monograph *Contribution à l'étude des Prépositions dans la langue du Nouveau Testament* (Paris, 1919).

παραβαίνω,

"pass on" occurs in P Ryl II. 77⁴¹ (A.D. 192) ὀφείλει εἰς τὴν κατεπείγο[υσα]ν ἀρχὴν παραβαίνειν, "he ought to pass on to the office immediately required" (Edd.). For the definitely metaphorical meaning "transgress," which alone is found in the NT (unless Ac 1²⁵), we may cite the following exx.: P Par 46¹² (B.C. 152) (= UPZ i. p. 338) παραβέβηκεν τοὺς ὅρκους, P Amh II. 35³⁰ (B.C. 132) παραβεβηκότος τὰ τῆς χειρογραφίας, P Bad 35³ (A.D. 87) πα[ρ]αβάς σου τὴν συνταγή[ν, BGU II. 638¹⁶ (A.D. 143) μὴ ἐξεῖναι δὲ μηθὲν τῶν προγεγρ αμμένων) παραβῆν[α]ι, and P Oxy III. 526¹⁰ (ii/A.D.) εἰ καὶ μὴ ἀ[νέ]βενε ἐγὼ τὸν λόγον μου οὐ παρέβενον, "even if he were not going I should not have broken my word" (Edd.). [For the omission of ἄν in this last sentence in the apodosis of unfulfilled condition, see s.v. ἄν, and *contra* Robertson, *Gr.* p. 920 f.]

Παραβαίνω is frequent in connexion with wills, e.g. P Oxy III. 494²⁵ (A.D. 156) where provision is made that anyone who shall disobey (τὸν παραβησόμενον) the conditions of a will shall forfeit to the party abiding by it (τῷ ἐμμένοντι) the damages and other sums. On the legal usages of παραβαίνω and ἐμμένω see Berger *Strafklauseln*, p. 5. For παραβαίνω used in a religious connexion, cf. Syll 574 (= ³689)³ (ii/B.C.) ὃς δ' ἂν παραβαίνηι, αὐτὸν αὐτὸν αἰτιάσεται, with reference to the temple of Artemis at Ephesus, and OGIS 569¹⁹ (iv/A.D.) μηδεμιᾷ σκαιᾷ τινι και[νο]υργίᾳ τὴν τιμὴν) τὴν τοῖς θεοῖς ὀφειλομένην παραβαίνειν.

παραβάλλω.

The RV rendering of Ac 20¹⁵ παρεβάλομεν εἰς Σάμον, "we touched at Samos," is supported by P Petr II. 13(5)⁴ (B.C. 258–253) ο[ὐ]κ ἔδει μὲν οὖν σε παραπορεύεσθαι ἀλλὰ καὶ πρὸς ἡμᾶς παραβαλεῖν ὥρ[ας] μόριον, where Mahaffy renders, "you ought, indeed, not to have passed us by in this way, but to have landed with us for a quarter of an hour"; but see Field, *Notes*, p. 131.

The verb in its wider sense "betake oneself," "go," may be illustrated by BGU IV. 1106⁴⁹ (B.C. 13) παραβαλε[ῖ δὲ] ἡ Θεοδότη πρὸς τὸν Μᾶρκον . . ἑκοῦσα καὶ τὸ παιδίον πρὸς τὸ ἐπιθεωρεῖσθαι ὑπ' αὐτοῦ, *ib.* III. 824¹⁴ (A.D. 55 6) παράβαλε οὖν ἐκεῖ, P Ryl II. 153⁵ (A.D. 138–161) παραβάλλου[τα] . . . εἰς τὸν τάφον μου, P Oxy VI 930²¹ (ii/iii A.D.) μελησάτω σοί τε καὶ τῷ παιδαγωγῷ σου καθήκοντι καθηγητῇ σε παραβάλλειν, "let it be the care of both you and your paedagogue to betake yourself to a suit-

able teacher," and *ib.* 937¹⁰ (iii/A.D.) παραγγέλλω σοι . . . ἵνα παραβάλῃς πρὸς τῇ πλατείᾳ τοῦ θεάτρου, "I bid you go to the street of the theatre." See also P Flor III. 312³ (A.D. 92) παραβέβλη[κ]α τὸν προκείμενον ὑπομνηματικόν.

In Aristeas 281 παραβάλλοντας τὸ ζῆν = "while risking their lives": see s.v. παραβολεύομαι. For the mid. of the verb cf. Syll 342 (= ³762)³⁹ (B.C. 48) ψυχῇ καὶ σ[ώ]ματι παραβαλλόμενος.

παράβασις.

P Flor III. 313¹⁵ (A.D. 449) ἀπὸ καταγνώσεως καὶ παραβάσε[ω]ς P Lond 1015¹¹ (vi/A.D.) (= III. p. 257) προστίμου καὶ παραβάσεως.

παραβάτης.

The remarkable tradition preserved in Cod. Bezae after Lk 6⁴ is perhaps the origin of the phrase παραβάτης νόμου in Paul and James: see Plummer *ad* Lk *l.c.*

παραβιάζομαι.

For the orig. meaning "urge," "press," against nature or law, cf. *Epicurea* ed. Usener p. 36² μήτε τὸ ἀδύνατον καὶ παραβιάζεσθαι. See also Polyb. xxii. 10. 7.

παραβολεύομαι.

"expose myself to danger" (cf. classical παραβάλλομαι), occurs in the NT only in Phil 2³⁰, but is cited by Deissmann (*LAE*, p. 84 n.⁵) from an Olbian inscr. of ii/A.D. which is under no suspicion of appropriating a coinage of a NT writer—*Latyschev* I. 21²⁶ ff., where it is said of a certain Carzoasus—ἀλλὰ καὶ (μέχρι) περάτων γῆς ἐμαρτυρήθη τοὺς ὑπὲρ φιλίας κινδύνους μέχρι Σεβαστῶν συμμαχία (for dat. see *Proleg.* p. 64) παραβολευσάμενος, "but also to the ends of the world it was witnessed of him that in the interests of friendship he had exposed himself to dangers as an advocate in (legal) strife (by taking his clients' causes even) up to emperors." The word is from παράβολος, "venturesome," the verbal part expressing the energy of βάλλω, instead of being static as in παραβολή: see s.v. παραβάλλω.

παραβολή.

Our sources throw no special light upon this word which in the NT is found only in the Synoptics = "parable," "similitude," and *bis* in Heb (9⁹, 11¹⁹) = "figure," "type." For Heb 11¹⁹, where Isaac's restoration was to Abraham a sort of resurrection, Moffatt (*ICC ad l.*) cites Aelian *Var. Hist.* iii. 33 describing Satyrus the flautist—τρόπον τινὰ τὴν τέχνην ἐκφαυλίζων παραβολῇ τῇ πρὸς φιλοσοφίαν. According to Quintil. v. 11. 23 "παραβολή, quam Cicero collationem vocat, longius res quae comparentur repetere solet." See further, especially for the Biblical usage, Hatch, *Essays*, p. 64 ff.

In P Flor III. 384⁶³ (v/A.D.?) τὰς τοῦ μηχανοστασίου παραβολάς, the editor understands π. as = "riparazioni."

παραγγελία,

"injunction," "command": P Lond 1231¹⁶ (A.D. 144) (= III. p. 109) ὅπως ἔχ[ω]ν ἔγραπτον παραγγελείαν πρόνοιαν ποιησῆται τῆς γε[ωρ]γείας τῶν [ἀρου]ρῶν αὐτ[ός, and P Oxy XII. 1411¹⁶ (A.D. 260) εἰ μὴ πειθαρχήσιαν τῇδε τ[ῇ παραγγελίᾳ, πειραθήσονται, . . . "if they disobey this injunction, they will experience the penalties . . ." (Edd.).

For the more technical meaning, a "summons" to appear in court, cf. P Oxy III. 484¹⁵ (A.D. 138) ὅπως ἔχων ἔγγραπτον παραγγελίαν παραγένηται ὅπου ἐὰν ὁ κράτιστος ἡγεμών . . . ἐπ᾽ ἀγαθῷ τὸν νομὸν διαλογίζηται, "in order that he may have a written notice and appear wherever his highness the praefect holds his auspicious court for the nome" (Edd.). The NT usage is discussed by Milligan, *Thess.* p. 47.

Παράγγελμα may be illustrated from P Amh II. 50⁵ (B.C. 106) ἐκ τοῦ παραγγέλ(ματος), "in accordance with the summons": see *Archiv* ii. p. 123 and cf. P Lond 904³⁶ (A.D. 104) (= III. p. 126, *Chrest.* I. p. 237).

παραγγέλλω

is common in Ptolemaic papyri to describe the official summons before a court, e.g. P Par 46¹⁷ (B.C. 153) (= UPZ i. p. 338) γέγραφά σοι, ὅπω[ς] Ἀπολλωνίωι παραγγείλῃς, P Grenf I. 40⁶ (ii/B.C.) (= *Chrest.* II. p. 21) ἔκρινον γράψαι σοι ὅπως εἰδὼς παραγγείλῃς καὶ τ[οῖς] ἄλλοις ἱερεῦσι ἑτοίμους εἶναι, and P Tebt I. 14⁵ (B.C. 114) ἔγραψας ἡμῖν Ἡρᾶν (ℓ. Ἡρᾶτι) . . . εὐθυνομένωι δὲ φόνωι καὶ ἄλλαις αἰτία(ι)ς παραγγείλαι ἀπαντᾶν ἐν ἡμέραι(ς) τρισὶν πρὸς τὴν περὶ τούτων ἐσομένην διεξαγωγήν, "you wrote to me that I was to give notice to Heras who is arraigned for murder and other offences to appear in three days' time for the decision to be made concerning these charges" (Edd.).

Miscellaneous uses of the verb are—P Amh II. 30⁴⁰ (ii/B.C.) παρηγγείλαμεν τῆι Θεμβῶτος (ℓ. Θεμβῶτι) ἐκχωρεῖν ἐκ τῆς οἰκίας, "we ordered Thembos to depart out of the house," P Tebt II. 386²² (B.C. 12) ἐν ἡμέραις τριάκοντα ἀφ᾽ ἧς ἐάν μοι παραγγίλῃ, "within thirty days from the day on which you give me notice," with reference to the repayment of a dowry following on a deed of divorce, P Ryl II. 81⁹ (c. A.D. 104) διὰ σοῦ αὐτοῖς παραγγείλας ἵν᾽ ὅσου ἐὰν χρείαν ἔχωσι ὕδατους (ℓ. ὕδατος) ἑαυ[τ]οῖς ἐπιχαλῶσι, "instructing them through you to draw off as much water as they need" (Edd.), the illiterate ib. 435 (ii/A.D.) where we have twice the formula παρήγκελκά συ (ℓ. παρήγγελκά σοι) ἄλλα ἅπαξ, "I have instructed you several time." (cf. *Archiv* vi. p. 379), and P Oxy VI. 937⁸ (iii/A.D.) κἂν νῦν οὖν παραγγέλλω σοι, ὦ κυρία μου ἀδελφή, ἵνα παραβάλῃς πρὸς τῇ πλατείᾳ τοῦ θεάτρου, "and for the present I bid you, my dear sister, go to the street of the theatre."

For the aoristic present παραγγέλλω in Ac 16¹⁸, see *Proleg.* p. 119. With παραγγέλλω in 1 Tim 6¹³ al. Ramsay (*Exp T* xiv. p. 159) compares the use in the inscrr. of Dionysopolis—παραγγέλλω πᾶσι μὴ καταφρονεῖν τοῦ θεοῦ. MGr παραγγένω.

παραγίνομαι.

The use of παραγίνομαι as a synonym for ἔρχομαι, which Thackeray (*Gr.* i. p. 267) thinks may be of Ionic origin, is common in the LXX and later Greek generally (cf. Glaser *De ratione,* p. 36 f.). In the NT it is mainly confined to the Lucan writings, but Harnack (*Sayings of Jesus,* p. 86) goes too far when he asserts that it is "a choicer (*gewählter*) word than ἦλθον": (cf. Lk 10³⁶˙³⁸). This is true to about the same extent as it is that *arrive* is "choicer" than *come.* In Witkowski's collection of Ptolemaic private letters παρα-

γίνομαι occurs some thirty times, four of them being in letters of men marked as "non-eruditorum"—e.g. P Eleph 13² (B.C. 223-2) (= Witkowski², p. 42) παραγενομένου Σανῶτος ἐκομισάμην τὴν παρὰ σοῦ ἐπιστολήν, P Oxy IV. 743²³ (B.C. 2) (= Witkowski², p. 129) παραγενομ(ένου) γὰρ Δαμᾶτος εἰς Ἀλεξάνδρειαν ἤλθαμεν ἐπὶ Ἐπαφρόδειτον.

Other exx. of παραγίνομαι from Ptolemaic times are—P Hib I. 55³ (B.C. 250) παραγενοῦ εἰς Ταλαὼν ἤδη, "come to Talao at once," P Lond 42¹²⁴ (B.C. 168) (= I. p. 30, UPZ i. p. 300, *Selections,* p. 10) ἐπὶ δὲ τῶι μὴ παραγίνεσθαί σε [πάντω]ν τῶν ἐκεῖ ἀπειλημμένων παραγεγο[νό]των ἀηδίζομαι, "but that you did not return when all those who were shut up with you returned distresses me" and P Par 43⁹ (B.C. 153) (= UPZ i p. 323) παραγενομένου (ℓ. παραγενοῦ) δὲ εἰς τὴν ἡμέραν, which Wilcken understands as an invitation to a marriage.

From Roman times we have—P Oxy II. 291⁹ (A.D. 25-26) μ[έχ]ρι ὑγια[ί]νων παρα[γ]ένωμαι, "until I come in peace," BGU II. 530¹⁰˙¹⁷ (A.D. 70-80) ἄχρι οὖ πα[ρ]αγενάμενος (for form cf. Blass-Debrunner § 81 3) ἐγ[ὼ] σώσωι . . . , P Ryl II. 232³ (ii/A.D.) ἅμα τῷ [παρα]γενέσθαι τὸν στρ[ατη]γὸν εἰς τὴν Ἡράκλειαν, "as soon as the strategus arrived at Heracleia," P Oxy IX. 1220²³ (iii/A.D.) ἐὰν παραγένῃ σὺν θεῷ, "if you come, D.V." (Ed.), and the Christian commendatory letter ib. VIII. 1162⁷ (iv/A.D.) τὸν ἀδελφὸ(=ό)ν ἡμῶν Ἀμμώνιον παραγινόμενον πρὸς ὑμᾶς συνδέξασθαι αὐτὸν ἐν ἰρήνῃ, "our brother Ammonius, who is coming to you, receive in peace" (Ed.). Notwithstanding AV and RV, the primary sense of the verb in 2 Tim 4¹⁶ is still "came," the idea of "help" arising from the use of the dat. here only in NT. From the inscrr. note *Syll* 554¹⁶ (beg. ii/B.C.) εἰς τὸ καθ᾽ ἑξάμηνον παραγινόμενον δικαστήριον, with reference to a six-monthly judicial circuit in Magnesia.

παράγω.

For the transitive use of παράγω (as in MGr) = "bring forward," which is not found in the NT, we may cite BGU IV. 1139¹⁹ (B.C. 5) where steps are taken to compel a certain Paris—παραγαγεῖν τὴν θυγατέρα ἡμῶν, [ἵν]α ἀποκομισθώμεθα αὐτὴν καὶ ὦμεν εὐεργετη(μένοι), and P Oxy VI. 971 (i/ii A.D.) where payment of so many obols is made to workmen—ἀντλ οὖσι καὶ παράγ ουσι) ὑδραγ(ωγόν).

For the meaning "pass by," as in Mt 20³⁰ al., cf. P Tebt I. 17⁴ (B.C. 114) τῇ δὲ ιϛ παράγειν τὴν κώμην, "on the 16th pass by the village." In P Magd 12⁷ (B.C. 217) the meaning passes into "lead astray," παρήγαγόν με οὐ βουλόμενοι σφραγίσασθαι τὴν συγγραφήν, "ils me dupent en refusant de sceller le bail" (Ed.): cf. Pindar *Nem.* vii. 23 σοφία δὲ κλέπτει παράγοισα μύθοις. In Mk 1¹⁶ παράγων is almost = "walking": note v.l. περιπατῶν. In P Lond 1109⁴⁵ (ii/A.D.) (= III. p. 45) καθ᾽ ἣν ἔσχε παραγω—, Wilcken (*Archiv* iv. p. 532) reads not παράγων but παραγωγήν in the sense of a "Passierschein" or "pass." The subst. is also found in BGU II. 302¹¹˙⁸ (A.D. 215) σὺν παραγωγῇ.

παραδειγματίζω.

In its sole NT occurrence, Heb 6⁶ (cf. Pss. Sol. 2¹³), this verb is used in the sense of "expose to public ignominy."

Cf. Plut. *Mor.* 520 where Archilochus is described as rendering himself infamous—ἑαυτὸν **παραδειγματίζοντος**—by the character of the verses he writes : cf. the use of the *simplex* in Mt 1[19], and see *s.v.* **δειγματίζω**.

We may cite one or two exx. of the subst. in the more ordinary sense of "example" : PSI IV. 422[38] (iii/B.C.) Ὡρός μω(==ο)ι τὸ **παράδειγμα** ἔδωκεν, P Fay 20[2] (Imperial edict—ii/A.D.) μοι παρέστη τὸ βούλευμα τοῦτο οὐδὲ ἀποδέοντι **παραδειγμάτων**, "I have formed this intention, not wanting in precedents " (Edd.), P Oxy II. 237[viii. 8] (A.D. 186) **παραδείγματι** τῷ καλλίστῳ χρώμενος, "following a most illustrious precedent," *OGIS* 508[8] (A.D. 162–3) ὡς μὴ ῥαιδίως ἀνάγεσθαί τινας τῶι **παραδείγματι**, and the epitaph to an athlete, *Kaibel* 940[4]—

> T]οιάδε τις δείξας παραδε[ί]γματα παισὶν ἑαυτοῦ
> μᾶλλον ὀρέξασθαι τῆς ἀρετῆς προτρέπει.

παράδεισος.

The essential features of this foreign (Iranian) word cling to it in its wide popular use and pass on into the applications found in the Bible. The modern Persian *pāēz* means a garden, as does **παράδεισος** from the earliest records we have of it in Greek (Xen. *Anab.* i. 2. 7 etc.). A garden of fruit-trees (protected presumably by a wall) is the general idea of it as seen in the papyri where it is very common. Thus we have P Petr III. 26[6] (iii/B.C.) εἰς ἀλλότριον κλῆρον ἢ **παράδεισον** ἢ κῆπον ἢ ἀμπ[ελῶ]να, bringing together " plot or orchard or garden or vineyard," P Tebt I. 5[54] (B.C. 118) τὰς ἀπομοίρας ἃς ἐλάμβαν[ο]ν ἔκ τε τ[ῶ]ν κ]τημάτων καὶ τῶν [π]αραδεί(σων), " the tithes which they (the temples) used to receive from the holdings and the orchards,"—and *OGIS* 90[15] (Rosetta stone—B C. 196) τὰς καθηκούσας ἀπομοίρας τοῖς θεοῖς ἀπό τε τῆς ἀμπελίτιδος γῆς καὶ τῶν **παραδείσων** καὶ τῶν ἄλλων τῶν ὑπαρξάντων τοῖς θεοῖς. In P Lond 933[12] (A.D. 211) (= III. p. 69) there is a payment on account of an " olive-orchard," ἐλαιωνοπαράδ(εισος). In P Petr I. 16[ii. 7] (B.C. 230) Mahaffy translates τὰ γενήματα τῶν ὑπαρχόντων μοι **παραδείσων**, " the produce of my parks," but the mere mention of *produce* shows that " orchards " are meant : see further Grenfell's note in P Rev L p. 94 ff and Wilcken *Ostr.* i. p. 157 f. From Genesis to Revelation fruit-trees are an essential part of the imagery connected with Eden. Milton's picture brings in the wall as well. And this part of the word's connotation suits strikingly the thought of that " fold " of God over whose jasper wall " great and high " the " first grand Thief " shall never climb. Deissmann (*BS* p. 148) finds the earliest ex. of the word in its technical Biblical meaning in 2 Cor 12[4], then Lk 23[43] and Rev 2[7] ; 4 Esdr 7[53], 8[52]. For the Jewish conception of the " garden " as the abode of the blessed cf. Enoch lxi. 12, and see Weber *Jüd. Theol.* pp. 341, 344.

παραδέχομαι.

" receive," " welcome," with a personal object, as in Heb 12[6] LXX : BGU I 27[10] (ii/iii A.D.) (= *Selections*, p. 101) **παρεδέξατο** ἡμᾶς ὁ τόπος ὡς ὁ θεὸς ἤθελεν, P Oxy XIV. 1676[28] (iii/A.D.) ἥδιστά σε **παραδεξόμεθα**, and PSI III. 208[5] (iv/A.D.) Ἡρακλῆν **παράδεξαι** [κ]ατὰ τὸ ἔθος. Hence the meaning " approve," " commend," in Aristeas 190 τοῦτον δὲ εὖ μάλα **παραδεξάμενος**.

The verb is common == " make allowance for," especially in leases—P Ryl II. 229[16] (A.D. 38) **παρεδεξάμην** σοι πάντα, " I have given you every allowance " (but see Olsson *Papyrusbriefe*, p. 81), P Amh II. 86[13] (A.D. 78) ἐὰν δέ τις ἄβροχο(s) γένηται **παραδεχθήσεταί** μοι κατὰ τὸ ἀνάλογον τοῦ φόρου, " if any of the land becomes unwatered, a proportionate allowance from the rent shall be made to me," P Oxy I. 101[25] (A.D. 142) ἐὰν δέ τις τοῖς ἑξῆς ἔτεσι ἄβροχος γένηται, **παραδεχθήσεται** τῷ μεμισθωμένῳ, " if in any of the years there should be a failure of water, an allowance shall be made to the lessee " (Edd.), and P Fay 125[10] (ii/A.D.) τὸ δαπανηθ[ὲν] **παραδέξομαι**, " I will make allowance for the expense." For a similar use of subst. **παραδοχή** see P. Oxy XIV. 1659[122] (A.D. 218–221) with the editors' note.

The verb is also found in receipts, e.g. *Preisigke* 3975[2] (iii/B.C.) **παραδέχεται**, and BGU VI. 1423[1] (ii/B.C.). For a similar use of the subst. cf. P Lond 1157 (A.D. 197–198?) (= III. p. 61 ff.) where, at the end of each monthly summary in a register of receipts in respect of certain taxes, the formula occurs—σύμφωνος πρὸς **παραδοχ(ήν)**, which " presumably means that the amount named tallies with the receipts " (Edd.). In P Flor I. 79[24] (A.D. 60) (= *Chrest.* I. p. *171*) εἴ[ν]αί με ἐν τῆι **παραδοχῆι** τῶν ἀπὸ τοῦ γυμνασίου, Wilcken understands **παραδοχή** as == " admission-list." As regards the adj. **παραδοχικός**, P Hib I. 87[13] (B.C. 256) σ]ῖτον καθα[ρὸ]ν μέτροις παραδ[ο]χικοῖς is translated by the editors " pure corn measured by the receiving measures," but Herwerden *Lex. s.v.* prefers the meaning " handed down by use," and therefore " legal." **Παραδόχιμος**, " hereditary," is found in P Tebt II. 298[10] (A.D. 107–8), *al.*

παραδιατριβή.

Παραδιατριβαί has only the support of a few minuscule MSS. in 1 Tim 6[5]. The true reading **διαπαρατριβαί** is understood by Field (*Notes*, p. 211) in the sense of " mutual irritations " : cf. for the sense of *reciprocity* the simple compd. in Polyb. ii. 36. 5 τὰ μὲν οὖν κατὰ Καρχηδονίους καὶ Ῥωμαίους ἐν ὑποψίαις ἦν πρὸς ἀλλήλους καὶ **παρατριβαῖς** (cited by Lock *ICC ad* 1 Tim *l.c.*).

παραδίδωμι.

(1) For this common verb in its ordinary meaning of " hand over " to another, cf. P Oxy IV. 742[7] (B.C. 2) **παράδος** δέ τινι τῶν φίλων ἀριθμῷ (see *s.v.*) αὐτὰς ἵνα πάλιν φ[ί]λος ἡμεῖν **παραδοῖ** (for form, Mayser *Gr.* p. 137) ἀσφ[αλῶς, " deliver a few of them (bundles of reeds) to one of our friends that a friend may deliver them to me safely," P Amh II. 93[22] (application for lease of an oil-press—A.D. 181) μετὰ τὸν χρόνον **παραδώσω** τὸ ἐλαιουργίον καθαρὸν σὺν ταῖς ἐναι(==ε)στώσαις θύραις καὶ κλεισί, ἐὰν φαίνεται μισθῶσαι, " at the end of the time I will deliver up the oil-press uninjured together with the doors and keys belonging to it, if you consent to the lease " (Edd.), P Tebt II. 406[9] (*c.* A.D. 266) an inventory of articles ἃ καὶ **παρεδόθη** Πασιγένη, " which were delivered to Pasigenes," and the Christian letter P Grenf II. 73[11] (late iii/A.D.) (= *Selections*, p. 118) τ]αύτην **παραδέδωκα** τοῖς καλοῖς καὶ πιστοῖς, with reference to the handing over of a woman to the care of certain good and faithful men until

her son arrives. It may be noted that in Ac 15²⁶ Field (*Notes*, p. 124) understands the verb of men "pledging" their lives : see also his note on 1 Cor 13³ (p. 176 f.).

(2) The use of **παραδίδωμι** with the correlative **παραλαμβάνω**, as in 1 Cor 11²·²³, 15³, may be illustrated from CP Herm I. 119ⁱⁱⁱ ²² (lease of a house) ἐν τέλει τοῦ χρόνου παραδώσω σὺν θύραις ὃν [ὡ]ς παρίληφα, BGU IV. 1018²⁴ (iii/A.D.) μετὰ τὸν χρόνον παραδώσω τὰς ἀρούρας καθαρὰς ὡς παρέλαβον, and P Thead 8²⁵ (A.D. 306) παραδώσω τούς τε αἴγας καὶ πρόβατα . . . εὐάρεστα πάντα καθὼς κἀγὼ παρέλαβον.

(3) The additional thought of " deliver up " to prison or judgment appears in such passages as P Petr III. 28 (*e*) *verso* (⁵)⁴ (iii/B.C.) παρεδόθη δὲ Παῶτι δεσμοφύλακι, " but he was handed over to Paos the gaoler," in connexion with the breaking into a house : cf. P Hib I. 54²¹ (*c*. B.C. 245) τὸ σῶμα δὲ εἰ συνείληφας παράδος [[αυτο]] Σεμφθεῖ ὅπως διακομίσηι ἡμῖν, "and if you have arrested the slave, deliver him to Semphtheus to bring to me " (Edd.), *ib.* 50³ᶠᶠ· (*c*. B.C. 245) ἀπόστειλον πρὸς ἡμᾶς μετὰ φυλακῆ[ς] τὴν παραδοθεῖσάν σοι ἔχουσαν τὸ κλέψιμον ἔλαιον καὶ τὸν παραδόντα σοι ἀπόστειλο[ν, " send to us under guard the woman who was delivered to you with the contraband oil in her possession, and send also the person who delivered her to you " (Edd.), and OGIS 660¹⁵ (i/A.D.) εἴς τε τὸ πρακτόρειόν τινας παρέδοσαν. It is further noteworthy that the language of 1 Cor 5⁵, 1 Tim 1²⁰, can be illustrated from pagan execratory formulas, e.g. the great magical Paris papyrus P Par 574¹²⁴⁷ (iii/A.D.) (= *Selections*, p. 114) παραδίδωμί σε εἰς τὸ μέλαν χάος ἐν ταῖς ἀπωλί(=εί)αις, " I shall give you over to black chaos in utter destruction," and P Lond 46³⁵ (iv/A.D.) (= I. p. 75) νεκυδαίμων . . . παραδίδωμί σοι τὸν δ(εῖνα), ὅπως . . . : see Deissmann *LAE*, p. 303 f. MGr παραδίδω, " surrender."

παράδοξος,

" unexpected " (as in Lk 5²⁶, cf. Aristeas 175) readily passes into the meaning " wonderful," " admirable." In this latter sense it was applied to one who was victor in both **πάλη** and **πένταθλον** (see Meyer on P Hamb I. 21³), and occurs as an athletic title in P Lond 1178⁵⁴ (A.D. 194) (= III. p. 217) πύκτον ἀλείπτου παραδόξου, and ⁵⁶ παλαιστοῦ παραδόξου, also P Oxy XIV. 1759 (ii/A.D.) where Demetrius wishes Theon, an athlete,⁴ νικᾶν πάντοτε, and concludes with the greeting ¹⁰ ἔ]ρρωσό μοι, παράδοξε. The word is used as a proper name in BGU II. 362ˣⁱᵛ· ¹⁰ (A.D. 215), and probably P Oxy IX. 1205¹ (A.D. 291).

For the adv. cf. OGIS 383²⁰ (mid. i/B.C.) κινδύνους μεγάλους παραδόξως διέφυγον.

παράδοσις

in itself signifies an act of " transmission " or " delivery " as in P Grenf II. 46 (*a*)⁵ (A.D. 139) παρέτυχον τῇ γενομένηι παραδόσει, in connexion with the official inspection of a freight, BGU IV. 1047ⁱᵛ· ²¹ (time of Hadrian) τὴν γεγονυ[ῖα]ν αὐτοῖς παράδοσιν, P Oxy X. 1262⁷ (A.D. 197) ἐπὶ παραλήμψεω(ς) καὶ παραδόσεως σπερμάτ[ων, " for the receiving and delivery of seed " (cf. Phil 4¹⁵), and P Fay 129² (iii/A.D.) ἐτάξατο πάντως καταβῆναι τῇ ἑνδεκάτῃ καὶ τὴν παράδοσιν ποιήσασθαι, " he appointed for certain the

eleventh for his coming down and making the delivery " (Edd.) : cf. also Bell in *Archiv* vi. p. 104 on the **παράδοσις** by the outgoing to the incoming **βιβλιοφύλακες**, and the similar use of the word to denote treasure lists and inventories handed over by one set of officers to their successors, cf. *Roberts-Gardner*, p. 256.

For the NT use of the word, see Burton *ICC ad Gal* 1¹⁴, and Mayor *Jude* pp. 23, 61 ff., and on the possibility that we have in the **παραδόσεις** of 2 Thess 2¹⁵ (cf. Rom 6¹⁷, 16¹⁷) reference to an early catechism or creed based on the sayings of Christ, see Seeberg *Katechismus*, pp. 1 ff., 41 f.

παραζηλόω.

In 1 Cor 10²² this verb must be understood not as a simple statement of fact, but as connoting the intention of the speaker—" *What! do we intend to rouse the Lord's jealousy?* " (Moffatt). In Ps 36⁶·⁷·⁸ μὴ παραζήλου, " fret not thyself," *noli aemulari*, is the thrice-repeated burden of the Psalm in view of " the infinite disorders of the world " (see Church *Cathedral Sermons*, p. 203 ff.). The subst. is used in a good sense in *Test. xii. patr.* Zab. ix. 8 of the Lord's bringing all the Gentiles εἰς παραζήλωσιν αὐτοῦ, " into zeal for Him."

παραθαλάσσιος,

" by the sea," in Mt 4¹³ finds a good parallel in *Syll* 326 (= ³ 709)²⁰ (*c*. B.C. 107) ἐπιστρέψας ἐπὶ τὰ παραθαλάσσια.

παραθεωρέω,

" overlook," " neglect," is found in an inscr. dealing with the right of asylum at the temple of Pnepheros at Theadelphia, *Chrest.* I. 70²¹ (B.C. 57—6) τούτου δὲ γενομένου ἔσται τὸ θεῖον μὴ παρατεθεωρημένον : cf. Ac 6¹.

παραθήκη

for the Attic **παρακαταθήκη** (see Nageli, p. 27) in the sense of " deposit " can be freely illustrated—P Par 54²¹ (B.C. 163—161) (= *UPZ* i. p. 388) ἀπέχω παρὰ Ἀφροδεισίῳ παραθήκην (δραχμὰς) Ἀφ, " I have received from Aphrodisius 1500 drachmae as deposit," P Hamb I. 2³ (A.D. 59) ὁμολογοῦμεν ἔχειν παρά σου διὰ χειρὸς δι᾽ ἐγ[γ]ύω[ν] ἀλλήλων εἰς ἔκτισιν παραθήκην ἀργυρίου . . . δραχμὰς ἑξακοσίας, P Ryl II. 324¹⁸ (A.D. 130) ἀργυρίου δραχμὰς ἑξήκοντα παραθήκην [ἀκί]νδυνον παντὸς [κι]νδύνου, BGU II. 520⁸ (Jan. A.D. 172) ὁμολογῶ ἔχω (*l*. ἔχειν) π[αρὰ σοῦ] ἐν παραθήκῃ 300 drachmae to be paid back in May-June, and P Lond 943⁹ (A.D. 227) (= III. p. 175) ἐκτείσ[ω κατ]ὰ τὸν τῶν παραθηκῶν νόμον a parallel to νόμος in Rom 7¹²). *Syll* 814 (= ³ 1199)⁴, a leaden tablet found in the temple of Demeter at Cnidus (Audollent *Defixiones* p. 5 cites authorities for dating it ii/i B.C.) devotes to Demeter and Kore and the other infernal gods τοὺς λαβόντας παρὰ Διοκλεῦς παραθή[κα]ν καὶ μὴ ἀποδιδόντας ἀλ[λ]᾽ ἀποστεροῦντας.

A special use is seen in *Syll* 848 (ii/B.C.), where Asandros of Beroea ἀνατίθησι τῶι Ἀπόλλωνι τῶι Πυθίωι ἐλευθέραν ἐμ παραθήκηι Εὐπορίαν τὴν αὐτοῦ παιδίσκην καταβεβληκυῖαν δραχμὰς Ἀλεξανδρείας διακοσίας. Dittenberger remarks that the practice of emancipation is varied : ἐμ

παραθήκηι implies that the freedom of Euporia is committed as a charge to Apollo's care.

For **παραθήκη** in the sense of "pledge," "security," we may refer to *Syll* 329 (=³742⁵¹ (B.C. 85) with Dittenberger's note.

παραινέω.

With the inf. construction of this verb. "exhort." "advise." as in Ac 27²², cf. BGU III. 747ⁱ·¹⁰ (A.D. 139) στρατιώταις . . . παραινῶν πείθε[σθ]αι τοῖς κελευομένοις, and see *Proleg.* p. 205. Cf. further BGU II. 372ⁱⁱ·⁴ (A.D. 154) ἵνα δὲ μὴ μόνον το[ύτ]οις ἀλλὰ [κ]αὶ ἑτέ[ρ]οις ταῦτά με παραινεῖν καὶ πράσσειν μάθωσι, the late P Iand 16⁴ (v/vi A.D.) ὑμέτερον οὖν τῶν σ[υ]μβ[ιωτῶν] ἐστιν τὸ παραινέσαι τῷ σοφωτάτῳ ὑμῶν ἀδελφῷ [τ.ὸ δίκαιο[ν] μου φ[υλ]άξαι ἐν τῇ κρίσει, and *Kaibel* 261¹⁷ (ii/A.D.) τοῦτ' Εὔοδος βροτοῖς πᾶσι παραινῶ. For the absol. use in Ac 27⁹ we may cite *Syll* 36 (=²89)⁴⁰ (B.C. 420) καθὰ παραινόσι Β[οττιαῖοι. The meaning "encouragement" usually given to παραίνεσις in Sap 8⁹ may perhaps be supported by *Syll* 256 (=³557)³³ (B.C. 207–6) διὰ τὴμ παρα[ίνεσιν τοῦ θε]οῦ.

παραιτέομαι,

"request," "entreat," is found in P Petr II. 58 (e)⁴⁸ (Ptol.) παραιτεῖ[σθαι] κ[ατα]πλεῖν εἰς [Ἀλε]ξανδρεί[αν : cf. Mk 15⁶ ABℵ (but see Field *Notes*, p. 43), Heb 12¹⁹. For the meaning "beg off from," as in Heb 12²⁵ (cf. Field *Notes*, p. 234), cf. BGU IV. 1040³² (ii/A.D.) τοὺς πράκτ[ορα]ς π[αρ]αιτίσθαι, "to beg off from the factors."

Hence the stronger sense "refuse," "decline" (1 Tim 4⁷, 5¹¹ ; cf. Aristeas 184), in P Lond 1231³ (A.D. 144) (= III. p. 108) παραιτούμενοι τὴν εἰς τὸ μ[έ]λλον with reference to "resigning" a lease of land, and BGU II. 625⁶ (beg. iii/A.D.) (as amended *Chrest.* I. p. 37) γείνωσκε, ἄδελφε, ἐκληρώθην (Eph 1¹¹) εἰς τὰ Βουκόλια· οὐκ ἠδυνάμην παρετῆσε (*l.* ἠδυνάμην παραιτήσασθαι). In an edict of Germanicus Caesar, Preisigke 3024³⁷ (A.D. 19), παραιτοῦμαι is directly contrasted with ἀποδέχομαι.

See also the letter of the Emperor Claudius to the Alexandrines, P Lond 1912¹⁰ (A.D. 41) ἀρχ[ι]ερέα δ' ἐμὸν καὶ ναῶν κατασκευὰς παρετοῦμε (*l.* παραιτοῦμαι), "I deprecate, however, the appointment of a high-priest to me and the erection of temples" (Bell).

παρακαθέζομαι,

"sit beside," occurs in the NT only in Lk 10³⁹. Its use there may have suggested the words put into the mouths of the women at the tomb of Jesus in Ev. Petr. 11 τίς δὲ ἀποκυλίσει ἡμῖν καὶ τὸν λίθον . . . ἵνα εἰσελθοῦσαι παρακαθεσθῶμεν αὐτῷ καὶ ποιήσωμεν τὰ ὀφειλόμενα ;

For the corresponding verb **παρακαθιζάνω** cf. *Syll*³ 717⁸⁵ (B.C. 100–99) ταῖς σχολαῖς παρακαθιζάνων, and for **παρακάθημαι** see PSI IV. 402¹⁰ (iii/B.C.).

παρακαλέω,

"ask." "beseech," as frequently in the NT, is a common formula in papyrus private letters, e.g. P Par 42⁸ (B.C. 156) (= *UPZ* i. p. 318) παρεκάλεσα αὐτὸν ἔρχεσθαι, περὶ ὧν ἂν βούληται, BGU IV. 1141¹⁰ (B.C. 14) ἐρωτῶ σε οὖν καὶ παρακαλῶι καὶ τὴν Καίσαρος τύ[χη]ν σε ἐξορκιζῶι, and

P Oxy IV. 744⁶ (B.C. 1) ἐρωτῶ σε καὶ παρακαλῶ σε ἐπιμελήθ-<ητ>-ι τῷ παιδίῳ.

For **παρακαλέω** c. semi-final ἵνα, as in 1 Thess 4¹ B, cf. P Ryl II. 229¹⁷ (A.D. 38) παρακάλεσον οὖν τὴν γυναῖκά σου τοῖς ἐμοῖς λόγοις, ἵνα ἐπιμελῆται τῶν χοιριδίων, and the Christian P Heid 6¹⁴ (iv/A.D.) (= *Selections*, p. 126) παρακαλῶ [ο]ὖν, δέσποτα, ἵνα μνημον[ε]ύῃς μοι εἰς τὰς ἁγίας σου εὐχάς : see *Proleg.* p. 206 ff.

Similarly **παρακληθείς** is used, much as we use "please" —P Fay 109³ (early i/A.D.) παρακληθεὶς τοὺς τρεῖς στατῆρες (= as) οὓς εἴρηκέ σοι Σέλευκος δῶναί μοι ἤδη δὸς Κλέωνι, "please give to Cleon the three staters which Seleucus told you to give me" (Edd.), and so¹⁰, P Ryl II. 230⁶ (A.D. 40) παρακληθ[εὶ]ς οὖν ἐκ παντὸς τρόπου ποίησον, "please do your utmost," and P Tebt II. 448 (ii/iii A.D.) παρακληθεὶς δέ, ἄδελφε, συνλαβοῦ τῷ ἀναδιδόντί σοι τὸ ἐπιστόλιον.

The somewhat stronger meaning "exhort," "urge," is seen in P Oxy VII. 1061⁴ (B.C. 22) ἀνάγκην ἔσχον παρακαλέσαι Πτολεμαῖον, "I have been obliged to urge Ptolemaeus," P Amh II. 130¹⁵ (A.D. 70) παρακέκλημαι ἐπὶ μίσονος (*l.* μείζονος) ναύλου, "I have been called on to pay (?) a higher freight," BGU III. 846¹⁰ (ii/A.D.) (= *Selections*, p. 94) παρακα[λ]ῶ σοι, μήτηρ, δ[ι]αλάγητί μοι, "I beg of you, mother, be reconciled to me," and P Oxy I. 117³ (ii/iii A.D.) κατ' ὄψιν σὲ παρακέκληκα, "I have urged you in person" (Edd.).

For 2 Cor 12⁸ Deissmann (*LAE*, p. 311) cites *Syll* 804 (= ³1170)³¹ where a man, who was cured at the shrine of Asclepius in Epidaurus, records regarding one of his ills— καὶ γὰρ περὶ τούτου παρεκάλεσα τὸν θεόν, "and concerning this thing I besought the god": see also P Leid K⁹ (B.C. 99) (= I. p. 52) πα[ρακα]λῶ δὲ κ[αὶ] αὐτοὺς τοὺς θεούς. ὅπως δῶσιν αὐτοῖς χ[άριν, and P Lond 1244⁶ (iv/A.D.) (= III. p. 244) εὐχόμενος καὶ παρακαλῶν τὸν θεόν.

With 1 Cor 4¹³ (cf. Ac 16³⁹) Lietzmann (*HZNT ad l.*) compares the use of the verb in Aristeas 220, 235, 238, 264. See also Menander *Fragm.* p. 241 –

> οὐχὶ παρακληθέντας ὑμᾶς δεῖ γὰρ ἡμῖν εὐνοεῖν,
> ἀλλ' ὑπάρχειν τοῦτο,

"you ought not to wait to be called on for goodwill to us : we should have that already."

A triple compd. **προσεπιπαρακαλέω** is found in BGU I. 248³ (i/A.D.), 246¹⁸ (ii/A.D.).

παρακαλύπτω,

"conceal," "veil," is found in the NT metaphorically only in Lk 9⁴⁵, where Grimm detects a Hebraism without any adequate cause.

παρακαταθήκη,

"trust," "deposit," which is read for **παραθήκη** in the TR of 1 Tim 6²⁰, 2 Tim 1¹⁴, may be illustrated from *Chrest.* I. 108¹⁷ (B.C. 240) ἐμ παρακαταθήκηι, BGU I. 114ⁱ·⁷ (ii/A.D.) ἀπαιτεῖν παρακαταθήκην ἐξ ὑπαρχόντων, ⁹ νοοῦμεν ὅτι αἱ παρακαταθῆκαι προῖκές ("gifts") εἰσιν, and P Oxy I. 71ⁱ·⁶ (A.D. 303) παρακαταθήκην ἀκίνδυνον καὶ ἀνυπόλογον. "a secure deposit, subject to no claim or charge." See also Artem. p. 4¹⁷ λαβὼν μνᾶς δέκα παρακαταθήκην ἐφύλαξεν and Plut. *Anten.* 21 where the word is used of "deposits" with the Vestal Virgins.

For the verb cf. P Oxy II. 237[ii.16] (A.D. 186) παρα-καταθέμενός τε τὸ ἀργύριον, "placing money on deposit," and BGU I. 326[ii.16] (A.D. 194) (= *Chrest.* II. p. 365) τῇ τε πίστι [α]ὐτῆς παρακατατίθομαι (*l.* παρακατατίθεμαι).

παράκειμαι.

For παράκειμαι, "lie to my hand," "am present," as in Rom 7[18.21], we may compare P Oxy III. 530[17 ff.] (ii/A.D.) where a son writes to his mother with reference to certain payments – εἰ πλεῖον δέ μοι παρέκει[το], πάλιν σοι ἀπεστάλ-κειν, καὶ τοῦτο πέ[μ]πων κέχρημαι, "if I had had more, I would have forwarded a further sum ; I have borrowed to send even this" (Edd.). Striking is the Christian prayer of iv/v A.D. written "in large rude uncials," P Oxy VII. 1058 –

> Ὁ θ εὸ\ς τῶν παρακει-
> μένων σταυρῶν,
> βοήθησον τὸν δο·
> ῦλόν σου Ἀπφουᾶν.
> ἀμήν.

"O God of the crosses that are laid upon us, help thy servant Apphouas. Amen" (Ed.). Cf. also *Kaibel* 703[3] (ii/iii A.D.) γαία πατρὶς ἢ παράκειμαι. Preisigke *Wörterbuch* s.v. gives a large number of Ptolemaic exx. of the word, e.g. P Tebt I. 61(*b*)[132] (B.C. 118–7) διὰ τὸ[ν ὄ]μβρον τῶν παρακειμένων ὑδάτων.

For a new trans. use of the verb = "bring in," "adduce," cf. P Fai 15[35] (B.C. 120) ἠρώτησεν τὸν Ἑρμίαν εἴ τινα ἀπόδειξιν παράκειται, P Tor I. 1[vi.4] (B.C. 116) παρακεῖσθαι αὐτὸν τὴν συνχώρησιν, and see Mayser *Gr.* II. i. p. 88.

παράκλησις.

For the primary meaning "appeal," "exhortation" (as in 1 Thess 2[3], 2 Cor 8[4]) cf. P Grenf I. 32[10] (B.C. 102) δι[ὰ τ]ὰς ἡμῶν παρακλήσεις, with reference to the "appeals" made to allow three soldiers to come to a certain spot, and P Tebt II. 392[26] (A.D. 134–5) of the insertion of a name in an agreement of indemnity at the instance of others—κα[τ]ὰ παράκλησιν γέγραπται αὐτῶν. See also the late P Flor III. 323[5] (A.D. 525) δεή]σεις καὶ παρακλή[σ]εις προσ[ε]νήνοχά σοι, and from the inscrr. *Syll* 552 (= [3]695)[12] (after B.C. 120) κατευχὴν καὶ παράκλησιν παντὸς τοῦ πλήθους ποιεῖσ[θαι.

On the semi-technical use of παράκλησις in Lk 2[25] with reference to the coming of the Messiah see Dalman *Words*, p. 109 f., and on the similar meaning "comfort" (not "invocation" as Hort *Ecclesia* p. 55) in Ac 9[31] see Swete *Holy Spirit in the NT* p. 96 f. As against the derivation of Βαρνάβας = υἱὸς παρακλήσεως, see s.v. Βαρνάβας.

παράκλητος.

orig. "one called in" to support, hence "advocate," "pleader," "a friend of the accused person, called to speak to his character, or otherwise enlist the sympathy of the judges" (Field *Notes*, p. 102). For the history of the word, which in the NT is confined to the Johannine writings, though the idea is present in Paul (Rom 8[26.34]), see the excellent summary by Hastings in *D.B.* iii. p. 665 ff. : cf. Lightfoot *On a Fresh Revision*[3] p. 56 ff., Zahn *Introd.* i.

p. 64 f., and Bauer *Joh.* p. 137 ff. (in *HZNT*). Useful reff. to the work of the "advocate" in the Hellenistic world will be found in Deissmann *LAE*, p. 340, where stress is rightly laid on the borrowing of the word in Heb. and Aramaic as evidence of its popular use.

The word is found in a very illiterate letter of ii/A.D., BGU II. 601[12] εὖ οὖν ποιήσῃς γράψον μοι περὶ τῆς οἰκίας, ὅτι τι ἔπραξας, καὶ τὸν ἀραβῶνα τοῦ Σαραπίωνος πάρακλος (*l.* παράκλητος) δέδωκα αὐτῷ, καὶ γράψον μοι περὶ τῆς ἀπα[= ὁ γραφῆς. In the previous sentence the writer says she has deposited in Demeter's temple καλαμεσιτὰ ἀσπ(= φ αλίσματα ("bonds written with a pen"?). Does she mean παρακληθεῖσα by her παράκλ(ητ)ος, i.e. "on being summoned"?

The negative of the verbal occurs in *OGIS* 248[25] (B.C. 175–161) "that the Demos (of Athens) may . . . show that it honours those who benefit itself and its friends ἀπαρακλή-τους," i.e. "uninvited."

παρακοή,

orig. "a failing to hear," "a hearing amiss" (*inauria*), and later active "disobedience" (*inobedientia*), as in Rom 5[19], where it is opposed to ὑπακοή. Cf. Trench *Syn.* p. 227 and see s.v. παρακούω. Two Byz. exx. of the subst. are found in P Lond IV. 1345[23], 1393[12] (cited by Preisigke *Wörterbuch* s.v.).

παρακολουθέω.

This important verb is used with various *nuances* of meaning which are closely related, and raise some interesting points of NT interpretation.

(1) Thus in the *v.l.* παρακολουθήσει for ἀκολουθήσει in [Mk] 16[17] the literal meaning "accompany," "follow closely" passes into the meaning "result," as may be illustrated by PSI III. 168[21] (B.C. 118) where it is stated that owing to the breaking down of a dyke οὐ κατὰ μικρὸν ἐλάττωμα παρακολουθεῖν τοῖς βασιλικοῖς: cf. P Rein 18[15] (B.C. 108) ὧν χάριν οὐκ ὀλί[γα] μοι βλάβη δι᾽ αὐτὸν παρηκολούθησεν, similarly *ib.* 19[12] (B.C. 108) and BGU IV. 1123[12] (time of Augustus), P Strass I. 22[10] (iii/A.D.) ἂν ἀλλαχόσε νομὴ παρακολουθήσῃ ἔχοντός τινος ἀφορμήν, P Lond 113 1[18] (vi/A.D.) (= I. p. 202) ἐδέησεν ταύτην τὴν ἔγγραφον ὁμολογίαν τῆς διαλύσεως μεταξὺ αὐτῶν παρακο-λουθῆσαι, and P Oxy VI. 942[2] (vi/vii A.D.) πάνυ δὲ ἡμᾶς ἠδίκησεν ἡ ἀδελφική σου λαμπρ(ότης) μηδὲν ἡμῖν σημάνασα τῶν παρακολουθησάντων, "we were much displeased with your brotherly excellency for not explaining to us any of the consequences" (Edd.). See also P Tebt I. 28[2] (*c.* B.C. 114) τῶν παρηκολουθηκότων ἐμποδι[σμὸν τῆ]ς καθ᾽ [ἡμᾶς] ἀσχολία[ς, "the hindrances placed in the way of the performance of our work" (Edd.).

(2) In Lk 1[3] the word is often understood = "investigate," as pointing to the evangelist's careful research into the facts he describes. And for this meaning we thought (*Exp.* VII. x. p. 286 f.) that we had found a good ex. in P Far 46[19] (= *UPZ* i. p. 338) (B.C. 152) where Apollonius appeals to his brother Ptolemaeus to examine personally into his grievance against a third party: νομίζω γὰρ μάλιστα τῶν ἄλλων παρακολουθήσαντά σε τῇι ἀληθείαι πικρότερον

προσενεχθήσεσθ' αὐτῶι, "for I think that you above all others when you have investigated the truth will deal more severely with him." But Cadbury in an elaborate article (*Exp* VIII. xxiv. p. 406), to which we are much indebted, points out that "Apollonius is not appealing for investigation, but is asking Ptolemaeus to summon the offending person to trial," adding that he will summon no other than Ptolemaeus as witness, seeing that of all concerned he is most "cognizant of the truth of the case." The verb, that is, "refers not to future inquiry but to past first-hand knowledge," a sense which, as Cadbury points out, may be further illustrated by such passages as PSI IV. 411³ (iii/B.C.) ὅπως οὖν παρακολουθῶν καὶ σὺ πρὸς ταῦτα ἐξαγάγῃς τοὺς λόγους γέγραφά σοι, and P Lond 23³⁶ (B.C. 158-7) (= *UPZ* i. p. 154) τῆς πρὸς Σώστρατον γραμματέα γεγραμένης ἐπιστολῆς τἀντίγραφον ὑποτετάχαμεν, ὅπως παρακολουθῇς. Add also *OGIS* 335¹⁴ (ii/i B.C.), where there are unfortunately many gaps—ὅτι οὐ͏κ ἐ͏ν τῶι παρόν[τι κα]ιρῶι μόνον οὐδ[ὲ . . . .]αὐτῶν, [ἀλλὰ] ἐκ παλαιω[ν χρ]όνων π[α]ρηκο[λούθησαν ἧι. . . . . εἰς τὸν ἡμέτερον δ]ῆμον ἔχ[ο]υσι προθυμίαι, and the subst. in M. Anton. iii 1 where we are exhorted to "press forward," διὰ τὸ τὴν ἐννόησιν τῶν πραγμάτων καὶ τὴν παρακολούθησιν προαπολήγειν, "because our insight into facts and our close touch of them is gradually ceasing even before we die" (Haines).

In view then of these passages we seem to be justified in understanding that Luke comes before us in his Preface not as one "having investigated" all his facts afresh, but as one "having acquired familiarity" with them, "having become cognizant" of them, for long (ἄνωθεν), and having so kept in touch with them, that his witness is practically contemporary witness.

In addition to Cadbury's *Exp* art. reference should be made to his "Commentary on the Preface of Luke" in Appendix C to *The Beginnings of Christianity* (edited by Jackson and Lake), Vol. ii. (1922), p. 489 ff., and to the useful list of articles and monographs dealing with the Preface, which will be found there.

(3) If then we are justified in taking παρακολουθέω in Lk 1² in the sense "am familiar with," may not this help us in the two passages in the Pastoral Epp., 1 Tim 4⁶, 2 Tim 3¹⁰, in which it occurs? In these the verb is usually taken as = "follow" a standard or rule of conduct, but with this there should at least be associated the prior idea of *familiarity with* the facts or truths, which lead to the conduct spoken of. In this connexion the following citations may prove helpful—P Tebt I. 6¹⁰ (B.C. 140-139) ὅπως παρακο[λουθήσας τῆι μεγίστηι σπο]υδῆι μηθὲν τῶν φροντίδος παραλίπη[ις (with reference to an ordinance previously referred to), *Syll* 664 (= ³ 718)⁹ (B.C. 98-7) ἐμφανίζου[σιν παρ]ηκολουθηκέναι αὐτὰς τοῖς ὑπ[ὸ τοῦ] δήμου ἐψηφισμέ]νοις πε]ρὶ τούτων πᾶσι, *ib.* 652 (= ³ 885)³² (c. A.D. 220) οἵ τε ἔφ[ηβοι] παρακολουθοῦντας τῆι περὶ τὸ θεῖον τῆς πόλεω[ς] θεραπείαι, and c. acc. *ib.* 790 (= ³ 1157)⁹⁰ (c. B.C. 100?) ὅπως πα[ρα]κολ[ουθῶσι οἱ παραγινόμενο]ι πάντες τὰ δεδογμένα, and *OGIS* 257¹⁷ (B.C. 125-96) ὅπως δὲ καὶ τὰ συγχωρηθέντα παρα]κολουθῆι, καλῶς ἔχειν [ἐκρίναμεν ἐπιστεῖλαί σοι (with Dittenberger's note). Thus meaning of παρακολουθέω is very common in Hellenistic philosophical writing, e.g. Epict. i. 7. 33, ii. 24. 19, both times c. dat.: cf. also 2 Macc 9²⁷ *v.l.*

παρακούω.

For παρακούω, "hear without heeding," "ignore," as in LXX, Mt 18¹⁷, Mk 5³⁶, cf. the end of a letter P Hib I. 170 (B.C. 247) (= Witkowski², p. 27) φρόντισον δέ, ὅπως μηκέτι ἀπὸ τούτων παρακούσει ἡμῶν, ἵνα μὴ ἀντὶ φιλίας ἔχθραν [ποιώ]μεθα, P Par 63¹³⁰ (B.C. 164) (= P Petr III. p. 28) πεῖραν λαμβάνειν τῶν ἐξακολουθού(=ό)των ἐπιτίμων τοῖς παρακούουσί τινος τῶν μετὰ σπουδῆς [ἐ]νθυμουμένων, where the verb means simply "ignore," as against Mahaffy's "wilfully misinterpret," and P Flor II. 148⁹ (A.D. 266-7) ἐὰν δέ τις τούτων μου τῶν γραμμάτων παρακούσῃ, οὐ συνοίσει αὐτῷ, "if any one of them pays no heed to these my letters, it will not go well with him."

See also for a stronger sense, as in LXX Isai 65¹², *Pap. Magique de Paris* 3037 διὰ τὸ παρακούειν αὐτόν, "because of his (Pharaoh's) refusal to hear," and *Syll* 256 (= ³ 557)²⁴ (c. B.C. 207 6) ὡς δὲ ἐπιβ[α]λόμενοι παρη[κο]ύσθησα[ν, "were refused": similarly *Test. xii. patr.* Dan. ii. 3. and for the meaning "disobey" see Musonius p. 82³. The verb is discussed by Field *Notes*, p. 28.

παρακύπτω.

In accordance with its derivation this verb suggests primarily looking at something not immediately in the line of vision, which may be seen e.g. by stretching or stooping, and, "when used figuratively, it commonly implies a rapid and cursory glance, never the contrary" (Hort *ad* 1 Pet 1¹²; see also his note on Jas 1²⁵). An instructive ex. is P Oxy III. 475²³ (A.D. 182) where a slave, anxious to catch a glimpse of castanet-players in the court below, is described as—βουληθεὶς ἀπὸ τοῦ δώματος τῆς αὐτῆς οἰκίας παρακύψαι: cf. Jn 20¹¹, Ev. Petr. 11. The verb is also found in P Lips I. 29¹⁰ (a will—A.D. 295) μηδὲ παρακ[ύ]π[τ]ειν ᾧτινιοῦν πράγμα[τ]ι δια[φ]έρον[τ]ί μοι. Παρακύπτω is discussed by Field *Notes* pp. 80 f., 235 f., and Abbott *Joh. Voc.* p. 300 ff. Ὑπερκύπτω occurs in *Syll* 802 (= ³ 1168)⁹¹ (c. B.C. 320) ὑπερέκυπτε εἰς τὸ ἄβατον. See also *s.vv.* κύπτω, ἀνακύπτω, κατακύπτω, and Epict. i. 1. 16 (cited by Sharp *Epict.* p. 75).

παραλαμβάνω

is the usual expression for receiving anything but money, for which ἀπέχω (aor. ἔσχον) is regularly used. Its correlative, as in the NT, is παραδίδωμι: thus *Syll* 588 (c. B.C. 180), a long account of ἀναθήματα in the Temple of Apollo at Delos, begins τάδε παρελάβομεν ἐν τῶι ναῶι τοῦ Ἀπόλλωνος παρὰ ἱεροποιῶν . . . καὶ παρέδομεν τοῖς μεθ' ἑαυτοὺς ἱεροποιοῖς. Cf. also the illiterate P Oxy IV. 742²ff. (B.C. 2) (= Witkowski², p. 127 f.) παράλαβε παρὰ Πόθου τὸν κάλαμ[ο]ν πανα[ρ](=ό)θμωι . . . ἀπόστειλόν μ[ο]ι πόσας δέσμας παρείληφες (for form, *Proleg.* p. 52) . . . παράδος δέ τινι τῶν φίλων ἀριθμῶ αὐτάς, "receive from Pothus the reeds all together, send me word how many bundles you have received, and deliver a few of them (see *s.v.* παραδίδωμι) to one of our friends."

Wilcken *Ostr.* i. p. 109 quotes a few instances of ἔλαβον in receipts with its correlative παρέλαβον in one place: on the relation of παρέλαβον to ἔλαβον in Jn 1¹² see *Proleg.* p. 115.

Other exx. of the verb are P Fay 123¹³ (c. A.D. 100)

παραλάβωμεν τὸ ἐλάδιον λυ(=οι)πὸν ἐὰν δόξῃ σοι, "let us get from him the rest of the oil if you agree" (Edd.), P Tebt II. 300²⁷ (A.D. 116–7) παρειλήφαμεν τὸ [βιβλίδιον, "we have received the account," and P Strass I. 45⁶⁴ (A.D. 312) παρελάβαμεν τὸ ἐνγεγραμμένον μέτρον τοῦ πυροῦ καὶ κριθῆς ὡς πρόκιται, "we received the registered amount of wheat and barley as agreed." With Jn 14³ Deissmann (*LAE* p. 169) compares an ancient epistolary formula: δόξα . . . τῷ . . . θεῷ . . . τὴν ψυχὴν ἡνίκα συμφέρει παραλαμβάνοντι.

The form παρελάβοσαν in 2 Thess 3⁶ ℵ* AD* has received increasing attestation since Moulton's note in *Proleg.* p. 52, and for the intruded nasal in παραλήμψομαι (Jn 14³), see the exx. in Mayser *Gr.* p. 194 f. P Amh II. 35¹⁵ (B.C. 132) shows ἐπὶ τὴν παράλημψιν τῶν ἐκφορίων, "for the collection of the rents"; cf. P Ryl II. 83³ (A.D. 138–161) π]ρὸς παράλημψ[ιν καὶ] καταγωγὴν βιβλί[ων, "for the receiving and forwarding of the accounts." For παραλημπτής see Preisigke *Fachwörter s.v.*: the μ is wanting in the "badly written and ill-spelled" receipt issued by "the receivers of public clothing"—οἱ . . . παραληπταὶ δημοσίο(υ) ἱματισμοῦ (P Ryl II. 189¹—A.D. 128).

παραλέγομαι.

For the meaning "coast along" in Ac 27⁸, Field (*Notes*, p. 143 f.) cites Diod. Sic. xiii. 3 κἀκεῖθεν ἤδη παρελέγοντο τὴν Ἰταλίαν, xiv. 55 αἱ δὲ τριήρεις ἔπλευσαν εἰς τὴν Λιβύην, παρελέγοντο δὲ τὴν γῆν. In BGU II. 665ⁱⁱ·¹⁴ (i/A.D.) ἐνετείλατο γὰρ θέων παρα[λ]έγων, the verb seems to refer to casual, incidental speech.

παράλιος,

"by the sea" (Lk 6¹⁷): cf. *Syll* 408 (= ³ 468)¹ (B.C. 244–3) στρατηγὸς ἐπὶ τὴν χώραν τὴν παραλίαν. According to Herwerden (*Lex. s.v.*) ἡ παραλία = ἡ πάραλος (ναῦς sc.) occurs rather frequently in Attic inscrr.

παραλλαγή.

The special meaning of a periodic "change" of a heavenly body which this word has in its only NT occurrence (Jas 1¹⁷), is illustrated by Hort *ad l.* from Dion Cass. lxxvi. 13, where it is said of the Emperor Severus in the North of Scotland —τήν τε τοῦ ἡλίου παράλλαξιν καὶ τὸ τῶν ἡμερῶν, τῶν τε νύκτων καὶ τῶν θερινῶν καὶ τῶν χειμερινῶν μέγεθος ἀκριβέστατα κατεφώρασεν. In Aristeas 75 παραλλαγή is used of stones arranged alternately—λίθων ἑτέρων παρ' ἑτέρους, τοῖς γένεσι παραλλαγὴν ἐχόντων. For the verb cf. Preisigke 4047¹ (love-charm—iii/A.D.) εἰς τὸ παραλλαγῆναι τὴν ψυχὴν αὐτῆς, Theophr. *H.P.* v. i. 3 αἱ πέψεις τῶν καρπῶν παραλλάττουσι, "times of ripeness vary."

παραλογίζομαι.

The first meaning "cheat in reckoning" which Hort (*ad* Jas 1²²) finds in this word is well illustrated by *OGIS* 665¹⁶ (A.D. 48) δαπάνας ἀδίκους καὶ παραλογισ[θείσ]ας ("fraudulently reckoned"). For the verb = "cheat," "delude," in general we may cite P Magd 29⁵ (B.C. 218) παραλελόγισταί με, P Amh II. 35¹² (B.C. 132) παραλογισάμενος τοὺς παρ' ἡμῶν γεωργούς. In P Oxy I. 34 *verso*ⁱⁱ·⁹ ((A.D. 127) ἐπεὶ

ὑπεύθυνός ἐστιν ὡς παραλογίσασθαί τι βουληθεὶς τῶν δεόντων, the reference is to a keeper of a state library, who had shown a willingness to "make a wrong use of" certain documents. Cf. Col 2⁴, where the verb points to drawing an erroneous conclusion from the reasoning submitted.

The subst. παραλογισμός seems always to point to *wilful* error; see e.g. P Lond 24²⁶ (B.C. 163) (= I. p. 32, *UPZ* i. p. 118) ἐφ' οἷς διαπέπρακται ἐπὶ παραλογισμῷ, "what he had carried through in a deceitful manner" P Oxy VIII. 1103⁵ (A.D. 360) τῶν νεολέκτων τῶν στρατευθέντων ὑφ' ἡμῶν ἐκ παραλογισμοῦ ἀνενεγκόντων ὡς μὴ πληρωθέντων τοῦ συνφώνου τοῦ πρὸς αὐτούς, "the new levies raised by us for military service had falsely represented themselves as not having received the sum agreed upon with them" (Ed.): cf. Aristeas 250 where womankind is said to be subject to sudden changes of opinion διὰ παραλογισμοῦ, "through fallacious reasoning." For παραλογεία cf. P Amh II. 33¹⁵ (c. B.C. 157) ἀδ.κημάτω[ν] καὶ παραλογειῶν σίτου τε καὶ χαλκοῦ, "misdeeds and peculations of both corn and money" (Edd.).

παραλυτικός.

For this rare word cf. Vett. Val. pp. 110²⁴, 127²¹. Παράλυτος is found in Artem. p. 244² ὁ ἐξ αὐτῆς γεννώμενος παράλυτος ἐγένετο, cf. *ib.*⁵

παραλύω.

For the literal sense "loose," "set free," cf. PSI IV. 435⁹ (B.C. 258–7) (as restored by Deissmann, *LO*⁴, p. 121) ἐμοῦ δὲ π[α]ρ[α]καλέσαντος τὸν θεὸν Σάραπιν,] ὅπως ἄμ με παραλύσῃ τοῦ ἐνταῦθα [ἔργο]ν, *Syll* 226 (= ³ 495)¹⁷ (c. B.C. 230) ἐξ ὧν ἀπέλυσε μὲν τὴμ πόλιν ὀφειλημάτων, παρέλυσε δὲ τόκων. The subst. παράλυσις occurs in Artem. p. 263²⁴.

παραμένω.

"remain beside," "stand by," is common: e.g. BGU IV. 1097¹⁵ (time of Claudius or Nero) οὐχο (= οὐκ) ὀλιγωρῶ ἀλλὰ εὐψυχοῦσα πα[ρα]μένω, P Ryl II. 234¹⁷ (ii/A.D.) εἰ βούλει παραμεῖναί με ἐνθάδε μετὰ τῶν ἀνθρώπων, P Oxy I. 120¹³ (iv/A.D.) ἀποστίλον μοί τινα . . . παραμένοντά μοι ἄχρις ἂν γνῶ πῶς τὰ κατ' αἰμαὶ ἀποτίθαιται (*l.* ἐμὲ ἀποτίθεται), "send someone to stay with me until I know the position of my affairs" (Edd.), *ib.* IX. 1222⁴ (iv/A.D.) παραμεῖναι τῇ ἀπετήσῃ (*l.* ἀπαιτήσει), "to stay for the collection."

In P Flor I. 44¹² (A.D. 158) parents offer in lieu of interest for a loan the services of their son παραμένοντα τῷ [Δ]ημητρ[ί]ῳ κ[αὶ ποιοῦν]τα τὰ ἐπιτασσόμενα αὐτ[ῷ. Vitelli notes that "παραμένειν (cf. παραμονή) is a common euphemism for *serve*": he quotes the will of Gregory Nazianzen, αὐτὴ παραμείνασα τὰς κόρας μέχρι τοῦ τῆς ζωῆς αὐτῆς χρόνου. Such a *nuance* would heighten the force of Phil 1²⁵, and still more that of Jas 1²⁵. For other exx. cf. P Petr III. 2²¹ (B.C. 236), where a man in his Will sets free certain slaves ἐάμ μοι παραμείνω[σ]ιν ἕ'ως ἂν ἐγὼ ζῶι, "if they remain with me as long as I live," BGU IV. 1126⁹ (B.C. 8) where a barmaid comes under the obligation ἐπὶ χρόνον ἔτη τρία . . . παραμένειν, "that she shall remain for the space of three years," in the beer-shop, in discharge of certain debts, P Tebt II. 384²¹ (contract of apprenticeship to a weaver—A.D. 10) παρεξόμεθα τὸν ἀδελφὸν ὑμῶν (l. ἡμῶν) Πασίωνα π[αραμέ]νοντα αὐτῷ ἐνιαυτὸν ἕνα, "we will produce our brother Pasion to remain with him (the weaver) for one year," P Oxy IV. 724¹³ (A.D. 155) παραμενεῖ δέ σ[ο]ι μετὰ [τὸ]ν χρό[νον] ὅσας ἐὰν ἀργήσῃ ἡμέρας ἢ μῆνας, where it is provided that an apprentice shall "remain" with his master for as many days or months as he may have played truant during his apprenticeship, and from the inscr. Syll 850⁵ (B.C. 173–2) παραμεινάτω δὲ παρὰ Ἀμύνταν Σωτήριχος ἔτη ὀκτὼ ἀνενκλήτως, of a slave, and ib. 840⁹ (= ³ 1200²⁴) (B.C. 101–100) ἀφῆκεν ἐλεύθερον παραμείναντα αὐτῷ τὸν τᾶς ζωᾶς χρόνον, of a slave boy manumitted, but to stay with his master as long as he lives. The service is clearly free: Vitelli's "euphemism" must not be pressed too far.

In late Greek παραμένω has come to mean "remain alive," cf. Schmid, Atticismus i. p. 132, who cites Dio Chrys. i 62. 8, al., and for the double compd. συνπαραμένω cf. PSI I. 64³ (i/B.C.?). The subst. παραμονή occurs in P Ryl II 128²⁰ (c A.D. 30) μὴ στοχασάμενος ὧν ὀφείλει μοι σὺν τῇ γυναικὶ αὐτοῦ κατὰ παραμονήν, "being oblivious of the debt which he and his wife owe me in accordance with a contract of engagement" (Edd.)—παραμονήν standing for παραμονῆς συγγραφήν: see also Preisigke Fachwörter s.v. Παραμονή = "durability" is found in P Lond V. 1764¹ (vi/A.D.) ἀναδεχόμενος τὴν τοῦ οἴνου καλλονὴν καὶ παραμονήν.

παραμυθέομαι.

The derived sense "comfort," "console," as in 1 Thess 5¹⁴, is well illustrated by the Christian letter written by a servant to his master regarding the illness of his mistress— P Oxy VI. 939²⁶ (iv/A.D.) (= Selections, p. 130) παραμυθούμ[εθα δὲ αὐτὴν ἑκάστης ὥρας ἐκδεχόμενοι τὴν [σ]ὴν ἄφιξιν, "but we are comforting her by hourly expecting your arrival." See also P Fay 19⁶ (ii/A.D.) παρα]μυθούμενον καὶ προτρέποντα, "comforting and tending" with reference to Antoninus' care of the Emperor Hadrian. The double compd. προσπαραμυθέομαι is found in Syll 312 (= ³ 762)²⁹ (c. B.C. 48) τὴν εὔνοιαν τοῦ [βασιλέ]ως πρὸς τὴν τ[ῆ]ς πόλεως σωτη[ρί]αν προσπαραμ[υθού]μενος.

παραμυθία

in its only occurrence in the NT, 1 Cor 14³ (cf. Sap 19¹²), refers to spiritual "encouragement" or "comfort." J. Weiss ad l. thinks that the idea may be derived from the tales which a mother or nurse relates to a child: cf. 1 Thess 2¹¹ and MGr παραμύθι, "fable," "tale." In the Christian P Oxy X. 1298² (iv/A.D.) the writer addresses his correspondent as—παραμυθίᾳ τῶν φίλων, "the consolation of his friends": cf. P Th ad 17¹⁷ (A.D. 352). In BGU IV. 1024⁷⁰ ¹²ff, a long legal report of the end of iv/A.D., we read of an old woman who sold her daughter πορνοβοσκῷ ἵνα δυνηθῶ διατραφῆναι. The girl is murdered, and the mother demands that the murderer παρασχεῖν αὐτῇ εἰς λόγον διατροφῶν ὀλ[ί]γην τινὰ τοῦ βίου παραμυθίαν. The word seems to have developed into the "comforts" of life, as with us—it is at any rate "consolation" in a money form that is suggested. Cf. the late use of the word = "gratuity"

(Lat. solatium) in P Lond V. 1785³ (vii/A.D.), and its technical use in monetary transactions, as illustrated in P Hamb I. p. 128 n¹.

παραμύθιον,

which in the NT is confined to Phil 2¹ (cf. Sap 3¹⁸), is explained by Moule (CG l' ad l.) as meaning "the converse which draws the mind aside (παρα —) from care; the aegrimoniae alloquium of Horace (Epod. xiii 18)," much in the sense of our "solace." Cf. P Flor III. 332¹⁹ (ii A.D.) when a mother writes to her son—γράφε μοι συνεχῶς περὶ τῆς ὑγίας ὑμῶν, ἵνα ἔχω παραμύθιον τῆς προελεύσεώς (" condition ") μου. In an epitaph of about Hadrian's time, Kaibel 051⁴, a son is described as πατρὸς καὶ μητρὸς . . παραμύθιον. An adj. παραμυθιακός (not in LS⁸) occurs in P Oxy XIV. 1631¹³ (contract for labour in a vineyard—A.D. 280) π[αραμυθιακὴ ἐργασία which the editors understand of keeping the vines well tended probably by digging, and quote Geop. iii. 5. 4 (May) παραμυθεῖται γὰρ ὁ σκάφος τὴν διψῶσαν ἄμπελον.

παρανομέω,

"act contrary to the law" (Ac 23³), is not so common as we might have expected, but see OGIS 765⁹ (ii/B.C.) οὐ μόνον δὲ ἐν τῆι χώραι εἰς το[ὺ]ς π]ο]λ[ί]τας παρε[ν]ό[μουν. Cf. also PSI IV. 330⁹ (B.C. 258–7) ἀδίκως μετὰ βίας παρανομηθείς, and the late P Oxy VIII. 1106⁹ (vi/A.D.), where certain lawbreakers are warned that a troop of soldiers may hand them over πρὸς τιμωρίαν ὧν ἂν παρανομῆσαι τολμήσειεν, "to be punished for any lawlessness upon which they may venture."

παρανομία.

In P Oxy VIII. 1119⁸ (A.D. 254) a petitioner complains of τὴν τόλμαν καὶ τὴν παρανομίαν, "the audacity and illegality," of a certain amphodogrammateus, and the same papyrus shows ¹⁰ ἐκ τοῦ παρανομήματος, "in consequence of his illegal action." For the adj. cf. Chrest. II. 372¹³ ²⁴ (ii/A.D.) τὸ ἀναγνωσθὲν δάνειον ἐκβάλλω ἐκ παρανόμου γάμου γενόμενον, and P Tebt II. 285⁴ (A.D. 239) where it is applied to "illegitimate" children. The adv. occurs in P Flor I. 36² (iv/A.D.) τὰ παρανόμως καὶ ῥιψο[κινδύνως ἐπ]ὶ τῶν τόπων τολμώμενα.

παραπικραίνω,

"provoke" (= παροργίζω, Hesych.), is regarded by Moffatt (ICC ad l Heb 3¹⁶) as a LXX coinage "to express 'rebellious' with a further sense of provoking or angering God." In Deut 32¹⁶ it is parallel to παροξύνω.

παραπικρασμός

occurs in the NT only in Heb 3⁸ ¹⁵ from Ps 94 (95)⁸: cf. Aq 1 Kingd 15²³, Sm Job 7¹¹, and Th Prov 17¹¹, and see Nestle's note in Exp T xxi. p. 94.

παραπίπτω.

The use of this verb in P Oxy I. 95³⁴ (A.D. 129) ἢν ἐὰν συμβῇ παραπεσεῖν ἢ ἄλλως πως διαφθαρ[ῆ]ναι. [. ., "if the terms of it (sc. a contract) should be broken or it in any other way be rendered invalid" (Edd.), supports the sinister meaning in Heb 6⁶ (cf. Sap 6⁹, 12²) : cf. also *Ostr.* 50³ (as amended *Ostr.* ii. p. 430—time of Trajan) **διὰ τὸ π(αρα)πεπτω κέναι) τὴν προτ(έραν) ἀποχ(ήν)**, where, in view of the foregoing ex., Wilcken (*Ostr.* i. pp. 78 f., 820) falls back on his earlier interpretation of the verb = "danebenfallen," "verlorengehen." See also P Oxy VIII. 1133¹² (A.D. 396) **διὰ τὸ παραπεπτοκένη** (*l.* **παραπεπτωκέναι) τὸ γρ(αμματ)ιόν σου καὶ μὴ εὑρίσκεσθαι δηλῶ τοῦτω**(= ο) **ἄκυρον**, "since your bond has been lost and cannot be found I declare that it is null" (Ed.), and BGU I. 214¹⁵ (A.D. 152) **διὰ τὸ φάσκειν παραπεπ[π]τωκέναι**.

For the meaning "fall into" c. dat. (as in 2 Macc 10⁴) cf. the Christian letter P Lond 1915² (c. A.D. 330–340) **τοῖ[ς ἐν . . . . .]ηφθονει συμφορᾳ παραπεσοῦσιν βοη[θεῖ]ν π[α]ρ[α]γγέλ⟨λ⟩εται ἡμῖν ὁ θεῖος λόγος**, "to those who have fallen into . . . misfortune the word of God exhorts us to give succour" (Bell) : cf.⁶ and *ib.* 1916²⁹. The verb occurs *ter* in Vett. Val., e.g. p. 73²⁵ **τῇ διανοίᾳ παραπίπτοντες**.

παραπλέω.

This NT ἅπ. εἰρ. = "sail past" (Ac 20¹⁶) is found in P Petr II. 45ⁱⁱ·² (B.C. 246) **παραπλεύσαντες εἰς ὅλους τοὺς [. . . . . .]υς ἀ[νέ]λαβον . . . .** [In P Lond 854¹ (i/ii A.D.) (= III. p. 206, *Selections*, p. 70) Wilcken (*Archiv* iv. p. 554) now reads **παρεπο[ιησ]άμην** for the editors' **παρεπ[λευσ]άμην**.] For the subst. see P Oxy III. 525¹ (early ii/A.D.) **ὁ παράπλους τοῦ Ἀνταιοπολίτου ὀχληρότατός ἐστιν**, "the voyage past the Antaeopolite nome is most troublesome."

παραπλήσιος.

P Par 63¹·⁹ (B.C. 164) (= P Petr III. p. 32) **τοὺς ἄλλ[ους] τοὺς παραπλησίους**, "other similar persons," P Tor 1. 1ⁱⁱⁱ·²² (B.C. 116) **καὶ τοῦ μὲν Φιλοκλέους παραπλήσια τοῖς διὰ τοῦ ὑπομνήματος προενεγκαμένου**, "Philocles brought forward matter similar to what was contained in the memorandum": cf. the adverbial use in Phil 2²⁷.

παραπλησίως.

With **παραπλησίως** in Heb 2¹⁴ = "similarly," *i.e.* almost "equally" or "also," Moffatt (*ICC ad l.*) compares Maxim. Tyr. vii. 2 **καὶ ἐστιν καὶ ὁ ἄρχων πόλεως μέρος, καὶ οἱ ἀρχόμενοι παραπλησίως**.

παραπορεύομαι.

"pass by" P Petr II. 13(5)³ (B.C. 258–253) **ο[ὐ]κ ἔδει μὲν οὖν σε παραπορεύεσθαι**, "you ought, indeed, not to have passed us by in this way" (Ed.), PSI IV. 354¹³ (B.C. 254–3) **ἐν τῶι παραπορεύεσθαι τὸν βασιλέα**: cf. Mt 27³⁹, *al.*

παράπτωμα.

In the royal ordinance P Tebt I. 5⁹¹ (B.C. 118) it is laid down that the measures used by revenue officers shall be tested, and that they must not exceed the government measure by more than the two [. .] allowed for errors, **τῶν εἰς τὰ παραπτώματα ἐ[π,]κεχωρημένω[ν . . β**: the editors suggest two hundredths of a **χοῖνιξ** A "slip" or "lapse" rather than a wilful "sin" is the connotation

suggested, and the same weakened sense may be found in P Lond 1917¹⁴ (c. A.D. 330–340) where the writer speaks of a **παράπτωμα διαβολική** (*sic*) into which he had fallen, but which, as Bell suggests, may not mean more than that he had stayed too long in the **κηπολάχανον** ("vegetable garden") mentioned just before. Needless to say, we do not propose to define the word in its NT occurrences from these instances : see Field *Notes*, p. 100 f.

παραρρέω.

For the verb used metaphorically "flow past," "drift away," in Heb 2¹, Moffatt (*ICC ad l.*) refers back to Prov 3²¹, and quotes Clem. *Paed.* III. xi. 58 **διὸ καὶ συστέλλειν χρὴ τὰς γυναῖκας κοσμίως καὶ περισφίγγειν** ("bind themselves round") **αἰδοῖ σώφρονι, μὴ παραρρυῶσι τῆς ἀληθείας διὰ χαυνότητα** ("vain conceit").

The subst. **παράρρυμα**, with reference apparently to a covering stretched along a ship's side for purposes of protection, is found in *Syll.*³ 969²⁶ (B.C. 347–6) **ποιήσει δὲ καὶ κιβωτοὺς τοῖς ἱστίοις καὶ τοῖς παραρρύμασιν τοῖς λευκοῖς**.

παράσημος.

Ramsay (*Luke*, p. 36 f.) describes the dat. absolute in Ac 28¹¹ **παρασήμῳ Διοσκούροις**, "with the Dioscuri as figure-head," as "the correct technical form, guaranteed by many examples in inscriptions," thus rendering unnecessary Blass's conjectural alteration **ᾧ ἦν παράσημον Διοσκούρων**. For this use of **παράσημος** cf. P Lond 256 *recto* (1)² (A.D. 15) (= II. p. 99) **ἧς παράσημος ἶβις**, P Tebt II. 486 (an account of corn-lading—ii/iii A.D.) **εἰς ἀνασείτησιν πλοί(ων) β. ὧν ἑνὸς μὲν οὐ παράσημον Θάλια . . καὶ λοιποῦ οὐ παράση[μον] γυμ[. .]**, and P Lond 948² (A.D. 236) (= III. p. 220) **κυβερνήτης ἰδίου πλοίου . . ἀσήμου**, where, however, the editor notes that the termination of **ἀσήμου** is doubtful, and has perhaps been altered. P Lille I. 22 and 23 (B.C. 221) concern two ships belonging to the Queen which have no figure-head (**ἀχάρακτος**) : see Wilcken *Archiv* v. p. 226.

In the Gnomon 104 (= BGU V. p. 31) the word is used in the general sense "mark" or "sign"—**μόνῳ προ . [.].αι ἐξὸν τὸ τῆς δικαιοσύνης παράσημον φορεῖν**. See also Aristeas 147, 158. For the verb **παρασημειόομαι** cf. P Oxy I. 34 *verso*ⁱⁱ·¹⁴ (A.D. 127) **παρασημιούσθ[ωσαν**, with reference to the "notes" made by the officials at the side of public documents, BGU I. 82¹¹ (A.D. 185) **παρασημιωσάμενος τὴν ἐπιστο[λή]ν**, "having taken note of the letter," and for the subst. cf. P Giss I. 40ⁱⁱ·⁶ (A.D. 212) **ἡ τῆς ἀτιμ[ί]ας παρασημεί[ω]σις**.

παρασκευάζω.

"prepare," "make ready." The verb is used in a causative sense in P Amh II. 145¹¹ (iv/v A.D.) **οὐδὲν ἕτε[ρον] παρασκευάζει πολλοὺς εἰδότας τὸ [σὸν] εἰς ἡμᾶς ἐνδιάθετον προσφεύγειν [μοι**, "no other reason causes many who know your feelings for me to come to me for help" (Edd.), PSI I. 50³ (iv/v A.D.) **σοι ἐδήλωσα ἵνα παρασκευάσῃς τοὺς σκυτέας** ("the leather workers") **τοῦ Ἀμμωνίου παρασχεῖν τῷ ταυρελάτῃ** ("the bull driver") **τὸ δέρμα**, and the late BGU I. 103³ (vi/vii A.D.) (= *Chrest.* I. p. 100) **καταξίωσον τούτους παρασκευάσε ἀμφοτέρους ἐλθῆν ἐνταῦθα**.

Other exx. of the verb are BGU IV. 1159[9] (time of Augustus) ἐργατῶν παρεσσκευακὼς (*l.* παρεσκευακὼς) μεγάλην, and from the inscrr. *Syll* 721 (= [3]662)[17] (B.C. 165-4) εὔχρηστον ἑαυτὸν παρασκευάζ[ειν, *ib.* 545 (= [3]707)[16] (ii/B.C.) τὰ πρὸς τὸν καιρὸν ἐμπείρως καὶ προθύμως παρεσκεύασεν. In 1 Cor 14[8] the mid. παρασκευάσεται is better understood intransitively " prepare," "make preparations," than reflexively "prepare himself" (AV, RV) : see *Proleg.* p. 156. Cf. also P Cairo Zen 59090[4] (B.C. 257) ὅπως τὰ πρὸς τὴν [παρουσίαν αὐτοῦ] παρασκευασώμεθα.

παρασκευή

is found in the general sense o. "preparation" in P Petr II. 45[iii 17] (B.C. 246) τοιαύτην παρασκευήν, P Strass I. 41[6] (A D. 250) αἰτοῦμε[ν δοθῆναι ἡμῖν ἡμέραν πρὸς] παρασκευὴν τῆς δίκης, and *Syll* 503 (= [3]506)[12] (c. B.C. 200) τῆ[ς τε τῶν σί]των παρ]ασκευῆς ἐφρόντισ[εν.

For παρασκευή as the technical designation for Friday (cf. MGr) see Didache viii. 1 ὑμεῖς δὲ νηστεύσατε τετράδα καὶ παρασκευήν. "but ye shall fast on the fourth day and the preparation day (Friday)": cf. Jos. *Antt.* XVI. 163 (vi. 2). The questions raised by the use of παρασκευή in the Synoptics and Jn lie outside our province, but see Abbott *Joh. Gr.* p. 92 f. Herwerden *Lex. s.v.* cites ἡ παρασκευή = *dies Veneris* from Clem. Al. p. 316, 15 (Sylb.).

παρατείνω,

"prolong" (Ac 20[7]): cf. P Oxy II 237 [viii. 10] (A.D. 186) παρατείνειν τὴν ἀπόδοσιν, "to postpone payment." The verb is used of distance in P Amh II. 68[31] (late i/A.D.) ἐφ' ὅσον παρατείνει νό(του), P Strass I. 29[2] (A.D. 289) λελον-χέναι . . . [τ]ῆς γῆς [ἐ]φ' ὅσον παρατίνουσιν νότον.

παρατηρέω,

For this verb "watch carefully," as in Mk 3[2] *al.*, cf. P Par 42[9] (B.C. 156) (= *UPZ* i. p. 318) χαριεῖ δὲ συμπαρα-στὰς ἡμῖν ἐν τοῖς λοιποῖς καὶ παρατηρήσας τοὺς ἀλάστορας, "you will do us a favour if for the future you will stand by us and keep a watchful eye on the criminals," and P Oxy VI. 937[16] (iii/A.D.) παραγγέλλω σοι ἵνα . . παραγγείλῃς πᾶσι τοῖς ἐκεῖ . . παρατηρεῖσθαι αὐτήν, "I bid you to bid all who are there to keep a strict watch on it (a stone bowl)."

In Lk 20[20] Field (*Notes*, p. 74) prefers to take the verb absolutely, "watching their opportunity.' Hobart p. 153 f. illustrates its use for close observation of an illness. *Tebt Ostr* 10 (ii/A D.) (= P Tebt II. p. 337) contains "a note of a number of days on which an unnamed person παρατηρῖ." For the verb with reference to the scrupulous (not "wrongful") observance of days and seasons in Gal 4[10], Burton (*ICC ad l.*) cites Dion Cass. xxxviii. 13 τὰ ἐκ τοῦ οὐρανοῦ γιγνόμενα παρατηρεῖν, and three passages from Josephus. See also Aristeas 246.

παρατήρησις,

"a watching for" (Lk 17[20]), like its verb, is claimed by Hobart p. 153 as a medical term. MGr παρατήρησι, "observation," "watchfulness."

παρατίθημι.

For παρατίθημι in its literal sense "place beside," "set before," as in Mk 6[41] *al.*, cf. P Oxy II. 326 (c. A.D. 45) π]αρατέθεικα τῆι μητρὶ Φιλου[μέν]ηι τὸ βροχίον τοῦ μέλανος ("the ink pot"). A literary ex. is afforded by Menander *Fragm.* 146 p. 43—

> ὡς ἀμυγδαλὰς
> ἐγὼ παρέθηκα,

"when I had set almonds before you." From this the transition is easy to "submit," "report," "bring forward by way of proof" (cf. Ac 17[3]), e.g. P Tor I. 1[ix. 28] (B.C. 116) ὧν καὶ παραθήσομαι ἀντίγραφα ἐπὶ τῆς καταστάσεως, P Oxy I. 33 *verso*[iii 12] (interview with an Emperor—late ii/A.D.) ὁ ἡβό[κατο]ς εὐθὺς δραμὼν παρέθετο [τῷ] κυρίῳ, "the veteran straightway ran and reported it to his lord," P Tebt II. 287[10] (A.D. 161-9) ἐνέτ[υ]χον τῷ στρατηγῷ π[α]ρατιθέμενοι . . . "they petitioned the strat gus adding a statement . . .," *ib.* 293[32] (A.D. 162) ταῦ]τ' ἐστὶν τὰ π[ερ]ὶ τοῦ γένους παρατεθέντα, "this is the evidence submitted concerning parentage" (Edd.), *ib.* 318[21] (A.D. 166) ἀκ[ο]λούθως οἷς παρεθ[έ]μην ἀντ[ιγρ]ά[φοις, "in accordance with the copies of the deeds submitted by me" (Edd.), PSI V. 447[16] (A.D. 167) ἅ τε παρέθοντο (cf. Blass-Debrunner, § 94. 1) δικαιώματα τῷ [πρ]ογεγρα(μμένῳ) Ἰουλίῳ, and P Thead 15[6] (A D. 280-281) τὴν δὲ βίαν πολλάκις παρεθέ-μεθα διὰ τῶν σῶν ὑπομνημάτων, where Jouguet (see his note *ad l.*) finds the meaning to be, "nous avons fait plusieurs fois consigner, à toutes fins utiles, le récit de ces actes dans ton journal." The subscription of *Chrest.* I. 26[33] (A.D. 156), for which Wilcken can find no exact parallel, runs—εἴ τινα δίκαια ἔχεις, τῷ στρατηγῷ παραθοῦ καὶ τὰ δέοντα ποιήσει.

The verb is common in connexion with the declaration and registration of claims on property, as when in P Oxy IV. 713 (A.D. 97) a claim of ownership addressed to the keepers of the records is headed—παρετέθ(η), "inserted in the register": cf. *ib.* II. 237[viii. 34] (A.D. 186) παρατιθέτωσαν δὲ καὶ αἱ γυναῖκες ταῖς ὑποστάσεσι τῶν ἀνδρῶν, "wives shall also insert copies in the property-statements of their husbands" (Edd.). For the mid. = "pledge," "deposit with another," see CPR I. 12[3] (A.D. 93) παρεθέμην σοι ἐνέχυρα περονείδων ("buckles"?) ζεῦγος, and the corresponding use of the subst. in P Oxy III. 533[9] (ii/iii A.D.) αἱ πρόσοδοί μου . . . παρὰ τῷ ταμείῳ ἐ[ν π]αραθέσει λογισθήτωσαν, and P Gen I. 44[24] (A.D. 260) διὰ τῆς παραθέσεως τῶν δραχμῶν.

Hence the thought of "commend" a person to the care of another, as in P Oxy XIV. 1663[3] (a letter of recommendation —ii/iii A.D.) Σωτῆρα . . . παρατίθεμαί σοι, and PSI I. 96[2] (v/A.D.) παραθέσθαι α[ὐτὸ]ν τοῖς πρωτοκ(ωμήταις ?): cf. Ac 14[23], 20[32], also Ps 30[6] (Lk 23[46]).

παρατυγχάνω,

"happen to be present," as in Ac 17[17] (cf. Field, *Notes* p. 125), may be illustrated from P Oxy I. 113[14] (ii/A.D.) χάριν ἔχω θεοῖς πᾶσιν γινώσκων [[ὅτι]] ὅτι μετέλαβον παρατετευχότα Πλουτίωνα εἰς τὸν Ὀξυρυγχείτην, "I thank all the gods to think that I came upon Plution in the Oxyrhynchite nome" (Edd.), *ib.* 76[11] (A.D. 179) πρὸς

καιρὸν παρατυγχάνων εἰς κώμην Νεμέρας, "happening at
the present time to be at the village of Nemerae" (Edd.).
The idea of "chance" is not necessarily implied, and is
often almost wholly wanting, see e.g. P Tebt II. 303¹⁵
(A.D. 176–180) ὅπως παρατύχῃ εἰς τὸν . . . διαλογισμόν,
"that he may be present at the assize," ib. 276¹⁵ (ii/iii A.D.)
ἡ δὲ Ἀφροδίτ]η παρατυγχάνουσα τῷ τοῦ ["Ἀρεως, "Venus
being in conjunction with Mars," P Lips I. 29¹² (A.D. 295)
οὐ β[ού]λ[ομ]αι αὐτὴν παρατ[υ]χ[εῖ]ν τοῖς ἡμετέροις
[πράγμασιν, "I do not wish that she should mix herself
up in our affairs," and Preisigke 421¹² (iii/A.D.) (= Deissmann LAE p. 372) ἵν' [ο]ὖν εἰδῇς καὶ παρατύχῃς . . . .
"in order that you may know and be present (at a festal
procession)."

For a new subst. παράτευξις = "intercourse," "personal
relations," see the early Christian letter P Amh I. 3 (a)ⁱⁱⁱ⁻²¹
(between A.D. 264 and 282) (= Deissmann LAE p. 195)
ὡς ἡμᾶς [ὠφέλησε πα]ράτευξιν πάπα, "as he hath profited
us by dealings with the Papas."

παραυτίκα.

P Oxy II. 237ᵛⁱⁱⁱ⁻¹⁴ (A.D. 186) μὴ παραυτίκα ἀρνη-
σάμενος ὀφείλειν, "not having immediately denied the
claim."

Hence the adjectival use in 2 Cor 4¹⁷ = "for the moment";
but cf. Field Notes p. 183. For the form πάραυτα (παρ'
αὐτά) see P Tebt I. 13¹⁵ (B.C. 114) πάραυτα δὲ συμψή-
σαντες ἀπὸ τῶν προγεγρ(αμμένων) ἕνα, "whereupon we
immediately seized one of the above-mentioned persons"
(Edd.), and cf. Mayser Gr. p. 486.

παραφέρω

is found in pass. in Heb 13⁹, Jude 12, = "am turned
aside." Similarly Field (Notes, p. 39) renders the act.
παρένεγκε in Mk 14³⁶ "turn aside, cause (or suffer) to pass
by,' and supports the rendering by various passages from
Plutarch, e.g. Vit. Pelop. ix. τοῦ δὲ Φυλλίδου παραφέροντος
τὸν λόγον, "letting the remark pass without notice." We
may add Plut. Arat. 43 τότε μὲν οὖν παρήνεγκε τὸ ῥηθέν,
"he let what was said pass without regarding it," which the
editor quotes for a similar meaning in P Eleph 11⁵ (B.C.
223–222) σὺ δὲ ἕως τοῦ νῦν παρενήν[οχ]ας ἐ[. . . . .]η
πάνθ' ὑπερθέμενος.

Παρήνεγκα καὶ παρέδωκα is a common formula in tax
receipts (Wilcken Archiv iii. p. 395): cf. also the interesting
papyrus dealing with the apotheosis of Apis, P Gen I. 36¹⁵
(A.D. 170) (= Chrest. I. p. 113) παρήνεγκα καὶ παρέδωκα
ὑπὲρ τοῦ προκειμένου ἱεροῦ ὑπὲρ ἀποθεώσεως "Ἀπιδος
Θαώϊτος βυσσοῦ στολίσματος πήχεις δέκα, and BGU III.
974⁵ (A.D. 380) (= Chrest. I. p. 500 f.) παρήνεγκα καὶ
παραδέδωκα ὑμῖν εἰς εὐθένειαν τῶν . . . στρατιωτῶν ἀπὸ
δηληγατίονος κανόνος . . . οἴνου ξέστας δισχειλίους.

For the meaning "bring forward," "produce," cf.
P Amh II 81¹² (A.D. 247) παρενενκεῖν αὐτὸν τοὺς β[ο]ηθοὺς
αὐτοῦ, and P Flor II. 127⁵ (A.D. 256) where a man writes
that, in view of his arrival, the bath should be heated, and
the wood for burning kept in readiness—καὶ δοκοὺς εἰς αὐτὸ
παρενεχθῆναι. See also the late P Oxy I. 131¹⁴ (vi/vii A.D.),
135²⁶ (A.D. 579), and cf. Aristeas 316.

παραφρονέω.

With 2 Cor 11²³ παραφρονῶν λαλῶ, "I am talking like
a madman," we may compare the account, written at earliest
about A.D. 200, of the trial of an Alexandrian gymnasiarch
before the Emperor Claudius, Chrest. I. 14ⁱⁱⁱ⁻¹⁴, where the
condemned man scornfully asks—τοί(=τί) γὰρ ἄλλο ἔχομεν
εἰ (= ἢ) παρα[φ]ρονοῦντι βασιλεῖ τόπον διδόναι; "for what
else is there to do except to give way to a mad king?"
Παραφροσύνη is similarly attributed to the Emperor Gaius
Caligula in Jos. Antt. XIX. 284 (v. 2) τοῦ διὰ τὴν πολλὴν
ἀπάνοιαν καὶ παραφροσύνην, ὅτι μὴ παραβῆναι ἠθέλησεν
τὸ Ἰουδαίων ἔθνος τὴν πάτριον θρησκείαν καὶ θεὸν προσαγορεύειν αὐτόν, ταπεινώσαντος αὐτούς.

παραφρονία.

We can cite no instance of this form as in 2 Pet 2¹⁶ (v.l.
παραφροσύνη), but for παραφρόνησις (as in LXX Zach 12⁴)
cf. BGU I. 310²¹ (Byz.) π[α]ραφρονήσεως.

παραχειμάζω,

"spend the winter" (Ac 27¹², 28¹¹, al.): cf. OGIS 544³⁰
(ii/A.D.) ἀποδεξάμεν[όν] τε στρατεύματα τὰ παραχειμά-
σα[ν]τα ἐν τῇ πόλει.

παραχειμασία,

"a wintering" (Ac 27¹²): cf. Syll 342 (= ³762)¹⁶ (A.D. 48)
κατὰ τὴν Γαΐου] Ἀντωνίου παραχειμασίαν.

παραχρῆμα,

"immediately": P Par 46¹⁸ (B.C. 152) (= UPZ i. p. 338)
παραχρῆμα παρέσομαι πρός σε, and P Fay 92¹⁸ (A.D. 126)
παραχρῆμα διὰ χιρός, "directly from hand to hand" (Edd.),
a common phrase in monetary transactions, see further
Berger Strafklauseln p. 78 f. The word is associated with
delay for a month in such a passage as P Amh II. 49² (B.C.
108) ἀποτεισάτωσαν ἐν τῷ ἐχομένωι μην(ὶ) ἡμιόλιον
παραχρῆμα. On the other hand notice the emphatic εὐθὺς
καὶ παραχρῆμα in P Strass I. 35¹⁷ (iv/v A.D.): cf. Dalman
Worte, p. 28 f.

πάρδαλις,

"a leopard" (Rev 13²): cf. the varied assortment of
animals in the charm P Lond I. 121⁷⁸³ (iii/A.D.) (= I. p. 109)
αἴλουρος (weasel) λέων πάρδαλις μυγαλός (shrewmouse).
For πάρδαλις as a type of roguery, see Headlam's note ad
Herodas III. 89.

παρεδρεύω,

lit. "have my seat beside." For the religious connotation
of the verb in its only NT occurrence 1 Cor 9¹³, we may cite
Syll 552 (= ³695)²⁷ (ii/B.C.) γινέσθω δὲ καὶ γυναικῶν ἔξοδος
εἰς τὸ ἱερὸν καὶ παρεδρευέτωσαν ἐν τῶι ἱερῶι τὴν ἐπιβάλλουσαν τιμὴν καὶ παρεδρείαν ποιούμεναι τῆς θεοῦ: cf.
ib. 521 (= ³717)³⁵ (B.C. 100–99) where the ephebi at Athens
are commended because παρήδρευσαν . . . ταῖς ἐκκλησ[ίαις
ἁπά]σαις ἐν ὅπλοις—they "attended" the meetings in arms,
although they were not allowed yet to speak or vote. The
Lat. adsideo is a close equivalent.

The newly discovered "historian" of the Trojan War,

Dictys the Cretan, tells us, P Tebt II 268⁷² (early iii/A.D.) τῇ δὲ πυρᾷ παρήδρευσεν Αἴ[ας, "Ajax kept vigil by the pyre" of Patroclus. See also the magic P Lond 121⁸⁹² (iii/A.D.) (= I. p. 112) πέμψον ἄγγελόν σου ἐκ τῶν παρε-δρευώ(=ό)ντων σου, and OGIS 473⁶ (A.D. 37 41) ταμίας ὁ παρεδρεύσας τὴν πρώτην ἐξάμηνον Φιλόδημος Ἑστιαί[ου. In Aristeas 81 τοῖς δὲ τεχνίταις παρήδρευεν ἐπιμελῶς, Thackeray renders "would carefully supervise the crafts-men." The subst. πάρεδρος, "assessor" (cf. Sap 9⁴), appears in OGIS 185⁹ (i/B.C.), where see Dittenberger's note.

πάρειμι

= (1) "am present": P Lille I. 12¹ (B.C. 250–249) ἐμνήσθην σοι καὶ παρόντι περὶ τῶν ρ̄ (ἀρουρῶν), "I have recalled to you in your presence (i.e by word of mouth) the affair of the hundred arourae," P Lond 42²² (B.C. 168) (= I. p. 30, UPZ i. p 3:o, Selections, p 10) ὡς ἔτι[s] σοῦ παρόντος πάντων ἐπεδεόμην, "while you were still at home I went short altogether," P Amh II 66³⁵ (A.D. 124) παρεῖναι τοὺς μαρτυρῆσαι δυναμένους τὸ[ν] φόν[ο]ν, "that there were present persons able to witness to the murder" (Edd.), and P Oxy VII 1070⁵⁰ (iii/A D.) κατ᾽ ὄψιν παρών, "when with you in person" (Ed.); (2) "have come": P Par 46¹⁸ (B.C. 153) (= UPZ i. p 338) παραχρῆμα παρέσομαι πρὸς σέ, P Ryl II. 77⁴ (A.D. 192) παρὼν εἶπ(εν), "came forward and said" Field (Notes, p. 65) prefers this latter meaning in Lk 13¹: see also Mt 26⁵⁰ al.

We may add a few exx. of prepositional phrases—P Tebt II. 423¹⁴ (early iii/A.D.) ἐν τῷ παρόντι, "at present," P Ryl II. 108⁷ (A.D. 110–1) ἐπὶ τοῦ παρόντος, "for the present," P Fay 122²¹ (c. A.D. 100) (as in Olsson Papyrus-briefe, p. 179) κατὰ παρό[ντα, "at present," P Giss I. 47¹⁰ (time of Hadrian) πρὸς τὸ παρόν, "with regard to the present" (cf. Heb 12¹¹) cf also P Ryl II. 109¹⁰ (A.D. 235) ἐπὶ παρόντι σοι διὰ βοηθοῦ, "you being represented by an assistant" (Edd.).

παρεισάγω,

lit. "bring in from the side," hence "introduce" (2 Pet 2¹): cf. P Tor I 1ᵛⁱⁱⁱ·⁴ (B.C. 116) προεφέρετο ἀλλότριον εἶναι τὸ παρεισαγόμενον ὑπ᾽ αὐτοῦ, where παρα- does not convey any idea of secrecy or stealth, cf. s.v. παρεισφέρω. This applies also to the verb in Aristeas 20 εἴ τινες προῆσαν ἢ μετὰ ταῦτα παρεισήχθησαν εἰς τὴν βασιλείαν, "any who were there before or had since been introduced into the kingdom" (Thackeray), and in Apol. Aristides 8.

παρείσακτος.

Like παρεισάγω, this word in its only occurrence in the NT, Gal 2⁴, need not necessarily have a sinister reference, but may simply mean that the brethren are "alien" to the body into which they have introduced themselves: see Burton ad Gal l.c. and cf. Suid. παρείσακτον· ἀλλότριον.

παρεισδύω.

The subst. occurs in P Strass I 22³⁰ (iii/A.D.) οὐδεμίαν παρείσδυσιν ἔχεις, ἡ γὰρ γ[υν]ὴ ἐν τῇ νομῇ γέγονεν πολλῷ χρόνῳ, "you cannot creep in, for the woman has been in possession for a long time": the sense is just that of Jude 4

παρεισεδύησαν (2 aor. pass. for 2 aor. act., Blass Gr. p. 43) γάρ τινες ἄνθρωποι. See also Vett. Val. p. 345⁸, and Linde Epic. p. 26.

παρεισέρχομαι,

lit. "come in from the side." The use of the verb in Rom 5²⁰ "come in to the side of a state of things already existing" (SH) shows that the idea of stealth is not neces-sarily present : cf. Vett. Val. p. 357⁹ τοῦτο δέ μοι παρεισῆλ-θεν περὶ τῆς προκειμένης ἀγωγῆς. On the other hand with Gal 2⁴ "who sneaked in to spy out our freedom" Burton (ICC ad l.) compares such a passage as Luc. Asin. 15 εἰ λύκος παρεισέλθοι.

The corr. double compd. παρεξέρχομαι occurs in the late P Lond 1075¹⁷ (vii/A.D.) (= III. p. 282) ἵνα μὴ τοῦ λοιπο[ῦ] παρεξέλθῃ τοῦ σκοποῦ ὑμῶν.

παρεισφέρω.

With the phrase in 2 Pet 1⁵ σπουδὴν πᾶσαν παρεισενέγ-καντες Deissmann compares the almost similar expression in the i/A.D Decree of Stratonicaea, CIG II. 2715 a¹⁰ πᾶσαν σπουδὴν ἰσφέρεσθαι, as pointing, to say the least, to a common use by the two writers "of the familiar forms and formulae of religious emotion"; see BS p. 360 ff., and especially p. 367 The phrase εἰσφέρομαι σπουδήν in late Greek is fully illustrated by Mayor ad 2 Pet l.c., but his claim that the addition of παρα- alters the sense can hardly be pressed in view of the above citation. See, however, the nuance "smuggle" in P Tebt I. 38¹² (B.C. 113) (= Chrest. I. p. 363) χάριν τῶν παρεισφερόντων εἰς τὴν κώμην καὶ παραπωλούντων Κολ[πιτ]ικὸν ἔλαιον καὶ κίκι, "owing to the smuggling into the village and illicit sale of Colpitic and castor oil " (Edd.).

παρεκτός.

This rare word used as a prep. c. gen. "apart from," "except" (quater in NT) is seen in Test. xii. patr. Zab i. 4 παρεκτὸς ἐννοίας. Didache vi. 1 παρεκτὸς Θεοῦ. For the form παρέξ cf. PSI I. 5³⁺²¹ (census return—A.D. 132 3) παρὲξ τῶν προγ(εγραμμένων), "apart from the persons written above," and P Oxy VIII. 1133⁹ (A.D. 396) τοὺς τέσσαρας χρυσίνους παρὲξ μυριάδων ἑξακοσίο(= ω ν, "four golden solidi less 600 myriads."

παρεμβάλλω.

The military use of παρεμβάλλω, which is common in the LXX = "encamp" (cf. Anz Subsidia, p. 311 f.) appears in Lk 19⁴³ ℵ (περιβαλοῦσιν AB) in the sense "cast up," "raise up." With this may be compared the technical use in P Fay 91⁶ (A.D. 99), where we have παρεμβάλλουσα used absolutely to describe a woman who puts olives into the press: similarly P Ryl II. 128⁹ (c. A.D. 30). See also P Oxy I. 129⁸ (vi/A.D.) ὅτι εἰς ἔκθεσμα πράγματά τινα παρεμβάλλεις ἑαυτόν, "that you are giving yourself over to lawless deeds" (Edd.).

παρεμβολή,

originally "insertion," "interpolation," came as early as Theophilus (fr. 9) or Diphilus (fr. 57) to be used of a

"camp" or "encampment." [Phryn. ed. Lob. p. 377
describes the word as δεινῶς Μακεδονικόν, but see Thumb
Hellen. p. 224.] It is so used in the LXX and *decies* in the
NT with slightly varying connotations.

Similar exx. from the papyri are BGU IV. 1097⁶ (time of
Claudius or Nero) ἀπῆλθεν εἰς παρεμβολὴν στρατεύσασθαι,
ib. I. 140⁵ (time of Hadrian) προε[τέθη ἥδε ἡ ἐπιστολ(ὴ)? ἐν
τῇ] π(α)ρεμβολ(ῇ) τῆ[ς] χειμασία[ς λεγιῶνο(ς) τρίτης, P Oxy
XII. 1481⁹ (a soldier to his mother— ii/A.D.) διότι ἐν παρεμ-
βολῇ ἡμί (*l.* εἰμί, and from the inscr. *Syll* 318 (= ³700)²⁰
(Thessalonica —B.C. 117) μετεπέμψατο εἰς τὴν παρενβολήν.
See also Kennedy *Sources*, p. 15

Interesting reff. to the great παρεμβολή near the suburb
of Nicopolis will be found in the letter on the Meletian
schism, P Lond 1914¹⁰ *al.* (A.D. 335?). For the village
named Παρεμβολή in the Arsinoite nome, see P Ryl II.
339 (A.D. 130), and the editor's note to P Hamb I. 2³
(A.D. 59).

παρενοχλέω.

For παρενοχλέω, "annoy," "trouble," c. dat. as in
Ac 15¹⁹, its only occurrence in the NT, cf. P Gen I. 31¹
(A.D. 145–6) Διόσκορος . . ἑκάστοτέ σοι κατ' ἐπιδημίαν
παρενοχλῶν. The more usual constr. in the Κοινή is c. acc.,
e.g. P Vat C¹⁷ (B.C. 161) (= *UPZ* i. p. 207) τόν τε βασιλέα
δι' ἐντεύξεων παρηνωχλήκαμεν, P Tebt I. 32³ (B.C. 145?)
στόχασαι οὖν ὅπως μ(ὴ) παρεν[ο]χλήσ[ῃς τὸν Ἀσ[κ-
ληπιάδην, *ib.* 34⁹ (c. B.C. 100) μὴ παρανοχλεί⟨σ⟩θω ὑπ'
οὐδενός, and the quaint injunction to certain village officials
P Lond 379² (iii/A.D.?) (= II. p. 162) μὴ παρενοχ-
λῖ(= εῖ)τε ἀκαιρί (*l.* ἀκαιρί, "do not give trouble at
inconvenient seasons." From the inscrr we may cite OGIS
139¹⁵ (B.C. 146–116) γράψαι Λόχωι . . . μὴ παρενοχλεῖν
ἡμᾶς πρὸς ταῦτα, and the new literary reference in
Menander's Θυρωρός, Demiańczuk, *Suppl. Com.* p. 56 οὐκ
ἀδελφός, οὐκ ἀδελφὴ παρενοχλήσει.

The verbal ἀπαρενόχλητος is found in P Tor I. 1ᵛⁱⁱⁱ ²³ (B.C.
116), P Oxy II. 286¹⁰ (A.D. 82) (see *s.v.* παρέχω), and BGU
II. 638¹³ (A.D. 143).

παρεπίδημος.

The sense of "a sojourner," or "a stranger" settled in a
particular district only for a time, which is confined in the
LXX to Gen 23⁴, Ps 38(39)¹², and in the NT to 1 Pet 1¹
(see Hort's note), 2¹¹, Heb 11¹³, can be well authenticated
in our documents. Thus in a Will, P Petr III. 7¹⁵ (B.C.
238–7), a bequest is made to a certain Apollonius—παρεπίδημον ὃς καὶ Συριστὶ Ἰωνάθας [καλεῖται, and in P Tor II.
8¹³ (B.C. 118) παρεπιδημοῦντες (*peregrini*) and κατοικοῦντες
(*incolae*) are distinguished. Cf. also OGIS 383¹⁵⁰ (mid.
i.B.C.) πλῆθος ἐπιχώριον καὶ παρεπίδημον, and Polyb. xxxii.
22. 4.

The corr. verb is common, e.g. P Petr II. 13(19)¹² (mid.
iii/B.C.) ὅπως τ[οῦτό]ν γε τὸν χρόνον παρεπιδημῇς, "in
order that for this season at least you may sojourn with us"
(Ed.), BGU I. 113¹² (A.D. 143) βουλόμενος παρεπιδημεῖν
πρὸς καιρόν. P Oxy III. 473² (A.D. 138–160) a decree in
honour of a gymnasiarch by the magistrates and people of
Oxyrhynchus together with the "resident" Roman and
Alexandrian citizens—Ῥ]ωμαίων καὶ Ἀλεξανδρέων τοῖς

παρεπιδημοῦσι, and Aristeas 110 προσέταξε μὴ πλέον
εἴκοσιν ἡμερῶν παρεπιδημεῖν. With Heb 11¹³ we may
compare *Is.PE* i. 22³⁷ τῶν παρεπιδημούντων ξένων. See
further Hicks *CR* i. p. 6, Deissmann *BS* p. 149, Wilcken
Papyruskunde I. i. pp. 49, 55, and Jouguet *Vie municipale*
p. 92 ff.

παρέρχομαι.

"pass by": P Giss I. 54¹¹ (iv/v A.D.) (= *Chrest.* I. p. 498)
πολλοὶ (*l.* πολλὰ) πλοῖα παρῆλθαν γομώμενα: cf. Lk 18³⁷.
For the constr. with διά as in Mt 8²⁸, cf. P Amh II. 154²
(vi/vii A.D.) μὴ παρελθεῖν τινα διὰ τῶν ἐποικείων αὐτοῦ,
"that no one should pass by the way of its farmsteads."
The verb is used in connexion with *time* in P Magd 25³ (B.C.
221) παρεληλυθότος τοῦ χρόν[ο]υ, and the Imperial edict
P Fay 20⁶ (iii/iv A.D.) ἐκ τοῦ παρελθόντος χρόνου: cf.
Mt 14¹⁵, where Wellhausen draws attention to the force of
παρα- in composition, and understands παρῆλθεν as "vor-
gerückt," *i.e.* "advanced," see *Proleg.* p. 247. For the
meaning "arrive," cf. P Gen I. 72¹ (ii/iii A.D.) εὐθέως οὖν
ἀρ[γ]ύριον ἑτοίμασον, ἵνα παρερχόμενος εὕρω πρ[ὸ] ἐμοῦ.

In other instances, such as Lk 12³⁷, παρέρχομαι, when
used participially with a finite verb, means little more than
our "come and . . ." In P Oxy I. 38¹¹ (A.D. 49–50) the
verb is used of an "application" to the strategus—καθὰ
π[α]ρῆλθον ἐπὶ τοῦ γενομένου τοῦ νομοῦ στρατηγοῦ Πασίωνος. See also *s.v.* ἀντιπαρέρχομαι.

πάρεσις.

Wetstein *ad* Rom 3²⁵ cites Dion. Hal. *Antt. Rom.* vii. 37
ὁλοσχερῆ πάρεσιν οὐχ εὕροντο, τὴν δὲ εἰς χρόνον ἀναβολὴν
ἔλαβον, in support of the meaning "remission of punishment," and Lietzmann (*HZNT ad l.*) adds a reference to
Xenophon *Hipparch.* vii. 10. To these two exx. of this
important NT ἅπ. εἰρ. Deissmann (*BS* p. 266) now supplies
a possible third. It occurs in BGU II. 624²¹ (time of Diocletian), where πάρεσει implies (temporary) "remission of
debt," cf. ¹⁹ ἱερᾶς μὴ ἀμέλει ὀφιλῆ[ς. If this is correct, it
may be taken as supporting Field's contention (*Notes*,
p. 153f.) that while both ἄφεσις and πάρεσις imply
remission, the former is more commonly used of the remission
or forgiveness of a sin, the latter of a debt: but see *s.v.*
ἄφεσις.

παρέχω.

This common verb appears both in the act. and mid. =
"provide," "supply": (1) act.—P Eleph 1⁴ (marriage-contract –B.C. 311–0) (= *Selections*, p. 2) παρεχέτω δὲ Ἡρακλείδης Δημητρίαι ὅσα προσήκει γυναικὶ ἐλευθέραι πάντα, "let
Heraclides provide for Demetria all things that are fitting
for a freeborn woman," P Amh II. 48⁹ (B.C. 106) παρεχέτω
οἶνον μόνιμον, "let him provide wine that will keep," BGU
II. 531ⁱⁱ ²⁰ (A.D. 70–80) ἐὰν δὲ ἀστοχήσῃς, [αἰω]νίαν μοι
λοίπην [π]αρέχιν μέλλις, "if you forget me, you will cause
me endless grief," P Oxy VI. 937²¹ (iii/A.D.) εἴ τινος χρήζει
ὁ Ἀντινοεὶς παρασχήσεις (for fut. cf. *Proleg.* p. 170 f.)
αὐτῷ, "if the man from Antinoopolis wants anything provide
him with it" (Edd.), P Gen I. 75¹⁸ (iii/iv A.D.) τόπον δὲ
αὐτοῖς παράσχες ποῦ μίνωσιν, and the Christian P Oxy
XIV. 1682⁶ (iv/A.D.) ἡ μὲν τοῦ θεοῦ πρόνοια παρέξει τὸ

μετὰ ὁλοκληρίας σε τὰ οἰκεῖα ἀπολαβεῖν, "may the divine providence grant that you may be restored in security to your home" (Edd.). For the phrase κόπους παρέχειν τινί, as in Mt 26[10] *al.*, see *s.v.* κόπος and add BGU III. 815[2] (ii/A.D.) ὁ προ[κου]ράτωρ μου κόπους [τινὰ]ς πα[ρ]έχῃ περὶ τῆς [δο]χῆς, and more particularly for Gal 6[17] the Leiden papyrus cited *s.v.* βαστάζω.

(2) mid.—P Hal I. 8[4] (B.C. 232) τὰς χρείας παρέχεσθαι, P Lond 1166[14] (A.D. 42) (= III. p. 105) χωρὶς τοῦ παρασχέσθαι τοὺς ὁμολοῦντας (*l.* ὁμολογοῦντας) τὴν καῦσιν καθὼς προκεῖται ἔτι, with reference to the heating of a gymnasium, P Oxy II. 275[26] (A.D. 66) (= *Selections*, p. 57) where it is provided that a father at the expiry of a contract of apprenticeship παρέξεται, "shall produce," his son to make good any days on which he may have played truant (ἀτακτήσῃ), *ib.* 286[9] (A.D. 82) παρέξεσθαι ἐμέ τε καὶ τὴν μητέρα μου Θαῆσιν ἀπαρενοχλήτους καὶ ἀνεισπράκτους κατὰ πάντα τρόπον, "would guarantee me and my mother against any trouble or liability whatsoever" (Edd.), BGU III. 846[11] (ii/A.D.) (= *Selections*, p. 94) οἶδα τί [ποτ'] αἰμαυτῷ παρέσχημαι, "I know what I have brought upon myself."

This prepares us for the further meaning "show" or "present oneself," as in Tit 2[7]: e.g. P Par 63[viii. 15] (B.C. 164) ἐμαυτὸν ἀμεμψιμοίρητον παρέσχημαι, P Oxy II. 281[13] (A.D. 20-50) παντελῶς ὄντα ἀνέγκλητον ἐματὴν ἐν ἁπάσει παρειχόμην, "I showed myself completely blameless in every respect," and the marriage contract CPR I. 27[14] (A.D. 190) αὐτῆς δὲ τῆς Θαϊσαρίου ἀμεμπτον καὶ ἀκατηγόρη[τον ἑαυτὴν παρ]εχομένη(= ς) ἐν τῇ συμβιώσει. Similarly in the inscrr. *Magn* 86[13] (ii/B.C.) πρό[θυμο]ν ἑα[υτὸν πρὸς τ]ὰ π[α]ρα[καλούμ]ενα παρέχεται, *Priene* 65[6] (c. B.C. 190) εὔνου[ν ἑαυτὸν] καὶ [ἐ]κτενῆ παρεχόμεν[ος διετέλει, and the exx. in Herwerden *Lex. s.v.* and Deissmann *BS* p. 254.

The technical use of παρέχω, "pay," is seen in P Petr I. 16(2)[13] (B.C. 230) where, with reference to the repayment of a sum of money, the person liable comes under an agreement—ἐὰν δὲ μὴ διαγράψω [καὶ] μὴ παρασχῶμαι τὸ λοιπὸν ἐμφανὲς ἀποτείσω ἡμιόλιον, "if the whole be not paid then I will pay 50 per cent. over and above the money (as fine)" (Ed.). So frequently in ostraca receipts, e.g. *Ostr* 1012[4] (end ii/A.D.) παρέσχες εἰς στρ(ατηγικὰς) χρείας εἴλης Ἡρακλειανῆς ἀχύ(ρου) . . . εἰς γ(όμον) ᾱ : cf. *Ostr.* i. p. 107 f.

παρηγορία,

"consolation" (Col 4[11]): cf. the two sepulchral inscrr. *Kaibel* 204[12] (i/B.C.)—

Οὐκ ἔπιον Λήθης Ἀιδωνίδος ἔσχατον ὕδωρ,
ὡς σὲ παρηγορίην κἄν φθιμένοισιν ἔχω,

and *ib.* 502[4] (iii/iv A.D.) βουλὴ ταὐτὸν ἔπραξε παρη[γορίην νἱ]οῖο. For the verb see the pagan letter of consolation on the occasion of a death P Oxy I. 115[11] (ii/A.D.) (= *Selections*, p. 96) παρηγορεῖτε οὖν ἑαυτούς, *Syll*[3] 806[29] (A.D. 153) παρηγορῆσαι αὐτοῦ τά τε τέκνα καὶ τοὺς συγγενεῖς . . . φέριν συνμέτρως τὰ τῆς λύπης, and *Kaibel* 261[19] (ii/A.D.) τὸν βίον τρυφῇ παρηγόρησον. As an ex. of the reciprocal middle we may cite MGr νὰ παρηγορηθοῦμε, "that we may comfort one another."

παρθενία,

"virginity" (Lk 2[36]): PSI I. 41[5] (iv/A.D.) ἀνδρὶ Παγένει ᾧ συνήφθην ἐκ παρθενίας, *Syll* 567 (=[3] 983)[18] (ii/A.D.) ἀπὸ παρθενείας. See also the illustrations from late literary sources in Field *Notes*, p. 50. MGr παρθενιά.

παρθένος,

"maiden," "virgin": cf. P Ryl II. 125[23] (A.D. 28-9) διὰ τῆς ἑατοῦ θυγατρὸς παρθένου, an P Lond 983[4] (iv/A.D.) (= III. p. 229), where a man complains of abusive language addressed τῇ ἡμετέρᾳ συμβίῳ καὶ τῇ παρθένῳ μου θυγατρί. In *Kaibel* 565[3] (not later than ii/A.D.) παρθένος is a child of five years of age. For the rare fem. form ἡ παρθένη (cf. MGr παρθένα), Hatzidakis (*Einl.* p. 24) cites a papyrus published in the *Journal des Savants*, 1873, p. 100. In farm accounts, P Fay 102[30] (c. A.D. 105), payments are made for παρθέ(νων) λικνιζουσῶ(ν), "girls winnowing." For αἱ παρθένοι αἱ ἱεραί, see the citation from *Michel* 694 *s.v.* εἶτεν, and cf. W. M. Ramsay *Ann. of Brit. School at Athens* xviii. p. 58.

The masc. used of men who have not known women in Rev 14[4] may be paralleled from *CIG* IV. 8784*b*—

Σκεῦος θεουργὸν (cf. Ac 9[15]) συλλαλείτω παρθένῳ
βλάβης σκέπεσθαι δεσπότην Κωνσταντῖνον :

cf. also *Joseph and Asenath* 3 ἐστὶν δὲ οὗτος ὁ Ἰωσὴφ ἀνὴρ θεοσεβὴς καὶ σώφρων καὶ παρθένος, *ib.* 6 ἄσπασον τὸν ἀδελφόν σου, διότι καὶ αὐτὸς παρθένος.

The adj. παρθέν(ε)ιος is found in the illiterate P Ryl II. 435[2] (ii/A.D.) παρηγκελκά συ (*l.* παρήγγελκά σοι) ἄλλα (for accentuation, *Archiv* vi. p. 379) ἅπαξ ὅτι ἆρεν (*l.* ἆρον) τὰ παρθένειά σου τέκνα, "I have charged you more than once 'Take away your children born of a maiden'": cf. παρθενικός in P Lond 47[41] (ii/A.D.) (= I. p. 82) δάφνη παρθε[νι]κή. See also P Par 57[ii. 21] (B.C. 156) where for παρθένην Wilcken (*UPZ* i. p. 445) suggests παρθενικήν or παρθένειον with ζώνην understood. For different forms of the word used as proper names see Preisigke *Namenbuch*.

παρίημι,

"let pass," "omit" (Lk 11[42]), cf. P Giss I. 43[23] (ii/A.D.) μηδ[έν]α παρεικέναι ἀναπόγρα(φον), P Oxy IX. 1202[15] (A.D. 217) παρεί[κε]ν τὸν ἡμέτερον υἱόν—a father's complaint that his son's name had been omitted from a list of ephebi, and *Syll* 326 (= [3] 709)[28] (B.C. 107) οὐδένα δὲ χρόνον ἀργὸν παρείς. In P Oxy IV. 713[26] (A.D. 97) ἐκ τῆς Θρασυμάχου παρειμένης (*sc.* γῆς), παρειμένης is a technical term applied to land, perhaps, as the editors suggest, in the sense of "conceded to" or "abandoned": cf. now *ib.* XII. 1549[14 55] (A.D. 240), also P Hib I. 53[5] (B.C. 246) with the editors' note, and see Heb 12[12]. For the meaning "admit" we may cite Aristeas 173 παρειμένοι δ' εἰς τὴν αὐλὴν . . . ἠσπασάμεθα τὸν βασιλέα, "on being admitted to the court, we greeted the king."

παριστάνω, παρίστημι.

The trans. sense of this verb "place beside," "present," "produce," is well seen in its use in connexion with judicial proceedings, as when in P Ryl II. 94[11] (A.D. 14-37) the head and the secretary of a guild of weavers become sureties for the production of five of their number against whom proceedings were pending—ἐπάναγκον παραστήσι⟨ν⟩ σοι αὐτού⟨s⟩ ὁπηνίκα ἐὰν ἐρῇ (l. αἰρῇ) ἐκδικοῦντες τὰ διὰ τοῦ ὑπομνήματος Πανινούτιος, "it is incumbent on us to produce them for you whenever you choose, to answer the claims stated in the petition of Paninoutis" (Edd.) : cf. P Oxy II 2 9[14] (A.D. 23) ἐὰν δὲ μὴ παριστῶ ἐν τα[ῖς] προκειμέναις ἡμέρα⟨ι⟩s ἐκτείσω τὰ προκείμενα⟨ις⟩ τῶν χρυσίων μν[α]ιήων δύο ἀνυπερθέτως, "if I do not produce him (a prisoner for whom he had become surety) within the said number of days, I will pay the said two minae of gold without delay" (Edd.), P Amh II. 66[40] (A.D. 124) οἱ ὑπὸ σοῦ παρασ τ]αθέντες μάρτυρες ὡμολόγησαν τὸν φόνον ἐγνωκέναι, "the witnesses produced by you acknowledged that they knew of the murder" (Edd.), and P Oxy VI. 807[10] (A.D. 340) ἐπέθετο ἡμῖν ἡ ὑμῶν ἐμμέλια ὥστε Χωοῦν . . . ἀναζητῆσαι καὶ παραστῆσαι, "your grace required us to search out and produce Choous" (Edd.).

This judicial sense helps us in 1 Cor 8[8] βρῶμα δὲ ἡμᾶς οὐ παραστήσει τῷ θεῷ, "food will not affect our standing with God" in the Day of Judgment to which the fut. tense points. Cf. P Hal I. 1[218] (mid. iii/B.C.) with reference to the oath by race or descent, ἄλλον δ' ὅρκον μηδένα ἐξέστω ὀμνύναι μη[δ]ὲ ὁρκ[ίζ]ειν μηδὲ γενεὰν παρίστασθαι : with the editors' note p. 121.

For the verb in connexion with sacrifice, as in Rom 12[1], cf. Priene 113[40] (after B.C. 84) τάς τε θυσίας τὰς εἰθισμέ[ν]ας καὶ τ]ὰς πατρίους τοῖς τῆς πόλεως πα[ρ]αστήσειν θεοῖς, and Magn 98[47] (beg. ii/B.C.) παριστανέτωσαν δὲ καὶ οἱ οἰκονόμοι . . . ἱερεῖα τρία, [ἃ] θύσουσιν τῶι τε Διί . . . [This last is apparently the earliest inscriptional evidence as yet known for the form παριστάνω : cf. Thieme, p. 13.] See also Deissmann BS, p. 254.

The rendering "is ready" (for the reaper) which Swete prefers for παρέστηκεν in Mk 4[29] may be supported by P Petr III. 43(3)[15] (iii/B.C.) ἔτι δὲ [οὐ]κ ἀγνοεῖς ὥς σοι διελέγην περὶ τοῦ ση[σ]άμου καὶ κρότωνος [ὅ]τι παρέστηκεν, "further you are well aware how I told you in conversation that the sesame and croton are ready" : cf. P Lille I 8[5] (iii/B.C.) γεωργῶ γῆν βασιλικὴν (ἀρουρῶν) ρξ, καὶ ἡ γῆ παρέστηκεν.

The intrans. sense "appear" is seen in P Oxy XIV. 1642[2] (appointment of a representative—A.D. 289) ἀποσυν-ίστημί σε κατὰ ταῦτά μου τὰ γράμματα παραστῆναι παρὰ σοὶ ἐν τῷ Ὀξυρυγχείτῃ, "I appoint you by this my deed to appear at home in the Oxyrhynchite nome as my representative" (Edd.). For the literal sense "am standing by," "am at hand," as in Lk 19[24], cf. Aristeas 19.

For the subst. παράστασις cf. P Magd 22[4] (B.C. 221) καταπλεῦσαί με εἰς τὴν πόλιν ἐπὶ τὴν παράστασιν τὴν γε[νομ]ένην ἡμῶ[ν, "pour notre comparation," P Oxy VII. 1033[8] (A.D. 392) ἀναγκαζόμεθα δὲ συνεχῶς ἕνεκεν τῆς παραστάσεως διαφόρων προσώπων, "we are often called upon for the production of various persons" (Edd.). The reference to the happily completed building of the Temple of Artemis in Magn 100 a[12] (2nd half of ii/B.C.) θείας ἐπιπνοίας καὶ παραστάσεως γενομένης τῷ σύμπαντι πλήθει τοῦ πολιτεύματος εἰς τὴν ἀποκατάστασιν τοῦ ναοῦ might serve, as Thieme remarks (ZNTW vii. (1906), p. 265 f.) for the dedication of a Christian church at the present day.

Παρμενᾶς.

This proper name (Ac 6[5]), a pet form of Παρμενίδης (cf. Jannaris Gr. § 287), occurs in a wall-scratching in the Serapeum at Memphis. Preisigke 2480 Διονύσιον Παρμενᾶνος (l. -ᾶτος) τὸν ἀδελφὸν Εὔπρας.

πάροδος.

With this NT ἅπ. εἰρ. (1 Cor 16[7]), cf. PSI IV. 354[3] (B.C. 254–3) ἐστὶν δὲ ἐν παρόδωι. See also OGIS 544[19] (ii/A.D.) ἐν τῆι τῶν ὄχλων παρόδωι, with Dittenberger's note. The LXX use of the word "passer-by," "traveller" (e.g. 2 Kingd 12[4]), is found in an epigram of the Imperial period cited by Deissmann LAE p. 296, where an old man Chrysogonus is represented as

παντὶ λέγων παρό-
δῳ· πεῖνε, βλέπις
τὸ τέλος,

"saying to each passer-by, 'Drink, for thou seest the end'."

Cf. also Kaibel 236[9] f. (ii/i B.C.)—

μᾶλλον δὲ κλαύσας, πάροδε, τὴν ἐμὴν τύχην
βαῖν' οὗ φίλον σοι καὶ τύχοις ὅσων θέλεις,

"rather having bewailed, passer-by, my fate, go where it is pleasant for you, and may you obtain all that you wish!"

In an account of early ii/A.D., P Amh II. 126[4], there are included παροδίων (δραχμαὶ) ρ, and in P Lond 318[2] (A.D. 156–7), 330[5] (A.D. 164) (= II. p. 87 f.) παρόδιον (not in LS[8]) is understood by the editor as "a pass or permit to travel." For the adj. παρόδιος cf. P Tebt I. 45[23] (B.C. 113) τὴν παρόδιον θύραν, "the street door," and so ib. 47[14], and for the verb παροδεύω (as in Sap 1[8]) see Kaibel 810[11]—

μή με μάτην, ξεῖνοι, παροδεύετε, γειτνιόωσαν
πόντῳ καὶ Νύμφαις Κύπριδα καὶ Βρομίωι,

i.e. subsistite viatores fruituri quae ab mari, ab fonte, a Baccho vobis bona parata sunt (Ed.).

παροικέω.

lit. "dwell beside," comes to be used in late Greek in the sense of "dwell transitorily," as compared with "dwell permanently" (κατοικέω : see the reff. in Lightfoot Col.[2] p. 159. The word is thus very suitable to describe the pilgrim nature of the Christian Church in relation to the locality in which it is situated : cf. Clem. R. ad Cor. inscr. ἡ ἐκκλησία τοῦ θεοῦ ἡ παροικοῦσα Ῥώμην τῇ ἐκκλησίᾳ τοῦ θεοῦ τῇ παροικούσῃ Κόρινθον (with Lightfoot's note), Polycarp ad Phil. inscr. τῇ ἐκκλησίᾳ τοῦ θεοῦ τῇ παροικούσῃ Φιλίππους. See also Philo de conf. linguarum 78 (ed. Wendland) πατρίδα μὲν τὸν οὐράνιον χῶρον ἐν ᾧ πολιτεύονται, ξένην δὲ τὸν περίγειον ἐν ᾧ παρῴκησαν νομίζουσαι. For the verb in a broken context, see PSI VI. 677[2] (iii/B.C.).

παροικία.

"a sojourn" in the spiritual sense, as in 1 Pet 1[17], is found in the Christian IGSI 531[7] τούτου τοῦ βίου τὴν παροικίαν. See further Hort 1 Pet. p. 154 ff.

In Pss. Sol. 17¹⁹ τίμιον ἐν ὀφθαλμοῖς παροικίας ψυχὴ σεσωσμένη ἐξ αὐτῶν we have "perhaps the earliest instance of παροικία applied to a *community* temporarily sojourning in a strange land," which has the further interest of showing that this use of παροικία was Jewish, before it was adopted by the Christian Church (see Ryle and James *ad l.*). In P Lips I. 64³ (A.D. 368-9) the true reading is ἀπὸ τῆς πόλεως καὶ τῆς ἀγροικίας (not παροικίας): see *Chrest.* I. p. 333.

πάροικος.

Hicks (*CR* i. p. 5 f.) has shown that πάροικος, while never losing the idea of "a sojourner," "a stranger" (see *s.vv.* παροικέω, παροικία), is often found in the inscrr. in the sense of the classical μέτοικος to denote "a licensed sojourner" in a town, "whose protection and status were secured by the payment of a small tax," as contrasted with ξένος, a mere passing stranger (cf. 1 ph 2¹⁹). Add to Hicks's reff., as bringing out the mixed character of the population in Graeco-Roman towns, an inscr. from Priene (cited by Rouffiac, p. 45), *Priene* 113³⁵ ff. (after B.C. 84), where Zosimus promises to invite τούς τε πολίτας πάντας καὶ παροίκους καὶ κατοίκους καὶ Ῥωμαίους καὶ ξένους καὶ δούλους, and later is praised for offering them a festival, 42 ff. δειπνεῖν γὰρ τοὺς πο[λ]ίτας πάντας κατὰ φυλὰς καὶ τοὺς ἐφηβευκότας τῶν παροίκων καὶ κατοίκων καὶ Ῥωμαίους πάντας καὶ τοὺς παρεπιδημοῦντας Ἀθηναίων κτλ. See also OGIS 55²⁹ (B.C. 247-221) with Dittenberger's note, along with Deissmann *BS* p. 227 f. and Kennedy *Sources* p. 102.

παροιμία.

In accordance with its derivation from παρά and οἶμος, παροιμία denotes literally "by the way." Apart from 2 Pet 2²², it is found in the NT only in Jn (10⁶, 16²⁵·²⁹), where Abbott (*Joh. Voc.* p. 219 f.) understands it as a brief, general (rather than a dark) saying. See also T. K. Abbott *Essays* p. 82 ff., and Headlam on Herodas II. 61 ἐγὼ δ' ὅκως ἂν μὴ μακρηγορέων ὑμέας . . . τῇ παροιμίῃ τρύχω. "Not to beat about the bush and weary you with general remarks and allusions *by the way*, but to get on the *main road* and come to the point."

πάροινος.

"one given to too much wine," is found *bis* in the Pastorals (1 Tim 3³ Tit 1⁷). For the corr. verb cf. PSI IV. 352⁶ (B.C. 254-3), where Artemidorus complains to Zeno regarding certain companions ἐν οἴνωι γάρ εἰσιν καὶ ἐμ πόρναις διὰ παντός, and not only so but ἐπαρώνησάμ (for augment, cf. Cronert *Mem. Herc.* p. 209 n.¹) με . . καὶ εἰς αὐτά με ἤγαγον, "they have made me drunken and led me on to the same thing." He then asks Zeno's aid, ἵνα μὴ πάλιν συμβαίνηι μοι . . . παροινεῖσθαι. Cf. P Lond 1014²⁷ (A.D. 335?) ἡμάρτησα καὶ ἐπαρυνήθην ἐν τῇ νυκτὶ ὅτι τοὺς ἀδελφοὺς ὕβρισα, "I sinned and was drunken in the night, in that I maltreated the brethren" (Bell). This prepares us for the wider meaning "assault with drunken violence," as in P Petr III 32 (g) *recto* (b)⁷ (Ptol.) ἐπι παραγενόμενος καὶ παροινήσας ἡμᾶς ἀφείλετο τὰ κτήνη, and P Eleph 12² (B.C. 223-2) γεγράφαμεν Πλειστάρχωι

τῶι φυλακίτηι περὶ τῶν παροινησάντων σε ἀποθέσθαι αὐτοὺς εἰς τὴν φυλακήν. For the subst. see Artem. p. 60¹². ἕπεται γὰρ ἀεὶ τῇ μέθῃ παροινία.

παροίχομαι,

which connotes time "gone by" in Ac 14¹⁶, is used in a similar context in P Ryl II. 153³⁵ (A.D. 138-161) τοῦ παρῳχημένου χρόνου, and *Syll* 652 (=³ 885)⁵ (*c.* A.D. 220) διὰ τῶν παρῳχημένων [χρόνων. Παρῳχηκότα occurs in BGU I. 288² (time of Antoninus Pius) in a broken context.

παρομοιάζω,

"am somewhat similar to," is found in Biblical Greek only in Mt 23²⁷: see *s.v.* παρόμοιος.

παρόμοιος,

"somewhat similar," as defined by Pollux: ὁ γὰρ παρόμοιος παρ' ὀλίγον ὅμοιός ἐστιν. The word, which in Biblical Greek is confined to Mk 7¹³, is common in classical and late writers: see the citations in Wetstein *ad l.*

παροξύνομαι,

For παροξύνομαι, "provoke" *in malam partem*, as in 1 Cor 13⁵, we may cite PSI I. 41¹³ (iv/A.D.), where a woman complains that her husband is being provoked against her by her sister, παροξυνόμενος ὑπὸ τ[ῆ]ς ὁμογνησίας αὐτοῦ [ἀδελφῆς, and the fragmentary BGU II. 588⁷ (i/A.D.) ὁ ὑπ' ἀνθρώ[. . .] παροξυνθείς. The verb is used *in bonam partem* in OGIS 48¹² (iii/B.C.) ἐφ' ο[ἷς] παροξυνόμενοι οἱ νεώτεροι καὶ οἱ ἄλλοι π[ολῖτ]αι ο[ἱ] αἱρο[ύμενοι] βέλτιον π[ολιτεύεσθ]αι κτλ. See also Jos. *Antt.* XVI. 125 (iv. 4) παροξῦναι δὲ τὴν εὔνοιαν, Xen. *Mem.* iii. 3. 13 φιλοτιμία ἥπερ μάλιστα παροξύνει πρὸς τὰ καλὰ καὶ ἔντιμα, and the other exx. in Field *Notes*, p. 231.

παροξυσμός.

Like its verb, παροξυσμός is used both *in bonam* (Heb 10²⁴) and *in malam partem* (Ac 15³⁹). For its use medically see P Tebt II. 272⁶ (late ii/A.D.) ἐν τοῖς παροξυσμοῖς, "during the paroxysms," and Artem. p. 100¹⁰ τοῖς δὲ νοσοῦσι παροξυσμοὺς σημαίνει καὶ φλεγμονὰς . . .

παροργίζω,

"provoke to anger" (Eph 6⁴). Over the door of a Church of S. George at Zorava in Syria, which was formerly a pagan temple, the inscr. runs—ὅπου θεὸς παρωργίζετο, νῦν θεὸς ἐξευμενίζεται, "where God was provoked to anger, God now shows Himself gracious" (OGIS 610⁴—vi/A.D.).

παροργισμός

does not seem to occur outside Biblical Greek. In the LXX it is used as a rule with an active meaning "provocation," but in its only NT occurrence, Eph 4²⁶, it points rather to a state of provocation, "wrath": see Armitage Robinson *Eph. ad l.*

παροτρύνω,

"urge on," which is confined to Ac 13⁵⁰ in Biblical Greek, is cited by Hobart p. 225 for its medical associations, but it is by no means uncommon in a more general sense in late Greek, e.g. Jos. *Antt.* VII. 118 (vi. 1) παρώτρυναν τὸν βασιλέα λέγοντες κατασκόπους πεπομφέναι . . . .

παρουσία.

For παρουσία in the general sense of "presence," "arrival," as in the later books of the LXX (Judith 10[15], 2 Macc 8[12], *al.*), it is sufficient to cite P Oxy III. 486[15] (A.D. 131) ἡ ἐπιμ[έ]λεια τῶν ὑπὸ τοῦ ποτ[α]μοῦ παρασεσυρμένων χρῄζει μου τῆς παρουσία[ς, "the repair of what has been swept away by the river requires my presence" (Edd.), *ib.* XIV. 1608[25] (iii/A.D.) τὴν ὑμῶν παρουσίαν ἐγδεχόμεθα, "we await your presence," a man to his "brothers," *ib.* I. 118[32] (late iii/A.D.) οὐδὲν γὰρ ὄφελος ὑστερησάντων (*l.* ὑστερήσαντος) τῶν χρειωδῶν τῇ παρουσίᾳ αὐτοῦ, "it is no use if a person comes too late for what required his presence" (Edd.), and *ib.* VI. 903[15] (iv/A.D.), where a woman declares that her husband ὤμοσεν ἐπὶ παρουσίᾳ τῶν ἐπισκόπων καὶ τῶν ἀδελφῶν αὐτοῦ ὅτι ἀπεντεῦθεν οὐ μὴ κρύψω αὐτῇ <ν> πάσας μου τὰς κλεῖς, "swore in the presence of the bishops and of his own brothers, 'Henceforward I will not hide all my keys from her'" (Edd.).

What however, more especially concerns us in connexion with the NT usage of παρουσία is the quasi-technical force of the word from Ptolemaic times onwards to denote the "visit" of a King, Emperor, or other person in authority, the official character of the "visit" being further emphasized by the taxes or payments that were exacted to make preparations for it. Thus in P Petr II. 39(*e*)[18] (iii/B.C.) mention is made of contributions for a "crown" (στεφάνου) to be presented to the King on his "arrival" (παρουσίας), and in a letter of B.C. 264 or 227, P Grenf II. 14(*b*)[2], a certain Appenneus writes that he has prepared ἐπὶ τὴν παρουσίαν τὴν Χρυσίππου, "for the visit of Chrysippus" (the dioecetes) by laying in a number of birds for his consumption. Other exx. from the papyri are P Par 26[1. 18] (B.C. 163-2) (= *Selections*, p. 15), where the Serapeum Twins lay their grievances before King Ptolemy Philometor and Queen Cleopatra on the occasion of their royal visits to Memphis—καθ' ἃς ἐποείσθ' ἐν Μέμφει παρουσίας, and P Tebt I. 48[14] (*c.* B.C. 113) τὴν ἐπιγεγραμμένην πρὸς τὴν τοῦ βασιλέως παρουσίαν ἀγορὰν (πυροῦ) (ἀρταβῶν) π̄, "the 80 artabae of wheat for the supplies imposed in connexion with the King's visit" (Edd.).

From the inscrr. we may cite *Syll* 226 (=[3] 495)[8] (Olbia, *c.* B.C. 230) τήν τε παρουσίαν ἐμφανισάντων τοῦ βασιλέως, and *OGIS* 139[9] (B.C. 146-116) ἀναγκάζουσι ἡμᾶς παρουσίας αὐτοῖς ποιεῖσθαι οὐχ ἑκόντας, where Dittenberger notes that the phrase παρουσίας ποιεῖσθαι is used "paullo insolentius" with reference to the demands which the visits entailed; and from the ostraca, *Ostr* 1481[2] (ii/B.C.) λόγος παρου(σίας) τῆ(ς) βασιλ(ίσσης), and *ib.* 1372[4] (A.D. 33), a receipt for payments made εἰς τὴν παρουσίαν Φλάκος ἡγημών (*l.* Φλάκκου ἡγεμόνος).

Wilcken in *Archiv* v. p. 284 notes a late papyrus which shows that Christians of vi/A.D. were conscious of the technical meaning of the word: P Aphrod Cairo 3 has a petition for the παρουσία of a *dux*, ἥν (*sc.* ἐξουσίαν, i.e. the *dux* himself) ἐκδέχομεν πρὸ πολλοῦ, οἷον οἱ ἐξ ᾍδου καραδο-

κοῦντες (cf. Rom 8[19]) τὴν τότε (ποτε?) τοῦ Χριστο)ῦ ἀενάου θ(εο)ῦ παρουσίαν. See further *Ostr.* i. p. 274 ff., and more particularly for the NT significance of the word Deissmann *LAE*. p. 372 ff. The relation of παρουσία to ἐπιφάνεια and ἀποκάλυψις is discussed by Milligan *Thess.* p. 145 ff

παροψίς.

For the late use of παροψίς in Mt 23[25] to denote the "dish" on which dainties were served rather than the dainties themselves (see Rutherford *NP*, p. 265 f.) cf. BGU III. 781[2] (as amended *Berichtigungen*, p. 66 i/A.D.) παροψίδων ἀναγλύπτων, so [6. 14]: also Artem. p. 67[6] πίνακες δὲ καὶ παροψίδες.

παρρησία.

In accordance with its etymology παρρησία is used especially of "freedom," "boldness," *in speech*, but it readily passes into the more general meaning "confidence," as in Heb 3[6], 1 Jn 2[28], Job 27[10], *Test. xii. patr.* Reub iv. 2. This may be illustrated from P Par 63[iii. 7] (B.C. 165) καλῶς ἔχειν ὑπέλαβον ταύτην ἔτι τὴν παρησίαν (for spelling, cf. Winer-Schmiedel *Gr.* p. 56) ἀγαγεῖν πρός σε P Oxy VIII. 1100[15] (A.D. 206) με]τὰ παρρησίας (cf. Ac 28[31]), unfortunately in a broken context, and *Kaibel* 1006[5] παρρησίαν ὁμοίαν οὐκ ἔχων βροτοῖς. Cf. also Aristeas 125 συμβουλευόντων παρρησίᾳ πρὸς τὸ συμφέρον τῶν φίλων, "since friends unreservedly offer advice for one's best interests" (Thackeray).

In *OGIS* 323[10] (B.C. 159-8) εὐδοκι[μη]κὼς ἐν ταῖς χρείαις ἁπάσαις κ[εκ]όσμηκε τὸν αὐτοῦ [β](ίον τῇ) καλλίστηι παρρησίαι, where the word seems to be equivalent to "liberality," and in Vett. Val. p. 6[3] ζωῆς καὶ θανάτου παρρησίαν ἔχοντες, the editor renders π. by *potentia*. See also Artem. p. 24[22] μέτωπον ὑγιὲς . . . παρρησίαν καὶ εὐανδρίαν σημαίνει.

παρρησιάζομαι

in the NT is confined to the free and bold proclamation of the Gospel, which is the right and privilege of the servant of Christ. See *s.v.* παρρησία. and cf. *Ep. Diogn.* xi. 2 οἷς ἐφανέρωσεν ὁ Λόγος φανείς, παρρησίᾳ λαλῶν.

πάσχα,

the general transliteration in the LXX of פֶּסַח, is applied in the NT to (1) the paschal lamb (Mk 14[12], 1 Cor 5[7]), or (b) the paschal supper (Mk 14[1]), or (c) the paschal festival as a whole (Lk 22[1]). For the form of the word see a note by Nestle in *Exp T* xxi. p. 521 f.

πάσχω.

For the neutral sense of this verb "am acted upon," "experience," as in Mt 17[15] (*v. l.*), cf. the common euphemism ἐάν τι πάσχω with reference to death, e.g. P Eleph 2[3] (B.C. 285-4) ἐὰν δέ τι πάσχηι Διονύσιος, P Petr I. 14[9] (a Will—B.C. 237) ἐὰν δέ τι ἀνθρώπινον πάσχω καταλιμπάνω τὰ ὑπ[άρχοντα κτλ., and P Ryl II. 68[22] (B.C. 89) where ἐὰν μέν τι πάθω is contrasted with ἐὰν δὲ περιγένωμαι, "if I survive." In a deed of divorce P Flor

I. 93¹¹ (A.D. 569), the parties complain—ἐκ σκαιοῦ πονηροῦ δαίμονος π[ε]πόνθαμεν. Note also πάσχω ἀπόκρισιν, which occurs *ter* in P Oxy XVI. 1855⁸·¹⁰·¹⁴ (vi/vii A.D.), and is understood by the editors, "get a favourable response" to certain demands. The document is late, but the curious phrase may perhaps be taken as illustrating the good sense which is sometimes given to the verb in Gal 3⁴.

For the meaning "experience ill treatment," "suffer" bodily or otherwise, we may cite P Amh II. 78⁴ (A.D. 184) βίαν πάσχων ἑκάστοτε ὑπὸ Ἐκύσεως, "I am constantly suffering violence from Hekusis," PSI IV. 299⁷ (iii/A.D.) τραχώματα ("roughnesses") ἔσχον καὶ δεινὰ πέπονθα (for form, see *Proleg.* p. 154), P Oxy VIII. 1120¹ (early iii/A.D.) περὶ ἧς (*sc.* ὕβρεως) πέπονθεν ἐπὶ τόπων ὁ ἀνὴρ τῆς θυγατρός μου Πολυδεύκης, "concerning the outrage suffered at his abode by my son-in-law Polydeuces" (Ed.), and the Christian P Fay 136³ (iv/A.D.) εἰδότες ὅτι ἔχετέ με ἰς ὅσ' ἂν πάσχετε, θεοῦ βοηθοῦντος, "knowing that you have me to aid in whatever you may suffer, the Lord helping you" (Edd.).

πατάσσω,

"strike," "smite." In P Hal I. 1¹⁹³ (mid. iii/B.C.) punishment is apportioned δούλωι ἐλεύθερον πατάξαντι: cf. P Par 50⁸ (B.C. 159) (= *UPZ* i p. 365) βουλόμενος πατάξαι αὐτόν, BGU IV. 1024ᵛⁱⁱ·¹⁷ (end iv/A.D.) ὁ δὲ ξίφ[ος] καταλαβὼν π[ατάσσ]ει τὴν φεύγο[υσαν, and the Christian P Hamb I. 22⁷ (iv/A.D.) ἐχθροὺς . . . πατάσσων, of God. We are reminded of the curses in Deut 28²²·²⁸ by *Syll* 891 (= ³1240)¹¹ (ii/A.D.) τοῦτόν τε θεὸς πατάξαι ἀπορίᾳ καὶ πυρετῷ. In the NT only the aor. and fut. are found in accordance with general Attic usage: see Wackernagel *Hellenistica*, p. 17 n¹.

πατέω.

For the intrans. use of this verb "tread," "walk," we may cite the new fragment of an uncanonical gospel, P Oxy V. 840, where a Pharisee is represented as saying to the Saviour in the temple,¹²ᶠᶠ τίς ἐπέτρεψέν σοι πατ[εῖν] τοῦτο τὸ ἁγνευτήριον . . . τ[όπον ὄν]τα καθαρόν, ὃν οὐδεὶς ἄ[λλος εἰ μὴ] λουσάμενος καὶ ἀλλά[ξας τὰ ἐνδύ]ματα πατεῖ; "who gave thee leave to walk in this place of purification, which is a pure place, wherein no other man walks except he has washed himself and changed his garments?" (Edd.).

The trans. use "tread on," "trample," is seen in such passages as P Flor II. 150⁵ (A.D. 267) πατῆσαι τὰ ἐν τῷ αἰγιαλῷ θέρη, "to tread the crops in the sand," P Oxy VI. 988 (A.D. 224) τὴν δὲ κριθὴν καλῶς πεπατημένην χωρὶς δίσης καὶ ἀθέρος. The verbal is common, e.g. BGU II. 591⁸² (A.D. 56–57) and P Flor III. 369¹² (A.D. 139(149)) φοίνικος ξηροῦ πατητοῦ, "dry pressed dates." For the subst. πατητής (*calcator*), "one who treads grapes with the feet," cf. BGU IV. 1039¹ (Byz.): in P Oxy VIII. 1142³ (late iii/A.D.) πάτημα is a kind of fodder, see the editor's note. The metaph. use of the verb is fully illustrated by Headlam *Herodas*, p. 392.

πατήρ.

For the looser use of πατήρ as a title of respect or honour, see P Oxy X. 1296 (iii/A.D.), where the writer

refers to two other men as "father" (¹⁵·¹⁸) in addition to his real "father" (cf. ²¹): cf. BGU I. 164² (ii/iii A.D.), P Oxy XIV. 1665² (iii/A.D.), *ib.* 1678¹⁹ (iii/A.D.), P Strass I. 26¹ (iv/A.D.), and for a literary reference *Menandrea*, p. 9¹³. In P Par 60³ (B.C. 154) Apollonius addresses his eldest brother as πατήρ, apparently as head of the family: see Wilcken's note in *UPZ* i. p. 321 where exception is taken to the view that the title indicates membership in the same religious community, as suggested in Otto *Priester* i. p. 124 n.³, *Selections*, p. 22. In P Lond 1178¹⁰ (A.D. 194) (= III. p. 216) the Emperor Claudius is designated πατὴρ πατρίδος (*pater patriae*).

With 1 Tim 5¹ we may compare the fragment of a Christian letter, P Oxy XII. 1592 (iii/iv A.D.), where a woman addresses her spiritual "father" as ³ κ(ύρι)έ μου π(άτε)ρ, and rejoices ⁵ ὅτι τοιοῦτός μου π(ατ)ὴρ τὴν μνήμην ποιεῖται. In the early Christian letter P Amh I. 3ⁱⁱ·¹⁶ (between A.D. 264 and 282) τὸν πατέρα Ἀπολλῶνιν, Harnack, *Geschichte* II. 2. p. 180, regards πατέρα as the title of the provincial bishop, but Deissmann (*LAE*, p. 196) thinks that the writer is speaking of his real father, and similarly Ghedini *Lettere*, p. 71 f. It may be noted that the idea of the Divine "Fatherhood" is fully discussed by Westcott *Epp. of St. John*, p. 27 ff.

For the anarthrous πατήρ cf. *Proleg.* pp. 71 f., 82 f., and Abbott *Joh. Gr.* p. 96 f., and for a probable use of πατήρ as voc. see P Par 51³⁶ (B.C. 159) (= *UPZ* i. p. 360). A form πάτρα or πατρά denoting probably "sister by the father's side" occurs in *C. and B.* ii. p. 394, No. 272: see Ramsay's note.

Exx. of πατρόθεν are *Syll* 216 (= ³426)¹⁰ (B.C. 270–261) ὅπως ἀναγραφῇ τὸ ὄνομα αὐ[τοῦ π]ατρόθεν ἐν τῆι στήληι, *ib.* 645 (= ³1047)⁴¹ (*c.* B.C. 100) ἀναγραψάντων . . . τὸ ὄνομα τοῦ δανεισαμένου πατρόθεν.

πατραλῴας.

See *s.v.* πατρολῴας.

πατριά

in Eph 3¹⁵ is used, as often in the LXX (Gen 12³ *al.*), of a group of persons united by descent from a common father or ancestor: hence the Lat. rendering *paternitas* in the collective sense of that word. Herwerden *s.v.* refers to a Delphic inscr. of v/B.C., where πατριαί are "genera, sive familiae, quibus phratria constat."

The adv. πατριαστί, "according to paternal descent," occurs in P Hal I. 1²⁴⁸ (mid. iii/B.C.); cf. *Syll* 614 (= ³1023)³² (*c.* B.C. 200) ἀπογραφέσθων . . . ἐν τριμήνωι τὸ ὄνομα πατριαστὶ ποτὶ τὸς ναοπόιας, where Herwerden (*Lex. s.v.*) understands πατριαστί rather in the sense of "addito nomine gentili."

πατριάρχης,

"patriarch" directly transferred to the NT (e.g. Ac 2²⁹) from the LXX, where it was "presumably formed . . . on the analogy of Heb. expressions with שׁאר ('head') and נשׂיא ('prince'), denoting leaders of tribes or families" (Kennedy *Sources*, p. 114).

πατρικός,

"paternal," "ancestral" (Gal 1¹⁴): P Par 22³³ (B.C. 163) (= *UPZ* i. p. 193) ἐπαναγκάσῃ δ᾽ αὐτήν, εἰ τ[ὸ] πατρικὸν ἡμῶν παρὰ λόγον ἔχει, ἀποδοῦναι, "and compel her, if she is wrongfully keeping our patrimony, to restore it," P Tebt I. 59⁷ (B.C. 99) (= Witkowski², p. 112) ἣν ἔχετε πρὸς ἡμᾶς ἄνωθεν πατρικὴν φιλίαν, "the hereditary friendship which you have for me of old," *ib.* II. 382⁹ (B.C. 30–A.D. 1) πατρικοὺς κλή(ρους), P Amh II. 74²¹ (A.D. 147) ὑπάρχ(ει) δὲ ἡ[μῖ]ν τὸ ἐπ[ιβ]άλλον ἥ[μ]ισυ μέρος πα-[τ]ρι[κ(ῆς) . . ., "we own a half share that has fallen to us of our father's" (Edd.), and Gnomon 46 (A.D. 150) (= BGU V. 1. p. 22) τ[ὰ] τέκνα τῷ πατρικῷ γένει ἀκολουθεῖ. The form πατρίκιος is found in P Tebt II. 567 (A.D. 53–4).

πατρίς,

"native place," "native town" rather than "native land" (cf. Mt 13⁵⁴, Lk 4²³ᶠ; Field *Notes*, p. 19): BGU IV. 1140⁷ (B.C. 4) κινδυνεύω οὐ μόνον τῆς ἰδίας πατρίδος στερηθῆναι ἀλλὰ . . ., P Ryl II. 153⁹ (a Will—A.D. 138–161) the testator bequeaths certain privileges to a freedman ἐπιμ[έ]νοντι ὡς προγέγραπται τῇ πατρίδι μου, "while he remains as aforesaid in my native city" (Edd.), P Oxy VIII. 1102¹⁰ (*c.* A.D. 146) an instruction to a man τὸ τέταρτον τῆς οὐσίας εἰσενενκεῖ⟨ν⟩ ὑπὲρ τῆς γυμνασ[ι]αρχίας τῇ αὐτοῦ πατρίδι, "to contribute the fourth part of the estate to his native city for the gymnasiarchy," P Ryl II. 77³⁴ (A.D. 192) πειθόμενος τῇ ἐμαυτοῦ πατρίδι ἐπιδέχομαι στεφα[νη]φόρον ἐξηγητείαν, "obedient to my native city, I offer to undertake the office of a crowned exegetes" (Edd.). Cf. also the important rescript of Caracalla, P Giss I. 40ⁱⁱ (A.D. 215) permitting those who had been banished to return to their own homes—ὑποστρεφέτωσαν πάντες εἰς τὰς πατρίδας τὰς ἰδίας, and the epitaph of Avircius Marcellus, Bishop of Hierapolis in Phrygia about A.D. 170, which closes with the warning that whoever disturbs his tomb shall pay χρηστῇ πατρίδι Ἱεράπολι χείλια χρυσᾶ, "1000 gold pieces to my excellent fatherland Hierapolis" (see W. M. Ramsay, *Exp.* III. ix. p. 265). For the mystical sense of πατρίς in Heb 11¹⁴ Moffatt (*ICC ad l.*) cites Philo *de Agric.* 65 (ed. Wendland).

For πατριότης see P Lond 1919 (a letter dealing with the Meletian schism—*c.* A.D. 330–340), where the postscript is added—³¹ᶠ ἐνδείξασθε οὖν τὴν ἔμφυτον ὑμῶν ἀγάπην καὶ εὐσπ(λ)αγχνία[ν] καὶ τὴν στοργὴν τῆς ὑμῶν πατριότητος, "show them the love and compassion that are native to you and the affection of your fatherliness" (Bell).

Πατρόβας.

Lightfoot (*Phil.²* p. 174 f.) recalls that this proper name (Rom 16¹⁴), an abbreviated form of Patrobius, was borne by a well-known freedman of Nero (Tac. *Hist.* i. 49, ii. 95), and cites two other exx. of it from the inscrr.: TI.CL.AUG. L.PATROBIUS (Grut. p 610. 3), and TI.CLAUDIO. PATROBIO (Murat. p. 1329. 3). Pallis (*ad Rom l.c.*) prefers the accentuation Πατροβᾶς, and regards the suffix as a contemptuous addition to the name when applied to slaves. He cites Blaydes *ad* Aristoph. *Eq.* 534: "Forma Κοννᾶς pro Κόννος contemptum exprimit."

πατρολῴας,

"a parricide," is confined in the NT to 1 Tim 1⁹, where TR reads πατραλῴας. With the list of vices in which it occurs Deissmann (*LAE*, p. 321 f.) compares the "scolding" of Ballio the pander in Plaut. *Pseud.* I. iii. 134, where it is said to the *parricida—verberasti patrem atque matrem*, with the scornful answer—*atque occide quoque potius quam cibum praehiberem*. The classical πατραλοίας seems to make "father-thrasher" (ἀλο(ι)άω) the original meaning.

πατροπαράδοτος.

To the few exx. of this NT ἅπ. εἰρ. (1 Pet 1¹⁸), "handed down from one's fathers," "inherited," Deissmann (*BS*, p. 266 f.) adds a Pergamene inscr., *Perg* 248⁶⁹ (B.C. 135–134), in which Attalus states that his mother Stratonike, who came originally from Cappadocia, had brought τὸν Δία τὸν Σαβάζιον πατροπαράδοτον to Pergamus. See also another Pergamene inscr. *Cagnat* IV. 293¹ ⁵¹ where a gymnasiarch is praised ἐπὶ [τ]οῖς προγεγραμμένοις καὶ ἐπὶ τῶι πατροπαράδοτ[ο]ν [ἔχ]ον[τα τὸ μεγαλο]μερὲς καὶ φιλόδοξον μηδένα καιρὸν παραλείπειν, and *Michel* 394⁴ (mid. i/B.C.) πατροπαράδοτον παρειληφὼς τὴν πρὸς τὸν δῆμ[ον] ἡμῶν εὔνοιαν.

πατρῷος,

"received from one's fathers," which occurs *ter* in Acts, may be illustrated by P Eleph 5²² (B.C. 284–3) ἔχω λόγον καὶ κεκόμιζμαι ἅπαντα τῶν πατρῴων, P Oxy III. 483²⁴ (A.D. 108) τοὺς πατρῴους θεούς (cf. Ac 24¹⁴), *Chrest.* I. 116⁴ (ii/iii A.D.) ἡγοῦ μάλιστα τοὺς πατρῴους καὶ σέ[β]ου Ἴσιν Σάραπιν κτλ., *ib.* 96¹¹˙²² (A.D. 215) εἰ]ς ἐπ[ιμέ]λ[ε]ι[α]ν τοῦ πατρῴου ἡμῶν θεοῦ, P Lond 973⁶ (iii A.D.) (= III. p. 213) προσκύνημά σου ποιῶ . . . παρὰ τοῖς πατρῴοις θεοῖς, P Oxy VII. 1025¹⁹ (late iii/A.D.) συνεορτάσοντες ἐν τῇ πατρῴᾳ ἡ[μῶν] ἑορτῇ γενεθλίῳ τοῦ Κρόνου θεοῦ μεγίστου. "in order to celebrate with us our traditional festival on the birthday of Cronus the most great god" (Ed.), and from the inscrr. *Syll* 571 (= ³987)³⁵ (iv/B.C.) το]ῦ Διὸς τοῦ Πατρῴιου.

Παῦλος.

The designation Σαῦλος ὁ καὶ Παῦλος of Ac 13⁹ is fully discussed by Deissmann *BS*, p. 313 ff., where it is shown that the Apostle was already in possession of the double name at the time referred to: cf. Ramsay *Paul*, p. 81 ff. Elsewhere (*Recent Discovery*, p. 356) Ramsay suggests that Paul's complete Roman name may have been "C. Julius Paullus," in view of the frequent conjunction of the names Julius Paullus in Lycaonia.

In the important letter on the Meletian Schism, P Lond 1914⁵⁹ (A.D. 335?), greetings are conveyed to Παῦλον τὸν ἀναγνώστην: the editor refers to a priest of the same name (ἀπὸ Τήεν⟨ε⟩ως) in *ib.* 1917⁴⁴ (*c.* A.D. 330–340), and to ὁ μακάριος Παῦλος in *ib* 1919²⁵ (same date). The name is not uncommon in the inscrr., see e.g. *Perg* 374 A¹⁶ (time of Augustus), where Ἀ. Καστρίκιος Παῦλος is included among the choristers of θεὸς Σεβαστὸς καὶ θεὰ Ῥώμη in Pergamum: cf. Thieme, p. 40. In Menander *Frag. Gr. Hist.* iv. 245 there is mention of Παῦλος ὁ Κίλιξ.

παύω.

For the mid. = "cease," as with one exception (1 Pet 3¹⁰) in the NT, cf. P Hib I. 59¹⁰ (c. B.C. 245) εἰ μὴ παύσει κ[α]κοποῶν ἐν τῆι κώμη[ι] μεταμελή[σ]ει σοι, "if you do not cease your malpractices in the village, you will be sorry for it," P Oxy VIII. 1121¹⁰ (A.D. 295) οὐκ ἐπαυσάμην τὰ πρέποντα γείνεσθαι ὑπὸ τέκνων γονεῦσι ἀναπληροῦσα, "I was assiduous in performing what is owing from children to parents" (Ed.), and P Lond 417¹¹ (c. A.D. 346) (= II. p. 299, *Selections*, p. 124) καὶ πάλειν, ἂμ μὴ παύσεται (*l.* ἐὰν μὴ παύσηται), ἔρχεται εἰς τὰς χεῖράς σου ἄλλω ἄβαξ (*l.* ἄλλο ἅπαξ), "and again, if he does not desist, he will come into your hands still another time." In an illiterate letter from parents to their son giving news regarding their health, P Oxy X. 1299⁵ᶠ. (iv/A.D.), they write—ἔπιτα ἀπὸ τοῦ νέω ἔτους πολλὰ ἐνοσοῦμεν, ἀλλὰ εὐχαριστῶ[μ]εν τῷ θεῷ ὅτι ἐπαυμένην (*l.* πεπαυμένοι) ἐσμέ<ν>, "next, since the new year we have been very ill, but we give thanks to God that we have recovered" (Edd.).

παχύνω,

"thicken," "fatten," which is used metaphorically in Mt 13¹⁵, Ac 28²⁷, occurs in a medical prescription, unfortunately very mutilated, P Tebt II. 273³³ (ii/iii A.D.) πρὸς πεπαχυ[σμέν]α[. .] . |. The subst. παχύτης is found in Aristeas 93 and πάχος *bis* in *ib.* 71, and its plur. in PSI VI. 601⁵ (iii/B.C.) τοῖς μεγέθεσι καὶ τοῖς πάχεσιν. For the corr. adj. see P Oxy VI. 921¹⁹ (iii/A.D.) σινδόνιον παχὺ ᾱ, "1 thick cambric," PSI IV. 364³ (B.C. 251-0) παχύτερον (ἱμάτιον), and P Petr II. 4(11)⁶ (B.C. 255-4) ξύλα . . . εὐμηκέστατα καὶ παχύτατα, "beams as long and thick as possible."

πέδη,

"a fetter" (Mk 5⁴, Lk 8²⁹): PSI IV. 406²¹ (iii/B.C.) ἀπάγεται εἰς φυλακὴν ἡμέρας ζ ἐμ πέδαις ὤν, P Lond 46¹³⁸ (iv/A.D.) (= I. p. 81) πέδας λύει—said of a charm. For the verb πεδάω see Artem. p. 261⁸.

πεδινός,

"level," "low-lying," is found in the NT only in Lk 6¹⁷ (Vg *in loco campestri*): cf. Aristeas 107 τινων μὲν πεδινῶν . . . τινων δὲ ὀρεινῶν. For the adj. πεδιακός see BGU III. 915¹⁷ (A.D. 49-50) πεδιακ(ῆς) ὁδο ῦ, for the subst. πεδίον, see P Tebt I. 56⁹ (late ii/B.C.) γείν[ωσ]κε δὲ περὶ τοῦ κατακεκλῦσθαι τὸ πεδίον ἡμῶν, "you must hear about our plain having been inundated" (Edd.), P Fay 36¹¹ (lease—A.D. 111-112) ἐποικίων καὶ πεδίων, "farmsteads and plains," and for πεδιοφύλαξ, "the guard of an estate," see *ib.* 113¹, 114⁶ (both A.D. 100).

πεζεύω.

On Ac 20¹³ Blass remarks: "πεζεύειν de terrestri (non necessario pedestri) itinere." An interesting parallel to the same passage is noted by Moffatt (*Exp* VIII. xvii. p. 237) from Plutarch's life of Marcus Cato (ix), where Cato states that one of the three things he regretted in life was πλεύσας ὅπου δυνατὸν ἦν πεζεῦσαι, "having once sailed to a place where he could have walked."

πεζῇ.

For the contrast in Mk 6³²ᶠ. between ἐν τῷ πλοίῳ, "in the boat," and πεζῇ (*sc.* ὁδῷ), "by land," cf. PSI V. 446¹³ (A.D. 133-7) μήτε πλέοντι μήτε πεζῇ βαδί([ζον]τι, and Artem. p. 182¹ τοῖς διαποροῦσι πότερον πεζῇ ἀπιτέον αὐτοῖς ἢ κατὰ πλοῦν συμβουλεύει πεζῇ. In P Tebt I. 5²⁸ (B.C. 118) the word is found with the two meanings "on foot" and "by land," ὁμ]οίως δὲ καὶ τοὺς πεζῇι ἀ[ν]απορε[υομένους] ἐκ τῆς πόλεως τὴν [ἄ]γουσαν πεζὴν ὁδὸν . . ., "likewise persons who travel on foot up the country from Alexandria by the land-route which leads . . ." (Edd.).

πεζός,

"on foot" or "by land": cf. P Fay 111¹⁰ (A.D. 95-6) πεζῶι [τὰ χ]υρίδια ἐλάσαι, "to drive the pigs on foot," P Meyer 19⁴ (ii/A.D.) ἐξελθὼν . . . πεζός. For a curious metaphorical usage cf. the contract of apprenticeship P Oxy IV. 724¹⁰ (A.D. 155), where payment is to be made to a shorthand teacher, τοῦ παιδὸς ἐκ παντὸς λόγου πεζοῦ γράφοντος καὶ ἀναγεινώσ[κον]τος ἀμέμπτως, "when the boy writes fluently in every respect and reads faultlessly" (Edd.).

πειθαρχέω.

The unusual constr. c. gen. = "obey" one in authority is found both in the papyri and in the inscrr., as in the marriage contracts P Tebt I. 104¹⁴ (B.C. 92) ἔ]στω δὲ Ἀπολλωνίαι π[α]ρὰ Φιλίσκωι πειθαρχοῦσα α[ὐ]τοῦ ὡς προσῆ[κό]ν ἐστιν γυναῖκα ἀνδρός, "Apollonia shall remain with Philiscus, obeying him as a wife should her husband" (Edd.), P Oxy II. 265¹³ (A.D. 81-95) ὅσ[α]δ[εῖ πειθαρχεῖν γαμετὴν γυναῖκα ἀνδρός, and in *Syll* 2 (= ³ 22)⁷ (B.C. 494) πυνθάνομαι σὲ τῶν ἐμῶν ἐπιταγμάτων οὐ κατὰ πάντα πειθαρχεῖν. For πειθαρχέω c. dat., as in Ac 27²¹, cf. P Oxy XII. 1411¹⁶ (A.D. 260) εἰ μὴ πειθαρχήσειαν τῇδε τ[ῇ παρ]αγγελίᾳ, and *Magn* 114⁸ πειθαρχεῖν δὲ π[άν]τως τοῖς ὑπὲρ τοῦ κοινῇ συμφέροντος ἐπιταττομένοις, and for the verb absolutely, as in Tit 3¹, cf. OGIS 483⁷⁰ (ii/A.D.) ἐὰν δὲ μηδ' οὕτω πειθαρχῶσιν οἱ ἰδιῶται, ἔκδοσιν ποιείσθωσαν κτλ.

πειθός,

"persuasive." For the spelling of this adj. (WH πιθός), which hitherto has not been found elsewhere than in 1 Cor 2⁴, cf. Moulton *Gr.* ii. p. 78, where the word is treated "as a new adj. straight from the verb-stem." See also Winer-Schmiedel, p. 135 n.²⁰, and Field *Notes*, p. 167.

For the subst., which is read in certain inferior authorities in 1 Cor 2⁴, see P Oxy III. 474³⁷ (A.D. 184?) ἀβουλίᾳ μᾶλλον ἢ πειθοῖ τῶν παρηγγελμένων χρωμένοις, "in defiance rather than obedience to the proclamations" (Edd.): cf. P Amh II. 31¹¹ (B.C. 112) πειθανάγκης προσαχθείσης περὶ τοῦ καθήκοντος προστίμου, "forcible persuasion being employed with regard to the proper fine" (Edd.).

πείθω.

For the conative present "apply persuasion," "seek to persuade," as in Ac 26²⁸, see *Proleg.* p. 147. The corresponding aor. ἔπεισα is seen in P Tor I. 1ᵛⁱⁱⁱ·³⁶ (B.C. 116) εἴπερ γε δὴ ἐνόμιζεν ἔχειν τι δίκαιον, δι' οὗ δύναται τὸν κριτὴν πεῖσαι, and BGU I. 164²⁶ (ii/iii A.D.) παρακαλῶ οὖν σε, φίλτατε, ἤδη ποτὲ πεῖσαι αὐτὸν τοῦ ἐλθεῖν. Cf. also P Oxy II. 294²² (A.D. 22) ἐὰν μή τι πίσωσι τὸν ἀρχιστάτορα δο[ῦν]αι εἰκανὸν ἕως ἐπὶ διαλογισμόν, "unless indeed they shall persuade the chief usher to give security for them until the inquiry." The 2nd perf. πέποιθα c. dat., which is rare in Hellenistic prose, is found in BGU IV. 1141¹⁷ (B.C. 14) πέποιθα γὰρ ἐματῶι, *persuasi mihi* : cf. 2 Cor 10⁷, Phil 1¹⁴, Philem²¹. In PSI V. 538⁷ (iii/B.C.) the intrans. πέποιθα is construed c. gen., which the editor attributes to Ionic influence—ἐπίστηι δὲ καὶ σὺ διότι τοῦ ὀψωνίου πεποίθαμεν, "sai anche tu che sull' ὀψώνιον facciamo assegnamento."

For the mid. or pass. "am persuaded," we may cite P Petr II. 11(1)⁴ (mid. iii/B.C.) (= *Selections*, p. 7) ἐὰν γὰρ σὺ παραγένηι, πέπεισμαι ῥαιδίως με τῶι βασιλεῖ συσταθήσεσθαι, "for, if you come, I am sure that I shall easily be introduced to the king," BGU IV. 1118⁴⁰ (B.C. 22) πείθεσθαι περὶ τῆς τούτων ἀξίας, P Oxy II. 268⁷ (A.D. 58) ὃ καὶ ἐπε[ίσθη]σαν κεφάλαιον. "the sum which they severally consented to accept" (Edd.), *ib.* X. 1293¹³ (A.D. 117-38) ἄλλος ξένος ἐστὶν οὗ δεῖ με πισθῆναι ὡς ἐσχήκατε. "another stranger whose word I have to take that you have received it" (Edd.). P Ryl II. 176³ (A.D. 201-11) ἃς ἐπείσθη{ν} λαβεῖν παρ' αὐτῆς, "the sum which she was induced to accept from her" (Edd.), and P Fay 133¹² (iv/A.D.) μὴ πισθεὶς οὖν τοῖς καρπώναις, "without being persuaded by the fruit-buyers."

In P Lips I. 28²⁸ (A.D. 381) εὐδοκῶ καὶ πίθομαι πᾶσι τοῖς ἐγγεγραμμένοις ὡς πρόκειται, the word passes into the meaning "obey": cf. the letter of Epicurus to a child ex vol. Hercul. 176 (iii/B.C.) (= *Selections*, p. 51.) –¹⁰ ε[ἰ ὑ]γιαίνεις . . . καὶ πάπαι καὶ Μάτρω[ν]ι πάντα πε[ί]θη[ι, and ¹⁴ ἐγὼ καὶ οἱ λοιποὶ πάντες σε μέγα φιλοῦμεν, ὅτι τούτοις πείθη πάντα, also P Ryl II. 77³⁴ (A.D. 192) πειθόμενος τῇ ἐμαυτοῦ πατρίδι, "being obedient to my native city."

Πειλᾶτος.

This proper name, with the spelling Πιλᾶτος, occurs several times in late papyri, e.g. P Lond V. 1661²⁹ (A.D. 553) or a νομικός, who acted as the scribe of various documents. [It is of interest to note that in this instance the scribe in appending his signature seems to have used a special form of notarial script: see the editor's note *ad l.*]

πεινάω,

"hunger": cf. P Flor I. 61⁵⁴ (A.D. 85) (= *Chrest.* II. p. 89) λειμοῦ γεν[ομ]ένου πε[ι]νῶν οὐκ ἀπῆ[τ]εις [τὸ]ν πυρόν : The construction c. acc. in Mt 5⁶ appears to be unique. For the reading πίνων not πινῶν in P Par 47²³ see *s.v.* πίνω, and for the disappearance of the -ήω verbs from the Κοινή see *Proleg.* p. 54, Thackeray *Gr.* i. p. 242.

πεῖρα.

The phrase πεῖραν λαμβάνειν, "make trial," "have experience of" in Heb 11²⁹,³⁶, is fully illustrated from late Greek writers by Field *Notes*, p. 232 f. We may add a few exx. from the Κοινή—P Par 63¹²⁹ (B.C. 164) (= P Petr III. p. 28) εἰ . . . μὴ βούλεσθε πεῖραν λαμβάνειν τῶν . . ἐπιτίμων, "if you do not wish to experience the penalties" (Mahaffy), P Oxy

XIV. 1681¹⁰ (iii/A.D.) ἀπὸ μέρους πεῖραν λαβόντας τῆς ἡμετέρας γνώμης. "because you have had a partial proof of my sentiments" (Edd.), and P Cairo Preis 2¹¹ (A.D. 362), where a man complains that after he had enjoyed three years of married life his mother-in-law had made sport of him συνέπεξέν με, asserting that his wife was experiencing (the evil effects of) a demon—ὡς τῆς γυναικός μου πῖραν λαβοῦσαν (*l.* πεῖραν λαβούσης) δέ[= αἵ]μονος.

Similar phrases occur in PSI IV. 377¹⁰ (B.C. 250-249) ἕως ἂν τούτου τοῦ (ἔτους) πεῖράν σοι ἀποδῶμεν, P Oxy XII. 1415²⁹ (late iii/A.D.) Πτολεμαῖος [π]εῖραν τῆς προαιρέσεως αὐτοῦ πολλάκις δέδωκεν, BGU IV. 1027ˣˣᵛⁱ ¹¹ (end iv/A.D.) οἷον ὀλέθρου πῖρας ἐροεῖτε . . . ἡ πῖρ[α] τῶν πραγμάτων ἐπιδείξει, and *Syll* 800 (=³ 1230)¹⁸ (ii/A.D.) πᾶσι τοῖς κακοῖς πε[ῖ]ραν δώσει. For a gen. πείρης, see Dieterich *Untersuchungen*, p. 172. In P Lond 1023⁵ (iv/A.D.) πειρατήριον occurs = "temptation"—διὰ τῶν ἁγίων σου εὐχῶν σωθήσομε(= αι) ἀπὸ παντὸς πι(= ει)ρατηρίου τοῦ διαβόλου.

πειράζω.

This poetic and late prose form of πειράω (*q.v.*), even when used in the general sense of "try," "test," has always the idea of probation associated with it : see the instances cited by Hort *ad* Jas 1² , especially Plut. *Moralia* 15, p. 230a where "Namertes being congratulated on the multitude of his friends asked the spokesman εἰ δοκίμιον ἔχει τίνι τρόπῳ πειράζεται ὁ πολύφιλος ; and when a desire was expressed to know he said Ἀτυχία." For a more sinister sense cf. Vett. Val. p. 17⁶ καθόλου δὲ κακεντρεχῶν τῇ διανοίᾳ, μάλιστα κατὰ τῶν πειραζόντων ἢ τῶν πονηρὰ δρώντων.

The Biblical usage is fully discussed by Hort *l.c.* See also Kennedy *Sources*, p. 106 f., and the exx. from late Greek in Anz *Subsidia*, p. 274. MGr πειράζω (Thumb *Hellen.* p. 218).

πειρασμός,

"trial," is confined to Biblical Greek and literature founded on it, except Diosc. p. 3B τοὺς ἐπὶ τῶν παθῶν πειρασμούς, "trials" made of drugs to see their effect in certain diseases: cf. Hort *ad* Jas 1². In *ZNTW* x. (1909), p. 246 ff. de Zwaan has suggested that the reading τὸν πειρασμόν (without ὑμῶν or other addition) in Gal 4¹⁴ may be taken, on the analogy of MGr, as = "the devil," "the demonic power."

πειράω,

usually found in mid. or pass. with act. meaning "try," "attempt," is confined to Ac 26² in NT, but can be freely illustrated from the Κοινή, e.g. PSI VI. 604¹⁶ (iii/B.C.) πειράσομαι ἀνέγκλητος εἶναι, P Vat A¹⁷ (B.C. 168) (= *UPZ* i. p. 303) ἀλλὰ πᾶς τις πειρᾶται, ὁπηνίκ' ἂν ἐκ κινδύνων διασωθῇ, ταχέως παραγίνεσθαι, "but everyone tries, whenever he has been delivered out of dangers, to come home quickly," P Par 49⁷ (B.C. 161) (= *UPZ* i. p. 308) πεπείραμαι (cf. 1 Kingd 17³⁹) . . . εἰς πᾶν τὸ σοι χρήσιμον ἐμαυτὸν ἐπιδιδόναι, P Fay 124⁷ (ii/A.D.) νῦν οὖν πάλειν ἐπιράθην (cf. 1 Macc 12¹⁰) γράφιν σ[ο]ι, "so now again I attempt to write to you," PSI IV. 299¹⁸ (iii/A.D.) αὐτὸς δὲ πειρῶμαι, ἐπὰν πλοίου εὐπορηθῶ, καταλαβεῖν ὑμᾶς, and

P Oxy I. 71¹·¹⁹ (A.D. 303) ἐπειράθη μέν τινα κακουργίαν ἐπὶ ἀποστερέσι τῇ ἡμετέρᾳ ποιήσασθαι διὰ τὸ ἀγράμματόν με εἶναι, "he attempted, owing to my being illiterate, to commit a fraud to my detriment" (Edd.).

πεισμονή

in Gal 5⁸ may be either act. "the act of persuasion," or pass. "the being persuaded": see Lightfoot or Burton (*ICC*) *ad l.* for exx. of both usages. For πεῖσμα see the vi/A.D. P Oxy VI. 945⁵ᶠ· Σερῆνος γὰρ . . . διὰ πίσματος γυναικὸς ἐδίωξεν Κόλλουθον τὸν εὐλαβέστατον ἐκ τοῦ λο⟨υ⟩τροῦ, καὶ ὅτε ἐποίησεν τὸ πῖσμα αὐτοῦ οὐ θέλει ἀποστῆναι, "for Serenus through the persuasion of his wife chased the most discreet Colluthus out of the bath, and having done what he was persuaded to do will not depart" (Edd.).

πέλαγος.

For πέλαγος, "the open sea" (note the conjunction with θάλασσα in Mt 18⁶), see *OGIS* 74³ (B.C. 247–221) Θεύδοτος Δωρίωνος Ἰουδαῖος σωθεὶς ἐκ πελ⟨άγ⟩ους, and cf. *ib.* 69¹ ff· σωθεὶς ἐγ μεγάλων κινδύνων ἐκπλεύσας ἐκ τῆς Ἐρυθρᾶς θαλάσσης. The adj. πελάγιος occurs in the sailor's song P Oxy XI. 1383 (late iii/A.D.) where the 2nd column begins –

Ῥοδίοις ἐκέλευον ἀνέμοις καὶ μέρεσι τοῖς πελαγίοις,
ὅτε πλέειν ἤθελον ἐγώ,

"I commanded the Rhodian winds and the seaward parts when I wished to sail."

πελεκίζω,

"cut off with an axe" (Rev 20⁴) : cf. Polyb. i. 7. 12 μαστιγώσαντες ἅπαντας κατὰ τὸ παρ' αὐτοῖς ἔθος ἐπελέκισαν, and the corr. verb πελεκάω in Apol. Arist. 13 πριζομένους καὶ πελεκουμένους. For πέλεκυς, "axe" (Lat. *securis*), cf. PSI V. 506⁷ (B.C. 257–6) εἰς τὴν ξυλοκοπίαν πελέκεις δέκα, and for πελέκημα, "chipped-stone," cf. P Oxy III. 498²⁴· ²⁶ (ii/A.D.). See also Luckhard *Privathaus*, p. 33 f.

πέμπτος.

It is hardly necessary to illustrate this word, but, as showing the housing conditions of the time, we may cite P Fay 31¹⁵ (c. A.D. 129) where a woman applies to the keepers of the archives at Arsinoe for leave to alienate πέμπτον μέρος, "the fifth part" of certain house property belonging to her. In the Gnomon 79 (= BGU V. 1. p. 31) it is laid down that in every temple (ἱερόν) where there is a shrine (ναός) there must be a prophet, who shall receive τῶν προσόδων τὸ π[έμ]πτον. For the form πέμπτος cf. *Ostr.* 3³, 4⁴ (both A.D. 17–18), and see Mayser *Gr.* p. 166.

πέμπω.

It is not necessary to do more than cite a few exx. of this common verb—P Hib I. 54¹⁹ (c. B.C. 245) (= *Chrest.* I. p. 563) κόμισαι δὲ καὶ τὸν ἔριφον παρὰ Ἀριστίωνος καὶ πέμψον ἡμῖν, "get the kid also from Aristion and send it to me," P Par 63¹·¹⁷ (B.C. 164) (= P Petr III. p. 18)

ἐν τῶι πεμφθέντι σοι παρ' ἡμῶν ὑπομνήματι, "in the minute sent to you by us," P Tebt I. 22⁶ (B.C. 112) πεπομφότες τῆι κ̄ᾱ ἐπὶ τὰ σπέρματα, "having sent on the 21st for the seed," *ib.* II. 414⁹ (ii/A.D.) ἰ μὴ ὅτι ἠσθένηκα, πάλαι πεπόνφην σοι, "had it not been for the fact that I was ill, I would have sent them to you long ago" (Edd.), and P Iand 10³ ᶠ (iii/A.D.) ἐπένσαμέν σοι ταύτην τὴν ἐπ]ιστολὴν διὰ τῶν φυλάκων [ἐκπορευομένων, ἐπειδὴ δι' ἄλλ]ου οὐ δυνάμεθα πένσαι σοι, with the editor's note, where there are also collected a number of instances of the dropping of the 2ᵈ π, e.g. P Oxy III. 528¹¹ (ii/A.D.) ἔπεμσας, ¹⁹ ἔπεμσε, and ²¹ ἔπεμσα. See also Deissmann's note *ad* P Meyer 20¹². MGr aor. ἔπεψα.

In the letter of Psenosiris, P Grenf II. 73¹⁰ (late iii/A.D.) (= *Selections*, p. 118), the "colourless" πέμπω is used to denote *banishment* into the Oasis—τὴν Πολιτικὴν τὴν πεμφθεῖσαν εἰς Ὄασιν ὑπὸ τῆς ἡγεμονίας. See also *Preisigke* 3815 where the label attached to a body forwarded for mummification runs—Βησοῦς πεμπομένη εἰς Πανῶ⟨ν⟩ καὶ παραδιδομένην ἀηταφιαστ̣ι τῶ Πανιοσᾶτι (*l.* παραδιδομένη ἐνταφιαστῇ τῷ Πανισᾶτι).

πένης,

"poor" (2 Cor 9⁹): P Oxy III. 471⁹⁵ (ii/A.D.) πένης ἄνθρωπος [ἐν] εὐτελέσιν ἱματίοις, "a poor man wearing cheap clothes" (Edd.), P Ryl II. 62¹¹ (transl. from Latin—iii/A.D.) δύναμαι χαρίσασθαι καὶ πένητι [πλοῦ]τον, PSI II. 120¹⁷ (a collection of sayings—iv/A.D.?) πένης ὢν πλουσίοις μὴ ὁμίλει, and BGU IV. 1024ᵛⁱⁱ· ⁹ (end iv/A.D.) τις γραῦς καὶ πένης. See also P Flor III. 296¹⁸ (vi/A.D.) π]ένητι καὶ πτωχῷ, which with its context recalls, as the editor points out, Ps 40·(41)². The words are also contrasted in Aristeas 249: for the subst. πενία cf. *ib.* 280. See further *s.v.* πτωχός.

πενθερά,

"a mother-in-law" (Mt 8¹⁴, *al.*) : cf. P Fay 126⁵ (ii/iii A.D.) ⟨ἐ⟩πεμψεν ἐπὶ τὴν πενθερά⟨ν⟩ σου χάριν τοῦ κτήματος, "he sent a message to your mother-in-law about the farm." MGr πεθερ(ι)ά.

πενθερός,

"a father-in-law" (Jn 18¹³) : cf. P Oxy II. 237ᵛⁱⁱ· ²¹ (A.D. 186) Σεμπρώνιον πενθερὸν ἑαυτο[ῦ, P Thead 13¹·² (A.D. 322 or 323) Ἥρων πενθερὸς αὐτῷ ἐτελεύτα, and P Lond 232⁸ (c. A.D. 346) (= II. p. 296) πενθερὸς γὰρ τυγχάνι Τιμοθέου.

πενθέω,

"mourn." The conjunction of πενθέω and κλαίω, as in Mk 16¹⁰ *al.*, is found in a very illiterate letter addressed by a man to his wife, P Oxy III. 528⁹ (ii/A.D.) γινόσκειν σε θέλω ἀφ' ὡς ἐ⟨κ⟩ξῆλθες ἀπ' ἐμοῦ πένθος ἡγούμην νυκτὸς κλέ(=αί)ων, ἡμέρας δὲ πενθῶ⟨ν⟩, "I wish you to know that ever since you left me I have been in mourning, weeping by night and mourning by day." See also P Par 22²¹ (B.C. 163) (= *UPZ* i. p. 193) ἐπιγενηθέντος δὲ τοῦ πένθους τοῦ Ἄπιος κατάγουσιν ἡμᾶς πενθεῖν τῶι θεῶι. In *Syll* 879 (= ³ 1219)⁵ (iii/B.C.) it is laid down τὰς οὔσας ἔχειν φαιὰν ἐσθῆτα μὴ κατερρυπωμένην, "that mourning women should wear dark raiment, not d."

θος,

mourning" (Jas 4⁹, *al.*): cf. P Tebt II. 332¹¹ (A.D. 176) ους ἀνδρὸς θυγατρός μου ἕνεκα, "on account of my rning for my daughter's husband," and from the inscrr. *S* 56¹³ (B.C. 238) τὰ πρὸς . . . τὴν τοῦ πένθους ἀπόλυ-(with the editor's note), and *Syll* 324 (= ³730)²² c.) χαλεπῶς μὲ]ν ἥνενκεν τὸ πένθος αὐτοῦ διὰ τὴν στότητα.

ιχρός,

poor" (Lk 21²), may be chronicled as occurring in J IV. 1024^viii. 12 (end of iv/A.D.): the old woman is ribed by the judge as πενιχρὰ καὶ πρεσβύτης, and ter as one ἥτις διὰ τὴν συνέχουσαν αὐτὴν πενίαν τὴν ῆς [θυγ]ατέρα[ν]] τῆς σωφροσύνης ἀπεστέρη[σεν. In tition addressed to the epimeletes, P Petr III. 36 (*a*)⁶ l.), a prisoner writes—μεγάλη ἡ ἀνάγκη ἐστιν καὶ τὸ χρὸν εἶναι καὶ ὁρᾶν [τ]ὸν θάνατον ὑποκείμενον [ἐν] τῆι ικῆι.

τακόσιοι.

Ryl II. 129¹³ (A.D. 30) ἥροσάν μου χόρτου δέσμας ακοσίας, "they carried off five hundred bundles of hay."

τε.

Tebt I. 56¹³ (*c.* B.C. 130–121) ἀρούρας πέ[ν]τε, "5 rae." For the form πέτε cf. P Iand 14⁶ (iv/A.D.)]ησα ἐκεῖ πέτε ἡ[μ]έρας.

τεκαιδέκατος.

Amh II. 131⁷ (early ii/A.D.) ἐλπίζω . . . μετὰ τὴν 'εκαιδεκάτην ἀναπλεύσειν, "I hope after the fifteenth :turn home."

τίκοντα.

'e may cite *Magn* 16²⁹ στέφανον διδόντες ἀπὸ πεντή-τα] χρ[υσῶν, if only because it is a good ex. of the titution in the Κοινή of ἀπό c. gen. for the gen. of e: see Radermacher *Gr.* p. 91.

τηκοστή.

'ith the use of this word to denote the Jewish Feast Pentecost" we are not at present concerned. It may noted, however, that in the ostraca πεντηκοστή is a , tax: see Wilcken *Ostr.* i. pp. 276 ff., 343 f., and the : *al OGIS* 46¹² (B.C. 285–247) τοὺς ὑποτεθέντας εἰς τὰς νας, τὴν πεντηκόστην καὶ τὸ γραφίον τῶν ὅρκων.

τοίθησις,

confidence," "trust," confined in the NT to Paul, is lemned by the Atticists, see Lob. *Phryn.* p. 294 f., herford *NP* p. 355. The subst. is found in the LXX in 4 Kingd 18¹⁹: for the verb see Thackeray *Gr.* i. 24 f.

περαιτέρω.

Good illustrations of the use of this compar. adv. = "further," "beyond," in Ac 19³⁹ are afforded by P Fay 124⁸ (ii/A.D.) γράφιν σ[ο]ι πρὶν ἤ τι περαιτέρ[ο]ν ἐνχιρήσω πο[ι]εῖν, "to write to you before taking further steps" (Edd.), and BGU II. 372^ii. 12 (A.D. 154) μ[η]δὲν περαιτέρω . . . ἐξετάζειν.

πέραν.

For πέραν c. gen., as in Jn 6¹, cf. P Amh II. 140⁵ (vi/A.D.) πέραν τῆς Ὀξυρυγχ(ιτῶν) πόλεως, "opposite the city of Oxyrhynchus." For τὸ πέραν, "the region beyond," as in Mt 8¹⁸, ²⁸ *al.*, cf. BGU IV. 1091⁴ (B.C. 14) ἐκ Σιναρὺ τοῦ πέραν, and *ib.* 1022²ᵃ (A.D. 196) εἰς τὸ πέραν. The form πέρα is found in P Leid W^vii. 26 (ii/iii A.D.) (= II. p. 103) διαπεράσεις τὸ πέρα, "you will cross to the other side," and P Oxy I. 117⁹ (ii/iii A.D.) τοῦ ἄντα καὶ . . . τοῦ πέρα, "of the near and the far (vineyard)."

πέρας,

"end": cf. P Giss I. 25⁷ (ii/A.D.) δεόμενος αὐτοῦ ὅπως πέρας ἐπιθῆι τῷ πράγματι, "asking him to put an end to the matter," BGU IV. 1019⁷ (mid. ii/A.D.) ὃς ἔδωκεν τὸν στρατηγὸν τοῦ νομοῦ εἰς τ[ὸ] πέρας ἐπιθεῖναι τ[ῆ] λογοθεσία, P Oxy II. 237^viii. 16 (A.D. 186) πέρας τῆς χρηματικῆς ἀμφισβητήσεως λαβούσης, "when the money-action has come to an end" (Edd.), and *OGIS* 669⁴⁰ (i/A.D.) οὐδὲν γὰρ ἔσται πέρας τῶν συκοφαντημάτων. See also the adverbial use in P Oxy II. 282¹¹ (A.D. 30–35) κατὰ πέρ[α]ς ἐξῆ[λθε, "finally she left the house," said of a dissatisfied wife, and *ib.* XIV. 1673²² (ii/A.D.) τὸ δὲ πέρας ᾔτησα τὴν μνᾶν, "in the end I asked for the mina."

Πέργαμον.

Along with this form of the name of the city (Strabo, Polyb. *al.*) is to be found (ἡ) Πέργαμος (Xen. Paus. *al.*). The two occurrences in the NT (Rev 1¹¹, 2¹²) are in the acc. and dat., leaving the nom. uncertain, and curiously no ex. of the nom. can be quoted from Frankel's Pergamene inscrr. (see *Perg* in Index III.) For features in the history and character of Pergamum, which make the message of Rev 2¹² ff. specially appropriate, see Ramsay *Letters*, p. 291 ff., and the art. in *EB s.v.* Pergamos.

The city gave its name to "parchment" (περγαμηνή, *charta pergamena*), which was first manufactured here: see Gardthausen *Griech. Palaeographie*² i. p. 93 ff.

περί.

While περί, literally "round about" as distinguished from ἀμφί (not in NT) "on both sides," is found c. dat. in classical Greek and the LXX, in the NT it occurs only c. gen. (291 times) and c. acc. (38 times): see *Proleg.* p. 105 and cf. p. 98.

1. For the commonest use c. gen. = "concerning," "about," see P Lille I. 17⁴ (mid. iii/B.C.) ἐπιστολὴν περὶ σιταρ[ί]ου, *ib.* 26¹ (iii/B.C.) ἔγραψάς μοι περὶ τῆς εἰς τὴν σησαμείαν γῆς, P Par 44⁷ (B.C. 153) ἀγωνιῶ γὰρ περὶ σου, P Lips I 104¹³ (B.C. 96–5) περὶ ὧν ἂν αἱρῆσθε, γράφετέ μοι, P Oxy IV. 743³¹ (B.C. 2) περὶ πάντων αὐτῷ τὴν ἐπι-

τροπὴν δέδωκα, "I have entrusted to him the care of the whole matter" (Edd.), *ib.* XII. 1583[11] (ii/A.D.) γράψον μοι περὶ τῶν ὄντων, "write me regarding the present state of affairs," and BGU II. 632[12] (ii/A.D.) (= *LAE.* p. 173) ο[ὐ]χ ὀκνῶ σοι γράψαι περὶ τῆ[ς] σωτηρίας μου καὶ τῶν ἐμῶν, "I am not delaying to write you regarding the health of me and mine." In P Par 48[5] (B.C. 153) (= Witkowski *Epp.*[2] p. 91) ἀκούσαντες . . τὰ περὶ σου συνβεβηκότα, we have a mixture of ἀκούσαντες περὶ σοῦ and ἀκούσαντες τά (σοι) συνβεβηκότα

Περί, "with regard to," at the beginning of a new clause (as in 1 Cor 7[1]) may be illustrated from the headings in the Mysteries inscr. from Andania *Syll* 653 (=[3] 736)[1] (B.C. 91) περὶ ἱε]ρῶν καὶ ἱερᾶν, *al.* See also P Eleph 13[4] (B.C. 223-2) περὶ δὲ τῶν εἴκοσι δραχμῶν οὔπω ἐκεκόμιστο Φίλων . . . περὶ δὲ τοῦ οἰναρίου Πραξιάδης οὔπω εἰσελήλυθεν ἐξ ἀγροῦ, BGU IV. 1097[5] (time of Claudius or Nero) περὶ δὲ Σαραπᾶτος τοῦ υἱοῦ οὐ καταλέλυκε παρ' ἐμὲ ὅλως, and *ib.* I. 246[13] (ii/iii A.D.) περὶ δὲ Νείλου οὐδ[ὲ π]αρασφαλίσματά μοι ἐδίδου οὐδὲ καταγραφήν . . [17] περὶ Ἑρμιόνης μελησάτω ὑμῖν, πῶς ἄλυπος ἦν.

The transition to the meaning "on account of," "for," is easy, when περί becomes practically identical with ὑπέρ (*q.v.*): cf. in the NT Mk 14[24], Gal 1[4], 1 Cor 1[13], Heb 5[3], *al.*, where the two words are *variae lectiones*, and for περί in this sense in the papyri see P Oxy X. 1298[4] (iv/A.D.) πρὸ πάντων εὔχομε τῷ κυρίῳ θεῷ περὶ τῆς ὁλοκληρίας σου καὶ τῶν φιλτάτων σου, and *ib.* XII. 1494[6] (early iv/A.D.) μά[[λ]]λειστα μὲν δεήσει καὶ ὑμᾶς εὔχεσθαι περὶ ἡμῶν, "it will be most necessary for you too t pray on my behalf" (Edd.). On the preposition placed after its noun in Ac 19[40] see Field *Notes,* p. 131.

Περί is frequent c. gen. of the articular inf., e.g. P Tebt I. 56[6] (*c.* B.C. 130-121) γε[ί]ν[ωσ]κε δὲ περὶ τοῦ κατακεκλῦσθαι τὸ πεδίον ὑμῶν (*l.* ἡμῶν), "you must hear about our plain having been inundated" (Edd.), and P Ryl II. 230[3] (A.D. 40) ἐκομισάμην ἐπιστολὴ(ν) περὶ τοῦ πέμψαι με ἐπὶ τοὺς ἄρτους τῇ ε, "I received a letter regarding my sending for the loaves on the 5th."

2. For the *local* use of περί c. acc. cf. P Tebt I. 56[12] (*c.* B.C. 130-121) ζητή[σ]α[ς] μοι περὶ τὴν κώμην σου εἰς τὴν τροφὴν ἡμῶν γῆς ἀρούρας πέ[ν]τε, "by seeking out in the neighbourhood of your village 5 arourae for our maintenance" (Edd.), P Oxy II. 246[14] (A.D. 66) περὶ τὴν αὐτὴν Φθῶχιν, "in the neighbourhood of the said Phthochis." See also from the inscr. *Preisigke* 1568[6] (ii/B.C.) οἱ περὶ αὐλήν ("court-officials").

With Mk 4[10] οἱ περὶ αὐτόν, "his disciples," cf. P Petr II. 45[ii 7] (B.C. 246) τοῖς περὶ τὸν Λαοδίκην, "to the party of Laodike," P Grenf I. 10[17] (B.C. 174) οἱ περὶ τὸν Δρύτωνα, and for the classical idiom in Ac 13[13] οἱ περὶ Παῦλον, "Paul and his company," cf. *ib.* I. 21[16] (B.C. 120) αἱ περὶ Ἀπολλωνίαν, "Apollonia and her sisters" a joint beneficiaries under a Will, and P Fay 34[11] (A.D. 161) τοῖ[ς] περὶ τὸν Πανεσνέα, "to Panesneus and his partners."

With Phil 2[23] τὰ περὶ ἐμέ, cf. P Par 44[6] (B.C. 153) τὰ περὶ Ἀπολλώνιον, and see also *ib.* 15[17] (B.C. 120) τῇ περὶ ἑαυτοὺς βίᾳ χρώμενοι, P Ryl II. 153[45] (A.D. 138-161) διὰ τὴν περὶ ἐμὲ ἀσθένιαν, and the magic formula P Oxy VI. 886[9] (iii/A.D.) ὁ δὲ τρόπος ἐστὶν τὰ περ[ὶ] τὰ γράμματα κθ, "the method is concerned with the 29 letters."

The *temporal* use of περί c. acc., as in Mt 20[3], Ac 10[3,9] *al.*, may be illustrated by BGU I. 246[20] (ii/iii A.D.) περὶ τὸν Χοιάκ, PSI III. 184[5] (A.D. 292) χθὲς περὶ ἕκτην ὥραν.

Further instances of the different uses of περί will be found in the monographs of Kuhring and Rossberg (see Abbreviations I.).

περιάγω.

For the trans. use of περιάγω, "lead around," as in 1 Cor 9[5], cf. P Cairo Zen 50033[2] (B.C. 257) ἐγὼ δὲ τοῖς ἐλθοῦσιν περιαγαγὼν πάντας τοὺς παραδείσους ἔδειξα. See also Diod. Sic. xvii. 77 πρὸς δὲ τούτοις τὰς παλλακίδας ("concubines") ὁμοίως τῷ Δαρείῳ περιῆγε, and *s.v.* χείρ.

περιαιρέω

in its literal sense "take away," "remove," may be illustrated from BGU IV. 1061[18] (B.C. 14) ἐξέδυσαν καὶ περιείλοντο αὐτοῦ πόκους ἐρίων ρν̅. Cf. P Tebt II. 300[11] (A.D. 151), where instructions are given that a priest who had died should be struck off the list—ἐπιδίδο(ω)μι ὤ(= ὅ)πως περιερεθῇ [τ]οῦτο τὸ ὄνομα, BGU IV. 1085[ii 7] (ii/A.D.) ἀξιούντων περιαιρεθῆναι αὐτὸν τῆς προκηρύξεω[ς, and the corresponding use of the act. in P Flor III. 308[7] (A.D. 203) ἀξιῶ αὐτὸν περιελεῖν ἐκ τῶν δημοσίων λόγων: see also Ac 28[13] and Field *Notes,* p. 149 f. For the metaph. usage, as in Ac 27[20], cf. M. Anton. xii. 2 τὸν πολὺν περισπασμὸν σεαυτοῦ περιαιρήσεις, "thou wilt free thyself from the most of thy distracting care" (Haines).

περιάπτω,

in the derived sense of "kindle," is found in the NT only in Lk 22[55] (cf. 3 Macc 3[7]). For the original meaning "tie about," "attach," see the magic P Lond 121[197] (iii/A.D.) (= I. p. 90) ἐπίγραφ(ε) εἰς χάρτ(ην) καὶ περίαπτε ρουραρβισαρου . . . as a charm against discharge from the eyes, *ib.*[219] p. 91) γράψον εἰς χάρτην καθαρὸν καὶ περίαψον ιαω σαβαωθ αδωναι . . . as a charm against ague, and Aristeas 159 ἐπὶ τῶν χειρῶν δὲ διαρρήδην τὸ σημεῖον κελεύει περιῆφθαι, "he expressly orders that the 'sign' be 'bound round upon the hands'" (Thackeray). The verb should perhaps be restored in this sense in PSI I. 64[7] (i/B.C. ?) π]εριη[ψάς μοι χρυ]σίον: see the editor's note. In Vett. Val. p. 285[32] περιάπτειν = *diffamare*.

περιαστράπτω.

Among the few reff. for this word, which in the NT is confined to Ac 9[3], 22[6], we may cite 4 Macc 4[10] ἄγγελοι περιαστράπτοντες τοῖς ὄχλοις.

περιβάλλω.

For a good parallel to the TR of Lk 19[43] cf. P Oxy IV. 707[32] (*c.* A.D. 136) where a man is charged with neglecting a vineyard—μηδὲ τὰς πλάτας περιβεβληκέναι, "not even to have built the enclosing walls." For the meaning "wrap about," "clothe myself," as in Mk 14[51] (cf. Field *Notes,* p. 40), see P Fay 12[15] (*c.* B.C. 103) ἐξέδυσαν ὁ περ[ιε]βεβλήμην ἱμάτιον, "they stripped me of the garment in which I was clothed," P Grenf I. 38[14] (ii/i B.C.) (as amended *Berichtigungen,* p. 182) ὅ τε περιεβλήμην ὀθόνιον κατέρηξεν, and the metaphor. use in PSI IV. 330⁷ (B.C. 258–7) οὗτος δὲ τῆι μεγίστηι με ἀτιμίαι περιβέβληκεν, ib. 435⁹ (iii/B.C.) (as read by Deissmann Exp VIII. xxiv. p. 421) εἰς ἀρρωσ[τ]ία[ν] μ[ε πε]ριέβαλεν μεγάλην, "he afflicted me with a great sickness," and Aristeas 208 αἰκίαις περιβάλλειν, "subject men to injuries." See also Menander Περικ. 36 εὐθὺς προσδραμών] ἐφίλει, περιέβαλλε.

περιβλέπομαι.

For the act. = "look round," cf. BGU IV. 1097³ (i/A.D.) ἠὰν δὲ ὁ ἀντίδικος ἀναβῇ, περιβλέπε αὐτόν. In the NT the verb is used only in the mid., and chiefly with reference to the quick, searching glance of Christ.

The verbal περίβλεπτος is common in late papyri as a form of address, e.g. P Oxy XVI. 1868 verso (vi/vii A.D.) τῷ τὰ πάντα λαμπρο(τάτῳ) καὶ περιβλέπτῳ κόμε(τι), "to the in all respects most illustrious and most admired comes": cf. the subst. in BGU II. 547³ (Byz.) παρακαλῶ τὴν ὑμετέραν περιβλεπτ[ότητα.

περιβόλαιον

in the wider sense of "covering," "clothing," rather than "veil" (AV marg.) in 1 Cor 11¹⁵ (cf. Ps 103(104)⁶) may be illustrated from Aristeas 158 ἐκ τῶν περιβολαίων παράσημον ἡμῖν μνείας δέδωκεν, "in our clothing, too, he has given us a symbol of remembrance" (Thackeray).

For περίβολος, "enclosure," we may cite the inscr. on the marble barrier of the inner court of the Temple at Jerusalem, OGIS 598¹ (i/A.D.) μηθένα ἀλλογενῆ εἰσπορεύεσθαι ἐντὸς τοῦ περὶ τὸ ἱερὸν τρυφάκτου καὶ περιβόλου, "that no foreigner enter within the screen and enclosure surrounding the sanctuary": see further Deissmann LAE p. 75, Otto Priester i. p. 282 ff.

περιδέω,

"bind around," as in Jn 11⁴⁴, occurs in the account of a healing at the temple of Asclepius in Epidaurus, Syll 802 (= ³1168)⁶² (c. B.C. 320) μετὰ δὲ τοῦτο τὸν θεὸν τὰν τοῦ Πανδάρου ταινίαν ("band") περιδῆσαι περὶ τὰ στίγματα.

For περίδεσμος as a prayer which was believed to fetter the object of imprecation, see Wünsch in Bliss and Macalister, Excavations in Palestine, 1902, p. 182.

περιεργάζομαι,

"am a busybody" (2 Thess 3¹¹: cf. Sir 3²³⁽²⁴⁾): cf. PSI V. 494⁷ (B.C. 258–7) περὶ δὲ τῶν . . . Ἀρχίου περιεργασάμην εἴς σε ἀπο . . φι δῶις ἢ γράψηις, the letter of the Emperor Claudius to the Alexandrines P Lond 1912⁹⁹ (A.D. 41) καὶ Ἰουδέοις δὲ ἄντικρυς κελεύωι μηδὲν πλῆωι ὧν πρότερον ἔσχον περιεργάζεσθαι. "and, on the other side, I bid the Jews not to busy themselves about anything beyond what they have held hitherto" (Bell), and P Giss I. 57³ (vi/vii A.D.) καταξιώση οὖν περιεργάσασθαι καὶ ποιῆσαι ἀποδοθῆναι τὰ γράμματα.

Very noteworthy from the inscrr. is Syll 633 (= ³1042)¹⁵ (ii/iii A.D.) ὃς ἂν δὲ πολυπραγμονήσῃ τὰ τοῦ θεοῦ ἢ περιεργάσηται, ἁμαρτίαν ὀφιλέτω Μηνὶ Τυράννωι. See also the magical citation s.v. περίεργος.

As illustrating the meaning of the verb it is customary to quote Plato Apol. 19 B, where it is said of Socrates in an

accusatory sense, περιεργάζεται ζητῶν τά τε ὑπὸ γῆς καὶ οὐράνια : cf. M. Anton. x. 2 τούτοις δὴ κανόσι χρώμενος, μηδὲν περιεργάζου, "apply these criteria to life, and do so without fuss" (Rendall). See also Test. xii. patr. Reub. iii. 10 μήτε περιεργάζεσθε πρᾶξιν γυναικῶν, "nor meddle with the affairs of womankind." In Aristeas 15 the verb is used in a good sense καθὼς περιείργασμαι, "as my research (into God's dealings) has taught me": but contrast 315.

περίεργος.

The idea of "curious, magical arts," which τὰ περίεργα has in Ac 19¹⁹, is well illustrated in P Leid Vᵛᵘ 19 (iii/iv A.D.) (= II. p. 30) διὰ τὴν τῶν πολλῶν περιεργίαν τὰς βοτάνας καὶ τὰ ἄλλα, οἷς ἐχρῶντο εἰς θεῶν εἴδωλα, ἐπέγραψαν, ὅπως μὴ συλ(= λλ)αβούμενοι περιεργάζωνται μηδέν, διὰ τὴν ἐξακολούθησιν τῆς ἁμαρτεί(= ί)ας, "ob vulgi curiositatem herbas et reliqua, quibus utebantur ad deorum simulacra, scriptis consignarant, ut non intellecturi reliqui homines) operarentur frustra propter investigationem erroris" (Ed.): see also the note on p. 73 f., and Deissmann BS p. 223 n.². Cf. the conjunction of words in Vett. Val. p. 7³⁰ φρόνιμοι, περίεργοι, ἀποκρύφων μύσται. For the meaning "busybody," as in 1 Tim 5¹³, cf. Menandrea pp. 11⁴⁵, 48⁸⁵, and Menander Fragm. p. 227, also Theophr. Char. x. (ed Jebb).

In the letter of a steward or bailiff, P Oxy IX. 1220²² (iii/A.D.), the word is used in a more general sense—οὐδὲν ἠφάνισεν ὁ ἱπποποτάμις, ἤ τι γάρ ἐστιν περιέργου, ἐφίσταμε (= αι) αὐτῶν, "the hippopotamus has destroyed nothing, for if there is any superfluity, I watch over the place" (Ed.).

περιέρχομαι.

With the use of this verb in 1 Tim 5¹³ we may compare P Oxy VII. 1033¹² (A.D. 392) μόνοι περιερχόμενοι τὴν πόλιν καὶ κατοπτεύοντες, "going about the city alone and keeping watch." The verb occurs in connexion with an inheritance in PSI V. 452³ (iv/A.D.) ἀνδράπ[οδ]α περιῆλθεν εἰς ἡμᾶς : cf. BGU IV. 1074³ (A.D. 275) ἠσθῆναι ἐπὶ τῷ εἰς ἐμὲ περιεληλυθέναι τὴν τῶν ὅλων κηδεμονίαν. Vett. Val. p. 40²⁸ ποικίλως τὸν βίον περιερχομένους.

περιέχω.

For the intrans. use, as in 1 Pet 2⁶ (cf. Blass-Debrunner § 308) we may quote P Oxy II. 249²¹ (A.D. 80) διαθήκη ὡς περιέχει, "in the will as it stands" or "as it is contained in the will": cf. ib. 285¹³ (A.D. 82) ἐφ' οἷς ἄλλοις ἡ ἀσφάλεια περιέχει, "with the other guarantees contained in the agreement" (Edd.), P Fay 96²⁰ (A.D. 122) μενούσης κυρίας τῆς μισθώσεως ἐφ' οἷς περιέχει πᾶσι, "the lease in all its provisions remaining valid" (Edd.), P Oxy I. 95²¹ (A.D. 129) ὡς καὶ ἡ ἰδιόγραφος πρᾶσις περιέχει, "as the autograph contract states" (Edd.), ib. IX. 1220²⁹ (iii/A.D.) the accounts will show the details ὡς περιέχει τὸ πι τ]τάκιον, "as contained in the memorandum," and Syll 929 (= ³685)²¹ (B.C. 139) καθότι τὰ . . . γράμματα περιέχει, also ³¹ τοῦ δόγματος περιέχοντος "the decree running thus" (words follow). In ib.⁷⁵ περιεχόμενον is pass. (c. dat. = "surrounded": cf. Lk 5⁹.

In P Lond 1178¹³ (A.D. 194) (= III. p. 216, Selections,

p. 99) the Emperor Claudius says χρυσοῦν σ[τέ|φ[α]νον ἡδέως ἔλαβον σύμβολον περιέχοντα τῆς ὑμετέρας πρός με εὐσεβείας, "I received with pleasure the golden crown as an expression of your loyal devotion towards me," which would illustrate the trans. use in the TR of Ac 23²³: cf. also P Tebt I. 44⁸ (B.C. 114) χάριν τῆς περιεχούσης με ἀρρωστίας, and Menander *Fragm.* 660² p. 193 περιέχων ἐγκώμιον, "containing commendation." Searles *Lexicographical Study* p. 102 cites a Delphic inscr. of A.D. 50, Collitz 2208¹⁰ εἰ δὲ μὴ παραμένοι καθὼς ἁ ὠνὰ περιέχει, where the verb has the unusual meaning "stipulate."

περιζώννυμι,

"gird round," is found in the pass., as in Rev 1¹³, 15⁶, in the magic charm P Lond 46¹⁵⁷ (iv/A.D.) (= I. p. 70) ἐγώ εἰμι ἡ χάρις τοῦ αἰῶνος ὄνομά μοι καρδία περιεζωσμένη ὄφιν: cf. Diod. Sic. i. 72. 2 περιεζωσμένοι.

For the subst. περίζωμα, "girdle," cf. P Par 10¹² (B.C. 145) περὶ τὸ σῶμα χλαμύδα καὶ περίζωμα, and P Oxy VI. 921¹⁰ (iii/A.D.) περίζωμα ἁ, "one girdle," in an inventory of property.

περιΐστημι.

OGIS 735¹⁰ (ii/B.C.) ἐν τοῖς νῦν περιστᾶσι και[ροῖς, "in present circumstances," as contrasted with ἔν τε τοῖς πρότερον χρόνοις mentioned just before. See also P Oxy VI. 899¹⁴ (A.D. 200) where a woman complains of having been reduced to extreme poverty—εἰς ἔνδειά]ν με οὐ τὴν τυχοῦσαν περιστῆναι, and *ib.* 902¹² (c. A.D. 465) εἰς τελείαν γὰρ ἀνατροπὴν καὶ εἰς αἰχάτην πεινων (*l.* ἐσχάτην πεῖναν) περιέστην, "I have been reduced to complete ruin and the extremity of hunger" (Edd.): cf. Vett. Val. p. 285³³ εἰς μεγίστας ἀτυχίας περιστάνουσιν.

The late use of the mid. = "turn oneself about" to avoid, "shun," c. acc., as in 2 Tim 2¹⁶, Tit 3⁹, may perhaps be illustrated from *Chrest.* II. 88^{iv. 39} (ii/A.D.) τῆς δὲ [ἀ]ντίας Δρουσίλλας περισταμένης τὴν λογο[θ]εσίαν. Other exx. of the mid. are BGU IV. 1019⁸ (mid. ii/A.D.) περι[έ]σταμένης δ' αὑτῆς, and the *florilegium* PSI II. 120³⁷ (iv/A.D. ?) μηδὲ εἰς πρᾶγμα περιίστασο ὅ σοι μὴ προσήκε.

περικάθαρμα,

a term of the deepest opprobrium, drawn from the "rinsing" of a dirty vessel. In the only place in which it occurs in the NT, 1 Cor 4¹³, there may be some reference to the fact that it was the most wretched and outcast, who used to be sacrificed as expiatory offerings: cf. Prov 21¹¹ and Epict. iii. 22. 78. "Possibly some cry of this sort, anticipating the 'Christiani ad leones' of the martyrdoms, had been raised against P(aul) by the Ephesian populace (cf. xv. 32; also Acts xxii. 22)" (Findlay *EGT ad* 1 Cor 4¹³). The word is fully illustrated by Wetstein *ad l.c.*: see also Lietzmann in *HZNT.*

The verb (Deut 18¹⁰) is found in Didache iii. 4 μηδὲ ἐπαοιδὸς μηδὲ μαθηματικὸς μηδὲ περικαθαίρων.

περικαθίζω.

For the meaning "sit around," "encircle," as in Lk 22⁵⁵ DG, cf. *Chrest.* I. 11 B.Fr.(a)¹⁰ (B.C. 123) εἰς τ[ὴ]ν πόλιν ἐπιβαλόντες μ[ετὰ τ]ῶν ἱκανῶν καὶ ἱ[ππ]έων περιεκάθισαν ἡμῶν τὸ φρούριον.

περίκειμαι.

For the literal sense "wear," "carry," c. acc., as in Ac 28²⁰ (cf. 4 Macc 12³), cf. *OGIS* 56⁶⁷ (B.C. 238) περικειμένων τὰς ἰδίας βασιλείας ("diadems") (cited by Mayser *Gr.* p. 34). The metaphorical usage is seen in the illiterate P Lond 1926¹³ (mid. iv/A.D.), where a certain Valeria asks for Paphnutius's prayers—μεγάλῳ γὰρ νόσῳ περίκιμε δυσπνήας δινῆς (*l.* περίκειμαι δυσπνοίας δεινῆς), "for I am afflicted with a great disease in the shape of a grievous shortness of breath" (Bell): cf. Heb 5², and from literary sources Theocritus xxiii. 13 f. φεῦγε δ' ἀπὸ χρῶς| ὕβριν τᾶς ὀργᾶς περικείμενος, *Anth. Pal.* xi. 38 πῖνε καὶ ἔσθιε καὶ περικεῖσο ἄνθεα.

περικεφαλαία,

"helmet"; cf. P Petr III. 140(a)³ (accounts—iii/B.C.) περικεφαλαίας καὶ θήκης ν̄, "60 dr. for a helmet and sheath," and *Syll* 522 (= ³ 958)²⁹f. (ii/B.C.), where a περικεφαλαία is first prize in a javelin-throwing contest, together with three λόγχαι, and is also offered, together with a κόντος ("the shaft of a pike"), as a prize for the best καταπαλταφέτης.

περικρατής,

"gaining the mastery over" (Ac 27¹⁶), is found in the apocryphal Sus (Θ) 39 A. For the verb see the *prooem.* to the Gnomon⁵ᶠ. (c. A.D. 150) (= BGU V. 1. p. 10) ὅπως . . . εὐχερ[ῶς] τῶν πραγμάτων περικ[ρ]ατῆς, "in order that you may easily master the business": cf. M. Anton. x. 8. 2.

περικρύπτω,

"conceal," "hide." Cf. Lk 1²⁴ περιέκρυβεν, a late impf. from a pres. περικρύβω, not found in the NT (see Blass *Gr.* p. 41). For the simplex see Ev. Petr. 7 ἐκρυβόμεθα. MGr κρύβω.

περικυκλόω,

"encircle" (Lk 19⁴³): cf. the iv/A.D. letter of a deacon to a bishop (see *Archiv* iv. p. 558), where the writer remarks—ἡ γὰρ εὐφημία σου, πάτερ, περιεκύκλωσεν τὸν κ[όσ]μον ὅλον ὡς ἀγαθὸν πατέρα (*l.* ἀγαθοῦ πατρός, Wilcken) (P Lond 981⁹ = III. p. 242, *Chrest.* I. p. 157). Περικυκλωθέν is used adverbially in the late P Lond 483¹⁷.⁷⁷ (A.D. 616) (= II. pp. 325, 328).

περιλείπομαι,

"am left over" (1 Thess 4¹⁵,¹⁷, with Milligan's note): cf. PSI IV. 409¹² (iii/B.C.) λοιποὶ περιελείφθησαν εἰς τὰς θυσίας, *ib.* VI. 571¹⁴ (iii/B.C.) οὐθέν μοι περιλείπεται, P Par 63¹³⁸ (B.C. 164) (= P Petr III. p. 32) βραχεῖα (*sc.* γῆ) παντελῶς ἀγεώργητος περιλειφθήσεται, "a very small portion of the land will be left uncultivated" (Mahaffy), and BGU IV. 1132¹² (B.C. 13) τὸ περιλελιμμένον αὐτῶι μέρος.

περιμένω,

"wait for" (Ac 1⁴): cf. P Giss I. 73¹ (time of Hadrian) ἐκομισάμην σου τὴν ἐπιστολὴν ἡδέως καὶ περιμένω σε, P Oxy XIV. 1762¹⁰ (ii/iii A.D.) οὔπω μέντοι εἰς διαλλαγὰς ἐλθεῖν ἠθέλησεν . . . σὲ περιμένων, and BGU II. 388ⁱⁱ ³⁹ (ii/iii A.D.) ἐ[ν] ἢ πλαστυγραφίᾳ περιμ[ένο]ν ἐστὶν τὸ ὄνομα.

πέριξ,

"round about" (Ac 5[16]), formerly a nom. sing. (Boisacq p. 772), and rare in Attic prose, cf. PSI IV. 317[5] (A.D. 95) πά]ντες οἱ πέριξ, and *Kaibel* 468[1] Λαίνεος στήλη με πέριξ ἔχει.

περιούσιος.

The appearance of]περιουσι[between hiatus in CP Herm I. 32[4] is tantalizing, as there is no indication in this tiny fragment what the meaning may be. The verb περίειμι, "survive," may be illustrated from P Oxy I. 37[i 28] (A.D. 49) (= *Chrest.* II p. 87, *Selections*, p. 50) <τῶν> στα]τήρων π[ερ]ιόντων, "the staters (forming a nurse's wages) remaining in my possession," *ib.* II. 243[10] (A.D. 79) ὁπότε περιῆν, "in her lifetime" (Edd.), and P Strass I. 52[8] (A.D. 151) τὰ . . . περιεσόμενα π[άν]τα εἰς τὸ ἴδιον.

For the subst. see P Fay 20[13] (Imperial rescript—iii/iv A.D.) οὐ διὰ περιουσίαν πλούτου, "not owing to a superfluity of wealth," and P Flor III. 367[12] (iii/A.D.) where the writer complains that his correspondent is despising his friends— πλούτῳ γαυρωθεὶς ("puffed up") [καὶ] πολλῇ χρημάτων περιουσίᾳ. In the important letter of Claudius to the Alexandrines, P Lond 1912 (A.D. 41), the Emperor enjoins the Jews to enjoy in a city not their own ⁹⁵ περιουσίας ἁπάντων ἀγαθῶν, "an abundance of all good things" (Bell). Cf. also Gnomon 6 (c. A.D. 150) (= BGU V. 1. p. 13) τετάρτου μέρους ἧς ἔχει περιουσίας, and P Oxy XIV. 1642[23] (A.D. 289) τῶ]ν ἐν περιουσίᾳ τυγχανόντων.

Reference should be made to Lightfoot *On a Fresh Revision*[3] App. I. p. 217 ff. "On the words ἐπιούσιος, περιούσιος."

περιοχή

in the literal sense of "compass," "circumference," occurs *quater* in connexion with certain measurements of a piece of land in BGU II. 492 (A.D. 148-9): cf. also the late P Hamb I. 23[20] (A.D. 569) μετὰ τῆς καθόλου αὐτοῦ περιοχῆς, "mit allem was dran und drum ist" (Preisigke). For the use in Ac 8[32] of a "passage" (of Scripture) see the reff. *s.v.* περιέχω, and cf. Cic. *ad Att.* xiii. 25. 3 *ergo ne Tironi quidem dictate, qui totas* περιοχάς *persequi solet, sed Spintharo syllabatim.* In the LXX περιοχή has the meaning "siege," and sometimes apparently "stronghold": see Conybeare and Stock *LXX Selections*, p. 305.

περιπατέω.

On the ethical use of this verb "conduct my life," corresponding to the Heb. הלך, see *Proleg.* p. 11. For the literal meaning "walk," "go about," cf. BGU III. 846[9] (ii/A.D.) (= *Selections*, p. 94) σαπρῶς παιριπατῶ (*l.* περιπατῶ), "I am going about in a disgraceful state," P Fay 126[2] (ii/iii A.D.) περ[ι]πατοῦντός μου σὺν τῷ πατρί, and BGU II. 380[13] (iii/A.D.) περπατω (*l.* περιπατῶ) μετὰ οὗ ἐὰν εὕρω. In P Lond 981[11] (iv/A.D.) (= III. p. 242, *Chrest.* I. p. 157) περιοδεύομεν καὶ περιπατοῦμεν νυκτήμαρ, the words are addressed apparently by subordinate church officials to a bishop: see Ghedini *Lettere*, p. 170 f.

See further, for an interesting parallel to Rev 3[1], *Kaibel* 387[2 f.] (III. fere saeculi)—

ὁ κτώμενος δὲ πολλὰ μὴ τρυφῶν [σ]ὺν τοῖς φίλοις
οὗτος τέ[θ]νηκε περιπατῶν καὶ ζῆ νεκρ[οῦ βίον.

In Menander Ἐπιτρ. 12 δίκας λέγοντες περιπατεῖτε, the verb is almost = "live." MGr περιπατῶ, περπατῶ, περβατῶ.

περιπείρω.

For the metaph. use of this verb "pierce" in 1 Tim 6[10], cf. Philo *Flacc.* 1 (ed. Cohn) ἀνηκέστοις περιέπειρε κακοῖς, and the other passages cited by Wetstein from late Greek.

περιπίπτω.

For περιπίπτω, "fall in with," as in all its NT occurrences (Lk 10[30], Ac 27[41], Jas 1[2]), cf. P Oxy XIV. 1630[20] (B.C. 73 or 44) ὅπου ἂν τῷ καθόλου περιπίπτῃς ἡμῖν, "in any place whatsoever where you may encounter us" (Edd.), P Tebt II. 278[52] (early i A.D.) θυμοῦ περιπεσεῖτε (= εῖται), "he will meet with anger," P Ryl I. 28[220] (mantic—iv/A.D.) ἐὰν δ[ὲ] ὁ ἐχόμενος μερίμναις πολλαῖς περιπεσεῖται καὶ κακοπαθίαις, "if the next (toe quiver) he will be involved in much anxiety and distress," and from the inscr. *Syll* 226 (= ³ 495[56] (c. B.C. 230) διότι μεγάλοις διαπτώμασι περιπεσεῖται ἡ πόλις, and the imprecatory formula to prevent violation of tombs as in *C. and B.* ii. p. 702, No. 636 (A.D. 234) ὃς ἂν κακουργέσι τοῦτο, τοιούταις (!) περιπέσοιτο συμφοραῖς.

The word is claimed as medical by Hobart p. 129 f., but for its wider usage cf. Wetstein *ad* Lk *l.c.*, Field *Notes* p. 61, and add *Pelagia-Legenden* p. 9[18], where it is stated that a harlot cannot be baptized without sponsors, ἵνα μὴ πάλιν ἐν τοῖς αὐτοῖς εὑρεθῇ περιπίπτουσα.

The 1 aor. is seen in a new comic fragment (? Menander: Demiańczuk *Suppl. Com.* p. 63):—

ἄνθρωπος γὰρ ὢν
ἀνθρωπίναις περιέπεσα συμφοραῖς.

περιποιέω.

For the mid. "make my own," "acquire for oneself," as in 1 Tim 3[13], see P Tor II. 8[70] (B.C. 119) (ἑαυτ)ῶι μεγάλην ἐξουσίαν περι(ποιούμενος), and cf. P Amh II. 34 (*d*)[2] (c. B.C. 157) πλεῖόν τι περιποιούμενοι τῶι βασιλεῖ, "gaining more for the king." For the corresponding use of the act. cf. P Oxy II. 279[3] (A.D. 44-5) βο]υλόμ(ενος) πλεῖον περιποιῆσαι τοῖς δη[μοσ]ίοις, *ib.* I. 58[9] (A.D. 288) ὄφελος μὲν οὐδὲν περιποιοῦσιν τῷ ταμείῳ, "they secure no advantage to the treasury" (Edd.), *ib.* XVI. 1892[34] (A.D. 581) τὸ ἱκανὸν [το]ῦ αὐτοῦ χρέους περιπ[οιῆ]σαι, "to make up the equivalent of the said debt" (Edd.), P Flor III. 295[5] (vi/A.D.) ἀζωτίαν ἑαυτοῖς περιποιοῦντες, and from the inscr. *Syll* 226 (= ³ 495.[134] (B.C. 230) οὐκ ὀλίγα χρήματα περιεποίησε τῆι πόλει. Cf. also *Pelagia-Legenden* p. 12[8]. In P Fay 111[8] (A.D. 95-6) (= *Selections*, p. 66) τῷ (*l.* τὸ) αἴτιωμα (cf. Ac 25[7]) περιεπύ(= οι)ησε is rendered by the editors "shifted the blame," in accordance with what seems to be the natural meaning of the context. In support of this unusual meaning for περιποιέω Dr. Hunt thinks that σοι must be understood, and refers us to the somewhat similar passage in Isocr. p. 150 E, where the common reading is μεγάλην αἰσχύνην τῇ πόλει περιποιοῦσιν (ποιοῦσιν Blass, περιαπτοῦσιν Cobet), and to Polyb. v. 58. 5 χωρὶς τῆς αἰσχύνης, ἣν περιποιεῖ νῦν τῇ βασιλείᾳ.

περιποίησις.

See P Rein 52² (iii/iv A.D.) ὑμῖν ἐγράφη τὴν περιποίησιν τοῦ σείτου καὶ τὴν ἀναπομπὴν δηλῶσαι, where the editor notes that περιποίησις means "soit acquisition ou production, soit conservation": here he doubtfully selects "production," but in view of the following ἀναπομπήν, "préservation" would be better (cf. P Flor II. p. 80). In P Tebt II. 317²⁶ (A.D. 174–5) τὸ τῆς περιποιήσεως δίκαιον is rendered "claim of ownership," which may be set by Eph 1¹⁴, where the "ownership" is *bought back* after alienation.

περιρχάίνω

(for form, cf. WH *Notes*², p. 139 f.), "sprinkle round about" (Rev 19¹³ ℵ*): cf. *Syll* 566 (= ³982)⁸ (after B.C. 133) ἀπὸ δὲ τάφου καὶ ἐκφορᾶς περιρασ(=ν)άμενοι, *ib*. 567 (= ³983)¹⁵ (ii/A.D.) ἀπὸ συνουσίας νομίμου αὐθημερὸν περιραναμένους καὶ πρότερον χρεισαμένους ἐλαίῳ—with reference to the purification required before entering sacred precincts. A περιραντήριον (for form cf. Kuhner-Blass ii. p. 281) is mentioned amongst temple furniture in *Syll* 754⁷. Cf. *Menandrea* p. 140³⁶ (after massage and purification with brimstone) ἀπὸ κρουνῶν τριῶν ὕδατι περίρραν(αι), "sprinkle yourself with water from three fountains."

περιρήγνυμι.

In Ac 16²² περιρρήξαντες is generally understood (AV, RV) of "stripping off" the garments of the prisoners in preparation for a beating (cf. 2 Macc 4³⁸). Ramsay, however, refers the action to the Praetors themselves, "rent their clothes in loyal horror, with the fussy, consequential airs that Horace satirises in the would-be Praetor of a country town (*Sat*. I. 5, 34)" (*Paul*, p. 219). The verb is thus taken as practically synonymous with the well-known διαρρήσσω with ἱμάτια, χιτῶνας (Mt 26⁶⁵, *al*.), as expressive of a gesture of horror. In support of this rendering Mr. K. L. Clarke kindly refers us to *Acta Thomae* 63 (Lipsius-Bonnet II ii. 180) τὴν ἐσθῆτα περιέρρηξα καὶ τὰς χεῖρας ἐπὶ τὴν ὄψιν ἐπάταξα, and cites Cyril's note on Ac 14¹⁴ ἔθος ἐστὶν Ἰουδαίοις ἐπὶ ταῖς κατὰ θεοῦ δυσφημίαις περιρηγνύναι τὰ ἱμάτια (Cramer's *Catena in loc*.).

περισπάω.

The late metaph. use of περισπάω="distract," "worry," in Lk 10⁴⁰ is well attested in the Κοινή—P Lond 24²¹ (B.C. 163) (= I. p. 32 f., *UPZ* i. p. 117 f.) δι' ἣν αἰτίαν περισπώμενος ὑπὸ τῆς Ταθήμιος, *ib*. ²⁴ ἀξιῶ οὖν σε μὴ ὑπεριδεῖν με περισπώμενον, and *ib*.²⁹ ὅπως καὶ αὐτὸς τῆι Ταθήμει ἀποδοὺς μὴ περισπῶμαι, "that I may be able to pay Tathemis and be no more worried," P Grenf I. 15⁵ (B.C. 146 or 135) ὅπ]ως μὴ περισπώμεθα ἐπὶ τὰ τὰ κριτήρια, P Tebt I. 43³⁸ (B.C. 118) ὅπως μηθενὶ ἐπιτρέπηι τ[.]νπ̣[. .]ον περὶ τῶν αὐτῶν παρενοχλεῖν ἡμᾶς μηδὲ περισπᾶν κατὰ μηδεμίαν παρεύρεσιν, "in order that no one may be allowed to molest us on the same charges or to annoy us on any pretext whatever" (Edd.), and *ib*.⁴⁵ ἐὰν ἦι οἷα προφ(έρ)εται προνοηθῆναι ὡς οὐ περισπασθή-σονται, "if the allegations are correct see that he is not molested," where we find παρενοχληθήσεται written above περισπασθήσονται, as if the verb in the sense of "distract"

was not sufficiently clear; cf. also P Oxy IV. 743³⁶ (B.C. 2) ἐν τῶ̣ δέ με περισπᾶσθαι (for constr. see *Proleg*. p. 14) οὐκ ἠδυνάσθην συντυχεῖν Ἀπολλω(νίῳ), "owing to my worries I was unable to meet Apollonius" (Edd.).

For the more literal sense "draw off," "draw away," cf. P Lond 43³¹ (B.C. 168) (= I. p. 31, *UPZ* i. p. 301, *Selections* p. 11) εἴπερ μὴ ἀναγκαιότερόν σ[ε] περισπᾶι, and P Tor I.ⁱᵛ.³⁶ (B.C. 116) προηνέγκατο τὸν Ἑρμίαν κατὰ κενὸν περιεσπακέναι, where in his note (p. 139) the editor describes περισπᾶν as "circumagere aliquem, eumque in diversa trahere decipiendi causa." In P Par 63⁹¹ (B.C. 164) (= P Petr III. p. 26) the verb is used of "distraining" furniture—τὰς ἀποσκευὰς . . . περισπᾶν. For the subst., as in Tob 10⁶ ℵ, cf. P Tebt II. 393¹⁶ (A.D. 150) περισπασμῶν χάρειν, "on account of his anxieties," and M. Anton. xii. 2 (quoted *s.v.* περιαιρέω). See also *s.v.* ἀπερισπάστως, and the citations from late Greek in Herwerden *Lex. s.v.* περι-σπάω.

περισσεία,

"superfluity," "surplus." Though Grimm-Thayer (p. 695) include this subst. in their list of so-called "Biblical" words, they inconsistently append the note "Inscr.," and Deissmann (*LAE*, p. 80) has now furnished two interesting exx. from this source. The first is from *CIG* I. 1378, where a president of the games is described as—τὴν περισσείαν ἀποδοὺς πᾶσαν τῇ πόλει τῶν ἀγωνοθετικῶν χρημάτων, "having handed over to the city the whole surplus of the money belonging to the presidents of the games." The second is again from a pagan inscr., *BCH* xxi. (1897), p. 65 ἐκ περισσειῶν (*l*. περισσειῶν), "from superfluous (money)." Add *IGSept* 322 ἐκ τῆς περισσήας.

περισσεύω,

with the meaning "remain over," as often in the NT (Mt 15³⁷, *al*.), occurs in *Syll* 306 (= ³672)¹⁹ (B.C. 162–0) εἰ δέ τι περισσεύοι ἀπὸ τῶν τόκων and *ib*. ³250ᴰ·³⁰ (B.C. 338–7) τῶν] σκευῶν τῶμ περισσευσάντω[ν σταδίου. The common Pauline sense "have abundance" survives in MGr περισσεύω.

περισσός,

"over and above," "superfluous," in popular Greek is often in its compve. and superlve. forms practically equiva-lent to πλείων, πλεῖστος, a usage which is fully developed in MGr.

Exx. of the word are P Tebt II. 459⁴ (B.C. 5) (= Wit-kowski², p. 126) καὶ ὃ ἐὰν περισσὸν γένηται, μέτρη[σ]ον αὐτοῖς κομισάμενος τὴν τιμὴν τοῦ λοιποῦ, P Fay 111¹¹ (A.D. 95–6) (= *Selections*, p. 66) περισσὸν [ἐν]ετιλάμ[η]ν σγ(=σοι) εἰς Διο[νυσι]άδα μ[εῖ]ναι, "I gave you strict charges to remain at Dionysias," *ib*. 117²³ (A.D. 108) περιτὸν γέγραπτα[ι, "more than enough has been written" *Chrest*. I. 238ⁱⁱ·⁴ (c. A.D. 117) περισσὸν ἡγοῦμαι διεξο(=ο δέστερον ὑμῖν γράφειν, "I count it superfluous to write you at greater length," and P Tebt II. 423¹⁵ (early iii/A.D.) ἐὰν εὕρης ἀγοραστὰς τῶν περισσῶν ὄνων, παραχώρησον μέχρι τρ(ι)ῶν, "if you find any purchasers of the surplus donkeys, get rid of as many as three" (Edd.). Add from inscr. *Cagnat* IV. 317⁸ (end i/B.C.) ἐκ τῶν περισσῶν τῆς [ἑορτῆς χρη]μάτων καθειέρωσεν, and *C. and B.* ii. p. 658, No. 611—

> τὸ ζῆν τροφὴ πό[τ]ος τε. ἠτι[μασμένα ;
> περισσὰ δέ ἐστι τὰ ἄλλα [ἃ ἀνθρώποις μέλει ;

For the compve. cf. P Flor II. 127²² (A.D. 256) πάντως περισσότερον, "in every possible way," and BGU II. 380¹⁰ (iii/A.D.) (= *Selections*, p. 105) where a mother writes to her sick son, ἐτολότην (*l.* ἐθολώθην), ὡς σου περισ(=σσ ό-τερον νωχελευομένου (cf. Aq Prov 18⁹, 24¹⁰, Job 2⁴), "I was troubled because you were only able to walk so slowly." See also Dieterich *Untersuchungen*, p. 181 n.², though we have not been able to trace his reference to BGU 13, 8.

περισσοτέρως,

in the strong sense "more exceedingly," as in 2 Cor 7¹⁵, may be illustrated by P Giss I. 25¹² (ii/A.D.) ἵνα περισσ[ο]τέρως αὐτῷ μελήσῃ διὰ τὸ ὑμῖς αὐτὸν προτρέπεσθαι.

περισσῶς.

For περισσῶς, "superfluously," with reference to what precedes, cf. P Amh II. 132² (early ii/A.D.) περισ⟨σ⟩ῶς μοι ἔγραψας περὶ τοῦ μισθοῦ τῶν ἐργατῶν, "it was unnecessary for you to write to me about the wages of the labourers" (Edd.). In P Tebt II. 488 (A.D. 121-2) περισσῶς καὶ νοῖν (*l.* νῦν) ἐνκαλεῖς the adv. has rather the meaning "exceedingly," as in Ac 26¹¹. See further Blass-Debrunner § 60, 3.

περιστερά

(a Semitic borrowing=bird of Istar) is common in the sense of "dove," cf. e.g. P Flor III. 361⁵ (A.D. 82-3) περιστερὰς ἑκατόν. The diminutive περιστέριον is found in BGU IV. 1095¹⁶ (A.D. 57) ἱμακάτιον περιστεραίων (*l.* ἡμικάδιον περιστερίων), "a half-jar of (preserved) pigeons," and περιστερίδιον in BGU II. 596⁷ (A.D. 84) (= *Selections*, p. 64) where the writer invites a friend to accompany the bearer of the letter, ὅπως εἰς τὴν ἑω(=ο)ρτὴν περιστερείδια ἡμεῖν ἀγοράσῃ, "that he may buy for us young pigeons for the feast," P Giss I. 80⁵ (ii A.D.) τὰ [π]εριστερίδι.[α καὶ ὀ]ρνυθάρια, ἃ οὐκ ἤωθα ἐσθεῖν, πέμ[ψον . . ., and P Lond ined. Inv. N. 1575 (iii/A.D.) (cited by Olsson *Papyrusbriefe*, p. 195) μνημονεύσατε τῶν περιστεριδίων ἡμῶν (a schoolboy to his father). In P Oxy VIII. 1127⁸ (A.D. 183) we have the lease of the upper-room of a house with a pigeon-cote—τὸν ὑπερῷον τόπον τῆς . . . οἰκίας καὶ ὃν ἔχει ἐκεῖ περιστερεῶνα : cf. Wilcken *Archiv* i. p. 120, Luckhard *Privathaus*, p. 90.

According to Plummer *ICC ad* Lk 3²², in ancient Jewish symbolism the dove is Israel, and not the Spirit, but see Nestle *ZNTW* vii. (1906), p. 358 f., and Abrahams *Studies in Pharisaism* i. p. 47 ff.

περιτέμνω

is always used in the LXX for the ceremonial act of circumcision, and Deissmann (*BS* p. 151 ff.) has suggested that the choice of this particular compound by the LXX translators may have been due to the fact that it was "in common use as a technical term for an Egyptian custom similar to the Old Testament *circumcision.*" He cites by

way of illustration P Lond 24¹² (B.C. 163) (= I. p. 32, *UPZ* i. p. 117) ὡς ἔθος ἐστὶ[ν] τοῖς Αἰγυπτίοις περι[[τε]]-τέμνεσθαι (see further below), and BGU I. 347¹·¹⁷ (A.D. 171) where we read of a boy—περιτ]μηθῆναι [κατὰ] τὸ ἔθος.

To this evidence we can now add a series of documents dealing with the priests of Soknebtunis, P Tebt II. 291-3: see especially 292²⁹ (A.D. 189-190), where a priest makes request to the strategus that κατὰ τὸ ἔθος ἐπι[στολὴν . . .] γραφῆναι ὑπὸ σοῦ τ[ῷ κρατίστῳ ἀρχιερεῖ ἵνα] συνχωρή-σαντος αὐτοῦ δυν[ηθῶσιν οἱ παῖδες] περιτμηθῆναι καὶ τὰς ἐπιβαλλο[ύσας ἱερουρ]γίας ἐπιτελεῖν, "in accordance with custom a letter should be written by you to his highness the high-priest in order that, his permission being given, the boys [his own son and another boy] may be able to be circumcised and to perform the sacred offices assigned to them" (Edd.).

Other documents of a similar character are P Tebt II. 314 (ii/A.D.), Preisigke 15 (A.D. 155-6), BGU I. 82 (A.D. 185) and PSI V. 454 (A.D. 320). See further Wilcken *Archiv* ii. p. 4 ff., and Otto *Priester* i. p. 213 ff.

It is clear, accordingly, that circumcision was in Egypt the necessary ritual preparation for a priest. The conception of Israel as a nation of priests is well illustrated by this connotation of the rite in a neighbouring land : we can recognize, moreover, how "uncircumcised" (ἀπερ-ίτμητος) means so clearly "unclean," when we see the rite applied to a class whose business it was to be capable of entering the presence of the gods. That circumcision in Egypt was not, however, confined to candidates for the priesthood is shown by P Lond *l.c.*, where it is applied to a girl on reaching puberty, and in preparation for marriage : see further Wilcken in *UPZ* i. p. 118.

περιτίθημι,

"place around," "clothe with," as in Mt 27²⁸, may be illustrated from PSI I. 64¹⁷ (i/B.C. ?), where a woman who has offered to live with a man as his wife promises not to carry off certain articles of adornment if she leaves him—ἐὰν ἄλλα χρυσίου κόσμου μετὰ τὰ προκείμεν[α . . .]. . ρησας μοι περιθῇς, οὐκ ἀπελε[ύ]σομαι αὐτ[ὰ] ἔχουσα. For the metaph. meaning "bestow," "confer," as in 1 Cor 12²³ (cf. Esth 1²⁰), see BGU IV. 1141¹⁹ (B.C. 14) εἰ σὺ μέν μοι καὶ τιμὴν περιτιθεῖς, P Giss I. 79¹¹ (c. A.D. 117) ὡς εἰμὶ γυνὴ [π]ᾶσαν σπουδὴν περιτίθεμαι, and OGIS 331²³ (mid. ii/B.C.) ὅπως δὲ καὶ σὺ εἰδῇς ὅτι περιτεθείκαμεν (cf. Meisterhans *Gr.* p. 189) τ[ὴν τ]ιμὴν καὶ ταύτ[ην] τῶι Ἀθηναίωι.

περιτομή.

P Tebt II. 314⁵ (ii/A.D.) πιστεύω σε μὴ ἀγνοεῖν ὅσον κάμ[α]τον ἤνεγκα ἕως τὴν [π]ερι[το]μὴν ἐκπλέξω ἐπιζη-τοῦντος τοῦ [ἀ]ρχιερέως τὸν παῖδα ε[ἰ]δῖν, "I believe you are aware how much trouble I had in getting the circumcision through, owing to the high-priest's desire to see the boy" (Edd.). See *s.v.* περιτέμνω.

περιτρέπω,

"turn round," "turn" (Ac 26²⁴) : cf. Jos. *Ant.* IX. 72 (iv. 4) ταῦτα τόν τε Ἰώραμον καὶ τοὺς παρόντας εἰς χαρὰν περιέτρεψε, and Plut. *Pyrrh.* 7 περιετρέψατο (for ἐτρέψατο, Herwerden *Lex.*) καὶ κατέβαλε τὸν Πάνταυχον.

περιτρέχω,

"run round" (Mk 6[55]: cf. Apoc. Petr. 5), is found in P Flor II. 120[7] (A.D. 254) περιτρέχων τὰ[ς] ἅλως, "going round the threshing floors": cf. PSI I. 99[27] (fragment of a comedy—ii/A.D.) περιδραμών.

περιφέρω.

With περιφέρω, "carry about," in 2 Cor 4[10], cf. P Oxy XIV. 1664[7] (iii/A.D.) [[ἁ]]πᾶσα γὰρ ἡμῶν ἡ ἡλικία ἐν τοῖς στέρνοις σε περιφέρει, "for our whole youth carries you in their hearts"—a friendly letter to a gymnasiarch. In *Syll* 803 (= [3] 1169)[66] (c. B.C. 320) it is said of a man blinded in battle—τὰν λόγχαν [ἐνιαυτὸν ἐν τῶι] προσώπωι περιέφερε. For the adj. see M. Anton. i. 15 τὸ κρατεῖν ἑαυτοῦ καὶ κατὰ μηδὲν περίφορον εἶναι, "self-mastery and stability of purpose" (Haines). P Tebt I. 12[17] (B.C. 118) περιφορὰν δὲ δὸς Διονυσίωι χά{ι}ριν τῆς εὐθυμετρίας is rendered by the editors, "give the turn-table (?) to Dionysius for the survey": cf. Eccles 2[12] א A, where περιφορά = "error." Περιφέρεια in its literal sense of "circumference" is found in the plur. in *Preisigke* 358[1] (iii/B.C.).

περιφρονέω,

"despise" (Tit 2[15]: cf. P Oxy I. 71[ii. 16] (A.D. 303), where a widow complains to the praefect regarding two overseers who περι[φ]ρονοῦντές μου τῆς ἀπραγμ[οσ]ύνης, "despising my inability," had mismanaged her affairs, and P Gen I. 14[11] (Byz.) (*Berichtigungsliste*, p. 159) διὰ τὸ μὴ περιφρονεῖν με περὶ τὰ ἔνδοξα πράγματα.

περίχωρος.

In Ac 14[6] ἡ περίχωρος (sc. γῆ) describes "the country that lies round" the two cities of Lystra and Derbe, "where there were no cities but only villages organized after the Anatolian style, not according to the Hellenic municipal fashion" (Ramsay *Recent Discovery*, p. 39 n.[1]: cf. CRE p. 47 ff.).

περίψημα,

as distinguished from περικάθαρμα (q.v.), the "rinsing," is the "scraping" of a dirty vessel. It is found in Tob 5[19], where the meaning may be either "offscouring" (cf. Ignat. *Eph*. xviii. 1) or "ransom." For this latter meaning cf. the phrase περίψημα ἡμῶν γενοῦ, which, according to Photius *Lex*., was pronounced over the criminal who at Athens was flung into the sea as a propitiatory offering to avert public calamity. From this, περίψημά σου came to be used as an epistolary formula much like "your humble and devoted servant": cf. Ignat. *Eph*. viii. 1 with Lightfoot's note *ad l.*, and especially the Festal Letter of Dionysius of Alexandria (Eus. *H.E.* vii. 22. 7), who says that this "popular saying which always seems a mere expression of courtesy" (τὸ δημῶδες ῥῆμα μόνης ἀεὶ δοκοῦν φιλοφροσύνης ἔχεσθαι) was translated into action by those Christians who, during the plague, gave their lives in tending the sick. In this connexion cf. the use of the word in an epitaph by a wife on her husband—εὐψύχει, κύριέ μου Μάξιμε, ἐγώ σου περίψημα τῆς καλῆς ψυχῆς (cited by Thieling *Der Hellenismus in Kleinafrika*, p. 34).

For the verb Herwerden (*Lex. s.v.* περιψῆν) cites an inscr. from Delos of B.C. 250, *BCH* xxvii. (1903), p. 74[84] σπόγγοι περιψῆσαι τὰ ἀναθήματα.

περπερεύομαι,

"play the braggart," which meets us first in 1 Cor 13[4], occurs later in M. Anton. v. 5, where it is associated with ἀρεσκεύομαι, "play the toady." Mr. W. K. L. Clarke kindly supplies us with a reference to Basil *Regulae* xlix. 423 A: τί ἐστὶ τὸ περπερεύεσθαι; πᾶν ὃ μὴ διὰ χρείαν, ἀλλὰ διὰ καλλωπισμὸν παραλαμβάνεται, περπερείας ἔχει κατηγορίαν. The compd. ἐνπερπερεύομαι is found in nearly the same sense in Cic. *ad Att.* i. 14. 4: cf. also Epict. ii. 1. 34. For the connexion of the verb with *parpti*, "puff up," see Boisacq, p. 774.

Πέρσις.

For this proper name (Rom 16[12]) Rouffiac (*Recherches*, p. 90) cites exx. not only from Rome (*IG* II. 768), but from Thespis (*IG* VII. 2074), and from Egypt (BGU III. 895[29] (ii/A.D.), as amended p. 8). No conclusive argument can therefore be drawn from it any more than from the other proper names in Rom 16 as to the *locale* of the Church to which they belonged: cf. Lightfoot *Philippians*[2] p. 171 ff., Lietzmann *HZNT ad* Rom 16, and Milligan *Documents*, p. 182 ff.

πέρυσι.

For the phrase ἀπὸ πέρυσι, "last year," cf. BGU II. 531[ii. 1] (ii/A.D.) εἰσὶν ἐν τῶι κεραμεῖ ἀπὸ πέρυσι (δραχμαὶ) ιβ, P Oxy I. 114[12] (ii/iii A.D.) ἀπὸ Τῦβι πέρυσι: see Deissmann *BS* p. 221. Πέρυσι alone is seen in P Petr II. 4(11)[2] (B.C. 255–4) ἣν ἐσκάψαμεν πέρυσι, "which we dug last year," P Giss I. 69[4] (A.D. 118–9) καὶ γὰρ πέρυσι ἐπὶ τὴν παράλημψιν τῶν ἱματίων αὐτὸν παρά σοι κατέλειψα καὶ νῦν δὲ . . . , P Oxy III. 488[31] (ii/iii A.D.) καὶ γὰρ καὶ πέρυσι πρὸς τούτοις ἕτερά με κακῶς παρέγραψεν, "for last year also he made other false entries in his register concerning me besides this" (Edd.), and P Fay 135[15] (iv/A.D.) χρεωστῖς γὰρ καὶ τοῦ πέρυσι λαχανοσπέρμου ἀρτάβην μίαν ἡμίσιαν, "for you have been using since last year one and a half artabae of vegetable seed" (Edd.).

The foregoing exx. appear to support the rendering "last year," rather than "a year ago" or "for a year past" in 2 Cor 8[10], 9[2] (cf. AV, RV). For the bearing of this upon the date of the Ep., see Lake *Earlier Epistles of St. Paul*, p. 141 f.

For the adj. περυσινός cf. PSI VI. 560[8] (B.C. 257–6?) ἐμπυ]ρ[ισ]μὸν τῆς περυσινῆς (sc. ξυλοκοπίας), "burning of last year's (cut wood)," and *Chrest.* I. 167[13] (B.C. 131) εἰ[ς] πλήρωσιν τῆς περυσινῆς [ἐγ]λήψεως ("collecting "). MGr πέρυσι, "of last year."

πετεινός,

"flying," or as a neut. subst. "a bird": *Ostr* 1523[9] (B.C. 127–6) ἔχω παρὰ σοῦ τὸ τέλος τῶν πετεινῶν, P Leid W[36] (ii/iii A.D.) (= II. p. 101) ἐὰν ἐπίπης (*l.* ἐπείπης) ἐπὶ πάντος πετι(= ει)νοῦ εἰς τὸ ὦτιον, τελευτήσει. See also the new Logion P Oxy IV. p. 5 (= White *Sayings*, p. 8).

πέτομαι.

P Iand 13²⁵ (iv/A.D.) χαρίζων μοι πετόμενος ἔρχοιο, "for my sake fly and come to me." The editor compares Cic. ad Att. ii. 24. 5 te rogo, ut plane ad nos advoles. For the literal use of the word we may cite an Ephesian inscr. from the beginning of v/B.C. relating to augury—Syll 801 (=³ 1167)¹⁸ ἐγ μὲν τῆς δεξιῆς ἐς τὴν ἀριστερὴν πετόμεν]ος, ἢμ μὲν ἀποκρύψε[ι], δε]ξιός, "in flying from right to left, if a bird conceal its wing, it is of good omen."

For the varied forms which this verb exhibits in Rev, the only book of the NT in which it is found, see Blass-Debrunner p. 60, where they are referred to an undefined pres. stem πετ—: cf. Helbing Gr. p. 83. See also the letter from a slave to her absent master, P Giss I. 17¹¹ (time of Hadrian) (= Chrest. I. p. 566) ὤφελον εἰ ἐδυνάμεθα πέτασθαι καὶ ἐλθεῖν καὶ προσκυνῆσαί σε, "would that I could fly and come and do obeisance to you!" where πέτασθαι may be pres. inf. from πέταμαι (late prose form), or possibly = πτάσθαι, 1 aor. of πέτομαι. MGr πετειοῦμαι, πετῶ.

πέτρα.

"a rock": PSI IV. 423²⁹ (iii/B.C.) λελατομεύκαμεν δὲ καὶ λίθους βασιλικοὺς ἐκ τῆς πέτρας. P Leid Wˣᴵˣ·³⁶ (ii/iii A.D.) (= II. p. 140) ἡ(= αἱ) πέτραι, καὶ τὰ ὄρη, καὶ ἡ θάλασσα. In PSI IV. 433 (B.C. 261-0) πέτρα is used rather of rocky ground, much like πετρώδης in Mt 13⁵ al., τὰ σκόρδα ("garlic") τὰ ἐπὶ τῆς πέτρας, ? οὐκ ἐφυτεύθη οὖν ἐπὶ τῆς πέτρας Ὀασιτικά : cf. the similar use of πετραῖος in P Tebt I. 84⁷·⁸ (B.C. 118).

For the catastrophic influence of the divine name we may cite the magic P Leid Vⁱⁱ ³¹ (iii/iv A.D.) (= II. p. 27) οὗ τὸ ὄνομα [οὗ] ἡ γῆ ἀκούσασα ἐλεύσεται, ὁ ἄδης ἀκούων ταράσσεται . . . αἱ πέτραι ἀκούσασαι ῥήγνυ(= νυν)ται : cf. Mt 27⁵¹. See also P Osl I. 1²⁶³ with the editor's note.

Πέτρος.

For the occurrence of the name Peter, both in Greek and Latin, among the inscrr. in the first-century catacomb of Priscilla at Rome, see Edmundson The Church in Rome, p. 52.

The name is found in such early Christian papyrus letters as P Iand 11⁹ (iii/A.D.) τῷ κυρίῳ μου ἀδελφῷ Πέτρῳ, PSI III. 208² (iii/iv A.D.) χαῖρε ἐν κ(υρί)ῳ, ἀγαπητὲ [ἄδ]ελφε Πέτρε.

πετρώδης.

See s.v. πέτρα.

πήγανον.

On the use of πήγανον, "rue," in Lk 11⁴² instead of ἄνηθον, "anise," in Mt 23²³, as a proof that Luke here used a Semitic source and misread שַׁבְּתָא for שִׁבְּתָא, see Nestle Exp T xv. p. 528, and ZNTW vii. (1906) p. 260 f.

πηγή.

"spring": cf. BGU IV. 1120⁴³ (B.C. 5) τὴν] ἐν τῇ ἀντλίᾳ πηγήν, "the spring in the ship's hold," OGIS 168⁹ (B.C. 116-81) ἡ τοῦ Νείλου πηγὴ ὀνομαζομέ[νη], and Aristeas 89 πηγῆς ἔσωθεν πολυρρύτου φυσικῶς ἐπιρρεούσης. The word is used metaphorically in Kaibel 403¹ (ii/iii A.D.) βέβηκα πηγὰς εἰς ἐμάς, "unde nata sum redeo," and in the Christian ib. 725²⁸—

    λαβὼ[ν πηγή]ν ἄμβροτον ἐν βροτέοις
    θεσπεσίων ὑδά[τω]ν τὴν σήν, φίλε, θάλπεο ψυχὴν
    ὕδασιν ἀενάοις πλουτοδότου σοφίης.

For the contrast with φρέαρ, "well," as in Jn 4¹¹ ff., cf. M. Anton. viii. 51 πῶς οὖν πηγὴν ἀέναον ἕξεις καὶ μὴ φρέαρ; "how then possess thyself of a living fountain and no mere well?" (Haines). See also Ramsay Recent Discovery p. 308 n.² MGr πηγή, πηγάδι, "fountain," "spring."

πήγνυμι,

which is used of "fixing" or "setting up" the tabernacle in Heb 8², is found = "plant" in P Lond 414¹⁸ (c. A.D. 346) (= II. p. 292) ἔπηξαν μὲν ἐρίχα[ν] ἀγρὶν (l. ἐρείκην ἀγρίαν) καὶ σῦκα. For the subst. πῆγμα see ib. 1177¹⁷⁶ (A.D. 113) (= III. p. 185) εἰς πήγματα, and for πῆξις cf. P Strass I. 32¹·⁴ (A.D. 261) ἥλους τέσσαρας εἰς τὴν τούτου πῆξιν.

πηδάλιον.

"rudder": P Oxy XIV. 1650¹¹ (freight account—i, ii A.D.) πηδαλίου (δρ.) ιδ (τετρώβολον), "rudder 14 dr. 4 ob.," ib. XII. 1449¹⁶ (return of temple property—A.D. 213-17) πηδάλιον) τῆς [Νεωτ(έρας)?, "a rudder representing Neotera" (Edd.), and for the plur., as in Ac 27⁴⁰, P Lond 1164(h)⁵ (A.D. 212) (= III. p. 164) σὺν . . πηδαλίοις δυσί, "with two rudders" (said of a boat).

πηλίκος,

"how great," is often used for ἡλίκος (Blass-Debrunner § 304), which is a v.l. in Gal 6¹¹ B* 33 : cf. Col 2¹ and see s.v. ἡλίκος. Πηλίκος occurs elsewhere in the NT only in Heb 7⁴ and in the LXX in Zech 2², 4 Macc 15²². On the meaning of πηλίκα γράμματα in Gal l.c. see s.v. γράμμα and cf. Milligan Documents p. 23 f.

πηλός,

"mud," "clay": cf. P Oxy XII. 1450⁴ (A.D. 249-250) τῶν ὀστράκων διὰ πηλοῦ, and the magic P Lond 121⁸⁷ (iii/A.D.) (= I. p. 112) λαβὼν πηλὸν ἀπὸ τρόχου [κε]ραμικοῦ μίξον μίγματος τοῦ θεοῦ . . . From the inscrr. see the law of astronomy carved at Pergamum in the time of Trajan, OGIS 483⁸¹ ἐάν τινες ἐν ταῖς ὁδοῖς χοῦν ὀρύσσωσιν ἢ λίθους ἢ πηλὸν ποιῶσιν, also Kaibel 646¹¹ f. (iii/iv A.D.), a sepulchral inscr. deprecating the giving of honours after death—

    ζῶντί μοι, εἴ τι ἔχεις, μεταδός, τέφραν δὲ μεθύσκων
    πηλὸν ποιήσεις καὶ οὐκ ὁ θανὼν πίεται,

and cf. Herodas II. 28 ff.—

    ὃν χρὴν ἑαυτὸν ὅστις ἐστὶ κἀκ ποίου
    πηλοῦ πεφύρητ᾽ εἰδότ᾽ ὡς ἐγὼ ζώειν
    τῶν δημοτέων φρίσσοντα καὶ τὸν ἥκιστον,

"who ought to know who he is, and of what clay he is mixed, and to live as I do, in awe of even the least of the burghers" (Knox).

A subst. πηλοποιία is found in P Petr II. 12(4 (B.C. 241), and an adj. πήλινος in ib. III. 45⁹ (iii/B.C.) τῶ]ν πηλίνων ἔργων καὶ τῶν πλινθίνων: cf. Luckhard *Privathaus* p. 26 ff. See also *CR* xxxiii. p. 2, where W. M. Ramsay publishes a iv/A.D. inscr., in which the head of a noble Anatolian family is described as τὸν [πήλ]ινο[ν χ]ιτῶνα ἐνταυθοῖ περιδυσάμενος, "putting off the mantle of clay (to consign it) to this place."

πήρα.

In Mt 10[10] *al.* πήρα is usually understood as "a travelling-bag" containing clothes or provisions for the journey; but Deissmann (*LAE*, p. 108 ff.) prefers to see in it "a collecting-bag" such as beggar-priests of pagan cults carried for receiving alms, and in support of this view cites an inscr. in which a slave of the Syrian goddess tells how he went begging for the "lady", adding—ἀ(π)οφόρησε ἑκάστη ἀγωγὴ πήρας ο, "each journey brought in seventy bags" (*BCH* xxi. (1897) p. 60—Imperial period). Consequently, as Deissmann's translator points out (*LAE l.c.* n.[3]), "wallet" is the right word in English, as seen e.g. in Shakespeare *Troilus and Cressida* III. iii. 145, "Time hath, my lord, a wallet at his back, Wherein he puts alms for oblivion." For the dim. πηρίδιον see Epict. iii. 22. 10, and *Menandrea* p. 14[111] πηρίδιον γνωρισμάτων, "a walletful of birth tokens." The etymology is uncertain.

πῆχυς.

For πῆχυς in its original meaning of "forearm," cf. P Amh II. 102[9] (A.D. 180) οὐλὴ π[ή]χι δεξιῷ, "a scar on the right forearm." As a measure of length, a "cubit," about one and a half feet (cf. Hultsch, *Archiv* iii. p. 438 ff.), the word hardly needs illustration, but we may cite one or two exx. of the contr. πηχῶν (for πηχέων), as in Jn 21[8], Rev 21[17]—P Petr II. 41[2f.] (iii/B.C.) πηχῶν ιθ πλάτος πηχῶν τῇ εἴσοδος, P Par 14[14] (B.C. 127) πηχῶν δέκα ἕξ, and P Lond 154[9] (A.D. 68) (= II. p. 179) ἔξοδος κοινὴ πλάτους πηχῶ[ν] τ[ριῶ]ν: other exx. in Mayser *Gr.* i. p. 267, and for the LXX usage see Thackeray *Gr.* i. p. 151. On the possibility that πῆχυς may refer to extension of *time* in Mt 6[27] (Lk 12[25]) see *s.v.* ἡλικία. A subst. πηχισμός, which LS describe as "Eccl.," is not uncommon in connexion with measurements, as of the ground-space occupied by a house in P Strass I. 9[8] (c. A.D. 307 or 352) μέτροις] καὶ πηχισμοῖς καὶ θεμελίοις καὶ τίχεσιν. MGr πῆχυ, "cubit": see Thumb *Handbook*, p. 57.

πιάζω.

This Doric form of πιέζω (*q.v.*) appears in all the NT occurrences of the verb except Lk 6[38], but always with the different meaning "seize," "lay hold of." For this meaning in the Κοινή we may cite the magic spell κλέπτην πιάσαι, "to catch a thief," in P Lond 46[172] (iv/A.D.) (= I. p. 70): cf. *Patr. Orient.* iv. 2, p. 132, where Wessely gives λῃστοπιάστης, "preneur de malfaiteurs" from a Roman papyrus of the time of Diocletian. Unfortunately the letter P Oxy IV. 812 (B.C. 5) is too fragmentary to decide the meaning of πεπίασται Λοκρίων in the post-script: but cf. P Hamb I. 6[18] (A.D. 128-9) οἱ δὲ ἀπὸ τῆς κώμης χρῶνται τοῖς αὐ[τ]οῖς ὑποδοχίοις, ὑφ' ὧν κ[αὶ] ὁ ἀπότακτος αὐτῶν φόρος διαγράφεται πιαζώμενος ὑπὸ σου

From a later period comes πιάσαι = λαβεῖν in P Lond 483[76] (A.D. 616) (= II. p. 328) πιάσαι ὀψάρια, cited by C. H. Muller in *Archiv* i. p. 439 as characteristic of the transition from ancient to modern Greek, in which ἔπιασα is aor. of πιάνω, "catch," "seize," "overtake." For Ac 3[7] we may quote (with Thayer) Theocritus iv. 35 τηνεῖ καὶ τὸν ταῦρον ἀπ' ὤρεος ἆγε πιάξας | τὰς ὁπλάς, "there he brought the bull from the mountain, seizing it by the hoof."

Thumb (*Hellen.* p. 67 n.[1]) accepts W. Schmid's view that πιάζω has been assimilated to the numerous verbs in -άζω: cf. also Schweizer *Perg.* p. 37. If the differentiation took place in one dialect—say that of the bucolics of Sicily —we can understand the word passing into the Κοινή as a kind of slang loanword, while πιέζω lived on awhile with its old meaning. The uses of πιάζω and πιέζω in the LXX are stated by Thackeray *Gr.* i. p. 282.

πιέζω

(see *s.v.* πιάζω) is found in Lk 6[38] with the original meaning "press down": cf. Micah 6[15] πιέσεις ἐλαίαν, and *Syll* 422 (= [3] 904)[7] (iv/A.D.) μ]ήτε ὁ βουλόμενος κεχρῆσθαι δι' ἄγνοιαν [ὑπ]ὸ τῆς ἀπειρίας πιεζείσθω. In *ib.* 587[304] (B.C. 329-8) the subst. πιεστήρ, which Dittenberger says means elsewhere *torcular vel prelum*, seems to have the force of μοχλός ("crowbar"), but the root meaning of *pressing* is still preserved. Πιέζω contains a reduced form of ἐπί and ἕζομαι: cf. πινυτός from ἐπί and the root of νόϝος (Boisacq *Dict. Étym.* pp. 782, 785).

πιθανολογία.

"Persuasive speech" in a somewhat depreciatory sense is evidently the meaning of this word in Col 2[4], its only occurrence in the Greek Bible: cf. the legal process, P Lips I. 40[iii. 7] (iv/v A.D.), where one of the parties declares with reference to certain things that had been seized—διὰ πειθανολογίας τὰ ἁρπαγέντα ζητοῦσι κατέχειν. The adj. π(ε)ιθανός, which has often a similar connotation, occurs in CP Herm I. 7[20]. See also Epict. i. 8. 7 ἡ πιθανολογική, "the art of persuasion."

πιθός.

See *s.v.* πειθός.

πικραίνω.

With the pass. "am embittered" in Col 3[19], cf. the compd. in P Lille I. 7[1.9] (iii/B.C.) προσπικρανθείς μοι.

πικρία

is properly "an embittered and resentful spirit which refuses reconciliation" (Robinson *ad* Eph 4[31]). For a weakened sense cf. BGU II. 417[5] (ii/iii A.D.), where a father counsels his son not to be too buoyed up in view of "the hardness of the times"—τὴν τοῦ καιροῦ πικρίαν. An interesting ex. of the word occurs in P Leid W[xi. 45] (ii/iii A.D.) (= II. p. 121) ἐφάνη διὰ τῆς πν.. ικρίας τοῦ Θεοῦ Νοῦς. We may add Vett. Val. p. 240[16] πικρίας δεσπόζει. MGr πίκρα, "bitterness," "sorrow."

πικρός,

"bitter," (1) literally: P Oxy VIII. 1088⁶⁴ (medical receipt—early i/A.D.) καρύων πικρῶ(ν), (2) metaphorically: P Par 63¹²¹ (B.C. 164) (= P Petr III. p. 28) τὸ . . . δοκοῦν εἶναι πικρόν, "what appears to be harsh" (Mahaffy) cf. Jas 3¹⁴), PSI I. 28⁸ (magic tablet—iii/iv A.D.) πικραῖς μάστιξιν, and Kaibel 640⁵ᶠ. (c. ii/A.D.)—

> ἑξηκοστὸν ἔτος πανελεύθερον ἐξεβίωσα
> καὶ καλὸν τὸ τύχης καὶ πικρὸν οἶδα βίου.

For a contrast with ὀξύς see Plut. Flam. xvii. 2 πικρὸς μὲν οὖν οὐδενί, πολλοῖς δὲ ὀξὺς ἐδόκει καὶ κοῦφος εἶναι τὴν φύσιν.

πικρῶς.

"bitterly": P Petr III. 42 H (8) f.⁸ (mid. iii/B.C.) (= Witkowski², p. 15) ὁ βασι[λεὺς ἐλθὼν εἰς τὴν λί]μνην πικρ[ῶ]ς σοι ἐχρήσατο. The compar. appears in P Par 46²⁰ (B.C. 152) (= UPZ i. p. 338) νομίζω γὰρ μάλιστα τῶν ἄλλων παρακολουθήσαντά σε τῆι ἀληθείαι πικρότερον προσενεχθήσεσθ' αὐτῶι, "denn ich glaube, dass Du ganz besonders vor den andern der Wahrheit die Ehre geben und ihn scharfer anfassen wirst" (Wilcken).

Πιλᾶτος.

See s.v. Πειλᾶτος.

πίμπλημι,

"fill." For the act. c. acc. and gen., as in Mt 27⁴⁸, cf. P Lond 453⁶ (iv/A.D.) (= II. p. 319) πλῆσον κεράμιον σινάπις(= εως) χλωροῦ, "fill the vessel with green mustard." The aor. pass. c. gen., as frequently in the Lukan writings, is seen in P Leid Wᵛⁱ·²² (ii/iii A.D.) (= II. p. 99) πλησθεὶς τῆς θεοσοφίας.

πίμπρημι,

which in the NT is confined to Lk (Ac 28⁶), is "the usual medical word for inflammation." see Hobart p. 50, where exx. are quoted from Hippocrates, Aretaeus, and Galen. and cf. Field Notes, p. 149. Hence the RV rendering "swell up" in Ac l.c. In Syll 813 (= ³1170¹⁵) εἴ τι[ς ἄλλος] τἀμὰ ἔχ[ει, πεπρη]μένος ἐξ[αγορεύ]ων, Dittenberger remarks that the force of πεπρημένος seems to be "igni quodam intestino, veluti febri, homines scelestos vexari et confici."

πινακίδιον.

With πινακίδιον, "a writing tablet," in Lk 1⁶³ cf. the form πινάκιον in P Hal I. 1²²⁵ (mid. iii/B.C.) ὁ δὲ καλεσά-μενος γραφέτω τὴν μαρτυρίαν εἰς π[ι]ν[ά]κι[ο]ν, P Amh II. 120³⁸ (account—early ii/A.D.) τιμῆ(ς) πινακίο(υ) (δραχμὴ) α (ὀβολοὶ δύο), and Syll 790 (= ³1157)⁴¹ (c. B.C. 100) ἀπο-δεχόμενοι τὰ πινάκια παρὰ τῶν μαντευομένων.

Πινακίς, which is a v.l. in Lk l.c., may be illustrated from P Ryl II. 144¹⁹ (A.D. 38) ἀπώλεσα πινακείδα, "I lost a writing-tablet," and P Leid Wⁱⁱⁱ·⁵ (ii/iii A.D.) (= II. p. 891) ἔχε δὲ πινακεῖτα (l. πινακίδα) εἰς ἣν μέλεις τρφιν (l. μέλλεις γράφειν) ὅσα σοι λέγει. See also Gnomon 36 (c. A.D. 150) (= BGU V. I. p. 13 κατὰ πινακίδας Ἑλληνικάς, "auf griechischen Tafeln," and Artem. p. 148²⁷.

πίναξ,

originally = "board," "plank," as e.g. in Syll 537 (= ³969)⁸³ (B.C. 347-6) ἐπὶ τούτων ἐπιθήσει πίνακας συνκολλήσας. Hence anything flat, as "a tablet," "a disc," and later "a dish" as in Mt 14⁸ al.: cf. P Tebt I. 112·¹ (accounts—B.C. 112) ἄρτου κε, πίνα(κος) ε, and BGU III. 781ᵛ·³⁶ (i/A.D.) πίναξ μέγας ἐν θήκῃ. For πίναξ, "a votive tablet," cf. Headlam Herodas p. 181 f.

πίνω.

In P Par 47²³ (as read in UPZ i. p. 332—B.C. 152-1) the strategus spends two days in the Anubieion πίνων, "drink-ing," apparently in connexion with some festival. The schoolboy who does not get his own way informs his father —οὐ μὴ φάγω οὐ μὴ πεῖν ταῦτα, "I won't eat, I won't drink: there now!" (P Oxy I. 119¹⁵ (= Selections, p. 103) —ii/iii A.D.). And the magical P Lond 121¹⁵⁰ (iii/A.D.) (= I. p. 99) supplies a recipe enabling a man πολλὰ πίνειν καὶ μὴ μεθύειν, "to drink much and not be drunk."

With 1 Cor 15³² Deissmann (LAE p. 296) compares a sepulchral epigram of the Imperial period in which the passer-by is exhorted —πεῖνε, βλέπις τὸ τέλος, "drink, thou seest the end." Cf. Kaibel 646¹² (iii/iv A.D.) οὐκ ὁ θανὼν πίεται, and Syll 804 (= ³1170¹⁵) (ii/A.D.) πιόντος μου γάλα μόνον, in connexion with a cure at the temple of Asclepius in Epidaurus. For Heb 6⁷ cf. Anacreontea xxi. 1 ἡ γῆ μέλαινα πίνει, and for the common phrase δοῦναι πιεῖν, as in Jn 4⁷, see the citations in Headlam Herodas, p. 55 f.

The NT form πεῖν is overwhelmingly attested in papyri of the Roman age—P Oxy VIII. 1088³⁵ (medical receipt—early i/A.D.) δὸς πεῖν (cf. Jn 4⁷, al.), P Flor I. 101⁸ (i/A.D.) ὕδωρ εἰς πεῖν, P Giss I. 31·² (end ii/A.D.) ἐμοὶ εἰς πεῖν (cf. Proleg. p. 81), and P Oxy XVI. 1945² (A.D. 517) παρασχοῦ εἰς πῖν. Deissmann (Urgeschichte p. 39 f.) has drawn attention to the bearing of this "vulgar" form upon the question of the Johannine vocabulary and style. The dissyllabic πιεῖν, which survives in Mt 27³⁴ (for LXX see Thackeray Gr. i. p. 64), may be seen in a series of accounts P Tebt I. 120¹³·ⁱ·ᵉᵗ. (B.C. 97 or 64) εἰς πιεῖν α. For the form πίομαι (Mk 10³⁹) cf. Proleg. p. 155, and for πίεσαι (Lk 17⁸), which in the LXX has entirely superseded πίῃ (Thackeray Gr. i. p. 218), cf. Proleg. p. 54.

πιότης,

"fatness" (Rom 11¹⁷): cf. Test. xii. patr. Levi viii. 8 ὁ πέμπτος κλάδον μοι ἐλαίας ἔδωκεν πιότητος.

πιπράσκω,

"sell," c. acc. rei: P Par 59⁴ (B.C. 159) (= UPZ i. p. 413) πέπρακα (cf. Mt 13⁴⁶: Blass Gr. § 59. 5) τὸ ὀθόνιον (δραχμὰς) φ, P Oxy XIV. 1672³ (A.D. 37-41) πεπράκαμεν χό ας) λβ ξένοις προσώποις, "we sold 32 choes to some strangers," BGU IV. 1079¹⁶ (A.D. 41) (= Selections, p. 39) παρὰ τάλαντόν σοι πέπρακα τὰ φο[ρτ]ία μου, "I have sold my wares for a talent," P Oxy II. 264² (A.D. 54) ὁμολογῶ πεπρακέναι σοι τὸν ὑπάρχοντά μοι ἱστὸν γερδι[ακόν, "I agree that I have sold to you the weaver's loom belonging to me," ib. IX. 1200⁴¹ (A.D. 266) πέπρακα τὸ ἐπιβαλόν μοι ψειλὸν τόπον καὶ ἀπέσχον τὴν τειμὴν ὡς

66

πρόκειται, "I have sold the free space falling to me and have received the price as aforesaid" (Ed.).

Other exx. of the verb are P Hib I. 41²³ (c. B.C. 261) ἐπιμέλειαν δὲ ποίησαι ὅπως καὶ τὸ ὑπάρχον ἔλαιον δι' αὐτοῦ ἤδη πραθῇ, "be careful to see that the existing store of oil be now sold by him" (Edd.), P Fay 131⁵ (iii/iv A.D.) ποίησον αὐτὰς πραθῆναι ἐκ (δραχμῶν) ιδ, "get them (artabae of barley) sold at 14 drachmae an artaba," and OGIS 484¹⁶ (ii/A.D.) ὅσα μέντοι τῶν λεπτῶν ὀψαρίων σταθμῷ πιπρασκόμενα τιμᾶται ὑπὸ τῶν ἀγορανόμων. The verbal πρατέος is found in the Christian P Oxy XII. 1494¹ (early iv/A.D.) εἴν' οὕτως θεοῦ θέλοντος τάχα τει πραταίον (l. τι πρατέον) γένηται, "in order that, if God so wills, there may perhaps be something to sell" (Edd.). The subst. πρᾶσις, "a selling," occurs in P Eleph 14²⁵ (iii/B.C.), and πρατήριον, "a market," in P Par 62^iii.15 (c. B.C. 170). For the compd. παραπιπράσκω (not in LS⁸) see Michel 809⁵ (iii/B.C.) and P bibl univ Giss 2²⁴ (ii/B.C.), and cf. Herwerden Lex. s.v. παράπρασις.

πίπτω,

"fall down." (1) of things—P Petr II. 13(3)² (B.C. 258-3) τὸ πρὸς νότον [τ]οῦ ὀχυρώματος τεῖχος μέρος μέν τι αὐτοῦ πεπτωκός ἐστιν, "the wall to the south of the prison, part of it has fallen" (Ed.); (2) of persons—P Oxy III. 475²⁵ (A.D. 182) ἔπεσεν καὶ ἐτελε[ύ]τησεν, "he fell and was killed," the report of an accident.

Πέπτωκεν is common = "paid" in documents of iii-ii B.C. : cf. P Lond 1200² (B.C. 192 or 168) (= III. p. 2) πέπτωκεν ἐπὶ τὴν ἐν Διοσπόλει τῇ μεγάλῃ τράπεζαν, "paid into the bank at Diospolis Magna," and P Fay 17¹ (B.C. 121), P Tebt I. 101¹ (B.C. 120) with the editors' notes. See also P Hib I. 66² (B.C. 228) (= Witkowski², p. 38) πίπτει [σοι] ("tibi solvitur") ἐν τοῖς κατὰ σὲ τόποις εἰκοστή, and Wilcken Ostr. i. p. 64. For a somewhat similar use of πέπτωκεν in dockets attached to contracts etc. cf. P Tebt II. 279¹ (B.C. 231) πέπτωκεν εἰς κιβωτὸν τὸ συνάλλαγμα ἐν Τεβτύνει, "there has been placed in the chest at Tebtunis the contract of nurture."

For the form πέσατε in Lk 23³⁰, Rev 6¹⁶, see Robertson Gr. p. 338 f., for the difficult ἐπέσαντο in Ev. Petr. 5, see Swete ad l., and for the timeless aorists in Lk 10¹⁸ (πεσόντα) and Rev 18² (ἔπεσεν), see Proleg. p. 134. Callimachus Ep. lvi. 4 (A.P. vi. 148) Ἕσπερε, πῶς ἔπεσες—a striking verbal resemblance to Isai 14¹².

Πισίδιος.

On "Pisidian" Antioch not "in" but "near" Pisidia (Ac 13¹⁴), see Ramsay CRE p. 25 ff.

πιστεύω.

The different constructions of πιστεύω in the NT are fully discussed by Moulton Proleg. pp. 67 f., 235 : see also Abbott Joh. Voc. p. 19 ff., and for the possibility that πιστεύω in Acts need not imply belief of a permanently religious character see Ramsay Teaching p. 445 ff., and Recent Discovery p. 164 ff.

For πιστεύω (a) c. dat. pers. cf. P Par 63¹¹⁰ (B.C. 164) (= P Petr III. p. 28) οἷς οὐδὲ βουλόμενοι προσίναι πρὸς τὴν γεωργίαν π[ιστ]εύ[σει]έ ἄν τις, "whom no one would trust,

even if they were willing to do the work" (Mahaffy), P Oxy VI. 898²⁹ (A.D. 123) οὐ πιστεύοντος οὔτε αὐτῇ οὐδὲ τῇ ἡλικίᾳ μου, "distrusting both her and my own youth" (Edd.), BGU III. 1011^ii.13 (ii/A.D.) κἂν τί σοι προσπίπτῃ περὶ τῶν ἐναντίων, ὧι πιστεύσειεν ἄ[ν] τις, διασάφει, and P Tebt II. 418¹⁵ (iii/A.D.) οὐδενὶ ἐπίστευσα [ὥ]στε αὐτῇ κομίσαι, "I have trusted no one to take it to her" : (b) c. acc. of thing, cf. PSI V. 494¹⁴ (B.C. 258-7) μηθὲν πίστευε ὧν λέγει, and P Par 47²⁹ (c. B.C. 152-1) (= UPZ i. p. 332, Selections, p. 23) πιστεύοντες τὰ ἐνύπνια : and (c) for the acc. and dat. we may cite the formula of manumission Syll 845⁷ (Delphi—B.C. 200-199) τὰν δὲ ὠνὰν ἐπίστευσε Νίκαια τῶι Ἀπόλλωνι ἐπ' ἐλευθερίαι, "the purchase, however, Nicaea hath committed unto Apollo, for freedom" (see Deissmann LAE, p. 327).

Πιστεύω is followed by acc. and inf. in P Tebt II. 314³ (ii/A.D.) πιστεύω σε μὴ ἀγνοεῖν ὅσον κάμ[α]τον ἤνεγκα, "I believe that you are aware how much trouble I had" (Edd.), and by ὅτι in P Lond 897¹² (A.D. 84) (= III. p. 207 as amended Berichtigungen, p. 288) κέκρικα γὰρ νὴ τοὺς θεοὺς ἐν Ἀλεξανδρείᾳ ἐπιμένειν· πιστεύωι γὰρ ὅτι δυνηθήσομαι ζῆν, ὃ μέντοι γε οὐ θέλω.

For the pass. cf. P Oxy III. 528²³ (ii/A.D.) ἥ(= ἵ)να μηκέτι [[φ]]πιστευθῶ μου τὴν ἐνβολ[ήν, "that I may no longer be believed with regard to my embarkation (?)," and ib. IX. 1223³⁶ (late iv/A.D.) οὐκέτι πιστευόμεθα, ἐὰν μὴ εὐγνωμονήσωμεν, "I am no longer trusted, unless I behave fairly" (Ed.).

With the Pauline use = "am entrusted with" the Gospel etc. (1 Thess 2⁴, Gal 2⁷, 1 Cor 9¹⁷, 1 Tim 1¹¹) Deissmann (LAE, p. 379) compares the designation of the Imperial secretary for Greek correspondence—τάξιν τὴν ἐπὶ τῶν Ἑλληνικῶν ἐπιστολῶν πεπιστευμένος (Jos. Antt. XX. 183 (viii. 9)).

See also BGU IV. 1159¹⁰ (time of Augustus) πεπιστευμένος ὑπὸ [[τοῦ]] αὐτοῦ Πτολεμαίου τὰς φυλακὰς τοῦ αὐτοῦ νόμου. Οἱ πιστεύομαι c. gen. as occasionally in late Greek (e.g. Polyb. vi. 56. 13 πιστευθεὶς ταλάντου) there is no instance in the NT.

πιστικός.

This rare word, confined in the NT to Mk 14³, Jn 12³, is sometimes derived (as by LS⁸) from πίνω in the sense of "liquid," but is better understood as from πιστός = "true," "genuine": see the discussion with interesting details in Winer-Schmiedel Gr. p. 138, and cf. ZNTW iii. p. 169 ff. where Nestle finds no ground for Naber's suggestion (Mnemosyne xxx. (1902), p. 1 ff.) that in the NT passages σπειστικῆς, ointment "that can be poured out," should be read for πιστικῆς. Abbott (Joh. Voc. p. 252), on the other hand, believes that the word in the original was some form of σπικάτον (not in LS⁸), and refers to Wetstein for illustrations of σπικάτον as an ointment in use among women of luxury.

For πιστικός, "faithful," applied to persons, commentators are in the habit of referring to the description of a good wife in Artem. p. 128²³ (c. A.D. 150)—πιστικὴν καὶ οἰκουρόν, but Hercher prefers to read πιστήν, as also in pp. 158³, 189¹⁷. We can, however, supply instances of this usage from the papyri, e.g. P Mon 1. 8² (last quarter vi/A.D.)

υἱοῦ μου γνησίου καὶ πιστικοῦ and ⁴ εἱλάσθαί σε ὡς πιστικόν, and for the more specialized sense of "one entrusted with the management of a ship," "a ship-master," see the introd. to the above papyrus, and Bell's note *ad* P Lond 1341¹² (A.D. 709). Cf. also P Flor III. 336³ (vii/A.D. ?), and possibly *ib.* 311² (A.D. 447). In Vett. Val. p. 10¹⁴ πιστικοί is followed as a term of praise by ἀγαθοὶ οἰκονόμοι.

πίστις.

In accordance with its common NT usage, πίστις is used of "faith," "confidence" in a person in such passages as P Strass I. 41²⁸ (c. A.D. 250), when in a legal process a witness is charged—ὡς πρεσβύτης καὶ πίστεως ἄξιος εἰπὲ ἃ οἶδας ἐν τῷ πρά[γματ]ι, and P Oxy XIV. 1627¹⁴ (A.D. 342) διὰ τὴν περὶ ἡμᾶς μετριότητα καὶ πίστις (*l.* πίστιν), "owing to your clemency to us and confidence in us" (Edd.). In P Lond 233¹¹ (A.D. 345) (= II. p. 273, *Chrest.* I. p. 68) the editor translates τῇ σῇ πίστ(ε)ι as apparently = "at your discretion" or "on your own credit." P Tebt II. 418¹⁵ (iii/A.D.) shows us—ἀπολάβῃς παρ' ἐμοῦ καλῇ πίστει, "receive it back from me in good faith" (Edd.): cf. P Oxy I. 71ⁱⁱ·¹¹ (A.D. 303) νομίζουσα τούτους τὴν καλήν μοι πίστιν ἀποσώζειν, "thinking that they would preserve my good name" (Edd.).

With the conjunction of πίστις and ἀλήθεια in 1 Tim 2⁷ cf. P Oxy I. 70⁴ᶠ (iii/A.D.) πᾶσα κυ[ρί]α ἔνγραφος συναλλαγὴ πίστιν καὶ ἀλήθ[ειαν ἔ]χει, "every valid written contract is credited and accepted" (Edd.), and P Flor I. 32 (*b*)¹⁴ (A.D. 298) ἐξόμνυμι . . . ἐξ ἀληθείας καὶ πίστεως τὴν ἀπογραφὴν πεποιῆσθαι: with 1 Tim 5¹² cf. *CIA* App. (Wünsch, praef. p. xv) ὑποκατέχετε ὑμεῖς αὐτὴν ταῖς ἐσχάταις τιμωρίαις ὅτι πρώτη ἠθέτησεν τὴν πίστιν πρὸς Φήλικα τὸν ἑαυτῆς ἄνδρα (cited by Parry *ad l.*): with 2 Tim 4⁷ cf. *Brit. Mus. Inscr.* Part III. No. 587 *b.*⁵ (ii/A.D.) ὅτι τὴν πίστιν ἐτήρησα, and *OGIS* 339⁴⁷ (c. B.C. 120) προχειρισαμένου τοὺς τὴν πίστιν εὐσεβῶς τε καὶ δικαίως τηρήσοντας: and with ἡ πίστις used of "the (Christian) faith" (Ac 6⁷, *al.*), cf. *Syll* 451 (=³ 932⁷) (ii/i B.C.) ἀξίως ἀνεστράφησαν αὐτῶν τε καὶ τᾶς ἐνχειρασθείσας αὐτοῖς πίστεως.

The passive sense "fidelity," "faithfulness," which is found in the LXX, and occasionally in the NT (Mt 23²², Gal 5²²), is common in our sources. See e.g. the illiterate P Fay 122²² (c. A.D. 100) ἐάν τινα εὕρῃς κατὰ παρό[ντας] ἔχοντα πείστην πολλήν, "if you find anyone quite trustworthy among those with you" (Edd.), P Oxy III. 494⁹ (A.D. 156) εὐνοούσῃ μοι καὶ πᾶσαν πίστιν μοι ἐνδεικνυμένη, "being well-disposed and showing entire faithfulness towards me" (Edd.), BGU I. 326ⁱⁱ·¹⁵ (a clause in a Will—A.D. 194) τῇ τε πίστι [α]ὐτῆς παρακατατίθομαι (cf. the Lat. formula *eius fidei committo*), and P Tebt II. 326¹⁰ (c. A.D. 266) εὐνοίᾳ καὶ πίστι καὶ τῇ τοῦ γένους οἰκειότητι, "owing to his kindness, fidelity, and ties of kinship" (Edd.).

For the sense of "guarantee," "pledge," as in Ac 17³¹, cf. the mantic P Ryl I. 28¹⁸⁷ (iv/A.D.) τοὺς ἀριστερὸς ἐὰν ἄλληται, σημαίνει αὐτὸν ἐπὶ λόγῳ καὶ πίστι πλανηθῆναι, "if the left foot quiver, it signifies that a man will be deceived over a promise and pledge" (Edd.).

Πίστις = "bond" or "mortgage" is found in such passages as P Tebt I. 14⁹ (B.C. 114) ἀναγραψάμενος αὐτοῦ τὰ ὑπάρχοντα συντάξαι θεῖναι ἐν πίστει, "making a list of his property and arranging for it to be placed in bond,"

P Reinach 18¹⁰ (B.C. 108) ἐθέμην αὐτῶι ἐν πίστει καθ' ὧν ἔχω ψιλῶν τό[π]ων συγγραφὴν ὑποθήκης, and P Oxy III. 486⁷ (A.D. 131) λαβοῦσα τὸν καθήκοντα τῆς ὠνῆς δημόσι[ον χρημα]τισμόν, ἔλεγεν ἐν πίστει με ἔχειν αὐτά, "although I had received the regular official contract of the sale, he said that I held this land on mortgage." The phrase ὠνὴ ἐν πίστει is discussed in *Philologus* lxiii. (N.F. xvii.), 1904, p. 498 ff. See also the references in Preisigke *Fachwörter s.v.* πίστις, and for NT usage Burton *Galatians* (in *ICC*), p. 478 ff.

πιστός.

For πιστός, "faithful," "trustworthy," as generally in the NT, cf. P Grenf II. 73¹² (late iii/A.D.) (= *Selections*, p. 118) τ]αύτην παραδέδωκα τοῖς καλοῖς καὶ πιστοῖς ἐξ αὐτῶν τῶν νεκροτάφων εἰς τήρησιν, "I have handed her over to the good and faithful men among the grave diggers themselves that they may take care of her" (cf. Mt 25²¹), and P Oxy I. 41ⁱⁱ·⁹ (iii/iv A.D.) ἁγνοὶ πιστοὶ σύνδικοι, "true and trustworthy advocates." In a deed of sale of a slave, published by Eitrem (*Sklavenkauf*, Christiania, 1916), the slave is described as ²⁷ πιστοῦ καὶ ἀδράστου, "faithful and not given to running away." A petitioner for release from prison οὕνεκα τοῦ θεοῦ καὶ τοῦ καλῶς ἔχοντος, "in the name of God and of fair play," describes himself, P Petr II. 19 I*a*)¹, as δοὺς τὰ πιστά, with reference apparently to certain required "pledges": cf. BGU IV. 1152²⁶ (B.C. 10) οὗ τὰ πιστὰ (reading almost certain—Ed.) πα[ρ]έδωκεν.

On the rare active use of πιστός, "trusting," "believing," which occurs first apparently in the NT (Gal 3⁹, 2 Cor 6¹⁵, and *sexies* in the Pastorals), see Hort *ad* 1 Pet 1²¹, where the usage is explained by the predominant sense of πίστις, "faith," "trust." It may be added that in 1 Cor 7²⁵ Lietzmann (*HZNT ad l.*) understands πιστός as = "Christian," with the meaning "I give my decision in accordance with my best Christian consciousness." He quotes in support a number of Syrian inscrr. where πιστός is used as a title. For Πίστος (note change of accent) as a common name for slaves, see the citations in Headlam *Herodas*, p. 329. For adv. πιστῶς, cf. P Lond 301⁷ (A.D. 138-161) (= II. p. 256) πιστῶς καὶ ἐπιμελῶς, P Oxy IX. 1187¹⁵ (A.D. 254) ὑγιῶς καὶ πιστῶς.

πιστόω

occurs in the pass. in the sense "am assured of" in 2 Tim 3¹⁴: cf. 3 Macc 4²⁰ and the *v.l.* in 2 Thess 1¹⁰ (cf. WH *Notes*², p. 128). For the mid. see *Syll*³ 633⁷⁷ (c. B.C. 180) εἶναι αὐτοὺς ἀτελεῖς πιστωσαμένους ὅρκωι, διότι ἐπὶ κτήσει ποιοῦνται τὴν διαγωγή[ν. A good ex. of the NT use of the verb is afforded by Aristeas 91 πεπεισμένος δὲ καὶ αὐτὸς τὴν τῶν ὑποδοχείων κατασκευὴν δηλώσω, καθὼς ἐπιστώθην, "such is my belief as to the nature of the reservoirs, and I will explain how it was confirmed" (Thackeray). We may note the late compd. πιστοφορέω (not in LS⁸): P Lond IV. 1338¹⁰ (A.D. 709) πιστοφορέθητι εἰς τοῦτο, "be sure of that." For the rare subst. πίστωμα, see Linde *Epi.* p. 104.

πλανάω.

For the metaph. use of πλανάω, "lead astray," "deceive," cf. P Par 47²⁸ (B.C. 152-1) (= *UPZ* i. p. 332,

Selections, p. 23) ἀποπεπτώκαμεν πλανό(= ώ)μενοι ὑπὸ τῶν θεῶν καὶ πιστεύοντες τὰ ἐνύπνια, P Flor I. 61¹⁶ (A.D. 85) (= *Chrest.* II. p. 88) ἐπλανήθη περὶ τὴν ἔντευξιν, P Oxy VI. 898⁸ (A.D. 123) πολλά μ[ε ἀ]δικοῦσα ἔτι καὶ πλανήσασά με, "injuring me much and ending by deceiving me," *ib.* II. 237ⁱⁱ·⁸ (A.D. 186) ὡς καὶ σὲ τὸν κύριον πλανῆσαι δυνάμενος, *ib.* I. 119¹² (ii/iii A.D.) (= *Selections*, p. 103) πεπλάνηκαν ἡμῶ(= ᾶ)ς ἐκε[ῖ], τῇ ἡμέρᾳ ιβ ὅτι(= ε) ἔπλευσε(= α)ς, "they deceived us there on the 12th, when you sailed," and the mantic P Ryl I. 28¹⁶⁸ (iv/A.D.) cited *s.v.* πίστις. *Kaibel* 351 (cited *s.v.* πλάνη) shows the verb—

⁴ἔκ[τ]εινεν δέ [μ]ε Ὑ[λ]εύς, ὃν οὐκ ἤσχυσα [πλ]ανῆσ[αι.

See also Menander Περικειρ. 70 f. εἰ δὲ καὶ νυνὶ πλανᾶς με —(Δα.) κρέμασον εὐθύς. εἰ πλανῶ τήμερον, and Ἐπιτρέπ. 269 ἐπλανήθη, "she strayed away," also Epict. iv. 6. 23 μὴ πλανᾶσθε, ἄνδρες, ἐμοὶ καλῶς ἐστίν (cf. Gal 6⁷, 1 Cor 6⁹).

πλάνη

has apparently the act. sense of "deceit" in BGU IV. 1208⁶ (B.C. 27–6) δι' οὗ [μοι] ἱστορεῖς τὴν [Καλατύ]τεως πλ[άν]ην, "by means of which (*sc.* a writing-tablet) you are acquainting me with the deceit of Kalatytis." Cf. *Kaibel* 351³ πάσα[ι]σ[ι] πλάνη[ς τ]έχν[αι]ς, where the editor understands the word as denoting the craft and stratagem which hunters use against wild beasts. See further *s.v.* πλανάω. In the NT πλάνη is generally, if not always, used in the pass. sense of "error": cf. Armitage Robinson *ad* Eph 4¹⁴.

πλανήτης.

For the ordinary use of πλανήτης, "planet," cf. the magic P Lond 121²¹³ (iii/A.D.) (= I. p. 100) γεννήσας τοὺς ε πλανήτας ἀστέρας οἵ εἰσιν οὐρανοῦ σπλάγχνα καὶ γῆς ἔντερα καὶ ὕδατος χύσις καὶ πυρὸς θράσος, and P Eud^vii. (cited by Mayser *Gr.* p. 441). In Jude 13, on the other hand, the imagery is clearly derived from Enoch (especially 18¹⁴ f.), and the reference is to "wandering stars," stars which have left their appointed orbits : see further Mayor *Comm. ad l.*

πλάνος,

"misleading," "deceiving" (1 Tim 4¹): Vett. Val. p. 74¹⁸ ποιεῖ γὰρ μάγους πλάνους θύτας.

πλάξ.

The late use of πλάξ (for στήλη) as a "tablet" for writing purposes (2 Cor 3³, Heb 9⁴) is seen in an inscr. giving the right of asylum to a Jewish synagogue, *Chrest.* I. 54¹ ff. βασιλίσσης καὶ βασιλέως προσταξάντων ἀντὶ τῆς προανακειμένης περὶ τῆς ἀναθέσεως τῆς προσευχῆς πλακὸς ἡ ὑπογεγραμμένη ἐπιγραφήτω Βασιλεὺς Πτολεμαῖος Εὐεργέτης τὴν προσευχὴν ἄσυλον. The date is uncertain, but Wilcken thinks the reference is to Euergetes I. (B.C. 246–221), and regards this usage of πλάξ as characteristic of the Egyptian Κοινή (cf. the LXX use of πλάκες for the tables of the Law; see his note *ad l.c.* and more recently *UPZ* i. p. 404. We may also note *OGIS* 672¹² (A.D. 80) ἐτέθησαν παρ' ἑκάτερα τῶν τοίχων πλάκες ἐπιγεγραμμέναι δεκατέσσαρες, *Kaibel* 828¹ (ii/A.D.) σοὶ πλάκα [τ]ήν[δ'] ἀν[έθ]ηκε, and P Osl I. 1³⁴⁰ (iv/A.D.) τὸν στρόβιλον τῆς πλακὸς τοῦ βαλανίου τούτου, "the top (cone) of the tablet of the bath," where, however, the exact meaning of πλάξ is by no means clear, see the editor's note. For πλάξ used of inscribed fragments of limestone, see Wilcken *Ostr.* i. p. 8 note. MGr πλάκα, "slab" (e.g. of a tomb).

πλάσμα,

"a thing moulded or formed" (Rom 9²⁰ LXX): cf. the magic P Lond 46³⁷⁸ (iv/A.D.) (= I. p. 77) πλ(άσμα) Ἑρμ(οῦ) χλαμυδηφόρου.

πλάσσω,

"mould," "form" (Rom 9²⁰ LXX): cf. P Tebt II. 342²² (late ii/A.D.) πεπλασμένα πλάσεως χειμερινῆς, "being of winter manufacture" (Edd.), with reference to pots, and PSI V. 472⁸ (A.D. 295) τῆς πλασσομ(ένης) πλίνθου. Cf. Artem. p. 175¹⁵ ἀνθρώπους πλάσσειν, and *Test. xii. patr.* Reub. iii. 5 πλάττειν λόγους (cf. 2 Pet 2³).

πλαστός.

A good ex. of the metaphorical use of πλαστός, "made up," "feigned," in 2 Pet 2³ is afforded by P Oxy II. 237^viii. 14 (A.D. 186) μὴ παραυτίκα πλαστὰ εἶναι τὰ γράμματα εἰπών, "not having immediately declared that the contract is forged": cf. Musonius p. 41¹⁶ πλαστοὶ καὶ οὐκ ἀληθινοὶ φίλοι. The more literal sense is seen in P Oxy IV. 729³⁰ (A.D. 137) τὴν ἐντὸς πλαστῶν χερσάμπε[λον, "the vineyard enclosed by a mud wall" (Edd.). For subst. πλάστης cf. P Giss I. 31ⁱⁱ·¹⁷ (end ii/A.D.).

πλατεῖα.

See *s.v.* πλατύς.

πλάτος,

"breadth": BGU IV. 1157⁹ (B.C. 10) πλάτους πηχῶν ἔνδεκα, and similarly P Oxy II. 242¹⁵ (A.D. 77), P Giss I. 42²·²¹ (A.D. 117). Cf. πλάτυμμα in BGU I. 162³ (ii/iii A.D.) ἄλλο πλάτυμμα ἓν χρυσοῦν, and πλάτυσμα, "tile," in Herodas III. 46.

πλατύνω.

The metaphorical use of this verb = "broaden," "enlarge," as in 2 Cor 6¹¹·¹³, finds at least a partial parallel in a fragment of an "Index" of the Digest, PSI I. 55⁴ (vi/A.D.) δύνατ(αι) . . . κατ' ἀρχὰς πλατύνεσθ(αι) ἡ ἀγω(γή).

πλατύς,

"broad." In P Par 10¹⁹ (B.C. 145) a reward is offered for a fugitive slave who is described as μεγέθει βραχύς, πλατὺς ἀπὸ τῶν ὤμων. Cf. P Fay 115¹⁷ (A.D. 101) a strap στερὴν (*l.* στερεὸν) καὶ πλατύ, "strong and broad," P Flor III. 333¹¹ (ii/A.D.) μέχρι πλατείας πύλης, and P Ryl II. 169¹⁶ (A.D. 196–7) πλατέων ἄρτων, "flat loaves." In P Lond 880²³ (B.C. 113) (= III. p. 9) we should read, according to P Strass II. 85²² note, πλατεῖα ὁδὸς τῶν θεῶν: cf. Mt 7¹³. This prepares us for the use of πλατεῖα as a subst. with or without any special name of the "street" or "public square" attached, e.g. P Oxy I. 51¹⁵ (A.D. 173) ἐ]π᾽ ἀμφόδου Πλατείας, "in the Broad Street quarter." *ib.* VI. 937[11] (iii/A.D.) παραγγέλλω σοι . . . ἵνα παραβάλῃς πρὸς τῇ πλατείᾳ τοῦ θεάτρου, "I bid you go to the street of the theatre," and P Amh II. 98[3] (ii/iii A.D.) ἐπ[ὶ] τὴν Σαραπιακ(ὴν) πλατ(εῖαν). Herwerden (*Lex. s.v.*) cites a Christian sepulchral inscr. *IGSI* 325[1] ἅπασα γέα καὶ πλατοῖς (*l.* πλατὺς) ἀὴρ γεν(ν)ᾷ σοι, θάνατε, but the reference appears to be wrong. See also Herodas VI. 53 τὴν πλατεῖαν ἐκβάντι, "as one leaves the Broad " (with Headlam's note). MGr πλατεῖα, "piazza," " square."

πλεῖστος,

"very large," plur. "very many," is generally elative in the papyri, e.g. P Petr III. 53 (*o*)[5] (iii/B.C.) θ]εῶι πλεί[στ]η χάρις, P Tebt I. 45[17] (B.C. 113) σὺν ἄλλοις πλείστοις, "with very many others," and P Oxy VI. 939[3] (iv/A.D.) (= *Selections*, p. 128) ὡς ἐν ἄλ]λοις πλείστοις, νῦν ἔτι μᾶλλον, "as on very many other occasions, so now still more." But for the genuine superlative sense we may cite such exx. as P Tebt I. 105[46] (B.C. 103) τὴν ἐσομένην πλείστην τιμὴν ἐν τῆι αὐτῆι κώμηι, "the highest price at which it may be sold at the said village" (Edd.), and P Fay 90[17] (A.D. 234) τὴν ἐπὶ τοῦ καιροῦ ἐσο|μένην) πλ[ί]στην τει(μήν), "the highest current price at the time being" (Edd.).

The word is common in greetings, e.g. P Oxy III. 533[1] (ii/iii A.D.) Ἀπίων Ἀπίωνι τῶι υἱῷ καὶ Ὡρίωνι τῶι φιλτάτῳ πλεῖστα χαίρειν, and intensified BGU III. 845[1] (ii/A.D.) .]ρεῖνος τῇ μητρὶ πλεῖστα πολλὰ χαίρι (= ει)ν. For τὰ πλεῖστα see P Tebt I. 22[5] (B.C. 112) διὰ σὲ τὰ πλεῖστα συνκάταινος ἐγενόμην, "for your sake I came to an agreement on most points" (Edd.), P Fay 35[12] (A.D. 150-1) Μύστης ἔγραψα τὰ πλεῖστα, "written for the most part by me, Mystes": cf. also Preisigke 8[7] (ii/A.D.) ἐδήλ(ωσεν) τοὺς . . . ἄνδρας ἐκ το[ῦ] πλείστου (cf. 1 Cor 14[27]) ἐγλελοιπέναι. Πλειστάκι, "repeatedly," occurs in P Ryl II. 130[13] (A.D. 31).

πλείων.

P Rev L[l. 12] (B.C. 258) τοῦ πλείονος καὶ τοῦ ἐλάσσονος κατὰ λόγον, "for more or less in proportion," P Petr II. 38(*b*)[2] (iii/B.C.) πλείονος τιμῆς, "at a higher price," PSI VI. 617[7] (iii/B.C.) ἵνα μὴ εἰς πλείονα ἀνηλώ[ματ]α ἐμπίπτω, P Lille I. 26[3] (iii/B.C.) (= Witkowski[2], p. 49) ἡ κώμη ἔρημος διὰ τὸ πλείω χρόνον μὴ βεβρέχθαι, and P Oxy I. 41[3] (iii/iv A.D.) ἐπὶ σοῦ τὰ ἀγαθὰ καὶ πλέον γίνεται, "under you our blessings increase ever more" (Edd.), acclamation to a prytanis at a public meeting.

Adverbial phrases are P Giss I. 47[10] (time of Hadrian) ἀντὶ πλείονος, "under its value," P Ryl II 65[15] (B.C. 67 ?) ἐπὶ πλεῖον, BGU I. 282[29] (after A.D. 175) ἐπὶ τὸ πλεῖον ἢ ἔλασσον, and PSI V. 514[5] (B.C. 252-1) σπούδασον μάλιστα μὲν πρὸ πλείονος, εἰ δὲ μή, τό γ᾽ ἐλάχιστον πρὸ τριῶν ἡμερῶν ἐν Ἀλεξανδρείᾳ καταστ[ῆναι? For the meaning " several," which is found in the phrase (ἐπὶ) πλείους ἡμέρας (*quater* in Ac), we may compare P Ryl II. 65[9] B.C. 67 ?) πλείονα σώματα, "several corpses." For πλέον ἔλαττον, *plus minus*, cf. BGU IV. 872[1] (Byz.).

The indeclinable πλείω in Mt 26[53] אBD (cf. Blass *Gr.* p. 108) can be paralleled from P Oxy II. 274[6] (A.D. 89-97)

πρὸς ὧι κεκλήρωται . . . πλείω πήχεις ἐννέα τέταρτον ὄγδοον—registration of property. As regards spelling Mayser (*Gr.* i. p. 69) has shown that πλείων has progressively ousted πλέων in B.C. papyri. The marked preponderance of the ει form in the NT (cf. WH *Notes*[2], p. 158) shows that in this particular our uncials faithfully represent their originals. In MGr a double comparative form πλειότερος is used, while πλέον (still used in the written language) takes the forms πλέο, πλιό, πιό.

πλέκω,

"plait," "weave" (Mt 27[29] *al.*): cf. Aristeas 70 κισσὸν ἀκάνθῳ πλεκόμενον, "ivy intertwined with acanthus." For the verbal cf. P Oxy III. 520[29] (A.D. 143) κύρτων πλεκτῶ(ν) η̄, "8 plaited fish-baskets," and the *fem.* πλεκτή *bis* in the same document = "rope." The subst. πλοκή occurs in P Giss I. 47[7] (time of Hadrian) (= *Chrest.* I. p. 383) where a θώραξ is described as τ]ὴν πλοκὴν λεπτότατος : cf. Aristeas 60, 67. The compd. περιπλοκή = "complication " is found in P Oxy III. 533[10] (ii/iii A.D.) μὴ ἔχωμεν περιπλοκὴν π[ρ]ὸς τὸν ἀντίδικον. In Vett. Val. pp. 109[32], 313[26], πλέκεσθαι = *perturbari*, and in *ib.* 110[22] = *misceri*. The verb survives in MGr with a by-form πλέκνω.

πλεονάζω.

For the generally intrans. use of this verb = "abound," "superabound," see P Rev L[lvn 13] (B.C. 258) τὸ πλεονάζον τοῦ προκηρυχθέντος, "in excess of the amount previously decreed," P Lille I. 1 *verso*[15] (B.C. 259-8) εἰς ὃ ἔσται βραχὺ τὸ ἀνάλωμα, ὥστε ἀντ᾽ ἐκείνου τοῦ πλεονάζοντος ἔργου ὧδε κομίζεσθαι, "la dépense sera donc peu élevée et de la sorte on balancera le supplément de travail indiqué plus haut " (Ed.), P Ryl II. 214[27] (ii/A.D.) με]τὰ τ᾽ὰς ἀπὸ μερισμοῦ] τοῦ ε (ἔτους) πε]πλεονακ(υίας) . . . (δραχμάς), "after deduction of the drachmae in excess of the assessment of the 5th year " (Edd.), and the Andanian inscr. relating to the mysteries *Syll* 653 (= [3] 736)[39] (B.C. 92) εἰ δὲ μή, μὴ ἐπιτρεπόντω οἱ ἱεροί, καὶ τὰ πλεονάζοντα ἱερὰ ἔστω τῶν θεῶν. Cf. also Aristeas 273 διὰ τὸ δύο πλεονάζειν τῶν ἑβδομήκοντα, "because their number exceeded seventy by two." The trans. use of πλεονάζω in 1 Thess 3[12] can be paralleled from the LXX (Numb 26[54], Ps 70(71)[21]). For the subst. πλεόνασμα cf. P Tebt I. 78[7] (B.C. 110-8) and for πλεονασμός cf. P Lond 604 B[34] (c. A.D. 47) (= III. p. 78) with the editor's note, and Wilcken *Ostr.* i. p. 280.

πλεονεκτέω.

For πλεονεκτέω, "take advantage of," "overreach," which in the NT is confined to Paul, cf. P Amh II. 78[13] (A.D. 184) (see *Berichtigungen*, p. 3) ἐν τοῖς κοινοῖς ἡμῶν ὑ[π]άρχουσι παντοδαπῶς μ[ου] πλεονεκτῖ ἄνθρωπος α[ὐ]θάδης, "in regard to our common property he, a self-willed man, takes all sorts of advantages over me ": see also Aristeas 270. In late Greek, as in 1 Thess 4[6], the verb is often followed by a direct object in the acc. (see *Proleg.* p. 65): for the pass., as in 2 Cor 2[11], cf. *OGIS* 484[27] (ii/A.D.) πλεονεκτεῖσθαι γὰρ καὶ τοὺς ὀλίγους (*qui humili conditione essent*) ὑπ᾽ αὐτῶν ἀνθρώπους δ῀ηλ]ον ἦν.

πλεονέκτης,

"covetous": cf. P Magd 5 *recto*[7] (B.C. 221) πλεονέκτης ὤν. The adv. πλεονεκτικῶς occurs in OGIS 665[16] (A.D. 48) ὑπὸ τῶν πλεονεκτικῶς καὶ ἀναιδῶς ταῖς ἐξουσίαις ἀποχρωμένων. On the fragment of a vellum leaf, P Oxy XV. 1828 *recto*[4], belonging probably to iii/A.D., and containing ethical instructions, reference is made to ὁ ψε[ύ]στης καὶ ὁ πλεονέκτης [καὶ ὁ ἀποστε]ρητής.

πλεονεξία,

"covetousness," in P Par 63[68] (B.C. 164) (= P Petr III. p. 24) μηδεμιᾶς ἐν τούτοις μήτε φιλοτιμίας, μήτε πλεονεξίας γενηθείσης keeps company with φιλοτιμία, which here represents a "grasping ambition": cf. PSI V. 446[9] (A.D. 133-7) τὸ δὲ στρατ[ι]ωτικὸν ἐπὶ πλεονεξίᾳ καὶ ἀδικίᾳ λαμβά[ν]εσθαι συνέβηκε. In Musonius p. 72[9] (ed. Hense) it is linked with βία—ἄπερ ἀπὸ βίας καὶ πλεονεξίας πέφυκε ζῆν, and in *ib.* p. 90[10] it accompanies ἡδονή—ὁ θεὸς . . . ἀήττητος μὲν ἡδονῆς, ἀήττητος δὲ πλεονεξίας, a remarkable parallel to the NT association with sins of the flesh, based on a saying of Jesus (Mk 7[22]) and repeated by at least three different NT writers (1 Cor 5[10], Heb 13[5], 2 Pet 2[14]). Bunyan's instinct rightly made Pickthank name together among Beelzebub's friends "my old Lord Lechery, Sir Having Greedy, with all the rest of our nobility." See also *Exp T* xxxvi. p. 478 f.

That πλεονεξία is a true vernacular word may be illustrated by its appearance in the illiterate P Fay 124[24] (ii/A.D.) μετάμελον σ[ο]ι πάλειν εἰσο[ίσ]ει ἡ πλεονεξ[ί]α σου, "your cupidity will again cause you regret" (Edd.): cf. P Oxy XII. 1469[4] (A.D. 298) ἐπείπερ ἐὰν πλεονεξία τις προχωρήσῃ καθ᾽ [ἡ]μῶν δι᾽ ἀδυναμείαν ἀναπόστατοι καταστη[σ]όμεθα, "since, if any advantage of us is taken, our weakness will leave us no escape" (Edd.)—a petition of certain village-representatives against a subordinate official, and *ib.* I. 67[19] (A.D. 338) ἵν᾽ οὕτως διχθῇ [αὐ]τῶν ἡ καθ᾽ ἡμῶν [πλεο]νεξία, "in this way their aggression against me will be made clear" (Edd.)—a dispute concerning property. For the word in a good sense cf. Epict. ii. 10. 9. In *Syll* 418(= ³ 888)[133] (A.D. 238) πλεονεκτήματα are simply "advantages," with ἐλαττώματα in antithesis.

πλευρά,

generally = the "side" of a human being: cf. P Oxy XII. 1414[26] (A.D. 270-5) τῆς πλευρᾶς [ῥ]έγχομαι, "I have a cough from my lung" (Edd.), and the magic P Osl I. 1[355] (iv/A.D.) ἄνυγον αὐτῆς τὴν δεξιὰν πλευράν. The neut. πλευρόν, which, along with πλευρά, is found in the LXX (Thackeray *Gr.* i. p. 157), may be illustrated from the astrological P Ryl II. 63[5] (iii/A.D.) Ἄρεως πλευρῶν, "the chest to Mars," and P Lond 121[266] (iii/A.D.) (= I. p. 93) εἰς τὸ δεξιὸν πλευρ[ὸ]ν μέρος. An unusual use of the word = "vessel" is found in P Fay 104[2] (late iii/A.D.) πλευρῶν ὑέλων, "glass vessels": see the editors' note.

πλέω.

P Grenf II. 14(*c*)[5] (iii/B.C.) οὐδ᾽ οὐκ ἔφυ (*l.* ὁ δ᾽ οὐκ ἔφη) δύνασθαι πλεῦσαι ἄνευ σου, "but he said that he could not sail without you," P Oxy IV. 726[10] (A.D. 135) οὐ δυνάμενος δι᾽ ἀ[σ]θένειαν (cf. Gal 4[13]) πλεῦσαι, "since he is unable

through sickness to make the voyage" (Edd.), *ib.* I. 110[13] (ii/iii A.D.) (= *Selections*, p. 103) πεπλάνηκαν ἡμῶ(= ᾶ s ἐκε[ῖ], τῇ ἡμέρᾳ ιβ ὅτι ἔπλευσε(= α)s, "they deceived us there on the 12th, when you sailed," *ib.* XIV. 1682[4] (iv/A.D.) ὁ ἀὴρ ἐναντίος ἡμεῖν ἦν ἀφ᾽ οὗ ἔπλευσας, "the wind was contrary to us since you sailed," and OGIS 572[30] (iii/A.D.) πλεύσει δὲ μόνα τὰ ἀπογεγραμμένα πλοῖα. For πλωτός, "navigable," see P Tebt I. 92[3] (late ii/B.C.). MGr πλέω (πλέγω), "swim," "travel."

πληγή,

"blow": cf. *Chrest.* II. 6[11] (B.C. 246) πληγάς μοι ἐνέβαλεν, P Tebt I. 44[19] (B.C. 114) ἔδωκεν πληγὰς πλείους ἧι [ε]ἶχεν ῥάβδωι, P Fay 12[17] (*c.* B.C. 103) ἤγαγον μεθ᾽ ὕβρεως καὶ πληγῶν, "they dragged me away with insults and blows," and P Tebt II. 331[10] (*c.* A.D. 131) ἐ]πήνεγκά[ν μο]ι πληγὰς εἰς πᾶν μέλ[ο]s το[ῦ σ]ώματος. Add from the law of astynomy at Pergamum, carved on stone in the time of Trajan, OGIS 483[177], αὐτὸς μαστιγούσθω ἐν τῶι κύφωνι ("the pillory") πληγαῖς πεντήκοντα, and see also *Syll* 737 (= ³ 1109)[54] (A.D. 178) ἐὰν δέ τις ἄχρι πληγῶν ἔλθῃ, ἀπογραφέστω ὁ πληγεὶς πρὸς τὸν ἱερέα ἢ τὸν ἀνθιερέα.

For the ellipsis of πληγάς in Lk 12[47], 2 Cor 11[24], cf. Herodas III. 77, V. 33 (with Headlam's notes).

πλῆθος

is used (1) of things—P Hib I. 52[5] (*c.* B.C. 245) τὰ ὀν]όματα κα[ὶ τὰ] πλήθη, "the names and the amounts," P Lille I. 3[76] (B.C. 241-0) ἱκανὰ πλήθη, "des sommes considérables" (Ed.), P Tebt II. 282[4] (late ii/B.C.) εἰ μὴ⟨ν⟩ παρειληφέναι τὰ ὑπογεγρ(αμμένα) πλήθηι, "that I have in truth received the hereinafter mentioned amounts" (Edd.), P Ryl II. 119[22] (A.D. 54-67) διὰ τὸ πλῆθος τῶν κατ᾽ ἔτος γενημάτων, "owing to its great yearly productivity" (Edd.): and (2) of persons—*Chrest.* I. 11A[i. 11] (B.C. 123) παραγενομένων τῶν αὐτῶν πληθῶν σὺν ὅπλοις, and P Tebt II. 310[8] (A.D. 186) τῷ πλήθι τῶν ἱερέων, "the corporation of priests" (Edd.).

πληθύνω,

"increase," "multiply": cf. *Poimandres* 3[3] (ed. Parthey) εἰς τὸ αὐξάνεσθαι ἐν αὐξήσει καὶ πληθύνεσθαι ἐν πλήθει (cited by Dibelius *HZNT ad* Col 2[19]). The verb is fully illustrated in Anz *Subsidia*, p. 296 f.

πλήθω.

See *s.v.* πίμπλημι.

πλημμύρα,

"a flooding," "flood." On the form πλημύρα in Lk 6[48] DW *al.*, as the older spelling, see Moulton *Gr.* ii. p. 101. The verb is found with a single μ in OGIS 666[8] (A.D. 54-68), where Egypt is described as πλημύρουσα πᾶσιν ἀγαθοῖς owing to the good deeds of the praefect Tiberius Claudius Balbillus, and in P Lond 924[10] (A.D. 187-188) (= iii. p. 134) πλημυρέντος τοῦ Νείλου. For double μ see Vett. Val. p. 344[12 f] and Artem. pp. 123[21] (of a well) πλημμυροῦντος τοῦ ὕδατος and 124[5] (of springs) ὕδατι καθαρῷ πλημμυροῦσαι.

πλήν

(1) as adv. introducing a clause (= ἀλλά, δέ) can be illustrated from Plato onwards (cf. Schmid *Atticismus* i. p. 133), and came to be regularly so used in common speech (cf. Blass-Debrunner § 449). With its use in Mt 11²² *al.*, cf. P Tebt II. 417⁸ (iii/A.D.) πλὴν ἀρξόμεθ[α] τοῦ ἔργου, "but we will begin the work," BGU IV. 1024ᵛⁱ·¹⁶ (end iv/A.D.) πλὴ<ν> συνέθετο ἀπολύσ[ειν] τὸν Διόδημον. See also P Ryl II. 163¹⁰ (A.D. 139) πλὴν εἰ μή, τὸν ἐπελευσόμενον τῷ ἐμῷ ὀνόματι . . . [ἀφισ]τάνειν με αὐτὸν παραχρῆμα, "otherwise if anyone shall make any claim in my name, I will repel him forthwith" (Edd.), P Fay 20¹⁶ (Imperial edict—iii/iv A.D.) οὐδὲ γὰρ τοῦτό μοι σπουδαιότε[ρο]ν ἐξ ἁπάντω[ν] χρηματίζεσθαι, πλὴν μᾶλλον φιλανθρωπίᾳ τε καὶ εὐεργεσίαις συναύξειν ταύτην τὴν ἀρχήν, "for it is not my aim to make money on all occasions, but rather by liberality and the conferring of benefits to increase the welfare of this empire" (Edd.). The classical collocation πλὴν ὅτι, "except that," occurs in the NT only in Ac 20²³, Phil 1¹⁸: cf. Artemidorus p. 53⁸ (after τὰ αὐτά).

(2) as a prep. c. gen. is seen in such passages as P Eleph 2⁷ (B.C. 285-4) καταλειπέτω τὰ ὑπάρχοντα πᾶσι τοῖς υἱοῖς πλὴν τῶν μερῶν, ὧν ἂν λαμβάνωσι παρὰ Δ. καὶ Κ., P Hib I. 90⁸ (B.C. 222) πλὴν τῆς χέρσου, P Lond 33²⁶ (B.C. 161) (= I. p. 20, *UPZ* i. p. 240) πλὴν τοῦ καταφθείρεσθαι, and P Leid Wᵛⁱⁱⁱ·¹³ (ii/iii A.D.) (= II. p. 107) πλὴν ἐμοῦ. In P Amh II. 93¹⁷ (A.D. 181) πλήν is construed c. acc.—πλὴν τέλος θυ[ε]ιῶν, "with the exception of the thyia-tax." Πλὴν τοῦ c. inf., which is not found in the NT, is illustrated in Mayser *Gr.* II. i. p. 327.

Πλήν is now connected not with πλέον, and hence = "more than," "beyond," but with πέλας, and hence = "besides," "apart from this": cf. the use of παρά, "beside," "except," and see Lightfoot on Phil 3¹⁶, Brugmann-Thumb *Gr.*⁴ p. 523, and Boisacq *Dict. Étym. s.v.*

πλήρης.

There are not a few traces of an indeclinable πλήρης, "full," in our NT texts—Mk 4²⁸ (C*—see WH *Notes²*, p. 24), Jn 1¹⁴ (all but D—cf. Deissmann *LAE*, p. 125 ff.), Ac 6⁵ (all but B), also Mk 8¹⁹ (AFGM *al.*), Ac 6³ (ΑΕΗΡ *al.*), 19²⁸ (AFL 33), 2 Jn⁸ (L). See further *Proleg.* p. 50, and for the interpretation of Jn 1¹⁴ cf. C. H. Turner *JTS* i. pp. 120 ff., 561 f.

Indeclinable πλήρης can now be abundantly illustrated from the papyri. Much our earliest ex. is P Leid Cⁱⁱⁱ·¹⁴ (B.C. 161) (= I. p. 118, *UPZ* i. p. 353) χαλκοῦς στατηρεί-ήους μαρσείπειον πλήρης. This is followed by the mummy-ticket *Preisigke* 3553⁷ (time of Augustus) ἔδωκα αὐτῷ τὰ ναῦλα πλήρης καὶ τὰς δαπάνας, "I have given him his full fare and money to spend," and P Lond 131 *recto*¹³³ (A.D. 78-79) (= I. p. 174) ἀρούρας πλήρη.

After i/A.D. exx. multiply rapidly, e.g. P Oxy III. 513⁵⁵ (A.D. 184) χαλκοῦς τρεῖς πλήρης, BGU I. 81²⁷ (as amended p. 356—A.D. 189) ἃς καὶ παραδώσω . . πλήρης, P Par 18 *bis*⁹ (ii/iii A.D.) τοῦ ναύλου δοθέντος ὑπ᾽ ἐμοῦ πλήρης, P Fay 88⁸ (iii/A.D.) ἔσχον παρὰ σοῦ τὸ ἐκφόριον . . . . πλήρης, P Grenf II. 69²⁹ (A.D. 265) διὰ τὸ πλήρη[ς α]ὐτὸν ἀπε[σ]χη-κέναι ὡ[ς] πρόκειτα[ι, BGU IV. 1064¹⁰ (A.D. 277-8) τὰ ἴσα τοῦ ἀργυρίου τάλαντα [δ]έκα πλήρης ἀριθμοῦ, *ib.* l. 13⁷

(A.D. 289) ἅπερ ἐντεῦθεν ἀπέσ[χ]αμεν παρὰ σοῦ πλήρης, *ib.* ll. 373²¹ (A.D. 298) ἔσχον τὴν τιμὴν πλήρης ὡς πρόκιται, and *Ostr* 1071² (A.D. 185) ἔσχ ομεν) τὸ τέλ(ος) πλήρης ἀπὸ Ἀθὺρ ἕως Μεχεὶρ κβ.

As regards the LXX Thackeray (*Gr.* i. p. 176 f.) thinks that the evidence for indeclinable πλήρης "is not as a rule so strong as to warrant our attributing the form to the autographs: in most cases it is certainly due to later scribes." The clearest exx., he thinks, are Job 21²⁴, Sir 19²⁶.

Other exx. of the adj. are P Ryl II. 145¹⁷ (A.D. 38) σάκκο(ν) πλήρη κνήκωι (*l.* κνήκου), and P Oxy III. 530⁸ (ii/A.D.) τ[ὸ δὲ] ναύβιον καὶ τὰ ἄλλα πάντα πλήρη διέγραψα, "but the naubion and the other taxes I have paid in full": and for the phrase ἐκ πλήρους see P Par 26¹·⁵ (B.C. 163-2) (= *Selections*, p. 14) οὐ κεκομισμέναι ἐκκ πλήρους, P Lond 1178⁴³ (A.D. 194) (= III. p. 217, *Selections* p. 100) ἀποδε-δωκότα τὸ κατὰ τὸν νόμ[ον ἐν]τάγιον πᾶν ἐκ πλήρους δηνάρια ἑκατόν, "on his payment of the legal fee amount-ing altogether to a hundred denarii." For the superl. see P Lond 77⁹ (end of vi A.D.) (= I. p. 232 f., *Chrest.* II. p. 370 f.) βεβαίᾳ [π]ίστει παντὶ πληρεστάτῳ δεσποτείᾳ: cf.³⁹.

πληροφορέω.

This verb occurs very rarely outside Biblical Greek, where its earliest occurrence is LXX Eccles 8¹¹. It is used of "accomplishing," "settling" legal matters in such a passage as P Amh II. 66¹² (A.D. 124), where the complainer is invited by the strategus to bring forward his witnesses, ἵνα δὲ καὶ νῦν πληροφορήσω, "in order that I may finish off the matter." Similarly in BGU III. 747ⁱ·²² (A.D. 139) αἱ[τ]ούμ[ε]νο[ς] π[λ]η[ρ]οφορε[ῖ]ν, the reference seems to be to a collector desiring to get in certain monies "in full." This prepares us for the verb in connexion with "paying off" debts, as in P Oxy III. 509¹⁰ (late ii/A.D.) τυγ[χά]νω δὲ πεπληροφορημένος τοῖς ὀφειλομένοις μοι, "but it happens that I have been paid the debt in full" (Edd.), and P Lond 1164(*g*)¹¹ (A.D. 212) (= III. p. 163) πεπληροφόρηται δὲ καὶ τῶν τόκων κατὰ μέρος διὰ χειρὸς πάντα εἰς περίλυσιν. Cf. also the expressive BGU II. 665ⁱⁱ·² (i/A.D.) ἐπληροφόρησα αὐτόν, the idea apparently being that the man to whom money has been entrusted satisfies the investor by the return he makes, and the magic P Lond 121⁹¹⁰ (iii/A.D.) (= I. p. 113) πληροφοροῦσα ἀγαπῶσα στέργουσα ἐμέ, pointing to an affection which is fully reciprocated. See further Whitaker *Exp* VIII. xx. p. 380 ff., and xxi. p. 239 f., where it is contended that πληροφορεῖσθαι "denotes not a conviction or assurance of the mind, but the result of such an assurance in life and conduct, the rich fruitfulness for which the conviction prepares the way." Hence in Rom 14⁵ the thought is that every Christian is to be "fully fruitful" in following out the course which his own mind shows him to be right. The verb is also discussed by Deissmann *LAE* p. 82 f., and by Lagrange *Bulletin d'ancienne littérature et d'archéo-logie chrétiennes* ii. (1912), p. 96 ff.

πληροφορία

does not occur in classical writers or the LXX, and in the NT appears as a rule to have passed into the meaning "full assurance," "confidence" (1 Thess 1⁵, Col 2², Heb 10²²):

cf. Clem. R. *Cor* 42 μετὰ **πληροφορίας** πνεύματος ἁγίου ἐξῆλθον εὐαγγελιζόμενοι. In Heb 6[11] the meaning is less subjective, "fulness" ("impletio sive consummatio," Grotius). The only instance of the subst. we can cite from the papyri is P Giss I. 87[25] τ]ὴν **πληροφο[ρίαν**, unfortunately in a very broken context.

πληρόω.

The original meaning "fill," "fill to the full" (MGr **πληρῶ**) may be illustrated from the phrase in *Syll* 633 (= [3]1042[20] (ii/iii A.D.) ἐὰν δέ τις τράπεζαν **πληρῶι** τῶι θεῶι, λαμβανέτωι τὸ ἥμισ[υ. The meaning "pay" is very common (MGr **πληρώνω**)—e.g. P Hib I. 40[11] (B.C. 261) δραχμὴν μίαν οὐθείς σοι μὴ **πληρ<ώσ>**ηι, "no one will pay so much as 1 drachma" (Edd.), BGU IV. 1055[23] (B.C. 13) μέχρει τοῦ **πληρωθῆναι** τὸ δάνηον, P Oxy I. 114[3] (ii/iii A.D.) κεῖται πρὸς β μνᾶς· **πεπλήρωκα** τὸν τόκον μέχρι τοῦ Ἐπείφ πρὸς στατῆρα τῆς μνᾶς, "it is pledged for two minae. I have paid the interest up to Epeiph, at the rate of a stater per mina" (Edd.), P Grenf II. 77[1] (iii/iv A.D.) (= *Selections*, p. 120) **ἐπλήρωσα** [αὐ]τὸν [το]ὺς μισθοὺς τῆς παρακομιδῆς τοῦ σώματος, "I paid him the costs of the carriage of the body"; P Oxy XII. 1489[5] (late iii/A.D.) ἐνοχλεῖς μοι ὅτι ὀφείλεις Ἀγαθὸς = ῷ) Δαίμονι χαλκόν· **πεπλήρω**σ[= κ]α αὐτόν, "you worry me about the money which you owe to Agathodaemon: I have paid him in full" (Edd.), P Fay 135[9] (iv/A.D.) ἐπισπούδασον **πληρῶσαι** ἵνα ἡ φιλία διαμίνη μετ' ἀλλήλων, "make haste to pay, in order that we may remain on good terms with each other" (Edd.), P Oxy VI. 902[16] (c. A.D. 465) ἐμοῦ ὡς προεῖπον ἑτοίμως ἔχοντος **πληρῶσαι** ὅσα ἐποφίλω αὐτῷ ἐγγράφως, "since I am ready, as aforesaid, to discharge any debt secured in writing" (Edd.), and *Syll* 737 (= [3]1109[48] (before A.D. 178) ἐὰν δὲ μὴ **πληροῖ** (*sc.* τὴν ὁρισθεῖσαν εἰς οἶνον φοράν). This usage may give us the clue to the translation of Phil 4[18] ἀπέχω δὲ πάντα . . . **πεπλήρωμαι**, "I have received payment," says Paul, "my account is settled"; see C. H. Dodd in *Exp* VIII. xv. p. 295, and cf. Moffatt "your debt to me is fully paid and more than paid!," and Goodspeed, "you have paid me in full, and more too."

The common NT use of **πληρόω** = "accomplish" a duty may be paralleled from P Lond 904[28] (A.D. 104) (= III. p. 125, *Selections*, p. 73) ἵνα . . τὴν συνήθη [οἰ]κονομίαν τῆ[ς ἀπο]γραφῆς **πληρώσωσιν**, "in order that they may carry out the regular order of the census": cf. P Oxy XIV. 1669[9] (iii A.D.) ἐνετειλάμην σοι ἐξετάσαι περὶ τοῦ συναγοραστικοῦ εἰ **πληροῦται**, "I bade you to inquire about the purchased corn, whether the amount is being completed" (Edd.). A Spartan inscr. in the *Annual of the British School at Athens* xii. p. 452, dated provisionally by H. J. W Tillyard in i/A.D., has ὃς ἕξει καὶ τὴν τοῦ ξυστάρχου τειμήν, **πληρῶν** τὰ εἰθισμέν[α, "discharging the usual offices": the editor cites *CIG* II. 2336 **πληρώσαντα** πᾶσαν ἀρχὴν καὶ λ[ε]ιτουργίαν. In the calendar inscr. *Priene* 105[34] (c. B.C. 9) Providence is stated to have filled the Emperor Augustus with virtue for the benefit of mankind, ὃν εἰς εὐεργε[σίαν ἀνθρώπων **ἐπλή]ρωσεν** ἀρετῆς (cf. Lk 2[40]).

The use of the verb in connexion with *time*, which Grimm treats as a "Hebraism," is found fully established in the Κοινή—P Lond 1108[10] (A.D. 18) (= III. p. 136) **πληρω**θέντος δὲ τοῦ χρόνου, P Oxy XIV. 1641[8] (A.D. 68) μέχρι τοῦ τὸν χρόνον **πληρωθῆναι**, and P Tebt II. 374[10] (A.D. 131) ὁ χρόνος τῆς μισθώσεως **ἐπληρό**(= ώ)θη εἰς τὸ διελη[λ]υθὸς ιδ (ἔτος), "the period of the lease expired in the past 14th year" (Edd.).

πλήρωμα.

This important word is not very common in the vernacular, but it can be illustrated in the sense of a full "company" or "complement." From Egypt we have P Petr III. 43(3)[13] (B.C. 240) ἔγραψάς μοι μὴ ἀποσπάσαι τὸ π[λή]ρωμα ἐκ Φιλωτέριδος ἕως οὗ τὰ ἔργα συντελέσαι, "you wrote me not to withdraw the gang from Philoteris before they had finished the work" (Ed.), cf.[15,19], and an inscr. from near Sebastopol *Syll* 326 (= [3]709[40] (c. B.C. 107) παραλαβὼν δὲ καὶ τῶν πολιτᾶν ἐπιλέκτους ἐμ **πληρώμασι** τρισί ("in three shiploads"). In P Hib I. 110[96] (c. B.C. 255) (= *Chrest.* I. p. 514) ἀπ[ὸ τοῦ] **πληρώματος**, Wilcken thinks the reference is to "the ship's crew": cf. Rom 11[25]. See also P Par 60 *Bis*[2] (c. B.C. 200) τὸ ἀνήλωμα εἰς Ἀλεξάνδρειαν ἀπὸ τῶν **πληρωμάτων** [ἀρ]χαίων.

The very common word **πλήρωσις** does not occur in the NT, but its restriction to commercial phraseology accounts for this: cf. *Ostr* 464[7] (A.D. 85–6), P Lips I. 105[3] (i/ii A.D.), and P Strass I. 19[5,12] (A.D. 105). That **πλήρωμα** should take its place as a *nomen actionis* (as in Rom 13[10]) is not strange, as the -σις and -μα nouns are drawing together a good deal: the shortened penultimate of θέμα, κρίμα, χρίσμα etc., due to the analogy of the -σις words, illustrates the closeness of association.

As against the so-called pass. sense of **πλήρωμα** for which Lightfoot contends (*Col.*[2] p. 257 ff., see the elaborate note by Armitage Robinson in *Eph.* p. 255 ff. Cf. also the art. "Pleroma" by W. Lock in Hastings *DB* iv. p. 1 f., and for illustrations of the word from Hermetic literature see Reitzenstein *Poimandres* p. 25 n[1].

πλησίον,

as adverb = "near" (Jn 4[5]): P Oxy III. 494[24] (A.D. 156) **πλησίον** τοῦ τάφου μου, *ib.* VIII. 1165[9] (vi/A.D.) κτήματι **πλησίον** τοῦ Μύρμηκος, "an estate near Murmux." For the adj. **πλησίος** cf. *OGIS* 736[5] (ii/i B.C.) (= *Fayûm Towns* p. 48) παρὰ τῶν **πλησίων** ἱερῶν.

πλησμονή

is best understood *in malam partem* "repletion," "satiety," in the difficult passage Col 2[23]: see Lightfoot's note *ad l.*, and to his citations add Euripides *Fr.* 887 ἐν **πλησμονῇ** τοι Κύπρις ἐν πεινῶντι δ' οὔ. Cf. also Artem. p. 199[18] **πλησμονῆς** ἢ ἐνδείας.

πλήσσω,

"strike," "smite" (Rev 8[12]): cf. P Ryl II. 68[10] (B.C. 89) ἔ[πληξέν] με ταῖς αὑτῆς χερσίν, BGU I. 163[7] (A.D. 108) ἄλλοι ὡς **πληγέντες** ὑπὸ αὐτοῦ ἀναφόριον δεδώκασι, "others have given information (from time to time) as having been assaulted by him," P Flor I. 59[4] (A.D. 225 or 241) ὥστε **πληγῆ]ναι** μέν με ἐσέσθ[αι (*l.* αἰσθέσθαι), P Lips I. 40[iii.3] (iv/v A.D.) ὅλον τὸ σῶμα αὐτοῦ **πεπληγμένον** ἐστίν, and *Kaibel* 280[3] (*tit. valde recens*) **πλη[γ]εὶς** ἐγκεφάλοιο κακὸν μόρον ἐ[ξ]ετέ[λ]ε(σ)σα[ς. For **πλῆγμα** cf. P Lips I. 40[7] (iv/v A.D.) and *ib.* 37[23] (A.D. 389).

πλοιάριον,

lit. "a little boat" (Mk 3⁹ : Vg *navicula*), but hardly to be distinguished from the ordinary πλοῖον (Jn 6²²·²⁴ : cf. *Ostr* 1051⁴ (A.D. 101) πλοιαρίου, and the late P Gen I. 14⁶ (Byz.) τὰ ναῦλα τοῦ μικροῦ πλοιαρίου. For the double dim. πλοιαρίδιον (not in LS⁸), cf. P Cairo Preis 48⁸ (ii/A.D.) where it is apparently interchangeable with πλοῖον—καὶ τὸ μὲν πλοῖόν σοι, ὡς ἠθέλησας, σκέψομαι. καλῶς δ᾽ ἔχει σε ἐνθάδε ἐλθόντα μετ᾽ ἐμοῦ μένειν μέχρι τὸ πλοιαρίδιον εὕρωμεν. Πλοιάριον refers to a lamp of some kind in P Grenf II. 111²⁶ (v/vi A.D.) πλοιάρ(ια) χαλκ(ᾶ) δ.

πλοῖον,

"boat." For this common word, which comes to be used for "ship" (Ac 20¹³) owing to the almost complete disappearance of ναῦς, cf. P Leid U^{ii. 6} (ii/B.C.) (= I. p. 123, UPZ i. p. 370) ἔδοξεν κατ᾽ ἐνύπνον (*l.* ἐνύπνιον) πλοῖον παπύρινον, ὃ καλεῖται ἀγυπτιστεὶ ῥῶψ, προσορμῆσαι εἰς Μέμφιν, P Hib I. 152 (c. B.C. 250) ἐμβαλοῦ εἰς τὸ πλοῖον ἅλας καὶ λωτὸν ὅπως ἔχωσιν [οἱ] ναυπηγοί, P Ryl II. 229¹¹ (A.D. 38) ἐρωτῶ σε ἐκ παντὸς τρόπου εὐθέως μοι πέ[μ]ψαι . . . τὸ ὀψάριον, ἐπεὶ ἐν πλοίῳ εἰμί, "I ask you therefore to do your utmost to send me the relish, as I am on board a boat," P Oxy I. 36^{ii. 8} (ii/iii A.D.) ἐ[ὰν] δὲ τελώνης ἐκφορ[τισθ]ῆναι τὸ πλοῖον ἐπιζητήσῃ, "but if the tax-farmer desire that the ship should be unloaded" (Edd.) (cf. Ac 21³), and *ib.* XIV. 1763⁴ (after A.D. 222) οὔπω μέχρι σήμερον τὰ πλοῖα τῆς ἀνῶνας ἐξῆλθεν. For the form cf. *ib.* 1773¹² (iii A.D.) ἀ]νῆλθα χάριν πλύου καὶ οὐκ εὗρον, and see Mayser *Gr.* p. 110 f.

πλόος, πλοῦς.

The late gen. πλοός, as in Ac 27⁹, occurs in *OGIS* 572²¹ (ii/A.D.) ὀφειλήσει τῷ δήμῳ ὑπὲρ ἑκάστου πλοός : cf. *ib.* 132⁹ (B.C. 130) ἐπὶ τῶν πλῶν, and see Blass-Debrunner § 52. Other exx. of the word are P Oxy IV. 727¹¹ (A.D. 154) οὐ δυν[ά]μενοι κατὰ τὸ παρὸν τὸν ἰς Αἴγυπτον πλοῦν ποιήσασθ[α]ι, and similarly P Tebt II. 317¹⁰ (A.D. 174-5) In an inscr. from Hierapolis, *Syll* 872 (= ³ 1229)³, we hear of a merchant who had made πλόας ἑβδομήκοντα δύο between Malea and Italy—an interesting ex. of the facilities of travel at the time.

πλούσιος,

"rich" : BGU IV. 1141²¹ (B.C. 14) το[ῖ]ς γεγονόσι πλουσίοις, *ib.* I. 248¹¹ (as amended *Berichtigungen,* p. 32 — i/A.D.) περὶ τοῦ πλουσίου, and P Oxy III. 471³⁹ (ii/A.D.) εὔμορφον καὶ πλούσιον μειράκιον, "handsome and rich stripling" : cf. 1 Tim 6¹⁷ (with Parry's note). With the metaph. usage in Jas 2⁵ *al.,* cf. Aristeas 15 τελείᾳ καὶ πλουσίᾳ ψυχῇ, and Antiphanes *fr.* 327 ψυχὴν ἔχειν δεῖ πλουσίαν.

πλουσίως.

In *OGIS* 767¹⁸ (i/B.C.) a certain Phaus Cyrenensis is commended for having performed his duties towards God ἐκτενῶς καὶ εὐσεβῶ(ι)ς, and his duties towards men μεγαλ[ο]ψύ(χ)ως καὶ πλουσίως ὑπὲρ δ(ύ)ναμιν.

PART VI.

πλουτέω.

For the aor. = "become rich," as in Rev 3¹⁸, cf. P Giss I. 13¹⁹ (not dated) ὅπω[ς] πλουτήσ]ῃς εἰς αἰῶ]να. The aor. is ingressive in 1 Cor 4⁸ ἤδη ἐπλουτήσατε; "have you already come into your wealth?" The pres. is seen in the Delphic precept, *Syll* 1268^{ii. 19} πλούτει δ[ικαίως.

πλουτίζω

is included by Anz (*Subsidia,* p. 297) in the class of verbs which, going back to the beginnings of Greek letters, disappear for a time from general use, only to come to light again in later Greek. This particular word is fairly common in the LXX and occurs *ter* in the NT.

πλοῦτος.

This masc. noun passes into the neuter declension in Hellenistic Greek (*Proleg.,* p. 60), and is so used *octies* by Paul, generally in a figurative sense. For the literal usage in 1 Tim 6¹⁷, cf. P Flor III. 367¹¹ (iii/A.D.) πλούτῳ γαυρωθείς, P Fay 20¹³ (iii/iv A.D.) οὐ διὰ περιουσίαν πλούτου, and *Syll* 553 (= ³ 589)³⁰ (B.C. 196) ὑπέρ τε εἰρήνης καὶ πλούτου καὶ σίτου φορᾶς.

πλύνω,

"wash" (Lk 5² *al.*). In a Zenon letter, PSI VI. 599⁷ (iii/B.C.) reference is made to πλῦναι καὶ διελξ[ι] (τὸν λίνον) as preliminaries in connexion with weaving cf. the medical receipt of early i/A.D. P Oxy VIII. 1088⁵ λίθου σχιστοῦ) πεπλ(υμένου) (δραχμὴ) ᾱ, "purified schist 1 dr.", and *OGIS* 483¹⁶⁹ (ii/B.C.) μήτε ἱμάτια πλύνειν μήτε σκεύος. The verb is used rhetorically in Herodas III. 93 ἴσσαι λάθοις τὴν γλάσσαν ἐς μέλι πλύνας, "Fie, sirrah! May you find that tongue of yours—dipped in honey" (Headlam : see note p. 161 f.). For subst. πλύνος see P Ryl II. 70⁸ (ii/B.C.) with the editor's note, and BGU VI. 1304² (B.C. 129-5), and for adj. πλύσιμος see P Sakkakini 59. 60. 94 *verso* (iii/B.C.) (cited Mayser *Gr.* II. i. p. 6). MGr πλύνω, πλένω, πλυνίσκω (Thumb *Handb.* p. 350).

πνεῦμα.

This is a notable ex. of those words, whose meaning has been so deepened and enriched through Christian influences, that we cannot expect our sources to throw much light on their use in the NT. One or two points may, however, be noted.

Thus for the more literal meaning of the word we may cite P Oxy VI. 904⁷ (v/A.D.) where a certain Flavius petitions a praeses on the ground ὡς λοιπὸν εἰς αὐτὸ τὸ τῆς σωτηρίας πνεῦμα δυστυχεῖν με, "so that at last the very breath of my life is in danger" (Edd.). In P Leid Wˣˣⁱⁱⁱ· ² (ii/iii A.D.) (= II. p. 157) reference is made to a book which περιέχει γέννησιν πνεύματος, πυρὸς καὶ σκότο(= ου)ς, "contains the creation of spirit, fire and darkness." The same document ˣˣⁱⁱⁱ· ⁴ shows οὐ ἀντιτάξεταί μοι πᾶν πνεῦμα, οὐ δαιμόνιον, οὐ συνάτ(=άντ)ημα. Reminiscent of LXX Numb 16²², 27¹⁶, is the Jewish "prayer for vengeance" from Rheneia, *Syll* 816 (= ³ 1181)²·, which opens—ἐπικαλοῦμαι καὶ ἀξιῶ τὸν θεὸν τὸν ὕψιστον, τὸν κύριον τῶν πνευμάτων καὶ πάσης σαρκός : see Deissmann's commentary in *LAE,*

67

p. 423 ff., and cf. Wünsch *AF* p. 15[7] (iii/A.D.) ὁρκίζω σε τὸν θεὸν τῶν ἀνέμων καὶ πνευμάτων Λαιλαμ ("god of the winds ").

The first words of an elaborate Christian charm of v/A.D. (?), P Oxy VIII. 1151, intended to ward off sickness and other evils, are Φεῦγε, πν(εῦμ)α μεμισι(=η)μένον, Χ(ριστό)ς σε διώκει· προέλαβέν σε ὁ υἱὸς τοῦ θ(εο)ῦ καὶ τὸ πν(εῦμ)α τὸ ἅγιον, "Fly, hateful spirit ! Christ pursues thee ; the Son of God and the Holy Spirit have outstripped thee " (Ed.): cf. the Christian amulet P Iand 6[10] (v/vi A.D.) directed πρὸς πᾶν ἀκάθαρτον πν(εῦμ)α, the familiar phrase of the Gospels.

To the injunction in the magic P Osl 1[169 f.] (iv/A.D.) φυλακτή[ρι]ον περιπόη (*l.* περιπόει), "do you put round yourself an amulet," there are added the words ἀλλὰ κρατί(=εί)σθω τῷ πνεύματι, "but let her be in the power of the spirit," where the editor (p. 76) thinks that τὸ πνεῦμα "seems here to have been used in a pregnant sense of the 'evil demon' in general." See also the description of a means for procuring an oracular response in P Lond 46[384] (iv/A.D.) (= I. p. 77) γράψον τὸν λό(γον) εἰς χάρτ(ην) ἱερατικὸν καὶ εἰς φῦσαν χήνειαν... καὶ ἔνθες εἰς τὸ ζῴδ(ιον) ἐνπνευματώσεως εἴνεκεν ("in order to fill it with πνεῦμα," i.e. spirit and life).

The trichotomy with which Paul has familiarized us in 1 Thess 5[23] (cf. Milligan *ad l.*) meets us in the Christian P Oxy VIII. 1161[6] (iv/A.D.) containing a prayer to "our gracious Saviour and to his beloved Son," ὅπως οὗτοι πάντες β[ο]ηθήσωσιν ἡμῶν τῷ σώματι, τῇ ψυχῇ, τῷ [[πν(εύματ)ι]] πν(εύματι), "that they all may succour our body, soul, and spirit." For the frequency of the trichotomy in Egyptian ritual in the order ψυχή, σῶμα, πνεῦμα, see F. E. Brightman in *JTS* ii. p. 273 f.

Reference should be made to the classical discussion of πνεῦμα by Burton *Galatians* (in *ICC*), p. 486 ff.

πνευματικός.

P Lond 46[25] (iv/A.D.) (= I. p. 66) ἐν συστροφῇ πρὸς πνευματικ(ὴν) ἀπειλή[ν, "shortly, for spiritual threatening" (Ed.). See also Vett. Val. pp. 1[11] πνευματικῆς ἤτοι αἰσθητικῆς κινήσεως, 231[20] περὶ καταδίκης καὶ πνευματικοῦ κινδύνου, and for πνευματώδης *ib.* 13[9] ψυχεινοί, πνευματώδεις.

πνέω,

"breathe," "blow": see the imprecatory tablet Wünsch *AF* 3[16], found in the grave of an official of Imperial times in the neighbourhood of Carthage, στρέβλωσον ("strain tight ") αὐτῶν τὴν ψυχὴν καὶ τὴν καρδίαν ἵνα μὴ[π]νέωσιν. With Ac 9[1], cf. Herodas VIII. 58 τὰ δεινὰ πνεῦσαι (and see Headlam's note p. 392).

πνίγω.

The nursery acrostic P Tebt II. 278[10] (i/A.D.) πνίξωι ἐματόν, ῥιγῶι γάρ, "I will choke myself, for it is cold " (Edd.), gives us the word in an elementary stage of educational achievement. Cf. Artem. p. 3[13] ἢ ἐμεῖν ἢ πνίγεσθαι. The subst. πνιγμός occurs in a Menander fragment published in PSI II. 126[50 f.] :—

τί παθών; χολή, λύπη τις, ἔκστασις φρενῶν,
πνιγμός.

πνικτός.

On πνικτός in the Apostolic Decree, Ac 15[20.29], see a note by Nestle in *ZNTW* vii. (1906), p. 254 ff., and more recently the elaborate discussion by Ropes in *Beginnings of Christianity* Part I. Vol. iii. p. 265 ff.

πνοή,

in the sense of "gust," "wind," as in Ac 2[2], occurs in the sundial inscr. *Preisigke* 358[13] (iii/B.C.) τ]ὸ ἄκρον τῆς σκιᾶς . . . ἐπὶ τῶν ἰῶτα φερόμενον [σ]ημαίνει ζεφύρου πνοήν: cf. Bacchylides v. 28 σὺν ζεφύρου πνοιαῖσιν.

ποδήρης,

"reaching to the feet," the termination -ήρης being perhaps derived from the root of ἀραρίσκω, though this would rather suggest "feet-fitting." The word is found in the NT only in Rev 1[13] (cf. *Proleg.* p. 49): but to the LXX exx. we may add Aristeas 96 χρυσοῖ γὰρ κώδωνες περὶ τὸν ποδήρη εἰσὶν αὐτοῦ, 'for there are 'bells of gold ' around *the border* of his 'long robe ' " (Thackeray).

πόθεν,

"whence": P Oxy II. 237[viii 33] (A.D. 186) δηλοῦντες πόθεν ἕκαστος τῶν ὑπαρχόντων καταβέβηκεν εἰς αὐτοὺς ἡ κτῆσ{ε}ις, "severally declaring the sources from which the property acquired has come into their possession " (Edd.). For the enclitic ποθέν, cf P Tebt II. 423[23] (early iii/A.D.) δή[λω]σόν μοι ταχ[έως] ἵνα π[έμ]ψω ποθὲν αὐτοῖς μέτρ[α τιν]ά, "tell me at once in order that I may send a few measures to them from somewhere " (Edd.), and for πόθεν = "how," see Mk 12[37], Jn 1[48] and 6[5] (Field *Notes*, p. 91).

ποία,

"grass." For the form cf. Moulton *Gr.* ii. p. 83, and see *Syll* 803 (= [3] 1169)[121] (from the Asclepieum—iii/B.C.), where a man with an injured eye describes the cure worked by the god—ἐδό]κει ὁ θεὸς ποίαν τρίψας ἐγχεῖν εἰς τ[ὸν ὀφθαλμόν τι· καὶ ὑγιὴς ἐγένετο. A new word πωολογία, whose meaning is obscure, occurs in P Lille I. 5[3 ff.] (iii/B.C.) Cronert and Wilcken suggest " Grünernte," which has led to a conjecture (*Exp* VII. x. p. 566) that in Jas 4[14] ποία may possibly = "green herb." rather than be taken as fem. of ποῖος.

ποιέω.

The phrase εὖ or καλῶς ποιήσεις is very common introducing a command or request, almost = our "please " or "kindly." It is generally followed by an aor. part., as in 3 Jn[6], e.g. P Oxy II. 294[12] (A.D. 22) εὖ οὖν ποιήσις γράψας μοι ἀντιφωνή[σ]ιν περὶ τούτων, "please write me an answer on these matters," *ib.* 300[5] (late i/A.D.) περὶ οὗ καλῶς ποιήσεις ἀντιφωνήσασά μοι ὅτι ἐκομίσου, "please send me an answer that you have received it," *ib.* III. 525[7] (early ii/A.D.) καλῶς ποιήσεις δοὺς λω[το]ῦ παρὰ Σαραπίωνος ἐκ τοῦ ἐ[μοῦ] λόγου, "pleas get some lotus (?) for him from Sarapion at my expense " (Edd.), *ib.* VI. 967 (ii/A.D.) ; but by the fut. ind. in *ib.* II. 297[3] (A.D. 54) καλῶς ποιήσεις γράψεις διὰ πιττακίων τὸν ἀπολογισμὸν τῶν [π]ρ[ο]βάτων, "kindly write me in a note the record of the sheep" (Edd.), *ib.* l. 113⁶ (ii/A.D.) εὖ ποιήσεις ἀγοράσεις μοι (δραχμὰς) β̄. In *ib.* VI. 929⁶·¹⁷ (ii/iii A.D.) καλῶς ποιήσεις is followed first by a part. ἀπαιτήσας, and then by ἀποκαταστῆσαι. The phrase μὴ ἄλλως ποιήσεις is used in cases of urgency as in the letter already quoted, *ib.* II. 294¹⁴ (A.D. 22) μὴ οὖν ἄλλως ποιήσις, ἐγὼ δὲ αὐτὸς οὔπω οὐδὲ ἐνήλειπα (= ἐναλήλιφα *sc.* ἐμαυτὸν) ἕως ἀκούσω φάσιν παρὰ σοῦ περὶ ἁπάντων, "be sure to do this ; I am not so much as anointing myself until I hear word from you on each point " (Edd.).

For the strong sense of ποιέω, "am effective," as in the "working" of charms, cf. P Osl I. 1⁶·⁴ (iv/A.D.) εἰς πάντα ποιῶν, with the editor's note. In P Oxy XII. 1480¹¹ (A.D. 32) πεπόητε εἰς τὸν ἐκλογιστήν, instead of the editors' rendering "he has made it (a delay spoken of) as far as the eclogistes is concerned (?)," Olsson (*Papyrusbriefe*, p. 75) thinks that ποιέω may be used for πράττω—"he has arranged it with the eclogistes."

The phrase ποιεῖν μετά τινος, "to act on someone's behalf," is common in the LXX (Gen 24¹² *al.*), but in the NT is confined to Luke (e.g. 1⁷², 10³⁷, Ac 14²⁷). It is often regarded as a Hebraism (Blass *Gr.* p. 134, Souter *Lex.* *s.v.*, but see Kühring, p. 35, *Proleg.* p. 106, Robertson *Gr.* p. 610 f.). The only instances we can quote from the papyri are late—BGU III. 648⁸ (iv/A.D.) καλιόστερεν (*l.* καλλιό-τερον) . . . ἐποίησα μετὰ σοῦ, *ib.* 798⁷ (Byz.) εἰς πάντα τὰ καλὰ ἃ ἐποίησεν μετὰ τῶν δούλων αὐτῆς. The Latin-ism τὸ ἱκανὸν ποιεῖν (Mk 15¹⁵) is illustrated *s.v.* ἱκανός.

For the meaning "remain," "abide," with an acc. of time as an adverbial addition, as in Ac 20³, Jas 4¹³, cf. PSI IV. 362¹⁵ (B.C. 251–0) ὁρῶν με πλείους ἡμέρας ἐκεῖ ποιοῦντα, γράφει μοι εἰς Ἀλεξάνδρειαν, P Par 47²¹ (*c.* B.C. 152–1) (= *UPZ* i. p. 332) δύο ἡμέρας ποιεῖ ἐν τῶι Ἀνυβιείωι πίνων, P Flor II. 137⁷ (A.D. 263) πρὸς τὴν μίαν ἡμέραν ἣν ποιεῖ ἐκεῖ, P Gen I. 54¹⁹ (iv/A.D.) ἐποιήσαμεν γὰρ τρῖς ἡμέρας ἐν τῇ Καρανίδι κοινώτεροι, and P Iand 14⁶ (iv/A.D.) : see also Mayser *Gr.* II. i. p. 81.

The meaning "celebrate," as in Mt 26¹⁸, Ac 18²¹ D, Heb 11²⁸, is seen in P Fay 117¹² (A.D. 108) ἐπὶ (= ἐὶ) Ἐρασο[s] τὰ Ἁρποχράτια ὧδε τάχα ιδ πυ[ή]σι, "since Erasus is going to celebrate the festival of Harpocrates so soon on the 14th" (Edd.).

The case against giving ποιέω a sacrificial sense in the NT (Lk 22¹⁹, 1 Cor 11²⁴) is stated at length by T. K. Abbott *Essays chiefly on the Original Texts of the Old and New Testaments*, p. 110 ff., see *contra* F. W. Mozley *Exp* VI. vii. p. 370 ff.

We may add a few miscellaneous exx.—PSI VI. 552¹⁹ (iii/B.C.) ἐὰν μὲν ποιῶσιν ἡδέως αὐτά, βέλτιστα, P Oxy II. 200⁸ (A.D. 50) ἐξ ἧς ἐποιησάμεθα πρὸ[s] ἑαυτοὺ<s> ἐπὶ τοῦ στρατηγοῦ, "in consequence of our confronting each other before the strategus" (Edd.), BGU I. 103⁷ (A.D. 108) φασὶ οἱ παρόντες ἐκεῖνον μᾶλλον τοῦτο πεποιηκέναι (for perf. cf. 2 Cor 11²⁵), καὶ γὰρ ἄλλοι ὡς πληγέντες ὑπὸ αὐτοῦ ἀναφόριον δεδώκασι, P Tebt II. 315²⁸ (ii/A.D.) where the writer promises to help in getting a friend's books through the scrutiny by the government inspector, πρὶν γὰρ [α]ὐτὸ[ν] π[ρό]s σε ἐλθῖν ἐγὼ αὐτὸν ποι[ήσ]ω ἐκπλέξαι σε, "for I will make him let you through before he comes to you" (Edd.), and *ib.* 407²¹ (A.D. 199?) where an ex-high-priest warns his wife and daughter that if they do not fall in with his wishes

he will leave certain property to the temple—πά[ν]τα ὅ[σα] ἐποίησα ἐπ' ὀνόματός σου εἶναι τοῦ [ἐν Ἀλεξανδρείᾳ θεοῦ] μεγ[ά]λου Σαράπιδος, "all that I placed in your name is the property of the great Serapis at Alexandria." In records of manumission, it is frequently stated that an enfranchised slave is free ποιεῖν ὃ κα θέλῃ, "to do whatever he wills"; see Deissmann (*LAE* p. 328f.), who compares Gal 5¹⁷.

For the forms ποῖσαι Lk 11⁴²ℵ, ποίσας Jn 5¹¹ W, see Moulton *Gr.* ii. p. 73, and cf. *Archiv* iv. p. 492. Πεποιή-κεισαν, as in Mk 15⁷, is found in *Magn* 93(b)²⁴ (a Senate decree—*c.* B.C. 190).

ποίημα,

"that which is made," plur. "pieces of work" (Rom 1²⁰) : cf. *Syll*³ 532⁵ (B.C. 218–7) ἐ[πιδείξεις] ἐποιήσατο τῶν ἰδίωμ ποιημάτων.

ποίησις,

"a doing," "a making" (Jas 1²⁵) : *Syll* 246 (=³ 547)⁴⁹ (B.C. 211–10) τῆς δὲ ποιήσεως τῆς εἰκό[ν]ος καὶ τῆς ἀναγο-ρεύσ[ε]ως ἐπιμεληθῆναι τὸν γραμματέα κτλ. MGr ποίησι, "poetry."

ποιητής,

readily passes into the special meaning "poet," like "maker" *Scottice* : see the reff. in Herwerden *Lex. s.v.*, and add *Preisigke* 595 (ii/A.D.) Π(ουβλίου) Αἰλίου Γλαυκίου ποιητοῦ γενομένου ἐξηγητοῦ, *ib.* 1005 Νεμεσιανὸς πολίτης τοῦ θείου ποιητοῦ Ὁμήρου, and *Cagnat* IV. 827⁵ Σεκοῦνδον παντὸ[s] μέτρου πυητὴν ἄριστον.

ποικίλος.

For the original meaning of this adj. "many-coloured," "variegated," cf. P Hib I. 120⁷ (B.C. 250–240), an account for goats which are classified as μέλαιναι, πυρραί, ποικίλαι, "black, red, streaked," similarly P Cairo Preis 37⁹ (iii/B.C.) τ[ρεῖ]s β[ό]ῦs, δύο μὲν [. . . . . .], ἕν[α δ]ὲ ποικίλον, and Artem. p. 234²⁴ ποικίλα καὶ κατάστικτα (ζῷα). In Herodas V. 67 Headlam (see note, p. 257) understands the word as "decorated with tattoo-marks." For the adv. cf. Olsson *Papyrusbriefe* 34²⁰ (time of Claudius) οἱ κονια[ταὶ ποικ]ίλως πάντα πεποιήκα[σι καὶ] ποι[ο]ῦσι, of plasterers decorating the walls of a house : see also Aristeas 17 πολλαχῶς καὶ ποικίλως.

In its NT occurrences (Mt 4²⁴ *al.*) the adj. is used meta-phorically "various," "manifold" : cf. Aelian *V.H.* ix. 8 ὁ δὲ . . . πολλαῖς καὶ ποικίλαις χρησάμενος βίου μετα-βολαῖς, and Herodas III. 80, where the meaning is "shift-ing," "artful," of character (see Headlam's note, p. 159 f.).

For the subst. ποικιλία (cf. Pss. Sol. 4⁸), see the calendar P Hib I. 27⁰⁹ (B.C. 301–240) ἡ τῶν μορίων ποικ[ιλία?], where, if the restoration is right, the reference is apparently to the multitude of the complicated fractions of the hours of the nights and days : see the editors' note. For ποικιλτής, "a broiderer," cf. BGU I. 34 *re* ¹⁵ⁱⁱ ²⁴, and for ποικιλτός (Exod 28⁶) "embroidered," cf. P Oxy X. 1277⁸ (A.D. 255).

ποιμαίνω,

"shepherd," "tend": cf. BGU III. 759¹¹ (A.D. 125) ἐπελθόντες μοι . . . ποιμαίνοντι θρέμματα Ἀνουβίωνος, P Ryl II. 114⁹ (c. A.D. 280) Συρίων . . . ἀναπίσας μου τὸν ἄν[δρα Γάνιδα ὀνό]ματι ποιμένιν αὐτοῦ τὰ πρόβατα, "Syrion persuaded my husband Ganis to pasture his flock," P Thead 15¹¹ (A.D. 280-1) ἀγανακτ[ή]σας ἐκέλευσας αὐτῷ τῷ Συρίωνι παραστῆσαι τοὺς ποιμένας μεθ᾽ [ὧ]ν ἐποίμανεν ὁ τῶν παίδων πατήρ, "in your indignation you have ordered Syrion himself to present at the tribunal the shepherds, along with whom the father of the children shepherded," and from the inscr. Syll 570 (=³ 980)³ (v/iv B.C.) ἐν τ]οῖς ἄλσεσιν μ[ὴ ποιμ]αίνειν μηδὲ κοπρ[έοε]ν (i.e. κοπρεύειν : editor).

Bauer (HZNT ad Jn 21¹⁵) sees no difference between βόσκω and ποιμαίνω in Jn 21¹⁵, ¹⁷ and ¹⁶, but refers to Philo Quod det. pot. ins. sol. p. 263²⁷ ff. ed. Cohn for a difference between them. From the idea of "pasturing," "feeding," the verb passes readily into the idea of "governing," "guiding" (Hort Ecclesia, p. 243): cf. Rev 2²⁷ with Swete's note.

ποιμήν,

"shepherd," is naturally common, and does not always occur in a very favourable light: cf. P Magd 6¹¹ (B.C. 221) προστάξαι Διοφάνει . . μὴ περιιδεῖμ με ἀνόμως ὑβριζόμενον ὑπὸ τῶν ποιμένων, P Ryl II. 152⁵ (A.D. 42) ἐπαφέντε ς) οἱ ποιμένες . . . ἃ ἔχουσι πρόβατα εἰς ἃς ἔχωι νομὰς ἐν ἐλαιῶ(νι) Θερμουθαρίου, "the shepherds let their flocks into the pasturage which I have in the olive-yard of Thermoutharion."

The word is also used of a lessee of sheep (μισθωτὴς προβάτων), cf. P Lond 851 (A.D. 216-219) (= III. p. 48), and the introd. to P Strass I. 24 (A.D. 118), also Archiv iv. p. 533.

ποίμνη.

Thumb (Hellen. p. 142 f.) cites φήμνης = ποίμνης from a wax tablet of iii/A.D. containing fragments of Babrius and published in JHS xiii. (1892-3). p. 294 ff.

ποίμνιον,

"a flock"—the diminutive meaning, as in late Greek generally, cannot be pressed, cf. P Ryl II. 114²⁰ (c. A.D. 280), where a widow complains to the praefect that her husband's former master had seized certain flocks belonging to the deceased, καὶ μέχρι τῆς σήμε[ρον οἰκειῶν τ]υγχάνει τὰ ἡμέτερα ποίμνια, "and until this day he remains in possession of our flocks" (Edd.). Cf. Aristeas 170 βουκολίων καὶ ποιμνίων, "herds and flocks."

ποῖος.

Hort ad 1 Pet 1¹¹ has pointed out that in Mt, Lk, Ac (23³⁴) and Rev ποῖος loses its classical force of "kind," "but only with reference to locality (including way) and time." Paul, on the other hand, keeps the proper sense "what manner," (Rom 3²⁷ al.), and so probably Jas 4¹⁴ and 1 Pet 1¹¹, 2²⁰.

For ποῖος in the weakened sense of "what" in indirect interrogation, see P Par 60⁷ (B.C. 154) (as read UPZ i. p. 321) ἀπόστιλόν μοι, πόσον ἔχει Πετευσοράπιος καὶ

ἀπὸ ποίου χρόνου, P Tebt I. 25¹⁸ (B.C. 117) διὰ τίνος καὶ ἀπὸ ποίου ἐπιδείγματος, P Amh II. 68⁷ (late i/A.D.) ἀπὸ ποίου ἔτους χερσεύουσιν, BGU II. 619ⁱ·⁸ (A.D. 155) ὑ[π]ὸ τίνων καὶ ἐπὶ ποίοις ὑπάρχουσι, and P Flor II. 254¹⁵ (A.D. 259) δήλωσόν μοι ἀπὸ ποίου κτήματος αὐτῷ παρέδωκες. MGr ποιός, "who?" "which?"

πολεμέω,

"make war with," is construed with μετά, as quater in Rev, in BGU IV. 1035⁹ (v/A.D.) (as read Chrest. I. p. 39) οἱ οὖν ἀπὸ Ὀξυρύγχων ἠθέλησαν . . . πολεμῆσαι μετὰ τῶν ἀπὸ Κερκῆσις, and in the Silko inscr. OGIS 201³ (vi/A.D.) ἅπαξ δύο ἐπολέμησα μετὰ τῶν Βλεμύων. Thumb (Hellen. p. 125) points out that there is no need to speak of Hebraism in view of MGr use, as in the popular song τρεῖς ὥρες ἐπολέμαε μὲ δεκοχτὼ χιλιάδες : cf. Abbott Songs, p. 44—

τὸ πῶς αὐτὸς 'πολέμησε μὲ τρεῖς χιλιάδα(ι)ς Τούρκους.

For the verb used hyperbolically of private quarrels, as in Jas 4², cf. Preisigke 4317¹² (c. A.D. 200) πολεμεῖ με διότι εἶπόν σοι εἰς ὄψιν, where the growth of the acc. construction may also be noted (cf. Proleg. p. 64). The pass. is seen in OGIS 748⁸ (iv/B.C.) πολεμηθείσης τῆς χώρας. MGr πολεμῶ, "fight," "struggle"; "endeavour" (Thumb Handb. p. 350).

πόλεμος

in the general sense of "war" may be illustrated from P Amh II. 30²⁷ (ii/B.C.) where in an inquiry regarding the ownership of a house proof is adduced Μαρρῆν . . κατεσχηκέναι τὴν οἰκίαν πρὸ τοῦ πολέμου, "that Marres had become owner of the house before the war," and from P Oxy IV. 705³³ (A.D. 200-2) where the Emperors Septimius Severus and Caracalla are reminded of the loyalty of the Oxyrhynchites in helping them in the war against the Jews— κατὰ τὸν πρὸς Εἰουδαίους πόλεμον συμμαχήσαντες. An interesting ex. of the word is found in the letter of the Emperor Claudius to the Alexandrines P Lond 1912⁷⁶ (A.D. 41) τῆς δὲ πρὸς Ἰουδαίους ταραχῆς καὶ στάσεως, μᾶλλον δ' εἰ χρὴ τὸ ἀληθὲς εἰπεῖν τοῦ πολέμου, πότεροι μὲν αἴτιοι κατέστησαν . . οὐκ ἐβουλήθην ἀκριβῶς ἐξελένξαι, "as to the question which of you were responsible for the riot and feud (or rather, if the truth must be told, the war) against the Jews, I was unwilling to commit myself to a decided judgment" (Bell). It may be noted that in the calendar inscr. Priene 105³⁶ (c. B.C. 9) the Emperor Augustus is signalized as σωτῆρα . . τὸν παύσαντα τὸν πόλεμον, κοσμήσαντα [δὲ πάντα.

For the meaning "battle," as in Lk 14³¹, 3 Kingd 22³⁴, al. see Field Notes, p. 67 f., and add the striking phrase 2 Kingd 11⁷ ἐπερωτᾶν . . εἰς εἰρήνην τοῦ πολέμου, "to ask how the battle progressed."

πόλις.

In the second Logia fragment, P Oxy IV. 654²¹, Blass suggested the restoration ὑμεῖς ἐστὲ ἡ πτό[λις (sc. τοῦ θεοῦ), and is followed by White (Sayings. p. 9). It may be worth while to note that this ancient by-form of πόλις occurs in three ostraca of the reign of Caligula as a proper name, Ostr 380¹ διαγεγρά(φηκεν) Πτόλις Ψενεν(ούφιος), ib. 381¹, 382¹, and similarly in PSI IV. 317¹⁶ (A.D. 95) Ἀσκληπιάδης Πτόλιδι τῷ φιλτάτῳ χαίρειν. This recalls the fact that πτόλεμος also survived in the royal name Πτολεμαῖος.

The distributive force which πόλις has in several Lucan passages (Ac 15²¹ *al.*) and in Tit 1⁵ is to be set against the very different meaning of the phrase in sundry documents of the new collection from Alexandria (reign of Augustus). Schubart, who edits the documents in BGU IV., notes (*Archiv* v. p. 38) that in a good many papers relating to the hire of a nurse (e.g. 1105⁷) it is stipulated that the child shall be kept ἔξω κατὰ πόλιν, "that is, outside the house of the person who gives the child in charge, but 'in the city'" of Alexandria. The phrase may be added to many others with art. dropped after a preposition, but required by the sense : see *Proleg.* p. 82.

For πόλις standing alone with reference to the city of the Gadarenes in Lk 8²⁷, cf. the similar usage in connexion with Alexandria in P Magd 22⁴ (B.C. 221) πρὶν τοῦ] καταπλεῦσαί με εἰς τὴν πόλιν, and P Tebt I. 50⁴ (B.C. 99) (= Witkowski², p. 112) καταντήσαντος γὰρ εἰς τὴν πόλιν Σοκονώφεως, much as in MGr πόλι is used specially of Constantinople, or we speak of "going up to town" (London). The word is also frequently used of the chief city of a district : see Jouguet *Vie Municipale*, p. 48 f. In PSI IV. 341³ (B.C. 256-5) certain weavers desire to settle in Philadelphia, ἀκούοντες . . . τὸ κλέος τῆς πόλεως.

The mingled Hebrew and Greek associations, which have gathered round the NT idea of the Heavenly City, are discussed and illustrated by Hicks *CR* i. p. 5, and reference should also be made to Souter *Lex. s.v.* For the Stoic conception of man as a member of the great commonwealth of the universe we may recall M. Anton. iii. 11. 2 πολίτην ὄντα πόλεως τῆς ἀνωτάτης, ἧς αἱ λοιπαὶ πόλεις ὥσπερ οἰκίαι εἰσίν.

πολιτάρχης.

This title is known from inscrr., as well as from Ac 17⁶ˑ⁸, to have been in use at Thessalonica and elsewhere : see E. De Witt Burton's art. in the *AJT* ii. (1898), p. 598 ff. (summarized in Hastings' *DB* iv. p. 315), where he prints seventeen inscrr., with two more in which the title (πολιτάρχης) or the verb (πολιταρχέω) is plausibly restored, showing that in Thessalonica there were 5 politarchs in the time of Augustus, and 6 in the time of Antoninus and Marcus Aurelius. Of the inscrr. 14 belong to Macedonia (5 of them to Thessalonica), 2 to Philippopolis in Thrace, and one each to Bithynia, Bosporus, and Egypt. To these we can now add a papyrus letter from Egypt, P Oxy IV. 745⁴ (c. A.D. 1), where the writer claims that his correspondent had made some promise through the "politarch" Theophilus—ὡς καὶ ὑπέσχου διὰ τοῦ πολειτάρχου Θεοφίλου. It is clear from Burton's citations that the title was essentially Macedonian. It would be brought into Egypt naturally by some early Ptolemy, but it is odd that it should be there at all and appear so seldom. The verb occurs in an inscr. from Cairo of iii/iv A.D., *Kaibel* 430⁷—

δισσῶν γάρ τε τόπων πολιταρχῶν αὐτὸς ἐτείμω.

πολιτεία.

In a letter of remonstrance, P Oxy VIII. 1119²¹ (A.D. 254), vindicating the privileges enjoyed by the Antinoites of immunity of public burdens outside their own city, the phrase occurs κατὰ το[ὺ]ς πατρίους τῆς ἡμετέρας πολιτείας νόμους, "in accordance with the ancestral usages of our constitution" (Ed.) : cf. Eph 2¹².

Wilcken (*Chrest.* I. i. p. 78) cites the following exx. from Egypt of πολιτεία practically = πόλις (*civitas*) : P Flor I. 95⁹ (Hermopolis Magna—A.D. 375) ὑπεδεξάμεθα [παρά σου] ὑπὲρ τῆς σῆς πολ[ιτ⟨ε⟩ι]ας, P Lips I. 62ⁱⁱˑ⁵ (Antinoopolis —A.D. 385) (= *Chrest.* I. p. 220) ὑπεδεξάμην παρά σου καὶ νῦν ὑπὲρ τῆς σῆς πολιτείας, and BGU I. 304³ (Fayûm— c. A.D. 640) παγάρχ(ῳ) τοῦ βορρ(ινοῦ) σκέλους ταύτης τῆς πολ[ι]τ(είας).

For πολιτεία = "citizenship," as in Ac 22²⁸, we may cite Gnomon 47 (c. A.D. 150) (= BGU V. 1. p. 23) ἀστὴ συνελθοῦσα Αἰ[γ]υ[πτίῳ] κατ' ἄγνοιαν ὡς ἀστῷ ἀνεύθυνός ἐστιν. ἐὰν δὲ καὶ ὑπὸ ἀμφοτέρ[ων ἀπ]αρχὴ τέκνων τεθῇ, τηρεῖται τοῖς τέκνοις ἡ πολιτεία, "if a woman, being a citizen [i.e. of Alexandria], marries an Egyptian in the mistaken belief that he is also a citizen, she is not liable to penalty : and if both parties present birth-certificates, their children preserve the status of citizens."

The religious sense which the word acquired (cf. the verb in Ac 23¹, Phil 1²⁷) is well seen in the Christian letter P Heid 6⁸ iv/A.D. (= *Selections*, p. 125 f.) πιστεύομεν γὰρ τὴν πολιτία'ν σ]ου ἐν οὐρανῷ. Deissmann *ad l.* cites Gregory of Nyssa σπεύδειν πρὸς τὴν ἐπουράνιον πολιτείαν (Migne 46, 597b), and Isidore of Pelusium ἡ οὐρανῷ πρέπουσα πολιτεία (*Epp.* 216 and 33).

πολίτευμα.

For πολίτευμα = "citizenship," or "franchise," we may compare *Syll* 238 (= ³ 543)⁶ (B.C. 210), where King Philip orders the authorities at Larisa to pass a vote giving πολιτεία to Thessalians or other Greeks resident in the city, until he shall have found others ἀξίους τοῦ παρ' ὑμῖν πολιτεύματος. This is followed by a further rescript, *ib.* 239⁷ (= ³ 543³²) (B.C. 214) in which Philip says that there are some States, ὧν καὶ οἱ Ῥωμαῖοί εἰσιν, οἳ καὶ τοὺς οἰκέτας ὅταν ἐλευθερώσωσιν προσδεχόμενοι εἰς τὸ πολίτευμα : he warns the Larisaeans to restore εἰς τὴν πολιτείαν those whose names they had erased. It seems that πολιτεία here is the actual "franchise" in the abstract, πολίτευμα being a less technical, more general word, rather like our "community" in its capacity of becoming either abstract or collective.

Other quotations all favour "community" or "commonwealth." Thus the famous decree set up by the Jewish community at Berenike in Cyrenaica in honour of the Roman Governor M. Tittius, *CIG* III. 5361 (B.C. 13), runs— ἔδοξε τοῖς ἄρχουσι καὶ τῷ πολιτεύματι τῶν ἐν Βερενίκῃ Ἰουδαίων : the names of the nine ἄρχοντες who stood at the head of the πολίτευμα are given at the head of the decree : cf. *OGIS* 658³ (B.C. 3), where there is a reference to a πολίτευμα which the Phrygians had set up in Alexandria : see also Aristeas 310 τῶν ἀπὸ τοῦ πολιτεύματος, "some members of the *Jewish* community" (Thackeray).

In *Syll* 472⁷ (i/B.C.) ὅπως [οὖν κ]αὶ ἡ πόλις τοὺς εὐνοοῦντας προ[καλ]εσαμένη πρὸς εὔνοιαν αὔξῃ τὸ [π]ολίτευμα τῶν προγόνων, the meaning, as Dittenberger notes, is "ut populus rem publicam ampliorem et opulentiorem reddat, quam a maioribus accepit." In a rescript of Alexander the Great, *ib.* 150 (= [3] 383[3]) (B.C. 333–2) we read **πολίτευμα δὲ [εἶ]ναι ἐν Χίωι δῆμον** = "that the constitution in Chios should be a democracy."

According to *Cos* p. 123 No. 74[5] (= *OGIS* 192) three officials put up a monument **ὑπὲρ τοῦ πολιτεύματος**: where, the editors note, the word **πολίτευμα** points to Africa and Egypt. We may also recall the inscr. found at Pompeii, but certainly of Egyptian origin, of date B.C. 3, cited by Hicks (*CR* i. p. 6), where **πολίτευμα** is "employed of an association of Phrygians, whom we must suppose to have resided in some Egyptian town or district in the enjoyment of their own laws, religion, and administration of justice." The inscr., *CIG* III. 5866 c, runs as follows –

> Γάϊος Ἰούλιος Ἡφαιστίωνος
> υἱὸς Ἡφαιστίων ἱερατεύσας
> τοῦ πολιτεύματος τῶν Φρυ-
> γῶν ἀνέθηκε Δία Φρύγιον, κτλ.

For a papyrus ex. of the word see P Tebt I. 32[9] (B.C. 145?), where reference is made to a letter written by Sosus and Aegyptus **τῶν . . . [προ]χειρισθέντων ὑπὸ τ[ο]ῦ πολιτεύ- ματ[ος τῶν Κρητῶν**, cf. [17]. See also *Archiv* iii. p. 129, v. p. 107.

The way was thus prepared for Paul's metaphorical application of the term in Phil 3[20] (RV "citizenship," RV marg. "commonwealth"). Holding that **πολίτευμα** sometimes denotes a settlement whose organization is modelled on that of the mother-city, many modern commentators would translate "we are a colony of heaven." But we should like clearer evidence that **πολίτευμα** can be used in this distinctive sense, and, further, such a translation reverses the relation presupposed between the colony and the mother-city.

πολιτεύομαι.

For this verb in its more official sense of "I live the life of a citizen," "I live the life of a member of a citizen body," cf. *Syll* 287 (= [3] 618)[12] (B.C. 188) **πολιτεύεσθαι κατὰ τοὺς ὑμετέρους νόμους**, *ib.* 325 (= [3]708)[25] (before B.C. 100) **τοῦτο βουλόμενος ἐμφαίνειν, ὅτι τοῖς εὐσεβέστατα καὶ κάλλιστα πολειτευομένοις καὶ παρὰ θεῶν τις χάρις καὶ παρὰ τῶν εὐεργετηθέντων ἐπακολούθει**—both Ac 23[1] and Phil 1[27] get some light from the parallel. See also *C. and B.* ii. p. 468, No. 305 (i/A.D.) **ο[ἱ] Γ]έροντες ἐτίμησαν Λούκιον Ἀτίλιον . . . ἔν τε ταῖς λοιπαῖς τῆς πόλεως καὶ τῆς γερουσίας χρείαις ἀγνῶς καὶ δικαίως ἐκ προγόνων πολιτευόμενον**. For **προπολιτεύομαι** see P Lond 233[4] (A.D. 345) (= II. p. 273, *Chrest.* I. p. 68).

Similarly we may cite from the papyri P Par 63[78] (B.C. 164) (= P Petr III. p. 24) **τοῖς καιροῖς πρεπόντως καὶ τοῖς ἀνθρώποις ἁρμόζοντως φαίνεσθαι πεπολιτευομένους**, "appearing to have administered your office in a manner befitting the circumstances and suitable to the population" (Mahaffy), P Amh II. 82[8] (iii/iv A.D.) where a man is described as unfitted for an official post— **ἀνεπιτήδειον ὄντα . . . οὐδὲ πολιτευσάμενόν ποτε**, P Oxy VI. 902[1] (c. A.D. 465) **τ]ῆ]ς μακαρίας μνήμης Φοιβ[ά]μμωνος τοῦ πολιτευσαμένου**, "Phoebammon, of blessed memory, member of the council" (Edd.), and P Iand 40[10] (v/vi A.D.) **Φιλόξενος πολιτευόμ(ενος)**, with the editor's note : "ur-

bium decuriones et curiales in papyris . . . **πολιτευόμενοι** vocantur."

Dibelius (*HZNT ad* Phil 1[27]) notes the more general sense which **πολιτεύομαι** sometimes has, almost = **περιπατέω**, and cites by way of illustration Clem. R. 6 **τούτοις τοῖς ἀνδράσιν ὁσίως πολιτευσαμένοις συνηθροίσθη πολὺ πλῆθος ἐκλεκτῶν**, and Proclus *typi epistolares* (Hercher *Epistologr. Graeci* p. 13) **οἶδα μὲν ὡς εὐσεβῶς ζῆς καὶ σεμνῶς πολιτεύῃ**.

πολίτης.

It is hardly necessary to illustrate this common word, but reference may be made to P Oxy I. 65[4] (iii/iv A.D.), where a *beneficiarius* sends an order to the comarchs of the village Teruthis—**παράδοτε τῷ ἀποσταλέντι ὑπηρέτ[ῃ] Παχούμιν Παχούμις(=ιος) ὃν κατεσχήκατε σήμερον καὶ κατηνέγκατε ἐν τῇ κώμῃ ὑμῶν πολίτην ὄντα**, "deliver up to my officer whom I have sent Pachoumis, son of Pachoumis, whom you have arrested to-day and brought to your village, being a citizen" (Edd.). See also the sepulchral epitaph, *Kaibel* 718[2], in which an inhabitant of Ephesus describes himself as **μεγά[λης θεοῦ εἰμι πολ]είτης**.

For the adj. **πολιτικός** cf. P Tebt I. 5[87] (B.C. 118) **τοὺς πρὸς χρείαις πάντας τῶν τε βασιλικῶν καὶ πολιτικῶν καὶ ἱερευτικῶν**, "all who are in charge of the Crown, State or sacred interests": see the editors' note. In support of their contention that **πολιτική** in P Grenf II. 73[9] (late iii/A.D.) denotes a woman of bad character (**πόρνη**), the editors are now able to appeal to P Oxy VI. 903[37] (iv/A.D.) **μετὰ μῆναν λαμβάνω πολιτικὴν ἐμαυτῷ**, "a month hence I will take a mistress." Deissmann (*Epistle of Psenosiris*, p. 30 f., *LAE*, p. 201) prefers to regard the word as a proper name **Πολιτική**: cf. *Selections*, p. 117 ff. See also *Archiv* viii. p. 60, where the name is associated with the social rank of the woman as a "citizeness."

πολλάκις,

"often": P Oxy III. 531[4] (ii/A.D.) **περὶ οὗ μοι παλλά- κεις (*l.* πολλάκις) γράφεις ἀνθρώπου**, "regarding the man about whom you write to me so often" (Edd.), P Ryl II. 75[9] (late ii/A.D.) **ἔκρεινα πολλάκις**, and P Flor III. 307[6] (iii/A.D.) **πολλάκις μου ἐπιστείλαντός σοι**. In P Lond 1914[38] (A.D. 335?) **πολλαχῶς**, "in many ways," seems to be used for **πολλάκις**.

πολλαπλασίων.

With this expressive compound = "having many folds," "many times over" in Mt 19[29], Lk 18[30], we may compare the form **πολλαπολλῶν** in P Oxy IV. 744[9] (B.C. 1) (= Witkowski[2], p. 132), where a husband writes to his wife—**ἐὰν πολλαπολλῶν τέκῃς**. The meaning of **πολλαπολλῶν** is far from clear, but Witkowski renders *quod bene vertat*, equivalent to our "by great good luck."

πολυλογία.

This NT ἅπ. εἰρ. (Mt 6[7]), "much speaking," is found in Vett. Val. p. 108[8] **τὰς πολυλογίας παραιτησάμενος**, and *ib.*[28] **πολυλογίαις καὶ ποικίλαις μεθόδοις χρησάμενοι**. See also *s.v.* **ματαιολογία**, and for the verb cf. *ib.* p. 175[31] **μή τις ἡμᾶς δόξῃ πολυλογεῖν ἢ διαπλέκειν τὴν αἵρεσιν**.

πολυμερῶς

(= πολυσχέδως, Hesych.) denotes "in many portions" as distinguished from πολυτρόπως, "in many manners" (Heb 1¹). For the adj., as in Sap 7²², cf. P Leid Wᵛⁱⁱ·⁴¹ (ii/iii A.D.) (= II. p. 105) where the god Fire is described as ἀόρατον καὶ πολυμερῆ. Both adj. and adv. are common in Vett. Val., e.g. p. 257¹⁹ ἐπεὶ οὖν τὸ συνεκτικώτατον κεφάλαιόν ἐστι τὸ περὶ χρόνων ζωῆς, πολυμερῶς [τε] οὕτως ἐν τοῖς ἔμπροσθεν συντέτακται.

πολυποίκιλος.

For the figurative use of πολυποίκιλος, as in Eph 3¹⁰, Armitage Robinson ad l. compares the Orphic hymns vi. 11 (τελετή), lxi. 4 (λόγος).

πολύς.

"much," plur. "many": P Petr I. 29² (iii/B.C.) χάρις τοῖς θεοῖς πολλή εἰ ὑγιαίνεις, "much thanks to the gods if you are well," P Ryl II. 243⁵ (ii/A.D.) τοῦτο οὐ μόνον ἡμεῖν γενάμενον ἀλλὰ καὶ πολλοῖς, "this has happened not to us only but to many" (Edd.), and ib. 238⁶ (A.D. 262) διὰ πολλὰς χρείας, "for various needs" (Edd.). The word is very common in epistolary greetings (πολλὰ χαίρειν: exx. from B.C. 118 to iii/iv A.D. in Exler Epistolography p. 27 f.) and in rhetorical prefaces (Sirach proem.), and consequently, as Cadbury suggests (in Jackson and Lake Beginnings of Christianity Part I. Vol. ii. p. 492 f.), πολλοί must not be pressed to mean "very many" in such passages as Lk 1¹, Ac 24³· ¹⁰.

For the adverbial πολλά, which "lies between πολύ and πολλάκις: it is 'much' with the idea of plurality and repetition introduced" (Hort ad Jas 3²), cf. P Heid 6²² (iv/A.D.) (= Selections, p. 127) πολλὰ προσαγορεύ(ω) πάντε = α)ς τοὺς ἀδελφοὺς ἡμῶν ἐν κ(υρί)ῳ, and the curious P Lond 1916²⁷ (c. A.D. 330–340) ἐπιδὴ τὰ πολλὰ πλεῖστα ἀργύρια χρεωστῖ, "since he owes much, very much money" (Bell). Deissmann (LAE, p. 317) supplies an interesting parallel to Rom 16⁶ from a Roman woman's praise of her husband in a sepulchral inscr. CIG IV. 9552⁵ τείς(= ὅστις) μοι πολλὰ ἐκοπίασεν, "who laboured much for me." And in P Leid C recto¹· ¹¹ (B.C. 161) (= UPZ i p. 353) ταῦτα πάντα τὰ πολλὰ ἐννήα εἰσί, Wilcken understands τὰ πολλά adverbially—"dies alles ist meistens neu."

Πολλοῦ, as gen. of price (Mt 26⁹) meets us in P Ryl II. 244¹⁰ (iii/A.D.) τὰ δὲ σωμάτια πολλοῦ ἐστιν ἐνθά[δ]ε, "slaves are very dear here." A good ex. of πολλῷ μᾶλλον (Lk 18³⁹) is afforded by P Par 26⁴⁷ (B.C. 162) (= UPZ i. p. 248, Selections p. 18) where the Serapeum Twins petition ἵνα, πᾶν τὸ ἑξῆς ἐχουσα, πολλῶι μᾶλλον τὰ νομιζόμενα τῶι Σαράπει καὶ τῆι Ἴσει ἐπιτελῶμεν, "that, when we have everything in order, we may be much better able to perform the usual ritual to Serapis and to Isis."

Ὥρας πολλῆς γενομένης in Mk 6³⁵ can be paralleled from Dion. Hal. ii. 54 ἐμάχοντο ἄχρι πολλῆς ὥρας, "to a late hour" (see Swete ad Mk l.c.). And the pendent nom. of time in Mk 8² meets us in P Oxy XIV. 1764⁴ (iii/A.D.) ἐπεὶ πολ[λ'αὶ ἡμέραι προσκαρτεροῦμεν Φιλέᾳ, where there is no need to correct with the editors into πολ[λ]ὰς ἡμέρας. The instrumental dat. πολλοῖς χρόνοις to denote duration of time is common, e.g. P Oxy I. 112⁸ (iii/iv A.D.) ἐρρῶσθ[αί

σε] εὔχομαι [πο]λλοῖς [χρόνοις, "I pray for your continued health" (Edd.).

In the account of a legal process at Alexandria in the 2nd half of iv/A.D., published in Archiv i. p. 298 ff., we find ¹¹·³ ὃς . . οὐ μετ' οὐ πολὺ ἥξει, "qui pourra se présenter dans peu de temps" (Ed.): cf. BGU II. 614¹² (A.D. 216) μετ' οὐ πολύ, "not long after." For ἐκ πολλοῦ χρόνου see P Strass I. 42¹⁶ (A.D. 310), and for ἐπὶ πολύ, see PSI IV. 299¹ (iii/A.D.), where Ghedini (Lettere p. 87) translates "a tal punto."

The LXX πολλοστός in the sense of "great," "powerful" (2 Kingd 23²⁰, Prov 5¹⁹), is discussed by Thackeray Gr. i. p. 185.

See also s.vv. πλείων, πλεῖστος.

πολύσπλαγχνος,

"very pitiful." This word, confined in the NT to Jas 5¹¹, is said to be found elsewhere only in Hermas Mand. iv. 3. 5. Sim. v. 7. 4. It is the equivalent of the LXX πολυέλεος (Ps 102⁸). See s.v. σπλάγχνον.

πολυτελής.

For the literal meaning "precious," "costly," as in Mk 14³, cf. PSI VI. 616² (iii/B.C.) τῶν πολυτελῆ(= ῶν) στρωμάτων, OGIS 90²⁵ᶠ (Rosetta stone—B.C. 196) τὸ Ἀπιεῖον ἔργοις πολυτελέσιν κατεσκεύασεν . . . λίθων πολυτελῶν πλῆθος οὐκ ὀλίγον ib. 132⁷ (B.C. 130) ἐπὶ τὴν συνα[γω]γὴν τῆς πολυτ[ε]λοῦς λιθείας, and Syll³ 783⁴¹ (after B.C. 27) μετὰ πάσης δαπάνης πολυτελοῦς.

For the comp. cf. PSI IV. 418¹⁹ (iii/B.C.) εἴ σοι ἡμῶν πολυτελέστερον τὸ τριβώνιον φαίνεται εἶναι, ὀθόνιόν τι ἡμῖν σύνταξον δοῦναι, "if our old cloak seems to you rather precious, give orders that a piece of linen cloth be given to us." The subst. πολυτέλεια occurs in OGIS 383⁶⁹ (mid. i/B.C.) εἰς θυσιῶν πολυτέλειαν.

πολύτιμος.

P Oxy VIII. 1121¹⁰ (A.D. 295) αἰσθῆτι πολυτειμοτάτῃ, "some very costly clothes." The meaning "much revered" may be illustrated from the ii/iii A.D. hymn Kaibel 1027³⁰—

Ἴδη χαῖρέ μοι, ὦ ἰώμενος, ὦ πολύ[τει]με,
π[α]ῖ[ζε, Τελ]εσφόρε.

Cf. Menander Frag. p. 33 πολύτιμοι θεοί, and similarly the verbal in BGU IV. 1208¹⁹ (B.C. 27–6) παρὰ τοῦ πολυτιμήτου Ποπλιος, and Menandrea p. 97⁵⁴ ὦ πολυτίμητοι θεοί.

πολυτρόπως.

See s.v. πολυμερῶς. For the adj. πολύτροπος cf. P Flor I. 33¹⁵ (iv/A.D.). In MGr πολύτροπος has a good sense, "adroit."

πόμα.

This late form of the Attic πῶμα, "drink," is seen in Kaibel 244⁹·⁴—

Φερσεφόνας δ' ἄδίαυλον ὑπὸ στυγερὸν δόμον ἦλθον
παυσιπόνῳ λάθας λουσαμένα πόματι.

Cf. Lob. Phryn. p. 456, and Thackeray Gr. i. p. 79.

πονηρία

is used in connexion with disease in P Tebt II. 272[8] (medical—late ii/A.D.) οὐ διὰ . . πονηρίαν καὶ συν[άρ]τησιν τῶν νόσων, "not because of the malignity or complication of the diseases" (Edd.): cf. OGIS 519[10] (c. A.D. 245) πάντων . . . ἤρεμον καὶ γαληνὸν τὸν βίον δια[γόντων, πο]νηρίας καὶ διασεισμῶν πε[π]αυμένων. In the vi/A.D. amulet, BGU III. 954[24] (= Selections, p. 134) the phrase in the Lord's Prayer is cited as—ῥῦσαι ἡμᾶς ἀπὸ τῆς πο[ν]ηρίας, which some may be tempted to quote in support of the AV of Mt 6[13].

The compound μειζοπονηρία (= μισοπονηρία) occurs in P Ryl II. 113[33] (A.D. 133) τοῦ οὖν πράγματος δεομένου τῆς σῆς μειζοπονηρίας, "since therefore the case requires the exercise of your hatred of wrongdoers" (Edd.).

πονηρός.

This adj. denoting the active exercise of evil is seen in BGU II. 372[ii. 1] (A.D. 154) πονηρ[ὸν κ]α[ὶ] λῃσ[τ]ρικὸν β[ίον, PSI V. 452[11] (iv/A.D.) πονηρὰ βουλευσαμέν[ου]s, and Syll 809 (= [3] 1175)[19] (iv/iii B.C.) ῥῆμα μοχθηρὸν ἢ πονηρὸν φθέγγεσθαι. With the Lat. sepulchral formula ab hoc monumento dolus malus abesto, cf. BGU I. 326[ii. 3] (A.D. 194) ταύτῃ τῇ διαθήκῃ δόλος πονηρὸς ἀπέστη(= ω). In the deed of divorce P Grenf II. 76[3] (A.D. 305-306) a couple are stated to have renounced their married life ἐκ τινὸς πονηροῦ δαίμονος, "owing to some evil deity," and similarly P Lips I. 34[3] (c. A.D. 375). The word is joined with ἀσεβεῖς in Jos. Antt. xii. 252, xiii. 34.

For the original meaning of πονηρός, "toilworn," "laborious" we may cite the description of Heracles, the type of the strenuous life—πονηρότατος καὶ ἄριστος (Hes. Fr. 43. 5).

πόνος,

"labour," "toil": P Grenf I. 1[18] (ii/B.C.) μέγαν ἔχει πόνον, "it is a toilsome matter." For the derived meaning "pain," "suffering," as in Rev 16[10f.], 21[4], cf. the medical prescriptions P Oxy II. 234[ii. 24, 27] (ii/iii A.D.) ἔνθετα εἰς τ[ὸ] οὖς πρὸς πόνους, "stoppings for the ear against earache," κλυσμοὶ ὠτὸς [πρὸς] πόνους, "clysters for the ear against earache": see also Syll 325 (= [3] 708)[11] (c. B.C. 107) σωματικῶν πόνων. An interesting inscr. from Adana (Syria, revue d'art oriental et d'archéologie ii. (1921), p. 217) runs—

οὐκέτι οὐδ[ὲν

βίος   τέλος

πόνος

"no more life, end, pain."

Vett. Val. p. 131[3] μετὰ πόνου καὶ μερίμνης καὶ βίας.

For the corresponding verb in its original meaning "labour," cf. P Fay 106[14] (c. A.D. 140) τ[ετρ]αε]τεῖ ἤδη χρόνωι ἐν τῇ χρ[είαι πονούμενος ἐξησθένησα, "after labouring for a period of four years at the post, I became very weak" (Edd.), and the Delphic precept Syll[3] 1268[ii. 7] πόνει μετ' εὐκλείας. The derived sense appears in BGU II. 380[3] (iii/A.D.) (= Selections, p. 104) εἰπέ μοι ὅτι τὸν πόδα πονεῖς ἀπὸ σκολάπου, "he told me that you had a sore foot from a splinter."

Cf. also Kaibel 1117[4 ff.]—

'Ὦ παῖ, φυλάσσου μὴ σφαλῇς· ἡ γλῶσσά τοι
αὐτὴ μὲν οὐδέν, ἡνίκ' ἂν λέγῃ, πονεῖ,
ὅταν δ' ἁμάρτῃ, πολλὰ προσβάλλει κακά.

For the Ionic forms πονέσω, ἐπόνεσα, πεπόνεκα, which are common in the LXX, see Thumb Archiv iv. p. 490.

Πόπλιος.

Ramsay (Paul, p. 343) points out that Πόπλιος (Ac 28[7 f.]) is the Greek form of the praenomen Publius, and that though it is not usual that an official should be called by his praenomen simply, "Publius" may have been so well known among the peasantry that Luke adopted their familiar mode of addressing him.

πορεία.

Unlike ὁδός, πορεία, "a journey," is rarely used in a metaphorical sense, but cf. Ps 67[25]. With reference to Jas 1[11] Hort, following Herder, makes the happy suggestion that the force lies in the idea of the rich man's perishing "while he is still on the move, before he has attained the state of restful enjoyment which is always expected and never arrives." In Syll[3] 1267[19] (iii/A.D.) Isis announces—ἐγὼ ἡλίου καὶ σελήνης πορείαν συνέταξα.

In P Grenf I. 43[8] (ii/B.C.) (= Witkowski[2], p. 109) πορεία denotes "passport" for a journey, and it is = "caravan" in P Lond 328[11] (A.D. 163) (= II. p. 75), where mention is made of camels provided—εἰς κυριακὰς χρείας τῶν ἀπὸ Βερνείκης γεινο(μένων) πορ(ε)ιῶν, "for Imperial service on the caravans that travel from Berenice" (Ed.).

For a wider use of the word cf. P Amh II. 97[11] (A.D. 180-192) καθὼς διὰ τῆς τοῦ ὁρισμοῦ πορείας δηλοῦ[τ]αι, "as is set forth in the survey" (Edd.). Πορεῖον is used collectively in P Cairo Zen 22[3] (B.C. 256): see Mayser Gr. II. i. p. 36.

πορεύομαι.

The act. of this verb is obsolete in late Greek. (1) For πορεύομαι = "journey," "go," cf. P Par 44[2] (B.C. 152) (= UPZ i. p. 327) γίνωσκέ με πεπορεῦσθαι (cf. Proleg. p. 229) εἰς Ἡρακλέους πόλιν ὑπὲρ τῆς οἰκίας, P Oxy VIII. 1143[2] (c. A.D. 1) τοῖς ἐκ τοῦ ἱεροῦ παστοφό(ροις) πορευομέ(νοις), ib. XII. 1480[7] (A.D. 32) ἐπορεύθην πρὸς Ἑρμογένην, P Ryl II. 234[3] (ii/A.D.) πορεύον, ἀντιφωνήσεται διὰ τῶν στρατηγῶν, "go, the answer will be given through the strategi" (Edd.), and P Oxy IX. 1219[4] (iii/A.D.) πορευόμενος εἰς τὴν Νεικίου, "on his way to the city of Nicias."

(2) With πορεύομαι of Christ's journeying to death in Lk 22[22] (and perhaps 13[33]), we may compare the usage in Ps 77[39]. See further Field Notes, p. 66, and for the relation of the verb to ὑπάγω, cf. Abbott Joh. Voc. p. 142 ff.

(3) An approximate ex. of the ethical use of πορεύομαι in 1 Pet 4[3] πεπορευμένους ἐν ἀσελγείαις is furnished by Sophocles O.T. 883: εἰ δέ τις ὑπέροπτα χερσὶν ἢ λόγῳ πορεύεται (cited by Kennedy Sources, p. 107).

A wider secondary use appears in P Tor I. 1[vi. 13] (B.C. 116) εἴπερ γε δὴ ἐνόμιζεν ἐκ τῆς ἀληθείας κατὰ νόμους ὁδῶι πορευόμενος τὸν ἐξ εὐθυδικίας λόγον συνίστασθαι, "si revera legitimae viae insistens recto ordine causam instituere voluisset" (Ed.). Cf. the compd. ἐπιπορεύομαι = "act" in *ib.* vii. 13, and in P Reinach 11¹⁹ (B.C. 111) ἐάν τε ἐπέλθῃ, ἥ τ' ἔφοδος Ὥρωι καὶ ⟨τῶι⟩ ὑπὲρ αὐτοῦ ἐπιπεπορευομένου ἄχυρος (*l.* ἐπιπορευομένωι ἄκυρος) ἔστωι, "s'il exerce une poursuite pareille, elle sera nulle pour Hôros et pour celui qui aura agi en son nom" (Ed.). See also *s.vv.* **παρα-πορεύομαι** and **προσπορεύομαι**.

πορθέω.

With a personal object this word = "destroy," "ravage," is classical only in poetry. The NT usage (Ac 9²¹, Gal 1¹³,²³, cf. 4 Macc 4²³, 11⁴) is paralleled in BGU II 588³ (i/A.D.) πορθοῦντες ὑμᾶς: cf. OGIS 201¹⁷ (vi/A.D.) ἐπόρθησα τὰς χώρας αὐτῶν, and for the compd. ἐκπορθέω see P Tebt I. 37¹⁴ (B.C. 73) ἐντέταλταί μοι παραλαβὼν στρατιώτας ἐκπορθῆσαι αὐτούς, "he has ordered me to take soldiers and ravage them."

πορισμός,

"means of gain," occurs in the NT only in 1 Tim 6⁵ᶠ (cf. Sap 13¹⁸, 14²): cf. for the thought Seneca *Ep.* 108 *qui philosophiam velut aliquod artificium venale didicerunt.* See also Artem. p 254²⁰ τὸ ἔργον λυσιτελὲς μὲν εἰς πορισμόν. Πόρος is found in the same sense in BGU II. 530¹⁴ (i/A.D.) κινδυνεύω ἐκστῆναι οὗ ἔχω πόρου, and *ib.* IV. 1189¹¹ (i/B.C. or i/A.D.) ἐπ[εὶ] οὖν οἱ σημαινόμενοι ἄνδρες πόρ[ο]ν ἔχουσι[ν] οἰ[κία]ς καὶ κλήρους κτλ. For πορίζομαι, "provide for myself," cf. P Par 63¹⁰² (B.C. 164) (= P Petrie III. p. 26) πορίζονται τὰ πρὸς τὸ ζῆν, "supply themselves with the means of life" (Mahaffy), P Oxy IX. 1203⁹ (late i/A.D.) ἐπορίσατο ἐκ τοῦ καταλογείου ὑπόμνημα, "provided himself with a memorandum from the bureau." The act. is seen in P Grenf II 14 (*a*)¹¹ (B.C. 270 or 233) πόρισόν μοι εἰς τὴν τροφήν, and P Lond 846¹¹ (A.D. 140) (= III. p. 131, *Chrest.* I. p. 582) μισθοῦ πορίζοντος τὸ ζῆν ἀπὸ τῆς γερδια[κ]ῆς. See also Field *Notes*, p. 211 f., and *Archiv* v. p. 30 f.

πορνεία.

Πορνεία (for form see WH *Notes*², p. 160), which is rare in classical Greek (LS⁸ refer only to Demosthenes) originally meant "prostitution," "fornication," but came to be applied to unlawful sexual intercourse generally. It was a wider term than μοιχεία, embracing the idea of "barter," "traffic" in sexual vice, though in the OT there was a tendency to assimilate in some respects the two terms: see R. H. Charles as cited *s.v.* μοιχεύω, and for an ex. of the word from the papyri P Tebt II. 276¹⁶ as cited *s.v.* μοιχεία.

πορνεύω,

"commit fornication," is found in the act. of the woman in Artem. p. 177²⁶ γυνὴ δὲ τὰς ἑαυτῆς σάρκας ἐσθίουσα πορνεύσει. For the subst. πόρνευμα cf. P Grenf I. 53²⁰ (iv/A.D.) εἰ δὲ θέλεις τὰ πορνεύματα τῶν θυγατέρων σου στέργειν ("acquiesce in"), μὴ ἐμὲ ἐξέταζε ἀλλὰ τ[ο]ὺ[ς] πρεσβυτέρους τῆς ἐκκλησίας.

πόρνη,

"prostitute." In PSI IV. 352⁴ (B.C. 254-3) Artemidorus writes to Zeno—ἐν οἴνωι γάρ εἰσιν καὶ ἐμ πόρναις διὰ

παντός, and in BGU IV. 1024⁸·⁴ᶠ (end iv/A.D.) a certain Diodemus is described as ἐρασθέντα πόρνης δημοσίας . . . συνεχῶς δὲ ἦσθ⟨έν⟩ει (see *Archiv* iii. p. 303) ὁ Διόδημος πρὸς τῆς πόρνη[ς] κατὰ τὰς [ἑ]σπερίνας ὥρας ὁ οὖν Διόδημος ἐφόνευσεν τὴν πόρνην—and in consequence was taken to prison. In P Oxy III. 528¹⁸ (ii/A.D.) a man quotes his sister (and wife) as saying, ὁ Κόλυβος δὲ πόρνην με πεπύ (= οἴ)ηκεν, "Colubus has made me a prostitute."

πόρνος,

literally a "male prostitute," but generally understood in the NT in the sense of a "fornicator." Deissmann (*LAE* p. 319 ff.) compares the list of the vicious, including πόρνοι, in 1 Cor 6⁹ᶠ, 1 Tim 1⁹ᶠ, with the corresponding designations inscribed on the counters of a popular game, which are also found in the "scolding" of Ballio the pander in Plautus *Pseudolus* 360 ff.

πόρρω,

"far off." This later Attic form is used in the LXX and NT for the older πρόσω (πόρσω): cf. also Aristeas 31. For πορρωτέρω see Thumb *Hellen.* p. 77.

πόρρωθεν.

In Lk 17¹² πόρρωθεν is used in the sense of μακράν, "at a distance," "afar off": cf. the more regular "from afar" in Heb 11¹³. For the form see Dieterich *Unter-suchungen*, p. 183 f.

πορφύρα.

For this common word = "purple dye" it is sufficient to cite P Oxy IV. 739¹⁷ (private account—*c.* A.D. 1) πορφύρας (δραχμαὶ) κ, "purple, 20 dr.," *ib.* VI. 931⁴ (ii/A.D.) τὴν οὐγκίαν τῆς πορφύρα[ς] ἔπεμψα, "I have sent the ounce of purple," and P Giss I. 47¹³ (time of Hadrian) τὸ ἡμιλεί[τρ]ιον τῆς πορφύρας ἀντὶ (δραχμῶν) ξ [(δραχμῶν)] σνβ, "the half pound of purple for 252 instead of 264 drachmae": see the editor's note. Πορφύρα is used of a "purple robe" in Aristeas 320, as in Mk 15¹⁷ *al.*, where however Souter (*Lex. s.v.*) understands "a red-coloured cloak," such as common soldiers wore.

πορφύρεος,

"dyed purple"; P Ryl II. 151¹⁴ (A.D. 40) χιτῶνα πορφυροῦν, P Oxy III. 531¹⁴ (ii/A.D.) τὰ ἱμάτια τὰ λευκὰ τὰ δυ[ν]άμενα μετὰ τῶν πορφυρῶν φορεῖσθαι φαινολίων, "the white robes which are to be worn with the purple cloaks" (Edd.). For the form πόρφυρος, hitherto regarded as poetic (LS⁸), cf. P Ryl II. 242⁹ (iii/A.D.) εἰς τὸ φόρφυρεν (*l.* πόρφυρον) [.] . . . ἱμάτιν μου αὐτὸ πωλῶ, "I am selling it for my purple cloak" (Edd.); for πορφύριον used as a subst. cf. P Oxy III. 520¹⁸ (A.D. 143) πορφυρίο υ στατή-(ρων) δ, "four staters of purple," P Lond 899³ (ii/iii A.D.) (= III. p. 208) τὸ πορφύριόν σοι ἔπεμψα: and for πορφύριν as a vulgar form (see Mayser *Gr.* p. 260) of πορφύριον cf. P Iand 9¹⁰ (ii/A.D.) σοῦ τὸ πορφύρ[ιν ἐπὶ σε ἀ]νέ-[πεμψα. For the adj. πορφυρικός see P Tebt I. 8³¹ (*c.* B.C. 201).

πορφυρόπωλις,

"a seller of purple fabrics" (Ac 16[14]) : cf. *Cos* p. 203, No. 309 —

Μάρκου Σπεδίου Νάσωνος πορφυροπώλου. Ἐλπίδος Σπεδίας πορφυροπώ[λιδος.

ποσάκις.

P Oxy III. 528[21] (ii/A.D.) ἰδοῦ ποσά{ρ}κεις (*l.* ἰδοῦ ποσάκις) ἔπεμσα ἐπὶ σέ, "see how many times I have sent to you !" (Edd.).

πόσις.

In the Tebtunis ostracon 3[1] (ii/A.D.) (= P Tebt II. p. 336) reference is made to πόσις ξύτου, "the drinking of beer" in connexion with a festival at the temple of Bubastus. In Jn 6[55], and probably in Rom 14[17], Col 2[16], the word is concrete = πόμα, "drink."

πόσος.

"how great ?" plur. "how many?": cf. P Oxy IV. 742[1] (B.C. 2) ἀπόστειλόν μ[ο]ι πόσας δέσμας παρείληφες, "send me word how many bundles you have received," P Fay 122[14] (*c.* A.D. 100) δήλωσόν μοι πόσαι ἐξέβησ[αν], "inform me how many (artabae) came out," P Tebt II. 417[18] (iii/A.D.) εἴδε πόσα μέτρα [ἔ]χι, "see how many measures there are," and the late P Amh II. 153[17] (vi-vii A.D.) γράψον μοι εὐθέως ὅτι π[ό]σα (*sc.* πρόβατα) ἀρρενικά ἐστιν καὶ πόσα θηλικά, "write me at once how many males there are, and how many females." For πόσου, "at what price," cf. PSI V. 508[5] (B.C. 250–5) πόσου ἕκαστόν ἐστιν, and P Oxy XII. 1491[8] (early iv/A.D.) ἀξιῶ σε μαθεῖν πόσου ἡμῖν συναλλάσσει κριθήν, "I beg you to find out at what price he is contracting to get barley for me." See also *Kaibel* 110[5] (ii/A.D.) ζω]ῆς δ' ἐς πόσον ἦλ[θες;

For the subst. ποσότης we may quote P Oxy X. 1293[9] (A.D. 117–38) περὶ τῆς ποσότητος τῶν ἐλαίω(ν), "about the amount of the oil" (Edd.), and P Ryl II. 240[6] (iii/A.D.) δήλωσόν μ[ο]ι τὴν ποσότητα ἵνα οὕτως [λημ]ματίσω, "inform me of the quantity that I may reckon it in" (Edd.).

ποταμός,

"the river," the Nile, is seen in P Petr II. 13.19/10 (B.C. 258–3) περὶ τὴ]ν ἀνα[χώ]ρησιν τοῦ ποταμοῦ, "at the falling of the river," OGIS 56[13] (B.C. 238) τοῦ τε ποταμοῦ ποτε ἐνλιπέστερον ἀναβάντος, "the river being somewhat backward in rising," while in *ib.* 672[8] (A.D. 80) we hear of the clearing of the Ἀγαθὸς Δαίμων ποταμός in length, breadth, and depth. Ποταμός is also applied in the inscrr. to an artificially constructed "canal," e.g. *ib.* 90[23] (Rosetta stone—B.C. 196) ὀχυρώσας τὰ στόματα τῶν ποταμῶν.

For the adj. ποτάμιος, see P Tebt II. 316[90] (A.D. 99) τ(έ)χνῃ (cf. Ac 18[3]) ἁλιεὺς ποτάμι(ο)ς, P Giss I. 40[ii. 18] (A.D. 215) (= *Chrest.* I. p. 38) ναῦται ποτά[μ]ιοι, for ποταμίτης, "a river-labourer," see P Oxy XIV. 1671[20] (iii/A.D.) with the references collected there, and for ἡ ποταμοφυλακίς (*sc.* ναῦς), "the river-watch-boat," see Wilcken *Ostr.* i. p. 282 ff.

ποταμοφόρητος.

Grimm's entry ("Besides only in Hesychius") would suggest that this compd. in Rev 12[15] = "carried away by a stream" was coined by John ; but it occurs as early as B.C. 110 in BGU VI. 1216[93, al] : cf. P Amh II. 85[16] (A.D. 78) ἐὰν δέ τι ἄβροχος γένηται ἢ καὶ ποταμοφόρητος ἢ ὕφαμμος, "if any part of the land becomes unwatered or is carried off by the river or covered by sand" (Edd.), also in P Tebt II. 610 (ii/A.D.), P Ryl II. 378[2] (ii/A.D.), and P Strass I. 5[10] (as read *Berichtigungen*, p. 404—A.D. 262) τῆς γῆς ταύτης [πο]ταμοφορήτου γενομέν[ης.

ποταπός.

This Hellenistic form of the classical ποδαπός, "of what country?" (cf. *Proleg.* p. 95), occurs in the Mime fragment, P Oxy III. 413[155] (Roman period) ποταπὰ περιπατεῖς ; "where are you walking from?" In the NT the word is never local, but = ποῖος; "of what sort?" "how great?": cf. the illiterate P Oxy XIV. 1678[16] (iii/A.D.) γράψον μν, ποταπὸν θέλεις ἐνήκω (*l.* ἐνέγκω), "write me what sort (of purple) you wish me to bring." The same usage occurs in Apoc. Petr. 2 ποταποί εἰσι τὴν μορφήν : see also Schmid *Atticismus* iii. p. 253, iv. p. 371.

πότε.

For πότε "at what time?" "when?" in indirect interrogative clauses, as in Mt 24[3] *al.*, see PSI V. 526[9] (iii/B.C.) διασαφήσας ἡμῖν πότε σοι ἔσται εὔκαιρον ἀποστεῖλαι, *ib.* VI. 650[9] (iii/B.C.) ἠρώτα με πότε διαγρά[ψω. Cf. *Syll* 385 (= [3] 832)[9] (A.D. 118) ἐκ πότε φέρειν αὐτὸ ἤρξασ[θε.

ποτέ,

an indefinite temporal particle = "at any time," "at some time," "once," "formerly": cf. PSI V. 484[2] (B.C. 258–7) ὡς ποτε αὐτῶι ἐδόκει, P Oxy IV. 745[7] (*c.* A.D. 1) οὐκ οἶδας γὰρ πῶς μοι ἐχρήσατο ἐν Ὀξυρύγχοις οὐχ ὡς λύσα⟨ν⟩τι ἀλλ' ὡς τινί ποτε ἀποστερηετῆι μὴ ἀποδεδωκότι, "you don't know how he treated me at Oxyrhynchus (?), not like a man who had paid but like a defrauder and a debtor" (Edd.), P Fay 110[26] (A.D. 94) Ἥρωνα τόν ποτε ἡγούμ(ενον), "Heron the former president," P Ryl II. 243[9] (ii/A.D.) ὅσα ποτε οὖν ἐὰν ἀνα{να}λώσῃς ἰς τὴν τοῦ κλήρου κατεργασίαν, ἡμεῖν ἐνλόγησον ἐπὶ λόγου. "put down to our account everything you expend on the cultivation of the holding" (Edd.), P Oxy VI. 928[6] (ii/iii A.D.) ὡμείλησάς δέ μοί ποτε περὶ τούτου, "you once had a conversation with me on this subject" (Edd.), P Par 574[1240] (iii/A.D.) (= *Selections*, p. 113) ἐξορκίζω σε. δαίμον, ὅστις ποτ' οὖν εἶ, and P Oxy XIV. 1680[13] (iii/iv A.D.) ὑπονοοῦμαι ὅτι πάντως πάλιν τί ποτε ἔχει πρὸς σέ, "I suspect that he must have some further claim against you" (Edd.).

In illustration of Rev 2[9] mention is sometimes made of CIG II. 3148 (time of Hadrian) οἱ ποτὲ Ἰουδαῖοι, "the quondam Jews," as if these were renegade Jews who had forsworn their faith, but Ramsay (*Letters*, p. 272), following Mommsen, is of opinion that they were "quondam" in the sense that they were "no longer recognised as a separate nation by the Roman law (as they had been before A.D. 70)."

For ἤδη ποτέ, *iam tandem*, as in Rom 1[10], cf. the ostracon letter published by Deissmann *LAE*, p. 186—[6] καὶ ἤδη ποτὲ δὸς τῇ ἐμῇ παιδίσκῃ τὰς τοῦ (πυροῦ) ᾶ ἕ, "and now at length give to my maid the 3¾ artabae of wheat." See further *s.v.* μήποτε.

πότερον.

For the adverbial use, as in Jn 7[17], cf. P Tebt II. 289[6] (A.D. 23) οὕτως γὰρ γνώσομαι πότερον ἐπὶ τόπων σε ἐάσω πράττοντά τι ἤ . . .., "for I shall thus know whether I shall leave you in employment where you are or . . ." (Edd.). The rare adjectival use (see *Proleg.* p. 77) is seen in P Lond 1912[74] (A.D. 41) in the address of the Emperor Claudius to the Alexandrines, τῆς δὲ πρὸς Ἰουδαίους ταραχῆς . . . πότεροι μὲν αἴτιοι κατέστησαν, "as to the question which of you were responsible for the riot against the Jews" (Bell).

ποτήριον.

P Tebt I. 6[27] (B.C. 140–139) φιάλας καὶ ποτήρια, "bowls and cups." P Ryl II. 127[31] (A.D. 29) ποτήρια κασσιδ(έρινα) β, "2 drinking-cups of tin," P Fay 127[12] (ii/iii A.D.) μικ⟨κ⟩ὸν ποτήριν Θεονᾶτι τῷ μικ⟨κ⟩ῷ (a Doric form: Thumb *Hellen.* p. 60), "a little cup for little Theonas," and from the inscr. *Syll* 226 (= ³495)[14] (*c.* B.C. 230) τὰ ἱερὰ ποτήρια. The word is fully illustrated in *SAM* iii. p. 142 ff. With Mt 23[25 ff.] we may compare ποτηροπλύτης, "washer of cups" in *Ostr* 1218[5] (Rom.).

ποτίζω.

For the meaning "irrigate," which is common in the LXX, cf. P Petr I. 29 *verso* (iii/B.C.) (=Witkowski[2], p. 31) ὀχιτεύομεν καὶ ποτίζομεν, "we are making conduits and irrigating," PSI V. 536[4] (iii/B.C.) τὴν γῆν τὴν καθαρὰν πᾶσαν . . . ποτίσας κατάσπειρον, BGU II. 530[23] (i/A.D.) (= *Selections*, p. 62) μόλις γὰρ μίαν πρασεὰν ποτίζι τὸ ὕδωρ, "for there is hardly a single plot which the water irrigates," P Fay 111[26] (A.D. 95–6) τῶν στίχον τὸν φυτὸν (*l.* τὸν στίχον τῶν φυτῶν) τῶν ἐν τῷ προφήτῃ πότισον, "water the row of trees 'at the prophet'" (Edd.), P Ryl II. 157[21] (A.D. 135) cited *s.v.* πούς, and P Oxy VI. 938[5] (iii/iv A.D.) τῆς γῆς . . . μὴ ποτιζομένης. For the subst. ποτισμός, as in Aq Prov 3[8], see *ib.* 934[14] (iii/A.D.) χάριν τῶν ποτισμῶν, "for the sake of the irrigation," *et saepe.* In MGr ποτίζω "make to drink," "water," is used with double acc.

Ποτίολοι,

"Puteoli": for the form of the name cf. Robertson *Gr.* p. 189, and see the citations in Wetstein *ad* Ac 28[13].

πότος

occurs in 1 Pet 4[3] = "a drinking bout": cf. the meaning "banquet" in Gen 19[3] *al.* and Aristeas 262. For the corresponding adj. used as a subst. in a more general sense, see PSI I. 64[21] (i/B.C.?), where a woman comes under a solemn promise not to administer philtres to her husband, nor to put anything hurtful μήτε ἐν ποτοῖς μήτε ἐν βρωτοῖς. Cf. also P Oxy XIV. 1673[12] (ii/A.D.) ἐκ δὲ τῶν ἐνκλισθέντων εὗρον ἐκ [τ]ῆς ᾱ λη(νοῦ) ποτή(ν) ᾱ, "of what was stored I found of the first vat 1 drinkable" (Edd.).

ποῦ,

originally a gen. of place (*Proleg.* p. 73), is seen = "where?" in P Fay 119[17] (*c.* A.D. 100) τ]ὴν διαγραφὴν τοῦ χόρτου ποῦ τέθικας; "where did you put the notice of payment for the hay?" (Edd.), and P Oxy XIV. 1671[22] (iii/A.D.) περὶ τῶν ποταμειτῶν . . . γράψον μοι ὅτι ποῦ εὑρίσκομεν, "as regards the river-workers write me where we may find them."

For ποῦ = ποῖ, as in Jn 7[35], 8[14], cf. Epict. i. 27. 9 ποῦ φύγω τὸν θάνατον; and the late Greek citations collected by Maidhof *Begriffsbestimmung* p. 298 ff., *e.g. Ausgewählte Martyrerakten* (ed. Knopf, 1901) 18. 7 ποῦ συνέρχεσθε ἢ εἰς ποῖον τόπον ἀθροίζεις τοὺς μαθητάς σου; In MGr besides "where?", ποῦ as the usual relative means "who," "which," and also "so that."

που.

For the enclitic που cf. PSI V. 485[5] (B.C. 258–7) ἐὰν οὖν που παραβάλῃι, *ib.* 484[6] (B.C. 258–7) ἴσως γάρ που καὶ ἡμεῖς πού σοι χρήσιμοι ἐσόμ[εθα] γράψαι φιλότιμον ἐπιστολὴν πρὸς Ζωίλον, ἵνα ἡμᾶς ἀφῇι, and P Oxy X. 1252 *verso*[1] (A.D. 288–95) καὶ πάλαι προ]σέταξα οἷς ἐὰν προσῇ που followed by a lacuna. With the usage in Heb 2[6], 4[4], cf. the fragment of a vi/A.D. petition, P Flor III. 296[17], where after a gap the words γά ?]ρ που διὰ τοῦ ἱεροψάλτου λέγων ὁ θ(εό)ς introduce a citation from Ps 40(41)[2 f.].

Πούδης,

"Pudens," a Roman Christian (2 Tim 4[21]). In BGU II. 455[4] (i/A.D.) we find the gen. Πούδεντος: cf. P Oxy XIV. 1626[2] (A.D. 325), and *JHS* xlvi. (1926), p. 46. For the untrustworthy legends which have grown up round the names of Pudens and Claudia, see *s.v.* Κλαυδία, and add Edmundson *The Church in Rome*, p. 244 ff.

πούς.

P Ryl II. 157[21] (A.D. 135) εἰ χρεία γείνοιτο [ποτίσαι ἐ]ν ἀναβάσει ἀπὸ ποδὸς τὴν αὐτὴν νοτίνην μερίδα, "if need arises at the inundation to water the same southern portion with the foot" (Edd.), a passage which recalls Deut 11[10]: similarly P Flor III. 309[7] (A.D. 130(149)) μέχρι τ[οῦ ἐ]σομένου ἀπὸ ποδὸς ποτισ[μ]οῦ. With Rev 3[9] cf. PSI IV. 298[20] (iv/A.D.) ἠπείχθη[ν π]ροσφυγεῖν τοῖς πο[σίν σου, δέσποτα, ἀξιῶν . . . In P Iand 18[3] (vi/vii A.D.) γράφω σοι κατὰ πόδα τούτων, the phrase = *brevissimo post* (Ed.), or "on the back of this," "immediately after this." Thackeray renders Aristeas 135 παρὰ πόδας ἔχοντες τὴν ἀναισθησίαν, "although their senselessness is obvious."

Commenting on Rev 1[9] (*ICC ad l.*) Charles points out that οἱ πόδες should be rendered "the legs," and supports this meaning by the secondary meaning of the Heb. רֶגֶל = "leg" (see *BDB Lex. s.v.*), and by the fact that in Palestinian Aramaic the word is used for the "thigh" of an animal. He adds "it is possible that this secondary meaning of πούς (when used as a rendering of the Hebrew) was not unexampled at the time." In these circumstances it is interesting to note that in the papyri there are instances of πούς, which imply "leg" rather than "foot," e.g. P Giss I. 43[14] (A.D. 118–119) οὐλ(ὴ) κνήμ(ῃι) ποδ(ὸς) ἀριστερῷ, "a wound on the calf of the left leg," P Flor I. 42[9] (A.D. 183) οὐλὴ μηρῷ [πο]δὸς δεξιοῦ, "a wound on the thigh (or leg-bone) of the right leg," and P Lips I. 12³ (iii/iv A.D.) οὐλὴ ἀντικνημίῳ δεξιοῦ ποδός.

πρᾶγμα.

(1) For the ordinary meaning, "an action," "a deed," cf. P Oxy VI. 938² (iii/iv A.D.) οὐκ ἀκόλουθον πρᾶγμα ἐποίησας ἐνεδρεύσας τὰς τροφὰς τῶν κτηνῶν, "it was an unfitting act of yours to intercept the fodder for the oxen" (Edd.), and ib. XII. 1477¹⁰ (question to an oracle—iii/iv A.D.) εἰ κερδαίνω ἀπὸ τοῦ πράγματ[ος; "am I to profit by the transaction?" (Edd.). The vaguer meaning "an affair," "a matter," is seen in P Ryl II. 153¹¹ (A.D. 138–161) ὑπηρετήσας πράγμασι ἡμῶν, "having been of service in our affairs," P Oxy IX. 1215³ (illiterate—ii/iii A.D.) καλῶς πυήσις ἐλθὼν πρὸς αἱμαὶ ἄχρι τὰ πράγματα κατασταλῆ, "please come to me until matters are arranged" (Ed.), and ib. XII. 1489⁷ (late iii/A.D.) οὐκ ἔχεις πρᾶγμα, "it is not your affair."

(2) The noun is common in the papyri = "lawsuit," as in 1 Cor 6¹, e.g. BGU I. 22⁹ (A.D. 114) ἁπλῶς μηδὲν ἔχουσα πρᾶγμα πρὸς ἐμέ, P Ryl II. 76¹⁴ (late ii/A.D.) λεγομένου τοῦ [π]ράγματος, "when the case is argued," ib. 113¹³ (A.D. 133) μὴ ἔχοντας πᾶν πρᾶγμα πρὸς ἐμέ, "not having any case against me," and P Strass I. 41³⁸ (an action regarding inheritance—A.D. 250) ὡς πρεσβύτης καὶ πίστεως ἄξιος εἰπὲ ἃ οἶδας ἐν τῷ πρά[γματ]ι, "as an old man and worthy of credit, say what you know in the matter."

(3) It is used in the weaker sense of "trouble," "difficulty" generally in P Oxy IV. 743¹⁹ (B.C. 2) εἰ καὶ π[ρ]ὸς ἄλλους εἶχον πρᾶγμα βοηθὸν αὐτοῦ γ[ε]νέσθαι διὰ ἢν ἔχομε[ν] πρὸς ἑατοὺς φιλίαν, "for although I (?) have had trouble with others you must assist him for the sake of our friendship" (Edd.), and ib. III. 525⁴ (early ii/A.D.) where, with reference to a troublesome voyage, the writer exclaims —λείαν τῷ πράγματι καταξύομαι, "I am extremely worn out with the matter" (Edd.): cf. P Magd 37 + 11⁶ (iii/B.C.) (= Archiv iv. p. 56) σχόντες πολλὰ πράγματα.

(4) An interesting ex. of πρᾶγμα = "business," "trade," is afforded by an inscr. on a sanctuary-temple in Theadelphia, Chrest. I. 70¹ (B.C. 57–6) ἄσυλον κατὰ πρόσταγμα, ᾧ μὴ πρᾶγμα, where the last clause must mean that within the boundaries of the temple all "business" ceases (see Wilcken's note ad l.). It is very doubtful, however, whether this meaning can be carried into ἐν τῷ πράγματι in 1 Thess 4⁶ (Vg in negotio, Luther im Handel): the reference would appear rather to be to "the matter on hand," viz. sins of the flesh (see Milligan ad l.).

For a possible instance of πρᾶγμα = "exaction," "recovery," like πρᾶξις, see P Lond V. 1732⁷ (A.D. 586?) with the editor's note. In MGr by a regular disappearance of γ before μ, the word becomes πρᾶμα, πρᾶμμα (Thumb Handb. p. 21).

πραγματεία.

See s.v. πραγματία.

πραγματεύομαι

is common with reference to government officials, e.g. P Petr III. 36 verso¹¹ (iii/B.C.) τ]οῖς ἄλ[λοις] τοῖς πραγματευομένοις, "to the others who are engaged in performing State

business," P Hib I. 66² (B.C. 228) παρὰ τῶν τὴν δωρεὰν πραγματευομένων, "with the managers of the δωρεά," P Grenf II. 37³ (ii/i B.C.) τοῖς τὰ βασιλικὰ πραγματευομένοις χαίρειν, P Tebt II. 350⁵ (A.D. 70–1) τοῖς τὸ ἐνκύκλιον πρᾶγμα(τευομένοις), "to the farmers of the tax on sales," and Syll 364 (= ³ 797)¹⁰ (A.D. 37) ἔδοξεν τῇ βουλῇ καὶ τοῖς πραγματευομένοις παρ' ἡμῖν Ῥωμαίοις. In ib. 492 (= ³ 382)⁵ (ii/B.C.) the verb is used of a poet, who πεπραγμ[ά]τευται περί τε τὸ ἱερὸν καὶ τὴ[ν] πόλιν τὴν Δηλίων καὶ τοὺς μύθου[ς] τοὺς ἐπιχωρίους γέγραφεν. In Gnomon 70 (= BGU V. 1 p. 28) it is laid down that those discharging public duties are not to buy or lend ἐν οἷς π[ρ]αγ[μ]ατεύο[ντ]αι τόποις, "in the places where they discharge their official functions."

In its only occurrence in the NT (Lk 19¹³) πραγματεύομαι means "trade," "do business" generally: cf. the ostracon Preisigke 2089 Ἡράκλειτος ὁ πραγματευόμενος τ[ὸ] συνηγορικὸν ("advocate's fee") καὶ ἐπι(δέκατον) . . ., and the subst. in P Oxy XVI. 1880⁵ (A.D. 427) Κῦρος . . πρ[α]γμ[α]τε[υ]τὴς ἀπὸ τῆς μεγα]λ[οπ]όλεως Ἀλεξ[α]νδρίας, "Cyrus trader of the metropolis Alexandria," where for the rendering "trader" the editors appeal to P Cairo Masp 67158¹⁷ ἐρ]γαστηριακῶν καὶ πραγματευτῶν, and P Lips I. 64³⁰ (c. A.D. 368) τοῦ πραγματευτικοῦ χρυσαργύρου, i.e. the trade-tax. For the verbal ἀπραγμάτευτος see P Par 33¹⁵ (B.C. 161) (= UPZ i. p. 240) Ἀπολλωνίου] . . . ἐν τῷ ἱερῷ ὄντο[ς ἀ]πραγματεύτου, where Wilcken understands the meaning to be that Apollonius was no longer occupied with the particular matter in hand. In P Lond 35²¹ (B.C. 161) (= I. p. 29) the editor prefers the meaning "inexperienced." For ἀπραγμοσύνη, see P Oxy I. 71ⁱⁱ·¹⁶ (A.D. 303) περι[φ]ρονοῦντές μου τῆς ἀπραγμ[οσύνης, and similarly P Amh II. 142¹⁴ (iv/A.D.).

πραγματία.

With 2 Tim 2⁴ ταῖς τοῦ βίου πραγματίαις, "the businesses which provide a livelihood," cf. the designation for officials in P Leid B^{ii. 19} (B.C. 164) (= I. p. 10, UPZ i. 20¹²) δεόμεθα οὖν ὑμῶν . . . μὴ ὑπεριδεῖν ἡμᾶς παρελκομένας ὑπὸ τῶν πρὸς τα[ῖ]ς πραγματείαις, and similarly P Tebt I. 5¹⁶¹ (B.C. 118). A wider meaning is found in PSI IV. 435¹⁶ (B.C. 258–7) ἀλλὰ περὶ πραγματείας ἧς καὶ ὡμολόγηκεις μοι, "only in the matter in which you had already given me assurance." See further s.v. πραγματεύομαι.

πραιτώριον

(a) Apart from Phil 1¹³ (see (b)) πραιτώριον is always used in the NT to denote the "palace" or "official residence" of a Governor: cf. Mk 15¹⁶, Ac 23³⁵. For this usage exx. can be freely supplied from our sources, e.g. BGU I. 288¹¹ (A.D. 138–161) κ[α]θημέγων ἐν συμβουλίῳ ἐν τῷ πραι τωρίῳ τοῦ κρατίστου ἡγ[εμόνος, P Oxy III. 471¹¹⁰ (ii/A.D.) where an official Maximus is charged with keeping a youth all day ἐν τῶι [πραι]τωρίωι, BGU I. 21ⁱ·¹⁶ (A.D. 340) ὑπατείας Σεπτιμίου Ἀκινδύνου τοῦ λαμπροτάτ[ου] ἐπάρχου τοῦ ἱεροῦ πραιτωρίου, similarly P Oxy IX. 1190¹⁶ (A.D. 347), ib. VIII. 1116² (A.D. 363), and from the inscr. Syll 932 (= ³ 880)⁶³ (A.D. 202) παραλα[νβ ά]ν[ι]ν τὰ πραιτώρια καὶ τὰ βαλανεῖα πανταχόθεν ὁλόκληρα. It may also be of interest to recall that an inscr. found in York and

printed in *IGSI* 2548 begins θεοῖς τοῖς τοῦ ἡγεμονικοῦ πραιτωρίου Σκριβ(ώνιος) Δη μ ήτριος.

(b) In Phil 1[13] the word has been frequently understood of
the "praetorian barracks or camp," but, as Lightfoot
Philippians pp. 97-102 has pointed out, clear instances of
this sense are wanting, and, further, such an interpretation
would be out of keeping with the words that follow (ἐν ὅλῳ
τῷ πραιτωρίῳ καὶ τοῖς λοιποῖς πᾶσιν). He prefers accordingly to give the word a personal application, and to think
of the imperial or praetorian guards, the *cohortes praetoriae*:
cf. Tac. *Hist.* iv. 46 militum et stipendia orant . . . igitur
in praetorium accepti, Suet. *Nero* 9 ascriptis veteranis e
praetorio, and from the inscr. *Mission Archéol. de Macédoine*
p. 325, No. 139 Τι. Κλαύδιον οὐετρανὸν στρατευσάμενον
ἐν πραιτωρίῳ, "a veteran, who served in the Guards": cf.
p. 326, No. 131.

With this Ramsay (*Teaching*, p. 363 f.) now agrees in
preference to his former view (*Paul*, p. 357), when following
Mommsen (*Berl. Sitzungsberichte*, 1895, p. 498 n.[1]: cf.
Hermes xxxv. (1900), p. 437 f.) he understood the reference
to be to "the whole body of persons connected with the
sitting in judgment," the law-officers of the Crown.

It should, however, be noted that, if the Epistle is to be
referred to an Ephesian rather than a Roman captivity of the
Apostle, as is now frequently the case, the view advocated
above would require modification.

πράκτωρ

is very common in the papyri = "a collector of revenue."
According to GH (*Fayûm Towns*, p. 100) the πράκτωρ in
Ptolemaic times was specially concerned with the exaction
of fines or payments (cf. Wilcken *Ostr.* i. p. 504), but during
the Roman period he was an ordinary collector of taxes.
Exx. are—P Petr II. 13(17)[2] (B.C. 258-253) παραγέγραμμαι
τῶι πράκτορι ὡς ὀ[φείλων] πρὸς τὰ ἀμπελικά . . . "I am
returned to the tax-agent (or public accountant) as owing
for the vine-tax . . . ," P Magd 41[5] (iii/B.C.) γράψας τῶι
ξενικῶι πράκτορι πρᾶξαι] καὶ ἀποδοῦναί μοι, P Fay 14[1]
(B.C. 124) οἱ προκεχιρισμένοι πράκτορες, "the appointed
collectors" of the crown-tax issue a notice—προσδιαγράψις
ἀργυρίου δραχμὰς τέσσαρας, "you are required to pay in
addition four drachmae," BGU II. 530[26] ff. (i/A.D.) (=
Selections, p. 62.) ἄλλως τε καὶ ἀπαιτῖται ὑπὸ τῶν
πρακτόρων ἱκανόν, "especially security is demanded by the
taxgatherers," and P Oxy IX. 1203[11] (late i/A.D.) ἐκ τοῦ
καταλογείου ὑπόμνημα πρὸς τὸν ἐνθάδε ξενικῶν πράκτορα,
"a memorandum from the bureau to the collector of external debts here" (Ed.: see note *ad l.*). In P Oxy XVI.
1829[5] (c. A.D. 577-9?) the variant πράκτηρ is found: see
the editors' note.

Πράκτωρ is still used technically in Lk 12[58], the only
place where it occurs in Biblical Greek, but the reference is
apparently not to a finance official, but to an "officer (usher)
of the court." For the juxtaposition of πράκτωρ and
ἀντίδικος, as in the Lukan passage, we may cite P Oxy III.
533[11, 23] (ii/iii A.D.). The same papyrus shows [21] πρακτο-
ρεία, "the post of collector."

πρᾶξις.

For the concrete plur. "doings," "deeds," cf. the mantic
P Ryl I. 28[121] (iv/A.D.) where it is decreed that, if both

a woman's legs quiver, δηλοῖ πράξεις καὶ ἀποδημίας, "it
denotes great achievements and travel." With the title
πράξεις (πρᾶξις D) ἀποστόλων (B) for our NT book, we
may compare the title of the *Res gestae Divi Augusti*
Cagnat III. 159, μεθηρμηνευμέναι ὑπεγράφησαν πράξεις τε
καὶ δωρεαὶ Σεβαστοῦ Θεοῦ. The Greek text of a iii/A.D.
Coptic spell from the great Paris magical papyrus, P Par
574 (= *Selections*, p. 113), is headed [1227] πρᾶξις γενναία
ἐκβάλλουσα δαίμονας, "a notable spell for driving out
demons": cf. Ac 19[13].

Πρᾶξις is common in the papyri in the legal sense of
"right of execution": e.g. P Eleph 1[12] (B.C. 311-10)
(= *Selections*, p. 3) ἡ δὲ πρᾶξις ἔστω καθάπερ ἐγ δίκης κατὰ
νόμον τέλος ἐχούσης, "and let the right of execution be
as if a formal decree of the court had been obtained," and
P Oxy II. 278[23] (A.D. 17) τῆς πράξεως [ο]ὔσης [τ]ῶι
Ἰσιδώρωι ἔκ τε τοῦ μεμισθωμένου κα[ὶ] ἐκ τῶν ὑπαρχόντων
αὐτῶι πάντων, "Isidorus having the right of execution upon
both the person and all the property of the lessee" (Edd.,
and *ib.* VI. 905[14] (A.D. 170) (= *Selections*, p. 87).

The adj. πράξιμος, which occurs in Polyb. xxi. 43. 17,
is found in P Giss I. 48[19] (A.D. 202-3) ἐν πραξίμ[οις]
ἱγηθῆναι.

πρασιά.

properly "a bed of garden herbs," or "of leeks" (if
derived from πράσον: cf. BGU II. 530[27] (i/A.D.) (= *Selections*, p. 62) μόλις γὰρ μίαν πρασιὰν ποτίζι τὸ ὕδωρ, "for
there is hardly a single plot which the water irrigates." In
the colloquial πρασιαὶ πρασιαί of Mk 6[40] the reference is to
regularity of arrangement rather than to variety of colouring:
Hesych. πρασιαί· αἱ ἐν τοῖς κήποις τετράγωνοι λαχανιαί.
For the reiteration πρασιαὶ πρασιαί (cf. also Mk 6[7, 39]) see
Proleg. p. 97 and Headlam's note to Herodas IV. 61
θερμὰ θερμὰ πηδεῖσαι. A Rabbinic explanation of Mk 6[40]
will be found in *Exp.* VIII. vii. p. 89 f.

πράσσω.

Like the Latin *ago* πράσσω suggests the acting of a moral
and responsible being rather than mere performance (*facio*):
cf. 1 Cor 5[2], 9[17], and for the juxtaposition of the two verbs
Jn 5[29], Rom 7[15]; see further Schmidt *Lat. u. Gr. Synonymik*,
p. 294 ff. The distinction cannot, however, always be
maintained.

For πράσσω in connexion with employment or the transaction of business, cf. P Tebt II. 289[7] (A.D. 23) where a
strategus writes to an official regarding a supplementary
report of tax-payments, οὕτως γὰρ γνώσομαι πότερον ἐπὶ
τόπων σε ἐάσω πράττοντά τι ἢ . . . ., "for I shall thus know
whether I shall leave you in employment where you are
or . . ." (Edd.), and the soldier's letter to his sister P Meyer
20[5] (1st half iii/A.D.) γεινώσκειν σε θέλω ὅτι ἐν τῷ Ἀρσι-
νοείτῃ πράσσω, "I wish you to know that I am on duty in
the Arsinoite district," and so [15, 4?].

From this comes the derived sense to *exact* tribute or
revenue (as in Lk 3[13], 19[23]): P Petr III. 53 (p)[19] (Ptol.)
καλῶς) οὖν (ποιήσεις) συ[ντάξαι] ἤδη πρᾶξαι τοὺς ἐγγύους
αὐτοῦ καὶ ἡμῖν ἀποκαταστῆσα[ι], "you will do well, therefore, to order that payment be exacted from his sureties and
restitution made to us" (Ed.), P Tebt I. 58[49] (letter of a

tax-gatherer—B.C. 111) (= Witkowski[2], p. 105) **τοὺς δὲ
λοιποὺς κω(μο)γρ(αμματεῖς) πρᾶξαι τὰς ΜΕ̄**, "and that
the rest of the komogrammateis should be made to pay
the 15000," and P Ryl II. 66[6] (late ii/B.C.) **πράσσειν τοὺς
προγεγραμμένους ἀκολούθως τοῖς ὑπὸ σοῦ κεκριμένοις**, "to
make the aforesaid persons pay in accordance with your
decisions" (Edd.). See also P Tor II. 3[41] (B.C. 127) with
Peyron's note.

With Ac 15[29], Eph 6[21], cf. P Oxy II. 292[13] (c. A.D. 25)
**πρὸ δὲ πάντων ὑγια(ί)νειν σε εὔχ[ο]μαι ἀβασκάντως τὰ
ἄριστα πράττων**, "before all else you have my good wishes
for unbroken health and prosperity" (Edd.), ib. VIII. 1155[3]
(A.D. 104) **εὗρον τὸν ἄνθρο(= ω)πον καλῶς πράσ⟨σ⟩οντα
τὰ μεγάλα**, "I found the man prospering in the main."
In P Oxy IV. 822 (c. A.D. 1) **εὖ πράσσειν** takes the place of
χαίρειν as an opening greeting: in ib. I. 115[12] (ii/A.D.)
(= *Selections*, p. 96) **εὖ πράττετε** is a closing greeting: cf.
Plato *Epp.* where **εὖ πράττειν** has the double meaning
"prosper" and "act rightly," and *Epicurea* ed. Usener
p. 131[17]; also M. Anton. vii. 36 **βασιλικὸν μὲν εὖ πράττειν,
κακῶς δὲ ἀκούειν.** In P Oxy VII. 1067[3] (iii/A.D.) **οὐ καλῶς
ἔπραξας μὴ ἐλθεῖν χάριν τοῦ ἀδελφοῦ σου. πράσσω** is
practically equivalent to **ποιέω** (see *supra*).

We may add the following miscellaneous exx.—P Eleph
1[15] (B.C. 311–10) (= *Selections*, p. 4) **τοὶ μετὰ Δημητρίας
πράσσοντες ἐπεγφέρωσιν κατὰ Ἡρακλείδου**, "let those
acting with Demetria bring the charge against Heraclides,"
P Oxy III. 532[15] (ii/A.D.) **ὅρα οὖν μὴ** (cf. Mt 18[10], 1 Thess
5[15]) **ἄλλως πράξῃς [[μὴ]] καὶ ποιήσῃς με πρὸς σὲ ἐλθεῖν
συνζητήσοντά σοι**, "mind that you do not fail and thereby
cause me to come to you and dispute with you about it"
(Edd.), and P Giss I. 34[4] (A.D. 265–6) **ἀξιῶ τὰ ἀκόλουθα
τοῖς γραφεῖσι πρᾶξαι.**

πραϋπάθεια.

"meekness," "gentleness of spirit," is found in the Greek
Bible only in 1 Tim 6[11]. Philo *de Abr.* (ed. Cohn) 213
applies it to Abraham, and it is also found in Ign. *Trall.* 8
**ὑμεῖς οὖν τὴν πραϋπάθειαν ἀναλαβόντες ἀνακτήσασθε
ἑαυτοὺς ἐν πίστει**, "do ye therefore arm yourselves with
gentleness and recover yourselves in faith" (Lightfoot).

πραΰς.

"meek," "gentle." In all its NT occurrences **πραΰς**
takes the place of the older form **πρᾶος** (cf. Blass-Debrunner
§ 26), but for the latter we may cite a sepulchral inscr. from
Pergamon, *Cagnat* IV. 504[9], where a certain Aelius Isidotus
is described as **ὁ πρᾶος ἰδίᾳ**, "meek in private life." Cf.
also Menander *Fragm.* 749, p. 211 [in Kock]—

    ὡς ἡδὺ πρᾶος καὶ νεάζων τῷ τρόπῳ | πατήρ.
    "how delightful is a father who is mild and
      young in heart."

The adv. **πραέως** occurs in P Par 63[xiii. 6] (B.C. 164)
εὐδιαλύ[τ]ως καὶ πραέως διατίθεσθαι.

πραΰτης.

"meekness," "gentleness." The older form **πραότης**
(see *s.v.* **πραΰς**) is found in P Lond 1912[101] (A.D. 41) **μετὰ
πραότητος καὶ φιλανθρωπείας**, "with mutual forbearance
and kindliness" (Ed.): cf. also the periphrasis in an inscr.

of about A.D. 350 from the Kara Dagh printed by W. M.
Ramsay in *The Thousand and One Churches* p. 518—

    λεύσεις, ὦ φίλε, τύμβον Ἀκυλείνου πραότητος.

"you behold, friend, the tomb of the meek Aquilinus," lit.
"the meekness of Aquilinus."

πρέπω.

A few exx. may be given of this common verb, which is
generally used impersonally (as in MGr) in the sense of what
is "fitting," "becoming" (Lat. *decorum*, see Cicero *de
Officiis*, i. 27. 93)—P Par 63[55] (B.C. 164) (= P Petr III.
p. 24) **τάχα γὰρ οὕτω πρέπει ῥηθέν**, "for that is perhaps the
proper expression" (Mahaffy), P Oxy I. 33[ii. 8] (late ii/A.D.)
**τῷ γὰρ θεῷ Ἀντωνείνῳ [τ]ῷ π[ατ]ρί σου ἔπρεπε αὐτο-
κρατορεύειν**, "the deified Antoninus, your father, deserved
imperial power" (Edd.), ib. VIII. 1121[11] (A.D. 295) **οὐκ
ἐπαυσάμην τὰ πρέποντα γείνεσθαι ὑπὸ τέκνων γονεῦσι
ἀναπληροῦσα**, "I was assiduous in performing what is owing
from children to parents" (Ed.), PSI I. 41[13] (iv/A.D.)
ἃ μὴ τοῖς ε[ὐ]γενέσι πρέπει, P Oxy I. 120[24] (iv/A.D.) **ὡς
πρέπον ἐστιν**, and *Syll* 325 (= [3]705[39] (c. B.C. 107) **ὥ[ς]
ἔπρεπεν ἀνδρὶ καλῷ καὶ ἀγαθῷ.**

For the adv. **πρεπόντως**, see P Par 63[77] (B.C. 164) (= P
Petr III. p. 24) **τοῖς καιροῖς πρεπόντως**, "befitting the
circumstances," and P Oxy VI. 907[17] (A.D. 276) where a
man bequeaths certain property to his wife—**πρεπόντως περὶ
τὴν συμβίωσιν ἀναστραφείσῃ**, "who has conducted herself
becomingly in our married life": cf. Aristeas 302.

πρεσβεία.

Hicks (*CR* i. p. 44) has drawn attention to the fact that
πρεσβεία, "the office of ambassador," was "in everyday use
in the intercourse between the Greek cities, and between
them and the kings"; this gives fresh point to its use in
Lk 14[32], 19[14]. See further *s.v.* **πρεσβεύω**, and for **πρεσβεία**
= "intercession," cf. P Oxy VIII. 1151[39] (v/A.D. ?) **εὔχεσθαι
πρεσβίαις τῆς δεσποίνης ἡμῶν τῆς θεοτόκου**, "pray through
the intercession of our lady the mother of God."

πρεσβεύω.

"I am an ambassador," was the regular word in the Greek
East for the Emperor's legate (cf. 2 Cor 5[20], Eph 6[20], and see
Deissmann *LAE*, p. 378 f.). Thus in the letter of the
Emperor Claudius to a Gymnastic Club, P Lond 1178[14]
(A.D. 194) (= III. p. 216, *Selections* p. 99), acknowledging
the "golden crown" they had sent him in commemoration
of his victorious campaign in Britain, we are told, **οἱ πρεσ-
βεύοντες ἦσαν Τιβ. Κλ. Ἑρμᾶς, Τιβ. Κλ. Κῦρος. . . .**
For other exx. of the verb in this sense see Magie p. 80, and
for its wider use in regard to embassies between town and
town, cf. *Priene* 108[164] (B.C. 129) **ἐπ]ρ[εσβ]ευσεν ὑπὲρ τοῦ
δήμου.** Amongst the questions addressed to an oracle in
iii/iv A.D., P Oxy XII. 1477[164], are the following—**εἰ
πρεσβεύσω; εἰ γίνομαι βουλευτής;** "shall I become an ambassador (?)? am I to become a senator?" (Edd.).

Like **πρεσβεία**, **πρεσβεύω** comes to be used of petition or
intercession, as perhaps in PSI VI. 571[7] (B.C. 252–250?)
**περὶ ὧν Μηνόδωρος ὁ ἀδελφὸς πρεσβεύσας ἀνήγγε{λ}λε{ι}ν
ἡμῖν ἀφεικέναι σε ἡμᾶς.**

πρεσβύτερος.

(1) For **πρεσβύτερος** in the literal sense of the "elder" of two, as in Lk 15[25], cf. P Oxy VII. 1061[15] (B.C. 22) of an elder brother, and *ib.* VIII. 1109[2] (A.D. 160-1) of an elder son. The fem. occurs in BGU II. 665[ii. 21] (i/A.D.) ἡ πρεσβυτέρα, Preisigke 1428 Ἀνουβιὰς πρεσβυτέρα Μέστου, and a curious double comparative in P Lond 177[15] (A.D. 40-1) (= II. p. 169) ἡ πρεσβυτερωτέρα ἡμῶν ἀδελφή.

(2) The use of **πρεσβύτερος** in 1 Tim 5[1] to denote an "elder," a "senior," as opposed to **νεώτερος**, may be illustrated from P Par 66[ii. 23] (Ptol. Rom.) where **πρεσβύτεροι καὶ ἀδύνατοι καὶ νεώτεροι** are employed as guardians in connexion with the work on canals and dykes: cf. further from the inscrr. *Priene* 117[5] (i/B.C.) ἀεί ποτε μὲν πρεσβυτέρους τιμῶν ὡς γονεῖς, τοὺς δὲ καθηλικας ὡς ἀδελφούς, τοὺς δὲ [νεωτέρους ὡς παῖδας, and *Latyschev* I. 22[28 ff.] (iii/A.D.) τοῖς μὲν ἡλικιώταις προσφερόμενος ὡς ἀδελφοῖς, τοῖς δὲ πρεσβυτέροις ὡς υἱός, τοῖς δὲ παισὶν ὡς πατήρ (cited by Dibelius *HZNT ad* 1 Tim *l.c.*). With the word, as in Heb 11[2], Moffatt (*ICC ad l.*) compares Philo *de Sobrietate* 16 (ed. Wendland) πρεσβύτερον . . . τὸν γέρως καὶ τιμῆς ἄξιον ὀνομάζει.

(3) We are not at present concerned with the precise force of **πρεσβύτερος** in the Jewish or Christian Church (see the discussions by Lightfoot *Dissertations on the Apostolic Age*, p. 135 ff., and Armitage Robinson in *The Early History of the Church and the Ministry* (Essays edited by Swete), p. 57 ff.), but in this connexion it is interesting to notice that the word was already familiar in Egypt as an honorific title with reference to certain village or communal officers. These varied in number according to the size of the villages, while their duties were of the most varied kind. Thus, to take two early exx., (1) in P Petr II. 4(6)[13] (B.C. 255-4) οἱ πρεσβύτεροι οἱ παρεστε.... η κότες interfere in the maintenance of order : (2) the corn required in connexion with a visit (**παρουσία**) of Soter II. is collected by the headman of the village and **τ[ῶν] πρεσβυτέρων τῶν γεω(ργῶν) τῆς αὐτῆς**, "the elders of the cultivators of the said village" (P Tebt I. 48[1]—c. B.C. 113). Similarly **πρεσβύτεροι** are appealed to in connexion with the rent of land (P Lips I. 106[14]—A.D. 98), the issuing of public notices (P Flor I. 99[3]—i/ii A.D. (= *Selections* p. 71), the lease of pasturage (P Lond 842[8]—A.D. 140) (= III. p. 141), payments of barley for military purposes (P Amh II. 107[5]—A.D. 185), and questions of taxation (BGU I. 334[1]—ii/iii A.D.).

In like manner, Deissmann has shown (*BS* p. 156) that "the Inscriptions of Asia Minor prove beyond doubt that **πρεσβύτεροι** was the technical term, in the most diverse localities, for the members of a corporation" : e.g. *Cos* 119[8] (possibly time of Claudius) γυμνασιαρχήσαντα τῶν πρεσβυτέρων σεμνῶς. Hicks (*CR* i. p. 44) had already reached the same conclusion : "All these terms [γερουσία, πρεσβύτεροι, συνέδριον], so familiar to us first in their Jewish, and afterwards in their Christian usage, had been commonly employed before, in a precisely analogous sense, in Graeco-Roman civic life."

(4) A still closer parallel to the Biblical usage, as Deissmann again has shown (*BS* p. 233 ff.), is afforded by the application of the term to the *priests* of pagan temples, as when the five presbyter-priests of the Socnopaeus temple (**τῶν ε πρεσβυτέρων ἱερέων πενταφυλίας θεοῦ Σοκνο[π]αίου**) inquire

into the conduct of a brother-priest (**συνιερέως**), who was charged with letting his hair grow too long (**κομῶντος** : cf. 1 Cor 11[14 f.]) and of wearing woollen garments (BGU I. 16 A.D. 159-160 (= *Selections*, p. 83 f.)) : cf. P Tebt II. 300[7] (A.D. 116-7) τ]οῖς δέκα πρεσβυτέροις (ἱερεῦσι, and see further Otto *Priester* i. p. 49 ff., Poland *Vereinswesen*, p. 373, and the literature referred to in Preisigke *Fachwörter*, s.v.

(5) We may add a few instances of **πρεσβύτερος** as it meets us in Christian papyri—P Grenf II. 73[1] (late iii/A.D.) (= *Selections*, p. 117) a letter addressed Ψενοσίρι πρεσβ[υτέ]ρῳ Ἀπόλλωνι πρεσβυτέρῳ ἀγαπητῷ ἀδελφῷ ἐν Κ(υρί)ῳ χαίρειν, *ib.* I. 53[23] (iv/A.D.) where with reference to a gross case of misconduct the writer says μὴ ἐμέν (for ἐμὲ) ἐξέταξε ἀλλὰ τ[ο]ὺ[ς] πρεσβυτέρους τῆς ἐκκλησίας, "if you do not believe me, ask the elders of the church" (Ed.), P Oxy VIII. 1162[1 ff.] (iv/A.D.) Λέων πρεσβύτερος τοῖς κατὰ τόπον συνλιτουργοῖ[ς] ("who share the local service") πρεσβυτέ[ροις καὶ διακώνοις, and P Strass I. 15[1 f.] (v/vi A.D.) Π(αρὰ) Θεοφίλου ὑποδιακ(όνου) καὶ ἐνοικολόγ(ου). Τῷ εὐλαβεστάτῳ Ἀνουβίωνι πρεσ(βυτέρῳ).

In addition to the literature already mentioned, reference should be made to the full discussion of **πρεσβύτερος** by H. Hauschildt in *ZNTW* iv. (1903), p. 235 ff. : cf. M. L. Strack *ib.* p. 213 ff.

πρεσβύτης

"an old man" : see P Strass I. 41[38] (A.D. 250) ὡς πρεσβύτης καὶ πίστεως ἄξιος εἰπὲ ἃ οἶδας ἐν τῷ πρά[γματ]ι, [41] πρεσβύτης ἄνθρωπός εἰμι, οὐκ ἐνιαυτὸς [δι]αγέγονεν οὐδὲ δύο οὐδὲ τρῖς, P Flor I. 50[62] (A.D. 268) Βίκτορα πρεσβύτην ὡς (ἐτῶν) ξη, and so[95]. In BGU IV. 1024[vi. 12] (end of iv/A.D.) the word is used of an old woman—Θεοδώρα δὲ αὐτῆς πενίχρα καὶ πρεσβύτης ἡ μήτηρ τῆς ἀπ[ελ]θούσης.

Πρεσβύτης = *senex* is written *quater* in the LXX for **πρεσβευτής** = *legatus* (see Thackeray *Gr.* i. p. 97), and a like confusion may have arisen in Philem 9, where Lightfoot, in accordance with the interchange of ευ and υ in the common dialect of the time, reads **πρεσβύτης** with the MSS., but renders "ambassador." It may be noted, however, that in P Oxy VI. 933[21] (late ii/A.D.) a letter addressed **πρεσβευτῇ**, the editors remark that an error for **πρεσβύτῃ** is unlikely : cf. Moulton *Gr.* i. p. 86 f. and see *s.v.* **πρεσβεύω**. On the use of **πρεσβευταί** for **πρέσβεις** in the inscrr. see Nachmanson p. 121, and Lafoscade *de Epistulis* p. 90.

πρεσβῦτις,

"an old woman." It is sometimes thought that the **πρεσβύτιδες** of Tit 2[3], the only place where the word occurs in the NT (cf. 4 Macc 16[14]), are the members of a priestly or organized class in view of the ἱεροπρεπεῖς which follows, see the citations *s.v.* **ἱεροπρεπής**; but the word need not imply more than that the **πρεσβύτιδες** "are to carry into daily life the demeanour of priestesses in a temple" (Lock *ICC ad l.*), and this meaning is strongly confirmed by the context (cf. *v.* 2).

πρηνής,

an Ionic form for Attic **πρανής** (cf. Moulton *Gr.* ii. p. 68), found in the NT only in Ac 1[18] **πρηνὴς** γενόμενος. As against the AV and RV "falling headlong" (supported by

Boisacq's derivation from πρό, p. 812), Chase (*JTS* xiii. (1912) p. 278 ff.) shows good reasons for taking πρηνής as a medical term = "swollen up" (cf. Sap 4[19]): see further Harnack *ThLZ* xxxvii. (1912), p. 235. If so, the root is prē, "burn": cf. Rendel Harris's suggestion (*AJ I* iv. (1900), p. 490 ff.) that for πρηνὴς γενόμενος we should read πρησθείς. A. D. Knox (*JTS* xxv. (1924), p. 289 f.) prefers to transpose πρηνής and μέσος, and to translate "when he arrived in the midst of it he fell headlong."

πρίζω.

This rare Hellenistic verb = πρίω, "saw asunder" (Heb 11[37]), is used of date-palms in CP Herm I. 28[11] φοίνικες . . ἄπρ[ιστοι π]επρισμ[ένοι: cf. P Oxy XIV. 1752[2] (A.D. 378), an order of payment to two πρίσταις, "sawyers," for repairs on a boat. For a curious word-play between πρῖνος and πρίζω see Th. Sus. 58 f.

πρίν.

1. adverb of time = "before," "formerly" (cf. 3 Macc 5[2], 6[4, 31]): P Oxy X. 1292[6] (c. A.D. 30) ὡς σὲ καὶ πρὶν ἠρώτησα, "as I asked you before," *ib.* XII. 1452[21] (A.D. 127-8) δηλῶ . . . Σαραπίωνα τετελ ευτηκέναι τὸ π ρὶν) ὄντα (δωδεκάδραχμον), "I declare that Serapion died some time ago being rated at 12 drachmae" (Edd.), *ib.* I 71[ii. 10] (A.D. 303) προσελαβόμην ἐμαυτῇ εἰς βοήθειαν . . τὸ πρὶν μὲν Σεκοῦνδόν τινα, ἔπιτα δὲ καὶ Τύραννον, "I engaged as my assistant first one Secundus, and subsequently Tyrannus besides" (Edd.), and *ib.* XIV. 1752[3] (A.D. 378) an order of payment of wine to two sawyers for repairing a boat —παρασχοῦ Πτολεμαίῳ καὶ τῷ κοινωνῷ πρίσταις εἰς λόγον δαπάνης ἀνανεώσεως τοῦ πλοίου τὸ πρὶν ὑπὸ Ἀπφοῦν οἴνου κνίδιον διπλοῦν ἕν.

2. conjunction = "before": (a) c. inf. with ἤ (cf. Mt 1[18]) P Oxy XII. 1473[12] (A.D. 201) πρὶν ἢ πληρωθῆναι τὸν Ὡρείωνα τοῖς προκειμένοις αὐτοῦ ταλάντοις δυσί "before Horion recovers the aforesaid 2 talents" (Edd.), P Strass I. 35[11] (iv/v A.D.) πρὶν ἢ ἐξελθεῖν αὐτόν. (b) c. inf. without ἤ (cf. Mt 26[34]) P Oxy VI. 928[8] (ii/iii A.D.) πρὶν προλημφθῆναι, "before she is entrapped," P Flor II. 242[13] (A.D. 254) πρὶν σε τὰ κτήνη ἐκεῖ πέμψαι, and the articular inf. in P Giss I. 105[31] (iv/A.D.) πρὶν τοῦ ἐμὲ ἐλθεῖν εἰς Ὄασιν.

The construction with ἄν and the subj., which in the NT is confined to Lk 2[26], is seen in P Oxy XII. 1413[36] (A.D. 270-5) πρὶν ἂν τὸ πᾶν ἀνάλωμα δοθῇ, and without ἄν in *ib.* I. 34[iii. 8] (A.D. 127) πρὶν αὐτῷ ἐπιστέλλη[τ]αι, P Fay 124[12] (ii/A.D.) πρὶν ἤ τι περαιότερο]ν ἐνχιρήσω πο[ι]εῖν, "before taking further steps" (Edd.), and P Lond 121[621] (iii/A.D.) (= I. p. 104) πρωὶ ἀνάστα πρὶν λαλῆς.

For πρίν as a preposition c. gen. cf. P Lond 121[418] (iii/A.D.) (= I. p. 97) πρὶν ἡλίου ἀν[α]τολῆς: it is construed c. acc. in Jn 11[55] D πρὶν τὸ πάσχα.

Πρίσκα, Πρίσκιλλα.

On the connexion of Prisca or Priscilla and her husband Aquila with the Roman Church, see SH p. 418 ff., supplemented by Edmundson *The Church in Rome*, p. 242 f., and for Harnack's suggestion that Priscilla may have been the author of the Ep. to the Hebrews, see *ZNTW* i. (1900), p. 16 ff.

πρό

is found 48 times in the NT, including 9 times with the articular inf., and always c. gen.

(1) For the *local* use "before," "in front of," which is rare in the NT (Ac[3], Jas[5]), we may cite P Petr II. 45[iii. 24] (B.C. 246) (= III. p. 334) πρὸ [τῆς πύλης] ὁδὸν ἐξήνεγκαν, and *OGIS* 50[12] (mid. iii/B.C.) ἀναθεῖναι πρὸ τοῦ νεὼ τοῦ Διονύσου. We have found no instances in our sources of the Hebraizing πρὸ προσώπου (Mt 11[10] (from LXX), Lk 9[52]), but for πρὸ ὀφθαλμῶν (2 Macc 8[17], 3 Macc 4[4]) cf. BGU II. 362[v. 8] (A.D. 215) πρὸ ὀφθαλμῶν θέμενος [τ]ὰ κελευσθέντα, similarly Aristeas 284, and *OGIS* 210[8] (c. A.D. 247) πρὸ ὀφθαλμῶν ἔχουσι τὰ περὶ τούτου κελευσθέντα: see Deissmann *LAE*, p. 183 f.

The thought of preference, as in Jas 5[12], 1 Pet 4[8], appears in the common epistolary phrase πρὸ πάντων—P Oxy II. 294[20] (A.D. 22) πρ]ὸ μὲν πάντων σεαυτοῦ ἐπιμέλου εἵν' ὑ[γιαίνῃς, *ib.* 292[11] (c. A.D. 25) πρὸ δὲ πάντων ὑγια<ί>νειν σε εὔχ[ο]μαι ἀβασκάντως τὰ ἄριστα πράττων, "before all else you have my good wishes for unbroken health and prosperity" (Edd.).

(2) For the *temporal* use "before," "earlier than," cf. P Hib I. 60[4] (c. B.C. 245) πρὸ ἕκτης ὥρας τῆι ιθ, "before the sixth hour on the 19th," P Fay 122[23] (c. A.D. 100) πρὸ ἡ]μερῶν τριῶν, "three days beforehand" (cf. 2 Cor 12[2]: *Proleg.* p. 101). BGU II. 592[3] (ii/A.D.) τετελεύτηκεν πρὸ δω[δε]καετίας, P Gen I. 47[4] (A.D. 346) πρὸ ὀλίγων ἡμερῶν τούτων, and from the inscrr. *OGIS* 56[45] (B.C. 238) πρὸ τοῦ νέου ἔτους, *ib.* 90[31] (Rosetta stone—B.C. 196) τῶν πρὸ αὐτοῦ βασιλέων. For the phrase πρὸ πολλοῦ cf. P Hib I. 170 (end of a letter—B.C. 247) τούτου γὰρ οὕνεκεν πρὸ πολλοῦ σοι γράφω, and P Oxy VIII. 1153[16] (i/A.D.) ἃ ἐδωρήσατό σοι Παυσανίας ὁ ἀδελφός σου πρὸ πολλοῦ ("some time ago"). Οἱ πρὸ ἡμῶν, "our predecessors," is supplied in P Tebt I. 61(*b*)[344] (B.C. 118-7): cf. also *ib.* 15[21] (B.C. 114) [[διὰ τῆς πρὸ ταύτης]] ἐπιστολῆς).

In 12[1] πρὸ ἓξ ἡμερῶν τοῦ πάσχα is often treated as a Latinism like *ante diem tertium Kalendas* (cf. Jannaris *Gr.* § 1651, Schulze *Graeca-Latina* p. 15) but Moulton (*Proleg.* p. 100 f.) regards the second gen. as practically an ablative = "starting from," and finds exx. of the construction in phrases which have nothing to do with the Latin formula. See e.g. the illiterate P Fay 118[15] (A.D. 110) πρὼ δύο ἡμερῶν ἀγόρασον τὰ ὀρνιθάρια τῆς ἑορτῆς καὶ πέμψεις αὐτά, "buy the fowls two days before the feast and send them," and the Mysteries inscr. from Andania *Syll* 653 (= [3]736)[70] (B.C. 92) πρὸ ἀμερᾶν δέκα τῶν μυστηρίων.

Similar exx. are supplied by Roussac p. 29—*Priene* 41[2] (decree of Senate—before B.C. 130) πρὸ ἡμερῶν πέντε εἰδυῶν Φεβροαρίων, and 105[23] (c. B.C. 9) πρ]ὸ ἐννέα καλανδῶν Ὀκτωβρίων, similarly [85]. See also Babrius xxviii. 4 πρὸ τῆς ὥρης.

(3) For πρό c. articular inf. (as in Mt 6[8] *al.*), cf. P Frankf 1[55] (B.C. 214-3) πρὸ τοῦ αὐτὸν ἢ τὰ ἐκφόρια κομίσασθαι, and for πρὸ τοῦ c. opt. or subj. cf. BGU III. 814[14] (iii/A.D.) πρὸ τοῦ [εἰσέ]λθοις εἰς τὴν παρεμπολήν σου, and P Fay 136[6] (iv/A.D.) πρὸ τοῦ τις ὑμᾶς ἐνέγκῃ, "before anyone fetches you." Cf. MGr προτοῦ (νά) c. aor. or pres. subj. (Thumb *Handb.*, p. 193).

προάγω.

For the intrans. use "go before," "precede," as in Mk 6⁴⁵, cf. *Syll* 316 (= ³684)²⁵ (*c.* B.C. 139?) Τιμόθεον . . . ἐ[κέλευσα] προάγειν εἰς Ῥώμην, "I bade Timothy go before me to Rome," P Leid Wˣⁱ·³⁰ (ii/iii A.D.) (= II. p. 119) προάγω σου κύριε, and Babrius vii. 7. For the pass. see BGU IV. 1060²⁵ (B.C. 14) ὅθεν καταπεπονημένοι προήγμεθα πρὸς ἀπειλαῖς, P Oxy II. 283¹⁶ (A.D. 45) διὸ προῆγμαι τὸ ὑπόμνημα ἐπιδοῦναι, "I am impelled, therefore, to present this petition," PSI IV. 299² (iii/A.D.) προήχθην γράψαι σο[ι τ]ὰ συμβάντα μοι, "I was impelled to write you what had happened to me," and from the inscrr. *Syll* 325 (= ³708)¹⁹ (before B.C. 100) τῇ τε ἡλικίᾳ προκόπτων καὶ προαγόμενος εἰς τὸ θεοσεβεῖν ὡς ἔπρεπεν αὐτῷ. The simple sense "preceding," "previous," belonging to the part. in Heb 7¹⁸, is shown in PSI V. 450⁵⁹ (ii/iii A.D.) τοῦ προάγοντος μηνός, P Hamb I. 18ⁱⁱ·¹³ (A.D. 222) τῆς προαγούσης βασιλείας, P Oxy VII. 1070⁷ (iii/A.D.) ἡ προάγουσα παρ' ἐμοῦ παρὰ πᾶσι θεοῖς εὐχή, "the prayer which I previously made to all the gods" (Ed.), and *IMAe* iii. 247 τὰ προάγοντα ψαφίσματα.

For the meaning "preside" cf. P Tor I. 1ᵛⁱⁱⁱ·²¹ (B.C. 116) προάγοντας τῆς κωμασίας, and for a possible absolute sense "excel," cf. P Oxy I. 42³ (A.D. 323) (= *Chrest.* I. p. 182) τὸ ἔθος ὁμοῦ τε καὶ ἡ πανήγυρις προάγουσα [σ]ημαίνει . . . , "tradition, no less than the distinguished character of the festival, requires . . ." (Edd.). See also *OGIS* 323⁶ (B.C. 159-138) συνέσει καὶ παιδείᾳ προάγιον.

The subst. **προαγωγή** in the sense of "advancement" occurs in a Delos decree of the time of Ptolemy Philometor published in *Archiv* vi. p. 9A⁴—Ἄγλαὸς . . τῆς μεγίστης τιμῆς καὶ προαγωγῆς ἠξιωμένος παρὰ βασιλ[εῖ] Πτολεμαίωι : see the other exx. cited on p. 18 f.

προαιρέω,

in its original meaning "bring forward," "produce," is seen in the illiterate P Fay 119²¹ (*c.* A.D. 100) σήμανόν μυ ποῦ [κ]ῖται εἵνα αὐτὰ προέλωι, "let me know where they (*sc.* documents) lie that I may get them out": *Menandrea* p. 44¹⁵ provides a new literary ex. For the mid **προαιρέομαι,** "prefer," "propose," as in 2 Cor 9⁷, cf. P Fay 12²⁵ (*c.* B.C. 103) προ[η]ρημένος ἐπεξελθεῖν, "having decided to proceed against them," and the letter of Vespasian confirming certain privileges granted by Claudius to a Gymnastic Club—P Lond 1178³⁶ (A.D. 194) (= III. p. 217) αὐτὸς φυλάττειν [π]ροαιροῦμαι. See also P Petr III. 53 (*g*)² (iii/B.C.) (= Witkowski², p. 44) εἰ ἔρρωσαι, μεθ' ὧν προαιρῖ ("vis") . . [ἔχοι] ἂν εὖ.

The subst. **προαίρεσις,** which is not found in the NT (cf. Carr *Hor. Bibl.* p. 132), may be illustrated by P Par 63³⁸ (B.C. 164) (= P Petr III. p. 20) παρὰ τὴν ἰδίαν προαί[ρεσιν, "contrary to our usual policy" (Mahaffy), P Oxy II. 237ᵛⁱ·³⁹ (A.D. 186) τῇ ἀπλανήτῳ προαιρέσει ἀνενεγκών, "exercising your unerring judgment" (Edd.), and the Imperial edict P Fay 20¹³ (iii/iv A.D.) διὰ τὴν ἐμαυτοῦ προαίρεσιν. It passes into the meaning "affection," "goodwill," in P Giss I. 68¹⁰ (time of Trajan/Hadrian) οἶδα τὴν προαίρεσιν ἣν εἶχες πρὸς αὐτόν, and P Oxy XIV. 1664⁸ (iii/A.D.) μεμνημένη τῆς ἀγαθῆς σου προαιρέσεως. For the προαιρέτης βιβλιοθήκης, see Preisigke *Girowesen*, p. 410.

PART VI.

προαιτιάομαι,

"I make a prior accusation," has not as yet been found elsewhere than in Rom 3⁹ (see *s.v.* αἰτιάομαι) ; but for προαιτία Herwerden (*Lex. s.v.*) now cites Damascius in Bekkeri *Anecdota* 1413.

προαμαρτάνω,

"sin before" (2 Cor 12²¹, 13²): cf. *OGIS* 751¹⁰ (ii/B.C.) θεωρῶν οὖν ὑμᾶς μετανενοηκότας τε ἐπὶ τοῖ[ς] προημαρτημένοις, with Dittenberger's notes.

προαύλιον,

in Mk 14⁶⁸, its only occurrence in the NT, denotes the "vestibule" leading from the street into the αὐλή or inner court. For the metaph. use of the plur. = *praeludia* Herwerden (*Lex. s.v.*) cites Theophyl. Sim. Hist. I. 19, 8 οὐκ ἄδοξα τὰ προαύλια τῆς ἡγεμονίας ἀπενεγκαμένοις, *al.*

προβαίνω,

"go forward," "advance," as in Mk 1¹⁹, is seen in BGU IV. 1209¹⁰ (B.C. 23) ἐπεὶ οὖν σὺν θεοῖς οὐδὲν μὲν προβέβη-(κεν), PSI I. 50¹⁵ (iv/v A.D.) καὶ προβῇ τὸ ἔργον τῆς μικρᾶς ξενίας τῆς περὶ τὴν ληνόν. For the metaph. use of "advance" in years, cf. P Par 15⁶² (B.C. 120) ἔτι δὲ καὶ προβεβηκότος ἤδη τοῖς ἔτεσι, and similarly P Tor I. 1ᵛⁱⁱ·²⁹ (B.C. 116): cf. Lk 1⁷·¹⁸, 2³⁶, where however ἐν is added before the datives.

προβάλλω,

"put forward" (Ac 19³³): cf. P Ryl II. 77⁴³ (A.D. 192) ἐμάθομεν τὸν Ἀχιλλέα προβαλόμενον ἑαυτὸν ("put himself forward") εἰς ἐξηγ(ητείαν), P Oxy XII. 1424⁵ (*c.* A.D. 318) φησὶν προβεβλῆσθαι εἰς λειτουργίαν, "he says that he has been appointed to a public office" (Edd.), and from the inscrr. *Syll* 732 (= ³1104)²⁹ (B.C. 37-6) ἡ σύνοδος . . . ὁμοθυμαδὸν προεβάλετο τοὺς εἰσοίσοντας αὐτοῖς τὰς καθηκούσας τιμάς, *ib.* 364 (= ³797)²³ (A.D. 37) φίλους τε κρινεῖν, οὓς ἂν αὐτὸς προαιρῆται, καὶ ἐχθρούς, οὓς ἂν αὐτὸς προβάληται. See also P Grenf I. 11ⁱ·¹⁴·ⁿ·¹³ (B.C. 157).

For προβολή, see P Tebt I. 5²² (B.C. 118) with the editors' note, also PSI VI. 666¹⁰ (iii/B.C.) and P Flor II. 153¹⁰ (A.D. 268).

προβατικός.

An interesting reference to Jn 5² is found in a Christian amulet, P Oxy VIII. 1151⁷ (v/A.D.?), where the invocation runs—ὁ θ(εὸ)ς τῆς προβατικῆς κολυμβήθρας, ἐξελοῦ τὴν δούλην σου Ἰωαννίαν . . . ἀπὸ παντὸς κακοῦ, "O God of the sheep-pool, deliver from every evil thy servant Joannia."

πρόβατον

is used of "sheep" collectively in such a passage as P Hib I. 32¹⁰ (B.C. 246) πρόβατα λη. (ὧν) ἔρσ[εν]ες η, ἄρνες ιγ ." "38 sheep, of which eight are rams, 13 lambs . . ." Other exx. of the word are P Petr II. 22⁶ (iii/B.C.) βοῦς(?) ἢ ὑποζύγιον ("ass") ἢ πρόβατον, P Oxy II. 244⁸ (A.D. 23) πρόβατα τριακόσια εἴκοσι καὶ αἶγας [ἑκατ]ὸν ἑξήκον[τ]α καὶ τοὺς ἐπακολουθ(οῦντας) ἄρνας [κ]αὶ ἐρίφους, P Fay

110¹³ (A.D. 94) ἵ[ν]α τὰ πρόβατα ἐκεῖ κοιμηθῆι, "that the sheep may be folded there," and CPR I. 40¹¹ (A.D. 301) (ἄρουραι) ᾶ πρὸς κατανομὴν προβάτων.

For the φόρος προβάτων, "sheep-tax," see Wilcken *Ostr.* i. p. 286. Πρόβατον occurs as a nickname (for a man?) in P Tebt I. 180 (B.C. 92 or 59). In P Ryl II. 73⁶ (B.C. 33–30) mention is made of a προβατοκτηνότροφος, "sheep-herdsman": cf. *OGIS* 655⁴ (B.C. 25–4), where Dittenberger's note now needs correction. Προβατών, "a sheep-pen," occurs in P Cairo Zen I. 59068² (B.C. 257), and προβατίων, "a sheep-stall," in BGU IV. 1130¹¹ (B.C. 11).

προβιβάζω.

The use of προβιβάζω in the LXX = "give instructions" (e.g. Exod 35³⁴, Deut 6⁷) may be held to determine the translation "being instructed" for προβιβασθεῖσα in Mt 14⁸: see Field *Notes*, p. 11, and add Musonius p. 60⁵ προβιβάζειν νέους εἰς φιλοσοφίαν. In *Kaibel* 947¹ προβιβασθείς is used apparently with the literal meaning "being led forward."

προβλέπομαι

in its only NT occurrence (Heb 11⁴⁰) is best rendered by "provide" (AV, RV): for the use of the mid. see Blass-Debrunner § 316. 1, and cf. the act. in the sepulchral inscr. *Kaibel* 326, in which a man states that he is providing a tomb for himself and his family—

 εὖ εἰδὼς κληρονόμων τὴν ἐπιλησμοσύνην
 καὶ κοινοῦ θανάτου μνημόσυνον προβλέπων.

In the LXX the verb is confined to Ps 36(37)¹³ in the sense "foresee." It is found *quater* in Vett. Val.

προγίνομαι,

confined in the NT to Rom 3²⁵, is seen in P Giss I. 50⁴ (A.D. 259) καψά[ρια πο]λειτικὰ δύο προγε[γονότ]α τῷ μετηλλαχότι [π]ατρί [μου, "two dressing-rooms in the town-baths which belonged formerly to my deceased father": cf. *Syll* 279 (= ³601)⁹ (B.C. 193) διὰ τὴν προγεγενημένην αὐτῶι δόξαν. In BGU III. 979¹ (A.D. 160–1) αἱ πρ[ογ]εγονυῖαι is unfortunately followed by an hiatus.

προγινώσκω.

For this verb = "foreknow," "know previously," as in the Apocrypha (Sap 6¹³ *al.*) and 2 Pet 3¹⁷, cf. BGU IV. 1141³⁹ (B.C. 14) διὰ τὸ προεγνωκέναι (corrected from προεγνωκώς) με περὶ τῶν δακτυλιδίων. In 1 Pet 1²⁰ Hort (*Comm. ad l.*) thinks the meaning is rather "designate before" to a position or function.

πρόγνωσις.

For πρόγνωσις, "foreknowledge," as in Ac 2²³, cf. the magical P Lond 121²⁸⁴ (iii/A.D.) (= I. p. 94) εἰς πρόγνωσιν κρειῶ (*l.* κριός), "for foreknowledge *Aries* (the ram)." In 1 Pet 1² Hort *ad l.* understands πρόγνωσις as "fore-knowledge" of a person not so much in himself, as in relation to a function: see also *s.v.* προγιγνώσκω. Προγνώστης occurs in P Lond 46⁴⁰ (iv/A.D.) (= I. p. 78) μοιρῶν προγνώστης.

πρόγονος.

The phrase ἀπὸ προγόνων, "from one's forefathers," as in 2 Tim 1³, is common in the inscrr., e.g. *OGIS* 485³ (i/A.D.) ἄνδρα . . . ἀπὸ προγόνων εὐσχήμονα καὶ ἤθει καὶ ἀγωγῇ κόσμιον, *ib.* 529¹ (A.D. 117–138) ἀπό τε τῶν [προ]γόνων διασημότατον κα[ὶ ἀ]πὸ τῶν ἰδίων αὐτοῦ φιλοτειμιῶν λαμπρότατον: cf. P Tor I. 1ᵛⁱⁱ·¹⁸ (B.C. 117–6) τῶν προγόνων προστάγματα περὶ τῶν κεκρατηκότων.

Πρόγονοι is used of *living* parents, as in 1 Tim 5⁴, in Plato *Legg.* xi. 931 E. In P Fay 48ⁱ·³ ᵃⁿᵈ ⁱⁱ·³ the editors, following Wilcken, now understand πρόγο(νος) = "step-son": see P Oxy IV. p. 263 and *Archiv* i. p. 552.

προγράφω.

For exx. of this verb meaning "write above," "write already," with the temporal force of the preposition much weakened as in Eph 3³, cf. P Petr III. 104¹¹ (B.C. 244–3) τὸ προγεγραμμένον ἐκφόριον, "the above-written rent," PSI I. 64²⁴ (i/B.C.?) θαὶς ὀμώμοκα τὸν προγεγραμμένον ὅρκον, P Amh II. 135¹² (early ii/A.D.) ὁ κύριος τῇ γ̄ προέγραψεν, "the master wrote on the third," and P Oxy I. 79¹⁷ (A.D. 181–192) (= *Selections*, p. 89) ὀμνύω . . . ἀληθῆ εἶν[αι] τὰ προ[γεγραμμένα.

The formulae of quotations in the NT may also be illustrated from the legal language of the time—καθότι προγέγραπται (P Tebt II. 386²⁴—marriage-contract, B.C. 12), κατὰ τὰ προγεγραμμένα (CPR I. 4²¹—deed of sale, A.D. 52–53).

For the forcible meaning "placard up" which, as Light-foot pointed out (*Comm. ad l.*), προγράφω has in Gal 3¹, we can now provide fresh exx. Thus in announcing that he will no longer be responsible for his son's debts a father directs that a public proclamation to that effect be set up, P Flor I. 99¹¹ (i/ii A.D.) (= *Selections*, p. 72) ἀ[ξιοῦμεν? π]ρογραφῆναι. To much the same effect we may quote from the inscrr. *IG* X. 4²¹ τόπος . . . ὃς προεγέγραπτο πωλούμενος . . . ἐν τῆι διόδωι τῆς ἀγορᾶς: cf. also the question to an oracle P Oxy XII. 1477¹¹ (iii/iv A.D.) εἰ προγράφεται τὰ ἐμά; "is my property to be sold by auction?" (Edd.), and P Tebt II. 411⁸ (ii/A.D.) οἷός τε ἦν καὶ προγράψαι εἰ μὴ ἐπηγγειλάμην σήμερόν σε παρέσασθαι, "he might even have proscribed you, had I not promised that you would be present to-day" (Edd.). See also Field *Notes*, p. 189. For the double comp¹· προαπογράφω, cf. P Ryl II. 102³⁹ (2nd half ii/A.D.).

The subst. πρόγραμμα is frequent with reference to official and other notices, e.g. P Tebt I. 35⁹ (B.C. 111) τὸ δ' ὑποκείμενον πρόγραμμα ἐκτεθήτω καὶ διὰ τῆς τοῦ κωμογραμματέως γνώμης, "let the following proclamation be published with the concurrence of the komogrammateus" (Edd.).

πρόδηλος.

In its NT occurrences (1 Tim 5²⁴ᶠ, Heb 7¹⁴) the προ-of πρόδηλος is *intensive* rather than *temporal*, "perfectly clear," "evident," cf. P Oxy II. 237ᵛⁱⁱ·⁹ (A.D. 186) τοῦ πράγματος πρ[ο]δήλου γενομένου, *Syll* 686 (= ³1073)²¹ (A.D. 117) ὡς πρόδηλον εἶναι τὴν ἐλπίδα τῆς (subst. omitted) ἐπὶ τὸν ἱερώτατον στέφανον αὐτῶι, and *IMAe* VII. 119, 120 ὁρᾷς θανάτου τὸ πρόδηλον. Similarly with the

verb—P Magd 21[10] (B.C. 221) τὴ]ν προδεδηλωμένην τιμήν,
P Ryl II. 109[6] (A.D. 235) πατὴρ τῶ[ν] δυεῖν προδεδ[η]-
λωμένων ἀφηλίκων, "father of the two minors aforesaid,"
and Aristeas 14 καθὼς προδεδήλωται, "as already explained."

προδίδωμι,

in the NT only in Rom 11[35], occurs in the same sense
of "give before," "give first," in P Oxy VIII. 1102[10]
(c. A.D. 146), with reference to a man's bequeathing part
of his estate to his native city, ὑφαιρουμένης τῆς προικὸς
τῆς προδεδομένης τῇ θυγ[ατρί, "with a deduction of the
dowry previously given to the daughter" (Ed.): cf. P Petr
II. 4(8)[4] (B.C. 255-4) τὸ γὰρ προδοθὲν αὐτοῖς δόμ[α, OGIS
266[61] (iii/B.C.) ο]ὐδὲ προδώσω ὑπεναντίως οὐθενὶ οὔτε αὐτοὺς
οὔτε αὐτ[ῶν τι, and Syll 246 (= ³ 547)[35] (after B.C. 211-0)
προδιδοὺς ἀργύριον εἰς ἐσθῆτα, with the editor's note. For
the meaning "deliver up" cf. P Thead 17[18] (A.D. 332)
where inhabitants of Theadelphia petition the Praefect τοὺς
[ὁ]μοκομήτας ἡμῖν προδοῦναι, "to deliver up to us certain
fellow-villagers" who had fled, in order that they might
escape taking their share in bearing the village burdens. In
Vett. Val. pp. 78[19], 240[15], προδίδωμι = perdo.

For the subst. πρόδομα of a payment in advance see
P Flor I. 20[28] (A.D. 127) (= Chrest. I. p. 422) τὰ ὑπὲρ
τῆ⟨ς⟩ ἀρούρης ἐκφόρια ἐκ προδόματος : cf. P Cairo Zen I.
59002[4] (B.C. 260).

προδότης,

"traitor," "treacherous." In LAE p. 217 Deissmann
quotes from BCH xxiii. (1899), p. 274, an imprecation, not
later than vi/A.D., on anyone who shall open the tomb
of a Christian deaconess at Delphi—ἔχοι τ]ὴν μερίδα τοῦ
Εἰούδα τοῦ [προδότου] τοῦ δεσπότου ἡμῶν Ἰ[ησοῦ Χριστ]οῦ,
"may he have the portion of Judas, the betrayer of our Lord
Jesus Christ." Cf. also Aristeas 270 ὃς γὰρ ἐπὶ τὸ πλεονεκτεῖν ὁρμᾶται, προδότης πέφυκε, "for the man who is
bent on advancing his own interests is a born traitor"
(Thackeray).

πρόδρομος.

This NT ἅπ. εἰρ. (Heb 6[20] : cf. Sap 12[8])="forerunner"
is cited by Herwerden from a Delos inscr. BCH xxix.
(1905) p. 448[7] τῆς δ' ὑφαιρεθείσης δοκοῦ τὸ χρήσιμον ὑπὸ
τὸν πρόδρομον τῆς κάτω παλαίστρας ὑπέθηκεν : see the
editor's note p. 453.

προεῖδον.

P Lond 354[22] (c. B.C. 10) (= II. p. 165). See s.v.
προοράω.

προεῖπον.

P Oxy VII. 1033[15] (A.D. 392) ὡς προείπαμεν, "as aforesaid" (Ed.), and the Christian letter of a slave to his master
regarding the illness of his mistress—P Oxy VI. 939[25]
(iv/A.D.) ἔδοξεν μὲν γὰρ ὡς προεῖπον ἀνεκτότερον ἐσχηκέναι
ἀνακαθεσθεῖσα, "for she seems, as I said before, to be in
a more tolerable state, in that she has sat up" (cf. Lk 7[15]).
Cf. from the inscrr. Syll 239 (= ³ 543)[38] (B.C. 214) τοῖς
μέντοι κατηγορεῖν τούτων μέλλουσιν προείπατε, ὅπως μὴ
φανῶσιν κτλ., and Kaibel 947[10] καὶ [σεμνῶ]ν εἰμ[ι]
προφήτης ὢν γε προεῖπα θεῶν. See s.v. προλέγω.

προεπαγγέλλομαι,

"promise beforehand" Rom 1[2], 2 Cor 9[5]), may be
illustrated from Priene 11[71] (B.C. 84) τὰ προεπηγγελμέν[α,
"what has been promised in advance," with reference to
certain rejoicings offered to the people by Zosimus : see
Rouffiac Recherches, p. 38.

προέρχομαι.

For the literal use of προέρχομαι, "go forward," "advance," cf. P Leid U[ii. 13] (B.C. 343) (= UPZ i. p. 371) ἕνα
δὲ προελθόντα εἰς τὸ μέσον. The word is common in a more
general sense like our "come forward," e.g. P Oxy II. 286[14]
(A.D. 82) τῆς δὲ Φιλουμένης παρ' ἕκαστα διοχλούσης με
προελθεῖν ἠνάγκασμαι, καὶ ἀξιῶ . . ., "since Philumene is
continually pressing me to repay, I have been forced to come
forward and request you . . ." (Edd.), ib. IX. 1203[18] (late
i/A.D.) ὅθεν ἀναγκαίως προερχόμενοι ἀξιοῦμεν τὸ μὲν ὑπόμνημα ἔχειν ἐν καταχωρισμῷ, "wherefore we perforce come
forward with the request that this memorandum should be
duly placed on record" (Ed.), ib. I. 68[20] (A.D. 131) δια-
γεγον[έ]ναι ἄλλα ἔτη πέντε καὶ μὴ τεθαρρηκαίναι (l.
τεθαρρηκέναι) τ[ὸν] Θέωνα προελθεῖν, "another five years
elapsed without Theon having dared to bring forward his
claim" (Edd.). For the double comp[d.] προαπέρχομαι, see
P Cairo Zen I. 59016[4] (B.C. 259) ἔφθασεν δέ με προαπελθὼν
Χάρμος.

προερῶ,

"say before" : P Par 63[39] (B.C. 164) (= P Petr III. p. 22)
πρὸς τοῖς προι(=ει)ρημένοις, "in addition to what has
just been said," P Amh II. 33[9] (c. B.C. 157) ἐν τῶι
προειρημένωι νομῶι (cf.[12]), P Tebt I. 27[44] (B.C. 113) πρὸς
ταῖς προειρημέναις χρείαις ("offices"), ib. 105[27] (B.C. 103)
πλὴν τῆς προειρημένης χέρσου ("dry ground"), and P Lond
232[9] (c. A.D. 346) (= II. p. 296) ἀδελφοῦ τοῦ προειρημένου
Παύλου. See s.v. προλέγω.

προευαγγελίζομαι,

"proclaim the glad tidings beforehand." For this verb,
which occurs in the Greek Bible only in Gal 3[8], Burton
(ICC ad l.) cites Philo Opif. mund. 34 (ed. Cohn), and
Mutat. nom. 158 (ed. Wendland).

προέχω.

Unfortunately we have as yet no such new light as F. B.
Westcott (St. Paul and Justification, p. 158 ff.) hoped for
from "some fortunate exhumed sherd, or strip of papyrus"
to help to explain the difficult προεχόμεθα of Rom 3[9]. He
himself thinks the meaning must be "are we in better
case?" but Field (Notes p. 152 f. : cf. Lightfoot Notes
p. 206 f., SH ad l.) inclines to treat the verb as pass. = "are
we excelled?" or "are we in worse case than they?"
(RV), and cites (from Wetstein) a clear ex. of this usage
from Plutarch II. p. 1038 C : ὥσπερ τῷ Διὶ προσήκει
σεμνύνεσθαι ἐπ' αὐτῷ τε καὶ τῷ βίῳ, καὶ μέγα φρονεῖν . . .
οὕτω τοῖς ἀγαθοῖς πᾶσι ταῦτα προσήκει, κατ' οὐδὲν προεχο-
μένοις ὑπὸ τοῦ Διός (cum nulla in re a Jove superentur).
We may give a few miscellaneous exx. of the use of the
verb in the act.: P Petr II. 12(4)[6] (B.C. 241) ὑπολόγησον ὃ
προέχουσι, "take into account what they have already"

(Ed.), BGU IV. 1121⁸ (B.C. 5) ὃ] προεῖχεν Ἱέραξ ὁ Ἱέρακος ἐπὶ τοῖς οὖσι ὁρίοις, P Lond 897²² (A.D. 84) (= III. p. 207) οὐκ ἔγραψα δὲ διὰ τῆς ἐ[π]ιστολῆς εἰδὼς ἐμαυτῶι ὅτι ἤδη [π]ροέσχη[κας] ἐν τῶι πράγματι, BGU III. 889⁹ (A.D. 151) ἃ προεῖχεν μισθῷ ὁ προγεγρ(αμμένος) Πτολ(εμαῖος), PSI V. 450¹⁷ (ii/iii A.D.) Πεκῦσις Διογένους προ[έσ]χον τὴν φερν[ήν, and Cagnat III. 103³ ἐν νομικῇ (iurisprudentia) προὔχοντα Κλεόμβροτον ἥρπασε μοῖρα.

προηγέομαι,

"give a lead to": cf. BGU IV. 1193¹¹ (B.C. 8) προῆγε(= η)μαι τὴν [τού]τ[ων] ἐπίδοσιν ποήσεσθαι. In P Lips I. 63⁶ (A.D. 388) παρὰ τοῦ προηγησαμένου Εὐσεβίου— the reference is to the immediately preceding praeses (see Wilcken Archiv iv. p. 226 f.). Cf. Syll 737 (= ³1109)⁸⁷ (A.D. 178) ψήφῳ οἱ ἰόβακχοι κρεινέτωσαν προηγουμένου τοῦ ἱερέως. For the otherwise unknown use of the verb in Rom 12¹⁰ in the sense of "account others better than or superior to oneself," a partial parallel may be found in the use of the simplex in Chrest. I. 116⁴ (ii/iii A.D.) ἡγοῦ μάλιστα τοὺς πατρῴους καὶ σὲ[β]ου°Ἴσιν Σαράπιν το[ὺς με]γίστους τῶν [θεῶν: cf. 1 Thess 5¹³.

The adv. προηγουμένως, "first of all," "above all," may be illustrated from such passages as P Oxy XIV. 1770⁴ (late iii/A.D.) προηγου[μένως εὔχομε(= αι) ὑμᾶς ὑγι[αίνειν, ib. 1774⁴ (early iv/A.D.) προηγουμένως ἀναγκε(= αῖ)ον ἦν προσαγορεύειν σαι(l. σε): cf. also Vett. Val. p. 264¹⁰ προηγουμένως δὲ συνορᾶν χρὴ τὸ ὡροσκοπικὸν κέντρον. The part. προηγούμενα used as an adj. meaning "principal" is common in Epictetus, e.g. i. 20. 1 πᾶσα τέχνη καὶ δύναμις προηγουμένων τινῶν ἐστι θεωρητική, "every art and faculty has certain principal things of which it is to take cognizance" (Matheson).

πρόθεσις.

The derived meaning "purpose," "plan," as in Ac 11²³, Eph 1¹¹, 2 Tim 3¹⁰ al., may be illustrated by P Tebt I. 27⁸¹ (B.C. 113) ἕκαστα χωρῆσαι κατὰ τὴν ἡμετέραν πρόθεσιν, "that everything should proceed according to the method prescribed by us" (Edd.), Syll 929 (= ³685)³⁸ (B.C. 139) τῆς δὲ προθέσεως ἡμῶν μὴ τελειουμένης. In P Amh II. 145¹² (A.D. 487) we have ἑτέραν μοι ἐνδοῦναι πρόθε[σ]ιν, "to grant me a further period" (Edd.), for the repayment of a loan. We may also note Arist. Rhet. xiii. 3. 3 where πρόθεσις and πίστις refer to the "statement of the case" and the "proof" respectively.

For a suggestion that the LXX phrase οἱ ἄρτοι τῆς προθέσεως, found in Mk 2²⁶ al. (cf. Heb 9² ἡ πρόθεσις τῶν ἄρτων), and indicating that the loaves were placed before God, may have been due to the reminiscence of a ceremonial custom of the time, see Deissmann BS p. 157.

προθεσμία,

lit. "a time-limit" for enforcement of claims which thereafter lapsed. Hence ἡ προθεσμία (sc. ἡμέρα), "the previously appointed day," is a common legal term, as in Gal 4² : cf. P Oxy I. 37¹·¹¹ (A.D. 49) (= Selections, p. 49) ἐνέστηι ἡ προθεσμία τοῦ δευτέρου ἐνιαυτοῦ," "there arrived the appointed time for the second year," ib. IV. 728¹⁸ (A.D. 142) τῇ ὡρισμένῃ προθεσμίᾳ, "the stipulated date" (Edd.), P Tebt

II. 294¹⁷ (A.D. 146) ταῖς συνήθεσι προθεσμίαις, "at the accustomed dates," and P Oxy IV. 724¹² (A.D. 155) οὐκ ἐκδέξομαι τὴν προκειμένην προθεσμ[ί]αν, "I will not wait for the aforesaid limit."

The word is used of "instalment" in P Ryl II. 100¹¹ (A.D. 238) τὸν φόρον ἀπο]δώσω ὑμῖν ἐν δυσὶ προθεσμί[αις, "I will deliver the rent to you in two instalments" (Edd.). For the compd. ἐκπρόθεσμος see P Oxy III. 533⁶ (ii/iii A.D.) ἵνα μὴ ἐκπρόθεσμα γένηται, "that they may not be later than the due time" (Edd.).

προθυμία,

"eagerness," "enthusiasm": P Par 63¹¹⁵ (B.C. 164) (= P Petr III. p. 30) τὴν πᾶσαν προσενεγκάμενοι σπουδὴν κ[αὶ] προθυμίαν, φροντίσαθ' ὅπως . . . "making use of the greatest zeal and eagerness, you must take precautions that . . . . ," Syll 735 (= ³1107)¹⁵ (c. B.C. 200) σπουδᾶς καὶ προθυμίας [ο]ὐθὲν ἐλλείποντες, and frequently in the inscrr., e.g. Magn 97⁷¹ (1st half ii/A.D.) τὰς . . τιμὰς . . [δέχεται μετ]ὰ πάσης προθυμίας : cf. Ac 17¹¹ and Deissmann BS p. 254 f.

For the verb cf. P Tebt I. 23¹¹ (c. B.C. 119 or 114) διὸ καὶ ἔτι καὶ νῦν καλῶς ποιήσεις φιλοτιμότερον προθυμηθεὶς ἵνα τὰ πρὸς αὐτὸν [. . . . .] διορθώσηι, "I shall therefore be glad if you will even now endeavour more earnestly to correct your behaviour towards him" (Edd.), and ib. 40¹¹ (B.C. 117) καὶ αὐτὸς προθυμούμενος εἶναι ἐκ τῆς οἰκίας, "and being myself eager to belong to your house."

πρόθυμος,

"eager": P Tebt I. 59⁹ (B.C. 99) (= Witkowski², p. 113) ἐν οἷς ἐὰν προσδέησθέ μου ἐπιτάσσοντές μοι προθυμότερον διὰ τὸ ἄνωθεν φοβεῖσθαι καὶ σέβεσθαι τὸ ἱερόν, "whatever you may require, do not hesitate to command my services, because of old I revere and worship the temple" (Edd.), P Oxy III. 473³ (A.D. 138-160) πολὺ προθυμότερος ὤφθη ἀλειμμάτων ἀφθόνῳ χορη[γίᾳ, "he appeared very eager in the unstinted provision of unguents," P Leid Wxiv.11 (ii/iii A.D.) (= II. p. 129) ἔλθε μοι πρόθυμος, ἱλαρός, ἀπήμαντος ("unharmed"), P Oxy I. 42⁴ (A.D. 323) προθυμότατα τοὺς ἐφήβους [τ]ὰ γυμνι[κὰ] ἐπιδείκνυσθαι προσήκει, and OGIS 221⁶¹ (beg. iii/B.C.) ὁρῶντες οὖν αὐτὸν εὔνουν ὄντα καὶ πρόθυμον εἰς τὰ ἡμέτερα πράγματα.

προθύμως,

"eagerly": PSI VI. 621⁷ (iii/B.C.) πᾶν γὰρ τὸ δυνατὸν καὶ προθύμως καὶ ἀόκνως ποιήσομεν, P Hib I. 82¹⁷ (B.C. 239-8) καλῶς οὖν [π]οιήσεις συναν[τι]λ[α]μβανόμενος προθύμως περὶ τοὺς ταῦτα συγκυρόντων, "please therefore to give your zealous co-operation in all that concerns this" (Edd.), and P Flor II. 157¹⁰ (iii/A.D.) ἵνα ὑπηρετούμενοι προθύμως ἡμῖν ἐργαζῶνται.

πρόϊμος,

as read by WH for the TR πρώϊμος in Jas 5⁷ LXX, is apparently derived from πρό and denotes "early" (in the year) as opposed to ὄψιμος: cf. for the LXX usage Thackeray Gr. i. p. 90. Πρώϊμος (cf. Mayser Gr. p. 136), however, is found in the Kanopic Decree OGIS 56⁶⁸ (B.C. 238) ὅταν ὁ πρώϊμος σπόρος παραστῆι, a passage which may also be cited along with Xen. *Oecon.* xvii. 4 in support of the application of Jas *l.c.* to early "crop" rather than to early "rain." The comp. **πρωιμώτερον** = "more punctually" occurs in P Tebt I. $27^{25, 76}$ (B.C. 113).

προΐστημι,

"put before," "set over," and intrans. "preside," "rule," "govern." The position of **προϊσταμένους** in 1 Thess 5^{12} between **κοπιῶντας** and **νουθετοῦντας** (cf. Rom 12^{8}), combined with the general usage of the verb in the NT, makes it practically certain that the word cannot be a technical term of office, even if the persons referred to are office-bearers of the Church (cf. Hort *Ecclesia*, p. 126 f.). This is further borne out by the wide and varied applications of the verb in the ordinary language of the time.

For a more or less official use cf. P Tebt I. 5^{58} (B.C. 118) where it is applied—**τοῖς προεστηκόσι τῶν ἱερῶν προσόδω[ν,** and *Chrest.* I. 70^{26} (B.C. 57–6) **διεδώκαμεν τὴν περὶ τούτων ἐπιτροπὴν Σωκράτῃ τῷ μάλιστα τοῦ ἱεροῦ διὰ παντὸς προϊσταμένῳ.**

In P Oxy VI. 891^{12} (A.D. 204) an exegetes is informed that he has been appointed to act in his official capacity on a date mentioned—**ἔδοξεν ὥστε σὲ μὲν προστῆναι,** "it was decided that you should preside" (Edd.), and in BGU IV. $1028^{ii. 8, 25}$ (ii/A.D.) we hear of the superintendents or heads of certain guilds—**προεστῶτι χαλκέων** and **Μαρείν[ῳ] καὶ τοῖς σὺν αὐτῷ προεστ(ῶσι).** Similarly the word is applied to estate agents—P Ryl II. 132^{3} (A.D. 32) a petition from **τοῦ προεστῶτος τῶν Εὐάνδ(ρου),** "the estate-agent of Evander," and to the heads of villages—P Oxy II. 239^{11} (A.D. 66) **ὀμνύω . . . μηδὲ μὴν ἀπὸ τοῦ νῦν προστήσε[σ]θ(αι) κώμης,** "I swear that henceforward I shall not become headman of a village," P Ryl II. 122^{6} (A.D. 127) **ἀξιῶ, ἐάν σοι δόξῃ, κελεῦσαι τοῖς προεστῶσει τῆς κώμης,** "I beg you, if you think fit, to give orders to the chief men of the village," and P Hamb I. 35^{3} (*c.* A.D. 160) **οἷς ἐκέλευσας προσταθῆναι κώμης Φιλαδελφεία[ς], τῶι κυρίωι χαίρειν.** In P Tebt II. 326^{10} (*c.* A.D. 266) a woman petitions that her brother be appointed guardian of her daughter on the ground that **προ[στ]ήσεσθαι γνησίως τοῦ παιδίου,** "he will honourably protect the child."

Other exx. of the verb are PSI IV. 341^{3} (B.C. 256–5) **ἀκούοντες γὰρ τὸ κλέος τῆς πόλεως καὶ σὲ τὸν προεστηκότα χρηστὸν καὶ δίκαιον εἶναι, ἐδοκιμάσαμεν . . . .,** P Lille I. 19^{8} (mid iii/B.C.) **π]αρὰ Σαραπίωνος τοῦ προεστηκότος τῆς Καλλιξέ[νους] δωρεᾶς,** P Petr II. $30(e)^{4}$ (iii/B.C.) **ὁ προεστηκὼς τοῦ Εἰρήνης ἀμ[πελῶνος,** *ib.* III. 73^{4} (iii/B.C.) **τοῦ π[ρο]εστηκότος τῆς λεγομένης Ἀρτεμιδώρου συνοικίας,** "the landlord of the lodging-house of Artemidorus, as it was called," and P Oxy X. 1275^{8} (iii/A.D.) **ὁ προεστὼς συμφωνίας αὐλητῶν καὶ μουσικῶν,** "chief of a company of flute-players and musicians."

Cf. also for still wider uses P Fay 13^{5} (B.C. 170?) **καλῶς ποιήσετε προστάντες Πετήσιος,** "please support Petesis" (Edd.), P Par 63^{40} (B.C. 164) (= P Petr III. p. 20) **ὑπὲρ τοῦ προστήσεσθαι τῶν κατὰ τὸν σπόρον μετὰ τῆς ἐνδεχομένης προσοχῆς,** "that you should attend to the seed-sowing with fitting care" (Mahaffy), and P Oxy XII. 1491^{5} (early iv/A.D.) **θαρρῶ . . . ὅτι ὄχλησις ἐὰν ᾖ προίστασαι ἡμῶν,** "I am confident that if there is any trouble you are supporting me" (Edd.). In the early Christian letter P Amh I. $3(a)^{iii. 23}$ (between A.D. 264 and 282) (= *LAE*, p. 195, Ghedini, p. 68) reference is made to certain business transactions carried through **πάπᾳ καὶ τοῖς κατ' α[ὐτὸν ἁγιω]τάτοις προ[εστῶσι,** "with the Papas and the most holy rulers who are before him," and in P Oxy I. 148^{1} (A.D. 556) *al.* the word is used of the head of a monastery. From the inscrr. cf. *OGIS* 728^{4} (B.C. 238–7) **προέστη τῶν κα[θ' αὐτὸν] ἀξίως τῆς πόλεως,** and *Syll* 318 (= ³700)^{7} (B.C. 118–7) where a certain **Μάαρκος** is described as **προϊστάμενος τῶν τε κατὰ κοινὸν πᾶσιν Μακεδόσιν συνφερόντων.**

We may add that while Field (*Notes*, p. 223 f.) is able to cite exx. from late Greek of **προΐστημι** with the meaning "manage some matter of business," he rejects the RV mg rendering of Tit 3^{8} "profess honest occupations" on the ground that **καλῶν ἔργων** must be taken in the usual sense of "good works." Field's objection may, however, be met so far by some such rendering as "make it their business to do good" (Goodspeed).

προκαλέω,

"call forth," "challenge," though occurring in classical writers from Homer downwards, is found only in Gal 5^{26} in Biblical Greek (except in 2 Macc 8^{11} A): but cf. BGU IV. $1024^{v. 5}$ (end of iv/A.D.) **τ[οῦτο] γὰρ προκαλ[εῖ] ἐμὲ τὸν δ[ι]κά[ζ]οντα.** In a letter addressed to the Smyrnaeans, *Syll* 414 (= ³876)^{6} (A.D. 198) (= *Lafoscade*, p. 33 f.) the Emperors Septimius Severus and Caracalla recall that, notwithstanding the immunity granted to sophists, a certain Claudius Rufinus had "at their summons" voluntarily undertaken a military command in view of his affection for his native land—**ὑμῶν αὐτὸν ἑκουσίῳ ἀνάγκῃ προκαλουμένων ὑφέστη τὴν στρατηγίαν κατὰ τὸ πρὸς τὴν πατρίδα φίλτρον.** The subst. **πρόκλησις** occurs in the fragmentary P Ryl II. 353 (iii/A.D.).

προκαταγγέλλω.

In illustration of this rare verb = "announce beforehand" (Ac 3^{18}, 7^{52}) Herwerden (*Lex. s.v.*) cites Clem. Al. p. 196, 4 Sylb. **ἡ προκατηγγελμένη γῆ.**

πρόκειμαι

in the participle is common = "set forth," "aforesaid," e.g. P Lond 44^{10} (B.C. 161) (= I. p. 34, *UPZ* i. p. 140) **τυγχάνω ἐν τῆι κατοχῆι γεγονὼς τὰ προκείμενα ἔτη,** P Tebt II. $294^{8 f.}$ (A.D. 146) **β[ούλομα]ι ὠνήσασθαι τὴν τοῦ προκιμένου ἱεροῦ προφη[τ]εία[ν] εἰς π[ρ]ᾶσιν π[ρ]οκιμένην ἔτι πάλαι,** "I wish to purchase the office of prophet in the aforesaid temple which has been for a long time offered for sale" (Edd.), *ib.* 293^{23} (*c.* A.D. 187) **ὤμοσα τὸν προκείμενον ὅρκον κ[α]θὼς πρόκειται,** "I have sworn the above oath as aforesaid" (Edd.), and the Gnostic charm P Oxy XII. 1478^{4} (iii/iv A.D.) **δὸς νείκην . . . τῷ προκειμένῳ Σαραπάμμωνι,** "give victory to the aforesaid Sarapammon": cf. also the letter regarding funeral expenses P Grenf II. 77^{28} (iii/iv A.D.) (= *Selections*, p. 121) **μισθοῦ ὡς πρόκ[ειται] (δραχμαὶ) τμ,** "cost (for the transport of the body) as set forth above 340 drachmae."

Πρόκειμαι passes readily into the meaning "am present," "am there," as in 2 Cor 8^{12}: cf. P Lond 1201^{2} (B.C. 161) (= III. p. 4) **διὰ τῆς προκειμένης συγγραφῆς,** and P Oxy II.

255¹⁷ (A.D. 48) (= *Selections*, p. 47) τὴ[ν π]ροκειμένην [γρα]φήν—with reference to a census.

προκηρύσσω,

literally "proclaim as a herald beforehand" (Ac 13²⁴): cf. PSI V. 486⁷ (B.C. 258-7) Ἀπολλώνιος προκεκήρυχεν στεγνὰ παρέξειν (sc. τὰ χώματα), P Petr II. 13(18b)¹⁰ (B.C. 258-3) ἔκθες οὖν ἔκθεμα καὶ προκήρυξον, "issue then a public notice and advertize," P Eleph 23¹⁵ (B.C. 223-2) ἣν (sc. γῆν) προκηρύσσεις ὡς οὖσαν Ψεντεῆτος τοῦ Ἐσθφήνιος, BGU III. 992¹·⁸ (B.C. 162) τῶν προτεθέντων εἰς πρᾶσιν καὶ προκηρυχθέντων ἐν Διοσπόλει, P Oxy I. 44²¹ (late i/A.D.) πολλάκις προκηρυχθεισῶν, of taxes put up to auction several times, *Chrest.* I. 81¹⁶ (A.D. 197) σὺ φρόντισον σὺν τῷ βασιλ(ικῷ) γρα(μματεῖ) τὰς τάξεις προκηρῦξαι, and P Lond 1910²⁹ (c. A.D. 330-340) ἐφάνη δὲ ἡ ἀγάπη ὑμῶν ἐν πᾶσι ἡ προκηρισσομένη (l. προκηρυσσομένη), "your love which is trumpeted abroad was shown in all things" (Bell). For the corresponding subst. = "auction," cf. P Oxy IV. 716²⁰ (A.D. 186) τὴν προκήρυξιν γενέσθαι, "that a public auction should be held."

προκοπή,

unlike its verb (προκόπτω), is not found in classical Greek (cf. Rutherford *NP*, p. 158), but is a *term. techn.* in Stoic philosophy for "progress towards wisdom" (cf. Zeller *Stoics*, p. 294). It occurs *ter* in the NT (Phil 1¹²,²⁵, 1 Tim 4¹⁵: cf. Sir 51¹⁷, 2 Macc 8⁸), and its colloquial use may be illustrated from P Ryl II. 233¹⁶ (ii/A.D.) εὔχομαί σε τὸν κύριον ἰδεῖν ἐν μείζοσι προκοπαῖς, ἐν ἀδραῖς εὐημερίαις, "I pray, my lord, that I may see your further advancement and ripe prosperity" (Edd.), P Giss I. 27⁷ (ii/A.D.) (= *Chrest.* I. p. 29) εὐαγγελίζοντι τὰ τῆς νείκης αὐτοῦ καὶ προκοπῆς (report of a victory over the Jews), P Tebt II. 276³⁹ (ii/iii A.D.) the fragment of an astrological work according to which, if the conjunction of certain planets takes place at the morning rising of Venus, ἀπὸ νε[ότ]ητος τὰς προκοπὰς ἀποτελοῦσιν, "they cause prosperity from youth upwards" (Edd.), and P Oxy XIV. 1631²⁰ (A.D. 280) κατὰ προκοπὴν τῶν ἔργων, "according to the progress of the works" (Edd.).

προκόπτω,

originally "cut forward" a way, is in late Greek always used intransitively "advance," "progress": cf. BGU II. 423¹⁷ (ii/A.D.) (= *Selections*, p. 91) a soldier to his father, ἐκ τούτου ἐλπίζω ταχὺ προκόσαι (l. προκόψαι) τῶν θε[ῶ]ν θελόντων, "on this account I hope to be quickly promoted, if the gods will," P Iand 3⁵ (astrological—ii/A.D.) τα[χέως μὲν περὶ τὴν παι]δείαν προκόπτει, P Gen I. 74³ (iii/A.D.) πρὸ μὲν πάντων εὔχομαί σε ὑγειαίνειν καὶ προκόπτειν, P Flor II. 175²⁶ (A.D. 255) δήλω[σ]όν μοι εἰ προέκοψεν ὑμῶν τὰ ἔργα, and P Oxy I. 122¹⁵ (iii/iv A.D.) ἐρ]ρῶσθαί σε . . . πολλοῖς χρόνοις καὶ προκόπτειν εὔχομαι, "I pray for your lasting health and prosperity": cf. Gal 1¹⁴. A striking parallel to Lk 2⁵² is afforded by *Syll* 325 (= ³708¹⁶ (before B.C. 100), where a certain Aristagoras is praised as τῇ] τε ἡλικίᾳ προκόπτων καὶ προαγόμενος εἰς τὸ θεοσεβεῖν. MGr προκόφτω, "come forward," "progress": cf. προκομμένος, "capable," "diligent."

πρόκριμα.

The phrase χωρὶς προκρίματος, "without prejudgment" in 1 Tim 5²¹, the only occurrence of πρόκριμα in the Greek Bible, occurs *ter* in P Flor I. 68 (A.D. 172), e.g. ¹³ μετέλα]βον [τ]ούτου τὸ ἴσον ὡς [κ]αθήκει χωρὶς προκρίμματος μένοντός μοι τοῦ [λόγου . . . . For the corresponding verb (only Sap 7⁸ in Greek Bible), cf. P Oxy III. 472⁷ (c. A.D. 130) θάνατον τοῦ ζῆν προκρείναντες, "preferring death to life," and *Syll*³ 783²⁰ (B.C. 27) τῆς κατ᾽ οἶκον ὠ[φε]λίας τὸν δημόσιον κόσμον προκρείνας.

προλαμβάνω,

"receive before": cf. P Petr III. 43(2) *recto*¹·²⁵ (iii/B.C.) τό τε ἀρ[γ]ύριον ὃ ἂν π[ροειλη]φότες ὦσιν, "the money which they have received previously," P Cairo Zen I. 59120² (B.C. 256) διὰ τὸ προλαβεῖν παρ᾽ αὐτοῦ κερμάτιον εἰς ἐφόδια, "because we have received from him in advance money for travelling expenses," *OGIS* 6²⁰ (iv/B.C.) ὁ δῆμος φαίνηται χάριν ἀποδιδοὺς ὧν προείληφεν ἀγαθῶν, and the immense inscr. of temple accounts from Eleusis *Syll* 587¹¹ (B.C. 328), money paid ἀρ]χι[τ]έκτονι, ὃ προέλαβεν Λυκούργου κελεύσαντος, "to the architect, which he received in advance at the bidding of Lycurgus." The sense of "anticipate" in Mk 14⁸, which Souter (*Lex. s.v.*) regards as perhaps an Aramaism, is apparently to be found in *IGSI* 2014¹ Σουλπικία, εὐψύχι· προέλαβές με κτλ. (cited by Herwerden *Lex. s.v.*). In P Cairo Zen I. 59060⁵ (B.C. 257) a boy athlete is described as τῶν νῦν ἀλιφομένων, οἳ προειλήφασιν χρόνον πολύν, πολὺ κρείττων, "far excelling those at present being trained, who had anticipated him by a considerable time."

For the derived meaning "overtake," "surprise," as in Gal 6¹ (cf. Sap 17¹⁷), see Field *Notes*, p. 190, and cf. P Oxy VI. 928⁸ (ii/iii A.D.) ἵνα ἐὰν δοκιμάσῃς ποιήσῃς πρὶν προλημφθῆναι, "that if you think fit you may act before she is entrapped "—said of a girl against whom a plot had been formed.

In *Syll* 804 (= ³1170) (ii/A.D.) from the Asclepieum at Epidaurus this word occurs *ter* meaning "eat" (or "drink"): ⁷τυρὸν καὶ ἄρτον προλαβεῖν, ⁹κιτρίου προλαμβάνειν τὰ ἄκρα, and ¹²γάλα μετὰ μέλιτος προλαβεῖν. Dittenberger quotes Wilamowitz to the effect that the temporal force of the προ- had worn off, and Baunack as finding the idea of *praeferre*, but he himself thinks προλαμβάνειν a mistake for προσλαμβάνειν, which is used in later Greek of taking food. One naturally thinks of 1 Cor 11²¹, where no part of the point lies in the "forestalling" of others: the gravamen of Paul's charge is that there was "no Lord's supper to eat," "everyone devours *his own* supper at the meal" (brought with him in a κίστη—cf. the last scene of Aristophanes' *Acharnians*).

The subst. πρόληψις is used in the sense of "preconception" in P Fay 124¹⁶ (ii/A.D.), as in Stoic philosophy. For πρόλημμα see BGU III. 775¹⁵ (ii/A.D.).

προλέγω.

The force of προ- in composition is raised again by this word, as e.g. in the marriage contract BGU IV. 1050³⁷ (time of Augustus): the contract is to be deposited ἐν ἡμέραις χρηματιζούσαις πέντε ἀφ᾽ ἧς ἂν ἀλλήλοις προείπωσιν, "within the five days named from the day on which they settle it with one another." Here the **προ-** simply implies that the terms of the contract have been discussed *beforehand*, and then embodied in the legal document. For this ordinary time sense in the NT, cf. 2 Cor 13[2], Gal 5[21], and 1 Thess 3[4] (with Milligan's note). In *Kaibel* 621[4] (ii/iii A.D.) ὃς προλέγει θνατοῖς εὐφροσύνης μετέχειν, the editor renders **προλέγει** by "hortatur" (see Index *s.v.*).

προμαρτύρομαι,

"summon (God) beforehand to witness," "call before-hand to witness." Hort *ad* 1 Pet 1[11] states that this verb is unknown elsewhere except in Theodorus Metochita, about A.D. 1300; but we can now add P Lond IV. 1356[32] (A.D. 710) προμαρτυρόμενος [αὑτοὺς εἰ]ς τὸ σχεῖν τὸν φόβον τοῦ Θεοῦ πρὸ ὀφθαλμῶν.

προνοέω,

"take thought for," "provide for": (1) act.—P Ryl II. 77[31] (A.D. 192) ἐπιστέλλεταί σοι ὅπως ἀκόλουθα τοῖς ἐπὶ σοῦ γενομένοις προνοήσαι(= ῃ) πρᾶξαι, "notice is given you in order that you may arrange to carry out the consequences of the proceedings before you" (Edd.). P Fay 130[7] (iii/A.D.) προνοῶ τοῦ χ[α]λκοῦ πά[ντη πάν]τως, "I am by all means looking after the copper," and *c.* acc., as in 2 Cor 8[21], P Lond 144[10] (ii/iii A.D.) (= II. p. 253, *Berichtigungen*, p. 266) παρακαλῶ προνοῆσαι ὀνάρ[ιον], ἵνα κτλ.: (2) mid.—P[?] V. 542[15] (iii/B.C.) σοι καθήκει ὑπὲρ τῶν τοιούτων προνοεῖσθαι, P Tebt I. 40[12] (B.C. 117) (= *Selections*, p. 28) διὰ τὸ μάλιστα ἐπιβάλλειν προνοεῖσθαι τῶν βασιλικῶν, "because it chiefly falls to you to look after the interests of the Crown," P Lond 1170 *verso*[267] (A.D. 258–259) (= III. p. 199) παρὰ Ἡρ[ω]νείνου προνο[ο]υμένου τῶν περὶ Θεαδελφίαν, P Oxy XII. 1491[14] (early iv/A.D.) ἵνα προνοήσωμαι ἀργυρίου, "in order that I may provide for the money," *OGIS* 495[20] ἀνθ' ὧν τῶν δημοσίων ἔργων μετὰ ἐπιμελείας προενοήσατο: (3) pass.—P Par 63[12] (B.C. 164) (= P Petr III. p. 18) τὴν πᾶσαν προσενεγκάμενος ἐκτένειαν καὶ π[ρο]νοηθείς, "using every effort and taking every precaution" (Mahaffy), BGU IV. 1024[vii. 5] (end iv/A.D.).

The verb is used in a weakened sense in P Oxy I 63[5] (ii/iii A.D.) προνόησον οὖν (σὺν—*Archiv* i. p. 128) πάσῃ σπουδῇ ἐνβαλέσθαι αὐτοῦ τὸν γόμον, "please to see that his freight is embarked with all despatch" (Edd.).

For **προνοητής**, "provider," cf P Grenf II. 67[1] (A.D. 237) (= *Selections*, p. 108) Θέωνι πρω(= ὁ νοη(τῇ) αὐλ(η-τρίδων), "to Theon provider of flute-girls." It is common in the sense of "steward," "manager," e.g. P Ryl II. 169[2] (application for a lease—A.D. 196–7) διὰ Ἰσιδώρου προνοητοῦ, P Lond 214[3] (A.D. 270–275) (= II. p. 161) προν[ο]ητὴς οὐσίας.

πρόνοια

= "providence" occurs first in the Greek Bible in Sap 14[3], but is not found in this sense in the NT, where it is = "forethought," "care" (Ac 24[3]: cf. Hesych. πρόνοια· προενθύμησις, ἐπιμέλεια, φροντίς): cf. P Hib I. 79[3] (*c.* B.C. 260) (= Witkowski[2], p. 25) ὧν πρόνοιαν ποιεῖ, "the objects of your care" (Edd.), BGU II. 531[i. 7] (ii/A.D.) τῇ προνοίᾳ [σο]υ εὐχαρισ[τῶ?], P Flor II. 131[7] (A.D. 257) τὴν τοῦ

χό[ρ]του πρόνοιαν, and the probably Christian P Oxy XIV. 1682[6] (iv/A.D.) (= Ghedini, p. 189) ἡ μὲν τοῦ θεοῦ πρόνοια παρέξει τὸ μετὰ ὁλοκληρίας σε τὰ οἰκεῖα ἀπολαβεῖν, "may the divine providence grant that you may be restored in security to your home" (Edd.). See also the Delphic precept *Syll*[3] 1268[i. 7] πρόνοιαν τ[ί]μα.

For the phrase **πρόνοιαν ποιοῦμαι**, as in Rom 13[14], cf. P Amh II. 40[12] (ii/B.C.) ὅθεν ὑμῶν μηδεμίαν πρόνοιαν ποησαμένων ἠναγκάσθην . . . ἀποστῆσαι τῆς γῆς τὸν Ἄρειον, "therefore as you had made no provision for your interests I was obliged to remove Arius" (Edd.), P Oxy VI. 899[17] (A.D. 200) ὅπως ὁ ἑκάστης κώμης πραγματικὸς πρόνοιαν ποιήση[ται], P Flor I. 2[207] (A.D. 265) τῆς τοῦ ἱ(ἐρωτά]του ταμείου ἀσφαλείας πρόνοιαν ποιήσ[η]σθε, and from the inscrr. *Priene* 71[28] (ii/B.C.) ἡ Πριηνέων πρόνοια ἥν ποιοῦνται: other exx. in Rouffiac *Recherches*, p. 72.

προοράω.

For this verb in the act. = "see beforehand," cf. BGU II. 372[ii. 9] (A.D. 154) (= *Chrest.* I. p. 33) προορῶντας καὶ προαπαντῶντας, and Vett. Val. p. 83[4] ἑκάστου οὖν ἀστέρος δεῖ τὰς φύσεις προορᾶν.

The mid. in the sense of "pay regard to," as in Ac 2[25] LXX, may be illustrated by P Par 26[i. 22] (B.C. 163–2) (= *Selections*, p. 15) οὐδεμίαν εὐλάβειαν προορωμένων, "paying no regard to religious scruple," P Flor I. 90[6] (i/ii A.D.) (= *Selections*, p. 72) οὗ χάριν προορώμεθα μήποτε ἐ[π]ηρεάσῃ ἡμεῖν, "wherefore we are paying heed lest he should deal despitefully with us," P Fay 20[20] (Imperial edict—iii/iv A.D.) προορᾶσθαι τῶν ἐθνῶν οἷς ἐφεστήκασι, "to pay regard to the interests of the people over whom they are placed," and *Syll*[3] 569[13] (B.C. 204–1) προορώμενος τάν τε τῶν ἐναντίων ἐπιβολάν. For the subst. **πρόοψις** see *ib.* 880[15] (A.D. 202) τῇ προόψει τῶν σταθμῶν ἠσθέ[ν]τες. An ex. of **προεῖδον** is given *s.v.*

προπάσχω.

"suffer previously." To the citations in LS[8] for this NT ἅπ. εἰρ. (1 Thess 2[2]) we may add Menander *Fragm.* p. 200, fr. 696.

[An interesting instance of the comp[l.] **προσπάσχω** occurs in the letter P Lond 1929 (mid. iv/A.D.), which the editor thinks may have been written by the great Athanasius him-self. After referring to the bad health of his mother, the writer proceeds—[13]ἀγὼν οὖν [μέγιστος πε]ρὶ ἐμοῦ [ἐστὶ] π[ρο]σπάσχοντος . . ., "so that there is very great anxiety concerning me, suffering [this?] in addition" (Ed.).]

προπάτωρ.

For this NT ἅπ. εἰρ. (Rom 4[1]: cf 3 Macc 2[21] A) = "forefather," cf. the fragment of a Gnostic Gospel, P Oxy VIII. 1081[37 f.] (early iv/A.D.) ὁ τῶν ὅλ]ων δεσπότης ο[ὐκ ἐστὶ] π(ατή)ρ ἀλλὰ προπά[τωρ· ὁ γὰ]ρ π(ατή)ρ [ἀρ]χὴ ἐ[σ]τ[ιν τῶν μ]ελλόντων. See also *Cagnat* III. 103[2] Ῥοῦφος ἐὼν προπάτωρ τῆς ἰδίης γενεῆς, and P Parth I. 342 f. ἴλαθί μοι προπάτωρ προγενέστερε αὐτογένεθλε cited by Wünsch *AF.* p. 18).

In Vett. Val. p. 3[22] τούς τε τούτων προπάτορας ἤ καὶ κυρίους, the editor suggests that the former title is perhaps = "inventores."

προπέμπω,

(1) lit. "send before," P Ryl II. 78¹⁵ (A.D. 157) ἀπόδε]σμον ἐπιστολῶν προπεμφθέντα ὑπ' ἐμοῦ, "packet of letters previously sent by me," cf.³⁶, PSI I. 97⁹ (letter of recommendation—vi/A.D.) προπέμψαι αὐτὰς μετὰ πάσης τιμῆς, and from the inscrr. OGIS 544³² (ii/A.D.) προπέμψαντα [τὰ] παροδεύοντα (στρατεύματα), and Kaibel 30² εἴ σε τύχη προὔπεμψε καὶ ἡλικίας ἐπέβησεν. (2) "set forward," "convoy," on a journey, as in all its NT occurrences, P Flor II. 206² (iii/A.D.) τοῖς προπέμπουσι καμήλοις οὖσι τὸν ἀριθμὸν ιδ Πολύκαρπον καὶ Πρωτῦν παράσχες τὰς συνήθεις τροφάς, "to the camels to the number of 14 which form the convoy of Polycarpus and Protys supply the customary foods."

προπετής.

To the exx. which Field (Notes, p. 131) has collected from late Greek to illustrate this adj. = "rash," "headlong," as in Ac 19³⁶, we may add ἡ προπετὴς μοῖρα from the epitaph Kaibel 478⁴ (ii/A.D.). For a new literary reference for the subst., cf. the work on the Trojan War attributed to Dictys Cretensis, P Tebt II. 268¹⁷ (early iii/A.D.) ἡ σὴ προπέτεια.

προπορεύομαι,

"go before," very common in the LXX, but in the NT confined to Luke (1⁷⁶, Ac 7⁴⁰ LXX). occurs ter in the temple-account P Oxy VIII. 1144 (i/ii A.D.), e.g.⁹ παστοφόρο[ι]s προπορευομ[ένοις] (δραχμαὶ) η.

πρός

is almost entirely confined in the NT to the acc. (679 times), as against 1 instance c. gen. (Ac 27³⁴) and 7 c. dat. (Mk 5¹¹, Lk 19²⁷, Jn 18¹⁶, 20¹¹·¹²⁽ᵇⁱˢ⁾, Rev 1¹³): cf. Proleg. pp. 106, 63.

(1) With the gen. constr. in Ac l.c., which is literary, = "on the side of," cf. P Flor III. 340¹³ (iii/A.D.) ἐκ τοῦ πρὸς βορρᾶ μέρους τοῦ προκειμέν[ου] τόπου.

(2) For the dat. constr. = "close at," "at," cf. P Petr II. 42 (b)⁵ (mid. iii/B.C.) (= Witkowski², p. 21) εἰμὶ γὰρ πρὸς τῶι ἀποδημεῖν, P Flor III. 382²⁷ (A.D. 222–3) πρὸς τῇ διαλογῇ αὐτοῦ, and ib. I. 5⁸ (A.D. 244–5) εἰς μὲν πρὸς τῷ πυλῶνι. The phrase οἱ πρός τινι, qui aliqua in re versantur, is seen in P Tebt I. 5⁸⁵ (B.C. 118) ἐ]πὶ προσπείπτει τοὺς πρὸς ταῖς σιτολο(γίαις) καὶ ἀντιγρ(αφείαις) μ[ίζοσι μέ[τ]ροις [πα]ρὰ τὰ εὖσ⟨ταθμα⟩ . . χα(λκᾶ, "since it sometimes happens that the sitologi and antigrapheis use larger measures than the correct bronze measures" (Edd.), ib. 39¹⁸ (B.C. 115) τῶν δὲ πρὸς ταῖς γραμματείαις ἀγνοούντων τὴν γεγονυῖαν περὶ ἐ[μο]ῦ οἰκονομίαν, "but the scribes being ignorant of this transaction affecting me" (Edd.), BGU II. 455² (i/A.D.) πρὸς τῇ ἐπιμελείᾳ τῶν χρηματιστῶν, and ib. III. 915⁹ (ii/A.D.) ὁ πρὸς ταῖς χρείαις.

(3) c. acc. (a) of motion towards—P Par 49²⁹ (B.C. 161–0) (= UPZ i. p. 309) παρακαλέσας αὐτὸν ἀπόστειλον πρὸς ἐμέ, BGU I. 246¹⁶ (ii/iii A.D.) ἵνα ἀπενέκκω (l. ἀπενέγκω) αὐτὸν πρὸς Σεραπίωνα, P Oxy XIV. 1773⁸ (iii/A.D.) οὐχ εὗρον πῶς ἔλθω πρὸς ὑμᾶς, P Grenf I. 61⁵ (vi/A.D.) εὐχὰς καὶ δεήσ[ε]ις ἀναπέμπω πρὸς τὸν Θεόν μου, and with

reference to place PSI IV. 311²⁶ (iv/A.D.?) πρ]ὸς τὴν Λαυδίκιαν τῆς κοίλης Συρία[ς. Headlam (on Herodas VII. 123) holds that τὰ πρὸς τὴν θύραν in Mk 2² "is surely idiomatic (not vulgar as Moulton thinks) 'spots which commanded the door'": cf. Mt 3¹⁰, Lk 3⁹. For πρός, "with," as in Jn 1¹ᶠ, Heb 4¹³, cf. Epict. iv. 9. 13 πρὸς ὃν οὐδείς ἐστί σου πιθανώτερος (see Sharp Epict. p. 92). And for the possibility that the difficult πρός in Mk 6³, 9¹⁹, 14⁴⁹, Jn 1¹, 1 Jn 1², is to be explained as an Aramaism, see Rendel Harris Prologue to S. John's Gospel p. 8 f., and Burney Aramaic Origin of the Fourth Gospel p. 28 f.

(b) of time = "for" (a time) and no longer—BGU I. 113¹² (A.D. 143) βουλόμενος παρεπιδημεῖν πρὸς καιρόν (cf. Lk 8¹³), P Oxy I. 67¹⁴ (A.D. 338) πρὸς ὀλίγον ἰσχύει, "withstands but for a short time" (cf. Jas 4¹⁴), and P Flor III. 282⁸ (A.D. 520) πρὸς ὅλον χρόνον.

(c) of mental direction, friendly or otherwise—P Hib I. 53³ (B.C. 246) πειρῶ οὖν ἀσφαλῶς διεγγυᾶν ὡς πρὸς σὲ τοῦ λό[γ]ου ἐσομένου, "do you therefore endeavour to obtain good security, knowing that you will be held accountable" (Edd.) (cf. Heb 4¹³), P Par 46¹² (B.C. 152) (= UPZ i. p. 338) οὓς (sc. ὅρκους) συνθέμενοι πρὸς ἑαυτό(= ούς (cf. Lk 23¹²), ib. 48⁷ (B.C. 152) (= UPZ i. p. 340) περὶ το[ῦ] ἀνθρώπου τοῦ πρὸς σὲ τὴν ἀηδείαν ποιήσαντος (cf. 2 Cor 7⁴), P Tebt I. 59⁷ (B.C. 99) ἣν ἔχετε πρὸς ἡμᾶς ἄνωθεν πατρικὴν φιλίαν, "the hereditary friendship which you have for me of old" (Edd.), P Oxy XIV. 1680¹⁵ (iii/iv A.D.) ὑπονοοῦμαι ὅτι πάντως πάλιν τί ποτε ἔχει πρὸς σέ, "I suspect that he must have some further claim against you" (Edd.), P Amh II. 145⁹ (iv/v A.D.) τὸ γνωστὸν τῆς πρὸς ἀλ[λήλο]υς συνηθείας, "the knowledge of our intimacy with one another" (cf. Jn 6⁶²), and from the inscrr. JHS xix. (1899) No. 302 (Christian) ὃς δὲ [ἂν κακὴν] κείραν (l. χεῖρα) προσενένκῃ, ἔστε(= αι) αὐτῷ πρὸς θεόν.

(d) = "with reference to," "in view of"—P Hib I. 54¹⁴ (c. B.C. 245) χρεία γάρ ἐστι ταῖς γυναιξὶν πρὸς τὴν θυσίαν, "for he is wanted by the women for the sacrifice" (Edd.), P Oxy I 115¹⁰ (letter of consolation—ii/A.D.) (= Selections, p. 96) ὅμως οὐδὲν δύναταί τις πρὸς τὰ τοιαῦτα, "yet no one can do anything in the face of such things."

(e) = "at the rate of"—P Oxy II. 237ᵛⁱ·²⁵ (A.D. 186) τὴν οὐσίαν ταύτην πρὸς ὅλα (τάλαντα) η, "this property for a total sum of 8 talents." ib. I. 114⁴ (ii/iii A.D.) τὸν τόκον . . . πρὸς στατῆρα τῆς μνᾶς, "interest, at the rate of a stater per mina."

(f) = "according to"—P Amh II. 43¹⁰ (B.C. 173) μέτρωι δικαίωι τῶι πρὸς τὸ βασιλικὸν χαλκοῦν, "by just measure calculated by the royal bronze standard" (Edd.): cf. Lk 12⁴⁷, 1 Cor 12⁵.

(g) with the articular inf. denoting purpose (as in Mk 13²², 1 Th 2⁹: Lightfoot Notes, p. 131)—P Ryl II. 69¹⁶ (B.C. 34) ἀποδοῦναι τὰς προκειμένας κνή κου (ἀρτάβας) ιε, πρὸς τὸ μηθὲν ἡμῖν ἐκφορίων διαπεσεῖν, "to restore to us the aforesaid 15 artabae of cnecus, so that the rents suffer no loss" (Edd.), BGU I 226²² (A.D. 99) ὅταν ὁ κράτιστος ἡγεμὼν . . . τὸν τοῦ νομοῦ διαλογισμὸν ποιῆται πρὸς τὸ τυχῖν με τῆς ἀπὸ σοῦ βοηθείας, "with a view to my obtaining your assistance," P Oxy II. 237ᵛⁱ·³⁵ (A.D. 186) ὅπως φροντίσῃς ἀκόλουθα πρᾶξαι τοῖς π[ε]ρὶ το[ύ]του πρότερον γραφεῖσι ὑπὸ Λογγαίου Ῥούφο[υ] τοῦ διασημοτάτο[υ] πρὸς τὸ μὴ π[ε]ρὶ τῶν αὐτῶν πάλιν αὐτὸν ἐντυγχάνειν, "see that the matter is decided in accordance with the previous instructions of his excellency Longaeus Rufus, in order that Chaeremon may not send any more petitions on the same subject" (Edd.), *ib.* xiii. 41 ἵνα] δ' [ο]ῦν β[εβ]αία τε καὶ εἰς ἅπαν διαμένῃ τῶν διαστρωμάτων ἡ χρῆσ[ε]ις πρὸς τὸ μὴ πάλιν ἀπογραφῆς δεηθῆναι, παραγγέλλω . . . "therefore in order that the use of the abstracts may become secure and permanent, and prevent the necessity of another registration, I command . . ." (Edd.).

(*h*) as a periphrasis for the adverb (as in Jas 4⁵ πρὸς φθόνον) cf. Jos. *Antt.* XII. 398 (x. 3) πρὸς ἡδονὴν ἑκάστῳ καὶ χάριν.

(*i*) = "in addition." In P Oxy I. 68²⁴ (A.D. 131) ἀργυρίου ταλάντων ἓξ καὶ πρὸς ἐπὶ τῷ αὐτὸν ἀποδο⟨ῦ⟩ναι τοῖς τοῦ Σαραπίωνος δανισταῖς τὰ ὑπὸ αὐτοῦ ὀφειλόμενα, the editors translate "six talents of silver with the further stipulation that (Dionysius) should repay Sarapion's creditors the debts owed to them," but suggest in their note that καὶ πρός might perhaps be connected with ἕξ, "six talents and upwards."

As in the case of all the prepositions, the monographs of Kuhring, Rossberg, and Regard (see Abbreviations I. General) should be consulted.

προσάββατον,

"the day before the Sabbath," in NT only Mk 15⁴² where it is an explanation of παρασκευή for the benefit of non-Jewish readers. The word occurs in Judith 8⁶, and in the titles of PSS 91(92) אּ, 92(93) אּB.

προσαγορεύω.

For the meaning "designate," as in Heb 5¹⁰, cf. P Leid Uⁱⁱ ¹⁴ (B.C. 343) (= I. p. 124, *UPZ* i. p. 371) τὸν προσαγορευόμενον αἰγυπτιστεὶ Ὀνοῦρει, ἑλληνιστεὶ (*l.* ἑλληνιστὶ) δὲ Ἄρης: cf. *Syll* 930 (= ³705)⁵⁵ (B.C. 112–1) ἄνδρας καλοὺς κα[ὶ] ἀγαθοὺς καὶ φίλους παρὰ δήμου καλοῦ κἀγαθοῦ . . . προσαγορεῦσαι, and *ib.* 349 (= ³764)⁵ (B.C. 45).

The LXX usage "greet," "salute," is seen in epistolary formulae such as P Oxy III. 526² (ii/A.D.) Χαίροις, Καλόκαιρε, Κύριλλός σε προσαγορεύω, "hail, Calocaerus: I, Cyrillus, greet you," *ib.* VI. 928¹⁴ (ii/iii A.D.) τὰ παιδία παρ' ἐμοῦ καὶ Ἰσιδωριῶνος προσαγόρε[υ]ε, "greet the children from me and Isidorion," *ib.* VII 1070⁴⁶ (iii/A.D.) τοὺς ἡμῶν πάντας κατ' ὄνομα προσαγόρευε καὶ ἄσπασε (= αι), P Amh II. 145²² (iv/v A.D.) προσαγορεύω [τὴν] σὴν διάθεσιν καὶ τὰ φίλτατά σου τὰ [πάν]τα, "I greet your highness and all those dearest to you," and the early Christian letter P Heid 6²³ (iv/A.D.) (= *Selections,* p. 127) πολλὰ προσαγορεύ(ω) πάντε(= ας) τοὺς ἀδελφοὺς ἡμῶν ἐν κῶ. In P Lond 1912²⁷ (A.D. 41) Γερμανικὸς Καῖσαρ γνησιωτέραις ὑμᾶς φωναῖς προσαγορεύσας, Bell thinks there is a reference "to some definite speech or speeches delivered by Germanicus."

προσάγω

is used in the general sense of "bring" in such passages as PSI IV. 435¹³ (B.C. 258–7) ὃς ἐνεχείρησεν οἰκοδομεῖν Σαραπιεῖον . . . καὶ προσαγηγόχει (for form, see Mayser *Gr.* p. 338) λίθους, P Magd 27⁴ (B.C. 218) πλίνθον προσ[ά]γων καὶ θεμέλιον σκάπτων.

From this it is an easy step to the meaning "collect,"

"add": e.g. P Tebt I. 58²⁰ (B.C. 111) ὑποσχνούμενος (*l.* ὑπισχνούμενον) προσάξι (= ειν ἀπὸ παντὸς εἴδους (πυροῦ) ὓ, "undertaking to collect from every class 400 artabae of wheat more" (Edd.), P Oxy II. 267⁷ (A.D. 36) αἷς (δραχμαῖς) οὐδὲν τῶι καθόλου προσῆκται, "to which nothing at all has been added" (Edd.), and P Ryl II. 96⁷ (iii/A.D.) ᾧ προσάγω ὑπ ἐρ] ἐπιθέματος, "to which I add as a further charge" (Edd.).

The verb is common = "present," "introduce," as in P Ryl II. 75⁵ (judicial proceedings—late ii A.D.) προσαχθέντων Γλύκωνος Διονυσίου καὶ Ἀπολλωνίου Γλύκωνος, similarly ¹⁴,²³, P Tebt II 292²⁷ (A.D. 189–190) Κρονίων . . . νυνεὶ ἐν Ἀλεξανδρείᾳ τυγχάνων προσάξι (= ει) τῷ κρα(τίστῳ) ἀρχιερεῖ, "Cronion, who now happens to be in Alexandria, will bring them before his highness the high-priest" (Edd.), P Oxy I. 71ⁱ ³ (A.D. 303) τὴν ἱκ[ετ]ηρίαν προσάγω εὔελπις, "I present my supplication with full confidence," and from the inscr. *OGIS* 519¹² (*c.* A.D. 245) τήνδε τὴν ἱκετεί[αν ὑ]μεῖν προσάγομεν: cf. Ac 16²⁰, 1 Pet 3¹⁸.

For the intrans. use of προσάγω = "approach," "draw near," as in Ac 27²⁷ אּA προσάγειν τινὰ αὐτοῖς χώραν, "that some land was drawing near to them," cf. Plut. *Cic.* v. 2 οὐκ ἠρέμα τῷ πρωτείῳ προσῆγεν, "he did not advance slowly to the primacy."

προσαγωγή.

Mahaffy in P Petr III. p. 262 says that προσαγωγή sometimes means "a landing-stage." This would agree with Pallis on Rom 5², who thinks that χάριν is there pictured as a haven, and that προσαγωγήν means "approach" in a nautical sense. In P Petr III. 112 (*f*) verso¹ⁱ ⁴ (p. 290) εἰς τομὴν καὶ προσαγωγὴν χάλικος, the word must mean "carting." In P Tebt I. 20⁶ (B.C. 113) ἐπὶ τῶν προσαγωγῶν refers to "additions" to the revenue, and in *ib.* 72¹¹⁹ (B.C. 114–3) τῆς προσαγωγῆς γεγονυίας to "increase" of rent. The gen. plur. προσαγωγίδων in P Petr III. 107(*a*)² and (*d*)¹ (iii/B.C.) is supposed by Mahaffy to be used as an adj. descriptive of ships, or possibly as connected with the meaning "landing-stages."

προσαιτέω,

"ask in addition," "ask besides," is seen in PSI IV. 349⁶ (B.C. 254–3) ἀπεστάλκαμεν . . . προσαιτοῦντες πρὸς τοῖς ξ με(τρηταῖς) τοῖς ἐνοφειλομένοις ἄλλους Σ.

προσαναβαίνω.

For the AV, RV rendering "go up higher" for προσανάβηθι in Lk 14¹⁰, Field (*Notes,* p. 66 f.) prefers "come up higher," in order to give προσ- its full force. For this meaning of approach to where the host is sitting cf. the use of the single comp⁴. ἀναβαίνω in Prov 25⁷, and the use of προσβαίνω in such passages as P Oxy VII. 1028¹¹ (A.D. 86) τοὺς προσβαίνοντ(ας) εἰς τοὺς (τεσσαρεσκαιδεκαετεῖς), "those approaching the age of 14," P Grenf II. 46⁵ (A.D. 141) Ἀνουβᾶ προσβ(άντος) εἰς ιδ (ἔτος) τῷ ἐνεστῶτι ε (ἔτει) Ἀντωνίνου.

προσαναλίσκω,

"spend in addition" (Lk 8⁴³ אּ A), is found in *Syll* 233 (= ³497)⁷ (after B.C. 229) καλῶς τὴν ἀγωνοθεσ[ίαν ἐκτελέσας] προσανήλωσεν οὐκ ὀλίγα χρήματα.

προσαναπληρόω.

For this double compd. = "fill up by adding" (2 Cor 9¹², 11⁹), cf. Philo *De praem.* 103 (ed. Cohn) τὴν ἐκείνων ἔνδειαν προσαναπληρούντων.

προσανατίθημι.

in mid. = "betake oneself to," "confer or communicate with," for the purpose of obtaining (Gal 1¹⁶) or giving (Gal 2⁶) instruction. In support of the former usage commentators refer to the employment of the verb for consulting sooth-sayers and the like, e.g. Diod. Sic. xvii. 116 τοῖς μάντεσι προσαναθέμενος περὶ τοῦ σημείου. In a report on taxation, P Tebt I. 99⁵ (c. B.C. 148) κα]ὶ προσανατιθέμεθα [τοῦ] ἀναφερομέν[ου ὑ]πὸ Παγκ[ρ]άτου ἀνειλῆφθαι κλῆρου, the reference is apparently to "setting forth in addition." The word is fully discussed by Zahn *Gal.* p. 64 f. and Burton *Gal.* p. 89 ff.

προσανέχω.

"rise up towards," is read in Ac 27²⁷ only in B³: cf. *s.vv.* προσάγω and προσαχέω.

προσαχέω.

"resound." For this Doric form (for προσηχέω) in Ac 27²⁷ B*, see Moulton *Gr.* ii. p. 71, where it is suggested that the word may have been appropriated as a kind of *term. tech.* from its use "by sailors from Crete, Cyprus, Lesbos, Corinth, or some other maritime country outside the Ionic-Attic area."

προσδαπανάω.

"spend in addition," occurs only in Lk 10³⁵ in Biblical Greek : cf. *Syll* 640 (= ³661)¹⁰ (B.C. 165–4) προσδαπανήσας εἰς ταῦτα πάντα οὐκ ὀλίγα (see *s.v.* ὀλίγος) ἐκ τῶν ἰδίων, and *Priene* 118¹¹ (i/B.C.) προσεδαπάνησεν μετὰ τῶν συναγ[ωνο]θετῶν δραχμάς. . . .

προσδέομαι.

In support of the view that in Ac 17²⁵ προσδέομαι means "need *in addition*," as against the AV, RV rendering "need," the following exx. of the verb may be cited : – P Petr II. 37ᵇ ¹ᵃ (iii/B.C.) (= p. [119]) ὁ γὰρ καιρὸς οὐδεμιᾶς ὑπερβολῆς προσδεῖται, "for the time allows of no *further* delay," P Lille I. 5¹³ (B.C. 260–59) διὰ τὸ προσδεῖσθαι μέρος τι τῆς γῆς αὐτοῦ πωολογίας, "because a part of his land has still need of poologia," P Flor I. 1⁶ (A.D. 153) μὴ προσδεομένοις ἀνανεώσεως, "needing no renewal," and *ib.* 56¹⁸ (A.D. 234) καὶ ἐν οἷς ἄλλοις αὐτοῦ προσδ[έομ]αι περὶ τούτων. Cf. P Ryl II. 155¹⁶ (A.D. 138–161) κα]ὶ μὴ προσδεομένη{ς} ἑτέρου [τινὸς αὐτῇ συναπογραφομένο]υ, "having no need of the concurrence of any other person" (Edd.), P Oxy IX. 1200³⁵ (A.D. 266) οὐ προσδεόμενος ἑτέρας μου εὐδοκήσεως ἢ μεταλήμψεως, "without requiring any further consent or concurrence from me" (Ed.). See also Field *Notes*, p. 127 f.

In other passages the force of προσ–, though not so obvious, is not excluded, e.g. P Par 63¹⁵⁴ (B.C. 154) (= P Petr III. p. 30) τῶν προσδεομένων κωμῶν, "the needy villages," i.e. "villages needing more than they have," P Tebt I. 59⁸ (B.C. 99) ἐν οἷς ἐὰν προσδεηθέ μου ἐπιτάσσοντές μοι προ-θυμότερον, "so, whatever you may require, do not hesitate to command my services" (Edd.), and P Oxy IV. 743³³ (B.C. 2) ἐν οἷς ἐὰν σοῦ προσδεῆται συνπροσγενέσθαι αὐτῶι, "whatever service he may require from you, stand by him" (Edd.). The subst. προσδέησις in *Epicurea* p. 28⁵ (ed. Usener) ἐν ἀσθενείᾳ καὶ φόβῳ καὶ προσδεήσει τῶν πλησίον ταῦτα γίνεται has the meaning "need," "want," the προσ– being apparently otiose.

προσδέχομαι.

For προσδέχομαι, "receive," "welcome," as in Lk 15², Rom 16², cf. *Syll* 236⁶ (= ³543³¹) (B.C. 214) οἳ καὶ τοὺς οἰκέτας ὅταν ἐλευθερώσωσιν προσδεχόμενοι εἰς τὸ πολίτευμα, and *Syll*³ 694²¹ (B.C. 129) ἀποδεξ[άμενος] τὴν εὔνοιαν προσ-[δέδεκ]ται τὸν δῆμ[ον] ἡμῶν πρός τε τὴν φ[ιλίαν] καὶ συμμα[χίαν.

The meaning "wait for" may be illustrated from P Oxy II. 295⁷ (c. A.D. 35) προσδέχου ἰς τὸν ἐνιαυτὸν Λουκία, "let Lucia wait until the year": cf. the illit. *Ostr* 1089⁵ (B.C. 135–4) προστέχομαι ἃς δέτωκας Ῥαδάνῳ (δραχμὰς) ῡῡ, "I am waiting for the 450 dr. you have given to Radanus," P Hib I. 58⁸ (B.C. 244) τοῦτο δέ σοι προσδέξομαι is rendered by the editors "and for this sum I will be responsible (?) to you" with reference to a proposed loan : they compare P Petr III. 64(b)⁶⁶ (ἐξεδέξατο) and 80(b)¹ (προσεδέξατο). In P Frankf 1³⁶, ³⁹ (B.C. 214–213) προσδέχομαι is intrans. The double compd. προσεισδέχομαι occurs *bis* in P Goodsp Cairo 7⁸, ¹³ (B.C. 119–118).

προσδοκάω.

"expect": cf. P Flor II. 127¹ (A.D. 256) σὺν θεῷ φάναι προσδόκα ἡμᾶς τῇ κ̄γ̄, P Oxy VIII. 1158⁴ (iii/A.D.) θα<μὰ> θῆς (*l.* τῆς) ἡμέρας προσδοκῶμέν σαι ἐλ[θεῖ]ν πρὸς ἡμᾶς, "many times in the day we expect you to come to us" (Ed.), and *Preisigke* 4317²⁴ (c. A.D. 200) προσδοκῶ σοι γεγύμνωμαι καὶ ὕβρισμαι <μαις> παρὰ πάντων τῶν συμπολιτῶν. In P Oxy VII. 1021⁶ (A.D. 54), a notification of the accession of Nero, the Emperor is described as ὁ δὲ τῆς οἰκουμένης καὶ προσδοκηθεὶς καὶ ἐλπισθείς, "the hope and expectation of the world": cf. the Christian P Lond 1028¹⁵ (mid. iv/A.D.) <ἢ> διὰ τοῦ κυρίου ἡμῶ(ν) Χρηστοῦ διὰ τῶν ὑμῶν εὐχῶν προσδοκο(= ω)μένη ἐλπίς. A unique constr. is found in Diog. Oenoand. (ed. William) p. 59⁷ μετὰ δὴ τοιούτων ἡμᾶς ἀγαθῶν προσδόκα, μῆτερ, χαίροντας αἰεί.

προσδοκία.

"expectation": P Tebt I. 24⁴¹ (B.C. 117) οὐκ ὀλίγω[ν] ἐν προσδοκίαι ὄντων, "there was a general expectation" (Edd.). A report from the Jewish War in the time of Trajan, *Chrest.* I. 16¹, begins with the statement that the last hope against the unholy Jews lay in the rising of the villagers—μία ἦν ἐλπὶς καὶ λοιπὴ προσδοκία ἡ τῶν ἀπὸ τοῦ νομοῦ ἡμῶν ἀθρόων κωμ[η]τῶν [πρὸ]ς τοὺς ἀνοσίους Ἰο[υ]δαίους [. .]. μη. The same document shows the adj. προσδόκιμος. In a deed of divorce, P Flor I. 93¹³ (A.D. 569), the couple announce that παρὰ προσδοκίαν, "contrary to expectation," their married life had suffered ἐκ σκαιοῦ πονηροῦ δαίμονος, "at the hands of a mischievous evil demon." In *Preisigke* 2011 Προσδοκία occurs as a proper name.

προσεάω.

We chronicle this verb from Ac 27⁷, where Ramsay renders "as the wind did not permit our straight course onwards," if only for the sake of drawing attention to the fact that it is one of the few words left in the NT of which Grimm's dictum holds good, "Not found elsewhere."

προσεργάζομαι.

"gain besides" by working, in the NT only in Lk 19¹⁶. For the double compd. **προσεξεργάζομαι**, see *Syll* 538 (= ³970)²¹ (B.C. 288) with reference to the pillars of a temple—**προσεξεργασαμένους σφόνδυλον ἑκάστωι τῶι κίονι**.

προσέρχομαι.

The semi-technical use of this verb of the approach of the worshipper to God is frequent in the LXX, and is found *septies* in Heb, twice (10¹· ²²) without an obj. : cf. P Giss I. 20²¹ (beg. ii/A.D.) (= *Chrest.* I. p. *124*) ἀξιώσεις οὖν δίστιχον αὐτῶι γραφῆναι, ἵνα ἀξίως σου καὶ τῶν θεῶν ἀόκνως προσέλθῃ, of worship to be performed at a private shrine of the Dioscuri. See also Dio Cassius lvi. 9 τοῖς θεοῖς προσερχώμεθα. The verb is similarly used of approach to a court in P Oxy VIII. 1119⁸ (A.D. 254) προσήλθομεν τῇ κρατίστῃ βουλῇ. Other exx. of προσέρχομαι c. dat. are P Oxy I. 76²² (A.D. 179) οὐκ οὖσα δὲ προαιρέσεως προσέρχεσθαι τῇ τούτου κληρονομίᾳ, "as I have no intention of entering on my inheritance" (Edd.) (cf. *adire hereditatem*, and P Ryl II. 234⁸ (ii/A.D.) μ[ετ' ὀ]λίγον δέ μου προσελθόντος τῷ γ[ραμ]ματεῖ. The absol. use is seen in P Oxy I. 40⁴ (ii/iii A.D.) προσελθ[ό]ντ[ος Ψάσνι]ος καὶ εἰπόντος, "Psasnis appeared and said."

No adequate parallel has yet been found to the meaning "consent to" required by the context in 1 Tim 6³: Field (*Notes*, p. 211) appears to favour Bentley's conjecture προσέχει for προσέρχεται, but see Parry *ad l.* A proverbial phrase is found in a new Comic Fragment (P Berol 9941¹⁴· ¹⁵) —ὄνος προσέρχεται (of one coming to a vacant seat at a banquet).

προσευχή.

For a pagan instance of **προσευχή** in the general sense of "prayer," "supplication," we can now cite the interesting letter, BGU IV. 1080⁴ (iii/A.D.) (= *Chrest.* I. p. *564*), in which a father congratulates his son on his marriage κατὰ τὰς κοινὰς ἡμῶν εὐχὰς καὶ προσευχάς.

Exx. of **προσευχή** as a Jewish "place of prayer," as in Ac 16¹³ (cf. 3 Macc 7²⁰), are readily forthcoming from both the papyri and the inscrr. Thus as early as B.C. 217 we have a petition from a village of the Fayûm, P Magd 35 (= *Chrest.* I. p. *80*), regarding a garment deposited⁵ ἐν τῆι προσευχῆι τῶν Ἰουδαίων, to await a judicial decision as to the rightful owner. And in P Tebt I. 86¹⁸ (late ii/B.C.) we read of a προσευχή Ἰουδαίων with a Διὸς παράδεισος) near at hand. From Roman times comes a series of accounts from the waterworks of the metropolis (? Hermopolis), P Lond 1177³⁷ (A.D. 113) (= III. p. 183) ἀρχόντων Ἰ[ου]δαίων προσευχῆς Θηβαίων μηνιαίω(ν) (δραχμῶν) ρκη, "the rulers of the *proseucha* of the Theban Jews 128 drachmae a month." The same document mentions ⁶⁰ a εὐχεῖον rated

at the same amount as the **προσευχή**, viz. 768 drachmae ; but there is nothing to determine how the two are related (cf. Moulton *Exp T* xix. p. 41).

Amongst the inscrr. a special interest is attached to the iii/B.C. inscr. cited *s.v.* πλάξ, *OGIS* 129⁹ (= *Chrest.* I. p. 79), where the right of asylum is granted to a Jewish *proseucha*—τὴν προσευχὴν ἄσυλον. See further *ib.* 726⁷ (B.C. 246–221) ὑπὲρ βασιλέως Πτολεμαίου καὶ βασιλίσσης Βερενίκης ἀδελφῆς καὶ γυναικὸς καὶ τῶν τέκνων τὴν προσευχὴν οἱ Ἰουδαῖοι, *ib.* 96⁶ (B.C. 205–181) οἱ ἐν Ἀθρίβει Ἰουδαῖοι τὴν προσευχὴν Θεῶ Ὑψίστῳ, and of a later date *ib.* 101⁶ Ἑρμίας καὶ Φιλω)τέρα ἡ γυνὴ καὶ τὰ παιδία τήνδε ἐξέδραν τῇ προσευχῇ(ι). Mention may also be made of a Jewish deed of manumission, *Latyschev* II. 52, where a Jewess announces the freedom bestowed on a slave ⁶ ἐπὶ τῆς [προ]σευχῆς, "in the *proseucha*," i.e. in the presence of the congregation. Noteworthy too are the further words of the same inscr. ¹³ χωρὶς ἰς τ[ὴ]ν προσ[ευχὴν θωπείας τε καὶ προσκα[ρτερ]ήσεως. "besides reverence and constancy towards the place of prayer," if only because of the association of προσευχή and προσκαρτέρησις (cf. Ac 1¹⁴ *al.*): see Schürer *Geschichte*³ iii. p. 53, Deissmann *LAE* p. 100 n⁴. From the above instances it will be seen that προσευχή is used = συναγωγή, but as Curtius (*Exp* VII. iv. p. 454) remarks "every προσευχή is not therefore a synagogue." Additional exx. will be found in Strack's paper on Ptolemaic inscrr. in *Archiv* ii. p. 537 ff., where he notes five Jewish "places of prayer" in Upper Egypt, and many in Lower.

For προσευχή, as a place of *heathen* worship, we may recall *Latyschev* I. 98⁷ (= *CIG* II. 2070) ἄρχ[οντες] τὴν προσευχὴν ἐ[πε]σκεύασαν τὴ ἑαυ[τ]ῶν προνοίᾳ στεγάσα[ντες] ἀπὸ τοῦ θεοῦ μέχρι... Boeckh (*CIG al l.*) defines προσευχήν as "sacellum adorando deo destinatum," the particular god being uncertain, but it should be noted that Schürer (*Geschichte*³, ii. p. 444) thinks that Jewish influence is possible in this case.

προσεύχομαι.

An interesting ex. of this verb, which is always used of prayer to the gods or to God, is afforded by P Cairo Zen 59034 (B.C. 257). A certain Zoilos had been ordered by the god Sarapis to inform a high State official Apollonios that a temple should be erected to him. Zoilos neglected the charge and in consequence was thrown into a serious illness —³ τ. εἰς ἀρρωσ[τ]ία[ν] μ[ε πε]ριέβαλεν μεγάλην ὥστε καὶ κινδυνεῦσαί [με. But on praying to the god and promising to do his bidding he was healed—¹⁹ᵗᵗ προσευξάμενος δ[ὲ] αὐ[τῶι, ἐ]ά[μ με ὑγιάσηι, διότι ὑπομενῶ τὴν λητου ργίαν καὶ ποιή[σει]ν τὸ ὑφ' αὐτοῦ προστασσόμενον (supply ὑγιάσθην). [An important commentary on the whole letter is supplied by Deissmann *Exp.* VIII. xxiv. p. 426 ff.]. Cf. *Preisigke* 3740 (i A.D.) Ἄττηος προσεύχεται τοῖς <ἐν> Ἀβύτῳ<ν> θεοῖς, ἵνα ὑγιαίνῃ. See also *s.v.* εὔχομαι.

προσέχω.

is used absol. = "attend to," "pay attention to" in P Magd 22⁹ (B.C. 221) ὁ δὲ οὐ προσέσχεν, and c. gen. in *ib.* 3 *recto*⁷ (B.C. 221) οὐ προσέσχηκεν ἡμῶν : cf. also P Par 45⁷ (B.C. 152) (= *UPZ* i. p. 329) προσέχων μὴ εὕρῃ τι κατὰ σοῦ ἱπῖν, "while I am taking heed lest he should find anything to say against you" : cf. Lk 21³⁴, Heb 2¹.

A good parallel to 1 Tim 4[13] is afforded by P Oxy III. 531[11] (ii/A.D.), where a father writes to his son τοῖς βιβλίοις σου αὐτὸ μόνον πρόσεχ[ε] φιλολογῶν, "give your undivided attention to your books, devoting yourself to learning" (Edd.) : cf. P Petr II. 20[ii. 1] (B.C. 252) μὴ προσεσχηκέναι τῆι . ἐπιστολῆι "has not attended to the letter" (cf. Ac 8[6]), P Tebt II. 410[4] (A.D. 16) Σωτηρίχω[ι] τῶι λάξωι . . [.] πρόσεχε, "give heed to Soterichus the stonemason," P Oxy VI. 930[11] (ii/iii A.D.) ἡμερίμνουν γὰρ περὶ αὐτοῦ εἰδυῖα ὅτι κατὰ δύν[α]μιν μέλλει σοι προσέχειν, "for I had no anxiety about him, knowing that he intended to look after you to the best of his ability" (Edd.), ib. XIV. 1682[12] (iv/A.D.) τὸ τέκνον σου τοῖς ἔργοις ἑαυτοῦ προσεχέτω. See also P Tor I. 1[vii. 35] (B.C. 117-116) μὴ προσεκτέον αὐτῶι παρ' ἕκαστα περισπᾶν τοὺς περὶ τὸν Ὧρον.

For the subst. προσοχή, as in Sap 6[18], cf. P Par 63[ii] (B.C. 164) (= P Petr III. p. 20) μετὰ τῆς ἐνδεχομένης προσοχῆς, "with fitting care," and P Tebt I. 27[75] (cited s.v. ἐνθυμέομαι.

προσηλόω,

"nail to" (Col 2[14] : cf. 3 Macc 4[9]) : Syll 588[200] (c. B.C. 180) ἄλλα χρυσᾶ παντοδαπά . . . . . προσ[η]λωμένα, ib. 349 (= [3]704)[6] (c. B.C. 45) ταῦτα ἐν δέλτωι χαλκῆι γεγραμμένα προσηλῶσαι ἵνα ἐξῆι, and ib. 366 (= [3]709)[26] (A.D. 38) τό τε ἐργαστήριον αὐτοῦ σανιδίοι[s] προσηλοῦσθαι. Cf. P Tebt II. 332[15] (A.D. 176) τὰς θύρ[α]s ἐξηλῶσαν[τ]ες, "extracting the nails from the doors."

προσήλυτος,

"a proselyte," lit. "one that has come to" Judaism from some Gentile religion, occurs quater in the NT, but is not found in classical literature, unless in the Scholium on Apoll. Rhod. i. 834 καθάπερ μετοίκους διατρίβειν καὶ προσηλύτους (cited by Hort 1 Pet. p. 154). A Cyrenaic inscr., Preisigke 1742, records some interesting names—Ἰωσῆς Κρίσπου . . . Λύκα Γαΐου . . Σάρρα προσήλυτος.

πρόσκαιρος,

which occurs first in 4 Macc 15[2. 8. 23], is used in the NT = "for a season," "transitory" (2 Cor 4[18]). The word is found in an edict of Caracalla, P Giss I. 40[ii. 26] (A.D. 215) (= Chrest. I. p. 39) πρ]αγματείας προ[σ]καίρου, with the meaning "in season," "opportune" : cf. OGIS 669[15] (i/A.D.) τὴν πρόσκαιρόν τινος ἀδικίαν μειμησάμενος, where the editor defines it as "temporis cuiusdam rationibus accommodatam," and Syll 737 (= [3]1109)[44] (A.D. 178) εἴ τις πρόσκαιρος ἑορτὴ τοῦ θεοῦ, with reference to a feast which took place on a special occasion. See also Pelagia-Legenden p. 12[26] ἐγὼ μὲν ἠλευθέρωσα ὑμᾶς ἀπὸ τῆς προσκαίρου δουλείας.

προσκαλέω.

For the mid. "call (someone) to myself," which alone is found in the NT (Mt 10[1] al.), cf. P Amh II. 35[22] (B.C. 132) προσκαλεσάμενος τὸν Παλᾶσιν, P Fay 12[3?] (c. B.C. 103) προσκαλεσάμενοι τόν τε Διοκλῆν καὶ Ἀμμώνι[ο]ν, Syll 177 (= [3]344)[42] (c. B.C. 303) ἐξ[έστω τὸν ἀποδημοῦντα πρ]οσκαλεῖσθαι ἀπὸ τοῦ ἀρχείου καὶ ἀπὸ τῆς οἰκίας, and see Proleg. p. 157. The pass. occurs in P Tebt I. 58[5] (B.C. 111) οὐδαμῶς προσκεκλήμεθα, "we have not yet been summoned."

προσκαρτερέω.

For προσκαρτερέω, "continue steadfastly" in a certain course of action, as in Ac 6[4], Rom 12[12], cf. the oath of a strategus on taking office, P Oxy I. 82[4] (iii/A.D.) προσκαρτερῶν τῇ στρατηγίᾳ ἀδιαλίπτως εἰς τὸ ἐν μηδενὶ μεμφθῆναι. Similarly P Lond 904[27] (A.D. 104) (= III. p. 125, Selections, p. 73), an order to certain persons to return home, in order that they may carry out the census and τῇ προσ[ηκού]σῃ αὐτοῖς γεωργίᾳ προσκαρτερήσω[σιν, "and continue steadfastly in the husbandry that belongs to them," and P Amh II. 65[3] (early ii/A.D.) a petition of two brothers, who had been chosen as cultivators of the royal domains, that one of them should be released ἵνα δυνηθῶμεν καὶ τῇ ἑαυτῶν γεωργίᾳ προσκαρτερεῖν, "in order that we may be able to attend to our own cultivation as well" (Edd.). Other exx. c. dat. rei are P Oxy III. 530[9] (ii/A.D.) ἐπὶ μάτη[ν] δὲ τῶι τοῦ Παυσιρίωνος τοσοῦτον χρόνον προσκαρτερ[ῶ, "I have been so long engaged with Pausirion's business to no purpose," Preisigke 4284[15] (A.D. 207) ταῖς ἐπιβα[λ]λούσαις ἡμε[ῖν] χρείαις προσκαρτερεῖν, and Vett. Val. 220[22] οὐ προσκαρτεροῦσι δὲ ἐλπίδι.

The verb is common = "attend" a court, e.g. P Oxy II. 261[12] (A.D. 55) οὐ δυναμένη προσκαρτερῆσαι τῷ κριτηρίῳ διὰ γυναικείαν ἀσθένειαν, ib. 260[14] (A.D. 59) προσκαρτερήσειν μέχρι οὗ ἂ ἔχωμεν προς ἑαυτοὺς ἐγ[β]ιβασθῆι, "remain until our suit is decided" (Edd.), and P Hamb I. 4[7] (A.D. 87) προσκαρτερήσι(= ει)ν τῷ ἱερωτάτῳ τοῦ κρατίστου ἡγεμόνος . . . βήματι (see the editor's note).

For the verb c. dat. pers. cf. P Giss I. 79[ii. 9] (c. A.D. 117) Ἐπαφρόδειτος ἕως τούτου οὐδὲν ἀμελέστερον ποιεῖ, ἀλλὰ προσκαρτερεῖ ἡμῖν καὶ πᾶσι τοῖς πράγμασι σου, P Lond 196[3] (c. A.D. 138-161) (= II. p. 153) προσ[κ]αρτερεῖν τῷ Νεοκύδει, and P Oxy XIV. 1764[4] (iii/A.D.) πολ[λ]αὶ ἡμέραι (nom. pend.) προσκαρτεροῦμεν Φιλέᾳ τῷ μοσχομαγ[ε]ίρῳ, "for many days we have been waiting for Phileas the butcher."

The verb is used absolutely in PSI VI. 598[7] (iii/B.C.) προσκαρτέρησον οὖν ἕως ἂν Ἐτέαρχος παραγένηται.

προσκαρτέρησις.

The only reference for this subst. in LS[8] is Eph 6[18], and Thayer includes it in his "Biblical" list. Two other exx. can, however, now be quoted from two deeds of manumission from Kertch (Panticapaeum) on the Black Sea. The earlier of these, Latyschev II. 53[13ff.] (A.D. 81), runs—χωρὶς ἰς τ[ὴ]ν προ[σ]ευχὴν θωπείας τε καὶ προσκα[ρτερ]ήσεως, "besides reverence and constancy towards the place of prayer" : see Deissmann LAE p. 100 f., and, independently, Hicks JTS x. p. 571 f.

προσκεφάλαιον,

"pillow," "cushion" (Mk 4[38] : cf. P Eleph 5[6] (B.C. 284-3) στρῶμα α̅, προσκεφάλαια α̅, P Oxy X. 1277[23] (A.D. 255) πέπρακα τὸ τρίκλινον καὶ τὰ προσκεφάλαια, "I have sold the couch and the cushions." In the Κολακεία of Theophrastus p. 40[32 f.] (ed. Jebb), the flatterer is represented as τοῦ παιδὸς ἐν τῷ θεάτρῳ ἀφελόμενος τὰ προσκεφάλαια αὐτὸς ὑποστρῶσαι, "taking the cushions from the slave in the theatre, and spreading them on the seat with his own hands."

προσκληρόω.

In Ac 17[4], the only occurrence of this verb in the NT, προσεκληρώθησαν is best understood with a pass. meaning answering to its pass. form, "were allotted to": cf. OGIS 257[5] (B.C. 109) Σελευκεῖς τοὺς ἐν Πιερίαι τῆς ἱερᾶς καὶ ἀσύλου [ἐξ ἀρχῆς] μὲν τῷ πατρὶ ἡμῶν προσκληρωθέντας. with Dittenberger's note. See also P Par 63[viii. 18] (B.C. 164) ἔδει μὲν οὖν δημοσίᾳ παιδήᾳ προσκεκληρωμένον καὶ μεμνημένον τῆς ἐκ παιδὸς πρός τε τὸν ἡμέτερον πατέρα κτλ.

πρόσκλησις.

For this word = "judicial summons," "invitation," which is read in 1 Tim 5[21] AD al., we may cite BGU IV. 1131[54] (B.C. 13) μὴ πρ[οσφέρειν] πρόσκλη[σιν) ἢ διαστολ(ήν). See s.v. πρόσκλισις.

προσκλίνω,

"incline towards," "attach myself," is found in the NT only in Ac 5[36] (cf. 2 Macc 14[24]), where Blass ad l. notes that "apparet de secta magis agi quam de seditione": cf. Clem. R. 47 προσεκλίθητε γὰρ ἀποστόλοις μεμαρτυρημένοις ("attested"), and the intrans. use of the verb in Polyb. iv. 51. 5.

πρόσκλισις.

Like its verb, πρόσκλισις is a NT ἅπ. εἰρ., 1 Tim 5[21], where it has the meaning of "partiality." It is found ter in Clem. R. (21, 47, 50).

προσκολλάω,

"stick to," "cleave to," is used metaphorically, as in Eph 5[31] (cf. Mk 10[7] D) quater in a vi/A.D. Will, P Oxy XVI. 1901, in which a man makes certain dispositions with regard to the wife who had been "joined" to him, e.g. [36] τὴν πρ]οσκολληθεῖσάν [μοι γυναῖκα. For the subst. προσκόλλησις see P Lond 1177[306] (A.D. 113) (= III. p. 189). Cf. s.v. κολλάω.

προσκόπτω.

The metaph. use of this word in the NT "stumble at," "take offence at," as in 1 Pet 2[8], may be illustrated by M. Anton. vi. 20, x. 30. The verb is found in Syll[3] 985[41] (i/A.D.), unfortunately in a broken context. For the adj. προσκοπτικός see Vett. Val. pp. 05[24], 68[22], 212[21].

προσκυνέω,

"do obeisance to," "worship," used generally of a god, as P Flor III. 332[11] (i/iA.D.) καὶ οὔ[τε ἐ]λουσάμην [οὔ]τε προσεκύνησα θεοὺς φοβουμένη σου τὸ μετέωρον. In Ptolemaic inscrr. the verb is construed with the acc., never the dat., as often in the NT (see Proleg., p. 64), e.g. OGIS 184[5] (i/B.C.) προσκεκύνηκα τὴν μεγίστην θεὰν κυρίαν Σώτειραν Ἶσιν.

P Giss I. 11[13] (A.D. 118) (= Chrest. I. p. 525) ἐπ<ε>ὶ ἐγὼ οὐ πάρειμι προσκυνῆσαί σε τὸν τιμιώτατον, ib. 17[11] (a slave to her master—time of Hadrian) (= Chrest. I. p. 566) ὥφελον εἰ ἐδυνάμεθα πέτασθαι καὶ ἐλθεῖν καὶ προσκυνῆσαί σε, BGU II. 423[15] (ii/A.D.) (= Selections, p. 91) ἵνα σου προσκυνήσω τὴν χῖραν, and P Tebt II. 286[22] (A.D. 121–

13[8] προσκυνεῖ[ν] ὀφείλοντες τὰς ἀναγνω[σ]θείσας τοῦ θεοῦ Τ[ρ]αιανοῦ . . . ἀποφ[ά]σεις, "as we are bound to respect the rescripts of the deified Trajan" (Edd.) are exx. of προσκυνέω with an object other than a god, though the last instance falls little short.

Often the verb is without object. Thus P Par 49[22] (before B.C. 161 or 160) (= UPZ i. p. 309) ἐ[ὰ]ν ἀναβῶ κἀγὼ προσκυνῆσαι—a very close parallel to Ac 24[11]: Syll[3] 807 (= [3] 1173)[2] (ii/A.D.) ἐχρημάτισεν (sc. Asclepius) ἐλθεῖν ἐπ[ὶ τὸ] ἱερὸν βῆμα καὶ προσκυνῆσαι: P Tebt II. 416[7] (iii/A.D.) ἐγενάμην εἰς Ἀλεξάνδριαν προσ[κ]υνῆσαι, "I came to Alexandria to pray" (Edd.). In MGr the meaning is weakened into "honour," "offer respects": see Thumb Handb. p. 352.

The subst. προσκύνημα, not in the NT, is used in innumerable pagan letters in the formula τὸ προσκύνημά σου ποιῶ παρὰ (τῷ δεῖνι) θεῷ and the like, e.g. BGU III. 846[2] (ii/A.D.) (= Selections, p. 93) τὸ προσκύνημά σου [ποι]ῶ κατ' αἰκάστην ἡμαίραν παρὰ τῷ κυρίῳ [Σερ]άπειδι: cf. P Oxy III. 528[5] (ii/A.D.) τὸ προσκύνημά σου πυῶ παρὰ τῇ σε φιλούσῃ Θοήρι, "I perform the act of veneration on your behalf to Thoeris who loves you" (Edd.). For a possible ex. of προσκύνημα ποιέω occurring in a Christian letter, see ib. XIV. 1775[2] (iv/A.D.) τὸ προσκύνημά σου ποιῶ καθ' ἑκάστην ἡμέραν παρὰ τῷ δεσπότῃ θεῷ ὅπως ὁλόκληρόν σε ἀπολάβω: see Ghedini Lettere, p. 254 f.

Προσκύνησις is found in the late P Oxy I. 128 verso[13] (vi/vii A.D.) ἡγείσθω τῆς ἐπιστο[λῆς ἡ ἐποφειλομένη κατὰ χρέος προσκύνησις τῇ ὑμετέρᾳ ἐνδοξότητι, "in the forefront of this letter we would place our due and fitting obeisance to your excellency" (Edd.).

προσκυνητής,

"a worshipper." For this word in Jn 4[23], Deissmann (LAE, p. 99) following Cremer (Addenda p. 1129) cites from pre-Christian Greek an inscr. from Apamea in Syria (Waddington 3,2720a) containing a decree drawn up in the interests of "the worshippers that come up"—τοῖς ἀνιοῦσι (ἀνιοῦσι, Cremer) προσκυνηταῖς. The word is again found in the iii/A.D. inscr. from the same district CIG IV. 4474[1].

προσλαλέω,

"speak to," in NT only in Ac 13[43], 28[20]: cf. Theophr. Char. p. 104[15] ed. Jebb, where the loquacious man is described as τοσαῦτα προσλαλῶν τοῖς παιδοτρίβαις καὶ διδασκάλοις, "chattering at this rate to the trainers and masters."

προσλαμβάνω

is found only in NT in mid. = "take to oneself," "receive": cf. BGU IV. 1141[37] (B.C. 14) δὶς προσελαβόμην αὐτὸν εἰς οἶκον παρ' ἐμέ (cf. Philem 17), P Fay 12[10] (c. B.C. 103) προσλαβόμενος συνεργὸ[ν] Ἀμμώνιον, P Amh II. 100[4] (A.D. 198–211) προσελάβετο τὸν Κορνήλιον κοινωνόν, P Oxy I. 71[ii. 2] (A.D. 303) προσελαβόμην ἐμαυτῇ εἰς βοήθειαν . . . Σεκοῦνδον, and P Leid W[viii. 22] (ii/iii A.D.) προσείλημμαι τὴν δύναμιν τοῦ Ἀβραάμ. In P Lond 23 recto[ii. 21] (B.C. 158) (= I. p. 38, UPZ i. p. 155) the verb is used as a t. t. for enrolment in the army, προσλαβέσθαι τὸν προωνομασμένον μου ἀδελφὸν Ἀπολλώνιον εἰς τὴν

Δεξειλάου σημέαν ("a band under one standard"). In *Menandrea* p. 3[32] the verb = "borrow."

προσμένω.

"remain," "stay on": P Vat A[16] (B.C. 168) (= *UPZ* i. p. 303) οὐ γὰρ πάντως δεῖ στενῶς ἐπανάγοντά σε προσμένειν ἕως τοῦ πορίσαι τι, "for, if you find yourself in difficulties, you ought not in any case to remain until you provide something," *Syll*[3] 615[7] (B.C. 180) ὅσον χρόνον ἀξιώσαν αὐτὸν τοὶ κατεσταμένοι ὑπὸ τὰς πόλιος, ἐπὶ ταῦτα ποτέμεινε.

προσορμίζω,

"bring to anchor" (Mk 6[53]): cf. the similar use of προσορμέω in P Leid U[ii. 7] (B.C. 343) (= I. p. 123, *UPZ* i. p. 370), where Nektonabos dreams in the Serapeum that he saw a papyrus boat (πλοῖον παπύρινον) προσορμῆσαι εἰς Μέμφιν, and P Goodsp Cairo 11[4] (iv/A.D.) ἐνεβάλου εἰς τὸ προσορμοῦν πλοῖον . . ξέστα[s] ἰταλικ(οὺs) ἑκατὸν τέσσαρας μόνους.

προσοφείλω.

This NT ἅπ. εἰρ. = "owe besides or in addition" (Philem 19: cf. Field *Notes*, p. 225) is common in our documents, although it is not always easy to distinguish it in meaning from the simple ὀφείλω: P Hib I. 110[30] (accounts—c. B.C. 270) προσωφείλησα σὺν [ἀνηλώμασιν], "I owed an additional sum with expenses," *ib.* 63[14] (c. B.C. 265) σὺ οὖν διόρθωσαι αὐτοῖς τὸ λ[ο]ιπὸν ὃ προσοφείλεις μοι, "do you therefore settle with them the remainder owing from you to me" (Edd.), PSI IV. 360[7] (B.C. 252-1) ἵνα κο[μ]ίσωνται τὸν προσοφειλόμενόν σοι σῖτον (with editor's note), P Par 26[11] (B.C. 162) (= *UPZ* i. p. 248, *Selections*, p. 17) ἐπιλαβόντα παρ' ἡμῶν τὴν γραφὴν τῶν ὀφειλομένων ἡμῖν δεόντων καὶ τίνα πρὸς τίνας χρόνους προσωφείληται καὶ ὑπὸ τίνων, "when he has received from us the written list of the necessaries owing to us and what further debts are due us along with the periods for which they have been owing and the persons who owe them," and P Oxy I. 101[42] (A.D. 142) ὃ δ' ἂν προσοφειλέσῃ ὁ μεμισθωμένος ἀποτεισάτω μεθ' ἡμιολίας, "any arrears owed by the lessee shall be paid with the addition of half their amount" (Edd.).

προσοχθίζω

occurs in Heb 3[10, 17] in citations from the LXX, where the verb denotes "am disgusted with," "abhor." For the subst. προσόχθισμα see 3 Kingd 16[32].

προσπαίω.

It is difficult to find any good parallel for the meaning "fell upon," "struck against" which προσέπεσαν requires in Mt 7[25] (but see Prov 25[20], Sm Ps 90(91)[12]). In these circumstances Lachmann has conjectured a reading προσέπαισαν, and is supported by Nestle *ZNTW* ix. (1908), p. 252 f.

πρόσπεινος,

"very hungry," Ac 10[10]: one of the rapidly decreasing number of NT words, of which it can be said, "Not found elsewhere" (Grimm).

προσπίπτω.

For the literal meaning "fall upon" in Mt 7[25] see *s.v.* προσπαίω, and for the derived sense "fall at one's feet," "supplicate," cf. the Christian amulet BGU III. 954[30] (vi/A.D.) (= *Selections*, p. 134) ἅγιε Σέρηνε, πρόσπεσε ὑπὲρ ἐμοῦ, ἵνα τελείως ὑγιανῶ.

The verb is common in our sources = "befall," "happen," e.g. PSI VI. 614[13] (iii/B.C.) γράφε δὲ καὶ Ἡραγόραι, ἐάν τί σοι προσπίπτηι τῶν καθ' αὐτόν, ἐπιμελῶς, *ib.* IV. 340[12] (B.C. 257-6) ὥ[στε] μηδεμίαν ὑποψίαν ἐκείνωι γε προσπεσεῖν, P Hib I. 78[4] (B.C. 244-3) ὅταν λειτουργία προσπέσηι ἀπολύειν αὐτούς, "to release them when service falls to their lot," P Par 39[9] (B.C. 161) (= *UPZ* i. p. 143) καθότι προσπίπτει μοι, BGU IV. 1206[16] (B.C. 28) ἐάν τι ἄλλο προσπέσῃ, σημανῶι σοι, and *ib.* III. 1011[ii. 12] (ii/A.D.) κἄν τί σοι προσπίπτηι περὶ τῶν ἐναντίων. In P Cairo Zen 59031[7] (B.C. 258) reference is made to some iron as a necessary part of a boat's equipment—τὸ[ν σ(]δη[ρ]ον ὃν [ἀ]ναγκαῖον ἦν ὑπάρχειν ἐν τῶι πλοίωι πρὸς τὰς προσπιπτούσας χρείας. P Petr II. 38 *verso* (c)[16] (Ptol.) τὰ προσπ[ίπτ]ον[τα describes cases "falling" to a judge to decide.

An interesting use of the verb shows it = "come to my ears or to my knowledge," e.g. P Par 63[30] (B.C. 164) (= P Petr III. p. 20) ἡμῖν προσπέπτωκεν, Witkowski[2] p. 96[8] (B.C. 131-0) (= P Revill Mél p. 205, *Archiv* ii. p. 518) προσπέπτωκεν ⟨γὰρ⟩ Παῶν ἀναπλεῖν ἐν τῶ Τῦβι ⟨μ(ηνί⟩, and P Oxy VII. 1027[7] (i/A.D.) προσέπεσέν μοι.

προσποιέω.

In P Oxy I. 121[21] (iii/A.D.) μὴ προσποιήσῃς πρὸς τοὺς κυρείους αὐτῶν, the editors translate "don't make over anything to their masters," but suggest that the verb may have the sense of the mid. "don't make any pretence." This is the meaning generally given in its only NT occurrence Lk 24[28] (cf. Job 19[14]), but see Plummer *ICC ad l.*

Other exx. from the Κοινή are P Oxy III. 531[5] (ii/A.D.) μηδὲν προσποιηθῇς ἕως ἐπ' ἀγαθῷ πρὸς σὲ παραγένο(=ω)μαι, "claim nothing until I come to you auspiciously" (Edd.), and the fragmentary PSI III. 220[8] (iii/A.D.) προσποιήθην. See also the description of the ironical man in Theophr. *Char.* p. 52[10] (ed. Jebb) προσποιήσασθαι ἄρτι παραγεγονέναι, "he will pretend that he has just arrived," cf.[11].

προσπορεύομαι,

"come near," "approach," is now read by Crönert and Wilcken (see *Berichtigungen*, p. 126) in P Eleph 18[5] (B.C. 223-22) προσπο[ρε]ύονται ἀγοράζοντες κτλ.: cf. P Magd 27[6] (B.C. 218) μὴ ἐπιτρέπηι προσπορεύεσθαι, P Par 50[3] (B.C. 159) (= *UPZ* i. p. 365) Ἀπολλώνιον εἶδον, προσπορεύεται μοι, P Amh II. 33[17] (c. B.C. 157) τοὺς προσπορευομένους συνηγόρους πρὸς τὰς προσοδικὰς κρίσεις, "advocates who take up revenue cases" (Edd.), and from the inscrr. *Syll* 177 (= [3] 314)[112] (c. B.C. 303) διὰ τὸ τὰ ἐκ τῶν προσόδων γινόμενα κατὰ χρόνους προσπορεύ[εσθαι ὑμῖν μακροτέρους.

In the NT the verb is used only in Mk 10[35], and is

one of many exx. of this writer's preference for compounds of πορεύομαι : indeed, except in 9³⁰, he does not use the simple verb at all. As Mark's Greek culture was manifestly small, Harnack's thesis in his "Sayings of Jesus" as to the connexion between culture and compound verbs cannot pass unchallenged : see further *Exp.* VII. vii. p. 411 f.

προσρήγνυμι.

"dash against," Lk 6⁴⁸⁴ : cf. M. Anton. iv. 49 ὅμοιον εἶναι τῇ ἄκρᾳ ᾗ διηνεκῶς τὰ κύματα προσρήσσεται, "be like the promontory whereon the waves break unceasingly."

προστάσσω.

"appoint," is read in the critical text of Ac 17²⁶ : cf. P Amh II. 29²⁹ (c. B.C. 250) βασιλέως προστάξαντος . . ., and P Tebt I. 7¹ (B.C. 114) βασιλέων προστάξάν[τ]ων μηθένα τῶν ἐπὶ τῶν κριτηρίων καὶ τῶν ἄλ[λ]ων τῶν πρὸς χρείαις δέχεσθαι ἐγκλήματα . . ., "the sovereigns decree that neither anyone who exercises judicial functions nor any of the other officials shall receive complaints . . .," where the editors note that the formula βασιλέων προστάξάντων "appears to be used in cases where the following decree is not quoted in its exact words, whether because it was extracted from a series or because the construction is altered to *oratio obliqua*." See also P Reinach 18²¹ (B.C. 108) παρὰ τὰ . . . προστεταγμένα. The verb is common in the inscrr., *e.g. Syll* 365 (= ³ 798)¹⁶ (A.D. 37) ὁ δὲ δῆμος . . . προσέταξε τοῖς ἄρχουσι ψήφισμα ὑπαντήσεως εἰσηγήσασθαι αὐτοῖς, and *ib.* 523 (= ³ 578)¹⁸ (ii/B.C.) μὴ ποιήσας τι τῶν προστεταγμένων ἐν τῶι νόμωι τῶιδε. For the subst. πρόσταγμα cf. P Cairo Zen 59034¹⁹ (B.C. 257) καλῶς οὖν ἔχει, Ἀπολλώνιε, ἐπακολουθῆσαί σε τοῖς ὑπὸ τοῦ θεοῦ προστάγμασιν, and for προσταγή cf. Diog. Oenoand. p. 18² (ed. William).

προστάτις.

We can supply no instance of the fem. προστάτις (Rom 16²), "protectress," "patroness," from our sources, but the masc. προστάτης is common in various connotations, e.g. BGU IV. 1130² (c. B.C. 11) Ἀπολλώνιος . . . Τρύφωνι . . . προστάτηι ἐράν[ω]ν χαίρειν, P Oxy II. 299⁴ (late i/A.D.) Διονυσίῳ προσ[τ]άτῃ Νεμερῶν κέκρηκα (δραχμὰς) η. "I have also lent Dionysius, the chief man of Nemerae, 8 drachmae" (Edd.), and *ib.* XI. 1150⁴ (vi/A.D.) ὁ θεὸς τοῦ προστάτου ἡμῶν τοῦ ἁγίου Φιλοξένου, "the god of Saint Philoxenus our patron." The title is applied to the office-bearer in a heathen religious association in Foucart *Associations Religieuses* p. 202, No. 20³⁴ (Imperial times) (= *CIG* I. 126) δοκιμα[ζέ]τω δὲ ὁ προστάτης [καὶ ὁ] ἀρχιερανιστὴς καὶ ὁ γραμματεὺς κα[ὶ οἱ] ταμίαι καὶ σύνδικοι : cf. SH *ad* Rom *l.c.*, and Otto *Priester* ii. p. 75, n.¹ See also *CR* i. p. 6, and Field *Notes* p. 166.

For the verb προστατέω, cf. P Petr II. 13 (19)⁴ (c. B.C. 252) (= Witkowski², p. 18) where a son writes to his father, οὐ] μὴν οὐθὲν ἐμοὶ [ἔσται με]ῖζον ἢ σοῦ προστατῆσα[ι τὸν] ἐ[π]ίλοιπον βίον, ἀξίως [μὲ]ν σοῦ, ἀξίως δ' ἐμοῦ, "there will be nothing of more importance for me than to look after you for the remainder of life, in a manner worthy of you, and worthy of me": for the subst. προστασία, cf. P Par 63¹¹³ (B.C. 164) (= P Petr III. p. 28) τοῦ προγεγραμμένου πλή-

θο]υς προστασίαι [π]ροσεδρεύων, "putting pressure on the leaders of the persons just described" (Mahaffy) : and for the adj προστατικός, cf. P Oxy XVI. 1857¹ (vi/vii A.D.) ἀπέστειλα τῇ ὑμετέρᾳ προστατικῇ μεγαλοπρεπείᾳ . . . "I send to your protecting magnificence . ."

προστίθημι.

"add." With Heb 12¹⁹ we may compare *Chrest.* II. 372ᵛ·¹¹ (ii/A.D.) καὶ προσέθηκεν· Ἐχθὲς ἔφης ἄλλους ἐσχηκέναι παῖδας,' and P Strass I. 41²¹ (A.D. 250) Σαραπίων ῥ]ήτωρ προσέθηκεν (his λόγος follows). Other exx. of the verb are P Oxy III. 471² (ii/A.D.) π]ροσθήσω τι κύριε περ[ὶ] οὖ θαυμάσεις οἶμαι, "I will add a fact, my lord, which will, I expect, excite your wonder" (Edd.), *ib.* VII. 1062⁴ (ii/A.D.) προσθεὶς ὅτι τὰ θέρεά ἐστιν τὰ κρείσσονα, "adding that the summer ones (*sc.* fleeces) were the best" (Ed.), P Ryl II. 153²⁷ (A.D. 138–161) ταῦτα οἱ προγεγραμμέ[νοι ἐπίτροποί] μου κα[ὶ κ]ληρονόμ[οι] μετελεύσονται καὶ προσθήσουσιν τῷ υἱῷ μου, "these (*sc.* certain allowances) shall be claimed by my aforesaid guardians and heirs and delivered to my son" (Edd.), BGU I. 84¹⁵ (A.D. 248) ἐδηλώ]θη προστεθεῖσθαι εἰ[ς ἀρίθμ]ησιν μην[ὸς Πα]ῦνι, and *Ostr* 1150³ (ii/iii A.D.) πρόσθες εἰς ὄνομ[α] Ἐπωνύχου), "put down to the account of Eponychus." With the use of the verb in Ac 2⁴¹ Preuschen (*HZNT ad l.*) compares Demosth. xviii. 39 ὅσα ἑκουσίως προσετίθετο τῶν πολισμάτων.

The confident assertion of Hebraism in the idiom προσέθετο πέμψαι, which Luke (20¹¹ al.) deliberately substitutes for the πάλιν ἀπέστειλε of Mk 12⁴, needs some reconsideration : see *Proleg.* p. 233. Helbing (*Gr.* p. iv.), goes so far as to call it "a good Greek construction," adding naturally that its extreme frequency in the LXX is due to "mechanical imitation of the original." The very fact that no other Hebraism has ever been discovered in Josephus (see Thumb *Hellen.* p. 125 f., Schmidt *Jos.* p. 514 ff., Deissmann *BS* p. 67 n.¹) might be fairly held to prove that the locution was really Greek.

προστρέχω.

"run up to," "approach": cf. the metaphorical use in P Oxy II. 247¹² (A.D. 90) ἀπογράφομ[αι τῷ ὁμογν]ησίῳ μου ἀδελ[φῷ] . . . προστρέχοντι τῇ ἐννόμῳ ἡλικίᾳ. "I register for my full brother who is approaching the legal age" (Edd.).

προσφάγιον.

In the private account P Oxy IV. 736¹⁶·⁸⁹ (c. A.D. 1) a half obol and 2½ obols respectively are set down for προσφάγιον, which the editors render "relish" (similarly in *ib.* 736¹⁰·¹²). In the same account ⁶¹·⁵²·⁶² ὄψον and ὀψάριον are translated "sauce." But the plentiful evidence from Hellenistic writers in Wetstein *ad* Jn 6⁹ would seem to show that ὄψον and ὀψάριον meant "fish" predominantly as early as Plato, and ordinarily in later times as in Athenaeus. In the same way, to judge from the papyrus evidence, προσφάγιον is best understood of some staple article of food of the *genus* fish, rather than of a mere "relish." Thus in P Oxy III. 498³³ (ii/A.D.) it is provided that a stone-cutter's wages are to be so many drachmae a day along with ἄρ]τον ἕνα καὶ προσφάγιον, and in P Grenf II. 77²¹ (iii/iv A.D.) (= *Selections*, p. 121) provision is made ὑπ(ὲρ)] δαπάνης ἐν ψωμίοις καὶ προσφαγίοις (δραχμαὶ) ϛ, "for outlays in delicacies and foods 16 drachmae." It would, therefore, be to one of the articles of an ordinary meal that Jesus' question referred in Jn 21⁵, where the RV rendering is supported by the Lewis Syriac, and by *d* of the Old Latin (*aliquid manducare*). See further Field *Notes*, p. 109, and Abbott *Joh. Gr.* p. 193 f.

πρόσφατος,

derived from πρός and the root of φόνος, ἔπεφνον etc., means originally "fresh-killed" (see Boisacq p. 816 for alternative derivations), but the second element in the compound died out quite early, and the word came to be used generally, "new," "fresh," "recent," as e.g. in the medical receipt P Oxy VIII. 1088²⁵ (early i/A.D.) ἐλλεβόρου λευκοῦ προσφατώτερον τρίψας, "pound fresh some white hellebore" (Ed.). In *Michel* 1501²¹ (B.C. 103-2) τὰς [ἐ]λ[άας τὰς προσ]φάτους, the adj. is used of "fresh," not salted, "olives": cf. Menander *Fragm.* p. 132 ἐν προσφάτοις ἰχθυδίοις τεθραμμένα, "brought up on fresh fish"

Phrynichus (p. 374, ed. Lob.) discusses whether in view of the word's etymology it is right to say πρόσφατον πρᾶγμα or only πρόσφατος νεκρός and the like, and finds an answer in a line of Sophocles *Andromeda*—

μηδὲν φοβεῖσθε προσφάτους ἐπιστολάς.

See also Rutherford *NP* p. 471 f. and Pearson on Soph. *fr.* 128.

προσφάτως,

"recently" (Ac 18²), occurs in P Par 63ᵛⁱⁱⁱ⁻¹⁰ (B.C. 164) ταύτην (*sc.* αἵρεσιν) γὰρ ἀπέγνωκα ἴδιον προσφάτως [π]ροσειληφθαι (*l.* —ῆφθαι) φίλον. It is also found in Polybius, LXX, and Aristeas, which demonstrates its genuine vernacular character, as P Par 63 by itself would not do. We can also cite it from *OGIS* 315²³ (B.C. 164-3) τῷ ἀδελφῷι ἐληλυθότ[ι] π[ροσ]φάτως ἐπὶ τ[ὸ] στ[ρα]τόπεδον: cf. Epicurus *Ep. ad matrem* fr. 11 B 4 (Linde p. 48) and Diog. Oenoand. p. 66¹ (ed. William), cf. p. xxvii. ff.

προσφέρω,

"bring to," "present," is seen in P Fay 21¹⁷ (A.D. 134) τὰ βιβλία προσφέροντες ο[ἷ]ς ὀφίλουσιν, "presenting their accounts to their creditors," P Giss I. 50¹⁸ (A.D. 259) προσφέρων τῇ πόλει . . . δραχμὰς δεκαεπτὰ ὀβολόν, and P Meyer 23³ (end iv/A.D.) παρὰ Τιθοῆτι τῷ προσφέροντί σοι ταῦτά μου τὰ γράμματα: cf. P Par 63¹² (B.C. 164) (= P Petr III. p. 18) καλῶς ποιήσεις τὴν πᾶσαν προσενεγκάμενος ἐκτένειαν, "you will do well in using every effort" (Mahaffy), and P Tebt I. 33¹⁵ (B.C. 112) (= *Selections*, p. 31) τὴν πᾶσαν προσενέγκαι σπουδή[ν.

The force seen in Heb 12⁷ appears in P Par 46²⁰ (B.C. 152) (= *UPZ* i. p. 338) where Apollonius appeals to his brother Ptolemaeus to examine personally into his grievance against a third party—νομίζω γὰρ μάλιστα τῶν ἄλλων παρακολουθηκοντά σε τῆι ἀληθείαι πικρότερον προσενεχθήσεσθ' αὐτῶι, "when you have investigated the truth you will deal with him most severely": cf. *Syll* 371 (= ³807 ¹³) (A.D. 54) προσενεχθεὶς φ[ι]λανθρώπως πᾶσι τοῖς πολείταις, and P Lond 1012⁶ (A.D. 41) ὁ(= οἱ) γὰρ ⟨ἄρ⟩χοντες . . .

μετριώτεροι ἡμεῖν προσενεχθήσονται τὸν ἐν ταῖς ἀρχαῖς χρόνον, "for the magistrates will behave with greater circumspection during their term of office" (Bell).

On the marriage contract P Oxy III. 496⁶ (A.D. 127) the editors remark that "προσφέρεσθαι is the word commonly used of property brought to the husband by the bride." So in the oldest extant Greek papyrus P Eleph 1⁴ (B.C. 311-10) (= *Selections*, p. 2) the bride is described as προσφερομένην εἱματισμὸν καὶ κόσμον valued at 1000 drachmae: similarly BGU IV. 1100¹¹ and 1104¹¹ (time of Augustus). In P Tebt II. 407¹⁰ (A.D. 199?) ἃ σοι] προσηνέχθη is "what was settled" upon the writer's daughter. A somewhat similar use is seen in *OGIS* 221¹¹ (B.C. 280-261) διὰ τὴν πρὸς ὑμᾶς εὔνοιαν προσενέγκασθαι πρὸς τὴν ὑμετέραν πόλιν, with reference to the gifting of royal land for the benefit of an adjoining city: see Dittenberger's note.

Grimm says the verb is "hardly to be found in native Greek writ." for *sacrificing*. Something very like it comes in the legal report BGU IV. 1024ᵛⁱⁱ⁻²⁵ (iv/v A.D.) of the poor girl whom her mother sold to shame, who ζῶσα [π]ροσεφέρετο τοῖς βου[λομένοις] ὡς νεκρά.

For the conative impf. in Heb 11¹⁷ προσέφερεν see *Proleg.* pp. 129, 238, 247, and for the double compound προσαναφέρω see P Tebt I. 16³ (B.C. 114) τυγχάνωι προσανενηνοχώ⟨s⟩ σοι δι' ἑτέρας ἐπισ(τολῆς), "I reported to you in another letter" (Edd.).

προσφιλής.

This Pauline word (Phil 4⁸) = "pleasing," "agreeable," is used of persons in PSI IV. 361⁹ (B.C. 251-0) πᾶσιν τοῖς παρ' αὐ[τ]οῦ προσφιλής εἰμι ὅσοι αὐτὸν σέβονται, and in the torn letter BGU IV. 1043²¹ (iii/A.D.) ὅλως π[ροσ]φιλής σου γεν[όμενος (?) . . . In a letter by Plotina, the wife of the Emperor Trajan, written in A.D. 121, she describes Trajan's successor Hadrian as ἐμοὶ . . προσφιλεστάτω[ι] κατὰ πάντα. The adj. is common in epitaphs, e.g. *Kaibel* 324⁹ Αὐρ[ηλ]ί[α] . . προσφιλής χαῖρε: cf. also Vett. Val. p. 121³³ περικτήσονται καὶ προσφιλεῖς γενήσονται. For the adv. cf. *OGIS* 331⁹ (mid. ii/B.C.) συντετελεκότος τὰ ἱερὰ . . . ἀξίως τοῦ θεοῦ, προσφιλῶς δὲ τῷ τε ἀδελφῷι καὶ ἡμῖγ.

προσφορά.

Like its verb, the subst. is used of dowry in marriage contracts, but not with the same frequency: cf. e.g. P Tebt II. 351¹ (ii/A.D.) προσφο(ρᾶς) οἰκί(ας) of the gift of a house from a mother to her daughter on the occasion of her marriage, and P Ryl II. 154¹⁰·²⁹ (A.D. 66); see also *Archiv* iv. p. 138, and the editors' introd. to P Ryl II. 155. In the medical P Tebt II. 272⁵ (late ii/A.D.) προσφορά has reference to the "increase" of bad symptoms, and apparently it is = "contribution" in P Oxy X. 1253⁹ (iv/A.D.), where it is associated with ἐξαγυρισμός (see also *ib.* 1322 (A.D 413)): cf. the similar use of the adj. in P Tebt I. 88¹⁵ (B.C. 115-4) ἄλλο πρόσφορον ("revenue") μηδὲν ἔχειν.

From a later date, P Oxy XVI. 1898²³ (A.D. 587), comes the receipt for a gift of wheat paid as τὴν ἁγίαν προσφοράν to an hospital. In their note *ad l.* the editors point out that in Byzantine times προσφορά is = (a) "a mass or other commemorative office for the dead, and so, eventually, the mass itself," and (b) "a gift made to a church or monastery for this purpose": see further the elaborate note at P Mon I. 8⁵.

προσφωνέω

is included by Mayser (*Gr.* p. 34) among the poetical verbs which have passed into the **Κοινή**. For the meaning "address," "give speech to," as in Ac 22², we may cite P Petr II. 38(b)³ (B.C. 242) παρὰ δέ σου οὐθ[ὲ]ν ἡμῖν προσπεφώνηται, "whereas from you not a word has been uttered" (Ed.), *Chrest.* I. 27 verso¹⁵ (ii/A.D.) περὶ τούτου ὡς ἔδοξε ν], προσφωνησάτω ἡμῖν ὁ πρυτανικός.

From this it is an easy transition to the more official sense of "report," as in P Ryl II. 83¹⁰ (A.D. 138–161) where a tax-collector states to the commission appointed to receive his accounts, προσφωνῶ περὶ τοῦ μηδέν μοι διαγεγρά(φθαι) ὑπὲρ [λ]ημμάτων ἰδίου λόγου, "I report to you that nothing has been paid to me on behalf of the revenues of the privy purse" (Edd.), BGU I. 16¹³ (A.D. 159–160) (= *Selections*, p. 84) ἐπιζητοῦσι ὑμ[ῖ]ν εἰ [οὕ]τως ἔχει προσφωνοῦμεν, "to your enquiries whether these things are so we report," with reference to certain charges against a priest, P Oxy I. 51⁹ (A.D. 173) a public physician is instructed to inspect the body of a man who had been hanged, and προσφωνῆσαι regarding it, and similarly *ib.* III. 475³ (A.D. 182), VI. 896³⁹ (A.D. 316): cf. 1 Esdr 2²¹. The account of Nero's speech to the Greeks on freedom in A.D. 67, *Syll* 376 (= ³814)³, is introduced with the words, συνελθόντων τῶν ὄχλων ἐν ἐκκλησίᾳ προσεφώνησεν τὰ ὑπογεγραμμένα.

The word is found associated with ὁμολογέω with the meaning "avow," "acknowledge," in P Gen I. 68¹ (A.D. 382) προσεφώ[ν]ησεν καὶ ὁμολόγησεν Αὐ[ρή]λιος Περγάμιος, and in P Leid G²⁰ (B.C. 99) (= I. p. 43) the editor (p. 47) thinks that προσφωνέω has the meaning *compellandi, cum reprehensione admonendi*.

For προσφώνησις cf. P Grenf I. 35⁸ (B.C. 99) ἐγράψαμεν ὑμῖν ὑπὲρ ὧν βουλόμεθα, μηδεμιᾶς προσφωνήσεως προσπεπτωκυίας, and see Preisigke *Fachwörter s.v.*

προσωπολημπτέω,

"have respect of persons," "favour specially" (Jas 2⁹). The verb and the two cognate substantives προσωπολήμπτης and προσωπολημψία are not found in the LXX, and may be reckoned amongst the earliest definitely Christian words. They belong to Palestinian Greek, being derived from πρόσωπον λαμβάνειν, the Hebraistic פָּנִים נָשָׂא, "lift the face" on a person, in the sense of being favourable to him, and hence, as always in the NT, to "show undue favour or partiality."

προσωπολήμπτης,

See *s.v.* προσωπολημπτέω.

προσωπολημψία,

See *s.v.* προσωπολημπτέω.

πρόσωπον,

"face": cf. P Par 47⁵ (B.C. 152–1) (= *UPZ* i. p. 332, *Selections* p. 22) ἱ μὴ μικρόν τι ἐντρέπομαι, οὐκ ἄν με ἴδες τὸ πόρσωπον, "but for the fact that I am a little ashamed,

you would never again have seen my face," and *ib.* 51³⁰⁶ (B.C. 159) (= *UPZ* i. p. 360) εἶχον πρόσωπον καλὸν « εἶχον » καὶ οὐκ ἤθελον οὔθενει δίξαί μου τὸ πόρσωπον διὰ τὸ καλὸν αὐτὸν εἶν[α]ι, where also note the form πόρσωπον by *metathesis* (Mayser *Gr.* p. 189). From this literal meaning it is an easy transition to the more general sense of "outward appearance," and thence to the frequent use of the word in the **Κοινή** as practically equivalent to our "person": see e.g. P Oxy XIV. 1072¹ (A.D. 37–41) ξένοις προσώποις, "to strangers," *ib.* II. 237ᵛⁱⁱ·³⁴ (A.D. 186) ὁμοίας ὑποθέσεως ἀκούσαντα [ἐξ] Αἰγυπτιακῶν προσώπων, "having heard a similar plea advanced by Egyptian witnesses" (Edd.), P Ryl I. 28⁸⁸ (iv/A.D.) ἐκ νεωτέρου προσώπου, "from a young person," P Oxy VIII. 1033³ (A.D. 392) ἕνεκεν τῆς παραστάσεως διαφόρων προσώπων, "for the production of various persons," *ib.* VI. 904³ (v/A.D.) ἡ δι' ἑαυτοῦ ἢ διὰ οἱουδήποτε προσώπου, "either by himself or by some other person," and *ib.* I. 135¹⁹ (A.D. 579) ἀποκρινόμενον εἰς ἅπαντα τὰ ὁρῶντα τὸ αὐτοῦ πρό[σ]ωπον ἤτοι τὴν τοῦ ἐναπογράφου τύχην, "responsible for all that regards his person or the fortunes of him who has been entered as a cultivator" (Edd.). See also *Philologus* lxiii. (N.F. xvii), 1904, p. 155 f. where Praechter quotes various passages from late Greek showing πρόσωπον = "soziale Persönlichkeit," "Ansehen," e.g. Polyb. v. 107. 3 ἐζήτουν ἡγέμονα καὶ πρόσωπον ὡς ἱκανοὶ βοηθεῖν ὄντες αὐτοῖς (said of the Egyptians, who desired to overthrow the rule of the Ptolemys).

For prepositional phrases with πρόσωπον, we may cite P Oxy VI. 903² (iv/A.D.) πολλὰ ἀσελγήματα λέγων εἰς πρόσωπόν μου, "using many terms of abuse to my face," a wife's accusation against her husband, BGU III. 909¹² (A.D. 359) πολλὰς ἐ[= αἰ][σ]χρολογίας εἰς πρόσωπόν μου ἐξειπών, P Petr III. 1ⁱ·⁵ (Ptol.) κα]τὰ πρόσωπον τοῦ ἱεροῦ, "in front of the temple," P Ryl II. 76¹² (late ii/A.D.) κατ' οἶκον εἶναι τὴν διαίρεσιν τῶν κτημάτων καὶ μὴ κατὰ πρόσωπον, "that the division of property should be made according to households and not individuals" (Edd.), similarly *ib.* 269¹ (ii/A.D.), P Lond 479⁶ (iii/A.D. ?) (= II. p. 256) ἐβουλόμην μὲν ἐγὼ ἐλθεῖν εἴ[γ]α σοι κατὰ [π]ρόσωπον ("face to face") διηγήσομαι τὰ συνβάντα μοι, P Oxy VII. 1071¹ (v/A.D.) καθὼς καὶ κατὰ πρόσωπον παρεκλήθης παρ' ἐμοῦ, "as you were urged in person by me" (Edd.), and *ib.* XVI. 1840¹ (vi/A.D.) πάντα ὅσα κατὰ πρόσωπον εἶπόν σοι. For κατὰ πρόσωπον as a *term. techn.* in judicial phraseology = *coram*, we may cite from the inscrr. *Magn.* 93 b¹¹ (after B.C. 190) κατὰ πρόσωπον λόγους ποιεῖσθαι, *Priene* 41⁶ (B.C. 139) λόγους ἐποήσαντο κατὰ πρό[σ]ωπον πρὸς Πριην[ε]ῖς, and *OGIS* 441⁶⁶ (B.C. 81) πρεσβευταῖς Στρατονικέων κατὰ πρόσωπον ἐν τῆι συγκλήτωι φιλανθρώπως ἀποκριθῆναι: cf. Ac 25¹⁶, 2 Cor 10¹. With πρὸ προσώπου (Ac 13²⁴) cf. Herodas VIII. 59 ἔρρ' ἐκ προσώπου, "out of my sight": see Headlam's note *ad l.*

For the extent to which these prepositional periphrases are to be regarded as Hebraistic in the NT cf. *Proleg.* pp. 14, 81, 99, and for the LXX cf. Thackeray *Gr.* i. p. 43 f.

προτάσσω,

"appoint beforehand," is read in the TR of Ac 17²⁶ (cf. 2 Macc 8³⁶): cf. P Oxy VIII. 1112¹⁵ (A.D. 188) Ἀπολλώνιο[ς] ὁ προτεταγμέ(νος), "Apollonius the aforesaid," *ib.* VI. 889¹⁵

71

(iv/A.D.) τοῦ προτεταγ[μένου] (sc. ἐπιστάλματος, or the like), and P Amh II. 145²⁴ (iv/v A.D.) τοῦτο γὰρ προτάττεσθαι εὔλογον, "for it is right that this should be put in the foremost place" (Edd.).

προτείνω.

In Ac 22²⁵, its only occurrence in the NT, this verb seems to be used not of binding or tying with thongs (AV, RV), but rather of "stretching forward" with thongs, so as to cause a tense posture for receiving blows (see Field *Notes*, p. 136 f.) : cf. P Leid Wˣˣᵛⁱⁱⁱ ³² (ii/iii A.D.) (= II. p. 145) ἰς τὸν βορρᾶ (*l.* εἰς τὸν βορρᾶν) τὴν μίαν πὺξ (*l.* πυγμὴν) προτί- (= εἰ)νας, "versus septentrionem unum pugnum extendens." For the derived meaning "put forward," "propose," cf. P Par 63¹⁶¹ (B.C. 164) (= P Petr III. p. 32) ἀσμένως ἐπιδέξασθαι τὸ προτεινόμενον, "to receive what is proposed cheerfully" (Edd.), and *OGIS* 315⁵³ (B.C. 164–159) χλωρὸς δ' εὐτονώτατος ἦν τὰ Ῥωμαϊκὰ προτείνων καὶ οὐθενὶ τρόπωι συμβουλεύων οὐθὲν ἄνευ 'κείνων πράσσειν.

πρότερος.

The comparative rarity of πρότερος in the NT, where it occurs only eleven times (never in Lk), as contrasted with the 200 appearances of πρῶτος, meets us again in the papyri. For the adj., as in Eph 4²², cf. P Fay 34⁹ (A.D. 161) κατὰ τὴν τῶν προτέρων ἐτῶν συνήθειαν, "according to the custom of former years," and for the neut. used adverbially see BGU IV. 1096⁴ (i/ii A.D.) ὃν (sc. γραμματέα) πρότερον εἶχον P Lond 1221¹⁹ (A.D. 105) (= III. p. 25) ἐν οἰ[κί]ᾳ πρότερον Κλαυδίας, and with the art. P Tebt II. 302⁶ (A.D. 71–2) ἀρούρας φδ τὸ πρότερον τῶν προκι[μένων θεῶν, "500¼ arourae which previously belonged to the aforesaid gods."

In view of these exx. we are probably right in understanding τὸ πρότερον in Gal 4¹³ in the general sense of "previously," "originally," rather than "on the former of two visits" (cf. Lake *Earlier Epp. of St. Paul*, p. 265 f.) : so also in all the other appearances of the phrase in the NT.

In the following exx. πρότερον is best rendered by our English "first"—P Petr I. 29¹⁵ (iii/B.C.) γίνωσκε δὲ καὶ ὅτι ὕδωρ ἕκαστος τῶν ὅρων τὴν ἄμπελον φυτευομένην πρότερον δεῖν φασίν, [ο]ὐ[δὲ ὑ]πάρχειν, "know, also, that each of the watchers says that the planted vines want water first, and that they have none" (Ed.), P Oxy X. 1281⁹ (A.D. 21) ἐφ' ᾧ κομιζομένου (τοῦ) Ἰωσήπου ταῦτα πρότερον δώσει λόγο[ν] τούτων, "on condition that when Joseph receives it he shall first render an account of it" (Edd.), and P Fay 32¹⁵ (A.D. 131) ἐὰν δέ τι κατὰ τοῦτ(ου) ἐξοικονομῶ πρότερον ἀποδίξω ὑπάρχειν, "if I alienate any of my rights over it, I will first establish my title to the ownership" (Edd.). See also *s.v.* πρῶτος.

προτίθημι

is very common in the papyri = "proclaim," "set forth" publicly, an edict or notice, e.g. P Oxy I, 34 *verso*ⁱⁱⁱ ¹⁴ (A.D. 127) προτεθήτω, "let this edict be publicly issued" (Edd.), *ib.* VIII. 1100² (A.D. 206) διατάγματος προτεθέντος ὑπ' ἐμοῦ ἐν τῇ λαμπροτάτ[ῃ πόλει τῶν Ἀλεξανδρέων] ἀντίγραφον, *ib.* XIV. 1633³⁷ (A.D. 275) δημ(οσίᾳ) προετέθ(η). Cf. P Tor I. 1ⁱⁱ ⁶ (B.C. 116) ἐνέβαλον ἔντευξιν εἰς τὸ προτεθὲν ("expositum") ὑπ' αὐτῶν ἀγγεῖον ("vas") ἐν τῇ Διοσπόλει,

P Amh II 85¹⁹ (A.D. 78) ἐὰν φαίνη<ται> προτεθ[ῆ]ναι τῆσδε τῆς μισθώσεως ἀντίγραφον ἐπὶ τὰς καθηκούσας ἡμέρας δέκα, "subject to your consenting to the publication of this lease for the legal period of ten days" (Edd.), BGU II. 372ⁱⁱ ¹⁸ (A.D. 154) ἔστω π[ρο]θεσμία [αὐτο]ῖς, ἐξ οὗ ἂν τοῦτ[ό] μου τὸ διάταγ[μ]α ἐν ἑκά[στ]ῳ νομῷ προτεθῇ μῆνες γ̄, "let their limit of time be three months from the date of publication of my edict in each several nome," and P Strass I. 22⁸ (iii/A.D.) προετέθη ἐν Ἀλεξανδ[ρ]είᾳ ἦ (ἔτει) Φαρμοῦθι κ̄δ̄.

This meaning of "set forth publicly" is preferred for προέθετο by SH *ad* Rom 3²⁵ (cf. Deissmann *BS* p. 124 ff.) : but Moulton on the strength of an inscr. suggests that the meaning may rather be "offered," or "provided" for a propitiatory gift. The inscr. is *Syll* 325 (= ³708)¹⁵ (before B.C. 100) τισὶν δὲ τῶν πολειτῶν ε[ἰς] λύτρα προτιθείς (sc. χρήματα) ἔδειξεν ἑαυτὸν πρὸς πᾶσαν ἀπάντησιν τῶν σωζομένων εὐομείλητον, which Moulton renders, "offering money for the ransom of other citizens, he showed himself gracious at every welcoming of those who from time to time safely returned." See further *Exp* VIII. i. p. 475 f.

A medical receipt for quartan fever, P Oxy VIII. 1088²⁷ (early i/A.D.), runs—φακὸν πρὸς τοὺς πόδας προτιθείς, καὶ σκεπάζειν ἱματίοις, "apply a warm bottle to the feet, and cover him up with blankets."

προτρέπω.

This NT ἅπ. εἰρ. lends itself easily to illustration in the same sense as in Ac 18²⁷, "urge forwards," "encourage" : P Par 63¹⁶⁵ (B.C. 164) (= P Petr III. p. 32) προτρεψαμένου τοὺς στρατηγοὺς καὶ τοὺς λαοὺς ἐ[πι]δέξασθαι τὰ τῆς ἀσχολίας, "instigated the strategi and the people to undertake the labour" (Mahaffy), P Ryl II. 77¹⁸ (A.D. 192) ἡμῶν δὲ προτρεπομένων αὐτὸν ἀναδέξασθαι τὴν κοσμητείαν, "but when we urged him to undertake the office of cosmetes" (Edd.), BGU I. 164¹⁷ (ii/iii A.D.) ἐὰν μὴ τοῦτο ποιήσῃς καὶ προτρέψῃς αὐτὸν ἐλθεῖν, *ib.* II. 450¹⁵ (ii/iii A.D.) προτρέψῃ αὐτὸν τ[α]κχέως παρ[αγ]ενέ[σ]θαι, P Oxy X. 1252 *verso*³³ (A.D. 288–95) προετρεψάμην Ἀμμώνιον . . ἐν τῷ μεταξὺ(= ὺ) ἀποδοῦναι, "I urged Ammonius to discharge this in the meantime," *OGIS* 339⁹⁰ (c. B.C. 120) ἵνα . . . ζηλωταὶ μὲν τῶν καλλίστων γίνωνται, προτρέπωνται δὲ πρὸς ἀρετήν, *Syll* 326 (= ³700)⁵ (c. B.C. 107) ἐπ[ὶ] τὰ κάλλιστα καὶ ἐνδοξότατα τὸν [βασ]ιλέα προτρεπόμενος, and *ib.* 686 (= ³1073)²⁷ (A.D. 117) ἐπὶ πλεῖστον ἀγωνίσεσθαι προτρεπόμενος. See also *Kaibel* 040⁵ *s.v.* παραδειγματίζω.

For the subst. see P Oxy X. 1252 *verso*²⁷ (A.D. 288–95) οὕ]τινες κατὰ μὲν τὴν προτροπὴν τῆς βουλῆς παρελθόντες, "who came forward at the behest of the senate," and for the adj. see Vett. Val. p. 55¹ προτρεπτικῶν καὶ διδασκαλικῶν λόγων.

προϋπάρχω.

"am before or previously." Like προτρέπω, this Lucan word (Lk 23¹², Ac 8⁹) is found in vernacular sources. Thus in a description of the repair of certain canal dykes, P Lille I. 1 *verso*¹ (B.C. 259–8), reference is made to the already existing dykes—τῶν δὲ προυπαρχόντων χωμάτων ἐν τοῖς διαπλευρισμοῖς τούτοις : cf. P Tebt I. 9³ (B.C. 119) κατασταθεὶς πρὸς [τ]ῆι προϋπαρχούση[ι] μοι κωμογραμματείας (*l.*—είαι), "on being appointed to the post of komogrammateus previously held by me" (Edd.), *ib.* 50[40] (B.C. 112–1) (= *Chrest.* I. p. 586) ἐκσκάψαι τὸν ὑδραγωγὸν καθὼς προϋπῆρξεν, "to dig out the conduit as it was before" (Edd.), and from the inscrr. *Syll* 462 (= [3]520)[32] (iii/B.C.) κα[τὰ τ]οὺς νόμους τοὺς προϋπ[άρχ]οντας, *ib.* 928 (= [3]679)[18] (B.C. 143) στήλην λεύ]κου λίθου, ἣν καὶ στησάτω πλησίον τῆς προϋπαρχούση[ς] (*sc.* στήλης). Vett. Val. p. 283[21] διὰ τὴν προϋπάρχουσαν ἔχθραν.

πρόφασις

is the "ostensible reason" for which a thing is done, and generally points to a false reason as opposed to the true, cf. Phil 1[18] εἴτε προφάσει εἴτε ἀληθείᾳ : see the classical parallels adduced *ad l.* by Wetstein, and add from the Κοινή such exx. as—P Tebt I. 27[72] (B.C. 113) (= *Chrest.* I. p. 520) οὔτε γὰρ βίαν οὔθ᾽ ἑτέραν ἡνδηποτοῦν πρόφασιν προσδεξόμεθα, BGU II. 648[11] (A.D. 164 or 196) βιαίως ἀντι[λ]αμβάνονται τ[ο]ῦ πατρικοῦ μου μέρους προφάσει γεωργίας βασιλικῆς γῆς. P Oxy VIII. 1119[11] (A.D. 254) ἀγνοίας πρ[ό]φασιν ὑποτεμνησάμενος, "pleading the excuse of ignorance," *ib.* VI. 903[3] (iv/A.D.) καὶ ταύτῃ τῇ προφάσει ἆραι εἴ τι ἔχω, "and on this pretext to take away whatever I have myself" (Edd.), BGU III. 941[15] (A.D. 376) ὁμολογῶ ἐντεῦθεν μηδένα λόγον ἔχειν πρὸς σὲ μηδὲ ἐπελθεῖν σοι μηδὲ ἐγκαλεῖν προφά[σει] τούτων, and PSI I. 52[23] (vi/A.D. ?) οἱασδηποτοῦν ἕνεκεν προφάσε(ως). In the early Christian letter P Amh I. 3[ii.7] (between A.D. 264 and 282) (= *LAE*, p. 193) we have the collocation προφάσε[ις] καὶ ἀναβολὰς καὶ ἀναδόσι[ς] (=εις) ποιη[σά]μενος, "though I made excuses and delays and puttings off."

For the more colourless meaning "occasion," cf. the Imperial edict P Fay 20[11] (iii/iv A.D.) ἐπὶ τῇ προφάσει τῆς ἐμαυτοῦ ἀρχῆς τῆς Αὐτοκράτορος, "on the occasion of my succession to the empire" (Edd.), BGU IV. 1024[vi.21] (iv/v A.D.) εὑρὼν οὖν πρόφασιν ὁ Ζεφύριο[ς] λέ[γει τοῖς πολιτευομέν[ο]ις᾽ οὐκ᾽έτι δύ]ναμαι ἀπο[λῦ]σαι Διόδημον, and the elegiac epitaph, *Kaibel* 204[5] (not later than i/B.C.) where a dead wife is invoked by her husband—

Ἀτθίς, ἐμοὶ ζή[σ]α[σ]α καὶ εἰς ἐμὲ πνεῦμα λιποῦσα
ὡς πάρος εὐφροσύνης, νῦν δακρύων πρόφασι.

The verb προφασίζομαι is found in PSI III. 207[25] (iii/iv A.D.), BGU III. 899[10] (iv/A.D. ?).

προφέρω

has the literal meaning "bring forth," "produce," in its only occurrence in the NT, Lk 6[45]. The verb lends itself readily to a variety of applications, as the following exx. will show—P Lond 21[15] (B.C. 162) (= I. p. 13, *UPZ* i. p. 213) ὅσα καὶ ἡμεῖς προεφερόμεθα, "all that we have also brought forward," P Amh II. 30[7] (ii/B.C.) δι᾽ οὗ προφέρ[οφερ]εται [τὸν ἑαυτοῦ πατέρα Μ]αρρῆν ἠγορακέναι [οἰκίαν, "in which (*sc.* a legal declaration) he sets forth that his father Marres had bought a house," P Ryl II. 125[27] (A.D. 28–9) ὃς καὶ ὡμολ[ό]γησεν τὴν πυξίδα ὡς προφέρεται κενήν, "moreover he acknowledges (having found) the box, but alleges that it was empty" (Edd.), P Oxy X. 1282[23] (A.D. 83) Thnas προφέρεται, "claims," that a right of execution for debt had descended to her, P Tebt II. 297[14] (*c.* A.D. 123) ἀντ[έγραψεν ὁ στρ]ατηγὸς τὸν κωμ[ο]γρ[α]μματέα ἐ[πὶ τ]ῆς ἐξετάσεως

προενηνοχ[έναι . . . "the strategus replied that the komogrammateus had represented at the inquiry . . ." (Edd.), *ib.* 291[43] (A.D. 162) ἐξ ἧς οἱ ἱερογραμματεῖς προήνεγκαν βίβλου ἱερατικῆς, "from a hieratic book produced by the sacred scribes" (Edd.), BGU IV. 1024[vi.4] (iv/v A.D.) ἠξίωσαν οὖν προεναι( ) [ἐ]χθ[ῆναι ἀ]πὸ τοῦ δ[ε]σμωτηρί[ου] καὶ ἀκουσθῆ[ναι αὐτό]ν, and P Oxy VIII. 1164[4] (vi/vii A.D.) προήνεγκαν οὐκ ὀλίγους ἄνδρας, μαρτυροῦντας ὡς αὐτῶν ἐστὶν ἡ κάμηλος, "they produced not a few persons testifying that the camel is theirs" (Edd.). MGr προφέρω, "utter," "give an opinion" (Thumb *Handbook*, p. 352).

προφητεία.

The noun is well established against Grimm's reduction of its vogue : thus P Tebt II. p. 448 (Index VI. *d*)) gives its occurrences in a series of documents (mostly ii A.D.) relating to the sales of the office of "prophet" at the temple of Soknebtunis, e.g. 294[5] (A.D. 146) where a certain Paknebkis offers ὠνήσασθαι τὴν τοῦ προκειμένου ἱεροῦ προφη[τ]εία[ν for the sum of 2200 drachmae, and *ib.* 295[10] (A.D. 126–138) where Marsisuchus offers 520 drachmae and extra payments τῆ[ς] τε προφητεί[ας κα]ὶ λεσωνίας τῆς καὶ βαιοφορίας, "for the post of prophet and lesones or palm-bearer." The history of the post is discussed by the editors p. 64 f.

προφητεύω.

In Gnomon 93 (= BGU V. p. 34) it is laid down : τοῖς θάπτουσι τὰ ἱερὰ ζῷ[α] οὐκ [ἐξ]ὸν προφητεύειν οὐδὲ ναὸν κωμάζειν ο[ὐ]δὲ τρέφειν ἱερὰ [ζ]ῷ[ι]α.

An interesting ex. of the verb is quoted by Boll *Offenbarung* p. 137 n[9].: π. κόσμου c. 1 ἡ ψυχὴ. . θείῳ ψυχῆς ὄμματι τὰ θεῖα καταλαβοῦσα τοῖς τε ἀνθρώποις προφητεύουσα : see also his reff. to Reitzenstein *Poimandres*, particularly pp. 154 n.[1], 203 f., and 220 ff.

The wrongly augmented form προεφήτευσεν is found in the LXX in 1 Kingd 18[19] A and Sir 46[20], but has disappeared from the critical text of the NT : cf. Winer-Schmiedel *Gr.* p. 102.

προφήτης.

OGIS 111[18] shows us a προφήτης in Upper Egypt in ii/B.C. : and in *Syll* 790 (= [3]1157[32] (*c.* B.C. 100?), a procession is ordered in honour of the oracle of Apollo Coropaeus (Corope in the Pagasaean Gulf). The procession is formed of an elected ἱερεύς of Apollo, one each from the colleges of στρατηγοί and νομοφύλακες, one of the πρυτάνεις and a ταμίας, preceding τὸν γραμματέα τοῦ θεοῦ καὶ τὸν προφήτην. The prophet is the interpreter of the oracle—"the composer" would come nearer to fact—and the γραμματεύς takes down the response he dictates.

See also the list of religious officials in the Canopic Decree *OGIS* 56[4] (B.C. 238) (cf. the Rosetta stone *ib.* 90[5]—B.C. 196) οἱ ἀρχιερεῖς καὶ προφῆται καὶ οἱ εἰς τὸ ἄδυτον εἰσπορευόμενοι πρὸς τὸν στολισμὸν τῶν θεῶν καὶ οἱ πτεροφόραι καὶ ἱερογραμματεῖς καὶ οἱ ἄλλοι ἱερεῖς. Dittenberger notes *ad l.* that the προφῆται are "interpretes oraculorum et scriptorum sacrorum," and for the title compares P Amh II. 50[5] (B.C. 146 or 135) Διόδωρος . . προφήτης Σοκνοπαίου θεοῦ μεγάλου Ἀμωνίωι χαίρειν, and similarly *ib.* 57[2]. From Roman times we may add *ib.* 128⁵⁶ (A.D. 128) προφήτη(s) ʾΙσιδο(s): cf. also BGU I. 149³ (ii/iii A.D.) τῷ προφήτῃ Σούχον θ[εοῦ μεγάλ]ου μεγάλου, and *ib.* II. 488³ (ii/A.D.) προφήτου. [. . . .] Συκατοίμεω[s, both passages cited by Deissmann *BS* p. 235 f., where also pointed attention is directed to the important fact that "in Egypt the *prophets* were priests." See also Otto *Priester* i. p. 80 ff., and in further illustration of the word in Hellenistic religious literature cf. Vett. Val. p. 63¹⁹ ὁ γεννώμενος ἔσται μακάριος εὐσεβής, προφήτης μεγάλου θεοῦ καὶ ἐπακουσθήσεται ὡς θεός, and p. 67²² ἐὰν δὲ ὁ τοῦ Διὸς συμπαρῇ αὐτῇ, ἔσται προφήτης εὐτυχὴς πλούσιος ἔνδοξος, πολλῶν ἀγαθῶν κυριεύσει.

The name of **προφήτης** is apparently given to a piece of land in P Fay 111²⁶ (A.D. 95–6) τῶν (*l.* τὸν) στίχον τὸν (*l.* τῶν) φυτον (*l.* φυτῶν) τῶν ἐν τῷ προφήτῃ πότισον, "water the row of trees at 'the prophet'" (Edd.).

προφῆτις.

"a prophetess" (Lk 2³⁶, Rev 2²⁰). In *Magn* 122 d³ (probably time of Diocletian) this word is conjecturally restored by the editor—ἐξ Εὐαγρίο[υ] Βαρίλλας προ(φήτι- δος?) Τραλλ(ιανοῦ): see Thieme p. 19 f. The proper name **Προφήτιλλα** is found in a sepulchral inscr. from Hierapolis, *C. and B.* i. p. 118, No. 27 (*c.* A.D. 200). Ramsay thinks that the name may be Christian, and that, if so, it was bestowed on this woman at a time when women-prophets were a feature of the Christianity of Anatolia, i.e. towards the close of ii/A.D.

προφθάνω.

P Lond 44¹⁶ (B.C. 161) (= I. p. 34, *UPZ* i. p. 140) τὴν μὲν θύραν τοῦ ἱεροῦ προφθάσαντός μου καὶ κλείσαντος, "when I had anticipated them and shut the temple door," spoken by a man taking refuge: cf. Mt 17²⁵.

προχειρίζομαι.

For the metaph. use of this verb "elect," "appoint," as in Ac 22¹⁴, 26¹⁶, cf. P Leid Li.³ (= I. p. 55) (Ptol.) ʾΑσκληπιάδης ὁ π[ρο]κεχειρισμένος πρὸ[s] τῇ γεωμετρίᾳ ὑπὸ Σαρ[α]πίωνος, P Fay 14¹ (B.C. 124) οἱ προκεχιρισμένοι πράκτορες, "the appointed collectors," P Amh II. 60² (A.D. 154) ʾΑφροδισίωι καὶ τοῖς σὺν αὐτῷ προχειρισθεῖσι πρὸς παράλημψ ιν) κ[αὶ κα]τακομιδὴν βιβλίως(= ν), "to Aphrodisius and those appointed with him to receive and transmit the accounts" (Edd.), P Lond 376⁵ (= II. p. 77) (A.D. 159) ἀντὶ τοῦ συνήθους προχιριζομένου ὑπὸ τοῦ κρατίστου ἐπι- στρατηγου, "instead of the usual person appointed by the epistrategus," and *Syll* 279 (= ³ 601)⁶ (B.C. 193) Μένιππος . . . προχειρισθεὶς καὶ ὑφ᾽ ὑμῶν πρεσβεῦσαι περὶ τῆς πόλεως.

For subst. προχειρισμός (not in LS⁸) see P Amh II. 39¹ (B.C. 103) (= Witkowski², p. 106).

προχειροτονέω.

"appoint beforehand," which in Biblical Greek is confined to Ac 10⁴¹, meets us in the official report BGU IV. 1191⁰ (*c.* end i/B.C.) τῶι προκεχειροτονημένωι. Cf. χειροτονέω.

πρύμνα,

"stern." In P Cairo Zen I. 59054⁸ (B.C. 257) a boat (κέρκουρος) is described as τοῦ ἄκρου συνοξῦναι τοῦ περὶ τὴν

πρύμναν πλάτος πήχεις βL, "being two and a half cubits broad at the narrow end round the stern" (Ed.). The same document shows us the adj. πρυμνητικός *bis.* For πρύμνα opposed to πρῷρα, cf. P Mon I. 4¹² (A.D. 581) ἀπὸ πρώρας μέχρι πρύμνης, "from prow to stern."

πρωΐ,

"early," "in the morning": cf. P Petr III. 42 II (8f.)⁶ (B.C. 250) (= Witkowski², p. 15) οἱ πρωῒ παραγενόμενοι, P Par 35¹⁷ (B.C. 163) (= *UPZ* i. p. 130) ἐπιστρέψας πρωΐ, and *ib.* 37ⁱ·²⁰ (B.C. 163) (= *UPZ* i. p. 128) πρωεί. The adverbial τὸ πρωΐ, which is common in the LXX (Gen 40⁶ *al.*) and is used in MGr, is found in PSI IV. 402¹⁰ (iii/B.C.) καὶ γὰρ τὸ πρωῒ εὐθέως παρακάθηνται τῆι φακῆι πωλοῦντες τὰς κολυκύνθας.

For πρώην (*sc.* ἡμέραν) see PSI IV. 352⁵ (B.C. 254–3) πρώην ἐν τῆι ἀπεγδόσει τῶν ἔργων, P Par 26²⁵ (B.C. 163) (= *Selections*, p. 16) ἀναβάντι πρώην εἰς τὸ ἱερόν, P Amh II. 66³⁹ (A.D. 124) πρώην οὐδὲν ἀπέδειξας, "the other day you proved nothing" (Edd.), P Oxy I. 59⁸ (A.D. 292) τοῦ πρώην αἱρεθέντος Θεοδώρου ἀντὶ ʾΑρείονος, "Theodore who was recently chosen in place of Arion," *ib.* VIII. 1104⁹ (A.D. 306) ἀκολ[ούθως] οἷς πρώην ἀναδέδωκά σοι γράμμασιν, "in accordance with the letters recently handed to you." Other exx. are *Chrest.* I. 122⁶ (A.D. 6) πρό(= ώ)ην, Preisigke 6⁹ (A.D. 216), and P Oxy IX. 1204¹⁸ (A.D. 299): cf. also BGU I. 303¹² (A.D. 586) ἀρούρας, ὅσας ἐὰν ὦσιν, ἃς καὶ ἐκ πρώην εἶχον.

πρωΐα,

"early morning" (Mt 27¹, Jn 21⁴): cf. BGU IV. 1206²⁰ (B.C. 28) (ἔτους) γ ʾΑθὺρ ̅ς̅ πρωίας, P Lond 1177⁶⁶ (A.D. 113) (= III. p. 183) ἀπὸ πρωίας ἕως ὀψέ.

πρώϊμος.

See s.v. πρόϊμος

πρωϊνός.

As distinguished from πρόϊμος, derived from πρό, πρωϊνός (Rev 2²⁸, 22¹⁶), derived from πρωΐ, means "belonging to the morning" in contrast to ἑσπερινός, "belonging to the even- ing" (see s.v.): cf. Thackeray *Gr.* i. p. 90.

πρῷρα,

"prow," is found in P Cairo Zen I. 59054¹⁵ (B.C. 257) and the corresponding adj. πρωιρατικός in *ib.*¹³·²⁷. For the gen. πρῴρης, as in Ac 27³⁰, cf. P Lond 122⁴⁰ (iv/A.D.) (= I. p. 117) ἐπὶ τῆς πλ(=ρ)ῴρης τοῦ ἱεροῦ πλοίου, and see Blass *Gr.* p. 25. See also s.v. πρύμνα.

πρωτεύω.

This NT ἅπ. εἰρ. (Col 1¹⁸) "hold the chief place," "am preeminent," may be illustrated from P Lips I. 40ⁱⁱ·¹⁶ (iv/v A.D.) ἀνὴρ ἀξιόπιστος ἐμαρτύρησεν πρωτεύων τῆς ʾΕρμουπολιτῶν, P Oxy XVI. 1083³ (A.D. 535) εὐκλεεστάτῳ πατρικίῳ πρωτεύοντι, *ib.* VIII. 1106⁶ (vi/A.D.) παρεγγύησον τοῖς πρωτεύουσιν ἀποσχέσθαι τοῦ τοιούτου τολμήματος, "instruct their leaders to abstain from any such outrage" (Ed.), and *Kaibel* 489² (iv/B.C.). With the use in Col *l.c.* we may compare Plut. *Mor.* p. 9 σπεύδοντες τοὺς παῖδας ἐν πᾶσι τάχιον πρωτεῦσαι. A less pleasing sentiment is found in Menander *Fragm.* p. 140—

> οἶκος δ' ἐν ᾧ τὰ πάντα πρωτεύει γυνή,
> οὐκ ἔστιν ὅστις πώποτ' οὐκ ἀπώλετο.

"never does a house fail to come to grief, where woman takes the lead in everything." For the similar form δευτερεύω (as in Esth 4⁸) cf. P Passalacqua¹³ (iii/B.C.) (= Witkowski², p. 54) περὶ Πετονοῦριν τὸν δευτερεύοντα : see P Par p. 405 f. The subst. πρωτεῖον occurs in *Kaibel* 569³ (i/A.D.).

πρωτοκαθεδρία.

See *s.v.* πρωτοκλισία.

πρωτοκλισία.

Like πρωτοκαθεδρία, πρωτοκλισία, "the chief place" at table, appears to be confined to the Gospels and writers who quote them, but for the title πρωτοκλίναρχος (not in LS*), see *Archiv* i. p. 413 f.

πρῶτος.

In the LXX regularly (Thackeray *Gr.* i. p. 183) and in the **Κοινή** frequently, especially in the Ptolemaic period, **πρῶτος** stands for πρότερος, so reversing the usual Hellenistic rule that the comparative does duty for both degrees of comparison. For an ex. almost contemporary with the NT we may cite P Oxy II. 297⁹ (A.D. 54), where a man asks for information for a supplementary return of lambs born since the first or former return for the year had been made— παρὰ τὴν πρώτην ἀπογραφήν. No stress can, therefore, be laid on the use of πρῶτος in Ac 1¹, as if Luke meant to write a *third* treatise (cf. Ramsay *Paul*, p. 28).

To illustrate Jn 1¹⁵, 15¹⁸, we may quote P Leid W^xii 49 (ii/iii A.D.) (= II. p. 125) ἰδὼν δὲ ὁ Φόβος αὐτοῦ ἰσχυρότερον ἀντέστη αὐτῷ, λέγων· σοῦ πρωτός εἰμι, "prior sum quam tu." Abbott (*Joh. Gr.* p. 510 f.) suggests that the Leiden papyrus may have been dependent on Jn 1¹⁵, and translates the latter passage "my Chief" (*ib.* p. 11 ff.), but see Moulton (*Proleg.* pp. 79, 245) in support of the ordinary rendering "before me."

That πρώτη in Ac 16¹² is not to be understood geographically (as Lightfoot *Philippians²* p. 49) but politically has been made clear by Ramsay in *C. and B.* ii. p. 420 (cf. *Paul*, p. 206 f.) in connexion with the rivalries of Greek cities to be regarded as "first" or "chief" of their respective districts. For the suggestion that the true reading in Ac *l.c.* is not πρώτη but πρώτης, see Field *Notes*, p. 124, Blass *Philology* p. 67 ff.

In P Hib I. 110⁷² (c. B.C. 255) (= *Chrest.* I. p. 514) a certain Phoenix is described as τῶν πρώτων Ἐσοπ[.].[. ., "one of the first company of E . . . ," and the editors compare for a similar military title an unpublished Tebtunis papyrus of iii/B.C.—τῶν Μενελάου πρώτων ἐκ τοῦ Ἑρμοπολίτου καὶ (ἑκατοντάρουρος : cf. also *IG* XIV. 601 cited *s.v.* Μελίτη. In P Oxy VIII. 1101³ (A.D. 367–70) π[αρ' ὀ]λίγων τῶν πρώτων is rendered by the editor "from a few first comers," and in *Syll* 523 (= ³578)¹⁰ (ii/B.C.) τὸ πρῶτον ἔργον is used in the sense of the highest class— class I—in connexion with the instruction of youths (see the editor's note).

The adverbial **πρῶτον** is seen in the soldier's letter to his father BGU II. 423¹² (ii/A.D.) (= *Selections* p. 91) γράψον μοι ἐπιστόλιον πρῶτον μὲν περὶ τῆς σωτηρίας σου, δεύτερον περὶ τῆς τῶν ἀδελφῶν μου, and τὸ πρῶτον, as in Jn 10⁴⁰ *al.*, in P Oxy IV. 811 (c. A.D. 1) καὶ τὸ πρῶτον ἔγραψά σο]ι εὐχαριστῶν Ἑρμίππου (*l.* Ἑρμίππῳ), where the meaning is either "at the first" or "earlier" (= πρότερον, see Olsson *Papyrusbriefe* p. 53.

For the double superlative πρώτιστος cf. P Eleph 10¹ (B.C. 223–2) ἀπὸ τοῦ πρωτίστου χρόνου, and BGU II. 665ⁱⁱ·¹⁶ (i/A.D.) ὅτι πρωτι[σ]τα λαμβάνει (*sc.* ὀψώνιον), and see *Proleg.* p. 236. In BGU III. 839⁵⁰ (i/A.D.) ἐγὼ γὰρ ἔχω τὸ προτερ[ικὸ]ν (*l.* πρωτερικόν), Herwerden understands πρωτερικόν as = "praeoptatio," "praerogativa (?)," but cf. Olsson *Papyrusbriefe* p. 198.

πρωτοστάτης.

For this word which is used metaphorically of a "leader" in Ac 24⁵, and nowhere else in the NT, see Poland *Vereinswesen*, p. 90.

πρωτότοκος,

"firstborn." As additional proof that this word is to be taken out of the list of purely "Biblical" words, Deissmann (*LAE*, p. 88) cites the undated pagan sepulchral inscr. *Kaibel* 460⁴ ἱερεὺς γάρ εἰμι πρωτοτόκων ἐκ τελεθ[ῶν?] (= τελετ[ῶν?]), "for I am a priest by the rites of the firstborn," and notes that the editor suggests that in the family of the deceased the firstborn always exercised the office of priest. He also refers to a Christian metrical epitaph from Rome of ii/iii A.D. *Kaibel* 730³ πρωτότοκον, διετές, with reference to a firstborn "sun-child" (ἡλιόπαις), i.e. child born on a Sunday, who died at the age of two years. Note further a sacrificial decree of c. B.C. 200, *Syll* 615 (= ³1024)¹⁷, in which mention is made of ὃν ἐνκύμονα πρωτότοκον, and a decree of adoption of A.D. 381, P Lips 598¹⁵ (= *Archiv* iii. p. 173) πρ[ὸ]ς τὸ εἶναί σου υἱὸ]ν γνήσιον καὶ πρωτότοκον ὡς ἐξ ἰδίου αἵματος γεννηθέντα σοι, and the magical P Osl I. 1³¹² (iv/A.D.) λαβὼν πρωτοτόκου κριοῦ ὀμφάλιον.

πρώτως.

For this *v.l.* in Ac 11²⁶ cf. P Par 63¹⁸¹ (B.C. 164) (= P Petr III. p. 34) ὥστ' ἐπὶ τ[ὴ]ν πρώτως παρισταμένην μετάγηται πάντα, "on the understanding that they then be all transferred to the land which provided them first" (Mahaffy), P Ryl II. 235¹¹ (ii/A.D.) ἀλλὰ οὐ πρώτως σου τὸ εἰκαῖον μανθάνομεν, "but it is not the first time that we learn your heedlessness" (Edd.), and P Oxy X. 1267¹⁰ (registration of a child—A.D. 209) βουλόμεθα πρώτως ἀπὸ τοῦ νῦν ἀναγραφῆναι ἐπὶ τοῦ ὑπάρχοντος ἐμοὶ . . . μέρους οἰκίας, "we wish that for the first time and henceforth he should be registered in the share of a house belonging to me": see the editors' note where πρώτως is taken as meaning that the new owner was making a return for the first time of his new acquisition. Cf. also from the inscrr. *C. and B.* ii. p. 459, No. 290 (A.D. 54–5), and see Preisigke *Fachwörter s.v.*

πταίω.

The metaph. use of **πταίω**, "stumble," in the NT (Rom 11¹¹ *al.*) may be illustrated from the vi/A.D. letter of an advocate, complaining about the treatment of certain cultivators in his employ—P Oxy VIII. 1165¹¹ **παρακληθῆτε οὖν, εἴτε ἔπταισαν εἴτε οὐκ ἔπταισαν, ποιῆσαι αὐτοὺς ἀπολυθῆναι**, "be persuaded, whether they made an error or whether they did not, to have them released" (Edd.). The verb is also found in PSI VII. 767³⁸ (A.D. 331?) **πτέ(= αί)σαντας τὴν τυχήν**, and *Syll* 350 (= ³768)¹⁰ (B.C. 31) **πταῖσαι**, and a subst. **πταῖμα** (for **πταῖσμα**) in *ib.*³ 456¹⁰ (c. B.C. 250) **πταίματός [τι]νος γενομένου**. Cf. M. Anton. vii. 22 **ἴδιον ἀνθρώπου φιλεῖν καὶ τοὺς πταίοντας**, "it is a man's especial privilege to love even those who stumble" (Haines), and Menander *Fragm.* p. 195 *fr.* 672². See also Deissmann *BS*, p. 68.

πτερύγιον.

"a little wing." hence "gable," "pinnacle" (Mt 4⁵, Lk 4⁹). For **πτερυγοειδῶς**, "in the form of a wing," in the technical language of magic, see Deissmann *LAE* p. 453 n.⁴

πτέρυξ,

"wing," is found several times in an oracle of iv/iii B.C., *Syll* 801 (= ³1107)¹⁻⁵, dealing with the auspices drawn from the flight of birds—**ἢν ἐπάρει τὴν εὐώνυμον (δεξιὴν) πτέρυγα.** In a food-account, P Oxy IV. 738¹⁰ (c. A.D. 1), the editors translate **πτέρυγες β.** "2 snipe (?)." MGr **φτερούγα**. For **πτερόω** in late Greek of spreading the oars or sails of a ship like wings, cf. Psaltes *Gr.* p. 323.

πτηνός,

"winged." For **τὰ πτηνά** used substantively, "winged creatures," "birds," as in I Cor 15³⁹, cf. Aristeas 145. 146. 147.

πτοέω,

in pass. "am terrified" (Lk 21⁹, 24³⁷): cf. P Leid Wᵛ·³³ (ii/iii A.D.) **ἰδὼν ὁ Θεὸς πάλιν ἐπτοήθη** ("obstupuit"), **ὡς ἰσχυρότερον θεωρήσας**: cf. *ib.*ˣᵛⁱⁱ·²⁹ **οὖ καὶ οἱ δαίμω(= ο)νες ἀκούοντες τὸ ὄνομα πτοῶ(= οῦ)νται.** The verb is restored by Deissmann (*LAE*, p. 439) in the second of the New Sayings of Jesus from Oxyrhynchus, P Oxy IV. 654²⁹⁴ **γνῶσ(= εσ)θε ἑαυτοὺς ἐν[ώπιον τῶν ἀνθρώπων,] καὶ ὑμεῖς ἐστέ, ἡ πτο[εῖσθε**, "know yourselves in the sight of men, and ye are there where ye are terrified"; but most editors prefer to read **ἡ πτό[λις θ(εο)ῦ]** in keeping with the context. The verb is used in a weaker sense in M. Anton. iv. 19 **ὁ περὶ τὴν ὑστεροφημίαν ἐπτοημένος**, "he whose heart flutters for after-fame" (Haines). See the exx. from classical and late Greek in Anz *Subsidia*, p. 298; and cf. Psaltes *Gr.* p. 227.

πτύον,

"winnowing-fan." This word from the vocabulary of "Q" (Mt 3¹², Lk 3¹⁷) appears in the letter of an illiterate landowner Gemellus, P Fay 120⁵ (c. A.D. 100) **εὖ πυήσις π[έ]μσ[ις] μυ θρ[ί]νακες δύωι καὶ λικμητρίδες δύωι καὶ πτύο>ν ἕν**, "please send me two forks and two shovels and a winnowing-fan" (Edd.).

πτύρομαι.

To the exx. of this verb "am frightened, terrified" (Phil 1²⁸) add Eus. *H.E.* v. 24 **οὐ πτύρομαι ἐπὶ τοῖς καταπλησσομένοις**, and the exx. from late Greek in Psaltes *Gr.* p. 225.

πτύσμα,

"spittle" (Jn 9⁶): cf. *Or. Sib.* i. 365 **πτύσματα φαρμακόεντα.**

πτύσσω.

With this verb used of "rolling up" a scroll in Lk 4²⁰, its only occurrence in the NT, cf. **πτυκτός**, "a folding writing-tablet," as in P Strass I. 37¹² (iii/A.D.) **πτυκτῶν τριῶν.** For the medical use of **πτύσσω** see Hobart p. 106 f. The compound **περιπτύσσω** occurs in P Lond 1925⁶ (mid. iv/A.D.) **αὐταῖς ὄψεσ{εσ}ίν σε περιπτύξασθαι**, "to embrace you with my very eyes."

πτύω,

"spit" (onomatopoetic, like Lat. *spuo*, Eng. *spew*: cf. **πυτίζω**—Boisacq, p. 824). For the use of "spittle," as in Mk 7³³, cf. Klostermann *HZNT ad l.*, and for the compound **ἐπιπτύω** see P Leid Wˣᵛⁱⁱ·³⁶ (ii/iii A.D.) (= II. p. 145) **ἰς τὴν γῆν ἐπιπτύων**, "in terram spuens." Cf. also Artem. p. 35 **μὴ ἐμεῖν δοκεῖν ἀλλὰ πτύειν (αἷμα)**, and the colloquial **πρὶν πτύσαι**, "before you can spit," in Menander **Περικ.** 202.

πτῶμα

in the NT is confined to its late sense (cf. Rutherford *NP* p. 472 f.) of "a dead body": cf. the collective sing., as in Rev 11⁸, in *Syll* 318 (= ³700)¹⁷ (B.C. 118) **ἐτρέ[ψ]ατο τοὺς ὑπεναντίους καὶ τοῦ τε πτώματος ἐκράτησεν καὶ πο[λ]λοὺς αὐτῶν ἀπέκτεινεν.** See also *Kaibel* 326⁵ where a man guards against **ἕτερον πτῶμα** being placed in his family tomb. For the meaning "ruin" of a building, cf. P Oxy I. 52¹² (A.D. 325) **ἐκ τοῦ συμβάντος πτώματος τῆς οἰκίας αὐτοῦ.** The word is also used of "payments" falling due as in P Eleph 11³ (B.C. 223–2) **ἐ[ν οἷς ἔτε]σιν τὰ πτώματα γέγονεν**, and in P Lond 3³⁷ (B.C. 146 or 135) (= I. p. 47). See further *Archiv* i. p. 87. In a series of farm-accounts, P Fay 102²⁰ (c. A.D. 105), certain boys are described as **διαλέγοντες πτῶμα**, which the editors think may refer to "gleaning."

πτωχεία,

literally "beggary," is not found in any Saying of our Lord recorded in the Gospels, but occurs in the fourth of the Oxyrhynchus Sayings, P Oxy I. 1 *recto*¹: cf. White *Sayings*, p. 34 f. In P Gen I. 14²³ (Byz.), a Christian begging-letter full of Biblical citations, we have **συγχώρησόν μοι τῷ ἐν πτωχεία.** The word denotes "poor-relief" in Justinian's Code, I. 3. 41. 23.

πτωχός.

"crouching," "cringing," hence "a beggar," was always used in a bad sense until it was ennobled by the Gospels. It occurs in P Petr III. 36 (a) recto⁷·¹⁸ (Ptol.) along with its comparative, but unfortunately in a very broken context: see also ib. 140¹ (private accounts) πτώχωι ν̣ γνάφει c. In Gal 4⁹ the translation "beggarly" is not very happy: the πτωχὰ στοιχεῖα are such that there is "nothing in them"— no one is the better for them: see Westcott St. Paul and Justification, p. 81. MGr φτωχός, "poor."

πυγμή.

literally "fist" (Suid.: σύγκλεισις δακτύλων): cf. the cognate pugnus, pungo, pugio (Boisacq, p. 827). We are unable to throw any light from our sources on the difficult πυγμῇ of Mk 7³ B, for which ℵ substitutes πυκνά (Vg crebro), but we may quote Palladius Hist. Lausiaca c. 55 νίψασθαι τὰς χεῖρας καὶ τοὺς πόδας πυγμῇ ὕδατι ψυχροτάτῳ, to which our attention has been drawn. According to Schulthess (ZNTW xxi. (1922) p. 233) the expression is best explained as a lightening of the regular ritualistic washing, by a simple rubbing over with the hand, or a dry washing. For such a practice, under the name of פֵּ֗ם, he refers to Krauss Archäol. I. 210, 269 N.6. The Islamic custom of ablution with dust or sand when water cannot be procured is described in Hughes' Dict. of Islam s.v. "Ablution" or "Tayammum."

πύθων.

For the use of this word in Ac 16¹⁶ in the sense of "ventriloquist," commentators generally appeal to Plut. de defectu Oraculorum 9 τοὺς ἐγγαστριμύθους . . . νῦν . . . πύθωνας προσαγορευομένους, the utterance being traced to the presence of a "familiar spirit" (πύθων) in the body of the speaker: cf. LXX Lev 10³¹, 1 Kingd 28⁷ al. Along with this the girl is described as having a certain prophetic power, μαντευομένη: cf. Suidas, πύθων· δαιμόνιον μαντικόν, and Knowling's note EGT ai Ac l.c.

πυκνός.

For the original meaning of this adj. "thick," "close," cf. P Fay 113⁸ (A.D. 100) ἐπὶ(=εἰ) Ἑρμόναξ ἐρώτησέ με, εἵνα ἐφίδῃ τὸν [ἐ]λαιῶνα αὐτοῦ τὸν ἐν Κερκεσούχ̣ο̣υ=οις ἐπὶ πυκνός ἐστιν τῇ=οῖς φυτῷ=οῖς, καὶ ἐξ αὐτὸ=ῶν ἐκκόψαι θέλι φυτά, "since Hermonax has asked me to allow him to look over his olive-yard at Kerkesucha, as it is overgrown with trees, and he wishes to cut down some of the trees" (Edd.): see also ib. 114¹³. Πυκνός = "frequent," as in 1 Tim 5²³, is found in Aristeas 90 πυκνὰ τὰ στόματα, "frequent outlets."

For the comparative of the adverb, as in Ac 24²⁶, = "very often," or "so much the oftener" (Blass Gr. p. 142), cf. P Oxy IV. 805 (B.C. 25) ἀξιῶ δὲ ἀντιφωνεῖν [μ]οι πυκνό-τερον: see also P Leid Wⁱⁱ·¹¹ (ii/iii A.D.) τῆς ὥρας πυκνό-τερον, similarly¹·³⁰, and Aristeas 318. The form πυκνοτέρως occurs in P Lond 1029⁶ (mid. iv/A.D.) παρακαλῶ οὖν πυκνο[τέ]ρως ἡμῶν μνήσθη[τι. For the verb πυκνόω, used intransitively, cf. Clem. Al. Paedagog. i. 6. 44 χειμῶνος μὲν πυκνοῦντος as against Cobet 277 πυκνοῦ ὄντος: cf.

Philologus lxiii. (N.F. xvii., 1904) p. 3. See also Polyb. xviii. 7. 8.

πυκτεύω.

With πυκτεύω = "box" in 1 Cor 9²⁶, cf. the sepulchral epitaph Kaibel 291¹ ὁ πυκ[τ]ε̣ύ̣σας [π]ο̣λλάκις ἐν [στα-δίοις. For subst. πύκτης cf. P Oxy VII. 1050ᵇ·¹ (ii/iii A.D.), an account for games, in which payment is made Κώφῳ πύκ[τῃ, and P Lond 1158⁵ (A.D. 226-227) (= III. p. 151) μακρὸς πύκτης, "a tall boxer." In ib. 1178¹² (A.D. 194) (= III. p. 217, Selections p. 100) notification is made of the admission to a Gymnastic Club of Ἑρμεῖνον, τὸν καὶ Μωρόν, [Ἑ]ρμοπολείτην πύ]κτην, "Herminus, also called Morus, boxer of Hermopolis."

πύλη.

P Oxy VI. 892¹ (A.D. 338) βορρινὴν πύλην τῆς πόλεως, "north gate of the city." For πύλη followed by the name of a village in custom-house receipts cf. P Fay 68¹ (A.D. 158) τετέλ εσται) δι(ὰ) πύλ(ης) Διονυσιάδος ἐρη μοφυλα-κίας, and see GH p. 195 ff. For the irregular dat. plur. in 3 Kingd 22¹⁰ A, see Psaltes Gr. p. 174.

πυλών.

"gateway" of a house (Mt 26⁷¹) or city (Ac 14¹³): P Tebt II. 331⁹ (c. A.D. 131) ἐπῆλθο[ν α]ὐθάδως εἰς ἣν ἔχω ἐν τῇ κώμῃ οἰκίαν . . ἐν τῷ πυλῶνι, "made a bold attack upon my house in the village . . at the gateway" (Edd.), P Ryl II. 233³ (ii/A.D.) κωμοκάτοικοί εἰσιν οἱ ἔ[χο]ντες πρὸ τοῦ πυλῶνός σου τὸν ψιλὸν τόπον, "the owners of the open plot in front of your gateway are villagers," and the illiterate P Oxy XII. 1480⁵ (late iii/A.D.) τὸ κιθώνιν ἐπιλέ-λισμε (l. ἐπιλέλησμαι) παρὰ Τεκοῦσαν εἰς τὸν πυλῶνα, "I have left my cloak behind with Tecusa at the gateway" (Edd.). Psaltes Gr. p. 24 n.¹ has collected exx. of the late form πυλεών. For πύλιον see Preisigke 2008², 5255³.

πυνθάνομαι,

"inquire," is common: P Petr II. 16¹³ (iii/B.C.) πευσό-μεσθα ἀκριβέστερον (cf. Ac 23²⁰), PSI VI. 614¹⁴ (iii/B.C.) πυνθάνεται εἴ τι ἥκει γράμμα παρά σου, P Cairo Zen I. 50044¹⁸ (B.C. 257) νῦν μὲν γὰρ αὐτὸν πυνθανόμεθα ὀλιγωρεῖσ-θαι, P Eleph 13³ (B.C. 223-2) ἐγὼ οὖν ἐπυνθανόμην τοῦ Σανῶτος, εἴ τι βούλοιτο ἐν τοῖς καθ' ἡμᾶς τόποις, P Lond 43¹ (ii/B.C.) (= I. p. 48, Chrest. I. p. 102) πυνθανομένη μανθάνειν σε Αἰγύπτια γράμματα συνεχάρην σοι καὶ ἐμαυτῇ, P Oxy VIII. 1102¹¹ (c. A.D. 146) πυνθανομένου μου οὐδὲν σαφές ἐδήλω[σ]έν, ib. VI. 930¹¹ (ii/iii A.D.) ἐμέλησε δέ μοι πέμψαι καὶ πυθέσθαι περὶ τῆς ὑγίας σου and ib. VII. 1065⁶ (ii/iii A.D.) ἐμ[ο]ῦ σου πυθομένου τί ἔπραξας.

πῦρ.

PSI III. 184⁷ (notice of a fire—A.D. 292) χθὲς περὶ ἕκτην ὥραν ἐξαίφνης καύματος ἐνόντος πῦρ ἐν σκυβάλοις χόρτου . . . ἀνεφάν]η. In P Oxy VI. 903⁵ (iv/A.D.) a wife amongst other charges against her husband alleges—πῦρ προσήνεγκεν ταῖς τροφίμαις μου γυμνώσας αὐτὰ[ς παντελῶς ἃ οὐ ποιοῦσι οἱ νόμοι, "he applied fire to my foster-daughters, having stripped them quite naked, which is contrary to the laws" (Edd.).

With τὸ πῦρ τὸ αἰώνιον (Mt 18⁸: cf. Dalman *Words*, p. 161) we may compare the magical papyrus P Lond 46¹⁴⁷ (iv/A.D.) (= I p. 70) where the enchanter, to impress the evil powers he desires to overcome, declares—ἐγώ εἰμι ὁ ἀκέφαλος δαίμων, ἐν τοῖς ποσὶν ἔχων τὴν ὅρασιν, ἰσχυρός, τὸ πῦρ τὸ ἀθάνατον, "I am the headless demon, having eyes in my feet, the strong one, the deathless fire": cf. Deissmann *LAE* p. 139. For the "fire of love" see P Leid Wᵛⁱⁱ ⁴⁹ (ii/iii A.D.) (= II. p. 105) ἐξορκίζω σε, πῦρ, δαίμων αἵρωτος ἀγείου (*l.* ἔρωτος ἁγίου), and P Osl I. 1¹¹⁰ (iv/A.D.), with the editor's note (p. 65). With Rev 8⁷ cf. *Orac. Sib.* v. 376 f. πῦρ γὰρ ἀπ' οὐρανίων δαπέδων βρέξει . . πῦρ καὶ αἷμα, and for Rom 12²⁰ see *Exp T* xxxvi. p. 478.

πύργος,

"a tower": cf. BGU IV. 1104⁹ (B.C. 27) τοῦ ἱεροῦ πύργου, P Ryl II. 138²⁰ (A.D. 34) ἐσύλησέν μου ἐν τῶι πύργωι ἱκανὰ ἀργαλε(ῖ)α, "he robbed me of a number of tools in the tower," and P Giss I. 67¹⁶ (time of Trajan/Hadrian), where reference is made to a sleeping-chamber (κοιτῶν) ἐπὶ τοῦ πύρ[γου. Πύργος is used of a "watch-tower" in a vineyard, as in Mt 21³³ *al.*, in BGU II. 650⁰ (A.D. 60-1) ἐν ᾧ ἐλαίων καὶ πύργος καὶ ἕτερα, and in P Oxy II. 243¹⁵ (A.D. 79) we hear of a πύργος δίστεγος, "a two-storied tower," cf. the οἰκία διπυργία in P Hamb I. 14⁹,²⁶ (A.D. 209-210). A Lycian inscr. (*JHS* xxxiv. (1914) p. 5 No. 10¹) shows πύργος apparently in the sense of a "tomb"—Ἐπάγαθος β ὁ τὸν πύργον ἐκ θεμελίων κατασκευάσας. The editors refer to the similar use of πυργίσκος in *CIG* III. 4207 *al.* This latter word is rendered "casket" by GH in P Oxy VI. 921²⁴ (iii/A.D.): cf. Artem. p.68¹.

It should be noted that in *Hermes* liv. p. 423 ff. F. Preisigke advocates the meaning "farm-building" for πύργος, and is supported by E. Meyer in *ib.* lv. p. 100 ff., where the suitability of this meaning for such NT passages as Mk 12¹, Lk 14²⁸, is shown. See also P Strass II. 110⁶ (iii/B.C.).

πυρέσσω,

"have fever" (Mt 8¹⁴, Mk 1³⁰): cf. Diog. Laert. *Antisth.* vi. 1. οἱ ἰατροί, φησί, μετὰ τῶν νοσούντων εἰσὶν ἀλλ' οὐ πυρέττουσιν. See also M. Anton. viii. 15, Artem. p. 221¹¹.

πυρετός,

"a fever." The Lucan combination with συνέχεσθαι (Lk 4³⁸, Ac 28⁸) is paralleled in P Oxy VI. 896²³ (A.D. 316) ὁρῶμε[ν αὐτό]ν τὸ̣ῦτ̣ον κλε̣[ινή]ρην ὄντα πυραι(= ε)τίοις . . . συνεχ[όμενον, "we saw the man himself lying on a bed seized with a slight . . . fever" (Edd.): note the technical plur. on which Hobart (p. 52) comments.

Πυρετός in the sing. is found in the heathen charm, BGU III. 956 (iii/A.D.), invoking protection ἀπὸ πα[ν]τὸς ῥίγου- ς - καὶ πυρετοῦ, cf. P Oxy VI. 924⁶ (iv/A.D.), *ib.* VIII. 1151³⁵ (v/A.D.?), and the curse *Syll* 800 (= ³ 1239)²⁰ (ii/A.D.) φρείκη [κ]α̣ὶ̣ πυρετῷ καὶ τεταρταίῳ καὶ ἐλέφα[ν]τ[ι: cf. also *ib.* 891 (= ³ 1240)¹⁰ (ii/A.D.). For the form πυρεσσός (not in LS⁸) see the fragment of a Gemellus letter P Fay 248 (*c.* A.D. 100).

πύρινος.

For this adj., "as of fire" (Rev 9¹⁷), cf. *Kaibel* 987 (A. 95), an inscr. on the right leg of the statue of Memnon Thebes—

Φθέγξαο, Λατοΐδα· σὸν γὰρ μέρος ὧδε κάθηται,
Μέμνων, ἀκτεῖσιν βαλλόμενος πυρίναις.

πυρόω,

"burn with fire," occurs in a Jewish-Greek sepulch. inscr. from Tell el Yehudieh, *ZNTW* xxii. (1923), p. 2 No. 18⁵ πατὴρ καὶ μήτηρ οἱ πυρώμενοι ἐννεαέτην, who Lietzmann thinks the reference is to "burning" the de body, and not to the parents' "burning with grief" (2 Cor 11²⁹). In the same list of inscrr. we find No. τρεῖς ὧδ[ε π]άρεσμεν, ὁ ἀνὴρ καὶ [ἡ θυγά]τηρ καὶ [π]επύρωκαν ἐγώ.

πυρράζω,

"am fiery red" (Mt 16²,³). For form see *s.v.* πυρρ The adj. πυρράκης, which occurs *ter* in the LXX, is fou in the description of a boy slave in P Cairo Zen I. 59076 (B.C. 257): cf. the exx. from Byzantine Greek in Psaltes G p. 302 n.¹

πυρρός,

literally "red as fire" (cf. 4 Kingd 3²²), is applied in t milder sense of "ruddy" to a witness to a will, P Petr 13(2)¹² (B.C. 237). In P Leid Wᵛⁱⁱ ⁴⁶ (ii/iii A.D.) we ha ποίσον(= ποίησον) ὑπποποτάμω(= ο]ν ἐκ κηροῦ πυρρ and in P Oxy VI. 922⁸ (vi/vii A.D.) ὑπὲρ τοῦ πυρροῦ ἵππ (cf. Rev 6⁴). The double ρρ is preserved in the LXX a NT as in the papyri, cf. BGU II. 408⁸ (A.D. 150) καμήλ ἄρρενος πυρροῦ, and see Mayser *Gr.* p. 221. It may noted that πυρ(ρ)ός and πυρ(ρ)άζω drop a ρ in Mt 16²C a late uncials, Rev 6⁴ APO46, 12³ CO46: see Moulton *Gr.* p. 101.

For the form πυρράκης, as in 1 Kingd 16¹², cf. P Petr 1.4³⁰ (B.C. 237), and see Mayser *Gr.* p. 455; and for πυρρ χρους cf. P Ryl II. 134¹⁵ (A.D. 34) ὗς τοκὰς ἐπίτοκος πυρρ χρους, "a brood-sow about to litter, tawny-coloured (Edd.).

Πύρρος.

According to the critical text Πύρρος is named in Ac 2 as the father of Sopater of Beroea. The name is by means rare in the papyri, and is spelt both with double a single ρ: e.g. P Oxy I. 47³ (late i/A.D.) ὑπὸ Πύρρου τ ἀσχολη), and *ib.* 43 recto²·⁹ (A.D. 295) Πύρῳ ὀπτίων other exx. in Preisigke *Namenbuch*.

πύρωσις,

"heat," "fiery test" (1 Pet 4¹²): cf. the Berlin mag papyrus 2ⁱⁱ·¹¹⁹ (ed. Parthey *Abh. d. Berl. Ak. d. Wissens* 1865, p. 153) δι' ἧς πέμπεις τὴν εἰς ἀέρα πύρωσιν, and s Linde *Epic.* p. 39.

πωλέω.

From meaning originally "put up for sale" (*vendito*) πωλέω came to mean simply "sell" (*vendo*). This later sense, which alone is found in the NT, can be fully illustrated from the papyri, e.g. PSI IV. 350² (B.C. 253–2) οὐθεὶς οὖν ἐν τοῖς τόποις πωλεῖ πρὸς σῖτον, ἀλλὰ πρὸς ἀργύριον, P Ryl II. 113⁷ (A.D. 133) μόλις πάντα τὰ ἐμαυτοῦ πωλήσας ἐδυνήθην πληρῶσαι, "I was with difficulty able to complete this by selling all my property" (cf. Mk 10²¹), P Oxy III. 494¹⁹ (a Will—A.D. 156) ἐξέστω δι' αὐτῆς πωλεῖν καὶ ὑποτίθεσθαι ἃ ἐὰν αἱρῆται, "she shall have the right to sell or mortgage on her own authority whatever she chooses," *ib.* VI. 932¹⁰ (late ii/A.D.) τὰ χοιρίδια χωρὶς μοῦ μὴ πώλι, "do not sell the young pigs without me," P Tebt II. 421⁷ (iii/A.D.) (= *Selections*, p. 106) θέλις αὐτὸ πωλῆσα[ι], πώλησον, "if you wish to sell it, sell it," and P Oxy I. 83¹⁵ (A.D. 327), where an egg-seller undertakes to offer his eggs only in the public market, and not "to sell secretly or in his own house"—κρυβῆ ἢ καὶ ἐν τῇ ἡμετέρᾳ οἰκίᾳ πωλῖν. For the rare pass. (cf. Rutherford *NP* p. 213) see the question to an oracle in *ib.* XII. 1477³ (iii/iv A.D.) εἰ πωλοῦμαι: "am I to be sold up?" (Edd.), and for the subst. πώλησις see BGU I. 184¹ (A.D. 72).

πῶλος.

For πῶλος = "foal," "colt," of an ass, as in the NT, cf. P Lille I. 8⁹ (iii/B.C.) ὄνους θηλείας β καὶ πώλους β. In P Oxy IX. 1222¹ (iv/A.D.) the writer instructs his son—δὸς τῷ ἀδελφῷ 'Αμ⟨μ⟩ωνιανῷ τὸν πῶλον εἷνα ἐνεχθῇ μοι, "give your brother Ammonianus the colt that it may be brought to me."

πώποτε,

"ever yet": P Par 47⁶ (B.C. 152–1) (= *UPZ* i. p. 332) οὐκ ἄν με ἴδις τὸ πόρσωπόν (*l.* πρόσωπόν) μου πόποτε (cf. Gen 43³), *ib.* 51²⁷ (B.C. 159) (= *UPZ* i. p. 360, *Selections* p. 21) ἐὰν μιανθῶσιν [οὐ μ]ὴ γένονται καθαραὶ πώποτε, "if they (women) are defiled, they shall never at all be pure." In BGU IV. 1205ⁱⁱ·¹¹ (B.C. 28) πέπρακα, πέπ[ο]τε [. . .]ο[ὐ πεπράκαμεν, Olsson *Papyrusbriefe* p. 30 proposes to read πώποτε [δ'] οὐ (?), "I have sold, but we have not yet (?) sold." For perfects with πώποτε, as in Jn 1¹⁸, expressing "a close nexus with present time," see *Proleg.* p. 144. For οὐδεπώποτε c. pres. cf. P Leid V ˣⁱ·³⁰ (iii/iv A.D.) (= II. p. 37) λύσιν οὐκ ἔχει τοῦτο οὐδεπώποτε.

πωρόω.

"petrify," "deaden." The subst. πῶρος occurs in *Syll* 540 (= ³1072⁵⁸·⁶⁶ (B.C. 175–2): cf. also M. Anton. ix. 36 πῶροι γῆς τὰ μάρμαρα, "marble but nodules of earth" (Haines). See *s.v.* πώρωσις.

πώρωσις.

For a full discussion of this word and its cognates, see Armitage Robinson *Ephesians*, p. 264 ff., where it is shown that in the NT "obtuseness or intellectual blindness is the meaning indicated by the context"; and that "this meaning is as a rule assigned by the ancient translators and commentators" (p. 273).

πῶς.

"how," "in what manner," (*a*) in direct questions— P Oxy IV. 744¹² (B.C. 1) (= *Selections*, p. 33) πῶς δύναμαί σε ἐπιλαθεῖν; "how can I forget you?" Cf. Ac 8³¹ πῶς γὰρ ἂν δυναίμην; which Field (*Notes*, p. 117) renders, "Why, how can I?" For the exclamatory πῶς, as in Mk 10²³, cf. Philemon *fr.* 2 ὦ πῶς πονηρόν ἐστιν ἀνθρώπου φύσις | τὸ σύνολον, Epict. *Man.* 24. 3 ὁρᾶτε ὑμεῖς, πῶς ἄνισοί ἐστε καὶ ἀγνώμονες; see further K. Rupprecht in *Philologus* lxxx. (N.F. xxxiv.), 1024, p. 207.

(*b*) in indirect discourse—P Oxy IV. 745⁶ (*c.* A.D. 1) οὐκ οἶδας γὰρ πῶς μοι ἐχρήσατο ἐν 'Οξυρύγχοις, "you don't know how he treated me at Oxyrhynchus(?)," P Tebt II. 408¹ (A.D. 3) ἐπιστάμενος πῶς σε τίθεμαι κὲ φιλῶ, "since you know how I esteem and love you" (Edd.) (cf. Ac 20¹⁸), P Oxy II. 294²¹ (A.D. 22) (= *Selections*, p. 36) γράψον μοι πῶς πάλιν ἄνω λαλαχεύεται, "write me how his hair is growing again on the top," P Ryl II. 235⁸ (ii/A.D.) οὐκ ἐδήλωσάς μοι περὶ τῆς εὐρωστίας σου καὶ πῶς διάγεις, "you did not inform me of your good health and how you are," P Oxy VI. 932¹ (late ii/A.D.) ἐρῖ σοι δὲ 'Απολινάρις πῶς τὰ θέματα καὶ τὰ δημόσια, "Apolinarius will tell you how the deposits and public dues stand," *ib.* 936²¹ (iii/A.D.) νῦν δὲ πῶς πλίονα γράψω περὶ αὐτῆς ἀπορῶ, "but now I am at a loss how I shall write more regarding her," and *ib.* I. 120¹¹ (iv/A.D.) ἄχρις ἂν γνῶ πῶς τὰ κατ' αἰμαὶ ἀποτίθαιται (*l.* ἐμὲ ἀποτίθεται), "until I know the position of my affairs" (Edd.).

We find already in the NT (e.g. 1 Thess 1⁹) the MGr tendency to use πῶς as equivalent to little more than ὅτι: cf. BGU I. 37⁸ (A.D. 50) οἶδας γὰρ πῶς αὐτοῦ ἑκάστης ὥρας χρῄζωι, P Ryl II. 235⁶ (ii/A.D.) ἐθ'αύμασε(=α) δὲ πῶς διὰ Λυπέρκου οὐκ ἐδήλωσάς μοι περὶ τῆς εὐρωστίας σου, "I was surprised that you did not inform me through Lupercus of your good health" (Edd.), and see Radermacher *Gr.* p. 159, Hatzidakis *Gr.* p. 19.

πῶς,

enclitic. "in some way," "in any way": P Oxy I. 95³⁸ (A.D. 129) ἄλλως πως, "in any other way," *ib.* 939¹³ (iv/A.D.) σπουδάζων] εἴ πως ἐκ παντὸς τρόπου δυνηθείης [πρὸς ἡμᾶς] ἀφικέσθαι, "being anxious that you should come to us by every possible means in your power" (Edd.), and *Syll* 510 (= ³864)²¹ (after B.C. 207) ἄν δὲ πως ἄλλως πρὸς αὐτοὺς ὁμολογήσωσιν. See also *s.v.* μήπως.

P

ῥαββεί—ῥακά (ῥαχά, Tisch.)

ῥαββεί.

For the accentuation ῥαββεί (ῥαββουνεί) in Cod. Vaticanus, showing that ει was regarded as a diphthong, cf. Nestle in *ZNTW* vii. (1906), p. 184. See also Dalman *Words*, pp. 324 ff., 340.

ῥαββουνεί.

See *s.v.* ῥαββεί.

ῥαβδίζω,

which is used of the Roman punishment "beat with a rod" in its two NT occurrences (Ac 16²², 2 Cor 11²⁵), is applied to "threshing" in P Ryl II. 148²⁰ (A.D. 40) ἐράβδισαν γόμους κ, "they threshed out 20 loads" of anise: cf. LXX Judg 6¹¹. For a similar use of the subst. ῥαβδισμός, see P Tebt I. 119⁴⁶ (B.C. 105-1), where the editors refer to *ib.* 229 (B.C. 97 or 62), and for ῥαβδιστής see BGU I. 115¹·¹⁵·²⁰ (ii/A.D.).

ῥάβδος,

"a rod": P Tebt I. 44²⁰ (B.C. 114) ἔδωκεν πληγὰς πλείους ἧι [ε]ἶχεν ῥάβδωι, "gave me many blows with the rod he was carrying": cf. P Lond 44¹² (B.C. 161) (= I. p. 34, *UPZ* i. p. 140), P Grenf I. 38¹² (ii/i B.C.). For a reminiscence of Ps 2⁹ (cf. Rev 2²⁷ al.) see the magical P Osl I. 1¹⁰⁸ (iv/B.C.) κατέχων ῥάβδον σιδηρᾶν, with the editor's note, and for a similar reminiscence of Exod 14¹⁶ see the leaden tablet from Hadrumetum, Wünsch *AF* 5¹⁰ (iii/A.D.) (= *Audollent*, p. 374) ὀρκίζω σε τὸν διαστήσαντα τὴν ῥάβδον ἐν τῇ θαλάσσῃ.

For the form ῥαύδους = ῥάβδους, cf. P Par 40²² (B.C. 158), 41²⁵ (B.C. 158-7) (= *UPZ* i. pp. 148, 150), and see Mayser *Gr.* p. 115.

ῥαβδοῦχος,

lit. "a rod-holder," is supplied by Wilcken in P Par 24⁶ (B.C. 164) (= *UPZ* i. p. 123) τῶν δ' ἐκ τοῦ ἱεροῦ ῥαβδο[ύ]χός τις Ζωίλος, with reference to a "temple-attendant" in the Serapeum at Memphis. For this usage (as distinguished from a *lictor* or attendant on Roman magistrates, as in Ac 16³⁵·³⁸) he refers to a ῥαβδοῦχος in the Roman Serapis worship in *IG* XIV. 1027, and to the ῥαβδοῦχοι in the temple service of Apollo in *Syll* 790 (= ³ 1157)²⁴ (c. B.C. 100?) whose duty is to keep in order the temple precincts—οἱ καὶ ἐχέτωσαν ἐξουσίαν κωλύειν τὸν ἀκοσμοῦντα. In P Oxy XIV. 1626⁹ (A.D. 325) the reference is again to an official of low rank who fills the single post of ῥαβδοῦχος of certain animals—χώραν μίαν ῥαβδούχου ἑνὸς τῶν αὐτῶν ζῴων: see the editors' note, and cf. *ib.* 1750¹² (A.D. 306) and *ib.* XVI. 1905¹⁶ (iv/v A.D.). Cf. the word ῥαβδοφόρος in P Petr II. 8(2) (*c*)⁹ (B.C. 246) and P Par 66¹⁸ (iii/B.C.). In the latter case the editor suggests that ῥαβδοφόροι may not be more than "conductors of works," but for the possibility that "police" were intended see *Archiv* vi. p. 416.

For the subst. ῥαβδουχία cf. P Oxy XVI. 1626²¹ (A.D. 325), and BGU I. 244¹⁴ (time of Gallienus).

ῥᾳδιουργία.

For ῥᾳδιουργία in the general sense of "false pretences," cf. P Oxy II. 237viii·¹⁵ (A.D. 186) εἴτε πλαστῶν γραμμάτων ἢ ῥᾳδιουργίας ἢ περιγραφῆς ἐνκαλεῖν, "to make a charge either of forgery or false pretences or fraud" (Edd.) (but see *Archiv* i. p. 182): cf. the wider usage in P Tor I. 1vi·³ (B.C. 116) (= *Chrest.* II. p. 36) κακοτρόπως καὶ ἐπὶ ῥᾳδιουργίαι παρακεῖσθαι αὐτὸν τὴν συνχώρησιν, Preisigke 5656¹² (A.D. 568) χωρὶς ῥᾳδιουργίας καὶ ἀταξίας, and P Strass I. 40³⁰ (A.D. 569) δίχα παντοίας μέμψεως καὶ καταγνώσεως καὶ ῥᾳδιουργίας. The special meaning of "theft" is seen in P Magd 35¹¹ (B.C. 216) (= *Mél. Nicole* p. 454) περὶ δὲ τῆς ῥᾳδιουργίας with reference to the theft of a mantle, and in BGU I. 220¹⁴ (A.D. 99).

For the verb see P Tebt I. 42¹⁶ (c. B.C. 114) (= *Chrest.* I. p. 385) ῥᾳδιουργηημένας (for form cf. Mayser *Gr.* pp. 120, 408), and P Flor III. 294⁵⁵ (vi/A.D.) ῥᾳδιουργῆσαι, and for the adj. ῥᾳδιουργός see P Lond IV. 1338²⁹ (A.D. 709), 1349³⁷ (A.D. 710).

ῥακά (ῥαχά, Tisch.)

in Mt 5²² is usually taken as a term of contempt transliterated from the Aramaic רֵיקָא, "empty": cf. Lightfoot *Hor. Hebr.* ii. p. 109. It is thus not so strong as μωρός, which denotes, according to Lightfoot *ib.* p. 112, "lightness of manner and life" rather than "foolishness": see Marriot *Sermon on the Mount*, p. 182. Mr. W. K. L. Clarke kindly supplies us with an interesting definition of ῥακά from Basil *Regulae* li. 432 C: τί ἐστι Ῥακά; ἐπιχώριον ῥῆμα ἠπιωτέρας ὕβρεως, πρὸς τοὺς οἰκειοτέρους λαμβανόμενον, "What is Ῥακά? a vernacular word of mild abuse, used in the family circle."

Various explanations of the word are discussed by Zorell *Lex. s.v.*, F. Schulthess *ZNTW* xxi. (1922) p. 241 ff., and Leipoldt *CQR* xcii. (1921), p. 38.

ῥάκος,

"a piece of cloth" (Mt 9[16], Mk 2[21]): cf. P Petr III. 42 H (8) f[27] (mid. iii/B.C.) ῥάκος λεπτόν, P Oxy I. 117[11] (ii/iii A.D.) ῥάκη δύο, P Lond 121[205] (iii/A.D.) (= I. p. 91) βύσσινον ῥάκος, *ib.*[359] (= p. 96) ῥάκος λινοῦν. See also Apoc. Petr. 15 ἄνδρες ῥάκη ῥυπαρὰ ἐνδεδύμενοι (cf. Jas 2[2]). In Artem. p. 18[8] the word is used of mummy wrappings—οἱ ἀποθανόντες ἐσχισμένοις ἐνειλοῦνται ῥάκεσι.

ῥαντίζω,

"sprinkle," equivalent to classical ῥαίνω, in Heb 9[13] *al.* is one of the exx. of "neues Sprachgut" in the Κοινή: cf. Thumb *Hellen.* p. 223. For ῥαντός, "sprinkled," "spotted," as in LXX Gen 30[32] D[sil], cf. PSI VI. 569[10] (iii/B.C.) θήλειαι μέλαιναι δ καὶ ῥαντὴ α, of birds.

ῥαντισμός,

"sprinkling": LXX, NT (Heb 12[24], 1 Pet 1[2] (cf. Hort *ad l.*) but not as yet found in any secular author: cf. however Vett. Val. p. 110[17] περὶ τὰς ὄψεις φακοὺς καὶ ῥαντίσματα ἔχοντες.

ῥαπίζω,

lit. "strike with a rod," *verbero,* came in late writers to be used in the sense of "strike (the face) with the palm of the hand" (Suidas: ῥαπίσαι· πατάσσειν τὴν γνάθον ἁπλῇ τῇ χειρί): see Lob. *Phryn.* p. 175, and cf. Rutherford *NP* p. 257 ff. This suits both the NT occurrences of the verb Mt 5[39], 26[67]: cf. LXX Hos 11[4], 1 Esdr 4[31].

ῥάπισμα,

"a blow on the cheek with the open hand": see *s.v.* ῥαπίζω and add Field *Notes.* pp. 40 f., 105 f. The word is used of a "scar," or the result of a blow, in a vi/A.D. account of the sale of a slave published in *Archiv* iii. p. 415 ff., see p. 419[33], and cf. Sudhoff *Ärztliches,* p. 143.

The difficult ῥαπίσμασιν αὐτὸν ἔλαβον in Mk 14[65] is fully discussed by Swete *ad l.,* where he translates "they caught Him with blows." The RV adopts the rendering "with blows of their hands" in the text, but puts the alternative "strokes of rods" in the margin. Blass (*Gr.* p. 118) describes the phrase as a "vulgarism," which at present can be paralleled only from a i/A.D. papyrus (αὐτὸν) κονδύλοις ("knuckles") ἔλαβεν, published in Fleckeis. *Jahrb. f. class. Philol.* xxxviii. (1892), pp. 29, 33.

ῥαφίς,

"needle," is found in a series of accounts P Oxy IV. 736[75] (c. A.D. 1) λίνου καὶ ῥαφίδος (ὀβολός), "thread and needle 1 ob."; cf. Mt 19[24], Mk 10[25]. On the relation of ῥαφίς to βελόνη (Lk 18[25]), see Rutherford *NP* p. 174 f.

ῥαχά.

See *s.v.* ῥακά.

ῥέδη.

For the substitution of ε for αι in this NT ἅπ. εἰρ. (Rev 18[13], = "a chariot," cf. Moulton *Gr.* ii. p. 81. According to Quintilian i. 5. 57 the ῥέδη came from Gaul and was a vehicle with four wheels.

Ῥεφάν.

See *s.v.* Ῥομφά.

ῥέω.

For ῥέω, "flow," which occurs in the NT only in Jn 7[38] (for fut. act. cf. *Proleg.* p. 154), see the traveller's account of his visit to the source of the Nile, P Lond 854[8] (i/ii A.D.) (= III. p. 206, Deissmann *LAE* p. 162) ὅθεν τ[υγ]χάνει Νεῖλος ῥέων, "whence the Nile flows out": cf. P Lond 121[436] (iii/A.D.) (= I. p. 98) παρὰ ῥέον βαλανείου and *Preisigke* 401[10] (A.D. 10-11) ποταμ[ὸν] . . ῥέοντα δι' ὅλης τῆς πόλεως.

For the subst. ῥεῦμα, cf. P Petr II. 37 2a *verso*[8] (iii/B.C.) ἐνκλείναντος τ[οῦ] ῥεύματος εἰς τὸ πρὸς βορρᾶν μέρος, and P Lond 46[263] (iv/A.D.) (= I. p. 73) ἐν τῷ ῥεύματι τοῦ ποταμοῦ εἰς τὴν θάλασσαν.

Ῥήγιον.

"Rhegium" (mod. "Reggio"), a town in Italy opposite Sicily. For the derivation of the name from ῥήγνυμι see the citations in Wetstein *ad* Ac 28[13].

ῥῆγμα.

For ῥῆγμα in the sense of "breach" in the Nile embankments see P Lond 131 *recto*[45, 60] (A.D. 78-9) (= I. p. 171 f.), and cf. PSI V. 450[11] (A.D. 270-82) ἐπὶ τοῦ πύργου. . ῥήγματα : cf. Lk 6[49], and for the medical use of the word = "rupture," see Hobart p. 50. The subst. ῥηγμός may be illustrated from *ib.* IV. 422[15] (iii/B.C.) ἡ δὲ γῆ ῥηγμῶν πλήρε(=η)ς ἐστὶν διὰ τὸ μήποτε αὐτὴν ἠρόσθαι.

ῥήγνυμι, ῥήσσω.

"rend," "break asunder": P Leid V[iii. 31] (iii/iv A.D.) (= II. p. 27) αἱ πέτραι ἀκούσασαι ῥήγνυνται (*l.* ῥήγνυνται). Ῥήσσω is claimed as Ionic by Winer-Schmiedel, p. 19. For ῥάσσω see Mk 9[18] D. In the LXX ῥάσσω is not an alternative of ῥήσσω, but a form of ἀράσσω: see Thackeray *Gr.* i. p. 76.

ῥῆμα.

For the ordinary meaning "word" in the NT, cf. P Giss I. 40[ii. 7] (A.D. 215) ἐκ τῶν ῥη[μά]των το[ῦ] προτέρου διατάγματος, P Amh II. 142[8] (iv/A.D.) ἀπρεπῆ ῥήματα, P Flor III. 309[4] (iv/A.D.) αἰσχρ[ο]ῖς ῥήμασι, and *Syll* 809 (= [3] 1175)[18] (iv/iii B.C.) ῥῆμα μοχθηρὸν ἢ πονηρὸν φθέγγεσθαι (contrasted with [20] κακόν τι ποῆσαι).

On the Hebraistic use = *res* in the LXX and in the more Hebraic parts of Luke's writings (Lk 1[37], 2[15], *al.*), see Thackeray *Gr.* i. p. 41. A somewhat similar use of λόγος has classical authority, e.g. Plato *Phil.* 33 C.

ῥήσσω.

See ῥήγνυμι.

ῥήτωρ.

The special meaning of "advocate," "barrister," which this word has in Ac 24[1], can be freely illustrated from our documents, e.g. P Oxy I. 37[i. 4] (A.D. 49) (= *Selections,* p. 48), the report of a lawsuit where the counsel for the plaintiff is introduced with the words—Ἀριστοκλῆς ῥήτωρ ὑπὲρ Πεσούριος, and *ib.* II. 237[vii. 23] (A.D. 186) Δίδυμος ῥήτωρ ἀπεκρείνατο μὴ χώρις λόγου τὸν Σεμπρώνιον κεκεινῆσθαι, "Didymus, advocate of Sempronius, replied that his client had had good reason for having been provoked" (Edd.), P Ryl II. 75[5. 16] (late ii/A.D.), PSI IV. 293[26. 33] (iii/A.D.), *et saepe.*

ῥητῶς.

For ῥητῶς, "explicitly," "in set terms" (1 Tim 4[1]), see P Par 63[62] (B.C. 164) (= P Petr III. p. 22) ῥητῶς τε διὰ τῆς π[ε]μ[φθεί]σης ὑμῖν ἐπιστολῆς, *OGIS* 515[39] (iii/A.D.) ῥητῶς τῆς ἀπογραφῆς [λεγούσης ὅτι συνάγ]εται ἡ βουλὴ διὰ τοῦτο, and cf. P Tebt II. 303[12] (A.D. 176–180) ἐπὶ τοῦ ῥητοῦ, "at the specified time," similarly *ib.* 332[19] (A.D. 176).

ῥίζα.

For the literal sense "root" cf. P Oxy XIV. 1674[5] (iii/A.D.) καῦσον τὴν ῥίζαν αὐτῆς, "burn its roots," with reference to an acacia tree. In P Lond 121[173] (iii/A.D.) (= I. p. 89) the eating of roots of bugloss, [ῥ]ί[ζ]ας βυγλου (i.e. βουγλώσσου), is recommended to prevent the breath from smelling after eating garlic. The metaphorical sense of "origin," "ancestry," is seen in *OGIS* 383[31] (mid. i/B.C.), where Antiochus I. refers to the Persians and Greeks as ἐμοῦ γένους εὐτυχεστάτη ῥίζα : cf. Rev 22[16].

ῥιζόω.

The rapid transition from the metaphor of "rooting" to that of "building" in Col 2[7] is rendered easier, as Lightfoot *ad l.* points out, by the use of ῥιζόω in connexion with cities and buildings, e.g. Plut. *Mor.* 321 D παρέσχε ῥιζῶσαι καὶ καταστῆσαι τὴν πόλιν. Similarly with reference to the building of a bridge, *Kaibel* 1078[7] αἰώνιος ἐρρίζωται.

ῥιπίζω.

To Hort's exx. *ad* Jas 1[6] of this word to denote the surface of the water blown upon by shifting breezes, rather than billows lashed by a storm, we may add Aristeas 70 where the workmanship bestowed on certain ornamental leaves is described as so life-like that if a breath of wind blew upon them— ῥιπιζόντος τοῦ κατὰ τὸν ἀέρα πνεύματος—the leaves stirred in their places. It should be noted that the verb is derived not from ῥιπή, "a rushing motion" (ῥίπτω), but from ῥιπίς, "a fire-fan."

ῥίπτω,

"throw off," "throw away": cf. P Tebt I. 48[23] (c. B.C. 113) ῥίψαντα τὸ ἱμάτιον εἰς φυγὴν ὁρμῆσαι, "so that he threw away his garment and took to flight" (Edd.), P Ryl II. 125[25] (A.D. 28–9) ἐκκενώσας τὰ προκείμενα ἔριψεν ἐν τῇ οἰκίᾳ μου τὴν πυξίδα κενήν, "having rifled the contents aforesaid he threw the box empty into my house" (Edd.). Both AV and RV adopt this meaning in Ac 22[23], but Field (*Notes,* p. 136), who is followed by various commentators, prefers the rendering "shake," "throw about," as if the verb = ῥιπτάζω : cf. the medical use in connexion with convulsive fits, etc., as illustrated by Hobart p. 2.

For the perf. pass., as in Mt 9[36], cf. P Petr II. 19 (2)[3] (iii/B.C.) καλῶς οὖμ ποιήσεις ἐ[πι]στροφήν [μου π]οιησάμενος, ἔρρειμαι γὰρ κακῶς διακείμενος ἀπ' ἐκείνου, and for the form ῥιπτέω see Radermacher *Gr.* p. 84. MGr ῥίφτω, ῥίχνω, ῥίχτω (ῥιμμένος ῥιχμένος), "throw," "cast away": see Thumb *Handb.* p. 353.

Ῥόδη.

For this proper name (Ac 12[13]) cf. the inscr. on a grave-stone at Alexandria of iii/B.C.—*Preisigke* 302 Ῥόδη Μύση μάμμη. Blass (*ad* Ac *l.c.*) points out that the name is found in myths and comedies: see e.g. Menander *Fragm.* 245[6], 546[5], Philemon *fr.* 84.

Ῥοδίνη is found as a proper name in the Christian inscr. *CIG* IV. 9484. The adj. ῥόδινος occurs in P Oxy III. 496[4] (articles in a dowry—A.D. 127) ζώνας δύο, σανδυκίνην, ῥοδίνην, "2 girdles, one red, the other rose-coloured," and P Goodsp Chicago 4[3] (medical prescription—ii/A.D.) κηρωτὴ ῥοδίνη, "wax-ointment scented with rose." See also P Petr II. 34 (*b*)[6] (an account for unguents—iii/B.C.) (= Sudhoff *Ärztliches,* p. 47) ῥοδίνου β.

ῥοιζηδόν.

"with crackling crash," is found in the NT only in 2 Pet 3[10]: see Wetstein and Mayor *ad l.*

Ῥομφά.

For the various forms which this proper noun takes in Ac 7[43] see WH *Notes[2]*, p. 92. In LXX Amos 5[26] from which the quotation in Ac is taken the form is Ῥειφάν or Ῥεφάν replacing כִּיּוּן of the Heb. text, and the word is understood as a corruption of the Assyrian name for the planet Saturn (= Chiun).

ῥομφαία.

For ῥομφαία, a Thracian weapon of large size, see Hastings' *DB* iv. p 634, where the different uses of the word are fully illustrated. In the NT it is found *sexies* in Rev, and once, metaphorically, in Lk 2[35].

ῥοπή

occurs as a *v.l.* for ῥιπή, "a moment," in 1 Cor 15[52] D*EFG 67**. For the original meaning, "a turn of the scale," as in Sap 18[12], cf. P Par 63[73] (B.C. 165) (as read P Petr III. p. 24) συμβαλεῖται ῥοπὴν εἰς τὸ προκείμενον, "it would turn the scale in favour of the matter in hand" (Mahaffy), and P Tebt I. 27[79] (cited *s.v.* ἐνθυμέομαι). See also Aristeas 90 ῥοπῇ καὶ νεύματι, "momento temporis et ad nutum," Vett. Val. p. 301[1] αἱ στιγμαὶ ἢ ῥοπαὶ τῶν ὡρῶν, and Herodas VII. 33 with Headlam's note.

Ῥοῦφος.

For the probable identification of the Ῥοῦφος of Rom 16[13] with the Ῥοῦφος of Mk 15[21], see SH p. 426 f. The name is very common: see e.g. P Hamb I. 29[5] (A.D. 89), and the reff. in Preisigke *Namenbuch s.v.*

ῥύμη.

For this word in its late Greek sense "street," "lane," which it has in its four occurrences in the NT (Mt 6[2],

Lk 14²¹, Ac 9¹¹, 12¹⁹), cf. P Par 51¹⁰ (B.C. 150) (= UPZ i.
p. 360, *Selections*, p. 20) ἔρχομαι εἰς τὴν ῥύβ(= μ)ην μετ᾽
αὐτῶν, BGU IV. 1037¹⁶ (A.D. 47) εἰς τὴν ἐκ λιβὸς ῥύμην
βασιλικήν, P Oxy I. 99⁹ (A.D. 55) ἀνὰ μέσον οὔσης τυφλῆς
ῥύμης ("blind alley"), and P Ryl II. 159¹ (ii/A.D.) δημοσίᾳ
ῥύμῃ. In an Alexandrian papyrus of the time of Augustus
we hear of a street named Εὐδαίμων—ἐν τῆι Εὐδαίμονος
λεγομένηι ῥύμηι (see *Archiv* v. p. 57 n.¹. For the diminutive ῥύμιον (not in LS) = "a little lane" or "alley," cf.
the direction in P Meyer 20 ⁵⁰ ⁵⁰ (1st half iii/A.D.) ἀντικρὺ
τοῦ [. . .] πωλίου ἥκεις ⟨εἰς⟩ τὸ ῥύμιον, "over against the
shop you come to the little lane."

See further Rutherford NP p. 487 f., and Kennedy *Sources*
p. 15 f., where the different stages in the history of ῥύμη are
stated.

ῥύομαι.

In the version of the Lord's Prayer which forms part
of the vi A.D. Christian amulet, BGU III. 954²³ (= *Selections*, p. 134), we find ῥῦσαι ἡμᾶς ἀπὸ τῆς πο[ν]ηρ[ί]ας,
in accordance with the AV interpretation of Mt 6¹³. Cf.,
however, the inscr. on a very old church in central Phrygia
—Ἀρχάγγελε Μιχαήλ, ἐλέησον τὴν πόλι σου κ[α]ὶ ῥῦσαι
αὐτὴν ἀπὸ τοῦ πονηρ[οῦ] (C. and B. ii. p. 741 No. 678).
As exx. of the verb we may add P Lond 413¹ (c. A.D. 346)
(= II. p. 301) ε[ὔχομ]αι σ[. .]ω τῷ θεῷ περὶ [τῆ]ς σ[ωτ]ηρίας
ἵνα ῥύσει σαι ἀπὸ.., and the inscr. on a statue in honour
of Hadrian erected A.D. 125, Syll 383 (= ³835 A) Αὐτοκρά-
τορι Ἀδριανῷ σωτῆρι, ῥυσαμένῳ καὶ θρέψαντι τὴν ἑαυτοῦ
Ἑλλάδα. The verb and its constructions are fully illustrated
by Chase *The Lord's Prayer* p. 71 ff. (in *Texts and Studies*
i. 3), and Anz *Subsidia* p. 275 f.

For the subst. ῥῦσις cf. *Kaibel* 204⁴ (Roman age) τοῦ
πικροῦ ῥῦσιν ἔχω θανάτου.

ῥυπαίνω

"make filthy," "defile," occurs in the NT only in Rev
22¹¹ ὁ ῥυπαρὸς ῥυπανθήτω ἔτι, where, as Swete points out
ad l., the aor. (not ῥυπαίνεσθαι) indicates the fixity of the
state into which the ῥυπαρός has entered. For the act. cf.
Jos. c. Ap. i. 220 ῥυπαίνειν τὴν εὐγένειαν. . .ἐπεχείρησαν,
and Vett. Val. p. 116⁸ ψύξει τοὺς γάμους ἢ ῥυπαίνει.

ῥυπαρία.

The moral significance of this word in Jas 1²¹, its only
occurrence in the NT, may be illustrated from *Pelagia-
Legenden* p. 6⁵⁰ ἀφῆκεν ἐν τῷ ὕδατι πᾶσαν αὐτῆς τὴν
ῥυπαρίαν—with reference to cleansing in Baptism. Mayor
ad Jas l.c. recalls that Plutarch (Mor. p. 60 D) uses
ῥυπαρία (like our "shabbiness") of "avarice," which
would suit the idea of a "debased" moral coinage : but see
s.v. ῥυπαρός. We may add two citations from Teles (ed.
Hense)—p. 33⁴ δι᾽ ἀνελευθερίαν καὶ ῥυπαρίαν (of rich men
not using their wealth), and p. 37⁵ διὰ ῥυπαρίαν καὶ
δειλίαν.

ῥυπαρός.

"shabby," "soiled," is applied to clothing in P Giss I.
76³ (ii/A.D.) τρίβωνα[ς] ῥυπαρὰς β καὶ στολὴν ὁμοίως
λευκήν, "two soiled cloaks and likewise a white robe," as

in Jas 2²; cf. P Fay 16¹⁰ (i/B.C.) σίτου ῥυπαροῦ, "dirty
(i.e. unwinnowed) corn," and P Ryl II. 72⁷¹ (B.C. 99-8)
κ(ριθῆς) ῥυπαρᾶς.

The adj. is very common in the papyri in connexion with
payments, and was generally understood as denoting
"debased" coin, e.g. P Tebt II. 545⁶ (A.D. 23) ἀργυρίου
ῥυπ(αροῦ) [δ]ρ[α]χμὰς δεκάδυο, "twelve dr. debased
silver" (Edd.), and P Fay 52 (a)³ (a receipt for poll-tax
—A.D. 101-2) ἐπὶ λ[ό]γου ῥυπαρᾶς δραχμὰς ὀκτώ. But,
according to Milne *Theban Ostraca* p. 104 (cf. *Annals of
Archaeology and Anthropology* vii. p. 64 ff.), "the word
does not appear to refer to any distinct class of coins—all
Roman tetradrachms of Alexandria might have been called
ῥυπαρά—and probably was a term of account, like the
'bad' piastre of some Turkish towns, e.g. Smyrna."
Hence in P Ryl II. 191³ ῥυπ(αρᾶς) (δραχμὰς) ἑπτὰ
ἡμιοβ(έλιον) the editors translate "7 drachmae of discounted
silver ½ obol."

ῥύπος.

"filth" (1 Pet 3²¹), is found = "wax" in superstitious
medicine, P Osl I. 1³⁰⁴ (iv/A.D.) μῖξον δὲ καὶ ταῖς κριθαῖς
καὶ ῥύπον ἀπὸ ὠτίου μούλας, "mix also with the barley-
corn the ear-wax of a female mule" (Ed.). In Isai 4¹ Γ the
noun is neuter. The adj. ῥυπώδης occurs in the medical
prescription P Oxy II. 234¹¹·¹⁸ (ii/iii A.D.) ὅταν ῥυπῶδες
γένηται, ἀνάλαβε, "when it becomes discoloured, draw the
liquor off."

ῥυπόω

is read in the TR of Rev 22¹¹ = "am filthy" morally.
For the literal sense of the compd. verb cf. Syll 879
(= ³1219)⁶ (iii/B.C.), where it is laid down τὰς πενθούσας
ἔχειν φαιὰν ἐσθῆτα μὴ κατερρυπωμένην, "that women in
mourning are to wear gray clothing not defiled."

ῥύσις

is very common of the "flow" or "yield" of wine at the
vintage, see e.g. P Giss I. 70⁰⁰·¹⁴ (c. A.D. 117) ἐὰν δ᾽ ὁ
θε[ὸ]ς ἐπιτρέψῃ πολλὴν ῥύσιν [ἔσεσθα]ι εἰς ἔτους, τάχα διὰ
τὴν ἐσομένην εὐωνίαν τοῦ γενήματος ἀθυμήσουσι οἱ
γ[εο]ῦχοι, and the other exx. collected by the editor ad l.
The noun seems to have a different meaning in P Bad 15³¹
(i/B.C.) εἰπὲ δὲ τῇ ἀδελφῇ πέμψαι μοι τὴν ῥύσιν, ἵνα
χειρογραφήσω. For its use in connexion with the "flow"
of blood, as in Mk 5²⁵, Lk 8⁴³, see Vett. Val. p. 285³⁰.
Ῥυτόν is applied to a drinking-horn in P Petr III. 42 H(7)³
(c. B.C. 250) (= Witkowski², p. 13).

ῥυτίς.

"a wrinkle" of age, which in Biblical Greek is confined
to Eph 5²⁷, may be illustrated from Plut. Mor. p. 789 D
οἷς ἡ γελωμένη πολιὰ καὶ ῥυτὶς ἐμπειρίας μάρτυς ἐπιφαί-
νεται : see Armitage Robinson ad Eph l.c.

Ῥωμαϊκός.

"Roman," as found in the TR of Lk 23³⁸, may be
illustrated from a Greek translation of an unknown Latin
work made by a certain Isidorianus, P Ryl II. 62 (iii/A.D.),
which ends—²⁴ Ὀλύμπ[ιος] Ἰσ[ι]δωριανὸς [. . . . . .]
ἑρμήνευσα ἀπὸ Ῥω[μα]ικῶν.

Ῥωμαϊστί,

"in the Latin language" (Jn 19⁵⁰): cf. Epict. i. 17. 16 ἴδε ἐπισκέψαι, πῶς τοῦτο λέγεται, καθάπερ εἰ Ῥωμαϊστί.

ῥώννυμι.

Ἔρρωσο, ἔρρωσθε (*vale*, *valete*), are regular closing formulae (as in Ac 15²⁹) in both private and official letters. Naturally they are much varied by the addition of terms of endearment and otherwise, particularly during the second and third centuries A.D. The following exx. must suffice: P Tebt II. 315²⁶ (ii/A.D.) ἔρρωσό μοι, τιμιώτατε, P Hamb I.

54ᵢᵢ·¹⁵ (ii/iii A.D.) ἔρρωσό μοι πολλοῖς χρόνοις ὑγιαίνων μετὰ καὶ τῶν σῶν, P Oxy XII. 1586¹⁵ (early iii/A.D.) ἐρρῶσθ(αι) εὔχομ(αι) [π]ανοικεί, *ib.* I. 122¹² (iii/iv A.D.) ἐρ]ρῶσθαί σε, κύριέ μου ἄδελφε, πολλοῖς χρόνοις καὶ προκόπτειν εὔχομαι. Many other exx. will be found in Exler *Epistolography* p. 74 ff. For the verb = "have strength" of persons cf. PSI V. 495²² (B.C. 258-7) βουλόμεθα γάρ σε τῶι τε σώματι ἐρρῶσθ[αι, and of trees cf. CP Herm I. 28¹¹ φοίνικες ἄλλοι ἐρ[ρω]μένοι.

The subst. ῥῶσις is used in connexion with praying for "strength" for anyone, e.g. *OGIS* 206⁴ εὐξάμενος ῥῶσιν καὶ τέκνοις καὶ γαμετῇ. See also in application to the body Vett. Val. p. 160¹³.

Σ

σαβαώθ—σάκκος

σαβαώθ.

This Heb. word = "hosts," "armies" Rom 9²⁹ LXX. Jas 5⁴) occurs as an invocation in the great Paris magical papyrus P Par 574¹²³⁵ (iii/A.D.) (= *Selections*. p. 113) Ἰαω Σαβαωθ, and in the amulet printed in *Archiv* i. p. 427 belonging to iii-v A.D. —

> Κύριε Σαβαωθ, ἀπόστρεψον
> ἀπ' ἐμοῦ . οτον (?) νόσον τῆς
> κεφαλ[ῆς

where Wilcken thinks that it cannot be determined with certainty whether it is the work of a Christian or a Jew or a Greek or an Egyptian. Cf. P Oxy VIII. 1152² (v/vi A.D.) with its magical, Jewish, and Christian elements —

> Ωρωρ φωρ ελωεί,
> ἀδωναεί, Ἰαω σα-
> βαώθ, Μιχαήλ, Ἰεσοῦ
> Χριστέ, βοήθι ἡμῖν
> καὶ τούτῳ οἴκῳ. ἀ-
> μήν.

and *ib.* VII. 1060¹ (vi/A.D.), a Gnostic charm against reptiles and other ills —

> Ἰαὼ σαβαωθ ἀδονέ
>
> ἀπάλλαξον τὸν οἶκον τοῦτον
> ἀπὸ παντὸς κακοῦ ἑρπετοῦ.

Also the leaden tablet, Wünsch *AF* No. 2 (ii/iii A.D.), on which is depicted an altar inscribed—Σεωθη | Σαβαωθ | Σαβαωθ, the thrice repeated name of the Jewish God. See further Deissmann *Urgeschichte* p. 23, and Cheyne's note on "Lord Sabaoth" in *Exp* III. i. p. 318 f.

σαββατισμός.

"a resting as on the Sabbath," found only in Heb 4⁹, where it may have been coined by the author : see Moffatt in *ICC ad l.*, who also refers to its possible occurrence in Plutarch *de superstit.* 166 A (βαπτισμούς, Bentley). The verb occurs in Exod 16³⁰: cf. Frankel *Vorstudien*, p. 8.

σάββατον

to denote the Heb. *Sabbath* is first found in the LXX. In the Pentateuch and elsewhere the plur. τὰ σάββατα is used both for "the Sabbath" and "the sabbaths": see Thackeray *Gr.* i. p. 35. In the LXX the dat. plur. is usually σαββάτοις, but in the critical text of the NT the form σάββασι occurs frequently: cf. πρόβασι for προβάτοις in P Lond 1171³ (B.C. 8) (= III. p. 178), and similar

exx. in Psaltes *Gr.* p. 176. For the significance of the added clause μηδὲ σαββάτῳ in Mt 24²⁰ see Boll *Offenbarung* p. 134, n.¹

σαγήνη.

a large "drag-net" (Mt 13⁴⁷) as distinguished from the smaller circular ἀμφίβληστρον (cf. Mk 1¹⁶), often identified with the *garf*. which is generally worked by two boats (cf. Lk 5⁷), which separate and then draw it in a sweep to the shore. It was consequently an expensive piece of machinery. and has been taken as evidence that some at least of the fishermen Apostles were fairly well-to-do (cf. *Exp T* xxviii. p. 229 f.).

σαίνω,

properly of dogs "wag the tail," "fawn" (e.g. *Od.* x. 217), then metaph. of persons "fawn upon," "beguile" (e.g. Aesch. *Choeph.* 186). This gives good sense in its only NT occurrence, 1 Thess 3³ τὸ μηδένα σαίνεσθαι ἐν ταῖς θλίψεσιν ταύταις: the Apostle dreaded that the Thessalonians would be "drawn aside," "allured," in the midst of the afflictions which were falling upon them, cf. Zahn *Einl.* i. p. 159 f. (Engl. Tr. i. p. 222). Others, however, prefer to read with FG σιένεσθαι *i.e.* σιαίνεσθαι, "to be disturbed," "troubled," in support of which Nestle (*ZNTW* vii. p. 361) cites two passages from the *Hist. Lausiaca* (ed. Butler, 1904), c. 24, p. 78, 10 and c. 35, p. 102, 16: Mercati adds further instances in *ZNTW* viii. p. 242. See also the quotations from papyri *s.v.* σιαίνομαι. Reference may be made to an art. by A. D. Knox in *JTS* xxv. (1924), p. 290 f., where a reading τὸ μηδένα παθαίνεσθαι is conjectured, = "that none break down in their afflictions."

For a new literary ex. of σαίνω, where it is used practically = θέλγω, see Bacchyl. I. 55 ὁ δ' εὖ ἔρδων θεοὺς ἐλπίδι κυδροτέρᾳ σαίνει κέαρ, "but he who is bountiful to the gods can cheer his heart with a loftier hope" (Jebb).

σάκκος,

a Semitic word, denoting "sackcloth," "sacking," a coarse cloth made of the hair of goats and other animals: cf. PSI IV. 427¹· ¹⁴ (iii/B.C.) γραφὴ σάκκων καὶ μαρσίππων . . . σάκκον τρίχινον ά, P Hamb 1. 10²⁹ (ii/A.D.) σάκκους τριχίνους. Other exx. of the word are P Reinach 17¹⁹ (B.C. 109) κιτὼν καὶ ἱμάτιον καὶ σάκκον, cf.²¹, P Ryl II. 145¹⁶ (A.D. 38) σάκκο(ν) πλήρηι κνήκωι, "a sack full of cnecus," BGU II. 597² (A.D. 75) τὸν σάκκον τοῦ πυροῦ, P Oxy VI. 932⁶ (late ii/A.D.) ἰς τοὺς σάκκους σφραγίσας, "sealing it (sc. vegetable seed) in the sacks," *ib.* XIV. 1733² (late iii/A.D.) τι(μὴ) σάκκων σιππίων (*l.* στυππίων "flax") (δρ.) σ̄. On reckoning loads by sacks, see Wilcken *Ostr.* i. p. 754.

For the dim. σακκίον, see P Ryl II. 245¹³ (iii/A.D.) ἐπεμψά σοι σακ[κίο]ν στιππείων, and cf. Menander *Fragm.* 544¹ p. 164 σακίον: for σακκούδιον. see P Oxy VI. 937²⁹ (iii/A.D.) δέξε (*l.* δέξαι) γ σακκούδια π(αρὰ) τοῦ ᾿Αντινοέως: and for σακκοφόρος, "a porter," see P Tebt I. 39²⁶ (B.C. 114). MGr σακκί, with dim. σακκούλι, σακουλά(κ ι.

Σαλαμίς.

For dat. Σαλαμῖνι in Ac 13⁵, אAEL read Σαλαμίνη, a form not unknown in Byz. Greek: cf. Blass-Debrunner *Gr.* § 57, and Psaltes *Gr.* p. 177.

σαλεύω.

lit. "agitate," "shake," as by winds and storms: see P Lond 46¹⁶² (iv/A.D.) (= I. p. 80) ἐπικαλοῦμαί σε τὸν . . . σαλε[ύσαντα] τὸν οὐρανόν, cf. Mt 24²⁹, *al.*, and the citations in Boll *Offenbarung*, p. 135. The verb is used figuratively, as in Heb 12²⁶¹, in the illiterate P Oxy III. 528¹³ (ii/A.D.) where a man writes to his sister (wife) ἐπεμσάς μυ ἐπιστολὰς δυναμένου λίθον σαλεῦσε, οὕτως ὁ λόγυ σου καικίνηκάν με, "you sent me letters which would have shaken a stone, so much did your words move me" (Edd.), and OGIS 515⁴⁷ (iii A.D.) σαλεύει γὰρ ὡς ἀλη[θῶς ἡ σωτηρία τῆς πόλε]ως ἐκ κακουργίας καὶ πανουργίας ὀλί[γων τινῶν αὐτῇ ἐπεμβα]ινόντων. Hence the derived meaning "dislodge," "drive away" from your sober senses, as in 2 Thess 2², where Lightfoot (*Notes on Epp. of S. Paul,* p. 109) compares Plut. *Mor.* 493 D ὄρεξιν τοῦ κατὰ φύσιν ἀποσαλεύουσαν followed almost immediately by ὡς ἐπ᾿ ἀγκύρας τῆς φύσεως σαλεύει.

For a weakened sense cf. PSI IV. 299⁴ (iii/A.D.) κατεσχέθην νόσῳ . . ὡς μὴ δύνασθαι μηδὲ σαλεύεσθαι, "I was held fast by illness, so as to be unable even to move myself": see also P Oxy III. 472⁷⁰ (*c.* A.D. 130) the request of a daughter to her mother—τι καὶ παρασχεῖν ὡς ἐπὶ ἑνὶ μόνῳ σαλευούσαν, "to give her something since she was dependent upon only a single source" (Edd.): cf. LS⁸ II. 2. MGr σαλεύω. "move," "stir."

σάλος.

is used of a "rough sea" in Lk 21²⁵: cf. Boll *Offenbarung*, p. 135.

σάλπιγξ.

"a trumpet": cf P Herm I. 124¹⁰ (iii/A.D.) ἐνίκησε τὸ] τῶν σαλπ[ίγγ]ων ἀγώνισμα, *Kaibel* 1049⁷ οὗ σάλπιγγος ἀκ[ούεται ἐνθάδ᾿ ὁμοκλή.

σαλπίζω.

"sound a trumpet," is often understood metaph. in Mt 6², as by Klostermann in *HZNT*, where he compares the use of the subst. in Achilles Tatius viii. 10 οὐχ ὑπὸ σάλπιγγι μόνον ἀλλὰ καὶ κήρυκι μοιχεύεται. For a defence of the literal meaning by a reference to the sounding of the ram's horn (*shofar*) on the occasion of public fasts, see Büchler in *JTS* x. (1909), p. 266 ff., also Klein in *ZNTW* vi. (1905), p. 203 f.

σαλπιστής.

"trumpeter." For this late form (for Attic σαλπιγκτής) in Rev 18²², cf. the inscr. *Syll*⁵ 1058¹ (ii/i B.C.) σαλπιστάς, and *Preisigke* 4591³ (Rom.) σαλπιστὴς χώρτης ᾿Ισπανό-ρου(μ. For σαλπικτής (= σαλπιγκτής) cf. P Oxy III. 519¹⁰ (ii/A.D.), where in an account of public games 4 drachmae are paid σαλπικτῇ.

Σαλω(ο)μών.

See *s.v.* Σολομών.

Σαμάρεια

(for spelling see Thackeray *Gr.* i. p. 167), "Samaria." The mention of a village of this name in the Fayum, as in P Petr II. 4 (11)² (B.C. 255–4), is proof of the early settlement of Jews in these districts (cf. P Petr I. p. 43 note*). See also P Tebt II. 566 (A.D. 131–2) Σαμάρεια, *ib.* 609 (ii A.D.) κώμης Σαμαρείας, and BGU I. 94⁴ (A.D. 289) περὶ κώμην Σαμάριαν.

Σαμαρείτης.

On the form, see WH *Notes²*, p. 161. Σαμαρεύς is also found in Byz. Greek: cf. Psaltes *Gr.* p. 254.

Σαμοθρᾴκη.

For the diphthong ᾳ in this place-name (Ac 16¹¹) see Meisterhans *Gr.* p. 64, 1.

Σαμουήλ.

In P Oxy VI. 994 (A.D. 499) an order for the payment of 12 artabae of corn to a monk is headed—Φοιβά[μμ]ων κόμ(ες) καὶ Σαμουὴλ περίβλ(επτος): other exx. of the name in Preisigke *Namenbuch s.v.*

σανδάλιον.

"a sandal." For the dim. (Mk 6⁹, Ac 12⁸), see *Syll* 754⁶, where σανδάλια are mentioned amongst the articles of the adornment of the statue of a god: cf. P Cornell 33¹ (iii/A.D.) σα[ν]δ άλια) βατ(= διστικὰ β, "2 walking-shoes." In P Oxy IV. 741¹⁰ (ii/A.D.) σανδάλια ὀνικ(ά), both the reading and meaning are doubtful, "donkey straps" (?) (Edd.).

σανίς.

"board," "plank," as in Ac 27⁴⁴, occurs in P Flor I. 69²¹ (iii/A.D.) (τοῖς) ἐξηλοῦσι σανίδες(= δας) [πλ]ατείας ἑτέρου τοίχου τοῦ προκ(ειμένου πλοίου: cf. ²¹. The word readily passes into the meaning of a "wooden tablet" for writing purposes, as in *Syll³* 975³⁰ (*c.* A.D. 250) ἀναγράψαντες εἰς τὴν σανίδα οὗ καὶ τὰ λοιπὰ γράμματα παραδό[τ ωσαν εἰς τὸ δημόσιον τῇ βουλῇ. In Herodas VII. 5 it denotes a wooden bench to sit upon. For the dim. σανίδιον see *Syll* 366 (=³790 ²⁵ (A.D. 38) τό τε ἐργαστήριον αὐτοῦ σανιδίο(ς προσηλοῦσθαι, and for the verb σανιδόω see P Lond 1104 (*h*)⁷ (A.D. 212) (= III. p. 164) πλοίον . . . σεσανιδ[ω]μένον διὰ νεὼς σὺν ἱστῷ.

Σαούλ.

See *s.v.* Σαῦλος.

σαπρός.

For the classical meaning "decayed," cf. the Attic inscr. *Syll* 587²¹ (B.C. 328) μισθωτεῖ τοῦ διατειχίσματος ἀνελόντι τὰ σαπρά with reference to "decayed" brickwork. In Hellenistic Greek the connexion with σήπω was lost, and it became "rotten," "corrupt," as in P Flor II. 176⁹ (A.D. 256) συκαρίων σαπρῶν, "rotten figs" (cf. Mt 7¹⁷). Similarly in P Lond 356¹¹ (i/A.D.) (= II. p. 252, *Selections*, p. 50) the adj. is applied to "stale" drugs as contrasted with drugs of "good" quality, τὸ καλόν. In P Fay 119⁴ (c. A.D. 100) χόρτου . . δύσμην σαπράν is "a stale bundle of hay," and in P Giss I. 21⁶ (time of Trajan) ἐξήτησα τὸ λακώνιον καὶ οὐχ εὗρον ἀλλὰ ἀτταλιανὸν σαπρόν, the reference is apparently to an article of clothing: cf. the adverb in BGU III. 846⁹ (ii/A.D.) (= *Selections*, p. 94) σαπρῶς παιριπατῶ. Later exx. are PSI VI. 718¹² (a receipt—iv/v A.D.) σαπρὸν ο[ἶ]νον ποιῆσε (= σαι) καλόν, and P Oxy XVI. 1849² (vi/vii A.D.) τὸ λάχανον ὅδε (l. ὧδε) σαπρόν ἐστι. Add Teles p. 27³ (of a house) σαπρὰ καὶ ῥέουσα καὶ καταπίπτουσα.

For the metaph. usage, as in Eph 4²⁹, cf. P Leid Wˣⁱᵛ·²⁸ (ii/iii A.D.) (= II. p. 131) ἀνάδυσόν μου τὴν σαπρὰν ἱ(= εἱ)μαρμένην, "withdraw from me the bitter fate," and Epict.iii. 16. 7. In Preisigke 5761²¹ (A.D. 91-6) ἔστι σαπρὸν γὰ.ρ] ὄνομα τῆς τοῦ μισθω[τοῦ] γυναικός, the word = "unpleasant," and in the astrological Vett. Val. p. 36³⁰ *al.* the editor understands it as = "periculosus." See further Rutherford *NP* p. 474.

Σαπφείρα.

"Sapphira." This proper name (Ac 5¹), which appears in various forms in the MSS., is probably derived from the Aramaic שַׁפִּירָא, "beautiful," and should be accented on the penultimate, see Winer-Schmiedel *Gr.* p. 76.

σάπφειρος.

This Semitic word (used by Theophrastus) = "a sapphire" (Rev 21¹⁹) appears under the form σαππίριν (σαπφείριον) in a list of colours and weights, P Oxy XIV. 1739¹ (ii/iii A.D.) σαππίριν μνᾶν ὁλκήν, cf. ⁷: see also P Tebt II. 405¹⁰ (iii/A.D.) δερματικὴ σαπιρίν(η) (l. δελματικὴ σαπφειρίνη), "a sapphire Dalmatian vest," and *Preisigke* 2251 (ostracon—iv/A.D.) σαππειρίου ὀνκ(ίαι) ι.

σαργάνη

in the sense of a flexible "mat-basket" occurs in the NT only in 2 Cor 11³³, but can be freely illustrated from the Κοινή. e.g. BGU II. 417¹¹ (ii/iii A.D.) π[ε]ρὶ ἐνοικίου κοφίνων καὶ τειμῆς σαργάνων, P Flor II. 260⁷ (A.D. 257) τὰς οἰνηγὰς καὶ τὰς σιτικὰς σαρ.γ.α[ν.ας, P Oxy VI. 938³ (iii/iv A.D.) δώδεκα σαργάνας χόρτου (cf. ⁶), and P Lond 236¹¹ (c. A.D. 346) (= II. p. 291) ἐλαίου σπάθια ("measures") δύο καὶ τὴν σαργάνην. In P Strass I. 37¹³ (iii/A.D.) τῆς ἡμῶν σαργάν[ης, the editor suggests that the reference may be to a "travelling-basket."

The dim. σαργάνιον is found in P Lips I. 21¹⁵ (A.D. 382) ἀχύρου σαργάνιον ἕν, and σαργανίτιον in BGU IV. 1095²¹ (A.D. 57): cf. also P Goodsp Cairo 30ˣˣⁱⁱ·¹² (A.D. 191-192) σαργανείλ[ω]ν.

σάρδιον.

"sard" (Rev 4³, 21²⁰), a red stone, perhaps the "cornelian": cf. *Syll* 588³ (c. B.C. 180) δακτύλιον χρυσοῦν σάρδιον.

σαρδόνυξ.

"sardonyx," a variety of onyx (Rev 21²⁰): cf. Pliny *H.N.* xxxvii. 23: "Sardonyches olim ut ex ipso nomine apparet intellegebantur candore in sarda, hoc est, velut carne ungui hominis imposita, et utroque translucido."

σαρκικός.

= "fleshly" (*carnalis*), with the nature and characteristics of σάρξ, as distinguished from σάρκινος, "fleshy" (*carneus*), made or composed of σάρξ; but in Hellenistic Greek the distinction between adjectives in -ικός and -ινος must not be pressed too far. See Lightfoot *Notes*, p. 184.

σάρκινος.

In a series of accounts P Lond 1177 (A.D. 113) (= III. p. 169) reference is made to "leather ropes," σχοινίων σαρκίνων, a curious use of the word.

σάρξ.

It lies outside our purpose to discuss the theological implications underlying the use of this important word in the NT. They are due partly to the influence of the LXX, and partly to the language-forming power of Christianity by which old terms were "baptized" into new conditions: see the full discussion of the term in Greek and Hebrew writings until A.D. 180 in Burton, "Spirit, Soul, and Flesh" (Chicago, 1918), and the same writer's "Commentary on Galatians" (in *ICC*) p. 492 ff., also Lightfoot *Notes*, p. 88 f. All that can be attempted here is to cite a few exx. of the word from the inscrr. It does not seem to occur in the papyri.

Thus for σάρξ = κρέας see *OGIS* 78¹⁶ (B.C. 221-205) διδῶν . . . σάρκα πεντάμναιον ἀπ.ὸ τῶ βμοὺς τῶ θυομένω τῶ Διὶ τῶ Σω[τηρ]ι, and, for the plur., *Syll* 645 (= ³1047)⁷ (c. B.C. 100) παρατιθέτω]σαν δὲ καὶ ἐ.π.ὶ τὴν τρά[πεζαν τοῦ μὲν βοὸς . . . . . καὶ] γλῶσσαν καὶ σάρκας τρεῖς (*tres carnium portiones*): cf. also *Preisigke* 4314⁶ (iii/B.C.) σάρκας ἔδευσε πυρί, and *Syll* 805 (= ³1171)⁵ (Rom.) ὥστε σάρκας ἐνπύου[ς καὶ] ἡμαγμένας δι' ὅλης ἡμέρας ἀ[πο]βάλλειν, in an account of healing worked by Aesculapius.

The common contrast between πνεῦμα and σάρξ is seen in the ii/i B.C. Jewish invocation for vengeance from Rheneia (Rhenea), which begins—

Ἐπικαλοῦμαι καὶ ἀξιῶ τὸν θεὸν τὸν
ὕψιστον, τὸν κύριον τῶν πνευμάτων
καὶ πάσης σαρκός.

See further Deissmann *LAE²*, p. 413 ff., and for a similar formula in Christian inscr. cf. *Preisigke* 2034² ὁ θ.εὸ)ς ὁ λ)ων π(νευ]μάτων καὶ πάσης σαρκός, and similarly 3901², 4049³. For the Hellenistic use of σάρξ instead of σῶμα in Epicurus, see *Sententiae* iv. and xx., with Bailey's notes, pp. 350, 360.

σαρόω,

a late form of σαίρω, "sweep." For the pass., as in Mt 12⁴⁴, cf. P Giss I. 11¹⁹ (A.D. 118) (= *Chrest.* I. p. *524*) ὥστε σαρωθῆναί σου τὸν νομόν. See also Herm. *Sim.* ix. 10. 3 αἱ δὲ παρθένοι λαβοῦσαι σάρους ἐσάρωσαν (cf. Lk 15⁸). The subst. is found in P Oxy XIV. 1602¹¹ (A.D. 188) σάρωσις φύλλων.

Σάρρα,

"Sarah": see *s.vv.* Ἰωσήφ and Ἰωσῆς, and add P Lond IV. 1450²⁵ (date uncertain), where there is mention of Abraam the son Σάρας, and P Oxy I. 134¹⁷ (A.D. 569), where John, the chief of the stonemasons, is described as νἱὸς Μηνᾶ μητρὸς Σάρας

On the possibility that καὶ αὐτὴ Σάρρα in Heb 11¹¹ is an interpolation from the margin, leaving Ἀβραάμ as the subject of both verses, see Field *Notes* p. 232, and Windisch *HZNT ad l.*

Σατανᾶς,

a Graecized transliteration of the Aramaic שָׂטָנָא, meaning originally "one lying in ambush for," and hence as a proper name "the adversary," "the accuser": cf. for the development of the Jewish belief *EB s.v.*, Bousset *Die Religion des Judentums*² (1906), p. 382 ff., also Hort *James*, p. 98 f.

In the magical incantation P Par 574¹²³⁶ (iii/A.D.) (= *Selections*, p. 113), Jesus the Christ is adjured to drive forth the devil from a man until this unclean demon of Satan—π ἀκάθαρτος ν δαίμων πι σαδανᾶς—shall flee before him. For the corresponding adj. cf. P Lond V. 1731¹¹ (A.D. 585) where a divorce is said to have taken place κατὰ διαβου = ο)λικὴν καὶ σατανικὴν ἐνέργειαν.

σάτον,

a word found in the LXX to denote a measure = 1⅓ modii, or nearly three English gallons (Mt 13³³, Lk 13²¹; Jos. *Ant.* IX. 85 (= ix. 4. 5)). Instead of connecting the word with the Aram. שָׂאתָא, Otto points to a root-form *σάτιον, corresponding to the Coptic *saïdion, "a wine-measure of Saïs": see *Archiv* iii. p. 448.

Σαῦλος,

the Graecized form of the Apostle Paul's Jewish name Σαούλ. For the phrase Σαῦλος ὁ καὶ Παῦλος (Ac 13⁹), see *s.v.* Παῦλος, and cf. the discussion on ὁ καί *s.v.* ὁ (10). No instances of the name Σαῦλος are given in Preisigke's *Namenbuch*, but an indecl. proper name Σαύλ is cited from P Flor III. 286¹⁷ (A.D. 514) τοῦ θαυμασ(ιωτάτου) Σαύλ ἀκτουαρίου.

σβέννυμι,

"extinguish," "put out," of fire etc.: cf. P Leid Wᵛⁱⁱ ²⁴ (ii/iii A.D.) (= II. p. 105) πῦρ σβέσαι (*l.* σβέσαι), and ³⁵ σβεσθηντι (*l.* σβέσθητι). For the metaph. use in 1 Thess 5¹⁹ cf. *Kaibel* 204⁴ (i/B.C.) ἀμφοτέροις ἡμῖν ἐσβέσας ἤλιον, and for the meaning "wash out," "erase," cf. the late P Mon I. 1⁴³ ἐσβέσθαι πᾶν σπέρμα δίκης, and *ib.* 14³⁷ (both vi/A.D.). MGr σβήνω, "extinguish," and intrans. "am extinguished." See also *s.v.* ζβέννυμι.

σεαυτοῦ,

"of thyself": cf. P Flor I. 61⁶⁰ (A.D. 85) (= *Chrest.* II. p. 89) ἄξιος μ[ὲ]ν ἦς μαστιγωθῆναι, διὰ σεαυτοῦ [κ]ατασχὼν ἄνθρωπον εὐσχήμονα καὶ γυν[αῖ]καν.

The contracted form σαυτοῦ is not found in the NT (but cf. Jas 2⁸ ¹⁹), but is common in the papyri, e.g. P Petr III. 53 (θ)⁸ (iii/B.C.) ἐπιμελό[μενό]ς τε σαυτοῦ, P Par 46²¹ (B.C. 152) (= *UPZ* i. p. 338) ἐ[πιμ]έλου με (*l.* δὲ) καὶ σαυτοῦ, BGU IV. 1079³¹ (A.D. 41) τὰ παρ(ὰ) σατῷ (*l.* σαυτοῦ), P Amh II. 132¹ (early ii/A.D.) σὺ γὰρ διὰ σαυτοῦ ἴ. "for you are acting for yourself" (Edd.), and BGU II. 380¹⁶ (iii/A.D.) εἰ δὲ οἶδες σατῷ, ὅτι ἔχεις ἔτι, γράψον μοι. See further *s.v.* αὐτοῦ, and Moulton *Gr.* ii. p. 180 f.

σεβάζομαι.

This rare verb is found in the NT only in Rom 1²⁵ where it is a stronger form of σέβομαι, "worship": cf. also Aq Hos 10⁵.

σέβασμα.

To the ordinary citations for this word = "object of worship" (Ac 17²³, 2 Thess 2⁴) we may add Arist. *Apol.* xii. οὐ γὰρ ἠρκέσθησαν [οἱ Αἰγύπτιοι] τοῖς τῶν Χαλδαίων καὶ Ἑλλήνων σεβάσμασιν.

For σεβασμός see M. Anton. iv. 16 τὸν σεβασμὸν τοῦ λόγου, "thy reverence of reason," and cf. Aristeas 170 σεβασμὸν ἀποδοῦναι, "to pay homage." The adj. σεβάσμιος with reference to an oath may be seen in P Amh II. 145¹⁰ (A.D. 349) ὀμνύν[τ]ες τὸν θεῖο ν κ]αὶ σ[ε]βάσμιον ὅρκο[ν τῶ]ν πάντα νικῶν[των] δεσποτῶν ἡμῶν Ἀγούστων, "swearing the divine and holy oath of our all-victorious masters the Augusti," and the other citations in Preisigke *Wörterb. s.v.* ὅρκος.

Σεβαστός,

the official Greek equivalent of *Augustus* = "worthy to be reverenced or worshipped." The title was bestowed on Octavian in B.C. 27, and was continued to his successors, e.g. Nero in Ac 25²¹·²⁵. Cf. P Oxy IV. 746¹² (A.D. 16), where a letter of recommendation is dated (ἔτους) γ Τιβερίου Καίσαρος Σεβαστοῦ Φαῶφι γ, "the 3rd year of Tiberius Caesar Augustus, Phaophi 3." In BGU IV. 1074² (A.D. 275) the Emperor Aurelian announces, τὰ δὲ [ὑ]πὸ το[ῦ] δ[ὲ τ]οῦ Σεβαστοῦ (viz. the Emperor Augustus) δ[εδ]ομένα ὑμῖν νόμιμα καὶ φιλάνθ[ρ]ωπα συντηρῶ. On the ἡμέραι Σεβασταί, held in honour of the Imperial family, see the note by GH *ad* P Oxy II. 288⁵, and on the Σεβαστὸν νόμισμα *ad ib.* 264⁸.

Following Usener (*Bull. dell' Inst. di Corrisp. Archeolog.*, 1874, p. 73 ff.), Lightfoot (*Apostolic Fathers*, Part II.² (1889), vol. i. p. 714) has pointed out that in Asia Minor and Egypt the title σεβαστή was applied to the first day of each month, probably "as the monthly commemoration of the birthday of Augustus," and others would extend this usage to a day of the week, not a day of the month. Deissmann suggests that the early Christian designation ἡ κυριακὴ ἡμέρα may have been intended in part at least as a protest against the Imperial cult: see *BS* p. 218 f., *LAE*² p. 358 ff., and *EB* 2816. Note further that F. H. Colson *The Week* (1920), p. 125 f., has shown, on the evidence of the papyri, that the σεβασταί ἡμέραι were not confined to any particular day of the week.

σέβομαι,

"reverence," "worship," is found in the NT only in the mid. (Mk 7⁷, Ac 16¹⁴, *al.*): cf. PSI IV. 361⁹ (B.C. 251–0) ὅσοι αὐτὸν σέβονται, P Tebt I. 59¹¹ (B.C. 99) διὰ τὸ ἄνωθεν φοβεῖσθαι καὶ σέβεσθαι τὸ ἱερόν, Chrest. I. 116² (sayings of Sansnos—ii/iii A.D.) σέβου τὸ θεῖον, and Syll 256 (= ³557⁷ (c. B.C. 207–6) τοῖς σεβ[β]ομένοις Ἀπ[ολλῶνα Πύθιον. We may add the claim of a worshipper of an obscure sect P Oxy XI. 1381²⁰² (ii/A.D.) Ἑλλην[ὶ]ς δὲ π[ᾶ]σα γλῶσσα τὴν σὴν λαλ[ή].[[. .]σε[ι] ἱστορίαν κ[αὶ] πᾶς Ἕλ[λ]ην ἀνὴρ τὸν τ[ο]ῦ Φθᾶ σεβήσεται Ἰμού[θ]ην, "every Greek tongue will tell thy story, and every Greek man will worship the son of Ptah, Imouthes" (Edd.). This reminds Reitzenstein (Hell. Myst. Rel. p. 70) of Phil 2¹¹ : see further Halliday Pagan Background of Early Christianity, p. 240.

The phrase οἱ σεβόμενοι (or φοβούμενοι) τὸν θεόν in the book of Acts to denote pagans in close touch with Jewish worship is discussed by Schürer Geschichte³ III. p. 123 ff. (= HJP II. ii. p. 314 ff.). Deissmann (LAE², p. 451 f.) cites an inscr. from a seat in the theatre of Miletus, dating from the Roman period, in which the Jews themselves are described as Θεοσέβιοι—

Τόπος Εἰουδέων τῶν καὶ Θεοσεβίον.

"Place of the Jews who are also called God-fearing."

The act. of the verb is seen in the libellus P Oxy XII. 1464² (A.D. 250) ἀεὶ μὲν θύειν καὶ [σπέ]νδειν καὶ σέβειν θεοῖς εἰθισμένοις, and in Kaibel 651⁶ (ii A.D.) σῶ[μα χ[ι]τὼν ψυχῆς· τὸν δὲ θεόν σέβε μου, where the editor notes that τὸν θεόν μου == τὸ θεῖόν μου, animam meam.

σειρά,

"a chain," is read in the TR of 2 Pet 2⁴ σειραῖς ζόφου, but not elsewhere in the Greek Bible, except Judg 16¹³, Prov 5²² : cf. Syll 588²⁰⁴ (c. B.C. 180) ἐκ τῆς σει[ρᾶς κρεμαμένων. See s.v. σειρός. On Σειραί, the Catenae of the Greek Church, see an art. by Nestle in Exp T X. p. 218 f.

σειρός,

"a pit," which takes the place of σειρά (q.v.) in the critical text of 2 Pet 2⁴, is found in P Leid Xᵛⁱⁱ ⁴⁸ (iii/iv A.D.) (= II. p. 225) ὕδατος ἀπὸ σειροῦ. For the spelling σιρός see P Lond 216¹¹ (A.D. 94) (= II. p. 186, Chrest. I. p. 224) σιροῖς κ(αὶ) τοῖς λοιποῖς χρηστηρίοις, where σιροί are vessels for holding grain : see also Moulton Gr. ii. p. 78 n.² The word is illustrated by Field Notes p. 241, and by Herwerden Lex. s.v. σιρός, which LS⁹ adopt as the correct spelling. It survives in French silo, "grain-pit."

σειρόω,

"exhaust," "empty," is not found in the NT, but in view of its occurrence in Sm Jerem 48¹² it may be illustrated from the curious P Fay 134⁷ (early iv/A.D.), where the writer asks a friend to bring an instrument for clipping coins, that, with the metal thus gained, καλὸν Μαρεωτικὸν δυν[ήσε]ι μοι σειρῶσαι ἐρχόμενος [τ]ῆς τιμῆς, "you will be able to strain me some good Mareotic wine, when you come, with the value" (Edd.).

σεισμός,

"earthquake" (Mt 24⁷, al.) : cf. Syll 744 (= ³1116)⁵ (ii A.D.) τῶν μναμείων τῶν πεσόντων ἐν τῶι σεισμῶι, and P Leid Wˣⁱᵛ ²⁴ (ii/iii A.D.) (= II. p. 149) ὃ ἐὰν εἴπω τέλειον, ἔσται σισμός ("terrae motus," Ed.). The word is used metaphorically in Preisigke 5075¹³ (B.C. 184 3) τ[οὺ]ς δὲ διαφορὰς ἢ σεισμοῦ χάριν καταπέ[μπετε] πρὸς ἡμᾶς παραχρῆμα, and P Par 15⁵⁷ (B.C. 120) ὁμολογουμένως δ᾽ ἐπὶ συκοφαντείᾳ καὶ σεισμῷ ἐπαγειοχό[τος . . .] ἔγκλημα : cf. σεῖσμα in P Tebt I. 41²² (c. B.C. 119) εἰσπραχθέντος τὰ σείσματα, "being made to refund his extortions" (Edd.). See also s.v. διασείω.

σείω,

"shake": P Lond 46¹¹³ (iv/A.D.) (= I. p. 70) ὁ σείσας τὴν οἰκουμένην, Kaibel 1046⁵⁵ σίσασα λόφον. The verb is used metaphorically in BGU I. 428⁹ (ii A.D.) ἔ]σεισεν τοὺς περὶ αὐτόν, and P Oxy X. 1252 verso³⁷ (A.D. 288–95) δηλοῦμεν ὡς μηδὲν ὑπ᾽ αὐτοῦ σεσεῖσθαι, "we affirm that nothing has been extorted from us by him": for the mixed construction the editors compare Ac 27¹⁰. MGr σείω (σείζω).

Σέκουνδος,

the name of a Thessalonian Christian and friend of Paul (Ac 20⁴). The same name occurs in the list of politarchs on the triumphal arch at Thessalonica, CIG II. 1967 (see s.v. πολιτάρχης), and again in a memorial inscr. of A.D. 15 discovered in a private house in the Jewish quarter of Thessalonica, Duchesne et Bayet p. 43, No. 59 Ἀπολλωνίῳ . . . Εὐτύχος Μαξίμου καὶ Σεκοῦνδα οἱ θρεπτοὶ τὸν βωμὸν μνείας χάριν κτλ. : cf. ib. p. 50, No. 78 Γάϊος Ἰούλιος Σεκοῦνδος Πρίμῳ τῷ ἰδίῳ τέκνῳ μνήμης χάριν. The name is common in the papyri, see Preisigke Namenbuch s.v.

σελήνη,

"the moon": P Hib I. 27¹² (calendar—B.C. 301–240) χρῶντ[αι] ταῖς κατὰ σελήνη[ν] ἡμέραις οἱ ἀστρολό[γοι, where the editors think that there is a loose mode of speaking of "the days of the month" without any real reference to the moon: see their note. The word occurs in the horoscopes BGU III. 957³ (B.C. 10), PSI IV. 312⁵ (A.D. 345), and in P Ryl I. 63¹ (iii/A.D.), where, in an imaginary astrological dialogue with Plato, a certain Egyptian prophet connects the moon with the left eye—Σελήνη ὁ εὐώνυμος. For the moon as the female principle of all physical life see P Osl I. p. 127, and for the importance of the rising moon, see ib. p. 93.

In P Leid Cⁱ ¹⁴ (B.C. 163) (= I. p. 118, UPZ i. p. 353) mention is made of the festival τὰ Σεληνεῖα (cf. Mayser Gr. i. pp. 75, 107, 448), and in the temple inventory BGU I. 162¹ (ii/iii A.D.) we hear of ἄλλα σελήναρια μεικρὰ χρυσᾶ β, by which Preisigke (Wörterb. s.v.) understands golden keys made in the form of a half moon. Hatzidakis (G. p. 59) notes that the word σελήνη is not now in popular use, the terms φεγγάρι and τὸ φέγγος taking its place. This does not, however, apply to the derivative σεληνιάζομαι, "am brought under the influence of the moon," "am epileptic," which is found everywhere, cf. Mt 4²⁴, 17¹⁵.

σεληνιάζομαι.

See s.v. σελήνη ad fin.

σεμίδαλις.

frequent in the LXX but in the NT confined to Rev 18[13] = "fine wheaten flour" (cf. Pliny *H.N* xiii. 21 "similago ex tritico fit laudatissimo"): cf. P Oxy IV. 736[82] (*c*. A.D. 1) σεμιδάρεως (*l.* σεμιδάλεως) ξηρᾶς (ἡμιωβέλιον), BGU IV. 1067[15] (A.D. 102) σεμιδάλεω(s) ἀρτάβας τρεῖ[s. and P Lond 190[15] (list of provisions—iii/A.D.?) = II. p. 255) σ[εμί]δαλιν. For σεμιδαλίτης ἄρτος, "fine wheaten bread," see P Petr III. 61 (*g*)[6] (iii/B.C.). Apparently σεμίδαλις, with Lat. *simila* of the same meaning, is borrowed from some Mediterranean tongue (Boisacq p. 850).

σεμνός.

For σεμνός, "august," "venerable," "worthy of respect," as applied to *persons*, cf. *Preisigke* 4004[5] (A.D. 8) ἐλθόντες πρὸς τὴν σεμνὴν Ἶσιν, and PSI I. 41[3] (iv/A.D.) where a wife describes herself as sprung ἐκ σεμνῶν γονέων καὶ ε[ὐδ]οκ[ί]μων. The adj. is very common in sepulchral inscr., e.g. *Kaibel* 558[ff.] (ii/A.D.)—

> Σεμνὴν Πηνελόπην ὁ πάλαι βίος, ἔσχε δὲ καὶ νῦν
> σεμνὴν Φιλικίταν, οὐ τάχα μιοτέρην,

ib. 635 Καλλίτεκνον σεμνὴν ὅδε τύμβος ἔχει σε, Ἀφροδείτη, 637[1] (ii A.D.), 642[12] (iii/iv A.D.), and 673[5] (iii/iv A.D.).

For σεμνός in relation to *places* we may cite P Ryl II. 110[3] (A.D. 259) where Hermopolis is described as πόλεως τῆς μεγάλης [ἀρχαίας λ]αμπρᾶς καὶ σεμνοτάτης "the great, ancient, illustrious and most august city": cf. P Lond 1157 *verso*[3] (A.D. 246) (= III. p. 110), and BGU IV. 1024[viii. 7] (iv/A.D.) τὸ σεμονὸν (*l.* σεμνὸν) τοῦ βουλευτηρίου.

σεμνότης

in the NT is confined to the Pastoral Epp., where it is translated *castitas* by the Vg in 1 Tim 2[2], 3[4], but better by *gravitas*, "seriousness," "dignity," in Tit 2[7]. Lock *ad* 1 Tim 2[2] in *ICC* cites Tert. *Praescr.* 43 *ubi metus in Deum, ibi gravitas honesta*, as indicating whence the "dignity" is derived. Cf. Aristeas 171 διὰ τὴν σεμνότητα καὶ φυσικὴν διάνοιαν τοῦ νόμου. Exx. of the word from the inscr. are *Syll* 371 (= [3]807)[11] (i/A.D.), where a doctor ἀνάλογον πεποίηται τὴν ἐπιδημίαν τῇ περὶ ἑαυτὸν ἐν πᾶσι σεμνότητι, and *OGIS* 567[19] (ii/A.D.) ἐπί τε συνηγορίαις καὶ σεμνότητι.

Σέργιος.

An inscr. found by Cesnola (*Cyprus*, p. 425: cf. Hogarth *Devia Cypria*, p. 114) at Soloi, a town on the north coast of Cyprus, is dated ἐπὶ Παύλου (ἀνθ)υπάτου, "in the proconsulship of Paulus." This Paulus is usually identified with the Sergius Paulus of Ac 13[7]: see especially Zahn *Intr.* iii. p. 463 ff., where, as showing the close connexion of the Sergian *gens* with Cyprus, mention is also made of another Cypriote inscr. found in 1887, *JHS* ix. (1888), p. 241, No. 50 Λ[ο]ύκιον Σέργιον . . . . Ἀρριανὸν συγκλητικὸν τριβοῦνον Σεργία Δημητρία τὸν ἀδελφόν.

σημαίνω.

"indicate," "signify": cf. P Par 63[xi. 63] (B.C. 165) διὰ τ[ῆ]s ἐπι[στο]λῆς προη . . . . σημῆναί μ[οι] τὴ[ν] φιλοτιμ[ί]αν, P Grenf I. 30[16] (B.C. 103) (= Witkowski[2], p. 107) διὰ γραμμάτων ἐκρίναμεν σημῆναι, BGU III. 1009[5]

(ii/B.C.) (= Witkowski[2], p. 111) περὶ μὲν [ο]ὖν τῶν ἄλλων [οὔ] σοι γέγραφα. Μ . . . ο]ς γάρ σοι σημα[ν]εῖ ἕκαστα, *ib.* IV. 1206[9] (B.C. 28) οὔπωι σεσήμαγκε τί ἐκβέβη[κ]ε, and *ib.* 1078[1] (A.D. 39) (= *Chrest.* I. p. 85) οὐ καλῶς δὲ ἐπόησας ἐκπορευομένων πολλῶν φίλων μὴ σημᾶναί μοι μηδὲ ἕν. For the two forms σημᾶναι and σημῆναι, see Mayser *Gr.* i. p. 360, Psaltes *Gr.* p. 223.

The pass. is seen in such passages as P Rein 7[10] (B.C. 141?) ἐν τῶι σημανθέντι χρόνωι, "within the stipulated time," P Amh II. 31[3] (B.C. 112) σημανθέντος, "it having been reported," P Oxy II. 283[12] (A.D. 45) τὸν σημαινόμενον δοῦλον, "the above-mentioned slave," P Tebt II. 278[12] (nursery acrostic—early i/A.D.) σημέ[= αί]νεταί μοι, τηρῖ μ[ε] γάρ, "he is indicated to me, for he watches me (?)" (Edd.). P Oxy I. 76[6] (A.D. 179) ὁ σημαινόμενός μου πατήρ, "my above-mentioned father," *ib.* 79[1] (notice of death—A.D. 181–192) (= *Selections*, p. 88) ὁ σημαινόμενός μου υἱός . . . ἄτεχνος ὢν ἐτελεύτησεν [τ]ῷ ἐνεστῶτι ἔτι, "my son who is here indicated died childless in the present year," and BGU I. 250[14] (after A.D. 130) (= *Chrest.* I. p. 115) προσφων[ῶ] . . τεθυκέναι με τὸν δηλούμ[εν]ον μόσχ[ο]ν τῷ σημαι[νο]μέ[ν]ῳ χρόνῳ.

The verb is used as a *term. tech.* for the pronouncement of the Delphic oracle by Heraclitus in Plut. *Mor.* 404 I. οὔτε λέγει, οὔτε κρύπτει, ἀλλὰ σημαίνει: Bauer *HZNT*[2] *ad* Jn 12[33] compares Jn 21[19], Rev 1[1], Ac 11[28], and Epict. i. 17. 18 f.

By a hitherto unknown usage the subst. σημασία is found introducing the "address" of the person to whom a letter is sent, e.g. P Oxy XIV. 1678[28] (iii/A.D.) σημασ[σ]ία ἐν Τευμενούτει ἐν τῷ ῥυμείῳ ἀντεὶ τοῦ φλητρος (*l.* φρέατος), "address, at the Teumenous quarter in the lane opposite the well" (Edd.): cf. *ib.* 1773[39] (iii/A.D.).

σημεῖον.

(1) "sign," "seal": cf. P Rev L[xxvi. 5] (B.C. 259–8) ἀποδειξάτωσαν] τὸ ἐπιβ[λ]ηθὲν σημεῖον ἀσινέ[s, "let them exhibit the seal which has been appended unbroken."

(2) "outward distinguishing mark": cf. P Par 18[bis 19] (Roman) ἔστιν δὲ σημεῖον τῆς ταφῆς, BGU II. 427[3] (A.D. 159) πέπρακα τὸν κάμηλον θήλιαν, ο[ὗ] τὸ σημεῖον πρόκιται, and Preisigke 5679[6] (A.D. 307) ὄνον λευ]κῆς οὔσης, ἐχούσης σημεῖον [ἐ]πὶ [τοῦ τραχή]λου. Similarly of a bodily "mark" disqualifying from the priesthood—*ib.* 15[27] (A.D. 155–6) Ἀγα[θ]οκλῆς ἐπύθετο, εἴ τινα σημεῖα ἔχουσιν [οἱ παῖδες ἐπὶ τοῦ σώματος, BGU I. 347[11] (A.D. 171) (= *Chrest.* I. p. 105) Σερηνια[νὸς] ἐπύθετο . . . εἰ [σ]ημ[εῖο]ν ἔχοι ὁ [παῖ]s. εἰπόντων αὐτῶν αὐτὸν εἶναι . . ἀρχιερεὺς . . ἐκέλευσεν τὸν παῖ[δα περιτ]μηθῆναι [κατὰ] τὸ ἔθος, and so *ib.* 82[9] (A.D. 185). In P Amh II. 39[2] (late ii/B.C.) a military corps of youths are described as οἱ [ἐκ] τοῦ σημείου νεανίσκοι, and for σημεῖον as an index of inward character, as in 2 Cor 12[12], cf. a rescript of Hadrian *Syll* 384 (= [3]831)[11] (A.D. 117) ἡγούμην σημεῖα ἀγαθῶν ἀνδρῶν τὰ τοιαῦτα εἶναι.

(3) In P Oxy II. 293[3] (A.D. 27) οὔτε διὰ γραπτοῦ οὔτε διὰ σημε[ί]ου, the editors understand the meaning to be "either by letter or by message," and so Wilcken *Archiv* iv. p. 259. Similarly in P Fay 128[6] (iii/A.D.), P Oxy IV. 724[3] (A.D. 155) of tachygraphic signs. In *ib.* XIV. 1635[9] (B.C.

44–37), a document dealing with the cession of catoecic land, τοῖς ἄλλοις σημείοις seems to refer to "boundary-marks" rather than to "title-deeds": cf. ib. III. 504[15] (early ii/A.D.) and the note to P Ryl II. 159[3]. See also Syll 929 (= [3] 685)[70, 75] (B.C. 139).

(4) For σημεῖον in its NT sense of "miracle" or "wonder" (Mt 12[38f], al.), we may cite Syll 326 (= [3] 709)[25] (c. B.C. 107) προεσάμανε μὲν τὰν μέλλουσαν γίνεσθαι πρᾶξιν [διὰ τ]ὸν ἐν τῶι ἱερῶι γενομένων σαμείων, and for the meaning "proof," see the illiterate P Oxy XIV. 1683[25] (late iv/A.D.) σημίου δὲ χάριν. Deissmann (LAE[2], p. 107) has pointed out that in 2 Thess 3[17] σημεῖον has the same force as the σύμβολον which in other cases was given to the bearer of a letter in proof of his commission, cf. e.g. P Passalacqua[15] (iii/B.C.) (= Witkowski Epp.[2], p. 54) ἀπεδόθη τάδ' αὐτῶι καὶ τὸ σύμβολον τῶν ἐγ.

σημειόω

In mid. = "mark for oneself," sometimes with the idea of disapprobation attached as in its only NT occurrence 2 Thess 3[14]: cf. Polyb. v. 78. 2 σημειωσάμενοι τὸ γεγονὸς with reference to a sinister omen, and see Lightfoot Notes, p. 133. The ordinary meaning is seen in such passages as Aristeas 148 παραδέδωκεν ὁ νομοθέτης σημειοῦσθαι τοῖς συνετοῖς εἶναι δικαίους, and OGIS 629[168] (A.D. 137) ὁ κράτιστος ἐσημ(ε)ιώσατο ἐν τῇ πρὸς Βάρβαρον ἐπιστολῇ.

The verb is regularly used for the signature to a receipt or formal notice in the papyri and the ostraca of the Imperial period (cf. Wilcken Ostr. i. p. 82 ff.): P Oxy I. 39[1] (A.D. 52) ἀντίγραφον ἀπολύσεως . . . Φαρμοῦθι κθ. σεσημ(ειωμένης), "copy of a release signed on Pharmouthi 29," ib. II. 237[viii. 29] (A.D. 186) where the prefect gives legal validity to the ὑπομνηματισμός by the words ἀνέγνων· σεσημ(είωμαι), ib. I. 65[6] (an order for arrest—iii iv A.D.) ὅρα μὴ κατάσχητε τὸν ὑπηρέτη(ν). σεση μείωμαι, "see that you do not detain the officer. Signed," and P Iand 37[25] (v vi A.D.) στιχι μοι [ταύ]την τὴν ἀποχὴν [σεσ]ημ(ε)ίωμαι ὡς πρόκ(ειται). The name is added in P Oxy XIV. 1750[17] (A.D. 306) Ἀ(π)φοῦς σεσημ(είωμαι). For the compd. συσσημειόω, not in LS[3], cf. P Tebt II. 383[61] (A.D. 46) Κρονίων συνσεσημίωμαι—an authenticating signature. It may be added that σημειῶσαι is used by the grammarians = "nota bene."

For the subst. σημείωσις cf. P Oxy II. 266[20] (A.D. 57) σημε(ι)ώσεω(ς) ἀντίγραφον, ib. IX. 1220[3] (iii/A.D.) διὰ σημει[ώ]σεως, "in some notes."

σήμερον.

This Ionic form for Attic τήμερον, "to-day," may be illustrated by P Hib I. 65[13] (c. B.C. 265) οὐκ ἐξέσται σοι σήμερ[ον μετ]ρεῖν, P Oxy VIII. 1153[3] (i/A.D.) σήμερον γὰ[ρ] παρεγένετο. "for he was here to-day," P Fay 123[23] (c. A.D. 100) εἴρηχεν ἡμῖν σήμερον. and P Oxy IX. 1216[9] (ii/iii A.D.) ἐνιαυτὸς σήμερον ἐκτὸς σου εἰμί, "a year to-day I have been away from you" (Ed.). The word is used more loosely in ib. VII. 1063[4] (ii/iii A.D.) σήμερον ὅτε ἔδωκά σοι ὀνόματα τρία . . . τῇ ἐξῆς ἐμ[ο]ῦ σου πυθομένου, "the other day when I gave you three names . . . the next day when I asked you" (Ed.); cf. Mt 27[19]. For ἡ σήμερον used as a subst. without ἡμέρα, as in Mt 11[23] al., cf. BGU II. 580[6] (ii A.D.)

νυκτὶ καὶ (l. τῇ) φερούσῃ εἰς τὴν σήμερον, P Oxy I. 121[5] (iii/A.D.) ἤδη ἐν τῇ σήμερον περειοργήτωσαν, "let them be dug round to-day" (Edd.), and P Ryl II. 114[19] (c. A.D. 280) μέχρι τῆς σήμερον. For the full phrase, as in Ac 20[26], see the Jewish prayer for vengeance Syll 816 (= [3] 1181)[11] (ii/i B.C.) LAE[2], p. 414 ff.) φ(. θεῷ) πᾶσα ψυχὴ ἐν τῇ σήμερον ἡμέραι ταπεινοῦτα[ι] μεθ' ἱκετείας. MGr (ἐ σήμερα.

σήπω.

"make to rot." The verb is found in the NT only in Jas 5[2] in 2nd perf. act. with an intrans. sense "am rotten" (cf. Proleg. p. 154): cf. P Oxy X. 1294[13] (ii/iii A.D.) μελη]σάτω δέ σοι τῶν ἐν τῷ χειλώματι ἵνα μὴ σαπῇ, "take care of the things in the box lest they rot" (Edd.), ib. XII. 1449[51] (A.D. 213–17) τὰ δὲ ἱμάτια πάντ(α) ἀπὸ τ(οῦ) χρ(όνου) σεση(μ)μένα ἄχρηστ(α), "and all the clothing decayed with age and useless" (Edd.), and the late P Amh II. 153[19] (vi vii A.D.) ἵνα ὁ θεός σήψῃ τὴν ψυχὴν σου ὡς διέσηψάς με εἰς τὴν κατ[α]γραφὴν ταύτην, "may God destroy your soul if you destroy me in the matter of this register" (Edd.).

For the subst. cf. BGU IV. 1116[26] (B.C. 13) πλὴν τριβῆς καὶ σήψεως, and the quotation from Photius Bibliotheca p. 513[36] (cited by Deissmann LAE[2] p. 68) οἱ γὰρ κόκκοι μετὰ τὴν ἐκ σήψεως νέκρωσιν καὶ φθορὰν ἀναζῶσι, "for the seeds come to life again after death and destruction by decay."

σηρικός.

See s.v. σιρικός.

σής.

"a moth." As a parallel to Mt 6[20] Lendrum cites (CR xx. (1906). p. 307) Pindar Fragm. 222—

Διὸς παῖς ὁ χρυσός·
κεῖνον οὐ σὴς οὐδὲ κὶς δάπτει.

σητόβρωτος.

"moth-eaten." Apart from Jas 5[2] the word occurs in the Greek Bible only in Job 13[28]. In secular Greek it has been found as yet only in Orac. Sib. proœm. 64 σητόβρωτα δέδορκε (of wooden idol-images).

σθενόω,

"strengthen" (1 Pet 5[10]). For the corr. subst. cf. P Leid G[14] (B.C. 181–145) (= I. p. 42) κράτος, σθένος, κυριείαν τῶν [ὑ]πὸ τὸν οὐρανὸν χώρω[ν], also P Oxy VIII. 1120[19] (early iii/A.D.) ὡς ἐν παντὶ σθένει βίαν με σχεῖν, "so that I am subjected to unmitigated violence" (Ed.), and ib. XII. 1557[9] (A.D. 255) ἀξιῶ ἐξαυτῆς παντὶ σθένει ἀναζητηθέντα τὰ κτήνη ἀποκατασταθῆναί μοι, "I desire that forthwith the cattle be sought with all one's might and restored to me." The phrase παντὶ σθένει is also common in treaties, e.g. Syll 61 (= [3] 122)[6] (B.C. 390–5) βοηθέν . . [π]αντὶ σθέ[νει] . . . [κατὰ τὸ δυνατόν].

σιαγών,

"a cheek." That this word, a specialty of Q (Mt 5[39], Lk 6[29]), is not of learned origin is shown by such passages as—P Cairo Zen I. 59070[12 f] (B.C. 257) σιαγόνες μείζους

καὶ φακοὶ ἐπὶ σιαγόνι δεξιᾶι, P Lond 909*a[7] (A.D. 136)
(III. p. 170) ὁμολογῶ πε[π]ρακέγε σοι κάμηλον ἄρσηνον
(l. ἄρρενα) . . . κεχαρακμένον τεξιὰν σιακόγην (l. σιαγόνα)
ταῦ ἄλφα, "I acknowledge to have sold to you a male
camel branded T.A, on its right cheek," P Ryl II. 88[28]
(A.D. 150) οὐλὴ σεαγό(νι) ἀριστ(ερᾷ), and ib. 63[9] (astrological—iii/A.D.) Π]αρθένου σιαγὼν ὀσφύες, "the cheek and
the loins to Virgo." A form σναγών occurs in BGU I. 100[5]
(A.D. 159).

σιαίνομαι.

For this verb = "am disturbed," which is read in 1 Thess
3[3] FG, we may cite two passages from late papyri—P Oxy
XVI. 1837[2] (early vi/A.D.) ἵνα μὴ ὁ ἀναγινόσκον (= ώσκων)
σιανθῇ, "lest he who reads should be annoyed" (Edd.),
and ib. 1840[2] (vi/vii A.D.) ἐπειδὴ τὸ λάχανον ὅδε (l. ὧδε)
σαπρόν ἐστι καὶ σιαίνομε (l. σιαίνομαι), "for the vegetables
here are rotten and disgust me" (Edd.). See s.v. σαίνω,
and for the new σιαντία see P Oxy XVI. 1855[13]
(vi/vii A.D.) ἀπαλλαγῆναι τῆς σιαντίας ταύτης, "to get rid
of this horrid business" (Edd.).

σιγάω.

The verb is restored (Berichtigungen, p. 322) in P Oxy
III. 471[11] (ii/A.D.), where an advocate asks—ταῦτ[α δὲ ἐκ]
τίνος αἰτ[ί]ας σ[εσίγη]κας; "what reason had you for being
silent regarding this?" For the compd κατασιγάω, "become silent," cf. CP Herm I. 25[ii.2] (iii/A.D.) οὔτε συσκευαζί[ι
οὔ]τε ἀπειλαὶ κατεσίγησαν μ[. . .
Herwerden (Lex. s.v.) cites the saying of Simonides apud
Plut. Mor. 125 D ἔλεγε μηδέποτ' αὐτῷ μεταμελῆσαι σιγή-
σαντι, φθεγξαμένῳ δὲ πολλάκις.

σιγή.

"silence": Kaibel 99[1] (iv/A.D.) πῶς κρυερὴ σιγή. For
the usage in Rev 8[1] cf. Dieterich Mithrasliturgie p. 42
σιγή, σιγή, σιγή, σύμβολον θεοῦ ζῶντος ἀφθάρτου φύλαξόν
με σιγή (cited by Wendland Urchr. Literaturformen,[2]
p. 382 n[3].). See Aristeas 95 for the σιγή which prevailed
during temple services. Reference may also be made to
G. Mensching Das Heilige Schweigen (Religionsgesch. Ver-
uche und Vorarbeiten, xx. 2), Giessen, 1926.

σιδήρεος.

"made of iron" (Ac 12[10], Rev 2[27], al.): P Eleph 5[7]
(B.C. 284–3) λυχνία σιδηρᾶ ᾱ, P Oxy III. 521[13 f] (ii/A.D.)
βάδιλλος σιδ[ηρούς], κάρκινος σιδη[ρούς, "iron shovel,
iron tongs," ib. VII. 1035[13] (A.D. 143) τὸ ὑπάρχον αὐτῷ
ξεῦγος κτενιστικὸν σιδηροῦν, "the combing instrument belonging to him, made of iron," and P Lond 1164(h)[9] (A.D.
212) (= III. p. 164) πλοῖον . . . ἀνκύραις σιδηραῖς σὺν
σπάθαις σιδηραῖς. The uncontracted form σιδηρέας occurs
in 4 Macc 9[28] א*, and σιδηραίαις in ib.[25]: see Thackeray
Gr. i. p. 173.

σίδηρος.

"iron" (Rev 18[12]): P Cairo Zen II. 59144[10] (B.C. 256)
τῶν ε̄ τα]λάντων) τ[οῦ σιδή]ου, "ten talents of iron,"
P Petr II. 13(1)[10] (B.C. 258–253) τὸν σίδηρον ἐνέχυρα
θήσουσιν, "they will put their iron (tools) in pledge" (Ed.),
and P Oxy I. 84[14] (A.D. 316) payment ὑπὲρ τιμῆς σιδή[ρο]υ

ἐνεργοῦ, "for the price of wrought iron." This last document shows us also σιδηροχαλκεύς, and P Lond 121[356]
(iii/A.D.) (= I. p. 95) σιδηρόψυχος, both adjectives new to
the lexicons. See also BGU I. 40[5] (undated) σιδηροφάγος
(not in LS[8]). For a subst. σιδήριον cf. P Oxy VII. 1066[20]
(iii/A.D.) τὰ σι]δήρια, "the iron tools," and for σιδήρωσις
"iron work" see ib. IX. 1208[14] (A.D. 291) with reference
to a machine fitted πάσῃ ξυλικῇ καταρτείᾳ καὶ σιδη[ρ]ώσει,
"with all wood-work and iron-work." The verb occurs in
the fragmentary P Lond 422 (c. A.D. 350) (= II. p. 318),
where directions are given to arrest a man and σιδηρῶσαι
αὐτόν, "put him in irons," on a charge of selling stolen
camels. MGr σίδερο.

Σιδών.

For the declension of this place-name in the LXX, see
Thackeray Gr. i. p. 169. In Mk 7[31] Wellhausen (Evang.
Marci, p. 60) thinks we should read εἰς Βηθσαιδάν for διὰ
Σιδῶνος: cf. also Allen Mark ad l.

σικάριος

(from Lat. sica, "stiletto"), "assassin" (Ac 21[38]), is
found several times in Josephus, e.g. Antt. XX. 186 (= xx.
8, 10). For σικάριον, a "dagger" or "knife," see P Oxy X.
1294[8] (ii/iii A.D.) ᾗ σικάρια ἐξ αὐτῶν σεαυτῇ ἓν ἄρον,
"three knives: of these take one for yourself" (Edd.).

σίκερα,

"strong drink," an indeclinable transcript from Aramaic
שִׁכְרָא, found in the NT only in Lk 1[15], but frequent in the
LXX (Thackeray Gr. i. p. 33). In P Tebt II. 413[11]
(ii/iii A.D.) for σικιωτεν Crönert suggests σικερώτιον, "a
jar for drinking σίκερα": see the editors' note, also s.v.
σκιά.

Σίλας,

or better Σιλᾶς (Winer-Schmiedel Gr. p. 74), a Semitic
name which is Latinized into Σιλουανός (q.v.). It is found
in a sepulchral inscr. Cagnat III. 817[1] Σίλα[ς Ν]ενησίος ὁ
καὶ Κλεόνεικος.

Σιλουανός

is read by WH in the NT occurrences of this proper name,
but the form Σιλβανός, which is found in certain MSS., is
otherwise well attested. An ex. of it, contemporary with the
NT writings, occurs in P Oxy II. 335 (c. A.D. 85), where a
Jew Silvanus buys part of a house in the Jewish quarter
from Paulus. Unfortunately the crucial letter is missing
(Σιλ[βα]νῷ—Edd.), but there does not seem room for ουα.
Σιλουανός occurs in P Lips I. 104 (A.D. 319), his own
signature at the foot having β; and in a Christian amulet,
BGU III. 954[4] (vi/A.D.), where we may presume the influence
of the Biblical name. P Lond 1157[16] (A.D. 197) (= III. p. 63)
is the earliest dated papyrus we know where the β is extant,
unless P Strass I. 27[69] (i/ii A.D.—Ed.) is older.
From inscrr. may be quoted Cagnat III. 705 (A.D. 147);
but Kaibel 432 (Syria—ii/A.D.) Σιλουανός, and similarly
Preisigke 674 (Alexandria—no date) and Cagnat III. 1188
(Syria—no date). Note also the Galatian Σ]ιλουανο[ῦ in
OGIS 533[50] (reign of Augustus). This is in keeping with
the fact that Avircius Marcellus in his famous epitaph,

C. and B. ii. p. 722 f. (c. A.D. 102), twice (³·¹⁷) calls himself
Ἀουίρκιος. Ramsay remarks (op. cit. p. 737) that "towards
the end of the second century, the use of β to represent
Latin v began; and in the third century it became almost
universal": cf. also his *Asian Elements*, p. 241. It must
be noted, however, that there are much earlier exx.: see
Viereck *Sermo Graecus*, p. 57, where instances are given
from i/B.C. Note also P Ryl II. 127²⁶ (A.D. 29) and 138¹
(A.D. 34), with **Λιβία** = *Livia*. There are some instances
of ο, as **Κοίντος, Οαλέριος.**

Σιλωάμ.

On this place-name see H. W. Sheppard in *JTS* xvi.
(1915), p. 414 ff., where the suggestion is made that the final
"m" in Siloam denotes a dual, applicable to the "two
pools"; but see *ib.* p. 555.

σιμικίνθιον,

on its only occurrence in the NT, Ac 19¹², is usually
rendered "apron" (so AV, RV), like the Lat. *semicinctium*
(Mart. 14. 153, Petr. 94. 8), but Nestle (*Exp T* xiii. p. 282)
thinks the reference must be, not to an apron worn above the
regular clothing, but to some article of underwear which had
been in actual contact with the Apostle's skin (**ἀπὸ τοῦ
χρωτὸς αὐτοῦ**), and compares the merit attached to the
Pope's "stockings" in certain Roman Catholic circles at
the present day. For the form **σιμικίνθιον** for **σημικίνθιον**
see Moulton *Gr.* ii. p. 172.

Σίμων,

a Greek name used as a substitute for **Συμεών** (*q.v.*) owing
to similarity of sound (cf. Deissmann *BS*, p. 315). The
name is common in the papyri and need not necessarily refer
to Jews, cf. P Lille I. 5³⁹ (B.C. 260–259), P Fay 14¹ (B.C. 124),
P Tebt I. 43¹⁵ (B.C. 118), BGU IV. 1129³ (B.C. 13), P Lond
1177²²⁹ (A.D. 113) (= III. p. 187), and BGU III. 913⁷
(A.D. 206).

σίναπι,

"mustard" (Mk 4³¹, *al.*): P Tebt I. 9¹³ (B.C. 119) (**ἀρτάβας**) **σινάπεως γ̄**, P Fay 122⁴ (c. A.D. 100) **εὖ ποιήσεις
μεταβαλόμενος τὸ παρὰ σοὶ σί[ν]απι . . τῷ κομίζοντί σοι
τὸ ἐπιστόλιον**, "please transfer the mustard that is with you
to the bearer of this letter" (Edd.), P Flor I. 20²¹ (A.D. 127)
(= *Chrest.* I. p. 422) **σποράν σὺν τῷ φυησομένῳ σινάπι**,
P Oxy VI. 936⁷ (iii/A.D.) **τριχοίνεικον σινάπεως**, "3
choinices of mustard," and P Lond 453⁶ (iv/A.D.) (= II.
p. 319) **πλήσον κεράμιον σινάπις χλωροῦ**. For a new adj.
σιναπηρός, see P Oxy XVII. 2148¹¹ (A.D. 27) **ὀψαρίδιν
σιναπηρόν**, "mustard relish." The spelling **σίνηπι** is found
in P Lips I. 97ˣˣˣⁱⁱⁱ·⁴·⁵ (A.D. 338). Like the Attic **νᾶπυ**, the
word is of Egyptian origin (Boisacq p. 657). MGr **σινάπι.**

σινδών,

"a fine linen cloth." The word is sometimes regarded as
of Semitic origin (so Boisacq p. 860), but see Thackeray *Gr.* i.
p. 36. Instances in our documents are common. In an
account of payments, P Tebt I. 182 (late ii B.C.), mention is
made of 2 talents 5000 (?) drachmae as paid **σινδόνων**: cf.
P Lond 203³ (B.C. 100) (= I. p. 163). A **σινδών** is described
as **καθαρά** (cf. Mt 27⁵⁹) in *ib.* 46²⁰⁶ (iv/A.D.) (= I. p. 71).

PART VII.

and P Leid Wᵘⁱ·ᴱ (ii/iii A.D. (= II. p. 89). In *Syll* 754¹
we read **σίνδονα ἐν ᾗ ἐξω[γ]ράφηται ἡ θεός**, and immediately afterwards **ἄλλας σινδόνας λαμπρᾶς τρεῖς.**

The use of the word for swathing dead bodies, as in Mt 27⁵⁹,
may be seen in the letter regarding funeral expenses, P Grenf
II. 77²⁷ (iii/iv A.D.) (= *Selections*, p. 121) **τιμ[ὴ] σινδόνος
(δραχμαὶ) κ̄**, "the price of a linen-cloth 20 drachmae." Cf.
P Par 18 *bis*¹⁰ (Rom.) a letter announcing the dispatch of a
dead body **ἔστιν δὲ σημεῖον τῆς ταφῆς· σινδών ἐστιν
ἐκτὸς ἔχων χρῆμα (*i.* χρῶμα ?) ῥόδινον.** **Σινδών** is further
illustrated by Field, *Notes*, p. 40. For the dim. **σινδόνιον,**
see P Gen I. 80⁶ (mid. iv A.D.), and P Bilabel II. 90⁶ (Byz.),
and for **σινδονίτης**, "a linen tunic," see *Syll* 653 (= ³ 736)¹⁷
(Andania—B.C. 92), also Menander *Sam.* 163. MGr **σεντόνι,**
"a linen napkin."

σινιάζω,

"sift," "shake in a sieve" (Lk 22³¹): cf. P Ryl II. 139⁶
(A.D. 34) **τὴν ἐπίσκεψιν ποιουμένου οὗ εἶχον σεννίου καὶ
ψυγμοῦ**, "making an inspection of my . . . and drying-
floor," where the editors think that the new word **σέννιον**
may be connected with **σινιάζω**, and compare P Strass I. 45¹¹
(A.D. 312) **εἰς τοὺς σεινίους τόπους**, and note. The verb,
like the late noun **σινίον** from which it comes, is of unknown
derivation (Boisacq p. 866).

σιρικός,

for **σηρικός**, "silken," is read by all uncials in Rev 18¹²:
cf. *IG* XIV. 785⁴ **σιρικοποιός**, and *IG* III. ii. 3513² (v/A.D.)
σιρικάριος. The adj. is formed from the name of the Indian
(or Chinese) people from whom silk was first obtained—**οἱ
Σῆρες.** Boisacq (p. 861 f.) suggests that both the fabric and
the tribe got their Greek names by popular etymology from
the native name of the fabric.

σιρός,

See *s.v.* **σειρός**, and for the spelling **σιρός** add *Syll*³ 83¹⁰
(B.C. 423–2).

σιτευτός,

"fattened" (Lk 15²³·ᵉᵗᶜ): cf. P Cairo Zen I. 59026 (a)⁴
(B.C. 258 or 257) **χῆνα[ς] σιτευτοὺς ϛ̄**, and similarly *ib.* II.
59210³ (B.C. 254), and P Grad 2⁹ (B.C. 225–4).

σιτίον,

"corn" (plur. "provisions," "food") is read by the
critical texts in Ac 7¹² in place of the TR **σῖτα.** The same
form is found in LXX Prov 24⁵⁷ (30²²) **ἐὰν . . ἄφρων
πλησθῇ σιτίων**, to which Field (*Notes*, p. 114) adds Aelian
V.H. v. 1. We can now cite P Giss I. 19⁶ (ii/A.D.), where
the writer, in token of mourning, declares—**οὔτε σιτίοις
ἡδέως προσέρχομαι**, "I have no pleasure in my food," and
P Oxy VIII. 1158¹¹ (iii/A.D.) **ἀγόρασον ἡμῖν σιτία εἰς τὴν
χρῆσιν ἡμῶν**, "buy us some provisions for our use." Also
Musonius p. 124⁴ **φαρμάκοις γὰρ οὐκ ἔοικεν, ἀλλὰ σιτίοις
ὑγιεινοῖς ἡ δύναμις αὐτοῦ.** In MGr the dim. survives as
σιτάρι (στάρι), "wheat."

For the verb **σιτέω** cf. P Ryl II. 143² (A.D. 38) **τῶν ἐν
τῷ Μουσείῳ σειτουμένων φιλοσόφων**, "the philosophers
maintained in the Museum" (see further *s.v.* **φιλόσοφος**),
and for the subst. **σιτ(ε)ία** cf. BGU IV. 1007¹⁴ (A.D. 101–2)
σιτίας ἄρτων.

74

σιτιστός,

"fattened," in the NT only in Mt 22⁴ (cf. Blass-Debrunner § 112), and rare elsewhere, but cf. Sm Ps 21(22)¹³, Jerem 46(26)²¹. For the subst. see P Lips I. 97ˣˣⁱ·¹⁷ (A.D. 338) ἡμερ[ι]ν(οῦ) σι(τισμοῦ).

σιτομέτριον,

"measure of corn," "allowance of corn" (Lk 12⁴²) occurs several times in Petrie papyri, e.g. III. 87 (a) recto¹⁷ (iii/B.C.) κατὰ τὴν σιτομετρίαν, ib. 140 (b)¹, ib. 141¹⁵. See also Deissmann LAE² p. 104 n.¹, where reference is made to an Opramoas inscr. of A.D. 149 at Rhodiapolis in Lycia, with the spelling σειτομέτριον.

For the subst. σιτομέτρης cf. P Flor II. 162² (iii/A.D.) διὰ τοῦ σοῦ σ[ι]τομέτρου, and Preisigke 1485 (a mummy tablet) Σισῶτος σιτομέτρης ἐβίωσεν ξ, and for the verb, as in Gen 47¹², see IG XII. vii. 515⁷⁰.

σῖτος,

"corn": cf. P Cairo Zen I. 59001⁹ (B.C. 273) τοῦτο δ' ἐστὶν ἡ τιμὴ τοῦ βασιλικοῦ σίτου, ib. 59004²⁵ (B.C. 259?) ἀπὸ τοῦ σιτοποιηθέντος σίτου, ib. 59049³ (B.C. 257) πρὸς τῆι συν]αγωγῆι τοῦ σίτου, P Cornell I³¹ (B.C. 256) εἰς τὸν ἑτοιμαζόμενον σῖτον εἰς τὴν ἑορτὴν κο τύλη] ᾱ, P Lond 42¹⁷ (B.C. 168) (= I. p. 30, UPZ i. p. 300, Selections, p. 10) εἰς πᾶν τι ἐληλυθυῖα διὰ τὴν τοῦ σίτου τιμήν, "having come to the last extremity because of the high price of corn," P Par 59⁶ (B.C. 159) (= UPZ i. p. 413) ἠγώρακα σίτου ἀρ(τάβας) β̄ (δραχμῶν) χ̄λ, and BGU I. 27¹⁵ (ii/A.D.) (= Selections, p. 101) ὥστε ἕως σήμερον μηδέν' ἀπολελύσθαι τῶν μετὰ σῖτον, "so that up till to-day no one of us in the corn service has been let go" (on this letter see W. M. Ramsay in Hastings' DB v. p. 381). In the Byzantine Aphrodito papyri σῖτος is several times distinguished from κριθή, and means especially "wheat," cf. P Lond IV. 1335⁷ (A.D. 709) with the editor's note. The τὰ σῖτα of Attic Greek is retained in the LXX in Job and Proverbs, see Thackeray Gr. i. p. 155. To the exx. of the very common adj. σιτικός we can now add P Bouriant 42⁵⁷ (A.D. 167), and 44 (ii/A.D.).

Σίων

is found as the name of a person in PSI I. 71² (vi/A.D.), al.

σιωπάω,

"keep silence," "am silent": P Oxy II. 237ᵛ·¹³ (A.D. 186) ὁ δὲ παρὼν ἀναγνωσθέντος τοῦ βιβλειδίου πρὸ βήματος ἐσιώπησεν, cf. c. acc. ib.ˣⁱ·³¹ σιωπήσας γὰρ . . τὴν τοῦ Ῥούφου ἐπιστολὴν ἐφ' ὅτῳ ἐγράφη, "ignoring entirely the circumstances under which the letter of Rufus was written" (Edd.). Other exx. are P Oxy XII. 1468²⁷ (c. A.D. 258) τ[ῆ]ς κ[α]κουργίας ταύτης μὴ σιωπη[σά]σῃ, "did not maintain silence about this fraud" (Edd.), P Lond 46²⁸² (iv/A.D.) (= I. p. 74) λαλούντων καὶ σιωπώντων, and Preisigke 4638⁸ (time of Philometor) κατὰ τὸ σιωπώμενον. Also Menander Fragm. 658² p. 193 διὰ τοῦ σιωπᾶν πλεῖστα περὶ αὐτῆς λέγει.

For the subst. σιωπή, see P Flor III. 309⁵ (iv/A.D.) οὐ χρὴ σ[ι]ωπῇ παραδίδοσθαι τὰ ὑπ' αὐτῆς εἰρημένα παρὰ τοὺς νόμους, and Syll 645 (= ³1047)²⁵ (ii/B.C.) σιωπὴν κατακηρύξας ὁ κῆρυξ. Herwerden (Lex. s.v.) cites Euri-

pides ap. Plut. Mor. 532 F τὴν σιωπὴν τοῖς σοφοῖς ἀπόκρισιν εἶναι.

σκανδαλίζω.

For the meaning "I set a trap for" rather than "I put a stumbling-block in the way of," for this important Biblical word, reference may be made to two recent discussions. The first by the Rev. A. Carr appeared in his Horae Biblicae (1903) p. 58 ff., where, after a survey of the evidence of the LXX, he comes to the conclusion that the underlying thought of enticement or temptation can hardly be dissociated from the word. And much the same conclusion is reached by Archdeacon Allen as the result of an independent inquiry in his St. Mark (1915) p. 190 ff., where, following out a hint by Dr. J. H. Moulton (Exp T xxvi. p. 331 f.), he again lays the emphasis on the idea of "snare" rather than of "stumbling-block." The etymological connexion of the word with Skr. skand, "leap," "spirt," Lat. scando, makes this clearer, leading on, as it does, to the Aristophanic use of σκανδάληθρον for "the stick of a mouse-trap" (cf. Acharn. 687 σκανδάληθρ' ἱστὰς ἐπῶν, "setting word-traps").

σκάνδαλον.

See s.v. σκανδαλίζω. Cf. also the Aphrodito papyri P Lond IV. 1338²⁷ (A.D. 709) πρόφασιν ἢ σκάνδαλον, 1339¹¹ (A.D. 709) μὴ διδῶν κατὰ σεαυτοῦ παντοῖον σκάνδαλον περὶ τούτου.

σκάπτω.

"dig," is confined in the NT to Luke (6⁴⁸, 13⁸, 16³). Exx. from the Κοινή are common, e.g. PSI VI. 672³ (iii/B.C.) ἐργάταις τοῖς σκάπτουσιν ἐν τῆι ἄμμωι, P Magd 27¹ (B.C. 218) θεμέλιον σκάπτων ὥστε οἰκοδομεῖν, BGU IV. 1120³⁰ (B.C. 5) σκ[ά]πτοντας καὶ ποτίζοντας, P Fay 110⁸ (A.D. 94) τὰ κύκλωι τοῦ ἐλαιουργίου ἔξωθεν σκάψον ἐπὶ βάθος, "dig a deep trench round the oil-press outside" (Edd.), BGU I. 14ⁱⁱ·¹⁸ (A.D. 255) σκάπτοντες ἐν χωρίῳ, and from the inscrr. Syll 531 (= ³963)⁹ (iv/B.C.) ἀμπέλους δ[ὲ σκ]άψει δίς.

For σκαφητός, a preliminary digging, see P Cornell 25 recto¹³ (B.C. 28–23), and P Oxy XIV. 1631¹⁰ (A.D. 280), and for a new word σκάφητρος, "a digging," see P Fay 112²·¹⁶ (A.D. 99), and P Ryl II. 245¹⁰ (iii/A.D.) ἐπ[ὶ] σκάφητρον τῶν ἐλαιώνων. Σκαφεῖον, "a hoe," occurs in P Tebt I. 45³⁹ (B.C. 113), ib. 47³⁶ (B.C. 113). MGr σκάφτω, σκάβω, "excavate." "dig out."

σκάφη,

"a small boat" (Ac 27¹⁶,³⁰,³²): cf. P Cairo Zen I. 59025⁵ (B.C. 28 or 29) σκάφης τρισκάλμου, "a boat with three sculls," BGU IV. 1157¹³ (B.C. 10) τρίτου μέρους τῆς δηλουμένης σκάφης, and P Lond 256 (a)¹ (A.D. 11–15) (= II. p. 99) κυβερνήτης σκάφης δημοσίας, "pilot of a public vessel." For the dim. σκαφίδιον see P Oxy VII. 1068⁷ (iii/A.D.) διαπέμψετό μοι σκαφίδιον ἀρταβῶν ἑξήκοντα, "he sent me a skiff of sixty artabae burden," as contrasted with πλοῖον, previously mentioned.

σκέλος,

"a leg." For the literal sense, as in Jn 19³¹ ff., cf. P Par 12¹⁶ (B.C. 157) σπασάμενος λέπει με τῇ μαχαίρᾳ εἰς τὸ σκέλος, P Lips I. 37²⁰ (A.D. 380) κατέκοψα[ν] π[ληγ]αῖς αὐτὸν κατά [τ]ε τῶν σκελῶν καὶ κατὰ τῶν ἄλλων μελῶ[ν] τοῦ σώματος, and Aristeas 151 ἡ γὰρ ἰσχὺς τῶν ὅλων σωμάτων μετ' ἐνεργείας ἀπέρεισιν ἐπὶ τοὺς ὤμους ἔχει καὶ τὰ σκέλη.

For the derived use of σκέλος in connexion with the building of irrigation works, cf. P Petr III. 39¹·³² (iii/B.C.) εἰς τὰ ἐντὸς σκέλη τῆς ἀφέσεως τῆς [ἐν τῆι ἐγ]βατηρίαι, and *ib.*ii. 9, iii. 9. Cf. also PSI IV. 437² (B.C. 247-6) περὶ τὰ σκεα τοῦ πλοίου, where the editor suggests a possible σκέλ<η> for σκεα, and cites Hesych. σκέλος· μέρος τι τῆς νεώς. We may add the late BGU I. 304³ (c. A.D. 640) τοῦ βορρ(ινοῦ) σκέλους ταύτης τῆς πολ ιτ είας. A verb σκελοκοπέω, unknown to the Lexicons, is found in Ev. Petr. 4.

σκέπασμα.

For σκέπασμα, "covering," with special reference to "clothing," as in 1 Tim 6⁸, cf. the corresponding use of σκέπη in Aristeas 140 βρωτῶν καὶ ποτῶν καὶ σκέπης, "meat and drink and raiment." The metaphorical use of the verb, as in Sap 5¹⁶, Sir 2¹³, may be illustrated by P Hib I. 35¹⁰ (c. B.C. 250) ὑπὸ ὑ[μῶ]ν σκεπαζόμε[θ]α, "we are protected by you," and by the similar use of σκεπάω in P Lond 897¹·⁸ (A.D. 84) (= III. p. 206) ἐὰν δὲ δύνημαι σκεπάσαι ἢ ὑπὸ σκέπην τινὰ γενέσθαι.

Σκευᾶς.

"Sceva," an inhabitant of Ephesus (Ac 19¹⁴). The name is found in CIG II. 2880, with reference to a Milesian gladiator.

For a suggestion that ἑπτά in Ac 19¹⁴, which changes unaccountably to "two" (ἀμφοτέρων) in ¹⁶, may be due to a gloss, Σκευᾶ = שבע = ἑπτά, see *Proleg.* pp. 80, 246.

σκευή,

which is applied to the "tackle" of a ship in Ac 27¹⁹, is used of a woman's "ornaments" in P Lond 1164(*f*)¹⁸ (A.D. 212) (= III. p. 161) γυναικιῶν αὐτῆς κοσμαρίων καὶ σκευῶν, and of "household plenishing," "goods," in BGU III. 775⁶ (ii/A.D.) παρ[α]δέδωκά συ (*l.* σοι) μου τὸ κλεδιν (*l.* κλειδίον) τῆς ὑκίας (*l.* οἰκίας) μου ὑπὸ τὴν σκευήν.

σκεῦος,

"a vessel" (Rom 9²¹ *al.*). This common noun is used with a variety of applications, e.g. P Eleph 14²¹ (iii/B.C.) ἐκ τε κτηνῶν καὶ σκευῶν, P Petr III. 107(*d*)¹·²⁵ (iii/B.C.) fares are paid for the conveyance τῶν 'Αγήνορος σκευῶν, "of Agenor's furniture," P Ryl II. 138²³ (A.D. 34) ἐρίων σταθμία ιε καὶ ἕτερα σκεύη, "15 measures of wool, as well as other implements," P Oxy I. 105¹ (A.D. 117-137) σκεύη καὶ ἔπιπλα, "movables and household stock," P Tebt II. 381¹³ (A.D. 123) (= *Selections*, p. 78) σκεύηι καὶ ἐνδομενίαν καὶ ἱματισμόν, "utensils and household-stock and clothing," and P Grenf II. 77¹⁴ (iii/iv A.D.) (= *Selections*, p. 120) χάριν τῶν σκευῶν αὐτοῦ, "on account of his goods."

For σκεῦος = "(a ship's) tackle," as in Ac 27¹⁷, cf. P Cairo Zen I. 59031¹⁰ (B.C. 258) ἀδύνατον γάρ μοι δοκεῖ εἶναι ἄνευ τῶν ἀναγκαίων σκευῶν πλεῖν τὰ πλοῖα, and *Syll* 537 (= ³969)⁵ (B.C. 347-6) σ]υνγραφαὶ τῆς σκευοθήκης τῆς λιθίνης τοῖς κρεμαστοῖς σκεύεσιν. In the new uncanonical

gospel, P Oxy V. 840¹⁴, τὰ ἅγια σκεύη are "the holy vessels" of the temple: cf. Heb 9²¹. See also Plut. *Mor.* 812 B σκεῦος ἱερόν. On σκεῦος = "body" rather than "wife" in 1 Thess 4⁴, see Milligan *ad l.*

For the dim. σκευάριον see P Lond 46²¹¹ (iv/A.D.) (= I. p. 72) σκευάριον καλλάϊνον μικρό[ν, and for σκευασία P Leid X*v. 33* (iii/iv A.D.) (= I. p. 217) χρυσοκόλλου σκευσία (*l.* σκευασία).

In P Petr II. 13 (10)⁵ (B.C. 258-253) Deissmann (*BS* p. 158) understands σκεοφύλακα as = σκευοφύλακα, "keeper of baggage" (cf. *ib.* 5(*a*)³), and in P Amh II. 62 (ii/B.C.) three persons called 'Απολλώνιος are distinguished as "the dark" (μέλας), "the fair" (λευκός), and "the baggage-carrier" (σκευοφ(όρος)).

σκηνή.

"tent": cf. P Cairo Zen I. 59013¹⁴ (B.C. 259) σκηνὴ δερματίνη, PSI V. 533² (iii/B.C.) σκηνὴν κατάγαγε ἡμῖν τετράκλινον ἢ πεντάκλινον, and P Leid W*xiii. 21* (ii/iii A.D.) (= II. p. 125) μὴ ἐξέλθῃς δὲ ἐκ τῆς σκηνῆς σου. The employment of σκηνή for οἰκία, καταγωγή, is said to be Asiatic in origin: see Menander *Fragm.* p. 201, No. 1065.

The editors understand σκηνή as = ship's "cabin" in P Hib I. 38⁷ (B.C. 252-1) τῶν συρίων ὑπὲρ τὴν σκηνὴ[ν] οὐσῶν, "the Syrian clothes being above the cabin," and so *ib.* 86⁷ (B.C. 248) ἀποκαταστήσω ἐπὶ σκηνὴν τοῖς ἰδίοις ἀνηλώμασιν, "I will restore it (*sc.* grain) at the cabin at my own expense."

We may recall the words which are sometimes ascribed to Democritus, ὁ κόσμος σκηνή, ὁ βίος πάροδος· ἦλθες, εἶδες, ἀπῆλθες. See also *Anth. Pal.* x. 72.

σκηνοπηγία.

lit. "feast of booth-making," and applied to the Jewish "Feast of Tabernacles" in Jn 7², is regarded by Winer-Schmiedel *Gr.* p. 23 as a coinage by Greek Jews, but it is found in Aristotle: see also the Cyrenaic inscr. CIG III. 5361¹ ἐπὶ συλλόγου τῆς σκηνοπηγίας. Σκανοπαγείσθων, "let them erect a booth," occurs in a Coan religious inscr. of ii/B.C.: see Deissmann's discussion in *LAE²*, p. 115 f.

σκηνοποιός,

in Biblical Greek is confined to Ac 18³, but for the verb σκηνοποιέω see Sm Isai 13²⁰, 22¹⁵, and for the subst. σκηνοποιία see Aq Deut 31¹⁰. In view of these passages there seems to be no reason to question the ordinary rendering "tentmaker" in Ac *l.c.*, but for explanations as to how the alternatives "landscape-painter" and "shoemaker" may have arisen, see notes by Ramsay and Nestle in *Exp T* viii. pp. 109, 153 f., 286.

σκῆνος.

For σκῆνος, "tent," "tabernacle," used metaph. of the body, as the dwelling-place of the soul, in 2 Cor 5¹·⁴, see the exx. from Pythagorean philosophy in Field *Notes*, p. 183, and the sepulchral epigram, *Brit. Mus. Inscr.* IV. (1916), No. 1114, placed over a recumbent skeleton—

Εἰπεῖν τίς δύναται, σκῆνος λιπόσαρκον ἀθρήσας,
εἴπερ "Υλας ἢ Θερσίτης ἦν, ὦ παροδεῖτα;

σκηνόω,

"dwell as in a tent," is confined in the NT to Jn (1[14], Rev 7[15] al.): cf. P Cairo Zen I. 59037[7] (B.C. 258-7) σκηνῶν ἐν τοῖς Ἀριστοβούλου, "living in the house of Aristobulus" (cf. Lk 2[49], PSI IV. 340[10] (B.C. 257-6) Ἀμύνταν δὲ ἔξω τε σκηνοῦντα [κ]αὶ γεγαμηκότα, and ib.[15] τῶι ἐν τῆι οἰκίαι σκηνοῦντι.

The thought of temporary dwelling is well brought out in Syll 177 (=[3] 344)[2] (Teos—B.C. 303) "every delegate (from Lebedos) sent to the Πανιώνιον we (i.e. King Antigonus) think should σκηνοῦν . . καὶ πανηγυράζειν and be treated as a Teian."

σκήνωμα.

With σκήνωμα, "tent" (Ac 7[46]), also used for the temporary abode of the soul (2 Pet 1[13 f.]), cf. σκήνωσις in Preisigke 3924[7] (edict of Germanicus—A.D. 19) ἐπὶ σκηνώσεις καταλαμβάνεσθαι ξενίας πρὸς βίαν.

σκιά,

"shade," is used of the shadow on a sun-dial in Preisigke 358[1] (iii/B.C.) μεθίσταται τὸ ἄκρον τῆς σκιᾶς ἐν ἡμέραις τριά κοντα. Other exx. of the word are P Oxy VIII. 1088[13] (medical receipt—early i/A.D.) ἐν τῆι σκιᾶι ξηράνας, "dry in the shade," and OGIS 201[20] (vi/A.D.) οὐκ ἀφῶ αὐτοὺς καθεσθῆναι εἰς τὴν σκιάν, εἰ μὴ (= ἀλλὰ) ὑπὸ ἡλίου ἔξω.

In BGU IV. 1141[11] (B.C. 13) Schubart thinks that σκιά is perhaps used in the sense of an "umbrella," but Olsson (Papyrusbriefe, p. 52) prefers the meaning "a variegated border," as in Syll 653 (=[3] 736)[20,24] (B.C. 92): cf. also P Oxy VI. 921[b] (iii/A.D.) σινδόνια σκιωτά, "cambrics with variegated borders" rather than "with shaded stripes," and the editors' suggestion ad l. that σικιωτεν in P Tebt II. 413[11] is perhaps for σκιωτόν.

With Heb 10[1] cf. Preisigke 344 Διόδωρος σκιὰν Ἀντιφίλου ἐποίησ[εν, and Vett. Val. p. 248[22] with reference to a picture which shows σκιὰν ἔργου καὶ ἀληθείας. Preisigke (Worterb. s.v.) cites the amulet P Masp II. 67188[5] (vi/A.D.) for σκιά = "an evil spirit"—παρ[α]φύλαξόν με ἀπὸ παντὸς πονηροῦ πν(εύμ)ατος, ὑπόταξόν μου πᾶν πν(εῦμ)α δαιμονίων φθειροποιῶν . . . καὶ πᾶσα σκιά (l. πᾶσαν σκιάν).

For the verb σκιάζω cf. P Cornell 50[10] (i/A.D.) ἵνα αἱ ἄμπελοι μὴ σκιάζωνται, and BGU I. 33[14] (ii/iii A.D.) τὰ δὲ οἰνάρια σκίασον, ἐὰν καιρὸς γένηται. For σκιατροφέω see Musonius p. 59[9]. The subst. σκιασμός occurs in Vett. Val. p. 210[5]. MGr ἴσκιος, "shade," "shadow," has a prothetic vowel : cf. s.v. στῆθος.

σκιρτάω,

"leap," "bound," is confined in the NT to Lk (1[41, 44], 6[23]): cf. Kaibel 271[6] σκιρτῶ καὶ τέρπομαι, ib. 649[3] (iii/A.D.)—

σκιρτῶσα γέγηθας
ἄνθεσιν ἐν μαλακοῖσι κακῶν ἔκτοσθεν ἁπάντων.

A new instance of the subst. σκίρτημα is found in the iv/A.D. Christian hymn, P Amh I. 2[19] Τὰ [δ]' ἀ[νάπ]αυλα (l. ἀνάπαυμα?) λυπο-<υ>μένων, Τὰ δὲ σκιρτήματα [.., "O the rest of the sorrowful, O the dancing of the . ." (cf. ZNTW ii. (1901), p. 73 ff.).

σκληρός.

The original meaning of this adj. was "hard," as in BGU III. 952[10] (ii/iii A.D.) τι]μῆς μαρμάρου ξηροῦ σκλ[ηροῦ, and from the inscr. Syll 540 (=[3]972)[96] (B.C. 175), which speaks of the working and building of the "hard" stone from Lebadeia, πέ]τρας σκληρᾶς: so OGIS 194[28] (B.C. 42) ἐκ σκληροῦ λίθου. But in this last inscr. [11] σκληροτέρας καὶ [μείζονος συμφορᾶς τοῦ ἀέρος describes (with some doubt from hiatus) a pestilent miasma in the atmosphere. See also P Cairo Zen II. 59275[9] (B.C. 251) σκ]ληρὰ κρέα. "bitter (or pickled) meats." BGU I. 140[24] (time of Hadrian) τ]οῦτο οὐκ ἐδόκει σκληρὸν [εἶ]ναι shows the metaph. sense which prevails in the NT: cf. Kaibel 942[2] (i/B.C.) θερμὸν πνεῦμα φέρων σκληρᾶς παῖς ἀπὸ πυγμαχίας, and Aristeas 289 where kings are described as ἀνήμεροί τε καὶ σκληροί, "inhuman and harsh." For σκληρουργός, "a mason," cf. P Ryl II. 410 (ii/A.D.), BGU III. 952[6] (ii/iii A.D.). For the history of σκληρός see an elaborate note by Dieterich in Rheinisches Museum N.F. lx. (1905), p. 236 ff.

σκληρότης

is found once (Rom 2[5]) in the NT = "obstinacy." For σκλήρωσις see P Leid X[ii.3] (iii/iv A.D.) (= II. p. 205) μολίβου κάθαρσις καὶ σλήρωσις (l. σκλήρωσις. Σκληρασία (not in LS[8]) is seen in ib.[xi. 4] (p. 233) κασσιτέρου σκληρασία.

σκληροτράχηλος.

This LXX word (Exod 33[3] al.) is quoted in the same metaph. sense of "stiff-necked," "obstinate," in its only NT occurrence Ac 7[51]. For the subst. σκληροτραχηλία see Test. xii. patr. Simeon vi. 2.

σκληρύνω,

"harden" (Heb 3[8] al.): cf. P Leid X[ii. 28] (iii/iv A.D.) (= II. p. 209) ἕως καταμιγῇ, καὶ σκλυρην (l. σκληρυνῇ). The verb is illustrated from Hippocrates and others by Anz Subsidia, p. 342 : for constr. c. articular inf. see Thackeray Gr. i. p. 54.

σκολιός,

"crooked," and hence metaph. "perverse" in the sense of "turning away from the truth" (Ac 2[40] al.): cf. Kaibel 244[1] Τύχη σκολιοῖς δόγμασιν ἠντίασεν. In Vett. Val. p. 250[23] διὰ τὸ σκολιὸν τῆς εἰσόδου, al., the editor renders the adj. "difficilis."

σκόλοψ.

The use of this word in BGU II. 380[9] (iii/A.D.) (= Selections, p. 105), where an anxious mother writes to her son— εἰπέ μοι, ὅτι τὸν πόδαν (l. πόδα) πονεῖς ἀπὸ σκολάπου (l. σκόλοπος), "he told me that you had a sore foot owing to a splinter," would seem to support the meaning "splinter" or "thorn" rather than "stake" (RV marg.) in the only occurrence of σκόλοψ in the NT, 2 Cor 12[7]. So in Syll 802 (=[3]1168)[92] (c. B.C. 320) a man falling from a tree περὶ σκόλοπάς τινας τοὺς ὀπτίλλους ἀμφέπαισε, and became blind, apparently not at once (κακῶς δὲ διακείμενος καὶ τυφλὸς γεγενημένος), where again we should think naturally of "splinters" or "thorns." This meaning appears still more clearly in the magical P Osl I. 1[152] (iv/A.D.), where the sorcerer says of the loved one—ἐὰν δὲ θέλῃ κοιμᾶσθαι, ὑποστρώσατε αὐτῇ στοιβὰς ἀκανθίνας, ἐπὶ δὲ τῶν κοτράφων σκόλοπας, "if she wants to lie down, strew beneath her prickly branches, and thorns upon her temples" (Ed.). See also Artem. p. 181[11] ἄκανθαι καὶ σκόλοπες ὀδύνας σημαίνουσι διὰ τὸ ὀξύ, and Babrius *Fab.* cxxii[3] ὄνος πατήσας σκόλοπα χωλὸς εἱστήκει: he appeals to a wolf[6f] χάριν δέ μοι δὸς ἀβλαβῆ τε καὶ κούφην,/ ἐκ τοῦ ποδός μου τὴν ἄκανθαν εἰρύσσας (cited by Field, *Notes* p. 187). It may be added that LXX usage (Numb 33[55], Ezek 28[24], Hos 2[6], Sir 43[19]) strongly confirms the rendering "thorn." We are not concerned here with the special metaph. application which Paul gives to the word in 2 Cor *l.c.*, but for a recent defence of the view that his "thorn" was epilepsy see Wendland *Kultur.* p. 125 f.

σκοπέω,

"look upon," "watch," "contemplate": cf. P Par 63[3] (B.C. 156) σκοπεῖτε ἵνα μηδὲν παρὰ ταῦτα γίνηται, P Oxy XII. 1420[2] (c. A.D. 129) ὁ στρατηγὸς σκεψάμενος ("after consideration") εἶπεν, *ib.* XIV. 1773[13] (iii/A.D.) νῦν οὖν ἐσκεψάμην τοὺς γόμους μου ἀρῖν εἰς Ἀντινόου, and *ib.* VI. 940[5] (v/A.D.) οὕτως σκοπῶ τὸ πρακτέον, "thus I shall see what is to be done" (Edd.). In Lk 11[35] σκόπει μὴ τὸ φῶς . . σκότος ἐστίν, we may render, "Look! perhaps the light is darkness" (cf. *Proleg.* p. 192). See also *s.vv.* ἐπισκοπέω and κατασκοπέω.

σκοπός.

For the metaph. meaning "aim," "object," as in Phil 3[14], we may cite the last Will and Testament of Bishop Abraham, P Lond 77[8] (end of vi/A.D.) (= I. p. 232, *Chrest.* II. p. 370), where the Bishop declares that he acts ἐξ οἰκεία[ς] προθέσεως καὶ σκοπῷ αὐθαιρέτῳ, and adds[48] συνήρηκεν τῷ ἐμῷ ἀγαθῷ σκοπ῀ῳ: cf. P Lips I. 38[17] (A.D. 390) σκοπὸν ἔχων, τὸν ἔνδικον . . . συντρίψαι, and Aristeas 251 κατορθοῦται γὰρ βίος, ὅταν ὁ κυβερνῶν εἰδῇ, πρὸς τίνα σκοπὸν δεῖ τὴν διέξοδον ποιεῖσθαι, "for life is then guided aright, when the steersman knows the port to which he must direct his course" (Thackeray).

For the lit. sense a "mark" to be aimed at, cf. Syll 670 (= ³ 1059 I.)[16] (ii/A.D.) σκοπῷ ἱππέων, 671 (= ³ 1059 II.)[11] (c. A.D. 1) σκοπῷ πεζῶν.

σκορπίζω,

"scatter," in Ionic and the vernacular for σκεδάννυμι (Rutherford *NP*, p. 295): cf. P Lond 131 *recto*[421] (A.D. 78-79) (= I. p. 182) σκόρ(πισον) τὴν κοπρὸ(ν) ἐν ταῖς αὐταῖς ἀρούρ(αις), CP Herm I. 7[11.15] (ii/A.D.) of young plums, ἐσκορπισμέναι ἐν τῷ χωρίῳ, so 28[14], P Flor II. 175[22] (A.D. 255) τὰ ὄντα καμήλια ἐσκορπίσαμεν, P Leid X[viii.39] (iii/iv A.D.) (= II. p. 227) μετὰ τὸ σκορπισθῆναι καὶ μόνον τὸν ἄργυρον καταλειφθῆναι, and *ib.* V[xi.29] (iii/iv A.D.) (= II. p. 37) σκορπίζων τὰς νεφέλας ἀπ᾽ ἀλλήλων. See also PSI V. 478[14] (v/A.D.) ἕως ἂν σκορπίσωσι τὸ πρᾶγμα. MGr σκορπίζω.

σκορπίος,

"a scorpion." On the mummy tablet *Preisigke* 1209 it is recorded that a certain Apollonius ἐτελεύτησεν ὑπὸ σκορπίου: cf. the sepulchral inscr. *ib.* 1267[6] (A.D. 8) πλ[α]γεῖσα . .

ὑπὸ σκορπίου μετήλλαξε, and P Lond 121[193] (iii/A.D.) (= I. p. 99) πρὸς σκορπίου πληγήν.

For the word as a sign of the Zodiac see the calendar P Hib I. 27[20] (B.C. 301-240) ε Σκορπίος ἑῶιος ἄρχ[ε]ται δύνειν, "5th, Scorpio begins to set in the morning," the horoscope PSI IV. 312[3] (A.D. 345) Σελήνη Σκορπίῳ, and the Gnostic charm against reptiles P Oxy VII. 1060[9] (vi A.D.) σκορπίε . . ἀπάλλαξον τὸν οἶκον τοῦτον ἀπὸ παντὸς κακοῦ ἑρπετοῦ ⟨καὶ⟩ πράγματος ταχὺ ταχύ.

σκοτεινός,

"dark": P Par 51[19] (B.C. 159) (= UPZ i. p. 360, *Selections*, p. 20) εἰς ⟨σ⟩κοτινὸν τόπον.

σκοτίζω.

The literal meaning "darken" (as in Mt 24[29], *al.*) is seen in Wunsch *AF* p. 16[13] (iii/A.D.) ὁρκίζω σε τὸν θεὸν τὸν φωτίζοντα καὶ σκοτίζοντα τὸν κόσμον. For the metaph. usage, as in Rom 1[21], cf. *Test. xii. patr.* Reub. iii. 8 οὕτως ἀπόλλυται πᾶς νεώτερος, σκοτίζων τὸν νοῦν αὐτοῦ ἀπὸ τῆς ἀληθείας, and see Lightfoot *Notes*, p. 253.

σκότος,

"darkness," always neut. in LXX and NT, as in MGr: cf. the magic P Lond 46[101] (iv A.D.) (= I. p. 68) καλῶ . . . σε τὸν κτίσαντα φῶς καὶ σκότος, *ib.*[164] ὁ χωρίσας τὸ φῶ[ς] ἀ]πὸ τοῦ σκότους, *ib.* 121[763] (iii A.D.) (= I. p. 108) ἀπὸ φωτὸς εἰς σκότος ἀπολήγουσα, and the vi/A.D. Christian letter of condolence P Oxy XVI. 1874[5] ἀνέγνοσα τὸ σκότος, unfortunately in a broken context.

σκοτόω,

"darken," used metaph. of the mind in Eph 4[18]: cf. P Oxy XVI. 1854[3] (vi/vii A.D.) νομίζω ὅτι τὸ μυστάριν ἤδη ἐσκότωσεν κάκείνους, "I think that the new wine has already blinded them" (Edd.). MGr σκοτώνω, "slay."

σκύβαλον.

"Dung," the prevailing sense of this word, may be explained by a popular association with σκώρ, with which it is impossible to connect it historically. That it was a vulgar coinage from ἐς κύνας βαλεῖν is likely enough (like σκορακίζω from ἐς κόρακας): its original meaning thus would be "refuse" (RV marg.); but "dung" is probably what Paul meant in Phil 3[8], the only occurrence of the word in the NT. This meaning is well illustrated by P Fay 119[7] (c. A.D. 100) where Gemellus informs his son that the donkey-driver has bought μικρὰν δύσμην καὶ χόρτον σαπρὸν καὶ ὅλον (*l.* ὅλον) λελυμένον ὡς σκύβαλον, "a little bundle and rotten hay, the whole of it decayed—no better than dung" (Edd.).

The word is found in the more general sense of "leavings," "gleanings," in P Ryl II. 149[22] (A.D. 39-40) κατενέμησαν ἀφ᾽ οὗ εἶχον λαχανοσπ έρμου σκυβάλου, "grazed them on the gleanings of my vegetable-seed crop" (Edd.), and PSI III. 184[7] (A.D. 292) ἐν σκυβάλοις χόρτου.

Σκύβαλος appears as a proper name in P Oxy I. 43 *verso*[iii.25] (A.D. 295) δ(ιὰ) Σκυβάλου βαφέως: cf. also CPR I. 175[16] (time of Commodus).

To the exx. of the word in late writers given by Wetstein add Vett. Val. p. 3[11] σκυβάλων ἐκκρίσεως, and for the thought of Phil 3⁸ note Plautus *Truc.* ii. 7. 5 *Amator qui bona sua pro stercore habet.* cited by Kennedy *EGT ad l.*

Σκύθης.

For Σκύθης used as a proper name see P Hib I. 55¹ (B.C. 250) Σκύθης Πτολεμαίωι χαίρειν, and *Preisigke* 4036 Εὔβιος Σκύθου.

σκυθρωπός.

"of a gloomy countenance" (Mt 6¹⁶, Lk 24¹⁷ (cf. Field *Notes*, p. 81 f.) : Gen 40⁷) : cf. P Leid W^vi 47 (ii/iii A.D.) (= II. p. 101) ἐὰν δὲ σκυθρωπὸς φάνῃ, λέγε· Δὸς ἡμέραν κτλ., Menander Ἐπιτρέπ. 43 σκυθρωπὸν ὄντα με | ἰδών, "τί σύννους," φησί, "Δᾶος ;" and Lucian *Hermotim.* 18 ὃς δ' ἂν μὴ ἔχῃ ταῦτα μηδὲ σκυθρωπὸς ᾖ. For the verb, as in Ps 37 (38)⁷, cf. PSI IV. 441³⁰ (iii/B.C.) ἐπ' ἐμοὶ σκυθρωπάζουσιν.

σκύλλω,

which in the classical period is physical, "flay," "skin," has become in late Greek almost entirely metaphorical, and has very different degrees of strength, like the English "distress," which answers to it very fairly all round.

(1) The verb has much its old physical sense in P Par 35¹³ (B.C. 163) (= UPZ i. p. 130) σκυλήσας τὸ ἱερόν. and BGU III. 757¹⁷ (A.D. 12) πυρίνων δραγμάτ(ων) σκύλαντες δράγμ(ατα) δέκα τρία, where it is = "plunder."

(2) For the meaning "distress," "harass," as in Mt 9³⁶, cf. P Par 63²⁵ (B.C. 164) (= P Petr III. p. 20) σκύλλεσθαι μὴ μετρίως, "harassed to no small extent" (Mahaffy), and P Leid G⁵ (B.C. 185-144) (= I. p. 42) π]αρ' ἕκαστ[ον σκ]ύλλεσθ[α]ι [ὑπ'] ἐνίων, "continuo vexari (se) a quibusdam," cf.¹⁴. With Mk 5³⁵, Lk 7⁶, cf. P Oxy II. 295⁵ (c. A.D. 35) μὴ σκ{λ}ύλλε ἑατὴν (l. σεαυτὴν) ἐνπῆναι (l. ἐμφῆναι ?), "don't trouble yourself to explain (?)" (Edd.), and ib. XIV. 1669¹³ (iii/A.D.) σ[κύληθι καὶ αὐτὸς ἐνθάδε, "do you yourself be at the pains of coming here" (Edd.). See also Diog. Oenoand. *fr.* 1¹·⁴ ὅτι μὴ δεόντως ὑπ' αὐτῆς σκύλλεται καὶ καταπονεῖται καὶ εἰς οὐκ ἀναγκαῖα σύρεται πράγματα, and cf. *Praef.* p. XXXIX.

(3) The meaning "worry," "trouble," is seen in such passages as P Tebt II. 421¹¹ (iii/A.D.) (= *Selections*, p. 107) μὴ σκύλῃς τὴν γ[υνα]ῖκά σου, "do not trouble your wife," P Flor III. 332¹⁵ (ii/A.D.) ἵνα κἀγὼ μὴ σκυλῶ εἰς τὰ δικαστήρια, and Preisigke 4317²² (c. A.D. 200) δι' αὐτῶν πέμψε ὃ θέλεις σὺν ἐπιστολίτιν, ἐὰν μὴ θέλῃς σκυλῆναι οὕτως.

(4) The verb is construed with πρός in the sense of "take the trouble of going to " in such passages as BGU III. 830⁶ (i/A.D.) τοὺς φίλακες (l. φύλακας) ἡμῶν σκῦλον πρὸς αὐ[τ]ήν, P Oxy I. 123¹⁰ (iii/iv A.D.) ποίησον αὐτὸν σκυλῆναι πρὸς Τιμόθεον, P Fay 134² (early iv/A.D.) παρακληθεὶς κύριε σκῦλον σεαυτὸν πρὸς ἡμᾶς, and P Oxy VI. 941² (vi/A.D.) ἐὰν σ[κ]υλῇς πρὸς τὸν υἱὸν τοῦ οἰκονόμου (with the editors' note).

A compd. συσκύλλω (not in LS⁸) occurs in P Oxy I. 65¹² (iii/iv A.D.) συνσκυλῆθι αὐτῷ, where the editors render "give him your best attention," and a verbal ἄσκυλτος in P Tebt II. 315⁹ (ii/A.D.) ἐγὼ γάρ σε ἄσκυλ[τον ποι]ήσω. "I will see that you are not worried" (Edd.), and P Oxy III. 532¹⁴ (ii/A.D.).

For the subst. σκυλμός = (*a*) "insolence" (corresponding to ὕβρις), cf. P Tebt I. 16¹⁵ (B.C. 114) μετὰ σκυλμοῦ, and *ib.* 41⁷ (c. B.C. 119) : (*b*) "fatigue," cf. P Fay 111³ (A.D. 95-6) (= *Selections*, p. 66) μένφομαί σαι μεγάλως ἀπολέσας χ[υ]ρίδια δύο ἀπὸ τοῦ σκυλμοῦ τῆς ὁδοῦ, "I blame you greatly for the loss of two pigs owing to the fatigue of the journey" (Edd.) : and (*c*) "distress," as in 3 Macc 3²⁵, 7³, cf. P Oxy I. 125¹⁴ (vi/A.D.), where it is joined with βλαβή, ζημία, and ὄχλησις. See also Artem. p. 125⁶ φροντίδας καὶ σκυλμούς, where the latter word has the sense of "vexations," as in Cicero's letters (cf. Abbott *Essays*, p. 87).

σκῦλον.

in plur. = "spoils" (Lk 11²²) : cf. P Hamb I. 91⁴ (B.C. 167) ἀπὸ τῶν γενομένων σκύλ[ω]ν ἐν Τεβέτνοι παρεδόθη μοι ὑπὸ τ[ῶν συν]στρατιω[τῶν αἰχμά]λωτα δ, and *ib.*³⁰ παραδοῦναί μοι τὰ σ[κύλ]α. Add from the inscrr. *Syll* 35 (= ³61)¹ (after B.C. 440) σκύλα ἀπὸ Θουρίον Ταραντῖνοι ἀνέθηκαν Διὶ Ὀλυμπίοι δεκάταν, OGIS 332⁵ (B.C. 138-2) ἄγαλμα . . βεβηκὸς ἐπὶ σκύλων ἐν τῶι ναῶι τοῦ Σωτῆρος Ἀσκληπιοῦ.

σκωληκόβρωτος.

"eaten by worms." This compd. found in the NT only in Ac 12²³ occurs in PSI V. 490¹¹ (B.C. 258-7)]τὴν γενομένην σκωληκόβρωτον, where the hiatus prevents our knowing what was "eaten by worms," perhaps κριθή. Cf. the use of the negative applied to grain in P Grad 7¹¹ (iii/B.C.) σπέρματος ἀσκωληκοβ[ρώ]του. The word is applied to diseased grain by Theophrastus (*C.P.* v. 9. 1), and hence was regarded by Hobart (p. 42 f.) as "medical," but the above citations show it in ordinary use (cf. Cadbury *JBL* xlv. (1926), p. 201). Add the occurrence of the subst. σκωληκοβρωσία in P Masp III. 67325 II. *verso*¹⁸ (Byz.) (cited by Preisigke *Wörterb. s.v.*), and the similar compd. ἰχθυόβρωτος in *Syll* 584 (= ³ 007)⁷ (i/B.C. ?) ὁ τούτων τι ποιῶν κακὸς κακῇ ἐξωλείᾳ ἀπόλοιτο, ἰχθυόβρωτος γενόμενος.

σκώληξ.

"a worm" (MGr σκουλήκι, σκωλήκι), comes from the same root as σκέλος : the linking notion is the meaning "bind," "twist" (Boisacq p. 882). For the metaph. use in Mk 9⁴⁸ LXX (cf. Sir 7¹⁶, Judith 16¹⁷) we may compare Apoc. Petr. 10 ἐπέκειντο δὲ αὐτοῖς σκώληκες ὥσπερ νεφέλαι σκότους. See also Teles p. 31³ κατορυχθέντα ὑπὸ σκωλήκων.

σμαράγδινος,

"emerald-green" (Rev 4³). To Deissmann's citation (*BS*, p. 267) of this adj. applied to a woman's garment in CPR I. 27⁸ (A.D. 190), we may add P Hamb I. 10²⁵ (ii/A.D.) ζμαράγδινον ὑπόζωνον.

σμάραγδος

is often regarded as = "rock crystal" (see Hastings' *DB* iv. p. 620), but, as Swete has shown *ad* Rev 21¹⁹, is to be identified rather with an "emerald" or other "green stone." The word occurs in the magic P Lond 46²²⁸ (iv/A.D.) (= I. p. 72) εἰς λίθον σμάραγδον : cf. Aristeas 66 ἀνθράκων τε καὶ σμαράγδων, "carbuncles and emeralds." In Sir 35⁶

we have the form ζσμαράγδου (cf. Thackeray *Gr.* i. p. 108).
In Menander *Fragm.* p. 108, No. 373 μάραγδος is used. For
the derivation of this foreign borrowing, see Boisacq p. 609.

σμύρνα,

"myrrh." For this spelling of the common noun which
is found in its two NT occurrences (Mt 2[11], Jn 19[39]) cf. the
medical prescription P Oxy II. 234[ii] (ii/iii A.D.) **σμύρναν
καὶ [στυ]πτηρίαν ἴσα τρί[ψας] ἔνθες.** "pound myrrh and
alum in equal quantities and insert" (Edd.), and *ib.* XIV.
1730[6] (ii/iii A.D.) **σμιρινῆαν**, which the editors regard as
= **σμυρναίαν**, *i.e.* **σμύρναν**?

To the exx. of ζμύρνα cited *s.v.* Ζμύρνα, we may add the
fragmentary P Cairo Zen I. 59009 (*b*)[11] (iii/B.C.) **ζμύρνης** [.
P Grenf I. 14[10] (B.C. 150 or 139) **κίστη μεγάλη** ξύλου
μεστὴ **ζμύρνης**, P Oxy VIII. 1088[37] (early i A.D.) **ζμύρνης
(δραχμαὶ)** ῑ, P Leid W[viii] 11 (ii/iii A.D.) (= II. p. 107)
προσμείξας αὐτο(= τῷ) **μέλαν καὶ ζμύρναν**, and, in connexion with the service of the temples, BGU I. 1[11] (iii A.D.)
τειμῆς μύρου κ[αὶ] ζμύρνης. As showing the price of myrrh,
which was a state monopoly, note P Tebt I. 35[4] (B.C. 111)
(= *Chrest.* I. p. 369) **τῆς ἀναδεδομένης κατὰ κώμην ζμύρνης
μηδένα πλεῖον πράσσε⟨⟨σι⟩⟩ν τῆς μνᾶς ἀργυ(ρίου) δραχμῶν μ,** "for the myrrh distributed in the villages no one
shall exact more than 40 drachmae of silver for a mina-
weight" (Edd.).

Σμύρνα.

See *s.v.* Ζμύρνα.

Σόδομα.

For the declension of this place-name see Thackeray *Gr.*
i. p. 68. It may be noted that the wall-scratchings *Sodoma,
Gomora* in Pompeii (see A. Mau *Pompeji in Leben und
Kunst,* Leipzig, 1900, p. 15 : Engl. Tr. p. 17) may be taken
as a trace of Christianity in that town, as well as a prophecy
of its end : cf. Nestle *ZNTW* v. (1904), p. 167 f.

Σολομών.

For the slips in the Hellenization of this proper name
Σαλωμών – Σαλωμῶν – Σολωμῶν, see Thackeray *Gr.* i. p.
165 f. To Preisigke's exx. of **Σολομών, Σολωμῶν** (*Namenbuch, s.vv.*), add P Bilabel 90[46] (iii A.D.) **Σολωμώ[ν.** See
also Wünsch *AF* p. 16[16] **ὁρκίζω σε τὸν θεὸν τ[ὸν] τοῦ
Σα[λομόνος Σοναρμιμωουθ,** with the editor's note.

σορός,

"a bier" (Lk 7[14]) : cf. P Lond 122[97] (iv A.D.) (= I.
p. 119) **ὁ ἐπὶ τῆς ζυρνίνη** (*l.* ζμυρνίνη) **σορῷ κατακείμενος,** and
ib. 121[236] (iii A.D.) (= I. p. 92) **ὁ ἐπὶ σωρῷ κατακείμενος.**
From the inscrr. we may cite the sepulchral *Kaibel* 336[2]
εἰμὶ δ' Ἀλεξανδρεύς. τῶν δὲ [σ]ορ[ῶν] ὁ μέσος, and *C. and
B.* ii. p. 717, No 651 (mid. iii A.D.), where two Christian
soldiers erect for themselves **τὸν βωμὸν καὶ τὴν κατ' αὐτοῦ
σορόν,** a symbolic bier carved on the altar, and in the usual
manner warn off intruders from the family vault : no one is
to place there **ξενὸν νεκρὸν ἢ σορόν.** *i.e.* "a strange body or
a bier that has carried it."

See also the inscr. on the tomb of a iv/A.D. Lycaonian
Bishop, as published by W. M. Calder in *Exp* VII. vi.

p. 387—[18] **ἐποίησα ἐμαυτῷ πέ[λ]τα τ]ε καὶ σορὸν ἐν ᾗ τὰ
προ[γεγραμένα] ταῦτα ἐποίησα ἐπιγρ[ά]φιν ἐμὸν τῆς τε
ἐκ[δοχῆς] τοῦ γένους μου.** "I made myself a monument
and sarcophagus on which I had the above engraved, on
this my tomb) and the tomb of the successors of my race,"
and *Cagnat* IV. 245[2] **ἔθηκα τὴν σορὸν ἐμαυτῷ [καὶ τῇ
συμβίῳ μου.** In P Hib I. 67[11] (B.C. 228) (= *Cnet* I.
p. 366) **σορώιον** is cloth used for burials.

σός,

"thy," "thine" : P Oxy IV. 811 (c. A.D. 1) **εἰς τὴν
σὴν καταλογήν,** BGU II. 665[ii.15] (i A.D.) **διὰ τὸ σὸν
ὀψώνι[ο]ν,** P Ryl II. 113[52] (A.D. 133) **τῆς σῆς μειζοπονηρίας**
("hatred of wrongdoers"), P Oxy XII. 1593[5] (iv A.D.)
ἀσπάζομαι τὸν πατέρα ἡμῶν, τουτέστιν σόν, ἄδελφε, P
Strass I. 35[7] (iv, v A.D.) **ἡ σὴ ἀρετή,** and P Amh II. 145[6]
(a title—c. A.D. 400) **τῇ σῇ τιμιότητι,** "to your honour."

The word is often used substantively, *e.g.* **ὁ σός,** "thy
household, agent, friend" (cf. Mk 5[19]— P Oxy IV. 743[42]
(B.C. 2) **ἐπίσκοπ(ού) τοὺς σοὺς πάντε(ς),** P Fay 123[5] (c.
A.D. 100) **ἐκθές σοι ἔγραψα διὰ Μάρδωνος τοῦ σοῦ,** "I
wrote to you yesterday by your servant Mardon," P Oxy
XIV. 1631[30] (A.D. 280) **τῶν σῶν ἐπακολουθούντων ἅπασι,**
"with the concurrence of your agents in everything"
(Edd.), and *ib.* IX. 1223[29] (late iv A.D.) **πέμπων δὲ δήλωσον
τοῖς σοῖς παρασχεῖν μοι τὴν ὑπ(ο)λοιπάδα[[ν]] τοῦ οἴνου,**
"send and tell your people to hand over to me the remainder of the wine" (Ed.) : **τὸ σόν,** "what is thine"
(cf. Mt 20[14])—Meyer *Ostr* 65[5] (iii A.D.) **ποίησον τὸ σὸν**
(*l.* σὸν) **ἐν τάχει :** and **τὰ σά,** "thy goods" (cf. Lk 6[30])—
P Cairo Zen I. 59076[3] (B.C. 257) **εἰ σύ τε ἔρρωσαι καὶ τὰ
σὰ πάντα . . . [κατὰ νοῦν ἐστιν.** PSI I. 64[4] (i B.C. ?)
οὐθ]ὲν παρορῶσα τῶν σῶν, BGU IV. 1040[5] (ii A.D.)
ε[ὐ]καρπεῖ τὰ σά, P Oxy VI. 903[11] (iv A.D.) **οὐδὲν τῶν σῶν
ἦρκεν,** "she has taken nothing of yours."

σουδάριον

(Lat. *sudarium* ; also naturalized in Aramaic), "a handkerchief" (Lk 19[20], *al.*). In the marriage contracts CPR
I. 27[7] (A.D. 190) and *ib.* 21[19] (A.D. 230) a **σουδάριον** is
included in the bride's dowry (cf. Deissmann *BS* p. 223),
and in P Lond 121[526] (iii A.D.) (= I. p. 110) the word occurs
in a charm for procuring dreams, **ἐντύλισσε τὰ φύλ[λα] ἐν
σουδαρίῳ κενῷ** (*l.* καινῷ) **καὶ τίθει ὑπὸ τὴν κεφαλήν σου.**
See also the magic P Osl I. 1[289] (iv A.D.) **σουδάριον
ὁλόλιτον,** "a *sudarium* of fine linen," with the editor's
note.

Σούσαννα.

This proper name (Lk 8[3]) occurs in a list of accounts
P Flor I. 78[25] (v/vi A.D. ?). See further exx. in Preisigke
Namenbuch s.v.

σοφία

appears as a title of honour in P Oxy VIII. 1165[8] (vi A.D.)
ἡ ὑμετέρα ἀδελφικὴ σοφία, "your fraternal wisdom," and
PSI VII. 790[14] (vi A.D. ?) **παρακαλῶ [τὴν] ὑμῶν σοφ[ί]αν
κελεῦσαι κτλ.** For the ordinary NT use of the word, see
Lightfoot *ad* Col 1[9], and *Notes* p. 317 f.

σοφίζω.

For the mid. σοφίζομαι, "devise cleverly" (2 Pet 1[16]), cf. PSI V. 452[11] (iv/A.D.) μᾶλλον δὲ σοφιζομένους δύνασθαι ἐκκλείνειν [τὸν δεσμὸν] τῆς δουλίας. See also the beginning of the uncanonical gospel P Oxy V. 840[1] (iv/A.D.) πρότερον πρὸ <τοῦ> ἀδικῆσαι πάντα σοφίζεται, "before he does wrong makes all manner of subtle excuses" (Edd.), Musonius p. 12[9] μελετῶσι λόγους καὶ σοφίζωνται καὶ ἀναλύωσι συλλογισμούς, and Vett. Val. p. 201[3] ἵνα δὲ μὴ δόξω πάλιν τὰ αὐτὰ σοφίζεσθαι.

σοφός.

From meaning "skilled," "clever," σοφός came to be applied from Plato onwards to "wise" theoretically: cf. the calendar P Hib I. 27[20] (B.C. 301–240) where ἀνὴρ σοφὸς καὶ ἡμῶν χρείαν ἔχων, "a wise man and a friend of mine" expounds πᾶσαν τὴν ἀλήθειαν, "the whole truth," and the sepulchral epigram PSI I. 17 III[3 f.] (iii/A.D.?)—

Τόνδ' ἐσορᾷς, ὦ ξεῖνε, τὸν ὄλβιον ἄνερα κεῖνον
τ(ὸν) σοφὸν Εὐπρέ[π]ιον καὶ βασιλεῦσι φίλον.

Immediately above σοφὸν the words πάντων ἁψάμενον γεράων have been inserted. Σοφός appears to have been a favourite word in sepulchral inscrr.: cf. Preisigke 3996[3] (time of Constantine) δάκρυσον . . . τὸν σοφὸν ἐν Μούσαις, C. and B. ii. p. 761, No. 704[1] ἄνδρ]α σοφὸν κε[δ]νήν [τ' ἄλ]οχον τόδε σῆμα [κέ]κευθεν: other exx. in S.A.M i. p. 31 n[1].

For the superlative in titles of address, see P Iand 16[1] (v/vi A.D.) τῷ σοφωτάτῳ ὑμῶν ἀδελφῷ (of an advocate), P Oxy I. 126[6] (A.D. 572) θυγάτηρ τ[οῦ σ]οφωτάτου σχολαστικοῦ Ἰ[ω]άννου, and ib. VIII. 1165[13] (vi/A.D.) δεσπό[τη] ἐμῷ τ(ῷ) πά(ντων) λαμπρ(οτάτῳ) σοφ(ωτάτῳ) π(άσης) προσκ(υνήσεως) ἀξ(ίῳ).

Σπανία.

For the probability that Paul accomplished his purpose of visiting Spain (Rom 15[24, 28]), see the evidence collected by Lightfoot Apost. Fathers Part I. vol. ii. p. 30 f.

σπαράσσω.

The only citation for this word which we can supply from our sources is P Petr II. 17 (4)[6] (iii/B.C.) ἐσπάρασσεν, but the broken nature of the context makes it impossible to determine the exact meaning. For the word = "throw on the ground" in Mk 1[26] see Swete's note ad l. In Herodas V. 57 the verb is = "maul," cf. ib. VIII. 25. A good example of the metaph. use is afforded by Teles p. 19[5] φαίνεται γὰρ ἡ Ξανθίππη ὀξυρεγμίᾳ σπαράσσειν ἡμᾶς (Socrates addressing Alcibiades). For the subst. σπάραγμα used collectively see Syll 583 (= [3] 996)[31] (c. i/A.D. ?) τὴν . . θεμελίωσιν ἐν τετραγώνῳ διὰ σπαράγματος.

σπαργανόω,

"swathe" (Lk 2[7, 12]). For the noun (as in Sap 7[4]) cf. Kaibel 314[6] (iii/A.D.) εἰς σπάργανά μ' αὐτὸς ἔθηκεν, and P Masp I. 67007 verso (D)[32] (Byz.) ταύτην ἐκ σπαργάνων θάλψας.

σπαταλάω,

"give myself to pleasure," "am wanton," is confined in the NT to 1 Tim 5[6] (Vg quae in deliciis est), Jas 5[5]. Hort James p. 107 ff. illustrates the word fully from the LXX and other sources, from which it appears that σπαταλάω is often combined with τρυφάω, with perhaps somewhat worse associations. But see Kaibel 646a[51] (p. 529)—

ὡς οὖν καιρὸν ἔχεις, λοῦσαι, μύρισαι, σπατάλησον
καὶ χάρισαι, δαπάνησον, ἅπερ δύνασαι· τίνι τηρεῖς;

For the subst. σπατάλη in its sense of "bracelet," see Syll[3] 1184[1].

σπάω,

generally used in mid. (Proleg. p. 157) "draw (my sword)" (Mk 14[47], Ac 16[27]): cf. P Tebt I. 48[19] (c. B.C. 113) (= Chrest. I. p. 457) σπασαμένων τὰς μαχαίρας, and similarly ib. 138 (late ii/B.C.). See also Preisigke 2134[5] ff. (time of the Antonines)—

Σὺ μὲν τέθνηκας καὶ ἐξέτεινας τὰ σκέλη,
ἐμοῦ δὲ πάππου τοῦ γέροντος ἔσπασας.
Ἀστὴρ οὐράνιος ὁ ἐπὶ ἀστέρι ἐπανατέλλων
ἐσπάσθη.

σπεῖρα,

gen. σπείρης (as in the NT and apparently always in the papyri: see Proleg. pp. 38, 48). The word meant originally "a coil," but came to be applied to a "maniple" or "cohort" of soldiers. For this, its only meaning in the NT, cf. P Oxy III. 477[3] (A.D. 132–3) γενομένῳ ἐπάρχῳ σπείρης πρώτης Δαμασ[κ]ηνῶν, "late praefect of the first cohort of the Damascenes," and similarly BGU I. 73[2] (A.D. 135), 136[22] (A.D. 135), al. See also PSI V. 447[11] (A.D. 167) οἱ ὑπογεγρα(μμένοι) στρατευσάμενοι ἐν εἴλαις καὶ σπείραις. In P Lond 755 verso[35] (iv/A.D.) (= III. p. 223), a list of buildings with measurements, σπ(ε)ῖραι = "base mouldings." In the inscrr. the word is used for θίασος: see Deissmann BS p. 186.

σπείρω,

"sow": cf. P Hamb I. 24[2] (B.C. 222) ἐσπαρκέναι ἐν τῶι ἰδίωι [κλήρωι, P Oxy II. 277[5] (B.C. 19) ὥστε σπεῖραι εἰς τὸ δωδέκατον ἔτος πυρῶι, ib. 280[12] (A.D. 88–9) σπεῖραι καὶ ξυλαμῆσαι ("reap"), BGU I. 1017 (A.D. 114–5) σπείρεσθαι καὶ καρπίζεσθαι καὶ ἀποφέρειν εἰς τὸ ἴδιον, P Ryl II. 243[9] (ii/A.D.) ἐλπίζοντες σὺν θεῷ τὸ πεδείον σπαρῆναι, P Fay 330 (ii/A.D.) ἐσπ αρμένου ἐδ(άφους), P Flor I. 21[14] (A.D. 239) εἰς τὴν ἐν πυρῷ σπειρομέν[η]ν γῆν, and the late ib. 131[17] (vi/vii A.D.) καθ' ἐνιαυτὸν σπείρω τὴν οὐσίαν μου.

σπεκουλάτωρ

(Lat. speculator), originally "scout," "courier," then "executioner": in NT only Mk 6[27] (see Swete's note). The word is found in a list of accounts P Cairo Goodsp 30 vii. 31 (A.D. 191–192) Θαι]σαρίῳ σπεκουλ(άτορι) (δραχμαὶ) δ, and ter in the Registri Familiarii P Flor I. 71[672, 763, 811] (iv/A.D.). Cf. also P Oxy IX. 1193[1] (iv A.D.) an order π[αρὰ] τοῦ σπεκουλ[άτορος] addressed to the chief of the police in a certain village, ib. 1223[21] (late iv/A.D.), and ib. 1214[2] (v/A.D.).

σπένδω.

"pour out an offering of wine," "make a libation" to a god: cf. P Hal I. 1²¹⁵ (mid. iii/B.C.) κ[αθ' ἱερ]ῶν σπένδων, P Par 22³ (B.C. 165) (= UPZ i. p. 102) where the Twins in the Serapeum are described as τῶι Ὀσοράπει (cf. Archiv iii. p. 250) χοὰς σπενδουσῶν ὑπέρ τε ὑμῶν καὶ τῶν ὑμετέρων τέκνων. P Tebt II. 600³ (iii/A.D.) οἴνου σπενδο[μέ]νου ἐν τῷ [ἱερῷ, and Syll 653 (= ³730)² (B.C. 92) ἱεροὺς . . . αἷμα καὶ οἶνον σπένδοντας.

The verb is similarly used in the libelli, or certificates of pagan worship, by which those who "poured out libations" to the gods obtained immunity: cf. BGU I. 287¹¹ (A.D. 250) (= Selections. p. 116) ἔθυσα [κα]ὶ ἔσ[πεισα] [κ]αὶ τῶν ἱ[ε]ρείων [ἐγευ]σάμην, and similarly P Oxy IV. 658⁷,¹¹, ib. XII. 1464⁵,⁷, P Ryl I. 12⁶ (all of date A.D. 250). Curtius (St. Paul in Athens, Exp VII. iv. p. 447) has drawn attention to the fact that this, the simplest form of old Pagan worship, is the only one which Paul takes over and applies directly to himself: see Phil 2¹⁷, 2 Tim 4⁶.

For the subst. σπονδή of a "libation" to a deified Emperor, cf. BGU IV. 1200¹² (i/B.C.) εἰς τὰς] ὑπὲρ τοῦ θε[οῦ] καὶ κυρίου Αὐτοκράτορος Κα[ίσαρος καθηκούσας] θυσίας καὶ σπονδάς. and similarly P Oxy VIII. 1143¹ (temple account—c. A.D. 1). Σπονδεῖον, the cup from which the libation is poured, occurs in BGU II. 388ⁱⁱ·²² (ii/iii A.D.) φιάλη ἀργυρῆ καὶ σπον[δ]εῖ[ο]ν καὶ θυμιατήριον, and ib. 590⁹ (A.D. 177-8).

It may be added that σπονδή came to be used of an additional impost, particularly on vine-land, levied nominally for a libation to Dionysus: cf. P Oxy VI. 917³ (ii/iii A.D.) σπ(ονδῆς) Διον(ύσου ?) (δραχμαὶ) η (τετρώβολον) χ(αλκοῦς) ᾱ, with the editors' note. From this the transition was easy to any "additional payment" or "gratification," e.g. P Oxy IV. 730¹³ (A.D. 130) σπονδῆς τῶν ὅλων παιδαρίοις δραχμὰς τέσσαρας, "4 drachmae for the slaves for a libation on account of all the land" (Edd.), ib. I. 101¹⁹ (A.D. 142), and ib. IX. 1207¹⁰ (A.D. 175-6). In P Lond 948¹² (A.D. 236) (= III. p. 220) a ship-master receives in addition to his pay a jar of wine ὑπὲρ σπονδῆς, as a pourboire: cf. P Oxy III. 610 (ii/A.D.) τὴν δὲ σπονδὴ(ν) χάρισαι and the similar use of the diminutive in ib. 525⁷ (early ii/A.D.) ἐὰν δέῃ τῷ ἀδελφῷ τῆς μητρὸ[ς] τῶν νίῶν Ἀχιλλᾶ δοθῆναι σπο[ν]δάριον καλῶς ποιήσεις δοὺς λω[το]ῦ, "if a gratuity must be given to the brother of the mother of Achillas' sons, please get some lotus (?)" (Edd.).

A figurative usage of the verb appears in the sepulchral inscr. Preisigke 4313¹⁵ (i/ii A.D.) ἄφθονον ἐνθάδε δάκρυ σπείσας ἐκ βλεφάρων κλαῖε . . .

σπέρμα,

"seed": P Cairo Zen I. 59097¹⁰ (B.C. 257) χόρτου σπέρμα, P Par 63¹¹⁰ (B.C. 165) (= P Petr III. p. 28) τὰ σπέρματα κατενεγκεῖν εἰς τοὺς ἀγρούς. "to carry the seed to the fields," BGU II. 507¹¹ (A.D. 75) ἀλλαξέτω σε αὐτὸν (sc. σάκκον) Πασίων καλοῖς σπέρμασι(= σι), P Tebt II. 341² (A.D. 140-1) δεήσει ἐπισταλῆναι εἰς δάνε[ι]α σπέρματα (l. σπερμάτων) κατασπ[ο]ρᾶς τοῦ ἐνεστῶτος δ (ἔτους) Ἀντωνίνου Καίσαρ . . . . "it will be necessary to send on account of loans of seed-corn for the sowing of the present 4ᵗʰ year of Antoninus Caesar . . ." (Edd.), and P Oxy I.

117¹¹ (ii/iii A.D.) σπέρματα σικυδίων σπουδαῖα ἔπεμψα ὑμεῖν, "I send you some good melon seeds" (Edd.).

For σπέρμα in the singular in Gal 3¹⁶, see Milligan Documents, p. 105; and for the subst. σπερματισμός see P Lond 604³ (A.D. 47) (= III. p. 71). We may note the proverb Kaibel 1038⁵ εἰς] πέλαγος σπέρμα βαλεῖν, of vain and empty toil, and Musonius p. 81 πρὸς καλοκἀγαθίαν καὶ σπέρμα ἀρετῆς. On the use of ἄτεκνος in Lk 20²⁹ as compared with οὐκ ἀφῆκεν σπέρμα in the parallel Mk 12²⁰ (cf. Mt 22²⁵), see H. Pernot La Langue des Évangiles (Paris, 1927), p. 17.

σπερμολόγος.

Although we have no fresh light to throw upon this NT ἅπ. εἰρ. (Ac 17¹⁸), it may be convenient to recall one or two facts in its history. Used originally of birds "picking up seed," it came to be applied in Athenian slang to an adventurer who gains a "hand-to-mouth" living in the markets by picking up anything that falls from the loads of merchandise which are being carried about. Hence it passed into the meaning of one gathering scraps of information and retailing them at second-hand without any real knowledge of their meaning. The AV, RV "babbler," which goes back to Tindale, is thus not far from the sense, one who talks idly to no definite purpose: see further Ramsay Paul p. 242 f., and Knowling ad Ac l.c. in EGT, and cf. Norden Agn. Theos p. 333, and E. Meyer Ursprung u. Anfänge iii. p. 91.

Some of the older definitions are recalled by Chase Credibility of Acts, p. 205—Etym. Magnum ὁ εὐτελὴς καὶ εὐκαταφρόνητος ἄνθρωπος καὶ ἴσως ἀπὸ τῶν ἀλλοτρίων διαζῶν: Hesych. φλύαρος: Suidas εὐρύλογος ἀκριτόμυθος: Onom. Vetus λάλος. Amongst modern renderings we may mention—"prater" (xixth century), "beggarly babbler" (Weymouth), "fellow with scraps of learning" (Moffatt), "rag-picker" (Goodspeed).

σπεύδω,

"hasten," is used (1) intransitively, as generally in the NT, in such passages as P Cairo Zen I. 59101¹⁰ (B.C. 257) ἵνα σπεύσηι περὶ Πτολεμαίου, P Tebt I. 19³ (B.C. 114) βεβουλήμεθα σπεῦσαι, "I am anxious to make haste" (Edd.), ib. II. 315²⁶ (ii/A.D.) ἔσπευσα δέ σοι γράψαι, P Oxy IX. 1216²⁰ (ii/iii A.D.) θεῶν γὰρ θελόντων σπεύδω ἐξορμῆσαι πρὸς ὑμᾶς, "for with the help of the gods I am hastening to set out to you," and P Gen I. 55¹ (iv/A.D.) ἔσπευσα προσαγορεῦσέ(= σαι) σου τὴν ἀμίμητον καλοκαγαθίαν: and (2) transitively in such passages as P Oxy I. 121¹² (iii/A.D.) σπεῦσον οἶν τοῦτο, ἵνα εἰδῶ, and Cagnat IV. 288 a¹⁰ τήν τε πατρίδα σπε[ύ]δων ὅσ[ο]ν ἐφ' ἑ[α]υ[τ]ῶι: cf. 2 Pet 3¹².

σπήλαιον.

Souter's note Lex. s.v. "a cave (especially as inhabited)," is supported by the Byzantine papyrus Preisigke 5295⁷. where in connexion with the letting of a house we hear of καμάραν μίαν ἐν τῷ σπηλαίῳ σου. MGr σπηλιά, σπήλιο, "cave": see also Thumb Handbook § 6. 6.

σπιλάς,

found in the NT only in Jude 12, is generally understood as = "rock," "reef," in accordance with its poetic classical

75

usage : cf. *Kaibel* 225[1] f. where it is said of a man who had precipitated himself from a rock—

Ὀστέα μὲν καὶ σάρκας ἐμὰς σπιλάδες διέχευαν
ὀξεῖαι, κρημνῶν ἄλμα ὑποδεξάμεναι.

Others prefer the rendering "spot," "stain," as if = σπῖλος (*q.v.*), which is found in the parallel passage 2 Pet 2[13] : cf. Lightfoot *Revision*, p. 152 f. More recently A. D. Knox has shown good ground (*JTS* xiv. (1913), p. 547 ff., xvi. (1915), p. 78) for taking the word as an adj. with ἄνεμος understood, "a dirty, foul wind," producing a correspondingly troubled and stormy effect on the water : cf. Isai 57[20].

σπῖλος,

originally "rock," came in late Greek to be used = Attic κηλίς, "spot," "stain" ; hence the metaph. usage in Eph 5[27]. With the application of σπῖλος to persons in 2 Pet 2[13] cf. Dion. Hal. *Antt.* iv. 24, p. 608 τοὺς δυσεκκαθάρτους σπίλους ἐκ τῆς πόλεως "the dregs of humanity from the city." See further Rutherford *NP* p. 87 f.

σπιλόω,

"stain," is confined in the NT to Jas 3[6], Jude[23] : cf. Sap 15[4] and *Test. xii. patr.* Aser ii. 7 ὁ πλεονεκτῶν . . . τὴν ψυχὴν σπιλοῖ, καὶ τὸ σῶμα λαμπρύνει.

σπλαγχνίζομαι,

"am moved as to the σπλάγχνα (*q.v.*), and hence "am filled with compassion, tenderness." Lightfoot on Phil 1[8] writes that the verb does not seem to be classical, and was "perhaps a coinage of the Jewish Dispersion," and Thumb, *Hellen.* p. 123 practically confirms this. It occurs in the fragmentary vi/A.D. petition P Flor III. 296[23] οὐκ ἐσπλαγχνίσθη ὁ εἰρημέ(νος), and we may note its appearance in the MGr sailor's prayer—

Σπλαγχίσου με, Βορέα μου,
Πατέρα μου Βορέα.

"O have pity on me, my North Wind, father North Wind" (see Abbott, *Songs* p. 164).

σπλάγχνον,

always plur. in NT (but see Phil 2[1]), the *viscera* (Ac 1[18]), and hence metaph. the "heart," the "affections," "compassion," "pity." For this, its more distinctively "Hebraic" usage (see *s.v.* σπλαγχνίζομαι), cf. BGU IV. 1139[17] (B.C. 5) ὑπὲρ σπλάγχνον, "for pity's sake," and its literal application to a part of the body, cf. the astrological P Ryl II. 63[6] (ii/A.D.) where the σπλάγχνα are dedicated to Jupiter—Διὸς [σπλ]άγχνα. See also from the inscrr. *Kaibel* 991[2] (ii/i B.C.) ζωὴ δὲ πλείων μητρὸς ἐν σπλάγχνοις ἐμή, and *ib.* 1034[5] τί[ν] ὑπὸ σπλάνχν[οις φροντίδα κεύθεις : Exx. of the word from various sources are collected in the notes *ad* Herodas I. 57 and III. 42 (ed. Headlam). For the corr. adj. see P Osl I. 1[149] (iv/A.D.) ἔρωτι σπλαγχνικῷ. The editor compares the use of εὔσπλαγχνος apparently in the sense of "benevolent" in P Leid V[is 3] (iii/iv A.D.) (= II. p. 31) : see Eph 4[32], 1 Pet 3[8].

"sponge" (Mt 27[48] *al.*) : cf. PSI V. 535[20] (iii/B.C.) σπόγγοι τραχεῖς, and *ib.* VI. 558[7] (B.C. 257-6) σφόγγων (for form see Lob. *Phryn.* p. 113). In P Oxy XI. 1384, a v/A.D. collection of medical recipes, two theological extracts are inserted "on account of their medical interest, perhaps as a kind of charm," say the editors ; but rather, according to Moffatt (*Exp T* xxvii. p. 424) as "illustrations . . . to show that specific remedies had religious justification." In the second "the angels of the Lord" are represented as having gone up to heaven to seek a remedy for their eyes—[24 ff.] ὀφθαλμοὺς πονο<ῦ>ντες καὶ σφόγγον κρατοῦντες, "suffering in their eyes and holding a sponge." MGr σφουγγάρι. In P Lond 113. 11 (*a*)[1] (vi/vii A.D.) (= I. p. 223) a certain Apollos has the cognomen σπογγοκέφαλος (a title not in LS[8]).

σποδός,

"ashes" : *Syll* 805 (= [3]1171)[12] κονίαν ἀπὸ τῆς ἱερᾶς σποδοῦ καὶ τοῦ ἱεροῦ ὕδατος,[13] τρώγει]ν σῦκα μετὰ σπο[δοῦ ἱερᾶς τῆς ἐκ τοῦ] βωμοῦ, ὅπου θ[ύουσι τῷ θεῷ : cf. Heb 9[13]. The adj. σπόδιαι, "ash-coloured," "grey," is applied to goats (αἶγες) in P Hib I. 120[9] (B.C. 250-49) : cf. PSI VI. 564[6] (B.C. 253-2).

σπορά

in its only NT occurrence, 1 Pet 1[23], has the quasi-collective meaning "seed" : cf. P Leid W[xi. 51] (ii/iii A.D.) (= II. p. 121) ἐφάνη γέννα . . . πάντων κρατοῦσα σποράν, δι᾽ ἧς τὰ πάντα ἐσπάρη, "semen, per quod omnia seminata sunt." For the more regular usage "a sowing" of seed, we may cite such passages as BGU II. 580[11] (no date) τὴν τοῦ [ἐ]νεστῶτος ἔτους σποράν, P Ryl II. 168[6] (A.D. 120) (ἄρουρας) τρεῖς εἰς σποράν λαχάνων, P Grenf II. 57 (A.D. 168) τὴν ἐπικει[μέν]ην σποράν, and P Oxy I. 103[9] (A.D. 316) ἄρουραν μείαν εἰς σποράν λινοκαλάμης ("fine flax" : cf. Josh 2[6]).

σπόριμος,

"ready for sowing" : cf. P Oxy XIV. 1635[6] (B.C. 44-37) κατοικικῆς γῆς σπορίμου, P Oxy I. 45[11] (A.D. 95) κατοικικῆς σειτοφόρου σπορίμου, "allotment corn land ready for sowing," P Amh II. 68[8] (late i/A.D.) ἀπὸ καθαρᾶς γῆς σπορίμης, and P Ryl II. 164[2] (A.D. 171) ἃς (*sc.* ἀρούρας) καὶ παραδώσω κατ᾽ ἀ[γρὸν] σπορίμας, "which also I will transfer severally in good condition for sowing" (Edd.). In P Lond 413[15] (*c.* A.D. 346) (= II. p. 302) the writer asks for nets since the gazelles are spoiling his crops, ἐπιδὴ τὰ δορκάδι[α] (cf. Isai 13[14]) ἀφανίζουσειν το (*l.* ἀφανίζουσι τὰ) σπόριμα : cf. Mk 2[23].

σπόρος.

(1) "Sowing" or "seed-time" : Ostr 1027[6] (Ptol.) ἐπιγένη(μα) οὗ ἐμίσθωσά σοι κλήρου εἰς τὸν σπόρον τοῦ κ̄ε ἔτους, "the increase of the lot that I have let to them, for the sowing of the year 25," P Lille I. 5[36] (B.C. 260-59) σπέρμα εἰς τὸν σπόρον, P Par 63[9] (B.C. 164) (= P Petr III. p. 19) ἡ περὶ τῶν κατὰ τὸν σπόρον [φ]ροντὶς κοινῇ πᾶσιν ἐπιβάλλει τοῖς τῶν πραγμ[ά]των κηδομένοις, "consideration for those engaged in sowing the seed is a common duty in-

cumbent on all those interested in the administration"
(Mahaffy), and P Tebt I. 60⁷¹ (B.C. 118) μετὰ τὸν σπόρον
τοῦ αὐτοῦ (ἔτους). In P Ryl II. 147²⁰ (A.D. 39) a complaint
is laid against shepherds for letting their sheep graze
down young barley and sheaves—κατενέμησαν ἀπὸ τῆς ἐν
σπόρῳ κρειθῆς καὶ δραγμάτων.

(2) "Seed" sown, "crop": P Grenf II. 36¹⁵ (B.C. 95)
(= Witkowski² p. 91) ἠκούσαμεν τὸν μῦν καταβεβρωκέναι
τὸν σπόρον, "we hear that mice have eaten up the crop,"
and BGU IV. 1189¹³ (i./B.C.–i./A.D.) οἱ σημαινόμενοι ἄνδρες
πόρ[ο]ν ἔχουσι[ν] οἰ[κία]ς καὶ κλήρους καὶ βοϊκὰ κτήνηι
καὶ σπόρους. The word is used in connexion with a report
on crops in P Tebt I. 24⁴² (B.C. 117) παρὰ τὸν ἐπιδεδομένον
ὑπ' αὐτῶν σπόρον, P Oxy XIV. 1661¹ (A.D. 74) διὰ σπόρου
ζ ἔτους ποιῶ αὐτὸν ὑπογέωργον, "by the list of crops of the
7th year, I make him a sub-lessee," and P Ryl II. 208¹
(ii./A.D.) ἀναγρα[φεῖσαι] διὰ σπ[όρου] εἰς Ἀπολλω[ν . . . ,
where the reference is to the list of crops registered for the
current year.

For ἄσπορος, "unsown," cf. BGU III. 703⁵ (ii./A.D.) of
land νυνὶ ἀσπόρου καὶ ἀβρόχ[ου.

σπουδάζω.

"make haste," and so "am eager," "give diligence,"
with the further idea of "effort," as in Gal 2¹⁰. For σπουδάζω followed by acc. c. inf., as in 2 Pet 1¹⁵ for which
Mayor ad l. can supply only one ex. [Plato] Ax. sec.
141 σπουδάσαντες τοῦτ' αὐτοῖς παραγενέσθαι, we can cite
BGU IV. 1080¹⁴ (iii./A.D.) σπουδάσωμεν ἡμᾶς καταξιῶσαι τῶν
ἴσ[ω]ν γραμμάτων, P Oxy VII. 1069¹⁹ (iii./A.D.) θέλω δὲ
εἰδένε πῶς σπουδάδεις (l. σπουδάζεις) αὐτῶ γενέστε (l. αὐτὸ
γενέσθαι), "I wish to know that you are hurrying on the
making of it" (Ed.), and ib. VI. 939¹⁸ (iv./A.D.) (= Selections. p. 129) ἕτερά σε γράμματα ἐπικαταλαβεῖν ἐσπούδασα
διὰ Εὐφροσύνου, "I am anxious that you should receive
another letter by Euphrosynus" (Edd.).

For the verb c. the simple inf. cf. ib. XIV. 1765⁸ (iii./A.D.)
σπούδασον γράψαι μοι, and P Amh II. 144⁷ (v./A.D.)
σπούδασον οὖν τὸ μικρὸ[ν] παιδίον ἡμῶν Ἀρτεμίδωρον [[.]]
θεῖναι ἐν ὑποθήκη, "make haste therefore and put our little
slave Artemidorus under pledge" (Edd.) ; and c. the acc.,
cf. P Fay 112¹⁵ (A.D. 99) μὴ σπουδασέτωσαν ἅλω ἀνταλομ-
μινα, "do not let them be in a hurry with the . . . threshing-floor," and P Bouriant 20³⁹ (after A.D. 350) σπουδασάτω
τὴν χορηγίαν. This last papyrus shows us also ³⁶ τοῦτο γὰρ
σπουδάζει, "car c'est le but qu'on se propose" (Ed.).

Other instances of the verb with varying meanings and
constructions are : P Hib I. 77¹ (B.C. 249) καθάπερ ὁ βασιλεὺς
σπουδάζει, "in accordance with the king's desire," P Oxy
VII. 1061¹⁶ (B.C. 22) συντύχηι καὶ σπουδάσει ἕως ὅτου
τελεσθῆ[ι, "that he may meet him and do his best until it is
effected" (Ed.) (for constr. see Blass-Debrunner § 399. 3),
P Oxy IV. 746⁸ (A.D. 16) τοῦτο οὖν ἐάν σοι φα[ί]νηται
σπουδάσεις κατὰ τὸ δίκαιον, "please therefore further him
in this matter, as is just" (Edd.), ib. I. 113²⁴ (ii./A.D.)
σπούδασον ἕως οὗ ἀγοράσῃ μοι Ὀννώφρις ἃ αὐτῶι εἴρηκεν
μήτ(ηρ) Εἰρήνης, "take care that Onnophris buys me what
Irene's mother told him" (Edd.), and from the inscr. Syll³
434 5¹² (B.C. 266–5) φανερός ἐστιν σπουδάζων ὑπὲρ τῆς
κοινῆς τ[ῶν] Ἑλλήνων ἐλευθερίας, and C. and B. ii. p. 470,

No. 399 σπουδασάντων κὲ τῶν συνβιωτῶν κὲ λβ ἄλλων, of
co-operation in the building of a tomb.

σπουδαῖος.

"zealous," "earnest": P Ryl II. 243⁵ (ii./A.D.) νῦν
ἐπιστάμεθα σου τὸ σπουδαῖον καὶ ὡς ἐπίκεισαι τοῖς ἔργοις
τοῦ κλήρου, "we now know your zeal and attentiveness
to the work of the holding" (Edd.). The adj. with the
corr. verb and noun are all seen in P Flor III. 338⁵⁻⁶
(iii./A.D.) ἄλλον γὰρ σπουδαῖον οὐκ ἔχωμεν μετὰ τούτου,
ὥστε, ἄδελφε, σπούδασον· καὶ νῦν τάχα ἡ σὴ σπουδὴ καὶ
φιλοστοργία κατανεικήσῃ τὴν ἐμὴν . . . ἀκαιρείαν. Σπουδαῖος is used in the wider sense of "good" in P Oxy I. 117¹²
(ii./iii A.D.) σπέρματα σικιδίων σπουδαῖα ἔπεμψα ὑμεῖν, "I
send you some good melon seeds" (Edd.), ib. VI. 929⁵
(ii./iii A.D.) εἰδώς σου τὸ [σ]πουδε[= αῖ]ον τὸ πρὸς πάντας,
"knowing your goodness to all" (Edd.), and similarly ib.
VII. 1064⁷ (iii./A.D.).

σπουδαίως.

"zealously," "earnestly": PSI VII. 742⁶ (v/vi A.D.)
σπουδαίως μεταδοῦναί μοι διὰ γρ[αμμάτων?] τὸ τῆς ὑποθέσεως. The compve σπουδαιοτέρως in Phil 2²⁸ is to be
taken as a superlve "with the utmost diligence" in accordance with a common practice in late Greek : cf. Blass Gr.
p. 33.

σπουδή.

(1) With σπουδή = "haste," "speed," as in Mk 6²⁵,
Lk 1³⁹, cf. P Ryl II. 231¹³ (A.D. 40) κατὰ σπουδὴν δέ σοι
ἔγραψα, P Tebt II. 315⁵ (ii A.D.) μετὰ σ[π]ο[υ]δῆς γράφω
ὅπως [μὴ μερ]ιμνῆς, "I am writing in haste that you may
not be over-anxious" and P Oxy I. 63⁵ (ii./iii A.D. (amended
Archiv i. p. 128) προνόησον σὺν πάσῃ σπουδῇ ἐνβαλέσθαι
αὐτοῦ τὸν γόμον, "please to see that his freight is embarked
with all despatch" (Edd.).

(2) The word passes readily into the meaning "zeal,"
"earnestness," as in 2 Cor 7¹¹·¹², cf. P Par 63¹²¹ (B.C. 164)
(= P Petr III. p. 28) πεῖραν λαμβάνειν τῶν ἐξακολουθούντων
ἐπιτίμων τοῖς παρακούουσί τινος τῶν μετὰ σπουδῆς [ἐ]νθυ-
μουμένων, "to experience the penalties which are inflicted
on those who wilfully misinterpret any of the regulations
which have been carefully conceived" (Mahaffy), ib.¹⁴ τὴν
πᾶσαν προσενεγκάμενοι σπουδὴν κ[αὶ] προθυμίαν, "making
use of the greatest zeal and forethought," P Tebt I. 33¹⁹
(B.C. 112) (= Selections. p. 31 τὴν πᾶσαν προσενέγκαι
σπουδὴ[ν, "display the utmost zeal," in preparations for a
Roman visitor, BGU IV. 1209⁷ (B.C. 23) οὐδὲν σπουδῆς
οὐδὲ κακοπαθίας παρέλιπον.

(3) The further meaning "good-will" may be illustrated
by P Tebt II. 314⁹ (ii./A.D.) τῆς δὲ τῶν φίλων σπουδῆς
τυχόντος ἐπετύχαμεν, "by means of the good offices of our
friends we attained it" (Edd.), P Oxy VI. 963 (ii./iii A.D.)
χάριν δέ σοι οἶδα, μῆτερ, ἐπὶ τῇ σπουδῇ τοῦ καθεδραρίου, a
woman thanking her mother for sending a stool, and ib. VII.
1068¹⁸ (iii./A.D.) παρακαλῶ οὖν, κύριέ μου, ὑπάρξε(= αι)
αὐτοῖς καὶ τὰ τῆς σῆς σπουδῆς, "so I urge you, my lord,
to supply them with the marks of your good will" (Ed.).

(4) The way for the religious connotation of the word, as
in 2 Cor 8⁷, cf. Rom 12¹¹·¹¹, Heb 6¹¹, may be said to be
prepared by such passages from the inscrr. as Magn 53⁶¹

(iii/B.C.) ἀπόδειξιν ποιούμενος τῆς περὶ τὰ μέγιστα σπουδῆς, and ib. 85¹² (ii/B.C.) ὅπ[ω]ς οὖν καὶ ἡ τοῦ [δή]μου πρός τε τ[ὴ]ν θεὰν ὁσιότης τε καὶ σπουδὴ ἐγδηλ[ος γένηται (cited by Thieme, p. 31).

(5) For the phrase πᾶσαν σπουδὴν ποιεῖσθαι, as in Jude³, cf. P Hib I. 44⁷ (B.C. 253) οὐ γὰρ ὡς ἔτυχεν περὶ τούτων τὴν σπουδὴν ποιεῖται ὁ διοικητής, "for the dioecetes is showing no ordinary anxiety with regard to this" (Edd.), PSI VI. 584²⁷ (ii/B.C.) περὶ τῆς κυνὸς πᾶσαν σπουδὴν ποίησαι· οὐ γάρ ἐστιν ἐμή, ib. IV. 340¹⁹ (B.C. 257-6) δεόμεθα πᾶσαν σπουδὴν ποιήσασθαι περὶ Πτολεμαίου, and P Hib I. 71⁸ (B.C. 245) ὡς ἂν οὖν λάβῃς τὰ γράμμ[ατα] τὴν πᾶσαν σπουδὴν ποίησαι ὅπ[ως ἀνα]ζητηθέντες ἀποσταλῶσι πρὸς [ἡμᾶς] μετὰ φυλακῆς, "as soon as you receive this letter use every effort to search for them (runaway slaves), and send them to me under guard" (Edd.). From the inscrr. Rouffiac (p. 53) cites Priene 53¹⁰ (ii/B.C.) πᾶσαν σπουδὴν ποιούμενος, ἵνα . . . , and, in illustration of 2 Pet 1⁵, ib. 118⁷ (i/B.C.) πᾶσαν εἰσφερόμενος σπ[ου]δὴν καὶ φιλοτιμίαν.

σπυρίς.

See s.v. σφυρίς.

στάδιος, στάδιον,

a measurement of distance = 600 Greek feet, or about 12 yards short of a "furlong," which is used to translate it in AV, RV of Lk 24¹³, al.: cf. Preisigke 401⁹ (A.D. 10-11) ἐπὶ σταδ[ίου]ς διακοσίου. As a stade was the length of the Olympic course, the word came to be used of "a racecourse," as in P Ryl II. 93¹⁶ (iii/A.D.) where σταδίου appears as the heading of a list of athletes: cf. 1 Cor 9²⁴. In ib. 157⁷ (A.D. 135) the words ἐν [σ]ταδίωι δευτέρωι occur in connexion with the measurement of a plot of land, but their meaning is "quite obscure" (Edd.).

στάμνος,

"an earthenware jar" for racking off wine, and then "a jar" generally, holding e.g. money, P Par 35²⁹ (B.C. 163) (= UPZ i. p. 130) στάμνον, ἐν ᾧ καὶ ἐνῆσαν χαλκοῖ, P Tebt I. 46³⁵ (B.C. 113) στάμνον ἐν ὧι χα(λκοῦ) Αχ, "a jar containing 1600 drachmae of copper"; wine, P Oxy I. 114¹⁰ (ii/iii A.D.) σιτέριον μέγα καὶ στάμνον, "a big tin flask and a wine-jar"; milk, BGU IV. 1055¹⁶ (B.C. 13) στάμμνον ὀκτωκαίδεκα κοτυρῶν γάλακτος; figs, Archiv v. p. 381, No. 56⁵ (late i/A.D.) στάμνον ἐν ᾧ ἦσαν ἑκατὸν πε[ν]τήκοντα ἰσχάδες, "a jar in which were a hundred and fifty dried figs"; and anything cooked, P Lond 664¹¹ (ii/iii A.D.) (= III. p. 212) ἀγόρασον στάμνον ἐψέματος.

It may be noted that the Doric ὁ στάμνος (cf. Exod 16³³) is more common in the papyri than the Attic ἡ στάμνος. For the dim. σταμνίον, see PSI IV. 413¹⁹ (iii B.C.) ταρίχου τὸ σταμνίον σύνταξ[ο]ν ἡμῖν ἐμπλῆσαι, P Caïro Zen I. 59012⁵⁸ (B.C. 259) τυροῦ Χίου στ[αμ]νίον α̅.

στασιαστής,

"a rebel," "a revolutionary" (Mk 15⁷): cf. PSI IV. 442⁴ (iii/B.C.) ὅς ἐστιν στασιαστής. For the verb στασιάζω (as in Judith 7¹⁵) see OGIS 665⁷⁰ (A.D. 48) ἐστασίασαν after a long lacuna, and Menander Ἐπιτρέπ. 640 f. κἀγώ σε ταῦτ' ἐμοὶ φρονεῖν ἀναγκάσω | καὶ μὴ στασιάζειν.

στάσις.

For the original meaning "a standing," as in Heb 9⁸, cf. the use of the plur. for "buildings," "erections" in P Petr III. 46 (3)¹ (iii/B.C.) εἰς τὰς στάσεις with the editor's note: see also Deissmann BS p. 158 f., and cf. Syll 700 (= ³1157)⁸³ (c. B.C. 100) ὁμοίω[ς δὲ κ]αὶ μὴ εἰσβάλλειν θρέμματα νομῆς ἕνεκεν μηδὲ στάσεως.

The usage in Ac 15², 23⁷⁻¹⁰ = "strife," "dissension," may be paralleled from P Rein 18¹⁶ (B.C. 108) ἐπ' ἀδίκου στάσεως ἱστάμενος, "soulever une querelle injuste," P Strass I. 20¹⁰ (iii/A.D.) where certain persons, who have been long at strife, agree στάσεις διαλύσασθαι, and P Oxy XVI. 1873² (late v/A.D.) ἔ[τι τὴ]ν Λυκοπολιτῶν στάσιν καὶ μ[α]νίαν φ[αντά]-ζομαι, "I still see in imagination the riots and madness at Lycopolis" (Edd.). See also P Lond 1912⁷³ (Claudius to the Alexandrines — A.D. 41) τῆς δὲ πρὸς Ἰουδαίους ταραχῆς καὶ στάσεως, Ostr 1151³ (iii/A.D.?) γράφω σοι τὴν στάσι(ν) περὶ τοῦ κλήρ(ου), and Menander Fragm. 560³ στάσις οἰκετῶν, "a wrangle among house-slaves." In P Lond 1177¹³³ (A.D. 113) (= III. p. 184) the word is used of a "shift" of workmen.

στατήρ.

"a stater," used in late writers = τετράδραχμον (Mt 17²⁷, 26¹⁵ Dalq): P Oxy I. 37¹·²³ (A.D. 49) (= Christ. II. p. 87) <τῶν> στα]τήρων π[ερ]ιόντων, "the staters remaining in my possession," P Fay 117²⁶ (A.D. 108) ὧτε τέσσαρες [στ]α[τ]ῆρας καθ' ὑμὸν γεγραφήκασι, "when they have charged you with four staters" (Edd.), and the curious alphabetical acrostic P Tebt II. 278²⁸ (early i/A.D.) δέκα στατήρων ἠγόρασ(τ)ε (l. ἠγόρασται), "it was bought for ten staters" (Edd.).

σταυρός.

"cross." The metaph. use of σταυρός in Lk 9²³, ἀράτω τὸν σταυρὸν αὐτοῦ καθ' ἡμέραν, finds an interesting illustration in a Christian prayer of iv/v A.D., P Oxy VII. 1058² ὁ θ εὸς τῶν παρακειμένων σταυρῶν, βοήθησον τὸν δοῦλόν σου Ἀπφοῦαν, "O God of the crosses that are laid upon us, help thy servant Apphouas" (Ed.). "God is apparently thought of as at once the sender and mitigator of trials" (Ed.). In P Lond 1917⁶ (c. A.D. 330-40) the writer calls upon his correspondent — ὅπως ἐφάρῃς τὰς χῖράς σ[ου πρὸς τὸν δεσ]πότην θαιὸν ὡς τοίπως σταυρῷ, "that you may lift up your hands to our Master God, in the semblance of a cross": see the editor's note and cf. ¹⁹.

The sign of the cross is frequently prefixed to Christian letters, e.g. P Iand I. 16 (v/vi A.D.), and in the late P Lips I. 90¹⁰ (Byz.) the scribe states that he has written the document for the original sender, but that the latter has affixed three authenticating crosses with his own hand — ἔγραψα ὑπὲρ αὐτοῦ γράμματα μὴ ἰδότος βαλόντος δὲ τῇ ἰδίᾳ αὐτοῦ χειρὶ τοὺς τρεῖς τιμίους σταυρούς †. A wall-scratching from Egypt, Preisigke 2273, shows Σταῦρος δῶν Χριστιανῶν.

σταυρόω

in its literal sense of "fence with pales" occurs in P Bilabel 30¹² (A.D. 577?) μετὰ τοῦ σταυρωμ[ένου . . . . where the reference appears to be to a room shut off with pales or laths: see the editor's note. The late use = "crucify," as in the NT, is seen in Polyb. i. 86. 4 ; and for the new verb **σταυρίσκω** cf. Εv. Petr. 2.

σταφυλή.

"a grape" (Rev 14[18]: see Swete's note *ad l.*): PSI IV. 345[12] (B.C. 256) Κριτίας σταφυλῆς φυλάκων, BGU IV. 1118[14] (B.C. 22) σταφυλῆς βότρυας, P Oxy I. 116[18] (as amended II. p. 319) κ[ί]στην σταφυλῆς λείαν καλῆς, "a box of exceedingly good grapes," and BGU II. 417[13] (ii/iii A.D.) περὶ τοῦ κοφίνου τῆς σταφυλῆς.

The word is used collectively in P Oxy XVI. 1834[3] (v/vi A.D.) ἡ σταφυλὴ ἐφανίσθη ε̣νεκεν τοῦ νέου ὕδατος, "the grapes have been destroyed owing to the inundation" (Edd.), *ib.* 1913[19] (c. A.D. 555?) εἰς χρ(είαν) τῆς σταφυλ(ῆς) τῶν πωμαρ(ίων) ἔξω τῆς πύλης, "for the requirements of the grapes of the orchards outside the gate" (Edd.). On an ostrakon-letter of mid. iii B.C., published in *Archiv* vi. p. 221, we have ἐκ τῶν κοφίνων σταφυλῆς βοτρ[.]οι β. A dim. σταφυλιων (σταφύλιον?) is found in P Fay 127[8] (ii/iii A.D.), and in P Tebt II. 585 (ii/A.D.) σταφυληγοῦντες and σακκηγοῦντες are mentioned.

στάχυς,

"an ear of corn" (Mt 12[1], *al.*), is found several times in the farm accounts P Lond 131 *recto* [40 al.] (A.D. 78–79) (= I. p. 184): cf. Aristeas 63 βοτρύων καὶ σταχύων, "vine clusters and corn-ears," and M. Anton. vii. 40 βίον θερίζειν, ὥστε κάρπιμον στάχυν, "our lives are reaped like the ripe ears of corn."

For the acc. plur. στάχυας, as in Gen 41[7], Mt 12[1], see Thackeray *Gr.* i. p. 147. Mayser (*Gr.* i. p. 267) cites as instance of the plur. στάχυς from a papyrus of B.C. 239. On the use of στάχυς in Judg 12[6], see Plater *Vulgate Grammar*, p. 13 n.[2] MGr στάχυ, or, with prothetic vowel, ἀστάχυ (a form that is found as early as Homer—*Il.* ii. 148 ἄσταχυς). Among cognate words with meaning "pointed," Boisacq (p. 904) notes the English "sting."

Στάχυς.

This proper name, as in Rom 16[9], is found in P Revill. Mel. p. 295[11] (B.C. 131–0) (= Witkowski[2], p. 97) Πέλοπα καὶ Στάχυν καὶ Σεναθῦριν. See also *Magn* 119[25].

στέγη,

"a roof" (Mk 2[4]), a poetical subst. which has passed into general use in the Κοινή, e.g. P Petr II. 12 (1)[11] (B.C. 241) καθε(= ῃ)ρηκότας τὰς στέγας, "having taken down the upper story" (Ed.)—an action on the part of the owners to avoid having Crown officials billeted on them (π]ρὸς τὸ μὴ ἐπισταθμεύεσθαι. Cf. BGU III. 1002[6] (B.C. 55) τῆς πρώτης στέγης τῆς οἰκίας, P Lond 1164 (*f*)[28] (A.D. 212) (= III. p. 162) ἡ οἰκία τῶν αὐτῶν στεγῶν, and P Flor I. 15[14. 16] (A.D. 563) ἐν τῇ πρώτῃ στέγῃ . . . ἐν τῇ δευτέρᾳ στέγῃ. In *Syll* 558 (= [3] 756)[11] (i/A.D.) τ(ὴ)ν ὀπίσω τοῦ προπύλου στέγην, the reference is to the covered vestibule adjoining the gate of the Temple of Asclepius: cf. *ib.*[18] στεγάσαι δὲ καὶ τοῦ προπύλου τὸ ὀπίσω μέρος. A neut. subst. is found in *Syll* 813 (= [3] 1179)[20] ἐπ[ὶ τὸ α]ὐτὸ στέγος ἐ[λθ]εῖν, and a dim. in P Oxy I. 109[20] (list of personal property—iii/iv A.D.) στέγαστρον καινὸν α, "1 new cover" (Edd.). For στεγανόμιον, "house-rent," see P Bouriant 20[6 al.] (after A.D. 350).

στέγω,

orig. "cover," and thence either "keep in" in the sense of "conceal," "hide," or "keep off" in the sense of "bear up under," "endure" (Hesych. : στέγει· κρύπτει, συνέχει, βαστάζει, ὑπομένει). A good ex. of the latter meaning, which is to be preferred in all the NT occurrences (1 Thess 3[1.5], 1 Cor 9[12], 13[7]), is afforded by P Oxy XIV. 1775[10] (iv/A.D.) ὁ γὰρ πατήρ μου πολλά μ[ο]ι κακὰ ἐποίησεν, καὶ ἔστεξα ἕως ἔλθῃς : cf. for a literary ex. the Alexandrian erotic fragment P Grenf I.[1.18] (ii/B.C.) ζηλοτυπεῖν γὰρ δεῖ, στέγειν, καρτερεῖν, also for the general use in late Greek Philo *in Flacc.* § 9 (ii. p. 526 M.) μηκέτι στέγειν δυνάμενοι τὰς ἐνδείας. The more literal sense of "ward off" is seen in *Syll* 318 (= [3] 700)[21] (ii B.C.) ἔστεξεν τὴν ἐπιφερομένην τῶν βαρβάρων ὁρμήν : cf. Polyb. iii. 53. 2 οὗτοι γὰρ ἔστεξαν τὴν ἐπιφορὰν τῶν βαρβάρων.

We may add one or two exx. of the corresponding verb στεγάζω = "cover," "roof over" : P Cairo Zen II. 59251[7] (B.C. 252) ἵνα . . . καταλάβωμεν αὐτὴν (sc. οἰκίαν) ἐστεγασμένην, P Lond 1204[18] (B.C. 113) (= III. p. 11) οἰκίας ᾠκοδομημένης καὶ ἐστεγασμένης, and P Ryl II. 233[1] (ii/A.D.) τὸ ἕτερον ὑδρ[ο]ψυγεῖον αὔριον στεγάζεται, "the second water-cooler is to be roofed over to-morrow" (Edd.). For the subst. στέγωσις = "roofing in," see P Oxy XII. 1450[9] (A.D. 249–250) ; the new word ἐπιστέγωσις with the same meaning is found in [10]. Στεγνός is used = "water-tight" of a boat in P Petr III. 46 (1)[4] (iii/B.C.). See also PSI V. 486[3] (B.C. 258–7), *ib.* 407[5] (B.C. 257–6).

στεῖρος,

"barren," of a childless woman in Lk 1[7] *al.*: for the form see Moulton *Gr.* ii. pp. 118, 157 f. Στεῖρα, i.e. [*] στερια, persists unchanged in MGr: see further Boisacq p. 906 f.

στέλλω.

(1) From the root meaning "set," "place", this verb comes to mean "send," as in P Tebt I. 24[12] (B.C. 117) τῶν δὲ σταλέν[των] διαφόρων, BGU III. 821[8] (ii/A.D.) πάντες γὰρ ἐστάλη[σα]ν, P Oxy XVI. 1843[18] (vi/vii A.D.) τὴν σταλεῖσάν μοι παρ' αὐτῆς μίαν ζυγὴν τῶν σαβάνων, "one pair of linen garments sent me by you" (Edd.).

(2) Hence "bring together," "make compact," as of setting or shortening the sails of a ship (Hom. *Il.* i. 433, *Od.* iii. 11), from which it is a natural transition to the more general meaning "restrain," "check," and in the mid. "draw or shrink back from" anything, whether from fear (Hesych. : στέλλεται· φοβεῖται) or any other motive, as in Malachi 2[5] ἀπὸ προσώπου ὀνόματός μου στέλλεσθαι αὐτόν, 3 Macc 1[19] αἱ δὲ καὶ προσαρτίως ἐσταλμέναι ("die sich ganz zurückgezogen halten," Kautsch) : cf. Hipp. *Vet. med.* 10 (ed. Foesius) οὔτ' ἄν ἀπόσχοιντο ὧν ἐπιθυμεούσιν, οὔτε στείλαιντο, and the old gloss quoted in Steph. *Thesaur. s.v.* where στέλλεσθαι is explained by ἀφίστασθαι ἀναχωρεῖν.

(3) This gives the clue to the meaning "hold aloof from," "avoid," in the two NT occurrences of the verb, 2 Thess 3[6] (Vg *ut subtrahatis vos*), and 2 Cor 8[20] (Vg *devitantes*). The compd. ὑποστέλλω is used in the same sense in Ac 20[20. 27], Gal 2[12], Heb 10[38].

(4) We may add two exx. of στέλλομαι = "set out"

from the inscr.—*Magn* 20⁸ ἔδοξεν δέ τισιν αὐτῶν ἐς τὰν Ἀσίαν ἀποικίαν στείλασθαι, and *Kaibel* 691⁴ πρώτην ὁδὸν δὲ στέλλομαι πρὸς Ἀΐδαν.

στέμμα

occurs in the NT only in Ac 14¹³, where it refers to the sacrificial garlands with which the victims were adorned (cf. Field *Notes*, p. 122). In P Ryl II. 77³¹ (A.D. 192) it is used in connexion with "guilds," οἱ διέπον[τες τὴν τ]ῶν στεμμάτων [διοίκησι]ν εἶπον, "the administrators of the guilds said" (see the editors' note), and in P Fay 87¹⁰ (A.D. 155) a sum is paid τῷ ἐπὶ τῶν στεμμάτων προκεχι(ρισμένῳ), "to the official in charge of the *stemmata*" (see the editors' note). The sepulchral *Kaibel* 858² shows στέμμασιν ἀθανάτοις. See further Headlam's elaborate note *ad* Herodas VIII. 11.

For the verb στέφω we may cite P Ryl II. 77³⁴ (A.D. 192) στεφέσθω Ἀχιλλεὺς κοσμητείαν, "let Achilles be crowned as cosmetes."

στεναγμός,

"a groan" (Ac 7³⁴, Rom 8²⁶), occurs in the magic P Lond 121⁷⁶⁷ (iii/A.D.) (= I. p. 100) between ποππυσμός and συρισμός: cf. the late *Preisigke* 4949¹² (A.D. 753) ὀδύνη] κ(αὶ) λύπη κ(αὶ) στενα[γμός, also *Kaibel* 707⁶ (ii/A.D.) λύπας καὶ στεναχά[ς.

στενάζω,

"groan": Mk 7³⁴, Jas 5⁹ ("the word denotes feeling which is internal and unexpressed," Mayor *ad l.*). Cf. *Preisigke* 2134¹³ (time of the Antonines) Ἡραΐδος θανούσης, ἐστέναξαν οἱ θεοί, P Leid Wˣˣⁱ·⁵⁰ (ii/iii A.D.) (= II. p 155) ἔπιτα στενάξας συριγμῷ ἀνταπόδος.

στενός,

For the literal sense "narrow," cf. P Lond 1164 (*e*)¹¹ (A.D. 212) (= III. p. 160) ῥύμη στενή: a ῥύμη δημοσία has been mentioned just before. See also Aristeas 118 διὰ τὸ στενὰς εἶναι τὰς παρόδους, "because the passes were narrow."

The metaph. use, as in Mt 7¹³, Lk 13²⁴, may be illustrated from an amnesty decree of the Emperor Caracalla of July 11th, 212, where to avoid a too "narrow" interpretation of a previous decree that all may return to their own homes (εἰς τὰς πατρίδας τὰς ἰδίας), it is emphasized that in reality all restrictions as to place of dwelling are abrogated, P Giss I. 40¹·⁷⁵ ἵνα μή τις στενότερον παρερμηνεύσῃ τὴν χάριτά μου ἐκ τῶν ῥη[μά]των το[ῦ] προτέρου διατάγματος κτλ. In the introduction the editor contrasts with στενότερον παρερμηνεύσῃ the φιλανθρωπότερ[ο]ν ἑρμηνεύω of an Epistle of Hadrian, BGU I. 140¹⁹⁵.

A similar use of the adv. occurs in P Vat A¹⁵ (B.C. 168) (= UPZ i. p. 303) οὐ γὰρ πάντως δεῖ στενῶς ἐπανάγοντά σε προσμένειν ἕως τοῦ πορίσαι τι καὶ κατενεγκεῖν, where Wilcken renders στενῶς ἐπανάγοντά σε, "wenn es dir schmal geht": see his note for other renderings. For the subst. στένωσις see the Christian P Gen I. 14⁶ (Byz.) διὰ τὴν πολλήν μου στένωσι[ν, and cf. P Flor III. 296²¹ (vi/A.D.), P Oxy XVI. 1869¹¹ (vi/vii A.D.) τοῦ βράδους τὸ αἴτιον τῇ στενώσει τῶν πραγμάτων ἀνεθέμ[ην, "I attributed the cause of the delay to the difficulty of the affairs."

στενοχωρέω.

For this late word, lit. "keep in a tight place," cf. P Petr II. 12 (1)¹³ (B.C. 241) ἐπεὶ στενοχωροῦμεν σταθμοῖς, "since we are short of billets" (Ed.). See also the Hawara papyrus in *Archiv* v. p. 381, No. 56³ (late i/A.D.) στενοχωρεῖν ἐν τῷ κα . . [.]ῳ οὐκ ἠδυνάσθη.

στενοχωρία,

which is joined with θλῖψις in Rom 8³⁵ in the sense of "anguish," "trouble," is common in the texts of Hellenistic astrology, e.g. Catal. VII. 169, 21: cf. Boll *Offenbarung*, p. 135. See also P Lond 1677¹¹ (A.D. 566-7) (= VI. p. 71) θλίψεις καὶ στενοχωρίας ἃς ὑπέμεινα.

στερεός,

lit. "firm," "solid," is frequently applied to grain in the sense of "hard," i.e. "ripe": P Oxy IV. 836 (i/B.C.) πυρὸν στερεὸν νέον καθαρὸν ἄδολον, *ib*. XIV. 1629¹² (B.C. 44) πυροῦ . . στερεοῦ ἀκρίθου, "of hard wheat, unmixed with barley" (Edd.). In P Reinach 8⁵ (B.C. 113-112) τοῦ προγεγραμμένου πυροῦ στερεοῦ, the editor renders στερεοῦ by "compacte": cf. *ib*. 9²⁰ (B.C. 112).

Other exx. of the adj. are P Petr II. 4 (1)³ (B.C. 255-4) εἰς τὴν στερεὰν πέτραν, BGU IV. 1205²⁸ (B.C. 28) στερεὸν μὴ κενόν, "strong not worthless," said of a counterpane, P Fay 121⁶ (c. A.D. 100) ζυγόδεσμον καινὸν στερεόν, "a new strong yoke-band" (Edd.), and the Christian P Hamb I. 22⁷ (iv/A.D.) ἐχθροὺς ἡμετέρους στερεαῖς ἐνὶ χερσὶ πατάσσων (cf. Ps 34 (35)¹⁰).

In P Lond 1204¹⁹ (B.C. 113) (= III. p. 11) πῆχυν στερεοῦ denotes a measurement which is understood by the editors to be akin to the πῆχυς οἰκοπεδικός = 100 square cubits or 1/100 of an aroura.

στερεόω,

"make firm" (Ac 3¹⁶): cf. Alex. Trall. II. p. 583 Putschm. (12th book), where as a charm against gout the sufferer is to write certain magic words on a gold leaf, and to add ὡς στερεοῦται ὁ ἥλιος ἐν τοῖς ὀνόμασι τούτοις καὶ ἀνακαινίζεται καθ' ἑκάστην ἡμέραν, οὕτω στερεώσατε τὸ πλάσμα τοῦτο . . . (the passage is cited in P Osl I. p. 88).

στερέωμα.

For the meaning "firmament," as in Gen 1⁶ ᶠᶠ·, cf. Wünsch *AF* p. 17²² (iii/A.D.) ὁρκίζω σε τὸν θεὸν τὸν τῶν οὐρανίων στερεωμάτων δεσπόζονται Ἰάω ιβοηα.

Στεφανᾶς.

This proper name (1 Cor 1¹⁶, 16¹⁵·¹⁷) is either a shortened form of Στεφανήφορος, or a development of Στέφανος (cf. Blass *Gr.* p. 71). See Lake *Earlier Epistles*, p. 328, on Στεφανᾶς as the ἀπαρχὴ τῆς Ἀχαίας.

Στέφανος.

It is hardly necessary to illustrate this common name, but cf. P Hib I. 112⁸¹ (c. B.C. 260) Σ]τέφανος Σατόκου, P Oxy III. 517¹¹ (A.D. 130) διὰ Στεφά(νου) γρ(αμμάτεως) σεση(μείωμαι), and P Giss I. 103¹ (Christian letter—iv/A.D.) Στεφάνῳ δι[ακόνῳ ἀγ]απητῷ υἱῷ.

στέφανος.

From denoting a "garland" or "wreath" generally, στέφανος came to denote a "crown of victory," and as such was applied by Paul to his converts, as in 1 Thess 2[19]. It should be noted, however, that the distinction between στέφανος, "crown of victory" ("Kranz") and διάδημα, "crown of royalty" ("Krone") must not be pressed too far as by Trench *Syn.* § xxiii., for στέφανος is not infrequently used in the latter sense : see Mayor's note on Jas 1[12], and add from our sources the use of στέφανος to denote the "crown-tax" (*aurum coronarium*) for the present made to a king on his accession or other important occasion, e.g. P Petr II. 30(e)[ii. 23] (iii/B.C.) (as amended Wilcken *Ostr.* i. p. 275) ἄλλου [..] στεφάνου) παρουσίας, P Cairo Zen I. 59036[26] (B.C. 257) where 3000 drachmae are collected as ὁ στέφανος τῶι βασιλεῖ, and P Fay 14[3] (B.C. 124) οἱ προκεχιρισμένοι πράκτορες τοῦ ἀναπεφωνημένου Νουμηνίῳ στεφάνου, "the appointed collectors of the crown-tax decreed for Numenius," a private individual. See further Wilcken *Ostr.* i. p. 295 ff., and for a more specific instance of "a crown of victory," see the interesting letter P Lond 1178 (= III. p. 215 f., *Selections*, p. 99), in which the Emperor Claudius acknowledges the "golden crown" sent to him by the Worshipful Gymnastic Club of Nomads on the occasion of his victory over the Britons —[12f.] τὸν πεμφθέντ[α μο]ι ὑφ᾽ ὑμῶν ἐπὶ τῇ κατὰ Βρετάννων νείκῃ χρυσοῦν σ[τέ]φ[α]νον. A member of this Club may be referred to in P Ryl II. 153[25] (A.D. 138–161), when "allowances" are made to an athlete on account of his "athletic crown"—ὑπὲρ οὗ ἔσχον ἀθλητικοῦ στεφάνου.

Στέφανος is used in a more general sense, "reward," "gratuity," in P Goodsp Cairo 5[5] (ii/B.C.), where Peteuris promises a reward of five talents of copper, εἰς στέφανον χαλκοῦ τάλαντα πέντε, on account of some special service (cf. *Archiv* ii. p. 578 f.). The dim. στεφάνιον is similarly used in P Petr III. 142[19] (iii/B.C.) στεφάνια τῶι Ἀδώνει, and P Par 42[12] (B.C. 156) (= *UPZ* i. p. 318) στεφάνιόν ἐστιν χαλκοῦ ταλάντων γ̄.

A good ex. of the metaph. use of the word, as in Phil 4[1], Rev 3[11], is afforded by PSI IV. 405[3] (iii/B.C.) μέγας γάρ σου ὁ στέφανός ἐστιν ὑπὸ πάντων . . . εὐλογεῖσθαι : see *Archiv* vi. p. 393. Some miscellaneous exx. of the word are—P Oxy IV. 736[56] (accounts—c. A.D. 1) γενεσίοις Τρυφᾶτος στεφά(νων) ὀβολοὶ δύο, "on the birthday of Tryphas, for garlands 2 ob.," ib. IX. 1211[6] (articles for a sacrifice—ii/A.D.) στέφανοι ῑϛ, P Lond 964[10] (preparations for a wedding feast—ii/iii A.D.) (= III. p. 212) μὴ ἐπιλάθῃ μηδὲν τοὺς στεφάνους κ̄ αὶ τὰ τάβλια, and ib. 1164(i)[21] (A.D. 212) (= III. p. 166) οἷς ἐνίκησα στεφάνοις.

Reference may be made to the monograph by Josef Köchling *De Coronarum apud antiquos vi atque usu* (in *Religionsgeschichtliche Versuche und Vorarbeiten* xiv. 2), Giessen, 1914.

στεφανόω.

In P Cairo Zen I. 59060[7] (B.C. 257) Hierokles writes to Zenon regarding a boy who was Zenon's nominee in the games. ἐλπίζω σε στεφανωθήσεσθαι, "I hope that you will be crowned (i.e. victorious) through him": cf. 2 Tim 2[5].

The verb is used technically of the ceremonial crowning of magistrates, e.g. P Oxy VIII. 1117[2] (c. A.D. 178) τῶν τοῦ ἔτους ἐστεφανωμένων ἀρχόντων, P Ryl II. 77[37] (A.D. 192) ὁ Ἀχιλλεὺς βούλεται στεφανωθῆναι ἐξηγητείαν, and *Preisigke* 4101[4] τὸν προφήτην ἐστεφάνωσε.

For the late sense "reward," cf. Polyb. xiii. 9. 5 ἐστεφάνωσαν τὸν Ἀντίοχον πεντακοσίοις ἀργυρίου ταλάντοις, and see *s.v.* στέφανος.

The compd. verb στεφανηφορέω is seen in P Oxy VII. 1021[15] (A.D. 54) στεφανηφοροῦντας καὶ βοιθυτοῦντας, "wearing garlands and with sacrifices of oxen," to celebrate Nero's accession : the subst. in P Giss I. 27[8] (Trajan/Hadrian (= *Chrest.* I. p. 29) στεφανηφορίαν ἄξω, to celebrate a victory ; and the adj. in P Ryl II. 77[31] (A.D. 192) στεφα[νη]φόρον ἐξηγητείαν, "the office of a crowned exegetes."

στῆθος.

"breast": P Magd 24[7] (B.C. 218) ὥστε καὶ ἀπογυμνωθῆναί μου τὸ στῆθος, P Tebt II. 310[12] (A.D. 90) οὐλὴ στήθ μέσῳ, and BGU II. 466[7] (A.D. 150–160) ἐν τῷ στήθι καυτήρ[ι]ον. In P Masp III. 67109[b. 17] (Byz.) στήθους ἐπιστ[άν]τος, the word appears to mean a small "hillock" of sand (cited by Preisigke *Wörterb.* s.v.). MGr στῆθι (ἀστήθι).

στήκω.

"stand," a new present (MGr στέκω) from the perf. ἕστηκα, and retaining the same meaning : cf. Blass-Debrunner *Gr.* § 73, Psaltes *Gr.* p. 245. The idea of emphasis usually associated with the verb can hardly be pressed in view of the late Greek love for such forms : cf. *Kaibel* 970 (iii/A.D. ?) where it is interchanged with ἕστανεν (from the late στα[ίνω]—

> Ο]ἷς ποτε γυμνασίῳ Φιλήμονος ἕστανεν Ἑρμῆν
> νῦν σ[τ]ήκω κἀ[ὶ] γὼ Τελέσφορος . . .

στηριγμός.

"support," and hence "steadfastness" in its only NT occurrence (2 Pet 3[17]). The word is found in a papyrus dealing with the heavenly bodies, P Par 10[bis 13] (A.D. 138) (p. 237) Κρόνος ἐν Ὑδροχῷ, μοιρῶν ῑ, λεπτῶν η̄, ἐν τῷ β στηριγμῷ, ἰδίῳ οἴκῳ, ὁρίοις Ἑρμοῦ. For στήριγμα cf. P Lond 121[869] (iii/A.D.) (= I. p. 100) ὁ ἐπὶ τοῦ ἁγίου στηρίγματος σεαυτὸν ἱδρύσας.

στηρίζω,

"fix firmly," "set fast," as in Lk 9[51], 16[26] cf. Dalman *Words*, p. 36 f.) : cf. P Leid V[ix. 24] (iii/iv A.D.) (= II. p. 31) φιλείας στηρείζειν (. φιλίας στηρίζειν), PSI V. 452[3] (iv A.D.) κανόνι στηρίξαι ὑπὸ θατέρου μέρους τῶν κοινω[νῶν].

The fut. and aor. forms in the NT are discussed by WH *Notes*[2]. p. 177, and Winer-Schmiedel *Gr.* p. 105 n[8]. For the LXX and late use of the verb see Anz *Subsidia*, p. 276 f.

στιβάς,

"a litter of reeds or rushes" (Mk 11[8], and hence "mattress," as in an account of a sale P Oxy III. 520[10] (A.D. 143) Ἰουλᾶτ[ος] στιβάδων γ, "Iulas, 3 mattresses." In *Syll* 737 (= [3]1109[52] (c. A.D. 178) ὁ προσδεχθησόμενος (εἰς τὴν στιβάδα, Dittenberger understands the word as = *sodalitas* (see his note *ad l.*).

στίγμα,

"mark," "brand," occurs in the NT only in Gal 6[17] τοῦ λοιποῦ κόπους μοι μηδεὶς παρεχέτω, ἐγὼ γὰρ τὰ στίγματα τοῦ Ἰησοῦ ἐν τῷ σώματί μου βαστάζω, where there is general agreement in understanding by the στίγματα the scars or wounds which Paul received in the course of his Apostolic labours (cf. 2 Cor 6[4b], 11[23-27]). The exact origin of the metaphor is, however, by no means clear, and though our sources do not help us much in the present instance, it may be well to refer to some of the interpretations which have been suggested.

(1) A common tendency is to derive the figure from the practice of branding slaves, especially those who had run away, or otherwise misbehaved. And here, to the numerous refl. in Wetstein *ad l.*, we may add two exx. of the corresponding verb in the papyri—P Lille I. 29[11] (iii/B.C.) μηθενὶ ἐξέστω σώματα πωλεῖν [ἐπ'] ἐξαγωγῆι, μηδὲ στίζειν, μηδ[ὲ] μα[στ]ι[ζ]ε[ι]ν, "let no one be permitted to sell slaves for export, nor to brand them, nor to scourge them," and P Par 10[8] (B.C. 156) (= *UPZ* i. p. 573), where a runaway slave is described as ἐστιγμένος τὸν δεξιὸν καρπὸν γράμμασι βαρβαρικοῖς δυσίν, "branded on the right wrist with two barbaric letters": cf. Herodas V. 66 with Headlam's note. But the idea of punishment is wholly alien to the thought of the passage before us. Nor is there any evidence that the practice of soldiers tattooing themselves with their commanders' names, which others prefer, was at all general.

(2) In his *BS* p. 349 ff. Deissmann works out at some length another line of interpretation with the aid of a bilingual Leyden papyrus of iii/A.D. The text runs—μή με δίωκε ὅδε . . . βαστάζω τὴν ταφὴν τοῦ Ὀσίρεως καὶ ὑπάγω κατα[στ]ῆσαι αὐτὴν ε(ἰ)ς Ἄβιδος . . . ἐάν μοι ὁ δεῖνα κόπους παράσχῃ, προσ(τ)ρέψω αὐτὴν αὐτῷ, "persecute me not, thou there! I carry the corpse of Osiris, and I go to convey it to Abydos. Should anyone trouble me, I shall use it against him." Without going into details, the general meaning, according to Deissmann, is clear: "the βαστάζειν of a particular amulet associated with a god acts as a *charm* against the κόπους παρέχειν on the part of an adversary." Similarly, he thinks, the Apostle counsels his Galatian converts, "Do be sensible, do not imagine that you can hurt me—I am protected by a *charm*." The explanation is ingenious and has gained the weighty support of Zahn *Galaterbrief*, p. 286: cf. also a note by J. H. Moulton in *Exp T* xxi. p. 283 f. But, apart from other objections, it is not easy to imagine the Apostle's deriving the suggestion of divine protection from a magical charm, or adopting a smiling, half-mocking attitude towards the Galatians, which Deissmann pictures, in a letter that is in general so severe. [For a discussion of the Leyden papyrus from a different point of view, see de Zwaan in *JTS* vi. (1905), p. 418 ff.]

(3) On the whole, accordingly, it would seem best to give the passage a wider and more general reference, and to take it as indicating simply the personal relation of Paul to his Master with all the security which that brought with

it. For such a meaning the commentators have supplied various parallels. Thus in Herod. ii. 113 it is provided that a slave in Egypt may secure virtual emancipation by going to a certain temple of Herakles and having branded upon him στίγματα ἱρά, to denote his consecration to the god (cf. T. R. Glover *Paul of Tarsus*, p. 98 f., citing L. R. Farnell *Greece and Babylon*, p. 194): similarly in Lucian *de Dea Syr.* 59 it is stated—στίζονται δὲ πάντες οἱ μὲν ἐς καρπούς, οἱ δὲ ἐς αὐχένας, καὶ ἀπὸ τοῦδε ἅπαντες Ἀσσύριοι στιγματηφορέουσι, and once more in 3 Macc 2[29] Ptolemy Philopator is described as compelling the Jews to be branded with the ivy-leaf of Dionysus—τούς τε ἀπογραφομένους χαράσσεσθαι, καὶ διὰ πυρὸς εἰς τὸ σῶμα παρασήμῳ Διονύσῳ κισσοφύλλῳ. [See also *s.v.* χάραγμα for σῆμα as a mark of identity in P Oxy XIV. 1680[11].] Most recently Wilcken in the *Festgabe für Adolf Deissmann* (Tübingen, 1927) p. 8 f. has revived the reference to the practice of the followers of the Syrian goddess, and thinks that the Galatian passage need not mean more than that Paul has given himself over to Jesus for His own ("dass er sich Jesu zu eigen gegeben habe").

An ex. of the medical use of στίγμα is afforded by the account of a cure in the temple of Aesculapius at Epidaurus, *Syll* 802 (= ³1168)[18] (c. B.C. 320) Πάνδαρ]ος Θεσσαλὸς στίγματα ἔχων ἐν τῶι μετώπωι· οὗτος [ἐγκαθεύδων ὄ]ψιν εἶδε, cf.[62].

στιγμή,

lit. a "prick" or "point," is used metaph. of time in Lk 4[5], Isai 29[5]: cf. Plut. 2. 13 D στιγμὴ χρόνου ὁ βίος, M. Anton. ii. 17, and the prepositional phrase ἐν στιγμῇ in Vett. Val. pp. 131[1], 239[11].

στίλβω,

"shine," "glisten" (Mk 9[3]): cf. *Kaibel* 918[1] Μαρκιανοῦ στίλβει τύπος Ἑλλάδος ἀνθυπάτοιο, *ib.* 810[4] ναοί μοι στίλβουσιν ὑπ' ἠόνος. In the epithalamium P Masp III. 67318[3] (Byz.) reference is made to σεμνὸν ἀεὶ στίλβοντα γάμον. See also Bacchyl. XVII. 55 ὀμμάτων δὲ στίλβειν ἄπο Λαμνίαν φοίνισσαν φλόγα, "a fiery light, as of the Lemnian flame, flashes from his eyes" (Jebb).

στοά.

For this word which is used of the covered "portico" or "colonnade" (AV, RV "porch") of the Temple in Jn 10[23], Ac 3[11], we may cite the following exx.—CP Herm I. 119 recto[iii. 16] πρὸς τῇ καμάρᾳ ὑπὸ στοὰν Ἀντινοϊτικῆς πλατίας, BGU IV. 1107[33] (B.C. 12) ἐν τῇ τετραγώ(νῳ) στοᾷ οἰκητηρίο(υ), *ib.* 1127[34] (B.C. 8) εἰς τὸ τῆς στοᾶς λογιστήριον, P Oxy XII. 1406[11] (edict of Caracalla—A.D. 213–17) προετέθη ἐν Β[αβυλῶνι?] ὑπὸ στ[ο]ᾷ δημοσίᾳ, "published at B[abylon?] in the public colonnade" (Edd.), *ib.* XVI.[13] (A.D. 505) ὑπ[ὸ τ]ὴν νοτιν[ὴ]ν δημοσίαν στοάν, *Michel* 1001[ii. 17] (c. B.C. 200) εἴ κα μή τις στοὰν οἰκοδομῆσαι προαιρεῖται, *Syll* 588[245] (c. B.C. 180) ἐνωπίωι τῶν στοῶν, and *C. and B.* i. p. 155. No. 61 (A.D. 136–7) τὴν ἐξέδραν καὶ τὴν στουὰν παρ' ἑαυτοῦ ἀποκαθέστησεν.

Στοϊκός.

See *s.v.* Στωϊκός.

στοιχεῖον.

It is not possible to trace here in detail the history of this interesting word. The utmost that can be attempted is to indicate some of its varied meanings, especially those which throw light on its NT occurrences.

The root meaning starts from στοῖχος, a "row" or "rank," and from this the word passes to denote sounds which can be arranged in a series such as the letters of the alphabet: cf. BGU III. 959² (A.D. 148 στοιχ(είου) ε̄ κολ λήματος) ῑζ̄, and see P Par 65¹¹⁶ (B.C. 164 στοιχειωδῶς, "letter by letter." Cf. *Anth. Pal.* ix. 547 (like Nos. 538, 539) to which Mr. H. Lang Jones kindly refers us, nonsense verses containing all the letters of the Greek alphabet—

ΑΔΗΛΟΝ

Τὰ εἴκοσι τέσσαρα στοιχεῖα
Τρηχὺν δ' ὑπερβὰς φραγμὸν ἐξήνθιζε κλώψ.

From this it is an easy transition to the thought of "elementary principles." the ABC of a science, as in Heb 5¹², and in this connexion attention has been drawn to Porphyry *ad Marcellam* c. 24, where the iii A.D. Neoplatonist writes—τέσσαρα στοιχεῖα μάλιστα κεκρατύνθω περὶ θεοῦ· πίστις, ἀλήθεια, ἔρως, ἐλπίς (cf. 1 Cor 15¹³).

The meaning of "the primary constituent elements" of the universe (cf. Suid.: στοιχεῖόν ἐστιν ἐξ οὗ πρώτου γίνεται τὰ γινόμενα καὶ εἰς ὅ ἔσχατον ἀναλύεται) which occurs in Sap 7¹⁷, 19¹⁸, 4 Macc 12¹³ is frequently found in 2 Pet 3¹⁰,¹², where the translation "elements" gives excellent sense. But M. R. James (*CGT ad l.*) prefers the rendering "luminaries," with which we may associate the word as an astrological term in P Lond 130¹⁹ (i/ii A.D.) (= I. p. 134) στοιχείωι Διός: cf. Diog. Laert. vi. 102 τὰ δώδεκα στοιχεῖα, the signs of the Zodiac. In this connexion, by the courtesy of Dr. Darwell Stone, we have been provided with a long list of passages from Patristic writers where, in addition to other uses, τὰ στοιχεῖα is applied to heavenly bodies, and to the planets in particular. The following exx. must suffice—Just. M. *Ap.* 2. 5. 2 τὰ οὐράνια στοιχεῖα εἰς αὔξησιν καρπῶν καὶ ὡρῶν κτλ., *Ep. ad Diogn.* 7. 2 οὗ τὰ μυστήρια πιστῶς πάντα φυλάσσει τὰ στοιχεῖα (mentioned after the heavens and the sea, before sun, moon, stars, Epiph. *adv. Haer.* 7 ἥλιον καὶ σελήνην καὶ τὰ ἄλλα ἄστρα καὶ τὰ κατ' οὐρανὸν στοιχεῖα, and the metaphorical application to distinguished men, "great lights," in Polycrates *apud* Eus. *H.E.* v. 24. 2 μεγάλα στοιχεῖα κεκοίμηνται, implying a literal use for sun or moon or planet.

Reference may also be made to Mr. F. H. Colson's Essay on "The Week" (Cambridge University Press, 1926), in which he suggests that the στοιχεῖα of Gal 4³ and Col 2⁸ may refer to the "seven planets," from which the days of the week are named (p. 95 ff.) and to A. Dieterich *Abraxas* (Leipzig, 1891) p. 60 ff., where there is an interesting statement regarding the application of στοιχεῖα to the physical elements in the magical papyri and the Orphic hymns, leading on to its application to the rulers and the gods. In *JTS* xxviii. (1927) p. 181 W. H. P. Hatch refers to four passages in a Syriac work entitled *The Book of the Laws of the Countries,* commonly

ascribed to Bardaiṣān, which show that in Mesopotamia in ii/iii A.D. στοιχεῖα were understood as "personal cosmic powers."

For an extension to the thought of "tutelary spirits," "angels," see Deissmann in *EB* s.v. "Elements," who applies it in the difficult NT passages Gal 4³ᵃ and Col 2⁸,²⁰, understanding by Gal 4³ "cosmic spiritual beings," the "angels" by whom according to 3¹⁹ the law was ordained, and by 4⁹ "the heathen deities" whom the Galatians had formerly served, while in Col 2⁸,²⁰ it is again personal powers who are thought of, "the principalities and the powers" of 2¹⁵. It may be added that this interpretation can also be illustrated from modern Greek usage, as when in Abbott *Songs* p. 178³ we read of τὸ στοιχειό τοῦ ποταμοῦ, "the spirit of the stream." Cf. Thumb *Handbook* p. 356: στοιχειό, "spirit," "ghost," and στοιχειώνω, "make a ghost of," "become a spirit."

στοιχέω.

From meaning "am in rows," "walk in line," στοιχέω came to be used metaphorically, "walk by or in," as a rule of life: cf. Phil 3¹⁶ (Vg *in eadem permaneamus regula*). A striking parallel to Rom 4¹² is afforded by *Syll* 325 (= ³708)⁶ (ii/B.C.) where a certain Aristagoras is praised for walking in the steps of his father and forbears—καὶ αὐτὸς στοιχεῖν βουλόμενος καὶ τοῖς ἐκείνων ἴχνεσιν ἐπιβαίνειν: cf. *ib.* 929 (= ³685)¹⁸ (B.C. 139) τῆς δὲ συνκλήτου στοιχούσης τῆι παρ' ἑαυ]τῆι πρὸς πάντας ἀνθρώ]πους ὑπαρχούσηι δικαιοσύνηι, and from the inscr. *Priene* 112¹¹³ (B.C. 84) στοιχεῖν τ[ῆ πρὸς τὸν δῆμον φιλαγαθίᾳ, and *ib.* 110²¹ (i/B.C.) ταῖς κατὰ τὴν ἡλικίαν [ἀρεταῖς] στοιχεῖν (see Rouffiac, p. 34). See also Musonius p. 102⁹ στοιχεῖν ἀρίστῳ ὄντι τῷ λόγῳ Σωκράτους. The construction with the dat., as in the NT, is thus amply attested: cf. Blass *Gr.* p. 110.

The verb is common in the phrase στοιχεῖ μοι, "agreed to by me," e.g. P Oxy I. 126⁵¹ (A.D. 572) στοιχῖ μοι τὸ παρὸν ἐπίσταλμα, *ib.* VIII. 1137⁷ (A.D. 502 3) στέχι με (*l.* στοιχεῖ μοι. Cf. also P Flor I. 65²² (A.D. 570–1?) Αὐρήλιος . . . στοιχῖ τοῦτο τὸ γρ[αμμάτιον ὡς π]ρόκειται, and BGU IV. 1020¹⁷ (vi/A.D.) Ἀβραὰμ Φοι βαμμῶνος) στοιχεῖ.

For the subst. στοῖχος, cf. P Oxy VIII. 1119¹² (A.D. 254) τοῦ στοίχου καταλαβόντος τὴν ἡμετέραν βουλὴν τῷ ἐνεστῶ[τι ἔτει, "since the turn has come to our senate in the present year" (Ed.), and for the compd. σύστοιχος, cf. BGU IV. 1205ⁱⁱ ⁹ (B.C. 28) οὐδὲ γὰρ σύνστοιχοι ἑατῶν [γ]ίνεσθε, "for you contradict yourselves."

στολή,

"a long robe": P Cairo Zen I. 59054³² (B.C. 257) ῥίσκον [χ]ωροῦντα ὅσον στ[ο]λὰς δέκα, "a trunk containing as much as ten robes," P Oxy IV. 839 (early i A.D.) ἦλθέ μοι γυμνὸς κεκινδυνευκώς. εὐθέως ἠγόρασα αὐτῶι στολήν, P Ryl II. 154⁸ (A.D. 66) ἱμα[τίω]ν σ[τ]ολὰ[ς] δύο, P Oxy XII. 1449¹³ (A.D. 213–17) στολὴ καλλαΐνη, "a green robe," and *Syll* 616 (= ³1025)¹⁰ (a liturgical calendar from Cos—c. B.C. 300) ὁ δὲ ἱερεὺς . . ἔχων τὰ]ν στο[λὰ]ν τὰν ἱεράν.

For στόλισμα see P Tebt II. 598 (A.D. 170–191) βύσσου στολ ίσματα), and for στολισμός (2 Chron 9¹ al., Aristeas 96 see BGU I. 1³ (iii/A.D.) εἰς [τ]ειμὴν ὀθονίων βυσσίνων στολισμῶ(ν).

στόμα.

For **στόμα** the "mouth" of a river or canal, cf. P Strass I. 55[9] (ii/A.D.) δίδομεν τοὺς ὑπογεγρα(μμένους) εἰς ἀφεσο-φυλακίαν ἀπὸ στώματο[s] (*l.* στόματο[s]) Ψι[α]ναλ( ) ("the canal Psinal( )") ἕως κτήματος ἀμπελ(ικοῦ) Ἰσίου Λεοντᾶτος, and *OGIS* 90[25] (Rosetta stone—B.C. 196) τὰ στόματα τῶν ποταμῶν, "the mouths of the canals."

For **στόμα** in prepositional phrases see P Giss I. 36[12] (B.C. 161) αἱ τέτταρες λέγουσαι ἐξ ἑνὸς στόματος γρα(μ-ματεῖ) Νεχούθει (with editor's note and cf. Ac 22[14]) and the common καθὼς καὶ ἐν στόματι ὑπηγόρευσα, as in P Mon I. 11[34] (A.D. 586). Στόμα πρὸς στόμα, as in 2 Jn[12], 3 Jn[14], occurs in the Berlin magic papyrus 1[39], ed. Parthey in *Abh. d. konigl. Akad. d. Wissenschaften*, Berlin, 1866, p. 121. The "Hebraisms" involved in such phrases are discussed by Moulton *Proleg.* p. 99 f.

στόμαχος,

in early Greek writers = "throat," but afterwards extended to "stomach," as in 1 Tim 5[23], its only NT occurrence: cf. P Leid W[xviii. 36] (ii/iii A.D.) (= II. p. 145) ἀμφοτέρας (*sc.* χεῖρας) ἐπὶ τοῦ στομάχου. The word is used metaph. in P Oxy III. 533[14] (ii/iii A.D.) ἵ[ν]α μὴ ἔχωμεν στομάχου[s] μηδὲ φθόνον, "that we may not be caused vexation and annoyance" (Edd.): cf. Vett. Val. p. 216[3] γέγονε στόμαχος ("anger") πρὸς δουλικὸν πρόσωπον.

στρατεία

(for the spelling, see Deissmann *BS* p. 181 f.) "military service": P Fay 91[11] (A.D. 99) Λυκίωι Βελλήνω Γεμέλλωι ἀπολυσ[ί]μωι ἀπὸ στρατείας, "to Lucius Bellenus Gemellus discharged from military service," BGU I. 140[11] (time of Hadrian) ο[ὓ]s οἱ γονεῖς αὐτῶν τῷ τῆς στρατείας ἀνείλα[ν]το χρόνῳ, Gnomon (= BGU V. 1) 34 (*c.* A.D. 150) τοῖς ἐν στρατείᾳ καὶ ἀπὸ στρατείας οὖσι συνκεχώρηται δια-τίθεσθα[ι] καὶ κατὰ Ῥωμαϊκὰς καὶ Ἑλληνικὰς διαθήκας, and *ib.* 62, and BGU II. 625[14] (beg. iii/A.D.), as read by Olsson *Papyrusbriefe* p. 114, ὕδατε (= οἴδατε) τὴν ἀνάγκην τῆς στρατείας. In the inscr. *Preisigke* 293[1] (Ptol.) ὁμοῦ τὴν τιμὴν τῆι θεῶν στρατείαι Ἄρηι συνμάχωι, Διὶ Ὀλυμπίωι κτλ., στρατείαι would seem to have the meaning "army" like στρατιά (*q.v.*), and this meaning is also given by the editors to the word in P Oxy I. 71[ii. 8] (A.D. 303) τῶν τε ἡμετέρων τέκνων ἐν στρατείᾳ ὄντων καὶ ἀπασχολ[ο]υμένων ἐπὶ τῆς ἀλλοδαπῆς, "my sons are in the army and absent upon foreign service," but the translation "on military service" is equally possible.

For the metaph. use of **στρατεία**, as in 2 Cor 10[4], 1 Tim 1[18], 4 Macc 9[23], cf. Epict. iii. 24. 34 στρατεία τίς ἐστιν ὁ βίος ἑκάστου καὶ αὕτη μακρὰ καὶ ποικίλη, and Maxim. Tyr. xix. 4 στρατηγὸν μὲν τὸν θεόν, στρατείαν δὲ τὴν ζωήν, ὁπλίτην δὲ τὸν ἄνθρωπον.

στράτευμα,

"a body of soldiers" (Mt 22[7], *al.*): cf. BGU I. 266[19] (A.D. 215 16) εἰς τὰς ἐν Συρίᾳ κυρι[α]κὰς ὑπηρεσίας τῶν γενναιοτάτω[ν] στρατευμάτων, *Ostr* 1595[4] (A.D. 258) ὑπὲρ τιμ[ῆς] ἐλαίου τῶν ἐνταῦθα στρατευμάτω[ν], and *Syll* 350 (= [3]768)[6] (B.C. 31) αὐτὸς (*Augustus*) δὲ μετὰ τ[οῦ] στρατεύ-ματος ὑγίαινον. For an important discussion of Lk 23[11]

σὺν τοῖς στρατεύμασιν = "with his forces," see A. W. Verrall in *JTS* X. (1909), p. 340 f.

στρατεύομαι

is common in the general sense "serve in the army," "am a soldier" (whether on active service or not). See e.g. P Rev L[xxiv. 6] (B.C. 259-8) τῶν στρατευομένων καὶ τοὺ[s ....] κλήρους πεφευκότων, P Tebt I. 5[168] (B.C. 118) τοὺς στρατευομένους Ἕλληνας, "the Greeks serving in the army" (Edd.), *ib.* 27[49] (B.C. 113) ἀπό τε τ[ῶ]ν στρατευομένων καὶ τῶν ἄλλων τῶν τόπους κατ[ο]ικούν-των, "from those in the army and the other inhabitants of the district" (Edd.), P Amh II. 32[1] (ii/B.C.) where certain στρατευόμενοι defend themselves against the charge of returning for taxation purposes their κλῆροι at less than their true value, P Lond 1171 *verso* (c)[7] (A.D. 42) (= III. p. 107) where a distinction is drawn between στρατευόμενοι "regu-lar soldiers" and μαχαιροφόροι "armed attendants upon officials" (see further the editors' note *ad* P Tebt I. 35[12]), P Hamb I. 31[18] (A.D. 103) ἀπογραφὴν περιέχουσαν ἐστρατεῦσθαι αὐτὸν [ἔ]τεσι κς, and P Oxy XIV. 1666[5] (iii/A.D.) φθάνω δὲ ὑμεῖν πρότερον γεγραφηκὼς περὶ τοῦ μικροῦ Παυσανίου ὡς εἰς λεγίωναν στρατευσάμενος, "I have previously written to you about the little Pausanias becoming a soldier of a legion" (Edd.).

The idea of *active* service seems to be implied in such passages as P Par 63[175] (B.C. 164) (= P Petr III. p. 34) where the cattle belonging ἄλλοις τοῖς στρατευομένοις are impressed into the service of the State, P Grenf I. 21[3] (Will—B.C. 126) τὸν μὲν ἵππον ἐφ' οὗ στρατεύομαι, BGU IV. 1097[7] (Claudius/Nero) ἀπῆλθεν εἰς παρεμβολὴν στρα-τεύσασθαι, cf. [8ff.], P Ryl II. 180[5] (A.D. 128) receipt for cloaks ἰς <σ>τρατιωτικὰς χρείας τῶν ἐν τῇ Ἰου[α]δαίᾳ στρατευομένων, "for the needs of the soldiers serving in Judaea" (Edd.), and P Oxy VIII. 1103[5] (A.D. 360) τῶν νεολέκτων τῶν στρατευθέντων, "the new levies raised by us for military service" (Ed.).

For the metaph. usage, as in 2 Cor 10[3] *al.*, cf. BGU IV. 1127[8] (B.C. 8) ἐὰν δὲ κατά τι στρατεύηται ὁ Ἀπολλώνιος ἐν τοῖς κατὰ τὴν παραχώρησιν, where Schubart notes that the meaning must be "Schwierigkeiten, Umstande machen," "make difficulties, troubles," comparing *ib.* 1131[20] (B.C. 17). This is rather like our phrase, "He has been in the wars." Cf. the use of μάχομαι in the sense of "quarrel" (*Scottice*, "fecht"), e.g. Menander *Fragm.* p. 86, No. 302[5] γυνὴ κρατεῖ πάντων, ἐπιτάττει, μάχετ' ἀεί. The use illustrates the large metaphorical application of the term in the NT. Cumont *Les Religions Orientales* p. xiv ff. (Engl. Tr. pp. xx, 213 f.) has collected a number of passages on the "Salvation Army" in ancient times. See also Harnack *Militia Christi* (1905), and Dibelius *HZNT ad* 1 Tim 1[18].

στρατηγός.

It would take us too far from our immediate object to discuss the various uses of **στρατηγός** as a civic and military title. Convenient reff. to the relevant literature will be found in Preisigke *Fachworter*, p. 158 f. See also J. G. Tait in *J. Eg. Arch.* viii. (1922), p. 166 ff. In NT usage the word is applied (1) to the commander of the Levitical guard of the temple (Ac 4[1] *al.*), a position next in honour to the High Priest, and to the Captains of the temple under him

(Lk 22⁴²: cf. Schürer *Geschichte* ii. p. 266 (= *HJP* Div. II. vol. i. p. 259)), and (2) to the governors or magistrates of the Roman colony at Philippi (Ac 16²⁰·²²). It is doubtful whether the **ἄρχοντες** of v. 19 and the **στρατηγοί** of v. 20 are the same officials according to their Greek or Latin forms of designation, or whether the **ἄρχοντες** are the chief magisterial authorities and the **στρατηγοί**, the local magistrates of the town. Ramsay (*St. Paul*, p. 217 f.) is inclined to distinguish between them on the ground that a concise writer like Luke would not likely have employed two clauses where one was sufficient. He adds that in the case of the Philippian magistrates the title "Praetors" was "not technically accurate," but was employed as a "courtesy title."

The designation **στρατηγός** = *praetor* is of constant occurrence in the papyri, and hardly needs illustration, but see P Oxy II. 294¹⁹ (A.D. 22) (= *Selections*, p. 35), BGU IV. 1095²⁵ (A.D. 57), and P Fay 118¹³ (A.D. 110).

στρατιά,

"army," "host": cf. P Bilabel 36¹¹ (time of Trajan) ἐὰν ἱκανὴ ἀνάβασις γένηται στρα[τιᾶς], μεθίστ[αν]ται καὶ βασιλικοὶ γ[εωργοὶ κτλ., and the fragmentary Preisigke 1481⁵ (ii A.D.)].ρατια εἶναι, which may represent ἐν σ]τρατιᾳ εἶναι. See also *s.v.* στρατεία.

στρατιώτης,

"a soldier": cf. P Amh II. 39⁴ (letter of a captain—late ii/B.C.) τοῖς ἄλλοις [στ]ρ[α]τιώται[ς] πᾶσι χαίρειν, P Oxy II. 240⁷ (A.D. 37) εἰ μὴν [μὴ συνε]ιδέναι με μηδενὶ διασεσεισμέ[νωι ἐπὶ] τῶν προκειμένων κωμῶν ὑπὸ [. . . . .]-ος στρατιώτου καὶ τῶν παρ' αὐτοῦ, "that I know of no one in the village aforesaid from whom extortions have been made by the soldier . . . or his agents" (Edd.) (cf. Lk 3¹⁴), *ib.* 276⁹ (A.D. 77) Κλαυδίου Κέλερος στρατιώτου λεγεῶνος δευτέρας, and *ib.* I. 64³ (iii/iv A.D.) ἐξαυτῆς παράδοτε τῷ ἀποσταλέντι ὑπ' ἐμοῦ στρατιώτῃ. In P Fay 135⁶ (iv A.D.) a son writes to his father urging him to pay a debt ἵνα μ[ὴ] δόξῃ μ[ο]ι στρατιώτας ἀποστῖλαι ἐπὶ σαὶ καὶ συνκλισθῆς ἄχρις ἂν πληρώσῃς, "that I may not have to send soldiers after you, and you be put in prison until you pay" (Edd.). Reference may also be made to P Lond 417 (c. A.D. 346) (= II. p. 299 f., *Selections*. p. 123 f.), where a praefect asks for the forgiveness of a deserter Παύλῳ τοῦ στρατιότῃ, under circumstances which closely recall the Ep. to Philemon. For a soldier in the service of the Church, apparently as its guardian and protector, see P Lond V. 1770¹ (vi–vii A.D.), with the editor's note. See also Dibelius *HZNT* at Eph 6¹⁰.

For the adj. **στρατιωτικός** see P Ryl II. 250³ (i B.C.) where a young man complains that he has been deprived of τὰ λειφθέν[τα μο]ι [πατ]ρικὴν στρατιωτικὴν μάχαιραν, *ib.* 189⁴ (A.D. 128) ἰς (σ)τρατιωτικὰς χρείας τῶν ἐν τῇ Ιου[α]δαίᾳ στρατευομένων παλλίωλα λευκὰ πέντε, "for the needs of the soldiers serving in Judaea five white cloaks" (Edd.), and P Oxy I. 71ⁱⁱ·⁷ (A.D. 303) στρατιωτικὰς εὐθηνίας, "supplies for the soldiers" (Edd.).

στρατολογέω,

"enlist in the army," in NT only in 2 Tim 2⁴. To the exx. in LS⁸ add Jos. *Bell.* v. 9. 4 βοηθὸν ἐστρατολόγησε.

στρατοπεδάρχης.

Mommsen (*Sitzungsb. d. preussischen Akademie*, 1895, No. XXVII) argues that this word, which occurs in the TR of Ac 28¹⁶, means there *princeps peregrinorum*, but in P Lond 196² (c. A.D. 138–161) (= II. p. 153) the editor prefers to understand the title as *princeps castrorum*, and compares Mommsen *l.c.* p. 498. See his note *ad l.* from which the foregoing is derived.

We may add references to Vett. Val. p. 76¹³ ποιοῦσι στρατοπεδάρχας ναυτικῶν τε καὶ πεζικῶν ἄρχοντας, and to *OGIS* 605⁴ (v A.D.).

στρατόπεδον.

For **στρατόπεδον** = "soldiers in camp," "army," as in its only occurrence in the NT (Lk 21²⁰), cf. *Preisigke* 4275⁷ (A.D. 216) Ἰουλίαν Δόμναν Σεβαστὴν τὴν μητέρα τῶν ἀν[ικήτων] στρατοπέδων, and similarly 5075³ (time of Caracalla). In BGU III. 903ⁱⁱ·⁷ (B.C. 128–7) ἐν τῶι τοῦ βασιλέως στρατοπέδωι, the word seems to have its ordinary meaning "camp."

στρεβλόω,

which is used metaph. = "pervert," "strain" in 2 Pet 3¹⁶, is found in a broken context in BGU I. 195¹³ (ii/A.D.) . . .] στρε[βλώ]σαν[τ]ες τοῦ στρατιωτικοῦ. [. . . See also Wünsch *AF* 3¹⁵ as cited *s.v.* πνέω. A new ex. of the lit. meaning "torture" occurs in Herodas II. 89 λαβών, Θαλῆ, στρέβλου με, "here, Thales, take me and torture me": cf. also *Vita Epicuri* VI. 118 κἂν στρεβλωθῇ δ' ὁ σοφὸς εἶναι αὐτὸν εὐδαίμονα, "and even if the wise man be put on the rack, he is happy" (Bailey).

στρέφω,

"turn": (1) act.—P Lond 121⁶²⁵ (iii A.D.) (= I. p. 106) ἄρκτε . . . ἡ στρέφουσα τὸν ἄξονα, (2) reflex. mid.—P Leid Wⁱⁱ·²⁷ (ii–iii A.D.) (= II. p. 101) λέγε στρεφόμενος, (3) reflex. pass.—P Oxy I. 33ⁱⁱⁱ·⁶ (late ii A.D.) στρ[α]φεὶς καὶ ἰδὼν Ἡλιόδωρον εἶπεν κτλ.

For the form ἐστρεμμένα (for ἐστραμμένα) in P Eud 281 (before B.C. 165) see Mayser *Gr.* i. pp. 49, 410. The verbal **στρεπτός** occurs with doubtful meaning in Aristeas 58. On the relation of στρέφω and its compds. to the Scriptural idea of "conversion," reference should be made to a paper by Field, *Notes* p. 246 ff. (see *s.v.* ἐπιστρέφω).

στρηνιάω,

first met with in the Middle Comedy (Rutherford *NP* p. 475) = "feel strong and hearty": cf. the cognate Lat. *strenuus*, Engl. "stern." According to Hesychius στρηνιῶντες = πεπλεγμένοι. δηλοῖ δὲ καὶ τὸ διὰ πλοῦτον ὑβρίζειν, καὶ βαρέως φέρειν. It is in this bad sense "wax wanton" through wealth etc. that the verb is used in Rev 18⁷·⁹: cf. P Meyer 20²³ (1ˢᵗ half iii A.D.) μὴ στρηνιάτω Λουκιᾶς, ἀλλὰ ἐργαζέσθω. The compd. καταστρηνιάω in 1 Tim 5¹¹ is rendered by Souter "exercise my youthful vigour against": for similar κατα-compds. see Blass-Debrunner *Gr.* § 181.

στρῆνος,

"wantonness," "luxury" (Rev 18³). Apparently the earliest instance of this word is in the iv/B.C. comic poet Nicostratus (see Kock *CAF* ii. p. 230, No. 42), if the fragment is genuine. Unfortunately the word stands alone without context. It occurs later in Lycophron 438 (iii/B.C.) and the LXX: cf. 4 Kingd 19²⁸ τὸ στρῆνός σου ἀνέβη ἐν τοῖς ὠσίν μου—said of the Assyrian King.

στρουθίον,

"a sparrow" (Mt 10²⁹·³¹, Lk 12⁶). The word is a dim. of στρουθός which is found in the food account P Oxy VI. 920⁸ (ii/iii A.D.) στρουτ(οῦ) (*l.* στρουθ(οῦ)) μεγάλ(ου) δραχμαὶ ἤ. The editors think that the reference is to an ostrich, and that the 8 drachmae may be part payment, in view of l.¹². They also refer to P Lips I. 97ˣˣᵛⁱⁱⁱ ¹⁸·²⁰; ˣˣⁱˣ·¹⁹,²¹ (A.D. 338), where there are entries of an artaba εἰς τὰ στρουθῶν. See also P Lond 239¹¹ (*c.* A.D. 346) (= II. p. 298). It must be added that from a fragment of the commercial law dealing with tariffs issued by the Emperor Diocletian in iii/A.D. it appears that of all birds used for food sparrows were the cheapest, thus throwing a fresh light upon our Lord's use of them in Mt 10²⁹ ᶠᶠ, Luke 12⁶ᶠ (see Deissmann *LAE*², p. 272 ff.).

For a proper name Στρουθεῖν (*-ίν* for *-ίον*) see *Letronne* 90¹ (i/B.C.) with the editor's note. In spite of the difference of meaning, στρουθός has been connected with Lat. *turdus*, Engl. "thrush," "throstle" (Boisacq, p. 920).

στρώννυμι, στρωννύω.

With the use of the pass. in Mk 14¹⁵ cf. P Lond 1164 (*h*)⁷ (A.D. 212) (= III. p. 164) πλοῖον . . . ἐστρωμένον καὶ σεσανιδ[ω]μένον, "a ship furnished and boarded over." In P Oxy I. 138²² ᵃⁿᵈ ³¹ (A.D. 610–11) a "contractor of the race-course" undertakes στρῶσαι τοῖς τε περιβλέπτοις διοικηταῖς καὶ λαμπροτάτοις χαρτουλαρίοις, "to find mounts for the noble superintendents and the most illustrious secretaries" (Edd.). Preisigke (*Wörterb. s.v.*) refers to an inscr. from Roman Egypt published in *Archiv* ii. p. 570, No. 150, Φιλαντῖνος ὁ καὶ Ἀμμώνιος ἔστρωσεν διὰ Διοσκύρου πατρὸς ἐκ τοῦ ἰδίου. The compd συνστρώννυμι is found in P Petr III. 43 (2) *recto*ⁱᵛ·¹⁵ (B.C. 246) συνστρώσας σχοινίοις, "having made a network of ropes," see the editor's note on p. 127 where for συνστρώννυμι = "pave," reference is made to *Syll* 537(= ³969)⁶¹ (B.C. 347–6) συνστρώσει τὸ ἔδαφος λίθοις. Καταστρώννυμι, "spread out," occurs in P Tor I. 1ᵛⁱⁱ·¹⁸ (B.C. 116): see *s.v.*

The subst. στρῶμα is common, e.g. PSI VI. 593⁸ (iii/B.C.) σκεύασόν μοι στρώματα τρία ἀνὰ μν(ᾶς) μ, P Bilabel 71⁵ (i/A.D.) ἀπέ[σ]τειλα ἐπιστολὰς περὶ τῆς] στρωμάτων κα[τασκευῆς, P Oxy X. 1277⁷ (A.D. 255) ὁμολογῶ πεπρακέναι σοι τρίκλιν[ο]ν στρωμάτων λινῶν, "I acknowledge that I have sold to you a three-sided couch with linen coverings" (Edd.). In a will of B.C. 123, published by GH in *Archiv* i. p. 63 ff., the testator bequeaths all his property to his wife, "except a mattress and a bed apiece" (πλὴν στρώματος ἑνὸς καὶ κλείνης) to his two sons—perhaps, as the editors suggest, the Egyptian method of "cutting off with a shilling."

For the dim. στρωμάτιον, cf. PSI IV. 401² (iii/B.C.) τὸ

στρωμάτιον ὑπὲρ οὗ σοι καὶ σήμερον διελεγόμην, and P Oxy XIV. 1645³ (A.D. 308) στρωμάτια τριβακὰ δύο, "two worn mattresses," and for στρῶσις cf. *ib.* 1631²⁷ (A.D. 280) τῆς στρώσεως τοῦ χοῦ, "the spreading of earth," and PSI III. 225⁵ (vi/A.D.) μίαν στρῶσιν ἀκκουβίτου, "one spreading of the couch" (cf. the verb in Ac 9³⁴).

στυγητός,

For this NT ἄπ. εἰρ. (Tit 3³) = "hateful," "hated," cf. Philo *de Decalogo* 131 (ed. Cohn) στυγητὸν καὶ θεομίσητον πρᾶγμα.

στυγνάζω,

"am gloomy," "am sad" (Mk 10²²): cf. P Leid Wᵛ·⁵ (ii/iii A.D.) (= II. p. 40) γελῶν ἐστύγνασε, and similarly xi 53, xii 1. For adj. στυγνός cf. PSI I. 28¹ (magic tablet—iii/iv A.D.?) στυγνοῦ σκότους, cf. ²⁰, and see Mt 16³; and for adv. στυγνοτέρως cf. BGU VI. 1301⁸ (ii/i B.C.) ἠγωνίασα μή ποτε στυγνοτέρω[ς ἔ]χεις τὰ πρὸς ἐμέ.

στύλος,

"pillar": BGU VII. 1713⁴ (ii/iii A.D.) στύλων μονολίθων, P Giss I. 69¹³ (A.D. 118–19) διὰ τὴν τοῦ πεντηκοντάποδος στύλου καταγωγὴν πλεῖστα κτήνη ἔχομεν, and BGU IV. 1028¹³ (ii/A.D.) πρὸς χρείαν τῶν τοὺς στύλ[ους ἐ]ργαζ[ο]μένων. See also the diminutives in P Iand 11⁸ (iii/A.D.) κόμισον δὲ ἕν στυλάριν and *OGIS* 332⁹ (B.C. 138–132) ἐπὶ στυλίδος μαρμαρίνης. A new adv. στυλοειδῶς, "in the form of a pillar," is found in Epicurus *Ep.* II. 104 (ed. Bailey).

The metaph. usage of στύλος, as in Gal 2⁹, is common to classical, Jewish, and Christian writers: see Suicer *Thes. s.v.*

Στωϊκός

is the original spelling in Ac 17¹⁸ B, the form Στοϊκός in ℵ ADE *al.* being due to the influence of στοά (cf. Moulton *Gr.* ii. p. 73).

σύ,

"thou" (for enclitic forms, cf. Blass *Gr.* p. 165). On the emphasis to be attached to the pronoun in the difficult Mt 26⁶⁴ σὺ εἶπας, "*you* say it," "the word is yours," see *Proleg.* p. 85 f. For the personal pronoun taking the place of the reflexive, cf. P Tebt I. 20³ (B.C. 113) χαριεῖ σὺν σοὶ αὐτὸν εἰσαγαγών, "you will do me a favour by personally introducing him" (Edd.), and *ib.* 30¹³ (B.C. 115) καλῶς ποιήσεις [[. .]] συντάξας καὶ παρὰ σοὶ ἀναγράφειν εἰς αὐτὸν ἀκολο[ύθω]ς, "please order the land to be entered accordingly on your list too under his name" (Edd.): see further Mayser *Gr.* II. i. p. 67, and for the indirect reflexive, see *ib.* pp. 68, 71.

One or two irregular forms which occur in the vernacular may be noted—σέ for σοί, P Oxy IV. 744⁶ (B.C. 1) (= *Selections*, p. 33) ἐὰν εὐθὺς ὀψώνιον λάβωμεν ἀποστελῶ σε ἄνω, *ib.* I. 119⁴ (ii/iii A.D.) (= *Selections*, p. 103) οὐ μὴ γράψω σε ἐπιστολήν, οὔτε λαλῶ σε, οὔτε νίγενω σε: σέν for σέ, P Lond 417¹⁰ (*c.* A.D. 346) (= II. p. 299, *Selections*, p. 124), ἐπειδὴ ἀσχολῶ ἐλθῖν πρὸ[ς] σὲν αὐτεημερέ (*l.* αὐταὶ ἡμέραι): ἐσοῦ for σοῦ, P Oxy III. 531³ (ii/A.D.) τοὺς μετ' ἐσοῦ πάντας, *ib.* I. 119⁴ (ii/iii A.D.) (= *Selections*, p. 103) ἢ οὐ θέλις ἀπενέκκειν (*l.* ἀπενεγκεῖν) μετ' ἐσοῦ εἰς 'Αλεξανδρίαν : cf. also Dieterich *Untersuch.* p. 100 ff. For the phrase τί ἐμοὶ καὶ σοί; in J² ⁴, see *s.v.* ἐγώ, and add a note by C. Lattey in *JTS* xx. (1919), p. 335 f., where the words are taken as = "let me be." See also Epict. iv. 2. 8 μηδέν σοι καὶ αὐτοῖς . . . ἔστω .

συγγένεια,

"kinship," and hence collectively "kinsfolk," "kindred" (Lk 1⁶¹, Ac 7³·¹⁴) : cf. P Oxy III. 487⁹ (A.D. 156), where a petitioner states that he had been appointed guardian to two minors seeing that neither on their father's nor on their mother's side had they any other persons who could undertake the duty from ties of kinship—ἐκ {κ} τῆς συγγενίας αὐτῶν, and P Bouriant 25¹⁵ (v/A.D.) προσαγόρευε πᾶσαν τὴν συγγένειαν ἡμῶν. See also the sepulchral inser. *Syll* 805 (= ³1245⁴ (iii/A.D.) ὁ πατήρ με ἀνέστησε ἥρωα συγγενείας cum *Lare familiari* Romanorum—Ed.).

συγγενεύς,

"relative." The dat. plur. συγγενεῦσι (Mk 6⁴, Lk 2⁴⁴, 1 Macc 10⁸⁹ A—WH *Notes²*, p. 165) can be cited from the Pisidian inser. *JHS* xxii. (1902), p. 358 No. 118 : but συγγενέσι is found in P Par 15²¹ (B.C. 120), P Tebt I. 61(*b*)⁷⁹ (B.C. 118–7), *al.*

συγγενής,

"relative," with reference to blood-relationship : cf. P Grenf II. 78¹³ (A.D. 307) συγγε[νεῖς ἀ]δελφοί, and P Fay I. 115¹ (A.D. 101) ἀγόρασον ἡμῖν δύωι συγγενῆ χυρίδια (*l.* συγγενῆ χοιρίδια), "buy us two pigs of a litter" (Edd.). See also Aristeas 7 οὐ μόνον κατὰ τὸ συγγενὲς ἀδελφῷ καθεστῶτι, "not only does thy character shew thee to be my brother by birth" (Thackeray).

The word is common along with κύριος in the sense of "guardian kinsman" : e.g. BGU III. 975¹³ (A.D. 45) (= *Selections*, p. 42) μετὰ γυρίου τοῦ ἑαυτῆς συγγηνὸς Σαταβοῦς, "along with her guardian kinsman Satabous," P Tebt II. 381⁵ (A.D. 123) (= *Selections*, p. 77) Θαῆσις . . . μετὰ κυρίου τοῦ ἑαυτῆς συγγενοῦς Κρονίωνος, *ib.* 311¹¹ (A.D. 134), and P Lond 903⁸ (early ii/A.D.) (= III. p. 116).

For the extension of the word to denote all of the same *nationality* (as in Rom 9³) or of the same *tribe* (as in Rom 16⁷·¹¹·²¹), see W. M. Ramsay *Cities* p. 177 f. For the first of these uses we may cite the difficult phrase συγγενεῖς κάτοικοι, as in P Tebt I. 61(*b*)⁷⁹ (B.C. 118–7) τῶν στρατευομένων ἐν τοῖς συγ[γ]ενέσι τῶν κατοίκων ἱππέων, *ib.* 62⁷⁸ (B.C. 119–8) συγγενῶν κατοίκων ἱππέων : see GH *ad ib.* 32⁹, where the suggestion is thrown out that the class referred to is perhaps to be connected with an arrangement by "nationalities." Schubart (*Archiv* ii. p. 153) thinks that the reference is rather to a special class of κάτοικοι, perhaps "a more distinguished regiment" ("ein vornehmeres Regiment").

In any case this may lead us to the use of συγγενής as the highest honorific title introduced by the Ptolemies : cf. the OT apocryphal books and the use of "cousin" by the King of England : see e.g. P Amh II. 36¹ (*c.* B.C. 135) βοήθω[ι] συγγενεῖ καὶ ἐπιστρα]τηγῶι καὶ στρα[τ]ηγῶι τῆς Θηβ[αίδ]ος, and from the inserr. OGIS 104² (*c.* B.C. 190) Χρύσερμον . . . τὸν συγγενῆ βασιλέως Πτολεμαίου καὶ ἐξηγητήν, *ib.*

137⁹ (B.C. 140–110) Λόχον τὸν συγγενέα [καὶ] στρατηγόν, and *Perg* 248²⁷ (B.C. 135–4) 'Αθήναιος ὁ Σωσάνδρου υἱός, τοῦ γενομένου ἱερέως τοῦ Καθηγεμόνος [Δι]ονύσου καὶ συντρόφου τοῦ πατρός μου, ὅτι μὲν ἡμῶν ἐστι συ[γ]γενής.

συγγενίς,

"kinswoman," a late form (Lob. *Phryn.* p. 451 f.), is found in the NT only in Lk 1³⁶ : cf. P Amh II. 78⁹ (A.D. 184) τῇ συγγενίδι μου . . . πρὸς γάμον συνελθ[ώ]ν, "being married to my kinswoman," and from the inser. *BCH* xxiv. (1900), p. 339¹⁷ συνγενίδος. See also Blass-Debrunner § 59. 3 and *Psalter Gr.* p. 152.

συγγνώμη.

See *s.v.* συνγνώμη.

συγκ—

See *passim* συνκ—

συγκυρία.

With the phrase κατὰ συγκυρίαν in Lk 10³¹ we may compare κατὰ δέ τινα συν[τυχεί]αν τελευτήσαντος αὐτοῦ ἐν τῆι Διο(σπόλ)ει in P Tor II. 8¹·³ (B.C. 110). For the verb see P Hib I. 82¹² (B.C. 239–8) περὶ τῶν εἰς ταῦτα συγκυρόντων, "in all that concerns this," and its common use in connexion with the "appurtenances" of a house, e.g. P Tebt II. 381¹² (A.D. 123) (= *Selections*, p. 78) οἰκίαν καὶ αὐλὴν καὶ τὰ συνκύρωντα (for form see OGIS p. 117) πάντα. Συγκυρέω is similarly used in P Oxy VI. 907⁹ (A.D. 276) χρηστήρια καὶ συνκυροῦντα πάντα, "utensils and all appurtenances." In the Greek Pentateuch συνκυροῦντα is one of the four terms to denote "suburbs" (see Thackeray *Gr.* i. p. 4 n.¹) : cf. P Lond 604² (A.D. 47) (= III. p. 71) παρὰ . . . Σωτη[ρίχ]ο[υ] κωμογραμμ[ατέως] Κροκοδείλων πόλεως καὶ τ[ῶν σ]υνκυρουσῶν κωμῶν.

συγχ—

See *passim* συνχ—

σύγχυσις,

"confusion," "disturbance" (Ac 19²⁹) : cf. P Flor I. 36¹⁰ (beg. iv/A.D.) τὸν γάμον ἐν συνχίσι (*l.* συγχύσ(ε)ι) ποιῆσαι, P Cairo Preis 4¹⁵ (A.D. 320) ἵνα μηδεμία σ[ύ]νχυσις κατὰ τοὺς αὐτοὺς (*sc.* καρποὺς) γένηται, ἐπιδίδωμι κτλ., and *Syll* 316 (= ³684)⁷ (B.C. 139?) ἀρχηγὸς τῆς ὅλης συγχύσεως. See also Epicurus *Ep.* II. 88 οὗ (*sc.* κόσμου) λυομένου πάντα τὰ ἐν αὐτῷ σύγχυσιν λήψεται, "whose dissolution will cause all within it to fall into confusion" (Bailey), and Cicero *ad Att.* vi. 9. 1 σύγχυσιν *litterarum*, vii. 8. 4 σύγχυσιν τῆς πολιτείας.

The verb συγχόω is seen in BGU II. 530¹⁰ (i A.D.) (= *Selections*, p. 61) ὁ ὑδραγωγὸς συνεχώσθη ὑπὸ τῆς ἄμμου, "the water-channel was choked with sand," and similarly P Tebt I. 50¹⁰·²¹ (B.C. 112–1). Cf. also P Lon i 1177³¹³ (A.D. 113) (= III. p. 189).

συζ—

See συνζ—

συκάμινος,

"a mulberry tree" (Lk 17⁶) : cf. P Cairo Zen I. 59083³ (B.C. 257) συκάμινος Ϲ, where Ϲ is perhaps = ἡμιωβέλιον,

P Leid C[iv. 14] (B.C. 160–150) (= *UPZ* i. p. 403) [[ζύτον]] συκαμίνου (δραχμὰς) ϛ, P Grenf II. 16[1] (B.C. 137) πεπρακέναι τὴν ὑπάρχουσαν αὐτοῖς συκάμινον, P Tebt II. 343[86] (ii/A.D.) συκάμινος α φοι(νικῶνος) ᾱ, BGU II. 492[7] (A.D. 148–9) π]ροκειμένη συκαμείνω κλάδο[. . ., and P Lond 121[223] (iii/A.D.) (= I. p. 91) γάλα συκαμίνου.

See also the form συκαμίνεον in P Flor I. 50[32, 66] (A.D. 268), and the compd. in P Hib I. 70 (*a*)[5] (B.C. 229–8) ἀρο(υρῶν) κ̅ συκαμινοακανθίνου λιτοῦ, "20 arourae of smooth (?) mulberry-acanthus land" (Edd.). The adj. συκαμίνινος is found in P Cairo Zen II. 50188[6] (B.C. 255) περὶ τοῦ πλοίου τοῦ συκαμινίνου συντάξαι, and P Flor II. 247[22] (A.D. 256) τὸ ξύλον τὸ συκαμείνινον. See also s.v. συκομορέα.

σνκῆ.

"fig-tree" (Mt 21[19], *al.*): PSI V. 499[6] (B.C. 257–6) σπούδασον δὲ καὶ κράδας ἀποστεῖλαι τῶν σύκων. For the adj. σύκινος see P Cairo Zen I. 50033[12] (B.C. 257) σύκινα Χῖα, "Chian jars containing figs," and P Tebt II. 513 (ii/iii A.D.) τὸ σύκινον ξυλάριον, τὸ ἐν τῷ πλινθουργίῳ κοπήτω.

σνκομορέα.

"a fig-mulberry" (Lk 19[4]), to be distinguished from συκάμινος (Lk 17[6]), "a mulberry." Hobart (p. 152) thinks that the distinction may be due to Luke's medical knowledge, seeing that both trees were used medicinally. For the spelling -έα for -αία, cf. Moulton *Gr.* ii. p. 84.

σῦκον.

"a fig": P Cairo Zen II. 50269[8] (B.C. 234) σ]ύκων καὶ ῥόων, "figs and roses," BGU IV. 1120[16] (B.C. 5) δισχίλια σῦκα, P Oxy III. 520[6] (ii/A.D.) σφυρίδιν τραγημάτων ἔχω (= οἶν ἀρίθμια σῦκα ρ, "a basket of dessert containing 100 figs" (Edd.), *ib.* XIV. 1631[24] (A.D. 280) σύκων θερινῶν . . τετρακοσίων, "400 summer figs," and P Flor II. 176[10] (A.D. 256) ἐκ τῆς τῶν σύκων κακίας. This last document shows us also the dimin. συκάριον—[9] τέσσαρα κερτύλλια συκαρίων σαπρῶν. With our "as like as two peas" cf. Herodas VI. 60 σῦκον εἰκάσαι σύκῳ. For συκῶν, "fig-garden," as in LXX Jer 5[17], see BGU II. 563[ii.3] (ii/A.D.).

σνκοφαντέω.

This verb, which is fairly common in the LXX, but in the NT occurs only in Lk 3[14], 19[8], is used in P Par 61[10] (B.C. 156), where an official warns a subordinate against certain persons who were making unfair claims—ἐνίων δὲ καὶ συκοφαντεῖσθαι προφερομένων—as being contrary to the humane rule of the Ptolemies ([11f.] ὅτι (ταῦτα) πάντα ἐστὶν ἀλλότρια τῆς τε ἡμῶν ἀγωγῆς): cf. *ib.* [16] μ]άλιστα δὲ τῶν συκοφαντεῖν ἐπιχειρούντων [τελωνῶν. The sense of "accuse falsely" rather than "exact wrongly" which Field (*Notes*, p. 56f.) prefers in the two NT passages (cf. W. M. Ramsay in Hastings' *DB* V. p. 396 note) comes out still more strongly in P Tebt I. 43[26] (B.C. 118) συκοφαντηθῶμεν, "be subject to false accusations" (Edd.): cf. *ib.* [36] συκοφαντίας τε καὶ διασισμοῦ χάριν, "for the sake of calumny or extortion" (Edd.), also P Oxy III. 472[33] (c. A.D. 130) οὐ γὰρ . . . τοῦτο αὐτοῖς εἰς συκοφαντίαν εὕρημα, "this does not afford them an excuse for calumnies"

(Edd.), and *OGIS* 383[157] (mid. i/B.C.) ὅπως ἕκαστος . . . ἀσυκοφάντητον ἔχῃ τὴν ἑορτὴν εὐωχούμενος, i.e. enjoy the feast undisturbed by the calumnies of men. The same sense appears in P Flor III. 382[57] (A.D. 222–3) ὑπὸ τοῦ πραγματικοῦ σε[[*]]συκοφαντη[μ]ένος as would appear from ὅπερ μου κα[τε]ψεύδετο in the next line.

Other exx. of the verb are P Cairo Zen II. 50212[4] (B.C. 254) ὅπως . . . [ὑπὸ μ]ηθενὸς συκοφαντηθῶσι, *Chrest.* I. 238[3] (c. A.D. 117) where the strategus writes warning his subordinate to see to it that the measuring of the seed should be so conducted that the native population shall not suffer, ὅπως μὴ βαρηθῶσιν ἢ παραπραχθῶσιν οἱ ἐνχώριοι ἢ συκοφαντηθῶσιν, and CPR I. 232[3] (ii/iii A.D.) where ὁμολό[γη]μα τοῖς συκοφαντουμένοις is followed by a reference to [6] ψευδο]μαρτυρίαν. The subst. occurs in P Flor I. 6[6] (A.D. 210) in connexion with fiscal matters, τὸ τακτὸν εἰς τὸ πρόστειμον τῆς συκοφαντίας: see the editor's note. On the origin of the term συκοφάντης, see A. B. Cook's art. in *CR* xxi. (1907) p. 133ff., in which he shows that the word means originally "one who shows the fig," i.e. "one who makes with his hand the sign known as 'the fig,'" a prophylactic gesture implying "misrepresent in an outrageous fashion."

σνλαγωγέω.

In Col 2[8], the only place where the verb occurs in the NT. Field (*Notes*, p. 195) prefers the translation "rob" to the RV "make spoil of," on the ground that the latter suggests "the idea of the Colossians themselves being carried off, instead of their (spiritual) treasures," and by way of illustration he points to Aristaen. *Ep.* II. 22 τοῦτον κατέλαβον, ἄνερ, ἐγχειροῦσα συλαγωγῆσαι τὸν ἡμέτερον οἶκον. But the RV rendering may find support from Heliodor. 10. 35 p. 307 Bekker οὗτός ἐστιν ὁ τὴν ἐμὴν θυγατέρα συλαγωγήσας (cited by Dibelius *HZNT ad l.*).

σνλάω,

"rob." Exx. of this NT ἅπ. εἰρ. (2 Cor 11[8]) are common in (*a*) the papyri—P Ryl II. 138[19] (A.D. 34) ἐσύλησέν μου ἐν τῶι πύργωι ἱκανὰ ἀργαλε⟨ῖ⟩α, "he robbed me of a number of tools in the tower" (Edd.), BGU IV. 1036[28] (A.D. 108) συλήσαντες ὅσα [ἔ]χωι ἐν τῇ κέλλαι, P Tebt II. 330[5] (ii/A.D.) εὗρον τὴν οἰκίαν μου σεσυλημένην, "I found my house pillaged," P Gen I. 47[9] (A.D. 346) μέχρι δεῦρο μηδὲν εὑρηκέναι με ἀπὸ τῶν συληθέντων, and P Lond 412[8] (A.D. 351) (= II. p. 280) ἐσύλησέν με ἔνδων τῆς οἰκείας: (*b*) the inscrr.—*Syll* 190 (= [3] 372)[5] (B.C. 288–281) ἐγχειρήσαντας συλῆσαι τὰ ἀναθήματ[α, *OGIS* 437[59] (i B.C.) ἐὰν δέ τις συλη[θ]ῆι ἢ ἀδικη[θῆι Σαρδιανῶν κτλ., and *Kaibel Addenda* 545 c[1] (= p. 528) Τίς Πλάταιαν σύλησεν;

For the subst. σύλησις see P Oxy VIII. 1121[6] (A.D. 295) ἐκείνοις τοῖς εὐχερῶς συλήσει καὶ ἁρπαγαῖς τῶν ἀλλοτρίων ἑαυτοὺς ἐπιδίδουσι, "those who lightly give themselves over to plunder and robbery of the property of others" (Ed.).

σνλλ—

See *passim* συνλ—

συλλαμβάνω,

(1) "arrest," "seize," as in Mt 26⁵⁵, *al.* : P Cairo Zen II. 59202² (B.C. 254) ὀρθῶς ἐποίησας συλλαβὼν τὸν ἐκ τοῦ ζυτοπωλίου ταμίαν, "You have done rightly in arresting the steward attached to the beer-house," P Hib I. 54²⁰ (*c.* B.C. 245) (= *LAE²*, p. 165) τὸ σῶμα δὲ εἰ συνείληφας παράδος [αὐτὸ]] Σεμφθεῖ, "if you have arrested the slave, deliver him to Semphtheus." P Ryl II. 145¹⁰ (A.D. 38) συνλαβὼν Ἀρτεμίδωρον, "having caught Artemidorus" with hostile intent, P Oxy II. 283¹² (A.D. 45) συνέλαβον τὸν σημαινόμενον δοῦλον, "I seized the above-mentioned slave," and P Tebt II. 304¹¹ (A.D. 167–8) τὸν ἀδελφόν μου Ὀννῶφρις (= ριν) συλ⟨λ⟩αβόντες τραυματιαιων(= αῖον) ἐποίησαν, "seizing my brother Onnophris they wounded him" (Edd.) ; (2) "help," "assist," as in Lk 5⁷, Phil 4³ ; P Giss I. 11¹² (A.D. 118) (= *Chrest.* I. p. *523*) καλῶς οὖν ποι[ήσ]ῃς, φίλτατε, σ[υ]νλαβόμενος τοὺς ἐμούς. *ib.* 25¹ (ii/A.D.) συνλαμβανόμενός μοι ἐν τῷ πράγματι, *ib.* 75³ (ii/A.D.) παρακ`αλῶ σε, ἄδελφε, συνλαβέσθαι [Ἀπολλ]ωνίωι, and P Oxy VII. 1064⁷ (iii/A.D.) γράφω σοι οὖν εἰδώς σου τὸ σπουδαῖον ὅπως συνλάβῃς τῷ Ἄπει, "so knowing your goodness I write to you that you may assist Apis" (Ed.) ; (3) "conceive," as in Lk 1²⁴, *al.* : see exx. from medical writers in Hobart p. 91 f.

Συνλήβδην, "in sum," "in general," occurs in P Fay 21⁷ (A.D. 134). For σύλληψις see *OGIS* 90¹⁷ (Rosetta stone— B.C. 196) with the editor's note, also Preisigke *Fachwörter* s.v., and for συλλήπτωρ see *OGIS* 654² (i/B.C.) N]είλωι συνλήπτορι χαριστήρια.

συλλέγω,

"bring together," "collect" : P Oxy IV. 743³¹ (B.C. 2) τὰ νῦν ἐπιπέπομφα αὐτὸν πάντα συνλέξαι, "now I have dispatched him to collect them all (*sc.* rents)," P Flor III. 356¹⁶ (i/ii A.D.) συλλέγω(ν) τὰ ἐ[κ]φόρια, *ib.* II. 127⁶ (A.D. 256) ἄχ[υρ]ον πανταχόθεν συλλέξας ἵνα θερμῶς λουσώμεθα` χειμῶνος ὄντος, "he collected chaff from all quarters that we might wash in hot water during winter," P Oxy VIII. 1160¹⁶ (iii/iv A.D.) τὰ σεσύλληχα (for συνεί- \ηχα) δὲ κέρμα⟨τα⟩ τηρῶ αὐτὰ εἰς τὴν δίκην, "I am keeping for the trial the money that I have collected" (Ed.), and P Grenf II. 77¹¹ (iii/iv A.D.) (= *Selections*, p. 120) σ[υ]νλέξαντες ὅσα εἶχεν καὶ οὕτως ἀπέστητε, "having collected all that he had you then went off."

For the verb with reference to speech, a use not found in the NT, see PSI IV. 368²¹ (iii/B.C.) συνέλεγον αὐτῶι 'ἀπ[όδ]ος τὸ ἐν[νό]μιον τῶν αἰγῶν,' and cf. *ib.* 382² (iii/B.C.) γινώσκεις ὅτι συνειπάμεθά σοι τὴν πρωίραν ἐπισκευὰν τοῦ πλοίου.

The subst. συλλογή is seen in the astrological P Tebt II. 276³² (ii/iii A.D.) συνλογὴν χρημά[των π]οιησάμενος ἐξωδιασμὸν αὐτῶν [ποιήσ]εται καὶ ἀπώλειαν, "after collecting a fortune he will spend and lose it" (Edd.), and P Cairo Preis 4¹² (A.D. 320) πρὸς τὴν τούτων συλλογήν, "for the collection of these (*sc.* fruits)."

συλλογίζομαι,

"reason together" (Lk 20⁵), is found with the meaning "compute" in such passages as P Tebt I. 82³ (B.C. 115),

P Lond 259¹³⁷ (A.D. 90–5) (= II. p. 41), and *Syll* 510 (= ³ 364)¹³ (after B.C. 207) συλλογισάμενοι τό τε δάνεον καὶ τὴν τίμη[σιν.

ουμβ—

See *passim* συνβ

συμβαίνω

is common of events = "come to pass," "happen" : P Petr II. 19 (2)⁸ (iii B.C.) δέομαι οὖν σου βοηθῆσαί μοι ἵνα μὴ συνβῆι μοι καὶ ἐν τῆι φυλακῆι καταφθαρῆναι, PSI IV. 340¹ (B.C. 257–6) νῦν οὖν συμβαίνει αὐτῶι ἀσχ[η]μονεῖν, P Hamb I. 27² (B.C. 250) συνέβη οὖν μοι ἐνοχληθῆναι ("be engaged"?) ἐμ Φιλαδελφείαι, BGU IV. 1060²³ (time of Augustus) ἡμᾶς δὲ συμβαίνει τὰ καθήκοντα αὐτῶν διορθοῦσθαι, P Oxy I. 105³ (Will—A.D. 117–137) ἐὰν δὲ συμβῆ . . . ἀδιάθετον τελευτῆσαι, "if I should happen to die with this will unchanged," P Tebt II. 335¹⁹ (mid. iii A.D.) ἐκεῖ οὐκοῦν συμβέβ`ηκε, "there therefore it happened," and P Oxy VII. 1065³ (iii/A.D.) διὰ τὰ συμβάντα μοι. In *ib.* I. 52¹¹ (A.D. 325) we have a report regarding a daughter who had been injured ἐκ τοῦ συμβάντος πτώματος τῆς οἰκίας αὐτοῦ, "by the fall of his (her father's) house which had occurred" (Edd.).

συμβουλεύω.

"advise," "counsel," (1) act. : cf. BGU IV. 1097⁸ (Claudius Nero) (as amended *Berichtigungen*, p. 97) οὐ καλῶς ἐπο[ί]ησας συνβουλεύσας αὐτῶι στρατεύσασθαι, P Oxy XIV. 1762¹¹ (ii/iii A.D.) ἵνα αὐτῷ περὶ τούτων συμβον[λε]ύσης ; cf. the pass. in *ib.* I. 118³ (late iii/A.D.) συμβουλευθέντες ὑπὸ τοῦ ἀξιολογωτάτου Ἀμμωνίωνος. (2) mid. : P Petr II. 13 (6)¹³ (B.C. 258–3) (as amended III. p. 110) ὡς ἂν σ[υ]νβουλευσαμένωι φα[ί]νηται, "as it shall appear to you after you have considered the matter," *OGIS* 441¹⁹ (B.C. 81) Λεύκιος . [. Σύλλας Ἐπαφρόδιτος δικτάτωρ συγκλήτωι συ[νεβούλευσατο πρὸ ἡμερῶν ἕξ], and see Herwerden *Lex. s.v.*

συμβούλιον.

This rare word = "council," as in Ac 25¹², is well illustrated by P Tebt II. 286¹⁵ (A.D. 121–138) where the presiding judge is described as ἀνασ[τὰ]ς εἰς [σ]υμ[β]ούλιον κ[αὶ σκεψάμ[ενος . . . (as restored by Wilcken *Archiv* v. p. 232) : cf. also Ac 26³⁰. Other instances of the word are BGU I. 288¹³ (A.D. 138–161) κ[α]θημένων ἐν συμβουλίῳ ἐν τῷ πραι[τωρίῳ, II. 511¹⁵ (written *c.* A.D. 200) ἐ]ν συμβουλείῳ . . . . ἐκάθισεν, and P Ryl II. 75²⁹ (judicial proceedings—late ii/A.D.) ἐν τῷ συμβουλίῳ εἶπεν.

Similarly we may cite *Syll* 316 (= ³ 684)¹¹ (ii/B.C.) μετὰ τοῦ πα[ρ]όν[το]ς (σ)υνβουλίου, *ib.* 328 (= ³741)⁸ (after B.C. 88) ἐπὶ τοῦ συνβουλίο[υ, = *coram consilio*, and *ib.* 334 (= ³747)⁷·²⁰ *al.* (B.C. 73).

σύμβουλος,

"counsellor," "adviser" (Rom 11³⁴ LXX) : P Petr II. 13 (6)¹¹ (B.C. 258–253) γέγραφα δέ σοι . . . [σύμ]βουλόν σε εἰς τὸ πρᾶγμα λαβεῖν, where the writer asks advice regarding a building contract. In a v/A.D. school-book PSI I. 19⁶ᶠᶠ the questions are put—Τίς στρατηγός ; Ἕκτωρ. Τίνες σύμβουλοι; Πολυδάμας καὶ Ἀ[γ]ήνωρ, and in a sepulchral inscr. at Alexandria *Preisigke* 1990 (A.D. 319) a certain Antoninus is addressed συνκοπιάτα σύνβουλε ἀγαθέ.

Συμεών.

This name is found in P Amh II. 152[11.22] (v/vi A.D.) : see also Preisigke *Namenbuch s.v.* Deissmann (*BS*, p. 310) suggests that the use of Συμεών (for Σίμων) in Ac 15[14] may be due to the solemn character of James's speech.

συμμ—

See *passim* συνμ—

συμμορφίζω,

"share the form of" (see *s.v.* μορφή), and hence "share the experience of," is found only in Phil 3[10] and ecclesiastical writers.

συμπ—

See *passim* συνπ—

συμπαθής,

"sharing the experiences" of others (1 Pet 3[8]) : cf. *OGIS* 456[66] (B.C. 27–11) προσενηνεγμένης αὐτῆς (*sc.* τῆς συγκλήτου) τῇ πόλει συμπαθέστατα. For the subst. cf. *ib.* 470[24] (time of Augustus) τῇ τῶν Ἑλλήνων συνπα[θείᾳ. In Epicurus συμπάθεια has often the general meaning "correspondence," e.g. *Ep.* I. 48, 50 (ed. Bailey). Συμπαθηθῆναι is one of the numerous list of passive aorists which are found in the Byzantine chronicles, though not in Attic Greek : see Psaltes *Gr.* p. 226.

συμπόσιον,

orig. "a drinking party," "a banquet," e.g. *Preisigke* 1100[5] (Ptol.) οἱ συνπόσιοι γενόμενοι φιλαγαθίας ἕνεκεν τῆς εἰς ἑαυτούς. From this it is an easy transition to the "room" in which the party was given (Hesych. : συμπόσιον· τόπος εὐωχίας καὶ πόσεως) : cf. P Ryl II. 233[5] (ii/A.D.) τοῦ μεικροῦ συμποσίου, "the small dining-room," P Oxy VIII. 1128[14] (A.D. 173), the lease at a rent of 20 drachmae per annum of a dining-room and the store-chamber within it— τὸ συμπόσιον καὶ τὴν ἐντὸς αὐτοῦ κέλλαν, *ib.* I. 76[19] (A.D. 179) συμπόσιον καὶ κοιτῶνα, and *ib.* VIII. 1159[26] (late iii/A.D.) ἔνεγκον τὸ τυλάριον τ[ὸ] παλαιὸν τὸ ἐν τῷ συμποσίῳ ἄνω, "bring the old cushion that is up in the dining-room" (Ed.). In P Flor I. 5[7] (A.D. 244–5) συμπόσιον ὑπερῷον, συμπόσιον appears to be used as an adj. In Mk 6[39] συμπόσια συμπόσια the word is extended to the "companies" of diners : the construction can no longer be regarded as Hebraistic, see *Proleg.* p. 97.

συμφ—

See *passim* συνφ—

συμφέρω.

From its trans. use "bring together," as in Ac 19[19], συμφέρω passes into the intrans. sense "come together," as e.g. of marriage union in P Oxy III. 496[10] (A.D. 127) σ]υνφερομένων δ' αὐτῶν εἴη μὲν ὑγεία, "when they come together, may they enjoy health," and so *ib.* 497[11] (early /A.D.).

The impers. συμφέρει, "it is expedient," is specially common, e.g. P Fay 112[17] (A.D. 99) συνφέρι γὰρ . . . . αὐτὸν [σ]καφῆναι, "for it is an advantage that it should be dug," P Oxy III. 471[14] (speech of an advocate—ii/A.D.) συνφέ[ρει τοί]νυν τοὔλαττο[ν μόν]ον ὁμολογεῖν, "it is best to acknowledge only the lesser fault" (Edd.), P Ryl II. 244[11] (iii/A.D.) οὐ συμφέρει ἀγοράσαι, "it is inexpedient to buy," P Oxy I. 121[21] (iii/A.D.) οὕτως ποίησον, καὶ συνφέρει, and *ib.* IX. 1220[19] (iii/A.D.) τοῦτο συνφέρι εἶνα (for constr. cf. Mt 5[29] : *Proleg.* p. 210) μὴ ἀπόληται ἀμελίᾳ, "this will be of use to prevent their perishing of neglect" (Ed.). For the participle, as in Ac 20[20], Heb 12[10], cf. PSI IV. 440[15] (iii/B.C.) πρὸς τὸ συμφέρον αὐτῶι, and P Amh II. 33[25] (c. B.C. 157) τούτου γὰρ γενομένου οὐθὲν τῶν ὑμῖν συμφερόντων διαπεσεῖται, "for if this is done, your interests will not suffer damage" (Edd.).

σύμφορος.

For τὸ σύμφορον used as a subst. = "profit," "advantage," as in 1 Cor 7[35], 10[33], cf. P Oxy XIV. 1676[25] (iii/A.D.) τὸ σύνφορόν σοι ποίει, "do what suits you" (Edd.). For συμφορά see P Oxy VIII. 1121[15] (A.D. 295) ὡς ἐμοῦ περὶ τὴν συμφορὰν οὔσης, "while I was occupied with my trouble" (Ed.), and Bacchyl. XIII. 31 συμφορὰ δ' ἐσθλόν τ' ἀμαλδύνει βαρύτλατος μολοῦσα, "fortune can crush worth, if she comes fraught with suffering" (Jebb).

συμφυλέτης.

"fellow-countryman." For the force of this word, which is found only in 1 Thess 2[14], cf. Milligan *Thess. ad l.* and Intr. p. liii. Rutherford *NP* p. 255 f. illustrates the frequency of similar compounds in late Greek.

σύμφυτος,

"cultivated," "planted" : cf. P Grenf II. 28[7] (B.C. 103) μερίδα ἀμπελῶ(νος) συνφύτου, BGU IV. 1120[36] (B.C. 5) τὰ μεμισθωμένα σύμφυτα καὶ εὐθηνοῦντα, "the land leased planted and flourishing," P Oxy IV. 729[22] (A.D. 137) σύνφυτο καὶ ἐπιμεμελημένα καὶ καθαρὰ ἀπό τε θρύου καὶ βοτάνης καὶ δείσης πάσης, "planted, well cared for, free from rushes, grass and weeds of all kinds" (Edd.), and *ib.* XIV. 1631[31] (A.D. 280) τὰ μισθούμενα σύμφυτα, "the land leased to us under cultivation." For σύμφυτος in Rom 6[5] = "grown along with," "united with," cf. Field *Notes*, p. 155, and for the subst. σύμφυσις see Kaibel 502[22] (iii/iv A.D.) μύσιν θεῶν τίς μοι δότω καὶ σύνφυσιν. The verb συμφύω occurs in P Ryl II. 427 Fr. 8[8].

συμφωνέω,

"agree with," "agree together" : P Lond 1166[4] (A.D. 42) (= III. p. 104) συνπεφωνηκέναι αὐτῶι, P Oxy II. 260[7] (A.D. 59) κα[τ]ὰ [τὰ] συ[μ]φωνηθέντα ἐμοὶ κα[ὶ] Ἀντ[ι]φ[ά]νει, "in accordance with what was agreed upon between me and Antiphanes" (cf. Ac 5[9]), *ib.* VIII. 1148[5] (question to the oracle—i/A.D.) εἰ βέλτειόν ἐστιν Φανίαν τὸν υἱό(ν) μου καὶ τὴν γυναῖκα αὐτοῦ μὴ συμφωνῆσαι νῦν τῷ πατρὶ α(ὐτοῦ) ἀλλὰ ἀντιλέγειν, "is it better for my son Phanias and his wife not to agree now with his father, but to oppose him?" (Ed.), *ib.* III. 530[23] (ii/A.D.) μὴ ἀγωνία δὲ περὶ ἡμῶν, οὐθὲν γὰρ φαῦλον περὶ ἡμᾶς ἐστ[ι]ν καὶ συμφωνοῦμεν ἀλλήλοις, "do not be anxious about us, for there is nothing the matter with us and we are at harmony with each other" (Edd.), *ib.* l. 133²⁵ (A.D. 550) **συμφωνῖ ἡμῖν πάντα τὰ ἐγεγραμμέ(να) ὡς πρόκιται**, " we agree to all that is herein contained, as it is above written " (Edd.), and *Syll* 540 (= ³972)⁸⁸ (B.C. 175-2) **συμφωνοῦντας πρὸς ἀλλήλους δοκίμως**.

The verb is used with reference to *price*, as in Mt 20¹³, in such passages as P Oxy XIV. 1672¹⁷ (A.D. 37-41) **ὁ φίλος συντυχὼν ἔλεγεν συμ[πε]φωνηκέναι τοῖς ἐκ τῆς κώ[μ]ης αὐτοῦ μετὰ χάριτος . . . ἐκ (δραχμῶν) λβ**, " our friend said that he had agreed with the people of his village thankfully at the rate of 32 drachmae " (Edd.), *ib.* IV. 728³⁷ (A.D. 142) **ἔσχον παρὰ σοῦ τὰς συνπεφωνημένας ὑπὲρ τιμῆς χόρτου ἀργυρί(ο)υ δραχμὰς διακοσίας ἑβδομήκοντα [ἕξ**. " I have received from you the 276 drachmae which were agreed upon for the price of the hay " (Edd.), and BGU II. 416⁵ (A.D. 150) **ἀπέχω τὴν συνπεπωνημένην (*l.* συνπεφωνημένην) τιμήν**, and *Syll* 241 (= ³535)⁹ (B.C. 217-6) **τὰ εἴκοσι τάλαντα τὰ συνφωνηθέντα ὑπὲρ τῶν αἰχμαλώτων**.

συμφώνησις,

" agreement," occurs in the NT only in 2 Cor 6¹⁵. For **συμφώνημα** see P Flor III. 379⁷ (ii/A.D.) in connexion with the settling of accounts.

συμφωνία

is fully discussed by Philipps Barry in *JBL* xxvii. part ii. (1908), p. 99 ff. (cf. also xxiii. part ii. (1904), p. 180 ff.), with the result that both in Dan 3³ and Lk 15²⁵ it is pronounced to be the name of a musical instrument, perhaps a " bagpipe." For the more general sense of " music," " symphony," cf. P Lond 968 (iii/A.D.) (= III. p. xlix) the fragment of an account, including an entry **ὑπὲρ συμφωνίας τυμπάνων**, and for the word = " a company of musicians," cf. P Flor II. 74⁵ (A.D. 181) **ὁμολογῶ παρειληφέναι ὑμᾶς μεθ' ἧς ἔχετε συμφωνίας πάσης μουσικῶν τε καὶ ἄλλων ὑπουργούντα[ς] . . . ἐν τῇ προκειμένῃ κώμῃ**, and P Oxy X. 1275⁹ (iii/A.D.) **ὁ προεστὼς συμφωνίας αὐλητῶν καὶ μουσικῶν**, cf.¹², ²⁴.

Συμφωνία is also found in a sense apparently unknown to classical Greek = " agreement " in such passages as P Oxy I. 104²⁰ (A.D. 96) **ὑπὲρ διαλύσεως καὶ συμφωνίας περὶ τῶν ὀφειλομένων ὑπ' ἐμοῦ τῷ . . . Ἀτρῇ**, P Rein 44¹⁵ (A.D. 104) **μετὰ τὸν τῆς συμφωνίας χρόνον τῆς γενομένης μεταξὺ αὐτοῦ καὶ Ἰσιδώρας**, and P Tebt II. 420⁹ (iii/A.D.) **(δραχμὰς) κη ὑπὲρ συμφωνίας τῆς ἀβρ<ό>χω(= ου)**, " 28 drachmae for the agreement concerning the unirrigated land."

σύμφωνος,

" agreeing ": cf. P Flor I. 48⁹ (A.D. 222) **συ]μφώνου γράμματος**, i.e. a contract agreeing with another contract already drawn up, P Gen I. 76¹⁹ (iii/iv A.D.) **οὐ σοινέθετο (*l.* συνέθετο) σύνφωνα**, and P Oxy VI. 914⁹ (A.D. 486) **κατὰ τὰ μεταξὺ [σύμφ]ωνα**, " according to the agreement between us." Cf. *Syll* 653 (= ³736)¹⁰¹ (B.C. 92) **σταθμοῖς καὶ μέτροις συμφώνοις ποτὶ τὰ δαμόσια**.

For the phrase **ἐκ συμφώνου**, " by agreement," as in 1 Cor 7⁵, cf. P Par 63¹⁵² (B.C. 164), CPR I. 11¹¹ (A.D. 108), P Ryl II. 162¹⁶ (A.D. 159) **καθὼς ἐκξυ(μ)φώνου ὑπηγό-**

PART VII.

ρευσαν, " as stated by mutual consent " (Edd.), and P Oxy XII. 1473²⁸ (A.D. 201). The corr. adv. **συμφώνως** occurs in P Oxy VII. 1032¹⁴ (A.D. 162).

συμψηφίζω.

For this verb, which is found in the NT only in Ac 19¹⁹ = " reckon up," cf. a London papyrus of A.D. 114-115 edited by H. I. Bell in *Archiv* vi. p. 102⁸ **ἕτεραν τόπον ἐπιτήδειον τοῦ εἰς τὴν ἀνοικοδομὴν συνεψηφίσθαι δραχμὰς τρι[σ]χιλείας κτλ**. For the adj. Preisigke (*Wörterb.*) recalls PSI V. 452²³ (iv/A.D.) **οὐδ' οὕτω ὁ λογιστὴς σύμψηφος αὐτῶν ταῖς εἰρωνίαις γίνεται**.

σύν.

This " aristocrat " among the prepositions as compared with **ἐν** the " maid of all work " is comparatively rare in the NT, having given place, as it did in Attic Greek, to **μετά** c. gen. (cf. Blass *Gr.* p. 132).

(1) For its general meaning " with," either " along with " or " in addition to," we may note—P Tebt I. 43⁸ (B.C. 118) **παρεγενήθημεν εἰς ἀπάντησιν σὺν τῶι τῆς κώμης κωμάρχωι [καὶ] τινων τῶν πρεσβυτέρων τῶν [γ]εωργῶν**, " we came to meet him together with the komarch of the village and some of the elders of the cultivators " (Edd.), *ib.* 13⁴ (B.C. 114) **ἐφοδεύοντός μου σὺν Ὥρωι κω(μάρχηι) καὶ Πατάνι . . . [[τὰ ἐν]] περὶ τὴν κώμην χωματικὰ ἔργα**, " as I was inspecting, in company with Horus the komarch and Patanis, the embankment works near the village " (Edd.), *ib.* 20² (B.C. 113) **πεπόμφ⟨α⟩με[ν] Ἀράχθην σὺν τοῖς κωμογραμματεῦσι ἐσόμενον μέχρι τοῦ με παραγενέσθαι**, " I have sent Arachthes to be with the komogrammateis until I come " (Edd.), BGU II. 393⁹ (A.D. 168) **ἐνοικίου τοῦ παντὸς κατ' ἔτος σὺν παντὶ λόγῳ** (*summa summarum*) **ἀργυρίου δραχμῶν εἴκοσι τεσσάρων**, P Flor I. 91¹⁸ (ii/A.D.) **ὅ[πως δυνηθῶ ἐν τῇ ἰ]δίᾳ συμμένων σὺν γυναικὶ καὶ τέκνοις**, " in order that I may be able to remain in my own house along with my wife and children," P Lond 343⁶ (A.D. 188) (= II. p. 214) **ὀφίλις μοι σὺν ἑτέροις ἐπὶ λόγου δραχμὰς διακοσίας**, PSI III. 208⁷ (iv/A.D.) **τοὺς σὺν σοι πάντας ἀδελφούς**, and the address of the Christian letter P Oxy XIV. 1774²¹ (early iv/A.D.) **κυρείᾳ μου ἀδελφῇ Ἀτιενατείη Διδύμη σὺν ταῖς ἀ[δελφαῖς**.

(2) The preposition is also further applied to those engaged in the same work or office—P Oxy II. 242³³ (A.D. 77) **Ἀρθοῶνις Ἀρθοώ(νιος) καὶ οἱ σὺν αὐτῷ ἱερεῖ(ς)**, BGU IV. 1028¹⁹ (ii/A.D.) **Νίννῳ καὶ τοῖς σὺν αὐτῷ ἡλοκόπ(οις)** (" nail-smiths ") **τειμὴν ἥ[λ]ων**, *ib.* III. 607⁶ (A.D. 140) **Ἰσχυρίων Ἀφροδ(ισίου) καὶ οἱ σὺν αὐτῷ ἐπιτη(ρηταί)**, P Gen I. 36¹⁰ (A.D. 170) (= *Chrest.* I. p. 112) **παρὰ Πεκύσιος Σαταβοῦτος ἱερέως σὺν ἑτέροις ἱερεῦ[σ]ι ἱεροῦ θεοῦ μεγίστου**, and P Oxy I. 91⁸ (A.D. 187) **ὁμολογῶ ἀπεσχηκέναι παρὰ σοῦ διὰ Ἡλιοδώρου καὶ τῶν σὺν αὐτῷ ἐπιτρηρητῶν**.

(3) For the thought of the assistance or the will of God, *deo volente*, we may cite the recurring **σὺν θεῷ** or **σὺν θεοῖς**—P Tebt I. 58 *recto*³⁵ (B.C. 111) (= *Chrest.* I. p. 358 f.) **ὥστ' ἂν σὺν τοῖς θεοῖς καταστοχήσαμεν αὐτοῦ**, " so by the grace of the gods we shall win him over(?)," and *ib.* *verso*⁵⁸ **σὺν τοῖς θεοῖς σχεδὸν ἔσται ὁ διάλογος ἕως τῆς λ τοῦ Παχών**, " by the grace of the gods the audit will take place about Pachon 30 " (Edd.), P Gen I. 46¹⁴

(A.D. 345) σ]ὺν θεῷ ὡς ἂν δυνηθ[ῶ] σ[οι] . . [ἐ]γγύας ἀποκαταστήσω, and P Amh II. 150²⁸ (A.D. 592) ἐκ νέων κ[αρπῶ]ν τῆς σὺν θεῷ δωδεκάτης ἐπινεμήσεως, "from the new crop of the, D.V., coming twelfth indiction" (Edd.). For a Christian ex. of the phrase see the well-known letter of Psenosiris, P Grenf II. 73¹⁶ (late iii A.D.) (= *Selections*, p. 118) ὅταν ἔλθῃ σὺν Θεῷ, "when he arrives by the help of God." For the rival theory that this letter refers not to the banishment of a Christian woman during the great persecution, but to the transport of a mummy for burial, see Cronert, *Raccolta Lumbroso*, p. 515 ff.

The preposition occasionally passes into what is almost an instrumental sense, as in P Par 12¹⁷ (B.C. 157) σὺν τοῖς θεοῖς καὶ τῇ σῇ τύχῃ ἐκ θανάτου σέσωμαι. See also P Tebt I. 20⁵ (B.C. 113) χαριεῖ σὺν σοὶ αὐτὸν εἰσαγαγών, "you will do me a favour by personally introducing him" (Edd.) (cf. 1 Cor 15¹⁰).

(4) Σύν = "in fellowship with," as a technical term in magic ritual, appears in such passages as P Par 574²⁹⁹⁰ (c. A.D. 300) λαμβάνω σε σὺν ἀγαθῇ Τύχῃ καὶ ἀγαθῷ Δαίμονι, and the cursing leaden tablet of iii B.C. *CIA* Append. (= *IG* III. iii.) 108 δήσω ἐγὼ κείνην . . . σὺν θ' Ἑκάτ(η)ι χθονίαι καὶ Ἐρινύσιν—both cited by Deissmann *LAE²*, pp. 255, 303.

For the NT formula σὺν Χριστῷ we must again refer to Deissmann, who in his monograph *Die neutestamentliche Formel "in Christo Jesu"* (Marburg, 1892) has shown that σὺν Χριστῷ "nearly always means the fellowship of the faithful with Christ after their death or after His coming." In this connexion he adduces elsewhere (see *LAE²* p. 303 n.¹) a striking parallel to Phil 1²³ in a *graffito* from Alexandria, probably of the Imperial period, where a deceased person is addressed in the words εὔχομαι κἀγὼ ἐν τάχυ σὺν σοὶ εἶναι, "I would that I were soon in fellowship with thee."

(5) For σύν c. gen. cf. *Ostr* 240⁵ (A.D. 159) σὺν Μηνοφίλου, and P Lond 113. 4¹⁹ (A.D. 595) (= I. p. 209) σὺν μισθοῦ ὅλου.

(6) For the pleonastic καί after μετά in Phil 4³ (cf. Deissmann *BS* p. 265 f.) we can now compare σὺν καί in *PAS* iii. 612 (Phrygia—Imperial) σὺν καὶ τῷ ἀνδρὶ αὐτῆς (cited by Hatch, *JBL* xxvii. (1908), p. 143).

συνάγω.

"bring or gather together." The verb is frequently used of the total amount, the full sum, received by sale or by purchase, e.g. P Oxy II. 285¹⁹ (c. A.D. 50) διέσισέν με ἄλλας δραχμὰς τέσσαρες . . . μηνῶν ἕξ, κατὰ μῆνα δραχμὰς δύο, αἵ συναγόμεναι (δραχμαί) κδ, "he also extorted from me four more drachmae, and two drachmae each month during six months . . .: total, 24 drachmae" (Edd.), P Tebt II. 296³ (A.D. 123) τὸ συναγ[ό]μενον τῆς προ[ο]σθήκης ἀνελήφθη, "the total amount of the increase was received," or P Oxy I. 55¹¹ (A.D. 283) where two joiners ask for payment of 4000 drachmae as the total amount of wages due to them in connexion with the construction of a street—τὰ συναγόμενα τῶν μισθῶν τοῦ ὅλου ἔργου. It would seem, therefore, that by συναγαγὼν πάντα in Lk 15¹³ we must understand with Field (*Notes*, p. 68) that the prodigal converted his goods into money, sold all off

and realized their full value, rather than that he "gathered all together" to take with him.

For the meaning "hospitably receive," "entertain," as in Mt 25³⁵, Ac 11²⁸ (cf. Hort *Ecclesia*, p. 61), and in several places in the LXX (with εἰς τὸν οἶκον or the like), cf. *OGIS* 130⁵ (B.C. 146-116) οἱ συνάγοντες ἐν Σήτει . . . βασιλισταί, where Dittenberger takes the verb transitively, and thinks the reference is to a club gathering or festal meal. He compares Athenaeus VIII. p. 365 c ἔλεγον δὲ συνάγειν καὶ τὸ μετ' ἀλλήλων πίνειν καὶ συναγώγιον τὸ συμπόσιον, and Theophrast. *Charact.* 30 (= xxvi. 36, ed. Jebb) συναγόντων παρ' αὐτῷ, "a club-dinner at his house." See also Kennedy *Sources*, p. 128, and Menander *Selections ad* Ἐπιτρέπ. 195.

Other exx. of the verb are P Alex 4⁸ (iii/B.C.) (= Witkowski², p. 51) ἔτι δὲ καὶ νῦν, εἰ μὴ τὴν μήκωνα συνάξεις, οὐδείς σε ἀνθρώπων μὴ ὠφειλήσηι, P Eleph 8⁷ (iii/B.C.) τὸ συναγόμενον εἰς τὸ ἱερὸν ἀργύριον, P Tebt II. 389¹⁵ (A.D. 141) σ]ὺν ταῖς συναγομέναις τόκου αὐτῶν δραχμαῖς τετρακ[ο]σίαις εἴκοσι, "with the interest accruing upon it, 420 drachmae" (Edd.), P Oxy XIV. 1701¹⁵ (iii/A.D.) τοὺς] δὲ συναχθέντας δραχμιαίους τόκους, BGU I. 08¹⁰ (A.D. 211 ὧν ἡ συναγομένη τιμὴ ἐν ἀργυρίῳ ἔ[με]ινεν.

[The originality in Lk 3¹⁷ of the vulgar aor. συνάξαι so (Nᵃ) as an element traceable to "Q" has been discussed by J. H. Moulton in *Exp* VII. vii. p. 413 and *Cambridge Biblical Essays*, p. 485 f., in connexion with the Synoptic Problem.]

συναγωγή.

(1) For συναγωγή in its literal sense of "a drawing together" cf. the description of the awning of a boat in P Cairo Zen I. 50054⁶ (B.C. 257) πρυμνητική . . . ἔχουσα συναγωγὴν εἰς πήχεις γ̄, i.e. "converging for a distance of three cubits" (Edd.) : also ²¹, ²².

(2) Hence, more generally, "a collecting," "a gathering" (a) of things—P Cairo Zen II. 59173²⁹ (B.C. 255 or 254) ὡς ἂν ἡ] συναγωγὴ τοῦ σίτου [γένηται, *Chrest.* I 304⁵ (iii/B.C.) εἰς τὴν συνα]γωγὴν τοῦ λοιποῦ (sc. κρότωνος), *Chrest.* I. 155² (a book catalogue from Memphis—beg. iii/A.D.) Σωκ[ρα]τικῶν ἐπιστο[λῶν)] συναγωγαί: cf. Cic. *ad Att.* xvi. 5. 5 *mearum epistularum nulla est* συναγωγή.

(b) Of persons. The use of συναγωγή in the LXX to denote an "assembly" for religious purposes, practically synonymous with ἐκκλησία, is prepared for by such passages from the inscrr. as *CIG* II. 2448 (Will of Epikteta—iii/ii B.C.), where συναγωγή is used of the "assembling" of the θίασος or corporation, and *Syll* 653 (= ³730)⁴⁹ (Andania decree—B.C. 92) ἐν τᾶι πρώται συννόμωι συναγωγᾶι τῶν συνέδρων, where the reference is to the senate of Andania. Both passages are cited by Hicks *CR* i. p. 43. See also the Ptolemaic inscr. of probably B.C. 112 reproduced by Strack (*Archiv* iii. p. 129) which begins ἐπὶ συναγωγῆς τῆς γενηθείσης ἐν τῶι ἄνω Ἀπολλ[ω]νιείωι τοῦ πολιτεύματος καὶ τῶν ἀπὸ τῆς πόλεως Ἰδουμαίων, where the συναγωγή is composed of τὸ πολίτευμα along with οἱ ἀπὸ τῆς πόλεως Ἰδουμαῖοι, BGU IV. 1137² (B.C. 6) ἐπὶ τῆς γε[νη]θείσης συναγωγῆς ἐν τῷ Παρατόμωι συνόδου Σεβάστης τοῦ θεοῦ αὐτοκράτορος Καίσαρος ἧς συνα[γωγεὺς] καὶ προστάτης Πρῖμος, an important document as expressly connecting a club or association, **σύνοδος**, with the Imperial cult (see *Archiv* v. p. 331 f.), and P Oxy IX. 1205⁷ (A.D. 291) [ὑπὲρ τῆς ἐλευθερώσεως καὶ ἀπολύσ᾿εως παρὰ τῆς συνα[γ]ωγῆς τῶν Ἰουδαίων is of interest as showing not only the existence of a Jewish colony at Oxyrhynchus, but the action of the synagogue in the manumission of certain Jews referred to in the document.

In a similar Jewish deed of enfranchisement from Kertch of date A.D. 81, *CIG* II. 2114 bb, reference is made to the joint-guardianship of the synagogue,¹⁸ σὺν [ἐ]πιτροπῇ τῆς συναγωγῆς τῶν Ἰουδαίων. In citing the inscr. Hicks (*CR* i. p. 4) notes that "the manumitted slave is pledged only to one obligation, that of diligent attendance at the synagogue worship."

On the inscr. συναγωγή Ἑβραίων discovered at Corinth see s.v. Ἑβραῖος, and note further the occurrence of the word to denote a "place of worship" (cf. Jas 2²) in an inscr. dated A.D. 318–319, which was discovered at Lebaba near Damascus and published by Le Bas and Waddington *Inscriptions grecques et latines* iii. No. 2558—

Συναγωγὴ Μαρκιωνιστῶν κώμ(ης)
Λεβάβων τοῦ κ(υρίο)υ καὶ σωτῆρος Ἰη(σοῦ) Χρηστοῦ
προνοία(ι) Παύλου πρεσβ(υτέρου)—τοῦ λχ ἔτους,

"the meeting-house of the Marcionists, in the village of Lebaba, of the Lord and Saviour Jesus Christ. Erected by the forethought of Paul a presbyter—In the year 630 (i.e. of the Seleucid era)" : cf. Schürer³ ii. p. 443 n.⁶² (= *HJP* II. ii. p. 69), Harnack *Mission and Expansion*,² p. 123 f., and Zahn *Intr.* i. p. 94 f. See also s.v. προσευχή.

συναγωνίζομαι,

"strive together with" (Rom 15³⁰) : *Syll* 193 (= ³367)¹⁸ (B.C. 290–289) συναγωνιζό[μ]ενος τῆι τοῦ δήμ]ου σωτηρίαι, *ib.* 286 (= ³606)⁷ (B.C. 190) συναγωνισάμενοι τὴν ἐν Λυδίαι . . μάχην, and *OGIS* 280³ (c. B.C. 228) οἱ συναγωνισάμενοι τὰς πρὸς τοὺς Γ[αλ]άτας καὶ Ἀντίοχον μάχας χαρισ[τ]ήρια. For the subst. see P Oxy XIV. 1676³⁶ (iii/A.D.) Δι]ονύσιος ὁ συναγωνισ[τής μο]υ, "Dionysius my fellow-worker," and BGU IV. 1074¹ (A.D. 275) τοῖς τούτων συναγωνισταῖς χαίρειν.

συναθροίζω,

"gather together," "assemble." This verb, which is confined to Ac 12¹², 19²⁵, in the NT, occurs in a military report P Oxy X. 1253⁵ (iv/A.D.) συνηθρυκέναι τούς τε τὰ κοινὰ διοικοῦν[τας] πρώτους [μ]ετὰ σὲ τιμήν, "have assembled the public magistrates next to yourself in rank" (Edd.).

συναίρω.

According to Grimm-Thayer this verb with λόγον in the sense of "settle accounts," "make a reckoning with," as in its NT occurrences (Mt 18²³ f., 25¹⁹), is "not found in Grk. auth." But numerous exx. can now be furnished from the papyri. e.g. P Lond 131 *recto*¹⁹⁴ (accounts—A.D. 78–79) (= I. p. 175) συ]ναίρων μετὰ Ἐπιμάχο[υ τὸν λόγον, BGU III. 775¹⁹ (ii/A.D.) τὰ ἤδη προλήμα (l. πρόλημμα) "what has already been advanced" ἄφὲς ἄχρης (l. ἄχρις) ἂν γένωμε ἐκῖ καὶ συνάρωμεν λόγον, PSI VII. 801³ (ii/A.D. ?)

παντὸς λόγο[υ] συνηρμένο[υ], and P Flor III. 372¹⁴ (iii/A.D.) ἕως Θὼθ παντὸς λόγο[υ] συνηρμένου ὀφίλω[.

For the mid. which is "more classical in spirit" (*Proleg.* p. 160) cf. P Ryl II. 229¹⁵ (A.D. 38) δοκῶ γὰρ συναιρόμενος πρὸς σὲ λογάριον, "I expect to make up an account with you" (Edd.), P Fay 109⁶ (early i/A.D.) ὅτι συνήρμαι λόγον τῷ πατρί, "for I have settled accounts with his (?) father" (Edd.), P Oxy I. 113²⁷ (ii/A.D.) ὅτι ἔδωκας αὐτῶι δήλωσόν μοι ἵνα συνάρωμαι αὐτῶι λόγον, "let me know what you have given him that I may settle accounts with him" (Edd.), and *ib.* XIV. 1669¹⁵ (iii/A.D.) ἵνα τοὺ]ς λόγους τῶν φόρων συνα[ιρώμεθ]α, "in order that we may make up the accounts of the rents" (Edd.).

Other exx. of the verb are P Rein 8⁷ (B.C. 113–2) ἀπὸ συναλλαγ[μάτων αὐτῶ]ι συνηρμένων, and *ib.* 31⁸ (B.C. 109), and BGU IV. 478⁹ (iii/A.D.) (= *Chrest.* I. p. 569), a father's letter of congratulation to his son on his marriage, ὅπως γενόμενοι παρ᾿ ὑμῖν συνάρωμεν διπλὴν ε[ἰ]λαπίνην ("banquet") τεθαλυῖαν.

For the subst. σύναρσις, hitherto attested only in Byz. writers, cf. *Ostr* 1135⁵ (A.D. 214) ἄχρι λόγου συνάρσεως, P Amh II. 101³ (early iii/A.D.) ἐκ συνάρσεως λόγων, and for συναίρεμα, "summary," see P Tebt II. 340⁵ (A.D. 206), and cf. BGU VII. 1613 B⁶ ¹⁶ (A.D. 69–70), 1626² (iii/A.D.).

συναιχμάλωτος,

one of Paul's numerous compounds in συν-: cf. Deissmann *Paul*², p. 240 f. Properly the word denotes "a fellow-prisoner of war," and in its Pauline occurrences can hardly be confined to the thought of *spiritual* captivity: cf. Abbott *ICC ad* Col 4¹⁰.

συνακολουθέω.

For the meaning "follow along with," as in Mk 14⁵¹, cf. the fragmentary P Petr II. 4 (2) (= p. [7]) συνακολουθείτω δέ τις παρὰ σοῦ τῆι ομ[, and P Tebt I. 30¹¹ (B.C. 114) συνε(= α)κολουθεῖν ἐπὶ τὴν σημαινομένην οἰκίαν, "to go along with him to the house alluded to." An interesting use of the verb is found in P Petr II. 13 (18ᵇ)¹⁶ (B.C. 258–253) περὶ] δὲ τοῦ κυρωθῆναι τὰ ἔργα γράψον Νέω[ν]ι? συ[να]κολουθεῖν τοῖς ἔργοις, where the editor renders "but as regards the audit (sanction) of the work, write to Neon? to keep his eye on the works."

συναλίζομαι.

We can cite no ex. of this rare verb from our sources, but reference should be made to Professor H. J. Cadbury's careful study in *JBL* xlv. (1926), p. 310 ff., where he sets aside both the ordinary interpretations of the verb in Ac 1⁴ —συναλίζω, "eat with," and συναλίζομαι, "gather" (transitive or intransitive), and regards συναλιζόμενος as simply another spelling for συναυλιζόμενος, with the consequent meaning "live with" in the sense of spending the night together. Such an orthographic change of α for αυ is, as he shows, common in the Κοινή, and may be illustrated from such passages as BGU III. 713¹² (A.D. 41–42) Τιβερίου Κρατίου (= Κλαυδίου), *ib.* IV. 1079²⁵ (A.D. 41) (= *Selections*, p. 40) βλέπε σατὸν (= σεαυτὸν) ἀπὸ τῶν Ἰουδαίων, and P Lond 1912⁹¹ (letter of Claudius to the Alexandrines—A.D. 41) ἀπολάοντας : see also Moulton *Proleg.* p. 47 and *Gr.* ii. p. 87. This would seem, on the whole, to be the best solution of this *crux interpretum*, but reference may also be made to Field *Notes*, p. 110 f., where συναλίζεσθαι is taken in its ordinary sense of *congregari* or *convenire*, and stress is laid on the *present* part., "'as he was assembling with them,' as he was on the way to meet them (some of them being in the same company with him) he gave them this charge."

συναλλάσσω,

"reconcile," found in the NT only in the conative impf. Ac 7²⁶ συνήλλασσεν αὐτοὺς εἰς εἰρήνην, "would have set them at one again" (AV, RV) (cf. Field *Notes*, p. 115). The following are exx. of the verb— BGU IV. 1120⁵³ (B.C. 5) μενεῖ ἡ τῶν καρπῶν συνάλλαξις . . . οἷς ἐὰν οἱ μεμισθωμένοι συναλλάξωσι, P Oxy I. 34 *verso*ⁱ·¹⁰ (A.D. 127) τὰ τῶν σ[υνα]λλασσόντων ὀνόματα, "the names of the contracting parties," *ib.* 237ᵛⁱⁱⁱ·³⁶ (A.D. 186) ἵνα οἱ συναλλάσσοντες μὴ κατ' ἄγνοιαν ἐνεδρεύονται, "in order that persons entering into agreements may not be defrauded through ignorance" (Edd.), P Tebt II. 413¹² (ii/iii A.D.) ταῦτά σοι συναλ<λ>άγη, "it was arranged with you" (Edd.), and BGU IV. 1062¹⁰ (A.D. 236-7) διὰ τοῦ αὐτοῦ . . . συνηλλαχέναι τῷ τε Ἀμόι καὶ Σύρῳ. For the subst. συνάλλαξις see P Fay 11²² (c. B.C. 115) κατανωτιζόμενος τ[ὸ] . . [. . .]ως ἔχον καὶ τὰς συναλλάξεις, "turning his back on (justice) and the contracts" (Edd.): for συναλλαγή, P Oxy I. 70⁴ (iii/A.D.) πᾶσα κυ[ρί]α ἔγγραφος συναλλαγὴ πίστιν καὶ ἀλήθ[ειαν ἔ]χει, "every valid written contract is credited and accepted" (Edd.): and for συνάλλαγμα, *ib.* 34 *verso*ⁱ·⁹ (A.D. 127) ἐγλογιζέσθωσαν τὰ συναλλάγματα (cf. *Archiv* ii. p. 492 ff.).

συναναβαίνω,

"go up with" (Mk 15⁴¹, Ac 13³¹): PSI IV. 410¹⁰ (iii/B.C.) καλῶς ποιήσε<τε> συναναβάντες Ἀπολλωνίῳ, P Tebt I. 21¹¹ (B.C. 115) ἐὰν δέ σοι κόπους παρέχηι συναναβαινε αὐτῶι, "if he gives you trouble go up with him" (Edd.), P Hamb I. 87¹⁸ (beg. ii/A.D.) πείθομαι γάρ, ὅτι καὶ Ἀ]στρανῶβις συναναβήσεταί σοι, and OGIS 632² (A.D. 141-2) οἱ συναναβάντες μετ' α[ὐ]τοῦ ἔμποροι.

συναναμίγνυμι,

"mix up together," thence metaph. in mid. "associate with" (1 Cor 5⁹·¹¹, 2 Thess 3¹⁴). For the corr. adj. συναναμιγος (not in LS⁸), see P Oxy IV. 718³⁶ (A.D. 180-192) προσεφώνησεν [τὰς τέσσαρας ταύ]τας ἀρούρας τῆς βασιλικῆς συναναμίγους εἶναι τῆι ὑπαρ[χούσῃ μοι γῇ τῶ]ν πεντήκοντα τριῶν, "stated that these 4 arourae of Crown land were included in the 53 arourae belonging to me" (Edd.). For the single comp⁴ cf. P Eleph 29¹¹ (iii/B.C.) ἕως τοῦ σοι συμμεῖξαι, and P Par 49²⁵ (c. B.C. 161) (= *UPZ* i. p. 309) ᾔσχυνται συμμεῖξαί μοι.

συναναπαύομαι,

In connexion with the use of this verb in Rom 15³² = "rest along with," "am refreshed in spirit with," it is worth recalling that in Eus. *H.E.* iv. 22. 2 Hegesippus is quoted as saying that he spent several days with the Corinthians, during which συνανεπάημεν τῷ ὀρθῷ λόγῳ, "we were mutually refreshed in the true doctrine." For a similar double comp¹ προσαναπαύομαι see Sap 8¹⁶.

συναντάω,

(1) "meet with," "encounter," as in Lk 9³⁷ *al.*, P Lille I. 6⁶ (iii/B.C.) συναντήσαντες (corrected from συναντες) τινές μοι ἔξω τῆς κώμης, P Cairo Zen I. 59056³ (B.C. 257) εἰς Καῦνον συνήντησεν ὅ τε πατήρ σου καὶ οἱ ἀδ[ελφοί, *ib.* II. 59179⁹ (B.C. 255) οἱ [συ]νταξάμενοι ("those who agreed to appear") οὐ συνήντησαν ἐπὶ τὴν [κρίσιν, P Lille I. 13² (B.C. 244-3) ὁ παρὰ Νίκωνος σιτολόγος οὐ συναντῶν ("ne se trouvant pas là"), PSI IV. 438²⁵ (iii/B.C.) διὸ οὐ συναντῶσιν, and P Hamb I. 25¹¹ (B.C. 238) ἀνακληθεὶς οὖν Κάλας τέτακται συναντήσεσθαι πρὸς σέ, and similarly¹⁶.

(2) "happen," "befall," as in Ac 20²², PSI IV. 392¹ (B.C. 242-1) εἰ ἔρρωσαι καὶ τἆλλά σοι κατὰ τρόπον συναντᾶι, and ¹⁰ συναντήσηι ἡμῖν τὰ παρὰ τοῦ βασιλέως κατὰ λ<όγ>ον : cf. *Syll* 279 (= ³601)¹⁴ (B.C. 193) ἐκ τῆς συναντωμένης ἡμῖν εὐμενείας διὰ ταῦτα παρὰ τοῦ δαιμονίου. Συναντάω does not seem to appear in Roman times, but καταντάω is common (e.g. P Tebt I. 59²—B.C. 99). See *Anz Subsidia*, p. 277 f. For the double comp¹ συναπαντάω, cf. PSI VI. 689⁹ (v/A.D.) π[ρ]ός σε συναπαντῆσαι ἅμα ται[ς] ἄλλαις ἐργάταις.

The subst. συνάντημα (lit. = "occurrence"), which in Exod 9¹⁴ is used to translate the Heb. word for "plague," is found in the same sinister sense in the magic P Leid Wˣᵛⁱⁱⁱ·⁴ (ii/iii A.D.) οὐ δαιμόνιον, οὐ συνάντημα (*l.* συνάντημα), οὐδὲ ἀλλό τι τῶν καθ' Ἅιδον πονηρόν, and in the Christian amulet P Iand 6¹⁶ (v/vi A.D.) πονηρὸν συ[ν]]νάντημα, see the editor's note.

συνάντησις,

"a going to meet," which is read for ὑπάντησις (*q.v.*) in the TR of Mt 8³⁴ (and LXX *saepe*) may be illustrated from *Pelagia-Legenden* p. 22²⁷ ἐξῆλθεν δὲ συνήθως ἡ τροφὸς εἰς συνάντησιν αὐτῆς.

συναντιλαμβάνομαι,

"lend a hand along with," "take an interest in" (Lk 10⁴⁰, Rom 8²⁶). Deissmann (*LAE²*, p. 87 f.) has shown that this word, which is included by Thayer in his "Biblical" list, can be traced throughout the whole of the Hellenistic world. Thus, in addition to its LXX occurrences (Exod 18²², *al.*), he quotes exx. from Delphi, *Syll* 250 (= ³412)⁷ (c. B.C. 260) συναντιλήψεσθαι τῶν τῆι πόλει συμφερόντων, "to help in things profitable for the city"; from Pergamum, *Perg* 18²⁶ (B.C. 263-241) τοὺς εἰς ταῦτα συναντιλαμβανομένους, "those helping in this": and from Egypt, P Hib I. 82¹³ (B.C. 239-8) καλῶς οὖν [π]οιήσεις συναν[τι]λ[α]μβανόμενος προθύμως περὶ τῶν εἰς ταῦτα συγκυρόντων, "thou wilt therefore do well to take part zealously in the things relating thereto." To these we may add PSI IV. 329⁶ (B.C. 258-7), *ib.* VI. 591¹² (iii/B.C.) καλῶς ἂν ο[ὖν ποιή]σαι<ς> συναντιλαβόμενό[ς μου?]. It will be noticed that all our exx. of this verb are from iii/B.C., but LS⁸ refer to a passage in Diod. 14. 8.

συναπάγω,

"lead away with," is used metaph. in the pass. "am carried away with" as with a flood: cf. Gal 2¹³, 2 Pet 3¹⁷. On the AV, RV rendering "condescend to" in Rom 12¹⁶ see Field *Notes*, p. 163, where the corresponding use of συμπεριφέρομαι, "comply with," "accommodate oneself to," as in Sir 25¹ γυνὴ καὶ ἀνὴρ ἑαυτοῖς συμπεριφερόμενοι, is cited.

συναποθνήσκω.

For this double compd. = "die along with" in 2 Cor 7³ (cf. Sir 19¹⁰) Wetstein *ad l.* cites Athenaeus vi. 249 B τούτους δ' οἱ βασιλεῖς ἔχουσι συζῶντας καὶ συναποθνήσκοντας. See also Cicero *ad Att.* vii. 20. 2.

συναπόλλυμαι.

"perish along with" (Heb 11³¹): cf. P Oxy III. 486³⁵ (A.D. 131) μὴ σὺ)ν τοῖς ὑπάρχουσί μου κἀγὼ λειμῷ συναπολῶμαι, "that I may not in addition to the loss of my property also perish with hunger" (Edd.).

συναποστέλλω.

"send along with." A good ex. of this NT ἅπ. εἰρ. (2 Cor 12¹⁸) is found in BGU IV. 1080¹⁸ (iii/A.D.?), where a father bids his son write, and (along with the letter) σ]υναπόστιλόν μοι σιππίου τρυφεροῦ λίτρας δέκα, "send me ten litres of delicate flax." Cf. also P Cairo Zen I. 59018³ (B.C. 258) συναπέστειλα [δὲ Στ]ράτωνι [παρ' ἡ]μῶν νεανίσκον καὶ ἐπιστολὴν ἔγρα]ψα πρὸς Ἰεδδοῦν, PSI IV. 377⁹ (B.C. 250–249) ἀξίωσον (l. ἀξίωσον), εἴ σοι δοκεῖ. συναποσταλῆναί μοί τινα ὅν ἂν δοκιμάζηις, P Hamb I. 27¹⁴ (B.C. 250) συναφέσταλκεν δὲ καὶ γεωργοὺς γ, and OGIS 5⁴ (B.C. 311) ὑπὲρ τούτων συναπεστείλαμε[ν μετὰ Δημά]ρχου Αἰσχύλου.

For a verb μεταποστέλλω (not in LS⁸), see BGU IV. 1207¹⁹ (B.C. 28) (= Olsson *Papyrusbriefe*, p. 34) ἐὰν οὖν πέμπῃς [ἀρ]γύριον, μεταπόστελλε (as read by Schubart) εἰκοστόν.

συναρμολογέω.

"fit together." For this expressive compd. (Eph 2²¹, 4¹⁶) we may cite the closely related συναρμόττω, as in *Syll* 537 (= ³969)⁶² (B.C. 347–6) λίθοις τὸ ἐντὸς ἅπαν συναρμόττουσι πρὸς ἀλλήλους.

συναρπάζω.

as a perfective of ἁρπάζω, denotes "seize and keep a firm hold of" in Lk 8²⁹ (see *Proleg.* p. 113): cf. PSI IV. 353¹² (B.C. 254–3) συναρπά[ξε]ι τὸν φυλακίτην, and P Masp III. 67295⁶ (Byz.) συναρπάζειν τὰ ἰάσ[ιμα τῶν ἀδεκ]άστων.

For the meaning "seize and carry away," as in Ac 27¹⁵, see P Ryl II. 119²⁹ (A.D. 54–67) κατὰ πᾶν οὖν συνηρπασμένοι ὑπὸ τούτου, "we have therefore been robbed on every side by this man" (Edd.). The subst. συναρπαγή is found in a deed of sale *Archiv* iii. p. 418¹⁶ (vi/A.D.) δίχα π]αντὸς δόλου καὶ φόβου καὶ βίας . . . καὶ περιγραφῆς πάσης καὶ συναρ[παγῆς: cf. P Lond 77⁷ (vi/A.D.) (= I. p. 232).

συναυξάνω.

"cause to increase (grow) together." An early ex. of this NT ἅπ. εἰρ. (Mt 13³⁰) may be cited—OGIS 233¹⁹ (iii B.C.) σπουδάζοντες συναυξῆσαι τὸν τῶν Ἀντιοχέων δῆμον. For the form συναύξω, *Syll* 295 (= ³629)² (B.C. 182) τὰν οὖσα)ν πρότερον ε]ὐνοιαν . . . φανερὸς γίνεται συναύξων, and P Fay 20¹⁶ (iv/A.D.) φιλανθρωπία τε καὶ

εὐεργεσίαις συναύξειν ταύτην τὴν ἀρχήν, "by liberality and the conferring of benefits to increase the welfare of this empire" (Edd.)—an edict now assigned to Julian (*Archiv* ii. p. 169).

συνβάλλω.

This favourite Lukan word is found with a variety of connotations—(1) "throw together" and hence "discuss," "confer" ἰ(sc. λόγους) c. dat , as in Lk 11⁵³ (*v.l.*), Ac 4¹⁵: P Fay 129² (iii/A.D.) Ἀπολλῶτι συνέβαλον καὶ ἐτάξατο πάντως καταβῆναι τῇ ἐνδεκάτῃ, "I arranged with Apollos and he appointed for certain the eleventh for his coming down" (Edd.), and OGIS 669²¹ (i/A.D.) ἵν[α μηδ]εὶς τῶι τοιούτωι συνβάλλῃ. (2) "meet with," "fall in with," as in Ac 20¹⁴: P Oxy XIV. 1668⁴ (iii/A.D.) συνέβαλον τῷ Σκωρῷ χάριν τῶν ἐργαστηρίων, "I had a meeting with Skorus respecting the workshops" (Edd.), and *ib.* 1669⁸ (iii/A.D.) ἐνετειλάμην σοι . . . συμβαλεῖν Πτολεμαίῳ τῷ σειτολόγῳ καὶ τὸν λόγον πέμψαι αὐτοῦ, "I bade you to meet Ptolemaeus the sitologus and send his account" (Edd.). (3) in mid. "contribute to," "help," as in Ac 18²⁷: P Hal I. 1¹⁰⁵ (mid. iii/B.C.) συμβαλλέσθω τὸ μέρος ἕκαστος [εἰ]ς τὸ ἀ[νάλωμα, "let each contribute his share towards the expense," P Par 63⁷³ (B.C. 164) (= P Petr III. p. 24) συμβαλεῖται ῥοπὴν εἰς τὸ προκείμενον, "it would turn the scale in favour of the matter in hand" (Mahaffy), P Tor I. 1ⁱⁱ ¹¹ (B.C. 116) (= *Chrest.* II. p. 34) μέγα τι συμβάλλεσθαι τεκμήριον, cf. *ib.*ᵛⁱⁱⁱ·²⁵ (p. 38 f.), P Lond 1915¹³ (c. A.D. 330–340) ὑμεῖς γνῶντες συμβάλλεσθε αὐτῷ, "you, knowing thereof, may help him," cf.³⁰, and *Syll* 187 (= ³346)⁴⁸ (B.C. 302–1) γνώμην δὲ συμβάλλεσθαι [τῆς βουλῆς ε]ἰ[ς] τὸν δῆμον.

συνβασιλεύω.

For this verb "reign together" (1 Cor 4⁸, 2 Tim 2¹²) cf. Polyb. xxx. 2. 4 κατὰ μὲν τὸ παρὸν συμβασιλεύει τ' ἀδελφῷ. Mention is made of συμβασιλισταί, apparently members of a royal military union (cf. Preisigke *Fachwörter s.v.* βασιλισταί), in an inscr. addressed to Ptolemy III., published in *Archiv* v. p. 158.

συνβιβάζω

has its ordinary Greek sense "bring together," "compact" in Eph 4¹⁶, Col 2²·¹⁹, but in 1 Cor 2¹⁶ συνβιβάσει (for form see Moulton *Gr.* ii. p. 187) the meaning is "instruct," as always in the LXX (Isai 40¹³ᶠ· *al.*): so Ac 19³³, and cf. Ac 9²², 16¹⁰.

For a similar development of meaning, cf. ἐκβιβάζω in such passages as P Oxy II. 200¹⁵ (A.D. 50) μέχρι οὗ ἂ ἔχωμεν πρὸς ἑαυτοὺς ἐγ[β]ιβασθῆι, "until our suit is decided" (Edd.), P Hamb I. 4¹⁰ (A.D. 87) μέχρι οὗ ἐκβιβάσω ἃ ἔχει πρός με, and P Oxy IX. 1195⁸ (A.D. 135) ἐκβιβάζων τὰ ἐνεστῶτ[ά μοι π]ρὸς Ἑρμ[α]ῖον, "in explanation of my case against Hermaeus" (Ed.).

συγγνώμη,

in NT only in 1 Cor 7⁶, with meaning "concession," "allowance" for circumstances (*ex concessione, non ex imperio*, Beza). From this there is an easy transition to the sense of "pardon": cf. P Cairo Zen I. 59044³⁷ (B.C. 257) καλῶς δ' ἂν ποιοῖς καὶ συγγνώμην ἡμῖν ἔχων, P Tebt I. 27⁴³

(B.C. 113) (= *Chrest.* I. p. 389) διαλαβὼν μηδεμιᾶς τεύξεσθαι συνγνώμης ὀλιγωρηθέντος τινός, "believing that you will receive no pardon for any neglect" (Edd.), P Flor I. 61[15] (A.D. 86–88) συ[γ]γνώμην αἰτούμενος ἐπεὶ ἐπλανήθη περὶ τὴν ἔντευξιν, P Oxy VI. 939[10] (iv/A.D.) (= *Selections*, p. 129) συγγνώμην δέ, κύριέ μου, σχοίης μοι [καὶ εὔνους] ἀποδέξῃ με, "but pray, my lord, do you pardon me and receive me kindly," and BGU III. 836[5] (time of Justinian) αἰτοῦντες συγγνώμην δοθῆναι αὐτοῖς.

σύνδεσμος

in its lit. sense of "fastening" (cf. Col 2[19]) occurs in Aristeas 85 τοῦ θυρώματος δὲ καὶ τῶν περὶ αὐτὸ συνδέσμων κατὰ τὰς φλιάς, "the great doorway and the fastenings which held it to the door-posts" (Thackeray). For the metaph. usage in Col 3[14] Wetstein cites from Simplicius in *Epictet.* p. 208 a parallel expression of the Pythagoreans: καλῶς οἱ Πυθαγορεῖοι περισσῶς τῶν ἄλλων ἀρετῶν τὴν φιλίαν ἐτίμων καὶ σύνδεσμον αὐτὴν πασῶν τῶν ἀρετῶν ἔλεγον. It may be noted that for τελειότητα in Col *l.c.* D*(Gdeg) read ἑνότητα. Σύνδεσις is used 'of the "continuation" of a text on the following page in P Oxy XIV. 1737[23] (ii/iii A.D.).

συνδέω,

"bind together." For the pass. in Heb 13[3], the only occurrence of the verb in the NT, cf. Preisigke 5282 (iii/A.D.), where Antinous asks his mother to hand over to Antipater τὸ συνδεδεμένον ἐπιστολίδιον, the letter made up of different papyrus sheets fastened together: cf. Herodian iv. 12. 11 πάντα τὸν σύνδεσμον τῶν ἐπιστολῶν. See also BGU I. 261[9] (ii/iii A.D.?) γράφεις μοι, ὅτι συνδέσσου (*l.* συνεδήσω) τὰς χέρες Ζωιδοῦτι (but Wilcken *Archiv* iv. p. 200 prefers to read σύνδες (= σύνθες) σου κτλ.), and CPR I. 232[17] (ii/iii A.D.) τὸν [σ]υνδέοντα πηλόν.

σύνδουλος,

"a fellow-slave": BGU IV. 1141[22] (B.C. 13) παρὰ (cf. Jannaris *Gr.* 1019[b]) τὸν σύνδουλόν σου καὶ συνεξελεύθερον, "except your fellow-slave and fellow-freedman," and *ib.*[30], P Lond 1213(*a*)[1] (A.D. 65–66) (= III. p. 121) μέτρησον Σόφῳ συνδούλῳ, *ib.* 157 *a.*[3] (ii/A.D.?) (= II p. 255) ἴδετε τ[ὴ]ν οἰκίαν τοῦ συνδούλ[ο]υ σου, and the late BGU II. 547[4] (Byz.) μὴ ὀχλῆσαι τῷ συνδούλῳ μου τῷ εὐλαβ(εστάτῳ) Πέτρῳ τῷ διακόνῳ.

The distinction drawn by Moeris (p. 273) that ὁμόδουλος is Attic and σύνδουλος Hellenistic cannot be maintained: see Headlam's note *ad* Herodas V. 56.

συνδρομή.

This NT ἅπ. λεγ. (Ac 21[30]: cf. LXX Judith 10[18], 3 Macc 3[8]) in the sense of "a tumultuous concourse" may be illustrated from Polyb. i. 67. 2 εὐθέως διαφορὰ καὶ στάσις ἐγεννᾶτο, καὶ συνδρομαὶ συνεχεῖς ἐγίγνοντο. For its medical sense of "a concourse" of symptoms, see the exx. in Hobart, p. 192.

συνέδριον

is used in late Greek to denote a "council" or "assembly" of any kind, though generally of a representative character. In the papyri the occurrences of the word are comparatively

rare, but see P Par 15[22] (a judicial process—B.C. 120) παραγγελέντος αὐτοῖς ἔρχεσθαι εἰς τὸ συνέδριον, P Tebt I. 27[31] (B.C. 113) (= *Chrest.* I. p. 388) δι’ ὧν ἐδηλοῦτο ἀναγκαῖον εἶναι μεταπεμφθέντων εἰς κοινὸν συνέδριον τῶν κατὰ κώμην δεκανῶν τῶν φ[υ]λακιτῶν, "in which it was stated to be necessary that the decani of the police in the villages should be summoned to a general meeting" (Edd.), CP Herm I. 7[ii.6] (ii/A.D.) ἐπεὶ ᾑρέθημεν ἐν τῷ συνεδρίῳ ἀκολ(ούθως) τοῖς ὑπομνημ(ατισθεῖσι) ἐπὶ τῆ[ς κ]ρατίστης βουλῆς κτλ., *ib.* 52[i.20] (iii/A.D.) πρὸς τὰ θεῖ[α] εὐσέβε[ιαν] ἐπινεύσειν τῇ δεήσει τοῦ κοινοῦ ἡμῶν συνεδρίου, *ib.* 52[ii.9] (iii/A.D.) δόξα]ν τῷ κοινῷ συνεδρίῳ ἐπὶ [τοῦ κρ]ατίστου δουκηναρίου, *OGIS* 222[27] (B.C. 266–1) ὅπως κατὰ τὸ δόγμα τ]οῦ συνεδρίου βουλεύσωνται [περὶ τῆς τοῦ ἱεροῦ οἰκοδομ]ῆς κτλ.—a decree of the Ionian States regarding the celebration of the birthday of Antiochus I. Soter, and *CIG* II. 3417 (Imperial period) where the συνέδριον τῶν πρεσβυτέρων is previously named γερουσία: see Deissmann *BS* p. 156, and cf. Hicks *CR* i. p. 44, "at Ephesus and elsewhere it is abundantly certain that οἱ πρεσβύτεροι and τὸ συνέδριον were convertible terms with γερουσία."

As showing the variety of applications of the word see the long list of exx. in *Syll*[3] Index, and the data in Schürer *Geschichte*[3] ii. p. 193 ff. (= *HJP* II. i. p. 169 f. note 461). In the NT the word is applied to Jewish local courts of justice attached to the Synagogue (Mt 10[17], Mk 13[9]), and hence to the great Council at Jerusalem, the Sanhedrin (Mt 5[22], *al.*). See also Burkitt *Syriac Forms*, p. 23.

συνείδησις,

(1) lit. "co-knowledge," hence "consciousness": P Par p. 422[7] (ii/A.D.) ὅ]ταν ἰσέλθῃς, καλὴ ὥρα, εὑρήσις συνίδησιν, "lorsque tu seras entré, à la bonne heure, tu trouveras les gens au courant de la chose (?)" (Ed.), P Ryl II. 116[9] (A.D. 194) θλειβομένη τῇ συνειδήσει περὶ ὧν ἐνοσφίσατο ἔν τε ἐνδομενείᾳ καὶ ἀποθέτοις, "oppressed by the consciousness of what she had appropriated both of the furniture and stored articles" (Edd.), P Flor III. 338[17] (iii/A.D.) οἶδα γὰρ ὅτι συνειδήσι ("coscenziosamente," Ed.) σπουδάζεις ἐμοί, P Oxy I. 123[13] (iii/iv A.D.) ἤδη γὰρ οἱ τῶν ἄλλων πόλεων συνείδησιν εἰσήνεγκαν τοῖς κολλήγαις αὐτῶν, εἰσῆλθαν, "already the notaries of the other towns have acquainted their colleagues, and they have come in" (Edd.), BGU IV. 1024[iii.7] (iv/A.D.) τὴν συνείδησιν τ[ῶν πεπραγμένων (?) . . ., and P Par 21[15] (A.D. 616) ὁμολογοῦμεν γνώμῃ ἑκουσίᾳ καὶ αὐθαιρέτῳ βουλήσει καὶ ἀδόλῳ συνειδήσει.

(2) The deeper sense of "conscience," which the word has in the Pauline writings, is often traced to the influence of popular Greek philosophy: "it is one of the few technical terms in St. Paul which seem to have Greek rather than Jewish affinities," say SH *ai* Rom 2[15]. But it should be noted that the word does not occur in Epictetus (*Fragm.* 97, Schweighäuser, is now pronounced non-genuine), nor in M. Antoninus (see Bonhöffer *Epiktet.* p. 156 f.). The word would seem, therefore, to have been "baptized" by Paul into a new and deeper connotation, and to have been used by him as equivalent to τὸ συνειδός, for which we may quote three exx. from our sources—P Oxy III. 532[23] (ii/A.D.) ὑπὸ κακοῦ συνειδότος κατεχόμενος, "being oppressed by an evil conscience" (cf. Sap 17[11]), P Reinach 52[5]

(ii/iv A.D.) ὑμεῖς δὲ ἠμελήσατε ἴσως οὐ καλῷ συνειδότι χρώμενοι, and *OGIS* 484[37] (ii/A.D.) τοὺς οὖν διὰ τὸ συνειδὸς ὀμνύναι μὴ δυναμένους διδόναι τι αὐτοῖς.

Συνείδησις occurs in Menander *Monost.* 597 ἅπασιν ἡμῖν ἡ συνείδησις θεός : cf. *ib.* 654 ; and for the comp[d]. εὐσυνείδητος, as in M. Anton. vi. 30, cf. Preisigke 4426[12] (c. A.D. 274) εὐσυνείδητον πρᾶγμα ποιῶν.

On συνείδησις see further Norden *Agnostos Theos* p. 136, n.[1], Bohlig *Geisteskultur von Tarsus*, p. 122 ff., and Bonhöffer *Epiktet.* p. 156 f.

συνεῖδον.

See s.v. σύνοιδα.

σύνειμι

(from εἰμί, "am"), "am with" (Lk 9[18], Ac 22[11]) : cf. P Flor I. 99[5] (i/ii A.D.) (= *Selections*, p. 71) τοῦ συνόντος ἀνδρός, "her present husband," P Oxy VI. 907[16] (A.D. 276) Πρείσκᾳ τῇ συνούσῃ μοι [γυναικί, "Prisca my present wife." The verb is very common of coming together in wedlock, e.g. P Tebt I. 104[29] (marriage contract—B.C. 92) μηδ᾽ ἄλλω[ι] ἀνδρ[ὶ] συνεῖναι, "not to have intercourse with another man," P Ryl II. 154[4] (A.D. 66) αὐ]τοῦ θυγατρὶ προούσῃ[ι] κ[αὶ] συνούσηι τοῦ Χα[ιρήμονος] γυναικὶ [Θαι]σαρίωι, "his daughter Thaisarion, who has formerly lived with Chaeremon as his wife" (Edd.), P Oxy II. 267[18] (A.D. 36) ἐπεὶ δὲ σύνεσμεν ἀλλήλοις ἀγράφω[ς], "and since we are living together without a marriage contract" (Edd.), *ib.* II. 237[viii. 43] (A.D. 186) τούτῳ τῷ ἀνδρὶ οὐθὲν [προσ]ήκ[ει] συνίναι, "she ought not to live with this man."

For the double comp[d]. συνένειμι, see P Oxy VI. 929[12] (ii/iii A.D.) ταῦτα δὲ πάντα συγνῆι εἰς τὸν χιτῶνα τὸν καροῖνον, "all these were inside the brown tunic."

σύνειμι

(from εἶμι, "go"), "come together," is found in the NT only in Lk 8[4]. All Preisigke's exx. from the papyri are late, e.g. P Lond V. 1674[49] (c. A.D. 570) and *ib.* 1686[31] (A.D. 565).

συνεισέρχομαι,

"enter together" (Jn 6[22], 18[15]) : cf. BGU II. 388[ii. 26] (2nd half ii/A.D.) (= *Chrest.* II. p. 109) με]τὰ δὲ δύο ἡμέ[ρ]α[ς] τοῦ συνεισ[ελθεῖν το]ὺς ἄρχοντας εἰς τὴ[ν οἰκία]ν, PSI I. 65[14] (vi/A.D.) συνεισέλθομεν εἰς τὴν παστάτ(= διὰ ("porch") τοῦ θ(εο)ῦ.

συνέκδημος,

"a travelling-companion" (Ac 19[29], 2 Cor 8[19]) : cf. *OGIS* 494[13] (i/ii A.D. ?) συν[έ]γδημος ἀναγραφεὶς ἐν [αἰ]ραρίῳ [Μ]εσσάλλα τοῦ γε[νο]μένου τῆς ᾿Ασίας ἀνθυπ[ά]του, where the editor notes that συνέγδημος = Lat. *comes*. See also *Syll* 657 (= [3]1052)[6] (i/B.C. *ad init.*) συνέγδαμοι, private individuals who had voluntarily accompanied a legation to Samothrace in connexion with initiation to the mysteries.

συνεκλεκτός,

"chosen together with," occurs in the NT only in 1 Pet 5[13] with ἐκκλησία understood. In P Strass I. 73[18]

(iii/A.D.) for ἐκπλέξας Keil reads <συν>εκλέξας, from συνεκλέγω, "raise or collect by borrowing."

συνεπιμαρτυρέω,

"bear witness together with" (Heb 2[4]) : cf. Aristeas 191 συνεπιμαρτυρήσας δὲ τούτῳ τὸν ἐχόμενον ἠρώτα, "he expressed his approval and asked the next" (Thackeray).

συνεπιτίθημι.

The aor. mid. of this double comp[d]., συνεπέθεντο, is found in Ac 24[9] = "joined in attacking." The verb is classical, and may also be illustrated from such passages in the LXX as Deut 32[27] ἵνα μὴ συνεπιθῶνται οἱ ὑπεναντίοι.

συνέπομαι,

"accompany" (Ac 20[4]) : see P Oxy XII. 1415[8] (late iii/A.D.) where the prytanis in submitting his case to the Senate adds, συ[ν]εσπόμενοι δὲ καὶ περὶ . . ., "and we will also add a statement regarding . . . ."

συνεργέω,

"work along with," "co-operate with"; P Lond 008[25] (A.D. 139) (= III. p. 133) δέον αὐτὸν ἀποδοῦναι συνεργῶν (*l.* συνεργοῦντα) τῇι γυναικί, P Leid W[xv. 18] (ii/iii A.D.) (= II. p. 133) τὸν συνεργοῦντα ᾿Απόλλωνα, "adjutorem Apolinem," P Amh II. 152[4] (v/vi A.D.) τοῦ θεοῦ συνεργήσαντος. Musonius p. 21[22] συνεργεῖ μὲν γὰρ καὶ τῇ πράξει ὁ λόγος, and M. Anton. vi. 42 πάντες εἰς ἓν ἀποτέλεσμα συνεργοῦμεν, "we are fellow-workers towards the fulfilment of one object" (Haines). For the trans. usage "cause to work together" see Rom 8[28] AB with note by SH, who for this use of συνεργεῖ compare *Test. xii. patr.* Issach. 3 and Gad 4. For the subst. συνέργεια, see P Lond 41 [recto]so[4] (ii/B.C.) (= I. p. 29, UPZ i. p. 280) σοῦ . . . ἐν τῇι τούτων ἐνεργείαι ἐπιταθέντος, and P Leid D[ii] (B.C. 162 = I. p. 25, UPZ i. p. 231) προσδεόμενος δ᾽ ἔτι τυχεῖν καὶ ἐν τοῦτο <ι>ς συνεργείας.

συνεργός,

"a fellow-worker": P Fay 12[10] (c. B.C. 103) προσλαβόμενος συνεργὸ[ν] ᾿Αμμώνιον, "having taken as a confederate Ammonius," BGU I. 361[iii. 19] (A.D. 184) ἡ Τασεὺς συνερ[γ]ὸς αὐτοῦ ἐγένετο, and *ib.* 168[15] (ii/iii A.D.). Other exx. are Teles p. 40[3] ἔχων συνεργὸν τὸν πλοῦτον τῇ αὐτοῦ κακίᾳ, Musonius p. 11[3] ὁμονοίας ἀγαθὴ συνεργός, Menander ᾿Επιτρέπ. 82 f. ποιμήν τις . . . τῶν τούτῳ συνεργῶν, "a certain shepherd, one of his mates" (Waddell).

The neut. plur. is used as a subst. = "tools." e.g. P Oxy VII. 1069[5] (iii/A.D.) εἵ[ν]α λάβῃς τὰ σίνεργά μου κα[ὶ] τὸν μεισθὸν τῶν γερζεγῶν, "so that you may receive my tools (?) and the wages of the weavers" (Ed.), *ib.* VIII. 1159[20] (late iii/A.D.) ἔασ[ο]ν δὲ παρ᾽ αὐτοῖς τὰ σίν[ερ]γα ἕως πέμψω τὰ ἀναλώματα, "leave the tools with them until I send the expenses" (Ed.).

συνέρχομαι,

"come together," "assemble": P Oxy IX. 1187[6] (A.D. 254) συνελθε[ῖ]ν σήμερον ἐν τῷ συνήθει τόπῳ, "to assemble to-day at the accustomed place" (Ed.): cf. Mk

3²⁰, *al.* The verb is common in connexion with marriage, as in Mt 1¹⁸, e.g. BGU IV. 1050⁶ (time of Augustus) συγχωροῦσιν Ἰσιδώρα καὶ Διονύσιος συνεληλυθέναι ἀλλήλοις πρὸς γάμο(ν), so *ib.* 1098⁸ (c. B.C. 20), 1105⁸ (c. B.C. 10), P Tebt II. 351² (ii/A.D.) οἰκί(ας) . . δοθείσης αὐτῆ . . . συνερχο(μένη) τῷ ὁμομητ(ρίῳ) ἀδελ(φῷ), "a house given to her on her marriage with her brother on the mother's side," *ib.* 334¹ (A.D. 200–1) σ[υ]νῆλθον πρὸς γάμον Ἑρμῇ, "I was united in marriage to Hermes" (Edd.): cf. also *Gnomon* 47 (= BGU V. p. 23) (c. A.D. 150) ἀστὴ συνελθοῦσα Αἰ[γ]υ[πτίῳ] κατ' ἄγνοιαν ὡς ἀστῷ ἀνεύθυνός ἐστιν, and the use of the subst. συνέλευσις in PSI V. 450¹⁰ (ii/iii A.D.), with which the editor compares P Oxy XII. 1473⁶ (A.D. 201) ἅμα τῇ τοῦ γάμ[ο]υ αὐτῶν προσελεύσει.

For the Lukan sense "accompany" (Lk 23⁵⁵, Ac 9³⁹), cf. BGU II. 596⁴ (A.D. 84) (= *Selections*, p. 64) καλῶς ποιήσεις συνελθὼν [Α]ἰλουρίωνι τῶι κομίζοντί σοι τὸ ἐπι[ι]στ[ό]λιον, "please accompany Ailourion who conveys this letter to you," and *ib.* 380¹³ (iii/A.D.) (= *Selections*, p. 105).

συνεσθίω,

"I eat in company with" (Lk 15², *al.*): cf. *Syll* 813(= ³1179)¹⁹ συμπιεῖν καὶ συμφαγεῖν καὶ ἐπ[ὶ τὸ α]ὐτὸ στέγος ἐ[λθ]εῖν.

σύνεσις

in its wider sense "intelligence," "understanding," as in Lk 2⁴⁷, is seen in such a passage as *OGIS* 323⁶ (B.C. 159–138) συνέσει καὶ παιδείαι προάγων. For its more "critical" aspect as distinguished from σοφία, the apprehension of general principles, see Abbott *ICC ad* Col 1⁹. The noun occurs = "decree" in the Andanian mystery inscr. *Syll*³ 736¹¹² (B.C. 92) σύνεσιν ἀνενεγκάντω εἰς τὸ πρυτανεῖον.

συνετός,

while sometimes pass. in earlier writers, is always act. in the NT, "intelligent," lit. "one who can put things together" (Mt 11²⁵ *al.*: *Proleg.* p. 222): cf. *Kaibel* 654¹ (iii/A.D.) τὴν συνετὸν ψυχὴν μακάρων εἰς ἀέρα δοῦσα, and Aristeas 148 παραδέδωκεν ὁ νομοθέτης σημειοῦσθαι τοῖς συνετοῖς, "the lawgiver has taught the understanding to note" (Thackeray). See also *s.v.* ἀσύνετος.

συνευδοκέω,

"approve of," "agree with." An early ex. of this common Hellenistic verb is found in P Grenf II. 26²³ (B.C. 103) συνευδοκοῦντες τῶν προγεγραμμένων. Cf. for the dat. constr., as in Lk 11⁴⁸, Rom 1³², P Oxy XIV. 1644²⁷ (B.C. 63–2) ἐπ[ὶ δ]ὲ πᾶσ[ι τ]οῖς προγεγραμμένοις συνευδοκοῦσιν [οἱ τ]ῶν ὁμ[ολο]γούντων μ[άρτυ]ρες, *ib.* II. 237ᵛⁱ·²¹ (A.D. 186) συνευδοκῆσαι βουληθείσαι<ς> αὐτῷ ὑποτιθεμένῳ τὴν οὐσίαν ταύτην, "when we wished to agree to his mortgaging the property in question" (Edd.). For the absol. use, as in Ac 22²⁰, cf. BGU IV. 1129⁶ (B.C. 13) ὡμολ(όγησεν) ὁ Πρώταρχ(ος) συνευδοκ(ούσης) καὶ τῆς γυναικ(ός). The subst. συνευδόκησις is seen in the sale contract P Oxy X. 1276¹⁹ (A.D. 249) οὐ προσδεόμενος με[τ]αδόσεως οὐδὲ ἑτέρας συνευδοκήσεως ἡμῶν,

"without requiring a notification or any further concurrence on our part" (Edd.), and similarly *ib.* XIV. 1638³¹ (A.D. 282).

συνευωχέομαι,

"feast along with," c. dat., as in 2 Pet 2¹³, occurs in BGU II. 596¹⁰ (A.D. 84) (= *Selections*, p. 64) ἐρωτηθεὶς κατελθὼν συνευωχηθῆ[ι] ἡμεῖν, "you are also invited to come down and feast along with us."

The simple verb εὐωχέομαι may be cited from *OGIS* 168¹¹ (B.C. 115) εὐωχηθεὶς ἐπὶ τοῦ Ἡραίου, *ib.* 383¹⁶⁷ (mid. i/B.C.) ὅπως ἕκαστος . . . ἔχῃ τὴν ἑορτὴν εὐωχούμενος ὅπου προαιρεῖται. For the subst. εὐωχία see P Oxy III. 494²¹ (A.D. 156) where a testator provides for a sum to be paid to his slaves and freedmen for a feast to be celebrated yearly at his tomb on his birthday— εἰς εὐωχίαν αὐτῶν ἣν ποιήσονται πλησίον τοῦ τάφου μου κατ' ἔτος τῇ γενεθλίᾳ μου.

συνέχω.

(1) For the literal meaning of this word "hold together," "keep together," cf. P Cairo Zen II. 59155⁵ (B.C. 256) μὴ πλείους δὲ πέντε ἡμερῶν σύσχῃς τὸ ὕδωρ, with reference to not keeping a piece of land flooded for more than five days; P Tebt II. 410¹¹ (A.D. 16) ἐρωτῶ σε ταχύτερον συσχεῖν τ[ὸ] πρᾶγμα, "I beg you to close the matter with all speed" (Edd.); and *ib.* 399²⁵ (A.D. 167) Ὀννῶφρις συν[έχ]ω τὰς δραχμὰς ἑγατὸν εἴκοσι τέσσαρας, "I Onnophris have received the 124 drachmae," in connexion with a loan on mortgage.

(2) With the usage of the verb in Lk 22⁶³ of the officers who held Jesus *in charge* Deissmann (*BS* p. 160) compares P Petr II. 20ⁱ·¹⁰ (B.C. 252) where in an official minute we read of certain sailors who went to Herakleopolis, καὶ συνέ[σ]χεν αὐτοὺς Ἡρακλείδης ὁ ἀρχιφυλακίτης, "and Herakleides, the chief of the police, arrested them." Add for the same sense P Magd 42² (B.C. 221) προσαπήγαγέν με εἰς τὴν φυλακὴν καὶ συνέσχεν ἐφ' ἡμέρας δ, P Lille I. 7¹⁵ (iii/B.C.) εἶπεν τῶι δεσμοφύ(λακι) δι' ἣν αἰτίαν συνέσχημαι, and cf. BGU IV. 1053ⁱ·³¹ and 1054⁹ (both B.C. 13) where συνέχεσθαι is used of debtors who are "held" until a loan is repaid, and P Lond 1014³⁸ (letter regarding the Meletian schism—A.D. 335 (?)) τοῦτ' οὖν ἤκουσεν Ἀθανάσιος ὅτι Ἀρχέλαος συνεσχέθη, πάνυ ἀθυμεῖ Ἀθανάσιος, "so Athanasius heard this news, that Archelaus was arrested, and Athanasius is very despondent" (Ed.).

(3) An interesting parallel to Lk 4³⁸ is afforded by P Oxy VI. 896⁹ (A.D. 316) where a man is described as πυραιτίοις . . . συνεχ[όμενον, "seized with a slight fever" (Edd.): cf. P Flor III. 296²² (vi/A.D.) τῇ συνεχούσῃ με ἀρρωστίᾳ.

(4) The more tropical sense of the word in Phil 1²³ may be illustrated by P Oxy II. 281²⁵ (A.D. 20–50) where a wife petitions the "Chief Justice" that her husband who had deserted her should be compelled "perforce" to pay back her dowry, ὅπως ἐπαναγκασθῇ συνεχόμενος ἀποδοῦναι κτλ. Field (*Notes*, p. 128) reading συνείχετο τῷ πνεύματι in Ac 18⁵ finds that the verb expresses "some strong internal feeling."

(5) With the description of the spirit of the Lord as τὸ συνέχον τὰ πάντα in Sap 1⁷ may be compared the

inscr. to Attis of A.D. 370, cited by Cumont *Les Religions Orientales* p. 77, cf. p. 267 (Eng. Tr. pp. 62, 226), as καὶ συνέχοντι τὸ πᾶν, and the further reference to Eleusis as συνέχοντα τὸ ἀνθρώπειον γένος ἁγιώτατα μυστήρια (Zosimus iv. 3. 2).

6) The adj. συνεχής may be illustrated by P Hamb I. 65¹³ (A.D. 141-2) ἐν δυ[σὶ σ]φρα[γ]ῖσι [συν]εχέσι ἀλλήλαις, and the adv. συνεχῶς by P Oxy II. 237ⁱ¹⁹ (A.D. 186) τοῦ Ὡρίωνος συνεχῶς ἐπαγγελλομένου ("continually threatening").

συνζάω,

"live along with" (Rom 6⁸ *al.*): cf. the ii/B.C. epigram on Menander discovered in Rome, *Kaibel* 1085¹¹—

  Ἐχρῆν μὲν στῆσαι σὺν Ἔρωτι φίλῳ σε, Μένανδρε,
  ᾧ συνζῶν ἐτέλεις ὄργια τερπνὰ θεοῦ.

See also Aristeas 130.

συνζεύγνυμι,

"yoke together," "join": P Giss I. 34³ (A.D. 265-6) (= *Archiv* v. p. 137) συνεζευγμένων τῶν γενομένων ἐπ' αὐτῷ ὑπομνημάτων, and Wünsch *AF* p. 20⁷⁵ (iii/A.D.) εἴ τις ἄλλος ἵππος τούτοις μέλλει συνζεύγνυσθαι.

The verb is used metaph. of union in wedlock, as in Mt 19⁶, Mk 10⁹, in P Flor I. 36⁹ (beg. iv/A.D.) τοὺς παῖδας [συ]νέ[ζ]ειξα, and *Kaibel* 372²² (c. iv/A.D.)—

  Κυριακὸν γὰρ ἐ[γ]ὼ λιπόμην ἐφ' ἐλπίσι ταύτης,
  Νόννης γαμετῆς συνζευχθῆναι θαλάμῳ.

συνζητέω.

For the NT meaning "discuss," "debate" (Mk 8¹¹ *al.*) cf. P Oxy III. 532¹⁷ (ii/A.D.) ποιήσῃς με πρὸς σὲ ἐλθεῖν συνζητήσοντά σοι, "cause me to come to you and dispute with you about it" (Edd.), and *ib.* XIV. 1673²⁰ (ii/A.D.) τοῖς τὸν ὄνον λαβοῦσι συνεζήτησα πολλὰ καὶ κατέπλεξα, "I had much discussion and complication with the men who took the donkey" (Edd.).

συνζήτησις,

"discussion" (in TR of Ac 28²⁹), is one of the Greek words used by Cicero, *ad Fam.* xvi. 21. 4 *non est enim seiunctus iocus a* φιλολογίᾳ *et quotidiana* συζητήσει. It is also found in Epicurus *Fr.* lxxiv. (ed. Bailey, p. 116).

σύνζυγος,

"yoke-fellow." We can produce no evidence for σύνζυγος as a proper name, though its use as such in Phil 4³ seems probable (WH marg.): see Kennedy *EGT ad l.* For its use as an appellative Thieme (p. 32) cites the Magnesian *graffito* 328 (prob. i A.D.) σ]ύζυγοι Βαίβιος Κάλλιπος: cf. 321.

συνήδομαι.

"delight in" (Rom 7²²): P Oxy XIV. 1663⁴ (ii/iii A.D.) συνήδομαί γε [τ]ῷ φίλῳ σο[υ] κηδεμόνι ἀγαθῷ καὶ ἐπι<ει>κεστάτῳ εἰς τὰ πραγμάτια, "I congratulate you on your dear protector who is good and capable in his affairs" (Edd.): cf. *OGIS* 453²⁹ (B.C. 39-35) ὑμεῖν τε συνήδομαι ἐπὶ τῷ ἔχειν τοιοῦτον πολείτην, *et saepe* in inscr.

PART VII.

συνήθεια

(1) "intimacy," "friendship," as in 4 Macc 2¹² *al.*, P Cairo Zen I. 59042² (B.C. 257) Ἀλέξανδρος . . οἰκεῖος καὶ αὐτῶι δέ μ̣οί εἰσι συ]νήθειαι, P Amh II. 145⁹ (iv/v A.D.) τὸ γνωστὸν τῆς πρὸς ἀλ[λήλο]υς συνηθείας, "the knowledge of our intimacy."

(2) "habit," "custom," as in Jn 15²⁹, P Fay 118¹⁴ (A.D. 110) οἷς ἔχομεν συνήθιαν πέμπιν, "for the persons we are accustomed to send them to" (Edd.), P Tebt II. 287⁵ (A.D. 161-9) κατὰ τὸν [γν]ώμονα καὶ τὴν συνήθειαν, "according to tariff and custom" (Edd.), *ib.* 37⁶¹⁹ (A.D. 162) ἀκολούθως τῇ τῶν ἀρουρῶν [συν]ηθείᾳ, "in accordance with the custom of the land," P Fay 34¹⁰ (A.D. 161) τὴν τῶν προτέρων ἐτῶν συνήθειαν, and *Syll* 418(= ³888)¹⁵⁴ (A.D. 238) κατωλιγωρήθη διὰ τὴν συνήθειαν τῆς τοιαύτης ἐνοχλήσεως. Cf. PSI I. 50⁶ (iv/v A.D.) κατὰ συνήθι[α]ν.

For a technical use of συνήθειαι to denote "customary gifts" to officials, see *Chrest.* I. 283 (vi/A.D.) and the numerous citations in Preisigke *Wörterb. s.v.*

A few exx. may be given of the adj. συνήθης—P Tebt II. 294¹⁷ (A.D. 146) ταῖς συνήθεσι προθεσμίαις, "at the accustomed dates," P Oxy XIV. 1662¹¹ (A.D. 188) μεταφορὰ τούτου εἰς τὸν συνήθη τόπον, P Fay 38³ (iii/iv A.D.) φροντίσατε ἐξαυτῆς τὴν συνήθη παραφυλακὴν γείνεσθαι, "see that you at once provide the necessary guard," and *Kaibel* 1002² ὡς συνήθεις καὶ φίλους ἠσπάζετο. For the adv. see P Amh II. 70ⁱ⁸ (c. A.D. 115) τὸ συνήθω[ς] διδόμ[ε]ν[ο]ν.

συνηλικιώτης.

For this NT ἅπ. εἰρ. (Gal 1¹⁴) = "a contemporary," Preisigke (*Wörterb. s.v.*) cites *CIG* III. 4929.

συνθάπτω.

For the lit. use of this compd. "bury along with," which is metaph. in Rom 6⁴, Col 2¹², cf. P Eleph 2¹² (a Will—B.C. 285-4) ἐὰν δέ τις αὐτῶν μὴ θέλῃ ἢ τραφεῖν ἢ συναποτείνειν ἢ μὴ συνθάπτωσιν, ἀποτεισάτω κτλ.

συνθλάω.

For συνθλάω "crush together," "break in pieces," of divine punishment, as in Mt 21⁴⁴, Lk 20¹⁸, cf. Pss 67(68)²², 109(110)⁵⁶.

συνθρύπτω.

According to Hobart p. 249 θρύπτω is a medical term for the crushing of a calculus, and he thinks that the compd. may have been similarly employed, and, in pursuance of his theme, points out that it is peculiar to Luke (Ac 21¹³) among Greek authors. But LS⁸ cite at least one other passage, Theod. Prodr. 4. 325 συνεθρύβη. For the simplex θρύπτω see P Oxy III. 471⁷⁹ (ii/A.D.) εὔμορφον καὶ πλούσιον μειράκιον ἐθρύπτετο, where the editors render, "this handsome and rich youth gave himself airs."

συνίημι.

For the metaph. meaning "perceive," "understand," which alone is found in the NT, see P Cairo Zen I. 59061⁶ (B.C. 257) συνίημι καὶ αὐ[τός, ἀλλὰ σὺ ἱκανὸς εἶ διοικῆσαι καὶ ἀποστεῖλαι ὡς ἀσφαλέστατα, where συνίημι takes the

78

place of ἐπίσταμαι in the closely parallel 5906⁰¹¹. The literal meaning "bring together" is probable in PSI VI. 665⁷ (iii/B.C.) γεωργοὺς δὲ οὓς οὐ συνίημι, but unfortunately the verb is followed by a lacuna.

συνίστημι

is very common in the papyri, and is used with a great variety of meanings. We can notice only the principal ones, and those most nearly related to the NT occurrences of the word.

(1) From its original meaning "set together," "combine," συνίστημι passes into the sense of "bring together as friends," "introduce," "recommend," as in 1 Petr II. 11(1)⁵ (iii/B.C.) (= *Selections*, p. 7) πέπεισμαι ῥαιδίως με τῶι βασιλεῖ συσταθήσεσθαι, "I am sure that I shall easily be introduced to the King," P Oxy IV. 787 (A.D. 16) ἐρωτῶ σε οὖν ἔχειν συνεσταμένον, "I ask you therefore to hold him as recommended," *ib.* II. 292⁶ (A.D. 25) παρακαλῶ σε μετὰ πάσης δυνάμεως ἔχειν αὐτὸν συνεσταμένον: cf. Rom 16¹, 2 Cor 3¹, *al.*

(2) The meaning "appoint," as a technical legal term, is seen in such passages as P Oxy II. 261¹³ (B.C. 55) where a woman states that she has appointed her grandson to act as her representative in a lawsuit—συνεστακέναι αὐτὴν τὸν προγεγραμμένον υἱωνὸν Χα[ιρ]ήμονα ἔγδικον, *ib.* I. 97²¹ (B.C. 115 ὁ) συνέστησα τὸν ἀδελφὸν ἐμοῦ Νικάνορα ἐπὶ πασει (*l.* πᾶσι) τοῖς προκειμένοις, and P Giss I. 25⁹ (ii/A.D.) συνέστησα γὰρ αὐτὸν διὰ τό σε τότε καταπεπλευκέναι. With this may be compared ὁ συνεσταμένος = "the nominee" in P Oxy II. 320 (A.D. 59) Σεκούνδου τοῦ συνεσταμένου ὑπὸ τῶν μετόχων ἀγο(ρανόμων), and 330 (A.D. 78-83).

See also P Tebt I. 27³⁵ (B.C. 113) ἐπὶ τοῦ συσταθέντος πρὸς σὲ διαλογισμοῦ, "at the inquiry instituted against you" (Edd.), P Amh II. 33⁶ (c. B.C. 157) σ]υνεστηκυίας ἡμῖν καταστάσεως ἐπὶ [Ζω]πύρου τοῦ ἐπι[μ]ελητοῦ, "a trial has been arranged before Zopyrus the epimeletes," and P Lond 1912²¹ (A.D. 41) εἴ ται καὶ συνείστασθαι τὴν ἀρχὴν δεῖ, "whether the order should be constituted" (Ed.).

(3) From this it is a natural transition to "establish," "prove," as in Rom 3⁵ *al.*, cf. BGU IV. 1062¹⁷ (A.D. 236-7) ἔτι δὲ καὶ συστήσασθαι τοὺς ταύτης λόγους.

(4) For the intrans. use "stand with (by)," as in Lk 9³² cf. the legal phrase μετὰ συνεστῶτος or συνεστώτων, of a person or persons "acting with" or "standing by" another, in such passages as P Oxy VI. 912⁴ (A.D. 235) ἐμίσθωσεν Αὐρηλία Βησοῦς . . . μετὰ συνεστῶτος Αὐρηλίου Θέωνος . . . Αὐρηλίῳ Πατύτι . . ., "Aurelia Besous, acting with Aurelius Theon, has leased to Aurelius Patus . . .," and P Ryl II. 165⁶ (A.D. 266), with the editors' notes. Also P Oxy X. 1273⁴⁸ (A.D. 260) Αὐρήλιος Θέων ὁ καὶ Νεπωτιανὸς συνέστην αὐτῇ καὶ ἔγραψα ὑπὲρ αὐ[τ]ῆς μὴ εἰδυίης γράμματα, and P Lond 978²⁰ (A.D. 331) (= III. p. 234) συνέστην τῇ συμβίᾳ μου. The verb is also intransitive in such passages as PSI II. 173¹² (ii/B.C.) τοῦ οὖν καιροῦ τῆς τῶν γενημάτων συναγωγῆς συνεστηκότος, BGU IV. 1102⁹ (deed of divorce—B.C. 13) τῆς συστ[ά]σης αὐτοῖς συνβιώσεως, and P Oxy III. 653¹⁹ (A.D. 162-3) συνέστηκ[ε]ν ὡς ἔκρινεν ὁ χιλίαρχο[ς, "the matter stood as the chiliarch decided."

(5) For the meaning "hold together," "cohere" in Col 1¹⁷ Lightfoot *ad l.* cites Philo *Quis rer. div. her.* 58 ed. Wendland (= I. p. 481) συνέστηκε καὶ ζωπυρεῖται προνοίᾳ θεοῦ, Clem. Rom. 27 ἐν λόγῳ τῆς μεγαλωσύνης αὐτοῦ συνεστήσατο τὰ πάντα, and for the meaning "consist" in 2 Pet 3⁵ see Field *Notes*, p. 242.

(6) Miscellaneous exx. of the verb are—P Amh II. 31⁷ (B.C. 112) ἐπὶ τῆς συσταθείσης πρακτορείας ἐν τοῖς Μεμνονείοις, of agents "engaged upon exacting payment in the Memnonia" (Edd.), P Ryl II. 69¹² (B.C. 34) συνέστησεν ἐπιδιδό(ναι) τὸ ὑπόμνημα, "obliged us to present this petition" (Edd.), P Oxy IX. 1188¹¹ (A.D. 13) ὡς πρὸς ὑμᾶ(ς) τοῦ περὶ τ(ῶν) ἀγνοη(θέντων) λόγ(ου) συστα(θησομένου), "knowing that you will be held accountable in any inquiry concerning facts that remain unknown" (Ed.), BGU I. 22¹⁵ (A.D. 114) (= *Selections*, p. 75) ἄλογόν μοι ἀηδίαν συνεστήσατο, "picked a senseless quarrel with me," so P Lond 342⁶ (A.D. 185) (= II. p. 174), and P Tebt II. 276²³ (ii/iii A.D.) τ[ὸ]ν βίον συστήσεται, "will gain his living."

For the subst. συστάτης = "delegate," see P Oxy VIII. 1116⁵ (A.D. 363), with the editor's note.

For the double comp. ἀποσυνίστημι, cf. P Hamb I. 27¹ (B.C. 250) ἔγραψάς μοι περὶ Πτολεμαίου . ., ὅτι ἐμοὶ αὐτὸν ἀποσυστήσαις, "you write me regarding Ptolemaeus, that you recommend him to me."

συνιστορέω,

"reckon together," is not found in the NT, but to the exx. cited *s.v.* ἱστορέω we may add P Par 15²² (B.C. 120) συνιστοροῦντες ἑαυτοῖς οὐδὲν βέβαιον ἔχουσι ἐξέκλιναν, P Tebt I. 24⁵¹ (B.C. 117) συνιστοροῦντες τὰ πλήθη τῶν ὑποστελλομένων, "reckoning up together the amounts of what had been concealed" (Edd.), and P Tor I. 1ᵛⁱⁱⁱ·¹² (B.C. 116).

συνκάθημαι,

"am sitting with." In a case heard before the Emperor Claudius, *Chrest.* I. 14ⁿ·⁵, certain senators sit along with the Emperor apparently as *assessors*—συνκα[θημένων αὐτῷ] συνκλητικ[ῶ]ν, and ¹³ συνεπένευ[σαν δὲ καὶ οἱ συν]καθήμενοι [π]άντες σ[υνκλητικοὶ εὖ?] εἰδότες κτλ.: cf. Ac 26³⁰. See also the record of lamp-oil in P Cornell 1⁹⁸ (B.C. 256) τοῖς παρὰ Διοσκουρίδου γραμματεῦσιν καὶ σ[υ]νκαθημένοις τὴν νύκτα ἐπὶ λύχνον κο(τύλαι) β.

συνκακουχέω,

"endure adversity with," c. dat. in Heb 11²⁵. According to Grimm-Thayer the verb "is not found elsewhere," but cf. the corr. form συνκακουργοῦντες in BGU I. 15ⁱⁱ·¹¹ (A.D. 194).

συνκαλέω,

"call together" (Mk 15¹⁶ *al.*): cf. BGU II. 511ⁱⁱ·⁵ (c. A.D. 200) συνκα[λέσας συμβούλειον(?) . . . .], and P Lond V. 1711⁵³ (A.D. 566-573) a marriage contract in which along with other interesting conditions a husband promises his wife not to introduce any unsuitable person into the house—προσομολογῶ ἐγὼ ὁ σὸς γαμέτης μὴ συγκαλέσαι τινὰ ἀνακόλουθον κατ' οἴκρν ἐπὶ σέ.

For ἡ σύνκλητος, "the senate," cf. P Oxy I. 33 verso[iv 8] (late ii/A.D.) ἄρα ἡ σύνκλητος ἦ σὺ ὁ λήσταρχος : "was it the senate, or you, the arch-pirate?" (Edd.) : cf. P Tebt I. 5[197] (B.C. 118) τὰ{ι} πορεῖα πρὸς τὴν σύνκλητον, "transport for the assembly."

συνκαλύπτω,

"veil completely" (Lk 12[2]) : cf. Syll 804(=[3] 1170)[6] (ii/A.D.) ἐπεὶ δὲ ἐγενόμην ἐν τῷ ἱερῷ, ἐκέλευσεν ἐπὶ δύο ἡμέρας συνκαλύψασθαι τὴν κεφαλήν.

συνκάμπτω,

"bend completely" (Rom 11[10]) : cf. Syll 802(=[3] 1168)[28] (c. iii/B.C.) συγκάμψας τὰν χῆρα.

συνκαταβαίνω,

"come down along with" (Ac 25[5]). For the late metaph. meaning "condescend," see Rutherford NP p. 485 f.

συνκατάθεσις.

With συνκατάθεσις = "agreement," "union," in 2 Cor 6[16], the only occurrence of the word in the NT, we may compare BGU I. 194[11] (A.D. 177) οἱ ἀπὸ τῆς κώμης ἀναδεξάμενοι ἐκ συνκαταθέσεως τὰς λειτουργείας ἐπιβαλλούσας αὐτοῖς, and P Flor I. 58 (iii/A.D.) δίχα γνώμης ἐμῆς καὶ συνκαταθέσε[ω]ς.

συνκατατίθημι.

For the lit. meaning "deposit together," cf. Kaibel 367[4] (iii/A.D.) ἐμαυτὴν ζῶσα συνκατέθηκα τάφῳ. From the idea of putting down the same vote or opinion with another, the verb came to be used in the middle = "agree with," as in P Lond 106[15] (c. A.D. 138–161) (= II. p. 153) Ἀγριππείνου συνκαταθεμένου Ἰουλιανὸς εἶπεν κτλ., BGU II. 388[ii. 34] (ii/iii A.D.) ἐπύθετο, εἰ γνώρι[μα] αὐτοῦ τὰ γράμματ[α], καὶ σ[υ]νκαταθεμένου [Πόστου]μος εἶπεν κτλ., and Cagnat IV. 330[20] (time of Trajan) περὶ πάντων ἃ ἐν αὐτ[ο]ῖς ἠξιώσατε συγκατεθέμην.

συνκαταψηφίζω.

According to Grimm-Thayer this verb = "number along with" is "not found elsewhere" than in Ac 1[26] : but for the form we may cite BGU IV. 1208[ii. 34] (B.C. 27–6) συνκαταριθμεῖσθαι.

συνκεράννυμι,

"mix together," "compound" (1 Cor 12[24] : cf. Kaibel 547[14] (i/A.D.) συνκεράσαι ψυχ[ῆ]ι πνεῦμα φιλανδροτάτηι, and for the pass., as in Heb 4[2], Syll[3] 783[33] (after B.C. 27) Ἐπιγόνη Ἀρτέμωνος αἰσ[ίοις] γάμοις συνκερασθεῖσα. See also Apoc. Petr. 3 συνκέκρατο δὲ τὸ ἐρυθρὸν αὐτῶν τῷ λευκῷ. The subst. σύνκρασις occurs in P Lond 121[512] (iii/A.D.) (= I. p. 100) ὁ ἔχων ἐν σεαυτῷ τὴν τῆς κοσμικῆς φύσεως σύγκρασι(ν).

συνκινέω.

With this verb = "move," "stir up," in Ac 6[12], its only NT occurrence, cf. Polyb. xv. 17. 1 συγκινεῖ πως ἕκαστον ἡμῶν ὁ ξενισμός.

συνκλείω

is used literally, as in Lk 5[6], in the sense of "shut together," "enclose," in such passages as P Fay 12[17] (c. B.C. 103) συνκλείσ[αν]τ[ὲ]ς με εἰς τὴν . . οἰκίαν, Preisigke 5280[11] (A.D. 158) Τούρβων . . κατασχών με εἰσήγαγ[ε]ν ἰς τὴν παρεμβολὴν καὶ συνέκλεισέν με, P Fay 135[7] (iv/A.D.) συνκλισθῆς ἄχρις ἂν πληρώσῃς, "you will be put in prison until you pay" (Edd.), and P Lond 237[9] (c. A.D. 346) (= II. p. 203) εἰς τὰ κάστρα τὰς ἀν[ν]ώνας οὐ συνέκλι = ει]σιν, "did not lock up the corn in the granaries."

For the verb with reference to time cf. Syll 320[18] (c. B.C. 107) τοῦ καιροῦ συγκλείοντος εἰς χειμῶνα (the constr. cf. Rom 11[32]). The subst. occurs in P Oxy II. 275[20] (A.D. 66) (= Selections, p. 56) ἐπὶ συνκλεισμῷ τοῦ ὅλου χρόνου, and P Flor I. 50[114] (A.D. 268) μέχρι συνκλεισμοῦ τοῦ διελθόντος α ἔτους.

συνκληρονόμος,

"fellow-heir," which occurs quater in the NT, is classed by Cremer[9] p. 584 as "unknown in profane Greek," but in addition to Cremer's own reference to Philo leg. ad Gaium § 10, Deissmann (LAE[2], p. 92) cites the word from an Ephesian inscr. of the Imperial period, Brit. Mus. Inscr. III. p. 240. No. 633 Εὐτυχίδος . . . . σ[υ]νκληρονό[μου αὐτ]οῦ, cf. especially 1 Pet 3[7]. Other exx. from Byzantine Greek are P Mon I. 6[12] (A.D. 583) συνκληρονόμον αὐτὸν ποιῆσαι, and P Masp III. 67340 verso[19] τῷ[ν με]τ᾽ ἐμὲ κληρονόμων ἢ [συνγ]κλη[ρο]νόμω[ν.

συνκοινωνός,

"fellow-sharer," "joint partaker," c. gen. pers. as in Phil 1[7], occurs in P Bilabel 19[6. 2] (A.D. 110) Δίδυμος Ἀπολλωνίου Ἀλλίωνι Ἀπολλωνίου συνκοινωνῶ χα[ίρειν).

συνκομίζω,

"bring together," "collect" : cf. P Ryl II. 122[4] (A.D. 127) συνκομισάμενος τὰ πλεῖσ[τα μ]έρη τῆς ἐκβάσεως τῶν ἐδαφῶν, "having gathered the greater part of the produce of the fields" (Edd.), P Tebt II. 501 (ii/iii A.D.) ἐγὼ γὰρ ἢ (l. εἰ) μὴ συνκομίσω τὸν χόρτον ἐν τρισὶ ἡμέραις οὐ δύναμε (l. -μαι) αὐτὰ καταλίψαι, and P Flor II. 150[9] (A.D. 267) ὅταν γὰρ δεήσει τὰ παρά σοι θέρη συνκομισθῆναι πλείονα ἕξει βοηθεῖν σε.

Souter (Lex. s.v.) suggests that in Ac 8[2] the verb may mean, not "take up" for burial (see Field Notes, p. 116 f.) but "get back," "recover" : cf. the use of the mid. in such passages as BGU II. 530[26] (A.D.) (= Selections, p. 62) μόνον διαγράφω τὰ δημόσια μηδὲν συνκομιζόμενος, "only I continue paying the public taxes without getting back anything in return," and P Flor I. 58 (iii/A.D.) τοὺς φόρους συνκομιζομένη : see also Job 5[6] ὥσπερ θιμωνιὰ ἅλωνος καθ᾽ ὥραν συνκομισθεῖσα.

For the subst. συνκομιδή cf. P Cairo Zen I. 50049[3] (see the editor's note), P Fay 135[3] (iv/A.D.) τοῦ καιροῦ καλέσαντος τῆς συγκομιδῆς, "as the season requires the gathering" (Edd.), and P Lond 1001[14] (A.D. 539) (= III. p. 271) καιρῷ συγκομιδῆς [κα]ρπ[ῶ]ν.

συνκρίνω.

In the difficult passage 1 Cor 2¹³ AV and RV follow the late usage of συνκρίνω = παραβάλλω (cf. Lob. *Phryn.* p. 278 f.) and translate "compare" (so also Field *Notes*, p. 168), but Lightfoot (*Notes*, p. 186 f.) prefers the meaning "combine" (cf. RV marg.) and cites Theod. Mops. *ad l.*: διὰ τῶν τοῦ πνεύματος ἀποδείξεων τὴν τοῦ πνεύματος διδασκαλίαν πιστούμεθα. Others take the verb as = "interpret," in keeping with its application in the LXX to the interpretation of dreams (Gen 40⁸·²², 41¹², Dan 5⁷: cf. Polyb. xiv. 3. 7 συνέκρινε καὶ διηρεύνα τὰ λεγόμενα).

We can produce no clear evidence bearing on any of these renderings from our sources, where the prevailing sense of the word is "decide," especially with reference to judicial decisions. A few exx. must suffice— P Lille I. 1 *verso*²⁷ (B.C. 259-8) ὕστερον δὲ ἐπισκοπούμενος τὸ περίχωμα συνέκρινεν ("a décidé") τὰ χώματα ποῆσαι, P Meyer 1⁴ (B.C. 144) περὶ τῶν αὐτῶν συγκρ[ιθ]έντων, P Fay 12³⁹ (c. B.C. 103) συνκρίνωσι πραθχῆναί (l. πραχθῆναί) μοι . . . τῆς ἀδίκου ἀγωγῆς, "give judgment that they shall perforce pay me for the illegal abduction" (Edd.), P Ryl II. 65¹⁶ (judicial sentence—B.C. 67?) συνεκρίναμεν, P Giss I. 61¹⁴ (A.D. 119) τοῦ τυράννου συνκρίναντ[ος τὸν] σωματισμόν, and P Flor I. 56⁷ (A.D. 234) συνέκρειψ[α γραφῆ]ναι καὶ πεμφ[θῆ]ναι τῆς ἐντεύξεως ἀντίγρα[φον).

For σύνκριμα cf. P Amh II. 68³⁴ (late i/A.D.) τῶι κυρίῳ συνκρ[ί]ματι, and for σύνκρισις cf. P Lond 359³ (i/ii A.D.) (= II. p. 150).

συνλαλέω.

For συνλαλέω, "talk together with," c. dat. pers., as in Mk 9⁴ *al.*, cf. P Hib I. 66⁴ (B.C. 228) συνλαλήσω σοι, "I will have a conversation with you," P Eleph 29⁵ (iii/B.C.) περὶ ὧν σοι συνελάλησα σοι (*sic*) ἐχθές, and CPR I. 18²³ (A.D. 124) Βλαίσιος . . . συλλαλήσας Ἀρτε[μι]δ[ώρῳ τ]ῷ νομ[ι]κῷ [π]ε[ρὶ το]ῦ πράγματος. See also from the inscr. OGIS 229²³ (mid. iii/B.C.) συνλελαλήκασιν ὑπὲρ ἀπάντων ἀκολ[ού]θως τοῖς ἐν τῇ ὁμολογίαι γεγραμμένοις.

συνμαθητής,

"fellow-disciple." For this NT ἅπ. εἰρ., Jn 11¹⁶, Bauer *HZNT ad l.* cites Plato *Euthyd.* 1 p. 272 ᶜ, Pollux VI. 159, Diog. Laert. VI. 2, Mart. Polyc. 17. 3. On compounds with συν- in late Greek, see Rutherford *NP*, p. 255 f.

συνμαρτυρέω,

"bear witness with" (Rom 2¹⁵ *al.*): cf. BGU I. 86¹¹ ff. (A.D. 155), where the signature of each attesting witness is accompanied by the words συνμαρτυρῶ καὶ συνσφρακίω. For the subst. σύμμαρτυς cf. BGU II. 600⁶ (ii/iii A.D.), and for συμμαρτύρομαι see the note to PSI VI. 696³ (iii/A.D.).

συνμερίζω,

"distribute in shares." The mid. occurs in 1 Cor 9¹³ in the sense "have a share in": cf. the subst. συμμεριστής, which is read by Preisigke (*Wörterb. s.v.*) in BGU II. 600⁶ (ii/iii A.D.) ἑκάσ]τοτε αὐτοῖς συνμεριστὴς γένομαι ἀκολούθως [τῇ] δι[α]θ[ήκη.

συνμέτοχος.

P Lond V. 1733⁵² (A.D. 594) ἅμα τῶν ἄλλων συμμετόχων ἡμῶν, with reference to the "joint-possessors" of a house

συνμιμητής.

One of Paul's favourite comp[d]ᵇ. in συν-, found only in Phil 3¹⁷ συνμιμηταί μου γίνεσθε, i.e. "vie with each other in imitating me," "one and all of you imitate me," so Lightfoot *ad l.*, comparing the verb συμμιμεῖσθαι in Plato *Polit.* p. 274 D.

συνοδεύω,

"journey along with" (Ac 9⁷): Vett. Val. p. 248⁷ συνοδεύουσα τῷ καταναγκάσαντι δαίμονι. A corresponding verb συνοδοιπορέω occurs in P Giss I. 27⁴ (ii/A.D.) (= *Chrest.* I. p. 29).

συνοδία,

"a company of travellers," is found in the NT only in Lk 2⁴⁴. For συνοδείτης cf. BGU IV. 1137⁹ (B.C. 6) ὑπὲρ Συντρόφου τοῦ Καίσαρος συνοδείτου, P Lond 1178⁴¹ (A.D. 194) (= III. p. 217, *Selections*, p. 99) γεινώσκετε] ὄντα [ἡμῶν] συνοδείτην Ἑρμεῖνον, where the reference is to the adoption of Herminus as the "member" of a gymnastic club, and *Preisigke* 4549¹⁰ (A.D. 226), where an inscr. dealing with a cult assembly ends— τὸ προσκύνημα [τῆς] συνόδου καὶ τῶν συνοδειτῶν καὶ τοῦ γράψαντος. See also *Kaibel* 613³ (ii/A.D.)—

> Ἤμην ποτὲ μουσικὸς ἀνήρ,
> ποιητὴς καὶ κιθαριστής,
> μάλιστα δὲ καὶ συνοδείτης.

σύνοδος.

This is not a NT word, but, in view of its later ecclesiastical importance, its use in Hellenistic Greek for a "club" or "society" may be illustrated as in the interesting diploma of membership in Ἡ ἱερὰ ξυστικὴ περιπολιστικὴ Ἀδριανὴ Ἀντωνιανὴ Σεπτιμιανὴ σύνοδος, "The Worshipful Gymnastic Club of Nomads under the patronage of Hadrian, Antoninus, Septimius" (P Lond 1178³⁸ (A.D. 194) (= III. p. 217, *Selections*, p. 99): cf. also P Oxy VI. 908⁹ (A.D. 199) where a certain Serapion claims that as a member of the Dionyseum and the sacred club—τῶν ἀπὸ τοῦ Διονυσείου καὶ τῆς ἱερᾶς συνόδου—he is exempt from taxation, P Grenf II. 67³ (A.D. 237) (= *Selections*, p. 108) a letter from the president of the village council of Bacchias—ἡγουμένου συνόδου κώ[μη]ς Βακχιάδος—regarding the hire of dancing girls, P Oxy XII. 1412¹⁹ (c. A.D. 284) ἐν τῇ παρούσῃ συνόδῳ, with reference to a special meeting of the Senate; and from the inscr. OGIS 480¹⁷ (beg. i/A.D.) ἡ σεβαστὴ σύνοδος τῶν νέων, and *ib.* 713⁹ (iii/A.D.) ἀπὸ τῆς ἱερᾶς θυμελικῆς καὶ ξυστικῆς συνόδου, "from the worshipful theatrical and gymnastic club."

For σύνοδος with definite religious associations see *s.v.* συναγωγή and Deissmann *LAE*² p. 375; and for an interesting parallel to 1 Cor 3³ see Reitzenstein *Poimandres*, p. 154 n³.

σύνοιδα,

perf. used as a present, "share my knowledge with," "am privy to"; cf. Ac 5[2], 1 Cor 4[4], and see such passages as BGU IV. 1141[10] (B.C. 14) χειρογραφῆσαί σε δεῖ περὶ τοῦ μὴ συνειδέναι τούτοις τὸν Ξύστον, "you must state in writing that Xystus knew nothing of these things," P Oxy II. 240[5] (A.D. 37) μὴ συνειδέναι με μηδενὶ διασεσεισμένωι, "that I know of no one from whom extortions have been made," ib. VI. 808[20] (A.D. 123) συνειδυῖα ἑαυτῇ πολλὰ τῶν ἐμῶν ἀνηρπακυίῃ, "being conscious of the theft of much of my property," Chrest. II. 88[5] (. A.D. 141) οἱ ἐπίτροποι συνειδότες ὡς ἀνόνητος αὐτοῖς ἐστὶν ἡ λογοθεσία, and Syll 807 (= [3]883 [7] n A.D.) μηδὲν αὐτοῖς δεινὸν συνειδότας—a condition of purity. See also s.v. συνείδησις.

συνοικέω.

"live together" of man and wife, as in its only NT occurrence 1 Pet 3[7]; PSI I. 64[4] (III/A.D.) συνοικήσουσά σοι ὡς γνησία γαμετή, P Oxy II. 237[50] (A.D. 186) εἰ συνοικεῖν ἀλλήλοις θέλοιεν, "if they wished to live together," and ib. XII. 1548[15] (A.D. 202-3) ἡ . . θυγά(τηρ) μου συνοικοῦσα τῷ ἀνδρὶ Ἀπολλωνίῳ. Cf. the similar use of συνοικισία in P Eleph 1[2] (B.C. 311-10), and of συνοικίσιον in P Oxy II. 266[11] (A.D. 66) κατὰ τὰ συ[ν]γραφὴν συνοικισίου, "in accordance with a contract of marriage," ib.

The verb is used more generally in P Amh II. 141[5] (A.D. 350) γνήσιός μου ἀδελφ[ό]ς . . . [ο]σσος συνοικ[εῖ] μοι, "my full brother . . . ssus lives with me," and Chrest. II. 96[8] (?after A.D. 350) ὁ παῖς καὶ συν[ο]ικ[εῖ] τῇ ἀδελφῇ. Cf. also συνοικίζω in Syll 709[10] (. B.C. 107) πόλιν ἐπὶ τοῦ τόπου συνοικίσας. A new verb συνοικιάζω occurs in P Lond V. 1735[11] (late vi A.D.), apparently in the sense of enlarging the house by adding new buildings to it (see the editor's note). For the subst. συνοικία cf. P Petr III. 65[a].[5] (iii B.C.), the report of a searcher for stolen goods ἐν τῇ Ἡρακλείτου συνοικίαι: in ib. 73[7] (iii B.C.) the word is = "lodging-house." Cf. also BGU VII. 1573[15] (A.D. 141-2) (τέταρτον μέρος συνοικίας, and the dim. συνοικίδιον in ib.[12].

συνοικοδομέω.

For the literal use of this verb = "build together," which is used metaphorically in its only NT occurrence (Eph 2[22]), cf. P Oxy XIV. 1648[69] (late ii A.D.) τὰ συνῳκοδομημένα βαφικὰ ἐργαστήρια, "dyeing-workshops constructed jointly" (Edd.), and Syll 431(= [3]913[16]) (before B.C. 330) ἡ νῦν οὖσα ἀγορὰ συνοικοδομῆται.

συνομιλέω.

"talk with" (Ac 10[27]); cf. BGU II. 401[13] (as amended p. 356) (A.D. 618) φανερῶς συνομειλῶν μετὰ Θεοδώρας, and for the adj. see Vett. Val. p. 109[4] σύνοικος καὶ συνόμιλος γενόμενος.

συνομορέω.

"border on," "am contiguous to," is found only in Ac 18[7]. For the simplex ὁμορέω, cf. P Amh II. 68[?] (late i A.D.) τῆς ἄλλης ὁμορούσης γῆς.

συνοχή.

lit. "compression" (as in Aristeas 61), came to be used metaph. in Biblical Greek = "straits," "anxiety" (Lk 21[25], 2 Cor 2[4]); cf. the magical P Lond 122[50] (iv A.D.) (= I. p. 117) διάσωσόν μου . . ἀπὸ πάσης συνοχῆς, Kaibel 1042[2] σ[υν]οχή τις ἔσται σοι κακῶν τε καὶ καλῶν, and Vett. Val. p. 2[?] κρυβάς, συνοχάς, δεσμά, πένθη, et saepe. An early ex. of the noun is afforded by P Lond 354[24] (c. b.c. 10) (= II. p. 165) where the sentence is apparently = "imprisonment." This is also the meaning in Didache i. 5 ἐν συνοχῇ δὲ γενόμενος ἐξετασθήσεται περὶ ὧν ἔπραξε. See further Deissmann LAE p. 95 n.5, and Bell Cyrenaica p. 135.

συνπαθέω.

We have no early exx. of this verb "suffer along with," as in Heb 4[15], 10[34], but cf. Menander Fragm. 227 No. 17 ὃς . . . ὁ Χριστὸς μόνος συνπαθήσει πλανωμένῳ κόσμῳ, and Philo Leg. ad Gaium p. 10[?] ἡ φιλανθρωπία αὐτοῦ . . . τοῦ θεοῦ ἀνείκαστος οὖσα συμπαθήσει τὸ πλῆθος τῶν ἀνομιῶν μου.

συνπαραγίνομαι.

"arrive along with"; PSI V. 532[11] (B.C. 257-6) ᾠχόμεθα πρὸς Ζωΐλον καὶ ἠξιοῦμεν αὐτὸν συμπαραγενέσθαι: cf. Lk 23[48] and the TR of 2 Tim 4[16]. See also the astrological Vett. Val. p. 64[22].

συνπαραλαμβάνω.

"take along with" (as helper), as in Ac 15[37] where Ramsay (Paul p. 253) points out that the word implies "a private companion or minister, who is not sent forth on the mission as an envoy, but is taken by the envoys on their own authority." Cf. BGU I. 220[12] (A.D. 69) περὶ ἧς ἐνεχίρισε συνπαραλαβὼν ἑαυτῷ τὸν τοῦ ἑτέρου μου ἀδελφοῦ Ἐριέως, and P Lond 358[?] (A.D. 150) (= II. p. 172) συμπαραλαβόντας αὐτοῖς Ἡρακλείδην ὑπηρέτην. See also P Ryl II. 189[?] (A.D. 128), where the verb appears bis in a receipt issued by the receivers of public clothing—Διογέν[η]ς παρέλαβα. Ὀνησᾶς συνπαρέλαβα. Φιλόξενος συνπαρέλαβα. "Received by me, Diogenes. Received also by me, Onesas. Received also by me, Philoxenus."

συνπάρειμι,

"am present along with" (Ac 25[24]); cf. PSI IV. 435[9] (B.C. 244-3) συμπαρῆν δὲ τούτοις καὶ Γλαυκίας, P Fay 12[14] (. B.C. 103) σὺν τούτοις καὶ ἑτέρους συμπαρόντας, "others besides themselves being present," BGU IV. 1137[5] (B.C. 6) συμπαρόντων τῶν πλείστων, and P Oxy I. 42[5] (A.D. 323) δι[π]λῇ τῶν θεατῶν συνπαρεσομένων τῇ τέρψει. "the spectators will be present at two performances" (Edd.). Other exx. in Mayser Gr. i. p. 503.

For a semi-technical use of συνπάρειμι, like συνίστημι (q.v.(4)), cf. P Ryl II. 120[?] (A.D. 167) συνπάρειμι α[ὐ]τῇ κα[ὶ] ἔγραψα ὑπὲρ αὐτῆς μὴ εἰδυίης [γράμματα, "I act as her representative, and write for her seeing that she does not know letters"; cf. [3] with the editors' note.

συνπάσχω,

"suffer together" (Rom 8¹⁷, 1 Cor 12²⁶): cf. P Oxy VI. 904⁷ (v/A.D.) μὴ υἱὸν δυνάμενον ἅμα μοι συνπαθῖν, and the epitaph of a pantomime *Kaibel* 608³ (ii/iii A.D.) συν‑πάσχων κείνοις [οἷσ]περ κεινεῖτο προσώποις. See also Cic. *ad Atticum* xii. 11. *Atticae hilaritatem libenter audio; commotiunculis* συμπάσχω.

συνπέμπω,

"send along with." For constr. c. acc. and dat., as in 2 Cor 8²², cf. P Oxy II. 237 ⁷ ²⁹ (A.D. 186) οὐδὲν δὲ ἧττον συνπέμψας τῇ ἐπιστολῇ. Other exx. of the verb are P Flor II. 215¹² (A.D. 250) τὸ δὲ ἐπιστόλιον ὃ συνέπεμψα πρὸς Ἥρωνα, and OGIS 315⁵⁰ (B.C. 164–159) συν[πε]μφθῆναί τινα αὐτῶι παρὰ σοῦ. For the meaning "send to the help of," see *Chrest.* I. 11⁴⁷ (B.C. 123) παρακα‑λέ[σα]ντες κα[ὶ] ἡμᾶς συ[ν]πέμψαι αὐτοῖς ἐξ ἡμῶν ε[ἰ]ς Ἑρμῶν⟨θιν⟩ τοὺς ἴσους ἄνδ ρας) θ.

συνπεριλαμβάνω.

The participle of this verb, which is = "embrace" in Ac 20¹⁰, is common in land-surveys in the sense of "in‑cluded," e.g. P Tebt I. 62⁴⁸ (B.C. 119–8) where it is stated that so many arourae are taken up by a shrine of Isis—Ἰσιεῖου συ[μπεριειλημμένου?): see the editors' note, where reference is made to *ib.* 81³⁰ (late ii/B.C.), 84⁹ (B.C. 118), *al.*

συνπίνω.

See *s.v.* συνεσθίω.

συνπίπτω.

For this verb = "fall together," "fall in," as in Lk 6⁴⁹, cf. P Oxy IX. 1188²⁴ (A.D. 13) ἀκάνθας συνπεπτωκ υίας) δύο, *ib.* II. 248²⁸ (A.D. 80) "two fallen acacia trees," *ib.* II. 248²⁸ (A.D. 80) κοινωνικῆς ἐπαύλεως συνπεπ[τω]κυίας, and *ib.* III. 510¹³ (A.D. 101) μέρεσι οἰκίας συμπεπτωκυίης, "shares of a house that has fallen in." Cf. the use of the subst. in BGU II. 475⁷ (ii/A.D.) ἄλλων (*sc.* τόπων) . . . δηλωθέντων εἶναι ἐν συμπτώσι, and of the adj. συμπτώσιμος in P Goodsp Cairo 13¹ (A.D. 341) ἀπὸ διαθ[έσε]ως παλαιᾶς συμπτωσίμοις (*l.* συμπτωσίμου) οἰκίας.

The verb is also used = "meet with anyone," as in P Par 49¹⁰ (before B.C. 161) (= *UPZ* i. 62¹⁰) τοῦ δὲ ἀδελφοῦ σου συμπεσόντος μοι, P Tebt I. 58⁵⁶ (B.C. 111) ἐὰν δεῖ συνπεσῖν τῶι Ἀνικήτωι σύνπεσαι, "if you must meet Anicetus, meet him."

A compd. συνεμπίπτω is seen in P Oxy II. 243³³ (A.D. 79) σὺν τοῖς καὶ εἰς τούτους συνεμπεσουμένοις φορτίοις πᾶσι, "together with all the fixtures that may be included in them" (Edd.).

συνπληρόω.

(1) For the Lukan usage (9⁵¹, Ac 2¹) "complete," "fulfil," with reference to time, cf. BGU IV. 1122²² (B.C. 13) ἐπὶ δὲ τοῦ συνπληρω(θῆναι) τοῦτον (*sc.* χρόνον), and the corresponding use of the subst. in P Grenf II. 33⁷ (B.C. 100) εἰς συμπλήρωσιν ἐτ[ῶν πέν]τε, P Giss I. 50²² (vi/A.D.) πρὸ συμπληρ(ώ σεως) το(ῦ) αὐτ(οῦ) δεκα⟨έ⟩τους [χρόνου: cf. P Oxy XIV. 1626¹⁶ (A.D. 325) τὰ δὲ φανησόμενα ἄχρι συνπληρώσεως τῆς ἐπιμελείας ἀπολήμψεται παρὰ τῶν αὐτῶν δεκανῶν, "and shall receive from the said *decani*

---

the sums found to have accrued up to the termination of his duties as superintendent" (Edd.).

(2) The verb in the sense of "accomplish," "make up," is seen in such passages as P Par 63⁶⁷ (B.C. 164) (= P Petr III. p. 22) ῥᾳδί[ω]ς τὰ τῆς χρίας σ[υ]νπληροῦν, "to accomplish with ease what was required" (Mahaffy), *Chrest.* I. 167²⁴ (B.C. 131) προνοήθητι ὡς μάλιστα μὲν συνπληρωθήσεται τὰ τοῦ παρελθόντος ἔτους κεφ[ά]λαια. Cf. P Petr II. 38(a)²² (iii/B.C.) ἤδη μιᾶς μὲν ἅλω συνπεπληρωμένης, "one threshing-floor being already filled" (cf. Lk 8²³), and the subst. in P Fay 44¹⁰ (B.C. 16?) εἰς συνπλήρωσιν χαλκοῦ (ταλάντων) πέντε, "making up a total of 5 talents of copper" (Edd.), P Tebt II. 573 (late i/B.C.) ἔκθεσις εἰς συνπλήρωσι[ν] (δραχμῶν) ιβ, P Oxy I. 114¹⁵ (ii/iii A.D.) πώλησον τὰ ψέλια εἰς συμ‑[[ρω]]πλήρωσιν τοῦ κέρματος, "sell the bracelets to make up the money" (Edd.), and *ib.* XIV. 1713¹⁴ (A.D. 279) εἰς δὲ τὴν συνπλήρωσιν τοῦ προκειμένου παντὸς κεφαλέου (= αίου).

συνπολίτης,

"fellow-citizen," a compd. condemned by the Atticists (Rutherford *NP* p. 255 f.), but found in Eph 2¹⁹: cf. BGU II. 632⁹ (ii/A.D.) παρὰ Ἀντωνε[ί]νου τοῦ συνπολ[ε]ίτου ἡμῶν, Preisigke 4317²⁵ (c. A.D. 200) ὕβρισμαι . . παρὰ πάντων τῶν συμπολιτῶν, and P Oxy VIII. 1119¹⁹ (A.D. 254) συμ]πολεῖται ἡμέτεροι προσῆλθον ἡμεῖν διὰ βιβλει‑δίων, "our fellow-citizens have approached us in a petition" (Ed.).

The verb occurs in what appears to be a school exercise written on the *verso* of P Oxy I. 79 (A.D. 181–192), where, after a reference to the death of someone, the writer continues σὺν τοῖς σ[τρ]ατιώταις . . . συμπολιτενόμεθα. See also OGIS 143⁶ (B.C. 146–116), with note.

συνπορεύομαι,

"journey together" (Lk 7¹¹ *al.*): PSI IV. 353¹³ (B.C. 254–3) τὸν μεθ' αὑτοῦ συμπορευόμενον.

συνπρεσβύτερος,

"fellow-elder" (1 Pet 5¹): cf. OGIS 339¹¹ (c. B.C. 120) πάντα τὰ συνφέροντα κατηργάσατο μετὰ τῶν συνπρεσ‑βευτῶν τῶι δήμωι.

συνσ—

See *passim* συσσ—

συνστέλλω,

which is used of time, "draw together," "shorten" in 1 Cor 7²⁹, is applied to the "curtailing" of expenses in P Amh II. 70(a)³ (c. A.D. 115) κελεύσαντος συσταλῆναι τὰ πολλὰ τῶν ἀγαλωμάτων τῆ[ς γυ]μνασιαρχίας, P Ryl II. 225⁴⁷ (ii/iii A.D.) δαπανῶν συσταλ(εισῶν) (δραχμαὶ) γ̄, and *Syll* 730 (= ³1102)¹¹ (B.C. 175–4) ἵνα συνσταλῶσιν αἱ λίαν ἄκαιροι δαπάναι.

συνστοιχέω,

as a military term "keep in line with," is found in Polyb. x. 23. 7 ἐφ' ὅσον συζυγοῦντας καὶ συστοιχοῦντας διαμένειν. For the metaph. usage "correspond exactly to" in Gal 4²³, cf. the adj. in BGU IV. 1205¹¹ (B.C. 28) οὐδὲ γὰρ σύνστοιχοι ("übereinstimmend") ἑατῶν [γ]ίνεσθε, and in Epicurus *Ep.* I. 76 τὰ σύστοιχα τούτοις, ' kindred phenomena to these " (Bailey).

συνστρατιώτης.

This expressive Pauline comp⁴. (Phil 2²⁵, Philem²) is found in a soldier's letter to his mother, where he mentions that he has borrowed money from a fellow-soldier, BGU III. 814²⁷ (iii/A.D.) κέχρημαι χαλκὸν π[α]ρὰ συστρατιώτου : cf. *Ostr* 1535¹ (ii/B.C.) τοῖς συνστρατιώταις αὐτοῦ, P Meyer 20¹⁴ (1st half iii/A.D.) ἔπεμσα διὰ Διοσκόρ[ο]υ συνστρατιώτου Διοπολείτου, and the Christian P Grenf I. 53⁶ (iv/A.D.) ἔπεμψά σοι διὰ Ἀπῶνος τοῦ συνσρατιώτου σοι γράμματα καὶ μάφορτιν ("a head-dress "). In *Menandrea* p. 120⁷¹ συ]στρατ[ιώτας is a probable supplement. For the verb see P Frankf 7¹·² (after B.C. 218-7).

συνσχηματίζω.

On συνσχηματίζεσθε in Rom 12² = "be ye outwardly conformed" as contrasted with μεταμορφοῦσθε, "be ye inwardly conformed," see Field *Notes.* p. 162.

σύνσωμος

is found in the NT only in Eph 3⁶, and may have been coined by Paul for the occasion. The word is usually understood as "fellow-member of the body," i.e. of the Church, but, as Preuschen has pointed out (*ZNTW* i. (1900), p. 85 f.), it cannot then be associated with the following gen. τῆς ἐπαγγελίας, nor is there any real sequence of thought in the three epithets συνκληρονόμα—σύνσωμα—συνμέτοχα. Accordingly, taking σῶμα in its sense of "slave" (see *s.v.*), he thinks that we have a term equivalent to σύνδουλος (Col 1⁷, *al.*), and that the meaning is that "the Gentiles are fellow-heirs and fellow-slaves, and so fellow-partakers of the promise."

συντάσσω,

"direct," "command": cf. P Cairo Zen II. 59155¹ (B.C. 256) ὁ βασιλεὺς συνέτασσεν ἡμῖν διπορῆσαι τὴν γῆν, "the King has been bidding me sow a second crop on the land," P Petr III. 61¹ᵇ (iii/B.C.) ἔγρ[αψ]εν Δῶρος αὐτοῦ συντάξαντος διὰ τὸ μὴ ἐπίστασθαι αὐ[τὸ]ν τὸν Ἀπολλώνιον] γράμματα, "Dorus wrote at his request because Apollonius cannot write," P Hib I. 147 (early iii/B.C.) σύντασσε [τοὺ]ς παρὰ σοὶ φ[ύ]λακας φυλάσσειν, P Tebt I. 40¹³ (B.C. 117) (= *Selections*, p. 28) ἀξιῶ συντάξαι γράψαι Δημητρίωι, "I beg you to give orders to write to Demetrius," P Oxy II. 278¹⁹ (A.D. 17) ὅπου [ἐ]ὰν συντάσσῃ ὁ Ἰσίδωρος ἐν Ὀξυρύγχων π[ό]λει, "at whatever spot in Oxyrhynchus Isidorus may require," *ib.* I. 106⁸ (A.D. 135) ἀπήγγειλα ὑμῖν . . Δημήτριον συντεταχέναι ἀναδοῦναι . . ., "I beg to inform you that Demetrius instructed me to give up . . . ." and P Meyer 8¹² (A.D. 151) πάντα [καταγραφῆναι] συνέταξεν εἰς τὸ τῆς γυναικὸς αὐτοῦ ὄνομα. P Leid B ¹¹·¹⁴ (B.C. 164) (= I. p. 10, *UPZ* i. 20³⁷) συντάγηι ἀποδοῦναι gives us an early ex. of the irrational ι adscript.

In P Cairo Zen II. 59179⁹ (B.C. 255) οἱ [συ]νταξάμενοι οὐ συνήντησαν ἐπὶ τὴν [κρίσιν] the editor renders οἱ συνταξάμενοι, "those who agreed to appear."

For συνταγή, see P Bilabel 35³ (A.D. 87) πα[ρ]αβὰς σου τὴν συνταγή[ν: for σύνταξις, see P Cairo Zen I. 59073¹¹ (B.C. 257) ὁ ἐπὶ τῆς συντάξεως ἐμ Μέμφ[ει (with the editor's note), and P Par 26⁶ (B.C. 162) (= *UPZ* i. p. 247, *Selections*, p. 13) τὴν καθήκουσαν ἡμῖν δίδοσθαι σύνταξιν τῶν δεόντων, "the contribution of the necessaries which it is fitting should be given to us," where the reference is to a contribution from the royal treasury for religious purposes (see Otto *Priester* i. p. 366 ff.): for συντάξιμος (not in LS⁸), see P Giss I. 94¹ (A.D. 60-7): and for ἀσυντάκτως, see P Par 32²⁵ (B.C. 161) (= Witkowski², p. 68, *UPZ* i. p. 305).

συντέλεια,

"consummation," "completion," in relation to time, as in the Jewish apocalyptic expression συντέλεια αἰῶνος, may be illustrated by P Oxy X. 1270¹² (A.D. 159) μέχρι συντελείας τοῦ δι̣ε(ληλυθότος πρώτου] καὶ εἰκοστοῦ ἔτους, "down to the end of and including the 21st year " (Edd.).

For the subst. in reference to completed work, cf. P Petr III. 42 F (c)⁵ (iii/B.C.) (as read p. x.) τὴ]ν συντέλειαν τῶν ἔργων, and the late use in *OGIS* 327⁶ (B.C. 159-138) ἀντὶ τῶν διὰ] τῆς τοῦ πολέμου συντελείας ἐπ̣[ιτευγμάτων ("contrivances"), with the editor's note. The common meaning of "joint-contribution" for public burdens is seen in such a passage as BGU III. 927⁴ (iii/A.D.) παρ̣εσχήκαμέν σοι εἰς λόγον συντελείας [κατὰ] κέλευσιν τοῦ διασημοτάτου μαγίστρου. For παγανικαὶ συντέλειαι, "heathen clubs or unions," see *Archiv* i. p. 410. For συντελείωσις cf. P Flor I. 6¹⁷ (A.D. 210) δ[εό]μεθα πλείονος χρόνου εἰς τὴν συντελείωσιν, and for συντελεστής = "contributor" to a tax, cf. the late P Flor III. 285³ (A.D. 536) and PSI IV. 283⁷ (A.D. 550) with the editors' notes.

συντελέω.

(1) For the ordinary sense "bring to an end," "complete," "finish," cf. P Cairo Zen I. 59124⁷ (B.C. 256) φροντίσας ἵνα τὰ ἔργα συντελῆται, P Petr II. 4(6)¹ᵇ (B.C. 255-4) οὐθὲν τῶν ἔργων συντελεσθήσεται, "no part of the work will be completed," *ib.* 9(3)⁶ (B.C. 241-39) τὰ συντετελεσμένα, and P Tebt I. 33¹⁰ (B.C. 112) (= *Selections*, p. 31) φρόντισον ὡς . . αἱ . . ἐμβα[τηριαι] . . . συντελεσθήσονται, "take care that the landing-stages be completed"—preparations for a visitor.

(2) The verb is a *terminus technicus* for the "supply" of certain fabrics which were government monopolies, as in P Hib I. 68⁸ (c. B.C. 228) εἰς τιμὰς ὀθονίων τῶν συντελουμέν[ω]ν εἰς τὸ βασιλικόν, and *OGIS* 90¹⁸ (Rosetta stone B.C. 196) τῶν τ' εἰς τὸ βασιλικὸν συντελουμένων ἐν τοῖς ἱεροῖς βυσσίνων ὀθονίων: cf. Wilcken *Ostr.* i. p. 266 ff.

Cf. also the verb = "contribute," "pay," certain imposts, as in P Oxy I. 127 *recto*¹ (late vi/A.D.) συντελεῖ ὁ ἔνδοξ[ος] οἶκ(ος) Ὀξυρυγχ(ιτῶν) ὑ(πὲρ) ἐμβολῆς, cf. ⁷ and *ib.* 126¹⁸ (A.D. 572).

(3) In P Lond 1179⁸⁰ (ii/A.D.) (= III. p. 146) τὸ βλάβος ἢ τὸ πῆμα ("calamity") συντελούμενον, the meaning seems to be "make good," while a weakened use of the verb is found in P Fay 12⁸ (c. B.C. 103) ἀδικήματα εἰς μ[ε] . . . συντελεσαμένον, "having done me various injuries " (Edd.), and P Ryl II. 145⁹ (A.D. 38) πλείστας ὕβ[ρι]ς τοῖς παρ' ἐμοῦ συντελῶν, "heaping

insults on my dependants" (Edd.). In PSI VI. 614¹ (iii B.C.) ἵνα περὶ ὧν καταπέπλευκας συντετελεσμένος τὸ τάχος ἀναπλεύσῃς, συντετελεσμένος is used in a middle sense.

In an interesting magical tablet (iv/A.D. ?) from Aschmunen published by the *Società Italiana per la Ricerca dei Papiri Greci in Egitto* in their "Omaggio" to the meeting of classicists in April, 1911, the incantation runs ναὶ κύριε βαλεῖ χθονίων θεῶν συντέλεσον τὰ ἐγγεγραμμένα τῷ πεδάλῳ τούτῳ (No. 5¹⁰), which recalls the Scriptural formula in Mk 13¹, Rom 9²⁸ (λόγον γὰρ συντελῶν καὶ συντέμνων ποιήσει Κύριος ἐπὶ τῆς γῆς).

συντέμνω.

For the metaph. use "cut down," "cut short," λόγον, as in Rom 9²⁸ LXX. cf. Gnomon *procem.* (= BGU V. p. 10) τὰ ἐν μέ[σ]ῳ [κεφ]άλαια συντεμὼν ὑπέταξ[ά] σοι. The subst. συντομή is used literally in P Oxy XIV. 1692¹². ¹⁵ (A.D. 188).

συντηρέω.

For this perfective of τηρέω (*Proleg.* pp. 113, 116) = "keep safe" (1) c. acc. pers., as in Mk 6²⁰. cf. P Tebt II. 410¹¹ (iii/A.D.) πᾶν ποίησον συντηρῆσαι τὴν γυναῖκά μου ἕως παραγένωμε (*l.* παραγένωμαι), "do everything possible to protect my wife until I arrive" (Edd.). P Oxy XII. 1418⁵ (A.D. 247) σ]υντηρῆσαι τὸν παῖδα, and the iv/A.D. Gnostic charm *ib.* VI. 924¹ ἦ μὴν φυλάξῃς καὶ συντηρήσῃς Ἀρίας ἀπὸ τοῦ ἐπιημερινοῦ φρικός, "verily guard and protect Aria from ague by day": and (2) c. acc. rei, as in Mt 9¹⁷, cf. P Bouriant 10¹² (B.C. 88) καλῶς ποιήσεις συντηρῶν τὸν τόπον, BGU IV. 1074² (A.D. 275) τὰ δὲ [ὑ]πὸ το[ῦ] δ[ὲ τ]οῦ Σεβαστοῦ δ[ε]δο[μ]ένα ὑμῖν νόμιμα καὶ φιλάν[θ]ωπα συντηρῶ, "I keep safe the laws and privileges granted to you by Augustus," and *Syll* 930 (= ³705) (B.C. 112) συντηρῆσαι τὰ ἐκ παλαιῶν χρόνων δεδομένα τίμια καὶ φιλάνθρωπα: see also *ib.* 655 (= ³820) (A.D. 83) μυστήρια ἀπὸ πλείστων ἐτῶν συντετηρημένα.

In P Tebt II. 282⁷ (late ii/B.C.) a guard declares that he will keep the best watch possible over other people's holdings—φυ[λακὴν] ἀλ[λο]τρ[ί]ων κλή[ρων] συντηρήσειν ἀπὸ το]ῦ βελτί(σ)του, and in BGU I. 180¹³ (ii/iii A.D.) a veteran claims that in view of his long military service, exemption from public burdens ought to be "strictly observed" in his case— ἐπ᾽ ἐμοῦ συντηρεῖσθαι ὀφείλι. Cf. also *ib.* IV. 1106³¹ (B.C. 13) ἅ τε ἐὰν λάβῃ ἢ πιστευθῇ σῶα συντηρήσειν(εἰν), and *ib.* 1126¹⁵ (B.C. 8), and for the subst. συντηρεία (not in LS⁸) cf. *Syll* 932 (= ³880)⁵² (A.D. 202) συν[τηρ]είας βουγαρίων.

συντίθημι.

(1) "place": P Oxy XIV. 1631¹⁷ (A.D. 280) ταῦτα λαβόντα τὸν οἶνον [σ]υνθήσομεν ἐν τῷ ἡλιαστηρίῳ, "we will put these (*sc.* jars), when they have been filled with wine, in the open-air shed" (Edd.).

(2) "provide," "furnish," "supply": P Cairo Zen I. 59020¹ (B.C. 258) αὐτοὶ δὲ συνεθήκαμε[ν αὐτῆι ὅσα ἠξίωσ]εν ἡμᾶς εἰς τὸν πλοῦν, "we supplied her with whatever she asked us for the voyage," P Petr II. 20 iii.⁸ (= III. 36⁵) (B.C. 252) πυνθανομένου δέ μου τῶν παρ᾽ αὐτοῦ, εἴ τι συντε-

θεικὼς αὐτῶι εἴ[η ἐπὶ σι . . . . and P Lille I. 15³ (B.C. 242–1) (= Witkowski *Epp.*² p. 30) κ̣μναίεία συνθεῖναι αὐτῶι. Cf. also P Hib I. 48¹² (B.C. 255) ἵνα μὴ ἐπικωλύωμαι τὸν λόγον συνθεῖναι, "that I may not be prevented from making up my account" (Edd.).

(3) in mid. and pass. "make a compact with," "covenant," "agree," as in Lk 22⁵, Jn 9²², Ac 23²⁰: P Cairo Zen I. 59052¹ (B.C. 257) οὐθὲν αὐτοῖς συνετέθη, P Fay 34²⁰ (A.D. 161) συνεθέμην πᾶσι τοῖς προκειμένοις, "I agreed to all the aforesaid terms," P Oxy VI. 908¹⁸ (A.D. 199) συ]νεθέμην πρὸς ὑμᾶς, "I made a compact with you," P Oxy XIV. 1668¹² (iii A.D.) οὔπω οὖν ἐγὼ αὐτῷ συνεθέμην περὶ τούτου, ἄχρι οὗ σοι δηλώσω, "I accordingly would not make an agreement with him about this before telling you" (Edd.), *ib.*¹⁵ οὐδ᾽ οὕτως συνέθεντο οἱ ἐργαζόμε[ν]οι, "the workmen had not agreed even on these terms" (Edd.), and *ib.* X. 1280⁵ (iv/A.D.) ὁμολογῶ ἑκουσίᾳ καὶ αὐθαιρέτῳ γνώμῃ συντεθεῖσθαί με πρὸς σὲ ἐπὶ τῷ μαι ἐπικοινωνῖν σοι εἰς τὸν ψυκτῆρα τοῦ καμηλῶνος, "I acknowledge that I have of my own free will covenanted with you to share with you in the arbour of the camel-shed" (Edd.). An unusual use of the word is found in P Oxy I. 78²³ (iii/A.D.) ἵν᾽ οὖν μὴ δόξω συνθέσθαι τῇ τοῦ πραγματικοῦ ἀγνοίᾳ, "to prevent the appearance of my having taken advantage of the tax-collector's ignorance" (Edd.).

For the subst. σύνθεσις see BGU III. 781 i.⁶ (i/A.D.) ἄλλη σύνθεσις πινακίων ἀναγλύπτων στρογγύλων δ, P Hamb I. 10¹³ (ii/A.D.) ἐβάσταξάν μου συνθέσις = εις) τελείας λευκὰς δεκατρεῖς, and P Oxy III. 496¹ (A.D. 127) ἱματίων συνθέσεις δύο, "two dresses." On σύνθημα in LXX Judg 12⁶, see Plater *Vulgate Gr.* p. 13, n.²

συντόμως.

The nearest parallel we can give to the NT usage "briefly" in Ac 24⁴ occurs in an astronomical treatise published in the Rylands papyri, I. 27³² (iii/A.D.) ἄλλως συντομώτερον ἀπὸ ἀρχῆς, "another shorter way, starting from the beginning" (Edd.). But cf. the adj. in a rhetorical fragment of iii/A.D., PSI I. 85² ἀπομνημόνευμα σύντομον ἐπὶ προσώπου τινὸς ἐπενετόν, also⁸.¹⁴, and the subst. in P Leid V⁸. ⁶ (iii/iv A.D.) (= II. p. 33) διὰ πάσης συνστομίας (*l.* συντομίας), "omni brevitate."

The reference of the word to time "quickly," "at once," is common :— P Cairo Zen II. 59201² (B.C. 254) Ἀπολλώνιον τὸν ἐργολάβον ("contractor") ἀποστελοῦμεν πρὸς σὲ συντόμ[ως, P Amh II. 37¹¹ (B.C. 196 or 172) παραγενήσ]ομαι συντόμως, and BGU III. 824¹⁵ (A.D. 55–56) παράβαλε οὖν ἐκεῖ, εἵνα συντόμως αὐτὸ ποιήσῃ καὶ καλόν. Cf. P Cairo Zen I. 59028⁸ (B.C. 258) ὅτι συντομώτατα, and P Grenf II. 94². ⁴ (vi/vii A.D.) διὰ συντόμου.

συντρέχω.

"run together" (Mk 6³³ *al.*): cf. P Lond 106¹⁹ (iii/B.C.) (= I. p. 61) συνδραμόντων πλειόνων, P Tor I. 1 v. ³² (B.C. 116 συντρέχειν ἔτη πρὸς τὰ πῆ, "fluxisse iam annos octo super octoginta," P Tebt I. 48²⁶ (c. B.C. 113) ἡμᾶς τε σὺν τοῖς λοιποῖς γεωργοῖς ὑπόπτως σχόντας συνδεδραμηκέναι, "we together with the rest of the cultivators having had our suspicions aroused ran off with him" (Edd.), PSI III. 174¹³ (ii/B.C.) συνδραμεῖν ἐπὶ τὸν ὅρμ[ι]ον, P Oxy I. 33 iii.⁸

(late ii/A.D.) συνδράμετε, Ῥωμ[α]ῖοι, and *Chrest.* II. 96[11] (after A.D. 350) Νόν]ναν τούτῳ τῷ λόγῳ συνδεδραμηκέναι. For a weakened sense see P Fay 133[7] (iv/A.D.) ἵνα καὶ τὰ κοῦφά σοι [σ]υνδράμῃ, "in order that you may collect the vessels," and similarly P Flor II. 134*[7] (A.D. 260).

A subst. συντρέχεια (not in LS[8]) occurs in P Flor III. 288[2] (vi/A.D.).

συντρίβω

is used figuratively "bruise," "crush," as in Rom 16[20], in P Petr II. 4(3)[5] (B.C. 255–4), where certain workmen complain, ἐλθόντων ἡμῶν ἐπὶ τὰ ἔργα συνετριβόμεθα. For the meaning "break down," "shatter," as in Mk 5[4], cf. P Par 35[23] (B.C. 163) (= *UPZ* i. p. 30) ἐσκύλησεν τὸν ναὸν ὥστε κινδυνεῦσαι καὶ συντρίψαι αὐτόν, and P Tebt I. 45[21] (B.C. 113) οὐδενὶ κόσμωι χρησάμενοι συντρίψαντες τὴν παρόδιον θύραν, "throwing off all restraint knocked down the street door" (Edd.), and so 47[13, 18].

We may add from the inscrr. *Syll* 807 (= [3]1173)[16] (after A.D. 138) where a blind soldier is enjoined to take blood of a white cock, together with honey, and συντρῖψαι καὶ ἐπὶ τρεῖς ἡμέρας ἐπιχρεῖσαι ἐπὶ τοὺς ὀφθαλμούς, "rub them into an eye-salve and anoint his eyes three days" (see Deissmann *LAE²*, p. 135), and *ib.* 802 (= [3]1168)[52] (c. A.D. 320) τὰ συντετριμμένα σ[κε]ύη. See also Menander Ἐπιτρέπ. 607 συντρίβει σε, "he plays havoc with you." With LXX 3 Kingd 19[11], cf. Wünsch *AF* p. 22[18] (iii/A.D.) ὁρκίζω σε τὸν συντρείβοντα τὰς πέτρας.

σύντριμμα,

"destruction," "ruin" (Rom 3[16]). For the meaning "fracture," as in Lev 21[19], cf. P Leid W [vi. 34] (ii/iii A.D.) (= II. p. 101) ἐὰν εἴπῃς ἐπὶ σπάσματος ἢ συντρίματος (*l.* συντρίμματος) τὸ (ὄνομα) γ̄, "in spasmo aut contusione." The subst. συντριβή occurs in the late Preisigke 5763[12] (A.D. 647) μὴ πρὸς τῇ τοιαύτῃ τῆς δίκης συντριβῇ ζημιωθῇ, and in Vett. Val. p. 74[4]: cf. Prov 16[18]. MGr συντρίμμια, "ruins."

σύντροφος.

For the lit. meaning "foster-brother" cf. PSI VI. 584[5] (iii/B.C.) ὁ ἀποδιδούς σοι τὴν ἐπιστολὴν τυγχάνει ὢν Βιαίου σύντροφος, P Oxy VII. 1034[2] (ii/A.D.) κληρονόμους καταλείπω τὴν θυγατέρ[α] μου τινὰ καὶ τὸν {τον} σύντροφον αὐτῆς τινα καί τινα, "I leave as my heirs my daughter *x* and her foster-brother *y* and *z*" (Ed.), P Ryl II. 106[3] (A.D. 158) παρὰ Καπίτωνος συντρόφου ἀπελευθέρου Πτολεμᾶς μητρὸς Τασουχαρίου, "from Capiton, foster-brother and freedman of Ptolema, his mother being Tasoucharion" (Edd.), and the Phrygian sepulchral inscr. cited by W. M. Ramsay (*Bearing*, p. 189)—

Μένανδρος Ἵππω-
νος καὶ Ἀμειὰς Τεί-
μωνι θρεπτῷ, καὶ
Ἀπολλώνιος
καὶ Διονύσιος συν-
τρόφῳ ὑπὲρ τῶν
ἰδίων Διὶ Βρον-
τῶντι,

"Menander son of Hippon and Amias to Timon their foster-child, and Apollonios and Dionysios to their foster-brother on behalf of the family's (salvation) to Zeus the Thunderer (a vow)." See an inscr. from Thyatira in *CR* iii. p. 138, No. 17 Πείλᾳ Νήφοντι νέῳ χρηστῷ συντρόφῳ μνείας χάριν.

The word is similarly rendered "foster-brother" in AV marg., RV, but from its widespread use as a court title, it is better understood as = "courtier" or "intimate friend": see e.g. the Pergamene inscr. *Cagnat* IV. 288[2] σύντροφ[ος] τοῦ βασιλέως, and the inscr. from Delos of the 1st half of ii/B.C., *OGIS* 247[2], where Heliodorus is described as τὸν σύντροφον τοῦ βασιλέως Σ[ελεύκου] Φιλοπάτορος: Dittenberger *ad l.* defines the word as denoting "hominem re vera una cum rege educatum." Cf. *OGIS* 372[2], and *Syll* 305 (= [3]708)[6] (A.D. 37) τοὺς Κότυος δὲ παῖδας Ῥοιμητάλκην καὶ Πολέμωνα καὶ Κότυν συντρόφους καὶ ἑταίρους ἑαυτῶι γεγονότας. The word occurs as a proper name in P Oxy I. 113[23] (ii/A.D.). See further Deissmann *BS* p. 310 ff. MGr σύντροφος, "companion."

συντυγχάνω,

"meet with," "fall in with" (Lk 8[19]): cf. P Oxy VII. 1061[9] (B.C. 22) ἔγραψα δὲ καὶ Δίωι τῷ τοῦ χιριστοῦ περὶ τούτου, ᾧ καὶ συντεύξηι, "I have written also to Dius, the son of the agent, about this: whom you will meet" (Ed.), *ib.* IV. 743[37] (B.C. 2) οὐκ ἠδυνάσθην συντυχεῖν Ἀπολλω.νίῳ, *ib.* VII. 1070[19] (iii/A.D.) ἐὰν οὖν [συ]ντύχητε καὶ δόξῃ τι ὑμεῖν περὶ αὐτῶν, "if therefore you meet and come to any conclusion about them" (Ed.), and *ib.* VIII. 1163[2] (v/A.D.) τῇ τετράδι καταλαβὼν . . συντυχὼν τῇ ἑξῆς τῷ δεσπότῃ μου, "I arrived on the 4th, and on the next day met my master."

Slightly different uses are seen in P Tebt I. 23[14] (c. B.C. 119 or 114) εἰ δέ τινα ἔξει[ς] πρὸς αὐτὸν λόγον σὺν αὐτῶι σύντυχε ἡμῖν, "if you have any grievance against him apply together with him to me" (Edd.), and P Oxy XIV. 1072[17] (A.D. 37–41) Μουνάτιος δὲ ὁ φίλος συντυχὼν ἔλεγεν συμ[πε]φωνηκέναι τοῖς ἐκ τῆς κώ[μ]ης αὐτοῦ, "our friend Munatius said that he had agreed with the people of his village" (Edd.).

For the subst. συντυχία, see P Flor II. 154 *verso* [3] (A.D. 268) χρηστὴν συντυχίαν, P Oxy XVI. 1860[5] (vi/vii A.D.) εἰς μέσον συντηχείας (*l.* συντυχίας), "in the course of conversation" (Edd.), and *OGIS* 331[19] (mid. ii/B.C.) κατ[ὰ] συντ[υ]χίαν.

Συντύχη

(for the accentuation see Winer-Schmiedel *Gr.* p. 71), the name of a woman member of the Church at Philippi (Phil 4[2]). It is found in the inscrr. *CIG* II. 2326[2], 3008[3-10], and in its masculine form is represented by the Latin Sintiches (*CIL* XII. 4703). On the superior position of women in Macedonia, see the inscriptional evidence brought forward in Lightfoot *Philippians²*, p. 54 ff. and on the possibility that Syntyche is to be identified with the Lydia of Acts, see Ramsay, *Bearing*, p. 309.

συνυποκρίνομαι

is generally understood in the sense "play a part with": cf. Aristeas 267 τὸ πρέπον ἑκάστῳ συνυποκρινόμενος, "acting the proper part towards each." But a different meaning has been found in Polyb. iii. 92. 5, where it is said of Fabius Cunctator that (having no intention of giving battle) συνυπεκρίνετο τοῖς προθύμως καὶ φιλοκινδύνως διακειμένοις. "he pretended to agree with the eager and adventurous spirits." This makes good sense in Gal 2[13]: the other Jews "pretended to agree with Peter," though they really did not.

συνφύω

is used in the 2 aor. pass. for 2 aor. act. = "grow up together with" in Lk 8[7]. For the act. see P Ryl II. 427 Fr. 8 τ]ῶν συνφυόντων. See also s.v. σύμφυτος.

συνχαίρω,

generally in the NT = "rejoice with": cf. P Lond 43[3] (ii/B.C.) (= I. p. 48, UPZ i. p. 635), where a mother writes to her son, πυνθανομένη μανθάνειν σε Αἰγύπτια γράμματα συνεχάρην σοι καὶ ἐμαυτῆι, "having ascertained that you are learning the Egyptian script, I rejoiced for you and for myself." and Syll 807 (= [3] 1173)[5] (after A.D. 138) ὀρθὸν ἀνέβλεψε τοῦ δήμου παρεστῶτος καὶ συνχαιρομένου, which the editor describes as "medii vel passivi usus barbarus," but cites the simplex in Aristoph. Pax 291 ὡς ἥδομαι καὶ χαίρομαι κεὐφραίνομαι, and ib. [10] ἐσώθη καὶ δημοσίᾳ ηὐχαρίστησεν τῷ θεῷ καὶ ὁ δῆμος συνεχάρη αὐτῷ. See also Proleg. p. 161, and Hatzidakis Gr. p. 200.

For the sense of "congratulate," which Lightfoot gives the verb in Phil 2[17 f.], we may cite the ironical P Tebt II. 424[5] (late iii/A.D.) εἰ μὲν ἐπιμένι(= εις σου τῆ ἀπονοίᾳ, συνχέ(= αί)ρω σοι, "if you persist in your folly, I congratulate you" (Edd.). Similarly BGU IV. 1080[2] (iii/A.D.) (= Chrest. I. p. 564), where a father congratulates his son on his happy marriage, ἀσπάζομαί σε συνχαίρων ἐπὶ τῇ ὑπαρχθείσῃ σοι ἀγαθῇ [ἐ]ςευβεῖ (l. εὐσεβεῖ) καὶ εὐτυχῆ (l. εὐτυχεῖ) [σ]υμβιώσι.

συνχέω,

lit. "pour together," "confuse," is used metaph. in Ac 21[27] = "stir up" a multitude: cf. P Leid W xix 38 (ii/iii A.D.) (= II. p. 149) ὁ κόσμος ὅλος συνχυνθήσεται, and P Oxy XVI. 1873[1] (late v/A.D.) ἔχω συνκεχυ[μ]ένος τοὺς λογισμούς, "I feel my reasoning faculties confused" (Edd.). See also OGIS 669[15] (i/A.D.) μηδὲ συν(χέ)ωσι τὴν κοινὴν πίστιν οἱ τῆι πρωτοπραξίᾳ πρὸς ἃ μὴ(ι) δεῖ καταχρώμενοι, and Syll 888(= [2] 1238)[13] (c. A.D. 160) where a curse is invoked on those who attempt ἢ συνθραῦσαι ἢ συγχέαι τῆς μορφῆς καὶ τοῦ σχήματος.

We may add from Menander Fragm. p. 217. No. 781— συνκέχυκε νῦν τὴν πίστιν ὁ καθ' ἡμᾶς βίος, "life nowadays has upset loyalty."

συνχράομαι,

"use together with." "associate with": cf. P Grenf II. 14(b)[4] (B.C. 264 or 227) συνκεχρήμε[θ'α δὲ καὶ τοὺς τεσσαράκοντα ὄνους, in the account of the preparations for the visit of the διοικητής. See also BGU IV. 1102[9] (Ptol./Aug.), 1208[23] (B.C. 27-6), and P Giss I. 41 ii. 1 (beg. of Hadrian's reign) (= Chrest. I. p. 50), where συνχρήσασθαι occurs in a broken context. In BGU IV. 1187[22] (c. B.C. 1) τῆι δὲ

περὶ ἑαυτὰς βίαι καὶ αὐθαδίᾳ [συ]νχρησάμενοι, the verb is practically = "resort to." It is found only once in the NT, Jn 4[9], where it suggests "treat with undue familiarity": cf. Ign. Magn. 3 πρέπει μὴ συνχρᾶσθαι τῇ ἡλικίᾳ τοῦ ἐπισκόπου, and Epict. i. 2. 7 ταῖς τῶν ἐκτὸς ἀξίαις συγχρώμεθα. Diog. Oenoand. fr. 64 iii. 9 shows the usual sense, familiariter uti aliquo.

συνχύννω,

"confound" (Ac 2[6] al.), is a Hellenistic form of συνχέω (q.v.), and survives in MGr: see Proleg. p. 45 n.[2]

συνωμοσία,

"conspiracy," "plot" (Ac 23[13]): cf. Syll 461 (= [3] 360)[45] (c. B.C. 300-280) εἴ τινά κα συνωμοσίαν αἴσ[θω]μαι ἐοῦσαν [ἢ γι]νομέναν, ἐξαγγελῶ τοῖς δαμ[ιορ]γοῖς, Cagnat IV. 914[10] καταλύσαντα συν[ω]μοσίαν μεγάλην.

Συράκουσαι

(sometimes accented Συρακοῦσαι), "Syracuse," a town in E. Sicily (Ac 28[12]). The plur. form was due to its being both a citadel and a settlement in the valley (see Souter Lex. s.v.), but in late Greek the sing. ἡ Συράκουσα is also found, perhaps owing to popular usage (see Psaltes Gr. p. 142).

Συρία.

The noun συρία is applied to "a Syrian cloth" in P Hib I. 51[5] (B.C. 245) συρίας λάμβανε ἐξ[αδρ]άχμους, "accept Syrian clothes at 6 drachmae": see the editors' note on l.[3]. and cf. ib. 38[7] (B.C. 252-1), P Cairo Zen I. 50010[20] (c. B.C. 259).

An interesting ex. of the private cult of the Συρία θεός in the Fayûm district is afforded by P Magd 2 (B.C. 222) (= Chrest. I. 101), where we hear of a soldier Μάχατας having erected a shrine in her honour, possibly, as Wilcken suggests, at the instigation of his foreign wife Ἀσία—[3] ἀνοικοδομήσαντος ἐν τῶι αὐτοῦ τόπωι ἱερὸν Συρίας Θεοῦ καὶ Ἀφροδίτης Βερενίκης. On the worship of the Syrian gods, see now U. Wilcken's paper in Festgabe für Adolf Deissmann (Tübingen, 1927), p. 1 ff.

Σύρος.

Mention is made of a κώμη Σύρων in the district of Alexandria in BGU IV. 1123[2], 1132[10] (both time of Augustus), and in the Oxyrhynchite district in P Oxy II. 270[22] (A.D. 94): see also GH in P Tebt II. p. 402. The adv. Συριστί is found in P Petr III. 7[15] (B.C. 238-7) ὃς καὶ Συριστὶ Ἰωνάθας [καλεῖται, "who is also called in the Syrian language Jonathan."

Συροφοινίκισσα,

"Syro-phoenician," Mk 7[26]. In their margin WH print Σύρα Φοινίκισσα. On the late form Φοινίκισσα (derived from the country Φοινίκη), see Winer-Schmiedel Gr. p. 135.

σύρω,

"draw," "drag" (Jn 21[8], Ac 8[3], Rev 12[4]). The word is used of oxen drawing wood in P Flor II. 158[7] (iii/A.D.) παράσχες . . τὸ ταυρικὸν ἵνα σύρῃ εἰς κώμ[η]ν τὰ ξύλα, *ib.* 227⁵ (A.D. 257) σύροντι ξύλα ἀπὸ τῆς διώρυγος. For an incorrect perf. part. = "attached," see P Lond V. 1686³³ (A.D. 505) μετὰ τῆς σεσυρομένης αὐταῖς συντελείας.

The word is read by Rendel Harris in Ev. Petr. 3 σύρωμεν (for εὕρωμεν) τὸν υἱὸν τοῦ θεοῦ, with which Robinson and James (p. 17) compare *Acts of Philip* (Tisch. p. 143) σύρατε τοὺς μάγους τούτους. The compd. παρασύρω occurs in P Oxy III. 486¹⁵ cited *s.v.* παρουσία.

σύσσημον.

This late Greek word = "sign," "signal," which is classed by Phrynichus (cf. Rutherford *NP* p. 492 f.) among κίβδηλα ἀμαθῆ, is apparently first found in Menander Περικειρ. 362, and is fully illustrated by Durham *Menander* p. 95. For its use in Mk 14⁴⁴, its only occurrence in the NT, see Swete *ad l.* who cites Wünsche *Neue Beiträge* p. 339 for a kiss as the customary method of saluting a Rabbi. A plur. συσσήματα is found in Byz. Greek: see Psaltes *Gr.* p. 176.

συστατικός.

"commendatory," occurs in P Oxy XII. 1587²⁰ (late iii/A.D.) συστατικῶν γραμμάτων: cf. 2 Cor 3¹ συστατικῶν ἐπιστολῶν. Good exx. of such letters are P Goodspeed 4 (ii/B.C.) (= *Selections*. p. 24). P Oxy IV. 787 (A.D. 16), *ib.* II. 294 (A.D. 22). *ib.* 292 (*c.* A.D. 25) (= *Selections*, p. 37).

Other exx. of the word are P Oxy III. 505² (ii/A.D.) κατὰ συστατικὸν γενόμενον, "by the terms of a deed of representation " (Edd.), and *ib.* 509¹² (late ii/A.D.) ὁμολο[γῶ] τὸ[ν] συστατικὸν πεπυῆσθαί σ[ο]ι, "I acknowledge that the contract of representation has been made with you" (Edd.), and in a more general sense P Tebt II. 315²⁹ (ii/A.D.) ἔχι γὰρ συστατικὰς [ὅ]πως τὸν ἀπιθοῦντα μετὰ φρουρᾶς τῷ ἀρχιερῖ πέμπιν, "for he has instructions to send recalcitrants under guard to the high-priest" (Edd.).

For συστάτης, "a delegate," cf. P Oxy VIII. 1116⁵ (A.D. 363) with note, and for σύστασις, "an appointment," cf. *ib.* II. 261¹⁷ (A.D. 55) εὐδοκεῖ γὰρ τῇδε τῇ συστάσει, and similarly P Tebt II. 317¹⁴ (A.D. 174–5). In P Flor I. 39⁴ (A.D. 396) συστάτης τῆς μελλούσης λιτου[ργεῖν φυ]λῆς, the word appears to mean "representative" (see the editor's note). See *s.v.* συνίστημι.

συστρέφω,

"gather together," "twist together," c. acc. rei, as in Ac 28³, is seen in P Oxy II. 234ⁱⁱ·³² (medical prescription for earache—ii/iii A.D.) οἰσυπηρὸν ἔριον περὶ μηλωτρίδα συστρέψας καὶ χλιαίνων ἔνσταξε, "twist some wool with the oil in it round a probe, warm, and drop in," and so³², also BGU VII. 1673¹⁵ (ii/A.D.) σ[υ]νέστρεψα, unfortunately in a broken context.

Cf. Wünsch *AF* p. 23¹⁹ (iii/A.D.) ὁρκίζω σε τὸν συνστρέφοντα τὴν γῆν ἐ[πὶ τ]ῶν θεμελίων αὐτῆς, where the verb = *conglobare* (cf. Prov 8²⁹). For the mid., apparently in the sense of "gather themselves together," cf. Mt 17²².

συστροφή.

With συστροφή = "concourse," "assembly" (Ac 19⁴⁰, 23¹²), cf. the metaph. application of the subst. to style in

P Lond 46²⁵ (iv/A.D.) (= I. p. 69) ἐν συστροφῇ πρὸς πνευματικ(ὴν) ἀπειλή[ν, "shortly, for spiritual threatening" (Ed.). and of the adv. συστρ[όφως] in Menander Κιθαρ. 92.

Συχέμ,

"Shechem" (Ac 7¹⁶). In addition to this indecl. form the LXX shows Σίκιμα, -α, -ων, -οις : see Thackeray *Gr.* i. p. 168.

σφάζω,

"slay," "slaughter": cf. BGU II. 388ⁱⁱ·²¹ (ii/iii A.D.) ὅτε ἐσημάνθη, ὅτι ἐσφάγη [Σ]εμπρώνιος, and *OGIS* 607⁶ ἐσφαγμένοι ἐν ὅρμῳ Πούχεως. See also the magic P Osl I. 1⁵ (iv/A.D.) ὁ τὸν ἴδιον ἀδελφὸν σφάξας (with the editor's note). For the form σφάττω (cf. Wackernagel *Hellenistica*, p. 24) see *Syll* 615 (= ³1024)⁵⁴ (B.C. 200) πρὸς τῶι β[ωμ]ῶι σ[φά]ττετ[αι] (*sc.* ἄμνος).

The verb is used hyperbolically in P Oxy II. 259⁸³ (A.D. 23) βλέπε με πῶς με ἡ μήτηρ ἡμῶν [ἔ]σφαξε χάριν τοῦ χειρογράφου : the editors compare the similar use of φονεύω in P Lond 113. 12(*1*)¹¹ (vi/vii A.D.) (= I. p. 227) ὁ χρεώστης ἐφ[ο]νευσέν με.

In Pontic and certain other dialects σπάζω takes the place of σφάζω: Thumb *Handbook*, p. 18. For σφαγιάζω cf. *Syll* 629 (= ³685)²⁷ (B.C. 139) σφαγιασθέντος ἱερείου.

σφόδρα,

"greatly," "exceedingly": (a) with verbs—P Oxy IV. 705⁷¹ (A.D. 200–2) κῶμαί τινες . . . σφ[ό]δρα ἐξησθένησαν, "certain villages are utterly exhausted," owing to public burdens, *ib.* I. 41¹⁷ (iii/iv A.D.) ἐπὶ τούτῳ σφόδρα χαίρω, *ib.* XIV. 1680¹³ (iii/iv A.D.) ἀκούω ὅτι σφόδρα Ἡράκλειος ὁ νῦν ἐπίτροπος ζητεῖ σε, "I hear that Heraclius the present overseer is vigorously searching for you" (Edd.), and PSI VII. 827²² (iv/A.D.) σφόδρα Θέωνα φιλῶ :

(b) with adjective—P Cairo Zen I. 59060⁶ (B.C. 257) σφόδρα ὀλίγου χρόνου. For the adj. σφοδρός see P Tebt II. 272⁷ (late ii/A.D.) δί[ψο]ς . . . σφοδρόν, BGU IV. 1024ⁱⁱ·¹⁹ (iv/v A.D.) σφοδρὰν (*l.* σφοδρὸν) ἔρωτα.

σφραγίζω,

"seal." In P Oxy VI. 932⁶ (late ii/A.D.) ἂν ἔρχῃ ἄφες ἀρτάβας ἕξ ἰς τοὺς σάκκους σφραγίσας λαχανοσπέρμου ἵνα πρόχιροι ὦσι, "if you come, take out six artabae of vegetable-seed, sealing it in the sacks in order that they may be ready" (Edd.), we have clear confirmation of Deissmann's view (*BS* p. 238 f.) that by Paul's καρπὸν σφραγίζεσθαι in Rom 15²⁸ we are to understand the Apostle as meaning that all the proper steps had been taken with regard to the collection. "If the *fruit* is *sealed*, then everything is in order : the sealing is the last thing that must be done prior to delivery." Cf. also P Hib I. 39¹⁵ (B.C. 265) where with reference to the embarkation upon a government transport of a quantity of corn, instructions are given that the shipmaster is to write a receipt, and further—δεῖγμα σφραγισάσ[θ]ω, "let him seal a sample," obviously to prevent the corn from being tampered with during its transit (Edd.).

Other exx. of the verb with varied applications are BGU I. 248²³ (i/A.D.) πέμψας μοι διὰ Σαβείνου ἐσφραγισμένας δραχμὰς εἴκοσι, P Oxy I. 116[17] (ii/A.D.) ἔπεμψα ὑμεῖν . . . κ[ί]στην σταφυλῆς λείαν καλῆς καὶ σφυρίδα φοίνικος καλοῦ ἐσφραγι(σμένας), "I send you a box of very excellent grapes and a basket of excellent dates under seal" (Edd.), ib. III. 528[16] (ii/A.D.) ἔδωκα τῇ ιβ μετὰ τῶν σῶν ἐπιστολῶν ἐσ(σ)φραγιζμένα, "I gave the letter sealed (to the messenger) on the 12th together with letters for you (?)" (Edd.), ib. VI. 929[13] (ii/iii A.D.) ταῦτα δὲ πάντα συνενῆι εἰς τὸν χιτῶνα τὸν καροῖνον, καὶ ἐσφραγίσθη γῇ λευκῇ, "all these were inside the brown tunic, and it was sealed with white clay" (Edd.) (cf. Job 38[14]). P Tebt II. 413[6] (ii/iii A.D.) τὸ χαρτάριν ἔλαβεν Σερηνίων ἐσ(σ)φραγισμένον, "Serenion took the papyrus sealed," P Lond 171 b[15] (iii/A.D.) (= II. p. 176) διέθετό μοι διαθήκην α[ὑ]τοῦ ἐσφραγισμένην, and P Oxy XIV. 1677[7] (iii/A.D.) τὸ ἐντολικὸν Πτολεμαῖος ὡς ἔδω[κ]εν μοι ἐσφραγισμένον, "the order for Ptolemais sealed as he gave it to me" (Edd.). From the idea of sealing for security, it is an easy transition to "seal up," "hide," "conceal," as in Rev 10[4], 22[10]. Again, the verb passes into the sense "distinguish," "mark," as when, in P Tebt II. 419[2] (iii/A.D.), an agent is instructed—πέμψον τὴν ὄνον ὅπως σφραγισθῇ, "send the ass to be branded" (cf. Rev 7[3 ff.]), and from this again into "confirm," "authenticate," as in Chrest. I. 89[5] (A.D. 149), where it is certified regarding an animal for sacrifice—κ[αὶ] δοκιμάσας ἐσφράγισα ὡς ἔστιν καθαρός (cf. Jn 6[27]).

The compd. ἐπισφραγίζω occurs in P Oxy III. 471[17] (ii/A.D.) ὁ μὲν γὰρ τελευταῖος ὑπομνημα[τ]ισμὸς [ἐ]πισφραγίζει τὴν δούλην αὐτοῦ, "for the last memorandum confirms (the question of) his slave (?)" (Edd.), and συνεσφραγίζω in BGU IV. 1204[3] (B.C. 28) τὰ πρὸς Πανίσκον γράμματα συνεσφράγισμαι ὑμεῖν, and P Ryl II. 90[6, 44] (early iii/A.D.).

In his Ant. Kunstprosa ii. p. 477 Norden advocates a connexion of the Pauline σφραγίζεσθαι with the language of the Greek mysteries, but see Anrich, Das Mysterienwesen, p. 120 ff.

Fine specimens of sealed rolls may be seen in the table attached to the edition of the Elephantine Papyri issued along with the Berlin Urkunden. Cf. also Archiv v. p. 384, No. 76. On sealing as a protection against falsification in the case of written documents, Erman's important art. in Mélanges Nicole, p. 126 ff. should be consulted.

σφραγίς,

"a seal": cf. P Oxy I. 113[21] (ii/A.D.) ἐρωτηθεὶς ἀγ[ό]ρασόν μοι σφραγ[ῖ]δα ἀργυροῦν, "I beg you to bring me a silver seal" (Edd.), ib. I. 117[15] (ii/iii A.D.) ῥάκη δύο κατασεσημημένα [τ]ῇ σφραγεῖδί μου, "two strips of cloth sealed with my seal." In ib. XVI. 1886[6] (v/vi A.D.) τοῦτο π[αραδοὺ]ς ἐδεξάμην τὴν αὐτοῦ σφραγῖ[δα, the editors understand the word as = either a "signet-ring" or a "bond." For the use of σφραγίς to denote the "impression" of a seal for attesting or closing, cf. P Oxy I. 106[22] (A.D. 135) where a certain Ptolema acknowledges the receipt of a Will ἐπὶ τῶν αὐτῶν σφραγείδων, "with the seals intact" (Edd.), which she had deposited ἐπὶ σφραγίδων, "under seals" in the archives, and now wished to revoke, and P Fay 122[8] (c. A.D. 100) τὰς δὲ λοιπὰς ὑπὸ τὴν ἀμφοτέρ[ω]ν σφραγεῖδα ἐάσας, "leaving the remaining

(artabae of mustard) under the seal of you both." See also Ev. Petr. 8 ἐπέχρισαν ἑπτὰ σφραγῖδας (as in Rev 5[1]).

For the use of σφραγίς to denote a "plot" of land, see the elaborate survey of Crown land in P Oxy VI. 918[8 al.] (ii/A.D.) with the editors' introduction, and cf. P Lond 163[11] (A.D. 88) (= II. p. 183) ἐν μιᾷ σφραγῖδι, "in one parcel (or lot)," a recurrent formula, and P Iand 27[5] (A.D. 100-101) with the editor's note.

For the later use of σφραγίς with reference to "baptism," see the reff. in Sophocles Lex. s.v., and cf. Lightfoot Apost. Fathers I. ii. p. 226.

σφυδρόν,

"ankle-bone." New instances of this rare form (for σφυρόν) in Ac 3[7] אּ* B* C* are cited by Cadbury (JBL xlv. (1926), p. 200) from the iii/A.D. (?) palmomantic P Flor III. 391[53, 56]. He rightly notes that "probably neither the common nor the uncommon spelling is distinctly medical" (contrast Hobart p. 35, Harnack Luke the Physician, p. 191).

σφυρίς,

"a basket," "a creel." Though LS[3] pronounce σφυρίς an Attic spelling for σπυρίς, it is the regular form in the papyri as in the NT (Mt 15[37], 16[10], Mk 8[8, 20], Ac 9[25]): cf. Mayser Gr. i. p. 173, Cronert Mem. Herc. p. 85 n.[3]. See e.g. P Cairo Zen I. 59013[12] (B.C. 259) κόκκωνος σφυρίδες δ, Ostr. 1152[3] (Ptol. Rom.) δύο σφυρίδων τῆς πίσση(ς), P Ryl II. 127[31] (A.D. 29) σφυρὶς ἐν ᾗ ἄρτο(ι) ν, "a basket in which were fifty loaves," P Oxy I. 116[19] (ii/A.D.) σφυρίδα φοίνικος καλοῦ, "a basket of good dates," ib. IV. 741[3] (ii/A.D.) σφυρὶς διπλῆ καρύων α, "1 double basket of nuts," ib. VII. 1070[31] (iii/A.D.) τραγη[μ]άτων ("sweetmeats") σφυρίδαν μεστὴν μίαν, and P Lond 1171[12] (B.C. 8) (= III. p. 178) σφυρίδων (ἀργυρίου δραχμὰς) η. For σπυρίς we can only cite P Par 62 v. 18 (c. B.C. 170) τιμὴν σπυρίδων.

For the dim. σφυρίδιον see P Oxy X. 1293[30] (A.D. 117-38) σφυρίδια δύο ἐσφρα(γισμένα), cf.[39], P Tebt II. 414[19] (ii/A.D.) τὸ σφυρίδιν (l. σφυρίδιον) μετὰ τῶν ἐνόντων κάτω, "the little basket with its contents at the bottom" (Edd.), P Oxy VI. 936[15] (iii/A.D.) σφυρίδιον Κανωπικὸν ὅπου ζεύγη ἄρτων δ. "a Canopic basket with 4 pairs of loaves," and ib. X. 1297[6] (iv/A.D.) σφυρίδια τέσ⟨σαρα⟩. It should be noted that in a fragmentary papyrus leaf as published by Mahaffy in P Petr II. p. 33 and amended ib. III. 72(e)[1] (= p. 202) we find σπυρίτων (= σπυρίδων) for σπυριδίου. See also the form σφυρίον in P Oxy XIV. 1058[6] (iv/A.D.) μεικρὸν σφυρίον.

σχεδόν,

"almost," "nearly": cf. P Tebt I. 58[58] (B.C. 111) (= Witkowski[2], p. 106) σὺν τοῖς θεοῖς σχεδὸν ἔσται ὁ διάλογος ἕως τῆς λ τοῦ Παχών, "by the grace of the gods the audit will take place about Pachon 30," P Ryl II. 81[7] (c. A.D. 104) σχεδὸν πᾶσαι (sc. θύραι) ἀφ' ὑδάτους εἰσί, P Giss I. 41 ii. 8 (beg. Hadrian's reign) (= Chrest. I. p. 30) σχεδὸν πά[ν]τ[α ὅσα] ἔχω ἔν τε ταῖ]ς κώμαις, P Oxy VII. 1033[1] (A.D. 392) πολλάκεις σχεδὸν εἰπε⟨ῖ⟩ν εἰς ψυχὴν ἐκεινδυνεύσαμεν, "we often run the risk almost of our lives." (Ed.), and from the inscr. *Priene* 105¹³ (*c.* B.C. 9) σχεδόν τ[ε] συ[μβαίνει.

σχῆμα.

The thought of "external bearing" or "fashion" which in general distinguishes this word from μορφή, "what is essential and permanent" (see *s.v.* μορφή), and which comes out so clearly in Phil 2⁸, may be illustrated by such passages as the following: P Tor I. 1 ᵛⁱⁱ·³² (B.C. 116) (= *Chrest.* II. p. 39) ἐμφανίστου σχῆμα, "delatoris more," P Leid Wⁱⁱⁱ·²⁰ (ii/iii A.D.) Αἰγυπτιακῷ σχήματι, so ˣᵛ·¹⁶ (= II. pp. 80, 133), P Giss I. 40²⁸ (A.D. 215) ὄψεις τε καὶ σχῆμα, P Lond 121⁷⁶⁰ (magic—iii/A.D.) (= I. p. 108) ὁ σχηματίσας εἰς τὰ εἴκοσι καὶ ὀκτὼ σχήματα τοῦ κόσμου, P Amh II. 142¹¹ (iv/A.D.) καταφρονήσαντες τῆς περὶ ἐμὲ ἀπραγμοσύνης καὶ τοῦ σχήματος, "despising my easiness of temper and bearing," and *Syll* 652 (= ³885)¹² (*c.* A.D. 220) με[τὰ τ]οῦ εἰθισμένου σχήμα[τος] τῆς ἅμα ἱεροῖς πομπ[ῆς].

In the sepulchral epigram PSI I. 17 *verso*¹ (iii/A.D.) ἀγ]γέλλει τὸ σχῆμα κ(αὶ) ἴ[νδαλμ' οὐ] βραχὺν ἄνδρα, the word appears to = "image," "statue": see further Calderini in *S.A.M.* i. p. 10 ff., where for the alternative meaning "(ceremonial) dress" he cites *Kaibel* 230³ ἁγνὸν ἐφήβου σχῆμα λαχών, and *ib. addenda* 874ᵃ⁵ (i/B.C.?) Ἐνναλίου κατ' ἔνοπλον σχῆμα, i.e. in martial panoply. Cf. Menander *Fragm.* p. 127, No. 430 εὐλοιδόρητον . . . φαίνεται τὸ τοῦ στρατιώτου σχῆμα, "the rôle of mercenary soldier lends itself to abuse."

For the astrological use of the word it must suffice to refer to the horoscope P Lond 130²¹ (i/ii A.D.) (= I. p. 133) λεπτὸν σχῆμα, and to the reff. in Vett. Val. Index II. *s.v.*

σχίζω.

For the lit. meaning "cleave," "rend," as in Mt 27⁵¹ *al.*, cf. PSI IV. 341⁷ (B.C. 256–5) σχιστοὺς (*s.* χιτῶνας : cf. Kock *CAF* iii. p. 291, No. 12 σχιστὸν χιτωνίσκον τιν' ἐνδέδυκας;), P Tebt II. 273⁴⁵·⁵² (ii/iii A.D.) λίθος σχισθ[είς, P Leid Wⁱⁱ·⁵¹ (ii/iii A.D.) (= II. p. 101) σχίσον ἰς δύο, *ib.* ⁱⁱⁱ·¹ (p. 103) σχισθήσεται, and Preisigke 1²⁰ (iii/A.D.) μιᾶς μέντοι κίσ[της εὑρε]θείης ἐ[σχι]σμένης. See also the new Logion, P Oxy I. p. 3, σχίσον τὸ ξύλον κἀγὼ ἐκεῖ εἰμί. The metaph. meaning in the pass. "am divided" into parties, as in Ac 14⁴, is illustrated from late Greek by Field *Notes,* p. 121.

The compd. ὑποσχίζω = "plough" is found in P Lond 1170 *verso*³⁰⁵ (A.D. 258–9) (= III. p. 200), and ὑποσχισμός = "ploughing" in P Fay 112³ (A.D. 99) τοὺς ὑποσχ[ει]σμοὺς καὶ διβολήτρους τῶν ἐλαιώνο(= ω)ν, "the ploughing up and hoeing of the olive-yards" (Edd.).

σχίσμα

= "ploughing" may be illustrated from the contract P Lond V. 1706⁷ (vi/A.D.), when the ploughing just proceeding is exempted from the contract—ἐκτὸς τοῦ νῦν σχ[ί]σματος τοῦ καὶ ὄντος. For σχίζα, "a splinter of wood," cf. P Cairo Zen II. 59101⁵ (B.C. 255) συ]να[πόσ]τε[ι]λον δὲ καὶ σχίζας ὅτι πλ[ε]ίστας, "send as large a supply of firewood as possible," and for a curious word-play with σχῖνος see the note *ad* Sus. 54 in Charles *Apocrypha* i. p. 650.

σχοινίον.

dim. of σχοῖνος, "a rush," and hence "a rope" made of rushes (Jn 2¹⁵, Ac 27³²) : cf. P Oxy III. 502³⁶ (A.D. 164) τοῦ προκειμένου φρέατος τροχελλέαν σὺν σχοινίῳ καινῷ, "the reel of the aforesaid well provided with a new rope" (Edd.), and *ib.* VI. 904⁶ (v/A.D.), a petition from a man who complains that he is καθ' ἑκάστην ἡμέραν μετεωριζ[ό]μενον σχοινίοις, "daily suspended by ropes."

The transition of σχοινίον to a term of "measurement," as in Ps 15⁶, appears in such passages as P Oxy XIV. 1635⁷ (B.C. 44–37) ἀπὸ μὲν ἀπηλιώτου εἰς λίβα σχοινία δύ[ο ἥ]μισυ, ἀπὸ δὲ νότ[ου] εἰς βορρᾶν σχοινία , where the editors note that "the σχοινίον was the side of an aroura and 100 cubits in length. Cf. BGU IV. 1000²¹ (B.C. 23–2) τὰ εἴκοσι σχοινία, P Fay 110²⁸ (A.D. 94) τὰς θύρας ἐπιστησάτωσαν οἱ τέκτονες· πέμπω δέ σοι τὰ σχινία, "let the carpenters put up the doors: I send you the measurements" (Edd.), and P Ryl II. 165¹⁷ (A.D. 266) sale of 4 arourae of catoecic land τῷ τῆς κατοικίας δικαίῳ σχοινίῳ, "measured by the just measurement of the settlement" (Edd.). See Preisigke *Fachwörter s.v.*

An interesting ex. of σχοῖνος = "a rope" is afforded by P Oxy I. 69⁸ (A.D. 190) where a theft of barley is detected ἐκ τοῦ . . ἀποσύρματος σχοί[νου, "from the marks of a rope dragged along" (Edd.). The word is used by Aquila in his version of Ps 44(45)² for "a pen" (LXX κάλαμος, Symmachus γραφεῖον): cf. Jerem 8⁸. For σχοινιοπλόκος, "a rope-weaver," see P Oxy VI. 934¹ (iii/A.D.), and for σχοινουργός with the same meaning, see P Lond 1171⁶⁴ (B.C. 8) (= III. p. 179). MGr σκοινί (σχοινί).

σχολάζω.

"have leisure": cf. P Hib I. 55⁶ (B.C. 250) ο]ὐ γὰρ σχολάζω μένειν πλείονα χρ[όνον, "for I have no leisure to remain longer" (Edd.), PSI V. 530⁷ (iii B.C.) καλῶς δ' ἂν ποήσαις ὑποζύγιον δοὺς ἐὰν ἦι σχολάζον, BGU I. 93¹³ (ii/iii A.D.) ἐὰ]ν . . δύνατόν σοι ἦ, μετ' αὐτῆς κατέλθης πρὸς ἐμέ, ἐὰν δὲ μὴ σχολάζης, διαπέμψεις αὐτὴν διὰ τῆς μητρός μου, *ib.* II. 424¹¹ (ii/iii A.D.) οὐ γὰρ ἐσχόλασον (*l.* ἐσχόλαζον) ἀπελθεῖν πρὸς αὐτὴν καὶ μέμφομαί σε πολλά, and P Oxy VII. 1070⁵⁶ (iii/A.D.) ἐν τῷ παρόντι οὐ σχολάζομεν ἑτέροις ἐξερχόμενοι, "at present we are not at leisure and are visiting others" (Ed.).

For the derived meaning "have leisure for," and hence "devote myself to," as in 1 Cor 7⁵, cf. P Lond V. 1836¹⁴ (iv/A.D.), where the writer asks that Sarapion should be freed from his present duties, and so τοῖς ἡμῶν [πρ]άγμασι σχολάζειν, "be at leisure for our affairs," and an unpublished Bremen papyrus of Roman times (cited by Gll *ad* P Oxy VII. 1065) ἴσθι δὲ ὅτι οὐ μέλλω θεῷ σχολάζειν, εἰ μὴ πρότερον ἀπαρτίσω τὸν υἱόν μου: cf. Preisigke 4284¹⁵ (A.D. 207) πρὸς τὸ ἐκ τῆς σῆς βοηθείας ἐκδικηθέντες δυνηθῶμεν (*sic*) τῇ γῇ σχολάζειν, P Par 69⁴·⁸ (day-book of a strategus—A.D. 232) (= *Chrest.* I. p. 91) τοῖ[ς διαφ]έρουσι ἐσχόλασεν, P Cornell 52³ (late iii/A.D.) ἐν τῇ χθὲς ἦλθον εἰς τὴν Τακόνα καὶ ἐσχόλασα τῇ καταστάσει τῶν ἄλλων λιτουργιῶν, "yesterday I came to Tacona and engaged in the induction of the other liturgical officials" (Edd.), also *OGIS* 569²³ (iv/A.D.) διατετάχθαι δὲ τ]ῇ τῶν ὁμογενῶν ὑμῶν θεῶν θρησκείᾳ σχολά[ζειν ἐμμενῶς ὑπὲρ] τῆς αἰωνίου καὶ ἀφθάρτου βασιλείας ὑμῶν, and *Test. xii. patr.* Jud. 20 δύο πνεύματα σχολάζουσι τῷ ἀνθρώπῳ, τὸ τῆς ἀληθείας καὶ τὸ τῆς πλάνης.

σχολή,

(1) "leisure" : cf. P Tebt II. 315[16] (ii/A.D.) ἐὰν μὲν οὖν σχολὴν ἄγῃς γράψας [σ]ου τὰ βιβλία ἄνελθε πρὸς ἐμέ, "so if you have time write up your books and come to me," in view of the visit of a government inspector, P Leid W [viii.] 21 (ii/iii A.D.) ἐγώ εἰμι ὁ ἐν (τῷ οὐρανῷ) σχολὴν (etiam) ἔχων, and P Flor II. 227[7] (A.D. 258) ἐγὼ γὰρ σχολὴν οὐκ ἔσχον πρὸς σὲ ἐλθεῖν. MGr σκόλη, "holiday." (2) "occupation" : cf. P Petr II. 11(1.[3]) (iii/B.C.) (= *Selections*, p. 7), where a son writes to his father, asking for an introduction to King Ptolemy, ὅπως τῆς ἐπὶ τοῦ παρόντος σχολῆς ἀπολυθῶ, "that I may be relieved from my present occupation." (3) "school," "lecture-hall," as in Ac 19[9], cf. P Giss I. 85[14] (Trajan/Hadrian) ἵνα μοι παρέξῃς τὰ ἐπιτήδια τῇ σχολῇ⟨s⟩. MGr σκολείο, "school."

For σχολαστικός = "advocate," see P Oxy VI. 902[1] (c. A.D. 465) with the editors' note, and *C. and B.* ii. p. 700, No. 609 with note.

σῴζω

(for the ι subscript see WH *Intr.*[2] p. 314, Blass-Debrunner *Gr.* § 26) is used like the English "save" with a variety of application, as the following miscellaneous exx. show—PSI IV. 395[13] (iii/B.C.) ἀντιλαβοῦ αὐτῶν καθ' ὁπόσον δύνῃι εἰς τὸ σῴζεσθαι αὐτούς, P Hib I. 77[7] (B.C. 249) συντετάγμεθα γὰρ . . . [τοῖς θε]οῖς [τὰ] ἱερὰ σωθήσεσθαι καθὰ καὶ πρότερον, "for we have received instructions that the sacred revenues (?) are to be preserved for the gods as in former times," P Amh II. 35[52] (B.C. 132) ἐπεὶ οὖν σέσωσαι ἐν τῆι ἀρρωστίαι ὑπὸ τοῦ Σοκνοπαίτος θεοῦ μεγάλου, "since, therefore, your life has been saved in sickness by the great god Socnopaeus," P Tebt I. 56[11] (late ii/B.C.) σῶσαι ψυχὰς πολλάς (from famine), *ib.* II. 302[16] (A.D. 71–2) τινων βιβλίων σ[ω]ζομένω[ν ἐν τῷ ἱερῷ, "certain documents preserved at the temple," BGU II. 423[8] (ii/A.D.) (= Deissmann *LAE*[2], p. 179) μου κινδυνεύσαντος εἰς θάλασσαν ἔσωσε εὐθέως, "when I was in danger at sea he saved me immediately" (cf. Mt 14[30 f.], P Oxy I. 33 *verso*[12] (interview with an Emperor—late ii/A.D.) π[ρῶτον μὲν Καῖσαρ ἔ]σωσε Κλεοπάτρ[αν] ἐκράτησεν βασιλείας, "in the first place Caesar saved Cleopatra's life when he conquered her kingdom," *ib.* VI. 935[7] (iii/A.D.) θεῶν συνλαμβανόντων . . ὁ ἀδελφὸς . . σῴζεται καὶ [ὑγι]αίνει, "with the assistance of heaven our brother is safe and well" (Edd.), *ib.* XII. 1414[22] (A.D. 270–5) σῷζόυ ἡμῖν, πρύτανι, καλῶς ἄρχις, "save yourself for us, prytanis; excellent is your rule" (Edd.), *ib.* XIV. 1644[2] (iii/A.D.) σε προσαγορεύω εὐχόμενός σε σῴζεσθαι πανοικησίᾳ καὶ εὖ διάγειν, "I salute you, praying that you may be preserved and prosper with all your household" (Edd.), and *ib.* I. 41[23] (acclamations to a praefect at a public meeting—iii/iv A.D.) δεόμ[ε]θα, καθολικαί, σῶσον πόλιν τοῖς κυρίοις, "we beseech you, ruler, preserve the city for our lords" (Edd.).

We may add from the inscrr. *Syll* 521 (= [3]717)[9] (B.C. 100–99) δι[ε]τήρησεν πάντας ὑγιαίνοντας καὶ σωζομένους,

ib. 762 (= [3]1130)[1] (after B.C. 167) σωθεὶς ἐκ πολλῶν καὶ μεγάλων κινδύνων . . θεοῖς συννάοις . . χαριστήριον, *OGIS* 69[4] (Ptol.) σωθεὶς ἐγ μεγάλων κινδύνων ἐκπλεύσας ἐκ τῆς Ἐρυθρᾶς θαλάσσης : cf. *ib.* 70[4], 71[3], and see Lumbroso *Archiv* viii. p. 61.

For σῴζειν εἰς, as in 2 Tim 4[18], cf. *Syll* 255 (= [3]521)[26] (iii/B.C.) διὰ τούτους σέσωιστα[ι] τὰ αἰχμάλωτα σώματα εἰς τὴν [ἰ]δίαν ἀπαθῆ.

The adj. σῶς is seen in such passages as BGU IV. 1106[31] (B.C. 13) ἅ τε ἐὰν λάβῃ ἢ πιστευθῇ σῶα συντηρήσειν (=σειν), P Lond 301[13] (A.D. 138–161) (= II. p. 257) παραδῷ[σω] τὸν γόμον σῶον καὶ ἀκακούργητον, "I will hand over the freight safe and unharmed," and BGU III. 802[29] (ii/A.D.) περιστερίδια ἑξήκ[οντα] σῶα καὶ ὑγιῆ, "sixty pigeons safe and sound."

For the relation of σῴζω to the Jewish-Aramaic אֱסָא see Wellhausen *Einleitung in die drei ersten Evangelien*, p. 33, and note the important article by W. Wagner "Über σῴζειν und seine Derivata im Neuen Testament " in *ZNTW* vi. (1905), p. 205 ff.

σῶμα,

"a body" (1) properly of the human body (a) "alive" : cf. P Cairo Zen I. 59034[20] (B.C. 257) μετὰ τῆς τοῦ σώματος ὑγιείας, and the common salutation, as in *ib.* 59036[9] (B.C. 257), εἰ τῶι τε σώματι ἔρρωσαι καὶ τἄλλα σοι κατὰ γνώμη[ν] ἐστίν, εἴη ἂν ὡς ἡμεῖς θέλομεν. See also BGU IV. 1208[18] (B.C. 27–26) τὰ δὲ ἄλλα χαριεῖ τοῦ σώμα[τος] [ἐπι]μελόμενος, ἵν' ὑγιαίνῃς, ὃ δὴ μέγιστον ἡγοῦμ[αι, PSI VII. 807[23] (A.D. 280) where a prisoner petitions ἔχειν τὸ σῶμα ἐλεύθερον καὶ ἀνύβριστον, and the magic P Lond 121[959] (iii/A.D.) (= I. p. 103) διαφύλασσέ μου τὸ σῶμα τὴν ψυχὴν ὁλόκληρον. Cf. Aristeas 139 ἁγνοὶ καθεστῶτες κατὰ σῶμα καὶ κατὰ ψυχήν. The tripartite division of 1 Thess 5[23] is found in P Oxy VIII. 1161[6] (iv/A.D.), where the writer (a Christian) prays to our God and the gracious Saviour and His beloved Son, ὅπως οὗτοι πάντες β[ο]ηθήσωσιν ἡμῶν τῷ σώματι, τῇ ψυχῇ, τῷ . . . πν(εύματι).

For the corresponding dim. σωμάτιον see the Christian letter P Oxy VI. 939[21] (iv/A.D.) (= *Chrest.* I. p. 156, *Selections*, p. 129) εἰ μὴ ἐπινόσως ἐσχήκει τὸ σωμάτιον τότε ὁ υἱὸς Ἀθανάσιος, αὐτὸν ἂν ἀπέστειλα πρός σε, "unless my son Athanasius had been then in a sickly state of body, I would have sent him to you," and *ib.*[25] νοσηλότερον δὲ ὅμως τὸ σωμάτιον ἔχει, "she is still in a somewhat sickly state of body."

(b) "dead," "a corpse," as in Mk 15[43] et saepe : cf. P Leid M[ii. 2] (ii/B.C.) (= I. p. 60) τὴν προστασίαν τῶν ἐπιβαλλόντων αὐτῷ σωμάτων, τῶν μεταγομένων εἰς τοὺς τάφους, and *ib.* W[vii.] 14 (ii/iii A.D.) a spell—Ἔγερσις σώματος νεκροῦ. In P Oxy I. 51[7] (A.D. 173) a public physician reports that he had been instructed ἐφιδεῖν σῶμα νεκρὸν ἀπηρτημένον, "to inspect the dead body of a man who had been found hanged," and in P Grenf II. 77[3] (iii/iv A.D.) the writer states that he has dispatched through the gravedigger τὸ σῶμα τοῦ [ἀδελφοῦ] Φιβίωνος, and has paid [το]ὺς μισθοὺς τῆς παρακομιδῆς τοῦ σώματος. Similarly σωμάτιον in the illiterate P Oxy VII. 1068[6] (iii A.D.), where the writer asks for a ship, ἵνα δυνηθῶ τὸ σωμάτιν κατενενκῖν ἐν Ἀλεξάνδριαν, "so that I might be able to carry the corpse down to Alexandria."

(2) For σώματα = "slaves," as in Rev 18[13] and frequently in the LXX, we can now produce many exx. The word stands alone in such passages as P Cairo Zen I. 50027[2] (B.C. 258) ὀψώνιον τοῖς σώμασιν, "wages for the slaves," P Hib I. 54[20] (c. B.C. 245) τὸ σῶμα δὲ εἰ συνείληφας, "but if you have arrested the slave" (Edd.), P Oxy III. 493[7] (a Will—early ii/A.D.) τὰ ἄπρατα τῶν σωμάτων, "unsold slaves," and BGU I. 187[12] (A.D. 159) Μελανᾶς ὁ προκίμενος [πέπ]ραχα τὸ σῶμα, where the context shows that a "slave" is intended.

For σῶμα in this sense but with a defining epithet cf. P Lond 401[9] (B.C. 116–111) (=II. p. 14) τῶν οἰκετικῶν σωμάτ[ων, P Oxy I. 94[9] (A.D. 83) πατρικὰ δοῦλα σώματα, BGU I. 168[9] (A.D. 169) δουλι[κ]ῶν σωμάτων, and P Lond 251[23] (A.D. 337–350) (= II. p. 317) τῶν δούλων σωμάτων.

The dim. σωμάτιον is correspondingly used in P Oxy I. 37[b. 7] (A.D. 49) ἀρρενικὸν σωμάτιον, "a male foundling," whom the next document in the vol. shows to have been a "slave"; and similarly the agreement for the nursing of a "slave-child" for two years, P Ryl II. 178[1] (early i/A.D.) μηδὲ ἕτερον σωμάτιον παρα[θηλάζειν παρὰ]ὰ τόδε, "and not to nurse another than this one"; and ib. 244[10] (iii/A.D.) τὰ δὲ σωμάτια πολλοῦ ἐστιν ἐνθά[δ]ε καὶ οὐ συμφέρει ἀγοράσαι, "slaves are very dear here, and it is inexpedient to buy" (Edd.).

(3) Σῶμα has also the general sense of "person," as when in the iii/B.C. census-paper, P Petr III. 59 (b)[2], σώματα ἐρσενικά are simply = "males," or in ib. 107, an account of fares and freights, where the word is applied repeatedly to "passengers." In P Petr II. 13 (3)[5] (B.C. 258–3) a warning is uttered that a prison wall may fall, and some of the prisoners perish—διαφανῆσαί τι τῶν σωμάτων. So in PSI IV. 359[6] (B.C. 252–1) a certain μισθωτός is referred to as τὸ σῶμα: cf. ib. 366[7] (B.C. 250–49), and the editor's introd. to ib. 423.

(4) Reference may also be made to the metaph. use of σῶμα to denote the "body" of a document, as in P Fay 34[20] (A.D. 161) Ἥρων ὁ προγεγρα[μμένος ἔγραψα τὸ σῶμα καὶ συνεθέμην πᾶσι τοῖς προκειμένοις καθὼς πρόκειται, "I, Heron, the above-mentioned, have written the body of the contract and agreed to all the aforesaid terms as is aforesaid" (Edd.): cf. P Lond 1132 b.[11] (A.D. 142) (= III. p. 142) ἔγρα]ψα τὸ σῶμα [αὐτοῦ τὸ ὄ]νομα ὑπογράφοντος ἔτους πέμπτ[ου] Ἀντωνίνου Καίσαρος.

σωματικός,

"bodily": cf. P Fay 21[10] (A.D. 134) εἴτ' ἐν γένεσιν εἴτ' ἐν ἀργυρίῳ εἴτ' ἐν σωματικαῖς ἐργασίαις, "whether in kind or in money or in bodily labour" (Edd.), P Flor I. 51[5] (A.D. 138–161) σ̣ωματικῆς ἀσθε[νεί]ας, and Syll 325 (= ³708)[11] (before B.C. 100) σωματικῶν πόνων. For the ὅρκος σωματικός, an oath taken by laying hands on corporeal objects such as a Bible or cross, see P Mon I. 6[56] (A.D. 583) with the editor's note.

σωματικῶς.

On σωματικῶς, "bodily-wise," "corporeally," "in concrete actuality" (Rawlinson), in Col 2[9] see Lightfoot's elaborate note ad l. A good ex. of the adv. is afforded

by OGIS 664[17] (i/A.D.) κατὰ [π]ᾶν ἢ ἀργυρικῶς ἢ σωματικῶς κολασθήσεται.

For σωματίζω and σωματισμός, which are not found in the NT, see Preisigke Fachwörter or Wörterbuch s.vv.

Σώπατρος,

a pet-form of Σωσίπατρος (q.v.), a Christian belonging originally to Beroea in Macedonia (Ac 20[4]).

σωρεύω

occurs in 2 Tim 3[6] in the sense of "overwhelm": see Field Notes, p. 217, and cf. Ep. Barn. iv. 6 ἐπισωρεύοντας ταῖς ἁμαρτίαις ὑμῶν.

The subst. σωρός, "a heap," is common in the papyri and ostraca, especially with reference to corn, e.g. P Flor III. 350[7] (A.D. 119) αὐτῆς (πυροῦ σωροῦ ἀρτάβαι) ι.

Σωσθένης.

This proper name (Ac 18[17], 1 Cor 1[1]) is found both in the papyri and the inscrr.—P Petr III. 112(c)[21] (iii/B.C.), P Lond 1044[39] (vi/A.D.) (= III. p. 255), Magn 118[6] (ii/A.D.) and Preisigke 678[39] (Egypt—c. A.D. 200).

Σωσίπατρος,

a Christian of Rome (Rom 16[21]), perhaps to be identified with Σώπατρος of Ac 20[4]. The name under both forms is common: see reff. in Preisigke's Namenbuch.

σωτήρ,

"saviour." Some vivid light by way of contrast is thrown on Jn 4[42] and 1 Jn 4[14] by the fact that the title σωτήρ was regularly given to the Ptolemies and to the Roman Emperors. Exx. are P Petr II. 8 (1) B[1] (c. B.C. 250) where the reign of Euergetes I. is alluded to in the words βασιλεύοντο[ς Πτ]ολεμαίου τ[οῦ Πτολεμα()ου σωτῆρος, and ib. III. 20[1.15] (B.C. 246) (= ib. II. 8 (2) revised), where the phrase πάν]των σωτῆρα is employed, cf. 1 Tim 4[10]. In Syll 347 (= ³760.[8], an Ephesian inscr. of A.D. 48, the Town Council of Ephesus and other cities acclaim Julius Caesar as θεὸν ἐπιφανῆ (see s.vv. θεός and ἐπιφανής) καὶ κοινὸν τοῦ ἀνθρωπίνου βίου σωτῆρα, and in a i/A.D. Egyptian inscr. (published in Archiv ii. p. 434. No. 24), reference is made to Nero as τῶι σωτῆρι καὶ εὐεργέτηι (cf. Lk 22[25]) τῆ[ς] οἰκουμένης: cf. the description of Vespasian in ib. No. 28 τὸν σωτῆρα καὶ εὐεργέτην.

The designation is further extended to leading officials, as when a complainant petitions a praefect in the words—ἐπὶ σὲ τοξευγω τὸν σωτῆρα τῶν δικαίων τυχεῖν, "(I turn) to you, my preserver, to obtain my just rights" (P Oxy I. 38[16] (A.D. 49–50) (= Selections, p. 54)), and similarly in the account of a public demonstration in honour of the prytanis at Oxyrhynchus, the multitude acclaim him—εὐτυχῆ ἡγεμώ[ν], σωτὴρ μετρίων, καθολικαί, "Prosperous praefect, protector of honest men, our ruler!" (ib. 41[22] (iii/iv A.D.).

The problem of Tit 2[13] cannot be discussed here, but Moulton (Proleg. p. 84) cites for what they are worth the Christian papyri BGU II. 366, 367, 368, 371, 395 (all vii/A.D.), which "attest the translation 'our great God and Saviour' as current among Greek-speaking Christians."

It may be further noted that following Hort, Parry, and Gore, Rawlinson (*Bampton Lect.* p. 172 n.[3]) regards δόξα as a Christological term, and translates " the 'epiphany' of Him Who is the Glory of our great God and Saviour, viz.: Jesus Christ."

In connexion with the belief that the death and resurrection of Attis each year secured a like renewal of life after their death to the faithful, we may add that a hymn dedicated to the god contains the following lines : θαρρεῖτε μύσται τοῦ θεοῦ σεσωσμένου, ἔσται γὰρ ὑμῖν ἐκ πόνων σωτηρία : see Cumont *Les Religions Orientales*, pp. 73, 266 (Engl. tr. pp. 50, 225).

See further the classic discussion on Σωτήρ by Wendland in *ZNTW* v. (1904), p. 335 ff.

σωτηρία

is common in the papyri in the general sense of " bodily health," " well-being," " safety," as in BGU II. 423[13] (ii/A.D.) (= *Selections*, p. 91) γράψον μοι ἐπιστόλιον πρῶτον μὲν περὶ τῆς σωτηρίας σου, δεύτερον περὶ τῆς τῶν ἀδελφῶν μου, *ib.* 632[13] (ii/A.D.) ο[ὐ]χ ὀκνῶ σοι γράψαι περὶ τῆ[ς] σωτηρίας μου καὶ τῶν ἐμῶν, *ib.* 380[6] (iii/A.D.) (= *Selections*, p. 104) ἐξέτασε (*l.* ἐξήτασα) περὶ τῆς σωτηρίας σου καὶ τῆς πε(αι)δίων σου, " I asked about your health and the health of your children," P Oxy VI. 939[20] (iv/A.D.) (= *Selections*, p. 129) νὴ γὰρ τὴν σὴν σωτηρίαν (cf. 1 Cor 15[31]), κύριέ μου, ἧς μάλιστά μοι μέλει, εἰ μὴ ἐπινόσως ἐσχήκει τὸ σωμάτιον τότε ὁ υἱὸς Ἀθανάσιος, αὐτὸν ἂν ἀπέστειλα πρός σε, " for by your own safety, my lord, which chiefly concerns me, unless my son Athanasius had then been in a sickly state of body, I would have sent him to you." P Oxy I. 138[21] (a contract—A.D. 610–11) ἐπὶ τούτοις πᾶσιν ἐπωμουσάμην (*l.* ἐπωμοσάμην) πρὸς τοῦ θεοῦ τοῦ παντοκράτορος, καὶ νίκης καὶ σωτηρίας καὶ διαμονῆς τῶν εὐσεβ(εστάτων) ἡμῶν δεσποτῶν Φλαουίου Ἡρακλείου καὶ Αἰλίας Φλαβίας, " to all this I swear by Almighty God and by the supremacy, salvation and preservation of our most pious sovereigns, Flavius Heraclius and Aelia Flavia " (Edd.).

With this may be compared the usage in Ac 27[34], Heb 11[7]. As a rule, however, in the NT σωτηρία, following its OT application to the great deliverances of the Jewish nation as at the Red Sea (Exod 14[13], 15[2]), etc., came to denote Messianic and spiritual salvation, either as a present possession (Lk 1[77] *al.*), or as to be realized fully hereafter (Rom 13[11] *al.*).

For σωτηρία as a pagan and Christian term, see Ramsay *Teaching*, p. 94 ff., and *Bearing* p. 173 ff., and for an early use of ἐλπὶς σωτηρίας (1 Thess 5[8]) in a non-religious sense cf. Menander Ἐπιτρέπ. 122.

σωτήριος

is used in the neut. as a subst. with reference to what produces σωτηρία, e.g. a sacrifice or a gift: cf. *Syll* 209 (= [3] 391)[22] (B.C. 281–0) θύσα]ι Σωτήρια ὑπὲρ Φιλοκλέους, *ib.* 640 (= [3] 384)[23] τεθύκασιν τὰ σω[τήρ]ια [τα]ῖς [θ]εα[ῖ]ς ὑπὲρ τῆς βουλῆς.

In the NT the word always occurs in a spiritual sense : see *s.vv.* σῴζω and σωτηρία.

σωφρονέω.

We can add nothing from our sources to Preisigke's (*Wörterb. s.v.*) iv/A.D. citations for this verb, P Lips I. 39[7] and PSI I. 41[7] and [23] σ)ωφρονεῖν καὶ ἡσυχάζειν, where the meaning is " am of sound mind," " am discreet," as in the NT occurrences (Mk 5[15] *al.*). See also Xen. *Oecon.* vii. 14 ἐμὸν δ' ἔφησεν ἡ μήτηρ ἔργον εἶναι σωφρονεῖν, the reference being to prudence in household management.

σωφρονίζω.

In the extraordinary interview with an Emperor, perhaps Commodus (P Oxy II. p. 310), the Emperor is represented as saying to a certain Appianus, who had addressed him in insulting language, ἰώθαμεν καὶ ἡμεῖς μαινομένους καὶ ἀπονενοημένους σωφρ( )ο)νίζειν, " we too are accustomed to bring to their senses those who are mad or beside themselves " (Edd.) (P Oxy I. 33 *verso* [iv.11]—late ii/A.D.) : cf. Tit 2[4], where, however, the RV understands the verb in the general sense of " train."

σωφρονισμός

by its termination suggests the trans. meaning " power to make σώφρων," but in its only occurrence in the NT, 2 Tim 1[7], the context clearly suggests the meaning " self-control," " self-discipline."

σωφροσύνη.

In an Imperial Edict regarding the remission of the *aurum coronarium*, P Fay 20 (iv/A.D.), the Emperor Julian (see *Archiv* ii. p. 169) claims that, ever since he became Caesar, he had striven to restore vigour to what was in decline,[14] οὐχ ὁρῶν ζητήσεσιν ἀλλὰ σωφρο[σύνῃ], μόνον οὐ πρὸς τὸ ἴδιον γινομένων ἀναλωμάτων, " not by acquisitions of territory (?) but by economy, limiting expenditure to public purposes " (Edd.). Later in the same document the word is used in the more general sense of " discretion," [21] μετὰ τοσαύτης κοσμιότητος καὶ σωφροσύνης καὶ ἐγκρατείας τὰ τῆς βασιλείας διοικοῦντα, " acting with so much propriety and discretion and moderation in the administration of his kingdom " (Edd.) : cf. Ac 26[25]. With this may be compared a sepulchral inscr. from Egypt published in *Archiv* v. p. 169, in which a certain woman Seratūs records the " good sense " of her mother and brother—ὧν καὶ ἡ σωφροσύνη κατὰ τὸν κόσμον λελάληται. See also *Syll* 344/5 (= [2] 757/8)[9] (B.C. 49–8), an inscr. in honour of Cornelia διά τε τὴν περὶ αὐτὴν σωφροσύνην καὶ τὴν πρὸς τὸν δῆμον εὔνοιαν, and *Preisigke* 5037 ἐκτανύσασα σωφροσύνῃ καὶ φιλανδρίᾳ.

With the meaning " self-control " in 1 Tim 2[9] may be compared the application to " chastity " in BGU IV. 1024[viii.15] (cited *s.v.* πενιχρός). Add Aristeas 237, 248, and see A. C. Pearson *Verbal Scholarship*, p. 21.

σώφρων.

In illustration of Tit 2[2.5] where the young women are exhorted φιλάνδρους εἶναι, φιλοτέκνους, σώφρονας, " loving to their husbands, loving to their children, soberminded," Deissmann (*LAE*[2], p. 315) has collected a number of exx.

of this same use of **σώφρων**, as an ideal of womanhood, e.g. *BCH* xxv. (1001) p. 88 ἡ **σόφρων** (*sic*) **καὶ φίλανδρος γυνὴ γενομένη**. and *ib.* xxii. (1808), p. 496, ἡ **φίλανδρος καὶ σ[ώ]φρων ἡ φιλόσοφος ζήσασα κοσμίως** (cf. 1 Tim 2⁹). In view of this, and of what is stated *s.v.* **σωφροσύνη**, we may be allowed to refer to a striking passage in Gilbert Murray's *Rise of the Greek Epic³*, p. 26, in which **σώφρων** or **σαόφρων**, "with saving thoughts," is contrasted with **ὀλοόφρων**, "with destructive thoughts." "There is a way of thinking which destroys and a way which saves. The man or woman who is *sōphrōn* walks among the beauties and perils of the world, feeling the love, joy, anger, and the rest ; and through all he has that in his mind which saves.—Whom does it save? Not him only, but, as we should say, the whole situation. It saves the imminent evil from coming to be."

Ταβειθά.

This feminine name (Ac 9^36, 40) under the form **Ταβιθά** is attested by Preisigke (*Namenbuch s.v.*) from several late papyri, e.g. P Lond IV. 1431^66 (A.D. 706-7) Ταβ[ι]θᾶ Δανείτ, "Tabitha daughter of David." For **Δορκάς**, the Greek form of the name, see *s.v.*

τάγμα.

For **τάγμα** = "company," "troop" in a military sense, see BGU IV. 1190^16 (late Ptol.) ἐ]κ τοῦ τάγματος αὐτοῦ: cf. 1 Cor 15^23 and Epicurus I. 71 φύσεως καθ' ἑαυτὰ τάγμα ἔχοντα, "having in themselves a place in the ranks of material existence" (Bailey). Other exx. of the word are P Oxy IX. 1202^18 (A.D. 217) my son being ἐκ τοῦ τάγματος τοῦ παρ' ἡμεῖν γυμνασίου, "on the roll of the gymnasium," *ib.* X. 1252 *verso*^24 (A.D. 288-95) τὸ τάγμα τὸ τῶν γυμνασιάρχων, and *ib.* VI. 891^15 (A.D. 294) τὰ δὲ ἀναλώματα ἀπὸ τοῦ κοινοῦ τῶν ἀπὸ τοῦ τάγματος δοθῆναι, "while the expenses should be paid by the whole body of those belonging to the order (of exegetae)" (Edd.).

τακτός,

"arranged," "fixed," of time, as in Ac 12^21, occurs in P Flor II. 133^1 (A.D. 257) τὰς τακτὰς ἡμέρας. Other exx. of the word are P Petr III. 104^8 (B.C. 243) (= *Chrest.* I. p. 394) ἐκφορίου τακτοῦ, "at a fixed rent," P Oxy I. 101^10 (A.D. 142) ἐπὶ μὲν τὰ τακτά, "on these conditions," P Flor I. 6^6 (A.D. 210) τὸ τακτὸν εἰς τὸ πρόστειμον τῆς συκοφαντίας, and P Giss I. 100^16 (iii/A.D.) ἀκολούθως ταῖς τα]κταῖς παρὰ σοῦ μεταβ[ολαῖς. For a military title τακτόμισθος (not in LS^8), cf. *UPZ* i. 31^3 (B.C. 162) with Wilcken's note.

ταλαιπωρία,

"wretchedness," "distress" (Rom 3^16 LXX): cf. P Tebt I. 27^10 (B.C. 113) ἐν τῆι αὐτῆι ταλαιπωρίαι διαμένεις, "you still continue in the same miserable condition" (Edd.). For plur. in Jas 5^1 cf. Aristeas 15 ἀπόλυσον τοὺς συνεχομένους ἐν ταλαιπωρίαις, and see Blass *Gr.* p. 84.

ταλαίπωρος,

"wretched," "miserable," is found in P Par 63^132 (B.C. 164) (= P Petr III. p. 30) τῶν μὲν ταλαιπώρων λαῶν . . . φείσεσθε, "you must spare the miserable populace" (Mahaffy), P Hawara 56^4 probably late i/A.D. (= *Archiv* v. p. 382) περὶ τῆς ταλαιπώρου [, and P Hamb I. 88^10 (mid. ii/A.D.) γράφεις μοι περὶ τῶν χρεωστῶν τοῦ ταλαιπώρου Ἰου[λ]ιανοῦ. The word occurs also in the

Jewish prayers for vengeance for the innocent blood of the two Jewish girls, Heraklea and Marthina, who were murdered in Rheneia (Magna Delos), *Syll* 816(=^3 1181)^5 ἐπικαλοῦμαι . . . ἐπὶ τοὺς . . . φαρμακεύσαντας τὴν ταλαίπωρον ἄωρον Ἡράκλεαν, now usually dated about B.C. 100 (see Deissmann *LAE*^2, p. 413 ff.).

ταλαντιαῖος,

"of a talent's weight or value" (cf. Moulton *Gr.* ii. p. 337), is found in the NT only in Rev 16^21; but, as Swete has pointed out *ad l.*, the word is well supported in later Greek, e.g. Polyb. ix. 41. 8, Joseph. *B.J.* v. 6. 3. See also the comic author Alcaeus of v/iv B.C., who speaks of νοσήματα ταλαντιαῖα (Kock *Fragm.* i. p. 759), and Crates of v B.C. (*ib.* p. 140).

τάλαντον,

a weight ranging from about 108 to 130 lbs., or a sum of money equivalent to a talent in weight. In a letter to a man in money difficulties BGU IV. 1079^16 (A.D. 41) (= *Selections*, p. 39) παρὰ τάλαντόν σοι πέπρακα τὰ φο[ρτ]ία μου, the meaning appears to be "for a talent I have sold my wares to you," or perhaps, "a talent (i.e. wares for a talent) excepted, I have sold my wares to you": cf. Olsson *Papyrusbriefe*, p. 94.

ταμεῖον,

"(inner) chamber," "store-chamber." The syncopated form ταμεῖον (for ταμιεῖον, which is found in the four NT occurrences of the word (Mt 6^6, 24^26, Lk 12^3, 24)), is the prevailing form in the papyri from i/A.D. onwards: see e.g. CPR I. 1^13 (A.D. 83-4) τραπέζ[ης] ταμείω[ν], "of the bank of the store-houses," and so^30, P Fay 110^7 (A.D. 94) ὃ λέγεις ταμε[ῖ]ον, "the storehouse you speak of," BGU I. 75^11 12 (ii/A.D.) εἰς τὸ ταμεῖον, P Oxy III. 533^9 (ii/iii A.D.) παρὰ τῷ ταμείῳ, and *ib.* VI. 886^1 (iii/A.D.) (= *Selections*, p. 111) ἐν τοῖς τοῦ Ἑρμοῦ ταμίοις, "in the archives of Hermes." In Menander Σαμ. 18 ταμείου probably stands for ταμειδίου.

The full form ταμιεῖον is seen in such passages from Ptolemaic times as P Petr II. 32^1 5 ἐργαζ[ομένου] μου ἐν τῶι βασιλικῶι ταμιείωι, "as I was working in the Royal Repository" (Edd.), *ib.* III. 73^7 (lease of a shop) ταμιεῖον εἰσιόντων ἐνδέξια ὄγδοον, "the eighth shop on the right as one enters" (Edd.), and P Hib I. 31^5 al. saep. (c. B.C. 270). From Roman times we can cite BGU I. 106^5 (A.D. 199) το[ῦ] ταμιείου, and P Flor I. 47^6 (A.D. 213-17) ἐντὸς ταμιείου οἰκίας. See further Thackeray *Gr.* i. p. 63 ff.

Ferguson, *Legal Terms*, p. 76 ff., gives exx. of both forms, ταμιεῖον and ταμεῖον.

For the verb ταμιεύομαι see P Magd 26⁵ (B.C. 217), where the editor reads τ]αμιευσόμεθα as against Wilcken's ἐκτ]αμιευσόμεθα. The same papyrus ⁵ ᵃⁿᵈ ⁹ provides other exx. of the comp^d.

τάξις.

(1) With Heb 5⁶ κατὰ τὴν τάξιν Μελχισεδέκ cf. the use of τάξις for a priestly "office" in P Tebt II. 297⁸ (c. A.D. 123) ὃς ἀπήνγ[ει]λεν τὴν τάξιν ὡς ὀφείλουσαν πραθῆναι, "who reported that the office ought to be sold" (Edd.). Cf. Diod. Sic. iii. 6 οἱ περὶ τὰς τῶν θεῶν θεραπείας διατρίβοντες ἱερεῖς, μεγίστην καὶ κυριωτάτην τάξιν ἔχοντες. Similarly of the post of water-guard in *ib.* 303¹⁰ (A.D. 150) τὴν ἐπιβάλλουσαν τῷ ὁμολογοῦντι Νείλῳ τάξιν τῆς [προ]κιμένης ὑδροφυλακίας. "the post of water-guard as aforesaid, which belongs to the contracting party Nilus" (Edd.). In *OGIS* 69⁵ the word is used of "garrisons"—ἡγέμων τῶν ἔξω τάξεων. Related exx. are—P Oxy VIII. 1120⁵ (early iii A.D.) βιβλείδια ἐπιδέδωκα ταῖς τάξεσι κατὰ τοῦ ὑβρίσαντος αὐτὸν Εὐδαίμονος, "I presented to the officials a petition against the perpetrator, Eudaemon" (Ed.). *ib.* XIV. 1670³ (iii/A.D.) αἰπὶ (*l.* ἐπεὶ) δὲ εἰς τὴν τάξιν τοῦ καθολικοῦ παρεδόθημεν, "when we were handed over to the staff of the catholicus" (Edd.), *ib.* IX. 1204¹⁷ (A.D. 299) ὑπηρετούμενος τῇ σῇ τοῦ ἐμοῦ κυρίου τάξει, "in obedience to your lordship's department" (Ed.), *ib.* X. 1261³ (A.D. 325) τάξ[ε]ως τοῦ διασημοτάτου καθολικοῦ, "on the staff of the most eminent catholicus" (Edd.), and *ib.* I. 120²³ (iv/A.D.) μάλιστα ἐπεὶ ξένης καὶ παρὰ τῇ τάξι ὄντα (*l.* ὤν), "especially as he was a stranger to the place and was engaged at his post" (Edd.).

(2) The word is also common = "list," as e.g. P Fay 29¹⁷ (A.D. 37) a notice of death, ὅπως ταγῇι τού[του] ὄν[ο]μα ἐν τῆι τῶν [τετ]ελευτηκότων τάξ[ει κατὰ] τὸ ἔ[θ]ος, "that his name may be placed upon the list of deceased persons, according to custom" (Edd.), similarly P Oxy II. 262¹² (A.D. 61), and PSI III. 164¹⁷ (A.D. 287), the enrolment of an ephebus ἐν τῇ τῶν ὁμηλίκων τάξει.

(3) The meaning "tax," "assessment," is very common in our documents, but, as this particular sense is not found in the NT, a very few exx. will suffice—BGU IV. 1096⁷ (i/ii A.D.) τὰ τῆς τάξεως βυβλία, "the accounts of the tax," similarly P Lond 300¹⁵ (A.D. 145) (= II. p. 119), P Fay 35¹⁰ (A.D. 150-1) ἀναδώσομεν σοι τὰς ἀποχὰς τῶν καταχωριζομένων βιβλείων τῆς τάξεως, "we will render to you the receipts among the documents for registration concerning the tax" (Edd.), and *Ostr* 1165⁵ (Rom.) ἐν τῇ αὐτῇ τάξει μεινάτωσαν.

(4) The derived meaning of "character," "quality," as in 2 Macc 9¹⁸, may be supported by P Tor I. 1 ᵛⁱⁱ ¹³ (B.C. 116) ἐμφανιστοῦ καὶ κατηγόρου τάξιν ἔχοντα παρακεῖσθαι, "was present in the character of an informer and an accuser": cf. Polyb. iii. 20. 5 οὐ γὰρ ἱστορίας, ἀλλὰ κουρεακῆς καὶ πανδήμου λαλιᾶς, ἐμοί γε δοκοῦσι τάξιν ἔχειν καὶ δύναμιν.

ταπεινός.

On the *verso* of P Oxy I. 79 (notification of death—A.D. 181-192) certain moral precepts have been written in a rude

hand, beginning μηδὲν ταπινὸν μηδὲ ἀγενὲς . . . πράξῃς, "do nothing mean or ignoble." Other exx. of the adj., which survives in MGr, are P Lond 131 *recto*³⁰⁹ (A.D. 78-9) (= I. p. 179) ἐν τοῖς ταπεινοῖς τόποις, *ib.* 1917⁷ (c. A.D. 330-340) a request for prayer διὰ ἐμοῦ τῷ ταπινῷ καὶ ταλεπώρῳ (*l.* τοῦ ταπεινοῦ καὶ ταλαιπώρου), "for me the humble and wretched," and P Gen I. 14⁷ (Byz.) μετὰ τῶν ταπεινῶν μου παίδων, and ¹⁵ τὰ ταπεινά μου ἄλογα.

It is hardly necessary to recall that "humility as a sovereign grace is the creation of Christianity" (W. E. Gladstone, *Life* iii. p. 466). Its history in pagan ethics may be illustrated in Epict. iii. 2. 14 ἄνθρωπον . . . ταπεινόν, μεμψίμοιρον, ὀξύθυμον, δειλόν κτλ., and iv. 1. 2 τίς θέλει ζῆν ἐξαπατώμενος, προπίπτων . . . μεμψίμοιρος, ταπεινός;

ταπεινόω,

"make low," is generally used metaphorically in the NT = "humble." By way of illustration we may again refer to the Jewish prayers cited *s.v.* ταλαίπωρος, where it is said with regard to God, ¹⁰⁸ ᾧ πᾶσα ψυχὴ ἐν τῇ σήμερον ἡμέρᾳ ταπεινοῦτα[ι] μεθ᾽ ἱκετείας, a phrase strikingly recalling Lev 23²⁹, and pointing, according to Deissmann *LAE²* p. 419, to a day not only of prayer, but of fasting. The literal sense of the verb (cf. Lk 3⁵ LXX) comes out well in Diod. i. 36 καθ᾽ ἡμέραν . . . ταπεινοῦται, with reference to the "falling" of the Nile: it "runs low."

ταπείνωσις

is seen in *OGIS* 383²⁰¹ (mid. i/B.C.) εἰς ὕβριν ἢ ταπείνωσιν ἢ κατάλυσιν, and P Leid Wˣ ¹⁷ (ii/iii A.D.) (= II. p. 115) ἡλίου ταπείνωσις. For ταπείνωμα, cf. the horoscope PSI IV. 312¹² (A.D. 345).

ταράσσω

in the metaph. sense "trouble," "disquiet," "perplex," as in Mt 2³ *al.*, is seen in P Tebt II. 315¹⁵ (ii/A.D.) τοιγαροῦν [μὴ]δὲν ταραχ[θ]ῇς, "do not be disturbed on this account" (Edd.), and *Syll* 373 (= ³ 810)¹³ (i/A.D.) οὓς ἐπὶ τῇ ψευδῶς ἐπι[σ]τολῇ πρὸς ὑμᾶς κομισθείσῃ τῷ τῶν ὑπάτων ὀνόματι ταραχθέντες πρός με ἐπέμψατε. For a somewhat more literal meaning "stir up," as in Ac 17⁸·¹³, cf. P Oxy II. 298²⁷ (i/A.D.) πάλι γὰρ πάντα ταράσσει, "for he is upsetting everything again" (Edd.), and P Giss I. 40ⁱⁱ·²⁰ (A.D. 212-5) (= *Chrest.* I. p. 38) ταράσσουσι τὴν πόλιν. MGr ταράζω(—άσσω), "perplex."

ταραχή,

"disturbance." In P Lond 1912⁷³ (A.D. 41) the Emperor Claudius writing to the Alexandrines declares himself unwilling to decide who was responsible for τῆς . . πρὸς Ἰουδαίους ταραχῆς καὶ στάσεως, μᾶλλον δ᾽ εἰ χρὴ τὸ ἀληθὲς εἰπεῖν τοῦ πολέμου, "the riot and feud (or rather, if the truth must be told, the war) against the Jews" (Ed.). In *OGIS* 90²⁰ (Rosetta stone—B.C. 196) ἐν τοῖς κατὰ τὴν ταραχὴν καιροῖς, the reference is to the Lycopolitan sedition, as in P Tor I. 1ᵛ·²⁹ (B.C. 116) ἐν τῇι γενομένηι ταραχῆι. See also *Syll* 316 (= ³ 684)¹³ (c. B.C. 139). P Amh II. 30¹¹ (ii/B.C.) ἐν δὲ τῇ[ι γενημένηι ταραχῆι refers most likely to the revolt in the Thebaid, instigated by Dionysius about B.C. 165, and this may again be the case in *UPZ* i. 14ⁿ·³ (B.C. 168): cf. p. 479.

τάραχος,

a late form of **ταραχή**, is found in Ac 12[18], 19[23], where it is masculine. For exx. of τὸ **τάραχος** in the LXX see Thackeray *Gr.* i. p. 159. According to Hobart (p. 93) the word is common in medical writers. Linde, *Epicurus* p. 24, quotes three passages from Epicurus for **τάραχος** (masc.) = "disturbance," "alarm," and notes two occurrences of the form **ταραχή**. See also Rutherford *NP.* p. 174.

Ταρσεύς,

"of Tarsus" (Ac 9[11], 21[39]). A new adj. **ταρσικούφικός** is found in connexion with the sale of a loom in P Oxy XIV. 1705[6] (A.D. 298) ἰστὸν ταρσικούφικόν, "a loom for Tarsian cloths."

ταρταρόω,

"I send to Tartarus," orig. "the place of punishment of the Titans," and hence appropriate in connexion with fallen angels in 2 Pet 2[4]. The word is cited elsewhere only from a scholion on *Il.* xiv. 295 (see LS).

For the subst. **τάρταρος** (cf. LXX Job 40[15], 41[23]) see *Acta Thomae* 32 where the serpent who tempted Eve says ἐγώ εἰμι ὁ τὴν ἄβυσσον τοῦ ταρτάρου οἰκῶν, and the other reff. in Mayor *ad* 2 Pet *l.c.* Add PSI I. 28[20] (magic tablet —iii/iv A.D.) ταρτάρου σκῆπτρα, and for **Ταρταροῦχος** see P Osl I. p. 33.

τάσσω,

"put in its place," "appoint," "enrol," is seen in such passages as P Par 26[20] (B.C. 162) (= *UPZ* i. p. 248, *Selections*, p. 15) τῶν δὲ πρὸς τοῖς χειρισμοῖς ἐν τῶι Σαραπιείωι . . τεταγμένων, "those who had been appointed to the administration in the Serapeum," P Oxy II. 259[3] (A.D. 23) τῷ τεταγμένῳ πρὸς τῇ τοῦ Διὸς φυλακῇ, "governor of the prison of Zeus," P Fay 29[15] (notice of death—A.D. 37) ὅπως ταγῇι τοῦ[του] ὄγ[ο]μα ἐν τῇι τῶν [τετ]ελευτηκότων τάξ[ει, "that his name may be placed on the list of deceased persons," so *ib.* 30[13] (A.D. 173), P Oxy X. 1252 *verso*[30] (A.D. 288–95) τετράμηνος γὰρ ἐφ' ἑκάστου τέτακται, "for a period of four months is allotted to each" (Edd.), and PSI IV. 298[8] (beg. iv/A.D.) τὸν τεταγμένον χρόνο(ν).

In P Oxy II. 274[7] (A.D. 89–97) ὧν καὶ τὸ τέλος ἔταξαν, the verb is used of "paying" the succession duty, which in ii/B.C. was 5% : cf. PSI IV. 388[51] (B.C. 244–3) ἃ δεῖ τάξασθαι εἰς τὸ βασιλικόν, *ib.* I. 56[10] (A.D. 107) ὧν καὶ τάξομαι τὸ καθῆκον τέλος.

For a weakened sense of the verb see P Oxy VIII. 1159[16] (late iii/A.D.) τάξαι τοῖς ἀνθρώποις ὅτι πέμπω τὰ ἀναλώματα αὐτῶν, "tell the men that I am sending the expenses for them" (Ed.).

The mid. is also used = "appoint for oneself" in P Fay 129[3] (iii/A.D.) Ἀπολλῶτι συνέβαλον καὶ ἐτάξατο πάντως καταβῆναι τῇ ἑνδεκάτῃ καὶ τὴν παράδοσιν ποιήσασθαι, "I arranged with Apollos, and he appointed for certain the eleventh for his coming down and making the delivery" (Edd.), *ib.* 130[8] (iii/A.D.) προνοῶ τοῦ χ[α]λκοῦ πά[ντη πάν]τως καθὼς ἐταξάμη[ν, "I am by all means looking after the copper, as I arranged" (Edd.) : cf. Mt 28[16], Ac 28[23]. Hence also the sense "enter into an agreement with" in such passages as P Hamb I. 25[11] (B.C. 238–7) Κάλως τέτακται

συναντήσεσθαι πρὸς σὲ τῆι κε τοῦ Χοίακ μηνό(ς), and P Magd I. 12[5] (B.C. 217) ταξάμενοί μοι ἐπὶ Διονυσίου, "they agreed verbally with me in the presence of Dionysius" (see the editor's note).

ταῦρος,

"a bull," "an ox" : P Oxy I. 121[14] (iii/A.D.) περεὶ τῶν ταύρων ἐργαζέσθωσαν, "as to the oxen, make them work." From the adj. form **ταυρικός** (not in LS[8]) comes τὸ **ταυρικόν**, "the oxen," as in P Fay 115[16] (A.D. 101) πέμψις μυ ψειρι τῶι ταυρικῶι, "send me a strap (?) for the oxen" (Edd.) : see also PSI IV. 429[25] (iii/B.C.) περὶ ταυρικῶν ζευγῶν ιβ, P Flor II. 134[1] (A.D. 260) (with the editor's note), which also shows **ταυρελάτης**, and P Ryl II. 240[5] (iii/A.D.) παράσχες χό[ρ]τον τῷ ταυρικῷ.

The classical adj. **ταύρειος** is found in the medical prescription P Oxy II. 234[45] (ii/iii A.D.) χολῇ ταυρείᾳ, "gall of an ox."

ταφή,

in the sense of "a mummy," or "mummy-wrappings," occurs in such passages as P Par 18 *bis*[10] ἔστιν δὲ σημεῖον τῆς ταφῆς· σινδὼν ἐστιν . . . . P Giss I. 68[7] (Trajan/ Hadrian) δεῖ αὐτὸν δευτέρᾳ ταφῇ ταφῆναι : cf. Deissmann *BS* p. 355 n.[2]

For the meaning "burial" (*sepultura*), as in Mt 27[7], cf. P Petr III. 2[19] (a Will—B.C. 236) τὰ δὲ λοι[πὰ κατα]λιμπάνω εἰς ταφὴν ἐμαυτοῦ, P Magd 13[6] (B.C. 217) ἐνδεεῖς δὲ γενόμενοι εἰς τὴν ταφὴν τὴν Φιλίππου (δραχμὰς) κε, P Tebt I. 5[77] (B.C. 118) τὰ εἰς τὴν ταφὴν τοῦ Ἄπιος καὶ Μνήσιος, "the expenses for the burial of Apis and Mnesis," BGU I. 183[24] (A.D. 85) τὴν προσήκουσα(= σαν) τῇ Σαταβοῦτος(= τι) ταφήν, P Amh II. 125[1] (late i/A.D.) λόγο(ς) δαπάνη(ς) ταφῆς, "account of funeral expenses," and P Tebt II. 479 (iii/A.D.) a woman's expenses in connexion with the death of her husband, including payments εἰς ἐγδίαν σιτολόγω[ν], εἰς ταφὴν αὐτοῦ.

τάφος,

"a tomb" : P Ryl II. 153[5] (a Will—A.D. 138–161) εἰς τὸν τάφον μου τὸν ἐπὶ τὴν ἄμμον τοῦ Σαρα[πιείον, a bequest payable on condition that the recipient goes "to my tomb in the sand of the Serapeum." In P Oxy III. 494[21] (A.D. 156) a testator makes provision for a feast (εἰς εὐωχίαν), which his slaves and freedmen are to observe yearly on his birthday πλησίον τοῦ τάφου μου : see J. G. Frazer, *Golden Bough*[3] i. p. 105.

From the inscrr. we may cite *OGIS* 335[116] (ii/i B.C.) ἕως [τοῦ] τάφου τοῦ πρὸς τῆι ὁδῶι [τοῦ ἐπικαλουμένου Ἐ]πικράτου, *Christ.* I. 70[17] (B.C. 57–6) μέχρι τῶν προσόντων ἀπὸ βορρᾶ τάφων τῶν ἀποθειωμένων ἱερῶν ζώων, and *Syll* 399 (= [3]858)[5] (after A.D. 161), where a memorial is described as οὐ τάφος, seeing that the body is laid elsewhere.

τάχα

is used of time in P Fay 117[12] (A.D. 108) τοὺς θιώτας πέμψις ἐπὶ Ἐρασο[ς] τὰ Ἀρποχράτια ὧδε τάχα ιδ πυ[ήσ]ι, "send the . . . since Erasus is going to celebrate the festival of Harpocrates so soon on the 14th."

For the meaning "perhaps," as in Rom 5[7], Philem[15], and in MGr, cf. BGU IV. 1079[11] (A.D. 41) (= *Selections*,

p. 30) τάχα δύναταί σε εὔλυτον ποῖσαι, and so [22], P Oxy I. 40[7] (ii/iii A.D.) τάχα κακῶς αὐτοὺς ἐθεράπευσας, "perhaps your treatment was wrong," ib. 121[23] (iii/A.D.) τάχα οὐδὲν δίδω, "I shall perhaps give him nothing" (Edd.), and so [19], and ib. VII. 1069[16] (iii/A.D.) τάχα γὰρ δυνασθῶμεν φο[ρ]υτρεῖσε(= ετρίσαι) σοι δύο καμήλους [πυ]ροῦ, "for we may be able to load two camels with wheat for you" (for δυνασθῶμεν equivalent to δυνησόμεθα see the editor's note, and Proleg. p. 185).

τάχε(ι)ον.

See s.v. ταχέως.

ταχέως,

"quickly": P Oxy I. 116[9] (ii/A.D.) ταχέως αὐτὸν ἀπολύσατε, "send him off quickly" (Edd.), P Fay 126[7] (ii/iii A.D.) ἄνελθε οὖν ταχέως ὅτι ἐπίγι, "do you therefore come back quickly, for it is pressing," and P Tebt II. 423[22] (early iii/A.D.) δή[λω]σόν μοι ταχ[έως, "tell me at once" (Edd.).

The compᵛᵉ τάχ(ε)ιον is always used with an elative force in the NT, except in Jn 20⁴: cf. P Lond Inv. No. 1501² (end i/A.D.) (= Olsson Papyrusbriefe, p. 210) πρὸ μὲν παντὸς εὔχομαί σε ὑγιαίνειν καὶ τάχειον ἀπολαβεῖν, "above all I pray that you may be in health and that I should receive you as soon as possible" (cf. Lk 15²⁷), P Oxy III. 531² (ii/A.D.) ἐὰν γὰρ θεοὶ θέλωσι, τάχιον πρὸς σὲ ἥξω, and BGU II. 417²⁵ (ii/iii A.D.) τάχειον δὲ καὶ σὺ παραγένου ἐπὶ τὸ τῶν Ταυρικῶν. See further Blass Gr. pp. 33, 141 f.

The compᵛᵉ ταχύτερον occurs in P Tebt II. 410¹¹ (A.D. 16) ἐρωτῶ σε ταχύτερον συσχεῖν τ[ὸ] πρᾶγμα, "I beg you to close the matter with all speed" (Edd.), BGU II. 615²³ (ii/A.D.) δήλωσόν μ[ο]ι ταχύτερον, and P Michigan Inv. No. 4527⁸ (c. A.D. 200) σύ μοι ταχύτερον ("at once," Ed.) δήλωσον περὶ τῆς ἀπροσκοπίας ("well-being": not in L.S.⁹) σου καὶ τῆς τῶν ἀδελφῶν μου. In MGr (Naxos) ταχυτέρου is used for "later" (adv.) (Thumb Handbook § 123, n.²).

For τάχιστα, as in Ac 17¹⁵, we may cite PSI IV. 360¹² (B.C. 252-1) ὡς ἂν τάχιστα λικμήσωμεν, "in order that we may winnow (the grain) as quickly as possible," ib. VII. 792¹⁰ (A.D. 136) ὡς [τ]άχιστά μοι δηλώσατε, and P Giss I. 27¹¹ (ii/A.D.) (= Chrest. I. p. 29) καλῶς οὖν ποιήσεις, τειμιώτατε, τάχιστά μοι δηλώσας. Cf. also the formula τὴν ταχίστην in 1 Macc 11²².

ταχινός.

For this adj. = "speedy" with the added idea of "sudden" in 2 Pet 1¹⁴, 2³, Herwerden Lex. s.v. cites CIA III. 1344³ ζωῆς καὶ καμάτου τέρμα δραμὼν ταχινόν.

τάχιστα.

See s.v. ταχέως.

τάχος,

"quickness": PSI IV. 326¹² (B.C. 261-0) ἔντειλαι τῶι παρά σου, ἵνα τὸ τάχος γέ[νη]ται, and P Oxy I. 59¹⁵ (A.D. 292) ἵν' . . . ἦ τάχος ἐκδημῆσαι, "in order that no time be lost in his departure" (Edd.): cf. PSI IV. 444¹¹

(iii/B.C.) πειρῶ δέ μοι ὅ τι τάχος γράψειν Ἔρρωσο, and P Bouriant 10²² (B.C. 88) ἀσ]φαλισάμενος [μέ]χρι τοῦ καὶ [ἡμᾶ]ς ὅτι τάχος [ἐπι]βαλεῖν πρὸς σέ.

The word is common in adverbial phrases with a preposition, e.g. P Oxy I. 62 verso¹⁸ (iii/A.D.) τὴν ἐμβολὴν ποιῆσαι διὰ τάχους, "to do the lading quickly" (Edd.). ib. VI. 892⁹ (A.D. 338) διὰ τάχεων ταῦτα ἐκκόψας παρενεχθῆναι, "with all speed to get the timber cut and delivered" (Edd.): PSI IV. 380¹⁴ (B.C. 249-8) καλῶς δ' ἂν ποιήσαις ἐν τάχει (cf. Lk 18⁸, al. αὐτὸν ἀποστείλας, P Giss I. 60¹⁰ (A.D. 118-9) πᾶσαν τὴν . . . [κ]ρειθὴν ἐν τάχει αὐτῶ ἐπιστεῖλαι, and P Oxy VII. 1069⁴ (iii/A.D.) καλῶς ποιήσεις ἀναγκάσε γενέστε ἢ ἀναγκάσαι γενέσθαι μου τὸ κειθώνε[ι]ν . . κιθώνιν) τὸ λευκὸν κατὰ τάχο[υ]ς, "you will do well to have my white tunic made quickly" (Ed.).

ταχύ

(neut. of ταχύς as adv.), "quickly" (Mt 5²⁵ al. and common in LXX). See P Par 45⁵ (B.C. 152) (= UPZ i. p. 329) κἄαυτὸς παρέσομαι ταχύ, P Oxy IV. 743¹¹ (B.C. 2) καλῶς δὲ γέγονεν τὸ ταχὺ αὐτὸν ἐλθεῖν, ὑφηγήσεται γάρ σοι, "it is well for him to come quickly, for he will instruct you" (Edd.), and BGU II. 423¹³ (soldier's letter to his father— ii/A.D.) (= Selections, p. 91) ἐκ τούτου ἐλπίζω ταχὺ προκόσαι l. προκόψαι) τῶν θε[ῶ]ν θελόντων, "in consequence of this I hope to be quickly promoted, if the gods will."

Ταχὺ ταχύ is a common formula in incantations, e.g. P Hawara 312⁵ (ii/A.D.) in Archiv v. p. 393 ἄρτι ἄρτι ταχὺ ταχὺ ἐξ ψυχῆς καὶ καρδίας, and the Gnostic amulet P Oxy VII. 1060⁸ (vi/A.D.) ἀπάλλαξον τὸν οἶκον τοῦτον ἀπὸ παντὸς κακοῦ ἑρπετοῦ <καὶ> πράγματος ταχὺ ταχύ, "free this house from every evil reptile and thing, quickly, quickly": see also Deissmann BS, p. 289, and LAE², p. 421, and for the repetition cf. Proleg. p. 97.

τε.

For this enclitic particle cf. BGU IV. 1132³ (B.C. 13) κατὰ τὰς διὰ τοῦ κριτηρίου τετελειωμένας ὑπό τε τοῦ Ἀμμωνίου καὶ ἔτι τοῦ μετηλλαχότος τοῦ Ἀλεξάνδρου ἀδελφοῦ, P Strass I. 14²¹ (A.D. 211) sale of a chamber καθαρὸν ἀπὸ παντὸς] ὀφ[ειλ]ήματος δ[ημο]σίου τε καὶ ἰδιωτι[κο]ῦ, and P Oxy XIV. 1038¹⁴ (A.D. 282) ἐφ' ᾧ τε καὶ τοὺς περὶ τὸν Ἀρὲτ [καὶ τὸν Σαρᾶν τελέσαι πάντα τὰ] . . . ὀφ[ε]ι>λήματα, "on condition that the party of Aret and Saras discharge all the debts" (Edd.).

For 2 Cor 10⁸ cf. Radermacher Gr.² pp. 5, 37. See also Kalker Quaest. p. 286 ff. Τε is one of the many particles which do not survive in MGr.

τεῖχος,

"a wall," especially the wall about a city (Ac 9²⁵ al.): cf. P Eleph 20⁵² (iii/B.C.) παστοφόριον ἐν Τεντύρει ἐντὸς τείχους, P Ryl II. 127¹³ (A.D. 29) τὸ ἀπὸ βορρᾶ τεῖχος τοῦ οἴκου, BGU III. 920¹ (ii/iii A.D. ?) μητροπόλεως ἐντὸς τείχους, P Flor I. 50⁴ (A.D. 268) ἐν[τὸς τειχῶν] καὶ ἐκτός, cf.³⁶, ⁸⁰, and P Strass I. 9⁸ (c. A.D. 307 or 352) θεμελίοις καὶ τίχεσιν.

For the dim. τειχίον see CPR I. 232¹⁴ (ii/iii A.D.) μέσο]υ [ὄν]τος τειχ[ίου, and for the form τειχάριον (not in L.S.⁹), see P Ryl II. 125⁷ (A.D. 28-9) κατασπασμὸν τειχαρίων παλαιῶ(ν). "demolition of old walls," and for the verb τειχίζω, see *ib.* 102⁹ (2ⁿᵈ half ii/A.D.) αὐλ( ) ἀ[π]ὸ βο[ρρ]ᾶ τετειχισμέ(ν).

τεκμήριον.

This strong word which AV renders "infallible proof" in Ac 1³ may be illustrated by an Ephesian inscr. *Syll* 656 (=³ 807)³⁷ (*c.* A.D. 160), where it is mentioned as μέγιστον τεκμήριον of the σεβασμός accorded to the goddess Artemis that a month is named after her. Cf. also *ib.* 929 (=³ 685)⁸⁴ (B.C. 139) μέγιστον καὶ ἰσχυρότατον τεκμήριον, and P Tor I. 1ⁱᵛ·¹¹ (B.C. 116) μέγα τι συμβάλλεσθαι τεκμήριον, also ᵛⁱⁱⁱ·³². In another Ptolemaic papyrus P Giss I. 39⁹ (B.C. 204–181) τεκμήριον stands beside ὅρκος.

The editors render P Ryl II. 150¹⁵ (A.D. 31–2) ἵν' ὑπάρχωσι τῇ [Ταχ]όιτι αἱ παραχωρούμεναι ἄ]ρουραι σὺν τοῖς ἄλλοις τε[κμηρίοις . . . , "in order that the arurae ceded may appertain to Tachois with all other titles" (i.e. "title-deeds"), but in their note they cite the parallel formula P Oxy III. 504¹⁹ (early ii/A.D.) σὺν τοῖς ἄλλοις σημίοι[ς, where the σημεῖα may possibly refer to "boundary-marks." It may be added that, according to Hobart p. 184, "Galen expressly speaks of the medical distinction between τεκμήριον—demonstrative evidence – and σημεῖον, stating that rhetoricians as well as physicians had examined the evidence."

For the verb τεκμαίρομαι, see P Ryl II. 74⁵ (A.D. 133–5) where a prefect declares that time will not permit his carrying out two purposes—τεκμαίρομαι τὸν χρόνον οὐ[χ ἱκανὸν εἶναι εἰ]ς ἀμφότερα.

τεκνίον.

For this dim. of τέκνον cf. P Oxy XIV. 1766¹⁴ (iii/A.D.) ἀσπάζομαι . . . τὰ ἀβάσκαντα τεκνία, "I greet your children, whom the evil eye will not harm."

τεκνογονέω.

With this NT ἄπ. εἰρ. (1 Tim 5¹⁴) = "bear a child," we may compare the similar compd. τεκνοποιέομαι in the marriage contract P Eleph 1⁹ (B.C. 311–10) (= *Selections*, p. 3), where the husband is bound down μηδὲ τεκνοποιεῖσθαι ἐξ ἄλλης γυναικός. "not to beget children by another woman." In *UPZ* i. 4⁵ (B.C. 164) ἕνεκ[α] τοῦ . . . τεκνοπ[ο]ήσασθα = θαι αὐτήν, the meaning is "adopt" (cf. Wilcken's note. See also *s.v.* τεκνογονία.

τεκνογονία.

Ramsay *Teaching* p. 170 ff. tries to show that, while τεκνογονέω is used in a physical sense in 1 Tim 5¹⁴, the abstract noun τεκνογονία in 1 Tim 2¹⁵ points rather to "the power of maternal instinct" or "motherhood." But it is by no means clear that the writer did not use the two words with the same connotation. In any case it is not likely that, with Ellicott and other commentators, we are to stress the article and in τῆς τεκνογονίας of 1 Tim 2¹⁵ find a reference to "the (great) child-bearing." i.e. the bearing of Jesus, foreshadowed in Gen. 3¹⁶.

τέκνον.

(1) The following may serve as exx. of this very common word = "a child"—P Amh II. 35⁵⁵ (B.C. 132) ὑπέρ τε τοῦ

βα(σιλέως) καὶ τῶν βα(σιλι)κῶν τέκνων, P Tor II. 11¹¹ ἕτερα τέκνα, "a second family," BGU IV. 1097²³ (time of Claudius/Nero) τὴν μητέρα καὶ Δήμητριν καὶ τὰ τέ[κ]να αὐτοῦ ἀσπάζου, BGU I. 234³¹ (*c.* A.D. 70–80) ὥσπερ ἰδ[ί]ων τέκνων, P Lond 807²³ (A.D. 84) (== III. p. 207) μέλει σοι πολλὰ περὶ ἐμοῦ μελ[ήσε]ι σοι δὲ ὡς ὑπὲρ ἰδίου τέκνου, P Oxy II. 237ᵛⁱⁱ· ³⁶ (A.D. 186) ἡ δὲ κτῆσις μετὰ θάνατον τοῖς τέκνοις κεκράτηται, "but the right of ownership after their death has been settled upon the children" (Edd.), and BGU II. 419¹⁵ (A.D. 276–7) οὐκ ἐπελεύσομα[ι] περὶ αὐτῶν το[ύτ]ων οὐδὲ οὐδεὶς τῶν παρ' ἐμοῦ οὐδὲ τέκνον τ[έ]κνου. As showing the oppression of the Egyptian middle-class, we may note the case of a certain Pamonthius, whose children had been seized by his creditors—οἵτινες οἱ ἀνελεήμονες ἐκεῖνοι καὶ ἄθεοι ἀπέσπασαν τὰ πάντα τὰ ἑαυτοῦ τέκνα νήπια κομιδῆ, "who, those pitiless and godless men, carried off all his children, being yet quite in their infancy" (Bell) (P Lond 1015²⁸—A.D. 330–340).

(2) Τέκνον is also used as a form of kindly address, even in the case of grown-up persons—P Oxy I. 33ⁱᵛ·¹¹ (late ii/A.D.) τρέχε, τέκνον, τελεύτα, P Giss I. 12⁵ (letter to a strategus— ii/A.D.) παρακαλῶ σε οὖν, τέκνον, . . . ἐντυπήν ("pattern") μοι πέμψον, similarly *ib.* 21²⁰ (time of Trajan) ἔρρωσο τέκνον, and P Oxy VII. 1065¹ (ii/iii A.D.) χαίροις, τέκνον 'Αμόι, "greeting, my son Amois!"

(3) Schaefer *ad* P Lond 13ⁿ has brought together various exx. of τέκνον and υἱός. e.g. P Gen I. 74¹ᶠᶠ (iii/A.D.) Ἡραῒς Ἀγριππί[ν]ῳ τῷ υἱῷ πλεῖστα χ(αίρειν). πρὸ μὲν πάντων εὔχομαί σε ὑγιαίνειν καὶ προκόπτειν. γε[ί]νωσκε, τέκνον, ἀπεληλυθέναι ἐμέ, P Amh II. 136¹¹ (iii/A.D.) 'Απίων Ὠρίωνι τῶι υἱῶι χαίρειν . . . . γράφω σοι, τέκνον, and P Oxy VI. 930⁸ (ii/iii A.D.) ὥστε οὖν, τέκνον, μελησάτω σοι, and on the *verso* Πτολεμαίω υἱῶι.

(4) For the Hebraistic idiom underlying the use of τέκνον with genitives of quality, as in Eph 5⁸ τέκνα φωτός, see Deissmann *BS* p. 161 ff., and *s.v.* υἱός.

τεκνοτροφέω.

With this NT ἄπ. εἰρ (1 Tim 5¹⁰) = "bring up children," cf. Epict. i. 23. 3 διὰ τί ἀποσυμβουλεύεις τῷ σοφῷ τεκνοτροφεῖν;

τέκτων.

The ordinary limitation of this word to "a worker in wood," "a carpenter," as in Mt 13⁵⁵, Mk 6³, is supported by P Fay 110²³ (A.D. 94) τὰς θύρας ἐπιστησάτωσαν οἱ τέκτονες. "let the carpenters put up the doors" (Edd.), P Flor II. 152⁹ (letter regarding the conveyance of wood— A.D. 268) τῷ τέκτονι τὴν συνήθη δ[α]πάνην, cf. *ib.* 158⁴ (iii/A.D.), and P Oxy I. 53² (A.D. 316), a report παρὰ τοῦ κοινοῦ τῶν τεκτόνων, from the guild of carpenters at Oxyrhynchus regarding a persea tree they had been commissioned to examine.

Other exx. of the word are P Fay 122¹⁹ (*c.* A.D. 100) ἀπαναγκάσεις Σισόιν τὸν τ[έκ]τονα ἀποτῖσαι, "make Sisois the carpenter pay up" (Edd.), *Ostr* 1597 (ii/A.D.) δὸς τοῖς τέκτοσι ζεύγη ἄρτων δέκα ἕν, P Oxy I. 121²⁵ (iii/A.D.) τοὺς τέκτονες(= ας) μὴ ἀφῇς ὅλως ἀργήσε(= σαι), "don't allow the carpenters to be wholly idle" (Edd.), PSI VII. 800⁴ (iv/A.D.) Φοιβάμμονι τέκτονι ἐργ(αζομένῳ) εἰς

. . ., and *ib.* 774[10] (v/A.D.) **τέκτων εἴτε κεραμεύς**. In Herodas IV. 22 the "craftsman" (**τέκτων**) is a sculptor. Cf. *s.v.* **ἀρχιτέκτων**.

For the adj. see P Oxy IV. 729[12] (A.D. 137), P Flor I. 16[21] (A.D. 239) **τεκτονικῶν μισθῶν**.

τέλειος,

lit. "having reached its end (**τέλος**)." Hence (1) "full-grown," "mature," (*a*) of *persons*—BGU IV. 1100[10] (marriage-contract—time of Augustus) **τ]έλιον οὖσα⟨ν⟩ πρὸς βίου κοινωνίαν [ἀν]δρί**, P Oxy III. 485[30] (A.D. 178) **κληρονόμοις [α]ὐ[τῆ]s τελεί[ο]ις**, "to her heirs being of age," *ib.* 11. 237[vii.15] (A.D. 186) **περὶ τοῦ τὰς ἤδη τελείας γυναῖκας γενομένας ἑαυτῶν εἶναι κυρίας, εἴτε βούλονται παρὰ τοῖς ἀνδράσιν μένειν εἴτε μή**, "all proving that women who have attained maturity are mistresses of their persons, and can remain with their husbands or not as they choose" (Edd.), (*b*) of *animals*—BGU IV. 1067[12] (A.D. 101–102) **ἀλεκτόρων τελείων τεσσάρων**, "four full-grown cocks," P Grenf II. 46[13] (A.D. 137) **πεπρακέναι αὐτῷ ὄνο[ν] θή-λ(ειαν) τελείαν**, and P Iand 35[6] (ii/iii A.D.) **βοῦν μελ[ά]νην τελίαν** (see note). (2) "in good working order or condition"—P Oxy II. 278[1] (A.D. 17) **μύλο]ν ἔν[α] τ[έ]λειο.]ν Θηβαεικόν**, "one perfect Theban mill" (Edd.), *ib.* IX. 1257[9] (A.D. 175–6?) **ἀλεκτρυόνων τελείων τεσσάρων, ὀρνείθων τελείων τοκάδων ὀκτώ**, "4 cocks in perfect condition, 8 laying hens in perfect condition" (Ed.), *ib.* VI. 999[18] (A.D. 225) **ἀκάνθας ἀριθμῷ τελείας δεκατέσσαρας**, "fourteen acacia-trees in good condition" (Edd.), P Tebt II. 406[12] (*c.* A.D. 266) **λυχνεία τελεία**, "a complete lamp-stand," and P Giss I. 122[1] (vi/A.D.) a receipt for the sale of certain arourae **τῆς πρὸς ἀλλήλους συμπεφωνημένης τελ[ε]ίας καὶ ἀξίας τιμῆς**. (3) "complete," "final"—P Tebt II. 361[6] (A.D. 132) **ἀριθμ(ητικοῦ) τελείο[υ] τ[ο]ῦ τ̅ς̅ (ἔτους)**, "for the full **ἀριθμητικόν** of the 16th year" (Edd.), *ib.* 335[8] (mid. iii A.D.) **τελείαν ἀπόφασιν**, "final verdict," P Oxy VI. 902[11] (*c.* A.D. 465) **εἰς τελείαν γὰρ ἀνατροπὴν καὶ εἰς αἰχάτην πεῖνον** (*l.* ἐσχάτην πεῖναν) **περιέστην**, "and I have been reduced to complete ruin and the extremity of hunger" (Edd.).

For the form **τέλεος**, see the interesting petition of a physician to the Praefect asking to be relieved from certain public duties on the ground of his profession, P Fay 106[21] (*c.* A.D. 140) **ὅπως] τέλεου ἀπολύονται τῶν [λειτουρ]γιῶν οἱ τὴν ἰατρικὴν ἐπιστή[μην] μεταχειριζόμενοι**, "that complete exemption from compulsory services be granted to persons practising the profession of physician" (Edd.). Reference may also be made to Knox's note in Herodas (ed. Headlam), p. 333 f.

For the relation of the epithet **τέλειος** in Paul to the language of the ancient mysteries, see Lightfoot *ad* Col 1[28], also the careful study of the word in Kennedy *St. Paul and the Mystery Religions*, p. 130 ff.

τελειότης,

"perfection," "completeness" (Col 3[14], Heb 6[1]): cf. the magic P Lond 121[770] (iii/A.D.) (= I. p. 109) **τελειότητος ἀναγκαστικὴ ἀπόρροια**.

τελειόω

is common in legal papyri = "execute": see e.g. P Oxy III. 485[20] (A.D. 108) **τελειῶσαι τὸν χρημα[τισμὸν] ὡς καθήκει**, "to execute the deed in the proper way" (Edd.), and P Giss I. 34[16] (A.D. 265–6) **ἐτελεί[ωσε]ν τὰ νόμιμα**. In P Oxy II. 238[9] (A.D. 72) it seems rather to have the meaning "complete" by the insertion of date and signatures—**προσέρχεσθαι τοῖς ἀγορανόμοις καὶ τε]λειοῦν] ταύτας [.. οἰκονομίας] ἐντὸς [. . . .**: see the editors' note.

On the use of the verb in connexion with martyrdom, as in 4 Macc 7[15] **ὃν πιστὴ θανάτου σφραγὶς ἐτελείωσεν**, see Moffatt *Heb.* p. 32, and cf. the Christian gravestone *Preisigke* 1600[3] **ἔνθα κατά[κει]ται ἡ μα. κα. ρία Π.[.]θία, ἐτελεώθη μη(νὶ) Θὼθ κα̅**. MGr **τελειώνω**, "finish."

τελείως

is found in the NT only in 1 Pet 1[13] **νήφοντες τελείως**, where Hort *Comm. ad l.* understands the phrase to mean "being sober with a perfect sobriety," a sobriety "entering into all their thoughts and ways," "the opposite of heedless drifting as in a mist." Cf. the fragmentary P Petr III. 42 H(8 c)[3] (iii/B.C.) **τελείως ποιήσεις**, P Flor I. 93[27] (deed of divorce—A.D. 509) **ἐξηλλάχθαι πρὸς ἀλλήλους καὶ διαλελύσθαι ἐντόνως καὶ τελείως**, and the Christian amulet BGU III. 954[30] (. vi A.D.) (= *Selections*, p. 134) ending **Ἅγιε Σέρηνε, πρόσπεσε ὑπὲρ ἐμοῦ, ἵνα τελείως ὑγιανῶ**, "O holy Serenus, supplicate on my behalf, that I may be in perfect health." In MGr the adv. has the form **τέλεια**.

τελείωσις,

"fulfilment," "completion" (Lk 1[45], Heb 7[11]): P Oxy II. 286[26] (A.D. 82) **πρὸς δὲ τὴν τοῦ χρηματισμοῦ τελείωσιν διαπέσταλμαι Ἡρακλείδην Ἡρακλείδου**, "I have dispatched as my agent Heraclides, son of Heraclides, to conclude the transaction" (Edd.), P Ryl II. 115[3] (A.D. 156) **εἰς τὸ τὰ τῆς [ἐνεχυρ]ασίας ἐπιτελεσθῆ[ν]αι πρὸς τελε[ίωσιν τῶν [νομί]μων**. Cf. further BGU IV. 1168[3] (B.C. 10) **πρὸς [τε]λείωσι(ν) τῆσδε τῆς] συγχωρήσεως**, P Flor I. 50[7] (A.D. 234) **πρὸς τ[ὴ]ν τοῦ χρηματ[ισμοῦ] τελείωσι(ν**, and *Test. xii. patr.* Reub. vi. 8 **μέχρι τελειώσεως χρόνων**, "until the consummation of the time." Also Epicurus II. 80 **ἕως τελειώσεως καὶ διαμονῆς**, "until the period of completion and stability" (Bailey).

τελεσφορέω,

"bring to maturity," only at Lk 8[14] in NT (cf. Hobart, p. 65). For the corresponding comp[d] **τελεσιουργέω**, see Epicurus I. 36 **τοῦ τετελεσιουργημένου**, "in the case of one fully initiated" (Bailey).

The adj. **τελεσιφόρος**, in the sense of "harlot," as in Deut 23[17], occurs in P Grenf II. 41[9] (A.D. 46), where we have reference to a tax on **ἑταῖραι**, cf. l.[28] **οἱ ἑτα(ιρισμάτων μισθ.ούμενοι**): see Wilcken *Ostr.* i. p. 219.

τελευτάω

is trans. = "bring to an end" in BGU I. 361[ii.35] (A.D. 184) **τελευτᾶν τ[ὸν] βίον**. For the general intrans. meaning "die," which the verb shows from v.B.C. onwards, it is enough to cite from the papyri such passages as P Magd 2[6]

(B.C. 222) ὁ ἀνήρ μου τετελεύτηκεν, P Fay 29⁹ (notice of
death—A.D. 37) ὁ ἀδ[ε]λφὸς Πενεοῦρις . . . τετελεύτηκεν
ἐν τῷ Μεσ[ο]ρὴ μην[ὶ] τοῦ πρώτο[υ] (ἔτους) Γαίου Καίσαρος
Σεβαστοῦ Γερμανικοῦ, "my brother Peneouris has died in
the month Mesore of the first year of Gaius Caesar Augustus
Germanicus," cf.¹⁶ ὅπως ταγῆι τοῦ[του] ὄν[ο]μα ἐν τῆι τῶν
[τετ]ελευτηκότων τάξ[ει κατὰ] τὸ ἔ[θ]ος, "in order that his
name may according to custom be placed in the list of
deceased persons," P Oxy III. 475²⁵ (A.D. 182) ἔπεσεν καὶ
ἐτελε[ύ]τησεν, ib. VI. 928³ (ii/iii A.D.) Ζωπύρου τελευτήσαντος, "now that Zopyrus is dead," P Strass I. 73¹³
(iii/A.D.) ὁ μικρὸς Μῖμος ἐτελεύτησεν, and from the inscrr.
Syll 895¹ ἐτελεύτησα ἐμβὰς (ε)ἰς ἔτη πέντε, and ib. 908
(= ³ 505,¹ (c. B.C. 227) τῶν κατὰ τὸν σεισμὸν τελευτασάντων.
The mummy-ticket Preisigke 3931³ (A.D. 123) shows the
impf. ἐτελεύτα.

In the florilegium PSI II. 120³¹ (iv/A.D. ?) it is suggested
that there is no cause to grieve over those who die (τοῖς
ἀποθνησκ[ο]υσιν), unless it be over those who end their
lives in a disgraceful manner (ἐπὶ τοῖς αἰσχρῶς τελευτῶσι).

τελευτή,

"death": cf. P Oxy II. 265²² (A.D. 81–95) πρὸς τὸ μετὰ
τὴν ἑαυτῆς τελευτὴν βεβαιῶσθαι, ib. I. 76²³ (A.D. 179) πρὸς
τὸ μετὰ τελευτὴν αὐτοῦ ἀνεύθυνόν με εἶναι, "to free me from
responsibility after his death," and P Cairo Preis 42⁹
(iii/iv A.D.), where a testator makes certain dispositions—
μετ' ἐμὴν τελευτήν. In P Ryl II. 106¹⁸ (A.D. 158) and
P Fay 30¹⁷ (A.D. 173) it is certified that notice has been
made to the scribes of the metropolis περὶ τελ[ευτῆς "concerning the death" of Harpocras and Aphrodisius respectively.

For the adj. τελευταῖος, "last," see P Lond 1912²⁵
(A.D. 41) εἴνα τὸ τελευταῖον εἴπω, and P Oxy VI. 940²
(v/A.D.) ἄχρι τῆς τελευταίας μερίδος, "until the last
holding."

τελέω,

(1) "complete," "accomplish," "fulfil": P Oxy VII.
1061¹² (B.C. 22) ἕως μοι τοῦτο τελέσητε, "until you accomplish this for me," ib.¹⁷ ἕως ὅτου τελεσθῇ[ι, "until it is
accomplished," P Giss I. 99¹¹ (ii/iii A.D.) θυσίαι τε λοῦνται.
The verb = "produce" in Chrest. I. 236⁶ (iii/A.D.) τελοῦσαι
ἀν[ὰ πυροῦ ἀ]ρτ[άβην] μί[αν.

(2) "pay": P Petr III. 59(b)³ (census paper—iii/B.C.)
ἀφ' ὧν ἐστὶν τῶν μὴ τελούντων ἱερὰ ἔθνη, "from this are to be
subtracted those priestly corporations which are exempt from
the tax" (Mahaffy), P Oxy IX. 1210² (i/B.C.–i/A.D.)
τελοῦντες λαογραφίαν Ὀξυρύγχίτου ἄνδ ρες), "men paying
poll-tax in the Oxyrhynchite nome," P Fay 36¹¹ (A.D. 111–2)
ὑφίσταμαι τελέσειν φόρου ἀργυρίου δραχμὰς ὀγδοήκοντα,
"I undertake to pay as rent eighty drachmae of silver"
(Edd.), P Oxy VII. 1037¹³ (A.D. 444) τελέσ[ω] σοι ὑπὲρ
ἐνοικίου, "I will pay you for rent," ib. VIII. 1130²² (A.D. 484)
ταῦτα τελέσω σοι, "I will pay you this sum." Receipts
are often introduced by the phrase τετέλεσται, usually written
in an abbreviated manner, e.g. P Grenf II. 50(a)(b)(c) al.
mostly belonging to ii/A.D. In BGU VI. 1211² (iii/B.C.)
the phrase τοὺς κατὰ τὴν χώραν τελοῦντα[ς] τῶι Διονύσωι,
referring to adherents of the Mysteries, has caused difficulty,
but, on the whole, Mayser (Gr. ii. p. 82) prefers to take the

verb in the sense of "paying." See also the very early
Christian letter P Amh I. 3(a)ⁱⁱ·¹² (between A.D. 264 and
282) (= Deissmann LAE², p. 207) ἰς τὸ καλῶς ἔχειν τ[ελ]εῖν
εὖ ἀνέχομαι, "for the sake of [my own] good feelings I will
gladly endure to pay" (Deissmann).

τέλος

(1) "end": P Eleph 1¹² (B.C. 311–0) (= Selections, p. 3)
ἐγ δίκης κατὰ νόμον τέλος ἐχούσης, "as if a formal decree
of the court had been obtained," P Petr II. 40(a)²³ (iii/B.C.)
(= Witkowski², p. 41) ἡ ἐλεφαντηγὸ[ς] ("the elephant-transport") ἡ ἐν Βερενίκηι τέλος ἔχει (= τετέλεσται), P Leid
Uⁱⁱⁱ·²⁰ (1st half ii/B.C.) (= I. p. 124) τέλος ἔχει πάντα, παρὲξ
τῆς ἐπιγραφῆς (cf. Lk 22³⁷, Field Notes, p. 76).

The various prepositional phrases formed with τέλος may
be illustrated by P Petr II. 13(19)⁸ (mid. iii/B.C.) (= Witkowski², p. 19) τὴν πᾶσαν σπουδὴν πόησαι [το]ῦ ἀφεθῆναί σε
διὰ τέλος, P Tebt I. 38¹¹ (B.C. 113) (= Chrest. I. p. 565) τῆς
ἐγλήμψεως εἰς τέλος καταλελ[ειμμέν]ης, "my enterprise has
been made a complete failure" (Edd.) (cf. 1 Thess 2¹⁶ with
Milligan's note, and Jn 13¹ with the discussion in Abbott JG,
p. 247 ff.), OGIS 90¹² (Rosetta-stone—B.C. 196) τινὰς μὲν
εἰς τέλος ἀφῆκεν, ἄλλας δὲ κεκούφικεν, P Tebt I. 14⁸
(B.C. 114) μέχρι δὲ τοῦ τὸ προκείμενον ἐπὶ τέλος ἀχθῆναι,
"until the matter was concluded" (Edd.), P Oxy IV. 724⁹
(A.D. 155) ἐπὶ τέλει τοῦ χρόνου, ib. VIII. 1128²⁰ (A.D. 173)
ἐπὶ τέλει ἑκάστου ἐνιαυτοῦ, "at the end of each year," ib.
XIV. 1694²³ (a lease—A.D. 280) ἐπὶ τέλει τοῦ χρόνου παραδότω τὴν οἰκίαν καθαρὰν ἀπὸ κοπρίων(—ιω), P Tebt II.
379¹⁷ (sale of a crop—A.D. 128) πρὸς ἡμᾶς ὄντων τῶν μέχρι
τέλους μερισμῶν, "being ourselves responsible throughout
for rates upon it" (Edd.), and ib. 420¹⁸ (iii/A.D.) ἀπὸ ἀρχῆς
μέχρι τέλους (cf. Heb 3⁶ אAC).

For τέλος, as in 1 Tim 1⁵, cf. Epict. Gnomol. 16 (ed.
Schenkl, p. 466) τέλος δὲ τοῦ μὲν (sc. καλῶς ζῆν) ἔπαινος
ἀληθής, τοῦ δὲ (sc. πολυτελῶς ζῆν) ψόγος, and for τὸ τέλος
κυρίον, as in Jas 5¹¹, cf. Bischoff in ZNTW vii. (1906),
p. 274 ff. See also PSI I 17 verso II. (iii/A.D. ?)—

> οὐ γάρ πω τοιοῦτος ἀνήλυθεν εἰς Ἀχέροντα·
> τῶν ὁσίων ἀνδρῶν Ἠλύσιον τὸ τέλος,
> ἔνθα διατρίβειν ἔλαχεν πάλαι ἔκ τινος ἐσθλῆς
> μοίρης· οὐδὲ θανεῖν τοὺς ἀγαθοὺς λέγεται.

(2) "tax," "toll": (a) sing., as in Rom 13⁷, in UPZ i. 115³
(ii/i(?)B.C.) τέλος οἰκίας καὶ αὐλῆς, "tax for house and court,"
Meyer Ostr 31³ (A.D. 32) (= Deissmann LAE², p. 111) ἀπέχων
(l. ἀπέχω) παρὰ σοῦ τόλες (l. τέλος) ἐπιξένου Θῶνθ καὶ
Φαῶφι (δραχμὰς) β, "I have received from you alien tax
(for the months) Thoyth and Phaophi 2 drachmae," P Lond
297b⁵ (A.D. 119) (= II. p. 111) τέλος ἐγκυκλίου(= —ον),
"general tax," ib. 468¹ (ii/A.D.) (= II. p. 81) τέλος
καμήλ(ων), P Oxy IX. 1200⁴⁵ (A.D. 266) τὸ τοῦ τειμήματος
τέλος, "the ad valorem tax" (Ed.): (b) plur., as in Mt 17²⁵,
in P Cairo Zen II. 59240⁷ (B.C. 253) ἵνα μή τι κατὰ τὰ τέλη
ἐνοχληθῶσιν, with reference to certain mules which were
not required to pay toll, and PSI III. 222¹⁰ (iii/A.D.)
στ]ιχεῖν τὰ τεταγμένα τέλη.

For subst. τέλεσμα cf. P Oxy VIII. 1123¹⁵ (A.D. 158–9)
περὶ τῶν τῆς αὐτῆς δημοσίας γῆς τελεσμάτ[ων] πάντων, "in
regard to all dues upon the said public land," and P Ryl II.
96⁷ (A.D. 117–8) s.v. τοσοῦτος.

Boisacq (p. 953) supports the theory that **τέλος**, "tax," is derived from **πλῆναι**, from Indo-Europ. *tel(ā)—, "bear," "endure": cf. the use of **φόρος**, "tribute." On the other hand, **τέλος**, "end," is cognate with **πέλω**, **πέλομαι**, from Indo-Europ. *quel—"turn," while a third **τέλος**, "company," comes from Indo-Europ. *queles—"herd," "family." In MGr **τέλος**, "end," survives: cf. the expression **τέλος πάντων**, "finally," "lastly."

τελώνης,

"tax-gatherer." P Par 61 (B.C. 156) throws a vivid light on the practices of tax-gatherers, as after special mention of **τῶν πρὸς ταῖς τελωνίαις ἐντυγχανόντων**, instructions are given that no one should be wronged (**ἀδικῆται**) by **τῶν συκοφαντεῖν** (cf. Lk 10[8]) **ἐπιχειρούντων [τελωνῶν** : see Wilcken *Ostr* i. p. 508, where reference is made to Herodas VI. 64 **τοὺς γὰρ τελώνας πᾶσα νῦν θύρη φρίσσει**. Cf. also P Petr III. 32(*f*)[17] (iii/B.C.) **ἐπισε< · ·>ν μοι Αἴθωνα τὸν τελώνην**, "to threaten me with Aithona the tax-gatherer," P Grenf II. 34[1] (B.C. 99) a docket to a contract showing that a tax of 10% had been paid **δι' Ἀπολλω(νίου) τελών(ου) καὶ τῶν μετό(χων)** on the price of a priest's lodging (**παστοφό-ριον**). P Oxy IV. 732[2] (A.D. 150) **τελῶναι ὠνῆς προθμίδων** (*l.* πορθμίδων) **πόλεως**, "farmers of the contract for the tax on ferry-boats at the city" (Edd.), and from the ostraca *Ostr* 1031 (A.D. 31) **τελώνης ὑικῆς** and 1040 (A.D. 58) **τελ(ῶ)ναι γερδ(ιακοῦ)**.

For the verb **τελωνέω**, cf. P Tebt I. 5[26] (B.C. 118) **τι τῶν μὴ τετελωνημέν[ων**, "something on which duty has not been paid" (Edd.), and *OGIS* 55[17] (B.C. 240): for the subst. **τελωνία**, cf. P Par 61[9] (B.C. 156) *ut supra*: and for the adj. **τελωνικός**, cf. P Rev L[AM 12] (B.C. 258) **ὅσα δ' ἐγκλήματα γίνεται ἐκ τ[ῶν νόμων] τῶν τελωνικῶν ἔστω καλεῖσθαι . . .**, "when disputes arise out of the laws concerning tax-farming, the Crown officials may bring an action . . ." (Ed.).

τελώνιον,

"revenue office," "custom-house" (Mt 9[9] *al.*): cf. P Par 62[viii. 3] (*c.* B.C. 170) (as revised P Rev L p. 181) **τὰς ἐκθέσε[ις ἐν τοῖς] τελωνίοις**, and *OGIS* 496[9] (A.D. 138–161) **τοῖς ἐπὶ τὸ τελώνιον τῆς ἰχθυϊκῆς πραγματευομένοις**. In P Petr II. 11(2 [3] (mid. iii B.C.) (= Witkowski[2], p. 6) **ἀπογέγραμμαι δὲ ἐπὶ τελώνιον τὸ οἰκόπεδον**, ἐπὶ τελώνιον does not refer to a place, but = "for the purpose of taxation." MGr **τελωνεῖον**.

τέρας,

For **τέρας** in its NT sense of "wonder," "portent," we may cite Vett. Val. p. 341[14] **ἐὰν δέ πως τὸ δωδεκατημόριον εἰς θηριῶδες ἐκπέσῃ ἢ τὸ τούτῳ διάμετρον ἢ οἱ τούτων κύριοι, τέρας ἢ ἄλογον ζῷον ἀποφαίνεσθαι**. For MGr **τέρατο**, "miracle," see Thumb *Handb.* § 105, n[1].

Τέρτιος,

"Tertius." The name of Paul's Roman (?) amanuensis, Rom 16[22], occurs in an inscr. in the i/A.D. Cemetery of Priscilla, *Dessau* 8002—

> ΤΕΡΤΙΑΔΕΛΦΕ
> ΕΥΨΥΧΙΟΥΔΙΣ
> ΑΘΑΝΑΤΟΣ

(cited by Edmundson *Church in Rome*, p. 22, n.[1]).

Τέρτυλλος,

dim. of **Τέρτιος**. The name occurs in ii/A.D. as the *agnomen* of Pliny's colleague Cornutus : see further Hastings' *DB* iv. p. 719 f. For the fem. "Tertulla," see *Dessau* 7998.

τέσσαρες,

"four." On the forms **τέσσαρες** and **τέσσερες** see WH *Notes*[2], p. 157. Moulton (*Proleg.* p. 36) notes that the characteristic Achaian acc. in -**ες** is well established in the vernacular, and that "in the NT **τέσσαρας** never occurs without some excellent authority for **τέσσαρες**." He adds to the discussion of **τέσσαρες** as accusative the reminder that the word "is isolated, as the only early cardinal which ever had a separate acc. form," and cites statistics from the ostraca to show how this indeclinable form predominated in business language before A.D. 200 (*ib.* p. 243 f.). The dat. pl. **τέτρασι** in Ac 11[5] D is interesting.

τεσσεράκοντα.

The spelling **τεσσεράκοντα** for **τεσσαράκοντα** is adopted in all the NT occurrences of the word, but is by no means common in the papyri during i–iii/A.D.: see however P Flor I. 61[62] (A.D. 85) (= *Chrest.* II. p. 89) **διὰ τεσ[σ]εράκοντα ἐτῶν**, *ib.* 86[9] (i/A.D.), P Gen I. 24[11] (A.D. 96), P Tebt II. 388[?.10] (A.D. 98), P Oxy XIV. 1685[15] (A.D. 158), and BGU III. 916[4] (Vespasian) **ὡς ἐτῶν τεσσεράκοντ[α**.

For the spelling **τεσσαράκοντα**, which is universal in Ptolemaic times and predominant till the Byzantine age, it is sufficient to note P Lond 262[5] (A.D. 11) (= II. p. 177) **ἐτῶν τεσσαράκοντα τριῶν** (but **τεσσερακόστου** in *l.* [?]), and P Fay 122[16] (*c.* A.D. 100) **ὑποδείγματα μεγάλων τεσσαρά-κοντα**, "forty specimens of the large sort."

The two forms **τεσσ]αράκοντα** and **τεσσεράκοντα** are found in the same document P Meyer 6[17. 18] (A.D. 125), evidence, as Deissmann has pointed out (*ut l.* p. 43 f.), that in non-literary texts (including the NT) a fixed form of spelling is not always to be looked for. See further Moulton *Gr.* ii. p. 66, and Thackeray *Gr.* i. pp. 62 f., 73 f.

τεσσαρεσκαιδέκατος,

"fourteenth" (Ac 27[27. 33]), is from iii/B.C. onwards the general form, cf. P Eleph 1[1] (B.C. 311) **ἔτει τεσσαρεσκαι-δεκάτωι**, P Tebt I. 106[1] (B.C. 101), and see *Proleg.* p. 96. The form **τεσσαρακαιδέκατος** is found only in Roman times : see Crönert *Mem. Herc.* p. 200. For **τεσσαρεσκαιδεκαέτης** see P Oxy IX. 1202[19] (A.D. 217).

τεταρταῖος,

"of the fourth day" (Jn 11[39]): cf. P Tebt II. 275[21] (a charm—iii/A.D.) **ἀπὸ παντὸς ῥίγους . . . τριταίου ἢ τεταρταίου**, "from every fever whether it be tertian or quartan" (Edd.), P Oxy VIII. 1151[37] (a charm—v/A.D. ?) **ἀποδίωξον καὶ φυγάδευσον ἀπ' αὐτῆς πάντα πυρετὸν κ(αὶ) παντοῖον ῥῆγος** (*l.* ῥῖγος) **ἀφημερινὸν τριτεον τεταρτεον** (*l.* τριταῖον τεταρταῖον) **καὶ πᾶν κακόν**, "chase from her and put to flight all fevers and every kind of chill, quotidian, tertian, and quartan, and every evil" (Ed.), and *Syll* 890(= [3] 1239)[20] (*c.* A.D. 100) **πυρετῷ καὶ τετα[ρ]ταίῳ καὶ ἐλέφα[ν]τ[ι**. See also Field *Notes*, p. 66.

τέταρτος,

"fourth" (Mt 14²⁵, al.): cf. P Cairo Zen II. 59258⁴ (B.C. 252) τοῦ τετάρ[του καὶ] τριακοστοῦ ἔτους, P Par 49²¹ (before B.C. 161) (= UPZ i. p. 309) σησάμου τέταρτον, P Oxy XIV. 1672¹⁴ (A.D. 37–41) τὰ (sc. οἰνάρια) τῆς [τ]ετάρτης ληνοῦ μόνης, "the wine of the fourth press only" (Edd.), ib. X. 1203²⁵ (A.D. 117–38) ὑστερῶ τέταρτα δ[ύ]ο, "I want two quarters (?)" (Edd.), ib. VIII. 1102⁹ (c. A.D. 146) τὸ τέταρτον τῆς οὐσίας, and PSI V. 450⁷⁹ (ii/iii A.D.) τέταρτον μέρ[ος] τῆς αὐτῆς [οἰ]κίας.

The classical τέτρας to denote the 4th day of the month is seen in such passages as P Ryl II. 197⁷ (late ii/A.D.) 'Αθὺρ . . . τετράδι. It is retained in the LXX proper, and is found in the title of the Ps 93 with reference to the fourth day of the week, as in MGr: see Thackeray Gr. i. p. 189.

τετραάρχης,

so read in the critical texts (see WH Notes², p. 152, where the form is put down as possibly "Alexandrian"), "a tetrarch" or governor of the fourth part of a district. The title is applied in the NT to Herod Antipas (Mt 14¹, al.). For the ordinary spelling see the 2ⁿᵈ declension form τέτραρχος Θεσσαλῶν in Syll³ 274 II. (B.C. 337), and Φιλίππου τετραρχίας ἔργον in ib. 220 (B.C. 346?) (with the editor's note): also CIG III. 4033 Τι. Σεουῆρον βασιλέων καὶ τετραρχῶν ἀπόγονον.

τετράγωνος,

"with four corners," "square" (Hesych. τετραντίας· τετράγωνος καὶ ἰσχυρός) occurs in Rev 21¹⁶: cf. PSI VI. 677¹¹ (iii/B.C.) στρω[?]μάτιον τετρά[γ]ωνον ᾱ, BGU IV. 1107³² (B.C. 12) ἐν τῇ τετραγώ(νῳ) στοᾷ, ib. I. 162¹² (temple-inventory—ii/iii A.D.) βωμίσκιον ἀργυροῦν μεικρὸ[ν τε]τράγωνον, P Lond 46⁴⁰¹ (hymn to Hermes—iv/A.D.) (= I. p. 78) στρογγύλε καὶ τετράγωνε λόγων ἀρχήγετα γλώσσης, and from the inscrr. OGIS 90¹⁵ (Rosetta stone—B.C. 196) ἐπὶ τοῦ περὶ τὰς βασιλείας τετραγώνου. MGr τετράγωνο, "square."

For τετραγωνίας in a personal description = "square-built," "robust," see P Petr III. 12²¹ (a Will—B.C. 234) λευκόχρως τετρα[γω]νίας τ[ετανός, and for τετραγωνισμός, "a squaring," see P Magd 29⁶ (B.C. 218) αὐτὸς δ[ὲ] ἐν τετραγωνισμῶι τὰ αὑτοῦ ἔχει, with reference to a partition of property.

τετράδιον,

"a group of four," applied to soldiers in Ac 12⁴, has reference to days in the heathen amulet BGU III. 956 (c. iii/A.D.) ἐξορκίζω ὑμᾶς . . ἀπὸ πα[ν]τὸς . . πυρετοῦ . . ἡμερι<νοῦ> ἢ τετρα[α δ<ί>ο<υ>, and to sheets of parchment in P Oxy XVII. 2156¹⁹ (iv/v A.D.) τὴν διφθέραν [τ]ῶν μεμβρανῶν ἐν τετραδίοις εἴκ[οσι]πέντε, "the skin of parchments in twenty-five quaternions" (Ed.).

τετρακισχίλιοι,

"four thousand" (Mt 15³⁸ al.): PSI V. 480⁷ (v/vi A.D.) εἰς πλή[ρ]ωσιν τ]ῶν τετ]ρακισχειλίων ἀρταβῶν τῶν πραθέντων αὐτῷ.

τετρακόσιοι,

"four hundred" (Ac 5³⁶ al.): PSI V. 462⁹ (A.D. 314) ἀργυρίου δραχμὰς δισχιλίας τετρακοσίας.

τετράμηνος,

"of four months" with χρόνος understood, and hence = "four months." Exx. are PSI IV. 408¹⁰ (iii/B.C.) ὀφείληται γάρ μοι τετράμηνον καὶ τοῦ ὀψωνίου μέρος (l. μέρος) τι, P Cairo Zen II. 59291² (B.C. 251–0) τοῖς ἔργοις προσέχειν τετράμηνον, P Grenf II. 41¹⁶ (A.D. 46) διὰ τετράμηνα, "every four months," P Oxy XII. 1482¹⁵ (ii/A.D.) μετὰ τετράμηνον, "after four months," and from the inscr. Syll 210(= ³410)⁴ (c. B.C. 274) τὴν πρώτην τετράμηνον.

For adj. τετραμήνιος (not in LS⁸) see P Oxy XII. 1418¹⁸ (A.D. 247) ἀν'αδέξομαι τῷ παιδὶ τετραμήνιον γυμνασιαρχίαν, "I shall undertake for my son the office of gymnasiarch for four months."

τετραπλόος,

"four-fold" (Lk 19⁸): cf. the form τετραπλάσιος in OGIS 665³⁰ (i/A.D.) τὸ τετραπλάσιον μέρος, and Syll 932(= ³880)⁸⁰ (A.D. 202) πρὸς δὲ δ[ιαλύ σωσ[ι] αὐτὰ τὰ ἐνπόρια εἰς τὸ [τε]τραπλάσιον τοῦ ἐνδεήσοντος.

τετράπους,

"four-footed" (for form see Thackeray Gr. i. p. 88, Moulton Gr. ii. § 107). For the neut. plur., as in Ac 10¹², 11⁶, Rom 1²³, cf. P Hib I. 95⁸ (B.C. 256) τετραπόδων 'Οξυρύγχων πόλεως, "four-footed animals at the city of Oxyrhynchus," P Strass I. 5¹⁵ (A.D. 262) τὰ θρέμματα καὶ τὰ τετράποδα τὰ ἡμέτερα ἀφήρπασ[α]ν, and P Thead 6¹⁰ (A.D. 322) βοϊκὰ καὶ πάντα τετράποδα. See also from nom. τετράποδος P Oxy III. 646 (A.D. 117–138) δίφρου [τετρ]απόδου, and ib. XIV. 1638⁵ (division of an inheritance—A.D. 282) τετραπόδοις καὶ δουλικοῖς σώμασι τέσσαρσι.

τεφρόω.

This rare word = "cover with ashes" or "reduce to ashes" is found in the NT only in 2 Pet 2⁶. Commentators cite Dio Cass. lxvi. p. 1094 τῶν ἐν μέσῳ κραυρουμένων ("being parched") καὶ τεφρουμένων ("being overwhelmed with ashes")—a description of an eruption of Vesuvius, and Lycophron Cass. 227 τεφρώσας γυῖα Λημναίῳ πυρί.

The adj. τεφρός, "ash-coloured," is used of a bird in PSI VI. 509⁶ (B.C. 253–2) ἄλλος (sc. ὄρνις) ἄρσην τεφρὸς ὀξυ[ωπής, cited by Preisigke Wörterb. s.v.

τέχνη.

For the meaning "trade," "profession," as in Ac 18³, cf. PSI VII. 854¹² (B.C. 258–7) διδάξαι τὴν τέχνην, P Tebt II. 316²⁰ (A.D. 99) τ<έ>χνη (l. τέχνη) ἁλιεὺς ποτάμι<ο>ς, "a river fisherman by trade," P Oxy X. 1263¹⁸ (A.D. 128–9) χρήσασθαι τῇ τῶν ἐργ[ατῶν] ποταμοῦ τέχ νη, "to practise the trade of a river worker" (Edd.), ib. XIV. 1647¹² (contract of apprenticeship—late ii/A.D.) πρ[ὸ]ς μάθησιν τῆς γερδι[α]κῆς τέχνης, "to learn the trade of weaving," ib. I. 40⁵ (ii/iii A.D.) ἰατρὸς ὑπάρχων τὴ[ν τέ]χνην, "being a doctor by profession," and ib. 83⁴ (A.D. 327) ὠοπώλου τὴν τέχνην, "an egg-seller by trade."

In *ib.* VII. 1029²⁶ (A.D. 107) certain hieroglyphic inscribers make a declaration μηδὲ ἔχει[ν] μαθητὰς ἢ ἐπιξένους χρω[ω]μένους τῇ τέχνῃ εἰς τὴν ἐνεστῶσαν ἡμέραν, "that we have no apprentices or strangers carrying on the art down to the present day" (Edd.) : cf. Ac 17²⁹.

For the sense of "artifice" cf. P Oxy XII. 1468³ (c. A.D. 258) τοῖς κακουργεῖν προχείρως ἔχουσιν τέχνῃ. "to those who are ready to commit crimes by artifice" : cf. *Kaibel* 38² (iv/A.D.) τέχνηι, οὐχὶ φύσει.

τεχνίτης,

"craftsman," "designer" (Ac 19²⁴, *al.*), is applied to God first in Alexandrian Judaism (Sap 13¹), and once in the NT Heb 11¹⁰ (see Moffatt *ICC ad l.*). From the papyri we may cite PSI VII. 854¹ (B.C. 258–7) ἃ δὲ οὐκ ἔφασαν δύνασθα[ι] τεχνίταις, *ib.* II. 152⁵ (ii/A.D.) οἱ τεχνεῖται πολλὰ ψευδογραφοῦνται, P Oxy VIII. 1117¹² (c. A.D. 178) τεχνειτῶν χρυσοχόων, *ib.* XII. 1413²⁷ (A.D. 270–5) ἄλλα δώδεκα τάλαντα δοθήτω τοῖς τεχνεῖτα[ι]ς, P Gen I. 62³ (iv/A.D.) τεχνίτας πρὸς τὴν ἐκκοπὴν τῶν ξύλων, and from the inscrr. *Syll* 540 (= ³072¹¹ (B.C. 175–172) ἐνεργῶν τεχνίταις ἱκανοῖς κατὰ τὴν τέχνην.

The very rare τεχνίτευμα "work of art," "art," is found in *OGIS* 51¹² (iii/B.C.) ἐκτενῶς ἑαυτὸν συνεπιδιδοὺς εἰς τὸ συναύξεσθαι τὸ τεχνίτευμα, cf. Aristeas 78 συνεχῶς ἐφ' ἕκαστον ἐπιβαλλούσης τῆς διανοίας τεχνίτευμα, "as the mind took in one by one each detail of the execution" (Thackeray), with reference to the completion of gold and silver bowls.

τήκω,

"melt," pass. "melt away," as in 2 Pet 3¹² where, according to Hort (*Notes²*, p. 105) τήκεται ℵABKL) may be a corruption for the rare τήξεται : cf. Hippocrates vi. p. 110, ed. Littré. In *C. and B.* i. p. 150 No. 45 ἐτήκω κολαθεῖσα ἐπὸ τοῦ θεοῦ, Ramsay notes that "ἐτήκω is probably for τήκομαι . . . 'waste away from fever or other formless disease.'" The comp¹· συντηκέτωσαν occurs in P Rev L¹· ¹⁷ (B.C. 258) of melting down lard.

τηλαυγῶς,

a NT ἅπ. εἰρ. (Mk 8²⁵ ℵᶜ ABDW : δηλαυγῶς ℵ*C), "clearly though at a distance," "clearly from afar." The force of the word is well brought out in a magical formula, P Oxy VI. 886 (iii/A.D.), which, after various directions for obtaining an omen, ends ²¹ χρηματισθήσῃ (*l.* χρηματισθήσῃ) τηλαυγῶς. "you will obtain an illuminating answer" (Edd.). See also *s.v.* δηλαυγῶς. For adj. τηλαυγής cf. Bacchyl. XVI. 5, also Vett. Val. p. 54³ τοῦτον τὸν τόπον οἱ παλαιοὶ μυστικῶς καὶ σκοτεινῶς διέγραψαν, ἡμεῖς δὲ τηλαυγέστερον. According to Moulton *Gr.* ii. p. 283 the meaning is "far-shining" or "far-discerned." "according as αὐγή or αὐγάζω is to guide our interpretation of the second part."

τηλικοῦτος,

"so large," "so great," is used of a person in the alphabetical nursery rhyme P Tebt II. 278³⁹ (early i/A.D.), where the writer complains that a stranger had stolen his garment—οὐθὲν τηλικούτωι, "it was nothing to one like him" (Edd.).

For the word, as in 2 Cor 1¹⁰ *al.*, cf. P Par 63³⁵ (B.C. 164) (= P Petr III. p. 20) τοσούτω[ν κ]αὶ τηλικούτων διαστολῶν, "so many and so extensive explanations" (Mahaffy), *ib.* ¹²⁶ ἐκ τηλικαύτης καταφθ[ο]ρᾶς, "from so great a distress," P Ryl II. 77²⁰ (A.D. 192 ἀ[δ]ικούμεν εἰς τηλικαύτην ὕβριν, P Oxy VI. 930¹¹ (iv/A.D.) = *Selections*, p. 129) ἐς τηλικαύτην σε [ἀγωνία]ν ἄκων ἐνέβαλον, "unwittingly I cast you into such distress," and P Grenf II. 82¹⁹ (*c.* A.D. 400) φυλάττειν τηλικούτῃ ἀρχοντικῇ ὑπηρεσίᾳ, "reserve him for the state galley" (Edd.).

τηρέω

(1) lit. "watch," "observe" : P Tebt II. 278¹³ (early i/A.D.) τηρῖ μ[ε] γάρ, "for he watches me (?)" (Edd.). (2) "guard," "protect" : PSI III. 168² (B.C. 118) τηροῦντός μου σὺν ἄλλοις ἐπὶ τοῦ ἐμ Ποχρίμει βασιλικοῦ χώματος, P Oxy VI. 985 (accounts—2ⁿᵈ half i/A.D.) ἐργάτῃ τηροῦντι τὸν οἶνον . . . δραχμαὶ) δ. (3) "keep," "preserve" : BGU IV. 1141²⁵ (B.C. 13) κἀγὼ τὴν φιλίαν σου θέλων ἄμεμπτ[ον] ἐματὸν ἐτήρησα (cf. 1 Thess 5²³), P Oxy XIV. 1757²¹ (ii A.D. after Hadrian) κόμισαι παρὰ Θέωνος μάγια ("vessels") δύο καὶ τήρησόν μοι αὐτὰ ἕως ἀναβῶ, *ib.* III. 533¹⁸ (ii/iii A.D.) ἵνα τηρήσωσι αὐτῶν τὴν δεξιάν, "that they should keep their pledge," *ib.* VIII. 1165¹⁶ (iii/iv A.D.) τὰ σεσύλληχα δὲ κέρμα (τα) τηρῶ αὐτὰ εἰς τὴν δίκην, "I am keeping for the trial the money that I have collected" (Edd.), and *ib.* X. 1298⁷ (iv A.D.) ἐγὼ μόνος (*l.* μόνον ?) πάνυ ἐμαυτὸν τηρῶν ὑπὲρ τὸν ἀσφαλήν, "I have been keeping myself quite alone beyond the point of safety" (Edd.).

A good parallel to 2 Tim 4⁷ is afforded by *Brit. Mus. Inscr.* Part III. No. 587 *b.⁵* (ii/A.D.) ὅτι τὴν πίστιν ἐτήρησα : cf. Deissmann *LAE²*, p. 309. See also *JTS* vi. (1905), p. 438, for the suggestion in Jn 2¹⁰ τηρέω = "maintain," "keep going" = "Thou hast kept going the good wine even until now." (4) "reserve," "set aside" : P Tebt II. 302²⁵ (A.D. 71–2) τὴν γῆν τὴν ἀντὶ συντάξεως ἡμεῖν ἐκ διαδοχῆς γονέων τετηρημένην, "this land which has been reserved to us instead of a subvention by inheritance from our ancestors" (Edd.), P Amh II. 71¹¹ (A.D. 178–9) ὧν ἡ [κ]αρπεία τοῦ (ἡμίσους) μέρους τετήρηται τῇ προγεγρ(αμμένῃ) μου μητρί, "the usufruct of the half part of which was reserved to my aforesaid mother" (Edd.), and cf. P Oxy II. 237ᵛⁱⁱⁱ·³⁵ (A.D. 186) οἷς ἡ μὲν χρῆσ[ε]ις διὰ δημοσίων τετήρηται χρηματισμῶν, "to whom the usufruct of the property has been guaranteed by public contracts" (Edd.).

τήρησις,

"keeping," "protection" : cf. P Tebt I. 27²³ (B.C. 113) τῶν κατ[ὰ] τὴν τήρησιν τῶν καρπῶν κατὰ τ[ὸ]ν ὑποδεικνύμενον τρόπον οἰκονομηθέντων, "that the protection of the crops be managed in the manner directed" (Edd.), P Oxy VII. 1070⁵¹ (iii/A.D.) μὴ ἀμελήσῃς μὴ ἄρα ποτὲ θέλῃς μ[ε]τὰ σ[ο]ῦ [Ἡρ]αείδι τὴν τήρησιν τῆς ὅλης οἰκίας παραδιδόναι, "do not neglect this, lest indeed you choose to hand over the keeping of the whole house to Herais" (Edd.), P Grenf II. 73¹¹ (late iii/A.D.) (= *Selections*, p. 118) τ]αύτην παραδέδωκα τοῖς καλοῖς καὶ πιστοῖς ἐξ αὐτῶν τῶν νεκροτάφων εἰς τήρησιν, "I have handed her over to the good and true men among the grave-diggers themselves that they may take care of her," and from the inscr. *Syll* 314 (= ³683⁶⁰ (B.C. 140) πρὸς τὴν τήρησιν τοῦ ὕδατος.

For τήρησις = "custody," "imprisonment," as in Ac 4³, 5¹⁸, cf. BGU II. 388ⁱⁱⁱ·⁷ (ii/iii A.D.) ἐκέλευσεν Σμάραγδον καὶ Εὔκαιρον εἰς τὴν τήρησιν παραδοθῆναι.

Τιβέριος.

For the transliteration of the vowels, see Blass-Debrunner § 41. 1. P Ryl II. 133 contains a petition addressed ἱερεῖ Τιβερίου Καίσαρος Σεβαστ[ο]ῦ, the first mention, according to the editors, of a priest of Tiberius in the papyri : see their note *ad l.*

τίθημι,

(1) "place," "set" : cf. P Oxy IV. 742⁵ (B.C. 2) ἀπόστειλόν μ[ο]ι πόσας δέσμας παρείληφες καὶ θ(ὲ)ς αὐτὰς εἰς τόπον ἀσφαλῶς, "send me word how many bundles you have received, and put them in a safe place" (Edd.), P Fay 110¹⁷ (c. A.D. 109) τ]ὴν διαγραφὴν τοῦ χόρτου ποῦ τέθικας ; "where did you put the notice of payment for the hay?" P Oxy XIV. 1674⁸ (iii/A.D.) θὲς τὴν ὀπτὴν πλίνθον π[α]ρὰ τὴν πλάτην, "put the baked bricks alongside the wall (?)" (Edd.).

(2) "put down," "lay down" : cf. P Cairo Zen II. 59218³² (B.C. 254) ὑπόμνημα τῶ[ν] ἱερέων τοῦ ἱεροῦ τῶν θέντων τὰ μέρη, "memorandum of the priests of the temple who have paid their portions," and P Fay 109⁵ (early i/A.D.) ἐάν σε δ<έ>η τὸ εἱμάτιόν σου θεῖναι ἐνέχυρον, "even if you have to pawn your cloak" (Edd.). See also Herodas V. 62 ἔθηκας, "you put off" (cf. Headlam's note with its reference to Lk 19²¹).

(3) "make," "appoint" : cf. P Oxy IV. 745² (c. A.D. 1) ὑπὲρ ὧν καὶ ἔθου χειρόγραφον [διὰ Ἀρ]τεμᾶτος, "for which you drew me up a bond through Artemas" (Edd.), *ib.* III. 482²⁹ (A.D. 109) ἀκολούθως ᾗ περιὼν ἔθετο, "in accordance with the will which he drew up in his lifetime" (Edd.), P Strass I. 4²¹ (A.D. 550) an attesting signatory— μαρτυρῶ τῇ μισθώσει ἀκούσας παρὰ τοῦ θεμέν(ου). See also P Tebt II. 408¹ (A.D. 3) ἐπιστάμενος πῶς σε τίθεμαι κὲ φιλῶ, "since you know how I esteem and love you" (Edd.).

(4) The word is used in financial transactions with reference to the borrower, e.g. P Grenf II. 31⁸ (B.C. 104) ὁμολογεῖ Χαιρήμων . . . ἀπέχειν παρὰ Παοῦτος τοῦ Ὥρου τὸ ἐπιβάλλον αὐτῷ μέρος δανείου οὖ ἔθετο Πατοῦς Ὥρου, and P Oxy XIV. 1044¹¹ (B.C. 63-62) περὶ οὖ ἔθετο ὁ Μοσχίων τῆι τῶν ὁμολογούντων μητρί, "concerning the money which Moschion borrowed from the mother of the acknowledging parties."

(5) Some grammatical forms may be noted. A form τιθέω (τιθῶ) is supposed by the comp⁴· ὑποτιθοῦσα in BGU I. 350¹³ (time of Trajan), and for a passive τίθομαι note the comp⁴· παρακατατίθομαι in *ib.* 326ⁱⁱ·¹⁶ (A.D. 189).

The aor. ἔθηκα is seen in *Magn* 67⁷ (c. B.C. 200?) : for ἔθησα see Radermacher *Gr.* p. 79. According to Meisterhans *Gr.* p. 180 τέθηκα is the only perfect found in Attic inscrr. from B.C. 400 to B.C. 200 : the form τέθεικα first makes its appearance in i/B.C. : but cf. from the papyri *UPZ* i. 62¹ (before B.C. 161 or 160) ἐκτέθεικα. The passive τέθειμαι, whose place is often taken by κεῖμαι, as in Phil 1¹⁶, may be illustrated from BGU IV. 1208²⁵ (B.C. 27-26) πέπομφά σοι ἣν τέθειται μίσθωσιν. See further Mayser

Gr. i. pp. 79, 370, Dieterich *Untersuchungen* p. 216 ff. MGr θέτω (θέχτω, θήκω, τέκνω) with aor. ἔθεκα beside the more common ἔθεσα (Thumb *Handb.* pp. 331, 140).

τίκτω.

For the ordinary sense "bear," "give birth to," cf. P Oxy IV. 744⁹ (B.C. 1) (= *Selections*, p. 33) ἐὰν πολλαπολλῶν τέκῃς . . ., "if—good luck to you !—you bear children . . .," BGU I. 261⁵ (ii/iii A.D.) ἐὰν Ἡροὶς τέκῃ εὐχόμεθα ἐλθεῖν πρός σε, P Oxy VII. 1069²¹ (iii/A.D.) ἐὰν γὰρ τέκῃ ἡ Ταμοῦν, ἀνάγκασον αὐτὴν τὸ βρέφος φειλοπονήσε (*l.* φιλοπονῆσαι), "if Tamun bear a child, make her be assiduous with it" (Edd.), *ib.* VIII. 1151¹² (Christian amulet—v/A.D.?) ἐξελοῦ τὴν δούλην σου Ἰωαννίαν, ἣν ἔτεκεν Ἀναστασία . . . ἀπὸ παντὸς κακοῦ, "deliver from every evil thy servant Joannia whom Anastasia bare," and similarly ³⁰. See also BGU II. 665ⁱⁱ·¹⁴ (i/A.D.) ἵνα ὧδε καταφθάσῃ τεκεῖν τὸ ἀναγκαῖον καὶ διὰ τὸ σὸν ὀψώνι[ο]ν.

The present participle ἡ τίκτουσα in Gal 4²⁷ LXX denotes a continuous relationship, practically equivalent to ἡ μήτηρ, see *Proleg.* p. 127 ; for the future middle τέξομαι in active sense (cf. Mt 1²³, see *ib.* p. 155 ; and for the late 1st aor. pass. ἐτέχθην (for Att. ἐγενόμην) in Mt 2², Lk 2¹¹, see Blass *Gr.* p. 44.

τίλλω

may be freely translated "prepare" in P Petr II. 32 (1,⁹ (= III. 36 (*d*)²) (Ptol.) κώιδι<. .>α τίλλοντες, "preparing hides by plucking the hairs from them : cf. the late P Oxy XVI. 1846¹ (vi/vii A.D.) θελήσῃ ἡ σὴ γνησία ἀδελφότης τὸ ἁλιευτικὸν ὃ λέγει τῷ τετιλμέ(νον) (?) [κ]αθοσιωμέ(νως?) παρασκευάσαι φιλοκαληθῆναι ; "will your true brotherliness kindly have the damaged fishing-vessel which you speak of repaired ?" (Edd.).

For the ordinary meaning "pluck," "pull," as in Mt 12¹ *al.*, see P Flor III. 321¹⁷ (iii/A.D.) τίλλαντες χόρτον τοῖς κτῆσι (*l.* κτήνεσι), and *ib.* 322²⁰ (A.D. 258?) τίλλοντες χόρτον (ἀρούρας) ξ, and ³⁶ δεσμεύοντες χόρτον τὰς τειλείσας (ἀρούρας) ε. Τιλήτωι is found after a lacuna in P Fay 131¹⁸ (iii–iv A.D.). See also Menander Ἐπιτρέπ. 271 τίλλουσ' ἑαυτῆς τὰς τρίχας, and Herodas II. 70 (with A. E. Housman's note in *CR* xxxvi. (1922), p. 109 f.).

For the uncommon subst. τίλσις, "a plucking out," see P Lond 113. 3⁵ (vi/A.D.) σπερμάτων καὶ κοπῆς ἢ καὶ τίλσεως ; for τιλμός in the same sense see P Oxy XIV. 1631⁹ (A.D. 280) τ]ιλμὸς καλάμου, and *ib.* 1692¹⁰ (A.D. 188) : and for τίλμα see Herodas II. 69.

Τιμαῖος.

This Aramaic proper name is fully discussed by Swete *ad* Mk 10⁴⁶ : see also Zorell *Lex. s.v.* The Greek name Τίμαιος ; (note accent) is common : see P Hib I. 111²³ (c. B.C. 250) τὰ πρὸς Τίμαιον (δραχμαὶ) κ, "the case against Timaeus, 20 drachmae," and the other reff. in Preisigke *Namenbuch s.v.*

τιμάω.

For τιμάω = "honour," as generally in the NT, cf. the decree in honour of a gymnasiarch P Oxy III. 473⁷ (A.D. 138-160) τιμῆσαι αὐτόν, *Chrest.* I. 41ⁱⁱⁱ·¹¹ (A.D. 232) τειμηθέντων τῶν Κ[ρατίστων Μαξιμίνου καὶ υἱο]ῦ Μαξίμου, and the inscrr. *saepe*. Τιμητός occurs in P Petr I. 24 (3)² (Ptol.).

The meaning "set a value upon," "price," as in Mt 27⁹ LXX, is seen in such passages as P Cairo Zen II. 59269¹³ (an account—B.C. 234) ἐ[ὰν δ]ὲ πλείονος ἢ ἐλάσσονος τ[ιμ]ῆται, αὐτῶι ὑπάρξει, "if the price be reckoned at more or less, it will be imputed to him accordingly," PSI IV. 382¹⁵ (B.C. 248-7) τιμῶσι δὲ αὐτὴν (*sc.* τὴν ἀκάνθην) δραχμῶν κη, P Par 58³ (B.C. 153-152) (= UPZ i. p. 325) τετίμηκα⟨ς⟩ τὴν βοῦν ταλάντων τρία ἥμισυ, and P Flor II. 206⁶ (iii/A.D.) ἅπ]αντα τίμησ[ο]ν.

τιμή

(1) "honour," as in Jn 4⁴⁴: P Tebt I. 33¹ (B.C. 112) (= *Selections*, p. 30) preparations for the visit of a Roman senator, who is described as ἐν μίζονι ἀξιώματι κα[ὶ] τιμῆι κείμενος, "occupying a position of highest rank and honour," and P Oxy I. 41¹⁷ (iii/iv A.D.) account of a popular demonstration in honour of the prytanis, who replies τὴν μὲν παρ' ὑμῶν τιμὴν ἀσπάζομαι καί γε ἐπὶ τούτῳ σφόδρα χαίρω, "I acknowledge with great pleasure the honour which you do me" (Edd.). Hence the phrase εἰς τὴν τιμήν, "out of regard for," in such passages as BGU III. 844¹⁹ (A.D. 83) (= Olsson *Papyrusbriefe*, p. 140) καλῶς δὲ ποιήσεις παρασχὼν Διοσκόρῳ χάας ῑ εἰς ἐμὴν τειμήν, and P Giss I. 66¹¹ (early ii/A.D.) ἐρωτῶ [σ]ε εἴς τε τὴν τῶν θεῶν εὐσέβειαν καὶ εἰς ἡμετέραν τιμὴν ἀπολῦσαι αὐτό(ν. With 1 Cor 12²³ we may compare BGU IV. 1141¹⁹ (B.C. 14) εἰ σὺ μέν μοι καὶ τιμὴν περιτιθεῖς.

In further reference to τιμή = "honour," "esteem," we may cite from the inscrr. *Priene* 105¹⁶ (c. B.C. 9) (= OGIS 458), where things are said to have been so arranged according to the divine will, ἵνα ἀφορμὴ γένοιτο τῆς εἰς τὸν Σεβαστὸν τιμῆς, "that there may be an opportunity of paying honour to the Emperor (Augustus)"; cf. 1 Tim 1¹⁷, Rev 4⁹, *al.*, and see Rouffiac *Recherches*, p. 11. In *C. and B.* i. p. 101 Ramsay notes that in Phrygia the erection of a gravestone is regarded as "a distinction and prerogative (τιμή) of the dead man and living god."

(2) "price," as in Mt 27⁶: P Petr II. 38 (b)² (iii/B.C.) προσπέπτωκέ μοι . . . τὸ ἔλαιον π[ωλ]εῖσθαι πλείονος τιμῆς τῆς ἐν τῶι προστάγμα[τι] διασεσαφημένης, "it has transpired to me that oil is sold at a higher price than that fixed in the Royal decree" (Ed.), P Lond 42¹⁷ (B.C. 168) (= I. p. 30, UPZ i. p. 300, *Selections*, p. 10) εἰς πᾶν τι ἐληλυθυῖα διὰ τὴν τοῦ σίτου τιμήν, "having come to the last extremity because of the high price of corn," P Fay 11³⁰ (c. B.C. 115) πραχθῆναί μοι αὐτὸν τ[ὴ]ν ὡρισμέν[η]ν τειμὴν τῆς ἀρ(τάβης), "that he shall be made to pay me the price fixed for each artaba" (Edd.), BGU IV. 1205¹⁸ (B.C. 28) πέπομφά σοι τιμὴν τοῦ ἐνκοιμήτρου (δραχμὰς) ρκ, *ib.* 1206¹⁴ (B.C. 28) διανδραγα[θ]εῖτε ἐν τῆι εἰσαγῆι τῆς τιμῆς [τ]οῦ φακοῦ καὶ ὁλώρας, P Ryl II. 229¹³ (A.D. 38) τοῦ λοιπ(οῦ) τῆς τιμῆ(ς) τοῦ χόρτου πρόχρησον ἕως οὗ παραγένωμαι, "as to the rest of the price for the hay make provision until I come" (Edd.), P Fay 122¹⁰ (c. A.D. 100) ἕως ἀπολάβω τὸ λοιπὸν τῆς τιμ[ῆ]ς πάλιν σοι γράψω, "until I get the remainder of the price and write to you again" (Edd.), *ib.* 90¹⁸ (A.D. 234) τὴν ἐπὶ τοῦ καιροῦ ἐσο(μένην) πλ[ε]ίστην τει(μήν), "the highest current price at the time being" (Edd.), P Grenf II. 67¹⁸ (A.D. 237) (= *Selections*, p. 109) ἀραβῶνος [τῇ τ]ιμῇ ἐλλογαυμέν[ο]υ σο]ι "earnest money to be reckoned by you in the price," *ib.* 77¹⁷,¹⁸ (iii/iv A.D.) (= *Selections*, p. 121) τιμ ἡ) φαρμάκου . . . τιμ(ὴ) οἴνου, "the price of medicine . . . the price of wine," in a note of funeral expenses.

Swete suggests that there may be a play on the double sense of τιμή in Ev. Petr. 3 where the multitude are described as scourging Jesus and saying Ταύτῃ τῇ τιμῇ τιμήσωμεν τὸν υἱὸν τοῦ θεοῦ, "with this honour let us honour," or "at this price let us apprize, the Son of God."

For τίμημα see P Grenf II. 67¹² (hire of dancing girls— A.D. 237) (= *Selections*, p. 108) ὑπὲρ τιμήμα[τος] πασῶν τῶν ἡμερῶν [πυρο]ῦ ἀρτάβας γ, "by way of payment for the whole period three artabae of wheat," PSI IV. 313³ (iii/iv A.D.) τὸ συνφωνηθὲν τίμημα μ[ετ]αξὺ μαρτύρων, and for τίμησις see *ib.* 327¹⁰ (B.C. 250-8) τίμησις ἣν ἐλάβομεν παρὰ Βουβάλου. Note also the adj. πρόστειμος (not in LS⁸) in P Ryl II. 244¹¹ (iii/A.D.) πάντα γὰρ πρόστειμα γέγονεν, "for everything has risen in price" (Edd.).

τίμιος

(1) "precious," "costly," of money value (Rev 17¹, *al.*). Cf. P Cairo Zen II. 59100¹⁰ (B.C. 255) a request to send some corn that the writer may not have to buy at a high price, ὅπως μὴ τίμιον ἀγαράζωμεν, and P Lond 77²¹ (Will— end of vi/A.D.) (= *Chrest.* II. p. 371) ἀπὸ τιμίου εἴδους ἕως ἐλαχίστου. The neut. is used as a subst. in P Oxy VII. 1025²⁰ (late iii/A.D.) τὰ τείμια, "the presents"; (2) "held in honour," "esteemed" (Ac 5³⁴, Heb 13⁴): cf. P Tebt II. 294²⁰ (A.D. 146) ἐπὶ τοῖς αὐτοῖς τιμίοις καὶ δικαίοις πᾶσει, "with all the same privileges and rights" (Edd.), P Lond 1178²³ (A.D. 194) (= III. p. 216) ἀνδράσι τειμίοις μο[υ καὶ] φίλοις, and from the inscr. *Syll* 930 (= ³ 695)¹⁸ (B.C. 112-1) συντηρῆσαι τὰ ἐκ παλαιῶν χρόνων δεδομένα τίμια καὶ φιλάνθρωπα.

The word is common in addresses, e.g. P Oxy II. 292¹ (c. A.D. 25) Θέων Τυράννωι τῶι τιμιωτάτωι πλεῖστα χαίρειν, *ib.* 290¹ (late i/A.D.) Ὧρος Ἀπίωνι τῶι τειμειωτάτωι χαίρειν. Cf. also PSI VII. 800³ (vi/A.D.) τὰ τίμια ἴχνη τῶν ποδῶν τῆς ὑμετέρας ἐνδόξου φιλανθρωπίας, and the MGr usage of τίμιος = "honest," "honourable."

τιμότης

"preciousness," "worth" (Rev 18¹⁹), is common as a title: cf. P Amh II. 145⁵ (iv/v A.D.) βούλο]μαι . . . μὴ φορτικός . . ὅμως γε[νέσ]θαι τῇ σῇ τιμιότητι περὶ οἱουδή- ποτε [πρά]γματος, "I desire nevertheless not to weary your honour on any subject" (Edd.).

Τιμόθεος

This common proper name is found also under the forms Τιμόθειος, Τιμώθεος: see the reff. in Preisigke *Namenbuch*.

Τίμων

one of the seven original "deacons," Ac 6³. Preisigke *Namenbuch* s.v. quotes only two exx. from our sources—P Petr III. 90(a)²⁶ (Ptol.) Ἀλέξανδρος Τίμωνος, and the wall-scratching *Preisigke* 1465 Ἀσπίδας Ἡρακλήου | τὸν κύριον Τίμων.

τιμωρέω.

For the usage of this verb "avenge oneself on," "punish," as in Ac 22^5, 26^11, cf. P Oxy I. 34^iii.14 (A.D. 127) τοὺς παρα-βάντας καὶ τοῦ[s] διὰ ἀπειθίαν κ[αὶ] ὡς ἀφορμὴν ζητοῦντας ἁμαρτημάτω[ν] τειμωρήσομαι, "any persons who violate it, whether from mere disobedience or to serve their own nefarious purposes, will receive condign punishment" (Edd.), and Syll 326 (=^3 709)^12 (c. B.C. 107) τοὺς δὲ αἰτίους τῆς ἐπαναστάσεο[s] τιμωρησάμενος.

In P Ryl II. 62^10 (iii/A.D.), a translation from an unknown Latin author, we have—ἀγρυπνεῖται καὶ κολάζεται [καὶ τι-]μωρεῖται καὶ παρηγορεῖται.

The adj. from which the verb is derived may be quoted from Syll 810 (=^3 1176)^7 εἰ δέ τι ἑκὼν ἐξαμ[αρτήσει], οὐκ ἐμὸν ἐπαρά[σασθαι], δίκη δὲ ἐπικρέματα[ί σοι] τιμωρὸς ἀπελθόν[τι] ἀπειθὴς Νεμέσε[ως]. "the inexorable avenging justice of Nemesis."

τιμωρία,

found in the NT only in Heb 10^29, conveys like the verb the idea of giving an offender his deserts, without the thought of discipline which normally attaches to κόλασις. So in P Lond 1171 verso (c) (A.D. 42) (=III. p. 107) κατὰ τούτου τῇ ἀνωτάτω χρήσομαι τειμωρίᾳ, a prefect threatens those who employ unauthorized violence and forced labour or extortion towards the natives, P Leid W^vii.28 (ii/iii A.D.) (= II. p. 105) ὁ κτίσας τὴν ἀναγκή(ν), καὶ τιμωρίαν, καὶ τὴν βάσανον, and BGU IV. 1024^iv.17 (iv/v A.D.) ἐκδέξι το[ίνυν] τὴ[η]ν ἕως κεφ[αλῆ]ς τ[ι]μωρίαν—a sentence of "capital punishment."

τίνω.

In its only appearance in the NT, 2 Thess 1^9, τίνω is used as in classical writers (e.g. Soph. Electra 298) with δίκην = "pay the penalty." For a similar phrase see P Fay 21^24f. (A.D. 134) τὴν προσήκουσαν δίκη[ν ὑ]πόσχωσι, "may pay the fitting penalty." The verb occurs in BGU I. 242^8 (time of Commodus) πλ]ηγαῖς πλίσταις με [ἐτ]είσατο, and in the Christian P Hamb I. 22^5 (iv/A.D.) τῖσον ἀπάντη . . . ἐχθροὺς ἡμετέρους, where the editor compares LXX Prov 20^22,22. The proper name Τεισάμενος occurs in P Petr III. 112(f)^20 (iii/B.C.). The subst. ἔκτισις, as in P Tebt II. 384^12 (A.D. 10). is merely the later spelling of ἔκτεισις, "payment in full," which has ει in all early inscrr. and papyri (see LS^8 s.v.). See also s.v. ἀποτίνω and Mayser Gr. i. p. 91.

τίς, τί,

"who?" "what?" (1) Exx. of this common interrog. pron. are—P Petr II. 40a^24 (iii/B.C.) γράψατέ μοι, τίς παρ' ὑμῖν τιμὴ ἐγένετο τοῦ σίτου, P Par 44^1 (B.C. 153) τί κε-λεύε[ι]s ὑπὲρ τούτων; BGU IV. 1078^7 (A.D. 30) ὄψομαι, τί με δεῖ ποιεῖν, P Grenf I. 53^33 (iv/A.D.) τίνος εὐγενό(= ε)σ-τερός ἐστι; and P Oxy I. 120^2 (iv/A.D.) λοιπὸν τί σοι γράψω οὐκ οἶδα.

(2) The use of τίς for ὅς, ὅστις, as in Mk 14^36, Lk 17^8, 1 Tim 1^7, and in LXX Gen 38^25, Lev 21^17, is fairly common in the papyri, e.g. BGU II. 665^iii.13 (i/A.D.) ο]ὐκ ἔχομεν διὰ τίνες (l. τίνος) πέμπωμεν, P Oxy VIII. 1155^13 (A.D. 104) αὐτὸ τὸ πρόγραμ[μ]α τοῦ ἡγεμόνος ἔπεψά σοι ἵνα

ἐπίγοις πρὸς τί σοί 'στι, "I send you the actual proclamation of the praefect in order that you may hasten to do what concerns you" (Ed.), ib. 1119^22 (A.D. 254) τίνα μοι ἐπέστει-λαν, BGU III. 822^5 (iii/A.D.) (cited s.v. ἑλκύω), and P Lond 239^10 (c. A.D. 346) (= II. p. 297) τίνος ἐὰν χρίαν ἔχῃς. See also Mayser Gr. II. i. p. 80.

(3) Occasionally τίς is used in the NT = πότερος, of two only (e.g. Mt 21^31, 27^17, Lk 22^27). In the LXX it has completely displaced πότερος which, it may be noted, hardly occurs at all in the papyri (see Proleg. p. 77 n.^1). In MGr τίς, τίνος, τίνα are rare: in their place the invariable τί is used (Thumb Handb. § 152).

τις

(indef. pron.), "someone," "something": P Vat A^17 (B.C. 168) (= UPZ i. p. 303) πᾶς τις πειρᾶται . . ., P Lond 42^16 (B.C. 168) (= Selections, p. 10) εἰς πᾶν τι ἐληλυθυῖα διὰ τὴν τοῦ σίτου τιμήν, "having come to the last extremity because of the high price of corn," P Oxy IV. 742^10 (B.C. 2) ἐάν τι δύνῃ . . . δὸς ἐργασία[ν, "if you can, give your attention to it" (Edd.), ib. I. 120^4 (iv/A.D.) τινα ὁρῶντα αἱαυτὸν (l. ἑαυτὸν) ἐν δυστυχίᾳ, "a man finding himself in adversity," [12] ἀποστίλον μοί τινα ἢ Γοῦγθον ἢ Ἀμμώνιον, "send someone to me, either Gunthus or Ammonius" (Edd.). P Oxy VI. 937^22 (iii/A.D.) γ]ράψον ἐκεῖ τὸ κατ' εἶδος ὅτι τι καὶ τι εἴληφας is translated by the editors "write the li-t there, that you have received so and so." They remark that it is simpler to take τι καὶ τι as analogous to τὸ καὶ τό than "to take τί καὶ τί as an indirect interroga-tive, ὅτι being redundant."

For τις used to denote an unspecified name, cf. P Oxy VII. 1034^11 (ii/A.D.) κληρονόμους καταλείπω τὴν θυγα-τέρ[α] μου τινὰ καὶ τὸν {τον} σύντροφον αὐτῆς τινα καὶ τινα, τὸν μέν τινα ἧς προυπήλλαξα . . . οἰκίας καὶ αὐλῆς, "I leave as my heirs my daughter x and her foster-brother y and z, of the house and court which I previously mortgaged" (Ed.), and ib. III. 500^1 (late ii/A.D.) τίς τινι χαίρει[ν, "A to B, greeting" (Edd.). A good parallel to Ac 5^36 is afforded by P Leid W^vii.25 (ii/iii A.D.) (= II. p. 103) δια-περάσεις τὸ πέρα, ὅτι ἐγώ ἰμί (l. εἰμί) τις: cf. also Herodas VI. 54 ἢν μέν κοτ', ἢν τις, ἀλλὰ νῦν γεγήρακε, "he once cut a figure, only now he has grown old" (see Headlam's note).

For τίς ποτε see P Oxy IV. 745^7 (c. A.D. 1) μοι ἐχρήσατο . . . οὐχ ὡς λύσα⟨ν⟩τι ἀλλ' ὡς τινι ποτε ἀποστερητῆι μὴ ἀποδεδωκότι, "he treated me not like a man who had paid but like a defrauder and a debtor" (Edd.), and ib. XIV. 1680^13ff. (iii/iv A.D.) ὑπονοοῦμαι ὅτι πάντως πάλιν τί ποτε ἔχει πρὸς σέ. [εἰ τ]ί ποτε αὐτῷ χρεωστεῖς . . ., "I suspect that he must have some further claim against you. If you owe him anything . . ." MGr has retained τίποτε (in a variety of forms, Thumb Handb. p. 358), while discarding most forms of τις (ib. p. 954).

With μήτιγε βιωτικά, "not to speak of mere affairs of daily life," in 1 Cor 6^3 cf. P Lond 42^23 (B.C. 168) (= I. p. 30, UPZ i. p. 300, Selections, p. 10) μὴ ὅτι γε τοσούτου χρόνου ἐπιγεγονότος, "not to speak of so much time having gone by": see Proleg. p. 240.

J. H. Moulton (Proleg. p. 59) thinks that the very difficult εἴ τις σπλάγχνα καὶ οἰκτιρμοί of Phil 2^1, involving as it does both number and gender, may be illustrated from

P Par 15[15] (B.C. 120) ἐπί τι μίαν τῶν . . οἰκιῶν, and BGU I. 326[11,2] (A.D. 194) εἰ δέ τι πε[ρ]ισσὰ γράμματα . . . [καταλίπω. He prefers, however, the suggestion of Blass, and independently of Kennedy (*EGT ad l.*, to read εἴ τι throughout in the sense of *si quid valet*: see also *Proleg.* p. 244 for Rouse's reference for indeclinable τι to MGr κάτι, as κάτι ἡσυχία, "a little rest."

τίτλος

(Lat. *titulus*, "inscription" Jn 19[19]). Hatch in *JBL* xxvii. (1908) p. 143 f. has collected several instances of this word = "epitaph" (as in Juv. *Sat.* vi. 230 from Christian inscr. from Iconium, dating probably from the Imperial period, e.g. *IMS* ii. 193 ἀνεστήσαμεν ζῶντες ἑαυτοῖς τὸν τίτλον, *ib.* 209 τίτλον ἐ(ν)ποίει, and *ib.* 215 ἀνεστήσαμεν τὸν τίτλον τοῦτον. Hatch adds a ref. to the neut. form τὸ τίτλον in *CIG* IV. 8621[19] (Taurian Chersonese). MGr retains τίτλος. "title."

Τίτος.

For this proper name, see the invitation to dinner εἰς τὰ Τίτου τοῦ (ἑκατοντάρχου) [ἀπὸ ὥρας] θ, "at the house of Titus the centurion at 9 o'clock" (P Fay 132[2]—iii/A.D.). Numerous other ref. are given by Preisigke *Namenbuch* s.v. On the probability that Titus, Paul's companion, was the brother of Luke, see Souter *Exp T* xviii. pp. 285, 335 f.

τοιγαροῦν,

"accordingly," "wherefore" (1 Thess 4[8], Heb 12[1]): P Tebt II. 315[14] (ii/A.D.) τοιγαροῦν [μη]δὲν ταραχ[θ]ῆς, ἐγὼ γάρ [σ]ε [ἀ]παλλάξω. "do not be disturbed on this account, as I will get you off" (Edd.), P Giss I. 3[7] (A.D. 117) (= *Chrest.* I. p. 571) χαίροντες τοιγαροῦν θύοντες τὰς ἑστίας ἀνάπτωμεν, and P Oxy I. 124[7] (a schoolboy's exercise—iii/A.D.) πέμψας τοιγαροῦν ὁ Ἄδραστος εἰς [Δε]λφοὺς ἐπυνθάνετο τὴν αἰτίαν, "Adrastus therefore sent to Delphi and inquired the cause" (Edd.).

τοίνυν,

"therefore." For τοίνυν after the first word of the sentence as in 1 Cor 9[26] (and in classical usage), cf. P Oxy III. 471[44] (speech of an advocate—ii/A.D.) συνφέ[ρει τοίνυν τοὐλάττο[ν μόν]ον ὁμολογεῖν, "it is best therefore to acknowledge only the lesser fault," *ib.* X. 1252 *verso*[18] (A.D. 288–95) αὐτὸς τοίνυν ἐγώ, ἡγ[ε]μὼν κύριε, ὑ[πογυ]ώ[ς χειροτονηθείς, "I myself therefore, my lord praefect, having been recently appointed" (Edd.), and *ib.* VI. 902[10] (c. A.D. 465) ἐπεὶ τοίνυν οἱ ἔκδικοι ἐπενοήθησαν ἐν ταῖς πόλεσιν, "therefore, since advocates have been devised in the cities" (Edd.). The word comes first, as in Lk 20[25], Heb 13[13], in *ib.* 940[9] (v/A.D.) τοίνυν, ὡς ἀνωτέρω εἴρηται, καταξίωσον ἐπέχειν τοῦ λογισμοῦ, "therefore, as stated above, please to delay the account-taking" (Edd.): see also the mime *ib.* III 413[225] ii/A.D. τοίνυν τὰ σεαυτῆς ἆρον.

τοιόσδε,

"of such a character," is found in Biblical Greek only in 2 Pet 1[17]. For the weaker τοῖος we may cite P Oxy VI. 903[11] (iv/A.D.) διὰ τὸν τρόφιμόν σου ἦλθας ἢ διὰ τὴν τοίαν ἦλθας λαλῆσαι ἐπάνω αὐτῆς; "have you come on account of your foster-son or of such a woman, to talk about her?"

τοιοῦτος,

"of such a kind," "such"; cf. P Vat A[13] (B.C. 168) (= *UPZ* i. p. 303) τοιούτους καιροὺς ἀνηντληκυῖα, P Lond 42[14] (B.C. 168) (= I. p. 30) ἐκ τοῦ τοιούτου καιροῦ cf. l.[21], *ib.* 807[11] (A.D. 84) (= III. p. 207) ἵνα μὴ πάλιν ἀναπλεύσωσι τὸν τοιοῦτον πόρον, P Fay 93[13] (A.D. 126) ὄνον θήλιαν πρωτοβόλον μυόχρουν τα[ύ]την τοιαύτην ἀναπόριφο[ν, "a female mouse-coloured donkey, shedding its first teeth, just as it is, free from blemish," P Oxy II. 237[viii,12] (A.D. 186) παραγγέλλω τῆς τοιαύτης πανουργίας ἀπέ[σ]χεσθαι, "I proclaim that such persons shall abstain from this form of knavery" (Edd.), P Flor II. 175[5] (A.D. 255) ἵνα [μ]ὴ ὡς τοιούτῳ σοι χρησώμε[θα, "in order that we may not have to treat him as such," i.e. as negligent, and P Oxy XII. 1502[5] (iii iv A.D.) ἠγαλλείασα ὅτει τοιοῦτός μου π(ατ)ὴρ τὴν μνήμην ποιεῖται.

For the neut. with the art. used as a substantive, cf. P Ryl II. 129[15] (A.D. 30) τοῖς τὸ τοιοῦτο διαπραξαντας, "those who have acted in this way," *ib.* 139[13] (A.D. 34) ὑπονοῶι οὖν τὸ τοιοῦτω (. τοιοῦτο) γεγονέναι ὑπὸ τῶν καταγινομένων ἐν τῆι Ληνῶι λεγομένῃ, "I suspect that this has been done by the inhabitants of the so-called Winepress" (Edd.).

τοῖχος,

"a wall," is used figuratively in Ac 23[3], its only occurrence in the NT (cf. τεῖχος). For its ordinary meaning, cf. P Magd 2 *recto*[11] (B.C. 221) (= *Chrest.* I. p. 431) ὑπάρχοντος δὲ τοίχου τινὸς ἡμιτελέστου . . . ἐμοῦ δὲ βουλομένης ἐπισυντελέσαι τὸν τοῖχον, ἵνα μὴ ὑπερβατὸν ἦι εἰς τὰ ἡμέτερα, *ib.* 29[3] (B.C. 218) ἐπιβὰς ὁ Θεοδόσιος ὠικοδόμησεν ἑαυτῶι τοίχους οἰκήσεω[ς, P Amh II. 54[3] (B.C. 112) οἶκος καθειρημένος ἧς οἱ τοῖχοι περίεισιν, "a dismantled house, of which the walls are standing" (Edd.), P Oxy III. 505[5] (ii/A.D.) οἱ λοιποὶ τῆς αὐτῆς αὐλῆς τοῖχοι, P Lond 46[72] (magic—iv/A.D.) (= I. p. 67) of writing εἰς τοῖχο(ν), Inscr. Delos 365–53 (iii/B.C.) ἐργολαβήσαντι ἀνοικοδομῆσαι πτῶμ[α] τοῦ τοίχου, and Herodas VI. 8 οὐ φέρουσιν οἱ τοῖχοι.

The word is used of the "side" of a ship in P Hib I. 38[8] (B.C. 252–1) συνέβη κλεῖναι τὸν δεξιὸν τοῖχον τοῦ πλοίου, "it came about that the right side of the ship listed" (Edd.): cf. P Flor I. 69[24, 25] (iii/A.D.).

τόκος,

"a bringing forth," and hence "offspring," and metaph. "interest," "usury," because it multiplies or "breeds" money the lexicons compare Shakespeare's *Merch. of Venice* I. 3 "breed of barren metal"). This metaph. usage occurs in the NT in Mt 25[27], Lk 19[23], and can be readily illustrated from the Κοινή. e.g. P Eleph 27a[24] (iii/B.C.) τετάγμεθα τὸ ἀργύριον καὶ τοὺς τόκους ἐπὶ τὴν βασιλικὴν τράπεζαν, P Grenf II. 18[17] (B.C. 127) τόκους διδράχμους τῆς μνᾶς τὸν μῆνα ἕκαστον, i.e. interest at 2 % a month (cf. *s.v.* δίδραχμον). BGU IV. 1171[21] (i/B.C.) τοὺς ὀφειλομένους τόκους. P Tebt II. 384[18] A.D.

10) ἀντὶ τῶν τούτων τόκων, "in return for the (remission of) interest upon this sum" (Edd.), P Bilabel 35⁵ (A.D. 87) με κ[υρίαν εἶναι] δραχμῶν κ̄ καὶ τὸν τόκον (cf.¹⁰), and P Oxy I. 114⁴ (ii/iii A.D.) πεπλήρωκα τὸν τόκον μέχρι τοῦ Ἐπεὶφ πρὸς στατῆρα τῆς μνᾶς, "I have paid the interest up to Epeiph, at the rate of a stater per mina" (Edd.). In the LXX τόκος renders ἡ . "oppression," by transliteration, as in Ps 71³⁴.

τολμάω,

"have courage," "am bold": P Par 22¹⁶ (B.C. 165) (= UPZ i. p. 193) μέχρι τοῦ νῦν οὐ τετόλμηκεν αὐτὸν ἡ Νέφορις θάψαι, BGU IV. 1209¹⁶ (B.C. 23) ἵνα πρὸς μὲν κατάπληξιν τῶν τολμησάντων ἔχωμεν α[ὐτο]ὺς ἑτοίμους πρὸς ἐντυχίαν, P Ryl II. 144²⁰ (A.D. 38) ἐτόλμησεν πθόνους (l. φθόνους) μοι ἐπαγαγεῖν αἰτίας τοῦ μὴ ὄντος, "moreover he had the audacity to bring baseless accusations of malice against me" (Edd.), P Oxy VIII. 1120¹⁵ (early iii A.D.) εἰσεπήδησεν εἰς τὴν οἰκίαν μου καὶ ἐτόλμησεν ἀποσπάσαι δούλην μου, "rushed into my house and dared to carry off my slave" (Ed.), ib. IX. 1204²⁹ (A.D. 299) τις 'Οξυρυγχείτης . . . ὁρμώμενος τετόλμηκεν αὐτὸν ὀνομάζειν εἰς δεκαπρωτείαν. "an Oxyrhynchite made a design upon him and ventured to nominate him for the decemprimate" (Ed.), and BGU III. 909¹⁸ (A.D. 359) ἐπὶ τοίνυν οὐχ ὀλίγ[α] ἐστὶν τὰ τολμηθέντα ὑπ' αὐτῶν κατ' ἐμοῦ.

On τολμάω in the sense of "take courage," as in Mk 15⁴³, see the exx. in Field Notes, p. 155, and for the meaning "submit to," as in Rom 5⁷, see ib. p. 44. For the form τορμάω cf. BGU III. 948⁷ (iv/v A.D.) οὐκ ἐτόρμηκας ἐμοὶ γράψεν (= -ειν), also ⁹· ¹¹ (see Mayser Gr. i. p. 188).

For the subst. τόλμη see P Oxy VIII. 1119⁵ (A.D. 254) ὑφηγησάμενοι τὴν τόλμαν καὶ τὴν παρανομίαν, "recounting the audacity and the illegality" of a certain official, and for τόλμημα see ib. 1106⁷ (vi/A.D.) ἀποσχέσθαι τοῦ τοιούτου τολμήματος, "to abstain from any such outrage" (Ed.).

τολμηρῶς,

"boldly" (comp⁽ᵉ⁾ Rom 15¹⁵): cf. Chrest. I. 461²⁵ (beg. iii/A.D.) τολμηρῶς ἐνεχθείς . . .

τολμητής,

By τολμητής in 2 Pet 2¹⁰ Mayor ad l. understands "a shameless and headstrong man." For a somewhat weaker sense cf. Jos. B.J. III. 475 (x. 2), ed. Niese 'Ιουδαῖοι μέν, εἰ καὶ σφόδρα τολμηταὶ καὶ θανάτου καταφρονοῦντες. ἀλλὰ πολέμων ἄπειροι.

τομός,

"sharp": the adj. is found in the NT only in Heb 4¹² (in the comp⁽ᵉ⁾), cf. the fragmentary PSI VI. 624¹ (iii/B.C.) τομώτερον, with reference to the culture of vines. Preisigke Wörterb. cites a form τόμιος from P Frankf 5⁷·¹⁷ (B.C. 242–1) ὓ]ς τοκὰς μία, ταύτης δ[έ]λφακες πέντε, τόμιοι δύο ("two geldings"), and PSI VI. 553² (a list of foods—B.C. 260–50) τομίας ᾱ.

τόξον,

"a bow." For this NT ἅπ. εἰρ. (Rev 6²), cf. P Eleph 5⁸ (B.C. 284–3) τόξον ᾱ φαρέτρα ᾱ, PSI IV. 340¹² (B.C. 257–6) λοιπὸν τὸ τόξον ἐπ' ἐμὲ τείνεται τῶι ἐν τῆι οἰκίαι σκηνοῦντι.

τοπάζιον,

"a topaz" (Rev 21²⁰), a highly prized green stone: cf. Ps 118¹²⁷ ἠγάπησα τὰς ἐντολάς σου ὑπὲρ τὸ χρυσίον καὶ τοπάζιον, and see Pliny H.N. xxxvii. 32 "egregia etiamnum sua topazo gloria est, virenti genere."

τόπος,

(1) "a place": P Cairo Zen II. 59193³ (B.C. 225) ἱππῶνα ("stable") οὐκ ἔχει ὁ τόπος, P Oxy IV. 742⁵ (B.C. 2) θ[ὲ]ς αὐτὰς εἰς τόπον ἀσφαλῶς, and BGU II. 595 (c. A.D. 70–80) εἵνα φιλάνθρωπον ("reward") εἰς δύο τόπους μὴ χορηγῆι Θέων. With τόπος as a "sitting-place" in Lk 14⁹, Deissmann (BS, p. 267) compares Perg 618, where τόπος means "seat in a theatre" (for further exx. see the editor's note). See also Magn. 237 where between the pillars of the temple of Artemis there have been scratched on the marble floor the words—ὁ τόπος τρικλείνου ἱερῶν αὐλητρίδων καὶ ἀκροβατῶν cited by Thieme p. 32, comparing 1 Cor 14¹⁶. Τόπος is also frequent in Christian (and pagan) sepulchral inscr. as in C. and B. ii. p. 554, No. 420 Τόπος Φιλοθέ[ου], where Ramsay compares the corresponding use of the Lat. locus, or loculus. With Jn 11⁴⁸ cf. MGr use of τόπος = "country," "nation."

(2) "a district": P Hib I. 66² (B.C. 228) ἐν τοῖς κατὰ σὲ τόποις, "in your district," P Tebt II. 281¹² (B.C. 125) παρὰ τῶν κτωμένων οἰκίας ἢ τόπους, "from acquirers of houses or spaces," P Oxy VIII. 1154⁴ (late i/A.D.) αὐτόπτης γάρ εἰμι τῶν τόπων καὶ οὐκ εἰμὶ ξέν[ο]ς τῶν ἐνθάδε, "for I am personally acquainted with these places and am not a stranger here" (Ed.), ib. II. 243¹⁴ (A.D. 79) ψιλῶν τόπων, "open plots of land," P Fay 100¹⁰ (A.D. 99) οἰκίας καὶ αὐλῆ[ς] καὶ τόπων ("grounds"), ib. 30⁷ (notice of death—A.D. 173) ἀναγρ(αφομένου) ἐπ' ἀμφόδου Λυσανίου Τόπων "registered in the quarter of Lysanias' District" (Edd.) P Oxy VIII. 1111ᵇ·⁸ (A.D. 203) ἥ[μισυ μέρος] τόπ(ου) περιτετειχισμ(ένου), "the half share of a walled space" (Ed.), and P Lond 954¹⁰ (A.D. 260) (= III. p. 153) ψιλὸν τόπον, "a vacant space."

See also such prepositional phrases as BGU IV. 1141⁹ (B.C. 13) εἰς ἐνφα[ν]ιστοῦ τόπον με ἔχειν, which is practically = εἰς ἐνφαντιστήν: similarly in Mt 21⁴⁶ εἰς προφήτην may be written εἰς προφήτου τόπον. P Par 47¹⁶ (c. B.C. 153) (as read UPZ i. p. 332) γίνωσκε ὅτι πιράσεται ὁ δραπέ[δ]ης μὴ ἀφῖναι ἡμᾶς ἐπὶ τῶν τόπων ἶναι ("an Ort und Stelle zu sein," Wilcken), P Tebt II. 289⁶ (A.D. 23) πότερον ἐπὶ τόπων σε ἐάσω πράττοντά τι, "whether I shall leave you in employment where you are" (Edd.), P Grenf II. 56¹⁷ (A.D. 162–3) money paid ἐπὶ τὴν ἐπὶ τόπων δημοσίαν τράπε[ζαν], "to the local public bank," and so P Tebt II. 294¹⁶ (A.D. 146), P Oxy VIII. 1120² (early iii A.D.) περὶ ἧς (sc. ὕβρεως) πέπονθεν ἐπὶ τόπων, "concerning the outrage suffered at his abode" (Ed.), ib. XIV. 1630⁵ (A.D. 222 (?)) ἐπικουρήσας τοῖς κατὰ τόπον γεωργοῖς τά τε σπέρματα [καὶ τὰς δαπάνας], "providing the local cultivators with both seed and expenses" (Edd.), ib. VII. 1068¹¹ (iii/A.D.) ἐφ' ᾧ μηδὶς ἐνοχλήσῃ αὐτῷ (l. αὐτοῖς) κατὰ τόπον, "to the intent that no one in the neighbourhood should trouble them (?)" (Ed.), and ib. VIII. 1162² (iv/A.D.) τοῖς κατὰ τόπον συνλιτουργοῖ[ς] πρεσβυτ[έ]ροις, "to the pres-

byters who share the local service" (Ed.).　For 1 Cor 14¹⁶
see G. H. Whitaker, *JTS* xxii. (1921), p. 268.

(3) metaph. "condition," as in Heb 12¹⁷: P Michigan
Inv. No. 4528¹⁰ (*c.* A.D. 200) ἐγὼ γὰρ εἰς καλὸν τόπον ἦλθον,
a soldier to his mother.　We may also note BGU I. 27¹¹
(ii/A.D.) (*Selections*, p. 101) where a ship-master writing
from Rome to his brother says, παρεδέξατο ἡμᾶς ὁ τόπος ὡς
ὁ θεὸς ἤθελεν.　Ghedini (*Lettere*, p. 51) commenting on the
passage suggests that the letter may be Christian, and τόπος
a term borrowed from pagan usage, denoting "la *schola
collegi*, il centro delle riunioni dei Christiani."　See further
ib. p. 127 f., *Aegyptus* ii. (1921), p. 337 f., *ib.* viii. (1927),
p. 175 (with reference to P Oxy XII. 1402¹¹ (iii/iv A.D.),
and for a different view Wilcken *Archiv* i. p. 436, iv.
p. 208 f., where τόπος is interpreted as *collegium navi-
cularioum* at Rome, and ὁ θεός as the god of the seamen's
guild.　According to Philo *de Somn.* i. 63 (ed. Wendland)—
ὁ θεὸς καλεῖται τόπος τῷ περιέχειν μὲν τὰ ὅλα.

τοσοῦτος

(1) of size, quantity, "so great," "so large": P Hib I.
51⁶ (B.C. 245) τοσοῦτο γὰρ ἔκκειται ἐν βασιλικοῦ, "for that
is the rate published by the government" (Ed.), P Ryl II.
96⁷ (A.D. 117-8) τοσοῦτο τέλεσμα οὐ βαστάζει, "it (*sc.*
crown-land) does not bear so great a charge" (Ed.), and
in a more general sense P Amh II. 141¹⁷ (A.D. 350) ἐπιδίδωμι . . . τάδε τὰ βιβλία [μο]υ τοσοῦτο μαρτυραμένη, "I
present this my petition bearing witness to the facts" (Ed.).

(2) of time, "so long": P Lond 42²³ (B.C. 168) (= I.
p. 30, *Selections* p. 10) τοσούτου χρόνου ἐπιγεγονότος, "so
long a time having elapsed," P Tebt II. 302¹⁸ (A.D. 71-2)
τ]οσούτων ἐτῶν, "for so many years," P Oxy III. 530⁹
(ii/A.D.) ἐπὶ μάτη[ν] δὲ τῶι τοῦ Παυσιρίωνος τοσοῦτον
χρόνον προσκαρτερῶ, "and that I have so long been
engaged with Pausirion's business to no purpose" (Ed.).

(3) The following prepositional phrases may be cited—
P Oxy XII. 1481² (early ii/A.D.) γεινώσκειν σ[ε] θέλω ὅτι
διὰ τοσούτου χρόνου οὐκ ἀπέσταλκά σοι ἐπιστόλιον διότι
. . ., "I would have you know that the reason why I have
been such a long time without sending you a letter is that
. . .": P Petr II. 11(2)⁴ (mid. iii/B.C.) (= Witkowski²,
p. 6) ἵνα ἐκ τοσούτου φέρωμεν τὴν εἰκοστήν: BGU IV. 1095¹³
(A.D. 57) πίθομαι γὰρ ὅτι ἐν τωσούτω με[τέ]πεμψαι(= — ψε)
ὁ Πτολεμαῖος, P Oxy VI. 940⁵ (v/A.D.) ἐν τοσούτῳ γράφεις
μοι, "meanwhile write to me"; BGU II. 665⁶ (i/A.D.)
(see *Berichtigungen*, p. 59) ἐπὶ τοσούτον (for ἐν τοσούτῳ)
ἔμε[λ]λε π]έμψιν Εὔπλουν, "meanwhile he will send
Euplous," P Tebt II. 304⁹ (A.D. 167-8) ἀητ[= δ]ίαν
συ<ν>ήψαν ἐπὶ τοσ[σ]οῦτον ὥστε μετὰ ξύλων ἐσπηδῆσαι,
"they picked a quarrel, going so far as to rush in with
staves" (Ed.), and the late P Lond 1075¹⁸ (vii/A.D.) (= III.
p. 282) πεπληροφόρημαι (cf. Rom 4²¹, *al.*) γὰρ σαφῶς ὅτι
οὐ θέλετε αὐτὸν εἶναι ἐπὶ τοσοῦτον ἀνεγκέφαλον, "for I am
fully persuaded that you do not wish him to be so brainless."

τότε,

"then," "at that time": cf. P Par 47¹³ (B.C. 152-1)
(= *UPZ* i. p. 332) κἄ[[ια]] ἴδης ὅτι μέλλομεν σωθῆναι, τότε
βαπτιζώμεθα, "if you have seen (in a dream) that we are

about to be saved, (just) then we are immersed in trouble,"
and P Oxy VI. 939²² (iv/A.D.) εἰ μὴ ἐπινόσως ἐσχήκει τὸ
σωμάτιον τότε ὁ υἱὸς Ἀθανάσιος, αὐτὸν ἂν ἀπέστειλα πρὸς
σέ, "if my son Athanasius had not then been ailing, I should
have sent him to you" (Ed.).

With 2 Pet 3⁶ ὁ τότε κόσμος (Vg *ille tunc mundus*), cf.
P Oxy X. 1273³⁰ (A.D. 200) τῆς τότε ἐσομένης αὐτῶν συντε-
μήσεως, "at the valuation that will then be made of them,"
and P Hamb I. 21⁹ (A.D. 315) ἐπὶ τοῦ τότε καιροῦ.　For
τότε little more than a connecting particle, cf. P Lond 807¹¹
(A.D. 84) (= III. p. 206) λαογραφίας τότε γὰρ ἐλασσωθεὶς
ὑπὸ τοῦ πρόοντος κωμογραμματέως ἐκ[ε]ῖνος μὲν [τ]ότε
ἐψεύσατο, and P Oxy XVII. 2116²¹ (A.D. 270).

The compd. ἔκτοτε occurs in PSI I. 104¹⁶ (ii/A.D.) ἔνθεν
ἔκτοτε ἄχρι τοῦ ῑ (ἔτους) ἐπεσχέθη: cf. the use of ἀπὸ τότε
in Mt 4¹⁷ *al.*, and in MGr (" since then ").

τουτέστι

= τοῦτ' ἔστι: P Flor II. 157¹ (iii/A.D.) εἰς τ[ὸ] ἔργον
ἐκεῖνο τὸ τῆς Θεω ξ'ενίδος, τουτέστιν τὸ τῆς ἄμμου ἀνελθεῖν,
P Oxy XII. 1424⁶ (*c.* A.D. 318) εἰς λειτουργίαν τῆς κώμης
Δωσιθέ[ο]υ, τουτέστιν εἰς ἀπαίτησιν στιχαρίων καὶ παλλίων,
"to a public office at the village of Dositheou, namely
the collectorship of tunics and cloaks" (Ed.), *ib.* 1593¹⁶
(iv/A.D.) ἀσπάζομαι τὸν πατέρα ἡμῶν, τουτέστιν σόν,
ἄδελφε, and from the inscrr. *Syll* 932 (= ³ 880)⁷⁰ (A.D. 202).

τράγος,

"a goat" (Heb 9¹² *al.*): P Hib I. 120³ (B.C. 250-40)
τῶν ὑπαρχουσῶν αἰγῶν καὶ τράγων, and P Frankf 5 *recto* ³⁴
(B.C. 242-1) ἐρίφους δύο, τράγον ἕνα.　Add *Preisigke* 285³
(Ptol.) ἥκω καὶ οἱ ὑπογεγραμμένοι κυνηγοὶ ἐπὶ τὴν θήραν
τῶν τράγων, and *ib.* 287³ (Ptol.).

τράπεζα,

(1) "a table," lit. "*four-footed* (table)": P Eleph 5¹²
(B.C. 284-3) τράπεζα ᾱ, PSI IV. 391⁴⁰ (B.C. 242-1)
τράπεζαν πυξίνην, "a table made of box-wood," *Chrest.* I.
11A³⁸ (B.C. 123) καὶ τούτων . . . συνκωθωνισθέντων καὶ
ἁλὸς [ἐπ]ὶ τραπέζης μεταξὺ ὄντων (*l.* ὄντος), and P Lond
46²⁰⁵ (iv/A.D.) (= I. p. 71) ἐπὶ παπυρίνης τραπέζης.

(2) From the "table" at which the money-changers sat,
τράπεζα came to mean "a bank," as in Mt 21¹², Lk 19²³
al.; P Eleph 27²³ (iii/B.C.) τετάγμεθα τὸ ἀργύριον καὶ τοὺς
τόκους ἐπὶ τὴν βασιλικὴν τράπεζαν, P Tebt II. 280² (B.C.
126) πέ(πτωκεν) ἐπὶ τὴν ἐν Κρο(κοδίλων) πό(λει) τρά-
(πεζαν) Ἡρακλείδει τρα πεζίτη ὥστε βασιλεῖ παρὰ
Σοκονώπιος . . . τέ(λος) τόπου ψιλο(ῦ) τοῦ ὄντος ἐν Τεβτύ-
(νει), "Sokonopis has paid into the bank at Crocodilopolis
to Heraclides the banker for the King the tax upon a vacant
space situated at Tebtunis" (Ed.), *ib.* 483 (A.D. 94) acknowledgment of a loan paid διὰ τῆς Ἀφροδισίου τραπέζης
Φανη[σί]ου, and P Tebt II. 204¹⁷ (A.D. 146) ἃς δραχμὰς)
κ[αὶ] διαγράψω κυρωθεὶς ἐπὶ τὴν ἐπὶ τόπων δημοσίαν
τράπεζαν τοῖς συνήθεσι προθεσμίαις, "which (drachmae I
will, as soon as my appointment is ratified, pay into the
local public bank at the accustomed dates" (Ed.).　In P
Fay 96¹ (A.D. 122) a receipt is issued διὰ τῆς Σαραπίωνος
τραπέζης stating that a certain payment had been made.
As the payment was not in money but in kind (" oil "), this

has led to the conjecture by Preisigke (*Girowesen*, p. 222) that the **τράπεζα** may not have been an ordinary bank but a revenue-office (see Wilcken's note *ad l. Chrest.* I. p. 372).

(3) For **τράπεζα** = "nether-stone" of a mill, see P Ryl II. 167¹² (A.D. 39) μυλαῖον ἐνεργὸν ἐν ᾧ μύλοι Θηβαικοὶ τρεῖς σὺν κώπαις καὶ τραπέζαις, "a mill in full working order, containing 3 Theban mill-stones, with handles and nether-stones," and the other exx. collected by the editors *ad l.* In the Christian P Grenf II. 111¹⁰ (v/vi A.D.) (= *Chrest.* I. p. 161) τράπεζ(α) μαρμαρ(ᾶ) ᾱ. τράπεζα refers to "the slab of the altar which was supported by the τρίπους (line 11)": see the editors' note. MGr τράπεζ, "table"; τράπεζα, "altar-table": see Thumb *Handb.* p. 358 f.

τραπεζ(ε)ίτης,

"money-changer," "banker" (Mt 25²⁷) : P Eleph 10⁴ (B.C. 223–2) ἐπιλαβὼν παρὰ τῶν τραπεζιτῶν τῶν ἐν τοῖς ἱεροῖς τ[ὰ] πεπτωκ[ό]τα εἰς τὸ ἐν Ἀπόλλων[ος] πόλει τῆι μ]εγάληι ἱερόν, where, however, Wilcken thinks the reference is to treasury officials rather than bankers (see *Chrest.* I. p. 275), P Oxy I. 50¹ (a receipt—A.D. 100) Θέων καὶ οἱ μέ[τοχοι] τρα(πεζῖται) τῷ ἀγο(ρανόμῳ) χαίρειν. τέτακ(ται) . . ., ib. X. 1284⁶ (A.D. 250) δημ[ο]σίων τραπ(ζιτῶν), "public bankers," and ib. 1253¹⁰ (iv/A.D.) certain δοθέντα αὐτοῖς διὰ Σαραπίωνος Εὐδαίμονος γενομ[ένου] τραπεζ[του], "paid through Sarapion son of Eudaemon, formerly banker."

τραῦμα,

"a wound" : *Ostr* 1150⁵ (B.C. 134) τὸ τραῦμα ὃ ἔχεις οὐ πεποίκαμέν (*l.* πεποιήκαμεν) σοι, PSI V. 455¹³ (A.D. 178) ἔχοντα ἐπὶ τῆς κεφαλῆς τραύματα τρία, P Oxy I. 52¹⁷ (A.D. 325) τ]οῦ δεξιοῦ γονατίου τραύματος, and from the inscrr. *Syll*³ 528¹⁰ (B.C. 221–19) πλείους ἐκ τ[ῶν] τραυμάτων ἀρρωστίαις . . . π[εριπε]σεῖν. In the NT the word is found only in Lk 10³⁴ (elsewhere πληγή is employed) : see Hobart, p. 28.

τραυματίζω,

"I wound" (Lk 20¹², Ac 19¹⁶) : P Petr III. 28 (*e*)⁷ (B.C. 260) Παγχοὴν ἐτραυμάτισα[ν, P Tebt I. 39³¹ (B.C. 114) ἐτραυμάτισαν τὴν γυναῖκά μου εἰς τὴν δεξιὰν χεῖρα, and P Par 68¹·⁹ (Rom.) τοὺς ἁρπασθέντ]ας ἐτραυμάτισαν.

An adj. **τραυματιαῖος**, not in LS⁸, is found in P Fay 108¹⁴ (*c.* A.D. 171) τραυματιαῖον ἐποίησαν τὸν [Πασίω]να, and PSI IV. 313¹² (iii/iv A.D.) τραυματιέόν μαι κατέστησε[ν. For ἄτρωτος, "inviolate," see P Lond 77⁵⁶ (end vi/A.D.) (= I. p. 234, *Chrest.* II. p. 372) εἴθ᾽ οὕτως ἐπάναγκες ἐμμεῖναι πᾶσι τοῖς ἐγγεγραμμένοις ταύτῃ τῇ ἀτρώτῳ διαθήκῃ.

τραχηλίζω

occurs in P Petr II. 15 (1) (*a*)² (B.C. 241–239) (= III 45 (3)²) εἰ δὲ μή, πάλι τραχηλιοῦσι ἐν τ[ῷ]ι β[. . . . .] ναύτας. πρότερον δὲ ἕκαστος τῶν λ[α]ῶν . . ., if we may separate Mahaffy's strange compound παλιτραχηλιοῦσι. The passage is peculiarly tantalizing from the gaps which prevent our getting the meaning of the verb, clearly used in a tropical sense.

In its only occurrence in the NT (Heb 4¹³) **τετραχηλισμένα** can only mean "laid open," "exposed," "open" (Vg *aperta*; Hesych. πεφανερωμένα), but the origin of the metaphor is very doubtful. Moffatt (*ICC Heb ad l.*) suggests "the practice of exposing an offender's face by pushing his head back," Souter (*Lex. s.v.*), with greater probability, prefers "the bending back of the head in sacrifice so as to expose the neck," like the Homeric αὐερύω (*Il.* i. 459).

The verb is found in Teles (ed. Hense) pp. 10⁹, 50⁹ : see also Philo *de Cherub.* 78 (ed. Cohn) πᾶσι τοῖς ἐπιτρέχουσι καὶ τραχηλίζουσι δεινοῖς ὑποβεβλημένος, and the compd. ἐκτραχηλίζω in *V. Leg. Alleg.* iii. 109, *Quod det. pot.* 19.

τράχηλος,

"neck" : cf. P Hal 1. 11¹¹ (B.C. 238) οὐλὴ τ]ραχήλωι κάτωι (for form see Mayser *Gr.* i. p. 136), P Tebt II. 385³ (A.D. 117) οὐλὴ τραχήλωι ἐξ ἀρισ[τ]ε[ρῶν, and P Par 18 *bis*⁶ (Rom.) dispatch of a corpse ἔχων (*l.* ἔχον) τάβλαν κατὰ τοῦ τραχήλου.

For Rom 16⁴ οἵτινες ὑπὲρ τῆς ψυχῆς μου τὸν ἑαυτῶν τράχηλον ὑπέθηκαν, Deissmann (*LAE*², p. 117 f.) finds an interesting parallel in a Herculaneum papyrus written after B.C. 150 (see *Berl. Sitzungsberichte*, 1900, p. 951), where it is said of the Epicurean Philonides—ὑπὲρ?] τοῦ μάλιστ᾽ ἀγαπωμένου τῶν ἀναγκαίων ἢ τῶν φίλων παραβάλοι ἂν ἑτοίμως τὸν τράχηλον, "for?] the most beloved of his relatives or friends he would readily stake his neck" (for the thought cf. also Rom 5⁷).

τραχύς,

"rough." For this adj., confined in the NT to Lk 3⁵ LXX, Ac 27²⁹, cf. the medical prescription, P Tebt II. 273 (ii/iii A.D.), which is headed—πρὸς τὰ τρ[α]χέα βλέφα[ρ]α (see the introd.). Other exx. are PSI V. 535²⁰ (iii/B.C.) σπόγγοι τραχεῖς, P Cairo Zen I. 50085³ (B.C. 257) χῆμαι λεῖαι καὶ τραχεῖαι, "smooth and rough cockles," and *Syll* 540 (=³ 972)⁷ (B.C. 175–172) ξοῖδος . . . τραχείας. The adj. is applied to a person in Vett. Val. p. 104¹¹, τραχεῖα μήτηρ.

τρεῖς.

The phraseology of such passages as Mk 6⁷ (δύο δύο),³⁹ (συμπόσια συμπόσια) and ⁴⁰ (πρασιαὶ πρασιαί) has hitherto been generally put down to Hebraistic influence. But apart from the fact that the idiom is found in classical Greek (Soph. *Fragm.* 201 μίαν μίαν, Aesch. *Persae* 980 μυρία μυρία), and the LXX (Gen 7¹⁵ δύο δύο, *al.*) and survives in MGr (cf. Thumb *Hellen.* p. 128, *Handb.* § 132), it can now be paralleled from the papyri. A good ex. is P Oxy I. 121¹⁹ (iii/A.D.) τοὺς κλάδους ἕνικον (*l.* ἔνεγκον) εἰς τὴν ὁδὸν πάντα (*l.* πάντας) εἵνα δήσῃ τρία τρία κὲ (*l.* καὶ) ἑλκύσῃ, "carry all the branches into the road and have them tied together by threes and dragged along" (Edd.) : cf. ib. VI. 886¹⁹ (iii/A.D.) ἔρε (*l.* αἶρε) κατὰ δύο δύο, "lift up (the leaves) two by two" (the editors compare Lk 10¹), and ib. 940⁶ (v/A.D.) ἔχε ἐγγὺς σοῦ μίαν μίαν, "keep him at hand together with you" (*una*: see the editors' note). But while this is true, the independence of Hebrew must not be carried too far. According to Robertson *Gr.* p. 284, "it is a vernacular idiom which was given fresh impetus from the Hebrew idiom." See the useful summary in Meecham *Letters*, p. 85, and cf. Headlam's note to Herodas IV. 61 θερμὰ θερμὰ πηδεῦσαι.

In P Cairo Zen II. 59236³ (B.C. 254 or 253) a petitioner complains that, in fixing his vineyard assessment, the officials had taken as a basis the average yield ἐκ τριῶν ἐτῶν, and not ἐκ δύο ἐτῶν as in his father's time. For the parenthetic nom. ἡμέραι τρεῖς in Mk 8², cf. P Oxy XIV. 1764¹ (iii/A.D.) ἐπεὶ πολ[λ]αὶ ἡμέραι προσκαρτεροῦμεν Φιλέᾳ : see also *s.v.* ἡμέρα and Meisterhans *Gr.* p. 203.

τρέμω,

"tremble" (Mk 5³³, *al.*): P Fay 124²⁷ (ii/A.D.) μὴ γὰρ ὑπολάβῃς τὴ[ἡ]ν μητέραν σου περὶ τούτων [τ]ρέμειν, "do not suppose that your mother has any alarm about this course" (Edd.): cf. Wünsch *AF* p. 19¹⁴ (iii/A.D.) εἴπω σοι καὶ τὸ ἀληθινὸν ὄνομα ὃ τρέμει Τάρταρα.

τρέφω,

"nourish," "feed." In P Eleph 2¹¹ (B.C. 285–4) provision is made for the maintenance of parents by their sons—τρεφέτωσαν αὐτοὺς οἱ υἱεῖς πάντες κοινῆι. Cf. PSI VI. 596¹ (iii B.C.) ἀφ' οὗ τε γεγόναμεν ἐν Φιλαδελφέαι σὺ ἡμᾶς τέτρεφας, *ib.* 604¹² (iii/B.C.) τέ[?]τροφα τοὺς ἵππους, P Oxy II. 275¹⁴ (contract of apprenticeship—A.D. 66) τοῦ παιδὸς τρεφομένου καὶ ἱματι[σ]ζομένου ἐπὶ τὸν ὅλον χρόνον, "the boy is to be fed and clothed during the whole period," *ib.* VI. 908²⁴ (A.D. 199) τρεφόντων ὑμῶν τὰ [κ]τήνη χόρτῳ τε καὶ κριθῇ, and P Lips I. 28¹⁸ (deed of adoption—A.D. 381) ὅνπερ θρέψω καὶ ἱματίζω (*l.* ἱματίσω) εὐγενῶς καὶ γνησίως ὡς υἱὸν γνήσιον καὶ φυσικὸν ὡς ἐξ ἐ[μ]οῦ γενόμενον. For the meaning "give suck," as in Lk 23²⁹, see P Ryl II. 178⁵ (agreement with a nurse—early i/A.D.) τοῦτο θρέψει ἐπὶ τὸν ἐνλείψοντα χρόνον, "she shall nurse it for the rest of the time." In P Oxy XII. 1415²² (date iii/A.D.) μέτριός εἰμι, παρὰ πατρὶ τρέφομα[ι, the editors render, "I am a man of moderate means, I live in my father's house."

τρέχω

in the lit. sense "run" occurs in a criminal process of an Alexandrian gymnasiarch before the Emperor Commodus, P Oxy I. 33 *verso* iii. 12 (= *Chrest.* I. p. 35) ὁ ἡβδ[κατο]ς εὐθὺς δραμὼν παρέθετο [τῷ] κυρίῳ λέγων, "κύριε, κάθῃ, Ῥωμαῖοι γονγύζο[υσ]ι," "the veteran forthwith ran and told his lord, saying, 'Lord, while you are sitting in judgment, the Romans are murmuring.'" The same document shows τρέχω in its derived sense "strive"—i. 11 τρέχε, τέκνον, τελεύτα. κλέος σοί ἐστιν ὑπὲρ τῆς γλυκυτάτης σου πατρίδος τελευτῆσαι, "onward, my son, to death, it is a glory for you to die for your beloved country" (Edd.). See also P Lond 130⁷⁷ (horoscope—i/ii A.D.) (= I. p. 135) μοίρας ἔτρεχε δεκατρεῖς, and *Menandrea* p. 73¹⁶⁷ ἵν' ἀναπηδήσας τρέχῃ. "that he might jump up and come at a run." We may add a wooden tablet, apparently for school use, published in *Mél. Nicole* p. 181 (= *Kaibel Praef.* p. xxii. 117(*b*)) in which the lines occur (with added accents)—

ᾧ μὴ δέδωκεν ἡ τύχη κοιμωμένῳ.
μάτην δραμεῖται, κἂν ὑπὲρ Λάδαν δράμῃ.

τρῆμα,

"opening," "hole," hence "eye" of a needle in Mt 19²⁴ (*v.l.* τρυπήματος), Lk 18²⁵. To the exx. of the word in medical writers given by Hobart p. 60, we may add the physiological fragment P Ryl I. 21 fragm. 3 ⁵ (i/B.C.) διὰ τῶν τρημάτων τῶν ἐν τῶι ἱερῶι ὀστῶι, and the parallel cited by Hunt P Berl A. iv. 1–2 διά τε τῶν] ἐν τῶι ἱερῶι ὀστῶι τρημάτων καὶ διὰ τῶν κοίλων τῶν ἐν τῷ ὀσφύι. The word also occurs in Aristeas 61 πάντες δ' ἦσαν διὰ τρημάτων κατειλημμένοι χρυσαῖς περόναις πρὸς τὴν ἀσφάλειαν, "and they (*sc.* precious stones) were all perforated and securely fastened to golden pins" (Thackeray). For the verb τετραίνω cf. *Syll* 540(= ³1072)⁷¹ (B.C. 175–172) τρήσας βαθύτερα καθαρμόσει. In Herodas III. 33 τετρημένη is used metaph. of slowness, "dribbles out": see Headlam's note.

τριάκοντα,

"thirty": P Fay 116¹ (A.D. 104) εὖ οὖν] ποιήσας σκέψῃ φάρο[υς] τριάκοντα, "please look out thirty fish(?)." A neo-Greek form τριάντα occurs in P Oxy XVI. 1874⁷ (vi/A.D.) τὰ τριάντα πέντε φορτία, "the thirty-five burdens" (see the editors' note). For τριακάς see P Oxy XVII. 2109⁴² (A.D. 261) ἀποδώσω τὸ ἐνοίκιον κατὰ μῆνα τριακάδι ἀνυπερθέτως, "I will pay the rent on the 30th of each month without delay."

τρίβολος,

"thistle," Mt 7¹⁶, Heb 6⁸. In his comment on the latter passage (*ICC ad l.*) Moffatt recalls Philo *Leg. Alleg.* 250 (ed. Cohn), where with reference to Gen 3¹⁸ Philo plays with the derivation of the word (like "trefoil")—ἕκαστον δὲ τῶν παθῶν τριβόλια εἴρηκεν, ἐπειδὴ τριττά ἐστιν, αὐτό τε καὶ τὸ ποιητικὸν καὶ τὸ ἐκ τούτων ἀποτέλεσμα.

τρίβος,

"a beaten track," "a path" (Mt 3³ *al.*, cf. Sir 2²) occurs in CPR I. 42¹⁴ (ἀρούρας δ ἐκ λιβὸς τρίβου, "4 arourae to the west of the path." See also the metrical inscr. of B.C. 145–116, *Archiv* i. p. 221²¹—

καὶ σοὶ δ' εὐοδίης τρίβον ὄλβιον εὔχομαι εἶναι,
πρός γ' ἔτι καὶ τέκνοις σοῖσι φιλοφροσύνοις.

For the verb τρίβω, see P Par 49²² (before B.C. 161) (= *UPZ* i. p. 309) ὅπως λαβὼν παρ' ἐμοῦ ἐν Μέμφει σησάμου τέταρτον τρίψῃ μοι ἐν Μέμφει τρίμμα, P Oxy II. 234 ii. 16 (medical prescription—ii/iii A.D.) ῥοῶν κυτίνους μεμυκότας τρίψας, "pound some closed calices of pomegranates" (Edd.), *ib.* IX. 1222² (iv/A.D.) δὸς τῷ ἀδελφῷ . . . τὸ ἅλας τὸ ἀμ<μ>ωνιακὸν τὸ τετριμ<μ>ένον καὶ τὸ ἄτριπτον, "give your brother the salt of ammonia, both the pounded and the unpounded" (Edd.), and P Flor III. 378¹⁹ (v/A.D.?) τὰ ἱμάτιά μοι ἐτρίβη. See also Herodas V. 62 τοῖς σφυροῖσι τρίβοντα, "burnishing with your ancles" certain Achaean wares (a euphemism for "fetters": *sc.* πέδας).

τριετία,

"a period of three years" (Ac 20³¹): P Giss I. 58 ii. 17 (A.D. 116) πληροῦντες τ[ὸ]ν τριετίας [χρόν]ον, P Tebt II.

488 (account of a trial—A.D. 121–2) ἠ]ξίου πρὸ πόσου χρόνου οἰκοδομῆσαι; Ἱέραξ· πρὸ τριετίας, ib. 342²¹ (late ii/A.D.) ἐπὶ τὴν λοιπ(ὴν) (τριετίαν), "for the remaining period of three years," and P Amh II. 100⁷ (A.D. 198–211) τῆς ὅλης τριετίας. The adj. τριετής occurs in ib. 68¹¹ (late i/A.D.) τῶι μὲν τῆς ἀτελείας τριετεῖ χρόνῳ, and the verb τριετίζω ter in Gen 15⁹. See also P Oxy XVII. 2105³ (A.D. 147–8) τριετηρικὸ[ς] ἀγῶ[ν, "a triennial contest."

τρίζω.

In its only occurrence in the NT, Mk 9¹⁸, τρίζω is used transitively, τοὺς ὀδόντας τρίζειν. "to gnash or grind the teeth"; see Blass-Debrunner § 148. 1.

τρίμηνος,

"lasting three months" (Heb 11²³): cf. P Cairo Zen II. 59155⁶ (B.C. 256) κατάσπειρε τὸν τρίμηνον πυρόν, "sow the three-month wheat." For τρίμηνος used as a subst. see P Lond 18¹⁰ (B.C. 161) (= I. p. 23) ἀπὸ Φαμενὼθ ᾱ ἕως Παχὼν λ γίνονται τῆς τριμήνου ὀλυρῶν κδ (ἀρτάβαι): the editor compares Herod. ii. 124. Similar exx. are BGU VII. 1717⁵ (ii/iii A.D.) and PSI VI. 689⁵·²⁰ (v/A.D. ?).

τρίς,

"thrice." With Ac 10¹⁶, 11¹⁰, cf. P Osl I. 1²⁷³ (iv/A.D.) ἐπὶ τρὶς ἀναποδίζων. "thrice stepping backwards."

τρίστεγος,

"of three stories" (Ac 20⁹). To the ii/A.D. warrant for this word in P Oxy I. 99⁵ (A.D. 55) μέρος ἥμισυ τῆς ὑπαρχούσης αὐτῷ μητρικῆς οἰκία[ς] τριστέγου, "one half of a three-storeyed house inherited from his mother" (cf. ¹⁵), and ib. VIII. 1105⁹ (A.D. 81–96) μερῶν τριῶν ἀπὸ μερῶν πέντε οἰκίας τριστέκου (l. τριστέγου), "three-fifths of a three-storeyed house" (Ed.): add ib. I. 75¹⁸ (A.D. 129) and from A.D. 212, P Lond 1164(e)⁷ (= III. p. 160) οἰκίας τριστέγου. This last papyrus shows us the corresponding forms δίστεγος and μονόστεγος.

τρίτον.

See s.v. τρίτος.

τρίτος,

"the third": P Petr III. 28 verso (b)⁷ (iii/B.C.) ἐδραγματοκλέπτει τρίτος ὤν, "with two others, he stole sheaves in gleaning" (Edd.): cf UPZ i. 13²¹ and 77¹¹·²⁵ (B.C. 161) with Wilcken's notes.

Other exx. of the adj. are P Cairo Zen II. 59236³ (B.C. 254 or 253) ἐκ τριῶν ἐτῶν τὰ γενήματα λαμβάνοντες, τὸ τρίτον μέρος ἐπέγραφον, meaning "they took the average yield of the last three years as an assessment for future taxation" (see note), BGU IV. 1078¹¹ (A.D. 39) γείνωσκε δὲ ἡγεμόνα εἰσεληλυθότα τῇ τρίτῃ [κ]αὶ εἰκάδι, ib. II. 596¹⁶ (A.D. 84) ἔτους τρίτου, and P Oxy VIII. 1114²⁴ (A.D. 237) περὶ ὥραν τρίτην.

For τρίτον = "thirdly" (as in 1 Cor 12²⁸), see BGU II. 423¹⁵ (ii/A.D.) (= Selections, p. 91) πρῶτον . . . δεύτερον . . . τρ[ί]τον, and for τὸ τρίτον, "for the third time," as in Mk 14⁴¹, cf. P Lips I. 33ⁱⁱ·¹⁵ (A.D. 368). Prepositional phrases are P Oxy XIV. 1640⁷ (A.D. 252) ἐκτείσω σοι τοῦ

ὑπερπεσόντος χρόνου διάφορον ἐκ τρίτου, "I will forfeit to you for the overtime an extra payment at the rate of one third" (Edd.), and P Lips I. 9⁹ (A.D. 233) κοινῶς ἐξ ἴσου κατὰ τὸ τ[ρ]ίτον.

τρίχινος.

For σάκκος τρίχινος, "sackcloth of hair," as in Rev 6¹², see s.v. σάκκος, and add PSI V. 533⁷ (iii/B.C.) λόφους τριχίνους, and P Goodsp Cairo 30ˣˣˣⁱˣ·¹⁶ (accounts—A.D. 191–92) σάκκου τριχ[ίν]ου. See also Pelagia-Legenden p. 4²⁵ τὸ στῆθος αὐτοῦ τύπτων ὅλον τὸ τρίχινον αὐτοῦ ἐπλήρωσεν τῶν δακρύων.

τρόμος,

"trembling" (Mk 16⁸ al.) occurs in the mythological fragment PSI II. 135¹⁰ (i/ii A.D.) ὑπὸ τρόμου.

τροπή,

"change." The plur. τροπάς is found apparently with reference to the "turnings" of water-wheels for irrigation purposes in P Flor II. 167¹⁵ (iii/A.D.): cf. ib. 214¹² (A.D. 255) μίαν τροπήν. For the common meaning "solstice," θερινή and χειμερινή, see P Hib I. 27¹²⁰ (calendar—B.C. 301–240) ἡλίου τροπαὶ εἰς θέρος, cf. ²¹⁰, P Ryl I. 27⁵⁷·⁴⁵ (astronomical treatise—iii A.D.), Syll 870 (= ³1264)¹ (iv/B.C.) τροπα[ὶ] χειμεριναί, and Preisigke 358⁴·⁶ (sun-dial—iii B.C.) ἀπὸ χειμερινῶν δὲ τροπῶν [ἐ]πὶ θερινὰς τροπὰς μεθιστάμενο[ν τ]ὸ ἄκρον τῆς σκιᾶς.

The verb τρέπω does not occur in the NT, but we may compare P Oxy VI. 935³ (iii/A.D.) θεῶν συνλαμβανόντων ἡ ἀδελφή ἐπὶ τ[ὸ] κομψότερον ἐτράπη, "with the assistance of heaven our sister has taken a turn for the better" (Edd.) with Jn 4⁵²: see also the Christian letter ib. 939¹⁷ (iv/A.D.) (= Selections. p. 129), where a dependent informs his master regarding his mistress—ἐπὶ τ]ὸ ῥᾷον ἔδοξεν τετράφθαι, "she seemed to have taken a turn for the better."

τρόπος,

"manner," "way." With the adverbial phrase καθ' ὃν τρόπον in Ac 15¹¹, 27²⁵, cf. the letter of the prodigal son BGU III. 846¹² (ii/A.D.) (= LAE², p. 187, Selections, p. 94) πεπαίδδευμαι καθ' ὃν δὶ τρόπον, where, if δι = δή, the meaning would be "punished I have been in any case." Wilcken, however, followed by Deissmann, suggests δι = δεῖ, "punished I have been as I ought"; cf. P Oxy II. 237ᵛⁱⁱⁱ·²⁹ (A.D. 186) καθ' ὃν ἔδει τρόπον. Similar phrases are P Frankf 1⁸¹ (B.C. 214–213) κ[αθ' ὅντ]ινοῦν τρόπον, P Grenf II. 31¹⁶ (B.C. 104) μὴ ἐπικαλεῖν περὶ τοῦ μέρους δανείου τρόπον μηδενί, P Ryl II. 229⁹ (A.D. 38) ἐκ παντὸς τρόπου, P Oxy II. 295¹³ (A.D. 77) κατὰ μηδένα τρόπον, ib. 286¹¹ (A.D. 82) κατὰ πάντα τρόπον (cf. Rom 3²), P Fay 21¹² (A.D. 134) ἄλλῳ ὁτῳδήτινι τρόπῳ, "any other way whatsoever" (Edd.), and P Oxy XVII. 2133¹⁶ (late iii/A.D.) καθ' ὁνδήποτ' οὖν τρόπον.

Michel 545⁷ (ii/B.C.) gives a good ex. of τρόπος = "manner of life," as in Heb 13⁵, if we can trust the supplement, ζηλωτὴς δὲ γινόμενος τῶν ἀρίστων συνῳκείου τὸν μὲν [τρό]πον ἀρετῇ καὶ σωφροσύνῃ, τό τε ἦθος κο[σ]μιότητι καὶ εὐσ[χη]μοσύνῃ: cf. also IG XII. 7 408⁸ ἤθους κοσμιότητι καὶ τρόπων ἐπιεικείᾳ.

τροποφορέω.

For this verb which is read in Ac 13[18] from LXX Deut 1[31] B* = "bear another's manner," cf. Cic. *ad Att.* xiii. 29. 2 τὸν τῦφόν μου, πρὸς θεῶν, τροποφόρησον. See *s.v.* τροφοφορέω.

τροφή.

"nourishment," "food" (Mt 3[4] *et saepe*) : cf. P Petr III. 46 (4)[3] (Ptol.) τῆς εἰς τὴν τροφὴν τῶν μόσχων ὀλύρας, "rye for the food of calves," P Tebt I. 56[8] (*c.* B.C. 130–121) οὐκ ἔχομεν ἕως τῆς τροφῆς τῶν κτηνῶν ἡμῶν, "we have not so much as food for our cattle" (Edd.), P Ryl II. 229[12] (A.D. 38) περὶ τῆς τροφῆς τῶν χοιριδίω ν, cf. [23], P Fay 115[5] (A.D. 101) ἀγόρασον ἡμῖν δύωι συγγενῆ χυρίδια εἰς τροφὴν εἰς ὕ(= οἶ)κον, "buy us two pigs of a litter to keep at the house" (Edd.), P Oxy IV. 705[7ª] (A.D. 210–20) εἰς συνωνὴν χ[όρτ]ου ἡ πρόσοδος κατατεθήσεται εἰς τροφὰς καὶ δ[απά]νας . . . , "for the purchase of hay, the revenue of which shall be devoted to the maintenance and support . . ." (Edd.), P Tebt II. 600[4] (iii/A.D.) ἀφ᾽ ὧν | ἀναλίσκομεν εἰς τροφὰς καὶ θυσίας, P Oxy VI. 938[2] (iii/iv A.D.) cited *s.v.* ἐνεδρεύω, and BGU IV. 1024[vii. 16] (iv/v A.D.) τῆς θυγατρός μου [τ]ελευτησάσης, ἀπεστερήθην τῶν τροφῶν, "when my daughter died, I was deprived of my means of support."

Ἡ τροφεία (not in LS[8]) in the same sense occurs frequently in the nursing-contracts BGU IV. 1058. 1106 *al.* (B.C. 13), and for τὰ τροφεῖα in a similar connexion see *ib.* I. 297[12] (A.D. 50) where a nurse acknowledges that she has received τὰ τροφεῖα καὶ τὰ ἔλαια καὶ τὸν ἱματισμὸν καὶ τἆλλα ὅσα καθήκει δίδοσθαι τροφῷ.

Τρόφιμος.

"Trophimus" (Ac 20[4] *al.*), as a proper name, occurs in P Oxy VIII. 1160[2] (late iii/iv A.D.) κυρίῳ μου πατρὶ Ὠριγένης Τρόφιμος πολλὰ χαίρειν, and in the inscrr. *Magn* 122 (*b*)[5] (not later than iv/A.D.), *PAS* ii. 38[69], *al.*

The word in its sense of "foster-child" may be illustrated from P Oxy X. 1284[12] (A.D. 250) ἀπὸ τῆς ἑαυτοῦ τροφίμ[ου] μη τρός, "from his foster-child's mother," *ib.* VI. 903[3] (iv/A.D.) ἅμα τῶν τροφίμ[ω]ν μου, "along with my foster-daughters." For ὁ τρόφιμος (as frequently in comedy), "the young heir," see Menander Ἐπιτρέπ. 100 : cf. *Fragm.* 531[1] where there is a *v.l.* Τρόφιμε.

τροφός.

For ἡ τροφός, which Paul uses with such effect in 1 Thess 2[7] (cf. LXX Gen 35[8], *al.*), note P Lond 951 *verso*[4] (late iii/A.D.) (= III. p. 213) where, with reference to a newly arrived infant the father-in-law or mother-in-law decrees—τ[ὸ] βρέφος ἐχέτω τροφόν· ἐγὼ γὰρ οὐκ ἐπιτ[ρέ]πω τῇ θυγατρί μου θηλάζειν. Cf. P Flor II. 179[2] (A.D. 263) Ἡραΐδι γενομένη τροφῷ ἀπόλυσον οἴνου δίχωρα δύο, and from the inscrr. *BCH* xviii. (1894). p. 145 (B.C. 240).

In *Kaibel* 247[7] (i/ii A.D.) τροφός = μήτηρ, but in *Pelagia-Legenden* p. 23[18] ἡ δὲ Πελαγία κάτω κύψασα ἐχωρίσθη τῆς ἑαυτοῦ τροφοῦ, the meaning must be simply "nurse" from the contrasted μήτηρ in the next line.

For a good ex. of a συγγραφὴ τροφῖτις or a contract entered into with the nurse (cf. *Archiv* i. p. 123) to supply her with the necessary τροφεῖα, see BGU IV. 1106 and the

documents which follow : also P Oxy I. 37[i. 16] (A.D. 49) (= *Selections*, p. 49) ἐγένετο ἐνθάδε ἡ τροφεῖτις εἰς υἱὸν (cf. Ac 7[21], Heb 1[5]) τοῦ Πεσούριος. τοῦ πρώτου ἐνιαυτοῦ ἀπέλαβεν τὰ τροφεῖα.

The Hellenistic τροφέω, which Phrynichus (ed. Lobeck, p. 580) views with such suspicion, is found in BGU III. 859[4] (ii/A.D.) ἐτρόφησεν καὶ ἐτιθήνησεν ἡ τοῦ Ἀμμωνίου δούλη Δημητροῦς, and [22] (cf. Radermacher *Gr.* p. 84 f.).

τροφοφορέω.

"bear like a nurse," takes the place of τροποφορέω (*q.v.*) in Ac 13[18], following LXX Deut 1[31] B*: but cf. Blass *ad* Ac *l.*—"non video quomodo formari potuerit τροφοφ."

τροχός.

"a wheel" (Jas 3[6] : see Hort *Comm. ad l.*, Field *Notes*, p. 237) : cf. P Oxy X. 1202[13] (A.D. 30) τὸν τροχὸν τῆς μηχανῆς, "the wheel of the machine," P Ryl II. 228[11] (ii/A.D.) ὄργανο(ν) τροχ οῦ. τὸ εἰς κόπτειν, "machinery of the wheel for cutting" (Edd.), P Flor II. 218[10] (A.D. 257) εἰς κατασκευὴν τροχοῦ ἑνὸς τοῦ . . κάρνου, "for the construction of one wheel of the car," P Oxy XII. 1475[16] (A.D. 267) ὁ τροχὸς ὁμοίως συνερευκὼς ἐκ μέρου[ς]ς. "the water-wheel likewise partly in disrepair" (Edd.), and P Lond 121[67] (a spell—iii A.D.) (= I. p. 112) λαβὼν πηλὸν ἀπὸ τροχοῦ [κε]ραμικοῦ μίξον . . .

For the verb τροχάζω, which is condemned by the Atticists (Lob. *Phryn.* p. 582 f.), cf. Preisigke 5748[6] (Christian) ἔσχον . . παρὰ σοῦ . . τὰς ἀννόνας ἃς τροχάζω ὑπὲρ τοῦ σοῦ μέρους, and for τροχίσκος *ib.* 5307[1] (Byz.). Τροχιλλέα or τροχελλέα, the "reel" of a mill occurs in BGU IV. 1116[24] (B.C. 13) μύλωι τε καὶ τροχιλλέα, and P Oxy III. 502[37] (A.D. 164) τοῦ προκειμένου φρέατος τροχελλέαν σὺν σχοινίῳ καινῷ, "the reel of the aforesaid well provided with a new rope" (Edd.).

τρύβλιον.

"bowl" rather than "dish" (AV. RV.) Mt 26[23], Mk 14[20], and LXX Numb 7[13] *al.* The word is found in Aristoph., e.g. *Ach.* 278 εἰρήνης ῥοφήσει τρύβλιον, and Alexis fr. 142[2. 4] (in a medical prescription).

τρυγάω.

"gather in " the crop (Lk 6[44], Rev 14[18 f]) : cf. P Petr II. 40 (*b*)[3] (iii/B.C.) γίνωσκέ με τρυγήσοντα τῆι θ τοῦ Παυνι, "take notice that I shall have my vintage on the 9th of Payni" (Edd.), PSI IV. 345[2] (B.C. 256-5) τρυγᾶν μέλλουσιν τῆι κ̅ϛ̅, P Ryl II. 130[10] (A.D. 31) ἐτρύγησαν ἐκ τῶν καρπῶν οὐκ ὀλίγην ἐλᾶν, "they gathered of the fruits a quantity of olives" (Edd.), P Flor II. 236[9] (A.D. 267) ἐπιμελῶς οὖν τρυγᾶτε, and P Oxy VI. 940[3] (v/A.D.) ἵνα μὴ δόξωμεν διώκειν τοὺς ἄλλους τοὺς μήπω τρυγήσαντας, "that we may not seem to press hardly upon the others who have not yet gathered the grapes" (Edd.).

For τρυγέω, see the late P Oxy XVI. 1859[4] (vi/vii A.D.) ἤρξαντο τρυγεῖν τὴν ἄμπελον αὐτῶν : for τρύγη, see P Ryl II. 157[18] (A.D. 135) πρ[ὸ]ς μόνας τὰς ἡμ[έ]ρας τῆς τρύγης, "for the days of the vintage only," P Fay 133[4] (iv/A.D.) ἵνα τὴν διαταγὴν τῆς τρύγης ποιήσηται, "that he may make arrangements about the vintage": for τρυγία, "new, raw wine," see BGU II. 417⁹ (ii/iii A.D.) τρυγία χρῶμαι: for τρύγησις, see PSI IV. 434 *verso* (B.C. 261–0), *ib.* VII. 807³⁷ (A.D. 280); and for τρυγητικός, see P Strass I. 40³⁹ (A.D. 569) ἑορτικὰ καὶ τρυγητικά. In MGr τρυγητής, "reaper," is popularly used for the month of September (Thumb *Handb.* p. 359).

τρυγών,

"turtle-dove" (Lk 2²⁴). In Aristeas 145 mention is made of περιστεραὶ τρυγόνες as winged creatures which may be eaten.

τρυμαλιά,

a LXX word denoting a "hole" or "perforation" in a rock (e.g. Judg 6²), is employed by Mk in the proverbial saying, 10²⁵: Mt (19²⁴) and Lk (18²⁵) substitute τρῆμα with τρύπημα as a *v.l.* in Mt (D Lω).

Τρύφαινα.

It is worth noting that this proper name, which is of interest in the early history of the Christian Church (Rom 16¹², *Acts of Paul and Thecla*; cf. Lightfoot *Philippians,* p. 173 f.) is found in a i/A.D. list of names belonging apparently to Crocodilopolis, P Lond 604B²³⁷ (c. A.D. 47) (= III. p. 84): it also occurs of three different persons in the Alexandrian papyri from the age of Augustus (BGU IV. 1105²·³, 1110⁷, 1162¹⁶): see further P Oxy II. 320 (A.D. 59), P Fay 40⁴ (A.D. 138), P Ryl II. 111⁵ (A.D. 101), and *ib.* 222⁶ (ii/A.D.).

The corresponding masculine name Τρύφων is also very common: e.g. P Oxy VIII. 1132⁴ (c. A.D. 162): it is interesting to observe that in BGU IV. 1008⁷ and 1140² (Augustus) it is the name of a Jew, as in Justin's Dialogue.

τρυφάω,

"live a luxurious life," occurs in the NT only in Jas 5⁵. The word appears on the left-hand margin of P Lond 973*b* (iii/A.D.) (= III. p. 213) —ν καὶ τρυφᾶν. Cf. the sepulchral epitaph *Kaibel* 362⁴⁴ (ii/iii A.D.)—

taῦτα τοῖς φίλοις λέγω·
παῖσον, τρύφησον, ζῆσον· ἀποθανεῖν σε δεῖ.

See also *s.v.* ἐντρυφάω.

τρυφή,

"luxury" (Lk 7²⁵, 2 Pet 2¹³): *Syll* 418 (=³ 888)¹²⁴ (A.D. 238) θερμῶν ὑδάτων λουτρὰ οὐ μόνον πρὸς τρυφὴν ἀλλὰ καὶ ὑγίαν καὶ θεραπείαν σωμάτων ἐπιτηδειότατα. For adj. τρυφερός, see BGU IV. 1080¹⁹ (iii/A.D.) σιππίου τρυφεροῦ.

Τρυφῶσα.

Like Τρύφαινα (*q.v.*). Τρυφῶσα is by no means confined to Rome (Rom 16¹²), see e.g. *Magn* 160⁵, 303¹, 304² (cited by Thieme, p. 41).

τρώγω,

orig. of animals, "munch," "crunch," "eat audibly," then of men, "eat vegetables, fruit, etc.," as in Herod. ii. 37, and then "eat" generally. The word, outside the Fourth Gospel (6⁵⁴ *al.*), is found in the NT only in Mt 24³⁸

(the Lukan parallel 17²⁷ here substitutes ἐσθίω): cf. *Syll* 805 (=³ 1171)¹⁰ ἔδωκεν εὔζωμον νήστῃ τρώγειν. Other exx. are P Lond 121⁷⁷ (iii/A.D.) (= I. p. 80) ψυχρὰ τρώγοντα κατακαίεσθαι, and *Preisigke* 5730⁵ (= P Bouriant 1¹⁶⁰) a school-exercise of iv/v A.D. containing a saying of Diogenes who, when he saw a certain man eating (ἔσθοντα), remarked ἡ νὺξ τὴν ἡμέραν τρώγει. There seems no good reason for assuming the survival of any difference in meaning between the two verbs that supplied a present stem for φαγεῖν: but see Haussleiter in *Archiv für lat. Lexicographie* ix. (1896), p. 300 ff. In MGr τρώ(γ)ω is the usual word for "eat."

In one of the Klepht ballads edited by Abbott *Songs* p. 22, the verb is used to denote security. The famous Andritsos, besieged in the great Monastery,¹¹ ἔτρωγε κ' ἔπινε, while his enemies stormed at the gate. For the comp¹. ἐπιτρώγω cf. P Oxy IX. 1185¹¹ (c. A.D. 200) παῖδα τὸν μεικρὸν δεῖ ἄρτον ἐσθίειν, ἄλας ἐπιτρώγειν, ὀψαρίου μὴ θιγγάνειν, "a little boy must eat bread, nibble besides some salt, and not touch the sauce" (Ed.). For τραγήματα = "the dessert" or δευτέρα τράπεζα (*secunda mensa, bellaria*), see Cagnat IV. 1000⁶ (ii/B.C.).

τυγχάνω.

(1) Τυγχάνω, properly "hit" as of hitting a mark, comes to be used in the sense "hit upon," "light upon," and thence "obtain" c. gen. rei, as in Ac 26²², 27³ *al.*: cf. P Petr II. 13 (19)⁶ (mid. iii/B.C.) τυχεῖν σε πάντων τῶν καλῶν, P Lond 42¹⁹ (B.C. 168) (= I. p. 30, *UPZ* i. p. 300) σοῦ παραγενομένου τεύξεσθαί τινος ἀναψυχῆς, P Ryl II. 65¹² (B.C. 67 ?) τυχεῖν δ' αὐτοὺς ὧν προσήκει, "that they should receive also the proper penalty" (Edd.), *ib.* 129¹⁶ (A.D. 30) τοὺς τὸ τοιοῦτο διαπράξαντας τυχεῖν ὧν προσῆκόν ἐστιν, "that the authors of the crime receive due punishment" (Edd.), and P Giss I. 4¹⁵ (A.D. 118) (= *Chrest.* I. p. 414) μόλ[ις τ]υχόντες ταύτης τῆς εὐεργεσίας.

(2) For the verb equivalent to little more than εἰμί, cf. P Oxy VII. 1070¹⁸ (iii/A.D.) σὺ αὐτὴ μήτη[ρ] τυγχάνουσα τοῦ τέκνου ἡμῶν, "you yourself as the mother of our child" (Edd.), and *ib.* X. 1265²⁰ (A.D. 336) κ[ἀ]κεῖν⟨ο⟩ν τυγχά(ν)οντος ἱερέως τῶν αὐτῶν ἱερέων, "who was himself one of the said priests" (Edd.).

(3) The verb is common in the papyri c. partic., though such a phrase as "I happen to be" is avoided by NT writers (see *Proleg.* p. 228): PSI V. 502¹³ (B.C. 257–6) Ζώιλος μὲν οὖν ἐτύγχανεν συμπεριοδεύων Τελέστῃ, P Lond 42²³ (B.C. 168) (= I. p. 31, *UPZ* i. p. 300) ἡ μήτηρ σου τυγχάνει βαρέως ἔχουσα, and P Strass I. 5¹⁰ (A.D. 262) ἐκ παλαιοῦ χρόνου τὴν γεωργίαν ἐνπιστευθεὶς τυγχάνων.

(4) For τυγχάνω c. inf. cf. P Petr III. 53(n)⁸ (iii/B.C.) ἀ[λ]λ' οὐ τυχὼν ἐπιδείξειν, [π]ρὸς βίαν ἔχεται, "but since he did not succeed in clearing himself, he is forcibly detained," PSI I. 39⁴ (A.D. 148) τυγχάνω ἠγορακέναι ἵπ⟨π⟩ον θήλειαν παρὰ Διοσκόρου, P Grenf II. 57⁸ (A.D. 168) τυγχάνεις ἔχειν ἐν μισθώσει τὴν ἐπικει[μέν]ην σποράν, and P Fay 136¹⁹ (Christian —iv/A.D.) ἄμινον ὑμᾶς ἐν τοῖς ἰδίοις οἷς ἐὰν τύχοι εἶναι ἢ ἐπὶ ξένης, "it is better for you to be in your homes whatever they may be, than abroad" (Edd.).

(5) The part. τυχών = "common," "ordinary," as in Ac 19¹¹, 28², 3 Macc 3⁷, may be illustrated by P Hib I. 44⁷

(B.C. 253) οὐ γὰρ ὡς ἔτυχεν περὶ τούτων τὴν σπουδὴν ποιεῖται ὁ διοικητής. "for the diœcetes is showing no ordinary anxiety with regard to this" (Edd.), P Tebt II. 283¹³ (B.C. 93 or 60) πληγὰς πλήους εἰς τὸ [ἐξ]τυχὸν μέρος τοῦ σώματος. "numerous blows upon various parts of the body" (Edd.), P Ryl II. 130¹² (A.D. 34) ὕβριν μοι συνεστησάτωι (= ήσατο) οὐ τὴν τυχοῦσαν, "he subjected me to no common outrage" (Edd.), BGU I. 36⁹ (ii/iii A.D.) ὕβριν οὐ τὴν τυχοῦσαν συνετελέσαντο, P Oxy VI. 899¹¹ (A.D. 200) εἰς ἔνδειά]ν με οὐ τὴν τυχοῦσαν περιστῆναι, "I am hence reduced to extreme poverty" (Edd.), and ib. VIII. 1121⁶ (A.D. 295) οὐκ ὀλίγος κίνδυνος οὐδὲ ἡ τυχοῦσα ἐπιστρέφεια. "no small danger and no ordinary severity" Ed.). Cf. τυχόντως in P Fay 12¹⁵ (c. B.C. 103) ο[ὐ] τυχόντως πλεῖστα κακολογηθείς, "being abused in the most unmeasured terms."

(6) The impersonal acc. abs. τυχόν (cf. 1 Cor 16⁶) occurs in the iv/B.C. letter, written on a leaden tablet, which Deissmann (LAE², p. 151) reproduces, where, in asking for certain articles of clothing, the writer adds—τυχὸν ἀποδώσω, "upon occasion I will return them." For the pleonastic τυχὸν ἴσως see Menander Ἐπιτρέπ. 287. MGr retains this use in τυχόν(ε), "perhaps."

(7) For the strong perf. τέτ(ε)υχα Heb 8⁹ א BD E. cf. PSI VII. 816¹⁰ (ii B.C.) ἔσομαι τετευχὼς τῆς παρ' ὑμῶν ἀ[ντιλήμψεως², similarly P Tebt II. 283²¹ (B.C. 93 or 60). and from the inscr. Priene 110⁹ τέ[τ]ευχεν (i/B.C.) and 108²⁸⁷ τετευχέναι (B.C. 129) (cited by Rouffiac Recherches p. 27). See also Deissmann BS p. 190, and Proleg. pp. 56, 154.

(8) It is significant that the word τύχη is not found in the NT. For the goddess Τύχη, as characteristic of the Hellenistic Age, see Rohde Griech. Roman., p. 276 ff., and for τύχη, "the good which a man obtains by the favour of the gods," see BGU IV. 1141¹⁰ (B.C. 13) ἐρωτῶ σε οὖν καὶ παρακαλῶι καὶ τὴν Καίσαρος τύ[χη]ν σε ἐξορκίζω, and similarly P Fay 24⁵ (A.D. 158).

τυμπανίζω.

The perfective of this expressive word (Heb 11³⁵) occurs in P Par 11 verso⁵ (B.C. 157) μὴ ἀποτυμπανισθῶσιν, "lest they should be tortured by beating": cf. Joseph. c. Apion. i. 148 ἀπετυμπανίσθη.

For the subst. τύμπανον, which in the LXX renders תֹף (cf. Thackeray Gr. i. p. 38), see P Hib I. 54¹² (c. B.C. 245) ἀπόστειλον δὲ ἡ[μ]ῖν καὶ Ζηνόβιον τὸν μαλακὸν (cf. 1 Cor 6⁹) ἔχοντα τύμπανον καὶ κύμβαλα καὶ κρόταλα, "send me also Zenobius the effeminate with a drum and cymbals and castanets" (Edd.). In the fragmentary P Lond 968 (iii/A.D.) (= III. p. xlix) there is an entry ὑπὲρ συμφωνίας τυμπάνων. Τυμπανιστής occurs in the late P Bilabel 95¹²⁵ (vii A.D.). In MGr τούμπανο is a "timbal."

τυπικῶς,

"by way of example" (1 Cor 10¹¹). Preisigke Wörterb. cites the corresponding adj. from P Masp II. 67154 verso²⁰ (vi A.D.) καὶ τὸν ὄρκον καὶ τὰ τυπικά, "ici le serment et les sceaux" (Ed.).

τύπος,

from meaning originally the "mark" of a blow (cf. Jn 20²⁵), came to denote the "stamp" or the "figure" which a stamp bears, and hence "pattern," "model," and finally "type" in the Biblical sense of a person or event prefiguring someone or something in the future (cf. Exp V. vi. p. 377 ff.). The word has equally varied meanings in the papyri. The following may serve as illustrations—

(1) "pattern": P Tebt II. 342²⁵ (late ii A.D.) κοῦφα ἀρεστὰ τύπῳ τῷ προκ[ειμένῳ], "pots in good order of the aforesaid pattern," and P Lond 1122¹³ (c. A.D. 254 268) (= III. p. 211, P Flor II. 187³) τὸν τύπον τον τοῦ ἐλαιουργοῦ π[α]ράδος, if the word is read correctly (see the editor's note).

See also P Lond 1017⁶ (c. A.D. 330-340) ὅπως ἐφάρῃς τὰς χῖρας σ[ου πρὸς τὸν δεσ]πότην θαιὸν ὡς τοίπως [.. τύπος σταυρ[, "that you may lift up your hands to our Master God, in the semblance of a cross" (Edd.; see his note).

(2) "plan": P Oxy XII. 1406¹² (A.D. 210-25) dues κα[ταχωρισθῆ]ναι τύπῳ τῷδε, "to be registered on the following plan," and P Flor III. 279¹⁸ (lease of land— A.D. 514) κατὰ τὸν αὐτὸν τύπον.

(3) "form," "manner of writing": P Flor I. 278¹¹·²⁰ (iii A.D.) τῷ αὐτῷ τύπῳ καὶ χρόνῳ, "of the same contents and date," with reference to a letter cf. Ac 23²⁵).

(4) "decree," "rescript": P Ryl II. 75⁵ (judicial proceedings—late ii A.D.) ζητηθήσεται ὁ πόρος αὐτο[ῦ], ἤδη μέντοι τύπος ἐστὶν καθ' ὃν ἔκρεινα πολλάκις, "let an inquiry be made into his means; only there is a principle according to which I have often judged" (Edd., who point out that τύπος may equally well be taken = "pattern", and the vi/vii A.D. P Lond 77¹⁷ (= I. p. 234) μηδὲ αἰτῆσαι θεῖον καὶ πραγματικὸν τύπον πρὸς τήνδε τὴν διαθήκην.

(5) "sentence," "decision": P Oxy VI. 893¹ (= Chrest. II. p. 122) τῷ τύπῳ τῶν ἀξιω[.]πίστων ἀνδρῶν, "by the sentence of the honourable men," and ib. XVI. 1911¹⁴³ δοῦναι τύπον εἰς τὴν συγχώρησιν, "give a decision." See also the difficult ib. 1829² (c. A.D. 577-02) with the editors' note.

(6) From the inscr. we may cite OGIS 383²¹² (mid. i/B.C.) τύπον δὲ εὐσεβείας . . . παισὶν ἐκγόνοις τε ἐμοῖς . . . ἐκτέθεικα, cf. 1 Tim 4¹², and the use of the word to denote the "models" in silver of different parts of the body presented as votive-offerings to the healing god: see Roberts—Gardner p. 191 with reference to CIA II. 403¹⁸ (iii/B.C.).

(7) For the verb τυπόω cf. P Oxy I. 67¹² (A.D. 338) φρόντισον τὰς κατὰ νόμους αὐτοῖς παραγγελίας ὑποδέξασθαι ποιῆσαι ἔνν[ο]μόν τε τυπωθῆν[αι] τὴν [το]ὺ δικαστηρίου προκατάρξειν(=ιν), "take care to enforce the precepts of the law, and to have the preliminary proceedings of the court conducted under legal forms" (Edd.), also the magical P Lond 121⁵⁵² (iii/A.D.) (= I. p. 102) ἵνα τυπώσηται τὴν ἀθάνατον μορφήν, and P Giss I. 54¹¹ (iv/v A.D.) (= Chrest. I. p. 408). In MGr τύπος is "type," "form of language," while τυπώνω = "I print" (Thumb Handb. p. 359).

τύπτω,

"strike," is not so common as we might have expected, but see P Lond 44²² (B.C. 161) (= I. p. 34, UPZ i. p. 140) ἀνῶσαί τε καὶ οὐ μετρίως σκύλαι ὑβρίζοντας καὶ τύπτοντας, P Ryl II. 77³⁹ (A.D. 192) πάσης τῆς ἐνεστώσης ἔτυψέ με ὁ Ἀχιλλεύς, ib.¹⁹ οὔτε ἔτυψα αὐτὸν οὔτε ὕβρισα, and P Grenf II. 78¹⁹ (A.D. 307) ἐπι[τυχόντ]ος τοῦ βοηθοῦ αὐτοῦ ἐμ[οὶ ὑ]π᾽ αὐτῶν αἰκιζο[μένῳ] καὶ τυπτομένῳ. For the vulgar form τυπτέω, see Radermacher Gr. p. 84.

Τύραννος,

"Tyrannus" (Ac 19⁹), as a proper name is common, e.g. P Oxy II. 292¹ (A.D. 25) (= Selections, p. 37), P Lond 919²² (A.D. 175) (III. p. 20), and BGU IV. 1015¹ (A.D. 222–3). The name is borne by a freedman of the Emperor Claudius, a physician, in Magn 113: see also ib. 122 c¹⁰, ¹¹. On its application to the Phrygian deity Mèn, cf. Cumont Relig. Orient. p. 75 (Engl. tr. p. 61). For Τυραννίς, as the name of a woman, see P Strass I. 73⁹ (iii/A.D.) with the editor's note.

τυφλός,

"blind" (1) literally : P Cornell 22⁷³ (census roll—early i/A.D.) Σωβθίτης τυφλός, P Oxy XII. 1446⁷ (A.D. 161–210) Ὥρου τυφλοῦ, P Hamb I. 22⁴ (Christian gravestone inscr.—iv/A.D.) Υ]ἱὲ θεοῦ μεγάλοιο . . . ὃς τυφλοῖσιν ἔδωκας ἰδεῖν φάος ἠελίοιο, and from the inscrr. Syll 802 (=³ 1168)³⁶ (c. B.C. 320) χωλοὺς καὶ τυφλοὺς ὑγιεῖς γίνεσθαι ἐνύπνιον ἰδόν[τας μό]νον. (2) metaphorically : P Oxy I. 99⁹ (A.D. 55)

τυφλῆς ῥύμης, "a blind alley," and similarly ib. X. 1276⁸ (A.D. 249).

τυφλόω,

"make blind." For a literal ex. of this verb, which in the NT is used only metaphorically (Jn 12⁴⁰ al.), see P Lond V. 1708⁸⁴ (A.D. 567?) ἐτυφλώθη δὲ ὁ αὐτὸς ἤτοι τῆς ὁράσεως ὑστερηθείς, and C. and B. ii. p. 386 No. 232¹⁵ (time of Caracalla or Alexander Severus) μηδεὶς δ᾽ οὖν πλούτῳ τυφλωθεὶς [κοῦ]φα φρονείτω. The subst. τύφλωσις occurs in Diog. Oenoand. p. 63⁹.

τυφόω,

metaphorically "am puffed up," "am haughty," is confined in the NT to the Pastoral Epp. (1 Tim 3⁶, al.). For the subst. τῦφος = "conceit," "vanity," cf. Cic. ad Att. xiii. 29. 2 (cited s.v. τροποφορέω), Vett. Val. p. 150² ἵνα μὴ δόξω διὰ τῦφον ταῦτα ποιεῖν, and for the adj. τυφώδης, see ib. pp. 2³, 12¹, and cf. Durham Menander, p. 97.

τυφωνικός,

"tempestuous" (Ac 27¹⁴). For Τυφῶν, "the malignant demon par excellence of magic," see P Osl I. 1⁴ (iv/A.D.) ἐλθέ, Τυφῶν, ὁ ἐπὶ τὴν ὑπτίαν πύλην καθήμενος, with the editor's note p. 35 ff.

Τύχικος,

οἱ Τυχικός, "Tychicus," a Christian "of Asia" (Ac 20⁴), and companion of Paul (Eph 6²¹, Col 4⁷). No ex. of the name is cited by Preisigke in his Namenbuch.

Υ

ὑακίνθινος—ὑγιαίνω

ὑακίνθινος.

In its only occurrence in the NT, Rev 9[17], ὑακίνθινος appears to denote a dusky blue colour as of sulphurous smoke (cf. πύρινος and θειώδης in the context). The adj. is found in PSI III. 183[5] (A.D. 484) διάλιθον διαφόρων ὑακ[ινθί]νων καὶ πιναρίων.

ὑάκινθος,

used of a precious stone in Rev 21[20], perhaps the "sapphire" (RV *marg.*). The word occurs as a proper name in P Giss I. 101[5] (iii/A.D.), PSI III. 194[1] (A.D. 566?).

ὑάλινος,

"glassy" (Rev 4[6], 15[2]): cf. the fragmentary P Petr III. 42 H (7)[3] (iii/B.C.)]ὑαλίνην γενέσθαι καὶ ῥυτόν, a gift from Philonides to the King, and *Syll*[3] 1106[153] (c. B.C. 300) ἀνέθηκα δὲ καὶ ὑαλίνα[ς φιά]λας τέσσαρας.

ὕαλος, ἡ,

"glass." This Attic form is retained in the NT (Rev 21[18, 21], cf. Job 28[17]). For the adj. cf. P Oxy X. 1294[6] (ii/iii A.D.) ὑάλαι λάγυνοι δ ὑγιειαι, "4 glass flasks in sound condition." In P Fay 134[3] (early iv/A.D.) the word is used of "some hard transparent stone" (Edd.). Note the irregular termination ὕαλας in P Lond 402 *verso*[13] (B.C. 152 or 141) (= II. p. 11), and the adj. ὑελοῦς in P Fay 104[4] (late iii/A.D.) λαγύνων ὑελῶν μεικ[ρῶν] πλευρῶν ὑελῶν δ. See also Moulton *Gr.* ii. p. 67.

ὑβρίζω.

The sense of wanton insult or contumely underlying this verb (cf. 1 Thess 2[2] with Milligan's note) is well brought out by P Tebt I. 16[7] (B.C. 114) ὡς ἦν ὑβρισμένος οὐ μετ[ρίως] ὑπὸ Ἀπολλοδώρου, "how he was grossly insulted by Apollodorus" (Edd.), P Oxy II. 281[17] (A.D. 20—50) οὐ διέλειπεν κακουχῶν με καὶ ὑβρί[ζ]ων καὶ τὰς χεῖρας ἐπιφέρων, "continually ill-treated and insulted me, using violence towards me" (Edd.)—a wife's complaint against her husband, P Oxy VIII. 1120[6] (early iii/A.D.) a petition by a "feeble widow woman" (γυνὴ χήρα καὶ ἀσθενής) against a man who had committed an outrage on her son-in-law—κατὰ τοῦ ὑβρίσαντος αὐτὸν Εὐδαίμονος, *ib.* XII. 1405[12] (iii/A.D.) a rescript of Severus guaranteeing the recipient against both loss of status and corporal punishment—ἡ δὲ ἐπιτειμία σου ἐκ τούτου οὐδὲν βλαβήσεται, οὐδὲ εἰς τὸ σῶμα ὑβρεισθήσει, "your citizenship, however, will in no way be injured thereby, nor will you be subjected to corporal punishment" (Edd.), Preisigke 4317[25] (c. A.D. 200) γεγύμνωμαι καὶ

ὕβρισμαι . . παρὰ πάντων τῶν συνπολιτῶν, P Lond 1014[1] (A.D. 335?) τὸν μονάριν Ἡρακλίδην δύ[σα]ντες (*l.* δήσαντες) καὶ ὑβρίσαντες, "Heraclides the keeper of the hostel they bound and maltreated" (Bell), P Oxy XVII. 2154[25] (iv/A.D.) ἵνα . . μὴ ὑβρισθῶ παρὰ τοὺς πάντας, "that I may not be insulted before them all," and *OGIS* 315[17f] (B.C. 164-3) ἡ θεὸς ἐπιστραφεῖσα τῶν ἑαυτῆς ἱερέων ὑβρισμένων καὶ ὑβριζομ[ένων]. A milder sense is found in BGU IV. 1141[14] (B.C. 14) ὑβρίσαι με πρὸς γέλωτά μοι τοῦτο ἔγραψας. MGr βρίζω, as well as ὑβρίζω, "I scold."

ὕβρις.

For this strong word (see *s.v.* ὑβρίζω), cf. the marriage contract P Eleph 1[8] (B.C. 311-10) (= *Selections*, p. 3) where it is provided that the husband shall not bring in another woman ἐφ' ὕβρει of his wife. See also P Fay 12[17] (c. B.C. 103) ἤγαγον μεθ' ὕβρεως καὶ πληγῶν, "they dragged me away with insults and blows," P Ryl II. 136[11] (A.D. 34) ὕβριν μοι συνεστησάτωι οὐ τὴν τυχοῦσαν, "he subjected me to no common outrage" (Edd.)—complaint of an assault, *ib.* 145[3] (A.D. 38) πλείστας ὕβ[ρι]ς τοῖς παρ' ἐμοῦ συντελῶν, "heaping insults on my dependants" (Edd.), P Oxy II. 237[viii. 15] (A.D. 186) οἰόμενος ἐκ (τού)του παύσασθαι αὐτὴν τῶν εἰς ἐμὲ ὕβρεων, "expecting that this would induce her to stop her insults" (Edd.).

For ὕβρις as nearly always "a sin of the strong and proud," see Murray *Greek Epic* p. 264 ff.: cf. Headlam *Herodas*, p. 86.

ὑβριστής

"emphasizes the element of outrageous disregard of other men's rights" (Parry *ad* 1 Tim 1[13]): cf. Rom 1[30] and a valuable note by Hort *Jas.* p. 95). The adj. ὑβριστικός occurs in Vett. Val. p. 172[2] in conjunction with ἀναιδής.

ὑγιαίνω,

"am in good health," is very common in private letters, *e.g.* (a) at the opening—BGU II. 423[3] (ii/A.D.) (= *Selections*, p. 90) πρὸ μὲν πάντων εὔχομαί σε ὑγιαίνειν, or (b) at the close—P Oxy IV. 745[10] (c. A.D. 1) ἀ[σ]πάζου πάντας τοὺς σοὺς καὶ σεαυτοῦ ἐπιμέλου ἵν' ὑγιαίνῃς : cf. Herodas VI. 97 ὑγίαινε, "good-bye" or "good-night," with Headlam's note.

For a metaph. usage, as in the Pastorals (1 Tim 1[10] al., cf. P Oxy II. 291[9] (A.D. 25-26) προέγραψ ά σοι] ἀνδραγαθί[ν] καὶ ἀπαιτεῖν μ[έχ]ρι ὑγια[ί]νων παρ[α]γένωμαι, "I have already written to you to be firm and demand payment

PART VIII.   647   83

until I come in peace" (Edd.), and *Menandrea* p. 77²²⁰ οὐ]χ ὑγιαίνεις, "you are not in your senses." MGr γιαίνω, "I heal, cure."

ὑγιής.

For ὑγιής, "sound," "whole," applied to material objects, cf. P Petr III. 46(1)¹⁶ (iii/B.C.) ὅση ἂν ἦι ὑγιής, "all the sound ones"—of bricks, P Oxy II. 278¹⁸ (hire of a mill—A.D. 17) τὸν μύλον ὑγιῆι καὶ ἀσινῆι, "the mill safe, and uninjured," *ib*. I. 113¹¹ (ii/A.D.) ἐκομισάμην πάνθ' ὅσα . . . ὑγιῆ, "I received everything safely," *Syll* 40 (=³ 98)² (B.C. 415–13) πίθ]οι . . . ὑγιές "whole wine-jars," and *ib*. 804 (=³ 1170)²⁶ (ii/A.D.?) ἐπέφλευσε τὴν χεῖρα . . μετ' ὀλίγον δὲ ὑγιὴς ἡ χεὶρ ἐγένετο (cf. Mt 12¹³).

With the metaph. usage in Tit 2⁸ cf. P Tebt I. 27⁶⁰ (B.C. 113) (= *Chrest.* I. p. 389) φροντίζειν, ὅπως καὶ τἄλ[λα γέν]ηται κατὰ θερείαν ἐξ ὑγιοῦς, "take care that all else is rightly done in the summer" (Edd.), P Amh II. 65³⁵ (late ii/A.D.) ὀμνύομεν . . . εἰ μὴν ἐξ ὑγειοῦς καὶ ἐπ' ἀληθείας ἐπιδεδωκ[έ]ναι τὴν παράδειξιν, and similarly P Oxy II. 255¹⁶ (A.D. 48), *ib*. VIII. 1110²¹ (A.D. 188). The corr. use of the adv. is frequent, *e.g. ib*. VII. 1024³³ (A.D. 129) where with reference to a grant of seed-corn to a cultivator it is provided ἣν καταθήσεται εἰς τὴν γῆν ὑγιῶς ἐπακολουθούντων τῶν εἰωθότων, "he shall sow it on the land in good faith under the observance of the usual officers" (Ed.), *ib*. 1031¹⁸ (a similar document—A.D. 228) ὑγιῶς καὶ πιστῶς, *ib*. I. 84¹ (mid. iii/A.D.), where a strategus on entering office undertakes to distribute the public λειτουργίαι ὑγιῶς καὶ πιστῶς, "honestly and faithfully," and *ib*. IX. 1187¹⁸ (A.D. 254). MGr γερός (from ὑγιηρός), "sound," "strong."

ὑγρός.

With the use of the adj. = "sappy," "green," in Lk 23³¹, cf. its application to "raw" pitch in BGU II. 544²⁰ (time of Antoninus) πίσσης ὑγρᾶς, and P Oxy XIV. 1753³ (A.D. 390). For the more general meaning "wet," "moist," cf. P Fay 331 (A.D. 125–6) ὑγροῦ λίτρον, "a litre of water," and the account of a cure at the temple of Asclepius in Epidaurus, *Syll* 804 (=³ 1170)²² (ii/A.D.) χρείμενος μὲν τοῖς ἁλσὶ καὶ τῶι νάπυ[ι] ὑγρῶι ἤλγησα. See also PSI IV. 442⁵ (ii/B.C.) with reference to an ἀμφίταπος or Egyptian rug (cf. Prov 7¹⁶) fraudulently damped to make it heavier—ὃ δὲ σταθεὶς ("weighed") ἐχθὲς ἔτι ὑγρὸς ἦν, and *Gnomon* 232 (*c.* A.D. 150) (= BGU V. p. 37) ἐπὶ ὑγροῖς ("Flüssigkeiten") οὐκ ἐξὸν δανίζε[ι]ν.

ὑδρία,

"a water-pot" (Jn 2⁶ *al.*): P Oxy III. 502³⁷ (A.D. 164) ὑδριῶν καὶ ὅλμου, "the water-pitchers and trough" (Edd.). The word is frequently extended to denote a "jar" or "pot" of any kind, even one for holding money: cf. PSI IV. 428⁸⁹ (iii/B.C.) ῥοῶν ("pomegranates") ὑδρία ᾱ, P Oxy I. 155¹ (vi/A.D.) ὑδρίας ἄρτου πέντε, "five pans of bread," *Michel* 833¹⁰⁰ (B.C. 270) χαλκοῦ ἐπισήμου παντοδαποῦ ἐν ὑδρίαι, and *Syll* 300 (=³ 646)⁵⁰ (B.C. 170) ὑδρίας σὺν ἀργυρίω[ι: see Rutherford *NP*, p. 23. The dim. ὑδρεῖον occurs in BGU I. 117² (A.D. 189) ὑ[πάρχ]ει μοι . . . ὑδρῖον.

ὑδροποτέω,

"drink water." For this NT ἅπ. εἰρ. (1 Tim 5²³), cf. Epict. iii. 13. 21 ἀσίτησον, ὑδροπότησον. On the more correct form ὑδροπωτέω, see Lob. *Phryn.* p. 456, Moeris p. 380.

ὑδρωπικός,

"afflicted with dropsy" (Lk 14²), one of the terms to which Hobart (p. 24) appeals in support of the "medical" vocabulary of Luke, but it should be noted that, in addition to the passages cited in LS⁸, the adj. occurs in Polyb. xiii. 2. 6: cf. *JBL* xlv. p. 205. For the subst. ὑδρωπία, not in LS⁸, see Vett. Val. p. 105²⁷.

ὕδωρ.

A few miscellaneous exx. should serve to illustrate this common word—P Cairo Zen III. 59467¹⁰ (iii/B.C.) τὸ ὕδωρ ἀφίομεν, "we release the water," PSI IV. 406³⁹ (iii/B.C.) χαλκία δύο ὕδατος, *ib*. 429³⁷ (iii/B.C.) τὸ ὕδωρ ἐκ τῆς διώρυγος, P Bilabel 49¹² (beg. ii/B.C.) ὤλκασσον ("draw") δὲ τὴν τρ[ο]φὴν ἐκ τοῦ ὕδατος, P Fay 110¹⁵ (A.D. 94) το[ὺ]ς ἐ[λαι]ῶνας τὸ δεύτερον [ὕ]δω[ρ] λου[σ]άτωσαν, "have the olive-yards washed over a second time" (Edd.), BGU I. 246⁹ (ii/iii A.D.) ἀλεῖ (*l.* ἁλὶ) καὶ ἄρτῳ καὶ ὕδατι, P Oxy II. 234ⁱⁱ·¹⁷ (medical prescription—ii/iii A.D.) κρόκον ὕδωρ ἐπιστάξας, "drop on saffron water" (Edd.), and P Amh II. 143¹⁷ (iv/A.D.) διὰ τὴν ἀφορμὴν τοῦ ὕδατος, "because of the flow of water."

ὑετός,

"rain." With Heb 6⁷ cf. the use of the corresponding verb in the prayer of the Athenians cited in M. Anton. v. 7 Ὗσον, ὗσον, ὦ φίλε Ζεῦ, κατὰ τῆς ἀρούρας τῆς Ἀθηναίων καὶ τῶν πεδίων, "Rain, rain, O dear Zeus, upon the corn-land of the Athenians and their meads" (Haines).

υἱοθεσία,

"adoption." Deissmann (*BS* p. 239) has drawn attention to the frequency of the phrase καθ' υἱοθεσίαν in the inscrr., which "lets us understand that Paul [Rom 8¹⁵, Gal 4⁵ *al.*] was availing himself of a generally intelligible figure when he utilised the term υἱοθεσία in the language of religion." Exx. are *Priene* 37² (ii/B.C.) Εὐφανίσκος Καλλιξείνου, καθ' υἱοθ[ε]σίαν δὲ Νικασιδάμου, *Syll* 269 (=³ 586)² (B.C. 196) Νικαγόρας Παμφ[ίλιδα, κα]θ' υἱοθεσίαν δὲ [Νικαγόρα, *ib*. 555 (=³ 977)⁷ (end ii/B.C.) Τιμ[ό]θεος Σωσικλεῦς, κατὰ δὲ υἱοθεσίαν Ἰσοπόλιος. See also Hicks *CR* i. p. 45 f., iii. p. 333, and for a literary ex. Diog. Laert. iv. 9. 53 νεανίσκων τινῶν υἱοθεσίας ποιεῖσθαι.

From the papyri we may cite P Oxy IX. 1206⁸ (A.D. 335) ὁμολογοῦμεν ἡμεῖς [μὲν ὅτ]ε Ἡρακλῆς καὶ ἡ γ[υ]νὴ Εἰσάριον ἐκδεδωκέναι σοί τῷ Ὡρίωνι τὸν ἐξ [ἡμ]ῶν υἱὸν Πατερ[μοῦθ]ιν ὡς ἐτῶν δύο εἰς υἱοθεσίαν, ἐμὲ δὲ [Ὡρίων]α ἔχειν [τοῦτ]ον γνήσιον υἱὸν πρὸς τὸ μένειν αὐτῷ τὰ ἀπ[ὸ τ]ῆς διαδοχῆς τῆς κληρονομίας μου δίκαια, "we agree, Heracles and his wife Isarion on the one part, that we have given away to you, Horion, for adoption our son Patermouthis, aged about two years, and I Horion on the other part, that I have him as my own son so that the rights proceeding from succession to my inheritance shall be maintained for him " (Ed.): cf. [14, 16, 20], and the editor's introduction. We may further cite P Lips I. 28[12] (A.D. 381) (= *Archiv* iii. p. 173 ff.) ὥσ]τ᾽ ἐμὲ τὸν [ἀ]δελ[φ]ὸν αὐτοῦ Σιλβανὸν . . . ἔχειν [πρὸς ?] υἱοθεσίαν : cf. [14, 17, 22, 24, 27]. This last papyrus shows also the verb υἱοθετέω,[22] τῶν ἐμῶν πραγμάτων κληρονόμον υἱοθετηθέντα μοι. For υἱοποιέομαι see Gnomon 41 (*c.* A.D. 150) (= BGU V. p. 21).

υἱός.

The literal sense of this word, "male issue," is too common to require illustration, but for a wider usage (as in the case of πατήρ, μήτηρ, τέκνον) we may cite such passages as P Giss I. 68[1] (time of Trajan/Hadrian) Ἄρσις Ἀπολλωνίῳ τῶι υἱῶι χαίρειν, and P Strass I. 2[1] (A.D. 217) διὰ τοῦ υἱ[ι]οῦ μου Αὐρηλίου, where the context makes it clear that it is not a son "after the flesh" who is intended, and similarly P Oxy IX. 1219[2] (iii/A.D.) with the editor's introduction.

Υἱός with the gen. in such expressions as υἱὸς τῆς βασιλείας, υἱὸς τοῦ φωτός, may be illustrated from the inscrr., e.g. *PAS* ii. 2 (reign of Nero) υἱὸς πόλεως, *Magn* 167[5] (time of Vespasian) υἱὸς τῆς πατρίδος, ib. 156[12] (iv/A.D.) υἱὸς τῆς πόλεως. The usage is naturally regarded as Hebraistic, but, as the above exx. prove, is not un-Greek, and may be explained on what Deissmann (*BS* p. 161 ff.) calls "the theory of analogical formations."

For a definitely spiritual sense of the word, cf. P Lond V. 1658[1 ff.] (iv/A.D.) τῷ αἱμήτῳ υἱῷ Ἄμ[μωνι] Ἀντώνιος ἐν κ(υρί)ῳ χαίρειν . . . ἀγαπητὲ υἱέ, P Giss I. 103[2] (iv/A.D.) Ἀπ[όλλων]ις Στεφάνῳ δι[ακόνῳ ἀγ]απητῷ υἱῷ [ἐν κ(υρί)ῳ χαίρειν, and P Grenf II. 93[1] (vi/vii A.D.) ὁ μεγαλοπρεπέστατος ὑμῶν υἱὸς ὁ κόμες ἔγραψέν μοι. It is startling to find the title ὁ υἱὸς τοῦ θεοῦ, round which so many sacred associations have gathered, applied to the Roman Emperors, as in the following reff. to Augustus—BGU II. 543[3] (B.C. 27) ὄμνυμι Καίσαρα Αὐτοκράτορα θεοῦ υἱόν, P Tebt II. 382[21] (B.C. 30-A.D. 1), P Grenf II. 40[4] (A.D. 9) ἔτους ἐνάτου καὶ τριακοστοῦ τῆς Καίσαρος κρατήσεως θεοῦ υἱοῦ, "the thirty-ninth year of the dominion of Caesar son of god," and *LMAe* iii. 174 (A.D. 5) Καῖσαρ θεοῦ υἱὸς Σεβαστός, interesting as coming from the Emperor himself. On the significance of the title as referred to Christ, see Deissmann *BS*, p. 166 f.

ὕλη.

Hort's contention (*ad* Jas 3[5], cf. p. 104 ff.) that ὕλη, when applied to living wood, "is either woodland as opposed to mountains and cultivated plains, specially the rough bushy skirts of the hills, or brushwood" may be supported by PSI VI. 577[8] (B.C. 248-7) τήν τε γῆν ἐ[κάθαρα ὑπάρχουσαν ?] ὕλης μεστήν. The word is used in the account of a purchase of wood P Cairo Zen I. 59112[1] (B.C. 257) ξύλων ὧν ἠγόρακεν ἐκ τῆς ὕλης: cf. also P Lond 166 *b*.[4] (A.D. 186) (= II. p. 106) ἐφ᾽ ὕλ(ης) καινῆς, wood for the sluice-gates of an embankment, and P Oxy XIV. 1674[4] (iii/A.D.) ποίησον τὴν ἄκανθαν καταβληθῆναι καὶ τὴν ὕλην αὐτῆς βάλε εἰς τὸν τρυγινον, "have the acacia tree cut down and throw the wood into the . . ." (Edd.). For the meaning "furniture," see

P Oxy XVI. 1901[30] (a Will—vi/A.D.) τὴν ἐν τῷ οἴκῳ μου πᾶσαν ὕλην ἀπὸ κεφαλαίου μέχρι ἐλαχίστου τινός, "all the furniture in my house from the chief pieces down to the smallest item" (Edd.). It may be noted that in P Par 47[9] (B.C. 152-1) (= *Selections*, p. 22) ἐνβέβληκαν ὑμᾶς εἰς ὕλην μεγάλην, Wilcken (*UPZ* i. p. 334) understands ὕλη as = "mud," "slime": cf. ὑλίζω, "I filter, strain," in P Lond 46[71] (iv/A.D.) (= I. p. 67).

Ὑμέναιος,

"Hymenaeus," a back-sliding Christian (1 Tim 1[20], 2 Tim 2[17]). For the adj. ὑμέναιος (from Ὑμήν, "the god of marriage") cf. the sepulchral inser. *Preisigke* 6706[4]—

> οὐδ᾽ ἐτέλεσσα
> νυμφιδίων θαλάμων εἰς ὑμέναια λέχη.

ὑμέτερος.

On the comparative rarity of the emphatic ὑμέτερος in the NT, cf. Blass *Gr.* p. 168: in Paul in particular it is largely ousted by ὑμῶν (in the position of the attribute). From the papyri it is sufficient to cite P Cairo Zen II. 59240[6] (B.C. 253) φροντίσας ὅπως ἀσφαλῶς μετὰ τῶν ὑμετέρων (sc. ἡμιόνων, "mules") ἀποσταλῶσιν ὡς ὄντες Ἀπολλωνίου.

ὑμνέω.

For the trans. use of this verb "sing to the praise of," as in Ac 16[25], cf. *OGIS* 56[50] (B.C. 238) ὑμνεῖσθαι δ᾽ αὐτήν (sc. τὴν θεάν), and *Syll* 721 (= [3] 662)[12] (c. B.C. 165-4) τούς τε θεοὺς . . . καὶ τὸν δῆμον τὸν Ἀθηναίων ὕμνησεν. For a curious ex. of a vi/A.D. Byzantine hymn, see P Lond 1029 (= III. p. 284): the verb ὑμνολογέω is found in line [9].

ὕμνος,

"a hymn": *OGIS* 56[69] (B.C. 238) οὓς ἂν ὕμνους οἱ ἱερογραμματεῖς γράψαντες δῶσιν τῶι ᾠδοδιδασκάλωι, P Giss I. 99[8] (ii/iii A.D.) ὕμνοι μὲν ᾄ[δονται] γλώττῃ ξενικῇ, and P Oxy I. 130[21] (vi/A.D.) ὕμνους ἀθανάτους ἀναπέμψω τῷ δεσπότῃ Χριστῷ. For the compound ὑμνῳδός, "singer of hymns," cf. *Perg* 523[10] ὑμνῳδ]οῦ θεοῦ Αἰγούστου, and *ib.* 374[4] ὑμνῳδοὶ θεοῦ Σεβαστοῦ καὶ θεᾶς Ῥώμης with Fränkel's commentary *ad l.* on the functions of the ὑμνῳδός. See also Deissmann *LAE*[2], p. 349.

ὑπάγω.

In its Johannine occurrences ὑπάγω is almost always = "go away," as distinguished from πορεύομαι "go on a journey": see Abbott *Joh. Voc.* p. 142 ff., where it is pointed out that before the Last Discourses our Lord never uses πορεύομαι of Himself, except in Jn 11[11], where the reference is primarily to a literal journey into Judaea. For ὑπάγω, "go away," "go back," in the vernacular we may cite P Oxy X. 1291[11] (A.D. 30) Ἀπολλῶς Θέωνος ὑπάγει αὔριον, BGU II. 450[4] (ii/iii A.D.) ὕπαγε ὅπου [ἐστὶ] Θᾶυς, ἵνα πέμψῃς [αὐτὸ]ν πρὸς ἐμέ, P Tebt II. 417[4] (illiterate—iii/A.D.) ἤδη εἴρηχέ σοι ὁ {α} πα[τ]ήρ σου [σ]ου ἐξερχομένου ὅτι ὕπαγε πρὸς τὸν Μῶρον καὶ εἶδε τί λέγει περὶ τῆς Ἀντινόου, "your father already told you, when you were leaving, to go to Morus and see what he says about Antinoe" (Edd.), and *ib.* 422⁹ (iii/A.D.) ἐρῖς Ταωσᾶτι ὕπαγε [[π]] μετὰ Μέλανος πρὸς Νεμεσᾶν, "tell Taosas to go with Melas to Nemesas," and P Oxy XII. 1477² (question to an oracle—iii/iv A.D.) εἰ μένω ὅπου ὑπάγω; "shall I remain where I am going?"

The word is avoided by Luke, perhaps, as Abbott (*ut s.*) suggests, because of its variety of usage in the vernacular, meaning "go on" or "come on," as well as "go back": see *e.g.* P Ryl II. 236⁷ (A.D. 256) ἄλλην μίαν τετραονίαν ἀπόστειλον εἰς τὴν πόλιν ἀντὶ τοῦ Ἄκη εἰς ὑπηρεσίαν τῶν ὑπαγόντων βαδιστῶν καὶ ἵππων, "send another team of four donkeys to the city in place of Akes to carry fodder for the riding donkeys and horses coming up" (Edd.).

In P Par 6²² (B.C. 120), if the restoration is correct, the verb is used of "raising" or "bringing up" a legal action—ἐπεὶ οὖν ὑπ[άγω] (?) κατὰ Ποήριος, "puisque j'intente action contre Poeris" (Ed.), and in P Michigan 338¹³ (iii/A.D.) it refers to the conduct of business—καλῶς γὰρ ὑπάγ(= ει), "for he is doing well." The same letter gives us another ex. of the sense "go away" (*ut supra*), ⁸ οὗ ἔπεμψα[ς] αὐτὸν ἐν πλ[ο]ίῳ ὑπάγοντι ἰς Ταπόσιριν, "where you sent him in a boat making for Taposiris" (Ed.).

For the trans. use, which does not occur in the NT, cf. the Klepht Ballad (Abbott *Songs*, p. 188)—

χίλιοι τὸν 'πήγαιναν 'μπροσθὰ καὶ πεντακόσιοι 'πίσω, "a thousand men led him in front and five hundred followed behind."

Besides πηγαίνω, παγαίνω, MGr has the forms πάγω, πάω, πάνω, "I go": see Thumb *Handbook*, p. 349.

ὑπακοή.

According to Grimm-Thayer this subst. = "obedience" (Rom 6¹⁶, *al.*) "is not found in prof. auth.," but we may cite, though it is late, P Strass I. 40⁴¹ (A.D. 569) μεθ' ὑπ[ερ]τάτης ἀρετῆς καὶ ὑπακοῆς ἐν πᾶσι τ[ο]ῖ[ς] ὀφελίμοις ἔργοις τε καὶ λόγοις. The word is found in Ev. Petr. 9 καὶ ὑπακοὴ ἠκούετο ἀπὸ σταυροῦ [ὅ]τι Ναί, where Swete understands it as = "response" or "refrain," in accordance with a common use of the verb in early Christian literature.

ὑπακούω.

(1) "listen," "attend": P Hib I. 78⁵ (B.C. 244–3) οὐδέποτε ὑ[πα]κήκοας ἡμῶν, "you have never listened to me" (Edd.) (cf. Ac 12¹³): cf. P Cairo Zen III. 59367¹⁵ (B.C. 240) εἰ μὲν οὖν διείλεξαι τῶι Κράτωνι καὶ ὑπακήκοε, "if therefore you have spoken to Kraton and he has given his assent." (2) "answer": P Petr III. 44(4)⁵ (iii/B.C.) Εὐρώται ἔγραψα, οὐθὲν [δὲ ὑ]πακούσαντος ἠναγκάσθην [τὴν θ]ύραν κλεῖσαι, P Oxy I. 87¹⁹ (A.D. 342) ὀμνύω . . ὑπακούοντα ἐν πᾶσι τοῖς πρός με ζητουμένοις περὶ τοῦ ναυκληρίου, "I swear that I will answer all inquiries made to me concerning the vessel" (Edd.). (3) "submit," "obey": P Tebt I. 24²⁶ (B.C. 117) οὐδ' οὕτως ὑπήκουσαν, "still they did not obey" (Edd.), P Hamb I. 29⁵ (A.D. 94) κληθέντων τινῶν . . καὶ μὴ ὑπακουσάντων, and similarly *l.* ⁷, P Flor I. 6²¹ (A.D. 210) ἐὰν οὖν . . . κληθεὶς μὴ ὑπακούσῃς ἔσται τὰ ἀκόλουθα . . ., "if, when you are called, you do not obey, the consequences will be . . .", P Oxy VI. 900⁹ (A.D. 322) ὑπακούειν καὶ ἡμεῖν τοῖς ἐνχιρισθεῖσι πλῖστα

δημόσια ἐπιτάγματα, "to render obedience to me who have been entrusted with so many public burdens" (Edd.), and P Lond V. 1711³⁵ (A.D. 566–573), where a husband describes his wife as ὑπακουούσης μοι καὶ φυλαττούσης μοι πᾶσαν εὔνοιαν, cf. *ib.* 1727¹² (A.D. 583–584).

ὕπανδρος,

"under the authority of a husband" (Rom 7²), is found in the LXX (Sir 9⁹), Polybius (x. 26. 3), and other late writers. Cf. MGr παντρεύω, "I marry."

ὑπαντάω,

"meet," c. dat. pers. (cf. *Proleg.* p. 64), as in Mt 8²⁸ *al.*: cf. P Lond 32⁸ (beg. viii/A.D.?) (= I. p. 230, *Chrest.* I. p. 40) ὅστις οὖν ὑπαν[τ]ήσῃ αὐτοῖς ἐκ τῶν ὑπουργῶν. Other exx. of the verb are P Oxy IX. 1196¹⁶ (A.D. 211–12) ὑπαντῶν τοῖς γεινομένοις μηνιαίοις, "presenting myself at the regular monthly statements" (Ed.), and BGU I. 321²⁹ (A.D. 216) τῇ δὲ ἀποδόσει μέχρι νῦν οὐχ ὑπήντησαν. Cf. also ὑπαπαντάω in P Strass II. 101⁴ (i/B.C.) καλῶς ποιήσεις ὑπαπαντήσας ἡμῖν τῆι ζ.

ὑπάντησις,

"a going to meet." For the verbal phrase construed c. dat., as in Jn 12¹³, cf. P Giss I. 74⁶ (ii/A.D.) Χαιρήμονα ἐξεληλυθ[έναι] εἰς ὑπάντησιν Οὐλπιανῶι (according to the amended reading in Preisigke's *Wörterb. s.v.* ὑπάντησις). The word seems to be synonymous with ἀπάντησις (*q.v.*: cf. *Proleg.* p. 14, n.⁴), though, according to Lightfoot (*Notes* p. 69) ἀπάντησις is simply "meeting," while ὑπάντησις involves the notion of "looking out for." Ὑπάντησις occurs *bis* in *Syll* 365 (= ³798)¹⁶ προσέταξε τοῖς ἄρχουσι ψήφισμα ὑπαντήσεως εἰσηγήσασθαι, ²³ ἀγαγεῖν δὲ ἐπὶ τὴν ὑπάντησιν καὶ τὸν ἐφήβαρχον τοὺς ἐφήβους.

ὕπαρξις.

For the late use of ὕπαρξις to denote "substance," "property," as in Heb 10³⁴, cf. P Oxy X. 1274¹⁴ (iii/A.D.) τὴν ὕπαρξιν αὐτοῦ πᾶσαν οὖσαν τιμήματος δουκηναρίας, "all his property valued at two hundred thousand sesterces" (Edd.). Cf. Teles p. 43⁹ ἢ ποία χρημάτων ὕπαρξις ⟨τῶν⟩ τοιούτων ἐπιθυμιῶν ἀπολύει: In MGr ὕπαρξι means "existence."

ὑπάρχω.

The idea of falling back upon a "basis," and hence of continuity with a previous state, which originally belonged this verb (cf. Hort *ad* Jas 2¹⁵), seems gradually to have faded in later Greek, as the following exx. show—P Petr III. 64 *b.*)¹² (iii/B.C.) τοῦτο (*sc.* τὸ ὀψώνιον) ὑπάρξει ἡ τιμὴ τῶν εὑρεθέ[ντων] παρὰ Τασύθει, "this will be made up by the price of the articles discovered in the possession of Tasuthis" (Edd.). P Hib I. 72¹⁸ (B.C. 241) τὴμ μὲν σφραγίδα ὡμολόγουν ὑπάρχειν ἐν τῶι ἀδύτωι, "confessed that the seal was in the sanctuary" (Edd.), P Oxy IX. 1189¹⁰ (*c.* A.D. 117) περὶ γραφῆς τῶν τοῖς ['Ι]ουδαίοις ὑπαρξάντων, "about a list of property which belonged to the Jews" (Ed.), *ib.* VI. 933¹⁷ (late ii/A.D.) πάντα αὐτῇ ὑπῆρκται, "everything was provided for her" (Edd.), *ib.* 905¹⁶ (A.D.

170) (= *Selections*, p. 87) a marriage contract, where the giver of the bride has the right of execution upon the husband and upon all his property—ἐκ τῶν ὑπαρχ[ό]ντων αὐτῷ πάντων (cf. Mt 19²¹, *al.*), P Tebt II. 418⁷ (iii/A.D.) εὐχόμενός σοι τὰ ἐν βίῳ κάλλιστα ὑπαρχθήσεσθαι, "praying that you may have life's greatest blessings" (Edd.), and the mantic P Ryl I. 28⁴³ (iii/iv A.D.) ἐν δανίοις δὲ ὑπάρχων ἀποδώσει (cf. Lk 7²⁵). It may be added that the new recension of Tobit 2 in P Oxy VIII. 1076 inserts in ver. 8 καὶ ἀπώλεσεν πάντα τὰ ὑπάρχο[ν]τα αὐτοῦ, which is reproduced in the Old Latin version with *et perdidit substantiam suam*.

In view of the above, the meaning "being originally" (RV marg.) cannot be pressed for ὑπάρχων in Phil 2⁶, though the thought is probably present. As showing how naturally it might arise, we may cite the letter of Claudius to the Alexandrines, P Lond 1912²³ (A.D. 41) φύσει μὲν εὐσεβεῖς περὶ τοὺς Σεβαστοὺς ὑπάρχοντες, "you are by disposition loyal to the Augusti" (Ed.), and *ib.* ¹⁰⁴. In MGr ὑπάρχω = "am present," "exist."

ὑπείκω,

"submit," is found in the NT only in Heb 13¹⁷. Moffatt (*ICC ad l.*) cites by way of illustration of the context, though the word itself is not found, Epict. *Fragm.* 27 τὸν προσομιλοῦντα . . . διασκοποῦ . . . εἰ μὲν ἀμείνονα, ἀκούειν χρὴ καὶ πείθεσθαι.

ὑπεναντίος.

The strong sense which Lightfoot gives to this word in Col 2¹⁴ ἐξαλείψας τὸ καθ' ἡμῶν χειρόγραφον τοῖς δόγμασιν, ὃ ἦν ὑπεναντίον ἡμῖν, "which was directly opposed to us," may be illustrated from an early second century Will, P Oxy III. 493¹⁰, where it is enacted that no one shall be permitted to set aside any of the provisions, or do anything opposed to them—τι ὑπεναντίως π[οιεῖν. Cf. also P Flor I. 1⁹ (A.D. 153) μηδ' ἄλλο τι περὶ αὐτῆς κακοτεχνεῖν ὑπεναντίον τούτοις τρόπῳ μηδενί, and an inscr. in C. and B. ii. p. 717, No. 651 (mid. iii/A.D.) εἰ δέ τις ὑπεναντίον ποιή[σει . . . A Christian amulet, P Oxy VIII. 1151⁵⁵ (v/A.D.?) designed to ward off fever and other ills, ends with the words—ὅτι τὸ ὄνομά σου, κ(ύρι)ε ὁ θ(εό)ς, ἐπικαλεσά[μ]ην τὸ θαυμαστὸν καὶ ὑπερένδοξον καὶ φοβερὸν τοῖς ὑπεναντίοις, "upon thy name, O Lord God, have I called, the wonderful and exceeding glorious name, the terror of thy foes" (Ed.) (cf. Heb 10²⁷).

ὑπέρ.

From its original locative meaning "over" (as in P Par 1¹⁴⁵ (B.C. 117) τὰ μὲν ὑπὲρ [γῆς], ταῦθ' ὑπὸ γῆς), ὑπέρ came to be applied in a variety of ways.

1. c. gen. (a) = "for," "on behalf of," "in the place of": P Tebt I. 6¹⁹ (B.C. 140–130) ἐπιτελεῖν τὰ νομιζόμενα τοῖς θεοῖς ὑπὲρ ἡμῶν καὶ τῶν τ[έκ]νων, "to pay the customary offerings to the gods on behalf of us and our children" (Edd.), P Oxy IV. 743²⁵ (B.C. 2) συνπροσγενέσθαι αὐτῶι ὡς ἀνθομολογη(σομένου) ὑπέρ σου οὕτως ὡς ὑπ[έρ] μου, "stand by him, as he will agree in everything for you just as for me" (Edd.), and BGU I. 246¹³ (ii/iii A.D.) νυκτὸς καὶ ἡμέρας ἐντυγχάνω τῷ θεῷ ὑπὲρ ὑμῶν. Cf. also

with Mk 9⁴⁰ the Christian P Iand I. 16⁸ (v/vi A.D.) τὸ νόμιμον ὑπὲρ ἡμῶν ἐστιν, and with 1 Cor 15²⁹ *Michel* 1001¹·¹⁰ (will of Epicteta—. B.C. 200) τοῦ καὶ κατασκευαξαμένου τὸ μουσεῖον ὑπὲρ τοῦ μεταλλαχότος ἁμῶν υἱοῦ Κρατησιλόχου.

From this it is an easy transition to ὑπέρ in a substitutionary sense, as when one man writes a letter for another, seeing that he is unable to write it for himself, e.g. P Tebt I. 104³⁹ (B.C. 92) ἔγραψεν ὑπὲρ αὐτοῦ Διονύσιος Ἑρμαίσκ ου ὁ προγεγραμμένος διὰ τ]ὸ αὐτὸν μὴ ἐπίστασθ αι γράμματα, *ib.* II. 373²³ (A.D. 110–1) γέ]γραφα ὑπὲρ αὐτοῦ φάσ[κοντος μὴ εἰδέναι γράμματα. Other exx. will be found *s.v.* ἀγράμματος, and see A. T. Robertson in *Exp* VIII. xviii. p. 321 ff., where the bearing of this use of ὑπέρ upon certain theological statements in the NT is discussed. Note also P Oxy IV. 722²⁵ (A.D. 91 or 107) οὐκ ἐξόντος τῷ 'Αχ ιλλεῖ οὐδ' ἄλλῳ ὑπὲρ αὐτοῦ ἀπαίτησιν ποιε[ῖσθαι] . . . τῶν προκει[μ]ένων λίτρων, where ὑπὲρ αὐτοῦ seems to imply acting in his name or on his behalf (cf. Wenger *Stellvertretung*, p. 12), and BGU I. 361ⁱⁱ·¹⁷ (A.D. 184) Φιλώτας ῥήτωρ ὑπὲρ Κασίου εἶπεν . . . : cf. In 11⁵⁰, Gal 3¹³, Philem¹³.

(b) = "concerning," "about," "as to," a somewhat colourless use of ὑπέρ, by which it is equivalent to little more than περί, for which it is often a *v.l.* in MSS. of the NT (see *s.v.* περί): P Par 45² (B.C. 152) (= *UPZ* i. p. 329) ἀπόντος μου πεφρόντικα ὑπὲρ σοῦ χρήσιμα τῶν σῶν πραγμάτων, P Tebt I. 6¹¹ (B.C. 140–130) καθάπερ οὖν καὶ πρ[ό]τερο[ν] προστετάχαμεν ὑπὲρ τῶν ἀνηκόντων τοῖς ἱερο[ῖς κομ ίζεσθαι, "in accordance therefore with our previous ordinance concerning the dues which belong to the temples" (Edd.), *ib.* I. 19¹ (B.C. 114) ὑπὲρ ὧν ἐσήμαινες πέμψαι γεωργῶν ἀπροσδεητοί ἐσμεν, "as for the cultivators whom you said you were sending, I do not require them" (Edd.), similarly ⁹, P Goodsp Cairo 4⁶ (ii/B.C.) (= *Selections*, p. 24) ὑπὲρ ὧν ἠβουλόμεθα, ἀπεστάλκαμεν πρὸς σέ Γλαυκίαν, "as regards those things we wished, we have sent to you Glaucias," and OGIS 5⁶⁹ (B.C. 311) ὑπὲρ δὴ τούτων καὶ γράψαι μοι ἐδόκει, 90³¹ (Rosetta-stone—B.C. 196) φροντίζων ὑπὲρ τῶν ἀνηκόντων εἰς αὐτοὺς διὰ παντός.

The preposition is common also in connexion with payments, e.g. P Eleph 5 *recto*¹⁹ (B.C. 284–3) ἐλογισάμην πρὸς 'Ερμαγόραν ὑπὲρ τοῦ οἴνου, P Oxy IV. 745² (c. A.D. 1) ὑπὲρ ὧν καὶ ἔθου χειρόγραφον, "for which (a purchase of wine) you drew me a bond," *ib.* II. 278¹⁰ (hire of a mill—A.D. 17) ὑπὲρ] τοῦ σημ[αι]νομένου μύλου ἑκάστου μ[ηνὸ]ς ἀργ υρίου δραχμὰς δύο τριώβολ(ον), *ib.* III. 522⁷ (ii/A.D.) ὑπ έρ) μισθ οῦ) ἐργ ατῶν) (δραχμαὶ) ιᾱ, *ib.* 514³ (A.D. 190–1) ἔσχον παρ' ὑμῶν ὑπὲρ ὀψωνίων ἀργ(υρίου) (δραχμὰς) υ, "I have received from you as my salary 400 drachmae" (Edd.), and P Iand 37⁷ (v/vi A.D.) ὑπὲρ συντιθείας τοῦ ῥιπαρ(ίου) with the editor's note. For the stronger ἀντί in connexion with the metaphor of purchase, cf. Mk 10⁴⁵ (= Mt 20²⁸) λύτρον ἀντὶ πολλῶν with 1 Tim 2⁶ ἀντίλυτρον ὑπὲρ πάντων: see *Proleg.* p. 105.

2. c. acc. = "over," "above," "beyond," lit. and metaph.: P Hib 1. 38⁷ (B.C. 252–1) τῶν συρίων ὑπὲρ τὴν σκηνὴ[ν] ῥύσων, "the Syrian cloths being above the cabin" (Edd.), P Petr III. 64³¹ (B.C. 230) ὑπὲρ ὀφρὺν δεξιάν, P Tor II. 8⁷⁹ (B.C. 119) ὑπὲρ ἑαυτὸν φρονῶν, P Flor I. 86¹

(i/A.D.) ἀπὸ Ἑρμοῦ πόλ[ε]ως τῆς ὑπὲρ Μέμφιν, P Ryl II. 74³ (A.D. 133–5) εἰς τοὺς ὑπὲρ Κόπτον ἀνε⟨λ⟩θεῖν, "to visit the regions beyond Coptos," P Flor I. 57⁶² (A.D. 223–5) ὑπὲρ τὸν ἀριθμ[ὸ]ν [τ]ῶν ἐβδομήκοντα ἐτῶν ἐγενόμην, and P Oxy X. 1298⁷ (iv/A.D.) ἐγὼ μόνος πάνυ ἐμαυτὸν τηρῶν ὑπὲρ τὸν ἀσφαλήν, "I have been keeping myself quite alone beyond the point of safety" (Edd.). Cf. also ib. XVI. 1840¹ (vi/vii A.D.) μίαν ὑπὲρ μίαν (sc. ἡμέραν), "day by day."

The gradual weakening of the construction of ὑπέρ c. acc. in late Greek is seen in the fact that in the NT this construction occurs only 19 times, as compared with 126 occurrences of ὑπέρ c. gen.: cf. Proleg. p. 105. For the use of διά (with gen. and with acc.) for ὑπέρ in late Greek, see Bell's note ad P Lond 1917⁷, where reference is also made to Jannaris Gr. §§ 1521, 1534(c).

See as usual the monographs on the prepositions by Kuhring, Rossberg, and Regard, as described in Abbreviations I. General.

ὑπεραίρω,

lit. "raise over." In BGU IV. 1085² (ii/A.D.), an advocate's plea, the plaintiff "does not press his claim beyond the two talents"—οὐκ ὑπεραίρει τὴ[ν] συντείμησιν τῶν δύο ταλάντων. The gen. here answers to ἐπί c. acc. in 2 Thess 2¹, a stronger opposition. See also BGU I. 1¹⁶ (ii/iii A.D.) (= Chrest. I. p. 122) ὑπὲρ ἐπικεφαλίο[υ] τῶν ὑπεραιρόντων ἱερέων, with reference to the poll-tax levied on the priests who "exceeded the number of the priests": cf. Wilcken Ostr. i. p. 241 f.

The verb is construed c. acc. in Syll³ 877.A⁵ (c. A.D. 200) τὸ]ν ὑπεράραντα [πάντας τοὺς] πρὸ ἑαυτοῦ ἡγε[μονεύσαντ]ας, and similarly in Aristeas 16, 290.

ὑπέρακμος,

"past the bloom of youth," "of full age": 1 Cor 7³⁶. Cf. the use of ὑπερετής (not in LS*) in P Ryl II. 105¹¹ (A.D. 136) Ταρμούθιος ὑπερετής, "Tarmouthis aged over 60" (Edd.), P Oxy VII. 1030⁵ (A.D. 212) Ἱστόρητος ὑπερετὴς ἄτεχ[νος], "Historetus, who was past age, having no handicraft," and similarly ib. IX. 1108⁸ (A.D. 150). For ὑπεργήρως, "exceedingly old," see P Giss I. 59ⁱᵛ·¹⁴ (A.D. 119–120).

ὑπεράνω,

"above": cf. the iii/A.D. Hadrumetum literary memorial, discussed by Deissmann BS p. 273 ff., where we find ²ᶠᶠ ὁρκίζω σε τὸν ὑπεράνω τῶν ὑπεράνω θεῶν: cf. LXX Ezek 10¹⁹. See also PSI II. 151⁴ (iii/A.D.) ἡ δὲ βασιλεὶς ἡ τού-[του] γυνὴ ὑπεράνω αὐτοῦ ἀνέκει[το, and cf. Teles p. 44¹ εἰ δὲ πάντων τις τῶν τοιούτων ὑπεράνω γένοιτο ἐν πολλῇ ἂν εἴη ἀδείᾳ. On ὑπεράνω for ὑπέρ in LXX Greek see Thackeray Gr. i. p. 25.

ὑπεραυξάνω.

Compounds of ὑπέρ are a marked feature of the Pauline vocabulary, especially in the second chronological group of the Epp.: see Ellicott ad Eph 3²⁰, and Lightfoot Notes, pp. 46 f., 294. The present verb is found intransitively in 2 Thess 1³ (Vg super.rescit, Beza vehementer augescat, Wycl.

over wexith): the lexicons cite Callisthenes ap. Stobaeus Flor. 100, 14.

ὑπερβαίνω

is found in the NT only in 1 Thess 4⁶, where it is best taken absolutely = "transgress." For the literal use cf. BGU III. 1007¹⁰ (iii/B.C.) πάντ[ες] ὑπερέβησαν εἰς τὴν αὐλήν μου, and for the trans. sense cf. PSI VI. 685⁶ (iv/A.D.) ὑπερβὰς τὰ ἑξή[κοντα ἔτη, P Lond 113. 1²³ (vi/A.D.) (= I. p. 201) ἔννομον ὑπ[ερβὰς] ἡλικίαν κατὰ τ[ὸν αὐτ]οῦ λόγον, and ib. V. 1711⁷⁶ (A.D. 566–573) εἰ ὑπερβήσωμαι ταῦτα τὰ ἐγγεγραμμένα. Also Aristeas 122 νομίζειν ὑπερφρονεῖν ἑτέρους ὑπερβεβηκότες, "the assuming of an air of superiority over others" (Thackeray). In one of the interesting letters belonging to the Gemellus correspondence, P Fay 110⁹ (A.D. 94), Gemellus gives instructions that a deep trench be dug round the oil-press, ἵνα μὴ εὖ ὑπερβατὸν ἦι τὸ ἐλαιουργῖον, "so that it may not be easy to walk into the oil-press" (Edd.): cf. P Ryl II. 138¹⁶ (A.D. 34) of a robber springing into a homestead ἐξ ὑπερβατῶν, "at a point where ingress was possible" (Edd.).

ὑπερβαλλόντως.

For this NT ἅπ. εἰρ. (2 Cor 11²³) = "above measure," cf. Syll 929 (=³ 685³⁵ (B.C. 139) διὰ τὸ ὑπερβαλλόντως αὐτοὺς τὴν πρὸς ἀλλήλους φιλονικίαν ἐνεστάσθαι.

ὑπερβάλλω.

The meaning "exceed," "surpass," as in 2 Cor 3¹⁰, al., is seen in Aristeas 84 χορηγίᾳ κατὰ πάντα ὑπερβαλλούσῃ, "with a prodigality beyond all precedent" (Thackeray), and the address P Lond 1925¹ (mid. iv/A.D.) τῷ ποθινοτ[άτῳ ἐ]πιστήμης ὑπερβάλλοντι ἅπα Παπνο[υτίῳ, "to the most desired, excellent in knowledge Apa Papnutius" (Bell).

In P Petr III. 30⁵ (iii/B.C.) ὑπερεβάλετο, said of a defendant in a case, is rendered by the editors "she applied for a postponement." For the meaning "outbid" at an auction, cf. P Hal I. 14³ (iii/B.C.) ὑπερβεβλή[σθ]αί με ὑπὸ Πετενύριος, P Oxy III. 513²⁵ (A.D. 184) ἕνεκα τοῦ ὑ[π]ερβεβλῆσθαι τὴν προκειμένην οἰκίαν ὑπὸ σοῦ, and ib. XIV. 1633⁵ (A.D. 275) βού]λομαι ὑπερ]βαλεῖν Αὐρήλιον Σερῆν[ον, "I wish to outbid Aurelius Serenus" (Edd.).

From the inscr. we may cite Syll 684 (=³ 1071) Βύβων τέτερει χερὶ ὑπερκεφαλά μ' ὑπερεβάλετο ὁ Φόρυ[ος ("Bybon, son of Phorys, threw me with one hand away over his head")—the words being cut in very ancient characters on a block of sandstone found in Olympia.

ὑπερβολή.

For the phrase καθ' ὑπερβολήν, "beyond measure," "exceedingly," as in Rom 7¹³, al., cf. P Tebt I. 23⁴ (B.C. 119 or 114) καθ' ὑπερβολὴν βεβαρυμμένοι, "I am excessively vexed" (Edd.), ib. 42⁵ (c. B.C. 114) ἠδικημένος καθ' ὑπερβολὴν ὑπ[ὸ] Ἁρμιύσιος, "I have been excessively unfairly treated by Harmiusis" (Edd.).

Other exx. of the word are P Amh II. 36¹³ (c. B.C. 135) λείπω τε τὴν ὑπερβολήν, "I do not exaggerate" (Edd.), P Lond 1916¹⁵ (c. A.D. 330–340) τῆς [ὑ]περβολῆς ὑμῶν, "your superfluity" (Bell), and, with reference to extension of time, "delay," P Petr II. 13 (18⁶·¹¹ (B.C. 258-253) οὐ[κέ?]τι ὕστερον ὑπερβολὴν δεξομένων, apparently of contractors' receiving no further extension of time, and ib. 37 1b recto¹⁷ (iii/B.C.) ὁ γὰρ καιρὸς οὐδεμίας ὑπερβολῆς προσδεῖται.

If we can trust the restoration, a striking ex. of ὑπερβολή occurs in the famous calendar inscr. *Prien* 105³⁴ (c. B.C. 9), where the birthday of the Emperor Augustus is referred to in the terms—

οὐδ' ἐν τοῖς ἐσομένοις ἐλπίδ[α λιπὼν ὑπερβολῆς], ἦρξεν δὲ τῶι κόσμωι τῶν δι' αὐτὸν εὐαγγελί[ων ἡ γενέθλιος] τοῦ θεοῦ,

"he has not left for those who will come after him any hope of surpassing him, but the birthday of the god was for the world the beginning of good tidings on his account."

ὑπερεῖδον,

"overlook," "look past" (Ac 17³⁰, cf. LXX Ps 26⁹, *al.*). The verb has the force of "look on with unconcern" in the following exx.—P Lond 24²¹ (B.C. 163) (= I. p. 32, *UPZ* i. p. 117) ἀξιῶ οὖν σε μὴ ὑπεριδεῖν με περισπώμενον, *UPZ* i. 15³³ (B.C. 156) διὸ ἀξιῶ, Ἥλιε βασιλεῦ, μὴ [ὑπερ]ιδεῖν με ἐν κατοχῆι [ὄντα, and P Meyer 1¹⁵ (B.C. 144) δεόμεθα ὑμῶν] τῶν μεγίστων θεῶν, μὴ ὑπεριδεῖν ἡμᾶς ἀπ' ὀλίγων [διαζῶντας κ]αὶ τοῖς ἰδίο⟨ι⟩ς ἐξησθενηκότας.

ὑπερέκεινα.

This compd. adv. (cf. ἐπέκεινα), "beyond yonder," is found only in 2 Cor 10¹⁶ and eccles. writers. For the form see Blass-Debrunner § 116. 3.

ὑπερεκπερισσοῦ,

"most exceedingly" (1 Thess 3¹⁰, 5¹³ (v.l.—ῶς), Eph 3²⁰): for the form see Blass-Debrunner § 12. 3.

ὑπερεκχύννω,

"pour out to overflowing," pass. "overflow," "run over," occurs in Lk 6³⁸, and as a v.l. in Joel 2²⁴. According to Grimm-Thayer the word is "not found elsewhere."

ὑπερεντυγχάνω,

"supplicate on behalf of" (Rom 8²⁶), does not seem to occur outside early Christian literature: cf. Clem. Alex. *Paed.* I. vi. 47, 4 (ed. Stählin). To the citations of ἐντυγχάνω (*q.v.*) we may add PSI IV. 340⁵, 347⁶, 353³ (all iii/B.C.), and P Hamb I. 27¹⁹ (B.C. 250) ἐπορεύθην πρὸς τὸν Φίλωνα εἰς τὴν Κοίτην καὶ ἐνέτυχον αὐτῶι περὶ τούτων, as illustrating further the wide reference of the verb in late Greek.

ὑπερευχαριστέω,

not a NT word, but found in Barnabas and Eusebius, now appears in P Tebt I. 12²¹ (B.C. 118) ὑπερευχαριστῶι, "I am overjoyed" (Edd.).

ὑπερέχω.

For the metaph. usage "surpass," "excel," c. gen., as in Phil 2³, cf. P Cairo Zen I. 59060⁶ (B.C. 257), where it is said of a boy being trained for the games—σφόδρα ὀλίγου χρόνου πολὺ ὑπερέξει αὐτῶν, "in an exceedingly short time

he will far excel them (*sc.* the other competitors)." Cf. Preisigke 4638¹⁵ (B.C. 181-145) ὑπὲρ ὧν πλειονάκι ἐντετευχυιῶν ὑπερέχων ἡμᾶς ἀπράκτους καθίστησι. In P Leid W col. 19 (ii/iii A.D.) (= II. p. 107) ὁ Αἰὼν Αἰῶνος is described as ὁ μόνος καὶ ὑπερέχων. From the inscr. we may cite *Syll* 540 (= ³072)⁷¹ (B.C. 175-172) ἐξελεῖ δὲ καὶ τὰ δέματα τὰ ὑπάρχοντα ἐν ταῖς στήλαις ὅσα ἂν ὑπερέχηι. Reference may also be made to the realistic description of Christ's Exaltation in Hermas *Sim.* ix. 6—ἀνήρ τις ὑψηλὸς τῷ μεγέθει, ὥστε τὸν πύργον ὑπερέχειν.

ὑπερηφανία.

For the sense "haughtiness," "arrogance," as in Mk 7²², cf. Aristeas 262 πῶς ἂν μὴ τραπείη τις εἰς ὑπερηφανίαν; "how should one keep oneself from pride?", and *ib.* 269. The verb is similarly used in P Flor III. 367¹² (iii/A.D.) πλούτῳ γαυρωθεὶς [καὶ] πολλῇ χρημάτων περιουσίᾳ ὑπ[ερη]φανεῖς τοῖς φίλοις, but has a weakened sense in P Oxy XIV. 1676¹⁶ (iii/A.D.) ἀλλὰ πάντως κρείττονα εἶχες· διὰ τοῦτο ὑπερηφάνηκας ἡμᾶς, "but you doubtless had better things to do; that was why you neglected us" (Edd.). See also the intrans. use of the verb in BGU I. 48¹⁹ (iii/A.D.) ἐὰν ἀναβῇς τῇ ἑορτῇ, ἵνα ὁμόσε γενώμεθα, καὶ μὴ ὑπερηφανήσῃς.

ὑπερήφανος

is always used in a bad sense in Biblical Greek, "haughty," "arrogant": cf. the adj. as a personal epithet in P Oxy III. 530²⁸ (ii/A.D.) ἀσπάζου . . . Λεοντᾶν τὸν ὑπερήφανον, "salute Leontas the proud," and the adv. in P Cairo Zen I. 59080⁴ (B.C. 257) μαστιγῶν ἐμὲ ὑπερηφ άνως. Commenting on Jas 4⁶, Hort has shown how readily the thought of personal arrogance passes into "insolence" or "scorn," the adj. thus standing midway between ἀλάζων and ὑβριστής (cf. Rom 1³⁰). See further Trench *Syn.* § 29.

ὑπερλίαν.

This rare compound, best written as one word (Blass *Gr.* p. 13 f.), is probably to be understood ironically in 2 Cor 11⁵, 12¹¹ τῶν ὑπερλίαν ἀποστόλων, "the super-apostles" (cf. Lietzmann *HZNT*² *ad ll.*).

ὑπερνικάω,

"am more than conqueror." With this NT ἅπ. εἰρ. in Rom 8³⁷, cf. the Christian epitaph *Kaibel* 1062, which begins—

δόξης] ὀρθατό[ν]ου ταμίης καὶ ὑπέρμαχος ἐσθλός.

ὑπέρογκος,

lit. "of excessive size," and thence extended to speech "big," "arrogant," in 2 Pet 2¹⁸, Jude¹⁶, the only occurrences in the NT: cf. *Assumption of Moses* vii. 9 *os eorum loquetur ingentia*, on which the passage in Jude depends.

ὑπεροχή.

For the metaph. use of this word "excellence," "pre-eminence," in 1 Tim 2² (cf. 2 Macc 3¹¹), Deissmann (*BS* p. 255) cites *Perg* 252²⁰ (after B.C. 133) τῶν ἐν ὑπεροχῇ ὄντων, with reference to persons of consequence. Add P

Michigan Inv. No. 191[11] (early ii/A.D.) (= *Classical Philology* xxii. (1927), p. 245), where a father flatters his son on his superiority over his brothers—οἶδας ὅτι πᾶν ῥά[διο]ν εἰς τ[οὺς ἀ]δελφούς σου διαφορά[ν ἔ]χεις καὶ ὑπεροχήν, "you know that in everything you easily differ from and hold pre-eminence over your brothers" (Ed.), and Aristeas 175 πόλεων ἐν ὑπεροχαῖς, "eminent cities."

The word readily comes to be used as a title of honour, e.g. P Oxy I. 130[20] (vi/A.D.) οὐκ ἔχω γὰρ ἄλλην καταφυγήν εἰ μὴ τὴν τοῦ δεσπότου Χριστοῦ καὶ τῆς ὑμετέρας ὑπεροχῆς, "for I have no other refuge than in the Lord Christ and your eminence" (Edd.), a petitioner addressing the *dux* of the Thebaid, and *ib.* XVI. 1829[14] (*c.* A.D. 577-9 (?)).

ὑπερπλεονάζω,

"abound exceedingly." For this NT ἅπ. εἰρ. (1 Tim 1[14]) we may cite Pss Sol 5[19] ἐὰν ὑπερπλεονάσῃ ὁ ἄνθρωπος, ἐξαμαρτάνει: cf. Vett. Val. p. 85[17]. The corr. adj. occurs in BGU II. 412[20] (iv/A.D.) μόνον τὸ γενόμενον κεφάλαιον αὐτῶν ἀπαίτησον καὶ μηδὲν λάβῃς παρ' αὐτῶ[ν ὑ]πέρπλεον.

ὑπερφρονέω,

"am high-minded" (Rom 12[3]), may be illustrated from Aristeas 122, where the LXX translators are praised as "cultivating the due mean" (τὸ μέσον ἐζηλωκότες κατάστημα), and being above conceit and the assuming of an air of superiority over others—ἀποτεθειμένοι . . . τὸ κατοίεσθαι καὶ νομίζειν ὑπερφρονεῖν ἑτέρους ὑπερβεβηκότες.

ὑπερῷον,

(τό, neut. of ὑπερῷος), "upper-chamber," "roof-chamber," Ac 1[13] *al.*: cf. BGU III. 999[ii 6] (B.C. 99) τὸ ἐν τῷ ἀπὸ λιβὸς μέρει ὑπερῶν (*l.* ὑπερῷον) a, and for a corr. use of the fem. P Flor III. 285[12] (A.D. 552) ἀνδρεῶνα . . . ἐν τῇ δευτέρᾳ στέγη σὺν [ὑ]περῴῳ.

Other exx. of the adj. are P Oxy I. 76[19] (A.D. 179), a woman declares that her father had certain rooms in a house belonging to her, including ὑπερῴους δύο, "two upper-chambers," *ib.* VIII. 1127[5] (A.D. 183) τὸν ὑπερῷον τόπον τῆς ὑπαρχούσης αὐτῷ . . . οἰκίας, Preisigke 6[13] (A.D. 216) ἡ δὲ αἰτία τῆς κλοπῆς ἐφάνη τοῦ τόπου ὑπερῴ[ο]υ ὄντος ἐκ τοῦ ποδώματος διατρ[ηθέ]ντος τὴν κακουργίαν γεγονέναι, P Lond V. 1874[12] (A.D. 605 or 613) ἀπὸ θ[εμελίων μέχρι τῶ]ν ὑπερῴων, and *Syll* 804 (= [3]1170)[11] (ii/A.D.) περιπάτῳ χρῆσθαι ὑπερῴῳ. See also Luckhard, *Privathaus*, p. 72 f.

ὑπέχω.

The metaph. usage "undergo," "suffer," of this verb in Jude[7], its only NT occurrence, can be readily illustrated from the common phrase τὸ δίκαιον ὑπέχειν, e.g. P Hal I. 1[163] (mid. iii/B.C.) λα[μ]βαν[έτ]ωσαν τὸ δ[ί]καιον [κ]αὶ ὑπεχέτω[σ]αν, P Petr II. 12 (3)[16] (B.C. 241) ἐπαναγκάσαι αὐτὸν τὸ δίκαιον ἡμῖν ὑποσχεῖν, "to force him to do us justice," and P Tebt I. 5[213] (B.C. 118) ὑπέχειν καὶ λαμβάνειν τὸ δίκαιον ἐπὶ τῶν χρηματιστῶν, "to give and receive satisfaction before the chrematistae": cf. P Fay 21[25] (A.D. 134) ὅπ]ως τῆς ἀποθίας ἐκίνοι τὴν προσήκουσαν δίκη[ν ὑ]πόσχωσι, "so that the creditors may pay the fitting penalty for their disobedience" (Edd.). See also BGU IV.

1022[24] (A.D. 196) λόγον αὐτὸν ὑποσχεῖν τῶν τετολμημένων, and P Oxy VIII. 1119[21] (A.D. 254) εἵνα . . . λόγον ὑπόσχῃ τ[ῆ]ς τε τῶν θείων νόμων καὶ τῶν ἡγεμο[ν]ικῶν κρίσεων [ὕβρεως, "that he may render an account for his outrage upon the Imperial laws and the judgements of praefects" (Ed.).

According to Mayser *Gr.* II. i. p. 98 ὑπέχομαι is first found with the meaning "offer," "make a tender," in Roman times, e.g. P Giss I. 6[b 5] (A.D. 117) ἐπεὶ οὖν τοσοῦτο τέλεσμ[α] οὐ βα[σ]τ[ά]ζουσι] . . . [ὑπ]έχομαι κατὰ τὴν εὐεργεσίαν τοῦ κυ[ρ]ίου Ἀδριανοῦ Καίσαρος γεωργήσειν τὰς προκιμένας (ἀρούρας), cf. ii. 11, iii. 9.

ὑπήκοος,

"obedient," "subject." In a panegyrical inscr. found on a marble throne at Adule on the Red Sea, Ptolemy III. is described as τοὺς μονάρχους τοὺς ἐν τοῖς τόποις πάντας ὑπηκόους καταστήσας (*OGIS* 54[17]-*c.* B.C. 247). Cf. CP Herm I. 52[b 18] (iii/A.D.) κατὰ τὴν ἔμφυτον αὐτοῦ πρὸς το[ὺ]ς ὑπηκόους φιλανθρωπίαν, P Lond 46[165] (iv/A.D.) (= I. p. 70) ὑπόταξόν μοι πάντα τὰ δημόνια, ἵνα μοι ἦν ὑπήκοος πᾶς δαίμων οὐράνιος, and *ib.* V. 1678[3] (A.D. 566-573) ? δούλ]ων ἡμῶν καὶ ὑπηκόων. For ὑπήκοος c. dat., as in Ac 7[39], cf. *Syll* 326 (= [3] 709)[13] (*c.* B.C. 107) σχεδὸν πάντας ὑπακόους συνέβα γεν[έ]σθαι [βα]σιλεῖ Μιθραδάται Εὐπάτορι.

ὑπηρετέω,

"serve," "minister to": (a) c. dat. pers.—P Tebt II. 420[19] (iii/A.D.) πάλιν σαι ὑπηρετῶ, "I will serve you again," P Oxy I. 58[24] (A.D. 288) appointment of treasury officials—δηλαδὴ δὲ τοιούτους αἱρεθῆναι ποιήσειτε (*l.* ποιήσετε) τούτοις φρον[τι]σταῖς ὑπηρετησομένους οἳ καὶ βασάνοις ὑποκείσονται, "you will of course take care that only such persons are appointed to assist these superintendents as are in a position to stand the test" (Edd.), and the curious magical spell, P Lond 125 *verso*[18] (v/A.D.) (= I. p. 124), for transforming a goddess into an old woman who shall declare—ἐγώ σοι ὑπηρετήσω.

(b) c. dat. rei—P Ryl II. 153[11] (A.D. 138-161) ὑπηρετήσας πράγμασι ἡμῶν καὶ ὠφέλιμος ἡμῖν, "has been of service in our affairs and useful to us," P Oxy I. 86[14] (A.D. 338) ν]αυτὴν παρασχεῖν . . . ὑπὲρ τοῦ δύνασθ[αι α]ὐτὸν [ὑπη]ρετήσασθαι τῇ δημοσίᾳ σιτ[ο]ποίᾳ, "to provide a boatman who shall help in the service of the public corn-supply" (Edd.).

See further P Oxy VI. 929[5] (ii/iii A.D.) εἰδώς σου τὸ [σ]πουδεον (*l.* σπουδαῖον) τὸ πρὸς πάντας καὶ νῦν ἐν τούτό με ὑπηρετήσεις, "knowing your goodness to all, I ask you now to do me this one service" (Edd.), P Grenf II. 77[34] (iii/iv A.D.) (= *Selections*, p. 122) πᾶν οὖν ποιήσετε ὑπηρετῆσαι τὸν μέλλοντα ἐνεγκ[εῖ]ν τὸ σῶμα ἐν ψωμίοις, "you will take every care therefore to entertain with delicacies the man who is to convey the body"—with reference to certain funeral arrangements.

For the subst. ὑπηρεσία it must be sufficient to cite the following miscellaneous exx.—P Tebt II. 302[39] (A.D. 71-2) ἐκτελοῦντες τὰς τῶν θεῶν λειτουργίας καὶ ὑπηρεσίας, "performing the services and ceremonies of the gods," *ib.* 303[12] (A.D. 150) appointment of Harpalus as guard on the desert canal—ποιοῦντα πᾶσαν τὴν ὑπηρε[σία]ν καὶ [ὑδροφ]υλακίαν, "performing all the duties and watching of the water" (Edd.), P Oxy XVII. 2123⁹ (nomination to office—A.D. 247–8) ἐ[ισ]δίδομεν εἰς ὑπηρεσίαν, "we present for service as assistant" (Ed.), P Ryl II. 238¹² (A.D. 262) ὃ εἶχαν βουρδωνάριον εἰς ἐμὴν ὑπηρεσίαν κατέσχον, "I have kept for my own use the mule which they had" (Edd.), P Flor II. 157⁷ (iii/A.D.) arrangements for the supply of bread and τὴν ἄλλην ὑπηρεσίαν for workmen that ὑπηρετούμενοι they may work with alacrity ἔχοντες τὸ ἀμέριμνον τῶν τροφῶν, and P Oxy I. 92² (A.D. 335?) παράσχες εἰς ὑπηρεσίαν τῆς γεουχ[ικῆ]ς οἰκίας οἴνου νέου κεράμια δέκα, "provide for the service of the landowner's house ten jars of new wine."

ὑπηρέτης.

The variety of uses of ὑπηρέτης connected with the general idea of "service" may again be illustrated from the papyri—P Hal I. 1¹⁷ (mid. iii/B.C.) ἐγγύος μὲν παρ' αὐτοῦ λαμβανέτω ὁ πράκτωρ ἢ ὁ ὑπηρέτης παραμονῆς, P Tebt I. 45⁵ (B.C. 113) ὑπηρέτου γεωργῶν τῶν ἐκ τῆς αὐτῆς (Κερκεοσίρεως), "assistant of the cultivators of the said (Kerkeosiris)," P Oxy II. 250¹³ (A.D. 23) διὰ Βίλλου διοικητικ[οῦ] ὑπηρέτ[ου, "through Billus, assistant to the dioecetes," P Fay 26²⁰ (A.D. 150) Σαραπίων ὑπηρέτης ("clerk") μεταδέδωκα Φαμ(ενὼθ) β, P Oxy VI. 899⁵⁰ (A.D. 200) ὑπηρέτης ἐπή[ν]εγκα, "I, assistant, have brought the petition," P Oxy I. 65²ᶠᶠ (iii/A.D.) παράδοτε τῷ ἀποσταλέντι ὑπηρέτ[ῃ] Παχούμιν . . . ὅρα μὴ κατάσχητε τὸν ὑπηρέτη⟨ν⟩, "deliver up to my officer whom I have sent Pachoumis. See that you do not detain the officer" (Edd.), and inscribed on a pillar in the market-place of Magnesia the words τόπος ὑπηρετῶν οἰκοδόμων ἐπὶ Πωλλίωνος κτλ. (Magn 239—time of Hadrian?): see Thieme, p. 33, where the common use of ὑπηρέτης as a cult-title along with διάκονος and μάγειρος is noted in illustration of Lk 4²⁰. In the same connexion Plummer (ICC ad l.) cites from Schürer Geschichte ii. p. 441, n.⁴² (= HJP II. ii. p. 66 f.) a Roman epitaph to a Jew who held a similar office—

Φλαβιος Ιουλιανος υπηρετης
Φλαβια Ιουλιανη θυγατηρ πατρι
Εν ειρηνη η κοιμησις σου.

ὕπνος.

For the significance of visions granted in sleep (cf. Gen 28¹⁰ᶠᶠ, 1 Kingd 3⁵ᶠᶠ), we may note the important PSI IV. 435⁵ (B.C. 258–7) (= Deissmann LAE², p. 153), where a certain Zoilus writes to his friend and patron Apollonius—ἐμοὶ συμβέβηκεν θεραπεύοντι τὸν θεὸν Σάραπιν περὶ τῆς σῆς ὑγιείας . . . τὸν Σάραπίμ μοι χρημα[τίζει]ν πλε[ον]άκ[ι]ς ἐν τοῖς ὕπνοις, ὅπως ἂν διαπλεύσω πρὸς σὲ καὶ ἐμ[φανίσω σοι τοῦτ]ο[ν] τὸ[ν] χρηματισμόν, "it happened to me, while serving the god Sarapis for thy health . . ., that Sarapis warned me many a time in sleep that I should sail over to thee and signify to thee this answer": cf. P Par 45⁶ (B.C. 153) (= Witkowski², p. 85, UPZ i. p. 320) ὁρῶ [[τον]] ἐν τῷ ὕπνῳ τὸν δραπέδην Μενέδημον ἀντικείμενον ἡμῖν, P Lond 121⁴¹⁰ (iii/A.D.) (= I. p. 97) εἰδέτω μοι . . . ἐν τοῖς ὕπνοις, a spell for making a person talk in his sleep. From the inscr. we may cite OGIS 610⁷ (vi/A.D.) from

above the door of a church dedicated to S. George in Syria Γεωργίου . . . τοῦ φανέντος αὐτῷ Ἰωάννῃ οὐ καθ' ὕπνον, ἀλλὰ φανερῶς.

In the private letter Preisigke 4317³ (c. A.D. 200) the writer complains to his correspondent—ὕπνος οὐ[κ] ἔρχεταί μοι διὰ νυκτὸς χάριν τῆς σῆς ⟨⟨σ⟩⟩απροεραίσει (l. ἀπροαιρέσεως, "inconsiderateness"). For the metaph. use applied to death see the sepulchral inscr. Kaibel 433 (ii/A.D.) beginning—ὕπνος ἔχει σε, μάκαρ. The verb is seen in such passages as BGU IV. 1141³⁵ (B.C. 14) μή τις ἔξω ὕπνωκε, and P Meyer 19¹ (ii/A.D.) (as read by Wilcken, Archiv vi. p. 407) ὕπνωσα εἰς Χῦσιν (= ἐν Χύσει, name of a village).

ὑπό.

1. c. gen. = "by" (a) of person or thing after passive verbs; P Hib I. 34¹ (B.C. 243–2) Ἀντίγονος ἀδικοῦμαι ὑπὸ Πάτρωνος, "I, Antigonus, am unjustly treated by Patron," P Giss I. 41ⁱⁱ·¹ (beginning of Hadrian's reign) (= Chrest. I. p. 30) οὐ γὰρ μόνον ὑπὸ τῆς μακρᾶς ἀποδημίας τὰ ἡμέτε[ρα] πα[ντ]άπασιν ἀμεληθέντα τυγχ[άνει, and P Grenf II. 73¹⁰ (late iii/A.D.) (= Selections, p. 118) τὴν Πολιτικὴν τὴν πεμφθεῖσαν εἰς Ὄασιν ὑπὸ τῆς ἡγεμονίας, "Politike who was sent into the Oasis by the government."

(b) after neuter verbs or active verbs which carry a passive meaning; P Oxy II. 239⁹ (A.D. 66) ὀμνύω . . . μηδεμίαν λογείαν γεγονέναι ὑπ' ἐμοῦ ἐν τῇ αὐτῇ κώμῃ, "I swear that I have levied no contributions for any purpose whatever in the said village" (Edd.), P Amh II. 78³ (A.D. 184) βίαν πάσχων ἑκάστοτε ὑπὸ Ἐκύσεως, "I am constantly suffering violence from Hekusis" (Edd.) (cf. Mt 17¹²), and Preisigke 1200 Ἀπολλώνιος . . . ἐτελεύτησεν ὑπὸ σκορπίου.

For further exx. of ὑπό denoting cause, cf. P Tebt I. 44²¹ (B.C. 114) ὑ[πὸ τ]ῶν πληγῶν κινδυν[εύω]ι τῶι ζῆν, "in consequence of the blows my life is in danger" (Edd.), P Par 26⁹ (B.C. 162) (= UPZ i. p. 247) ὑπὸ τῆς λιμοῦ διαλυόμεναι, and ib. 47²⁵ (c. B.C. 152–1) (= UPZ i. p. 332, Selections p. 23) οὐκ ἔστι ἀνακύψαι με πόποτε ἐν τῇ Τρικομίαι ὑπὸ τῆς αἰσχύνης, "it is not possible ever to look up again in Tricomia for very shame."

2. c. acc. in the sense of "under," "subject to"; P Hib I. 44² (B.C. 253) περὶ τῶν μαχίμων τῶν ὄντων ἐν τοῖς ὑπὸ σὲ τόποις, "concerning the native soldiers in the districts under you" (Edd.), PSI IV. 384² (B.C. 248–7) τῶν ὑπὸ σὲ τὴν ὑικὴν πραγματευομένων (= -ένων), P Petr II. 46(b)¹ (B.C. 200) οὔπω ὑπὸ ἱππάρχην, "not yet under a cavalry colonel," P Tebt I. 5² (B.C. 118) τοὺς ὑ[πὸ] τὴ[ν] βασιλείαν ὄ[ν]ταντας, P Oxy I. 60⁸ (A.D. 323) τοῖς ὑπὸ Οὐαλεριανὸν πραιπόσιτον νυνὶ ἐκεῖσε διατρίβουσι, P Amh II. 130³ (A.D. 350) τοῦ ὑπὸ σὲ πάγου, "the pagus under your jurisdiction," and P Grenf II. 97³ (vi/A.D.) τοῦ ὑπὸ σὲ κτήματος.

Note also the construction, said to be of Egyptian origin (Thumb Hellen. p. 124), by which ὑπό is used of the "lading" of an animal, e.g. Fay Ostr 14² (A.D. 1) ὑπ(ὸ) κριθ(ὴν) ὄνον ἕνα, "one ass laden with barley," Meyer Ostr 81² (A.D. 23) ὑπ(ὸ) λαχανό(σπερμον) ὄγον ἕνα, "one ass laden with vegetable seed," BGU I. 248²⁶ (A.D. 70–80) ὀνάριον ὑπὸ τρίχωρο(ν) οἴνου, "an ass laden with three chores of wine," and P Tebt II. 423¹⁷ (early iii/A.D.) κτήνη ὑπὸ χόρτον, "the animals laden with hay."

3. Ὑπό is used of time = "about," only in Ac 5²¹ in NT. cf. P Tebt I. 50¹⁸ (B.C. 112) ὑπὲρ ὧν ὑπὸ τὸν καιρὸν παραλαβὼν σέ τε καὶ Ὧρον, "I therefore at the time took you and Horus" (Edd.), and PSI II. 156⁷ (iv/A.D. ?) ὑπὸ δὲ τὴν ὥρα[ν.

4. For the construction with the acc. cf. also such miscellaneous exx. as P Oxy I. 94¹² (A.D. 83), price received for slaves ἤτοι ὑφ' ἕν ἢ καθ' ἕνα, "for one or both of them," ib. III. 494⁶ (A.D. 156) a Will in which an owner sets free certain slaves ὑπὸ Δία Γῆν Ἥλιον, "under sanction of Zeus, Earth and Sun" (Edd.), similarly ib. I. 48⁶ (A.D. 86) and 49⁸ (A.D. 100), both as amended, P Giss I. 47²⁴ (time of Hadrian) (= Chrest. I. p. 383) τῆς πεμφθείσης σοι ὑπὸ τὰ ζώδια ξυλίνης θήκης, where the editor understands the reference to be to a wooden box set off with figures of small beasts, P Oxy I. 76¹⁴ (A.D. 179) ἔχων ὑφ' ἑαυτὸν πρὸς οἴκησιν, "owning as a place of residence," and P Ryl II. 238¹⁹ (A.D. 262) κτηνύδριον δὲ αὐτοῖς ἓν γοργὸν τῶν ὑπὸ σὲ παράσχες, "give them one spirited donkey from those in your charge" (Edd.).

5. c. dat. This construction, though common in the classical historians, is unknown to the NT, but may be illustrated from our sources, e.g. OGIS 54²⁰ (B.C. 247) τὴν λοιπὴν (γῆν) πᾶσαν ἕως Βακτριανῆς ὑφ' ἑαυτῶι ποιησάμενος, P Petr III. 7²⁴ (B.C. 238-237) ὑπὸ γεννείωι, P Giss I. 11⁵ (A.D. 118) (= Chrest. I. p. 525) ἐπεστάλην εἰς τὸν ὑπό σοι νομὸν μόνος, P Oxy IV. 708³ (A.D. 188) τοῦ] καταχθέντος γόμου ἐκ τοῦ ὑπὸ σοὶ νομοῦ, "the cargo dispatched from the nome under you" (Edd.), and P Ryl II. 87² (early iii/A.D.) arourae covered ὑπ' ἄμμω.

The monographs by Kuhring, Rossberg, and Regard (see Abbreviations I. General) should be consulted.

ὑποβάλλω

in the rare sense of "suborn" is found in the NT only in Ac 6¹¹, where Field (Notes, p. 113) cites from Stephanus Appian B.C. i. 74 ἐπὶ δὲ τούτοις, ἡ ὑπόκρισιν ἀρχῆς ἐννόμου, μετὰ τοσούσδε φόνους ἀκρίτους ἐπεβλήθησαν κατήγοροι τῷ ἱερεῖ τοῦ Διὸς Μερόλα. For a somewhat similar use of ὑπόβλητος, cf. P Oxy II. 257⁴² (A.D. 94-5) ὀμν[ύω] . . . εἶνα[ι ἐκ τῆς] Ἰσιδώρας τὸν Θεογένην. [. . . . . . .] καὶ μὴ θέσει μ[ηδ]ὲ ὑπόβλητο[ν, "I swear that Theogenes is the son of Isidora, and neither adopted nor supposititious" (Edd.), similarly ib. X. 1206³⁴ (A.D. 68), and ib. XIV. 1639⁹ (A.D. 222?) Ἰσιδότου ὑποβλήτῳ χρησαμένου (= -ένου) [ὀνόματι?, "Isidotus using a false name." In Gnomon 70 (= BGU V. p. 28) ὑπόβλητοι refers to "dummy" persons.

Ὑποβάλλω in the more literal sense of "subject," "submit," occurs in P Oxy XII. 1408⁷ (c. A.D. 258) τοῖς κακουργεῖν προχείρως ἔχουσιν τέχνη . . . τοῖς ἐκ τῶν νόμων ὡρισμένοις ἐπιτιμίοις ὑποβάλλει ἡ σὴ εὔτονος καὶ περὶ πάντα ἀκοίμητος πρόνοια, "the wicked designs of those who are ready to commit crimes by artifice are subjected to the decreed penalties of the laws by your active and in all cases unresting vigilance" (Edd.), ib. VIII. 1101²⁵ (A.D. 367-70) ἐὰν δὲ ᾖ] βουλευτὴς, δημεύσει ὑποβάλλω, "and if he is a senator, I subject him to confiscation of property" (Ed.).

For the meaning "suggest," "prompt," cf. ib. XVI. 1837⁸ (early vi/A.D.) ὑποβάλλι τῷ μεγαλοπρε[πεστάτῳ, "he is suggesting to his magnificence" (Edd.). From this it is an easy transition to "nominate," as in ib. VI. 900⁶ (A.D. 332) ὑποβληθέντος ἔτι εἰς κονδουκτορίαν, "being nominated besides as contractor," and ⁶ ὑπὲρ τῶν ἐνιαυσίως εἰς τοῦτο ὑπ[ο]βαλλομένων, "on behalf of the annual nominees to this office."

ὑπογραμμός,

"writing-copy," and hence "example" in 1 Pet 2²¹, its only NT occurrence. We can cite no ex. of the word from our sources, but ὑπογραφή and ὑπογράφω are very common, e.g. P Hib I. 51¹ (B.C. 245) ὑπογέγρ[απτα]ι τῆς . . . ἐπιστολῆς . . τἀντίγραφ[ον, followed by a copy of the letter, and P Goodsp Cairo 3⁸ (iii/B.C.) (= Witkowski Epp.² p. 47) Αἰγυπτιστὶ δὲ ὑπέγραψα, ὅπως ἀκριβῶς εἰδῆις, with Witkowski's note, and the note by Wilcken in Archiv iii. p. 115 f. See also Deissmann BS p. 250. The formation in -μός is discussed s.v. ἁρπαγμός.

ὑπόδειγμα.

For ὑπόδειγμα, "example," as in Jas 5¹⁰, cf. BGU III. 747ⁱⁱ·¹³ (A.D. 139) ὑπόδιγμα ἀπειθίας, Priene 117⁵⁷ (i/B.C.) πολί[τ]ου καλὸν ὑπόδειγμα [παραστήσας. OGIS 383²¹⁸ (mid. i/B.C.) νομίζω τε αὐτοὺς καλὸν ὑπόδειγμα μιμήσασθαι. Kaibel 435² καλῶν ὑπόδειγμα φιλάνδρων, and Aristeas 143 χάριν δὲ ὑποδείγματος, "for the sake of illustration."

The word is used of a "specimen" in BGU IV. 1141¹³ (B.C. 14) πρὸς ὃ ἐδειξέ σοι ὑπόδειγμα, and P Fay 122¹⁶ (c. A.D. 100) ἔπεμψά σοι ὑποδείγματα μεγάλων τεσσαράκοντα, "I sent you forty specimens of the large sort" (Edd.: cf. Olsson, p. 180). On the use in common Greek of ὑπόδειγμα for παράδειγμα, see Rutherford NP p. 62.

ὑποδείκνυμι,

(1) "point out," "show": P Tebt I. 28¹⁵ (c. B.C. 114) ἀξιοῦμεν ἐμβλέψαντα εἰς τὰ ὑποδεδειγμένα, "we beg you to look into the matters indicated" (Edd.), BGU IV. 1138⁵ (B.C. 18) ἐκ τῶν ὑποδειχθέντ(ων) σοί.

(2) "inform," "warn" (Mt 3⁷, Lk 3⁷): P Goodsp Cairo 4¹² (ii/B.C.) (= Selections, p. 25) χαριεῖ οὖν ἀκούσας αὐτοῦ καὶ περὶ ὧν παραγέγονεν ὑποδείξας, "please therefore give him a hearing, and inform him regarding those things he has come about," P Oxy IV. 743³⁰ (B.C. 2) ἵνα αὐτῷ αὐτὰ ταῦτα ὑποδείξω, "in order to inform him of this," BGU II. 417¹³ (ii/iii A.D.) ὑποδείξας αὐτῷ π[ερὶ ἐνοικίου κοφίνων, and Aristeas 112 διὰ τὸ καλῶς ὑμῖν τὸν Ἐλεάζαρον ὑποδεδειχέναι τὰ προειρημένα, "because Eleazar has given us an admirable exposition of the principles just mentioned" (cf. 2 Chron 15³ A).

ὑποδέχομαι.

Hort's translation of ὑποδεξαμένη, "hospitably entertained," in Jas 2²⁵ is supported by the use of the verb in Michel 159⁶ (B.C. 127-126), where a gymnasiarch is praised because ὑπεδέξατο τοὺς ἀλειφομένους πάντας, "he entertained all who were in training": cf. ib. 1010¹⁶·³⁸ (beg. i/B.C.) ὑπεδέξατο τὴν σύνοδον ἐκ τῶν ἰδίων. For exx. from the papyri see P Bilabel 48² (B.C. 120) εὔχομαι δὲ τοῖς θεοῖς, ἵν' ὑγιαίνοντά σε ὑποδέξωμαι κατὰ πολλοὺς τρόπους, P Oxy XIV. 1643[12] (A.D. 298) to bring a charge πρὸς τοὺς ὑποδεξα-[μένους αὐτὸν] καὶ αἰτεῖσθαι ἐκδικείαν, "against those who harboured him (sc. a fugitive slave), and demand satisfaction," and ib. XII. 1408[23] (c. A.D. 210–14) τὸ ? τοὺς λῃστὰς κα]θαι[ρ]εῖν χωρὶς τῶν ὑποδεχομένων μὴ δύνασθαι πᾶ[σι φανερόν, "that it is impossible to exterminate robbers apart from those who shelter them is evident to all" (Edd.), cf.[25,26]

For the more general sense "receive," cf. ib. 1412[10] (c. A.D. 284) τῶν πλοίων ἤδη τῶν ὑπ[ο]δεχομένων τὰ εἴδη ἐφορμούντων, "the boats to receive the supplies are already at anchor" (Edd.), and for the subst. ὑποδοχή, "amount received" in connexion with taxes, see P Lond V. 1667[3] (early vi/A.D.) with the editor's note, and for ὑποδοχεῖον, "a receptacle," see P Petr II. 20[ii.] 4 (B.C. 252) λέμβου . . . ἐν τῶι βα[σιλικῶι ὑποδοχίωι, "boat in the Royal dock," BGU I. 301[11] (A.D. 151) ἀρούρας . . ἐν αἷς οἰκόπεδα καὶ ὑποδοχὶ (l. ὑποδοχεῖα), and the numerous exx. cited ad P Hamb I. 6[7]. Ὑποδέκτης, "steward," is seen in P Oxy I. 136[15] (A.D. 583): cf. Archiv ii. p. 260 f. For the meaning "collector of taxes" in late Greek, cf. P Grenf II. 94[5] (vi/vii A.D.) ὑποδέκτῃ Ἑρμουπόλεως.

ὑποδέω,
"bind under": mid. "put on," especially of foot-gear, as in P Lond 121[729] (iii/A.D.) (= I. p. 107) ὑποδησάμενος Λύκια ὑποδήματα: cf. Eph 6[15].

ὑπόδημα,
"shoe," "sandal": P Goodsp Cairo 30[xxxi. 14] (A.D. 191–2) ὑ(πὲρ) τιμ(ῆς) ὑποδ(ημάτων), P Oxy VI. 936[25] (iii/A.D.) ἔνε⟨γ⟩κόν μοι . . ὑπόδημα, "send me some(?) shoes" (Edd.), PSI I. 50[6] (iv/v A.D.) παρασχεῖν τῷ ταυρελάτῃ τὸ δέρμα καὶ τὸ ὑπόδημα, and from the inscrr. Syll 560 (=[3] 338)[25] (iv/iii B.C.) μηδὲ ὑποδήματα ἐσφερέτω, "let him not take shoes" into the sacred enclosure, and similarly ib. 653 (=[3] 736)[22], where in the regulations regarding the Andanian mysteries it is enacted that in the processions the sacred women are not to wear ὑποδήματα εἰ μὴ πίλινα ("made of felt") ἢ δερμάτινα ἱερόθυτα.

ὑπόδικος,
For the forensic ὑπόδικος = "answerable to," "bring under the cognizance of," rather than "guilty before," as in Rom 3[19], cf. Michel 1009[86] (c. B.C. 275) ἐὰν δέ τις πα[ρὰ ταῦτα ποιῇ, ὑπόδικος ἔστω ἐν Ἀμφικ[τί]οσιν, and ib. 1357[39] (B.C. 300–299) ὑπόδικος ἔστω Διόδωρος ἐάν τι π[ροσ]οφείλει τῆς μισθώσεως. See also P Hal I. 1[101] (mid. iii/B.C.) ὁ δὲ μ[ὴ ποιῶν κατὰ τὰ γεγραμ]μένα ὑπόδικο[ς ἔσ]τω τοῦ βλάβους (τῶι ἀδικουμένωι), and P Fay 22[9] (i/A.D.) where, amongst other Ptolemaic marriage enactments, certain officials are held answerable—ο[ἱ]π όδικοι (l. ὑπόδικοι) ἔσ[τωσαν—apparently for the dowry.

ὑποζύγιον,
"a beast of burden," confined in the LXX and NT (Mt 21[5] LXX, 2 Pet 2[16]) to a he-ass, cf. P Cairo Zen I. 59075[4] (B.C. 257) (= Deissmann LAE[2], p. 162) ἀπέσταλκα . . τὸν παρ' ἡμῶν . . [ἄγοντα τὸν δεῖνα] ἵππους δύο . . . ὑποζύγια

[Ἀ]ραβικὰ λευκὰ δύο . . ., "I have sent N.N., one of our men, bringing two horses, two white Arabian asses . . ." (Deissmann), and P Hib I. 34[5] (B.C. 243–2), and 73[9] (same date), where ὑποζύγιον and ὄνος are interchanged. See also P Petr III. 26[5] (iii/B.C.) βοῦς ἢ ὑποζύγιον ἢ πρόβατον, and other exx. in Mayser Gr. II. i. p. 31.

The reference may be more general in such passages as PSI IV. 359[6] (B.C. 252–1) ὑποζύγια καὶ σάκκους, P Lille I. 13[2] (B.C. 244–3) ὑποζυγίων πεντήκοντα ἐφεστηκότων, and P Tebt II. 92[13] (late ii/B.C.) ἐντ[εῦθ]εν κατάγεται δι' ὑποζυγίων, "(the corn) is thence transported by beasts of burden" (Edd.).

ὑποζώννυμι,
"undergird," "frap" a ship (Ac 27[17]): see Hastings DB v. p. 367. For the subst. ὑποζώνη, "a girdle," cf. BGU III. 717[10] (A.D. 149) (see Berichtigungen, p. 4) ὑποζώνην ὀναγρί(νην) μίαν, ib. 816[24] (iii/A.D.) ζεῦγος ὑποζωνῶν, and for the form ὑπόζωνον, not in LS[8], P Hamb I. 10[23] (ii/A.D.) ζμαράγδινον ὑπόζωνον καὶ πάλλιον. Ὑπόζωμα is found in Syll 537 (=[3] 969)[74] (B.C. 347–6) μεσόμνας ("shafts"), ἐφ' ὧν κείσεται τὰ ὑποζώματα καὶ τἆλλα σκεύη: see Dittenberger's note.

ὑποκάτω,
"below," "under," "underneath," as prep. c. gen., P Petr III. 37[b]5·2 (iii/B.C.) ὑποκά]τω τοῦ παλαιο]ῦ χώμ[α]τ[ος, P Lond 46[318] (iv/A.D.) (= I. p. 70) ὑποκάτω τοῦ κρίκου, and P Oxy VI. 922[21] (vi/vii A.D.) τὸ φοράδιν τὸ ἀποθανὼν ὑποκάτω Μηνᾶ μειζοτέρ ου, "the mare which died belonged to Menas the official" (Edd.). See also PSI V. 488[10] (B.C. 258–7) τὰ ἐπάνω τ ῆς ?] Ἡφαίστου κρηπῖδος καὶ τὰ ὑποκάτω, P Tebt I. 106[19] (B.C. 101) ἡ ἐπάνωι ἢ ἡ ὑποκάτωι γῆι, and P Lond 46[230] (iv/A.D.) (= I. p. 72) τὸ ὑποκάτω.

ὑποκρίνομαι.
With this verb = "feign," "pretend," in Lk 20[20], cf. Pss. Sol. iv. 22 ἐκκόψειαν κόρακες ὀφθαλμοὺς ἀνθρώπων ὑποκρινομένων, "let ravens peck out the eyes of the men that work hypocrisy" (Ryle and James).

ὑπόκρισις.
For the literal meaning "play-acting" cf. M. Anton. xi. 1 where ὑποκρίσεως is placed between ὀρχήσεως and τῶν τοιούτων. The word is found in the LXX (2 Macc 6[25]) and the NT only in its metaph. sense: cf. Pss. Sol. iv. 7 ἐξάραι ὁ θεὸς τοὺς ἐν ὑποκρίσει ζῶντας μετὰ ὁσίων, "let God destroy them that live in hypocrisy in the company of the saints" (Ryle and James).

ὑποκριτής,
again only metaph. in LXX (Job 34[30], 36[13]) and NT. For the lit. meaning "play-actor" we may cite from the inscrr. Syll 709 (=[3] 1080)[5] (B.C. 307–6) ὑποκριτὴς τραγωι-δοῖς ἐνίκ[α, and from the papyri P Cairo Zen I. 59004[44] (a flour account—B.C. 259?) Κλέωνι ὑποκριτῆι ἀλεύρων ἀρ(τάβη) α. See also Aristeas 219.

ὑπολαμβάνω.

The derived meaning "take up in the mind," "assume," "suppose," which this verb has in Lk 7⁴³, Ac 2¹⁵, may be illustrated from such passages as P Cairo Zen II. 59251³ (B.C. 252) ὑπελαμβάνομεν ταχέως παρέσασθαι πρὸς ὑμᾶς, P Tebt I. 15¹⁶ (B.C. 114) καλῶς ἔχειν ὑπελάβομεν διασαφῆσαι ἵν' εἰδῆς, "therefore I thought it well to report the matter for your information" (Edd.), P Grenf II. 36¹⁰ (B.C. 95) ὑπελαμβάνοσαν φονευθήσεσθαι, "they expected to be killed," and P Fay 124²⁵ (ii/A.D.) μὴ γὰρ ὑπολάβῃς τ[ὴ]ν μητέραν σου περὶ τούτων [τ]ρέμειν, "do not suppose that your mother has any alarm about this course" (Edd.).

For the more literal "take up and carry away" (cf. Ac 1⁹), see CPR I. 1²¹ (A.D. 83–4) ὅτι δ' ἂν τούτων παραβῇ ἡ Πτολεμ]αῒς ἀποτίσ[εται τῷ Μάρωνι παρ]αχρῆμα ὃ ὑπείληφεν . . . κεφαλαῖον μεθ' ἡμιολίας, and BGU III. 709¹⁹ (time of Anton. Pius) ἀποτισάτω ἃς ὑπείληφεν δραχμάς.

ὑπολαμπάς.

In Ac 20⁸ D substitutes for λαμπάδες the exceedingly rare word ὑπολαμπάδες, on which see a note by H. Smith in *Exp T* xvi. p. 478. The story of Phylarchus (iii/B.C.—*ap.* Athenaeus 536 E) of a gouty King who κατεῖδε διά τινων ὑπολαμπάδων τοὺς Αἰγυπτίους παρὰ τὸν πόταμον ἀριστοποιουμένους, "saw through certain windows Egyptians picnicing by the river," and wished that he were one of them, is the only authority in LS⁸ for the word, but we can add an inscr. from Delos *Syll* 588²¹⁹ (c. B.C. 180) where money is paid ἐπισκευάσαντι τὸ κλεῖθρον τῆς ὑπολαμπάδος Εὐ[κρ]άτει, the translation "window" being again consistent with the context. On the whole, however, there seems no sufficient reason for setting aside the ordinary reading λαμπάδες in Ac *l.c.*: "many lamps" may readily exercise a soporific tendency.

ὑπόλειμμα,

(or ὑπόλιμμα, WH), "remnant." This NT ἅπ. εἰρ. (Rom 9²⁷) occurs in a broken context in a wine account, PSI VII. 866⁸ (iii/B.C.).

ὑπολείπω,

"leave behind," "leave remaining": P Petr II. 11(1)⁶ (iii/B.C.) (= *Selections*, p. 8) ἀπὸ τούτου τὸ μὲν ἥμυσυ εἰς τὰ δέοντα ὑπελιπόμην, "half of this I have kept by me for necessaries," P Hib I. 45¹⁶ (B.C. 257) ὅπως μηθὲν ὑπολείψεσθε ἐν αὐτῶι, "in order that you shall not have anything owing from him," *ib.* 50⁴ (c. B.C. 257) σὺ [ο]ὖν ὑπολειπόμενος σαυτῶι ταύτην τὴν ὄλυραν, "do you therefore leave this olyra for yourself" (Edd.), P Cairo Zen III. 59327⁵³ (B.C. 249) ὑπολιποῦ τόπον, "leave a space," P Tebt II. 288¹⁴ (A.D. 226) μηδεμιᾶς προφάσεως ὑμεῖν ὑπολειπομένης, "no pretext being left to you," P Oxy VI. 886²⁰ (iii/A.D.) (= *Selections*, p. 112) τὸ δὲ ὑπολιπό[μ]ενον ἔσχατον ἀνάγνωτι, "read that which is left at the last," and PSI I. 76⁶ (A.D. 574–8) ἡ ὑπολειφθεῖσά μοι ἀκίνητος οὐσία.

For the adj. ὑπόλοιπος, see P Oxy VI. 602⁸ (c. A.D. 465) τὸ ὑπόλοιπον τῶν ἐμῶν ζώων, "the remainder of my kine," Preisigke 5208² (Byz.) τὸ ὑπόλοιπον τῶν χωρίων αὐτῆς.

ὑπολήνιον,

denoting the "lower trough" or "pit" into which the juice ran from the ληνός (cf. Mk 12¹) occurs in a iv/A.D. account, P Oxy XIV. 1735⁵ ὑπολήνια δι(πλο)κ(έραμον) ᾱ.

ὑπολιμπάνω,

"leave behind." For this Ionic form of ὑπολείπω in I Pet 2²¹ cf. P Hib I. 45¹³ (B.C. 257) τὰ λοιπὰ πειρᾶσθε συνάγειν καὶ μὴ ὑπολιμπάνεσθε, "try to levy the rest and do not leave any arrears," and PSI IV. 392¹ (B.C. 242–1) ὃ ὑπελιμπανόμεθα [κερ]μάτιον.

ὑπομένω.

For the trans. use of this verb "bear up," "endure," cf. PSI IV. 435¹¹ (B.C. 258–7) (= Deissmann *LAE²*, p. 153) προσευξάμενος δ[ὲ] αὐ[τῶι, ἐ]ά[μ με] ὑγιάσηι, διότι ὑπομενῶ τὴν λῃτο[υργ]ίαν, "but having prayed to him, if he would heal me, I said that I would endure my ministry," P Oxy II. 237 viii. 35 (A.D. 186) δίκην ὑπομενοῦσι τὴν προσήκουσαν, "will suffer the due penalty of their disobedience" (Edd.), P Hamb I. 22² (Christian—iv/A.D.) ὃς κακὰ πόλλ' ὑπέμεινε μιῆς ἐπίηρα θυγάτρος, "who suffered many ills for the sake of his only daughter," P Oxy IX. 1186³ (iv/A.D.) τὸ τὴν διὰ τῶν ἱμάντων . . . αἰκείαν ὑπομένειν ἐστὶν μὲν καὶ ἐπὶ τῶν δουλικὴν τύχην εἰληχότων ἀνιαρόν, "subjection to the punishment of scourging is even for those of servile estate lamentable" (Edd.), cf. ⁷ τοιαύτην ὕβρειν ὑπομένειν, and *ib.* VI. 904⁵ (v/A.D.) αὐτὸν τὸ ἀζήμιον πληροῖν τοῖ[ς] τὴν βλάβην ὑπομένουσιν, "that he would himself make up the loss to those who suffered injury" (Edd.).

The intrans. meaning "stay behind" (as in Lk 2⁴³, Ac 17¹⁴) is seen in P Petr III. 43(3)¹⁴ (iii/B.C.) διὰ τὸ Θεόδωρον ἀξιῶσαί με ὑπομεῖναι [ἕως Παῦνι ῑ, "because Theodorus directed me to remain till the 10th of Pauni" (Edd.), and PSI IV. 322⁴ (B.C. 266–5) ὑπόμεινον οὖν ἕω[ς ἄν] παραγένηται *sc.* τὸ πλοῖον).

Further exx. of the verb are—P Fay 11²¹ (c. B.C. 115) ο]ὐχ ὑπομένει ἑκουσίως ἀποδιδόναι, "he persistently refuses to pay voluntarily" (Edd.), P Amh II. 130²⁰ (A.D. 350) ἡμεῖς αὐτοὶ τὸν ὑπὲρ αὐτοῦ λόγον ὑπομενοῦμεν, "we ourselves will be answerable for him" (Edd.), a similar formula in P Lond 974¹⁰ (A.D. 305–306) (= III. p. 116), and from the inscr. *OGIS* 484³⁸ (ii/A.D.) ὥστε μὴ τὴν τοῦ ὀμνύναι ἀνάγκην ὑπομένειν.

ὑπομιμνήσκω,

"remind": cf. P Hib I. 49¹¹ (c. B.C. 257) παρὰ Φίλωνος τοῦ Λυσανίου ὑπόμνησον ὅπως ἂν λάβῃ τὰς ἐλαίας τὰς καλάς, "remind him that he is to receive from Philon son of Lysanias the fine olives" (Edd.), P Cairo Zen I. 59132³ (B.C. 256) νῦν δὲ καλῶς ἔχ[ειν ὑ]πέλαβον ὑπομνῆσαί σε, P Lond 33²³ (B.C. 161) (= I. p. 20, *UPZ* i. p. 239) ὑπομνήσαντά σε εὐκαίρως, P Tebt II. 423² (early iii/A.D.) ἄλλοτέ σοι ἔγραψα ὑπομιμνήσκων περὶ τῶν ἔργων, "I have written to you on other occasions to remind you about the work," P Oxy XVII. 2152⁴ (iii/A.D.) καλῶς ποιήσεις ὑπομνήσας αὐτὸν ἐν τάχει μοι ἀντιγράψαι, "you will do well to remind him to reply to me quickly," and *ib.* I. 125¹⁷ (A.D. 560) συγχωρήσω αὐτὴν ὑπομνησθῆναι παρ' οἱουδήποτε προσώπου ὑπὲρ ἐμοῦ, "I should permit you to be reminded of your suretyship for me by any person whatsoever" (Edd.).

ὑπόμνησις,

"remembrance," especially as prompted from without (see Ellicott *ad* 2 Tim 1⁵): cf. P Oxy XII. 1593⁶ (iv/A.D.) περὶ ὅ{ι} οἶδες οὐδεμίαν ὑπόμνησίν μοι ἐδηλώσας, "you have not put me in remembrance of what you know": cf. 2 Pet 1¹³, 3¹.

For ὑπόμνημα, not in the NT, we may cite P Lille 8¹ (iii/B.C.) where the word is used of a "reminder" addressed to a strategus with reference to an ἔντευξις already presented to him, P Petr III. 51³ (iii/A.D.) τὰ ἴδια ὑπομνήματα, "his private memoranda," and P Oxy I. 68⁵ (A.D. 131) ἀντί-γραφον οὗ οὐ [δεόν]τως ἐτελείωσεν τῷ καταλογείῳ ὑπο[μνή]-ματος, "a copy of a memorandum which he has wrongfully executed in the record office" (Edd.), and similarly³¹. In P Fay 28¹² (A.D. 150-1) (= *Selections*. p. 82) the word refers to the official "intimation" of a birth—τὸ τῆς ἐπιγενήσεως ὑπόμνημα, and in P Tebt II. 300 *verso* (A.D. 151) of a death—ὑπόμ(νημα) τελευτ(ῆς) Ψύφις Παῶπις. For ὑπομνηματισμός, the official "minute" of court pro-ceedings, cf. P Oxy I. 37 ⁱ ¹ (A.D. 49) (= *Selections*. p. 48). See further Laqueur *Quaestiones*, p. 8 ff.

ὑπομονή,

"steadfast endurance," denoting "an inward feeling, as well as outward conduct, but directed only towards aggres-sion" (Hort *ad* Rev 2²: cf. also Lightfoot *Notes*, p. 11, and Ropes *ICC ad* Jas 1³). Hence in late Jewish literature the word is frequently applied to the virtue shewn by martyrs, e.g. 4 Macc 1¹¹ θαυμασθέντες . . . ἐπὶ τῇ ἀνδρίᾳ καὶ τῇ ὑπομονῇ : cf Pss. Sol. ii. 40 ὅτι χρηστὸς ὁ κύριος τοῖς ἐπικα-λουμένοις αὐτὸν ἐν ὑπομονῇ. In *Test. xii. patr.* Jos. x. 1 ὁρᾶτε . . . πόσα κατεργάζεται ἡ ὑπομονή, the reference is to resistance to the wiles of the Egyptian woman.

ὑπονοέω.

For this verb, which is found *ter* in Acts (13²⁵, 25¹⁸, 27²⁷) = "suppose," cf. P Ryl II. 139¹³ A.D. 34 ὑπονοῶι οὖν τὸ τοιουτω (*l.* τοιοῦτο) γεγονέναι ὑπὸ τῶν καταγινομένων ἐν τῆι Ληνῶι λεγομένῃ, "I suspect that this has been done by the inhabitants of the so-called Winepress" (Edd.), P Oxy I. 69⁶ (A.D. 190) an account of the theft of 10 artabae of barley, ἃς καὶ ὑπονενοηκέναι καθεῖσθαι κατὰ μέρος, "which we guessed had been removed piecemeal," and *ib.* XIV. 1680¹⁴ (iii/iv A.D.) ὑπονοοῦμαι ὅτι πάντως πάλιν τί ποτε ἔχει πρὸς σέ, "I suspect that he must have some further claim against you" (Edd.). A double comp¹ καθυπονοέω is seen in P Oxy XII. 1465⁷ (i/B.C.) καθυπονοῶν οὖν εἰς Σαραπίωνα, "I have suspicions against Sarapion," and P Ryl II. 146¹⁸ (A.D. 39) καθυπονοῶ δὲ τοὺς ἐν τῷ ἐποικίῳ καταγεινομένους, "and I suspect the residents in the farmstead."

ὑπόνοια.

This subst., which is found in the NT only in 1 Tim 6⁴ (cf. Sir 3²⁴) = "suspicion," may be illustrated from P Lond 1912⁹⁷ (Claudius to the Alexandrines—A.D. 41) ἐξ οὗ

μείζονας ὑπονοίας ἀναγκασθήσομε (*l.* ἀναγκασθήσομαι) λαμβάνειν, "thus compelling me to receive the greater suspicion" (Ed.), Chrest. I. 238³ (c. A.D. 117) τὴν ὑπόνοιαν ταύτην χωρεῖτε, P Oxy III. 472³ (c. A.D. 130) οὐδ' ὅλως ὑπόνοιαν οὐδεμίαν ἔσχεν, "nor had the least suspicion," *ib.* X. 1272¹³ (A.D. 144) ὑπόνοιαν οὖν ἔχουσα κατὰ [τ]ῶν γειτόνων μου, "having the same suspicion against my neighbours," and BGU III. 984²⁷ (iv/A.D.) (as read *Archiv* ii. p. 387) ἐρρωμένον σε [ὁ θεὸς κ]αθ' ὑπόνοια[ν . . διαφυλάξι (*l.* διαφυλάξῃ) ἐν ἀφθο[ν . . .

ὑποπλέω.

For this word "sail under the lee of" (Ac 27⁴·⁷), Her-werden *Lex. s.v.* cites Philostr. *Im.* p. 305¹ (ed. Kayser) τὸ μὲν ὑποπλεῖται τοῦ ζεύγματος.

ὑποπόδιον,

"footstool," is first found in the LXX (Ps 98⁵, *al.*), and is sometimes claimed as a Jewish formation (cf. Winer-Schmiedel *Gr.* p. 23), but, as showing that the word may already have been current in the popular tongue, Deissmann (*BS*, p. 223) cites two exx. from ii/A.D. marriage-contracts, CPR I. 22⁸ (reign of Antoninus Pius) καθέδραν σὺν ὑπο-ποδίωι, and similarly *ib.* 27¹¹ (A.D. 190). To these we may add from an earlier date P Tebt I. 45³⁸ (B.C. 113) ὑποπόδιον in a list of stolen articles, and the ostracon *Preisigke* 4292³ (Rom. : cf. *Archiv* iv. p. 248) ὑποπόδια δύο.

ὑπόστασις.

For this important word we may begin by citing a few exx. of the common meaning "substance," "property," "effects": P Oxy III. 488¹⁷ (ii/iii A.D.) πλέον τῆς ὑποστά-σεώς μου ἐν ὅλῃ ἀρούρῃ μιᾷ, "more land than I actually possess by one whole aroura" (Edd.), *ib.* X. 1274¹³ (iii/A.D.) ἀπὸ δὲ ταύτης τῆ[ς] ὑποστάσεως δηλῶ ὀφείλειν τὸν ἄνδρα μου ἐμοὶ . . ., "and out of this estate I declare that my husband owes me . . .," (Edd.), P Flor I. 50⁹ (A.D. 268) τέταρτον μ[έρος ὑποστάσεως, P Oxy I. 138⁵ (A.D. 610-611) κινδύνῳ ἐμῷ καὶ τῆς ἐμῆς ὑποστάσεως, "at the risk of myself and my property," similarly³¹, and *ib.* 139¹⁸ (A.D. 612), and P Lond IV. 1343¹ (A.D. 709) σὺν ταῖς φαμηλίαις καὶ ὑποστ[άσεσιν, "with their families and effects." Note also P Petr III. 69 (*a*), p. 195. The document unfortunately is much mutilated, but it has been taken as meaning that "the owner of certain dovecots had underestimated their value in his ὑπόστασις, and that the officials were directed to sell his property and pay the difference to the treasury." In P Tebt I. 61 (*b*) ¹⁹⁴ (B.C. 118) τῆς ἐν τῶι κγ (ἔτει) ἀπὸ τῶν ἀπολειπου]σῶν παρὰ τὰς ὑπο[στάσεις τοῦ ιβ ἔτους], the editors translate, "concerning the land which was returned in the 23rd year as part of that which failed to come up to the *expectations* formed in the 12th": the same phrase occurs in *ib.* 72¹³¹ (B.C. 114-3).

On P Eleph 15³ (B.C. 223) οἱ δ' ὑπογεγραμμένοι γεωργοὶ ἐπέδωκαν ἡμῖν ὑπόστασιν, Rubensohn remarks that ὑπό-στασις is the substantive of ὑφίστασθαι in a corresponding sense: it seems to mean a written *undertaking*. Cf. also P Cornell 50⁶ (i/A.D.) κἂν μὲν ὑπόστασιν λάβῃς, δήλωσόν μοι, where, as the editors point out, the context requires "agreement of sale," rather than "declaration of pro-

perty." For the latter meaning we may cite P Tebt II.
336⁷ (c. A.D. 190) ἔστιν ὑποστάσεως τῆς κώ[μης . . .
"the amount standing in the name of the village . . ."
(Edd.), and the fragmentary P Fay 343 (ii/A.D.), a list of
villages with amounts in kind under the heading ὑπόστασις. Still one other passage may be noted, P Oxy II.
237 ᵛⁱⁱⁱ·²⁶ (A.D. 186) ταῖς τῶν ἀνδρῶν ὑποστάσεσιν, where,
according to GH (p. 176), ὑπόστασις stands for "the
whole body of documents bearing on the ownership of a
person's property, deposited in the archives, and forming
the evidence of ownership."

These varied uses are at first sight somewhat perplexing,
but in all cases there is the same central idea of something
that *underlies* visible conditions and guarantees a future
possession. And as this is the essential meaning in Heb 11¹,
we venture to suggest the translation "Faith is the *title-
deed* of things hoped for." In Heb 1³, on the other hand,
the notion of *underlying* is applied in a different way.
The history of the theological term "substance" is discussed by T. B. Strong in *JTS* ii. (1901), p. 224 ff., and
iii. (1902), p. 22 ff.

For an ex. of the adj. cf. the Andania mysteries-inscr.
Syll 653 (= ³736)⁵⁹ (B.C. 92) καὶ ἀπὸ τῶν πρωτομυστᾶν
τὸ ὑποστατικόν, where Dittenberger notes: "Ab ὑποστῆναι, 'subire, in se suscipere.' Pecunia est quam πρωτο-
μύσται dare debent cum haec dignitas in eos confertur"—
a fee on *undertaking* office.

ὑποστέλλω.

In his farewell address to the elders of the Church in
Ephesus, Paul lays stress on the fact that he had "kept
back" nothing of the whole counsel of God, using this verb
(οὐδὲν ὑπεστειλάμην, Ac 20²⁰): cf. Field *Notes*, p. 132):
cf. P Oxy II. 246²⁶ (A.D. 66), where a sender of a property-
return swears by the Emperor Nero μὴ ὑπεστά[λθ]αι, "not
to have prevaricated" or "kept back anything." See also
P Cairo Zen III. 50412²⁴ (iii/B.C.) οὐ ἕνεκεν ὑπεσταλμένοι
εἰσίν, where the meaning may be "have been concealed" or
"withdrawn" (see the editor's note), P Tebt I. 24⁵¹ (B.C.
117) συνιστοροῦντες τὰ πλήθη τῶν ὑποστελλομένων, "reckoning up together the amounts of what had been concealed"
(Edd.), and P Oxy III. 486²² (A.D. 131) περὶ ὑπα[ρχό]ντων
τινῶν ἐλογοποιήσατο ὡς ὑποστελλόντων αὐτῷ, "invented a
claim with regard to certain property of which he said he
was defrauded" (Edd.). Add from the inscr. *Syll* 246
(= ³547)¹⁰ (B.C. 211–210) οὔτε κακοπά[θ]ιαν οὐδεμίαν οὔτε
κί[ν]δυνον ὑποστελλόμενος.

For the intrans. usage = "come under," "belong to,"
cf. P Oxy VIII. 1102¹⁴ (c. A.D. 146) ἄρουραι . . . δοκοῦσιν
τῇ συνγραφοδιαθήκῃ μὴ ὑποστέλλειν, "arourae appear not
to come under the testamentary covenant" (Ed.), *ib.*
XVII. 2131¹³ (A.D. 207) μηδ' ὅλως ὑποστέλλων τῷ [ν]υνὶ
ἀμφοδογραμματεῖ, "am not at all subject to the present
district-scribe" (Ed.), P Gen I. 16¹⁶ (A.D. 207) (= *Chrest.*
I. p. 417) πάντα τὰ ὑποστέλλοντα τῇ κώμῃ, and PSI III.
187⁷ (iv/A.D.) ἀπὸ τ[ῶν ὑ]ποστελλόντων τῇ δεκαπρωτείᾳ.

ὑποστολή

is found in the NT only in Heb 10³⁹, where it derives the
meaning "drawing back" from the preceding ὑποστείληται.

In Jos. *Antt.* XVI. 112 (= iv. 3) δι' ἃς οὐδεμίαν ὑποστολὴν
ποιοῦνται κακοηθείας, Whiston renders "as makes them
leave no sort of mischief untried."

ὑποστρέφω,

"turn back," "return." For this verb, which is a favourite
with Lk, cf. P Giss I. 40ⁱⁱ·⁵ (A.D. 215) ὑποστρεφέτωσαν
πάντες εἰς τὰς πατρίδας τὰς ἰδίας, P Flor II. 247¹⁰ (A.D.
256) δύναται ἐξαυτῆς ὑποστρέψαι, P Oxy I. 122⁸ (iii/iv A.D.)
Ἐπ[. . .].ς ὑπέστρεφεν, "E. went back," and P Masp I.
67004⁹ (Byz.). See also Vett. Val. p. 288³² αὐτὸς δὲ τῆς
ἐλπίδος σφαλεὶς ὑπέστρεψεν ὀλίγα ὠφεληθείς.

ὑποστρώννύω,

"spread underneath" c. acc. rei, as in Lk 19³⁶ : P Lond
46²⁰⁷ (iv/A.D.) (= I. p. 71) σινδόνα καθαρὰν καὶ ἐλάϊνα
ὑποστρώσας, and the magic P Osl I. 1¹⁵¹ (iv/A.D.) ὑποστρώσατε αὐτῇ στοίβας ἀκανθίνας. For the pass. see P Leid
Wˣᵛⁱ·⁷ (ii/iii A.D.) (= II. p. 137) κίμενος ἐπὶ ψιέθρῳ (*l.*
ψιάθῳ) θρυίνῃ, ὑπεστρωμένη σοι χαμαί.

ὑποταγή,

"subjection" (2 Cor 9¹³): BGU I. 96⁷ (2ⁿᵈ half iii/A.D.)
where a certain Noumenius is described—ὡς ἐν ὑποταγῇ
[τ]υγχάνοντα. For ὑποταγή = *servitus*, see Vett. Val. p.
106⁸, *al.*

ὑποτάσσω.

With Jas 4⁷ ὑποτάγητε οὖν τῷ θεῷ, "submit yourselves
therefore to God," Hort (Comm. *ad l.*) compares, in addition
to various passages from the LXX, the use of the verb in
Epict. iii. 24. 65 ὡς τοῦ Διὸς διάκονον ἔδει, ἅμα μὲν
κηδόμενος, ἅμα δ' ὡς τῷ θεῷ ὑποτεταγμένος, and iv. 12 11
ἐγὼ δ' ἔχω τίνι με δεῖ ἀρέσκειν, τίνι ὑποτετάχθαι, τίνι
πείθεσθαι, τῷ θεῷ καὶ τοῖς μετ' ἐκεῖνον. He further notes
that "human submission to God" is spoken of only here
and Heb 12⁹ in the NT. Note also such passages as P Leid
Wˣˣⁱⁱ·⁵⁴ (ii/iii A.D.) (= II. p. 127) πάντα ὑποτέτακταί σου
(*l.* σοι), and from the inscr. *OGIS* 654⁷ (i/B.C.) σύμπασαν
τὴ[ν] Θηβαΐδα μὴ ὑποταγεῖσαν τοῖς βασιλεῦσι[ν], ὑποτάξας.

The verb is very common in the papyri in the sense of
"append" to a document, e.g. P Oxy I. 34 *verso*ⁱⁱ·⁷ (A.D.
127) αὐτὸ τὸ πρόγραμμα ἐκγραψάμενος ὑπέταξα τῇ [ἐ]πι-
στολῇ, "I have copied out the proclamation and append
it to this letter," P Ryl II. 104⁷ (A.D. 167) ὑπέταξα τὰ
ἀμφοτέρων ἡμῶν δίκαια, "I append the claims of both of
us," and P Oxy I. 67⁹ (A.D. 338) ὥς γε τὰ ὑποτεταγμένα
διαβεβεοῦται, "as at least the appended document testifies."
See also Laqueur *Quaestiones*, pp. 7, 24 f.

For the "ingressive" fut. ὑποταγήσεται in 1 Cor 15²⁸,
see *Proleg.* p. 149, and for the "reflexive" ὑποτάσσεσθε in
Col 3¹⁸, see *ib.* p. 163.

ὑποτίθημι.

We are primarily concerned with this verb only in so far
as we can throw light upon its usage in the NT. In this
connexion it is interesting to notice that Field's statement
(*Notes*, p. 208 f.) that in 1 Tim 4⁶ ὑποτίθεσθαι "does not
appear to contain the idea of *reminding* a person of something that he knew before, but simply of *suggesting* or *ad-*

rising" may be supported by a private letter of i/ii A.D.
BGU VI. 1301[15] γινώσκων ὅτι εἰς πᾶν σοι συνκ[ατα]βήσομαι ἐὰν ὑποτιθέ[να]ι̣ βο̣ύ̣ληι ἑκόντι ὡς ἄλλως . . .

The difficult phrase in Rom 10[1] τὸν ἑαυτῶν τράχηλον ὑπέθηκαν, "laid down their own necks" in the sense of "risked their own lives" is confirmed by Deissmann (*LAE*[2], p. 117 f.) from a Herculaneum papyrus (after B.C. 150), where, however, παραβάλλω takes the place of ὑποτίθημι— ὑπὲρ ?] τοῦ μάλιστ᾽ ἀγαπωμένου τῶν ἀναγκαίων ἢ τῶν φίλων παραβάλοι ἂν ἑτοίμως τὸν τράχηλον, "for (?) the most beloved of his relatives or friends he would readily stake his neck."

For the legal usage "mortgage" it is sufficient to cite P Petr II. 46(*b*)[5] (B.C. 200) ὑποτίθημι τὴν ὑπάρχουσάν μοι οἰκίαν, P Oxy III. 494[19] (a Will—A.D. 156) γυναικὶ . . . ἐξέστω δι᾽ αὑτῆς πωλεῖν καὶ ὑποτίθεσθαι ἃ ἐὰν αἱρῆται, "my wife shall have the right to sell and mortgage on her own authority anything she chooses" (Edd.), and P Ryl II. 162[28] (A.D. 159) πωλοῦσα καὶ ὑποτιθοῦσα (for form cf. Deissmann *BS*, p. 193) καὶ μετα]διδοῦσα, "having the power of sale, mortgage, gift." In P Oxy X. 1260[30] (list of property—early ii/A.D.) we hear of κιτῶνα ὑποτεθειμένον Τνεφερσόιτι πρὸς δραχμὰς ὀκτώ, "a tunic pledged to Tnephersoitis for eight drachmas" (Edd.). See also P Cairo Zen III. 59361[9] (B.C. 242) τὸν δὲ (χιλιάρουρον) ὑποτιθέμεθα ἐπὶ τὸ ἔλαττον (δραχμὰς) ᾽Α. "we assess at the reduced sum of 1000 drachmae" (Ed.).

ὑποτρέχω,

"run in under," hence of navigators "run under the lee of" (Ac 27[16]). For a metaph. usage see P Tebt I. 24[67] (B.C. 117) τὰς ὑποδεδραμημέ[να]ι̣ς ἐπι[σ]τατείαις (*l.* ὑποδεδραμμένας ἐπιστατείας) κατακεχωρ[ηκότων, "have handed over the posts of epistatae into which they have crept" (Edd.), and cf. P Giss I. 79[iv. 1] (*c*. A.D. 117) σὲ ὑποδραμ[εῖν καὶ παραγρά]φειν αὐτούς, "dass du heimlich entwichen bist und sie prellst."

ὑποτύπωσις

is found in the NT only in 1 Tim 1[16], 2 Tim 1[13], where it denotes not "pattern," but "sketch in outline," "the outline without the substance," "summary account": cf. Galen 19, 11 ὑποτυπώσεσί τε καὶ ὑπογραφαῖς (cf. 1 Pet 2[21]) χρῶνται· καλοῦσι δὲ οὕτως αὐτοὶ τοὺς λόγους ὅσοι διὰ βραχέων ἑρμηνεύουσι τὴν ἔννοιαν τοῦ πράγματος (cited by Parry *ad* 2 Tim *l.c.*). For the verb see PSI IV. 429[19] (iii/B.C.) τὴν πρὸς ᾽Απολλόδωρον συγγραφὴν ὑποτυπώσασθαι καὶ γράψαι.

ὑποφέρω.

In its NT occurrences (1 Cor 10[13], 2 Tim 3[11], 1 Pet 2[19]) the word is used metaphorically = "endure": cf. Preisigke 5238[22] (A.D. 12) οὐ δυνάμενος ὑποφέρειν τὰς [ἀ]ικ[ε]ίας ἀδικίας, and for the wider sense "bear" the use of the adj. ὑπόφορος with reference to corn-bearing land in *ib.* 5659[8] (A.D. 201). Other exx. of the verb are P Oxy III. 488[19] (ii/iii A.D.) ἐκ τούτου οὐκ ὀλίγην βλάπην ὑποφέρει, "in consequence he inflicts much loss upon me" (Edd.), and P Flor III. 362[19] (iv/A.D.) οὐ γὰρ αὐτὸς ὑποφέρω κίνησιν, "for I do not set myself in motion."

ὑποχωρέω,

"withdraw" (Lk 5[16], 9[10]): cf. P Oxy I. 67[19] (A.D. 338) εἰ τὴν δεσποτίαν αὐτοῖς ἐνγράφως ὑπεχώρησεν, "whether she made any written cession of them to these men" (Edd.)—a dispute regarding property. For the subst. ὑποχώρησις, see *ib.*[20]. The verb is found, unfortunately before a lacuna, in *Syll* 603 (=[3] 1017)[16] (iii/B.C.).

ὑποπιάζω.

The subst. ὑπώπιον, from which this verb is derived, denotes primarily "the part of the face under the eyes," and hence "a blow in the face," or "a bruise" generally: cf. P Lips I. 39[13] (A.D. 390) (= *Chrest.* II. p. 141), where a complaint is lodged of an attack—ὡς καὶ τὰ ὑπώπια ἔχω ἀφ᾽ ὅλων τῶν ω.[. . .] καὶ τῶν προσ[. . . . . The verb is to be understood = "treat severely" in 1 Cor 9[27] (cf. Field *Notes*, p. 174), but passes into the meaning of "weary" in Lk 18[5] (cf. *ib.* p. 71). See also Lob. *Phryn.* p. 461.

ὗς,

"a sow" (2 Pet 2[22]): P Cairo Zen II. 59152[17] (B.C. 256) οὐ[θ]ὲν γὰρ κακὸν ἔχε[ι ἡ] ὗς, and P Ryl II. 134[11] (A.D. 34) ὗς τοκὰς ἐπίτοκος, "a brood sow about to litter" (Edd.). In *Archiv* v. p. 384, No. 76[10] (i B.C.) ἐὰν εὕρῃς οἶν ἕως μ. (*sc.* δραχμῶν) ἀγόρασόν μοι κάλλα, οἶν is probably = ὗν. See also Radermacher *Gr.*[2] p. 59, and Hatzidakis *Gr.* p. 176.

For the adj. ὑικός, cf. PSI IV. 431[1] (iii/B.C.) ἱερεῖα ὑικὰ γ̅—for sacrifice, and BGU III. 757[10] (A.D. 12) ἃ βόσκουσιν ὑικὰ κτήνηι. Add P Ryl II. 193[1] (A.D. 132-5) ὑικ ῆς) μίαν (τετρώβολον), "for pig-tax one drachma four obols," and the editors' note for the varying sums paid under this tax.

ὑσσός,

See *s.v.* ὕσσωπος.

ὕσσωπος,

ὁ and ἡ (cf. Thackeray *Gr.* i. p. 140).

In P Cairo Goodsp 30[xlii. 8] (A.D. 191-2) ὑσσίπου (*l.* ὑσσώπου) (τετρώβολον) the editor translates "caper plant": cf. Heb 9[19]. In Jn 19[29] ὑσσώπῳ is probably a graphic error for ὑσσῷ, "a pike," "a javelin": see Field *Notes*, p. 106 ff.

ὑστερέω,

(1) "come late," "am late" (Heb 4[1], cf. P Oxy I. 118 *verso*[30] (late iii/A.D.) οὐδὲν γὰρ ὄφελος ὑστερησάντων τῶν χρειωδῶν τῇ παρουσίᾳ αὐτοῦ, "it is no use if a person comes too late for what required his presence" (Edd.); (2) "come short" (*a*) c. acc.: P Hib I. 45[7] (B.C. 261) ἵνα οὖν μηθὲν ὑστερῇ τὰ ἐ[λ]αιουργία φρόντισον, "take care then that the oil-presses do not fall short" (Edd.), *ib.* 65[9] (*c*. B.C. 265) ἵνα μη̣θὲ̣ν [εἰς ἐ]μὲ ὑστερήσῃ, "in order that there may be no arrears against me" (Edd.), P Oxy X. 1293[21] (A.D. 117-38) ἐπειδὴ ὑστερῶ τέταρτα δ[ύ]ο, "since I want two quarters (?)," and BGU IV. 1074[7] (A.D. 275) ὡς μήτε ὑστερεῖν τι ὑμῖν τῶν ὑπαρχόντων δικαίων: (*b*) c. gen.:

P Cairo Zen II. 59270⁵ (B.C. 251) ξύλων ἀκανθίνων οὐχ ὑστεροῦσι, ib. III. 59311⁵ (B.C. 250) ἐπιμελὲ[ς] ποιησάμενος ἵνα μὴ ὑστερήσηι τοῦ Ἡρακλεοδώρου τὸ μέλ[ι, P Oxy XIV. 1678⁵ (illiterate—iii/A.D.) ἢ [ὑστ]ερείσι (l. εἰ ὑστερήσει) τῆς πρωτοκερείας, μετὰ {υ} ταῦτα εἴδη ἄλλην ἐλπείδαν οὐκ ἔχομεν, "if it misses the early season we have no other hope after this produce" (Edd.). See also PSI IV. 432³ (iii/B.C.) ἵνα μὴ ὑστερῶμεν τοῖς καιροῖς, "that we may not miss the season," with reference to certain seed-sowing operations, and P Cairo Zen III. 59307²³ (B.C. 250) ὅπως ὁ κλῆρος ποτίζηται καὶ μὴ ὑστερῶμεν. MGr ὑστερῶ, "I deprive."

ὕστερον,

adv. (instead of ὑστέρως), "later," "afterwards": P Cairo Zen III. 59404¹² (iii/B.C.) ὕστερον οὖν ἐλθὼν ἡμᾶς ἐκάλει, PSI IV. 435¹¹ (B.C. 258-7) ὕστερον δὲ ἀπεῖπεν αὐτῶι ὁ θεὸς μὴ οἰκοδομεῖν, P Oxy VII. 1062⁸ (ii/A.D.) ὕστερον δέ μοι [ἔγρ]α[ψ]ας, ib. IV. 718¹¹ (A.D. 180-192) χρόνῳ δὲ παμπόλλῳ ὕστε[ρον, "a very long while afterwards," and P Ryl II. 237⁵ (mid. iii/A.D.) ὕστερον ὁ στρατηγὸς εἶπέ] μοι· διάγραψον τοῦτο καὶ αὐτῷ συνφέρει. For ὕστερον = "lastly," see Blass-Debrunner Gr. § 62.

ὕστερος.

For the prepositional phrase εἰς ὕστερον cf. P Lond 908³² (A.D. 139) (= III. p. 133) ὅσα ἐὰν εἰς ὕστερον μεταδῷ, P Oxy II. 237ᵛⁱⁱⁱ·⁴⁰ (A.D. 186) εἴ τις γένοιτο ζήτησις εἰς ὕστερον, "if any inquiry be made hereafter," and for ἐξ ὑστέρου cf. P Hib I. 52¹⁰ (c. B.C. 245) ὅπως μηθὲν δι[ά]πτωμα ἐξ ὑστέρου γίνη[ται, "in order that there may be no subsequent loss" (Edd.), P Oxy VIII. 1118¹² (i/ii A.D.) ἐξ ὑστέρου, "for the future."

For a form ὑστέρω for ὑστέρως see Radermacher Gr.², p. 64. The superl. ὕστατον (cf. 3 Macc 5¹⁹) occurs in P Iand 27⁵ (A.D. 100-101).

ὑφαίρω,

"weave," confined in the NT to Lk 12²⁷: cf. P Cairo Zen III. 59423⁹ (iii/B.C.) ὃν ἐξ ἀρχῆς ἀναλύσαντες ὑφάναμεν, of an old carpet unloosed and partly rewoven, P Oxy I. 113⁹ (ii/A.D.) ἐπεὶ ὁ κιτὼν ὑφανθῆναι μέλλει "for the tunic is to be woven immediately," and ib. XII. 1414¹¹ (A.D. 270-5) οἱ λινοῦφοι οἱ μέλλοντες ὑφαίνειν τὴν ὀθόνην τοῦ ἱεροῦ, "the cloth-weavers who are to weave the linen of the temple."

ὑφαντός,

"woven" (Jn 19²³): cf. P Amh II. 135¹⁵ (early ii/A.D.) πρὶν δὲ ὑφαντῶν, "as for the woven stuffs." Related words are ὕφασμα, "woven material," as in P Oxy XII. 1428¹⁰ (iv/A.D.) τὴν ἐσθῆτα ἀνεπι[κλή]τοις τοῖς ὑφάσμασιν κατασκευάσαι, "to manufacture the clothing in irreproachable (?) materials" (Edd.); and ὑφάντης, "weaver," as in P Hib I. 67⁵ (B.C. 228) τοῖς ἐν Ἀγκύρων πόλει [ὑ]πογεγραμμένοις ὑφάνταις.

The compd. ἐξυφαίνω, "finish weaving," is seen in P Cairo Zen II. 59263³ (B.C. 251) ἔγραψέν μοι Μαιανδρία ὅτι χλαμύδα αὐτὴν κελεύεις ἐξυφᾶναι.

ὑψηλός,

"high": BGU IV. 1185²¹ (B.C. 94-93?) γεωμετρίαν δύσβροχον δ[ι]ὰ τὸ λείαν ὑψηλὴν εἶναι, of height above the water level, P Thead 16⁶ (after A.D. 307) ἐν ὑψηλοῖς τόποις. The reference is to bodily height in P Flor II. 142⁵ (A.D. 264) ὄνους δύο θηλείας ὑψηλάς, "two tall female asses." MGr ψηλός, "high."

ὕψιστος,

For this distinctively Jewish title of the "most high" God, we may cite from the inscrr. OGIS 96⁷ (ii/i B.C.) οἱ ἐν Ἀθρίβει Ἰουδαῖοι τὴν προσευχὴν θεῷ Ὑψίστῳ, Archiv v. p. 163, No. 10² (B.C. 29) Θεῶι μεγάλω<ι> μεγάλω<ι> ὑψίστω<ι>, where Rubensohn thinks that the reference is again to Jehovah, JHS xxii. (1902), p. 124, No. 58³ ἦεν ἐν ἀνθρώποις ἱερεὺς θεοῦ ὑψίστου, and C. and B. ii. p. 652, No. 563 ἐὰν δέ τις ἕτερον σῶμα εἰσενέγκῃ ἔσ]ται αὐτῷ πρὸς τὸν θεὸν τὸν ὕψιστον (see the editor's note). Other references will be found in Herwerden Lex. s.v.

The Christian use of the word appears in the following exx. selected from Ghedini's Lettere Christiane—P Lips I. 111³ (iv/A.D.) πρὸ μὲν [πά]ντων εὔχομαι τῷ ὑψίστῳ θε[ῷ] περὶ τῆς σῆς ὑγίας, P Lond 1244³ (iv/A.D.) (= III. p. 244) π]ροσαγορεύω νυκτὸς [κ]αὶ ἡμέραις τῷ ὑψίστῳ θεῷ, and P Iand I. 14³ (iv/A.D.) πρὸ μ[ὲν] πάντων [εὔ]χομαι τῷ ἐν ὑψίσ[τ]ῳ θεῷ (cf. Lk 2¹⁴).

See also the magical P Lond 46¹⁶ (iv/A.D.) (= I. p. 66) διατήρησόν με καὶ τὸν παῖδα τοῦτον ἀπημάντους ἐν ὀνόματι τοῦ ὑψίστου θεοῦ, the Pagan prayer for vengeance in Preisigke 1323 (ii/A.D.) Θεῷ ὑψίστῳ καὶ πάντων ἐπόπτῃ καὶ Ἡλίῳ καὶ Νεμέσεσι αἴρει Ἀρσεινόη ἄωρος τὰς χεῖρας, and OGIS 755, 756, two stones from a sanctuary at Miletus τοῦ ἁγιωτάτου Θεοῦ Ὑψίστου, which were afterwards built into a Christian church in the beginning of the Byzantine age.

ὕψος,

"height": P Tebt I. 5¹⁵³ (B.C. 118) τὰ ἱερὰ ἀνοικοδομεῖν ἕως ὕψους π(ηχῶν) ι, "rebuild the temples to the height of 10 cubits," CPR I. 88⁹ (iii/A.D.) ἀπὸ ἐ]δάφους μέχ[ρ]ι παντὸς ὕψους, P Oxy XII. 1409¹⁶ (A.D. 278) ὥστε ἐπενεχθῆναι εἰς τὸ τεταγμένον ὕψος τε καὶ πλάτος τὰ χώματα, "so that the dykes are raised to the ordained height and breadth" (Edd.), and Syll 537 (= ³ 969)⁴⁸ (B.C. 347-6) ὕψος ἐννέα παλαστῶν ἐκ τοῦ ὑψηλοτέρου.

ὑψόω,

"lift," "raise up": P Leid Wˣ ¹⁰ (ii/iii A.D.) (= II. p. 115) κατὰ πρόσθεσιν τῶν φωτῶν ὑψωθέντων, ib. xii. 43 (= p. 123) τοῦ δὲ φανέντος ἐκύρτανεν ἡ γῆ καὶ ὑψώθη πολλοι (l. πολλού), "hoc autem (dracone) apparente curvavit se terra et elevata est multum" (Ed.).

ὕψωμα,

"height," "exaltation" (Rom 8³⁹): P Lond 110¹⁴ (horoscope—A.D. 138) (= I. p. 131) ὑψώματι Ἡλ[ίου] ταπινώματι Κρόνου, P Leid Wˣ (ii/iii A.D.) (= II. p. 113) τῷ ἰδίῳ ὑψώματι, and Preisigke 5114⁸ (A.D. 613-40) ἐν τῷ ὑψώματι τῆς π[όλεως. For ὕψωμα = ὕψωσις see Vett. Val. p. 62²⁹, and for the force of the metaphor in 2 Cor 10⁵, see Lightfoot Revision³, p. 159.

Φ

φάγος—Φανουήλ

φάγος,

"a glutton," is joined with οἰνοπότης in Mt 11¹⁹, Lk 7³⁴. A new verb φαγονέω, " am fat, sluggish," occurs in P Lond IV. 1380⁹ (A.D. 711) οὐκ ἀπεστείλαμέν σε σχολάσαι εἰς τὸ φαγονὶν, μᾶλλον δε . . . φοβῖσθαι τὸν Θεόν.

φαιλόνης.

See *s.v.* **φελόνης.**

φαίνω

is used in the sense of δοκεῖ (videtur), as in Mk 14⁶⁴, Lk 24¹¹, in P Par 62²³ (before B.C. 161) (= *UPZ* i. p. 309) ὁ δὲ φαίνεται τὴν ἡμέραν ἐκείνην ἀσχοληθείς, "but he seems to have been engaged on that day," BGU IV. 1141¹⁶ (B.C. 13) ἐγὼ μὲν οὐ δοκῶι ἄξιος εἶναι ὑβρίζεσθαι . . . οὐδὲ γὰρ ἡμάρτηκά τι εἰς σέ, οὐδὲ τοῖς σοῖς φίλοις φανή(σεται) ὑβρίζεσθαί με, P Oxy IV. 811 (*c.* A.D. 1) εἴ σοι φαί[νε]ται γράφον αὐτῶι, *ib.* 745⁸ (A.D. 16) τοῦτο οὖν ἐὰν σοι φα[ί]νηται σπουδάσεις κατὰ τὸ δίκαιον, "if it seems good to you, further him in this matter, as is just," P Ryl II. 125²⁹ (A.D. 28–29) διὸ ἀξιῶ, ἐὰν φαίνηται, ἀχθῆναι τὸν ἐγκαλούμενο(ν) ἐπὶ σέ, "wherefore I ask, if it seems good to you, that the accused be brought before you" (Edd.), and P Oxy I. 37³¹ ⁷ (report of a lawsuit—A.D. 49) φαίνεταί μοι κατὰ τὰ ὑπὸ τοῦ κυρίου ἡγεμόνος κριθέντα, "I give judgment in accordance with the decision of our lord the praefect" (Edd.). For a wider usage, see *ib.* XIV. 1626⁴ (A.D. 325) εἰς ἔκτισιν τῶν φανη[σο]μένων μισθῶν, "to pay in full the sums found to have accrued", cf. *l.*¹⁶ τὰ δὲ φανησόμενα ἄχρι συνπληρώσεως τῆς ἐπιμελείας, "the sums found to have accrued up to the termination of his duties as superintendent" (Edd.).

For the pass. "appear," "am manifest," cf. the restoration in *Priene* 105³⁶ (*c.* B.C. 9) φανεὶς δὲ ὁ Καῖσαρ τὰς ἐλπίδας τῶν προλαβόντων . . . , "César, par son apparition, (a realise) les espérances des ancêtres " (Routhac).

φανερός,

"clear," "manifest," is often found with γίνεσθαι, as in BGU IV. 1141⁴¹ (B.C. 14) φανερόν μοι ἐγενήθη, or with ποιέω, as in P Oxy VI. 928⁷ (ii/iii A.D.) φανερόν σοι ποιῶ, "I inform you," P Tebt II. 333¹² (A.D. 216) ἐπιδίδωμι αὐτὸ τοῦτο φανερόν σοι ποιοῦσα, "I present this statement, making this matter known to you " (Edd.).

The adj. is variously applied to a number of objects such as ἀργύριον (PSI II. 229⁶, iii/A.D.), χρέος (*Chrest.* II. 71³, A.D. 462, where see the editor's note), πρᾶγμα (P Oxy VI. 902³, *c.* A.D. 465), κεφάλαιον (P Lond 992¹¹, A.D. 507

(= III. p. 253)), ἀννῶνα (BGU III. 836³, vi/A.D.), and κεράτιον (P Iand 20⁸, vi/vii A.D.).

For the comp⁵⁶, see P Fay 20⁵ (Imperial edict—iii/iv A.D.) πολὺ ἄν φανερωτέραν τὴν ἐμαυτοῦ μεγαλοψυχίαν ἐπιδεικ[ν]ύμενος, "I should have made a much more conspicuous display of my magnanimity " (Edd.); and for the super¹⁵, P Oxy VIII. 1100³ (A.D. 206) ἐν τοῖς τῶν νομῶν φανερωτάτοις τόποις.

φανερόω,

"make clear," "make known": P Goodsp Cairo 15¹⁹ (A.D. 362) ἐφανέρωσα τῇ μονῇ καὶ τῷ βοηθῶ [το]ῦ πραιποσίτου, "I have made known both to the establishment of the *praepositus* and to his assistant " (Ed.). See also the Christian prayer P Oxy VI. 925⁴ (v/vi A.D.) (= *Selections*, p. 131) ὁ θ(εὸ)ς . . . φανέρωσόν μοι τὴν παρὰ σοὶ ἀλήθιαν εἰ βούλη με ἀπελθεῖν εἰς Χιούτ, "O God, reveal to me thy truth, whether it be thy will that I go to Chiout " (Edd.).

φανερῶς,

"openly": P Leid B¾ ₄ (B.C. 164) (= *UPZ* i. p. 109) ὥστ' ἄν φανερῶς λέγειν τοὺς πλείστους τῶν ἀγνοούντων, BGU II. 401¹⁵ (A.D. 618) μήτε κ[ρυ]πτῶς μήτε φανερῶς.

φανέρωσις,

"manifestation " (1 Cor 12⁷, 2 Cor 4²), is found along with εἴδησις in P Lond IV. 1350¹³ (A.D. 710), similarly 1339¹⁷, 1343⁸.

φανός,

"a link or torch consisting of strips of resinous wood tied together," but in late Greek also used for a "lantern" (Rutherford *NP* p. 131 f.): see Jn 18³ where it is joined with λαμπάς, as in P Lond 1159⁵⁹ (A.D. 145–147) (= III. p. 113, *Chrest.* I. p. 492) ἐπὶ ξύλ ων καὶ ἀνθράκων καὶ φανῶ ν καὶ λαμπάδων οἱ προόντες, account of the preparations for an official visit of the prefect. See also P Par 35¹⁵ (B.C. 163) (= *UPZ* i. p. 130) ὀψὲ τῆς ὥρας καὶ ἐχόντων φα[νόν, and similarly *ib.* 37¹⁸.

Φανουήλ,

indecl., "Phanouel " (Lk 2³⁶). Deissmann (*BS* p. 77, n.³) has pointed out that Philo *De confusione ling.* 129 (ed. Wendland) ἔστι δὲ ὡς μὲν Ἑβραῖοι λέγουσι Φανουήλ, ὡς δὲ ἡμεῖς ἀποστροφὴ θεοῦ, "is of great interest in regard to Philo's opinion as to his own language : he felt himself to be a Greek."

φαντάζω.

In its only occurrence in the NT (Heb 12²¹) the pass. participle of this verb is used, as in classical Greek, = "appearing": cf. the magic P Lond 121⁸⁸⁸ (iii/A.D.) (= I. p. 112) φανταζομένη ἀγρυπνοῦσα, in an address to the moon-goddess. For the sense "make visible," see P Oxy XVI. 1873² (late v/A.D.), a letter in hightown language describing a riot at Lycopolis—ἔ]τι τὴν Λυκοπολιτῶν στάσιν καὶ μ[α]νίαν φ[αντά]ζομαι, "I still see in imagination the riots and madness at Lycopolis" (Edd.). Cf. also M. Anton. x. 28 φαντάζου πάντα τὸν ἐφ' ὁτινιοῦν λυπούμενον, "picture to thyself every one that is grieved at any occurrence whatever" (Haines).

φαντασία.

For the meaning "pomp," "dignity," as in Ac 25²³, cf. Vett. Val. p. 38²⁶ εὐπόρους δὲ καὶ πλουσίους καὶ μετὰ πλείστης φαντασίας διεξάγοντας, et saepe. The word is used of idols in ib. p. 67⁶ ὑπὸ δαιμονίων καὶ φαντασίας εἰδώλων χρηματισθήσονται. For its philosophic use see Epict. i. 1. 15 δῆλον ὅτι ἡ χρηστικὴ δύναμις ταῖς φαντασίαις, "clearly it (sc. reason) is the faculty which can deal with our impressions" (Matheson), and for its use by medical writers to denote the "appearance" or "manifestation" of disease, see Hobart, p. 205.

φάντασμα,

"appearance," "apparition" (Mt 14²⁶, Mk 6⁴⁹): cf. the charm P Lond 121²⁷⁹ (iii/A.D.) (= I. p. 102) φυλακτήριον σωματοφύλαξ πρὸς δαίμονας πρὸς φαντάσματα πρὸς πᾶσαν νόσον κτλ., and the corresponding use of φαντασμός in ib. 124²⁵ (iv/v A.D.) (= I. p. 122) θυμοκάτοχον . . πρὸς ἐχθροὺς . . καὶ φόβους καὶ φαντασμοὺς ὀνείρων, a spell for defeating the malice of enemies.

φάραγξ,

"ravine" (Lk 3⁵ LXX). Preisigke (Wört. s.v.) identifies this word with the φάλαγξ of BGU I. 282¹⁸ (after A.D. 175) according to the better reading φάλαγξ for Φάλαγξ (see ib. p. 358): cf. l.²⁷. The verb φαραγγόω is found in P Tebt I. 151 (a survey-list—late ii/B.C.) with reference to land ploughed up in furrows—ἀρούρης πεφαραγγωμένης.

Φαραώ.

"Pharaoh." For the form Φαραώθης, as in Josephus, see Deissmann BS p. 327.

φαρμακ(ε)ία

in its general sense "practice of drugging," may be illustrated from P Cairo Zen I. 59018⁵ (B.C. 258) (= Preisigke 0710⁵), where a man states that having taken a dose of medicine he is unable to leave the house—ἄρρωστ]ος ἐτύγχανον ἐκ φαρμακείας ὤν. In P Oxy III. 486²¹ (A.D. 131) it has the sinister sense of "poisoning"—τῇ μητρί μου Ἑρμιόνη φαρμακείας ἐγκαλῶν, "charging my mother Hermione with poisoning": cf. Vett. Val. p. 11¹, et saepe. From this it is an easy transition to "sorcery," "witchcraft," as in Gal 5²⁰; see Lightfoot's note ad l., also Burton ICC Gal. p. 306.

φάρμακον

in its only NT occurrence (Rev 9²¹) has the evil meaning "drug," "enchantment," "sorcery": cf. P Tebt I. 43¹⁹ (B.C. 118) ἐπανείρηται αὐτὸν (l. ἐπανήρηται αὐτὸς) φαρμάκωι, "he has been poisoned," and PSI I. 64²⁰ (i/B.C.?), where a wife solemnly promises that she will not mix noxious drugs with her husband's drink or food—μηδὲ ποι[ή]σειν εἰς σε φάρμακα φίλτρα μηδὲ κακοποιὰ μήτε ἐν ποτοῖς μήτε ἐν βρωτοῖς, with which may be compared Syll 815 (= ³1180)² cited s.v. θανάσιμος, the sepulchral Kaibel 595³ where a physician is praised as πολλούς τε σώσας φαρμάκοις ἀνωδύνοις, and the magic P Lond 122³³ (iv/A.D.) (= I. p. 117) διασῶσόν μου πάνδοτε εἰς τὸν αἰῶνα ἀπὸ φαρμάκων καὶ δολίων. See also the prayer for vengeance Preisigke 1323 (ii/A.D.), and compare Musonius p. 124⁴ φαρμάκοις γὰρ οὐκ ἔοικεν, ἀλλὰ σιτίοις ὑγιεινοῖς ἡ δύναμις αὐτοῦ. A dim. φαρμάκιον is found in P Petr III. 42 II (8)²⁵ (mid. iii/B.C.) (= Witkowski², p. 16).

For φάρμακον in a healing sense, "physic," "medicine" we may cite P Lond 356⁶ (i/A.D.) (= II. p. 252, Selections p. 59) καλῶς ποιήσεις ἰδίωι κινδύνω τὸ καλὸν πωλήσας ἐξ ὧν ἐάν σοι εἴπῃ φαρμάκων ἔχειν χρείαν Σῶτας ὁ φίλος μου, "be so good as to sell at your own risk good quality of whatever drugs my friend Sotas says that he has need," P Flor II. 222¹¹ (A.D. 256) τὸ φάρμακον . . εἰς τὸν παρ' ἐμοὶ ταῦρον, "medicine for my bull," P Grenf II. 77¹⁷ (funeral expenses—iii/iv A.D.) (= Selections, p. 121) ἔστι δὲ τὰ ἀναλώματα τιμ(ὴ) φαρμάκου παλ(αιαὶ) (δραχμαὶ) ξ κτλ., "the expenses are—the price of medicine 60 old drachmae," etc. See also Sir 6¹⁶, Test. xii. patr. Jos. ii. 7 μέγα φάρμακόν ἐστιν ἡ μακροθυμία, and Ign. Eph. xx. φάρμακον ἀθανασίας, of the Eucharist.

φαρμακός,

"a sorcerer" (Rev 21⁸). For the corr. verb φαρμακεύω, cf. P Oxy III. 472¹ (c. A.D. 130) καὶ γὰρ ἀπὸ τῆς ἐκείνου οἰκίας ἐξεληλύθει πεφαρμακεῦσθαι λέ[γω]ν, "for it was from his house that he came out saying that he had been poisoned" (Edd.), and similarly ib. A striking ex. is also afforded by the Jewish prayers invoking vengeance on the murderers or poisoners of two innocent girls, e.g. Syll 816 (= ³1181)⁵ (ii/B.C.—i/B.C.) (= Deissmann LAE², p. 414)—

Ἐπικαλοῦμαι καὶ ἀξιῶ τὸν θεὸν τὸν ὕψιστον, τὸν κύριον τῶν πνευμάτων καὶ πάσης σαρκός, ἐπὶ τοὺς δόλωι φονεύσαντας ἢ φαρμακεύσαντας τὴν ταλαίπωρον ἄωρον Ἡράκλεαν ἐγχέαντας αὐτῆς τὸ ἀναίτιον αἷμα ἀδίκως κτλ.

"I call upon and pray the Most High God, the Lord of the spirits and of all flesh, against those who with guile murdered or poisoned the wretched, untimely lost Heraclea, shedding her innocent blood wickedly," etc. (Deissmann).

The verb φαρμακόω occurs in P Oxy XII. 1477²⁰ (iii/iv A.D.) where a petitioner addresses to an oracle the question—εἰ πεφαρμάκωμαι; "have I been poisoned?"

φάσις,

"information" (Ac 21³¹). The word is common, e.g. P Oxy IV. 805 (B.C. 25) ἐν δὲ τοῖς ἐρχομένοις πλ[ο]ίοις καλαὶ φάσεις ἐλεύσονται παρ᾽ [ἐ]μοῦ, *ib.* II. 294¹⁵ (A.D. 22) ἐγὼ δὲ αὐτὸς οὔπω οὐδὲ ἐνήλεπα ἕως ἀκούσω φάσιν παρὰ σοῦ περὶ ἀπάντων, "I am not so much as anointing myself until I hear word from you on each point" (Edd.). P Ryl II. 231⁶ (A.D. 40) πέμψας μοι φάσιν ἵνα πέμψω ἐπὶ αὐτούς, "send me word in order that I may send for them" (Edd.), similarly Preisigke 7258⁶, and P Oxy X. 1274⁶ (iii/A.D.) ἐπεὶ ἀπευκταίας μ[ο]ι καταγγελείσης φάσ[ε]ως περὶ τελευτῆς τοῦ μακαρείτου μου ἀνδ[ρός, "in consequence of the lamentable news announced to me concerning the death of my beloved husband" (Edd.).

For the word in a horoscope cf. P Lond 130²¹ (i/ii A.D.) (= I. p. 133) πρός τε μοῖραν καὶ λεπτὸν σχῆμά τε καὶ φάσιν. In P Tor I. 1ⁱˣ ⁸ (B.C. 116) (= *Chrest.* II. p. 39) φάσεσι δὲ καὶ λόγωι προφερομένου εἶναι αὐτοῦ τὴν οἰκίαν, φάσεσι = "verbis tantum."

φάσκω,

"assert," "allege" (Ac 24⁹. 25¹⁹, Rom 1²²) : cf. P Par 35⁹ (B.C. 163) (= *UPZ* i. p. 129) τῶν δ᾽ οὖν φασκόντων εἶναι ἐν τῷ[ι] τόπωι ὅπλα, Meyer *Ostr* 58⁹ (B.C. 144) διὰ τὸ φάσκειν αὐτὸν μὴ εἰδέναι γράμματα (a common phrase), P Oxy III. 486²⁶ (A.D. 131) φάσκων κατὰ πίστιν . . [. .] ἐγγεγράφθαι, "asserting that it had been registered in security," and P Ryl II. 117¹⁹ (A.D. 269) φάσκων εἶναι αὐτὸν δ[α]νιστὴν ἐκείνου, "professing that he was a creditor of his" (Edd.) (cf. Rev 2²).

φάτνη.

That the traditional rendering "manger," "feeding-trough," in Lk 2⁷·¹²·¹⁶, 13¹⁵, is correct may be confirmed by P Lille I. 17¹⁵ (iii/B.C.) (as read in *Berichtigungen*, p. 202) τὸ σ[ειτ]άριον ἐγὶ φάτ[ν]ηι, and P Oxy XIV. 1734ⁱ⁴ (ii/iii A.D.), where mention is made of εἰς φάτνας and χορ]τοθήκης. See, however, Cadbury in *JBL* xlv. (1926), p. 317 ff., who comes to the conclusion that "this much at least is probable, that φάτνη is a place in the open and that the clause which follows emphasizes the absence of shelter."

Thumb (*Hellen.* p. 71) conjectures that the form πάθνη, which survives in MGr, is an Ionism taken over by the Κοινή: see Thackeray *Gr.* i. p. 106, and Herwerden *Lex.* s.v. In P Lips I. 106⁹ (A.D. 98) Πάθνη is apparently a place-name.

φαῦλος.

For the idea of "worthlessness" (rather than "active moral evil") often associated with this word, we may compare its weakened sense in such passages as P Oxy III. 530²² (ii/A.D.) οὐθὲν γὰρ φαῦλον περὶ ἡμᾶς ἐστ[ι]ν, "for there is nothing the matter with us" (Edd.), *ib.* XIV. 1768⁸ (iii/A.D.) ὅπως εὐθυμῆτε ὡς οὐδέν ἐστιν [φ]αῦλον πε[ρὶ ἡμ]ᾶς, P Flor II. 208⁸ (A.D. 256) μὴ τὰ ἐν αὐτῦς (= οἷς) φαῦλα, "not the things of no moment in them (*sc.* baskets)," and *ib.* 247¹⁷ (A.D. 256) ἵνα μὴ χρεία γένηται πρός σε φαύλων γραμμάτων, "harsh letters." In P Reinach 54¹¹·¹³ (iii/iv A.D.) the adj. is applied to "bad" wine.

The stronger meaning, as generally in the NT (Jn 3²⁰, *al.*), is seen in P Leid W ˣⁱᵛ·¹⁶ (ii/iii A.D.) (= II. p. 129) ἐὰν εἴπῃ

τι φαῦλον, λέγε "si dicat quid mali, dic," and perhaps P Oxy IX. 1220¹¹ (iii A.D.) οὐδὲν βλέπω φαύλου παρ᾽ ἐμοί, "I see nothing bad in my behaviour" (Ed.).

The adverb is seen in Menander Σαμία 165 ὅτε φαύλως ἔπραττες, "when you were poor" (Allinson).

φείδομαι,

"spare," c. gen. pers., as in Ac 20²⁹, *al.*: cf. P Par 63¹³³ (B.C. 164) (= P Petr III. p. 31) τῶν ἄλλων ἀδυνατούντων φείσεσθε, "you must spare the others who are incapable" (Mahaffy), and P Oxy VII. 1065⁶·⁶ (iii/A.D.) ὥσπερ [ο]ἱ θεοὶ οὐκ ἐφίσαντό μ[ο]υ, οὕτως κἀγὼ θεῶ[ν] οὐ φί[σ]ομαι, "as the gods have not spared me, so will I not spare the gods," an interesting passage as illustrating "the tendency in the popular religion to regard the relationship between gods and men as one of strict reciprocity" (Ed.).

See also P Oxy VII. 1070²⁶ (iii A.D.) μηδενὸς ὧν ἔχομεν αὐτῶν φειδομένη, "sparing nothing that we have" (Ed.), P Fay 20¹⁹ (iii/iv A.D.) μεθ᾽ ὅσης αὐτοὺς προθυμίας φείδεσθαι, "how much zeal it is their duty to show in exercising thrift" (Edd.), and from the inscr. *Syll* 325 (= ³708)³⁰ (before B.C. 100) οὐδενὸς φεισάμενος οὔτε τῶν πρὸς τοὺς θεοὺς οὔτε τῶν πρὸς τοὺς πολείτας δικαίων, where Herwerden (*Lex. s.v.*) understands the verb in the sense "rationem habere."

φειδομένως.

This rare adv., which in Biblical Greek is confined to 2 Cor 9⁶ (but see Prov 21¹⁴) occurs in Plut. *Alex.* xxv. νῦν δὲ φειδομένως χρῶ τοῖς παροῦσι, "now, however, use sparingly what thou hast."

φελόνης,

"cloak" (*paenula*). The word appears in the above form in 2 Tim 4¹³, its only NT occurrence, cf. P Fay 347 (ii/A.D.), payment for various articles including φελονῶν. The dim. appears in P Gen I. 80¹⁴ (mid. iv/A.D.) φ[ε]λόνιον ᾱ.

Other forms are (1) φαινόλης, as in the private account P Oxy IV. 736⁴ (c. A.D. 1) φαινόλ[ο]υ Κοράξου (δραχμαὶ) ῑ, and similarly ¹⁰·⁷⁷, *ib.* XII. 1583⁶ (ii/A.D.) γενοῦ παρὰ Ἰσίδωρον χάριν τοῦ [φαι]νόλου καὶ τοῦ ἐπικαρσίου ("cross-band"), P Hamb I. 10¹⁹ (ii/A.D.) φαινόλην λευκοσπανὸν τέλειον, and P Oxy XIV. 1737⁹ (ii/iii A.D.) ιβ φαινόλ(αι) ϛ. (2) φαινόλιον, as in P Oxy III. 531¹⁴ (ii/A.D.) τὰ ἱμάτια τὰ λευκὰ τὰ δυ[ν]άμενα μετὰ τῶν πορφυρῶν φορεῖσθαι φαινολίων, "the white robes which are to be worn with the purple cloaks," *ib.* XII. 1584⁷ (ii/A.D.) περὶ τῶν φαινολίων, *ib.* VI. 936¹⁸ (iii/A.D.) ὁ ἠπητὴς λέγει ὅτι οὐ δίδω οὔτε τὸν χαλκὸν οὔτε τὸ φαινόλιν (for φαινόλιον) ἄτερ Ἰούστου, "the cobbler says that he will not give up either the money or the cloak without Justus," and *ib.* ¹⁹ οὔπω λελύτρωται τὸ φαινόλιν, "the cloak has not yet been redeemed." (3) φαιλόνιον, as in *ib.* 933³⁰ (late ii/A.D.) εἰ ἠγόρασεν τῷ παιδίῳ σου τὸ φαιλόνιον, "whether he bought the cloak for your child": cf. P Giss I. 12³ (ii/A.D.) ἐπεμψάς μοι ὑγιῶς τὸν στήμονα καὶ τὴν κρόκην τῶν φαιλωνίων.

In view of the above usage it does not seem possible to understand the word other than as "cloak" in 2 Tim *l.c.*;

but see E. Maunde Thompson *Greek and Latin Palaeography* (Oxford, 1912), pp. 31 f., 47: cf. also Birt *Das antike Buchwesen*, p. 65. There is an interesting discussion of the word in Field *Notes*, p. 217 f.

φέρω.

(1) "bring," "carry": P Tebt II. 418⁹ (iii/A.D.) καλῶς ποιήσεις, ἄδελφε, [ἐ]ὰν εἰσέρχῃ ἐνεγκὼν μετὰ σεαυτοῦ τὴν γυναῖκά μου, "you will do well, brother, to come up and bring my wife with you" (Edd.), *ib.* 421⁶·⁸ (iii/A.D.) (= *Selections*, p. 106) τὸ κιτώνιον αὐτῆς τὸ λευκὸν τὸ παρὰ σοὶ ἔνιγκον ἐρχ[ό]μενος, τὸ δὲ καλλάινον μ[ὴ] ἐνίγκῃς, "her tunic, the white one which you have, bring when you come, but the turquoise one do not bring," P Grenf II. 73⁸ (late iii/A.D.) (as now read by Deissmann *LAE*² p. 214) οἱ νεκροτάφοι ἐνηνόχασιν (cf. *Proleg.* p. 154) ἐνθάδε εἰς Τοετὼ τὴν Πολιτικὴν τὴν πεμφθεῖσαν εἰς Ὄασιν ὑπὸ τῆς ἡγεμονίας, "the grave-diggers have brought here to Toëto Politika, who had been sent into the Oasis by the government," P Fay 134³ (early iv/A.D.) φέρων εἰ δόξαν σοι τὴν ὕαλον, "bring, if you please, the crystal" (Edd.), and *ib.* 136⁷ (iv/A.D.) ἀπαντήσατε ἀπ' ἑαυτῶν πρὸ τοῦ τις ὑμᾶς ἐνέγκῃ, "return from where you are before some one fetches you" (Edd.).

(2) For the derived sense "bring by announcing," "announce," cf. P Oxy VIII. 1148⁹ (i/A.D.) where a question addressed to an oracle ends—τοῦτό μοι σύμφωνον ἔνεγκε, "tell me this truly." Hunt *ad l.* cites in further illustration of this meaning P Fay 138³ (i/ii A.D.) ἢ κρείνεται αὐτὸν ἀπελθεῖν ἰς πόλειν: τοῦτο ἐκξένεγκον, and BGU I. 229¹ (ii/iii A.D.) ἢ μὲν σοθήσωι (*l.* μὴν σωθήσομαι) . . . , τοῦτό[ν] μοι ἐξένικον, where the sense is not "bring this to pass," but "deliver an oracle," "give an answer" (cf. LS⁹ *s.v.* ἐκφέρω II. 3). The point is not without interest for Heb 9¹⁶ ὅπου γὰρ διαθήκη, θάνατον ἀνάγκη φέρεσθαι τοῦ διαθεμένου, where φέρεσθαι may = "to be made publicly known" rather than "be brought" or "be brought in." See the discussion of the whole verse in Field *Notes*, p. 220 f.

(3) "endure": P Grenf I. 42⁵ (ii/B.C.) (= *Chrest.* I. p. 528) κινδύνους [μεγάλους . . . . ἐνην]οχότων, and P Tebt II. 314¹ (ii/A.D.) πιστεύω σε μὴ ἀγνοεῖν ὅσον κάμ[α]τον ἤνεγκα ἕως τὴν [π]ερι[το]μὴν ἐκπλέξω. "I believe you are aware how much trouble I had in getting the circumcision through": cf. Heb 12²⁰, 13¹³.

(4) For φέρω εἰς, "lead to," as in Ac 12¹⁰, cf. P Oxy I. 69¹ (A.D. 190) (θύραν) φέρουσαν εἰς δημοσίαν ῥύμην, and *ib.* 99⁷·¹⁷ (A.D. 55). See also P Tebt I. 54⁸ (B.C. 86) τῆι νυκτὶ τῆι φερούσηι εἰς τὴν κε̄ τοῦ Φαῶφι, "on the night which led to the 25ᵗʰ of Phaophi," the "day" began with sunrise, and similarly P Ryl II. 120⁵ (A.D. 30), BGU II. 589⁶ (ii/A.D.). MGr φέρνω, as well as φέρω.

φεύγω,

"flee," "escape": Preisigke 6757¹⁸ (B.C. 240-8) κατελάβομεν δὲ τὸν Ἀτφεῖν πεφευγότα, P Oxy II. 295¹ (c. A.D. 35) γίνωσκε ὅτι Σέλευκος ἐλθὼν ὧδε πέφευγε, "I must tell you that Seleucus came here and has fled" (Edd.), *ib.* XII. 1415⁸ (late iii/A.D.) ἵνα μὴ φεύγωσιν, "lest they run away," to avoid a certain duty laid upon them, P Grenf II.

84⁴ (v/vi A.D.) πατέραν φονεύσας (*l.* πατέρα φονεύσας) νόμους φοβηθεὶς ἔφυγεν εἰς ἐρημίαν, "having killed his father, in fear of the laws he fled into the desert," and the Christian amulet P Oxy VIII. 1151¹ (v/A.D.?) φεῦγε πν(εῦμ)α μεμισιμένον, Χ(ριστό)s σε διώκει, "fly, hateful spirit! Christ pursues thee" (Ed.).

A somewhat weakened sense is found in P Giss I. 40ⁱⁱ·¹⁶ (A.D. 215) Αἰ[γύπτι]οι πάντες, οἵ εἰσιν ἐν Ἀλεξανδρείᾳ, καὶ μάλιστα ἄ[γ]ροικοι, οἵτινες πεφε[ύγασιν] ἄλ[λοθεν, and *ib.*²³ οἵτινες φεύγουσι τὰς χώρας τὰς ἰδίας.

Φῆλιξ.

For this common proper name cf. P Oxy IV. 800 (c. A.D. 153), where it is the name of a prefect.

φήμη,

"report," "rumour" (Mt 9²⁶, Lk 4¹⁴): the word is doubtfully restored in BGU IV. 1024ᵛⁱⁱ·²⁸ (end iv/A.D.). A late ex. is afforded by P Masp I. 67097 *verso* D⁸⁹ (Byz.).

φημί.

A few miscellaneous exx. will suffice for this common verb—P Lille I. 5⁷ (B.C. 260-59) εἰς σπέρμα, πρὸς αἷς φ[ησι]ν ἔχειν πυρ οῦ πγ̄, "pour semence, en plus des 83 artabes de blé qu'il dit avoir" (Ed.), P Tebt II. 280¹¹ (B.C. 126) ὧν ἔφη ἠγορα(κέναι) κατὰ συ(γγραφήν). "which (space) he stated he had bought by a contract," P Amh II. 30¹¹ (ii/B.C.) ἔφη ἐκχωρήσει(ν) ἐκ τῆς οἰκίας ἐν ἡ[μ]έραις ῑ, P Flor I. 49⁶ (A.D. 209) Σαραπίωνος, ὥς φη(σιν), [ἀπὸ τῆ]ς μητροπόλεως, and *ib.* 127² (A.D. 256) σὺν θεῷ φάναι προσδόκα ἡμᾶς, "if God pleases, expect us."

For the part. we may cite P Petr III. 30⁶ (iii/B.C.) φαμένη καταστήσεσθαι πρός [με, "though she said that she would appear against me" (Edd.), and its frequent occurrence in the subscriptions of letters in such phrases as— P Ryl II. 155²³ (A.D. 138-61) ἔγρα]ψα ὑ[πὲ]ρ αὐτῆς κα[ὶ] τοῦ κυρίου φαμένων μὴ εἰδέ[ν]αι γράμ[ματα, and *ib.* 88²⁷ (A.D. 156) ἐγράφη διὰ Ἀμμωνίου νομογρά(φου) καὶ ἔστιν [ὁ] Διωγᾶς φάμενος μὴ εἰδέναι γράμ(ματα), "written by Ammonius, scribe of the nome; Diogas, professing to be illiterate" (Edd.).

φημίζω,

"spread a report," a *v.l.* for διαφημίζω (*q.v.*) in Mt 28¹⁵: cf. P Giss I. 19⁴ (ii/A.D.) μεγάλως ἀγωνιῶσα περί σου διὰ τὰ ὄν[τα τ]οῦ καιροῦ φημιζόμενα.

Φῆστος,

the name of a certain ἔπαρχος εἴλης, in P Lond 904³³ (A.D. 104) (= III. p. 126). The document itself is interesting as a specimen of an official letter copy-book (cf. Deissmann *LAE*² p. 235).

φθάνω.

1. The original meaning "anticipate," "precede," old Engl. "prevent," as in 1 Thess 4¹⁵ (cf. Sap 4⁷, 6¹³, 16²⁸) may be illustrated from such passages as P Ryl II. 119¹⁶ (A.D. 54-67) ἀπολυθῆναί τε τὸν Μουσαῖον ὧν ἔφθη λαβεῖν

ἐκφορίων, "and that Musaeus should receive a discharge from the rents previously obtained" (Edd.), P Oxy II. 237[vi. 30] (A.D. 186) ὅτι φθάνει τὸ πρᾶγμα ἀκρειβῶς [ἐξ]ητασμένον, "the fact that a searching inquiry into the affair had already been held" (Edd.), ib. [vii. 42] εἰ ἔφθακας (cf. 2 Thess 2[16] ἔφθακεν BD* 31) ἅπαξ προῖκα δ[οὺς τ[ῇ] θυγ]ατρί σου, ἀποκατάστησον, "if you have already once given a dowry to your daughter, you must restore it," (Edd.), ib. XIV. 1666[3] (iii/A.D.) φθάνω δὲ ὑμεῖν πρότερον γεγραφηκὼς περὶ τοῦ μεικροῦ Παυσανίου ὡς εἰς λεγιῶνα στρατευσάμενον, "I have previously written to you about the little Pausanias becoming a soldier of a legion" (Edd.), ib. VI. 907[11] (a Will—A.D. 276) τῇ Πτολεμαΐδι βεβαιῶ διὰ τούτου μου τοῦ βουλήματος ἣν φθάσας ἐπιδέδωκα αὐτῇ προῖκα, "and I also confirm to Ptolemais by this will the dowry which I previously gave her" (Edd.), ib. 935[20] (iii/A.D.) ἔφθανε γὰρ προβαστάξας τὰς ἐν ταῖς (ἀρούραις ?) ζ., "he has already taken away those (sc. bundles) in the 7 [?] arourae" (Edd.), ib. VIII. 1103[5] (A.D. 360) φθάσαντες ἡμεῖς ἐπληρώσαμεν αὐτούς, "we had previously paid them" (Ed.), and P Grenf I. 53[32] (iv/A.D.) (= Chrest. I. p. 158) καὶ ταῦτα πάλιν φθάνομεν ἀποδείξειν.

2. Apart from 1 Thess 4[15], the verb in the NT has lost its sense of priority, and means simply "come," "arrive," as in Mt 12[28], 1 Thess 2[16], Rom 9[31], 2 Cor 10[14] (but see RV marg.), and Tob 5[19] ἀργύριον τῷ ἀργυρίῳ μὴ φθάσαι, "let not money come (or be added) to money" (see Thackeray Gr. i. p. 289): cf. P Amh II. 72[9] (A.D. 246) ἧς κληρον[ο]μ[ίας φθάσασα διεπεμψάμην τῷ λαμπροτάτῳ ἡγεμόνι, "of this inheritance I at once announced the succession to his excellency the praefect" (Edd.), P Tebt II. 417[10] (iii/A.D.) πλὴν ἀρξόμεθ[α] τοῦ ἔργου, ἐπὶ γὰρ ἐ[ὰν φθάσωμεν ἐπιλαβέσθαι τοῦ ἔργου δυνόμεθα αὐτ[ὸ ἀ]φῖνε (l. ἀφεῖναι), "but we will begin the work, for as soon as we make haste to set ourselves to it we can finish it completely (?)" (Edd.), and P Flor I. 9[9] (A.D. 255) (= p. 28) φθάσαντός μου πρὸς τοῖς μναιμίοις (l. μνημείοις), "when I had arrived at the tombs." Cf. P Lond IV. 1343[24] (A.D. 709) φθάσαι τὰ ἔσκατα (l. ἔσχατα), "passing their wildest expectations" (Ed.).

For φθάνω εἰς, as in Rom 9[31], Phil 3[16], cf. BGU II. 522[6] (ii/A.D.) τῆς εἰς ἅπαντός (= -ας) σου φιλανθρωπία[ς] κύριε φθανούσης (gen. abs.), P Par 18[11] (ii/A.D.) ἔτι δύο ἡμέρας ἔχομεν καὶ φθάσωμεν εἰς Πηλ[οὔ]σι, and see the rare usage ἔφθασα τὸ Σκέλος, "perveni ad Scelos," in P Iand 21[3] (vi/vii A.D.) (with the editor's note).

In Sir 30[25] ἐν εὐλογίᾳ Κυρίου ἔφθασα, καὶ ὡς τρυγῶν ἐπλήρωσα ληνόν, the meaning apparently is "I attained my object," not "I outstripped others" (see Sanday Inspiration, p. 261 n[1].). Note the colloquial ἔφθασα, "here I am" in MGr, and φτάνω, "arrive," "comprehend."

φθέγγομαι,

"utter" c. acc. as in 2 Pet 2[15]: cf. P Leid W[xix. 19] (ii/iii A.D.) (= II. p. 147) ἐπικαλοῦμαί σε . . . οὗ τὸ ὄνομα οὐδὲ θεοὶ δύναται (l. δύνανται) φθέγγεσθαι. For the absol. use of the verb, as in Ac 4[18], see the epigram PSI I. 17 iv.[1 f.] (iii/A.D. ?)—

Εἰ καὶ τὴν φωνὴν ὁ ζωγράφος ὧδ' ἐνέθηκεν,
εἶπες ἂν ὡς ἤδη φθέγγεται Εὐπρέπιος.

The reference is to abusive language in P Lond 983[13] (iv/A.D.) (= III. p. 229), a petition that a certain woman should be called to account—ὧν καθ' ἡμῶν ἐφθέγξατο, similarly P Flor III. 309[11] (iv/A.D.), and from the inserr. Syll 809 (=[3] 1175)[6] (iv/iii B.C.) ῥῆμα μοχθηρὸν φθέγγεσθαι.

φθείρω.

For the metaph. sense "corrupt," "injure," as in 1 Cor 3[17], al., we may point to the common clause in marriage-contracts forbidding the wife φθείρειν τὸν κοινὸν οἶκον (P Tebt I. 104[29] (B.C. 92), BGU IV. 1050[22] (time of Augustus), P Oxy III. 497[1] (early ii/A.D.), al.): cf. 1 Cor 3[17].

A literal sense is seen in certain nursing contracts, where provision is made against the nurse's "spoiling" her milk, e.g. BGU IV. 1058[29] (B.C. 13) μὴ φθίρουσαν τὸ γάλα. In P Strass I. 24[15] (A.D. 118) the pass. ἐφθάρη[σ]α[ιν is used of the destruction of cattle. Cf. also P Cairo Zen I. 59037[7] (B.C. 258-7) where a man is described as ἐν Ἀλεξανδρείᾳ φθειρόμενος, "in Alexandria wasting his time."

φθινοπωρινός,

derived from φθινόπωρον (cf. P Cairo Zen I. 59020[1]—B.C. 258), a compound from φθίνουσα ὀπώρα, "the concluding portion of the ὀπώρα," and hence "autumnal": cf. Moulton Gr. ii. § 106, p. 279 f. In Jude[12] the epithet is applied to false teachers, δένδρα φθινοπωρινὰ ἄκαρπα, "autumn trees without fruit" (RV): they were barren at the very time when fruit might be expected (cf. Lk 13[6 ff.]). See the full discussion of the word with many reff. in Mayor Ep. of Jude, p. 55 ff., and add from the papyri the calendar P Hib I. 27[170] (B.C. 301-240) κγ̅ ἰσημερία φθινοπωρινή. MGr φθινοπωρινός, "autumnal."

φθόγγος,

"utterance," "sound" (1 Cor 14[7]): cf. the magical P Lond 121[774] (iii/A.D.) (= I. p. 109) φθόγγος ἐναρμόνιος, and [777] φθόγγος [ἀ]ναγκαστικός, also P Leid V[vhi. 6] (iii/iv A.D.) (= II. p. 29) πρὸς ἁρμονίαν τῶν ἑπτὰ φθόγγων ἐχόντων φωνὰς πρὸς τὰς κη φῶτα τῆς σελήνης.

φθονέω.

For φθονέω, "envy," c. dat. as in Gal 5[26], cf. P Flor III. 373[6] (iii/A.D.) ἐμοὶ ἐφθόνεσεν (l. ἐφθόνησεν) ὡς συνειδότι τῷ δούλῳ καὶ τὰ μέρη αὐτοῦ λαμβάνων, and P Masp I. 67121[9] (Byz.) πονη[ρ]οῦ δ[αί]μων[ο]ς φθονήσαντος (τῷ ἡμ]ετέρῳ συνεκεσίῳ (l. συνοικεσίῳ). See also P Grenf I. 53[29] (iv/A.D.) (= Chrest. I. p. 158) ἐξ ὧν φθονοῦσιν ὅτι σου χάρω (for χάριν) αὐτὰ προστεθείκαμεν, where the editor translates, "they (sc. the daughters) are angry because for your own sake we have told you what has happened."

φθόνος,

"envy": cf. P Ryl II. 144[21] (A.D. 38) ἔτι δὲ καὶ ἐτόλμησεν πθόνους (l. φθόνου) μοι ἐπαγαγεῖν αἰτίας τοῦ μὴ ὄντος, "moreover he had the audacity to bring baseless accusations of malice against me" (Edd.), P Oxy II. 237[vi. 21] (A.D. 186) ἐπὶ φθόνῳ δὲ μόνῳ [λο]ιδορούμενος, "but malice was the root of his abuse" (Edd.: but see their note ad l.), *ib.* III. 533[14] (ii/iii A.D.) ἵ[ν]α μὴ ἔχωμεν στομάχου[s] μηδὲ φθόνον, "that we may not be caused vexation and annoyance" (Edd.), P Thead 14[34] (iv/A.D.) οὐδὲν βεβάστακται· οὗτοι φθόνῳ περὶ κληιδίου κατα[γορεύουσιν?, "nothing has been taken. These accuse us from jealousy." Hort (*Jas.* p. 93 f.) thinks that the difficult πρὸς φθόνον in Jas 4[5] must be understood as = "jealously" or "with jealousy" (cf. the RV marginal renderings): see also the elaborate note in the *Revue Biblique* xii. (1915), p. 35 ff., and for a suggestion to read φόνον for φθόνον, see J. A. Findlay in *Exp T* xxxvii. (1926), p. 381 f. For Phil 1[15] the commentators cite by way of illustration the comic poet Philemon (Meineke iv. p. 55) πολλά με διδάσκεις ἀφθόνως διὰ φθόνον.

φθορά.

(1) "loss": P Tebt I. 105[3] (B.C. 103) ἀνυ(πόλογον) πά(σης) φθο(ρᾶς), "subject to no deduction for loss," with reference to a lease of land, and P Strass I. 24[26] (A.D. 118) (γίγνονται) φθορᾶς ε̄, "total, 5 by death," with reference to the death of cattle. In *Syll* 316 (=[3] 684)[7] (B.C. 139?) the noun is united with ἔμπρησις—λέγω δὲ ὑπὲρ τῆς ἐμπρήσεως καὶ φθορᾶς τῶν ἀρχ(εί)ων καὶ τῶν δημοσίων γραμμάτων.

(2) "corruption," "decay": *Priene* 105[2] (c. B.C. 9), where it is stated that the world would have suffered speedy φθορᾶν, had it not been for the birth of Augustus: cf. Rom 8[21].

The word is used of "abortion" in *Syll* 633 (=[3] 1042)[7] (ii/A.D.); see the editor's note with its references to Ps.Pauli *Apoc.* 60 αὗταί εἰσιν αἱ φθείρασαι ἑαυτὰς καὶ τὰ βρέφη αὐτῶν ἀποκτείνασαι, and to ἀπὸ φθορείων in *Syll* 567 (=[3] 983)[12] (ii/A.D.).

φιάλη,

"bowl." The Attic spelling φιάλη, which the LXX and the NT (Rev 5[8], *al.*) retain instead of the Hellenistic φιέλη, is found also in the Κοινή, e.g. P Cairo Zen I. 59021[16] (B.C. 258) φιάλας τουδέ με οὐκ ἐώντος δέχεσθαι, P Tebt I. 6[27] (B.C. 140–139) φιάλας καὶ ποτήρια, "bowls and cups," P Oxy III. 521[17] (ii/A.D.) φιάλη χαλκῆ, P Fay 127[9] (ii/iii A.D.) ἔπεμψα ὑμῖν γ̄ [ζεύ]γη φιαλῶν, "I have sent you three pairs of bowls," and P Oxy VI. 937[12] (iii/A.D.) τῆς φιάλης τῆς λιθίνης, "the stone bowl." In PSI IV. 306[8] (ii/iii A.D.) ἑκάστης φιάλλης (*l.* φιάλης) the reference is to a "cistern."

φιλάγαθος,

"loving what is good" (Tit 1[8]). In P Oxy I. 33[ii. 11] (late ii/A.D.) a certain Appianus taunts an Emperor, perhaps Commodus (see P Oxy II. p. 319), by extolling the superior virtues of his predecessor Marcus Aurelius—ἄκουε, τὸ μὲν πρῶτον ἦ[ν] φιλόσοφος, τὸ δεύτερον ἀφιλάργυρος, τ[ὸ] τρίτον φιλάγαθος, "listen; in the first place he was a lover of wisdom, secondly, he was no lover of gain, thirdly, he was a lover of virtue" (Edd.).

For the corr. subst., which is common in the inscrr., cf. *Preisigke* 1106[6] (Ptol.) οἱ συνπόσιον γενόμενοι φιλαγαθίας ἕνεκεν τῆς εἰς ἑαυτούς, *ib.* 6117[4] (B.C. 18) φιλαγαθίας χάριν, and for the verb cf. P Tebt I. 124[17] (c. B.C. 118) ἣι ἔχομεν ἀπὸ τῆς ἀρχῆς εὐγνοίαι φιλαγαθήσαντες.

Φιλαδελφία,

For this city of the Roman province Asia (Rev 1[11], 3[7]), see Ramsay *Letters*, p. 391 ff. A village of the same name is found in the Arsinoite nome, see P Lond 166 *b*[6] (A.D. 186) (= II. p. 106), BGU II. 356[6] (A.D. 213).

φιλαδελφία.

In profane Greek and the LXX φιλαδελφία is confined to the love of those who are brothers by common descent, e.g. Luc. *dial. deor.* xxvi. 2, 4 Macc 13[23, 26], 14[1], and cf. P Lond V. 1708[101] (A.D. 567 ?) τῇ ἐμῇ φιλαδελφίᾳ, of kindness to sisters; but in the NT the word is used in the definite sense of "love of the brethren," i.e. the Christian brotherhood (Rom 12[10], Heb 13[1], 1 Pet 1[22], 2 Pet 1[7]).

φιλάδελφος,

"loving one's (Christian) brothers," 1 Pet 3[8]. For a brother loving his actual brother (see *s.v.* φιλαδελφία), cf. the inscr. on a tomb *Preisigke* 313[3] (ii/A.D.?) Εἰσίων φιλάδελφε χρηστὲ χαῖρε, and similarly *ib.* 6234[2] (B.C. 33), *al.*

φίλανδρος.

is common in epitaphs of a wife "loving her husband" (Tit 2[4]): cf. *Perg* 604 (about the time of Hadrian) cited by Deissmann *LAE*[2], p. 314—

Ἰούλιος Βάσσος
Ὀτακιλίᾳ Πώλλῃ
τῇ γλυκυτάτῃ
[γ]υναικί, φιλάνδρ[ῳ]
καὶ φιλοτέκνῳ
συνβιωσάσῃ
ἀμέμπτως
ἔτη λ̄.

"Julius Bassus to Otacilia Polla, his sweetest wife. Loving her husband, and loving her children, she lived with him unblamably 30 years." Cf. *Preisigke* 330 Δ[ιονυσά]ριον παν[ά]ρετε φίλανδρε φιλότ[ε]κνε εὐψύ[χ]ει, and the citation from *BCH* xxii. *s.v.* φιλόσοφος : the corr. subst. occurs in *Preisigke* 5037 Εὐψύχι Ταῆσι μητρώων μόρον ἐκτανύσασα σωφροσύνη καὶ φιλανδρίᾳ.

φιλανθρωπία.

This common word occurs only *bis* in the NT (Ac 28[2], Tit 3[4]), and is best understood in the sense of "kindness," "humanity," rather than "philanthropy" or "the love of mankind" in general (cf. Field *Notes*, p. 147 f.).

For the phrase τυγχάνω φιλανθρωπίας (cf. Ac 28[2], Esther 8[13], 2 Macc 6[22]) we may cite P Petr III. 29 (e)[13] (iii/B.C.) ἵνα τύχω τῆ[ς παρ]ά σου φιλαν[θρωπί]ας, "in order that I may meet with consideration at your hands" (Edd.), P Magd 28[12] (B.C. 217) τούτου γὰρ γενομένου, ἐπὶ σὲ καταφυγών, βασιλεῦ . . . ἐγώ τε ἔσομαι τῆς παρὰ σοῦ φιλανθρωπίας τετευχώς, and similarly P Leid G[21] (B.C. 181–145) (= I. p. 43), P Tebt I. 30[20] (B.C. 115).

Other exx. of the subst. are—P Michigan Inv. No. 2798[3] (time of Hadrian) (= *Class. Phil.* xxii. p. 248) χάριν σοι ἔχω τῇ φιλαν[θ]ρωπίᾳ περὶ τοῦ ἐλαίου, "I thank you for your kindness about the olive-oil" (Ed.), P Ryl II. 296

(ii/A.D.) τῇ σῇ φιλανθρωπείᾳ, as a title of address to a high official, P Fay 20[16] (Imperial edict—iii/iv A.D.) φιλανθρωπίᾳ τε καὶ εὐεργεσίαις συναύξειν ταύτην τὴν ἀρχήν, "by liberality and the conferring of benefits to increase the welfare of this kingdom" (Edd.), and OGIS 130[21] (B.C. 145–116), where the priests of Philae commemorate certain relief granted them by Ptolemy Euergetes II. by erecting a pillar—ἐν ἧι ἀναγράψομεν τὴν γεγονυῖαν ἡμῖν ὑφ' ὑμῶν περὶ τούτων φιλανθρωπίαν: cf. Aristeas 265 where ἀνθρωπία and ἀγάπησις are said to be the most necessary possessions for a king, and see further Wendland ZNTW v. (1904), p. 345 n².

The adj. (in Greek Bible only Sap 1[6]) is similarly used of the virtues of rulers in such inscrr. as Magn 18[17] (letter of Antiochus III—B.C. 205) ἔχοντες οὖν ἐξ ἀρχῆς π[ερὶ] τοῦ δήμου τὴν φιλανθρωποτάτην διάλ[η]ψιν διὰ τὴν εὔνοιαν, ib. 201² τ]ὸν θειότατον καὶ μέ[γ]ιστον καὶ φιλανθρωπότατον βασιλέα, with reference to the Emperor Julian. Cf. from the papyri P Oxy IV. 705[69] (A.D. 200–2) ὦ φιλανθρωπότατοι Αὐτοκράτορες, with reference to Septimius Severus and Caracalla, and in the same document the words of the petitioner who states that he has before him[75] καὶ τοῦ φιλανθρώπου καὶ τοῦ χρησίμου, "a both humane and useful object," and the Christian prayer ib. VI. 925² (v/vi A.D.) (= Selections, p. 131), which begins—Ὁ θε(ὸ)ς ὁ παντοκράτωρ ὁ ἅγιος ὁ ἀληθινὸς φιλάνθρωπος καὶ δημιουργός.

For φιλάνθρωπα = "ordinances of special favour," as in 2 Macc 4[11], cf. P Meyer 1[24] (B.C. 144) μένειν [δὲ κύρια τὰ φ]ιλάνθρωπα, with the editor's note, and see also P Ryl II. 155[7] (A.D. 138–161), again with the editor's note. In BGU II. 595[7] (A.D. 70–80) εἵνα φιλάνθρωπον εἰς δύο τόπους μὴ χορηγῇι, the word is apparently = "a douceur," "that he did not need to give a douceur on two occasions."

We may add one or two exx. of the verb φιλανθρωπέω: P Tebt I. 31[21] (B.C. 112) ἵν' ὦ] πεφιλανθρωπημένος, "that I may obtain redress," in connexion with a change of ownership, similarly ib. II. 397[27] (A.D. 198), P Oxy III. 532[20] (ii/A.D.) βουλόμενόν σε φιλανθρωπω[[ση]]σαι (l. φιλανθρωπῆσαι), "wishing to welcome you," and OGIS 90[12] (Rosetta stone—B.C. 196) ταῖς τε ἑαυτοῦ δυνάμεσιν πεφιλανθρώπηκε πάσαις, where φιλανθρωπέω is used intransitively = φιλάνθρωπον εἶναι, as the editor notes.

As against Hobart's claim (p. 296 f.) that φιλανθρωπία (Ac 28²) and φιλανθρώπως (Ac 27³) were part of Luke's "medical" vocabulary, Cadbury (JBL xlv. (1926) p. 201 f.) has pointed out that the words occur over 40 times in Dittenberger's Syll³ Index s.vv. φιλανθρωπία, -ος.

φιλανθρώπως.

For the somewhat weakened sense of "kindly" in Ac 27³, cf. OGIS 51³(B.C. 239) τοῖς τε τεχνίταις φιλανθρώπως ἅπαντα ("throughout") χρῆται, Priene 47[4] (B.C. 200) ἔν τε τοῖς ἄλλοις φι⟨λ⟩ανθρώπως χρώμενος διατελεῖ, and Preisigke 6185[10] (iii/A.D.) εὐμεν[ῶ]ς καὶ φιλαν[θρώπως.

φιλαργυρία.

To the numerous illustrations of 1 Tim 6[10] given by the commentators may be added (as by Lock) Test. xii. patr.

Jud. xix. 1 ἡ φιλαργυρία πρὸς εἰδωλολατρείαν ὁδηγεῖ. For the corr. verb see Syll 278 (= ³595)[12] (B.C. 195–4) ὅτι τελέως ἐν οὐθενὶ φιλαργυρήσ[α]ι βεβουλήμεθα.

φιλάργυρος,

"loving money" (Lk 16[14], 2 Tim 3²), is found in an imperfect context in P Petr III. 53 (j) (iii/B.C.). The word appears as a proper name in P Oxy XIV. 1678[12] (iii/A.D.).

φίλαυτος,

"loving self," occurs in Bibl. Greek only in 2 Tim 3²: cf. Philo Leg. Allegr. i. 49 (ed. Cohn) φίλαυτος δὲ καὶ ἄθεος ὁ νοῦς οἰόμενος ἴσος εἶναι θεῷ. For the corr. subst. see P Par 26[i. 10] (B.C. 163) (= UPZ i. p. 247, Selections, p. 14) δι' ὀλίων (l. ὀλίγων) τὴν τῶν ἀδικούντων ἡμᾶς φιλαυτίαν ἐχθεῖναι. For φίλαυτος and φιλαυτία, Waddell (Selections, p. 178) refers to Plato Laws 731 D and the discussion in Aristot. Eth. N. ix. 8.

φιλέω,

"love": P Tebt II. 408³ (A.D. 3) ἐπιστάμενος πῶς σε τίθεμαι κὲ φιλῶ, "since you know how I esteem and love you" (Edd.), BGU II. 531[ii. 19] (A.D. 70–80) α[ἰ]σθόμενος πῶς με φιλεῖς, P Tebt II. 294[24] (A.D. 146) ἵνα καὶ αἱ ὀφ[ε]ιλ[ό]μεναι ἱερουργίαι τῶν σε φιλούντων θεῶν ἐπιτελῶνται, "in order that the due services of the gods who love you may be performed" (Edd.), P Oxy III. 528[6] (ii/A.D.) τὸ προσκύνημά σου πυῶ (l. ποιῶ) παρὰ τῇ σε φιλούσῃ Θοήρι, "I perform the act of veneration on your behalf to Thoeris who loves you" (Edd.). We may add the iii/A.D. love-spell Preisigke 4947[6] ὁρκίζω σε, νεκυδαῖμον, . . . διακόνησόν μοι εἰς Ἀπλωνοῦν, ἣν ἔτεκεν Ἀρσινόη . . . ἵνα με φιλῇ καὶ ὃ ἐὰν αὐτὴν αἰτῶ, ἐπήκοός μοι ᾖ⟨⟨ν⟩⟩.

The verb is followed by an inf., as in Mt 6⁵, in P Giss I. 84[13] (ii/A.D. ad init.) φι]λοῦσι νῦν οὗτοι τὴν ἀλήθ[ε]ιαν εἰπεῖν, Chrest. II.[ii. 14] (ii/A.D.) τοῦτο δὲ ἐπὶ πολλῶν φιλεῖν γενέσθαι.

With the closing greeting ἄσπασαι τοὺς φιλοῦντας ἡμᾶς ἐν πίστει in Tit 3[15] cf. P Fay 119[23] (c. A.D. 100) ἀσπάζου Ἐπάγαθον καὶ τοὺς φιλοῦντες ἡμᾶς πρὸς ἀλήθιαν, and BGU III. 814[38] (iii/A.D.) ἀσπάζομαι καὶ το]ὺς φιλοῦντο(= α)ς ἡμᾶς πάντες.

It is possible, however, that, following Wilcken's suggestion (Archiv vi. p. 379), we should in both these passages read ὑμᾶς for ἡμᾶς in keeping with the form the greeting takes elsewhere, as P Fay 118[26] (A.D. 110) ἀσπάζου τοὺς φιλοῦντές σε πάντες πρὸς ἀλήθιαν, PSI I. 94[11] (ii/A.D.) ἄσπασαι Τερεῦν καὶ τοὺς φιλοῦντάς σε πάντας, and P Giss I. 12³ (ii/A.D.) ἐπισκοποῦμαι τὴν σὴν σύνβιον καὶ τοὺς φιλοῦντάς σε πάντας. In any case Wilcken (l.c.; cf. Ziemann Epist. p. 329 f.) regards this use of ὑμᾶς [σε] φιλοῦντας for ἡμᾶς φιλοῦντας, which we might have expected, as one of the finer touches of these ancient letters, even if it had become largely stereotyped and formal. He knows no instance of its use earlier than about A.D. 100.

If φιλέω and ἀγαπάω (q.v.) are to be distinguished in the NT, the former is probably the love of friendship, the latter reverential love: but there appears to be a growing tendency to regard the two verbs as synonymous, even in Jn 21¹⁵: cf. *ib.* 13²³ with 20², and see *ib.* 11³. ⁵. ³⁶.

The meaning "kiss," which **φιλέω** has in Mk 14⁴⁴ *al.*, is seen in PSI I. 26¹³ (act of martyrs—v/A.D.) ἐκράτησ[εν αὐτοῦ τὴν] χεῖραν καὶ ἐφίλησεν.

For an exhaustive discussion on "The Terminology of Love in the New Testament," see B. B. Warfield in *The Princeton Theological Review* xvi. (1918), pp. 1 ff., 153 ff.

φιλήδονος,

"loving pleasure." An interesting parallel to 2 Tim 3⁴, the only place in the NT where this word is found, is afforded by Philo *de Agric.* 88 (ed. Wendland) φιλήδονον καὶ φιλοπαθῆ μᾶλλον ἢ φιλάρετον καὶ φιλόθεον ἀνὰ κράτος ἐργάσηται (cited by Wetstein). See also Vett. Val. pp. 7¹² συντηρητικοί, φιλήδονοι, φιλόμουσοι, 9³, 40⁵.

φίλημα,

"a kiss." For the φίλημα ἅγιον (Rom 16¹⁶, *al.*), see Lightfoot *Notes* p. 90 f. and Milligan *Thess.* p. 80.

Φιλήμων,

For the connexion of this name (Philem¹) with Phrygia it is enough to refer to the legend of Philemon and Baucis: see Lightfoot *Colossians*², p. 304. For other exx. of the name cf. P Hib I. 70 (*a*)⁸ (B.C. 229–8), P Oxy I. 43 *verso*¹ᵛ. ⁵ (A.D. 295), and from the inscr. *Magn* 117⁸, where it is the title of the ἄππας of Dionysus, and *Perg* 341⁴ Φιλήμων Ἄνθου σκουτλάριος (both cited by Thieme, p. 41).

Φίλητος,

For this proper name (2 Tim 2¹⁷) cf. the property return P Oxy I. 72¹⁷ (A.D. 90) διὰ Τιβερίου Ἰουλίου Φιλήτου.

φιλία,

"friendship" is found in the NT only in Jas 4⁴, but occurs several times in Prov and the Apocrypha. The word is opposed to ἔχθρα in P Hib I. 170² (B.C. 247) φρόντισον . . . . ἵνα μὴ ἀντὶ φιλίας ἔχθραν [ποιώ]μεθα. Other exx. are PSI IV. 415⁷ (iii/B.C.) ὁ κομίζων σοι τὴν ἐπιστ[ο]λήν ἐστιν ἡμῖν ἐν φιλίαι, P Grenf I. 1⁴ (Alexandrian erotic fragment—ii/B.C.) ὁ τὴν φιλίαν ἐκτικὼς ἔλαβέ με ἔρως, "love the stablisher of friendship overcame me" (Ed.), P Tebt I. 59⁸ (B.C. 99) ὑποδεικνυ̣όντ̣ ὧν ἦν ἔχετε πρὸς ἡμᾶς ἄνωθεν πατρικὴν φιλίαν, "intimating to me the hereditary friendship which you have for me of old" (Edd.), BGU IV. 1141²⁵ (B.C. 14) κἀγὼ τὴν φιλίαν σου θέλων ἀμεμπτ[ον] ἐμαυτὸν ἐτήρησα, P Lond 897⁹ (A.D. 84) (= III. p. 207) εἵνα μὴ τὴν πρός σε φιλείαν καταλείψωι, P Tebt II. 616 (ii/A.D.) ἐνεργίας καὶ σπουδῆς καὶ φιλείας, P Oxy IV. 705³³ (A.D. 200–2) ἡ πρὸς Ῥωμαίους εὔν[οι]ά τε καὶ πίστις καὶ φιλία ἣν ἐνεδείξαντο, and P Fay 135¹ᵛ (iv/A.D.) ἐπισπούδασον πληρῶσαι ἵνα ἡ φιλία διαμίνῃ μετ' ἀλλήλων, "make haste to pay, in order that we may remain on good terms with each other" (Edd.).

Φιλία is used as a title in such passages as PSI I. 97¹ (vi/A.D.) ἡ ὑμ̣ε[τ]έρα λαμπρὰ καὶ ἀδελφικὴ φιλία, *ib.* 98³

(vi/A.D.) ἡ **πανάρετός σου φιλία**, and P Amh II. 154¹. ⁶ (vi/vii A.D.). We may note also the adv. **φιλικῶς** in a closing greeting in the letter Preisigke 6782¹⁵ (B.C. 259) ποιήσομεν γὰρ φιλικῶ[s]. Ἔρρ[ω]σο.

Φιλιππήσιος.

This Latin form (*Philippensis*) for the pure Greek Φιλιππεύς (cf. *Syll*³ 267A³—after B.C. 347–6, with note) or Φιλιππηνός, is found in the title of the Ep. to the Philippians, and again in ch. 4¹⁵. W. M. Ramsay (*JTS* i. (1900), p. 116) draws attention to this as "one of the little noticed indications of Paul's preference for technical Latin forms to indicate Roman administrative ideas."

Φίλιπποι.

For Philippi, a Roman colony, and consequently "a miniature likeness of the great Roman people," see Lightfoot *Philippians*², p. 49 f., and for the description of it as πρώτη τῆς μερίδος Μακεδονίας πόλις in Ac 16¹², see *s.v.* μέρις.

Φίλιππος,

For this common name see P Hib I. 62¹ (B.C. 245) Φίλιππος Πτολεμαίωι χαίρειν, and the other citations in Preisigke's *Namenbuch*. In *C. and B.* ii. p. 552 W. M. Ramsay cites an inscr. Εὐγένιος ὁ ἐλάχιστος ἀρχιδιάκ(ονος) κὲ ἐφεστ(ὼς) τοῦ ἁγίου κὲ ἐνδόξου ἀποστόλου κὲ θεολόγου Φιλίππου, as affording "a clear proof that a church (doubtless *the* church) of Hierapolis was dedicated to St. Philip." The inscr. further shows that "the local tradition was attached to Philip the Apostle."

φιλόθεος,

"loving God." For this NT ἅπ. εἰρ., 2 Tim 3⁴, see the citation from Philo *de Agric.* *s.v.* **φιλήδονος**. Cf. Vett. Val. p. 17⁹, *al.*

Φιλόλογος,

a Roman Christian (Rom 16¹⁵). The name is common as a slave name, see SH *ad Rom l.c.*: cf. Lightfoot *Philippians*², p. 175. In P Lond 256 *recto* (*a*)¹⁶ (A.D. 15) (= II. p. 99, *Chrest.* I. p. 522) it is the name of a consignee of corn from the interior of Egypt to the coast.

An interesting ex. of the verb occurs in P Oxy III. 531¹¹ (ii/A.D.), where a father writes to his son—τοῖς βιβλίοις σου αὐτὸ μόνον πρόσεχ[ε] φιλολογῶν, "give your undivided attention to your books, devoting yourself to learning" (Edd.). See also *Syll* 804 (=³ 1170²⁹ συνέβη οὖν φιλολογήσαντί μοι συνπληρωθῆναι.

φιλον(ε)ικία,

For Lk 22²⁴, the only occurrence of this word in the NT, Field (*Notes*, p. 75 f.) prefers the rendering "emulation" to "strife" (AV) or "contention" (RV), and this may be supported by the late P Oxy XVI. 1860⁷ (vi/vii A.D.) εἰ θέλει ἡ ἀγαθὴ ἡμῶν (*l.* ὑμῶν) φ[ι]λ[ο]γε[ικία] γνωρίσαι αὐτὴν τὸ περὶ τῆς [ἀ]ληθείας, "if your good ambition desires to ascertain for yourself the truth" (Edd.).

The thought of "dispute" is uppermost in such passages from the papyri as P Lond 992¹¹ (A.D. 507) (= III. p. 253) πρὸ δίκης καὶ φιλονικείας ἔδοξεν ἡμῖν κτλ., an agreement to submit certain matters at dispute to arbitration. P Oxy I. 157¹ (vi/A.D.) ἐπιδὲ φιλονικία γέγονεν μεταξὺ Παπνουθίου τοῦ μονάζοντος καὶ τοῦ γραμματευς (= -τέως)—with reference to a dispute between a monk and a scribe, and from the inscrr. as *Syll* 929 (=³ 685)³⁶ (B.C. 139) διὰ τὸ ὑπερβαλλόντως αὑτοὺς τὴν πρὸς ἀλλήλους φιλονικίαν ἐνεστάσθαι. This last ex. shows the correct spelling of the word φιλονικία, derived from φίλος and νίκη, "victory," see Blass *Gr.* p. 8; cf. also *Magn* 105⁸ (B.C. 138). For the verb φιλονικέω cf. a fragment of Demosth. *de Pace* preserved in PSI II. 129¹⁴ (iv/A.D.).

φιλοξενία,

"love of strangers," "hospitality" (Rom 12¹³, Heb 13²): cf. the curious P Lond 1917¹ (c. A.D. 330-340) where the writer addresses his correspondent—ταῦτα τὰ γ[ρά]μματα ἡ[μῶν ἔγρα]ψα ἐν τῷ χαρτίῳ τούτῳ ἵν' αὐτὰ ἀνάγνοις μαιτὰ χαρᾶς . . . καὶ [[π]] μαιτὰ φιλοξε[[ν]]νίας μακροθυμίας πεπληρωμαίνη (*l.* πεπληρωμένος) πνεύμ̣ατος ἁγίου, "this our letter I wrote on this papyrus that you might read it with joy, and with entertainment of long-suffering filled with the Holy Ghost" (Bell), and similarly *l.*¹⁴. We may also cite the inscr. on a statue to the rhetorician Herodes Atticus, *Syll*³ 859.4 (c. A.D. 150) ἡ πόλις ἡ Δελφῶν φιλίας καὶ [φιλο]ξενίας ἕνεκα.

φιλόξενος.

With this adj. in 1 Tim 3² Dibelius (*HZNT ad l.*) compares Hermas *Sim.* ix. 27. 2 ἐπίσκοποι καὶ φιλόξενοι, οἵτινες ἡδέως εἰς τοὺς οἴκους ἑαυτῶν πάντοτε ὑπεδέξαντο τοὺς δούλους τοῦ θεοῦ ἄτερ ὑποκρίσεως.

φιλοπρωτεύω,

"I love the chief place," "I desire to be first" (3 Jn⁹). The instance of this verb cited by Deissmann (*BS* p. 178) from Blass *Gr* p. 68 is now stated to be erroneous (*LAE*², p. 76, n.¹), but we can give one or two exx. of the corresponding φιλοπονέω, "I love labour," "I am industrious" —P Oxy VII. 1069²⁰ (iii/A.D.) τὴν πεδείσκην μου δὲ πρὸ λόγον ἀνάγκασον φιλοπονεῖστε (*l.* φιλοπονεῖσθαι, and ²³, *ib.* X. 1296⁷ (a son to his father—iii/A.D.) φιλοπονοῦμεν καὶ ἀναψύχομεν, καλῶς ἡμε[ῖ]ν ἔστᾳι, "I am industrious and take relaxation: all will be well with me" (Edd.), and P Lond 130⁵ (i/ii A.D.) (= I. p. 133), where a master of astrology, writing to his pupil, recalls that the ancient Egyptians laboriously devoted themselves to the art— γ]νησίως τε περ[ὶ] τὰ οὐράνια φιλοπονήσαντες.

φίλος,

"a friend": Preisigke 6817¹ (letter of commendation—B.C. 255) πυνθανόμενος δέ σε εἶναι ἐπιε[ι]κὴ ἠξίωσάν τινές με τῶν φίλων γράψαι [σο]ι, P Vat A²⁰ (B.C. 168) (= Witkowski², p. 66) ἀσπάζεσθαι τὴν γυναῖκα καὶ τὰ παιδία καὶ τοὺς φίλους, BGU IV. 1209⁶ (B.C. 23) ἡμῶν δὲ φίλου γενομένου Πετεχῶντος, "our late friend Petechon," P Oxy IV. 742¹ᶠᶠ. (B.C. 2) παράδος δέ τινι τῶν φίλων ἀριθμῷ αὐτὰς (*sc.* δέσμας) ἵνα πάλιν φ[ί]λος ἡμεῖ παραδοῖ ἀσφ[αλῶς, "deliver a few of them (*sc.* bundles of reeds) to

PART VIII.

one of our friends, that a friend may deliver them to me safely," *ib.* XIV. 1672¹⁷ (A.D. 37-41) Μουνάτιος δὲ ὁ φίλος συντυχὼν ἔλεγεν συμ[πε]φωνηκέναι τοῖς ἐκ τῆς κώ[μ]ης αὐτοῦ μετὰ χάριτος, "our friend Munatius said that he had agreed with the people of his village thankfully" (Edd.), P Tebt II. 314⁹ (ii/A.D.) τῆς δὲ τῶν φίλων σπουδῆς τυχόντος ἐπετύχαμεν, "but by means of the good offices of our friends we achieved it" (Edd.), *ib.* 410 co σ?(iii/A.D.) Ὠριγένει παρὰ Σωτηρίχου φίλου, and P Fay 131¹⁴ (iii/iv A.D.) τὸ Δεκασίου τοῦ φίλου λάχανον πάντως πότισον, "by all means water the vegetables of our friend Decasius" (Edd.).

For a legal proceeding carried through παρόντων φίλων δύο. see P Meyer 6³² (A.D. 125) with the editor's note: for the designation οἱ πρῶτοι φίλοι, see *ib.* 1¹² (B.C. 144) Ἀπολλοδώρωι τῶν ἃ φίλων καὶ ἐπ(ιστάτει) καὶ γρα[μματεῖ, similarly¹⁷, P Tebt I. 30¹⁵ (B.C. 115), *Preisigke* 6665² ⁴ (B.C. 255-4?), and *OGIS* 90³ (ii/B.C. *ad init.*) τὸν Πτολεμαίου τῶν πρώτων φίλων καὶ ἀρχικυνήγου υἱόν·with the editor's note: and for the title φίλος τοῦ Καίσαρος, as in Jn 19¹² see *CIG* II. 3499⁵, 3500⁴.

Φίλτατος, which does not occur in the NT, is very common in epistolary addresses, e.g. P Tebt II. 408² (A.D. 3) Ἱππόλιτος Ἀκουσιλάῳ τῷ φ[ι]λτάτῳ πλεῖστα χαίρειν. So stereotyped has the formula become that it is used even in letters of reproof, such as P Flor II. 226 (iii/A.D.), where the writer, addressing himself to his "dearest" Heroninus, goes on to accuse him of unsocial behaviour—οὐ σήμερον οὖν οἶδα σ[οῦ] ἀπάνθρωπον, ἀλλὰ ἀεὶ οἶδα.

φιλοσοφία

occurs in the NT only in Col 2⁸, where it is not "philosophy" in general that is condemned, but the particular system (note the art.), associated as it was with κενὴ ἀπάτη : see Hort *Judaistic Christianity*, p. 119. For the word in its direct application to mode of life, cf. Musonius p. 10⁷ ἐπιστήμη δὲ περὶ βίον οὐχ ἑτέρα τις ἢ φιλοσοφία ἐστι.

φιλόσοφος.

For this word in the wide sense of "a lover of wisdom," cf. P Oxy I. 33ⁱⁱ ¹⁷ cited *s.v.* φιλάγαθος, and the inscr. *BCH* xxii. (1898), p. 400, in which a woman is described as ἡ φίλανδρος καὶ σ[ώ]φρων ἡ φιλόσοφος ζήσασα κοσμίως, "loving her husband and sober-minded, a lover of wisdom, she lived modestly."

The more technical sense may be illustrated by P Ryl II. 143³ (A.D. 38) Διδύμῳ . . . τῶν ἐν τῷ Μουσείωι σειτουμένων φιλοσόφων ἀτελῶν στρατηγῶι, "to Didymus . . . one of the philosophers maintained in the Museum immune from charges, strategus," and by the inscr. *OGIS* 714⁵ with the editor's note. See also the private letter P Hamb I. 37³ᶠᶠ. (ii/A.D.) in which the writer addresses his friend— ἀναγκαῖον γάρ ἐστι μνημίσκεσθαι (*l.* μιμνήσκεσθαι) . . τοῦ ἤθους σου τοῦ ἀληθινοῦ⟨s⟩ φιλοσόφου. Σὺ γὰρ ἀληθινὸς φιλόσοφος καὶ εὐσχήμων γεγένη[σαι] . . . καὶ ἡμεῖς ὑ[πὸ σοῦ βελτίο]ν παιδευόμεθα ἢ ὑ[πὸ συμπάντων] τῶν φιλοσόφων.

φιλόστοργος,

"loving warmly" (Rom 12¹⁰) : cf. Vett. Val. p. 76²⁷ τοὺς μὲν γὰρ εὐνουστέρους καὶ φιλοστοργοτέρους θανάτῳ χωρί-

86

ζουσι. The subst. **φιλοστοργία** is common in Wills, where bequests are made **κατὰ φιλοστοργίαν**, see e.g. P Oxy III. 490⁴ (A.D. 124), 492⁶ (A.D. 130). Other exx. of the subst. are P Tebt II. 408⁷ (A.D. 3) **τῆι φιλοστοργίᾳ τῶν περὶ Σωτήριχον**, "out of their regard for Soterichus and his people" (Edd.), P Oxy III. 495¹² (A.D. 181–9) **μητρικῇ φιλοστοργίᾳ**, P Flor III. 338¹¹ (iii/A.D.) **καὶ νῦν τάχα ἡ σὴ σπουδὴ καὶ φιλοστοργεία κατανεικήσῃ τὴν ἐμὴν . . ἀκαιρείαν**, and *Chrest.* II. 361¹⁶ (A.D. 360) **ἐνέδειξών** (l. **ἐνέδειξάν**) **μοι εὔνοιαν καὶ φιλοστοργείαν**.

For the adverb cf. *OGIS* 257⁴ (B.C. 109) **σοῦ ἐμνημονεύο- μεν [φιλοστ]όργως**, and Preisigke 5294⁹ (A.D. 235) **ε[ὐ]νοίως καὶ φιλοστόργ[ως]**. A good ex. of the verb occurs in *Syll*³ 1267²³ (ii/iii A.D.) (= Deissmann *LAE*², p. 140) **ἐγὼ ὑπὸ τέκνων γονεῖς φιλοστοργεῖσθαι ἐνομοθέτησα**—an Isis inscr. from Ios.

φιλότεκνος,

"loving one's children" (Tit 2⁴), is common in memorial inscr., e.g. *Perg* 604 cited *s.v.* **φίλανδρος**, *Archiv* v. p. 167—

> Δράκων Ἀπίωνος χρηστὲ φιλό-
> τεκνε φιλόπιλε ὡς ἐτῶν πεντ[ή]-
> κοντα[

and *Preisigke* 330¹ **Δ[ι]ονυσά]ριον παν[ά]ρετε φίλανδρε φιλό- τ[ε]κνε, εὐψ[ύ]χει**, and *ib.* 350² **Σάμβυ φιλ[ό]τεκνε χρηστ[ὲ] χαῖρε.**

φιλοτιμέομαι

is found in the NT in Rom 15²⁰, 2 Cor 5⁹, 1 Thess 4¹¹, and in all three passages seems to have lost its original idea of emulating ("am ambitious"), and to mean little more than "am zealous," "strive eagerly," in accordance with its usage in late Greek: cf. P Petr III. 42 H.(8)¹³ (iii/B.C.) **ἐφιλοτιμοῦ με παραγε[νέσθαι πρὸς σὲ καὶ] ἧλθον**, PSI IV. 375¹ (B.C. 250–40) **ὃν τρόπον ἐφιλοτιμήθης περὶ ἡμῶν**, P Cairo Zen III. 59305⁴ (B.C. 250), and P Tebt II. 410¹⁰ (i/A.D.) **μν[ή]σθητι ὡ[ς] ἐν τῷ Τρ[ι]στόμῳ με ἐφιλοτ[ι]μοῦ σὺν ἐμοὶ μεῖναι**, "remember how zealous you were at Tristomos to remain with me" (Edd.).

The verb is also common in honorary decrees, where its general meaning is "act with public spirit," e.g. *CIA* II. 444²³ᶠᶠ (ii/B.C.) **ὅπως οὖν καὶ ἡ βουλὴ καὶ ὁ δῆμος μνημο- νεύοντες φαίνωνται τῶν εἰς ἑαυτοὺς φιλοτιμουμένων**, *OGIS* 117⁸ (ii/B.C.) **ὁ δῆμος ὁ Ἀθηναίων εὐχάριστος ὢν διατελεῖ τοῖς εἰς ἑαυτὸν φιλοτιμουμένοις**, and *ib.* 118¹⁰ (ii/B.C.), 233¹⁵ (iii/B.C.). See further Hicks *CR* i. p. 46, Field *Notes* p. 165, and Lightfoot *Notes* p. 60 f.

For the subst. **φιλοτιμία** cf. P Par 63⁶³ (B.C. 164) (= P Petr III. p. 24) **μήτε φιλοτιμίας μήτε πλεονεξίας γενηθείσης**, "no undue [official] competition or grasping being per- mitted" (Mahaffy), P Oxy VIII. 1153¹⁵ (i/A.D.) **ἃ ἐδωρήσατό σοι Παυσανίας ὁ ἀδελφός σου πρὸ πολλοῦ ἐκ φιλοτιμίας αὐτοῦ κατηρτισμένα**, "which (sc. wrist-bands) your brother Pausanias went to the expense of having made some time ago and presented to you" (Ed.), and *ib.* XVI. 1913¹⁴ (c. A.D. 555?) **λόγῳ φιλοτιμίας**, "by way of largesse" (Edd.).

For the adj. **φιλότιμος** cf. P Petr I. 29¹² (iii/B.C.), where

the writer says that he had borrowed from Dynis 4 artabae of wheat, which he had offered and "was pressing" (**φιλο- τίμου ὄντος**) to lend, P Giss I. 3¹³ (A.D. 117) (= *Chrest.* I. p. *571*) **φιλότιμόν τε τὸ πρὸς [ἡμᾶς**, P Ryl II. 77³⁴ (A.D. 192) **μιμοῦ τὸν πα[τ]έρα τὸν φιλότιμον τὸν [γ]έροντα φῶτα**, "imitate your father the lover of office, the brave old man" (Edd.), and for the compve. PSI IV. 392¹³ (B.C. 242–1) **εὐχαριστήσεις δέ μοι φιλοτιμότερον γράψας ἐνταῦθα οἷς ἂν ὑπολαμβάνῃς ἐπιτήδεον εἶναι**, P Tebt I. 23¹⁰ (c. B.C. 119 or 114) **διὸ καὶ ἔτι καὶ νῦν καλῶς ποιήσεις φιλοτιμότερον προθυμηθεὶς ἵνα τὰ πρὸς αὐτὸν [. . . . .] διορθώσῃι**, "I shall therefore be glad if you will even now endeavour more earnestly to correct your behaviour towards him" (Edd.), and for the adv. **φιλοτίμως**, PSI IV. 412¹⁹ (iii/B.C.) **ἐντειλαι οὖν φιλοτίμως**, *ib.* VI. 568⁶ (B.C. 253–2) **ποιήσομε]ν γὰρ φιλοτίμως**, and P Cairo Zen III. 59401³ (iii/B.C.).

φιλοφρόνως,

"kindly," "with friendliness" (Ac 28⁷): cf. P Grenf I. 30⁵ (B.C. 103) **ἐντετάλμεθ[α] ἀσπάσεσθαι ὑμᾶς παρ' ἡμῶν φιλοφρόνως**, BGU III. 1009³ (ii/B.C.), and from the inscrr. *Magn* 103⁵⁰ (2nd half ii/B.C.).

For the subst. cf. BGU I. 248² (A.D. 70–80) **τῆς] εἰς μὲ φιλοφροσύνης**, *ib.* 249¹⁹ (ii/A.D.), and *ib.* II. 531⁸ (ii/A.D.).

φιμόω,

after appearing in Aristoph. (*Nub.* 592), does not appear again until the LXX and NT, perhaps because it was regarded as a non-literary or even slang word. It is found in the sense of "muzzle" in a quotation from the LXX in 1 Cor 9⁹, 1 Tim 5¹⁸, and metaphorically = "put to silence" in Mt 22³⁴ *al.* (cf. Lucian *De Mort. Per.* 15).

According to Rohde *Psyche* II. p. 424 (Engl. Tr. p. 604) **φιμοῦν** and **φιμωτικόν** are used in rude Egypto-Syrian Greek as equivalent to **καταδεῖν**, **κατάδεσμος** in denoting the *binding* of a person by means of a spell, so as to make him powerless to harm. Exx. of this magical usage are—P Lond 121⁹⁶⁷ (iii/A.D.) (= I. p. 114) **δεῦρό μοι . . . καὶ φίμωσον, ὑπόταξον, καταδούλωσον τὸν δεῖνα**, an appeal to a god, *ib.* ³⁹⁶ **φιμωτικὸν καὶ ὑποτακτικὸν γενναῖον καὶ κάτοχος**, *ib.* 123⁴ (iv/v A.D.) (= I. p. 120) **καθυπόταξον φίμωσον κατα- δούλωσον πᾶν γένος ἀνθρώπων**, and P Osl I. 1¹⁶⁴ (iv/A.D.) **φιμώσαται τὰ στόματα τὰ κατ' ἐμοῦ.** These instances, as Eitrem has pointed out, make "an effective background" for the usage in Mk 1²⁵, 4³⁹.

The subst. **φίμωσις** occurs in Vett. Val. p. 257¹³ **πρὶν φθάσαι τὴν φίμωσιν**, apparently with reference to the silence of death.

Φλέγων,

"Phlegon," the name of a Roman Christian, Rom 16¹⁴. According to Lietzmann (*HZNT ad l.*) this name, which is given to a dog in Xenophon (*Cyneg.* 7, 5), came later to be applied to slaves, see *CIL* II. 2017.

φλογίζω,

"set on fire" (Jas 3⁶). We have no ex. of **φλογίζω** from our sources, but for **φλέγω** see the magic tablet PSI I. 28¹² (iii/iv A.D.?) **διὰ τούτου τοῦ ναικυονδαίμονος φλέξον τὴν καρδίαν**, and ¹⁵.

φλόξ,

"a flame" (Lk 16²⁴, *al.*): P Leid Wᵛⁱⁱ·³⁵ (ii/iii A.D.) (= II. p. 105) ἀποσκεδασθήτω μου πᾶσα φηλόξ (*l.* φλόξ), P Lond 122⁷⁵ (hymn to the Sun—iv/A.D.) (= I. p. 118) ἥλιε χρυσόκομα διέπων φλογὸς ἀκάματον φῶς, and from the inscrr. *Preisigke* 5620 (amulet) φῶς πῦρ φλόξ. and *Syll* 804 (= ³ 1170)²⁴ (ii/A.D.) φλὸξ ἀναδραμοῦσα ἐπέφλευσε τὴν χεῖρα. For a form φλώξ see P Oxl I. 1³⁵⁶ (iv/A.D.) ὡς φλώξ καομένη, with the editor's note.

φλυαρέω

c. acc = "prate against" in 3 Jn¹⁰. For the more general meaning "talk nonsense," cf. P Cairo Zen III. 59300⁷ (B.C. 250) δικαίως οὖν Ἀπολλωνίδει φλυαρεῖν ἐπέρχεται, *ib.*⁹ οὐκ ἂν νῦν διὰ κενῆς ἐφλυάρει, and the Christian P Heid 6¹² (iv/A.D.) (= *Selections*, p. 126) ἵνα οὖν μὴ πολλὰ γράφω καὶ φλυαρήσω (*l.* φλυαρήσω), "that I may not by much writing prove myself an idle babbler."

φοβέομαι

(act. obsolete): (1) "fear," "dread," (a) absol., P Lips I. 40ⁱⁱ·²² (iv/v A.D.) κἀγὼ αὐτὸς φοβοῦμαι, ἐπειδὴ ἀπών ἐστιν ὁ ἑταῖρός μου, OGIS 669⁵⁹ (i/A.D.) ὅσοι μὲν γὰρ ἐφοβήθησαν ἀκούσαντες περὶ . . . ; (b) c. acc., P Oxy II. 237ᵛⁱⁱⁱ·¹¹ (A.D. 186) φοβηθέντας τὸν κίνδυνον, "through fear of the danger" (Edd.), P Flor III. 332¹² (ii/A.D.) οὔ]τε προσεκύνησα θεοὺς φοβουμένη σου τὸ μετέωρον, P Grenf II. 84³ (v/vi A.D.) τοὺς νόμους φοβηθεὶς ἔφυγεν εἰς ἐρημίαν (said of a patricide); (c) c. μή and conj., P Magd 9³ (iii/B.C.) φοβουμένη μὴ συμπέσηι (of a sanctuary in a dangerous state), BGU IV. 1097⁴ (time of Claudius or Nero) (= Olsson, p. 113) φοβοῦμαι γὰρ μὴ σχάσῃ. νε[ν]ανσίακε [γ]άρ, "for I am afraid that he will give up, for he has become sick," P Tebt II. 318¹⁸ (A.D. 166) φο[βου]μένη δ[ὲ] μὴ λάθω [κατὰ] τὸ εἰς με δίκαι[ον] οἰκονομεῖ[ας, "as I am afraid that my right of procedure may escape notice" (Edd.), *ib.* 335⁸ (mid. iii/A.D.) φοβούμενος μὴ ἄρα εὑρεθείη ἐν αὐτοῖς ἐπιλημψι[ς, "from fear that they might disclose a claim by seizure" (Edd.). In Gal 4¹¹ φοβοῦμαι ὑμᾶς μή πως εἰκῆ κεκοπίακα, "I am afraid about you: perhaps I have toiled in vain," we have an ex. of μή used in cautious assertions : see *Proleg.* pp. 192 f., 248. (d) On the translation-Hebraism φοβοῦμαι ἀπό, as in Mt 10²⁸ (= Lk 12⁴), see *Proleg.* pp. 102, 104, and Thackeray *Gr.* i. p. 46 f.

(2) "reverence," P Tebt I. 59¹⁰ (B.C. 99) (= Witkowski², p. 113) an official writes to the priests of Tebtunis assuring them of his good will διὰ τὸ ἄνωθεν φοβεῖσθαι καὶ σέβεσθαι τὸ ἱερόν, "because of old I revere and worship the temple."

In illustration of the φοβούμενος τὸν θεόν of Ac 10², *al.*, Deissmann (*LAE*², p. 451) cites the inscr. from the theatre of Miletus—

> Τόπος Εἰουδέων τῶν καὶ Θεοσεβίον.

"Place of the Jews, who also are called God-fearing."

φοβερός,

"fearful" (Heb 10²⁷, *al.*): BGU II. 428⁸ (ii/A.D.) φοβερὸς ἐγένετο before a lacuna, P Leid Wˣⁱⁱ·⁹ (ii/iii A.D.) (= II. p. 121) ἐκλήθη δὲ ὀνόματι ἁγίῳ ἀναγραμματιζόμενον (= -ένῳ) φωβερῷ καὶ φρεικτῷ (*l.* φοβερῷ καὶ φρικτῷ), and

the magic PSI I. 28²¹ (iii/iv A.D. ?). The Christian amulet P Oxy VIII. 1151¹² (v/A.D. ?) closes with the words ὅτι τὸ ὄνομά σου κ(ύρι)ε ὁ θ(εό)ς, ἐπικαλεσά[μ]ην τὸ θαυμαστὸν καὶ ὑπερένδοξον καὶ φοβερὸν τοῖς ὑπεναντίοις, "upon thy name, O Lord God, have I called, the wonderful and exceeding glorious name, the terror of thy foes" (Ed.): cf. Ps 110 (111)⁹, *al.*

φόβηθρον,

"that which causes terror," is so read by WH, following BD, in its only occurrence in the NT. Luke 21¹¹: see Blass Debrunner *Gr.* § 35. 3. The word is cited by Hobart (p. 164) from Hippocrates *Morb. Sacr.* 303, as denoting "fearful objects that present themselves to the imagination of the sick."

φόβος,

"fear": OGIS 339¹⁷ (ii. B.C. 120) διά τε τὸν ἀπὸ τῶν γειτνιώντων Θραικῶν φόβον, P Fay 21²¹ (A.D. 134) τῷ τοῦ προστίμου φόβω, "by the fear of incurring penalties," P Oxy XIV. 1668¹⁹ (iii/A.D.) ὁ ἡγεμὼν ἀμνησίαν ἔπεμψεν ἐνθάδε, καὶ οὐκέτι φόβος οὐδὲ εἷς ἔνει, "the praefect has sent an amnesty here, and there is no longer any fear at all" (Edd.), and BGU II. 547¹ (Byz.) μέγας φόβος ἐπίκειται ἡμῖν. For the plur. as in 2 Cor 7⁵, see *Syll* 168 (= ³ 326)²¹ (B.C. 307–6) καὶ φόβων κ[αὶ κινδύνων μεγάλων τοὺς] Ἕλληνας περιστάντων.

The reverential fear towards God, which appears in such a passage as Ac 9³¹, may be illustrated from P Lond 1014¹² (A.D. 335 ?) (= IV. p.) φόβον θεοῦ ἔχοντες ἐν τῇ καρδίᾳ: cf. *ib.* IV. 1393¹⁸. In 2 Cor 5¹¹ Field (*Notes*, p. 183) prefers the rendering "terror," as against RV "fear."

Φοίβη.

This proper name (Rom 16¹) is found as the name of a slave in P Flor I. 50⁶¹ (A.D. 268): cf. *Syll* 399 (= ³ 805)¹⁰ (c. A.D. 54) Κλαυδία Φοίβη τὸν ἑαυτῆς ἄνδρα καὶ εὐεργέτην ἀρετῆς ἔνεκα καὶ εὐνοίας, *Magn* 122 (a)¹¹ (time of Diocletian), and the v/vi A.D. inscr. from the Mount of Olives cited *s.v.* κοιμάομαι. For a note by Mrs. M. D. Gibson on the NT Phoebe as a kind of Lady Bountiful, see *Exp T* xxiii. p. 281.

Φοινίκισσα.

See *s.v.* Συροφοινίκισσα.

φοῖνιξ,

"a palm tree" (Jn 12¹³), or the fruit of a palm tree "dates": cf. P Hal I. 7⁷ (B.C. 232) αἴτησον δὲ . . . ὥστε εἰς [ξέ]νια φοίνικας, P Amh II. 31⁸ (B.C. 112) τόπους περιειλημμένους εἰς φυτείαν φοινίκων, "pieces of land which had been enclosed for the purpose of growing palms" (Edd.), and so ¹⁶, BGU IV. 1095⁹ (A.D. 57) περὶ δὲ τοῦ φοίνικος παλαιὸν οὐχ εὕραμεν, "as regards the dates, we did not find any old." P Ryl II. 172¹² (A.D. 208) φοίνικος μονοξύλου, "dates on single stems" (Edd.), and P Flor I. 50² (division of property—A.D. 268) σὺν τοῖς ἐ[νοῦσι φοί]νιξι καὶ φυτοῖς.

Related words are φοινικών, "a palm garden" (P Tebt II. 343⁵—ii/A.D.), φοινίκινος, "made of palm-wood"

(P Oxy XIV. 1658¹—iv/A.D.), and **φοινικηγός**, "date-measure" (P Ryl II. 172¹³—A.D. 208). For the tax on dates, see Wilcken *Ostr.* i. p. 313 ff.

φονεύς,

"a murderer" (Mt 22⁷, *al.*): P Lips I. 37²⁹ (A.D. 389) Ἰωᾶν τὸν προκίμενον φονέα ἀποδεῖξαι, BGU IV. 1024ᵛⁱⁱⁱ·¹¹ (iv/v A.D.) ξίφι σαι (*l.* ξίφει σε) [κα]ταβληθῆναι ὡς φονέα.

φονεύω,

"murder." The document just cited *s.v.* φονεύς, BGU IV. 1024, shows the corr. verb several times, e.g. ᵛⁱ·⁷ ὁ οὖν Διόδημος ἐφόνευσεν τὴν πόρνην. Other exx. are P Grenf II. 36¹¹ (B.C. 95) μὴ λυπεῖσθε ἐπὶ τοῖς χωρισθεῖσι. ὑπελαμβάνοσαν φονευθήσεσθαι, "do not grieve over the departed. They expected to be killed" (Edd.), *ib.* 84² (v/vi A.D.) υἱὸς τὸν εἴδιον πατέραν φωνεύσας καὶ τοὺς νόμους φοβηθεὶς ἔφυγεν εἰς ἐρημίαν, P Oxy XVI. 1885¹¹ (A.D. 509) ἐπιθεωρῆσαι [τὸν σχεδὸν φο]νευθέντα Σουροῦς, "to inspect the nearly murdered Sourous" (Edd.), and the hyperbolical use in P Lond 113. 12 (*d*)¹¹ (vi/vii A.D.), where a petitioner for redress of injuries complains that he has been murdered—ὁ χρεώστης ἐφ[ό]νευσέν με. See also *s.vv.* σφάζω and φαρμακός. [Is it possible that the above use of φονεύω throws light on the difficult Jas 4²?]

In Ev. Petr. 2 γέγραπται γὰρ ἐν τῷ νόμῳ ἥλιον μὴ δῦναι ἐπὶ πεφονευμένῳ, "πεφονευμένῳ is strangely attributed to Herod, from whom we should have expected κεκρεμασμένῳ or the like : but it agrees with the anti-Judaic tone of the fragment" (Swete).

φόνος,

"murder": cf. P Tebt I. 5⁵ (B.C. 118), where an amnesty is granted by Ptolemy and Cleopatra to all their subjects π]λὴν τ[ῶν φόν]ους ἑκουσίοις καὶ ἱεροσυλίαις ἐνεχομ[ένων, "except to persons guilty of wilful murder or sacrilege" (Edd.). In *ib.* 14¹ (B.C. 114) notice is sent to a certain Heras εὐθυνομένωι ("arraigned") . . . φόνωι καὶ ἄλλαις αἰτία(ι)ς, where the reference may be to "manslaughter" rather than to actual "murder": see *Archiv* ii. p. 498 f. Add P Amh II. 60³⁴ (A.D. 124) Στοτοήτιος λέγοντος ἐνκεκλ[η]κέναι τοῖς [π]ερὶ Σαταβοῦν φόνου ἐπ[ὶ] τῶι ἀδελφῶι αὐτοῦ, "Stotoetis stated that he had accused Satabous and his friends of murder committed against his brother" (Edd.), and Gnomon 36 (*c.* A.D. 150) (= BGU V. p. 20) τῶν ἐπὶ φόνοις ἢ μίζοσιν ἁμαρτήμασιν κολαζομένων.

φορέω.

For the common NT sense "wear" (Mt 11⁸, *al.*) cf. P Oxy III. 531²⁴ʰ (ii/A.D.) κομ[ί]σαι διὰ Ὀννώφρα τὰ ἱμάτια τὰ λευκὰ τὰ δυ[ν]άμενα μετὰ τῶν πορφυρῶν φορεῖσθαι φαινολίων, τὰ ἄλλα μετὰ τῶν μουρσίνων φορέσεις, "receive by Onnophris the white robes which are to be worn with the purple cloaks, the others you should wear with the myrtle-coloured (?) ones" (Edd.), P Giss I. 47⁸ (time of Hadrian) (= *Chrest.* I. p. 383) ὡς μὴ κάμνειν τὸν φοροῦντα αὐτόν, with reference to a breastplate, and the enactment in connexion with the Andanian mysteries, *Syll* 653 (= ³ 736)⁷⁷ (B.C. 92) φορούντω δὲ οἱ δέκα ἐν τοῖς μυστηρίοις στρόφιον πορφύριον. See also P Michigan

Inv. No. 1367³³ (iii/iv A.D.) (= Preisigke 7247) ἔνεγκον ἐρχομένη σου τὰ χρυσία, ἀλλὰ μὴ αὐτὰ φορέσῃς ἐν τῷ πλο[ί]ῳ, "when you come, bring your gold ornaments, but do not wear them on the boat."

φόρον,

(Lat. *forum*), "Forum" (Ac 28¹⁵): see P Lond 992¹³ (A.D. 507) (= III. p. 253) τοὺς ἐλλογιμωτάτους σχολαστικοὺς φόρου Θηβαίδος, where the editors note that "the expression appears to be new," and similarly *ib.* V. 1707⁶ (A.D. 566).

φόρος,

in the wide sense of "payment," "rent," may be illustrated by such passages as P Giss I. 95⁴ (A.D. 95) φ[ό]ρου οὗ ἐμίσθωσά σ[οι] ἐλαιουργίου, "rent of the vineyard which I let to you," P Oxy X. 1279¹⁹ (A.D. 139) φόρου τῶν ⟨ν⟩ομῶν κατ' ἔτος σὺν παντὶ δραχμῶν τεσσάρων, "at the annual rent for the pastures of four drachmae in all" (Edd.), *ib.* XVII. 2141² (A.D. 208?) ἐξοδίασον εἰς φόρους ἐδαφῶν . . . ἀργυρίο[υ] δραχμὰ[ς] τριακοσίας, "pay for rent of lands three hundred drachmae of silver," and P Tebt II. 377²⁵·²⁷ (A.D. 210), which illustrates the common distinction between ἐκφόριον ("rent in kind") and φόρος ("rent in money"), in leases of the Roman period ; for exceptions see the editor's note, and *ib.* 424⁶ (late iii/A.D.) ἴσθε δὲ ὅτι ὀφίλις φόρους καὶ ἀποφορὰς ἑπτὰ ἐτῶν, ὡς ἐὰ⟨ν⟩ μὴ ἀποκαταστασίας [δ]ὴ πέμψῃς [ο]ἶδάς σου τὸ[ν] κίνδυνον, "let me tell you that you owe seven years' rent and dues, so unless you now send discharges you know your danger." (Edd.). In P Iand I. 26¹⁵ (A.D. 98) we have the phrase φόρου τοῦ παντός, "the total rent," for which the editor compares P Lond 906¹⁰ (A.D. 128) (= III. p. 108), P Fay 93¹³ (A.D. 161), *al.* See also Preisigke *Fachwörter s.v.*

φορτίζω,

"load" (Lk 11⁴⁶: for double acc. see Blass-Debrunner § 155.7). Preisigke (*Wörterb.*) cites for the related verb φορτόω, P Amh II. 150²¹ (A.D. 592) χόρτου ξ[ηρο]ῦ σῶα πεφο[ρτομ]ένα (*l.* ζῷα πεφορτωμένα), "fifty beasts loaded with dry hay," similarly ²³·³⁹, and P Flor III. 293¹⁵ (vi/A.D.) τῶν πλοίων πεφορτωμένων τῶν γενημάτων.

φορτίον,

(1) "burden," "load": P Oxy VII. 1049³ (account of transport—late ii/A.D.) ὄνο(ι) θ φο(ρτία) θ, "9 donkeys, 8 loads" (see the editor's note). (2) "freight," "cargo," as in Ac 27¹⁰ (TR φόρτος): P Oxy VIII. 1153⁹ (i/A.D.) payment by Heraclas the boatman (ὁ ναυτικός) of 600 drachmae (ὑπὲρ) τῶν φορτίων αὐτοῦ, "for his freights," P Lond 948⁷ (A.D. 236) (= III. p. 220), the shipmaster is to receive 100 drachmae for freightage, 40 paid in advance and the remaining 60 on the safe delivery of the cargo—ἅπερ φορτία παραδώσει σῶα καὶ ἀκακούργητα. The hitherto rare form **φόρετρον** is found = "freight" in P Petr II. 30 (*a*)¹³ (Ptol.), P Ryl II. 209⁵·²⁴ (early iii/A.D.), P Oxy XII. 1589¹⁸ (early iv/A.D.), and numerous exx. in Preisigke III. Index p. 341, and the new verb **φορετρίζω** in P Oxy VII. 1069¹⁶ (iii/A.D.), and *ib.* XII. 1589¹⁶ (early

iv/A.D.). (3) "wares," "merchandise": BGU IV. 1118¹⁹ (B.C. 22) τὰ δὲ ἐκ τῆς μισθώσεως φορτία πάντα, *ib.* 1079¹⁷ (A.D. 41) (= *Selections*, p. 40) παρὰ τάλαντόν σοι πέπρακα τὰ φο[ρτ]ία μου, " I have sold you my wares, for a talent," a letter to a man in money-difficulties. (4) "fixture": P Oxy II. 243²⁷ (A.D. 79) house and land property σὺν τ[ο]ῖς ἐμπεσουμένοις εἰς τούτους [φ]ορτίοις πᾶσι, "with all fixtures which may be included in them." For this use of φορτία the editors compare *ib.* 242¹⁵ (A.D. 77), and CPR I. 206⁶. (5) The word is used metaph., as in Mt 11³⁰, *al.*, in P Oxy XVI. 1874⁷ (vi/A.D.), a Christian letter of condolence, in which reference is made to τὰ τριάντα πέντε φορτία, "the thirty-five burdens," apparently a proverbial expression (see the editors' note). For the metaph. use of the adj. φορτικός, see P Amh II. 145⁷ (iv/v A.D.), a Christian letter in which the writer expresses the hope that he will not be "wearisome" (φορτικός) to his correspondent, P Oxy VI. 904⁹ (v/A.D.) a petition to be released from an office which had proved "so severe and onerous"—τ]ὴν τοιαύτην ἀπαρέτητον καὶ φορτικωτάτην λειτουργίαν. In the letter ascribed to the Emperor Hadrian, P Fay 19⁵, the phrase φ[ο]ρτικὸν λόγο[ν is used with reference to the conventional reasons of philosophy, as contrasted with a simple statement of facts.

Φορτουνᾶτος

(TR Φουρ-: cf. Mayser *Gr.* p. 116 f.), "Fortunatus," a Christian of Corinth (1 Cor 16¹⁷), who is perhaps to be identified with the Fortunatus of Clem. Rom. *1 Cor.* lxv. The name, however, is very common: see Lightfoot *Apost. Fathers* Part I. Vol. I p. 187, n.¹⁰, and the exx. collected in *ib.* p. 29, n.³ and p. 62, n.¹. Add *OGIS* 707⁵ Φορτουνᾶτος Σεβασ[τοῦ] ἀπελ(εύθερος).

φραγέλλιον

(Lat. *flagellum*), "a scourge" (Jn 2¹⁵): cf. P Lond 191¹¹ (an inventory—A.D. 103-117) (= II. p. 265) φλαγγέλιον καλάμου ἰνδικοῦ. The word is an ex. of the transliterated Latin words which found their way into Mark's Greek vocabulary from his residence in Rome.

φραγελλόω

(Lat. *flagello*), "scourge" (Mt 27²⁶, Mk 15¹⁵): cf. *Test. xii. Patr.* Benj. ii. 3.

φραγμός

prop. "a fencing in," and hence "a fence" (as always in the NT, Mt 21³³ *al.*). Exx. are BGU IV. 1119³² (a lease—B.C. 5) τὸν φραγμὸν ὑγιᾶ οἷον καὶ παρείληφεν, P Oxy III. 580 (ii/A.D.) εἰς ἐπιτήρησιν φόρου φραγμοῦ Παεβύθεως, and P Giss I. 50¹² (vi/A.D.) καλαμουργίαν καὶ τοὺς σφραγμούς (*l.* φραγμούς). For the μεσότοιχον τοῦ φραγμοῦ of Eph 2¹⁴ we may recall the inscr. on the Temple barrier *OGIS* 598 cited *s.v.* ἀλλογενής. The form φράγμα is found in P Bilabel 95¹⁵⁹ (A.D. 7).

φράζω

"declare," "explain" (Mt 13³⁶). In P Rev Lxxix 6 (B.C. 259-8) owners of orchards are called upon to register themselves, φράζον[τες τό τε] αὐτῶν ὄνομα καὶ ἐν ἧι κώμηι οἰκοῦσιν, "stating their names and the village in which they live." See also *Syll* 537 (= ³ 960)⁹⁵ (B.C. 347-6) πρὸς τὸ παράδειγμα ὃ ἂν φράξηι ὁ ἀρχιτέκτων, and the sepulchral inscr. *Preisigke* 5705¹² (iii/iv A.D.) ἀλλὰ σύ, ὦ παροδεῖτα, ἰδὼν ἀγαθοῦ τάφον ἀνδρός, ὅν τε κατευφημῶν κοῖα φράσας ἄπιθι.

φράσσω

"fence in" is used metaph. in Rom 3¹⁹, 2 Cor 11¹⁰. For the lit. sense cf. P Oxy I. 69¹ (A.D. 190) a complaint of a robbery—θυρίδα συμ]πεφρεγμένην πλίνθοις φέρουσαν εἰς δημοσίαν ῥύμην ἀνατρέψαντας, "they broke down a door that led into the public street and had been blocked up with bricks" (Edd.), and from the inscr. *Syll* 531 (= ³ 963)¹⁹ (iv/B.C.) φράξει τὰ ἐφ᾽ ὁδοῦ τειχία ἅπαντα καὶ πεφρ[α]γμ.εν.α [κα]ταλείψει ἀπιών: cf. Heb 11³³.

φρέαρ

"a well" (Lk 14⁵, *al.*): P Grenf I. 21⁸ (B.C. 126) a Will in which the testator leaves amongst other bequests ἔδα(φος) ἀμπελῶ(νος), καὶ τὰ ἐν τούτωι φρέατα ἐξ ὅπης πλίνθου, "a vineyard and the wells of baked brick in it," P Oxy VIII. 1105¹⁰ (A.D. 81-96) φρέατ[ρ]ος λιθίνου, "a stone well," *ib.* III. 502³⁵ (a lease—A.D. 164) καὶ τοῦ προκειμένου φρέατος τροχελλέαν σὺν σχοινίῳ καινῷ, "the reel of the aforesaid well provided with a new rope" (Edd.), *ib.* XIV. 1678²⁵ (iii/A.D.) a letter having on the *verso* ἀπό(δος) παρὰ Θέων[ος] σημασ[σ]ία ἐν Τευμενούτει ἐν τῷ ῥυμείῳ ἀντεὶ τοῦ φλήτρος (*l.* φρέατος), "deliver from Theon: address, at the Teumenous quarter in the lane opposite the well" (Edd.), and P Giss I. 49¹¹ (iii/A.D.) καμάραι δύο καὶ φρέαρ.

For the form φρήτα for φρέατα, see P Cairo Zen III. 59499¹² (iii B.C.), with the editor's note. A dim. φρεάτιον occurs in PSI IV. 423³⁹ (iii/B.C.) περὶ τῶν φρεατίων.

φρεναπατάω

"deceive one's own mind," first found in Gal 6³, but see *s.v.* φρεναπάτης.

φρεναπάτης

"deceiver." In the NT only in Tit 1¹⁰: cf. a woman's description of her former lover in P Grenf I. 1¹⁰ (ii/B.C.) ὁ φρεναπάτης ὁ πρὰ τοῦ μέγα φρονῶν, where the context seems to require the meaning "deceiver," rather than "one who deceives *his own* mind," "conceited," as Blass *Gr.* p. 68, n.²: cf. Burton *ad ICC* Gal 6³. See also P Lond V. 1677²² (A.D. 566-567).

φρήν

From its physical sense of "midriff" or "the parts about the heart," φρήν comes to be applied to the "heart" or "mind" itself, in the plur. as in 1 Cor 14²⁰: cf. the magic PSI I. 28²² (iii/iv B.C.?) σὰς φρένας τέρπει, P Leid Wˣᵛⁱⁱ ⁴⁸ (ii/iii A.D.) ὄνομά σου καὶ πνεῦμά σου ἐπ᾽ ἀγαθοῖς (*l.* ἀγαθοῖς) εἰσέλθοις τὸν ἐμὸν (*l.* ἐμὴν) νοῦν καὶ τὰς {ἐμὲ} ἐμὰς φρένας, P Lond 46³²⁷ (iv/A.D.) (= I. p. 75) καταδεσμεύω δὲ αὐτοῦ τὸν νοῦν καὶ τὰς φρένας, and Wünsch *AF* p. 20⁵⁶ (iii/A.D.) βασάνισον αὐτῶν τὴν διάνοιαν τὰς φρένας τὴν αἴσθησιν.

φρίσσω,

which is "specially used of awe of a mysterious Divine power" (Hort *ad* Jas 2[19]), is well illustrated by P Leid V[iv 12] (iii/iv A.D.) (= II. p. 17) τὸ μέγα ὄνομα λέγειν· Αωθ, ὃν (*l.* ὃ) πᾶς θεὸς προσκύνει, καὶ π[ᾶ]ς δαίμων φρείσσει (*l.* φρίσσει). Cf. Herodas VI. 44 τοὺς γὰρ τελώνας πᾶσα νῦν θύρη φρίσσει, "for every door now-a-days shudders at the tax-gatherers" (Knox).

The verbal φρικτός is common in magical papyri, e.g. P Leid W[v 10] (ii/iii A.D.) (= II. p. 95) ὀνόματι ἀγείῳ (ἁγίῳ) . . φοβερῷ καὶ φρικτῷ, P Lond 121[311] (iii/A.D.) (= I. p. 94) ὀνεί[ρ]ους τε φρικτούς, *ib.* 46[80] (iv/A.D.) (= I. p. 68) κατὰ τῶν φρικτῶν ὀνομάτων, so[176 f.], and *ib.* 123[10] (iv/v A.D.) (= I. p. 121) κατὰ τῆς φρικτῆς ἀνάγκης. See also Deissmann *BS* p. 288, and the magic P Osl I. 1[9] (iv/A.D.) τόν σου υἱὸν φροῖξον, "shudder at thine own son" with the editor's note (p. 36) that "φρίσσειν (cf. τὰ φρικτὰ ὀνόματα) is constantly used of the effect that the sorcerer wishes to bring about by means of his magic." The verb occurs in two poems on the death of a dog, Preisigke 6754[5, 20] (iii/B.C.) (= *Archiv* vi. p. 453 f.). See also the reff. in Preuschen-Bauer, *Wörterb. s.v.*

For the subst. φρίξ, cf. the Gnostic charm P Oxy VI. 924[5] (iv/A.D.) συντηρήσῃς Ἀρίας (*l.* Ἀρίαν) ἀπὸ τοῦ ἐπιημερινοῦ (*l.* τῆς ἐφημερινῆς) φρικός, "protect Aria from ague by day," and [4 f.], and *Syll*[890] (=[3] 1239)[19] (ii/A.D.) where a tomb is entrusted to the care of the καταχθόνιοι θεοί with the prayer that whoever violates it shall be submitted to various ills καὶ φρείκῃ [κ]α[ὶ] πυρετῷ κτλ.

φρονέω.

According to Kennedy (*EGT ad* Phil 1[7]) φρονέω "seems always to keep in view the *direction* which thought (of a practical kind) takes." Hence its use c. acc. in such passages as P Ryl II. 128[10] (*c.* A.D. 30) Σονῆρις . . ἀλλότρια φρονήσασα ἐνκαταλιποῦσα τὸ ἐλαιούργιον ἀπηλλάγη, "Soueris changed her mind, left the mill, and departed" (Edd.), and P Oxy II. 282[9] (A.D. 30–5) ἡ δὲ ἀλλότρια φρονήσασα τῆς κοινῆς συμβιώ[σεως] κατὰ πέρ[α]ς ἐξῆ[λ]θε, "but she became dissatisfied with our union, and finally left the house" (Edd.).

For τὸ ἐν φρονεῖν in Phil 2[2] Deissmann (*BS* p. 256) cites the sepulchral epitaph *IMAe* 149 (Rhodes – ii/B.C.) in which it is said of a married couple—ταὐτὰ λέγοντες ταὐτὰ φρονοῦντες ἤλθομεν τὰν ἀμέτρητον ὁδὸν εἰς Ἀίδαν. Cf. also *OGIS* 669[36] (i/A.D.) ἐὰν δὲ καὶ δύο ἔπαρχοι τὸ αὐτὸ πεφρονηκότες ὦσι.

The phrase νοῶν καὶ φρονῶν, "being sane and in my right mind," is common in Wills : see *s.v.* νοέω.

φρόνημα,

"the content of φρονεῖν, the general bent of thought and motive" (SH *ad ICC* Rom 8[6]) : cf. Vett. Val. p. 100[2] ἐὰν οὖν τις Ὀδυσσέως φρόνημα λαβὼν παραπλεύσῃ τούτους, καταλείπει σεμνὴν ἐν τῷ βίῳ τὴν ἐπιστήμην.

φρόνησις,

"prudence" leading to right action, as compared with the more theoretical σοφία : cf. Eph 1[8]. See further Lightfoot *ad* Col 1[9], and *Notes* p. 317 f., also *OGIS* 332[25] (B.C. 138–2)

ἀρετῆς ἕνεκεν καὶ φρονήσεως τῆς συναυξούσης τὰ πράγ[μα]τα, and Wunsch *AF*, p. 6[1] (i/ii A.D.) ψ[υ]χὴν [δι]άνοιαν φρόνησιν αἴσθησιν ζοὴν [καρδ]ίαν.

In the trimeter PSI IV. 280 (iv/v A.D.) φρόνησις is contrasted with τύχη—

ὅστις νομίζει διὰ φρόνησιν εὐτυχεῖν
μάταιός ἐστι· πάντα γὰρ τὰ τοῦ βίου
οὐ διὰ φρόνη[σ]ιν, διὰ τύχην δὲ γείνεται.

For a subst. φρονιμότης see *ib.* I. 94[2] (ii/A.D.) ἐξαιτ[εῖ ?]ται δέ με πλέον ἡ φρονιμότης αὐτ[ο]ῦ πρὸς τὸ μαρτυρῆσαι ὑμεῖν τὴν φιλανθρωπίαν μου.

φρόνιμος,

"prudent," is frequent in the NT as denoting fitness for God's service (Mt 7[24], 10[16], *al.* : Swete *Parables of the Kingdom*, p. 123) : cf. *OGIS* 383[106] (mid. i/B.C.) διαμονῆς δὲ τούτων ἕνεκεν, ἣν ἐμ φρονίμοις ἀνδράσι εὐσεβὲς ἀεὶ τηρεῖν. The word is common as a proper name, e.g. P Oxy III. 531[23, 25] (ii/A.D.).

φρονίμως.

P Lond 1927[36] (mid. iv/A.D.) φρονίμως ἔδιξας τὸ γεννεότατον ἄθλον, "you prudently showed forth your most noble contest," with reference to manner of life: cf. Lk 16[8].

φροντίζω,

"am careful," "give heed," is found in the NT only in Tit 3[8], where it is followed by inf. (see *Proleg.* p. 206 f.) : cf. P Ryl II. 78[26] (A.D. 157) φρόντισον εὐθέως πέμψαι τὸν λῆψόμενον αὐτόν, "take care to send somebody at once to take it" (Edd.), and P Grenf II. 77[15] (iii/iv A.D.) (= *Selections*, p. 121) φροντίσατε οὖν τὰ ἀναλωθέντα ἑτοιμάσαι, "see to it therefore that you furnish the sums expended."

Elsewhere the verb is construed (1) c. gen., as in BGU I. 249[20] (ii/A.D.) φρόντισον δ᾽ ἐμοῦ χορίου δερμάτ[ων] ἑξακοσίων, *ib.* 300[1] (A.D. 148) φροντιοῦντά μου τῶν ἐν Ἀρσινοείτῳ ὑπαρχόντων, P Oxy VII. 1072[8] (v/vi A.D.) σπούδασον φροντίσαι τοῦ νέου λάκκου τοῦ γιγνομένου σὺν θεῷ ἐν τῳ κτήματι ἱερέων, "hasten to give heed to the new pond which is being made by the help of God in the priests' estate" (Ed.). (2) c. acc., as in P Lond 28[5] (*c.* B.C. 162) (= I. p. 43, *UPZ* i. p. 343) φροτίσαι (*l.* φροντίσαι) μοι σιτάριον, P Par 45[2] (B.C. 152) (= *UPZ* i. p. 329) πεφρόντικα ὑπὲρ τοῦ χρήσιμα τῶν σῶν πραγμάτων. (3) c. ἵνα as in P Tebt I. 33[2] (B.C. 112) (= *Selections*, p. 30) φρόν]τισον οὖν ἵνα γένη(ται) ἀκολούθως, "take care that its instructions are followed" (with reference to a letter), and so[4]. (4) c. ὅπως (μή), as in P Hib I. 170[1] (B.C. 247) (= Witkowski[2], p. 27) φρόντισον δέ, ὅπως μηκέτι ἀπὸ τούτων παρακούσει ἡμῶν, and (5) c. ὡς, as in P Tebt I. 10[6] (B.C. 119) φρόντισον ὡς τὰ τῆς ὑποσχέσεως ἐκπληρωθήσεται, "take care that the terms of his agreement are fulfilled" (Edd.).

For the subst. φροντίς, cf. P Tebt I. 33[17] (B.C. 112) (= *Selections*, p. 31) τὴν μεγίστην φροντίδα ποιουμένου, "taking the greatest care." P Amh II. 135[6] (early ii/A.D.) τὴ(ν) φροντίδα πάντων ποιεῖν ὡς ἰδίων σου, "look after everything as if it were your own" (Edd.), and for φροντιστής, see Preisigke *Fachwörter*, p. 170, and *Wörterbuch s.v.*

φρουρέω

is used literally "guard," "protect," in such passages as P Amh II. 43[17] (B.C. 173) where a contract is witnessed by six persons, τῶν ἐν τῆι Σοκνοπαίου Νήσωι φρουρούντων καὶ μισθο(φόρων), "belonging to the guard at Soenopaei Nesus and in receipt of pay," P Lilabel 9[6] (B.C. 103) τοῖ]ς ἐν Κρο(κοδείλων) πό(λει) φερομένοις φρου(ρούσιν), and P Tebt I. 92[2] (late ii/B.C.) Κερκεοσίρεως τῆς μὴ φρουρουμένης μηδ' οὔσης ἐπὶ τοῦ μεγάλου ποταμοῦ, "at Kerkeosiris, which is unguarded and is not situated upon the great river" (Edd.): cf. 2 Cor 11[32] and Field Notes, p. 186 f. See also an important note by E. L. Hicks in CR i. p. 7 f.: in the other NT passages (Gal 3[23], Phil 4[7], 1 Pet 1[5]) he prefers the idea of "a garrison keeping ward over a town" to the idea of "soldiers keeping guard either to prevent escape, or to protect the weak."

For φρουρός, cf. P Oxy IX. 1193[4] (iv/A.D.) ὄνον ἕνα πα[ράσχου] μετὰ καὶ ἑνὸς φύλακος τῷ ἀποσταλέντι φρ⟨ο⟩υρῷ, "supply one donkey together with one guard to the sentinel whom I have sent" (Ed.): for φρουρά, cf. P Tebt II. 315[31] (ii/A.D.) ἔχι γὰρ συστατικὰς [ὅ]πως τὸν ἀπιθοῦντα μετὰ φρουρᾶς τῷ ἀρχιερεῖ πέμπιν, "he has instructions to send recalcitrants under guard to the high-priest" (Edd.): and for φρούριον, cf. P Amh II. 31[25] (B.C. 112) περίστασις τοῦ φρουρίου, "the free space round the guardhouse."

In P Petr I. 29[14] (iii/B.C.) τῶν ὅρων apparently applies to the "watchers" of a vineyard, and Mahaffy following Bury regards ὅροι as the word from which φρουροί (προ-οροι) is derived, and compares the Homeric οὖρος.

φρυάσσω.

From denoting the "vehement neighing" of horses, this verb came to be used of the "haughtiness" or "insolence" of men (cf. "prancing proconsuls"), as in Ac 4[25] from Ps 2[1]. In M. Anton. iv. 48 μετὰ δεινοῦ φρυάγματος, the reference is to the "revolting insolence" with which tyrants have exercised their power of life and death.

φρύγανον,

"brushwood" (Ac 28[3]), as in P Cairo Zen III. 59517[3] (iii/B.C.), wages to workmen εἰς συναγωγὴν φρυγάνων, "for the gathering of brushwood." In Syll 568 (=[3] 984)[6] (end of iv/B.C.) a priest undertakes μηδὲ [φ]έρει(ν) ξύλα μηδὲ κοῦρον ("branches with leaves") μηδὲ φρύγανα μηδ[ὲ] φυλλόβολα ("branches shedding leaves") ἐκ τοῦ ἱεροῦ.

For the new παραφρυγάνισμος, see P Petr II. 6[11] (c. B.C. 250), where Mahaffy takes the meaning to be the piling of brushwood bound with clay to raise the banks of the canal. In his Introduction to the vol. p. 28 f. he supplies an interesting parallel from Wood's Sources of the Oxus, p. 22, where we are told that, when the river threatens to cut away its banks, the natives protect them with branches of tamarisk, in order to break the force of the water.

Φρυγία,

"Phrygia, an ethnic district in Asia Minor, the north-western part of which was in the Roman province Asia,

and the south-eastern part in the Roman province Galatia: in Ac. xvi. 6 Φρυγίαν is adj." (Souter Lex s.v.). See further W. M. Ramsay Cities and Bishoprics of Phrygia (Oxford, 1895, 1897), and the same writer in Hastings DB iii. p. 863 ff.

Φύγελος,

not Φύγελλος (see WH Notes[2], p. 166), a Christian who deserted Paul (2 Tim 1[15]). A proper name Φυγέλιος occurs in CIG II. 3027.

φυγή,

"flight" (Mt 24[20]): P Tebt I. 48[24] (c. B.C. 113) ῥίψαντα τὸ ἱμάτιον εἰς φυγὴν ὁρμῆσαι, "throwing away his garment took to flight," Gnomon 36 (c. A.D. 150) (= BGU V. p. 20) αὐθέ[[ιερ]]ρετον (l. αὐθαίρετον) φυγὴν ἑλομένου, "having taken to flight of their own accord," BGU III. 909[14] (A.D. 359) τῶν ἀπὸ τῆς κώμης φυγὴ(ν) ποιησαμένων, and P Oxy XVI. 1876[5] (c. A.D. 480) διὰ τῆς φυγῆς περιγράφειν τὸ χρέος ἐσπούδασαν, "they attempted by flight to evade payment of the debt" (Edd.).

For a weaker sense cf. ib. VIII. 1121[26] (A.D. 295) ἐμοῦ ἤδη τὴν πρ[ὸς τὸν μ]ίζονα φυγὴν ποιουμένη(ς), "since I am already having recourse to the official" (Ed.), in connexion with a petition.

φυλακή.

(1) For φυλακή in the general sense of "care," "charge," of a thing: P Lille 1. 7[8] (iii/B.C.) ἐπιζητήσαντος αὐτοῦ βυβλάριά τινα, ἃ ἐδεδώκειν ἐν φυ(λακῆι) "il me réclama de petits livres qu'il m'avait donnés en garde."

(2) "watch," "guard": P Tebt II. 282[7] (late ii/B.C.) a guard declares that he will keep the best watch possible upon other people's holdings—φυ λακὴν ἀλ[λο]τρ[ί]ων κλή(ρων) συντηρήσειν ἀπὸ τ[ο]ῦ βελτί[σ]του, Priene 28[4] (soon after B.C. 200) ὅπως δὲ ἡ χ[ώ]ρα ἡ Μιλησίων καὶ Πριηνέων ἐμ φυλακῆι καὶ σωτηρίαι ὑπάρχηι.

(3) = "a guard," i.e. "persons keeping guard" (Lat. custodia), as in Ac 12[10]: P Giss I. 19[16] (ii/A.D.), a sister begs her brother not to face some danger (perhaps connected with the Jewish war) without a guard—μὴ μόνος τὸν κίνδυνον [ἄνευ] φυλακῆς ὑπόμεινε (l. ὑπόμενε).

(4) = "a prison" (Mt 14[10], al.): BGU IV. 1138[18] (B.C. 18) ἀπολεί[ψ]ομαι τὸν Παπία(ν) ἐκ τῆς φυλακῆ(ς), P Oxy II. 259[45] (A.D. 23), a declaration τῷ τεταγμένῳ πρὸς τῇ τοῦ Διὸς φυλακῇ, "by the surety for a man who had been arrested for debt that he will restore ὃν ἐνγεγύημαι . . . ἐκ [τ]ῆς πολιτικῆς φυλα[κ]ῆς "the man whom I bailed out of the public prison," P Giss I. 84[18] (A.D. 83) Ἀσκλᾶν εἰς τὴν φυλακὴν παρ[α]δοθῆναι (cf. Ac 8[3]), PSI VII. 832[7] (v/A.D.) εἰς τὴν δημοσίαν φυλακήν.

(5) the time during which a watch was kept, as in Mt 24[43] al.: P Petr II. 45[i. 15] (B.C. 246) (= Chrest. I. p. 5) πρώτης φυλακῆς ἀρχομένης.

For the subst. φυλακία cf. P Oxy XVI. 1627[12] (A.D. 342) an appointment εἰς φυλακίαν ἱεροῦ Θοήριου, "to the guarding of the temple of Thoeris."

φυλακτήριον,

lit. "a guarded post" or "fortification," came to be used by the Jews as a technical term for the "prayer-fillet," a strip of parchment inscribed with portions of the Law, and worn as an "amulet" or "protective-mark" on the forehead or next the heart, as in Mt 23⁵: cf. the golden φυλακτήρια worn by the kings of Egypt, *OGIS* 90⁴⁵ (Rosetta stone—B.C. 196) ἐπιθεῖναι δὲ καὶ ἐπὶ τοῦ περὶ τὰς βασιλείας τετραγώνου κατὰ τὸ προειρημένον βασίλειον φυλακτήρια χρυ[σᾶ, "to place on the square surface round the crowns, beside the afore-mentioned crown, golden phylacteries" (Mahaffy).

Other exx. of the word are P Leid Wˣᵛⁱⁱⁱ·² (ii/iii A.D.) (= II. p. 143) τὸ γὰρ ὄνομά σου ἔχω ε φυλακτήριων (*l.* ἔχω ὡς φυλακτήριον) ἐν καρδίᾳ τῇ ἐμῇ,ˣˣ·²⁴ ἐν τὸ ἀργύρῳ πετάλου (*l.* ἐν τῷ ἀργύρου πετάλῳ) τὰ ζ (*sc.* vocales). πρὸς τὸν φυλκτήρον (*l.* τὸ φυλακτήριον), and P Lond 121²⁹⁸ (iii/A.D.) (= I. p. 94) φυλακτήρια λέων—a spell for the times when the moon is in the several signs of the Zodiac. See also Deissmann *BS*, p. 352.

φύλαξ,

"a guard": P Hib I. 147 (early iii/B.C.) σύντασσε [τοὺς] παρὰ σοὶ φ[ύ]λακας φυλάσσειν καὶ προ[σ]έχειν ἵνα κτλ., P Oxy II. 803 (late i/B.C.) τοὺς ἀπὸ τοῦ νομοῦ φύλακας, BGU III. 830²⁴ (i/A.D.) τοὺς φιλακες (*l.* φύλακας) ἡμῶν σκύλον πρὸς αὐ[τ]ήν, *ib.* 720¹¹ (A.D. 137) ὃν δὲ ἐὰν βούληται ὁ Σαραπίων ὀπωροφύλακα φυλάσσι⟨ν⟩ τῷ τῆς ὀπώρας καιρῷ φύλακα πέμψει, "Sarapion shall send any guard whom he chooses in order to protect the fruit at the time of bearing" (Edd.), and *ib.* VI. 931⁶ (ii/A.D.) ἔπεμψα διὰ τοῦ κομίσαντος [τ]ὸ ἀπὸ σοῦ ἐπιστόλιον φύλακος . . . "I have sent by the guard who brought the letter from you . . ."

For the different orders of φύλακες see Jouguet *Vie Municipale*, p. 261 ff., and for φύλακτρον, "police-tax," see P Oxy III. 502¹³ (A.D. 164) with the editors' note.

φυλάσσω,

(1) "guard," "protect": P Par 66²² (i/B.C.) πρεσβύτεροι οἱ τὰ χώματα καὶ περιχώματα φυλάσσοντες, P Oxy VI. 924¹ (iv/A.D.) ἦ μὴν φυλάξῃς καὶ συντηρήσῃς Ἀρίας ἀπὸ τοῦ ἐπιημερινοῦ (*l.* Ἀρίαν . . . τῆς ἐφημερινῆς) φρικός, "verily guard and protect Aria from ague by day" (Edd.).

(2) "keep," "observe": *Cagnat* IV. 661¹³ (A.D. 85) τοῦτο δὲ τὸ ψήφισμα νενομοθετῆσθαι τῷ αἰῶνι τῆς Ῥωμαίων ἡγεμονίας φυλαχθησόμενον (cf. Ac 7⁵³, *al.*), P Ryl II. 177¹¹ (A.D. 246) τὸ δὲ ὑπηλλαγμένον [ἥμισυ μέρος οἰκίας φυ]λάξομ(εν) ἀνεξαλλοτρίωτον, "the mortgaged half share of the house we will preserve unalienated" (Edd.). Cf. also P Ryl II. 116²⁰ (A.D. 194) λόγου μοι φυλασσομένου περὶ ὧν ἔχω δικαίων πάντων, "account being kept of all my claims" (Edd.), *ib.* 86⁸ (A.D. 195) λόγου φυλασσομένου τῇ πόλει πε[ρ]ὶ [ο]ὗ [ἔ]χει παντὸς δ[ικαίο]υ, "without prejudice to any right claimed by the city" (Edd.).

The verb is common of observing the duties of marriage, e.g. P Oxy VI. 905⁹ (A.D. 170) συμβιούτωσαν [οὖν ἀλλήλοις οἱ γ]αμοῦντες φυλάσσοντες τὰ τοῦ γάμου δί-

καια, and so *ib.* X. 1273²³ (A.D. 260), XII. 1473¹¹ (A.D. 201).

With φ. ἀπό, as in Lk 12¹⁵, cf. P Lond IV. 1349³⁵ (A.D. 710) παραφυλάξαι δι[ὰ] τ[ῆς] διοικήσεως σου ἀπὸ τῶν προσφευγόντων ἐν αὐτῇ φυγάδω[ν: cf. Blass *Gr.* p. 87 f.

φυλή,

"a tribe," especially one of the twelve tribes of Israel (Mt 19²⁸ *al.*), and extended by analogy to the tribes of the earth (Mt 24³⁰ *al.*). For the priestly tribes in Egypt, cf. P Tebt II. 299³ (c. A.D. 50), where a certain Psoiphis, τῶν ἀ[πὸ τῆς κώ]μης πέμπτη[ς φυλῆς] ἱερέος (*l.* ἱερέως) τῶν ἐν [τῇ κώμῃ] θεῶν, "priest of the fifth tribe of the gods at the village," asks that the birth of a son be registered, P Ryl II. 170⁵ (A.D. 127) Πακῦσις . . . ἱερεὺς πρώτης φυλῆς Σοκνοπαίου θεοῦ μεγάλου, and similarly ⁹·²⁷. See further Otto *Priester* i. p. 23 ff.

In Claudius's address to the Alexandrines P Lond 1912⁴¹ (A.D. 41) a φυλὴ Κλαυδιανά, not known elsewhere, is mentioned : see the editor's note, where reference is made to Schubart *Archiv* v. p. 94 f. for the Alexandrian tribe-names of the Roman period. Cf. also Preisigke *Fachwörter s.v.* φυλή.

φύλλον,

"a leaf" (Mt 21¹⁹, *al.*). In the magical P Oxy VI. 886¹⁴ᶠᶠ (iii/A.D.) (= *Selections* p. 111 f.) the petitioner for an omen is instructed—λαβὼν φύνικος ἄρσενος φύλλα κθ ἐπίγρ(αψον) ἐν ἑκάστῳ τῶν φύλλων τὰ τῶν θεῶν ὀνόματα κὲ ἐπευξάμενος ἆρε (*l.* αἶρε) κατὰ δύο δύο, τὸ δὲ ὑπολιπό[μ]ενον ἔσχατον ἀνάγνωτι κὲ εὑρήσις σου τὴν κληδόνα, ἐν οἷς μέτεστιν, "take 29 leaves of a male palm, and write upon each of the leaves the names of the gods, and having prayed lift them up two by two, and read that which is left at the last, and you will find in what things your omen consists." See also the ostrakon letter of the middle of iii/B.C. *Archiv* vi. p. 221¹⁷ ἔχουσι δὲ αἱ πεταλίαι ἐπιγραφὴν ἐν φύλλοις.

In the papyri φύλλον is common in the collective sense of "crops," e.g. P Tebt I. 38³ (B.C. 113) τῆς κατὰ φύλλον γεωμετρίας, "the land survey according to crops." For the verb φυλλολογέω see P Hamb I. 23²⁷ (A.D. 569) βοτανολογῆσαι καὶ φυλλολογῆσαι, and for the corr. subst. P Oxy XIV. 1631¹³ (contract for labour—A.D. 280) φυλλολογίαι αἱ ἐνχρήζουσαι, "needful thinnings of foliage" (Edd.).

φύραμα,

"a mixture," and hence "a lump" (Rom 11¹⁶, *al.*): cf. the account of a beer-seller P Tebt II. 401²⁷ (early i/A.D.) in which reference is made to—φυράμ(ατος) (ἀρτάβαι) ε (δραχμαί), and P Lond 46³⁷⁸ (iv/A.D.) (= I. p. 77) εἰς ὅλο(ν) τὸ φύραμα.

For the verb φυράω cf. the medical receipt P Oxy VIII. 1088²² (early i/A.D.) μάνναν φύρασον χυλῶι πράσωι καὶ ἐνάλιψον τὸν χυλὸν ἔνδόθεν, "mix frankincense with onion-juice and apply the juice inside" (Ed.), to stop nose-bleeding, *ib.* XIV. 1692²¹ (A.D. 188) φυράσι τὸν Πηλουσι-[ακὸν οἶνον ?. The compd. ἀναφυράω, "mix up well," occurs in *Syll* 807 (= ³ 1173)⁹ (not earlier than A.D. 138) τέφραν μετ' οἴνου ἀναφυρᾶσαι.

φυσικός.

In Rom 1²⁶ᶠ φυσικός is "natural," "according to nature," as opp. to παρὰ φύσιν, "against nature": cf. P Lips I. 28¹⁸ (A.D. 381) ὅνπερ θρέψω καὶ ἱματίζω εὐγενῶς καὶ γνησίως ὡς υἱὸν γνήσιον καὶ φυσικὸν ὡς ἐξ ἐ[μ]οῦ γενόμενον, in a deed of adoption. In 2 Pet 2¹² Mayor renders γεγεννημένα φυσικά "born creatures of instinct," as against RV "born mere animals." Cf. also Aristeas 171 τὴν σεμνότητα καὶ φυσικὴν διάνοιαν τοῦ νόμου = "the sanctity and natural (or inward) meaning of the Law" according to Thackeray, who however pronounces the exact sense "uncertain."

φυσιόω.

For the metaph. use of this verb = "puff up," as in 1 Cor 4⁶ ἵνα μὴ εἷς ὑπὲρ τοῦ ἑνὸς φυσιοῦσθε (for form, cf. *Proleg.* p. 54), see Cic. *ad Att.* v. 20. 6 πεφύσηημαι. This form φυσάω occurs in Herodas II. 32 τῇ γενῇ φυσῶντες, "priding themselves on their birth," and Menander Ἐπιτρέπ. 529.

φύσις,

"nature," is applied to (1) "birth," "physical origin," as in Gal 2¹⁵, Rom 2²⁷: cf. P Oxy X. 1266³³ (A.D. 98) εἶναι δ' ἐμοῦ καὶ τῆς Θερμουθίου φύσ[ει υἱὸν τὸ]ν Πλουτίωνα καὶ μὴ θέ[σει, "that Plution is the son of myself and Thermouthion by birth and not by adoption," and the letter ascribed to the Emperor Hadrian P Fay 19¹¹ (ii/A.D.) ὁ μὲν φύσει πατὴρ γενόμεν[ος .... τεσσαρά]κοντα βιώσας ἔτη ἰδιώτης μετ[ήλλαξε, "my father by birth died at the age of forty a private person."

(2) "innate properties or powers," what belongs to persons or things in view of their origin, as in 2 Pet 1⁴: cf. the Kommagenian inser., from mid. i/B.C. cited by Deissmann *BS* p. 368 n.², ἵνα .. γένησθε θείας κοινωνοὶ φύσεως, P Leid Wᵛⁱ·⁴³ (ii/iii A.D.) (= II. p. 101) ἀνὰ μέσον τῶν δύο φυσέων, (οὐρανοῦ) καὶ γῆς, P Lond 121⁵¹² (iii/A.D.) (= I. p. 100) τῆς κοσμικῆς φύσεως, and the amulet *Preisigke* 5620¹⁹ ὁ τὴν ἐνουράνιον τῆς ἐωνίου φύσεως κεκληρωμένος ἀνάγκην.

For the adverbial phrase κατὰ φύσιν, as in Rom 11²¹, ²⁴, cf. P Tebt II. 288⁶ (A.D. 226) τὰ [ὀνό]ματα τῶν κατὰ φύσιν ⟨γε⟩γεωργηκ[ότ]ων δημοσίων γεωργῶν καὶ κληρ[ο]ύχων, "the names of the public cultivators and owners who have planted the different kinds" (Edd.). [See also W. M. Ramsay *Pauline and other Studies* (1906), p. 219 ff.]

φυτεία,

prop. "a planting," as in P Petr II. 32 (2 *a*)⁵ (iii/B.C.) ἡμῶν ἐπιδικνυόντων σοι τὴν φυτήαν Θεοδότου, P Tebt I. 5²⁰⁴ (B.C. 118) τὴν δὲ φυτείαν ποιεῖσθαι ἀπὸ τοῦ ν̅β̅ (ἔτους), BGU IV. 1185²¹ (B.C. 04-3?) εἰς ἀμπέλου καὶ παραδείσων φυτ[[η]]εῖαν, and P Oxy VII. 1032¹⁹ (A.D. 162)

τοὺς δὲ τόπους εἶναι ἐν φυτεία. In its only NT occurrence (Mt 15¹³) the word is used of the thing planted, "a plant," cf. *OGIS* 606⁷ τὰς περὶ αὐτὸν (*sc.* τὸν ναὸν) φυτείας πάσας ἐφύ[τευσεν ἐκ τ]ῶν ἰδίων ἀναλ[ωμάτων.

φυτεύω,

"plant": P Petr I. 29¹ (iii/B.C.) (= Witkowski², p. 30) πεφύτευται δὲ καὶ ἡ ἄμπελος πᾶσα, *so* ¹⁵, PSI IV. 433⁶ (B.C. 261-0) οὐκ ἐφυτεύθη οὖν ἐπὶ τῆς πέτρας Ὀασιτικά, P Flor II. 148¹² (A.D. 266-7) τῶν φυτευομένων τόπων, and P Oxy XVI. 1911¹⁰⁴ (A.D. 557) ὑπὲρ (ἀρου.) β̅ φυτευθ(εισῶν) ἐν ἀμπέλ(ῳ).

In his note on 1 Cor 3⁶ (*Notes*, p. 187 f.) Lightfoot refers to the application by the Fathers of ἐφύτευσα to the work of educating the catechumens as a significant ex. of "a general fault of patristic exegesis, the endeavour to attach a technical sense to words in the NT which had not yet acquired this meaning."

φύω,

"grow," "grow up": P Grenf II. 28³ (B.C. 103) τῶν φυομένων δένδρων, P Flor I. 20²⁰ (A.D. 127) (= *Chrest.* I. p. 422) σὺν τῷ φυησομένωι σινάπι, PSI VI. 607¹² (ii/A.D.) ὅλου τοῦ κ[ή]που σὺ[ν] τοῖς φυτοῖς φ[υ]ομένοις πᾶσι ἐν ἑκάστ[η] μέρ]ίδι.

For the trans. use "bring forth," "produce," see *Preisigke* 6648¹ εἰμεὶ ἐγὼ Ἰησοῦς, ὁ φὺς δὲ Φαμεῖς, παροδεῖτα, where the editor understands ὃν φύσε Φαμεῖς or ὁ φύσ[ας] Φ.: cf. Lk 8⁶·⁸, and note the new 2 aor. pass. ἐφύην in place of the intrans. act. ἔφυν (cf. Blass-Debrunner § 76. 2).

The subst. φυτόν is very common. e.g. PSI VI. 568³ (B.C. 253-2?) φυτὰ παντοδαπά, BGU II. 530³¹ (i/A.D.) (= *Selections*, p. 62) ἐπὶ κινδυνεύει τὰ φυτὰ διαφωνῆσαι, "otherwise there is a risk that the plants perish," P Fay 111²⁵ (A.D. 95-6) (= *Selections*, p. 67) τῶν (*l.* τὸν) στίχον τὸν φυτῶν (*l.* τῶν φυτῶν) τὸν ἐν τῷ προφήτῃ πότισον, "water the row of trees in 'the prophet'" (apparently the name of a piece of land), P Ryl II. 99⁵ (iii/A.D.) ὑδρεύματα καὶ φυτά, "irrigators and trees," and P Hamb I. 23¹⁹ (A.D. 209) σὺν φυτοῖς παντοίοις ἐγκάρποις τε καὶ ἀκάρποις. See also φυή in such passages as BGU III. 708¹ (A.D. 104-5) ἀπέχ[ο]μεν πα[ρά σου τιμ]ὴν χόρτου φυῆς [τοῦ ἐνεστ]ῶτος ε (ἔτους).

φωλεός,

"a hole," "den," "lair": a late Greek word fully illustrated by Wetstein *ad* Mt 8²⁰. A verb φωλεύω is used by a translator of Job 38⁴⁰. MGr φωλιά, "nest."

φωνέω,

"cry out," "shout": cf. BGU III. 925³ (iii/A.D.) μετὰ τὴ⟨ν⟩ [ἀ]ν[άγ]ν[ωσιν] ἡ βουλὴ ἐφώνησεν· Ἕλλειμμά ἐστιν ...., and P Oxy XVII. 2110⁶ (A.D. 370) οἱ βουλευταὶ ἐφώνησαν· κύριον τὸ κατὰ κῆραν, "The senators cried, 'What is on the tablet is valid'" (Ed.).

The word, which is used of the "crowing" of a cock in Mt 26³⁴ *al.*, gives place to κοκκύζω in the new Rainer fragment (*Mittheilungen aus der Sammlung der Papyrus*

Erzherzog Rainer, i. p. 53 ff., ii. p. 41 f.: cf. Milligan *Here and There*, p. 123 ff.).

From the inscrr. we may cite *Syll* 737 (= ³ 1109)[108] (after A.D. 178) μηδεὶς δ' ἔπος φωνείτω, and for the meaning "address" followed by a nom. of the title, as in Jn 13[13], see Blass-Debrunner §§ 143, 147.

φωνή,

"a sound," "a voice": cf. P Lond 1912[27] (A.D. 41) γνησιωτέραις ὑμᾶς φωναῖς προσαγορεύσας, "addressing you more frankly by word of mouth," P Ryl II. 77[46] (A.D. 192) ἔχομεν δὴ φωνὴν τοῦ Ἀσπιδᾶ, "we now have the declaration of Aspidas" (Edd.). In one of the family letters of Paniskos (iii/iv A.D.) from the Michigan papyri edited by J. G. Winter in the *Journ. Egypt. Arch.* xiii. p. 72[21] we find πολλάκι[ς] φωνὴν αὐ[τῷ] ἐβά[λομ]εν ἵνα ἔλ[θῃ] πρὸς τὸν ἐπανορθωτὴ(ν) Ἀχιλλ[έα], "we sent him word repeatedly that he might come to the epanorthotes Achilles" —a phrase for which the editor can find no parallel.

For the power of the divine voice cf. Wünsch *AF* p. 23[24] (iii/A.D.) διὰ φωνῆς προστάγματος, where the editor compares Ps 32[9] αὐτὸς εἶπεν, καὶ ἐγενήθησαν. The word is used of Coptic speech in P Lond 77[13] (end vi/A.D.) (= I. p. 232) τῇ τῶν Αἰγυπτίων φωνῇ: cf. also P Giss I. 40[ii. 27] (A.D. 215) (= *Chrest.* I. p. 39).

φῶς.

For "light" opposed to "darkness," see P Leid W[vi. 44] (ii/iii A.D.) (= II. p. 101) φωτὸς καὶ σκότους. In the imprecatory curse *Syll* 891 (= ³ 1240)[20] the prayer is uttered that the victim shall enjoy μηδὲ οἴκου, μὴ φωτός, μὴ χρήσεως, μηδὲ κτήσεως. The plur. is applied to "window-lights" in P Lond 1170[62] (ii/A.D.) (= III. p. 146) φῶτα θυρίδων, and to "torches," as in Ac 16[29], in BGU III. 909[15] (A.D. 359) ἐπελθόντες . . . τῇ ἡμετέρᾳ οἰκίᾳ καὶ φῶτα ἐπενεγκ[όν]τες ἐνέπρησαν αὐτὴν ἐκ θεματίου: cf. *ib.* IV. 1201[10] (A.D. 2) where φωτί takes the place of πυρί or φλογί -εὕρωμεν τὰς θύρας τοῦ ἱεροῦ Σαραπείδος θεοῦ μεγίστου ὑφημένας (*l.* ὑφημμένας) φωτί. This last passage may illustrate Mk 14[54] θερμαινόμενος πρὸς τὸ φῶς, where we should translate with the AV "warmed himself at the fire": see C. H. Turner *Comm. ad l.* in Gore's *New Commentary*.

The subst. is applied metaph. to those who impart light, as in *Syll* 888 (= ³ 1238)[2] (c. A.D. 160) where a wife is described as τὸ φῶς τῆς οἰκίας, and in P Ryl II. 77[34] (A.D. 192) μιμοῦ τὸν πα[τ]έρα τὸν φιλότιμον τὸν [γ]έροντα φῶτα. See also the Christian sepulchral inscr. P Hamb I. 22[4] (iv/A.D.), where Christ is invoked—ὃς τυφλοῖσιν ἔδωκας ἰδεῖν φάος ἠελίοιο (cf. Mt 9[27 ff.], *al.*), and the Christian amulet BGU III. 954[28] (vi/A.D.) (= *Selections*, p. 134)—

> ὁ φῶς ἐκ φωτός, θ(εὸ)ς ἀληθινὸς χάρισον
> ἐμὲ τὸν δοῦλόν σου τὸ φῶς.

Φῶς is naturally common in the magic papyri, e.g. P Lond 121[563] (iii/A.D.) (= I. p. 102) ἐν φωτὶ κραταιῷ καὶ ἀφθάρτῳ: cf. the *verso* of BGU II. 597[33] (A.D. 75) cited *s.v.* φωσφόρος.

φωστήρ,

"a luminary" (Phil 2[15], Rev 21[11]: cf. Gen 1[16]): cf. P Leid W[vii. 25] (ii/iii A.D.) (= II. p. 105) δόξα τοῦ ἐντίμου φωστῆρος, Wünsch *AF* p. 23[23] (iii/A.D.) ὁρκίζω σε τὸν φωστῆρα καὶ ἄστρα ἐν οὐρανῷ ποιήσαντα, and Vett. Val. p. 110[22] περὶ τοὺς φωστῆρας ἀδικούμενοι, where the editor understands φωστῆρες as = "oculi."

φωσφόρος,

"light-bringing": thence as a subst. "day-star" (probably the planet Venus). In Biblical Greek the word is found only in 2 Pet 1[19] (see Mayor's note), applied metaphorically to the rising of the kingdom of God in the heart. An interesting ex. of the word is found in BGU II. 597[32] (A.D. 75), where on the *verso* of a private letter there has been added in uncial characters the hexameter line— Φωσφόρε φωσφορεοῦσα φίλων (*l.* φίλον) φῶς φῶς φέρε λαμπάς. The words, according to Olsson (*Papyrusbriefe* p. 139), are probably an extract from an Orphic hymn. The same epithet is found in the magic P Lond 46[175, 300] (iv/A.D.) (= I. pp. 70, 74) φωσφόρ' ἰαω. In P Rein 10[8] (B.C. 111) it is applied to the priestess of Queen Cleopatra— φωσφόρου βασιλίσσης Κλεοπάτρας, "sous la phosphore (prêtresse) de la reine Cléopâtre": cf. Otto *Priester* ii. p. 320.

For φωσφόριον, "a window," see P Ryl II. 162[26] (A.D. 159), and P Hamb I. 15[8] (A.D. 209).

φωτεινός

(or φωτινός, WH), "shining," "bright" (Mt 6[22] *al.*). The superl[ve.] is applied to a person in the address P Lond 1917[1] (c. A.D. 330–340) τῷ γνησιωτάτῳ καὶ φω[τ]ινωτάτῳ μ[α]καριωτάτῳ . . . . ἄπα Παιηρῦ, ἐν δεσπό[τον Ἰη]σοῦ Χριστοῦ χαῖραι (*l.* χαῖρε), "to the most genuine and most enlightened, most blessed Apa Paieôu, greeting in our Master Jesus Christ" (Ed.). Cf. also the vi/A.D. biblical scholion PSI I. 65[13] οἱ (*l.* εἰ ?) πειστοὶ κροιγορούντες (*l.* πιστοὶ γρηγορούντες) ἐσώ(=ό)μεθα, λαμπάτ(=δ)ες ὑ(=ή)μων φωτινὲ (*l.* φωτειναὶ) ἐν ἐλαίῳ.

In a Christian Greek inscr. from Nubia of ix/A.D., published in *J. Eg. Arch.* xiii. p. 227, the prayer occurs—ὁ θ(εὸ)ς ἀνάπαυσον τ[ὴ]ν ψυχὴν αὐτ(ο)ῦ ἐν κόλποις Ἀβραὰμ κ(αὶ) Ἰσαὰκ κ(αὶ) Ἰακὼβ ἐν τόπῳ φωτινῷ ἐν τόπῳ ἀναψύξεως ἔνθα ἀπέδρα ὀδύνη κ(αὶ) λύπη κ(αὶ) στεναγμός, "O God, give rest to his soul in the bosom of Abraham and Isaac and Jacob, in a place of light, in a place of refreshment, from which pain and grief and lamentation have fled away" (Ed.). See also P. D. Scott-Moncrieff *Paganism and Christianity in Egypt*, p. 104, where reference is made to a funeral tablet (Berlin, No. 11820), which runs "Taêsai lived 28 years. She has gone to the shining (land)." The φωτινὸς τόπος may be either the Christian heaven, or the place of the "illuminated ones" of the old pagan religion.

φωτίζω.

For the literal sense "enlighten," "illumine," as in Lk 11[36], cf. Wünsch *AF* p. 16[13] (iii/A.D.) ὁρκίζω σε τὸν θεὸν τὸν φωτίζοντα καὶ σκοτίζοντα τὸν κόσμον. The metaph. usage "bring to light," "make known," as in 2 Tim 1[10] (cf. LXX 4 Kingd 17³⁷ᶠ), may be illustrated by Polyb. xxx. 8. 1, Epict. i. 4. 31.

For the mystical sense of spiritual illumination, as in Eph 1¹⁸, see *s.v.* **φωτισμός**.

φωτισμός,

like its verb (*q.v.*), is applied to spiritual illumination in 2 Cor 4⁴·⁶, and the corr. use of both verb and subst. in the OT (Pss 18(19)⁸, 26(27)¹) makes it unnecessary with Reitzenstein (*Hellen. Mysterien Religionen*² p. 142 ff) to look for an explanation of the metaphor in Hellenistic Mystery-Religion. See further Kennedy *St. Paul and the Mystery Religions*, p. 107 f. For the application to "baptism" in ecclesiastical usage, see Justin M. *Apol.* 61E. ὁ **φωτιζόμενος** λούεται, 65C εὐχὰς ποιησάμενοι ὑπὲρ τοῦ **φωτισθέντος**.

X

χαίρω—χάλκεος

χαίρω,

"rejoice": P Eleph 13³ (B.C. 223–222) ἐκομισάμην τὴν παρὰ σοῦ ἐπιστολήν, ἣν ἀναγνοὺς ἐχάρην (cf. *Proleg.* p. 161) ἐπὶ τῶι με αἰσθέσθαι τὰ κατὰ σέ, P Berol 11662³ (time of Claudius) (= Olsson, p. 100) πρὸ μὲν πάντων ἐχάρην μεγάλως λαβών σου [ἐ]πιστολήν, ὅτι ὑγιαίνεις, similarly P Giss I. 21³ (time of Trajan), BGU II. 531ⁱ·⁴ (ii/A.D.), and P Oxy I. 41¹⁷ (iii/iv A.D.) ἐπὶ τούτῳ σφόδρα χαίρω.

It should be noted that in Phil 3¹, 4¹, RV marg. renders χαίρετε by "farewell." Lightfoot (*Comm. ad ll.*) combines the two meanings "farewell" and "rejoice," but the latter is generally preferred by the commentators.

The verb is very common in the opening address of letters, as in Ac 15²³, 23²⁶, cf. Jas 1¹, e.g. P Eleph 10¹ (B.C. 223–222) Εὐφρόνιος Μίλωνι χαίρειν (for imper. inf. see *Proleg.* p. 179f.), P Oxy II. 292² (c. A.D. 25) Θέων Τυράννωι τῶι τιμιωτάτωι πλεῖστα χαίρειν, P Ryl II. 157³ (A.D. 135) ἀλλήλαις χα[ί]ρειν, "mutual greetings," and the official petition to a strategus P Oxy VIII. 1119²² (A.D. 254) Ἀντώνιος Ἀλέξανδρος στρατηγῷ Ὀξυρυγχείτου χαίρειν. Wilcken cites *UPZ* i. 62¹ (before the end of B.C. 161 (or 160)) Διονύσι[ος Πτολε]μαίωι χαίρειν καὶ ἐρρῶσθαι, as the oldest ex. of that combination. Cf. P Oxy IV. 746² (A.D. 16) Θέων Ἡρακλείδηι τῶι ἀδελφῶι πλεῖστα χαίρειν καὶ ὑγιαίνειν. In *ib.* 822 (c. A.D. 1) εὖ πράσσειν is substituted for χαίρειν.

The imper. takes the place of the inf. in such greetings as P Oxy XIV. 1664¹ (iii/A.D.) Χαῖρε, κύριέ μου Ἀπίων. "Greeting, my lord Apion," and similarly *ib.* 1667¹ (iii/A.D.), *ib.* IX. 1185¹³ (c. A.D. 200), *ib.* XII. 1492¹³ (Christian—iii/iv A.D.) Χα[ῖ]ρε, ἱερ[ὲ υἱὲ] Δημητρι[ανέ. Occasionally, during the Roman period, we have χαίροις for χαῖρε, as P Oxy III. 526¹ (ii/A.D.) Χαίροις Καλόκαιρε, Κύριλλός σε προσαγορεύω, "Greeting, Calocaerus: I, Cyrillus, address you," *ib.* I. 112¹ (iii/iv A.D.), and P Iand I. 12¹ (iii/iv A.D.) (see the editor's note).

For epistolary phrases with χαίρω, see further G. A. Gerhard *Untersuchungen zur Geschichte des Griech. Briefes* (Heidelberg, 1903), Ziemann *Epist.* (see Abbreviations I. General), Exler *Epistolography* (see *ib.*), and the note "On some current epistolary phrases" by J. A. Robinson *Ephesians*, p. 275 ff.

A good ex. of χαιρετίζω, as in LXX Tob 7¹, is supplied by P Oxy X. 1242³⁵ (early iii/A.D.), cited *s.v.* χαλεπός. For ἐπιχαίρω of malignant exulting, see the prayer for vengeance *Preisigke* 1323 (ii/A.D.) ἥ τις αὐτή (*sc.* the suppliant) φάρμακα ἐποίησε ἢ καὶ ἐπέχαρέ τις αὐτῆς τῷ θανάτῳ ἢ ἐπιχαρεῖ, μετέλθετε αὐτούς.

χάλαζα,

"hail" (Rev 8⁷, 11¹⁹, 16²¹): cf. Epicurus *Epist.* II. §§ 106, 107 (ed. Bailey).

χαλάω,

"slacken," "let down" (Mk 2⁴, *al.*): cf. P Lond 131*¹² (A.D. 78) (= I. p. 189) persons περὶ τὸ ὄργανον χαλῶντ(ες) τὰς τριχ(ίας), and the compd. ἐπιχαλάω in P Ryl II. 81¹¹ (c. A.D. 104) ἵν᾽ ὅσον ἐὰν χρείαν ἔχωσι ὑδάτους (= -ος) ἑαυ[τοῖς ἐ]πιχαλῶσι, "that they may draw off for themselves as much water as they need" (Edd.). The subst. χάλασμα occurs in Preisigke 428⁷ (B.C. 99), *al.* In MGr χαλάω = "break to pieces" and χάλασμα = "ruin."

χαλεπός,

"hard," "difficult,": cf. P Oxy X. 1242³⁶ (early iii/A.D.), an account of an audience granted by Trajan to certain Greek and Jewish envoys from Alexandria, when the Emperor does not return the salute of the Alexandrian envoys but exclaims—χαιρετίζετέ με ὡς ἄξειοι τυγχάνοντ[ες] τοῦ χαίρειν, τοιαῦτα χαλεπὰ τολμήσαντε[ς] Ἰουδαίοις; "do you give me greeting like men deserving to receive one, when you are guilty of such outrages to the Jews?" (Edd.): see also *Syll* 356 (=³ 780)³¹ (c. B.C. 6) αὐτοῖς ἐδόξ[ατε] χαλεποὶ γεγονέναι, where the adj. = "harsh," "fierce," as in Mt 8²⁸.

χαλιναγωγέω,

"bridle," hence "check," "restrain." No earlier exx. of this word have been found than Jas 1²⁶, 3². For the metaph. cf. Lucian *Tyrannicida* 4 τὰς τῶν ἡδονῶν ὀρέξεις χαλιναγωγούσης.

χαλινός,

"a bridle" (Jas 3³, Rev 14²⁰): PSI V. 543⁵⁰ (iii/B.C.) χαλινοῦ τοῦ ἀργυροῦ κατασκευή. For the common phrase ἀχάλινον στόμα, see Aristoph. *Ran.* 838.

χάλκεος,

"made of bronze," "bronze" (Rev 9²⁰): P Hamb I. 31⁹ (ii/A.D.) δ]έλτον χαλκῆν, "a bronze writing-tablet," CPR I. 232¹² (ii/iii A.D.) κ]άδον ("jar") καὶ ἕτε[ρον] εἶδος χάλκεον, P Lond 1177⁹² (A.D. 113) (= III. p. 183) κ[άδ]ων χαλκῶ(ν), and ³⁰³.

χαλκεύς,

"a worker in bronze" (2 Tim 4¹⁴): P Tebt I. 103³³ (taxing-list—B.C. 94 or 61) Ὠφελίων χαλκεύς, P Oxy I. 113¹⁸ (ii/A.D.) διὰ τὸ τὸν χαλκέα μακρὰν ἡμῶν εἶναι, "because the smith is a long way from us," and BGU IV. 1028⁸ (ii/A.D.) (τῷ) προεστῶτι χαλκέων κ[αὶ τοῖς σὺν αὐτῷ τειμὴν] ψαλλίδ[ων.

χαλκίον,

"a bronze vessel," "a kettle" (Mk 7⁴): P Fay 95¹¹ (ii/A.D.) μηχαναὶ δύο καὶ χαλκίον, "two machines and a caldron" (Edd.), P Tebt II. 405²¹ (c. A.D. 266) χαλκίον τέλειον μολυβοῦν, "a leaden kettle in good condition," ib.²² χαλκίον μικρόν: cf. the ostracon Preisigke 4293² (Rom.), and for χάλκινος see P Meyer 20¹¹ (1st half iii/A.D.).

χαλκός.

From meaning "bronze" generally (1 Cor 13¹, Rev 18¹²), χαλκός comes to be applied to "bronze-money" (Mk 6⁸, 12⁴¹): cf. P Lips I. 106¹⁹ (A.D. 98) βλέπε δέ, μηδενὶ ἄλλῳ δοῖς (l. δῷς) χαλκόν, P Tebt II. 414²⁹ (ii/A.D.) πέμψῃ μοι τὸν χαλκόν, ἔπι ἔρχομαι, "send me the money, since I am coming" (Edd.), and P Oxy X. 1295¹⁷ (ii/iii A.D.) δήλωσόν μοι πόσου χαλκοῦ δέδωκες αὐτῶι, "let me know how much money you have given to him" (Edd.).

χαμαί

in its two NT occurrences (Jn 9⁶, 18⁶) means "to the ground," cf. P Lips I. 40ᵇ·²⁹ (iv/v A.D.) εἶδεν τὰς θύρας χαμαὶ ἐρριμένας and ib.iii·³⁴ ἄλλος ἔβαλεν αὐτὸν χαμαί. The same papyrus shows the other meaning "on the ground," c.15 ἡ ἔσω(?) καὶ ἡ ἔ]ξω θύρα χαμαὶ κεῖνται, and iii·14.

Χαναναῖος,

"a Canaanite": an old Biblical name which Mt (15²²) employs in preference to Mk's (7²⁶) Ἑλληνίς, "a Gentile" (RV mg.). For the different forms which the name takes in the LXX, see Thackeray Gr. i. pp. 164, 170 f., and cf. Burkitt Syriac Forms, p. 5.

χαρά,

"joy": BGU IV. 1141³ (B.C. 14) μετὰ πολλῆς [χ]αρᾶς, P Fay 20¹ (iii/iv A.D.) an edict, perhaps of the Emperor Julian (see Archiv ii. p. 169) which begins—ὅ[πω]ς μὴ διὰ τὸ τῆς χαρᾶς τῆ[ς] ἑαυτῶν δήλωσιν ποιήσασθαι ε . . . νην ἐπ' ἐμοὶ παρελθόντι ἐπὶ τὴν ἀρχὴν . . ., "lest for the sake of making a manifestation of their joy at my accession to empire . . ." (Edd.), P Iand I. 13¹⁸ (iv/A.D.) ἵνα μετὰ χαρᾶς σε ἀπολάβωμεν (cf. Mt 13²⁰), and the inscr. Preisigke 991⁶ (A.D. 290) μετὰ πάσης χαρᾶς καὶ ἱλαρίας. In the Christian P Oxy VIII. 1162⁵ Λέων πρεσβύτερος τοῖς . . . πρεσβυτ[έ]ροις καὶ διακώνοις ἀ[γ]απητοῖ[ς] ἀδελφοῖς ἐν κ(υρί)ῳ θ(ε)ῷ χαρὰ χα[ί]ρειν, "Leon, presbyter, to the presbyters and deacons, beloved brothers in the Lord God, fullness of joy"(Ed.), we have an ex. of the cogn. dat., as in Jn 3²⁹: for a corresponding usage in the LXX, cf. Thackeray Gr. i. p. 48 ff.

Χαρά is common as a proper name: see Preisigke Namenbuch s.v. In MGr the word is used for a "festival," "wedding."

χάραγμα

in the sense of the impress made by a stamp occurs septies in Rev, ter with special reference to "the mark of the beast" (13¹⁷, 16², 19²⁰). The exact meaning of the figure has been much discussed. Deissmann (BS, p. 240 ff.) suggests that an explanation may be found in the fact that, according to papyrus texts, it was customary to affix to bills of sale or official documents of the 1st and 2nd centuries of the Empire a seal giving the year and name of the reigning Emperor, and possibly his effigy. Thus on the back of CPR I. 11 (A.D. 108), an agreement regarding a house, there can still be deciphered a red seal with the inscr. (ἔτους) ιβ Αὐτοκράτορος Καίσαρος Νέρουα Τραιανοῦ. But no evidence has been produced of a similar seal being attached to persons, and Swete (Comm. ad Rev 3¹⁶) is content to find an explanation of the mysterious "mark" in the general symbolism of the book. "As the servants of God receive on their foreheads (vii. 3) the impress of the Divine Seal, so the servants of the Beast are marked with the 'stamp' of the Beast."

Χάραγμα is also used in connexion with the attestation of the copy of a document or writing, e.g. Preisigke 5275¹¹ (A.D. 11) ἀντίγραφον ἀπ' ἀντιγράφου χαράγματος καὶ ὑπαγραφῆς Ἑλληνικοῖς γράμμασι, and similarly 5231¹¹ (A.D. 11) and 5247³¹ (A.D. 47).

Other exx. of the word are BGU IV. 1088⁵ (A.D. 142) a female camel χαλ[αγ]μέ[νην) Ἀραβικοῖς χαράγμασ[ιν, similarly P Grenf II. 50(a)⁴ (A.D. 142), and the closing words of a letter P Lond V. 1658⁸ (iv/A.D.) (= Ghedini, p. 151) διὰ χαραγμάτων εὔχο[μαι, which Ghedini understands as = "I pray for your health in this letter." In P Oxy I. 144⁶ (A.D. 580) χρυσοῦ ἐν ὀβρύζῳ χαράγματι the reference is to gold in pure coin or stamped money.

For the subst. χαραγμός, cf. P Ryl II. 160(a)¹⁹ (A.D. 14-37) ἀντίγρ(αφον) χ]αραγμοῦ: for χάραξις, cf. ib. 164¹⁸ (A.D. 171) καθ]αρὸν ἀπὸ [ἀλίφατος καὶ ἐπιγραφῆς καὶ χαράξ[εως· and for the verb χαράσσω, cf. ib. 160⁶ (A.D. 28-9) τ]ῷ πρὸς τὸ γρ[αφε]ῖον χαράξαντι ἀποδοῦναι, "to pay the clerk of the record-office when he has endorsed the deed" (Edd.), (cf. 3 Macc 2²⁹).

We may add two interesting exx. of the compd. verb ἐγχαράσσω. The first is P Lond 854¹¹ (i/ii A.D.) (= III. p. 206, Selections p. 70), where in making the Nile tour a traveller announces that he had engraved the names of his friends on the temples—τῶν φίλων [ἐ]μ[ῶν τ]ὰ ὀνόματα ἐνεχάραξα τοῖς ἱ[ε]ροῖς. And the second is P Oxy XIV. 1680¹² (iii/iv A.D.), where a son anxious for his father's safety owing to the general insecurity writes—σῆ[μα ἠ]θέλησα ἐνχαράξαι σοι, "I wanted to stamp a mark on you."

χαρακτήρ.

From denoting "the tool for engraving," χαρακτήρ came to be used of the "mark," "impress" made, with special reference to any distinguishing peculiarity, and hence = "an exact reproduction." The word is found in the NT only in Heb 1³, cf. OGIS 383⁶⁰ (mid. i/B.C.) χαρακτῆρα μορφῆς ἐμῆς, of a statue.

Other exx. are Syll.² 226 (= ³495¹⁵ c. B.C. 320) τοῦ δὲ ξένου φέροντος ἐπὶ τὸν χαρακτῆρα, P Flor I. 61²¹ (A.D. 85)

(= *Chrest.* II. p. *88*) οὐ τῶν χαρα[κτή]ρων μόνων κληρο[ν]όμους δεῖ εἶναι, and P Leid W xxiv. 11 (ii/iii A.D.) (= II. p. 159) τέλει τέ μοι κύριε, τὸν μέγαν, κύριον, ἄφθεγτον χαρακτῆρα ("notam"), ἵνα αὐτὸν ἔχω. In the case of *Syll*[3] 783²³ (after B.C. 27) μέχρι τῶν Σεβαστείων εὐπλόησεν χαρακτήρων, Deissmann (*LAE*[2] p. 341 n.¹) translates "he made a successful voyage to the August Persons (Augustus and Livia)," taking χαρακτήρ thus early in the transferred sense of "person." See also notes on the word by J. Geffcken in *Exp T* xxi. p. 426 f., and by A. Körte in *Hermes* lxiv. (1929), p. 69 ff.

χάραξ.

For the meaning "palisade," as in Lk 19¹³, cf. BGU III. 830⁵ (i/A.D.) συμβαλὼν χάρ[ακα] περὶ τοῦ ἐ[λαιῶν]ος: and see *Syll*[3] 363¹ (B.C. 297) οἱ ἐν τῶι χάρακι, where the reference is to a fortified camp. The word has its earlier meaning of "stake," "vine-prop" in PSI IV. 393⁶ (B.C. 242–1) χάρακος καλαμίνου μυριάδες τρεῖς, BGU IV. 1122¹⁷ (B.C. 13) τὸ φυτὸν καὶ χάρακας καὶ φλοῦν.

χαρίζομαι.

The two meanings usually assigned to this verb, "show kindness to" and "graciously bestow," can hardly be separated as the following miscellaneous exx. show— P Lond 42³² (B.C. 168) (= I. p. 31, *UPZ* i. p. 301, *Selections*, p. 11) χάριε (*l.* χαριεῖ) δὲ καὶ τοῦ σώματος ἐπιμε[λό]μενος, ἵν᾿ ὑγιαίνηις, P Tebt I. 56¹⁶ (*c.* B.C. 130–121) τοῦτο δὲ ποιήσας ἔσῃ μοι κεχαρισμένος εἰς τὸν ἅπαντα χρόν[ον, "if you do this I shall be eternally obliged to you" (Edd.), P Oxy II. 292³ (*c.* A.D. 25) χαρίεσαι (see below) δέ μοι τὰ μέγιστα, P Tebt II. 509 (i/ii A.D.) μεθ᾿ ἃς ἐχαρισάμην αὐτῶι ἀπὸ λοι[π(ῶν)] κοπ(ῆς) χόρτ(ου) (δραχμὰς) κ, P Oxy I. 33 *verso* iii. 4 (late ii/A.D.) καὶ τοῦτο ἡμεῖν χάρ[ισ]αι, κύριε Καῖσαρ, "grant me this one favour, lord Caesar" (Edd.), P Grenf II. 68³ (A.D. 247) ὁμολογῶ χαρίζεσθ[αι] σοι χάριτι ἀναφαιρέτῳ καὶ ἀμετανοήτῳ . . . a deed of gift, *Chrest.* I. 461¹⁵ (beg. iii/A.D.) εὐεργεσίας ἧς ἐχαρί[σαντο τοῖς ἀπολυθεῖ]σι στρατιώταις, Aristeas 38 βουλομένων δ᾿ ἡμῶν καὶ τούτοις χαρίζεσθαι, "since we desire to confer a favour not on these only," the favour being the LXX translation of the Law, and the Christian amulet BGU III. 954²⁸ (vi/A.D.) (= *Selections*, p. 134) ὁ φῶς ἐκ φωτός, θ(εὸ)ς ἀληθινὸς χάρισον ἐμὲ τὸν δοῦλόν σου τὸ φῶς, "O Light of light, very God, graciously give thy servant light."

A striking linguistic parallel to our Lord's trial before Pilate occurs in P Flor I. 61 (A.D. 85), where a Prefect, after stating to an accused man, ⁵⁹f ἄξιος μ[ὲ]ν ἧς μαστιγωθῆναι, "thou art worthy to be scourged" (cf. Jn 19¹), adds ⁶¹ χαρίζομαι δέ σε τοῖς ὄχλοις, "but I give you freely to the multitude" (cf. Mk 15¹⁵): see Deissmann *LAE*[2], p. 269 f.

For the form χαρίεσαι = χαριεῖσαι, as in P Oxy 292 *supra,* cf. P Grenf II. 14 (c)³ (iii/B.C.) χαρίεσαί μοι τοῦτο ποιήσας, and see *Proleg.* p. 53 f., where Moulton shows that this formation of the 2nd sing. pres. mid., like the similar NT formations καυχᾶσαι, ὀδυνᾶσαι, has been "formed afresh in the Κοινή with the help of the -σαι

that answers to 3rd sing. -ται in the perfect." MGr χαρίζω, "present," "give."

χάριν,

"for the sake of," "by reason of." In classical Greek χάριν generally follows its case, and so always in the NT, except in 1 Jn 3¹². In the LXX, on the other hand, it generally precedes, and similarly in the papyri, e.g. P Oxy IV. 743²⁹ (B.C. 2) χάριν τῶν ἐκφορίων, "for the rents," P Tebt II. 410¹ (A.D. 16) χάριν οὗ παρορίζεται ὑπὸ γίτονος, "on account of the encroachments being made on him by a neighbour" (Edd.), P Oxy XII. 1583⁶ (ii/A.D.) χάριν τοῦ [φαι]νόλου, and *ib.* VI. 934¹² (iii/A.D.) χάριν τῶν ποτισμῶν. In *ib.* XIV. 1683¹⁸ (late iv/A.D.) χάριν follows— σημί (= εἰ)ου δὲ χάριν, "and in proof": and in *ib.* VII. 1068 (iii/A.D.) it is found both before and after its case— ¹⁶ χάριν ἀναγκέας χρίας, and ²¹ Σιμίου χάριν, "for Simias's sake." See also the illiterate BGU III. 948¹ (iv/v A.D.) εὔχομε τὸν παντοκράτορον θεὸν τὰ πε[ρὶ τ]ῆς ὑγίας σου καὶ ὁλοκληρίας σου χαιριν (*l.* χάριν), and cf. P Tebt II. 393¹⁶ (A.D. 150) περισπασμῶν χάρειν, "on account of his anxieties."

Χάριν in the weakened sense of "about" is seen in P Fay 126⁵ (ii/iii A.D.) (ἔ)πεμψεν ἐπὶ τὴν πενθερά(ν) σου χάριν τοῦ κτήματος ἐπὶ μελ<λ>ι ὁρίζεσθαι, "he had sent a message to your mother-in-law about the farm, since the boundaries are to be fixed" (Edd.).

χάρις.

The utmost we can attempt with this important word is to illustrate some of its meanings from our sources with the view of showing how readily it lent itself to the deeper Christian implications involved in its NT use.

1. "grace," "graciousness": *OGIS* 383⁹ (Commagene rescript—mid. i/B.C.) ἔργα χάριτος ἰδίας: cf Lk 4²².

2. "favour": P Leid D i. 11 (B.C. 162–161) (= I. p. 25, *UPZ* i. p. 231) περὶ μὲν οὖν τούτων δοῖ σοι ὁ Σάραπις καὶ ἡ Ἶσις ἐπαφροδισί[α]ν χάριν μορφὴν πρὸς τὸν βασιλέα καὶ τὴν βασίλισσαν, similarly *ib.* K¹⁰ (*c.* B.C 99) (= I. p. 52), P Lips I. 104¹⁴ (ii/i B.C.) χάριν σοι ἔχω ἐφ᾿ αἷς γράφεις ἐπι[σ]τολαῖς, and *ib.*²¹, BGU I. 19 i. 21 (A.D. 135) ἠξίου προσφυγεῖν τῇ χάριτι τοῦ θεοῦ ἐπιφανεστάτου Αὐτοκράτορος, *ib.* IV. 1085⁵ (time of Marcus) κατὰ τὴν χάριν τοῦ θεοῦ Αἰλ[ί]ου Ἀντων[ε]ίνου δύνονται ἔχειν τὸν τάφον, P Grenf II. 68⁴ (A.D. 247) ὁμολογῶ χαρίζεσθ[αι] σοι χάριτι ἀναφαιρέτῳ καὶ ἀμετανοήτῳ, P Oxy XIV. 1664¹³ (iii/A.D.) τὰς γὰρ ἐντολάς σου ἥδιστα ἔχων ὡς χάριτας λήμψομαι, "for I shall be most pleased to accept your commands as favours" (Edd.), and P Fay 136⁸ (iv/A.D.) (= Ghedini p. 242) in which the writer summons those whom he is addressing to return to their homes πρὸ τοῦ τις ὑμᾶς ἐνέγκῃ καὶ οὐκ ἔστιν οὐκέτι ἐν ὑμῖν χάρις, "before some one compels them, and there is no longer favour extended to them": cf. Lk 1³⁰, 2⁵², Ac 2⁴⁷, *al.*

3. "thanks," "gratitude": P Oxy VII. 1021¹⁸ (A.D. 54) διὸ πάντες ὀφείλομεν . . . θεοῖς πᾶσι εἰδέναι χάριτας, "therefore ought we all to give thanks to all the gods," notification of the accession of Nero, BGU II. 596¹³ (A.D. 84) τοῦτ[ο] οὖν ποιήσας ἔσῃ μοι μεγάλην χάριταν (= -ιτα), P Oxy VI. 963 (ii/iii A.D.) χάριν δέ σοι οἶδα,

μῆτερ, ἐπὶ τῇ σπουδῇ τοῦ καθεδραρίου ("stood"), ἐκομισάμην γὰρ αὐτό, and the constantly recurring χάρις τοῖς θεοῖς,
as in P Petr I. 20² (iii/B.C.) (= Witkowski², p. 30) χάρις
τοῖς θε(ο)ῖς πολλή, εἰ ὑγιαίνεις, P Hib I. 79⁶ (c. B.C. 260)
εἰ ἔρρωσαι . . . εἴ⟨η⟩ ἄν ὡς ἐγὼ θέλω καὶ τοῖς θεοῖς πολλὴ
χά[ρι]ς, "if you are well, it would be as I wish, and much
gratitude would be due to the gods" (Edd.), BGU III. 843⁶
(i–ii A.D.) χάρις τοῖς θεοῖς ἱκάμ ην εἰς) ᾽Αλεξανδρίαν, P Fay
124¹⁶ (ii/A.D.) τοῖ[ς] θεο]ι[ς] ἐστ[ι]ν χάρις ὅτι οὐδεμία
ἐστὶν πρόλημψις ἡμεῖν γεγενημένη. "thank heaven, there
is no preconceived principle on our part" (Edd.), PSI I. 94⁶
(ii/A.D.) θεοῖς δὲ χάρις ὅτι ἤρεσε καὶ τῷ παιδὶ ἡ ποδίς, καὶ
προσεδρεύει ἰς τὰ μαθήματα, P Giss I. 17⁶ (time of Hadrian)
(= Chrest. I. p. 566) χάρις τοῖς θεοῖς πᾶσι ὅτι σε διαφυλάσσουσι ἀπρόσκοπον, and the Christian P Oxy VI. 939⁶
(iv/A.D.), where a servant writes to his master regarding the
illness of his mistress, εἴη διὰ παντὸς ἡμᾶς χάριτας ὁμο-
[λογοῦντα]ς διατελεῖν ὅτι ἡμῖν ἵλεως ἐγένετο . . διασώσας
ἡμῖν [τὴν ἡμῶν] κύριαν, "may it be granted us to continue
for ever to acknowledge our thanks to Him because He was
gracious to us by preserving for us our mistress" (Edd.) : cf.
Lk 17⁹, Rom 6¹⁷, 1 Tim 1¹², 2 Tim 1³, Heb 12²⁸, al. See
also Epict. iv. iv. 7 τότε καὶ ἐγὼ ἡμάρτανον νῦν δ᾽ οὐκέτι,
χάρις τῷ Θεῷ, "then I too was faulty, but, thanks to God,
not now" (cited by Sharp), and for the χάρις
ascribed to the Emperors, cf. Syll 365 (=³ 798⁷ᶠᶠ (A.D. 37)
τῆς ἀθανάτου χάριτος . . . θεῶν δὲ χάριτες τούτῳ διαφέρουσιν ἀνθρωπίνων διαδοχῶν, ᾧ ἡ νυκτὸς ἥλιος καὶ τὸ ἄφθαρτον
θνητῆς φύσεως—said of Caligula! Other exx. are cited by
Wendland in ZNTW v. (1904), p. 345 n².

4. We may note one or two prepositional phrases—P Par
63 (B.C. 164) (= P Petr III. p. 22) διὰ χάριν, "through
favouritism" (Mahaffy), BGU IV. 1135¹⁶ (B.C. 10) κα]τὰ
χάριν, P Oxy XIV. 1672⁶ (A.D. 37–41) μετὰ χάριτος, with
reference to a profitable sale of wine, almost = μετὰ χαρᾶς,
"with joy" (see Olsson, p. 78), ib. IX. 1188⁵ (A.D. 13)
στοχα(σάμενος) τοῦ μηδ(ὲν) ἀγνοηθῆναι μηδὲ πρὸς χά[ρ]ιν
οἰκονομηθ[ῆναι), "making it your aim that nothing be concealed or done by favour" (Ed.).

5. The favourite Pauline greeting χάρις καὶ εἰρήνη may
have been suggested by the union of the ordinary Greek and
Hebrew forms of salutation, but both are deepened and
spiritualized, χαίρειν (cf. Ac 15²³, 23²⁶, Jas 1¹) giving place
to χάρις, and εἰρήνη (cf. Ezra 4¹⁷, Dan 4¹) pointing to the
harmony restored between God and man (cf. Jn 14²⁷). See
further Hort 1 Pet. p. 25 f., and the discussion on the
Apostolic Greeting by F. Zimmer in Luthardt's Zeitschrift
1886, p. 443 ff.

Reference should be made to the Note "On the meanings
of χάρις and χαριτοῦν" in Robinson Eph. p. 221 ff., and to
the exhaustive monograph "Charis. Ein Beitrag zur
Geschichte des ältesten Christentums" by G. P. von Wetter
(Leipzig, 1913).

χάρισμα,

which in Pauline usage "includes all spiritual graces and
endowments" (Lightfoot Notes, p. 148 f.), is used of "gifts"
generally in BGU IV. 1044⁵ (iv/A.D.) οἴδατε τὰ χαρίσματα
ὧν ποιηκὼς ἡμῖν (l. ἃ πεποίηκα ὑμῖν).

The other exx. which Preisigke (Wört.) cites for the word

are late, e.g. the Will of Abraham of Hermonthis, P Lond
77²⁴ (end vi A.D.) (= Chrest. II. p. 371), in which he
describes his property as acquired ἀπὸ ἀγορασίας καὶ
χαρίσματος.

χαριτόω.

The only ex. of this word we can produce from our
sources is the iv/A.D. charm BGU IV. 1026ˣˣⁱⁱⁱ ²⁴, where, after
various invocations such as δ ὸ]ς μοι χάριν, ποίη[σόν] με
καλόν, the whole is concluded with χαριτώσο[μαι, "I will
bestow favour upon thee." For the NT usage (Lk 1²⁸,
Eph 1⁶), see Lightfoot Notes p. 315, and Robinson Eph.
p. 226 ff. Some various renderings of Eph 1⁶ are brought
together in Exp T xxix. p. 501. Cf. MGr χαριτωμένος,
"charming."

χάρτης,

"paper," made from the pith of the papyrus-plant by a
process described by Pliny N.H. xiii. 11–13 (cf. V. Gardthausen Griechische Palaeographie² (Leipzig, 1911), p. 45 ff.,
E. Maunde Thompson An Introduction to Greek and Latin
Palaeography (Oxford, 1912), p. 21 ff. and the other literature
cited in Selections, p. xxi. ff.).

The word χάρτης occurs only once in the NT (2 Jn¹²),
but is naturally common in our sources, e.g. P Lille I. 3¹⁵
(after B.C. 241–0), where payment is made ὅπως [ἔ]χωμεν
χορηγεῖν εἴς τε τὴ[ν] γραμματεί[αν) καὶ χάρτας, P Cairo
Zen III. 59317⁴ (B.C. 250) ἀνηλώσω δὲ εἰς ταῦτα χάρτας δ,
"I shall require 4 papyrus rolls for these things" (sc. the
keeping of certain accounts), P Oxy II. 300 (i/A.D.) payment of 1 drachma 3 obols χάρτου, P Tebt II. 347¹²
(ii/A.D.) ἀποθήκη τιμὴν χαρτῶν δραχμαὶ) δ : the editors
compare ib. 542, "where 9 dr. for τιμῆ(ς) χάρτου are
deducted from the receipts on account of a tax," ib. 420⁵
(iii/A.D.) ἡγόρασα β χάρτας, "I bought two sheets of
papyrus," P Flor III. 307⁷ (iii/A.D.) πολλάκις μου . . .
χάρτας ἐπιστολικο[ὺ]ς ἀποσ]τείλαντος, ἵν᾽ εὐπορῆς (?). Ας
11²⁹, τοῦ γρά[φειν] μοι, P Oxy VI. 805¹² (A.D. 305) τιμῆς
χάρτου καὶ γράπ[τρων . . . , "for the price of papyrus and
writing-materials," and so¹⁴. For χάρτης ἱερατικός "sacred
paper," cf. P Lond 46³⁰⁴ (iv/A.D.) (= I. p. 74).

It may be of interest to add some related words—χάρτη,
as in BGU III. 822 verso (iii/A.D.) πέμψον μοι ἄγραφον
χάρτην, ἵνα εὕρο[με]ν ἐπιστολ[ὴν] γράψαι; χαρτίον, as in
P Cairo Zen III. 59470⁵ (mid iii/B.C.) περὶ δὲ τῶν χαρτίων
ἔγραψα μέν σοι, P Gen I. 52³ χαρτίον (so read by Wilcken
Archiv iii. p. 399) καθαρὸν μὴ εὑρὼν πρὸς τὴν ὥραν εἰς
τοῦ[τ]ον ἔγραψα, "not having found a clean sheet of paper,
for the moment I have written on this"; χαρτάριον, as in
P Tebt II. 413⁵ (ii/iii A.D.) τὸ χαρτάριν (l. χαρτάριον)
ἔλαβεν Σερηνίων ἐσ[σ]φραγισμένον, "Serenion took the
papyrus sealed"; χαρτοπώλης, as read in P Tebt I. 112⁶²
(B.C. 112) (as amended Berichtigungen, p. 425); and ἐπί-
χάρτη, "an extra sheet," as in P Oxy I. 34 verso¹⁵
(A.D. 127).

For the light thrown by contemporary papyrus documents on
the outward form and method of the NT Epistles, reference
may be permitted to the Excursus on "St. Paul as a Letter-
writer" in Milligan Thess. p. 121 ff., and Here and There,
p. 27 ff.

χεῖλος,

(1) "a lip," as in Mt 15[8] *al.*, cf. the personal descriptions. P Petr III. 10[22] (B.C. 234) οὐλὴ παρὰ χείλη, P Grenf II. 23[a][ii. 6] (B.C. 107) οὐλὴ χείληι τῶι κάτω, Preisigke 5314[7] (Byz.) διὰ τῶν χιλέων μου, (2) "edge," "brink," of things, as in Heb 11[12], cf. BGU III. 781[ii. 11] (i/A.D.) ἄλλα λουτη-ρίδια ὠτάρια ἔχον[τ]α ἐπὶ τοῦ χείλους, and Aristeas 70.

Χείλωμα, which LS[8] cite from the LXX (? Aq. Ex 37(38)[2]) in the sense of "a lip," "rim," occurs in P Oxy X. 1294[5. 12] (ii./iii A.D.), where GH understand "a receptacle" of some kind, perhaps connected with χηλός.

χειμάζω,

"raise a storm," occurs in an agreement regarding a canal *Syll* 542 (=[3] 973[5] (B.C. 338–322) χρήσιμος ὁ λουτρῶν ὅταν χειμάζει ὁ θεός. For the pass., as in Ac 27[18], see *Inscr. ins. mar. Aeg.* II., 119, where certain persons being storm-tossed at sea make an offering to the most high god—χειμασθέντες ἐν πελάγει θεῶ ὑψίστω χρηστήριον.

The verb is used metaphorically in a letter from a tax-farmer P Tebt I. 58[31] (B.C. 111) βεβουλεύμεθα ἐκσπάσαι τὸ ἐπιδεδομένον ὑπόμνη μα) μή ποτε ἐπὶ τοῦ διαλόγου χειμασ-θῶμεν. "we have determined to extract the memorandum in order that we may not come to grief at the audit" (Edd.), BGU III. 844[4] (A.D. 83) γ]εινώσκειν σε θέλω, ὅτει [ε,ὐθέω,ς] ἀναβ[ὰς] ἐχειμάσ[θ]ην πολλά . . . : cf. Preisigke 7208 (time of Trajan) ἐπεὶ χειμάζομαι προτάσεσί τισι τεθειμέναις μοι γεομετρικαῖς, and P Oxy XVI. 1873[5] (late v/A.D.).

χείμαρρος,

"winter-torrent" (Jn 18[1]): Suid. ὁ ἐν τῷ χειμῶνι ῥέων. Cf. Aristeas 117 ἄλλοι δὲ χείμαρροι λεγόμενοι κατίασι, "other winter-torrents, as they are called, flow down (into the plain)." For the form as compared with the longer χειμάρρους, see Thackeray *Gr.* i. p. 144.

χειμών,

(1) "winter" (Jn 10[22]): P Lille I. 1 *recto*[34] (B.C. 259–8) ἐὰν μὲν κατὰ χειμῶνα συντελῆται τὰ ἔργα, τίθεμεν ἔσεσθαι εἰς ὅ τοῦ στατῆρος. "if the works are completed during the winter we reckon them at the rate of 70 (naubia) to the stater," P Tebt II. 278[46] (early i/A.D.) χιμῶν γάρ ἐστι, ψύχος πολύ, "it is winter, there is great cold," P Flor II. 127[7] (A.D. 256) the heating of a bath-chamber ἵνα θερμῶς λουσώμεθα χειμῶνος ὄντος, and from the inscr. *Priene* 112[98] (after B.C. 84) heating of the gymnasium διὰ τοῦ χειμῶνος ὅλου δ[ι]' ἡμέρ(α)s. See also *s.v.* θέρος.

(2) "storm," "tempest" (Mt 16[3], Ac 27[20]): *Preisigke* 998 (A.D. 16–17) Λούκιος Μάγας Στράτωνος ἀπὸ Σουήνης ὑπάγων ἰς Πιρ . . . ἀπὸ χιμῶνος ἐλασθείς ὧδε, and similarly 997 (iv/A.D.). For the adj. χειμερινός, cf. P Iand I. 28[5] (A.D. 104) ἀρουρῶν χειμερινῶν καὶ θερινῶν, P Lond 842[12] (A.D. 140) (= III. p. 141) ὁμολογοῦμεν πεπρακέναι . . . νομὰς προ-βάτων . . . ἐφ' ἐνιαυτὸν ἕνα θερινὰς καὶ χειμερινὰς ἀπὸ μηνός . . . , and P Tebt II. 342[23] (late ii/A.D.) κούφων . . . πλάσεως χειμερινῆς, "pots being of winter manufacture" (Edd.).

χείρ,

"a hand." The grammatical forms of this common noun are fully illustrated by Mayser *Gr.* p. 282 f. For its varied uses we may cite—P Par 63[208] (B.C. 164) (= P Petr III. p. 36) φροντίζεσθ' ὅπως μηθεὶς ἐπ[ι]βάλληι τὰ[ς] χεῖρας τοῖς τοιούτοις κατὰ μηδεμίαν π[αρ]εύρε[σιν, "take care that no one lay violent hands on such persons on any pretext whatever" (Mahaffy): *Perg* 268 C[11] (B.C. 98) τὸν παρακα]-λέσοντα δοῦναι τ[ὰ]s χεῖρας ἡμῖν εἰ[ς σύλλυσιν, "to give the hands towards an agreement to be brought about by us," a usage for which Deissmann (*BS* p. 251) can find no other ex., but compares Gal 2[9] δεξιὰς ἔδωκαν . . . κοινωνίας, and similar phrases in 1 and 2 Macc.: P Tebt II. 391[26] (A.D. 99) ἡ χὶρ ἤδη κυρία ἔστω ὡς ἐν δημοσίωι κατακεχωρισμένη, "this bond shall be valid, as if it had been publicly regis-tered" (Edd.), similarly *ib.* 379[18] (A.D. 128): BGU II. 423[16] (ii/A.D.) (= *Selections*, p. 91) ἵνα σου προσκυνήσω τὴν χεῖραν (see *Proleg.* p. 49), a son to his father: P Oxy I. 119[6] (ii/iii A.D.) (= *Selections*, p. 103) οὐ μὴ λάβω χεῖραν παρά [σ]οῦ, "I won't take your hand," another boy to his father: and *ib.* IX. 1208[6] (A.D. 291) Αὐ[ρή]λιος . . . μ[ετ]ὰ συνβεβαιωτοῦ τοῦ πατρὸς τοῦ καὶ ἔχοντος αὐτὸν ὑπὸ τῇ χειρὶ κατὰ τοὺς Ῥωμαίων ν[ό]μους, "Aurelius with his father, who has him under power according to Roman law, as co-guarantor" (Ed.).

For χείρ in prepositional phrases cf. ἀνὰ χεῖρα in P Ryl II. 88[21] (A.D. 156) οὐδὲν δέ μοι ὀ[φείλεται ὑπὲρ τ]ῶν ἀνὰ χεῖρα χρόνων, "nothing is owing to me for the current period" (Edd.), *ib.* 997 (ii/A.D.) τῇ ἀνὰ χεῖρα (πενταετίᾳ), "during the current period of 5 years" (Edd.): ἀπὸ χερός in P Cairo Zen II. 59155[3] (B.C. 256) πότισον τὴν γῆν ἀπὸ χερός, "water the ground by hand" ("i.e. by means of buckets or *nattals*," Ed.): διὰ χερός (Mk 6[2], *al.*) in P Magd 25[2] (B.C. 221) ὀφείλων γάρ μ[ο]ι διὰ χερὸς κριθῶν (ἀρτάβας) ιε̅, "il m'a emprunté de la main à la main et me doit quinze artabes d'orge" (Ed.), P Oxy II. 268[7] (A.D. 58) ἀπεσχηκυῖαι [παρὰ τοῦ Ἀντ]ιφάνους διὰ χειρὸς ἐ[ξ οἴκου ὁ καὶ ἐπε[ίσθη]-σαν κεφάλαιον, "have received from Antiphanes from hand to hand in cash the sum which they severally consented to accept" (Edd.), P Fay 92[18] (A.D. 126) δραχμὰς πεντήκοντα ἐξ παραχρῆμα διὰ χιρὸς ἐξ οἴκ[ου: ἐν χερσί (Gal 3[19]) in BGU IV. 1095[12] (A.D. 57) τὰ δὲ νῆα (*l.* νέα) ἐν χερσὶ γέγοναι, *ib.* III. 844[6] (A.D. 83) ὁ ἐὰν [ἔχηι]s ἐν χερσίν: μετὰ χεῖρας in P Oxy XVI. 1876[2] (c. A.D. 480) λίβελλον . . . ἔχων μετὰ χεῖρας ἀναγνώσομ[αι, "the *libellus* I hold in my hands and will read" (Edd.). For χείρ in "Hebraic" locutions, see *Proleg.* p. 99 f.

For healing by touch of hand, as in Mk 1[41], see Herodas IV. 18 (ed. Headlam), where an offering is made for a cure in the temple of Asclepius with the words—

ἤιτρα
νούσων ἐποιεύμεσθα τὰς ἀπέψησας
ἐπ' ἠπίας σὺ χεῖρας, ὦ ἄναξ, τείνας,

"we have made payment for the cure, for thou, Lord, hast wiped away our sickness by laying on us thy gentle hands." And for lifting up hands in prayer, as in 1 Tim 2[8], see the uplifted hands on the stones containing the Jewish prayers for vengeance found at Rheneia, discussed and illustrated by Deissmann in *LAE*[2], p. 413 ff. Cf. also Dibelius *HZNT ad* 1 Tim *l.c.*

The verb χειρίζω is seen in P Ryl II. 151[16] (A.D. 40) ἀπηνέγκατο ἀφ' ὧν χιρίζω τοῦ γυμνα[σ]ιάρχ[ου] ἀργυ(ρίου) ρ̄, "he carried off 100 drachmae from the money of the gymnasiarch which I administer" (Edd.), ib. 225[18] (ii/iii A.D.) μετόχοις χειριζομένοις πρακτο]ρείαν, "associate tax-collectors" (Edd.): and χειρισμός in P Par 26[19] (B.C. 163–2) (= Wilcken UPZ i. p. 247, Selections p. 15) τῶν δὲ πρὸς τοῖς χειρισμοῖς ἐν τῷ Σαραπιείῳ καὶ Ἀσκληπιείῳ τεταγμένων, "those who had been appointed to the administration in the Serapeum and Asclepeum," BGU IV. 1141[49] (B.C. 13) μή τι παραναπείσῃ αὐτὸν εἰς τὸ δηλῶσαί τι ἐν τῶι χειρισμῶι, where Olsson (p. 52) prefers the rendering "matter" or "account": and χειριστής in PSI V. 537[10] (iii/B.C.) χειριστὴν ἐπαποστείλον, P Oxy XII. 1578[19] (iii/A.D.) περὶ ὧν ἐπέστειλα Ἀσκληπιάδῃ χειριστῇ.

χειραγωγέω,

"lead by the hand," "guide" (Ac 9[8], 22[11], cf. Judg 16[16] A, Tobit 11[16] ℵ): P Par 6[35] (B.C. 104 (= P Petr III. p. 22) ὥσ[τ]ε καὶ τὸν πάντων ἀπειρότατον ὑπ' αὐτῶν [τ]ῶν πραγμάτ[ων] χειραγωγούμενον, "so that even the most inexperienced person in the world being guided by the facts themselves" (Mahaffy). Cf. Musonius p. 79[7] χειραγωγούντων τοὺς γονεῖς, and Ev. Petr. 9 τοῦ δὲ χειραγωγουμένου ὑπ' αὐτῶν ὑπερβαίνουσαν τοὺς οὐρανούς, "and (the head) of him that was led by them overpassed the heavens."

χειραγωγός,

"one who leads by the hand" (Ac 13[11]). For the subst. Preisigke (Wörterb. s.v.) cites P Lond IV. 1340[7] (A.D. 710) μετὰ ἐπιηκείας καὶ χειραγωγείας, and for χειραγώγιμος P Lond 220ii.[21] (B.C. 133) (= II. p. 6).

χειρόγραφον,

properly "written with the hand," "a signature," is very common in the sense of "a written agreement," or more technically "a certificate of debt," "a bond." Exx. of the word are P Oxy IV. 745[2] (c. A.D. 1) ὑπὲρ ὧν καὶ ἔθου χειρόγραφον, "for which you drew me up a bond," in connexion with a purchase of wine, ib. II. 269[ii. 7] (A.D. 57) ἐὰν δύνῃ ἐρωτηθεὶς ὄχλησον Διόσκορον καὶ ἔκπραξον αὐτὸν τὸ χειρόγραφον, "if you can, please worry Dioscorus and exact from him his bond" (Edd.), BGU I. 300[12] (A.D. 148) τ[ὸ] χειρόγραφον τοῦτο δισσὸν γραφὲν ὑπ' ἐμοῦ κύρι[ο]ν ἔστω, "let this bond written by me in duplicate be valid," P Oxy VIII. 1132[16] (c. A.D. 162) τὸ δὲ κεφάλαιον δανεισθέν σοι ὑπ' ἐμοῦ κατὰ χειρόγραφ[ον], "the capital sum lent to you by me in accordance with a note of hand," and ib. IV. 710[30] (A.D. 193) βου[λόμενος οὖν] ἐν δημοσίῳ γενέσθαι τὸ αὐθεντικὸν χειρόγραφον, "being therefore desirous that the authentic bond should be publicly registered" (Edd.).

For Col 2[14], the only occurrence of the word in the NT, we may cite BGU III. 717[24] (A.D. 149) χειρόγρα[φον] . . . χωρὶς ἀλίφατος καὶ ἐπιγραφῆς, "a decree neither washed out nor written over" (cf. Milligan Documents, p. 16, Here and There, p. 5).

Exx. of original χειρόγραφα are BGU I. 179 (time of

Anton. Pius) and 272 (A.D. 138–6), both crossed out and cancelled: cf. P Flor I. 61[63] (A.D. 85) (= Chrest. II. p. 89), where in connexion with a trial the governor of Egypt ἐκ[έ]λευσε τὸ χειρό[γ]ραφον χιασθῆναι, "gave orders that the bond be crossed out": see further Deissmann BS, p. 247, and LAE[2], p. 334.

It may be well to add a few instances of the corr. subst. and verb. Thus for χειρογραφία, cf. P Oxy III. 477[17] (A.D. 132–3) μ[ο]υ χειρογραφία[ν μεθ'] ὅρκ]ου ἀληθῆ εἶναι τὰ προκείμε[να, "my declaration on oath that the foregoing statements are true," and P Giss I. 15[8] (time of Hadrian) τὰς χειρογραφίας [προέ]σθαι with the editor's elaborate note in the introd. p. 60 f. And for χειρογραφέω, cf. P Petr III. 104[9] (B.C. 244–3) (= Chrest. I. p. 393) κεχει[ρ]ογραφήκασι τὸν εἰθισμένον ὅρκον τοσούτου μεμισθῶσθαι, "they have written under their hands the usual oath that it was let for this amount" (Edd.), and P Oxy I. 37[ii. 4] (A.D. 49) (= Selections, p. 51) ἐὰν χειρογραφήσῃι . . . ἐκεῖνο τὸ ἐνχειρισθὲν αὐτῆι σωμάτιον . . . τετελευτηκέναι, "if she will make a written declaration that the foundling handed over to her is dead," report of a lawsuit. See also Mayser Gr. p. 461.

χειροποίητος,

"made by hands," in the LXX applied only to idols, but in the NT used of material temples (Ac 7[48], 17[24]): cf. Orac. Sib. xiv. 62 ναῶν ἱδρύματα χειροποιήτων. In the travel-letter, P Lond 854[4] (i/ii A.D.) (= III. p. 205, Selections, p. 70), the writer remarks that many go by ship ἵνα τὰς χε[ι]ροπ[οιή]τους τέ]χνας ἱστορήσωσι, "in order that they may visit works of art made by hands," on the banks of the Nile.

χειροτονέω,

lit. "stretch out the hand," then "elect by show of hands," and then "elect," "appoint" generally (cf. Ac 14[23], 2 Cor 8[19]): see P Fay 26[11] (A.D. 150) ὑπό [τ]ε ἐμοῦ . . . καὶ τοῦ κεχειροτονη[μέν]ο[υ π]ρὸς τοῦτο, P Ryl II. 77[37] (A.D. 192) ⟨οὐχ⟩ ἧττον ἑαυτὸν ἐχειροτόνησεν εἰς τὴν κατεπείγουσαν ἀρχὴν κοσμητείαν, "he none the less nominated himself for the office immediately required, that of cosmetes" (Edd.), Chrest. II. 88[4. 19] (ii/A.D.) χειροτονηθήσονται δὲ ἐντὸς κ ἡμερῶν ὑπὸ τοῦ στρατηγοῦ ⟨τοῦ⟩ νομοῦ, P Flor I. 6[14] (A.D. 210) ἐπισκέπτης γὰρ ἐχειροτονήθην and P Oxy X. 1252verso[18] (A.D. 288–95) ὑ[πογύω]ς χειροτονη[θείς] . . . εἰς τὴν παρὰ Ὀξυρυγχ[είταις] πρυτανείαν, "having been recently appointed to the prytany at Oxyrhynchus."

For χειροτονέω in its later ecclesiastical sense of "ordain," cf. the vi/A.D. P Giss I. 55[5] where a bishop writes to a brother-bishop ἠξιώθην . . . γράψαι πρ[ὸ]ς τὴν σὴν ἁγιότητα π[ερὶ Σανσνεῦτ]ός τινος πρὸ πολλοῦ χειροτονηθέν]τος π[αρὰ τοῦ τῆς μ]α[καρίας μνήμης Φοιβάδίου τοῦ ἐπισκ[όπου, and see the Coptic ostracon regarding the ordination of deacons in Crum Coptic Ostraca, No. 29 reproduced by Deissmann LAE[2], p. 221 ff.

The corr. subst. appears in such passages as P Oxy IX. 1191[5] (A.D. 280) περὶ τῆς τῶν ἐπιμελητῶν χειροτονίας, "concerning the election of administrators," ib. 1204[24] (A.D. 299) τὸ βιβλίον τῆς χειροτονείας παρασχεθήτω, "let

the document containing the appointment be produced"
(Ed.), and *Syll* 192 (= ³485)¹⁷ (B.C. 236–5) ἄξιον ἑαυτὸν
παρέξειν τῆς τε το[ῦ δή]μου χειροτονίας.

χείρων,

"worse," is fairly common in the NT: cf. BGU IV.
1118³¹ (B.C. 22) οὐδενὶ χείρον[α, *ib.* 1208¹·²⁸ (B.C. 27: τὸ
δὲ [πά]ντων χείρῳ (*l.* χεῖρον), where, however, the word
is uncertain, P Oxy II. 237ᵛⁱⁱ·⁴³ (A.D. 186) χεῖρόν ἐστι
ἀνδρὸς ἀφαι[ρεῖ]σθαι, "it is worse to take away (a wife)
from her husband (than a dowry from a daughter?)" (Edd.),
and *Syll* 588¹²² (c. B.C. 180) τοῦ χείρονος χρυσίου πρῶτον
χύμα. For the superl⁰ see *ib.* 316 (= ³684)¹² (B.C. 139?)
τῆς χειρίστης κα[τασ]τάσεως [καὶ] ταραχῆς, and P Amh
II. 40⁹ (ii/B.C.).

χερουβείν,

"cherubin" (Heb 9⁵), transliterated from the Aramaic
(-εῖμ, Hebrew): cf. Wunsch *AF* p. 12²⁵ τοῦ καθημένου
ἐπὶ τῶν χερουβί, P Lond 121²⁶⁴ (iii/A.D.) (= I. p. 93) ἐπὶ
χερουβὶν καθήμενον, and similarly ⁶³⁴. See also *Revue
Biblique* xxxv. (1926), pp. 328 ff., 421 ff., and the other reff.
in Preuschen-Bauer *Worterb. s.v.*

χήρα,

"a widow": cf. *Syll* 408 (= ³531)¹⁷ (iii/B.C.) χήρα
ἐλευ[θέρα καὶ ἐξ] ἐλευθέ[ρων, BGU II. 522⁷ (ii/A.D.) αὐτὴ
δέομαι, γυ[νὴ] χήρα καὶ ἀθοήτητος (*l.* ἀβοήθητος) ἐπι-
τ̣υχεῖν τῆς αὐτῆς φιλανθρωπίας, P Oxy VIII. 1120¹²
(a petition—early iii/A.D.) κατὰ τοῦτο μαρτύρομαι τὴν
βίαν γυνὴ χήρα καὶ ἀσθενής, "I accordingly testify to his
violence, being a feeble widow woman," P Ryl II. 114⁵
(c. A.D. 280) τὸ μετριοφιλές σου αἰσθομένη, [δέσποτά μου
ἡ]γεμών, καὶ περὶ πάντας κηδεμονίαν, [μαλιστα περὶ
γυ]ναῖκας καὶ χήρας τὴν προσέλευσιν ποι[οῦμαί σοι . . .,
"perceiving your love of equity, my lord praefect, and your
care for all, especially women and widows, I approach
you . . ." (Edd.), and BGU II. 412⁶ (iv/A.D.). For the
ordo viduarum, see Lock *ICC* at 1 Tim 5¹·¹¹, and for "they
which devour widows' houses" (Mk 12⁴⁰), see Abrahams
Studies in Pharisaism i. p. 79 ff.

χθές,

For this form, which is read in TR Jn 4⁵², Ac 7²⁸,
Heb 13⁸, see *s.v.* ἐχθές, and to the ex. of χθές from the
Κοινή given there, add PSI III. 184⁴ (A.D. 292) χθὲς περὶ
ἕκτην ὥραν, P Oxy VI. 901⁶ (A.D. 336) ἑσπερινες ὥρες
(*l.* ἑσπερίναις ὥραις) τῇ χθὲς ἡμέρᾳ, "in the evening time
of yesterday" (Edd.), and Preisigke 6003⁴ (A.D. 316). Other
exx. in Preisigke *Worterb. s.v.*

χιλίαρχος,

lit. "the ruler of a thousand men," the Roman *tribunus
militum*. This form (in Herodotus and elsewhere χης)
prevails in the NT (Jn 18¹², *al.*), and is found in the
inscr., e.g. *Magn* 157 (b)¹⁵ (i/A.D.) χιλίαρχος λεγιῶνος,
Preisigke 173³ (c. A.D. 200), and OGIS 119³ (where see
Dittenberger's note). See also P Oxy III. 653 (A.D.
162–3) and the corr. verb in *ib.* 477² (A.D. 132–3).

χιλιάς,

We may note P Oxy IV. 742¹³ (B.C. 2) (as amended
Berichtigungen p. 328) ὅ]ρα ἐμὲ ἠγορακέναι παρ[ὰ Πόθο]υ
τὴν χιλίαν δέσμην (δραχμῶν) δ[εκάπ]εντε, "see I have
bought from Pothus the thousand bundles for fifteen
drachmae." But Witkowski (*Epp.*² p. 128) understands
τὴν χιλίαν δέσμην = ἑκάστην τὴν χιλιάδα δεσμῶν, as
meaning "at fifteen drachmae for a bundle of a thousand."

χιτών,

"a tunic," "an undergarment," as distinguished from
ἱμάτιον (*q.v.*): cf. Preisigke 6717⁹ (B.C. 258 or 257)
χιτῶνα καὶ ἱμάτιον, PSI I. 64¹⁰ (i/B.C. ?) ἱμάτιον ταλάντων
πέντε χιτῶνα [δὲ or τε ? δραχμῶν] τετρακισχιλίων ἑξακοσίων, and Musonius p. 107⁷.

The form χιτών, which occurs throughout in the NT,
may be seen further in Preisigke 6783⁴ (B.C. 257) χιτὼν
βύ[σσινος, and P Oxy I. 114⁶ (ii/iii A.D.) χιτὼν καὶ
μαφόρτιν λευκόν, "a tunic and a white veil." For other
forms, which are frequent in the Κοινή, we may note the
Ionic κιτών, as in Mk 14⁶³ B* (cf. *Proleg.* p. 38), in BGU
I. 22¹⁶ (A.D. 114) (= *Selections*, p. 75) περιέσχισέ μοι τὸν
κιτῶνα καὶ τὸ πάλλιον, "she stripped off my tunic and
mantle," P Oxy I. 113⁸ (ii/A.D.) ὁ κιτὼν ὑφανθῆναι
μέλλει, "the tunic is to be woven immediately," *ib.* X.
1299³⁰ (early ii/A.D.), *s.v.* ὑποτίθημι, and P Fay
108¹⁷·²¹ (A.D. 171): κίθων in P Oxy II. 298¹¹ (i/A.D.)
ἰς κιθῶ[να], P Giss I. 77⁶ (ii/A.D.) ἔπεμ[ψ]ας μοι τὸν
κιθῶναν, and P Ryl II. 440⁹ (iii/A.D.) πέμψον μοι τὸν
τριβακὸν κιθῶνα: the dim. κιτώνιον in P Tebt II. 421⁵
(iii/A.D.) τὸ κιτώνιον αὐτῆς τὸ λευκὸν παρὰ σοὶ ἔνιγκον
(*l.* ἔνεγκον), "bring the white tunic of hers that you have":
and the dim. κιθώνιον in P Oxy X. 1310 (iii/A.D.) κιθώνιον
ἀργέντιον καὶ μαφόρτιον, and *ib.* XII. 1480²·⁸ (late
iii/A.D.).

The word was formerly regarded as of Semitic origin, but
is now traced to Asia Minor: see Wilcken *UPZ* i. p.
390, n¹.

χιών,

"snow" (Mt 28³, Rev 1¹⁴) occurs in the magic papyri
P Lond 121³⁸² (iii/A.D.) (= I. p. 90) χιὼν γένου, *ib.* 46¹⁹
(iv/A.D.) (= I. p. 65) σὺ γὰρ εἶ ὁ καταδείξας φῶς καὶ
χιόνα, and *ib.* 122³⁰ (iv/A.D.) (= I. p. 117) τῷ κυρίῳ τῶν
χιόνων.

χλαμύς,

"a cloak" worn over the χιτών (Mt 27²⁸·³¹): P Cairo
Zen II. 59263² (B.C. 251) ἔγραψέν μοι Μαιανδρία ὅτι
χλαμύδα αὐτὴν κελεύεις ἐξυφᾶναι, "Maiandria wrote me
that you are ordering her to weave a cloak," P Par 10¹²
(B.C. 145) περὶ τὸ σῶμα χλαμύδα καὶ περίζωμα, P Oxy I.
123¹⁹ (iii/iv A.D.) ἐκ[ε]λεύσθημεν γὰρ μετὰ τῶν χλαμύδων
εἰσβῆναι, "for the orders which we received were to wear
cloaks when we entered" (Edd.), with reference to an
official function, and *ib.* X. 1288⁴ (private account—iv/A.D.)
χλαμύδος καὶ στιχάρ[ι]ον (= -ου) (τάλ.) ιζ, "for a short
cloak and tunic 17 tal."

The word occurs in the epitaph of a prematurely deceased youth, *Kaibel* 222³⁴ (Rom.)—

ἄρτι γὰρ ἐκ χ[λ]αμύδος νεοπενθὴς ᾤχετ' ἐς "Αδα
ὀκτωκαιδεχέτης,

where the reference is to the cloak which the *ephebi* wore (see Herwerden, *Lex. s.v.*).

χλευάζω.

For this NT ἅπ. εἰρ. (Ac 17³²) = "mock," "scoff," see the document quoted *s.v.* Ἰουδαῖος *sub fine*, PSI V. 481⁹ (v/vi A.D.) χλευάσας ἑαυτόν, and P Masp I. 67002¹⁰ (Byz.) νῦν δὲ ἐχλευάσθην παρ' αὐτοῦ. See also Menander Ἐπιτρέπ. 215.

The corr. subst. occurs in P Oxy VI. 904² (v/A.D.), a petition by an old man "who has suffered a breach of contract and mockery" ἀσυνθηκεὶ διαπεπονθότα καὶ χλεύην, and Preisigke 5763⁵¹ (A.D. 647) δίχα δόλου τινος καὶ χλεύης καὶ βίας.

χλιαρός,

"lukewarm," occurs in the NT only in Rev 3¹⁶, where WH (*Notes*², p. 157) admit a possible alternative spelling χλιερός (ℵ*): cf. Moulton *Gr* ii. p. 67.

Χλόη,

"the Verdant," an epithet of Demeter, which may have led to its use as a proper name, especially among members of the freedmen class (like Phoebe, Hermes and Nereus, Rom 16¹,¹⁴,¹⁵). Hence Lightfoot (*Notes*, p. 152) thinks that Chloe of 1 Cor 1¹¹ was a freedwoman: cf. the mention of the slave Chloe in Hor. *Od*. iii. 9. 9. "me nunc Thressa Chloe regit." More recently F. R. Montgomery Hitchcock in *JTS* xxv. (1924), p. 163ff. has taken the view that οἱ Χλόης in 1 Cor *l.c.* were a pagan body, probably followers of Demeter. The noun under the form χλούη (= χλόη). "green corn or grass," occurs *bis* in P Tebt I. 112¹⁶,⁹⁴ (B.C. 112).

χλωρός,

"green" (Mk 6³⁹, al.): P Lond 287¹⁵ (A.D. 90) (= II. p. 202) χόρτου χλωρ[οῦ, P Oxy XVII. 2137²² (A.D. 226) τὸ λοιπὸν ἐν χλωροῖς γενόμενον ἡμισυ μέρος, "the remaining half share that has been put under green crops," P Flor II. 127²¹ (A.D. 256) τὰ γὰρ ἐργατικά μου κτήνη χλωρὸν ἐσθίει, and ²³ χλωρὸ[ν χ]όρτον ποιῆσον ἐνεχθῆναι, and P Lond 453⁷ (iv/A.D.) (= II. p. 319) πλῆσον κεράμιον σίναπις χλωροῦ. Other exx. of the adj. are BGU IV. 1118²⁰ (B.C. 22), P Lond 171a⁴ (A.D. 102) (= II. p. 102), P Oxy IX. 1211⁸ (ii/A.D.), and ib. VI. 910¹¹ (A.D. 197).

χοϊκός.

For the meaning "made of dust" in 1 Cor 15⁴⁷ff, see Field *Notes*, p. 179f. The Lexicons cite *Rhetor. Graec.* i. p. 613⁴ (ed. Walz) γυμνοὶ τούτους τοῦ χοικοῦ βάρους.

χοῖνιξ,

"a choenix," a Greek dry measure, equivalent to 1·92 pints (Rev 6⁶): cf. the note *ad* P Petr II. 25(a) (iii/B.C.). In CPR I. 242⁹ (A.D. 40) σὺν χοινίκεσιν δοισί, the editor thinks that the reference is to the two nave boxes of an oil-mill.

χοῖρος,

"a pig": P Tebt I. 199 (early i/B.C.) τιμὴν χοίρου (δραχμαὶ) ἤ, *Chrest.* I. 73⁵ (A.D. 247-8) an order that πάντας τοὺς χοίρους ἐξελασθῆναι ἀπὸ ἱεροῦ κώμης Τάλμεως, in order that the sacred service may not be disturbed cf. OGIS 210, P Flor II. 166⁴ (iii A.D.) τὸν χοῖρον καὶ τὰ δελφάκια ("sucking pigs") τὰ β καλὰ παράδος Γρηγωρίῳ τῷ μαγείρῳ μου, ἀλλὰ ἤτω ὁ χοῖρος καλός, and P Oxy VI. 901⁵ (A.D. 336) ἡμέτεροι χῦροι δύο τὴν ὁρμὴν ποιούμενοι ἐπὶ ἡμέτερον ἔδαφος (cf. Mk 5¹³).

For dim. χοιρίδιον, see P Ryl II. 229¹² (A.D. 38) περὶ δὲ τῆς τροφῆς τῶν χοιριδίω(ν), and similarly ¹⁹, P Fay 111¹⁰ (A.D. 95-6) πεζῶι [τὰ χ]υρίδια ἐλάσαι, "to drive the pigs on foot," ib. 115⁷ (A.D. 101) μέλλομεν .... χυρίδια θύειν εἰς τὰ γενέσια Σαβίνου, "we intend to sacrifice pigs on the birthday feast of Sabinus" (Edd.), and P Oxy VI. 932¹⁰ (late ii/A.D.) τὰ χοιρίδια χωρὶς μοῦ μὴ πώλι, "do not sell the young pigs without me" (Edd.).

The adj. χοίρειος, "(flesh) of a pig" occurs in P Magd 4⁸ (B.C. 221) πρᾶξαι αὐτοὺς τὴν τιμὴν τ[ῶν χοι]ρείων.

χολάω,

"am angry with" c. dat. pers. Jn 7²³. For χολόω see *Preisigke* 4531, an inscr. stating that the defilement of a sacred spot ἕξει τὸν Σέραπιν κεχολωμένον. In Menander Ἐπιτρέπ. 170 χολάω occurs in its original sense "am mad."

χολή.

For χολή, "gall," "bile," as in Mt 27³⁴, cf. PSI III. 211⁴ (v/A.D.) τὸν τῆς [σ]ἰχολῆς νοσήσαντα. See also Ev. Petr. 5 ποτίσατε αὐτὸν χολὴν μετὰ ὄξους, with Swete's illustrative note. The power of "gall" in medical and magical receipts is discussed by Olsson ad P Osl I. 1²⁵⁴ (iv/A.D.) (p. 104f.). In Herodas III. 70 (ed. Headlam) δότω τις ἐς τὴν χεῖρα πρὶν χολὴ βῆξαι, the editor translates "put it into my hand before I choke with choler": (see the note p. 150).

χόος.

See χοῦς.

χορηγέω

(for form cf. Moulton *Gr.* ii. p. 68), orig. "lead a chorus," "supply a chorus," is used in late Greek in the general sense "furnish," "supply," with the further idea of "lavishly," "abundantly," c. acc. as in 2 Cor 9¹⁰ (see *Proleg.* p. 65). From the papyri we may cite BGU IV. 1051¹⁵ (marriage contract—time of Augustus) ἀπὸ τοῦ νῦν χορηγεῖν αὐτὸν τῇ Λυκαίνῃ τὰ δέοντα πάντα, similarly ib. 1099¹¹, P Ryl II. 153²⁴ (a Will—A.D. 138-161) αὐτὸς χορηγήσει τοῖς αὐτοῖς τὰς αὐτὰς ἐφ' ὃν ἕκαστον αὐτῶν περίεστιν [χρόνον, "he himself shall supply to the said persons the said provisions as long as each of them survives" (Edd.), similarly ²⁰,³⁰, and ib. 181³ (c. A.D. 203-4) χορηγεῖσθαι ὑφ' ὑμῶν τῶν υἱῶν χορηγιά τινα κατ' ἔτος, "that a certain annual allowance should be furnished in perpetuity by you his sons" (Edd.), an agreement to compound an annuity. From the inscrr. we may add *Priene* 108[151] (after B.C. 129) τὴν εἰς αὐτοὺς μισθοφορὰν [ἐ]κ [τῶ]ν ἰδίων χορηγῶν, and *OGIS* 248[16] (B.C. 175-164) χρήμασι χορηγήσαντες, where note the constr. c. dat. and see Dittenberger's note.

The subst. χορηγία may be illustrated from P Fay 124[20] (ii/A.D.), a complaint that a man does not pay his mother her allowance in a fair manner—εἰ μὴ . . . τὴν χορηγίαν τῇ μητρὶ εὐγνωμόνως ἀποδίδυς (*l.* ἀποδίδοις), and χορήγησις from BGU IV. 1208[ii. 18] (B.C. 27-26) χορήγησιν ποιεῖσθαι. See also *s.v.* ἐπιχορηγέω.

χορός,

in the sense of a "choir" or "band of singers," may be illustrated by the Christian sepulchral inscr. *Preisigke* 3013[8] ὁ θεὸς ἀναπαύσεως τὴν ψυχὴν αὐτοῦ καὶ τοῦ χοροῦ τῶν ἀγγέλων.

χορτάζω,

"feed to the full," "satisfy," used originally of animals. but extended in colloquial Greek to men, when it becomes in the mid. practically = ἐσθίω : cf. Mk 7[27] and see Kennedy *Sources*, p. 82. The verb is read in P Petr III. 42 D (1)[5] (B.C. 254). According to Nägeli (p. 58), its occurrence in Phil 4[12] is one of the few vulgarisms Paul permits himself. MGr χορτάζω, χορταίνω, "satiate."

χόρτασμα

occurs in Ac 7[11] in the plur. = "food," "sustenance": cf. PSI IV. 354[5] (B.C. 254) ἑτοιμάζειν ἀγορὰν ("supplies") καὶ χορτάσματα, *ib.* 400[15] (iii/B.C.) ὥστε καὶ τὰ κτήνη σου ἔχειν χορτάσματα δωρεάν, P Hamb I. 27[17] (B.C. 250) ὥστε λυσιτελεῖ μισθώσασθαι ἢ χορτάσματα ζητεῖν, and P Lond 1220[7] (A.D. 145) (= III. p. 142) ὑπὲρ τιμῆς χορτασμάτων.

χόρτος,

"grass," "hay": P Petr III. 62(*b*)[5] (iii/B.C.) χόρτου ξηροῦ, P Lille 5[63] (B.C. 260-259) χόρτου σπέρματος, P Ryl II. 129[12] (A.D. 30) ἤρωσάν μου χόρτου δέσμας πεντηκοσίας, "they carried off five hundred bundles of my hay," BGU I. 248[2] (i/A.D.) δήλωσον δέ μοι, πόσου εἰς κοπὴν ὁ χόρτος πιπράσκεται, P Fay 110[6] (c. A.D. 100) χόρτον σαπρόν, "rotten hay," P Oxy III. 499[15] (A.D. 121) ὥστε ξυλαμῆσαι χόρτον εἰς κοπὴν καὶ ἐπινομήν, "so as to be cultivated with grass for cutting and grazing," P Flor I. 127[23] (A.D. 256) χλωρὸ[ν χ]όρτον ποιῆσον ἐνεχθῆναι, and P Oxy VIII. 1107[3] (v/vi A.D.) χόρτον, "green crops" (Edd.). For the adj. see PSI VI. 579[6] (B.C. 246-5) τὴν χορτοφόρον γῆν παραδείξας Ἰάσονι.

Χουζᾶς,

"Chuza," a house-steward of Herod Antipas (Lk 8[3]) The name has been found in a Nabataean inscr. making it probable that Chuza was not a Jew but a Nabataean : see F. C. Burkitt in *Exp* V. ix. p. 118 ff. (cf. *Syriac Forms*, p. 6), where also Blass's contention (*Philology of the Gospels*,

p. 152 f.) on the evidence of *l.* a vii/A.D. Old Latin version, that Chuza was also called Cydias, is criticized.

χοῦς,

abbreviated from χόος. The original meaning "earth," "earth dug out," is seen in P Tebt I. 13[11] (B.C. 114) τὸν ἀπ' αὐτοῦ χοῦν ἀναβεβληκότας εἰς τὰ τοῦ σημαινο(μένου) Φιλοναύ(του) κλή(ρου) χώματα, "had heaped the earth from it (*sc.* a dyke) on to the mounds of the holding of the said Philonautes" (Edd.), P Oxy VI. 985 (accounts—2nd half i/A.D.) ἐργά(ταις) δυσὶ σκάπτοντ(ι) χοῦν ("a mound"), *ib.* XIV. 1758[10] (ii/A.D.) καλῶς .ποιήσεις κατενγυήσας τὸν χοῦν ὃ ἐξέσκαψεν Ἀτρῆς ὁ γεωργός μου ἀπὸ τῶν ἐδαφῶν μου, and P Tebt II. 342[27] (late ii/A.D.) ψ[ι]λοῦ τόπου εἰς ἐκσκαφὴν χοὸς καὶ χαινογείου καὶ ἄμμου, "a vacant space for digging earth. porous clay and sand" (Edd.). The meaning "dust," as in Mk 6[11], Rev 18[19], may be seen in *Syll* 500 (=[3] 313)[26] (B.C. 320-319) τοὺς τὸν [χ]οῦν κατα-[βε]βληκότας εἰς τὰς ὁδ[ο]ὺς ταύτας [ἀ]ναι[ρ]εῖν.

χράομαι,

from χρή, "necessity." "make for myself what is necessary with something," hence c. dat. as in Ac 27[17] *al.* : cf. P Magd 11[7] (B.C. 221) πρὸς τὸ μὴ δύνασθαι τοῖς ἱστίοις ἔτι χράσθαι (for form, Mayser *Gr.* p. 247), P Tebt I. 45[21] (B.C. 113) οὐδενὶ κόσμωι χρησάμενοι συντρίψαντες τὴν παρόδιον θύραν, "throwing off all restraint knocked down the street door" (Edd.), P Ryl II. 148[17] (A.D. 40) ληστρικῶι τρόπωι χρησάμενοι, P Oxy VIII. 1153[27] (i/A.D.) ἐντοπίᾳ δὲ πορφύρᾳ χρήσασθ(αι) μέλλομεν, "we are going to use local purple" (Ed.), *ib.* X. 1266[36] (A.D. 98) μηδ' ἀλλοτρίαις [ἀσφα]ε[ί]αις ἢ ὁμωνυμίᾳ κεχρῆ[σ]-θαι, "that I have not availed myself of credentials belonging to others or identity of names" (Edd.), *ib.* 1263[12] (A.D. 128-9) χρήσασθαι τῇ τῶν ἐργ(ατῶν) ποταμοῦ τέχ[νῃ, "to practise the trade of a river-worker," P Giss I. 40[26] (iii/A.D.) χράσθωσαν τ[οῖς] προκειμένοις τόποι[ς ἀκω-λ]ύτως, and PSI VIII. 872[6] (vi/A.D.).

For the verb c. dat. pers. = "treat," as in Ac 27[3], cf. P Petr III. 42 H(8)f.[8] (iii/B.C.) πικρ[ῶ]ς σοι ἐχρήσατο, P Oxy IV. 745[5] (c. A.D.) οὐκ οἶδας γὰρ πῶς μοι ἐχρήσατο ἐν Ὀξυρύγχοις, "you don't know how he treated me at Oxyrhynchus (?)" (Edd.), and P Flor II. 187[3] (iii/A.D.) ἀσπουδάστως ἐχρήσω μοι. C. H. Dodd (*JTS* xxvi. (1924), p. 77 f.) draws attention to a useful parallel to the absolute use of χρῆσαι in 1 Cor 7[21] from P Oxy XVI. 1865[ff.] (vi/vii A.D.) καὶ πολλάκις ἐξῆ[ν γράψαι σοι περὶ τοῦ] κεφαλαίου τούτου, καὶ προσδόκον (*l.* προσδοκῶν) καθ' ἑκάστην καταλαμβά[νειν ἐκεῖσε ?] τούτου ἕνεκεν οὐκ ἐχρη-σάμην ἄλλην γράψαι ἄλλος γράμμα[σι] . . . . .[? f.] καὶ πρὸς τὸ γνῶναι τὸν ἐμὸν δεσπότην ἐχρησάμην παρακαλῶν διὰ τούτον (*l.* τούτων) μου τῶν γραμμάτων, "I had many opportunities of writing to you concerning this matter, and, expecting each day to come thither, for that reason did not avail myself of them to write another letter over again. That my master may know this I took the opportunity of exhorting you by this my writing" (Edd.). "The late date," as Dodd points out, "detracts somewhat from the value of the comparison, but for what it is worth it favours the rendering of the Pauline passage—'If you actually have before you the

possibility of becoming free, avail yourselves of it by preference.'"

The constr. c. acc. in 1 Cor 7³¹ is difficult, as it seems for
the most part to be confined to much later writers, but see
Sap 7¹⁴ B and the note in *Proleg*. p. 245. Lightfoot (*Notes*,
p. 233) cites an ex. from a Cretan inscr. of iii/ii B.C., *CIG*
II. p. 405. See also Radermacher *Gr*.², pp. 121, 133.

χράω.

See κίχρημι.

χρεία,

(1) "necessity," "need," or "occasion of need": P Hib
I. 54¹³ (c. B.C. 245) χρεία γάρ ἐστι ταῖς γυναιξὶν πρὸς τὴν
θυσίαν, "for he is wanted by the women for the sacrifice"
(Edd.), P Grenf II. 14(*a*)⁶ (iii B.C.) πρὸς τινὰ χρείαν ἀναγκαίαν (cf. Tit 3¹⁴), P Fay 117⁵ (A.D. 108) πέμσαι αὐτῷ . .
εἰκθύδιν (*l.* ἰχθύδιον), ἐπὶ (*l.* ἐπεὶ) χρίαν αὐτοῦ ἔχωμον
(*l.* ἔχομεν), "send him some fish, as we want to make use
of him" (Edd.), P Michigan Inv. No. 2798³ (time of
Hadrian) περ]ὶ ὧν ἐὰν χρείαν ἔχῃς γράφε μοι, "do you
write to me about what you may need," P Tebt II. 410¹⁷
(iii/A.D.) μετάδες (*l.* μετάδος) καὶ ᾿Ακουτᾶτι τῷ ἀδελφῷ ὅτι
ἐὰν χρίαν τινὸς ἔχῃ ἡ γυνή μου ποίησον αὐτῆς τὴν χρίαν
ἕως ἔλθω, μηδὲν ἐπιζητείτω, "tell my brother Akoutas
also to do anything that my wife requires until I come, and let
her want for nothing" (Edd.), and P Grenf II. 72⁶ (A.D.
290–304) εἰς ἰδίαν μου χρείαν . . . τάλαντα δύο.

For χρείαν ἔχω treated as an active verb and followed by
the acc., as in Rev 3¹⁷, cf. P Oxy VII. 1068²⁰ (iii A.D.) εἴ τι
ἂν ἄλλου (*l.* ἄλλο) σου χρίαν σκῶσιν (*l.* σχῶσιν), "with
anything else they may need from you" (Ed.), *ib*. XIV.
1683¹⁷ (late iv/A.D.) δὸς οὖν αὐτά, ἐπιδὲ χρείαν αὐτὰ ὁ
υἱός μου ⟨ἔχει⟩, "give them to her, since my son needs
them," *ib*. XVI. 1929³ (iv/v A.D.) χρίαν ἔχομεν τὰ πλοία,
and P Lond 1018¹⁶ (A.D. 330–340) εἴ τι χρείαν ἔχεις πέμψον
σοι, with Bell's note.

(2) "matter in hand," "business" (Ac 6³: cf. 1 Macc
12⁴⁵, 2 Macc 7³⁴, Judith 12¹⁰): P Tebt I. 35² (B.C. 111)
τοῖς ἐπὶ χρειῶν τεταγμένοις χαίρειν, "to the other officials,
greeting," BGU I. 18¹⁴ (A.D. 169) παραγ[γ]έλεται (*l.* παραγ-
γέλλεται) ἀντιλαμβάνεσθαι τῆς ἐνχιρισθίσης α[ὐ]τοῖς χρε[ί]α]ς
ὑγιῶς καὶ πιστῶς, P Iand 33¹² (time of Commodus) ὀμνύομεν . . . ἀντιλήμψασθαι τῆς χρίας καὶ φυλάξιν (= -ειν)
διὰ νυκτὸς τὴν κώμ[ην] ἀνεγκλή]τως, P Tebt II. 327²³ (late
ii/A.D.) κε]κελευσμένον οὖν, κύριε, γ[υ]ναίκας ἀφεῖσθαι τῶν
τ[οιο]ύτων χρειῶν, "wherefore, my lord, it has been decreed
that women should be freed from such burdens" (Edd.), and
P Oxy VII. 1063⁵ (ii/iii A.D.) εἶπας οὐδένα ἐκείνων εἰς τὴν
χρείαν ἔδωκα, "you said 'I have not given in any of them
sc. certain names for the office'" (Ed.).

In Mk 11³, Mt 21³, Lk 19³¹·³⁴ ὁ κύριος αὐτοῦ (αὐτῶν)
χρείαν ἔχει, Nicklin (*CR* xv. (1901), p. 203) thinks that, in
view of the order of the words, the natural translation is,
"Its (their) owner needs (it or them)." Various translations
of Eph 4²⁹ ἀλλ᾿ εἴ τις ἀγαθὸς πρὸς οἰκοδομὴν τῆς χρείας
are discussed by Field, *Notes* p. 192, with a preference for
"that which is good for the improvement of the occasion."
J. A. Robinson (*Comm. ad l.*) renders "for building up as
the matter may require" or "*as need may be*."

χρεοφιλέτης

(not χρεωφειλέτης, see WH *Notes*², pp. 159, 161) "a
debtor" Lk 7⁴¹, 16⁵): cf. *Syll* 326 (= ³ 742)⁵³ (c. B.C. 85)
ἀπέλυσαν τοὺς χρεωφ(ε)ιλέτας, where, according to the
editor's note, the inscr. shows **ΧΡΕΟΦΙΛΕΤΑΣ**.

For χρέος, see BGU IV. 1113²³ (B.C. 14) ὡς ἴδιον χρέος
ἀργυρ[ίο]υ δραχ[μὰ]ς χι̣λ̣ί̣[α]ς̣, and for χρεώστης, see *ib*.
III. 786¹¹·⁶ (ii/A.D.) ὄντα χρεώστην το[ῦ] ταμείου.

χρή

occurs in the NT only in Jas 3¹⁰ (but cf. Prov 25²⁷,
4 Macc 8²⁶ A), where Hort (*Comm. ad l.*) notes that "it is
a somewhat vague word, apparently starting from the sense
'there is need.'" This is borne out by such exx. as the
following—P Hib I. 64¹⁹ (B.C. 264) χρὴ δὲ καὶ [γρά]φειν
μοι π̣[ερ]ὶ ὧν ἂν χρείαν ἔχῃς, "and you must write to
me about anything which you require" (Edd.), BGU III.
830¹⁸ (i A.D.) χρ[ὴ] οὖν ἑτοιμάσ[ε]ιν (*l.* ἑτοιμάσαι) καὶ
προαιρ[εῖν], ἵν᾿ ἔχῃ (*l.* ἔχῃ) τοῦ π[ωλ]εῖν, "it is therefore
necessary to prepare and bring forward, in order that he
may be able to sell," P Flor III. 309⁵ (iv/A.D.) οὐ χρὴ σ̣[ι]ωπῇ
παραδίδοσθαι τὰ ὑπ᾿ αὐτῆς εἰρημένα, P Oxy I. 120⁵
(iv/A.D.) χρὴ γὰρ τινα ὁρῶντα αἰαυτὸν (*l.* ἑαυτὸν) ἐν
δυστυχίᾳ κἂν ἀναχωρεῖν, "when a man finds himself in
adversity he ought to give way" (Edd., *ib*. VIII. 1163³
(v/A.D.) ἐρωτηθὶς παρὰ τῆς αὐτοῦ μεγαλοπρεπίας ὅσα
ἐχρῆν ἀνεδίδαξα αὐ[τὸ]ν περὶ τῆς ὑμετέρας μεγαλοπρεπίας,
"on the inquiry of his magnificence I told him what was
fitting about your magnificence" (Ed.). See also the
Attic inscr. *Prienejc* 421¹⁰ (= *LAE*², p. 397) χρή,
τιμιώτατε, τὰς θεάς (or θέας) κωμάζεσθαι, "it is necessary,
O most honourable, that the goddesses (or spectacles) be
celebrated in festal procession."

χρῄζω,

"need," "have need," (1) c. gen. pers. (Rom 16²)
—BGU I. 37⁷ (A.D. 50) οἶδας γὰρ πῶς αὐτοῦ ἑκάστης
ὥρας χρῄζωι, P Flor I. 138⁶ (A.D. 264) ἄνελθε ἐπεὶ
ἀναγκαίως σου χρῄζω: (2) c. gen. rei (Mt 6³², *al*.)—P
Strass I. 32¹⁷ (A.D. 261) χρῄζει ταύτης τῆς ὑπηρεσίας,
P Oxy VII. 1066¹⁴ (iii/A.D.) εἴ τινος δὲ χρῄζεις ἀντίγραφόν
μοι: (3) c. acc. rei—P Oxy I. 113²² (ii/A.D.) ταῦτα ἐμοῦ
χρῄζοντος εἰς ἑορτήν, "especially when I wanted it for a
festival" (Edd.): (4) absolutely—P Ryl II. 81²³ (c. A.D.
104) ἐκ τούτου δὲ [φανε]ρόν ἐστιν [καὶ] μηδένα χρῄζειν,
"it is evident from this that nobody wants it" (Edd.),
ib. 239¹³ mid. iii/A.D.) κἂν πάλιν χρῄζεις, δηλώσεις [μ]οι,
"and if you have need again, let me hear" (Edd.).

χρῆμα.

For the plur. = "moneys," "property," "possessions,"
as in Mk 10²³, *al*., cf. the letter of a freedman to his patron,
BGU IV. 1141²¹ (B.C. 13) θέλεις με εἶναι ἄνθρωπ . . . καὶ
συνέστησας καὶ συνδούλοις καὶ συνεξελευθέροις, ὅπερ ἐμοὶ
χρήματά ἐστιν παρά σοί, "you wish me to be a man (?)
and you have stood by both my fellow-slaves and fellow-
freedmen, which for me means the same as money from
you (?)," P Oxy III. 473⁴ (A.D. 138–160) τά τε [θε]ωρικὰ

χρήματα, "funds for theatrical displays, *ib.* I. 55[15] (A.D. 283) ἀξιοῦμεν ἐπιστειλέ σαι (*l.* ἐπιστείλαί σε) τῷ ταμίᾳ τῶν πολιτικῶν χρημάτων τὸν ἐξοδιασμὸν ἡμεῖν ποιήσασθαι κατὰ τὸ ἔθος, "we beg you to instruct the public treasurer to pay us in full, as is usual" (Edd.), and P Fay 20[12] (iii/iv A.D.) ἀντὶ τῶν χρυσῶν στεφάνων χρήματα, "the sums due in place of golden crowns" (Edd.). The sing., as in Ac 4[37], appears in P Oxy III. 474[41] (A.D. 184?) μὴ ἐφάπτεσθαι τοῦ κυριακοῦ χρήματος (with the editors' note), P Tebt II. 353[25] (A.D. 192) στεφανικοῦ χρήματος.

χρηματίζω,

(1) "negotiate," "transact business": P Lille I. 26[6] (iii/B.C.) ἐξέσται ἡμᾶς λαβεῖν καὶ χρηματίσασθ[αι τὴν] παρὰ τοῦ βασιλικοῦ χορηγίαν, and *ib.*[8] where the same verb = "assign," "distribute," P Oxy XII. 1479[8] (late i/B.C.) ἀφ᾽ οὗ κεχώρισαι τῇ ιϛ [κ]εχρημάτικεν Σαβεῖνος, "since you went away on the 16th, Sabinus has been acting in the business" (Edd.), P Ryl II. 105[10] (A.D. 260) Ἰουλιανῇ . . χρηματιζούσῃ χωρὶς [κυρίου, and P Oxy IX. 1199[7] (iii/A.D.) Αὐρηλίας . . χρηματιζούσῃ⟨ς⟩ δικαίῳ τέκνων, "Aurelia acting in virtue of her children" (*sc.* without a guardian).

(2) "take a name from," "am called," as in Ac 11[26], Rom 7[3], so frequently in the phrase ὡς χρηματίζει following a description, e.g. P Oxy II. 268[2] (A.D. 58) παρὰ Ἀμμωναρί[ο]ν τῆς Ἀμμω[νί]ου . . . ὡς . . . χρηματί[ζ]ει, "from Ammonarion, daughter of Ammonius, and however she is described," and P Ryl II. 110[3] (A.D. 259) Ἀλεξάνδρῳ ἀρχιπροφήτῃ . . . καὶ ἐπ᾽ ἄλλων ταξέων κα[ὶ] ὡς χρη-(ματίζει), "to Alexander, chief prophet holding other posts and however he is styled" (Edd.). According to Schubart (*Archiv* v. p. 114) χρηματίζω always denotes an official description as compared with ἐπικαλεῖσθαι, λέγεσθαι. Note also its occurrence in connexion with attesting signatures— P Oxy II. 242[30] (A.D. 77) Κλαύδιος Ἀντώνινος χρη-(μάτισον), P Amh II. 47[18] (B.C. 113) Ἡλιόδω[ρος] κεχρη(μάτικα).

(3) "make answer," "instruct," "warn," as in Mt 2[12], Job 40[3]: cf. P Fay 137[2] (i/A.D.) (= *Selections*, p. 69) Σοκωννωκοννῖ (*l.* Σοκανοβκονεῖ) θεῶι με⟨γά⟩λο μεγάλωι. χρημάτισόν μοι, ἢ μείνωι ἐν Βακχιάδι; "to Sokanobkoneus the great, great god. Answer me, Shall I remain in Bacchias?" Similarly in the passive, P Giss I. 20[18] (ii/A.D.) ἐχρη[μ]ατίσθην ὑπὸ τῶν Διοσκούρων τῆς κτήσεώς σου, and P Oxy VI. 886[24] (iii/A.D.) (= *Selections*, p. 112) a magical formula followed by the assurance, καὶ χρηματισθήσῃ τηλαυγῶς, "and you will receive a clear answer." Cf. also P Par 46[3] (B.C. 152) (= Witkowski[2], p. 86, *UPZ* i. p. 337) εἰ ἔρρωσαι καὶ τὰ παρὰ τῶν θεῶν κατὰ λόγον σοι χρηματίζεται, εἴη ἄν, ὡς βούλομαι, and *ib.* 26[21] (B.C. 162) (= *UPZ* i. p. 248, *Selections*, p. 15) τὰ ὑφ᾽ ὑμῶν ἡμῖν χρηματιζόμενα, "the privileges conferred on us by you."

It should be noted, however, that Moulton (*Gr.* ii. p. 265) ascribes this meaning to an entirely different verb χρηματίζω from the foregoing, that being associated with χρήματα, "business," this with an equivalent of χρησμός, "oracle."

In MGr χρηματίζω is used for the subst. verb "am."

χρηματισμός

is commonly used to denote a "report," as in P Lond 20[22] (B.C. 162) (= I. p. 9, *UPZ* i. p. 207) ἀξιῶ σε . . ἀναλαβόντα τὸν παρὰ Δωρίωνος χρηματισμὸν ἐπιτελέσαι ἀκολούθως, *ib.* 17[11] (B.C. 162) (= I. p. 10, *UPZ* i. p. 209) τὸ ἀντίγραφον σὺν τῶι γεγονότι πρὸς αὐτὴν χρηματισμῶι προσήφαμεν, and [18] ἐπισταλέντος τοῦ καθήκοντος χρηματισμοῦ. In its only NT occurrence, Rom 11[4], it is used of "a divine response," "an oracle": see *s.v.* χρηματίζω.

χρήσιμος,

"useful": in NT only 2 Tim 2[14]. Cf. P Cairo Zen III. 59301[5] (B.C. 250) ἔστιν γὰρ ἄνθρωπος ἡμῖν χρήσιμος, P Alex 4[5] (iii/B.C.) (= Witkowski[2], p. 51) πρὸς τὸ μὴ γίνεσθαι τῶι βασιλεῖ τὸ χρήσιμον, ἀποδείξομέν σε, P Par 45[2] (B.C. 152) (= *UPZ* i. p. 329) ἀπόντος μου πεφρόντικα ὑπὲρ σοῦ χρήσιμα τῶν σῶν πραγμάτων, P Oxy IV. 705[75] (A.D. 200-2) καὶ τοῦ φιλανθρώπου καὶ τοῦ χρησίμου στοχαζ[όμε]νος, "having before me a both humane and useful object," P Ryl II. 114[34] (c. A.D. 280) πρὸς τὸ τοῖς φόροις χρήσιμον, "with a view to what is expedient for the revenues" (Edd.).

From the inscrr. we may cite a Coan decree of iii/B.C. conferring a gold crown on a physician for services during an epidemic, that all may recognize that the citizens honour those who practise the healing art—ὅπως εἰδῶντι [πάντες ὅτι ὁ δᾶμ]ος [τὸ]ὺς χρησίμους ὄντας κα[ὶ] εὔνους τῶν π]ολιτᾶν καταξίω]ς τ[ιμᾶι . . . (*Cos* 5[26] = *Syll* 490 (= [3] 943[26]). For the word as a proper name see e.g. *Preisigke* 729[1] (i/A.D. ?) Χρήσιμος ἀγαθὸς ἄωρος, *ib.* 928.

χρῆσις,

"use," is found in the NT only in a sexual sense, Rom 1[26 f]. For a more general meaning, cf. P Cairo Zen III. 59349[4] (B.C. 244) wine εἰς χρῆσιν, "for use," i.e. for present consumption, P Oxy I. 105[5] (a Will—A.D. 117-137) ἐπὶ τῷ αὐτὴν ἔχειν ἐπὶ τὸν τῆς ζωῆς αὐτῆς χρόνον τὴν χρῆσιν . . . τῆς αὐτῆς οἰκίας, "with the condition that she shall have for her lifetime the right of using the said house" (Edd.). This prepares us for the meaning "loan," as in BGU IV. 1065[11] (A.D. 97) τῆς συμπεφωνημ(ένης) χρήσεως ἀργυρίου, P Tebt II. 388[13] (A.D. 98) διὰ χειρὸς ἐξ οἴκου χρῆσιν πυροῦ νέου . . ., "from hand to hand out of the house a loan of new wheat," P Flor I. 44[14] (A.D. 158) χρῆσιν κεφαλ[α]ί[ου ἀργυρί]ου δραχμὰς ἑκατὸν εἴκο[σι . . ., and P Oxy VIII. 1130[5] (A.D. 484) ἐν χρήσει, "as a loan." See also PSI VIII. 929[11, 29] (A.D. 111).

χρηστεύομαι,

"am kind," is found in the NT only in 1 Cor 13[4]. Harnack (*Exp.* VIII. iii. p. 406) suggests that Paul may have derived it from a recension of Q, which was used and quoted by Clemens Romanus.

χρηστολογία

in the NT only in Rom 16[18] in the sense of "fair and insinuating speech." The commentators quote Jul. Capitolinus *Pertinax* 13: χρηστόλογον *eum appellantes qui bene loqueretur et male faceret.*" The word is also found in a good sense in eccles. writers.

χρηστός,

"virtuous," "excellent," as in 1 Cor 15[33], is well illustrated by P Oxy III. 642 (ii/A.D.) ἀπολαύσωμεν τῷ χρηστῷ ὑμῶν ἤθει, *ib.* XIV. 1663[11] (ii/iii A.D.) διὰ τὸ ἦθος τὸ χρηστόν, "on account of his excellent character," and *ib.* VII. 1070[10] (iii/A.D.), a pompous letter from a man to his wife in which he speaks of τῶν χρηστῶν ἐλπίδων τῶν ἐν ἀνθρώποισι νε[[σ]]νομισμένων, "the good hopes that are held by mankind" (Ed.). See also the citation from the Avircius inscr. *s.v.* πατρίς.

The thought of "gracious," as in Lk 6[35], appears in P Leid W[vii. 26] (ii/iii A.D.) (= I. p. 103) κλῦτί μοι (*l.* κλῦθί μοι), ὁ χρηστὸς ἐν βαζάνοις (*l.* βασ-), βοήθησον ἐν ἀνάγκαις, and in such a προσκύνημα as *Preisigke* 158[1] Ἀνδρόμαχος . . ἀφίκετο πρὸς Ἀμενώθην χρηστὸν θεὸν . . . καὶ ὁ θεὸς αὐτῶι ἐβοήθησε. Note also the common use of the adj. as a descriptive epithet in sepulchral inscrr., e.g. *Preisigke* 9[4] ἄωρε χρηστὲ χαῖρε, 10[5], *al.* and its occurrence as a proper name in P Grenf I. 49[12] (A.D. 220-1) ὑπὸ τοῦ λαμπροτάτου ἡγεμόνος Γεμεινίου Χρήστου, *al.* See also *s.v.* Χριστιανός.

Its use with reference to things may be seen in P Cairo Zen III. 59340[7] (B.C. 244) εἰ ἔστιν ἤδη χρηστόν, "if it is now fit for use," of a jar of wine, P Oxy XVII. 2148[1] (A.D. 27) ἐκομισάμην τὴν σεμίδ[αλ]ιν χρηστὴν οὖσαν, "I received the fine flour which was good" (Ed.), [16] ἐάν τι ποιῇς χρηστόν, περιποίησον εἰς οἶκον ἀδελ[φ]ῶν, "if you make anything good, make an extra amount for your brothers' house" (Ed.), and *ib.* VI. 937[28] (iii/A.D.) δικότυλον ἐλαίου χρηστοῦ, "two cotylae of good oil" (Edd.).

χρηστότης,

"kindness." This subst., which is confined in the NT to the Pauline writings, may be illustrated by BGU II. 372[18] (A.D. 154) εὐ[μ]εν[εί]ας καὶ χρη[σ]τότητος, and *Syll* 324 (= ³ 730)[21] (i B.C. *ad init.*) χαλεπῶς μὲν ἤνεγκεν τὸ πένθος αὐτοῦ διὰ τὴν χρηστότητα. Note also the common use as a title of address like our "your Grace," e.g. BGU III. 084[3] (iv/A.D.) ἔγραψα . . [τ]ῇ χρηστ[ότ]ητί σου, P Heid 6[6] (iv/A.D.) (= *Selections*, p. 125), and P Giss I. 7[15] with the other exx. collected there. For the combination χρηστότης καὶ φιλανθρωπία, as in Tit 3[4], cf. Field *Notes*, p. 222 f.

χρῖσμα

(for accent see Blass-Debrunner § 13) is found in the NT in 1 Jn 2[20. 27], where it is variously understood of "the act of anointing" (Brooke *ICC*) or "that with which the anointing is performed" (Westcott *Comm.*). The word occurs in P Lond 121[874] (iii/A.D.) (= I. p. 112) τῷ σεληνιακῷ χρίσματι, and [879]. See also *s.v.* χρίω.

Χριστιανός,

a word of Latin formation (cf. Pompeiani, Caesariani), apparently invented by the Antiochenes as a nickname for the partisans or followers of Christ, Ac 11[26], cf. 26[3], 1 Pet 4[16]. From the fact that in these, the only instances of its use in the NT, Codex Sinaiticus writes the word Χρηστιανοί, Blass thinks that this was the original form (cf. *Hermes* xxx. (1895), p. 465 ff.), but the difference in spelling may be due

simply to a confusion of sound between Χριστ- and χρηστ-: cf. Radermacher *Gr.*², p. 45.

The common use of Χρηστός as a proper name may, however, also be recalled, see *s.v.* χρηστός. Deissmann (*LAE*², p. 377), following Winer-Schmiedel *Gr.* § 16, 2c, n.[18] (p. 135), draws attention to the analogy on linguistic grounds between Χριστιανός and Καισαριανός, "Caesarian," "Imperial (slave)": cf. P Lond 256 *recto*¹ (A.D. 11-15) (= II. p. 96, *Chrest.* I. p. 407) Φαῦστος Πρίσκου Καίσαρος, one of the imperial slaves. As an ex. of the word from the inscrr., we may cite a wall-scratching from Egypt, *Preisigke* 2273 Σταῦρος δῶν Χριστιανῶν.

See further R. A. Lepsius *Über den Ursprung und ältesten Gebrauch des Christennamens* (Jena, 1873), also the art. "Christian" in Hastings *DB* i. p. 384 ff. and A. Carr *Exp* V. vii. p. 456 ff.

χριστός (Χρ-).

We cannot expect our sources to throw much light on this important verbal, but we may note that apparently the earliest ex. of its use as a title is to be found in Pss. Sol. xvii. 36 καὶ βασιλεὺς αὐτῶν χριστὸς κύριος, where we should probably read χριστὸς κυρίου, "and their King shall be the Lord's Anointed."

For full discussions of the Jewish and the Christian use of the word, see Dalman *Words of Jesus*, p. 289 ff., Burton *Gal.* (in *ICC*), p. 395 ff., and *New Testament Word Studies* (Chicago, 1927), p. 27 ff. and Preuschen-Bauer *Wörterb. s.v.*

Attention may be drawn here to G. Ghedini's collection of *Lettere Christiane dai Papiri Greci del III. e IV. Secolo* (Milan, 1923), and to C. Wessely's *Les plus anciens Monuments du Christianisme écrits sur Papyrus*, being *Patrologia Orientalis* IV. 2 and XVIII. 3 (Paris, 1907, 1924).

χρίω,

"anoint with oil," is applied to camels in P Flor III. 364[21] (iii/A.D.) ἐχρίσθησαν οἱ προκείμενοι κάμ(ηλοι): see also *s.v.* ἀλείφω *sub fin.* For the meaning "provide oil," cf. P Oxy XII. 1413[19] (A.D. 270-5), where the gymnasiarch is reported as saying that so-and-so promised εἰς τὴ]ν τριακάδα τοῦ Μεσορὴ χρεῖσαι, τῇ μὲν τριακάδι οὐκ ἔχρεισεν, ἀλλὰ τῇ ἑξῆς νεομηνίᾳ δι᾽ ἐμοῦ ἔ[χρεισε]ν, "to provide oil on Mesore 30. On Mesore 30 he failed to provide oil, but on the first day of the following month he provided it through me" (Edd.). The word is common in the magic papyri. See also P Leid W[vii. 26, 44] (= II. pp. 99, 101).

From the inscrr. cf. *Syll* 507 (= ³ 983)[16] (ii/A.D.) where worshippers in a temple are described as πρότερον χρεισαμένους ἐλαίῳ, and *ib.* 804 (= ³ 1170)[18] (ii/A.D.) νάπωι καὶ ἁλσὶν κεχρειμένος, the account of a cure. The subst. χρίσις occurs in P Petr II. 25(*a*)[13] (iii/B.C.) εἰς χρίσιν ἐλαίου, "for the lotion of oil."

χρονίζω.

For the general meaning "delay," see P Masp I. 67002¹ [10] (vi/A.D.) ἐχρόνισεν γὰρ ὁ αὐτὸς Διόσκορ[ο]ς ἰδικῶς ἀτουργῶν (= αὐτ-) τα[ῦτα᾽ς μετὰ θάνατον τοῦ πατρὸς αὐτοῦ, and cf. the compl. ἀναχρονίζω in P Tebt II. 413[14] (ii/iii A.D.) ἀναχρονίζομέν [σ]οι πέμποντες ἐπιστόλια, "we are late in sending you letters" (Edd.).

The word is not infrequent in the papyri in the sense "date" a letter or other document, e.g. BGU I. 347[ii.9] (A.D. 171) ἐ]πιστολ[ὴν] . . . κεχρονισμένην εἰς τὸ διεληλυθὸ[ς ι] (ἔτος) Φαρμοῦθι ιϛ, P Oxy XII. 1451[23] (A.D. 175) δέλτους] μαρτυροποιή[σεως δύο ἐπὶ σφρα]γείδων κεχρονισμένας τὴν μὲν Λουκιλλιαν[οῦ ιϛ (ἔτει)] θεοῦ Ἀντωνίνου, [τὴν δὲ Μαρκέλλης] δ ἔτει Αὐρηλίου Ἀντωνίνου, "two tablets of evidence under seal, dated, that of Lucilianus in the 16th year of the deified Antoninus, and that of Marcella in the 4th year of Aurelius Antoninus" (Edd.), and ib. I. 57[7] (iii/A.D.).

χρόνος,

"time," "a time," "a period": P Petr II 40 (a)[14] (iii/B.C.) ὀλίγος γὰρ χρόνος ὑμῖν ἐστιν, P Strass I. 74[7ff] (A.D. 126) τοῦ χρόνου πληρωθέντος οὐκέτι βούλομαι αὐτὰς (sc. ἀρούρας) γεωργεῖν ἀποδεδωκὼς πάντα τὰ ἐκφόρια τῶν ἔμπρ[ο]σθεν χρόνων, P Lond 1231[10] (A.D. 144) (= III. p. 109) τοῦ χρόνου τῆς μισθώσεως πεπληροκότος, and P Oxy I. 101[60] (A.D. 142) χρό(νος) ὁ α(ὐτός), "the same date."

For the acc. of duration of time, as in Mk 2[19] al., cf. P Petr II. 12 (3)[18] (B.C. 241) οὐ τὸν πλείω χρόνον καταφθαρησόμεθα, "we shall no longer be harried," BGU IV. 1055[30] (B.C. 30) τὸν μεμερισμένον αὐτῷ χρόνον, a common phrase in Alexandrian contracts: and for the instr. dat. of extension of time, as in Lk 8[27.29] al. (cf. Proleg. p. 75), cf. P Strass I. 22[31] (iii/A.D.) οὐδεμίαν παρείσδυσιν ἔχεις, ἡ γὰρ γ[υν]ὴ ἐν τῇ νομῇ γέγονεν πολλῷ χρόνῳ, and the recurrent formula in private letters ἐρρῶσθαί σε εὔχομαι πολλοῖς χρόνοις, e.g. P Oxy VI. 936[52] (iii/A.D.), ib. I. 112[8] (iii/iv A.D.), and P Lond 417[14] (c. A.D. 346) (= II. p. 299, Selections, p. 124).

These last exx. show the approach to the MGr meaning "year": cf. P Gen I. 50[21f.] (iv/A.D.) ἐρρῶσθα[ί σε] ὡς πλείστ[οι]ς ἔτεσιν εὔχομαι, where ἔτεσιν takes the place of the usual χρόνοις, and the Christian inscr. JHS xxii. 1902), p. 399f. (cited s.v. διχοτομέω), in which the writer says of his wife—τῇ συνζησάσᾳ μοι χρόνους ὀλίγους ἐπι[τ]ίμως. For numerous exx. in late Greek of χρόνος = "year," see Sophocles Lex. s.v.

For χρόνος with prepositions, see P Oxy I. 68[10] (A D 131) ἀπὸ τῶν ἔνπροσθεν χρόνων: P Lille I. 26[3] (iii/B.C.) διὰ τὸ πλείω χρόνον, P Lips I. 110[29] (iii/iv A.D.) διὰ πολλοῦ χρόνου: P Tebt I. 50[17] (late ii/B.C.) εἰς τὸν ἅπαντα χρόν[ον, P Fay 117[23] (A.D. 108) εἰς τὸν ἀεὶ χρόνον: P Strass I. 5[10] (A.D. 262) ἐκ παλαιοῦ χρόνου, OGIS 90[14] (Rosetta stone—B.C. 196) ἐκ πολλοῦ χρόνου: CPR I. 13[2] ἐν τοῖς ἐν[πρ]οσθε[ν] χρόν[οι]ς, ib. 23[23] ἐν τοῖς τῆς συνβιώσεως χρόνοις: BGU IV. 1126[8] (B.C. 8) ἐπὶ χρόνον ἔτη τρία ἀπὸ Μεχεὶρ τοῦ ἐνεστῶτος . . . ἔτους, and so ib. 1021[9] (iii/A.D.), P Oxy II. 275[19] (A.D. 66) ἐπὶ τὸν ὅλον χρόνον, P Tebt II. 381[19] (A.D. 123) ἐφ' ὅν . . χρόνον: BGU IV. 1128[8] (B.C. 14) ἕως τοῦ προκ(ειμένου) χρό(νου): P Petr II. 13(19)[10] (B.C. 258–253) καθ' ὃν χρόνον, P Giss I. 48[9] (A.D. 202–203) τὰ κατὰ χρόνους δοθέντα ἐπιθέματα: P Oxy XIV. 1641[17] (A.D. 68) μετὰ τὸν χρόνον, "at the end of the period": CPR I. 104[17] (iii A D) μέχρι τοῦ τῆς κυρώσεως χρόνου: P Flor III. 282[9] (A.D. 520) πρὸς ὅλον χρόνον: and P Ryl II. 180[7] (A.D. 124) ὑπὲρ τῶν ἔμπροσθεν χρόνων μέχρι

τῆς ἐνεστώσης ἡμέρας, "for the past down to the present day."

For the conjunction of χρόνος and καιρός as in Ac 1[7], 1 Thess 5[1], cf. P Lond 42[23] (B.C. 168) (= I. p. 30, UPZ i. p. 300, Selections, p. 10), where a woman writes to her husband urging him to return home in view of the suffering through which she had passed, μὴ ὅτι γε τοσούτου χρόνου ἐπιγεγονότος καὶ τοιούτων καιρῶν, "to say nothing of so long time having passed and such times!"—the two words bringing out respectively the period and the occurrences by which it was marked. See further s.v. καιρός, and to the reff. there add K. Dieterich Rhein. Museum N.F. lix. (1904), p. 233 ff., and E. Curtius Gesch. Abhandlungen ii. p. 187 ff.

χρονοτριβέω.

For this NT ἅπ. εἰρ. = "spend time" (Ac 20[16]) Preisigke (Wörterb. s.v.) cites two exx.—UPZ i. 39[29] (= P Lond I. p. 20) λειτουργίαν τοιαύτην παρεχωμένας χρονοτριβεῖσθαι, and similarly ib. 40[20] (= P Par 33[ii.2]), both of B.C. 162–161.

χρύσεος

(for contracted form in LXX, see Thackeray Gr. i. p. 172 f., and in NT, see Proleg. p. 48), "made of gold," "golden": P Ryl II. 124[30] (i/A.D.) ἐνώδιον χρυσοῦν, "a golden ear-ring," ib. 125[17] (A.D. 28–9) μηνίσκο(ν) χρυσο(ῦν), "a golden crescent," BGU II. 423[10] (ii/A.D.) (= Selections, p. 91) ἔλαβα βιάτικον παρὰ Καίσαρος χρυσοῦς τρεῖς, "I received my travelling money from Caesar, three gold pieces."

For the form χρύσεος in late Greek, see the reff. in Glaser De ratione, p. 22, and cf. Radermacher Gr.[2], p. 58.

χρυσίον,

"gold," is used of (a) "gold coin," as in Ac 3[6] al., in P Cairo Zen III. 59351[2] (B.C. 243) χρυσίου δραχμὰς υ. "four hundred drachmae of gold," P Oxy II. 259[14] (A.D. 23) τῶν χρυσίων μν[α]ιήων δύο, "two minae of gold."

(b) "gold ornaments," as in 1 Pet 3[3], in P Michigan Inv. No. 1367[32] (iii/A.D.) (= Journ. of Egypt. Arch. xiii. p. 62) ἐνεγκον ἐρχομένη σου τὰ χρυσία ἀλλὰ μὴ αὐτὰ φορέσῃς ἐν τῷ πλο[ί]ῳ, "when you come bring your gold ornaments, but do not wear them in the boat," P Oxy X. 1273[28] (A.D. 260) τὰ μὲν χρυσία, the gold objects of a dowry.

χρυσοδακτύλιος,

"wearing a gold ring," does not seem to occur except in Jas 2[2], but cf. the similar use of χρυσόχειρ in Lucian Tim. 20, and Epict. i. 22. 18 γέρων πολιὸς χρυσοῦς δακτυλίους ἔχων πολλούς.

χρυσόλιθος,

a sparkling gem of bright yellow colour, perhaps "yellow jasper" (Rev 21[20]): see Swete Apoc. p. 288 f., Hastings' DB iv. p. 620. The word is included in a list of painters' colours in P Lond 928[13] (ii/A.D.) (= III. p. 191).

χρυσόπρασος.

a leek-coloured gem, akin to the beryl (Rev 21[20]) : cf. Pliny *H.N.* xxxvii. 32 "vicinum genus huic est pallidius, et a quibusdam proprii generis existimatur vocaturque chrysoprasus."

χρυσός,

"gold." For the *aurum coronarium* cf. *Ostr* 675[2] (ii/iii A.D.) ὑπ(ὲρ) στεφάνου χρυσοῦ β (δραχμάς), and similarly *ib.* 683[1] *al.* and see Wilcken *Ostr.* i. p. 299f.

The various epithets applied to χρυσός are seen in such passages as CPR I. 12[6] (A.D. 83) χρυσοῦ δοκιμίου, "gold of full value," similarly *ib.* 24[5] (A.D. 136), P Oxy VI. 995[3] (A.D. 170) χρυσοῦ μὲν κοινοῦ, "common gold," similarly *ib.* X. 1273[6.17] (A.D. 260), and *ib.* VIII. 1121[19] (A.D. 205) χρυσῷ οὐκ ὀλίγῳ, "a considerable amount of gold."

χρυσόω,

"overlay with gold" (Rev 17[4], 18[16]) : cf. P Oxy III. 521[7] (ii/A.D.) ξύλινον κεχρυσωμένον, cf. [2].[4], and *Syll* 583 (= [3]996)[25] (i/A.D. ?) κλεῖν κεχρυσωμένην.

χωλός,

"lame." A good ex. of this adj. is afforded by the personal description in a note of sale, Preisigke 428[6] (B.C. 99) εὐθύρ(ρ)ινος ὑποσκνιφο[ῦ] χωλοῦ, "straight-nosed, near-sighted, lame." See also BGU IV. 1196[97] (B.C. 10), III. 712[3.8.20] (ii/A.D.), and P Cairo Goodsp 30[xxxi.21] (A.D. 191-2), and for a metaph. usage Herodas I. 71 (ed. Headlam)—

χωλὴν δ' ἀείδειν χώλ' ἂν ἐξεπαίδευσα,

"I would have taught her to sing her lame song to a limp."

χώρα.

For this word in its widest sense of the "terrestrial region," cf. P Leid G[14] (B.C. 181-143) (= I. p. 42) κυριείαν τῶν [ὑ]πὸ τὸν οὐρανὸν χωρῶ[ν. In P Cairo Zen III. 59451[4] (iii/B.C.) it refers to exemption from compulsory labour κατὰ τὴν χώραν, "throughout the country" or "district," and for a similar geographical sense we may refer to P Oxy IV. 709[3] (c. A.D. 50) τοὺς δὲ λοιποὺς τῆς κάτωι χώρας ν[ομοὺς εἰς Ἀλεξανδρείαν, with reference to the Delta, and *ib.* X. 1274[3] (iii A.D.) βασιλικὴ γραμματεία Ἀλεξανδρέων χώρας, "basilico-grammateus of the territory of the Alexandrians." Note also the comp[d]. in P Oxy VI. 936[5] (iii/A.D.) τὸ προσκύνημά σου ποιῶ παρὰ τοῖς ἐπιχωρίοις θεοῖς, "I perform the act of worship on your behalf to the gods of the country" (Edd.), a son to his father.

The thought of the "country" as opposed to the town (cf. Lk 21[21], Jn 4[35], Jas 5[4]) is seen in P Tebt II. 416[11] (iii/A.D.) μὴ οὖν ἀκούσῃς ἀνθρώπων ὅτι μέλλω μένιν ἐνθάδε, ἐν τά[χι παραγείνομε πρ[ὸ]ς σὲ εἰς τὴν χώραν, "do not therefore listen to people who say that I intend to remain here (in Alexandria) : I am coming speedily into the country to you" (Edd.).

For the metaph. sense "place," "position," which does not occur in the NT, it is sufficient to cite P Oxy XII.

1466[9] (A.D. 213-217) ἐ[ὰ]ι παλλά[ξεται καὶ εἰς ἄτιμον χώραν [καταστή]σεται, "he shall be deprived of his rank and set in a position of dishonour" (Edd.), *ib.* VI. 909[8] (A.D. 322) τοὺς ἐξ ἔθους ταύτην τὴν χώραν ἀποπληροῦντας, "those who customarily discharge such services," (Edd.), *ib.* XIV. 1626[9] (A.D. 325) χώραν μίαν ῥαβδούχου, "the single post of ῥαβδοῦχος." *ib.* VIII. 1134[9] (A.D. 421) ἀποπληρῶν χώραν προνοητοῦ, "discharging the function of an agent" (Edd.).

MGr χώρα : see K. Dieterich in *Rhein. Museum N.F.* lix. (1904), p. 226 ff.

χωρέω

is used with the same variety of connotation in ordinary usage as in the NT., as the following exx. will show :—

(1) "go away," "withdraw," followed by εἰς (Mt 15[17], 2 Pet 3[9]) : P Oxy VII. 1021[8] (A.D. 54) ὁ μὲν ὀφειλόμενος τοῖς προγόνοις καὶ ἐνφανὴς θεὸς Καῖσαρ εἰς αὐτοὺς κεχώρηκε, "the Caesar who had to pay his debt to his ancestors, god manifest, has joined them" (Ed.), with reference to the decease of the Emperor Claudius : cf. BGU III. 700[9] (ii/A.D.) ἄχυρα τὰ καὶ χωροῦντα ἰς ὑπόκαυσιν τοῦ με[γά]λου γυμ[νασίου, P Tebt II. 397[27] (A.D. 198) τῶν δραχμῶν χωρουσῶν ἰς τὸ δημόσιον ὑπέρ τιμῆς πυροῦ, "the drachmae are being paid to the treasury as the price of wheat" (Edd.), *ib.* 423[1] (early ii/A.D.) χωρησάτω εἰς τὴν Τβεκλῦτιν χορτάρακός τε καὶ ἄρακος μ[ο]ναχὸς εἰς σπέρματα, "let the grass aracus and the aracus go alone to Tbeklutis for seed," P Oxy X. 1278[23] (A.D. 214) τὸ[ν κ[ό]προν χωρῆσαι κατ' ἔ[τος εἰς τὸ προκείμ[εν]ον α[ὐ]τῶν ἀμπελ[ι]κὸν κτῆμα, "the dung is to go annually to their aforesaid vineyard" (Edd.), and P Ryl II. 236[25] (A.D. 256) ποίησον . . . ὥμους δύο ἐλαιουργικοὺς κοπῆναι ἵνα χωρήσωσιν εἰς τὸ ἐλαιουργίον Ἀμμωνίου, "have two beams(?) cut for oil-presses so that they may go to the press of Ammonius."

(2) "pass," "pass muster" : P Lond 356[3] (ii/A.D.) (= II. p. 252, *Selections.* p. 50) σαπρὸν αὐτῷ δοῦγαι τὸ μὴ χωροῦν ἐν τῇ Ἀλεξανδρείᾳ, "gave him stale stuff, which will not pass muster in Alexandria," with reference to drugs.

(3) "give place to," "make room for," lit., P Cairo Zen III. 59509[10] (iii/B.C.) ὁ γὰρ ὑ[πάρχων (sc. θησαυρὸς) οὐχ ἱκαν[ός ἐστι] χωρεῖν τὸν σῖτον, of a granary which is not large enough to hold the crop, and metaph., as in 2 Cor 7[2], *Chrest.* I. 238[8] (? A.D. 117) ἐπεὶ οὔτε ὑμεῖς τὴν ὑπόνοιαν ταύτην χωρεῖτε, and *Syll* 376 (= [3]814)[11] (A.D. 67) χαρίζομαι τοσαύτην ὅσην οὐκ ἐχωρήσατε αἰτεῖσθαι, Nero's speech regarding Greek liberty.

χωρίζω,

"separate," "divide" : cf. Wünsch *AF* p. 12[21] ἐξορκίζω ὑμᾶς κατὰ τοῦ ἐπάν[ω] τοῦ οὐρανοῦ θεοῦ . . . ὁ διορίσας τὴν γῆν καὶ χωρίσας τὴν θάλασσαν : cf. Gen 1[?], Isai 45[18]. See also P Fay 110[10] (A.D. 94) χώρισον τὸ κόπριον εἰς τὴν κοπρηγίαν, "take away the manure to the manureheap" (Edd.).

In mid. and pass. the verb passes into the meaning "separate oneself from," "depart," as in P Tor I. 1[8.31]

(B.C. 116) (= *Chrest.* II. p. 32) τοῦ δὲ Δημητρίου χωριζομένου, "abiit Demetrias," *ib.* viii. 10 ἔλεγεν πολύ τι κεχωρίσθαι, "respondet longe abs re esse," P Oxy XII. 1479⁷ (late i/B.C.) ἀφ' οὗ κεχώρισαι τῇ ιϛ, "since you went away on the 16th," P Grenfell II. 36⁹ (B.C. 95) μὴ λυπεῖσθε ἐπὶ τοῖς χωρισθεῖσι. ὑπελαμβάνοσαν φονευθήσεσθαι, "do not grieve over the departed. They expected to be killed" (Edd.), BGU IV. 1204⁶ (B.C. 28) τὴν οὖν ἀπάντων ἀντιφώνησιν ἐν τάχ[ει πέμ]ψον διὰ τὸ πλοῖον χωρίζεσθαι, and P Ryl II. 125¹⁰ (A.D. 28-9) ἐμοῦ χωρισθέντος εἰς ἀποδημίαν βιωτ[ι]κῶν χάριν, "when I had left home on business concerning my livelihood" (Edd.).

The word has almost become a technical term in connexion with divorce, as in 1 Cor 7¹⁰. ¹¹. ¹⁵; cf. BGU IV. 1102⁹ (B.C. 13) συνχωροῦσιν Ἀ[πο]λλωνία καὶ Ἑρμογένης κεχ[ω]ρίσθαι ἀπ' ἀλλήλων τῆς συστ[ά]σης αὐτοῖς συνβιώσεως, P Ryl II. 154²⁵ (A.D. 66) ἐὰν δὲ διαφορᾶς αὐτοῖς γεναμένης [χ]ωρίζωνται ἀπ' ἀλλήλων . . ., "but if any difference arises between them and they separate the one from the other . . ." (Edd.), BGU I. 251⁶ (A.D. 81), and *ib.* IV. 1045²² (A.D. 154): and for the subst. in a similar context, see P Ryl II. 154³⁰ (A.D. 66) κατὰ] τὸν ἀπ' ἀλλ[ή]λων τῶν [γα]μούντω[ν χ]ωρ[ι]σμό[ν.

χωρίον,

"a piece of land," "a field": P Hal I. 1⁸⁵ (mid. iii/B.C.) ἐάν τι]ς ὀφρύηνην [παρὰ] ἀλλότριον χω[ρίον οἰ]κοδομῇ, τὸν [ὅρον μὴ π]αραφαινέτω, P Oxy VI. 985 (2nd half i/A.D.) εἰς τὸ ἀπηλιωτικὸν χῶμα τοῦ χωρίον, *ib.* VIII. 1141⁶ (iii/A.D.) τὰ κατεπείγοντα ἄλ(λα) ἔργ(α) χωρ(ίου) Γαϊανοῦ, "the other pressing work at the farmstead of Gaianus" (Ed.), *ib.* IX. 1220²³ (iii/A.D.) περὶ τῶν χωρίων, ἐὰν παραγένῃ σὺν θεῷ, μαθήσι τὴν διάθεσιν αὐτῶν, "about the fields, if you come, D.V., you will learn their condition" (Ed.), P Lond 214⁹ (A.D. 270-275) (= II. p. 161, *Chrest.* I. p. 200) γενόμενος εἰς ἀμπελικὸν χωρίον καλούμενον Ἐλαιῶνα, and *Syll* 429 (= ³ 911)²⁰ (B.C. 300-250) ἐπισκοπῶνται τά τε χωρία εἰ γεωργεῖται κατὰ τὰς συνθήκας: cf. *Preisigke* 1973, a list of place names on ostraca from Oxyrhynchus—3¹¹ χωρίον Ἄνδρ έου), χωρίον Παρορίου, *al.*

For the use of "local" plants for magical purposes cf. P Osl I. 1²³⁸ (iv/A.D.) κρέμασον εἰς κάλαμον χωρίου, "suspend it (*sc.* a frog) on a reed taken from the spot," with the editor's note.

χωρίς

1. as adv. "separately," Jn 20⁷: Bauer (*HZNT ad l.*) aptly compares Ignat. *Trall.* 11 οὐ δύναται οὖν κεφαλὴ χωρὶς γεννηθῆναι ἄνευ μελῶν, "now it is not possible that a head should be born separately without members." For an ex. from the *Κοινή* cf. the medical receipt P Oxy VIII. 1088⁴¹ (early i/A.D.) λῆα ποιήσας καὶ χωρὶς ἕκαστον ἀναπλάσας μεθ' ὕδατος, "pound and work them up separately with water" (Ed.).

2. as prep. c. gen. "apart from," "without": (a) of persons—P Oxy VI. 932¹⁰ (late ii/A.D.) τὰ χοιρίδια χωρὶς μοῦ μὴ πώλι, "do not sell the young pigs without me" (Edd.), and BGU III. 920¹ (A.D. 180-181) χωρὶς κυρίου κατὰ τὰ Ῥωμαί[ων ἔθη. (b) of things—P Tebt I. 61 (*a*)¹⁸⁶ (B.C. 118-117) χωρὶς σπέρματος καὶ τῆς ἄλλης δα(πάνης), P Oxy IX. 1211¹¹ (medical receipt—ii/A.D.) πᾶν ἄρωμα χωρὶς λιβάνου, "every spice except frankincense." (c) of abstract nouns (cf. Philem¹⁴, and the equivalent P Tebt I. 104²⁸ (B.C. 92) ἄνευ τῆς Φιλίσκου γνώ[μ]ης—P Oxy II. 237ᵛⁱⁱ. ²⁶ (A.D. 186) χωρὶς λόγου, *ib.* VIII. 1128²¹ (A.D. 173) χωρὶς ὑπερθέσεως, "without delay," and *ib.* VIII. 1130¹⁹ (A.D. 484) χωρὶς ἐγγραφοῦς ἐντάγιον (= -ίου), "without a written deed."

3 = "besides": (a) the object being excluded—P Oxy VIII. 1124¹⁶ (A.D. 26) χωρὶς τῶν προκειμένων, "apart from the amounts aforesaid," P Ryl II. 138¹³ (A.D. 34) χωρὶς δὲ τούτου κατέλαβα τοῦτον . . ., "over and beyond this I detected him . . ." (Edd.), P Amh II. 85⁹ (A.D. 78) χωρὶς τῆς κατ' ἄρουραν ἀρταβιήας, "excluding the tax of an artaba on each aroura" (Edd.), *ib.* 86¹⁰ (A.D. 78) χωρὶς γνησίων δημοσίων, "excluding public charges proper" (Edd.), P Oxy I. 101¹² (A.D. 142) σπεῖραι καὶ ξυλαμῆσαι οἷς ἐὰν αἱρῆται χωρὶς ἰσάτεως καὶ ὀχομενίου, the lessee "may sow and gather whatever crops he chooses with the exception of woad and coriander (?)" (Edd.), *ib.* IV. 724⁸ (A.D. 155) apprenticeship to a shorthand-writer at a certain salary χωρὶς ἑορτικῶν, "excluding holidays."

(b) the object being included, as in Mt 14²¹, 15³⁸, 2 Cor 11²⁸:—P Oxy II. 249⁷ (supplementary property return—A.D. 80) ἀπογράφομαι . . χωρὶς τῶν προαπεγραψάμην . . ., "I register in addition to what I have previously registered . . .," P Ryl II. 175²² (A.D. 168) χωρὶς ἄλλων ὧν ὀφείλουσι, "apart from other sums which they owe" (Edd.), and BGU II. 393¹³ (A.D. 168) ἄλλο δὲ οὐδὲ ἁπλῶς τελέσω τῷ καθόλου χωρὶς τῶν προκειμένων.

4. For χωρὶς c. inf. cf. P Lond 1166¹⁴ (A.D. 42) (= III. p. 105) χωρὶς τοῦ παράσχεσθαι τοὺς ὁμολογοῦντας (*l.* ὁμολογοῦντας) τὴν καῦσιν—with reference to the heating of baths, and BGU III. 859¹⁷ (ii/A.D.) ἐπελε[ύ]σεσθαι τρόπῳ μηδενί . . . χωρὶς τοῦ μένειν κύρια καὶ τὰ προγεγρ αμμένα).

With 1 Cor 14⁵ ἐκτὸς εἰ μὴ διερμηνεύῃ (cf. 15², 1 Tim 5¹⁹), cf. *C. and B.* ii. p. 391, No. 254 χωρὶς εἰ μή τι πάθῃ ἡ θυγάτηρ μου.

Mayser *Gr.* p. 245 cites a shortened form χῶρι from P Amh II. 113²² (A.D. 157) χῶρι ἄλλων, but the same document shows χωρὶς a few lines further down, ³⁶ χω[ρὶ]s ἄλλων.

As in the case of all the prepositions, the monographs of Kuhring, Rossberg, and Regard (see Abbreviations I. General) should be consulted.

χῶρος,

(Lat. *caurus*), "the north-west wind," and hence the quarter from which it comes, Ac 27¹²: see Ramsay *Paul*, p. 321 f.

Ψ

ψάλλω—ψηλαφάω

ψάλλω,

properly = "play on a harp," but in the NT, as in Jas 5[13], = "sing a hymn": cf. *Syll* 523 (= [3] 578)[18] (ii/B.C.) διδάξει . . . κιθαρίζειν ἢ ψάλλειν, *Pelagia-Legenden* p. 14[23] ἤρξατο ψάλλειν τὴν τρίτην [ὥραν, and Menander Ἐπιτρέπ. 260 ἔψαλλον κόραις. See *s.v.* ψαλμός. MGr ψάλλω, ψέλνω, "sing."

ψαλμός,

"psalm" or "song," sung to a harp accompaniment: see *Syll* 524 (= [3] 959)[10] (ii/A.D.), where κιθαρισμός and ψαλμός are distinguished, the former, according to the editor, being "de eo qui plectro utitur," the latter "de eo qui ipsis digitis chordas pulsat." See also Preuschen-Bauer *Wörterb. s.v.*

ψευδής,

"false," "untrue": P Cairo Zen II. 59140[14] (B.C. 256) γνώριζε οὖν Κριτίαν γράφοντά σοι ψευδῆ, P Tebt I. 73[6] (B.C. 113-11) ἀνεγηνέχθαι ἐν ψευ[δ]έσι, and BGU III. 1011[ii. 16] (ii/B.C.) διότι γὰρ πολ[λὰ] ληρώ[δη] καὶ ψευδῆ προσαγ[γ]έλ[λε]ται κατανοεῖς καὶ αὐτός. Exx. of a later date seem to be rare, but cf. *OGIS* 669[54] (i/A.D.) ἐάν τι εὑρεθῶσι ψευδὲς ἢ ⟨ι⟩ παρὰ τὸ δέον παραγεγραφότες, and CPR I. 232[10] (ii/iii A.D.) ψευδεῖς αἰτίας ἡμῖν ἐπιφέρειν. The word is supplied in the Byzantine papyrus P Masp III. 67295[6].

For the adj. ψευδοπόρφυρος, "of false purple," see P Oxy VII. 1051[15] (iii/A.D.).

ψευδολόγος,

"speaking false things" (1 Tim 4[2]). For the corr. subst. cf. CPR I. 19[15] (A.D. 330) ἀντεπιστάλματα . . . μετὰ ψευδολογίας, "replies full of false statements."

ψεύδομαι,

"speak falsely," "deceive by lies": P Par 47[6] (*c.* B.C. 152-1) (as read by Wilcken *UPZ* i. p. 332) ὅτι ψεύδηι πάντα καὶ οἱ παρὰ σὲ θεοὶ ὁμοίως, "for you lie in all things and your gods likewise," P Lond 897[ii. 2] (A.D. 84) (== III. p. 206) ἐκ[ε]ῖνος μὲν [τ]ότε ἐψεύσατο, νυνεὶ δὲ ὑμεῖς τὴν ἀλήθειαν γράφεται (*l.* γράψατε), P Oxy II. 237[iv. 24, v. 22] (A.D. 186), and *OGIS* 669[28] (i/A.D.) ἐὰν δέ τις ἐλεγχθῆι ψευσά[μενος, and the late P Oxy XVI. 1868[3] (vi/vii A.D.) οἴδαμεν καὶ πεπίσμεθα τὴν σὴν γνησίαν λαμπρότητα [μὴ] ψευδομένην, μάλιστα καὶ ὅταν ὁμώσης (*l.* ὁμόσης), "we know and are persuaded that your true illustriousness does not speak falsely, especially when you have sworn" (Edd.).

The verb is common in such phrases as P Oxy X. 1260[32] (A.D. 98) ὀμνύω Αὐτοκράτορα Καίσαρα Νέρουαν . . . μὴ ἐψεῦσθαι, *ib.* 1264[20] (A.D. 272) ὀμνύω τὸν ἔθιμον Ῥωμαίοις ὅρκον μὴ ἐψεῦσθα[ι, "I swear the oath customary with Romans that I have not made a false statement" (Edd.).

ψευδομαρτυρέω,

"bear false witness" (Mt 19[18] *al.*): cf. the compd. ψευδογραφέω in P Tebt I. 78[17] (B.C. 110-8) μηθὲν ἐψ[ευ]δογραφηκέναι, "I have made no false statement" (Edd.).

ψευδομαρτυρία,

"false witness." The subst. ψευδομαρτύριον occurs *sexies* in P Hal I. 1 (mid. iii/B.C.), e.g.[11] ἀπὸ μὲν τοῦ δικαστηρίου ἐπιφερέτω ὁ [εἰσ]αγωγεὺς ἐπὶ τὴν τοῦ ψευδομαρτυρίου.

ψεῦδος,

"falsehood," "untruth": cf. *Chrest.* I. 110A[18] (B.C. 110) οὐθὲν ψεῦδος ἐν τῷ ὅρκῳ ἐστίν, and the Delphic precept *Syll*[3] 1268[27] ψεῦδος αἰσχύνο[υ. In 2 Thess 2[11] τῷ ψεύδει is contrasted with τῆς ἀληθείας (ver. 10). Note that "among the Persians 'the Lie' (*Dranga*, akin to the Avestan demon *Druj*) is a comprehensive term for all evil" (Moulton *Exp T* xviii. p. 537).

ψευδώνυμος,

"falsely named" (1 Tim 6[20]), cf. *Kaibel* 42[1]—

ψευδώνυμον ἀλλά με δαίμων
θῆκεν ἀφαρπάξας ὠκύτατ' εἰς Ἄιδα.

ψεύστης,

"a liar." On the place which ψεύστης occupies in the primitive Christian lists of vices, corresponding to Jewish or pagan lists, see Deissmann *LAE*[2]. p. 315 ff.

ψηλαφάω.

From meaning "feel," "touch" (as in Lk 24[39], cf. Gen 27[12]), ψηλαφάω comes in late Greek to denote "examine closely," as in Polyb. viii. 18. 4 πᾶσαν ἐπίνοιαν ἐψηλάφα, and P Lond IV. 1396[1] (A.D. 709-714): cf. Thumb *Hellen.* p. 250. See also an interesting official letter of the Arab period, edited by H. I. Bell in *Journ. of Egypt. Archaeology* xii. (1926), p. 273 (= Preisigke III. p. 251) ἐπείπερ ψηλαφήσαντός μου τὸν λόγον τῶν ἐπιζητουμένων δι' ὑμῶν ἀπὸ διαγράφου, "whereas, on my examining the register of sums demanded of you in respect of poll-tax." For the difficult

Heb 12[18] E. C. Selwyn (*JTS* xii. p. 133 f.) suggests a conjectural reading πεφεψαλωμένῳ (ὄρει) = "a calcined volcano."

ψηφίζω,

"count up," "reckon" (lit. with pebbles): P Oxy I. 55[12] (A.D. 283) ἀ]κολού(θω]ς τοῖς ψυφιστιση ἐν τῇ γρατίστη (*l.* ψηφισθεῖσι . . . κρατίστῃ) βουλῇ, "in accordance with the vote of the high council" (Edd.), *ib.* 41[7] (report of a public meeting—iii/iv A.D.) ψηφισθήτω ὁ πρύ(τανις) ἐν τυαύτη (*l.* τοιαύτη) [ἡμέρ]ᾳ, "let the president receive the vote on this great day" (Edd.), and P Fay 20[abbot] (iii/iv A.D.) ὁπόσα . . . ἐψηφίσμεθα . . . καὶ ἔτι ψηφισθησόμεθα, "what sums I have been voted and shall yet be voted." For constr. c. inf. *OGIS* 48[13] (B.C. 240) ἐψηφίσαν[το] ἐξ ἐπιλέκτων ἀνδρῶν τὴν βουλὴν [καὶ τὰ] δικαστή[ρια αἱρεῖσ]θαι. In P Cairo Zen III. 50328[111] (B.C. 248) ψηφίσας ταῦτα, the verb has the meaning "calculate."

For the subst. ψήφισμα, cf. P Oxy I. 41 as cited *supra*, where the citizens acclaim the president, [8] πολλῶν ψηφισμάτων ἄξιος, πολλῶν ἀγαθῶν ἀπολαύομεν διὰ σαί, πρύτανι, "many votes do you deserve, for many are the blessings which we enjoy through you, O president" (Edd.). The ψηφίσματα in P Tebt I. 6[23] (B.C. 140–139) (= *Chrest.* I. p. 507) are decrees of the priests (see *Archiv* iv. p. 500), and not royal decrees as the editors think probable, referring to P Tor I. 1[iii. 8] (B.C. 116) (= *Chrest.* II. p. 37) κατὰ τοὺς πολιτικοὺς νόμους καὶ τὰ ψηφίσματα. See further Preisigke *Fachwörter s.v.*

MGr ψηφίζω, ψηφῶ, "I observe, esteem."

ψῆφος.

For ψῆφος, "a pebble," as in Rev 2[17], cf. P Petr II. 13(6)[15] (B.C. 258–253) where, with reference to a stone contract, mention is made of removing τὰς ψήφους, by which the editor understands "the pebbles lying over the rock to be quarried."

From the use of pebbles in voting, the word comes readily to mean "vote," "number": cf. P Lips I. 105[19] (i/ii A.D.) (= *Chrest.* I. p. 276) μὴ καταγειοχέναι (*l.* καταγηοχέναι) ἑκάστ[ου] εἴδους τὴν ψῆφον, and *ib.* 64[38] (c. A.D. 368) (= *Chrest.* I. p. 353) ὡς λίτραν χρυσίου ταῖς ταμιακαῖς ψήφοις δοῦναι προσταχθήσει.

For Rev 13[18] cf. an inscr. edited by Cumont in *REGr* xv. (1902), p. 5, which concludes—ἐν) ὀνόματι οὗ ἐστιν ψῆφος τξε: see Wünsch *AF*, p. 23. Note also P Par 63[xiii. 25] (B.C. 164) τὴν ἐν χρόνῳ [βο]υλευομ[ένη]ν ψῆφον ἐ[ξε]τάσοντα.

ψιθυριστής,

lit. "a whisperer," but used with special reference to secret attacks on a person's character, as compared with κατάλαλος, an open detractor.

For the combination in Rom 1[29] (cf. 2 Cor 12[20]) Lightfoot (*Notes*, p. 256) cites Tac. *Ann.* vi. 7 "cum primores senatus infimas etiam delationes exercerent, alii propalam, multi per occultum."

ψιχίον,

"a crumb" (Mt 15[27], Mk 7[28]) is "not found in Grk. auth.," according to Grimm: cf. MGr ψίχα.

ψυχή.

As in the case of σάρξ (*q.v.*), no attempt can be made here to treat fully this important word; but a few miscellaneous exx. may be given to illustrate its varied uses in the Κοινή.

1. (a) = "breath of life": Wünsch *AF*, p. 11[15] στρέβλωσον αὐτῶν τὴν ψυχὴν καὶ τὴν καρδίαν ἵνα μὴ (π]νέωσιν, P Leid W[xii. 29] (ii/iii A.D.) (= II. p. 123) αἰσθησάμενος (*l.* ἀσθμασάμενος) καὶ ἐγένετο Ψυχὴ καὶ πάντα ἐκεινήθη (*l.* ἐκινήθη) "anhelitu ducto, et nata est Anima, et omnia mota sunt" (Ed.).

(b) = "life": P Tebt I. 56[11] (late ii/B.C.) καλῶς οὖν ποιήσῃς εὐχαριστῆσαι πρῶτον μὲν τοῖς θεοῖς, δεύτερον δὲ σῶσαι ψυχὰς πολλάς, "please therefore in the first place to give thanks to the gods and secondly to save many lives," by providing for their maintenance, P Oxy XII. 1409[22] (A.D. 278) ἐὰν γὰρ τοιοῦτο ἐπιχειρ[ῆσ]αι τολμή[σ]η . . . ἴστω . . . περὶ αὐτῆς τῆς ψυχῆς τὸν ἀγῶνα ἕξει, "if any one dare to attempt exactions, let him know that his life will be at stake" (Edd.), *ib.* VII. 1033[11] (A.D. 392) μὴ ἐχόντων ἡμῶν τὴν βοήθειαν εἴτ' οὖν τοὺς δημοσίους καὶ τοὺς ἐφοδευτὰς πολλάκεις σχεδὸν εἰπε⟨ῖ⟩ν εἰς ψυχὴν ἐκεινδυνεύσαμεν, "having no assistance either of public guards or inspectors we often run the risk almost of our lives" (Ed.). *Syll* 342 (= [3] 762)[39] (B.C. 48) ψυχῇ καὶ σ[ώ]ματι παραβαλλόμενος, and Herodas III. 3 (ed. Headlam) of a schoolmaster flogging a pupil ἄχρις ἡ ψυχή] αὐτοῦ ἐπὶ χειλέων μοῦνον ἡ κακὴ λειφθῆι, "till his life—curse it—remain hanging on his lips."

2. = "the soul," as the seat of the feelings, desires: P Grenf I. 1[i. 9] (Alexandrian Erotic Fragment—ii/B.C.) συνοδηγὸν ἔχω τὸ πολὺ πῦρ ἐν τῇ ψυχῇ μου καιόμενον, BGU IV. 1040[21] (ii/A.D.) καθαρὰ]ν γὰρ ἔχων τὴν ψυχήν, P Giss I. 3[9] (A.D. 117) (= *Chrest.* I. p. 571) γέλωσι καὶ μέθαις ταῖς ἀπὸ κρήνης τὰς ψυχὰς ἀνέντες, in connexion with Hadrian's accession to the throne, *Archiv* v. p. 393, No. 312[9] (a magic spell—ii/A.D.) ἄρτι ἄρτι ταχὺ ταχὺ ἐκ ψυχῆς καὶ καρδίας (cf. Eph 6[5]), P Oxy VI. 903[33] (iv/A.D.) καὶ περὶ Ἀντίλλας τῆς δούλης αὐτοῦ ἔμεινεν θλίβων τὴν ψυχήν μου, "he also persisted in vexing my soul about his slave Antilla" (Edd.), an accusation against a husband, *ib.* XVI. 1873[3] (late v/A.D.) χιμαζομένης δέ μου τῆς ψυχῆς, "while my soul is tempest-tossed" (Edd.), *ib.* 1874[16. 17] (vi/A.D.) a Christian letter of condolence in which the writer prays that it may be granted to the mourners to sing with the departed in Paradise ὅτι κρίνοντε (*l.* ὅτε κρίνονται ἑ ψυχὲ (*l.* αἱ ψυχαί) τῶν ἀνθρώπων, "when the souls of men are judged," and adds παρακαλῶ σε, κύριέ μου, μὲ βάλης [?λύπη]ν εἰς τὸ ψυχί σου καὶ ἀπολήσις τὸ (*l.* ἀπολέσῃς τὰ) πράγματά σου, "I exhort you, my lord, not to put grief into your soul and ruin your fortunes" (Edd.), and P Grenf I. 61[4] (vi/A.D.) a letter apparently from a slave addressed τῷ δεσπότῃ μου τῆς ψυχῆς γλυκυτάτῳ καὶ τιμιωτάτῳ.

The word is naturally common in memorial inscrr., e.g. *Kaibel* 701[1] μνησθείης, ἀγαθὴ ψυχή, Γερμανικέ, *Preisigke* 6008[2] (v/vi A.D.) εὐχαριστήριον Ταριτσένης ὑπὲρ ἀναπαύσεως ψυχῆς Διδύμου, *ib.* 6089[1] ἀνάπαυσον τὴν ψυχὴν αὐτοῦ [ε]ἰς κώλπης Ἀβ]ραὰμ κτλ. The Christian gravestones from Old Dongola, referred to by F. C. Burkitt in

JTS iv. (1903), p. 585 ff. may be noted as showing the name of the dead person in apposition to **ψυχή** (see below). Cf. also the curse in P Amh II. 153¹⁹ (vi/vii A.D.) ἵνα ὁ θεὸς σήψῃ τὴν ψυχήν σου ὡς διέσηψάς με εἰς τὴν κατ[α]γραφὴν ταύτην, "may God destroy your soul, if you destroy me in the matter of this register" (Edd.).

3. In BGU IV. 1141²⁴ (B.C. 13) (= Olsson, p. 45) οὐδὲ γὰρ ἐφιλίασά σοι εἰς τὸ ἀφαρπάσαι τι, ἀλλὰ ἡ σὴ ψυχὴ ἐπίσταται, ὅτι ὡς δοῦλος ἐπ᾽ ἐλευθερίᾳ θέλει ἀρέσαι οὕτω κτλ., Olsson (p. 50) notes that ἡ σὴ ψυχή = σύ, and compares Ac 2⁴¹˙⁴³, 27³⁷. Note also the interchange of τὴν ψυχὴν αὐτοῦ and ἑαυτόν in Lk 9²⁴˙²⁵, and see *Proleg.* pp. 87, 105 n².

4. With the trichotomy in 1 Thess 5²³, cf. the fragment of a Christian letter P Oxy VIII. 1161⁶ (iv/A.D.) (= Ghedini, p. 226)] . . ας καὶ τῷ ἀγαθ[ῷ ἡμῶ]ν σωτῆρι καὶ τῷ οι[ί]ῷ (*l.* υ[ἱ]ῷ) αὐτοῦ τῷ ἠγαπημένῳ ὅπως οὗτοι πάντες β[ο]ηθήσωσιν ἡμῶν τῷ σώματι, τῇ ψυχῇ, τῷ [[πν]ευματ]ι] πν(εύματ)ι, " . . . (to our God) and gracious Saviour and to his beloved Son, that they all may succour our body, soul, and spirit " (Ed.), and see further Milligan *Thess.* p. 78 f., and H. A. A. Kennedy *St. Paul and the Mystery-Religions*, p. 142, where evidence is adduced from Philo and the Liturgy of Mithras showing the assimilation of ψυχή to πνεῦμα.

For the expressive **ψυχαγωγέω** cf. P Hamb I. 91²² (B.C. 167) ἡ αἰχμάλ]ωτος ψυχαγωγηθεῖσα ὑπὸ τῶν ἐκ τῆς κώμης ἱερείων . . . . P Ryl II. 128¹² (*c.* A.D. 30) complaint of a breach of contract by a mill-hand ἀλλότρια φρονήσασα ἐνκαταλιποῦσα τὸ ἐλαιούργιον ἀπηλλάγη ψοιχαγωγηθεῖσα ὑπὸ τοῦ πατρὸς αὐτῆς, "who changed her mind, left the mill, and departed, persuaded by her father" (Edd.). The subst. in the sense of "gratification," "enchantment," is found in Aristeas 78 ψυχαγωγία τις ἦν μετὰ θαυμασμοῦ.

ψυχικός,

the "natural" as opposed to **πνευματικός** the "spiritual" man in 1 Cor 2¹⁴, cf. 15⁴⁴˙⁴⁶. According to Souter *Lex. s.v.* the reference is to ψυχή in the sense of "the principle of life and the basis of its emotional aspect, animating the present body of flesh, in contrast to the higher life." Cf. the opening prayer of the Liturgy of Mithras with its reference to ἀνθρωπίνης μου ψυχικῆς δυνάμεως, "my human natural powers," as cited by H. A. A. Kennedy *St. Paul and the Mystery-Religions*, p. 143.

For the contrast with **σωματικός**, see *Syll* 303 (= ³ 656)²⁰ (*c.* B.C. 166) ψυχικὴν ἅμα καὶ σω[ματικὴν] ὑπέμειναν [κ]α[κ]οπαθίαν. The adj. also occurs in *Kaibel* 815⁴ ψυχικὰ δῶρα, of gifts to Mercury on behalf of a deceased wife.

ψῦχος,

"cold" (Jn 18¹⁸ *al.*), as in the i/A.D. acrostic P Tebt II. 278¹⁶ᶠ —

χιμὼν γάρ ἐστι,
ψῦχος πολύ.

Cf. *Syll* 537 (= ³969⁹²) (B.C. 347-6) ὅπως δ᾽ ἂν καὶ ψῦχος

ἦι ἐν τῆι σκευοθήκηι. The form ψῦξις occurs in the household account Preisigke 5304³ (Byz.), perhaps in the sense of "wine-cooler."

ψυχρός,

"cold": neut. "cold water" (Mt 10⁴²): cf. the inscr. found in a burial chamber Preisigke 335 δίδοι σοι] Ὄσιρις τὸ ψυχρὸν ὕδωρ, and so often. The adj. appears alone in the medical *Syll* 804 (= ³1170)²⁹ ἀναγαργαρίζεσθαι ψυχρῷ πρὸς τὴν σταφυλήν, "to be used as a gargle with cold water for the uvula," and for ψυχροφόρος cf. P Oxy VI. 896¹¹ (A.D. 316) τῶν δύο ψυχροφόρων, "the two cold water conductors," in connexion with baths.

ψύχω

is used metaph. in pass. in Mt 24¹² = "am become cool." For the act. "make cool," see P Petr II. 14 3˙⁸ (iii/B.C.) (as read p. 30) εἰς τὸ θεμέλιον ψῦξαι, "for drying the foundation"—with reference to certain building operations. See Lob. *Phryn.* p. 318.

ψωμίζω.

For ψωμίζω which in late Greek has come to be used = "feed," "nourish," generally (cf. Rom 12²⁰, 1 Cor 13³), cf. the subst. ψώμισμα in the food-contract BGU IV. 1058¹⁵ (B.C. 13) (as read *Chrest.* II. p. 181) σὺν ἐλαίωι καὶ ψωμίσματι, "with oil and bread."

ψωμίον,

"a little bit," "morsel," of food. For an early ex. of this diminutive, prior to Jn 13²⁶ᶠ, see P Tebt I. 33¹⁴ (B.C. 112) τὸ γεινόμενον . . . τοῖς κροκο[δείλοις] ψωμίον, "the customary tit-bits for the crocodiles." Other exx. are P Grenf II. 67¹¹ (A.D. 237) (= *Selections*, p. 109) ὑπὲρ τιμήμα[τος] . . . ψωμίων ζε[ύ]γη ιε, "by way of payment 15 couples of delicacies," in connexion with the hire of dancing girls, P Oxy XII. 1489⁵ (late iii/A.D.) ἤ (*l.* εἰ) πεποι⟨ή⟩κατε ψωμία, πέμψον μοι, "if you have made any cakes, send them to me" (Edd.), and similarly *ib.* 1591⁷ (iv/A.D.), P Grenf II. 77²⁰ (letter regarding funeral expenses —iii/iv A.D.) (= *Selections*, p. 121) ὑπ ἐρ] δαπάνης ἐν ψωμίοις καὶ προσφαγίοις (δραχμαὶ) ιϛ, "for outlay in delicacies and foods 16 drachmae," so²⁶, and *Preisigke* 1975 (ostrakon—v/A.D.) ψωμία εἴκοσι.

The use of ψωμίον for "bread" (see *s.v.* ἄρτος) may be seen in P Lond 1014¹⁹ (A.D. 335?) (= III. p. 266) μὴ ἀμελήσηται οὖν περὶ ἡμῶν, ἄδελφοι, ἐπιδὴ τὰ ψωμία ἀφήκαν ὀπίσω, "do not neglect us then, brethren, since they left behind the bread," cf.³² ἀποστίλατέ μοι ὀλίγα ψωμία, "send me a few loaves" (see the editor's note, and cf. *J. Eg. Arch.* xiii. p. 118, where reference is made to an art. by Kretschmer on *Brot und Wein im Neugriechischen* in *Glotta* xv. (1926), p. 60 ff.), and P Oxy VII. 1071⁵ (v/A.D.) ἐὰν κελεύεις ἵνα ποιήσουσιν αὐτὰ ψωμία ἐνταῦθα κ[α]ὶ πέμψουσιν αὐτὰ εἰς τὴν Ἰβιόνος, γράψον αὐτοῖς, "if you order them to make the bread here and send it to the village of Ibion, write to them" (Ed.).

A curious ex. of the word is afforded by a letter of the farmer Gemellus, P Fay 119³⁴ (c. A.D. 100), where writing to his son he enjoins—πέμσις τὰ κτήνη κοπρηγεῖν εἰς τὸ λάχανον . . ἐπὶ κράζει Πᾶσις εἴνα μὴ εἰς ψωμὶν γένηται διὰ τὸ ὕδωρ, "send the animals to carry manure at the vegetable-ground, for Pasis is crying out that we must not allow it (apparently manure!) to be dissolved by the water"

(Edd.). The letter, it will be noted, is illiterate. MGr ψωμί, dim. ψωμάκι.

ψώχω,

"rub." The fact that up till now ψώχω is attested only in Lk 6¹, and (in the middle) in Nicander *Theriaca*, 619, cannot be stressed for Luke's medical knowledge, but is rather a mere statistical accident : see Cadbury *JBL* xlv. (1926), p. 199.

Ω

ὦ—ὠνέομαι

ὦ.

For ὦ as interj. c. voc., as in Ac 1¹ *al.*, cf. BGU II. 665ⁱⁱⁱ·⁸ (i/A.D.) ἐρρῶσθ[αί σε] εὔχ(ομαι) ὦ πάτερ. Moulton in *Proleg.* p. 71 discusses the progressive omission of ὦ in Hellenistic as compared with classical Greek : cf. Blass-Debrunner § 146.

ὧδε.

(1) "here" : P Grenf II. 36¹⁷ (B.C. 95) ὧδε, ἢ ἐν Διοσπόλει, "here, or in Diospolis," P Oxy IV. 736⁹² (*c.* A.D. I) ὅ]τε ὧδε ἐδείπνει, "when he was dining here," BGU IV. 1097¹¹ (time of Claudius or Nero) ὧδέ ἐστιν παρ' [ἐ]μοί, P Fay 123¹⁰ (*c.* A.D. 100) ὡς ἔχωι ὧδε ἡμέρας ὀλίγας, "as I am staying here a few days," P Oxy VIII. 1160¹¹(iii/iv A.D.) διμήνου δὲ ἤργηκα ὡδη (*l.* ὧδε), "I have been idle here for two months" (Ed.), and *ib.* IX. 1222³ (iv/A.D.) εἵνα θεραπεύσω αὐτὸν ὧδε ἔξω, "in order that I may doctor him away here" (Ed.).

For the metaph. usage = "in this circumstance or connexion," as in 1 Cor 4² *al.*, cf. P Fay 117¹² (A.D. 108) ἐπὶ Ἐρασο[ς] τὰ Ἀρποχράτια ὧδε τάχα ιδ πγ[ήσ]ι, "since Erasus is going to celebrate the festival of Harpocrates so soon on the 14th" (Edd.), and P Meyer 22⁶ (iii/iv A.D.) λήσωμε (*l.* λήμψομαι) ὧδε χαλκῶν (*l.* χαλκόν), "I shall in this way receive the money."

(2) "hither" : PSI VI. 599³ (iii/B.C.) ἥκαμεν ὧδε ὥστε ἐργάζεσθαι, "we have come hither to work," P Oxy II. 295⁴ (*c.* A.D. 35) γίνωσκε ὅτι Σέλευκος ἐλθὼν ὧδε πέφευγε, "know that Seleucus came hither and has fled," *Preisigke* 998³ (A.D. 16-17) ἀπὸ χιμῶνος ἐλασθεὶς ὧδε, and the wall-scratching *ib.* 1854 Ἄσελλος ὧδε γέγον[α.

ᾠδή.

"a song" (Eph 5¹⁹, *al.*) : cf. the Ephesian tomb inscr. *Kaibel* Add. 297a³—

> δακρύοις τε καὶ ᾠδαῖς
> τειμῶσιν τὸν σόν, Μαρκελλεῖνε, τάφον,

and *Syll* 615 (= ³1024)¹⁶ (*c.* B.C. 200) ἐπὶ ᾠδῆι ὑπὲρ καρποῦ Δήμητρι, with reference to a hymn sung in the course of a sacrifice.

For ᾠδός, "a singer," see *OGIS* 56⁶⁹ (B.C. 238) τούς τε ᾠδοὺς ἄνδρας καὶ τὰς γυναῖκας, *ib.* 352¹¹ (B.C. 163 130) διδόναι τῶν ᾠδῶν τῶι νικήσα[ντι . . .

ὠδίν.

For the late form ὠδίν (cf. Blass-Debrunner § 46. 4) = "birth-pangs," as in 1 Thess 5³, cf. the sepulchral inscr.

Preisigke 4312⁴ᶠ (Ptol.) θνήσκω δ' ἄλγεσ[ι πικροτάτοις ὠδῖνας προφυγοῦσα συναίμον[ς . . ., also *Kaibel* 145⁴ (ii/A.D.)—

> τοῦ με χάριν προφυγόντα πικρὰν ὠδῖνα τεκούσης
> ἠγάγετε ἱμερτοῦ πρὸς φάος ἠελίου.

On the force of λύσας τὰς ὠδῖνας τοῦ θανάτου in Ac 2²⁴, see Field *Notes*, p. 112.

ὠδίνω,

"have birth-pangs," "travail" (Gal 4²⁷, *al.*) : cf. *Kaibel* 321¹² παῦσον δ' ὠδείν[ουσ]α, and *ib.* 1103², an inscr. from a Pompeian sleeping-room—

> Ὁ θρασὺ[ς] ἀνθέστακεν Ἔρως [τῷ Πανὶ παλαίων,
> χἁ Κύπρις ὠδείνει,

where the editor understands ὠδείνει as = "anxia est."

ὦμος,

"shoulder" (Mt 23⁴, Lk 15⁵) : P Hamb I. 105¹⁵ (iii/B.C.) τὸν ἀριστερὸν ὦμον, and PSI V. 455¹⁶ (A.D. 178) a public physician reports—ἐφ[ι]δὸν τοῦτον . . ἔχοντα . . . ἐπὶ τῆς ἀριστερᾶς ὠμοπλάτης καὶ τοῦ ὦμου τύμματα πληγῶν. Cf. P Cairo Zen III. 59381³ (iii/B.C.), where amongst other articles of meat we read of—ὦμος ᾱ σκέλος ᾱ, and *Syll* 633 (= ³1042)¹⁸ (ii/iii A.D.) for the same combination in connexion with a sacrifice.

The word is apparently used = "beam" in P Ryl II. 236²³ (A.D. 256) ποίησον δὲ ἐξαυτῆς ὤμους δύο ἐλαιουργικοὺς κοπῆναι, "have two beams (?) cut at once for oil-presses" (Edd.) : cf. P Flor II. 233³ (A.D. 263) τέσσαρας ὤμους, with the editor's note.

ὠνέομαι,

"buy" (for the form, see Rutherford *NP* p. 210 ff.), is confined in the NT to a citation from the LXX in Ac 7²⁶. The verb is very common in our sources, e.g. P Tor I. 1ᵛ·⁷ (B.C. 116) (= *Chrest.* II. p. 35) ἐώνητο παρὰ Ἑλήκιος . . . πήχεις οἰκοπεδικοὺς ἑπτὰ ἥμισυ, P Gen I. 20⁶ (B.C. 109) ἥν (*sc.* μερίδα γῆς) ἐώνήσατο ἐγ βασιλικοῦ, BGU IV. 1146⁸ (B.C. 19) ἧς ἐώνηνται παρ' αὐ[τοῦ, P Oxy IX. 1188¹⁹ (A.D. 13) βούλομαι ὠνή[σασθαι] . . . ξύλα ἐξηραμμέ[να], "I wish to purchase some dried logs" (Ed.), P Tebt II. 410⁶ (A.D. 16) χάριν οὗ παρορίζεται ὑπὸ γίτονος ἐωνημένου τῶν γιτνιωσῶν αὐτῷ, "on account of the encroachments being made on him by a neighbour who has bought some of the adjoining property" (Edd.), P Oxy I.

701

78¹² (iii/A.D.) ἔναγχος ἐωνημένος παρά τ(ινος?) τὰς ὑπογεγραμμένας (ἀρούρας), "having lately bought from some one the hereinafter described land (?)" (Edd.), and *ib.* VI. 914⁸ (A.D. 486) διαφόρων βαμμάτων [ὧν ἐ]ώνημαι παρὰ σοῦ, "various dyes which I have bought from you."

The subst. ὠνητής occurs in P Cairo Zen III. 59303² (iii/B.C.) ὠνητὴς περὶ τοῦ ἵππου τοῦ μεγάλου, "purchaser of the big horse," and for ὠνή, cf. P Oxy III. 486⁷ (A.D. 131) τὸν καθήκοντα τῆς ὠνῆς δημόσι[ον χρημα]τισμόν, "the regular official contract of the sale" (Edd.).

Reference may also be made to the Delphic inscr. of B.C. 200–199, *Syll* 845¹⁴, where, with regard to the manumission of a slave, the words occur—τὰν τιμὰν ἀπέχει. τὰν δὲ ὠνὰν ἐπίστευσε Νίκαια τῶι Ἀπόλλωνι ἐπ' ἐλευθερίαι, "the price he (viz. the previous vendor) hath received. The purchase, however, Nicaea hath committed unto Apollo, for freedom." See Deissmann *LAE*² p. 323 ff., where the usage referred to is discussed as illustrating the Pauline conception of Christian freedom.

ᾠόν,

"an egg" (Lk 11¹²) (for form, Blass-Debrunner § 26). An interesting ex. of this common word is afforded by P Oxy I. 83⁸ (A.D. 327), the declaration by an egg-seller that he will not sell eggs except in the public market—ὁμολογῶ . . . τὴν διάπρασίν μοι τῶν ὠῶν (*l.* ᾠῶν) ποιήσασθαι ἐπὶ τῆς ἀγορᾶς δημοσίᾳ. Other exx. are P Petr III. 142³ (an account—Ptol.) ᾠά, P Oxy IX. 1207¹⁰ (A.D. 175–6) ὠῶν ἑκατόν, P Oxy X. 1339 (account of expenses—iii/A.D.) ὑπ(ὲρ) τι(μῆς) λαχάνων καὶ ὠῶν (δρ.) τ̄, P Oxy VI. 936⁶ (iii/A.D.) κλονίον (for κλουβίον or κλωβίον) ὠῶν π, "a basket of 80 eggs," and for the dim. ᾠάριον, see BGU III. 781ˣ·⁶ (i/A.D.).

For the use of eggs in magic see P Osl I¹⁴⁹ (iv/A.D.) τὰ ἀνόμιμα ᾠά θύεται, "the lawless eggs are sacrificed," with the editor's note.

ὥρα

(1) "an hour": P Oxy II. 235⁷ (A.D. 20–50) ὥρᾳ τετάρτῃ τῆς νυκτός, P Ryl II. 234³ (ii/A.D.) ὥρᾳ ᾱ, "at the first hour," P Hamb I. 96³ (date of a horoscope—A.D. 145) ὀγδόου Ἀντωνείνου Φαρμοῦτι κατ' ἀρχαίους ῑδ̄ ὥρα τρίτῃ νυκτός, P Ryl II. 109¹¹ (A.D. 235) τῇ κη̄ τοῦ ὄντος Μεσορὴ μηνὸς ὥρας ἀρχομένης τετάρτης, and P Oxy IX. 1214⁷ (v/A.D.) ὥρ(ας) ζ, "at 7 o'clock." With ἡ ὥρα = "the fatal hour," as in Mt 26¹⁵, cf. P Leid Wᵛⁱⁱ ²⁷ (ii/iii A.D.) (= II. p. 193) βοήθησον ἐν ἀνάγκαις, ἐλεήμων ἐν ὥραις βιαίος (*l.* βιαίαις).

(2) As the hour was the shortest period of time known to the ancients, ὥρα came to be used much as we use "in one second," "in one moment," "instantly," e.g. P Tebt II. 411³ (ii/A.D.) ἅμα τῷ λαβεῖν μου τὴν ἐπιστολὴν αὐτῇ ὥρᾳ ἄνελθε, "immediately after receiving my letter, come up instantly" (Edd.), and similarly P Oxy IX. 1193² (iv/A.D.): cf. Lk 2³⁸, and for the added significance that this usage gives to Rev 17¹² see Ramsay *Teaching*, p. 57. In P Iand I. 42¹ (vi/A.D.) ὥρα = "now" stands alone: the editor can supply no parallel. For the acc. denoting a point of time, as in Jn 4⁵², Rev 3³, cf. BGU IV. 1079¹¹ (A.D. 41)

(= *Selections*, p. 39) ἀκολούθει δὲ Πτολλαρίωνι πᾶσαν ὥραν, "stick to Ptollarion constantly," and see *Proleg.* pp. 63, 245.

(3) The word = "age" in P Lond 24¹¹ (B.C. 163) (= I. p. 32, *UPZ* i. p. 117), where a mother represents that her daughter Tathemis has reached the age when circumcision was usual—τὴν Ταθῆμιν ὥραν ἔχειν ὡς ἔθος ἐστὶ[ν] τοῖς Αἰγυπτίοις περι[τε]τέμνεσθαι, and similarly in P Ryl II. 101⁶ (A.D. 63) a request for the examination of a youth—ὥραν [ἔχοντα τῆς εἰς το]ὺς ἐφή[β]ους εἰσκρίσεως, "having reached the age for admission as an ephebus" (Edd.).

(4) For prepositional phrases we may cite the following—P Oxy III. 523¹ (ii/A.D.) (= *Selections*, p. 97) an invitation to dinner ἐν τοῖς Κλαυδ(ίου) Σαραπίω(νος) τῆι ῑς̄ ἀπὸ ὥρας θ, "in the house of Claudius Serapion on the 16th at 9 o'clock": *ib.* VI. 935¹⁷ (iii/A.D.) διὸ γ[ράφ]ω σοι . . . διὰ ὥρας γράφ[ῃς] μο[ι] π[ε]ρὶ τούτου, "I write to you therefore to ask you to write to me at once about him (?)" (Edd.): *ib.* I. 41²⁹ (iii/iv A.D.) ἰς (*l.* εἰς) ὥρας πᾶσι τοῖς τὴν πόλιν φιλοῦσιν, "Hurrah for all who love the city" (Edd.): BGU IV. 1208³¹ (B.C. 27–26) ἐν τῆι ὥραι ἐπεχώρησεν: P Oxy XVI. 1844¹ (vi/vii A.D.) εὐθέως καὶ κατ' αὐτὴν τὴν ὥραν, "immediately and at the very moment": P Lips I. 105⁷ (i/ii A.D.) (= *Chrest.* I. p. 270) ὃν μετὰ μίαν ὥραν πέμψω, "which (*sc.* "a reckoning") I shall send within an hour": P Oxy IV. 804 (horoscope—A.D. 4) περὶ ὥρα ν) γ̄ τῆς ἡμέρα(ς), *ib.* VII. 1114²⁴ (A.D. 237) περὶ ὥραν τρίτην, "at the third hour of the day" (Ed.): P Gen I. 52¹ (*c.* A.D. 346) χαρτίον καθαρὸν μὴ εὑρὼν πρὸς τὴν ὥραν εἰς τοῦ[τ]ον ἔγραψα, "not having found a clean sheet of paper at the moment, I wrote on this": and P Oxy II. 306 (late i/A.D.) ἐπεὶ δὲ μετρίως εἶχε ὑπὸ τὴν ὥραν ἐνεσημάνθη οὐκ εἴσχυσέ σοι γρ[ά]ψαι.

ὡραῖος,

lit. "in season" (Mt 23²⁷, *al.*): cf. PSI V. 535¹¹ (Ptol.) ταρίχου ὡραίων ἀπολέκτων πεπονηκὸς Θάσι⟨ον⟩ κερ(άμιον) ᾱ, *ib.* 558⁷ (B.C. 257–6) σφόγγων ὡραίου κερ(άμιον) ἓν δέδωκεν, *ib.* 504¹² (iii/B.C.) ὡραίων κεράμια β, and *Kaibel* 812¹ (ii/A.D.)—

ὅπως ῥᾳδ]ινὴ διὰ παντός
ἄμπελος ὡραῖον καρπὸν ἔχῃ βοτρύων.

In P Goodsp Cairo 2¹·⁴ (ii/A.D.) we have a medical fragment containing a warning against τῶν ὡραίων, "ripe fruits," where the editor notes the generally colourless character of ὡραῖος, and cites Athenaeus *Deipnosophistae* 116E ὡραῖα *sc.* ταρίχη, meaning fish "pickled in the season." For the derived meaning "in the bloom of youth" "beautiful," cf. the magic P Lond 125 *verso*¹³ (v/A.D.) (= I. p. 124) γυναῖκαν . . . ὡραίαν καὶ [ν]έαν. In *Syll*³ 668⁴ (B.C. 160–59) ἐν ὡραί[αι] ἐκκλησίαι, the editor understands the adj. in the sense of ἔννομος, νόμιμος. For the adj. ὥριμος, see P Tebt I. 54⁶ (B.C. 86) κλήρου ἀρο ρῶν) ῑ . . ὡρίμου σπαρῆναι, "the holding of 10 arourae ready for sowing."

ὠρύομαι,

"roar," "howl." The use of the verb in 1 Pet 5⁸ is probably derived from Ps 21(22)¹¹ ὡς λέων ὁ ἀρπάζων καὶ ὠρυόμενος. For the thought Moffatt (*NT Comm. ad l.*) cites Latimer's *Sermon of the Plough* where the text is quoted to prove that the devil is "the most diligent prelate and preacher in England."

ὡς.

1. = "as": P Goodsp Cairo 4[1] (ii/B.C.) (= *Selections*, p. 24) εἰ ἔρρωσαι . . . εἴη ἂν ὡς αἱρούμεθα, "if you are well, it will be as we desire," BGU I. 163[7] (A.D. 108) καὶ γὰρ ἄλλοι ὡς πληγέντες ὑπὸ αὐτοῦ ἀναφόριον δεδώκασι, "for others have given information (from time to time) as having been assaulted by him," P Flor I. 56[18] (A.D. 234) ὡς καθήκει, and BGU IV. 1024[viii. 11] (iv/v A.D.) κα]ταβληθῆναι ὡς φονέα.

2. = "that," "how," after verbs of saying, thinking, etc.: P Tebt I. 10[6] (B.C. 119) φρόντισον ὡς τὰ τῆς ὑποσχέσεως ἐκπληρωθήσεται, "take care that the terms of his agreement are fulfilled" (Edd.), and P Tebt II. 410[19] (i/A.D.) μν[ή]σθητι ὡ[ς] ἐν τῷ Τριστόμῳ με ἐφιλοτ[ι]μοῦ σὺν ἐμοὶ μεῖναι, "remember how zealous you were at Tristomos to remain with me" (Edd.).

3. c. ind. with ἄν, as in 1 Cor 12[2], cf. P Par 46[18] (B.C. 152) ὡς ἂν εὐκαιρήσω, παραχρῆμα παρέσομαι πρός σε.

4. c. conj. with ἄν, as in Rom 15[24], 1 Cor 11[34], Phil 2[23], = "as soon as," "when": P Hib I. 44[5] (B.C. 253) ὡς ἂν οὖν λάβηις τὴν ἐπιστολὴν . . . ἀπόστειλον, "as soon as you receive the letter, send," *ib.* 66[4] (B.C. 228) ὡ[ς δ'] ἂν παραγένωμαι . . . συνλαλήσω σοι, "as soon as I arrive, I will have a conversation with you," and with ἐάν (= ἄν) P Fay 111[16] (A.D. 95–6) ὡς ἐὰν βλέπηις [τ]ὴν τιμὴν παντὸς ἀγόρασον τὰς τοῦ λωτίνου (ἀρτάβας) κ, "as soon as you learn the price, be sure to buy the 20 artabae of lotus": see *Proleg.* p. 167 f.

5. c. inf.: P Giss I. 47[a] (time of Hadrian) (= *Chrest.* I. p. 383) where reference is made to a θώραξ made ὡς μὴ κάμνειν τὸν φοροῦντα αὐτόν, "so as not to weary the person carrying it," and P Oxy VIII. 1120[19] (early iii/A.D.), where a widow complains that a certain Thonis had carried off her slave Theodora μὴ ἔχων κατ' αὐτῆς ἐξουσίαν, ὡς ἐν παντὶ σθένει βίαν με σχεῖν, "though he had no power over her, so that I am subjected to unmitigated violence" (Ed.): cf. Lk 9[52]. The literary phrase ὡς ἔπος εἰπεῖν (in NT only Heb 7[9]) occurs in a would-be literary papyrus, a dispute concerning property, P Oxy I. 67[14] (A.D. 338) πάντα μέν, ὡς ἔπος ἐστὶν εἰπεῖν, ὅσα ἰσχύειν τι δύν[α]τ[αι] παρὰ τὴν τῶν νόμων [ἰσχὺ]ν πρὸς ὀλίγον ἰσχύει, "everything, it may be said, that is able to withstand the power of the law withstands but for a short time" (Edd.).

6. = ὅτι: P Oxy XVII. 2110[6] (A.D. 370) παρατίθημι ἐν ὑμῖν ὡς οὐ χρὴ λύεσθαι τὰ διατυπωθέντα, "I put it to you that the ordinances should not be infringed" (Edd.), *ib.*[34] ὀνε[ι]δίζομεν ὡς οὐ προσήκει αὐτὸν ἐνοχλεῖσθαι προφάσει ἐπιμελείας τῆς αὐτῆς ἐρεᾶς ἐσθῆτος, "we find fault saying that it is not right that he should be burdened on the score of the administration of the said woollen clothing" (Edd.).

7. ὡς ὅτι (2 Thess 2[2], 2 Cor 5[19], 11[21]: Lightfoot *Notes* p. 110) in later Greek is practically = simple ὅτι, e.g. Dion. Hal. *Antt.* ix. 14 ἐπιγνοὺς ὡς [om. ὡς, Kiessling] ὅτι ἐν ἐσχάτοις εἰσὶν οἱ κατακλεισθέντες ἐν τοῖς λόφοις, CPR I. 19[3] (iv/A.D.) πρώην βιβλία ἐπιδέδωκα τῇ σῇ ἐπιμελείᾳ ὡς ὅτι ἐβουλήθην τινὰ ὑπάρχοντά μου ἀποδόσθαι: see further *Proleg.* p. 212, Jannaris *Gr.* § 1754.

8. = "about," as in P Amh II. 72[12] (A.D. 246) δηλῶ τὰ καταλειφθέντα ὑπ' α[ὐ]τοῦ σύνπαντα ἄξια εἶναι ὡς ταλάντων τριῶν, "I declare that the property left by him is worth in all about three talents" (Edd.). This usage is specially common in notifications of age, e.g. P Tebt II. 381[1] (a Will—A.D. 123) (= *Selections*, p. 77) Θαῆσις . . . ἐτῶν ἑβδομήκοντα ὀκτώ, "Thaesis being about seventy-eight years of age": cf. Lk 3[23], and see Deissmann's note in P Meyer, p. 26.

ὡσαννά,

orig. a cry for help (Ps 118[25]), but as used by the Evangelists a shout of praise (Mt 21[9], Mk 11[9]: see Dalman *Words of Jesus*, p. 220 ff. It is because of Luke's omission of ὡσαννά in 19[38] that Jerome calls him "inter omnes evangelistas Graeci sermonis eruditissimus" (*Ep.* 20. 4 to Pope Damasus). For a discussion of the cry *Hosanna*, see F. C. Burkitt in *JTS* xvii. (1916), p. 139 ff., and cf. Preuschen-Bauer, *Wörterb. s.v.*

ὡσαύτως,

"in like manner," "likewise": P Hamb I. 25[14] (B.C. 238) Καλᾶς τέτακται συναντήσεσθαι πρός σε . . . ὡσαύτως δὲ καὶ τῶι Ἀκολούθωι παρηγγείλαμεν συναντᾶν πρός σε, P Eleph 29[10] (iii/B.C.) ὡσαύτως παστοφόριον ἐν Τεντύρει ἐντὸς τείχους, P Tebt II. 4[11] (iii B.C.) ὡσαύτως δὲ καὶ σχοινία ρ, ἐὰν δὲ ὑπάρχηι πλέω σ, "likewise, too, 100 ropes, but if you have plenty, 200," in connexion with building operations, P Ryl II. 130[12] (A.D. 31) ἔτι δὲ καὶ πλεῖστάκι ὡσαύτως ἐτρύγησαν καὶ ἀπηνέγκαντο, "moreover they repeatedly gathered them in the same way and carried them off," of thieves in an olive-yard, P Oxy II. 267[19] (agreement of marriage—A.D. 36) προσομολογῶι ἐὰν ὡσαύτως ἐκ διαφορᾶς ἀπ[αλλαγ]ῶμεν ἀπ' ἀλλήλ[ων . . . ., "I further agree if as aforesaid owing to a quarrel we separate from each other . . ." (Edd.), similarly *ib.* III. 496[14] (A.D. 127), and Preisigke 5114[17] (A.D. 613–640).

ὡσεί,

(1) "as if," "as it were," "like": PSI IV. 343[10] (B.C. 256–5) ὡσεὶ καὶ παρόντος σου ὁ λόγος συντεθήσεται, P Tebt I. 58[26] (letter of a tax-farmer—B.C. 111) θεωρήσας με ὡς προσεδρεύοντα καθ' ἡμέραν ὡσεὶ δεδίλανται, "seeing me in daily attendance he has as it were turned coward" (Edd.), and P Fay 118[21] (A.D. 110) σησ τρίδια ὡσὶ εἰς ξυλαμήν, "sieves as it were for mowing."

(2) "about" with numbers: Preisigke 5115[1] (B.C. 145) ὠνῆς ψηλοῦ τόπου ὡσεὶ π(ήχεως) ᾱ, P Tebt I. 15[2] (B.C. 114) ὡσεὶ περὶ ὥραν ιᾱ, "at about the eleventh hour," and P Oxy XVI. 1870[11] (v/A.D.) στ[αμνίο]ν ἐν χωροῦν ὡσεὶ ξέστα[ς δύο?, "one vessel containing about two *xextae*."

ὥσπερ,

"even as," "as": PSI V. 486[5] (B.C. 258–7) ἵνα τὰ χώματα τὰ ἐν τ[ῆι] γῆι αὐτῶν χωννύηται ὥσπε[ρ] καὶ τὰ λοιπά, P Fay 109[24] (. A.D. 140) a physician pleads that members of his profession should be exempted from certain compulsory services, μάλ[ι]στα [δὲ οἱ δε]δοκιμασμένοι ὥσπερ κἀγώ, "especially those who have passed the examination like myself," P Oxy VII. 1065[6] (iii/A.D.) ἐὰν δὲ ὀλιγωρήσῃς, ὥσπερ [ο]ἱ θεοὶ οὐκ ἐφίσαντό μ[ο]υ οὕτως κἀγὼ θεῶ[ν] οὐ φί[σ]ομαι, "if you neglect this, as the gods have not spared me so will I not spare the gods" (Ed.); cf. 1 Cor 8[5], and see von Dobschütz *ZNTW* xxiv. (1925), p. 50.

In P Oxy VIII. 1121[12] (A.D. 295) ὥσπερ ταύτης πρὸ ὀλίγου τούτων ἡμερῶν τὸν βίον ἀναπαυσαμένης ἀδιαθέτου, "when a few days ago she died intestate" (Ed.). ὥσπερ is little more than a connecting particle. For the emphatic ὥσπερ, see Meisterhans *Gr.* p. 257.

ὡσπερεί.

With ὡσπερεί, "as it were," in 1 Cor 15[8], cf. ὡσπεροῦν in PSI I. 76[3] (A.D. 574–578) ἡ πίστις τῶν συναλλαγμάτων . . . ὡσπεροῦν καὶ τἀναντία καταπατουμένη, σαφῶς ἀπεργάζεται.

ὥστε.

1. For the construction c. inf. denoting result "so as to," the stress being laid on the dependence of the result on its cause (cf. Mt 8[24], Lk 4[29], *al.*) we may cite BGU I. 27[13] (ii/A.D.) (= *Selections*, p. 101) καθ' ἡμέραν προσδεχόμ[ε]θα διμι[σ]σωρίαν, ὥστε ἕως σήμερον μηδέν' ἀπολελύσθαι τῶν μετὰ σῖτον, "daily we are waiting for our discharge, so that up till to-day no one of us in the corn service has been let go," P Oxy X. 1279[11] (A.D. 139) ἐπιδέχομαι μισθώσασθαι ἐκ τοῦ δημοσίου . . . ἀρούρας τρεῖς . . . ὥστε κατ' ἔτος σπεῖραι καὶ ξυλαμῆσαι οἷς ἐὰν αἱρῶμαι, "I consent to lease from the State three arourae, on condition that I may sow and plant the land with any crop which I choose" (Edd.), *ib.* 1255[7] (A.D. 202) ἐπιτεθειμένου σου ἡμῖν ὥστε ἐν ἀσφαλεῖ ἔχειν τοὺς καρποὺς ἐν ταῖς ἁλωνίαις, "having been enjoined by you to keep in safety the crops at the threshing floors" (Edd.), *ib.* VI. 801[12] (A.D. 294) ἔδοξεν ὥστε σὲ μὲν προστῆναι, "it was decided you should preside" (Edd.). For the omission of ὥστε before the inf. (as in Ac 5[2], Col 4[6], Heb 5[5], 6[10]), cf. P Oxy III. 526[4] (ii/A.D.) οὐκ ἤμην ἀπαθὴς ἀλόγως σε καταλείπιν, "I was not so unfeeling as to leave you without reason" (Edd.).

2. For the strict consecutive ὥστε c. ind. (as in Jn 3[16], Gal 2[13]), cf. P Oxy XIV. 1672[6] (A.D. 37–41) πεπράκαμεν χό(ας) λβ ξένοις προσώποις ἐν οἷς ἦν καὶ πολλὰ λέα οἰνάρια [[ὥστε]] ἐκ (δραχμῶν) ε μετὰ χάριτος, ὥστε αἱ πράσεις ἡμῶν καλλιότεραι γεγ[ό]νασι λείαν, καὶ ἐλπίζομεν ὅτι καλλιότεραι τούτων γενήσονται, "we sold 32 choes to some strangers, including a quantity of quite thin wine, at the rate of 5 drachmae, thankfully, so that our sales have become much more favourable, and we hope that they will become more favourable than this" (Edd.).

3. The consecutive ὥστε c. subj., as in 1 Cor 5[8], may be illustrated by BGU III. 874[1] (Byz.) ἄλλοτε γεγράφηκα ὑμῖν ὥστε πέμψηται (*l.* πέμψητε) εἰς Παρμοῦθιν καὶ δέξηται (*l.* δέξησθε) τὰ δύο χρύσινα παρὰ τοῦ διάκονος, and with the imper., as in 1 Cor 3[21], by P Oxy X. 1293[13] (A.D. 117–138) ἔδει αὐτῶι διδῶναι (*l.* διδόναι)· ὥστε τοῦ λοιποῦ

γράφεται (*l.* γράφετε), "you ought to have given him (a letter); so in future write" (Edd.).

4. Some miscellaneous exx. may be added. For ὥστε = "namely," cf. P Ryl II. 75[11] (late ii/A.D.) an account of judicial proceedings, where the prefect decides, τύπος ἐστὶν καθ' ὃν ἔκρεινα πολλάκις καὶ τοῦτο δίκαιον εἶναί μοι φαίνεται ἐπὶ τῶν ἐ[[κ]]ξιστανο-[[με]]μένων, ὥστε, εἴ τι ἐπὶ περιγρ[α]φῇ τῶν δανιστῶν ἐποίησαν, ἄκοιρον εἶναι, "there is a principle according to which I have often judged and which seems to me fair in the case of those who resign their property, namely, that if they have done anything to defraud their creditors, the resignation shall not be valid" (Edd.). For ὥστε = ὡς, cf. *ib.* 155[21] (A.D. 138–161) ὥστε ἐὰν αἱρῆται, "as she pleases." For ὥστε εἰς, cf. P Hal I. 7[1] (B.C. 232) ὥστε εἰς [ξέ]νια φοίνικας, "dates for gifts to guests." With this last passage cf. the banker's receipt P Tebt II. 280[3] (B.C. 126) Ἡρακλείδει τραπεζίτῃ ὥστε βασιλεῖ παρὰ Σοκονῶπιος, "Sokonobis to Heraclides the banker for the king" (Edd.), and P Lond 848 *verso*[2] (A.D. 213?) (= III. p. 209) δὸς Λάδωνι ὥστε τῇ γυναῖκι Ἀγαθείνου ἐρίων πόκους πέντε, "give to Ladon for the wife of Agathinus five fleeces."

ὠτάριον,

which in the NT (Mk 14[47], Jn 18[10]) is used of "an ear," is found in the papyri = "handle," e.g. BGU III. 781[i. 15] (i/A.D.) σὺν ποδίοις καὶ ὠταρίοις ἤ, *ib.*[ii. 1] ὠτάρια ἔχοντα σατύρια, *et saepius.*

ὠτίον,

For this dimin. of οὖς, "an ear" (Mt 26[51], *al.*), reference may be made to the new Saying of Jesus, P Oxy I. 1[20a], which, as restored by White *Sayings* p. xviii., runs—λέγει Ἰησοῦς· ἀκούεις εἰς τὸ ἓν ὠτίον σου, τὸ δὲ ἕτερον συνέκλεισας.

For other exx. of ὠτίον cf. P Oxy I. 108[17] (meat bill of a cook—A.D. 183 or 215) ὠτίον ᾱ, ἄκρον ᾱ, νεφρία β, "1 ear, 1 trotter, 2 kidneys," P Leid W[vi. 36] (ii/iii A.D.) (= II. p. 101) ἐὰν ἐπίπῃς (*l.* ἐπείπῃς) ἐπὶ παντὸς πετεινοῦ (*l.* πετεινοῦ) εἰς τὸ ὠτίον, τελευτήσει, and Preisigke 6003[10] (A.D. 316) τοῦ] ἀριστεροῦ ὠτί[ου. Like ὠτάριον, ὠτίον is used = "handle," as in BGU III. 781[i. 3 al.] (i/A.D.), and P Oxy XIV. 1658[13] (iv/A.D.) ὠτίον χαλκίου, "a handle of a kettle" (Edd.).

ὠφέλ(ε)ια,

"advantage," "benefit." The form ὠφέλια, which is read in Rom 3[1], Jude[16], was already classical, and is also found in the papyri and inscrr. (always in Attic inscrr., Meisterhans *Gr.* p. 56), e.g. P Oxy XII. 1409[11] (A.D. 278) τὴν γὰρ ἀπὸ τῶν ἔργων τούτων γεινομένην ὠφ[έλ]ιαν πάντας ε[ἰδέναι πέ]πεισμαι, "for I am persuaded that every one is aware of the benefit resulting from these works (*sc.* repairing of the dykes)" (Edd.), *ib.* 1477[4] (question to an oracle—iii/iv A.D.) εἰ ἔχω ὠφέλιαν ἀπὸ τοῦ φίλου; "am I to obtain benefit from my friend?" *Priene* 11[5] (c. B.C. 297) ὑ[πὸ τῆ]ς ὠφελίας, and Cagnat IV. 946[11].

ὠφελέω,

"help," "benefit," c. acc. pers. as in Heb 4², Preisigke 4305¹⁰ (iii/B.C.) εἰ μὴ τὴν μήκωνα ("the poppy") συνάξεις, μ[η]δείς σε ἀνθρώπων μὴ ὠφελήσηι, P Oxy IX. 1219¹² (iii/A.D.) οἶδα ὅτι καὶ ταῦτά μου τὰ γράμματα πόλλ' αὐτὸν ὠφελήσει, "I know that this letter of mine also will be of much help to him," and ib. XII. 1490⁴ (late iii/A.D.) λέγει γὰρ ὅτι ὠφέλησα αὐτὸν μεγάλως καὶ ἐν τῇ ἀννώνῃ, "he says 'I helped him greatly in the matter of the annona.'"

For the verb = "instruct," as frequently in early ecclesiastical writers, cf. Pelagia-Legenden p. 3²⁰ οἱ ἐπίσκοποι . . . ἠρώτων τὸν κύριον Νόννον εἰπεῖν καὶ ὠφελῆσαι αὐτούς. According to Field (Notes, p. 21) the meaning "prevail," which is attached to the verb by AV, RV, in Mt 27²⁴,

Jn 12¹⁹. seems to require confirmation. MGr φελῶ, "I assist, am useful"; ὠφελεῖ, "it is useful, advantageous."

ὠφέλιμος,

"useful," confined in the NT to the Pastorals: cf. P Ryl II. 153¹¹ (A.D. 138–161) ὠφέλιμος ἡμεῖν γενόμενος [παρ]ὰ τὴν ἡμῶ[ν] εἰς τοὺς ἔξω [τό]πους ἀποδημυλη (l. ἀποδημίαν), "having been useful to us on the occasion of our absence abroad." The phrase ἐν πᾶσι καλοῖς καὶ ὠφελίμοις ἔργοις is common in contracts, e.g. P Lond V. 1711³⁶ (A.D. 566–573), and the Byzantine papyri, P Masp II. 67158¹⁸, 67150²³. See also Syll³ 1165³ (an oracle) αἴ ἐστι αὐτοῖ προβατεύοντι ὄναιον (= ἄρειον Hesych.) καὶ ὠφέλιμον.

CPSIA information can be obtained
at www.ICGtesting.com
Printed in the USA
BVHW021659050423
661817BV00012B/449